LAW, DIVERSITY, AND BUSINESS: MANAGERIAL IMPLICATIONS

Marriage Equality and the Constitution 52

Increased Diversity in the Federal Judiciary 62

Derogatory Trademarks 131

Native Americans and Criminal Justice 162

Respecting Cultural Differences in Foreign Markets 203

Equal Opportunity in Public Contracting 261

Reverse Redlining in the Mortgage Market 574

Combating Appearance-Based Discrimination 656

Can a Person Who Is Not a Member of a Protected Class Sue for Discrimination? 732

The Worldwide Lack of Women on Boards of Directors 818

How Should Airlines Deal with "Customers of Size"? 863

LINKING BUSINESS LAW to . . .

Linking Business Law to Management:
Dealing with Administrative Law 20

Linking Business Law to Marketing:
Trademarks and Service Marks 151

Linking Business Law to Accounting and Finance:
Managing a Company's Reputation 206

Linking Business Law to Marketing:
Customer Relationship Management 276

Linking Business Law to Corporate Management:
Quality Control 457

Linking Business Law to Accounting and Finance:
Banking in a Period of Crisis 513

Linking Business Law to Corporate Management:
What Can You Do to Prepare for a Chapter 11 Reorganization? 569

Linking Business Law to Corporate Management:
Human Resource Management 674

Linking Business Law to Accounting and Finance:
Sources of Funds 768

Standard Edition

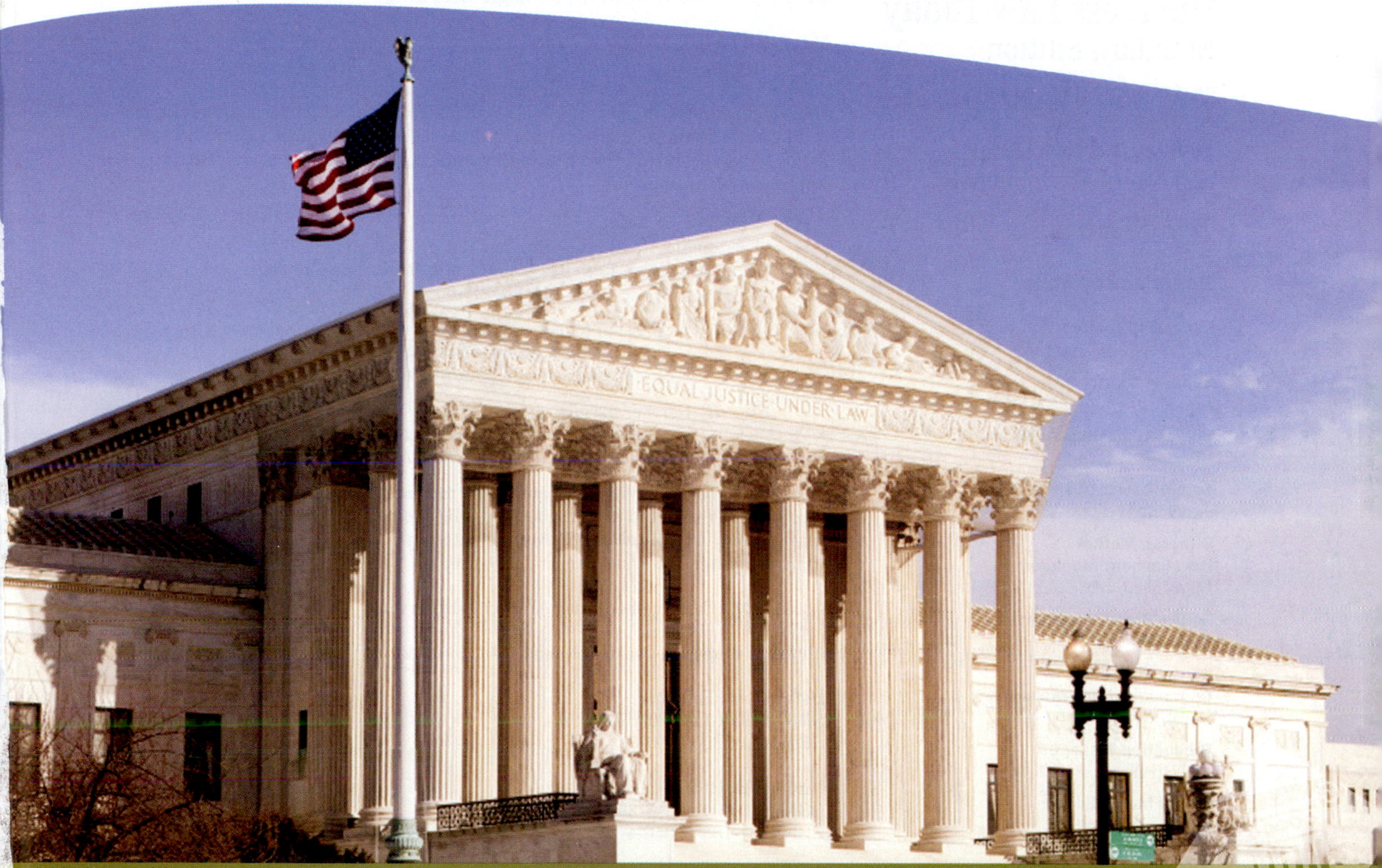

(BackyardProduction/iStockphoto.com)

Business Law Today

Text & Summarized Cases

DIVERSE, ETHICAL, ONLINE, AND GLOBAL ENVIRONMENT

Tenth Edition

Roger LeRoy Miller
Institute for University Studies
Arlington, Texas

Australia • Brazil • Japan • Korea • Mexico • Singapore • Spain • United Kingdom • United States

Business Law Today
Standard Edition

TEXT & SUMMARIZED CASES

Diverse, Ethical, Online, and Global Environment

TENTH EDITION

Roger LeRoy Miller

Editorial Director:
Erin Joyner

Editor-in-Chief:
Rob Dewey

Senior Acquisitions Editor:
Vicky True-Baker

Senior Developmental Editor:
Jan Lamar

Director, Market Development Manager:
Lisa Lysne

Senior Brand Manager:
Kristen Hurd

Senior Marketing Communications Manager:
Sarah Greber

Production Manager:
Bill Stryker

Senior Media Editor:
Kristen Meere

Manufacturing Planner:
Kevin Kluck

Editorial Assistant:
Tristann Jones

Compositor:
Parkwood Composition Service

Senior Art Director:
Michelle Kunkler

Cover and Internal Designer:
Stratton Design

Cover Image:
© Comstock Images/Getty Images, Inc.

Library of Congress Control Number: 2012952002

Instructor's Edition:
ISBN 13: 978-1-285-06071-2
ISBN 10: 1-285-06071-7

Student Edition:
ISBN 13: 978-1-133-27356-1
ISBN 10: 1-133-27356-4

South-Western Cengage Learning
5191 Natorp Blvd.
Mason, OH 45040
USA

Cengage Learning products are represented in Canada by Nelson Education, Ltd.

For your course and learning solutions, visit **www.cengage.com**.

Purchase any of our products at your local college store or at our preferred online store **www.cengagebrain.com**.

Printed in the United States
2 3 4 5 6 7 16 15 14

Contents in Brief

UNIT 1 The Legal Environment of Business 1

Chapter 1 The Legal Environment 3
Chapter 2 Constitutional Law 33
Chapter 3 Courts and Alternative Dispute Resolution 60
Chapter 4 Torts and Cyber Torts 95
Chapter 5 Intellectual Property and Internet Law 126
Chapter 6 Criminal Law and Cyber Crime 155
Chapter 7 Ethics and Business Decision Making 190
Chapter 8 International Law in a Global Economy 210

UNIT 2 Contracts 237

Chapter 9 Nature and Classification 239
Chapter 10 Agreement in Traditional and E-Contracts 257
Chapter 11 Consideration, Capacity, and Legality 281
Chapter 12 Defenses to Contract Enforceability 305
Chapter 13 Third Party Rights and Discharge 327
Chapter 14 Breach and Remedies 352

UNIT 3 Commercial Transactions 381

Chapter 15 The Formation of Sales and Lease Contracts 383
Chapter 16 Performance and Breach of Sales and Lease Contracts 413
Chapter 17 Warranties and Product Liability 437
Chapter 18 Negotiable Instruments: Transferability and Liability 462
Chapter 19 Checks and Banking in the Digital Age 494
Chapter 20 Secured Transactions 519
Chapter 21 Creditors' Rights and Bankruptcy 542
Chapter 22 Mortgages and Foreclosures after the Recession 573

UNIT 4 Agency and Employment Law 595

Chapter 23 Agency Relationships in Business 597
Chapter 24 Employment, Immigration, and Labor Law 624
Chapter 25 Employment Discrimination and Diversity 654

UNIT 5 Business Organization 683

Chapter 26 Sole Proprietorships and Private Franchises 685
Chapter 27 All Forms of Partnership 702
Chapter 28 Limited Liability Companies and Special Business Forms 725
Chapter 29 Corporate Formation, Merger, and Termination 743
Chapter 30 Corporate Directors, Officers, and Shareholders 773

Chapter 31 Investor Protection, Insider Trading, and Corporate Governance 799

UNIT 6 Government Regulation 831

Chapter 32 Antitrust Law and Promoting Competition 833
Chapter 33 Consumer and Environmental Law 856
Chapter 34 Liability of Accountants and Other Professionals 882

UNIT 7 Property and Its Protection 907

Chapter 35 Personal Property and Bailments 909
Chapter 36 Real Property and Landlord-Tenant Law 931
Chapter 37 Insurance, Wills, and Trusts 949

APPENDICES

A How to Brief Cases and Analyze Case Problems A–1
B The Constitution of the United States A–3
C The Uniform Commercial Code (Excerpts) A–11
D The Sarbanes-Oxley Act (Excerpts and Explanatory Comments) A–131
E Answers to *Issue Spotters* A–138
F Answers to Even-Numbered *For Review* Questions A–144
G Sample Answers for *Questions with Sample Answer* A–152
H Sample Answers for *Case Problems with Sample Answer* A–158
I Case Excerpts for *Case Analysis Questions* A–165

Glossary G–1
Table of Cases TC–1
Index I–1

Contents

UNIT 1 The Legal Environment of Business 1

CHAPTER 1 The Legal Environment 3

Business Activities and the Legal Environment 4
Sources of American Law 6
The Common Law Tradition 11
Adapting the Law to the Online Environment: *How the Internet Has Expanded Precedent* 13
Landmark in the Law: *Equitable Principles and Maxims* 15
Classifications of Law 16
Beyond Our Borders: *National Law Systems* 18
Linking Business Law to Management: *Dealing with Administrative Law* 20
Appendix to Chapter 1: Finding and Analyzing the Law 24

CHAPTER 2 Constitutional Law 33

The Constitutional Powers of Government 34
Landmark in the Law: *Gibbons v. Ogden* (1824) 36
Classic Case: *Heart of Atlanta Motel v. United States* (1964) 37
Business and the Bill of Rights 40
Beyond Our Borders: *The Impact of Foreign Law on the United States Supreme Court* 42
Adapting the Law to the Online Environment: *Vulgar Facebook Photos Receive First Amendment Protection* 43
Case: *Bad Frog Brewery, Inc. v. New York State Liquor Authority* (1998) 45
Case: *Mitchell County v. Zimmerman* (2012) 48
Due Process and Equal Protection 49
Law, Diversity, and Business: Managerial Implications *Marriage Equality and the Constitution* 52
Privacy Rights 52
Business Application: *Is "Pretexting" Illegal?* 56

CHAPTER 3 Courts and Alternative Dispute Resolution 60

The Judiciary's Role in American Government 61
Basic Judicial Requirements 61
Law, Diversity, and Business: Managerial Implications *Increased Diversity in the Federal Judiciary* 62
Landmark in the Law: *Marbury v. Madison* (1803) 63
Case: *Southern Prestige Industries, Inc. v. Independence Plating Corp.* (2010) 64
Spotlight Case: *Gucci America, Inc. v. Wang Huoqing* (2011) 68
The State and Federal Court Systems 70
Beyond Our Borders: *Islamic Law Courts Abroad and at Home* 72
Following a State Court Case 75
Adapting the Law to the Online Environment: *The Duty to Preserve Electronic Evidence for Discovery* 79
The Courts Adapt to the Online World 82
Alternative Dispute Resolution 83
Case: *Cleveland Construction, Inc. v. Levco Construction, Inc.* (2012) 86
Business Application: *To Sue or Not to Sue?* 90

CHAPTER 4 Torts and Cyber Torts 95

The Basis of Tort Law 96
Intentional Torts against Persons 97
Case: *Shoyoye v. County of Los Angeles* (2012) 99
Case: *Orlando v. Cole* (2010) 101
Beyond Our Borders: *"Libel Tourism"* 102
Intentional Torts against Property 107

Adapting the Law to the Online Environment: *Facebook Uses Privacy Concerns to "Smear" Google 108*
Unintentional Torts (Negligence) 111
Landmark in the Law: *Palsgraf v. Long Island Railroad Co. (1928) 115*
Spotlight Case: Taylor v. Baseball Club of Seattle, L.P. (2006) 116
Strict Liability 118
Cyber Torts 119
Business Application: *How Important Is Tort Liability to Business? 122*

CHAPTER 5 Intellectual Property and Internet Law 126

Trademarks and Related Property 127
Classic Case: Coca-Cola Co. v. Koke Co. of America (1920) 127
Adapting the Law to the Online Environment: *Using Online Shame in Trademark Disputes 130*
Law, Diversity, and Business: Managerial Implications *Derogatory Trademarks 131*
Cyber Marks 135
Spotlight Case: Hasbro, Inc. v. Internet Entertainment Group, Ltd. (1996) 137
Patents 138
Copyrights 140
Landmark in the Law: *The Digital Millennium Copyright Act of 1998 145*
Trade Secrets 146
International Protection for Intellectual Property 147
Beyond Our Borders: *The Anti-Counterfeiting Trade Agreement 148*
Case: Golan v. Holder (2012) 149
Linking Business Law to Marketing: *Trademarks and Service Marks 151*

CHAPTER 6 Criminal Law and Cyber Crime 155

Civil Law and Criminal Law 156
Criminal Liability 158
Types of Crimes 161
Law, Diversity, and Business: Managerial Implications *Native Americans and Criminal Justice 162*
Spotlight Case: People v. Sisuphan (2010) 164
Defenses to Criminal Liability 168
Constitutional Safeguards and Criminal Procedures 170
Case: Messerschmidt v. Millender (2012) 172
Criminal Process 175
Landmark in the Law: *Miranda v. Arizona (1966) 176*
Cyber Crime 178
Case: United States v. Oliver (2011) 180
Beyond Our Borders: *Hackers Hide in Plain Sight in Russia 182*
Adapting the Law to the Online Environment: *Prosecuting Those Who Post False Information on the Internet 184*
Business Application: Protecting Your Company against Hacking of Your Bank Accounts 185

CHAPTER 7 Ethics and Business Decision Making 190

Business Ethics 191
Case: Johnson Construction Co. v. Shaffer (2012) 192
Case: Mathews v. B and K Foods, Inc. (2011) 194
Ethical Transgressions by Financial Institutions 196
Approaches to Ethical Reasoning 198
Making Ethical Business Decisions 201
Practical Solutions to Corporate Ethics Questions 202
Business Ethics on a Global Level 202
Law, Diversity, and Business: Managerial Implications *Respecting Cultural Differences in Foreign Markets 203*
Adapting the Law to the Online Environment: *Corporate Reputations under Attack 204*
Linking Business Law to Accounting and Finance: *Managing a Company's Reputation 206*

CHAPTER 8 International Law in a Global Economy 210

International Law—Sources and Principles 211
Case: Spectrum Stores, Inc. v. Citgo Petroleum Corp. (2011) 213
Doing Business Internationally 215
Regulation of Specific Business Activities 217
Commercial Contracts in an International Setting 220
Case: S&T Oil Equipment & Machinery, Ltd. v. Juridica Investments, Ltd. (2012) 222
Payment Methods for International Transactions 223
Beyond Our Borders: *Arbitration versus Litigation 224*
U.S. Laws in a Global Context 225

Spotlight Case: Khulumani v. Barclay National Bank, Ltd. (2007) 226
Business Application: How to Choose and Use a Lawyer 228
Unit 1—Business Case Study with Dissenting Opinion: Paduano v. American Honda Motor Co. 233

UNIT 2 Contracts 237

CHAPTER 9 Nature and Classification 239

An Overview of Contract Law 240
Elements of a Contract 241
Types of Contracts 242
Case: Schwarzrock v. Remote Technologies, Inc. (2011) 244
Adapting the Law to the Online Environment: Can a Disclaimer Prevent an E-Mail from Forming an Agreement? 247
Quasi Contracts 248
Case: Seawest Services Association v. Copenhaver (2012) 248
Interpretation of Contracts 250
Spotlight Case: Wagner v. Columbia Pictures Industries, Inc. (2007) 251

CHAPTER 10 Agreement in Traditional and E-Contracts 257

Agreement 258
Classic Case: Lucy v. Zehmer (1954) 259
Law, Diversity, and Business: Managerial Implications Equal Opportunity in Public Contracting 261
Spotlight Case: Basis Technology Corp. v. Amazon.com, Inc. (2008) 262
Case: Powerhouse Custom Homes, Inc. v. 84 Lumber Co. (2011) 266
E-Contracts 268
Adapting the Law to the Online Environment: The Validity of E-Signatures on Agreements with Online Colleges and Universities 269
The Uniform Electronic Transactions Act 272
Linking Business Law to Marketing: Customer Relationship Management 276

CHAPTER 11 Consideration, Capacity, and Legality 281

Consideration 282
Landmark in the Law: Hamer v. Sidway (1891) 283
Promissory Estoppel 286
Case: Harvey v. Dow (2011) 287
Contractual Capacity 288
Legality 291
Case: Sturdza v. United Arab Emirates (2011) 293
Adapting the Law to the Online Environment: An Increasing Amount of Online Gambling Is in Our Future 294
Spotlight Case: Comedy Club, Inc. v. Improv West Associates (2009) 295
The Effect of Illegality 298
Business Application: Should Retailers Enter into Contracts with Minors and Intoxicated Persons? 300

CHAPTER 12 Defenses to Contract Enforceability 305

Voluntary Consent 306
Case: L&H Construction Co. v. Circle Redmont, Inc. (2011) 307
Adapting the Law to the Online Environment: Misrepresentation in Online Personals 309
Case: Fazio v. Cypress/GR Houston I, LP (2012) 311
The Statute of Frauds—Writing Requirement 313
Beyond Our Borders: The Statute of Frauds and International Sales Contracts 317
The Statute of Frauds—Sufficiency of the Writing 318
Case: Beneficial Homeowner Service Corp. v. Steele (2011) 319
The Parol Evidence Rule 320
Business Application: When E-Mails Become Enforceable Contracts 323

CHAPTER 13 Third Party Rights and Discharge 327

Assignments 328
Case: Hosch v. Colonial Pacific Leasing Corp. (2012) 329
Spotlight Case: Gold v. Ziff Communications Co. (2001) 332
Delegations 332

Third Party Beneficiaries 335
Contract Discharge 338
Case: *Pack 2000, Inc. v. Cushman (2011) 339*
Beyond Our Borders: *Impossibility or Impracticability of Performance in Germany 347*
Business Application: *Dealing with Third Party Rights 348*

CHAPTER 14 Breach and Remedies 352

Damages 353
Adapting the Law to the Online Environment: *The Effect of Breaching an Online Testing Service's Terms of Use 354*
Case: *Jamison Well Drilling, Inc. v. Pfeifer (2011) 355*
Landmark in the Law: *Hadley v. Baxendale (1854) 357*
Spotlight Case: *B-Sharp Musical Productions, Inc. v. Haber (2010) 359*
Equitable Remedies 359
Case: *Emerick v. Cardiac Study Center, Inc. (2012) 362*
Recovery Based on Quasi Contract 363
Contract Provisions Limiting Remedies 364
Business Application: *What Do You Do When You Cannot Perform? 366*
Appendix to Chapter 14: An Annotated Employment Contract 370

Unit 2—Business Case Study with Dissenting Opinion: *Braddock v. Braddock 376*

UNIT 3 Commercial Transactions 381

CHAPTER 15 The Formation of Sales and Lease Contracts 383

The Scope of the UCC and Articles 2 (Sales) and 2A (Leases) 384
Landmark in the Law: *The Uniform Commercial Code 385*
Adapting the Law to the Online Environment: *Local Governments Attempt to Tax Online Travel Companies 386*
The Formation of Sales and Lease Contracts 389
Case: *WPS, Inc. v. Expro Americas, LLC (2012) 393*
Classic Case: *Jones v. Star Credit Corp. (1969) 399*
Title and Risk of Loss 400
Case: *United States v. 2007 Custom Motorcycle (2011) 402*
Contracts for the International Sale of Goods 407
Business Application: *Who Bears the Risk of Loss—the Seller or the Buyer? 408*

CHAPTER 16 Performance and Breach of Sales and Lease Contracts 413

Performance Obligations 414
Obligations of the Seller or Lessor 414
Case: *Wilson Sporting Goods Co. v. U.S. Golf & Tennis Centers, Inc. (2012) 416*
Classic Case: *Maple Farms, Inc. v. City School District of Elmira (1974) 418*
Obligations of the Buyer or Lessee 421
Anticipatory Repudiation 422
Remedies of the Seller or Lessor 423
Remedies of the Buyer or Lessee 426
Beyond Our Borders: *The CISG's Approach to Revocation of Acceptance 429*
Spotlight Case: *Fitl v. Strek (2005) 430*
Limitation of Remedies 431
Business Application: *What Can You Do When a Contract Is Breached? 432*

CHAPTER 17 Warranties and Product Liability 437

Warranties 438
Classic Case: *Webster v. Blue Ship Tea Room, Inc. (1964) 440*
Lemon Laws 444
Product Liability 445
Landmark in the Law: *MacPherson v. Buick Motor Co. (1916) 446*
Strict Product Liability 446
Spotlight Case: *Bruesewitz v. Wyeth, LLC (2011) 447*
Beyond Our Borders: *Imposing Product Liability as Far Away as China 449*
Case: *Johnson v. Medtronic, Inc. (2012) 451*
Adapting the Law to the Online Environment: *The Supreme Court Takes a Stand on Warning Labels for Video Games 453*
Defenses to Product Liability 454

Linking Business Law to Corporate Management: Quality Control 457

CHAPTER 18 Negotiable Instruments: Transferability and Liability 462

Types of Instruments 463
Requirements for Negotiability 466
Case: Reger Development, LLC v. National City Bank (2010) 469
Spotlight Case: Las Vegas Sands, LLC v. Nehme (2011) 471
Transfer of Instruments 472
Beyond Our Borders: Severe Restrictions on Check Indorsements in France 474
Case: Hammett v. Deutsche Bank National Co. (2010) 475
Holder in Due Course (HDC) 477
Signature and Warranty Liability 481
Defenses, Limitations, and Discharge 485
Landmark in the Law: Federal Trade Commission Rule 433 487
Business Application: Pitfalls When Writing and Indorsing Checks 488

CHAPTER 19 Checks and Banking in the Digital Age 494

Checks 495
Case: MidAmerica Bank v. Charter One Bank (2009) 496
The Bank-Customer Relationship 497
Bank's Duty to Honor Checks 498
Case: Michigan Basic Property Insurance Association v. Washington (2012) 503
Bank's Duty to Accept Deposits 504
Landmark in the Law: Check Clearing in the 21st Century Act (Check 21) 506
Case: Cumis Mutual Insurance Society, Inc. v. Rosol (2011) 508
Electronic Fund Transfers 509
E-Money and Online Banking 511
Adapting the Law to the Online Environment: Smartphone-Based Payment Systems 512
Linking Business Law to Accounting and Finance: Banking in a Period of Crisis 513

CHAPTER 20 Secured Transactions 519

The Terminology of Secured Transactions 520
Creation of a Security Interest 520
Adapting the Law to the Online Environment: Secured Transactions Online 521
Perfection of a Security Interest 522
Case: In re Baker (2012) 525
Case: In re Camtech Precision Manufacturing, Inc. (2011) 527
The Scope of a Security Interest 529
Priorities 531
Case: Citizens National Bank of Jessamine County v. Washington Mutual Bank (2010) 532
Rights and Duties of Debtors and Creditors 533
Default 535

CHAPTER 21 Creditors' Rights and Bankruptcy 542

Laws Assisting Creditors 542
Spotlight Case: Wilson Court Limited Partnership v. Tony Maroni's, Inc. (1998) 546
Protection for Debtors 548
Bankruptcy Proceedings 549
Landmark in the Law: The Bankruptcy Reform Act of 2005 550
Adapting the Law to the Online Environment: Live Chatting with Your State's Bankruptcy Court 551
Chapter 7—Liquidation 551
Chapter 11—Reorganization 562
Bankruptcy Relief under Chapter 12 and Chapter 13 564
Case: Ransom v. FIA Card Services, N.A. (2011) 566
Case: United Student Aid Funds, Inc. v. Espinosa (2010) 567
Linking Business Law to Corporate Management: What Can You Do to Prepare for a Chapter 11 Reorganization? 569

CHAPTER 22 Mortgages and Foreclosures after the Recession 573

Mortgages 574
Law, Diversity, and Business: Managerial Implications Reverse Redlining in the Mortgage Market 574
Real Estate Financing Law 578
Case: In re Kitts (2011) 580
Foreclosures 581
Spotlight Case: McLean v. JPMorgan Chase Bank, N.A. (2012) 584
Case: Mitchell v. Valteau (2010) 586

Unit 3—Business Case Study with Dissenting Opinion: First Bank v. Fischer & Frichtel, Inc. 592

UNIT 4
Agency and Employment Law 595

CHAPTER 23 Agency Relationships in Business 597

Agency Relationships 598
How Agency Relationships Are Formed 601
Case: Laurel Creek Health Care Center v. Bishop (2010) 602
Duties of Agents and Principals 604
Agent's Authority 606
Adapting the Law to the Online Environment:
What Happens When an Agent Breaches Company Policy on the Use of Electronic Data? 608
Spotlight Case: Lundberg v. Church Farm, Inc. (1986) 609
Liability in Agency Relationships 610
Case: Williams v. Pike (2011) 611
Landmark in the Law:
The Doctrine of Respondeat Superior 614
Beyond Our Borders:
Islamic Law and Respondeat Superior 616
How Agency Relationships Are Terminated 616
Business Application:
How Can an Employer Use Independent Contractors? 619

CHAPTER 24 Employment, Immigration, and Labor Law 624

Employment at Will 625
Case: Waddell v. Boyce Thompson Institute for Plant Research, Inc. (2012) 626
Wages, Hours, and Layoffs 627
Beyond Our Borders: Brazil Requires Employers to Pay Overtime for Use of Smartphones after Work Hours 628
Family and Medical Leave 630
Worker Health and Safety 631
Income Security 632
Employee Privacy Rights 635
Adapting the Law to the Online Environment:
Social Media in the Workplace Come of Age 636
Case: National Aeronautics and Space Administration v. Nelson (2011) 638
Immigration Law 639
Labor Unions 642
Case: Local Joint Executive Board of Las Vegas v. National Labor Relations Board (2008) 645
Business Application:
How to Develop a Policy on Employee Use of the Internet and Social Media 649

CHAPTER 25 Employment Discrimination and Diversity 654

Title VII of the Civil Rights Act of 1964 655
Law, Diversity, and Business: Managerial Implications
Combating Appearance-Based Discrimination 656
Case: Morales-Cruz v. University of Puerto Rico (2012) 663
Beyond Our Borders:
Sexual Harassment in Other Nations 665
Discrimination Based on Age 665
Case: Mora v. Jackson Memorial Foundation, Inc. (2010) 666
Discrimination Based on Disability 667
Case: Rohr v. Salt River Project Agricultural Improvement and Power District (2009) 669
Defenses to Employment Discrimination 671
Affirmative Action 672
Linking Business Law to Corporate Management:
Human Resource Management 674

Unit 4—Business Case Study with Dissenting Opinion:
EEOC v. Greater Baltimore Medical Center, Inc. 678

UNIT 5
Business Organization 683

CHAPTER 26 Sole Proprietorships and Private Franchises 685

Sole Proprietorships 686
Adapting the Law to the Online Environment:
Can a Sole Proprietor Change His Name to Match His Domain Name? 686

Spotlight Case: *Garden City Boxing Club, Inc. v. Dominguez (2006)* 688

Franchises 689

Beyond Our Borders: *Franchising in Foreign Nations* 690

The Franchise Contract 692

Termination of the Franchise 694

Case: *Mac's Shell Service, Inc. v. Shell Oil Products Co. (2010)* 695

Case: *Holiday Inn Franchising, Inc. v. Hotel Associates, Inc. (2011)* 696

Business Application: *What Problems Can a Franchisee Anticipate?* 698

CHAPTER 27 All Forms of Partnership 702

Basic Partnership Concepts 703

Partnership Formation 705

Beyond Our Borders: *Doing Business with Foreign Partners* 705

Partnership Operation, Dissociation, and Termination 707

Classic Case: *Meinhard v. Salmon (1928)* 709

Case: *Russell Realty Associates v. Russell (2012)* 714

Limited Liability Partnerships 716

Limited Partnerships 717

Case: *Craton Capital, LP v. Natural Pork Production II, LLP (2011)* 720

CHAPTER 28 Limited Liability Companies and Special Business Forms 725

Landmark in the Law: *Limited Liability Company (LLC) Statutes* 726

Limited Liability Companies 726

Case: *ORX Resources, Inc. v. MBW Exploration, LLC (2010)* 728

LLC Operation and Management 730

Beyond Our Borders: *Limited Liability Companies in Other Nations* 731

Law, Diversity, and Business: Managerial Implications *Can a Person Who Is Not a Member of a Protected Class Sue for Discrimination?* 732

Case: *Polk v. Polk (2011)* 732

Dissociation and Dissolution of an LLC 733

Case: *Venture Sales, LLC v. Perkins (2012)* 734

Special Business Forms 736

Business Application: *How Do You Choose between an LLC and an LLP?* 739

CHAPTER 29 Corporate Formation, Merger, and Termination 743

Corporate Nature and Classification 744

Landmark in the Law: *Citizens United v. Federal Election Commission (2010)* 745

Case: *Rubin v. Murray (2011)* 749

Corporate Formation and Powers 750

Piercing the Corporate Veil 756

Case: *Brennan's, Inc. v. Colbert (2012)* 757

Corporate Financing 758

Adapting the Law to the Online Environment: *The New Era of Crowdfunding* 759

Mergers and Acquisitions 761

Case: *American Standard, Inc. v. OakFabco, Inc. (2010)* 765

Corporate Termination 766

Linking Business Law to Accounting and Finance: *Sources of Funds* 768

CHAPTER 30 Corporate Directors, Officers, and Shareholders 773

Directors and Officers 774

Duties and Liabilities of Directors and Officers 777

Adapting the Law to the Online Environment: *Software to Help Officers Spot Potential Embezzlers* 778

Case: *Henrichs v. Chugach Alaska Corp. (2011)* 779

Classic Case: *Guth v. Loft, Inc. (1939)* 780

Shareholders 782

Rights of Shareholders 786

Beyond Our Borders: *Derivative Actions in Other Nations* 789

Case: *McCann v. McCann (2012)* 790

Duties and Liabilities of Shareholders 791

Major Business Forms Compared 792

Business Application: *Creating a Retention Policy for E-Documents* 794

CHAPTER 31 Investor Protection, Insider Trading, and Corporate Governance 799

Landmark in the Law:
The Securities and Exchange Commission 800
Securities Act of 1933 800
Case: Litwin v. Blackstone Group, LP (2011) 807
Securities Exchange Act of 1934 808
Classic Case: Securities and Exchange Commission v. Texas Gulf Sulphur Co. (1968) 809
Spotlight Case: Dura Pharmaceuticals, Inc. v. Broudo (2005) 812
State Securities Laws 815
Corporate Governance 816
Beyond Our Borders:
Corporate Governance in Other Nations 817
Law, Diversity, and Business: Managerial Implications
The Worldwide Lack of Women on Boards of Directors 818
Online Securities Fraud 821
Unit 5—Business Case Study with Dissenting Opinion:
Notz v. Everett Smith Group, Ltd. 827

UNIT 6 Government Regulation 831

CHAPTER 32 Antitrust Law and Promoting Competition 833

The Sherman Antitrust Act 834
Landmark in the Law:
The Sherman Antitrust Act of 1890 835
Section 1 of the Sherman Act 836
Adapting the Law to the Online Environment:
The Justice Department Goes after E-Book Pricing 838
Section 2 of the Sherman Act 840
Case: E.I. DuPont de Nemours and Co. v. Kolon Industries, Inc. (2011) 841
Spotlight Case: Weyerhaeuser Co. v. Ross-Simmons Hardwood Lumber Co. (2007) 844
The Clayton Act 845
Enforcement and Exemptions 848
U.S. Antitrust Laws in the Global Context 850
Case: Carrier Corp. v. Outokumpu Oyj (2012) 850
Beyond Our Borders: The European Union's Expanding Role in Antitrust Litigation 851
Business Application:
How Can You Avoid Antitrust Problems? 852

CHAPTER 33 Consumer and Environmental Law 856

Consumer Law 857
Case: Hypertouch, Inc. v. ValueClick, Inc. (2011) 858
Adapting the Law to the Online Environment:
A Consumer Privacy Bill of Rights 862
Law, Diversity, and Business: Managerial Implications
How Should Airlines Deal with "Customers of Size"? 863
Environmental Law 868
Case: Natural Resources Defense Council, Inc. v. County of Los Angeles (2011) 872
Case: Sackett v. Environmental Protection Agency (2012) 873
Business Application:
The Proper Way to Use Credit Reporting Services 877

CHAPTER 34 Liability of Accountants and Other Professionals 882

Potential Common Law Liability to Clients 883
Landmark in the Law:
The SEC Adopts Global Accounting Rules 884
Case: Kelley v. Buckley (2011) 887
Case: Walsh v. State (2009) 888
Potential Liability to Third Parties 889
The Sarbanes-Oxley Act 891
Potential Statutory Liability of Accountants under Securities Laws 892
Spotlight Case: Overton v. Todman & Co., CPAs (2007) 895
Potential Criminal Liability 897
Confidentiality and Privilege 897
Unit 6—Business Case Study with Dissenting Opinion:
Department of Environmental Quality v. Worth Township 903

UNIT 7 Property and Its Protection 907

CHAPTER 35 Personal Property and Bailments 909

Property Ownership 910
Acquiring Ownership of Personal Property 911
Adapting the Law to the Online Environment: *The Exploding World of Virtual and Digital Property* 912
Case: Goodman v. Atwood (2011) 913
Classic Case: In re Estate of Piper (1984) 914
Mislaid, Lost, and Abandoned Property 916
Bailments 918
Case: Bridge Tower Dental, P.A. v. Meridian Computer Center, Inc. (2012) 922
Business Application: *What Should You Do with Lost Property?* 926

CHAPTER 36 Real Property and Landlord-Tenant Law 931

The Nature of Real Property 931
Ownership Interests in Real Property 933
Transfer of Ownership 936
Spotlight Case: Stambovsky v. Ackley (1991) 937
Case: Town of Midland v. Morris (2011) 941
Leasehold Estates 942
Landlord-Tenant Relationships 943

CHAPTER 37 Insurance, Wills, and Trusts 949

Insurance 950
Case: Valero v. Florida Insurance Guaranty Association, Inc. (2011) 954
Wills 956
Case: In re Estate of Johnson (2011) 959
Case: In re Estate of Melton (2012) 959
Adapting the Law to the Online Environment: *Social Media Estate Planning* 963
Trusts 965
Business Application: *How Can You Manage Risk in Cyberspace?* 970
Unit 7—Business Case Study with Dissenting Opinion: *Kovarik v. Kovarik* 976

APPENDICES

A How to Brief Cases and Analyze Case Problems A–1
B The Constitution of the United States A–3
C The Uniform Commercial Code (Excerpts) A–11
D The Sarbanes-Oxley Act (Excerpts and Explanatory Comments) A–131
E Answers to *Issue Spotters* A–138
F Answers to Even-Numbered *For Review* Questions A–144
G Sample Answers for *Questions with Sample Answer* A–152
H Sample Answers for *Case Problems with Sample Answer* A–158
I Case Excerpts for *Case Analysis Questions* A–165

Glossary G–1
Table of Cases TC–1
Index I–1

Preface to the Instructor

Today's business and legal environment is changing at a pace never before experienced. In many instances, technology is both driving and facilitating this change. The expanded use of the Internet for both business and personal transactions has led to new ways of doing business in the twenty-first century. Other factors that have affected the legal environment include the recent economic recession and our nation's ongoing struggle to regain financial stability, combat joblessness, and reduce the national debt.

In the midst of this evolving environment, however, one thing remains certain: For those entering the business world, an awareness of business law and the legal environment is critical. *Business Law Today,* Tenth Edition, provides the information your students need in an interesting and contemporary way. The Tenth Edition of *Business Law Today* continues its established tradition of being the most up-to-date text on the market.

I have spent a great deal of effort incorporating the latest legal developments and giving this book a visual appeal that will encourage students to learn the law. The law presented in *Business Law Today* includes new statutes, regulations, and cases, as well as recent developments in cyberlaw.

What's New in the Tenth Edition

Instructors have come to rely on the coverage, accuracy, and applicability of *Business Law Today.* To make sure that the text engages your students' interest, solidifies their understanding of the legal concepts presented, and provides the best teaching tools available, the following items are now offered either in the text or in conjunction with the text.

New *Spotlight Cases* and *Spotlight Case Problems*

For the Tenth Edition of *Business Law Today,* certain cases and case problems have been carefully chosen to spotlight as good teaching cases. ***Spotlight Cases*** **and** ***Spotlight Case Problems*** are labeled either by the name of one of the parties or by the subject involved. Some examples include *Spotlight on Amazon, Spotlight on Apple, Spotlight on the Seattle Mariners, Spotlight on Commercial Speech,* and *Spotlight on Internet Porn.*

Instructors will find these *Spotlight Cases* useful to illustrate the legal concepts under discussion, and students will enjoy studying these cases because they involve interesting and memorable facts.

Suggested answers to all case-ending questions and case problems are included in both the *Instructor's Manual* and the *Answers Manual* for this text.

New Focus on Diversity

This Tenth Edition of *Business Law Today* recognizes the tremendous impact of diversity on the business world and legal environment today. Therefore, the text includes a special new feature entitled ***Law, Diversity, and Business: Managerial Implications*** that emphasizes diversity issues. These features address important topics such as marriage equality laws, appearance-discrimination legislation, and discriminatory mortgage lending. The new *Law, Diversity, and Business: Managerial Implications* features include the following:

- *Derogatory Trademarks* (Chapter 5)
- *Native Americans and Criminal Justice* (Chapter 6)
- *The Worldwide Lack of Women on Boards of Directors* (Chapter 31)
- *How Should Airlines Deal with "Customers of Size"?* (Chapter 33)

New *Appendix to Chapter 14* Focuses on Reading and Analyzing Contracts

Because reading and analyzing contracts is such a crucial skill for businesspersons, **a special new Appendix to Chapter 14** has been added. This appendix follows the last contracts chapter and explains how to read and analyze a contract. Then, it presents an example of an employee noncompetition and nondisclosure agreement. The sample contract is annotated so that students can quickly see what each contract provision means.

New *Debate This* Feature

To encourage student participation and motivate students to think critically about the rationale underlying the law on a particular topic, a new feature has been created for the Tenth Edition. Entitled *Debate This,* it consists of a brief statement or question concerning the chapter material that can be used to spur lively classroom or small group discussions. It can also be used as a written assignment. This feature follows the *Reviewing* feature (discussed shortly) at the end of each chapter. **Suggested pro and con responses to the *Debate This* features can be found in both the *Instructor's Manual* and the *Answers Manual* for this text.**

New Cases and Case Problems

The Tenth Edition of *Business Law Today* is filled with new cases and case problems. Nearly every chapter features at least one new case and new case problem from 2011 and 2012. Many chapters include two recent case summaries and problems. That means more than 75 percent of the cases are new to this edition.

The new cases have been carefully selected based on these criteria: (1) they illustrate important points of law, (2) they are of high interest to students and instructors, and (3) they are simple enough factually for business law students to understand. I have made it a point to find recent cases that enhance learning. I have also eliminated cases that are too difficult procedurally or factually.

New *Group Projects*

For instructors who want to have their classes perform group projects, each chapter of the Tenth Edition includes a **new *Business Law Critical Thinking Group Assignment.*** Each project begins by describing a business scenario and then requires each group of students to answer a specific question pertaining to the scenario based on the information that they learned in the chapter. These projects may be used in class to spur discussion or as homework assignments.

I have also created **a new *Group Project*** for the end of every unit. These projects require students, as a group, to apply the concepts they learned in the previous chapters. These projects can be useful for reviewing materials in class prior to a test. **Suggested answers to all group assignments are included in both the *Instructor's Manual* and the *Answers Manual* for this text.**

A New Chapter on *Mortgages and Foreclosures after the Recession*

The Tenth Edition includes an entirely new chapter (Chapter 22) entitled ***Mortgages and Foreclosures after the Recession.*** This chapter examines some of the mortgage-lending practices that contributed to the Great Recession that began in 2008 and discusses the legal reforms enacted in response to it.

New Coverage of Current Significant Topics

To pique student interest from the outset, many chapters in the Tenth Edition open with the latest news related to important legal topics. For example:

- Chapter 2 covers the constitutional challenge to the Obama administration's Patient Protection and Affordable Care Act and the United States Supreme Court's 2012 decision in that matter.
- Chapter 5 discusses the patent infringement lawsuit that Apple, Inc., filed against Samsung for allegedly imitating the iPhone and iPad too closely.
- Chapter 24 mentions the United States Supreme Court's 2012 decision on the extent to which federal law preempts the states from enacting immigration legislation.

Coverage of the latest developments in the topics under discussion is a priority throughout the text.

Practical and Effective Learning Tools

Today's business leaders must often think "outside the box" when making business decisions. For this reason, I have included numerous critical-thinking elements in the Tenth Edition that are designed to challenge students' understanding of the materials beyond simple retention. I have also retained, improved, and streamlined the many practical features of this text to help students learn how the law applies to business.

Highlighted and Numbered *Case Examples*

One of the most appreciated features of *Business Law Today* has always been the highlighted numbered examples that appear throughout the book to illustrate the legal principles under discussion. Further, many instructors use cases to illustrate how the law applies to business. For this reason, the in-text numbered examples have been expanded to include ***Case Examples.***

These *Case Examples* are integrated appropriately throughout the text and present the facts, issues, and rulings from actual court cases. These are especially useful to simplify difficult areas of law. Students can read through the case examples and quickly see how courts apply the legal principles under discussion in the real world.

Linking Business Law to . . . Feature

The Tenth Edition of *Business Law Today* also includes a **special feature entitled *Linking Business Law to* . . . [one of the six functional fields of business].** As will be discussed in Chapter 1, the six functional fields of business are *corporate management, production and transportation, marketing, research and development, accounting and finance,* and *human resources management.*

This feature appears in selected chapters to underscore how the law relates to other fields of business. Some of the new *Linking Business Law to . . .* features include:

- *Linking Business Law to Marketing*—Trademarks and Service Marks (Chapter 5)
- *Linking Business Law to Corporate Management*—Quality Control (Chapter 17)
- *Linking Business Law to Corporate Management*—What Can You Do to Prepare for a Chapter 11 Reorganization? (Chapter 21)
- *Linking Business Law to Accounting and Finance*—Sources of Funds (Chapter 29)

Business Application

Many chapters end with a ***Business Application* feature** that focuses on practical considerations related to the chapter's contents. This feature concludes with a **checklist** of tips for the businessperson. For example, these topics include the following:

- *Protecting Your Company against Hacking of Your Bank Accounts* (Chapter 6)
- *How to Choose and Use a Lawyer* (Chapter 8)
- *What Can You Do When a Contract Is Breached?* (Chapter 16)
- *How to Develop a Policy on Employee Use of the Internet and Social Media* (Chapter 24)

Preventing Legal Disputes

The Tenth Edition of *Business Law Today* continues the emphasis on providing practical information in every chapter through a special feature entitled ***Preventing Legal Disputes.*** These brief, integrated sections offer sensible guidance on steps that businesspersons can take in their daily transactions to avoid legal disputes and litigation in a particular area.

Adapting the Law to the Online Environment

The Tenth Edition contains many new ***Adapting the Law to the Online Environment*** features, which examine cutting-edge cyberlaw issues coming before today's courts. Here are some examples of these features:

- *Vulgar Facebook Photos Receive First Amendment Protection* (Chapter 2)
- *The Validity of E-Signatures for Online Colleges and Universities* (Chapter 10)
- *The Supreme Court Takes a Stand on Warning Labels for Video Games* (Chapter 17)
- *Live Chatting with Your State's Bankruptcy Court* (Chapter 21)
- *Social Media in the Workplace Come of Age* (Chapter 24)
- *The New Era of Crowdfunding* (Chapter 29)
- *The Justice Department Goes after E-Book Pricing* (Chapter 32)

Each feature concludes with a *Critical Thinking* question that asks the student to analyze some facet of the issues discussed in the feature. **Suggested answers to these questions are included in both the *Instructor's Manual* and the *Answers Manual* for this text.**

Summarized Case Presentation

Each case is presented in a certain format, which begins with the case title and citation (including parallel citations). Whenever possible, a URL that can be used to access the case online appears just below the case citation (a footnote to the URL explains how to find the specific case at that Web site). I then briefly outline the facts of the dispute, the legal issue presented, and the court's decision.

To enhance student understanding, I paraphrase the reason for the court's decision and provide bracketed explanations for any unfamiliar terms. Each case concludes with a question, which may include a *Critical Thinking, What If the Facts Were Different?* or *Why Is This Case Important?* question. *Classic Cases* include a special section entitled *Impact of This Case on Today's Law* to clarify the relevance of the case to modern law. **Suggested answers to all case-ending questions are included in both the *Instructor's Manual* and the *Answers Manual* for this text.**

Critical-Thinking and Legal Reasoning Elements

The chapter-ending materials include a separate section of questions that focus on critical thinking and writing. This section includes the *Business Law Critical Thinking Group Assignment* (discussed previously) and may also include one or more of the following:

- ***Critical Legal Thinking*** questions require students to think critically about some aspect of the law discussed in the chapter.
- ***Business Law Writing*** questions require students to compose a written response to a business-oriented critical-thinking question.

- ***Case Analysis Questions*** are sometimes included to improve students' ability to analyze cases and perform legal reasoning. Students read through a case excerpt that is provided in *Appendix I* at the end of this text, brief the case, and then answer a series of questions relating to the case.

Reviewing . . . Features

Each chapter in this text ends with a ***Reviewing . . .* feature** that helps solidify students' understanding of the chapter materials. Each of these features presents a hypothetical scenario and then asks a series of questions that require students to identify the issues and apply the legal concepts discussed in the chapter. The questions are intended to help students review the chapter materials in a simple and interesting way.

An instructor can use this feature as the basis for a lively in-class discussion or can encourage students to use it for self-study and assessment prior to completing homework assignments.

ExamPrep Sections

Following the chapter summary in every chapter is an ***ExamPrep* section that includes two *Issue Spotters* related to the chapter's topics** that facilitate student learning and review of the chapter materials. For this edition, the answers to the *Issue Spotters* are provided in *Appendix E* at the end of this text.

Beyond Our Borders

The ***Beyond Our Borders*** feature gives students an awareness of the global legal environment by indicating how international laws or the laws of other nations deal with specific legal concepts or topics being discussed in the chapter. This feature always concludes with a *Critical Thinking* question. **Suggested answers to these questions are included in both the *Instructor's Manual* and the *Answers Manual* for this text.**

Landmark in the Law

The ***Landmark in the Law*** feature discusses a landmark case, statute, or other legal development that has had a significant effect on business law. Each of these features has a section titled ***Application to Today's World,*** which indicates how the law discussed in the feature affects the legal landscape of today's world.

Sample Answers

Each chapter includes a ***Question with Sample Answer*** that is answered in *Appendix G* and a ***Case Problem with Sample Answer*** that is based on an actual case and answered in *Appendix H.* Students can compare their own answers to the answers provided to determine whether they have applied the law correctly and to learn what needs to be included when answering the end-of-chapter *Business Scenarios and Case Problems.*

Ethical Issues

In addition to a full chapter on ethics, chapter-ending ethical questions, and the ***Ethical Considerations*** in many of the *Critical Thinking* questions in the cases, this text includes a feature called ***Ethical Issues.*** This feature, which is closely integrated with the text, opens with a question addressing an ethical dimension of the topic being discussed. The feature is designed to make sure that students understand that ethics is an integral part of a business law course.

Business Law Today on the Web

The Web site for the Tenth Edition of *Business Law Today* can be found by going to www.cengagebrain.com and entering ISBN 9781133273561. The Web site offers a broad array of teaching/learning resources, including the following:

- ***Practice quizzes*** for every chapter in this text.
- ***Appendix A: How to Brief Cases and Analyze Case Problems***
- ***Legal reference materials*** including a "Statutes" page that offers links to the full text of selected statutes referenced in the text, a Spanish glossary, and other important legal resources.
- ***CourseMate*** access can also be purchased by the students, where they will find additional study tools, such as an e-Book, additional quizzes, flashcards, key terms, and PowerPoint slides.

Other Pedagogical Devices within Each Chapter

- ***Learning Objectives*** (a series of brief questions at the beginning of each chapter provide a framework for the student as he or she reads through the chapter). *For this edition, to facilitate learning, I repeat the Learning Objective question in the margin adjacent to where the question is answered in the text.*
- ***Chapter Outline*** (an outline of the chapter's first-level headings).
- ***Margin definitions.***
- ***Margin Quotations.***
- ***Exhibits.***
- ***Photographs (often with critical-thinking questions) and cartoons.***

Chapter-Ending Pedagogy

- ***Reviewing . . .* feature** (in every chapter).
- ***Debate This*** (in every chapter).
- ***Key Terms*** (with appropriate page references).
- ***Chapter Summary*** (in table format with page references).
- ***ExamPrep*** (including two *Issue Spotters* for each chapter that are answered in *Appendix E*).
- ***For Review*** (the questions set forth in the chapter-opening *Learning Objectives* section are presented again to aid students in reviewing the chapter. For this edition, answers to the even-numbered questions for each chapter are provided in Appendix F.).
- ***Business Scenarios and Case Problems*** (every chapter includes a *Question with Sample Answer* (answered in *Appendix G*), a *Case Problem with Sample Answer* (answered in *Appendix H*), *A Question of Ethics*, and a *Business Law Critical Thinking Group Assignment*. Selected chapters also include a *Spotlight Case Problem*.)

Unit-Ending Pedagogy

Each of the seven units in the Tenth Edition of *Business Law Today* concludes with the following features:

- ***Business Case Study with Dissenting Opinion***—This feature focuses on a court case that relates to a topic covered in the unit. It opens with an introductory section, discusses the case background and significance, and then provides excerpts from the court's majority opinion and from a dissenting opinion as well. The case study portion ends with *Questions for Analysis*—a series of questions that prompt the student to think critically about the legal, ethical, economic, international, or general business implications of the case.

- ***Business Scenario***—This feature presents a hypothetical business situation and then asks a series of questions about how the law applies to various actions taken by the firm. To answer the questions, the student must apply the laws discussed throughout the unit.
- ***Group Project***—The final portion of the unit-ending pedagogy is the new *Group Project* that was discussed earlier in this preface.

Suggested answers to all unit-ending questions are included in both the *Instructor's Manual* and the *Answers Manual* for this text.

Supplemental Teaching Materials

This edition of *Business Law Today* is accompanied by an expansive number of teaching and learning supplements, which are available on the *Instructor's Resource CD-ROM,* or IRCD, as well as on the password-protected portion of the companion Web site. Individually and in conjunction with a number of colleagues, I have developed supplementary teaching materials that I believe are the best available today. The many components of the supplements package are listed below.

Instructor's Resource CD-ROM (IRCD)

The IRCD includes the following supplements:

- ***Instructor's Manual*** (includes at least one **additional case on point** per chapter, answers to all *Critical Thinking* questions, *Reviewing* features, *Business Law Critical Thinking Group Assignments, Business Case Studies with Dissenting Opinions, Business Scenarios,* and *Group Projects*).
- ***Answers Manual*** (includes answers to all the *Business Scenarios and Case Problems, Critical Thinking* questions, and unit-ending questions in the text, and ***Alternate Problem Sets with Answers***).
- A comprehensive ***Test Bank.***
- **Case-Problem Cases.**
- **Case Printouts.**
- **ExamView.**
- **PowerPoint slides.**
- *Instructor's Manual* for the *Drama of the Law* video series.
- *Handbook of Landmark Cases and Statutes in Business Law and the Legal Environment.*
- *Handbook on Critical Thinking in Business Law and the Legal Environment.*
- *A Guide to Personal Law.*

Software, Video, and Multimedia Supplements

- ***Business Law Digital Video Library***—Provides access to ninety videos that spark class discussion and clarify core legal concepts. Access is available as an optional package with each new text at no additional cost. You can access the *Business Law Digital Video Library,* along with corresponding *Video Questions,* at **login.cengage.com**.
- **Westlaw®**—Ten free hours on Westlaw are available to qualified adopters.
- ***CengageNOW*** for *Business Law Today* (at an additional cost)—Arguably the most comprehensive online learning and assessment tool for business law and the legal environment on the market today. For more information, contact your South-Western/Cengage Learning Sales Representative. For a demo of this complete online learning system, go to **www.cengage.com/now**.

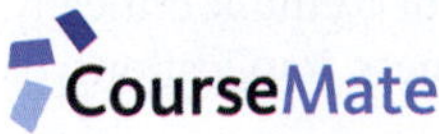

- ***CourseMate***—Brings business law concepts to life with interactive learning, study, and exam preparation tools that support this printed textbook. Built-in engagement tracking tools allow you to assess your students' study activities. Additionally, *CourseMate* includes an interactive e-Book, which contains the entire contents of this printed textbook enhanced by the many advantages of a digital environment.

For Users of the Ninth Edition

I thought that those of you who have been using *Business Law Today* would like to know some of the major changes that have been made for the Tenth Edition.

New Features and Special Pedagogy

I have added the following entirely new elements for the Tenth Edition:

- *Law, Diversity, and Business: Managerial Implications* feature in selected chapters.
- *Spotlight Cases* and *Spotlight Case Problems* in selected chapters.
- An *Appendix to Chapter 14* on reading and analyzing contracts.
- A *Debate This* feature in every chapter.
- A *Business Law Critical Thinking Group Assignment* in every chapter.
- A *Group Project* at the end of each unit.
- *Appendix E* (Answers to the *Issue Spotters*), *Appendix F* (Answers to Even-Numbered *For Review* Questions), and *Appendix H* (Sample Answers for *Case Problems with Sample Answer*).

Significantly Revised Chapters

Every chapter of the Tenth Edition has been revised as necessary to incorporate new developments in the law, and to simplify or streamline the presentations. Other major changes and additions made for this edition include the following:

- **Chapter 2 (Constitutional Law)**—This chapter has been thoroughly updated and revised. It opens with a discussion of the constitutional issue raised by the Obama administration's Patient Protection and Affordable Care Act and considers how the United States Supreme Court's decision in the matter will affect business. The privacy concerns raised by social networking Web sites are also discussed. A feature addresses First Amendment rights and postings on Facebook, and another feature examines the legal issues presented by same-sex marriage and marriage equality laws.
- **Chapter 5 (Intellectual Property and Internet Law)**—The materials on intellectual property rights have been thoroughly revised and updated. The chapter incorporates the major changes to patent law made by the America Invents Act, which make the first person to file for a patent application the holder. A new subsection addresses patent infringement lawsuits and high-tech companies, and the suit filed by Apple, Inc., against Samsung over iPhones, iPads, and Android software is discussed. Coverage of domain names and cybersquatting has been updated. Numerous updates and new examples have been added to illustrate how intellectual property laws apply in the digital world. A *Spotlight on Internet Porn* case covers trademark dilution by a porn site using a toymaker's domain name. There is also a discussion of the 2012 United States Supreme Court decision addressing Congress's authority to restore copyright protection to foreign works that were already in the public domain. A *Beyond Our Borders* feature outlines the provisions of a new international treaty to combat global counterfeiting and piracy.
- **Chapter 6 (Criminal Law and Cyber Crime)**—This chapter has been substantially revised to deal with the growing problem of cyber crime, including many types of Internet fraud, identity theft, phishing, and hacking. It also covers some of the difficulties involved in prosecuting cyber crime. The chapter incorporates recent United States Supreme Court decisions on whether police can attach a GPS tracking device to a suspect's vehicle and whether police

officers can be held personally liable for performing an illegal search. New features examine whether a person can be prosecuted for posting fake photos on Facebook and provide guidance on how businesspersons can prevent their bank accounts from being hacked.

- **Chapters 9 through 14 (the Contracts unit)**—The discussion of online contracting and electronic signatures has been merged with the coverage of traditional contracts. More examples, case examples, updates throughout, and streamlined coverage have been added. Numerous *Spotlight Cases* have been added to this unit, including *Spotlight on Amazon, Spotlight on Columbia Pictures, Spotlight on the Improv,* and *Spotlight on PC Magazine.*
- **Chapters 15 through 22 (the Commercial Transactions unit)**—This entire unit deals with commercial transactions and aspects of the Uniform Commercial Code, including sales and lease law, negotiable instruments, banking, secured transactions, and bankruptcy. This edition includes an entirely new chapter on Mortgages and Foreclosures after the Recession (Chapter 22). Chapter 22 provides a timely look at the mortgage crisis, predatory lending practices, and the laws enacted to address some of the problems that became evident during the recession.
- **Chapter 24 (Employment, Immigration, and Labor Law)**—This chapter has been thoroughly revised and updated to include discussions of legal issues facing employers today. A feature covers the use of social media in the workplace, and another feature explains how to develop policies on social media and Internet use. The chapter includes a section on immigration law, a topic of increasing importance to employers, and discusses the United States Supreme Court's decision on whether federal law preempts state immigration laws. The chapter also includes an updated discussion of the Family and Medical Leave Act, employee privacy rights and electronic monitoring of employees—including social media communications—drug testing, rights of union workers, strikes, and lockouts (such as the recent NFL and NBA lockouts).
- **Chapter 25 (Employment Discrimination and Diversity)**—The chapter covering employment discrimination has been significantly updated and now emphasizes diversity. A feature was added on combating appearance-based discrimination. The materials on sexual harassment and retaliation have been revised to incorporate recent case law.
- **Chapters 26 through 31 (the Business Organizations unit)**—This unit has been reworked to simplify and streamline the presentation of the materials and to focus on diversity. Features address whether a person who is not a member of a protected class can sue for discrimination (Chapter 28) and why so few women are included on corporate boards of directors (Chapter 31). Chapter 29 includes a new feature on crowdfunding and a *new Landmark in the Law* feature on the *Citizens United* case. Chapter 30 features cover shareholder access rules and software designed to help corporate officers spot potential embezzlers. Chapter 31 has been substantially reworked to simplify complex materials into basic concepts. The materials on insider trading, Ponzi schemes, and fraud have been updated, new examples have been added, and a new *Spotlight Case* focuses on securities fraud.
- **Chapter 32 (Antitrust Law and Promoting Competition)**—The materials in this chapter have been reworked to focus on overriding principles of antitrust law and provide concrete information. The chapter includes updated figures on interlocking directorates and an updated discussion of global antitrust law. Features cover the Justice Department's concern about pricing of e-books for Kindles and iPads, and whether cable and other TV programmers violate the Sherman Act by bundling services. A *Spotlight Case on the Weyerhaeuser Company* was added.
- **Chapter 33 (Consumer and Environmental Law)**—The chapter has been thoroughly updated and incorporates recent changes to menu labeling requirements, the recent health-care reforms, and new federal credit-card rules. New features have been added on how airlines deal with "customers of size," the new Consumer Privacy Bill of Rights, and the proper way to use credit reporting services.

- **Chapters 35 through 37 (the Property and Its Protection unit)**—These three chapters have been updated to deal with issues surrounding virtual and digital property and social media estate planning. A *Spotlight on Haunted Houses* case appears in Chapter 36.

Acknowledgments

Numerous careful and conscientious users of *Business Law Today* were kind enough to help me revise the book. In addition, the staff at South-Western/Cengage Learning went out of their way to make sure that this edition came out early and in accurate form. In particular, I wish to thank Rob Dewey and Vicky True-Baker for their countless new ideas, many of which have been incorporated into the Tenth Edition. I also extend special thanks to Jan Lamar, my longtime developmental editor, for her many useful suggestions and for her efforts in coordinating reviews and ensuring the timely and accurate publication of all supplemental materials. I am particularly indebted to Lisa Lysne for her support and excellent marketing advice.

My production manager and designer, Bill Stryker, made sure that I came out with an error-free, visually attractive edition. I will always be in his debt. I thank my photo researcher, Ann Hoffman, for providing an amazingly varied number of choices of photographs for this edition. I am also indebted to the staff at Parkwood Composition, the compositor. Their ability to generate the pages for this text quickly and accurately made it possible for me to meet my ambitious printing schedule.

I must especially thank Katherine Marie Silsbee for her management of the project, as well as for the application of her superb research and editorial skills. I also wish to thank William Eric Hollowell, coauthor of the *Instructor's Manual, Study Guide,* and *Test Bank,* for his excellent research efforts. The copyediting services of Pat Lewis were invaluable, and the proofreading by Maggie Jarpey and Sue Bradley will not go unnoticed. I thank, too, Lavina Leed Miller, for her indexing expertise. I also thank Vickie Reierson and Roxanna Lee for their proofreading and other assistance, which helped to ensure an error-free text. Finally, my appreciation goes to Suzanne Jasin for her many special efforts on the projects.

Acknowledgments for Previous Editions

John J. Balek
Morton College, Illinois

John Jay Ballantine
University of Colorado, Boulder

Lorraine K. Bannai
Western Washington University

Marlene E. Barken
Ithaca College, New York

Daryl Barton
Eastern Michigan University

Denise A. Bartles
Missouri Western State University

Merlin Bauer
Mid State Technical College, Wisconsin

Donna E. Becker
Frederick Community College, Maryland

Richard J. Bennet
Three Rivers Community College, Connecticut

Anne Berre
Schreiner University, Texas

Brad Botz
Garden City Community College, Kansas

Teresa Brady
Holy Family College, Philadelphia

Lee B. Burgunder
California Polytechnic University—San Luis Obispo

Bradley D. Childs
Belmont University, Tennessee

Dale Clark
Corning Community College, New York

Peter Clapp
St. Mary's College, Moraga, California

Tammy W. Cowart
University of Texas, Tyler

Stanley J. Dabrowski
Hudson County Community College, New Jersey

Sandra J. Defebaugh
Eastern Michigan University

Patricia L. DeFrain
Glendale College, California

Julia G. Derrick
Brevard Community College, Florida

Joe D. Dillsaver
Northeastern State University, Oklahoma

Claude W. Dotson
Northwest College, Wyoming

Larry R. Edwards
Tarrant County Junior College, South Campus, Texas

Jacolin Eichelberger
Hillsborough Community College, Florida

George E. Eigsti
Kansas City, Kansas, Community College

Florence E. Elliott-Howard
Stephen F. Austin State University, Texas

Tony Enerva
Lakeland Community College, Ohio

Benjamin C. Fassberg
Prince George's Community College, Maryland

Jerry Furniss
University of Montana

Elizabeth J. Guerriero
Northeast Louisiana University

Phil Harmeson
University of South Dakota

Nancy L. Hart
Midland College, Texas

Janine S. Hiller
Virginia Polytechnic Institute & State University

Karen A. Holmes
Hudson Valley Community College, New York

Fred Ittner
College of Alameda, California

Susan S. Jarvis
University of Texas, Pan American

Jack E. Karns
East Carolina University, North Carolina

Sarah Weiner Keidan
Oakland Community College, Michigan

Richard N. Kleeberg
Solano Community College, California

Bradley T. Lutz
Hillsborough Community College, Florida

Darlene Mallick
Anne Arundel Community College, Maryland

John D. Mallonee
Manatee Community College, Florida

Joseph D. Marcus
Prince George's Community College, Maryland

Woodrow J. Maxwell
Hudson Valley Community College, New York

Beverly McCormick
Morehead State University, Kentucky

William J. McDevitt
Saint Joseph's University, Pennsylvania

John W. McGee
Aims Community College, Colorado

James K. Miersma
Milwaukee Area Technical Institute, Wisconsin

Susan J. Mitchell
Des Moines Area Community College, Iowa

Jim Lee Morgan
West Los Angeles College, California

Jack K. Morton
University of Montana

Solange North
Fox Valley Technical Institute, Wisconsin

Jamie L. O'Brien
South Dakota State University

Ruth R. O'Keefe
Jacksonville University, Florida

Robert H. Orr
Florida Community College at Jacksonville

George Otto
Truman College, Illinois

Thomas L. Palmer
Northern Arizona University
David W. Pan
University of Tulsa, Oklahoma
Victor C. Parker, Jr.
North Georgia College and State University
Donald L. Petote
Genessee Community College, New York
Francis D. Polk
Ocean County College, New Jersey
Gregory Rabb
Jamestown Community College, New York
Brad Reid
Abilene Christian University, Texas
Anne Montgomery Ricketts
University of Findlay, Ohio
Donald A. Roark
University of West Florida
Hugh Rode
Utah Valley State College
Dr. William J. Russell
Northwest Nazarene University, Idaho
William M. Rutledge
Macomb Community College, Michigan
Martha Wright Sartoris
North Hennepin Community College, Minnesota
Anne W. Schacherl
Madison Area Technical College, Wisconsin
Edward F. Shafer
Rochester Community College, Minnesota
Lance Shoemaker
West Valley College, California
Lou Ann Simpson
Drake University, Iowa
Denise Smith
Missouri Western State College
Hugh M. Spall
Central Washington University
Catherine A. Stevens
College of Southern Maryland
Maurice Tonissi
Quinsigamond Community College, Massachusetts
James D. Van Tassel
Mission College, California
Russell A. Waldon
College of the Canyons, California
Frederick J. Walsh
Franklin Pierce College, New Hampshire
James E. Walsh, Jr.
Tidewater Community College, Virginia
Randy Waterman
Richland College, Texas
Jerry Wegman
University of Idaho
Edward L. Welsh, Jr.
Phoenix College, Arizona
Clark W. Wheeler
Santa Fe Community College, Florida
Lori Whisenant
University of Houston, Texas
Kay O. Wilburn
The University of Alabama at Birmingham
John G. Williams
Northwestern State University, Louisiana
James L. Wittenbach
University of Notre Dame, Indiana
Joseph Zavaglia, Jr.
Brookdale Community College, New Jersey

I also wish to extend special thanks to the following individuals for their valuable input for the new Chapter 22 and for helping revise Chapter 36:

Robert C. Bird
University of Connecticut
Dean Bredeson
University of Texas at Austin
Corey Ciocchetti
University of Denver
Thomas D. Cavenagh
North Central College, Illinois
Joan Gabel
Florida State University
Eric D. Yordy
Northern Arizona University

Acknowledgments for the Tenth Edition

John Jay Ballantine
University of Colorado, Boulder

Laura Barnard
Lakeland Community College, Ohio

Bonnie S. Bolinger
Ivy Tech Community College, Wabash Valley Region, Indiana

Sandra Defebaugh
Eastern Michigan University

Joseph L. Flack
Washtenaw Community College, Michigan

Mo Hassan
Cabrillo College, California

Andy E. Hendrick
Coastal Carolina University, South Carolina

Diane MacDonald
Pacific Lutheran University, Washington

Susan Mitchell
Des Moines Area Community College, Iowa

Annie Laurie I. Myers
Northampton Community College, Pennsylvania

Jamie L. O'Brien
South Dakota State University

Gerald M. Rogers
Front Range Community College, Colorado

I know that I am not perfect. If you or your students find something you don't like or want me to change, use the "Contact Us" button on this text's Web site. In the alternative, pass along your thoughts to your South-Western/Cengage Learning sales representative. Your comments will help us make *Business Law Today* an even better book in the future.

Roger LeRoy Miller

Dedication

To Debbie and Gary,
Great friends and partners are rare.

R.L.M.

UNIT 1

(BackyardProduction/iStockphoto.com)

The Legal Environment of Business

UNIT CONTENTS

1. The Legal Environment
2. Constitutional Law
3. Courts and Alternative Dispute Resolution
4. Torts and Cyber Torts
5. Intellectual Property and Internet Law
6. Criminal Law and Cyber Crime
7. Ethics and Business Decision Making
8. International Law in a Global Economy

CHAPTER 1

(JustASC/Shutterstock.com)

The Legal Environment

CHAPTER OUTLINE

- Business Activities and the Legal Environment
- Sources of American Law
- The Common Law Tradition
- Classifications of Law

LEARNING OBJECTIVES

The five learning objectives below are designed to help improve your understanding of the chapter. After reading this chapter, you should be able to answer the following questions:

1. What are four primary sources of law in the United States?
2. What is the common law tradition?
3. What is a precedent? When might a court depart from precedent?
4. What is the difference between remedies at law and remedies in equity?
5. What are some important differences between civil law and criminal law?

"Laws should be like clothes.
They should be made to fit the people they are meant to serve."
—Clarence Darrow, 1857–1938 (American lawyer)

In the chapter-opening quotation, Clarence Darrow asserts that law should be created to serve the public. As you are part of that public, the law is important to you. Those entering the world of business will find themselves subject to numerous laws and government regulations. A basic knowledge of these laws and regulations is beneficial—if not essential—to anyone contemplating a successful career in today's business environment.

Law A body of enforceable rules governing relationships among individuals and between individuals and their society.

Although the law has various definitions, they all are based on the general observation that **law** consists of *enforceable rules governing relationships among individuals and between individuals and their society.* In some societies, these enforceable rules consist of unwritten principles of behavior, while in other societies they are set forth in ancient or contemporary law codes. In the United States, our rules consist of written laws and court decisions created by modern legislative and judicial bodies. Regardless of how such rules are created, they all have one feature in common: *they establish rights, duties, and privileges that are consistent with the values and beliefs of a society or its ruling group.*

In this introductory chapter, we look first at an important question for any student reading this text: How do business law and the legal environment affect business decision making? Next, we describe the basic sources of American law, the common law tradition, and some schools of legal thought. We conclude the chapter with a discussion of some general classifications of law.

Business Activities and the Legal Environment

As those entering the business world will learn, laws and government regulations affect all business activities—hiring and firing decisions, workplace safety, the manufacturing and marketing of products, and business financing, to name just a few. To make good business decisions, a basic understanding of the laws and regulations governing these activities is essential. Moreover, in today's setting, simply being aware of what conduct can lead to legal liability is not enough. Businesspersons must develop critical thinking and legal reasoning skills so that they can evaluate how various laws might apply to a given situation and determine the potential result of their course of action. Businesspersons are also under increasing pressure to make ethical decisions and to consider the consequences of their decisions for stockholders and employees (as will be discussed in Chapter 7).

Many Different Laws May Affect a Single Business Transaction

As you will note, each chapter in this text covers a specific area of the law and shows how the legal rules in that area affect business activities. Although compartmentalizing the law in this fashion facilitates learning, it does not indicate the extent to which many different laws may apply to just one transaction. This is where the critical thinking skills that you will learn throughout this book become important. You need to be able to identify the various legal issues, apply the laws that you learn about, and arrive at a conclusion on the best course of action.

EXAMPLE 1.1 Suppose that you are the president of NetSys, Inc., a company that creates and maintains computer network systems for other business firms. NetSys also markets software for internal computer networks. One day, Janet Hernandez, an operations officer for Southwest Distribution Corporation (SDC), contacts you by e-mail about a possible contract involving SDC's computer network. In deciding whether to enter into a contract with SDC, you need to consider, among other things, the legal requirements for an enforceable contract. Are the requirements different for a contract for services and a contract for products? What are your options if SDC **breaches** (breaks, or fails to perform) the contract? The answers to these questions are part of contract law and sales law.

Breach The failure to perform a legal obligation.

Other questions might concern payment under the contract. How can you guarantee that NetSys will be paid? For example, if SDC pays with a check that is returned for insufficient funds, what are your options? Answers to these questions can be found in the laws that relate to negotiable instruments (such as checks) and creditors' rights. Also, a dispute may arise over the rights to NetSys's software, or there may be a question of liability if the software is defective. There may even be an issue as to whether you and Hernandez had the authority to make the deal in the first place. Resolutions of these questions may be found in the laws that relate to intellectual property, e-commerce, torts, product liability, agency, business organizations, or professional liability. ●

Finally, if any dispute cannot be resolved amicably, then the laws and the rules concerning courts and court procedures spell out the steps of a lawsuit. Exhibit 1.1 on the facing page illustrates the various areas of the law that may influence business decision making.

Exhibit 1.1 Areas of the Law That May Affect Business Decision Making

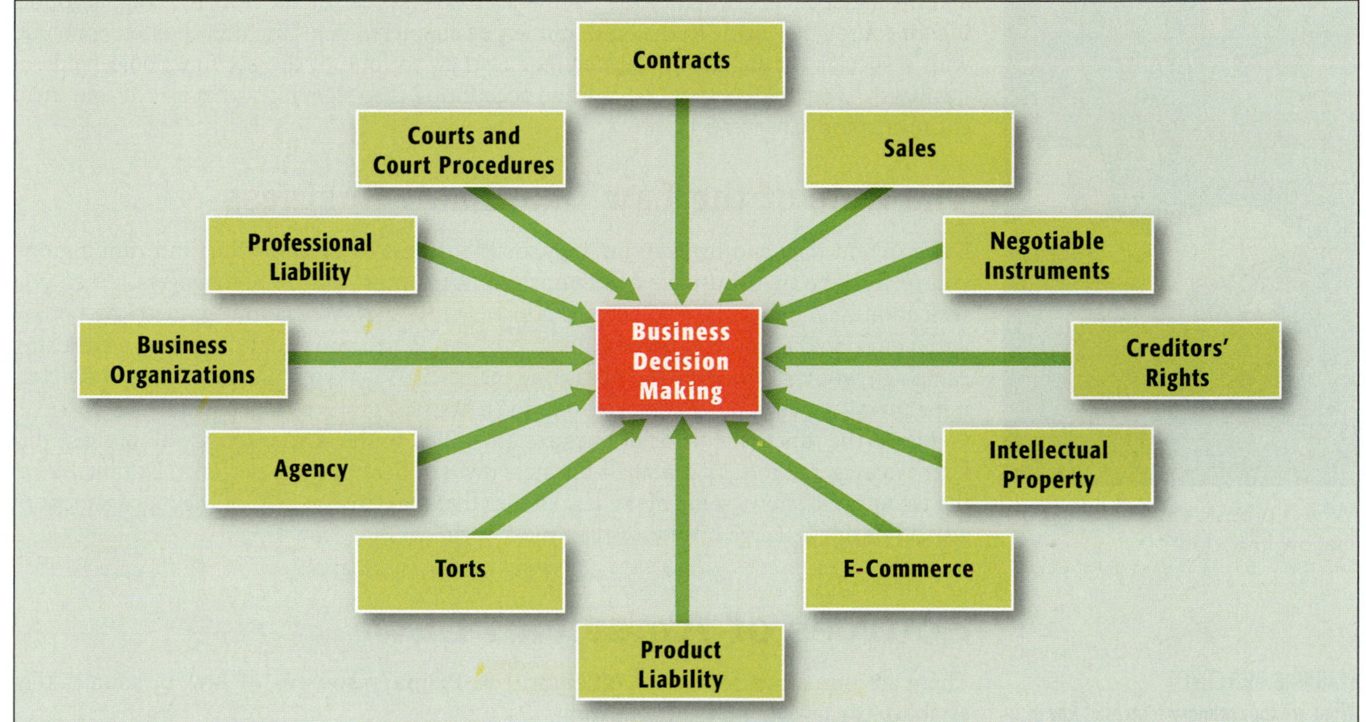

PREVENTING LEGAL DISPUTES

To avoid potential legal disputes, be aware of the many different laws that may apply to a single business transaction. Become familiar with the laws that affect your business operations, but always consult an expert. Attorneys must keep up with the myriad rules and regulations that govern the conduct of business in the United States. When you need to choose an attorney, obtain recommendations from friends, relatives, or business associates who have had long-standing relationships with their attorneys. If that fails, contact your local or state bar association, or check FindLaw's online directory (at lawyers.findlaw.com).

Linking Business Law to the Six Functional Fields of Business

In all likelihood, you are taking a business law or legal environment course because you intend to enter the business world, though some of you may also plan to become full-time practicing attorneys. Many of you are taking other business school courses and may therefore be familiar with the functional fields of business listed below:

1. Corporate management.
2. Production and transportation.
3. Marketing.
4. Research and development.
5. Accounting and finance.
6. Human resource management.

(Kzenon/Shutterstock.com)

Why is a basic understanding of the law important?

One of our goals in this text is to show how legal concepts can be useful for managers and businesspersons, whether their activities focus on management, marketing, accounting, or some other field. To that end, numerous chapters, including this chapter, conclude with a special feature called "*Linking Business Law to* [one of the six functional fields of business]." The link between the law and accounting is so significant that it is treated in an entire chapter (Chapter 34).

The Role of the Law in a Small Business

Some of you may end up working in a small business or even owning and running one yourselves. The small business owner/operator is the most general of managers. When you seek additional financing, you become a finance manager. When you "go over the books" with your bookkeeper, you become an accountant. When you decide on a new advertising campaign, you are suddenly the marketing manager. When you hire employees and determine their salaries and benefits, you become a human resources manager.

Just as the functional fields of business are linked to the law, so too are all of these different managerial roles that a small-business owner/operator must perform. Exhibit 1.2 on the facing page shows some of the legal issues that may arise as part of the management of a small business. Large businesses face most of these issues, too.

Sources of American Law

LEARNING OBJECTIVE 1
What are four primary sources of law in the United States?

Primary Source of Law A document that establishes the law on a particular issue, such as a constitution, a statute, an administrative rule, or a court decision.

There are numerous sources of American law. **Primary sources of law,** or sources that establish the law, include the following:

- The U.S. Constitution and the constitutions of the various states.
- Statutes, or laws, passed by Congress and by state legislatures.
- Regulations created by administrative agencies, such as the federal Food and Drug Administration.
- Case law (court decisions).

We describe each of these important primary sources of law in the following pages. (See the appendix at the end of this chapter for a discussion of how to find statutes, regulations, and case law.)

Secondary Source of Law A publication that summarizes or interprets the law, such as a legal encyclopedia, a legal treatise, or an article in a law review.

Secondary sources of law are books and articles that summarize and clarify the primary sources of law. Legal encyclopedias, compilations (such as *Restatements of the Law,* which summarize court decisions on a particular topic), official comments to statutes, treatises, articles in law reviews published by law schools, and articles in other legal journals are examples of secondary sources of law. Courts often refer to secondary sources of law for guidance in interpreting and applying the primary sources of law discussed here.

Constitutional Law

Constitutional Law The body of law derived from the U.S. Constitution and the constitutions of the various states.

The federal government and the states have separate written constitutions that set forth the general organization, powers, and limits of their respective governments. **Constitutional law** is the law as expressed in these constitutions.

The U.S. Constitution is the supreme law of the land. As such, it is the basis of all law in the United States. A law in violation of the U.S. Constitution, if challenged, will be declared unconstitutional and will not be enforced, no matter what its source. Because of its paramount importance in the American legal system, we discuss the U.S. Constitution at length in Chapter 2 and present the complete text of the U.S. Constitution in Appendix B.

Exhibit 1.2 Linking Business Law to the Management of a Small Business

Business Organization
What is the most appropriate business organizational form, and what type of personal liability does it entail?

↓

Taxation
How will the small business be taxed, and are there ways to reduce those taxes?

↓

Intellectual Property
Does the small business have any patents or other intellectual property that needs to be protected, and if so, what steps should the firm take?

↓

Administrative Law
What types of government regulations apply to the business, and what must the firm do to comply with them?

↓

Employment
Does the business need an employment manual, and does management have to explicitly inform employees of their rights?

↓

Contracts, Sales, and Leases
Will the firm be regularly entering into contracts with others, and if so, should it hire an attorney to review those contracts?

↓

Accounting
Do the financial statements created by an accountant need to be verified for accuracy?

↓

Finance
What are appropriate and legal ways to raise additional capital so that the business can grow?

The Tenth Amendment to the U.S. Constitution reserves to the states all powers not granted to the federal government. Each state in the union has its own constitution. Unless it conflicts with the U.S. Constitution or a federal law, a state constitution is supreme within that state's borders.

Statutory Law

Statutory Law The body of law enacted by legislative bodies (as opposed to constitutional law, administrative law, or case law).

Laws enacted by legislative bodies at any level of government, such as the statutes passed by Congress or by state legislatures, make up the body of law generally referred to as **statutory law.** When a legislature passes a statute, that statute ultimately is included in

Citation A reference to a publication in which a legal authority—such as a statute or a court decision—or other source can be found.

Ordinance A regulation enacted by a city or county legislative body that becomes part of that state's statutory law.

the federal code of laws or the relevant state code of laws. Whenever a particular statute is mentioned in this text, we usually provide a footnote showing its **citation** (a reference to a publication in which a legal authority—such as a statute or a court decision—or other source can be found). In the appendix following this chapter, we explain how you can use these citations to find statutory law.

Statutory law also includes local **ordinances**—statutes (laws, rules, or orders) passed by municipal or county governing units to administer matters not covered by federal or state law. Ordinances commonly have to do with city or county land use (zoning ordinances), building and safety codes, and other matters affecting only the local governing unit.

A federal statute, of course, applies to all states. A state statute, in contrast, applies only within the state's borders. State laws thus may vary from state to state. No federal statute may violate the U.S. Constitution, and no state statute or local ordinance may violate the U.S. Constitution or the relevant state constitution.

Uniform Laws

During the 1800s, the differences among state laws frequently created difficulties for businesspersons conducting trade and commerce among the states. To counter these problems, a group of legal scholars and lawyers formed the National Conference of Commissioners on Uniform State Laws (NCCUSL, online at www.nccusl.org) in 1892 to draft **uniform laws** ("model statutes") for the states to consider adopting. The NCCUSL still exists today and continues to issue uniform laws: it has issued more than two hundred uniform acts since its inception.

Uniform Law A model law developed by the National Conference of Commissioners on Uniform State Laws for the states to consider enacting into statute.

Each state has the option of adopting or rejecting a uniform law. *Only if a state legislature adopts a uniform law does that law become part of the statutory law of that state.* Furthermore, a state legislature may choose to adopt only part of a uniform law or to rewrite the sections that are adopted. Hence, even though many states may have adopted a uniform law, those laws may not be entirely "uniform."

The Uniform Commercial Code (UCC)

One of the most important uniform acts is the Uniform Commercial Code (UCC), which was created through the joint efforts of the NCCUSL and the American Law Institute.[1] The UCC was first issued in 1952 and has been adopted in all fifty states,[2] the District of Columbia, and the Virgin Islands. The UCC facilitates commerce among the states by providing a uniform, yet flexible, set of rules governing commercial transactions. Because of its importance in the area of commercial law, we cite the UCC frequently in this text. We also present excerpts of the UCC in Appendix C. (For a discussion of the creation of the UCC, see the *Landmark in the Law* feature on page 385 in Chapter 15.)

Administrative Law

Administrative Law The body of law created by administrative agencies in order to carry out their duties and responsibilities.

Administrative Agency A federal or state government agency created by the legislature to perform a specific function, such as to make and enforce rules pertaining to the environment.

Another important source of American law is **administrative law,** which consists of the rules, orders, and decisions of administrative agencies. An **administrative agency** is a federal, state, or local government agency established to perform a specific function. Rules issued by various administrative agencies now affect almost every aspect of a business's operations, including the firm's capital structure and financing, its hiring and firing procedures, its relations with employees and unions, and the way it manufactures and markets its products. (See this chapter's *Linking Business Law to Management* feature on page 20.)

1. This institute was formed in the 1920s and consists of practicing attorneys, legal scholars, and judges.
2. Louisiana has adopted only Articles 1, 3, 4, 5, 7, 8, and 9.

"Laws and institutions, like clocks, must occasionally be cleaned, wound up, and set to true time."

Henry Ward Beecher, 1813–1887
(American clergyman and abolitionist)

Federal Agencies

At the national level, numerous *executive agencies* exist within the cabinet departments of the executive branch. For example, the Food and Drug Administration is within the U.S. Department of Health and Human Services. Executive agencies are subject to the authority of the president, who has the power to appoint and remove their officers.

There are also major *independent regulatory agencies* at the federal level, including the Federal Trade Commission, the Securities and Exchange Commission, and the Federal Communications Commission. The president's power is less pronounced in regard to independent agencies, whose officers serve for fixed terms and cannot be removed without just cause.

State and Local Agencies

There are administrative agencies at the state and local levels as well. Commonly, a state agency (such as a state pollution-control agency) is created as a parallel to a federal agency (such as the Environmental Protection Agency). Just as federal statutes take precedence over conflicting state statutes, so do federal agency regulations take precedence over conflicting state regulations. Because the rules of state and local agencies vary widely, we focus here exclusively on federal administrative law.

Agency Creation

Because Congress cannot possibly oversee the actual implementation of all the laws it enacts, it must delegate such tasks to others, especially when the legislation involves highly technical matters, such as air and water pollution. Congress creates an administrative agency by enacting **enabling legislation**, which specifies the name, composition, purpose, and powers of the agency being created.

Enabling Legislation A statute enacted by Congress that authorizes the creation of an administrative agency and specifies the name, composition, purpose, and powers of the agency being created.

EXAMPLE 1.2 The Federal Trade Commission (FTC) was created in 1914 by the Federal Trade Commission Act.[3] This act prohibits unfair and deceptive trade practices. It also describes the procedures the agency must follow to charge persons or organizations with violations of the act, and it provides for judicial review (review by the courts) of agency orders. Other portions of the act grant the agency powers to "make rules and regulations for the purpose of carrying out the Act," conduct investigations of business practices, obtain reports from interstate corporations concerning their business practices, investigate possible violations of the act, publish findings of its investigations, and recommend new legislation. The act also empowers the FTC to hold trial-like hearings and to **adjudicate** (resolve judicially) certain kinds of disputes involving its regulations. •

Adjudicate To render a judicial decision. Adjudication is the trial-like proceeding in which an administrative law judge hears and resolves disputes involving an administrative agency's regulations.

Note that the powers granted to the FTC incorporate functions associated with the legislative branch of government (rulemaking), the executive branch (investigation and enforcement), and the judicial branch (adjudication). Taken together, these functions constitute **administrative process**, which is the administration of law by administrative agencies.

Administrative Process The procedure used by administrative agencies in administering the law.

Rulemaking

A major function of an administrative agency is **rulemaking**—formulating new regulations. When Congress enacts an agency's enabling legislation, it confers the power to make **legislative rules**, or substantive rules, which are legally binding on all businesses. The Administrative Procedure Act of 1946 (APA)[4] imposes strict procedural requirements that agencies must follow in legislative rulemaking and other functions. **EXAMPLE 1.3** The Occupational Safety and Health Act of 1970 authorized the Occupational Safety and Health Administration (OSHA) to develop and issue rules governing safety in the workplace. When OSHA wants to formulate rules regarding safety in the steel industry, it has to follow specific procedures outlined by the APA. •

Rulemaking The process by which an administrative agency formally adopts a new regulation or amends an old one.

Legislative Rule An administrative agency's rule that carries the same weight as a congressionally enacted statute.

3. 15 U.S.C. Sections 45–58.
4. 5 U.S.C. Sections 551–706.

Legislative Rules Legislative rulemaking commonly involves three steps. First, the agency must give public notice of the proposed rulemaking proceedings, where and when the proceedings will be held, the agency's legal authority for the proceedings, and the terms or subject matter of the proposed rule. The notice must be published in the *Federal Register,* a daily publication of the U.S. government. Second, following this notice, the agency must allow ample time for interested parties to comment in writing on the proposed rule. The agency takes these comments into consideration when drafting the final version of the regulation. The third and last step is the drafting of the final rule and its publication in the *Federal Register.* (See the appendix at the end of this chapter for an explanation of how to find agency regulations.)

Interpretive Rule A nonbinding rule or policy statement issued by an administrative agency that explains how it interprets and intends to apply the statutes it enforces.

Interpretive Rules In addition to making *legislative rules,* which are subject to the procedural requirements of the APA, agencies also issue **interpretive rules**—rules that specify how the agency will interpret and apply its regulations. The APA does not apply to interpretive rulemaking. Interpretive rules are not legally binding on all businesses but simply indicate how an agency plans to interpret and enforce its statutory authority. **EXAMPLE 1.4** The Equal Employment Opportunity Commission periodically issues interpretive rules indicating how it plans to interpret the provisions of certain statutes, such as the Americans with Disabilities Act. These informal rules provide enforcement guidelines for agency officials. ●

Investigation and Enforcement

Agencies have both investigatory and prosecutorial powers. An agency can request that individuals or organizations hand over specified books, papers, electronic records, or other documents. In addition, agencies may conduct on-site inspections, although a search warrant is normally required for such inspections. Sometimes, a search of a home, an office, or a factory is the only means of obtaining evidence needed to prove a regulatory violation. Agencies investigate a wide range of activities, including coal mining, automobile manufacturing, and the industrial discharge of pollutants into the environment.

After investigating a suspected rule violation, an agency may decide to take action against an individual or a business. Most administrative actions are resolved through negotiated settlement at their initial stages without the need for formal adjudication. If a settlement cannot be reached, though, the agency may issue a formal complaint and proceed to adjudication.

Administrative Law Judge (ALJ) One who presides over an administrative agency hearing and has the power to administer oaths, take testimony, rule on questions of evidence, and make determinations of fact.

Adjudication

Agency adjudication involves a trial-like hearing before an **administrative law judge (ALJ).** Hearing procedures vary widely from agency to agency. After the hearing, the ALJ renders a decision in the case. The ALJ can fine the charged party or prohibit the party from carrying on some specified activity. Either the agency or the charged party may appeal the ALJ's decision to the commission or board that governs the agency. If the party fails to get relief there, appeal can be made to a federal court. If neither side appeals the case, the ALJ's decision becomes final.

ETHICAL ISSUE

Do administrative agencies exercise too much authority? Administrative agencies, such as the Federal Trade Commission, combine in a single governmental entity functions normally divided among the three branches of government. They create rules, conduct investigations, and prosecute and pass judgment on violators. Yet administrative agencies' powers often go unchecked by the other branches, causing some businesspersons to suggest that it is unethical for agencies—which are not even mentioned in the U.S. Constitution—to wield so many powers.

Although agency rulemaking must comply with the requirements of the Administrative Procedure Act (APA), the act applies only to legislative, not interpretive, rulemaking. In addition, the APA is largely procedural and aimed at preventing arbitrariness. It does little to ensure that the rules passed by agencies are fair or correct. Even on those rare occasions when an agency's ruling is challenged and later reviewed by a court, the court cannot reverse the agency's decision unless the agency exceeded its authority or acted arbitrarily. Courts typically are reluctant to second-guess an agency's rules, interpretations, and decisions.[5] Moreover, once an agency has final regulations in place, it is difficult to revoke or alter them. President Barack Obama discovered this when he tried to change some of the rules that agencies had put into place in the last few months of the administration of his predecessor, President George W. Bush.

Case Law and Common Law Doctrines

Case Law The rules of law announced in court decisions. Case law interprets statutes, regulations, constitutional provisions, and other case law.

The rules of law announced in court decisions constitute another basic source of American law. These rules of law include interpretations of constitutional provisions, of statutes enacted by legislatures, and of regulations created by administrative agencies. Today, this body of judge-made law is referred to as **case law.** Case law—the doctrines and principles announced in cases—governs all areas not covered by statutory law or administrative law and is part of our common law tradition. We look at the origins and characteristics of the common law tradition in some detail in the pages that follow.

The Common Law Tradition

LEARNING OBJECTIVE 2
What is the common law tradition?

Because of our colonial heritage, much of American law is based on the English legal system. A knowledge of this tradition is crucial to understanding our legal system today because judges in the United States still apply common law principles when deciding cases.

Early English Courts

After the Normans conquered England in 1066, William the Conqueror and his successors began the process of unifying the country under their rule. One of the means they used to do this was the establishment of the king's courts, or *curiae regis*. Before the Norman Conquest, disputes had been settled according to the local legal customs and traditions in various regions of the country. The king's courts sought to establish a uniform set of rules for the country as a whole. What evolved in these courts was the beginning of the **common law**—a body of general rules that applied throughout the entire English realm. Eventually, the common law tradition became part of the heritage of all nations that were once British colonies, including the United States.

Common Law The body of law developed from custom or judicial decisions in English and U.S. courts, not attributable to a legislature.

LEARNING OBJECTIVE 3
What is a precedent? When might a court depart from precedent?

Precedent A court decision that furnishes an example or authority for deciding subsequent cases involving identical or similar facts.

Courts developed the common law rules from the principles underlying judges' decisions in actual legal controversies. Judges attempted to be consistent, and whenever possible, they based their decisions on the principles suggested by earlier cases. They sought to decide similar cases in a similar way and considered new cases with care because they knew that their decisions would make new law. Each interpretation became part of the law on the subject and served as a legal **precedent**—that is, a court decision that furnished an example or authority for deciding subsequent cases involving identical or similar legal principles or facts.

In the early years of the common law, there was no single place or publication where court opinions, or written decisions, could be found. Beginning in the late thirteenth and early fourteenth centuries, however, portions of significant decisions from each year were gathered together and recorded in *Year Books*. The *Year Books* were useful references for lawyers and judges. In the sixteenth century, the *Year Books* were discontinued, and other reports of cases became available. (See the appendix to this chapter for a discussion of how cases are reported, or published, in the United States today.)

5. See, for example, *Citizens' Committee to Save Our Canyons v. Krueger*, 513 F.3d 1169 (10th Cir. 2008). See the appendix at the end of this chapter for an explanation of how to read legal citations.

Stare Decisis

The practice of deciding new cases with reference to former decisions, or precedents, eventually became a cornerstone of the English and U.S. judicial systems. The practice forms a doctrine called ***stare decisis***[6] ("to stand on decided cases").

Stare Decisis A common law doctrine under which judges are obligated to follow the precedents established in prior decisions.

The Importance of Precedents in Judicial Decision Making

Under the doctrine of *stare decisis,* once a court has set forth a principle of law as being applicable to a certain set of facts, that court and courts of lower rank must adhere to that principle and apply it in future cases involving similar fact patterns. *Stare decisis* has two aspects: (1) decisions made by a higher court are binding on lower courts, and (2) a court should not overturn its own precedents unless there is a strong reason to do so.

Controlling precedents in a *jurisdiction* (an area in which a court or courts have the power to apply the law) are referred to as binding authorities. A **binding authority** is any source of law that a court must follow when deciding a case. Binding authorities include constitutions, statutes, and regulations that govern the issue being decided, as well as court decisions that are controlling precedents within the jurisdiction. United States Supreme Court case decisions, no matter how old, remain controlling until they are overruled by a subsequent decision of the Supreme Court, by a constitutional amendment, or by congressional legislation.

Binding Authority Any source of law that a court *must* follow when deciding a case.

KNOW THIS

Courts normally must follow the rules set forth by higher courts in deciding cases with similar fact patterns.

Stare Decisis *and Legal Stability* The doctrine of *stare decisis* helps the courts to be more efficient because if other courts have carefully reasoned through a similar case, their legal reasoning and opinions can serve as guides. *Stare decisis* also makes the law more stable and predictable. If the law on a given subject is well settled, someone bringing a case to court can usually rely on the court to make a decision based on what the law has been.

Departures from Precedent Although courts are obligated to follow precedents, sometimes a court will depart from the rule of precedent. If a court decides that a precedent is simply incorrect or that technological or social changes have rendered the precedent inapplicable, the court may rule contrary to the precedent. Cases that overturn precedent often receive a great deal of publicity.

CASE EXAMPLE 1.5 In *Brown v. Board of Education of Topeka,*[7] the United States Supreme Court expressly overturned precedent when it concluded that separate educational facilities for whites and blacks, which had been upheld as constitutional in numerous previous cases,[8] were inherently unequal. The Supreme Court's departure from precedent in the *Brown* decision received a tremendous amount of publicity as people began to realize the ramifications of this change in the law. •

Persuasive Authority Any legal authority or source of law that a court may look to for guidance but need not follow when making its decision.

School integration occurred after *Brown v. Board of Education of Topeka.*

(Library of Congress)

When There Is No Precedent At times, a case may raise issues that have not been raised before in that jurisdiction, so the court has no precedents on which to base its decision. When deciding such cases, called "cases of first impression," courts often look at precedents established in other jurisdictions for guidance. Precedents from other jurisdictions, because they are not binding on the court, are referred to as **persuasive authorities.** A court may also consider other factors, including legal principles and policies underlying previous court decisions or existing statutes, fairness, social values and customs, public policy, and data and concepts drawn from the social sciences.

6. Pronounced *stahree* dih-*si*-sis.
7. 347 U.S. 483, 74 S.Ct. 686, 98 L.Ed. 873 (1954).
8. See *Plessy v. Ferguson,* 163 U.S. 537, 16 S.Ct. 1138, 41 L.Ed. 256 (1896).

ADAPTING THE LAW TO THE ONLINE ENVIRONMENT

HOW THE INTERNET HAS EXPANDED PRECEDENT

The notion that courts should rely on precedents to decide the outcome of similar cases has long been a cornerstone of U.S. law. Nevertheless, the availability of "unpublished opinions" over the Internet has changed what the law considers to be precedent. An *unpublished opinion* is a decision issued by an appellate (reviewing) court that is not intended for publication in a reporter (the bound books that contain court opinions).[a] Courts traditionally did not consider unpublished opinions to be "precedents," binding or persuasive, and often did not allow attorneys to refer to (cite) these decisions in their arguments.

Increased Online Availability of Unpublished Decisions

The number of court decisions not published in printed books has risen dramatically in recent years. Nearly 80 percent of the decisions of the federal appellate courts are unpublished, and the number is equally high in some state court systems. Even though certain decisions are not intended for publication, they are posted ("published") almost immediately in online legal databases, such as Westlaw and Lexis. With the proliferation of free legal databases and court Web sites, the general public also has almost instant access to the unpublished decisions of most courts. This situation has caused many to question why these opinions have no precedential effect.

Prior to the Internet, not considering unpublished decisions as precedent might have been justified on the grounds of fairness. How could lawyers know about decisions if they were not printed in the case reporters? Now that opinions are so readily available on the Web, however, this justification is no longer valid. Moreover, it now seems unfair *not* to consider these decisions as precedent because they are so publicly accessible. Some claim that unpublished decisions could make bad precedents because these decisions frequently are written by staff attorneys and law clerks, rather than by judges, so the reasoning may be inferior. If the decision is considered merely as persuasive precedent, however, judges who disagree with the reasoning are free to reject the conclusion.

The Federal Rules Now Allow Judges to Consider Unpublished Opinions

The United States Supreme Court made history in 2006 when it announced that it would allow lawyers to cite unpublished decisions in all federal courts. Rule 32.1 of the Federal Rules of Appellate Procedure states that federal courts may not prohibit or restrict the citation of federal judicial opinions that have been designated as "not for publication," "nonprecedential," or "not precedent." The rule applies only to federal courts and only to unpublished opinions issued after January 1, 2007. It does not specify what weight a court must give to its own unpublished opinions or to those from another court.

Basically, Rule 32.1 establishes a uniform rule for all of the federal courts that allows attorneys to cite—and judges to consider as persuasive precedent—unpublished decisions.

Critical Thinking

Only a few states, such as Massachusetts, have followed the federal courts in allowing unpublished decisions to be used as persuasive precedent. The other states claim that doing so would increase the already heavy workload of their courts. Under the current system, a judge who designates an opinion as unpublished does not have to take the time to provide a complete set of facts, references, and views. Does this argument justify the different treatment for unpublished opinions in the state and federal courts? Explain.

a. Recently decided cases that are not yet published are also sometimes called *unpublished opinions*, but because these decisions will eventually be printed in reporters, we do not include them here.

Can a court consider unpublished decisions as persuasive precedent? See this chapter's *Adapting the Law to the Online Environment* feature above for a discussion of this issue.

Equitable Remedies and Courts of Equity

Remedy The relief given to an innocent party to enforce a right or compensate for the violation of a right.

A **remedy** is the means given to a party to enforce a right or to compensate for the violation of a right. **EXAMPLE 1.6** Elena is injured because of Rowan's wrongdoing. If Elena files a lawsuit and is successful, a court can order Rowan to compensate Elena for the harm by paying her a certain amount. The compensation is Elena's remedy. ●

LEARNING OBJECTIVE 4

What is the difference between remedies at law and remedies in equity?

The kinds of remedies available in the early king's courts of England were severely restricted. If one person wronged another, the king's courts could award as compensation either money or property, including land. These courts became known as *courts of law,* and the remedies were called *remedies at law.* Even though this system introduced uniformity in the settling of disputes, when a person wanted a remedy other than economic compensation, the courts of law could do nothing, so "no remedy, no right."

Remedies in Equity

Equity is a branch of law, founded on what might be described as notions of justice and fair dealing, that seeks to supply a remedy when no adequate remedy at law is available. When individuals could not obtain an adequate remedy in a court of law, they petitioned the king for relief. Most of these petitions were referred to the *chancellor,* an adviser to the king who had the power to grant new and unique remedies. Eventually, formal chancery courts, or *courts of equity,* were established. Thus, two distinct court systems were created, each having its own set of judges and its own set of remedies. The remedies granted by the chancery courts were called *remedies in equity.*

Plaintiff One who initiates a lawsuit.

Defendant One against whom a lawsuit is brought, or the accused person in a criminal proceeding.

Plaintiffs (those bringing lawsuits) had to specify whether they were bringing an "action at law" or an "action in equity," and they chose their courts accordingly. **EXAMPLE 1.7** A plaintiff might ask a court of equity to order the **defendant** (the person against whom a lawsuit is brought) to perform within the terms of a contract. A court of law could not issue such an order because its remedies were limited to the payment of money or property as compensation for damages. A court of equity, however, could issue a decree for *specific performance*—an order to perform what was promised. A court of equity could also issue an *injunction,* directing a party to do or refrain from doing a particular act. In certain cases, a court of equity could allow for the *rescission* (cancellation) of the contract, thereby returning the parties to the positions that they held prior to the contract's formation. • Equitable remedies will be discussed in greater detail in Chapter 14.

The Merging of Law and Equity

Today, in most states, the courts of law and equity have merged, and thus the distinction between the two courts has largely disappeared. A plaintiff may now request both legal and equitable remedies in the same action, and the trial court judge may grant either form—or both forms—of relief.

KNOW THIS

Even though courts of law and equity have merged, the principles of equity still apply, and courts will not grant an equitable remedy unless the remedy at law is inadequate.

The distinction between legal and equitable remedies remains significant, however, because a court normally will grant an equitable remedy only when the remedy at law (monetary damages) is inadequate. To request the proper remedy, a businessperson (or her or his attorney) must know what remedies are available for the specific kinds of harms suffered. Exhibit 1.3 below summarizes the procedural differences (applicable in most states) between an action at law and an action in equity.

Exhibit 1.3 Procedural Differences between an Action at Law and an Action at Equity

PROCEDURE	ACTION AT LAW	ACTION IN EQUITY
Initiation of lawsuit	By filing a complaint.	By filing a petition.
Decision	By jury or judge.	By judge (no jury).
Result	Judgment.	Decree.
Remedy	Monetary damages.	Injunction, specific performance, or rescission.

Equitable Principles and Maxims General propositions or principles of law that have to do with fairness (equity).

Equitable Principles and Maxims

Over time, the courts have developed a number of **equitable principles and maxims** that provide guidance in deciding whether plaintiffs should be granted equitable relief. Because of their importance, both historically and in our judicial system today, these principles and maxims are set forth in this chapter's *Landmark in the Law* feature below.

Schools of Legal Thought

Jurisprudence The science or philosophy of law.

How judges apply the law to specific cases, including disputes relating to the business world, depends on their philosophical approaches to law, among other things. The study of law, often referred to as **jurisprudence,** includes learning about different schools of legal thought and discovering how each school's approach to law can affect judicial decision making.

Natural Law The oldest school of legal thought, based on the belief that the legal system should reflect universal ("higher") moral and ethical principles that are inherent in human nature.

The Natural Law School

Those who adhere to the **natural law** theory believe that a higher, or universal, law exists that applies to all human beings and that written laws should imitate these inherent principles. If a written law is unjust, then it is not a true (natural) law and need not be obeyed.

LANDMARK IN THE LAW

Equitable Principles and Maxims

In medieval England, courts of equity were expected to use discretion in supplementing the common law. Even today, when the same court can award both legal and equitable remedies, it must exercise discretion. Students of business law should know that courts often invoke equitable principles and maxims when making their decisions. Here are some of the most significant equitable principles and maxims:

1. *Whoever seeks equity must do equity.* (Anyone who wishes to be treated fairly must treat others fairly.)
2. *Where there is equal equity, the law must prevail.* (The law will determine the outcome of a controversy in which the merits of both sides are equal.)
3. *One seeking the aid of an equity court must come to the court with clean hands.* (Plaintiffs must have acted fairly and honestly.)
4. *Equity will not suffer a wrong to be without a remedy.* (Equitable relief will be awarded when there is a right to relief and there is no adequate remedy at law.)
5. *Equity regards substance rather than form.* (Equity is more concerned with fairness and justice than with legal technicalities.)
6. *Equity aids the vigilant, not those who rest on their rights.* (Equity will not help those who neglect their rights for an unreasonable period of time.)

The last maxim has come to be known as the *equitable doctrine of laches.* The doctrine arose to encourage people to bring lawsuits while the evidence was fresh. If they failed to do so, they would not be allowed to bring a lawsuit. What constitutes a reasonable time, of course, varies according to the circumstances of the case. Time periods for different types of cases are now usually fixed by *statutes of limitations*—that is, statutes that set the maximum time period during which a certain action can be brought. After the time allowed under a statute of limitations has expired, no action can be brought, no matter how strong the case was originally.

Application to Today's World *The equitable maxims listed above underlie many of the legal rules and principles that are commonly applied by the courts today—and that you will read about in this book. For example, in Chapter 10 you will read about the* doctrine of promissory estoppel. *Under this doctrine, a person who has reasonably and substantially relied on the promise of another may be able to obtain some measure of recovery, even though no enforceable contract, or agreement, exists. The court will estop (bar, or impede) the one making the promise from asserting the lack of a valid contract as a defense. The rationale underlying the doctrine of promissory estoppel is similar to that expressed in the fourth and fifth maxims listed on the left.*

The natural law tradition is one of the oldest and most significant schools of jurisprudence. It dates back to the days of the Greek philosopher Aristotle (384–322 B.C.E.), who distinguished between natural law and the laws governing a particular nation. According to Aristotle, natural law applies universally to all humankind.

The notion that people have "natural rights" stems from the natural law tradition. Those who claim that certain nations, such as China and North Korea, are depriving many of their citizens of their human rights are implicitly appealing to a higher law that has universal applicability. The question of the universality of basic human rights also comes into play in the context of international business operations. For example, U.S. companies that have operations abroad often hire foreign workers as employees. Should the same laws that protect U.S. employees apply to these foreign employees? This question is rooted implicitly in a concept of universal rights that has its origins in the natural law tradition.

Legal Positivism A school of legal thought centered on the assumption that there is no law higher than the laws created by a national government. Laws must be obeyed, even if they are unjust, to prevent anarchy.

Legal Positivism

In contrast, *positive,* or national, law (the written law of a given society at a particular point in time) applies only to the citizens of that nation or society. Those who adhere to **legal positivism** believe that there can be no higher law than a nation's positive law. According to the positivist school, there is no such thing as "natural rights." Rather, human rights exist solely because of laws. If the laws are not enforced, anarchy will result. Thus, whether a law is morally "bad" or "good" is irrelevant. The law is the law and must be obeyed until it is changed—in an orderly manner through a legitimate lawmaking process.

A judge with positivist leanings probably would be more inclined to defer to an existing law than would a judge who adheres to the natural law tradition.

Historical School A school of legal thought that looks to the past to determine what the principles of contemporary law should be.

The Historical School

The **historical school** of legal thought emphasizes the evolutionary process of law by concentrating on the origin and history of the legal system. This school looks to the past to discover what the principles of contemporary law should be. The legal doctrines that have withstood the passage of time—those that have worked in the past—are deemed best suited for shaping present laws. Hence, law derives its legitimacy and authority from adhering to the standards that historical development has shown to be workable.

Followers of the historical school are more likely than those of other schools to adhere strictly to decisions made in past cases.

Legal Realism A school of legal thought that holds that the law is only one factor to be considered when deciding cases and that social and economic circumstances should also be taken into account.

Legal Realism

In the 1920s and 1930s, a number of jurists and scholars, known as *legal realists,* rebelled against the historical approach to law. **Legal realism** is based on the idea that law is just one of many institutions in society and that it is shaped by social forces and needs. This school holds that because the law is a human enterprise, judges should look beyond the law and take social and economic realities into account when deciding cases. Legal realists also believe that the law can never be applied with total uniformity. Given that judges are human beings with unique experiences, personalities, value systems, and intellects, different judges will obviously bring different reasoning processes to the same case. Female judges, for instance, might be more inclined than male judges to consider whether a decision might have a negative impact on the employment of women or minorities.

Substantive Law Law that defines, describes, regulates, and creates legal rights and obligations.

Procedural Law Law that establishes the methods of enforcing the rights established by substantive law.

Classifications of Law

The law may be broken down according to several classification systems. For example, one classification system divides law into **substantive law** (all laws that define, describe, regulate, and create legal rights and obligations) and **procedural law** (all laws that establish the methods of enforcing the rights established by substantive law).

EXAMPLE 1.8 A state law that provides employees with the right to workers' compensation benefits for any on-the-job injuries they sustain is a substantive law because it creates legal rights (workers' compensation laws will be discussed in Chapter 24). Procedural laws, in contrast, establish the method by which an employee must notify the employer about an on-the-job injury, prove the injury, and periodically submit additional proof to continue receiving workers' compensation benefits. Note that a law concerning workers' compensation may contain both substantive and procedural provisions. •

Other classification systems divide law into federal law and state law or private law (dealing with relationships between persons) and public law (addressing the relationship between persons and their governments). Frequently, people use the term **cyberlaw** to refer to the emerging body of law that governs transactions conducted via the Internet.

Cyberlaw An informal term used to refer to all laws governing electronic communications and transactions, particularly those conducted via the Internet.

Cyberlaw is not really a classification of law, nor is it a new *type* of law. Rather, it is an informal term used to describe traditional legal principles that have been modified and adapted to fit situations that are unique to the online world. Of course, in some areas new statutes have been enacted, at both the federal and state levels, to cover specific types of problems stemming from online communications. Throughout this book, you will read about how the law is evolving to govern specific legal issues that arise in the online context.

LEARNING OBJECTIVE 5

What are some important differences between civil law and criminal law?

Civil Law and Criminal Law

Civil Law The branch of law dealing with the definition and enforcement of all private or public rights, as opposed to criminal matters.

Civil law spells out the rights and duties that exist between persons and between persons and their governments, and the relief available when a person's rights are violated. Typically, in a civil case, a private party sues another private party (although the government can also sue a party for a civil law violation) to make sure that the other party complies with a duty or pays for the damage caused by the failure to comply with a duty. **EXAMPLE 1.9** If a seller fails to perform a contract with a buyer, the buyer may bring a lawsuit against the seller. The purpose of the lawsuit will be either to compel the seller to perform as promised or, more commonly, to obtain monetary damages for the seller's failure to perform. •

Civil Law System A system of law derived from Roman law that is based on codified laws (rather than on case precedents).

Criminal Law The branch of law that defines and punishes wrongful actions committed against the public.

Much of the law that we discuss in this text is civil law. Contract law, for example, which we will discuss in Chapters 9 through 14, is civil law. The whole body of tort law (see Chapter 4) is civil law. Note that *civil law* is not the same as a *civil law system.* As you will read shortly, a **civil law system** is a legal system based on a written code of laws.

Criminal law has to do with wrongs committed against society for which society demands redress. Criminal acts are proscribed by local, state, or federal government statutes (see Chapter 6 and many of the laws discussed in Chapters 31 through 34). Thus, criminal defendants are prosecuted by public officials, such as a district attorney (D.A.), on behalf of the state, not by their victims or other private parties. Whereas in a civil case the object is to obtain a remedy (such as monetary damages) to compensate the injured party, in a criminal case the object is to punish the wrongdoer in an attempt to deter others from similar actions. Penalties for violations of criminal statutes consist of fines and/or imprisonment—and, in some cases, death. We will discuss the differences between civil and criminal law in greater detail in Chapter 6.

A witness points out someone in the courtroom to the judge.

(Junial Enterprises/Shutterstock.com)

National and International Law

Although the focus of this book is U.S. business law, increasingly businesspersons in this country engage in transactions that extend beyond our national borders. In these situations, the laws of other nations or the laws governing relationships among nations may come into play. For this reason, those who pursue a career in business today should have an understanding of the global legal environment (discussed further in Chapter 8).

National Law Law that pertains to a particular nation (as opposed to international law).

National Law

The law of a particular nation, such as the United States or Sweden, is **national law.** National law, of course, varies from country to country because each country's law reflects the interests, customs, activities, and values that are unique to that nation's culture. Even though the laws and legal systems of various countries differ substantially, broad similarities do exist, as discussed in this chapter's *Beyond Our Borders* feature below.

International Law The law that governs relations among nations.

International Law

In contrast to national law, international law applies to more than one nation. **International law** can be defined as a body of written and unwritten laws

BEYOND OUR BORDERS National Law Systems

Despite their varying cultures and customs, almost all countries have laws governing torts, contracts, employment, and other areas. Two types of legal systems predominate around the globe today. One is the common law system of England and the United States, which we have discussed elsewhere. The other system is based on Roman civil law, or "code law," which relies on the legal principles enacted into law by a legislature or governing body.

Civil Law Systems

Although national law systems share many commonalities, they also have distinct differences. In a *civil law system,* the primary source of law is a statutory code, and case precedents are not judicially binding, as they normally are in a common law system. Although judges in a civil law system commonly refer to previous decisions as sources of legal guidance, those decisions are not binding precedents (*stare decisis* does not apply).

Exhibit 1.4 below lists some countries that today follow either the common law system or the civil law system. Generally, those countries that were once colonies of Great Britain have retained their English common law heritage. The civil law system, which is used in most continental European nations, has been retained in the countries that were once colonies of those nations. In the United States, the state of Louisiana, because of its historical ties to France, has in part a civil law system, as do Haiti, Québec, and Scotland.

Islamic Legal Systems

A third, less prevalent legal system is common in Islamic countries, where the law is often influenced by *sharia,* the religious law of Islam. Islam is both a religion and a way of life. *Sharia* is a comprehensive code of principles that governs the public and private lives of Islamic persons and directs many aspects of their day-to-day life, including politics, economics, banking, business law, contract law, and social issues.

Although *sharia* affects the legal codes of many Muslim countries, the extent of its impact and its interpretation vary widely. In some Middle Eastern nations, aspects of *sharia* have been codified in modern legal codes and are enforced by national judicial systems.

Critical Thinking

Does the civil law system offer any advantages over the common law system, or vice versa? Explain.

Exhibit 1.4 The Legal Systems of Selected Nations

CIVIL LAW		COMMON LAW	
Argentina	Indonesia	Australia	Nigeria
Austria	Iran	Bangladesh	Singapore
Brazil	Italy	Canada	United Kingdom
Chile	Japan	Ghana	United States
China	Mexico	India	Zambia
Egypt	Poland	Israel	
Finland	South Korea	Jamaica	
France	Sweden	Kenya	
Germany	Tunisia	Malaysia	
Greece	Venezuela	New Zealand	

observed by independent nations and governing the acts of individuals as well as governments. It is a mixture of rules and constraints derived from a variety of sources, including the laws of individual nations, customs developed among nations, and international treaties and organizations. Each nation is motivated not only by the need to be the final authority over its own affairs, but also by the desire to benefit economically from trade and harmonious relations with other nations. In essence, international law is the result of centuries-old attempts to strike a balance between these competing needs.

The key difference between national law and international law is that government authorities can enforce national law. If a nation violates an international law, however, enforcement is up to other countries or international organizations, which may or may not choose to act. If persuasive tactics fail, the only option is to take coercive actions against the violating nation. Coercive actions range from the severance of diplomatic relations and boycotts to, as a last resort, war. We will examine the laws governing international business transactions in later chapters (including all of Chapter 8 and parts of Chapters 15 and 16, which cover contracts for the sale and lease of goods).

Reviewing . . . The Legal Environment

Suppose that the California legislature passes a law that severely restricts carbon dioxide emissions from automobiles in that state. A group of automobile manufacturers files a suit against the state of California to prevent the enforcement of the law. The automakers claim that a federal law already sets fuel economy standards nationwide and that these standards are essentially the same as carbon dioxide emission standards. According to the automobile manufacturers, it is unfair to allow California to impose more stringent regulations than those set by the federal law. Using the information presented in the chapter, answer the following questions.

1. Who are the parties (the plaintiffs and the defendant) in this lawsuit?
2. Are the plaintiffs seeking a legal remedy or an equitable remedy? Why?
3. What is the primary source of the law that is at issue here?
4. Read through the appendix that follows this chapter, and then answer the following question: Where would you look to find the relevant California and federal laws?

DEBATE THIS: Under the doctrine of *stare decisis,* courts are obligated to follow the precedents established in their jurisdiction unless there is a compelling reason not to do so. Should U.S. courts continue to adhere to this common law principle, given that our government now regulates so many areas by statute?

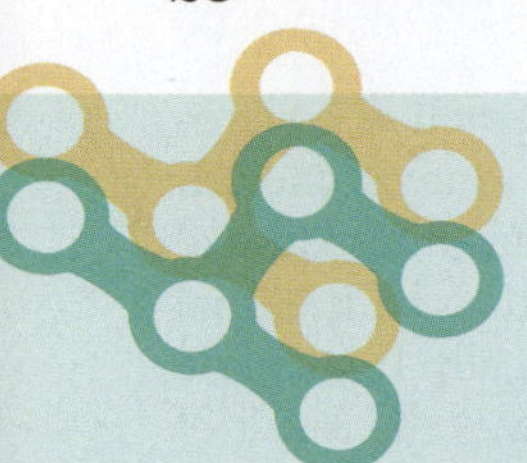

LINKING BUSINESS LAW to Management

Dealing with Administrative Law

Whether you work for a large corporation or own a small business, you will be dealing with multiple aspects of administrative law. Recall from page 8 that administrative law involves all of the rules, orders, and decisions of administrative agencies. All federal, state, and local government administrative agencies create rules that have the force of law. As a manager, you probably will need to pay more attention to administrative rules and regulations than to laws passed by local, state, and federal legislatures.

Federal versus State and Local Agency Regulations

The three levels of government create three levels of rules and regulations though their respective administrative agencies. At the federal level, these include the Food and Drug Administration, the Equal Employment Opportunity Commission, and the Occupational Safety and Health Administration. At the state level, there are often agencies that govern business activities in a manner similar to federal agencies.

As a manager, you will have to learn about agency regulations that pertain to your business activities. It will be up to you, as a manager or small-business owner, to discern which of those regulations are most important and could potentially create the most liability if you violate them.

When Should You Participate in the Rulemaking Process?

All federal agencies and many state agencies invite public comments on proposed rules. Suppose that you manage a large construction company and your state occupational safety agency proposes a new rule requiring every employee on a construction site to wear hearing protection. You believe that the rule will lead to a *less* safe environment because your employees will not be able to communicate easily with one another.

Should you spend time offering comments to the agency? As an efficient manager, you make a trade-off calculation. First, you determine the value of the time that you would spend attempting to prevent or at least alter the proposed rule. Then you compare this implicit cost with your estimate of the potential benefits your company would receive if the rule is *not* put into place.

Be Prepared for Investigations

All administrative agencies have investigatory powers. Agencies' investigators usually have the power to search business premises, although normally they first have to obtain a search warrant. As a manager, you often have the choice of cooperating with agency investigators or providing just the minimum amount of assistance. If your business is routinely investigated, you will often opt for cooperation. In contrast, if your business is rarely investigated, you may decide that the on-site proposed inspection is overreaching. Then you must contact your company's attorney for advice on how to proceed.

If an administrative agency cites you for a regulatory violation, you will probably negotiate a settlement with the agency rather than take your case before an administrative law judge. Again, as a manager, you have to weigh the cost of the negotiated settlement with the potential cost of fighting the enforcement action.

Critical Thinking

Why are owner/operators of small businesses at a disadvantage relative to large corporations when they attempt to decipher complex regulations that apply to their businesses?

Key Terms

adjudicate 9
administrative agency 8
administrative law 8
administrative law judge (ALJ) 10
administrative process 9
binding authority 12
breach 4
case law 11
citation 8
civil law 17
civil law system 17
common law 11
concurring opinion 30
constitutional law 6
criminal law 17
cyberlaw 17
defendant 14
dissenting opinion 30
enabling legislation 9
equitable principles and maxims 15
historical school 16
international law 18
interpretive rule 10
jurisprudence 15
law 3
legal positivism 16
legal realism 16
legislative rule 9
majority opinion 30
national law 18
natural law 15
ordinance 8

per curiam opinion 30
persuasive authority 12
plaintiff 14
plurality opinion 30
precedent 11
primary source of law 6
procedural law 16
remedy 13
rulemaking 9
secondary source of law 6
stare decisis 12
statutory law 7
substantive law 16
uniform law 8

Chapter Summary: The Legal Environment

Sources of American Law (See pages 6–11.)	1. *Constitutional law*—The law as expressed in the U.S. Constitution and the various state constitutions. The U.S. Constitution is the supreme law of the land. State constitutions are supreme within state borders to the extent that they do not violate the U.S. Constitution or a federal law. 2. *Statutory law*—Laws or ordinances created by federal, state, and local legislatures and governing bodies. None of these laws can violate the U.S. Constitution or the relevant state constitutions. Uniform laws, when adopted by a state legislature, become statutory law in that state. 3. *Administrative law*—The rules, orders, and decisions of federal or state government administrative agencies. Federal administrative agencies are created by enabling legislation enacted by the U.S. Congress. Agency functions include rulemaking, investigation and enforcement, and adjudication. 4. *Case law and common law doctrines*—Judge-made law, including interpretations of constitutional provisions, of statutes enacted by legislatures, and of regulations created by administrative agencies. The common law—the doctrines and principles embodied in case law—governs all areas not covered by statutory law or administrative law.
The Common Law Tradition (See pages 11–16.)	1. *Common law*—Law that originated in medieval England with the creation of the king's courts, or *curiae regis,* and the development of a body of rules that were common to (or applied in) all regions of the country. 2. *Stare decisis*—A doctrine under which judges "stand on decided cases"—or follow the rule of precedent—in deciding cases. *Stare decisis* is the cornerstone of the common law tradition. 3. *Remedies*—A remedy is the means by which a court enforces a right or compensates for a violation of a right. Courts typically grant legal remedies (monetary damages) but may also grant equitable remedies (specific performance, injunction, or rescission) when the legal remedy is inadequate or unavailable. 4. *Schools of legal thought*—Judges' decision making is influenced by their philosophy of law. The following are four important schools of legal thought, or legal philosophies: a. Natural law tradition—One of the oldest and most significant schools of legal thought. Those who believe in natural law hold that there is a universal law applicable to all human beings and that this law is of a higher order than positive, or conventional, law. b. Legal positivism—A school of legal thought centered on the assumption that there is no law higher than the laws created by the government. Laws must be obeyed, even if they are unjust, to prevent anarchy. c. Historical school—A school of legal thought that stresses the evolutionary nature of law and looks to doctrines that have withstood the passage of time for guidance in shaping present laws. d. Legal realism—A school of legal thought that generally advocates a less abstract and more realistic approach to the law that takes into account customary practices and the circumstances in which transactions take place.
Classifications of Law (See pages 16–19.)	The law may be broken down according to several classification systems, such as substantive or procedural law, federal or state law, and private or public law. Two broad classifications are civil and criminal law, and national and international law. Cyberlaw is not really a classification of law but a term that is used for the growing body of case and statutory law that applies to Internet transactions.

ExamPrep

ISSUE SPOTTERS

1. The First Amendment to the U.S. Constitution provides protection for the free exercise of religion. A state legislature enacts a law that outlaws all religions that do not derive from the Judeo-Christian tradition. Is this law valid within that state? Why or why not? **(See page 6.)**
2. Apples & Oranges Corporation learns that a federal administrative agency is considering a rule that will have a negative impact on the firm's ability to do business. Does the firm have any opportunity to express its opinion about the pending rule? Explain. **(See page 10.)**

—Check your answers to the Issue Spotters against the answers provided in Appendix E at the end of this text.

BEFORE THE TEST

Go to www.cengagebrain.com, enter the ISBN 9781133273561, and click on "Find" to locate this textbook's Web site. Then, click on "Access Now" under "Study Tools," and select Chapter 1 at the top. There, you will find a Practice Quiz that you can take to assess your mastery of the concepts in this chapter, as well as Flashcards, a Glossary of important terms, and Video Questions (when assigned).

For Review

Answers to the even-numbered questions in this For Review section can be found in Appendix F at the end of this text.

1. What are four primary sources of law in the United States?
2. What is the common law tradition?
3. What is a precedent? When might a court depart from precedent?
4. What is the difference between remedies at law and remedies in equity?
5. What are some important differences between civil law and criminal law?

Business Scenarios and Case Problems

1–1 Binding versus Persuasive Authority. A county court in Illinois is deciding a case involving an issue that has never been addressed before in that state's courts. The Iowa Supreme Court, however, recently decided a case involving a very similar fact pattern. Is the Illinois court obligated to follow the Iowa Supreme Court's decision on the issue? If the United States Supreme Court had decided a similar case, would that decision be binding on the Illinois court? Explain. **(See page 12.)**

1–2 Remedies. Arthur Rabe is suing Xavier Sanchez for breaching a contract in which Sanchez promised to sell Rabe a Van Gogh painting for $150,000. **(See page 14.)**

1. In this lawsuit, who is the plaintiff, and who is the defendant?
2. If Rabe wants Sanchez to perform the contract as promised, what remedy should Rabe seek?
3. Suppose that Rabe wants to cancel the contract because Sanchez fraudulently misrepresented the painting as an original Van Gogh when in fact it is a copy. In this situation, what remedy should Rabe seek?
4. Will the remedy Rabe seeks in either situation be a remedy at law or a remedy in equity?
5. Suppose that the court finds in Rabe's favor and grants one of these remedies. Sanchez then appeals the decision to a higher court. Read through the subsection entitled "Parties to Lawsuits" in the appendix following this chapter. On appeal, which party in the Rabe-Sanchez case will be the appellant (or petitioner), and which party will be the appellee (or respondent)? **(See page 30.)**

1–3 Question with Sample Answer—Sources of Law. Under a Massachusetts state statute, large wineries could sell their products through wholesalers or to consumers directly, but not both. Small wineries could use both methods. Family Winemakers of California filed a suit against the state, arguing that this restriction gave small wineries a competitive advantage in violation of the U.S. Constitution. The court agreed that the statute was in conflict with the Constitution. Which source of law takes priority, and why? [*Family Winemakers of California v. Jenkins,* 592 F.3d 1 (1st Cir. 2010)] **(See page 6.)**

—For a sample answer to Question 1–3, go to Appendix G at the end of this text.

1–4 Philosophy of Law. After World War II ended in 1945, an international tribunal of judges convened at Nuremberg, Germany. The judges convicted several Nazi war criminals of "crimes against humanity." Assuming that the Nazis who were convicted had not disobeyed any law of their country and had merely been following their government's (Hitler's) orders, what law had they violated? Explain. **(See page 15.)**

1–5 Reading Citations. Assume that you want to read the court's entire opinion in the case of *State v. Allen,* 268 P.3d 1198 (Kan. 2012). Read the section entitled "Finding Case Law" in the appendix that follows this chapter, and then explain specifically where you would find the court's opinion. **(See page 25.)**

1–6 Case Problem with Sample Answer—Law around the World. Karen Goldberg's husband was killed in a terrorist bombing in Israel. She filed a suit in a U.S. federal court against UBS AG, a Switzerland-based global financial services company. She claimed that UBS aided her husband's killing because it provided services to the terrorists. UBS argued that the case should be transferred to another country. Like many nations, the United States has a common law system. Other nations have civil law systems. What are the key differences between these systems? [*Goldberg v. UBS AG,* 690 F.Supp.2d 92 (E.D.N.Y. 2010)] **(See page 18.)**

—For a sample answer to Problem 1–6, go to Appendix H at the end of this text.

1–7 **Spotlight on AOL—Common Law.** AOL, LLC, mistakenly made public the personal information of 650,000 of its members. The members filed a suit, alleging violations of California law. AOL asked the court to dismiss the suit on the basis of a "forum-selection" clause in its member agreement that designates Virginia courts as the place where member disputes will be tried. Under a decision of the United States Supreme Court, a forum-selection clause is unenforceable "if enforcement would contravene a strong public policy of the forum in which suit is brought." California has declared in other cases that the AOL clause contravenes a strong public policy. If the court applies the doctrine of *stare decisis,* will it dismiss the suit? Explain. [*Doe 1 v. AOL, LLC,* 552 F.3d 1077 (9th Cir. 2009)] **(See page 12.)**

1–8 **A Question of Ethics—*Stare Decisis.*** On July 5, 1884, Dudley, Stephens, and Brooks—"all able-bodied English seamen"—and a teenage English boy were cast adrift in a lifeboat following a storm at sea. They had no water with them in the boat, and all they had for sustenance were two one-pound tins of turnips. On July 24, Dudley proposed that one of the four in the lifeboat be sacrificed to save the others. Stephens agreed with Dudley, but Brooks refused to consent—and the boy was never asked for his opinion. On July 25, Dudley killed the boy, and the three men then fed on the boy's body and blood. Four days later, the men were rescued by a passing vessel. They were taken to England and tried for the murder of the boy. If the men had not fed on the boy's body, they would probably have died of starvation within the four-day period. The boy, who was in a much weaker condition, would likely have died before the rest. [*Regina v. Dudley and Stephens,* 14 Q.B.D. (Queen's Bench Division, England) 273 (1884)] **(See pages 16–17.)**

1. The basic question in this case is whether the survivors should be subject to penalties under English criminal law, given the men's unusual circumstances. You be the judge and decide the issue. Give the reasons for your decision.
2. Should judges ever have the power to look beyond the written "letter of the law" in making their decisions? Why or why not?

Critical Thinking and Writing Assignments

1–9 **Business Law Writing.** John's company is involved in a lawsuit with a customer, Beth. John argues that for fifty years higher courts in that state have decided cases involving circumstances similar to his case in a way that indicates he can expect a ruling in his company's favor. Write at least one paragraph discussing if this is a valid argument. Write another paragraph discussing whether the judge in this case must rule as those other judges did, and why. **(See page 12.)**

1–10 **Business Law Critical Thinking Group Assignment—Court Opinions.** Read through the subsection entitled "Decisions and Opinions" in the appendix following this chapter. **(See page 30.)**

1. One group will explain the difference between a concurring opinion and a majority opinion.
2. Another group will outline the difference between a concurring opinion and a dissenting opinion.
3. A third group will explain why judges and justices write concurring and dissenting opinions, given that these opinions will not affect the outcome of the case at hand, which has already been decided by majority vote.

Appendix to Chapter 1:
Finding and Analyzing the Law

The statutes, agency regulations, and case law referred to in this text establish the rights and duties of businesspersons engaged in various types of activities. The cases presented in the following chapters provide you with concise, real-life illustrations of how the courts interpret and apply these laws. Because of the importance of knowing how to find statutory, administrative, and case law, this appendix offers a brief introduction to how these laws are published and to the legal "shorthand" employed in referencing these legal sources.

Finding Statutory and Administrative Law

When Congress passes laws, they are collected in a publication titled *United States Statutes at Large*. When state legislatures pass laws, they are collected in similar state publications. Most frequently, however, laws are referred to in their codified form—that is, the form in which they appear in the federal and state codes. In these codes, laws are compiled by subject.

United States Code

The *United States Code* (U.S.C.) arranges all existing federal laws of a public and permanent nature by subject. Each of the fifty subjects into which the U.S.C. arranges the laws is given a title and a title number. For example, laws relating to commerce and trade are collected in "Title 15, Commerce and Trade." Titles are subdivided by sections. A citation to the U.S.C. includes title and section numbers. Thus, a reference to "15 U.S.C. Section 1" means that the statute can be found in Section 1 of Title 15. ("Section" may be designated by the symbol §, and "Sections" by §§.) In addition to the print publication of the U.S.C., the federal government also provides a searchable online database of the *United States Code* at **www.gpo.gov** (click on "Libraries" and then "Core Documents of Our Democracy" to find the *United States Code*).

Commercial publications of these laws are available and are widely used. For example, West Group publishes the *United States Code Annotated* (U.S.C.A.). The U.S.C.A. contains the complete text of laws included in the U.S.C., notes of court decisions that interpret and apply specific sections of the statutes, and the text of presidential proclamations and executive orders. The U.S.C.A. also includes research aids, such as cross-references to related statutes, historical notes, and other references. A citation to the U.S.C.A. is similar to a citation to the U.S.C.: "15 U.S.C.A. Section 1."

State Codes

State codes follow the U.S.C. pattern of arranging laws by subject. The state codes may be called codes, revisions, compilations, consolidations, general statutes, or statutes, depending on the state. In some codes, subjects are designated by number. In others, they are designated by name. For example, "13 Pennsylvania Consolidated Statutes Section 1101" means that the statute can be found in Title 13, Section 1101, of the Pennsylvania code. "California Commercial Code Section 1101" means the statute can be found in Section 1101 under the subject heading "Commercial Code" of the California code. Abbreviations may be used. For example, "13 Pennsylvania Consolidated Statutes Section 1101" may be abbreviated

"13 Pa. C.S. § 1101," and "California Commercial Code Section 1101" may be abbreviated "Cal. Com. Code § 1101."

Administrative Rules

Rules and regulations adopted by federal administrative agencies are compiled in the *Code of Federal Regulations* (C.F.R.). Like the U.S.C., the C.F.R. is divided into fifty titles. Rules within each title are assigned section numbers. A full citation to the C.F.R. includes title and section numbers. For example, a reference to "17 C.F.R. Section 230.504" means that the rule can be found in Section 230.504 of Title 17.

Finding Case Law

Before discussing the case reporting system, we need to look briefly at the court system (which will be discussed in detail in Chapter 3). There are two types of courts in the United States: federal courts and state courts. Both the federal and state court systems consist of several levels, or tiers, of courts. *Trial courts,* in which evidence is presented and testimony is given, are on the bottom tier (which also includes lower courts handling specialized issues). Decisions from a trial court can be appealed to a higher court, which commonly would be an intermediate *court of appeals,* or an *appellate court.* Decisions from these intermediate courts of appeals may be appealed to an even higher court, such as a state supreme court or the United States Supreme Court.

State Court Decisions

Most state trial court decisions are not published. Except in New York and a few other states that publish selected opinions of their trial courts, decisions from state trial courts are merely filed in the office of the clerk of the court, where the decisions are available for public inspection. (Increasingly, they can be found online as well.)

Written decisions of the appellate, or reviewing, courts, however, are published and distributed. As you will note, most of the state court cases presented in this book are from state appellate courts. The reported appellate decisions are published in volumes called *reports* or *reporters,* which are numbered consecutively. State appellate court decisions are found in the state reporters of that particular state.

Additionally, state court opinions appear in regional units of the *National Reporter System,* published by West Group. Most lawyers and libraries have the West reporters because they report cases more quickly and are distributed more widely than the state-published reports. In fact, many states have eliminated their own reporters in favor of West's National Reporter System. The National Reporter System divides the states into the following geographic areas: *Atlantic* (A. or A.2d), *North Eastern* (N.E. or N.E.2d), *North Western* (N.W. or N.W.2d), *Pacific* (P., P.2d, or P.3d), *South Eastern* (S.E. or S.E.2d), *South Western* (S.W., S.W.2d, or S.W.3d), and *Southern* (So., So.2d, or So.3d). (The *2d* and *3d* in the abbreviations refer to *Second Series* and *Third Series,* respectively.) The states included in each of these regional divisions are indicated in Exhibit 1A.1 on the following page, which illustrates West's National Reporter System.

After appellate decisions have been published, they are normally referred to (cited) by the name of the case; the volume, name, and page number of the state's official reporter (if different from West's National Reporter System); the volume, name, and page number of the *National Reporter;* and the volume, name, and page number of any other selected reporter. This information is included in the *citation.* (Citing a reporter by volume number, name, and page number, in that order, is common to all citations.) When more than one reporter is cited for the same case, each reference is called a *parallel citation.* Note that some states have adopted a "public domain citation system" that uses a somewhat different format for

Exhibit 1A.1 West's National Reporter System—Regional/Federal

Regional Reporters	Coverage Beginning	Coverage
Atlantic Reporter (A., A.2d, or A.3d)	1885	Connecticut, Delaware, District of Columbia, Maine, Maryland, New Hampshire, New Jersey, Pennsylvania, Rhode Island, and Vermont.
North Eastern Reporter (N.E. or N.E.2d)	1885	Illinois, Indiana, Massachusetts, New York, and Ohio.
North Western Reporter (N.W. or N.W.2d)	1879	Iowa, Michigan, Minnesota, Nebraska, North Dakota, South Dakota, and Wisconsin.
Pacific Reporter (P., P.2d, or P.3d)	1883	Alaska, Arizona, California, Colorado, Hawaii, Idaho, Kansas, Montana, Nevada, New Mexico, Oklahoma, Oregon, Utah, Washington, and Wyoming.
South Eastern Reporter (S.E. or S.E.2d)	1887	Georgia, North Carolina, South Carolina, Virginia, and West Virginia.
South Western Reporter (S.W., S.W.2d, or S.W.3d)	1886	Arkansas, Kentucky, Missouri, Tennessee, and Texas.
Southern Reporter (So., So.2d, or So.3d)	1887	Alabama, Florida, Louisiana, and Mississippi.
Federal Reporters		
Federal Reporter (F., F.2d, or F.3d)	1880	U.S. Circuit Courts from 1880 to 1912; U.S. Commerce Court from 1911 to 1913; U.S. District Courts from 1880 to 1932; U.S. Court of Claims (now called U.S. Court of Federal Claims) from 1929 to 1932 and since 1960; U.S. Courts of Appeals since 1891; U.S. Court of Customs and Patent Appeals since 1929; U.S. Emergency Court of Appeals since 1943.
Federal Supplement (F.Supp. or F.Supp.2d)	1932	U.S. Court of Claims from 1932 to 1960; U.S. District Courts since 1932; U.S. Customs Court since 1956.
Federal Rules Decisions (F.R.D.)	1939	U.S. District Courts involving the Federal Rules of Civil Procedure since 1939 and Federal Rules of Criminal Procedure since 1946.
Supreme Court Reporter (S.Ct.)	1882	United States Supreme Court since the October term of 1882.
Bankruptcy Reporter (Bankr.)	1980	Bankruptcy decisions of U.S. Bankruptcy Courts, U.S. District Courts, U.S. Courts of Appeals, and the United States Supreme Court.
Military Justice Reporter (M.J.)	1978	U.S. Court of Military Appeals and Courts of Military Review for the Army, Navy, Air Force, and Coast Guard.

NATIONAL REPORTER SYSTEM MAP

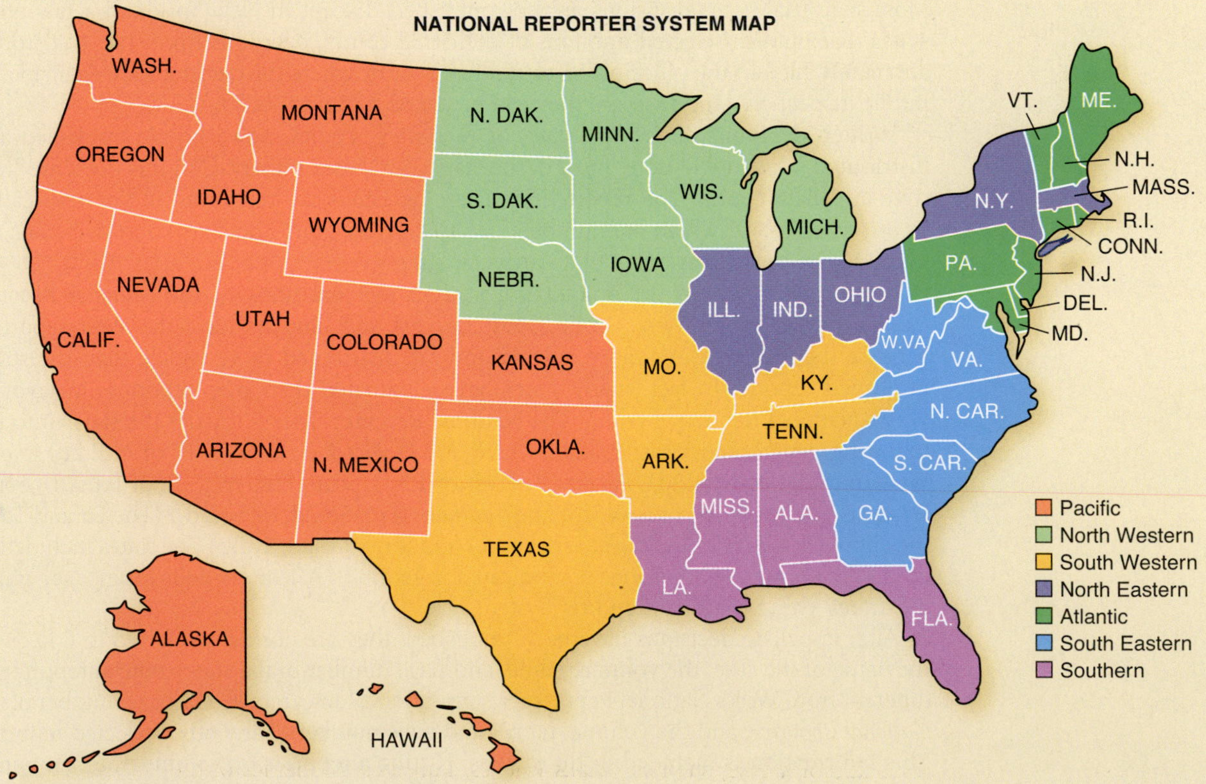

- Pacific
- North Western
- South Western
- North Eastern
- Atlantic
- South Eastern
- Southern

the citation. For example, in Wisconsin, a Wisconsin Supreme Court decision might be designated "2012 WI 23," meaning that the decision was the twenty-third issued by the Wisconsin Supreme Court in the year 2012. Parallel citations to the *Wisconsin Reports* and West's *North Western Reporter* are still included after the public domain citation.

Consider the following citation: *Goldstein v. Lackard,* 81 Mass.App.Ct. 1112, 961 N.E.2d. 163 (2012). We see that the opinion in this case can be found in Volume 81 of the official *Massachusetts Appellate Court Reports,* on page 1112. The parallel citation is to Volume 961 of the *North Eastern Reporter, Second Series,* page 163. When we present opinions in this text (starting in Chapter 2), in addition to the reporter, we give the name of the court hearing the case and the year of the court's decision. Sample citations to state court decisions are listed and explained in Exhibit 1A.2 on pages 28–29.

Federal Court Decisions

Federal district (trial) court decisions are published unofficially in the *Federal Supplement* (F. Supp. or F.Supp.2d), and opinions from the circuit courts of appeals (federal reviewing courts) are reported unofficially in the *Federal Reporter* (F., F.2d, or F.3d). Cases concerning federal bankruptcy law are published unofficially in West's *Bankruptcy Reporter* (Bankr. or B.R.).

The official edition of United States Supreme Court decisions is the *United States Reports* (U.S.), which is published by the federal government. Unofficial editions of Supreme Court cases include West's *Supreme Court Reporter* (S.Ct.) and the *Lawyers' Edition of the Supreme Court Reports* (L.Ed. or L.Ed.2d). Sample citations for federal court decisions are also listed and explained in Exhibit 1A.2.

Unpublished Opinions

Many court opinions that are not yet published or that are not intended for publication can be accessed through Westlaw® (abbreviated in citations as "WL"), an online legal database. When no citation to a published reporter is available for cases cited in this text, we give the WL citation (such as 2012 WL 573109, which means it was case number 573109 decided in the year 2012). Sometimes, both in this text and in other legal sources, you will see blanks left in a citation. This occurs when the decision will be published, but the particular volume number or page number is not yet available.

Old Cases

On a few occasions, this text cites opinions from old, classic cases dating to the nineteenth century or earlier. Some of these cases are from the English courts. The citations to these cases may not conform to the descriptions given above because they were published in reporters that are no longer used today.

Reading and Understanding Case Law

The cases in this text have been condensed from the full text of the courts' opinions and paraphrased by the authors. For those wishing to review court cases for future research projects or to gain additional legal information, the following sections will provide useful insights into how to read and understand case law.

Case Titles and Terminology

The title of a case, such as *Adams v. Jones,* indicates the names of the parties to the lawsuit. The *v.* in the case title stands for *versus,* which means "against." In the trial court, Adams was the plaintiff—the person who filed the suit. Jones was the defendant. If the case is appealed, however, the appellate court will sometimes place the name of the party

Exhibit 1A.2 How to Read Citations

STATE COURTS

282 Neb. 990, 808 N.W.2d 48 (2012)[a]

N.W. is the abbreviation for West's publication of state court decisions rendered in the *North Western Reporter* of the National Reporter System. *2d* indicates that this case was included in the *Second Series* of that reporter. The number 808 refers to the volume number of the reporter; the number 48 refers to the page in that volume on which this case begins.

Neb. is an abbreviation for *Nebraska Reports,* Nebraska's official reports of the decisions of its highest court, the Nebraska Supreme Court.

204 Cal.App.4th 112, 138 Cal.Rptr.3d 519 (2012)

Cal.Rptr. is the abbreviation for West's unofficial reports—titled *California Reporter*—of the decisions of California courts.

93 A.D.3d 493, 940 N.Y.S.2d 75 (2012)

N.Y.S. is the abbreviation for West's unofficial reports—titled *New York Supplement*—of the decisions of New York courts.

A.D. is the abbreviation for *Appellate Division,* which hears appeals from the New York Supreme Court—the state's general trial court. The New York Court of Appeals is the state's highest court, analogous to other states' supreme courts.

313 Ga.App. 804, 723 S.E.2d 39 (2012)

Ga.App. is the abbreviation for *Georgia Appeals Reports,* Georgia's official reports of the decisions of its court of appeals.

FEDERAL COURTS

___ U.S. ___, 132 S.Ct. 1201, 182 L.Ed.2d 42 (2012)

L.Ed. is an abbreviation for *Lawyers' Edition of the Supreme Court Reports*, an unofficial edition of decisions of the United States Supreme Court.

S.Ct. is the abbreviation for West's unofficial reports—titled *Supreme Court Reporter*—of decisions of the United States Supreme Court.

U.S. is the abbreviation for *United States Reports*, the official edition of the decisions of the United States Supreme Court. The blank lines in this citation (or any other citation) indicate that the appropriate volume of the case reporter has not yet been published and no page number is available.

a. The case names have been deleted from these citations to emphasize the publications. It should be kept in mind, however, that the name of a case is as important as the specific page numbers in the volumes in which it is found. If a citation is incorrect, the correct citation may be found in a publication's index of case names. In addition to providing a check on errors in citations, the date of a case is important because the value of a recent case as an authority is likely to be greater than that of older cases from the same court.

Exhibit 1A.2 How to Read Citations, Continued

FEDERAL COURTS (Continued)

668 F.3d 1148 (9th Cir. 2012)

9th Cir. is an abbreviation denoting that this case was decided in the U.S. Court of Appeals for the Ninth Circuit.

___ F.Supp.2d ___ (S.D. Fla. 2012)

S.D. Fla. is an abbreviation indicating that the U.S. District Court for the Southern District of Florida decided this case.

ENGLISH COURTS

9 Exch. 341, 156 Eng.Rep. 145 (1854)

Eng.Rep. is an abbreviation for *English Reports, Full Reprint,* a series of reports containing selected decisions made in English courts between 1378 and 1865.

Exch. is an abbreviation for *English Exchequer Reports*, which includes the original reports of cases decided in England's Court of Exchequer.

STATUTORY AND OTHER CITATIONS

18 U.S.C. Section 1961(1)(A)

U.S.C. denotes *United States Code*, the codification of *United States Statutes at Large*. The number 18 refers to the statute's U.S.C. title number and 1961 to its section number within that title. The number 1 in parentheses refers to a subsection within the section, and the letter A in parentheses to a subsection within the subsection.

UCC 2–206(1)(b)

UCC is an abbreviation for *Uniform Commercial Code*. The first number 2 is a reference to an article of the UCC, and 206 to a section within that article. The number 1 in parentheses refers to a subsection within the section, and the letter b in parentheses to a subsection within the subsection.

***Restatement (Third) of Torts,* Section 6**

Restatement (Third) of Torts refers to the third edition of the American Law Institute's *Restatement of the Law of Torts*. The number 6 refers to a specific section.

17 C.F.R. Section 230.505

C.F.R. is an abbreviation for *Code of Federal Regulations*, a compilation of federal administrative regulations. The number 17 designates the regulation's title number, and 230.505 designates a specific section within that title.

appealing the decision first, so the case may be called *Jones v. Adams.* Because some reviewing courts retain the trial court order of names, it is often impossible to distinguish the plaintiff from the defendant in the title of a reported appellate court decision. You must carefully read the facts of each case to identify the parties.

The following terms and phrases are frequently encountered in court opinions and legal publications. Because it is important to understand what these terms and phrases mean, we define and discuss them here.

Parties to Lawsuits

As mentioned in Chapter 1, the party initiating a lawsuit is referred to as the *plaintiff* or *petitioner,* depending on the nature of the action, and the party against whom a lawsuit is brought is the *defendant* or *respondent*. Lawsuits frequently involve more than one plaintiff and/or defendant. When a case is appealed from the original court or jurisdiction to another court or jurisdiction, the party appealing the case is called the *appellant*. The *appellee* is the party against whom the appeal is taken. (In some appellate courts, the party appealing a case is referred to as the *petitioner,* and the party against whom the suit is brought or appealed is called the *respondent*.)

Judges and Justices

The terms *judge* and *justice* are usually synonymous and are used to refer to the judges in various courts. All members of the United States Supreme Court, for example, are referred to as justices. And justice is the formal title usually given to judges of appellate courts, although this is not always the case. In New York, a justice is a judge of the trial court (which is called the Supreme Court), and a member of the Court of Appeals (the state's highest court) is called a judge. The term *justice* is commonly abbreviated to J., and *justices* to JJ. A Supreme Court case might refer to Justice Sotomayor as Sotomayor, J., or to Chief Justice Roberts as Roberts, C.J.

Decisions and Opinions

Most decisions reached by reviewing, or appellate, courts are explained in written *opinions.* The opinion contains the court's reasons for its decision, the rules of law that apply, and the judgment. When all judges or justices unanimously agree on an opinion, the opinion is written for the entire court and can be deemed a *unanimous opinion.* When there is not unanimous agreement, a **majority opinion** is written. The majority opinion outlines the views of the majority of the judges or justices deciding the case. Sometimes, the majority agrees on the result, but not the reasoning. The opinion joined by the largest number of judges or justices, but less than a majority, is called a **plurality opinion.**

Majority Opinion A court opinion that represents the views of the majority (more than half) of the judges or justices deciding the case.

Plurality Opinion A court opinion that is joined by the largest number of the judges or justices hearing the case, but less than half of the total number.

Concurring Opinion A court opinion by one or more judges or justices who agree with the majority but want to make or emphasize a point that was not made or emphasized in the majority's opinion.

Dissenting Opinion A court opinion that presents the views of one or more judges or justices who disagree with the majority's decision.

***Per Curiam* Opinion** A court opinion that does not indicate which judge or justice authored the opinion.

Often, a judge or justice who strongly wishes to make or emphasize a point that was not made or emphasized in the unanimous or majority opinion will write a **concurring opinion.** This means the judge or justice agrees (concurs) with the judgment given in the unanimous or majority opinion but for different reasons. When there is not a unanimous opinion, a **dissenting opinion** presents the views of one or more judges who disagree with the majority's decision. (See the *Unit 1: Business Case Study with Dissenting Opinion* on page 233 for an example of a dissenting opinion.) The dissenting opinion is important because it may form the basis of the arguments used years later in overruling the precedential majority opinion. Occasionally, a court issues a ***per curiam* opinion** (*per curiam* is Latin for "of the court"), which does not indicate which judge or justice authored the opinion.

A Sample Court Case

Knowing how to read and analyze a court opinion is an essential step in undertaking accurate legal research. A further step involves "briefing" the case. Legal researchers routinely brief cases by summarizing and reducing the texts of the opinions to their essential elements. Briefing cases facilitates the development of critical thinking skills that are crucial for businesspersons when evaluating relevant business law. (For instructions on how to brief a case, go to Appendix A at the end of this text.)

The cases contained within the chapters of this text have already been analyzed and briefed by the authors, and the essential aspects of each case are presented in a convenient format consisting of four basic sections: *Facts, Issue, Decision,* and *Reason,* as shown in Exhibit 1A.3 below, which has also been annotated (see the next page) to illustrate the kind of information that is contained in each section.

Throughout this text, in addition to this basic format, we sometimes include a special introductory section entitled *Historical and Social [Economic, Technological, Political,* or *other] Setting.* In some instances, a *Company Profile* is included in place of the introductory setting. These profiles provide background on one of the parties to the lawsuit.

Each case is followed by a question or section that is designed to enhance your analysis. *Critical Thinking* sections, such as the one shown in Exhibit 1A.3, present a question about some issue raised by the case. *Why Is This Case Important?* sections explain the significance of the case. *What If the Facts Were Different?* questions alter the facts slightly and ask you to consider how this would change the outcome. A section entitled *Impact of This Case on Today's Law* concludes each of the *Classic Cases* that appear throughout the text to indicate the significance of the case for today's legal landscape.

Exhibit 1A.3 A Sample Court Case

Sample Case

United States v. Jones

1

Supreme Court of the United States 2

3 ___ U.S.___, 132 S.Ct. 945, 181 L.Ed.2d 911(2012).
www.supremecourt.gov/opinions/11pdf/10-1259.pdf

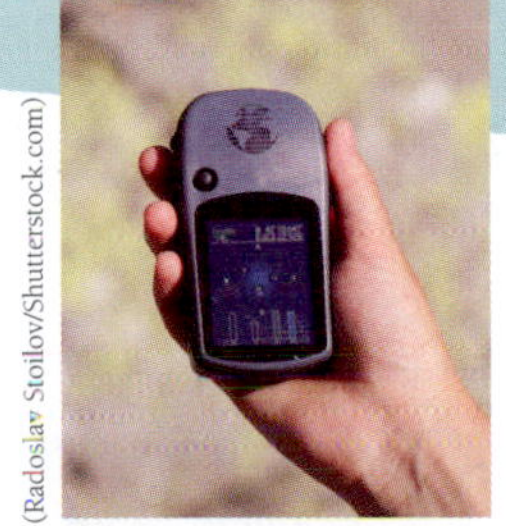
(Radoslav Stoilov/Shutterstock.com)

Tracking device for automobiles.

4 **FACTS** Antoine Jones owned and operated a nightclub in the District of Columbia and was suspected of drug trafficking. As part of an investigation, the government installed a Global Positioning System (GPS) tracking device underneath a vehicle belonging to Jones's wife. Although it did not have a valid warrant, the government tracked the vehicle for four weeks, ultimately gathering enough evidence of drug trafficking to obtain an indictment. Before the trial, Jones filed a motion to suppress the evidence obtained with the device, arguing that the government had violated his Fourth Amendment rights by subjecting him to an unlawful "search." The district court held that most of the evidence was admissible, and Jones was convicted and sentenced to life in prison. A federal appellate court reversed the conviction, and the government appealed to the United States Supreme Court.

5 **ISSUE** Did the government engage in a "search" within the meaning of the Fourth Amendment by installing the GPS tracking device and then monitoring the vehicle's movements?

6 **DECISION** Yes. The United States Supreme Court affirmed the judgment of the federal appellate court. The government engaged in a Fourth Amendment "search" by installing and using the tracking device.

7 **REASON** The Fourth Amendment prohibits "unreasonable searches and seizures" based on "the right of the people to be secure in their persons, houses, papers, and effects." A vehicle is an "effect," and the government's installation and use of the tracking device constituted a "search." Traditionally, the Supreme Court recognized the Fourth Amendment's close connection to property rights and found a "search" only if the government's conduct would have amounted to trespass under English common law. In 1967, however, the Supreme Court ruled that the Fourth Amendment also protects a person's "reasonable expectation of privacy."

Whether or not Jones had a reasonable expectation of privacy in either the vehicle's undercarriage or its movements on public streets was irrelevant in this situation. The Court reasoned that its precedent on privacy did not eliminate the traditional rule that a common law trespass may also establish a search. In this case, the government engaged in trespass, and therefore a search, by installing the tracking device without consent.

8 **CRITICAL THINKING—Ethical Consideration** *Was the government's conduct ethical? Why or why not?*

Continued

Review of Sample Court Case

1 The name of the case is *United States v. Jones.* The government prosecuted Jones in federal court, and now the government is appealing, or challenging, a decision by the U.S. Court of Appeals for the District of Columbia (the federal appellate court).

2 The court deciding this case is the United States Supreme Court.

3 The case citation includes a citation to the *Supreme Court Reporter,* which contains only decisions of the United States Supreme Court. The case can be found in Volume 132 of the *Supreme Court Reporter,* beginning on page 945. The heading also provides a Web address at which you can view the opinion.

4 The *Facts* section identifies the parties, summarizes the relevant facts, and explains the procedural history leading up to the decision being summarized.

5 The *Issue* section presents the central issue(s) that the court must decide. In this case, for example, the United States Supreme Court must determine whether the government's conduct constituted a "search" for purposes of the Fourth Amendment. Most cases address more than one issue, but this textbook's authors have edited many cases to focus on just one issue.

6 The *Decision* section summarizes the court's decision about an issue. The decision reflects the opinion of the judge or, if a panel heard the case, the majority's opinion. For an appellate court case, the *Decision* section will frequently explain whether the appellate court "affirmed" or "reversed" a lower court's ruling. In either situation, the appellate court may remand the case, meaning it sends the case back for further proceedings consistent with its decision.

7 The *Reason* section explains how the court arrived at its decision, summarizing the key legal principles and authorities. In the *Jones* case, for example, the Supreme Court held that the government performed a Fourth Amendment search by installing and using a GPS tracking device. The Court found that a search may occur if the government violates either a reasonable expectation of privacy or a person's property rights.

8 The *Critical Thinking* section raises a question relating to the summarized case. Here, the question concerns an "ethical" consideration. Other cases in this text raise critical thinking questions that focus on diversity, e-commerce, economics, global, legal environment, political, social, or technological issues.

CHAPTER 2

Constitutional Law

(Creativeye99/iStockphoto.com)

CHAPTER OUTLINE

- The Constitutional Powers of Government
- Business and the Bill of Rights
- Due Process and Equal Protection
- Privacy Rights

LEARNING OBJECTIVES

The five learning objectives below are designed to help improve your understanding of the chapter. After reading this chapter, you should be able to answer the following questions:

1. What is the basic structure of the U.S. government?
2. What constitutional clause gives the federal government the power to regulate commercial activities among the various states?
3. What constitutional clause allows laws enacted by the federal government to take priority over conflicting state laws?
4. What is the Bill of Rights? What freedoms do the First Amendment guarantee?
5. Where in the Constitution can the due process clause be found?

"The United States Constitution has proved itself the most marvelously elastic compilation of rules of government ever written."
—Franklin D. Roosevelt, 1882–1945 (Thirty-second president of the United States, 1933–1945)

The U.S. Constitution is brief. (See Appendix B for the full text of the U.S. Constitution.) It contains only about seven thousand words—less than one-third of the number of words in the average state constitution. Perhaps its brevity explains, in part, why the Constitution has proved to be so "marvelously elastic," as Franklin Roosevelt pointed out in the chapter-opening quotation, and why it has survived for more than two hundred years—longer than any other written constitution in the world.

Laws that govern business have their origin in the lawmaking authority granted by the Constitution, which is the supreme law in this country. As mentioned in Chapter 1, neither Congress nor any state can enact a law that is in conflict with the Constitution. Constitutional disputes frequently come before the courts. For example, numerous states have challenged the Obama administration's Affordable Care Act [1] on constitutional grounds. The United States

1. *National Federation of Independent Business v. Sebelius*, ___ U.S. ___, 132 S.Ct. 2566, 183 L.Ed.2d 450 (2012).

Supreme Court had to decide if the provisions of this law that require most Americans to have health insurance by 2014 exceed the constitutional authority of the federal government. In 2012, the Court upheld the constitutionality of this provision—a decision that significantly impacts business because many individuals obtain insurance through their employers.

In this chapter, we first look at some basic constitutional concepts and clauses and their significance for business. Then, we examine how certain fundamental freedoms guaranteed by the Constitution affect businesspersons and the workplace. We also examine the constitutional protection of privacy rights. In recent years, many users of online social networks have become concerned at the amount of their personal information that exists in cyberspace and the possibility that it might be misused. Such concerns recently led the Federal Trade Commission to charge Facebook, Twitter, and Google with misleading users about the way their personal data were being used. All three companies agreed to revise their privacy policies as a result.

The Constitutional Powers of Government

Following the Revolutionary War, the states created a *confederal* form of government in which the states had the authority to govern themselves and the national government could exercise only limited powers. When problems arose because the nation was facing an economic crisis and state laws interfered with the free flow of commerce, a national convention was called, and the delegates drafted the U.S. Constitution. This document, after its ratification by the states in 1789, became the basis for an entirely new form of government.

A Federal Form of Government

The new government created by the Constitution reflected a series of compromises made by the convention delegates on various issues. Some delegates wanted sovereign power to remain with the states, whereas others wanted the national government alone to exercise sovereign power. The end result was a compromise—a **federal form of government** in which the national government and the states *share* sovereign power.

Federal Form of Government A system of government in which the states form a union and the sovereign power is divided between the central government and the member states.

The Constitution sets forth specific powers that can be exercised by the national government and provides that the national government has the implied power to undertake actions necessary to carry out its expressly designated powers. All other powers are "reserved" to the states. The broad language of the Constitution, though, has left much room for debate over the specific nature and scope of these powers. Generally, it has been the task of the courts to determine where the boundary line between state and national powers should lie—and that line changes over time. In the past, for instance, the national government met little resistance from the courts when extending its regulatory authority over broad areas of social and economic life. Today, the courts are sometimes willing to curb the national government's regulatory powers.

The Separation of Powers

LEARNING OBJECTIVE 1
What is the basic structure of the U.S. government?

To make it difficult for the national government to use its power arbitrarily, the Constitution divided the national government's powers among the three branches of government. The legislative branch makes the laws, the executive branch enforces the laws, and the judicial branch interprets the laws. Each branch performs a separate function, and no branch may exercise the authority of another branch.

The U.S. Constitution provides for a system of checks and balances. How does the president check the power of Congress? In what ways can Congress check the power of the president?

(Jim Young/Reuters /Landov)

Checks and Balances The principle under which the powers of the national government are divided among three separate branches—the executive, legislative, and judicial branches—each of which exercises a check on the actions of the others.

Additionally, a system of **checks and balances** allows each branch to limit the actions of the other two branches, thus preventing any one branch from exercising too much power. The following are examples of these checks and balances:

1. The legislative branch (Congress) can enact a law, but the executive branch (the president) has the constitutional authority to veto that law.
2. The executive branch is responsible for foreign affairs, but treaties with foreign governments require the advice and consent of the Senate.
3. Congress determines the jurisdiction of the federal courts, and the president appoints federal judges, with the advice and consent of the Senate, but the judicial branch has the power to hold actions of the other two branches unconstitutional.[2]

LEARNING OBJECTIVE 2

What constitutional clause gives the federal government the power to regulate commercial activities among the various states?

The Commerce Clause

Commerce Clause The provision in Article I, Section 8, of the U.S. Constitution that gives Congress the power to regulate interstate commerce.

To prevent states from establishing laws and regulations that would interfere with trade and commerce among the states, the Constitution expressly delegated to the national government the power to regulate interstate commerce. Article I, Section 8, of the U.S. Constitution expressly permits Congress "[t]o regulate Commerce with foreign Nations, and among the several States, and with the Indian Tribes." This clause, referred to as the **commerce clause,** has had a greater impact on business than any other provision in the Constitution.

Initially, the commerce power was interpreted as being limited to *interstate* commerce (commerce among the states) and not applicable to *intrastate* commerce (commerce within a state). In 1824, however, in the case of *Gibbons v. Ogden* (see the chapter's *Landmark in the Law* feature on the following page), the United States Supreme Court held that commerce

2. See the *Landmark in the Law* feature on page 61 in Chapter 3 on the case of *Marbury v. Madison* (1803), in which the doctrine of judicial review was clearly enunciated by Chief Justice John Marshall.

LANDMARK IN THE LAW

Gibbons v. Ogden (1824)

The commerce clause of the U.S. Constitution gives Congress the power "[t]o regulate Commerce with foreign Nations, and among the several States, and with the Indian Tribes." Prior to the commerce clause, states tended to restrict commerce within and beyond their borders, which made trade more costly and inefficient. The goal of the clause was to unify the states' commerce policies and improve the efficiency of exchanges.

The problem was that although the commerce clause gave Congress some authority to regulate trade among the states, the extent of that power was unclear. What exactly does "to regulate commerce" mean? What does "commerce" entail? These questions came before the United States Supreme Court in 1824 in the case of *Gibbons v. Ogden.*[a]

Background In 1803, Robert Fulton, the inventor of the steamboat, and Robert Livingston, who was the ambassador to France, secured a monopoly from the New York legislature on steam navigation on the waters in the state of New York. Their monopoly extended to interstate waters—waterways between New York and another state. Fulton and Livingston licensed Aaron Ogden, a former governor of New Jersey and a U.S. senator, to operate steam-powered ferryboats between New York and New Jersey.

Thomas Gibbons already operated a ferry service between New Jersey and New York, which had been licensed by Congress under a 1793 act regulating the coasting trade. Although the federal government had licensed Gibbons to operate boats in interstate waters, he did not have the state of New York's permission to compete with Ogden in that area. Ogden sued Gibbons. The New York state courts granted Ogden's request for an injunction—an order prohibiting Gibbons from operating in New York waters. Gibbons appealed the decision to the United States Supreme Court.

Marshall's Decision The issue before the Court was whether the law regulated commerce that was "among the several states." The chief justice on the Supreme Court was John Marshall, an advocate of a strong national government. Marshall defined the word *commerce* as used in the commerce clause to mean all commercial intercourse—that is, all business dealings that affect more than one state. This broader definition included navigation.

In addition to expanding the definition of commerce, Marshall also validated and increased the power of the national legislature to regulate commerce. Said Marshall, "What is this power? It is the power . . . to prescribe the rule by which commerce is to be governed." Marshall held that the power to regulate interstate commerce is an exclusive power of the national government and that this power includes the power to regulate any intrastate commerce that substantially affects interstate commerce. Accordingly, the Court held in favor of Gibbons.

Application to Today's World *Marshall's broad definition of the commerce power established the foundation for the expansion of national powers in the years to come. Today, the national government continues to rely on the commerce clause for its constitutional authority to regulate business activities. Marshall's conclusion that the power to regulate interstate commerce was an exclusive power of the national government has also had significant consequences. By implication, this means that a state cannot regulate activities that extend beyond its borders, such as out-of-state online gambling operations that affect the welfare of in-state citizens. It also means that state regulations over in-state activities normally will be invalidated if the regulations substantially burden interstate commerce.*

a. 22 U.S. (9 Wheat.) 1, 6 L.Ed. 23 (1824).

within a state could also be regulated by the national government as long as the commerce *substantially affected* commerce involving more than one state.

The Commerce Clause and the Expansion of National Powers

In *Gibbons v. Ogden,* the commerce clause was expanded to regulate activities that "substantially affect interstate commerce." As the nation grew and faced new kinds of problems, the commerce clause became a vehicle for the additional expansion of the national government's regulatory powers. Even activities that seemed purely local came under the regulatory reach of the national government if those activities were deemed to substantially affect interstate commerce. **CASE EXAMPLE 2.1** In 1942, in *Wickard v. Filburn,*[3] the

3. 317 U.S. 111, 63 S.Ct. 82, 87 L.Ed. 122 (1942).

Supreme Court held that wheat production by an individual farmer intended wholly for consumption on his own farm was subject to federal regulation. The Court reasoned that the home consumption of wheat reduced the market demand for wheat and thus could have a substantial effect on interstate commerce. ●

The following *Classic Case* involved a challenge to the scope of the national government's constitutional authority to regulate local activities.

Classic Case 2.1

Heart of Atlanta Motel v. United States

Supreme Court of the United States,
379 U.S. 241, 85 S.Ct. 348, 13 L.Ed.2d 258 (1964).
www.law.cornell.edu/supct/cases/name.htm[a]

(© Bettmann/Corbis)

Morton Rolleston in front of his Heart of Atlanta Motel.

HISTORICAL AND SOCIAL SETTING *In the first half of the twentieth century, state governments sanctioned segregation on the basis of race. In 1954, the United States Supreme Court held that racially segregated school systems violated the Constitution. In the following decade, the Court ordered an end to racial segregation imposed by the states in other public facilities, such as beaches, golf courses, buses, parks, auditoriums, and courtroom seating. Privately owned facilities that excluded or segregated African Americans and others on the basis of race were not subject to the same constitutional restrictions, however. Congress passed the Civil Rights Act of 1964 to prohibit racial discrimination in "establishments affecting interstate commerce." These facilities included "places of public accommodation."*

FACTS The owner of the Heart of Atlanta Motel, in violation of the Civil Rights Act of 1964, refused to rent rooms to African Americans. The motel owner brought an action in a federal district court to have the Civil Rights Act declared unconstitutional on the ground that Congress had exceeded its constitutional authority to regulate commerce by enacting the statute. The owner argued that his motel was not engaged in interstate commerce but was "of a purely local character." The motel, however, was accessible to state and interstate highways. The owner advertised nationally, maintained billboards throughout the state, and accepted convention trade from outside the state (75 percent of the guests were residents of other states). The district court ruled that the act did not violate the Constitution and enjoined (prohibited) the owner from discriminating on the basis of race. The owner appealed. The case ultimately went to the United States Supreme Court.

ISSUE Did Congress exceed its constitutional power to regulate interstate commerce by enacting the Civil Rights Act of 1964?

DECISION No. The United States Supreme Court upheld the constitutionality of the act.

REASON The Court noted that the act was passed to correct "the deprivation of personal dignity" accompanying the denial of equal access to "public establishments." Testimony before Congress leading to the passage of the act indicated that African Americans in particular experienced substantial discrimination in attempting to secure lodging while traveling. This discrimination impeded interstate travel and thus impeded interstate commerce.

As for the owner's argument that his motel was "of a purely local character," the Court said that even if this was true, the motel affected interstate commerce. According to the Court, "if it is interstate commerce that feels the pinch, it does not matter how local the operation that applies the squeeze." Therefore, under the commerce clause, "the power of Congress to promote interstate commerce also includes the power to regulate the local incidents thereof, including local activities."

IMPACT OF THIS CASE ON TODAY'S LAW *If the United States Supreme Court had invalidated the Civil Rights Act of 1964, the legal landscape of the United States would be much different today. The act prohibits discrimination based on race, color, national origin, religion, or gender in all "public accommodations," including hotels and restaurants. The act also prohibits discrimination in employment based on these criteria. Although state laws now prohibit many of these forms of discrimination as well, the protections available vary from state to state—and it is not certain whether such laws would have been passed had the outcome in this case been different.*

a. This is the "Historic Supreme Court Decisions—by Party Name" page within the "Supreme Court" collection that is available at the Web site of the Legal Information Institute. Click on the "H" link, or scroll down the list of cases to the entry for the *Heart of Atlanta* case. Click on the case name, and select the format in which you wish to view the case.

The Commerce Clause Today

Today, at least theoretically, the power over commerce authorizes the national government to regulate almost every commercial enterprise in the United States. The breadth of the commerce clause permits the national government to legislate in areas in which Congress has not explicitly been granted power.

In the last twenty years, the Supreme Court has on occasion curbed the national government's regulatory authority under the commerce clause. In 1995, the Court held—for the first time in sixty years—that Congress had exceeded its regulatory authority under the commerce clause. The Court struck down an act that banned the possession of guns within one thousand feet of any school because the act attempted to regulate an area that had "nothing to do with commerce."[4] Subsequently, the Court invalidated key portions of two other federal acts on the ground that they exceeded Congress's commerce clause authority.[5]

In one notable case, however, the Supreme Court did allow the federal government to regulate noncommercial activities taking place wholly within a state's borders. **CASE EXAMPLE 2.2** About a dozen states, including California, have adopted laws that legalize marijuana for medical purposes. Marijuana possession, however, is illegal under the federal Controlled Substances Act (CSA).[6] After the federal government seized the marijuana that two seriously ill California women were using on the advice of their physicians, the women filed a lawsuit. They argued that it was unconstitutional for the federal statute to prohibit them from using marijuana for medical purposes that were legal within the state. The Supreme Court, though, held that Congress has the authority to prohibit the *intra*state possession and noncommercial cultivation of marijuana as part of a larger regulatory scheme (the CSA).[7] In other words, state medical marijuana laws do not insulate the users from federal prosecution. •

The Regulatory Powers of the States

As part of their inherent sovereignty, state governments have the authority to regulate affairs within their borders. This authority stems in part from the Tenth Amendment to the Constitution, which reserves to the states all powers not delegated to the national government. State regulatory powers are often referred to as **police powers.** The term encompasses not only the enforcement of criminal law but also the right of state governments to regulate private activities in order to protect or promote the public order, health, safety, morals, and general welfare. Fire and building codes, antidiscrimination laws, parking regulations, zoning restrictions, licensing requirements, and thousands of other state statutes have been enacted pursuant to a state's police powers. Local governments, including cities, also exercise police powers.[8] Although a state may not directly regulate interstate commerce, it may indirectly affect interstate commerce through the reasonable exercise of its police powers. Generally, state laws enacted pursuant to a state's police powers carry a strong presumption of validity.

Police Powers Powers possessed by the states as part of their inherent sovereignty. These powers may be exercised to protect or promote the public order, health, safety, morals, and general welfare.

Because the Constitution reserves to the states all powers not delegated to the national government, the states can and do regulate many types of commercial activities within their borders. So, too, do municipalities. One of these powers is the imposition of building codes. What is the general term that applies to such powers?

(AP Photo/Lenny Ignelzi)

The "Dormant" Commerce Clause

The United States Supreme Court has interpreted the commerce clause to mean that the national government has the *exclusive* authority to regulate commerce that substantially affects trade and commerce among the

4. The Court held the Gun-Free School Zones Act of 1990 to be unconstitutional in *United States v. Lopez,* 514 U.S. 549, 115 S.Ct. 1624, 131 L.Ed.2d 626 (1995).
5. See *Printz v. United States,* 521 U.S. 898, 117 S.Ct. 2365, 138 L.Ed.2d 914 (1997), involving the Brady Handgun Violence Prevention Act of 1993; and *United States v. Morrison,* 529 U.S. 598, 120 S.Ct. 1740, 146 L.Ed.2d 658 (2000), concerning the federal Violence Against Women Act of 1994.
6. 21 U.S.C. Sections 801 *et seq.*
7. *Gonzales v. Raich,* 545 U.S. 1, 125 S.Ct. 2195, 162 L.Ed.2d 1 (2005).
8. Local governments derive their authority to regulate their communities from the state because they are creatures of the state. In other words, they cannot come into existence unless authorized by the state to do so.

(Juanmonino/iStockphoto.com)

Can state and city governments regulate the ingredients in fast food?

states. This express grant of authority to the national government, which is often referred to as the "positive" aspect of the commerce clause, implies a negative aspect—that the states do *not* have the authority to regulate interstate commerce. This negative aspect of the commerce clause is often referred to as the "dormant" (implied) commerce clause.

The dormant commerce clause comes into play when state regulations affect interstate commerce. In this situation, the courts normally weigh the state's interest in regulating a certain matter against the burden that the state's regulation places on interstate commerce. Because courts balance the interests involved, predicting the outcome in a particular case can be extremely difficult.

CASE EXAMPLE 2.3 Tri-M Group, LLC, a Pennsylvania electrical contractor, was hired to work on a veteran's home in Delaware that was partially state funded. Delaware's regulations allowed contractors on state-funded projects to pay a lower wage rate to apprentices if the contractors had registered their apprenticeship programs in the state. Out-of-state contractors, however, were not eligible to pay the lower rate unless they maintained a permanent office in Delaware. Tri-M filed a suit in federal court claiming that Delaware's regulations discriminated against out-of-state contractors in violation of the dormant commerce clause. The state argued that the regulations were justified because it had a legitimate interest in safeguarding the welfare of all apprentices by requiring a permanent place of business in Delaware. But the court held that the state had not overcome the presumption of invalidity that applies to discriminatory regulations and that nondiscriminatory alternatives existed for ensuring the welfare of apprentices. Therefore, the regulations violated the dormant commerce clause.[9] ●

The Supremacy Clause

Supremacy Clause The requirement in Article VI of the U.S. Constitution that provides that the Constitution, laws, and treaties of the United States are "the supreme Law of the Land."

Preemption A doctrine under which certain federal laws preempt, or take precedence over, conflicting state or local laws.

Article VI of the Constitution provides that the Constitution, laws, and treaties of the United States are "the supreme Law of the Land." This article, commonly referred to as the **supremacy clause,** is important in the ordering of state and federal relationships. When there is a direct conflict between a federal law and a state law, the state law is rendered invalid. Because some powers are *concurrent* (shared by the federal government and the states), however, it is necessary to determine which law governs in a particular circumstance.

Preemption occurs when Congress chooses to act exclusively in a concurrent area. In this circumstance, a valid federal statute or regulation will take precedence over a conflicting state or local law or regulation on the same general subject. Often, it is not clear whether Congress, in passing a law, intended to preempt an entire subject area against state regulation. In these situations, the courts determine whether Congress intended to exercise exclusive power over a given area. No single factor is decisive as to whether a court will find preemption. Generally, congressional intent to preempt will be found if a federal law regulating an activity is so pervasive, comprehensive, or detailed that the states have little or no room to regulate in that area. Also, when a federal statute creates an agency—such as the National Labor Relations Board—to enforce the law, matters that may come within the agency's jurisdiction will likely preempt state laws.

LEARNING OBJECTIVE 3
What constitutional clause allows laws enacted by the federal government to take priority over conflicting state laws?

CASE EXAMPLE 2.4 The United States Supreme Court ruled on a case involving a man who alleged that he had been injured by a faulty medical device (a balloon catheter that had been inserted into his artery following a heart attack). The Court noted that the Medical Device Amendments of 1976 had included a preemption provision. The medical device had passed the U.S. Food and Drug Administration's rigorous premarket approval process. Therefore, the Court ruled that the federal regulation of medical devices preempted the man's state law claims for negligence, strict liability, and implied warranty (see Chapters 4 and 17).[10] ●

9. *Tri-M Group, LLC v. Sharp,* 638 F.3d 406 (3d Cir. 2011). Sharp was the name of the secretary of the Delaware Department of Labor.

10. *Riegel v. Medtronic, Inc.,* 552 U.S. 312, 128 S.Ct. 999, 169 L.Ed.2d 892 (2008).

LEARNING OBJECTIVE 4
What is the Bill of Rights? What freedoms does the First Amendment guarantee?

Bill of Rights The first ten amendments to the U.S. Constitution.

Business and the Bill of Rights

The importance of having a written declaration of the rights of individuals eventually caused the first Congress of the United States to enact twelve amendments to the Constitution and submit them to the states for approval. The first ten of these amendments, commonly known as the **Bill of Rights,** were adopted in 1791 and embody a series of protections for the individual against various types of interference by the federal government.[11]

Some constitutional protections apply to business entities as well. For example, corporations exist as separate legal entities, or legal persons, and enjoy many of the same rights and privileges as natural persons do. Summarized here are the protections guaranteed by these ten amendments (see the Constitution in Appendix B for the complete text of each amendment):

1. The First Amendment guarantees the freedoms of religion, speech, and the press and the rights to assemble peaceably and to petition the government.
2. The Second Amendment guarantees the right to keep and bear arms.
3. The Third Amendment prohibits, in peacetime, the lodging of soldiers in any house without the owner's consent.
4. The Fourth Amendment prohibits unreasonable searches and seizures of persons or property.
5. The Fifth Amendment guarantees the rights to *indictment* (formal accusation) by a grand jury, to due process of law, and to fair payment when private property is taken for public use. The Fifth Amendment also prohibits compulsory self-incrimination and double jeopardy (trial for the same crime twice).
6. The Sixth Amendment guarantees the accused in a criminal case the right to a speedy and public trial by an impartial jury and with counsel. The accused has the right to cross-examine witnesses against him or her and to solicit testimony from witnesses in his or her favor.
7. The Seventh Amendment guarantees the right to a trial by jury in a civil (noncriminal) case involving at least twenty dollars.[12]
8. The Eighth Amendment prohibits excessive bail and fines, as well as cruel and unusual punishment.
9. The Ninth Amendment establishes that the people have rights in addition to those specified in the Constitution.
10. The Tenth Amendment establishes that those powers neither delegated to the federal government nor denied to the states are reserved for the states.

We will look closely at several of these amendments in Chapter 6, in the context of criminal law and procedures. In this chapter, we examine two important guarantees of the First Amendment—freedom of speech and freedom of religion—after we look at how the Bill of Rights puts certain limits on government.

KNOW THIS

Although most of the rights in the Bill of Rights apply to actions of the states, some of them apply only to actions of the federal government.

Limits on Federal and State Governmental Actions

As originally intended, the Bill of Rights limited only the powers of the national government. Over time, however, the United States Supreme Court "incorporated" most of these rights

11. One of the proposed amendments was ratified more than two hundred years later (in 1992) and became the Twenty-seventh Amendment to the Constitution. See Appendix B.
12. Twenty dollars was forty days' pay for the average person when the Bill of Rights was written.

(Johanna Leguerre/AFP/Getty Images)

The European Court of Human Rights meets in the French city of Strasbourg on a regular basis. Most lawsuits heard by these seven judges involve appeals concerning actions by European governments. Should judges and justices in the United States give deference to decisions made by this foreign court?

into the protections against state actions afforded by the Fourteenth Amendment to the Constitution. That amendment, passed in 1868 after the Civil War, provides, in part, that "[n]o State shall . . . deprive any person of life, liberty, or property, without due process of law." Starting in 1925, the Supreme Court began to define various rights and liberties guaranteed in the national Constitution as constituting "due process of law," which was required of state governments under the Fourteenth Amendment. Today, most of the rights and liberties set forth in the Bill of Rights apply to state governments as well as to the national government.

The rights secured by the Bill of Rights are not absolute. Many of the rights guaranteed by the first ten amendments are described in very general terms. For example, the Second Amendment states that people have a right to keep and bear arms, but it does not explain the extent of this right. As the Supreme Court noted in 2008, this does not mean that people can "keep and carry any weapon whatsoever in any manner whatsoever and for whatever purpose."[13] Legislatures can prohibit the carrying of concealed weapons or certain types of weapons, such as machine guns. Ultimately, it is the Supreme Court, as the final interpreter of the Constitution, that gives meaning to these rights and determines their boundaries. (For a discussion of how the Supreme Court may consider other nations' laws when determining the appropriate balance of individual rights, see this chapter's *Beyond Our Borders* feature on the following page.)

The First Amendment—Freedom of Speech

A democratic form of government cannot survive unless people can freely voice their political opinions and criticize government actions or policies. Freedom of speech, particularly political speech, is thus a prized right, and traditionally the courts have protected this right to the fullest extent possible.

Symbolic Speech Nonverbal expressions of beliefs. Symbolic speech, which includes gestures, movements, and articles of clothing, is given substantial protection by the courts.

Symbolic speech—gestures, movements, articles of clothing, and other forms of expressive conduct—is also given substantial protection by the courts. The Supreme Court held that the burning of the American flag to protest government policies is a constitutionally protected form of expression.[14] Similarly, wearing a T-shirt with a photo of a presidential candidate would be a constitutionally protected form of expression. The test is whether a reasonable person would interpret the conduct as conveying some sort of message. **EXAMPLE 2.5** As a form of expression, Nam has gang signs tattooed on his torso, arms, neck, and legs. If a reasonable person would interpret this conduct as conveying a message, then it might be a protected form of symbolic speech. ●

KNOW THIS

The First Amendment guarantee of freedom of speech applies only to *government* restrictions on speech.

Reasonable Restrictions

Expression—oral, written, or symbolized by conduct—is subject to reasonable restrictions. A balance must be struck between a government's obligation to protect its citizens and those citizens' exercise of their rights. Reasonableness is analyzed on a case-by-case basis.

Content-Neutral Laws Laws that regulate the time, manner, and place, but not the content, of speech receive less scrutiny by the courts than do laws that restrict the content of expression. If a restriction imposed by the government is content neutral, then a court may allow it. To be content neutral, the restriction must be aimed at combating some secondary

13. *District of Columbia v. Heller,* 554 U.S. 570, 128 S.Ct. 2783, 171 L.Ed.2d 637 (2008).
14. See *Texas v. Johnson,* 491 U.S. 397, 109 S.Ct. 2533, 105 L.Ed.2d 342 (1989).

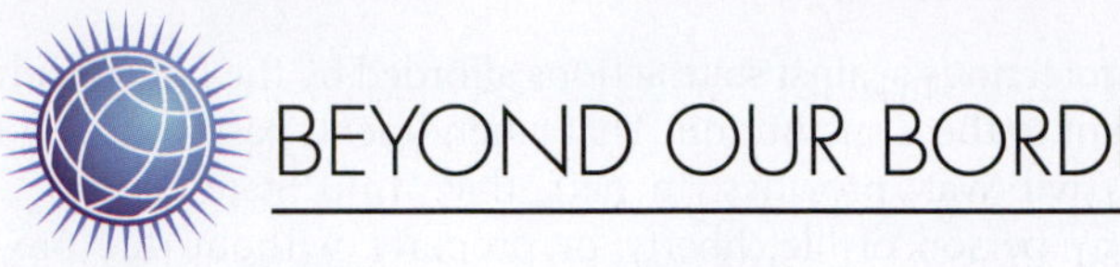

The Impact of Foreign Law on the United States Supreme Court

The United States Supreme Court interprets the rights provided in the U.S. Constitution. Changing public views on controversial topics, such as privacy in an era of terrorist threats or the rights of gay men and lesbians, may affect the way the Supreme Court decides a case. But should the Court also consider other nations' laws and world opinion when balancing individual rights in the United States?

Justices on the Supreme Court have increasingly considered foreign law when deciding issues of national importance. This trend started in 2003 when, for the first time ever, foreign law was cited in a majority opinion of the Supreme Court. The case was a controversial one in which the Court struck down laws that prohibited oral and anal sex between consenting adults of the same gender. In the majority opinion (an opinion that the majority of justices have signed), Justice Anthony Kennedy mentioned that the European Court of Human Rights and other foreign courts have consistently acknowledged that homosexuals have a right "to engage in intimate, consensual conduct."[a] The Supreme Court again looked at foreign law when deciding whether the death penalty was an appropriate punishment for persons who were juveniles when they committed their crimes.[b]

The practice of looking at foreign law has many critics, including Justice Antonin Scalia and other more conservative members of the Supreme Court, who believe that foreign views are irrelevant to rulings on U.S. law. Other Supreme Court justices, however, including Justice Stephen Breyer and Justice Ruth Bader Ginsburg, have publicly stated that in our increasingly global community we should not ignore the opinions of courts in the rest of the world.

a. *Lawrence v. Texas,* 539 U.S. 558, 123 S.Ct. 2472, 156 L.Ed.2d 508 (2003).

b. *Roper v. Simmons,* 543 U.S. 551, 125 S.Ct. 1183, 161 L.Ed.2d 1 (2005).

Critical Thinking

Should U.S. courts, and particularly the United States Supreme Court, look to other nations' laws for guidance when deciding important issues—including those involving rights granted by the Constitution? If so, what impact might this have on their decisions? Explain.

---

societal problem, such as crime, and not be aimed at suppressing the expressive conduct or its message.

Courts have often protected nude dancing as a form of symbolic expression. Nevertheless, the courts typically allow content-neutral laws that ban *all* public nudity. **CASE EXAMPLE 2.6** Ria Ora was charged with dancing nude at an annual "anti-Christmas" protest in Harvard Square in Cambridge, Massachusetts. Ora argued that the statute was overbroad and unconstitutional, and a trial court agreed. On appeal, a state appellate court reversed. The court found that the statute was constitutional because it banned public displays of open and gross lewdness in situations in which there was an unsuspecting or unwilling audience.[15] •

Compelling Government Interest A test of constitutionality that requires the government to have convincing reasons for passing any law that restricts fundamental rights, such as free speech, or distinguishes between people based on a suspect trait.

Laws That Restrict the Content of Speech If a law regulates the content of the expression, it must serve a compelling state interest and must be narrowly written to achieve that interest. Under the **compelling government interest** test, the government's interest is balanced against the individual's constitutional right to be free of law. For the statute to be valid, there must be a compelling governmental interest that can be furthered only by the law in question.

The United States Supreme Court has held that schools may restrict students' speech at school events. **CASE EXAMPLE 2.7** Some high school students held up a banner saying "Bong Hits 4 Jesus" at an off-campus but school-sanctioned event. The majority of the Court ruled that school officials did not violate the students' free speech rights when they confiscated the banner and suspended the students for ten days. Because the banner could reasonably be interpreted as promoting drugs, the Court concluded that the school's actions were justified. Several justices disagreed, however, noting that the majority's

15. *Commonwealth v. Ora,* 451 Mass. 125, 883 N.E.2d 1217 (2008).

holding creates a special exception that will allow schools to censor any student speech that mentions drugs.[16]

Can a high school suspend teenagers from extracurricular activities because they posted suggestive photos of themselves online at social networking sites? For a discussion of this issue, see this chapter's *Adapting the Law to the Online Environment* below.

16. *Morse v. Frederick*, 551 U.S. 393, 127 S.Ct. 2618, 168 L.Ed.2d 290 (2007).

ADAPTING THE LAW TO THE ONLINE ENVIRONMENT

VULGAR FACEBOOK PHOTOS RECEIVE FIRST AMENDMENT PROTECTION

A federal judge in Indiana ruled that a high school did not have the right to punish students for posting raunchy photos of themselves on the Internet. According to the court, "the case poses timely questions about the limits school officials can place on out-of-school speech by students in the information age where Twitter, Facebook, MySpace, texts, and the like rule the day."[a]

High School Suspended the Teens from Extracurricular Activities

T.V. and M.K. were both entering the tenth grade at a public high school. During summer sleepovers, the girls took photos of each other pretending to suck penis-shaped rainbow-colored lollipops and holding them in various suggestive positions. They later posted the photos on Facebook, MySpace, and Photo Bucket to be seen by persons granted "friend" status or given a password. The images did not identify the school that the girls attended.

When a parent complained to the school about the provocative online display, school officials suspended both girls from extracurricular activities for a portion of the upcoming school year. Both T.V. and M.K. were members of the high school's volleyball team, and M.K. was also a member of the cheerleading squad and the show choir. Through their parents, the girls filed a lawsuit claiming that the school had violated their First Amendment rights.

Can Online Photos Qualify as Symbolic Speech?

Expressive conduct is entitled to First Amendment protection if it meets a two-part intent-plus-perception test. Conduct is symbolic speech if the "intent to convey a particularized message was present" and if "the likelihood was great that the message would be understood by those who viewed it."[b] Here, both girls testified that they were just trying to be funny when they took the photos and posted them online for their friends to see. Although the photos were suggestive, the girls were fully clothed, and the images were not pornographic or obscene. The court reasoned that the conduct depicted in the photos was intended to be humorous and would be understood as such by their teenage audience. Therefore, the photos were entitled to First Amendment protection as symbolic speech, even if they were "juvenile and silly."

Did the Off-Campus Speech Substantially Disrupt School Activities?

Although schools can restrict students' speech at times, this was not one of those times, according to the court. The conduct took place off campus and did not substantially disrupt the work and discipline of the high school. Schools generally can punish students only for off-campus speech that becomes an in-school problem, such as bullying, but here, the photos had only a minimal effect on the volleyball team. (Some of the other players and two parents had complained that the photos were inappropriate.) The court also struck down the provision in the student handbook banning out-of-school conduct that brings discredit or dishonor on the school, finding that it was impermissibly broad and vague.

Critical Thinking

How might the outcome of this case have been different if the girls had posted the photos on the high school's public Web site for all to see?

a. *T.V. ex rel. B.V. v. Smith-Green Community School Corp.*, 807 F.Supp.2d 767 (N.D.Ind. 2011).

b. See *Texas v. Johnson*, 491 U.S. 397, 109 S.Ct. 2533, 105 L.Ed.2d 342 (1989).

These policemen look on at the Occupy Portland encampment set up in a public place. When the mayor of Portland, Oregon, ordered the demonstrators to "pull up stakes," was he violating their right to free speech?

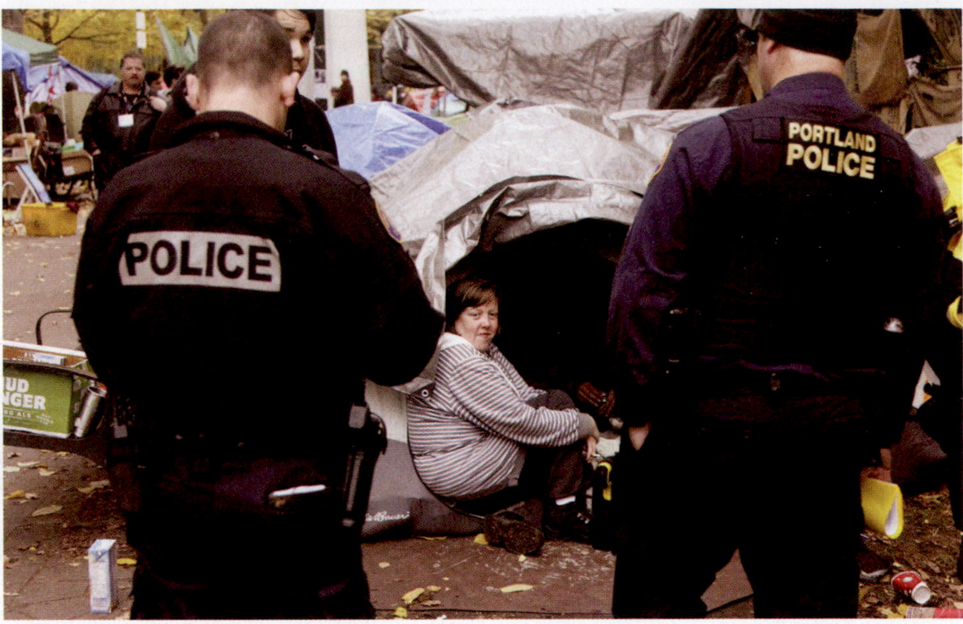

(AP Photo/Rick Bowmer)

Corporate Political Speech Political speech by corporations also falls within the protection of the First Amendment. **CASE EXAMPLE 2.8** Many years ago, the United States Supreme Court reviewed a Massachusetts statute that prohibited corporations from making political contributions or expenditures that individuals were permitted to make. The Court ruled that the Massachusetts law was unconstitutional because it violated the right of corporations to freedom of speech.[17] • The Court has also held that a law prohibiting a corporation from using bill inserts to express its views on controversial issues violated the First Amendment.[18]

Corporate political speech continues to be given significant protection under the First Amendment. In 2010, the Supreme Court overturned a twenty-year-old precedent when it ruled that corporations can spend freely to support or oppose candidates for president and Congress.[19] (See the *Landmark in the Law* feature in Chapter 29 for a discussion of this issue.)

"If the freedom of speech is taken away, then dumb and silent we may be led like sheep to the slaughter."

George Washington, 1732–1799 (First president of the United States, 1789–1797)

Commercial Speech The courts also give substantial protection to *commercial speech,* which consists of communications—primarily advertising and marketing—made by business firms that involve only their commercial interests. The protection given to commercial speech under the First Amendment is not as extensive as that afforded to noncommercial speech, however. A state may restrict certain kinds of advertising, for instance, in the interest of protecting consumers from being misled. States also have a legitimate interest in the beautification of roadsides, and this interest allows states to place restraints on billboard advertising. **CASE EXAMPLE 2.9** Café Erotica, a nude dancing establishment, sued the state after being denied a permit to erect a billboard along an interstate highway in Florida. The state appellate court decided that because the law directly advanced a substantial government interest in highway beautification and safety, it was not an unconstitutional restraint on commercial speech.[20] •

Generally, a restriction on commercial speech will be considered valid as long as it (1) seeks to implement a substantial government interest, (2) directly advances that interest, and (3)

17. *First National Bank of Boston v. Bellotti,* 435 U.S. 765, 98 S.Ct. 1407, 55 L.Ed.2d 707 (1978).
18. *Consolidated Edison Co. v. Public Service Commission,* 447 U.S. 530, 100 S.Ct. 2326, 65 L.Ed.2d 319 (1980).
19. *Citizens United v. Federal Election Commission,* 558 U.S. ___, 130 S.Ct. 876, 175 L.Ed.2d 753 (2010).
20. *Café Erotica v. Florida Department of Transportation,* 830 So.2d 181 (Fla.App. 1 Dist. 2002); review denied, *Café Erotica/We Dare to Bare v. Florida Department of Transportation,* 845 So.2d 888 (Fla. 2003).

goes no further than necessary to accomplish its objective. A substantial government interest is a significant or important connection or concern of the government with respect to a particular matter. Examples of such interests are given in *Case Example 2.9* in the previous paragraph. This substantial-interest requirement limits the power of the government to regulate commercial speech.

At issue in the following *Spotlight Case* was whether a government agency had unconstitutionally restricted commercial speech when it prohibited the inclusion of a certain illustration on beer labels.

Spotlight on Commercial Speech

Case 2.2

Bad Frog Brewery, Inc. v. New York State Liquor Authority

United States Court of Appeals, Second Circuit, 134 F.3d 87 (1998).
www.findlaw.com/casecode/index.html[a]

(Courtesy of Bad Frog Beer)

Can a label be too offensive?

FACTS Bad Frog Brewery, Inc., makes and sells alcoholic beverages. Some of the beverages feature labels with a drawing of a frog making the gesture generally known as "giving the finger." Bad Frog's authorized New York distributor, Renaissance Beer Company, applied to the New York State Liquor Authority (NYSLA) for brand label approval, as required by state law before the beer could be sold in New York. The NYSLA denied the application, in part, because "the label could appear in grocery and convenience stores, with obvious exposure on the shelf to children of tender age." Bad Frog filed a suit in a federal district court against the NYSLA, asking for, among other things, an injunction against the denial of the application. The court granted summary judgment in favor of the NYSLA. Bad Frog appealed to the U.S. Court of Appeals for the Second Circuit.

ISSUE Was the NYSLA's ban of Bad Frog's beer labels a reasonable restriction on commercial speech?

DECISION No. The U.S. Court of Appeals for the Second Circuit reversed the judgment of the district court and remanded the case for judgment to be entered in favor of Bad Frog.

REASON The appellate court held that the NYSLA's denial of Bad Frog's application violated the First Amendment. The ban on the use of the labels lacked a "reasonable fit" with the state's interest in shielding minors from vulgarity, and the NYSLA did not adequately consider alternatives to the ban. The court acknowledged that the NYSLA's interest "in protecting children from vulgar and profane advertising" was "substantial." The question was whether banning Bad Frog's labels "directly advanced" that interest. "In view of the wide currency of vulgar displays throughout contemporary society, including comic books targeted directly at children, barring such displays from labels for alcoholic beverages cannot realistically be expected to reduce children's exposure to such displays to any significant degree." The court concluded that a commercial speech limitation must be "part of a substantial effort to advance a valid state interest, not merely the removal of a few grains of offensive sand from a beach of vulgarity." Finally, as to whether the ban on the labels was more extensive than necessary to serve this interest, the court pointed out that there were "numerous less intrusive alternatives." For example, the NYSLA could have placed restrictions on the permissible locations where the appellant's products could be displayed in stores.

WHAT IF THE FACTS WERE DIFFERENT? *If Bad Frog had sought to use the label to market toys instead of beer, would the court's ruling likely have been the same? Explain your answer.*

a. Under the heading "US Court of Appeals," click on "2nd." Enter "Bad Frog Brewery" in the "Party name:" box, and click on "Search." On the resulting page, click on the case name to access the opinion.

Unprotected Speech

The United States Supreme Court has made it clear that certain types of speech will not be given any protection under the First Amendment. Speech that harms the good reputation of another, or defamatory speech (see Chapter 4), will not be protected. Speech that violates criminal laws (such as threatening speech) is not constitutionally protected. Other unprotected speech includes "fighting words," or words that are likely to incite others to respond violently.

Obscene Speech The First Amendment, as interpreted by the Supreme Court, also does not protect obscene speech. Establishing an objective definition of obscene speech has proved difficult, however, and the Court has grappled with this problem from time to time.

In a 1973 case, *Miller v. California,*[21] the Supreme Court created a test for legal obscenity, which involved a set of requirements that must be met for material to be legally obscene. Under this test, material is obscene if (1) the average person finds that it violates contemporary community standards; (2) the work taken as a whole appeals to a prurient (arousing or obsessive) interest in sex; (3) the work shows patently offensive sexual conduct; and (4) the work lacks serious redeeming literary, artistic, political, or scientific merit.

Because community standards vary widely, the *Miller* test has had inconsistent application, and obscenity remains a constitutionally unsettled issue. Numerous state and federal statutes make it a crime to disseminate and possess obscene materials, including child pornography.

Online Obscenity Congress's first two attempts at protecting minors from pornographic materials on the Internet—the Communications Decency Act (CDA) of 1996[22] and the Child Online Protection Act (COPA) of 1998[23]—failed. Ultimately, the United States Supreme Court struck down both the CDA and COPA as unconstitutional restraints on speech, largely because the wording of these acts was overbroad and would restrict non-pornographic materials.[24]

In 2000, Congress enacted the Children's Internet Protection Act (CIPA),[25] which requires public schools and libraries to block adult content from access by children by installing **filtering software.** Such software is designed to prevent persons from viewing certain Web sites by responding to a site's Internet address or its **meta tags,** or key words. CIPA was also challenged on constitutional grounds, but in 2003 the Supreme Court held that the act did not violate the First Amendment. The Court concluded that because libraries can disable the filters for any patrons who ask, the system is reasonably flexible and does not burden free speech to an unconstitutional extent.[26]

Filtering Software A computer program that is designed to block access to certain Web sites, based on their content. The software blocks the retrieval of a site whose URL or key words are on a list within the program.

Meta Tag A key word in a document that can serve as an index reference to the document. On the Web, search engines return results based, in part, on the tags in Web documents.

In 2003, Congress enacted the Prosecutorial Remedies and Other Tools to End the Exploitation of Children Today Act (Protect Act).[27] The act makes it a crime to knowingly advertise, present, distribute, or solicit "any material or purported material in a manner that reflects the belief, or that is intended to cause another to believe, that the material or purported material" is illegal child pornography. Thus, it is a crime to intentionally distribute virtual child pornography, which uses computer-generated images, not actual people. In a case challenging the constitutionality of the Protect Act, the Supreme Court held that the statute was valid because it does not prohibit a substantial amount of protected speech.[28] Rather, the act generally prohibits offers to provide, and requests to obtain, child pornography—both of which are unprotected speech. Nevertheless, because of the difficulties of policing the Internet, as well as the constitutional complexities of prohibiting online obscenity through legislation, it remains a problem worldwide.

---

21. 413 U.S. 15, 93 S.Ct. 2607, 37 L.Ed.2d 419 (1973).

22. 47 U.S.C. Section 223(a)(1)(B)(ii).

23. 47 U.S.C. Section 231.

24. See *Reno v. American Civil Liberties Union,* 521 U.S. 844, 117 S.Ct. 2329, 138 L.Ed.2d 874 (1997); *Ashcroft v. American Civil Liberties Union,* 535 U.S. 564, 122 S.Ct. 1700, 152 L.Ed.2d 771 (2002); and *American Civil Liberties Union v. Ashcroft,* 322 F.3d 240 (3d Cir. 2003).

25. 17 U.S.C. Sections 1701–1741.

26. *United States v. American Library Association,* 539 U.S. 194, 123 S.Ct. 2297, 156 L.Ed.2d 221 (2003).

27. 18 U.S.C. Section 2252A(a)(5)(B).

28. *United States v. Williams,* 553 U.S. 285, 128 S.Ct. 1830, 170 L.Ed.2d 650 (2008).

The First Amendment—Freedom of Religion

The First Amendment states that the government may neither establish any religion nor prohibit the free exercise of religious practices. The first part of this constitutional provision is referred to as the *establishment clause,* and the second part is known as the *free exercise clause.* Government action, both federal and state, must be consistent with this constitutional mandate.

Establishment Clause The provision in the First Amendment that prohibits the government from establishing any state-sponsored religion or enacting any law that promotes religion or favors one religion over another.

The Establishment Clause

The **establishment clause** prohibits the government from establishing a state-sponsored religion, as well as from passing laws that promote (aid or endorse) religion or show a preference for one religion over another. Although the establishment clause involves the separation of church and state, it does not require a complete separation.

Establishment clause cases often involve such issues as the legality of allowing or requiring school prayers, using state-issued vouchers to pay tuition at religious schools, and teaching creation theories versus evolution. Federal or state laws that do not promote or place a significant burden on religion are constitutional even if they have some impact on religion. For a government law or policy to be constitutional, it must not have the primary effect of promoting or inhibiting religion.

(AP Photo/Denis Poroy)

This large cross on Mount Soledad can be viewed by freeway drivers in San Diego. Because the land on which it sits became public property, should it be removed as a violation of the establishment clause?

Religious displays on public property have often been challenged as violating the establishment clause, and the United States Supreme Court has ruled on a number of such cases. Generally, the Court has focused on the proximity of the religious display to nonreligious symbols, such as reindeer and candy canes, or to symbols from different religions, such as a menorah (a nine-branched candelabrum used in celebrating Hanukkah). The Supreme Court eventually took a slightly different approach when it held that public displays having historical, as well as religious, significance do not necessarily violate the establishment clause.[29]

CASE EXAMPLE 2.10 Mount Soledad is a prominent hill near San Diego. There has been a forty-foot cross on top of Mount Soledad since 1913. In the 1990s, a war memorial was constructed next to the cross that included six walls listing the names of veterans. The site was privately owned until 2006, when Congress authorized the property's transfer to the federal government "to preserve a historically significant war memorial." Shortly after that, Steve Trunk and the Jewish War Veterans filed lawsuits claiming that the cross display violated the establishment clause because it endorsed the Christian religion. A federal appellate court agreed, finding that the primary effect of the memorial as a whole sent a strong message of endorsement and exclusion (of non-Christian veterans). The court noted that although not all cross displays at war memorials violate the establishment clause, the cross in this case physically dominated the site, was originally dedicated to religious purposes, had a long history of religious use, and was the only portion visible to drivers on the freeway below.[30] •

Free Exercise Clause The provision in the First Amendment that prohibits the government from interfering with people's religious practices or forms of worship.

The Free Exercise Clause

The **free exercise clause** guarantees that a person can hold any religious belief that she or he wants, or a person can have no religious belief. The constitutional guarantee of personal religious freedom restricts only the actions of the government, however, and not those of individuals or private businesses.

When religious *practices* work against public policy and the public welfare, though, the government can act. For instance, the government can require a child to receive certain types of vaccinations or medical treatment when a child's life is in danger—regardless

29. See *Van Orden v. Perry,* 545 U.S. 677, 125 S.Ct. 2854, 162 L.Ed.2d 607 (2005). The Court held that a six-foot-tall monument of the Ten Commandments on the Texas state capitol grounds did not violate the establishment clause because the Ten Commandments had historical significance.

30. *Trunk v. City of San Diego,* 629 F.3d 1099 (9th Cir. 2011).

(AP Photo/Bill Haber)

A large and heavy monument showing the Ten Commandments is being removed from a state government building. Why would a federal judge order that it be moved from public view?

of the child's or parent's religious beliefs. When public safety is an issue, an individual's religious beliefs often have to give way to the government's interests in protecting the public. **EXAMPLE 2.11** According to the Muslim faith, a woman should not appear in public without a scarf, known as a *hijab*, over her head. Due to public safety concerns, many courts today do not allow the wearing of any headgear (hats or scarves) in courtrooms. In Douglasville, Georgia, a Muslim woman was prevented from entering a courthouse with her husband because she refused to remove her scarf. As she left, she uttered an expletive at the court official and was arrested and brought before the judge, who ordered her to serve ten days in jail. Similar incidents have occurred in other states. •

According to the United States Supreme Court, the free exercise clause protects the use of a controlled substance in the practice of a sincerely held religious belief. **CASE EXAMPLE 2.12** A religious sect in New Mexico follows the practices of a Brazil-based church. Its members ingest hoasca tea as part of a ritual to connect with and better understand God. Hoasca tea, which is brewed from plants native to the Amazon rain forest, contains an illegal hallucinogenic drug, dimethyltryptamine (DMT), which is regulated by the federal Controlled Substances Act. When federal drug agents confiscated the church's shipment of hoasca tea as it entered the country, the church members filed a lawsuit claiming that the confiscation violated their right to freely exercise their religion. Ultimately, the Supreme Court agreed, ruling that the government had failed to demonstrate a sufficiently compelling interest in barring the sect's sacramental use of hoasca.[31] •

KNOW THIS

The free exercise clause applies only to the actions of the state and federal governments, not to private employers. Private employers may nonetheless be required to accommodate their employees' religious beliefs.

In the following case, the court had to decide whether a county ordinance that prohibited the use of steel cleats on tires was a violation of a church's right to freely exercise its religion.

31. *Gonzales v. O Centro Espirita Beneficente Uniao Do Vegetal*, 546 U.S. 418, 126 S.Ct. 1211, 163 L.Ed.2d 1017 (2006).

Case 2.3

Mitchell County v. Zimmerman

Supreme Court of Iowa,
810 N.W.2d 1 (2012).

(Lingbeek/iStockphoto.com)

Some Mennonites still use animal power.

FACTS Members of the Old Order Groffdale Conference Mennonite Church generally use horses and buggies for transportation. About forty years ago, they started using tractors, particularly for hauling their agricultural products to market. To ensure that the tractors are not used for pleasure purposes (thereby displacing the horse and buggy), their tires have to be fitted with steel cleats that slow down the tractors. Thus, it is a religious requirement of the Mennonites that any motorized tractor driven by a church member be equipped with steel cleats. To minimize road damage, over time the steel cleats have been made wider and are mounted on rubber belts to provide cushioning. Nevertheless, in 2009, finding that the Mennonites' steel cleats tended to damage newly resurfaced roads, Mitchell County adopted a road protection ordinance: "No tire on a vehicle moved on a highway is allowed to have any block, stud, flange, cleat, or spike, or any other protuberances of any material other than rubber." Eli Zimmerman, a Mennonite, received a citation for violating this ordinance.

Case 2.3—Continued

Zimmerman filed a motion to dismiss, which the trial court denied. Zimmerman appealed.

ISSUE Was Mitchell County's ordinance a violation of the free exercise clause of the First Amendment?

DECISION Yes. The reviewing court reversed the trial court's decision and remanded the case for entry of an order of dismissal.

REASON The First Amendment states, in part, that Congress shall make no law "prohibiting the free exercise" of religion. The First Amendment was made applicable to the states by the Fourteenth Amendment. Consequently, "laws that are not neutral or of general applicability require heightened scrutiny. They must be justified by a compelling governmental interest and must be narrowly tailored to advance that interest." The court first observed that the ordinance's language on the use of steel cleats was nonreligious and therefore neutral. Nevertheless, the court found that the ordinance was not *operationally* neutral because it was adopted specifically to address the Mennonites' use of steel cleats despite their forty-year religious practice of using such cleats.

Finally, the ordinance was not *generally applicable* because it contained exceptions for tire chains for snowy weather and steel-studded snow tires. In other words, Mitchell County chose "to prohibit only a particular source of harm to the roads that had a religious origin." The ordinance was not clearly tailored to achieve the stated objective of road preservation. "The question here is whether the County's goal of road preservation can be accomplished less restrictively without banning the tractors' use by the Mennonites. On the record, we believe it can." The court therefore concluded that the application of the ordinance to Zimmerman violated his right to free exercise of religion.

WHAT IF THE FACTS WERE DIFFERENT? *Suppose that Mitchell County had passed an ordinance that allowed the Mennonites to continue to use steel cleats on the newly resurfaced roads provided that the drivers paid a $5 fee each time they were on the road. Would the court have ruled differently? Why or why not?*

Due Process and Equal Protection

LEARNING OBJECTIVE 5

Where in the Constitution can the due process clause be found?

Two other constitutional guarantees of great significance to Americans are mandated by the due process clauses of the Fifth and Fourteenth Amendments and the equal protection clause of the Fourteenth Amendment.

Due Process

Due Process Clause The provisions in the Fifth and Fourteenth Amendments that guarantee that no person shall be deprived of life, liberty, or property without due process of law. State constitutions often include similar clauses.

Both the Fifth and the Fourteenth Amendments provide that no person shall be deprived "of life, liberty, or property, without due process of law." The **due process clause** of each of these constitutional amendments has two aspects—procedural and substantive. Note that the due process clause applies to "legal persons," such as corporations, as well as to individuals.

Procedural Due Process

Procedural due process requires that any government decision to take life, liberty, or property must be made fairly. This means that the government must give a person proper notice and an opportunity to be heard, and that it must use fair procedures in determining whether a person will be subjected to punishment or have some burden imposed on him or her.

Fair procedure has been interpreted as requiring that the person have at least an opportunity to object to a proposed action before a fair, neutral decision maker (who need not be a judge). **EXAMPLE 2.13** In most states, a driver's license is construed as a property interest. Therefore, the state must provide some sort of opportunity for the driver to object before suspending or terminating the person's license. ●

PREVENTING LEGAL DISPUTES

Many of the constitutional protections discussed in this chapter have become part of our culture in the United States. Due process, especially procedural due process, has become synonymous with what Americans consider "fair." For this reason, if you wish to avoid legal disputes, consider giving due process to anyone who might object to some of your business decisions or actions, whether that person is an employee, a partner, an affiliate, or a customer. For instance, provide ample notice of new policies to all affected persons, and give them at least an opportunity to express their opinions on the matter. Providing an opportunity to be heard is often the ideal way to make people feel that they are being treated fairly. People are less likely to sue a businessperson or firm that they believe is fair and listens to both sides of an issue.

Substantive Due Process

Substantive due process protects an individual's life, liberty, or property against certain government actions regardless of the fairness of the procedures used to implement them. Substantive due process limits what the government may do in its legislative and executive capacities. Legislation must be fair and reasonable in content and must further a legitimate governmental objective. Only when state conduct is arbitrary or shocks the conscience, however, will it rise to the level of violating substantive due process.

"Our Constitution protects aliens [extraterrestrials], drunks, and U.S. senators."

Will Rogers, 1879–1935
(American humorist)

If a law or other governmental action limits a fundamental right, the courts will hold that it violates substantive due process unless it promotes a compelling or overriding state interest. Fundamental rights include interstate travel, privacy, voting, marriage and family, and all First Amendment rights. Thus, a state must have a substantial reason for taking any action that infringes on a person's free speech rights. In situations not involving fundamental rights, a law or action does not violate substantive due process if it rationally relates to any legitimate governmental end. It is almost impossible for a law or action to fail the "rationality" test. Under this test, almost any government regulation of business will be upheld as reasonable.

Equal Protection

Equal Protection Clause The provision in the Fourteenth Amendment that requires state governments to treat similarly situated individuals in a similar manner.

Under the Fourteenth Amendment, a state may not "deny to any person within its jurisdiction the equal protection of the laws." The United States Supreme Court has used the due process clause of the Fifth Amendment to make the **equal protection clause** applicable to the federal government as well. Equal protection means that the government must treat similarly situated individuals in a similar manner.

Both substantive due process and equal protection require review of the substance of the law or other governmental action rather than review of the procedures used. When a law or action limits the liberty of all persons to do something, it may violate substantive due process. When a law or action limits the liberty of some persons but not others, it may violate the equal protection clause. **EXAMPLE 2.14** If a law prohibits all advertising on the sides of trucks, it raises a substantive due process question. If the law makes an exception to allow truck owners to advertise their own businesses, it raises an equal protection issue. •

In an equal protection inquiry, when a law or action distinguishes between or among individuals, the basis for the distinction—that is, the classification—is examined. Depending on the classification, the courts apply different levels of scrutiny, or "tests," to determine whether the law or action violates the equal protection clause. The courts use one of three standards: strict scrutiny, intermediate scrutiny, or the "rational basis" test.

Strict Scrutiny

If a law or action prohibits or inhibits some persons from exercising a fundamental right, the law or action will be subject to "strict scrutiny" by the courts. A classification based on a *suspect trait*—such as race, national origin, or citizenship

(kevinruss/iStockphoto.com)

Does the equal protection clause protect the homeless? If so, how?

status—will also be subject to strict scrutiny. Under this standard, the classification must be necessary to promote a *compelling government interest* (see page 42). Compelling state interests include remedying past unconstitutional or illegal discrimination, but do not include correcting the general effects of "society's discrimination."

EXAMPLE 2.15 For a city to give preference to minority applicants in awarding construction contracts, it normally must identify past unconstitutional or illegal discrimination against minority construction firms. Because the policy is based on suspect traits (race and national origin), it will violate the equal protection clause *unless* it is necessary to promote a compelling state interest. • Generally, few laws or actions survive strict-scrutiny analysis by the courts.

Intermediate Scrutiny

Another standard, that of "intermediate scrutiny," is applied in cases involving discrimination based on gender or legitimacy. Laws using these classifications must be *substantially related to important government objectives.* **EXAMPLE 2.16** An important government objective is preventing illegitimate teenage pregnancies. Because males and females are not similarly situated in this regard—only females can become pregnant—a law that punishes men but not women for statutory rape will be upheld even though it treats men and women unequally. •

The state also has an important objective in establishing time limits (called *statutes of limitation*) for how long after an event a particular type of action can be brought. Nevertheless, the limitation period must be substantially related to the important objective of preventing fraudulent or outdated claims. **EXAMPLE 2.17** A state law requires illegitimate children to bring paternity suits within six years of their births in order to seek support from their fathers. A court will strike down this law if legitimate children are allowed to seek support from their parents at any time because distinguishing between support claims on the basis of legitimacy is not related to the important government objective of preventing fraudulent or outdated claims. •

The "Rational Basis" Test

In matters of economic and social welfare, a classification will be considered valid if there is any conceivable "rational basis" on which the classification might relate to a *legitimate government interest.* It is almost impossible for a law or action to fail the rational basis test. **EXAMPLE 2.18** A city ordinance that in effect prohibits all pushcart vendors, except a specific few, from operating in a particular area of the city will be upheld if the city offers a rational basis—such as reducing traffic in that area—for the ordinance. In contrast, a law that provides for unemployment benefits to be paid only to people over six feet tall would clearly fail the rational basis test because it could not further any legitimate government interest. •

"There was, of course, no way of knowing whether you were being watched at any given moment."

George Orwell, 1903–1950
(English author,
from his famous novel *1984*)

Privacy Rights

The U.S. Constitution does not explicitly mention a general right to privacy. In a 1928 Supreme Court case, *Olmstead v. United States,*[32] Justice Louis Brandeis stated in his dissent that the right to privacy is "the most comprehensive of rights and the right most valued by civilized men." The majority of the justices at that time, however, did not agree with Brandeis.

It was not until the 1960s that a majority on the Supreme Court endorsed the view that the Constitution protects individual privacy rights. In a landmark 1965 case, *Griswold v. Connecticut,*[33] the Supreme Court invalidated a Connecticut law that effectively prohibited

32. 277 U.S. 438, 48 S.Ct. 564, 72 L.Ed. 944 (1928).
33. 381 U.S. 479, 85 S.Ct. 1678, 14 L.Ed.2d 510 (1965).

the use of contraceptives on the ground that it violated the right to privacy. The Supreme Court held that a constitutional right to privacy was implied by the First, Third, Fourth, Fifth, and Ninth Amendments.

Today, privacy rights receive protection under various federal statutes as well the U.S. Constitution. State constitutions and statutes also secure individuals' privacy rights, often to a significant degree. Privacy rights are also protected to an extent under tort law (see Chapter 4), consumer law (see Chapter 33), and employment law (see Chapter 24). In this section, after a brief look at some of the most important federal statutes protecting the privacy of individuals, we examine some current topics related to privacy rights. One such topic, the debate over marriage equality laws, is discussed in this chapter's *Law, Diversity, and Business: Managerial Implications* feature below.

Federal Statutes Protecting Privacy Rights

In the last several decades, Congress has enacted a number of statues that protect the privacy of individuals in various areas of concern. Most of these statues deal with personal information collected by governments or private businesses. Here, we look first at some

LAW, DIVERSITY, AND BUSINESS: MANAGERIAL IMPLICATIONS

MARRIAGE EQUALITY AND THE CONSTITUTION

The debate over whether to allow same-sex marriage has been raging across the country for many years. The legal issues raised by marriage equality involve both the privacy rights protected by state and federal constitutions and the full faith and credit clause of the U.S. Constitution, which requires states to enforce judicial decisions (and marriage decrees) issued in other states.

A Business Example Although marriage equality may not appear at first glance to be business related, it is a pertinent legal issue for managers, as Target Corporation learned in 2010. The company contributed $150,000 to a political group backing the Republican candidate in the Minnesota gubernatorial race, who had taken a stand against same-sex marriage. Although Target insisted that it made its donation because of the candidate's probusiness stance, boycotts of Target stores sprang up across the country.

State Laws A few states have enacted laws that allow gay marriage, most of which have been challenged in court. For example, in 2011, just days after New York's same-sex marriage law took effect, a conservative group filed a lawsuit seeking to overturn all of the marriages performed under authority of that law. Numerous other states have passed statutes that define marriage solely as a union between a man and a woman.

In California, where same-sex couples could obtain marriage certificates in the past, voters in 2008 enacted Proposition 8 to restrict marriage to one man and one woman. Then, in 2012, a federal appellate court struck down Prop 8 as a violation of the equal protection clause, reasoning that it was not rationally related to California's interests. "Although the Constitution permits communities to enact most laws they believe to be desirable," the court stated, "it requires that there be at least a legitimate reason for the passage of a law that treats different classes of people differently." In the court's view, Prop 8 served no legitimate purpose other than to "lessen the status and human dignity of gay men and lesbians in California."[a]

Business Implications *In this era of social networking, a company's policies can almost instantly become public—the boycotts of Target mentioned earlier were largely organized via Facebook. Consequently, businesspersons must carefully consider and address the rights and needs of their colleagues and employees who have different sexual orientations.*

At a minimum, managers should formulate policies that clearly specify how same-sex partners will be treated in terms of family and medical leave, health insurance coverage, pensions, and other benefits. Managers will need to evaluate their company's policies taking into account such factors as the firm's size, location, composition, and client base.

a. *Perry v. Brown*, 671 F.3d 1052 (9th Cir. 2012).

of the most important federal statutes protecting individuals' privacy and then examine in more detail the protection given to the important area of medical information.

Federal Privacy Legislation

In the 1960s, Americans were sufficiently alarmed by the accumulation of personal information in government files that they pressured Congress to pass laws permitting individuals to access their files. Congress responded in 1966 with the Freedom of Information Act, which allows any person to request copies of any information on her or him contained in federal government files. In 1974, Congress passed the Privacy Act, which also gives persons the right to access such information. These and other major federal laws protecting privacy rights are listed and described in Exhibit 2.1 on the following page. (See the *Business Application* on page 56 for a discussion of some laws pertaining to the collection of personal information by businesses.)

(sjlocke/iStockphoto.com)

Hospital patients are always informed about privacy rights under HIPAA.

Medical Information

Responding to the growing need to protect the privacy of individuals' health records—particularly computerized records—Congress passed the Health Insurance Portability and Accountability Act (HIPAA) of 1996.[34] This act defines and limits the circumstances in which an individual's "protected health information" may be used or disclosed.

HIPAA requires health-care providers and health-care plans, including certain employers who sponsor health plans, to inform patients of their privacy rights and of how their personal medical information may be used. The act also generally states that a person's medical records may not be used for purposes unrelated to health care—such as marketing—or disclosed to others without the individual's permission.

In 2009, Congress expanded HIPAA's provisions to apply to *vendors* (those who maintain personal health records for health-care providers) and to electronic records shared by multiple medical providers. Congress also authorized the Federal Trade Commission to enforce HIPAA and pursue violators.[35]

Technological Advances and Privacy Rights

Although advances in technology offer many benefits, they may also raise privacy issues. At the beginning of this chapter, we noted the concerns raised by the personal data collected by social networking sites. Here, we look briefly at two other areas in which technological developments are raising privacy issues today—the online dissemination of court records and the U.S. government's efforts to combat terrorism.

Court Records

The online dissemination of information concerning civil and criminal cases raises new privacy issues. Although court proceedings have always been a matter of public record, previously people had to go to a courthouse to examine the physical records. Now, technological improvements in information sharing allow civil and criminal justice records to be shared, synthesized, sold, and analyzed electronically. From anywhere in the world, private individuals, businesses, and other organizations can instantly access court records either directly in a state database or from a private data firm.

---

34. HIPAA was enacted as Pub. L. No. 104-191 (1996) and is codified in 29 U.S.C.A. Sections 1181 *et seq.*

35. These provisions were part of the American Recovery and Reinvestment Act (ARRA) of 2009, popularly known as the stimulus law. See 45 C.F.R. Sections 164.510 and 164.512(f)(2).

Exhibit 2.1 Federal Legislation Relating to Privacy

TITLE OF ACT	PROVISIONS CONCERNING PRIVACY
Freedom of Information Act (1966)	Provides that individuals have a right to obtain access to information about them collected in government files.
Family and Educational Rights and Privacy Act (1974)	Limits access to computer-stored records of education-related evaluations and grades in private and public colleges and universities.
Privacy Act (1974)	Protects the privacy of individuals about whom the federal government has information. Under this act, agencies that use or disclose personal information must make sure that the information is reliable and guard against its misuse. Individuals must be able to find out what data concerning them the agency is compiling and how the data will be used. In addition, the agency must give individuals a means to correct inaccurate data and must obtain their consent before using the data for any other purpose.
Tax Reform Act (1976)	Preserves the privacy of personal financial information.
Right to Financial Privacy Act (1978)	Prohibits financial institutions from providing the federal government with access to a customer's records unless the customer authorizes the disclosure.
Electronic Communications Privacy Act (1986)	Prohibits the interception of information communicated by electronic means.
Driver's Privacy Protection Act (1994)	Prevents states from disclosing or selling a driver's personal information without the driver's consent.
Health Insurance Portability and Accountability Act (1996)	Prohibits the use of a consumer's medical information for any purpose other than that for which such information was provided, unless the consumer expressly consents to the use.
Financial Services Modernization Act (Gramm-Leach-Bliley Act) (1999)	Prohibits the disclosure of nonpublic personal information about a consumer to an unaffiliated third party unless strict disclosure and opt-out requirements are met.

Moreover, states earn substantial revenues by selling certain records—such as residents' criminal history and tax records—to private data firms. These revenues make it unlikely that the states will refrain from selling such information in the future. Although most states have some privacy protections in place, once the information leaves the state's control, it can be given to anyone and used for any purpose. Additionally, if a state sells inaccurate or incomplete information to a company, there may be no way of correcting inaccuracies after the information has been sold.

"The things most people want to know about are usually none of their business."

George Bernard Shaw, 1856–1950 (Irish dramatist and socialist)

The advent of electronically available court documents raises difficult questions about how to protect a person's privacy. Court records (and police reports) frequently disclose the names and addresses of witnesses and victims, and may also include their date of birth, ethnicity, Social Security number, credit information, and details about their children and family. Criminals might use this information to perpetrate identity theft (see Chapter 6) or to intimidate or harass a witness or victim. Employers and landlords may use the information to screen potential applicants. An employer might decide not to hire a person who was involved in a civil or criminal case, and a landlord might not rent property to that person. (Even the victims in domestic violence cases, for example, may find that employers are reluctant to offer them jobs.) Furthermore, when mistakes occur, they can be devastating, as when a person's Social Security number is associated with a criminal or a person is misidentified as a sex offender.

The USA Patriot Act The USA Patriot Act was passed by Congress in the wake of the terrorist attacks of September 11, 2001, and then reauthorized in 2006.[36] The Patriot

36. The Uniting and Strengthening America by Providing Appropriate Tools Required to Intercept and Obstruct Terrorism Act of 2001, also known as the USA Patriot Act, was enacted as Pub. L. No. 107-56 (2001) and reauthorized by Pub. L. No. 109-173 (2006).

Act has given government officials increased authority to monitor Internet activities (such as e-mail and Web site visits) and to gain access to personal financial information and student information. Law enforcement officials may now track the telephone and e-mail communications of one party to find out the identity of the other party or parties.

To gain access to these communications, the government must certify that the information likely to be obtained by such monitoring is relevant to an ongoing criminal investigation, but it does not need to provide proof of any wrongdoing.[37] Privacy advocates argue that this law adversely affects the constitutional rights of all Americans, and it has been widely criticized in the media.

ETHICAL ISSUE

Does the threat of terrorism justify the U.S. government's use of body scanners at airports? The Transportation Security Administration (TSA) screens all persons seeking to board commercial airline flights for weapons, explosives, or other dangerous substances. In 2010, the TSA started using advanced imaging technology (AIT), or full-body scanners, as the primary screening device at many airports. Many travelers complained that they were being forced to undergo an electronic strip search because the scanners showed every part of one's body. Privacy advocates brought a lawsuit against the U.S. Department of Homeland Security, arguing that AIT was overly invasive and violated the Fourth Amendment's prohibition against unreasonable searches.

In 2011, a federal appellate court held that the use of full-body scanners at airports was constitutional. The court balanced the intrusiveness of a full-body scan against a scan's ability to further a compelling governmental interest. Here, the government had a critical need to ensure airline safety, and the full-body scanners, which can detect liquids and powders in addition to traditional weapons, furthered that interest. The court also found, however, that the TSA had violated the Administrative Procedure Act by changing its regulations to require AIT without following formal rulemaking procedures (see page 9 in Chapter 1). Therefore, the court ordered the TSA to open itself up for public comments on the use of the scanners.[38]

---

37. See, for example, *American Civil Liberties Union v. National Security Agency,* 493 F.3d 644 (6th Cir. 2007).

38. *Electronic Privacy Information Center v. U.S. Department of Homeland Security,* 653 F.3d 1 (D.C.Cir. 2011).

Reviewing . . . Constitutional Law

A state legislature enacted a statute that required any motorcycle operator or passenger on the state's highways to wear a protective helmet. Jim Alderman, a licensed motorcycle operator, sued the state to block enforcement of the law. Alderman asserted that the statute violated the equal protection clause because it placed requirements on motorcyclists that were not imposed on other motorists. Using the information presented in the chapter, answer the following questions.

1. Why does this statute raise equal protection issues instead of substantive due process concerns?
2. What are the three levels of scrutiny that the courts use in determining whether a law violates the equal protection clause?
3. Which level of scrutiny or test would apply to this situation? Why?
4. Applying this standard or test, is the helmet statute constitutional? Why or why not?

DEBATE THIS Legislation aimed at protecting people from themselves concerns the individual as well as the public in general. Protective helmet laws are just one example of such legislation. Should individuals be allowed to engage in unsafe activities if they choose to do so?

BUSINESS APPLICATION

Is "Pretexting" Illegal?*

Most businesses, institutions, and organizations gather information from and about their customers, constituents, or members. Many businesses also want information about potential customers and may obtain names from a mailing list of some other business or organization. Unless the owner of the list has a privacy policy that prohibits the sharing of certain information without the person's consent, a business may purchase the list and proceed to offer its product or service to all the people on it. Locating potential customers in this manner may be completely legal, depending on how the information was obtained in the first place. Pretexting is a method of collecting personal information that skirts the boundary between legal and illegal.

What Is "Pretexting"?

A *pretext* is a false motive put forth to hide the real motive, and *pretexting* is the process of obtaining information by false means. The term *pretexting* was first used in the 1990s when scammers obtained Social Security numbers by claiming that they were from the Social Security Administration and that their computer had broken down. Pretexters may try to obtain personal data by claiming that they are taking a survey for a research firm, a political party, or even a charity. Then they proceed to ask for information such as the person's insurance or telephone company, where he or she banks, and perhaps the name of his or her broker. Once they obtain the information, the pretexters sell it to a data broker, who in turn sells it to someone else, who may be a legitimate businessperson, a private investigator, or an individual intent on identity theft.

Pretexting Legislation

In 1999, Congress passed the Gramm-Leach-Bliley Act, which made pretexting to obtain financial information illegal. Initially, it was not clear whether that law prohibited lying to obtain *nonfinancial* information for purposes other than identity theft.

Fueling the debate over pretexting was a scandal involving Hewlett-Packard's board of directors. To find out who had leaked confidential company information to the press, Hewlett-Packard chair, Patricia C. Dunn, hired private investigators who used false pretenses to gain access to individuals' personal cell phone records. Dunn claimed that she was not aware of the investigators' methods and had assumed that they had obtained the information from public records. Although criminal charges that were brought against her were later dropped, several civil lawsuits followed. The company eventually paid $14.5 million in fines to settle a lawsuit filed by the California attorney general. In 2008, Hewlett-Packard reached a settlement with the New York Times Company and three *BusinessWeek* magazine journalists in connection with the scandal.

To clarify the law on pretexting to gain access to phone records, Congress enacted the Telephone Records and Privacy Protection Act. This act makes it a federal crime to pretend to be someone else or to make false representations for the purpose of obtaining another person's confidential phone records. The act also prohibits the buying, selling, transferring, or receiving of such phone records without the phone owner's permission. The Federal Trade Commission investigates and prosecutes violators, who can be fined and sentenced to up to ten years in prison.

Checklist for Providing or Securing Customer Information

1. *Make sure that your company has a privacy policy. If it does not, one should be created.*
2. *Never provide a third party with information unless your company's privacy policy specifically allows you to do so.*
3. *If you wish to acquire personal information on potential customers from a third party, make sure the data broker is legitimate, and find out how the information was acquired.*
4. *Treat all pretexting as illegal.*

*This *Business Application* is not meant to substitute for the services of an attorney who is licensed to practice law in your state.

Key Terms

Bill of Rights 40
checks and balances 35
commerce clause 35
compelling government interest 42
due process clause 49
equal protection clause 50
establishment clause 47
federal form of government 34
filtering software 46
free exercise clause 47
meta tags 46
police powers 38
preemption 39
supremacy clause 39
symbolic speech 41

Chapter Summary: Constitutional Law

The Constitutional Powers of Government (See pages 34–35.)	The U.S. Constitution established a federal form of government, in which government powers are shared by the national government and the state governments. At the national level, government powers are divided among the legislative, executive, and judicial branches.
The Commerce Clause (See pages 35–39.)	1. *The expansion of national powers*—The commerce clause expressly permits Congress to regulate commerce. Over time, courts expansively interpreted this clause, thereby enabling the national government to wield extensive powers over the economic life of the nation. 2. *The commerce power today*—Today, the commerce power authorizes the national government, at least theoretically, to regulate almost every commercial enterprise in the United States. In recent years, the Supreme Court has reined in somewhat the national government's regulatory powers under the commerce clause. 3. *The regulatory powers of the states*—The Tenth Amendment reserves to the states all powers not expressly delegated to the national government. Under their police powers, state governments may regulate private activities in order to protect or promote the public order, health, safety, morals, and general welfare. 4. *The "dormant" commerce clause*—If state regulations substantially interfere with interstate commerce, they will be held to violate the "dormant" commerce clause of the U.S. Constitution. The positive aspect of the commerce clause, which gives the national government the exclusive authority to regulate interstate commerce, implies a "dormant" aspect—that the states do *not* have this power.
The Supremacy Clause (See page 39.)	The U.S. Constitution provides that the Constitution, laws, and treaties of the United States are "the supreme Law of the Land." Whenever a state law directly conflicts with a federal law, the state law is rendered invalid.
Business and the Bill of Rights (See pages 40–49.)	The Bill of Rights, which consists of the first ten amendments to the U.S. Constitution, was adopted in 1791 and embodies a series of protections for individuals—and, in some instances, business entities—against various types of interference by the federal government. Today, most of the protections apply against state governments as well. Freedoms guaranteed by the First Amendment that affect businesses include the following: 1. *Freedom of speech*—Speech, including symbolic speech, is given the fullest possible protection by the courts. Corporate political speech and commercial speech also receive substantial protection under the First Amendment. Certain types of speech, such as defamatory speech and lewd or obscene speech, are not protected under the First Amendment. Government attempts to regulate unprotected forms of speech in the online environment have, to date, met with numerous challenges. 2. *Freedom of religion*—Under the First Amendment, the government may neither establish any religion (the establishment clause) nor prohibit the free exercise of religion (the free exercise clause).
Due Process and Equal Protection (See pages 49–51.)	1. *Due process*—Both the Fifth and the Fourteenth Amendments provide that no person shall be deprived of "life, liberty, or property, without due process of law." Procedural due process requires that any government decision to take life, liberty, or property must be made fairly, using fair procedures. Substantive due process focuses on the content of legislation. Generally, a law that limits a fundamental right violates substantive due process unless the law promotes a compelling state interest, such as public safety. 2. *Equal protection*—Under the Fourteenth Amendment, a law or action that limits the liberty of some persons but not others may violate the equal protection clause. Such a law may be upheld, however, if there is a rational basis for the discriminatory treatment of a given group or if the law substantially relates to an important government objective.
Privacy Rights (See pages 51–55.)	Americans are increasingly becoming concerned about privacy issues raised by Internet-related technology. The Constitution does not contain a specific guarantee of a right to privacy, but such a right has been derived from guarantees found in several constitutional amendments. A number of federal statutes protect privacy rights. Privacy rights are also protected by many state constitutions and statutes, as well as under tort law.

ExamPrep

ISSUE SPOTTERS

1. Can a state, in the interest of energy conservation, ban all advertising by power utilities if conservation could be accomplished by less restrictive means? Why or why not? **(See pages 44–45.)**
2. Suppose that a state imposes a higher tax on out-of-state companies doing business in the state than it imposes on in-state companies. Is this a violation of equal protection if the only reason for the tax is to protect the local firms from out-of-state competition? Explain. **(See pages 50–51.)**

—Check your answers to the Issue Spotters against the answers provided in Appendix E at the end of this text.

BEFORE THE TEST

Go to www.cengagebrain.com, enter the ISBN 9781133273561, and click on "Find" to locate this textbook's Web site. Then, click on "Access Now" under "Study Tools," and select Chapter 2 at the top. There, you will find a Practice Quiz that you can take to assess your mastery of the concepts in this chapter, as well as Flashcards, a Glossary of important terms, and Video Questions (when assigned).

For Review

Answers to the even-numbered questions in this For Review section can be found in Appendix F at the end of this text.

1. What is the basic structure of the U.S. government?
2. What constitutional clause gives the federal government the power to regulate commercial activities among the various states?
3. What constitutional clause allows laws enacted by the federal government to take priority over conflicting state laws?
4. What is the Bill of Rights? What freedoms do the First Amendment guarantee?
5. Where in the Constitution can the due process clause be found?

Business Scenarios and Case Problems

2–1 **Freedom of Speech.** A mayoral election is about to be held in Bay City. One of the candidates is Donita Estrella, and her supporters wish to post campaign signs on streetlights and utility posts. A Bay City ordinance prohibits the posting of signs on public property. The purpose of the ordinance is to improve the appearance of the city. Estrella's supporters contend that the ordinance violates their rights to free speech. What factors might a court consider in determining the constitutionality of this ordinance? **(See page 41.)**

2–2 **Question with Sample Answer—The Free Exercise Clause.** Thomas worked in the nonmilitary operations of a large firm that produced both military and nonmilitary goods. When the company discontinued the production of nonmilitary goods, Thomas was transferred to the plant producing military equipment. Thomas left his job, claiming that it violated his religious principles to participate in the manufacture of goods to be used in destroying life. In effect, he argued, the transfer to the military equipment plant forced him to quit his job. He was denied unemployment compensation by the state because he had not been effectively "discharged" by the employer but had voluntarily terminated his employment. Did the state's denial of unemployment benefits to Thomas violate the free exercise clause of the First Amendment? Explain. **(See page 47.)**

—For a sample answer to Question 2–2, go to Appendix G at the end of this text.

2–3 **The Equal Protection Clause.** With the objectives of preventing crime, maintaining property values, and preserving the quality of urban life, New York City enacted an ordinance to regulate the locations of commercial establishments that featured adult entertainment. The ordinance expressly applied to female, but not male, topless entertainment. Adele Buzzetti owned the Cozy Cabin, a New York City cabaret that featured female topless dancers. Buzzetti and an anonymous dancer filed a suit in a federal district court against the city, asking the court to block the enforcement of the ordinance. The plaintiffs argued, in part, that the ordinance violated the equal protection clause. Under the equal protection clause, what standard should the court apply in considering this ordinance? Under this test, how should the court rule? Why? **(See page 51.)**

2–4 **Spotlight on Plagiarism—Due Process.** The Russ College of Engineering and Technology of Ohio University announced in a press conference that it had found "rampant and flagrant plagiarism" in the theses of mechanical engineering graduate students. Faculty singled out for "ignoring their ethical responsibilities" included Jay Gunasekera, chair of the department. Gunasekera was prohibited from advising students. He filed a suit against Dennis Irwin, the dean of Russ College, for violating his due process rights. What does due process require in these circumstances? Why? [*Gunasekera v. Irwin,* 551 F.3d 461 (6th Cir. 2009)] **(See page 49.)**

2–5 **The Commerce Clause.** Under the federal Sex Offender Registration and Notification Act (SORNA), sex offenders must register and update their registration as sex offenders when they travel from one state to another. David Hall, a convicted sex offender in New York, moved to Virginia, where he did not update his registration. He was charged with violating SORNA. He claimed that the statute is unconstitutional, arguing that Congress cannot criminalize interstate travel if no commerce is involved. Is that reasonable? Why or why not? [*United States v. Guzman,* 591 F.3d 83 (2d Cir. 2010)] **(See page 35.)**

2–6 Case Problem with Sample Answer—Establishment Clause. Judge James DeWeese hung a poster in his courtroom showing the Ten Commandments. The American Civil Liberties Union (ACLU) filed a suit, alleging that the poster violated the establishment clause. DeWeese responded that his purpose was not to promote religion but to express his view about "warring" legal philosophies—moral relativism and moral absolutism. "Our legal system is based on moral absolutes from divine law handed down by God through the Ten Commandments." Does this poster violate the establishment clause? Why or why not? [*American Civil Liberties Union of Ohio Foundation, Inc. v. DeWeese,* 633 F.3d 424 (6th Cir. 2011)] **(See page 47.)**

—For a sample answer to Problem 2–6, go to Appendix H at the end of this text.

2–7 The Dormant Commerce Clause. In 2001, Puerto Rico enacted a law that requires specific labels on cement sold in Puerto Rico and imposes fines for any violations of these requirements. The law prohibits the sale or distribution of cement manufactured outside Puerto Rico that does not carry a required label warning that the cement may not be used in government-financed construction projects. Antilles Cement Corp., a Puerto Rican firm that imports foreign cement, filed a complaint in federal court, claiming that this law violated the dormant commerce clause. (The dormant commerce clause doctrine applies not only to commerce among the states and U.S. territories, but also to international commerce.) Did the 2001 Puerto Rican law violate the dormant commerce clause? Why or why not? [*Antilles Cement Corp. v. Fortuno,* 670 F.3d 310 (1st Cir. 2012)] **(See page 38.)**

2–8 A Question of Ethics—Free Speech. Aric Toll owns and manages the Balboa Island Village Inn, a restaurant and bar in Newport Beach, California. Anne Lemen lives across from the Inn. Lemen complained to the authorities about the Inn's customers, whom she called "drunks" and "whores." Lemen told the Inn's bartender Ewa Cook that Cook "worked for Satan." She repeated her statements to potential customers, and the Inn's sales dropped more than 20 percent. The Inn filed a suit against Lemen. [*Balboa Island Village Inn, Inc. v. Lemen,* 40 Cal.4th 1141, 156 P.3d 339 (2007)] **(See page 45.)**

1. Are Lemen's statements about the Inn's owners and customers protected by the U.S. Constitution? In whose favor should the court rule? Why?
2. Did Lemen behave unethically in the circumstances of this case? Explain.

Critical Thinking and Writing Assignments

2–9 Business Law Writing. The United States Supreme Court originally interpreted the commerce clause to allow the federal government to regulate interstate commerce. Over time, however, the Supreme Court has made it clear that the commerce clause applies not only to interstate commerce, but also to commerce that is purely intrastate (within one state). Today, the federal government has the power to regulate almost every commercial enterprise in the United States. Write a page discussing what expanded federal government power over commerce means for commercial businesses that operate only within the borders of one state. Does it promote or discourage intrastate commerce? **(See page 35.)**

2–10 Business Law Critical Thinking Group Assignment. For many years, New York City has had to deal with the vandalism and defacement of public property caused by unauthorized graffiti. In an effort to stop the damage, the city banned the sale of aerosol spray-paint cans and broad-tipped indelible markers to persons under twenty-one years of age. The new rules also prohibited people from possessing these items on property other than their own. Within a year, five people under age twenty-one were cited for violations of these regulations, and 871 individuals were arrested for actually making graffiti.

Lindsey Vincenty and other artists wished to create graffiti on legal surfaces, such as canvas, wood, and clothing. Unable to buy her supplies in the city or to carry them in the city if she bought them elsewhere, Vincenty and others filed a lawsuit on behalf of themselves and other young artists against Michael Bloomberg, the city's mayor, and others. The plaintiffs claimed that, among other things, the new rules violated their right to freedom of speech.

1. One group will argue in favor of the plaintiffs and provide several reasons why the court should hold that the city's new rules violate the plaintiffs' freedom of speech. **(See page 41.)**
2. Another group will develop a counterargument that outlines the reasons why the new rules do not violate free speech rights. **(See page 41.)**
3. A third group will argue that the city's ban violates the equal protection clause because it applies only to persons under age twenty-one. **(See page 50.)**

3 CHAPTER

Courts and Alternative Dispute Resolution

CHAPTER OUTLINE

- The Judiciary's Role in American Government
- Basic Judicial Requirements
- The State and Federal Court Systems
- Following a State Court Case
- The Courts Adapt to the Online World
- Alternative Dispute Resolution

LEARNING OBJECTIVES

The five learning objectives below are designed to help improve your understanding of the chapter. After reading this chapter, you should be able to answer the following questions:

1 What is judicial review? How and when was the power of judicial review established?

2 Before a court can hear a case, it must have jurisdiction. Over what must it have jurisdiction? How are the courts applying traditional jurisdictional concepts to cases involving Internet transactions?

3 What is the difference between a trial court and an appellate court?

4 What is discovery, and how does electronic discovery differ from traditional discovery?

5 What are three alternative methods of resolving disputes?

(Alina555/iStockphoto.com)

"An eye for an eye will make the whole world blind."
—Mahatma Gandhi, 1869–1948 (Indian political and spiritual leader)

Every society needs to have an established method for resolving disputes. Without one, as Mahatma Gandhi implied in the chapter-opening quotation, the biblical "eye for an eye" would lead to anarchy. This is particularly true in the business world—almost every businessperson will face a lawsuit at some time in his or her career. For this reason, anyone involved in business needs to have an understanding of court systems in the United States, as well as the various methods of dispute resolution that can be pursued outside the courts.

In this chapter, after examining the judiciary's overall role in the American governmental scheme, we discuss some basic requirements that must be met before a party may bring a lawsuit before a particular court. We then look at the court systems of the United States in some detail and, to clarify judicial procedures, follow a hypothetical case through a state court system. Because Islamic legal systems are prevalent in many parts of the world, some judges in this country have been asked to accept some Islamic law. You will read later in this chapter about this controversy.

Throughout this chapter, we indicate how court doctrines and procedures are being adapted to the needs of a cyber age. The chapter concludes with an overview of some alternative methods of settling disputes, including online dispute resolution.

The Judiciary's Role in American Government

As you learned in Chapter 1, the body of American law includes the federal and state constitutions, statutes passed by legislative bodies, administrative law, and the case decisions and legal principles that form the common law. These laws would be meaningless, however, without the courts to interpret and apply them. This is the essential role of the judiciary—the courts—in the American governmental system: to interpret and apply the law. (For a discussion of the impact of increased diversity on our nation's court system, see this chapter's *Law, Diversity, and Business: Managerial Implications* feature on the following page.)

LEARNING OBJECTIVE 1

What is judicial review? How and when was the power of judicial review established?

Judicial Review The process by which a court decides on the constitutionality of legislative enactments and actions of the executive branch.

Judicial Review

As the branch of government entrusted with interpreting the laws, the judiciary can decide, among other things, whether the laws or actions of the other two branches are constitutional. The process for making such a determination is known as **judicial review.** The power of judicial review enables the judicial branch to act as a check on the other two branches of government, in line with the checks-and-balances system established by the U.S. Constitution. (Today, nearly all nations with constitutional democracies, including Canada, France, and Germany, have some form of judicial review.)

(Library of Congress)

James Madison (1751–1836) wrote in favor of the states' adopting the new Constitution. What did he think of judicial review?

The Origins of Judicial Review in the United States

The U.S. Constitution does not mention judicial review, but the concept was not new at the time the nation was founded. Indeed, before 1789 state courts had already overturned state legislative acts that conflicted with state constitutions. Additionally, many of the founders expected the United States Supreme Court to assume a similar role with respect to the federal Constitution. Alexander Hamilton and James Madison both emphasized the importance of judicial review in their essays urging the adoption of the new Constitution. How was the doctrine of judicial review established? See this chapter's *Landmark in the Law* feature on page 63 for the answer.

Basic Judicial Requirements

Before a court can hear a lawsuit, certain requirements must first be met. These requirements relate to jurisdiction, venue, and standing to sue. We examine each of these important concepts here.

Jurisdiction The authority of a court to hear and decide a specific case.

Jurisdiction

In Latin, *juris* means "law," and *diction* means "to speak." Thus, "the power to speak the law" is the literal meaning of the term **jurisdiction.** Before any court can hear a case, it must have jurisdiction over the person (or company) against whom the suit is brought (the defendant) or over the property involved in the suit. The court must also have jurisdiction over the subject matter of the dispute.

LAW, DIVERSITY, AND BUSINESS: MANAGERIAL IMPLICATIONS

INCREASED DIVERSITY IN THE FEDERAL JUDICIARY

The United States Supreme Court first met in 1790, but the first female associate justice—Sandra Day O'Connor—was not appointed until 1981. In the Court's two-hundred-twenty-year history, only three other women have been appointed—Ruth Bader Ginsburg in 1993; Sonia Sotomayor in 2009, who was also the first Hispanic on the Court; and Elena Kagan in 2010. When Kagan joined the Court, for the first time in its history, one-third of the justices were women.

Obama's Judicial Nominations Set a Record for Women and Minorities As president, Barack Obama moved at a historic pace to diversify the federal judiciary. Nearly three of every four individuals confirmed for the federal bench have been women or members of minority groups. Indeed, he is the first president who has not selected a majority of white males for lifetime judgeships. During the first three years of Obama's presidency, 21 percent of his nominees who were confirmed were African American, 11 percent were Hispanic, and 7 percent were Asian American. Almost half were women.

The Benefits of a More Diverse Judiciary According to the Alliance for Justice, the more diverse the courts, the more confidence people have in our judicial system. Having a diverse judiciary enriches the decision-making process.

Does having more women on the bench change the way the law is interpreted? Yes, according to Vanderbilt University law professor Tracey George. She cites research that suggests including a woman in a decision-making group influences the behavior of the rest of the group. In particular, some academic studies have found evidence that in gender discrimination lawsuits, if a three-judge panel of a federal appeals court includes a woman, the court is more likely to rule in favor of the person asserting discrimination.

Business Implications *A more diverse federal judiciary will mean that managers must be more conscientious about their employment decisions and make sure that they are not motivated by gender or racial discrimination. Business owners and managers should also establish internal decision-making and record-keeping procedures that are fair and neutral, to avoid any appearance of bias at the workplace. If allegations of discrimination arise, managers should promptly investigate and evaluate the company's conduct, and consider the possibility of settling the claim before trial.*

Jurisdiction over Persons or Property

Generally, a court can exercise personal jurisdiction (*in personam* jurisdiction) over any person or business that resides in a certain geographic area. A state trial court, for example, normally has jurisdictional authority over residents (including businesses) in a particular area of the state, such as a county or district. A state's highest court (often called the state supreme court)[1] has jurisdiction over all residents of that state.

A court can also exercise jurisdiction over property that is located within its boundaries. This kind of jurisdiction is known as *in rem* jurisdiction, or "jurisdiction over the thing." **EXAMPLE 3.1** A dispute arises over the ownership of a boat in dry dock in Fort Lauderdale, Florida. The boat is owned by an Ohio resident, over whom a Florida court normally cannot exercise personal jurisdiction. The other party to the dispute is a resident of Nebraska. In this situation, a lawsuit concerning the boat could be brought in a Florida state court on the basis of the court's *in rem* jurisdiction. •

Long Arm Statute A state statute that permits a state to exercise jurisdiction over nonresident defendants.

Long Arm Statutes Under the authority of a state **long arm statute,** a court can exercise personal jurisdiction over certain out-of-state defendants based on activities that took place within the state. Before exercising long arm jurisdiction over a nonresident, however, the court must be convinced that the defendant had sufficient contacts, or *minimum*

1. As will be discussed shortly, a state's highest court is frequently referred to as the state supreme court, but there are exceptions. For example, in New York, the supreme court is a trial court.

LANDMARK IN THE LAW

Marbury v. Madison (1803)

The power of judicial review was established in the Supreme Court's decision in the case of *Marbury v. Madison*.[a] Though the decision is widely viewed as a cornerstone of constitutional law, the case had its origins in early U.S. politics. When Thomas Jefferson defeated the incumbent president, John Adams, in the presidential elections of 1800, Adams feared the Jeffersonians' antipathy toward business and toward a strong national government. Adams thus rushed to "pack" the judiciary with loyal Federalists (those who believed in a strong national government) by appointing what came to be called "midnight judges" just before he left office. But Adams's secretary of state (John Marshall) was able to deliver only forty-two of the fifty-nine judicial appointment letters by the time Jefferson took over as president. Jefferson refused to order his secretary of state, James Madison, to deliver the remaining commissions.

Marshall's Dilemma William Marbury and three others to whom the commissions had not been delivered sought a writ of *mandamus* (an order directing a government official to fulfill a duty) from the United States Supreme Court, as authorized by the Judiciary Act of 1789. As fate would have it, John Marshall had just been appointed as chief justice of the Supreme Court. Marshall faced a dilemma: If he ordered the commissions delivered, the new secretary of state (Madison) could simply refuse to deliver them—and the Court had no way to compel him to act. At the same time, if Marshall simply allowed the new administration to do as it wished, the Court's power would be severely eroded.

a. 5 U.S. (1 Cranch) 137, 2 L.Ed. 60 (1803).

Marshall's Decision Marshall masterfully fashioned his decision to enlarge the power of the Supreme Court by affirming the Court's power of judicial review. He stated, "It is emphatically the province and duty of the Judicial Department to say what the law is. . . . If two laws conflict with each other, the Courts must decide on the operation of each. . . . [I]f both [a] law and the Constitution apply to a particular case, . . . the Court must determine which of these conflicting rules governs the case."

Marshall's decision did not require anyone to do anything. He concluded that the highest court did not have the power to issue a writ of *mandamus* in this particular case. Although the Judiciary Act of 1789 specified that the Supreme Court could issue writs of *mandamus* as part of its original jurisdiction, Article III of the Constitution, which spelled out the Court's original jurisdiction, did not mention writs of *mandamus*. Because Congress did not have the right to expand the Supreme Court's jurisdiction, this section of the Judiciary Act of 1789 was unconstitutional—and thus void. The *Marbury* decision stands to this day as a judicial and political masterpiece.

Application to Today's World *Since the* Marbury v. Madison *decision, the power of judicial review has remained unchallenged and today is exercised by both federal and state courts. If the courts did not have the power of judicial review, the constitutionality of Congress's acts could not be challenged in court—a congressional statute would remain law unless changed by Congress. The courts of other countries that have adopted a constitutional democracy often cite this decision as a justification for judicial review.*

contacts, with the state to justify the jurisdiction.[2] Generally, this means that the defendant must have enough of a connection to the state for the judge to conclude that it is fair for the state to exercise power over the defendant. If an out-of-state defendant caused an automobile accident or sold defective goods within the state, for instance, a court will usually find that minimum contacts exist to exercise jurisdiction over that defendant.

CASE EXAMPLE 3.2 After an Xbox game system caught fire in Bonnie Broquet's home in Texas and caused substantial personal injuries, Broquet filed a lawsuit in a Texas court against Ji-Haw Industrial Company, a nonresident company that made the Xbox components. Broquet alleged that Ji-Haw's components were defective and had caused the fire. Ji-Haw argued that the Texas court lacked jurisdiction over it, but in 2008, a state appellate court held that the Texas long arm statute authorized the exercise of jurisdiction over the out-of-state defendant.[3] •

2. The minimum-contacts standard was established in *International Shoe Co. v. State of Washington,* 326 U.S. 310, 66 S.Ct. 154, 90 L.Ed. 95 (1945).

3. *Ji-Haw Industrial Co. v. Broquet,* 2008 WL 441822 (Tex.App.—San Antonio 2008).

(Jacob Kepler/Bloomberg via Getty Images)

Suppose that a young gamer is injured because Microsoft's Xbox, shown above, released an electrical shock. Who can the parents sue?

Similarly, a state may exercise personal jurisdiction over a nonresident defendant who is sued for breaching a contract that was formed within the state, even when that contract was negotiated over the phone or through correspondence. **EXAMPLE 3.3** Sharon Mills, a California resident, forms a corporation to distribute a documentary film on global climate change. Brad Cole, an environmentalist who lives in Ohio, loans the corporation funds that he borrows from an Ohio bank. A year later, the film is still not completed. Mills agrees to repay Cole's loan in a contract arranged through phone calls and correspondence between California and Ohio. When Mills does not repay the loan, Cole files a lawsuit in an Ohio court. In this situation, the Ohio court can likely exercise jurisdiction over Mills because her phone calls and letters have established sufficient contacts with the state of Ohio. •

Corporate Contacts Because corporations are considered legal persons, courts use the same principles to determine whether it is fair to exercise jurisdiction over a corporation.[4] A corporation normally is subject to personal jurisdiction in the state in which it is incorporated, has its principal office, and is doing business. Courts apply the minimum-contacts test to determine if they can exercise jurisdiction over out-of-state corporations.

The minimum-contacts requirement is usually met if the corporation advertises or sells its products within the state, or places its goods into the "stream of commerce" with the intent that the goods be sold in the state. **EXAMPLE 3.4** A business is incorporated under the laws of Maine but has a branch office and manufacturing plant in Georgia. The corporation also advertises and sells its products in Georgia. These activities would likely constitute sufficient contacts with the state of Georgia to allow a Georgia court to exercise jurisdiction over the corporation. •

Some corporations do not sell or advertise products or place any goods in the stream of commerce. Determining what constitutes minimum contacts in these situations can be more difficult. In the following case, the question before the court was whether a New Jersey firm had minimum contacts with a North Carolina firm.

4. In the eyes of the law, corporations are "legal persons"—entities that can sue and be sued. See Chapter 29.

Case 3.1

Southern Prestige Industries, Inc. v. Independence Plating Corp.

Court of Appeals of North Carolina, 690 S.E.2d 768 (2010). www.nccourts.org[a]

(J van der Wolf/Shutterstock.com)

Many parts in these jets must be metal coated.

FACTS Independence Plating Corporation (the defendant) is a New Jersey corporation that provides metal-coating services. Its only office and all of its personnel are located in New Jersey. It does not advertise out of state, but it had a longstanding business relationship with Kidde Aerospace in North Carolina (filing under the name Southern Prestige Industries, Inc.). For almost a year, Independence and Kidde engaged in frequent transactions. On November 18, 2008, Kidde initiated an action for breach of contract in a North Carolina state court, alleging defects in the metal-plating process carried out by Independence. Independence filed a motion to dismiss for lack of personal jurisdiction, which the trial court denied.

a. In the right-hand column of the page, click on "Court Opinions." When that page opens, select the year 2010 under the heading "Court of Appeals Opinions." Scroll down to February 2, 2010, and click on the case title under "Unpublished Opinions" to access the opinion. The North Carolina court system maintains this Web site.

Case 3.1—Continued

Independence appealed, arguing that it had insufficient contacts with North Carolina for the state to exercise jurisdiction.

ISSUE Did Independence Plating Corporation have sufficient minimum contacts with North Carolina for the state to exercise personal jurisdiction?

DECISION Yes. The North Carolina appellate court affirmed the trial court's decision. Independence had sufficient minimum contacts with North Carolina to satisfy the due process of law requirements necessary for the state to exercise jurisdiction.

REASON In determining whether minimum contacts existed, the court looked at several factors, including the number of contacts and their nature and quality, as well as the interests of North Carolina, the forum state. In this case, thirty-two separate purchase orders were exchanged between the two parties in a period of less than twelve months. Independence sent invoices totaling more than $21,000, and these invoices were paid from Southern's corporate bank account. "North Carolina has a single 'manifest interest' in providing the plaintiff with 'a convenient forum for redressing injuries inflicted by' [the] defendant, an out-of-state merchant."

CRITICAL THINKING—Ethical Consideration *Was it fair for the North Carolina courts to require a New Jersey company to litigate in North Carolina? Explain.*

Jurisdiction over Subject Matter

Jurisdiction over subject matter is a limitation on the types of cases a court can hear. In both the federal and state court systems, there are courts of *general* (unlimited) *jurisdiction* and courts of *limited jurisdiction*. An example of a court of general jurisdiction is a state trial court or a federal district court. An example of a state court of limited jurisdiction is a probate court. **Probate courts** are state courts that handle only matters relating to the transfer of a person's assets and obligations after that person's death, including matters relating to the custody and guardianship of children. An example of a federal court of limited subject-matter jurisdiction is a bankruptcy court. **Bankruptcy courts** handle only bankruptcy proceedings, which are governed by federal bankruptcy law (discussed in Chapter 21).

Probate Court A state court of limited jurisdiction that conducts proceedings relating to the settlement of a deceased person's estate.

Bankruptcy Court A federal court of limited jurisdiction that handles only bankruptcy proceedings, which are governed by federal bankruptcy law.

A court's jurisdiction over subject matter is usually defined in the statute or constitution creating the court. In both the federal and state court systems, a court's subject-matter jurisdiction can be limited not only by the subject of the lawsuit but also by the amount in controversy, by whether a case is a felony (a more serious type of crime) or a misdemeanor (a less serious type of crime), or by whether the proceeding is a trial or an appeal.

Original and Appellate Jurisdiction

The distinction between courts of original jurisdiction and courts of appellate jurisdiction normally lies in whether the case is being heard for the first time. Courts having original jurisdiction are courts of the first instance, or trial courts—that is, courts in which lawsuits begin, trials take place, and evidence is presented. In the federal court system, the *district courts* are trial courts. In the various state court systems, the trial courts are known by various names, as will be discussed shortly.

The key point here is that any court having original jurisdiction is normally known as a trial court. Courts having appellate jurisdiction act as reviewing courts, or appellate courts. In general, cases can be brought before appellate courts only on appeal from an order or a judgment of a trial court or other lower court.

KNOW THIS

Federal courts do not have the power to hear every case. They have jurisdiction to hear a dispute only when it raises a federal question or when the parties are residents of different states (or countries) and the amount involved in the controversy exceeds $75,000.

Jurisdiction of the Federal Courts

Because the federal government is a government of limited powers, the jurisdiction of the federal courts is limited. Federal courts have subject-matter jurisdiction in two situations.

Federal Questions Article III of the U.S. Constitution establishes the boundaries of federal judicial power. Section 2 of Article III states that "[t]he judicial Power shall extend to all Cases, in Law and Equity, arising under this Constitution, the Laws of the United States, and Treaties made, or which shall be made, under their Authority." This clause means that whenever a plaintiff's cause of action is based, at least in part, on the U.S. Constitution, a treaty, or a federal law, then a **federal question** arises, and the federal courts have jurisdiction. Any lawsuit involving a federal question, such as a person's rights under the U.S. Constitution, can originate in a federal court. Note that in a case based on a federal question, a federal court will apply federal law.

Federal Question A question that pertains to the U.S. Constitution, an act of Congress, or a treaty and provides a basis for federal jurisdiction in a case.

Diversity of Citizenship Federal district courts can also exercise original jurisdiction over cases involving **diversity of citizenship.** The most common type of diversity jurisdiction has two requirements:[5] (1) the plaintiff and defendant must be residents of different states, and (2) the dollar amount in controversy must exceed $75,000. For purposes of diversity jurisdiction, a corporation is a citizen of both the state in which it is incorporated and the state in which its principal place of business is located. A case involving diversity of citizenship can be filed in the appropriate federal district court. If the case starts in a state court, it can sometimes be transferred, or "removed," to a federal court. A large percentage of the cases filed in federal courts each year are based on diversity of citizenship.

Diversity of Citizenship A basis for federal court jurisdiction over a lawsuit between citizens of different states and countries.

As noted, a federal court will apply federal law in cases involving federal questions. In a case based on diversity of citizenship, in contrast, a federal court will apply the relevant state law (which is often the law of the state in which the court sits).

Exclusive versus Concurrent Jurisdiction

When both federal and state courts have the power to hear a case, as is true in lawsuits involving diversity of citizenship, **concurrent jurisdiction** exists. When cases can be tried only in federal courts or only in state courts, **exclusive jurisdiction** exists. Federal courts have exclusive jurisdiction in cases involving federal crimes, bankruptcy, patents, and copyrights; in suits against the United States; and in some areas of admiralty law (law governing transportation on the seas and ocean waters). State courts also have exclusive jurisdiction over certain subject matter—for instance, divorce and adoption.

Concurrent Jurisdiction Jurisdiction that exists when two different courts have the power to hear a case.

Exclusive Jurisdiction Jurisdiction that exists when a case can be heard only in a particular court or type of court.

When concurrent jurisdiction exists, a party may bring a suit in either a federal court or a state court. A number of factors can affect the decision of whether to litigate in a federal or a state court, such as the availability of different remedies, the distance to the respective courthouses, or the experience or reputation of a particular judge. For instance, if the dispute involves a trade secret, a party might conclude that a federal court—which has exclusive jurisdiction over copyrights, patents, and trademarks—would have more expertise in the matter.

A resident of another state might also choose a federal court over a state court if he or she is concerned that a state court might be biased against an out-of-state plaintiff. In contrast, a plaintiff might choose to litigate in a state court if it has a reputation for awarding substantial amounts of damages or if the judge is perceived as being pro-plaintiff. The concepts of exclusive and concurrent jurisdiction are illustrated in Exhibit 3.1 on the facing page.

Jurisdiction in Cyberspace

The Internet's capacity to bypass political and geographic boundaries undercuts the traditional basis on which courts assert personal jurisdiction. As already discussed, for a court to compel a defendant to come before it, there must be at least minimum contacts—the

5. Diversity jurisdiction also exists in cases between (1) a foreign country and citizens of a state or of different states and (2) citizens of a state and citizens or subjects of a foreign country. These bases for diversity jurisdiction are less commonly used.

Exhibit 3.1 Exclusive and Concurrent Jurisdiction

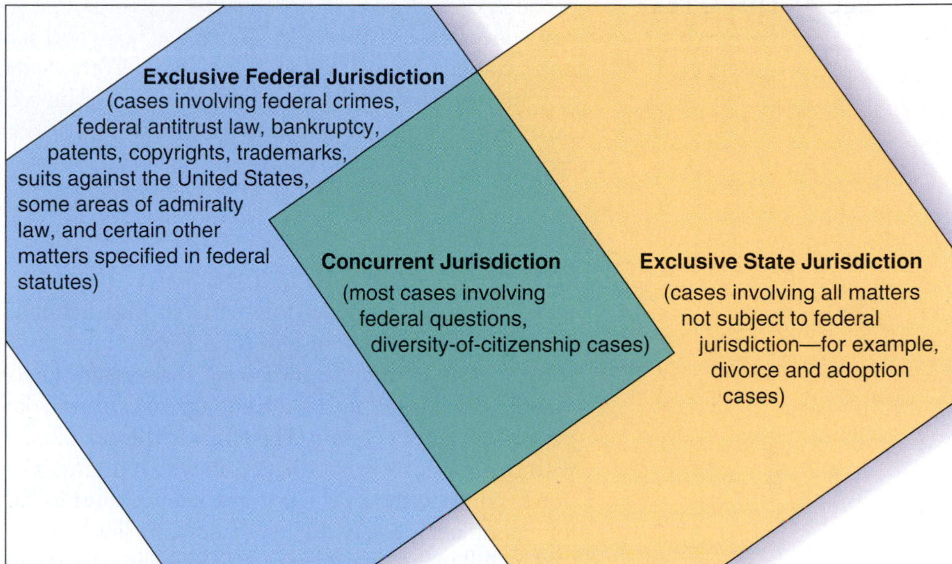

presence of a salesperson within the state, for example. Are there sufficient minimum contacts if the defendant's only connection to a jurisdiction is an ad on a Web site originating from a remote location?

LEARNING OBJECTIVE 2

Before a court can hear a case, it must have jurisdiction. Over what must it have jurisdiction? How are the courts applying traditional jurisdictional concepts to cases involving Internet transactions?

The "Sliding-Scale" Standard

The courts have developed a standard—called a "sliding-scale" standard—for determining when the exercise of jurisdiction over an out-of-state defendant is proper. In developing this standard, the courts have identified three types of Internet business contacts: (1) substantial business conducted over the Internet (with contracts and sales, for example), (2) some interactivity through a Web site, and (3) passive advertising. Jurisdiction is proper for the first category, improper for the third, and may or may not be appropriate for the second.[6] An Internet communication is typically considered passive if people have to voluntarily access it to read the message, and active if it is sent to specific individuals.

In certain situations, even a single contact can satisfy the minimum-contacts requirement. **CASE EXAMPLE 3.5** Daniel Crummey purchased a used recreational vehicle (RV) from sellers in Texas after viewing numerous photos of it on eBay. The sellers' statements on eBay claimed that "everything works great on this RV and will provide comfort and dependability for years to come. This RV will go to Alaska and back without problems!" Crummey picked up the RV in Texas, but on the drive home, the RV quit working. He filed a suit in Louisiana against the sellers alleging that the vehicle was defective, but the sellers claimed that the Louisiana court lacked jurisdiction. Because the sellers had used eBay to market and sell the RV to a Louisiana buyer—and had regularly used eBay to sell vehicles to remote parties in the past—the court found that jurisdiction was proper.[7] ●

6. For a leading case on this issue, see *Zippo Manufacturing Co. v. Zippo Dot Com, Inc.*, 952 F.Supp. 1119 (W.D.Pa. 1997).

7. *Crummey v. Morgan*, 965 So.2d 497 (La.App.1 Cir. 2007). But note that a single sale on eBay does not necessarily confer jurisdiction. Jurisdiction depends on whether the seller regularly uses eBay as a means for doing business with remote buyers. See *Boschetto v. Hansing*, 539 F.3d 1011 (9th Cir. 2008).

PREVENTING LEGAL DISPUTES

Those of you with an entrepreneurial spirit may be eager to establish Web sites to promote products and solicit orders. Be aware, however, that you can be sued in states in which you have *never* been physically present if you have had sufficient contacts with residents of those states over the Internet. Before you create a Web site that is the least bit interactive, you need to consult an attorney to find out whether you will be subjecting yourself to jurisdiction in every state. Becoming informed about the extent of your potential exposure to lawsuits in various locations is an important part of preventing litigation.

International Jurisdictional Issues

Because the Internet is global in scope, it obviously raises international jurisdictional issues. The world's courts seem to be developing a standard that echoes the minimum-contacts requirement applied by U.S. courts. Most courts are indicating that minimum contacts—doing business within the jurisdiction, for example—are enough to compel a defendant to appear and that a physical presence is not necessary. The effect of this standard is that a business firm has to comply with the laws in any jurisdiction in which it targets customers for its products. This situation is complicated by the fact that many countries' laws on particular issues—free speech, for example—are very different from U.S. laws

The following case illustrates how federal courts apply a sliding-scale standard to determine if they can exercise jurisdiction over a foreign defendant whose only contact with the United States is through a Web site.

Spotlight on Gucci

Case 3.2

Gucci America, Inc. v. Wang Huoqing

United States District Court, Northern District of California, ___ F.Supp.3d ___ (2011).

(Alessia Pierdomenico/ Bloomberg via GettyImages)

Gucci luxury leather products are often counterfeited. Can Gucci sue an Asian company in the United States, nonetheless?

FACTS Gucci America, Inc., is a New York corporation headquartered in New York City. Gucci manufactures and distributes high-quality luxury goods, including footwear, belts, sunglasses, handbags, and wallets, which are sold worldwide. In connection with its products, Gucci uses twenty-one federally registered trademarks (trademark law will be discussed in Chapter 5). Gucci also operates a number of boutiques, some of which are located in California. Wang Huoqing, a resident of the People's Republic of China, operates numerous Web sites. When Gucci discovered that Huoqing's Web sites were selling counterfeit goods—products with Gucci's trademarks but not genuine Gucci articles—it hired a private investigator in San Jose, California, to buy goods from the Web sites. The investigator purchased a wallet that was labeled Gucci but was counterfeit. Gucci filed a trademark infringement lawsuit against Huoqing in a federal district court in California seeking damages and an injunction to prevent further infringement. Huoqing was notified of the lawsuit via e-mail (see the discussion of *service of process* on page 76) but did not appear in court. Gucci asked the court to enter a default judgment—that is, a judgment entered when the defendant fails to appear—but the court first had to determine whether it had personal jurisdiction over Huoqing based on the Internet sales.

ISSUE Can a U.S. federal court exercise personal jurisdiction over a resident of China whose only contact with the United States was through an interactive Web site that advertised and sold counterfeit goods?

DECISION Yes. The U.S. District Court for the Northern District of California held that it had personal jurisdiction over the foreign defendant, Huoqing. The court entered a default judgment against Huoqing and granted Gucci an injunction.

REASON The court reasoned that the due process clause allows a federal court to exercise jurisdiction over a defendant who has had sufficient minimum contacts with the court's forum—the place where the court exercises jurisdiction.

Case 3.2—Continued

Specifically, jurisdiction exists when (1) the nonresident defendant engages in some act or transaction with the forum "by which he purposefully avails himself of the privilege of conducting activities in the forum, thereby invoking the benefits and protections of its laws; (2) the claim must be one which arises out of or results from the defendant's forum-related activities; and (3) exercise of jurisdiction must be reasonable." To determine whether Huoqing had purposefully conducted business activities in Gucci's district, the court used a sliding-scale analysis. Under this analysis, passive Web sites do not create sufficient contacts for such a finding, but interactive sites may do so. Huoqing's Web sites were fully interactive. In addition, Gucci presented evidence that Huoqing had advertised and sold the counterfeited goods within the court's district, and that he had made one actual sale within the district—the sale to Gucci's private investigator.

WHAT IF THE FACTS WERE DIFFERENT? *Suppose that Gucci had not presented evidence that Huoqing had made one actual sale through his Web site to a resident (the private investigator) of the court's district. Would the court still have found that it had personal jurisdiction over Huoqing? Why or why not?*

Venue

Venue The geographic district in which a legal action is tried and from which the jury is selected.

Jurisdiction has to do with whether a court has authority to hear a case involving specific persons, property, or subject matter. **Venue**[8] is concerned with the most appropriate physical location for a trial. Two state courts (or two federal courts) may have the authority to exercise jurisdiction over a case, but it may be more appropriate or convenient to hear the case in one court than in the other.

Basically, the concept of venue reflects the policy that a court trying a suit should be in the geographic neighborhood (usually the county) where the incident leading to the lawsuit occurred or where the parties involved in the lawsuit reside. Venue in a civil case typically is where the defendant resides, whereas venue in a criminal case normally is where the crime occurred. Pretrial publicity or other factors, though, may require a change of venue to another community, especially in criminal cases when the defendant's right to a fair and impartial jury has been impaired.

EXAMPLE 3.6 Police raid a compound of religious polygamists in Texas and remove many children from the ranch. Authorities suspect that some of the girls were being sexually and physically abused. The raid receives a great deal of media attention, and the people living in the nearby towns are likely influenced by this publicity. In this situation, if the government files criminal charges against a member of the religious sect, that individual may request—and will probably receive—a change of venue to another location. •

Standing to Sue

Standing to Sue The legal requirement that an individual must have a sufficient stake in a controversy before he or she can bring a lawsuit.

Justiciable Controversy A controversy that is not hypothetical or academic but real and substantial; a requirement that must be satisfied before a court will hear a case.

Before a person can bring a lawsuit before a court, the party must have **standing to sue**, or a sufficient "stake" in the matter to justify seeking relief through the court system. In other words, to have standing, a party must have a legally protected and tangible interest at stake in the litigation. The party bringing the lawsuit must have suffered a harm, or have been threatened by a harm, as a result of the action about which she or he has complained. Standing to sue also requires that the controversy at issue be a **justiciable**[9] **controversy**—a controversy that is real and substantial, as opposed to hypothetical or academic. As Chief Justice John Roberts recently noted in a United States Supreme Court decision, a lack of

---

8. Pronounced *ven*-yoo.

9. Pronounced jus-*tish*-uh-bul.

standing is like Bob Dylan's line in the song "Like a Rolling Stone": "When you got nothing, you got nothing to lose."[10]

CASE EXAMPLE 3.7 James Bush visited the office of the Federal Bureau of Investigation (FBI) in San Jose, California, on two occasions. He filled out forms indicating that he was seeking records under the Freedom of Information Act (FOIA—see Chapter 33) regarding a police brutality claim and the FBI's failure to investigate it. Bush later filed a suit against the U.S. Department of Justice in an attempt to compel the FBI to provide the requested records. The court dismissed the lawsuit on the ground that no justiciable controversy existed. Because Bush had not complied with the requirements of the FOIA, the FBI was not obligated to provide any records, and thus there was no actual controversy for the court to decide.[11] •

Note that in some situations a person may have standing to sue on behalf of another person, such as a minor or a mentally incompetent person. **EXAMPLE 3.8** Three-year-old Emma suffers serious injuries as a result of a defectively manufactured toy. Because Emma is a minor, her parent or legal guardian can bring a lawsuit on her behalf. •

The State and Federal Court Systems

As mentioned earlier in this chapter, each state has its own court system. Additionally, there is a system of federal courts. Even though there are fifty-two court systems—one for each of the fifty states, one for the District of Columbia, plus a federal system—similarities abound. Exhibit 3.2 on the facing page illustrates the basic organizational structure characteristic of the court systems in many states. The exhibit also shows how the federal court system is structured. Keep in mind that the federal courts are not superior to the state courts. They are simply an independent system of courts, which derives its authority from Article III, Sections 1 and 2, of the U.S. Constitution. We turn now to an examination of these court systems, beginning with the state courts.

The State Court Systems

Typically, a state court system will include several levels, or tiers, of courts. As indicated in Exhibit 3.2 on the facing page, state courts may include (1) trial courts of limited jurisdiction, (2) trial courts of general jurisdiction, (3) appellate courts, and (4) the state's highest court (often called the state supreme court). Generally, any person who is a party to a lawsuit has the opportunity to plead the case before a trial court and then, if he or she loses, before at least one level of appellate court. If the case involves a federal statute or a federal constitutional issue, the decision of a state supreme court on that issue may be further appealed to the United States Supreme Court.

The states use various methods to select judges for their courts. Generally, judges are elected, but in some states, they are appointed. Usually, states specify the number of years that a judge will serve. In contrast, as you will read shortly, judges in the federal court system are appointed by the president of the United States and, if confirmed by the Senate, hold office for life—unless they engage in blatantly illegal conduct.

Trial Courts

Trial courts are exactly what their name implies—courts in which trials are held and testimony taken. State trial courts have either general or limited jurisdiction.

---

10. The chief justice stated, "The absence of any substantive recovery means that respondents cannot benefit from the judgment they seek and thus lack Article III standing." He then quoted Bob Dylan's lyrics from "Like a Rolling Stone," on *Highway 61 Revisited* (Columbia Records 1965). This was the first time that a member of the Supreme Court cited rock lyrics in an opinion. See *Sprint Communications Co. v. APCC Services, Inc.*, 554 U.S. 269, 128 S.Ct. 2531, 171 L.Ed.2d 424 (2008).

11. *Bush v. Department of Justice*, 2008 WL 5245046 (N.D.Cal. 2008).

Exhibit 3.2 The State and Federal Court Systems

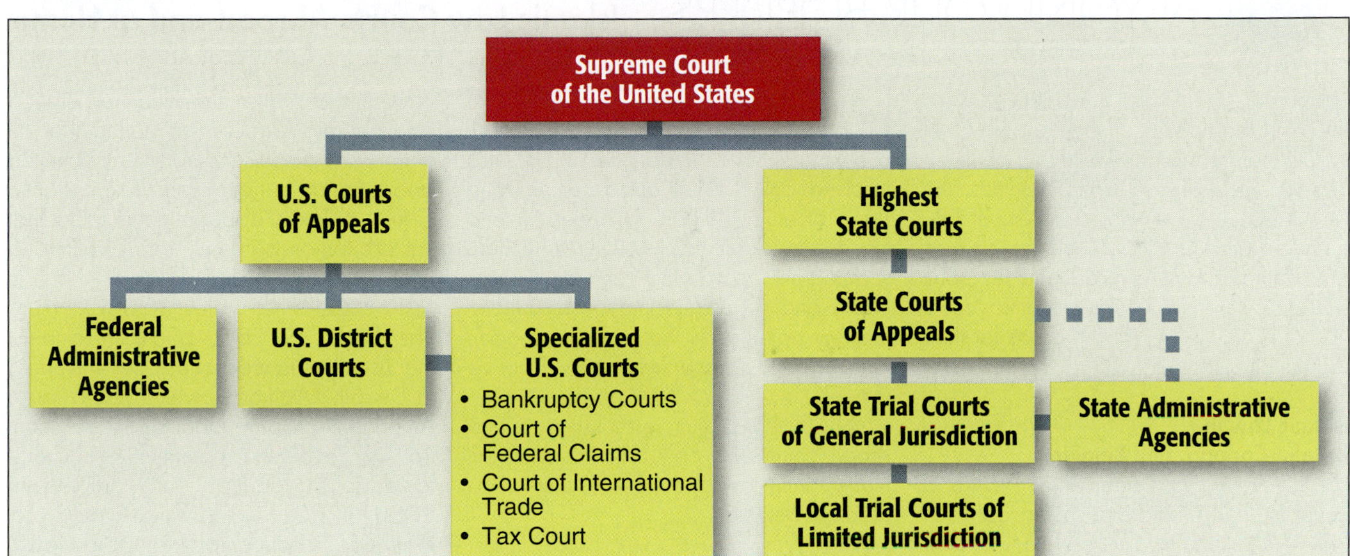

Trial courts that have general jurisdiction as to subject matter may be called county, district, superior, or circuit courts.[12] The jurisdiction of these courts is often determined by the size of the county in which the court sits. State trial courts of general jurisdiction have jurisdiction over a wide variety of subjects, including both civil disputes and criminal prosecutions. (In some states, trial courts of general jurisdiction may hear appeals from courts of limited jurisdiction.)

Small Claims Court A special court in which parties can litigate small claims without an attorney.

Some courts of limited jurisdiction are called special inferior trial courts or minor judiciary courts. **Small claims courts** are inferior trial courts that hear only civil cases involving claims of less than a certain amount, such as $5,000 (the amount varies from state to state). Suits brought in small claims courts are generally conducted informally, and lawyers are not required (in a few states, lawyers are not even allowed).

Another example of an inferior trial court is a local municipal court that hears mainly traffic cases. Decisions of small claims courts and municipal courts may sometimes be appealed to a state trial court of general jurisdiction. Other courts of limited jurisdiction as to subject matter include domestic relations or family courts, which handle primarily divorce actions and child-custody disputes, and probate courts, as mentioned earlier. A few states have even established Islamic law courts, which are courts of limited jurisdiction that serve the American Muslim community. (See this chapter's *Beyond Our Borders* feature on the following page for a discussion of the rise of Islamic law courts.)

Appellate, or Reviewing, Courts

Every state has at least one court of appeals (appellate court, or reviewing court), which may be an intermediate appellate court or the state's highest court. About three-fourths of the states have intermediate appellate courts. Generally, courts of appeals do not conduct new trials, in which evidence is submitted to the court and witnesses are examined. Rather, an appellate court panel of three or more judges reviews the record of the case on appeal, which includes a transcript of the trial proceedings, and determines whether the trial court committed an error.

12. The name in Ohio is court of common pleas, and the name in New York is supreme court.

BEYOND OUR BORDERS Islamic Law Courts Abroad and at Home

As discussed in Chapter 1, Islamic law is one of the world's three most common legal systems, along with civil law and common law systems. In most Islamic countries, the law is based on *sharia,* a system of law derived from the Qur'an and the sayings and doings of Muhammad and his companions. Today, many non-Islamic countries are establishing Islamic courts for their Muslim citizens.

Islamic Law in Britain, Canada, and Belgium

For several years, Great Britain has had councils that arbitrate disputes between British Muslims involving child custody, property, employment, and housing. These councils do not deal with criminal law or with any civil issues that would put *sharia* in direct conflict with British statutory law. Most Islamic law cases involve marriage or divorce. Starting in 2008, Britain officially sanctioned the authority of *sharia* judges to rule on divorce and financial disputes of Muslim couples. Britain now has eighty-five officially recognized *sharia* courts that have the full power of their equivalent courts within the traditional British judicial system.

In Ontario, Canada, a group of Canadian Muslims established a judicial tribunal using *sharia.* To date, this tribunal has resolved only marital disagreements and some other civil disputes. Under Ontario law, the regular judicial system must uphold such agreements as long as they are voluntary and negotiated through an arbitrator. Any agreements that violate Canada's Charter of Rights and Freedoms will not be upheld.

In 2011, Belgium established its first *sharia* court. This court also handles primarily family law disputes for Muslim immigrants in Belgium.

Islamic Law Courts in the United States

The use of Islamic courts in the United States has been somewhat controversial. The legality of arbitration clauses that require disputes to be settled in Islamic courts has been upheld by regular state courts in some states, including Minnesota and Texas.

In the Texas case, an American Muslim couple was married and was issued an Islamic marriage certificate. Years later, a dispute arose over marital property and the nonpayment of a "dowry for the bride." The parties involved had signed an arbitration agreement stating that all claims and disputes were to be submitted to arbitration in front of the Texas Islamic Court. A Texas appeals court ruled that the arbitration agreement was valid and enforceable.[a]

In some other states, however, there has been a public backlash against the use of Islamic courts. For instance, in Detroit, Michigan, which has a large American Muslim population, a controversy over the community's attempt to establish Islamic courts erupted in 2008. In 2011, a law that would prohibit judges from enforcing foreign laws, including *sharia,* was proposed in the Michigan state legislature.

Critical Thinking

One of the arguments against allowing sharia *courts in the United States is that we would no longer have a common legal framework within our society. Do you agree or disagree? Why?*

a. *Jabri v. Qaddura,* 108 S.W.3d 404 (Tex.App.—Fort Worth 2003).

Question of Fact In a lawsuit, an issue that involves only disputed facts, and not what the law is on a given point.

Question of Law In a lawsuit, an issue involving the application or interpretation of a law.

Focus on Questions of Law Appellate courts generally focus on questions of law, not questions of fact. A **question of fact** deals with what really happened in regard to the dispute being tried—such as whether a party actually burned a flag. A **question of law** concerns the application or interpretation of the law—such as whether flag-burning is a form of speech protected by the First Amendment to the U.S. Constitution. Only a judge, not a jury, can rule on questions of law.

Defer to the Trial Court's Findings of Fact Appellate courts normally defer (or give weight) to a trial court's findings on questions of fact because the trial court judge and jury were in a better position to evaluate testimony by directly observing witnesses' gestures, demeanor, and nonverbal behavior during the trial. At the appellate level, the judges review the written transcript of the trial, which does not include these nonverbal elements.

LEARNING OBJECTIVE 3
What is the difference between a trial court and an appellate court?

An appellate court will challenge a trial court's finding of fact only when the finding is clearly erroneous (that is, when it is contrary to the evidence presented at trial) or when there is no evidence to support the finding. **EXAMPLE 3.9** A jury concludes that a manufacturer's product harmed the plaintiff, but no evidence was submitted to the court to support that conclusion. In this situation, the appellate court will hold that the trial court's decision was erroneous. • The options exercised by appellate courts will be discussed further later in this chapter.

KNOW THIS

The decisions of a state's highest court are final on questions of state law.

Highest State Courts

The highest appellate court in a state is usually called the supreme court but may be called by some other name. For example, in both New York and Maryland, the highest state court is called the court of appeals. The decisions of each state's highest court are final on all questions of state law. Only when issues of federal law are involved can a decision made by a state's highest court be overruled by the United States Supreme Court.

The Federal Court System

The federal court system is basically a three-tiered model consisting of (1) U.S. district courts (trial courts of general jurisdiction) and various courts of limited jurisdiction, (2) U.S. courts of appeals (intermediate courts of appeals), and (3) the United States Supreme Court.

Unlike state court judges, who are usually elected, federal court judges—including the justices of the Supreme Court—are appointed by the president of the United States and confirmed by the U.S. Senate. All federal judges receive lifetime appointments because under Article III they "hold their offices during Good Behavior."

ETHICAL ISSUE

Can justice be served when courts are underfunded? The economic downturn that started a few years ago has led to massive budget cuts for many of this nation's court systems. In California, for example, which is experiencing unsustainable state government budget deficits, court funding has been reduced by hundreds of millions of dollars. As a consequence, a typical civil lawsuit may take several years to be heard by a court. Nationwide, the American Bar Association found that in the last several years most states have cut court funding by almost 15 percent. Twenty-six states have stopped filling judicial vacancies. Some have even forced judges to take a leave of absence without pay. One municipal court in Ohio stopped accepting new cases because it could not buy paper.

The end result is that the courts are limiting access to the justice system. According to Rebecca Love Kourlis of the Institute for the Advancement of the American Legal System, our traditional idea that everyone has an equal right to justice is being threatened. The American Bar Association reports that its members fear that "the underfunding of our judicial system threatens the fundamental nature of our tripartite system of government." That brings to mind the words of Judge Learned Hand, who said in 1951: "If we are to keep our democracy, there must be one commandment: Thou shalt not ration justice."

U.S. District Courts

At the federal level, the equivalent of a state trial court of general jurisdiction is the district court. There is at least one federal district court in every state. The number of judicial districts can vary over time, primarily owing to population changes and corresponding caseloads. Today, there are ninety-four federal judicial districts. U.S. district courts have original jurisdiction in federal matters. Federal cases typically originate in district courts. Federal courts with original, but special (or limited), jurisdiction include the bankruptcy courts and others shown in Exhibit 3.2 on page 71.

U.S. Courts of Appeals

In the federal court system, there are thirteen U.S. courts of appeals—also referred to as U.S. circuit courts of appeals. The federal courts of appeals for twelve of the circuits, including the U.S. Court of Appeals for the District of Columbia Circuit, hear appeals from the federal district courts located within their respective judicial circuits. The Court of Appeals for the Thirteenth Circuit, called the Federal Circuit, has national appellate jurisdiction over certain types of cases, such as cases involving patent law and cases in which the U.S. government is a defendant.

The decisions of the circuit courts of appeals are final in most cases, but appeal to the United States Supreme Court is possible. Exhibit 3.3 below shows the geographic boundaries of the U.S. circuit courts of appeals and the boundaries of the U.S. district courts within each circuit.

The United States Supreme Court

The highest level of the three-tiered model of the federal court system is the United States Supreme Court. According to the language of Article III of the U.S. Constitution, there is only one national Supreme Court. All other courts in the federal system are considered "inferior." Congress is empowered to create other inferior courts as it deems necessary. The inferior courts that Congress has created include the second tier in our model—the U.S. courts of appeals—as well as the district courts and any other courts of limited, or specialized, jurisdiction.

The United States Supreme Court consists of nine justices. Although the Supreme Court has original, or trial, jurisdiction in rare instances (set forth in Article III, Section 2), most of its work is as an appeals court. The Supreme Court can review any case decided by any of the federal courts of appeals, and it also has appellate authority over some cases decided in the state courts.

Writ of *Certiorari* A writ from a higher court asking a lower court for the record of a case.

Appeals to the Supreme Court To bring a case before the Supreme Court, a party requests that the Court issue a writ of *certiorari*. A **writ of *certiorari***[13] is an order issued by

13. Pronounced sur-shee-uh-*rah*-ree.

Exhibit 3.3 Boundaries of the U.S. Courts of Appeals and U.S. District Courts

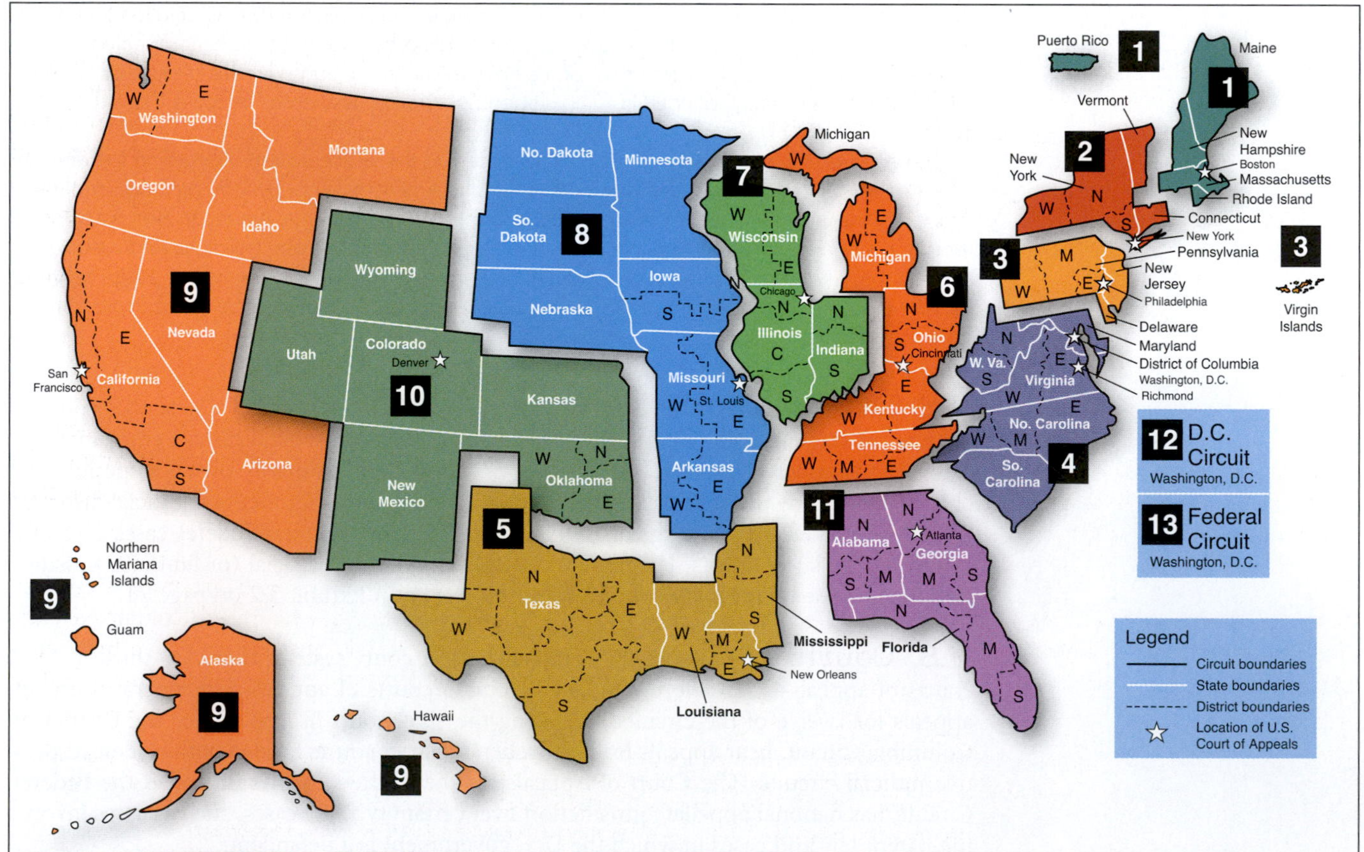

Source: Administrative Office of the United States Courts.

Rule of Four A rule of the United States Supreme Court under which the Court will not issue a writ of *certiorari* unless at least four justices approve of the decision to issue the writ.

the Supreme Court to a lower court requiring that court to send the record of the case for review. Under the **rule of four,** the Court will not issue a writ unless at least four of the nine justices approve. Whether the Court will issue a writ of *certiorari* is entirely within its discretion. The Court is not required to issue one, and most petitions for writs are denied. (Although thousands of cases are filed with the Supreme Court each year, it hears, on average, fewer than one hundred of these cases.)[14] A denial is not a decision on the merits of a case, nor does it indicate agreement with the lower court's opinion. Furthermore, a denial of the writ has no value as a precedent.

Petitions Granted by the Court Typically, the Court grants petitions when cases raise important constitutional questions or when the lower courts are issuing conflicting decisions on a significant issue. The justices, however, never explain their reasons for hearing certain cases and not others, so it is difficult to predict which type of case the Court might select.

Following a State Court Case

"Lawsuit: A machine which you go into as a pig and come out of as a sausage."

Ambrose Bierce, 1842–1914 (American journalist)

To illustrate the procedures that would be followed in a civil lawsuit brought in a state court, we present a hypothetical case and follow it through the state court system. The case involves an automobile accident in which Kevin Anderson, driving a Lexus, struck Lisa Marconi, driving a Hyundai Genesis. The accident occurred at the intersection of Wilshire Boulevard and Rodeo Drive in Beverly Hills, California. Marconi suffered personal injuries and incurred medical and hospital expenses as a result, as well as lost wages for four months. Anderson and Marconi are unable to agree on a settlement, and Marconi sues Anderson. Marconi is the plaintiff, and Anderson is the defendant. Both are represented by lawyers.

Litigation The process of resolving a dispute through the court system.

During each phase of the **litigation** (the process of working a lawsuit through the court system), Marconi and Anderson will have to observe strict procedural requirements. A large body of law—procedural law—establishes the rules and standards for determining disputes in courts. Procedural rules are very complex, and they vary from court to court and from state to state. In addition to the various sets of rules for state courts, the federal courts have their own rules of procedure. Additionally, the applicable procedures will depend on whether the case is a civil or criminal proceeding. Generally, the Marconi-Anderson civil lawsuit will involve the procedures discussed in the following subsections. Keep in mind that attempts to settle the case may be ongoing throughout the trial.

The Pleadings

Pleadings Statements by the plaintiff and the defendant that detail the facts, charges, and defenses of a case.

The complaint and answer (and the counterclaim and reply)—all of which are discussed next—taken together are called the **pleadings.** The pleadings inform each party of the other's claims and specify the issues (disputed questions) involved in the case. The style and form of the pleadings may be quite different in different states.

Complaint The pleading made by a plaintiff alleging wrongdoing on the part of the defendant. When filed with a court, the complaint initiates a lawsuit.

The Plaintiff's Complaint

Marconi's suit against Anderson commences when her lawyer files a **complaint** with the appropriate court. The complaint contains a statement alleging (1) the facts necessary for the court to take jurisdiction, (2) a brief summary of the facts necessary to show that the plaintiff is entitled to relief (a remedy),[15] and

14. From the mid-1950s through the early 1990s, the United States Supreme Court reviewed more cases per year than it has in the last few years. In the Court's 1982–1983 term, for example, the Court issued opinions in 151 cases. In contrast, in its 2011–2012 term, the Court issued opinions in only 77 cases.

15. The factual allegations in a complaint must be enough to raise a right to relief above the speculative level. They must plausibly suggest that the plaintiff is entitled to a remedy. See *Bell Atlantic Corp. v. Twombly,* 550 U.S. 544, 127 S.Ct. 1955, 167 L.Ed.2d 929 (2007).

(3) a statement of the remedy the plaintiff is seeking. Complaints may be lengthy or brief, depending on the complexity of the case and the rules of the jurisdiction.

Summons A document informing a defendant that a legal action has been commenced against her or him and that the defendant must appear in court on a certain date to answer the plaintiff's complaint.

Default Judgment A judgment entered by a court against a defendant who has failed to appear in court to answer or defend against the plaintiff's claim.

Answer Procedurally, a defendant's response to the plaintiff's complaint.

Counterclaim A claim made by a defendant in a civil lawsuit against the plaintiff. In effect, the defendant is suing the plaintiff.

Reply Procedurally, a plaintiff's response to a defendant's answer.

Motion to Dismiss A pleading in which a defendant admits the facts as alleged by the plaintiff but asserts that the plaintiff's claim to state a cause of action has no basis in law.

Motion for Judgment on the Pleadings A motion by either party to a lawsuit at the close of the pleadings requesting the court to decide the issue solely on the pleadings without proceeding to trial. The motion will be granted only if no facts are in dispute.

Service of Process

After the complaint has been filed, the sheriff, a county deputy, or another *process server*—that is, one who delivers a complaint and summons—serves a **summons** and a copy of the complaint on defendant Anderson. The summons notifies Anderson that he must file an answer to the complaint with both the court and the plaintiff's attorney within a specified time period (usually twenty to thirty days). The summons also informs Anderson that failure to answer may result in a **default judgment** for the plaintiff, meaning the plaintiff could be awarded the damages sought in her complaint. Service of process is essential in our legal system. No case can proceed to trial unless the plaintiff can prove that he or she has properly served the defendant.

The Defendant's Answer

The defendant's **answer** either admits the statements or allegations set forth in the complaint or denies them and outlines any defenses that the defendant may have. If Anderson admits to all of Marconi's allegations in his answer, the court will enter a judgment for Marconi. If Anderson denies any of Marconi's allegations, the litigation will go forward.

Anderson can deny Marconi's allegations and set forth his own claim that Marconi was negligent and therefore owes him compensation for the damage to his Lexus. This is appropriately called a **counterclaim.** If Anderson files a counterclaim, Marconi will have to answer it with a pleading, normally called a **reply,** which has the same characteristics as an answer.

Anderson can also admit the truth of Marconi's complaint but raise new facts that may result in dismissal of the action. This is called raising an *affirmative defense.* For example, Anderson could assert the expiration of the time period under the relevant *statute of limitations* (a state or federal statute that sets the maximum time period during which a certain action can be brought or rights enforced) as an affirmative defense.

Motion to Dismiss

A **motion to dismiss** requests the court to dismiss the case for stated reasons. Grounds for dismissal of a case include improper delivery of the complaint and summons, improper venue, and the plaintiff's failure to state a claim for which a court could grant relief. For instance, if Marconi had suffered no injuries or losses as a result of Anderson's negligence, Anderson could move to have the case dismissed because Marconi would not have stated a claim for which relief could be granted.

If the judge grants the motion to dismiss, the plaintiff generally is given time to file an amended complaint. If the judge denies the motion, the suit will go forward, and the defendant must then file an answer. Note that if Marconi wishes to discontinue the suit because, for example, an out-of-court settlement has been reached, she can likewise move for dismissal. The court can also dismiss the case on its own motion.

Pretrial Motions

Either party may attempt to get the case dismissed before trial through the use of various pretrial motions. We have already mentioned the motion to dismiss. Two other important pretrial motions are the motion for judgment on the pleadings and the motion for summary judgment.

At the close of the pleadings, either party may make a **motion for judgment on the pleadings,** or on the merits of the case. The judge will grant the motion only when there is no dispute over the facts of the case and the sole issue to be resolved is a question of law. In deciding on the motion, the judge may consider only the evidence contained in the pleadings.

Motion for Summary Judgment A motion requesting the court to enter a judgment without proceeding to trial. The motion can be based on evidence outside the pleadings and will be granted only if no facts are in dispute.

In contrast, in a **motion for summary judgment,** the court may consider evidence outside the pleadings, such as sworn statements (affidavits) by parties or witnesses, or other documents relating to the case. Either party can make a motion for summary judgment. Like the motion for judgment on the pleadings, a motion for summary judgment will be granted only if there are no genuine questions of fact and the sole question is a question of law.

LEARNING OBJECTIVE 4

What is discovery, and how does electronic discovery differ from traditional discovery?

Discovery

Discovery A method by which the opposing parties obtain information from each other to prepare for trial.

Before a trial begins, each party can use a number of procedural devices to obtain information and gather evidence about the case from the other party or from third parties. The process of obtaining such information is known as **discovery.** Discovery includes gaining access to witnesses, documents, records, and other types of evidence.

The Federal Rules of Civil Procedure and similar rules in the states set forth the guidelines for discovery. Generally, discovery is allowed regarding any matter that is not privileged and is relevant to the claim or defense of any party. Discovery rules also attempt to protect witnesses and parties from undue harassment and to safeguard privileged or confidential material from being disclosed. If a discovery request involves privileged or confidential business information, a court can deny the request and can limit the scope of discovery in a number of ways. For instance, a court can require the party to submit the materials to the judge in a sealed envelope so that the judge can decide if they should be disclosed to the opposing party.

Discovery prevents surprises at trial by giving parties access to evidence that might otherwise be hidden. This allows both parties to learn what to expect during a trial before they reach the courtroom. Discovery also serves to narrow the issues so that trial time is spent on the main questions in the case.

Deposition The testimony of a party to a lawsuit or a witness taken under oath before a trial.

Depositions and Interrogatories

Discovery can involve the use of depositions or interrogatories, or both. A **deposition** is sworn testimony by a party to the lawsuit or any witness. The person being deposed (the deponent) answers questions asked by the attorneys, and the questions and answers are recorded by an authorized court official and sworn to and signed by the deponent. (Occasionally, written depositions are taken when witnesses are unable to appear in person.) The answers given to depositions will, of course, help the attorneys prepare for the trial. They can also be used in court to impeach (challenge the credibility of) a party or a witness who changes her or his testimony at the trial. In addition, a witness's deposition can be used as testimony if he or she is not available for the trial.

Interrogatories A series of written questions for which written answers are prepared by a party to a lawsuit, usually with the assistance of the party's attorney, and then signed under oath.

Interrogatories are written questions for which written answers are prepared and then signed under oath. The main difference between interrogatories and written depositions is that interrogatories are directed to a party to the lawsuit (the plaintiff or the defendant), not to a witness, and the party can prepare answers with the aid of an attorney. The scope of interrogatories is broader because parties are obligated to answer the questions, even if that means disclosing information from their records and files.

Requests for Other Information

A party can serve a written request on the other party for an admission of the truth on matters relating to the trial. Any matter admitted under such a request is conclusively established for the trial. For example, Marconi can ask Anderson to admit that he was driving at a speed of forty-five miles an hour. A request for admission saves time at trial because the parties will not have to spend time proving facts on which they already agree.

A party can also gain access to documents and other items not in her or his possession in order to inspect and examine them. Likewise, a party can gain "entry upon land" to inspect the premises. Anderson's attorney, for example, normally can gain permission to inspect and photocopy Marconi's car repair bills.

When the physical or mental condition of one party is in question, the opposing party can ask the court to order a physical or mental examination, but the court will do so only if the need for the information outweighs the right to privacy of the person to be examined. If the court issues the order, the opposing party can obtain the results of the examination.

Electronic Discovery

Any relevant material, including information stored electronically, can be the object of a discovery request. The federal rules and most state rules now specifically allow all parties to obtain electronic "data compilations." Electronic evidence, or **e-evidence,** includes all types of computer-generated or electronically recorded information, such as e-mail, voice mail, tweets, blogs, spreadsheets, as well as documents and other data stored on computers. E-evidence can reveal significant facts that are not discoverable by other means. For example, computers automatically record certain information about files—such as who created the file and when, and who accessed, modified, or transmitted it—on their hard drives. This information can be obtained only from the file in its electronic format—not from printed-out versions.

E-Evidence A type of evidence that consists of all computer-generated or electronically recorded information.

E-Discovery Procedures Amendments to the Federal Rules of Civil Procedure that took effect in 2006 deal specifically with the preservation, retrieval, and production of electronic data. Although traditional means, such as interrogatories and depositions, are still used to find out about the e-evidence, a party must usually hire an expert to retrieve evidence in its electronic format. The expert uses software to reconstruct e-mail exchanges and establish who knew what and when they knew it. The expert can even recover files that the user thought had been deleted from a computer.

"The judicial system is the most expensive machine ever invented for finding out what happened and what to do about it."

Irving R. Kaufman, 1910–1992 (American jurist)

Advantages and Disadvantages Electronic discovery has significant advantages over paper discovery. Back-up copies of documents and e-mail can provide useful—and often quite damaging—information about how a particular matter progressed over several weeks or months. E-discovery can uncover the proverbial smoking gun that will win the lawsuit, but it is also time consuming and expensive, especially when lawsuits involve large firms with multiple offices. Also, many firms are finding it difficult to fulfill their duty to preserve electronic evidence from a vast number of sources. For a discussion of some of the problems associated with preserving electronic evidence for discovery, see this chapter's *Adapting the Law to the Online Environment* feature on the facing page.

Pretrial Conference

Either party or the court can request a pretrial conference, or hearing. Usually, the hearing consists of an informal discussion between the judge and the opposing attorneys after discovery has taken place. The purpose of the hearing is to explore the possibility of a settlement without trial and, if this is not possible, to identify the matters that are in dispute and to plan the course of the trial.

Jury Selection

A trial can be held with or without a jury. The Seventh Amendment to the U.S. Constitution guarantees the right to a jury trial for cases in *federal* courts when the amount in controversy exceeds $20, but this guarantee does not apply to state courts. Most states have similar guarantees in their own constitutions (although the threshold dollar amount is higher than $20). The right to a trial by jury does not have to be exercised, and many cases are tried without a jury. In most states and in federal courts, one of the parties must request a jury in a civil case, or the judge presumes that the parties waive the right.

KNOW THIS

Picking the "right" jury is often an important aspect of litigation strategy, and a number of firms now specialize in jury consulting services.

ADAPTING THE LAW TO THE ONLINE ENVIRONMENT

THE DUTY TO PRESERVE ELECTRONIC EVIDENCE FOR DISCOVERY

Today, less than 0.5 percent of new information is created on paper. Instead of sending letters and memos, people send e-mails and text messages, creating a massive amount of electronically stored information (ESI). The law requires parties to preserve ESI whenever there is a "reasonable anticipation of litigation."

Why Companies Fail to Preserve E-Evidence

Preserving e-evidence can be a challenge, though, particularly for large corporations that have electronic data scattered across multiple networks, servers, desktops, laptops, iPhones, iPads, and other smartphones and tablets. Although many companies have policies regarding back-up of office e-mail and computer systems, these may cover only a fraction of the e-evidence requested in a lawsuit.

Technological advances further complicate the situation. Users of BlackBerrys, for example, can configure them so that messages are transmitted with limited or no archiving rather than going through a company's servers and being recorded. How can a company preserve e-evidence that is never on its servers? In one case, the court held that a company had a duty to preserve transitory "server log data," which exist only temporarily on a computer's memory.[a]

Potential Sanctions and Malpractice Claims

A court may impose sanctions (such as fines) on a party that fails to preserve electronic evidence or to comply with e-evidence requests. A firm may be sanctioned if it provides e-mails without the attachments, does not produce all of the e-discovery requested, overwrites the contents of files, or fails to suspend its automatic e-mail deletion procedures.[b] Sanctions for e-discovery violations have become increasingly common in recent years.[c] Attorneys who fail to properly advise their clients concerning the duty to preserve e-evidence or who fail to supervise vendors, contract attorneys, or subordinates who work for the clients also often face sanctions and malpractice claims.[d]

Lessons from Intel

A party that fails to preserve e-evidence may even find itself at such a disadvantage that it will settle a dispute rather than continue litigation. For instance, Advanced Micro Devices, Inc. (AMD), sued Intel Corporation, one of the world's largest microprocessor suppliers, for violating antitrust laws. Immediately after the lawsuit was filed, Intel began collecting and preserving the ESI on its servers. Although the company instructed its employees to retain documents and e-mails related to competition with AMD, many employees saved only copies of the e-mails that they had received and not e-mails that they had sent.

In addition, Intel did not stop its automatic e-mail deletion system, causing other information to be lost. In the end, although Intel produced data that were equivalent to "somewhere in the neighborhood of a pile 137 miles high" in paper, its failure to preserve e-discovery led it to settle the dispute.[e]

Critical Thinking

How might a large company protect itself from allegations that it intentionally failed to preserve electronic data?

a. See *Columbia Pictures v. Brunnell*, 2007 WL 2080419 (C.D.Cal. 2007).

b. See, for example, *Io Group, Inc. v. GLBT, Ltd*, 2011 WL 4974337 (N.D.Cal. 2011); *E. I. Du Pont de Nemours & Co. v. Kolon Industries, Inc.*, 803 F.Supp.2d 469 (E.D.Va. 2011); *Genger v. TR Investors, LLC*, 26 A.3d 180 (Del.Supr. 2011); *PIC Group, Inc. v. LandCoast Insulation, Inc.*, 2011 WL 2669144 (S.D.Miss. 2011).

c. Elizabeth E. McGinn and Karen M. Morgan, "New Ethical Issues and Challenges in E-Discovery," *New York Law Journal*, October 5, 2011.

d. See, for example, *Surowiec v. Capital Title Agency, Inc.*, 790 F.Supp.2d 997 (D.Ariz. 2011).

e. See *In re Intel Corp. Microprocessor Antitrust Litigation*, 2008 WL 2310288 (D.Del. 2008). See also *Net2Phone, Inc. v. eBay, Inc.*, 2008 WL 8183817 (D.N.J. 2008).

Voir Dire An important part of the jury selection process in which the attorneys question prospective jurors about their backgrounds, attitudes, and biases to ascertain whether they can be impartial jurors.

Before a jury trial commences, a jury must be selected. The jury selection process is known as ***voir dire***.[16] During *voir dire* in most jurisdictions, attorneys for the plaintiff and the defendant ask prospective jurors oral questions to determine whether a potential jury member is biased or has any connection with a party to the action or with a prospective witness. In some jurisdictions, the judge may do all or part of the questioning based on written questions submitted by counsel for the parties.

During *voir dire*, a party may challenge a prospective juror *peremptorily*—that is, ask that an individual not be sworn in as a juror without providing any reason. Alternatively, a party

16. Pronounced vwahr *deehr*.

KNOW THIS

A prospective juror cannot be excluded solely on the basis of his or her race or gender.

may challenge a prospective juror *for cause*—that is, provide a reason why an individual should not be sworn in as a juror. If the judge grants the challenge, the individual is asked to step down. A prospective juror may not be excluded from the jury by the use of discriminatory challenges, however, such as those based on racial criteria or gender.

At the Trial

At the beginning of the trial, the attorneys present their opening arguments, setting forth the facts that they expect to prove during the trial. Then the plaintiff's case is presented. In our hypothetical case, Marconi's lawyer would introduce evidence (relevant documents, exhibits, and the testimony of witnesses) to support Marconi's position. The defendant has the opportunity to challenge any evidence introduced and to cross-examine any of the plaintiff's witnesses.

Motion for a Directed Verdict A motion for the judge to take the decision out of the hands of the jury and to direct a verdict for the party making the motion on the ground that the other party has not produced sufficient evidence to support her or his claim.

Directed Verdicts

At the end of the plaintiff's case, the defendant's attorney has the opportunity to ask the judge to direct a verdict for the defendant on the ground that the plaintiff has presented no evidence that would justify the granting of the plaintiff's remedy. This is called a **motion for a directed verdict** (known in federal courts as a *motion for judgment as a matter of law*). If the motion is not granted (it seldom is granted), the defendant's attorney then presents the evidence and witnesses for the defendant's case. At the conclusion of the defendant's case, the defendant's attorney has another opportunity to make a motion for a directed verdict. The plaintiff's attorney can challenge any evidence introduced and cross-examine the defendant's witnesses.

Award The monetary compensation given to a party at the end of a trial or other proceeding.

Closing Arguments and Awards

After the defense concludes its presentation, the attorneys present their closing arguments, each urging a verdict in favor of her or his client. The judge instructs the jury in the law that applies to the case (these instructions are often called *charges*), and the jury retires to the jury room to deliberate a verdict. In the Marconi-Anderson case, the jury will not only decide for the plaintiff or for the defendant but, if it finds for the plaintiff, will also decide on the amount of the **award** (the compensation to be paid to her).

Posttrial Motions

Motion for Judgment *N.O.V.* A motion requesting the court to grant judgment in favor of the party making the motion on the ground that the jury's verdict against him or her was unreasonable and erroneous.

Motion for a New Trial A motion asserting that the trial was so fundamentally flawed (because of error, newly discovered evidence, prejudice, or another reason) that a new trial is necessary to prevent a miscarriage of justice.

After the jury has rendered its verdict, either party may make a posttrial motion. If Marconi wins and Anderson's attorney has previously moved for a directed verdict, Anderson's attorney may make a **motion for judgment *n.o.v.*** (from the Latin *non obstante veredicto,* which means "notwithstanding the verdict"—called a *motion for judgment as a matter of law* in the federal courts). Such a motion will be granted only if the jury's verdict was unreasonable and erroneous. If the judge grants the motion, the jury's verdict will be set aside, and a judgment will be entered in favor of the opposite party (Anderson).

Alternatively, Anderson could make a **motion for a new trial**, asking the judge to set aside the adverse verdict and to hold a new trial. The motion will be granted if, after looking at all the evidence, the judge is convinced that the jury was in error but does not feel that it is appropriate to grant judgment for the other side. A judge can also grant a new trial on the basis of newly discovered evidence, misconduct by the participants or the jury during the trial, or error by the judge.

The Appeal

Assume here that any posttrial motion is denied and that Anderson appeals the case. (If Marconi wins but receives a smaller monetary award than she sought, she can appeal also.) Keep in mind, though, that a party cannot appeal a trial court's decision simply because he

The members of the California Supreme Court, that state's highest court, ready themselves for a hearing. Do all parties to legal disputes have a right to be heard by an appellate court?

(AP Photo/Paul Sakuma)

or she is dissatisfied with the outcome of the trial. A party must have legitimate grounds to file an appeal. In other words, he or she must be able to claim that the lower court committed an error. If Anderson has grounds to appeal the case, a notice of appeal must be filed with the clerk of the trial court within a prescribed time. Anderson now becomes the appellant, or petitioner, and Marconi becomes the appellee, or respondent.

Filing the Appeal

Anderson's attorney files the record on appeal with the appellate court. The record includes the pleadings, the trial transcript, the judge's rulings on motions made by the parties, and other trial-related documents. Anderson's attorney will also provide the reviewing court with a condensation of the record, known as an *abstract,* and a brief. The **brief** is a formal legal document outlining the facts and issues of the case, the judge's rulings or jury's findings that should be reversed or modified, the applicable law, and arguments on Anderson's behalf (citing applicable statutes and relevant cases as precedents).

Brief A written summary or statement prepared by one side in a lawsuit to explain its case to the judge.

Marconi's attorney will file an answering brief. Anderson's attorney can file a reply to Marconi's brief, although it is not required. The reviewing court then considers the case.

Appellate Review

As explained earlier, a court of appeals does not hear evidence. Instead, the court reviews the record for errors of law. Its decision concerning a case is based on the record on appeal, the abstracts, and the attorneys' briefs. The attorneys can present oral arguments, after which the case is taken under advisement.

After reviewing a case, an appellate court has the following options:

1. The court can *affirm* the trial court's decision.
2. The court can *reverse* the trial court's judgment if it concludes that the trial court erred or that the jury did not receive proper instructions.
3. The appellate court can *remand* (send back) the case to the trial court for further proceedings consistent with its opinion on the matter.
4. The court might also affirm or reverse a decision *in part.* For example, the court might affirm the jury's finding that Anderson was negligent but remand the case for further proceedings on another issue (such as the extent of Marconi's damages).

5. An appellate court can also *modify* a lower court's decision. If the appellate court decides that the jury awarded an excessive amount in damages, for example, the court might reduce the award to a more appropriate, or fairer, amount.

Appeal to a Higher Appellate Court If the reviewing court is an intermediate appellate court, the losing party may decide to appeal to the state supreme court (the highest state court). Such a petition corresponds to a petition for a writ of *certiorari* from the United States Supreme Court. Although the losing party has a right to ask (petition) a higher court to review the case, the party does not have a right to have the case heard by the higher appellate court.

Appellate courts normally have discretionary power and can accept or reject an appeal. Like the United States Supreme Court, state supreme courts generally deny most appeals. If the appeal is granted, new briefs must be filed before the state supreme court, and the attorneys may be allowed or requested to present oral arguments. Like the intermediate appellate court, the supreme court may reverse or affirm the appellate court's decision or remand the case. At this point, the case typically has reached its end (unless a federal question is at issue and one of the parties has legitimate grounds to seek review by a federal appellate court).

Enforcing the Judgment

The uncertainties of the litigation process are compounded by the lack of guarantees that any judgment will be enforceable. Even if a plaintiff wins an award of damages in court, the defendant may not have sufficient assets or insurance to cover that amount. Usually, one of the factors considered before a lawsuit is initiated is whether the defendant has sufficient assets to pay the damages sought, should the plaintiff win the case. What other factors should be considered when deciding whether to bring a lawsuit? See this chapter's *Business Application* feature on page 90 for answers to this question.

The Courts Adapt to the Online World

We have already mentioned that the courts have attempted to adapt traditional jurisdictional concepts to the online world. Not surprisingly, the Internet has also brought about changes in court procedures and practices, including new methods for filing pleadings and other documents and issuing decisions and opinions. Some jurisdictions are exploring the possibility of cyber courts, in which legal proceedings could be conducted totally online.

Electronic Filing

The federal court system has now implemented its electronic filing system, Case Management/Electronic Case Files (CM/ECF), in nearly all of the federal courts. The system is available in federal district, appellate, and bankruptcy courts, as well as the U.S. Court of International Trade and the U.S. Court of Federal Claims. More than 33 million cases are on the CM/ECF system. Users can create a document using conventional document-creation software, save it as a PDF (portable digital file), then log on to a court's Web site and submit the PDF to the court via the Internet. Access to the electronic documents filed on CM/ECF is available through a system called PACER (Public Access to Court Electronic Records), which is a service of the U.S. Judiciary.

More than 60 percent of the states have some form of electronic filing. Some states, including Arizona, California, Colorado, Delaware, Mississippi, New Jersey, New York, and Nevada, offer statewide e-filing systems. Generally, when electronic filing is made available, it is optional. Nonetheless, some state courts have now made e-filing mandatory in certain types of disputes, such as complex civil litigation.

Courts Online

Docket The list of cases entered on a court's calendar and thus scheduled to be heard by the court.

Most courts today have sites on the Web. Of course, each court decides what to make available at its site. Some courts display only the names of court personnel and office phone numbers. Others add court rules and forms. Many appellate court sites include judicial decisions, although the decisions may remain online for only a limited time. In addition, in some states, including California and Florida, court clerks offer **docket** (the court's schedule of cases to be heard) information and other searchable databases online.

Appellate court decisions are often posted online immediately after they are rendered. Recent decisions of the U.S. courts of appeals, for example, are available online at their Web sites. The United States Supreme Court also has an official Web site and publishes its opinions there immediately after they are announced to the public. In fact, even decisions that are designated as "unpublished" opinions by the appellate courts are usually published online (as discussed in the *Adapting the Law to the Online Environment* feature in Chapter 1 on page 13).

Cyber Courts and Proceedings

Someday, litigants may be able to use cyber courts, in which judicial proceedings take place only on the Internet. The parties to a case could meet online to make their arguments and present their evidence. This might be done with e-mail submissions, through video cameras, in designated chat rooms, at closed sites, or through the use of other Internet and social media facilities. These courtrooms could be efficient and economical. We might also see the use of virtual lawyers, judges, and juries—and possibly the replacement of court personnel with computer software.

Already the state of Michigan has passed legislation creating cyber courts that will hear cases involving technology issues and high-tech businesses. The state of Wisconsin has also enacted a rule authorizing the use of videoconferencing in both civil and criminal trials, at the discretion of the trial court.[17] In some situations, a Wisconsin judge can allow videoconferencing even if the parties object, provided that certain operational criteria are met.

The courts may also use the Internet in other ways. For instance, some bankruptcy courts in Arizona, New Mexico, and Nevada recently began offering online chatting at their Web sites, which you will read about in Chapter 23. The model for these online chats came from retailers in the private sector, and chatting may eventually be offered on all federal bankruptcy court Web sites. Other courts are ordering parties to use the Internet as part of their judgments. A Florida county court granted "virtual" visitation rights in a couple's divorce proceedings so that the child could visit with each parent online (through a videoconferencing system or Skype, for instance) during stays at the other parent's residence.

Alternative Dispute Resolution

Alternative Dispute Resolution (ADR) The resolution of disputes in ways other than those involved in the traditional judicial process, such as negotiation, mediation, and arbitration.

Litigation is expensive. It is also time consuming. Because of the backlog of cases pending in many courts, several years may pass before a case is actually tried. For these and other reasons, more and more businesspersons are turning to **alternative dispute resolution (ADR)** as a means of settling their disputes.

The great advantage of ADR is its flexibility. Methods of ADR range from the parties sitting down together and attempting to work out their differences to multinational corporations agreeing to resolve a dispute through a formal hearing before a panel of experts. Normally, the parties themselves can control how they will attempt to settle their dispute, what procedures will be used, whether a neutral third party will be present or make a decision, and whether that decision will be legally binding or nonbinding.

---

17. Wisconsin Statute Section 751.12.

Today, more than 90 percent of cases are settled before trial through some form of ADR. Indeed, most states either require or encourage parties to undertake ADR prior to trial. Many federal courts have instituted ADR programs as well. In the following pages, we examine the basic forms of ADR. Keep in mind, though, that new methods of ADR—and new combinations of existing methods—are constantly being devised and employed.

Negotiation

Negotiation A process in which parties attempt to settle their dispute informally, with or without attorneys to represent them.

The simplest form of ADR is **negotiation,** in which the parties attempt to settle their dispute informally, with or without attorneys to represent them. Attorneys frequently advise their clients to negotiate a settlement voluntarily before they proceed to trial. Parties may even try to negotiate a settlement during a trial or after the trial but before an appeal. Negotiation traditionally involves just the parties themselves and (typically) their attorneys. The attorneys, though, are advocates—they are obligated to put their clients' interests first.

Mediation

Mediation A method of settling disputes outside the courts by using the services of a neutral third party, who acts as a communicating agent between the parties and assists them in negotiating a settlement.

In **mediation,** a neutral third party acts as a mediator and works with both sides in the dispute to facilitate a resolution. The mediator talks with the parties separately as well as jointly and emphasizes their points of agreement in an attempt to help the parties evaluate their options. Although the mediator may propose a solution (called a *mediator's proposal*), he or she does not make a decision resolving the matter. States that require parties to undergo ADR before trial often offer mediation as one of the ADR options or (as in Florida) the only option.

LEARNING OBJECTIVE 5
What are three alternative methods of resolving disputes?

One of the biggest advantages of mediation is that it is not as adversarial as litigation. In a trial, the parties "do battle" with each other in the courtroom, trying to prove each other wrong, while the judge is usually a passive observer. In mediation, the mediator takes an active role and attempts to bring the parties together so that they can come to a mutually satisfactory resolution. The mediation process tends to reduce the hostility between the disputants, allowing them to resume their former relationship without bad feelings. For this reason, mediation is often the preferred form of ADR for disputes involving business partners, employers and employees, or other parties involved in long-term relationships.

EXAMPLE 3.10 Two business partners, Mark Shalen and Charles Rowe, have a dispute over how the profits of their firm should be distributed. If the dispute is litigated, Shalen and Rowe will be adversaries, and their respective attorneys will emphasize how the parties' positions differ, not what they have in common. In contrast, when the dispute is mediated, the mediator emphasizes the common ground shared by Shalen and Rowe and helps them work toward agreement. The two men can work out the distribution of profits without damaging their continuing relationship as partners. ●

Arbitration

Arbitration The settling of a dispute by submitting it to a disinterested third party (other than a court), who renders a decision.

In **arbitration,** a more formal method of ADR, an arbitrator (a neutral third party or a panel of experts) hears a dispute and imposes a resolution on the parties. Arbitration differs from other forms of ADR in that the third party hearing the dispute makes a decision for the parties. Exhibit 3.4 on the facing page outlines the basic differences among the three traditional forms of ADR. Usually, the parties in arbitration agree that the third party's decision will be *legally binding,* although the parties can also agree to *nonbinding* arbitration. (Arbitration that is mandated by the courts often is nonbinding.) In nonbinding arbitration, the parties can go forward with a lawsuit if they do not agree with the arbitrator's decision.

In some respects, formal arbitration resembles a trial, although usually the procedural rules are much less restrictive than those governing litigation. In the typical arbitration,

Exhibit 3.4 Basic Differences in the Traditional Forms of Alternative Dispute Resolution

TYPE OF ADR	DESCRIPTION	NEUTRAL THIRD PARTY PRESENT	WHO DECIDES THE RESOLUTION
Negotiation	The parties meet informally with or without their attorneys and attempt to agree on a resolution.	No	The parties themselves reach a resolution.
Mediation	A neutral third party meets with the parties and emphasizes points of agreement to help them resolve their dispute.	Yes	The parties decide the resolution, but the mediator may suggest or propose a resolution.
Arbitration	The parties present their arguments and evidence before an arbitrator at a hearing, and the arbitrator renders a decision resolving the parties' dispute.	Yes	The arbitrator imposes a resolution on the parties that may be either binding or nonbinding.

the parties present opening arguments and ask for specific remedies. Both sides present evidence and may call and examine witnesses. The arbitrator then renders a decision.

The Arbitrator's Decision

The arbitrator's decision is called an *award.* It is usually the final word on the matter. Although the parties may appeal an arbitrator's decision, a court's review of the decision will be much more restricted in scope than an appellate court's review of a trial court's decision. The general view is that because the parties were free to frame the issues and set the powers of the arbitrator at the outset, they cannot complain about the results. A court will set aside an award only in the event of one of the following:

1. The arbitrator's conduct or "bad faith" substantially prejudiced the rights of one of the parties.
2. The award violates an established public policy.
3. The arbitrator exceeded her or his powers—that is, arbitrated issues that the parties did not agree to submit to arbitration.

Arbitration Clauses

Just about any commercial matter can be submitted to arbitration. Frequently, parties include an **arbitration clause** in a contract. The clause provides that any dispute that arises under the contract will be resolved through arbitration rather than through the court system. Parties can also agree to arbitrate a dispute after a dispute arises.

Arbitration Clause A clause in a contract that provides that, in the event of a dispute, the parties will submit the dispute to arbitration rather than litigate the dispute in court.

Arbitration Statutes

Most states have statutes (often based in part on the Uniform Arbitration Act of 1955) under which arbitration clauses will be enforced, and some state statutes compel arbitration of certain types of disputes, such as those involving public employees. At the federal level, the Federal Arbitration Act (FAA), enacted in 1925, enforces arbitration clauses in contracts involving maritime activity and interstate commerce (though its applicability to employment contracts has been controversial, as discussed in a later subsection). Because of the breadth of the commerce clause (see Chapter 2), arbitration agreements involving transactions only slightly connected to the flow of interstate commerce may fall under the FAA.

CASE EXAMPLE 3.11 Buckeye Check Cashing, Inc., cashes personal checks for consumers in Florida. Buckeye would agree to delay submitting a consumer's check for payment if the consumer paid a "finance charge." For each transaction, the consumer signed an agreement that included an arbitration clause. A group of consumers filed a lawsuit claiming that Buckeye was charging an illegally high rate of interest in violation of state law. Buckeye filed a motion to compel arbitration, which the trial court denied, and the case was appealed. The plaintiffs argued that the entire contract—including the arbitration clause—was illegal and therefore arbitration was not required. The United States Supreme Court found that the arbitration provision was *severable,* or capable of being separated, from the rest of the contract. The Court held that when the challenge is to the validity of a contract as a whole, and not specifically to an arbitration clause within the contract, an arbitrator must resolve the dispute. Even if the contract itself later proves to be unenforceable, arbitration will still be required because the FAA established a national policy favoring arbitration and that policy extends to both federal and state courts.[18] •

In the following case, the parties had agreed to arbitrate disputes involving their contract, but a state law allowed one party to void a contractual provision that required arbitration outside the state. The court had to decide if the FAA preempted the state law.

18. *Buckeye Check Cashing, Inc. v. Cardegna,* 546 U.S. 440, 126 S.Ct. 1204, 163 L.Ed.2d 1038 (2006).

Case 3.3

Cleveland Construction, Inc. v. Levco Construction, Inc.

Court of Appeals of Texas, First District, 359 S.W.3d 843 (2012).
law.justia.com[a]

(Bertold Werkmann/Shutterstock.com)
An excavation machine.

FACTS Cleveland Construction, Inc. (CCI), was the general contractor on a project to build a grocery store in Houston, Texas. CCI hired Levco Construction, Inc., as a subcontractor to perform excavation and grading. The contract included an arbitration provision stating that any disputes would be resolved by arbitration in Ohio. When a dispute arose between the parties, Levco filed a suit against CCI in a Texas state court. CCI sought to compel arbitration in Ohio under the Federal Arbitration Act (FAA), but a Texas statute allows a party to void a contractual provision that requires arbitration outside Texas. The Texas court granted an emergency motion preventing arbitration. CCI appealed.

ISSUE Does the FAA preempt the Texas statute, which denies enforcement of arbitration clauses that require a party to submit to arbitration outside Texas?

DECISION Yes. The Texas appellate court reversed the trial court, holding that the FAA preempts the Texas statute.

REASON The FAA requires courts to enforce valid arbitration agreements, and it "preempts . . . inconsistent state laws . . . under the Supremacy Clause of the United States Constitution." (See page 39 in Chapter 2.) In this case, the Texas statute provided that an agreement to arbitrate was voidable if it required arbitration outside Texas. Thus, if the court applied the Texas statute, it would void the parties' agreement to arbitrate any disputes in Ohio. Voiding the agreement, however, the court found "would undermine the declared federal policy of rigorous enforcement of arbitration agreements." The court ruled that the parties had a valid arbitration agreement, so the FAA preempted the Texas statute.

CRITICAL THINKING—Legal Consideration *How would business be affected if each state could pass a statute, like the one in Texas, allowing parties to void out-of-state arbitrations?*

a. In the search box, type "Cleveland Construction v. Levco Construction" and click on "Search Justia." On the page that opens, click on the link to access this case opinion. Justia Company maintains this Web site.

The Issue of Arbitrability

Notice that in the preceding *Case Example 3.11*, the issue before the United States Supreme Court was *not* the basic controversy (whether the interest rate charged was illegally high) but rather the issue of arbitrability—that is, whether the matter had to be resolved by arbitration under the arbitration clause. Actions over arbitrability often occur when a dispute arises over an agreement that contains an arbitration clause: one party files a motion to compel arbitration, while the other party wants to have the dispute settled by a court, not by arbitration. If the court finds that the dispute is covered by the arbitration clause, it may compel the other party to submit to arbitration, even though his or her claim involves the violation of a statute, such as an employment statute. Usually, if the court finds that the legislature, in enacting the statute, did not intend to prohibit arbitration, the court will allow the claim to be arbitrated.

No party will be ordered to submit a particular dispute to arbitration, however, unless the court is convinced that the party consented to do so.[19] Additionally, the courts will not compel arbitration if it is clear that the prescribed arbitration rules and procedures are inherently unfair to one of the parties.

The terms of an arbitration agreement can limit the types of disputes that the parties agree to arbitrate. When the parties do not specify limits, however, disputes can arise as to whether a particular matter is covered by the arbitration agreement. Then it is up to the court to resolve the issue of arbitrability.

Mandatory Arbitration in the Employment Context

A significant question in the last several years has concerned mandatory arbitration clauses in employment contracts. Many claim that employees' rights are not sufficiently protected when workers are forced, as a condition of being hired, to agree to arbitrate all disputes and thus waive their rights under statutes specifically designed to protect employees. The United States Supreme Court, however, has generally held that mandatory arbitration clauses in employment contracts are enforceable.

KNOW THIS

Litigation—even of a dispute over whether a particular matter should be submitted to arbitration—can be time consuming and expensive.

CASE EXAMPLE 3.12 In a landmark decision, *Gilmer v. Interstate Johnson Lane Corp.*,[20] the Supreme Court held that a claim brought under a federal statute prohibiting age discrimination (see Chapter 25) could be subject to arbitration. The Court concluded that the employee had waived his right to sue when he agreed, as part of a required registration application to be a securities representative with the New York Stock Exchange, to arbitrate "any dispute, claim, or controversy" relating to his employment. •

Since the *Gilmer* decision, some courts have refused to enforce one-sided arbitration clauses on the ground that they are unconscionable (see Chapter 11).[21] Thus, businesspersons considering using arbitration clauses in employment contracts should be careful that they are not too one sided—especially provisions on how the parties will split the costs of the arbitration procedure.

Private Arbitration Proceedings

In 2011, the Delaware Chancery Court established a new confidential arbitration process, which allows parties to arbitrate their disputes in private. Because many companies are headquartered in Delaware, the court's caseload is heavy, and its influence on the business environment is significant. Delaware's decision to authorize secret arbitration proceedings has been controversial.

EXAMPLE 3.13 Two smartphone makers were the first to use Delaware's confidential arbitration procedures to reach a settlement of their dispute. Skyworks Solutions, Inc.,

---

19. See, for example, *Wright v. Universal Maritime Service Corp.*, 525 U.S. 70, 119 S.Ct. 391, 142 L.Ed.2d 361 (1998).

20. 500 U.S. 20, 111 S.Ct. 1647, 114 L.Ed.2d 26 (1991).

21. See, for example, *Macias v. Excel Building Services, LLC*, 767 F.Supp.2d 1002 (N.D.Cal. 2011), citing *Davis v. O'Melveny & Myers, LLC*, 485 F.3d 1066 (9th Cir. 2007), and *Nagrampa v. MailCoups, Inc.*, 469 F.3d 1257 (9th Cir. 2006).

makes technology that transmits signals from smartphones, and Advanced Analogic Technologies, Inc. (AATI), makes power management devices for smartphones. Skyworks had agreed to a merger deal with AATI for $262.5 million, but then backed out, claiming that AATI had not properly accounted for revenue. Both parties filed lawsuits and ended up arbitrating using Delaware's new process. The two reached a settlement to complete the merger for $256 million, without disclosing the details of their agreement. •

Other Types of ADR

The three forms of ADR just discussed are the oldest and traditionally the most commonly used. In recent years, several new types of ADR have emerged. Some parties today are using *assisted negotiation,* in which a third party participates in the negotiation process. The third party may be an expert in the subject matter of the dispute. In *early neutral case evaluation,* the parties explain the situation to an expert, and the expert assesses the strengths and weaknesses of each party's claims. Another form of assisted negotiation is the *mini-trial,* in which the parties present arguments before the third party (usually an expert), who renders an advisory opinion on how a court would likely decide the issue. This proceeding is designed to assist the parties in determining whether they should settle or take the dispute to court.

Other types of ADR combine characteristics of mediation and arbitration. In *binding mediation,* for example, the parties agree that if they cannot resolve the dispute, the mediator may make a legally binding decision on the issue. In *mediation-arbitration,* or "med-arb," the parties agree to attempt to settle their dispute through mediation. If no settlement is reached, the dispute will be arbitrated.

Summary Jury Trial (SJT) A method of settling disputes by holding a trial in which the jury's verdict is not binding but instead guides the parties toward reaching an agreement during the mandatory negotiations that immediately follow.

Today's courts are also experimenting with a variety of ADR alternatives to speed up (and reduce the cost of) justice. Numerous federal courts now hold **summary jury trials (SJTs),** in which the parties present their arguments and evidence and the jury renders a verdict. The jury's verdict is not binding, but it does act as a guide to both sides in reaching an agreement during the mandatory negotiations that immediately follow the trial. Other alternatives being employed by the courts include summary procedures for commercial litigation and the appointment of special masters to assist judges in deciding complex issues.

Providers of ADR Services

ADR services are provided by both government agencies and private organizations. A major provider of ADR services is the American Arbitration Association (AAA), which was founded in 1926 and now handles more than 200,000 claims a year in its numerous offices worldwide. Most of the largest U.S. law firms are members of this nonprofit association. Cases brought before the AAA are heard by an expert or a panel of experts in the area relating to the dispute and are usually settled quickly. The AAA has a special team devoted to resolving large, complex disputes across a wide range of industries.

Hundreds of for-profit firms around the country also provide various forms of dispute-resolution services. Typically, these firms hire retired judges to conduct arbitration hearings or otherwise assist parties in settling their disputes. The judges follow procedures similar to those of the federal courts and use similar rules. Usually, each party to the dispute pays a filing fee and a designated fee for a hearing session or conference.

Online Dispute Resolution

Online Dispute Resolution (ODR) The resolution of disputes with the assistance of organizations that offer dispute-resolution services via the Internet.

An increasing number of companies and organizations offer dispute-resolution services using the Internet. The settlement of disputes in these online forums is known as **online dispute resolution (ODR).** The disputes have most commonly involved disagreements over the rights to domain names or over the quality of goods sold via the Internet, including goods sold through Internet auction sites.

ODR may be best suited for resolving small- to medium-sized business liability claims, which may not be worth the expense of litigation or traditional ADR. Rules being developed in online forums may ultimately become a code of conduct for everyone who does business in cyberspace. Most online forums do not automatically apply the law of any specific jurisdiction. Instead, results are often based on general, universal legal principles. As with most offline methods of dispute resolution, any party may appeal to a court at any time.

Interestingly, some local governments are using ODR to resolve claims. **EXAMPLE 3.14** New York City has used Cybersettle.com to resolve auto accident, sidewalk, and other personal-injury claims made against the city. Parties with complaints submit their demands, and the city submits its offers confidentially online. If an offer exceeds a demand, the claimant keeps half the difference as a bonus. ●

Reviewing . . . Courts and Alternative Dispute Resolution

Stan Garner resides in Illinois and promotes boxing matches for SuperSports, Inc., an Illinois corporation. Garner created the promotional concept of the "Ages" fights—a series of three boxing matches pitting an older fighter (George Foreman) against a younger fighter, such as John Ruiz or Riddick Bowe. The concept included titles for each of the three fights ("Challenge of the Ages," "Battle of the Ages," and "Fight of the Ages"), as well as promotional epithets to characterize the two fighters ("the Foreman Factor"). Garner contacted George Foreman and his manager, who both reside in Texas, to sell the idea, and they arranged a meeting at Caesar's Palace in Las Vegas, Nevada. At some point in the negotiations, Foreman's manager signed a nondisclosure agreement prohibiting him from disclosing Garner's promotional concepts unless they signed a contract. Nevertheless, after negotiations between Garner and Foreman fell through, Foreman used Garner's "Battle of the Ages" concept to promote a subsequent fight. Garner filed a lawsuit against Foreman and his manager in a federal district court in Illinois, alleging breach of contract. Using the information presented in the chapter, answer the following questions.

1. On what basis might the federal district court in Illinois exercise jurisdiction in this case?
2. Does the federal district court have original or appellate jurisdiction?
3. Suppose that Garner had filed his action in an Illinois state court. Could an Illinois state court exercise personal jurisdiction over Foreman or his manager? Why or why not?
4. Assume that Garner had filed his action in a Nevada state court. Would that court have personal jurisdiction over Foreman or his manager? Explain.

DEBATE THIS In this age of the Internet, when people communicate via e-mail, tweets, FaceBook, and Skype, is the concept of jurisdiction losing its meaning?

BUSINESS APPLICATION

To Sue or Not to Sue?*

Inadvertently or intentionally, wrongs are committed every day in the United States. Sometimes, businesspersons believe that wrongs have been committed against them by other businesspersons, by consumers, or by the government. If you are deciding whether to sue for a wrong committed against you or your business, you must consider many issues.

The Question of Cost

Competent legal advice is not inexpensive. Commercial business law attorneys charge $100 to $600 an hour, plus expenses. It is almost always worthwhile to make an initial visit to an attorney who has skills in the area in which you are going to sue to get an estimate of the expected costs of pursuing redress for your grievance. Note that less than 10 percent of all corporate lawsuits go to trial—the rest are settled beforehand. You may end up settling for far less than you think you are "owed" simply because of the length of time a lawsuit would take and the cost of going to court. And then you might not win, anyway!

Basically, you must do a cost-benefit analysis to determine whether you should sue. Your attorney can give you an estimate of the dollar costs involved in litigating the dispute. Realize, though, that litigation also involves nondollar costs such as time away from your business, stress, inconvenience, and publicity. You can "guesstimate" the benefits by multiplying the probable size of the award by the probability of obtaining that award.

*This *Business Application* is not meant to substitute for the services of an attorney who is licensed to practice law in your state.

The Alternatives before You

Negotiation, mediation, arbitration, and other ADR forms are becoming increasingly attractive alternatives to court litigation because they usually yield quick results at a comparatively low cost. Most disputes relating to business can be mediated or arbitrated through the American Arbitration Association (AAA).

There are numerous other ADR providers as well. You can obtain information on ADR from the AAA, courthouses, chambers of commerce, law firms, state bar associations, or the American Bar Association. The Yellow Pages in large metropolitan areas usually list agencies and firms that can help you settle your dispute out of court. You can also locate providers on the Web by using a general search engine and searching for arbitration providers in a specific city.

Checklist for Deciding Whether to Sue

1. *Are you prepared to pay for going to court? Make this decision only after you have consulted an attorney to get an estimate of the costs of litigating the dispute.*
2. *Do you have the patience to follow a court case through the judicial system, even if it takes several years?*
3. *Is there a way for you to settle your grievance without going to court? Even if the settlement is less than you think you are owed, you may be better off settling now for the smaller figure.*
4. *Can you use some form of ADR? Investigate these alternatives—they are usually cheaper and quicker to use than the courts.*

Key Terms

alternative dispute resolution (ADR) 83
answer 76
arbitration 84
arbitration clause 85
award 80
bankruptcy court 65
brief 81
complaint 75
concurrent jurisdiction 66
counterclaim 76
default judgment 76
deposition 77
discovery 77
diversity of citizenship 66
docket 83
e-evidence 78
exclusive jurisdiction 66
federal question 66
interrogatories 77
judicial review 61
jurisdiction 61
justiciable controversy 69
litigation 75
long arm statute 62
mediation 84
motion for a directed verdict 80
motion for a new trial 80
motion for judgment *n.o.v.* 80
motion for judgment on the pleadings 76
motion for summary judgment 77
motion to dismiss 76
negotiation 84
online dispute resolution (ODR) 88
pleadings 75
probate court 65
question of fact 72
question of law 72
reply 76
rule of four 75
small claims court 71
standing to sue 69
summary jury trial (SJT) 88
summons 76
venue 69
voir dire 79
writ of *certiorari* 74

Chapter Summary: Courts and Alternative Dispute Resolution

The Judiciary's Role in American Government (See page 61.)	The role of the judiciary—the courts—in the American governmental system is to interpret and apply the law. Through the process of judicial review—determining the constitutionality of laws—the judicial branch acts as a check on the executive and legislative branches of government.
Basic Judicial Requirements (See pages 61–70.)	1. *Jurisdiction*—Before a court can hear a case, it must have jurisdiction over the person against whom the suit is brought or the property involved in the suit, as well as jurisdiction over the subject matter. a. Limited versus general jurisdiction—Limited jurisdiction exists when a court is limited to a specific subject matter, such as probate or divorce. General jurisdiction exists when a court can hear any kind of case. b. Original versus appellate jurisdiction—Original jurisdiction exists when courts have authority to hear a case for the first time (trial courts). Appellate jurisdiction is exercised by courts of appeals, or reviewing courts, which generally do not have original jurisdiction. c. Federal jurisdiction—Arises (1) when a federal question is involved (when the plaintiff's cause of action is based, at least in part, on the U.S. Constitution, a treaty, or a federal law) or (2) when a case involves diversity of citizenship (citizens of different states, for example) and the amount in controversy exceeds $75,000. d. Concurrent versus exclusive jurisdiction—Concurrent jurisdiction exists when two different courts have authority to hear the same case. Exclusive jurisdiction exists when only state courts or only federal courts have authority to hear a case. 2. *Jurisdiction in cyberspace*—Because the Internet does not have physical boundaries, traditional jurisdictional concepts have been difficult to apply in cases involving activities conducted via the Web. Gradually, the courts are developing standards to use in determining when jurisdiction over a Web site owner or operator located in another state is proper. 3. *Venue*—Venue has to do with the most appropriate location for a trial, which is usually the geographic area where the event leading to the dispute took place or where the parties reside. 4. *Standing to sue*—A requirement that a party must have a legally protected and tangible interest at stake sufficient to justify seeking relief through the court system. The controversy at issue must also be a justiciable controversy—one that is real and substantial, as opposed to hypothetical or academic.
The State and Federal Court Systems (See pages 70–75.)	1. *Trial courts*—Courts of original jurisdiction, in which legal actions are initiated. a. State—Courts of general jurisdiction can hear any case. Courts of limited jurisdiction include domestic relations courts, probate courts, traffic courts, and small claims courts. b. Federal—The federal district court is the equivalent of the state trial court. Federal courts of limited jurisdiction include the U.S. Tax Court, the U.S. Bankruptcy Court, and the U.S. Court of Federal Claims. 2. *Intermediate appellate courts*—Courts of appeals, or reviewing courts, which generally do not have original jurisdiction. Many states have an intermediate appellate court. In the federal court system, the U.S. circuit courts of appeals are the intermediate appellate courts. 3. *Supreme (highest) courts*—Each state has a supreme court, although it may be called by some other name. Appeal from the state supreme court to the United States Supreme Court is possible only if the case involves a federal question. The United States Supreme Court is the highest court in the federal court system and the final arbiter of the U.S. Constitution and federal law.
Following a State Court Case (See pages 75–82.)	Rules of procedure prescribe the way in which disputes are handled in the courts. Rules differ from court to court, and separate sets of rules exist for federal and state courts, as well as for criminal and civil cases. A civil court case in a state court would involve the following procedures: 1. *The pleadings*— a. Complaint—Filed by the plaintiff with the court to initiate the lawsuit. The complaint is served with a summons on the defendant. b. Answer—A response to the complaint in which the defendant admits or denies the allegations made by the plaintiff. The answer may assert a counterclaim or an affirmative defense. c. Motion to dismiss—A request to the court to dismiss the case for stated reasons, such as the plaintiff's failure to state a claim for which relief can be granted. 2. *Pretrial motions (in addition to the motion to dismiss)*— a. Motion for judgment on the pleadings—May be made by either party. It will be granted if the parties agree on the facts and the only question is how the law applies to the facts. The judge bases the decision solely on the pleadings. b. Motion for summary judgment—May be made by either party. It will be granted if the parties agree on the facts and the sole question is a question of law. The judge can consider evidence outside the pleadings when evaluating the motion.

Continued

Chapter Summary: Courts and Alternative Dispute Resolution—Continued

Following a State Court Case—Continued	3. *Discovery*—The process of gathering evidence concerning the case. Discovery involves depositions (sworn testimony by a party to the lawsuit or any witness), interrogatories (written questions and answers to these questions made by parties to the action with the aid of their attorneys), and various requests (for admissions, documents, and medical examinations, for example). Discovery may also involve electronically recorded information, such as e-mail, voice mail, word-processing documents, and other data compilations. Although electronic discovery has significant advantages over paper discovery, it is also more time consuming and expensive and often requires the parties to hire experts. 4. *Pretrial conference*—Either party or the court can request a pretrial conference to identify the matters in dispute after discovery has taken place and to plan the course of the trial. 5. *Trial*—Following jury selection *(voir dire),* the trial begins with opening statements from both parties' attorneys. The following events then occur: a. The plaintiff's introduction of evidence (including the testimony of witnesses) supporting the plaintiff's position. The defendant's attorney can challenge evidence and cross-examine witnesses. b. The defendant's introduction of evidence (including the testimony of witnesses) supporting the defendant's position. The plaintiff's attorney can challenge evidence and cross-examine witnesses. c. Closing arguments by the attorneys in favor of their respective clients, the judge's instructions to the jury, and the jury's verdict. 6. *Posttrial motions*— a. Motion for judgment *n.o.v.* ("notwithstanding the verdict")—Will be granted if the judge is convinced that the jury was in error. b. Motion for a new trial—Will be granted if the judge is convinced that the jury was in error. The motion can also be granted on the grounds of newly discovered evidence, misconduct by the participants during the trial, or error by the judge. 7. *Appeal*—Either party can appeal the trial court's judgment to an appropriate court of appeals. After reviewing the record on appeal, the abstracts, and the attorneys' briefs, the appellate court holds a hearing and renders its opinion.
The Courts Adapt to the Online World (See pages 82–83.)	A number of state and federal courts now allow parties to file litigation-related documents with the courts via the Internet or other electronic means. Nearly all of the federal appellate courts and bankruptcy courts and a majority of the federal district courts have implemented electronic filing systems. Almost every court now has a Web page offering information about the court and its procedures, and increasingly courts are publishing their opinions online. In the future, we may see cyber courts, in which all trial proceedings are conducted online.
Alternative Dispute Resolution (See pages 83–89.)	1. *Negotiation*—The parties come together, with or without attorneys to represent them, and try to reach a settlement without the involvement of a third party. 2. *Mediation*—The parties themselves reach an agreement with the help of a neutral third party, called a mediator. The mediator may propose a solution but does not make a decision resolving the matter. 3. *Arbitration*—A more formal method of ADR in which the parties submit their dispute to a neutral third party, the arbitrator, who renders a decision. The decision may or may not be legally binding, depending on the circumstances. 4. *Other types of ADR*—These include assisted negotiation, early neutral case evaluation, mini-trials, and summary jury trials (SJTs). 5. *Providers of ADR services*—The leading nonprofit provider of ADR services is the American Arbitration Association. Hundreds of for-profit firms also provide ADR services. 6. *Online dispute resolution*—A number of organizations and firms are now offering negotiation, mediation, and arbitration services through online forums. These forums have been a practical alternative for the resolution of domain name disputes and e-commerce disputes in which the amount in controversy is relatively small.

ExamPrep

ISSUE SPOTTERS

1. Sue contracts with Tom to deliver a quantity of computers to Sue's Computer Store. They disagree over the amount, the delivery date, the price, and the quality. Sue files a suit against Tom in a state court. Their state requires that their dispute be submitted to mediation or nonbinding arbitration. If the dispute is not resolved, or if either party disagrees with the decision of the mediator or arbitrator, will a court hear the case? Explain. **(See page 84.)**
2. At the trial, after Sue calls her witnesses, offers her evidence, and otherwise presents her side of the case, Tom has at least two choices between courses of action. Tom can call his first witness. What else might he do? **(See page 80.)**

—Check your answers to the Issue Spotters against the answers provided in Appendix E at the end of this text.

BEFORE THE TEST

Go to www.cengagebrain.com, enter the ISBN 9781133273561, and click on "Find" to locate this textbook's Web site. Then, click on "Access Now" under "Study Tools," and select Chapter 3 at the top. There, you will find a Practice Quiz that you can take to assess your mastery of the concepts in this chapter, as well as Flashcards, a Glossary of important terms, and Video Questions (when assigned).

For Review

Answers to the even-numbered questions in this For Review section can be found in Appendix F at the end of this text.

1. What is judicial review? How and when was the power of judicial review established?
2. Before a court can hear a case, it must have jurisdiction. Over what must it have jurisdiction? How are the courts applying traditional jurisdictional concepts to cases involving Internet transactions?
3. What is the difference between a trial court and an appellate court?
4. What is discovery, and how does electronic discovery differ from traditional discovery?
5. What are three alternative methods of resolving disputes?

Business Scenarios and Case Problems

3–1 Standing to Sue. Jack and Maggie Turton bought a house in Jefferson County, Idaho, located directly across the street from a gravel pit. A few years later, the county converted the pit to a landfill. The landfill accepted many kinds of trash that cause harm to the environment, including major appliances, animal carcasses, containers with hazardous content warnings, leaking car batteries, and waste oil. The Turtons complained to the county, but the county did nothing. The Turtons then filed a lawsuit against the county alleging violations of federal environmental laws pertaining to groundwater contamination and other pollution. Do the Turtons have standing to sue? Why or why not? **(See page 69.)**

3–2 Question with Sample Answer—Jurisdiction. Marya Callais, a citizen of Florida, was walking along a busy street in Tallahassee when a large crate flew off a passing truck and hit her. Callais sustained numerous injuries. She incurred a great deal of pain and suffering plus significant medical expenses, and she could not work for six months. She wishes to sue the trucking firm for $300,000 in damages. The firm's headquarters are in Georgia, although the company does business in Florida. In what court may Callais bring suit—a Florida state court, a Georgia state court, or a federal court? What factors might influence her decision? **(See page 69.)**

—For a sample answer to Question 3–2, go to Appendix G at the end of this text.

3–3 Discovery. Advance Technology Consultants, Inc. (ATC), contracted with RoadTrac, LLC, to provide software and client software systems for the products of global positioning satellite (GPS) technology being developed by RoadTrac. RoadTrac agreed to provide ATC with hardware with which ATC's software would interface. Problems soon arose, however, and RoadTrac filed a lawsuit against ATC alleging breach of contract. During discovery, RoadTrac requested ATC's customer lists and marketing procedures. ATC objected to providing this information because RoadTrac and ATC had become competitors in the GPS industry. Should a party to a lawsuit have to hand over its confidential business secrets as part of a discovery request? Why or why not? What limitations might a court consider imposing before requiring ATC to produce this material? **(See page 77.)**

3–4 Case Problem with Sample Answer—Arbitration. Kathleen Lowden sued cellular phone company T-Mobile USA, Inc., contending that its service agreements were not enforceable under Washington state law. Lowden moved to create a class-action lawsuit, in which her claims would extend to similarly affected customers. She contended that T-Mobile had improperly charged her fees beyond the advertised price of service and charged her for roaming calls that should not have been classified as roaming. T-Mobile moved to force arbitration in accordance with provisions that were clearly set forth in the service agreement. The agreement also specified that no class-action lawsuit could be brought, so T-Mobile asked the court to dismiss the class-action request. Was T-Mobile correct that Lowden's only course of action would be to file for arbitration personally? Explain. [*Lowden v. T-Mobile USA, Inc.*, 512 F.3d 1213 (9th Cir. 2008)] **(See page 86.)**

—For a sample answer to Problem 3–4, go to Appendix H at the end of this text.

3–5 Venue. Brandy Austin used powdered infant formula to feed her infant daughter shortly after her birth. Austin claimed that a can of Nestlé Good Start Supreme Powder Infant Formula was contaminated with *Enterobacter sakazakii* bacteria, which can cause infections of the bloodstream and central nervous system, in particular, meningitis (inflammation of the tissue surrounding the brain or spinal cord). Austin filed an action against Nestlé in Hennepin County District Court in Minnesota. Nestlé argued for a change of venue because the alleged tortious action on the part of Nestlé occurred in South Carolina. Austin is a South Carolina resident and gave birth to her daughter in that state. Should the case be transferred to a South Carolina venue? Why or why not? [*Austin v. Nestle USA, Inc.*, 677 F.Supp.2d 1134 (D.Minn. 2009)] **(See page 69.)**

3–6 **Arbitration.** PRM Energy Systems owned patents licensed to Primenergy, LLC, to use in the United States. Their contract stated that "all disputes" would be settled by arbitration. Kobe Steel of Japan was interested in using the technology represented by PRM's patents. Primenergy agreed to let Kobe use the technology in Japan without telling PRM. When PRM learned about the secret deal, the firm filed a suit against Primenergy for fraud and theft. Does this dispute go to arbitration or to trial? Why? [*PRM Energy Systems v. Primenergy, LLC*, 592 F.3d 830 (8th Cir. 2010)] **(See page 85.)**

3–7 **Spotlight on National Football—Arbitration.** Bruce Matthews played football for the Tennessee Titans. As part of his contract, he agreed to submit any dispute to arbitration. He also agreed that Tennessee law would determine all matters related to workers' compensation. After Matthews retired, he filed a workers' compensation claim in California. The arbitrator ruled that Matthews could pursue his claim in California but only under Tennessee law. Should this award be set aside? Explain. [*National Football League Players Association v. National Football League Management Council*, 2011 WL 1137334 (S.D.Cal. 2011)] **(See pages 84–87.)**

3–8 **Minimum Contacts.** Seal Polymer Industries sold two freight containers of latex gloves to Med-Express, Inc., a company based in North Carolina. When Med-Express failed to pay the $104,000 owed for the gloves, Seal Polymer sued in an Illinois court and obtained a judgment against Med-Express. Med-Express argued that it did not have minimum contacts with Illinois and therefore the Illinois judgment based on personal jurisdiction was invalid. Med-Express stated that it was incorporated under North Carolina law, had its principal place of business in North Carolina, and therefore had no minimum contacts with Illinois. Was this statement alone sufficient to prevent the Illinois judgment from being collected against Med-Express in North Carolina? Why or why not? [*Seal Polymer Industries v. Med-Express, Inc.*, 725 S.E.2d 5 (N.C.App. 2012)] **(See pages 62–64.)**

3–9 **A Question of Ethics—Agreement to Arbitrate.** Nellie Lumpkin, who suffered from dementia, was admitted to the Picayune Convalescent Center, a nursing home. Because of her mental condition, her daughter, Beverly McDaniel, signed the admissions agreement. It included a clause requiring the parties to submit any dispute to arbitration. After Lumpkin left the center two years later, she filed a suit against Picayune to recover damages for mistreatment and malpractice. [*Covenant Health & Rehabilitation of Picayune, LP v. Lumpkin*, 23 So.2d 1092 (Miss. App. 2009)] **(See page 87.)**

1. Is it ethical for this dispute—involving negligent medical care, not a breach of a commercial contract—to be forced into arbitration? Why or why not? Discuss whether medical facilities should be able to impose arbitration when there is generally no bargaining over such terms.
2. Should a person with limited mental capacity be held to the arbitration clause agreed to by her next of kin who signed on her behalf? Why or why not?

Critical Thinking and Writing Assignments

3–10 **Business Law Critical Thinking Group Assignment.** Assume that a statute in your state requires that all civil lawsuits involving damages of less than $50,000 be arbitrated and allows such a case to be tried in court only if a party is dissatisfied with the arbitrator's decision. The statute also provides that if a trial does not result in an improvement of more than 10 percent in the position of the party who demanded the trial, that party must pay the entire costs of the arbitration proceeding.

1. One group will argue that the state statute violates litigants' rights of access to the courts and to trial by jury.
2. Another group will argue that the statute does not violate litigants' rights of access to the courts.
3. A third group will evaluate how the determination on rights of access would be changed if the statute was part of a pilot program and affected only a few judicial districts in the state.

CHAPTER 4

Torts and Cyber Torts

(Oxford/iStockphoto.com)

CHAPTER OUTLINE

- The Basis of Tort Law
- Intentional Torts against Persons
- Intentional Torts against Property
- Unintentional Torts (Negligence)
- Strict Liability
- Cyber Torts

LEARNING OBJECTIVES

The five learning objectives below are designed to help improve your understanding of the chapter. After reading this chapter, you should be able to answer the following questions:

1. What is the purpose of tort law? What types of damages are available in tort lawsuits?
2. What are two basic categories of torts?
3. What is defamation? Name two types of defamation.
4. Identify the four elements of negligence.
5. What is meant by strict liability? In what circumstances is strict liability applied?

"Two wrongs do not make a right."
—English Proverb

Tort A wrongful act (other than a breach of contract) that results in harm or injury to another and leads to civil liability.

Business Tort Wrongful interference with another's business rights and relationships.

Torts are wrongful actions (the word *tort* is French for "wrong"). Most of us agree with the chapter-opening quotation—two wrongs do not make a right. Through tort law, society tries to ensure that those who have suffered injuries as a result of the wrongful conduct of others receive compensation from the wrongdoers. Although some torts, such as assault and trespass, originated in the English common law, the field of tort law continues to expand. As technological advances such as the Internet provide opportunities to commit new types of wrongs, the courts are extending tort law to cover these wrongs. For instance, not too long ago, Google announced that it was starting a competing service similar to Facebook's. The unveiling of Google+ was met with praise and some very damning criticisms that turned out to have been initiated by a public relations firm that Facebook regularly used. Was a cyber tort committed? You'll decide later in this chapter.

As you will see in later chapters of this book, many of the lawsuits brought by or against business firms are based on the tort theories discussed in this chapter. Some of the torts examined here can occur in any context, including the business environment. Others, traditionally referred to as **business torts**, involve wrongful interference with the business rights of others. Business torts include such vague concepts as *unfair competition* and *wrongfully interfering with the business relations of another.*

Cyber Tort A tort committed in cyberspace.

Torts committed via the Internet are sometimes referred to as **cyber torts.** We look at how the courts have applied traditional tort law to wrongful actions in the online environment in the concluding pages of this chapter.

The Basis of Tort Law

Two notions serve as the basis of all torts: wrongs and compensation. Tort law is designed to compensate those who have suffered a loss or injury due to another person's wrongful act. In a tort action, one person or group brings a personal suit against another person or group to obtain compensation (monetary **damages**) or other relief for the harm suffered.

Damages A monetary award sought as a remedy for a breach of contract or a tortious action.

The Purpose of Tort Law

LEARNING OBJECTIVE 1

What is the purpose of tort law? What types of damages are available in tort lawsuits?

Generally, the purpose of tort law is to provide remedies for the invasion of various *protected interests.* Society recognizes an interest in personal physical safety, and tort law provides remedies for acts that cause physical injury or interfere with physical security and freedom. Hence, society recognizes an interest in protecting real and personal property. Tort law provides remedies for acts that cause destruction or damage to property. Society also recognizes an interest in protecting certain intangible interests, such as personal privacy, family relations, reputation, and dignity. Consequently, tort law provides remedies for invasion of these interests.

Damages Available in Tort Actions

Because the purpose of tort law is to compensate the injured party for the damage suffered, it is important to have a basic understanding of the types of damages that plaintiffs seek in tort actions.

Compensatory Damages A monetary award equivalent to the actual value of injuries or damage sustained by the aggrieved party.

Compensatory Damages

Compensatory damages are intended to compensate or reimburse plaintiffs for actual losses—to make the plaintiffs whole and put them in the same position that they would have been in had the tort not occurred. Compensatory damages awards are often broken down into *special damages* and *general damages.*

Special damages compensate the plaintiff for quantifiable monetary losses, such as medical expenses, lost wages and benefits (now and in the future), extra costs, the loss of irreplaceable items, and the costs of repairing or replacing damaged property. **CASE EXAMPLE 4.1** Seaway Marine Transport operates the *Enterprise,* a large cargo ship with twenty-two hatches for storing coal. When the *Enterprise* moved into position to receive a load of coal on the shores of Lake Erie in Ohio, it struck a land-based coal-loading machine operated by Bessemer & Lake Erie Railroad Company. A federal court found Seaway liable for negligence and awarded $522,000 in special damages to compensate Bessemer for the cost of repairing the damage to the loading machine.[1] •

General damages compensate individuals (not companies) for the nonmonetary aspects of the harm suffered, such as pain and suffering. A court might award general damages for physical or emotional pain and suffering, loss of companionship, loss of consortium (losing the emotional and physical benefits of a spousal relationship), disfigurement, loss of reputation, or loss or impairment of mental or physical capacity.

Punitive Damages Monetary damages that may be awarded to a plaintiff to punish the defendant and deter similar conduct in the future.

Punitive Damages

Occasionally, **punitive damages** may also be awarded in tort cases to punish the wrongdoer and deter others from similar wrongdoing. Punitive damages are appropriate only when the defendant's conduct was particularly egregious (bad)

1. *Bessemer & Lake Erie Railroad Co. v. Seaway Marine Transport,* 596 F.3d 357 (6th Cir. 2010).

or reprehensible (unacceptable). Usually, this means that punitive damages are available mainly in intentional tort actions and only rarely in negligence lawsuits (*intentional torts* and *negligence* will be explained later in the chapter). They may be awarded, however, in suits involving *gross negligence,* which can be defined as an intentional failure to perform a manifest duty in reckless disregard of the consequences of such a failure for the life or property of another. (See this chapter's *Business Application* feature on page 122 for steps businesses can take to avoid tort liability and the large damages awards that may go with it.)

Courts exercise great restraint in granting punitive damages to plaintiffs in tort actions because punitive damages are subject to the limitations imposed by the due process clause of the U.S. Constitution (discussed in Chapter 2). The United States Supreme Court has held that a punitive damages award that is grossly excessive furthers no legitimate purpose and violates due process requirements.[2] Consequently, an appellate court will sometimes reduce the amount of punitive damages awarded to a plaintiff because the amount was excessive and thereby violates the due process clause.

Tort Reform

Although tort law performs a valuable function by enabling injured parties to obtain compensation, critics contend that certain aspects of today's tort law encourage too many trivial and unfounded lawsuits, which clog the courts and add unnecessary costs. They say that damages awards are often excessive and bear little relationship to the actual damage suffered, which inspires more plaintiffs to file lawsuits. The result, in the critics' view, is a system that disproportionately rewards a few plaintiffs while imposing a "tort tax" on business and society as a whole. Among other consequences, physicians and hospitals order more tests than necessary in an effort to avoid medical malpractice suits, thereby adding to the nation's health-care costs.

Measures to reduce the number of tort cases include (1) limiting the amount of both punitive damages and general damages that can be awarded, (2) capping the amount that attorneys can collect in contingency fees (attorneys' fees that are based on a percentage of the damages awarded to the client), and (3) requiring the losing party to pay both the plaintiff's and the defendant's expenses.

The Class Action Fairness Act (CAFA) of 2005[3] shifted jurisdiction over large interstate tort and product liability class-action lawsuits (lawsuits filed by a large number of plaintiffs) from the state courts to the federal courts. The intent was to prevent plaintiffs' attorneys from *forum shopping*—looking for a state court known to be sympathetic to their clients' cause and predisposed to award large damages. At the state level, more than thirty states have limited damages, especially in medical malpractice suits.

Classifications of Torts

LEARNING OBJECTIVE 2
What are two basic categories of torts?

There are two broad classifications of torts: *intentional torts* and *unintentional torts* (torts involving negligence). The classification of a particular tort depends largely on how the tort occurs (intentionally or negligently) and the surrounding circumstances. In the following pages, you will read about these two classifications of torts.

Intentional Torts against Persons

Intentional Tort A wrongful act knowingly committed.

Tortfeasor One who commits a tort.

An **intentional tort**, as the term implies, requires *intent.* The **tortfeasor** (the one committing the tort) must intend to commit an act, the consequences of which interfere with the personal or business interests of another in a way not permitted by law. An evil or harmful

2. *State Farm Mutual Automobile Insurance Co. v. Campbell,* 538 U.S. 408, 123 S.Ct. 1513, 155 L.Ed.2d 585 (2003).
3. 28 U.S.C. Sections 1453, 1711–1715.

motive is not required—in fact, the person committing the action (the actor) may even have a beneficial motive for committing what turns out to be a tortious act.

KNOW THIS

In intentional tort actions, the defendant must intend to commit the act, but need not have intended to cause harm to the plaintiff.

In tort law, intent means only that the actor intended the consequences of his or her act or knew with substantial certainty that certain consequences would result from the act. The law generally assumes that individuals intend the *normal* consequences of their actions. Thus, forcefully pushing another—even if done in jest and without any evil motive—is an intentional tort if injury results, because the object of a strong push can ordinarily be expected to fall down.

We now discuss intentional torts against persons, which include assault and battery, false imprisonment, infliction of emotional distress, defamation, invasion of the right to privacy, appropriation, misrepresentation, abusive or frivolous litigation, and wrongful interference.

Assault and Battery

Assault Any word or action intended to make another person fearful of immediate physical harm—a reasonably believable threat.

An **assault** is any intentional and unexcused threat of immediate harmful or offensive contact, including words or acts that create in another person a reasonable apprehension of harmful contact. An assault can be completed even if there is no actual contact with the plaintiff, provided the defendant's conduct causes the plaintiff to have a reasonable apprehension of imminent harm. Tort law aims to protect individuals from having to expect harmful or offensive contact.

Battery Unexcused, harmful or offensive, physical contact with another that is intentionally performed.

If the act that created the apprehension is *completed* and results in harm to the plaintiff, it is a **battery,** which is defined as an unexcused and harmful or offensive physical contact *intentionally* performed. **EXAMPLE 4.2** Ivan threatens Jean with a gun and then shoots her. The pointing of the gun at Jean is an assault. The firing of the gun (if the bullet hits Jean) is a battery. • The contact can be harmful, or it can be merely offensive (such as an unwelcome kiss). Physical injury need not occur. The contact can involve any part of the body or anything attached to it—for example, a hat, a purse, or a wheelchair in which one is sitting. The contact can also occur as a result of some force set in motion by the defendant, such as throwing a rock. Whether the contact is offensive or not is determined by the *reasonable person standard.*[4]

Defense A reason offered and alleged by a defendant in an action or lawsuit as to why the plaintiff should not recover or establish what she or he seeks.

If the plaintiff shows that there was contact, and the jury (or judge, if there is no jury) agrees that the contact was offensive, the plaintiff has a right to compensation. A plaintiff may be compensated for the emotional harm resulting from a battery, as well as for physical harm. The defendant may raise a number of legally recognized **defenses** (reasons why plaintiffs should not obtain what they are seeking) that justify his or her conduct, including self-defense and defense of others.

False Imprisonment

False imprisonment is the intentional confinement or restraint of another person's activities without justification. False imprisonment interferes with the freedom to move without restraint. The confinement can be accomplished through the use of physical barriers, physical restraint, or threats of physical force. Moral pressure or threats of future harm do not constitute false imprisonment. It is essential that the person under restraint does not wish to be restrained.

Businesspersons are often confronted with suits for false imprisonment after they have attempted to confine a suspected shoplifter for questioning. Under the "privilege to detain" granted to merchants in most states, a merchant can use *reasonable force* to detain or delay a person suspected of shoplifting the merchant's property. Although the details of the

4. The reasonable person standard is an objective test of how a reasonable person would have acted under the same circumstances. See "The Duty of Care and Its Breach" later in this chapter.

privilege vary from state to state, generally laws require that any detention be conducted in a *reasonable* manner and for only a *reasonable* length of time. Undue force or unreasonable detention can lead to liability for the business.

Cities and counties may also face lawsuits for false imprisonment if they detain individuals without reason. In the following case, a man sued the County of Los Angeles for false imprisonment.

Case 4.1

Shoyoye v. County of Los Angeles

Court of Appeal of California, Second District, 203 Cal.App.4th 947, 137 Cal.Rptr.3d 839 (2012).

(photobank.kiev.ua/Shutterstock.com)

Cities and counties can be sued for false imprisonment.

FACTS Adetokunbo Shoyoye was lawfully arrested in 2007 when he was at a police station reporting an unrelated incident. The police discovered that he had two outstanding warrants: one for an unpaid subway ticket, and another for grand theft, which was actually issued because a former roommate had stolen his identity and been convicted of grand theft under Shoyoye's name. Shoyoye was incarcerated. Shortly thereafter, he appeared before a magistrate who ordered him released on the first warrant. A few days later, a different court released him on the second warrant.

A Los Angeles County employee mistakenly attached information related to another person—who was scheduled to be sent to state prison for violating his parole—to Shoyoye's paperwork. Subsequently, this erroneous information was entered into the computer system under Shoyoye's name. As a result, instead of being released as ordered, Shoyoye was held in jail for sixteen days, subjected to strip searches, required to wait naked in line to shower in close proximity to other inmates, and shackled. During this time, Shoyoye made numerous attempts to explain to various officials that he was being detained for no reason. He was housed in a large dormitory with hundreds of inmates, many of whom were gang members, and witnessed criminal activity and fights. He feared that he might be sent to prison, be put into "the hole" for discipline, or become a victim of violence. After his release, he sued the County of Los Angeles for, among other things, false imprisonment. A jury awarded him $22,700 in economic damages (for past and future lost earnings and property loss), and $180,000 in noneconomic damages (for past and future pain and suffering). The County of Los Angeles appealed.

ISSUE Did the County of Los Angeles wrongfully detain Shoyoye because of its clerical errors?

DECISION Yes. The reviewing court found that Shoyoye had experienced false imprisonment and held that the jury award for economic damages and noneconomic damages was appropriate under the circumstances.

REASON "The elements of a tortious claim of false imprisonment are: (1) the non-consensual, intentional confinement of a person, (2) without lawful privilege, and (3) for an appreciable period of time, however brief." The court concluded that the evidence presented at trial "was clearly sufficient to establish these elements." Had any county employees simply looked at the paper file on Shoyoye rather than the computer records, they would have realized that the "hold" on Shoyoye did not pertain to him. The erroneous paperwork on Shoyoye resulted in sixteen days of undeserved detention in a less-than-desirable environment.

CRITICAL THINKING—Ethical Consideration *Shoyoye asked numerous county employees to verify that he had been wrongfully detained. What obligation did those employees have to attempt to discover "the truth"?*

Intentional Infliction of Emotional Distress

Actionable Capable of serving as the basis of a lawsuit. An actionable claim can be pursued in a lawsuit or other court action.

The tort of *intentional infliction of emotional distress* can be defined as an extreme and outrageous act, intentionally committed, that results in severe emotional distress to another. To be **actionable** (capable of serving as the ground for a lawsuit), the conduct must be so extreme and outrageous that it exceeds the bounds of decency accepted by society.

Outrageous Conduct

Courts in most jurisdictions are wary of emotional distress claims and confine them to truly outrageous behavior. Generally, repeated annoyances (such as those experienced by a person who is being stalked), coupled with threats, are sufficient to support a claim. Acts that cause indignity or annoyance alone usually are not enough.

EXAMPLE 4.3 A father attacks a man who has had consensual sexual relations with the father's nineteen-year-old daughter. The father handcuffs the man to a steel pole and threatens to kill him unless he leaves town immediately. The father's conduct may be sufficiently extreme and outrageous to be actionable as an intentional infliction of emotional distress. ●

Limited by the First Amendment

Note that when the outrageous conduct consists of speech about a public figure, the First Amendment's guarantee of freedom of speech also limits emotional distress claims. **CASE EXAMPLE 4.4** *Hustler* magazine once printed a fake advertisement that showed a picture of the Reverend Jerry Falwell and described him as having lost his virginity to his mother in an outhouse while he was drunk. Falwell sued the magazine for intentional infliction of emotional distress and won, but the United States Supreme Court overturned the decision. The Court held that creators of parodies of public figures are protected under the First Amendment from claims of intentional infliction of emotional distress. (The Court applied the same standards that apply to public figures in defamation lawsuits, discussed next.)[5] ●

Defamation

LEARNING OBJECTIVE 3
What is defamation? Name two types of defamation.

As discussed in Chapter 2, the freedom of speech guaranteed by the First Amendment to the U.S. Constitution is not absolute. In interpreting the First Amendment, the courts must balance free speech rights against other strong social interests, including society's interest in preventing and redressing attacks on reputation. (Nations with fewer free speech protections have seen an increase in defamation lawsuits targeting U.S. citizens and journalists as defendants. See this chapter's *Beyond Our Borders* feature on page 102 for a discussion of this trend.)

Defamation Anything published or publicly spoken that causes injury to another's good name, reputation, or character.

Libel Defamation in writing or another form having the quality of permanence (such as a digital recording).

Slander Defamation in oral form.

Defamation of character involves wrongfully hurting a person's good reputation. The law has imposed a general duty on all persons to refrain from making *false,* defamatory *statements of fact* about others. Breaching this duty in writing or some other permanent form (such as a digital recording) constitutes the tort of **libel.** Breaching this duty orally is the tort of **slander.** As you will read later in this chapter, the tort of defamation can also arise when a false statement of fact is made about a person's product, business, or legal ownership rights to property.

Statement of Fact Requirement

Often at issue in defamation lawsuits (including online defamation, discussed later in this chapter) is whether the defendant made a statement of fact or a *statement of opinion.*[6] Statements of opinion normally are not actionable because they are protected under the First Amendment. In other words, making a negative statement about another person is not defamation unless the statement is false and represents something as a fact (for example, "Lane cheats on his taxes") rather than a personal opinion (for example, "Lane is a jerk").

Whether an attorney's statement to a reporter about another attorney constituted fact or opinion was at issue in the following case.

---

5. *Hustler Magazine, Inc. v. Falwell,* 485 U.S. 46, 108 S.Ct. 876, 99 L.Ed.2d 41 (1988). For another example of how the courts protect parody, see *Busch v. Viacom International, Inc.,* 477 F.Supp.2d 764 (N.D.Tex. 2007), involving a fake endorsement of televangelist Pat Robertson's diet shake.

6. See, for example, *Lott v. Levitt,* 469 F.Supp.2d 575 (N.D.Ill. 2007).

Case 4.2

Orlando v. Cole

Appeals Court of Massachusetts,
76 Mass.App.Ct. 1112, 921 N.E.2d 566 (2010).

High school women's basketball remains popular.

(Jamie Roach/Shutterstock.com)

FACTS Joseph Orlando, an attorney, was representing a high school student who had sued her basketball coach for sexual assault. The coach, Thomas Atwater, was apparently an acquaintance of Orlando's. Before he had retained an attorney, Atwater approached Orlando and admitted that he had committed the assault. Atwater signed an affidavit to that effect and then made a full confession to the police. A few days later, Orlando spoke to two newspaper reporters, gave them a copy of Atwater's affidavit, and explained the circumstances under which Atwater gave the affidavit. The reporters then asked Garrick Cole, who was now representing Atwater, for comments. Cole responded that the affidavit was "inaccurate" and called Orlando's actions "deceitful" and "fraudulent." The newspaper published an article that quoted both Orlando and Cole, and also indicated that Cole would not say what he thought was inaccurate in the affidavit. Both Orlando's and Cole's comments were reported together in various publications. Orlando sued Cole for slander, alleging that Cole's comments were false, described conduct undertaken by Orlando in his profession and business, and imputed "an unfitness for or a misconduct in his office or employment." Orlando claimed that he had suffered harm to his reputation as an attorney as a result of Cole's comments. The trial court granted Cole's motion to dismiss the complaint, and Orlando appealed.

ISSUE Did Cole's statements that another attorney filed an "inaccurate" affidavit and engaged in "fraudulent" and "deceptive" conduct with regard to a case constitute statements of fact that give rise to a defamation claim?

DECISION Yes. The Appeals Court of Massachusetts reversed the trial court's judgment and held that Cole's statements were "reasonably susceptible of a defamatory connotation [implication]." The appellate court remanded the case to allow for a jury trial.

REASON The reviewing court reasoned that the dismissal was premature because "a statement is defamatory in the circumstances if it discredits a person in the minds of any considerable and respectable class of the community." The terms that Cole had used—"inaccurate," "fraudulent," and "deceitful"—implied professional misconduct. Further, those statements are capable of being proved false in a trial. The comments were not offered simply as opinions, nor did any cautionary language accompany them. They appeared to be based on undisclosed defamatory facts. A jury should be allowed to decide whether defamation had occurred.

CRITICAL THINKING—Legal Consideration *Orlando sued Cole for slander. Why didn't he sue Cole for libel, given that the comments were reported in various news publications?*

The Publication Requirement The basis of the tort of defamation is the publication of a statement or statements that hold an individual up to contempt, ridicule, or hatred. *Publication* here means that the defamatory statements are communicated to persons other than the defamed party. **EXAMPLE 4.5** If Thompson writes Andrews a private letter falsely accusing him of embezzling funds, the action does not constitute libel. If Peters falsely states that Gordon is dishonest and incompetent when no one else is around, the action does not constitute slander. In neither instance was the message communicated to a third party. •

The courts have generally held that even dictating a letter to a secretary constitutes publication, although the publication may be privileged (privileged communications will be discussed shortly). Moreover, if a third party overhears defamatory statements by chance, the courts usually hold that this also constitutes publication. Defamatory statements made via the Internet are also actionable, as you will read later in this chapter. Note further that anyone who republishes or repeats defamatory statements is liable even if that person reveals the source of the statements.

BEYOND OUR BORDERS "Libel Tourism"

As mentioned earlier, U.S. plaintiffs sometimes engage in forum shopping by trying to have their complaints heard by a particular state court that is likely to be sympathetic to their claims. *Libel tourism* is essentially forum shopping on an international scale. Rather than filing a defamation lawsuit in the United States where the freedoms of speech and press are strongly protected, a plaintiff files it in a foreign jurisdiction where there is a greater chance of winning.

The Threat of Libel Tourism

Libel tourism can have a chilling effect on the speech of U.S. journalists and authors because the fear of liability in other nations may prevent them from freely discussing topics of profound public importance. Libel tourism could even increase the threat to our nation's security if it discourages authors from writing about persons who support or finance terrorism or other dangerous activities.

The threat of libel tourism captured media attention when Khalid bin Mahfouz, a Saudi Arabian businessman, sued U.S. resident Dr. Rachel Ehrenfeld in London, England. Ehrenfeld had written a book on terrorist financing that claimed Mahfouz financed Islamic terrorist groups. Mahfouz filed the case in England because English law assumes that the offending speech is false (libelous), and the author must prove that the speech is true in order to prevail.

The English court took jurisdiction because twenty-three copies of the book had been sold online to residents of the United Kingdom. Ehrenfeld did not go to England to defend herself, and the court entered a judgment of $225,000 against her. She then countersued Mahfouz in a U.S. court in an attempt to show that she was protected under the First Amendment and had not committed libel, but that case was dismissed for lack of jurisdiction.[a]

The U.S. Response

In response to the *Ehrenfeld* case, the New York state legislature enacted the Libel Terrorism Reform Act in 2008.[b] That act enables New York courts to assert jurisdiction over anyone who obtains a foreign libel judgment against a writer or publisher living in New York State. It also prevents courts from enforcing foreign libel judgments unless the foreign country provides equal or greater free speech protection than is available in the United States and New York. In 2010, the federal government passed similar legislation that makes foreign libel judgments unenforceable in U.S. courts unless they comply with the First Amendment.[c]

Critical Thinking

Why do we need special legislation designed to control foreign libel claims against U.S. citizens? Explain.

a. *Ehrenfeld v. Mahfouz,* 518 F.3d 102 (2d Cir. 2008).

b. McKinney's Consolidated Laws of New York, Sections 302 and 5304.

c. Securing the Protection of our Enduring and Established Constitutional Heritage Act, 28 U.S.C. Sections 4101–4105.

Damages for Libel Once a defendant's liability for libel is established, general damages are presumed as a matter of law. As mentioned earlier, general damages are designed to compensate the plaintiff for nonspecific harms such as disgrace or dishonor in the eyes of the community, humiliation, injured reputation, and emotional distress—harms that are difficult to measure. In other words, to recover damages in a libel case, the plaintiff need not prove that she or he was actually harmed in any specific way as a result of the libelous statement.

Damages for Slander In contrast to cases alleging libel, in a case alleging slander, the plaintiff must prove *special damages* to establish the defendant's liability. In other words, the plaintiff must show that the slanderous statement caused the plaintiff to suffer actual economic or monetary losses. Unless this initial hurdle of proving special damages is overcome, a plaintiff alleging slander normally cannot go forward with the suit and recover any damages. This requirement is imposed in cases involving slander because slanderous statements have a temporary quality. In contrast, a libelous (written) statement has the quality of permanence, can be circulated widely, especially through tweets and blogs, and usually results from some degree of deliberation on the part of the author.

Exceptions to the burden of proving special damages in cases alleging slander are made for certain types of slanderous statements. If a false statement constitutes "slander *per se,*" no proof of special damages is required for it to be actionable. The following four types of false utterances are considered to be slander *per se:*

"My initial response was to sue her for defamation of character, but then I realized that I had no character."

Charles Barkley, 1963–present (National Basketball Association player, 1984–2000)

1. A statement that another has a loathsome disease (historically, leprosy and sexually transmitted diseases, but now also including allegations of mental illness).
2. A statement that another has committed improprieties while engaging in a business, profession, or trade.
3. A statement that another has committed or has been imprisoned for a serious crime.
4. A statement that a person (usually only unmarried persons and sometimes only women) is unchaste or has engaged in serious sexual misconduct.

Defenses against Defamation

Truth is normally an absolute defense against a defamation charge. In other words, if the defendant in a defamation suit can prove that his or her allegedly defamatory statements were true, normally no tort has been committed. Other defenses to defamation may exist if the statement is privileged or concerns a public figure. Note that the majority of defamation actions in the United States are filed in state courts, and the states may differ both in how they define defamation and in the particular defenses they allow, such as privilege (discussed next).

Privilege A special right, advantage, or immunity granted to a person or a class of persons, such as a judge's absolute privilege to avoid liability for defamation over statements made in the courtroom during a trial.

Privileged Communications In some circumstances, a person will not be liable for defamatory statements because she or he enjoys a **privilege**, or immunity. Privileged communications are of two types: absolute and qualified.[7] Only in judicial proceedings and certain government proceedings is an absolute privilege granted. Thus, statements made in a courtroom by attorneys and judges during a trial are absolutely privileged, as are statements made by government officials during legislative debate.

In other situations, a person will not be liable for defamatory statements because he or she has a *qualified,* or conditional, privilege. An employer's statements in written evaluations of employees are an example of a qualified privilege. Generally, if the statements are made in good faith and the publication is limited to those who have a legitimate interest in the communication, the statements fall within the area of qualified privilege. **EXAMPLE 4.6** Jorge worked at Facebook for five years and was being considered for a management position. His supervisor, Lydia, wrote a memo about Jorge's performance to those evaluating him for the management position. The memo contained certain negative statements. As long as Lydia honestly believed that what she wrote was true and limited her disclosure to company representatives, her statements would likely be protected by a qualified privilege. ●

Actual Malice The deliberate intent to cause harm that exists when a person makes a statement with either knowledge of its falsity or reckless disregard of the truth. Actual malice is required to establish defamation against public figures.

Public Figures Politicians, entertainers, professional athletes, and other persons who are in the public eye are considered *public figures.* In general, public figures are considered fair game, and false and defamatory statements about them that appear in the media will not constitute defamation unless the statements are made with **actual malice.**[8] To be made with actual malice, a statement must be made *with either knowledge of its falsity or a reckless disregard of the truth.*

Statements about public figures, especially when made via a public medium, are usually related to matters of general interest. They are made about people who substantially affect all of us. Furthermore, public figures generally have some access to a public medium

7. Note that the term *privileged communication* in this context is not the same as privileged communication between a professional, such as an attorney, and his or her client. The latter type of privilege will be discussed in Chapter 34, in the context of the liability of professionals.
8. *New York Times Co. v. Sullivan,* 376 U.S. 254, 84 S.Ct. 710, 11 L.Ed.2d 686 (1964).

Lynne Spears, mother of singer Britney Spears, wrote a "tell all" book entitled *Through the Storm: A Real Story of Fame and Family in a Tabloid World.*

for answering disparaging (belittling, discrediting) falsehoods about themselves, whereas private individuals do not. For these reasons, public figures have a greater burden of proof in defamation cases (they must prove actual malice) than do private individuals.

CASE EXAMPLE 4.7 Lynne Spears, the mother of pop star Britney Spears, wrote a book in which she claimed that Sam Lutfi, Britney's former business manager, contributed to a mental breakdown that Britney experienced in 2008. Among other things, the book stated that Lutfi added psychiatric drugs to Britney's food, disabled her cars and phones, and stole funds from her bank accounts. Lutfi filed a lawsuit for defamation and asserted that Lynne's statements were untrue, disparaging, and made with actual malice. A court found that Lutfi was a public figure but had presented enough evidence in his complaint for the case to go forward to trial. Lynne appealed, but the appellate court affirmed the ruling and refused to dismiss Lufti's complaint.[9] •

Invasion of the Right to Privacy and Appropriation

A person has a right to solitude and freedom from prying public eyes—in other words, to privacy. As discussed in Chapter 2, the Supreme Court has held that a fundamental right to privacy is implied by various amendments to the U.S. Constitution. Some state constitutions also explicitly provide for privacy rights. In addition, a number of federal and state statutes have been enacted to protect individual rights in specific areas. Tort law also safeguards these rights through the torts of *invasion of privacy* and *appropriation.*

Invasion of Privacy

Four acts qualify as an invasion of privacy:

1. *Intrusion into an individual's affairs or seclusion.* Invading someone's home or illegally searching someone's briefcase is an invasion of privacy. The tort has been held to extend to eavesdropping by wiretap, the unauthorized scanning of a bank account, compulsory blood testing, and window peeping. **EXAMPLE 4.8** A female sports reporter for ESPN was digitally videoed while naked through the peephole in the door of her hotel room. She subsequently won a lawsuit against the man who took the video and posted it on the Internet. •
2. *False light.* Publication of information that places a person in a false light is also an invasion of privacy. For example, writing a story about a person that attributes ideas and opinions not held by that person is an invasion of privacy. (Publishing such a story could involve the tort of defamation as well.) **EXAMPLE 4.9** An Arkansas newspaper printed an article with the headline "Special Delivery: World's oldest newspaper carrier, 101, quits because she's pregnant!" Next to the article was a picture of a ninety-six-year-old woman who was not the subject of the article (and not pregnant). She sued the paper for false light and won. •
3. *Public disclosure of private facts.* This type of invasion of privacy occurs when a person publicly discloses private facts about an individual that an ordinary person would find objectionable or embarrassing. A newspaper account of a private citizen's sex life or financial affairs could be an actionable invasion of privacy, even if the information revealed is true, because it should not be a matter of public concern.
4. *Appropriation of identity.* Under the common law, using a person's name, picture, or other likeness for commercial purposes without permission is a tortious invasion of privacy. An individual's right to privacy normally includes the right to the exclusive use of her or his identity. **EXAMPLE 4.10** An advertising agency asks a singer with a distinctive voice and stage presence to do a marketing campaign for a new automobile. The singer rejects the offer. If the agency then uses someone who imitates the singer's voice and dance moves in the ad, this would be actionable as an appropriation of identity. •

9. *Lutfi v. Spears,* 2010 WL 4723437 (2010).

Appropriation In tort law, the use by one person of another person's name, likeness, or other identifying characteristic without permission and for the benefit of the user.

Appropriation

Most states today have codified the common law tort of appropriation of identity in statutes that establish the distinct tort of **appropriation** or right of publicity. **CASE EXAMPLE 4.11** Vanna White, the hostess of the popular television game show *Wheel of Fortune,* brought an appropriation action against Samsung Electronics America, Inc. Without White's permission, Samsung had included in one of its advertisements a depiction of a robot dressed in a wig, gown, and jewelry, posed in a scene that resembled the *Wheel of Fortune* set, in a stance for which White is famous. The court held in White's favor, reasoning that Samsung's robot ad left "little doubt" as to the identity of the celebrity whom the ad was meant to depict.[10] •

States differ as to the degree of likeness that is required to impose liability for appropriation, however. Some courts have held that even when an animated character in a video or a video game is made to look like an actual person, there are not enough similarities to constitute appropriation.

CASE EXAMPLE 4.12 The Naked Cowboy, Robert Burck, has been a street entertainer in New York City's Times Square for years. He performs for tourists wearing only a white cowboy hat, white cowboy boots, and white underwear and carrying a guitar strategically placed to give the illusion of nudity. Burck has become a well-known persona, appearing in television shows, movies, and video games, and has licensed his name and likeness to various companies, including Chevrolet. When Mars, Inc., the maker of M&Ms candy, installed a video on billboards in Times Square that depicted a blue M&M dressed exactly like The Naked Cowboy, Burck sued for appropriation. A federal district court held that Mars's use of a cartoon character dressed in The Naked Cowboy's signature costume did not amount to appropriation by use of Burck's "portrait or picture." (Burck was allowed to continue his lawsuit against Mars for allegedly violating trademark law—to be discussed in Chapter 5.)[11] •

Fraudulent Misrepresentation

Fraudulent Misrepresentation Any misrepresentation, either by misstatement or by omission of a material fact, knowingly made with the intention of deceiving another and on which a reasonable person would and does rely to his or her detriment.

A misrepresentation leads another to believe in a condition that is different from the condition that actually exists. This is often accomplished through a false or incorrect statement. Although persons sometimes make misrepresentations accidentally because they are unaware of the existing facts, the tort of **fraudulent misrepresentation,** or fraud, involves *intentional* deceit for personal gain. The tort includes several elements:

1. The misrepresentation of facts or conditions with knowledge that they are false or with reckless disregard for the truth.
2. An intent to induce another to rely on the misrepresentation.
3. Justifiable reliance by the deceived party.
4. Damage suffered as a result of the reliance.
5. A causal connection between the misrepresentation and the injury suffered.

Puffery A salesperson's often exaggerated claims concerning the quality of property offered for sale. Such claims involve opinions rather than facts and are not legally binding promises or warranties.

For fraud to occur, more than mere **puffery,** or *seller's talk,* must be involved. Fraud exists only when a person represents as a fact something she or he knows is untrue. For example, it is fraud to claim that a roof does not leak when one knows it does. Facts are objectively ascertainable, whereas seller's talk is not. "I am the best accountant in town" is seller's talk. The speaker is not trying to represent something as fact because the term *best* is a subjective, not an objective, term.[12]

---

10. *White v. Samsung Electronics America, Inc.*, 971 F.2d 1395 (9th Cir. 1992).

11. *Burck v. Mars, Inc.*, 571 F.Supp.2d 446 (S.D.N.Y. 2008). Also see *Kirby v. Sega of America, Inc.*, 144 Cal.App.4th 47, 50 Cal.Rptr.3d 607 (2006).

12. In contracts for the sale of goods, Article 2 of the Uniform Commercial Code distinguishes, for warranty purposes, between statements of opinion (puffery) and statements of fact. See Chapter 17 for a further discussion of this issue.

Statement of Fact versus Opinion

Normally, the tort of misrepresentation or fraud occurs only when there is reliance on a *statement of fact.* Sometimes, however, the tort may involve reliance on a *statement of opinion* if the individual making the statement has a superior knowledge of the subject matter. For instance, when a lawyer makes a statement of opinion about the law in a state in which the lawyer is licensed to practice, a court would construe reliance on that statement to be equivalent to reliance on a statement of fact. We will examine fraudulent misrepresentation in further detail in Chapter 12, in the context of contract law.

Negligent Misrepresentation

Sometimes, a tort action can arise from misrepresentations that are made negligently rather than intentionally. The key difference between intentional and negligent misrepresentation is whether the person making the misrepresentation had actual knowledge of its falsity. Negligent misrepresentation requires only that the person making the statement or omission did not have a reasonable basis for believing its truthfulness. Liability for negligent misrepresentation usually arises when the defendant who made the misrepresentation owed a duty of care to the particular plaintiff to supply correct information. Statements or omissions made by attorneys and accountants to their clients, for example, can lead to liability for negligent misrepresentation.

Abusive or Frivolous Litigation

Persons or businesses generally have a right to sue when they have been injured, but they do not have a right to file meritless lawsuits or use the legal system simply to harass others. Tort law recognizes that people have a right not to be sued without a legally just and proper reason, and therefore it protects individuals from the misuse of litigation. Torts related to abusive litigation include malicious prosecution and abuse of process.

If a person initiates a lawsuit out of malice and without probable cause (a legitimate legal reason), and ends up losing the suit, he or she can be sued for *malicious prosecution.* In some states, the plaintiff (who was the defendant in the first proceeding) must also prove injury beyond the normal costs of litigation, such as lost profits. *Abuse of process* can apply to any person using a legal process against another in an improper manner or to accomplish a purpose for which it was not designed. The key difference between the torts of abuse of process and malicious prosecution is the level of proof required to succeed.

Abuse of process does not require the plaintiff to prove malice or show that the defendant (who was previously the plaintiff) lost in a prior legal proceeding. In addition, an abuse of process claim is not limited to prior litigation. It can be based on the wrongful use of subpoenas, court orders to attach or seize real property, or other types of formal legal process.

Wrongful Interference

Business torts involving wrongful interference are generally divided into two categories: wrongful interference with a contractual relationship and wrongful interference with a business relationship.

Wrongful Interference with a Contractual Relationship

Three elements are necessary for wrongful interference with a contractual relationship to occur:

1. A valid, enforceable contract must exist between two parties.
2. A third party must know that this contract exists.
3. The third party must *intentionally* induce a party to breach the contract.

CASE EXAMPLE 4.13 A landmark case involved an opera singer, Joanna Wagner, who was under contract to sing for a man named Lumley for a specified period of years. A man named Gye, who knew of this contract, nonetheless "enticed" Wagner to refuse to carry out the agreement, and Wagner began to sing for Gye. Gye's action constituted a tort because it wrongfully interfered with the contractual relationship between Wagner and Lumley.[13] (Of course, Wagner's refusal to carry out the agreement also entitled Lumley to sue Wagner for breach of contract.) •

The body of tort law relating to intentional interference with a contractual relationship has expanded greatly in recent years. In principle, any lawful contract can be the basis for an action of this type. The contract could be between a firm and its employees or a firm and its customers. Sometimes, a competitor draws away one of a firm's key employees. To recover damages from the competitor, the original employer must show that the competitor knew of the contract's existence and intentionally induced the breach.

Wrongful Interference with a Business Relationship

Businesspersons devise countless schemes to attract customers, but they are prohibited from unreasonably interfering with another's business in their attempts to gain a share of the market. There is a difference between *competitive methods* and *predatory behavior*—actions undertaken with the intention of unlawfully driving competitors completely out of the market.

Attempting to attract customers in general is a legitimate business practice, whereas specifically targeting the customers of a competitor is more likely to be predatory. **EXAMPLE 4.14** A shopping mall contains two athletic shoe stores: Joe's and Ultimate Sport. Joe's cannot station an employee at the entrance of Ultimate Sport to divert customers by telling them that Joe's will beat Ultimate Sport's prices. This type of activity constitutes the tort of wrongful interference with a business relationship, which is commonly considered to be an unfair trade practice. If this activity were permitted, Joe's would reap the benefits of Ultimate Sport's advertising. •

Defenses to Wrongful Interference

A person can avoid liability for the tort of wrongful interference with a contractual or business relationship by showing that the interference was justified or permissible.

Bona fide competitive behavior is a permissible interference even if it results in the breaking of a contract. **EXAMPLE 4.15** If Antonio's Meats advertises so effectively that it induces Sam's Restaurant to break its contract with Burke's Meat Company, Burke's will be unable to recover against Antonio's Meats on a wrongful interference theory. After all, the public policy that favors free competition in advertising outweighs any possible instability that such competitive activity might cause in contractual relations. •

Although luring customers away from a competitor through aggressive marketing and advertising obviously interferes with the competitor's relationship with its customers, courts typically allow such activities in the spirit of competition. (For a discussion of Facebook's advertising campaign that alleged sweeping privacy violations by Google's social network, see this chapter's *Adapting the Law to the Online Environment* on the next page.)

KNOW THIS

What society and the law consider permissible often depends on the circumstances.

Intentional Torts against Property

Intentional torts against property include trespass to land, trespass to personal property, conversion, and disparagement of property. These torts are wrongful actions that interfere with individuals' legally recognized rights with regard to their land or personal property.

13. *Lumley v. Gye,* 118 Eng.Rep. 749 (1853).

ADAPTING THE LAW TO THE ONLINE ENVIRONMENT

FACEBOOK USES PRIVACY CONCERNS TO "SMEAR" GOOGLE

With close to one billion users, Facebook is the largest social network in the world. Although Facebook has had various competitors, none has posed as much of a threat as Google. Several years ago, Google added a social-networking feature called Social Circles that eventually became part of Google+. Today, Google+ has more than 100 million users and is growing faster than Facebook.

Privacy Policies Matter

For many users of social networks, privacy is a major concern. Facebook has faced a number of complaints about its privacy policy and has changed its policy several times to satisfy its critics and to ward off potential government investigations. One of Google's main advertising points has been its social network's ability to keep "conversations" private and limited to as few individuals as users desire.

As the rivalry between Google and Facebook intensified, Facebook hired Burson-Marsteller, a public relations firm, to plant anonymous stories raising questions about Google's privacy policy. Although Facebook later claimed that Burson-Marsteller was only supposed to investigate how Social Circles collected and used data, several influential bloggers reported that they were approached by Burson-Marsteller and asked to publish negative stories about privacy concerns on Social Circles. In some instances, Burson-Marsteller even offered to supply the stories—one would have claimed that Social Circles "enables people to trace their contacts' connections and profile information by crawling and scraping the sites you and your contacts use, such as Twitter, YouTube, and Facebook."

The Campaign Backfires

If Facebook's goal was to discredit Google, the plan failed dramatically. Bloggers across the Web responded with a mixture of derision and amazement. Some pointed out that planting anonymous stories violated Facebook's privacy policy for its own site, while others said that Facebook's effort to attack Google showed that the social-networking giant was running scared. Writing in *Wired* magazine, Steven Levy concluded that "Facebook was running a smear campaign against itself."[a]

Critical Thinking

If you were part of Google's legal team, on what basis might you think that you could sue Facebook and its public relations firm?

a. Steven Levy, "Facebook's Stealth Attack on Google Exposes Its Own Privacy Problem," *Wired*, May 12, 2011. See also Sam Gustin, "Burson-Marsteller Deletes Critical Facebook Posts, Spares Google-Smear Flacks," *Wired*, May 13, 2011; David Sarno, "Sibling Rivalry? Facebook vs. Google," *Los Angeles Times*, May 13, 2011; and Barbara Ortutay, "Facebook-Google Rivalry Intensifies with PR Fiasco," *Huffington Post*, May 12, 2011.

The law distinguishes real property from personal property (see Chapters 35 and 36). *Real property* is land and things "permanently" attached to the land. *Personal property* consists of all other items, which are basically movable. Thus, a house and lot are real property, whereas the furniture inside the house is personal property. Cash and stocks and bonds are also personal property.

Trespass to Land

Trespass to Land Entry onto, above, or below the surface of land owned by another without the owner's permission or legal authorization.

A **trespass to land** occurs anytime a person, without permission, enters onto, above, or below the surface of land that is owned by another; causes anything to enter onto the land; or remains on the land or permits anything to remain on it. Actual harm to the land is not an essential element of this tort because the tort is designed to protect the right of an owner to exclusive possession of her or his property.

Common types of trespass to land include walking or driving on someone else's land, shooting a gun over the land, throwing rocks at a building that belongs to someone else, building a dam across a river and thereby causing water to back up on someone else's land, and constructing a building so that part of it is on an adjoining landowner's property.

Trespass Criteria, Rights, and Duties

Before a person can be a trespasser, the real property owner (or other person in actual and exclusive possession of the property) must establish that person as a trespasser. For example, "posted" trespass signs expressly establish as a trespasser a person who ignores these signs and enters onto the property. A guest in your home is not a trespasser—unless she or he has been asked to leave but refuses. Any person who enters onto your property to commit an illegal act (such as a thief entering a lumberyard at night to steal lumber) is established impliedly as a trespasser, without posted signs.

At common law, a trespasser is liable for any damage caused to the property and generally cannot hold the owner liable for injuries sustained on the premises. This common law rule is being abandoned in many jurisdictions in favor of a *reasonable duty of care* rule that varies depending on the status of the parties. For instance, a landowner may have a duty to post a notice that guard dogs patrol the property. Also, under the *attractive nuisance* doctrine, children do not assume the risks of the premises if they are attracted to the property by some object, such as a swimming pool, an abandoned building, or a sand pile. Trespassers normally can be removed from the premises through the use of reasonable force without the owner being liable for assault, battery, or false imprisonment.

Defenses against Trespass to Land

One defense to a claim of trespass to land is to show that the trespass was warranted—for instance, that the trespasser entered the property to assist someone in danger. Another defense is for the trespasser to show that he or she had a license to come onto the land. A *licensee* is one who is invited (or allowed to enter) onto the property of another for the licensee's benefit. A person who enters another's property to read an electric meter, for example, is a licensee. When you purchase a ticket to attend a movie or sporting event, you are licensed to go onto the property of another to view that movie or event.

Note that licenses to enter are *revocable* by the property owner. If a property owner asks a meter reader to leave and the meter reader refuses to do so, the meter reader at that point becomes a trespasser.

Trespass to Personal Property

Trespass to Personal Property
Wrongfully taking or harming the personal property of another or otherwise interfering with the lawful owner's possession of personal property.

Whenever an individual wrongfully takes or harms the personal property of another or otherwise interferes with the lawful owner's possession of personal property, **trespass to personal property** occurs (also called *trespass to chattels* or *trespass to personalty*[14]). In this context, harm means not only destruction of the property, but also anything that diminishes its value, condition, or quality.

Trespass to personal property involves intentional meddling with a possessory interest (the right to possess), including barring an owner's access to personal property. **EXAMPLE 4.16** Kelly takes Ryan's business law book as a practical joke and hides it so that Ryan is unable to find it for several days before the final examination. Here, Kelly has engaged in a trespass to personal property. (Kelly has also committed the tort of *conversion*—to be discussed next.) •

A complete defense to a claim of trespass to personal property is to show that the trespass was warranted. Most states, for example, allow automobile repair shops to retain a customer's car (under what is called an *artisan's lien*—see Chapter 21) when the customer refuses to pay for repairs already completed.

14. Pronounced *per*-sun-ul-tee.

Conversion

Conversion Wrongfully taking or retaining possession of an individual's personal property and placing it in the service of another.

Whenever a person wrongfully possesses or uses the personal property of another without permission, the tort of **conversion** occurs. Any act that deprives an owner of personal property or the use of that property without that owner's permission and without just cause can be conversion. Even the taking of electronic records and data can be a form of conversion.[15]

KNOW THIS

It is the *intent* to do an act that is important in tort law, not the motive behind the intent.

Often, when conversion occurs, a trespass to personal property also occurs because the original taking of the personal property from the owner was a trespass, and wrongfully retaining it is conversion. Conversion is the civil side of crimes related to theft, but it is not limited to theft. Even if the rightful owner consented to the initial taking of the property, so there was no theft or trespass, a failure to return the personal property may still be conversion. **EXAMPLE 4.17** Chen borrows Mark's iPad to use while traveling home from school for the holidays. When Chen returns to school, Mark asks for his iPad back. Chen tells Mark that she gave it to her little brother for Christmas. In this situation, Mark can sue Chen for conversion, and Chen will have to either return the iPad or pay damages equal to its replacement value. •

Even if a person mistakenly believed that she or he was entitled to the goods, the tort of conversion may occur. In other words, good intentions are not a defense against conversion. In fact, conversion can be an entirely innocent act. Someone who buys stolen goods, for example, can be liable for conversion even if he or she did not know that the goods were stolen. If the true owner brings a tort action against the buyer, the buyer must either return the property to the owner or pay the owner the full value of the property, despite having already paid the purchase price to the thief. A successful defense against the charge of conversion is that the purported owner does not, in fact, own the property or does not have a right to possess it that is superior to the right of the holder.

Disparagement of Property

Disparagement of Property An economically injurious falsehood about another's product or property.

Slander of Quality (Trade Libel) The publication of false information about another's product, alleging that it is not what its seller claims.

Slander of Title The publication of a statement that denies or casts doubt on another's legal ownership of any property, causing financial loss to that property's owner.

Disparagement of property occurs when economically injurious falsehoods are made about another's product or property, not about another's reputation. Disparagement of property is a general term for torts specifically referred to as *slander of quality* or *slander of title*. Publication of false information about another's product, alleging that it is not what its seller claims, constitutes the tort of **slander of quality,** or **trade libel.** To establish trade libel, the plaintiff must prove that the improper publication caused a third party to refrain from dealing with the plaintiff and that the plaintiff sustained economic damages (such as lost profits) as a result.

An improper publication may be both a slander of quality and defamation of character. For example, a statement that disparages the quality of a product may also, by implication, disparage the character of the person who would sell such a product.

When a publication denies or casts doubt on another's legal ownership of any property, and the property's owner suffers financial loss as a result, the tort of **slander of title** may exist. Usually, this is an intentional tort that occurs when someone knowingly publishes an untrue statement about property with the intent of discouraging a third party from dealing with the property's owner. For instance, a car dealer would have difficulty attracting customers after competitors published a notice that the dealer's stock consisted of stolen automobiles.

15. See, for example, *Thyroff v. Nationwide Mutual Insurance Co.*, 8 N.Y.3d 283, 864 N.E.2d 1272, 832 N.Y.S.2d 873 (2007).

Unintentional Torts (Negligence)

Negligence The failure to exercise the standard of care that a reasonable person would exercise in similar circumstances.

The tort of **negligence** occurs when someone suffers injury because of another's failure to live up to a required *duty of care*. In contrast to intentional torts, in torts involving negligence, the tortfeasor neither wishes to bring about the consequences of the act nor believes that they will occur. The actor's conduct merely creates a *risk* of such consequences. If no risk is created, there is no negligence. Moreover, the risk must be foreseeable—that is, it must be such that a reasonable person engaging in the same activity would anticipate the risk and guard against it. In determining what is reasonable conduct, courts consider the nature of the possible harm.

LEARNING OBJECTIVE 4

Identify the four elements of negligence.

Many of the actions discussed earlier in the chapter in the section on intentional torts constitute negligence if the element of intent is missing. **EXAMPLE 4.18** Juan walks up to Maya and intentionally shoves her. Maya falls and breaks an arm as a result. In this situation, Juan has committed an intentional tort (assault and battery). If Juan carelessly bumps into Maya, however, and she falls and breaks an arm as a result, Juan's action will constitute negligence. In either situation, Juan has committed a tort. •

To succeed in a negligence action, the plaintiff must prove each of the following:

1. *Duty.* That the defendant owed a duty of care to the plaintiff.
2. *Breach.* That the defendant breached that duty.
3. *Causation.* That the defendant's breach caused the plaintiff's injury.
4. *Damages.* That the plaintiff suffered a legally recognizable injury.

We discuss each of these four elements of negligence next.

The Duty of Care and Its Breach

Duty of Care The duty of all persons, as established by tort law, to exercise a reasonable amount of care in their dealings with others. Failure to exercise due care, which is normally determined by the reasonable person standard, constitutes the tort of negligence.

Reasonable Person Standard The standard of behavior expected of a hypothetical "reasonable person." It is the standard against which negligence is measured and that must be observed to avoid liability for negligence.

Central to the tort of negligence is the concept of a **duty of care.** The basic principle underlying the duty of care is that people in society are free to act as they please so long as their actions do not infringe on the interests of others.

When someone fails to comply with the duty to exercise reasonable care, a potentially tortious act may have been committed. Failure to live up to a standard of care may be an act (setting fire to a building) or an omission (neglecting to put out a campfire). It may be a careless act or a carefully performed but nevertheless dangerous act that results in injury. Courts consider the nature of the act (whether it is outrageous or commonplace), the manner in which the act was performed (cautiously versus heedlessly), and the nature of the injury (whether it is serious or slight).

"Do you have any picture books that could help a child understand tort reform?"

The Reasonable Person Standard

Tort law measures duty by the **reasonable person standard.** In determining whether a duty of care has been breached, the courts ask how a reasonable person would have acted in the same circumstances. The reasonable person standard is said to be (though in an absolute sense it cannot be) objective. It is not necessarily how a particular person would act. It is society's judgment on how people *should* act. If the so-called reasonable person existed, he or she would be careful, conscientious, even tempered, and honest.

The courts frequently use this hypothetical reasonable person in decisions relating to other areas of law as well. That individuals are required to exercise a reasonable standard of care in their activities is a pervasive concept in business law, and many of the issues discussed in subsequent chapters of this text have to do with this duty.

In negligence cases, the degree of care to be exercised varies, depending on the defendant's occupation or profession, her or his relationship with the plaintiff, and other factors. Generally, whether an action constitutes a breach of the duty of care is determined on a case-by-case basis. The outcome depends on how the judge (or jury, if it is a jury trial) decides a reasonable person in the position of the defendant would act in the particular circumstances of the case.

ETHICAL ISSUE

Does a pharmacist's duty of care include a duty to warn customers of certain adverse effects when filling prescriptions? Pharmacists typically discuss the potential side effects of prescription medications with the customer when they first fill a prescription. Under what is known as the "learned intermediary doctrine," pharmacists are generally *immune* from liability for any negative effects resulting from medications that were prescribed by the customer's physician (the intermediary). Nevertheless, according to the Nevada Supreme Court, pharmacists may have a duty to warn a customer in some situations, if they are aware of certain customer-specific risks, such as allergies. The case involved a pharmacist at a Walgreen drugstore who filled a prescription for a woman even though the pharmacy's computer indicated that she was allergic to the medication prescribed. The woman subsequently died when her condition worsened. The court concluded that the pharmacist should have either warned the customer or notified the prescribing physician. The court noted, however, that the duty to warn exists only when the pharmacist *knows* of a possible adverse effect for the specific customer.[16]

"A little neglect may breed great mischief."

Benjamin Franklin, 1706–1790
(American politician and inventor)

The Duty of Landowners

Landowners are expected to exercise reasonable care to protect persons coming onto their property from harm. As mentioned earlier, in some jurisdictions, landowners are held to owe a duty to protect even trespassers against certain risks. Landowners who rent or lease premises to tenants (see Chapter 36) are expected to exercise reasonable care to ensure that the tenants and their guests are not harmed in common areas, such as stairways, entryways, and laundry rooms.

Business Invitee A person, such as a customer or a client, who is invited onto business premises by the owner of those premises for business purposes.

Duty to Warn Business Invitees of Risks Retailers and other firms that explicitly or implicitly invite persons to come onto their premises are usually charged with a duty to exercise reasonable care to protect those persons, who are considered **business invitees.** **EXAMPLE 4.19** Liz enters a supermarket, slips on a wet floor, and sustains injuries as a result. If there was no sign warning that the floor was wet when Liz slipped, the owner of the supermarket would be liable for damages. A court would hold that the business owner was negligent because the owner failed to exercise a reasonable degree of care in protecting the store's customers against foreseeable risks about which the owner knew or *should have known.* That a patron might slip on the wet floor and be injured was a foreseeable risk, and the owner should have taken care to avoid this risk or to warn the customer of it (by posting a sign or setting out orange cones, for example). •

The landowner also has a duty to discover and remove any hidden dangers that might injure a customer or other invitee. Store owners have a duty to protect customers from potentially slipping and injuring themselves on merchandise that has fallen off the shelves, for instance.

Obvious Risks Are an Exception Some risks, of course, are so obvious that the owner need not warn of them. For instance, a business owner does not need to warn customers to open a door before attempting to walk through it. Other risks, however, may seem obvious to a business owner but may not be so to someone else, such as a child. In addition, even if a risk is obvious, that does not necessarily excuse a business owner from the duty to protect its customers from foreseeable harm.

---

16. *Klasch v. Walgreen Co.,* 264 P.3d 1155 (Nev. 2011).

CASE EXAMPLE 4.20 Giorgio's Grill in Hollywood, Florida, is a restaurant that becomes a nightclub after hours. At those times, traditionally, as the manager of Giorgio's knew, the staff and customers throw paper napkins into the air as the music played. The napkins land on the floor, but no one picks them up. One night, Jane Izquierdo went to Giorgio's. Although she had been to the club on other occasions and knew about the napkin-throwing tradition, she slipped on a napkin and fell, breaking her leg. She sued Giorgio's for negligence but lost at trial because the jury found that the risk of slipping on the napkins was obvious. A state appellate court reversed, however, holding that the obviousness of a risk does not discharge a business owner's duty to its invitees to maintain the premises in a safe condition.[17] ●

PREVENTING LEGAL DISPUTES

It can be difficult to determine whether a risk is obvious. Because you can be held liable if you fail to discover hidden dangers on business premises that could cause injuries to customers, you should post warnings of any conceivable risks on the property. Be vigilant and frequently reassess potential hazards. Train your employees to be on the lookout for possibly dangerous conditions at all times and to notify a superior immediately if they notice something. Remember that a finding of liability in a single lawsuit can leave a small enterprise close to bankruptcy. To prevent potential negligence liability, make sure that your business premises are as safe as possible for all persons who might be there, including children, senior citizens, and individuals with disabilities.

The Duty of Professionals

If an individual has knowledge, skill, or training superior to that of an ordinary person, the individual's conduct must be consistent with that status. Because professionals—such as physicians, dentists, architects, engineers, accountants, and lawyers—are required to have a certain level of knowledge and training, a higher standard of care applies. In determining whether professionals have exercised reasonable care, the law takes their training and expertise into account. Thus, an accountant's conduct is judged not by the reasonable person standard, but by the reasonable accountant standard.

If a professional violates her or his duty of care toward a client, the professional may be sued for **malpractice**, which is essentially professional negligence. For example, a patient might sue a physician for *medical malpractice*. A client might sue an attorney for *legal malpractice*. We will discuss the liability of accountants and attorneys in more detail in Chapter 34.

Malpractice Professional misconduct or the lack of the requisite degree of skill as a professional. Negligence—the failure to exercise due care—on the part of a professional, such as a physician, is commonly referred to as malpractice.

Causation

Another necessary element in a negligence action is *causation*. If a person fails in a duty of care and someone suffers an injury, the wrongful act must have caused the harm for the act to be considered a tort.

Courts Ask Two Questions

In deciding whether there is causation, the court must address two questions:

1. *Is there causation in fact?* Did the injury occur because of the defendant's act, or would it have occurred anyway? If an injury would not have occurred without the defendant's act, then there is causation in fact. **Causation in fact** can usually be determined by the use of the *but for* test: "but for" the wrongful act, the injury would not have occurred. Theoretically, causation in fact is limitless. One could claim, for example, that "but for"

Causation in Fact An act or omission without which an event would not have occurred.

17. *Izquierdo v. Gyroscope, Inc.*, 946 So.2d 115 (Fla.App. 2007).

the creation of the world, a particular injury would not have occurred. Thus, as a practical matter, the law has to establish limits, and it does so through the concept of proximate cause.

Proximate Cause Legal cause. It exists when the connection between an act and an injury is strong enough to justify imposing liability.

2. *Was the act the proximate cause of the injury?* **Proximate cause,** or legal cause, exists when the connection between an act and an injury is strong enough to justify imposing liability. Courts use proximate cause to limit the scope of the defendant's liability to a subset of the total number of potential plaintiffs that might have been harmed by the defendant's actions. **EXAMPLE 4.21** Ackerman carelessly leaves a campfire burning. The fire not only burns down the forest but also sets off an explosion in a nearby chemical plant that spills chemicals into a river, killing all the fish for a hundred miles downstream and ruining the economy of a tourist resort. Should Ackerman be liable to the resort owners? To the tourists whose vacations were ruined? These are questions of proximate cause that a court must decide. •

KNOW THIS

Proximate cause can be thought of in terms of a question of social policy. Should the defendant be made to bear the loss instead of the plaintiff?

Both of these questions regarding causation in fact and proximate cause must be answered in the affirmative for liability in tort to arise. If a defendant's action constitutes causation in fact but a court decides that the action was not the proximate cause of the plaintiff's injury, the causation requirement has not been met—and the defendant normally will not be liable to the plaintiff.

Foreseeability

Questions of proximate cause are linked to the concept of foreseeability because it would be unfair to impose liability on a defendant unless the defendant's actions created a foreseeable risk of injury. Probably the most cited case on proximate cause is the *Palsgraf* case, which is discussed in this chapter's *Landmark in the Law* feature on the facing page. In determining the issue of proximate cause, the court addressed the following question: Does a defendant's duty of care extend only to those who may be injured as a result of a foreseeable risk, or does it also extend to a person whose injury could not reasonably be foreseen?

The Injury Requirement and Damages

For a tort to have been committed, the plaintiff must have suffered a *legally recognizable* injury. To recover damages (receive compensation), the plaintiff must have suffered some loss, harm, wrong, or invasion of a protected interest. Essentially, the purpose of tort law is to compensate for legally recognized injuries resulting from wrongful acts. If no harm or injury results from a given negligent action, there is nothing to compensate—and no tort exists. **EXAMPLE 4.22** If you carelessly bump into a passerby, who stumbles and falls as a result, you may be liable in tort if the passerby is injured in the fall. If the person is unharmed, however, there normally cannot be a suit for damages because no injury was suffered. •

Compensatory damages are the norm in negligence cases. As noted earlier, a court will award punitive damages only if the defendant's conduct was grossly negligent, reflecting an intentional failure to perform a duty with reckless disregard of the consequences to others.

Injuries from car accidents can cause handicaps that last a lifetime. Do such injuries satisfy the injury requirement for a finding of a negligence tort?

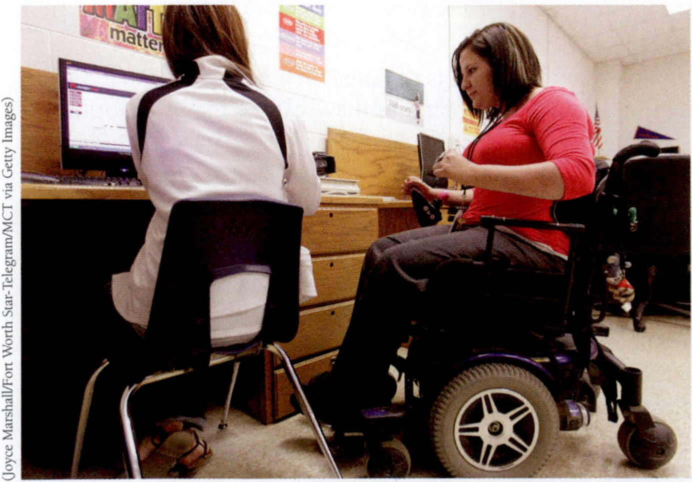

(Joyce Marshall/Fort Worth Star-Telegram/MCT via Getty Images)

Defenses to Negligence

Defendants often defend against negligence claims by asserting that the plaintiffs failed to prove the existence of one or more of the required elements for negligence. Additionally,

LANDMARK IN THE LAW

Palsgraf v. Long Island Railroad Co. (1928)

In 1928, the New York Court of Appeals (that state's highest court) issued its decision in *Palsgraf v. Long Island Railroad Co.*,[a] a case that has become a landmark in negligence law and proximate cause.

The Facts of the Case The plaintiff, Helen Palsgraf, was waiting for a train on a station platform. A man carrying a small package wrapped in newspaper was rushing to catch a train that had begun to move away from the platform. As the man attempted to jump aboard the moving train, he seemed unsteady and about to fall. A railroad guard on the train car reached forward to grab him, and another guard on the platform pushed him from behind to help him board the train. In the process, the man's package fell on the railroad tracks and exploded, because it contained fireworks. The repercussions of the explosion caused scales at the other end of the train platform to fall on Palsgraf, who was injured as a result. She sued the railroad company for damages in a New York state court.

The Question of Proximate Cause At the trial, the jury found that the railroad guards were negligent in their conduct. On appeal, the question before the New York Court of Appeals was whether the conduct of the railroad guards was the proximate cause of Palsgraf's injuries. In other words, did the guards' duty of care extend to Palsgraf, who was outside the zone of danger and whose injury could not reasonably have been foreseen?

The court stated that the question of whether the guards were negligent *with respect to Palsgraf* depended on whether her injury was *reasonably foreseeable* by the railroad guards. Although the guards may have acted negligently with respect to the man boarding the train, this had no bearing on the question of their negligence with respect to Palsgraf. This was not a situation in which a person commited an act so potentially harmful (for example, firing a gun at a building) that he or she would be held responsible for any harm that resulted. The court stated that here "there was nothing in the situation to suggest to the most cautious mind that the parcel wrapped in newspaper would spread wreckage through the station." The court thus concluded that the railroad guards were not negligent with respect to Palsgraf because her injury was not reasonably foreseeable.

Application to Today's World *The* Palsgraf *case established foreseeability as the test for proximate cause. Today, the courts continue to apply this test in determining proximate cause—and thus tort liability for injuries. Generally, if the victim of a harm or the consequences of a harm done are unforeseeable, there is no proximate cause. Note, though, that in the online environment, distinctions based on physical proximity, such as the "zone of danger" cited by the court in this case, are largely inapplicable.*

a. 248 N.Y. 339, 162 N.E. 99 (1928).

there are three basic *affirmative* defenses in negligence cases (defenses that a defendant can use to avoid liability even if the facts are as the plaintiff states): (1) assumption of risk, (2) superseding cause, and (3) contributory and comparative negligence.

Assumption of Risk A defense to negligence. A plaintiff may not recover for injuries or damage suffered from risks he or she knows of and has voluntarily assumed.

Assumption of Risk

A plaintiff who voluntarily enters into a risky situation, knowing the risk involved, will not be allowed to recover. This is the defense of **assumption of risk.** The requirements of this defense are (1) knowledge of the risk and (2) voluntary assumption of the risk. This defense is frequently asserted when the plaintiff is injured during recreational activities that involve known risk, such as skiing and skydiving. Note that assumption of risk can apply not only to participants in sporting events, but also to spectators and bystanders who are injured while attending those events.

The risk can be assumed by express agreement, or the assumption of risk can be implied by the plaintiff's knowledge of the risk and subsequent conduct. Courts do not apply the assumption of risk doctrine in emergency situations, though.

In the following case, the issue was whether a spectator at a baseball game voluntarily assumed the risk of being hit by an errant ball thrown while the players were warming up before the game.

Spotlight on the Seattle Mariners

Case 4.3

Taylor v. Baseball Club of Seattle, L.P.

Court of Appeals of Washington, 132 Wash.App. 32, 130 P.3d 835 (2006).

(Otto Greule Jr./Allsport/Getty Images)

Many fans arrive at baseball games early so they can watch the players warm up.

FACTS Delinda Middleton Taylor went to a Mariners baseball game at Safeco Field with her boyfriend and two minor sons. Their seats were four rows up from the field along the right field foul line. They arrived more than an hour before the game began so that they could see the players warm up and get their autographs. When she walked in, Taylor saw that Mariners pitcher Freddy Garcia was throwing a ball back and forth with José Mesa right in front of their seats. As Taylor stood in front of her seat, she looked away from the field, and a ball thrown by Mesa got past Garcia and struck her in the face, causing serious injuries. Taylor sued the Mariners for the allegedly negligent warm-up throw. The Mariners filed a motion for a summary judgment in which they argued that Taylor, a Mariners fan, was familiar with baseball and the inherent risk of balls entering the stands, and therefore assumed the risk of her injury. The trial court granted the motion and dismissed Taylor's case. Taylor appealed.

ISSUE Was the risk of injury from an errant baseball thrown during pregame warm-up foreseeable to a reasonable person with Taylor's familiarity with baseball?

DECISION Yes. The state intermediate appellate court affirmed the lower court's judgment. Taylor, as a spectator in an unprotected area of seats, voluntarily undertook the risk associated with being hit by an errant baseball thrown during warm-ups before the start of the game.

REASON The court observed that there was substantial evidence that Taylor was familiar with the game. She was a seasoned Mariners fan, and both of her sons had played baseball for at least six years. "She attended many of her sons' baseball games, she witnessed balls entering the stands, she had watched Mariners' games both at the Kingdome and on television, and she knew that there was no screen protecting her seats, which were close to the field. In fact, as she walked to her seat she saw the players warming up and was excited about being in an unscreened area where her party might get autographs from the players and catch balls." It was not legally relevant that the injury occurred during the pregame warm-up because "it is the normal, every-day practice at all levels of baseball for pitchers to warm up in the manner that led to this incident." The Mariners had satisfied their duty to protect spectators from balls entering the stands by providing a protective screen behind home plate. Taylor chose not to sit in the protected area and thus knowingly put herself at risk.

CRITICAL THINKING—Ethical Consideration *Would the result in this case have been different if Taylor's minor son, rather than Taylor herself, had been struck by the ball? Should courts apply the doctrine of assumption of risk to children? Discuss.*

Superseding Cause An unforeseeable intervening event may break the connection between a wrongful act and an injury to another. If so, the event acts as a *superseding cause*—that is, it relieves a defendant of liability for injuries caused by the intervening event. **EXAMPLE 4.23** While riding his bicycle, Derrick negligently hits Julie, who is walking on the sidewalk. As a result of the impact, Julie falls and fractures her hip. While she is waiting for help to arrive, a small plane crashes nearby and explodes, and some of the fiery debris hits her, causing her to sustain severe burns. Derrick will be liable for Julie's fractured hip because the risk of hitting her with his bicycle was foreseeable. Normally, Derrick will not be liable for the burns caused by the plane crash—because the risk of a plane's crashing nearby and injuring Julie was not foreseeable. •

Contributory Negligence A rule in tort law, used in only a few states, that completely bars the plaintiff from recovering any damages if the damage suffered is partly the plaintiff's own fault.

Contributory and Comparative Negligence All individuals are expected to exercise a reasonable degree of care in looking out for themselves. In the past, under the common law doctrine of **contributory negligence**, a plaintiff who was also negligent (failed to exercise a reasonable degree of care) could not recover anything from the defendant. Under this rule, no matter how insignificant the plaintiff's negligence was relative to the defendant's negligence, the plaintiff was precluded from recovering any damages. Today, only a few jurisdictions still hold to this doctrine.

Comparative Negligence A rule in tort law, used in the majority of states, that reduces the plaintiff's recovery in proportion to the plaintiff's degree of fault, rather than barring recovery completely.

In most states, the doctrine of contributory negligence has been replaced by a **comparative negligence** standard. Under this standard, both the plaintiff's and the defendant's negligence are computed, and the liability for damages is distributed accordingly. Some jurisdictions have adopted a "pure" form of comparative negligence that allows the plaintiff to recover, even if the extent of his or her fault is greater than that of the defendant. For example, if the plaintiff was 80 percent at fault and the defendant 20 percent at fault, the plaintiff may recover 20 percent of his or her damages. Many states' comparative negligence statutes, however, contain a "50 percent" rule that prevents the plaintiff from recovering any damages if she or he was more than 50 percent at fault. Under this rule, a plaintiff who is 35 percent at fault could recover 65 percent of his or her damages, but a plaintiff who is 65 percent (more than 50 percent) at fault could recover nothing.

Special Negligence Doctrines and Statutes

There are a number of special doctrines and statutes relating to negligence. We examine a few of them here.

Res Ipsa Loquitur A doctrine under which negligence may be inferred simply because an event occurred, if it is the type of event that would not occur in the absence of negligence. Literally, the term means "the facts speak for themselves."

Res Ipsa Loquitur

Generally, in lawsuits involving negligence, the plaintiff has the burden of proving that the defendant was negligent. In certain situations, however, under the doctrine of ***res ipsa loquitur***[18] (meaning "the facts speak for themselves"), the courts may infer that negligence has occurred. Then the burden of proof rests on the defendant—to prove she or he was *not* negligent. This doctrine is applied only when the event creating the damage or injury is one that ordinarily would occur only as a result of negligence.

CASE EXAMPLE 4.24 Mary Gubbins undergoes abdominal surgery and following the surgery has nerve damage in her spine near the area of the operation. She is unable to walk or stand for months, and even after regaining some use of her legs through physical therapy, her mobility is impaired and she experiences pain. In her subsequent negligence lawsuit, Gubbins can assert *res ipsa loquitur,* because the injury would never have occurred in the absence of the surgeon's negligence.[19] •

Negligence *Per Se* An action or failure to act in violation of a statutory requirement.

Negligence *Per Se*

Certain conduct, whether it consists of an action or a failure to act, may be treated as **negligence *per se*** (*per se* means "in or of itself"). Negligence *per se* may occur if an individual violates a statute or ordinance and thereby causes the kind of harm that the statute was intended to prevent. The statute must clearly set out what standard of conduct is expected, when and where it is expected, and of whom it is expected. The standard of conduct required by the statute is the duty that the defendant owes to the plaintiff, and a violation of the statute is the breach of that duty.

CASE EXAMPLE 4.25 A Delaware statute states that anyone "who operates a motor vehicle and who fails to give full time and attention to the operation of the vehicle" is guilty of inattentive driving. Michael Moore was cited for inattentive driving after he collided with Debra Wright's car when he backed a truck out of a parking space. Moore paid the ticket, which meant that he pleaded guilty to violating the statute. The day after the accident, Wright began having back pain, which eventually required surgery. She sued Moore for damages, alleging negligence *per se.* The Delaware Supreme Court ruled that the inattentive driving statute set forth a sufficiently specific standard of conduct to warrant application of negligence *per se.*[20] •

---

18. Pronounced *rehz ihp-suh low-kwuh-tuhr.*

19. *Gubbins v. Hurson,* 885 A.2d 269 (D.C. 2005).

20. *Wright v. Moore,* 931 A.2d 405 (Del.Supr. 2007).

"Danger Invites Rescue" Doctrine

Sometimes, a person who is trying to avoid harm—such as an individual who swerves to avoid a head-on collision with a drunk driver—ends up causing harm to another (such as a cyclist riding in the bike lane) as a result. In those situations, the original wrongdoer (the drunk driver in this scenario) is liable to anyone who is injured, even if the injury actually resulted from another person's attempt to escape harm. The "danger invites rescue" doctrine extends the same protection to a person who is trying to rescue another from harm—the original wrongdoer is liable for injuries to an individual attempting a rescue. The idea is that the rescuer should not be held liable for any damages because he or she did not cause the danger and because danger invites rescue.

EXAMPLE 4.26 Ludley drives down a street but fails to see a stop sign because he is trying to quiet his squabbling children in the car's back seat. Salter, who is standing on the curb, realizes that Ludley is about to hit a pedestrian and runs into the street to push the pedestrian out of the way. If Ludley's vehicle hits Salter instead, Ludley will be liable for Salter's injury, as well as for any injuries the other pedestrian sustained. • Whether rescuers injure themselves, the person rescued, or even a stranger, the original wrongdoer will still be liable.

Good Samaritan Statute A state statute stipulating that persons who provide emergency services to, or rescue, someone in peril cannot be sued for negligence unless they act recklessly, thereby causing further harm.

Good Samaritan Statutes

Most states have enacted what are called **Good Samaritan statutes.**[21] Under these statutes, someone who is aided voluntarily by another cannot turn around and sue the "Good Samaritan" for negligence. These laws were passed largely to protect physicians and medical personnel who voluntarily render medical services in emergency situations to those in need, such as individuals hurt in car accidents. Indeed, the California Supreme Court has interpreted the state's Good Samaritan statute to mean that only a person who renders medical aid is immune from liability.[22] Thus, only medical personnel and persons rendering medical aid in emergencies are protected in California.

Dram Shop Act A state statute that imposes liability on the owners of bars and taverns, as well as those who serve alcoholic drinks to the public, for injuries resulting from accidents caused by intoxicated persons when the sellers or servers of alcoholic drinks contributed to the intoxication.

Dram Shop Acts

Many states have also passed **dram shop acts,**[23] under which a tavern owner or bartender may be held liable for injuries caused by a person who became intoxicated while drinking at the bar or who was already intoxicated when served by the bartender. Some states' statutes also impose liability on *social hosts* (persons hosting parties) for injuries caused by guests who became intoxicated at the hosts' homes. Under these statutes, it is unnecessary to prove that the tavern owner, bartender, or social host was negligent. **EXAMPLE 4.27** Selena hosts a Super Bowl party at which Raul, a minor, sneaks alcoholic drinks. Selena is potentially liable for damages resulting from Raul's drunk driving after the party. •

LEARNING OBJECTIVE 5

What is meant by strict liability? In what circumstances is strict liability applied?

Strict Liability Liability regardless of fault, which is imposed on those engaged in abnormally dangerous activities, on persons who keep dangerous animals, and on manufacturers or sellers that introduce into commerce defective and unreasonably dangerous goods.

Strict Liability

Another category of torts is called **strict liability,** or *liability without fault.* Intentional torts and torts of negligence involve acts that depart from a reasonable standard of care and cause injuries. Under the doctrine of strict liability, liability for injury is imposed for reasons other than fault.

---

21. These laws derive their name from the Good Samaritan story in the Bible. In the story, a traveler who had been robbed and beaten lay along the roadside, ignored by those passing by. Eventually, a man from the country of Samaria (the "Good Samaritan") stopped to render assistance to the injured person.
22. *Van Horn v. Watson,* 45 Cal.4th 322, 197 P.3d 164, 86 Cal.Rptr.3d 350 (2008).
23. Historically, a *dram* was a small unit of liquid, and spirits were sold in drams. Thus, a dram shop was a place where liquor was sold in drams.

Abnormally Dangerous Activities

Strict liability for damages proximately caused by an abnormally dangerous or exceptional activity is one application of this doctrine. Courts apply the doctrine of strict liability in such cases because of the extreme risk of the activity. For instance, even if blasting with dynamite is performed with all reasonable care, there is still a risk of injury. Because of the potential for harm, the person who is engaged in an abnormally dangerous activity—and benefits from it—is responsible for paying for any injuries caused by that activity. Although there is no fault, there is still responsibility because of the dangerous nature of the undertaking.

Other Applications of Strict Liability

The strict liability principle is also applied in other situations. Persons who keep wild animals, for example, are strictly liable for any harm inflicted by the animals. In addition, an owner of domestic animals may be strictly liable for harm caused by those animals if the owner knew, or should have known, that the animals were dangerous or had a propensity to harm others.

A significant application of strict liability is in the area of *product liability*—liability of manufacturers and sellers for harmful or defective products. Liability here is a matter of social policy and is based on two factors: (1) the manufacturer or seller can better bear the cost of injury because it can spread the cost throughout society by increasing prices of goods and services, and (2) the manufacturer or seller is making a profit from its activities and therefore should bear the cost of injury as an operating expense. We will discuss product liability in greater detail in Chapter 17.

Cyber Torts

Torts can also be committed in the online environment. One of the most common types of *cyber torts* is online defamation, as we discuss next. We also discuss how the courts are attempting to address the problems associated with bulk, unsolicited, junk e-mails, or spam.

Identifying the Author of Online Defamation

An initial issue raised by online defamation was simply discovering who was committing it. In the real world, identifying the author of a defamatory remark generally is an easy matter, but suppose that a business firm has discovered that defamatory statements about its policies and products are being posted in an online forum. Such forums allow anyone—customers, employees, or crackpots—to complain about a firm that they dislike while remaining anonymous.

Therefore, a threshold barrier to anyone who seeks to bring an action for online defamation is discovering the identity of the person who posted the defamatory message. An Internet service provider (ISP)—a company that provides connections to the Internet—can disclose personal information about its customers only when ordered to do so by a court. Consequently, businesses and individuals are increasingly bringing lawsuits against "John Does" (John Doe, Jane Doe, and the like are fictitious names used in lawsuits when the identity of a party is not known or when a party wishes to conceal his or her name for privacy reasons). Then, using the authority of the courts, the plaintiffs can obtain from the ISPs the identity of the persons responsible for the defamatory messages.

(AP Photo/Joel Ryan)

Woody Allen sued a clothing company for using his image on the Web. Can the Internet service provider through which the offending ads were directed be held liable?

Liability of Internet Service Providers

Recall from the discussion of defamation earlier in this chapter that those who repeat or otherwise disseminate defamatory statements made by others can be held liable for defamation. Thus, newspapers, magazines, and radio and television stations can be subject to liability for defamatory content that they publish or broadcast, even though the content was prepared or created by others. Applying this rule to cyberspace, however, raises an important issue: Should ISPs be regarded as publishers and therefore be held liable for defamatory messages that are posted by their users in online forums or other arenas?

Before 1996, the courts grappled with this question. Then Congress passed the Communications Decency Act (CDA), which states that "[n]o provider or user of an interactive computer service shall be treated as the publisher or speaker of any information provided by another information content provider."[24] Thus, under the CDA, ISPs generally are treated differently from publishers in other media and are not liable for publishing defamatory statements that come from a third party.[25] Although the courts generally have construed the CDA as providing a broad shield to protect ISPs from liability for third-party content, some courts have started establishing some limits to CDA immunity.[26]

The Spread of Spam

Businesses and individuals alike are targets of *spam,* or unsolicited "junk e-mails" that flood virtual mailboxes with advertisements, solicitations, and other messages. Considered relatively harmless in the early days of the Internet, by 2012 spam accounted for roughly 75 percent of all e-mails.

State Regulation of Spam

In an attempt to combat spam, thirty-six states have enacted laws that prohibit or regulate its use. Many state laws that regulate spam require the senders of e-mail ads to instruct the recipients on how they can "opt out" of further e-mail ads from the same sources. For instance, in some states an unsolicited e-mail ad must include a toll-free phone number or return e-mail address that the recipient can use to contact the sender to request that no more ads be e-mailed.

The Federal CAN-SPAM Act

In 2003, Congress enacted the Controlling the Assault of Non-Solicited Pornography and Marketing (CAN-SPAM) Act, which took effect on January 1, 2004. The legislation applies to any "commercial electronic mail messages" that are sent to promote a commercial product or service. Significantly, the statute preempts state antispam laws except for those provisions in state laws that prohibit false and deceptive e-mailing practices.

"Speech is not free when it comes postage due."

Jim Nitchals, 1962–1998
(Spam fighter and computer programmer)

Generally, the act permits unsolicited commercial e-mail but prohibits certain spamming activities, including the use of a false return address and the inclusion of false, misleading, or deceptive information in e-mail. The statute also prohibits "dictionary attacks"—sending messages to randomly generated e-mail addresses—and the "harvesting" of e-mail addresses from Web sites with specialized software.

CASE EXAMPLE 4.28 In 2007, federal officials arrested Robert Alan Soloway, considered one of the world's most prolific spammers. Soloway, known as the "Spam King," had been using botnets (automated spamming networks—see Chapter 6) to send out hundreds of millions of unwanted e-mails. In 2008, Soloway pleaded guilty to mail fraud and failure to pay taxes.[27] •

---

24. 47 U.S.C. Section 230.

25. See, for example, *Fair Housing Council of San Fernando Valley v. Roommate.com, LLC,* 521 F.3d 1157 (9th Cir. 2008).

26. See, for example, *Chicago Lawyers' Committee for Civil Rights Under Law, Inc. v. Craigslist, Inc.,* 519 F.3d 666 (7th Cir. 2008); *Anthony v. Yahoo, Inc.,* 421 F.Supp.2d 1257 (N.D.Cal. 2006); and *Almeida v. Amazon.com, Inc.,* 456 F.3d 1316 (11th Cir. 2006).

27. See www.usdoj.gov/usao/waw/press/2008/mar/soloway.html.

The U.S. Safe Web Act After the CAN-SPAM Act prohibited false and deceptive e-mails originating in the United States, spamming from servers located in other nations increased. These cross-border spammers generally were able to escape detection and legal sanctions because the Federal Trade Commission (FTC) lacked the authority to investigate foreign spamming.

Congress sought to rectify the situation by enacting the U.S. Safe Web Act of 2006 (also known as the Undertaking Spam, Spyware, and Fraud Enforcement with Enforcers Beyond Borders Act). The act allows the FTC to cooperate and share information with foreign agencies in investigating and prosecuting those involved in Internet fraud and deception, including spamming and spyware. It also provides ISPs with a "safe harbor" (immunity from liability) for supplying information to the FTC concerning possible unfair or deceptive conduct in foreign jurisdictions.

There is some evidence that the U.S. Safe Web Act—in conjunction with the increased efforts of federal law enforcement and security experts—has been effective. The number of spam messages sent appeared to have decreased somewhat between 2010 and 2011, although spam still flows at a rate of 70 billion messages per day. The Federal Bureau of Investigation has worked with dozens of ISPs to stop some of the automated spamming networks and has also been actively cooperating with other nations, leading to the arrest of several major spammers located in the Netherlands and Russia.

Reviewing . . . Torts and Cyber Torts

Two sisters, Darla and Irene, are partners in an import business located in a small town in Rhode Island. Irene is also campaigning to be the mayor of their town. Both sisters travel to other countries to purchase the goods they sell at their retail store. Irene buys Indonesian goods, and Darla buys goods from Africa. After a tsunami destroys many of the towns in Indonesia to which Irene usually travels, she phones one of her contacts there and asks him to procure some items and ship them to her. He informs her that it will be impossible to buy these items now because the townspeople are being evacuated due to a water shortage. Irene is angry and tells her contact that if he cannot purchase the goods, he should simply take them without paying for them after the town has been evacuated. Darla overhears her sister's instructions and is outraged. They have a falling-out, and Darla decides that she no longer wishes to be in business with her sister. Using the information presented in the chapter, answer the following questions.

1. Suppose that Darla tells several of her friends about Irene's instructing her contact to take goods without paying for them after the tsunami. If Irene files a tort action against Darla alleging slander, will her suit be successful? Why or why not?
2. Now suppose that Irene wins the election and becomes the city's mayor. Darla then writes a letter to the editor of the local newspaper disclosing Irene's misconduct. If Irene accuses Darla of committing libel, what defenses could Darla assert?
3. If Irene accepts goods shipped from Indonesia that were wrongfully obtained, has she committed an intentional tort against property? Explain.
4. Suppose now that Darla was in the store one day with an elderly customer, Betty Green, who was looking for a graduation gift for her granddaughter. When Darla went to the counter to answer the phone, Green continued to wander around the store and eventually went through an open door into the stockroom, where she fell over some boxes on the floor and fractured her hip. Green files a negligence action against the store. Did Darla breach her duty of care? Why or why not?

DEBATE THIS Because of the often anonymous nature of the Internet, defamation has become an outdated legal concept. It's now too difficult to track down the person responsible for the defamatory statement.

BUSINESS APPLICATION

How Important Is Tort Liability to Business?*

Although there are more claims for breach of contract than for any other category of lawsuits, the dollar amount of damages awarded in tort actions is typically much higher than the awards in contract claims. Tort claims are also commonplace for businesses.

Because of the potential for large damages awards for intentional and unintentional acts, businesspersons should take preventive measures to avoid tort liability as much as possible. Remember that injured persons can bring most tort actions against a business as well as against another person. In fact, if given a choice, plaintiffs often sue a business rather than an individual because the business is more likely to have "deep pockets" (the ability to pay large damages awards). Moreover, sometimes businesses can be held liable for torts that individuals cannot.

The Extent of Business Negligence Liability

A business can be exposed to negligence liability in a wide variety of instances. Liability to business invitees is a clear example. A business that fails to warn invitees that its floor is slippery after a rainstorm, or that its parking lot is icy after snow, may be liable to an injured customer. Indeed, business owners can be liable for nearly any fall or other injury that occurs on business premises.

Even the hiring of employees can lead to negligence liability. For example, a business can be liable if it fails to do a criminal background check before hiring a person to supervise a child-care center when an investigation would have revealed that the person had previously been convicted of sexual assault. Failure to properly supervise or instruct employees can also lead to liability for a business.

Liability for Torts of Employees and Agents

A business can also be held liable for the negligence or intentional torts of its employees and agents. As you will learn in Chapters 23, 24, and 25, a business is liable for the torts committed by an employee who is acting within the scope of his or her employment or an agent who is acting with the authority of the business. Therefore, if a sales agent commits fraud while acting within the scope of her or his employment, the business will be held liable.

Checklist for Minimizing Business Tort Liability

1. *Constantly inspect the premises and look for areas where customers or employees might trip, slide, or fall. Take corrective action whenever you find a problem.*
2. *Train employees on the importance of periodic safety inspections and the procedures for reporting unsafe conditions.*
3. *Routinely maintain all business equipment (including vehicles).*
4. *Check with your liability insurance company for suggestions on improving the safety of your premises and operations.*
5. *Make sure that your general liability policy will adequately cover the potential exposure of the business, and reassess your coverage annually.*
6. *Review the background and qualifications of individuals you are considering hiring as employees or agents.*
7. *Investigate and review all negligence claims promptly. Most claims can be settled at low cost before a lawsuit is filed.*

*This *Business Application* is not meant to substitute for the services of an attorney who is licensed to practice law in your state.

Key Terms

actionable 99
actual malice 103
appropriation 105
assault 98
assumption of risk 115
battery 98
business invitee 112
business tort 95
causation in fact 113
comparative negligence 117
compensatory damages 96
contributory negligence 116
conversion 110
cyber tort 96
damages 96
defamation 100
defense 98
disparagement of property 110
dram shop act 118
duty of care 111
fraudulent misrepresentation 105
Good Samaritan statute 118
intentional tort 97
libel 100
malpractice 113
negligence 111
negligence *per se* 117
privilege 103
proximate cause 114
puffery 105
punitive damages 96
reasonable person standard 111
res ipsa loquitur 117
slander 100
slander of quality (trade libel) 110
slander of title 110
strict liability 118
tort 95
tortfeasor 97
trespass to land 108
trespass to personal property 109

Chapter Summary: Torts and Cyber Torts

Intentional Torts against Persons (See pages 97–107.)	1. *Assault and battery*—An assault is an unexcused and intentional act that causes another person to be apprehensive of immediate harm. A battery is an assault that results in physical contact. 2. *False imprisonment*—The intentional confinement or restraint of another person's movement without justification. 3. *Intentional infliction of emotional distress*—An extreme and outrageous act, intentionally committed, that results in severe emotional distress to another. 4. *Defamation (libel or slander)*—A false statement of fact, not made under privilege, that is communicated to a third person and that causes damage to a person's reputation. For public figures, the plaintiff must also prove actual malice. 5. *Invasion of the right to privacy*—Includes four acts: wrongful intrusion into a person's private activities; publication of information that places a person in a false light; disclosure of private facts that an ordinary person would find objectionable; and appropriation of identity, which involves the use of a person's name, likeness, or other identifying characteristic, without permission and for a commercial purpose. Most states have enacted statutes establishing appropriation of identity as the tort of *appropriation* or right of publicity. Courts differ on the degree of likeness required. 6. *Misrepresentation (fraud)*—A false representation made by one party, through misstatement of facts or through conduct, with the intention of deceiving another and on which the other reasonably relies to his or her detriment. Negligent misrepresentation occurs when a person supplies information without having a reasonable basis for believing its truthfulness. 7. *Abusive or frivolous litigation*—When a person initiates a lawsuit out of malice and without probable cause, and loses the suit, he or she can be sued for the tort of *malicious prosecution*. When a person uses a legal process against another improperly or to accomplish a purpose for which it was not designed, she or he can be sued for *abuse of process*. 8. *Wrongful interference*—The knowing, intentional interference by a third party with an enforceable contractual relationship or an established business relationship between other parties for the purpose of advancing the economic interests of the third party.
Intentional Torts against Property (See pages 107–110.)	1. *Trespass to land*—The invasion of another's real property without consent or privilege. 2. *Trespass to personal property*—Unlawfully damaging or interfering with the owner's right to use, possess, or enjoy her or his personal property. 3. *Conversion*—Wrongfully taking or using the personal property of another without permission. 4. *Disparagement of property*—Any economically injurious falsehood that is made about another's product or property. The term includes the torts of *slander of quality* and *slander of title*.
Unintentional Torts (Negligence) (See pages 111–118.)	1. *Negligence*—The careless performance of a legally required duty or the failure to perform a legally required act. Elements that must be proved are that a legal duty of care existed, that the defendant breached that duty, that the breach caused the plaintiff's injury, and that the plaintiff suffered a legally recognizable injury. 2. *Defenses to negligence*—The basic affirmative defenses in negligence cases are assumption of risk, superseding cause, and contributory or comparative negligence. 3. *Special negligence doctrines and statutes*— a. *Res ipsa loquitur*—A doctrine under which a plaintiff need not prove negligence on the part of the defendant because "the facts speak for themselves." b. Negligence *per se*—A type of negligence that may occur if a person violates a statute or an ordinance and the violation causes another to suffer the kind of injury that the statute or ordinance was intended to prevent. c. Special negligence statutes—State statutes that prescribe duties and responsibilities in certain circumstances. Violation of these statutes will impose civil liability. Dram shop acts and Good Samaritan statutes are examples of special negligence statutes.
Strict Liability (See pages 118–119.)	Under the doctrine of strict liability, a person may be held liable, regardless of the degree of care exercised, for damages or injuries caused by her or his product or activity. Strict liability includes liability for harms caused by abnormally dangerous activities, by dangerous animals, and by defective products (product liability).
Cyber Torts (See pages 119–121.)	General tort principles are being extended to cover cyber torts, or torts that occur in cyberspace, such as online defamation. Federal and state statutes may also apply to certain forms of cyber torts. For example, under the federal Communications Decency Act of 1996, Internet service providers (ISPs) are not liable for defamatory messages posted by their subscribers.

ExamPrep

ISSUE SPOTTERS

1. Jana leaves her truck's motor running while she enters a Kwik-Pik Store. The truck's transmission engages and the vehicle crashes into a gas pump, starting a fire that spreads to a warehouse on the next block. The warehouse collapses, causing its billboard to fall and injure Lou, a bystander. Can Lou recover from Jana? Why or why not? **(See pages 111–114.)**
2. A water pipe bursts, flooding a Metal Fabrication Company utility room and tripping the circuit breakers on a panel in the room. Metal Fabrication contacts Nouri, a licensed electrician with five years' experience, to check the damage and turn the breakers back on. Without testing for short circuits, which Nouri knows that he should do, he tries to switch on a breaker. He is electrocuted, and his wife sues Metal Fabrication for damages, alleging negligence. What might the firm successfully claim in defense? **(See pages 112, 115–117.)**

—Check your answers to the Issue Spotters against the answers provided in Appendix E at the end of this text.

BEFORE THE TEST

Go to www.cengagebrain.com, enter the ISBN 9781133273561, and click on "Find" to locate this textbook's Web site. Then, click on "Access Now" under "Study Tools," and select Chapter 4 at the top. There, you will find a Practice Quiz that you can take to assess your mastery of the concepts in this chapter, as well as Flashcards, a Glossary of important terms, and Video Questions (when assigned).

For Review

Answers to the even-numbered questions in this For Review section can be found in Appendix F at the end of this text.

1. What is the purpose of tort law? What types of damages are available in tort lawsuits?
2. What are two basic categories of torts?
3. What is defamation? Name two types of defamation.
4. Identify the four elements of negligence.
5. What is meant by strict liability? In what circumstances is strict liability applied?

Business Scenarios and Case Problems

4–1 Liability to Business Invitees. Kim went to Ling's Market to pick up a few items for dinner. It was a stormy day, and the wind had blown water through the market's door each time it opened. As Kim entered through the door, she slipped and fell in the rainwater that had accumulated on the floor. The manager knew of the weather conditions but had not posted any sign to warn customers of the water hazard. Kim injured her back as a result of the fall and sued Ling's for damages. Can Ling's be held liable for negligence? Discuss. **(See page 112.)**

4–2 Question with Sample Answer—Negligence. Shannon's physician gives her some pain medication and tells her not to drive after taking it because the medication induces drowsiness. In spite of the doctor's warning, Shannon decides to drive to the store while on the medication. Owing to her lack of alertness, she fails to stop at a traffic light and crashes into another vehicle, causing a passenger in that vehicle to be injured. Is Shannon liable for the tort of negligence? Explain. **(See pages 113–114.)**

—For a sample answer to Question 4–2, go to Appendix G at the end of this text.

4–3 Spotlight on Intentional Torts—Defamation. Sharon Yeagle was an assistant to the vice president of student affairs at Virginia Polytechnic Institute and State University (Virginia Tech). As part of her duties, Yeagle helped students participate in the Governor's Fellows Program. The *Collegiate Times,* Virginia Tech's student newspaper, published an article about the university's success in placing students in the program. The article's text surrounded a block quotation attributed to Yeagle with the phrase "Director of Butt Licking" under her name. Yeagle sued the *Collegiate Times* for defamation. She argued that the phrase implied the commission of sodomy and was therefore actionable. What is *Collegiate Times*'s defense to this claim? [*Yeagle v. Collegiate Times,* 497 S.E.2d 136 (Va. 1998)] **(See page 100.)**

4–4 Case Problem with Sample Answer—Libel and Invasion of Privacy. The *Northwest Herald,* a newspaper, received regular e-mail reports from police departments about criminal arrests. When it received a report that Caroline Eubanks had been charged with theft, the *Herald* published the information. Later, the police sent an e-mail that retracted the report about Eubanks. The *Herald* published a correction.

Eubanks filed a suit against the paper for libel and invasion of privacy. Does Eubanks have a good case for either tort? Why or why not? [*Eubanks v. Northwest Herald Newspapers,* 397 Ill. App.3d 746, 922 N.E.2d 1196 (2010)] **(See pages 102–104.)**

—For a sample answer to Problem 4–4, go to Appendix H at the end of this text.

4–5 Proximate Cause. Galen Stoller was killed at a railroad crossing when an Amtrak train hit his car. The crossing was marked with a stop sign and a railroad-crossing symbol but there were no flashing lights. Galen's parents filed a suit against National Railroad Passenger Corporation (Amtrak) and Burlington Northern & Santa Fe Railroad Corp alleging negligence in the design and maintenance of the crossing. The defendants argued that Galen had not stopped at the stop sign. Was Amtrak negligent? What was the proximate cause of the accident? [*Henderson v. National Railroad Passenger Corp.,* ___ F.3d ___ (10th Cir. 2011)] **(See page 114.)**

4–6 Business Torts. Medtronic, Inc., is a medical technology company that competes for customers with St. Jude Medical S.C., Inc. James Hughes worked for Medtronic as a sales manager. His contract prohibited him from working for a competitor for one year after leaving Medtronic. Hughes sought a position as a sales director for St. Jude. St. Jude told Hughes that his contract with Medtronic was unenforceable and offered him a job. Hughes accepted. Medtronic filed a suit, alleging wrongful interference. Which type of interference was most likely the basis for this suit? Did it occur here? Explain. [*Medtronic, Inc. v. Hughes,* __ N.W.2d __ (Minn.App. 2011)] **(See pages 106–107.)**

4–7 Intentional Infliction of Emotional Distress. While living in her home country of Tanzania, Sophia Kiwanuka signed an employment contract with Anne Margareth Bakilana, a Tanzanian living in Washington, D.C. Kiwanuka traveled to the United States to work as a babysitter and maid in Bakilana's house. When Kiwanuka arrived, Bakilana confiscated her passport, held her in isolation, and forced her to work long hours under threat of having her deported. Kiwanuka worked seven days a week without breaks and was subjected to regular verbal and psychological abuse by Bakilana. Kiwanuka filed a complaint against Bakilana for intentional infliction of emotional distress, among other claims. Bakilana argued that Kiwanuka's complaint should be dismissed because the allegations were insufficient to show outrageous intentional conduct that resulted in severe emotional distress. If you were the judge, in whose favor would you rule? Why? [*Kiwanuka v. Bakilana,* 2012 WL 593065 (D.D.C. 2012)] **(See pages 99–100.)**

4–8 A Question of Ethics—Wrongful Interference. White Plains Coat & Apron Co. and Cintas Corp. are competitors. White Plains had five-year exclusive contracts with some of its customers. As a result of Cintas's soliciting of business, dozens of White Plains' customers breached their contracts and entered into rental agreements with Cintas. White Plains filed a suit against Cintas, alleging wrongful interference. [*White Plains Coat & Apron Co. v. Cintas Corp.,* 8 N.Y.3d 422, 867 N.E.2d 381 (2007)] **(See pages 106–107.)**

1. What are the two policies at odds in wrongful interference cases? When there is an existing contract, which of these interests should be accorded priority? Why?
2. Is a general interest in soliciting business for profit a sufficient defense to a claim of wrongful interference with a contractual relationship? What do you think? Why?

Critical Thinking and Writing Assignments

4–9 Business Law Critical Thinking Group Assignment. Assume that your business partner, Gayanne Zokhrabov, was at the train station when a train, traveling at more than 70 mph, hit eighteen-year-old Hiroyuki Joho, who was running across the tracks. The impact killed Joho and flung parts of his body about 100 feet into the air. Some of them landed on Gayanne and knocked her to the ground. As a result, she hurt her shoulder and broke her leg and wrist. She has not been able to work and has hired an attorney to file a negligence lawsuit against Joho's estate. (The attorney believes that Gayanne cannot successfully sue Amtrak because of a lack of proximate cause—it was not reasonably foreseeable that Joho would run across the tracks and his body parts would cause injuries to others.)

1. One group should analyze whether Joho had a *duty* to Gayanne and whether his decision to run in front of the train was a *breach* of that duty because she was in the zone of danger.
2. A second group should consider proximate cause: Was it reasonably foreseeable that a train accident could send Joho's body parts into crowds of waiting passengers?
3. A third group should discuss whether it is ethical to sue the dead man's estate over flying body parts. Further, what impact might the case and the publicity surrounding it have on you and your partner's business reputation?

4–10 Case Analysis Question. Go to Appendix I at the end of this text and examine the excerpt of Case No. 1, *Lott v. Levitt.* Review and then brief the case, making sure that your brief answers the following questions.

1. **Issue:** At the center of the dispute in this case was a distinction between what types of speech?
2. **Rule of Law:** What difference does it make what type of speech a particular statement is?
3. **Applying the Rule of Law:** How does a court determine to which type of speech a certain statement belongs?
4. **Conclusion:** In this case, how was the speech at issue classified, and why? What effect did that decision have on the parties' suit?

5 CHAPTER

Intellectual Property and Internet Law

CHAPTER OUTLINE

- Trademarks and Related Property
- Cyber Marks
- Patents
- Copyrights
- Trade Secrets
- International Protection for Intellectual Property

LEARNING OBJECTIVES

The five learning objectives below are designed to help improve your understanding of the chapter. After reading this chapter, you should be able to answer the following questions:

1 What is intellectual property?

2 Why is the protection of trademarks important?

3 How does the law protect patents?

4 What laws protect authors' rights in the works they create?

5 What are trade secrets, and what laws offer protection for this form of intellectual property?

(Login/Shutterstock.com)

"The Internet is just a world passing around notes in a classroom."
—Jon Stewart, 1962–present (American comedian and host of *The Daily Show*)

Intellectual Property Property resulting from intellectual and creative processes.

LEARNING OBJECTIVE 1
What is intellectual property?

Intellectual property is any property resulting from intellectual, creative processes—the products of an individual's mind. Although it is an abstract term for an abstract concept, intellectual property is nonetheless familiar to almost everyone. The information contained in books and computer files is intellectual property. The apps for your iPhone and iPad, the movies you watch, and the music you listen to are all forms of intellectual property. Although the need to protect creative works was first recognized in Article I, Section 8, of the U.S. Constitution (see Appendix B), statutory protection of these rights began in the 1940s and continues to evolve to meet the needs of modern society.

Of significant concern to businesspersons is the need to protect their rights in intellectual property, which may be more valuable than their physical property, such as machines and buildings. Consider, for instance, the importance of intellectual property rights to technology companies, such as Apple, Inc., the maker of the iPhone and iPad. In today's world, intellectual property rights can be a company's most valuable assets, which is why

Apple sued rival Samsung Electronics Company in 2011. Apple claimed that Samsung's Galaxy line of mobile phones and tablets (those that run Google's Android software) copy the look, design, and user interface of Apple's iPhone and iPad. Although Apple is one of Samsung's biggest customers and buys many of its components from Samsung, Apple also needs to protect its iPhone and iPad revenues from competing Android products. You will read about the verdict in this case on pages 139 and 140.

In today's global economy, however, protecting intellectual property in one country is no longer sufficient, and the United States is participating in various international agreements to secure ownership rights in intellectual property in other countries. Because the Internet allows the world to "pass around notes" so quickly, as Jon Stewart joked in the chapter-opening quotation on the facing page, protecting these rights in today's online environment has proved particularly challenging.

Trademarks and Related Property

Trademark A distinctive word, symbol, or design that identifies the manufacturer as the source of particular goods and distinguishes its products from those made or sold by others.

A **trademark** is a distinctive word, symbol, sound, or design that identifies the manufacturer as the source of particular goods and distinguishes its products from those made or sold by others. At common law, the person who used a symbol or mark to identify a business or product was protected in the use of that trademark. Clearly, by using another's trademark, a business could lead consumers to believe that its goods were made by the other business. The law seeks to avoid this kind of confusion. (For information on how companies use trademarks and service marks, see this chapter's *Linking Business Law to Marketing* feature on page 151.)

LEARNING OBJECTIVE 2

Why is the protection of trademarks important?

In the following *Classic Case* concerning Coca-Cola, the defendants argued that the Coca-Cola trademark was not entitled to protection under the law because the term did not accurately represent the product.

Classic Case 5.1

Coca-Cola Co. v. Koke Co. of America

Supreme Court of the United States,
254 U.S. 143, 41 S.Ct. 113, 65 L.Ed. 189 (1920).
www.findlaw.com/casecode/supreme.html[a]

(Rob Wilson / Shutterstock.com)

How is Coca-Cola protected?

COMPANY PROFILE *John Pemberton, an Atlanta pharmacist, invented a caramel-colored, carbonated soft drink in 1886. His bookkeeper, Frank Robinson, named the beverage Coca-Cola after two of the ingredients, coca leaves and kola nuts. Asa Candler bought the Coca-Cola Company in 1891 and, within seven years, had made the soft drink available throughout the United States and in parts of Canada and Mexico as well. Candler continued to sell Coke aggressively and to open up new markets, reaching Europe before 1910. In doing so, however, he attracted numerous competitors, some of whom tried to capitalize directly on the Coke name.*

FACTS The Coca-Cola Company brought an action in a federal district court to enjoin (prevent) other beverage companies from using the words *Koke* and *Dope* for their products. The defendants contended that the Coca-Cola trademark was a fraudulent representation and that Coca-Cola was therefore not entitled to any help from the courts. By using the Coca-Cola name, the defendants alleged, the Coca-Cola Company represented that the beverage contained cocaine (from coca leaves). The district court granted the injunction, but the federal appellate court reversed. The

a. This is the "US Supreme Court Opinions" page within the Web site of the "FindLaw Internet Legal Resources" database. This page provides several options for accessing an opinion. Because you know the citation for this case, you can go to the "Citation Search" box, type in the appropriate volume and page numbers for the *United States Reports* ("254" and "143," respectively, for the *Coca-Cola* case), and click on "Search."

Classic Case 5.1—Continues next page ➡

Classic Case 5.1—Continued

Coca-Cola Company appealed to the United States Supreme Court.

ISSUE Did the marketing of products called Koke and Dope by the Koke Company of America and other firms constitute an infringement on Coca-Cola's trademark?

DECISION Yes for Koke, but no for Dope. The United States Supreme Court enjoined the competing beverage companies from calling their products Koke but did not prevent them from calling their products Dope.

REASON The Court noted that before 1900 the Coca-Cola beverage had contained a small amount of cocaine. This ingredient had been deleted from the formula by 1906 at the latest, however, and the Coca-Cola Company had advertised to the public that no cocaine was present in its drink. Coca-Cola was a widely popular drink "to be had at almost any soda fountain." Because of the public's widespread familiarity with Coca-Cola, the retention of the name (referring to coca leaves and kola nuts) was not misleading: "Coca-Cola probably means to most persons the plaintiff's familiar product to be had everywhere rather than a compound of particular substances." The name *Coke* was found to be so common a term for the trademarked product Coca-Cola that the defendants' use of the similar-sounding *Koke* as a name for their beverages was disallowed. The Court could find no reason to restrain the defendants from using the name *Dope,* however.

WHAT IF THE FACTS WERE DIFFERENT? *Suppose that Coca-Cola had been trying to make the public believe that its product contained cocaine. Would the result in the case likely have been different? Explain your answer.*

IMPACT OF THIS CASE ON TODAY'S LAW *In this early case, the United States Supreme Court made it clear that trademarks and trade names (and nicknames for those marks and names, such as "Coke" for "Coca-Cola") that are in common use receive protection under the common law. This holding is significant historically because it is the predecessor to the federal statute later passed to protect trademark rights (the Lanham Act of 1946, discussed below).*

Statutory Protection of Trademarks

Statutory protection of trademarks and related property is provided at the federal level by the Lanham Act of 1946.[1] The Lanham Act was enacted in part to protect manufacturers from losing business to rival companies that used confusingly similar trademarks. The act incorporates the common law of trademarks and provides remedies for owners of trademarks who wish to enforce their claims in federal court. Many states also have trademark statutes.

KNOW THIS

Trademark dilution laws protect the owners of distinctive marks from unauthorized uses even when the defendant's use involves noncompeting goods or is unlikely to cause confusion.

Trademark Dilution

Before 1995, federal trademark law prohibited only the unauthorized use of the same mark on competing—or on noncompeting but "related"—goods or services. Protection was given only when the unauthorized use would likely confuse consumers as to the origin of those goods and services. In 1995, Congress amended the Lanham Act by passing the Federal Trademark Dilution Act,[2] which allowed trademark owners to bring a suit in federal court for trademark *dilution*.

Trademark dilution laws protect "distinctive" or "famous" trademarks (such as Rolls Royce, McDonald's, Dell, and Apple) from certain unauthorized uses even when the use is on noncompeting goods or is unlikely to confuse. More than half of the states have also enacted trademark dilution laws.

Use of a Similar Mark May Constitute Trademark Dilution

A famous mark may be diluted not only by the use of an *identical* mark but also by the use of

1. 15 U.S.C. Sections 1051–1128.
2. 15 U.S.C. Section 1125.

a *similar* mark, provided that it reduces the value of the famous mark.[3] **CASE EXAMPLE 5.1** A woman opened a coffee shop under the name "Sambuck's Coffeehouse" in Astoria, Oregon, even though she knew that "Starbucks" was one of the largest coffee chains in the nation. When Starbucks Corporation filed a dilution lawsuit, the federal court ruled that use of the "Sambuck's" mark constituted trademark dilution because it created confusion for consumers. Not only was there a "high degree" of similarity between the marks, but also both companies provided coffee-related services through "stand-alone" retail stores. Therefore, the use of the similar mark (Sambuck's) reduced the value of the famous mark (Starbucks).[4] •

(AP Photo/The Daily Astorian, Kara Hansen)

When an Oregon woman opened this store, its sign read "Sambuck's." On what ground did Starbuck's sue her so that she had to change the store's name?

Trademark Registration

Trademarks may be registered with the state or with the federal government. To register for protection under federal trademark law, a person must file an application with the U.S. Patent and Trademark Office in Washington, D.C. A mark can be registered (1) if it is currently in commerce or (2) if the applicant intends to put the mark into commerce within six months.

In special circumstances, the six-month period can be extended by thirty months, giving the applicant a total of three years from the date of notice of trademark approval to make use of the mark and to file the required use statement. Registration is postponed until the mark is actually used. Nonetheless, during this waiting period, the applicant's trademark is protected against any third party who has neither used the mark previously nor filed an application for it. Registration is renewable between the fifth and sixth years after the initial registration and every ten years thereafter (every twenty years for trademarks registered before 1990).

Trademark Infringement

KNOW THIS

To prove trademark infringement, the trademark owner must show that the other party's use of the mark created a likelihood of confusion about the origin of that party's goods or services.

Registration of a trademark with the U.S. Patent and Trademark Office gives notice on a nationwide basis that the trademark belongs exclusively to the registrant. The registrant is also allowed to use the symbol ® to indicate that the mark has been registered. Whenever someone else uses that trademark in its entirety or copies it to a substantial degree, intentionally or unintentionally, the trademark has been *infringed* (used without authorization).

When a trademark has been infringed, the owner has a cause of action against the infringer. To succeed in a lawsuit for trademark infringement, the owner must show that the defendant's use of the mark created a likelihood of confusion about the origin of the defendant's goods or services. The owner need not prove that the infringer acted intentionally or that the trademark was registered (although registration does provide proof of the date of inception of the trademark's use). See this chapter's *Adapting the Law to the Online Environment* feature on the following page for a discussion of how some companies are turning first to Internet forums, before they resort to costly trademark litigation.

The remedy most commonly granted for trademark infringement is an *injunction* to prevent further infringement. Under the Lanham Act, a trademark owner that successfully proves infringement can recover actual damages, plus the profits that the infringer wrongfully received from the unauthorized use of the mark. A court can also order the destruction of any goods bearing the unauthorized trademark. In some situations, the trademark owner may also be able to recover attorneys' fees.

---

3. See *Moseley v. V Secret Catalogue, Inc.*, 537 U.S. 418, 123 S.Ct. 1115, 155 L.Ed.2d 1 (2003).

4. *Starbucks Corp. v. Lundberg*, 2005 WL 3183858 (D.Or. 2005).

Distinctiveness of the Mark

A central objective of the Lanham Act is to reduce the likelihood that consumers will be confused by similar marks. For that reason, only those trademarks that are deemed sufficiently distinctive from all competing trademarks will be protected. (In addition, a trademark may not be derogatory, as the *Law, Diversity, and Business: Managerial Implications* feature on the facing page explains.)

Strong Marks

Fanciful, arbitrary, or suggestive trademarks are generally considered to be the most distinctive (strongest) trademarks. Because they are normally taken from outside the context of the particular product, strong marks provide the best means of distinguishing one product from another. Fanciful trademarks include invented words, such as *Xerox* for one manufacturer's copiers and *Google* for search engines. Arbitrary trademarks use common words that would not ordinarily be associated with the product, such as *Dutch Boy* as a name for paint.

A single letter used in a particular style can be an arbitrary trademark. **CASE EXAMPLE 5.2** Sports entertainment company ESPN, Inc., sued Quiksilver, Inc., a maker of youth-oriented clothing, alleging trademark infringement. ESPN claimed that

ADAPTING THE LAW TO THE ONLINE ENVIRONMENT

USING ONLINE SHAME IN TRADEMARK DISPUTES

Claims of trademark infringement have risen 5 percent each year for the past several years and will exceed four thousand in 2013. Trademark litigation is costly and can drag on for years. Small businesses, particularly start-ups, typically do not have the resources to engage in such lengthy litigation. Yet claims of infringement, even when they seem dubious, must be addressed. Some entrepreneurs are finding that online publicity and the shame it can bring are an effective alternative to going to federal court to resolve trademark disputes.

Can a Company Trademark the Letter "K"?

When Phil Michaelson created the Web site KeepRecipes.com to provide an Internet cookbook where people could collect and share recipes, he never thought the word "Keep" and the letter "K" could be someone's trademarks. On his site, users click on "K," short for "Keep," when they want to save the instructions for a recipe. Nevertheless, AdKeeper, a New York–based service company, immediately sent Michaelson a cease-and-desist letter. AdKeeper claimed that the use of "K" and "Keep," as well as the Web site name KeepRecipes.com, constituted "blatant trademark infringement."

Online Publicity Provides a Solution

Michaelson did not have the resources to engage in a prolonged legal battle with AdKeeper, even though he thought its claims had no merit. Instead, he turned to Chillingeffects.org, a Web site created by several universities to foster lawful online activity. Soon after he described his problem and posted the cease-and-desist letter, several lawyers who deal with Web site issues offered to represent him in his trademark dispute at no charge.

Using Social Media

Other small entrepreneurs facing lawsuits are turning to social media, especially Facebook and Twitter, where large companies' threats to sue small companies for trademark infringement are generally met with displeasure. When the restaurant company Chick-fil-A, Inc., threatened Vermont T-shirt manufacturer Bo Muller-Moore with a lawsuit, he created a Facebook page. Chick-fil-A claimed that Muller-Moore had infringed its trademarked slogan "Eat Mor Chikin" when he used the slogan "Eat More Kale" on his T-shirts—even though Muller-Moore used correct spelling and kale and chicken would seem to be rather different foods. Several thousand supporters regularly look at Muller-Moore's Facebook page and have donated $10,000 for his defense.

Critical Thinking

As social media becomes ever more pervasive in our lives, what do you expect to occur with respect to trademark disputes?

LAW, DIVERSITY, AND BUSINESS: MANAGERIAL IMPLICATIONS

DEROGATORY TRADEMARKS

When determining whether a trademark is sufficiently distinctive to warrant protection, the U.S. Patent and Trademark Office (USPTO) also considers whether the mark might be offensive to any of the diverse groups in our society. Under the Lanham Act, the USPTO must deny registration to trademarks that "may disparage or falsely suggest a connection with persons, living or dead, institutions, beliefs, or national symbols, or bring them into contempt, or derision."[a]

A Disparaging Mark Can Be Costly Sometimes, the USPTO fails to recognize a potentially disparaging mark and approves its registration. Discovering too late that it has chosen the wrong trademark can be very expensive for a business. Biggby Coffee, one of the nation's fastest-growing coffee franchises, spent nearly $1 million to change its name from Beaner's Coffee to Biggby Coffee after it became aware that the word *beaners* is sometimes used as a disparaging term for Hispanic Americans.

Names of Sports Teams One of the most controversial issues involving trademarks has to do with the use of American Indian names and mascots for sports teams. Many Native Americans find the use of these names highly offensive and demeaning. In 1992, seven Native Americans petitioned the Trademark Trial and Appeal Board, which hears appeals of USPTO decisions, and asked it to cancel six trademarks of the Washington Redskins football team that had been registered since the late 1960s and 1970s. The board agreed that the use of the term *redskins* was offensive and canceled the marks. The team's owner appealed to a federal court, setting off a long-running legal battle that did not end until 2009 when a federal appellate court found that the Native Americans had waited too long to bring their suit. The United States Supreme Court subsequently declined to hear the case.[b]

Native Americans were more successful in their long struggle to end the use of the name *Fighting Sioux* for the University of North Dakota's teams. The National Collegiate Athletic Association (NCAA) had put the University of North Dakota (UND) on a list of schools with names and mascots that it found objectionable. All of the other schools on the list either changed their teams' names or obtained permission from Native Americans to keep them. After several months of debate and controversy, in June 2012, the citizens of North Dakota overwhelming voted to get rid of the UND's team name, and the state's board of higher education officially voted to remove it as well.

Business Implications *As society becomes more sensitive to diversity issues, businesses can expect that their trademarks will be subject to increased scrutiny. When choosing a trademark, logo, or motto, a business must consider the diverse groups in our society.*

a. 15 U.S.C. Section 1052(a).

b. *Pro-Football Inc. v. Harjo*, 565 F.3d 880 (2009; *cert.* denied, *Harjo v. Pro-Football, Inc.*, 130 S. Ct. 631 (2009).

Quiksilver had used on its clothing the stylized "X" mark that ESPN uses in connection with the "X Games" (competitions in extreme action sports). Quiksilver filed counterclaims for trademark infringement and dilution, arguing that it had a long history of using the stylized X on its products. ESPN created the X Games in the mid-1990s, and Quiksilver has used the X mark since 1994. ESPN asked the court to dismiss Quiksilver's counterclaims, but the court refused, holding that the X on Quiksilver's clothing was clearly an arbitrary mark. The court found that the two Xs were "similar enough that a consumer might well confuse them."[5]

Suggestive Trademarks Suggestive trademarks bring to mind something about a product without describing the product directly. For instance, "Dairy Queen" suggests an association between its products and milk, but it does not directly describe ice cream. "Blu-ray" is a suggestive mark that is associated with the high-quality, high-definition video contained on a particular optical data storage disc. Although blue-violet lasers are used to read blu-ray discs, the term *blu-ray* does not directly describe the disc.

5. *ESPN, Inc. v. Quiksilver, Inc.*, 586 F.Supp.2d 219 (S.D.N.Y. 2008).

Secondary Meaning

Descriptive terms, geographic terms, and personal names are not inherently distinctive and do not receive protection under the law *until* they acquire a secondary meaning. **CASE EXAMPLE 5.3** Frosty Treats, Inc., sells frozen desserts out of ice cream trucks. The video game series Twisted Metal depicted an ice cream truck with a clown character on it that was similar to the clowns on Frosty Treats' trucks. In the last game of the series, the truck bears the label "Frosty Treats." Frosty Treats sued for trademark infringement, but the court held that "Frosty Treats" is a descriptive term that is not protected by trademark law unless it has acquired a secondary meaning. To establish secondary meaning, Frosty Treats would have to show that the public recognizes its trademark and associates it with a single source. Because Frosty Treats failed to do so, the court entered a judgment in favor of the video game producer.[6] •

A secondary meaning arises when customers begin to associate a specific term or phrase, such as "London Fog," with specific trademarked items (coats with "London Fog" labels) made by a particular company. Whether a secondary meaning becomes attached to a term or name usually depends on how extensively the product is advertised, the market for the product, the number of sales, and other factors. Once a secondary meaning is attached to a term or name, a trademark is considered distinctive and is protected. Even a color can qualify for trademark protection, such as the color schemes used by four state university sports teams, including Ohio State University and Louisiana State University.[7]

Generic Terms

Generic terms are terms that refer to an entire class of products, such as *bicycle* and *computer.* Generic terms receive no protection, even if they acquire secondary meanings. A particularly thorny problem for a business arises when its trademark acquires generic use. For instance, *aspirin* and *thermos* were originally trademarked products, but today the words are used generically. Other trademarks that have acquired generic use include *escalator, trampoline, raisin bran, dry ice, lanolin, linoleum, nylon,* and *cornflakes.*[8]

Service, Certification, and Collective Marks

Service Mark A trademark that is used to distinguish the services (rather than the products) of one person or company from those of another.

Certification Mark A mark used by one or more persons, other than the owner, to certify the region, materials, mode of manufacture, quality, or other characteristic of specific goods or services.

Collective Mark A mark used by members of a cooperative, association, union, or other organization to certify the region, materials, mode of manufacture, quality, or other characteristic of specific goods or services.

A **service mark** is essentially a trademark that is used to distinguish the *services* (rather than the products) of one person or company from those of another. For instance, each airline has a particular mark or symbol associated with its name. Titles and character names used in radio and television are frequently registered as service marks.

Other marks protected by law include certification marks and collective marks. A **certification mark** is used by one or more persons, other than the owner, to certify the region, materials, mode of manufacture, quality, or other characteristic of specific goods or services. Certification marks include such marks as "Good Housekeeping Seal of Approval" and "UL Tested."

When used by members of a cooperative, association, labor union, or other organization, a certification mark is referred to as a **collective mark.** **EXAMPLE 5.4** Collective marks appear at the end of a movie's credits to indicate the various associations and organizations that participated in making the movie. The labor union marks found on the tags of certain products are also collective marks. •

Trade Dress

Trade Dress The image and overall appearance ("look and feel") of a product that is protected by trademark law.

The term **trade dress** refers to the image and overall appearance of a product. Trade dress is a broad concept that can include all or part of the total image or overall impression created by a product or its packaging. **EXAMPLE 5.5** The distinctive decor, menu, and style of

6. *Frosty Treats, Inc. v. Sony Computer Entertainment America, Inc.*, 426 F.3d 1001 (8th Cir. 2005).
7. *Board of Supervisors of LA State University v. Smack Apparel Co.*, 438 F.Supp.2d 653 (2006). See also *Qualitex Co. v. Jacobson Products Co.*, 514 U.S. 159, 115 S.Ct. 1300, 131 L.Ed.2d 248 (1995).
8. See, for example, *Boston Duck Tours, LP v. Super Duck Tours, LLC*, 531 F.3d 1 (1st Cir. 2008).

service of a particular restaurant may be regarded as the restaurant's trade dress. Similarly, trade dress can include the layout and appearance of a mail-order catalogue, the use of a lighthouse as part of a golf hole, the fish shape of a cracker, or the G-shaped design of a Gucci watch. •

Basically, trade dress is subject to the same protection as trademarks. In cases involving trade dress infringement, as in trademark infringement cases, a major consideration is whether consumers are likely to be confused by the allegedly infringing use.

Counterfeit Goods

Counterfeit goods copy or otherwise imitate trademarked goods but are not genuine. The importation of goods bearing counterfeit (fake) trademarks poses a growing problem for U.S. businesses, consumers, and law enforcement. It is estimated that nearly 7 percent of the goods imported into the United States are counterfeit. In addition to having negative financial effects on legitimate businesses, sales of certain counterfeit goods, such as pharmaceuticals and nutritional supplements, can present serious public health risks.

Although Congress has enacted statutes against counterfeit goods (discussed next), the United States cannot prosecute foreign counterfeiters because our national laws do not apply to them. Instead, one effective tool that U.S. officials are using to combat online sales of counterfeit goods is to obtain a court order to close down the domain names of Web sites that sell such goods. **EXAMPLE 5.6** In 2011, U.S. agents shut down 150 domain names on the Monday after Thanksgiving ("Cyber Monday," the online version of "Black Friday," the day after Thanksgiving when the holiday shopping season begins). Although the criminal enterprises may continue selling counterfeit versions of brand-name products under different domain names, shutting down the Web sites, particularly on key shopping days, prevents some counterfeit goods from entering the United States. •

Stop Counterfeiting in Manufactured Goods Act

In 2006, Congress enacted the Stop Counterfeiting in Manufactured Goods Act[9] (SCMGA) to combat counterfeit goods. The act made it a crime to intentionally traffic in, or attempt to traffic in,

9. Pub. L. No. 109-181 (2006), which amended 18 U.S.C. Sections 2318–2320.

A federal customs officer displays about $4 million of counterfeit goods that were seized in the Los Angeles area. Is it possible to control the foreign sources of such merchandise?

(AP Photo/Nick Ut)

counterfeit goods or services, or to knowingly use a counterfeit mark on or in connection with goods or services. Before this act, the law did not prohibit the creation or shipment of counterfeit labels that were not attached to products.[10] Therefore, counterfeiters would make labels and packaging bearing a fake trademark, ship the labels to another location, and then affix them to inferior products to deceive buyers. The SCMGA closed this loophole by making it a crime to traffic in counterfeit labels, stickers, packaging, and the like, whether or not they are attached to goods.

Penalties for Counterfeiting

Persons found guilty of violating the SCMGA may be fined up to $2 million or imprisoned for up to ten years (or more if they are repeat offenders). If a court finds that the statute was violated, it must order the defendant to forfeit the counterfeit products (which are then destroyed), as well as any property used in the commission of the crime. The defendant must also pay restitution to the trademark holder or victim in an amount equal to the victim's actual loss.

CASE EXAMPLE 5.7 Wajdi Beydoun pleaded guilty to conspiring to import cigarette-rolling papers from Mexico that were falsely marked as "Zig-Zags" and sell them in the United States. The defendant was sentenced to prison and ordered to pay $566,267 in restitution. On appeal, the court affirmed the prison sentence but ordered the trial court to reduce the amount of restitution because it exceeded the actual loss suffered by the legitimate sellers of Zig-Zag rolling papers.[11] ●

Trade Names

Trade Name A name that a business uses to identify itself and its brand. A trade name is directly related to a business's reputation and goodwill and is protected under trademark law.

Trademarks apply to *products*. The term **trade name** is used to indicate part or all of a *business's name,* whether the business is a sole proprietorship, a partnership, or a corporation. Generally, a trade name is directly related to a business and its goodwill. Trade names may be protected as trademarks if the trade name is the same as the company's trademarked product—for example, Coca-Cola. Unless it is also used as a trademark or service mark, a trade name cannot be registered with the federal government.

Trade names are protected under the common law, however. As with trademarks, words must be unusual or fancifully used if they are to be protected as trade names. For instance, the courts held that the word *Safeway* was sufficiently fanciful to obtain protection as a trade name for a grocery chain.

Licensing

License An agreement by the owner of intellectual property to permit another to use a trademark, copyright, patent, or trade secret for certain limited purposes.

One way to make use of another's trademark or other form of intellectual property, while avoiding litigation, is to obtain a license to do so. A **license** in this context is an agreement permitting the use of a trademark, copyright, patent, or trade secret for certain limited purposes. The party that owns the intellectual property rights and issues the license is the *licensor,* and the party obtaining the license is the *licensee.*

A license grants only the rights expressly described in the license agreement. A licensor might, for example, allow the licensee to use the trademark as part of its company name, or as part of its domain name, but not otherwise use the mark on any products or services. Disputes frequently arise over licensing agreements, particularly when the license involves Internet uses.

Typically, license agreements are very detailed and should be carefully drafted. **CASE EXAMPLE 5.8** George V Restauration S.A. and others owned and operated the Buddha Bar Paris, a restaurant with an Asian theme in Paris, France. In 2005, one of the owners

10. See, for example, *Commonwealth v. Crespo,* 884 A.2d 960 (Pa. 2005).

11. *United States v. Beydoun,* 469 F.3d 102 (5th Cir. 2006).

allowed Little Rest Twelve, Inc., to use the Buddha Bar trademark and its associated concept in New York City under the name *Buddha Bar NYC*. Little Rest paid royalties for its use of the Buddha Bar mark and advertised Buddha Bar NYC's affiliation with Buddha Bar Paris, a connection also noted on its Web site and in the media. When a dispute arose, the owners of Buddha Bar Paris withdrew their permission for Buddha Bar NYC's use of their mark, but Little Rest continued to use it. The owners of the mark filed a suit in a New York state court against Little Rest, and ultimately a state appellate court granted an injunction preventing Little Rest from using the mark.[12]

PREVENTING LEGAL DISPUTES

Consult with an attorney before signing any licensing contract to make sure that the wording of the contract is very clear as to what rights are or are not being conveyed. This can help to avoid litigation. Moreover, to prevent misunderstandings over the scope of the rights being acquired, determine whether any other parties hold licenses to use that particular intellectual property and the extent of those rights.

Cyber Marks

Cyber Mark A trademark in cyberspace.

In cyberspace, trademarks are sometimes referred to as **cyber marks.** We turn now to a discussion of how new laws and the courts are addressing trademark-related issues in cyberspace.

Domain Names

Domain Name Part of an Internet address, such as "cengage.com." The part to the right of the period is the top level domain and indicates the type of entity that operates the site, and the part to the left of the period, called the second level domain, is chosen by the entity.

As e-commerce expanded worldwide, one issue that emerged involved the rights of a trademark owner to use the mark as part of a domain name. A **domain name** is part of an Internet address, such as "cengage.com." Every domain name ends with a top level domain (TLD), which is the part to the right of the period that indicates the type of entity that operates the site (for example, "com" is an abbreviation for "commercial").

The second level domain (SLD)—the part of the name to the left of the period—is chosen by the business entity or individual registering the domain name. Competition for SLDs among firms with similar names and products has led to numerous disputes. By using the same, or a similar, domain name, parties have attempted to profit from a competitor's goodwill, sell pornography, offer for sale another party's domain name, or otherwise infringe on others' trademarks.

The Internet Corporation for Assigned Names and Numbers (ICANN), a nonprofit corporation, oversees the distribution of domain names and operates an online arbitration system. Due to numerous complaints, ICANN completely overhauled the domain name distribution system. In 2012, ICANN started selling new generic top level domain names (gTLDs) for an initial price of $185,000 plus an annual fee of $25,000. Whereas TLDs were limited to only a few terms (such as "com," "net," and "org"), gTLDs can take any form. ICANN anticipates that many companies and corporations will want gTLDs based on their brands. For example, Apple, Inc., might want to use "ipad or "imac" as a gTLD, and Coca-Cola might want "coke."

Cybersquatting The act of registering a domain name that is the same as, or confusingly similar to, the trademark of another and then offering to sell that domain name back to the trademark owner.

One of the goals of the new system is to alleviate the problem of *cybersquatting*. **Cybersquatting** occurs when a person registers a domain name that is the same as, or confusingly similar to, the trademark of another and then offers to sell the domain name back to the trademark owner.

12. *George V Restauration S.A. v. Little Rest Twelve, Inc.*, 58 A.D.3d 428, 871 N.Y.S.2d 65 (2009).

Anti-cybersquatting Legislation

During the 1990s, cybersquatting led to so much litigation that Congress passed the Anticybersquatting Consumer Protection Act (ACPA), which amended the Lanham Act—the federal law protecting trademarks discussed earlier. The ACPA makes it illegal to "register, traffic in, or use" a domain name (1) if the name is identical or confusingly similar to the trademark of another and (2) if the person registering, trafficking in, or using the domain name has a "bad faith intent" to profit from that trademark.

The Ongoing Problem of Cybersquatting

Despite the ACPA, cybersquatting continues to present a problem for businesses, largely because more TLDs are now available and many more companies are registering domain names. Indeed, domain name registrars have proliferated. Registrar companies charge a fee to businesses and individuals to register new names and to renew annual registrations (often through automated software). Many of these companies also buy and sell expired domain names.

Although all registrars are supposed to relay information about these transactions to ICANN and the other companies that keep a master list of domain names, this does not always occur. The speed at which domain names change hands and the difficulty in tracking mass automated registrations have created an environment in which cybersquatting can flourish.

Cybersquatters have also developed new tactics, such as *typosquatting* (registering a name that is a misspelling of a popular brand, for example, hotmial.com). Because many Internet users are not perfect typists, Web pages using these misspelled names can generate significant traffic. More traffic generally means increased profits (advertisers often pay Web sites based on the number of unique visits, or hits), which in turn provides incentive for more cybersquatters. Also, if the misspelling is significant, the trademark owner may have difficulty proving that the name is identical or confusingly similar to the owner's mark, as required by the ACPA.

Cybersquatting is costly for businesses, which must attempt to register all variations of a name to protect their domain name rights from would-be cybersquatters. Large corporations may have to register thousands of domain names across the globe just to protect their basic brands and trademarks.

Applicability of the ACPA and Sanctions under the Act

The ACPA applies to all domain name registrations of trademarks. Successful plaintiffs in suits brought under the act can collect actual damages and lost profits or elect to receive statutory damages that range from $1,000 to $100,000.

Although some companies have been successful suing under the ACPA, there are roadblocks to pursuing such lawsuits. Some domain name registrars offer privacy services that hide the true owners of Web sites, making it difficult for trademark owners to identify cybersquatters. Thus, before bringing a suit, a trademark owner has to ask the court for a subpoena to discover the identity of the owner of the infringing Web site. Because of the high costs of court proceedings, discovery, and even arbitration, many disputes over cybersquatting are settled out of court.

Meta Tags

Search engines compile their results by looking through a Web site's key-word field. *Meta tags,* or key words (see Chapter 2 on page 46), may be inserted into this field to increase the likelihood that a site will be included in search engine results, even though the site may have nothing to do with the inserted words. Using this same technique, one site may appropriate the key words of other sites with more frequent hits so that the appropriating site appears in the same search engine results as the more popular sites. Using another's trademark in a meta tag without the owner's permission, however, normally constitutes trademark infringement.

Some uses of another's trademark as a meta tag may be permissible if the use is reasonably necessary and does not suggest that the owner authorized or sponsored the use. **CASE EXAMPLE 5.9** Terri Welles, a former model who had been "Playmate of the Year" in *Playboy* magazine, established a Web site that used the terms *Playboy* and *Playmate* as meta tags. Playboy Enterprises, Inc., which publishes *Playboy,* filed a suit seeking to prevent Welles from using these meta tags. The court determined that Welles's use of Playboy's meta tags to direct users to her Web site was permissible because it did not suggest sponsorship and there were no descriptive substitutes for the terms *Playboy* and *Playmate.*[13] •

Dilution in the Online World

As discussed earlier, trademark *dilution* occurs when a trademark is used, without authorization, in a way that diminishes the distinctive quality of the mark. Unlike trademark infringement, a claim of dilution does not require proof that consumers are likely to be confused by a connection between the unauthorized use and the mark. For this reason, the products involved do not have to be similar, as the following *Spotlight Case* illustrates.

13. *Playboy Enterprises, Inc. v. Welles,* 279 F.3d 796 (9th Cir. 2002). See also *Canfield v. Health Communications, Inc.,* 2008 WL 961318 (C.D.Cal. 2008).

Spotlight on Internet Porn

Case 5.2

Hasbro, Inc. v. Internet Entertainment Group, Ltd.

United States District Court, Western District of Washington, 1996 WL 84853 (1996).

(Reuters/Hasbro/Ray Stubblebine/Landov)

Candy Land is a children's board game. Why did its parent company, Hasbro, Inc., sue a Web site?

FACTS Hasbro, Inc., the maker of Candyland, a children's board game, owns the Candyland trademark. The defendants, Brian Cartmell and the Internet Entertainment Group, Ltd., used *candyland.com* as a domain name for a sexually explicit Internet site. Any person who performed an online search for "candyland" was directed to this adult Web site. Hasbro filed a trademark dilution claim in a federal court, seeking a permanent injunction to prevent the defendants from using the Candyland trademark.

ISSUE Did the defendants' use of the word *candyland* in connection with a sexually explicit Web site violate Hasbro's trademark rights?

DECISION Yes. The district court granted Hasbro a permanent injunction and ordered the defendants to remove all content from the *candyland.com* Web site and to stop using the Candyland mark.

REASON The court reasoned that Hasbro had shown that the defendants' use of the Candyland mark and the domain name candyland.com in connection with their Internet site was causing irreparable injury to Hasbro. As required to obtain an injunction, Hasbro had demonstrated a likelihood of prevailing on its claims that the defendants' conduct violated both the federal and the Washington State statutes against trademark dilution. "The probable harm to Hasbro from defendants' conduct outweighs any inconvenience that defendants will experience if they are required to stop using the CANDYLAND name."

WHY IS THIS CASE IMPORTANT? *This was the first case alleging dilution on the Web. The court precluded the use of* candyland.com *as a URL for an adult site, even though consumers were not likely to confuse an adult Web site with a children's board game.*

Patents

Patent A property right granted by the federal government that gives an inventor an exclusive right to make, use, sell, or offer to sell an invention in the United States for a limited time.

LEARNING OBJECTIVE 3
How does the law protect patents?

A **patent** is a grant from the government that gives an inventor the exclusive right to make, use, and sell an invention for a period of twenty years. Patents for designs, as opposed to inventions, are given for a fourteen-year period.

Until recently, patent law in the United States differed from the laws of many other countries because the first person to invent a product or process obtained the patent rights rather than the first person to file for a patent. It was often difficult to prove who invented an item first, however, which prompted Congress to change the system in 2011 by passing the America Invents Act.[14] Now the first person to file an application for a patent on a product or process will receive patent protection. In addition, the new law established a nine-month limit for challenging a patent on any ground.

The period of patent protection begins on the date when the patent application is filed, rather than when the patent is issued, which can sometimes be years later. After the patent period ends (either fourteen or twenty years later), the product or process enters the public domain, and anyone can make, sell, or use the invention without paying the patent holder.

(www.uspto.gov)

This is the home page of the U.S. Patent and Trademark Office. Is its database searchable?

Searchable Patent Databases

A significant development relating to patents is the availability online of the world's patent databases. The Web site of the U.S. Patent and Trademark Office (www.uspto.gov) provides searchable databases covering U.S. patents granted since 1976. The Web site of the European Patent Office (www.epo.org) provides online access to 50 million patent documents in more than seventy nations through a searchable network of databases. Businesses use these searchable databases in many ways. Because patents are valuable assets, businesses may need to perform patent searches to list or inventory their assets.

What Is Patentable?

Under federal law, "[w]hoever invents or discovers any new and useful process, machine, manufacture, or composition of matter, or any new and useful improvement thereof, may obtain a patent therefor, subject to the conditions and requirements of this title."[15] Thus, to be patentable, an invention must be *novel, useful,* and *not obvious* in light of current technology.

Almost anything is patentable, except the laws of nature,[16] natural phenomena, and abstract ideas (including algorithms[17]). Even artistic methods and works of art, certain business processes, and the structures of storylines are patentable, provided that they are novel and not obvious.[18]

KNOW THIS

A patent is granted to inventions that are novel (new) and not obvious in light of prior discoveries.

Plants that are reproduced asexually (by means other than from seed), such as hybrid or genetically engineered plants, are patentable in the United States, as are genetically engineered (or cloned) microorganisms and animals. **CASE EXAMPLE 5.10** Monsanto, Inc., has been selling its patented genetically modified (GM) seeds to farmers as a way to achieve higher yields from crops using fewer pesticides. Monsanto requires farmers who buy GM seeds to sign licensing agreements promising to plant the seeds for only one crop and to

---

14. The full title of this law is the Leahy-Smith America Invents Act, Pub. L. No. 112-29 (2011), which amended 35 U.S.C. Sections 1, 41, and 321.

15. 35 U.S.C. 101.

16. *Laboratory Corporation of America Holdings v. Metabolite Laboratories, Inc.,* 548 U.S. 124, 126 S.Ct. 2921, 165 L.Ed.2d 399 (2006).

17. An *algorithm* is a step-by-step procedure, formula, or set of instructions for accomplishing a specific task—such as the set of rules used by a search engine to rank the listings contained within its index in response to a particular query.

18. For a United States Supreme Court case discussing the obviousness requirement, see *KSR International Co. v. Teleflex, Inc.,* 550 U.S. 398, 127 S.Ct. 1727, 167 L.Ed.2d 705 (2007). For a discussion of business process patents, see *In re Bilski,* 535 F3d 943 (Fed.Cir. 2008).

pay a technology fee for each acre planted. To ensure compliance, Monsanto has assigned seventy-five employees whose job is to investigate and prosecute farmers who use the GM seeds illegally. Monsanto has filed more than ninety lawsuits against nearly 150 farmers in the United States and has been awarded more than $15 million in damages (not including out-of-court settlement amounts).[19] •

"To invent, you need a good imagination and a pile of junk."

Thomas Edison, 1847–1931 (American inventor)

Patent Infringement

If a firm makes, uses, or sells another's patented design, product, or process without the patent owner's permission, it commits the tort of patent infringement. Patent infringement may occur even though the patent owner has not put the patented product in commerce. Patent infringement may also occur even though not all features or parts of an invention are copied. (To infringe the patent on a process, however, all steps or their equivalent must be copied.)

(Seongjoon Cho/Bloomberg via Getty Images)

Galaxy Tab 10.1 tablet computer at the company's Galaxy Zone showroom in Seoul, Korea.

Patent Infringement Suits and High-Tech Companies

Obviously, companies that specialize in developing new technology stand to lose significant profits if someone "makes, uses, or sells" devices that incorporate their patented inventions. Because these firms are the holders of numerous patents, they are frequently involved in patent infringement lawsuits (as well as other types of intellectual property disputes). Many companies that make and sell electronics and computer software and hardware are based in foreign nations (for example, Samsung Electronics Company is a Korean firm). Foreign firms can apply for and obtain U.S. patent protection on items that they sell within the United States, just as U.S. firms can obtain protection in foreign nations where they sell goods.

Nevertheless, as a general rule, no patent infringement occurs under U.S. law when a patented product is made and sold in another country. The United States Supreme Court has narrowly construed patent infringement as it applies to exported software.

CASE EXAMPLE 5.11 AT&T Corporation holds a patent on a device used to digitally encode, compress, and process recorded speech. AT&T brought an infringement case against Microsoft Corporation, which admitted that its Windows operating system incorporated software code that infringed on AT&T's patent. The case reached the United States Supreme Court on the question of whether Microsoft's liability extended to computers made in another country. The Court held that it did not. Microsoft was liable only for infringement in the United States and not for the Windows-based computers produced in foreign locations. The Court reasoned that Microsoft had not "supplied" the software for the computers but had only electronically transmitted a master copy, which the foreign manufacturers then copied and loaded onto the computers.[20] •

Apple, Inc. v. Samsung Electronics Company

As mentioned in the chapter introduction, Apple sued Samsung in federal court alleging that Samsung's Galaxy mobile phones and tablets infringe on Apple's patents. The complaint also included allegations of trade dress violations (that Samsung copied the "look and feel" of iPhones and iPads) and trademark infringement (that the icons used for many of the apps on Samsung's products are nearly identical to Apple's apps).

Apple claimed that its design patents cover the graphical user interface (the display of icons on the home screen), the device's shell, and the screen and button design. It also claimed that its patents cover the way information is displayed on iPhones and other

19. See, for example, *Monsanto Co. v. Scruggs*, 459 F.3d 1328 (2006); *Monsanto Co. v. McFarling*, 2005 WL 1490051 (E.D.Mo. 2005); and *Sample v. Monsanto Co.*, 283 F.Supp.2d 1088 (2003).

20. *Microsoft Corp. v. AT&T Corp.*, 550 U.S. 437, 127 S.Ct. 1746, 167 L.Ed.2d 737 (2007).

"The patent system . . . added the fuel to the fire of genius."

Abraham Lincoln, 1809–1865 (The sixteenth president of the United States, 1861–1865)

devices, the way windows pop open, and the way information is scaled and rotated, among other things. Apple argued that Samsung's phones and tablets that use Google's HTC Android operating system violate all of these patents.

In 2012, a jury issued a verdict in favor of Apple and awarded more than $1 billion in damages.[21] The jury found that Samsung had willfully infringed five of Apple's patents and had "diluted" Apple's registered iPhone trade dress. The jury's award was one of the largest ever in a patent case. The case also provides an important precedent for Apple in its legal attacks against Android devices made by other companies because for every iPhone sold worldwide, more than three Android-based smartphones are sold.

Remedies for Patent Infringement

If a patent is infringed, the patent holder may sue for relief in federal court. The patent holder can seek an injunction against the infringer and can also request damages for royalties and lost profits. In some cases, the court may grant the winning party reimbursement for attorneys' fees and costs. If the court determines that the infringement was willful, the court can triple the amount of damages awarded (treble damages).

In the past, permanent injunctions were routinely granted to prevent future infringement. In 2006, however, the United States Supreme Court ruled that patent holders are not automatically entitled to a permanent injunction against future infringing activities. According to the Supreme Court, a patent holder must prove that it has suffered irreparable injury and that the public interest would not be *disserved* by a permanent injunction.[22] This decision gives courts discretion to decide what is equitable in the circumstances and allows them to consider the public interest rather than just the interests of the parties.

CASE EXAMPLE 5.12 In the first case applying this rule, a court found that although Microsoft had infringed on the patent of a small software company, the latter was not entitled to an injunction. According to the court, the small company was not irreparably harmed and could be adequately compensated by monetary damages. Also, the public might suffer negative effects from an injunction because the infringement involved part of Microsoft's widely used Office suite software.[23] •

LEARNING OBJECTIVE 4
What laws protect authors' rights in the works they create?

Copyrights

Copyright The exclusive right of an author or originator of a literary or artistic production to publish, print, sell, or otherwise use that production for a statutory period of time.

A **copyright** is an intangible property right granted by federal statute to the author or originator of certain literary or artistic productions. The Copyright Act of 1976,[24] as amended, governs copyrights. Works created after January 1, 1978, are automatically given statutory copyright protection for the life of the author plus 70 years. For copyrights owned by publishing companies, the copyright expires 95 years from the date of publication or 120 years from the date of creation, whichever is first. For works by more than one author, the copyright expires 70 years after the death of the last surviving author.

Copyrights can be registered with the U.S. Copyright Office (www.copyright.gov) in Washington, D.C. A copyright owner no longer needs to place a © or *Copr.* or *Copyright* on the work, however, to have the work protected against infringement. Chances are that if somebody created it, somebody owns it.

KNOW THIS

If a creative work does not fall into a certain category, it might not be copyrightable, but it may be protected by other intellectual property law.

21. *Apple, Inc. v. Samsung Electronics Co.*, Case Nos. CV 11-1846 and CV 12-0630 (N.D. Cal. August 24, 2012).
22. *eBay, Inc. v. MercExchange, LLC*, 547 U.S. 388, 126 S.Ct. 1837, 164 L.Ed.2d 641 (2006).
23. See *Z4 Technologies, Inc. v. Microsoft Corp.*, 434 F.Supp.2d 437 (2006).
24. 17 U.S.C. Sections 101 *et seq.*

(Jewel Samad/AFP/Getty Images)

Artist Shepard Fairey created a poster portrait of Barack Obama. It was clearly based on an Associated Press file photo taken by Manny Garcia. Did Fairey violate copyright law?

What Is Protected Expression?

Works that are copyrightable include books, records, films, artworks, architectural plans, menus, music videos, product packaging, and computer software. To be protected, a work must be "fixed in a durable medium" from which it can be perceived, reproduced, or communicated. Protection is automatic. Registration is not required.

To obtain protection under the Copyright Act, a work must be original and fall into one of the following categories:

1. Literary works (including newspaper and magazine articles, computer and training manuals, catalogues, brochures, and print advertisements).
2. Musical works and accompanying words (including advertising jingles).
3. Dramatic works and accompanying music.
4. Pantomimes and choreographic works (including ballets and other forms of dance).
5. Pictorial, graphic, and sculptural works (including cartoons, maps, posters, statues, and even stuffed animals).
6. Motion pictures and other audiovisual works (including multimedia works).
7. Sound recordings.
8. Architectural works.

Section 102 Exclusions

It is not possible to copyright an idea. Section 102 of the Copyright Act specifically excludes copyright protection for any "idea, procedure, process, system, method of operation, concept, principle, or discovery, regardless of the form in which it is described, explained, illustrated, or embodied." Thus, others can freely use the underlying ideas or principles embodied in a work.

What is copyrightable is the particular way in which an idea is *expressed.* Whenever an idea and an expression are inseparable, the expression cannot be copyrighted. Generally, anything that is not an original expression will not qualify for copyright protection. Facts widely known to the public are not copyrightable. Page numbers are not copyrightable because they follow a sequence known to everyone. Mathematical calculations are not copyrightable.

ETHICAL ISSUE

Should the federal Copyright Act preempt plaintiffs from bringing "idea-submission" claims under state law? In the past, federal courts generally held that the Copyright Act preempted (or superseded—see Chapter 2) claims in state courts alleging the theft of ideas. In 2011, however, a federal appellate court's decision in the case, *Montz v. Pilgrim Films,*[25] opened the door to such claims. The plaintiff, Larry Montz, had presented representatives from NBC Universal with a concept for a reality-style television program that would follow two paranormal investigators who search for evidence of ghosts. A number of meetings and discussions took place during which Montz provided scripts, videos, and other materials for the proposed show. Ultimately, the studio decided that it was not interested. Three years later, however, NBC partnered with Pilgrim Films to produce *Ghost Hunters,* a series on the Syfy channel that depicts a team of investigators who travel around the country looking for paranormal activity. Montz sued the producers for copyright infringement, breach of contract, and breach of confidence. He claimed that he had expressly conditioned the disclosure of his idea on an expectation that he would be a partner with NBC on the production and would receive a share of any profits.

The lower court dismissed his case, but the appellate court reversed, finding that the Copyright Act did not preempt Montz's two state law claims (breach of an implied contract and breach of confidence). The court reasoned that the state claims asserted rights that are qualitatively different from the rights protected by copyright. The contract claim survived preemption because it required proof of an extra element—the implied agreement of payment for use of a concept—which is

25. 649 F.3d 975 (9th Cir. 2011). See also *Gross v. Miramax Film Corp.,* 383 F.3d 965 (9th Cir. 2004), *cert.* denied, 546 U.S. 824, 126 S.Ct. 361, 163 L.Ed.2d 68 (2005).

a personal right that is different from copyright law. Similarly, the breach of confidence claim required the extra element of a confidential relationship between the parties.

Compilations of Facts Unlike ideas, *compilations* of facts are copyrightable. Under Section 103 of the Copyright Act, a compilation is a work formed by the collection and assembling of preexisting materials or of data that are selected, coordinated, or arranged in such a way that the resulting work as a whole constitutes an original work of authorship.

The key requirement for the copyrightability of a compilation is originality. The White Pages of a telephone directory do not qualify for copyright protection because they simply list alphabetically names and telephone numbers. The Yellow Pages of a directory can be copyrightable, provided that the information is selected, coordinated, or arranged in an original way. Similarly, a court held that a compilation of information about yachts listed for sale may qualify for copyright protection.[26]

Copyright Infringement

Whenever the form or expression of an idea is copied, an infringement of copyright occurs. The reproduction does not have to be exactly the same as the original, nor does it have to reproduce the original in its entirety. If a substantial part of the original is reproduced, copyright infringement has occurred.

"Don't worry about people stealing an idea. If it's original and it's any good, you'll have to ram it down their throats."

Howard Aiken, 1900–1973 (Engineer and pioneer in computing)

Remedies for Copyright Infringement Those who infringe copyrights may be liable for damages or criminal penalties. These range from actual damages or statutory damages, imposed at the court's discretion, to criminal proceedings for willful violations. Actual damages are based on the harm caused to the copyright holder by the infringement, while statutory damages, not to exceed $150,000, are provided for under the Copyright Act. In addition, criminal proceedings may result in fines and/or imprisonment. In some instances, a court may grant an injunction against the infringer.

CASE EXAMPLE 5.13 Rusty Carroll operated an online term paper business, R2C2, Inc., that offered up to 300,000 research papers for sale on nine different Web sites. Individuals whose work was posted on these Web sites without their permission filed a lawsuit against Carroll for copyright infringement. A federal district court in Illinois ruled that an injunction was proper because the plaintiffs had shown that they had suffered irreparable harm and that monetary damages were inadequate to compensate them. Because Carroll had repeatedly failed to comply with court orders regarding discovery, the court found that the copyright infringement was likely to continue unless an injunction was issued. The court therefore issued a permanent injunction prohibiting Carroll and R2C2 from selling any term paper without sworn documentary evidence that the paper's author had given permission.[27] •

The "Fair Use" Exception An exception to liability for copyright infringement is made under the "fair use" doctrine. In certain circumstances, a person or organization can reproduce copyrighted material without paying royalties (fees paid to the copyright holder for the privilege of reproducing the copyrighted material). Section 107 of the Copyright Act provides as follows:

> [T]he fair use of a copyrighted work, including such use by reproduction in copies or phonorecords or by any other means specified by [Section 106 of the Copyright Act], for purposes such as criticism, comment, news reporting, teaching (including multiple copies for classroom use), scholarship, or research, is not an infringement of copyright. In determining whether the use

26. *BUC International Corp. v. International Yacht Council, Ltd.*, 489 F.3d 1129 (11th Cir. 2007).
27. *Weidner v. Carroll*, No. 06-782-DRH, U.S. District Court for the Southern District of Illinois, January 21, 2010.

made of a work in any particular case is a fair use the factors to be considered shall include—

(1) the purpose and character of the use, including whether such use is of a commercial nature or is for nonprofit educational purposes;
(2) the nature of the copyrighted work;
(3) the amount and substantiality of the portion used in relation to the copyrighted work as a whole; and
(4) the effect of the use upon the potential market for or value of the copyrighted work.

What Is Fair Use? Because these guidelines are very broad, the courts determine whether a particular use is fair on a case-by-case basis. Thus, anyone reproducing copyrighted material may be committing a violation. In determining whether a use is fair, courts have often considered the fourth factor to be the most important.

CASE EXAMPLE 5.14 The owner of copyrighted music, BMG Music Publishing, granted a license to Leadsinger, Inc., a manufacturer of karaoke devices. The license gave Leadsinger permission to reproduce the sound recordings, but not to reprint the song lyrics, which appeared at the bottom of a TV screen when the karaoke device was used. BMG demanded that Leadsinger pay a "lyric reprint" fee and a "synchronization" fee. Leadsinger refused to pay, claiming that its use of the lyrics was educational and thus did not constitute copyright infringement under the fair use exception. A federal appellate court disagreed. The court held that Leadsinger's display of the lyrics was not a fair use because it would have a negative effect on the value of the copyrighted work.[28] •

The First Sale Doctrine Section 109(a) of the Copyright Act—also known as the first sale doctrine—provides that "the owner of a particular copy or phonorecord lawfully made under [the Copyright Act], or any person authorized by such owner, is entitled, without the authority of the copyright owner, to sell or otherwise dispose of the possession of that copy or phonorecord." In other words, once a copyright owner sells or gives away a particular copy of a work, the copyright owner no longer has the right to control the distribution of that copy. Thus, for example, a person who buys a copyrighted book can sell it to another person.

Until 2011, it was unclear whether the first sale doctrine applied to the promotional CDs that music companies often send to individuals in the music industry, such as music critics and radio programmers. **CASE EXAMPLE 5.15** Universal Music Group (UMG) regularly ships promotional CDs to people in the music industry. The labels state that the CDs are "the property of the record company," "licensed to the intended recipient," and for "Promotional Use Only—Not for Sale." Troy Augusto obtained some of these promotional CDs from various sources and sold them through online auction sites. When UMG filed a copyright infringement lawsuit, Augusto argued that the music company had given up its right to control further distribution of the CDs under the first sale doctrine.

Ultimately, a federal appellate court held that UMG had conveyed title of the copyrighted promotional CDs to the recipients, rather than simply creating licenses. The court reasoned that the promotional CDs were dispatched to the recipients without any prior arrangement as to those particular copies. Furthermore, because the recipients had not agreed to a license, the written restriction placed on the CD labels was insufficient to create one. •

Copyright Protection for Software

In 1980, Congress passed the Computer Software Copyright Act, which amended the Copyright Act of 1976 to include computer programs in the list of creative works protected by federal copyright law.

---

28. *Leadsinger, Inc. v. BMG Music Publishing*, 512 F.3d 522 (9th Cir. 2008).

Generally, the courts have extended copyright protection not only to those parts of a computer program that can be read by humans, such as the high-level language of a source code, but also to the binary-language object code of a computer program, which is readable only by the computer. Additionally, such elements as the overall structure, sequence, and organization of a program have been deemed copyrightable. Not all aspects of software are protected, however. For the most part, though, courts have not extended copyright protection to the "look and feel"—the general appearance, command structure, video images, menus, windows, and other screen displays—of computer programs. (Note that copying the "look and feel" of another's product may be a violation of trade dress or trademark laws, as Apple, Inc., alleged in its iPhone lawsuit discussed on page 139.)

Copyrights in Digital Information

Copyright law is probably the most important form of intellectual property protection on the Internet, largely because much of the material on the Web (software, for example) is copyrighted and, in order to be transferred online, it must be "copied." Technology has vastly increased the potential for copyright infringement. Generally, anytime a party downloads software or music into a device's random access memory, or RAM, without authorization, a copyright is infringed.

CASE EXAMPLE 5.16 In one case, a rap song that was included in the sound track of a movie had used only a few seconds from the guitar solo of another's copyrighted sound recording without permission. Nevertheless, a federal appellate court held that digitally sampling a copyrighted sound recording of any length constitutes copyright infringement.[29]

In 1998, Congress passed additional legislation to protect copyright holders—the Digital Millennium Copyright Act (DMCA). Because of its significance in protecting against the piracy of copyrighted materials in the online environment, this act is presented as this chapter's *Landmark in the Law* feature on the facing page.

Despite the DMCA and other efforts to combat online piracy, it has continued unabated and even grown, as downloading e-books and movies has become more popular. As media industries complained that counterfeit products were costing both profits and American jobs, two measures to curb piracy were introduced in Congress—the Stop Online Piracy Act (SOPA) in the House and the Protect IP Act (PIPA) in the Senate. Both versions were highly controversial, however.

MP3 and File-Sharing Technology

Soon after the Internet became popular, a few enterprising programmers created software to compress large data files, particularly those associated with music, so that they could be more easily transmitted online. The best-known compression and decompression system is MP3, which enables music fans to download songs or entire CDs onto their computers or onto a portable listening device, such as an iPod. The MP3 system also made it possible for music fans to access other fans' files by engaging in file-sharing via the Internet.

Peer-to-Peer (P2P) Networking The sharing of resources (such as files, hard drives, and processing styles) among multiple computers.

Distributed Network A network used by persons located (distributed) in different places to share computer files.

File-Sharing

File-sharing is accomplished through **peer-to-peer (P2P) networking.** The concept is simple. Rather than going through a central Web server, P2P involves numerous personal computers (PCs) that are connected to the Internet. Individuals on the same network can access files stored on a single PC through a **distributed network,** which has parts dispersed in many locations. Persons scattered throughout the country or the world can work together on the same project by using file-sharing programs. A popular method

29. *Bridgeport Music, Inc. v. Dimension Films,* 410 F.3d 792 (6th Cir. 2005).

LANDMARK IN THE LAW

The Digital Millennium Copyright Act of 1998

The United States leads the world in the production of creative products, including books, films, videos, recordings, and software. Exports of U.S. creative products surpass those of every other U.S. industry in value.

Given the importance of intellectual property to the U.S. economy, the United States has actively supported international efforts to protect ownership rights in intellectual property, including copyrights. In 1996, to curb unauthorized copying of copyrighted materials, the member nations of the World Intellectual Property Organization (WIPO) adopted a treaty to upgrade global standards of copyright protection, particularly for the Internet.

Implementing the WIPO Treaty Congress implemented the provisions of the WIPO treaty by enacting a new statute to update U.S. copyright law. The law—the Digital Millennium Copyright Act of 1998 (DCMA)—is a landmark step in the protection of copyright owners and, because of the leading position of the United States in the creative industries, serves as a model for other nations. Among other things, the DCMA established civil and criminal penalties for anyone who circumvents (bypasses) encryption software or other technological antipiracy protection. Also prohibited are the manufacture, import, sale, and distribution of devices or services for circumvention.

The act provides for exceptions to fit the needs of libraries, scientists, universities, and others. In general, the law does not restrict the "fair use" of circumvention methods for educational and other noncommercial purposes. For example, circumvention is allowed to test computer security, conduct encryption research, protect personal privacy, and enable parents to monitor their children's use of the Internet. The exceptions are to be reconsidered every three years.

Limiting the Liability of Internet Service Providers The DCMA also limited the liability of Internet service providers (ISPs). Under the act, an ISP is not liable for any copyright infringement by its customer *unless* the ISP is aware of the subscriber's violation. An ISP may be held liable only if it fails to take action to shut the subscriber down after learning of the violation. A copyright holder has to act promptly, however, by pursuing a claim in court, or the subscriber has the right to be restored to online access.

Application to Today's World *Without the DCMA, copyright owners would have a more difficult time obtaining legal redress against those who, without authorization, decrypt and/or copy copyrighted materials. Nevertheless, problems remain, particularly because of the global nature of the Internet.*

of sharing very large files over the Internet uses torrenting programs such as the technology first developed by BitTorrent.

Cloud Computing A Web-based service that extends a computer's software or storage capabilities by allowing users to remotely access excess storage and computing capacity as needed.

A newer method of sharing files via the Internet is **cloud computing,** which is essentially a subscription-based or pay-per-use service that extends a computer's software or storage capabilities. Cloud computing can deliver a single application through a browser to multiple users, or it may be a utility program to pool resources and provide data storage and virtual servers that can be accessed on demand. Amazon, Apple, Facebook, Google, IBM, and Sun Microsystems are using and developing additional cloud computing services.

Sharing Stored Music Files

When file-sharing is used to download others' stored music files, copyright issues arise. Recording artists and their labels are losing large amounts of royalties and revenues because few CDs are purchased and then made available on distributed networks, from which everyone can download them for free. **CASE EXAMPLE 5.17** The issue of file-sharing infringement has been the subject of an ongoing debate since highly publicized cases against two companies (Napster, Inc. and Grokster, Ltd.) that created software used for copyright infringement. In the first case, Napster operated a Web site with free software that enabled users to copy and transfer MP3 files via the Internet. Firms in the recording industry sued Napster. Ultimately, the court held that Napster was liable for contributory and vicarious[30] (indirect) copyright infringement. As technology evolved, Grokster, Ltd., and several other companies created and distributed new types of file-sharing software that did not maintain a central index of content, but allowed P2P network users to share stored music files. The court held that because the companies distributed file-sharing software "with the object of promoting its use to infringe the copyright," they were liable for the resulting acts of infringement by third-party users.[31] •

Trade Secrets

Trade Secret A formula, device, idea, process, or other information used in a business that gives the owner a competitive advantage in the marketplace.

The law of trade secrets protects some business processes and information that are not or cannot be protected under patent, copyright, or trademark law against appropriation by a competitor. A **trade secret** is basically information of commercial value. Trade secrets may include customer lists, plans, research and development, pricing information, marketing techniques, and production methods—anything that makes an individual company unique and that would have value to a competitor.

Unlike copyright and trademark protection, protection of trade secrets extends both to ideas and to their expression. (For this reason, and because there are no registration or filing requirements for trade secrets, trade secret protection may be well suited for software.) Of course, the secret formula, method, or other information must be disclosed to some persons, particularly to key employees. Businesses generally attempt to protect their trade secrets by having all employees who use the process or information agree in their contracts, or in confidentiality agreements, never to divulge it.[32]

State and Federal Law on Trade Secrets

Under Section 757 of the *Restatement of Torts,* those who disclose or use another's trade secret, without authorization, are liable to that other party if (1) they discovered the secret by improper means or (2) their disclosure or use constitutes a breach of a duty owed to the other party. The theft of confidential business data by industrial espionage, as when a business taps into a competitor's computer, is a theft of trade secrets without any contractual violation and is actionable in itself.

LEARNING OBJECTIVE 5
What are trade secrets, and what laws offer protection for this form of intellectual property?

Although trade secrets have long been protected under the common law, today most states' laws are based on the Uniform Trade Secrets Act, which has been adopted in forty-seven states. Additionally, in 1996 Congress passed the Economic Espionage Act, which made the theft of trade secrets a federal crime. We will examine the provisions and significance of this act in Chapter 6, in the context of crimes related to business.

Trade Secrets in Cyberspace

Today's computer technology undercuts a business firm's ability to protect its confidential information, including trade secrets. For instance, a dishonest employee could e-mail trade secrets in a company's computer to a competitor or a future employer. If e-mail is not an option, the employee might walk out with the information on a flash pen drive.

30. *Vicarious (indirect) liability* exists when one person is subject to liability for another's actions. A common example occurs in the employment context, when an employer is held vicariously liable by third parties for torts committed by employees in the course of their employment.

31. *A&M Records, Inc. v. Napster, Inc.,* 239 F.3d 1004 (9th Cir. 2001); and *Metro-Goldwyn-Mayer Studios, Inc. v. Grokster, Ltd.,* 545 U.S. 913, 125 S.Ct. 2764, 162 L.Ed.2d 781 (2005). Grokster, Ltd., later settled this dispute out of court and stopped distributing its software.

32. See, for example, *Verigy US, Inc. v. Mayder,* 2008 WL 5063873 (N.D.Cal. 2008); and *Gleeson v. Preferred Sourcing, LLC,* 883 N.E.2d 164 (Ind.App. 2008).

A former employee's continued use of a Twitter account after leaving the company may be the grounds for a suit alleging misappropriation of trade secrets. **CASE EXAMPLE 5.18** Noah Kravitz worked for a company called PhoneDog for four years as a product reviewer and video blogger. PhoneDog provided him with the Twitter account "@PhoneDog_Noah." Kravitz's popularity grew, and he had approximately 17,000 followers by the time he quit in 2010. PhoneDog requested that Kravitz stop using the Twitter account. Although Kravitz changed his handle to "@noahkravitz," he continued to use the account. PhoneDog subsequently sued Kravitz for misappropriation of trade secrets, among other things. Kravitz moved for a dismissal, but the court found that the complaint adequately stated a cause of action for misappropriation of trade secrets and allowed the suit to continue.[33] ●

For a summary of trade secrets and other forms of intellectual property, see Exhibit 5.1 below.

International Protection for Intellectual Property

For many years, the United States has been a party to various international agreements relating to intellectual property rights. For example, the Paris Convention of 1883, to which about 173 countries are signatory, allows parties in one country to file for patent and trademark protection in any of the other member countries. Other international agreements

33. *PhoneDog v. Kravitz*, 2011 WL 5415612 (N.D.Cal. 2011).

Exhibit 5.1 Forms of Intellectual Property

	DEFINITION	HOW ACQUIRED	DURATION	REMEDY FOR INFRINGEMENT
Patent	A grant from the government that gives an inventor exclusive rights to an invention.	By filing a patent application with the U.S. Patent and Trademark Office and receiving its approval.	Twenty years from the date of the application; for design patents, fourteen years.	Monetary damages, including royalties and lost profits, *plus* attorneys' fees. Damages may be tripled for intentional infringements.
Copyright	The right of an author or originator of a literary or artistic work, or other production that falls within a specified category, to have the exclusive use of that work for a given period of time.	Automatic (once the work or creation is put in tangible form). Only the *expression* of an idea (and not the idea itself) can be protected by copyright.	For authors: the life of the author, plus 70 years. For publishers: 95 years after the date of publication or 120 years after creation.	Actual damages plus profits received by the party who infringed *or* statutory damages under the Copyright Act, *plus* costs and attorneys' fees in either situation.
Trademark (service mark and trade dress)	Any distinctive word, name, symbol, or device (image or appearance), or combination thereof, that an entity uses to distinguish its goods or services from those of others. The owner has the exclusive right to use that mark or trade dress.	1. At common law, ownership created by use of the mark. 2. Registration with the appropriate federal or state office gives notice and is permitted if the mark is currently in use or will be within the next six months.	Unlimited, as long as it is in use. To continue notice by registration, the owner must renew by filing between the fifth and sixth years, and thereafter, every ten years.	1. Injunction prohibiting the future use of the mark. 2. Actual damages plus profits received by the party who infringed (can be increased under the Lanham Act). 3. Destruction of articles that infringed. 4. *Plus* costs and attorneys' fees.
Trade Secret	Any information that a business possesses and that gives the business an advantage over competitors (including formulas, lists, patterns, plans, processes, and programs).	Through the originality and development of the information and processes that constitute the business secret and are unknown to others.	Unlimited, so long as not revealed to others. Once revealed to others, it is no longer a trade secret.	Monetary damages for misappropriation (the Uniform Trade Secrets Act also permits punitive damages if willful), *plus* costs and attorneys' fees.

include the Berne Convention, the Trade-Related Aspects of Intellectual Property Rights (known as the TRIPS agreement), and the Madrid Protocol.

To learn about a new international treaty that will affect international property rights, see this chapter's *Beyond Our Borders* feature below.

The Berne Convention

Under the Berne Convention of 1886, an international copyright agreement, if a U.S. citizen writes a book, every country that has signed the convention must recognize her or his copyright in the book. Also, if a citizen of a country that has not signed the convention first publishes a book in one of the 163 countries that have signed, all other countries that have signed the convention must recognize that author's copyright. Copyright notice is not needed to gain protection under the Berne Convention for works published after March 1, 1989.

This convention and other international agreements have given some protection to intellectual property on a worldwide level. None of them, however, has been as significant and far reaching in scope as the TRIPS agreement, discussed in the next subsection.

In 2011, the European Union agreed to extend the period of royalty protection for musicians from fifty years to seventy years. This decision aids major record labels as well as performers and musicians who previously faced losing royalties from sales of their older recordings. The profits of musicians and record companies have been shrinking in recent years because of the sharp decline in sales of compact discs and the rise in digital downloads (both legal and illegal).

In the following case, the United States Supreme Court had to decide if Congress had exceeded its authority under the U.S. Constitution when it enacted a law that restored copyright protection to many foreign works that were already in the public domain.

BEYOND OUR BORDERS — The Anti-Counterfeiting Trade Agreement

After several years of negotiations, in 2011 Australia, Canada, Japan, Korea, Morocco, New Zealand, Singapore, and the United States signed a new international treaty to combat global counterfeiting and piracy. The European Union, Mexico, Switzerland, and other nations that support the treaty are still developing domestic procedures to comply with its provisions. Once a nation has adopted appropriate procedures, it can ratify the treaty.

Provisions and Goals

The treaty, called the Anti-Counterfeiting Trade Agreement (ACTA), will have its own governing body. The goal of ACTA is to increase international cooperation, facilitate the best law enforcement practices, and provide a legal framework to combat counterfeiting.

The treaty applies not only to counterfeit physical goods, such as medications, but also to pirated copyrighted works being distributed via the Internet. The idea is to create a new standard of enforcement for intellectual property rights that goes beyond the TRIPS agreement and encourages international cooperation and information sharing among signatory countries.

Border Searches

Under ACTA, member nations are required to establish border measures that allow officials, on their own initiative, to search commercial shipments of imports and exports for counterfeit goods. The treaty neither requires nor prohibits random border searches of electronic devices, such as laptops and iPads, for infringing content. If border authorities reasonably believe that any goods in transit are counterfeit, the treaty allows them to keep the suspect goods unless the owner proves that the items are authentic and noninfringing.

The treaty allows member nations, in accordance with their own laws, to order online service providers to furnish information about (including the identity of) suspected trademark and copyright infringers.

Critical Thinking

Why will product counterfeiting always exist?

Case 5.3

Golan v. Holder

Supreme Court of the United States,
___ U.S. ___, 132 S.Ct. 873, 181 L.Ed.2d 835 (2012).

(criben/Shutterstock.com)

Why do U.S. entertainers now have to pay royalties on older European compositions?

FACTS The United States joined the Berne Convention in 1989, but it failed to give foreign copyright holders the same protections enjoyed by U.S. authors. Contrary to the Berne Convention, the United States did not protect any foreign work that had already entered the public domain. In 1994, Congress enacted the Uruguay Round Agreements Act (URAA), which "restored" copyright protection for many foreign works that were already in the public domain. The URAA put foreign and domestic works on the same footing, allowing their copyrights to extend for the same terms. Lawrence Golan, along with a group of musicians, conductors, and publishers, filed a suit against Eric Holder, in his capacity as the U.S. Attorney General, challenging the URAA and claiming that it violated the copyright clause of the U.S. Constitution. These individuals had enjoyed free access to foreign works in the public domain before the URAA's enactment and argued that Congress had exceeded its constitutional authority in passing the URAA. A federal appellate court held that Congress did not violate the copyright clause by passing the URAA. The petitioners appealed. The United States Supreme Court granted *certiorari* to resolve the matter.

ISSUE Does the URAA violate the copyright clause in the U.S. Constitution by restoring copyright protection for foreign works in the public domain?

DECISION No. The United States Supreme Court affirmed the judgment of the federal appellate court. Thus, Golan and the others could no longer use, without permission, any of the previous public domain foreign works, which are indeed protected by the URAA. By passing the URAA in the United States, Congress, in effect, took the foreign works that Golan and others had been using out of the public domain. Henceforth, U.S. copyright and patent laws cover all such foreign intellectual property.

REASON The copyright clause empowers Congress "to promote the Progress of Science . . . by securing for limited Times to Authors . . . the exclusive Right to their Writings." The Court concluded that Congress is not barred from protecting works in the public domain simply because a copyright must exist for only a "limited time." The Court relied heavily on the precedent set by its decision in an earlier case in which it held that Congress did not violate the copyright clause by extending existing copyrights by twenty years.[a] In that case, the Court declined to interpret the text of the copyright clause as requiring that a "time prescription, once set, becomes forever 'fixed' or 'inalterable.'" In passing the URAA, Congress did not create perpetual copyrights. Therefore, the URAA does not violate the copyright clause.

CRITICAL THINKING—Global Consideration *What does the Court's decision in this case mean for copyright holders in the United States who want copyright protection in other countries? Will other nations be more or less inclined to protect U.S. authors? Explain.*

a. See *Eldred v. Ashcroft*, 537 U.S. 186, 123 S.Ct. 769, 154 L.Ed.2d 683 (2003).

The TRIPS Agreement

Representatives from more than one hundred nations signed the TRIPS agreement in 1994. The agreement established, for the first time, standards for the international protection of intellectual property rights, including patents, trademarks, and copyrights for movies, computer programs, books, and music. The TRIPS agreement provides that each member country must include in its domestic laws broad intellectual property rights and effective remedies (including civil and criminal penalties) for violations of those rights.

Generally, the TRIPS agreement forbids member nations from discriminating against foreign owners of intellectual property rights (in the administration, regulation, or adjudication of such rights). In other words, a member nation cannot give its own nationals (citizens) favorable treatment without offering the same treatment to nationals of all member countries. **EXAMPLE 5.19** A U.S. software manufacturer brings a suit for the infringement of intellectual property rights under Germany's national laws. Because Germany is a member of the TRIPS agreement, the U.S. manufacturer is entitled to receive the same treatment as a German manufacturer. ● Each member nation must also ensure that legal procedures are available for parties who wish to bring actions for infringement of intellectual property rights. Additionally, a related document established a mechanism for settling disputes among member nations.

The Madrid Protocol

In the past, one of the difficulties in protecting U.S. trademarks internationally was that it was time consuming and expensive to apply for trademark registration in foreign countries. The filing fees and procedures for trademark registration vary significantly among individual countries. The Madrid Protocol, however, which was signed into law in 2003, may help to resolve these problems. The Madrid Protocol is an international treaty that has been signed by seventy-three countries. Under its provisions, a U.S. company wishing to register its trademark abroad can submit a single application and designate other member countries in which it would like to register the mark. The treaty was designed to reduce the costs of obtaining international trademark protection by more than 60 percent.

Although the Madrid Protocol may simplify and reduce the cost of trademark registration in foreign nations, it remains to be seen whether it will provide significant benefits to trademark owners. Even with an easier registration process, the question of whether member countries will enforce the law and protect the mark still remains.

Reviewing . . . Intellectual Property and Internet Law

Two computer science majors, Trent and Xavier, have an idea for a new video game, which they propose to call "Hallowed." They form a business and begin developing their idea. Several months later, Trent and Xavier run into a problem with their design and consult with a friend, Brad, who is an expert in creating computer source codes. After the software is completed but before Hallowed is marketed, a video game called Halo 2 is released for both the Xbox and Playstation 3 systems. Halo 2 uses source codes similar to those of Hallowed and imitates Hallowed's overall look and feel, although not all the features are alike. Using the information presented in the chapter, answer the following questions.

1. Would the name *Hallowed* receive protection as a trademark or as trade dress?
2. If Trent and Xavier had obtained a business process patent on Hallowed, would the release of Halo 2 infringe on their patent? Why or why not?
3. Based only on the facts presented above, could Trent and Xavier sue the makers of Halo 2 for copyright infringement? Why or why not?
4. Suppose that Trent and Xavier discover that Brad took the idea of Hallowed and sold it to the company that produced Halo 2. Which type of intellectual property issue does this raise?

DEBATE THIS Congress has amended the Copyright Act several times. Copyright holders now have protection for many decades. Was Congress justified in extending the copyright time periods? Why or why not?

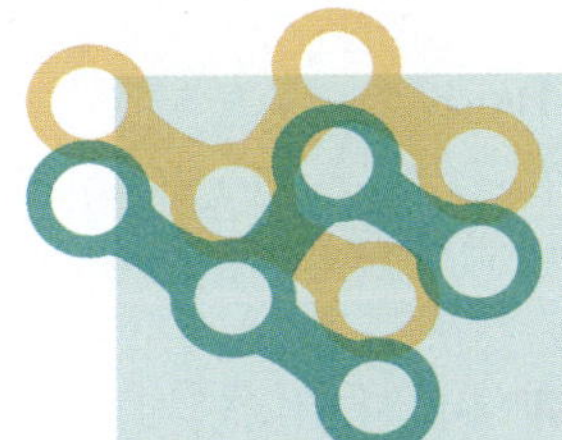

LINKING BUSINESS LAW to Marketing

Trademarks and Service Marks

In your marketing courses, you have learned or will learn about the importance of trademarks. If you become a marketing manager, you will be involved in creating trademarks or service marks for your firm, protecting the firm's existing marks, and ensuring that you do not infringe on anyone else's marks.

The Broad Range of Trademarks and Service Marks

The courts have held that trademarks and service marks consist of much more than well-known brand names, such as Apple or Amazon. As a marketing manager, you will need to be aware that parts of a brand or other product identification often qualify for trademark protection.

- **Catchy Phrases**—Certain brands have established phrases that are associated with them, such as Nike's "Just Do It!" As a marketing manager for a competing product, you will have to avoid such catchy phrases in your own marketing program. Note, though, that not all phrases can become part of a trademark or service mark. When a phrase is extremely common, the courts normally will not grant trademark or service mark protection to it.
- **Abbreviations**—The public sometimes abbreviates a well-known trademark. For example Budweiser beer is known as Bud and Coca-Cola as Coke. As a marketing manager, you should avoid using any name for a product or service that closely resembles a well-known abbreviation, such as Koke for a cola drink.
- **Shapes**—The shape of a brand name, a service mark, or a container can take on exclusivity if the shape clearly aids in product or service identification. For example, just about everyone throughout the world recognizes the shape of a Coca-Cola bottle. As a marketing manager, you would do well to avoid using a similar shape for a new carbonated drink.
- **Ornamental Colors**—Sometimes color combinations can become part of a service mark or trademark. For example, FedEx established its unique identity with the use of bright orange and purple. The courts have protected this color combination. The same holds for the black-and-copper color combination of Duracell batteries.
- **Ornamental Designs**—Symbols and designs associated with a particular mark are normally protected. Marketing managers should not attempt to copy them. Levi's places a small tag on the left side of the rear pocket of its jeans. Cross uses a cutoff black cone on the top of its pens.
- **Sounds**—Sounds can also be protected. For example, the familiar roar of the Metro-Goldwyn-Mayer (MGM) lion is protected.

When to Protect Your Trademarks and Service Marks

Every business should register its logo as a trademark, and perhaps also its business name and Web site address, to provide the company with the highest level of protection. A trademark will discourage counterfeiting and will give your firm the advantage in the event of future infringement.

Once your company has established a trademark or a service mark, as a manager, you will have to decide how aggressively you wish to protect those marks. If you fail to protect them, your company faces the possibility that they will become generic. Remember that *aspirin, cellophane, thermos, dry ice, shredded wheat,* and many other familiar terms were once legally protected trademarks. Protecting exclusive rights to a mark can be expensive, however, so you will have to determine how much it is worth to your company to protect your rights. If you work in a small company, making major expenditures to protect your trademarks and service marks might not be cost-effective.

Critical Thinking

The U.S. Patent and Trademark Office requires that a registered trademark or service mark be put into commercial use within three years after the application has been approved. Why do you think the federal government established this requirement?

Key Terms

certification mark 132
cloud computing 145
collective mark 132
copyright 140
cyber mark 135
cybersquatting 135
distributed network 144
domain name 135

intellectual property 126
license 134
patent 138
peer-to-peer (P2P) networking 144
service mark 132
trade dress 132
trade name 134
trade secret 146
trademark 127

Chapter Summary: Intellectual Property and Internet Law

Trademarks and Related Property (See pages 127–135.)	1. A *trademark* is a distinctive word, symbol, or design that identifies the manufacturer as the source of the goods and distinguishes its products from those made or sold by others. 2. The major federal statutes protecting trademarks and related property are the Lanham Act of 1946 and the Federal Trademark Dilution Act of 1995. Generally, to be protected, a trademark must be sufficiently distinctive from all competing trademarks. 3. *Trademark infringement* occurs when one uses a mark that is the same as, or confusingly similar to, the protected trademark, service mark, trade name, or trade dress of another without permission when marketing goods or services.
Cyber Marks (See pages 135–137.)	A *cyber mark* is a trademark in cyberspace. Trademark infringement in cyberspace occurs when one person uses, in a domain name or in meta tags, a name that is the same as, or confusingly similar to, the protected mark of another.
Patents (See pages 138–140.)	1. A *patent* is a grant from the government that gives an inventor the exclusive right to make, use, and sell an invention for a period of twenty years (fourteen years for a design patent) from the date when the application for a patent is filed. To be patentable, an invention (or a discovery, process, or design) must be genuine, novel, useful, and not obvious in light of current technology. Computer software may be patented. 2. Almost anything is patentable, except the laws of nature, natural phenomena, and abstract ideas (including algorithms). Even business processes or methods are patentable if they relate to a machine or transformation. 3. *Patent infringement* occurs when one uses or sells another's patented design, product, or process without the patent owner's permission. The patent holder can sue the infringer in federal court and request an injunction, but must prove irreparable injury to obtain a permanent injunction against the infringer. The patent holder can also request damages and attorneys' fees. If the infringement was willful, the court can grant treble damages.
Copyrights (See pages 140–146.)	1. A *copyright* is an intangible property right granted by federal statute to the author or originator of certain literary or artistic productions. The Copyright Act of 1976, as amended, governs copyrights. Computer software may be copyrighted. 2. *Copyright infringement* occurs whenever the form or expression of an idea is copied without the permission of the copyright holder. An exception applies if the copying is deemed a "fair use." 3. To protect copyrights in digital information, Congress passed the Digital Millennium Copyright Act of 1998. 4. Technology that allows users to share files via the Internet on distributed networks often raises copyright infringement issues. 5. The courts have ruled that companies that provide file-sharing software to users can be held liable for contributory and vicarious copyright liability.
Trade Secrets (See pages 146–147.)	*Trade secrets* include customer lists, plans, research and development, and pricing information. Trade secrets are protected under the common law and, in some states, under statutory law against misappropriation by competitors. The Economic Espionage Act of 1996 made the theft of trade secrets a federal crime (see Chapter 6).
International Protection for Intellectual Property (See pages 147–150.)	Various international agreements provide international protection for intellectual property. A landmark agreement is the 1994 agreement on Trade-Related Aspects of Intellectual Property Rights (TRIPS), which provides for enforcement procedures in all countries signatory to the agreement.

ExamPrep

ISSUE SPOTTERS

1. Global Products develops, patents, and markets software. World Copies, Inc., sells Global's software without the maker's permission. Is this patent infringement? If so, how might Global save the cost of suing World for infringement and at the same time profit from World's sales? **(See pages 135 and 139.)**
2. Eagle Corporation began marketing software in 2001 under the mark "Eagle." In 2012, Eagle.com, Inc., a different company selling different products, begins to use *eagle* as part of its URL and registers it as a domain name. Can Eagle Corporation stop this use of *eagle*? If so, what must the company show? **(See page 137.)**

— Check your answers to the Issue Spotters against the answers provided in Appendix E at the end of this text.

BEFORE THE TEST

Go to www.cengagebrain.com, enter the ISBN 9781133273561 and click on "Find" to locate this textbook's Web site. Then, click on "Access Now" under "Study Tools," and select Chapter 5 at the top. There, you will find a Practice Quiz that you can take to assess your mastery of the concepts in this chapter, as well as Flashcards, a Glossary of important terms, and Video Questions (when assigned).

For Review

Answers to the even-numbered questions in this For Review section can be found in Appendix F at the end of this text.

1. What is intellectual property?
2. Why is the protection of trademarks important?
3. How does the law protect patents?
4. What laws protect authors' rights in the works they create?
5. What are trade secrets, and what laws offer protection for this form of intellectual property?

Business Scenarios and Case Problems

5–1 Patent Infringement. John and Andrew Doney invented a hard-bearing device for balancing rotors. Although they obtained a patent for their invention from the U.S. Patent and Trademark Office, it was never used as an automobile wheel balancer. Some time later, Exetron Corp. produced an automobile wheel balancer that used a hard-bearing device with a support plate similar to that of the Doneys' device. Given that the Doneys had not used their device for automobile wheel balancing, does Exetron's use of a similar device infringe on the Doneys' patent? **(See page 139.)**

5–2 Question with Sample Answer—Copyright Infringement. In which of the following situations would a court likely hold Maruta liable for copyright infringement? Why? **(See page 142.)**

1. At the library, Maruta photocopies ten pages from a scholarly journal relating to a topic on which she is writing a term paper.
2. Maruta makes leather handbags and sells them in her small shop. She advertises her handbags as "Vutton handbags," hoping that customers will mistakenly assume that they were made by Vuitton, the well-known maker of high-quality luggage and handbags.
3. Maruta teaches Latin American history at a small university. She has a digital video recorder and frequently records television programs relating to Latin America and puts them on DVDs. She then takes the DVDs to her classroom so that her students can watch them.

—For a sample answer to Question 5–2, go to Appendix G at the end of this text.

5–3 Trade Secrets. Briefing.com offers Internet-based analyses of investment opportunities to investors. Richard Green is the company's president. One of Briefing.com's competitors is StreetAccount, LLC (limited liability company), whose owners include Gregory Jones and Cynthia Dietzmann. Jones worked for Briefing.com for six years until he quit in March 2003, and he was a member of its board of directors until April 2003. Dietzmann worked for Briefing.com for seven years until she quit in March 2003. As Briefing.com employees, Jones and Dietzmann had access to confidential business data. For instance, Dietzmann developed a list of contacts through which Briefing.com obtained market information to display online. When Dietzmann quit, however, she did not return all of the contact information to the company. Briefing.com and Green filed a suit in a federal district court against Jones, Dietzmann, and StreetAccount, alleging that they appropriated these data and other "trade secrets" to form a competing business. What are trade secrets? Why are they protected? Under what circumstances is a party liable at common law for their appropriation? How should these principles apply in this case? [*Briefing.com v. Jones,* 2006 WY 16, 126 P.3d 928 (2006)] **(See pages 146–147.)**

5–4 Licensing. Redwin Wilchcombe composed, performed, and recorded a song called *Tha Weedman* at the request of Lil Jon, a member of Lil Jon & the East Side Boyz (LJESB), for LJESB's album *Kings of Crunk.* Wilchcombe was not paid, but was given credit on the album as a producer. After the album had sold two million copies, Wilchcombe filed a suit against LJESB, alleging copyright infringement. The defendants claimed that they had a license to use the song. Do the facts support this claim? Explain. [*Wilchcombe v. TeeVee Toons, Inc.,* 555 F.3d 949 (11th Cir. 2009)] **(See page 134.)**

5–5 Case Problem with Sample Answer—Trade Secrets. Jesse Edwards, an employee of Carbon Processing and Reclamation, LLC (CPR), put unmarked boxes of company records in his car. Edwards's wife, Channon, who suspected him of hiding financial information from her, gained access to the documents. William Jones, the owner of CPR, filed a suit, contending that Channon's unauthorized access to the files was a theft of trade secrets. Could the information in the documents be trade secrets? Should liability be imposed?

Why or why not? [*Jones v. Hamilton,* 59 So.3d 134 (Ala.Civ. App. 2010)] **(See page 146.)**

—For a sample answer to Problem 5–5, go to Appendix H at the end of this text.

5–6 **Spotlight on Macy's—Copyright Infringement.** United Fabrics International, Inc., bought a fabric design from an Italian designer and registered a copyright to it with the U.S. Copyright Office. When Macy's, Inc., began selling garments with a similar design, United filed a copyright infringement suit against Macy's. Macy's argued that United did not own a valid copyright to the design and so could not claim infringement. Does United have to prove that the copyright is valid to establish infringement? Explain. [*United Fabrics International, Inc. v. C & J Wear, Inc.,* 630 F.3d 1255 (9th Cir. 2011)] **(See page 142.)**

5–7 **Theft of Trade Secrets.** Hanjuan Jin, a citizen of the People's Republic of China, began working at Motorola in 1998. He worked as a software engineer in a division that created proprietary standards for cellular communications. In 2004 and 2005, in contradiction to Motorola's policies, Jin also began working as a consultant for Lemko Corp. Lemko introduced Jin to Sun Kaisens, a Chinese software company. During 2005, Jin returned to Beijing on several occasions and began working with Sun Kaisens and with the Chinese military. The following year, she started corresponding with Sun Kaisens's management about a possible full-time job in China. During this period, she took several medical leaves of absence from Motorola. In February 2007, after one of these medical leaves, she returned to Motorola. During the next several days at Motorola, she accessed and downloaded thousands of documents on her personal laptop as well as on pen drives. On the following day, she attempted to board a flight to China but was randomly searched by U.S. Customs and Border Protection officials at Chicago's O'Hare International Airport. Ultimately, U.S. officials discovered the thousands of downloaded Motorola documents. Are there any circumstances under which Jin could avoid being prosecuted for theft of trade secrets? If so, what are these circumstances? Discuss fully. [*United States v. Hanjuan Jin,* 833 F.Supp.2d 977 (N.D.Ill. 2012)] **(See pages 146–147.)**

5–8 **A Question of Ethics—Copyright Infringement.** Custom Copies, Inc., prepares and sells coursepacks, which contain compilations of readings for college courses. A teacher selects the readings and delivers a syllabus to the copy shop, which obtains the materials from a library, copies them, and binds the copies. Blackwell Publishing, Inc., which owns the copyright to some of the materials, filed a suit, alleging copyright infringement. [*Blackwell Publishing, Inc. v. Custom Copies, Inc.,* 2006 WL 152950 (N.D.Fla. 2006)] **(See pages 142–144.)**

1. Custom Copies argued, in part, that it did not "distribute" the coursepacks. Does a copy shop violate copyright law if it only copies materials for coursepacks? Does the fair use doctrine apply in these circumstances? Discuss.
2. What is the potential impact if copies of a book or journal are created and sold without the permission of, and the payment of royalties or a fee to, the copyright owner? Explain.

Critical Thinking and Writing Assignments

5–9 **Business Law Writing.** Sync Computers, Inc., makes computer-related products under the brand name "Sync," which the company registers as a trademark. Without Sync's permission, E-Product Corp. embeds the Sync mark in E-Product's Web site, in black type on a blue background. This tag causes the E-Product site to be returned at the top of the list of results on a search engine query for "Sync." Write three paragraphs explaining why E-Product's use of the Sync mark as a meta tag without Sync's permission constitutes trademark infringement. **(See pages 136–137.)**

5–10 **Business Law Critical Thinking Group Assignment.** After years of research, your company develops a product that might revolutionize the green (environmentally conscious) building industry. The product is made from relatively inexpensive and widely available materials combined in a unique way that can substantially lower the heating and cooling costs of residential and commercial buildings. The company has registered the trademark it intends to use on the product, and has filed a patent application with the U.S. Patent and Trademark Office.

1. One group should provide three reasons why this product does or does not qualify for patent protection.
2. Another group should develop a four-step procedure for how your company can best protect its intellectual property rights (trademark, trade secret, and patent) and prevent domestic and foreign competitors from producing counterfeit goods or cheap knockoffs.
3. Another group should list and explain three ways your company can utilize licensing.

CHAPTER 6

(AlexKosev/iStockphoto.com)

Criminal Law and Cyber Crime

CHAPTER OUTLINE

- Civil Law and Criminal Law
- Criminal Liability
- Types of Crimes
- Defenses to Criminal Liability
- Constitutional Safeguards and Criminal Procedures
- Criminal Process
- Cyber Crime

LEARNING OBJECTIVES

The five learning objectives below are designed to help improve your understanding of the chapter. After reading this chapter, you should be able to answer the following questions:

1. What two elements normally must exist before a person can be held liable for a crime?
2. What are five broad categories of crimes? What is white-collar crime?
3. What defenses can be raised to avoid liability for criminal acts?
4. What constitutional safeguards exist to protect persons accused of crimes?
5. How has the Internet expanded opportunities for identity theft?

"The crime problem is getting really serious. The other day, the Statue of Liberty had both hands up."
—Jay Leno, 1950–present (American comedian and television host)

Criminal law is an important part of the legal environment of business. Various sanctions are used to bring about a society in which businesses can compete and flourish. These sanctions include damages for various types of tortious conduct (see Chapter 4), damages for breach of contract (see Chapter 14), and various equitable remedies (see Chapter 1). Additional sanctions are imposed under criminal law. Many statutes regulating business provide for criminal as well as civil sanctions.

In this chapter, after a brief summary of the major differences between criminal and civil law, we look at the elements that must be present for criminal liability to exist. We then examine various categories of crimes, the defenses that can be raised to avoid liability for criminal actions, and the rules of criminal procedure. Advances in technology allow authorities to trace phone calls and track vehicle movements with greater ease and precision. One such technique is attaching tracking devices to a suspect's vehicle. Is such an action a violation of the constitutional rights of those suspects who are being tracked? You will discover what the courts have to say on this question later in this chapter.

Civil Law and Criminal Law

Remember from Chapter 1 that *civil law* spells out the duties that exist between persons or between persons and their governments, excluding the duty not to commit crimes. Contract law, for example, is part of civil law. The whole body of tort law, which deals with the infringement by one person on the legally recognized rights of another, is also an area of civil law.

Crime A wrong against society proclaimed in a statute and, if committed, punishable by society through fines, imprisonment, or death.

Criminal law, in contrast, has to do with crime. A **crime** can be defined as a wrong against society proclaimed in a statute and, if committed, punishable by society through fines and/or imprisonment—and, in some cases, death. As mentioned in Chapter 1, because crimes are *offenses against society as a whole,* criminals are prosecuted by a public official, such as a district attorney (D.A.), rather than by the crime victims. Victims often report the crime to the police, but ultimately it is the D.A.'s office that decides whether to file criminal charges and to what extent to pursue the prosecution or carry out additional investigation.

Key Differences between Civil Law and Criminal Law

Because the state has extensive resources at its disposal when prosecuting criminal cases, and because the sanctions can be so severe, there are numerous procedural safeguards to protect the rights of defendants. We look here at one of these safeguards—the higher burden of proof that applies in a criminal case—and at the sanctions imposed for criminal acts. Exhibit 6.1 below summarizes these and other key differences between civil law and criminal law.

Burden of Proof

In a civil case, the plaintiff usually must prove his or her case by a *preponderance of the evidence.* Under this standard, the plaintiff must convince the court that, based on the evidence presented by both parties, it is more likely than not that the plaintiff's allegation is true.

Beyond a Reasonable Doubt The standard of proof used in criminal cases.

In a criminal case, in contrast, the state must prove its case **beyond a reasonable doubt.** If the jury views the evidence in the case as reasonably permitting either a guilty or a not guilty verdict, then the jury's verdict must be *not* guilty. In other words, the government (prosecutor) must prove beyond a reasonable doubt that the defendant has committed every essential element of the offense with which she or he is charged. If the jurors are not convinced of the defendant's guilt beyond a reasonable doubt, they must find the defendant not guilty.

Note also that in a criminal case, the jury's verdict normally must be unanimous—agreed to by all members of the jury—to convict the defendant.[1] (In a civil trial by jury, in contrast, typically only three-fourths of the jurors need to agree.)

1. Note that there are exceptions—a few states allow jury verdicts that are not unanimous. Arizona, for example, allows six of eight jurors to reach a verdict in criminal cases. Louisiana and Oregon have also relaxed the requirement of unanimous jury verdicts.

Exhibit 6.1 **Key Differences between Civil Law and Criminal Law**

ISSUE	CIVIL LAW	CRIMINAL LAW
Party who brings suit	The person who suffered harm.	The state.
Wrongful act	Causing harm to a person or to a person's property.	Violating a statute that prohibits some type of activity.
Burden of proof	Preponderance of the evidence.	Beyond a reasonable doubt.
Verdict	Three-fourths majority (typically).	Unanimous (almost always).
Remedy	Damages to compensate for the harm or a decree to achieve an equitable result.	Punishment (fine, imprisonment, or death).

Criminal Sanctions The sanctions imposed on criminal wrongdoers are also harsher than those applied in civil cases. Remember from Chapter 4 that the purpose of tort law is to allow persons harmed by the wrongful acts of others to obtain compensation from the wrongdoer rather than to punish the wrongdoer.

In contrast, criminal sanctions are designed to punish those who commit crimes and to deter others from committing similar acts in the future. Criminal sanctions include fines as well as the much harsher penalty of the loss of one's liberty by incarceration in a jail or prison. The harshest criminal sanction is, of course, the death penalty.

Civil Liability for Criminal Acts

Some torts, such as assault and battery, provide a basis for a criminal prosecution as well as a tort action. **EXAMPLE 6.1** Carlos is walking down the street, minding his own business, when suddenly a person attacks him. In the ensuing struggle, the attacker (assailant) stabs Carlos several times, seriously injuring him. A police officer restrains and arrests the wrongdoer. In this situation, the attacker may be subject both to criminal prosecution by the state and to a tort lawsuit brought by Carlos. •

Exhibit 6.2 below illustrates how the same act can result in both a tort action and a criminal action against the wrongdoer.

Exhibit 6.2 Tort Lawsuit and Criminal Prosecution for the Same Act

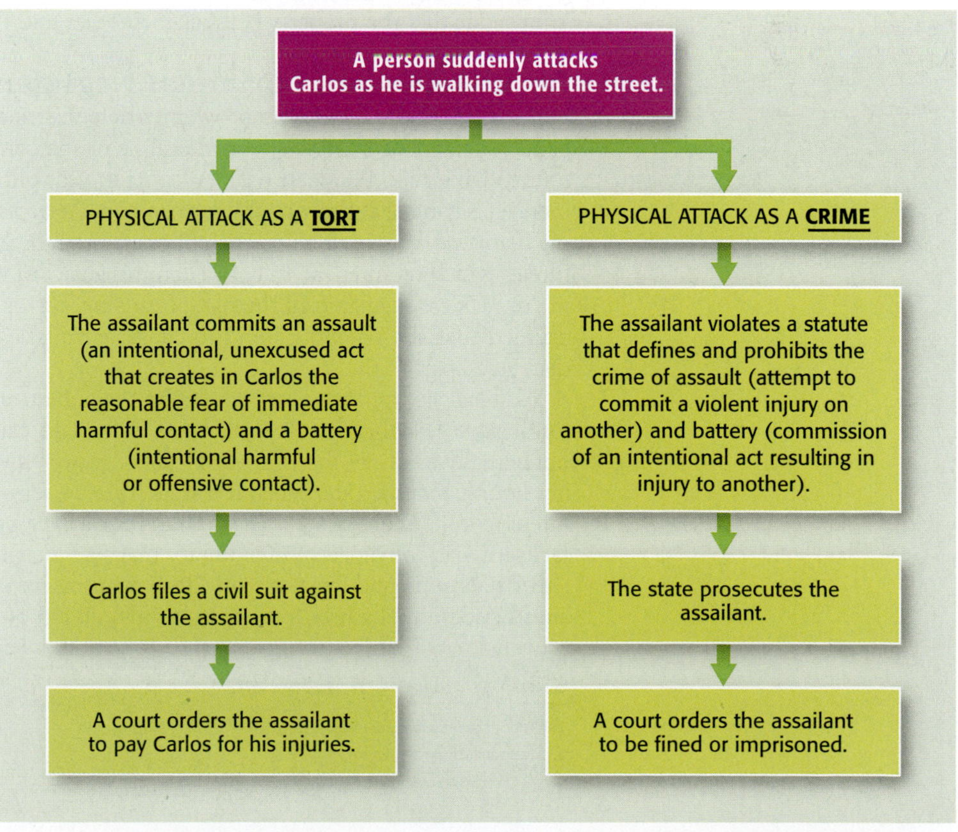

Criminal Liability

LEARNING OBJECTIVE 1
What two elements normally must exist before a person can be held liable for a crime?

Two elements normally must exist simultaneously for a person to be convicted of a crime: (1) the performance of a prohibited act and (2) a specified state of mind or intent on the part of the actor. Note that to establish criminal liability, there must be a *concurrence* between the act and the intent. In other words, these two elements must occur together.

The Criminal Act

Actus reus A guilty (prohibited) act. The commission of a prohibited act is one of the two essential elements required for criminal liability, the other element being the intent to commit a crime.

Every criminal statute prohibits certain behavior. Most crimes require an act of *commission*. That is, a person must *do* something in order to be accused of a crime. In criminal law, a prohibited act is referred to as the ***actus reus***,[2] or guilty act. In some situations, an act of *omission* can be a crime, but only when a person has a legal duty to perform the omitted act, such as failing to file a tax return.

The *guilty act* requirement is based on one of the premises of criminal law—that a person is punished for harm done to society. For a crime to exist, the guilty act must cause some harm to a person or to property. Thinking about killing someone or about stealing a car may be wrong, but the thoughts do no harm until they are translated into action. Of course, a person can be punished for attempting murder or robbery, but normally only if he or she took substantial steps toward the criminal objective.

State of Mind

Mens rea The wrongful mental state ("guilty mind"), or intent, that is one of the key requirements to establish criminal liability for an act.

A wrongful mental state ***(mens rea)***[3] is generally required to establish criminal liability. What constitutes such a mental state varies according to the wrongful action. For murder, the act is the taking of a life, and the mental state is the intent to take life. For theft, the guilty act is the taking of another person's property, and the mental state involves both the knowledge that the property belongs to another and the intent to deprive the owner of it.

Recklessness and Criminal Negligence

A court can also find that the required mental state is present when a defendant's acts are reckless or criminally negligent. A defendant is *criminally reckless* if he or she consciously disregards a substantial and unjustifiable risk. **EXAMPLE 6.2** A fourteen-year-old New Jersey girl posted a Facebook message saying that she was going to launch a terrorist attack on her high school and asking if anyone wanted to help. The police arrested the girl for the crime of making a terrorist threat, which requires the intent to commit an act of violence with "the intent to terrorize" or "in reckless disregard of the risk of causing" terror or inconvenience. Although the girl claimed that she did not intend to cause harm, she was prosecuted under the "reckless disregard" part of the statute. •

Criminal negligence occurs when the defendant takes an unjustified, substantial, and foreseeable risk that results in harm. A defendant can be negligent even if she or he was not actually aware of the risk but *should have been aware* of it.[4] A homicide is classified as *involuntary manslaughter* when it results from an act of criminal negligence and there is no intent to kill. **EXAMPLE 6.3** Dr. Conrad Murray, the personal physician of pop star Michael Jackson, was convicted of involuntary manslaughter in 2011 for prescribing the drug that led to Jackson's sudden death in 2009. Murray had given Jackson propofol, a powerful anesthetic normally used in surgery, as a sleep aid on the night of his death, even though Murray knew that Jackson had already taken other sedatives. •

2. Pronounced *ak*-tuhs *ray*-uhs.
3. Pronounced *mehns ray*-uh.
4. Model Penal Code Section 2.02(2)(d).

(Frederick M. Brown/Getty Images)

Why was Dr. Conrad Murray convicted of involuntary manslaughter in the death of pop star Michael Jackson?

Strict Liability and Overcriminalization

In recent years, an increasing number of laws and regulations have imposed criminal sanctions for strict liability crimes—that is, offenses that do not require a wrongful mental state, or malice, to establish criminal liability.

Federal Crimes The federal criminal code now lists more than four thousand criminal offenses, many of which do not require a specific mental state. There are also at least ten thousand federal rules that can be enforced through criminal sanctions, and many of these rules do not require intent. **EXAMPLE 6.4** Eddie Leroy Anderson, a retired logger and former science teacher, and his son went digging for arrowheads near a campground in Idaho. They did not realize that they were on federal land and that it is a crime to take artifacts off federal land without a permit. Although the penalty could be as much as two years in prison, father and son pleaded guilty and were sentenced to probation and a $1,500 fine each. •

Strict liability crimes are particularly common in environmental laws, laws aimed at combating illegal drugs, and other laws related to public health, safety, and welfare. Under federal law, for instance, tenants can be evicted from public housing if one of their relatives or guests used illegal drugs—regardless of whether the tenant knew or should have known about the drug activity.

State Crimes Many states have also enacted laws that punish behavior as criminal without the need to show criminal intent. **EXAMPLE 6.5** Under Arizona law, a hunter who shoots an elk outside the area specified by his or her permit has committed a crime. Criminal liability is imposed regardless of the hunter's intent or knowledge of the law.[5] •

Overcriminalization Proponents of laws that establish strict liability crimes argue that they are necessary to protect the public and the environment. Critics say that the laws have led to *overcriminalization,* or the use of criminal law to attempt to solve social problems, such as illegal drug use. They argue that when the requirement of intent is removed from criminal offenses, people are more likely to commit crimes unknowingly—and perhaps even innocently. When an honest mistake can lead to a criminal conviction, the role of criminal law as a deterrent to future wrongful conduct is undermined.

Corporate Criminal Liability

As will be discussed in Chapter 29, a *corporation* is a legal entity created under the laws of a state. At one time, it was thought that a corporation could not incur criminal liability because, although a corporation is a legal person, it can act only through its agents (corporate directors, officers, and employees). Therefore, the corporate entity itself could not "intend" to commit a crime. Over time, this view has changed. Obviously, corporations cannot be imprisoned, but they can be fined or denied certain legal privileges (such as necessary licenses).

Liability of the Corporate Entity

Today, corporations are normally liable for the crimes committed by their agents and employees within the course and scope

5. See, for example, *State v. Slayton,* 214 Ariz. 511, 154 P.3d 1057 (2007).

of their employment.[6] For such criminal liability to be imposed, the prosecutor typically must show that the corporation could have prevented the act or that a supervisor within the corporation authorized or had knowledge of the act. In addition, corporations can be criminally liable for failing to perform specific duties imposed by law (such as duties under environmental laws or securities laws).

CASE EXAMPLE 6.6 A prostitution ring, the Gold Club, was operating out of motels in West Virginia. A motel manager, who was also an officer in the corporation that owned the motels, gave discounted rates to Gold Club prostitutes, and they paid him in cash. The corporation received a portion of the funds generated by the Gold Club's illegal operations. At trial, the jury found that the corporation was criminally liable because a supervisor within the corporation—the motel manager—had knowledge of the prostitution and the corporation had allowed it to continue.[7]

(AP Photo/Seth Wenig)

Gary Foster, formerly a Citigroup vice president, embezzled $22 million from his employer. Are corporate officers liable for their crimes?

Liability of Corporate Officers and Directors

Corporate directors and officers are personally liable for the crimes they commit, regardless of whether the crimes were committed for their personal benefit or on the corporation's behalf. Additionally, corporate directors and officers may be held liable for the actions of employees under their supervision. Under the *responsible corporate officer doctrine,* a court may impose criminal liability on a corporate officer regardless of whether she or he participated in, directed, or even knew about a given criminal violation.[8]

CASE EXAMPLE 6.7 The Roscoe family owned the Customer Company, which operated an underground storage tank that leaked gasoline. After the leak occurred, an employee, John Johnson, notified the state environmental agency, and the Roscoes hired an environmental services firm to clean up the spill. The clean-up did not occur immediately, however, and the state sent many notices to John Roscoe, a corporate officer, warning him that the company was violating federal and state environmental laws. Roscoe gave the letters to Johnson, who passed them on to the environmental services firm, but the spill was not cleaned up. The state eventually filed criminal charges against the corporation and the Roscoes individually, and they were convicted. On appeal, the court affirmed the Roscoes' convictions under the responsible corporate officer doctrine. The Roscoes were in positions of responsibility, they had influence over the corporation's actions, and their failure to act constituted a violation of environmental laws.[9]

PREVENTING LEGAL DISPUTES

If you become a corporate officer or director at some point in your career, you need to be aware that you can be held liable for the crimes of your subordinates. You should always be familiar with any criminal statutes relevant to the corporation's particular industry or trade. Also, make sure that corporate employees are trained in how to comply with the multitude of applicable laws, particularly environmental laws and health and safety regulations, which frequently involve criminal sanctions.

6. See Model Penal Code Section 2.07.
7. As a result of the convictions, the motel manager was sentenced to fifteen months in prison, and the corporation was ordered to forfeit the motel property. *United States v. Singh,* 518 F.3d 236 (4th Cir. 2008).
8. For a landmark case in this area, see *United States v. Park,* 421 U.S. 658, 95 S.Ct. 1903, 44 L.Ed.2d 489 (1975).
9. The Roscoes and the corporation were sentenced to pay penalties of $2,493,250. *People v. Roscoe,* 169 Cal.App.4th 829, 87 Cal.Rptr.3d 187 (3 Dist. 2008).

Types of Crimes

LEARNING OBJECTIVE 2
What are five broad categories of crimes? What is white-collar crime?

Federal, state, and local laws provide for the classification and punishment of hundreds of thousands of different criminal acts. Traditionally, though, crimes have been grouped into five broad categories: violent crime (crimes against persons), property crime, public order crime, white-collar crime, and organized crime. Within each of these categories, crimes may also be separated into more than one classification. Note also that many crimes may be committed in cyberspace, as well as the physical world. When they occur in the virtual world, we refer to them as cyber crimes, as discussed later in the chapter.

Violent Crime

Robbery The act of forcefully and unlawfully taking personal property of any value from another.

Crimes against persons, because they cause others to suffer harm or death, are referred to as *violent crimes.* Murder is a violent crime. So, too, is sexual assault, or rape. **Robbery**—defined as the taking of cash, personal property, or any other article of value from a person by means of force or fear—is another violent crime. Typically, states have more severe penalties for *aggravated robbery*—robbery with the use of a deadly weapon.

Assault and battery, which were discussed in Chapter 4 in the context of tort law, are also classified as violent crimes. Recall that assault can involve an object or force put into motion by a person. **EXAMPLE 6.8** On the anniversary of a landmark abortion rights decision, Paul drives his sport utility vehicle into a local abortion clinic. The police arrest him for aggravated assault even though no one is injured by his act. •

Each of these violent crimes is further classified by degree, depending on the circumstances surrounding the criminal act. These circumstances include the intent of the person committing the crime, whether a weapon was used, and (in cases other than murder) the level of pain and suffering experienced by the victim. (For a discussion of why some violent crimes committed on Indian reservations are not being prosecuted, see this chapter's *Law, Diversity, and Business: Managerial Implications* feature on the following page.)

Property Crime

The most common type of criminal activity is property crime—crimes in which the goal of the offender is some form of economic gain or the damaging of property. Robbery is a form of property crime, as well as a violent crime, because the offender seeks to gain the property of another. We look here at a number of other crimes that fall within the general category of property crime. (Note also that many types of cyber crime, discussed later in this chapter, are forms of property crime as well.)

Burglary The unlawful entry or breaking into a building with the intent to commit a felony.

Burglary

Traditionally, **burglary** was defined under the common law as breaking and entering the dwelling of another at night with the intent to commit a felony. Originally, the definition was aimed at protecting an individual's home and its occupants. Most state statutes have eliminated some of the requirements found in the common law definition. The time of day at which the breaking and entering occurs, for example, is usually immaterial. State statutes frequently omit the element of breaking, and some states do not require that the building be a dwelling. When a deadly weapon is used in a burglary, the person can be charged with *aggravated burglary* and punished more severely.

Larceny The wrongful taking and carrying away of another person's personal property with the intent to permanently deprive the owner of the property.

Larceny

Under the common law, the crime of **larceny** involved the unlawful taking and carrying away of someone else's personal property with the intent to permanently deprive the owner of possession. Put simply, larceny is stealing, or theft. Whereas robbery involves force or fear, larceny does not. Therefore, picking pockets is larceny, not robbery.

LAW, DIVERSITY, AND BUSINESS: MANAGERIAL IMPLICATIONS

NATIVE AMERICANS AND CRIMINAL JUSTICE

Thanks to freedom from state antigambling laws and "sin" taxes on alcohol and cigarettes, Native American reservations are often considered to be somewhat outside the law. Indeed, Vernon Roanhorse, a Navajo tribal official, calls his reservation a "lawless land." The problems, however, go much deeper than casinos and cheap cigarettes.

In its earliest days, the U.S. government treated the various Native American tribes as individual sovereign nations. Ever since, the government has allowed Native Americans a considerable amount of self-rule. Nevertheless, tribal leaders do not have complete jurisdiction over all events that occur on tribal lands, including crimes.

Problems with Criminal Jurisdiction As far as criminal law is concerned, the 275 tribes operate in a jurisdictional void. They run their own court systems, but federal law denies tribal courts criminal jurisdiction over defendants who are not Indians or are Indians from a different tribe.

Furthermore, Native American courts *cannot prosecute felonies* (the most serious crimes) under any circumstances. For these crimes, they must rely on the Federal Bureau of Investigation (FBI) to act as their police force and U.S. attorneys to act as their prosecutors.

Lack of Federal Enforcement The federal government's record in this area is dismal. About 200 criminal charges involving Native Americans are dismissed each year because FBI agents fail to file arrest reports. For their part, U.S. attorneys decline to prosecute about two-thirds of all Indian Country cases.

According to a 2011 report by the National Organization for Women, Native American women experience the highest rate of violence of any group in the United States. Domestic violence, sexual abuse, and stalking crimes are common. More than 80 percent of Native American rape victims identify their assailant as non-Indian, which means that these suspects are out of the reach of Native American jurisdiction and can be apprehended only by the often unresponsive federal criminal justice system.

Business Implications *In today's legal environment, many crimes do not involve violence, but rather are violations of corporate, consumer, environmental, or intellectual property laws. Those who do business with Native Americans should be aware of the jurisdictional problems that affect criminal prosecutions, particularly with felony offenses. In contracts with Native Americans, businesspersons should consider using arbitration or forum-selection clauses that specify how and where any disputes will be resolved.*

Similarly, an employee who takes company products and supplies home for personal use without authorization commits larceny. (Note that a person who commits larceny generally can also be sued under tort law because the act of taking possession of another's property involves a trespass to personal property.)

Most states have expanded the definition of property that is subject to larceny statutes. Stealing computer programs may constitute larceny even though the "property" is not physical (see the discussion of computer crime later in this chapter). So, too, can the theft of natural gas or Internet and television cable service.

Obtaining Goods by False Pretenses

Obtaining goods by means of false pretenses is a form of theft that involves trickery or fraud, such as paying for an iPad with a stolen credit-card number. Statutes dealing with such illegal activities vary widely from state to state. They often apply not only to acquiring property, but also to obtaining services or funds by false pretenses—for example, selling an iPad that you claim is yours when you actually do not own it.

Receiving Stolen Goods

It is a crime to receive goods that a person knows or should have known were stolen or illegally obtained. To be convicted, the recipient of such goods need not know the true identity of the owner or the thief, and need not have paid for the goods. All that is necessary is that the recipient knows or should have known that the goods were stolen, and intended to deprive the true owner of those goods.

Arson The intentional burning of a building.

Arson

The willful and malicious burning of a building (and, in some states, vehicles and other items of personal property) is the crime of **arson.** At common law, arson traditionally applied only to burning down another person's house. The law was designed to protect human life. Today, arson statutes have been extended to cover the destruction of any building, regardless of ownership, by fire or explosion.

Every state has a special statute that covers the act of burning a building for the purpose of collecting insurance. **EXAMPLE 6.9** Benton owns an insured apartment building that is falling apart. If he sets fire to it or pays someone else to do so, he is guilty not only of arson but also of defrauding the insurer, which is attempted larceny. • Of course, the insurer need not pay the claim when insurance fraud is proved.

Forgery The fraudulent making or altering of any writing in a way that changes the legal rights and liabilities of another.

Forgery

The fraudulent making or altering of any writing (including electronic records) in a way that changes the legal rights and liabilities of another is **forgery.** **EXAMPLE 6.10** Without authorization, Severson signs Bennett's name to the back of a check made out to Bennett and attempts to cash it. Severson has committed the crime of forgery. • Forgery also includes changing trademarks, falsifying public records, counterfeiting, and altering a legal document.

Public Order Crime

Historically, societies have always outlawed activities that are considered to be contrary to public values and morals. Today, the most common public order crimes include public drunkenness, prostitution, gambling, and illegal drug use. These crimes are sometimes referred to as victimless crimes because they normally harm only the offender. From a broader perspective, however, they are deemed detrimental to society as a whole because

This West Hollywood, California, carport fire was one of twelve such fires that were set by an individual during a short time period. What type of crime was that person guilty of committing?

(Gene Blevins/Reuters/Landov)

(Lucas JACKSON/Reuters /Landov)

Bernard Madoff (right) perpetuated the largest fraudulent investment scheme in modern history.

White-Collar Crime Nonviolent crime committed by individuals or corporations to obtain a personal or business advantage.

Embezzlement The fraudulent appropriation of funds or other property by a person who was entrusted with the funds or property.

they may create an environment that gives rise to property and violent crimes.

EXAMPLE 6.11 A man flying from Texas to California on a commercial airliner becomes angry and yells obscenities at a flight attendant when a beverage cart strikes his knee. After the pilot diverts the plane and makes an unscheduled landing at a nearby airport, police remove the passenger and arrest him. If the man is later found guilty of the public order crime of interfering with a flight crew, he may be sentenced to more than two years in prison. ●

White-Collar Crime

Crimes that typically occur only in the business context are popularly referred to as **white-collar crimes.** Although there is no official definition of white-collar crime, the term is commonly used to mean an illegal act or series of acts committed by an individual or business entity using some nonviolent means. Usually, this kind of crime is committed in the course of a legitimate occupation. Corporate crimes fall into this category. In addition, certain property crimes, such as larceny and forgery, may also be white-collar crimes if they occur within the business context.

Embezzlement

When a person who is entrusted with another person's funds or property fraudulently appropriates it, **embezzlement** occurs. Typically, embezzlement is carried out by an employee who steals funds. Banks are particularly prone to this problem, but embezzlement can occur in any firm. In a number of businesses, corporate officers or accountants have fraudulently converted funds for their own benefit and then "fixed" the books to cover up their crime. Embezzlement is not larceny, because the wrongdoer does not physically take the property from another's possession, and it is not robbery, because force or fear is not used.

Embezzlement occurs whether the embezzler takes the funds directly from the victim or from a third person. If the financial officer of a corporation pockets checks from third parties that were given to her to deposit into the corporate account, she is embezzling. Frequently, an embezzler takes a relatively small amount at one time but does so repeatedly over a long period. The embezzler might underreport income or deposits and keep the remaining amount, for example, or create fictitious persons or accounts and write checks to them from the corporate account. An employer's failure to remit state withholding taxes that were collected from employee wages can also constitute embezzlement.

The intent to return embezzled property—or its actual return—is not a defense to the crime of embezzlement, as the following *Spotlight Case* illustrates.

Spotlight on White-Collar Crime

Case 6.1

People v. Sisuphan

Court of Appeal of California, First District,
181 Cal.App.4th 800, 104 Cal.Rptr.3d 654 (2010).

(Joe Raedle/Getty Images)

A Toyota dealership employee committed embezzlement but returned the funds. Is this a defense?

FACTS Lou Sisuphan was the director of finance at a Toyota dealership. Sisuphan complained repeatedly to management about another employee, Ian McClelland. The general manager, Michael Christian, would not terminate McClelland "because he brought a lot of money into the dealership." To jeopardize McClelland's employment, Sisuphan took and kept an envelope containing a payment of nearly $30,000 from one of McClelland's customers that McClelland had tried to deposit in the company's safe. Later, Sisuphan told the dealership what he had done, adding that he had "no intention of stealing the money"

Spotlight Case 6.1—Continued

and returned it. Christian fired Sisuphan the next day, and the district attorney later charged Sisuphan with embezzlement. After a jury trial, Sisuphan was found guilty. Sisuphan appealed.

ISSUE Did Sisuphan take the funds with the intent to defraud his employer?

DECISION Yes. The appellate court affirmed Sisphan's conviction for embezzlement. Sisuphan had the required intent at the time he took the funds, and the evidence that he repaid the dealership was properly excluded.

REASON The court reasoned that evidence of repayment is admissible only if it shows that a defendant's intent at the time of the taking was not fraudulent. In determining whether Sisuphan's intent was fraudulent at the time of the taking, the main issue was not whether he intended to spend the funds that he had taken, but whether he intended to use the payment "for a purpose other than that for which the dealership entrusted it to him." Sisuphan's stated purpose was to get McClelland fired. Because this purpose was beyond the scope of his responsibility, it was "outside the trust afforded him by the dealership" and indicated that he had fraudulent intent.

CRITICAL THINKING—Legal Consideration *Why was Sisuphan convicted of embezzlement instead of larceny? What is the difference between these two crimes?*

Mail and Wire Fraud

One of the most potent weapons against white-collar criminals are the federal laws that prohibit mail fraud[10] and wire fraud.[11] These laws make it a federal crime to devise any scheme that uses the U.S. mail, commercial carriers—such as FedEx or UPS—or wire, including telegraph, telephone, television, e-mail, or online social media, with the intent to defraud the public. These laws are often applied when persons send out advertisements or e-mails with the intent to obtain cash or property by false pretenses.

CASE EXAMPLE 6.12 Cisco Systems, Inc., offers a warranty program to authorized resellers of Cisco parts. Iheanyi Frank Chinasa and Robert Kendrick Chambliss formulated a scheme to use this program to defraud Cisco by obtaining replacement parts to which they were not entitled. The two men sent numerous e-mails and Internet service requests to Cisco to convince the company to ship them new parts via commercial carriers. Ultimately, Chinasa and Chambliss were convicted of mail and wire fraud, and conspiracy to commit mail and wire fraud.[12] •

"It was beautiful and simple as all truly great swindles are."

O. Henry, 1862–1910
(American writer)

The maximum penalty under these statutes is substantial. Persons convicted of mail, wire, and Internet fraud may be imprisoned for up to twenty years and/or fined. If the violation affects a financial institution or involves fraud in connection with emergency disaster-relief funds, the violator may be fined up to $1 million, imprisoned for up to thirty years, or both.

Bribery

The crime of bribery involves offering something of value to someone in an attempt to influence that person, who is usually, but not always, a public official, to act in a way that serves a private interest. Three types of bribery are considered crimes: bribery of public officials, commercial bribery, and bribery of foreign officials. As an element of the crime of bribery, intent must be present and proved. The bribe itself can be anything the recipient considers to be valuable. Realize that the *crime of bribery occurs when the bribe is offered*—it is not required that the bribe be accepted. *Accepting a bribe* is a separate crime.

Commercial bribery involves corrupt dealings between private persons or businesses. Typically, people make commercial bribes to obtain proprietary information, cover up an

10. The Mail Fraud Act of 1990, 18 U.S.C. Sections 1341–1342.
11. 18 U.S.C. Section 1343.
12. *United States v. Chinasa*, 789 F.Supp.2d 691 (E.D.Va. 2011).

inferior product, or secure new business. Industrial espionage sometimes involves commercial bribes. **EXAMPLE 6.13** Kent works at the firm of Jacoby & Meyers. He offers to pay Laurel, an employee in a competing firm, if she will give him her firm's trade secrets and pricing schedules. Kent has committed commercial bribery. • So-called kickbacks, or payoffs for special favors or services, are a form of commercial bribery in some situations.

Bankruptcy Fraud

Federal bankruptcy law (see Chapter 21) allows individuals and businesses to be relieved of oppressive debt through bankruptcy proceedings. Numerous white-collar crimes may be committed during the many phases of a bankruptcy proceeding. A creditor may file a false claim against the debtor. Also, a debtor may attempt to protect assets from creditors by fraudulently transferring property to favored parties. For instance, a company-owned automobile may be "sold" at a bargain price to a trusted friend or relative. Closely related to the crime of fraudulent transfer of property is the crime of fraudulent concealment of property, such as hiding gold coins.

Theft of Trade Secrets

As discussed in Chapter 5 on page 146, trade secrets constitute a form of intellectual property that can be extremely valuable for many businesses. The Economic Espionage Act of 1996[13] made the theft of trade secrets a federal crime. The act also made it a federal crime to buy or possess trade secrets of another person, knowing that the trade secrets were stolen or otherwise acquired without the owner's authorization.

Violations of the act can result in steep penalties. An individual who violates the act can be imprisoned for up to ten years and fined up to $500,000. If a corporation or other organization violates the act, it can be fined up to $5 million. Additionally, the law provides that any property acquired as a result of the violation, such as airplanes and automobiles, and any property used in the commission of the violation, such as servers and other electronic devices, are subject to criminal *forfeiture*—meaning that the government can take the property. A theft of trade secrets conducted via the Internet, for example, could result in the forfeiture of every computer or other device used to commit or facilitate the crime.

Insider Trading

An individual who obtains "inside information" about the plans of a publicly listed corporation can often make stock-trading profits by purchasing or selling corporate securities based on the information. **Insider trading** is a violation of securities law and will be considered more fully in Chapter 31. Generally, the rule is that a person who possesses inside information and has a duty not to disclose it to outsiders may not profit from the purchase or sale of securities based on that information until the information is made available to the public.

Insider Trading The purchase or sale of securities on the basis of *inside information* (information that has not been made available to the public).

Organized Crime

As mentioned, white-collar crime takes place within the confines of the legitimate business world. *Organized crime,* in contrast, operates *illegitimately* by, among other things, providing illegal goods and services. For organized crime, the traditional preferred markets are gambling, prostitution, illegal narcotics, and loan sharking (lending at higher than legal interest rates), along with counterfeiting and credit-card scams.

Money Laundering

Organized crime and other illegal activities generate many billions of dollars in profits each year from illegal drug transactions and, to a lesser extent, from racketeering, prostitution, and gambling. Under federal law, banks and other financial institutions are required to report currency transactions involving more than $10,000. Consequently, those who engage in illegal activities face difficulties when they try to deposit their cash profits from illegal transactions.

13. 18 U.S.C. Sections 1831–1839.

Money Laundering Engaging in financial transactions to conceal the identity, source, or destination of illegally gained funds.

As an alternative to simply storing cash from illegal transactions in a safe-deposit box, wrongdoers and racketeers launder their "dirty" money to make it "clean" by passing it through a legitimate business. **Money laundering** is engaging in financial transactions to conceal the identity, source, or destination of illegally gained funds.

EXAMPLE 6.14 Harris, a successful drug dealer, becomes a partner with a restaurateur. Little by little, the restaurant shows increasing profits. As a partner in the restaurant, Harris is able to report the "profits" of the restaurant as legitimate income on which he pays federal and state taxes. He can then spend those funds without worrying that his lifestyle may exceed the level possible with his reported income. •

The Racketeer Influenced and Corrupt Organizations Act

To curb the entry of organized crime into the legitimate business world, Congress enacted the Racketeer Influenced and Corrupt Organizations Act (RICO).[14] The statute, which was enacted as part of the Organized Crime Control Act, makes it a federal crime to (1) use income obtained from racketeering activity to purchase any interest in an enterprise, (2) acquire or maintain an interest in an enterprise through racketeering activity, (3) conduct or participate in the affairs of an enterprise through racketeering activity, or (4) conspire to do any of the preceding activities.

(Debbie Egan-Chin/*NY Daily News* via Getty Images)

Vincent Gotti (center) is one of sixty alleged mobsters—members of organized crime—in New York and Sicily, Italy. What types of crimes are the most commonly committed by such individuals?

Broad Application of RICO The broad language of RICO has allowed it to be applied in cases that have little or nothing to do with organized crime. RICO incorporates by reference twenty-six separate types of federal crimes and nine types of state felonies[15] and declares that if a person commits two of these offenses, he or she is guilty of "racketeering activity." Under the criminal provisions of RICO, any individual found guilty is subject to a fine of up to $25,000 per violation, imprisonment for up to twenty years, or both. Additionally, the statute provides that those who violate RICO may be required to forfeit (give up) any assets, in the form of property or cash, that were acquired as a result of the illegal activity or that were "involved in" or an "instrumentality of" the activity.

Penalties In the event of a RICO violation, the government can seek civil penalties, such as the divestiture of a defendant's interest in a business (called forfeiture) or the dissolution of the business. Moreover, in some cases, the statute allows private individuals to sue violators and potentially to recover three times their actual losses (treble damages), plus attorneys' fees, for business injuries caused by a violation of the statute. This is perhaps the most controversial aspect of RICO and one that continues to cause debate in the nation's federal courts. The prospect of receiving treble damages in civil RICO lawsuits has given plaintiffs a financial incentive to pursue businesses and employers for violations.

Classification of Crimes

Felony A crime—such as arson, murder, rape, or robbery—that carries the most severe sanctions, ranging from more than one year in a state or federal prison to the death penalty.

In addition to being grouped into the five categories just discussed, crimes are also classified as felonies or misdemeanors depending on their degree of seriousness. **Felonies** are serious crimes punishable by death or by imprisonment for more than a year. Many states

14. 18 U.S.C. Sections 1961–1968.
15. See 18 U.S.C. Section 1961(1)(A).

also define different degrees of felony offenses and vary the punishment according to the degree. **Misdemeanors** are less serious crimes, punishable by a fine or by confinement for up to a year. In most jurisdictions, **petty offenses** are considered to be a subset of misdemeanors. Petty offenses are minor violations, such as jaywalking or violations of building codes. Even for petty offenses, however, a guilty party can be put in jail for a few days, fined, or both, depending on state or local law.

Misdemeanor A lesser crime than a felony, punishable by a fine or incarceration in jail for up to one year.

Petty Offense The least serious kind of criminal offense, such as a traffic or building-code violation.

Defenses to Criminal Liability

LEARNING OBJECTIVE 3
What defenses can be raised to avoid liability for criminal acts?

Persons charged with crimes may be relieved of criminal liability if they can show that their criminal actions were justified under the circumstances. In certain circumstances, the law may also allow a person to be excused from criminal liability because she or he lacks the required mental state. We look at several of the defenses to criminal liability here.

Note that procedural violations, such as obtaining evidence without a valid search warrant, may also operate as defenses. As you will read later in this chapter, evidence obtained in violation of a defendant's constitutional rights normally may not be admitted in court. If the evidence is suppressed, then there may be no basis for prosecuting the defendant.

Justifiable Use of Force

Self-Defense The legally recognized privilege to do what is reasonably necessary to protect oneself, one's property, or someone else against injury by another.

Probably the best-known defense to criminal liability is **self-defense.** Other situations, however, also justify the use of force: the defense of one's dwelling, the defense of other property, and the prevention of a crime. In all of these situations, it is important to distinguish between deadly and nondeadly force. *Deadly force* is likely to result in death or serious bodily harm. *Nondeadly force* is force that reasonably appears necessary to prevent the imminent use of criminal force.

Generally speaking, people can use the amount of nondeadly force that seems necessary to protect themselves, their dwellings, or other property or to prevent the commission of a crime. Deadly force can be used in self-defense if the defender *reasonably believes* that imminent death or grievous bodily harm will otherwise result. In addition, normally the attacker must be using unlawful force, and the defender must not have initiated or provoked the attack.

Traditionally, deadly force could be used to defend a dwelling only when the unlawful entry was violent and the person believed deadly force was necessary to prevent imminent death or great bodily harm. Today, however, in some jurisdictions, deadly force can also be used if the person believes it is necessary to prevent the commission of a felony in the dwelling. Many states are expanding the situations in which the use of deadly force can be justified. Florida, for example, allows the use of deadly force to prevent the commission of a "forcible felony," including robbery, carjacking, and sexual battery. Similar laws have been passed in at least seventeen other states.

Necessity

Sometimes, criminal defendants are relieved of liability if they can show that a criminal act was necessary to prevent an even greater harm. **EXAMPLE 6.15** Trevor is a convicted felon and, as such, is legally prohibited from possessing a firearm. While he and his wife are in a convenience store, a man draws a gun, points it at the cashier, and demands all the cash. Afraid that the man will start shooting, Trevor grabs the gun and holds on to it until police arrive. In this situation, if Trevor is charged with possession of a firearm, he can assert the defense of necessity. •

(AP Photo/The Huntsville Times, Glenn Baeske)

Amy Bishop, shown with her attorney, killed three of her fellow college professors and wounded three more. She pleaded not guilty by reason of insanity. What does she have to prove to prevail at trial?

Insanity

A person who suffers from a mental illness may be incapable of the state of mind required to commit a crime. Thus, insanity can be a defense to a criminal charge. Note that an insanity defense does not allow a person to avoid prison. It simply means that if the defendant successfully proves insanity, she or he will be placed in a mental institution.

The courts have had difficulty deciding what the test for legal insanity should be, however, and psychiatrists as well as lawyers are critical of the tests used. Almost all federal courts and some states use the relatively liberal substantial-capacity test set forth in the Model Penal Code:

> A person is not responsible for criminal conduct if at the time of such conduct as a result of mental disease or defect he [or she] lacks substantial capacity either to appreciate the wrongfulness of his [or her] conduct or to conform his [or her] conduct to the requirements of the law.

Some states use the *M'Naghten* test,[16] under which a criminal defendant is not responsible if, at the time of the offense, he or she did not know the nature and quality of the act or did not know that the act was wrong. Other states use the irresistible-impulse test. A person operating under an irresistible impulse may know an act is wrong but cannot refrain from doing it. Under any of these tests, proving insanity is extremely difficult. For this reason, the insanity defense is rarely used and usually is not successful.

Mistake

KNOW THIS

"Ignorance" is a lack of information. "Mistake" is a confusion of information, which can sometimes negate criminal intent.

Everyone has heard the saying "Ignorance of the law is no excuse." Ordinarily, ignorance of the law or a mistaken idea about what the law requires is not a valid defense. A *mistake of fact*, as opposed to a *mistake of law*, can excuse criminal responsibility if it negates the mental state necessary to commit a crime.

EXAMPLE 6.16 If Oliver Wheaton mistakenly walks off with Julie Tyson's briefcase because he thinks it is his, there is no crime. Theft requires knowledge that the property belongs to another. (If Wheaton's act causes Tyson to incur damages, however, she may sue him in a civil action for trespass to personal property or conversion—torts that were discussed in Chapter 4.) •

Duress

Duress Unlawful pressure brought to bear on a person, causing the person to perform an act that she or he would not otherwise perform.

Duress exists when the *wrongful threat* of one person induces another person to perform an act that she or he would not otherwise perform. In such a situation, duress is said to negate the mental state necessary to commit a crime because the defendant was forced or compelled to commit the act.

Duress can be used as a defense to most crimes except murder. The states vary in how duress is defined and what types of crimes it can excuse, however. Generally, to successfully assert duress as a defense, the defendant must reasonably believe in the immediate danger, and the jury (or judge) must conclude that the defendant's belief was reasonable.

16. A rule derived from *M'Naghten's* Case, 8 Eng.Rep. 718 (1843).

Entrapment

Entrapment A defense in which a defendant claims that he or she was induced by a public official to commit a crime that he or she would otherwise not have committed.

Entrapment is a defense designed to prevent police officers or other government agents from enticing persons to commit crimes so that they can later be prosecuted for criminal acts. In the typical entrapment case, an undercover agent *suggests* that a crime be committed and pressures or induces an individual to commit it. The agent then arrests the individual for the crime.

For entrapment to succeed as a defense, both the suggestion and the inducement must take place. The defense is not intended to prevent law enforcement agents from ever setting a trap for an unwary criminal. Rather, its purpose is to prevent them from pushing the individual into a criminal act. The crucial issue is whether the person who committed a crime was predisposed to commit the illegal act or did so only because the agent induced it.

Statute of Limitations

With some exceptions, such as for the crime of murder, statutes of limitations apply to crimes just as they do to civil wrongs. In other words, the state must initiate criminal prosecution within a certain number of years. If a criminal action is brought after the statutory time period has expired, the accused person can raise the statute of limitations as a defense.

Immunity

Self-Incrimination Giving testimony in a trial or other legal proceeding that could expose the person testifying to criminal prosecution.

Accused persons are understandably reluctant to give information if it will be used to prosecute them, and they cannot be forced to do so. The privilege against **self-incrimination** is granted by the Fifth Amendment to the U.S. Constitution, which reads, in part, "nor shall [any person] be compelled in any criminal case to be a witness against himself." When the state wishes to obtain information from a person accused of a crime, the state can grant *immunity* from prosecution or agree to prosecute for a less serious offense in exchange for the information. Once immunity is given, the person can no longer refuse to testify on Fifth Amendment grounds because he or she now has an absolute privilege against self-incrimination.

Plea Bargaining The process by which a criminal defendant and the prosecutor work out an agreement to dispose of the criminal case, subject to court approval.

Often, a grant of immunity from prosecution for a serious crime is part of the **plea bargaining** between the defendant and the prosecuting attorney. The defendant may be convicted of a lesser offense, while the state uses the defendant's testimony to prosecute accomplices for serious crimes carrying heavy penalties.

Constitutional Safeguards and Criminal Procedures

LEARNING OBJECTIVE 4

What constitutional safeguards exist to protect persons accused of crimes?

Criminal law brings the power of the state, with all its resources, to bear against the individual. Criminal procedures are designed to protect the constitutional rights of individuals and to prevent the arbitrary use of power by the government.

The U.S. Constitution provides specific safeguards for those accused of crimes, as mentioned in Chapter 2. Most of these safeguards protect individuals against state government actions, as well as federal government actions, by virtue of the due process clause of the Fourteenth Amendment. These protections are set forth in the Fourth, Fifth, Sixth, and Eighth Amendments.

Fourth Amendment Protections

Search Warrant An order granted by a public authority, such as a judge, that authorizes law enforcement personnel to search particular premises or property.

The Fourth Amendment protects the "right of the people to be secure in their persons, houses, papers, and effects." Before searching or seizing private property, law enforcement officers must obtain a **search warrant**—an order from a judge or other public official authorizing the search or seizure.

Should the police be able to use high-tech tracking devices without a search warrant? Police increasingly are using new technologies for surveillance. In particular, a Global Positioning System (GPS) tracker can easily be attached to a suspect's car while it is parked on a public street. If police do this without obtaining a search warrant, have they conducted an unreasonable search in violation of the Fourth Amendment? According to the United States Supreme Court, they have. In *United States v. Jones,*[17] a unanimous Court said that the government "physically occupied private property [the car] for the purpose of obtaining information. We have no doubt that such physical intrusion would have been considered a 'search' within the meaning of the Fourth Amendment when it was adopted." In other words, attaching a GPS tracker to a car is analogous to entering a person's home to make a search. Both require search warrants.

Undoubtedly, there will be continued debate about how technology can legally be used to track people's movements. How much surveillance should society accept? Should the Supreme Court's decision be extended to cell phones and other digital devices? For instance, federal and local law enforcement agents routinely engage in secret cell phone tracking by using devices called Stingrays. Does such tracking violate the Fourth Amendment? It may, given that the Supreme Court expressed concern about the invasion of privacy represented by the GPS tracker in the *Jones* case.

17. ___ U.S. ___, 132 S.Ct. 945, 181 L.Ed.2d 911 (2012). This case was presented in Exhibit 1A.3 on page 31.

(AP Photo/Paul Sakuma)

Federal Bureau of Investigation (FBI) agents remove numerous boxes of documents from Solyndra, a bankrupt solar energy company in Fremont, California. U.S. taxpayers lost $535 million in loan guarantees because of the bankruptcy. Because of the Fourth Amendment, did the FBI have to first obtain a search warrant to enter the company's offices?

Probable Cause Reasonable grounds for believing that a search should be conducted or that a person should be arrested.

Search Warrants and Probable Cause

To obtain a search warrant, law enforcement officers must convince a judge that they have reasonable grounds, or **probable cause,** to believe a search will reveal a specific illegality. Probable cause requires the officers to have trustworthy evidence that would convince a reasonable person that the proposed search or seizure is more likely justified than not.

Furthermore, the Fourth Amendment prohibits general warrants. It requires a particular description of what is to be searched or seized. General searches through a person's belongings are impermissible. The search cannot extend beyond what is described in the warrant. Although search warrants require specificity, if a search warrant is issued for a person's residence, items in that residence may be searched even if they do not belong to that individual.

CASE EXAMPLE 6.17 Paycom Billing Services, Inc., an online payment service, stores vast amounts of customer credit-card information in its computers. Christopher Adjani, a former employee, threatened to sell Paycom's confidential client information if the company did not pay him $3 million. The FBI obtained a search warrant to search Adjani's person, automobile, and residence, including computer equipment. When the FBI agents served the warrant, they discovered evidence of the criminal scheme on a computer in Adjani's residence. The computer belonged to Adjani's live-in girlfriend. Adjani filed a motion to suppress this evidence, claiming that because he did not own the computer, it was beyond the scope of the warrant. A federal appellate court disagreed, however, and held that the search of the computer was proper, given the alleged involvement of computers in the crime.[18] •

In the following case, police officers obtained a search warrant and conducted a search of a gang member's foster mother's home for weapons. A judge later ruled that the warrant was not supported by probable cause, and the homeowners sued individual police officers for executing an illegal search warrant.

18. *United States v. Adjani,* 452 F.3d 1140 (9th Cir. 2006).

Case 6.2

Messerschmidt v. Millender

Supreme Court of the United States,
___ U.S. ___, 132 S.Ct. 1235,
182 L.Ed.2d 47 (2012).

(Mario Villafuerte/Getty Images)

Police officers conduct a search.

FACTS The Los Angeles County Sheriff's Department was protecting a woman from Jerry Ray Bowen when he tried to kill her with a sawed-off shotgun. The woman told the police that she and Bowen used to date, that Bowen was a gang member, and that she thought Bowen was staying at the home of Augusta Millender, his foster mother. After investigating the incident further, the police prepared a warrant to search the foster mother's home for all guns and gang-related material, and a judge approved it. When police officers, including Curt Messerschmidt, served the search warrant, they discovered that Bowen was not at the home but searched it anyway. Millender sued individual police officers in federal court for subjecting her to an illegal search. A federal appellate court held that the police lacked probable cause for such a broad search and that the police officers could be held personally liable. The police officers appealed. The United States Supreme Court granted *certiorari* to determine whether the police officers were immune from personal liability.

ISSUE Assuming that the search violated the Fourth Amendment to the U.S. Constitution, are the police officers immune from liability?

DECISION Yes. The United States Supreme Court reversed the decision of the federal appellate court, granting the officers immunity from liability.

REASON The doctrine of qualified immunity "gives government officials breathing room to make reasonable but

Case 6.2—Continued

mistaken judgments." The Court explained that immunity depends on whether an official "acted in an objectively reasonable manner." Here, the police officers acted reasonably, in part, because a neutral judge approved the search warrant. Moreover, a reasonable police officer could have believed that the warrant was proper. For example, even if the warrant was too broad because it authorized a search for all guns rather than just the one Bowen fired, a reasonable police officer could conclude that Bowen had other guns. After all, the Court reasoned, he owned a sawed-off shotgun, he was a known gang member, and he had just tried to kill a woman for calling the police. Similarly, one could reasonably conclude that there was probable cause to search for gang-related material because it would be helpful in prosecuting Bowen for attacking his ex-girlfriend. Finally, the officers conducted a detailed investigation and had the warrant application reviewed three times before submitting it to the judge.

CRITICAL THINKING—Legal Consideration *How would police officers behave if they could always be held personally liable for executing unconstitutional warrants? Would they be more or less inclined to apply for and execute search warrants? Explain.*

Searches and Seizures in the Business Context

Because of the strong governmental interest in protecting the public, a warrant normally is not required for seizures of spoiled or contaminated food. Nor are warrants required for searches of businesses in such highly regulated industries as liquor, guns, and strip mining.

Generally, however, government inspectors do not have the right to search business premises without a warrant, although the standard of probable cause is not the same as in nonbusiness contexts. The existence of a general and neutral plan of enforcement will justify the issuance of a warrant. Lawyers and accountants frequently possess the business records of their clients, and inspecting these documents while they are out of the hands of their true owners also requires a warrant. Inspecting a physician's medical records also generally requires a warrant, although an exception may be made if the physician agrees to allow the search.[19]

Fifth Amendment Protections

The Fifth Amendment offers significant protections for accused persons. One is the guarantee that no one can be deprived of "life, liberty, or property without due process of law." Two other important Fifth Amendment provisions protect persons against double jeopardy and self-incrimination.

Due Process of Law

Remember from Chapter 2 on page 49 that *due process of law* has both procedural and substantive aspects. Procedural due process requirements underlie criminal procedures. The law must be carried out in a fair and orderly way. In criminal cases, due process means that defendants should have an opportunity to object to the charges against them before a fair, neutral decision maker, such as a judge. Defendants must also be given the opportunity to confront and cross-examine witnesses and accusers and to present their own witnesses.

Double Jeopardy The Fifth Amendment requirement that prohibits a person from being tried twice for the same criminal offense.

Double Jeopardy

The Fifth Amendment also protects persons from **double jeopardy** (being tried twice for the same criminal offense). The prohibition against double jeopardy means that once a criminal defendant is acquitted (found "not guilty") of a particular crime, the government may not retry him or her for the same crime.

19. See, for example, *United States v. Moon*, 513 F.3d 527 (2008).

The prohibition against double jeopardy does not preclude the crime victim from bringing a civil suit against that same defendant to recover damages, however. In other words, a person found "not guilty" of assault and battery in a state criminal case can be sued for damages by the victim in a civil tort case.

Additionally, a state's prosecution of a crime will not prevent a separate federal prosecution relating to the same activity (and vice versa), provided the activity can be classified as a different crime. **CASE EXAMPLE 6.18** Professional football player Michael Vick was convicted in federal court for operating a dogfighting ring and sentenced to serve twenty-three months in federal prison. A year later, the state where the crime took place, Virginia, filed its own charges against Vick for dogfighting. He pleaded guilty to those charges and received a *suspended sentence* (meaning that the judge reserved the option of imposing a sentence later if circumstances, such as future violations, warranted it).[20]

Self-Incrimination

As explained earlier, the Fifth Amendment grants a privilege against self-incrimination. Thus, in any criminal proceeding, an accused person cannot be compelled to give testimony that might subject her or him to any criminal prosecution.

KNOW THIS The Fifth Amendment protection against self-incrimination does not cover partnerships or corporations.

The Fifth Amendment's guarantee against self-incrimination extends only to natural persons. Because a corporation is a legal entity and not a natural person, the privilege against self-incrimination does not apply to it. Similarly, the business records of a partnership do not receive Fifth Amendment protection. When a partnership is required to produce these records, it must do so even if the information incriminates the persons who constitute the business entity. Sole proprietors and sole practitioners (those who fully own their businesses) who have not incorporated normally cannot be compelled to produce their business records. These individuals have full protection against self-incrimination because they function in only one capacity—there is no separate business entity (see Chapter 26).

Protections under the Sixth and Eighth Amendments

The Sixth Amendment guarantees several important rights for criminal defendants: the right to a speedy trial, the right to a jury trial, the right to a public trial, the right to confront witnesses, and the right to counsel. The Sixth Amendment right to counsel is one of the rights of which a suspect must be advised when he or she is arrested. In many cases, a statement that a criminal suspect makes in the absence of counsel is not admissible at trial unless the suspect has knowingly and voluntarily waived this right.

The Eighth Amendment prohibits excessive bail and fines, as well as cruel and unusual punishment. Under this amendment, prison officials are required to provide humane conditions of confinement, including adequate food, clothing, shelter, and medical care. If a prisoner has a serious medical problem, for instance, and a correctional officer is deliberately indifferent to it, a court could find that the prisoner's Eighth Amendment rights were violated. Critics of the death penalty claim that it constitutes cruel and unusual punishment.[21]

The Exclusionary Rule and the *Miranda* Rule

Two other procedural protections for criminal defendants are the exclusionary rule and the *Miranda* rule.

Exclusionary Rule A rule that prevents evidence that is obtained illegally or without a proper search warrant—and any evidence derived from illegally obtained evidence—from being admissible in court.

The Exclusionary Rule

Under what is known as the **exclusionary rule**, all evidence obtained in violation of the constitutional rights spelled out in the Fourth, Fifth,

20. See *United States v. Kizeart*, 2010 WL 3768023 (S.D.Ill. 2010), for a discussion of the Michael Vick dogfighting case.

21. For an example of a case challenging the constitutionality of the death penalty, see *Baze v. Rees*, 552 U.S. 597, 128 S.Ct. 1520, 170 L.Ed.2d 420 (2008).

and Sixth Amendments, as well as all evidence derived from illegally obtained evidence, normally must be excluded from the trial. Evidence derived from illegally obtained evidence is known as the "fruit of the poisonous tree." For example, if a confession is obtained after an illegal arrest, the arrest is "the poisonous tree," and the confession, if "tainted" by the arrest, is the "fruit."

The purpose of the exclusionary rule is to deter police from conducting warrantless searches and engaging in other misconduct. The rule is sometimes criticized because it can lead to injustice. Many a defendant has "gotten off on a technicality" because law enforcement personnel failed to observe procedural requirements. Even though a defendant may be obviously guilty, if the evidence of that guilt was obtained improperly (without a valid search warrant, for example), it normally cannot be used against the defendant in court.

KNOW THIS

Once a suspect has been informed of his or her rights, anything that person says can be used as evidence in a trial.

The *Miranda* Rule In *Miranda v. Arizona,* a case decided in 1966, the United States Supreme Court established the rule that individuals who are arrested must be informed of certain constitutional rights, including their Fifth Amendment right to remain silent and their Sixth Amendment right to counsel. If the arresting officers fail to inform a criminal suspect of these constitutional rights, any statements the suspect makes normally will not be admissible in court. Although the Supreme Court's *Miranda* ruling was controversial, the decision has survived attempts by Congress to overrule it.[22] Because of its importance in criminal procedure, the *Miranda* case is presented as this chapter's *Landmark in the Law* feature on the following page.

Exceptions to the *Miranda* Rule Over time, as part of a continuing attempt to balance the rights of accused persons against the rights of society, the United States Supreme Court has carved out numerous exceptions to the *Miranda* rule. For example, the Court has recognized a "public safety" exception, holding that certain statements—such as statements concerning the location of a weapon—are admissible even if the defendant was not given *Miranda* warnings. Additionally, to stop police questioning, a suspect must unequivocally and assertively request to exercise his or her right to counsel. Saying "Maybe I should talk to a lawyer" during an interrogation after being taken into custody is not enough. Police officers are not required to decipher the suspect's intentions in such situations.

Criminal Process

As mentioned, as a result of the effort to safeguard the rights of the individual against the state, a criminal prosecution differs from a civil case in several respects. Exhibit 6.3 on page 177 summarizes the major procedural steps in processing a criminal case. Here, we discuss three phases of the criminal process—arrest, indictment or information, and trial—in more detail.

Arrest

Before a warrant for arrest can be issued, there must be probable cause to believe that the individual in question has committed a crime. As discussed earlier, *probable cause* can be defined as a substantial likelihood that the person has committed or is about to commit a crime. Note that probable cause involves a likelihood, not just a possibility. An arrest can be made without a warrant if there is no time to get one, but the action of the arresting officer is still judged by the standard of probable cause.

22. *Dickerson v. United States,* 530 U.S. 428, 120 S.Ct. 2326, 147 L.Ed.2d 405 (2000).

LANDMARK IN THE LAW

Miranda v. Arizona (1966)

The United States Supreme Court's decision in *Miranda v. Arizona*[a] has been cited in more court decisions than any other case in the history of U.S law. Through television shows and other media, the case has also become familiar to most of the adult population in the United States.

The case arose after Ernesto Miranda was arrested in his home on March 13, 1963, for the kidnapping and rape of an eighteen-year-old woman. Miranda was taken to a police station in Phoenix, Arizona, and questioned by two police officers. Two hours later, the officers emerged from the interrogation room with a written confession signed by Miranda.

Rulings by the Lower Courts The confession was admitted into evidence at the trial, and Miranda was convicted and sentenced to prison for twenty to thirty years. Miranda appealed his conviction, claiming that he had not been informed of his constitutional rights. He did not assert that he was innocent of the crime or that his confession was false or made under duress. He claimed only that he would not have confessed if he had been advised of his right to remain silent and to have an attorney. The Supreme Court of Arizona held that Miranda's constitutional rights had not been violated and affirmed his conviction. In its decision, the court emphasized that Miranda had not specifically requested an attorney.

a. 384 U.S. 436, 86 S.Ct. 1602, 16 L.Ed.2d 694 (1966).

The Supreme Court's Decision The *Miranda* case was subsequently consolidated with three other cases involving similar issues and reviewed by the United States Supreme Court. In its decision, the Court stated that whenever an individual is taken into custody, "the following measures are required: He must be warned prior to any questioning that he has the right to remain silent, that anything he says can be used against him in a court of law, that he has the right to the presence of an attorney, and that if he cannot afford an attorney one will be appointed for him prior to any questioning if he so desires." If the accused waives his or her rights to remain silent and to have counsel present, the government must be able to demonstrate that the waiver was made knowingly, intelligently, and voluntarily.

Application to Today's World *Today, both on television and in the real world, police officers routinely advise suspects of their "Miranda rights" on arrest. When Ernesto Miranda himself was later murdered, the suspected murderer was "read his Miranda rights." Interestingly, this decision has also had ramifications for criminal procedure in Great Britain. British police officers are required, when making arrests, to inform suspects, "You do not have to say anything. But if you do not mention now something which you later use in your defense, the court may decide that your failure to mention it now strengthens the case against you. A record will be made of everything you say, and it may be given in evidence if you are brought to trial."*

Indictment A formal charge by a grand jury that there is probable cause to believe that a named person has committed a crime.

Grand Jury A group of citizens who decide, after hearing the state's evidence, whether a reasonable basis (probable cause) exists for believing that a crime has been committed and that a trial ought to be held.

Information A formal accusation or complaint (without an indictment) issued in certain types of actions (usually criminal actions involving lesser crimes) by a government prosecutor.

Indictment or Information

Individuals must be formally charged with having committed specific crimes before they can be brought to trial. If issued by a grand jury, this charge is called an **indictment.**[23] A **grand jury** usually consists of more jurors than the ordinary trial jury. A grand jury does not determine the guilt or innocence of an accused party. Rather, its function is to hear the state's evidence and to determine whether a reasonable basis (probable cause) exists for believing that a crime has been committed and that a trial ought to be held.

Usually, grand juries are used in cases involving serious crimes, such as murder. For lesser crimes, an individual may be formally charged with a crime by what is called an **information,** or criminal complaint. An information will be issued by a government prosecutor if the prosecutor determines that there is sufficient evidence to justify bringing the individual to trial.

23. Pronounced in-*dyte*-ment.

Exhibit 6.3 **Major Procedural Steps in a Criminal Case**

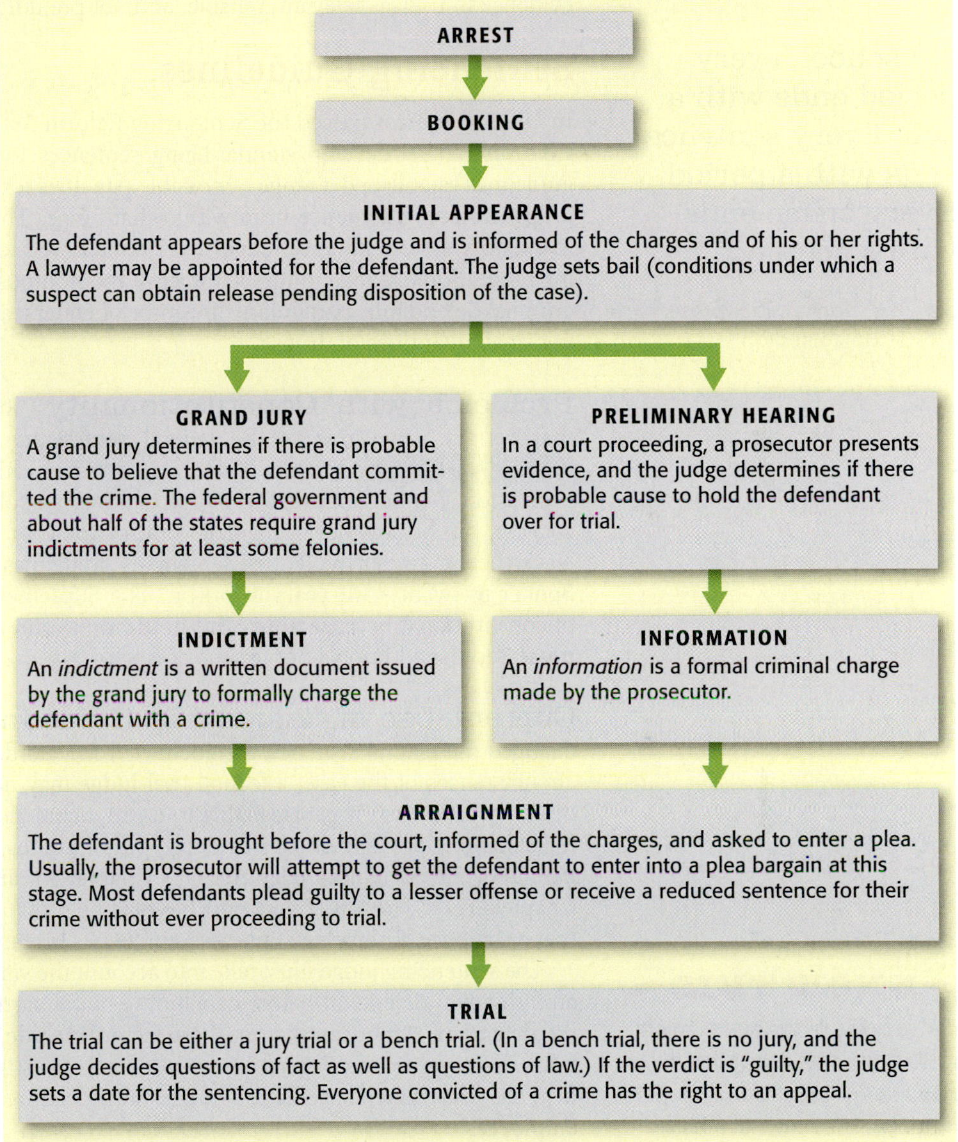

Trial

At a criminal trial, the accused person does not have to prove anything—the entire burden of proof is on the prosecutor (the state). As mentioned earlier, the prosecution must show that, based on all the evidence presented, the defendant's guilt is established *beyond a reasonable doubt.* If there is a reasonable doubt as to whether a criminal defendant committed the crime with which she or he has been charged, then the verdict must be "not guilty." Note that giving a verdict of "not guilty" is not the same as stating that the defendant is innocent. It merely means that not enough evidence was properly presented to the court to prove guilt beyond a reasonable doubt.

Courts have complex rules about what types of evidence may be presented and how the evidence may be brought out in criminal cases. These rules are designed to ensure that evidence in trials is relevant, reliable, and not prejudicial toward the defendant.

"In school, every period ends with a bell. Every sentence ends with a period. Every crime ends with a sentence."

Steven Wright, 1955–present (American comedian)

Sentencing Guidelines

In 1984, Congress passed the Sentencing Reform Act, which created the U.S. Sentencing Commission to develop standardizing sentences for federal crimes. The commission's guidelines established a range of possible penalties for each federal crime and required the judge to select a sentence from within that range. The guidelines originally established a mandatory system because judges were not allowed to deviate from the specified sentencing range. Some federal judges felt uneasy about imposing long prison sentences on certain criminal defendants, particularly first-time offenders, and in illegal substances cases involving small quantities of drugs.[24]

Problems with Constitutionality

In 2005, the Supreme Court held that certain provisions of the federal sentencing guidelines were unconstitutional. **CASE EXAMPLE 6.19** Freddie Booker was arrested with 92.5 grams of crack cocaine in his possession. Booker admitted to police that he had sold an additional 566 grams of crack cocaine, but he was never charged with, or tried for, possessing this additional quantity. Nevertheless, under the federal sentencing guidelines the judge was required to sentence Booker to twenty-two years in prison. The Supreme Court ruled that this sentence was unconstitutional because a jury did not find beyond a reasonable doubt that Booker had possessed the additional 566 grams of crack.[25] •

Current Use of Sentencing Guidelines

Essentially, the Court's ruling changed the federal sentencing guidelines from mandatory to advisory. Depending on the circumstances of the case, a federal trial judge may now depart from the guidelines if he or she believes that it is reasonable to do so. Sentencing guidelines still exist and provide for enhanced punishment for certain types of crimes, including white-collar crimes, violations of the Sarbanes-Oxley Act (see Chapter 7), and violations of securities laws (see Chapter 31).[26] The Supreme Court has also held that a sentencing judge cannot presume that a sentence within the applicable guidelines is reasonable.[27]

The sentencing judge must take into account the various sentencing factors that apply to an individual defendant before concluding that a particular sentence is reasonable. When the defendant is a business firm, these factors include the company's history of past violations, management's cooperation with federal investigators, and the extent to which the firm has undertaken specific programs and procedures to prevent criminal activities by its employees.

KNOW THIS

When determining the appropriate sentence for a business firm, courts focus on three things: previous violations, cooperation with authorities, and good faith efforts to avoid violations.

Cyber Crime

Computer Crime The unlawful use of a computer or network to take or alter data, or to gain the use of computers or services without authorization.

The U.S. Department of Justice broadly defines **computer crime** as any violation of criminal law that involves knowledge of computer technology for its perpetration, investigation, or prosecution. A number of the white-collar crimes discussed earlier in this chapter, such as fraud, embezzlement, and the theft of intellectual property, are now often committed with the aid of computers and are thus considered computer crimes.

24. See, for example, *United States v. Angelos*, 345 F.Supp.2d 1227 (D. Utah 2004).

25. *United States v. Booker*, 543 U.S. 220, 125 S.Ct. 738, 160 L.Ed.2d 621 (2005).

26. The sentencing guidelines were amended in 2003, as required under the Sarbanes-Oxley Act, to impose stiffer penalties for corporate securities fraud—see Chapter 31.

27. *Nelson v. United States*, 555 U.S. 350, 129 S.Ct. 890, 172 L.Ed.2d 719 (2009).

Cyber Crime A crime that occurs in the online environment rather than in the physical world.

Many computer crimes fall under the broad label of **cyber crime,** which describes any criminal activity occurring via a computer in the virtual community of the Internet. Most cyber crimes are not "new" crimes. Rather, they are existing crimes in which the Internet is the instrument of wrongdoing. Here, we look at several types of activity that constitute cyber crimes against persons or property. Other cyber crimes will be discussed in later chapters as they relate to particular topics, such as consumer law or investor protection.

Cyber Fraud

Cyber Fraud Any misrepresentation knowingly made over the Internet with the intention of deceiving another for the purpose of obtaining property or funds.

As mentioned in Chapter 4, fraud is any misrepresentation knowingly made with the intention of deceiving another and on which a reasonable person would and does rely to her or his detriment. **Cyber fraud** is fraud committed over the Internet. Frauds that were once conducted solely by mail or phone can now be found online, and new technology has led to increasingly creative ways to commit fraud.

EXAMPLE 6.20 The "Nigerian letter fraud scam" is perhaps the longest-running Internet fraud. Swindlers send e-mails asking recipients if they will send funds to help fictitious officials from Nigeria transfer millions of nonexistent dollars to Western banks. The e-mails promise that the recipients will be reimbursed and will also receive compensation (a fee or percentage) for transferring the funds. Variations of the scam reflect current events. For instance, the e-mails may ask for financial help in retrieving the fortune of a loved one or an associate who perished in the conflict in Iraq or Afghanistan or during the earthquake and tsunami in Japan. ●

Online Auction Fraud

Online auction fraud, in its most basic form, is a simple process. A person puts up an expensive item for auction, on either a legitimate or a fake auction site, and then refuses to send the product after receiving payment. Or, as a variation, the wrongdoer may send the purchaser an item that is worth less than the one offered in the auction.

The larger online auction sites, such as eBay, try to protect consumers against such schemes by providing warnings about deceptive sellers or offering various forms of insurance. The nature of the Internet, however, makes it nearly impossible to completely block fraudulent auction activity. Because users can assume multiple identities, it is very difficult to pinpoint fraudulent sellers—they will simply change their screen names with each auction.

A state government official examines counterfeit jewelry, much of which would have been sold online.

(AP Photo/Paul Sakuma)

Online Retail Fraud

Somewhat similar to online auction fraud is online retail fraud, in which consumers pay directly (without bidding) for items that are never delivered. As with other forms of online fraud, it is difficult to determine the actual extent of online sales fraud, but anecdotal evidence suggests that it is a substantial problem. **CASE EXAMPLE 6.21** Jeremy Jaynes grossed more than $750,000 per week selling nonexistent or worthless products such as "penny stock pickers" and "Internet history erasers." By the time he was arrested, he had amassed an estimated $24 million from his various fraudulent schemes.[28] ●

Cyber Theft

In cyberspace, thieves are not subject to the physical limitations of the "real" world. A thief can steal data stored in a networked computer with Internet access from anywhere on the globe. Only the speed of the connection and the thief's computer equipment limit the quantity of data that can be stolen.

28. *Jaynes v. Commonwealth of Virginia,* 276 Va.App. 443, 666 S.E.2d 303 (2008).

Identity Theft The illegal use of someone else's personal information to access the victim's financial resources.

LEARNING OBJECTIVE 5
How has the Internet expanded opportunities for identity theft?

Identity Theft

Not surprisingly, there has been a marked increase in identity theft in recent years. **Identity theft** occurs when the wrongdoer steals a form of identification—such as a name, date of birth, or Social Security number—and uses the information to access the victim's financial resources. This crime existed to a certain extent before the widespread use of the Internet. Thieves would rifle through garbage to find credit-card or bank account numbers and then use those numbers to purchase goods or to withdraw funds from the victims' accounts.

The Internet has provided even easier access to private data. Frequent Web surfers surrender a wealth of information about themselves without knowing it. Many Web sites use "cookies" to collect data on those who visit their sites. The data may include the areas of the site the user visits and the links on which the user clicks.

Furthermore, Web browsers often store information such as the consumer's name and e-mail address. Finally, every time a purchase is made online, the item is linked to the purchaser's name, allowing Web retailers to amass a database of who is buying what. Of course, the database also includes purchasers' credit-card numbers. Cyber criminals who steal people's identities normally do not use the identifying information themselves. Instead, they sell the credit-card numbers and other information on the Internet.

In the following case, the court had to decide whether to suppress evidence of an identity theft crime that officers found at a defendant's girlfriend's house.

Case 6.3

United States v. Oliver

United States Court of Appeals, Fifth Circuit, 630 F.3d 397 (2011).

(pixinity/Shutterstock.com)

Identity theft often leads to various types of fraud.

FACTS Lonnie Oliver, Jr., was arrested by officers investigating a scheme to file fraudulent claims for unemployment benefits. Oliver and others were suspected of gaining access to people's names and Social Security numbers and using this information to receive unemployment benefits. After he was read his *Miranda* rights, Oliver confessed to his role in the scheme. Oliver also consented to a search of his car, but he refused to consent to a search of his home. Oliver's co-defendant then told the police that Oliver had stored a laptop computer and a cardboard box containing items related to the scheme at the apartment of Erica Armstrong, Oliver's girlfriend. Acting on this information, agents went to Armstrong's apartment, and she gave them the box and the laptop computer. Inside the box, officers found hundreds of personal identifiers of victims, along with credit and debit cards. They also found a notebook labeled "business ideas" with Oliver's notes for the scheme.

After the laptop was seized, officers obtained a warrant to search its contents and found evidence that Oliver had used it to submit fraudulent unemployment claims. Oliver filed a motion to suppress the evidence in the cardboard box on the ground that it had been obtained unconstitutionally because he had not consented to the search. Further, he claimed that the evidence found on the laptop should also be excluded as "fruit of the poisonous tree" (see page 175) because the warrant to search the laptop was issued on the basis of an affidavit that relied, in part, on the evidence in the box. The district court denied the motion. Oliver appealed.

ISSUE Were the searches of Oliver's laptop and box lawful under the Fourth Amendment?

DECISION Yes. A federal appellate court affirmed the lower court's decision that the search was legal and that the evidence in the box and on the laptop computer was admissible.

REASON The court explained that the private search doctrine legitimized the search of the box and that the independent source doctrine applied to the computer. Under the private search doctrine, when a private individual examines the contents of a closed container, a subsequent search of the container by government officials does not constitute an unlawful search for purposes of the Fourth Amendment. In this case, Armstrong

Case 6.3—Continued

testified that she had looked through the contents of the box before the police came to her apartment. Even though the officers were unaware of her actions at that time, the private search doctrine applied to and legitimized the officers' search.

As for the laptop, under the independent source doctrine, evidence obtained through a legal, independent source need not be suppressed. Both Oliver and his co-defendant had admitted to using a laptop computer to submit fraudulent unemployment claims. Therefore, police had an independent source for obtaining a warrant to search the laptop, whether or not its original seizure was legal.

WHAT IF THE FACTS WERE DIFFERENT? *Suppose that Armstrong had not looked through the cardboard box before the police searched it. Would the box's contents have been admissible? Why or why not?*

Phishing An e-mail fraud scam in which the messages purport to be from legitimate businesses to induce individuals into revealing their personal financial data, passwords, or other information.

Phishing

A distinct form of identity theft known as **phishing** has added a different wrinkle to the practice. In a phishing attack, the perpetrators "fish" for financial data and passwords from consumers by posing as a legitimate business such as a bank or credit-card company. The "phisher" sends an e-mail asking the recipient to "update" or "confirm" vital information, often with the threat that an account or some other service will be discontinued if the information is not provided. Once the unsuspecting individual enters the information, the phisher can use it to masquerade as that person or to drain his or her bank or credit account.

EXAMPLE 6.22 Customers of Wells Fargo Bank receive official-looking e-mails telling them to input personal information on an online form to complete a mandatory installation of a new Internet security certificate. But the Web site is bogus. When the customers complete the forms, their computers are infected and funnel their data to a computer server. The cyber criminals then sell the data. •

Employment Fraud

Cyber criminals also look for victims at online job-posting sites. Claiming to be an employment officer in a well-known company, the criminal sends bogus e-mails to job seekers. The message asks the unsuspecting job seeker to reveal enough information to allow for identity theft. **EXAMPLE 6.23** The job site Monster.com had to ask all of its users to change their passwords after cyber thieves broke into its databases and stole user identities, passwords, and other data. The theft of 4.5 million users' personal information from Monster.com was one of Britain's largest cyber theft cases. •

Credit-Card Theft

As mentioned, identity theft often includes credit-card theft. An important point to note, however, is that stolen credit-card numbers are much more likely to hurt merchants and credit-card issuers (such as banks) than consumers. In most situations, the legitimate holders of credit cards are not held responsible for the costs of purchases made with a stolen number (see Chapter 33). That means the financial burden must be borne either by the merchant or by the credit-card company. Most credit-card issuers require merchants to cover the costs—especially if the address to which the goods are sent does not match the billing address of the credit card.

Additionally, companies take risks by storing their online customers' credit-card numbers. By doing so, companies can provide quicker service because a consumer can make a purchase by providing a code or clicking on a particular icon without entering a lengthy card number. These electronic warehouses are quite tempting to cyber thieves, however. **EXAMPLE 6.24** A cyber thief was able to gain access to computerized records at CardSystems Solutions, a company in Tucson, Arizona, that processes credit-card transactions for small Internet businesses. The breach exposed 40 million credit-card numbers. •

Hacking

Hacker A person who uses computers to gain unauthorized access to data.

Botnet A network of compromised computers connected to the Internet that can be used to generate spam, relay viruses, or cause servers to fail.

A **hacker** is someone who uses one computer to break into another. (Smartphones can be hacked, too.) The danger posed by hackers has increased significantly because of **botnets,** or networks of computers that have been appropriated by hackers without the knowledge of their owners. A hacker will secretly install a program on thousands, if not millions, of personal computer "robots," or "bots," that allows him or her to forward transmissions to an even larger number of systems. To read about a group of well-known hackers in Russia, see this chapter's *Beyond Our Borders* feature below.

EXAMPLE 6.25 In 2011, a hacker broke into Sony Corporation's PlayStation 3 video gaming and entertainment networks. The incident forced the company to temporarily shut down its online gaming services and affected more than 100 million online accounts that provide gaming, chat, and music streaming services. •

Malware Malicious software programs, such as viruses and worms, that are designed to cause harm to a computer, network, or other device.

Worm A software program that automatically replicates itself over a network but does not alter files and is usually invisible to the user until it has consumed system resources.

Virus A software program that can replicate itself over a network and spread from one device to another, altering files and interfering with normal operations.

Malware

Botnets are one of the latest forms of **malware,** a term that refers to any program that is harmful to a computer or, by extension, its user. A **worm,** for example, is a software program that is capable of reproducing itself as it spreads from one computer to the next. **EXAMPLE 6.26** Within three weeks, the computer worm called "Conflicker" spread to more than 1 million personal computers around the world in 2009. It was transmitted to some computers through the use of Facebook and Twitter. This worm also infected servers and devices plugged into infected computers via USB ports, such as iPods, iPhones, iPads, and USB flash drives. •

A **virus,** another form of malware, is also able to reproduce itself, but must be attached to an "infested" host file to travel from one computer network to another. For example, hackers are now capable of corrupting banner ads that use Adobe's Flash Player. When an Internet user clicks on the banner ad, a virus is installed. Worms and viruses can be programmed to perform a number of functions, such as prompting host computers to continually "crash" and reboot, or otherwise infect the system.

Service-Based Hacking

A recent trend in business computer applications is the use of "software as a service." Instead of buying software to install on a computer, the user connects to Web-based software. The user can write e-mails, edit spreadsheets, and

BEYOND OUR BORDERS Hackers Hide in Plain Sight in Russia

According to the security software maker Symantec, few Internet users and businesses have completely avoided computer crime. Consumers alone lose about $120 billion a year worldwide because of hackers and e-fraudsters.

The KoobFace Gang

A group of at least five men who live comfortably in St. Petersburg, Russia, started hacking four years ago—and they are still at it. Calling themselves KoobFace, they created a system of illegal botnets that includes 800,000 infected personal computers. Via this system, they have succeeded in using the KoobFace worm to infiltrate Facebook accounts. The KoobFace gang continues to make $2 million to $5 million a year from this venture. KoobFace is considered a pioneer in the criminal exploitation of social networks.

Knowing the Perpetuators Does Not Lead to Convictions

Authorities worldwide know the identities of the members of KoobFace, yet so far none of them has been charged with a crime. No law enforcement agencies have even confirmed that the group is under investigation. Because Western law officials do not have the resources to tackle even well-known hackers, the Russians hackers are free to continue their activities. It is not surprising that Russia has gained a reputation as a "hacker haven."

Critical Thinking

Why might it be difficult for U.S. authorities to ever investigate the KoobFace gang?

> "A hacker does for love what others would not do for money."
>
> Laura Creighton (Computer programmer and entrepreneur)

the like using his or her Web browser. Cyber criminals have adapted this method and now offer "crimeware as a service."

A would-be thief no longer has to be a computer hacker to create a botnet or steal banking information and credit-card numbers. He or she can rent the online services of cyber criminals to do the work on such sites as NeoSploit. The thief can even target individual groups, such as U.S. physicians or British attorneys. The cost of renting a Web site to do the work is only a few cents per target computer. (For some tips on protecting a company against hackers, see the *Business Application* on page 185.)

Cyberterrorism

Cyberterrorists, as well as hackers, may target businesses. Whereas the goals of a hacker might include theft of data, such as a merchant's customer files, or monitoring a server to discover a business firm's plans and transactions, a cyberterrorist would aim to do more immediate damage. For instance, by inserting false codes or data, a cyberterrorist might change the processing control system of a food manufacturer to alter the levels of ingredients so that consumers of the food would become ill.

A cyberterrorist attack on a major financial institution, such as the New York Stock Exchange or a large bank, could leave securities or money markets in flux and seriously affect the daily lives of millions of citizens. Similarly, any prolonged disruption of computer, cable, satellite, or telecommunications systems due to the actions of expert hackers would have serious repercussions on business operations—and national security—on a global level.

Prosecution of Cyber Crime

Cyber crime has raised new issues in the investigation of crimes and the prosecution of offenders. Determining the "location" of a cyber crime and identifying a criminal in cyberspace are two significant challenges for law enforcement.

Jurisdiction and Identification Challenges A threshold issue is, of course, jurisdiction. Jurisdiction is normally based on physical geography, as discussed in Chapter 3 on page 61, and each state and nation has jurisdiction over crimes committed within its boundaries. But geographic boundaries simply do not apply in cyberspace. A person who commits an act against a business in California, where the act is a cyber crime, might never have set foot in California but might instead reside in New York, or even in Canada, where the act may not be a crime.

Identifying the wrongdoer can also be difficult. Cyber criminals do not leave physical traces, such as fingerprints or DNA samples, as evidence of their crimes. Even electronic "footprints" (digital evidence) can be hard to find and follow. For example, e-mail may be sent through a remailer, an online service that guarantees that a message cannot be traced to its source.

For these reasons, laws written to protect physical property are often difficult to apply in cyberspace. Nonetheless, governments at both the state and the federal level have taken significant steps toward controlling cyber crime, both by applying existing criminal statutes and by enacting new laws that specifically address wrongs committed in cyberspace. California, for instance, which has the highest identity theft rate in the nation, established a new eCrime unit in 2011 to investigate and prosecute cyber crimes. Other states, including

Florida, Louisiana, and Texas, also have special law enforcement units that focus solely on Internet crimes.

The Computer Fraud and Abuse Act Perhaps the most significant federal statute specifically addressing cyber crime is the Counterfeit Access Device and Computer Fraud and Abuse Act of 1984.[29] This act is commonly known as the Computer Fraud and Abuse Act, or CFAA.

Among other things, the CFAA provides that a person who accesses a computer online, without authority, to obtain classified, restricted, or protected data (or attempts to do so) is subject to criminal prosecution. Such data could include financial and credit records, medical records, legal files, military and national security files, and other confidential information in government or private computers. The crime has two elements: accessing a computer without authority and taking the data.

This theft is a felony if it is committed for a commercial purpose or for private financial gain, or if the value of the stolen information exceeds $5,000. Penalties include fines and imprisonment for up to twenty years. For a discussion of whether it should be a violation of the CFAA to post fake pictures on the Internet's social media sites, see this chapter's *Adapting the Law to the Online Environment* feature below.

29. 18 U.S.C. Section 1030.

ADAPTING THE LAW TO THE ONLINE ENVIRONMENT

PROSECUTING THOSE WHO POST FALSE INFORMATION ON THE INTERNET

As discussed in the text, the Computer Fraud and Abuse Act (CFAA) was enacted nearly thirty years ago. At that time, the new law was aimed at computer hacking. Since then, Congress has greatly expanded the act's reach. Today, the CFAA criminalizes any computer use that "exceeds authorized access" to any computer.

Posting Fake Photos Can Be a Crime

Just a few years ago, the Justice Department prosecuted a woman for supposedly violating the "terms of service" of MySpace.com. The woman had set up a MySpace account pretending to be a sixteen-year-old boy and had used the account to harass a thirteen-year-old girl (who subsequently committed suicide). Because the woman's profile did not use her actual photo, she was charged with conspiracy to violate the CFAA because MySpace's terms of service require that all profile information be truthful.[a] Another defendant was prosecuted for posing as someone else and posting sexually inappropriate messages on Facebook that purported to be from her.[b] In both instances, many suggested that the prosecutors were attempting to criminalize actions that, however blameworthy they may have been, were hardly crimes under the law.

a. *United States v. Drew,* 259 F.R.D. 449 (C.D.Cal. 2009).

b. *In re Rolando S.,* 197 Cal.App.4th 936, 129 Cal.Rptr.3d 49 (2011).

Civil Suits Filed by Private Parties

In addition to potential criminal penalties, the CFAA also allows private parties to bring civil suits against other private parties. An employer can sue a former employee for excessive Internet usage while at work. In other words, if the employer can prove (through keystroke monitoring, for example) that the employee visited Facebook and sent too many personal e-mails from work, the employer has grounds to sue. In one case, the terms of service on a company's Web site stated that no competitors could visit it. When one of them did, the company sued that competitor.

Have We Gone Too Far?

Agreements are breached every day. Employees routinely ignore their bosses' instructions. If such actions involve a computer or the Internet, however, they become federal crimes. In other words, the law today gives computer owners the power to criminalize any computer use with which they disagree.

Critical Thinking

Is the expansion of the 1984 Computer Fraud and Abuse Act part of the overcriminalization trend in this country? Why or why not?

Reviewing . . . Criminal Law and Cyber Crime

Edward Hanousek worked for Pacific & Arctic Railway and Navigation Company (P&A) as a roadmaster of the White Pass & Yukon Railroad in Alaska. As an officer of the corporation, Hanousek was responsible "for every detail of the safe and efficient maintenance and construction of track, structures, and marine facilities of the entire railroad," including special projects. One project was a rock quarry, known as "6-mile," above the Skagway River. Next to the quarry, and just beneath the surface, ran a high-pressure oil pipeline owned by Pacific & Arctic Pipeline, Inc., P&A's sister company. When the quarry's backhoe operator punctured the pipeline, an estimated 1,000 to 5,000 gallons of oil were discharged into the river. Hanousek was charged with negligently discharging a harmful quantity of oil into a navigable water of the United States in violation of the criminal provisions of the Clean Water Act (CWA). Using the information presented in the chapter, answer the following questions.

1. Did Hanousek have the required mental state *(mens rea)* to be convicted of a crime? Why or why not?
2. Which theory discussed in the chapter would enable a court to hold Hanousek criminally liable for violating the statute regardless of whether he participated in, directed, or even knew about the specific violation?
3. Could the quarry's backhoe operator who punctured the pipeline also be charged with a crime in this situation? Explain.
4. Suppose that, at trial, Hanousek argued that he could not be convicted because he was not aware of the requirements of the CWA. Would this defense be successful? Why or why not?

DEBATE THIS Because of overcriminalization, particularly by the federal government, Americans may be breaking the law regularly without knowing it. Should Congress rescind many of the more than four thousand federal crimes now on the books?

BUSINESS APPLICATION

Protecting Your Company against Hacking of Your Bank Accounts*

Each year, conventional, old-fashioned crooks rob banks to the tune of about $50 million. In contrast, every year cybercrooks steal billions of dollars from the bank accounts of small and mid-size companies in Europe and the United States. Why? The reason is that small businesses tend to be lax in protecting themselves from hackers. They keep their accounts in community or regional banks, have only rudimentary security measures, and usually fail to hire an on-site cyber security expert.

You May Not Receive Compensation for Your Losses

Many small-business owners believe that if their bank accounts are hacked and disappear, their banks will reimburse them. That is not always the case, however. Just ask Mark Patterson, the owner of Patco Construction in Stanford, Maryland. He lost more than $350,000 to cyberthieves. When People's United Bank would not agree to a settlement, Patterson sued, claiming that the bank should have monitored his account. So far, federal judges have agreed with the bank—that its protections were "commercially reasonable," which is the only standard that banks have to follow.

*This *Business Application* is not meant to substitute for the services of an attorney who is licensed to practice law in your state.

Insurance May Not Be the Answer

Similarly, small-business owners often think that their regular insurance policy will cover cyber losses at their local banks. In reality, unless there is a specific "rider" to a business's insurance policy, its bank accounts are not covered. So, just because your business will be reimbursed if thieves break in and steal your machines and network servers, that does not mean you will be covered if cybercrooks break into your bank account.

Checklist for Preventing Cyberthefts of Your Bank Accounts

1. *Meet with your bank managers and discuss what you can do to protect your company's bank accounts.*
2. *Have your company sign up for identity-theft services. Many large banks provide these.*
3. *Change your company's passwords frequently. Always use long, complicated passwords.*
4. *Instruct your employees never to reply to unknown e-mail requests, particularly if they ask for any information about the company.*
5. *Have a computer expert test the firewalls safeguarding your internal computer network.*

Key Terms

actus reus 158
arson 163
beyond a reasonable doubt 156
botnet 182
burglary 161
computer crime 178
crime 156
cyber crime 179
cyber fraud 179
double jeopardy 173
duress 169
embezzlement 164
entrapment 170
exclusionary rule 174
felony 167
forgery 163
grand jury 176
hacker 182
identity theft 180
indictment 176
information 176
insider trading 166
larceny 161
malware 182
mens rea 158
misdemeanor 168
money laundering 167
petty offense 168
phishing 181
plea bargaining 170
probable cause 172
robbery 161
search warrant 171
self-defense 168
self-incrimination 170
virus 182
white-collar crime 164
worm 182

Chapter Summary: Criminal Law and Cyber Crime

Civil Law and Criminal Law (See pages 156–157.)	1. *Civil law*—Spells out the duties that exist between persons or between persons and their governments, excluding the duty not to commit crimes. 2. *Criminal law*—Has to do with crimes, which are wrongs against society proclaimed in statutes and, if committed, punishable by society through fines and/or imprisonment—and, in some cases, death. Because crimes are *offenses against society as a whole,* they are prosecuted by a public official, not by the victims. 3. *Key differences*—An important difference between civil and criminal law is that the standard of proof is higher in criminal cases (see Exhibit 6.1 on page 156 for other differences between civil and criminal law). 4. *Civil liability for criminal acts*—A criminal act may give rise to both criminal liability and tort liability (see Exhibit 6.2 on page 157 for an example of criminal and tort liability for the same act).
Criminal Liability (See pages 158–160.)	1. *Guilty act*—In general, some form of harmful act must be committed for a crime to exist. 2. *Intent*—An intent to commit a crime, or a wrongful mental state, is generally required for a crime to exist.
Types of Crimes (See pages 161–168.)	1. Crimes fall into five general categories: violent crime, property crime, public order crime, white-collar crime, and organized crime. a. Violent crimes are those that cause others to suffer harm or death, including murder, assault and battery, sexual assault (rape), and robbery. b. Property crimes are the most common form of crime. The offender's goal is to obtain some economic gain or to damage property. This category includes burglary, larceny, obtaining goods by false pretenses, receiving stolen property, arson, and forgery. c. Public order crimes are acts, such as public drunkenness, prostitution, gambling, and illegal drug use, that a statute has established are contrary to public values and morals. d. White-collar crimes are illegal acts committed by a person or business using nonviolent means to obtain a personal or business advantage. Usually, such crimes are committed in the course of a legitimate occupation. Examples include embezzlement, mail and wire fraud, bribery, bankruptcy fraud, theft of trade secrets, and insider trading. e. Organized crime is a form of crime conducted by groups operating illegitimately to satisfy the public's demand for illegal goods and services (such as gambling or illegal narcotics). This category of crime also includes money laundering and racketeering (RICO) violations. 2. Crimes may also be classified according to their degree of seriousness. Felonies are serious crimes punishable by death or by imprisonment for more than one year. Misdemeanors are less serious crimes punishable by fines or by confinement for up to one year.
Defenses to Criminal Liability (See pages 168–170.)	Defenses to criminal liability include justifiable use of force, necessity, insanity, mistake, duress, entrapment, and the statute of limitations. Also, in some cases defendants may be relieved of criminal liability, at least in part, if they are given immunity.
Constitutional Safeguards and Criminal Procedures (See pages 170–175.)	1. *Fourth Amendment*—Provides protection against unreasonable searches and seizures and requires that probable cause exist before a warrant for a search or an arrest can be issued. 2. *Fifth Amendment*—Requires due process of law, prohibits double jeopardy, and protects against self-incrimination. 3. *Sixth Amendment*—Guarantees a speedy trial, a trial by jury, a public trial, the right to confront witnesses, and the right to counsel.

Chapter Summary: Criminal Law and Cyber Crime—Continued

Constitutional Safeguards and Criminal Procedures—Continued	4. *Eighth Amendment*—Prohibits excessive bail and fines, and cruel and unusual punishment. 5. *Exclusionary rule*—A criminal procedural rule that prohibits the introduction at trial of all evidence obtained in violation of constitutional rights, as well as any evidence derived from the illegally obtained evidence. 6. *Miranda rule*—A rule set forth by the Supreme Court in *Miranda v. Arizona* holding that individuals who are arrested must be informed of certain constitutional rights, including their right to counsel.
Criminal Process (See pages 175–178.)	1. *Arrest, indictment, and trial*—Procedures governing arrest, indictment, and trial for a crime are designed to safeguard the rights of the individual against the state. See Exhibit 6.3 on page 177 for a summary of the procedural steps involved in prosecuting a criminal case. 2. *Sentencing guidelines*—The federal government has established sentencing laws or guidelines, which are no longer mandatory but provide a range of penalties for each federal crime.
Cyber Crime (See pages 178–184.)	1. *Cyber fraud*—Occurs when misrepresentations are knowingly made over the Internet to deceive another. Two widely reported forms are online auction fraud and online retail fraud. 2. *Cyber theft*—In cyberspace, thieves can steal data from anywhere in the world. Identity theft is made easier by the fact that many e-businesses store information such as the consumer's name, e-mail address, and credit-card numbers. Phishing and employment fraud are variations of identity theft. The financial burden of stolen credit-card numbers falls more on merchants and credit-card issuers than on consumers. 3. *Hacking*—A hacker is a person who uses one computer to break into another. Malware is any program that is harmful to a computer or, by extension, a computer user. Worms, viruses, and botnets are examples. 4. *Cyberterrorism*—Cyberterrrorists aim to cause serious problems for computer systems. A cyberterrorist attack on a major U.S. financial institution or telecommunications system could have serious repercussions, including jeopardizing national security. 5. *Prosecution of cyber crime*—Prosecuting cyber crime is more difficult than prosecuting traditional crime. Identifying the wrongdoer through electronic footprints left on the Internet is complicated, and jurisdictional issues may arise when the suspect lives in another jurisdiction or nation. A significant federal statute addressing cyber crime is the Computer Fraud and Abuse Act of 1984.

ExamPrep

ISSUE SPOTTERS

1. Daisy takes her roommate's credit card, intending to charge expenses that she incurs on a vacation. Her first stop is a gas station, where she uses the card to pay for gas. With respect to the gas station, has she committed a crime? If so, what is it? **(See pages 160–163.)**
2. Without permission, Ben downloads consumer credit files from a computer belonging to Consumer Credit Agency. He then sells the data to Dawn. Has Ben committed a crime? If so, what is it? **(See page 184.)**

—Check your answers to the Issue Spotters against the answers provided in Appendix E at the end of this text.

BEFORE THE TEST

Go to www.cengagebrain.com, enter the ISBN 9781133273561, and click on "Find" to locate this textbook's Web site. Then, click on "Access Now" under "Study Tools," and select Chapter 6 at the top. There, you will find a Practice Quiz that you can take to assess your mastery of the concepts in this chapter, as well as Flashcards, a Glossary of important terms, and Video Questions (when assigned).

For Review

Answers to the even-numbered questions in this *For Review* section can be found in Appendix F at the end of this text.

1. What two elements normally must exist before a person can be held liable for a crime?
2. What are five broad categories of crimes? What is white-collar crime?
3. What defenses can be raised to avoid liability for criminal acts?
4. What constitutional safeguards exist to protect persons accused of crimes?
5. How has the Internet expanded opportunities for identity theft?

Business Scenarios and Case Problems

6–1 Double Jeopardy. Armington, while robbing a drugstore, shot and seriously injured Jennings, a drugstore clerk. Armington was subsequently convicted of armed robbery and assault and battery in a criminal trial. Jennings later brought a civil tort suit against Armington for damages. Armington contended that he could not be tried again for the same crime, as that would constitute double jeopardy, which is prohibited by the Fifth Amendment to the U.S. Constitution. Is Armington correct? Explain. **(See pages 173–174.)**

6–2 Question with Sample Answer—Cyber Fraud. Kayla, a student at Learnwell University, owes $20,000 in unpaid tuition. If Kayla does not pay the tuition, Learnwell will not allow her to graduate. To obtain the funds to pay the debt, she sends e-mails to people that she does not know asking them for financial help to send her child, who has a disability, to a special school. In reality, Kayla has no children. Is this a crime? If so, which one? **(See pages 165 and 179.)**

—For a sample answer to Question 6–2, go to Appendix G at the end of this text.

6–3 White-Collar Crime. Helm Instruction Co. hired Patrick Walsh to work as its comptroller. Walsh convinced Helm's president, Richard Wilhelm, to hire Shari Price as Walsh's assistant. Wilhelm was not aware that Walsh and Price were engaged in an extramarital affair. Over the next five years, Walsh and Price spent more than $200,000 of Helm's funds on themselves. Among other things, Walsh drew unauthorized checks on Helm's accounts to pay his personal credit-card bills. Walsh also issued unauthorized salary increases, overtime payments, and tuition reimbursement payments to Price and himself, altering Helm's records to hide the payments. After an investigation, Helm officials confronted Walsh. He denied the affair with Price and argued that his unauthorized use of Helm's funds was an "interest-free loan." Walsh claimed that it was less of a burden on the company to pay his credit-card bills than to give him the salary increases to which he felt he was entitled. Did Walsh commit a crime? If so, what crime did he commit? Discuss. [*State v. Walsh,* 113 Ohio St.3d 1515, 866 N.E.2d 513 (6 Dist. 2007)] **(See pages 164–165.)**

6–4 Cyber Crime. Jiri Klimecek was a member of a group that overrode copyright protection in movies and music to make them available for download online. Klimecek bought and installed a server and paid to connect it to the Internet. He knew that users could access the server to upload and download copyrighted works. He obtained access to movies and music to make them available. When charged with copyright infringement, he claimed that he had not understood the full scope of the operation. Did Klimecek commit a crime? Explain. [*United States v. Klimecek,* __ F.3d __ (7th Cir. 2009)] **(See pages 158–159.)**

6–5 Case Problem with Sample Answer—Search and Seizure. Three police officers, including Maria Trevizo, pulled over a car with suspended registration. One of the occupants, Lemon Johnson, wore clothing consistent with membership in the Crips gang. Trevizo searched him "for officer safety" and found a gun. Johnson was charged with illegal possession of a weapon. What standard should apply to an officer's search of a passenger during a traffic stop? Should a warrant be required? Could a search proceed solely on the basis of probable cause? Would a reasonable suspicion short of probable cause be enough? Discuss. [*Arizona v. Johnson,* 555 U.S. 323, 129 S.Ct. 781, 172 L.Ed.2d 694 (2009)] **(See page 172.)**

—For a sample answer to Problem 6–5, go to Appendix H at the end of this text.

6–6 Search. Charles Byrd was in a minimum-security county jail awaiting trial. A team of sheriff's deputies wearing T-shirts and jeans took Byrd and several other inmates into a room for a strip search without any apparent justification. Byrd was ordered to remove all his clothing except his boxer shorts. A female deputy searched Byrd while several male deputies watched. One of the male deputies videotaped the search. Byrd filed a suit against the sheriff's department. Did the search violate Byrd's rights? Discuss. [*Byrd v. Maricopa County Sheriff's Department,* 629 F.3d. 1135 (9th Cir. 2011)] **(See page 172.)**

6–7 Credit- and Debit-Card Theft. Jacqueline Barden was shopping for school clothes with her children when her purse and automobile were taken. In Barden's purse were her car keys, credit and debit cards for herself and her children, as well as the children's Social Security cards and birth certificates needed for enrollment at school. Immediately after the purse and car were stolen, Rebecca Mary Turner attempted to use Barden's credit card at a local Exxon gas station, but the card was declined. The gas station attendant recognized Turner because she had previously written bad checks and used credit cards that did not belong to her. Turner was later arrested while attempting to use one of Barden's checks to pay for merchandise at a Walmart—where the clerk also recognized Turner from prior criminal activity. Turner claimed that she had not stolen Barden's purse or car, and that a friend had told her he had some checks and credit cards and asked her to try using them at Walmart. Turner was convicted at trial. She appealed, claiming that there was insufficient evidence that she committed credit- and debit-card theft. Was the evidence sufficient to uphold her conviction? Why or why not? [*Turner v. State of Arkansas,* 2012 Ark.App. 150 (2012)] **(See page 162.)**

6–8 A Question of Ethics—Identity Theft. Twenty-year-old Davis Omole had earned good grades in high school and played on the football and chess team. He then went on to college. Omole worked at a cell phone store where he stole customers' personal information. He used the stolen identities to create a hundred different accounts on eBay and held more than three hundred auctions listing for sale items that he did not own (including cell phones, plasma televisions, and stereos). From these auctions, he collected $90,000. To avoid getting caught, he continuously closed and opened the eBay accounts, activated and deactivated cell phone and e-mail accounts, and changed mailing addresses and post office boxes. Omole, who had previously been convicted in a state court for Internet fraud, was convicted in a federal district court of identity theft and wire fraud. [*United States v. Omole,* 523 F.3d 691 (7th Cir. 2008)] **(See page 180.)**

1. Omole displayed contempt for the court and ridiculed his victims, calling them stupid for having been cheated. What does this behavior suggest about Omole's ethics?
2. Under federal sentencing guidelines, Omole could have been imprisoned for more than eight years, but he received only three years, two of which were the mandatory sentence for identity theft. Was this sentence too lenient? Explain.

Critical Thinking and Writing Assignments

6–9 **Critical Legal Thinking.** Ray steals a purse from an unattended car at a gas station. Because the purse contains money and a handgun, Ray is convicted of grand theft of property (cash) and grand theft of a firearm. On appeal, Ray claims that he is not guilty of grand theft of a firearm because he did not know that the purse contained a gun. Can Ray be convicted of grand theft of a firearm even though he did not know that the gun was in the purse? Explain. **(See page 161.)**

6–10 **Business Law Critical Thinking Group Assignment.** Cyber crime costs consumers millions of dollars every year, and it costs businesses, including banks and other credit-card issuers, even more. Nonetheless, when cyber criminals are caught and convicted, they are rarely ordered to pay restitution or sentenced to long prison terms.

1. One group should argue that stiffer sentences would reduce the amount of cyber crime.
2. A second group should determine how businesspersons can best protect themselves from cyber crime and avoid the associated costs.

7 CHAPTER

Ethics and Business Decision Making

CHAPTER OUTLINE

- Business Ethics
- Ethical Transgressions by Financial Institutions
- Approaches to Ethical Reasoning
- Making Ethical Business Decisions
- Practical Solutions to Corporate Ethics Questions
- Business Ethics on a Global Level

LEARNING OBJECTIVES

The five learning objectives below are designed to help improve your understanding of the chapter. After reading this chapter, you should be able to answer the following questions:

1. What is business ethics, and why is it important?
2. How can business leaders encourage their companies to act ethically?
3. How do duty-based ethical standards differ from outcome-based ethical standards?
4. What are six guidelines that an employee can use to evaluate whether his or her actions are ethical?
5. What types of ethical issues might arise in the context of international business transactions?

(pixdeluxe/iStockphoto.com)

"New occasions teach new duties."
—James Russell Lowell, 1819–1891 (American editor, poet, and diplomat)

Ethics scandals erupted throughout corporate America during the first decade of the 2000s. Heads of major corporations were tried for fraud, conspiracy, grand larceny, and obstruction of justice. For example, Jeffrey Skilling, the head of Enron Corporation (a multibillion-dollar enterprise that ended in one of the largest bankruptcies in U.S. history), was convicted of securities fraud and insider trading for deceiving investors and covering up losses.

Ethical problems plagued many U.S. financial institutions and Wall Street firms as well. These ethical scandals contributed to the onset of the deepest recession since the Great Depression of the 1930s. In the economic crisis that began in 2008, not only did some $9 trillion in investment capital evaporate, but millions of workers lost their jobs. Many people lost their life savings in a Ponzi scheme (an illegal pyramid operation) perpetrated for decades by Bernard Madoff, who pleaded guilty in 2009 to bilking investors out of more than $65 billion.

In short, the scope and scale of corporate unethical behavior, especially in the financial sector, skyrocketed (with enormous repercussions worldwide). As the chapter-opening quotation states, "New occasions teach new duties." The ethics scandals of the last several years have taught everyone that business ethics cannot be taken lightly. How businesspersons should act and whose interests they should consider—the firm, its executives, its employees, its shareholders, and more—are the focus of this chapter on business ethics.

Business Ethics

Ethics Moral principles and values applied to social behavior.

As you might imagine, business ethics is derived from the concept of ethics. **Ethics** can be defined as the study of what constitutes right or wrong behavior. It is the branch of philosophy that focuses on morality and the way in which moral principles are derived and applied to one's conduct in daily life. Ethics has to do with questions relating to the fairness, justness, rightness, or wrongness of an action.

Business Ethics What constitutes right or wrong behavior and the application of moral principles in a business context.

Business ethics focuses on what constitutes right or wrong behavior in the business world and on how businesspersons apply moral and ethical principles to situations that arise in the workplace. Because business decision makers often address more complex ethical dilemmas than they face in their personal lives, business ethics is more complicated than personal ethics.

LEARNING OBJECTIVE 1
What is business ethics, and why is it important?

Why Is Business Ethics Important?

To see why business ethics is so important, think about the corporate executives who were sentenced to prison for the crimes that you read about in the first paragraphs of this chapter. They could have avoided this outcome had they engaged in ethical decision making during their careers. As a result of their crimes, all of their companies suffered losses, and some were forced to enter bankruptcy, causing thousands of workers to lose their jobs.

Moral Minimum The minimum degree of ethical behavior expected of a business firm, which is usually defined as compliance with the law.

If the executives had acted ethically, the corporations, shareholders, and employees of those companies would not have paid such a high price. Thus, an in-depth understanding of business ethics is important to the long-run viability of a corporation. It is also important to the well-being of individual officers and directors and to the firm's employees. Finally, unethical corporate decision making can negatively affect suppliers, consumers, the community, and society as a whole.

"Have you noticed ethics creeping into some of these deals lately?"

The Moral Minimum

The minimum acceptable standard for ethical business behavior—known as the **moral minimum**—normally is considered to be compliance with the law. In many corporate scandals, had most of the businesspersons involved simply followed the law, they would not have gotten into trouble. Note, though, that in the interest of preserving personal freedom, as well as for practical reasons, the law does not—and cannot—codify all ethical requirements.

As they make business decisions, businesspersons must remember that just because an action is legal does not necessarily make it ethical. For instance, no law specifies the salaries that public corporations can pay their officers. Nevertheless, if a corporation pays its officers an excessive amount relative to other employees, or to what officers at other corporations are paid, the executives' compensation might be challenged by some as unethical. (Executive bonuses can also present ethical problems—see the discussion later in this chapter.)

In the following case, the court had to determine if a repair shop was entitled to receive full payment of an invoice or some lesser amount given its conduct in the matter.

Case 7.1

Johnson Construction Co. v. Shaffer

Court of Appeal of Louisiana, Second Circuit, 87 So.3d 203 (2012).

(AlexKZ/Shutterstock.com)

Can an auto repair shop hold a truck "hostage" during a payment dispute with its owner?

FACTS A truck owned by Johnson Construction Company needed repairs. So John Robert Johnson, Jr., took the truck with its attached fifteen-ton trailer to Bubba Shaffer, doing business as Shaffer's Auto and Diesel Repair, LLC. The truck was supposedly fixed, and Johnson paid the bill. Thereafter, though, the truck continued to leak oil and water. Johnson returned the truck to Shaffer who again claimed to have fixed the problem. Johnson paid the second bill. The problems with the truck continued, however, so Johnson returned the truck and trailer to Shaffer a third time. Johnson was given a verbal estimate of $1,000 for the repairs, but Shaffer ultimately sent an invoice for $5,863. Johnson offered to settle for $2,480, the amount of the initial estimate ($1,000), plus the costs of parts and shipping. Shaffer refused the offer and would not return Johnson's truck or trailer until full payment was made. Shaffer retained possession for almost four years and also charged Johnson a storage fee of $50 a day and 18 percent interest on the $5,863.

Johnson Construction filed a suit against Shaffer alleging unfair trade practices. The trial court determined that Shaffer had acted deceptively and wrongfully in maintaining possession of Johnson Construction's trailer, on which it had performed no work. The trial court awarded Johnson $3,500 in general damages plus $750 in attorneys' fees. Shaffer was also awarded the initial estimate of $1,000. Shaffer appealed.

ISSUE Was Shaffer entitled to receive the full amount of his invoice ($5,863) and reasonable storage fees for the truck and trailer?

DECISION No. The reviewing court affirmed the trial court's decision and also assessed Shaffer all costs of the appeal.

REASON The reviewing court examined the testimony with respect to the verbal estimate of $1,000 for the repairs of the truck. In Louisiana, to enforce an oral agreement pertaining to something priced in excess of $500, the contract must be authenticated by at least one additional witness or other corroborating circumstances. Johnson testified that he had agreed to the initial $1,000 estimate but he had not authorized Shaffer to perform additional repairs or tear down the engine. A mechanic employed by Shaffer testified that Johnson had not authorized additional repairs to the truck. Thus, those repairs were not part of any agreement because they involved tearing down the engine. The trial court had not been in error when it viewed Shaffer's testimony on the issue as "disingenuous." The court noted, "As for the amount that Shaffer contends is due for storage, had it invoiced Mr. Johnson the amount of the original estimate in the first place, there would have been no need to store the truck or trailer." Therefore, the reviewing court rejected the request for storage fees.

Finally, that Shaffer kept the trailer for nearly four years even though no work had been done on it was viewed by the court as holding the trailer "hostage in an effort to force payment for unauthorized repairs." The award of $3,500 in general damages to Johnson Construction seemed appropriate for such lengthy unlawful conversion of the trailer.

WHAT IF THE FACTS WERE DIFFERENT? *Suppose that Shaffer had invoiced Johnson for only $1,500. Would the outcome have been different? Explain your answer.*

Short-Run Profit Maximization

Some people argue that a corporation's only goal should be profit maximization, which will be reflected in a higher market valuation. When all firms strictly adhere to the goal of profit maximization, resources tend to flow to where they are most highly valued by society. Thus, in theory, profit maximization ultimately leads to the most efficient allocation of scarce resources.

Corporate executives and employees have to distinguish, however, between *short-run* and *long-run* profit maximization. In the short run, a company may increase its profits by continuing to sell a product, even though it knows that the product is defective. In the long run, though, because of lawsuits, large settlements, and bad publicity, such unethical conduct will cause profits to suffer. Thus, business ethics is consistent only with long-run profit maximization. An overemphasis on short-term profit maximization is the most common reason that ethical problems occur in business.

CASE EXAMPLE 7.1 When the powerful narcotic painkiller OxyContin was first marketed, its manufacturer, Purdue Pharma, claimed that it was unlikely to lead to drug addiction or abuse. Internal company documents later showed, however, that the company's executives knew that OxyContin could be addictive, but they kept this risk a secret to boost sales and maximize short-term profits. Purdue Pharma and three former executives pleaded guilty to criminal charges that they misled regulators, patients, and physicians about OxyContin's risks. Purdue Pharma agreed to pay $600 million in fines and other payments. The three former executives agreed to pay $34.5 million in fines and were barred from federal health programs for a period of fifteen years. Thus, the company's focus on maximizing profits in the short run led to unethical conduct that hurt profits in the long run.[1] ●

"It's easy to make a buck. It's a lot tougher to make a difference."

Tom Brokaw, 1940–present
(American television journalist)

"Gray Areas" in the Law

In many situations, business firms can predict with a fair amount of certainty whether a given action would be legal. For instance, firing an employee solely because of that person's race or gender would clearly violate federal laws prohibiting employment discrimination. In some situations, though, the legality of a particular action may be less clear. In part, this is because there are so many laws regulating business that it is increasingly possible to violate one of them without realizing it. The law also contains numerous "gray areas," making it difficult to predict with certainty how a court will apply a given law to a particular action.

KNOW THIS

When it is not entirely clear how a law applies, a company's best defense to allegations of misconduct is to show that the firm acted honestly and responsibly under the circumstances.

In addition, many rules of law require a court to determine what is "foreseeable" or "reasonable" in a particular situation. Because a business has no way of predicting how a specific court will decide these issues, decision makers need to proceed with caution and evaluate an action and its consequences from an ethical perspective. The same problem often occurs in cases involving the Internet because it is often unclear how a court will apply existing laws in the context of cyberspace. Generally, if a company can demonstrate that it acted in good faith and responsibly in the circumstances, it has a better chance of successfully defending its action in court or before an administrative law judge.

LEARNING OBJECTIVE 2
How can business leaders encourage their companies to act ethically?

The Importance of Ethical Leadership

Talking about ethical business decision making is meaningless if management does not set standards. Furthermore, managers must apply the same standards to themselves as they do to the employees of the company.

If a company discovers that a manager has behaved unethically or engaged in misconduct, the company should take prompt remedial action. The following case illustrates what can happen when a manager fails to follow the standards that apply to other employees.

1. *United States v. Purdue Frederick Co.*, 495 F. Supp.2d 569 (W.D.Va. 2007).

Case 7.2

Mathews v. B and K Foods, Inc.

Missouri Court of Appeals,
332 S.W.3d 275 (2011).

(Robyn Mackenzie/Shutterstock.com)

Many employees fill out timesheets for payroll purposes.

FACTS Dianne Mathews was employed by B and K Foods, Inc., as a floral manager. In 2010, she was terminated for submitting falsified timesheets. She filed for unemployment compensation (see Chapter 24), but B and K objected, arguing that Mathews was not entitled to unemployment benefits because she had been discharged for misconduct in connection with work. At an employment commission hearing, the chief executive officer of B and K testified that it was company policy to pay employees who worked through their lunch breaks. To be paid, a person turned in a "no-lunch sheet." Mathews, however, turned in "no-lunch sheets" when she ran personal errands.

She admitted to knowing about the policy, but she contended that her conduct was warranted. She claimed that a former employee who was a higher-level manager at B and K had told her that it was unnecessary to adjust her timesheet when she spent a few minutes on a personal errand. The employment commission ruled that Mathews could not receive unemployment compensation benefits. Mathews appealed.

ISSUE Was it misconduct for Mathews to be paid for time spent running personal errands when this was against company policy?

DECISION Yes. A state intermediate appellate court affirmed the employment commission's decision that Mathews should not receive unemployment benefits.

REASON According to the court, "'work-related misconduct' must involve a willful violation of the rules or standards of the employer." The employer met its burden of proving such misconduct. B and K presented substantial evidence that Mathews had falsified time cards by turning in "no-lunch" sheets for time she had spent running personal errands. Mathews admitted that she was familiar with the company's no-lunch policy. Furthermore, she was responsible for seeing that her subordinate employees followed the policy. The court accepted the B and K executive's statement that "they had no choice but to terminate [Mathews] because she was in a higher position and had a responsibility to enforce the lunch policy."

WHAT IF THE FACTS WERE DIFFERENT? *Suppose that Mathews had not admitted to knowing about the "no-lunch sheet" policy. Would the result in this case have been different? Why or why not?*

Attitude of Top Management

One of the most important ways to create and maintain an ethical workplace is for top management to demonstrate its commitment to ethical decision making. A manager who is not totally committed to an ethical workplace rarely succeeds in creating one. Management's behavior, more than anything else, sets the ethical tone of a firm. Employees take their cues from management. **EXAMPLE 7.2** Devon, a BioTek employee, observes his manager cheating on her expense account. Later, when Devon is promoted to a managerial position, he "pads" his expense account as well, knowing that he is unlikely to face sanctions for doing so. •

KNOW THIS

One of the best ways to encourage good business ethics at a workplace is to take immediate corrective action in response to any unethical conduct.

Managers who set unrealistic production or sales goals increase the probability that employees will act unethically. If a sales quota can be met only through high-pressure, unethical sales tactics, employees will try to act "in the best interest of the company" and will continue to behave unethically.

A manager who looks the other way when she or he knows about an employee's unethical behavior also sets an example—one indicating that ethical transgressions will be accepted. Managers have found that discharging even one employee for ethical reasons has a tremendous impact as a deterrent to unethical behavior in the workplace.

Behavior of Owners and Managers

Business owners and managers sometimes take more active roles in fostering unethical and illegal conduct. This may indicate to their co-owners, co-managers, employees, and others that unethical business behavior will be tolerated. **EXAMPLE 7.3** Lawyer Samir Zia Chowhan posted a help-wanted ad on Craigslist seeking an "energetic woman" for the position of legal secretary. The ad stated that the position included secretarial and paralegal work, as well as "additional duties" for two lawyers in the firm. Applicants were asked to send pictures and describe their physical features. When a woman applied for the job, Chowhan sent her an e-mail saying that "in addition to the legal work, you would be required to have sexual interaction with me and my partner, sometimes together sometimes separate." He also explained that she would need to perform sexual acts on them at the job interview so that he and his partner could determine whether she would be able to handle these duties. The woman filed a complaint with the Illinois Bar Association, which suspended Chowhan's law license for a year for making false statements about the ad. Because the bar association's ethics rules prohibited attorneys from having sex with their clients, but not with potential employees, Chowhan could only be disciplined for lying. •

Creating Ethical Codes of Conduct

"What you do speaks so loudly that I cannot hear what you say."

Ralph Waldo Emerson, 1803–1882 (American essayist and poet)

One of the most effective ways of setting a tone of ethical behavior within an organization is to create an ethical code of conduct. A well-written code of ethics explicitly states a company's ethical priorities and demonstrates the company's commitment to ethical behavior.

This chapter concludes with a foldout exhibit showing the code of ethics of Costco Wholesale Corporation as an example. This code of conduct indicates Costco's commitment to legal compliance, as well as to the welfare of its members (those who purchase its goods), employees, and suppliers. The code also details some specific ways in which the interests and welfare of these different groups will be protected. You will also see that Costco acknowledges that by protecting these groups' interests, it will realize its "ultimate goal"—rewarding its shareholders with maximum shareholder value.

Providing Ethics Training to Employees For an ethical code to be effective, its provisions must be clearly communicated to employees. Most large companies have implemented ethics training programs, in which managers discuss with employees on a face-to-face basis the firm's policies and the importance of ethical conduct. Smaller firms should also offer some form of ethics training to employees because if a firm is accused of an ethics violation, the court will consider the presence or absence of such training in evaluating the firm's conduct.

Some firms hold periodic ethics seminars during which employees can openly discuss any ethical problems that they may be experiencing and learn how the firm's ethical policies apply to those specific problems. Other companies require their managers to meet individually with employees and grade them on their ethical (or unethical) behavior.

Global companies are finding that they need to communicate their ethics policies to their foreign suppliers as well as their domestic employees. **EXAMPLE 7.4** Like other high-tech companies, Apple, Inc., relies heavily on foreign suppliers for components and assembly of many of its products. Following a number of high-profile labor problems with its foreign suppliers and manufacturers, Apple started to evaluate practices at companies in its supply chain and to communicate its ethics policies to them. After its audits revealed numerous violations, in 2012 Apple released a list of its suppliers for the first time. Apple's five-hundred-page "Supplier Responsibility Report" showed that sixty-seven facilities had docked worker pay as a disciplinary measure. Some had falsified pay records and forced workers to use machines without safeguards. Others had engaged in unsafe environmental practices, such as dumping wastewater on neighboring farms. Apple terminated its relationship with one supplier and turned over its findings to the Fair Labor Association for further inquiry. •

PREVENTING LEGAL DISPUTES

To avoid disputes over ethical violations, you should first create a written ethical code that is expressed in clear and understandable language. The code should establish specific procedures that employees can follow if they have questions or complaints. It should assure employees that their jobs will be secure and that they will not face reprisals if they do file a complaint. A well-written code might also include examples to clarify what the company considers to be acceptable and unacceptable conduct. You should also hold periodic training meetings so that you can explain to employees face to face why ethics is important to the company. If your company does business internationally, you might also communicate the code to firms in your supply chain and make sure they follow your ethics policies.

The Sarbanes-Oxley Act and Web-Based Reporting Systems

Congress enacted the Sarbanes-Oxley Act[2] to help reduce corporate fraud and unethical management decisions. The act requires companies to set up confidential systems so that employees and others can "raise red flags" about suspected illegal or unethical auditing and accounting practices. (The Sarbanes-Oxley Act will be discussed in more detail in Chapters 31 and 34, and excerpts and explanatory comments on this important law appear in Appendix D of this text.)

Some companies have implemented online reporting systems to accomplish this goal. In one system, employees can click on an icon on their computers that anonymously links them with EthicsPoint, an organization based in Portland, Oregon. Through EthicsPoint, employees can report suspicious accounting practices, sexual harassment, and other possibly unethical behavior. EthicsPoint, in turn, alerts management personnel or the audit committee at the designated company to the possible problem. Those who have used the system say that it is less inhibiting than calling a company's toll-free number.

Ethical Transgressions by Financial Institutions

"Never let your sense of morals prevent you from doing what is right."

Isaac Asimov, 1920–1992
(Russian-born writer and scientist)

One of the best ways to learn the ethical responsibilities inherent in operating a business is to look at the mistakes made by other companies. In the following subsections, we describe some of the most egregious ethical failures of financial institutions during the last decade. Many of these ethical wrongdoings received wide publicity and raised public awareness of the need for ethical leadership throughout all businesses.

Corporate Stock Buybacks

During the economic crisis that started in 2008, many of the greatest financial companies in the United States either went bankrupt, were taken over by the federal government, or had to be bailed out by U.S. taxpayers. What many people do not know is that those same corporations were using their own cash funds to prop up the value of their stock in the years just before the economic crisis.

Stock Buyback The purchase of shares of a company's own stock by that company on the open market.

The theory behind a **stock buyback** is simple—the management of a corporation believes that the market price of its shares is "below their fair value." Therefore, instead of issuing dividends to shareholders or reinvesting profits, management uses the company's funds to buy its shares in the open market, thereby boosting the price of the stock. From 2005 to 2007, stock buybacks for the top five hundred U.S. corporations added up to $1.4 *trillion.*

2. 15 U.S.C. Sections 7201 *et seq.*

Stock Option An agreement that grants the owner the option to buy a given number of shares of stock at a set price, usually within a specific time period.

Who benefits from stock buybacks? The main individual beneficiaries are corporate executives who have been given **stock options,** which enable them to buy shares of the corporation's stock at a set price. When the market price rises above that level, the executives can profit by selling their shares. Although stock buybacks are legal and can serve legitimate purposes, they can easily be abused if managers use them just to increase the stock price in the short term so that they can profit from their options without considering the long-term needs of the company.

In the investment banking business, which almost disappeared in the latter half of 2008, stock buybacks were particularly egregious. EXAMPLE 7.5 Goldman Sachs, an investment bank, bought back $15 billion of its stock in 2007. Yet by 2009, U.S. taxpayers had provided $10 billion in bailout funds to that same company. Lehman Brothers Holdings had also bought back large amounts of stock before it filed for bankruptcy in 2008. •

Startling Executive Decisions at American International Group

American International Group (AIG) was once a respected, conservative worldwide insurance company based in New York. Then it decided to enter an area in which it had little expertise—the issuance of insurance contracts guaranteeing certain types of complicated financial contracts. When many of those insured contracts failed, AIG experienced multibillion-dollar losses. Finally, the company sought a federal bailout that eventually amounted to almost $200 billion of U.S. taxpayers' funds.

While some company executives were testifying before Congress after receiving the funds, other AIG executives spent almost $400,000 on a retreat at a resort in California. In essence, U.S. taxpayers were footing the bill.

Executive Bonuses

Until the economic crisis began in 2008, the bonuses paid in the financial industry did not make headlines. After all, times were good, and why shouldn't those responsible for record company earnings be rewarded? When investment banks and commercial banks began to fail, however, or had to be bailed out or taken over by the federal government, executive bonuses became an important issue.

Richard Fuld, a former head of investment bank Lehman Brothers, earned $500 million in bonuses during the seven years before the company's bankruptcy.

(Kevin Dietsch/UPI/Landov)

The industry had been profiting from the sale of risky assets to investors. Executives and others in the industry who had created and sold those risky assets suffered no liability—and even received bonuses. Of course, some of those firms that had enjoyed high short-run returns from their risky investments—and paid bonuses based on those profits—found themselves facing bankruptcy. EXAMPLE 7.6 Lehman Brothers' chief executive officer earned almost $500 million between 2000 and the firm's demise in 2008. Even after Lehman Brothers entered bankruptcy, its new owners, Barclays and Nomura, legally owed $3.5 billion in bonuses to employees still on the payroll. In 2006, Goldman Sachs awarded its employees a total of $16.5 billion in bonuses, or an average of almost $750,000 for each employee. •

Public outrage at the bonuses paid by firms receiving taxpayer funds subsequently caused Congress to include a provision in the American Recovery and Reinvestment Tax Act of

2009 to change the compensation system in the financial industry. The provision did not cap executive salaries but did severely restrict the bonuses that could be paid by firms that had received bailout funds under the Troubled Asset Relief Program (TARP).[3] Although cash bonuses to Wall Street executives fell, the total compensation for financial service firms increased in 2010 to nearly $150 billion.

Approaches to Ethical Reasoning

Ethical Reasoning A reasoning process in which an individual links his or her moral convictions or ethical standards to the particular situation at hand.

Each individual, when faced with a particular ethical dilemma, engages in **ethical reasoning**—that is, a reasoning process in which the individual examines the situation at hand in light of his or her moral convictions or ethical standards. Businesspersons do likewise when making decisions with ethical implications.

How do business decision makers decide whether a given action is the "right" one for their firms? What ethical standards should be applied? Broadly speaking, ethical reasoning relating to business traditionally has been characterized by two fundamental approaches. One approach defines ethical behavior in terms of duty, which also implies certain rights. The other approach determines what is ethical in terms of the consequences, or outcome, of any given action. We examine each of these approaches here.

In addition to the two basic ethical approaches, several theories have been developed that specifically address the social responsibility of corporations. Because these theories also influence today's business decision makers, we conclude this section with a short discussion of the different views of corporate social responsibility.

LEARNING OBJECTIVE 3
How do duty-based ethical standards differ from outcome-based ethical standards?

Duty-Based Ethics

Duty-based ethical standards often are derived from revealed truths, such as religious precepts. They can also be derived through philosophical reasoning.

Religious Ethical Standards

In the Judeo-Christian tradition, the Ten Commandments of the Old Testament establish fundamental rules for moral action. Other religions have their own sources of revealed truth. Religious rules generally are absolute with respect to the behavior of their adherents. The commandment "Thou shalt not steal" is an absolute mandate for a person who believes that the Ten Commandments reflect revealed truth. Even a benevolent motive for stealing (such as Robin Hood's) cannot justify the act because the act itself is inherently immoral and thus wrong.

"When I do good, I feel good. When I do bad, I feel bad. And that's my religion."

Abraham Lincoln, 1809–1865
(Sixteenth president of the United States, 1861–1865)

Kantian Ethics

Duty-based ethical standards may also be derived solely from philosophical reasoning. The German philosopher Immanuel Kant (1724–1804), for example, identified some general guiding principles for moral behavior based on what he believed to be the fundamental nature of human beings. Kant believed that human beings are qualitatively different from other physical objects and are endowed with moral integrity and the capacity to reason and conduct their affairs rationally. Therefore, a person's thoughts and actions should be respected. When human beings are treated merely as a means to an end, they are being treated as the equivalent of objects and are being denied their basic humanity.

Categorical Imperative An ethical guideline developed by Immanuel Kant under which an action is evaluated in terms of what would happen if everybody else in the same situation, or category, acted the same way.

A central theme in Kantian ethics is that individuals should evaluate their actions in light of the consequences that would follow if *everyone* in society acted in the same way. This **categorical imperative** can be applied to any action. **EXAMPLE 7.7** Suppose that you are deciding whether to cheat on an examination. If you have adopted Kant's categorical imperative, you will decide *not* to cheat because if everyone cheated, the examination (and the entire education system) would be meaningless. ●

3. 12 U.S.C. Section 5211.

Principle of Rights The belief that human beings have certain fundamental rights. Whether an action or decision is ethical depends on how it affects the rights of various groups, such as owners, employees, consumers, suppliers, the community, and society.

The Principle of Rights

Because a duty cannot exist without a corresponding right, duty-based ethical standards imply that human beings have basic rights. The principle that human beings have certain fundamental rights (to life, liberty, and the pursuit of happiness, for example) is deeply embedded in Western culture. As discussed in Chapter 1, the natural law tradition embraces the concept that certain actions (such as killing another person) are morally wrong because they are contrary to nature (the natural desire to continue living).

Those who adhere to this **principle of rights,** or "rights theory," believe that a key factor in determining whether a business decision is ethical is how that decision affects the rights of others. These others include the firm's owners, its employees, the consumers of its products or services, its suppliers, the community in which it does business, and society as a whole.

Conflicting Rights A potential dilemma for those who support rights theory, however, is that there are often conflicting rights and people may disagree on which rights are most important. When considering all those affected by a business decision to downsize a firm, for example, how much weight should be given to employees relative to shareholders? Which employees should be laid off first, those with the highest salaries or those who have worked there for less time (and have less senority)? How should the firm weigh the rights of customers relative to the community, or employees relative to society as a whole?

Resolving Conflicts In general, rights theorists believe that whichever right is stronger in a particular circumstance takes precedence. **EXAMPLE 7.8** A firm can either keep a manufacturing plant open, saving the jobs of twelve workers, or shut the plant down and avoid contaminating a river with pollutants that would endanger the health of tens of thousands of people. In this situation, a rights theorist can easily choose which group to favor. (Not all choices are so clear-cut, however.) •

Outcome-Based Ethics: Utilitarianism

Utilitarianism An approach to ethical reasoning in which an action is evaluated in terms of its consequences for those whom it will affect. A "good" action is one that results in the greatest good for the greatest number of people.

"The greatest good for the greatest number" is a paraphrase of the major premise of the utilitarian approach to ethics. **Utilitarianism** is a philosophical theory developed by Jeremy Bentham (1748–1832) and modified by John Stuart Mill (1806–1873)—both British philosophers. In contrast to duty-based ethics, utilitarianism is outcome oriented. It focuses on the consequences of an action, not on the nature of the action itself or on any set of preestablished moral values or religious beliefs.

Cost-Benefit Analysis A decision-making technique that involves weighing the costs of a given action against the benefits of that action.

Under a utilitarian model of ethics, an action is morally correct, or "right," when, among the people it affects, it produces the greatest amount of good for the greatest number. When an action affects the majority adversely, it is morally wrong. Applying the utilitarian theory thus requires (1) a determination of which individuals will be affected by the action in question; (2) a **cost-benefit analysis,** which involves an assessment of the negative and positive effects of alternative actions on these individuals; and (3) a choice among alternative actions that will produce maximum societal utility (the greatest positive net benefits for the greatest number of individuals).

Corporate Social Responsibility

Corporate Social Responsibility The idea that corporations can and should act ethically and be accountable to society for their actions.

For many years, groups concerned with civil rights, employee safety and welfare, consumer protection, environmental preservation, and other causes have pressured U.S. corporations to behave in a responsible manner with respect to these causes. Thus was born the concept of **corporate social responsibility**—the idea that those who run corporations can and should act ethically and be accountable to society for their actions. Just what constitutes corporate social responsibility has been debated for some time, however, and there are a number of different theories today.

Stakeholder Approach

One view of corporate social responsibility stresses that corporations have a duty not just to shareholders, but also to other groups affected by corporate decisions ("stakeholders"). Under this approach, a corporation would consider the impact of its decision on the firm's employees, customers, creditors, suppliers, and the community in which the corporation operates. The reasoning behind this "stakeholder view" is that in some circumstances, one or more of these other groups may have a greater stake in company decisions than the shareholders do. Although this may be true, as mentioned earlier, it is often difficult to decide which group's interests should receive greater weight if the interests conflict.

During the last few years, layoffs numbered in the millions. Nonetheless, some corporations succeeded in reducing labor costs without layoffs. To avoid slashing their workforces, these employers turned to alternatives such as (1) four-day workweeks, (2) unpaid vacations and voluntary furloughs, (3) wage freezes, (4) pension cuts, and (5) flexible work schedules. Some companies asked their workers to accept wage cuts to prevent layoffs, and the workers agreed. Companies finding alternatives to layoffs included Dell (extended unpaid holidays), Cisco Systems (four-day end-of-year shutdowns), Motorola (salary cuts), and Honda (voluntary unpaid vacation time).

Corporate Citizenship

Another theory of social responsibility argues that corporations should be good citizens by promoting goals that society deems worthwhile and taking positive steps toward solving social problems. The idea is that because business controls so much of the wealth and power of this country, business, in turn, has a responsibility to society to use that wealth and power in socially beneficial ways.

Under a corporate citizenship view, companies are judged on how much they donate to social causes, as well as how they conduct their operations with respect to employment discrimination, human rights, environmental concerns, and similar issues. **EXAMPLE 7.9** Google has teamed up with investment firm Kohlberg Kravis Roberts to develop four solar energy farms that will serve the Sacramento Municipal Utility District in California. The four solar farms reportedly cost $95 million and will provide enough power for more than 13,000 average U.S. homes. •

Microsoft founder Bill Gates and his wife, Melinda, are shown below with financier Warren Buffett (right) after Buffett gave $40 billion to the Bill and Melinda Gates Foundation.

(Keith Meyers/The New York Times/Redux)

A Way of Doing Business

A survey of U.S. executives undertaken by the Boston College Center for Corporate Citizenship found that more than 70 percent of those polled agreed that corporate citizenship must be treated as a priority. More than 60 percent said that good corporate citizenship added to their companies' profits. Strategist Michelle Bernhart has argued that corporate social responsibility cannot attain its maximum effectiveness unless it is treated as a way of doing business rather than as a special program.

Not all socially responsible activities can benefit a corporation, however. Corporate responsibility is most successful when a company undertakes activities that are relevant and significant to its stakeholders and related to its business operations. **EXAMPLE 7.10** A Brazilian mining firm invested more than $150 million in social projects, including health care, infrastructure, and education. At the same time, it invested more than $300 million in environmental protection. One of its projects involves the rehabilitation of native species in the Amazon Valley. To that end, it is planting almost 200 million trees in an attempt to restore 1,150 square miles of land where cattle breeding and farming have caused deforestation. ● (See the *Linking Business Law to Accounting and Finance* feature at the end of this chapter for more examples of corporate responsibility.)

"Next to doing the right thing, the most important thing is to let people know you are doing the right thing."

John D. Rockefeller, 1839–1897 (American industrialist and philanthropist)

Making Ethical Business Decisions

The George S. May International Company has provided six basic guidelines to help corporate employees judge their actions. Each employee—no matter what her or his level in the organization—should evaluate her or his actions using the following six guidelines:

LEARNING OBJECTIVE 4
What are six guidelines that an employee can use to evaluate whether his or her actions are ethical?

1. *The law.* Is the action you are considering legal? If you do not know the laws governing the action, then find out. Ignorance of the law is no excuse.
2. *Rules and procedures.* Are you following the internal rules and procedures that have already been laid out by your company? They have been developed to avoid problems. Is what you are planning to do consistent with your company's policies and procedures? If not, stop.
3. *Values.* Laws and internal company policies reinforce society's values. You might wish to ask yourself whether you are attempting to find a loophole in the law or in your company's policies. Next, you have to ask yourself whether you are following the "spirit" of the law as well as the letter of the law or the internal policy.
4. *Conscience.* If you feel any guilt, let your conscience be your guide. Alternatively, ask yourself whether you would be happy to be interviewed by the national news media about the actions you are going to take.
5. *Promises.* Every business organization is based on trust. Your customers believe that your company will do what it is supposed to do. The same is true for your suppliers and employees. Will your actions live up to the commitments you have made to others, both inside the business and outside?
6. *Heroes.* We all have heroes who are role models for us. Is what you are planning on doing an action that your "hero" would take? If not, how would your hero act? That is how you should be acting.

ETHICAL ISSUE

Should you do the right thing even when it puts your job at risk? Dean Krehmeyer, executive director of the Business Roundtable's Institute for Corporate Ethics, once said, "Evidence strongly suggests being ethical—doing the right thing—pays." Sometimes, however, being ethical in the business world costs an employee his or her job. For instance, Michael Woodford was chief executive officer for Olympus Corporation, a Tokyo-based camera maker. He had worked thirty years for Olympus when he discovered that the company had been engaging in questionable accounting practices. After confronting management in 2011 about excessive spending on certain acquisitions, Woodford was fired from the board of directors.

He then resigned as chair and called for the other board members to resign and for a shareholders' meeting to be held to select a new board. Olympus initially denied any wrongdoing but later acknowledged a $687 million payment for financial advice and expensive acquisitions to cover up investment losses. Many speculate that the company falsified a large amount of information in its financial reports over the years. Olympus's bookkeeping is now under investigation in Japan, the United States, and Great Britain. But Woodford, who did the right thing by encouraging the company to come clean about the cover-up, no longer works for the company. He plans to sue Olympus, but because it is a Japanese company, he may never be compensated for losing his job.

Practical Solutions to Corporate Ethics Questions

Corporate ethics officers and ethics committees require a practical method to investigate and solve specific ethics problems. Ethics consultant Leonard H. Bucklin of Corporate-Ethics.US has devised a procedure that he calls Business Process Pragmatism.[4] It involves the following five steps:

"If you are uncertain about an issue, it's useful to ask yourself, 'Would I be absolutely comfortable for my actions to be disclosed on the front page of my hometown newspaper?'"

Warren E. Buffett, 1930–present (American businessperson and philanthropist)

1. *Inquiry.* Of course, an understanding of the facts must be the initial action. The parties involved might include the mass media, the public, employees, or customers. At this stage of the process, the ethical problem or problems are specified. A list of relevant ethical principles is created.
2. *Discussion.* Here, a list of action options is developed. Each option carries with it certain ethical principles. Finally, resolution goals should also be listed.
3. *Decision.* Working together, those participating in the process craft a consensus decision, or a consensus plan of action for the corporation.
4. *Justification.* Does the consensus solution withstand moral scrutiny? At this point in the process, reasons should be attached to each proposed action or series of actions. Will the stakeholders involved accept these reasons?
5. *Evaluation.* Do the solutions to the corporate ethics issue satisfy corporate values, community values, and individual values? Ultimately, can the consensus resolution to the corporate ethics problem withstand the moral scrutiny of the decisions taken and the process used to reach those decisions?

Business Ethics on a Global Level

Given the various cultures and religions throughout the world, it is not surprising that conflicts in ethics frequently arise between foreign and U.S. businesspersons. For instance, in certain countries, the consumption of alcohol and specific foods is forbidden for religious reasons. Under such circumstances, it would be thoughtless and imprudent for a U.S. businessperson to invite a local business contact out for a drink.

The role played by women in other countries may also present some difficult ethical problems for firms doing business internationally. Equal employment opportunity is a fundamental public policy in the United States, and Title VII of the Civil Rights Act of 1964 prohibits discrimination against women in the employment context (see Chapter 25). Some other countries, however, offer little protection for women against gender discrimination in the workplace, including sexual harassment. (See this chapter's *Law, Diversity, and Business: Managerial Implications* feature on the facing page for a discussion of the impact of cultural differences on global marketing strategies.)

We look here at how laws governing workers in other countries, particularly developing countries, have created some especially difficult ethical problems for U.S. sellers of goods manufactured in foreign countries. We also examine some of the ethical ramifications of laws prohibiting U.S. businesspersons from bribing foreign officials to obtain favorable business contracts.

Monitoring the Employment Practices of Foreign Suppliers

LEARNING OBJECTIVE 5
What types of ethical issues might arise in the context of international business transactions?

Many U.S. businesses now contract with companies in developing nations to produce goods, such as shoes and clothing, because the wage rates in those nations are significantly lower than wages in the United States. Yet what if a foreign company exploits its

4. Corporate-Ethics and Business Process Pragmatism are registered trademarks.

LAW, DIVERSITY, AND BUSINESS: MANAGERIAL IMPLICATIONS

RESPECTING CULTURAL DIFFERENCES IN FOREIGN MARKETS

Today, more businesses engage in global activities than ever before. Certainly, anyone developing marketing strategies for a foreign market needs to be aware of all aspects of culture, including religion, language, values, and customs.

Global Marketing and the Need to Consider Each Culture Separately No matter how "small" the world has become, countries still have different sets of shared values that affect their citizens' preferences. Samsonite, for example, made a major cultural blunder when it used an advertisement showing its luggage being carried on a "magic" flying carpet. Most Middle Eastern consumers thought that Samsonite was selling carpets. As another example, Green Giant learned to its dismay that it could not use its logo with a man in a green hat in certain parts of Asia. Why not? The reason was that in those areas a green hat signifies a man who has an unfaithful wife.

The Translation of Names and Slogans Can Be a Problem, Too In the same vein, the translation of slogans and names into other languages is fraught with pitfalls. Toyota had to drop the "2" from its model MR2 in France because the combination of sounds was very close to a French swear word. Mitsubishi Motors had to rename one of its models in Spanish-speaking countries because the original name described a sexual activity.

Can Global Marketing Standardization Work in a Diverse World? Many multinationals have adopted global marketing standardization, meaning that they try to adapt product features, advertising, and packaging so that they are usable throughout the world. Those in favor of such standardization—a global vision, as it were—contend that advances in communications and technology have created a small, interconnected world. Consumers everywhere want the same items that they see in popular movies. Coca-Cola, Colgate-Palmolive, and McDonald's, for example, tend toward global marketing standardization.

Business Implications *Managers in any company wishing to do business abroad have to be aware that their marketing campaigns may offend potential consumers (and even governments). Given that almost 15 percent of U.S. production is sold abroad, this issue is an important one and will become more important as standards of living increase in poorer parts of the globe. Higher standards of living usually lead to more imports. Many of those imports will come from the United States and will have to be marketed carefully.*

workers—by hiring women and children at below-minimum-wage rates, for example, or by requiring its employees to work long hours in a workplace full of health hazards? What if the company's supervisors routinely engage in workplace conduct that is offensive to women? What if plants that are operated abroad routinely violate labor and environmental standards?

EXAMPLE 7.11 Apple, Inc., owns Pegatron Corporation, a subsidiary company based in China, that supplies parts for iPads and other Apple products. In December 2011, dozens of employees at the Pegatron factory in Shanghai were injured when aluminum dust created from polishing cases for iPads caught fire and exploded. Apple did not respond to allegations that conditions at the factory violated labor and environmental standards. •

Given today's global communications network, few companies can assume that their actions in other nations will go unnoticed by "corporate watch" groups that discover and publicize unethical corporate behavior. (For a discussion of how the Internet has increased the ability of critics to publicize a corporation's misdeeds, see this chapter's *Adapting the Law to the Online Environment* feature on the following page.) As a result, U.S. businesses today usually take steps to avoid such adverse publicity—either by refusing to deal with certain suppliers or by arranging to monitor their suppliers' workplaces to make sure that the employees are not being mistreated.

ADAPTING THE LAW TO THE ONLINE ENVIRONMENT

CORPORATE REPUTATIONS UNDER ATTACK

In the pre-Internet days, disgruntled employees and customers wrote letters of complaint to corporate management or to the editors of local newspapers. Occasionally, an investigative reporter would write an exposé of alleged corporate misdeeds. Today, those unhappy employees and customers have gone online. To locate them, just type in the name of any major corporation. You will find electronic links to blogs, wikis, message boards, and online communities—many of which post harsh criticisms of corporate giants. Some disgruntled employees and consumers have even created rogue Web sites that mimic the look of the target corporation's official Web site—except that the rogue sites feature chat rooms and postings of "horror stories" about the corporation.

Damage to Corporate Reputations

Clearly, by providing a forum for complaints, the Internet has increased the potential for damage to the reputation of any major (or minor) corporation. Now a relatively small number of unhappy employees, for example, may make the entire world aware of a single incident that is not at all representative of how the corporation ordinarily operates.

Special Interest Groups Go on the Attack

Special interest groups are also using the Internet to attack corporations they do not like. Rather than writing letters or giving speeches to a limited audience, a special interest group can now go online and mercilessly "expose" what it considers to be a corporation's "bad practices." Wal-Mart and Nike in particular have been frequent targets for advocacy groups that believe that those corporations exploit their workers.

Online Attacks: Often Inaccurate, but Probably Legal

Corporations often point out that many of the complaints and charges leveled against them are unfounded or exaggerated. Sometimes, management has tried to argue that the online attacks are libelous. The courts, however, disagree. To date, most courts have regarded online attacks as simply the expression of opinion and therefore a form of speech protected by the First Amendment.

In contrast, if employees breach company rules against the disclosure of internal financial information or trade secrets, the courts have been willing to side with the employers. Note, also, that companies that succeed in lawsuits against inappropriate employee online disclosures always have a clear set of written guidelines about what employees can do when they blog or generate other online content.

Critical Thinking

How might online attacks actually help corporations in the long run? (Hint: Some online criticisms might be accurate.)

The Foreign Corrupt Practices Act

"Never doubt that a small group of committed citizens can change the world; indeed, it is the only thing that ever has."

Margaret Mead, 1901–1978 (American anthropologist)

Another ethical problem in international business dealings has to do with the legitimacy of certain "side" payments to government officials. In the United States, most contracts are formed within the private sector. In many countries, however, government regulation and control over trade and industry are much more extensive than in the United States, so government officials make the decisions on most major construction and manufacturing contracts. Side payments to government officials in exchange for favorable business contracts are not unusual in such countries, where they are not considered to be unethical. In the past, U.S. corporations doing business in these countries largely followed the dictum "When in Rome, do as the Romans do."

In the 1970s, however, large side payments by U.S. corporations to foreign representatives for the purpose of securing advantageous international trade contracts led to a number of scandals. In response, in 1977 Congress passed the Foreign Corrupt Practices Act[5] (FCPA), which prohibits U.S. businesspersons from bribing foreign officials to secure advantageous contracts.

5. 15 US.C. Sections 78 dd-1 *et seq.*

Prohibition against the Bribery of Foreign Officials The first part of the FCPA applies to all U.S. companies and their directors, officers, shareholders, employees, and agents. This part prohibits the bribery of officials of foreign governments if the purpose of the payment is to induce the officials to act in their official capacity to provide business opportunities.

The FCPA does not prohibit payment of substantial sums to minor officials whose duties are ministerial. These payments are often referred to as "grease," or facilitating payments. They are meant to accelerate the performance of administrative services that might otherwise be carried out at a slow pace. Thus, for example, if a firm makes a payment to a minor official to speed up an import licensing process, the firm has not violated the FCPA. Generally, the act, as amended, permits payments to foreign officials if such payments are lawful within the foreign country. The act also does not prohibit payments to private foreign companies or other third parties unless the U.S. firm knows that the payments will be passed on to a foreign government in violation of the FCPA. Business firms that violate the FCPA may be fined up to $2 million. Individual officers or directors who violate the act may be fined up to $100,000 (the fine cannot be paid by the company) and may be imprisoned for up to five years.

Accounting Requirements In the past, bribes were often concealed in corporate financial records. Thus, the second part of the FCPA is directed toward accountants. All companies must keep detailed records that "accurately and fairly" reflect the company's financial activities. In addition, all companies must have an accounting system that provides "reasonable assurance" that all transactions entered into by the company are accounted for and legal. These requirements assist in detecting illegal bribes. The FCPA further prohibits any person from making false statements to accountants or false entries in any record or account.

Reviewing . . . Ethics and Business Decision Making

Isabel Arnett was promoted to be chief executive officer of Tamik, Inc., a pharmaceutical company that manufactures a vaccine called Kafluk, which supposedly provides some defense against bird flu. The company began marketing Kafluk throughout Asia. After numerous media reports that bird flu might soon become a worldwide epidemic, the demand for Kafluk increased, sales soared, and Tamik earned record profits. Arnett then began receiving disturbing reports from Southeast Asia that in some patients, Kafluk had caused psychiatric disturbances, including severe hallucinations, and heart and lung problems. She was also informed that six children in Japan had committed suicide by jumping out of windows after receiving the vaccine. To cover up the story and prevent negative publicity, Arnett instructed Tamik's partners in Asia to offer cash to the Japanese families whose children had died in exchange for their silence. Arnett also refused to authorize additional research within the company to study the potential side effects of Kafluk. Using the information presented in the chapter, answer the following questions.

1. This scenario illustrates one of the main reasons why ethical problems occur in business. What is that reason?
2. Would a person who adheres to the principle of rights consider it ethical for Arnett not to disclose potential safety concerns and to refuse to perform additional research on Kafluk? Why or why not?
3. If Kafluk prevented fifty Asian people who were exposed to bird flu from dying, would Arnett's conduct in this situation be ethical under a utilitarian cost-benefit analysis? Why or why not?
4. Did Tamik or Arnett violate the Foreign Corrupt Practices Act in this scenario? Why or why not?

DEBATE THIS Executives in large corporations are ultimately rewarded if their companies do well, particularly as evidenced by rising stock prices. Consequently, shouldn't we just let those who run corporations decide what level of negative side effects of their goods or services is "acceptable"?

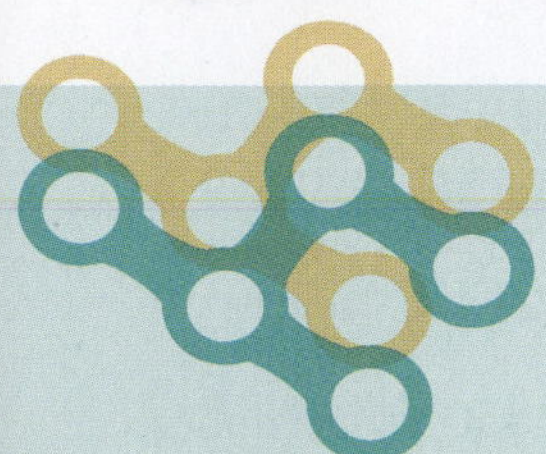

LINKING BUSINESS LAW to Accounting and Finance

Managing a Company's Reputation

While in business school, all of you must take basic accounting courses. Accounting generally is associated with developing balance sheets and profit-and-loss statements, but it can also be used as a support system to provide information that can help managers do their jobs correctly. Enter managerial accounting, which involves the provision of accounting information for a company's internal use. Managerial accounting is used within a company for planning, controlling, and decision making.

Increasingly, managerial accounting is also being used to *manage corporate reputations.* To this end, more than 2,500 multinationals now release to the public large quantities of managerial accounting information.

Internal Reports Designed for External Scrutiny

Some large companies refer to the managerial accounting information that they release to the public as their corporate sustainability reports. Dow Chemical Company, for example, issues its Global Reporting Initiative Sustainability Report annually. So does Waste Management, Inc., which calls its report "The Color of Our World."

Other corporations call their published documents social responsibility reports. The antivirus software company Symantec Corporation issued its first corporate responsibility report in 2008. The report demonstrated the company's focus on critical environmental, social, and governance issues. Among other things, Symantec pointed out that it had adopted the Calvert Women's Principles, the first global code of corporate conduct designed to empower, advance, and invest in women worldwide.

A smaller number of multinationals provide what they call citizenship reports. For example, in 2011 General Electric (GE) released its Seventh Annual Citizenship Report, which it calls "Sustainable Growth." GE's emphasis is on energy and climate change, demographics, growth markets, and financial markets. It even has a Web site that provides detailed performance metrics (www.ge.com/citizenship).

The Hitachi Group releases an Annual Corporate Social Responsibility Report, which outlines its environmental strategy, including its attempts to reduce carbon dioxide emissions (so-called greenhouse gases). It typically discusses human rights policy and its commitment to human rights awareness.

Why Use Managerial Accounting to Manage Reputations?

We live in an age of information. Any news, whether positive or negative, about a corporation will be known throughout the world almost immediately given the 24/7 cable and online news networks, social media, Internet bloggers, and smartphones. Consequently, corporations want to manage their reputations by preparing and releasing the news that the public, their shareholders, and government officials will receive. In a world in which corporations are often blamed for anything bad that happens, corporations are finding that managerial accounting information can provide a useful counterweight. To this end, some corporations have combined their social responsibility reports with their traditional financial accounting information. When a corporation's reputation is on the line, the future is at stake.

Critical Thinking

Valuable company resources are used to create and publish corporate social responsibility reports. Under what circumstances can a corporation justify such expenditures?

Key Terms

business ethics 191
categorical imperative 198
corporate social responsibility 199
cost-benefit analysis 199
ethical reasoning 198
ethics 191
moral minimum 191
principle of rights 199
stock buyback 196
stock option 197
utilitarianism 199

Chapter Summary: Ethics and Business Decision Making

Business Ethics (See pages 191–196.)	1. *Ethics*—Business ethics focuses on how moral and ethical principles are applied in the business context. 2. *The moral minimum*—Lawful behavior is the moral minimum. The law has its limits, though, and some actions may be legal but not ethical. 3. *Short-term profit maximization*—One of the most pervasive reasons why ethical breaches occur is the focus on short-term profit maximization. Executives should distinguish between short-run and long-run profit goals and focus on maximizing profits over the long run because only long-run profit maximization is consistent with business ethics. 4. *Legal uncertainties*—It may be difficult to predict with certainty whether particular actions are legal, given the numerous and frequent changes in the laws regulating business and the "gray areas" in the law. 5. *The importance of ethical leadership*—Management's commitment and behavior are essential in creating an ethical workplace. Management's behavior, more than anything else, sets the ethical tone of a firm and influences the behavior of employees. 6. *Ethical codes*—Most large firms have ethical codes or policies and training programs to help employees determine whether specific actions are ethical. In addition, the Sarbanes-Oxley Act requires firms to set up confidential systems so that employees and others can report suspected illegal or unethical auditing or accounting practices.
Ethical Transgressions by Financial Institutions (See pages 196–198.)	During the first decade of the 2000s, corporate wrongdoing among U.S. financial institutions escalated. A number of investment banking firms, such as Goldman Sachs, were nearly bankrupted by their risky investments, and others, such as Lehman Brothers, were forced into bankruptcy. Earlier these same firms had engaged in the abusive use of stock buybacks and stock options. AIG, an insurance giant, was also on the brink of bankruptcy when the government stepped in with federal bailout funds. Exorbitant bonuses paid to Wall Street executives added to the financial industry's problems and fueled public outrage. U.S. taxpayers paid the price through the federal bailouts and a deepening nationwide recession.
Approaches to Ethical Reasoning (See pages 198–201.)	1. *Duty-based ethics*—Ethics based on religious beliefs; philosophical reasoning, such as that of Immanuel Kant; and the basic rights of human beings (the principle of rights). A potential problem for those who support this approach is deciding which rights are more important in a given situation. Management constantly faces ethical conflicts and trade-offs when considering all those affected by a business decision. 2. *Outcome-based ethics (utilitarianism)*—Ethics based on philosophical reasoning, such as that of Jeremy Bentham and John Stuart Mill. Applying this theory requires a cost-benefit analysis, weighing the negative effects against the positive and deciding which course of action produces the better outcome. 3. *Corporate social responsibility*—A number of theories based on the idea that corporations can and should act ethically and be accountable to society for their actions. These include the stakeholder approach and corporate citizenship.
Making Ethical Business Decisions (See page 201.)	Making ethical business decisions is crucial in today's legal environment. Doing the right thing pays off in the long run, both by increasing profits and by avoiding negative publicity and the potential for bankruptcy. We provide six guidelines for making ethical business decisions on page 201.
Practical Solutions to Corporate Ethics Questions (See page 202.)	Corporate ethics officers and ethics committees require a practical method to investigate and solve specific ethics problems. For a five-step pragmatic procedure to solve ethical problems recommended by one expert, see page 202.
Business Ethics on a Global Level (See pages 202–205.)	Businesses must take account of the many cultural, religious, and legal differences among nations. Notable differences relate to the role of women in society, employment laws governing workplace conditions, and the practice of giving side payments to foreign officials to secure favorable contracts.

ExamPrep

ISSUE SPOTTERS

1. Delta Tools, Inc., markets a product that under some circumstances is capable of seriously injuring consumers. Does Delta have an ethical duty to remove this product from the market, even if the injuries result only from misuse? Why or why not? **(See pages 192–193.)**
2. Acme Corporation decides to respond to what it sees as a moral obligation to correct for past discrimination by adjusting pay differences among its employees. Does this raise an ethical conflict between Acme and its employees? Between Acme and its shareholders? Explain your answers. **(See page 201.)**

—Check your answers to the Issue Spotters against the answers provided in Appendix E at the end of this text.

BEFORE THE TEST

Go to www.cengagebrain.com, enter the ISBN 9781133273561, and click on "Find" to locate this textbook's Web site. Then, click on "Access Now" under "Study Tools," and select Chapter 7 at the top. There, you will find a Practice Quiz that you can take to assess your mastery of the concepts in this chapter, as well as Flashcards, a Glossary of important terms, and Video Questions (when assigned).

For Review

Answers to the even-numbered questions in this **For Review** ***section can be found in Appendix F at the end of this text.***

1. What is business ethics, and why is it important?
2. How can business leaders encourage their companies to act ethically?
3. How do duty-based ethical standards differ from outcome-based ethical standards?
4. What are six guidelines that an employee can use to evaluate whether his or her actions are ethical?
5. What types of ethical issues might arise in the context of international business transactions?

Business Scenarios and Case Problems

7–1 Business Ethics. Jason Trevor owns a commercial bakery in Blakely, Georgia, that produces a variety of goods sold in grocery stores. Trevor is required by law to perform internal tests on food produced at his plant to check for contamination. Three times in 2011, the tests of food products that contained peanut butter were positive for salmonella contamination. Trevor was not required to report the results to U.S. Food and Drug Administration officials, however, so he did not. Instead, Trevor instructed his employees to simply repeat the tests until the outcome was negative. Therefore, the products that had originally tested positive for salmonella were eventually shipped out to retailers. Five people who ate Trevor's baked goods in 2011 became seriously ill, and one person died from salmonella. Even though Trevor's conduct was legal, was it unethical for him to sell goods that had once tested positive for salmonella? If Trevor had followed the six basic guidelines for making ethical business decisions, would he still have sold the contaminated goods? Why or why not? **(See page 201.)**

7–2 Question with Sample Answer—Ethical Duties. Shokun Steel Co. owns many steel plants. One of its plants is much older than the others. Equipment at that plant is outdated and inefficient, and the costs of production at that plant are now twice as high as at any of Shokun's other plants. The company cannot raise the price of steel because of competition, both domestic and international. The plant employs more than a thousand workers and is located in Twin Firs, Pennsylvania, which has a population of about 45,000. Shokun is contemplating whether to close the plant. What factors should the firm consider in making its decision? Will the firm violate any ethical duties if it closes the plant? Analyze these questions from the two basic perspectives on ethical reasoning discussed in this chapter. **(See page 198.)**

—For a sample answer to Question 7–2, go to Appendix G at the end of this text.

7–3 Spotlight on Pfizer—Corporate Social Responsibility. Methamphetamine (meth) is an addictive drug made chiefly in small toxic labs (STLs) in homes, tents, barns, or hotel rooms. The manufacturing process is dangerous, often resulting in explosions, burns, and toxic fumes. Government entities spend time and resources to find and destroy STLs, imprison meth dealers and users, treat addicts, and provide services for affected families. Meth cannot be made without ingredients that are also used in cold and allergy medications. Arkansas has one of the highest numbers of STLs in the United States. To recoup the costs of fighting the meth epidemic, twenty counties in Arkansas filed a suit against Pfizer, Inc., which makes cold and allergy medications. What is Pfizer's ethical responsibility here, and to whom is it owed? Why? [*Ashley County, Arkansas v. Pfizer, Inc.*, 552 F.3d 659 (8th Cir. 2009)] **(See page 200.)**

7–4 Case Problem with Sample Answer—Ethics and the Law. Prudential Insurance Co. of America has a company guideline not to change the amount of a salesperson's commission once a client has been quoted a price for insurance. Despite this principle, in order to reduce the quoted price for insurance offered to York International Corp., Prudential cut the fee that it paid to a broker. A competing broker, Havensure, LLC, filed a suit, arguing that the reduced quote caused it to lose York as a potential customer. Is a company's violation of its own policy unethical? Is it a basis for legal liability? Explain. [*Havensure, LLC v. Prudential Insurance Co. of America*, 595 F.3d 312 (6th Cir. 2010)] **(See page 195.)**

—For a sample answer to Problem 7–4, go to Appendix H at the end of this text.

7–5 Ethical Leadership. David Krasner, who worked for HSH Nordbank AG, complained that his supervisor, Roland Kiser, fostered an atmosphere of sexism that was demeaning to women. Among other things, Krasner claimed that career advancement was based on "sexual favoritism." He objected to Kiser's relationship with a female employee, Melissa Campfield, who was promoted before more qualified employees, including Krasner. How do a manager's attitudes and actions affect the workplace? [*Krasner v. HSH Nordbank AG,* 680 F.Supp.2d 502 (S.D.N.Y. 2010)] **(See pages 194–195.)**

7–6 Ethical Misconduct. Frank Pasquale used his father's Social Security number to obtain a credit card. Later, pretending to act on behalf of his father's firm, Pasquale borrowed $350,000. When he defaulted on the loan and his father confronted him, he produced forged documents that showed the loan had been paid. Adams Associates, LLC, which held the unpaid loan, filed a suit against both Pasquales. Should the court issue a judgment against the father and the son? Discuss. [*Adams Associates, LLC v. Frank Pasquale Limited Partnership,* __ A.3d __ (N.J.Super. A.D. 2011)] **(See pages 196–197.)**

7–7 A Question of Ethics—Copyrights. Steven Soderbergh is the Academy Award–winning director of *Erin Brockovich, Traffic,* and many other films. CleanFlicks, LLC, filed a suit in a federal district court against Soderbergh, fifteen other directors, and the Directors Guild of America. The plaintiff asked the court to rule that it had the right to sell DVDs of the defendants' films altered without the defendants' consent to delete scenes of "sex, nudity, profanity and gory violence." CleanFlicks sold or rented the edited DVDs under the slogan "It's About Choice" to consumers, sometimes indirectly through retailers. It would not sell to retailers that made unauthorized copies of the edited films. The defendants, with DreamWorks LLC and seven other movie studios that own the copyrights to the films, filed a counterclaim against CleanFlicks and others engaged in the same business, alleging copyright infringement. Those filing the counterclaim asked the court to enjoin (prevent) CleanFlicks and the others from making and marketing altered versions of the films. [*CleanFlicks of Colorado, LLC v. Soderbergh,* 433 F.Supp.2d 1236 (D.Colo. 2006)] **(See page 201.)**

1. Movie studios often edit their films to conform to content and other standards and sell the edited versions to network television and other commercial buyers. In this case, however, the studios objected when CleanFlicks edited the films and sold the altered versions directly to consumers. Similarly, CleanFlicks made unauthorized copies of the studios' DVDs to edit the films, but objected when others made unauthorized copies of the altered versions. Is there anything unethical about these apparently contradictory positions? Why or why not?
2. CleanFlicks and its competitors asserted, in part, that they were making "fair use" of the studios' copyrighted works. They argued that by their actions "they are criticizing the objectionable content commonly found in current movies and that they are providing more socially acceptable alternatives to enable families to view the films together, without exposing children to the presumed harmful effects emanating from the objectionable content." If you were the judge, how would you view this argument? Is a court the appropriate forum for making determinations of public or social policy? Explain.

Critical Thinking and Writing Assignments

7–8 Critical Legal Thinking. Human rights groups, environmental activists, and other interest groups concerned with unethical business practices have often conducted publicity campaigns against various corporations that those groups feel have engaged in unethical practices. Can a small group of well-organized activists dictate how a major corporation conducts its affairs? Should a small group be able to do so? Discuss fully. **(See page 202.)**

7–9 Business Law Writing. Assume that you are a high-level manager for a shoe manufacturer. You know that your firm could increase its profit margin by producing shoes in Indonesia, where you could hire women for $100 a month to assemble them. You also know that human rights advocates recently accused a competing shoe manufacturer of engaging in exploitative labor practices because the manufacturer sold shoes made by Indonesian women for similarly low wages. You personally do not believe that paying $100 a month to Indonesian women is unethical because you know that in their country, $100 a month is a better-than-average wage rate. Write one page explaining whether you would have the shoes manufactured in Indonesia and make higher profits for the company or avoid the risk of negative publicity and its potential adverse consequences for the firm's reputation. Are there other alternatives? Discuss fully. **(See page 202.)**

7–10 Business Law Critical Thinking Group Assignment. In the 1990s, Pfizer, Inc., developed a new antibiotic called Trovan (trovafloxacin mesylate). Tests showed that in animals Trovan had life-threatening side effects, including joint disease, abnormal cartilage growth, liver damage, and a degenerative bone condition. In 1996, an epidemic of bacterial meningitis swept across Nigeria. Pfizer sent three U.S. physicians to test Trovan on children who were patients in Nigeria's Infectious Disease Hospital. Pfizer did not obtain the patients' consent, alert them to the risks, or tell them that Médecins Sans Frontières (Doctors without Borders) was providing an effective conventional treatment at the same site. Eleven children died in the experiment, and others were left blind, deaf, paralyzed, or brain damaged. Rabi Abdullahi and other Nigerian children filed a suit in a U.S. federal court against Pfizer, alleging a violation of a customary international law norm prohibiting involuntary medical experimentation on humans. [*Abdullahi v. Pfizer, Inc.,* 562 F.3d 163 (2d Cir. 2009)]

1. One group should use the principles of ethical reasoning discussed in this chapter to develop three arguments on how Pfizer's conduct was a violation of ethical standards.
2. A second group should take a pro-Pfizer position and argue that the company did not violate any ethical standards (and counter the first group).
3. A third group should come up with proposals for what Pfizer might have done differently to avert the consequences.

8 CHAPTER

International Law in a Global Economy

CHAPTER OUTLINE

- International Law—Sources and Principles
- Doing Business Internationally
- Regulation of Specific Business Activities
- Commercial Contracts in an International Setting
- Payment Methods for International Transactions
- U.S. Laws in a Global Context

LEARNING OBJECTIVES

The five learning objectives below are designed to help improve your understanding of the chapter. After reading this chapter, you should be able to answer the following questions:

1. What is the principle of comity, and why do courts deciding disputes involving a foreign law or judicial decree apply this principle?
2. What is the act of state doctrine? In what circumstances is this doctrine applied?
3. Under the Foreign Sovereign Immunities Act, in what situations is a foreign state subject to the jurisdiction of U.S. courts?
4. What are three clauses commonly included in international business contracts?
5. What federal law allows U.S. citizens, as well as citizens of foreign nations, to file civil actions in U.S. courts for torts that were committed overseas?

(AP Photo/Shuji Kajiyama)

"The merchant has no country."
—Thomas Jefferson, 1743–1826 (Third president of the United States, 1801–1809)

International business transactions are not unique to the modern world. Indeed, commerce has always crossed national borders, as President Thomas Jefferson noted in the chapter-opening quotation. What is new in our day is the dramatic growth in world trade and the emergence of a global business community. Because exchanges of goods, services, and intellectual property on a global level are now routine, students of business law and the legal environment should be familiar with the laws pertaining to international business transactions.

Laws affecting the international legal environment of business include both international law and national law. As discussed in Chapter 1, *international law* is defined as a body of law—formed as a result of international customs, treaties, and organizations—that governs relations among or between nations. International law may be public, creating standards for the nations themselves. It may also be private, establishing international standards for private transactions that cross national borders. *National law,* as pointed out in Chapter 1, is the law of a particular nation, such as Brazil, Germany, Japan, or the United States.

Because there is so much uncertainty with one of our largest trading partners, the European Union (EU), issues in international law are going to be in the news for years to come. When we trade with many EU countries, we buy their goods in euros, their common currency. What will happen if some countries leave the euro zone and go back to their former domestic currencies? We can't pretend to tell you the answer, but you'll learn enough in this chapter to be able to follow the arguments.

International Law—Sources and Principles

The major difference between international law and national law is that government authorities can enforce national law. What government, however, can enforce international law? By definition, a *nation* is a sovereign entity—meaning that there is no higher authority to which that nation must submit. If a nation violates an international law and persuasive tactics fail, other countries or international organizations have no recourse except to take coercive actions—from severance of diplomatic relations and boycotts to, as a last resort, war—against the violating nation.

In essence, international law attempts to reconcile the need of each country to be the final authority over its own affairs with the desire of nations to benefit economically from trade and harmonious relations with one another. Sovereign nations can, and do, voluntarily agree to be governed in certain respects by international law for the purpose of facilitating international trade and commerce, as well as civilized discourse. As a result, a body of international law has evolved.

Sources of International Law

Basically, there are three sources of international law: international customs, treaties and international agreements, and international organizations and conferences. We look at each of these sources here.

International Customs

One important source of international law consists of the international customs that have evolved among nations in their relations with one another. Article 38(1) of the Statute of the International Court of Justice refers to an international custom as "evidence of a general practice accepted as law." The legal principles and doctrines that you will read about shortly are rooted in international customs and traditions that have evolved over time in the international arena.

Treaties and International Agreements

Treaties and other explicit agreements between or among foreign nations provide another important source of international law. A **treaty** is an agreement or contract between two or more nations that must be authorized and ratified by the supreme power of each nation. Under Article II, Section 2, of the U.S. Constitution, the president has the power "by and with the Advice and Consent of the Senate, to make Treaties, provided two-thirds of the Senators present concur."

Treaty A formal international agreement negotiated between two nations or among several nations. In the United States, all treaties must be approved by the Senate.

A *bilateral* agreement, as the term implies, is an agreement formed by two nations to govern their commercial exchanges or other relations with one another. A *multilateral* agreement is formed by several nations. For example, regional trade associations such as the Andean Common Market (ANCOM), the Association of Southeast Asian Nations (ASEAN), and the European Union (EU) are the result of multilateral trade agreements.

International Organization An organization that is composed mainly of member nations and usually established by treaty—for example, the United Nations. More broadly, the term also includes nongovernmental organizations (NGOs) such as the Red Cross.

International Organizations

In international law, the term **international organization** generally refers to an organization that is composed mainly of member nations

(AP Photo/Haraz N. Ghanbari)

General-Secretary of the United Nations (UN) Ban Ki-moon shakes hands with U.S. Secretary of State Hillary Clinton. Why do governments support the UN?

and usually established by treaty. The United States is a member of more than one hundred bilateral and multilateral organizations, including at least twenty through the United Nations. These organizations adopt resolutions, declarations, and other types of standards that often require nations to behave in a particular manner. The General Assembly of the United Nations, for example, has adopted numerous nonbinding resolutions and declarations that embody principles of international law.

Disputes involving these resolutions and declarations may be brought before the International Court of Justice. That court, however, normally has authority to settle legal disputes only when nations voluntarily submit to its jurisdiction.

The United Nations Commission on International Trade Law has made considerable progress in establishing uniformity in international law as it relates to trade. One of the commission's most significant creations to date is the 1980 Convention on Contracts for the International Sale of Goods (CISG). As will be discussed in Chapter 15, the CISG is similar to Article 2 of the Uniform Commercial Code. It is designed to settle disputes between parties to sales contracts if the parties have not agreed otherwise in their contracts. The CISG governs only sales contracts between trading partners in nations that have ratified the CISG, however.

International Principles and Doctrines

Over time, a number of legal principles and doctrines have evolved and have been employed by the courts of various nations to resolve or reduce conflicts that involve a foreign element. The three important legal principles discussed next are based primarily on courtesy and respect, and are applied in the interests of maintaining harmonious relations among nations.

Comity The principle by which one nation defers to and gives effect to the laws and judicial decrees of another nation. This recognition is based primarily on respect.

LEARNING OBJECTIVE 1

What is the principle of comity, and why do courts deciding disputes involving a foreign law or judicial decree apply this principle?

The Principle of Comity

Under the principle of **comity,** one nation will defer to and give effect to the laws and judicial decrees of another country, as long as they are consistent with the law and public policy of the accommodating nation.

CASE EXAMPLE 8.1 Karen Goldberg's husband was killed in a terrorist bombing in Israel. She filed a lawsuit in a federal court in New York against UBS AG, a Switzerland-based global financial services company with many offices in the United States. Goldberg claimed that UBS was liable under the U.S. Anti-Terrorism Act for aiding and abetting the murder of her husband because it provided financial services to the international terrorist organizations responsible for his murder. UBS argued that the case should be transferred to a court in Israel, which would offer a remedy "substantially the same" as the one available in the United States. The court refused to transfer the case, however, because that would require an Israeli court to take evidence and judge the emotional damage suffered by Goldberg, "raising distinct concerns of comity and enforceability." U.S. courts hesitate to impose U.S. law on foreign courts when such law is "an unwarranted intrusion" on the policies governing a foreign nation's judicial system.[1] •

One way to understand the principle of comity (and the *act of state doctrine,* which will be discussed shortly) is to consider the relationships among the states in our federal form of government. Each state honors (gives "full faith and credit" to) the contracts, property deeds, wills, and other legal obligations formed in other states, as well as judicial decisions

1. *Goldberg v. UBS AG,* 690 F.Supp.2d 92 (E.D.N.Y. 2010).

with respect to such obligations. On a worldwide basis, nations similarly attempt to honor judgments rendered in other countries when it is feasible to do so. Of course, in the United States the states are constitutionally required to honor other states' actions, whereas internationally, nations are not *required* to honor the actions of other nations.

Act of State Doctrine A doctrine providing that the judicial branch of one country will not examine the validity of public acts committed by a recognized foreign government within its own territory.

The Act of State Doctrine

The **act of state doctrine** provides that the judicial branch of one country will not examine the validity of public acts committed by a recognized foreign government within its own territory.

A government controls the natural resources, such as oil reserves, within its territory. It can decide to utilize the resources or preserve them, or to establish a balance between utilization and preservation. Does the act of state doctrine apply to such decisions even though they may affect market prices in other countries? That was the question in the following case.

Case 8.1

Spectrum Stores, Inc. v. Citgo Petroleum Corp.

United States Court of Appeals, Fifth District, 632 F.3d 938 (2011). www.ca5.uscourts.gov[a]

(Photo by Scott Olson/Getty Images)

Citgo is a Venezuelan state-owned oil company.

FACTS Spectrum Stores, Inc., and other U.S. gasoline retailers (the plaintiffs) filed a suit against Citgo Petroleum Corporation and other oil production companies in a federal district court. The plaintiffs alleged that the defendants had conspired to fix the prices of crude oil and refined petroleum products in the United States, primarily by limiting the production of crude oil. Citgo is owned by the national oil company of Venezuela, and most of the other defendants are owned entirely or in part by Venezuela or Saudi Arabia. Both nations are members of the Organization of Petroleum Exporting Countries (OPEC), which was formed by several oil-rich nations "to ensure the stabilization of oil markets in order to secure an efficient, economic and regular supply of petroleum." Spectrum sought damages, an injunction, and other relief. The court dismissed the suit, and Spectrum appealed.

ISSUE Does the act of state doctrine prevent a federal court from considering claims that companies owned by foreign governments illegally conspired to fix oil prices in the United States?

DECISION Yes. The U.S. Court of Appeals for the Fifth Circuit affirmed the lower court's dismissal. The act of state doctrine bars consideration of Spectrum's claims.

REASON The court reasoned that under the act of state doctrine, a U.S. court will not rule on the validity of a foreign government's acts within its own territory. It is the sovereign right of each nation to decide how to exploit its own resources. Granting relief to Spectrum would effectively have ordered foreign governments to dismantle their chosen means of exploiting the resources within their own territories. Such a decision would also have had the effect of "embarrassing" the diplomacy carried out by the executive and legislative branches of the U.S. government. In other words, a ruling in this case would have interfered with the political branches' policy of engaging with the OPEC nations through diplomacy rather than litigation to affect the global supply of oil.

CRITICAL THINKING—Legal Consideration *If the judicial branch does not have the authority to rule on matters of foreign policy, which branch of government does? Explain.*

a. In the left column, in the "Opinions" section, click on "Opinions Page." On the next page, in the "Search for opinions where:" section, in the "and/or Docket number is:" box, type "09-20084" and click on "Search." Then click on the docket number to access this case opinion. (The title listed is *In re: Refined Petro, et.al.*) The U.S. Court of Appeals for the Fifth Circuit maintains this Web site.

When a Foreign Government Takes Private Property The act of state doctrine can have important consequences for individuals and firms doing business with, and investing in, other countries. This doctrine is frequently employed in situations involving expropriation or confiscation.

Expropriation A government's seizure of a privately owned business or personal property for a proper public purpose and with just compensation.

Confiscation A government's taking of a privately owned business or personal property without a proper public purpose or an award of just compensation.

Expropriation occurs when a government seizes a privately owned business or privately owned goods for a proper public purpose and awards just compensation. When a government seizes private property for an illegal purpose or without just compensation, the taking is referred to as a **confiscation.** The line between these two forms of taking is sometimes blurred because of differing interpretations of what is illegal and what constitutes just compensation.

EXAMPLE 8.2 Flaherty, Inc., a U.S. company, owns a mine in Argentina. The government of Argentina seizes the mine for public use and claims that the profits that Flaherty realized from the mine in preceding years constitute just compensation. Flaherty disagrees, but the act of state doctrine may prevent the company's recovery in a U.S. court. • Note that in a case alleging that a foreign government has wrongfully taken the plaintiff's property, the defendant government has the burden of proving that the taking was an expropriation, not a confiscation.

LEARNING OBJECTIVE 2

What is the act of state doctrine? In what circumstances is this doctrine applied?

Doctrine May Immunize a Foreign Government's Actions When applicable, both the act of state doctrine and the doctrine of *sovereign immunity* (to be discussed next) tend to immunize (protect) foreign governments from the jurisdiction of U.S. courts. This means that firms or individuals who own property overseas often have diminished legal protection against government actions in the countries in which they operate.

The Doctrine of Sovereign Immunity

Sovereign Immunity A doctrine that immunizes foreign nations from the jurisdiction of U.S. courts when certain conditions are satisfied.

When certain conditions are satisfied, the doctrine of **sovereign immunity** immunizes foreign nations from the jurisdiction of U.S. courts. In 1976, Congress codified this rule in the Foreign Sovereign Immunities Act (FSIA).[2] The FSIA exclusively governs the circumstances in which an action may be brought in the United States against a foreign nation, including attempts to attach a foreign

2. 28 U.S.C. Sections 1602–1611.

These are employees of Owens Illinois, a glass company. The president of Venezuela expropriated this firm. What is the difference between expropriation and confiscation?

nation's property. Because the law is jurisdictional in nature, a plaintiff has the burden of showing that a defendant is not entitled to sovereign immunity.

Section 1605 of the FSIA sets forth the major exceptions to the jurisdictional immunity of a foreign state. A foreign state is not immune from the jurisdiction of U.S. courts in the following situations:

LEARNING OBJECTIVE 3
Under the Foreign Sovereign Immunities Act, in what situations is a foreign state subject to the jurisdiction of U.S. courts?

1. When the foreign state has waived its immunity either explicitly or by implication.
2. When the foreign state has engaged in commercial activity within the United States or in commercial activity outside the United States that has "a direct effect in the United States."[3]
3. When the foreign state has committed a tort in the United States or has violated certain international laws.

In applying the FSIA, questions frequently arise as to whether an entity is a "foreign state" and what constitutes a "commercial activity." Under Section 1603 of the FSIA, a *foreign state* includes both a political subdivision of a foreign state and an instrumentality of a foreign state. Section 1603 broadly defines a *commercial activity* as a commercial activity that is carried out by a foreign state within the United States, but it does not describe the particulars of what constitutes a commercial activity. Thus, the courts are left to decide whether a particular activity is governmental or commercial in nature.

Doing Business Internationally

Export The sale of goods and services by domestic firms to buyers located in other countries.

A U.S. domestic firm can engage in international business transactions in a number of ways. The simplest way is for U.S. firms to **export** their goods and services to markets abroad. Alternatively, a U.S. firm can establish foreign production facilities so as to be closer to the foreign market or markets in which its products are sold. The advantages may include lower labor costs, fewer government regulations, and lower taxes and trade barriers. A domestic firm may engage in manufacturing abroad by licensing its technology to an existing foreign company or by establishing overseas subsidiaries or joint ventures.

"Commerce is the great civilizer. We exchange ideas when we exchange fabrics."

Robert G. Ingersoll, 1833–1899
(American politician and orator)

Exporting

Exporting can take two forms: direct exporting and indirect exporting. In *direct exporting,* a U.S. company signs a sales contract with a foreign purchaser that provides for the conditions of shipment and payment for the goods. (How payments are made in international transactions will be discussed later in this chapter.) If sufficient business develops in a foreign country, a U.S. corporation may set up a specialized marketing organization in that foreign market by appointing a foreign agent or distributor. This is called *indirect exporting.*

When a U.S. firm desires to limit its involvement in an international market, it will typically establish an *agency relationship* with a foreign firm. (*Agency* will be discussed in Chapter 23.) The foreign firm then acts as the U.S. firm's agent and can enter into contracts in the foreign location on behalf of the principal (the U.S. company).

Distribution Agreement A contract between a seller and a distributor of the seller's products setting out the terms and conditions of the distributorship.

Distributorships

When a foreign country represents a substantial market, a U.S. firm may wish to appoint a distributor located in that country. The U.S. firm and the distributor enter into a **distribution agreement,** which is a contract between the seller and the distributor setting out the terms and conditions of the distributorship. These terms and conditions—for example, price, currency of payment, availability of supplies, and method of payment—primarily involve contract law. Disputes concerning distribution agreements

3. See, for example, *O'Bryan v. Holy See,* 556 F.3d 361 (6th Cir. 2009).

(AP Photo)

Chinese workers assemble cars at a Ford plant in Chongqing, China. Why would Ford build a plant outside the United States?

may involve jurisdictional or other issues, as well as contract law, which will be discussed later in this chapter.

The National Export Initiative

Although the United States is one of the world's major exporters, exports make up a much smaller share of annual output in the United States than they do in our most important trading partners. In the past, the United States has not promoted exports as actively as many other nations have.

In an effort to increase U.S. exports, in 2010 the Obama administration created the National Export Initiative (NEI) with a goal of doubling U.S. exports by 2015. Some commentators believe that another goal of the NEI is to reduce outsourcing—the practice of having manufacturing or other activities performed in lower-wage countries such as China and India.

Export Promotion An important component of the NEI is the Export Promotion Cabinet, which includes officials from sixteen government agencies and departments. All cabinet members must submit detailed plans to the president, outlining the steps that they will take to increase U.S. exports.

The U.S. Commerce Department plays a leading role in the NEI, and hundreds of its trade experts serve as advocates to help some twenty thousand U.S. companies increase their export sales. In addition, the Commerce Department and other cabinet members work to promote U.S. exports in the high-growth developing markets of Brazil, China, and India. The members also identify market opportunities in fast-growing sectors, such as environmental goods and services, biotechnology, and renewable energy.

Increased Export Financing Under the NEI, the Export-Import Bank of the United States increased the financing that it makes available to small and medium-sized businesses by 50 percent. In the initial phase, the bank added hundreds of new small-business clients that sell a wide variety of products, from sophisticated polymers to date palm trees and nanotechnology-based cosmetics.

PREVENTING LEGAL DISPUTES

In light of the National Export Initiative, managers in companies that are now outsourcing or thinking of doing so may wish to reconsider. Increasingly, the federal government is taking a stance against outsourcing. As long as unemployment remains high in the United States, the emphasis will be on the creation of jobs at home. These efforts will often be backed by subsidies and access to federally supported borrowing initiatives.

Manufacturing Abroad

An alternative to direct or indirect exporting is the establishment of foreign manufacturing facilities. Typically, U.S. firms establish manufacturing plants abroad if they believe that doing so will reduce their costs—particularly for labor, shipping, and raw materials—and enable them to compete more effectively in foreign markets. Foreign firms have done the same in the United States. Sony, Nissan, and other Japanese manufacturers have established U.S. plants to avoid import duties that the U.S. Congress may impose on Japanese products entering this country.

(Imaginechina via AP Images)

What type of legal agreement do the distributors of Coca-Cola in China have with the Coca-Cola Company?

Licensing A U.S. firm may license a foreign manufacturing company to use its copyrighted, patented, or trademarked intellectual property or trade secrets. Like any other licensing agreement (see Chapters 5 and 10), a licensing agreement with a foreign-based firm calls for a payment of royalties on some basis—such as so many cents per unit produced or a certain percentage of profits from units sold in a particular geographic territory.

EXAMPLE 8.3 The Coca-Cola Bottling Company licenses firms worldwide to use (and keep confidential) its secret formula for the syrup used in its soft drink. In return, the foreign firms licensed to make the syrup pay Coca-Cola a percentage of the income earned from the sale of the soft drink. • Once a firm's trademark is known worldwide, the firm may experience increased demand for other products it manufactures or sells. As will be discussed in Chapter 26, franchising is a well-known form of licensing.

Subsidiaries A U.S. firm can also expand into a foreign market by establishing a wholly owned subsidiary firm in a foreign country. When a wholly owned subsidiary is established, the parent company, which remains in the United States, retains complete ownership of all the facilities in the foreign country, as well as complete authority and control over all phases of the operation. A U.S. firm can also expand into international markets through a joint venture. In a joint venture, the U.S. company owns only part of the operation. The rest is owned either by local owners in the foreign country or by another foreign entity. All of the firms involved in a joint venture share responsibilities, as well as profits and liabilities (joint ventures will be discussed in Chapter 28).

Regulation of Specific Business Activities

Doing business abroad can affect the economies, foreign policies, domestic policies, and other national interests of the countries involved. For this reason, nations impose laws to restrict or facilitate international business. Controls may also be imposed by international agreements. Here, we discuss how different types of international activities are regulated.

Investment Protections

Firms that invest in foreign nations face the risk that the foreign government may take possession of the investment property. Expropriation, as already mentioned, occurs when property is taken and the owner is paid just compensation for what is taken. Expropriation does not violate generally observed principles of international law. Such principles are normally violated, however, when a government confiscates property without compensation (or without adequate compensation). Few remedies are available for confiscation of property by a foreign government. Claims are often resolved by lump-sum settlements after negotiations between the United States and the taking nation.

To counter the deterrent effect that the possibility of confiscation may have on potential investors, many countries guarantee that foreign investors will be compensated if their property is taken. A guaranty can take the form of statutory laws or provisions in international treaties. As further protection for foreign investments, some countries provide insurance for their citizens' investments abroad.

KNOW THIS

Countries restrict exports for several reasons including these: to protect national security, to further foreign policy objectives, and to conserve resources (or raise their prices).

Export Controls

The U.S. Constitution provides in Article I, Section 9, that "No Tax or Duty shall be laid on Articles exported from any State." Thus, Congress cannot impose any export taxes. Congress can, however, use a variety of other devices to control exports. Congress may set export quotas

"The notion dies hard that in some sort of way exports are patriotic but imports are immoral."

Lord Harlech, 1918–1985 (British writer)

on various items, such as grain being sold abroad. Under the Export Administration Act of 1979,[4] the flow of technologically advanced products and technical data can be restricted.

While restricting certain exports, the United States (and other nations) also uses devices such as export incentives and subsidies to stimulate other exports and thereby aid domestic businesses. Under the Export Trading Company Act of 1982,[5] U.S. banks are encouraged to invest in export trading companies, which are formed when exporting firms join together to export a line of goods. The Export-Import Bank of the United States provides financial assistance, consisting primarily of credit guaranties given to commercial banks that in turn lend funds to U.S. exporting companies.

Import Controls

Import restrictions include strict prohibitions, quotas, and tariffs. Under the Trading with the Enemy Act of 1917,[6] for instance, no goods may be imported from nations that have been designated enemies of the United States.

Other laws prohibit the importation of illegal drugs and agricultural products that pose dangers to domestic crops or animals. The import of goods that infringe U.S. patents is also prohibited. The International Trade Commission investigates allegations that imported goods infringe U.S. patents and imposes penalties if necessary.

Quota A set limit on the amount of goods that can be imported.

Tariff A tax on imported goods.

Quotas and Tariffs

Limits on the amounts of goods that can be imported are known as **quotas.** At one time, the United States had legal quotas on the number of automobiles that could be imported from Japan. Today, Japan "voluntarily" restricts the number of automobiles exported to the United States (but it builds most cars in U.S. factories).

Tariffs are taxes on imports. A tariff usually is a percentage of the value of the import, but it can be a flat rate per unit (for example, per barrel of oil). Tariffs raise the prices of goods, causing some consumers to purchase more domestically manufactured goods and fewer imported goods.

Political Factors

Sometimes, countries impose tariffs on goods from a particular nation in retaliation for political acts. **EXAMPLE 8.4** A few years ago, Mexico imposed tariffs of 10 to 20 percent on ninety products exported from the United States in retaliation for the Obama administration's cancellation of a cross-border trucking program. The program had been instituted to comply with a provision in the North American Free Trade Agreement (to be discussed shortly) intended to eventually grant Mexican trucks full access to U.S. highways.

U.S truck drivers opposed the program, however, and consumer protection groups claimed that the Mexican trucks posed safety issues. Because the Mexican tariffs were imposed annually on $2.4 billion of U.S. goods, in 2011 President Barack Obama negotiated a deal that allowed Mexican truckers to enter the United States. In exchange, Mexico agreed to suspend half of the tariffs immediately and the remainder when the first Mexican hauler complied with the new U.S. requirements. •

Dumping The sale of goods in a foreign country at a price below the price charged for the same goods in the domestic market.

Antidumping Duties

The United States has specific laws directed at what it sees as unfair international trade practices. **Dumping,** for instance, is the sale of imported goods at "less than fair value." "Fair value" is usually determined by the price of those goods in the exporting country. Foreign firms that engage in dumping in the United States hope to undersell U.S. businesses to obtain a larger share of the U.S. market. To prevent this, an extra tariff—known as an *antidumping duty*—may be assessed on the imports.

---

4. 50 U.S.C. Sections 2401–2420.
5. 15 U.S.C. Sections 4001, 4003.
6. 12 U.S.C. Section 95a.

Minimizing Trade Barriers

Restrictions on imports are also known as *trade barriers*. The elimination of trade barriers is sometimes seen as essential to the world's economic well-being. Most of the world's leading trading nations are members of the World Trade Organization (WTO), which was established in 1995.

Normal Trade Relations (NTR) Status A legal trade status granted to member countries of the World Trade Organization.

To minimize trade barriers among nations, each member country of the WTO is required to grant **normal trade relations (NTR) status** to other member countries. This means each member is obligated to treat other members at least as well as it treats the country that receives its most favorable treatment with regard to imports or exports. Various regional trade agreements and associations also help to minimize trade barriers between nations.

The European Union (EU)

The European Union (EU) arose out the 1957 Treaty of Rome, which created the Common Market, a free trade zone comprising the nations of Belgium, France, Italy, Luxembourg, the Netherlands, and West Germany. Today, the EU is a single integrated trading unit made up of twenty-seven European nations.

The EU has gone a long way toward creating a new body of law to govern all of the member nations—although some of its efforts to create uniform laws have been confounded by nationalism. The EU's council and commission issue regulations, or directives, that define EU law in various areas, such as environmental law, product liability, anticompetitive practices, and corporations. The directives normally are binding on all member countries.

The North American Free Trade Agreement (NAFTA)

The North American Free Trade Agreement (NAFTA) created a regional trading unit consisting of Canada, Mexico, and the United States. The goal of NAFTA is to eliminate tariffs among these three countries on substantially all goods by reducing the tariffs incrementally over a period of time. NAFTA gives the three countries a competitive advantage by retaining tariffs on goods imported from countries outside the NAFTA trading unit.

Additionally, NAFTA provides for the elimination of barriers that traditionally have prevented the cross-border movement of services, such as financial and transportation services. NAFTA also attempts to eliminate citizenship requirements for the licensing of accountants, attorneys, physicians, and other professionals.

The Central America–Dominican Republic–United States Free Trade Agreement (CAFTA-DR)

The Central America–Dominican Republic–United States Free Trade Agreement (CAFTA-DR) was formed by Costa Rica, the Dominican

A commercial truck crosses the border between Mexico and the United States. What treaty made this possible?

(AP Photo/*The Laredo Morning Times*, Ricardo Santos)

(Georges Gobet/AFP/Getty Images)

Flags from European countries fly in front of the European Parliament in Strasbourg, France.

Republic, El Salvador, Guatemala, Honduras, Nicaragua, and the United States. Its purpose is to reduce tariffs and improve market access among all of the signatory nations, including the United States. Legislatures in all seven countries have approved the CAFTA-DR, despite significant opposition in certain nations.

The Republic of Korea–United States Free Trade Agreement (KORUS FTA) In 2011, the United States ratified its first free trade agreement with South Korea—the Republic of Korea–United States Free Trade Agreement (KORUS FTA). The treaty's provisions will eliminate 95 percent of each nation's tariffs on industrial and consumer exports within five years. KORUS is the largest free trade agreement the United States has entered since NAFTA, and may boost U.S. exports by more than $10 billion a year. It will benefit U.S. automakers, farmers, ranchers, and manufacturers by enabling them to compete in new markets.

Also in 2011, Congress ratified free trade agreements with Colombia and Panama. The Colombian trade agreement included a provision requiring an exchange of tax information, and the Panama bill incorporated labor rights assurances. The Obama administration spent years negotiating these treaties in an effort to boost U.S. exports, reduce prices for U.S. consumers, and help our sluggish economy recover. The administration also hoped that the agreements will provide an impetus for continuing the negotiation of the trans-Pacific trade initiative, aimed at increasing exports to Japan and other Asian nations.

Bribing Foreign Officials

Giving cash or in-kind benefits to foreign government officials to obtain business contracts and other favors is often considered normal practice. To reduce such bribery by representatives of U.S. corporations, Congress enacted the Foreign Corrupt Practices Act in 1977.[7] This act and its implications for American businesspersons engaged in international business transactions were discussed in Chapter 7 on page 204.

Commercial Contracts in an International Setting

Like all commercial contracts, an international contract should be in writing. For an example of an actual international sales contract from Starbucks Coffee Company, refer to the foldout exhibit at the end of Chapter 15.

Contract Clauses

LEARNING OBJECTIVE 4
What are three clauses commonly included in international business contracts?

Language and legal differences among nations can create special problems for parties to international contracts when disputes arise. To avoid these problems, parties should include special provisions in the contract that designate the language of the contract, the jurisdiction where any disputes will be resolved, and the substantive law that will be applied in settling any disputes. Parties to international contracts should also indicate in their contracts what acts or events will excuse the parties from performance under the contract and whether disputes under the contract will be arbitrated or litigated.

Choice-of-Language Clause A deal struck between a U.S. company and a company in another country normally involves two languages. Typically, many phrases in one language are not readily translatable into another. Consequently, the complex contractual terms involved may not be understood by one party in the other party's language. To

7. 15 U.S.C. Sections 78m–78ff.

make sure that no disputes arise out of this language problem, an international sales contract should have a **choice-of-language clause** designating the official language by which the contract will be interpreted in the event of disagreement.

Choice-of-Language Clause A clause in a contract designating the official language by which the contract will be interpreted in the event of a disagreement over the contract's terms.

Note also that some nations have mandatory language requirements. In France, for instance, certain legal documents, such as the prospectuses used in securities offerings (see Chapter 29), must be written in French. In addition, contracts with any departmental or local authority in France, instruction manuals, and warranties for goods and services offered for sale in France must also be written in French.

Forum-Selection Clause

When a dispute arises, litigation may be pursued in courts of different nations. There are no universally accepted rules as to which court has jurisdiction over a particular subject matter or parties to a dispute. Consequently, parties to an international transaction should always include in the contract a **forum-selection clause** indicating what court, jurisdiction, or tribunal will decide any disputes arising under the contract. It is especially important to indicate the specific court that will have jurisdiction. The forum does not necessarily have to be within the geographic boundaries of the home nation of either party.

Forum-Selection Clause A provision in a contract designating the court, jurisdiction, or tribunal that will decide any disputes arising under the contract.

CASE EXAMPLE 8.5 Garware Polyester, Ltd., based in Mumbai, India, made plastics and high-tech polyester film. Intermax Trading Corporation, based in New York, acted as Garware's North American sales agent and sold its products on a commission basis. Garware and Intermax had executed a series of agency agreements with provisions stating that the courts of Mumbai, India, would have exclusive jurisdiction over any disputes relating to the agreements. When Intermax fell behind in its payments to Garware, Garware filed a lawsuit in a U.S. court to collect the balance due, claiming that the forum-selection clause did not apply to sales of warehoused goods. The court, however, sided with Intermax. Because the forum-selection clause was valid and enforceable, Garware had to bring its complaints against Intermax in a court in India.[8] •

Choice-of-Law Clause

A contractual provision designating the applicable law—such as the law of Germany or the United Kingdom or California—is called a **choice-of-law clause.** Every international contract typically includes a choice-of-law clause. At common law (and in European civil law systems), parties are allowed to choose the law that will govern their contractual relationship, provided that the law chosen is the law of a jurisdiction that has a substantial relationship to the parties and to the international business transaction.

Choice-of-Law Clause A clause in a contract designating the law (such as the law of a particular state or nation) that will govern the contract.

Under Section 1–105 of the Uniform Commercial Code, parties may choose the law that will govern the contract as long as the choice is "reasonable." Article 6 of the United Nations Convention on Contracts for the International Sale of Goods (discussed in Chapter 15), however, imposes no limitation on the parties' choice. Similarly, the 1986 Hague Convention on the Law Applicable to Contracts for the International Sale of Goods—often referred to as the Choice-of-Law Convention—allows unlimited autonomy in the choice of law. The Hague Convention indicates that whenever a contract does not specify a choice of law, the governing law is that of the country in which the *seller's* place of business is located.

Force Majeure Clause

Every contract, particularly those involving international transactions, should have a ***force majeure* clause.** *Force majeure* is a French term meaning "impossible or irresistible force"—sometimes loosely identified as "an act of God." In international business contracts, *force majeure* clauses commonly stipulate that in addition to acts of God, a number of other eventualities (such as government orders or embargoes, for example) may excuse a party from liability for nonperformance.

***Force Majeure* Clause** A provision in a contract stipulating that certain unforeseen events—such as war, political upheavals, or acts of God—will excuse a party from liability for nonperformance of contractual obligations.

8. *Garware Polyester, Ltd. v. Intermax Trading Corp.*, 2001 WL 1035134 (S.D.N.Y. 2001). See also *Laasko v. Xerox Corp.*, 566 F.Supp.2d 1018 (C.D.Cal. 2008).

Civil Dispute Resolution

International contracts frequently include arbitration clauses. By means of such clauses, the parties agree in advance to be bound by the decision of a specified third party in the event of a dispute, as discussed in Chapter 3. (For an example of an arbitration clause in an international contract, refer to the foldout exhibit at the end of Chapter 15.) The United Nations Convention on the Recognition and Enforcement of Foreign Arbitral Awards (often referred to as the New York Convention) assists in the enforcement of arbitration clauses, as do provisions in specific treaties among nations. The New York Convention has been implemented in nearly one hundred countries, including the United States.

If a sales contract does not include an arbitration clause, litigation may occur. If the contract contains forum-selection and choice-of-law clauses, the lawsuit will be heard by a court in the specified forum and decided according to that forum's law. If no forum and choice of law have been specified, however, proceedings will be more complex and legally uncertain. For instance, litigation may take place in two or more countries, with each country applying its own choice-of-law rules to determine the substantive law that will be applied to the particular transactions. Even if a plaintiff wins a favorable judgment in the plaintiff's country, there is no way to predict whether courts in the defendant's country will enforce the judgment. (For further discussion of this issue, see this chapter's *Beyond Our Borders* feature on page 224.)

In the following case, the court had to decide whether an agreement was enforceable even though one party was a U.S. citizen and the other may have had its principal place of business in the United States.

Case 8.2

S&T Oil Equipment & Machinery, Ltd. v. Juridica Investments, Ltd.

United States Court of Appeals, Fifth Circuit, 2012 WL 28242 (2012).
www.ca5.uscourts.gov[a]

(Roberto Giobbi/Shutterstock.com)

Oil-pumping equipment built by S&T Oil.

FACTS Juridica Investments, Ltd. (JIL), entered into a financing contract with S&T Oil Equipment & Machinery, Ltd., a U.S. company. The contract included an arbitration provision stating that any disputes would be arbitrated in Guernsey, which is one in a group of British islands in the English Channel. The contract also stated that it was executed in Guernsey and that it would be fully performed there. When a dispute arose between the parties, JIL initiated arbitration in Guernsey. Nevertheless, S&T filed a suit in federal district court in the United States. When JIL filed a motion to dismiss in favor of arbitration, the court granted the motion and compelled arbitration under the Convention on the Recognition and Enforcement of Foreign Arbitral Awards—an international agreement also known as the New York Convention. S&T appealed.

ISSUE Was arbitration required under the New York Convention?

DECISION Yes. The U.S. Court of Appeals for the Fifth Circuit affirmed the district court's judgment compelling arbitration.

REASON The court explained that the New York Convention requires arbitration if "(1) there is a written agreement to arbitrate the matter; (2) the agreement provides for arbitration in a Convention signatory nation; (3) the agreement arises out of a commercial legal relationship; and (4) a party to the agreement is not an American citizen." Here, the first three requirements were clearly satisfied, but there was some question about whether JIL was an American citizen based on its principal place of business. Nevertheless, under the statute implementing the Convention, an arbitration agreement between U.S. citizens is enforceable if it "involves property abroad, envisages performance or

a. In the left-hand column, click on "Opinions Page." Then, in the "and/or Docket number is:" box, type "11-20400" and click on "Search." In the result, click on the docket number to access the opinion.

Case 8.2—Continued

enforcement abroad, or has some other reasonable relation with one or more foreign states." In this case, JIL and S&T executed their contract in Guernsey and agreed that it would be fully performed there. Thus, the parties had a reasonable relation with a foreign state beyond the arbitration agreement itself. Arbitration was therefore required under the Convention.

CRITICAL THINKING—Global Consideration *What would happen if Congress did not require a reasonable relationship with a foreign state for arbitration agreements between U.S. citizens? Would there be more or fewer agreements to arbitrate disputes abroad?*

(Ralf Siemieniec/Shutterstock.com)

How do businesses pay foreign firms?

Payment Methods for International Transactions

Currency differences between nations and the geographic distance between parties to international sales contracts add a degree of complexity to international sales that does not exist in the domestic market. Because international contracts involve greater financial risks, special care should be taken in drafting these contracts to specify both the currency in which payment is to be made and the method of payment.

Monetary Systems

Although our national currency, the U.S. dollar, is one of the primary forms of international currency, any U.S. firm undertaking business transactions abroad must be prepared to deal with one or more other currencies. After all, a Japanese firm may want to be paid in Japanese yen for goods and services sold outside Japan. Both firms therefore must rely on the convertibility of currencies.

Foreign Exchange Market A worldwide system in which foreign currencies are bought and sold.

Currencies are convertible when they can be freely exchanged one for the other at some specified market rate in a **foreign exchange market.** Foreign exchange markets make up a worldwide system for the buying and selling of foreign currencies. The foreign exchange rate is simply the price of a unit of one country's currency in terms of another country's currency. For instance, if today's exchange rate is eighty Japanese yen for one dollar, that means that anybody with eighty yen can obtain one dollar, and vice versa. Like other prices, the exchange rate is set by the forces of supply and demand.

Correspondent Bank A bank in which another bank has an account (and vice versa) for the purpose of facilitating fund transfers.

Frequently, a U.S. company can rely on its domestic bank to take care of all international transfers of funds. Commercial banks often transfer funds internationally through their **correspondent banks** in other countries. **EXAMPLE 8.6** A customer of Citibank wishes to pay a bill in euros to a company in Paris. Citibank can draw a bank check payable in euros on its account in Crédit Agricole, a Paris correspondent bank, and then send the check to the French company to which its customer owes the funds. Alternatively, Citibank's customer can request a wire transfer of the funds to the French company. Citibank instructs Crédit Agricole by wire to pay the necessary amount in euros. •

Letters of Credit

Letter of Credit A written document in which the issuer (usually a bank) promises to honor drafts or other demands for payment by third persons in accordance with the terms of the instrument.

Because buyers and sellers engaged in international business transactions are frequently separated by thousands of miles, special precautions are often taken to ensure performance under the contract. Sellers want to avoid delivering goods for which they might not be paid. Buyers desire the assurance that sellers will not be paid until there is evidence that the goods have been shipped. Thus, **letters of credit** are frequently used to facilitate international business transactions.

BEYOND OUR BORDERS Arbitration versus Litigation

Businesspersons often find it advantageous to include arbitration clauses in their international contracts because arbitration awards are usually easier to enforce than court judgments. A problem in collecting court judgments is that the application of the principle of comity varies from one nation to another. Many nations have not signed bilateral agreements with the United States agreeing to enforce judgments rendered in U.S. courts.

When Constitutional Rights Are Involved

Even when the United States has an agreement with another nation, a judgment by a court in that nation may not be enforced in the United States if it conflicts with U.S. laws or policies, especially if the case involves important constitutional rights such as freedom of the press or freedom of religion.

For instance, a U.S. federal appellate court refused to enforce a French default judgment against a U.S. firm, Viewfinder, Inc., on constitutional grounds. Viewfinder operated a Web site that posted photographs from fashion shows and information about the fashion industry. Several French clothing designers filed an action in a French court alleging that the Web site showed photos of their clothing designs. Because Viewfinder defaulted and did not appear in the French court to contest the allegations, the French court awarded the designers the equivalent of more than $175,000.

When the designers came to the United States to enforce the judgment, Viewfinder asserted a number of arguments as to why the U.S. court should not enforce the French judgment. Ultimately, Viewfinder convinced the U.S. court that its conduct on the Web site was protected expression under the First Amendment.[a]

Arbitration Can Also Prevent Enforcement of a Judgment

Sometimes, arbitration can also be used to prevent a judgment from being collected. Consider a dispute between Chevron Corporation and Ecuador. After years of litigation (that Chevron inherited when it merged with Texaco), a group of thirty thousand Amazon Indians and farmers won an $18.2 billion verdict in an Ecuadoran court against Chevron for dumping toxic waste into the rivers and rain forests of Ecuador.

But Chevron did not own any property in Ecuador that the government could seize to collect the debt. Chevron filed an action in a New York federal court and convinced the judge that the Ecuadoran trial was tainted by fraud and corruption. Meanwhile, Chevron also took its case to an arbitration panel for the United Nations Commission on International Trade Law (UNCITRAL), which blocked the plaintiffs from collecting on the Ecuadoran judgment. UNCITRAL issued an order that bans enforcement of the Ecuadoran judgment in the United States or anywhere else in the world.[b]

Critical Thinking

What might be some advantages of arbitrating disputes involving international transactions? Are there any disadvantages?

a. *Sarl Louis Feraud International v. Viewfinder, Inc.*, 489 F.3d 474 (2d Cir. 2007).

b. *In re Chevron Corp.*, 650 F.3d 276 (3d Cir. 2011).

Parties to a Letter of Credit In a simple letter-of-credit transaction, the *issuer* (a bank) agrees to issue a letter of credit and to ascertain whether the *beneficiary* (seller) performs certain acts. In return, the *account party* (buyer) promises to reimburse the issuer for the amount paid to the beneficiary. The transaction may also involve an *advising bank* that transmits information and a *paying bank* that expedites payment under the letter of credit. See Exhibit 8.1 on the facing page for an illustration of a letter-of-credit transaction.

Under a letter of credit, the issuer is bound to pay the beneficiary (seller) when the beneficiary has complied with the terms and conditions of the letter of credit. The beneficiary looks to the issuer, not to the account party (buyer), when it presents the documents required by the letter of credit.

Typically, the letter of credit will require that the beneficiary deliver a *bill of lading* to the issuing bank to prove that shipment has been made. A letter of credit assures the beneficiary (seller) of payment and at the same time assures the account party (buyer) that payment will not be made until the beneficiary has complied with the terms and conditions of the letter of credit.

KNOW THIS

A letter of credit is independent of the underlying contract between the buyer and the seller.

The Value of a Letter of Credit The basic principle behind letters of credit is that payment is made against the documents presented by the beneficiary and not against the facts that the documents purport to reflect. Thus, in a letter-of-credit transaction, the issuer does not police the underlying contract. A letter of credit is independent of the underlying contract between the buyer and the seller. Eliminating the need for banks (issuers) to inquire

Exhibit 8.1 A Letter-of-Credit Transaction

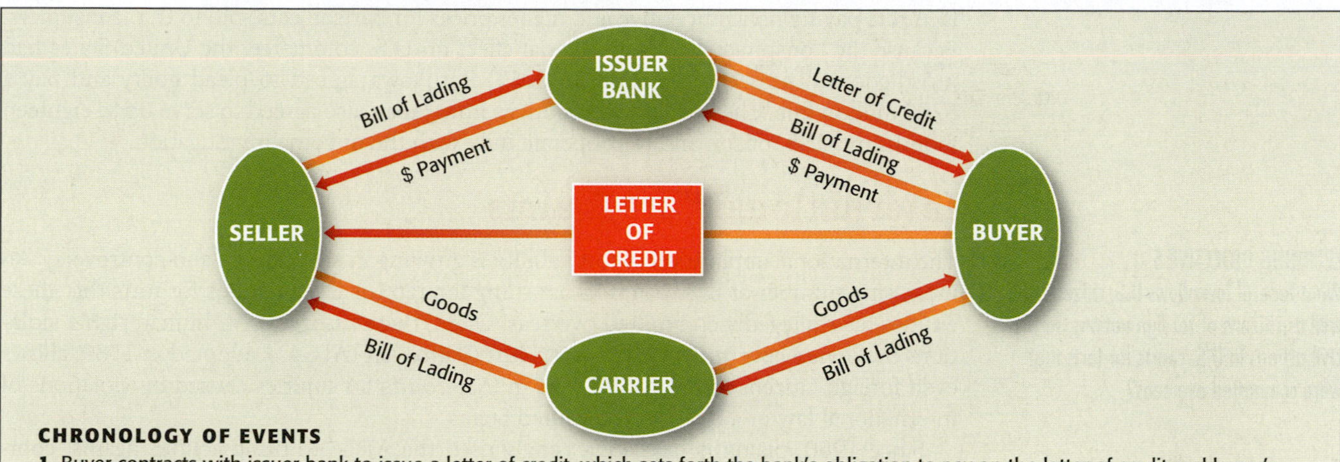

CHRONOLOGY OF EVENTS

1. Buyer contracts with issuer bank to issue a letter of credit, which sets forth the bank's obligation to pay on the letter of credit and buyer's obligation to pay the bank.
2. Letter of credit is sent to seller informing seller that on compliance with the terms of the letter of credit (such as presentment of necessary documents—in this example, a bill of lading), the bank willl issue payment for the goods.
3. Seller delivers goods to carrier and receives a bill of lading.
4. Seller delivers the bill of lading to issuer bank and, if the document is proper, receives payment.
5. Issuer bank delivers the bill of lading to buyer.
6. Buyer delivers the bill of lading to carrier.
7. Carrier delivers the goods to the buyer.
8. Buyer settles with issuer bank.

into whether actual contractual conditions have been satisfied greatly reduces the costs of letters of credit. Moreover, the use of a letter of credit protects both buyers and sellers.

U.S. Laws in a Global Context

The internationalization of business raises questions about the extraterritorial application of a nation's laws—that is, the effect of the country's laws outside its boundaries. To what extent do U.S. domestic laws apply to other nations' businesses? To what extent do U.S. domestic laws apply to U.S. firms doing business abroad? Here, we discuss the extraterritorial application of certain U.S. laws, including antitrust laws, tort laws, and laws prohibiting employment discrimination. (Because these issues can be quite complex, consulting an attorney may be advisable—see the *Business Application* feature at the end of this chapter.)

U.S. Antitrust Laws

U.S. antitrust laws (to be discussed in Chapter 32) have a wide application. They may *subject* firms in foreign nations to their provisions, as well as *protect* foreign consumers and competitors from violations committed by U.S. citizens. Section 1 of the Sherman Act—the most important U.S. antitrust law—provides for the extraterritorial effect of the U.S. antitrust laws.

The United States is a major proponent of free competition in the global economy. Thus, any conspiracy that has a *substantial effect* on U.S. commerce is within the reach of the Sherman Act. The law applies even if the violation occurs outside the United States, and foreign governments as well as businesses can be sued for violations.

EXAMPLE 8.7 An investigation by the U.S. government revealed that a Tokyo-based auto parts supplier, Furukawa Electric Company, and its executives conspired with competitors in an international price-fixing agreement (an agreement to set prices—see Chapter 32). The agreement lasted more than ten years and resulted in automobile manufacturers paying noncompetitive and higher prices for parts in cars sold to U.S. consumers. Because the conspiracy had a substantial effect on U.S. commerce, the United States had jurisdiction to prosecute the case. In 2011, Furukawa agreed to plead guilty and pay a $200 million fine. The Furukawa executives from Japan also agreed to serve up to eighteen months in a U.S. prison and to cooperate fully with the ongoing investigation. •

International Tort Claims

LEARNING OBJECTIVE 5
What federal law allows U.S. citizens, as well as citizens of foreign nations, to file civil actions in U.S. courts for torts that were committed overseas?

The international application of tort liability is growing in significance and controversy. An increasing number of U.S. plaintiffs are suing foreign (or U.S.) entities for torts that these entities have allegedly committed overseas. Often, these cases involve human rights violations by foreign governments. The Alien Tort Claims Act (ATCA),[9] adopted in 1789, allows even foreign citizens to bring civil suits in U.S. courts for injuries caused by violations of international law or a treaty of the United States.

Since 1980, plaintiffs have increasingly used the ATCA to bring actions against companies operating in other countries. ATCA actions have been brought against companies doing business in various nations including Colombia, Ecuador, Egypt, Guatemala, India, Indonesia, Nigeria, and Saudi Arabia. Some of these cases have involved alleged environmental destruction. In addition, mineral companies in Southeast Asia have been sued for collaborating with oppressive government regimes.

The following *Spotlight Case* involved claims against hundreds of corporations that allegedly "aided and abetted" the government of South Africa in maintaining its apartheid (racially discriminatory) regime.

9. 28 U.S.C. Section 1350.

Spotlight on International Torts Claims

Case 8.3
Khulumani v. Barclay National Bank, Ltd.
United States Court of Appeals, Second Circuit, 504 F.3d 254 (2007).[a]

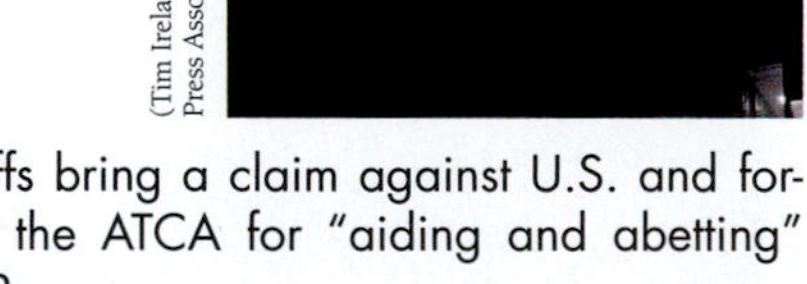

(Tim Ireland/PA Wire/ Press Association via AP Images)

FACTS A group of plaintiffs (the Khulumani plaintiffs), along with other plaintiff groups, filed class-action claims on behalf of victims of apartheid-related atrocities, human rights violations, crimes against humanity, and unfair and discriminatory forced-labor practices. The plaintiffs brought this action in federal district court under the Alien Tort Claims Act (ATCA) against a number of corporations, including Bank of America, Barclay National Bank, Citigroup, Credit Suisse Group, General Electric, and IBM. The district court dismissed the plaintiffs' complaints in their entirety. The court held that the plaintiffs had failed to establish subject-matter jurisdiction under the ATCA. The plaintiffs appealed to the U.S. Court of Appeals for the Second Circuit.

ISSUE Can the plaintiffs bring a claim against U.S. and foreign companies under the ATCA for "aiding and abetting" human rights violations?

DECISION Yes. The U.S. Court of Appeals for the Second Circuit vacated the district court's dismissal of the plaintiffs' claims and remanded the case for further proceedings. According to the reviewing court, a plaintiff may plead a theory of aiding and abetting liability under the ATCA.

REASON The court stated that the district court "erred in holding that aiding and abetting violations of a customary international law cannot provide a basis for ATCA jurisdiction."

a. See also 509 F.3d 148 (2d Cir. 2007), in which the court denied the defendants' motion for a stay; and *American Isuzu Motors, Inc. v. Ntsebeza*, 553 U.S. 1028, 128 S.Ct. 2424, 171 L.Ed.2d 225 (2008), in which the United States Supreme Court had to affirm the Second Circuit's decision in this case because it was unable to hear the appeal in the following term.

Spotlight Case 8.3—Continued

The court reasoned that the United States Supreme Court has instructed courts in this nation to exercise caution and carefully evaluate international norms and potential adverse foreign policy consequences in deciding whether to hear ATCA claims. Thus, "the determination whether a norm is sufficiently definite to support a cause of action should (indeed, inevitably must) involve an element of judgment about the practical consequences of making that cause available to litigants in the federal courts." The court rejected the defendants' argument that an adjudication of the case by the U.S. court "would offend amicable working relationships with a foreign country."

CRITICAL THINKING—Ethical Consideration *Should the companies cited as defendants in this case have refused all business dealings with South Africa during the era of apartheid when the country's white government severely limited the rights of the majority black African population? Why or why not?*

ETHICAL ISSUE

Should U.S. courts allow "forum-shopping" plaintiffs to sue companies for aiding and abetting global terrorism? Some plaintiffs are bringing actions in U.S. courts alleging that certain banks and other companies in foreign countries have aided and abetted terrorist activities. Foreign plaintiffs may assert claims for aiding and abetting under the ATCA, while U.S. nationals may also bring claims under the Anti-Terrorism Act (ATA).[10]

In 2009, some 1,600 plaintiffs, including both U.S. and foreign nationals, brought claims against Arab Bank, PLC, alleging that the bank knowingly provided financial services to terrorist organizations that attacked Israel. A U.S. district court held that it had jurisdiction to hear the claims.[11] Similarly, in 2010, a federal court held that it had jurisdiction to hear a case brought by a U.S. citizen against a Switzerland-based financial institution for helping fund the terrorists that killed her husband, a Canadian citizen, in Israel.[12]

Although punishing those who aid terrorists is certainly desirable, some have suggested that such rulings may encourage international "forum shopping." Victims of global terrorism may bring lawsuits in U.S. courts against foreign defendants that have little or no contact with the United States because of the potential for large damages awards—and treble damages if the victims are U.S. nationals.

Antidiscrimination Laws

Laws in the United States prohibit discrimination on the basis of race, color, national origin, religion, gender, age, and disability, as will be discussed in Chapter 25. These laws, as they affect employment relationships, generally apply extraterritorially. U.S. employees working abroad for U.S. employers are protected under the Age Discrimination in Employment Act of 1967. The Americans with Disabilities Act of 1990, which requires employers to accommodate the needs of workers with disabilities, also applies to U.S. nationals working abroad for U.S. firms.

In addition, the major law regulating employment discrimination—Title VII of the Civil Rights Act of 1964—also applies extraterritorially to all U.S. employees working for U.S. employers abroad. U.S. employers must abide by U.S. discrimination laws unless to do so would violate the laws of the country where their workplaces are located. This "foreign laws exception" prevents employers from being subjected to conflicting laws.

10. 18 U.S.C. Sections 2331 *et seq.*

11. *Almog v. Arab Bank, PLC,* 471 F.Supp.2d 257 (E.D.N.Y. 2007). See also *Litle v. Arab Bank, PLC,* 611 F.Supp.2d 233 (E.D.N.Y. 2009).

12. *Goldberg v. UBS AG,* 690 F.Supp.2d 92 (E.D.N.Y. 2010). See *Case Example 8.1* on page 212 for further discussion of this case.

Reviewing . . . International Law in a Global Economy

Robco, Inc., was a Florida arms dealer. The armed forces of Honduras contracted to purchase weapons from Robco over a six-year period. After the government was replaced and a democracy installed, the Honduran government sought to reduce the size of its military, and its relationship with Robco deteriorated. Honduras refused to honor the contract by purchasing the inventory of arms, which Robco could sell only at a much lower price. Robco filed a suit in a federal district court in the United States to recover damages for this breach of contract by the government of Honduras. Using the information provided in the chapter, answer the following questions.

1. Should the Foreign Sovereign Immunities Act preclude this lawsuit? Why or why not?
2. Does the act of state doctrine bar Robco from seeking to enforce the contract? Explain.
3. Suppose that prior to this lawsuit, the new government of Honduras had enacted a law making it illegal to purchase weapons from foreign arms dealers. What doctrine might lead a U.S. court to dismiss Robco's case in that situation?
4. Now suppose that the U.S. court hears the case and awards damages to Robco, but the government of Honduras has no assets in the United States that can be used to satisfy the judgment. Under which doctrine might Robco be able to collect the damages by asking another nation's court to enforce the U.S. judgment?

DEBATE THIS The U.S. federal courts are accepting too many lawsuits initiated by foreigners that concern matters not relevant to this country.

BUSINESS APPLICATION

How to Choose and Use a Lawyer*

Most people in today's business world will sooner or later need to obtain legal advice from an attorney. Indeed, it is almost impossible for nonexperts to keep up with the myriad rules and regulations that govern business in the United States and around the globe. The application of laws in an international context, in particular, involves complex legal principles, treaties, jurisdictional issues, conflicts of law, political events, and customary rules and practices. Making informed business decisions in light of these factors may be difficult without the assistance of an attorney.

Weighing Costs and Benefits

Although lawyers may seem expensive—anywhere from $100 to $500 or more per hour—cautious businesspersons will make sure that they are not "penny wise and pound foolish." The consultation fee paid to an attorney can be insignificant compared with the potential liability facing a business. It is increasingly possible for businesspersons to incur penalties for violating laws or regulations of which they are totally unaware. Consider, for instance, the federal criminal laws discussed in Chapter 6 or the international tort claims explained in this chapter.

Obtaining competent legal advice *before* a dispute arises may enable a businessperson to avoid potentially costly mistakes. It may also enable the business to keep a beneficial relationship with a trade partner or customer regardless of a dispute. Keep in mind that sometimes higher-priced attorneys from larger firms may be worth the extra expense. They may have more expertise in the field that is relevant to your business concern, such as international or patent law. Higher-priced attorneys may also have better relationships with firms in a particular industry, more contacts, or more clout in the legal community to wield on your behalf.

Selecting an Attorney

In selecting an attorney, you can ask friends, relatives, or business associates to recommend someone. Alternatively, you can call the local or state bar association to obtain the names of several lawyers or check the Yellow Pages in your local telephone directory for listings. FindLaw has an online database containing biographies of attorneys throughout the country, listed by area of specialty and by state. You can find attorneys in your area by accessing the FindLaw

*This *Business Application* is not meant to substitute for the services of an attorney who is licensed to practice law in your state.

Lawyer Directory online at lawyers.findlaw.com. You might also investigate legal clinics and prepaid legal service plans.

For your initial meeting with an attorney you are considering hiring, prepare a written list of your questions and a brief summary of the problem for which you need legal advice. Also, bring copies of any relevant documents that the lawyer might need to see. While at the meeting, ask about legal fees, discuss the legal problem you are facing (or anticipate facing), and clarify the scope of what you want the lawyer to do for you. Remember that almost everything you say at this meeting is protected by the attorney-client privilege of confidentiality.

Evaluating Your Attorney

Before hiring the attorney, ask yourself the following questions after your first meeting: Did the attorney seem knowledgeable about what is needed to address your concerns? Did she or he seem willing to investigate the law and the facts further to ensure an accurate understanding of your legal situation? Did the attorney have insight into how to approach the problem, and who to contact first on your behalf? Did you communicate well with each other? Did the attorney perceive which issues were of foremost concern to you and address those issues to your satisfaction? Did the attorney "speak your language" when explaining the legal implications of those issues?

Checklist for Choosing and Using a Lawyer

1. *If you ever think that you need legal advice, you probably do.*
2. *When choosing an attorney, try to get recommendations from friends, relatives, or business associates who have had long-standing relationships with their attorneys. If that fails, check with your local or state bar association, FindLaw's online directory, or the Yellow Pages.*
3. *When you initially consult with an attorney, bring a written list of questions to which you want answers, perhaps a summary of your problem, and copies of relevant documents.*
4. *Do not hesitate to ask about the legal fees that your attorney will charge, and be sure to clarify the scope of the work to be undertaken by the attorney. Ask any and all questions that you feel are necessary to ensure that you understand your legal options.*
5. *Even after you hire the attorney, continue to evaluate the relationship over time. For many businesspersons, relationships with attorneys last for decades, so it pays to make sure that the relationship is a fruitful one.*

Key Terms

act of state doctrine 213
choice-of-language clause 221
choice-of-law clause 221
comity 212
confiscation 214
correspondent bank 223
distribution agreement 215
dumping 218
export 215
expropriation 214
force majeure clause 221
foreign exchange market 223
forum-selection clause 221
international organization 211
letter of credit 223
normal trade relations (NTR) status 219
quota 218
sovereign immunity 214
tariff 218
treaty 211

Chapter Summary: International Law in a Global Economy

International Law—Sources and Principles (See pages 211–215.)	1. *Principle of comity*—Under this principle, nations give effect to the laws and judicial decrees of other nations for reasons of courtesy and international harmony. 2. *Act of state doctrine*—Under this doctrine, U.S. courts avoid passing judgment on the validity of public acts committed by a recognized foreign government within its own territory. 3. *Doctrine of sovereign immunity*—When certain conditions are satisfied, foreign nations are immune from U.S. jurisdiction under the Foreign Sovereign Immunities Act of 1976. Exceptions are made when a foreign state (a) has waived its immunity either explicitly or by implication, (b) has engaged in commercial activity within the United States, or (c) has committed a tort within the United States.
Doing Business Internationally (See pages 215–217.)	U.S. domestic firms may engage in international business transactions in several ways including (1) exporting, which may involve foreign agents or distributors, and (2) manufacturing abroad through licensing arrangements, franchising operations, wholly owned subsidiaries, or joint ventures.
Regulation of Specific Business Activities (See pages 217–220.)	In the interests of their economies, foreign policies, domestic policies, or other national priorities, nations impose laws that restrict or facilitate international business. Such laws regulate foreign investments, exporting, and importing. The World Trade Organization attempts to minimize trade barriers among nations, as do regional trade agreements and associations, including the European Union and the North American Free Trade Agreement.

Continued

Chapter Summary: International Law in a Global Economy—Continued

Commercial Contracts in an International Setting (See pages 220–223.)	International business contracts often include choice-of-language, forum-selection, and choice-of-law clauses to reduce the uncertainties associated with interpreting the language of the agreement and dealing with legal differences. Most domestic and international contracts include *force majeure* clauses. They commonly stipulate that acts of God and certain other events may excuse a party from liability for nonperformance of the contract. Arbitration clauses are also frequently found in international contracts.
Payment Methods for International Transactions (See pages 223–225.)	1. *Currency conversion*—Because nations have different monetary systems, payment on international contracts requires currency conversion at a rate specified in a foreign exchange market. 2. *Correspondent banking*—Correspondent banks facilitate the transfer of funds from a buyer in one country to a seller in another. 3. *Letters of credit*—Letters of credit facilitate international transactions by ensuring payment to sellers and assuring buyers that payment will not be made until the sellers have complied with the terms of the letters of credit. Typically, compliance occurs when a bill of lading is delivered to the issuing bank.
U.S. Laws in a Global Context (See pages 225–227.)	1. *Antitrust laws*—U.S. antitrust laws may be applied beyond the borders of the United States. Any conspiracy that has a substantial effect on commerce within the United States may be subject to the Sherman Act, even if the violation occurs outside the United States. 2. *Tort laws*—U.S. tort laws may be applied to wrongful acts that take place in foreign jurisdictions under the Alien Tort Claims Act. This act allows even foreign citizens to bring civil suits in U.S. Courts for injuries caused by violations of international law or a treaty of the United States. 3. *Antidiscrimination laws*—The major U.S. laws prohibiting employment discrimination, including Title VII of the Civil Rights Act of 1964, the Age Discrimination in Employment Act of 1967, and the Americans with Disabilities Act of 1990, cover U.S. employees working abroad for U.S. firms—*unless* to apply the U.S. laws would violate the laws of the host country.

ExamPrep

ISSUE SPOTTERS

1. Café Rojo, Ltd., an Ecuadoran firm, agrees to sell coffee beans to Dark Roast Coffee Company, a U.S. firm. Dark Roast accepts the beans but refuses to pay. Café Rojo sues Dark Roast in an Ecuadoran court and is awarded damages, but Dark Roast's assets are in the United States. Under what circumstances would a U.S. court enforce the judgment of the Ecuadoran court? **(See page 212.)**
2. Gems International, Ltd., is a foreign firm that has a 12 percent share of the U.S. market for diamonds. To capture a larger share, Gems offers its products at a below-cost discount to U.S. buyers (and inflates the prices in its own country to make up the difference). How can this attempt to undersell U.S. businesses be defeated? **(See page 218.)**

—Check your answers to the Issue Spotters against the answers provided in Appendix E at the end of this text.

BEFORE THE TEST

Go to www.cengagebrain.com, enter the ISBN 9781133273561, and click on "Find" to locate this textbook's Web site. Then, click on "Access Now" under "Study Tools," and select Chapter 8 at the top. There, you will find a Practice Quiz that you can take to assess your mastery of the concepts in this chapter, as well as Flashcards, a Glossary of important terms, and Video Questions (when assigned).

For Review

Answers to the even-numbered questions in this For Review section can be found in Appendix F at the end of this text.

1. What is the principle of comity, and why do courts deciding disputes involving a foreign law or judicial decree apply this principle?
2. What is the act of state doctrine? In what circumstances is this doctrine applied?
3. Under the Foreign Sovereign Immunities Act, in what situations is a foreign state subject to the jurisdiction of U.S. courts?
4. What are three clauses commonly included in international business contracts?
5. What federal law allows U.S. citizens, as well as citizens of foreign nations, to file civil actions in U.S. courts for torts that were committed overseas?

Business Scenarios and Case Problems

8–1 **Letters of Credit.** Antex Industries, a Japanese firm, agreed to purchase 92,000 electronic integrated circuits from Electronic Arrays. The Swiss Credit Bank issued a letter of credit to cover the transaction. The letter of credit specified that the chips would be transported to Tokyo by ship. Electronic Arrays shipped the circuits by air. Payment on the letter of credit was dishonored because the shipment by air did not fulfill the precise terms of the letter of credit. Should a court compel payment? Explain. **(See pages 223–225.)**

8–2 **Question with Sample Answer—Dumping.** U.S. pineapple producers alleged that producers of canned pineapple from the Philippines were selling their canned pineapple in the United States for less than its fair market value (dumping). The Philippine producers also exported other products, such as pineapple juice and juice concentrate, which used separate parts of the same fresh pineapple, so they shared raw material costs, according to the producers' own financial records. To determine fair value and antidumping duties, the plaintiffs argued that a court should calculate the Philippine producers' cost of production and allocate a portion of the shared fruit costs to the canned fruit. The result of this allocation showed that more than 90 percent of the canned fruit sales were below the cost of production. Is this a reasonable approach to determining the production costs and fair market value of canned pineapple in the United States? Why or why not? **(See page 218.)**

—For a sample answer to Question 8–2, go to Appendix G at the end of this text.

8–3 **Case Problem with Sample Answer—Comity.** Jan Voda, M.D., a resident of Oklahoma City, Oklahoma, owns three U.S. patents related to guiding catheters for use in interventional cardiology, as well as corresponding foreign patents issued by the European Patent Office, Canada, France, Germany, and Great Britain. Voda filed a suit in a federal district court against Cordis Corp., a U.S. firm, alleging infringement of the U.S. patents under U.S. patent law and of the corresponding foreign patents under the patent law of the various foreign countries. Cordis admitted, "[T]he XB catheters have been sold domestically and internationally since 1994. The XB catheters were manufactured in Miami Lakes, Florida, from 1993 to 2001 and have been manufactured in Juarez, Mexico, since 2001." Cordis argued, however, that Voda could not assert infringement claims under foreign patent law because the court did not have jurisdiction over such claims. Which of the important international legal principles discussed in this chapter would be most likely to apply in this case? How should the court apply it? Explain. [*Voda v. Cordis Corp.*, 476 F.3d 887 (Fed.Cir. 2007)] **(See pages 212–213.)**

—For a sample answer to Problem 8–3, go to Appendix H at the end of this text.

8–4 **Sovereign Immunity.** When Ferdinand Marcos was president of the Republic of the Philippines, he put assets into a company called Arelma. Its holdings are in New York. A group of plaintiffs, referred to as the Pimentel class, brought a class-action suit in a U.S. district court for human rights violations by Marcos. They won a judgment of $2 billion and sought to attach Arelma's assets to help pay the judgment. At the same time, the Republic of the Philippines established a commission to recover property wrongfully taken by Marcos. A court in the Philippines was determining whether Marcos's property, including Arelma, should be forfeited to the Republic or to other parties. The Philippine government, in opposition to the Pimentel judgment, moved to dismiss the U.S. court proceedings. The district court refused, and the U.S. Court of Appeals for the Ninth Circuit agreed that the Pimentel class should take the assets. The Republic of the Philippines appealed. What are the key international legal issues? [*Republic of the Philippines v. Pimentel*, 553 U.S. 851, 128 S.Ct. 2180, 171 L.Ed.2d 131 (2008)] **(See pages 214–215.)**

8–5 **Dumping.** The fuel for nuclear power plants is low enriched uranium (LEU). LEU consists of feed uranium enriched by energy to a certain assay—its percentage of the isotope necessary for a nuclear reaction. The amount of energy is described by an industry standard as a "separative work unit" (SWU). A nuclear utility may buy LEU from an enricher, or the utility may provide an enricher with feed uranium and pay for the SWUs necessary to produce LEU. Under an SWU contract, the LEU returned to the utility may not be exactly the particular uranium the utility provided. This is because feed uranium is fungible and trades like a commodity (such as wheat or corn), and profitable enrichment requires the constant processing of undifferentiated stock. LEU imported from foreign enrichers, including Eurodif, S.A., was purportedly being sold in the United States for "less than fair value." Does this constitute dumping? Explain. If so, what could be done to prevent it? [*United States v. Eurodif, S.A.*, 555 U.S. 305, 129 S.Ct. 878, 172 L.Ed.2d 679 (2009)] **(See page 218.)**

8–6 **International Agreements and Jurisdiction.** U.S. citizens who were descendants of victims of the Holocaust (the mass murder of 6 million Jews by the Nazis during World War II) in Europe filed a claim for breach of contract in the United States against an Italian insurance company, Assicurazioni Generali, S.P.A. (Generali). Before the Holocaust, the plaintiffs' ancestors had purchased insurance policies from Generali, but Generali refused to pay them benefits under the policies. Due to certain agreements among nations after World War II, such lawsuits could not be filed for many years. In 2000, however, the United States agreed that Germany could establish a foundation—the International Commission on Holocaust-Era Insurance Claims, or ICHEIC—that would compensate victims who had suffered losses at the hands of the Germans during the war. Whenever a German company was sued in a U.S. court based on a Holocaust-era claim, the U.S. government would inform the court that the matter should be referred to the ICHEIC as the exclusive forum and remedy for the resolution. There was no such agreement with Italy, however, so the federal district court dismissed the suit. The plaintiffs appealed. Did the plaintiffs have to take their claim to the ICHEIC rather than sue in a U.S. court? Why or why not? [*In re Assicurazioni Generali, S.P.A.*, 592 F.3d 113 (2d Cir. 2010)] **(See page 222.)**

8–7 **Sovereign Immunity.** Bell Helicopter Textron, Inc., designs, makes, and sells helicopters with distinctive and famous trade dress that identifies them as Bell aircraft. Bell also owns the helicopters' design patents. Bell's Model 206 Series includes the Jet Ranger. Thirty-six years after Bell developed the Jet Ranger, the Islamic Republic of Iran began to make and sell counterfeit Model 206 Series helicopters and parts. Iran's counterfeit versions—the Shahed 278 and the Shahed 285—used Bell's *trade dress* (see Chapter 5). The Shahed aircraft was promoted at an international air show in Iran to aircraft customers. Bell filed a suit in a U.S. district court against Iran, alleging violations of trademark and patent laws. Is Iran—a foreign nation—exempt in these circumstances from the jurisdiction of U.S. courts? Explain. [*Bell Helicopter Textron, Inc. v. Islamic Republic of Iran*, 764 F.Supp.2d 122 (D.D.C. 2011)] **(See pages 214–215.)**

8–8 **Commercial Activity Exception.** Technology Incubation and Entrepreneurship Training Society (TIETS) entered into a joint-venture agreement with Mandana Farhang and M.A. Mobile to develop and market certain technology for commercial purposes. Farhang and M.A. Mobile filed a suit in a federal district court in California, where they both were based, alleging claims under the joint-venture agreement and a related nondisclosure agreement. The parties agreed that TIETS was a "foreign state" covered by the Foreign Sovereign Immunities Act because it was a part of the Indian government. Nevertheless, Farhang and M.A. Mobile argued that TIETS did not enjoy sovereign immunity because it had engaged in a commercial activity that had a direct effect in the United States. Could TIETS still be subject to the jurisdiction of U.S. courts under the commercial activity exception even though the joint venture was to take place outside the United States? If so, how? [*Farhang v. Indian Institute of Technology*, 2012 WL 113739 (N.D.Cal. 2012)] **(See page 215.)**

8–9 **A Question of Ethics—Terrorism.** On December 21, 1988, Pan Am Flight 103 exploded 31,000 feet in the air over Lockerbie, Scotland, killing all 259 passengers and crew on board and 11 people on the ground. Among those killed was Roger Hurst, a U.S. citizen. An investigation determined that a portable radio-cassette player packed in a brown Samsonite suitcase smuggled onto the plane was the source of the explosion. The explosive device was constructed with a digital timer specially made for, and bought by, Libya. Abdel Basset Ali Al-Megrahi, a Libyan government official and an employee of the Libyan Arab Airline (LAA), was convicted by the Scottish High Court of Justiciary on criminal charges that he planned and executed the bombing in association with members of the Jamahiriya Security Organization (JSO)—an agency of the former Libyan government that performed security and intelligence functions—or the Libyan military. Members of the victims' families filed a suit in a U.S. federal district court against the JSO, the LAA, Al-Megrahi, and others. The plaintiffs claimed violations of U.S. federal law, including the Anti-Terrorism Act, and state law, including the intentional infliction of emotional distress. [*Hurst v. Socialist People's Libyan Arab Jamahiriya*, 474 F.Supp.2d 19 (D.D.C. 2007)] **(See pages 226–227.)**

1. Under what doctrine, codified in which federal statute, might the defendants have claimed to be immune from the jurisdiction of a U.S. court? Should this law include an exception for "state-sponsored terrorism"? Why or why not?
2. The defendants agreed to pay $2.7 billion, or $10 million per victim, to settle all claims for "compensatory death damages." The families of eleven victims, including Hurst, were excluded from the settlement because they were "not wrongful death beneficiaries under applicable state law." These plaintiffs continued the suit. The defendants filed a motion to dismiss. Should the motion have been granted on the ground that the settlement barred the plaintiffs' claims? Explain.

Critical Thinking and Writing Assignments

8–10 **Business Law Critical Thinking Group Assignment.** Assume that you are manufacturing iPad accessories and that your business is becoming more successful. You are now considering expanding operations into another country.

1. One group will explore the costs and benefits of advertising on the Internet.
2. Another group will examine whether to take in a partner from a foreign nation and explain the benefits and risks of taking in a partner.
3. A third group will discuss what problems will arise if you want to manufacture in a foreign location.

UNIT 1 The Legal Environment of Business

Business Case Study with Dissenting Opinion

Paduano v. American Honda Motor Co.

The effect and importance of the U.S. Constitution's supremacy clause were discussed in Chapter 2. When there is a direct conflict between a federal law and a state law, the state law is rendered invalid. If Congress has chosen to act exclusively in an area, the federal statute will take precedence over a conflicting state law on the same subject under the doctrine of preemption.

There is a strong presumption against preemption, however, because the states are independent "sovereigns" in our federal system. In areas in which the states have traditionally exercised their police power, such as consumer protection, for example, this presumption applies with particular force.

In this *Business Case Study with Dissenting Opinion,* we review *Paduano v. American Honda Motor Co.,*[1] a case in which the buyer of a new car complained about the vehicle's inability to achieve the fuel economy advertised in the automaker's brochure. The defendant contended that federal law preempted the plaintiff's claims, which were founded on state law.

Case Background

Gaetano Paduano bought a new Honda Civic Hybrid in California in June 2004. The Environmental Protection Agency's (EPA's) fuel economy estimate stated on the federally mandated new car label was forty-seven miles per gallon (mpg) for city driving and forty-eight mpg for highway driving. Honda's sales brochure repeated the fuel economy estimate and added, "Just drive the Hybrid like you would a conventional car and save on fuel bills."

Paduano drove the vehicle for about a year but was frustrated with its fuel economy performance, which was less than half of the EPA estimate. A service employee at a Honda dealership told him that to achieve the estimate he would have to drive differently. The employee said, "It is very difficult to get MPG on [the] highway and to drive with traffic in a safe manner." The required "special" manner "would create a driving hazard." Paduano asked American Honda Motor Company to repurchase the vehicle. Honda refused.

Paduano filed a suit in a California state court against the automaker, alleging, among other things, deceptive advertising in violation of the state's Consumer Legal Remedies Act and Unfair Competition Law. Honda argued that the federal Energy Policy and Conservation Act, which prescribed the EPA fuel economy estimate, preempted Paduano's claims. The court issued a summary judgment in Honda's favor. Paduano appealed to a state intermediate appellate court.

Majority Opinion

AARON, J. [Judge]

* * * *

The basic rules of preemption are not in dispute: *Under the supremacy clause of the United States Constitution, Congress has the power to preempt state law concerning matters that lie within the authority of Congress.* In determining whether federal law preempts state law, a court's task is to discern congressional intent. Congress's express intent in this regard will be found when Congress explicitly states that it is preempting state authority. [Emphasis added.]

* * * *

Honda * * * argues that [the EPCA] prevents Paduano from pursuing his * * * claims. That provision states in pertinent part,

> When a requirement under [the EPCA] is in effect, a State or a political subdivision of a State may adopt or enforce a law or regulation on disclosure of fuel economy or fuel operating costs for an automobile covered by [the EPCA] only if the law or regulation is identical to that requirement.

1. 169 Cal.App.4th 1453, 88 Cal.Rptr.3d 90 (4 Dist. 2009).

Business Case Study with Dissenting Opinion—Continues next page

Business Case Study with Dissenting Opinion—Continued

* * * Honda goes on to assert that "Paduano's deceptive advertising and misrepresentation claims would impose *non* identical disclosure requirements."

Contrary to Honda's characterization * * *, Paduano's claims are based on statements Honda made in its advertising brochure to the effect that one may drive a Civic Hybrid in the same manner as one would a conventional car, and need not do anything "special," in order to achieve the beneficial fuel economy of the EPA estimates. * * * Paduano is challenging * * * Honda's * * * commentary in which it alludes to those estimates in a manner that may give consumers the misimpression that they will be able to achieve mileage close to the EPA estimates while driving a Honda hybrid in the same manner as they would a conventional vehicle. Paduano does not seek to require Honda to provide "additional alleged facts" regarding the Civic Hybrid's fuel economy, as Honda suggests, but rather, seeks to prevent Honda from making misleading claims about how easy it is to achieve better fuel economy. Contrary to Honda's assertions, if Paduano were to prevail on his claims, Honda would not have to do anything differently with regard to its disclosure of the EPA mileage estimates.

* * * *

* * * [The EPCA's] express preemption provisions do not purport to take away states' power to regulate the advertising of new vehicles, even when that advertising includes the EPA mileage estimates. *As long as a state's regulation does not require a manufacturer to provide a fuel estimate different from the EPA fuel economy estimate, or to make claims that go beyond, or are contrary to, what the federal scheme requires, the EPCA does not preempt such regulation.* * * * Allowing states to regulate false advertising and unfair business practices may further the goals of the EPCA, and we reject Honda's claim. [Emphasis added.]

* * * *

* * * We * * * conclude that federal law does not preempt Paduano's claims concerning Honda's advertising.

* * * *

The summary judgment is reversed. * * * The matter is remanded to the trial court for further proceedings.

Dissenting Opinion

O'ROURKE, J., [Judge] * * * DISSENTING * * * .

* * * In my view, Paduano's false advertising claims under the Consumer Legal Remedies Act (CLRA) and Unfair Competition Law (UCL) are * * * preempted by the Energy Policy and Conservation Act of 1975 (EPCA) because those claims are necessarily predicated on Honda's representations about fuel economy and the Honda Civic Hybrid's asserted failure to meet the federal Environmental Protection Agency's (EPA) estimates as to fuel economy. * * * Paduano seeks to impose a legal duty on Honda to change its disclosures concerning fuel economy to something different from the EPA estimate. In such a case, the EPCA expressly preempts enforcement of his UCL and CLRA causes of action. * * * Accordingly, I respectfully dissent from * * * the majority opinion.

* * * *

Because Paduano's sought-after relief would require that Honda change its advertising to either eliminate or reduce the EPA mileage estimate, or include additional disclosures relating to the EPA mileage estimate and his car's fuel economy, his state law false advertising claims fail under express preemption principles as imposing a legal obligation related to fuel economy standards or they fail because they would impose disclosure requirements concerning fuel economy that are not identical to the EPCA.

This conclusion as to preemption is not impacted by the fact that Paduano's claims are made under consumer protection laws. A presumption against preemption is characteristically applied where the field is one that the states have traditionally occupied and regulated, but such a presumption is not triggered when the state regulates in an area where there has been a history of significant federal presence. In my view, the EPCA and its corresponding federal regulations reflect a significant federal presence with respect to the measurement and disclosure of automobile fuel economy estimates and standards, as well as the advertising concerning a new vehicle's fuel economy.

Business Case Study with Dissenting Opinion—Continued

Questions for Analysis

1. **Law** What was the majority's decision on the principal issue before the court in this case? What were the reasons for this decision?
2. **Law** How would the dissent apply the law to the facts differently than the majority did? What were the dissent's reasons?
3. **Ethics** Suppose that the defendant automaker opposed this action solely to avoid paying for a car that had proved to be a "lemon." Would this have been unethical? Explain.
4. **Economic Dimensions** Is the majority's ruling or the dissent's position more favorable for the auto market? Why?
5. **Implications for the Businessperson** What does the interpretation of the law in this case suggest to businesspersons who sell products labeled with statements mandated by federal or state law?

UNIT 1 The Legal Environment of Business

Business Scenario

CompTac, Inc., which is headquartered in San Francisco, California, is one of the leading software manufacturers in the United States. The company invests millions of dollars to research and develop new software applications and computer games that are sold worldwide. It also has a large service department and takes great pains to offer its customers excellent support services.

1. **Jurisdiction.** CompTac routinely purchases some of the materials necessary to produce its computer games from a New York firm, Electrotex, Inc. A dispute arises between the two firms, and CompTac wants to sue Electrotex for breach of contract. Can CompTac bring the suit in a California state court? Can CompTac bring the suit in a federal court? Explain. **(See pages 62–65.)**
2. **Negligence.** A customer at one of CompTac's retail stores stumbles over a crate in the parking lot and breaks her leg. Just moments earlier, the crate had fallen off a CompTac truck that was delivering goods from a CompTac warehouse to the store. The customer sues CompTac, alleging negligence. Will she succeed in her suit? Why or why not? **(See page 111.)**
3. **Wrongful Interference.** Roban Electronics, a software manufacturer and one of CompTac's major competitors, has been trying to convince one of CompTac's key employees, Jim Baxter, to come to work for Roban. Roban knows that Baxter has a written employment contract with CompTac, which Baxter would breach if he left CompTac before the contract expired. Baxter goes to work for Roban, and the departure of its key employee causes CompTac to suffer substantial losses due to delays in completing new software. Can CompTac sue Roban to recoup some of these losses? If so, on what ground? **(See page 107.)**
4. **Cyber Crime.** One of CompTac's employees in its accounting division, Alan Green, has a gambling problem. To repay a gambling debt of $10,000, Green decides to "borrow" from CompTac to cover the debt. Using his knowledge of CompTac account numbers, Green electronically transfers $10,000 from a CompTac account into his personal checking account.

Business Scenario—Continues next page ➡

Business Scenario—Continued

A week later, he is luckier at gambling and uses the same electronic procedures to transfer funds from his personal checking account back to the CompTac account. Has Green committed any crimes? If so, what are they? **(See pages 178–180.)**

5. **Ethical Decision Making.** One of CompTac's best-selling products is a computer game that includes some extremely violent actions. Groups of parents, educators, and consumer activists have bombarded CompTac with letters and e-mail messages calling on the company to stop selling the product. CompTac executives are concerned about the public outcry, but at the same time, they realize that the game is CompTac's major source of profits. If it ceased marketing the game, the company could go bankrupt. If you were a CompTac decision maker, what would your decision be in this situation? How would you justify your decision from an ethical perspective? **(See page 201.)**
6. **Intellectual Property.** CompTac wants to sell one of its best-selling software programs to An Phat Company, a firm located in Ho Chi Minh City, Vietnam. CompTac is concerned, however, that after an initial purchase, An Phat will duplicate the software without permission (in violation of U.S. copyright laws) and sell the illegal bootleg software to other firms in Vietnam. How can CompTac protect its software from being pirated by An Phat Company? **(See page 148.)**

UNIT 1 The Legal Environment of Business

Group Project

Drawing on your knowledge of *Paduano v. American Honda Motor Co.*, assume that your group makes decisions for an automaker that sells cars in every state and that each state has slightly different consumer protection statutes.

1. One group will list two underlying reasons why there is a strong presumption against preemption.
2. One group will evaluate the truth or falsity of the majority's conclusion that "as long as a state's regulation does not require a manufacturer to provide a fuel estimate different from the EPA fuel economy estimate," there is no preemption.
3. Another group will develop the dissent's argument that a presumption against preemption is not triggered when the state regulates in an area where there has been a "history of significant federal presence."

UNIT 2

(Edhar/Shutterstock.com)

Contracts

UNIT CONTENTS

9. Nature and Classification
10. Agreement in Traditional and E-Contracts
11. Consideration, Capacity, and Legality
12. Defenses to Contract Enforceability
13. Third Party Rights and Discharge
14. Breach and Remedies

CHAPTER 9

Nature and Classification

(nuno/iStockphoto.com)

CHAPTER OUTLINE

- An Overview of Contract Law
- Elements of a Contract
- Types of Contracts
- Quasi Contracts
- Interpretation of Contracts

LEARNING OBJECTIVES

The five learning objectives below are designed to help improve your understanding of the chapter. After reading this chapter, you should be able to answer the following questions:

1 What is a contract? What is the objective theory of contracts?

2 What are the four basic elements necessary to the formation of a valid contract?

3 What is the difference between express and implied contracts?

4 How does a void contract differ from a voidable contract? What is an unenforceable contract?

5 What rules guide the courts in interpreting contracts?

"All sensible people are selfish, and nature is tugging at every contract to make the terms of it fair."
—Ralph Waldo Emerson, 1803–1882 (American poet)

Promise A declaration that binds a person who makes it (the promisor) to do or not to do a certain act.

As Ralph Waldo Emerson observed in the chapter-opening quotation, people tend to act in their own self-interest, and this influences the terms they seek in their contracts. Contract law must therefore provide rules to determine which contract terms will be enforced and which promises must be kept. A **promise** is a declaration by a person (the *promisor*) to do or not to do a certain act. As a result, the person to whom the promise is made (the *promisee*) has a right to expect or demand that something either will or will not happen in the future.

Like other types of law, contract law reflects our social values, interests, and expectations at a given point in time. It shows, for example, what kinds of promises our society thinks should be legally binding. It distinguishes between promises that create only *moral* obligations (such as a promise to take a friend to lunch) and promises that are legally binding (such as a promise to pay for merchandise purchased).

Increasingly, contracts are formed online. While some believe that we need a new body of law to cover e-contracts, others point out that we can apply existing contract law quite easily.

Through the following chapters you will see how in fact contract law can be used to resolve online disputes. For instance, in this chapter you will read about the validity of the *disclaimers* that you often see on e-mails that you receive from professionals (or even nonprofessionals!).

An Overview of Contract Law

Before we look at the numerous rules that courts use to determine whether a particular promise will be enforced, it is necessary to understand some fundamental concepts of contract law. In this section, we describe the sources and general function of contract law and introduce the objective theory of contracts.

Sources of Contract Law

The common law governs all contracts except when it has been modified or replaced by statutory law, such as the Uniform Commercial Code (UCC),[1] or by administrative agency regulations. Contracts relating to services, real estate, employment, and insurance, for example, generally are governed by the common law of contracts. (See the appendix at the end of Chapter 14 for an example of a common law contract used in employment.)

Contracts for the sale and lease of goods, however, are governed by the UCC—to the extent that the UCC has modified general contract law. The relationship between general contract law and the law governing sales and leases of goods will be explored in detail in Chapter 15. In this unit covering the common law of contracts (Chapters 9 through 14), we indicate briefly in footnotes the areas in which the UCC has significantly altered common law contract principles.

The Function of Contracts

No aspect of modern life is entirely free of contractual relationships. You acquire rights and obligations, for example, when you borrow funds, buy or lease a house, obtain insurance, form a business, and purchase goods or services. Contract law is designed to provide stability and predictability for both buyers and sellers in the marketplace.

Promisor A person who makes a promise.

Promisee A person to whom a promise is made.

Contract law assures the parties to private agreements that the promises they make will be enforceable. Clearly, many promises are kept because the parties involved feel a moral obligation to do so or because keeping a promise is in their mutual self-interest. The **promisor** (the person making the promise) and the **promisee** (the person to whom the promise is made) may decide to honor their agreement for other reasons. Nevertheless, the rules of contract law are often followed in business agreements to avoid potential problems.

By supplying procedures for enforcing private agreements, contract law provides an essential condition for the existence of a market economy. Without a legal framework of reasonably assured expectations within which to plan and venture, businesspersons would be able to rely only on the good faith of others. Duty and good faith are usually sufficient, but when dramatic price changes or adverse economic conditions make it costly to comply with a promise, these elements may not be enough. Contract law is necessary to ensure compliance with a promise or to entitle the innocent party to some form of relief.

Definition of a Contract

Contract A set of promises constituting an agreement between parties, giving each a legal duty to the other and also the right to seek a remedy for the breach of the promises or duties.

A **contract** is an agreement that can be enforced in court. It is formed by two or more parties who agree to perform or to refrain from performing some act now or in the future. Generally, contract disputes arise when there is a promise of future performance. If the

1. See Chapter 1 on page 8 and Chapter 15 for further discussions of the significance and coverage of the Uniform Commercial Code. Excerpts from the UCC are presented in Appendix C at the end of this book.

LEARNING OBJECTIVE 1
What is a contract?
What is the objective theory of contracts?

contractual promise is not fulfilled, the party who made it is subject to the sanctions of a court (see Chapter 14). That party may be required to pay monetary damages for failing to perform the contractual promise and, in certain limited instances, may be required to perform the promised act.

The Objective Theory of Contracts

Objective Theory of Contracts The view that contracting parties shall only be bound by terms that can objectively be inferred from promises made.

In determining whether a contract has been formed, the element of intent is of prime importance. In contract law, intent is determined by what is referred to as the **objective theory of contracts,** not by the personal or subjective intent, or belief, of a party. The theory is that a party's intention to enter into a contract is judged by outward, objective facts as interpreted by a *reasonable person,* rather than by the party's secret, subjective intentions.

Objective facts include (1) what the party said when entering into the contract, (2) how the party acted or appeared, and (3) the circumstances surrounding the transaction. As will be discussed later in this chapter, in the section on express versus implied contracts, intent to form a contract may be manifested by conduct, as well as by words, oral or written.

Freedom of Contract and Freedom from Contract

As a general rule, the law recognizes everyone's ability to enter freely into contractual arrangements. This recognition is called *freedom of contract,* a freedom protected in Article I, Section 10, of the U.S. Constitution. Because freedom of contract is a fundamental public policy of the United States, courts rarely interfere with contracts that have been voluntarily made.

Of course, as in other areas of the law, there are many exceptions to the general rule that contracts voluntarily negotiated will be enforced. For example, illegal bargains, agreements that unreasonably restrain trade, and certain unfair contracts made between one party with a great amount of bargaining power and another with little power are generally not enforced. In addition, as you will read in Chapter 11, certain contracts and clauses may not be enforceable if they are contrary to public policy, fairness, and justice. These exceptions provide *freedom from contract* for persons who may have been pressured into making contracts unfavorable to their interests.

Elements of a Contract

The many topics that will be discussed in the following chapters on contract law require an understanding of the basic elements of a valid contract and the way in which a contract is created. You will also need an understanding of the types of circumstances in which even legally valid contracts will not be enforced. (See the sample contract on pages 372–375.)

Requirements of a Valid Contract

The following list briefly describes the four requirements that must be met for a valid contract to exist. If any of these elements is lacking, no contract will have been formed. (Each item will be explained more fully in subsequent chapters.)

LEARNING OBJECTIVE 2
What are the four basic elements necessary to the formation of a valid contract?

1. *Agreement.* An agreement to form a contract includes an *offer* and an *acceptance.* One party must offer to enter into a legal agreement, and another party must accept the terms of the offer (see Chapter 10).
2. *Consideration.* Any promises made by the parties must be supported by legally sufficient and bargained-for consideration (something of value received or promised to convince a person to make a deal) (see Chapter 11).

3. *Contractual capacity.* Both parties entering into the contract must have the contractual capacity to do so, meaning that the law must recognize them as possessing characteristics that qualify them as competent parties (see Chapter 11).
4. *Legality.* The contract's purpose must be to accomplish some goal that is legal and not against public policy (see Chapter 11).

Defenses to the Enforceability of a Contract

Even if all of the elements of a valid contract are present, a contract may be unenforceable if the following requirements are not met.

1. *Voluntary consent.* The apparent consent of both parties must be voluntary. For instance, if a contract was formed as a result of fraud, mistake, or duress (coercion), the contract may not be enforceable.
2. *Form.* The contract must be in whatever form the law requires. Some contracts must be in writing to be enforceable.

The failure to fulfill either requirement may be raised as a defense to the enforceability of an otherwise valid contract. Both requirements will be explained in more detail in Chapter 12.

Types of Contracts

There are numerous types of contracts. They are categorized based on legal distinctions as to their *formation, performance,* and *enforceability.*

Contract Formation

Contracts are classified based on how and when a contract is formed. Exhibit 9.1 below illustrates three classifications of contracts based on their mode of formation. The best way to explain each type of contract is to compare one type with another, as we do in the following pages.

Offeror A person who makes an offer.

Offeree A person to whom an offer is made.

Bilateral versus Unilateral Contracts

Every contract involves at least two parties. The **offeror** is the party making the offer. The **offeree** is the party to whom the offer is made. The offeror always promises to do or not to do something and thus is also a

Exhibit 9.1 Classifications Based on Contract Formation

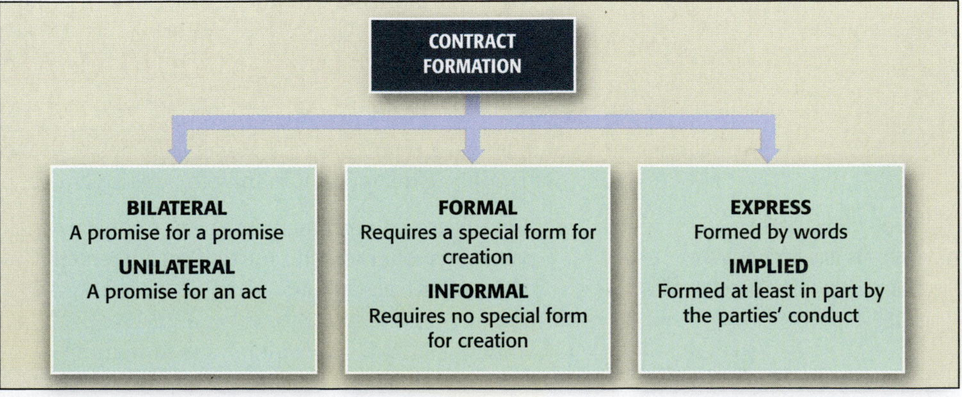

promisor. Whether the contract is classified as *bilateral* or *unilateral* depends on what the offeree must do to accept the offer and bind the offeror to a contract.

Bilateral Contract A type of contract that arises when a promise is given in exchange for a return promise.

Bilateral Contracts If the offeree can accept simply by promising to perform, the contract is a **bilateral contract.** Hence, a bilateral contract is a "promise for a promise." An example of a bilateral contract is a contract in which one person agrees to buy another person's automobile for a specified price. No performance, such as the payment of funds or delivery of goods, need take place for a bilateral contract to be formed. The contract comes into existence at the moment the promises are exchanged. (The appendix to Chapter 14 includes an example of a bilateral contract.)

EXAMPLE 9.1 Javier offers to buy Ann's Android-based smartphone for $200. Javier tells Ann that he will give her the cash for the phone on the following Friday, when he gets paid. Ann accepts Javier's offer and promises to give him the phone when he pays her on Friday. Javier and Ann have formed a bilateral contract. •

Unilateral Contract A contract that results when an offer can be accepted only by the offeree's performance.

Unilateral Contracts If the offer is phrased so that the offeree can accept only by completing the contract performance, the contract is a **unilateral contract.** Hence, a unilateral contract is a "promise for an act." In other words, the contract is formed not at the moment when promises are exchanged but rather when the contract is *performed.* **EXAMPLE 9.2** Reese says to Kata, "If you drive my car from New York to Los Angeles, I'll give you $1,000." Only on Kata's completion of the act—bringing the car to Los Angeles—does she fully accept Reese's offer to pay $1,000. If she chooses not to accept the offer to drive the car to Los Angeles, there are no legal consequences. •

Contests, lotteries, and other competitions offering prizes are also examples of offers for unilateral contracts. If a person complies with the rules of the contest—such as by submitting the right lottery number at the right place and time—a unilateral contract is formed, binding the organization offering the prize to a contract to perform as promised in the offer.

Can a company that sponsors a contest change the prize from what it originally advertised? Courts have historically treated contests as unilateral contracts, which typically cannot be modified by the offeror after the offeree has begun to perform. But this principle may not always apply to contest terms or advertisements. For instance, John Rogalski entered a poker tournament conducted by Little Poker League, LLC (LPL). The tournament lasted several months as players competed for spots in a winner-take-all final event. During the final event, Rogalski and the other contestants signed a "World Series of Poker (WSOP) Agreement," which stated that LPL would pay the $10,000 WSOP entry fee on the winner's behalf and provide $2,500 for travel-related expenses. The agreement also stated that if the winner did not attend the WSOP, he or she would relinquish the WSOP seat and return the expense money to LPL.

Rogalski won the poker tournament and took the $2,500 for travel expenses, but he did not attend the WSOP tournament. He then filed a suit for $10,000 against LPL, arguing that it had advertised that the winner could choose to receive the cash value of the prizes ($12,500) instead of attending the WSOP tournament. Rogalski claimed that by participating in LPL's tournament, he had accepted the advertised offer to take the cash in lieu of entering the WSOP tournament, and that the later agreement was an invalid contract modification. LPL filed a counterclaim to recover the $2,500 in expenses. The court ruled in favor of LPL, finding that the contract was formed when Rogalski signed the WSOP agreement, and not when he began participating in the contest. Under the contest rules as stated in the WSOP agreement, Rogalski had to return the $2,500 to LPL.[2]

In the following case, the court was asked to resolve a dispute that arose from an employer's refusal to pay a bonus to a former employee. The court's decision depended, in part, on whether the parties' employment contract was bilateral or unilateral.

---

2. *Rogalski v. Little Poker League, LLC*, 2011 WL 589636 (Minn.App. 2011).

Case 9.1

Schwarzrock v. Remote Technologies, Inc.

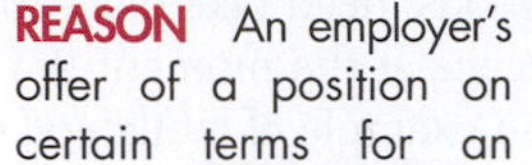
Court of Appeals of Minnesota,
2011 WL 68262 (2011).

(Brian A Jackson/Shutterstock.com)

Is an employment agreement a unilateral contract?

FACTS Nick Schwarzrock applied for a job at Remote Technologies, Inc., a Minnesota-based manufacturer of home-theater and home-automation controls. Remote wrote a letter to Schwarzrock offering him a job for an annual salary of $60,000, plus a bonus. The day after he started work, Schwarzrock signed an employment agreement (EA) that expressly "superseded all previous correspondence." The EA stated that "any bonus to Employee shall rest in the sole discretion of the employer." When Remote fired Schwarzrock, he filed a lawsuit to recover the bonus that he believed he was owed under a bilateral contract. Remote argued that the bonus was discretionary and that when Schwarzrock accepted the EA, he created a binding unilateral contract.

ISSUE Was Schwarzrock's EA an enforceable unilateral contract?

DECISION Yes. The state appellate court affirmed the lower court's judgment that the EA was a unilateral contract, not a bilateral contract.

REASON An employer's offer of a position on certain terms for an indefinite period becomes a unilateral contract on the employee's acceptance. The court reasoned that the EA was a unilateral offer of employment by Remote that specifically made any bonus subject to the employer's discretion. Schwarzrock accepted this offer when he signed the EA and continued working. Both the letter and Remote's EA expressed the employer's intent to offer a salary and a potential bonus to Schwarzrock. The letter may have implied that the bonus was not discretionary, but the EA clarified or modified the offer by clearly stating that it was.

WHAT IF THE FACTS WERE DIFFERENT? *Suppose that the court had ruled that Schwarzrock was employed under a bilateral contract, as he alleged. Would the result have been different? Explain.*

Revocation of Offers for Unilateral Contracts A problem arises in unilateral contracts when the promisor attempts to *revoke* (cancel) the offer after the promisee has begun performance but before the act has been completed. **EXAMPLE 9.3** Seiko offers to buy Jin's sailboat, moored in San Francisco, on delivery of the boat to Seiko's dock in Newport Beach, three hundred miles south of San Francisco. Jin rigs the boat and sets sail. Shortly before his arrival at Newport Beach, Jin receives a message from Seiko withdrawing her offer. Seiko's offer is to form a unilateral contract, and only Jin's delivery of the sailboat at her dock is an acceptance. •

In contract law, offers are normally *revocable* (capable of being taken back, or canceled) until accepted. Under the traditional view of unilateral contracts, Seiko's revocation would terminate the offer. Because of the harsh effect on the offeree of the revocation of an offer to form a unilateral contract, the modern-day view is that once performance has been *substantially* undertaken, the offeror cannot revoke the offer. Thus, in our example, even though Jin has not yet accepted the offer by complete performance, Seiko is prohibited from revoking it. Jin can deliver the boat and bind Seiko to the contract.

Formal versus Informal Contracts

Formal Contract An agreement that by law requires a specific form for its validity.

Another classification system divides contracts into formal contracts and informal contracts. **Formal contracts** are contracts that require a special form or method of creation (formation) to be enforceable.[3] For example, *negotiable instruments,* which include checks, drafts, promissory notes, and certificates of deposit (as will be discussed in Chapter 18), are formal contracts because, under the Uniform Commercial Code, a special form and language are required to create them.

3. See *Restatement (Second) of Contracts,* Section 6, which explains that formal contracts include (1) contracts under seal, (2) recognizances, (3) negotiable instruments, and (4) letters of credit. As mentioned in Chapter 1, *Restatements of the Law* are books that summarize court decisions on a particular topic and that courts often refer to for guidance.

Letters of credit, which are frequently used in international sales contracts (as discussed in Chapter 8), are another type of formal contract.

Informal Contract A contract that does not require a specific form or method of creation to be valid.

Informal contracts (also called *simple contracts*) include all other contracts. No special form is required (except for certain types of contracts that must be in writing), as the contracts are usually based on their substance rather than their form. Typically, businesspersons put their contracts in writing to ensure that there is some proof of a contract's existence should problems arise.

Express versus Implied Contracts

Express Contract A contract in which the terms of the agreement are stated in words, oral or written.

Implied Contract A contract formed in whole or in part from the conduct of the parties.

Contracts may also be categorized as express or implied by the conduct of the parties. In an **express contract**, the terms of the agreement are fully and explicitly stated in words, oral or written. A signed lease for an apartment or a house is an express written contract. If a classmate accepts your offer to sell your textbooks from last semester for $75, an express oral contract has been made.

A contract that is implied from the conduct of the parties is called an **implied contract**. This type of contract differs from an express contract in that the *conduct* of the parties, rather than their words, creates and defines at least some of the terms of the contract. For an implied contract to arise, certain requirements must be met.

Requirements for Implied Contracts

Normally, if the following conditions exist, a court will hold that an implied contract was formed:

1. The plaintiff furnished some service or property.
2. The plaintiff expected to be paid for that service or property, and the defendant knew or should have known that payment was expected (based on the objective theory of contracts discussed on page 241).
3. The defendant had a chance to reject the services or property and did not.

LEARNING OBJECTIVE 3
What is the difference between express and implied contracts?

EXAMPLE 9.4 Oleg, a small-business owner, needs an accountant to complete his tax return. He drops by a local accountant's office, explains his situation to the accountant, and learns what fees she charges. The next day, he returns and gives the receptionist all of the necessary documents to complete his return. Then he walks out without saying anything further to the accountant. In this situation, Oleg has entered into an implied contract to pay the accountant the usual fees for her services. The contract is implied because of Oleg's conduct and hers. She expects to be paid for completing the tax return, and by bringing in the records she will need to do the job, Oleg has implied an intent to pay her. •

Mixed Contracts with Express and Implied Terms

Note that a contract can be a mixture of an express contract and an implied contract. In other words, a contract may contain some express terms, while others are implied. During the construction of a home, for instance, the homeowner often asks the builder to make changes in the original specifications.

Danica Patrick signs a contract to drive full-time in the NASCAR Nationwide Series circuit and select Sprint Cup.

(AP Photo/Paul Connors)

CASE EXAMPLE 9.5 Lamar Hopkins hired Uhrhahn Construction & Design, Inc., for several projects during the construction of his home. Each project was based on a cost estimate and specifications, and had a signed contract that required modifications to be in writing. When work was in progress, however, Hopkins made several requests for changes. There was no written record of these changes, but Uhrhahn performed the work and Hopkins paid for it. A dispute arose after Hopkins requested that Uhrhahn use Durisol blocks rather than cinder blocks. Uhrhahn orally agreed to the modification, but then demanded extra payment because the Durisol blocks were more complicated and costly to install. Hopkins refused to pay. Uhrhahn sued and won. The court found that that there was an implied contract for the Durisol blocks. The builder did the work, and the buyer accepted the work. Such oral modification of the original contract creates an enforceable contract, and payment is due for the extra work.[4] •

4. *Uhrhahn Construction & Design, Inc. v. Hopkins*, 179 P.3d 808 (Utah App. 2008).

Contract Performance

Executed Contract A contract that has been fully performed by both parties.

Executory Contract A contract that has not yet been fully performed.

Contracts are also classified according to their state of performance. A contract that has been fully performed on both sides is called an **executed contract.** A contract that has not been fully performed on either side is called an **executory contract.** If one party has fully performed but the other has not, the contract is said to be executed on the one side and executory on the other, but the contract is still classified as executory.

EXAMPLE 9.6 You agreed to buy ten tons of coal from Western Coal Company. Western has delivered the coal to your steel mill, where it is now being burned. At this point, the contract is an executory contract—it is executed on the part of Western and executory on your part. After you pay Western for the coal, the contract will be executed on both sides. ●

Contract Enforceability

Valid Contract A contract that results when the elements necessary for contract formation (agreement, consideration, legal purpose, and contractual capacity) are present.

A **valid contract** has the four elements necessary for contract formation: (1) an agreement (offer and acceptance) (2) supported by legally sufficient consideration (3) for a legal purpose and (4) made by parties who have the legal capacity to enter into the contract. As mentioned, we will discuss each of these elements in the following chapters. (See this chapter's *Adapting Law to the Online Environment* feature on the facing page for a discussion of how businesses today frequently include disclaimers on their e-mail messages to avoid the potential of enforceable obligations.)

LEARNING OBJECTIVE 4
How does a void contract differ from a voidable contract? What is an unenforceable contract?

As you can see in Exhibit 9.2 below, valid contracts may be enforceable, voidable, or unenforceable. Additionally, a contract may be referred to as a *void contract.* We look next at the meaning of the terms *voidable, unenforceable,* and *void* in relation to contract enforceability.

Voidable Contract A contract that may be legally avoided at the option of one or both of the parties.

Voidable Contracts

A **voidable contract** is a *valid* contract but one that can be avoided at the option of one or both of the parties. The party having the option can elect either to avoid any duty to perform or to *ratify* (make valid) the contract. If the contract is avoided, both parties are released from it. If it is ratified, both parties must fully perform their respective legal obligations.

As a general rule, for example, contracts made by minors are voidable at the option of the minor (as will be discussed in Chapter 11). Additionally, contracts entered into under

Exhibit 9.2 Enforceable, Voidable, Unenforceable, and Void Contracts

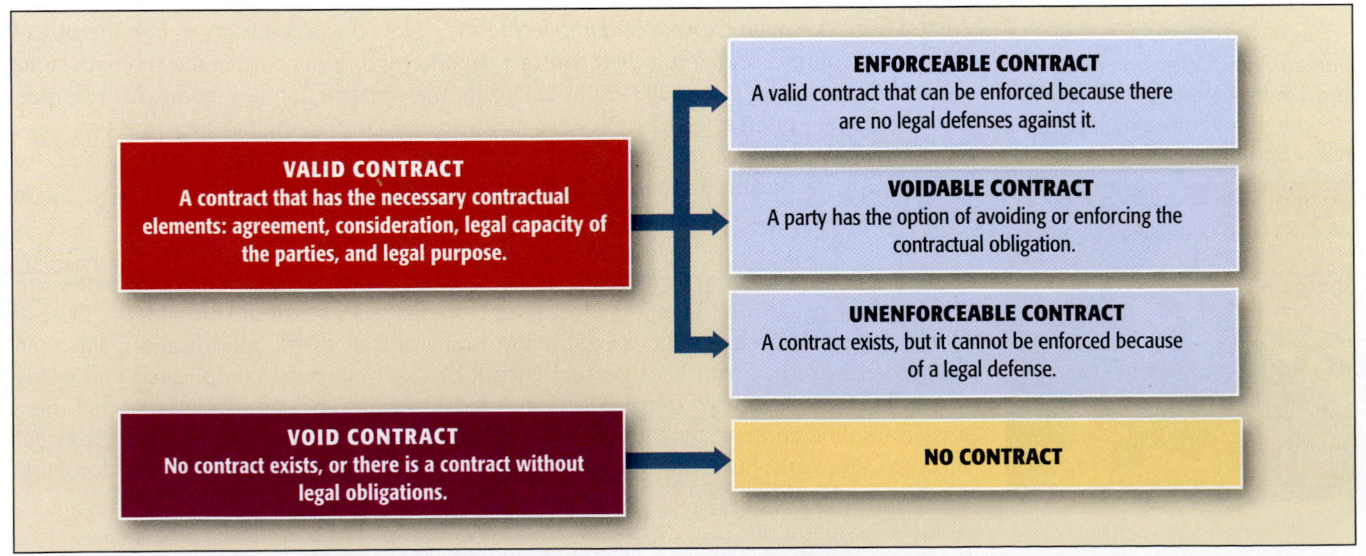

ADAPTING THE LAW TO THE ONLINE ENVIRONMENT

CAN A DISCLAIMER PREVENT AN E-MAIL FROM FORMING AN AGREEMENT?

When you receive an e-mail from a business, the e-mail will usually include a list of disclaimers, which may be longer than the message itself. Indeed, disclaimers have grown longer over the years, but does that make them more enforceable?

Simple in the Beginning but Longer and More Complex Today

About twenty years ago, when e-mail first began to be used in business, disclaimers simply stated that the information contained in the e-mail was privileged, confidential, or proprietary. The typical disclaimer further said (and continues to say) that any use, distribution, copying, or disclosure to another person of the e-mail was strictly prohibited. Finally, the disclaimer generally told the recipient to destroy the message if it was not intended for him or her and to notify the sender by reply e-mail.

Today, disclaimers may also include automatic digital signatures with the sender's contact information and perhaps a reminder to be "green" and protect the environment by not printing the e-mail. In addition, disclaimers are likely to include a number of warnings, such as the e-mail could contain viruses and the recipient is responsible for guarding against them, the recipient should not rely on any professional advice contained in the e-mail, and the e-mail does not constitute a contractual offer or acceptance.

Are All E-Mail Disclaimers Enforceable?

Relatively few cases have dealt with the issue of whether e-mail disclaimers are enforceable, and the court decisions have not yet answered the question of enforceability. Another issue is whether e-mails with no disclaimers are less protected than ones without them.

One issue that can easily arise is whether a series of e-mails creates a contract. Although e-mails may seem to impose a contractual obligation between the sender and the recipient, the courts generally deem unilateral contracts unenforceable. Thus, a disclaimer stating that an e-mail is not intended as an offer or an acceptance might be useful. The disclaimer should be carefully worded, however.

A court in Scotland, for example, held that an e-mail disclaimer did not extend to a detailed proposal attached to the e-mail. Therefore, the attached proposal was deemed a valid offer.[a]

As disclaimers are added to more and more e-mails, the less likely it is that a judge will be convinced that e-mails with disclaimers are more privileged or confidential than others. In addition, making the disclaimers longer does not guarantee that the e-mails to which the disclaimers are attached will be considered more privileged and confidential than others.

In 2012, for instance, the investment bank Nomura Group attached a nearly three-thousand-word disclaimer to a Federal Reserve report that it had e-mailed to its clients. One phrase in the disclaimer stated that the opinions expressed in the e-mail were subject to change without notice.

Critical Thinking

One commentator likened e-mail disclaimers to the tags on new mattresses that forbid removal of the tags under penalty of law or to twenty-page booklets on safety that accompany new products. No one reads the tags or the booklets, and no one cares. Why do e-mail disclaimers continue to proliferate nonetheless and become ever longer?

---

a. *Baillie Estates Limited v. Du Pont (UK) Limited* (June 30, 2009).

fraudulent conditions are voidable at the option of the defrauded party. Contracts entered into under legally defined duress or undue influence are also voidable (see Chapter 12).

Unenforceable Contract A valid contract rendered unenforceable by some statute or law.

Unenforceable Contracts

An **unenforceable contract** is one that cannot be enforced because of certain legal defenses against it. It is not unenforceable because a party failed to satisfy a legal requirement of the contract. Rather, it is a valid contract rendered unenforceable by some statute or law. For example, some contracts must be in writing (see Chapter 12), and if they are not, they will not be enforceable except in certain exceptional circumstances.

Void Contract A contract having no legal force or binding effect.

Void Contracts

A **void contract** is no contract at all. The terms *void* and *contract* are contradictory. None of the parties has any legal obligations if a contract is void. A contract can be void because, for example, one of the parties was previously determined by a court to be legally insane and thus lacked the legal capacity to enter into a contract. Or, a contract can be void because the purpose of the contract was illegal, such as contracting to rob a bank or burn down a building (arson).

Quasi Contracts

Quasi Contract An obligation or contract imposed by law (a court), in the absence of an agreement, to prevent the unjust enrichment of one party.

Quasi contracts, or contracts *implied in law*, are wholly different from actual contracts. Express contracts and implied contracts are actual or true contracts formed by the words or actions of the parties. The word *quasi* is Latin for "as if." Quasi contracts are not true contracts because they do not arise from any agreement, express or implied, between the parties themselves. Rather, quasi contracts are fictional contracts that courts can impose on the parties "as if" the parties had entered into an actual contract. They are equitable rather than legal contracts.

When the court imposes a quasi contract, a plaintiff may recover in *quantum meruit*,[5] a Latin phrase meaning "as much as he or she deserves." *Quantum meruit* essentially describes the extent of compensation owed under a quasi contract.

Usually, quasi contracts are imposed to avoid the *unjust enrichment* of one party at the expense of another. The doctrine of unjust enrichment is based on the theory that individuals should not be allowed to profit or enrich themselves inequitably at the expense of others.

In the following case, the parties did not have an express contract, but one party enjoyed the benefits of the other party's services. The court had to decide if the parties had a quasi contract.

5. Pronounced *kwahn*-tuhm *mehr*-oo-wit.

Case 9.2

Seawest Services Association v. Copenhaver

Court of Appeals of Washington, 2012 WL 255857 (2012). www.courts.wa.gov[a]

(LordRunar/iStockphoto.com)

What purpose does a water meter serve?

FACTS Seawest Services Association owned and operated a water-distribution system that served homes both inside and outside a housing development. Seawest had two classes of members. Full members owned property in the housing development, and limited members received water services for homes outside the development. Both full and limited members paid water bills and, as necessary, assessments for work performed on the water system. In 2001, the Copenhavers purchased a home outside the housing development. They did not have an express contract with Seawest, but they paid water bills for eight years and paid one $3,950 assessment for water system upgrades. In 2009, a dispute arose between the parties, and the Copenhavers began refusing to pay their water bills and assessments. Seawest sued the Copenhavers in a Washington state court. The trial court found that the Copenhavers were limited members of Seawest and thus were liable for the unpaid water bills and assessments. The Copenhavers appealed.

ISSUE Did the Copenhavers have a quasi contract with Seawest?

DECISION Yes. The Washington appellate court affirmed the decision of the trial court, holding that the Copenhavers were liable to Seawest for breach of a quasi contract.

REASON The court explained that a quasi contract exists when a person knowingly receives a benefit from another party and it would be "inequitable for the [person] to retain the benefit without the payment of its value." The Copenhavers enjoyed the benefits of Seawest's water services and even paid for them before their dispute arose. The court found that "the Copenhavers would be unjustly enriched if they could retain benefits provided by Seawest without paying for them." After all, the court reasoned, they purchased a home that received water services, and they knew that they could not receive water without being a limited member of Seawest.

CRITICAL THINKING—Ethical Consideration *In recognizing quasi contracts, does the law try to correct for unethical behavior? Discuss.*

a. In the left-hand column, click on "Court Opinions." In the page that opens, type "Seawest Services" in the "Search Opinions" box and click on "Search." In the result, click on the link to access the case. The Administrative Office of the Washington Courts administers this Web site.

Limitations on Quasi-Contractual Recovery

Although quasi contracts exist to prevent unjust enrichment, in some situations, the party who obtains a benefit is not liable for its fair value. Basically, a party who has conferred a benefit on someone else unnecessarily or as a result of misconduct or negligence cannot invoke the doctrine of quasi contract. The enrichment in those situations will not be considered "unjust."

CASE EXAMPLE 9.7 Qwest Wireless, LLC, provides wireless phone services in Arizona and thirteen other states. Qwest marketed and sold handset insurance to its wireless customers, although it did not have a license to sell insurance in Arizona or in any other state. Patrick and Vicki Van Zanen sued Qwest in a federal court for unjust enrichment based on its receipt of sales commissions for the insurance. The court agreed that Qwest had violated the insurance-licensing statute, but found that the sales commissions did not constitute unjust enrichment because the customers had, in fact, received the handset insurance. Also, Qwest had not retained a benefit (the commissions) without paying for it (providing insurance). Therefore, the Van Zanens and other customers did not suffer unfair detriment.[6] •

When an Actual Contract Exists

The doctrine of quasi contract generally cannot be used when an actual contract covers the area in controversy. In this situation, a remedy already exists if a party is unjustly enriched because the other fails to perform—the nonbreaching party can sue the breaching party for breach of contract.

EXAMPLE 9.8 Fung contracts with Cameron to deliver a furnace to a building owned by Bateman. Fung delivers the furnace, but Cameron never pays Fung. Bateman has been unjustly enriched in this situation, to be sure. Nevertheless, Fung cannot recover from Bateman in quasi contract because Fung had an actual contract with Cameron. Fung already has a remedy—he can sue for breach of contract to recover the price of the furnace from Cameron. In this situation, the court does not need to impose a quasi contract to achieve justice. •

Interpretation of Contracts

Sometimes, parties agree that a contract has been formed but disagree on its meaning or legal effect. One reason that this may happen is that one of the parties is not familiar with the legal terminology used in the contract. To an extent, *plain language laws* have helped to avoid this difficulty. Sometimes, though, a dispute may still arise over the meaning of a contract simply because the rights or obligations under the contract are not expressed clearly—no matter how "plain" the language used.

In this section, we look at some common law rules of contract interpretation. These rules, including the *plain meaning rule* and various other rules that have evolved over time, provide the courts with guidelines for deciding disputes over how contract terms or provisions should be interpreted. Exhibit 9.3 on the following page provides a brief graphic summary of how these rules are applied.

PREVENTING LEGAL DISPUTES

To avoid disputes over contract interpretation, make sure your intentions are clearly expressed in your contracts. Careful drafting of contracts not only helps prevent potential disputes over the meaning of certain terms but may also be crucial if the firm brings a lawsuit or needs to defend against a lawsuit for breach of contract. By using simple, clear language and avoiding legalese, you can take a major step toward avoiding contract disputes.

6. *Van Zanen v. Qwest Wireless, LLC*, 522 F.3d 1127 (10th Cir. 2008).

Exhibit 9.3 **Rules of Contract Interpretation**

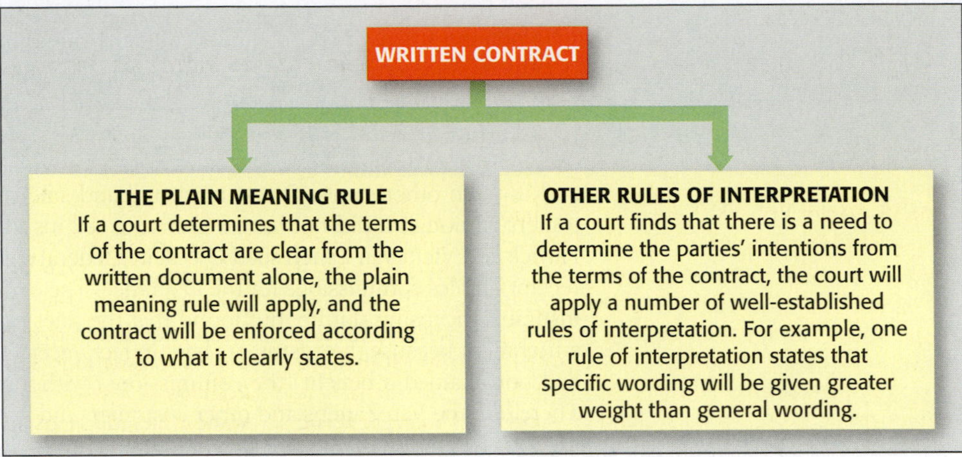

Plain Language Laws

The federal government and a majority of the states have enacted plain language laws to regulate legal writing and eliminate "legalese." All federal agencies are required to use plain language in most of their forms and written communications. Plain language requirements have been extended to agency rulemaking as well. States frequently have plain language laws that apply to consumer contracts, which are those made primarily for personal, family, or household purposes. The legal profession has also moved toward plain English, and court rules in many jurisdictions require attorneys to use plain language in court documents.

The Plain Meaning Rule

KNOW THIS

No one can avoid contractual obligations by claiming that she or he did not read the contract. A contract normally is interpreted as if each party read every word carefully.

When a contract's language is clear and unequivocal, a court will enforce the contract according to its obvious terms. The meaning of the terms must be determined from *the face of the instrument*—from the written document alone. This is sometimes referred to as the *plain meaning rule.*

The words—and their plain, ordinary meaning—determine the intent of the parties at the time that they entered into the contract. A court is bound to give effect to the contract according to this intent. The importance of each word or phrase in a contract will also be discussed in the Appendix to Chapter 14: An Annotated Employment Contract.

Ambiguity

A court will consider a contract to be ambiguous in the following situations:

1. When the intent of the parties cannot be determined from its language.
2. When it lacks a provision on a disputed issue.
3. When a term is susceptible to more than one interpretation.
4. When there is uncertainty about a provision.

Extrinsic Evidence

If a contract term is ambiguous, a court may consider *extrinsic evidence* (outside evidence), or it may interpret the ambiguity against the party who drafted the contract term. Extrinsic evidence is any evidence not contained in the document itself, and may include the testimony of the parties, additional agreements or communications, or other information relevant to determining the parties' intent.

Whether extrinsic evidence is considered can significantly affect how a court interprets ambiguous contractual provisions and thus can affect the outcome of litigation. When the contract is clear and unambiguous, a court cannot consider evidence outside the contract. The following *Spotlight Case* illustrates these points.

Spotlight on Columbia Pictures

Case 9.3

Wagner v. Columbia Pictures Industries, Inc.

California Court of Appeal, Second District, 146 Cal.App.4th 586, 52 Cal.Rptr.3d 898 (2007).

(Photo by John M. Heller/Getty Images)

Actor Robert Wagner had the rights to the TV series, *Charlie's Angels.*

FACTS Actor Robert Wagner entered into an agreement with Spelling-Goldberg Productions (SGP) "relating to *Charlie's Angels* (herein called the 'series')." The contract entitled Wagner to 50 percent of the net profits that SGP received from broadcasting the series and from all ancillary, music, and subsidiary rights in connection with the series. SGP hired Ivan Goff and Ben Roberts to write the series, under a contract subject to the Writers Guild of America Minimum Basic Agreement (MBA).[a] The MBA stipulated that the writer of a television show retains the right to make and market films based on the material, subject to the producer's right to buy this right if the writer decides to sell it within five years.

The first *Charlie's Angels* episode aired in 1976. In 1982, SGP sold its rights to the series to Columbia Pictures Industries, Inc. Thirteen years later, Columbia bought the movie rights to the material from Goff's and Roberts's heirs. In 2000 and 2003, Columbia produced and distributed two *Charlie's Angels* movies. Wagner filed a suit in a California state court against Columbia, claiming a share of the profits from the films. The court granted Columbia's motion for summary judgment. Wagner appealed to a state intermediate appellate court.

ISSUE Did the language of Wagner's contract with SGP entitle Columbia to all of the profits from the two *Charlie's Angels* movies?

DECISION Yes. The state intermediate appellate court affirmed the lower court's judgment.

REASON Wagner offered evidence to show that a previous contract with SGP involving a property titled *Love Song* had been intended to give him half of the net profits that SGP received from the property from all sources without limitation as to source or time. Wagner argued that because the profits provision in the *Charlie's Angels* agreement used identical language, the provision should be interpreted to give him the same share. The court stated that an "agreement is the writing itself." Extrinsic evidence is not admissible "to show intention independent of an unambiguous written instrument." The court reasoned that even if the parties intended Wagner to share in the profits from all sources, "they did not say so in their contract." Under the language of the contract, Wagner was not entitled to share in the profits from the exercise of the movie rights to *Charlie's Angels* if those rights were acquired separately. SGP did not acquire the movie rights to *Charlie's Angels* by exercising this right within the five-year period. Columbia obtained those rights separately more than five years later.

CRITICAL THINKING—Legal Consideration *How might the result in this case have been different if the court had allowed Wagner's extrinsic evidence of the prior contract regarding* Love Song *to be used as evidence in this dispute?*

a. The Writers Guild of America is an association of screen and television writers that negotiates industry-wide agreements with motion picture and television producers to cover the rights of its members.

Other Rules of Interpretation

LEARNING OBJECTIVE 5

What rules guide the courts in interpreting contracts?

Generally, a court will interpret the language to give effect to the parties' intent *as expressed in their contract.* This is the primary purpose of the rules of interpretation—to determine the parties' intent from the language used in their agreement and to give effect to that intent. A court normally will not make or remake a contract, nor will it normally interpret the language according to what the parties *claim* their intent was when they made the contract.[7]

7. Nevertheless, if a court finds that, even after applying the rules of interpretation, the terms are susceptible to more than one meaning, the court may admit extrinsic evidence to prove what the parties intended. See, for example, *Langdon v. United Restaurants, Inc.*, 105 S.W.3d 882 (Mo.Ct.App. 2003).

Rules the Courts Use The courts use the following rules in interpreting contractual terms:

1. Insofar as possible, a reasonable, lawful, and effective meaning will be given to all of a contract's terms.
2. A contract will be interpreted as a whole. Individual, specific clauses will be considered subordinate to the contract's general intent. All writings that are a part of the same transaction will be interpreted together.
3. Terms that were the subject of separate negotiation will be given greater consideration than standardized terms and terms that were not negotiated separately.
4. A word will be given its ordinary, commonly accepted meaning, and a technical word or term will be given its technical meaning, unless the parties clearly intended something else.
5. Specific and exact wording will be given greater consideration than general language.
6. Written or typewritten terms prevail over preprinted terms.
7. Because a contract should be drafted in clear and unambiguous language, a party that uses ambiguous expressions is held to be responsible for the ambiguities. Thus, when the language has more than one meaning, it will be interpreted *against* the party that drafted the contract.
8. Evidence of *trade usage, prior dealing,* and *course of performance* may be admitted to clarify the meaning of an ambiguously worded contract. (We will define and discuss these terms in Chapter 15.) What each of the parties does pursuant to the contract will be interpreted as consistent with what the other does and with any relevant usage of trade and course of dealing or performance.

"The difference between the right word and the almost right word is the difference between lightning and a lightning bug."

Mark Twain, 1835–1910
(American author and humorist)

Express Terms Usually Given Most Weight Express terms (terms expressly stated in the contract) are given the greatest weight, followed by course of performance, course of dealing, and custom and usage of trade—in that order. When considering custom and usage, a court will look at the trade customs and usage common to the particular business or industry and to the locale in which the contract was made or is to be performed.

CASE EXAMPLE 9.9 Jessica Robbins bought a house in Tennessee. U.S. Bank financed the purchase, and Tennessee Farmers Mutual Insurance Company issued the homeowner's insurance policy. The policy included a standard mortgage clause that promised payment to the bank unless the house was lost due to an "increase in hazard" that the bank knew about but did not tell the insurer. When Robbins fell behind on her mortgage payments, the bank started foreclosure proceedings (see Chapter 22). No one told the insurer. Robbins filed for bankruptcy, which postponed foreclosure. Meanwhile, the house was destroyed in a fire. The bank filed a claim under the policy, but the insurer refused to pay on the ground that it had not been told by the bank of an "increase in hazard"—the foreclosure. The bank then filed a lawsuit. The court found that the plain meaning of the words "increase in hazard" in the policy referred to physical conditions on the property that posed a risk, not to events such as foreclosure. Thus, the bank was not required to notify the insurer under the terms of the policy, and the lack of notice did not invalidate the coverage.[8] •

8. *U.S. Bank, N.A. v. Tennessee Farmers Mutual Insurance Co.,* 277 S.W.3d 381 (Tenn.Sup.Ct. 2009).

Reviewing . . . Nature and Classification

Mitsui Bank hired Ross Duncan as a branch manager in one of its Southern California locations. At that time, Duncan received an employee handbook informing him that Mitsui would review his performance and salary level annually. In 2010, Mitsui decided to create a new lending program to help financially troubled businesses stay afloat. It hired Duncan as the credit development officer (CDO) and gave him a written compensation plan. Duncan's compensation was to be based on the new program's success and involved a bonus and commissions based on new loans and sales volume. The written plan also stated, "This compensation plan will be reviewed and potentially amended after one year and will be subject to such review and amendment annually thereafter." Duncan's efforts as CDO were successful, and the business-lending program he developed grew to represent 25 percent of Mitsui's business in 2011 and 40 percent by 2012. Nevertheless, Mitsui not only refused to give Duncan a raise in 2011 but also amended his compensation plan to significantly reduce his compensation and to change his performance evaluation schedule to every six months. When he had still not received a raise by 2012, Duncan retired as CDO and filed a lawsuit claiming breach of contract. Using the information presented in the chapter, answer the following questions.

1. What are the four requirements of a valid contract?
2. Did Duncan have a valid contract with Mitsui for employment as credit development officer? If so, was it a bilateral or a unilateral contract?
3. What are the requirements of an implied contract?
4. Can Duncan establish an implied contract based on the employment manual or the written compensation plan? Why or why not?

DEBATE THIS Companies should be able to make or break employment contracts whenever and however they wish.

Key Terms

bilateral contract 243
contract 240
executed contract 246
executory contract 246
express contract 245
formal contract 244
implied contract 245
informal contract 245
objective theory of contracts 241
offeree 242
offeror 242
promise 239
promisee 240
promisor 240
quasi contract 248
unenforceable contract 247
unilateral contract 243
valid contract 246
void contract 247
voidable contract 246

Chapter Summary: Nature and Classification

An Overview of Contract Law (See pages 240–241.)	1. *Sources of contract law*—The common law governs all contracts except when it has been modified or replaced by statutory law, such as the Uniform Commercial Code (UCC), or by administrative agency regulations. The UCC governs contracts for the sale or lease of goods (see Chapter 15). 2. *The function of contracts*—Contract law establishes what kinds of promises will be legally binding and supplies procedures for enforcing legally binding promises, or agreements. 3. *Definition of a contract*—A contract is an agreement that can be enforced in court. It is formed by two or more competent parties who agree to perform or to refrain from performing some act now or in the future. 4. *Objective theory of contracts*—In contract law, intent is determined by objective facts, not by the personal or subjective intent, or belief, of a party.

Continued

Chapter Summary: Nature and Classification—Continued

Elements of a Contract (See pages 241–242.)	1. *Requirements of a valid contract*—The four requirements of a valid contract are agreement, consideration, contractual capacity, and legality. 2. *Defenses to the enforceability of a contract*—Even if the four requirements of a valid contract are met, a contract may be unenforceable if it lacks voluntary consent or is not in the required form.
Types of Contracts (See pages 242–247.)	1. *Bilateral*—A promise for a promise. 2. *Unilateral*—A promise for an act (acceptance is the completed—or substantial—performance of the contract by the offeree). 3. *Formal*—Requires a special form for contract formation. 4. *Informal*—Requires no special form for contract formation. 5. *Express*—Formed by words (oral, written, or a combination). 6. *Implied*—Formed at least in part by the conduct of the parties. 7. *Executed*—A fully performed contract. 8. *Executory*—A contract not yet fully performed. 9. *Valid*—A contract that has the four necessary contractual elements of agreement, consideration, capacity, and legality. 10. *Voidable*—A contract in which a party has the option of avoiding or enforcing the contractual obligation. 11. *Unenforceable*—A valid contract that cannot be enforced because of a legal defense. 12. *Void*—No contract exists, or there is a contract without legal obligations.
Quasi Contracts (See pages 248–249.)	A quasi contract, or a contract implied in law, is a contract that is imposed by law to prevent unjust enrichment.
Interpretation of Contracts (See pages 249–252.)	Increasingly, plain language laws require contracts to be written in plain language so that the terms are clear and understandable to the parties. Under the plain meaning rule, a court will enforce the contract according to its plain terms, the meaning of which must be determined from the written document alone. Other rules applied by the courts when interpreting are set out on page 252.

ExamPrep

ISSUE SPOTTERS

1. Joli signs and returns a letter from Kerin, in which he said that he had a book at a certain price. When Kerin delivers the book, Joli sends it back, claiming that they do not have a contract. Kerin claims they do. What standard determines whether these parties have a contract? **(See page 241.)**
2. Dyna tells Ed that she will pay him $1,000 to set fire to her store so that she can collect under a fire insurance policy. Ed sets fire to the store, but Dyna refuses to pay. Can Ed recover? Why or why not? **(See page 247.)**

—Check your answers to the Issue Spotters against the answers provided in Appendix E at the end of this text.

BEFORE THE TEST

Go to www.cengagebrain.com, enter the ISBN 9781133273561, and click on "Find" to locate this textbook's Web site. Then, click on "Access Now" under "Study Tools," and select Chapter 9 at the top. There, you will find a Practice Quiz that you can take to assess your mastery of the concepts in this chapter, as well as Flashcards, a Glossary of important terms, and Video Questions (when assigned).

For Review

Answers to the even-numbered questions in this For Review section can be found in Appendix F at the end of this text.

1. What is a contract? What is the objective theory of contracts?
2. What are the four basic elements necessary to the formation of a valid contract?
3. What is the difference between express and implied contracts?

4. How does a void contract differ from a voidable contract? What is an unenforceable contract?
5. What rules guide the courts in interpreting contracts?

Business Scenarios and Case Problems

9–1 Unilateral Contract. Rocky Mountain Races, Inc., sponsors the "Pioneer Trail Ultramarathon" with an advertised first prize of $10,000. The rules require the competitors to run 100 miles from the floor of Blackwater Canyon to the top of Pinnacle Mountain. The rules also provide that Rocky reserves the right to change the terms of the race at any time. Monica enters the race and is declared the winner. Rocky offers her a prize of $1,000 instead of $10,000. Did Rocky and Monica have a contract? Explain. **(See page 243.)**

9–2 Question with Sample Answer—Implied Contract. Janine was hospitalized with severe abdominal pain and placed in an intensive care unit. Her doctor told the hospital personnel to order around-the-clock nursing care for Janine. At the hospital's request, a nursing services firm, Nursing Services Unlimited, provided two weeks of in-hospital care and, after Janine was sent home, an additional two weeks of at-home care. During the at-home period of care, Janine was fully aware that she was receiving the benefit of the nursing services. Nursing Services later billed Janine $4,000 for the nursing care, but Janine refused to pay on the ground that she had never contracted for the services, either orally or in writing. In view of the fact that no express contract was ever formed, can Nursing Services recover the $4,000 from Janine? If so, under what legal theory? Discuss. **(See page 245.)**

—For a sample answer to Question 9–2, go to Appendix G at the end of this text.

9–3 Contract Classification. For employment with the Firestorm Smokejumpers—a crew of elite paratroopers who parachute into dangerous situations to fight fires—applicants must complete a series of tests. The crew chief sends the most qualified applicants a letter stating that they will be admitted to Firestorm's training sessions if they pass a medical exam. Jake Kurzyniec receives the letter and passes the exam, but a new crew chief changes the selection process and rejects him. Is there a contract between Kurzyniec and Firestorm? If there is a contract, what type of contract is it? **(See pages 242–243.)**

9–4 Spotlight on Taco Bell—Implied Contract. Thomas Rinks and Joseph Shields developed Psycho Chihuahua, a caricature of a Chihuahua dog with a "do-not-back-down" attitude. They promoted and marketed the character through their company, Wrench, LLC. Ed Alfaro and Rudy Pollak, representatives of Taco Bell Corp., learned of Psycho Chihuahua and met with Rinks and Shields to talk about using the character as a Taco Bell "icon." Wrench sent artwork, merchandise, and marketing ideas to Alfaro, who promoted the character within Taco Bell. Alfaro asked Wrench to propose terms for Taco Bell's use of Psycho Chihuahua. Taco Bell did not accept Wrench's terms, but Alfaro continued to promote the character within the company. Meanwhile, Taco Bell hired a new advertising agency, which proposed an advertising campaign involving a Chihuahua. When Alfaro learned of this proposal, he sent the Psycho Chihuahua materials to the agency. Taco Bell made a Chihuahua the focus of its marketing but paid nothing to Wrench. Wrench filed a suit against Taco Bell in a federal court claiming that it had an implied contract with Taco Bell and that Taco Bell breached that contract. Do these facts satisfy the requirements for an implied contract? Why or why not? [*Wrench, LLC. v. Taco Bell Corp.*, 256 F.3d 446 (6th Cir. 2001), *cert.* denied, 534 U.S. 1114, 122 S.Ct. 921, 151 L.Ed.2d 805 (2002)] **(See page 245.)**

9–5 Quasi Contract. Kim Panenka asked to borrow $4,750 from her sister, Kris, to make a mortgage payment. Kris deposited a check for that amount into Kim's bank account. Hours later, Kim asked to borrow another $1,100. Kris took a cash advance on her credit card and deposited this amount into Kim's account. When Kim did not repay Kris, the sister filed a suit, arguing that she had "loaned" Kim the money. Can the court impose a contract between the sisters? Explain. [*Panenka v. Panenka,* 331 Wis.2d 731, 795 N.W.2d 493 (2011)] **(See pages 248–249.)**

9–6 Interpretation of Contracts. Lisa and Darrell Miller had a son, Landon. When the Millers divorced, they entered into a "Joint Plan" (JP). Under the JP, Darrell agreed to "begin setting funds aside for Landon to attend college." After Landon's eighteenth birthday, Lisa asked a court to order Darrell to pay the boy's college expenses based on the JP. Darrell contended that the JP was not clear on this point. Do the rules of contract interpretation support Lisa's request or Darrell's contention? Explain. [*Miller v. Miller,* 1 So.3d 815 (La.App. 2009)] **(See pages 249–252.)**

9–7 Case Problem with Sample Answer—Quasi Contract. Robert Gutkowski, a sports marketing expert, met with George Steinbrenner, the owner of the New York Yankees, many times to discuss the Yankees Entertainment and Sports Network (YES). Gutkowski was paid as a consultant. Later, he filed a suit, seeking an ownership share in YES. There was no written contract for the share, but he claimed that there were discussions about him being a part owner. Does Gutkowski have a valid claim for payment? Discuss. [*Gutkowski v. Steinbrenner,* 680 F.Supp.2d 602 (S.D.N.Y. 2010)] **(See pages 248–249.)**

—For a sample answer to Problem 9–7, go to Appendix H at the end of this text.

9–8 A Question of Ethics—Unilateral Contracts. International Business Machines Corp. (IBM) hired Niels Jensen as a software sales representative. According to the brochure on IBM's "Sales Incentive Plan" (SIP), "the more you sell, the more earnings for you." But "the SIP program does not constitute a promise by IBM. IBM reserves the right to modify the program at any time." Jensen was given a "quota letter" that said he would be paid $75,000 as a base salary and, if he attained his quota, an additional $75,000 as incentive pay. Jensen closed a deal worth more than $24 million to IBM. When IBM paid him less than $500,000 as a commission, Jensen filed a suit. He argued that the SIP was a unilateral offer that became a binding contract when he closed the sale. [*Jensen v. International Business Machines Corp.*, 454 F.3d 382 (4th Cir. 2006)] **(See pages 243–244.)**

1. Would it be fair to the employer for the court to hold that the SIP brochure and the quota letter created a unilateral contract if IBM did not *intend* to create such a contract? Would it be fair to the employee to hold that *no* contract was created? Explain.
2. The "Sales Incentives" section of IBM's brochure included a clause providing that "management will decide if an adjustment to the payment is appropriate" when an employee closes a large transaction. Does this affect your answers to the above questions? From an ethical perspective, would it be fair to hold that a contract exists despite this statement? Explain.

Critical Thinking and Writing Assignments

9–9 Business Law Critical Thinking Group Assignment. Review the basic requirements for a valid contract listed at the beginning of this chapter. Now consider the relationship entered into when a student enrolls in a college or university.

1. One group should analyze and discuss whether a contract has been formed between the student and the college or university.
2. A second group should assume that there is a contract and explain whether it is bilateral or unilateral.

CHAPTE

(Khafizov Ivan Harisovich/Shutterstock.com)

Agreement in Traditional and E-Contracts

CHAPTER OUTLINE

- Agreement
- E-Contracts
- The Uniform Electronic Transactions Act

LEARNING OBJECTIVES

The five learning objectives below are designed to help improve your understanding of the chapter. After reading this chapter, you should be able to answer the following questions:

1. What elements are necessary for an effective offer? What are some examples of nonoffers?
2. In what circumstances will an offer be irrevocable?
3. What are the elements that are necessary for an effective acceptance?
4. How do shrink-wrap and click-on agreements differ from other contracts? How have traditional laws been applied to these agreements?
5. What is the Uniform Electronic Transactions Act? What are some of the major provisions of this act?

"It is necessity that makes laws."
—Voltaire, 1649–1778 (French intellectual and writer)

Voltaire's statement that it is "necessity that makes laws" is certainly true in regard to contracts. In Chapter 9, we pointed out that promises and agreements, and the knowledge that some of those promises and agreements will be legally enforced, are essential to civilized society. The homes we live in, the food we eat, the clothes we wear, and the cars we drive—all of these have been purchased through implicit or explicit contractual agreements. Contract law developed over time, through the common law tradition, to meet society's need to know with certainty what kinds of promises, or contracts, will be enforced and the point at which a valid and binding contract is formed.

For a contract to be valid and enforceable, the requirements listed in Chapter 9 must be met. In this chapter, we look closely at the first of these requirements, *agreement*. Agreement is required to form a contract, regardless of whether it is formed in the traditional way by exchanging paper documents or created online by exchanging electronic messages or documents, as many contracts are formed today. We discuss online offers and acceptances and examine some laws that have been created to apply to electronic contracts, or *e-contracts,* in the latter part of the chapter. Can a series of e-mails bind Amazon.com to a contract? You will see what the court had to say when you read the *Spotlight Case* on page 262.

Agreement

Agreement A mutual understanding or meeting of the minds between two or more individuals regarding the terms of a contract.

An essential element for contract formation is **agreement**—the parties must agree on the terms of the contract. Ordinarily, agreement is evidenced by two events: an *offer* and an *acceptance*. One party offers a certain bargain to another party, who then accepts that bargain.

Because words often fail to convey the precise meaning intended, the law of contracts generally adheres to the *objective theory of contracts,* as discussed in Chapter 9 on page 241. Under this theory, a party's words and conduct are held to mean whatever a reasonable person in the offeree's position would think they meant.

Requirements of the Offer

Offer A promise or commitment to perform or refrain from performing some specified act in the future.

An **offer** is a promise or commitment to perform or refrain from performing some specified act in the future. As discussed in Chapter 9, the party making an offer is called the *offeror,* and the party to whom the offer is made is called the *offeree.*

Three elements are necessary for an offer to be effective:

LEARNING OBJECTIVE 1
What elements are necessary for an effective offer? What are some examples of nonoffers?

1. There must be a serious, objective intention by the offeror.
2. The terms of the offer must be reasonably certain, or definite, so that the parties and the court can ascertain the terms of the contract.
3. The offer must be communicated to the offeree.

Once an effective offer has been made, the offeree's acceptance of that offer creates a legally binding contract (providing the other essential elements for a valid and enforceable contract are present).

Intention

The first requirement for an effective offer is a serious, objective intention on the part of the offeror. Intent is not determined by the *subjective* intentions, beliefs, or assumptions of the offeror. Rather, it is determined by what a reasonable person in the offeree's position would conclude the offeror's words and actions meant. Offers made in obvious anger, jest, or undue excitement do not meet the requirement of a serious, objective intent. Because these offers are not effective, an offeree's acceptance does not create an agreement.

EXAMPLE 10.1 You ride to school each day with Julio in his new automobile, which has a market value of $20,000. One cold morning, the car will not start. Julio yells in anger, "I'll sell this car to anyone for $500!" You drop $500 in his lap. A reasonable person, taking into consideration Julio's frustration and the obvious difference in value between the car's market price and the purchase price, would declare that Julio's offer was not made with serious and objective intent and that you do not have an agreement. ●

The concept of intention can be further clarified through an examination of the types of statements that are *not* offers. We look at these expressions and statements in the subsections that follow.

In the *Classic Case* presented next, the court considered whether an offer made "after a few drinks" met the serious-intent requirement.

Classic Case 10.1

Lucy v. Zehmer

Supreme Court of Appeals of Virginia,
196 Va. 493, 84 S.E.2d 516 (1954).

(dcwcreations/Shutterstock.com)

A farm that might be for sale.

FACTS W. O. Lucy and A. H. Zehmer had known each other for fifteen to twenty years. For some time, Lucy had been wanting to buy Zehmer's farm, but Zehmer had always said that he was not interested in selling. One night, Lucy stopped in to visit with the Zehmers at a restaurant they operated. Lucy said to Zehmer, "I bet you wouldn't take $50,000 for that place." Zehmer replied, "Yes, I would, too; you wouldn't give fifty." Throughout the evening, the conversation returned to the sale of the farm. All the while, the parties were drinking whiskey.

Eventually, Zehmer wrote up an agreement, on the back of a restaurant check, for the sale of the farm, and he asked his wife, Ida, to sign it—which she did. When Lucy brought an action in a Virginia state court to enforce the agreement, Zehmer argued that he had been "high as a Georgia pine" at the time and that the offer had been made in jest: "two doggoned drunks bluffing to see who could talk the biggest and say the most." Lucy claimed that he had not been intoxicated and did not think Zehmer had been, either, given the way Zehmer handled the transaction. The trial court ruled in favor of the Zehmers, and Lucy appealed.

ISSUE Did the agreement meet the serious-intent requirement despite the claim of intoxication?

DECISION Yes. The agreement to sell the farm was binding.

REASON The court held that the evidence given about the nature of the conversation, the appearance and completeness of the agreement, and the signing all tended to show that a serious business transaction, not a casual jest, was intended. The court had to look into the objective meaning of the Zehmers' words and acts: "An agreement or mutual assent is of course essential to a valid contract, but the law imputes to a person an intention corresponding to the reasonable meaning of his words and acts. If his words and acts, judged by a reasonable standard, manifest an intention to agree, it is immaterial what may be the real but unexpressed state of mind."

WHAT IF THE FACTS WERE DIFFERENT? *Suppose that the day after Lucy signed the agreement, he decided that he did not want the farm after all, and Zehmer sued Lucy to perform the contract. Would this change in the facts alter the court's decision that Lucy and Zehmer had created an enforceable contract? Why or why not?*

IMPACT OF THIS CASE ON TODAY'S LAW *This is a classic case in contract law because it so clearly illustrates the objective theory of contracts (see page 241) with respect to determining whether an offer was intended. Today, the courts continue to apply the objective theory of contracts and routinely cite the* Lucy v. Zehmer *decision as a significant precedent in this area.*

KNOW THIS

An opinion is not an offer and not a contract term. Goods or services can be "perfect" in one party's opinion and "poor" in another's.

Expressions of Opinion An expression of opinion is not an offer. It does not demonstrate an intention to enter into a binding agreement. **CASE EXAMPLE 10.2** Hawkins took his son to McGee, a physician, and asked McGee to operate on the son's hand. McGee said that the boy would be in the hospital three or four days and that the hand would *probably* heal a few days later. The son's hand did not heal for a month, but nonetheless the father did not win a suit for breach of contract. The court held that McGee did not make an offer to heal the son's hand in three or four days. He merely expressed an opinion as to when the hand would heal.[1] •

Statements of Future Intent A statement of an *intention* to do something in the future is not an offer. **EXAMPLE 10.3** If Samir says, "I *plan* to sell my stock in Novation, Inc., for $150 per share," no contract is created if John "accepts" and gives Samir $150 per share for the

1. *Hawkins v. McGee*, 84 N.H. 114, 146 A. 641 (1929).

stock. Samir has merely expressed his intention to enter into a future contract for the sale of the stock. If John accepts and hands over the $150 per share, no contract is formed, because a reasonable person would conclude that Samir was only *thinking about* selling his stock, not *promising* to sell it. ●

(alexskopje/Shutterstock.com)

When a contractor submits a bid proposal, is that proposal binding on the entity to whom the bid was addressed?

Preliminary Negotiations A request or invitation to negotiate is not an offer. It only expresses a willingness to discuss the possibility of entering into a contract. Examples are statements such as "Will you sell Forest Acres?" and "I wouldn't sell my car for less than $8,000." A reasonable person in the offeree's position would not conclude that such statements indicated an intention to enter into binding obligations.

Likewise, when the government and private firms need to have construction work done, they invite contractors to submit bids. The *invitation* to submit bids is not an offer, and a contractor does not bind the government or private firm by submitting a bid. (The bids that the contractors submit are offers, however, and the government or private firm can bind the contractor by accepting the bid.) For a discussion of some problems with programs designed to promote equal opportunity in government contracting, see this chapter's *Law, Diversity, and Business: Managerial Implications* feature on the facing page.

Advertisements, Catalogues, and Circulars In general, advertisements, catalogues, price lists, and circular letters (meant for the general public) are treated as invitations to negotiate, not as offers to form a contract.[2] This applies whether the ads and the like are in traditional media or online. **CASE EXAMPLE 10.4** An ad on *Science*NOW's Web site asked for "news tips." Erik Trell, a professor and physician, submitted a manuscript in which he claimed to have solved a famous mathematical problem. When *Science*NOW did not publish his solution, Trell filed a lawsuit for breach of contract. He claimed that *Science*NOW's ad was an offer, which he had accepted by submitting his manuscript. The court dismissed Trell's suit, holding that an ad is only an invitation for offers, and not an offer itself. Hence, responses to an ad are not acceptances—instead, the responses are the offers. Thus, Trell's submission of the manuscript for publication was the offer, which *Science*NOW did not accept.[3] ●

Price lists are another form of invitation to negotiate or trade. A seller's price list is not an offer to sell at that price. It merely invites the buyer to offer to buy at that price. In fact, the seller usually puts "prices subject to change" on the price list. Only in rare circumstances will a price quotation be construed as an offer.

Although most advertisements and the like are treated as invitations to negotiate, this does not mean that an advertisement can never be an offer. On some occasions, courts have construed advertisements to be offers because the ads contained definite terms that invited acceptance (such as an ad offering a reward for the return of a lost dog).

KNOW THIS

Advertisements are not binding, but they cannot be deceptive.

Agreements to Agree In the past, agreements to agree—that is, agreements to agree to the material terms of a contract at some future date—were not considered to be binding contracts. The modern view, however, is that agreements to agree may be enforceable agreements (contracts) if it is clear that the parties intended to be bound by the agreements. In other words, today the emphasis is on the parties' intent rather than on form.

CASE EXAMPLE 10.5 After a customer nearly drowned on a water ride at one of its amusement parks, Six Flags, Inc., filed a lawsuit against the manufacturer that had designed the ride. The manufacturer claimed that the parties did not have a binding contract but had only engaged in preliminary negotiations that were never formalized into a contract to

2. *Restatement (Second) of Contracts*, Section 26, Comment b.

3. *Trell v. American Association for the Advancement of Science*, 2007 WL 1500497 (W.D.N.Y. 2007).

LAW, DIVERSITY, AND BUSINESS: MANAGERIAL IMPLICATIONS

EQUAL OPPORTUNITY IN PUBLIC CONTRACTING

Cities and states put projects out for bids. Undoubtedly, there has been discrimination against minorities and female contractors in such bidding processes in the past. The city of San Francisco, California, along with other cities, such as Seattle, Washington, and Madison, Wisconsin, created a system to "make up" for such past discrimination.

San Francisco's Public Contracting Policy San Francisco has allowed its city government officials to treat bids from businesses owned by women or members of minority groups as though the bids were as much as 10 percent lower than bids from other businesses. Hence, if a bid from a minority-owned construction company was, say, $1 million, city officials could consider it to be only $900,000 when comparing it with bids from nonminority-owned businesses.

Proposition 209 Changes the Policy In 1996, the voters of California approved Proposition 209, known as the California Civil Rights Initiative. The proposition amended the state constitution to prohibit state government institutions from considering ethnicity, race, and gender in the areas of public contracting, public employment, and public education. Thus, San Francisco's preferential treatment of minority- and female-owned companies in public contracting was viewed as a violation of Proposition 209. When the California Supreme Court reviewed San Francisco's preferential bidding procedure, it ruled that the process was indeed a violation of the state constitution, as amended.[a]

Seattle, perhaps not wishing to be challenged in court, changed its preferential bidding system by replacing race and gender preferences with geographic preferences for "small" and "disadvantaged" businesses.

Business Implications *Without using preferential bidding, how might managers ensure that their bidding procedure is fair to all businesses, including those that may be suffering the effects of past discrimination?*

a. *Coral Construction, Inc. v. San Francisco*, 50 Cal.4th 315, 235 P.3d 947 (2010).

construct the ride. The court, however, held that a faxed document specifying the details of the ride, along with the parties' subsequent actions (beginning construction and handwriting notes on the fax), was sufficient to show an intent to be bound. Because of the court's finding, the manufacturer was required to provide insurance for the water ride at Six Flags, and its insurer was required to defend Six Flags in the personal-injury lawsuit that arose out of the incident.[4]

Preliminary Agreements Increasingly, the courts are holding that a preliminary agreement constitutes a binding contract if the parties have agreed on all essential terms and no disputed issues remain to be resolved.[5] In contrast, if the parties agree on certain major terms but leave other terms open for further negotiation, a preliminary agreement is binding only in the sense that the parties have committed themselves to negotiate the undecided terms in good faith in an effort to reach a final agreement.

In the following *Spotlight Case,* one party claimed that the agreement formed via e-mail was binding, and the other party claimed that it was merely an agreement to agree or to work out the terms of a settlement in the future.

4. *Six Flags, Inc. v. Steadfast Insurance Co.*, 474 F.Supp.2d 201 (D.Mass. 2007).

5. See, for example, *Tractebel Energy Marketing, Inc. v. AEP Power Marketing, Inc.*, 487 F.3d 89 (2d Cir. 2007); and *Barrand v. Whataburger, Inc.*, 214 S.W.3d 122 (Tex.App.—Corpus Christi 2006).

Spotlight on Amazon.com

Case 10.2

Basis Technology Corp. v. Amazon.com, Inc.

Appeals Court of Massachusetts, 71 Mass.App.Ct. 29, 878 N.E.2d 952 (2008).

(Koichi Kamoshida/Liaison/Getty Images)

Jeff Bezos, the founder and CEO of Amazon.com, with a Japanese manager.

FACTS Basis Technology Corporation created software and provided technical services for a Japanese-language Web site operated by Amazon.com, Inc. The agreement between the two companies allowed for separately negotiated contracts for additional services that Basis might provide to Amazon. At the end of 1999, Basis and Amazon entered into stock-purchase agreements. Later, Amazon objected to certain actions related to the securities that Basis sold. Basis sued Amazon for various claims involving these securities and for failing to pay for services performed by Basis that were not included in the original agreement. During the trial, the two parties appeared to reach an agreement to settle out of court via a series of e-mail exchanges outlining the settlement. When Amazon reneged, Basis served a motion to enforce the proposed settlement. The trial judge entered a judgment against Amazon, which appealed.

ISSUE Did the agreement that Amazon entered into with Basis via e-mail constitute a binding settlement contract?

DECISION Yes. The Appeals Court of Massachusetts affirmed the trial court's finding that Amazon intended to be bound by the terms of the e-mail exchanges.

REASON The court examined the evidence consisting of e-mails between the two parties. It pointed out that in open court and on the record, counsel "reported the result of the settlement without specification of the terms." Amazon claimed that the e-mail terms were incomplete and were not definite enough to form an agreement. The court noted, however, that "provisions are not ambiguous simply because the parties have developed different interpretations of them." In the exchange of e-mails, the essential business terms were indeed resolved. Afterward, the parties were simply proceeding to record the settlement terms, not to create them. The e-mails constituted a complete and unambiguous statement of the parties' desire to be bound by the settlement terms.

WHAT IF THE FACTS WERE DIFFERENT? *Assume that, instead of exchanging e-mails, the attorneys for both sides had a phone conversation that included all of the terms to which they actually agreed in their e-mail exchanges. Would the court have ruled differently? Why or why not?*

PREVENTING LEGAL DISPUTES

To avoid potential legal disputes, be cautious when drafting a memorandum that outlines a preliminary agreement or understanding with another party. If all the major terms are included, a court might hold that the agreement is binding even though you intended it to be only a tentative agreement. One way to avoid being bound is to include in the writing the points of disagreement, as well as those points on which you and the other party agree. Alternatively, you could add a disclaimer to the memorandum stating that, although you anticipate entering a contract in the future, neither party intends to be legally bound to the terms that were discussed. That way, the other party cannot claim that you have already reached an agreement on all essential terms.

Definiteness The second requirement for an effective offer involves the definiteness of its terms. An offer must have reasonably definite terms so that a court can determine if a breach has occurred and give an appropriate remedy.[6] The specific terms required depend, of course, on the type of contract. Generally, a contract must include the following terms, either expressed in the contract or capable of being reasonably inferred from it:

6. *Restatement (Second) of Contracts,* Section 33. The UCC has relaxed the requirements regarding the definiteness of terms in contracts for the sale of goods. See UCC 2–204(3).

"I fear explanations explanatory of things explained."

Abraham Lincoln, 1809–1865
(Sixteenth president of the United States, 1861–1865)

1. The identification of the parties.
2. The identification of the object or subject matter of the contract (also the quantity, when appropriate), including the work to be performed, with specific identification of such items as goods, services, and land.
3. The consideration to be paid.
4. The time of payment, delivery, or performance.

An offer may invite an acceptance to be worded in such specific terms that the contract is made definite. **EXAMPLE 10.6** Nintendo of America, Inc., contacts your Play 2 Win Games store and offers to sell "from one to twenty-five Nintendo 3DS gaming systems for $75 each. State number desired in acceptance." You agree to buy twenty systems. Because the quantity is specified in the acceptance, the terms are definite, and the contract is enforceable. •

Communication

A third requirement for an effective offer is communication—the offer must be communicated to the offeree. **EXAMPLE 10.7** Tolson advertises a reward for the return of her lost cat. Dirk, not knowing of the reward, finds the cat and returns it to Tolson. Ordinarily, Dirk cannot recover the reward because an essential element of a reward contract is that the one who claims the reward must have known it was offered. A few states would allow recovery of the reward, but not on contract principles—Dirk would be allowed to recover on the basis that it would be unfair to deny him the reward just because he did not know about it. •

Termination of the Offer

The communication of an effective offer to an offeree gives the offeree the power to transform the offer into a binding, legal obligation (a contract) by an acceptance. This power of acceptance does not continue forever, though. It can be terminated by either the *action of the parties* or by *operation of law.* Termination by the action of the parties can involve a revocation by the offeror or a rejection or counteroffer by the offeree.

Termination by Action of the Offeror

The offeror's act of withdrawing an offer is referred to as **revocation**. Unless an offer is irrevocable, the offeror usually can revoke the offer (even if he or she has promised to keep it open), as long as the revocation is communicated to the offeree before the offeree accepts. Revocation may be accomplished by an express repudiation of the offer (such as "I withdraw my previous offer of October 17") or by the performance of acts that are inconsistent with the existence of the offer and that are made known to the offeree.

Revocation The withdrawal of a contract offer by the offeror. Unless an offer is irrevocable, it can be revoked at any time prior to acceptance without liability.

EXAMPLE 10.8 Misha offers to sell some land to Gary. A month passes, and Gary, who has not accepted the offer, learns that Misha has sold the property to Liam. Because Misha's sale of the land to Liam is inconsistent with the continued existence of the offer to Gary, the offer to Gary is effectively revoked. •

The general rule followed by most states is that a revocation becomes effective when the offeree or the offeree's *agent* (a person who acts on behalf of another—see Chapter 23) actually receives it. Therefore, a statement of revocation sent via FedEx on April 1 and delivered at the offeree's residence or place of business on April 2 becomes effective on April 2.

Termination by Action of the Offeree

If the offeree rejects the offer—by words or by conduct—the offer is terminated. Any subsequent attempt by the offeree to accept will be construed as a new offer, giving the original offeror (now the offeree) the power of acceptance.

Like a revocation, a rejection of an offer is effective only when it is actually received by the offeror or the offeror's agent. **EXAMPLE 10.9** Goldfinch Farms offers to sell specialty

Maitake mushrooms to a Japanese buyer, Kinoko Foods. If Kinoko rejects the offer by sending a letter via U.S. mail, the rejection will not be effective (and the offer will not be terminated) until Goldfinch receives the letter. ●

KNOW THIS

The way in which a response to an offer is phrased can determine whether the offer is accepted or rejected.

Inquiries about an Offer Merely inquiring about an offer does not constitute rejection. **EXAMPLE 10.10** Your friend offers to buy your Inkling digital pen—which automatically remembers whatever is drawn with it on any kind of paper—for $100. You respond, "Is that your best offer?" A reasonable person would conclude that you have not rejected the offer but have merely made an inquiry. You could still accept and bind your friend to the $100 price. ●

Counteroffer An offeree's response to an offer in which the offeree rejects the original offer and at the same time makes a new offer.

Mirror Image Rule A common law rule that requires that the terms of the offeree's acceptance adhere exactly to the terms of the offeror's offer for a valid contract to be formed.

Counteroffers A **counteroffer** is a rejection of the original offer and the simultaneous making of a new offer. **EXAMPLE 10.11** Burke offers to sell his home to Lang for $270,000. Lang responds, "Your price is too high. I'll offer to purchase your house for $250,000." Lang's response is called a counteroffer because it rejects Burke's offer to sell at $270,000 and creates a new offer by Lang to purchase the home at a price of $250,000. ●

At common law, the **mirror image rule** requires that the offeree's acceptance match the offeror's offer exactly. In other words, the terms of the acceptance must "mirror" those of the offer. If the acceptance materially changes or adds to the terms of the original offer, it will be considered not an acceptance but a counteroffer— which, of course, need not be accepted. The original offeror can, however, accept the terms of the counteroffer and create a valid contract.[7]

Termination by Operation of Law

The power of the offeree to transform the offer into a binding, legal obligation can be terminated by operation of law through the occurrence of any of the following events:

1. Lapse of time.
2. Destruction of the specific subject matter of the offer.
3. Death or incompetence of the offeror or the offeree.
4. Supervening illegality of the proposed contract. (A statute or court decision that makes an offer illegal automatically terminates the offer.)

Lapse of Time An offer terminates automatically by law when the period of time *specified in the offer* has passed. If the offer states that it will be left open until a particular date, then the offer will terminate at midnight on that day. If the offer states that it will be left open for a number of days, this time period normally begins to run when the offer is actually *received* by the offeree, not when it is formed or sent.

If the offer does not specify a time for acceptance, the offer terminates at the end of a *reasonable* period of time. A reasonable period of time is determined by the subject matter of the contract, business and market conditions, and other relevant circumstances. An offer to sell farm produce, for instance, will terminate sooner than an offer to sell farm equipment because produce is perishable and subject to greater fluctuations in market value.

Destruction or Death An offer is automatically terminated if the specific subject matter of the offer (such as an iPad or a house) is destroyed before the offer is accepted. An offeree's power of acceptance is also terminated when the offeror or offeree dies or becomes legally incapacitated (capacity will be discussed in Chapter 11), *unless the offer is irrevocable.*

---

7. The mirror image rule has been greatly modified in regard to sales contracts. Section 2–207 of the UCC provides that a contract is formed if the offeree makes a definite expression of acceptance (such as signing the form in the appropriate location), even though the terms of the acceptance modify or add to the terms of the original offer (see Chapter 15).

LEARNING OBJECTIVE 2
In what circumstances will an offer be irrevocable?

Irrevocable Offers

Although most offers are revocable, some can be made irrevocable. Increasingly, courts refuse to allow an offeror to revoke an offer when the offeree has changed position because of justifiable reliance on the offer (under the doctrine of *promissory estoppel*—see Chapter 11). In some circumstances, "firm offers" made by merchants may also be considered irrevocable. We will discuss these offers in Chapter 15.

Option Contract A contract under which the offeror cannot revoke the offer for a stipulated time period (because the offeree has given consideration for the offer to remain open).

Another form of irrevocable offer is an option contract. An **option contract** is created when an offeror promises to hold an offer open for a specified period of time in return for a payment (consideration) given by the offeree. An option contract takes away the offeror's power to revoke an offer for the period of time specified in the option. If no time is specified, then a reasonable period of time is implied.

Option contracts are frequently used in conjunction with the sale of real estate. **EXAMPLE 10.12** Tyrell agrees to lease a house from Jackson, the property owner. The lease contract includes a clause stating that Tyrell is paying an additional $15,000 for an option to purchase the property within a specified period of time. If Tyrell decides not to purchase the house after the specified period has lapsed, he loses the $15,000, and Jackson is free to sell the property to another buyer. ●

Acceptance

Acceptance The act of voluntarily agreeing, through words or conduct, to the terms of an offer, thereby creating a contract.

An **acceptance** is a voluntary act by the offeree that shows assent, or agreement, to the terms of an offer. The offeree's act may consist of words or conduct. The acceptance must be unequivocal and must be communicated to the offeror. Generally, only the person to whom the offer is made or that person's agent can accept the offer and create a binding contract.

LEARNING OBJECTIVE 3
What are the elements that are necessary for an effective acceptance?

Unequivocal Acceptance

To exercise the power of acceptance effectively, the offeree must accept unequivocally. This is the *mirror image rule* previously discussed. If the acceptance is subject to new conditions or if the terms of the acceptance materially change the original offer, the acceptance may be deemed a counteroffer that implicitly rejects the original offer.

When an offer is rejected, it is terminated.

Certain terms included in an acceptance will not change the offer sufficiently to constitute rejection. **EXAMPLE 10.13** In response to an art dealer's offer to sell a painting, the offeree, Ashton Gibbs, replies, "I accept. Please send a written contract." Gibbs is requesting a written contract but is not making it a condition for acceptance. Therefore, the acceptance is effective without the written contract. In contrast, if Gibbs replies, "I accept *if* you send a written contract," the acceptance is expressly conditioned on the request for a writing, and the statement is not an acceptance but a counteroffer. (Notice how important each word is!)[8] ●

Silence as Acceptance

Ordinarily, silence cannot constitute acceptance, even if the offeror states, "By your silence and inaction, you will be deemed to have accepted this offer." This general rule applies because an offeree should not be put under a burden of liability to act affirmatively in order to reject an offer. No consideration—that is, nothing of value (see Chapter 11)—has passed to the offeree to impose such a liability.

In some instances, however, the offeree does have a duty to speak. If so, his or her silence or inaction will operate as an acceptance. Silence may be an acceptance when an offeree takes the benefit of offered services even though he or she had an opportunity to reject them and knew that they were offered with the expectation of compensation.

8. As noted in footnote 7, in regard to sales contracts, the UCC provides that an acceptance may still be effective even if some terms are added. The new terms are simply treated as proposals for additions to the contract, unless both parties are merchants. If the parties are merchants, the additional terms (with some exceptions) become part of the contract [UCC 2–207(2)].

EXAMPLE 10.14 Juan earns extra income by washing store windows. Juan taps on the window of a store, catches the attention of the store's manager, and points to the window and raises his cleaner, signaling that he will be washing the window. The manager does nothing to stop him. Here, the store manager's silence constitutes an acceptance, and an implied contract is created. The store is bound to pay a reasonable value for Juan's work. •

Silence can also operate as an acceptance when the offeree has had prior dealings with the offeror. If a merchant, for instance, routinely receives shipments from a supplier and in the past has always notified the supplier when defective goods are rejected, then silence constitutes acceptance. Also, if a buyer solicits an offer specifying that certain terms and conditions are acceptable, and the seller makes the offer in response to the solicitation, the buyer has a duty to reject—that is, a duty to tell the seller that the offer is not acceptable. Failure to reject (silence) will operate as an acceptance.

KNOW THIS

A bilateral contract is a promise for a promise, and a unilateral contract is performance for a promise.

Communication of Acceptance

In a bilateral contract, communication of acceptance is necessary because acceptance is in the form of a promise (not performance), and the contract is formed when the promise is made (rather than when the act is performed). Communication of acceptance is not necessary if the offer dispenses with the requirement, however, or if the offer can be accepted by silence.[9]

Because a unilateral contract calls for the full performance of some act, acceptance is usually evident, and notification is unnecessary. Nevertheless, exceptions do exist, such as when the offeror requests notice of acceptance or has no way of determining whether the requested act has been performed.

In the following case, the court had to decide whether a party's failure to respond to a settlement offer constituted acceptance.

9. Under UCC 2–206(1)(b), an order or other offer to buy goods that are to be promptly shipped may be treated as either a bilateral or a unilateral offer and can be accepted by a promise to ship or by actual shipment.

Case 10.3

Powerhouse Custom Homes, Inc. v. 84 Lumber Co.

Court of Appeals of Georgia, 307 Ga.App. 605, 705 S.E.2d 704 (2011).

(gmnicholas/iStockphoto.com)

A custom home being built.

FACTS Powerhouse Custom Homes, Inc., entered into a credit agreement with 84 Lumber Company under which Powerhouse owed $95,260.42. When Powerhouse failed to pay, 84 Lumber filed a suit to collect. During mediation, the parties agreed to a deadline for objections to whatever agreement they might reach. If there was no objection, the agreement would be binding. Powerhouse then offered to pay less than the amount owed, and 84 Lumber did not respond. Powerhouse argued that 84 Lumber accepted the offer by not objecting to it within the deadline.

ISSUE Did 84 Lumber, by its failure to object to Powerhouse's proposal to settle the debt for less than was owed, unequivocally accept the offer?

DECISION No. The court held that for a contract to be formed, an offer must be accepted unequivocally. Without such an acceptance, there is no enforceable contract.

REASON Powerhouse made an offer of a proposed settlement, but 84 Lumber did not communicate its acceptance. Thus, the court reasoned that the parties did not reach an agreement. Because 84 Lumber had not agreed to Powerhouse's proposal, the ten-day deadline did not apply. Powerhouse was liable for the entire debt, plus interest, attorneys' fees, and costs.

CRITICAL THINKING—Economic Consideration *Why do judgments often include awards of interest, attorneys' fees, and costs?*

Mode and Timeliness of Acceptance

Acceptance in bilateral contracts must be timely. The general rule is that acceptance in a bilateral contract is timely if it is made before the offer is terminated. Problems may arise, though, when the parties involved are not dealing face to face. In such situations, the offeree should use an authorized mode of communication.

Mailbox Rule A common law rule that acceptance takes effect, and thus completes formation of the contract, at the time the offeree sends or delivers the acceptance via the communication mode expressly or impliedly authorized by the offeror.

The Mailbox Rule Acceptance takes effect, and thus completes formation of the contract, at the time the offeree sends or delivers the acceptance via the mode of communication expressly or impliedly authorized by the offeror. This is the so-called **mailbox rule,** also called the *deposited acceptance rule,* which the majority of courts follow. Under this rule, if the authorized mode of communication is the mail, then an acceptance becomes valid when it is dispatched (placed in the control of the U.S. Postal Service)—not when it is received by the offeror.

The mailbox rule does not apply to instantaneous forms of communication, such as when the parties are dealing face to face, by phone, by fax, and usually by e-mail. Under the Uniform Electronic Transactions Act (UETA—see page 273 later in this chapter), e-mail is considered sent when it either leaves the sender's control or is received by the recipient. This rule, which takes the place of the mailbox rule if the parties have agreed to conduct transactions electronically, allows an e-mail acceptance to become effective when sent.

Authorized Means of Communication A means of communicating acceptance can be expressly authorized by the offeror or impliedly authorized by the facts and circumstances of the situation. An acceptance sent by means not expressly or impliedly authorized normally is not effective until it is received by the offeror.

When an offeror specifies how acceptance should be made, such as by overnight delivery, the contract is not formed unless the offeree uses that mode of acceptance. Both the offeror and the offeree are bound in contract the moment the specified means of acceptance is employed. **EXAMPLE 10.15** Motorola Mobility, Inc., offers to sell 144 Atrix 4G smartphones and 72 Lapdocks to Call Me Plus phone stores. The offer states that Call Me Plus must accept the offer via FedEx overnight delivery. The acceptance is effective (and a binding contract is formed) the moment that Call Me Plus gives the overnight envelope containing the acceptance to the FedEx driver. •

If the offeror does not expressly authorize a certain mode of acceptance, then acceptance can be made by *any reasonable means.*[10] Courts look at the prevailing business usages and the surrounding circumstances to determine whether the mode of acceptance used was reasonable. Usually, the offeror's choice of a particular means in making the offer implies that the offeree can use the *same or a faster* means for acceptance. **EXAMPLE 10.16** If the offer is made via Priority U.S. mail, it would be reasonable to accept the offer via Priority mail or by a faster method, such as e-mail, fax, or overnight delivery. •

Substitute Method of Acceptance If the offeror authorizes a particular method of acceptance, but the offeree accepts by a different means, the acceptance may still be effective if the substituted method serves the same purpose as the authorized means. The use of a substitute method of acceptance is not effective on dispatch, though, and no contract will be formed until the acceptance is received by the offeror. Thus, if an offer specifies FedEx overnight delivery but the offeree accepts by overnight delivery from another carrier, such as UPS, the acceptance will still be effective, but not until the offeror receives it.

---

10. Note that UCC 2–206(1)(a) states specifically that an acceptance of an offer for the sale of goods can be made by any medium that is *reasonable* under the circumstances.

E-Contracts

E-Contract A contract that is formed electronically.

Numerous contracts are formed online. Electronic contracts, or **e-contracts,** must meet the same basic requirements (agreement, consideration, contractual capacity, and legality) as paper contracts. Disputes concerning e-contracts, however, tend to center on contract terms and whether the parties voluntarily agreed to those terms.

Online contracts may be formed not only for the sale of goods and services but also for *licensing.* The "sale" of software generally involves a license, or a right to use the software, rather than the passage of title (ownership rights) from the seller to the buyer. **EXAMPLE 10.17** Galynn wants to obtain software that will allow her to work on spreadsheets on her BlackBerry. She goes online and purchases GridMagic. During the transaction, she has to click on several on-screen "I agree" boxes to indicate that she understands that she is purchasing only the right to use the software and will not obtain any ownership rights. After she agrees to these terms (the licensing agreement), she can download the software. •

As you read through the following subsections, keep in mind that although we typically refer to the offeror and the offeree as a *seller* and a *buyer,* in many online transactions these parties would be more accurately described as a *licensor* and a *licensee.*

Online Offers

Sellers doing business via the Internet can protect themselves against contract disputes and legal liability by creating offers that clearly spell out the terms that will govern their transactions if the offers are accepted. All important terms should be conspicuous and easy to view.

Displaying the Offer

The seller's Web site should include a hypertext link to a page containing the full contract so that potential buyers are made aware of the terms to which they are assenting. The contract generally must be displayed online in a readable format such as in a twelve-point typeface.

All provisions should be reasonably clear. **EXAMPLE 10.18** Netquip sells a variety of heavy equipment, such as trucks and trailers, online at its Web site. Because Netquip's pricing schedule is very complex, the schedule must be fully provided and explained on the Web site. In addition, the terms of the sale (such as any warranties and the refund policy) must be fully disclosed. •

"If two men agree on everything, you can be sure one of them is doing the thinking."

Lyndon Baines Johnson, 1908–1973 (Thirty-sixth president of the United States, 1963–1969)

Provisions to Include

An important rule to keep in mind is that the offeror (seller) controls the offer and thus the resulting contract. The seller should therefore anticipate the terms she or he wants to include in a contract and provide for them in the offer. In some instances, a standardized contract form may suffice. At a minimum, an online offer should include the following provisions:

1. *Acceptance of terms.* A clause that clearly indicates what constitutes the buyer's agreement to the terms of the offer, such as a box containing the words "I accept" that the buyer can click on to indicate acceptance. (Mechanisms for accepting online offers will be discussed in detail later in this chapter.)
2. *Payment.* A provision specifying how payment for the goods (including any applicable taxes) must be made.
3. *Return policy.* A statement of the seller's refund and return policies.
4. *Disclaimer.* Disclaimers of liability for certain uses of the goods. For example, an online seller of business forms may add a disclaimer that the seller does not accept responsibility for the buyer's reliance on the forms rather than on an attorney's advice.

5. *Limitation on remedies.* A provision specifying the remedies available to the buyer if the goods are found to be defective or if the contract is otherwise breached. Any limitation of remedies should be clearly spelled out.
6. *Privacy policy.* A statement indicating how the seller will use the information gathered about the buyer. (See the *Linking Business Law to Marketing* feature on page 276 for a discussion of how the information may be used.)
7. *Dispute resolution.* Provisions relating to dispute settlement, such as an arbitration clause.

Dispute-Settlement Provisions Online offers frequently include provisions relating to dispute settlement. For example, the offer might include an arbitration clause specifying that any dispute arising under the contract will be arbitrated in a designated forum. (For a discussion of how students enrolling in online education courses may agree to arbitration of any future disputes, see this chapter's *Adapting the Law to the Online Environment* below.)

ADAPTING THE LAW TO THE ONLINE ENVIRONMENT

THE VALIDITY OF E-SIGNATURES ON AGREEMENTS WITH ONLINE COLLEGES AND UNIVERSITIES

The number of online institutions offering bachelor's, master's, and even doctorate degrees has grown dramatically over the past decade. The enrollment procedures for these online colleges and universities are conducted online. Most, if not all, of these schools ask enrolling students to agree that any disputes will be solved by arbitration. How valid are these enrollment agreements when the students simply indicate their assent via what the online universities call e-signatures?

At Least Two Online Students Claimed That Their E-Signatures Were Invalid

Scott Rosendahl alleged that online Ashford University's enrollment adviser misleadingly claimed that Ashford offered one of the cheapest undergraduate degree programs in the country. In fact, it did not. Veronica Clarke enrolled in the doctor of psychology program at the online University of the Rockies. She alleged that its enrollment adviser told her that the doctor of psychology program would qualify her to become a clinical psychologist in the U.S. military, but that statement was false.

Rosendahl and Clarke sued their respective universities for violation of unfair competition laws and false advertising laws, fraud, and negligent misrepresentation.

The Online Universities Argued for Arbitration

The universities pointed out that each student electronically agreed to the enrollment agreement that clearly contained a requirement that all disputes be arbitrated. Each agreement stated, "Such arbitration shall be the sole remedy for the resolution of any dispute or controversies between the parties to this agreement."

One issue was whether the e-signatures on the agreement were valid. Each application form had an "acknowledgment and signature" paragraph that stated, "My signature on this application certifies that I have read, understood, and agreed to my rights and responsibilities as set forth in this application."

Both students had to click on an electronic box acknowledging that they had read the agreement and consented to it. When they clicked on the box, the phrase "Signed by E-Signature" appeared on the signature line.

The Court Ruled in Favor of the Online Universities

The universities submitted copies of Rosendahl's and Clarke's online application forms to the court. Both forms contained the arbitration agreement and were signed with e-signatures. Rosendahl and Clarke provided no proof that they did not consent to the enrollment agreements. Thus, the court held that the online universities had proved the existence of valid arbitration agreements.[a]

Critical Thinking

Did the fact that the arbitration agreements were valid prevent Rosendahl and Clarke from pursuing their claims for negligent misrepresentation and fraud? Why or why not?

---

a. *Rosendahl v. Bridgepoint Education, Inc.*, 2012 WL 667049 (S.D.Cal. 2012).

Many online contracts also contain a *forum-selection clause* (see page 221 in Chapter 8) indicating the forum, or location (such as a court or jurisdiction), for the resolution of any dispute arising under the contract. As discussed in Chapter 3 on page 68, significant jurisdictional issues may occur when parties are at a great distance, as they often are when they form contracts via the Internet. A forum-selection clause will help to avert future jurisdictional problems and also help to ensure that the seller will not be required to appear in court in a distant state.

Some online contracts may also include a *choice-of-law clause* specifying that any dispute arising out of the contract will be settled in accordance with the law of a particular jurisdiction, such as a state or country. Choice-of-law clauses are particularly common in international contracts, but they may also appear in e-contracts to specify which state's laws will govern in the United States.

Online Acceptances

The *Restatement (Second) of Contracts*—a compilation of common law contract principles—states that parties may agree to a contract "by written or spoken words or by other action or by failure to act."[11] The Uniform Commercial Code (UCC), which governs sales contracts, has a similar provision. Section 2–204 of the UCC states that any contract for the sale of goods "may be made in any manner sufficient to show agreement, including conduct by both parties which recognizes the existence of such a contract."

Click-On Agreement An agreement that arises when an online buyer clicks on "I agree," or otherwise indicates her or his assent to be bound by the terms of an offer.

Click-On Agreements

The courts have used these provisions to conclude that a binding contract can be created by conduct, including the act of clicking on a box indicating "I accept" or "I agree" to accept an online offer. The agreement resulting from such an acceptance is often called a **click-on agreement** (sometimes, *click-on license* or *click-wrap agreement*). Exhibit 10.1 on the facing page shows a portion of a click-on agreement that accompanies a software package.

Generally, the law does not require that the parties have read all of the terms in a contract for it to be effective. Therefore, clicking on a box that states "I agree" to certain terms can be enough. The terms may be contained on a Web site through which the buyer is obtaining goods or services, or they may appear on a computer screen when software is loaded from a CD-ROM or DVD or downloaded from the Internet.

LEARNING OBJECTIVE 4
How do shrink-wrap and click-on agreements differ from other contracts? How have traditional laws been applied to these agreements?

CASE EXAMPLE 10.19 Facebook, Inc., is headquartered in California. The "Terms of Use" that govern Facebook users' accounts include a forum-selection clause that provides for the resolution of all disputes in a court in Santa Clara County. Potential Facebook users cannot become actual users unless they click on an acknowledgment that they have agreed to this term. Mustafa Fteja was an active user of facebook.com when his account was disabled. He sued Facebook in a federal court in New York, claiming that it had disabled his Facebook page without justification and for discriminatory reasons. Facebook filed a motion to transfer the case to California under the forum-selection clause. The court found that the forum-selection clause in Facebook's online contract was binding and transferred the case. Fteja had been informed of the consequences of his click—he would be bound to the forum-selection clause. When he clicked on the button and became a Facebook user, he agreed to resolve all disputes with Facebook in Santa Clara County, California.[12] •

Shrink-Wrap Agreement An agreement whose terms are expressed in a document located inside a box in which goods (usually software) are packaged.

Shrink-Wrap Agreements

A **shrink-wrap agreement** (or *shrink-wrap license*) is an agreement whose terms are expressed inside a box in which the goods are packaged. (The term *shrink-wrap* refers to the plastic that covers the box.) Usually, the party who opens the box is told that she or he agrees to the terms by keeping whatever is in the box. Similarly, when the purchaser opens a software package, he or she agrees to abide by the terms of the limited license agreement.

---

11. *Restatement (Second) of Contracts,* Section 19.
12. *Fteja v. Facebook, Inc.,* 841 F.Supp.2d 829 (S.D.N.Y. 2012).

Exhibit 10.1 A Click-On Agreement

This exhibit illustrates an online offer to form a contract. To accept the offer, the user simply scrolls down the page and clicks on the "I Accept" button.

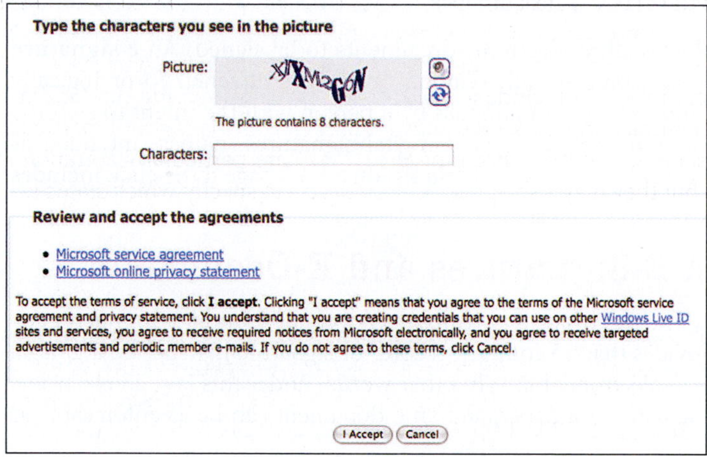

Type the characters you see in the picture

Picture: XJXM2G6N

The picture contains 8 characters.

Characters:

Review and accept the agreements

- Microsoft service agreement
- Microsoft online privacy statement

To accept the terms of service, click **I accept**. Clicking "I accept" means that you agree to the terms of the Microsoft service agreement and privacy statement. You understand that you are creating credentials that you can use on other Windows Live ID sites and services, you agree to receive required notices from Microsoft electronically, and you agree to receive targeted advertisements and periodic member e-mails. If you do not agree to these terms, click Cancel.

I Accept | Cancel

EXAMPLE 10.20 Arial orders a new iMac from Big Dog Electronics, which ships it to her. Along with the iMac, the box contains an agreement setting forth the terms of the sale, including what remedies are available. The document also states that Arial's retention of the iMac for longer than thirty days will be construed as an acceptance of the terms. ●

In most instances, a shrink-wrap agreement is not between a retailer and a buyer, but between the manufacturer of the hardware or software and the ultimate buyer-user of the product. The terms generally concern warranties, remedies, and other issues associated with the use of the product.

Shrink-Wrap Agreements and Enforceable Contract Terms In some cases, the courts have enforced the terms of shrink-wrap agreements in the same way as the terms of other contracts. These courts have reasoned that by including the terms with the product, the seller proposed a contract that the buyer could accept by using the product after having an opportunity to read the terms. Thus, a buyer's failure to object to terms contained within a shrink-wrapped software package may constitute an acceptance of the terms by conduct.

Shrink-Wrap Terms That May Not Be Enforced Sometimes, however, courts have refused to enforce certain terms included in shrink-wrap agreements because the buyer did not expressly consent to them. An important factor is when the parties form their contract.

Suppose that a buyer orders a product over the telephone. If the contract is formed at that time and the seller does not mention terms such as an arbitration clause or forum-selection clause, clearly the buyer has not expressly agreed to these terms. If the clauses are then included in the shrink-wrap agreement, a court may conclude that those terms were only proposals for additional terms, and not part of the original contract. After all, the buyer did not discover them until *after* the contract was formed.

ETHICAL ISSUE

Is it fair to enforce shrink-wrap and click-wrap terms that buyers were not aware of at the time they agreed to a purchase? Most people realize that if they sign a written contract without reading it, they can be held to its terms. But are most people aware that they can be legally bound by a whole host of conditions included in the packaging of electronics or software, not to mention the music, movies, and software they download from the Web? Simply by buying and keeping the latest electronic gadgets, we enter into binding contracts with the manufacturers that include rather one-sided terms. The terms may be unfair, but the law says we are bound. For instance, just by installing or downloading certain software today, users routinely agree to allow the companies to install tracking software on their computers.

Moreover, many software programs—including some that are designed to combat *malware* (see Chapter 6 on page 182)—automatically delete files from the users' hard drives. Consumers and businesspersons are often unaware of these consequences, and yet by buying and installing the software, they have agreed that they will not hold the manufacturer liable.

Browse-Wrap Term A term or condition of use that is presented when an online buyer downloads a product but the buyer does not have to agree to before installing or using the product.

Browse-Wrap Terms

Like the terms of a click-on agreement, **browse-wrap terms** can occur in a transaction conducted over the Internet. Unlike a click-on agreement, however, browse-wrap terms do not require the buyer or user to assent to the terms before, say, downloading or using certain software. In other words, a person can install the software without clicking "I agree" to the terms of a license. Browse-wrap terms are often unenforceable because they do not satisfy the agreement requirement of contract formation.[13]

E-Signature Technologies

E-Signature An electronic sound, symbol, or process attached to or logically associated with a record and adopted by a person with the intent to sign the record.

Today, numerous technologies allow electronic documents to be signed. An **e-signature** has been defined as "an electronic sound, symbol, or process attached to or logically associated with a record and executed or adopted by a person with the intent to sign the record."[14] Thus, e-signatures include encrypted digital signatures, names (intended as signatures) at the ends of e-mail messages, and "clicks" on a Web page if the click includes the identification of the person.

Federal Law on E-Signatures and E-Documents

In 2000, Congress enacted the Electronic Signatures in Global and National Commerce Act (E-SIGN Act),[15] which provides that no contract, record, or signature may be "denied legal effect" solely because it is in electronic form. In other words, under this law, an electronic signature is as valid as a signature on paper, and an e-document can be as enforceable as a paper one.

(Terry Davis/Shutterstock.com)

Many e-signatures are legally binding today.

For an e-signature to be enforceable, the contracting parties must have agreed to use electronic signatures. For an electronic document to be valid, it must be in a form that can be retained and accurately reproduced.

The E-SIGN Act does not apply to all types of documents, however. Contracts and documents that are exempt include court papers, divorce decrees, evictions, foreclosures, health-insurance terminations, prenuptial agreements, and wills. Also, the only agreements governed by the UCC that fall under this law are those covered by Articles 2 and 2A and UCC 1–107 and 1–206. Despite these limitations, the E-SIGN Act significantly expanded the possibilities for contracting online.

Partnering Agreements

Partnering Agreement An agreement between a seller and a buyer who frequently do business with each other concerning the terms and conditions that will apply to all subsequently formed electronic contracts.

One way that online sellers and buyers can prevent disputes over signatures in their e-contracts, as well as disputes over the terms and conditions of those contracts, is to form partnering agreements. In a **partnering agreement,** a seller and a buyer who frequently do business with each other agree in advance on the terms and conditions that will apply to all transactions subsequently conducted electronically. The partnering agreement can also establish special access and identification codes to be used by the parties when transacting business electronically.

A partnering agreement reduces the likelihood that disputes will arise under the contract because the buyer and the seller have agreed in advance to the terms and conditions that will accompany each sale. Furthermore, if a dispute does arise, a court or arbitration forum will be able to refer to the partnering agreement when determining the parties' intent.

The Uniform Electronic Transactions Act

Although most states have laws governing e-signatures and other aspects of electronic transactions, these laws are far from uniform. In an attempt to create more uniformity among the states, in 1999 the National Conference of Commissioners on Uniform State

13. See, for example, *Jesmer v. Retail Magic, Inc.,* 863 N.Y.S.2d 737 (2008).
14. This definition is from the Uniform Electronic Transactions Act on page 273.
15. 15 U.S.C. Sections 7001 *et seq.*

Record Information that is either inscribed on a tangible medium or stored in an electronic or other medium and is retrievable.

Laws and the American Law Institute promulgated the Uniform Electronic Transactions Act (UETA). The UETA has been adopted, at least in part, by forty-eight states.

The primary purpose of the UETA is to remove barriers to e-commerce by giving the same legal effect to electronic records and signatures as is given to paper documents and signatures. As mentioned earlier, the UETA broadly defines an *e-signature* as "an electronic sound, symbol, or process attached to or logically associated with a record and executed or adopted by a person with the intent to sign the record."[16] A **record** is "information that is inscribed on a tangible medium or that is stored in an electronic or other medium and is retrievable in perceivable [visual] form."[17]

The Scope and Applicability of the UETA

LEARNING OBJECTIVE 5

What is the Uniform Electronic Transactions Act? What are some of the major provisions of this act?

The UETA does not create new rules for electronic contracts but rather establishes that records, signatures, and contracts may not be denied enforceability solely due to their electronic form. The UETA does not apply to all writings and signatures. It covers only electronic records and electronic signatures *relating to a transaction.* A *transaction* is defined as an interaction between two or more parties relating to business, commercial, or governmental activities.[18]

The act specifically does not apply to wills or testamentary trusts or to transactions governed by the UCC (other than those covered by Articles 2 and 2A).[19] In addition, the provisions of the UETA allow the states to exclude its application to other areas of law.

The Federal E-SIGN Act and the UETA

When Congress passed the E-SIGN Act in 2000, a year after the UETA was presented to the states for adoption, a significant issue was to what extent the federal E-SIGN Act preempted the UETA as adopted by the states. The E-SIGN Act[20] refers explicitly to the UETA and provides that if a state has enacted the uniform version of the UETA, it is not preempted by the E-SIGN Act. In other words, if the state has enacted the UETA without modification, state law will govern.

The problem is that many states have enacted nonuniform (modified) versions of the UETA, largely for the purpose of excluding other areas of state law from the UETA's terms. The E-SIGN Act specifies that those exclusions will be preempted to the extent that they are inconsistent with the E-SIGN Act's provisions.

The E-SIGN Act, however, explicitly allows the states to enact alternative requirements for the use of electronic records or electronic signatures. Generally, however, the requirements must be consistent with the provisions of the E-SIGN Act, and the state must not give greater legal status or effect to one specific type of technology. Additionally, if a state enacts alternative requirements *after* the E-SIGN Act was adopted, the state law must specifically refer to the E-SIGN Act.

The relationship between the E-SIGN Act and the UETA is illustrated in Exhibit 10.2 on the following page.

Highlights of the UETA

The UETA will not apply to a transaction unless each of the parties has previously agreed to conduct transactions by electronic means. The agreement need not be explicit, however, and it may be implied by the conduct of the parties and the surrounding circumstances.[21]

16. UETA 102(8).
17. UETA 102(15).
18. UETA 2(12) and 3.
19. UETA 3(b).
20. 15 U.S.C. Section 7002(2)(A)(i).
21. UETA 5(b).

Exhibit 10.2 The E-SIGN Act and the UETA

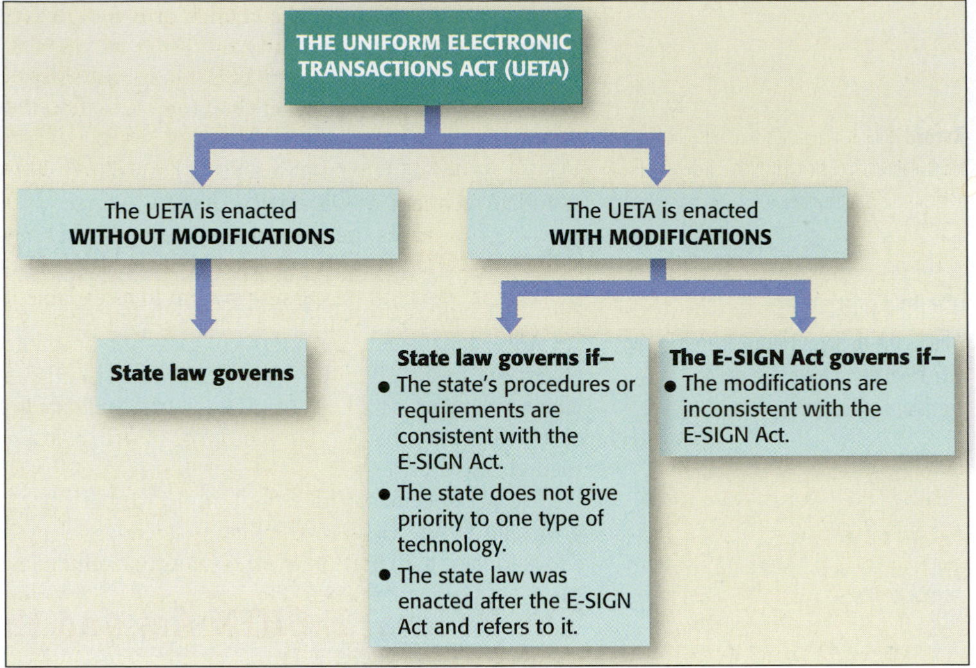

It may be reasonable to infer that a person who gives out a business card with an e-mail address on it has consented to transact business electronically.[22] The party's agreement may also be inferred from a letter or other writing, as well as from some verbal communication. A person who has previously agreed to an electronic transaction can also withdraw his or her consent and refuse to conduct further business electronically.

Attribution Under the UETA, if an electronic record or signature is the act of a particular person, the record or signature may be attributed to that person. If a person types her or his name at the bottom of an e-mail purchase order, that name will qualify as a "signature" and be attributed to the person whose name appears. In some contexts, a record may have legal effect even if no one has signed it. **EXAMPLE 10.21** J. P. Darby sends a fax to Corina Scott. The fax contains a letterhead identifying Darby as the sender, but Darby's signature does not appear on the faxed document. Depending on the circumstances, the fax may be attributed to Darby. •

Authorized Signatures The UETA does not contain any express provisions about what constitutes fraud or whether an agent is authorized to enter a contract. Under the UETA, other state laws control if any issues relating to agency, authority, forgery, or contract formation arise. If existing state law requires a document to be notarized, the UETA provides that this requirement is satisfied by the electronic signature of a notary public or other person authorized to verify signatures.

The Effect of Errors The UETA encourages, but does not require, the use of security procedures (such as encryption) to verify changes to electronic documents and to

22. UETA 5, Comment 4B.

correct errors. If the parties have agreed to a security procedure and one party does not detect an error because he or she did not follow the procedure, the conforming party can legally avoid the effect of the change or error. To avoid the effect of errors, a party must promptly notify the other party of the error and of her or his intent not to be bound by the error. In addition, the party must take reasonable steps to return any benefit received. Parties cannot avoid a transaction if they have benefited.

Timing An electronic record is considered *sent* when it is properly directed to the intended recipient in a form readable by the recipient's computer system. Once the electronic record leaves the control of the sender or comes under the control of the recipient, the UETA deems it to have been sent. An electronic record is considered *received* when it enters the recipient's processing system in a readable form—*even if no individual is aware of its receipt.*

Reviewing . . . Agreement in Traditional and E-Contracts

Ted and Betty Hyatt live in California, a state that has extensive statutory protection for consumers. The Hyatts decided to buy a computer so that they could use e-mail to stay in touch with their grandchildren, who live in another state. Over the phone, they ordered a computer from CompuEdge, Inc. When the box arrived, it was sealed with a brightly colored sticker warning that the terms enclosed within the box would govern the sale unless the customer returned the computer within thirty days. Among those terms was a clause that required any disputes to be resolved in Tennessee state courts. The Hyatts then signed up for Internet service through CyberTool, an Internet service provider. They downloaded CyberTool's software and clicked on the "quick install" box that allowed them to bypass CyberTool's "Terms of Service" page. It was possible to read this page by scrolling to the next screen, but the Hyatts did not realize this. The terms included a clause stating that all disputes were to be submitted to a Virginia state court. As soon as the Hyatts attempted to e-mail their grandchildren, they experienced problems using CyberTool's e-mail service, which continually stated that the network was busy. They also were unable to receive the photos sent by their grandchildren. Using the information presented in the chapter, answer the following questions.

1. Did the Hyatts accept the list of contract terms included in the computer box? Why or why not? What is this type of e-contract called?
2. What type of agreement did the Hyatts form with CyberTool?
3. Suppose that the Hyatts experienced trouble with the computer's components after they had used the computer for two months. What factors will a court consider in deciding whether to enforce the forum-selection clause? Would a court be likely to enforce the clause in this contract? Why or why not?
4. Are the Hyatts bound by the contract terms specified on CyberTool's "Terms of Service" page that they did not read? Which of the required elements for contract formation might the Hyatts claim were lacking? How might a court rule on this issue?

DEBATE THIS The terms and conditions in click-on agreements are so long and detailed that no one ever reads the agreement. Therefore, the act of clicking on "Yes, I agree" is not really an acceptance.

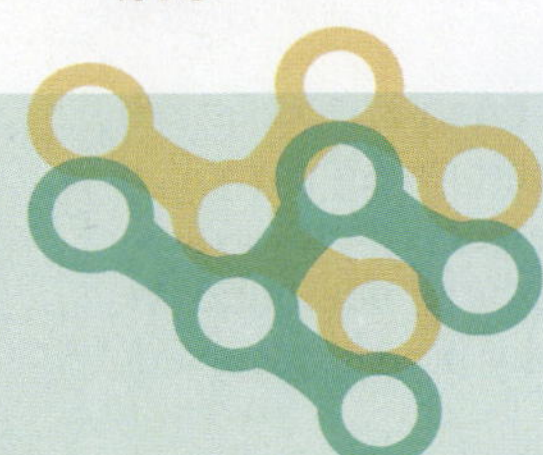

LINKING BUSINESS LAW to Marketing

Customer Relationship Management

As you learned in this chapter, increasingly the contracting process is moving online. Large and small e-commerce Web sites offer to sell millions of goods and services. The vast amount of data collected from online shoppers has pushed *customer relationship management* (CRM) to the fore. CRM is a marketing strategy that allows companies to acquire information about customers' wants, needs, and behaviors. The companies can then use that information to build customer relationships and loyalty. The focus of CRM is understanding customers as individuals rather than simply as a group of consumers. As Exhibit 10.3 shows, CRM is a closed system that uses feedback from customers to build relationships with those customers.

Two Examples—Netflix and Amazon

If you are a customer of Netflix.com, you choose Blu-ray discs and DVDs that are sent to you by mail or streamed online based on your individual tastes and preferences. Netflix asks you to rate movies you have rented (or even seen in theaters) on a scale of one to five stars. Using a computer algorithm, Netflix then creates an individualized rating system that predicts how you will rate thousands of different movies. As you rate more movies, the predictive reliability becomes more accurate. By applying your individual rating system to movies you have not seen, Netflix is able to suggest movies that you might like.

Amazon.com uses similar technology to recommend books and music that you might wish to buy. Amazon sends out numerous "personalized" e-mails to its customers with suggestions based on those customers' individual buying habits.

Thus, CRM allows both Netflix and Amazon to use a focused marketing effort, rather than the typical shotgun approach used by spam advertising on the Internet.

CRM in Online versus Traditional Companies

For online companies such as Amazon and Netflix, all customer information has some value because the cost of obtaining it, analyzing it, and utilizing it is so small. In contrast, traditional companies often must use a different process that is much more costly to obtain data to be used for CRM. An automobile company, for example, obtains customer information from a variety of sources, including dealers, customer surveys, online inquiries, and the like. Integrating, storing, and managing such information generally makes CRM much more expensive for traditional companies than for online companies.

Exhibit 10.3 A Customer Relationship Management Cycle

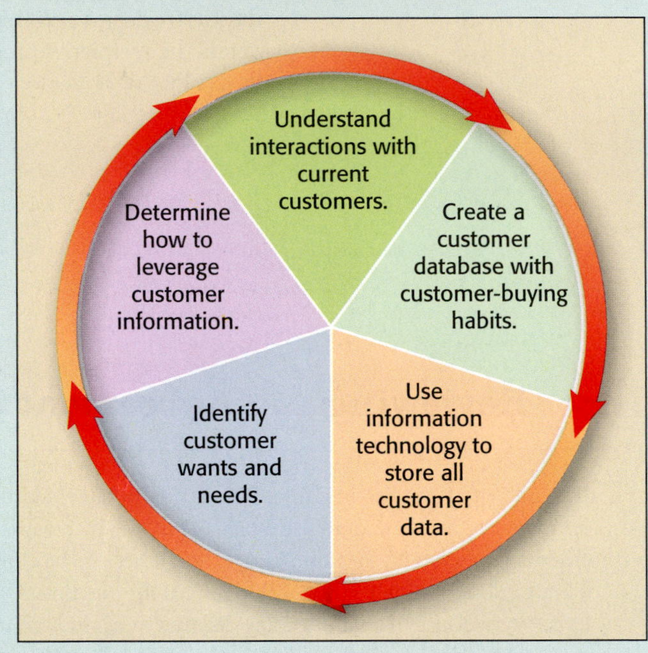

Critical Thinking

Online companies such as Amazon not only target individual customers but also utilize each customer's buying habits to create generalized marketing campaigns. Might any privacy issues arise as an online company creates a database to be used for generalized marketing campaigns?

Key Terms

acceptance 265
agreement 258
browse-wrap term 271
click-on agreement 270
counteroffer 264
e-contract 268
e-signature 272
mailbox rule 267
mirror image rule 264
offer 258
option contract 265
partnering agreement 272
record 273
revocation 263
shrink-wrap agreement 270

Chapter Summary: Agreement in Traditional and E-Contracts

Requirements of the Offer (See pages 258–263.)	1. *Intent*—There must be a serious, objective intention by the offeror to become bound by the offer. Nonoffer situations include (a) expressions of opinion; (b) statements of future intent; (c) preliminary negotiations; (d) generally, advertisements, catalogues, price lists, and circulars; and (e) traditionally, agreements to agree in the future. 2. *Definiteness*—The terms of the offer must be sufficiently definite to be ascertainable by the parties or by a court. 3. *Communication*—The offer must be communicated to the offeree.
Termination of the Offer (See pages 263–265.)	1. *By action of the parties*— a. Revocation—Unless the offer is irrevocable, it can be revoked at any time before acceptance without liability. Revocation is not effective until received by the offeree or the offeree's agent. Some offers, such as a merchant's firm offer and option contracts, are irrevocable. b. Rejection—Accomplished by words or actions that demonstrate a clear intent not to accept the offer. A rejection is not effective until it is received by the offeror or the offeror's agent. c. Counteroffer—A rejection of the original offer and the making of a new offer. 2. *By operation of law*— a. Lapse of time—The offer terminates (1) at the end of the time period specified in the offer or (2) if no time period is stated in the offer, at the end of a reasonable time period. b. Destruction of the specific subject matter of the offer—Automatically terminates the offer. c. Death or incompetence of the offeror or offeree—Terminates the offer unless the offer is irrevocable. d. Illegality—Supervening illegality terminates the offer.
Acceptance (See pages 265–267.)	1. Can be made only by the offeree or the offeree's agent. 2. Must be unequivocal. Under the common law (mirror image rule), if new terms or conditions are added to the acceptance, it will be considered a counteroffer. 3. Acceptance of a unilateral offer is effective on full performance of the requested act. Generally, no communication is necessary. 4. Except in a few situations, an offeree's silence does not constitute an acceptance. 5. Acceptance of a bilateral offer can be communicated by the offeree by any authorized mode of communication and is effective on dispatch. If the offeror does not specify the mode of communication, acceptance can be made by any reasonable means. Usually, the same means used by the offeror or a faster means can be used.
Online Offers (See pages 268–270.)	The terms of contract offers presented via the Internet should be as inclusive as the terms in an offer made in a written (paper) document. The offer should be displayed in an easily readable format and should include some mechanism, such as an "I agree" or "I accept" box, by which the customer may accept the offer. Because jurisdictional issues frequently arise with online transactions, the offer should include dispute-settlement provisions, as well as a forum-selection clause.
Online Acceptances (See pages 270–272.)	1. *Click-on agreement*— a. Definition—An agreement created when a buyer, completing a transaction on a computer, is required to indicate her or his assent to be bound by the terms of an offer by clicking on a box that says, for example, "I agree." The terms of the agreement may appear on the Web site through which the buyer is obtaining goods or services, or they may appear on a computer screen when software is downloaded. b. Enforceability—The courts have enforced click-on agreements, holding that by clicking on "I agree," the offeree has indicated acceptance by conduct. Browse-wrap terms (terms in a license that an Internet user does not have to read prior to downloading the product, such as software), however, may not be enforced on the ground that the user is not made aware that he or she is entering into a contract. 2. *Shrink-wrap agreement*— a. Definition—An agreement whose terms are expressed inside a box in which the goods are packaged. The party who opens the box is informed that, by keeping the goods that are in the box, he or she agrees to the terms of the shrink-wrap agreement. b. Enforceability—The courts have often enforced shrink-wrap agreements, even if the purchaser-user of the goods did not read the terms of the agreement. A court may deem a shrink-wrap agreement unenforceable, however, if the buyer learns of the shrink-wrap terms after the parties entered into the agreement.
E-Signatures (See page 272.)	The Uniform Electronic Transactions Act (UETA) defines an e-signature as "an electronic sound, symbol, or process attached to or logically associated with a record and executed or adopted by a person with the intent to sign the record." 1. *E-signatures*—E-signatures may include encrypted digital signatures, names at the ends of e-mail messages, and clicks on a Web page.

Continued

Chapter Summary: Agreement in Traditional and E-Contracts—Continued

E-Signatures—Continued	2. *Federal law on e-signatures and e-documents*—The Electronic Signatures in Global and National Commerce Act (E-SIGN Act) of 2000 gave validity to e-signatures by providing that no contract, record, or signature may be "denied legal effect" solely because it is in an electronic form.
The Uniform Electronic Transactions Act (UETA) (See pages 272–275.)	This uniform act has been adopted, at least in part, by most states, to create rules to support the enforcement of e-contracts. 1. *Scope and applicability*—Under the UETA, contracts entered into online, as well as other documents, are presumed to be valid. The UETA does not apply to certain transactions governed by the UCC or to wills or testamentary trusts. 2. *State laws governing e-signatures*—Although most states have laws governing e-signatures, these laws are not uniform. The UETA provides for the validity of e-signatures and may ultimately create more uniformity among the states in this respect.

ExamPrep

ISSUE SPOTTERS

1. Fidelity Corporation offers to hire Ron to replace Monica, who has given Fidelity a month's notice of intent to quit. Fidelity gives Ron a week to decide whether to accept. Two days later, Monica decides not to quit and signs an employment contract with Fidelity for another year. The next day, Monica tells Ron of the new contract. Ron immediately faxes a formal letter of acceptance to Fidelity. Do Fidelity and Ron have a contract? Why or why not? **(See page 263.)**
2. Applied Products, Inc., does business with Beltway Distributors, Inc., online. Under the Uniform Electronic Transactions Act, what determines the effect of the electronic documents evidencing the parties' deal? Is a party's "signature" necessary? Explain. **(See pages 272–275.)**

—Check your answers to the Issue Spotters against the answers provided in Appendix E at the end of this text.

BEFORE THE TEST

Go to www.cengagebrain.com, enter the ISBN 9781133273561 and click on "Find" to locate this textbook's Web site. Then, click on "Access Now" under "Study Tools," and select Chapter 10 at the top. There, you will find a Practice Quiz that you can take to assess your mastery of the concepts in this chapter, as well as Flashcards, a Glossary of important terms, and Video Questions (when assigned).

For Review

Answers to the even-numbered questions in this For Review section can be found in Appendix F at the end of this text.

1. What elements are necessary for an effective offer? What are some examples of nonoffers?
2. In what circumstances will an offer be irrevocable?
3. What are the elements that are necessary for an effective acceptance?
4. How do shrink-wrap and click-on agreements differ from other contracts? How have traditional laws been applied to these agreements?
5. What is the Uniform Electronic Transactions Act? What are some of the major provisions of this act?

Business Scenarios and Case Problems

10–1 Agreement. Ball writes to Sullivan and inquires how much Sullivan is asking for a specific forty-acre tract of land Sullivan owns. Ball then receives a letter from Sullivan stating, "I will not take less than $60,000 for the forty-acre tract as specified." Ball immediately sends Sullivan a fax stating, "I accept your offer for $60,000 for the forty-acre tract as specified." Discuss whether Ball can hold Sullivan to a contract for sale of the land. **(See page 258.)**

10–2 Online Acceptance. Anne is a reporter for *Daily Business Journal,* a print publication consulted by investors and other businesspersons. She often uses the Internet to perform research for the articles that she writes for the publication. While visiting the Web site of Cyberspace Investments Corp., Anne reads a pop-up window that states, "Our business newsletter, *E-Commerce Weekly,* is available at a one-year subscription rate of $5 per issue. To subscribe, enter your e-mail address below and click 'SUBSCRIBE.' By subscribing, you agree to the terms of the subscriber's agreement. To read this agreement, click 'AGREEMENT.' " Anne enters her e-mail address but does not click on "AGREEMENT" to read the terms. Has Anne entered into an enforceable contract to pay for *E-Commerce Weekly*? Explain. **(See page 270.)**

10–3 Question with Sample Answer—Acceptances. Chernek, the sole owner of a small business, has a large piece of used farm equipment for sale. He offers to sell the equipment to Bollow for $10,000. Discuss the legal effects of the following events on the offer. **(See page 264.)**

1. Chernek dies prior to Bollow's acceptance, and at the time she accepts, Bollow is unaware of Chernek's death.
2. The night before Bollow accepts, a fire destroys the equipment.
3. Bollow pays $100 for a thirty-day option to purchase the equipment. During this period, Chernek dies, and Bollow accepts the offer, knowing of Chernek's death.
4. Bollow pays $100 for a thirty-day option to purchase the equipment. During this period, Bollow dies, and Bollow's estate accepts Chernek's offer within the stipulated time period.

—For a sample answer to Question 10–3, go to Appendix G at the end of this text.

10–4 Shrink-Wrap Agreements. TracFone Wireless, Inc., sells phones and wireless service. The phones are sold for less than their cost, which TracFone recoups by selling prepaid airtime for their use on its network. Software in the phones prohibits their use on other networks. The phones are sold subject to the condition that the buyer agrees "not to tamper with or alter the software." This is printed on the packaging. Bequator Corp. bought at least 18,616 of the phones, disabled the software so that they could be used on other networks, and resold them. Is Bequator liable for breach of contract? Explain. [*TracFone Wireless, Inc. v. Bequator Corp.,* __ F.Supp.2d __ (S.D.Fla. 2011)] **(See pages 270–271.)**

10–5 Spotlight on Crime Stoppers—Communication. The Baton Rouge Crime Stoppers (BCS) offered a reward for information about the "South Louisiana Serial Killer." The information was to be provided via a hot line. Dianne Alexander had survived an attack by a person suspected of being the killer. She identified a suspect in a police photo lineup and later sought to collect the reward. BCS refused to pay because she did not provide information to them via the hot line. Did Alexander comply with the terms of the offer? Explain. [*Alexander v. Lafayette Crime Stoppers, Inc.,* 38 So.3d 282 (La.App. 3 Dist. 2010)] **(See pages 266–267.)**

10–6 Case Problem with Sample Answer—Acceptance. Troy Blackford smashed a slot machine while he was gambling at Prairie Meadows Casino. He was banned from the premises. Despite the ban, he later gambled at the casino and won $9,387. When he tried to collect his winnings, the casino refused to pay. He filed a suit for breach of contract, arguing that he and the casino had a contract because he had accepted its offer to gamble. Is there a contract between the casino and Blackford? Discuss. [*Blackford v. Prairie Meadows Racetrack and Casino,* 778 N.W.2d 184 (Iowa 2010)] **(See page 265.)**

—For a sample answer to Problem 10–6, go to Appendix H at the end of this text.

10–7 Online Acceptances. Heather Reasonover opted to try Internet service from Clearwire Corp. Clearwire sent her a confirmation e-mail that included a link to its Web site. Clearwire also sent her a modem. In the enclosed written materials, at the bottom of a page, in small type was the Web site URL. When Reasonover plugged in the modem, an "I accept terms" box appeared. Without clicking on the box, Reasonover quit the page. A clause in Clearwire's "Terms of Service," accessible only through its Web site, required its subscribers to submit any dispute to arbitration. Is Reasonover bound to this clause? Why or why not? [*Kwan v. Clearwire Corp.,* 2012 WL 32380 (W.D.Wash. 2012)] **(See page 270.)**

10–8 A Question of Ethics—Dispute-Settlement Provisions. Dewayne Hubbert, Elden Craft, Chris Grout, and Rhonda Byington bought computers from Dell Corp. through its Web site. Before buying, Hubbert and the others configured their own computers. To make a purchase, each buyer completed forms on five Web pages. On each page, Dell's "Terms and Conditions of Sale" were accessible by clicking on a blue hyperlink. A statement on three of the pages read, "All sales are subject to Dell's Term[s] and Conditions of Sale," but a buyer was not required to click an assent to the terms to complete a purchase. The terms were also printed on the backs of the invoices and on separate documents contained in the shipping boxes with the computers. Among those terms was a "Binding Arbitration" clause.

The computers contained Pentium 4 microprocessors, which Dell advertised as the fastest, most powerful Intel Pentium processor available at that time. Hubbert and the others filed a suit in an Illinois state court against Dell, alleging that this marketing was false, misleading, and deceptive. The plaintiffs claimed that the Pentium 4 microprocessor was slower and less powerful, and provided less performance, than either a Pentium III or an AMD Athlon, and at a greater cost. Dell asked the court to compel arbitration. [*Hubbert v. Dell Corp.,* 359 Ill.App.3d 976, 835 N.E.2d 113, 296 Ill.Dec. 258 (5 Dist. 2005)] **(See pages 269–272.)**

1. Should the court enforce the arbitration clause in this case? If you were the judge, how would you rule on this issue?
2. In your opinion, do shrink-wrap, click-on, and browse-wrap terms impose too great a burden on purchasers? Why or why not?
3. An ongoing complaint about shrink-wrap, click-on, and browse-wrap terms is that sellers (often large corporations) draft them and buyers (typically individual consumers) do not read them. Should purchasers be bound in contract by terms that they have not even read? Why or why not?

Critical Thinking and Writing Assignments

10–9 Case Analysis Question. Go to Appendix I at the end of this text and examine the excerpt of Case No. 2, *Feldman v. Google, Inc.* Review and then brief the case, making sure that your brief answers the following questions.

1. **Issue:** The dispute between the parties to this case centered on what agreement and asked which question?
2. **Rule of Law:** What rule concerning the existence of a contract did the court apply in this case?
3. **Applying the Rule of Law:** How did the language in the parties' agreement and its context affect the application of the rule of law?
4. **Conclusion:** In whose favor did the court rule? Why?

10–10 Business Law Critical Thinking Group Assignment. To download a specific app to your smartphone or tablet device, you usually have to check a box indicating that you agree to the company's terms and conditions. Most individuals do so without ever reading those terms and conditions. Print out a specific set of terms and conditions from the same downloaded app to use in this assignment.

1. One group will determine which of these terms and conditions are favorable to the company.
2. Another group will determine which of these terms and conditions conceivably will be favorable to the individual.
3. A third group will determine which terms and conditions, on net, favor the company too much.

CHAPTER 11

Consideration, Capacity, and Legality

(pixdeluxe/iStockphoto.com)

CHAPTER OUTLINE

- Consideration
- Promissory Estoppel
- Contractual Capacity
- Legality
- The Effect of Illegality

LEARNING OBJECTIVES

The five learning objectives below are designed to help improve your understanding of the chapter. After reading this chapter, you should be able to answer the following questions:

1 What is consideration? What is required for consideration to be legally sufficient?

2 In what circumstances might a promise be enforced despite a lack of consideration?

3 Does a minor have the capacity to enter into an enforceable contract? What does it mean to disaffirm a contract?

4 Under what circumstances will a covenant not to compete be enforced? When will such covenants not be enforced?

5 What is an exculpatory clause? In what circumstances might exculpatory clauses be enforced? When will they not be enforced?

"Liberty of contract is not an absolute concept. It is relative to many conditions of time and place and circumstance."
—Benjamin Cardozo, 1870–1938 (Associate justice of the United States Supreme Court, 1932–1938)

Courts generally want contracts to be enforceable, and much of the law is devoted to aiding the enforceability of contracts. Before a court will enforce a contractual promise, however, it must be convinced that there was some exchange of consideration underlying the bargain.

Furthermore, as indicated in the chapter-opening quotation, "liberty of contract" is not absolute. In other words, not all people can make legally binding contracts at all times. Contracts entered into by persons lacking the capacity to do so may be voidable. Similarly, contracts calling for the performance of an illegal act are illegal and thus void—they are not contracts at all. In this chapter, we first examine the requirement of consideration and then look at contractual capacity and legality.

As more commerce is done online, the issues of consideration, capacity, and legality have become the subject of many disputes. Should people be able to exchange organs for transplants on Craigslist? Should online gambling be allowed? These are some current topics you will learn about in this chapter.

Consideration

Consideration The value given in return for a promise or performance in a contractual agreement.

In every legal system, some promises will be enforced, and other promises will not be enforced. The simple fact that a party has made a promise does not necessarily mean that the promise is enforceable. Under the common law, a primary basis for the enforcement of promises is consideration. **Consideration** usually is defined as the value given in return for a promise.

Often, consideration is broken down into two parts: (1) something of *legally sufficient value* must be given in exchange for the promise, and (2) there must be a *bargained-for exchange*.

Legally Sufficient Value

LEARNING OBJECTIVE 1
What is consideration? What is required for consideration to be legally sufficient?

To be legally sufficient, consideration must be something of value in the eyes of the law. The "something of legally sufficient value" may consist of any of the following:

1. A promise to do something that one has no prior legal duty to do (to pay on receipt of certain goods, for example).
2. The performance of an action that one is otherwise not obligated to undertake (such as providing accounting services).
3. The refraining from an action that one has a legal right to undertake (called a **forbearance**).

Forbearance The act of refraining from an action that one has a legal right to undertake.

Consideration in bilateral contracts normally consists of a promise in return for a promise, as explained in Chapter 9. In a contract for the sale of goods, for instance, the seller promises to ship specific goods to the buyer, and the buyer promises to pay for those goods when they are received. Each of these promises constitutes consideration for the contract.

In contrast, unilateral contracts involve a promise in return for a performance. **EXAMPLE 11.1** Anita says to her neighbor, "If you paint my garage, I will pay you $800." Anita's neighbor paints the garage. The act of painting the garage is the consideration that creates Anita's contractual obligation to pay her neighbor $800. ●

What if, in return for a promise to pay, a person refrains from pursuing harmful habits, such as the use of tobacco and alcohol? Does such forbearance create consideration for the contract? This was the issue in the 1891 case *Hamer v. Sidway* that we present as this chapter's *Landmark in the Law* feature on the facing page.

Bargained-for Exchange

"Understanding does not necessarily mean agreement."

Howard Vernon, 1918–1992 (American author)

The second element of consideration is that it must provide the basis for the bargain struck between the contracting parties. The item of value must be given or promised by the promisor (offeror) in return for the promisee's promise, performance, or promise of performance.

This element of bargained-for exchange distinguishes contracts from gifts. **EXAMPLE 11.2** Sheng-Li says to his son, "In consideration of the fact that you are not as wealthy as your brothers, I will pay you $5,000." The fact that the word *consideration* is used does not, by itself, mean that consideration has been given. Indeed, Sheng-Li's promise is not enforceable because the son need not do anything to receive the $5,000 promised. Because the son does not need to give Sheng-Li something of legal value in return for his promise, there is no bargained-for exchange. Rather, Sheng-Li has simply stated his motive for giving his son a gift. ●

LANDMARK IN THE LAW

Hamer v. Sidway (1891)

In *Hamer v. Sidway*,[a] the issue before the court arose from a contract created in 1869 between William Story, Sr., and his nephew, William Story II. The uncle promised his nephew that if the nephew refrained from drinking alcohol, using tobacco, and playing billiards and cards for money until he reached the age of twenty-one, the uncle would pay him $5,000 (about $75,000 in today's dollars). The nephew, who indulged occasionally in all of these "vices," agreed to refrain from them and did so for the next six years. Following his twenty-first birthday in 1875, the nephew wrote to his uncle that he had performed his part of the bargain and was thus entitled to the promised $5,000 (plus interest). A few days later, the uncle wrote the nephew a letter stating, "[Y]ou shall have the five thousand dollars, as I promised you." The uncle said that the money was in the bank and that the nephew could "consider this money on interest."

The Issue of Consideration The nephew left the money in the care of his uncle, who held it for the next twelve years. When the uncle died in 1887, however, the executor of the uncle's estate refused to pay the $5,000 (plus interest) claim brought by Hamer, a third party to whom the promise had been *assigned.* (The law allows parties to assign, or transfer, rights in contracts to third parties—see Chapter 13.) The executor, Sidway, contended that the contract was invalid because there was insufficient consideration to support it. The uncle had received nothing, and the nephew had actually benefited by fulfilling the uncle's wishes. Therefore, no contract existed.

The Court's Conclusion Although a lower court upheld Sidway's position, the New York Court of Appeals reversed and ruled in favor of the plaintiff, Hamer. "The promisee used tobacco, occasionally drank liquor, and he had a legal right to do so," the court stated. "That right he abandoned for a period of years upon the strength of the promise of the testator [one who makes a will] that for such forbearance he would give him $5,000. We need not speculate on the effort which may have been required to give up the use of those stimulants. It is sufficient that he restricted his lawful freedom of action within certain prescribed limits upon the faith of his uncle's agreement."

Application to Today's World *Although this case was decided more than a century ago, the principles enunciated by the court remain applicable to contracts formed today, including online contracts. For a contract to be valid and binding, consideration must be given, and that consideration must be something of legally sufficient value.*

a. 124 N.Y. 538, 27 N.E. 256 (1891).

Adequacy of Consideration

Adequacy of consideration involves "how much" consideration is given. Essentially, adequacy of consideration concerns the fairness of the bargain. On the surface, fairness would appear to be an issue when the items exchanged are of unequal value. In general, however, a court will not question the adequacy of consideration if the consideration is legally sufficient.

Under the doctrine of freedom of contract (see Chapter 9 on page 241), parties are usually free to bargain as they wish. The determination of whether consideration exists does not depend on the comparative value of the things exchanged. If people could sue merely because they had entered into an unwise contract, the courts would be overloaded with frivolous suits.

Nevertheless, a large disparity in the amount or value of the consideration exchanged may raise a red flag, causing a court to look more closely at the bargain. Shockingly inadequate consideration can indicate that fraud, duress, or undue influence was involved. (Defenses to enforceability will be discussed in Chapter 12.) Judges are uneasy about enforcing unequal bargains, and it is their task to make certain that there was not some defect in the contract's formation that negated voluntary consent.

KNOW THIS

A consumer's signature on a contract does not always guarantee that the contract will be enforced. The contract must also comply with state and federal consumer protection laws.

Agreements That Lack Consideration

Sometimes, one or both of the parties to a contract may think that they have exchanged consideration when in fact they have not. Here, we look at some situations in which the parties' promises or actions do not qualify as contractual consideration.

Preexisting Duty

Under most circumstances, a promise to do what one already has a legal duty to do does not constitute legally sufficient consideration. A sheriff, for example, cannot collect a reward for information leading to the capture of a criminal if the sheriff already has a legal duty to capture the criminal.

(TFoxFoto/Shutterstock.com)

Are there circumstances under which a contractor, who has performed cement work, can legally demand a payment amount that is greater than what was stated in the contract?

Likewise, if a party is already bound by contract to perform a certain duty, that duty cannot serve as consideration for a second contract. **EXAMPLE 11.3** Bauman-Bache, Inc., begins construction on a seven-story office building and after three months demands an extra $75,000 on its contract. If the extra $75,000 is not paid, the firm will stop working. The owner of the land, having no one else to complete construction, agrees to pay the extra $75,000. The agreement is not enforceable because it is not supported by legally sufficient consideration—Bauman-Bache had a preexisting contractual duty to complete the building. ●

Unforeseen Difficulties

The preexisting duty rule is intended to prevent extortion and the so-called holdup game. Nonetheless, if, during performance of a contract, extraordinary difficulties arise that were totally unforeseen at the time the contract was formed, a court may allow an exception to the rule.

Suppose that in *Example 11.3* above, Bauman-Bache had asked for the extra $75,000 because it encountered a rock formation that no one knew existed, and the landowner had agreed to pay the extra amount to excavate the rock. In this situation, the court may refrain from applying the preexisting duty rule and enforce the agreement to pay the extra $75,000.

Note, however, that for the rule to be waived, the difficulties must be truly unforeseen and not be the types of risks ordinarily assumed in business. In *Example 11.3,* if the construction was taking place in an area where rock formations were common, a court would likely enforce the preexisting duty rule on the basis that Bauman-Bache had assumed the risk that it would encounter rock.

Rescission A remedy whereby a contract is canceled and the parties are returned to the positions they occupied before the contract was made.

Rescission and New Contract

The law recognizes that two parties can mutually agree to rescind, or cancel, their contract, at least to the extent that it is *executory*—that is, not yet performed by both parties. **Rescission**[1] is the unmaking of a contract so as to return the parties to the positions they occupied before the contract was made.

Sometimes, parties rescind a contract and make a new contract at the same time. When this occurs, it is often difficult to determine whether there was consideration for the new contract or whether the parties had a preexisting duty under the previous contract. If a court finds there was a preexisting duty, then the new contract will be invalid because there was no consideration.

Past Consideration An act that takes place before the contract is made and that ordinarily, by itself, cannot be consideration for a later promise to pay for the act.

Past Consideration

Promises made in return for actions or events that have already taken place are unenforceable. These promises lack consideration in that the element of bargained-for exchange is missing. In short, you can bargain for something to take place now or in the future but not for something that has already taken place. Therefore, **past consideration** is no consideration.

CASE EXAMPLE 11.4 Jamil Blackmon became friends with Allen Iverson when Iverson was a high school student who showed tremendous promise as an athlete. Blackmon

1. Pronounced reh-*sih*-zhen.

suggested that Iverson use "The Answer" as a nickname in the league said that Iverson would be "The Answer" to the National Basketball Ass attendance. Later, Iverson said that he would give Blackmon 25 perce from the merchandising of products that used "The Answer" as a logo o Iverson's promise was made in return for past consideration (Blackmon's earlier suggestion), it was unenforceable. In effect, Iverson stated his intention to give Blackmon a gift.[2]

Illusory Promises

If the terms of the contract express such uncertainty of performance that the promisor has not definitely promised to do anything, the promise is said to be *illusory*—without consideration and unenforceable. **EXAMPLE 11.5** The president of Tuscan Corporation says to his employees, "All of you have worked hard, and if profits remain high, a 10 percent bonus at the end of the year will be given—if management thinks it is warranted." This is an *illusory promise,* or no promise at all, because performance depends solely on the discretion of the president (the management). There is no bargained-for consideration. The statement declares merely that management may or may not do something in the future.

Option-to-cancel clauses in contracts for specified time periods sometimes present problems in regard to consideration. **EXAMPLE 11.6** Abe contracts to hire Chris for one year at $5,000 per month, reserving the right to cancel the contract at any time. On close examination of these words, you can see that Abe has not actually agreed to hire Chris, as Abe can cancel without liability before Chris starts performance. Abe has not given up the opportunity of hiring someone else. This contract is therefore illusory.

If worded correctly, option-to-cancel contracts can also create enforceable obligations. **EXAMPLE 11.7** Now suppose that Abe contracts to hire Chris for a one-year period at $5,000 per month, reserving the right to cancel the contract at any time after Chris has begun performance by giving Chris thirty days' notice. Abe, by saying that he will give Chris thirty days' notice, is relinquishing the opportunity (legal right) to hire someone else instead of Chris for a thirty-day period. If Chris works for one month, and Abe then gives him thirty days' notice, Chris has a valid and enforceable contractual claim for $10,000 for two months' salary.

Settlement of Claims

KNOW THIS

Businesspersons should consider settling potential legal disputes to save both their own time and resources and those of the courts.

Businesspersons and others often enter into contracts to settle legal claims. It is important to understand the nature of the consideration given in these settlement agreements, or contracts. Claims are commonly settled through an *accord and satisfaction,* in which a debtor offers to pay a lesser amount than the creditor says is owed. Claims may also be settled by the signing of a *release* or a *covenant not to sue.*

Accord and Satisfaction A common means of settling a disputed claim, whereby a debtor offers to pay a lesser amount than the creditor purports to be owed.

Liquidated Debt A debt whose amount has been ascertained, fixed, agreed on, settled, or exactly determined.

Accord and Satisfaction

In an **accord and satisfaction,** a debtor offers to pay, and a creditor accepts, a lesser amount than the creditor originally claimed was owed. The *accord* is the agreement under which one of the parties promises to give or perform, and the other to accept, in satisfaction of a claim, something other than that on which the parties originally agreed. *Satisfaction* is the performance (usually payment), which takes place after the accord is executed. A basic rule is that there can be no satisfaction unless there is first an accord. For accord and satisfaction to occur, the amount of the debt *must be in dispute.*

If a debt is *liquidated,* accord and satisfaction cannot take place. A **liquidated debt** is one whose amount has been ascertained, fixed, agreed on, settled, or exactly determined. **EXAMPLE 11.8** Barbara Kwan signs an installment loan contract with her banker. In the

2. *Blackmon v. Iverson,* 324 F.Supp.2d 602 (E.D.Pa. 2003).

(gmnicholas/iStockphoto.com)

Is it possible to limit one's liability after a car accident?

contract, Kwan agrees to pay a specified rate of interest on a specified amount of borrowed funds at monthly intervals for two years. Because both parties know the precise amount of the total obligation, it is a liquidated debt. ●

In the majority of states, acceptance of (an accord for) a lesser sum than the entire amount of a liquidated debt is not satisfaction, and the balance of the debt is still legally owed. The reason for this rule is that the debtor has given no consideration to satisfy the obligation of paying the balance to the creditor—because the debtor has a preexisting legal obligation to pay the entire debt.

Unliquidated Debts

An *unliquidated debt* is the opposite of a liquidated debt. The amount of the debt is *not* settled, fixed, agreed on, ascertained, or determined, and reasonable persons may differ over the amount owed. In these circumstances, acceptance of payment of the lesser sum operates as a satisfaction, or discharge, of the debt because there is valid consideration—the parties give up a legal right to contest the amount in dispute.

Release

Release An agreement in which one party gives up the right to pursue a legal claim against another party.

A **release** is a contract in which one party forfeits the right to pursue a legal claim against the other party. It bars any further recovery beyond the terms stated in the release. Releases will generally be binding if they are (1) given in good faith, (2) stated in a signed writing (required by many states), and (3) accompanied by consideration.[3] Clearly, parties are better off if they know the extent of their injuries or damages before signing releases.

EXAMPLE 11.9 Kara's car is damaged in an accident caused by Raoul's negligence. Raoul offers to give Kara $3,000 if she will release him from further liability resulting from the accident. Kara believes that this amount will cover her repairs, so she agrees and signs the release. Later, Kara discovers that the repairs will cost $4,200. Can she collect the balance from Raoul? Normally, the answer is no— Kara is limited to the $3,000 in the release. Why? The reason is that a valid contract existed. Kara and Raoul both voluntarily consented to the terms (hence, agreement existed), and sufficient consideration was present. The consideration was the legal detriment Kara suffered (she forfeited her right to sue to recover damages, should they be more than $3,000) in exchange for Raoul's promise to give her $3,000. ●

Covenant Not to Sue

Covenant Not to Sue An agreement to substitute a contractual obligation for some other type of legal action based on a valid claim.

Unlike a release, a **covenant not to sue** does not always prevent further recovery. The parties simply substitute a contractual obligation for some other type of legal action based on a valid claim. Suppose (in the preceding example) that Kara agrees with Raoul not to sue for damages in a tort action if he will pay for the damage to her car. If Raoul fails to pay, Kara can bring an action for breach of contract.

Promissory Estoppel

Promissory Estoppel A doctrine that can be used to enforce a promise when the promisee has justifiably relied on it and when justice will be better served by enforcing the promise.

Sometimes, individuals rely on promises, and their reliance may form a basis for a court to infer contract rights and duties. Under the doctrine of **promissory estoppel** (also called *detrimental reliance*), a person who has reasonably and substantially relied on the promise of another can obtain some measure of recovery. Promissory estoppel is applied in a variety of contexts and allows a party to recover on a promise even though it was made *without consideration.* Under this doctrine, a court may enforce an otherwise unenforceable promise to avoid an injustice that would otherwise result.

3. Under the Uniform Commercial Code (UCC), a written, signed waiver or renunciation by an aggrieved party discharges any further liability for a breach, even without consideration [UCC 1–107].

LEARNING OBJECTIVE 2

In what circumstances might a promise be enforced despite a lack of consideration?

Requirements to Establish Promissory Estoppel

For the doctrine of promissory estoppel to be applied, the following elements are required:

1. There must be a clear and definite promise.
2. The promisor should have expected that the promisee would rely on the promise.
3. The promisee reasonably relied on the promise by acting or refraining from some act.
4. The promisee's reliance was definite and resulted in substantial detriment.
5. Enforcement of the promise is necessary to avoid injustice.

Estopped Barred, impeded, or precluded.

If these requirements are met, a promise may be enforced even though it is not supported by consideration. In essence, the promisor (the offeror) will be **estopped** (barred or prevented) from asserting lack of consideration as a defense.

Promissory estoppel is similar in some ways to the doctrine of quasi contract that was discussed in Chapter 9 on pages 248–249. In both situations, a court is acting in the interests of equity and imposes contract obligations on the parties to prevent unfairness even though no actual contract exists. In quasi contracts, however, no promise at all was made, whereas with promissory estoppel, a promise was made and relied on, but it was unenforceable.

Application of Promissory Estoppel

Promissory estoppel was originally applied to situations involving gifts (I promise to pay you $1,000 a week so that you will not have to work) and donations to charities (I promise to contribute $50,000 a year to the All Saints orphanage). Later, courts began to apply the doctrine to avoid inequity or hardship in other situations, including business transactions.

EXAMPLE 11.10 An employer, Jay Bailey, orally promises to pay each of his five employees $2,000 a month for the remainder of their lives after they retire. When Sal Hernandez retires, he receives the monthly amount for two years, but then Bailey stops paying. Under the doctrine of promissory estoppel, Hernandez can sue Bailey in an attempt to enforce his promise. ●

In the following case, a daughter built a house on her parents' land with their help and permission. When the parents refused to deed the land on which the house was built to her, she filed a lawsuit against them on a claim of promissory estoppel.

Case 11.1

Harvey v. Dow

Supreme Judicial Court of Maine, 2011 ME 4, 11 A.3d 303 (2011).

(George Muresan/Shutterstock.com)

When must a property owner transfer a deed to his or her child?

FACTS Jeffrey and Kathryn Dow owned 125 acres of land in Corinth, Maine. The Dows regarded the land as their children's heritage, and the subject of the children's living on the land was often discussed within the family. With the Dows' permission, their daughter, Teresa, installed a mobile home and built a garage on the land. After Teresa married Jarrod Harvey, the Dows agreed to finance the construction of a house on the land for the couple.

When Jarrod died in a motorcycle accident, however, Teresa financed the house with life insurance proceeds. The construction cost about $200,000. Jeffrey performed a substantial amount of work on the house, doing general carpentry and much of the foundation work, and helping to install the underground electrical lines. Teresa then asked her parents for a

Case 11.1—Continues next page

Case 11.1—Continued

deed to the property so that she could obtain a mortgage. They refused. Teresa filed a suit in a Maine state court against her parents. The court rejected the claim that she was entitled to a judgment on a theory of promissory estoppel. Teresa appealed.

ISSUE Did Teresa Harvey detrimentally rely on her parents' promise to convey the land to her when she and her husband built a house on it?

DECISION Yes. The Supreme Judicial Court of Maine vacated the lower court's judgment and remanded the case for the entry of a judgment in Teresa's favor. The state's highest court held that the Dows showed a present commitment to transfer land to their daughter or to forgo a challenge to her ownership of it.

REASON The court reasoned that the Dows' support and encouragement of their daughter's construction of a house on the land "conclusively demonstrated" their intent. For years, they had made general promises to convey the land to their children, including Teresa. In addition, Jeffrey had approved the site for the house, obtained the building permit, and built much of the house himself. The court explained, "Statements or conduct representing a present commitment to do or refrain from doing something in the future reasonably can be expected to induce reliance and the promisee's reliance on such statements is reasonable."

CRITICAL THINKING—Legal Consideration *On remand, the lower court was ordered to determine the appropriate remedy. Should Teresa be awarded specific performance to compel a transfer of the land? Or should she obtain damages? Discuss.*

Contractual Capacity

Contractual Capacity The capacity required by the law for a party who enters into a contract to be bound by that contract.

Contractual capacity is the legal ability to enter into a contractual relationship. Courts generally presume the existence of contractual capacity, but in some situations, capacity is lacking or may be questionable. A person who has been determined by a court to be mentally incompetent, for example, cannot form a legally binding contract with another party. In other situations, a party may have the capacity to enter into a valid contract but may also have the right to avoid liability under it. For example, minors—or *infants,* as they are commonly referred to in the law—usually are not legally bound by contracts.

In this section, we look at the effect of youth, intoxication, and mental incompetence on contractual capacity.

Minors

Today, in almost all states, the *age of majority* (when a person is no longer a minor) for contractual purposes is eighteen years—the so-called coming of age.[4] In addition, some states provide for the termination of minority on marriage.

Emancipation In regard to minors, the act of being freed from parental control.

Minority status may also be terminated by a minor's **emancipation,** which occurs when a child's parent or legal guardian relinquishes the legal right to exercise control over the child. Normally, minors who leave home to support themselves are considered emancipated. Several jurisdictions permit minors to petition a court for emancipation. For business purposes, a minor may petition a court to be treated as an adult.

LEARNING OBJECTIVE 3

Does a minor have the capacity to enter into an enforceable contract? What does it mean to disaffirm a contract?

The general rule is that a minor can enter into any contract an adult can, provided that the contract is not one prohibited by law for minors (for example, the sale of alcoholic beverages or tobacco products). A contract entered into by a minor, however, is voidable at the option of that minor, subject to certain exceptions (to be discussed shortly). To exercise the option to avoid a contract, a minor need only manifest (clearly show) an intention not to be bound by it. The minor "avoids" the contract by disaffirming it.

4. The age of majority may still be twenty-one for other purposes, such as the purchase and consumption of alcohol.

Disaffirmance The legal avoidance, or setting aside, of a contractual obligation.

Disaffirmance

The legal avoidance, or setting aside, of a contractual obligation is referred to as **disaffirmance.** To disaffirm, a minor must express, through words or conduct, his or her intent not to be bound to the contract. The minor must disaffirm the entire contract, not merely a portion of it. For instance, a minor cannot decide to keep part of the goods purchased under a contract and return the remaining goods. When a minor disaffirms a contract, the minor can recover any property that she or he transferred to the adult as consideration for the contract, even if it is then in the possession of a third party.[5]

A contract can ordinarily be disaffirmed at any time during minority[6] or for a reasonable time after the minor comes of age. What constitutes a "reasonable" time may vary. If an individual fails to disaffirm an executed contract within a reasonable time after reaching the age of majority, a court will likely hold that the contract has been ratified (*ratification* will be discussed shortly).

Note that an adult who enters into a contract with a minor cannot avoid his or her contractual duties on the ground that the minor can do so. Unless the minor exercises the option to disaffirm the contract, the adult party normally is bound by it.

A Minor's Obligations on Disaffirmance

Although all states' laws permit minors to disaffirm contracts (with certain exceptions), including executed contracts, state laws differ on the extent of a minor's obligations on disaffirmance. Courts in most states hold that the minor need only return the goods (or other consideration) subject to the contract, provided the goods are in the minor's possession or control. Even if the minor returns damaged goods, the minor often is entitled to disaffirm the contract and obtain a refund of the purchase price.

A growing number of states place an additional duty on the minor to restore the adult party to the position she or he held before the contract was made. These courts may hold a minor responsible for damage, ordinary wear and tear, and depreciation of goods that the minor used prior to disaffirmance.

CASE EXAMPLE 11.11 Sixteen-year-old Joseph Dodson bought a truck for $4,900 from a used-car dealer. Although the truck developed mechanical problems nine months later, Dodson continued to drive it until the engine blew up and the truck stopped running. Dodson then disaffirmed the contract and attempted to return the truck to the dealer for a refund of the full purchase price. The dealer refused to accept the truck or to provide a refund. Dodson filed a suit. Ultimately, the Tennessee Supreme Court allowed Dodson to disaffirm the contract but required him to compensate the seller for the depreciated value—not the purchase price—of the truck.[7] •

Exceptions to a Minor's Right to Disaffirm

State courts and legislatures have carved out several exceptions to the minor's right to disaffirm. Some contracts, such as marriage contracts and contracts to enlist in the armed services, cannot be avoided on the ground of public policy. Other contracts may not be disaffirmed for different reasons.

Although ordinarily minors can disaffirm contracts even when they have misrepresented their age, a growing number of states have enacted laws to prohibit disaffirmance in such situations. Some state laws also prohibit minors from disaffirming contracts entered into by a minor who is engaged in business as an adult.

---

5. Section 2–403(1) of the UCC allows an exception if the third party is a "good faith purchaser for value." See Chapter 16.

6. In some states, however, a minor who enters into a contract for the sale of land cannot disaffirm the contract until she or he reaches the age of majority.

7. *Dodson by Dodson v. Shrader,* 824 S.W.2d 545 (Tenn. 1992).

Necessaries Necessities required for life, such as food, shelter, clothing, and medical attention.

Ratification The acceptance or confirmation of an act or agreement that gives legal force to an obligation that previously was not enforceable.

KNOW THIS

A minor's station in life (including financial position, social status, and lifestyle) is important in determining whether an item is a necessary or a luxury. For instance, clothing is a necessary, but if a minor from a low-income family contracts for the purchase of a $2,000 leather coat, a court may deem the coat a luxury. In this situation, the contract would not be for "necessaries."

In addition, a minor who enters into a contract for necessaries may disaffirm the contract but remains liable for the reasonable value of the goods. **Necessaries** are basic needs, such as food, clothing, shelter, and medical services, at a level of value required to maintain the minor's standard of living or financial and social status. Thus, what will be considered a necessary for one person may be a luxury for another.

Ratification

In contract law, **ratification** is the acceptance or confirmation of an act or agreement that gives legal force to an obligation that previously was not enforceable. A minor who has reached the age of majority can ratify a contract expressly or impliedly. *Express* ratification occurs when the individual, on reaching the age of majority, states orally or in writing that she or he intends to be bound by the contract. *Implied* ratification takes place when the minor, on reaching the age of majority, behaves in a manner inconsistent with disaffirmance.

EXAMPLE 11.12 Lin enters into a contract to sell her laptop to Andrew, a minor. Andrew does not disaffirm the contract. If, on reaching the age of majority, he writes a letter to Lin stating that he still agrees to buy the laptop, he has expressly ratified the contract. If, instead, Andrew takes possession of the laptop as a minor and continues to use it well after reaching the age of majority, he has impliedly ratified the contract. •

If a minor fails to disaffirm a contract within a reasonable time after reaching the age of majority, then a court must determine whether the conduct constitutes implied ratification or disaffirmance. Generally, courts presume that a contract that is *executed* (fully performed by both parties) was ratified. A contract that is still executory is normally considered to be disaffirmed.

Parents' Liability

As a general rule, parents are not liable for the contracts made by minor children acting on their own, except contracts for necessaries, which the parents are legally required to provide. This is why businesses ordinarily require parents to cosign any contract made with a minor. The parents then become personally obligated to perform the conditions of the contract, even if their child avoids liability. (See the *Business Application* feature on page 300 for additional tips on dealing with minors.)

Intoxicated Persons

Intoxication is a condition in which a person's normal capacity to act or think is inhibited by alcohol or some other drug. A contract entered into by an intoxicated person can be either voidable or valid (and thus enforceable).

If the person was sufficiently intoxicated to lack mental capacity, then the transaction may be voidable at the option of the intoxicated person even if the intoxication was purely voluntary. If, despite intoxication, the person understood the legal consequences of the agreement, the contract is enforceable. Courts look at objective indications of the situation to determine if the intoxicated person possessed or lacked the required capacity.

For the contract to be voidable, the person must prove that the intoxication impaired her or his reason and judgment so severely that she or he did not comprehend the legal consequences of entering into the contract. In addition, the person claiming intoxication must be able to return all consideration received.

Mentally Incompetent Persons

Contracts made by mentally incompetent persons can be void, voidable, or valid. If a court has previously determined that a person is mentally incompetent and has appointed a guardian to represent the person, any contract made by that mentally incompetent person is *void*—no contract exists. Only the guardian can enter into a binding contract on behalf of the mentally incompetent person.

If a court has not previously judged a person to be mentally incompetent, the contract may be *voidable*. A contract is voidable if the person did not know that he or she was entering into the contract or lacked the mental capacity to comprehend its nature, purpose, and consequences. In such situations, the contract is voidable (or can be ratified) at the option of the mentally incompetent person but not at the option of the other party.

A contract entered into by a mentally incompetent person (whom a court has not previously declared incompetent) may also be *valid* if the person had capacity *at the time the contract was formed*. Some people who are incompetent due to age or illness have *lucid intervals*—temporary periods of sufficient intelligence, judgment, and will—during which they will be considered to have legal capacity to enter into contracts.

Legality

For a contract to be valid and enforceable, it must be formed for a legal purpose. Legality is the fourth requirement for a valid contract to exist. A contract to do something that is prohibited by federal or state statutory law is illegal and, as such, is void from the outset and thus unenforceable. Additionally, a contract to commit a tortious act (see Chapter 4 on page 96) or to commit an action that is contrary to public policy is illegal and unenforceable.

ETHICAL ISSUE

Should advertisements to buy or sell human organs be made legal on Web sites such as Craigslist? According to the United Network for Organ Sharing, between 4,500 and 5,000 people die each year in the United States while waiting on organ transplant lists. Increasingly, though, patients who need an organ transplant are sidestepping these traditional lists and advertising for organs on Web sites, such as Craigslist.com. The organ most requested is a kidney because most individuals have two but can survive with just one.

For example, Salina Hodge posted a plea for help on Craigslist asking for someone to donate a kidney. She received more than eight hundred responses from all over the world. One came from a young woman who lived just a few miles away. The transplant was successful, and both donor and donee are leading normal lives.

Federal law prohibits the sale or purchase of any organ for a payment that exceeds the donor's travel and hospital expenses. Nonetheless, individuals facing death will often try desperate means, and some ads posted on Craigslist clearly violate the law—for example, an offer to buy a kidney in exchange for $250,000 worth of paintings. Because the purchase or sale of an organ is illegal, such a contract would not be enforceable.

Some commentators argue that the law should be changed to allow an open market in human organs. They point out that dying patients and their families and friends will continue to offer side payments to obtain organs, even though the payments are technically illegal. Furthermore, some poor individuals will always be willing to provide a kidney for, say, $100,000. Proponents of a legal market in organs claim that such a market would be preferable to a black market where there is nothing to prevent those living in poverty from being exploited.

Contracts Contrary to Statute

Statutes often set forth rules specifying which terms and clauses may be included in contracts and which are prohibited. Thus, a contract to sell illegal drugs in violation of criminal laws is unenforceable, as is a contract to hide a corporation's violation of the Sarbanes-Oxley Act (see Chapter 31). Similarly, a contract to smuggle undocumented workers from another country into the United States for an employer is illegal (see Chapter 24), as is a contract to dump hazardous waste in violation of environmental laws (see Chapter 33).

If the object or performance of a contract is rendered illegal by statute *after* the contract has been formed, the contract is considered to be discharged by law. (See the discussion in Chapter 13.)

Usury Charging an illegal rate of interest.

Usury

Almost every state has a statute that sets the maximum rate of interest that can be charged for different types of transactions, including ordinary loans. A lender who makes a loan at an interest rate above the lawful maximum commits **usury.** Although usurious contracts are illegal, most states simply limit the interest that the lender may collect on the contract to the lawful maximum interest rate in that state. In a few states, the lender can recover the principal amount of the loan but no interest.

Although usury statutes place a ceiling on allowable rates of interest, exceptions are made to facilitate business transactions. For example, many states exempt corporate loans from the usury laws. In addition, almost all states have special statutes allowing much higher interest rates on small loans to help those borrowers who need funds and could not otherwise obtain loans.

Note, though, that in 2009 the federal government placed some restrictions on the interest rates and fees that banks and credit-card companies can legally charge consumers, particularly for late payments (discussed in Chapter 33).

Gambling

Gambling is the creation of risk for the purpose of assuming it. Any scheme that involves the distribution of property by chance among persons who have paid valuable consideration for the opportunity (chance) to receive the property is gambling. Traditionally, the states have deemed gambling contracts illegal and thus void. It is sometimes difficult, however, to distinguish a gambling contract from the risk sharing inherent in almost all contracts. (For a discussion of how the federal government has changed its interpretation of the laws pertaining to online gambling, see the *Adapting the Law to the Online Environment* feature on page 294.)

All states have statutes that regulate gambling, and many states allow certain forms of gambling, such as horse racing, video poker machines, and charity-sponsored bingo. In addition, nearly all states allow state-operated lotteries and gambling on Native American reservations. Nevertheless, even in states that permit certain types of gambling, courts often find that gambling contracts are illegal.

CASE EXAMPLE 11.13 Video poker machines are legal in Louisiana, but their use requires the approval of the state video gaming commission. Gaming Venture, Inc., did not obtain this approval before agreeing with Tastee Restaurant Corporation to install poker machines in some of its restaurants. For this reason, when Tastee allegedly reneged on the deal by refusing to install poker machines, a state court held that their agreement was an illegal gambling contract and therefore void.[8] •

Licensing Statutes

All states require members of certain professions—including physicians, lawyers, real estate brokers, accountants, architects, electricians, and stockbrokers—to have licenses. Some licenses are obtained only after extensive schooling and examinations, which indicate to the public that a special skill has been acquired. Others require only that the particular person be of good moral character and pay a fee.

Whether a contract with an unlicensed person is legal and enforceable depends on the purpose of the licensing statute. If the statute's purpose is to protect the public from unauthorized practitioners, then a contract involving an unlicensed practitioner generally is illegal and unenforceable. If the purpose is merely to raise government revenues, however, a contract with an unlicensed person may be enforced (and the unlicensed practitioner fined).

EXAMPLE 11.14 A state requires a stockbroker to be licensed and to file a bond with the state to protect the public from fraudulent transactions in stocks. Because the purpose of the statute is to protect the public, a court will deem a contract with an unlicensed stockbroker in that state to be illegal and unenforceable. •

8. *Gaming Venture, Inc. v. Tastee Restaurant Corp.*, 996 So.2d 515 (La.App. 5 Cir. 2008).

Can a member of a profession licensed in one jurisdiction recover on a contract to perform professional services in another jurisdiction? What if the contract was the result of a winning entry in an international competition? The court in the following case was asked these questions.

Case 11.2

Sturdza v. United Arab Emirates

District of Columbia Court of Appeals, 11 A.3d 251 (2011).

(.shock/Shutterstock.com)

A team of architects checking its plans.

FACTS The United Arab Emirates (UAE) held a competition for the design of a new embassy in Washington, D.C. Elena Sturdza—an architect licensed in Maryland but not in the District of Columbia—won. Sturdza and the UAE exchanged proposals, but the UAE stopped communicating with her before the parties had signed a contract. Two years later, Sturdza learned that the UAE had contracted with a District of Columbia architect to use another design. Sturdza filed a suit against the UAE, alleging breach of contract.

ISSUE Can an architect who is not licensed in the District of Columbia sue to enforce a contract under which she was to perform architectural services in the District of Columbia?

DECISION No. According to the licensing statute, an architect cannot recover on a contract to perform architectural services in the District of Columbia if she or he lacks a District of Columbia license.

REASON Sturdza argued that the licensing statute should not apply to architects who submit plans in international architectural design competitions. The court held, however, that licensing requirements are necessary to ensure the safety of those who work in and visit buildings in the District of Columbia, as well as the safety of neighboring buildings. Besides, the statute contains no exception for international design competitions or any other type of client or service. "We must apply the statute as it is written and not create *ad hoc* [impromptu] exceptions by judicial decree based on nebulous [unclear] policy considerations."

CRITICAL THINKING—Global Consideration *The architectural services at the center of this case were to be performed for a foreign embassy. Should the court have made an exception for such a circumstance? Why or why not?*

Contracts Contrary to Public Policy

Although contracts involve private parties, some are not enforceable because of the negative impact they would have on society. These contracts are said to be *contrary to public policy.* Examples include a contract to commit an immoral act, such as selling a child, and a contract that prohibits marriage. **EXAMPLE 11.15** Everett offers a young man $10,000 if he will refrain from marrying Everett's daughter. If the young man accepts, no contract is formed (the contract is void) because it is contrary to public policy. Thus, if the man marries Everett's daughter, Everett cannot sue him for breach of contract. • Business contracts that may be contrary to public policy include contracts in restraint of trade and unconscionable contracts or clauses.

LEARNING OBJECTIVE 4
Under what circumstances will a covenant not to compete be enforced? When will such covenants not be enforced?

Contracts in Restraint of Trade The United States has a strong public policy favoring competition in the economy. Thus, contracts in restraint of trade (anticompetitive agreements) generally are unenforceable because they are contrary to public policy. Typically, such contracts also violate one or more federal or state antitrust laws (these laws will be discussed in Chapter 32). An exception is recognized when the restraint is reasonable and is an ancillary (secondary, or subordinate) part of the contract. Such restraints often are included in contracts for the sale of an ongoing business and employment contracts.

ADAPTING THE LAW TO THE ONLINE ENVIRONMENT

AN INCREASING AMOUNT OF ONLINE GAMBLING IS IN OUR FUTURE

Until very recently, the federal government interpreted the Wire Act of 1961[a] as prohibiting all forms of interstate transmission of gambling-related communications. Presumably, that law meant that all online gambling was effectively illegal when it became a reality more than three decades later. In 2006, Congress passed the Unlawful Internet Gambling Enforcement Act[b] to further reduce the amount of online gambling. That act essentially prohibited credit-card companies from collecting online bets for online gambling companies.

The Justice Department Releases a Game Changer

In 2011, Illinois and New York asked the Office of Legal Counsel of the U.S. Justice Department to clarify the interpretation of the Wire Act of 1961. In response, the department declared that the Wire Act applies only to bets or wagers on sporting events or contests and that it does not cover purely *intra*state communications. In short, under the Obama administration's interpretation of the Wire Act, almost all federal antigambling legislation no longer applies to gaming that is legal under state laws. The decision will pave the way for all states to legalize Internet poker and certain other types of online betting.

a. 18 U.S.C. Section 1084.
b. 31 U.S.C. Section 5361–5367.

The District of Columbia and Nevada Are Just Starting Points

As of 2012, only two jurisdictions had legalized online gambling—the District of Columbia and Nevada. Therefore, start-up online gambling businesses can be expected to increase dramatically in the next few years in those jurisdictions.

Other jurisdictions are also seeking additional revenues to reduce their budget deficits. Several states, including California, are already considering changing their laws to allow legal in-state Internet gambling. The lure of taxing billions of online gambling profits each year is very tempting.

Expect More Mobile Gambling Apps

For the last two years, the residents of Nevada have been able to utilize a mobile gambling app. Even bettors who do not live in Nevada can use an app that allows them to place sports bets via their phones. The first mobile app was created by America Wagering, Inc., for BlackBerry mobile phone devices.

Today, a number of casinos in Nevada offer mobile gambling apps that work on iPhones and Android-based smartphones. More apps will follow as more states legalize online gaming.

Critical Thinking

Why do you think that the Justice Department still believes that the Wire Act of 1961 applies to betting on sporting events or contests?

Covenant Not to Compete A contractual promise of one party to refrain from conducting business similar to that of another party for a certain period of time and within a specified geographical area.

Covenants Not to Compete and the Sale of an Ongoing Business Many contracts involve a type of restraint called a **covenant not to compete,** or a restrictive covenant (promise). A covenant not to compete may be created when a seller agrees not to open a new store in a certain geographic area surrounding the old store. Such an agreement enables the seller to sell, and the purchaser to buy, the goodwill and reputation of an ongoing business without having to worry that the seller will open a competing business a block away. Provided the restrictive covenant is reasonable and is an ancillary part of the sale of an ongoing business, it is enforceable.

Employment Contract A contract between an employer and an employee in which the terms and conditions of employment are stated.

Covenants Not to Compete in Employment Contracts Agreements not to compete can also be included in **employment contracts.** (See the annotated contract at the end of Chapter 14 for an example of an employment contract containing a noncompete clause.) People in middle-level and upper-level management positions commonly agree not to work for competitors or not to start a competing business for a specified period of time after terminating employment. Such agreements are generally legal in most states so long as the specified period of time (of restraint) is not excessive in duration and the geographic restriction is reasonable. What constitutes a reasonable time period may be shorter in the online environment than in conventional employment contracts because the restrictions would apply worldwide.

To be reasonable, a restriction on competition must protect a legitimate business interest and must not be any greater than necessary to protect that interest.[9] **CASE EXAMPLE 11.16** Safety and Compliance Management, Inc. (SCMI), provides drug-testing services. When SCMI hired Angela to pick up test specimens, she signed a covenant not to compete "in any area of SCMI business." Angela later quit SCMI's employ to work in a hospital where she sometimes collected patient specimens. SCMI claimed this was a breach of their noncompete agreement. A court ruled that the covenant was unreasonable because it imposed a greater restriction on Angela than was necessary to protect SCMI.[10]

The contract in the following *Spotlight Case* provided an exclusive license to open and operate comedy clubs under a certain famous trademark. It also included a covenant not to compete. The question was whether the restraint was reasonable.

9. See, for example, *Gould & Lamb LLC v. D'Alusio*, 949 So.2d 1212 (Fla.App. 2007), and *Freeman v. Brown Hiller, Inc.*, 102 Ark.App. 76, 281 S.W.3d 749 (2008).

10. *Stultz v. Safety and Compliance Management, Inc.*, 285 Ga.App. 799, 648 S.E.2d 129 (2007).

Spotlight on the Improv

Case 11.3

Comedy Club, Inc. v. Improv West Associates

United States Court of Appeals, Ninth Circuit, 553 F.3d 1277 (2009).
www.ca9.uscourts.gov[a]

(Ralph Notaro/Getty Images)

How much control over the name Improv Comedy Club does its owner have?

FACTS Improv West Associates is the founder of the Improv Comedy Club and owner of the "Improv" trademark. Comedy Club, Inc. (CCI), owns and operates restaurants and comedy clubs. Improv West granted CCI an exclusive license to open four Improv clubs per year in 2001, 2002, and 2003. Their agreement prohibited CCI from opening any non-Improv comedy clubs "in the contiguous United States" until 2019. When CCI failed to open eight clubs by the end of 2002, Improv West commenced arbitration. The arbitrator's award in 2005 stated that CCI had forfeited its right to open Improv clubs, but that the parties' agreement had not terminated and the covenant not to compete was enforceable—CCI could not open any new comedy clubs for its duration. A federal district court confirmed the award, and CCI appealed.

ISSUE Is a covenant not to compete in the comedy club business for fourteen years in forty-eight states too broad to be enforced?

DECISION Yes. The U.S. Court of Appeals for the Ninth Circuit reversed part of the lower court's confirmation of the award and remanded the case.

REASON The court said that terminating CCI's exclusive right to open Improv clubs due to its inadequate performance of the parties' contract "makes sense" and that Improv West should be protected from "improper" competition. But the covenant not to compete in this case has "dramatic geographic and temporal [relating to time] scope. . . . For more than fourteen years the entire contiguous United States comedy club market, except for CCI's current Improv clubs, is off limits to CCI." The effect would be to foreclose competition in a substantial share of the comedy club business. This restraint is "too broad to be countenanced." The covenant should be tailored to cover only the areas in which CCI is operating Improv clubs under the parties' agreement. It should allow CCI to open non-Improv clubs in "all those counties" where it does not operate an Improv club.

WHY IS THIS CASE IMPORTANT? *Competition is a paramount principle of our capitalist economic system. But business competitiveness requires the support of our laws if it is to be a reality. This case shows the multifaceted role that the law can play to encourage competition by removing unfair restraints and by enforcing proper limits to prevent its abuse.*

a. In the left-hand column, in the "Opinions" pull-down menu, click on "Published." On that page, click on "Advanced Search." Then, in the "by Case No.:" box, type "05-55739" and click on "Search." In the result, click on the "01/29/2009" link to access the opinion.

Enforcement Problems The laws governing the enforceability of covenants not to compete vary significantly from state to state. California prohibits the enforcement of all covenants not to compete. In some states, such as Texas, such a covenant will not be enforced unless the employee has received some benefit in return for signing the noncompete agreement. This is true even if the covenant is reasonable as to time and area. If the employee receives no benefit, the covenant will be deemed void.

Occasionally, depending on the jurisdiction, courts will *reform* covenants not to compete. If a covenant is found to be unreasonable in time or geographic area, the court may convert the terms into reasonable ones and then enforce the reformed covenant. This presents a problem, however, in that the judge has implicitly become a party to the contract. Consequently, courts usually resort to contract **reformation** only when necessary to prevent undue burdens or hardships.

Reformation A court-ordered correction of a written contract so that it reflects the true intentions of the parties.

PREVENTING LEGAL DISPUTES

A business clearly has a legitimate interest in having employees sign covenants not to compete and in preventing them from using the valuable skills and training provided by the business for the benefit of a competitor. The problem is that these covenants frequently lead to litigation. Moreover, it is difficult to predict what a court will consider reasonable in a given situation. Therefore, you need to be aware of the difficulties in enforcing noncompete agreements. Seek the advice of counsel in the relevant jurisdiction when drafting covenants not to compete. Avoid overreaching in terms of time and geographic restrictions, particularly if you are the manager of a high-tech or Web-based company. Consider using noncompete clauses only for key employees and, if necessary, offer some compensation (consideration) for signing the agreement. If an employee signed a noncompete clause when he or she was hired, be sure to discuss the meaning of that clause and your expectations with the employee at the time of termination.

Unconscionable Contracts or Clauses

Ordinarily, a court does not look at the fairness or equity of a contract, or, as discussed earlier, inquire into the adequacy of consideration. Persons are assumed to be reasonably intelligent, and the courts will not come to their aid just because they have made unwise or foolish bargains. In certain circumstances, however, bargains are so oppressive that the courts relieve innocent parties of part or all of their duties. Such bargains are deemed **unconscionable**[11] because they are so unscrupulous or grossly unfair as to be "void of conscience."

Unconscionable (Contract or Clause) A contract or clause that is void on the basis of public policy because one party was forced to accept terms that are unfairly burdensome and that unfairly benefit the stronger party.

The Uniform Commercial Code (UCC) incorporates the concept of unconscionability in its provisions with regard to the sale and lease of goods.[12] A contract can be unconscionable on either procedural or substantive grounds, as discussed in the following subsections and illustrated graphically in Exhibit 11.1 on the facing page.

"Better a friendly refusal than an unwilling consent."

Spanish Proverb

Procedural Unconscionability Procedural unconscionability often involves inconspicuous print, unintelligible language ("legalese"), or the lack of an opportunity to read the contract or ask questions about its meaning. This type of unconscionability typically arises when a party's lack of knowledge or understanding of the contract terms deprived him or her of any meaningful choice.

Procedural unconscionability can also occur when there is such a disparity in bargaining power between the two parties that the weaker party's consent is not voluntary. This type of situation often involves an **adhesion contract**, which is a standard-form contract written exclusively by one party (the dominant party, usually the seller or creditor) and presented to the other (the adhering party, usually the buyer or borrower) on a take-it-or-leave-it basis. In

Adhesion Contract A standard-form contract in which the stronger party dictates the terms.

11. Pronounced un-*kon*-shun-uh-bul.
12. See UCC 2–302 and 2–719.

Exhibit 11.1 Unconscionability

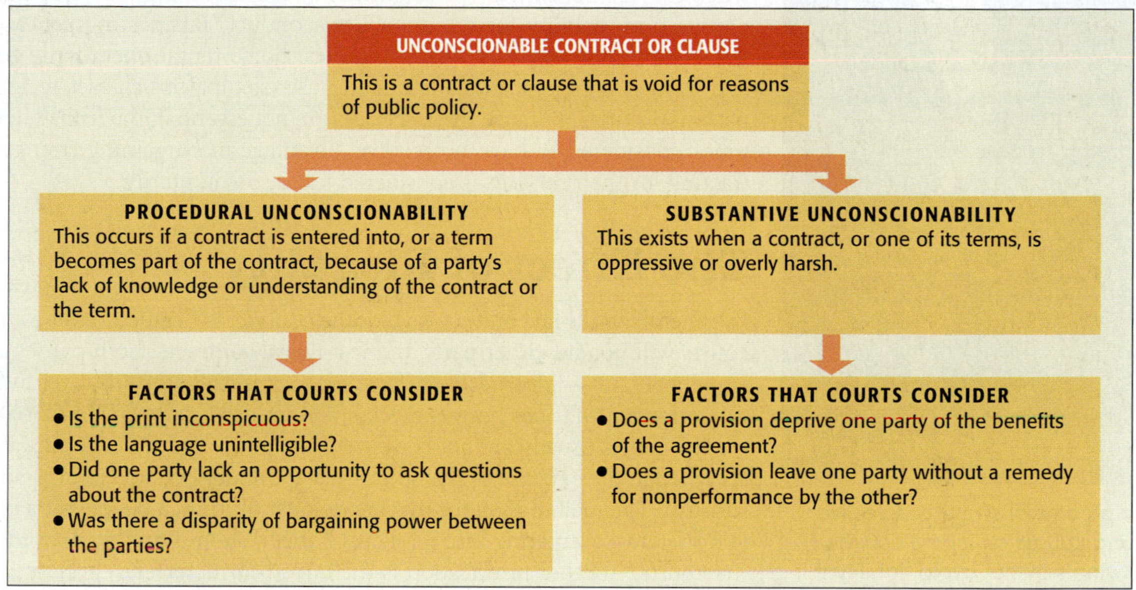

other words, the adhering party has no opportunity to negotiate the terms of the contract. Not all adhesion contracts are unconscionable, only those that unreasonably favor the drafter.[13]

Substantive Unconscionability Substantive unconscionability occurs when contracts, or portions of contracts, are oppressive or overly harsh. Courts generally focus on provisions that deprive one party of the benefits of the agreement or leave that party without remedy for nonperformance by the other. **CASE EXAMPLE 11.17** A person with little income and only a fourth-grade education agrees to purchase a refrigerator for $4,500 and signs a two-year installment contract. The same type of refrigerator usually sells for $900 on the market. Despite the general rule that the courts will not inquire into the adequacy of the consideration, some courts have held that this type of contract is unconscionable because the contract terms are so oppressive as to "shock the conscience" of the court.[14] •

Substantive unconscionability can arise in a wide variety of business contexts. For example, a contract clause that gives the business entity unrestricted access to the courts but requires the other party to arbitrate any dispute with the firm may be unconscionable. Similarly, contracts drafted by cell phone providers and insurance companies have been struck down as substantively unconscionable when they included provisions that were overly harsh or one sided.[15]

LEARNING OBJECTIVE 5

What is an exculpatory clause? In what circumstances might exculpatory clauses be enforced? When will they not be enforced?

Exculpatory Clause A clause that releases a contractual party from liability in the event of monetary or physical injury, no matter who is at fault.

Exculpatory Clauses

Often closely related to the concept of unconscionability are **exculpatory clauses**, which release a party from liability in the event of monetary or physical injury, *no matter who is at fault.* Indeed, courts sometimes refuse to enforce such clauses because they deem them to be unconscionable. Exculpatory clauses found in rental agreements for commercial property are frequently held to be contrary to public policy, and such clauses are almost always unenforceable in residential property leases. Exculpatory clauses in the employment context may be deemed unconscionable when they attempt to remove the employer's potential liability for injuries to employees.

13. See, for example, *Thibodeau v. Comcast Corp.*, 2006 PA Super. 346, 912 A.2d 874 (2006).
14. See, for example, *Jones v. Star Credit Corp.*, 59 Misc.2d 189, 298 N.Y.S.2d 264 (1969). This classic case will be presented in Chapter 15 as Case 15.2 on pages 398–399.
15. See, for example, *Gatton v. T-Mobile USA, Inc.*, 152 Cal.App.4th 571, 61 Cal.Rptr.3d 344 (2007); and *Aul v. Golden Rule Insurance Co.*, 2007 WL 1695243 (Wis.App. 2007).

(dwphotos/iStockphoto.com)

If a carnival swing is defective and causes an injury, can the swing's owner avoid liability if it had made each participant sign an exculpatory clause?

Although courts view exculpatory clauses with disfavor, they do enforce such clauses when they do not contravene public policy, are not ambiguous, and do not claim to protect parties from liability for intentional misconduct. Businesses such as health clubs, racetracks, amusement parks, skiing facilities, horse-rental operations, golf-cart concessions, and skydiving organizations frequently use exculpatory clauses to limit their liability for patrons' injuries. Because these services are not essential, the firms offering them are sometimes considered to have no relative advantage in bargaining strength, and anyone contracting for their services is considered to do so voluntarily.

The Effect of Illegality

In general, an illegal contract is void: the contract is deemed never to have existed, and the courts will not aid either party. In most illegal contracts, both parties are considered to be equally at fault—*in pari delicto*. If the contract is executory (not yet fulfilled), neither party can enforce it. If it has been executed, neither party can recover damages.

The courts usually are not concerned if one wrongdoer in an illegal contract is unjustly enriched at the expense of the other—except under certain circumstances (to be discussed shortly). The main reason for this hands-off attitude is a belief that a plaintiff who has broken the law by entering into an illegal bargain should not be allowed to obtain help from the courts. Another justification is the hoped-for deterrent effect: a plaintiff who suffers a loss because of an illegal bargain will presumably be deterred from entering into similar illegal bargains in the future.

There are exceptions to the general rule that neither party to an illegal bargain can sue for breach and neither party can recover for performance rendered. We look at these exceptions here.

Justifiable Ignorance of the Facts

When one of the parties to a contract is relatively innocent (has no reason to know that the contract is illegal), that party can often recover any benefits conferred in a partially executed contract. In this situation, the courts will not enforce the contract but will allow the parties to return to their original positions.

A court may sometimes permit an innocent party who has fully performed under a contract to enforce the contract against the guilty party. **EXAMPLE 11.18** A trucking company contracts with Gillespie to carry crated goods to a specific destination for a normal fee of $5,000. The trucker delivers the crates and later finds out that they contained illegal goods. Although the shipment, use, and sale of the goods are illegal under the law, the trucker, being an innocent party, can normally still legally collect the $5,000 from Gillespie. ●

Members of Protected Classes

When a statute protects a certain class of people, a member of that class can enforce an illegal contract even though the other party cannot. **EXAMPLE 11.19** Statutes prohibit certain employees (such as flight attendants or pilots) from working more than a specified number of hours per month. These employees thus constitute a class protected by statute. An employee who is required to work more than the maximum can recover for those extra hours of service. ●

Blue Sky Laws State laws that regulate the offering and sale of securities for the protection of the public.

Other examples of statutes designed to protect a particular class of people are **blue sky laws**—state laws that regulate the offering and sale of securities for the protection of the public (see Chapter 31)—and state statutes regulating the sale of insurance. If an insurance company violates a statute when selling insurance, the purchaser can nevertheless enforce the policy and recover from the insurer.

Withdrawal from an Illegal Agreement

If the illegal part of a bargain has not yet been performed, the party rendering performance can withdraw from the contract and recover the performance or its value. **EXAMPLE 11.20** Marta and Ande decide to wager (illegally) on the outcome of a boxing match. Each deposits $1,000 with a stakeholder, who agrees to pay the winner of the bet. At this point, each party has performed part of the agreement, but the illegal part of the agreement will not occur until the winner is paid. Before such payment occurs, either party is entitled to withdraw from the agreement by giving notice to the stakeholder of his or her withdrawal. •

Severable, or Divisible, Contracts

A contract that is *severable,* or divisible, consists of distinct parts that can be performed separately, with separate consideration provided for each part. With an *indivisible* contract, in contrast, the parties intended that complete performance by each party would be essential, even if the contract contains a number of seemingly separate provisions.

If a contract is divisible into legal and illegal portions, a court may enforce the legal portion but not the illegal one, so long as the illegal portion does not affect the essence of the bargain. This approach is consistent with the basic policy of enforcing the legal intentions of the contracting parties whenever possible. **EXAMPLE 11.21** Cole signs an employment contract that includes an overly broad and thus illegal covenant not to compete. In this situation, a court might allow the employment contract to be enforceable but reform the unreasonably broad covenant by converting its terms into reasonable ones. Alternatively, the court could declare the covenant illegal (and thus void) and enforce the remaining employment terms. • (See the appendix to Chapter 14 that starts on page 374 for an example of how some contracts include a clause indicating that the parties intend the contract terms to be enforced to the "fullest extent possible.")

Fraud, Duress, or Undue Influence

Often, one party to an illegal contract is more at fault than the other. When a party has been induced to enter into an illegal bargain through fraud, duress, or undue influence on the part of the other party to the agreement, the first party will be allowed to recover for the performance or its value.

Reviewing . . . Consideration, Capacity, and Legality

Renee Beaver started racing go-karts competitively in 2009, when she was fourteen. Many of the races required her to sign an exculpatory clause to participate, which she or her parents regularly signed. In 2012, right before her birthday, she participated in the annual Elkhart Grand Prix, a series of races in Elkhart, Indiana. During the event in which she drove, a piece of foam padding used as a course barrier was torn from its base and ended up on the track. A portion of the padding struck Beaver in the head, and another portion was thrown into oncoming traffic, causing a multikart collision during which she sustained severe injuries. Beaver filed an action against the race organizers for negligence. The organizers could not locate the exculpatory clause that Beaver was supposed to have signed. Race organizers argued that she must have signed one to enter the race, but even if she had not signed one, her actions showed her intent to be bound by its terms. Using the information presented in the chapter, answer the following questions.

1. Did Beaver have the contractual capacity to enter a contract with an exculpatory clause? Why or why not?
2. Assuming that Beaver did, in fact, sign the exculpatory clause, did she later disaffirm or ratify the contract? Explain.
3. Now assume that Beaver had stated that she was eighteen years old at the time that she signed the exculpatory clause. How might this affect Beaver's ability to disaffirm or ratify the contract?

Continued

4. Now suppose that Beaver can prove that she did not actually sign an exculpatory clause and this convinces race organizers to pursue a settlement. They offer to pay Beaver one-half of the amount that she is claiming in damages if she now signs a release of all claims. Because Beaver is young and the full effects of her injuries may not be clear at this time, what other type of settlement agreement might she prefer? What is the consideration to support any settlement agreement that Beaver enters into with the race organizers?

DEBATE THIS After agreeing to an exculpatory clause or purchasing some item, such as an iPad, minors often seek to avoid the contracts. Today's minors are far from naïve and should not be allowed to avoid their contractual obligations.

BUSINESS APPLICATION

Should Retailers Enter into Contracts with Minors and Intoxicated Persons?*

Sales personnel, particularly those who are paid on a commission basis, are often eager to make contracts. Sometimes, however, these salespersons must deal with minors and intoxicated persons, both of whom have limited contractual capacity. Therefore, if you are a retailer, you should make sure that your employees are acquainted with the law governing contracts with minors and intoxicated persons.

Contracts with Minors

If your business involves selling consumer durables, such as cell phones, electronics, gaming equipment, appliances, furniture, or automobiles, your sales personnel must be careful in forming contracts with minors and should heed the adage, "When in doubt, check." Remember that a contract signed by a minor (unless it is for necessaries) normally is voidable, and the minor may exercise the option to disaffirm the contract. Employees should demand proof of legal age when they have any doubt about whether a customer is a minor. If the customer is a minor, the employees should insist that an adult (such as a parent) be the purchaser or at least cosign any sales contract.

In addition, because the law governing minors' rights varies substantially from state to state, you should check with your attorney concerning the laws governing disaffirmance in your state. You and those you hire to sell your products should know, for example, what the consequences will be if a minor disaffirms the sale or has misrepresented his or her age when forming a sales contract. Similarly, you need to find out whether and in what circumstances a minor, on disaffirming a contract, can be required to pay for damage to goods sold under the contract.

Dealing with Intoxicated Persons

Little need be said about a salesperson's dealings with obviously intoxicated persons. If the customer, despite intoxication, understands the legal consequences of the contract being signed, the contract is enforceable. Nonetheless, it may be extremely difficult to establish that the intoxicated customer understood the consequences of entering into the contract if the customer claims that she or he did not understand. Therefore, the best advice is, "When in doubt, don't." In other words, if you suspect a customer may be intoxicated, do not sign a contract with that customer.

Checklist for the Retailer

1. *When in doubt about the age of a customer to whom you are about to sell major consumer durable goods or anything other than necessaries, require proof of legal age.*
2. *If such proof is not forthcoming, require that a parent or guardian sign the contract.*

*This *Business Application* is not meant to substitute for the services of an attorney who is licensed to practice law in your state.

Key Terms

accord and satisfaction 285
adhesion contract 296
blue sky laws 298
consideration 282
contractual capacity 288
covenant not to compete 294
covenant not to sue 286
disaffirmance 289
emancipation 288
employment contract 294
estopped 287
exculpatory clause 297
forbearance 282
liquidated debt 285
necessaries 290
past consideration 284
promissory estoppel 286
ratification 290
reformation 296
release 286
rescission 284
unconscionable 296
usury 292

Chapter Summary: Consideration, Capacity, and Legality

Consideration (See pages 282–286.)	1. *Elements of consideration*— a. Something of *legally sufficient value* must be given in exchange for a promise. b. There must be a bargained-for exchange. 2. *Legal sufficiency and adequacy of consideration*—Legal sufficiency means that something of legal value must be given in exchange for a promise. Adequacy relates to "how much" consideration is given and whether a fair bargain was reached. Courts will inquire into the adequacy of consideration only when fraud, undue influence, duress, or unconscionability may be involved. 3. *Contracts that lack consideration*—Consideration is lacking in the following situations: a. Preexisting duty—A promise to do what one already has a legal duty to do is not legally sufficient consideration for a new contract. b. Past consideration—Actions or events that have already taken place do not constitute legally sufficient consideration. c. Illusory promises—When the nature or extent of performance is too uncertain, the promise is rendered illusory (without consideration and unenforceable). 4. *Settlement of claims*—Disputes may be settled by the following, which are enforceable provided there is consideration: a. Accord and satisfaction—An *accord* is an agreement in which a debtor offers to pay a lesser amount than the creditor claims is owed. *Satisfaction* takes place when the accord is executed. b. Release—An agreement in which, for consideration, a party forfeits the right to seek further recovery beyond the terms specified in the release. c. Covenant not to sue—An agreement not to sue on a present, valid claim.
Promissory Estoppel (See pages 286–288.)	The equitable doctrine of promissory estoppel applies when a promisor should have expected a promise to induce definite and substantial action or forbearance by the promisee, and the promisee does act in reliance on the promise. Such a promise is binding, even though there is no consideration, if injustice can be avoided only by enforcement of the promise. Also known as the doctrine of *detrimental reliance.*
	CONTRACTUAL CAPACITY
Minors (See pages 288–290.)	1. *General rule*—Contracts with minors are voidable at the option of the minor. 2. *Disaffirmance*—The legal avoidance of a contractual obligation. a. Disaffirmance can take place (in most states) at any time during minority and within a reasonable time after the minor has reached the age of majority. b. The minor must disaffirm the entire contract, not just part of it. c. When disaffirming executed contracts, the minor has a duty to return the received goods if they are still in the minor's control or (in some states) to pay their reasonable value. d. A minor who has committed an act of fraud (such as misrepresenting her or his age) will be denied the right to disaffirm by some courts. e. A minor may disaffirm a contract for necessaries but remains liable for the reasonable value of the goods. 3. *Ratification*—The acceptance, or affirmation, of a legal obligation. a. Express ratification—Occurs when the minor, in writing or orally, explicitly assumes the obligations imposed by the contract. b. Implied ratification—Occurs when the conduct of the minor is inconsistent with disaffirmance or when the minor fails to disaffirm an executed contract within a reasonable time after reaching the age of majority. 4. *Parents' liability*—Generally, except for contracts for necessaries, parents are not liable for the contracts made by minor children acting on their own. Parents may be liable for minors' torts in certain circumstances, however. 5. *Emancipation*—Occurs when a child's parent or legal guardian relinquishes the legal right to exercise control over the child. Normally, minors who leave home to support themselves are considered emancipated. In some jurisdictions, minors are permitted to petition a court for emancipation for limited purposes.

Continued

Chapter Summary: Consideration, Capacity, and Legality—Continued

Intoxicated Persons (See page 290.)	1. A contract entered into by an intoxicated person is voidable at the option of the intoxicated person if the person was sufficiently intoxicated to lack mental capacity, even if the intoxication was voluntary. 2. A contract with an intoxicated person is enforceable if, despite being intoxicated, the person understood the legal consequences of entering into the contract.
Mentally Incompetent Persons (See pages 290–291.)	1. A contract made by a person previously judged by a court to be mentally incompetent is void. 2. A contract made by a person who is mentally incompetent, but has not been previously declared incompetent by a court, is voidable at the option of that person.
LEGALITY	
Contracts Contrary to Statute (See pages 291–294.)	1. *Usury*—Usury occurs when a lender makes a loan at an interest rate above the lawful maximum, which varies from state to state. 2. *Gambling*—Gambling contracts that contravene (go against) state statutes are deemed illegal and thus void. 3. *Licensing statutes*—Contracts entered into by persons who do not have a license, when one is required by statute, will not be enforceable unless the underlying purpose of the statute is to raise government revenues (and not to protect the public from unauthorized practitioners).
Contracts Contrary to Public Policy (See pages 294–298.)	1. *Contracts in restraint of trade*—Contracts to reduce or restrain free competition are illegal and prohibited by statutes. An exception is a *covenant not to compete.* Such covenants usually are enforced by the courts if the terms are secondary to a contract (such as a contract for the sale of a business or an employment contract) and are reasonable as to time and area of restraint. Courts tend to scrutinize covenants not to compete closely and, at times, may reform them if they are overbroad rather than declaring the entire covenant unenforceable. 2. *Unconscionable contracts and clauses*—When a contract or contract clause is so unfair that it is oppressive to one party, it may be deemed unconscionable. As such, it is illegal and cannot be enforced. 3. *Exculpatory clauses*—An exculpatory clause is a clause that releases a party from liability in the event of monetary or physical injury, no matter who is at fault. In certain situations, exculpatory clauses may be contrary to public policy and thus unenforceable.
EFFECT OF ILLEGALITY	
General Rule (See page 298.)	In general, an illegal contract is void, and the courts will not aid either party when both parties are considered to be equally at fault *(in pari delicto)*. If the contract is executory, neither party can enforce it. If the contract is executed, neither party can recover damages.
Exceptions (See pages 298–299.)	Several exceptions exist to the general rule that neither party to an illegal bargain will be able to recover. In the following situations, the court may grant recovery: 1. *Justifiable ignorance of the facts*—When one party to the contract is relatively innocent. 2. *Members of protected classes*—When one party to the contract is a member of a group of persons protected by statute, such as employees. 3. *Withdrawal from an illegal agreement*—When either party seeks to recover consideration given for an illegal contract before the illegal act is performed. 4. *Severable, or divisible, contracts*—When the court can divide the contract into illegal and legal portions and the illegal portion is not essential to the bargain. 5. *Fraud, duress, or undue influence*—When one party was induced to enter into an illegal bargain through fraud, duress, or undue influence.

ExamPrep

ISSUE SPOTTERS

1. In September, Sharyn agrees to work for Totem Productions, Inc., at $500 a week for a year beginning January 1. In October, Sharyn is offered $600 a week for the same work by Umber Shows, Ltd. When Sharyn tells Totem about the other offer, they tear up their contract and agree that Sharyn will be paid $575. Is the new contract binding? Explain. **(See page 284.)**

2. Sun Airlines, Inc., prints on its tickets that it is not liable for any injury to a passenger caused by the airline's negligence. If the cause of an accident is found to be the airline's negligence, can it use the clause as a defense to liability? Why or why not? **(See pages 297–298.)**

—Check your answers to the Issue Spotters against the answers provided in Appendix E at the end of this text.

BEFORE THE TEST

Go to www.cengagebrain.com, enter the ISBN 9781133273561 and click on "Find" to locate this textbook's Web site. Then, click on "Access Now" under "Study Tools," and select Chapter 11 at the top. There, you will find a Practice Quiz that you can take to assess your mastery of the concepts in this chapter, as well as Flashcards, a Glossary of important terms, and Video Questions (when assigned).

For Review

Answers to the even-numbered questions in this For Review section can be found in Appendix F at the end of this text.

1. What is consideration? What is required for consideration to be legally sufficient?
2. In what circumstances might a promise be enforced despite a lack of consideration?
3. Does a minor have the capacity to enter into an enforceable contract? What does it mean to disaffirm a contract?
4. Under what circumstances will a covenant not to compete be enforced? When will such covenants not be enforced?
5. What is an exculpatory clause? In what circumstances might exculpatory clauses be enforced? When will they not be enforced?

Business Scenarios and Case Problems

11–1 Contracts by Minors. Kalen is a seventeen-year-old minor who has just graduated from high school. He is attending a university two hundred miles from home and has contracted to rent an apartment near the university for one year at $500 per month. He is working at a convenience store to earn enough income to be self-supporting. After living in the apartment and paying monthly rent for four months, he becomes involved in a dispute with his landlord. Kalen, still a minor, moves out and returns the key to the landlord. The landlord wants to hold Kalen liable for the balance of the payments due under the lease. Discuss fully Kalen's liability in this situation. **(See pages 288–290.)**

11–2 Question with Sample Answer—Past Consideration. Daniel, a recent college graduate, is on his way home for the Christmas holidays from his new job. He gets caught in a snowstorm and is taken in by an elderly couple who provide him with food and shelter. After the snowplows have cleared the road, Daniel proceeds home. Daniel's father, Fred, is most appreciative of the elderly couple's action and in a letter promises to pay them $500. The elderly couple, in need of funds, accept Fred's offer. Then, because of a dispute with Daniel, Fred refuses to pay the elderly couple the $500. Discuss whether the couple can hold Fred liable in contract for the services rendered to Daniel. **(See page 284.)**

—For a sample answer to Question 11–2, go to Appendix G at the end of this text.

11–3 Past Consideration. Access Organics, Inc., hired Andy Hernandez to sell organic produce. Later, Hernandez signed an agreement not to compete with Access for two years following the termination of his employment. He did not receive a pay increase or any other new benefits in return for signing the agreement. When Access encountered financial trouble, Hernandez left and began to compete with his former employer. Access filed a lawsuit against Hernandez. Is the noncompete agreement enforceable? Discuss. [*Access Organics, Inc. v. Hernandez,* 341 Mont. 73, 175 P.3d 899 (2008)] **(See page 284.)**

11–4 Spotlight on Arbitration Clauses—Unconscionable Contracts or Clauses. Roberto Basulto and Raquel Gonzalez, who did not speak English, responded to an ad on Spanish-language television sponsored by Hialeah Automotive, LLC, which does business as Potamkin Dodge. Potamkin's staff understood that Basulto and Gonzalez did not speak or read English and conducted the entire transaction in Spanish. They explained the English-language contract, but did not explain an accompanying arbitration agreement. This agreement limited the amount of damages that the buyers could seek in court to less than $5,000, but did not limit Potamkin's right to pursue greater damages. Basulto and Gonzalez bought a Dodge Caravan and signed the contract in blank—that is, leaving some terms to be filled in later. Potamkin later filled in a lower trade-in allowance than agreed and refused to change it. The buyers returned the van—having driven it a total of seven miles—and asked for a return of their trade-in vehicle, but it had been sold. The buyers filed a suit in a Florida state court against Potamkin. The dealer sought arbitration. Was the arbitration agreement unconscionable? Why or why not? [*Hialeah Automotive, LLC v. Basulto,* 22 So.3d 586 (Fla.App. 3 Dist. 2009)] **(See page 296.)**

11–5 **Disaffirmance.** J.T., a minor, is a motocross competitor. At Monster Mountain MX Park, he signed a waiver of liability to "hold harmless the park for any loss due to negligence." Riding around the Monster Mountain track, J.T. rode over a blind jump, became airborne, and crashed into a tractor that he had not seen until he was in the air. To recover for his injuries, J.T. filed a suit against Monster Mountain, alleging negligence for its failure to remove the tractor from the track. Does the liability waiver bar this claim? Explain. [*J.T. v. Monster Mountain, LLC,* 754 F.Supp.2d 1323 (M.D.Ala. 2010)] **(See page 289.)**

11–6 **Case Problem with Sample Answer—Unconscionable Contracts or Clauses.** Geographic Expeditions, Inc. (GeoEx), which guided climbs up Mount Kilimanjaro, required climbers to sign a release to participate in an expedition. The form required any disputes to be submitted to arbitration in San Francisco and limited damages to the cost of the trip. GeoEx told climbers that the terms were nonnegotiable and that other travel firms imposed the same terms. Jason Lhotka died on a GeoEx climb. His mother filed a suit against GeoEx. GeoEx sought arbitration. Was the arbitration clause unconscionable? Why or why not? [*Lhotka v. Geographic Expeditions, Inc.,* 181 Cal.App.4th 816, 104 Cal. Rptr.3d 844 (1 Dist. 2010)] **(See page 297.)**

—For a sample answer to Problem 11–6, go to Appendix H at the end of this text.

11–7 **Mental Incompetence.** Dorothy Drury suffered from dementia and chronic confusion. When she became unable to manage her own affairs, including decisions about medical and financial matters, her son Eddie arranged for her to move to an assisted living facility. During admission, she signed a residency agreement, which included an arbitration clause. After she sustained injuries in a fall at the facility, a suit was filed to recover damages. The facility asked the court to compel arbitration. Was Dorothy bound to the residency agreement? Discuss. [*Drury v. Assisted Living Concepts, Inc.,* 245 Or.App. 217, 262 P.3d 1162 (2011)] **(See page 290.)**

11–8 **Licensing Statutes.** PEMS Co. International, Inc., agreed to find a buyer for Rupp Industries, Inc., for a commission of 2 percent of the purchase price, which was to be paid by the buyer. Using PEMS's services, an investment group bought Rupp for $20 million and changed its name to Temp-Air, Inc. PEMS asked Temp-Air to pay a commission on the sale. Temp-Air refused, arguing that PEMS had acted as a broker in the deal without a license. The applicable statute defines a broker as any person who deals with the sale of a business. If this statute was intended to protect the public, can PEMS collect its commission? Explain. [*PEMS Co. International, Inc. v. Temp-Air, Inc.,* __ N.W.2d __ (Minn.App. 2011)] **(See page 292.)**

11–9 **A Question of Ethics—Promissory Estoppel.** Claudia Aceves borrowed $845,000 from U.S. Bank to buy a home. Less than two years into the loan, she could no longer afford the monthly payments. The bank notified her that it planned to foreclose on her home. (Foreclosure is a process that allows a lender to repossess and sell the property that secures a loan—see Chapter 22.) The bank offered to modify Aceves's mortgage if she would forgo bankruptcy. In reliance on the bank's promise, she agreed. Once she withdrew the filing, however, the bank foreclosed and began eviction proceedings. Aceves filed a suit against the bank for promissory estoppel. [*Aceves v. U.S. Bank, N.A.,* 192 Cal.App.4th 218, 120 Cal.Rptr.3d 507 (2 Dist. 2011)] **(See page 286.)**

1. Could Aceves succeed in her claim of promissory estoppel? Why or why not?
2. Did Aceves or U.S. Bank behave unethically? Discuss.

Critical Thinking and Writing Assignments

11–10 **Critical Legal Thinking.** Are legalized forms of gambling, such as state-operated lotteries, consistent with a continuing public policy against the enforcement of gambling contracts? Why or why not? **(See page 292.)**

11–11 **Business Law Critical Thinking Group Assignment.** Assume that you are a group of executives at a large software corporation. The company is considering whether to add covenants not to compete to its employment contracts. You know that there are some issues with the enforceability of these covenants and want to make an informed decision.

1. One group should make a list of interests that are served by enforcing covenants not to compete.
2. A second group should create a list of interests that are served by refusing to enforce covenants not to compete.
3. A third group should discuss whether a court that determines that a covenant not to compete is illegal should reform (and then enforce) the covenant. The group should present arguments for and against reformation.

CHAPTER 12

Defenses to Contract Enforceability

(vladek/Shutterstock.com)

CHAPTER OUTLINE

- Voluntary Consent
- The Statute of Frauds—Writing Requirement
- The Statute of Frauds—Sufficiency of the Writing
- The Parol Evidence Rule

LEARNING OBJECTIVES

The five learning objectives below are designed to help improve your understanding of the chapter. After reading this chapter, you should be able to answer the following questions:

1. In what types of situations might voluntary consent to a contract's terms be lacking?
2. What is the difference between a mistake of value or quality and a mistake of fact?
3. What are the elements of fraudulent misrepresentation?
4. What contracts must be in writing to be enforceable?
5. What is parol evidence? When is it admissible to clarify the terms of a written contract?

"Understanding is a two-way street."

—Eleanor Roosevelt, 1884–1962 (First Lady of the United States, 1933–1945)

An otherwise valid contract may still be unenforceable if the parties have not genuinely agreed to its terms. As mentioned in Chapter 9, a lack of voluntary consent is a *defense* to the enforcement of a contract. As Eleanor Roosevelt stated in the chapter-opening quotation, "Understanding is a two-way street." If one party does not voluntarily consent to the terms of a contract, then there is no genuine "meeting of the minds," and the law will not normally enforce the contract, as we discuss in the first part of this chapter.

A contract that is otherwise valid may also be unenforceable if it is not in the proper form. For example, if a contract is required by law to be in writing and there is no written evidence of the contract, it may not be enforceable. In the second part of this chapter, we examine the kinds of contracts that require a writing under what is called the *Statute of Frauds.* This chapter concludes with a discussion of the parol evidence rule, under which courts determine the admissibility at trial of evidence extraneous (external) to written contracts.

Voluntary Consent

LEARNING OBJECTIVE 1
In what types of situations might voluntary consent to a contract's terms be lacking?

Voluntary consent (assent) may be lacking because of mistake, fraudulent misrepresentation, undue influence, or duress. Generally, a party who demonstrates that he or she did not genuinely agree to the terms of a contract can choose either to carry out the contract or to rescind (cancel) it and thus avoid the entire transaction.

This is one reason why many contracts include definitions of important terms (see the *Appendix to Chapter 14: An Annotated Employment Contract* for an example).

Mistakes

We all make mistakes, so it is not surprising that mistakes are made when contracts are created. In certain circumstances, contract law allows a contract to be avoided on the basis of mistake. It is important to distinguish between *mistakes of fact* and *mistakes of value or quality.* Only a mistake of fact may allow a contract to be avoided.

LEARNING OBJECTIVE 2
What is the difference between a mistake of value or quality and a mistake of fact?

EXAMPLE 12.1 Paco buys a violin from Beverly for $250. Although the violin is very old, neither party believes that it is valuable. Later, however, an antiques dealer informs the parties that the violin is rare and worth thousands of dollars. Here, both parties were mistaken, but the mistake is a mistake of *value* rather than a mistake of *fact* that warrants contract rescission. Therefore, Beverly cannot rescind the contract. •

Mistakes of fact occur in two forms—*unilateral* and *bilateral (mutual).* A unilateral mistake is made by only one of the contracting parties, whereas a mutual mistake is made by both. We look next at these two types of mistakes and illustrate them graphically in Exhibit 12.1 on the facing page.

Unilateral Mistakes

A unilateral mistake occurs when only one party is mistaken as to a *material fact*—that is, a fact important to the subject matter of the contract. Generally, a unilateral mistake does not give the mistaken party any right to relief from the contract. In other words, the contract normally is enforceable against the mistaken party.

EXAMPLE 12.2 Elena intends to sell her motor home for $17,500. When she learns that Chin is interested in buying a used motor home, she sends him an e-mail offering to sell the vehicle to him. When typing the e-mail, however, she mistakenly keys in the price of $15,700. Chin immediately sends an e-mail to Elena, accepting her offer. Even though Elena intended to sell her motor home for $17,500, she has made a unilateral mistake and is bound by the contract to sell the vehicle to Chin for $15,700. •

This rule has at least two exceptions, however.[1]

KNOW THIS

What a party to a contract knows or should know can determine whether the contract is enforceable.

When the Other Party Has Reason to Know That a Mistake Was Made If the *other* party to the contract knows or should have known that a mistake of fact was made, the contract may not be enforceable. **EXAMPLE 12.3** In *Example 12.2,* if Chin knew that Elena intended to sell her motor home for $17,500, then Elena's unilateral mistake (stating $15,700 in her offer) may render the resulting contract unenforceable. •

Mathematical Mistakes The second exception arises when a unilateral mistake of fact was due to a mathematical mistake in addition, subtraction, division, or multiplication and was made inadvertently and without gross (extreme) negligence. If a contractor's bid was significantly low because he or she made a mistake in addition when totaling the estimated costs, any contract resulting from the bid normally may be rescinded. Of course, in both situations, the mistake must still involve some *material fact* (one that is important and central to the contract).

Bilateral (Mutual) Mistakes

A bilateral mistake is a "mutual misunderstanding concerning a basic assumption on which the contract was made."[2] When both parties

1. The *Restatement (Second) of Contracts,* Section 153, liberalizes the general rule to take into account the modern trend of allowing avoidance in some circumstances even though only one party has been mistaken.
2. *Restatement (Second) of Contracts,* Section 152.

Exhibit 12.1 Mistakes of Fact

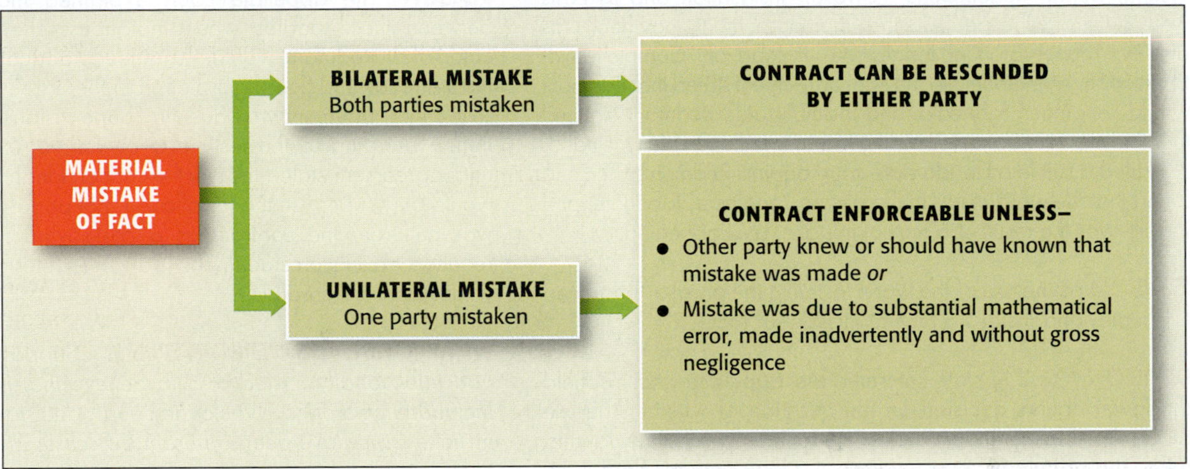

are mistaken about the same material fact, the contract can be rescinded by either party. Note that, as with unilateral mistakes, the mistake must be about a material fact. When a bilateral mistake occurs, normally the contract is voidable by the adversely affected party and can be rescinded, or canceled.

"Mistakes are the inevitable lot of mankind."

Sir George Jessel, 1824–1883 (English jurist)

A word or term in a contract may be subject to more than one reasonable interpretation. If the parties to the contract attach materially different meanings to the term, their mutual misunderstanding may allow the contract to be rescinded.

CASE EXAMPLE 12.4 In a classic case, Wichelhaus purchased a shipment of cotton from Raffles to arrive on a ship called the *Peerless* sailing from Bombay, India. Wichelhaus meant a ship called *Peerless* leaving Bombay in October, but Raffles meant a different ship also named *Peerless* leaving Bombay in December. When the goods arrived on the December *Peerless* and Raffles tried to deliver them, Wichelhaus refused to accept them. The British court held for Wichelhaus, concluding that a mutual mistake had been made because the parties had attached materially different meanings to an essential term of the contract (which ship *Peerless* was to transport the goods).[3] •

In the following case, the court had to grapple with the question of whether a mutual mistake of fact had occurred.

3. *Raffles v. Wichelhaus*, 159 Eng.Rep. 375 (1864).

Case 12.1

L&H Construction Co. v. Circle Redmont, Inc.

District Court of Appeal of Florida, Fifth District, 55 So.3d 630 (2011).
www.5dca.org/opinions.shtml[a]

(© Jerry McCrea/Star Ledger/Corbis)
The Thomas Edison historic site in West Orange, New Jersey.

FACTS L&H Construction Company was a general contractor involved in the renovation of the Thomas Edison historic site in West Orange, New Jersey, for the National Park Service. L&H contracted with Circle Redmont, Inc. (Redmont), which is based in Melbourne, Florida, to make a cast-iron staircase and a glass flooring system. Redmont's original proposal was to "engineer, fabricate, and install" the staircase and flooring

a. In the "Search Opinions" section, in the "Search for this:" box, type "5D09-2609" and click on "Submit." In the result, click on the appropriate link to view the opinion. The Florida Fifth District Court of Appeal maintains this Web site.

Case 12.1—Continues next page

Case 12.1—Continued

system. During negotiations, however, installation and its costs were cut from the deal. In the final agreement, payment was due on "Supervision of Installation" instead of "Completion of Installation." Nevertheless, the final agreement stated that Redmont would "engineer, fabricate, and install." Later, Redmont claimed that this was a mistake. L&H insisted that installation was included. L&H filed a suit in a Florida state court against Redmont. The court found that the word *install* in the phrase "engineer, fabricate, and install" was the result of a mutual mistake. L&H appealed.

ISSUE Was the use of the word *install* in the phrase "engineer, fabricate, and install" a mutual mistake of fact?

DECISION Yes. A state intermediate appellate court upheld the lower court's decision on the question of whether the use of the word *install* in the parties' agreement was a mutual mistake. The appellate court reversed the lower court's final judgment in Redmont's favor on other grounds, however.

REASON The appellate court explained that the contract between these parties was ambiguous. The proposal indicated that Redmont would "engineer, fabricate, and install" the staircase and flooring system, but the agreement stated that L&H's final payment was due on "Supervision" of the installation. According to the testimony of Redmont's witnesses, the final agreement stated the parties' understanding that Redmont would only supervise the installation, not perform it. Installation was cut from the contract as a cost-saving measure at the request of L&H's president. The trial court determined that these witnesses were credible.

WHAT IF THE FACTS WERE DIFFERENT? *Suppose that Redmont had intentionally misled L&H to believe that installation was included in the price. Would the court's decision on the mutual mistake issue have been different? Discuss.*

Fraudulent Misrepresentation

Although fraud is a tort (see Chapter 4), the presence of fraud also affects the authenticity of the innocent party's consent to a contract. When an innocent party is fraudulently induced to enter into a contract, the contract usually can be avoided because she or he has not *voluntarily* consented to the terms.[4] Normally, the innocent party can either rescind (cancel) the contract and be restored to her or his original position or enforce the contract and seek damages for any harms resulting from the fraud.

LEARNING OBJECTIVE 3
What are the elements of fraudulent misrepresentation?

Generally, fraudulent misrepresentation refers only to misrepresentation that is consciously false and is intended to mislead another. Typically, fraud involves three elements:

1. A misrepresentation of a material fact must occur.
2. There must be an intent to deceive.
3. The innocent party must justifiably rely on the misrepresentation.

Additionally, to collect damages, a party must have been harmed as a result of the misrepresentation.

KNOW THIS
To collect damages in almost any lawsuit, there must be some sort of injury.

Fraudulent misrepresentation can occur in the online as well as the offline environment. For a case involving allegations that Yahoo fraudulently posted online personal ads, see this chapter's *Adapting the Law to the Online Environment* feature on the facing page. Because curbing Internet fraud is a major challenge in today's world, we will explore the topic further in Chapter 33 in the context of consumer law.

Misrepresentation Has Occurred

The first element of proving fraud is to show that misrepresentation of a material fact has occurred. This misrepresentation can occur by words or actions. For instance, an art gallery owner's statement "This painting is a Picasso" is a misrepresentation of fact if the painting was done by another artist. Similarly, if a customer asks to see only Jasper Johns paintings and the owner immediately leads the customer over to paintings that were not done by Johns, the owner's actions can be a misrepresentation.

4. *Restatement (Second) of Contracts,* Sections 163 and 164.

ADAPTING THE LAW TO THE ONLINE ENVIRONMENT

MISREPRESENTATION IN ONLINE PERSONALS

If you type "online personals" into any search engine, you will get more than 15 million hits. In the past, a major player in the online personals matching business was Yahoo! Personals. Indeed, for a time, it called itself the "top online dating site." It offered two options—one for casual dates and another for people who wanted serious relationships. The latter was called Yahoo! Personals Primer. Users had to take a relationship test and then used Yahoo's matching system software to "zero in on marriage material."

Misrepresentation Reared Its Ugly Head

Everyone who uses online dating services is aware that people tend to exaggerate their positive features and downplay their negatives when they create their profiles. But users generally assume that the profiles are not completely made up. A few years ago, however, a disgruntled user of Yahoo! Personals Primer brought a lawsuit claiming that Yahoo had done exactly that. The suit alleged fraud and negligent misrepresentation, among other things.

Robert Anthony claimed that Yahoo deliberately and intentionally originated, created, and perpetuated false and/or nonexistent profiles. Not only did many profiles use the exact same phrases to describe people, but the same photo appeared for different profiles. Anthony also claimed that when a subscription term neared its end, Yahoo would send the subscriber a fake profile, heralding it as a "potential new match."

The Court Disagreed with Yahoo

Yahoo asked the court to dismiss the complaint on the ground that it was barred by the Communications Decency Act (CDA) of 1996,[a] which protects Internet service providers from liability for material supplied by their users. The court rejected that argument and held that Yahoo had become an information content provider itself when it created bogus user profiles. The case was allowed to continue.[b]

a. 47 U.S.C. Section 230.

b. *Anthony v. Yahoo!, Inc.*, 421 F.Supp.2d 1257 (N.D.Cal. 2006). See also *Doe v. SexSearch.com*, 502 F.Supp.2d 719 (N.D. Ohio 2007); and *Fair Housing Council of San Fernando Valley v. Roommate.com, LLC*, 521 F.3d 1157 (9th Cir. 2008).

(fazon1/iStockphoto.com)

When is misrepresentation actionable on online dating Web sites?

Match.com Faced Similar Charges

Earlier, Match.com, another large online dating service, faced a similar lawsuit. Matthew Evans claimed that he had obtained a date through Match.com with a woman who later confessed that she was actually an employee. The lawsuit claimed that Match.com "secretly employs people as 'date bait' to send bogus e-mails and to go on as many as 300 dates a month in order to keep customers paying for the use of the site." That suit was dismissed, however.

A class-action suit brought in 2009 accused Match.com of matching customers with individuals who were nonpaying customers or who were not customers at all. This suit has not yet been resolved.

As of 2010, Match.com became the exclusive online dating service provider for Yahoo!, Inc. The co-branded site is called Match.com on Yahoo!

Critical Thinking

Assume that a user of Match.com on Yahoo! discovered that each profile exaggerated the person's physical appearance, intelligence, and occupation. Would that user prevail if she or he brought a lawsuit for fraudulent misrepresentation? Why or why not?

Misrepresentation by Conduct Misrepresentation also occurs when a party takes specific action to conceal a fact that is material to the contract.[5] For instance, if a seller, by her or his actions, prevents a buyer from learning of some fact that is material to the contract, the seller's behavior constitutes misrepresentation by conduct.

5. *Restatement (Second) of Contracts,* Section 160.

CASE EXAMPLE 12.5 Actor Tom Selleck contracted to purchase a horse named Zorro for his daughter from Dolores Cuenca. Cuenca acted as though Zorro was fit to ride in competitions, when in reality the horse suffered from a medical condition. Selleck filed a lawsuit against Cuenca for wrongfully concealing the horse's condition, and a jury awarded Selleck more than $187,000 for Cuenca's misrepresentation by conduct.[6] ●

Another example of misrepresentation by conduct is the untruthful denial of knowledge or information concerning facts that are material to the contract when such knowledge or information is requested.

"If a man smiles all the time, he's probably selling something that doesn't work."

George Carlin, 1937–2008 (American comedian)

Statements of Opinion Statements of opinion and representations of future facts (predictions) are generally not subject to claims of fraud. Every person is expected to exercise care and judgment when entering into contracts, and the law will not come to the aid of one who simply makes an unwise bargain. Statements such as "This land will be worth twice as much next year" and "This car will last for years and years" are statements of opinion, not fact. Contracting parties should recognize them as opinions and not rely on them. A fact is objective and verifiable, whereas an opinion is usually subject to debate. Therefore, a seller is allowed to use *puffery* to sell her or his goods without being liable for fraud.

Nevertheless, in certain situations, such as when a naïve purchaser relies on an opinion from an expert, the innocent party may be entitled to rescission or reformation. (Reformation is an equitable remedy by which a court alters the terms of a contract to reflect the true intentions of the parties.)

CASE EXAMPLE 12.6 In a classic case, an instructor at an Arthur Murray dance school told Audrey Vokes, a widow without family, that she had the potential to become an accomplished dancer. The instructor sold her 2,302 hours of dancing lessons for a total amount of $31,090.45 (equivalent to $142,000 in 2013). When it became clear to Vokes that she did not, in fact, have the potential to be an excellent dancer, she sued the school for fraudulent misrepresentation. The court held that because the dance school had superior knowledge about a person's dance potential, the instructor's statements could be considered statements of fact rather than opinion.[7] ●

Should an architect have greater knowledge about building codes than the person paying for the project?

(shotbydave/iStockphoto.com)

Misrepresentation of Law Misrepresentation of law *ordinarily* does not entitle a party to be relieved of a contract. **EXAMPLE 12.7** Tanya has a parcel of property that she is trying to sell to Lev. Tanya knows that a local ordinance prohibits building anything higher than three stories on the property. Nonetheless, she tells Lev, "You can build a condominium one hundred stories high if you want to." Lev buys the land and later discovers that Tanya's statement is false. Lev generally cannot avoid the contract because under the common law, people are assumed to know state and local laws. ●

Exceptions to this rule occur, however, when the misrepresenting party is in a profession known to require greater knowledge of the law than the average citizen possesses, such as real estate brokers or lawyers.

Misrepresentation by Silence Ordinarily, neither party to a contract has a duty to come forward and disclose facts, and a contract normally will not be set aside because certain pertinent information has not been volunteered. **EXAMPLE 12.8** Jude is selling a car that has been in an accident and has been repaired. He does not need to volunteer this information to a potential buyer. If, however, the buyer asks him if the car has had extensive bodywork and he lies, Jude has committed fraudulent misrepresentation. ●

In general, if the seller knows of a serious defect or a serious potential problem that the buyer cannot reasonably be expected to discover, the seller may have a duty to speak.

6. *Selleck v. Cuenca*, Case No. GIN056909, North County of San Diego, California, decided September 9, 2009.
7. *Vokes v. Arthur Murray, Inc.*, 212 So.2d 906 (Fla.App. 1968).

Normally, the seller must disclose only *latent defects*—that is, defects that could not readily be ascertained. Because a buyer of a house could easily discover the presence of termites through an inspection, for instance, termites may not qualify as a latent defect. Also, when the parties are in a *fiduciary relationship*—one of trust, such as partners, physician and patient, or attorney and client—there is a duty to disclose material facts. Failure to do so may constitute fraud.

In the following case, the issue of misrepresentation by silence was at the heart of the dispute. A real estate investor sued for fraud after a seller failed to disclose material facts about the property's value.

Case 12.2

Fazio v. Cypress/GR Houston I, LP

Court of Appeals of Texas, First District, 2012 WL 5324842 (2012).

(jnatkin/iStockphoto.com)

What does a rent-reduction request from a shopping mall's main tenant indicate?

FACTS Peter Fazio began talks with Cypress/GR Houston I, LP, to buy retail property whose main tenant was a Garden Ridge store. In performing a background investigation, Fazio and his agents became concerned about Garden Ridge's financial health. Nevertheless, after being assured that Garden Ridge had a positive financial outlook, Fazio sent Cypress a letter of intent to buy the property for $7.67 million "[b]ased on the currently reported absolute net income of $805,040.00." Cypress then agreed to provide all information in its possession, but it failed to disclose that (1) a consultant for Garden Ridge had recently requested a $240,000 reduction in the annual rent as part of a restructuring of the company's real estate leases and (2) Cypress's bank was so concerned about Garden Ridge's financial health that it had required a personal guaranty of the property's loan. The parties entered into a purchase agreement, but Garden Ridge went into bankruptcy shortly after the deal closed. Fazio sued Cypress for fraud after he was forced to sell the property for only $3.75 million. A jury found in Fazio's favor, but the trial court awarded a *judgment notwithstanding the verdict* (see page 80) to Cypress. Fazio appealed.

ISSUE Was Fazio fraudulently induced to enter into the purchase agreement?

DECISION Yes. The Texas appellate court reversed the trial court and held that Cypress was liable to Fazio for fraud.

REASON The court found that Cypress had engaged in fraud as a matter of law. Before the parties entered into the purchase agreement, Cypress had agreed to provide all information in its possession. Cypress knew that Fazio had been concerned about Garden Ridge's financial health and that he had based the purchase price on the anticipated income from the property. Moreover, a reasonable person in Fazio's position would have attached significance to Garden Ridge's recent request for a $240,000 rent reduction and to the fact that Cypress had been required to provide a personal guaranty of the property's loan. Finally, in the purchase agreement, Fazio did not disclaim his reliance on Cypress's misrepresentations or waive possible claims for fraud.

CRITICAL THINKING—Ethical Consideration *Was Cypress's conduct unethical? Why or why not?*

Scienter Knowledge by a misrepresenting party that material facts have been falsely represented or omitted with an intent to deceive.

Intent to Deceive

The second element of fraud is knowledge on the part of the misrepresenting party that facts have been misrepresented. This element, usually called **scienter,**[8] or "guilty knowledge," generally signifies that there was an intent to deceive. *Scienter* clearly exists if a party knows that a fact is not as stated. *Scienter* also exists if a party

8. Pronounced *sy-en-ter*.

makes a statement that he or she believes not to be true or makes a statement recklessly, without regard to whether it is true or false. Finally, this element is met if a party says or implies that a statement is made on some basis, such as personal knowledge or personal investigation, when it is not.

CASE EXAMPLE 12.9 Robert Sarvis applied for a position as a business law professor two weeks after his release from prison. On his résumé, he said that he had been a corporate president for fourteen years and had taught business law at another college. After he was hired, his probation officer alerted the school to Sarvis's criminal history. The school immediately fired him, and Sarvis sued for breach of his employment contract. The court concluded that by not disclosing his history, Sarvis clearly exhibited an intent to deceive and that the school had justifiably relied on his misrepresentations. Therefore, the school could rescind Sarvis's employment contract.[9]

Justifiable Reliance on the Misrepresentation The third element of fraud is *justifiable reliance* on the misrepresentation of fact. The deceived party must have a justifiable reason for relying on the misrepresentation, and the misrepresentation must be an important factor (but not necessarily the sole factor) in inducing the party to enter into the contract.

KNOW THIS

An opinion is neither a contract offer, nor a contract term, nor fraud.

Reliance is not justified if the innocent party knows the true facts or relies on obviously extravagant statements. **EXAMPLE 12.10** If a used-car dealer tells you, "This old Cadillac will get over sixty miles to the gallon," you normally would not be justified in relying on this statement. Suppose, however, that Merkel, a bank director, induces O'Connell, a co-director, to sign a statement that the bank has sufficient assets to meet its liabilities by telling O'Connell, "We have plenty of assets to satisfy our creditors." This statement is false. If O'Connell knows the true facts or, as a bank director, should know the true facts, he is not justified in relying on Merkel's statement. If O'Connell does not know the true facts, however, *and has no way of finding them out,* he may be justified in relying on the statement.

Injury to the Innocent Party Most courts do not require a showing of harm when the action is to rescind (cancel) the contract. These courts hold that because rescission returns the parties to the positions they held before the contract was made, a showing of injury to the innocent party is unnecessary.

To recover damages caused by fraud, however, proof of an injury is universally required. The measure of damages is ordinarily equal to the property's value had it been delivered as represented, less the actual price paid for the property. Courts may also award *punitive, or exemplary, damages,* which compensate a plaintiff over and above the amount of the actual loss. As discussed on pages 96 and 97 of Chapter 4, the public-policy consideration underlying punitive damages is to punish the defendant and thereby set an example that will deter similar wrongdoing by others.

PREVENTING LEGAL DISPUTES

If you are selling products or services, assume that all clients and customers are naïve and that they rely on your representations. Instruct employees to phrase their comments so that customers understand that any statements that are not factual are the employee's opinion. If someone asks a question that is beyond the employee's knowledge, it is better to say that he or she does not know than to guess and have the customer rely on a representation that turns out to be false. This can be particularly important when the questions concern topics such as compatibility or speed of electronic and digital goods, software, or related services.

9. *Sarvis v. Vermont State Colleges,* 172 Vt. 76, 772 A.2d 494 (2001).

Undue Influence

Undue influence arises from relationships in which one party can greatly influence another party, thus overcoming that party's free will. A contract entered into under excessive or undue influence lacks voluntary consent and is therefore voidable.[10]

In various types of relationships, one party may have an opportunity to dominate and unfairly influence another party. Minors and elderly people, for instance, are often under the influence of guardians (persons who are legally responsible for others). If a guardian induces a young or elderly ward (a person whom the guardian looks after) to enter into a contract that benefits the guardian, the guardian may have exerted undue influence. Undue influence can arise from a number of confidential or fiduciary relationships, including attorney-client, physician-patient, guardian-ward, parent-child, husband-wife, and trustee-beneficiary.

The essential feature of undue influence is that the party being taken advantage of does not, in reality, exercise free will in entering into a contract. It is not enough that a person is elderly or suffers from some mental or physical impairment. There must be clear and convincing evidence that the person did not act out of her or his free will.

Duress

Agreement to the terms of a contract is not voluntary if one of the parties is forced into the agreement. The use of threats to force a party to enter into a contract constitutes *duress*,[11] as does blackmail or extortion to induce consent to a contract. Duress is both a defense to the enforcement of a contract and a ground for rescission of a contract.

To establish duress, there must be proof of a threat. The threatened act must be wrongful or illegal and must render the person incapable of exercising free will. A threat to exercise a legal right, such as the right to sue someone, ordinarily does not constitute duress.

The Statute of Frauds—Writing Requirement

LEARNING OBJECTIVE 4

What contracts must be in writing to be enforceable?

Another defense to the enforceability of a contract is *form*—that is, some contracts must be in writing. Every state has a statute that stipulates that certain types of contracts must be in writing or be evidenced by a written memorandum or electronic record that is signed by the party against whom enforcement is sought, unless certain exceptions apply. Although the statutes vary slightly from state to state, their primary purpose is to ensure that, for certain types of contracts, there is reliable evidence of the contracts and their terms. In this text, we refer to these statutes collectively as the **Statute of Frauds**.

Statute of Frauds A state statute that requires certain types of contracts to be in writing to be enforceable.

The following types of contracts are said to fall "within" or "under" the Statute of Frauds and therefore require a writing:

1. Contracts involving interests in land.
2. Contracts that cannot by their terms be performed within one year from the day after the date of formation.
3. Collateral contracts, such as promises to answer for the debt or duty of another.
4. Promises made in consideration of marriage.
5. Under the Uniform Commercial Code (UCC—see Chapter 15), contracts for the sale of goods priced at $500 or more.

---

10. *Restatement (Second) of Contracts,* Section 177.

11. *Restatement (Second) of Contracts,* Sections 174 and 175.

The actual name of the Statute of Frauds is misleading because it does not apply to fraud. Rather, in an effort to prevent fraud, the statute denies *enforceability* to certain contracts that do not comply with its requirements. The name derives from an English act passed in 1677 that was titled "An Act for the Prevention of Frauds and Perjuries."

Contracts Involving Interests in Land

Under the Statute of Frauds, a contract involving an interest in land must be evidenced by a writing to be enforceable.[12] **EXAMPLE 12.11** If Carol contracts orally to sell Seaside Shelter to Axel but later decides not to sell, Axel cannot enforce the contract. Similarly, if Axel refuses to close the deal, Carol cannot force Axel to pay for the land by bringing a lawsuit. The Statute of Frauds is a defense to the enforcement of this type of oral contract. ●

A contract for the sale of land ordinarily involves the entire interest in the real property (discussed in Chapter 36), including buildings, growing crops, vegetation, minerals, timber, and anything else permanently attached to the land. Therefore, a *fixture* (personal property so affixed or so used as to become a part of the realty) is treated as real property.

The Statute of Frauds requires written contracts not just for the sale of land but also for the transfer of other interests in land, such as mortgages, easements, and leases. We describe these other interests in Chapters 22 and 36.

"A verbal contract isn't worth the paper it's written on."

Samuel Goldwyn, 1879–1974 (Hollywood motion picture producer)

The One-Year Rule

Contracts that cannot, *by their own terms,* be performed within one year *from the day after* the contract is formed must be in writing to be enforceable. Because disputes over such contracts are unlikely to occur until some time after the contracts are made, resolution of these disputes is difficult unless the contract terms have been put in writing.

Time Period Starts the Day after the Contract Is Formed The one-year period begins to run *the day after the contract is made.* **EXAMPLE 12.12** Superior University forms a contract with Kimi San stating that San will teach three courses in history during the coming academic year (September 15 through June 15). If the contract is formed in March, it must be in writing to be enforceable—because it cannot be performed within one year. If the contract is not formed until July, however, it will not have to be in writing to be enforceable—because it can be performed within one year. ●

Exhibit 12.2 on the facing page graphically illustrates the one-year rule.

Is Performance within One Year Possible? Normally, the test for determining whether an oral contract is enforceable under the one-year rule of the Statute of Frauds is whether performance is *possible* within one year from the day after the date of contract formation—not whether the agreement is *likely* to be performed within one year. When performance of a contract is objectively impossible during the one-year period, the oral contract will be unenforceable.

EXAMPLE 12.13 Bankers Life orally contracts to lend $40,000 to Janet Lawrence "as long as Lawrence & Associates operates its financial consulting firm in Omaha, Nebraska." The contract does not fall within the Statute of Frauds—no writing is required—because Lawrence & Associates could go out of business in one year or less. In this event, the contract would be fully performed within one year. Similarly, an oral contract for lifetime employment does not fall within the Statute of Frauds. Because an employee who is hired

12. In some states, the contract will be enforced if each party admits to the existence of the oral contract in court or admits to its existence during discovery before trial (see Chapter 3).

Exhibit 12.2 The One-Year Rule

Under the Statute of Frauds, contracts that by their terms are impossible to perform within one year from the day after the date of contract formation must be in writing to be enforceable. Put another way, if it is at all possible to perform an oral contract within one year from the day after the contract is made, the contract will fall outside the Statute of Frauds and be enforceable.

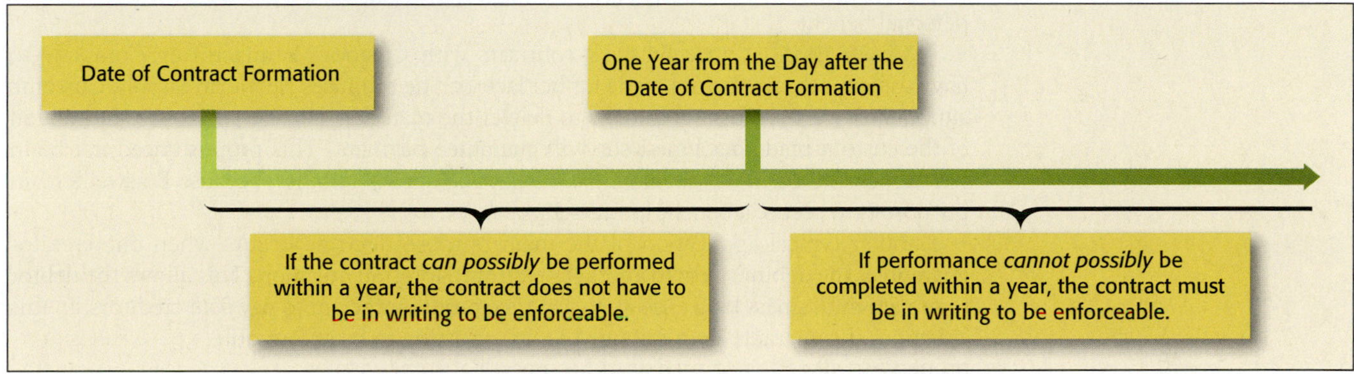

"for life" can die within a year, the courts reason that the contract can be performed within one year. ●

Collateral Promises

Collateral Promise A secondary promise to a primary transaction, such as a promise made by one person to pay the debts of another if the latter fails to perform. A collateral promise normally must be in writing to be enforceable.

A **collateral promise,** or secondary promise, is one that is ancillary (subsidiary) to a principal transaction or primary contractual relationship. In other words, a collateral promise is one made by a third party to assume the debts or obligations of a primary party to a contract if that party does not perform. Any collateral promise of this nature falls under the Statute of Frauds and therefore must be in writing to be enforceable. To understand this concept, it is important to distinguish between primary and secondary promises and obligations.

Primary versus Secondary Obligations A contract in which a party assumes a primary obligation normally does not need to be in writing to be enforceable. **EXAMPLE 12.14** Kareem orally contracts with Joanne's Floral Boutique to send his mother a dozen roses for Mother's Day. He agrees to pay when he receives the bill from Joanne's. Because Kareem is a direct party to this contract and has incurred a *primary* obligation to Joanne's, this contract does not have to be in writing under the Statute of Frauds. If Kareem fails to pay and the florist sues him for payment, Kareem cannot raise the Statute of Frauds as a defense. He cannot claim that the contract is unenforceable because it was not in writing. ●

In contrast, a contract in which a party assumes a secondary obligation does have to be in writing to be enforceable. **EXAMPLE 12.15** Kareem's mother borrows $10,000 from the Medford Trust Company on a promissory note payable in six months. Kareem promises the bank officer handling the loan that he will pay the $10,000 *if his mother does not pay the loan on time.* Kareem, in this situation, becomes what is known as a *guarantor* on the loan. He is guaranteeing to the bank (the creditor) that he will pay the loan if his mother fails to do so. This kind of collateral promise, in which the guarantor states that he or she will become responsible only if the primary party does not perform, must be in writing to be enforceable. ● We will return to the concept of guaranty and the distinction between primary and secondary obligations in Chapter 21 in the context of creditors' rights.

An Exception—The "Main Purpose" Rule An oral promise to answer for the debt of another is covered by the Statute of Frauds *unless* the guarantor's purpose in accepting secondary liability is to secure a personal benefit. Under the "main purpose" rule, this type of contract need not be in writing.[13] The assumption is that a court can infer from the circumstances of a case whether a "leading objective" of the promisor was to secure a personal benefit.

EXAMPLE 12.16 Carrie Braswell contracts with Custom Manufacturing Company to have some machines custom made for her factory. She promises Newform Supply, Custom's supplier, that if Newform continues to deliver the materials to Custom for the production of the custom-made machines, she will guarantee payment. This promise need not be in writing, even though the effect may be to pay the debt of another, because Braswell's main purpose is to secure a benefit for herself. •

Another typical application of the main purpose doctrine occurs when one creditor guarantees the debtor's debt to another creditor to forestall litigation. This allows the debtor to remain in business long enough to generate profits sufficient to pay *both* creditors. In this situation, the guaranty does not need to be in writing to be enforceable.

Promises Made in Consideration of Marriage

A unilateral promise to make a monetary payment or to give property in consideration of marriage must be in writing. **EXAMPLE 12.17** Baumann promises to pay Joe Villard $10,000 if Villard marries Baumann's daughter. Because the promise is in consideration of marriage, it must be in writing to be enforceable. •

Prenuptial Agreement An agreement made before marriage that defines each partner's ownership rights in the other partner's property. Prenuptial agreements must be in writing to be enforceable.

The same rule applies to **prenuptial agreements**—agreements made before marriage (also called *antenuptial agreements*) that define each partner's ownership rights in the other partner's property. A prospective wife or husband may wish to limit the amount the prospective spouse can obtain if the marriage ends in divorce. Prenuptial agreements must be in writing to be enforceable. Generally, courts tend to give more credence to prenuptial agreements that are accompanied by consideration.

EXAMPLE 12.18 After a divorce from actor Tom Cruise, actress Nicole Kidman entered into a prenuptial agreement with her second husband, country singer Keith Urban. Kidman agreed that in the event of a divorce, she would pay Urban $640,000 for every year they were married, unless Urban relapsed and used drugs again (then he would receive nothing). •

"Wallace, have you forgotten our prenuptial contract? No whistling!"

Contracts for the Sale of Goods

The Uniform Commercial Code (UCC—see Chapter 15) includes Statute of Frauds provisions that require written evidence or an electronic record of a contract. Section 2–201 requires a writing or memorandum for the sale of goods priced at $500 or more under the UCC (this low threshold amount may be increased in the future). To satisfy the UCC requirement, a writing need only state the quantity term. Other terms agreed on do not have to be stated "accurately" in the writing, as long as they adequately reflect both parties' intentions.

The contract will not be enforceable, however, for any quantity greater than that set forth in the writing. In addition, the writing must have been signed by the person to be charged—that is, by the person who refuses to perform or the one being sued. Beyond

13. *Restatement (Second) of Contracts,* Section 116.

these two requirements, the writing need not designate the buyer or the seller, the terms of payment, or the price. (See this chapter's *Beyond Our Borders* feature below to learn whether other countries have requirements similar to those in the Statute of Frauds.)

Exceptions to the Statute of Frauds

Exceptions to the applicability of the Statute of Frauds are made in certain situations. We describe those situations here.

Partial Performance When a contract has been partially performed and the parties cannot be returned to their positions prior to the contract, a court may grant *specific performance* (an equitable remedy that requires a contract to be performed according to its precise terms—see Chapter 14).

In cases involving oral contracts for the transfer of interests in land, courts usually look at whether justice is better served by enforcing the oral contract when partial performance has taken place. For instance, if the purchaser has paid part of the price, taken possession, and made valuable improvements to the property, a court may grant specific performance. The parties still have to prove that an oral contract existed, however.

In some states, mere reliance on certain types of oral contracts is enough to remove them from the Statute of Frauds. Under the UCC, an oral contract for goods priced at $500 or more is enforceable to the extent that a seller accepts payment or a buyer accepts delivery of the goods.[14]

Admissions In some states, if a party against whom enforcement of an oral contract is sought admits in pleadings, testimony, or otherwise in court proceedings that a contract for sale was made, the contract will be enforceable.[15] A contract subject to the UCC will be enforceable, but only to the extent of the quantity admitted.[16]

EXAMPLE 12.19 The president of Ashley Corporation admits under oath that an oral agreement was made with Com Best to pay $10,000 for certain business equipment. In this situation, a court will enforce the agreement only to the extent admitted (the $10,000), even if Com Best claims that the agreement involved $20,000 of equipment. ●

14. UCC 2–201(3)(c). See Chapter 15.
15. *Restatement (Second) of Contracts,* Section 133.
16. UCC 2–201(3)(b). See Chapter 15.

BEYOND OUR BORDERS The Statute of Frauds and International Sales Contracts

As you will read in Chapter 15, the Convention on Contracts for the International Sale of Goods (CISG) provides rules that govern international sales contracts between citizens of countries that have ratified the convention (agreement). Article 11 of the CISG does not incorporate any Statute of Frauds provisions. Rather, it states that a "contract for sale need not be concluded in or evidenced by writing and is not subject to any other requirements as to form."

Article 11 accords with the legal customs of most nations, which no longer require contracts to meet certain formal or writing requirements to be enforceable. Ironically, even England, the nation that enacted the original Statute of Frauds in 1677, has repealed all of it except the provisions relating to collateral promises and to transfers of interests in land. Many other countries that once had such statutes have also repealed all or parts of them. Civil law countries, such as France, have never required certain types of contracts to be in writing. Obviously, without a writing requirement, contracts can take on any form.

Critical Thinking

If a country does not have a Statute of Frauds and a dispute arises over an oral agreement, how can the parties substantiate their positions?

Promissory Estoppel In some states, an oral contract that would otherwise be unenforceable under the Statute of Frauds may be enforced under the doctrine of promissory estoppel (see page 286 in Chapter 11). Section 139 of the *Restatement (Second) of Contracts* provides that an oral promise can be enforceable, notwithstanding the Statute of Frauds, if the promisee has justifiably relied on it to her or his detriment. For the contract to be enforceable, the reliance must have been foreseeable to the person making the promise, and enforcing the promise must be the only way to avoid injustice.

Special Exceptions under the UCC Special exceptions to the applicability of the Statute of Frauds exist for sales contracts. Oral contracts for customized goods may be enforced in certain circumstances. Another exception has to do with oral contracts *between merchants* that have been confirmed in writing. We will examine these exceptions in Chapter 15.

Exhibit 12.3 below graphically summarizes the types of contracts that fall under the Statute of Frauds and the various exceptions that apply.

The Statute of Frauds—Sufficiency of the Writing

A written contract will satisfy the writing requirement of the Statute of Frauds. (See the Appendix to Chapter 14 for an example of a written contract and descriptions of the meaning of its terms.) A *written memorandum* (written or electronic evidence of the oral contract) signed by the party against whom enforcement is sought will also satisfy the writing requirement.

The signature need not be placed at the end of the document but can be anywhere in the writing. It can even be initials rather than the full name. As mentioned in Chapter 10, in today's business world, there are many ways to create signatures electronically, and electronic signatures generally satisfy the Statute of Frauds.

What Constitutes a Writing?

A writing can consist of any confirmation, invoice, sales slip, check, fax, or e-mail—or such items in combination. The written contract need not consist of a single document to constitute an enforceable contract. One document may incorporate another document by expressly referring to it. Several documents may form a single contract if they are physically

Exhibit 12.3 Contracts Subject to the Statute of Frauds

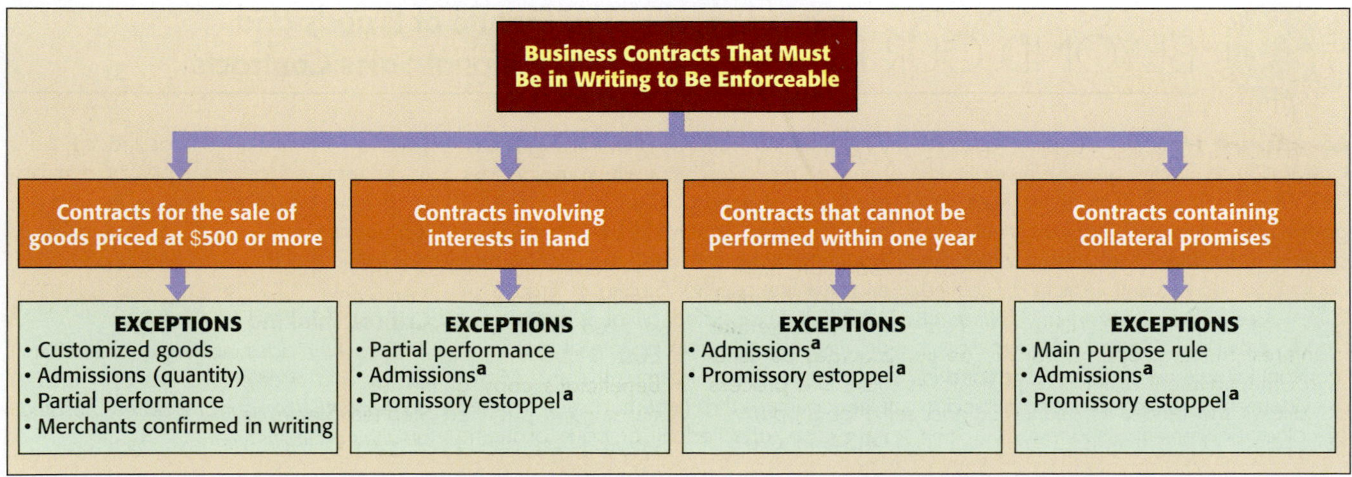

a. Some states follow Section 133 (on admissions) and Section 139 (on promissory estoppel) of the *Restatement (Second) of Contracts.*

attached—such as by staple, paper clip, or glue—or even if they are only placed in the same envelope. (See the *Business Application* feature on page 323.)

EXAMPLE 12.20 Simpson orally agrees to sell some land next to a shopping mall to Terro Properties. Simpson gives Terro an unsigned memo that contains a legal description of the property, and Terro gives Simpson an unsigned first draft of their contract. Simpson sends Terro a signed letter that refers to the memo and to the first and final drafts of the contract. Terro sends Simpson an unsigned copy of the final draft of the contract with a signed check stapled to it. Together, the documents can constitute a writing sufficient to satisfy the Statute of Frauds and bind both parties to the terms of the contract as evidenced by the writings. ●

"The pen is mightier than the sword, and considerably easier to write with."

Marty Feldman, 1934–1982 (English actor and comedian)

What Must Be Contained in the Writing?

A memorandum or note evidencing the oral contract need only contain the essential terms of the contract, not every term. There must, of course, also be some indication that the parties voluntarily agreed to the terms. A faxed or e-mailed memo of the terms of an agreement could be sufficient if it showed that there was a meeting of the minds and that the terms were not just part of the preliminary negotiations.[17] Under the UCC, in regard to the sale of goods, the writing need only state the quantity and be signed by the party against whom enforcement is sought.

Because only the party against whom enforcement is sought must have signed the writing, a contract may be enforceable by one of its parties but not by the other. **EXAMPLE 12.21** Rock orally agrees to buy Betty Devlin's lake house and lot for $350,000. Devlin writes Rock a letter confirming the sale by identifying the parties and the essential terms of the sales contract—price, method of payment, and legal address—and signs the letter. Devlin has made a written memorandum of the oral land contract. Because she signed the letter, she normally can be held to the oral contract by Rock. Devlin cannot enforce the agreement against Rock, however. Because he has not signed or entered into a written contract or memorandum, Rock can plead the Statute of Frauds as a defense. ●

In the following case, the court was presented with a written document that the plaintiff sought to enforce. The writing, however, was missing at least one element needed to satisfy the Statute of Frauds—the signatures of the parties against whom the enforcement was being sought.

17. See, for example, *Coca-Cola Co. v. Babyback's International, Inc.*, 841 N.E.2d 557 (Ind.App. 2006).

Case 12.3

Beneficial Homeowner Service Corp. v. Steele

Supreme Court of New York, Suffolk County, 2011 WL 61728 (2011).

(Feverpitched/iStockphoto.com)

Lenders foreclose on many houses and then sell them.

FACTS Beneficial Homeowner Service Corporation filed a suit against Stephen and Susan Steele to foreclose on a mortgage. (A mortgage is a written instrument that gives a creditor an interest in the property that the debtor provides as security for the payment of the loan, and foreclosure is a process that allows the lender to repossess and sell that property—see Chapter 22.) Beneficial sought $91,614.34 in unpaid principal, plus interest, and claimed that the loan was secured by real property in East Hampton, New York. Beneficial's copy of the loan agreement identified Stephen Steele as the sole obligor (the party owing the debt); however, it had not been signed.

Case 12.3—Continues next page

Case 12.3—Continued

ISSUE Does the Statute of Frauds require the borrowers' signatures on a contract that gives the lender an interest in real property (a mortgage loan)?

DECISION Yes. The court concluded that the agreement was unenforceable.

REASON Because a mortgage involves the transfer of an interest in real property, the mortgage agreement and its underlying obligation must be in writing to satisfy the Statute of Frauds. To be enforceable, the writing must be signed by the parties to be charged. Beneficial was seeking to foreclose on a mortgage that purportedly constituted security for a certain loan agreement. Beneficial sought to enforce the agreement against two parties—Stephen and Susan Steele—who had not signed it. In fact, Susan was not even mentioned in the agreement as a party to it. The lender's assertions about the document were "painfully obvious misstatements of facts" and meant that the agreement was most likely unenforceable. The court ordered a hearing to determine whether Beneficial had acted in good faith.

WHAT IF THE FACTS WERE DIFFERENT? *Suppose that at the hearing, the Steeles admitted they had an obligation to pay the outstanding loan amount. Would the result have been different? Explain.*

The Parol Evidence Rule

Parol Evidence Rule A rule of contracts under which a court will not receive into evidence prior or contemporaneous oral statements and agreements that contradict the terms of the parties' written contract.

LEARNING OBJECTIVE 5
What is parol evidence? When is it admissible to clarify the terms of a written contract?

Sometimes, a written contract does not include—or contradicts—an oral understanding reached by the parties before or at the time of contracting. For instance, a landlord might tell a person who agrees to rent an apartment that she or he can have a cat, whereas the lease contract clearly states that no pets are allowed. In determining the outcome of such disputes, the courts look to a common law rule governing the admissibility in court of oral evidence, or *parol evidence*.

Under the **parol evidence rule**, if a court finds that a written contract represents the complete and final statement of the parties' agreement, then it will not allow either party to present parol evidence (testimony or other evidence of communications between the parties that is not contained in the contract itself). In other words, a party normally cannot introduce in court evidence of the parties' prior negotiations, prior agreements, or contemporaneous oral agreements if that evidence contradicts or varies the terms of the parties' written contract.[18]

Exceptions to the Parol Evidence Rule

Because of the rigidity of the parol evidence rule, courts make several exceptions. These exceptions include the following:

1. *Contracts subsequently modified.* Evidence of a *subsequent modification* of a written contract can be introduced in court. Keep in mind that the oral modifications may not be enforceable if they come under the Statute of Frauds—for example, if they increase the price of the goods for sale to $500 or more or extend the term for performance to more than one year. Also, oral modifications will not be enforceable if the original contract provides that any modification must be in writing.[19]
2. *Voidable or void contracts.* Oral evidence can be introduced in all cases to show that the contract was voidable or void (for example, induced by mistake, fraud, or misrepresentation). In this situation, if deception led one of the parties to agree to the terms of a written contract, oral evidence indicating fraud should not be excluded. Courts frown on bad faith and are quick to allow the introduction at trial of parol evidence when it establishes fraud.
3. *Contracts containing ambiguous terms.* When the terms of a written contract are ambiguous, evidence is admissible to show the meaning of the terms.
4. *Incomplete contracts.* Evidence is admissible when the written contract is incomplete in that it lacks one or more of the essential terms. The courts allow evidence to "fill in the gaps" in the contract.

18. *Restatement (Second) of Contracts,* Section 213.
19. UCC 2–209(2), (3). See Chapter 15.

5. *Prior dealing, course of performance, or usage of trade.* Under the UCC, evidence can be introduced to explain or supplement a written contract by showing a prior dealing, course of performance, or usage of trade.[20] When buyers and sellers deal with each other over extended periods of time, certain customary practices develop. These practices are often overlooked in the writing of the contract, so courts allow the introduction of evidence to show how the parties have acted in the past. Usage of trade—practices and customs generally followed in a particular industry—can also shed light on the meaning of certain contract provisions, and thus evidence of trade usage may be admissible. We will discuss these terms in further detail in Chapter 15, in the context of sales contracts.
6. *Contracts subject to an orally agreed-on condition precedent.* As you will read in Chapter 13, sometimes the parties agree that a condition must be fulfilled before a party is required to perform the contract. This is called a *condition precedent.* If the parties have orally agreed on a condition precedent and the condition does not conflict with the terms of a written agreement, then a court may allow parol evidence to prove the oral condition. The parol evidence rule does not apply here because the existence of the entire written contract is subject to an orally agreed-on condition. Proof of the condition does not alter or modify the written terms but affects the *enforceability* of the written contract.

   EXAMPLE 12.22 A city leases property for an airport from a well-established helicopter business. The lease is renewable every five years. During the second five-year lease, a dispute arises, and the parties go to mediation (see Chapter 3 on page 84). They enter into a settlement memorandum under which they agree to amend the lease agreement subject to the approval of the city council. The city amends the lease, but the helicopter business refuses to sign it, contending that the council has not given its approval. In this situation, the council's approval is a condition precedent to the formation of the settlement memorandum contract. Therefore, the parol evidence rule does not apply, and oral evidence is admissible to show that no agreement exists as to the terms of the settlement. •
7. *Contracts with an obvious or gross clerical (or typographic) error.* When an *obvious* or *gross* clerical (or typographic) error exists that clearly would not represent the agreement of the parties, parol evidence is admissible to correct the error. **EXAMPLE 12.23** Davis agrees to lease 1,000 square feet of office space from Stone Enterprises at the current monthly rate of $3 per square foot. The signed written lease provides for a monthly lease payment of $300 rather than the $3,000 agreed to by the parties. Because the error is obvious, Stone Enterprises would be allowed to admit parol evidence to correct the mistake. •

KNOW THIS

The parol evidence rule and its exceptions relate to the rules concerning the *interpretation* of contracts.

Integrated Contracts

Integrated Contract A written contract that constitutes the final expression of the parties' agreement. Evidence extraneous to the contract that contradicts or alters the meaning of the contract in any way is inadmissible.

The determination of whether evidence will be allowed basically depends on whether the written contract is intended to be a complete and final statement of the terms of the agreement. If it is so intended, it is referred to as an **integrated contract,** and extraneous evidence (evidence from outside the contract) is excluded. For an example of an integration clause within a contract, see Paragraph 19 on page 374 in the Appendix to Chapter 14.

CASE EXAMPLE 12.24 The Pittsburgh Steelers sent Ronald Yocca a brochure offering to sell the right to buy season tickets to Steelers games at their new football stadium. Prices and locations of seats were indicated in diagrams. Yocca responded, listing his seating preferences. The Steelers sent him the tickets with a diagram that showed different seating sections than were shown in the brochure. Also enclosed was a document that read, "This agreement contains the entire agreement of the parties." Yocca was asked to sign and return the document. Later, when Yocca went to the first game, he discovered that his seat was not where he expected it to be based on the brochure. He sued for breach of contract. The court, however, concluded that the brochure was not part of the parties' contract and dismissed the suit. Under the parol evidence rule, the signed document could not be supplemented by evidence of previous negotiations or agreements.[21] •

20. UCC 1–205, 2–202. See Chapter 15.

21. *Yocca v. Pittsburgh Steelers Sports, Inc.*, 578 Pa. 479, 854 A.2d 425 (2004).

Exhibit 12.4 The Parol Evidence Rule

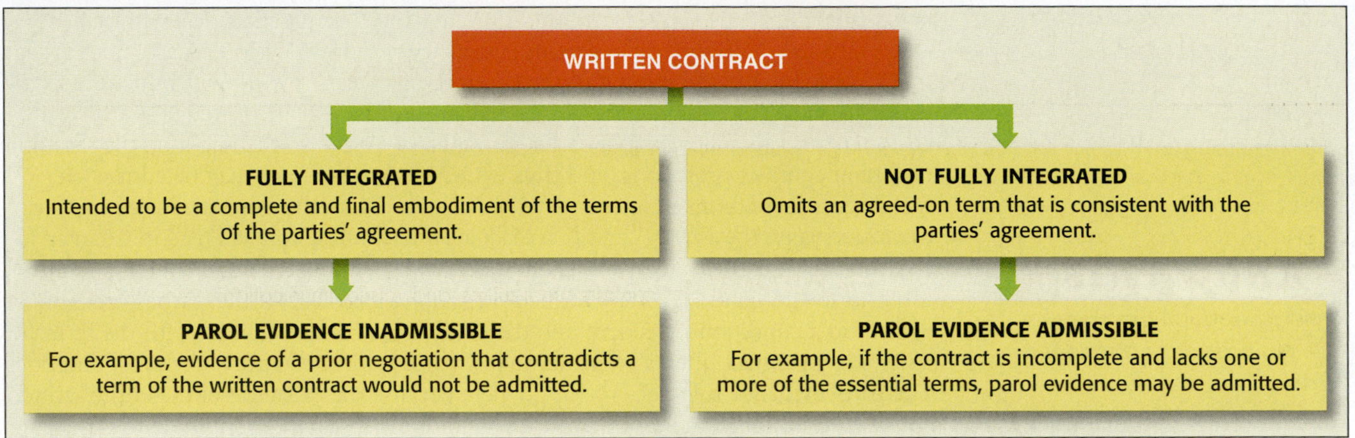

An integrated contract can be either completely or partially integrated. If it contains all of the terms of the parties' agreement, then it is completely integrated. If it contains only some of the terms that the parties agreed on and not others, it is partially integrated. If the contract is only partially integrated, evidence of consistent additional terms is admissible to supplement the written agreement.[22] Note that for both completely and partially integrated contracts, courts exclude any evidence that *contradicts* the writing and allow parol evidence only to add to the terms of a partially integrated contract.

Exhibit 12.4 above illustrates the relationship between integrated contracts and the parol evidence rule.

22. *Restatement (Second) of Contracts,* Section 216.

Reviewing . . . Defenses to Contract Enforceability

Charter Golf, Inc., manufactures and sells golf apparel and supplies. Ken Odin had worked as a Charter sales representative for six months when he was offered a position with a competing firm. Charter's president, Jerry Montieth, offered Odin a 10 percent commission "for the rest of his life" if Ken would turn down the offer and stay on with Charter. He also promised that Odin would not be fired unless he was dishonest. Odin turned down the competitor's offer and stayed with Charter. Three years later, Charter fired Odin for no reason. Odin sued, alleging breach of contract. Using the information presented in the chapter, answer the following questions.

1. Would a court likely decide that Montieth's employment contract with Odin falls within the Statute of Frauds? Why or why not?
2. Assume that the court does find that the contract falls within the Statute of Frauds and that the state in which the court sits recognizes every exception to the Statute of Frauds discussed in the chapter. What exception provides Odin with the best chance of enforcing the oral contract in this situation?
3. Now suppose that Montieth had taken out a pencil, written "10 percent for life" on the back of a register receipt, and handed it to Odin. Would this satisfy the Statute of Frauds? Why or why not?
4. Assume that Odin had signed a written employment contract at the time he was hired by Charter, but it was not completely integrated. Would a court allow Odin to present parol evidence of Montieth's subsequent promises? Why or why not?

DEBATE THIS Many countries have eliminated the Statute of Frauds except for sales of real estate. The United States should do the same.

BUSINESS APPLICATION

When E-Mails Become Enforceable Contracts*

Most business students must take a course in business communication. These courses cover the planning and preparation of oral and written communications, including electronic messages. Indeed, e-mails have become so pervasive that an increasing number of contracts are created via e-mail.

Voluntary Consent and Mistakes

One possible defense to contract enforceability is a lack of voluntary consent, sometimes due to mistakes. Often, when a mistake is unilateral, the courts will still enforce the contract. Consequently, the e-mail communications that you create can result in an enforceable contract even if you make a typographic error in, say, a dollar amount.

If you are making an offer or an acceptance via e-mail, you should treat that communication as carefully as if you were writing or typing it on a sheet of paper. Unfortunately, many individuals in the business world treat e-mails somewhat casually. When you realize that you are creating an enforceable contract if you make an offer or an acceptance via e-mail, then you know that you have to reread your e-mails several times before you hit the send button.

The Sufficiency of the Writing

In this chapter, you learned about the Statute of Frauds. The legal definitions of written memoranda and signatures have changed in our electronic age. Today, an e-mail definitely constitutes a writing.

A writing can also be a series of e-mail exchanges between two parties. In other words, five e-mail exchanges taken together may form a single contract. (In the past, before e-mails and faxes, this rule applied to written communications on pieces of paper that were stapled or clipped together.) If one or more e-mails name the parties, identify the subject matter, and lay out the consideration, a court normally will accept those e-mails as constituting a writing sufficient to satisfy the Statute of Frauds.

The Importance of Clear, Precise E-Mail Language

In addition to typographic errors, casually written e-mails may contain ambiguities and miscommunications. Nevertheless, those e-mails may create an enforceable contract, whether you intended to create one or not. Therefore, all of your business e-mails should be carefully written.

Checklist for the Businessperson

1. **Create a precise and informative subject line.** *Rather than saying "we should discuss" or "important information," be specific in the subject line of the e-mail, such as "change delivery date for line portable generators."*
2. **Repeat the subject matter within the body of the e-mail message.** *In the actual e-mail message, avoid phrases with indefinite antecedents such as "This is . . . ." Good business e-mail communication involves a repetition of most of the subject line. That way, if your recipient skips the subject line, the message will still be clear.*
3. **Focus on a limited number of subjects, usually one.** *Do not ramble and discuss a variety of topics in your e-mail. If necessary, send several e-mails on several different topics.*
4. **Create e-mails that are just as attractive as communications written on letterhead.** *Obviously, e-mails that have no particular format, no paragraphs, bad grammar, misspellings, and incorrect punctuation create a negative impression. More important, if your language is not precise, you may find that you have created an enforceable contract when you did not intend to do so. At a minimum, use the spelling and grammar checkers in your word-processing program.*
5. **Proof your work.** *This aspect of e-mail communication is so important that it is worth repeating. Proofreading your e-mails before you hit the send button is the most important step that you can take to avoid contract misinterpretations.*

*This *Business Application* is not meant to substitute for the services of an attorney who is licensed to practice law in your state.

Key Terms

collateral promise 315
integrated contract 321
parol evidence rule 320
prenuptial agreement 316
scienter 311
Statute of Frauds 313

Chapter Summary: Defenses to Contract Enforceability

VOLUNTARY CONSENT	
Mistakes (See pages 306–308.)	1. *Unilateral*—Generally, the mistaken party is bound by the contract *unless* (a) the other party knows or should have known of the mistake or (b) the mistake is an inadvertent mathematical error—such as an error in addition or subtraction—committed without gross negligence. 2. *Bilateral (mutual)*—When both parties are mistaken about the same material fact, such as identity, either party can avoid the contract.
Fraudulent Misrepresentation (See pages 308–312.)	When fraud occurs, usually the innocent party can enforce or avoid the contract. The following elements are necessary to establish fraud: 1. A misrepresentation of a material fact must occur. 2. There must be an intent to deceive. 3. The innocent party must justifiably rely on the misrepresentation.
Undue Influence (See page 313.)	Undue influence arises from special relationships, such as fiduciary or confidential relationships, in which one party's free will has been overcome by the undue influence exerted by the other party. Usually, the contract is voidable.
Duress (See page 313.)	Duress is the tactic of forcing a party to enter a contract under the fear of a threat—for example, the threat of violence or serious economic loss. The party forced to enter the contract can rescind the contract.
FORM	
The Statute of Frauds—Writing Requirement (See pages 313–318.)	1. *Applicability*—The following types of contracts fall under the Statute of Frauds and must be in writing to be enforceable: a. Contracts involving interests in land, such as sales, leases, or mortgages. b. Contracts that cannot by their terms be fully performed within one year from (the day after) the contract's formation. c. Collateral promises, such as contracts made between a guarantor and a creditor whose terms make the guarantor secondarily liable. *Exception:* the "main purpose" rule. d. Promises made in consideration of marriage, including promises to make a monetary payment or give property in consideration of a promise to marry and prenuptial agreements made in consideration of marriage. e. Contracts for the sale of goods priced at $500 or more under the Statute of Frauds provision in Section 2–201 of the Uniform Commercial Code. 2. *Exceptions*—Partial performance, admissions, and promissory estoppel.
The Statute of Frauds—Sufficiency of the Writing (See pages 318–320.)	To constitute an enforceable contract under the Statute of Frauds, a writing must be signed by the party against whom enforcement is sought, name the parties, identify the subject matter, and state with reasonable certainty the essential terms of the contract. Under the UCC, a contract for a sale of goods is not enforceable beyond the quantity of goods shown in the contract.
The Parol Evidence Rule (See pages 320–322.)	The parol evidence rule prohibits the introduction at trial of evidence of the parties' prior negotiations, prior agreements, or contemporaneous oral agreements that contradicts or varies the terms of the parties' written contract. The written contract is assumed to be the complete embodiment of the parties' agreement. Exceptions are made in the circumstances listed on pages 320–321.

ExamPrep

ISSUE SPOTTERS

1. Elle, an accountant, certifies several audit reports for Flite Corporation, her client, knowing that Flite intends to use the reports to obtain loans from Good Credit Company (GCC). Elle believes that the reports are true and does not intend to deceive GCC, but she does not check the reports before certifying them. Can Elle be held liable to GCC? Why or why not? **(See pages 309 and 310.)**
2. My-T Quality Goods, Inc., and Nu! Sales Corporation orally agree to a deal. My-T's president has the essential terms written up on company letterhead stationery, and the memo is filed in My-T's office. If Nu! Sales later refuses to complete the transaction, is this memo a sufficient writing to enforce the contract against it? Explain your answer. **(See page 318.)**

—Check your answers to the Issue Spotters against the answers provided in Appendix E at the end of this text.

BEFORE THE TEST

Go to www.cengagebrain.com, enter the ISBN 9781133273561 and click on "Find" to locate this textbook's Web site. Then, click on "Access Now" under "Study Tools," and select Chapter 12 at the top. There, you will find a Practice Quiz that you can take to assess your mastery of the concepts in this chapter, as well as Flashcards, a Glossary of important terms, and Video Questions (when assigned).

For Review

Answers to the even-numbered questions in this For Review section can be found in Appendix F at the end of this text.

1. In what types of situations might voluntary consent to a contract's terms be lacking?
2. What is the difference between a mistake of value or quality and a mistake of fact?
3. What are the elements of fraudulent misrepresentation?
4. What contracts must be in writing to be enforceable?
5. What is parol evidence? When is it admissible to clarify the terms of a written contract?

Business Scenarios and Case Problems

12–1 Voluntary Consent. Jerome is an elderly man who lives with his nephew, Philip. Jerome is totally dependent on Philip's support. Philip tells Jerome that unless Jerome transfers a tract of land he owns to Philip for a price 30 percent below market value, Philip will no longer support and take care of him. Jerome enters into the contract. Discuss fully whether Jerome can set aside this contract. **(See page 313.)**

12–2 Question with Sample Answer—Statute of Frauds. Gemma promises a local hardware store that she will pay for a lawn mower that her brother is purchasing on credit if the brother fails to pay the debt. Must this promise be in writing to be enforceable? Why or why not? **(See pages 313–316.)**

—For a sample answer to Question 12–2, go to Appendix G at the end of this text.

12–3 The Parol Evidence Rule. Evangel Temple Assembly of God leased a facility from Wood Care Centers, Inc., to house evacuees who had lost their homes in a hurricane. The lease stated that Evangel could end it at any time by giving notice and paying 10 percent of the rent that would otherwise be paid over the rest of the term. The lease also stated that if the facility did not retain its tax exemption—which was granted to it on Evangel's behalf as a church—Evangel could end the lease without making the 10 percent payment. Is parol evidence admissible to interpret this lease? Why or why not? [*Wood Care Centers, Inc. v. Evangel Temple Assembly of God of Wichita Falls,* 307 S.W.3d 816 (Tex.App.—Fort Worth 2010)] **(See page 320.)**

12–4 Case Problem with Sample Answer—Contract Involving Interests in Land. Mohammad Salim offered to sell a convenience store and gas station to Talat Solaiman and Sabina Chowdhury. The prospective buyers drafted a "Purchase Agreement" that described its object as "the property and business known as BP Food Mart" at a specific address. The parties signed the agreement. Later, the buyers wanted out of the deal. Is the property description sufficient for the seller to enforce the agreement? Explain. [*Salim v. Solaiman,* 302 Ga.App. 607, 691 S.E.2d 389 (2010)] **(See page 314.)**

—For a sample answer to Problem 12–4, go to Appendix H at the end of this text.

12–5 Mutual Mistake. When Steven Simkin divorced Laura Blank, they agreed to split their assets equally. They owned an account with Bernard L. Madoff Investment Securities estimated to be worth $5.4 million. Simkin kept the account and paid Blank more than $6.5 million—including $2.7 million to offset the amount of the funds that they believed were in the account. Later, they learned that the account actually contained no funds due to its manager's fraud. Could their agreement be rescinded on the basis of a mistake? Discuss. [*Simkin v. Blank,* 80 A.D.3d 401, 915 N.Y.S.2d 47 (1 Dept. 2011)] **(See pages 306–307.)**

12–6 Misrepresentation. Charter One Bank owned a fifteen-story commercial building. A fire inspector told Charter that the building's drinking-water and fire-suppression systems were linked. Without disclosing this information, Charter sold the building to Northpoint Properties, Inc. Northpoint spent $280,000 to repair the water and fire-suppression systems and filed a suit against Charter One. Is the seller liable for not disclosing the building's defects? Discuss. [*Northpoint Properties, Inc. v. Charter One Bank,* 2011-Ohio-2512 (Ohio App. 8 Dist. 2011)] **(See pages 308–312.)**

12–7 Statute of Frauds. Newmark & Co. Real Estate, Inc., contacted 2615 East 17 Street Realty, LLC, to lease certain real property on behalf of a client. Newmark e-mailed the landlord a separate agreement for the payment of Newmark's commission. The landlord e-mailed it back with a separate demand to pay the commission in installments. Newmark revised the agreement and e-mailed a final copy to the landlord. Do the parties have an agreement that qualifies as a writing under the Statute of Frauds? Explain. [*Newmark & Co. Real Estate, Inc. v. 2615 East 17 Street Realty,* LLC, 80 A.D.3d 476, 914 N.Y.S.2d 162 (1 Dept. 2011)] **(See page 318.)**

12–8 The Parol Evidence Rule. Rimma Vaks and her husband, Steven Mangano, executed a written contract with Denise Ryan and Ryan Auction Co. to auction their furnishings. The six-page contract provided a detailed summary of the parties' agreement. It addressed the items to be auctioned, how reserve prices would be determined, and the amount of Ryan's commission. When a dispute arose between the parties, Vaks and Mangano sued Ryan for breach of contract. Vaks and Mangano asserted that, before they executed the contract, Ryan had made various oral representations that were inconsistent with the terms of their written agreement. Assuming that their written contract was valid, can Vaks and Mangano recover for breach of an oral contract? Why or why not? [*Vaks v. Ryan,* 2012 WL 194398 (Mass.App. 2012)] **(See pages 320–322.)**

12–9 A Question of Ethics—Bilateral Mistake. On behalf of BRJM, LLC, Nicolas Kepple offered Howard Engelsen $210,000 for a parcel of land known as lot five on the north side of Barnes Road in Stonington, Connecticut. Engelsen's company, Output Systems, Inc., owned the land. Engelsen had the lot surveyed and obtained an appraisal. The appraiser valued the property at $277,000, after determining that it was three acres and thus could not be subdivided because it did not meet the town's minimum legal requirement of 3.7 acres for subdivision. Engelsen responded to Kepple's offer with a counteroffer of $230,000, which Kepple accepted. The parties signed a contract. When Engelsen refused to go through with the deal, BRJM filed a suit against Output, seeking specific performance and other relief. Output asserted the defense of mutual mistake on at least two grounds. [*BRJM, LLC v. Output Systems, Inc.,* 100 Conn.App. 143, 917 A.2d 605 (2007)] **(See pages 306–307.)**

1. In the counteroffer, Engelsen asked Kepple to remove from their contract a clause requiring written confirmation of the availability of a "free split," which meant that the property could be subdivided without the town's prior approval. Kepple agreed. After signing the contract, Kepple learned that the property was *not* entitled to a free split. Would this circumstance qualify as a mistake on which the *defendant* could avoid the contract? Why or why not?
2. After signing the contract, Engelsen obtained a second appraisal that established the size of lot five as 3.71 acres, which meant that it could be subdivided, and valued the property at $490,000. Can the defendant avoid the contract on the basis of a mistake in the first appraisal? Explain.

Critical Thinking and Writing Assignments

12–10 Critical Legal Thinking. Describe the types of individuals who might be capable of exerting undue influence on others. **(See page 313.)**

12–11 Business Law Critical Thinking Group Assignment. Jason Novell, doing business as Novell Associates, hired Barbara Meade as an independent contractor. The parties orally agreed on the terms of employment, including payment of a share of the company's income to Meade, but they did not put anything in writing. Two years later, Meade quit. Novell then told Meade that she was entitled to $9,602—25 percent of the difference between the accounts receivable and the accounts payable as of Meade's last day of work. Meade disagreed and demanded more than $63,500—25 percent of the revenue from all invoices, less the cost of materials and outside processing, for each of the years that she had worked for Novell. Meade filed a lawsuit against Novell for breach of contract.

1. The first group will evaluate whether the parties had an enforceable contract.
2. The second group will decide whether the parties' oral agreement falls within any exception to the Statute of Frauds.
3. The third group will discuss how the lawsuit would be affected if Novell admitted that the parties had an oral contract under which Meade was entitled to 25 percent of the difference between the accounts receivable and payable as of the day Meade quit.

CHAPTER 13

Third Party Rights and Discharge

(Muellek Josef/Shutterstock.com)

CHAPTER OUTLINE

- Assignments
- Delegations
- Third Party Beneficiaries
- Contract Discharge

LEARNING OBJECTIVES

The five learning objectives below are designed to help improve your understanding of the chapter. After reading this chapter, you should be able to answer the following questions:

1. What is an assignment? What is the difference between an assignment and a delegation?
2. In what situations is the delegation of duties prohibited?
3. What factors indicate that a third party beneficiary is an intended beneficiary?
4. How are most contracts discharged?
5. What is a contractual condition, and how might a condition affect contractual obligations?

"The laws of a state change with the changing times."
—Aeschylus, 525–456 B.C.E. (Greek dramatist)

Privity of Contract The relationship that exists between the promisor and the promisee of a contract.

Because a contract is a private agreement between the parties who have entered into that contract, it is fitting that these parties alone should have rights and liabilities under the contract. This concept is referred to as **privity of contract**, and it establishes the basic principle that third parties have no rights in contracts to which they are not parties.

You may be convinced by now that for every rule of contract law, there is an exception. As times change, so must the laws, as indicated in the chapter-opening quotation. When justice cannot be served by adherence to a rule of law, exceptions to the rule must be made.

In this chapter, we look at some exceptions to the rule of privity of contract. These exceptions include *assignments, delegations,* and *third party beneficiary contracts.* We also examine how contractual obligations can be *discharged*. Normally, contract discharge is accomplished by both parties performing the acts promised in the contract. In the latter part of the chapter, we look at the degree of performance required to discharge a contractual obligation, as well as at some other ways that contract discharge can occur.

Assignments

LEARNING OBJECTIVE 1

What is an assignment? What is the difference between an assignment and a delegation?

Assignment The transfer to another of all or part of one's rights arising under a contract.

In a bilateral contract, the two parties have corresponding rights and duties. One party has a *right* to require the other to perform some task, and the other has a *duty* to perform it. Sometimes, though, a party will transfer her or his rights under the contract to someone else. The transfer of contract *rights* to a third person is known as an **assignment.** (The transfer of contract duties is a *delegation,* as will be discussed later in this chapter.)

Assignments are important because they are often used in business financing. Lending institutions, such as banks, frequently assign the rights to receive payments under their loan contracts to other firms, which pay for those rights. If you obtain a loan from your local bank to purchase a car, you may later receive a notice stating that your bank has transferred (assigned) its rights to receive payments on the loan to another firm and that you should make your payments to that other firm.

Lenders that make *mortgage loans* (loans to allow prospective home buyers to purchase real estate—see Chapter 22) often assign their rights to collect the mortgage payments to a third party, such as Chase Home Mortgage Company. Following an assignment, the home buyer is notified that future payments must be made to the third party, rather than to the original lender. Billions of dollars change hands daily in the business world in the form of assignments of rights in contracts.

Effect of an Assignment

Assignor A party who transfers (assigns) his or her rights under a contract to another party (called the *assignee*).

Assignee A party to whom the rights under a contract are transferred, or assigned.

Obligee One to whom an obligation is owed.

Obligor One who owes an obligation to another.

In an assignment, the party assigning the rights to a third party is known as the **assignor,**[1] and the party receiving the rights is the **assignee.**[2] Other terms traditionally used to describe the parties in assignment relationships are the **obligee** (the person to whom a duty, or obligation, is owed) and the **obligor** (the person who is obligated to perform the duty). Exhibit 13.1 on the facing page illustrates assignment relationships.

Extinguishes the Rights of the Assignor

When rights under a contract are assigned unconditionally, the rights of the *assignor* (the party making the assignment) are extinguished.[3] The third party (the *assignee,* or the party receiving the assignment) has a right to demand performance from the other original party to the contract (the *obligor,* the person who is obligated to perform).

EXAMPLE 13.1 Brent (the obligor) owes Alex $1,000, and Alex, the obligee, assigns to Carmen the right to receive the $1,000 (thus, Alex is now the assignor). Here, a valid assignment of a debt exists. Carmen, the assignee, can enforce the contract against Brent, the obligor, if Brent fails to perform (pay the $1,000). ●

In the following case, a lender assigned its rights to loan payments from a borrower. The court had to decide whether the borrower owed the payments to the assignee.

1. Pronounced uh-*sye*-nore.
2. Pronounced uh-*sye*-nee.
3. *Restatement (Second) of Contracts,* Section 317.

Case 13.1

Hosch v. Colonial Pacific Leasing Corp.

Court of Appeals of Georgia,
313 Ga.App. 873, 722 S.E.2d 778 (2012).
www.findlaw.com/casecode/index.html[a]

(wolv/iStockphoto.com)

Can a loan for equipment be assigned without notice?

FACTS Edward Hosch entered into four loan agreements with Citicapital Commercial Corporation to finance the purchase of heavy construction equipment. A few months later, Citicapital merged into Citicorp Leasing, Inc., which was then renamed GE Capital Commercial, Inc. One year later, GE Capital assigned the loans to Colonial Pacific Leasing Corporation. When Hosch defaulted on the loans, Colonial Pacific served him with a notice of default and demanded payment. Hosch failed to repay the loans, so Colonial Pacific sued to collect. The trial court granted summary judgment to Colonial Pacific and entered final judgment against Hosch. On appeal, Hosch argued that there was insufficient evidence that the loans were assigned to Colonial Pacific.

ISSUE Is Hosch liable to Colonial Pacific?

DECISION Yes. The Georgia appellate court affirmed the trial court's judgment in favor of the assignee, Colonial Pacific.

REASON The court stated that "a party may assign a contractual right to collect payment, including the right to sue to enforce the right." To be enforceable, the assignment must be in writing. In this case, there was sufficient evidence that GE Capital assigned Hosch's loans to Colonial Pacific. Significantly, the record included a written assignment, other documents showing that the loans had been assigned, and affidavits of a GE litigation specialist.

Against that evidence, Hosch merely asserted that he had not been notified of the assignment. Under the loan agreements, however, GE Capital could assign its rights without Hosch's knowledge or consent.

CRITICAL THINKING—Legal Consideration *Do borrowers benefit when lenders may freely assign their rights under loan agreements? If so, how?*

a. Under "State Resources," click on "Georgia." On the next page, under "State Court Opinions," click on "Georgia Court of Appeals Opinions." In the "Party name:" box, enter "Hosch" and click on "Search." In the result, click on the case name to access the opinion.

Exhibit 13.1 Assignment Relationships

In the assignment relationship illustrated here, Alex assigns his *rights* under a contract that he made with Brent to a third party, Carmen. Alex thus becomes the *assignor* and Carmen the *assignee* of the contractual rights. Brent, the *obligor,* now owes performance to Carmen instead of to Alex. Alex's original contract rights are extinguished after the assignment.

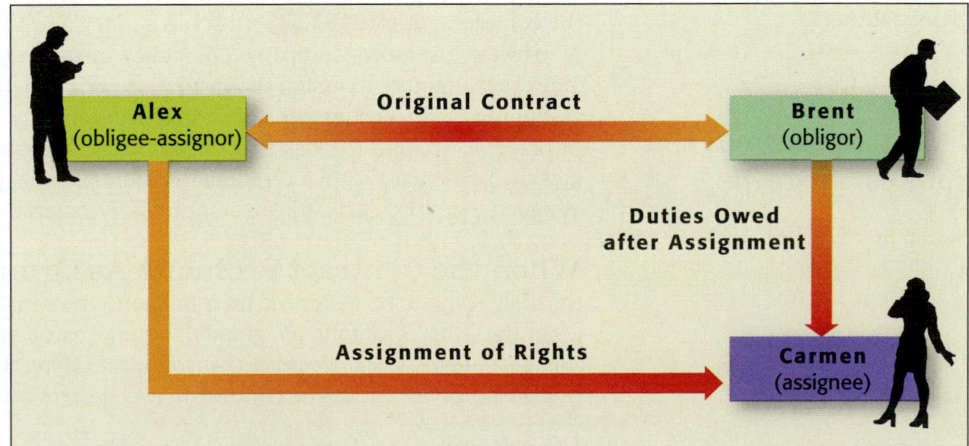

Assignee Takes Rights Subject to Defenses

The assignee obtains only those rights that the assignor originally had. Also, the assignee's rights are subject to the defenses that the obligor has against the assignor.

EXAMPLE 13.2 Brent owes Alex $1,000 under a contract in which Brent agreed to buy Alex's MacBook Pro laptop. Alex assigns his right to receive the $1,000 to Carmen. Brent, in deciding to purchase the laptop, relied on Alex's fraudulent misrepresentation that the computer had 8 megabytes of memory. When Brent discovers that the computer has only 4 megabytes of memory, he tells Alex that he is going to return the laptop and cancel the contract. Even though Alex has assigned his "right" to receive the $1,000 to Carmen, Brent need not pay Carmen the $1,000—Brent can raise the defense of Alex's fraudulent misrepresentation to avoid payment. •

Rights That Cannot Be Assigned

As a general rule, all rights can be assigned. Exceptions are made, however, in the following special circumstances.

(AISPIX/Image Source/Shutterstock.com)

This piano teacher has signed a contract to give weekly piano lessons. Can the teacher then assign this contract to another piano teacher?

When a Statute Expressly Prohibits Assignment

If a statute expressly prohibits assignment, the particular right in question cannot be assigned. **EXAMPLE 13.3** Marn is a new employee of CompuFuture, Inc. CompuFuture is an employer governed by workers' compensation statutes (see Chapter 24) in this state, so Marn is a covered employee. Marn has a rather high-risk job. In need of a loan, she borrows from Stark, assigning to Stark all workers' compensation benefits due her should she be injured on the job. A state statute prohibits the assignment of *future* workers' compensation benefits, and thus such rights cannot be assigned. •

When a Contract Is Personal in Nature

When a contract is for personal services, the rights under the contract normally cannot be assigned unless all that remains is a monetary payment.[4] **EXAMPLE 13.4** Brent signs a contract to be a tutor for Alex's children. Alex then attempts to assign to Carmen his right to Brent's services. Carmen cannot enforce the contract against Brent. Brent may not like Carmen's children or for some other reason may not want to tutor them. Because personal services are unique to the person rendering them, rights to receive personal services cannot be assigned. •

When an Assignment Will Significantly Change the Risk or Duties of the Obligor

A right cannot be assigned if assignment will significantly increase or alter the risks or the duties of the obligor (the party owing performance under the contract).[5] **EXAMPLE 13.5** Alex has a hotel, and to insure it, he takes out a policy with Northwest Insurance Company. The policy insures against fire, theft, floods, and vandalism. Alex attempts to assign the insurance policy to Carmen who also owns a hotel. The assignment is ineffective because it may substantially alter the insurance company's duty of performance and the risk that the company undertakes. An insurance company evaluates the particular risk of a certain party and tailors its policy to fit that risk. If the policy is assigned to a third party, the insurance risk is materially altered. •

"Man, an animal that makes bargains."

Adam Smith, 1723–1790
(Scottish economist and author)

When the Contract Prohibits Assignment

If a contract stipulates that the right cannot be assigned, then *ordinarily* it cannot be assigned. (For an example of a contract that prohibits assignment by one party, see page 374, Paragraph 12, of the *Annotated Employment Contract* that follows Chapter 14.) **EXAMPLE 13.6** Brent agrees to build a house for Alex. The contract between Brent and Alex states, "This contract cannot

4. *Restatement (Second) of Contracts,* Sections 317 and 318.
5. See Section 2–210(2) of the Uniform Commercial Code (UCC).

be assigned by Alex without Brent's consent. Any assignment without such consent renders this contract void, and all rights hereunder will thereupon terminate." Alex then assigns his rights to Carmen without first obtaining Brent's consent. Carmen cannot enforce the contract against Brent. • This rule has several exceptions:

1. A contract cannot prevent an assignment of the right to receive funds. This exception exists to encourage the free flow of funds and credit in modern business settings.
2. The assignment of ownership rights in real estate often cannot be prohibited because such a prohibition is contrary to public policy in most states. Prohibitions of this kind are called restraints against **alienation** (the voluntary transfer of land ownership).
3. The assignment of negotiable instruments (see Chapter 18) cannot be prohibited.
4. In a contract for the sale of goods, the right to receive damages for breach of contract or for payment of an account owed may be assigned even though the sales contract prohibits such an assignment.[6]

Alienation The of transfer of land out of one's possession (thus "alienating" the land from oneself).

Notice of Assignment

Once a valid assignment of rights has been made to a third party, the third party should notify the obligor of the assignment (for example, in Exhibit 13.1 on page 329, Carmen should notify Brent). Giving notice is not legally necessary to establish the validity of the assignment because an assignment is effective immediately, whether or not notice is given. Two major problems arise, however, when notice of the assignment is *not* given to the obligor.

Priority Issues If the assignor assigns the same right to two different persons, the question arises as to which one has priority—that is, which one has the right to the performance by the obligor. The rule most often observed in the United States is that the first assignment in time is the first in right.

Nevertheless, some states follow the English rule, which basically gives priority to the first assignee who gives notice. **EXAMPLE 13.7** Brent owes Alex $5,000 on a contractual obligation. On May 1, Alex assigns this monetary claim to Carmen, but she does not give notice of the assignment to Brent. On June 1, for services Dorman has rendered to Alex, Alex assigns the same monetary claim (to collect $5,000 from Brent) to Dorman. Dorman immediately notifies Brent of the assignment. In the majority of states, Carmen would have priority because the assignment to her was first in time. In some states, however, Dorman would have priority because he gave first notice. •

Potential for Discharge by Performance to the Wrong Party

Until the obligor has notice of an assignment, the obligor can discharge his or her obligation by performance to the assignor, and this performance constitutes a discharge to the assignee. Once the obligor receives proper notice, only performance to the assignee can discharge the obligor's obligations.

EXAMPLE 13.8 Suppose that Alex, in the above example, assigns to Carmen his right to collect $5,000 from Brent, and Carmen does not give notice to Brent. Brent subsequently pays Alex the $5,000. Although the assignment was valid, Brent's payment to Alex is a discharge of the debt, and Carmen's failure to notify Brent of the assignment causes her to lose the right to collect the $5,000 from Brent. (Note that Carmen still has a claim against Alex for the $5,000.) If Carmen had given Brent notice of the assignment, however, Brent's payment to Alex would not have discharged the debt. •

In the following *Spotlight Case,* the parties disputed whether the right to buy advertising space in publications at a steep discount was validly assigned from the original owner to companies that he later formed.

6. UCC 2–210(2).

Spotlight on PC Magazine

Case 13.2
Gold v. Ziff Communications Co.

Appellate Court of Illinois, First District,
322 Ill.App.3d 32, 748 N.E.2d 198, 254 Ill. Dec. 752 (2001).

(Dusan Jankovic/Shutterstock.com)

Ziff bought *PC Magazine* from its founder, Anthony Gold.

FACTS Ziff Communications Company publishes specialty magazines. In 1982, Ziff bought *PC Magazine* from its founder, Anthony Gold, for more than $10 million. As part of the deal, Ziff gave Gold, or a company that he "controlled," "ad/list rights"—rights to advertise at an 80 percent discount on a limited number of pages in Ziff publications and free use of Ziff's subscriber lists. Gold then formed Software Communications, Inc. (SCI), a mail-order software business that he wholly owned, to use the ad/list rights. In 1987 and 1988, Gold formed two new mail-order companies, Hanson & Connors, Inc., and PC Brand, Inc. Gold told Ziff that he was allocating his ad/list rights to Hanson & Connors, which took over most of SCI's business, and to PC Brand, of which Gold owned 90 percent. Ziff's other advertisers complained about this "allocation."

Ziff refused to run large ads for Hanson & Connors or to release its subscriber lists to the company. Ziff also declared PC Brand ineligible for the ad discount because it "was not controlled by Gold." Gold and his companies filed a suit in an Illinois state court against Ziff, alleging breach of contract. The court ordered Ziff to pay more than $88 million in damages and interest. Ziff appealed, arguing in part that Gold had not properly assigned the ad/list rights to Hanson & Connors and PC Brand.

ISSUE Was there a valid assignment of rights from Gold and SCI to Hanson & Connors and PC Brand?

DECISION Yes. The state intermediate appellate court affirmed the lower court's decision on this issue. The appellate court remanded the case, however, for a new trial on the amount of the damages, reasoning that some parts of the award "were not within the reasonable contemplation of the parties."

REASON The court explained, "We agree with plaintiffs that assignments can be implied from circumstances. No particular mode or form . . . is necessary to effect a valid assignment, and any acts or words are sufficient which show an intention of transferring or appropriating the owner's interest. In the instant case, it is undisputed that Gold owned 100 [percent] of SCE. In a letter dated May 13, 1988, Gold, as president of SCI, instructed Ziff that he was allocating the ad/list rights to Hanson and PC Brand. Additionally, SCI stopped using the ad/list rights when PC Brand and Hanson were formed. . . . Gold's behavior toward his companies and his conduct toward the obligor, Ziff, implied that the ad/list rights were assigned to PC Brand and Hanson."

FOR CRITICAL ANALYSIS—Social Consideration *Would the assignments in this case have been valid if Gold had not notified Ziff? Explain.*

PREVENTING LEGAL DISPUTES

Providing notice of assignment, though not legally required, is one of the best ways to avoid potential legal disputes over assignments. Whether you are the assignee or the assignor, you should inform the obligor of the assignment. An assignee who does not give notice may lose the right to performance, but failure to notify the obligor may have repercussions for the assignor as well. If no notice is given and the obligor performs the duty for the assignor, the assignee, to whom the right to receive performance was assigned, can sue the assignor for breach of contract. Litigation may also ensue if the assignor has assigned a right to two different parties, as may happen when rights that overlap (such as rights to receive various profits from a given enterprise) are assigned.

Delegation of Duties The transfer to another of all or part of one's duties arising under a contract.

Delegator A party who transfers (delegates) her or his obligations under a contract to another party (called the *delegatee*).

Delegations

Just as a party can transfer rights to a third party through an assignment, a party can also transfer duties. Duties are not assigned, however. They are *delegated.* Normally, a **delegation of duties** does not relieve the party making the delegation (the **delegator**) of the obligation

Delegatee A party to whom contractual obligations are transferred, or delegated.

to perform in the event that the party to whom the duty has been delegated (the **delegatee**) fails to perform. No special form is required to create a valid delegation of duties. As long as the delegator expresses an intention to make the delegation, it is effective. The delegator need not even use the word *delegate*. Exhibit 13.2 below graphically illustrates delegation relationships.

Duties That Cannot Be Delegated

LEARNING OBJECTIVE 2

In what situations is the delegation of duties prohibited?

As a general rule, any duty can be delegated. This rule has some exceptions, however. Delegation is prohibited in the following circumstances:

1. When performance depends on the personal skill or talents of the obligor.
2. When special trust has been placed in the obligor.
3. When performance by a third party will vary materially from that expected by the obligee (the one to whom performance is owed) under the contract.
4. When the contract expressly prohibits delegation.

When the Duties are Personal in Nature

When special trust has been placed in the obligor or when performance depends on the obligor's personal skill or talents, contractual duties cannot be delegated. EXAMPLE 13.9 Horton, who is impressed with Brower's ability to perform veterinary surgery, contracts with Brower to have her perform surgery on Horton's prize-winning stallion in July. Brower later decides that she would rather spend the summer at the beach, so she delegates her duties under the contract to Kuhn, who is also a competent veterinary surgeon. The delegation is not effective without Horton's consent, no matter how competent Kuhn is, because the contract is for *personal* performance. •

In contrast, nonpersonal duties may be delegated. Assume that Brower contracts with Horton to pick up and deliver heavy construction machinery to Horton's property. Brower delegates this duty to Kuhn, who is in the business of delivering heavy machinery. This delegation is effective because the performance required is of a *routine* and *nonpersonal* nature.

Exhibit 13.2 Delegation Relationships

In the delegation relationship illustrated here, Brent delegates his *duties* under a contract that he made with Alex to a third party, Carmen. Brent thus becomes the *delegator* and Carmen the *delegatee* of the contractual duties. Carmen now owes performance of the contractual duties to Alex. Note that a delegation of duties normally does not relieve the delegator (Brent) of liability if the delegatee (Carmen) fails to perform the contractual duties.

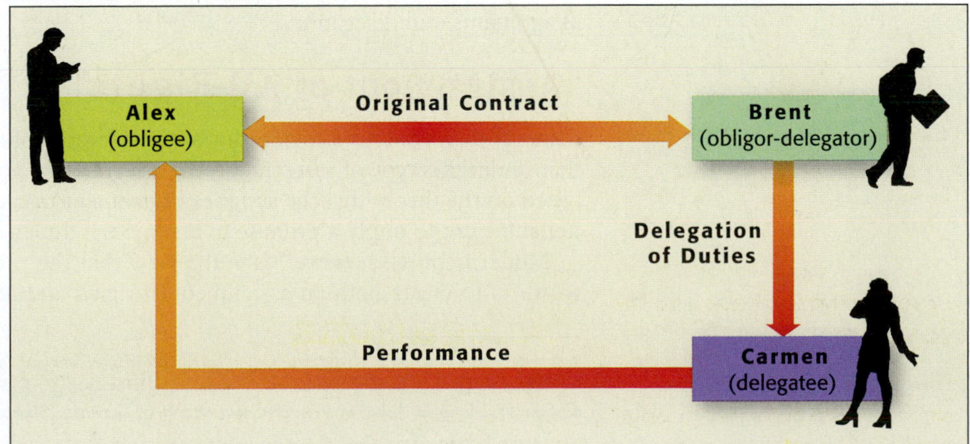

When Performance by a Third Party Will Vary Materially from That Expected by the Obligee

When performance by a third party will vary materially from that expected by the obligee under the contract, contractual duties cannot be delegated. **EXAMPLE 13.10** Jared, a wealthy investor, established the company Heaven Sent to provide grants of capital to struggling but potentially successful businesses. Jared contracted with Merilyn, whose judgment Jared trusted, to select the recipients of the grants. Later, Merilyn delegated this duty to Donald. Jared did not trust Donald's ability to select worthy recipients. This delegation is not effective because it materially alters Jared's expectations under the contract with Merilyn. •

When the Contract Prohibits Delegation

When the contract expressly prohibits delegation by including an *antidelegation clause,* the duties cannot be delegated. **EXAMPLE 13.11** Dakota Company contracted with Belisario, a certified public accountant, to perform its audits. Because the contract prohibited delegation, Belisario could not delegate the duty to perform the audits to another accountant—not even an accountant at the same firm. •

Effect of a Delegation

If a delegation of duties is enforceable, the *obligee* (the one to whom performance is owed) must accept performance from the delegatee (the one to whom the duties are delegated). **EXAMPLE 13.12** Brent has a duty to pick up and deliver heavy construction machinery to Alex's property. Brent delegates his duty to Carmen. In this situation, Alex (the obligee) must accept performance from Carmen (the delegatee) because the delegation is effective. The obligee can legally refuse performance from the delegatee only if the duty is one that cannot be delegated. •

KNOW THIS

In an assignment, the assignor's original contract rights are extinguished after the assignment. In a delegation, the delegator remains liable for performance under the contract if the delegatee fails to perform.

A valid delegation of duties does not relieve the delegator of obligations under the contract.[7] Although there are many exceptions, the general rule today is that the obligee can sue both the delegatee and the delegator.

EXAMPLE 13.13 In the situation in *Example 13.12,* if Carmen (the delegatee) fails to perform, Brent (the delegator) is still liable to Alex (the one to whom performance is owed). The obligee can also hold the delegatee liable if the delegatee made a promise of performance that will directly benefit the obligee. In this situation, there is an "assumption of duty" on the part of the delegatee, and breach of this duty makes the delegatee liable to the obligee. For instance, if Carmen (the delegatee) promised Brent (the delegator), in a contract, to pick up and deliver the construction equipment to Alex's property but fails to do so, Alex (the obligee) can sue Brent, Carmen, or both. •

Exhibit 13.3 on the facing page summarizes the basic principles of the laws governing assignments and delegations.

"Assignment of All Rights"

Sometimes, a contract provides for an "assignment of all rights." The traditional view was that under this type of assignment, the assignee did not assume any duties. This view was based on the theory that the assignee's agreement to accept the benefits of the contract was not sufficient to imply a promise to assume the duties of the contract.

Modern courts, however, take the view that the probable intent in using such general words is to create both an assignment of rights and an assumption of duties.[8] Therefore,

7. For a classic case on this issue, see *Crane Ice Cream Co. v. Terminal Freezing & Heating Co.,* 147 Md. 588, 128 A. 280 (1925).

8. See UCC 2–210(1), (4); and *Restatement (Second) of Contracts,* Section 328.

Exhibit 13.3 **Assignments and Delegations**

Which rights can be assigned, and which duties can be delegated?	All rights can be assigned *unless:* 1. A statute expressly prohibits assignment. 2. The contract is for personal services. 3. The assignment will materially alter the obligor's risk or duties. 4. The contract prohibits assignment.	All duties can be delegated *unless:* 1. Performance depends on the obligor's personal skills or talents, or special trust has been placed in the obligor. 2. Performance by a third party will vary materially from that expected by the obligee. 3. The contract prohibits delegation.
What if the contract prohibits assignment or delegation?	No rights can be assigned *except:* 1. Rights to receive funds. 2. Ownership rights in real estate. 3. Rights to negotiable instruments. 4. Rights to payments under a sales contract or to damages for breach of a sales contract.	No duties can be delegated.
What is the effect on the original party's rights?	On a valid assignment, effective immediately, the original party (assignor) no longer has any rights under the contract.	On a valid delegation, if the delegatee fails to perform, the original party (delegator) is liable to the obligee (who may also hold the delegatee liable).

when general words are used (for example, "I assign the contract" or "all my rights under the contract"), the contract is construed as implying both an assignment of rights and an assumption of duties.

Third Party Beneficiaries

Third Party Beneficiary One for whose benefit a promise is made in a contract but who is not a party to the contract.

Intended Beneficiary A third party for whose benefit a contract is formed. An intended beneficiary can sue the promisor if the contract is breached.

As mentioned earlier in this chapter, to have contractual rights, a person normally must be a party to the contract. In other words, privity of contract must exist. An exception to the doctrine of privity exists when the original parties to the contract intend, *at the time of contracting,* that the contract performance directly benefit a third person. In this situation, the third person becomes a **third party beneficiary** of the contract. As an **intended beneficiary** of the contract, the third party has legal rights and can sue the promisor directly for breach of the contract.

Who Is the Promisor?

Who, though, is the promisor? In bilateral contracts, both parties to the contract are promisors because they both make promises that can be enforced. In third party beneficiary contracts, courts determine the identity of the promisor by asking which party made the promise that benefits the third party—that person is the promisor. In effect, allowing the third party to sue the promisor directly circumvents the "middle person" (the promisee) and thus reduces the burden on the courts. Otherwise, the third party would sue the promisee, who would then sue the promisor.

Indeed, at one time, this circuitous route was the rule. The reason was that the third party beneficiary was not a party to the contract and thus, under the doctrine of privity of contract, had no legal rights under the contract.

CASE EXAMPLE 13.14 In the classic case of *Lawrence v. Fox*[9]—decided in 1859—a court for the first time departed from the doctrine of privity of contract and allowed a third party to sue the promisor directly. The case involved three parties—Holly, Lawrence, and Fox. Holly had borrowed \$300 from Lawrence. Shortly thereafter, Holly loaned \$300 to Fox. In return, Fox promised Holly that he would pay Holly's debt to Lawrence on the following day. But Fox did not pay Lawrence, so Lawrence filed a suit against Fox to recover the

9. 20 N.Y. 268 (1859).

amount of the debt. The issue before the court was whether Lawrence, who was not a party to the Holly-Fox contract, could sue Fox directly to recover the $300. The court held that Lawrence could do so, thereby establishing the modern rule that an intended beneficiary can sue the promisor directly. •

Types of Intended Beneficiaries

Two of the most common types of intended beneficiaries are creditor beneficiaries and donee beneficiaries. We discuss both types of beneficiaries next.

Creditor Beneficiary

One type of intended beneficiary is a *creditor beneficiary.* Like the plaintiff in *Lawerence v. Fox,* a creditor beneficiary benefits from a contract in which one party (the promisor) promises another party (the promisee) to pay a debt that the promisee owes to a third party (the creditor beneficiary). As an intended beneficiary, the creditor beneficiary can sue the promisor directly to enforce the contract.

CASE EXAMPLE 13.15 Autumn Allan owned a condominium unit in a Texas complex located directly beneath a condo unit owned by Aslan Koraev. Over the course of two years, Allan's unit suffered eight incidents of water and sewage incursion as a result of plumbing problems and misuse of appliances in Koraev's unit. Allan sued Koraev for breach of contract and won. Koraev appealed, arguing that he had no contractual duty to Allan. The court found that Allan was an intended third party beneficiary of the contract between Koraev and the condominium owner's association. Because the governing documents stated that each owner had to comply strictly with their provisions, failure to comply created grounds for an action by the condominium association or an aggrieved (wronged) owner. Here, Allan was clearly an aggrieved owner and could sue Koraev directly for his failure to perform his contract duties to the condominium association.[10] •

Donee Beneficiary

Another type of intended beneficiary is a *donee beneficiary.* When a contract is made for the express purpose of giving a *gift* to a third party, the third party (the donee beneficiary) can sue the promisor directly to enforce the promise.[11]

The most common donee beneficiary contract is a life insurance contract. **EXAMPLE 13.16** Ang (the promisee) pays premiums to Standard Life, a life insurance company, and Standard Life (the promisor) promises to pay a certain amount on Ang's death to anyone Ang designates as a beneficiary. The designated beneficiary is a donee beneficiary under the life insurance policy and can enforce the promise made by the insurance company to pay her or him on Ang's death. •

When the Rights of an Intended Beneficiary Vest

An intended third party beneficiary cannot enforce a contract against the original parties until the third party's rights have *vested,* meaning that the rights have taken effect and cannot be taken away. Until these rights have vested, the original parties to the contract—the promisor and the promisee—can modify or rescind the contract without the consent of the third party.

When do the rights of third parties vest? Generally, the rights vest when one of the following occurs:

1. When the third party demonstrates express consent to the agreement, such as by sending a letter or note acknowledging awareness of, and consent to, a contract formed for her or his benefit.

---

10. *Allan v. Nersesova,* 307 S.W.3d 564 (Tx.App—Dallas 2010).

11. This principle was first enunciated in *Seaver v. Ransom,* 224 N.Y. 233, 120 N.E. 639 (1918).

2. When the third party materially alters his or her position in detrimental reliance on the contract, such as when a donee beneficiary contracts to have a home built in reliance on the receipt of funds promised to him or her in a donee beneficiary contract.
3. When the conditions for vesting are satisfied. For instance, the rights of a beneficiary under a life insurance policy vest when the insured person dies.

Incidental Beneficiaries

Incidental Beneficiary A third party who benefits from a contract even though the contract was not formed for that purpose. An incidental beneficiary has no rights in the contract and cannot sue to have it enforced.

Sometimes, a third person receives a benefit from a contract even though that person's benefit is not the reason the contract was made. Such a person is known as an **incidental beneficiary.** Because the benefit is unintentional, an incidental beneficiary cannot sue to enforce the contract.

CASE EXAMPLE 13.17 Spectators at the infamous boxing match in which Mike Tyson was disqualified for biting his opponent's ear sued Tyson and the fight's promoters for a refund on the basis of breach of contract. The spectators claimed that they were third party beneficiaries of the contract between Tyson and the fight's promoters. The court, however, held that the spectators could not sue because they were not in contractual privity with the defendants. Any benefits they received from the contract were incidental to the contract, and according to the court, the spectators got what they paid for: "the right to view whatever event transpired."[12]

LEARNING OBJECTIVE 3
What factors indicate that a third party beneficiary is an intended beneficiary?

Intended versus Incidental Beneficiaries

In determining whether a party is an intended or an incidental beneficiary, the courts focus on the parties' intent, as expressed in the contract language and implied by the surrounding circumstances. Any beneficiary who is not deemed an intended beneficiary is considered incidental.

Exhibit 13.4 below graphically illustrates the distinction between intended and incidental beneficiaries.

12. *Castillo v. Tyson*, 268 A.D.2d 336, 701 N.Y.S.2d 423 (Sup.Ct.App.Div. 2000).

Exhibit 13.4 Third Party Beneficiaries

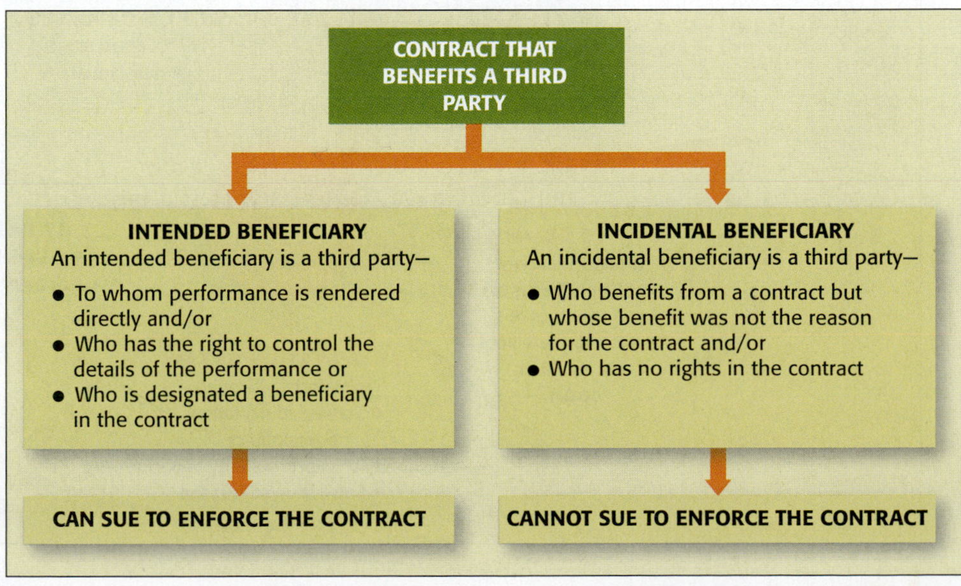

Reasonable Person Test Although no single test can embrace all possible situations, courts often apply the *reasonable person* test: Would a reasonable person in the position of the beneficiary believe that the promisee intended to confer on the beneficiary the right to enforce the contract?

Other Factors Indicating an Intended Beneficiary In addition, the presence of one or more of the following factors strongly indicates that the third party is an intended beneficiary of the contract:

1. Performance is rendered directly to the third party.
2. The third party has the right to control the details of performance.
3. The third party is expressly designated as a beneficiary in the contract.

LEARNING OBJECTIVE 4
How are most contracts discharged?

Discharge The termination of an obligation, such as occurs when the parties to a contract have fully performed their contractual obligations.

Performance The fulfillment of one's duties under a contract—the normal way of discharging one's contractual obligations.

Contract Discharge

The most common way to **discharge**, or terminate, one's contractual duties is by the **performance** of those duties. The duty to perform under a contract may be *conditioned* on the occurrence or nonoccurrence of a certain event, or the duty may be *absolute.* As shown in Exhibit 13.5 below, in addition to performance, a contract can be discharged in numerous other ways, including discharge by agreement of the parties and discharge by operation of law.

Conditions of Performance

In most contracts, promises of performance are not expressly conditioned or qualified. Instead, they are *absolute promises.* They must be performed, or the party promising the act will be in breach of contract. EXAMPLE 13.18 JoAnne contracts to sell Alfonso a painting for $10,000. The parties' promises are unconditional: JoAnne will transfer the painting to

Exhibit 13.5 Contract Discharge

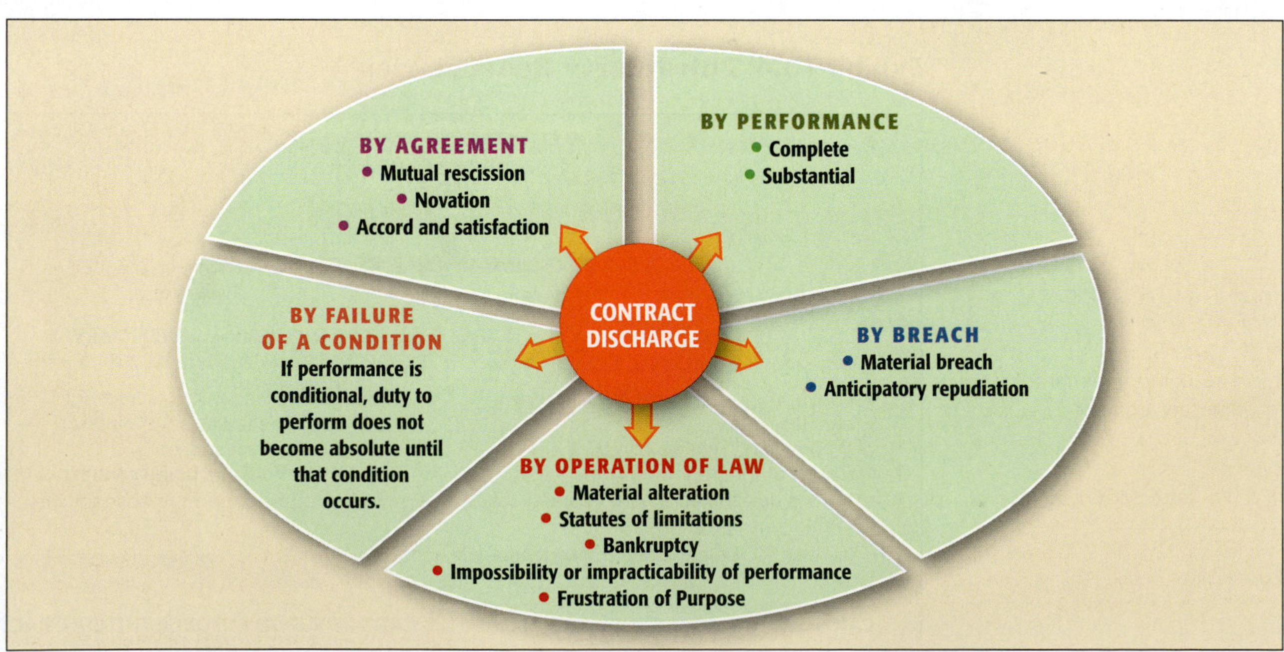

Alfonso, and Alfonso will pay $10,000 to JoAnne. The payment does not have to be made if the painting is not transferred. •

Condition A qualification, provision, or clause in a contractual agreement, the occurrence or nonoccurrence of which creates, suspends, or terminates the obligations of the contracting parties.

In some situations, however, contractual promises are conditioned. A **condition** is a qualification in a contract based on a possible future event, the occurrence or nonoccurrence of which will trigger the performance of a legal obligation or terminate an existing obligation under a contract. If the condition is not satisfied, the obligations of the parties are discharged.

EXAMPLE 13.19 Alfonso, in *Example 13.18,* offers to purchase JoAnne's painting only if an independent appraisal indicates that it is worth at least $10,000. JoAnne accepts Alfonso's offer. Their obligations (promises) are conditioned on the outcome of the appraisal. Should this condition not be satisfied (for example, if the appraiser deems the value of the painting to be only $5,000), their obligations to each other are discharged and cannot be enforced. •

LEARNING OBJECTIVE 5

What is a contractual condition, and how might a condition affect contractual obligations?

We look next at three types of conditions that can be present in any given contract: *conditions precedent, conditions subsequent,* and *concurrent conditions.*

Condition Precedent A condition in a contract that must be met before a party's promise becomes absolute.

Conditions Precedent

A condition that must be fulfilled before a party's promise becomes absolute is called a **condition precedent.** The condition precedes the absolute duty to perform, as in the JoAnne-Alfonso example just given. For instance, insurance contracts frequently specify that certain conditions, such as passing a physical examination, must be met before the insurance company will be obligated to perform under the contract.

Sometimes, a lease of real property (see Chapter 36) includes an option to buy that property. The lease in the following case required timely rent payments as a condition of exercising such an option, but the lessee often failed to make the payments on time. The court had to decide whether the lessee could still exercise the option even though it had not strictly complied with the condition precedent.

Case 13.3

Pack 2000, Inc. v. Cushman

Appellate Court of Connecticut,
126 Conn.App. 339, 11 A.3d 181 (2011).
www.jud.ct.gov/index.asp[a]

(leezsnow/iStockphoto.com)

An employee works at a Midas muffler shop.

FACTS Eugene Cushman agreed to transfer two Midas muffler shops to Pack 2000, Inc. The deal included leases for the real estate on which the shops were located. Each lease provided Pack with an option to buy the leased real estate subject to certain conditions. Pack was to pay rent by the first day of each month, make payments on the notes by the eighth day of each month, and pay utilities and other accounts on time. Pack, however, was often late in making these payments. The utility and phone companies threatened to cut off services, an insurance company canceled Pack's liability coverage, and other delinquencies prompted collection calls and letters. When Pack sought to exercise the options to buy the real estate, Cushman responded that Pack had not complied with the conditions. Pack filed a suit in a Connecticut state court against Cushman, seeking specific performance of the options. The court rendered a judgment in Pack's favor. Cushman appealed.

ISSUE Can Pack exercise its option to buy the leased real estate even though it did not strictly comply with the condition precedent that required it to make payments on time?

DECISION No. A state intermediate appellate court reversed the lower court's judgment and remanded the case for the entry

a. In the left column, in the "Opinions" pull-out menu, click on "Appellate Court." On that page, in the "Search the Archives:" section, click on "Appellate Court Archive." In the result, click on "2011." Scroll to the "Published in Connecticut Law Journal—2/1/11" section, and click on the docket number next to the title of the case to view the opinion. The Connecticut judicial branch maintains this Web site.

Case 13.3—Continues next page ➡

Case 13.3—Continued

of a judgment for Cushman. A party retains its right to exercise an option to buy real estate only by complying strictly with any conditions precedent to its exercise of the option.

REASON The leases provided Pack with the option to buy the leased real estate. But to take advantage of the options, Pack had to comply with the condition precedent of making periodic payments to Cushman and to certain third parties by specific dates. Pack was often late in making these payments and thus did not strictly comply with the condition. The court reasoned that because of this failure of strict compliance, Pack lost the right to exercise the options to buy the real estate.

WHAT IF THE FACTS WERE DIFFERENT? *Suppose that Pack had not made any late payments. Would the result have been different? Explain.*

Condition Subsequent A condition in a contract that, if it occurs, operates to terminate a party's absolute promise to perform.

Conditions Subsequent

When a condition operates to terminate a party's absolute promise to perform, it is called a **condition subsequent.** The condition follows, or is subsequent to, the absolute duty to perform. If the condition occurs, the party need not perform any further. **EXAMPLE 13.20** A law firm hires Julia Darby, a recent law school graduate and a newly licensed attorney. Their contract provides that the firm's obligation to continue employing Darby is discharged if she fails to maintain her license to practice law. This is a condition subsequent because a failure to maintain the license will discharge a duty that has already arisen. •

Generally, conditions precedent are common, and conditions subsequent are rare. The *Restatement (Second) of Contracts* omits the terms *condition subsequent* and *condition precedent* and refers to both simply as "conditions."[13]

Concurrent Conditions Conditions that must occur or be performed at the same time—they are mutually dependent. No obligations arise until these conditions are simultaneously performed.

Concurrent Conditions

When each party's absolute duty to perform is conditioned on the other party's absolute duty to perform, **concurrent conditions** are present. These conditions exist only when the parties expressly or impliedly are to perform their respective duties *simultaneously.*

EXAMPLE 13.21 If a buyer promises to pay for goods when they are delivered by the seller, each party's absolute duty to perform is conditioned on the other party's absolute duty to perform. The buyer's duty to pay for the goods does not become absolute until the seller either delivers or attempts to deliver the goods. Likewise, the seller's duty to deliver the goods does not become absolute until the buyer pays or attempts to pay for the goods. Therefore, neither can recover from the other for breach without first tendering performance. •

Discharge by Performance

Tender An unconditional offer to perform an obligation by a person who is ready, willing, and able to do so.

The contract comes to an end when both parties fulfill their respective duties by performing the acts they have promised. Performance can also be accomplished by tender. **Tender** is an unconditional offer to perform by a person who is ready, willing, and able to do so. Therefore, a seller who places goods at the disposal of a buyer has tendered delivery and can demand payment according to the terms of the agreement. A buyer who offers to pay for goods has tendered payment and can demand delivery of the goods.

Once performance has been tendered, the party making the tender has done everything possible to carry out the terms of the contract. If the other party then refuses to perform, the party making the tender can consider the duty discharged and sue for breach of contract.

13. *Restatement (Second) of Contracts,* Section 224. Note that the difference between conditions precedent and conditions subsequent can be important procedurally, because a plaintiff must prove a condition precedent whereas the defendant normally proves a condition subsequent.

(1001nights/istockphoto.com)
When is a deal to sell a new car completed?

Complete Performance When a party performs exactly as agreed, there is no question as to whether the contract has been performed. When a party's performance is perfect, it is said to be complete.

Normally, conditions expressly stated in the contract must fully occur in all aspects for complete performance (strict performance) of the contract to take place. Any deviation breaches the contract and discharges the other party's obligations to perform.

For instance, most construction contracts require the builder to meet certain specifications. If the specifications are conditions, complete performance is required to avoid material breach. (*Material breach* will be discussed shortly.) If the conditions are met, the other party to the contract must then fulfill her or his obligation to pay the builder.

For some construction contracts, specifications are not explicitly stated as conditions. In such situations, sometimes the builder fails to meet the specifications and that means the performance is not complete. What effect does that failure have on the other party's obligation to pay? The answer is part of the doctrine of *substantial performance.*

Substantial Performance A party who in good faith performs substantially all of the terms of a contract can enforce the contract against the other party under the doctrine of substantial performance. Note that good faith is required. Intentionally failing to comply with the terms is a breach of the contract.

To qualify as *substantial performance,* the performance must not vary greatly from the performance promised in the contract, and it must create substantially the same benefits as those promised in the contract. If the omission, variance, or defect in performance is unimportant and can easily be compensated by awarding damages, a court is likely to hold that the contract has been substantially performed. Courts decide whether the performance was substantial on a case-by-case basis, examining all of the facts of the particular situation. If performance is substantial, the other party's duty to perform remains absolute (except that the party can sue for damages due to the minor deviations).

CASE EXAMPLE 13.22 Wisconsin Electric Power Company (WEPCO) contracted with Union Pacific Railroad to transport coal to WEPCO from mines in Colorado. The contract required WEPCO to notify Union Pacific monthly of how many tons of coal (below a certain maximum) it wanted to have shipped the next month. Union Pacific was to make "good faith reasonable efforts" to meet the schedule. The contract also required WEPCO to supply the railcars. When WEPCO did not supply the railcars, Union Pacific used its own railcars and delivered 84 percent of the requested coal. In this situation, a federal court held that the delivery of 84 percent of the contracted amount constituted substantial performance.[14] •

Performance to the Satisfaction of Another Contracts often state that completed work must personally satisfy one of the parties or a third person. The question is whether this satisfaction becomes a condition precedent, requiring actual personal satisfaction or approval for discharge, or whether the test of satisfaction is performance that would satisfy a *reasonable person* (substantial performance).

When the subject matter of the contract is *personal,* a contract to be performed to the satisfaction of one of the parties is conditioned, and performance must actually satisfy that party. For instance, contracts for portraits and works of art are considered personal. Therefore, only the personal satisfaction of the party fulfills the condition—unless a court

14. *Wisconsin Electric Power Co. v. Union Pacific Railroad Co.*, 557 F.3d 504 (7th Cir. 2009).

finds that the party is expressing dissatisfaction to avoid payment or otherwise is not acting in good faith.

Most other contracts need to be performed only to the satisfaction of a reasonable person unless they *expressly state otherwise.* When such contracts require performance to the satisfaction of a third party (such as, "to the satisfaction of Robert Ames, the supervising engineer"), the courts are divided. A majority of courts require the work to be satisfactory to a reasonable person, but some courts hold that the personal satisfaction of the third party designated in the contract (here, Robert Ames) must be met. Again, the personal judgment must be made honestly, or the condition will be excused.

Breach of Contract The failure, without legal excuse, of a promisor to perform the obligations of a contract.

Material Breach of Contract

A **breach of contract** is the nonperformance of a contractual duty. A breach is *material* when performance is not at least substantial.[15] If there is a material breach, the nonbreaching party is excused from the performance of contractual duties and can sue for damages caused by the breach. If the breach is *minor* (not material), the nonbreaching party's duty to perform may sometimes be suspended until the breach is remedied, but the duty is not entirely excused. Once the minor breach is cured (corrected), the nonbreaching party must resume performance of the contractual obligations.

(AP Photo/Chris Pizzello)

If Paris Hilton agrees to attend a large party in exchange for $3,000, is she in breach of contract if she leaves after ten minutes?

Any breach entitles the nonbreaching party to sue for damages, but only a material breach discharges the nonbreaching party from the contract. The policy underlying these rules is that contracts should go forward when only minor problems occur, but that contracts should be terminated if major problems arise.[16]

CASE EXAMPLE 13.23 Su Yong Kim sold an apartment building in Portland, Oregon. At the time of the sale, the building's plumbing violated the city's housing code. The contract therefore provided that Kim would correct the violations within eight months after signing the contract. A year later, Kim still had not made the necessary repairs, and the buyers were being fined by the city for the code violations. The buyers stopped making payments under the contract, and the dispute ended up in court. The court found that Kim's failure to make the repairs was a material breach of the contract because it defeated the purpose of the contract. The buyers had purchased the building to lease it out to tenants, but instead they were losing tenants and paying fines to the city due to the substandard plumbing. Because Kim's breach was material, the buyers were not obligated to continue to perform their obligation to make payments under the contract.[17] •

ETHICAL ISSUE

Is it a material breach for a hospital to accept a country singer's donation but then refuse to honor its commitment to name a new women's health center after the singer's mother? Country singer Garth Brooks was born in Yukon, Oklahoma. Since he has become famous, he has made generous contributions to charities in that town. When his mother, Colleen Brooks, died, he donated $500,000 to Integris Rural Health, Inc., in Yukon with the intention that the funds would be used to build a new women's health center named after his mother. Several years passed after Brooks's donation, but the health center was not built. Integris claimed that it intended to do something to honor Colleen Brooks but insisted that it had never promised to build a new health center. When Integris refused to return the $500,000, Garth Brooks sued for breach of contract.

Was the hospital's failure to build a women's health center and name it after Brooks's mother a material breach of the contract? A jury thought so. In January 2012, a jury in Rogers County, Oklahoma, awarded Brooks $500,000 in actual damages for breach of contract. The jury also awarded Brooks another $500,000 because it found the hospital guilty of reckless disregard and intentionally acting with malice toward others.

---

15. *Restatement (Second) of Contracts,* Section 241.
16. See UCC 2–612, which deals with installment contracts for the sale of goods.
17. *Kim v. Park,* 192 Or.App. 365, 86 P.3d 63 (2004).

Anticipatory Repudiation An assertion or action by a party indicating that he or she will not perform a contractual obligation.

Anticipatory Repudiation of a Contract

Before either party to a contract has a duty to perform, one of the parties may refuse to perform her or his contractual obligations. This is called **anticipatory repudiation.**[18]

Repudiation Is a Material Breach When anticipatory repudiation occurs, it is treated as a material breach of the contract, and the nonbreaching party is permitted to bring an action for damages immediately, even though the scheduled time for performance under the contract may still be in the future.[19] Until the nonbreaching party treats this early repudiation as a breach, however, the breaching party can retract the anticipatory repudiation by proper notice and restore the parties to their original obligations.

An anticipatory repudiation is treated as a present, material breach for two reasons. First, the nonbreaching party should not be required to remain ready and willing to perform when the other party has already repudiated the contract. Second, the nonbreaching party should have the opportunity to seek a similar contract elsewhere and may have the duty to do so to minimize his or her loss.

KNOW THIS

The risks that prices will fluctuate and values will change are ordinary business risks for which the law does not provide relief.

May Occur When Market Prices Fluctuate Quite often, an anticipatory repudiation occurs when a sharp fluctuation in market prices creates a situation in which performance of the contract would be extremely unfavorable to one of the parties.

EXAMPLE 13.24 Shasta Corporation contracts to manufacture and sell 100,000 laptop computers to New Age, Inc., a retailer of computer equipment. Delivery is to be made two months from the date of the contract. One month later, three suppliers of computer parts raise their prices to Shasta. Because of these higher prices, Shasta stands to lose $500,000 if it sells the computers to New Age at the contract price. Shasta writes to New Age, stating that it cannot deliver the 100,000 computers at the contract price. Even though some may sympathize with Shasta, its letter is an anticipatory repudiation of the contract. New Age can treat the repudiation as a material breach and immediately pursue remedies, even though the contract delivery date is still a month away. •

Discharge by Agreement

Any contract can be discharged by agreement of the parties. The agreement can be contained in the original contract, or the parties can form a new contract for the express purpose of discharging the original contract.

Discharge by Mutual Rescission

As mentioned in previous chapters, rescission occurs when the parties cancel the contract and are returned to the positions they occupied prior to the contract's formation. For *mutual rescission* to take place, the parties must make another agreement that also satisfies the legal requirements for a contract—there must be an *offer,* an *acceptance,* and *consideration.* Ordinarily, if the parties agree to rescind the original contract, their promises not to perform those acts promised in the original contract will be legal consideration for the second contract.

Oral agreements to rescind executory contracts (that neither party has performed) are enforceable even if the original agreement was in writing. Under the Uniform Commercial Code, however, an agreement rescinding a contract for the sale of goods, regardless of price, must be in writing when the contract requires a written rescission. Also, agreements to rescind contracts involving transfers of realty must be evidenced by a writing.

---

18. *Restatement (Second) of Contracts,* Section 253; and UCC 2–610.

19. The doctrine of anticipatory repudiation first arose in the landmark case of *Hochster v. De La Tour,* 2 Ellis and Blackburn Reports 678 (1853), when an English court recognized the delay and expense inherent in a rule requiring a nonbreaching party to wait until the time of performance before suing for an anticipatory repudiation.

When one party has fully performed, an agreement to rescind the original contract usually is not enforceable unless additional consideration or restitution is made. Because the performing party has received no consideration for the promise to call off the original bargain, additional consideration is necessary.

Novation The substitution, by agreement, of a new contract for an old one, with the rights under the old one being terminated.

Discharge by Novation

The process of **novation** substitutes a third party for one of the original parties. Essentially, the parties to the original contract and one or more new parties get together and agree to the substitution. The requirements of a novation are as follows:

1. The existence of a previous, valid obligation.
2. Agreement by all of the parties to a new contract.
3. The extinguishing of the old obligation (discharge of the prior party).
4. A new, valid contract.

EXAMPLE 13.25 Union Corporation contracts to sell its pharmaceutical division to British Pharmaceuticals, Ltd. Before the transfer is completed, Union, British Pharmaceuticals, and a third company, Otis Chemicals, execute a new agreement to transfer all of British Pharmaceuticals' rights and duties in the transaction to Otis Chemicals. As long as the new contract is supported by consideration, the novation will discharge the original contract (between Union and British Pharmaceuticals) and replace it with the new contract (between Union and Otis Chemicals). •

A novation expressly or impliedly revokes and discharges a prior contract. The parties involved may expressly state in the new contract that the old contract is now discharged. If the parties do not expressly discharge the old contract, it will be impliedly discharged if the new contract's terms are inconsistent with the old contract's terms.

Discharge by Accord and Satisfaction

As Chapter 11 explained, in an *accord and satisfaction,* the parties agree to accept performance different from the performance originally promised. An *accord* is an executory contract (one that has not yet been performed) to perform some act to satisfy an existing contractual duty that is not yet discharged.[20] A *satisfaction* is the performance of the accord agreement. An *accord* and its *satisfaction* discharge the original contractual obligation.

Once the accord has been made, the original obligation is merely suspended until the accord agreement is fully performed. If it is not performed, the party to whom performance is owed can bring an action on the original obligation or for breach of the accord. **EXAMPLE 13.26** Shea obtains a judgment of $8,000 against Marla. Later, both parties agree that the judgment can be satisfied by Marla's transfer of her automobile to Shea. This agreement to accept the auto in lieu of $8,000 in cash is the accord. If Marla transfers her automobile to Shea, the accord agreement is fully performed, and the $8,000 debt is discharged. If Marla refuses to transfer her car, the accord is breached. Because the original obligation is merely suspended, Shea can sue to enforce the judgment for $8,000 in cash or bring an action for breach of the accord. •

"Law is a practical matter."

Roscoe Pound, 1870–1964
(American jurist)

Discharge by Operation of Law

Under some circumstances, contractual duties may be discharged by operation of law. These circumstances include material alteration of the contract, the running of the relevant statute of limitations, bankruptcy, and impossibility of performance.

Material Alteration

To discourage parties from altering written contracts, the law allows an innocent party to be discharged when one party has materially altered a

20. *Restatement (Second) of Contracts,* Section 281.

written contract without the knowledge or consent of the other party. If a party alters a material term of the contract—such as the quantity term or the price term—without the knowledge or consent of the other party, the party who was unaware of the alteration can treat the contract as discharged or terminated.

Statutes of Limitations

As mentioned earlier in this text (see Chapter 1 on page 15), statutes of limitations limit the period during which a party can sue on a particular cause of action. After the applicable limitations period has passed, a suit can no longer be brought. The period for bringing lawsuits for breach of oral contracts is usually two to three years, and for written contracts, four to five years. Lawsuits for breach of a contract for the sale of goods must be brought within four years after the cause of action has accrued. In their original contract, the parties can agree to reduce this four-year period to not less than one year. They cannot, however, agree to extend it beyond four years.

Bankruptcy

A proceeding in bankruptcy attempts to allocate the debtor's assets to the creditors in a fair and equitable fashion. Once the assets have been allocated, the debtor receives a *discharge in bankruptcy* (see Chapter 21). A discharge in bankruptcy ordinarily bars the creditors from enforcing most of the debtor's contracts.

Impossibility of Performance A doctrine under which a party to a contract is relieved of his or her duty to perform when performance becomes objectively impossible or totally impracticable.

Impossibility of Performance

After a contract has been made, performance may become impossible in an objective sense. This is known as **impossibility of performance** and may discharge the contract.[21] The doctrine of impossibility of performance is applied only when the parties could not have reasonably foreseen, at the time the contract was formed, the event or events that rendered performance impossible. Performance may also become so difficult or costly due to some unforeseen event that a court will consider it commercially unfeasible, or impracticable, as will be discussed later in the chapter.

Objective impossibility ("It cannot be done") must be distinguished from subjective impossibility ("I'm sorry, I cannot do it"). An example of subjective impossibility occurs when a party cannot deliver goods on time because of railcar shortages or cannot make payment on time because the bank is closed. In effect, the nonperforming party is saying, "It is impossible for *me* to perform," rather than "It is impossible for *anyone* to perform." Accordingly, such excuses do not discharge a contract, and the nonperforming party is normally held in breach of contract.

The star dancer below has a contract to appear in five ballets during the winter season. If he breaks his leg before the season, is he still bound by the contract?

(Yuri Arcurs/Shutterstock.com)

When Performance Is Impossible

Three basic types of situations will generally qualify as grounds for the discharge of contractual obligations based on impossibility of performance:[22]

1. *When a party whose personal performance is essential to the completion of the contract dies or becomes incapacitated prior to performance.* **EXAMPLE 13.27** Fred, a famous dancer, contracts with Ethereal Dancing Guild to play a leading role in its new ballet. Before the ballet can be performed, Fred becomes ill and dies. His personal performance was essential to the completion of the contract. Thus, his death discharges the contract and his estate's liability for his nonperformance. •
2. *When the specific subject matter of the contract is destroyed.* **EXAMPLE 13.28** A-1 Farm Equipment agrees to sell Gudgel the green tractor on its lot and promises to have the tractor ready for Gudgel to pick up on Saturday. On Friday night, however, a truck veers off the nearby highway and smashes into the tractor, destroying it beyond repair. Because the contract was for this specific tractor, A-1's performance is rendered impossible owing to the accident. •

21. *Restatement (Second) of Contracts,* Section 261.
22. *Restatement (Second) of Contracts,* Sections 262–266; and UCC 2–615.

3. *When a change in the law renders performance illegal.* **EXAMPLE 13.29** Russo contracts with Playlist, Inc., to create a Web site through which users can post and share movies, music, and other forms of digital entertainment. Russo goes to work. Before the site is operational, however, Congress passes the No Online Piracy in Entertainment (NOPE) Act. The NOPE Act makes it illegal to operate a Web site on which copyrighted works are posted without the copyright owners' consent. In this situation, the contract is discharged by operation of law. The purpose of the contract has been rendered illegal, and contract performance is objectively impossible. •

Temporary Impossibility An occurrence or event that makes performance temporarily impossible operates to suspend performance until the impossibility ceases. Ordinarily, the parties must then perform the contract as originally planned. Only if the lapse of time and the change in circumstances surrounding the contract make it substantially more burdensome for the parties to perform the promised acts will the contract be discharged.

CASE EXAMPLE 13.30 On August 22, Keefe Hurwitz contracted to sell his home in Louisiana to Wesley and Gwendolyn Payne for a price of $241,500. On August 26—just four days after the parties signed the contract—Hurricane Katrina made landfall and caused extensive damage to the house. The cost of repairs was estimated at $60,000, and Hurwitz would have to make the repairs before the closing date (see Chapter 36). Hurwitz refused to pay $60,000 for the repairs only to sell the property to the Paynes for the previously agreed-on price of $241,500. The Paynes sued to enforce the contract. Hurwitz claimed that Hurricane Katrina had made it impossible for him to perform and had discharged his duties under the contract. The court ruled that Hurricane Katrina had caused only a temporary impossibility. Therefore, Hurwitz had to pay for the necessary repairs and to perform the contract as written. He could not obtain a higher purchase price to offset the cost of the repairs.[23] •

KNOW THIS

The doctrine of commercial impracticability does not provide relief from such events as ordinary price increases or easily predictable changes in the weather.

Commercial Impracticability

Courts may excuse parties from their performance obligations when the performance becomes much more difficult or expensive than the parties originally contemplated at the time the contract was formed. For someone to invoke the doctrine of **commercial impracticability** successfully, however, the anticipated performance must become *extremely* difficult or costly.[24]

Commercial Impracticability A doctrine that may excuse the duty to perform a contract when performance becomes much more difficult or costly due to forces that neither party could control or contemplate at the time the contract was formed.

The added burden of performing not only must be extreme but also *must not have been known by the parties when the contract was made.* For instance, in one classic case, a court held that a contract could be discharged because a party would have to pay ten times more than the original estimate to excavate a certain amount of gravel.[25] In another case, a power failure during a wedding reception relieved the owner of a banquet hall from the duty to perform a contract.[26] (See this chapter's *Beyond Our Borders* feature on the facing page for a discussion of Germany's approach to impracticability and impossibility of performance.)

Frustration of Purpose

Closely allied with the doctrine of commercial impracticability is the doctrine of **frustration of purpose.** In principle, a contract will be discharged if supervening circumstances make it impossible to attain the purpose both parties had in mind when making the contract. As with commercial impracticability, the supervening event must not have been foreseeable at the time of the contracting.[27]

Frustration of Purpose A court-created doctrine under which a party to a contract will be relieved of her or his duty to perform when the objective purpose for performance no longer exists (due to reasons beyond that party's control).

23. *Payne v. Hurwitz,* 978 So.2d 1000 (La.App. 1st Cir. 2008).
24. *Restatement (Second) of Contracts,* Section 264.
25. *Mineral Park Land Co. v. Howard,* 172 Cal. 289, 156 P. 458 (1916).
26. *Facto v. Panagis,* 390 N.J.Super. 227, 915 A.2d 59 (2007).
27. See, for example, *East Capitol View Community Development Corp. v. Robinson,* 941 A.2d 1036 (D.C.App. 2008).

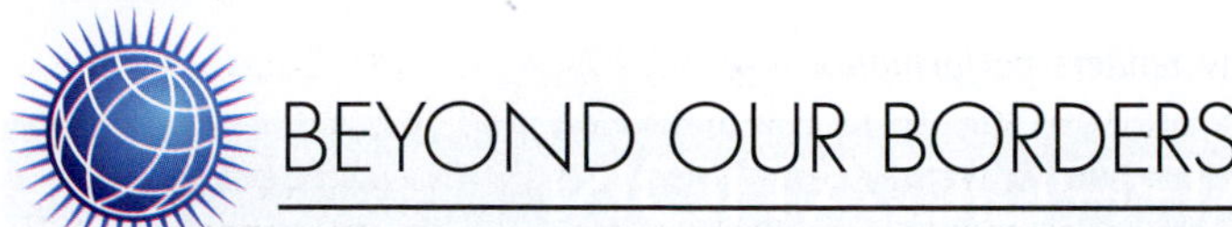

Impossibility or Impracticability of Performance in Germany

In the United States, when a party alleges that contract performance is impossible or impracticable because of circumstances unforeseen at the time the contract was formed, a court will either discharge the party's contractual obligations or hold the party to the contract. In other words, if a court agrees that the contract is impossible or impracticable to perform, the remedy is to rescind (cancel) the contract. Under German law, however, a court may adjust the terms of (reform) a contract in light of economic developments. If an unforeseen event affects the foundation of the agreement, the court can alter the contract's terms to align with the parties' original expectations, thus making the contract fair to the parties.

Critical Thinking

When a contract becomes impossible or impracticable to perform, which remedy would a businessperson prefer—rescission or reformation? Why? Explain your answer.

Reviewing . . . Third Party Rights and Discharge

Val's Foods signs a contract to buy 1,500 pounds of basil from Sun Farms, a small organic herb grower, as long as an independent organization inspects the crop and certifies that it contains no pesticide or herbicide residue. Val's has a contract with several restaurant chains to supply pesto and intends to use Sun Farms' basil in the pesto to fulfill these contracts. When Sun Farms is preparing to harvest the basil, an unexpected hailstorm destroys half the crop. Sun Farms attempts to purchase additional basil from other farms, but it is late in the season and the price is twice the normal market price. Sun Farms is too small to absorb this cost and immediately notifies Val's that it will not fulfill the contract. Using the information presented in the chapter, answer the following questions.

1. Suppose that Sun Farms supplies the basil that survived the storm but the basil does not pass the chemical-residue inspection. Which concept discussed in the chapter might allow Val's to refuse to perform the contract in this situation?
2. Under which legal theory or theories might Sun Farms claim that its obligation under the contract has been discharged by operation of law? Discuss fully.
3. Suppose that Sun Farms contacts every basil grower in the country and buys the last remaining chemical-free basil anywhere. Nevertheless, Sun Farms is able to ship only 1,475 pounds to Val's. Would this fulfill Sun Farms' obligations to Val's? Why or why not?
4. Now suppose that Sun Farms sells its operations to Happy Valley Farms. As part of the sale, all three parties agree that Happy Valley will provide the basil as stated under the original contract. What is this type of agreement called?

DEBATE THIS The doctrine of commercial impracticability should be abolished.

BUSINESS APPLICATION

Dealing with Third Party Rights*

Assignments of contractual rights and delegations of duties are common in the business world. As you discovered in this chapter, third party rights and duties stem from the law on assignments, delegations, and third party beneficiaries. A third party may not even be aware that he or she has rights in a contract, as can happen when a person is the beneficiary of a life insurance policy. In certain situations, businesses may wish to attempt to prohibit a third party from acquiring such rights.

The general rule, though, is that any contractual right or duty can be assigned or delegated unless the assignment or delegation is prohibited by (1) the contract, (2) a statute, or (3) other limitations.

For example, a tenant under a long-term lease contract may assign the lease to another party. To avoid such assignments, property owners often prohibit the assignment of the balance of a lease term unless the property owner's consent is obtained. (See Chapter 36).

* This *Business Application* is not meant to substitute for the services of an attorney who is licensed to practice law in your state.

When a contract calls for the manufacture and sale of goods, the manufacturer may assign or delegate the production of such goods to a third party unless prohibited by the contract. Consequently, most purchase orders (contracts) have a clause that prohibits such assignments or delegations without the buyer's consent.

Checklist for the Businessperson

1. *Determine whether you can assign or delegate your rights or duties under a contract to a third party.*
2. *If you can assign or delegate your contract rights or performance, attempt to determine your benefits and obligations, such as notice to customers, if you do make the assignment or delegation.*
3. *If you do not want your contract rights or duties to be assigned or delegated, insert a contract clause that prohibits assignment or delegation without your consent.*
4. *Whenever you might be a third party beneficiary to a contract, such as a creditor beneficiary, take steps to determine your rights.*

Key Terms

alienation 331
anticipatory repudiation 343
assignee 328
assignment 328
assignor 328
breach of contract 342
commercial impracticability 346
concurrent conditions 340
condition 339
condition precedent 339
condition subsequent 340
delegatee 333
delegation of duties 332
delegator 332
discharge 338
frustration of purpose 346
impossibility of performance 345
incidental beneficiary 337
intended beneficiary 335
novation 344
obligee 328
obligor 328
performance 338
privity of contract 327
tender 340
third party beneficiary 335

Chapter Summary: Third Party Rights and Discharge

THIRD PARTY RIGHTS	
Assignments (See pages 328–332.)	1. An assignment is the transfer of rights under a contract to a third party. The person assigning the rights is the *assignor,* and the party to whom the rights are assigned is the *assignee.* The assignee has a right to demand performance from the other original party to the contract. 2. Generally, all rights can be assigned. For exceptions, see Exhibit 13.3 on page 335. 3. The assignee should notify the obligor of the assignment. Although not legally required, notification avoids two potential problems: a. If the assignor assigns the same right to two different persons, generally the first assignment in time is the first in right, but in some states the first assignee to give notice takes priority. b. Until the obligor is notified of the assignment, the obligor can tender performance to the assignor. If the assignor accepts the performance, the obligor's duties under the contract are discharged without benefit to the assignee.

Continued

Chapter Summary: Third Party Rights and Discharge—Continued

Delegations (See pages 332–335.)	1. A delegation is the transfer of duties under a contract to a third party (the *delegatee*), who then assumes the obligation of performing the contractual duties previously held by the one making the delegation (the *delegator*). 2. As a general rule, any duty can be delegated, except in the circumstances listed in Exhibit 13.3 on page 335. 3. A valid delegation of duties does not relieve the delegator of obligations under the contract. If the delegatee fails to perform, the delegator is still liable to the obligee. 4. An "assignment of all rights" or an "assignment of the contract" is often construed to mean that both the rights and the duties arising under the contract are transferred to a third party.
Third Party Beneficiaries (See pages 335–338.)	A third party beneficiary contract is one made for the purpose of benefiting a third party. 1. *Intended beneficiary*—One for whose benefit a contract is created. When the promisor (the one making the contractual promise that benefits a third party) fails to perform as promised, the third party can sue the promisor directly. Examples of third party beneficiaries are creditor and donee beneficiaries. 2. *Incidental beneficiary*—A third party who indirectly (incidentally) benefits from a contract but for whose benefit the contract was not specifically intended. Incidental beneficiaries have no rights to the benefits received and cannot sue to have the contract enforced.
	CONTRACT DISCHARGE
Conditions of Performance (See pages 338–340.)	Contract obligations may be subject to the following types of conditions: 1. *Condition precedent*—A condition that must be fulfilled before a party's promise becomes absolute. 2. *Condition subsequent*—A condition that, if it occurs, operates to terminate a party's absolute promise to perform. 3. *Concurrent conditions*—Conditions that must be performed simultaneously. Each party's absolute duty to perform is conditioned on the other party's absolute duty to perform.
Discharge by Performance (See pages 340–343.)	A contract may be discharged by complete (strict) performance or by substantial performance. In some instances, performance must be to the satisfaction of another. Totally inadequate performance constitutes a material breach of the contract. An anticipatory repudiation of a contract allows the other party to sue immediately for breach of contract.
Discharge by Agreement (See pages 343–344.)	Parties may agree to discharge their contractual obligations in several ways: 1. *By rescission*—The parties mutually agree to rescind (cancel) the contract. 2. *By novation*—A new party is substituted for one of the primary parties to a contract. 3. *By accord and satisfaction*—The parties agree to render and accept performance different from that on which they originally agreed.
Discharge by Operation of Law (See pages 344–346.)	Parties' obligations under contracts may be discharged by operation of law owing to one of the following: 1. Contract alteration. 2. Statutes of limitations. 3. Bankruptcy. 4. Impossibility of performance. 5. Impracticability of performance. 6. Frustration of purpose.

ExamPrep

ISSUE SPOTTERS

1. Eagle Company contracts to build a house for Frank. The contract states that "any assignment of this contract renders the contract void." After Eagle builds the house, but before Frank pays, Eagle assigns its right to payment to Good Credit Company. Can Good Credit enforce the contract against Frank? Why or why not? **(See page 330.)**
2. Ready Foods contracts to buy two hundred carloads of frozen pizzas from Speedy Distributors. Before Ready or Speedy starts performing, can the parties call off the deal? What if Speedy has already shipped the pizzas? Explain your answers. **(See pages 343–344.)**

—Check your answers to the Issue Spotters against the answers provided in Appendix E at the end of this text.

BEFORE THE TEST

Go to www.cengagebrain.com, enter the ISBN 9781133273561, and click on "Find" to locate this textbook's Web site. Then, click on "Access Now" under "Study Tools," and select Chapter 13 at the top. There, you will find a Practice Quiz that you can take to assess your mastery of the concepts in this chapter, as well as Flashcards, a Glossary of important terms, and Video Questions (when assigned).

For Review

Answers to the even-numbered questions in this For Review section can be found in Appendix F at the end of this text.

1. What is an assignment? What is the difference between an assignment and a delegation?
2. In what situations is the delegation of duties prohibited?
3. What factors indicate that a third party beneficiary is an intended beneficiary?
4. How are most contracts discharged?
5. What is a contractual condition, and how might a condition affect contractual obligations?

Business Scenarios and Case Problems

13–1 Third Party Beneficiaries. Wilken owes Rivera $2,000. Howie promises Wilken that he will pay Rivera the $2,000 in return for Wilken's promise to give Howie's children guitar lessons. Is Rivera an intended beneficiary of the Howie-Wilken contract? Explain. **(See pages 336–338.)**

13–2 Question with Sample Answer—Assignment. Aron, a college student, signs a one-year lease agreement that runs from September 1 to August 31. The lease agreement specifies that the lease cannot be assigned without the landlord's consent. In late May, Aron decides not to go to summer school and assigns the balance of the lease (three months) to a close friend, Erica. The landlord objects to the assignment and denies Erica access to the apartment. Aron claims that Erica is financially sound and should be allowed the full rights and privileges of an assignee. Discuss fully whether the landlord or Aron is correct. **(See page 330.)**

—For a sample answer to Question 13–2, go to Appendix G at the end of this text.

13–3 Spotlight on Drug Testing—Third Party Beneficiaries. Bath Iron Works (BIW) offered a job to Thomas Devine, contingent on Devine's passing a drug test. The testing was conducted by NorDx, a subcontractor of Roche Biomendical Laboratories. When NorDx found that Devine's urinalysis showed the presence of opiates, a result confirmed by Roche, BIW refused to offer Devine permanent employment. Devine sued Roche, claiming that the ingestion of poppy seeds can lead to a positive result and that he tested positive for opiates only because of his daily consumption of poppy seed muffins. Devine argued that he was a third party beneficiary of the contract between his employer (BIW) and NorDx (Roche). Is Devine an intended third party beneficiary of the BIW—NorDx contract? Why or why not? Do drug-testing labs have a duty to the employees to exercise reasonable care in conducting the tests? Explain. [*Devine v. Roche Biomedical Laboratories*, 659 A.2d 868 (Me. 1995)] **(See pages 335–336.)**

13–4 Assignments. Senna Hills, Ltd., granted Southern Union Co. the right to distribute propane in a residential subdivision developed by Senna in exchange for a fee. Under their agreement, Senna's "right to receive a Fee shall continue for so long as the Propane System is owned by Southern Union." The agreement also allowed Southern Union to assign the distribution right. Later, Sonterra Energy Corp. bought the distribution system and was assigned the distribution right, but did not pay the fee to Senna. Did Sonterra breach the propane service agreement? Why or why not? [*Senna Hills, Ltd. v. Sonterra Energy Corp.*, __ S.W.3d __ (Tex.App.—Austin 2010)] **(See pages 328–332.)**

13–5 Duties That Cannot Be Delegated. Bruce Albea Contracting, Inc., the contractor on a highway project, subcontracted the asphalt work to APAC-Southeast, Inc. Their contract prohibited any delegation without Albea's consent. In midproject, APAC delegated its duties to Matthews Contracting Co. Although Albea allowed Matthews to finish the work, Albea did not pay APAC for its work on the project. Albea argued that APAC had violated the antidelegation clause, rendering their contact void. Is Albea correct? Explain. [*Western Surety Co. v. APAC-Southeast, Inc.*, 302 Ga.App. 654, 691 S.E.2d 234 (2010)] **(See page 333.)**

13–6 Case Problem with Sample Answer—Conditions of Performance. James Maciel leased an apartment in Regent Village, a university-owned housing facility for Regent University (RU) students in Virginia Beach, Virginia. The lease ran until the end of the fall semester. Maciel had an option to renew the lease semester by semester as long as he maintained his status as an RU student. When Maciel completed his coursework for the spring semester, he told RU that he intended to withdraw. The university told him that he could stay in the apartment until May 31, the final day of the spring semester. Maciel asked for two additional weeks, but the university denied the request. On June 1, RU changed the locks on the apartment. Maciel entered through a window and e-mailed the university that he planned to stay "for another one or two weeks." When he was charged with trespassing, Maciel argued that he had "legal authority" to occupy the apartment. Was Maciel correct? Explain. [*Maciel v. Commonwealth*, __ S.E.2d __ (Va.App. 2011)] **(See pages 338–340, 342.)**

—For a sample answer to Problem 13–6, go to Appendix H at the end of this text.

13–7 Notice of Assignment. Arnold Kazery was the owner of a hotel leased to George Wilkinson. The lease included renewal options of ten years each. When Arnold transferred his interest in the property to his son Sam, no one notified Wilkinson. For the next twenty years, Wilkinson paid the rent to Arnold and renewed the lease by notice to Arnold. When Wilkinson wrote to Arnold that he was exercising another option to renew, Sam filed a suit against him, claiming that the lease was void. Did Wilkinson give proper notice to renew? Discuss. [*Kazery v. Wilkinson*, 52 So.3d 1270 (Miss.App. 2011)] **(See page 331.)**

13–8 A Question of Ethics—Assignment and Delegation. Premier Building & Development, Inc., entered a listing agreement giving Sunset Gold Realty, LLC, the exclusive right to find a tenant for some commercial property. The terms of the listing agreement stated that it was binding on both parties and "their * * * assigns." Premier Building did not own the property at the time, but had the option to purchase it. To secure financing for the project, Premier Building established a new company called Cobblestone Associates. Premier Building then bought the property and conveyed it to Cobblestone the same day. Meanwhile, Sunset Gold found a tenant for the property, and Cobblestone became the landlord. Cobblestone acknowledged its obligation to pay Sunset Gold for finding a tenant, but it later refused to pay Sunset Gold's commission. Sunset Gold then sued Premier Building and Cobblestone for breach of the listing agreement. [*Sunset Gold Realty, LLC v. Premier Building & Development, Inc.*, 133 Conn.App. 445, 36 A.3d 243 (2012)] **(See pages 328–335.)**

1. Is Premier Building relieved of its contractual duties if it assigned the contract to Cobblestone? Why or why not?
2. Given that Sunset Gold performed its obligations under the listing agreement, did Cobblestone behave unethically in refusing to pay Sunset Gold's commission? Why or why not?

Critical Thinking and Writing Assignments

13–9 Critical Legal Thinking. The concept of substantial performance permits a party to be discharged from a contract even though the party has not fully performed her or his obligations according to the contract's terms. Is this fair? Why or why not? What policy interests are at issue here? **(See page 341.)**

13–10 Business Law Critical Thinking Group Assignment. ABC Clothiers, Inc., has a contract with John Taylor, owner of Taylor & Sons, a retailer, to deliver one thousand summer suits to Taylor's place of business on or before May 1. On April 1, John receives a letter from ABC informing him that ABC will not be able to make the delivery as scheduled. John is very upset, as he had planned a big ad campaign.

1. The first group will discuss whether John Taylor can immediately sue ABC for breach of contract (on April 2).
2. Now suppose that John Taylor's son, Tom, tells his father that they cannot file a lawsuit until ABC actually fails to deliver the suits on May 1. The second group will decide who is correct, John or Tom.
3. Assume that Taylor & Sons can either file immediately or wait until ABC fails to deliver the goods. The third group will evaluate which course of action is better, given the circumstances.

14 CHAPTER

Breach and Remedies

CHAPTER OUTLINE

- Damages
- Equitable Remedies
- Recovery Based on Quasi Contract
- Contract Provisions Limiting Remedies

LEARNING OBJECTIVES

The five learning objectives below are designed to help improve your understanding of the chapter. After reading this chapter, you should be able to answer the following questions:

1 What is the standard measure of compensatory damages when a contract is breached? How are damages computed differently in construction contracts?

2 What is the difference between compensatory damages and consequential damages? What are nominal damages, and when do courts award nominal damages?

3 Under what circumstances is the remedy of rescission and restitution available?

4 When do courts grant specific performance as a remedy?

5 What is a limitation-of-liability clause, and when will courts enforce it?

(Philip Hunton/Shutterstock)

"There's a remedy for everything except death."
—Miguel de Cervantes, 1547–1616 (Spanish author)

Normally, people enter into contracts to secure some advantage. When it is no longer advantageous for a party to fulfill her or his contractual obligations, that party may *breach,* or fail to perform, the contract.[1] Once one party breaches the contract, the other party—the nonbreaching party—can choose one or more of several remedies. A *remedy* is the relief provided to an innocent party when the other party has breached the contract. It is the means employed to enforce a right or to redress an injury. Although it may be an exaggeration to say there is a remedy for "everything" in life, as in the chapter-opening quotation, there is a remedy available for nearly every contract breach.

The most common remedies available to a nonbreaching party under contract law include damages, rescission and restitution, specific performance, and reformation. As discussed in Chapter 1 on pages 13–14, courts distinguish between *remedies at law* and *remedies in equity.* Today, the remedy at law is normally monetary damages. We discuss this

1. A *breach of contract* occurs when one party fails to perform part or all of the required duties under a contract. *Restatement (Second) of Contracts,* Section 235(2).

remedy in the first part of this chapter. Equitable remedies include rescission and restitution, specific performance, and reformation, all of which we examine later in the chapter. Usually, a court will not award an equitable remedy unless the remedy at law is inadequate. In the final pages of this chapter, we look at some special legal doctrines and concepts relating to remedies.

Damages

KNOW THIS

The terms of a contract must be sufficiently definite for a court to determine the amount of damages to award.

A breach of contract entitles the nonbreaching party to sue for monetary damages. As you read in Chapter 4, tort law damages are designed to compensate a party for harm suffered as a result of another's wrongful act. In the context of contract law, damages are designed to compensate the nonbreaching party for the loss of the bargain. Often, courts say that innocent parties are to be placed in the position they would have occupied had the contract been fully performed.[2]

Types of Damages

There are basically four broad categories of damages:

1. Compensatory (to cover direct losses and costs).
2. Consequential (to cover indirect and foreseeable losses).
3. Punitive (to punish and deter wrongdoing).
4. Nominal (to recognize wrongdoing when no monetary loss is shown).

Compensatory and punitive damages were discussed in Chapter 4 in the context of tort law. Here, we look at these types of damages, as well as consequential and nominal damages, in the context of contract law. (See this chapter's *Adapting the Law to the Online Environment* feature on the following page for a discussion of the effect of breaching the terms of use in an online service contract.)

LEARNING OBJECTIVE 1

What is the standard measure of compensatory damages when a contract is breached? How are damages computed differently in construction contracts?

Compensatory Damages

Damages that compensate the nonbreaching party for the *loss of the bargain* are known as *compensatory damages.* These damages compensate the injured party only for damages actually sustained and proved to have arisen directly from the loss of the bargain caused by the breach of contract. They simply replace what was lost because of the wrong or damage.

In general, the standard measure of compensatory damages is the difference between the value of the breaching party's promised performance under the contract and the value of her or his actual performance. This amount is reduced by any loss that the injured party has avoided.

EXAMPLE 14.1 You contract with Marinot Industries to perform certain personal services exclusively for Marinot during August for a payment of $4,000. Marinot cancels the contract and is in breach. You are able to find another job during August but can earn only $3,000. You normally can sue Marinot for breach and recover $1,000 as compensatory damages. You may also recover from Marinot the amount that you spent to find the other job. • Expenses that are directly incurred because of a breach of contract—such as those incurred to obtain performance from another source—are called **incidental damages.**

Incidental Damages Damages that compensate for expenses directly incurred because of a breach of contract, such as those incurred to obtain performance from another source.

The measurement of compensatory damages varies by type of contract. Certain types of contracts deserve special mention—contracts for the sale of goods, contracts for the sale of land, and construction contracts.

2. *Restatement (Second) of Contracts,* Section 347.

ADAPTING THE LAW TO THE ONLINE ENVIRONMENT

THE EFFECT OF BREACHING AN ONLINE TESTING SERVICE'S TERMS OF USE

Increasingly, online testing services are available for almost any subject. Employers, for example, use online behavioral testing to evaluate the employability of applicants. Schools and counseling services can administer an online test to assess the probability that an adolescent is chemically dependent.

California uses an online test to establish a driver impairment index for those who have been arrested for drunk driving.

Typical Terms and Conditions of Use

The majority of online testing services have a relatively short list of terms and conditions for using their tests. For example, most testing services require that fees be paid for each test and for its scoring.

Also, the school, employer, or other entity that is using the online test usually must agree that the persons who administer the test are qualified. In addition, the test user must agree that no decision or diagnosis can be made solely on the basis of the online test results.

Violation of the Online Terms

If the test user violates any of the terms and conditions, the implied contract with the testing service has been breached. The following is a typical provision from an online testing service:

> When You Breach This Agreement: Each time you administer a test, the agreement granted herein will automatically terminate once the scoring has been provided to you. The Company has the right to terminate the authorization granted to you if you breach the terms and conditions of use for any test or if you violate the terms and conditions and obligations under this agreement. Once you breach your duties under this agreement, the Company will suffer immediate and irreparable damages. You therefore acknowledge that injunctive relief will be appropriate.

Critical Thinking

What possible "immediate and irreparable" damages might an online testing service experience if the test user breaches the contract?

Under what circumstances will a court award monetary damages for a breached sale-of-land contract?

(CHRISsadowski/iStockphoto.com)

Sale of Goods In a contract for the sale of goods, the usual measure of compensatory damages is the difference between the contract price and the market price.[3] **EXAMPLE 14.2** Medik Laboratories contracts to buy ten model UTS 400 network servers from Cal Industries for $4,000 each, but Cal Industries fails to deliver the servers. The market price of the servers at the time Medik learns of the breach is $4,500. Therefore, Medik's measure of damages is $5,000 (10 × $500), plus any incidental damages (expenses) caused by the breach. • When the buyer breaches and the seller has not yet produced the goods, compensatory damages normally equal the seller's lost profits on the sale, rather than the difference between the contract price and the market price.

Sale of Land Ordinarily, because each parcel of land is unique, the remedy for a seller's breach of a contract for a sale of real estate is specific performance—that is, the buyer is awarded the parcel of property for which he or she bargained (*specific performance* will be discussed more fully later in the chapter). When this remedy is unavailable (because the property has been sold, for example) or when the buyer is the party in breach, the measure of damages is typically the difference between the contract price and the market price of the land. The majority of states follow this rule.

3. This is the difference between the contract price and the market price at the time and place at which the goods were to be delivered or tendered. See Sections 2–708, 2–713, and 2–715(1) of the Uniform Commercial Code (UCC).

Construction Contracts The measure of damages in a building or construction contract depends on which party breaches and when the breach occurs. If the owner breaches *before performance has begun,* the contractor can recover only the profits that would have been made on the contract—that is, the total contract price less the cost of materials and labor. If the owner breaches *during performance,* the contractor can recover the profits plus the costs incurred in partially constructing the building. If the owner breaches *after the construction has been completed,* the contractor can recover the entire contract price plus interest.

"A long dispute means that both parties are wrong."

Voltaire, 1694–1778 (French author)

When the contractor breaches the construction contract—either by failing to begin construction or by stopping work partway through the project—the measure of damages is the cost of completion, which includes reasonable compensation for any delay in performance. If the contractor finishes late, the measure of damages is the loss of use. Exhibit 14.1 on the next page summarizes the rules for the measure of damages in breached construction contracts. (The *Business Application* feature on page 366 offers some suggestions on what to do if you cannot perform.)

How should a court rule when the performance of both parties—the construction contractor and the owner—falls short of what their contract required? That was the issue in the following case.

Case 14.1

Jamison Well Drilling, Inc. v. Pfeifer

Court of Appeals of Ohio, Third District, 2011 Ohio 521 (2011).

(temmuzcan/iStockphoto.com)

A water well-drilling system.

FACTS Jamison Well Drilling, Inc., contracted to drill a water well for Ed Pfeifer in Crawford County, Ohio, for $4,130 in labor and supplies. Jamison drilled the well and installed a storage tank. The Ohio Department of Health requires that a well be lined with a minimum of twenty-five vertical feet of casing, but Jamison installed only eleven feet of casing in the drilled well. The county health department later tested the water in the well for bacteria and repeatedly found that the levels were too high. The state health department investigated and discovered that the well's casing did not comply with its requirements. The department ordered that the well be abandoned and sealed. Pfeifer used the storage tank but paid Jamison nothing. Jamison filed a suit in an Ohio state court against Pfeifer to recover the contract price and other costs. The court entered a judgment for Jamison for $970 for the storage tank. Jamison appealed.

ISSUE Does the owner have to pay the full contract price to the contractor that drilled a well and installed a storage tank when the well cannot be used because it does not meet health department standards?

DECISION No. A state appellate court affirmed the lower court's decision. The judgment had struck a balance that took into consideration that the completed construction project had value and the storage tank was functional, but the well was not usable.

REASON The court reasoned that the parties entered into a contract for the drilling of a well for a certain price. The work included the installation of a storage tank. The drilled well was not in compliance with state law and consequently had to be sealed and abandoned. Pfeifer may have assumed the risk that the well could not be used due to inadequate water production, but he did not assume the risk that it would have to be sealed for noncompliance with state law. Thus, Jamison was not entitled to the full contract price of $4,130. Yet the storage tank was usable, and Pfeifer had kept it. Because it would not be fair to allow Pfeifer to keep the tank without paying for it, Jamison should recover the cost of the tank.

WHAT IF THE FACTS WERE DIFFERENT? *Suppose that Pfeifer had paid Jamison for the work before the well was ordered to be sealed and had later filed a suit to recover for breach of contract. What would have been the measure of damages?*

Exhibit 14.1 Measurement of Damages— Breach of Construction Contracts

PARTY IN BREACH	TIME OF BREACH	MEASUREMENT OF DAMAGES
Owner	Before construction has begun.	Profits (contract price less cost of materials and labor).
Owner	During construction.	Profits plus costs incurred up to time of breach.
Owner	After construction is completed.	Full contract price, plus interest.
Contractor	Before construction has begun.	Cost in excess of contract price to complete work.
Contractor	Before construction is completed.	Generally, all costs incurred by owner to complete.

LEARNING OBJECTIVE 2
What is the difference between compensatory damages and consequential damages? What are nominal damages, and when do courts award nominal damages?

Consequential Damages Foreseeable damages that result from a party's breach of contract but are caused by special circumstances beyond the contract itself.

Consequential Damages

Foreseeable damages that result from a party's breach of contract are called **consequential damages,** or *special damages*. They differ from compensatory damages in that they are caused by special circumstances beyond the contract itself and flow from the consequences, or results, of a breach.

When a seller fails to deliver goods, knowing that the buyer is planning to use or resell those goods immediately, a court may award consequential damages (in addition to compensatory damages) for the loss of profits from the planned use or resale. **EXAMPLE 14.3** Gilmore contracts to have a specific machine part shipped to her—one that she desperately needs to repair her printing press. In her contract with the shipper, Gilmore states that she must receive the part by Monday, or she will not be able to print her paper and will lose $3,000. If the shipper is late, Gilmore normally can recover the consequential damages caused by the delay (that is, the $3,000 in losses). •

KNOW THIS
To avoid the risk of consequential damages, a seller can limit the buyer's remedies via contract.

For the nonbreaching party to recover consequential damages, the breaching party must know (or have reason to know) that special circumstances will cause the nonbreaching party to suffer an additional loss.[4] See this chapter's *Landmark in the Law* feature on the facing page for a discussion of the nineteenth-century English case that established this rule on consequential damages.

Punitive Damages

Punitive, or exemplary, damages, generally are not awarded in an action for breach of contract. Such damages have no legitimate place in contract law because they are, in essence, penalties, and a breach of contract is not unlawful in a criminal sense. A contract is simply a civil relationship between the parties. The law may compensate one party for the loss of the bargain—no more and no less.

In a few situations, when a person's actions cause both a breach of contract and a tort, punitive damages may be available. Overall, though, punitive damages are almost never available in contract disputes.

Nominal Damages A small monetary award (often one dollar) granted to a plaintiff when no actual damage was suffered.

Nominal Damages

When no actual damage or financial loss results from a breach of contract and only a technical injury is involved, the court may award **nominal damages** to the innocent party. Nominal damages awards are often small, such as one dollar, but they do establish that the defendant acted wrongfully. Most lawsuits for nominal damages are brought as a matter of principle under the theory that a breach has occurred and some damages must be imposed regardless of actual loss.

EXAMPLE 14.4 Hernandez contracts to buy potatoes at fifty cents a pound from Stanley. Stanley breaches the contract and does not deliver the potatoes. Meanwhile, the price of

4. UCC 2–715(2). See Chapter 16.

LANDMARK IN THE LAW

Hadley v. Baxendale (1854)

The rule that requires a breaching party to have notice of special ("consequential") circumstances that will result in additional loss to the nonbreaching party before consequential damages can be awarded was first enunciated in *Hadley v. Baxendale*,[a] a landmark case decided in 1854.

Case Background This case involved a broken crankshaft used in a flour mill run by the Hadley family in Gloucester, England. The crankshaft attached to the steam engine in the mill broke, and the shaft had to be sent to a foundry in Greenwich so that a new shaft could be made to fit the engine.

The Hadleys hired Baxendale, a common carrier, to transport the shaft from Gloucester to Greenwich. Baxendale received payment in advance and promised to deliver the shaft the following day. It was not delivered for several days, however. The Hadleys had no extra crankshaft on hand to use, so they had to close the mill during those days. The Hadleys sued Baxendale to recover the profits they lost during that time. Baxendale contended that the loss of profits was "too remote."

In the mid-1800s, it was common knowledge that large mills, such as that run by the Hadleys, normally had more than one crankshaft in case the main one broke and had to be repaired. It is against this background that the parties presented their arguments on whether the damages resulting from the loss of profits while the crankshaft was out for repair were "too remote" to be recoverable.

a. 9 Exch. 341, 156 Eng.Rep. 145 (1854).

The Issue before the Court and the Court's Ruling The crucial issue for the court was whether the Hadleys had informed the carrier, Baxendale, of the special circumstances surrounding the crankshaft's repair. Specifically, did Baxendale know at the time of the contract that the mill would have to shut down while the crankshaft was being repaired?

In the court's opinion, the only circumstances communicated by the Hadleys to Baxendale at the time the contract was made were that the item to be transported was a broken crankshaft of a mill and that the Hadleys were the owners and operators of that mill. The court concluded that these circumstances did not reasonably indicate that the mill would have to stop operations if the delivery of the crankshaft was delayed.

Application to Today's World *Today, the rule enunciated by the court in this case still applies. When damages are awarded, compensation is given only for those injuries that the defendant could reasonably have foreseen as a probable result of the usual course of events following a breach. If the alleged injury is outside the usual and foreseeable course of events, the plaintiff must show specifically that the defendant had reason to know the facts and foresee the injury. This rule applies to contracts in the online environment as well. For example, suppose that a Web merchant loses business (and profits) due to a computer system's failure. If the failure was caused by malfunctioning software, the merchant normally may recover the lost profits from the software maker if these consequential damages were foreseeable.*

potatoes falls. Hernandez is able to buy them in the open market at half the price he agreed to pay Stanley. Hernandez is clearly better off because of Stanley's breach. Thus, because Hernandez sustained only a technical injury and suffered no monetary loss, if he sues for breach of contract and wins, the court will likely award only nominal damages. •

Mitigation of Damages

In most situations, when a breach of contract occurs, the injured party is held to a duty to mitigate, or reduce, the damages that he or she suffers. Under this doctrine of **mitigation of damages**, the required action depends on the nature of the situation.

Mitigation of Damages The requirement that a plaintiff do whatever is reasonable to minimize the damages caused by the defendant.

Employment Contracts

In the majority of states, a person whose employment has been wrongfully terminated has a duty to mitigate damages incurred because of the employer's breach of the employment contract. In other words, a wrongfully terminated employee has a duty to take a similar job if one is available. If the person fails to do this, the damages received will be equivalent to the person's former salary less the income he or she would have received in a similar job obtained by reasonable means. Normally, a terminated employee is under no duty to take a job that is not of the same type and rank.

CASE EXAMPLE 14.5 Harry De La Concha was employed by Fordham University. He claimed that he was injured in an fight with Fordham's director of human resources and filed for workers' compensation benefits (which are available for on-the-job injuries regardless of fault—see Chapter 24). Fordham then fired De La Concha, who argued that he had been terminated in retaliation for filing a workers' compensation claim. The New York state workers' compensation board held that De La Concha had failed to mitigate his damages because he had not even looked for another job, and a state court affirmed the decision. Because De La Concha had failed to mitigate his damages, any compensation he received for wrongful termination would be reduced by the amount he *could have obtained* from other employment.[5] •

Rental Agreements

Some states require a landlord to use reasonable means to find a new tenant if a tenant abandons the premises and fails to pay rent. If an acceptable tenant becomes available, the landlord is required to lease the premises to this tenant to mitigate the damages recoverable from the former tenant. The former tenant is still liable for the difference between the amount of the rent under the original lease and the rent received from the new tenant. If the landlord has not taken reasonable steps to find a new tenant, a court will likely reduce any award by the amount of rent the landlord could have received had he or she done so.

Liquidated Damages versus Penalties

Liquidated Damages An amount, stipulated in a contract, that the parties to the contract believe to be a reasonable estimation of the damages that will occur in the event of a breach.

Penalty A contract clause that specifies a certain amount to be paid in the event of a default or breach of contract but is unenforceable because it is designed to punish the breaching party rather than to provide a reasonable estimate of damages.

A **liquidated damages** provision in a contract specifies that a certain dollar amount is to be paid in the event of a future default or breach of contract. (*Liquidated* means determined, settled, or fixed.)

Liquidated damages differ from penalties. A **penalty** specifies a certain amount to be paid in the event of a default or breach of contract and is designed to penalize the breaching party. Liquidated damages provisions normally are enforceable. In contrast, if a court finds that a provision calls for a penalty, the agreement as to the amount will not be enforced, and recovery will be limited to actual damages.[6]

Determining Enforceability

To determine whether a particular provision is for liquidated damages or a penalty, the court must answer two questions:

1. At the time the contract was formed, was it apparent that damages would be difficult to estimate in the event of a breach?
2. Was the amount set as damages a reasonable estimate and not excessive?[7]

If the answers to both questions are yes, the provision normally will be enforced. If either answer is no, the provision usually will not be enforced.

In the following *Spotlight Case,* the court had to decide whether a clause in a contract was an enforceable liquidated damages provision or an unenforceable penalty.

---

5. *De La Concha v. Fordham University,* 814 N.Y.S.2d 320, 28 A.3d 963 (2006).
6. This is also the rule under the UCC. See UCC 2–718(1).
7. *Restatement (Second) of Contracts,* Section 356(1).

Spotlight on Liquidated Damages

Case 14.2

B-Sharp Musical Productions, Inc. v. Haber

New York Supreme Court, 27 Misc.3d 41, 899 N.Y.S.2d 792 (2010).

(oleg66/iStockphoto.com)

Bands contract their performance dates months in advance.

FACTS B-Sharp Musical Productions, Inc., and James Haber entered into a contract under which B-Sharp was to provide a band on a specified date to perform at Haber's son's bar mitzvah. Haber was to pay approximately $30,000 for the band's services. The contract contained a liquidated damages clause stating, "If [the contract] is terminated in writing by [Haber] for any reason within ninety (90) days prior to the engagement, the remaining balance of the contract will be immediately due and payable. If [the contract] is terminated in writing by [Haber] for any reason before the ninety (90) days period, 50% of the balance will be immediately due and payable."

Within ninety days before the date of the bar mitzvah, Haber sent a letter to B-Sharp stating that he was canceling the contract. When Haber refused to pay the remaining amount due under the contract—approximately $25,000—B-Sharp sued Haber and his wife in a New York state court to recover the damages. The court granted B-Sharp's motion for summary judgment, enforcing the liquidated damages clause, and the defendants appealed.

ISSUE Was the liquidated damages clause, which specified the amount to be paid in the event that the performance was canceled, enforceable?

DECISION Yes. The appellate court upheld the trial court's judgment. The clause in question was "not an unenforceable penalty." It was a reasonable estimate of damages, given that B-Sharp would be unlikely to book another engagement that close to the performance.

REASON The clause used an estimate of B-Sharp's probable loss in the event of a cancellation as the measure of loss. This estimate reflected an understanding that "although the expense and possibility of rebooking a cancelled [performance] could not be ascertained with certainty, as a practical matter, the expense would become greater, and the possibility would be less, the closer to the [performance] the cancellation was made, until a point was reached, [ninety] days before the [performance], that any effort to rebook could not be reasonably expected."

CRITICAL THINKING—Ethical Consideration *Were there ethical reasons for the court to enforce the liquidated damages clause in this case? Explain.*

Liquidated Damages in Construction Contracts

Liquidated damages provisions are frequently used in construction contracts because it is difficult to estimate the amount of damages that would be caused by a delay in completing the work.

EXAMPLE 14.6 Ray Curl, a builder, enters into a contract with a developer to build a home in a new subdivision. The contract includes a clause that requires Curl to pay $300 for every day he is late in completing the project. This is a liquidated damages provision that is enforceable because it specifies a reasonable amount that Curl must pay to the developer if his performance is late. •

Equitable Remedies

Sometimes, damages are an inadequate remedy for a breach of contract. In these situations, the nonbreaching party may ask the court for an equitable remedy. Equitable remedies include rescission and restitution, specific performance, and reformation.

LEARNING OBJECTIVE 3

Under what circumstances is the remedy of rescission and restitution available?

Rescission and Restitution

As discussed in Chapter 13, *rescission* is essentially an action to undo, or cancel, a contract—to return nonbreaching parties to the positions that they occupied prior to the transaction.[8] When fraud, mistake, duress, undue influence, lack of capacity, or failure of consideration is present, rescission is available. Rescission may also be available by statute.[9] The failure of one party to perform under a contract entitles the other party to rescind the contract. The rescinding party must give prompt notice to the breaching party.

Restitution An equitable remedy under which a person is restored to his or her original position prior to loss or injury, or placed in the position he or she would have been in had the breach not occurred.

Restitution

To rescind a contract, both parties generally must make **restitution** to each other by returning goods, property, or funds previously conveyed.[10] If the property or goods can be returned, they must be. If the property or goods have been consumed, restitution must be made in an equivalent dollar amount.

KNOW THIS

Restitution offers several advantages over traditional damages. First, restitution may be available in situations when damages cannot be proved or are difficult to prove. Second, restitution can be used to recover specific property. Third, restitution sometimes results in a greater overall award.

Essentially, restitution involves the recapture of a benefit conferred on the defendant that has unjustly enriched her or him. **EXAMPLE 14.7** Andrea pays $32,000 to Miles in return for his promise to design a house for her. The next day, Miles calls Andrea and tells her that he has taken a position with a large architectural firm in another state and cannot design the house. Andrea decides to hire another architect that afternoon. Andrea can require restitution of $32,000 because Miles has received an unjust benefit of $32,000. •

Restitution Is Not Limited to Rescission Cases

Restitution may be required when a contract is rescinded, but the right to restitution is not limited to rescission cases. Because an award of restitution basically gives back, or returns, something to its rightful owner, a party can seek restitution in actions for breach of contract, tort actions, and other types of actions. For instance, restitution can be obtained when funds or property has been transferred by mistake or because of fraud or incapacity. Similarly, restitution might be available when there has been misconduct by a party with a special relationship with the other party. Even in criminal cases, a court can order restitution of funds or property obtained through embezzlement, conversion, theft, or copyright infringement.

LEARNING OBJECTIVE 4

When do courts grant specific performance as a remedy?

Specific Performance An equitable remedy in which a court orders the parties to perform as promised in the contract. This remedy normally is granted only when the legal remedy (monetary damages) is inadequate.

Specific Performance

The equitable remedy of **specific performance** calls for the performance of the act promised in the contract. This remedy is attractive to a nonbreaching party because it provides the exact bargain promised in the contract. It also avoids some of the problems inherent in a suit for monetary damages, such as collecting a judgment and arranging another contract. Moreover, the actual performance may be more valuable (to the promisee) than the monetary damages.

Normally, however, specific performance will not be granted unless the party's legal remedy (monetary damages) is inadequate.[11] For this reason, contracts for the sale of goods rarely qualify for specific performance. Monetary damages ordinarily are adequate in sales contracts because substantially identical goods can be bought or sold in the market. Only if the goods are unique will a court grant specific performance. For instance, paintings, sculptures, and rare books and coins are often unique, and monetary damages will not enable a buyer to obtain substantially identical substitutes in the market.

Former Detroit mayor Kwame Kilpatrick (below) at his restitution hearing.

(AP Photo/Paul Sancya, File)

8. The rescission discussed here refers to *unilateral* rescission, in which only one party wants to undo the contract. In *mutual* rescission, which we discussed in Chapter 13, both parties agree to undo the contract. Mutual rescission discharges the contract, whereas unilateral rescission is generally available as a remedy for breach of contract.

9. Many states have laws that allow individuals who enter into "home solicitation contracts" to rescind these contracts within three business days for any reason. See, for example, California Civil Code Section 1689.5.

10. *Restatement (Second) of Contracts,* Section 370.

11. *Restatement (Second) of Contracts,* Section 359.

(dimdimich/iStockphoto.com)

Why would specific performance be preferred when antiques are the item in dispute?

Sale of Land A court may grant specific performance to a buyer in an action for a breach of contract involving the sale of land. In this situation, the legal remedy of monetary damages will not compensate the buyer adequately because every parcel of land is unique, as was discussed on page 354. The same land in the same location obviously cannot be obtained elsewhere. Only when specific performance is unavailable (for example, when the seller has sold the property to someone else) will damages be awarded instead.

CASE EXAMPLE 14.8 Howard Stainbrook entered into a contract to sell Trent Low forty acres of mostly timbered land for $45,000. Low agreed to pay for a survey of the property and other costs in addition to the price. He gave Stainbrook a check for $1,000 to show his intent to fulfill the contract. One month later, Stainbrook died. His son David became the executor of the estate. After he discovered that the timber on the property was worth more than $100,000, David asked Low to withdraw his offer to buy the forty acres. Low refused and filed a suit against David seeking specific performance of the contract. The court found that because Low had substantially performed his obligations under the contract and offered to perform the rest, he was entitled to specific performance.[12] ●

Contracts for Personal Services Personal-service contracts require one party to work personally for another party. Courts normally refuse to grant specific performance of contracts for personal services. This is because ordering a party to perform personal services against his or her will amounts to a type of involuntary servitude, which is contrary to the public policy expressed in the Thirteenth Amendment to the U.S. Constitution (see Appendix B). Moreover, the courts do not want to monitor contracts for personal services, which usually require the exercise of personal judgment or talent.

EXAMPLE 14.9 If Mikhail contracts with a surgeon to perform brain surgery and she later refuses to perform, the court will not compel (nor would Mikhail want) the surgeon to perform under these circumstances. There is no possible procedure that the court can assure meaningful performance in such a situation.[13] ●

If a contract is not deemed personal, the remedy at law of monetary damages may be adequate if substantially identical service (for instance, lawn mowing) is available from other persons.

"Controversy equalizes fools and wise men—and the fools know it."

Oliver Wendell Holmes, 1809–1894 (American author)

Reformation

Reformation is an equitable remedy used when the parties have *imperfectly* expressed their agreement in writing. Reformation allows a court to rewrite the contract to reflect the parties' true intentions.

Fraud or Mutual Mistake Courts order reformation most often when fraud or mutual mistake is present. **EXAMPLE 14.10** If Carson contracts to buy a forklift from Yoshie but the written contract refers to a crane, a mutual mistake has occurred. Accordingly, a court could reform the contract so that the writing conforms to the parties' original intention as to which piece of equipment is being sold. ● Exhibit 14.2 on page 362 graphically presents the remedies, including reformation, that are available to the nonbreaching party.

Written Contract Incorrectly States the Parties' Oral Agreement A court will also reform a contract when two parties enter into a binding oral contract but

12. *Stainbrook v. Low*, 842 N.E.2d 386 (Ind.App. 2006).

13. Similarly, courts often refuse to order specific performance of construction contracts because courts are not set up to operate as construction supervisors or engineers.

Exhibit 14.2 Remedies for Breach of Contract

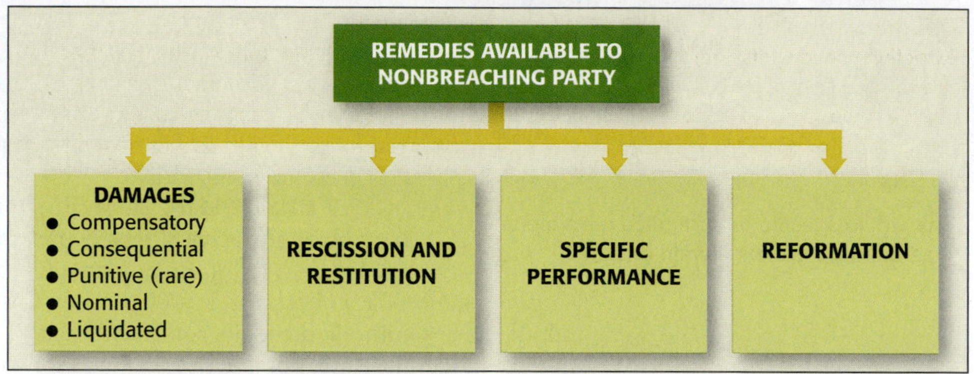

later make an error when they attempt to put the terms into writing. Usually, the court will allow into evidence the correct terms of the oral contract, thereby reforming the written contract.

Covenants Not to Compete Courts also may reform contracts when the parties have executed a written covenant not to compete (see page 294 of Chapter 11). If the covenant not to compete is for a valid and legitimate purpose (such as the sale of a business) but the area or time restraints are unreasonable, some courts will reform the restraints by making them reasonable and will enforce the entire contract as reformed. Other courts, however, will throw out the entire restrictive covenant as illegal.

In the following case, a physician claimed that the covenant not to compete he signed was unreasonable and should therefore be declared illegal.

Case 14.3

Emerick v. Cardiac Study Center, Inc.

Court of Appeals of Washington, Division 2, 166 Wash.App. 1039 (2012).

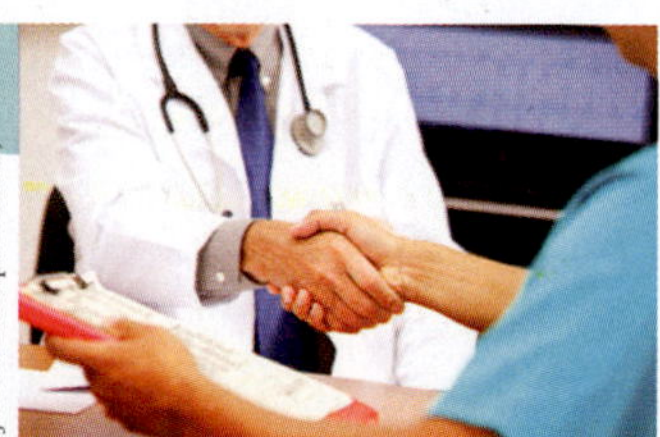
(sjlocke/iStockphoto.com)

Can a covenant not to compete apply to physician-shareholders in a medical group?

FACTS Cardiac Study Center, Inc., is a medical practice group of approximately fifteen cardiologists. In 2002, Cardiac hired Dr. Robert Emerick as an employee. In 2004, Emerick became a shareholder of Cardiac. He signed a shareholder employment agreement, which included a covenant not to compete. The covenant stated that a physician who left the group promised not to practice competitively in the surrounding area for a period of five years. In 2005, patients and other medical providers began to complain to Cardiac about Emerick's conduct. Some physicians stopped referring patients to Cardiac as a result. Finally, Cardiac terminated Emerick's employment in 2009. Emerick sued Cardiac seeking a declaration that the covenant not to compete was unenforceable. He prevailed at trial, and Cardiac appealed.

ISSUE Was the Cardiac Study Center's covenant not to compete unenforceable as against public policy?

DECISION No. The state appellate court held that the covenant not to compete was reasonable.

REASON The reviewing court examined the reasonableness of the covenant not to compete in terms of how it protected the employer's business or goodwill. The court pointed out that "an employee who joins an established business gains access to his employer's customers and acquires valuable information as to the nature and character of the business." Further, an employer has a "legitimate interest in protecting its existing client base and prohibiting the employee from taking its clients." Cardiac had provided Emerick with an immediate client base and established referral sources when he moved to the area. Emerick had access to Cardiac's

Case 14.3—Continued

business model and goodwill. Finally, the reviewing court explained that many Washington courts have held that restrictive covenants among physicians are enforceable. Indeed, "restrictive covenants are common among professionals because they allow a new professional to step in to an already established practice while protecting the employer from future competition."

WHY IS THIS CASE IMPORTANT? *Many covenants not to compete are found to be unenforceable. Nonetheless, if businesspersons create restrictive covenants that are reasonable, do not extend to a very large geographic area, and do not last for decades, courts will often hold that they are enforceable. The ability to use enforceable covenants encourages businesses to hire employees who will have access to client lists and unique business models.*

Recovery Based on Quasi Contract

In some situations, when no actual contract exists, a court may step in to prevent one party from being unjustly enriched at the expense of another party. As discussed in Chapter 9, *quasi contract* is a legal theory under which an obligation is imposed in the absence of an agreement. A quasi contract is not a true contract but rather a fictional contract that is imposed on the parties to prevent unjust enrichment.

When Quasi Contract Is Used

Quasi contract allows a court to act as if a contract exists when there is no actual contract or agreement between the parties. Therefore, if the parties have entered into a contract concerning the matter in controversy, a court normally will not impose a quasi contract. A court can also use the doctrine when the parties entered into a contract, but it is unenforceable for some reason.

KNOW THIS

The function of a quasi contract is to impose a legal obligation on a party who made no actual promise.

Quasi-contractual recovery is often granted when one party has partially performed under a contract that is unenforceable. Quasi contracts provide an alternative to suing for damages and allow the party to recover the reasonable value of the partial performance. **EXAMPLE 14.11** Ericson contracts to build two oil derricks for Petro Industries. The derricks are to be built over a period of three years, but the parties do not create a written contract. Therefore, the Statute of Frauds will bar the enforcement of the contract.[14] After Ericson completes one derrick, Petro Industries informs him that it will not pay for the derrick. Ericson can sue Petro Industries under the theory of quasi contract. •

The Requirements of Quasi Contract

To recover on a quasi contract theory, the party seeking recovery must show the following:

1. The party conferred a benefit on the other party.
2. The party conferred the benefit with the reasonable expectation of being paid.
3. The party did not act as a volunteer in conferring the benefit.
4. The party receiving the benefit would be unjustly enriched if allowed to retain the benefit without paying for it.

Applying these requirements to *Example 14.11* above, Ericson can sue in quasi contract because all of the conditions for quasi-contractual recovery have been fulfilled. Ericson

14. Contracts that by their terms cannot be performed within one year from the day after the date of contract formation must be in writing to be enforceable (see Chapter 12).

conferred a benefit on Petro Industries by building the oil derrick. Ericson build the derrick with the reasonable expectation of being paid. He did not intend to act as a volunteer. Petro Industries would be unjustly enriched if it was allowed to keep the derrick without paying Ericson for the work. Therefore, Ericson should be able to recover the reasonable value of the oil derrick that was built (under the theory of *quantum meruit*[15]—"as much as he or she deserves"). The reasonable value is ordinarily equal to the fair market value.

KNOW THIS

Exculpatory clauses may be held unconscionable, depending on the relative bargaining positions of the parties and the importance to the public interest of the business seeking to enforce the clause.

Contract Provisions Limiting Remedies

A contract may include provisions stating that no damages can be recovered for certain types of breaches or that damages will be limited to a maximum amount. The contract may also provide that the only remedy for breach is replacement, repair, or refund of the purchase price. The contract can also provide that one party can seek injunctive relief if the other party breaches the contract (see Paragraph 11 on page 374 in the *Annotated Employment Contract* that follows this chapter). Provisions stating that no damages can be recovered are called *exculpatory clauses* (see Chapter 11). Provisions that affect the availability of certain remedies are called *limitation-of-liability clauses.*

The UCC Allows Sales Contracts to Limit Remedies

The Uniform Commercial Code (UCC) provides that remedies can be limited in a contract for the sale of goods. We will examine the UCC provisions on limitation-of-liability clauses in Chapter 16, in the context of the remedies available on the breach of a contract for the sale or lease of goods.[16]

Enforceability of Limitation-of-Liability Clauses

LEARNING OBJECTIVE 5

What is a limitation-of-liability clause, and when will courts enforce it?

Whether a limitation-of-liability clause in a contract will be enforced depends on the type of breach that is excused by the provision. Normally, a provision excluding liability for fraudulent or intentional injury will not be enforced. Likewise, a clause excluding liability for illegal acts or violations of law will not be enforced.

A clause excluding liability for negligence may be enforced in certain situations, however. When an exculpatory clause for negligence is contained in a contract made between parties who have roughly equal bargaining positions, the clause usually will be enforced.

CASE EXAMPLE 14.12 Engineering Consulting Services, Ltd. (ECS), contracted with RSN Properties, Inc., a real estate developer, to perform soil studies for $2,200 and render an opinion on the use of septic systems in a residential subdivision being developed. A clause in the contract limited ECS's liability to RSN to the value of the engineering services or the sum of $50,000, whichever was greater. ECS concluded that most of the lots were suitable for septic systems, so RSN proceeded with development. RSN completed roads and waterline construction in reliance on ECS's conclusions, which turned out to be incorrect. The county refused to approve further development of the lots because they were unsuitable for septic systems. RSN sued ECS for breach of contract and argued that the limitation-of-liability clause was against public policy and unenforceable. The court, however, held that the "contract represented a reasonable allocation of risks in an arm's-length business transaction, and did not violate public policy for professional engineering practice." The court therefore enforced the limitation-of-liability clause.[17] ●

---

15. Pronounced *kwahn-tuhm mehr-oo-wuht.*

16. UCC 2–719.

17. *RSN Properties, Inc. v. Engineering Consulting Services, Ltd.*, 301 Ga.App. 52, 686 S.E.2d 853 (2009).

ETHICAL ISSUE

Should courts enforce a limitation-of-liability clause in a contract that cruise ship passengers are required to sign? In 2012, a cruise ship carrying 4,200 passengers and crew capsized off the coast of Italy, killing more than thirty people. Captain Francesco Schettino, the captain of the ship *Costa Concordia,* was blamed for causing the accident because he brought the ship too close to shore where it struck a rock that punctured its hull. Passengers have attempted to sue the corporate owner of the ship, Carnival Cruise Lines, over the incident. But Carnival included a carefully drafted limitation-of-liability clause in its contract, which each passenger is required to sign when purchasing a ticket. The clause limits the kind of suits that can be brought, where they can be filed, and how much passengers can ultimately recover from Carnival.

U.S. courts have upheld similar limitations of liability in other cruise ship cases. Because no U.S. port was involved with the Italian cruise ship's accident, however, the contract specifies that litigation must take place in Italy. Thus, no U.S. court will be involved. Under international law, limitations on liability can be set aside only if the ship's owner engaged in egregious (highly unacceptable) acts. The captain's acts were arguably egregious. For instance, he increased the *Costa Concordia's* speed in shallow waters, in the dark, despite the proximity of obstacles, to make up for time he had spent having dinner with a woman. Then he abandoned the ship while passengers were stranded aboard. Nevertheless, the ship's owner, Carnival Cruise Lines, claims that it was unaware of the captain's reckless conduct until after the accident. Unless the passengers can persuade a court that Carnival is responsible for the acts of its captain, their recovery from the cruise line is likely to be limited.

Reviewing . . . Breach and Remedies

Kyle Bruno enters into a contract with X Entertainment to be a stuntman in a movie being produced. Bruno is widely known as the best motorcycle stuntman in the business, and the movie to be produced, *Xtreme Riders,* has numerous scenes involving high-speed freestyle street-bike stunts. Filming is set to begin August 1 and end by December 1 so that the film can be released the following summer. Both parties to the contract have stipulated that the filming must end on time in order to capture the profits from the summer movie market. The contract states that Bruno will be paid 10 percent of the net proceeds from the movie for his stunts. The contract also includes a liquidated damages provision, which specifies that if Bruno breaches the contract, he will owe X Entertainment $1 million. In addition, the contract includes a limitation-of-liability clause stating that if Bruno is injured during filming, X Entertainment's liability is limited to nominal damages. Using the information presented in the chapter, answer the following questions.

1. One day, while Bruno is preparing for a difficult stunt, he gets into an argument with the director and refuses to perform any stunts. Can X Entertainment seek specific performance of the contract? Why or why not?
2. Suppose that while performing a high-speed wheelie on a motorcycle, Bruno is injured by an intentionally reckless act of an X Entertainment employee. Will a court be likely to enforce the limitation-of-liability clause? Why or why not?
3. What factors would a court consider to determine if the $1 million liquidated damages clause is valid or is a penalty?
4. Suppose that there was no liquidated damages clause (or the court refused to enforce it) and X Entertainment breached the contract. The breach caused the release of the film to be delayed until after summer. Could Bruno seek consequential (special) damages for lost profits from the summer movie market in that situation? Explain.

DEBATE THIS Courts should always uphold limitation-of-liability clauses, whether or not the two parties to the contract had equal bargaining power.

BUSINESS APPLICATION

What Do You Do When You Cannot Perform?*

Not every contract can be performed. If you are a contractor, you may take on a job that, for one reason or another, you cannot or do not wish to perform. Simply walking away from the job and hoping for the best normally is not the most effective way to avoid litigation—which can be costly, time consuming, and emotionally draining. Instead, you should consider various options that may reduce the likelihood of litigation.

For example, suppose that you are a building contractor and you sign a contract to build a home for the Andersons according to a set of plans that they provided. Performance is to begin on June 15. On June 1, Central Enterprises offers you a position that will pay you two and a half times as much net income as you could earn as an independent builder. To take the job, you have to start on June 15. You cannot be in two places at the same time, so to accept the new position, you must breach the contract with the Andersons.

Consider Your Options

What can you do in this situation? One option is to subcontract the work to another builder and oversee the work yourself to make sure it conforms to the contract. Another option is to negotiate with the Andersons for a release. You can offer to find another qualified builder who will build a house of the same quality at the same price. Alternatively, you can offer to pay any additional costs if another builder takes the job and is more expensive. In any event, this additional cost would be one measure of damages that a court would impose on you if the Andersons prevailed in a suit for breach of contract (in addition to any costs the Andersons suffer as a result of the breach, such as costs due to the delay in construction). Thus, by making the offer, you might be able to avoid the expense of litigation—if the Andersons accept your offer.

Settlement Offers

Often, parties are reluctant to propose compromise settlements because they fear that what they say will be used against them in court if litigation ensues. Generally, however, offers for settlement will not be admitted in court to prove that you are liable for a breach of contract (though they are at times admissible to prove a party breached the duty of good faith).

Checklist for When You Cannot Perform

1. *Consider a compromise.*
2. *Subcontract out the work and oversee it.*
3. *Offer to find an alternative contractor to fulfill your obligation.*
4. *Make a cash offer to "buy" a release from your contract. Work with an attorney in making the offer unless the amount involved is insignificant.*

*This *Business Application* is not meant to substitute for the services of an attorney who is licensed to practice law in your state.

Key Terms

consequential damages 356
incidental damages 353
liquidated damages 358
mitigation of damages 357
nominal damages 356
penalty 358
restitution 360
specific performance 360

Chapter Summary: Breach and Remedies

COMMON REMEDIES AVAILABLE TO NONBREACHING PARTY	
Damages (See pages 353–359.)	The legal remedy designed to compensate the nonbreaching party for the loss of the bargain. By awarding monetary damages, the court tries to place the parties in the positions that they would have occupied had the contract been fully performed. The nonbreaching party frequently has a duty to *mitigate* (lessen or reduce) the damages incurred as a result of the contract's breach. There are four broad categories of damages. In addition, a contract may contain a provision for liquidated damages. 1. *Compensatory damages*—Damages that compensate the nonbreaching party for injuries actually sustained and proved to have arisen directly from the loss of the bargain resulting from the breach of contract.

Chapter Summary: Breach and Remedies—Continued

Damages—Continued	a. In breached contracts for the sale of goods, the usual measure of compensatory damages is the difference between the contract price and the market price. b. In breached contracts for the sale of land, the measure of damages is ordinarily the same as in contracts for the sale of goods. c. In breached construction contracts, the measure of damages depends on which party breaches and at what stage of construction the breach occurs. 2. *Consequential damages*—Damages that result from special circumstances beyond the contract itself. The damages flow only from the consequences of a breach. For a party to recover consequential damages, the damages must be the foreseeable result of a breach of contract, and the breaching party must have known at the time the contract was formed that special circumstances existed that would cause the nonbreaching party to incur additional loss on breach of the contract. Also called *special damages*. 3. *Punitive damages*—Damages awarded to punish the breaching party. Usually not awarded in an action for breach of contract unless a tort is involved. 4. *Nominal damages*—Damages small in amount (such as one dollar) that are awarded when a breach has occurred but no actual injury has been suffered. Awarded only to establish that the defendant acted wrongfully. 5. *Liquidated damages*—Damages that may be specified in a contract as the amount to be paid to the nonbreaching party in the event the contract is breached. Clauses providing for liquidated damages are enforced if the damages were difficult to estimate at the time the contract was formed and if the amount stipulated is reasonable. If the amount is construed to be a penalty, the clause will not be enforced.
Rescission and Restitution (See page 360.)	1. *Rescission*—A remedy whereby a contract is canceled and the parties are restored to the original positions that they occupied prior to the transaction. Available when fraud, a mistake, duress, or failure of consideration is present. The rescinding party must give prompt notice of the rescission to the breaching party. 2. *Restitution*—When a contract is rescinded, both parties must make restitution to each other by returning the goods, property, or funds previously conveyed. Restitution prevents the unjust enrichment of the parties.
Specific Performance (See pages 360–361.)	An equitable remedy calling for the performance of the act promised in the contract. This remedy is available only in special situations—such as those involving contracts for the sale of unique goods or land—when monetary damages would be an inadequate remedy. Specific performance is not available as a remedy for breached contracts for personal services.
Reformation (See pages 361–362.)	An equitable remedy allowing a contract to be "reformed," or rewritten, to reflect the parties' true intentions. Available when an agreement is imperfectly expressed in writing.
Recovery Based on Quasi Contract (See pages 363–364.)	An equitable theory imposed by the courts to obtain justice and prevent unjust enrichment in a situation in which no enforceable contract exists. The party seeking recovery must show the following: 1. A benefit was conferred on the other party. 2. The party conferring the benefit did so with the expectation of being paid. 3. The benefit was not volunteered. 4. The party receiving the benefit would be unjustly enriched if allowed to retain the benefit without paying for it.
CONTRACT DOCTRINES RELATING TO REMEDIES	
Contract Provisions Limiting Remedies (See pages 364–365.)	A contract may provide that no damages (or only a limited amount of damages) can be recovered in the event the contract is breached. Under the Uniform Commercial Code, remedies may be limited in contracts for the sale of goods. Clauses excluding liability for fraudulent or intentional injury or for illegal acts cannot be enforced. Clauses excluding liability for negligence may be enforced if both parties hold roughly equal bargaining power.

ExamPrep

ISSUE SPOTTERS

1. Greg contracts to build a storage shed for Haney, who pays Greg in advance, but Greg completes only half the work. Haney pays Ipswich $500 to finish the shed. If Haney sues Greg, what would be the measure of recovery? **(See page 355.)**
2. Lyle contracts to sell his ranch to Marley, who is to take possession on June 1. Lyle delays the transfer until August 1. Marley incurs expenses in providing for cattle that he bought for the ranch. When they made the contract, Lyle had no reason to know of the cattle. Is Lyle liable for Marley's expenses in providing for the cattle? Why or why not? **(See page 356.)**

—Check your answers to the Issue Spotters against the answers provided in Appendix E at the end of this text.

BEFORE THE TEST

Go to www.cengagebrain.com, enter the ISBN 9781133273561, and click on "Find" to locate this textbook's Web site. Then, click on "Access Now" under "Study Tools," and select Chapter 14 at the top. There, you will find a Practice Quiz that you can take to assess your mastery of the concepts in this chapter, as well as Flashcards, a Glossary of important terms, and Video Questions (when assigned).

For Review

Answers to the even-numbered questions in this For Review section can be found in Appendix F at the end of this text.

1. What is the standard measure of compensatory damages when a contract is breached? How are damages computed differently in construction contracts?
2. What is the difference between compensatory damages and consequential damages? What are nominal damages, and when do courts award nominal damages?
3. Under what circumstances is the remedy of rescission and restitution available?
4. When do courts grant specific performance as a remedy?
5. What is a limitation-of-liability clause and when will courts enforce it?

Business Scenarios and Case Problems

14–1 Liquidated Damages. Carnack contracts to sell his house and lot to Willard for $100,000. The terms of the contract call for Willard to make a deposit of 10 percent of the purchase price as a down payment. The terms further stipulate that if the buyer breaches the contract, Carnack will retain the deposit as liquidated damages. Willard makes the deposit, but because her expected financing of the $90,000 balance falls through, she breaches the contract. Two weeks later, Carnack sells the house and lot to Balkova for $105,000. Willard demands her $10,000 back, but Carnack refuses, claiming that Willard's breach and the contract terms entitle him to keep the deposit. Discuss who is correct. **(See pages 358–359.)**

14–2 Question with Sample Answer—Mitigation of Damages. Lauren Barton, a single mother with three children, lived in Portland, Oregon. Cynthia VanHorn also lived in Oregon until she moved to New York City to open and operate an art gallery. VanHorn asked Barton to manage the gallery under a one-year contract for an annual salary of $72,000. To begin work, Barton relocated to New York. As part of the move, Barton transferred custody of her children to her husband, who lived in London, England. In accepting the job, Barton also forfeited her husband's alimony and child-support payments, including unpaid amounts of nearly $30,000. Before Barton started work, VanHorn repudiated the contract. Unable to find employment for more than an annual salary of $25,000, Barton moved to London to be near her children. Barton filed a suit in an Oregon state court against VanHorn, seeking damages for breach of contract. Should the court hold, as VanHorn argued, that Barton did not take reasonable steps to mitigate her damages? Why or why not? **(See pages 357–358.)**

—For a sample answer to Question 14–2, go to Appendix G at the end of this text.

14–3 Spotlight on Types of Damages—Compensatory Damages. Tyna Ek met Russell Peterson in Seattle, Washington. Peterson persuaded Ek to buy a boat that he had once owned, the *O'Hana Kai,* which was in Juneau, Alaska, for $43,000. Ek and Peterson then entered into a contract under which Peterson was to make the boat seaworthy so that it could be transported to Seattle within a month, where he would pay its moorage costs and renovate the boat at his own expense. In return, Peterson would receive a portion of the profit on its resale the following year. On the sale, Ek would recover her costs, and then Peterson would be reimbursed for his. Ek loaned Peterson her cell phone so that they could communicate while he prepared the vessel for the trip to Seattle. In March, Peterson, who was still in Alaska, borrowed $4,000 from Ek. Two months later, Ek began to receive unanticipated, unauthorized bills for vessel parts and moorage, the use of her phone, and charges on her credit card. She went to Juneau to take possession of the boat. Peterson moved it to Petersburg, Alaska, where he registered it under a false name, and then to Taku Harbor, where the police seized it. Ek filed a suit in an Alaska state court against Peterson, alleging breach of contract and seeking damages. If the court finds in Ek's favor, what should her damages include? Discuss. [*Peterson v. Ek,* 93 P.3d 458 (Alaska 2004)] **(See page 353.)**

14–4 Quasi Contract. Middleton Motors, Inc., a struggling Ford dealership in Wisconsin, sought managerial and financial assistance from Lindquist Ford, Inc., a successful Ford dealership in Iowa. While the two dealerships negotiated the terms for the services and a cash infusion, Lindquist sent Craig Miller, its general manager, to assume control of Middleton. After a year, the parties had not agreed on the terms, Lindquist had not invested any funds, Middleton had not made a profit, and

Miller was fired without being paid. Can Miller recover pay for his time on a quasi-contract theory? Why or why not? Which of the quasi-contract requirements is most likely to be disputed in this case? Why? [*Lindquist Ford, Inc. v. Middleton Motors, Inc.*, 557 F.3d 469 (7th Cir. 2009)] **(See pages 363–364.)**

14–5 **Liquidated Damages.** Planned Pethood Plus, Inc. (PPP), a veterinary clinic, borrowed $389,000 from KeyBank. The term of the loan was ten years. A "prepayment penalty" clause provided a formula to add an amount to the balance due if PPP offered to repay its loan early. The additional amount depended on the time of the prepayment. Such clauses are common in loan agreements. After one year, PPP offered to pay its loan. KeyBank applied the formula to add $40,525.92 to the balance due. Is this a penalty or liquidated damages? Explain. [*Planned Pethood Plus, Inc. v. KeyCorp, Inc.*, 228 P.3d 262 (Colo.App. 2010)] **(See page 358.)**

14–6 **Damages.** Before buying a house, Dean and Donna Testa hired Ground Systems, Inc. (GSI), to inspect the sewage and water disposal system. GSI reported a split system with a watertight septic tank, a wastewater tank, a distribution box, and a leach field. The Testas bought the house. Later, Dean saw that the system was not as GSI described—there was no distribution box or leach field, and there was only one tank, which was not watertight. The Testas arranged for the installation of a new system and sold the house. Assuming that GSI is liable for breach of contract, what is the measure of damages? [*Testa v. Ground Systems, Inc.*, 206 N.J. 330, 20 A.3d 435 (App.Div. 2011)] **(See pages 353–354.)**

14–7 **Case Problem with Sample Answer—Consequential Damages.** After submitting the high bid at a foreclosure sale, David Simard entered into a contract to purchase real property in Maryland for $192,000. Simard defaulted (failed to pay) on the contract, so a state court ordered the property to be resold at Simard's expense, as required by state law. The property was then resold for $163,000, but the second purchaser also defaulted on his contract. The court then ordered a second resale, resulting in a final price of $130,000. Assuming that Simard is liable for consequential damages, what is the extent of his liability? Is he liable for losses and expenses related to the first resale? If so, is he also liable for losses and expenses related to the second resale? Why or why not? [*Burson v. Simard*, 35 A.3d 1154 (Md. 2012)] **(See page 356.)**

—For a sample answer to Problem 14–7, go to Appendix H at the end of this text.

14–8 **A Question of Ethics—Performance and Damages.** On a weekday, Tamara Cohen, a real estate broker, showed a townhouse owned by Ray and Harriet Mayer to Jessica Seinfeld, the wife of comedian Jerry Seinfeld. On the weekend, when Cohen was unavailable because her religious beliefs prevented her from working, the Seinfelds revisited the townhouse on their own and agreed to buy it. The contract stated that the "buyers will pay buyer's real estate broker's fees." [*Cohen v. Seinfeld*, 15 Misc.3d 1118(A), 839 N.Y.S.2d 432 (Sup. 2007)] **(See page 353.)**

1. Is Cohen entitled to payment even though she was not available to show the townhouse to the Seinfelds on the weekend? Explain.
2. What obligation do parties involved in business deals owe to each other with respect to their religious beliefs? How might the situation in this case have been avoided?

Critical Thinking and Writing Assignments

14–9 **Critical Legal Thinking.** Review the discussion of the doctrine of mitigation of damages in this chapter. What are some of the advantages and disadvantages of this doctrine? **(See pages 357–358.)**

14–10 **Business Law Critical Thinking Group Assignment.** Frances Morelli agreed to sell Judith Bucklin a house in Rhode Island for $177,000. The sale was supposed to be closed by September 1, when the parties were to exchange the deed for the price. The contract included a provision that "if Seller is unable to convey good, clear, insurable, and marketable title, Buyer shall have the option to: (a) accept such title as Seller is able to convey without reduction of the Purchase Price, or (b) cancel this Agreement and receive a return of all Deposits."

An examination of the public records revealed that the house did not have marketable title. Bucklin offered Morelli additional time to resolve the problem, and the closing did not occur as scheduled. Morelli decided "the deal is over" and offered to return the deposit. Bucklin refused and, in mid-October, decided to exercise her option to accept the house without marketable title. She notified Morelli, who did not respond. She then filed a lawsuit against Morelli in a state court.

1. One group will discuss whether Morelli has breached the contract, and will decide in whose favor the court should rule.
2. A second group will assume that Morelli did breach the contract and will determine what the appropriate remedy is in this situation.

Appendix to Chapter 14

An Annotated Employment Contract

As the text and cases in this unit have indicated, businesses use contracts to make their transactions more predictable. Contracts allow parties to clarify their obligations in great detail. Businesses also use contracts to resolve anticipated problems or conflicts and to clarify responsibility in the event of a breach. An understanding of what is in a typical contract is crucial to using contracts effectively.

Being able to read and understand a contract takes some practice, however. Contract terms often are highly technical and complex, and sometimes the vocabulary and phrasing can be unfamiliar. Nevertheless, businesspersons need to be able to understand the meaning of various contract provisions so that they will know what their business's obligations and rights are under the contract.

Reading a Contract

A contract is generally intended to serve two purposes:

1. To achieve some commercial purpose—such as, a sale of goods, a lease of property, or an employment agreement.
2. To prevent future conflict by clarifying the obligations and rights of the parties.

Parties should address the details of the business agreement and also should think strategically about how a conflict should be resolved if something goes awry.

Different types of contracts will have different provisions. Sales contracts should contain information on the products being sold, the quantity, the price, and delivery terms. Employment contracts may contain information on the term of employment, employment duties, confidentiality and nondisclosure of the employer's documents and information, and restrictions on competing with the employer after leaving the position.

Although standard forms exist for many types of contracts, the parties to a particular contract may have specific requirements and thus may need to tailor the contract to fit their transaction. A larger transaction or more specialized goods or real estate will require a more specific and probably a longer contract. For example, a sales contract between Airbus and American Airlines for the sale of an Airbus S.A.S. plane was more than 109 pages, not counting the eleven exhibits that followed the main contract.[1]

Regardless of the specificity of the contract provisions, it is important for a businessperson to read and evaluate the responsibilities or commitments of both parties to the contract. Sometimes, a single word or phrase can make an enormous difference. For example, a rental contract for a house may state that the owner is responsible for any plumbing issues, or it may specify that the renter is the responsible party. If a plumber has to be called to deal with clogged pipes on a holiday, that single phrase in the contract will determine who has to pay the plumber's very high holiday rates.

1. "Sample Business Contracts." *Onecle.com*. 14 July 2012. Web.

Usually, someone signs a contract after having reviewed it in detail (or after one's attorney has reviewed it).

(Denis Opolja/Shutterstock.com)

Contract Analysis Exercise

The sample contract on pages 372–375 is based on an actual employment-related contract between a company called Boulder Dry and its chief financial officer (CFO). As you read the contract, think about the following questions:

1. Which party seems to have had the stronger bargaining position, and why?
2. Which specific provisions favor the employer?
3. Which specific provisions favor the employee?
4. The parties' main intentions in signing this contract were to protect the firm's confidential information and to explain how the CFO could use that information. Which provisions are related to those two purposes?
5. Which provisions seem entirely unrelated to the main purposes? Why are these other provisions included in the contract? What do they do for the parties?
6. What terms in the contract do you find difficult to understand?
7. As a potential employee being asked to sign this agreement, what concerns might you have?
8. If after one year the employee resigns from Boulder Dry, what provisions of this contract should the employee have reviewed before resigning because they would affect his or her future? When leaving the company, what actions would the employee take to ensure that he or she was in compliance with all obligations?

SEE SAMPLE CONTRACT ON THE FOLLOWING PAGES.

EMPLOYEE NONCOMPETITION AND NONDISCLOSURE AGREEMENT

In consideration of my employment or continued employment, with Boulder Dry (the "Company"), and the compensation received from the Company, I hereby agree as follows:

1. ***Proprietary Information and Inventions:*** I understand and acknowledge that:
   - A. The Company is engaged in research, development, production, marketing, and servicing. I am expected to make new contributions and inventions of value to the Company as part of my employment.
   - B. My employment creates a relationship of trust between the Company and me with respect to information that may be made known to me or learned by me during my employment.
   - C. The Company possesses information that has been discovered or developed by the Company that has commercial value to the Company and is treated by the Company as confidential. All such information is hereinafter called "Proprietary Information," which term shall include, but shall not be limited to, systems, processes, data, computer programs, discoveries, marketing plans, strategies, forecasts, new products, unpublished financial statements, licenses, and customer and supplier lists. The term "Proprietary Information" shall not include any of the foregoing that is in the public domain.
   - D. All existing confidential lists of customers of the Company, and all confidential lists of customers developed during my employment, are the sole and exclusive property of the Company and I shall not have any right, title, or interest therein.
2. ***Ownership of Proprietary Information:*** All Proprietary Information shall be the sole property of the Company, including patents, copyrights, and trademarks. I hereby assign to the Company any rights I may have or acquire in such Proprietary Information. Both during and after my employment, I will keep in strictest confidence and trust all Proprietary Information. I will not use or disclose any Proprietary Information without the written consent of the Company, except as may be necessary in performing my duties as a Company employee.
3. ***Commitment to Company and Other Employment:*** During my employment, I will devote substantially all of my time to the Company, and I will not, without the Company's prior written consent, engage in any employment or business other than for the Company.
4. ***Documentation:*** Upon the termination of my employment, I will deliver to the Company all documents, computer programs, data, and other materials of any nature pertaining to my work with the Company. I will not take any originals or reproductions of the foregoing that are embodied in a tangible medium of expression.
5. ***Disclosure of Inventions:*** I will promptly disclose to the Company all discoveries, designs, inventions, blueprints, computer programs, and data ("Inventions") made by me, either alone or jointly with others, during my employment. Inventions include by definition those things that are related to the business of the Company or that result from the use of property owned, leased, or contracted for by the Company.
6. ***Ownership of Inventions:*** All Inventions shall be the sole property of the Company, and the Company shall be the sole owner of all patents, copyrights, trademarks, and other rights. I assign to the Company any rights I may have or acquire in such Inventions. I shall assist the Company to obtain and enforce patents, copyrights, trademarks, and other rights and protections relating to Inventions. This obligation shall continue beyond the termination of my employment, but the Company shall compensate me at a reasonable rate after my termination.
7. ***Other Agreements:*** I represent and warrant that this Agreement and the performance of it do not breach any other agreement to which I am a party. I have not entered into and shall not enter into any agreement in conflict with this Agreement.
8. ***Use of Confidential Information of Other Persons:*** I have not brought and will not bring with me to the Company any materials or documents of an employer or a former employer that are not generally available to the public. If I desire or need to use any materials from a prior employer, I will obtain express written authorization from such employer.
9. ***Restrictive Covenant:*** I hereby acknowledge my possession of Proprietary Information and the highly competitive nature of the business of the Company. I will not, during my employment and for three (3) years following my termination, directly or indirectly engage in any competitive business or assist others in engaging in any competitive business. I understand that this Section is not meant to prevent me from earning a living. It does intend to prevent any competitive business from gaining any unfair advantage from my knowledge of Proprietary Information. I understand that by making my new employer aware of the provisions of this Section 9, that employer can take such action as to avoid my breaching the provisions hereof and to indemnify me in the event of a breach.

COMMENTS TO CONTRACT PARAGRAPHS

Paragraph 1A. This is essentially a broad description of the employee's role at the company and explains why this agreement is necessary. Often, a clause like this precedes a statement indicating that the employer gets to keep any value that the employee adds to the firm.

Paragraph 1B. This paragraph establishes that a relationship of trust and confidence exists between employer and employee. Through this clause, both parties are agreeing they owe duties to each other related to information that benefits the company. The clause implies that that there will be negative consequences for the employee if he or she breaks that relationship.

Paragraph 1C. This paragraph establishes what the term "Proprietary Information" means. In contracts, terms that are capitalized and placed in quotation marks (sometimes in parentheses as well) are called "defined terms." Whenever the term "Proprietary Information" appears throughout the rest of the contract, it will have the definition set out in this paragraph. The definition is extremely broad and captures almost any intellectual property, data, and similar items. The contract asserts that this information is important to the business and gives the company some strategic advantage.

Paragraph 1D. This clause clarifies that customer lists belong to the employer even if the employee develops or expands the lists in some way. This may become important if the employee leaves the company because the clause clarifies that the employee may not recruit or "steal" customers.

Paragraph 2. Here, we see the defined term "Proprietary Information" again. This paragraph documents that the employer owns all Proprietary Information, as defined, even if it was created by the employee. Further, the employee agrees to give the employer any legal rights that the employee may obtain to any Proprietary Information.

Paragraph 3. In this clause, the employee promises that he or she will work full-time for the employer and will not take any additional employment without the employer's permission.

Paragraph 4. This clause further asserts that the company takes the confidential nature of the Proprietary Information seriously. Here, the employee promises that if he or she leaves the company's employment, he or she will turn over any work-related material to the company.

Paragraph 5. If the employee creates something of any kind at work, he or she must tell the employer about it, and the employer will receive any disclosures confidentially. The contract goes out of its way to ensure that almost anything the employee invents at work or that is related to work fits under this paragraph. Such items are given a new term called "Inventions." Note that the definition of inventions includes the same items that are in the definition of Proprietary Information as well as some additional ones. The paragraphs discussing Proprietary Information deal with information that the company already possesses and will continue to possess and that the employee will access or need. This paragraph expands the obligations of the employee to what could be called new proprietary information, defined as "Inventions."

Paragraph 6. Just as the employee agreed to give any right in already existing information (such as a modified customer list) to the employer, here the employee promises to give all legal rights to inventions to the employer. In addition, because the rights may originally belong to the employee, the employee promises to help the employer secure any rights or protections necessary to increase the value of the invention. This obligation to help the employer continues to exist after the employee leaves the firm, and the employer agrees to pay for the work required in that situation. The employer is making sure that it can keep anything the employee invents during work time or with company resources.

Paragraph 7. The employer wants to ensure that this contract does not conflict with any others the employee may have already signed. Here, the employee affirms that he or she has made no conflicting agreements. The clause implies that the employee will be responsible for any consequences that arise from such conflicts.

Paragraph 8. The employer does not want to become involved in a dispute with another company by hiring this employee. In this clause, the employee states that he or she is not bringing the employer any confidential information belonging to someone else.

Paragraph 9. This paragraph is a covenant not to compete, one of the most important provisions from the perspective of the employee. Employers worry that former employees will join a rival company and take their information and expertise with them. A covenant not to compete helps prevent that from happening. In short, a covenant not to compete prohibits an employee from working for a competing business for a specified time. This covenant applies regardless of whether the employee leaves the company or is terminated. Covenants not to compete have to be carefully drafted. A court will not enforce a covenant that is too broad in its coverage or that lasts for too long. Three years, the length of this covenant not to compete, is not unduly long. If the covenant is challenged, however, the employer will have to show that this length of time was necessary to protect its business interests. Employees do not appreciate covenants not to compete, but find that they are an inevitable part of employment in information-sensitive industries.

10. *Agreement Not to Solicit Customers:* During the course of my employment and for a period of three (3) years following my termination, I will not attempt to solicit any person, firm, or corporation that has been a customer account of the Company.
11. *Remedies:* I acknowledge that a remedy at law for any breach or threatened breach of the provisions of this Agreement would be inadequate. I therefore agree that the Company shall be entitled to injunctive relief in addition to any other available rights and remedies in case of any such breach or threatened breach. Nothing contained herein shall be construed as prohibiting the Company from pursuing any other remedies available for any such breach or threatened breach.
12. *Assignment:* This Agreement and the rights and obligations of the parties hereto shall bind and inure to the benefit of any successor(s) of the Company, whether by reorganization, merger, consolidation, sale of assets, or otherwise. Neither this Agreement nor any rights or benefits hereunder may be assigned by me.
13. *Interpretation:* It is the desire and intent of the parties hereto that the provisions of this Agreement shall be enforced to the fullest extent permissible. Accordingly, if any provision of this Agreement shall be adjudicated to be invalid or unenforceable, such provision shall be deemed deleted. Such deletion will apply only to the deleted provision in the particular jurisdiction in which such adjudication is made. If any provision contained herein shall be held to be excessively broad as to duration, geographical scope, activity, or subject, it shall be construed by limiting and reducing it so as to be enforceable.
14. *Notices:* All notices pursuant to this Agreement shall be given by personal delivery or by certified mail, return receipt requested. Notices to the Employee shall be addressed to the Employee at the address of record with the Company. Notices to the Company shall be addressed to its principal office. The date of personal delivery or the date of mailing any such notice shall be deemed to be the date of delivery thereof.
15. *Waivers:* Any waiver of breach of any provision of this Agreement shall not thereby be deemed a waiver of any preceding or succeeding breach of the same or any other provision of this Agreement.
16. *Headings:* The headings of the sections hereof are inserted for convenience only and shall not be deemed to constitute a part hereof nor to affect the meaning hereof.
17. *Governing Law:* This Agreement shall be governed by and construed and enforced in accordance with the laws of the State of New Hampshire.
18. *No Employment Agreement:* I acknowledge that this Agreement does not constitute an employment agreement. This Agreement shall be binding upon me regardless of whether my employment shall continue for any length of time and whether my employment is terminated for any reason whatsoever. This is true whether my employment is terminated by the Company or by me.
19. *Complete Agreement, Amendments, and Prior Agreements:* The foregoing is the entire agreement of the parties with respect to the subject matter hereof and may not be amended, supplemented, canceled, or discharged except by written instrument executed by both parties hereto. This Agreement supersedes any and all prior agreements between the parties hereto with respect to the matters covered hereby.

Date: ________________ Employee: ______________________________

Accepted and agreed to as of this date by Company:

Date: ______________ By: ______________________________

Name: ______________________________________

Title: ______________________________________

Paragraph 10. Similar to a covenant not to compete, this clause prohibits an employee from soliciting the company's customers during his or her employment or for up to three years afterward. Without such protection, an employer would be vulnerable to any former employee taking customer lists and using them to solicit customers at a new employer or at his or her own business.

Paragraph 11. This paragraph allows the employer to seek injunctive relief against the employee, should it be necessary. Here, the employee agrees that the employer not only may seek monetary damages from the employee in the event that this agreement is breached but may also prohibit him or her from engaging in whatever behavior violates the contract. Recall that typically the first line of remedies is damages to compensate for injury. Here the parties are acknowledging in advance (for the benefit of any court that later is involved) that the harm caused by a breach of the contract cannot be compensated or corrected with monetary damages.

Paragraph 12. Companies change, and so do their owners. This paragraph states that the contract will survive even if ownership of the company changes due to a merger, reorganization, or other reason. The employee cannot avoid this contract simply because the owner that signed the agreement later sells the company to someone else. This paragraph and many of the subsequent paragraphs are often referred to as "boilerplate language," meaning provisions that appear in some form in many contracts. They are included because conflicts have arisen over these points in the past and courts have interpreted contracts without this language in a way that the parties want to avoid. Boilerplate language can be very dangerous because parties may see the headings and not read further because the language is similar from contract to contract. But boilerplate language can make a difference in which party later wins a dispute (because the language spells out the law that will be used to interpret the contract, where a case must be brought, the proper way to give notice of changes, and the like).

Paragraph 13. Employers know that even the most carefully drafted agreements can sometimes be rendered unenforceable by a reviewing court. Laws change over time, and so do attitudes toward contract terms. This paragraph states that if part of this contract is rendered unenforceable for some reason, the rest of the contract will survive intact (that is, the unenforceable part of the contract is severable). The paragraph specifically references the covenant not to compete and the prohibition against solicitation. If a court rejects those terms as too broad in scope or too lengthy, the parties agree that the court should adjust the clause in order to make it enforceable under the law.

Paragraph 14. This paragraph deals with notices. If the employer or the employee wants to communicate about the contract, the communication must be sent by personal delivery or registered/certified mail. Note that this means that an e-mail is not sufficient notice under this agreeement.

Paragraph 15. This paragraph says "any party," but it is really meant to protect the employer. Sometimes, through generosity or neglect, employers fail to enforce every clause of a contract. For example, an employer may allow a former employee to start a competing business earlier than the contract states or permit an employee to take a second job. This paragraph ensures that if the employer allows some action that is prohibited in the contract, that does not mean that the contract term is waived forever. Just because the employer does not fully enforce the contract every time does not necessarily mean the employer is barred from doing so in the future.

Paragraph 16. This clause is meant to clarify that the headings are just headings and do not change the interpretation of the language in the paragraphs or the overall meaning of the contract.

Paragraph 17. This contract will be interpreted using the law of the state of New Hampshire. It is likely that the employer selected New Hampshire for some particular reason. Typically, an employer chooses a state where the law provides the most benefits for the employer. For example, employers typically choose the law of a particular state because it is their geographic home state and the employer's lawyers are familiar with its law. Employers may also choose a legal jurisdiction because its laws create a climate that is more favorable to the employer than the employee.

Paragraph 18. In this paragraph, the employee acknowledges that this contract is about nondisclosure of information and does not constitute an employment agreement that promises any length of service or any promise of continued employment.

Paragraph 19. This paragraph states that this contract is the complete agreement between the employer and the employee. Any other side agreements, e-mails, conversations, or other communications are irrelevant. The employee cannot rely on a manager's promise of a particular salary or terms of a covenant not to compete. This agreement is the final statement of the relationship between the employer and the employee.

UNIT 2 Contracts

Business Case Study with Dissenting Opinion

Braddock v. Braddock

Fraudulent misrepresentation (discussed in Chapter 12) is one of the events that may cause a contract to lack voluntary consent. For a misrepresentation to be fraudulent, it must misrepresent a present, material fact. A representation, or prediction, of a future fact does not qualify. The misrepresentation must be consciously false and intended to mislead an innocent party, who must justifiably rely on it. When an innocent party is fraudulently induced to enter into a contract, the party can rescind the contract and be restored to her or his original position or enforce the contract and seek damages for injuries resulting from the fraud.

In this *Business Case Study with Dissenting Opinion,* we set out *Braddock v. Braddock,*[1] a case involving an individual who gave up his career and relocated his home and family based on his cousin's representations about a newly formed entrepreneurial venture. The individual's position in the new enterprise, however, was not what the cousin had told him it would be. Were the cousin's statements fraudulent? Or were they simply expressions of expectation—predictions of future possibilities—subject to contingencies that neither party could control?

Case Background

David Braddock wanted to form Broad Oak Energy, Inc. (BOE), to tap oil and gas reserves in Louisiana and Texas. He asked his cousin John, an investment banker in New York, to find an investor to provide BOE with $75 to $150 million and also asked John to come to work for BOE. David assured John that he would be BOE's chief financial officer (CFO) and land manager and that he would receive half as much stock in the company as would be issued to David, who would serve as the company's chief executive officer. John quit his job, agreed to accept a significantly reduced fee to find an investor for BOE, and moved his family to Texas. As a result of John's efforts, Warburg Pincus, LLC, agreed to provide $150 million in start-up capital.

Two weeks later, David told John that Warburg Pincus insisted that John not be made CFO or land manager. Instead, David offered him the position of landman, a substantially reduced position with lesser salary, benefits, and terms. Surprised, John nevertheless cooperated. He signed "engagement agreements" to accept the lesser position as an "employee at will," subject to discharge for any reason at any time. Stress soon began to take a toll on his health, and he was granted a conditional medical leave of absence. The next month, BOE terminated his employment.

John filed a suit in a New York state court against David, asserting that these circumstances constituted fraud. The court dismissed the complaint. John appealed to a state intermediate appellate court.

Majority Opinion

SAXE, J. [Judge]

* * * *

To plead a claim for [fraud], a plaintiff must assert the misrepresentation of a material fact, which was known by the defendant to be false and intended to be relied on when made, and that there was justifiable reliance and resulting injury. The complaint here sufficiently sets forth these elements. [Emphasis added.]

* * * *

[John's] allegations satisfy the particularity requirement for a fraud claim.

* * * *

* * * Since David and John are cousins, John's reliance on David's good faith may be found to be reasonable even where it might not be reasonable in the context of an arm's length transaction with a stranger. Family members stand in a fiduciary relationship [one of trust] toward one another in a co-owned business venture. * * * Under the

1. 60 A.D.3d 84, 871 N.Y.S.2d 68 (1 Dept. 2009).

Business Case Study with Dissenting Opinion—Continued

circumstances alleged here, John had reason to believe that David would treat him, in their interaction, with good faith and integrity.

* * * *

The situation presented here should be distinguished from cases in which a plaintiff who was involved in a business deal claims that, in the original discussions of the deal, misrepresentations were made as to its terms but the falsity of those representations was revealed by the time the deal was executed. In such cases, the ultimate terms of the deal, if agreed upon, are all that the plaintiff is entitled to, and he will not be permitted to seek damages based upon the original misrepresentations, because he did not rely on them in electing to go through with the deal. Here, in contrast, John's subsequent execution of documents that fundamentally altered the originally promised terms of his position with the company was not merely an election to enter into the deal anyway. First of all, even before he executed * * * the agreements * * * , the deal was essentially under way, at least on his part, in that he had already sacrificed his former life and undertaken tasks to forward the venture, and he was no longer in a position to reject the offered terms or even to negotiate effectively. Indeed, when the allegations are understood in the context of an ongoing attempt by John to salvage something from his dashed expectations, the fact that he subsequently acceded to new and lesser terms should not justify holding * * * that he did not reasonably rely on his cousin's alleged misrepresentations and false assurances, to his own severe detriment.

If all these interactions had been between strangers conducting an arm's length business transaction, strict reliance on the signed written documents, to the exclusion of the parties' words and conduct, would be appropriate. But the expectation of the good faith of a family member in circumstances such as these may justify some reliance on assurances that are not incorporated into written documents drafted and executed later.

* * * *

Here, * * * the issues of material misrepresentation and reasonable reliance are not subject to summary disposition [settlement], and the fiduciary relationship between the parties, with its concomitant [associated] mutual obligation to act in good faith, makes John's reliance on David's assurances all the more reasonable.

* * * *

* * * Defendants' motion to dismiss the complaint for failure to state a cause of action * * * [is] denied * * * so as to reinstate the [plaintiff's fraud] cause of action.

Dissenting Opinion

LIPPMAN, P.J. [Presiding Judge], (DISSENTING).

* * * *

* * * It is, in essence, alleged that John's entire course of conduct in providing investment banking services for a discounted fee, giving up his lucrative New York employment as an investment banker and advisor, moving to Texas and agreeing to take the non-executive position with BOE from which he was eventually dismissed * * * was induced by David's * * * assurances.

* * * *

* * * At the time of David's nominal assurances, BOE was but an unfunded shell requiring for its viability an enormous infusion of capital. And, while John was confident of procuring financing for the venture, there had been, at the time, neither a commitment of funds nor even the emergence of a leading candidate to provide such a commitment. Moreover, John, in addition to being an experienced investment banker and financial consultant, was, by reason of his own prior professional involvement in oil and gas ventures and his extensive familial connections to the industry, particularly well aware of the risks such ventures entailed. * * * In these circumstances, * * * no promise of high executive-level employment in the company * * * could reasonably have been viewed as an "assurance" or a "guarantee." * * * What he now terms "assurances" and "guarantees" could have been reasonably understood as only expressions of expectation or intent, the realization of which would depend upon contingencies not within the power of the parties to foreseeably accommodate to their stated objectives.

* * * While he may have had a moral claim to rely upon his cousin even when objective circumstances counseled otherwise, there is no legal right to recovery in fraud that may be vindicated upon such a predicate.

Accordingly, I would affirm the dismissal of plaintiffs' fraud cause of action.

Business Case Study with Dissenting Opinion—Continues next page

Business Case Study with Dissenting Opinion—Continued

Questions for Analysis

1. **Law** What did the majority conclude on the issue before the court in this case? What reasoning supported this conclusion?
2. **Law** On what important point did the dissent disagree with the majority, and why?
3. **Ethics** How do you view David's statements and John's actions? Did David take unethical advantage of his cousin, luring him in bad faith? Was John too willing to rely on assurances of events that he should have known from experience might not occur? Discuss.
4. **Economic Dimensions** What does this case indicate about employment and employment contracts?
5. **Implications for the Investor** Why would an investor like Warburg Pincus not want someone like John in an executive role in an enterprise for which the investor was providing significant capital?

UNIT 2 Contracts

Business Scenario

Alberto Corelli offers to pay $2,500 to purchase a painting titled *Moonrise* from Tara Shelley, an artist whose works have been causing a stir in the art world. Shelley accepts Corelli's offer. Assuming that the contract has met all of the requirements for a valid contract, answer the following questions.

1. **Minors.** Corelli was a minor when he purchased the painting. Is the contract void? Is it voidable? What is the difference between these two concepts? A month after his eighteenth birthday, Corelli decides that he would rather have the $2,500 than the painting. He informs Shelley that he is disaffirming the contract and requests that Shelley return the $2,500 to him. When she refuses to do so, Corelli brings a court action to recover the $2,500. What will the court likely decide in this situation? Why? **(See page 288.)**
2. **Statute of Frauds.** Both parties are adults, the contract is oral, and the painting is still in progress. Corelli pays Shelley the $2,500 in return for her promise to deliver the painting to his home when it is finished. A week later, after Shelley finishes the painting, a visitor to her gallery offers her $3,500 for it. Shelley sells the painting to the visitor and sends Corelli a signed letter explaining that she is "canceling" their contract for the *Moonrise* painting. Corelli sues Shelley to enforce the contract. Is the contract enforceable? Explain. **(See page 313.)**
3. **Capacity.** Both parties are adults, and the contract, which is in writing, states that Corelli will pay Shelley the $2,500 the following day. In the meantime, Shelley allows Corelli to take the painting home with him. The next day, Corelli's son returns the painting to Shelley, stating that he is canceling the contract. He explains that his father has been behaving strangely lately, that he seems to be mentally incompetent at times, and that he clearly was not acting rationally when he bought the painting, which he could not afford. Is the contract enforceable? Discuss fully. **(See pages 290–291.)**
4. **Impossibility of Performance.** Both parties are adults, and the contract is in writing. The contract calls for Shelley to deliver the painting to Corelli's gallery in two weeks. Corelli has already arranged to sell the painting to a third party for $4,000, for a $1,500 profit, but it must be available for the third party in two weeks or the sale will not go through. Shelley knows this but does not deliver the painting at the time promised. Corelli sues Shelley for $1,500 in

Business Scenario—Continued

damages. Shelley claims that performance was impossible because her mother fell seriously ill and required Shelley's care. Who will win this lawsuit, and why? **(See page 345.)**

5. **Agreement in E-Contracts.** Both parties are adults, and Shelley, on her Web site, offers to sell the painting for $2,500. Corelli accepts the offer by clicking on an "I accept" box on the computer screen displaying the offer. Among other terms, the online offer includes a forum-selection clause stating that any disputes under the contract are to be resolved by a court in California, the state in which Shelley lives. After Corelli receives the painting, he notices a smear of paint across the lower corner of the painting that was not visible in the digitized image that appeared on Shelley's Web site. Corelli calls Shelley, tells her about the smear, and says that he wants to cancel the contract and return the painting. When Shelley refuses to cooperate, Corelli sues her in a Texas state court, seeking to rescind the contract. Shelley claims that any suit against her must be filed in a California court in accordance with the forum-selection clause. Corelli maintains that the forum-selection clause is unconscionable and should not be enforced. What factors will the court consider in deciding this case? What will the court likely decide? Would it matter whether Corelli read the terms of the online offer before clicking on "I accept"? **(See page 268.)**

UNIT 2 Contracts

Group Project

RiotGear, LLC, contracts with Standard Transit, Inc., to distribute RiotGear's "Occupy Earth/Global Movement" line of apparel to retail outlets for a certain price. RiotGear promises to donate a share of the proceeds from the sale of the "Occupy Earth/Global Movement" line to The Cause, a charitable organization dedicated to supporting those who seek social and economic change through protest. In reliance on the expected donation, The Cause contracts for medical and other supplies. When Standard increases the distribution cost, RiotGear tells The Cause that there will be no donation.

1. While the goods are in transit, RiotGear receives this tweet from Standard: "Price increase of 99 percent or no delivery." RiotGear agrees and pays, but later sues Standard for the increase over the original price. The first group will identify the rule that a court would apply in this situation and decide whether RiotGear is entitled to the difference in price.
2. The second group will determine whether The Cause can enforce RiotGear's original promise despite the lack of consideration. What doctrine might a court apply in this situation, and what are the requirements to enforce a promise?

UNIT 3

(Blend_Images/iStockphoto.com)

Commercial Transactions

UNIT CONTENTS

15. The Formation of Sales and Lease Contracts
16. Performance and Breach of Sales and Lease Contracts
17. Warranties and Product Liability
18. Negotiable Instruments: Transferability and Liability
19. Checks and Banking in the Digital Age
20. Secured Transactions
21. Creditors' Rights and Bankruptcy
22. Mortgages and Foreclosures after the Recession

CHAPTER 15

The Formation of Sales and Lease Contracts

(Matthew Staver/Landov)

CHAPTER OUTLINE

- The Scope of the UCC and Articles 2 (Sales) and 2A (Leases)
- The Formation of Sales and Lease Contracts
- Title and Risk of Loss
- Contracts for the International Sale of Goods

LEARNING OBJECTIVES

The five learning objectives below are designed to help improve your understanding of the chapter. After reading this chapter, you should be able to answer the following questions:

1. How do Article 2 and Article 2A of the UCC differ? What types of transactions does each article cover?
2. In a sales contract, if an offeree includes additional or different terms in an acceptance, will a contract result? If so, what happens to these terms?
3. What exceptions to the writing requirements of the Statute of Frauds are provided in Article 2 and Article 2A of the UCC?
4. Risk of loss does not necessarily pass with title. If the parties to a contract do not expressly agree when risk passes and the goods are to be delivered without movement by the seller, when does risk pass?
5. What law governs contracts for the international sale of goods?

"I am for free commerce with all nations."

—George Washington, 1732–1799 (First president of the United States, 1789–1797)

The chapter-opening quotation echoes a sentiment that most Americans believe—free commerce will benefit our nation. This is particularly true with respect to the Uniform Commercial Code (UCC). The UCC facilitates commercial transactions by making the laws governing sales and lease contracts uniform and, as far as possible, clear, simple, and readily applicable to the numerous difficulties that can arise during such transactions.

Recall from Chapter 1 that the UCC is one of many uniform (model) acts drafted by the National Conference of Commissioners on Uniform State Laws and submitted to the states for adoption. Once a state legislature has adopted a uniform act, the act becomes statutory law in that state. Thus, when we turn to sales and lease contracts, we move away from common law principles and into the area of statutory law.

The Scope of the UCC and Articles 2 (Sales) and 2A (Leases)

The UCC attempts to provide a consistent, integrated framework of rules to deal with all phases ordinarily arising in a commercial sales or lease transaction. For example, consider the following events, all of which may occur during a single transaction:

1. *A contract for the sale or lease of goods is formed and executed.* Article 2 and Article 2A of the UCC provide rules governing all aspects of this transaction.
2. *The transaction may involve a payment—by check, electronic fund transfer, or other means.* Article 3 (on negotiable instruments), Article 4 (on bank deposits and collections), Article 4A (on fund transfers), and Article 5 (on letters of credit) cover this part of the transaction.
3. *The transaction may involve a bill of lading or a warehouse receipt that covers goods when they are shipped or stored.* Article 7 (on documents of title) deals with this subject.
4. *The transaction may involve a demand by the seller or lender for some form of security for the remaining balance owed.* Article 9 (on secured transactions) covers this part of the transaction.

The UCC has been adopted in whole or in part by all of the states.[1] Because of its importance in the area of commercial transactions, we present the UCC as this chapter's *Landmark in the Law* feature on the facing page.

Article 2—Sales

Sales Contract A contract for the sale of goods.

Article 2 of the UCC governs **sales contracts,** or contracts for the sale of goods. To facilitate commercial transactions, Article 2 modifies some of the common law contract requirements that were discussed in Chapters 9 through 14. To the extent that it has not been modified by the UCC, however, the common law of contracts also applies to sales contracts.

In general, the rule is that when a UCC provision addresses a certain issue, the UCC governs, but when the UCC is silent, the common law governs. The relationship between general contract law and the law governing sales of goods is illustrated in Exhibit 15.1 on the facing page. (For a discussion of an issue involving state taxation of sales that take place over the Internet, see this chapter's *Adapting the Law to the Online Environment* feature on page 386.)

Keep in mind that Article 2 deals with the sale of *goods*—it does not deal with real property (real estate), services, or intangible property such as stocks and bonds. Thus, if a dispute involves real estate or services, the common law applies. Also note that in some situations, the rules under the UCC can vary quite a bit depending on whether the buyer or the seller is a merchant. We look now at how the UCC defines a *sale, goods,* and *merchant status.*

Sale The passing of title to property from the seller to the buyer for a price.

What Is a Sale?

The UCC defines a **sale** as "the passing of title [evidence of ownership] from the seller to the buyer for a price" [UCC 2–106(1)]. The price may be payable in cash (or its equivalent) or in other goods or services.

Tangible Property Property that has physical existence and can be distinguished by the senses of touch and sight.

Intangible Property Property that cannot be seen or touched but exists only conceptually, such as corporate stocks. Such property is not governed by Article 2 of the UCC.

What Are Goods?

To be characterized as a *good,* the item of property must be *tangible,* and it must be *movable.*

Tangible and Movable Property

Tangible property has physical existence—it can be touched or seen. **Intangible property**—such as corporate stocks and bonds, patents and

1. Louisiana has not adopted Articles 2 and 2A, however.

LANDMARK IN THE LAW

The Uniform Commercial Code

Of all the attempts to produce a uniform body of laws relating to commercial transactions in the United States, none has been as comprehensive or successful as the Uniform Commercial Code (UCC).

The Origins of the UCC The UCC was the brainchild of William A. Schnader, president of the National Conference of Commissioners on Uniform State Laws (NCCUSL). The drafting of the UCC began in 1945. The most significant individual involved in the project was its chief editor, Karl N. Llewellyn of the Columbia University Law School. Llewellyn's intellect, continuous efforts, and ability to compromise made the first version of the UCC—completed in 1949—a legal landmark. Over the next several years, the UCC was substantially accepted by almost every state in the nation.

Periodic Changes and Updates Various articles and sections of the UCC are periodically changed or supplemented to clarify certain rules or to establish new rules when changes in business customs render the existing UCC provisions inapplicable. For example, because of the increasing importance of leases of goods in the commercial context, Article 2A governing leases was added to the UCC. To clarify the rights of parties to commercial fund transfers, particularly electronic fund transfers, Article 4A was issued. Articles 3 and 4, on negotiable instruments and banking relationships, underwent significant revision in the 1990s. Because of other changes in business and in the law, the NCCUSL has recommended the repeal of Article 6 (on bulk transfers) and has offered a revised Article 6 to those states that prefer not to repeal it. The NCCUSL has also revised Article 9, covering secured transactions. The revised Article 9, which has been adopted by all of the states, will be discussed at length in Chapter 20.

Application to Today's World *By periodically revising the UCC's articles, the NCCUSL has been able to adapt its provisions to changing business customs and practices. UCC provisions governing sales and lease contracts have also been extended to contracts formed in the online environment.*

Exhibit 15.1 The Law Governing Contracts

This exhibit graphically illustrates the relationship between general contract law and statutory law (UCC Articles 2 and 2A) governing contracts for the sale and lease of goods. Sales contracts are not governed exclusively by Article 2 of the UCC but are also governed by general contract law whenever it is relevant and has not been modified by the UCC.

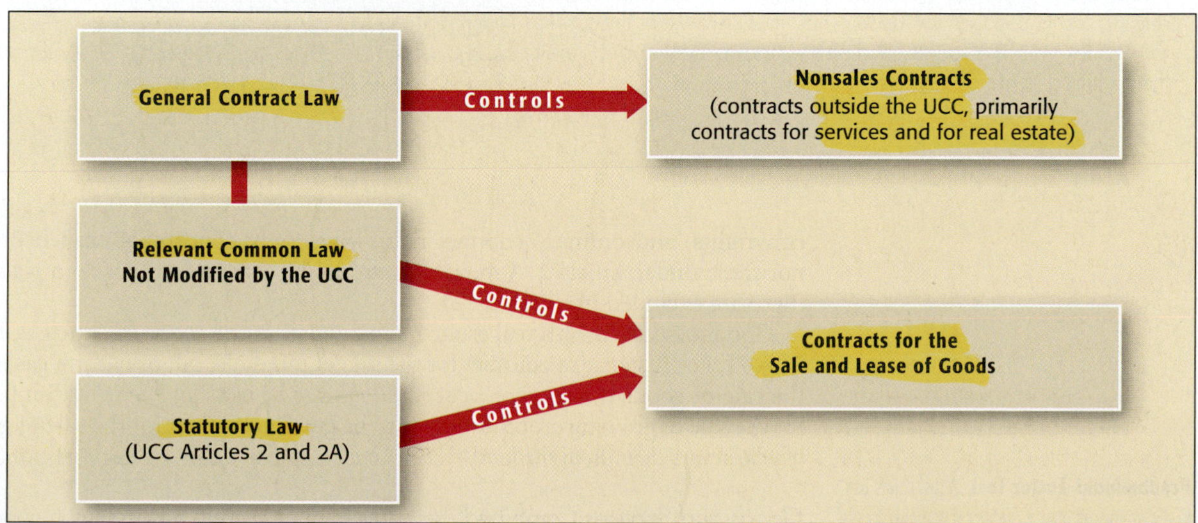

ADAPTING THE LAW TO THE ONLINE ENVIRONMENT

LOCAL GOVERNMENTS ATTEMPT TO TAX ONLINE TRAVEL COMPANIES

A battle is raging across the United States between state and local governments and online retailers. The online retailers claim that because they do not have a physical presence in a state, they should not have to collect state and local taxes for the goods and services they sell. Although most states have laws that require their residents to report online purchases and pay taxes on them (so-called use taxes), few U.S. consumers comply with these laws.

Local Governments Sue Online Travel Companies

Travelocity, Priceline.com, Hotels.com, and Orbitz.com are online travel companies (OTCs) that offer, among other things, hotel booking services. By 2013, more than twenty cities, including Atlanta, Charleston, Philadelphia, and San Antonio, had filed suits claiming that the OTCs owed taxes on hotel reservations that they had booked. All of the cities involved in the suits impose a hotel occupancy tax, which is essentially a sales tax.

The issue is not whether the OTCs should pay the tax but rather how it should be assessed and collected. OTCs typically purchase blocks of hotel rooms at a wholesale rate and then resell the rooms to customers at a marked-up resale rate, keeping the difference as profit. The OTCs forward to the hotels an amount intended to cover the hotel occupancy tax (sales tax) based on the wholesale prices of the rooms sold. The hotels then remit to the city taxing authority the tax on the rooms sold by the OTCs.

The cities claim, however, that the OTCs should assess the occupancy tax rates on the retail prices that they charge, rather than on the wholesale prices of the rooms. Of course, the retail prices are higher, so the cities would collect more tax if the retail price is used as the base. The cities also want the OTCs to register with the local jurisdictions and to collect and remit the required taxes directly.

The Cities Are Losing in Court

When these lawsuits were first brought a few years ago, city governments generally obtained favorable rulings, both in federal district courts[a] and in state courts.[b] In contrast, when some of these suits were retried or reviewed by higher courts, the OTCs prevailed. In 2012, for example, the city of Goodlettsville, Tennessee, lost its continuing case against Priceline.com and nine other OTCs. In siding with the OTCs, the court said, "If the Tennessee legislature intends to permit its political subdivisions to tax the retail rate paid by the consumers to the OTCs for hotel bookings, the legislature may do so through appropriate statutory language."[c]

In contrast, when the South Carolina Department of Revenue sued Travelscape, LLC, the Supreme Court of South Carolina held that the OTC had to remit taxes based on the retail price of the hotel rooms sold.[d] The South Carolina decision reflected a minority opinion, however. As of early 2012, the OTCs had prevailed in fifteen of nineteen cases nationwide.

Critical Thinking

What are possible benefits if cities and states do not impose a sales tax on the difference between the wholesale price of rooms and the retail price of rooms sold by OTCs?

---

a. See, for example, *City of Goodlettsville v. Priceline.com, Inc.*, 605 F.Supp.2d 982 (M.D.Tenn. 2009).

b. See *City of Atlanta v. Hotels.com, L.P.*, 285 Ga. 231, 674 S.E.2d 898 (2009).

c. *City of Goodlettsville v. Priceline.com, Inc.*, 2012 WL 573681 (M.D.Tenn. 2012).

d. *Travelscape, LLC v. South Carolina Department of Revenue*, 391 S.C. 89, 705 S.E.2d 28 (2011).

copyrights, and ordinary contract rights—has only conceptual existence and thus does not come under Article 2. A movable item can be carried from place to place (real estate is therefore excluded from Article 2).

Goods *associated* with real estate often fall within the scope of Article 2, however [UCC 2–107]. For instance, a contract for the sale of minerals, oil, or natural gas is a contract for the sale of goods if *severance, or separation, is to be made by the seller.* Similarly, a contract for the sale of growing crops or timber to be cut is a contract for the sale of goods *regardless of who severs them from the land.*

Predominant-Factor Test A test courts use to determine whether a contract is primarily for the sale of goods or for the sale of services.

Goods and Services Combined In cases involving contracts in which goods and services are combined, courts generally use the **predominant-factor test** to determine whether a

(Marquis/Shutterstock.com)

If a couple buys a concessions business that includes a truck, trailer, and tables and chairs, would this purchase be a sale of goods or of services?

contract is primarily for the sale of goods or for the sale of services.[2] This determination is important because the UCC will apply to services provided under a mixed contract that is predominantly for goods, even though the majority of courts treat services as being excluded by the UCC.

If Contract Is Primarily for Goods, UCC Applies to All Disputes If a court decides that a mixed contract is primarily a goods contract, *any* dispute, even a dispute over the services portion, will be decided under the UCC. **CASE EXAMPLE 15.1** Gene and Martha Jannusch agreed to sell Festival Foods, a concessions business, to Lindsey and Louann Naffziger for a price of $150,000. The deal included a truck, a trailer, freezers, roasters, chairs, tables, a fountain service, signs, and lighting. The Naffzigers paid $10,000 down with the balance to come from a bank loan. They took possession of the equipment and began to use it immediately in Festival Foods operations at various events.

After six events, the Naffzigers returned the truck and all the equipment and wanted out of the deal because the business did not generate as much income as they expected. The Jannusches sued the Naffzigers for the balance due on the purchase price, claiming that the Naffzigers could no longer reject the goods under the UCC. The Naffzigers claimed that the UCC did not apply because the deal primarily involved the sale of a business rather than the sale of goods. The court found that the UCC governed under the predominant-factor test. The primary value of the contract was in the goods, not the value of the business. The parties had agreed on the essential terms of the contract (such as the price). Thus, a contract had been formed, and the Naffzigers had breached it. The Naffzigers took possession of the business and had no right to return it.[3] ●

Who Is a Merchant?

Article 2 governs the sale of goods in general. It applies to sales transactions between all buyers and sellers. In a limited number of instances, however, the UCC presumes that certain special business standards ought to be imposed on merchants because they possess a relatively high degree of commercial expertise.[4] Such standards do not apply to the casual or inexperienced seller or buyer (a "consumer"). Section 2–104 sets out three ways in which merchant status can arise:

1. A merchant is a person who *deals in goods of the kind* involved in the sales contract. Thus, a retailer, a wholesaler, or a manufacturer is a merchant of those goods sold in the business. A merchant for one type of goods is not necessarily a merchant for another type. For instance, a sporting equipment retailer is a merchant when selling tennis rackets but not when selling a used iPad.
2. A merchant is a person who, by occupation, *holds himself or herself out as having special knowledge and skill* related to the practices or goods involved in the transaction. Note that this broad definition may include banks or universities as merchants.
3. A person who *employs a merchant as a broker, agent, or other intermediary* has the status of merchant in that transaction. Hence, if an art collector hires a broker to purchase or sell art for her, the collector is considered a merchant in the transaction.

Merchant Under the UCC, a person who deals in goods of the kind involved in the sales contract or who holds herself or himself out as having skill or knowledge peculiar to the practices or goods being purchased or sold.

In summary, a person is a **merchant** when she or he, acting in a mercantile (commercial) capacity, possesses or uses an expertise specifically related to the goods being sold. This basic distinction is not always clear-cut. For instance, state courts appear to be split on whether farmers should be considered merchants.

2. UCC 2–314(1) does stipulate that serving food or drinks is a "sale of goods" for purposes of the implied warranty of merchantability, as will be discussed in Chapter 17. The UCC also specifies that selling unborn animals and rare coins qualifies as a "sale of goods."
3. *Jannusch v. Naffziger,* 379 Ill.App.3d 381, 883 N.E.2d 711 (2008).
4. The provisions that apply only to merchants deal principally with the Statute of Frauds, firm offers, confirmatory memorandums, warranties, and contract modifications. These special rules reflect expedient business practices commonly known to merchants in the commercial setting. They will be discussed later in this chapter.

ETHICAL ISSUE

Should merchants be allowed to use buying patterns to learn personal information about their customers, such as whether they are pregnant? Whether you shop on the Internet or in stores, most major retailers compile information about you based on what, when, and how you buy. Sometimes, based on your purchases, you will instantly be given printed coupons at the cash register. These customized coupons reflect your preferences based on past behavior. If you regularly use Amazon.com, for instance, you receive customized offers every time you visit that site.

Target Brands, Inc., uses a very sophisticated data collection process that assigns each shopper a unique guest identification code. Over time, a shopper's habits become the source of predictions for future consumer behavior. For example, Target can accurately predict which female shoppers are pregnant based on their recent purchases of vitamin and mineral supplements. When Target's system detects a buying pattern suggesting that a customer is pregnant, it starts offering coupons for baby-related products and services.

A father in Minneapolis, Minnesota, complained to a Target manager that his daughter was receiving such coupons for no reason. In reality, Target's system had accurately discovered his daughter's pregnancy. The father was even more furious that his daughter had lied to him. Was Target's action legal? Probably, it was. Target had complied with the relevant federal and state privacy laws. Current laws even allow retailers to share their customer data with affiliate companies.

LEARNING OBJECTIVE 1

How do Article 2 and Article 2A of the UCC differ? What types of transactions does each article cover?

The Scope of Article 2A—Leases

Lease Under Article 2A of the UCC, a transfer of the right to possess and use goods for a period of time in exchange for payment.

Leases of personal property (goods) have become increasingly common. In this context, a **lease** is a transfer of the right to possess and use goods for a period of time in exchange for payment. Article 2A of the UCC was created to fill the need for uniform guidelines in this area.

Article 2A covers any transaction that creates a lease of goods, as well as subleases of goods [UCC 2A–102, 2A–103(1)(k)]. Except that it applies to leases, rather than sales, of goods, Article 2A is essentially a repetition of Article 2 and varies only to reflect differences between sales and lease transactions. (Note that Article 2A is not concerned with leases of real property, such as land or buildings. The laws governing leases of real property will be discussed in Chapter 36.)

Lease Agreement An agreement in which one person (the lessor) agrees to transfer the right to the possession and use of property to another person (the lessee) in exchange for rental payments.

Lessor A person who transfers the right to the possession and use of goods to another in exchange for rental payments.

Lessee A person who acquires the right to the possession and use of another's goods in exchange for rental payments.

Definition of a Lease Agreement

Article 2A defines a **lease agreement** as the bargain between a lessor and a lessee with respect to the lease of goods, as found in their language and as implied by other circumstances, including course of dealing and usage of trade or course of performance [UCC 2A–103(1)(k)]. A **lessor** is one who transfers the right to the possession and use of goods under a lease [UCC 2A–103(1)(p)]. A **lessee** is one who acquires the right to the temporary possession and use of goods under a lease [UCC 2A–103(1)(o)].

In other words, the lessee is the party who is leasing the goods from the lessor. Article 2A applies to all types of leases of goods, including commercial leases and consumer leases. Special rules apply to certain types of leases, however, including consumer leases.

Consumer Leases

Under UCC 2A–103(1)(e), a *consumer lease* involves three elements:

1. A lessor who regularly engages in the business of leasing or selling.
2. A lessee (except an organization) who leases the goods "primarily for a personal, family, or household purpose."
3. Total lease payments that are less than a dollar amount set by state statute.

To ensure special protection for consumers, certain provisions of Article 2A apply only to consumer leases. For instance, one provision states that a consumer may recover attorneys' fees if a court finds that a term in a consumer lease contract is unconscionable [UCC 2A–108(4)(a)].

The Formation of Sales and Lease Contracts

In regard to the formation of sales and lease contracts, Article 2 and Article 2A of the UCC modify common law contract rules in several ways. Remember, though, that parties to sales contracts are normally free to establish whatever terms they wish.

The UCC comes into play only when the parties have failed to provide in their contract for a contingency that later gives rise to a dispute. The UCC makes this clear time and again by using such phrases as "unless the parties otherwise agree" or "absent a contrary agreement by the parties."

Offer

In general contract law, the moment a definite offer is met by an unqualified acceptance, a binding contract is formed. In commercial sales transactions, the verbal exchanges, correspondence, and actions of the parties may not reveal exactly when a binding contractual obligation arises. The UCC states that an agreement sufficient to constitute a contract can exist even if the moment of its making is undetermined [UCC 2–204(2), 2A–204(2)].

Open Terms

Remember from pages 262 and 263 of Chapter 10 that under the common law of contracts, an offer must be definite enough for the parties (and the courts) to ascertain its essential terms when it is accepted. In contrast, the UCC states that a sales or lease contract will not fail for indefiniteness even if one or more terms are left open as long as (1) the parties intended to make a contract and (2) there is a reasonably certain basis for the court to grant an appropriate remedy [UCC 2–204(3), 2A–204(3)].

KNOW THIS

Under the UCC, it is the actions of the parties that determine whether they intended to form a contract.

The UCC provides numerous *open-term* provisions (discussed next) that can be used to fill the gaps in a contract. Thus, if a dispute occurs, all that is necessary to prove the existence of a contract is an indication (such as a purchase order) that there is a contract. Missing terms can be proved by evidence, or a court can presume that the parties intended whatever is reasonable under the circumstances.

The *quantity* of goods involved must be expressly stated in the contract, however. If the quantity term is left open, the courts will have no basis for determining a remedy.

Open Price Term

If the parties have not agreed on a price, the court will determine a "reasonable price at the time for delivery" [UCC 2–305(1)]. If either the buyer or the seller is to determine the price, the price is to be fixed (set) in good faith [UCC 2–305(2)]. Under the UCC, *good faith* means honesty in fact and the observance of reasonable commercial standards of fair dealing in the trade [UCC 2–103(1)(b)]. The concepts of *good faith* and *commercial reasonableness* permeate the UCC.

Sometimes, the price fails to be fixed (specified) through the fault of one of the parties. In that situation, the other party can treat the contract as canceled or specify a reasonable price. **EXAMPLE 15.2** Perez and Merrick enter into a contract for the sale of unfinished doors and agree that Perez will determine the price. Perez refuses to specify the price. Merrick can either treat the contract as canceled or set a reasonable price [UCC 2–305(3)]. ●

Open Payment Term

When parties do not specify payment terms, payment is due at the time and place at which the buyer is to receive the goods [UCC 2–310(a)]. The buyer can tender payment using any commercially normal or acceptable means, such as a check or credit card. If the seller demands payment in cash, however, the buyer must be given a reasonable time to obtain it [UCC 2–511(2)].

KNOW THIS

The common law requires that the parties make their terms definite before they have a contract. The UCC applies general commercial standards to make the terms of a contract definite.

CASE EXAMPLE 15.3 Max Alexander agreed to purchase hay from Wagner's farm. Alexander left his truck and trailer at the farm for the seller to load the hay. Nothing was said about when payment was due, and the parties were unaware of the UCC's rules. When Alexander came back to get the hay, a dispute broke out. Alexander claimed that he had been given less hay than he had ordered and argued that he did not have to pay at that time. Wagner refused to release the hay (or the vehicles on which the hay was loaded) until Alexander paid for it. Eventually, Alexander jumped into his truck and drove off without paying for the hay—for which he was later prosecuted for the crime of theft (see Chapter 6). Because the parties had failed to specify when payment was due, UCC 2–310(a) controlled, and payment was due at the time Alexander picked up the hay.[5] •

Open Delivery Term When no delivery terms are specified, the buyer normally takes delivery at the seller's place of business [UCC 2–308(a)]. If the seller has no place of business, the seller's residence is used. When goods are located in some other place and both parties know it, delivery is made there. If the time for shipment or delivery is not clearly specified in the sales contract, the court will infer a "reasonable" time for performance [UCC 2–309(1)].

"Business, more than any other occupation, is a continual dealing with the future. It is a continual calculation, an instinctive exercise in foresight."

Henry R. Luce, 1898–1967
(U.S. editor and publisher)

Duration of an Ongoing Contract A single contract might specify successive performances but not indicate how long the parties are required to deal with each other. In this situation, either party may terminate the ongoing contractual relationship. Principles of good faith and sound commercial practice call for reasonable notification before termination, however, to give the other party time to make substitute arrangements [UCC 2–309(2), (3)].

Options and Cooperation Regarding Performance When the contract contemplates shipment of the goods but does not specify the shipping arrangements, the *seller* has the right to make these arrangements in good faith, using commercial reasonableness in the situation [UCC 2–311].

When a sales contract omits terms relating to the assortment of goods, the *buyer* can specify the assortment. **EXAMPLE 15.4** Petry Drugs, Inc., agrees to purchase one thousand toothbrushes from Marconi's Dental Supply. The toothbrushes come in a variety of colors, but the contract does not specify color. Petry, the buyer, has the right to take six hundred blue toothbrushes and four hundred green ones if it wishes. Petry, however, must exercise good faith and commercial reasonableness in making its selection [UCC 2–311]. •

Requirements and Output Contracts

Normally, if the parties do not specify a quantity, a court will have no basis for determining a remedy. No contract is formed because there is almost no way to determine objectively what is a reasonable quantity of goods for someone to buy (whereas a court can objectively determine a reasonable price for particular goods by looking at the market). Nevertheless, the UCC recognizes two exceptions involving requirements and output contracts [UCC 2–306(1)].

Requirements Contract An agreement in which a buyer agrees to purchase and the seller agrees to sell all or up to a stated amount of what the buyer needs or requires.

Requirements Contracts In a **requirements contract,** the buyer agrees to purchase and the seller agrees to sell all or up to a stated amount of what the buyer *needs* or *requires*. **EXAMPLE 15.5** Umpqua Cannery forms a contract with Al Garcia. The cannery agrees to purchase from Garcia, and Garcia agrees to sell to the cannery, all of the green beans that the cannery needs or requires during the following summer. •

There is implicit consideration in a requirements contract because the buyer (the cannery, in this situation) gives up the right to buy goods (green beans, in this example) from any other seller, and this forfeited right creates a legal detriment (that is, consideration).

Requirements contracts are common in the business world and normally are enforceable. In contrast, if the buyer promises to purchase only if the buyer *wishes* to do so, or

5. *State v. Alexander,* 186 Or.App. 600, 64 P.3d 1148 (2003).

if the buyer reserves the right to buy the goods from someone other than the seller, the promise is illusory (without consideration) and unenforceable by either party.

Output Contract An agreement in which a seller agrees to sell and a buyer agrees to buy all or up to a stated amount of what the seller produces.

Output Contracts In an **output contract,** the seller agrees to sell and the buyer agrees to buy all or up to a stated amount of what the seller *produces*. **EXAMPLE 15.6** Al Garcia forms a contract with Umpqua Cannery. Garcia agrees to sell to the cannery, and the cannery agrees to purchase from Garcia, all of the beans that Garcia produces on his farm during the following summer. ● Again, because the seller essentially forfeits the right to sell goods to another buyer, there is implicit consideration in an output contract.

The UCC imposes a *good faith limitation* on requirements and output contracts. The quantity under such contracts is the amount of requirements or the amount of output that occurs during a *normal* production year. The actual quantity purchased or sold cannot be unreasonably disproportionate to normal or comparable prior requirements or output [UCC 2–306(1)].

PREVENTING LEGAL DISPUTES

If a business owner leaves certain terms of a sales or lease contract open, the UCC allows a court to supply the missing terms. Although this rule can sometimes be advantageous (to establish that a contract existed, for instance), it can also be a major disadvantage. If a party fails to state a price in the contract offer, for example, a court will impose a reasonable price by looking at the market price of similar goods *at the time of delivery*. Thus, instead of receiving the usual price for the goods, a business will receive what a court considers a reasonable price when the goods are delivered. Therefore, when drafting contracts for the sale or lease of goods, make sure that the contract clearly states any terms that are essential to the bargain, particularly the price. It is generally better to establish the terms of a contract than to leave it up to a court to determine what terms are reasonable after a dispute has arisen.

Merchant's Firm Offer

Under regular contract principles, an offer can be revoked at any time before acceptance. The major common law exception is an *option contract* (discussed in Chapter 10), in which the offeree pays consideration for the offeror's irrevocable promise to keep the offer open for a stated period. The UCC creates a second exception for firm offers made by a merchant to sell, buy, or lease goods.

Firm Offer An offer (by a merchant) that is irrevocable without the necessity of consideration for a stated period of time or, if no definite period is stated, for a reasonable time (neither period to exceed three months).

A **firm offer** arises when a merchant-offeror gives *assurances* in a *signed writing* that the offer will remain open. The offer must be both *written* and *signed* by the offeror.[6] When a firm offer is contained in a form contract prepared by the offeree, the offeror must also sign a separate assurance of the firm offer. A merchant's firm offer is irrevocable without the necessity of consideration[7] for the stated period or, if no definite period is stated, a reasonable period (neither period to exceed three months) [UCC 2–205, 2A–205].

EXAMPLE 15.7 Osaka, a used-car dealer, e-mails Saucedo on January 1 stating, "I have a 2013 Kia Sportage on the lot that I'll sell you for $18,000 any time between now and January 31." This e-mail creates a firm offer, and Osaka will be liable for breach if he sells that Kia Sportage to someone other than Saucedo before January 31. ●

KNOW THIS

The UCC provides that acceptance can be made by any means that is reasonable under the circumstances—including prompt shipment of the goods.

Acceptance

Acceptance of an offer to buy, sell, or lease goods generally may be made in any reasonable manner and by any reasonable means. The UCC permits acceptance of an offer to buy goods "either by a prompt *promise* to ship or by the prompt or current shipment of

6. *Signed* includes any symbol executed or adopted by a party with a present intention to authenticate a writing [UCC 1–201(39)]. A complete signature is not required. Therefore, initials, a thumbprint, a trade name, or any mark used in lieu of a written signature will suffice, regardless of its location on the document.

7. If the offeree pays consideration, then an option contract (not a merchant's firm offer) is formed.

conforming or nonconforming goods" [UCC 2–206(1)(b)]. *Conforming goods* accord with the contract's terms, whereas *nonconforming goods* do not.

The prompt shipment of nonconforming goods constitutes both an acceptance, which creates a contract, and a breach of that contract. This rule does not apply if the seller **seasonably** (within a reasonable amount of time) notifies the buyer that the nonconforming shipment is offered only as an *accommodation,* or a favor. The notice of accommodation must clearly indicate to the buyer that the shipment does not constitute an acceptance and that, therefore, no contract has been formed.

Seasonably Within a specified time period or, if no period is specified, within a reasonable time.

EXAMPLE 15.8 McFarrell Pharmacy orders five cases of Johnson & Johnson 3-by-5-inch gauze pads from H.T. Medical Supply, Inc. If H.T. ships five cases of Xeroform 3-by-5-inch gauze pads instead, the shipment acts as both an acceptance of McFarrell's offer and a *breach* of the resulting contract. McFarrell may sue H.T. for any appropriate damages. If, however, H.T. notifies McFarrell that the Xeroform gauze pads are being shipped *as an accommodation*—because H.T. has only Xeroform pads in stock—the shipment will constitute a counteroffer, not an acceptance. A contract will be formed only if McFarrell accepts the Xeroform gauze pads. •

Notice of Acceptance Required

Under the common law, because a unilateral offer invites acceptance by a performance, the offeree need not notify the offeror of performance unless the offeror would not otherwise know about it. In other words, a unilateral offer can be accepted by beginning performance.

The UCC is more stringent than the common law in this regard because it requires notification. Under the UCC, if the offeror is not notified within a reasonable time that the offeree has accepted the contract by beginning performance, then the offeror can treat the offer as having lapsed before acceptance [UCC 2–206(2), 2A–206(2)].

LEARNING OBJECTIVE 2
In a sales contract, if an offeree includes additional or different terms in an acceptance, will a contract result? If so, what happens to these terms?

Additional Terms

Recall from page 264 of Chapter 10 that under the common law, the *mirror image rule* requires that the terms of the acceptance exactly match those of the offer. Thus, if Alderman makes an offer to Beale, and Beale accepts but in the acceptance makes some slight modification to the terms of the offer, there is no contract.

To avoid these problems, the UCC dispenses with the mirror image rule. Generally, the UCC takes the position that if the offeree's response indicates a *definite* acceptance of the offer, a contract is formed even if the acceptance includes additional or different terms from those contained in the offer [UCC 2–207(1)]. Whether the additional terms become part of the contract depends, in part, on whether the parties are nonmerchants or merchants.

In the following case, a party conditioned its acceptance of an offer on the other parties' agreement to additional terms by a specific date. When the parties agreed to the most important terms after the deadline, the court had to decide if there was an enforceable contract.

Case 15.1

WPS, Inc. v. Expro Americas, LLC

Court of Appeals of Texas, First District,
2012 WL 310937 (2012).
www.findlaw.com/casecode[a]

(teekid/iStockphoto.com)

FACTS In April 2006, WPS, Inc., submitted a formal proposal to manufacture equipment for Expro Americas, LLC, and Surface Production Systems, Inc. (SPS). Expro and SPS then submitted two purchase orders. WPS accepted the first purchase order in part and the second order conditionally. Among other things, WPS required that, by April 28, 2006, Expro and SPS give their "full release to proceed" and agree "to pay all valid costs associated with any order cancellation." The parties' negotiations continued, and Expro and SPS eventually submitted a third purchase order on May 9,

a. Under "Popular State Resources," click on "Texas Caselaw." Under "Browse Texas Courts," click on "Court of Appeals of Texas." In the result, enter "WPS, Inc." in the "Party name:" box and click on "Search." When that page opens, click on the case name to access the opinion.

Case 15.1—Continued

2006. The third purchase order did not comply with all of WPS's requirements, but it did give WPS full permission to proceed and agreed that Expro and SPS would pay all cancellation costs. With Expro and SPS's knowledge, WPS then began work under the third purchase order. Expro and SPS soon canceled the order, however, so WPS sent them an invoice for the cancellation costs. At trial, the jury and court concluded that there was a contract and found in WPS's favor. Expro and SPS appealed.

ISSUE Did the parties have a contract even though Expro and SPS did not comply with all the requirements of WPS's conditional acceptance?

DECISION Yes. The Texas appellate court affirmed the judgment for WPS.

REASON The court found that the parties had a contract based on WPS's conditional acceptance and Expro and SPS's third purchase order. It did not matter that Expro and SPS submitted the third purchase order after WPS's deadline of April 28, 2006. Regardless of what WPS originally required, the parties continued their negotiations and "operated as if they had additional time to resolve the outstanding differences." Moreover, Expro and SPS agreed to nearly everything that WPS requested. Most important, they gave WPS "full release to proceed" and agreed "to pay all valid costs associated with any order cancellation." Those terms had been holding up the contract, and SPS's vice president conceded that the "release to proceed" "basically means that one party is in agreement." A jury could have reasonably concluded that, since the parties were in agreement, WPS was contractually obligated to move forward with its work.

CRITICAL THINKING—Legal Consideration *By allowing a party to condition its acceptance on additional terms, does contract law make negotiations more or less efficient? Explain.*

Rules When One Party or Both Parties Are Nonmerchants If one (or both) of the parties is a *nonmerchant*, the contract is formed according to the terms of the original offer submitted by the original offeror and not according to the additional terms of the acceptance [UCC 2–207(2)].

EXAMPLE 15.9 Tolsen offers in writing to sell his laptop and printer to Valdez for $1,500. Valdez replies to Tolsen stating, "I accept your offer to purchase your laptop and printer for $1,500. I *would like* a box of laser printer paper and two extra toner cartridges to be included in the purchase price." Valdez has given Tolsen a definite expression of acceptance (creating a contract), even though the acceptance also *suggests* an added term for the offer. Because Tolsen is not a merchant, the additional term is merely a proposal (suggestion), and Tolsen is not legally obligated to comply with that term. ●

Rules When Both Parties Are Merchants The drafters of the UCC created a special rule for merchants to avoid the "battle of the forms," which occurs when two merchants exchange separate standard forms containing different contract terms.

Under UCC 2–207(2), in contracts *between merchants,* the additional terms *automatically* become part of the contract unless one of the following conditions exists:

1. The original offer expressly limited acceptance to its terms.
2. The new or changed terms materially alter the contract.
3. The offeror objects to the new or changed terms within a reasonable period of time.

Generally, if the modification does not involve any unreasonable element of surprise or hardship for the offeror, the court will hold that the modification did not materially alter the contract. Courts also consider the parties' prior dealings and course of performance when determining whether the alteration is material.

Conditioned on Offeror's Assent Regardless of merchant status, the UCC provides that the offeree's expression cannot be construed as an acceptance if it contains additional or different terms that are explicitly conditioned on the offeror's assent to those terms

[UCC 2–207(1)]. **EXAMPLE 15.10** Philips offers to sell Hundert 650 pounds of turkey thighs at a specified price and with specified delivery terms. Hundert responds, "I accept your offer for 650 pounds of turkey thighs *on the condition that you give me ninety days to pay for them."* Hundert's response will be construed not as an acceptance but as a counteroffer, which Philips may or may not accept. •

Additional Terms May Be Stricken The UCC provides yet another option for dealing with conflicting terms in the parties' writings. Section 2–207(3) states that conduct by both parties that recognizes the existence of a contract is sufficient to establish a contract for the sale of goods even though the writings of the parties do not otherwise establish a contract. In this situation, "the terms of the particular contract will consist of those terms on which the writings of the parties agree, together with any supplementary terms incorporated under any other provisions of this Act."

In a dispute over contract terms, this provision allows a court simply to strike from the contract those terms on which the parties do not agree. **EXAMPLE 15.11** SMT Marketing orders goods over the phone from Brigg Sales, Inc., which ships the goods with an acknowledgment form (confirming the order) to SMT. SMT accepts and pays for the goods. The parties' writings do not establish a contract, but there is no question that a contract exists. If a dispute arises over the terms, such as the extent of any warranties, UCC 2–207(3) provides the governing rule. •

Consideration

The common law rule that a contract requires consideration also applies to sales and lease contracts. Unlike the common law, however, the UCC does not require a contract modification to be supported by new consideration. An agreement modifying a contract for the sale or lease of goods "needs no consideration to be binding" [UCC 2–209(1), 2A–208(1)]. Of course, a contract modification must be sought in good faith [UCC 1–304].

In some situations, an agreement to modify a sales or lease contract without consideration must be in writing to be enforceable. If the contract itself prohibits any changes to the contract unless they are in a signed writing, for instance, then only those changes agreed to in a signed writing are enforceable.

If a consumer (nonmerchant buyer) is dealing with a merchant and the merchant supplies the form that contains a prohibition against oral modification, the consumer must sign a separate acknowledgment of such a clause [UCC 2–209(2), 2A–208(2)]. Also, any modification that brings a sales contract under Article 2's Statute of Frauds provision (discussed next) usually must be in writing to be enforceable.

The Statute of Frauds

KNOW THIS

It has been proposed that the UCC be revised to eliminate the Statute of Frauds.

The UCC contains Statute of Frauds provisions covering sales and lease contracts. Under these provisions, sales contracts for goods priced at $500 or more and lease contracts requiring payments of $1,000 or more must be in writing to be enforceable [UCC 2–201(1), 2A–201(1)]. (These low threshold amounts may eventually be raised.)

Sufficiency of the Writing

The UCC has greatly relaxed the requirements for the sufficiency of a writing to satisfy the Statute of Frauds. A writing or a memorandum will be sufficient as long as it indicates that the parties intended to form a contract and as long as it is signed by the party (or agent of the party—see Chapter 23) against whom enforcement is sought. The contract normally will not be enforceable beyond the quantity of goods shown in the writing, however. All other terms can be proved in court by oral testimony. For leases, the writing must reasonably identify and describe the goods leased and the lease term.

Special Rules for Contracts between Merchants Once again, the UCC provides a special rule for merchants in sales transactions (there is no corresponding rule that applies to leases under Article 2A). Merchants can satisfy the Statute of Frauds if, after the parties have agreed orally, one of the merchants sends a signed written confirmation to the other merchant within a reasonable time. The communication must indicate the terms of the agreement, and the merchant receiving the confirmation must have reason to know of its contents. Unless the merchant who receives the confirmation gives written notice of objection to its contents within ten days after receipt, the writing is sufficient against the receiving merchant, even though she or he has not signed anything [UCC 2–201(2)]. Generally, courts even hold that it is sufficient if a merchant sends an e-mail confirmation of the agreement.[8]

(Csaba Vanyi/Shutterstock.com)

The buyer and the seller of aircraft parts are both merchants.

EXAMPLE 15.12 Alfonso is a merchant-buyer in Cleveland. He contracts over the telephone to purchase $4,000 worth of spare aircraft parts from Goldstein, a merchant-seller in New York City. Two days later, Goldstein sends a written and signed confirmation detailing the terms of the oral contract, and Alfonso subsequently receives it. If Alfonso does not notify Goldstein in writing of his objection to the contents of the confirmation within ten days of receipt, Alfonso cannot raise the Statute of Frauds as a defense against the enforcement of the oral contract. •

Exceptions In addition to the special rules for merchants, the UCC defines three exceptions to the writing requirements of the Statute of Frauds. An oral contract for the sale of goods priced at $500 or more or the lease of goods involving total payments of $1,000 or more will be enforceable despite the absence of a writing in the circumstances discussed in the following subsections [UCC 2–201(3), 2A–201(4)].

These exceptions and other ways in which sales law differs from general contract law are summarized in Exhibit 15.2 on the next page.

LEARNING OBJECTIVE 3
What exceptions to the writing requirements of the Statute of Frauds are provided in Article 2 and Article 2A of the UCC?

Specially Manufactured Goods An oral contract is enforceable if (1) it is for goods that are specially manufactured for a particular buyer or specially manufactured or obtained for a particular lessee, (2) these goods are not suitable for resale or lease to others in the ordinary course of the seller's or lessor's business, and (3) the seller or lessor has substantially started to manufacture the goods or has made commitments for their manufacture or procurement. In this situation, once the seller or lessor has taken action, the buyer or lessee cannot repudiate the agreement claiming the Statute of Frauds as a defense.

EXAMPLE 15.13 Womach orders custom-made draperies for her new boutique. The price is $6,000, and the contract is oral. When the merchant-seller manufactures the draperies and tenders delivery to Womach, she refuses to pay for them even though the job has been completed on time. Womach claims that she is not liable because the contract was oral. Clearly, if the unique style and color of the draperies make it improbable that the seller can find another buyer, Womach is liable to the seller. Note that the seller must have made a substantial beginning in manufacturing the specialized item prior to the buyer's repudiation. (Here, the manufacture was completed.) Of course, the court must still be convinced by evidence of the terms of the oral contract. •

Admissions An oral contract for the sale or lease of goods is enforceable if the party against whom enforcement of the contract is sought admits in pleadings, testimony, or

8. See, for example, *Bazak International Corp. v. Tarrant Apparel Group*, 378 F.Supp.2d 377 (S.D.N.Y. 2005); and *Great White Bear, LLC v. Mervyns, LLC*, 2007 WL 1295747 (S.D.N.Y. 2007).

other court proceedings that a contract for sale or lease was made. In this situation, the contract will be enforceable even though it was oral, but enforceability will be limited to the quantity of goods admitted.

CASE EXAMPLE 15.14 Gerald Lindgren, a farmer, agreed by phone to sell his crops to Glacial Plains Cooperative. The parties reached four oral agreements: two for the delivery of soybeans and two for the delivery of corn. Lindgren made the soybean deliveries and part of the first corn delivery, but he sold the rest of his corn to another dealer. Glacial Plains bought corn elsewhere, paying a higher price, and then sued Lindgren for breach of contract. In papers filed with the court, Lindgren acknowledged his oral agreements with Glacial Plains and admitted that he did not fully perform. The court applied the admissions exception and held that the four agreements were enforceable.[9] •

Partial Performance An oral contract for the sale or lease of goods is enforceable if payment has been made and accepted or goods have been received and accepted. This is the "partial performance" exception. The oral contract will be enforced at least to the extent that performance *actually* took place.

"Whatever is not nailed down is mine. Whatever I can pry loose is not nailed down."

Collis P. Huntington, 1821–1900 (U.S. railroad builder and owner)

EXAMPLE 15.15 Jamal orally contracts to lease to Opus Enterprises a thousand chairs at $2 each to be used during a one-day concert. Before delivery, Opus sends Jamal a check for $1,000, which Jamal cashes. Later, when Jamal attempts to deliver the chairs, Opus refuses delivery, claiming the Statute of Frauds as a defense, and demands the return of its $1,000. Under the UCC's partial performance rule, Jamal can enforce the oral contract by tender of delivery of five hundred chairs for the $1,000 accepted. Similarly, if Opus had made no payment but had accepted the delivery of five hundred chairs from Jamal, the oral contract would have been enforceable against Opus for $1,000, the lease payment due for the five hundred chairs delivered. •

Parol Evidence

Recall from page 320 in Chapter 12 that *parol evidence* is testimony or other evidence of the parties' prior negotiations, prior agreements, or contemporaneous oral agreements. When the parties to a sales contract set forth its terms in a confirmatory memorandum

9. *Glacial Plains Cooperative v. Lindgren*, 759 N.W.2d 661 (Minn.App. 2009).

Exhibit 15.2 Major Differences between Contract Law and Sales Law

TOPIC	CONTRACT LAW	SALES LAW
Contract Terms	Contract must contain all material terms.	Open terms are acceptable, if parties intended to form a contract, but the contract is not enforceable beyond quantity term.
Acceptance	Mirror image rule applies. If additional terms are added in acceptance, counteroffer is created.	Additional terms will not negate acceptance unless acceptance is made expressly conditional on assent to the additional terms.
Contract Modification	Modification requires consideration.	Modification does not require consideration.
Irrevocable Offers	Option contracts (with consideration).	Merchants' firm offers (without consideration).
Statute of Frauds Requirements	All material terms must be included in the writing.	Writing is required only for the sale of goods of $500 or more, but contract is not enforceable beyond quantity specified. Merchants can satisfy the requirement by a confirmatory memorandum evidencing their agreement. *Exceptions:* 1. Specially manufactured goods. 2. Admissions by party against whom enforcement is sought. 3. Partial performance.

or in other writing that is intended as a complete and final statement of their agreement, the contract is considered *fully integrated,* and the *parol evidence rule* applies. The terms of a fully integrated contract cannot be contradicted by evidence of any prior agreements or contemporaneous oral agreements.

If, however, the writing contains some of the terms the parties agreed on but not others, the contract is not fully integrated. When a court finds that the terms of a sales contract are *not fully integrated* or are ambiguous, the court may allow evidence of *consistent additional terms* to explain or supplement the terms stated in the contract. The court may also allow the parties to submit evidence of *course of dealing, usage of trade,* or *course of performance* [UCC 2–202, 2A–202]. A court will not under any circumstances allow the parties to submit evidence that contradicts the stated terms (this is also the rule under the common law).

Course of Dealing and Usage of Trade

Under the UCC, the meaning of any agreement, evidenced by the language of the parties and by their actions, must be interpreted in light of commercial practices and other surrounding circumstances. In interpreting a commercial agreement, the court will assume that the course of prior dealing between the parties and the usage of trade were taken into account when the agreement was phrased.

Course of Dealing Prior conduct between the parties to a contract that establishes a common basis for their understanding.

Course of Dealing A **course of dealing** is a sequence of previous actions and communications between the parties to a particular transaction that establishes a common basis for their understanding [UCC 1–303(b)]. A course of dealing is restricted to that previous sequence of actions and communications. Under the UCC, a course of dealing between the parties is relevant in ascertaining the meaning of the parties' agreement. It may give particular meaning to specific terms of the agreement, and may supplement or qualify the terms of its agreement [UCC 1–303(d)]. (Usage of trade and course of performance may be relevant for the same purposes, as will be discussed next.)

Usage of Trade Any practice or method of dealing that is so regularly observed in a place, vocation, or trade that parties justifiably expect it will be observed in their transaction.

Usage of Trade Any practice or method of dealing that is so regularly observed in a place, vocation, or trade that the parties justifiably expect (or should expect) it to be observed in their transaction is a **usage of trade** [UCC 1–303(c)].

EXAMPLE 15.16 Phat Khat Loans, Inc., hires Title Review, LLC, to search the public records for prior claims on potential borrowers' assets. Title's invoice states, "Liability limited to amount of fee." In the search industry, liability limits are common. After conducting many searches for Phat Khat, Title reports that there are no claims with respect to Main St. Autos. Phat Khat loans $100,000 to Main, with payment guaranteed by Main's assets. When Main defaults on the loan, Phat Khat learns that another lender has priority to Main's assets under a previous claim. In Phat Khat's suit against Title for breach of contract, Title's liability is limited to the amount of its fee. The statement in the invoice was part of the contract between Phat Khat and Title, according to the usage of trade in the industry and the parties' course of dealing. •

Course of Performance The conduct that occurs under the terms of a particular agreement, which indicates what the parties to that agreement intended it to mean.

Course of Performance

A **course of performance** is the conduct that occurs under the terms of a particular agreement [UCC 1–303(a)]. Presumably, the parties themselves know best what they meant by their words, and the course of performance actually undertaken under their agreement is the best indication of what they meant [UCC 2–208(1), 2A–207(1)].

EXAMPLE 15.17 Janson's Lumber Company contracts with Barrymore to sell Barrymore a specified number of "two-by-fours." The lumber does not in fact measure 2 inches by 4 inches but rather 1⅞ inches by 3¾ inches. Janson's agrees to deliver the lumber in five deliveries, and Barrymore, without objection, accepts the lumber in the first three deliveries.

On the fourth delivery, however, Barrymore objects that the two-by-fours do not measure 2 inches by 4 inches.

The course of performance in this transaction—that is, Barrymore's acceptance of three deliveries without objection under the agreement—is relevant in determining that here the term *two-by-four* actually means "1⅞ by 3¾." Janson's can also prove that two-by-fours need not be exactly 2 inches by 4 inches by applying course of prior dealing, usage of trade, or both. Janson's can, for example, show that in previous transactions, Barrymore took 1⅞-by-3¾-inch lumber without objection. In addition, Janson's can show that in the lumber trade, two-by-fours are commonly 1⅞ inches by 3¾ inches. •

Rules of Construction The UCC provides *rules of construction* for interpreting contracts. Express terms, course of performance, course of dealing, and usage of trade are to be construed together when they do not contradict one another. When such a construction is unreasonable, however, the following order of priority controls: (1) express terms, (2) course of performance, (3) course of dealing, and (4) usage of trade [UCC 1–303(e), 2–208(2), 2A–207(2)].

Unconscionability

As discussed on page 296 in Chapter 11, an unconscionable contract is one that is so unfair and one sided that it would be unreasonable to enforce it. The UCC allows the court to evaluate a contract or any clause in a contract, and if the court deems it to have been unconscionable at the time it was made, the court can (1) refuse to enforce the contract, (2) enforce the remainder of the contract without the unconscionable clause, or (3) limit the application of any unconscionable clauses to avoid an unconscionable result [UCC 2–302, 2A–108].

The following *Classic Case* illustrates an early application of the UCC's unconscionability provisions.

Classic Case 15.2

(JazzIRT/iStockphoto.com)

Can a retailer sell a freezer at four times its wholesale price?

Jones v. Star Credit Corp.

Supreme Court of New York, Nassau County, 59 Misc.2d 189, 298 N.Y.S.2d 264 (1969).

HISTORICAL AND ECONOMIC SETTING *In the sixth century, Roman civil law allowed the courts to rescind a contract if the goods that were the subject of the contract had a market value that was less than half the contract price. This same ratio has appeared over the last decade in many cases in which courts have found contract clauses to be unconscionable under UCC 2–302 on the ground that the price was excessive. Most of the litigants who have used UCC 2–302 successfully have been consumers who were poor or otherwise at a disadvantage. In a Connecticut case, for example, the court held that a contract requiring a person who was poor to make payments totaling $1,248 for a television set that ordinarily sold for $499 was unconscionable.*[a] *The seller had not told the buyer the full purchase price. In a New York case, the court held that a contract requiring a Spanish-speaking consumer to make payments totaling nearly $1,150 for a freezer that had a wholesale price of less than $350 was unconscionable.*[b] *The contract was in English, and the salesperson did not translate or explain it.*

FACTS The Joneses, the plaintiffs, agreed to purchase a freezer for $900 as the result of a salesperson's visit to their home. Tax and financing charges raised the total price to $1,234.80. At trial, the freezer was found to have a maximum retail value of approximately $300. The plaintiffs, who had made payments totaling $619.88, brought a suit in a New York state court

a. *Murphy v. McNamara*, 36 Conn.Supp. 183, 416 A.2d 170 (1979).

b. *Frostifresh Corp. v. Reynoso*, 52 Misc.2d 26, 274 N.Y.S.2d 757 (1966), reversed on issue of damages, 54 Misc.2d 119, 281 N.Y.S.2d 946 (1967).

Classic Case 15.2—Continued

to have the purchase contract declared unconscionable under the UCC.

ISSUE Could this contract be denied enforcement on the ground of unconscionability?

DECISION Yes. The court held that the contract was not enforceable as it stood, and the contract was reformed so that no further payments were required.

REASON The court relied on UCC 2–302(1), which states that if "the court as a matter of law finds the contract or any clause of the contract to have been unconscionable at the time it was made, the court may . . . so limit the application of any unconscionable clause as to avoid any unconscionable result." The court then considered the disparity between the $900 purchase price and the $300 retail value, as well as the fact that the credit charges alone exceeded the retail value. These excessive charges were exacted despite the seller's knowledge of the plaintiffs' limited resources. The court reformed the contract so that the plaintiffs' payments, amounting to more than $600, were regarded as payment in full.

IMPACT OF THIS CASE ON TODAY'S LAW *This early case illustrates the approach that many courts today take when deciding whether a sales contract is unconscionable—an approach that focuses on "excessive" price and unequal bargaining power.*

Title and Risk of Loss

"To win, you have to risk loss."

Jean-Claude Killy, 1943–present (French Alpine skier)

Before the creation of the UCC, *title*—the right of ownership—was the central concept in sales law and controlled all issues of rights and remedies of the parties to a sales contract. In some situations, title is still relevant under the UCC, and the UCC has special rules for determining who has title. (These rules do not apply to leased goods, obviously, because title remains with the lessor, or owner, of the goods.) In most situations, however, the UCC has replaced the concept of title with three other concepts: (1) identification, (2) risk of loss, and (3) insurable interest.

Identification

Identification In a sale of goods, the express designation of the goods provided for in the contract.

Before any interest in specific goods can pass from the seller or lessor to the buyer or lessee, the goods must exist and be identified as the specific goods designated in the contract. **Identification** takes place when specific goods are designated as the subject matter of a sales or lease contract.

Title and risk of loss cannot pass from seller to buyer unless the goods are identified to the contract. (Remember that title to leased goods does not pass to the lessee.) Identification is important because it gives the buyer or lessee the right to insure the goods and the right to recover from third parties who damage the goods.

The parties can agree in their contract on when identification will take place (although it will not effectively pass title and risk of loss to the buyer on future goods, such as unborn cattle). If the parties do not so specify, however, the UCC provisions discussed here determine when identification takes place [UCC 2–501(1), 2A–217].

Existing Goods

If the contract calls for the sale or lease of specific goods that are already in existence, identification takes place at the time the contract is made. **EXAMPLE 15.18** You contract to purchase or lease a fleet of five cars designated by their vehicle identification numbers (VINs). Because the cars are identified by their VINs, identification has taken place, and you acquire an insurable interest in them at the time of contracting. ●

Future Goods

Goods that are not both existing and identified to the contract are called *future goods*. For instance, if a sale involves unborn animals to be born within twelve months after contracting, identification takes place when the animals are conceived. If a lease involves any unborn animals, identification also occurs when the animals are conceived. If a sale involves crops that are to be harvested within twelve months (or the next harvest season occurring after contracting, whichever is longer), identification takes place when the crops are planted. Otherwise, identification takes place when the crops begin to grow.

In a sale or lease of any other future goods, identification occurs when the goods are shipped, marked, or otherwise designated by the seller or lessor as the goods to which the contract refers.

Goods That Are Part of a Larger Mass

As a general rule, goods that are part of a larger mass are identified when the goods are marked, shipped, or somehow designated by the seller or lessor as the particular goods that are the subject of the contract. **EXAMPLE 15.19** A buyer orders 1,000 cases of beans from a 10,000-case lot. Until the seller separates the 1,000 cases of beans from the 10,000-case lot, title and risk of loss remain with the seller. •

Fungible Goods Goods that are alike by physical nature, agreement, or trade usage.

A common exception to this rule involves fungible goods. **Fungible goods** are goods that are alike by physical nature, by agreement, or by trade usage. They are usually stored in large containers—for example, specific grades or types of wheat, oil, and inexpensive wine. If two or more persons own an interest in fungible goods as *tenants in common* (see Chapter 36), one of those persons can pass title and risk of loss to a buyer without an actual separation of the goods. The buyer replaces the seller as an owner in common [UCC 2–105(4)].

Passage of Title

Once goods exist and are identified, the provisions of UCC 2–401 apply to the passage of title. In nearly all subsections of UCC 2–401, the words "unless otherwise explicitly agreed" appear, meaning that any explicit understanding between the buyer and the seller determines when title passes. Without an explicit agreement to the contrary, *title passes to the buyer at the time and the place the seller performs by delivering the goods* [UCC 2–401(2)]. For instance, if a person buys cattle at a livestock auction, title will pass to the buyer when the cattle are physically delivered to him or her (unless, of course, the parties agree otherwise).

If a seller gives up possession or control of goods, but keeps a "Certificate of Origin" supposedly showing ownership, has there been a delivery sufficient to pass title? That was the question in the following case.

Case 15.3

United States v. 2007 Custom Motorcycle

United States District Court, District of Arizona, __ F.Supp.2d __ (2011).

(Margo Harrison/Shutterstock.com)

When does passage of title occur?

FACTS Timothy Allen commissioned a custom motorcycle from Indy Route 66 Cycles, Inc. Indy built the motorcycle and issued a "Certificate of Origin." Two years later, federal law enforcement officers arrested Allen on drug charges and seized his home and other property. The officers also seized the Indy-made motorcycle from the garage of the home of Allen's sister, Tena. The government alleged that the motorcycle was subject to forfeiture as the proceeds of drug trafficking. Indy filed a claim against the government, arguing that it owned the motorcycle, as evidenced by the "Certificate of Origin," which the company still possessed. Indy claimed that it had been keeping the motorcycle in storage. The government filed a motion to strike the claim, asserting that title to the motorcycle had passed when it was delivered to Allen.

ISSUE Did ownership to the motorcycle pass at the time that Indy gave Allen possession and control over it?

Case 15.3—Continued

DECISION Yes. The district court issued a ruling in the government's favor and granted the motion to strike Indy's claim.

REASON Under UCC 2–401(2), "unless otherwise explicitly agreed, title passes to the buyer at the time and place at which the seller completes his performance with reference to the physical delivery of the goods." In the sales transaction in this case, the parties did not "otherwise explicitly agree" to different terms. Thus, the critical question was whether Indy had delivered the cycle to Allen. Testimony by Indy's former vice president, Vince Ballard, was "inconclusive" but implied that Indy had delivered the motorcycle to Allen. The cycle was found in Tena's garage, which also indicated that Indy had delivered it to Allen. Thus, Indy had given up possession of the cycle to Allen. This was sufficient to pass title even though Indy had kept a "Certificate of Origin." As a consequence, the motorcycle was subject to forfeiture as the proceeds of drug trafficking.

WHAT IF THE FACTS WERE DIFFERENT? *Suppose that Indy had given the "Certificate of Origin" to Allen and had kept the motorcycle. Would the result have been different? Explain.*

Shipment Contract A contract for the sale of goods in which the seller is required or authorized to ship the goods by carrier. The seller assumes liability for any losses or damage to the goods until they are delivered to the carrier.

Destination Contract A contract for the sale of goods in which the seller is required or authorized to ship the goods by carrier and tender delivery of the goods at a particular destination. The seller assumes liability for any losses or damage to the goods until they are tendered at the destination specified in the contract.

Document of Title A paper exchanged in the regular course of business that evidences the right to possession of goods (for example, a bill of lading or a warehouse receipt).

LEARNING OBJECTIVE 4

Risk of loss does not necessarily pass with title. If the parties to a contract do not expressly agree when risk passes and the goods are to be delivered without movement by the seller, when does risk pass?

Shipment and Destination Contracts

Unless otherwise agreed, delivery arrangements can determine when title passes from the seller to the buyer. In a **shipment contract,** the seller is required or authorized to ship goods by carrier, such as a trucking company. Under a shipment contract, the seller is required only to deliver conforming goods into the hands of a carrier, and title passes to the buyer at the time and place of shipment [UCC 2–401(2)(a)]. Generally, *all contracts are assumed to be shipment contracts if nothing to the contrary is stated in the contract.*

In a **destination contract,** the seller is required to deliver the goods to a particular destination, usually directly to the buyer, but sometimes to another party designated by the buyer. Title passes to the buyer when the goods are *tendered* at that destination [UCC 2–401(2)(b)]. As you will read in Chapter 16, *tender of delivery* occurs when the seller places or holds conforming goods at the buyer's disposal (with any necessary notice), enabling the buyer to take possession [UCC 2–503(1)].

Delivery without Movement of the Goods

When the sales contract does not call for the seller to ship or deliver the goods (when the buyer is to pick up the goods), the passage of title depends on whether the seller must deliver a **document of title,** such as a bill of lading or a warehouse receipt, to the buyer. A *bill of lading* is a receipt for goods that is signed by a carrier and serves as a contract for the transport of the goods. A *warehouse receipt* is a receipt issued by a warehouser for goods stored in a warehouse.

When a document of title is required, title passes to the buyer *when and where the document is delivered.* Thus, if the goods are stored in a warehouse, title passes to the buyer when the appropriate documents are delivered to the buyer. The goods never move. In fact, the buyer can choose to leave the goods at the same warehouse for a period of time, and the buyer's title to those goods will be unaffected.

When no documents of title are required and delivery is made without moving the goods, title passes at the time and place the sales contract is made, if the goods have already been identified. If the goods have not been identified, title does not pass until identification occurs [UCC 2–401(3)]. **EXAMPLE 15.20** Juarez sells lumber to Bodan. They agree that Bodan will pick up the lumber at the lumberyard. If the lumber has been identified (segregated, marked, or in any other way distinguished from all other lumber), title passes to Bodan when the contract is signed. If the lumber is still in large storage bins at the lumberyard, title does not pass to Bodan until the particular pieces of lumber to be sold under this contract are identified. •

Sales or Leases by Nonowners

Problems occur when a person who acquires goods with *imperfect* title attempts to sell or lease them. Sections 2–402 and 2–403 of the UCC deal with the rights of two parties who lay claim to the same goods, sold with imperfect title. Generally, a buyer acquires at least whatever title the seller has to the goods sold.

Void Title

A buyer may unknowingly purchase goods from a seller who is not the owner of the goods. If the seller is a thief, the seller's title is *void*—legally, no title exists. Thus, the buyer acquires no title, and the real owner can reclaim the goods from the buyer. If the goods were leased, the same result would occur because the lessor has no leasehold interest to transfer.

EXAMPLE 15.21 If Saki steals diamonds owned by Maren, Saki has a *void title* to those diamonds. If Saki sells the diamonds to Shannon, Maren can reclaim them from Shannon even though Shannon acted in good faith and honestly was not aware that the goods were stolen. • (Article 2A contains similar provisions for leases.)

Voidable Title

A seller has *voidable title* if the goods that she or he is selling were obtained by fraud, paid for with a check that is later *dishonored*—that is, returned for insufficient funds—purchased from a minor, or purchased on credit when the seller was insolvent. Under the UCC, a person is **insolvent** when that person ceases to pay his or her debts in the ordinary course of business, cannot pay his or her debts as they come due, or is insolvent within the meaning of federal bankruptcy law [UCC 1–201(23)].

Insolvent A condition in which a person cannot pay his or her debts as they become due or ceases to pay debts in the ordinary course of business.

Good Faith Purchaser A purchaser who buys without notice of any circumstance that would cause a person of ordinary prudence to inquire as to whether the seller has valid title to the goods being sold.

In contrast to a seller with *void title,* a seller with *voidable title* has the power to transfer good title to a good faith purchaser for value. A **good faith purchaser** is one who buys without knowledge of circumstances that would make a person of ordinary prudence inquire about the validity of the seller's title to the goods. One who purchases *for value* gives legally sufficient consideration (value) for the goods purchased. The real, or original, owner cannot recover goods from a good faith purchaser for value [UCC 2–403(1)].[10] If the buyer of the goods is not a good faith purchaser for value, then the actual owner of the goods can reclaim them from the buyer (or from the seller, if the goods are still in the seller's possession). Exhibit 15.3 on the facing page illustrates these concepts.

The Entrustment Rule

According to Section 2–403(2), when goods are entrusted to a merchant *who deals in goods of that kind,* the merchant has the power to transfer all rights to *a buyer in the ordinary course of business.* This is known as the **entrustment rule.** Entrusted goods include both goods that are turned over to the merchant and purchased goods left with the merchant for later delivery or pickup [UCC 2–403(3)]. Article 2A provides a similar rule for leased goods [UCC 2A–305(2)].

Entrustment Rule The rule that entrusting goods to a merchant who deals in goods of that kind gives that merchant the power to transfer those goods and all rights to them to a buyer in the ordinary course of business.

A buyer in the ordinary course of business is a person who, in good faith and without knowledge that the sale violates the ownership rights or security interest of a third party, buys in ordinary course from a person (other than a pawnbroker) in the business of selling goods of that kind [UCC 1–201(9)]. (A *security interest* is any interest in personal property that secures the payment of or the performance of an obligation—see Chapter 20.)

KNOW THIS

The purpose of holding most goods in inventory is to turn those goods into revenues by selling them. That is one of the reasons for the entrustment rule.

EXAMPLE 15.22 Jan leaves her watch with a jeweler to be repaired. The jeweler sells new and used watches. The jeweler sells Jan's watch to Kim, a customer, who is unaware that the jeweler has no right to sell it. Kim, as a good faith buyer, gets good title against Jan's claim of ownership.[11] Kim, however, obtains only those rights held by the person entrusting the goods (here, Jan). Suppose that Jan had stolen the watch from Greg and then left it with the jeweler to be repaired. The jeweler then sells it to Kim. In this situation, Kim gets good title against Jan, who entrusted the watch to the jeweler, but not against Greg (the real owner), who neither entrusted the watch to Jan nor authorized Jan to entrust it. •

---

10. The real owner could, of course, sue the person who initially obtained voidable title to the goods.

11. Jan, of course, can sue the jeweler for the tort of trespass to personalty or conversion (see Chapter 4) for the equivalent cash value of the watch.

Exhibit 15.3 Void and Voidable Titles

If goods are transferred from their owner to another by theft, the thief acquires no ownership rights. Because the thief's title is *void*, a later buyer can acquire no title, and the owner can recover the goods. If the transfer occurs by fraud, the transferee acquires a *voidable* title. A later good faith purchaser for value can acquire good title, and the original owner cannot recover the goods.

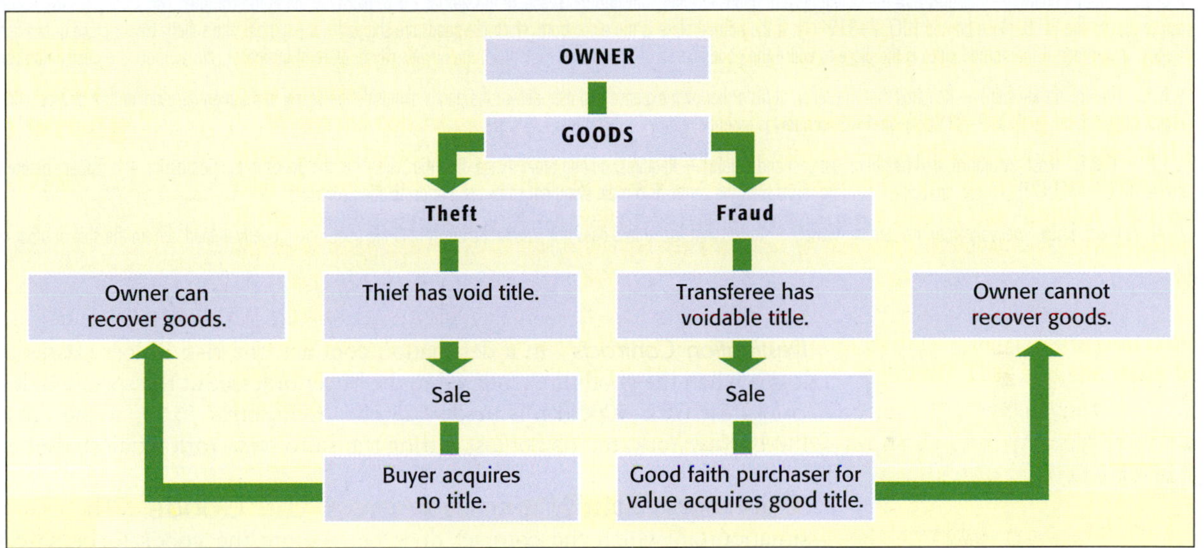

Risk of Loss

Under the UCC, risk of loss does not necessarily pass with title. When risk of loss passes from a seller or lessor to a buyer or lessee is generally determined by the contract between the parties. Sometimes, the contract states expressly when the risk of loss passes. At other times, it does not, and a court must interpret the performance and delivery terms of the contract to determine whether the risk has passed.

Delivery with Movement of the Goods—Carrier Cases

When the contract involves movement of the goods through a common carrier but does not specify when risk of loss passes, the courts first look for specific delivery terms in the contract.

The terms that have traditionally been used in contracts within the United States are listed and defined in Exhibit 15.4 on the following page. These terms determine which party will pay the costs of delivering the goods and who bears the risk of loss. If the contract does not include these terms, then the courts must decide whether the contract is a shipment or a destination contract.

Shipment Contracts In a shipment contract, the seller or lessor is required or authorized to ship goods by carrier, but is not required to deliver them to a particular final destination. The risk of loss in a shipment contract passes to the buyer or lessee when the goods are delivered to the carrier [UCC 2–319(1)(a), 2–509(1)(a), 2A–219(2)(a)].

EXAMPLE 15.23 A seller in Texas sells five hundred cases of grapefruit to a buyer in New York, F.O.B. Houston (free on board in Houston—that is, the buyer pays the transportation charges from Houston). The contract authorizes shipment by carrier. It does not require that the seller tender the grapefruit in New York. Risk passes to the buyer when conforming goods are properly placed in the possession of the carrier. If the goods are damaged in transit, the loss is the buyer's. (Actually, buyers have recourse against carriers, subject to certain limitations, and buyers usually insure the goods from the time the goods leave the seller.) •

Exhibit 15.4 Contract Terms—Definitions

The contract terms listed and defined in this exhibit help to determine which party will bear the costs of delivery and when risk of loss will pass from the seller to the buyer.

F.O.B. (free on board)—Indicates that the selling price of goods includes transportation costs to the specific F.O.B. place named in the contract. The seller pays the expenses and carries the risk of loss to the F.O.B. place named [UCC 2–319(1)]. If the named place is the place from which the goods are shipped (for example, the seller's city or place of business), the contract is a shipment contract. If the named place is the place to which the goods are to be shipped (for example, the buyer's city or place of business), the contract is a destination contract.

F.A.S. (free alongside ship)—Requires that the seller, at his or her own expense and risk, deliver the goods alongside the vessel in the manner usual in that port or on a dock designated and provided by the buyer [UCC 2–319(2)]. An F.A.S. contract is essentially an F.O.B. contract for ships.

C.I.F. or **C.&F.** (cost, insurance, and freight or just cost and freight)—Requires, among other things, that the seller "put the goods in the possession of a carrier" before risk passes to the buyer [UCC 2–320(2)]. (These are basically pricing terms, and the contracts remain shipment contracts, not destination contracts.)

Delivery ex-ship (delivery from the carrying vessel)—Means that risk of loss does not pass to the buyer until the goods are properly unloaded from the ship or other carrier [UCC 2–322].

Destination Contracts In a destination contract, the risk of loss passes to the buyer or lessee when the goods are tendered to the buyer or lessee at the specified destination [UCC 2–319(1)(b), 2–509(1)(b), 2A–219(2)(b)]. In *Example 15.23,* if the contract had been F.O.B. New York, the risk of loss during transit to New York would have been the seller's.

Delivery without Movement of the Goods

The UCC also addresses situations in which the contract does not require the goods to be shipped or moved. Frequently, the buyer or lessee is to pick up the goods from the seller or lessor, or the goods are held by a bailee.

Bailee Under the UCC, a party who, by a bill of lading, warehouse receipt, or other document of title, acknowledges possession of goods and/or contracts to deliver them.

Under the UCC, a **bailee** is a party who, by a bill of lading, warehouse receipt, or other document of title, acknowledges possession of goods and/or contracts to deliver them. A warehousing company, for example, or a trucking company that normally issues documents of title for the goods it receives is a bailee.[12]

Goods Held by the Seller When the seller keeps the goods for pickup, a document of title usually is not used. If the seller is a merchant, risk of loss to goods held by the seller passes to the buyer when the buyer *actually takes physical possession of the goods* [UCC 2–509(3)]. In other words, the merchant bears the risk of loss between the time the contract is formed and the time the buyer picks up the goods.

If the seller is not a merchant, the risk of loss to goods held by the seller passes to the buyer on *tender of delivery* [UCC 2–509(3)]. This means that the seller bears the risk of loss until he or she makes the goods available to the buyer and notifies the buyer that the goods are ready to be picked up. With respect to leases, the risk of loss passes to the lessee on the lessee's receipt of the goods if the lessor is a merchant. Otherwise, the risk passes to the lessee on tender of delivery [UCC 2A–219(2)(c)].

Goods Held by a Bailee When a bailee is holding goods for a person who has contracted to sell them and the goods are to be delivered without being moved, the goods are usually represented by a document of title, such as a bill of lading or a warehouse receipt.

Risk of loss passes to the buyer when (1) the buyer receives a negotiable document of title for the goods, (2) the bailee acknowledges the buyer's right to possess the goods, or (3) the buyer receives a nonnegotiable document of title or a writing (record) directing the bailee to deliver the goods *and* has had a *reasonable time* to present the document to the bailee and demand the goods. Obviously, if the bailee refuses to honor the document, the risk of loss remains with the seller [UCC 2–503(4)(b), 2–509(2)].

12. Bailments will be discussed in Chapter 35.

With respect to leases, if goods held by a bailee are to be delivered without being moved, the risk of loss passes to the lessee on acknowledgment by the bailee of the lessee's right to possession of the goods [UCC 2A–219(2)(b)].

Risk of Loss When the Contract Is Breached

When a sales or lease contract is breached, the transfer of risk operates differently depending on which party breaches. Generally, the party in breach bears the risk of loss.

Cure The rights of a party who tenders nonconforming performance to correct his or her performance within the contract period.

When the Seller or Lessor Breaches If the goods are so nonconforming that the buyer has the right to reject them, the risk of loss does not pass to the buyer until (1) the defects are **cured**—that is, until the goods are repaired, replaced, or discounted in price by the seller or (2) the buyer accepts the goods in spite of their defects (thus waiving the right to reject). **EXAMPLE 15.24** A buyer orders ten stainless steel refrigerators from a seller, F.O.B. the seller's plant. The seller ships white refrigerators instead. The white refrigerators (nonconforming goods) are damaged in transit. The risk of loss falls on the seller. Had the seller shipped stainless steel refrigerators (conforming goods) instead, the risk would have fallen on the buyer [UCC 2–510(1)]. •

If a buyer accepts a shipment of goods and later discovers a defect, acceptance can be revoked. Revocation allows the buyer to pass the risk of loss back to the seller, at least to the extent that the buyer's insurance does not cover the loss [UCC 2–510(2)].

When the Buyer or Lessee Breaches The general rule is that when a buyer or lessee breaches a contract, the risk of loss immediately shifts to the buyer or lessee. This rule has three important limitations:

1. The seller or lessor must already have identified the contract goods.
2. The buyer or lessee bears the risk for only a commercially reasonable time after the seller or lessor has learned of the breach.
3. The buyer or lessee is liable only to the extent of any deficiency in the seller's insurance coverage [UCC 2–510(3), 2A–220(2)].

Insurable Interest

Parties to sales and lease contracts often obtain insurance coverage to protect against damage, loss, or destruction of goods. Any party purchasing insurance, however, must have a sufficient interest in the insured item to obtain a valid policy. Insurance laws—not the UCC—determine sufficiency (see Chapter 37). The UCC is helpful, however, because it contains certain rules regarding insurable interests in goods.

Insurable Interest A property interest in goods being sold or leased that is sufficiently substantial to permit a party to insure against damage to the goods.

Insurable Interest of the Buyer or Lessee

A buyer or lessee has an **insurable interest** in identified goods. The moment the contract goods are identified by the seller or lessor, the buyer or lessee has a special property interest that allows the buyer or lessee to obtain necessary insurance coverage for those goods even before the risk of loss has passed [UCC 2–501(1), 2A–218(1)]. Buyers obtain an insurable interest in crops at the time of identification. **EXAMPLE 15.25** In March, a farmer sells a cotton crop that he hopes to harvest in October. When the crop is planted, the buyer acquires an insurable interest in it because those goods (the cotton crop) are identified to the sales contract between the seller and the buyer. •

Insurable Interest of the Seller or Lessor

A seller has an insurable interest in goods if she or he retains title to the goods. Even after title passes to the buyer, a seller who has a security interest in the goods (a right to secure payment—see Chapter 20) still has an insurable interest and can insure the goods [UCC 2–501(2)]. Hence, both a buyer and a seller can have an insurable interest in the same goods at the same time. Of course, the buyer or seller must sustain an actual loss to have the right to recover from an insurance company. In regard to leases, the lessor retains an insurable interest in leased goods until the lessee exercises an option to buy and the risk of loss has passed to the lessee [UCC 2A–218(3)]. (See the *Business Application* feature on page 408 for a discussion of insurance coverage and other measures that buyers and sellers can take to protect against losses.)

Contracts for the International Sale of Goods

LEARNING OBJECTIVE 5
What law governs contracts for the international sale of goods?

International sales contracts between firms or individuals located in different countries are governed by the 1980 United Nations Convention on Contracts for the International Sale of Goods (CISG). The CISG governs international contracts only if the countries of the parties to the contract have ratified the CISG and if the parties have not agreed that some other law will govern their contract. As of 2012, the CISG had been adopted by seventy-eight countries, including the United States, Canada, Mexico, some Central and South American countries, and most European nations.

Applicability of the CISG

Essentially, the CISG is to international sales contracts what Article 2 of the UCC is to domestic sales contracts. As discussed earlier, in domestic transactions the UCC applies when the parties to a contract for a sale of goods have failed to specify in writing some important term concerning price, delivery, or the like. Similarly, whenever the parties subject to the CISG have failed to specify in writing the precise terms of a contract for the international sale of goods, the CISG will be applied.

Unlike the UCC, *the CISG does not apply to consumer sales.* Neither the UCC nor the CISG applies to contracts for services.

Businesspersons must take special care when drafting international sales contracts to avoid problems caused by distance, including language differences and varying national laws. The fold-out exhibit for this chapter, which shows an actual international sales contract used by Starbucks Coffee Company, illustrates many of the special terms and clauses that are typically contained in international contracts for the sale of goods. Annotations in the exhibit explain the meaning and significance of specific clauses in the contract. (Other laws that frame global business transactions were discussed in Chapter 8.)

A Comparison of CISG and UCC Provisions

The provisions of the CISG, although similar for the most part to those of the UCC, differ from them in certain respects. We have already mentioned some of these differences. In the *Beyond Our Borders* feature in Chapter 12 on page 317, for example, we pointed out that the CISG does not include any Statute of Frauds provisions. Under Article 11 of the CISG, an international sales contract does not need to be evidenced by a writing or to be in any particular form. We look here at some differences between the UCC and the CISG with respect to contract formation.

Offers

Some differences between the UCC and the CISG have to do with offers. For instance, the UCC provides that a merchant's firm offer is irrevocable, even without consideration, if the merchant gives assurances in a signed writing.

In contrast, under the CISG, an offer can become irrevocable without a signed writing. Article 16(2) of the CISG provides that an offer will be irrevocable if the merchant-offeror simply states orally that the offer is irrevocable or if the offeree reasonably relies on the offer as being irrevocable. In both of these situations, the offer will be irrevocable even without a writing and without consideration.

Another difference is that, under the UCC, if the price term is left open, the court will determine "a reasonable price at the time for delivery" [UCC 2–305(1)]. Under the CISG, however, the price term must be specified, or at least provisions for its specification must be included in the agreement. Otherwise, normally no contract will exist.

Acceptances Like UCC 2–207, the CISG provides that a contract can be formed even though the acceptance contains additional terms, unless the additional terms materially alter the contract. Under the CISG, however, the definition of a "material alteration" includes virtually any change in the terms. If an additional term relates to payment, quality, quantity, price, time and place of delivery, extent of one party's liability to the other, or the settlement of disputes, the CISG considers the added term a "material alteration." In effect, then, the CISG requires that the terms of the acceptance mirror those of the offer.

Additionally, under the UCC, an acceptance is effective on dispatch. Under the CISG, however, a contract is not created until the offeror receives the acceptance. (The offer becomes irrevocable, however, when the acceptance is sent.) Also, in contrast to the UCC, the CISG provides that acceptance by performance does not require that the offeror be notified of the performance.

Reviewing . . . The Formation of Sales and Lease Contracts

Guy Holcomb owns and operates Oasis Goodtime Emporium, an adult entertainment establishment. Holcomb wanted to create an adult Internet system for Oasis that would offer customers adult theme videos and "live" chat room programs using performers at the club. On May 10, Holcomb signed a work order authorizing Crossroads Consulting Group (CCG) "to deliver a working prototype of a customer chat system, demonstrating the integration of live video and chatting in a Web browser." In exchange for creating the prototype, Holcomb agreed to pay CCG $64,697. On May 20, Holcomb signed an additional work order in the amount of $12,943 for CCG to install a customized firewall system. The work orders stated that Holcomb would make monthly installment payments to CCG, and both parties expected the work would be finished by September. Due to unforeseen problems largely attributable to system configuration and software incompatibility, the project required more time than anticipated. By the end of the summer, the Web site was still not ready, and Holcomb had fallen behind in the payments to CCG. CCG was threatening to cease work and file suit for breach of contract unless the bill was paid. Rather than make further payments, Holcomb wanted to abandon the Web site project. Using the information presented in the chapter, answer the following questions.

1. Would a court be likely to decide that the transaction between Holcomb and CCG was covered by the Uniform Commercial Code (UCC)? Why or why not?
2. Would a court be likely to consider Holcomb a merchant under the UCC? Why or why not?
3. Did the parties have a valid contract under the UCC? Explain.
4. Suppose that Holcomb and CCG meet in October in an attempt to resolve their problems. At that time, the parties reach an oral agreement that CCG will continue to work without demanding full payment of the past-due amounts and Holcomb will pay CCG $5,000 per week. Assuming that the contract falls under the UCC, is the oral agreement enforceable? Why or why not?

DEBATE THIS The UCC should require the same degree of definiteness of terms, especially with respect to price and quantity, as general contract law does.

BUSINESS APPLICATION

Who Bears the Risk of Loss—the Seller or the Buyer?*

The shipment of goods is a major aspect of commercial transactions. Many issues arise when an unforeseen event, such as fire or theft, causes damage to goods in transit. At the time of contract negotiation, both the seller and the buyer should determine the importance of the risk of loss. In some circumstances, risk is relatively unimportant (such as when ten boxes of copier paper are being sold), and the delivery terms should simply reflect costs and price. In other circumstances, risk is extremely important (such as when a fragile piece of pharmaceutical testing equipment is being sold), and the parties will need an express agreement as to the moment risk is to pass so that they can insure the goods accordingly. Risk should always be considered before a loss occurs, not after.

A major consideration relating to risk is when to insure goods against possible losses. Buyers and sellers should determine the point at which risk passes so that they can obtain insurance coverage to protect themselves against loss when they have an insurable interest in the goods.

Checklist to Determine Risk of Loss

The UCC uses a three-part checklist to determine risk of loss:

1. If the contract includes terms allocating the risk of loss, those terms are binding and must be applied.
2. If the contract is silent as to risk and either party breaches the contract, the breaching party is liable for the risk of loss.
3. If the contract makes no reference to risk and the goods are to be shipped or delivered, the risk of loss is borne by the party having control over the goods (delivery terms) if neither party breaches.

*This *Business Application* is not meant to substitute for the services of an attorney who is licensed to practice law in your state.

If You Are the Seller

If you are a seller of goods to be shipped, realize that as long as you have control over the goods, you are liable for any loss unless the buyer is in breach or the contract contains an explicit agreement to the contrary. When there is no explicit agreement, the delivery terms in your contract can serve as a basis for determining control. Thus, if goods are shipped "F.O.B. buyer's business," risk of loss does not pass to the buyer until there is a tender of delivery at the destination—the buyer's business. Any loss or damage in transit falls on the seller because the seller has control until proper tender has been made.

If You Are the Buyer

If you are a buyer of goods, it is important to remember that most sellers prefer "F.O.B. seller's business" as a delivery term. Under this term, once the goods are delivered to the carrier, the buyer bears the risk of loss. Thus, if conforming goods are completely destroyed or lost in transit, the buyer not only suffers the loss but is obligated to pay the seller the contract price.

Checklist for the Seller or the Buyer

1. *Before entering into a contract, determine the importance of the risk of loss for a given sale.*
2. *If risk is extremely important, the contract should expressly state the moment the risk of loss will pass from the seller to the buyer. This clause could even provide that risk will not pass until the goods are "delivered, installed, inspected, and tested (or in running order for a period of time)."*
3. *If an express clause is not included, delivery terms determine the passage of risk of loss.*
4. *When appropriate, either party or both parties should consider procuring insurance.*

Key Terms

bailee 404
course of dealing 397
course of performance 397
cure 405
destination contract 401
document of title 401
entrustment rule 402
firm offer 391
fungible goods 400
good faith purchaser 402
identification 399
insolvent 402
insurable interest 405
intangible property 384
lease 388
lease agreement 388
lessee 388
lessor 388
merchant 387
output contract 391
predominant-factor test 386
requirements contract 390
sale 384
sales contract 384
seasonably 392
shipment contract 401
tangible property 384
usage of trade 397

Chapter Summary: The Formation of Sales and Lease Contracts

The Scope of the UCC and Articles 2 (Sales) and 2A (Leases) (See pages 384–388.)	1. *The UCC*—The UCC attempts to provide a consistent, uniform, and integrated framework of rules to deal with all phases *ordinarily arising* in a commercial sales or lease transaction, including contract formation, passage of title and risk of loss, performance, remedies, payment for goods, warehoused goods, and secured transactions. 2. *Article 2 (sales)*—Article 2 governs contracts for the sale of goods (tangible, movable personal property). The common law of contracts also applies to sales contracts to the extent that the common law has not been modified by the UCC. If there is a conflict between a common law rule and the UCC, the UCC controls. 3. *Article 2A (leases)*—Article 2A governs contracts for the lease of goods. Except that it applies to leases, instead of sales, of goods, Article 2A is essentially a repetition of Article 2 and varies only to reflect differences between sales and lease transactions.
The Formation of Sales and Lease Contracts (See pages 389–398.)	1. *Offer*— a. Not all terms have to be included for a contract to be formed (only the subject matter and quantity term must be specified). b. The price does not have to be included for a contract to be formed. c. Particulars of performance can be left open. d. A written and signed offer by a *merchant,* covering a period of three months or less, is irrevocable without payment of consideration. 2. *Acceptance*— a. Acceptance may be made by any reasonable means of communication. It is effective when dispatched. b. An offer can be accepted by a promise to ship or by prompt shipment of conforming goods, or by prompt shipment of nonconforming goods if not accompanied by a notice of accommodation. c. Acceptance by performance requires notice within a reasonable time. Otherwise, the offer can be treated as lapsed. d. A definite expression of acceptance creates a contract even if the terms of the acceptance differ from those of the offer, unless the additional or different terms in the acceptance are expressly conditioned on the offeror's assent to those terms. 3. *Consideration*—A modification of a contract for the sale of goods does not require consideration. 4. *The Statute of Frauds*— a. All contracts for the sale of goods priced at $500 or more must be in writing. A writing is sufficient as long as it indicates a contract between the parties and is signed by the party against whom enforcement is sought. A contract is not enforceable beyond the quantity shown in the writing. b. When written confirmation of an oral contract *between merchants* is not objected to in writing by the receiver within ten days, the contract is enforceable. c. For exceptions to the Statute of Frauds, see Exhibit 15.2 on page 396. 5. *Parol evidence rule*— a. The terms of a clear and complete written contract cannot be contradicted by evidence of prior agreements or contemporaneous oral agreements. b. Evidence is admissible to clarify the terms of a writing if the contract terms are ambiguous or if evidence of course of dealing, usage of trade, or course of performance is necessary to learn or to clarify the parties' intentions. 6. *Unconscionability*—An unconscionable contract is one that is so unfair and one sided that it would be unreasonable to enforce it. If the court deems a sales contract to have been unconscionable at the time it was made, the court can (a) refuse to enforce the contract, (b) refuse to enforce the unconscionable clause, or (c) limit the application of any unconscionable clauses to avoid an unconscionable result.
Title and Risk of Loss (See pages 399–406.)	1. *Shipment contract*—In the absence of an agreement, title and risk pass on the seller's or lessor's delivery of conforming goods to the carrier [UCC 2–319(1)(a), 2–401(2)(a), 2–509(1)(a), 2A–219(2)(a)]. 2. *Destination contract*—In the absence of an agreement, title and risk pass on the seller's or lessor's *tender* of delivery of conforming goods to the buyer or lessee at the point of destination [UCC 2–319(1)(b), 2–401(2)(b), 2–509(1)(b), 2A–219(2)(b)]. 3. *Delivery without movement of the goods*—In the absence of an agreement, if the goods are not represented by a document of title, title passes on the formation of the contract, and risk passes on the buyer's or lessee's receipt of the goods if the seller or lessor is a merchant or on the tender of delivery if the seller or lessor is a nonmerchant. 4. *Sales and leases by nonowners*—Between the owner and a good faith purchaser or between the lessee and a sublessee: a. Void title—Owner prevails [UCC 2–403(1)]. b. Voidable title—Buyer prevails [UCC 2–403(1)]. c. Entrusted to a merchant—Buyer or sublessee prevails [UCC 2–403(2), (3); 2A–305(2)].

Continued

Chapter Summary: The Formation of Sales and Lease Contracts—Continued

Title and Risk of Loss—Continued	5. *Risk of loss when the contract is breached*— a. If the seller or lessor breaches by tendering nonconforming goods that are rejected by the buyer or lessee, the risk of loss does not pass to the buyer or lessee until the defects are cured (unless the buyer or lessee accepts the goods in spite of their defects, thus waiving the right to reject) [UCC 2–510(1), 2A–220(1)]. b. If the buyer or lessee breaches the contract, the risk of loss immediately shifts to the buyer or lessee for goods that are identified to the contract. The buyer or lessee bears the risk for only a commercially reasonable time after the seller or lessor has learned of the breach [UCC 2–510(3), 2A–220(2)].
Contracts for the International Sale of Goods (See pages 406–407.)	International sales contracts are governed by the United Nations Convention on Contracts for the International Sale of Goods (CISG)—if the countries of the parties to the contract have ratified the CISG (and if the parties have not agreed that some other law will govern their contract). Essentially, the CISG is to international sales contracts what Article 2 of the UCC is to domestic sales contracts. Whenever parties who are subject to the CISG have failed to specify in writing the precise terms of a contract for the international sale of goods, the CISG will be applied.

ExamPrep

ISSUE SPOTTERS

1. E-Design, Inc., orders 150 computer desks. Fav-O-Rite Supplies, Inc., ships 150 printer stands. Is this an acceptance of the offer or a counteroffer? If it is an acceptance, is it a breach of the contract? What if Fav-O-Rite told E-Design it was sending the printer stands as "an accommodation"? **(See pages 391–394.)**
2. Truck Parts, Inc. (TPI), often sells supplies to United Fix-It Company (UFC), which services trucks. Over the phone, they negotiate for the sale of eighty-four sets of tires. TPI sends a letter to UFC detailing the terms and two weeks later ships the tires. Is there an enforceable contract between them? Why or why not? **(See pages 389–391.)**

—Check your answers to the Issue Spotters against the answers provided in Appendix E at the end of this text.

BEFORE THE TEST

Go to www.cengagebrain.com, enter the ISBN 9781133273561, and click on "Find" to locate this textbook's Web site. Then, click on "Access Now" under "Study Tools," and select Chapter 15 at the top. There, you will find a Practice Quiz that you can take to assess your mastery of the concepts in this chapter, as well as Flashcards, a Glossary of important terms, and Video Questions (when assigned).

For Review

Answers to the even-numbered questions in this For Review section can be found in Appendix F at the end of this text.

1. How do Article 2 and Article 2A of the UCC differ? What types of transactions does each article cover?
2. In a sales contract, if an offeree includes additional or different terms in an acceptance, will a contract result? If so, what happens to these terms?
3. What exceptions to the writing requirements of the Statute of Frauds are provided in Article 2 and Article 2A of the UCC?
4. Risk of loss does not necessarily pass with title. If the parties to a contract do not expressly agree when risk passes and the goods are to be delivered without movement by the seller, when does risk pass?
5. What law governs contracts for the international sale of goods?

Business Scenarios and Case Problems

15–1 Statute of Frauds. Fresher Foods, Inc., orally agreed to purchase one thousand bushels of corn for $1.25 per bushel from Dale Vernon, a farmer. Fresher Foods paid $125 down and agreed to pay the remainder of the purchase price on delivery, which was scheduled for one week later. When Fresher Foods tendered the balance of $1,125 on the scheduled day of delivery and requested the corn, Vernon refused to deliver it. Fresher Foods sued Vernon for damages, claiming that Vernon had breached their oral contract. Can Fresher Foods recover? If so, to what extent? **(See pages 394–396.)**

15–2 **Question with Sample Answer—Merchant's Firm Offer.** On September 1, Jennings, a used-car dealer, wrote a letter to Wheeler, stating, "I have a 1955 Thunderbird convertible in mint condition that I will sell you for $13,500 at any time before October 9. [signed] Peter Jennings." By September 15, having heard nothing from Wheeler, Jennings sold the Thunderbird to another party. On September 29, Wheeler accepted Jennings's offer and tendered the $13,500. When Jennings told Wheeler he had sold the car to another party, Wheeler claimed Jennings had breached their contract. Is Jennings in breach? Explain. **(See page 391.)**

—For a sample answer to Question 15–2, go to Appendix G at the end of this text.

15–3 **Spotlight on Goods and Services—The Statute of Frauds.** Fallsview Glatt Kosher Caterers ran a business that provided travel packages, including food, entertainment, and lectures on religious subjects, to customers during the Passover holiday at a New York resort. Willie Rosenfeld verbally agreed to pay Fallsview $24,050 for the Passover package for himself and his family. Rosenfeld did not appear at the resort and never paid the money owed. Fallsview sued Rosenfeld for breach of contract. Rosenfeld claimed that the contract was unenforceable because it was not in writing and violated the UCC's Statute of Frauds. Is the contract valid? Explain. [*Fallsview Glatt Kosher Caterers, Inc. v. Rosenfeld,* 794 N.Y.S.2d 790 (N.Y. Super. 2005)] **(See pages 394–396.)**

15–4 **Case Problem with Sample Answer—Passage of Title.** Kenzie Godfrey was a passenger in a taxi when it collided with a car driven by Dawn Altieri. Altieri had originally leased the car from G.E. Capital Auto Lease, Inc. By the time of the accident, she had bought it, but she had not fully paid for it or completed the transfer-of-title paperwork. Godfrey suffered a brain injury and sought to recover damages from the owner of the car that Altieri was driving. Who had title to the car at the time of the accident? Explain. [*Godfrey v. G.E. Capital Auto Lease, Inc.,* 89 A.D.3d 471, 933 N.Y.S.2d 208 (1 Dept. 2011)] **(See page 400.)**

—For a sample answer to Problem 15–4, go to Appendix H at the end of this text.

15–5 **Additional Terms.** B.S. International, Ltd. (BSI), makes costume jewelry. JMAM, LLC, is a wholesaler of costume jewelry. JMAM sent BSI a letter with the terms for orders, including the necessary procedure for obtaining credit for items that customers rejected. The letter stated, "By signing below, you agree to the terms." Steven Baracsi, BSI's owner, signed the letter and returned it. For six years, BSI made jewelry for JMAM, which resold it. Items rejected by customers were sent back to JMAM, but were never returned to BSI. BSI filed a suit against JMAM, claiming $41,294.21 for the unreturned items. BSI showed the court a copy of JMAM's terms. Across the bottom had been typed a "PS" requiring the return of rejected merchandise. Was this "PS" part of the contract? Discuss. [*B.S. International, Ltd. v. JMAM, LLC,* 13 A.3d 1057 (R.I. 2011)] **(See page 392.)**

15–6 **Delivery without Movement of the Goods.** Aleris International, Inc., signed a contract to buy a John Deere loader from Holt Equipment Co. The agreement provided that "despite physical delivery of the equipment, title shall remain in the seller until" Aleris paid the full price. The next month, Aleris filed for bankruptcy. Holt asserted that it was the owner of the loader and filed a claim with the court to repossess it. Who is entitled to the loader, and why? [*In re Aleris International, Ltd.,* __ Bankr. __ (D.Del. 2011)] **(See page 401.)**

15–7 **Goods Held by the Seller or Lessor.** Douglas Singletary bought a manufactured home from Andy's Mobile Home and Land Sales. The contract stated that the buyer accepted the home "as is where is." Singletary paid the full price, and his crew began to ready the home to relocate it to his property. The night before the home was to be moved, however, it was destroyed by fire. Who suffered the loss? Explain. [*Singletary, III v. P&A Investments, Inc.,* 712 S.E.2d 681 (N.C.App. 2011)] **(See page 404.)**

15–8 **Partial Performance and the Statute of Frauds.** After a series of e-mails, Jorge Bonilla, the sole proprietor of a printing company in Uruguay, agreed to buy a used printer from Crystal Graphics Equipment, Inc., in New York. Crystal Graphics, through its agent, told Bonilla that the printing press was fully operational, contained all of its parts, and was in excellent condition except for some damage to one of the printing towers. Bonilla paid $95,000. Crystal Graphics sent him a signed, stamped invoice reflecting this payment. The invoice was dated six days after Bonilla's conversation with the agent. When the printing press arrived, Bonilla discovered that it was missing parts and was damaged. Crystal Graphics sent replacement parts, but they did not work. Ultimately, Crystal Graphics was never able to make the printer operational. Bonilla sued, alleging breach of contract, breach of the implied covenant of good faith and fair dealing, breach of express warranty, and breach of implied warranty. Crystal Graphics claimed that the contract was not enforceable because it did not satisfy the Statute of Frauds. Can Crystal Graphics prevail on this basis? Why or why not? [*Bonilla v. Crystal Graphics Equipment, Inc.,* 2012 WL 360145 (S.D.Fla. 2012)] **(See page 396.)**

15–9 **A Question of Ethics—Statute of Frauds.** Daniel Fox owned Fox & Lamberth Enterprises, Inc., a kitchen remodeling business. Fox leased a building from Carl Hussong. When Fox planned to close his business, Craftsmen Home Improvement, Inc., expressed an interest in buying his assets. Fox set a price of $50,000. Craftsmen's owners agreed and gave Fox a list of the desired items and a "Bill of Sale" that set the terms for payment. Craftsmen expected to negotiate a new lease with Hussong and modified the premises, including removal of some of the displays. When Hussong and Craftsmen could not agree on new terms, Craftsmen told Fox that the deal was off. [*Fox & Lamberth Enterprises, Inc. v. Craftsmen Home Improvement, Inc.*, __ N.E.2d __ (2 Dist. 2006)]

1. In Fox's suit for breach of contract, Craftsmen raised the Statute of Frauds as a defense. What are the requirements of the Statute of Frauds? Did the deal between Fox and Craftsmen meet these requirements? Did it fall under one of the exceptions? Explain. **(See pages 394–396.)**
2. Craftsmen also claimed that the "predominant factor" of its agreement with Fox was a lease for Hussong's building. What is the predominant-factor test? Does it apply here? In any event, is it fair to hold a party to a contract to buy a business's assets when the buyer is unable to negotiate a favorable lease of the premises on which the assets are located? Discuss. **(See pages 386–387.)**

Critical Thinking and Writing Assignments

15–10 **Case Analysis Question.** Go to Appendix I at the end of this text and examine the excerpt of Case No. 3, *Spray-Tek, Inc. v. Robbins Motor Transportation, Inc.* Review and then brief the case, making sure that your brief answers the following questions.

1. **Issue:** What contract provision was at the heart of the dispute between the parties to this case, and why?
2. **Rule of Law:** What rule of law did the court apply to interpret this provision?
3. **Applying the Rule of Law:** How did the court apply this rule to interpret the provision at the center of this case?
4. **Conclusion:** Did the court resolve the dispute between the parties with respect to determining who suffered the loss and how much that loss was? Explain.

15–11  **Business Law Critical Thinking Group Assignment.** Mountain Stream Trout Co. agreed to buy "market size" trout from trout grower Lake Farms, LLC. Their five-year contract did not define *market size*. At the time, in the trade, *market size* referred to fish of one-pound live weight. After three years, Mountain Stream began taking fewer, smaller deliveries of larger fish, claiming that *market size* varied according to whatever its customers demanded and that its customers now demanded larger fish. Lake Farms filed a suit for breach of contract.

1. The first group will decide whether parol (outside) evidence is admissible to explain the terms of this contract. Are there any exceptions that could apply?
2. A second group will determine the impact of course of dealing and usage of trade on the interpretation of contract terms.
3. A third group will discuss how parties to a commercial contract can avoid the possibility that a court will interpret the contract terms in accordance with trade usage.

CHAPTER 16

(Bobby Yip/Reuters/Landov)

Performance and Breach of Sales and Lease Contracts

CHAPTER OUTLINE

- Performance Obligations
- Obligations of the Seller or Lessor
- Obligations of the Buyer or Lessee
- Anticipatory Repudiation
- Remedies of the Seller or Lessor
- Remedies of the Buyer or Lessee
- Limitation of Remedies

LEARNING OBJECTIVES

The five learning objectives below are designed to help improve your understanding of the chapter. After reading this chapter, you should be able to answer the following questions:

1. What are the respective obligations of the parties under a contract for the sale or lease of goods?
2. What is the perfect tender rule? What are some important exceptions to this rule that apply to sales and lease contracts?
3. What options are available to the nonbreaching party when the other party to a sales or lease contract repudiates the contract prior to the time for performance?
4. What remedies are available to a seller or lessor when the buyer or lessee breaches the contract? What remedies are available to a buyer or lessee if the seller or lessor breaches the contract?
5. In contracts subject to the UCC, are parties free to limit the remedies available to the nonbreaching party on a breach of contract? If so, in what ways?

"Gratitude is as the good faith of merchants: it holds commerce together."
—François de la Rochefoucauld, 1613–1680 (French author)

The performance required of the parties under a sales or lease contract consists of the duties and obligations each party has under the terms of the contract. Keep in mind that a party's "duties and obligations" include those specified by the agreement, by custom, and by the Uniform Commercial Code (UCC). Because, as the chapter-opening quotation indicates, good faith "holds commerce together," the UCC also imposes a duty of good faith on the parties involved in commercial contracts. This duty basically requires honesty and fair dealing. In this chapter, we examine the performance obligations of the parties under a sales or lease contract.

Sometimes, circumstances make it difficult for a person to carry out the promised performance, and the contract is breached. When breach occurs, the aggrieved party looks for remedies—which we discuss in the second half of the chapter.

Performance Obligations

As discussed in previous chapters and noted in this chapter's introduction, the standards of good faith and commercial reasonableness are read into every contract. These standards provide a framework for the entire agreement. If a sales contract leaves open some particulars of performance, for instance, the parties must exercise good faith and commercial reasonableness when later specifying the details.

LEARNING OBJECTIVE 1
What are the respective obligations of the parties under a contract for the sale or lease of goods?

In the performance of a sales or lease contract, the basic obligation of the seller or lessor is to *transfer and deliver conforming goods.* The basic obligation of the buyer or lessee is to *accept and to pay for conforming goods* in accordance with the contract [UCC 2–301, 2A–516(1)]. Overall performance of a sales or lease contract is controlled by the agreement between the parties. When the contract is unclear and disputes arise, the courts look to the UCC and impose standards of good faith and commercial reasonableness.

Obligations of the Seller or Lessor

Conforming Goods Goods that conform to contract specifications.

Tender of Delivery A seller's or lessor's act of placing conforming goods at the disposal of the buyer or lessee and providing whatever notification is reasonably necessary to enable the buyer or lessee to take delivery.

The major obligation of the seller or lessor under a sales or lease contract is to tender conforming goods to the buyer or lessee. Goods that conform to the contract description in every way are called **conforming goods.** To fulfill the contract, the seller or lessor must either deliver or tender delivery of conforming goods to the buyer or lessee. **Tender of delivery** occurs when the seller or lessor makes conforming goods available to the buyer or lessee and provides whatever notification is reasonably necessary to enable the buyer or lessee to take delivery [UCC 2–503(1), 2A–508(1)].

Tender must occur at a *reasonable hour* and in a *reasonable manner.* In other words, a seller cannot call the buyer at 2:00 A.M. and say, "The goods are ready. I'll give you twenty minutes to get them." Unless the parties have agreed otherwise, the goods must be tendered for delivery at a reasonable hour and kept available for a reasonable period of time to enable the buyer to take possession of them [UCC 2–503(1)(a)].

Normally, all goods called for by a contract must be tendered in a single delivery, unless the parties have agreed that the goods may be delivered in several lots or *installments* [UCC 2–307, 2–612, 2A–510]. Hence, an order for 1,000 shirts cannot be delivered 2 shirts at a time. If, however, the parties agree that the shirts will be delivered in four lots of 250 each as they are produced (for summer, fall, winter, and spring stock), then delivery may occur in this manner.

Fresh produce is loaded for delivery. Under what circumstances can the buyer reject this produce?

(AP Photo/Mike Groll)

Place of Delivery

As noted in Chapter 15, the UCC provides for the place of delivery pursuant to a contract only if the contract does not. The buyer and seller (or lessor and lessee) may agree that the goods will be delivered to a particular destination where the buyer or lessee will take possession. If the contract does not designate the place of delivery, then the goods must be made available to the buyer at the *seller's place of business* or, if the seller has none, at the seller's residence [UCC 2–308(a)]. If, at the time of contracting, the parties know that the goods identified to the contract are located somewhere other than the seller's business, then *the location of the goods* is the place for their delivery [UCC 2–308(b)].

EXAMPLE 16.1 Li Wan and Jo Boyd both live in San Francisco. In San Francisco, Wan contracts to sell Boyd five used trucks, which both parties know are located in a Chicago warehouse. If nothing more is specified in the contract, the place of delivery for the trucks is Chicago. Wan may tender delivery either by giving Boyd a negotiable or nonnegotiable document of title or by obtaining the bailee's (warehouser's) acknowledgment that the buyer is entitled to possession.[1] ●

KNOW THIS

Documents of title include bills of lading, warehouse receipts, and any other documents that, in the regular course of business, entitle a person holding these documents to obtain possession of, and title to, the goods covered.

Delivery via Carrier

In many instances, it is clear from the surrounding circumstances or delivery terms in the contract (such as F.O.B. or F.A.S. terms, shown in Exhibit 15.4 on page 404) that the parties intended the goods to be moved by a carrier. In carrier contracts, the seller fulfills the obligation to deliver the goods through either a shipment contract or a destination contract.

Shipment Contracts Recall from Chapter 15 that a *shipment contract* requires or authorizes the seller to ship goods by a carrier, rather than to deliver them at a particular destination [UCC 2–319, 2–509(1)(a)]. Under a shipment contract, unless otherwise agreed, the seller must do the following:

1. Put the goods into the hands of the carrier.
2. Make a contract for their transportation that is reasonable according to the nature of the goods and their value. (For example, certain types of goods require refrigeration in transit.)
3. Obtain and promptly deliver or tender to the buyer any documents necessary to enable the buyer to obtain possession of the goods from the carrier.
4. Promptly notify the buyer that shipment has been made [UCC 2–504].

"Resolve to perform what you ought. Perform without fail what you resolve."

Benjamin Franklin, 1706–1790 (American politician and inventor)

If the seller fails to notify the buyer that shipment has been made or fails to make a proper contract for transportation, the buyer can treat the contract as breached and reject the goods, but only if a *material loss* of the goods or a *significant delay* results. Of course, the parties can agree that a lesser amount of loss or that any delay will be grounds for rejection.

Destination Contracts In a *destination contract,* the seller agrees to deliver conforming goods to the buyer at a particular destination. The seller must provide the buyer with any documents of title necessary to enable the buyer to obtain delivery from the carrier [UCC 2–503].

The Perfect Tender Rule

LEARNING OBJECTIVE 2
What is the perfect tender rule? What are some important exceptions to this rule that apply to sales and lease contracts?

As previously noted, the seller or lessor has an obligation to ship or tender *conforming goods,* and the buyer or lessee is required to accept and pay for the goods according to the terms of the contract. Under the common law, the seller was obligated to deliver goods that conformed to the terms of the contract in every detail. This was called the *perfect tender* doctrine.

The UCC preserves the perfect tender doctrine by stating that if the goods or tender of delivery fail *in any respect* to conform to the contract, the buyer or lessee has the right to accept the goods, reject the entire shipment, or accept part and reject part [UCC 2–601, 2A–509].

The corollary to this rule is that if the goods conform in every respect, the buyer or lessee does not have a right to reject the goods, as the following case illustrates.

1. If the seller delivers a nonnegotiable document of title or merely instructs the bailee in a writing (or electronic record) to release the goods to the buyer without the bailee's *acknowledgment* of the buyer's rights, this is also a sufficient tender, unless the buyer objects [UCC 2–503(4)]. Risk of loss, however, does not pass until the buyer has a reasonable amount of time in which to present the document or to give the bailee instructions for delivery, as discussed in Chapter 15.

Case 16.1

Wilson Sporting Goods Co. v. U.S. Golf & Tennis Centers, Inc.

Court of Appeals of Tennessee, 2012 WL 601804 (2012).

(cscredon/iStockphoto.com)

FACTS U.S. Golf & Tennis Centers, Inc., operates two retail sporting goods stores that specialize in golf and tennis equipment. U.S. Golf agreed to buy 96,000 golf balls from Wilson Sporting Goods Company for a total price of $20,000. The parties negotiated the agreement via fax, and Wilson affirmed that U.S. Golf was receiving the lowest price ($5 per two-dozen unit) "that Wilson offered to any one in the market." Wilson shipped golf balls to U.S. Golf that conformed to the contract in quantity and quality, but it did not receive payment. U.S. Golf claimed that it had learned that Wilson had sold the product for $2 a unit to another buyer and asked Wilson to reduce the contract price of the balls to $4 per unit (for a total of $16,000). Wilson refused and filed a suit to collect the $20,000. The trial court entered judgment in favor of Wilson for $33,099.28, which included the contract price, interest, attorneys' fees, and certain allowable expenses. U.S. Golf appealed.

ISSUE When a seller has tendered conforming goods, can the buyer reject the goods and cancel the contract?

DECISION No. The state appellate court affirmed the lower court's judgment in favor of Wilson. When a seller tenders conforming goods, the buyer is obligated to accept and pay for the goods.

REASON Because it was undisputed that the shipment of golf balls conformed in quantity and quality to the contract specifications, U.S. Golf was obligated to accept the goods and pay the agreed-on price. U.S. Golf argued that Wilson had breached the contract by misrepresenting the price of the golf balls as its lowest price, but the court was not convinced. Evidence showed that the parties had agreed on a price of $20,000. U.S. Golf did not present any evidence to contradict the price term in the parties' agreement or to establish that Wilson had engaged in misrepresentation. Therefore, the perfect tender rule applied, and U.S. Golf was not entitled to reject the goods or cancel the contract.

WHAT IF THE FACTS WERE DIFFERENT? *Suppose that U.S. Golf had presented as evidence a contract between Wilson and another buyer a month after this shipment was delivered to U.S. Golf. In that contract, Wilson agreed to sell the same golf balls for $4 per unit to a different buyer. Would the court have ruled differently in this dispute? Why or why not?*

Exceptions to the Perfect Tender Rule

Because of the rigidity of the perfect tender rule, several exceptions to the rule have been created, some of which are discussed here.

Agreement of the Parties

Exceptions to the perfect tender rule may be established by agreement. If the parties have agreed, for example, that defective goods or parts will not be rejected if the seller or lessor is able to repair or replace them within a reasonable period of time, the perfect tender rule does not apply.

Cure

The UCC does not specifically define the term *cure,* but it refers to the right of the seller or lessor to repair, adjust, or replace defective or nonconforming goods [UCC 2–508, 2A–513].

Timing and Reasonable Grounds When any tender of delivery is rejected because of nonconforming goods and the time for performance has not yet expired, the seller or lessor can notify the buyer or lessee promptly of the intention to cure and can then do so *within the contract time for performance* [UCC 2–508(1), 2A–513(1)]. Once the time for

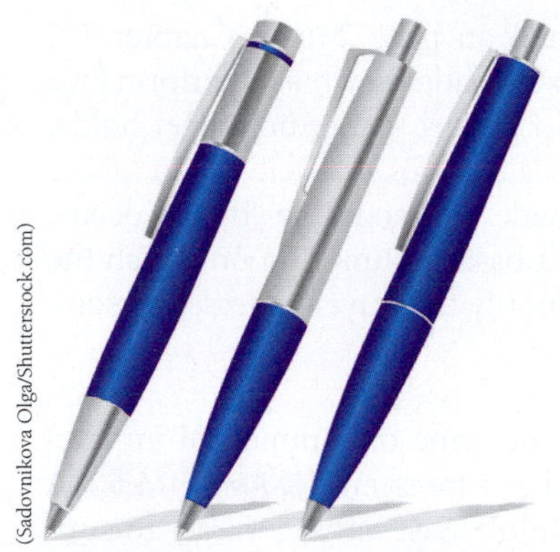
(Sadovnikova Olga/Shutterstock.com)

If a buyer has accepted these blue pens in the past when she ordered black pens, is the seller justified in shipping blue pens again?

performance has expired, the seller or lessor still has a reasonable time in which to cure if, at the time of delivery, he or she had *reasonable grounds to believe that the nonconforming goods would be acceptable to the buyer or lessee* [UCC 2–508(2), 2A–513(2)].

EXAMPLE 16.2 In the past, EZ Office Supply frequently accepted blue pens when the seller, Baxter's Wholesale, did not have black pens in stock. In this context, Baxter's has reasonable grounds to believe that EZ will again accept such a substitute. Even if EZ rejects the substituted goods on a particular occasion, because Baxter's had reasonable grounds to believe that the substitution would be acceptable, it will have a reasonable time to cure by tendering black pens. •

A seller or lessor may sometimes tender nonconforming goods with a price allowance (discount), which can also serve as "reasonable grounds" to believe the buyer or lessee will accept the nonconforming tender.

Nature of Defect Must Be Disclosed The right to cure means that, to reject goods, the buyer or lessee must inform the seller or lessor of a particular defect. For instance, if a lessee refuses a tender of goods as nonconforming but does not disclose the nature of the defect to the lessor, the lessee cannot later assert the defect as a defense if the defect is one that the lessor could have cured. Generally, buyers and lessees must act in good faith and state specific reasons for refusing to accept goods [UCC 2–605, 2A–514].

KNOW THIS

If goods never arrive, the buyer or seller usually has at least some recourse against the carrier. Also, a buyer normally insures the goods from the time they leave the seller's possession.

Substitution of Carriers

When an agreed-on manner of delivery (such as the carrier to be used to transport the goods) becomes impracticable or unavailable through no fault of either party, but a commercially reasonable substitute is available, the seller must use this substitute performance, which is sufficient tender to the buyer [UCC 2–614(1)].

EXAMPLE 16.3 A sales contract calls for a large generator to be delivered via Roadway Trucking Corporation on or before June 1. The contract terms clearly state the importance of the delivery date. The employees of Roadway Trucking go on strike. The seller is required to make a reasonable substitute tender, perhaps by rail if that is available. Note that the seller normally will be responsible for any additional shipping costs, unless other arrangements have been made in the sales contract. •

Installment Contract A contract that requires or authorizes delivery in two or more separate lots to be accepted and paid for separately.

Installment Contracts

An **installment contract** is a single contract that requires or authorizes delivery in two or more separate lots to be accepted and paid for separately. With an installment contract, a buyer or lessee can reject an installment *only if the nonconformity substantially impairs the value* of the installment and cannot be cured [UCC 2–307, 2–612(2), 2A–510(1)]. If the buyer or lessee subsequently accepts a nonconforming installment and fails to notify the seller or lessor of cancellation, however, the contract is reinstated [UCC 2–612(3), 2A–510(2)].

Unless the contract provides otherwise, the entire installment contract is breached only when one or more nonconforming installments *substantially* impair the value of the *whole contract*. **EXAMPLE 16.4** A contract calls for the parts of a machine to be delivered in installments. The first part is necessary for the operation of the machine, but when it is delivered, it is irreparably defective. The failure of this first installment will be a breach of the whole contract because the machine will not operate without the first part. The situation would likely be different, however, if the contract had called for twenty carloads of plywood and only 6 percent of one carload had deviated from the thickness specifications in the contract. It is unlikely that a court would find that a defect in 6 percent of one installment substantially impaired the value of the whole contract. •

The point to remember is that the UCC significantly alters the right of the buyer or lessee to reject the entire contract if the contract requires delivery to be made in several installments. The UCC strictly limits rejection to cases of *substantial* nonconformity.

Commercial Impracticability As mentioned on page 346 in Chapter 13, occurrences unforeseen by either party when a contract was made may make performance commercially impracticable. When this occurs, the rule of perfect tender no longer holds. According to UCC 2–615(a) and 2A–405(a), a delay in delivery or nondelivery in whole or in part is not a breach when performance has been made impracticable "by the occurrence of a contingency the nonoccurrence of which was a basic assumption on which the contract was made." The seller or lessor must, however, notify the buyer or lessee as soon as practicable that there will be a delay or nondelivery.

"Obstacles are those frightful things you see when you take your eyes off your goal."

Henry Ford, 1863–1947
(Founder of Ford Motor Company)

Foreseeable versus Unforeseeable Contingencies The doctrine of commercial impracticability extends only to problems that could not have been foreseen. **EXAMPLE 16.5** A major oil company that receives its supplies from the Middle East has a contract to supply a buyer with 100,000 barrels of oil. Because of an oil embargo by the Organization of Petroleum Exporting Countries, the seller is unable to secure oil supplies to meet the terms of the contract. Because of the same embargo, the seller cannot secure oil from any other source. This situation comes under the commercial impracticability exception to the perfect tender doctrine. •

Can unanticipated increases in a seller's costs, which make performance "impracticable," constitute a valid defense to performance on the basis of commercial impracticability? The court dealt with this question in the following *Classic Case*.

Classic Case 16.2

Maple Farms, Inc. v. City School District of Elmira

Supreme Court of New York,
76 Misc.2d 1080, 352 N.Y.S.2d 784 (1974).

(princessdlaf/iStockphoto.com)
School districts often make long-term contracts for milk deliveries.

FACTS On June 15, 1973, Maple Farms, Inc., formed an agreement with the city school district of Elmira, New York, to supply the school district with milk for the 1973–1974 school year. The agreement was in the form of a requirements contract, under which Maple Farms would sell to the school district all the milk the district required at a fixed price—which was the June market price of milk. By December 1973, the price of raw milk had increased by 23 percent over the price specified in the contract. This meant that if the terms of the contract were fulfilled, Maple Farms would lose $7,350. Because it had similar contracts with other school districts, Maple Farms stood to lose a great deal if it was held to the price stated in the contracts. When the school district would not agree to release Maple Farms from its contract, Maple Farms brought an action in a New York state court for a declaratory judgment (a determination of the parties' rights under a contract). Maple Farms contended that the substantial increase in the price of raw milk was an event not contemplated by the parties when the contract was formed and that, given the increased price, performance of the contract was commercially impracticable.

ISSUE Could Maple Farms be released from the contract on the ground of commercial impracticability?

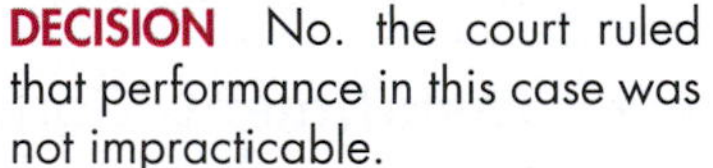
DECISION No. the court ruled that performance in this case was not impracticable.

REASON The court reasoned that commercial impracticability arises when an event occurs that is totally unexpected and unforeseeable by the parties. The increased price of raw milk was not totally unexpected, given that in the previous year the price of milk had risen 10 percent and that the price of milk had traditionally varied. Additionally, the general inflation of prices in the United States should have been anticipated. Maple Farms had reason to know these facts and could have included a clause in its contract with the school district to protect itself from its present situation. The court also noted that, for the school district, the primary purpose of the contract was to protect itself (for budgeting purposes) against price fluctuations.

WHAT IF THE FACTS WERE DIFFERENT? *Suppose that the court had ruled in the plaintiff's favor. How might that ruling have affected the plaintiff's contracts with other parties?*

IMPACT OF THIS CASE ON TODAY'S LAW *This case is a classic illustration of the UCC's commercial impracticability*

Classic Case 16.2—Continued

doctrine. Under this doctrine, parties who freely enter into contracts normally will not be excused from their contractual obligations simply because changed circumstances make performance difficult or unprofitable. Rather, to be excused from performance, a party must show that the changed circumstances were unforeseeable by both parties at the time the contract was formed. This principle continues to be applied today.

Partial Performance Sometimes, an unforeseen event only *partially* affects the capacity of the seller or lessor to perform, and the seller or lessor is thus able to fulfill the contract *partially* but cannot tender total performance. In this situation, the seller or lessor is required to allocate in a fair and reasonable manner any remaining production and deliveries among those to whom it is contractually obligated to deliver the goods, and this allocation may take into account its regular customers [UCC 2–615(b), 2A–405(b)]. The buyer or lessee must receive notice of the allocation and has the right to accept or reject it [UCC 2–615(c), 2A–405(c)].

EXAMPLE 16.6 A Florida orange grower, Best Citrus, Inc., contracts to sell this season's crop to a number of customers, including Martin's grocery chain. Martin's contracts to purchase two thousand crates of oranges. Best Citrus has sprayed some of its orange groves with a chemical called Karmoxin. When studies show that persons who eat products sprayed with Karmoxin may develop cancer, the Department of Agriculture issues an order prohibiting the sale of these products. Best Citrus picks only those oranges not sprayed with Karmoxin, but there are not enough to meet all the contracted-for deliveries. In this situation, Best Citrus is required to allocate its production. It notifies Martin's that it cannot deliver the full quantity specified in the contract and indicates the amount it will be able to deliver. Martin's can either accept or reject the allocation, but Best Citrus has no further contractual liability. ●

ETHICAL ISSUE

Is it appropriate to use the latest global economic crisis as a reason to escape contractual obligations? Starting as early as 2007 and lasting through at least 2012, many companies were hit hard by the global economic crisis. When economic conditions make it difficult (or even impossible) for parties to perform, should the courts void agreements because of commercial impracticability? Many companies have argued that the latest economic crisis was the equivalent of a natural disaster (an act of God), but in general, financial difficulties do not excuse a defaulting party's breach. Sometimes, however, the courts make exceptions. One exception involved the automaker Chrysler.

In 1999, Chrysler entered into an agreement with the city of Twinsburg, Ohio, and the county in which it is located. Chrysler received a 50 percent tax exemption on certain property for a ten-year period. In exchange, the company was to invest about $125 million in a stamping plant in Twinsburg and maintain about three hundred full-time employment positions there. When the auto industry crashed during the financial crisis, Chrysler filed for bankruptcy in 2009. As part of its restructuring, Chrysler planned to close the Twinsburg plant. Under its agreement with the city, Chrysler could do so if its changed circumstances were due to changed economic conditions beyond its reasonable control. When the city challenged the plant's closing, the bankruptcy court determined that the closing was in fact caused by a change in economic conditions that were beyond Chrysler's control.[2] Thus, the global economic slowdown was equivalent to an act of God, at least in terms of commercial impracticability.

---

2. *In re Old Carco, LLC*, 452 Bankr. 100 (2011). The court used the name *Old Carco* to designate the prebankrupt Chrysler Company.

(AP Photo/Joseph Kaczmarek)

What happens to a contract for the sale of goods when those goods identified to the contract are completely destroyed by fire?

Destruction of Identified Goods Sometimes, an unexpected event, such as a fire, totally destroys goods through no fault of either party and before risk passes to the buyer or lessee. In such a situation, *if the goods were identified at the time the contract was formed,* the parties are excused from performance [UCC 2–613, 2A–221]. If the goods are only partially destroyed, however, the buyer or lessee can inspect them and either treat the contract as void or accept the goods with a reduction of the contract price.

EXAMPLE 16.7 Atlas Sporting Equipment agrees to lease to River Bicycles sixty bicycles of a particular model that has been discontinued. No other bicycles of that model are available. River specifies that it needs the bicycles to rent to tourists. Before Atlas can deliver the bicycles, they are destroyed by a fire. In this situation, Atlas is not liable to River for failing to deliver the bicycles. The goods were destroyed through no fault of either party, before the risk of loss passed to the lessee. The loss was total, so the contract is avoided. Clearly, Atlas has no obligation to tender the bicycles, and River has no obligation to make the lease payments for them. •

Assurance and Cooperation

Two other exceptions to the perfect tender doctrine apply equally to parties to sales and lease contracts: the right of assurance and the duty of cooperation.

The Right of Assurance The UCC provides that if one party to a contract has "reasonable grounds" to believe that the other party will not perform as contracted, he or she may *in writing* "demand adequate assurance of due performance" from the other party. Until such assurance is received, he or she may "suspend" further performance (such as payments due under the contract) without liability. What constitutes "reasonable grounds" is determined by commercial standards. If such assurances are not forthcoming within a reasonable time (not to exceed thirty days), the failure to respond may be treated as a *repudiation* of the contract [UCC 2–609, 2A–401].

CASE EXAMPLE 16.8 Two companies that make road-surfacing materials, Koch Materials Company and Shore Slurry Seal, Inc., enter into a contract. Koch obtains a license to use Novachip, a special material made by Shore, and Shore agrees to buy all of its asphalt from Koch for the next seven years. A few years into the contract term, Shore notifies Koch that it is planning to sell its assets to Asphalt Paving Systems, Inc. Koch demands assurances that Asphalt Paving will continue the deal, but Shore refuses to provide assurances. In this situation, Koch can treat Shore's failure to give assurances as a repudiation and file a suit against Shore for breach of contract.[3] •

PREVENTING LEGAL DISPUTES

Whenever you have doubts about the other party's ability or willingness to perform a sales contract, you should demand adequate assurances. Rather than requiring a party to "wait and see" (and possibly incur significant losses as a result), the UCC allows a party with reasonable suspicions to seek adequate assurance of performance from the other party. If the other party fails to give assurance, you can treat it as an anticipatory repudiation (a breach, as will be discussed shortly) and pursue damages.

Perhaps more important, the other party's failure to give assurance allows you to suspend further performance, which can save your business from sustaining substantial losses that could be recovered only through costly and lengthy litigation. Ultimately, it may be better simply to withdraw from a deal when the other party will not provide assurances of performance than to continue performing under a contract that is likely to be breached anyway.

The Duty of Cooperation Sometimes, the performance of one party depends on the cooperation of the other. The UCC provides that when such cooperation is not forthcoming,

3. *Koch Materials Co. v. Shore Slurry Seal, Inc.*, 205 F.Supp.2d 324 (D.N.J. 2002).

the other party can suspend her or his own performance without liability and hold the uncooperative party in breach or proceed to perform the contract in any reasonable manner [UCC 2–311(3)].

EXAMPLE 16.9 Aman is required by contract to deliver 1,200 Samsung washing machines to various locations in California on or before October 1. Farrell, the buyer, is to specify the locations so that the deliveries can be made on time. Aman repeatedly requests the delivery locations, but Farrell does not respond. On October 1, the washing machines are ready to be shipped, but Farrell still refuses to give Aman the locations. Aman does not ship on October 1. Can Aman be held liable? The answer is no. Aman is excused for any resulting delay of performance because of Farrell's failure to cooperate. •

Obligations of the Buyer or Lessee

The main obligation of the buyer or lessee under a sales or lease contract is to pay for the goods tendered in accordance with the contract. Once the seller or lessor has adequately tendered delivery, the buyer or lessee is obligated to accept the goods and pay for them according to the terms of the contract.

Payment

"Death, they say, acquits us of all obligations."

Michel de Montaigne, 1533–1592 (French writer and philosopher)

In the absence of any specific agreements, the buyer or lessee must make payment at the time and place the goods are *received* [UCC 2–310(a), 2A–516(1)]. When a sale is made on credit, the buyer is obligated to pay according to the specified credit terms (for example, 60, 90, or 120 days), not when the goods are received. The credit period usually begins on the *date of shipment* [UCC 2–310(d)]. Under a lease contract, a lessee must make the lease payment that was specified in the contract [UCC 2A–516(1)].

Payment can be made by any means agreed on by the parties—cash or any other method generally acceptable in the commercial world. If the seller demands cash when the buyer offers a check, credit card, or the like, the seller must permit the buyer reasonable time to obtain legal tender [UCC 2–511].

Right of Inspection

Unless the parties otherwise agree, or for C.O.D. (collect on delivery) transactions, the buyer or lessee has an absolute right to inspect the goods before making payment. This right allows the buyer or lessee to verify, before making payment, that the goods tendered or delivered are what were contracted for or ordered. If the goods are not what were ordered, the buyer or lessee has no duty to pay. *An opportunity for inspection is therefore a condition precedent to the right of the seller or lessor to enforce payment* [UCC 2–513(1), 2A–515(1)].

Inspection can take place at any reasonable place and time and in any reasonable manner. Generally, what is reasonable is determined by custom of the trade, past practices of the parties, and the like. The buyer bears the costs of inspecting the goods (unless otherwise agreed), but if the goods are rejected because they are not conforming, the buyer can recover the costs of inspection from the seller [UCC 2–513(2)].

Acceptance

A buyer or lessee demonstrates acceptance of the delivered goods by doing any of the following:

1. If, after having had a reasonable opportunity to inspect the goods, the buyer or lessee signifies to the seller or lessor that the goods either are conforming or are acceptable in spite of their nonconformity [UCC 2–606(1)(a), 2A–515(1)(a)].

2. If the buyer or lessee has had a reasonable opportunity to inspect the goods and has *failed to reject* them within a reasonable period of time, then acceptance is presumed [UCC 2–602(1), 2–606(1)(b), 2A–515(1)(b)].
3. In sales contracts, if the buyer *performs any act inconsistent with the seller's ownership,* then the buyer will be deemed to have accepted the goods. For example, any use or resale of the goods—except for the limited purpose of testing or inspecting the goods—generally constitutes an acceptance [UCC 2–606(1)(c)].

Partial Acceptance

If some of the goods delivered do not conform to the contract and the seller or lessor has failed to cure, the buyer or lessee can make a *partial* acceptance [UCC 2–601(c), 2A–509(1)]. The same is true if the nonconformity was not reasonably discoverable before acceptance. (In the latter situation, the buyer or lessee may be able to revoke the acceptance, as will be discussed later in this chapter.)

A buyer or lessee cannot accept less than a single commercial unit, however. The UCC defines a *commercial unit* as a unit of goods that, by commercial usage, is viewed as a "single whole" for purposes of sale, and its division would materially impair the character of the unit, its market value, or its use [UCC 2–105(6), 2A–103(1)(c)]. A commercial unit can be a single article (such as a machine), a set of articles (such as a suite of furniture or an assortment of sizes), a quantity (such as a bale, a gross, or a carload), or any other unit treated in the trade as a single whole.

LEARNING OBJECTIVE 3
What options are available to the nonbreaching party when the other party to a sales or lease contract repudiates the contract prior to the time for performance?

Anticipatory Repudiation

What if, before the time for contract performance, one party clearly communicates to the other the intention not to perform? As discussed in Chapter 13, such an action is a breach of the contract by anticipatory repudiation.

Suspension of Performance Obligations

When anticipatory repudiation occurs, the nonbreaching party has a choice of two responses: (1) treat the repudiation as a final breach by pursuing a remedy or (2) wait to see if the repudiating party will decide to honor the contract despite the admitted intention to renege [UCC 2–610, 2A–402]. In either situation, the nonbreaching party may suspend performance.

A Repudiation May Be Retracted

The UCC permits the breaching party to "retract" his or her repudiation (subject to some limitations). This retraction can be done by any method that clearly indicates the party's intent to perform. Once retraction is made, the rights of the repudiating party under the contract are reinstated. There can be no retraction, however, if since the time of the repudiation the other party has canceled or materially changed position or otherwise indicated that the repudiation is final [UCC 2–611, 2A–403].

EXAMPLE 16.10 On April 1, Cora VanMeter, who owns a small inn, purchases a suite of furniture from Robert Horton, who owns Horton's Furniture Warehouse. The contract states, "Delivery must be made on or before May 1." On April 10, Horton informs VanMeter that he cannot make delivery until May 10 and asks her to consent to the modified delivery date. In this situation, VanMeter has the option of either treating Horton's notice of late delivery as a final breach of contract and pursuing a remedy or agreeing to the changed delivery date. Suppose that VanMeter does neither for two weeks. On April 24, Horton informs VanMeter that he will be able to deliver the furniture by May 1 after all. In effect, Horton has retracted his repudiation, reinstating the rights and obligations of the parties under the original contract. Note that if VanMeter had indicated after Horton's repudiation that she was canceling the contract, Horton would not have been able to retract his repudiation. •

LEARNING OBJECTIVE 4

What remedies are available to a seller or lessor when the buyer or lessee breaches the contract? What remedies are available to a buyer or lessee if the seller or lessor breaches the contract?

Remedies of the Seller or Lessor

When the buyer or lessee is in breach, the seller or lessor has numerous remedies available under the UCC. Generally, the remedies available to the seller or lessor depend on the circumstances at the time of the breach, such as which party has possession of the goods, whether the goods are in transit, and whether the buyer or lessee has rejected or accepted the goods.

When the Goods Are in the Possession of the Seller or Lessor

Under the UCC, if the buyer or lessee breaches the contract before the goods have been delivered to her or him, the seller or lessor has the right to pursue the following remedies:

1. Cancel (rescind) the contract.
2. Resell the goods and sue to recover damages.
3. Sue to recover the purchase price or lease payments due.
4. Sue to recover damages for the buyer's nonacceptance.

The Right to Cancel the Contract If the buyer or lessee breaches the contract, the seller or lessor can choose to cancel (rescind) the contract [UCC 2–703(f), 2A–523(1)(a)]. The seller must notify the buyer or lessee of the cancellation, and at that point all remaining obligations of the seller or lessor are discharged. The buyer or lessee is not discharged from all remaining obligations, however. She or he is in breach, and the seller or lessor can pursue remedies available under the UCC for breach.

KNOW THIS

A buyer or lessee breaches a contract by wrongfully rejecting the goods, wrongfully revoking acceptance, refusing to pay, or repudiating the contract.

The Right to Withhold Delivery In general, sellers and lessors can withhold or discontinue performance of their obligations under sales or lease contracts when the buyers or lessees are in breach. This is true whether a buyer or lessee has wrongfully rejected or revoked acceptance of contract goods (rejection and revocation of acceptance will be discussed later), failed to make a payment, or repudiated the contract [UCC 2–703(a), 2A–523(1)(c)]. The seller or lessor can also refuse to deliver the goods to a buyer or lessee who is insolvent (unable to pay debts as they become due), unless the buyer or lessee pays in cash [UCC 2–702(1), 2A–525(1)].

The Right to Resell or Dispose of the Goods When a buyer or lessee breaches or repudiates a sales contract while the seller or lessor is still in possession of the goods, the seller or lessor can resell or dispose of the goods. The seller can retain any profits made as a result of the sale and can hold the buyer or lessee liable for any loss [UCC 2–703(d), 2–706(1), 2A–523(1)(e), 2A–527(1)]. The seller must give the original buyer reasonable notice of the resale, unless the goods are perishable or will rapidly decline in value [UCC 2–706(2), (3)].

When the Goods Are Unfinished When the goods contracted for are unfinished at the time of breach, the seller or lessor can either (1) cease manufacturing the goods and resell them for scrap or salvage value or (2) complete the manufacture and resell or dispose of them, holding the buyer or lessee liable for any *deficiency* (the amount less than the contract price).

In choosing between these two alternatives, the seller or lessor must exercise reasonable commercial judgment to mitigate the loss and obtain maximum value from the unfinished goods [UCC 2–704(2), 2A–524(2)]. Any resale of the goods must be made in good faith and in a commercially reasonable manner.

Incidental Damages All costs resulting from a breach of contract, including all reasonable expenses incurred because of the breach.

When the Resale Price Is Insufficient In sales transactions, the seller can recover any deficiency between the resale price and the contract price, along with **incidental damages**, defined as the costs resulting from the breach [UCC 2–706(1), 2–710]. In lease transactions, the lessor may lease the goods to another party and recover from the original lessee, as damages, any unpaid lease payments up to the beginning date of the lease term under the new lease. The lessor can also recover any deficiency between the lease payments due under the original lease contract and those due under the new lease contract, along with incidental damages [UCC 2A–527(2)].

The Right to Recover the Purchase Price or the Lease Payments Due

Under the UCC, an unpaid seller or lessor can bring an action to recover the purchase price or payments due under the lease contract, plus incidental damages [UCC 2–709(1), 2A–529(1)]. If a seller or lessor is unable to resell or dispose of goods and sues for the contract price or lease payments due, the goods must be held for the buyer or lessee. The seller or lessor can resell or dispose of the goods at any time before collection (of the judgment) from the buyer or lessee, but must credit the net proceeds from the sale to the buyer or lessee.

EXAMPLE 16.11 Southern Realty contracts to purchase one thousand pens with its name inscribed on them from Gem Point. When Gem Point tenders delivery of the pens, Southern Realty wrongfully refuses to accept them. In this situation, Gem Point can bring an action for the purchase price because it delivered conforming goods, but Southern Realty refused to accept or pay for the goods. Gem Point obviously cannot resell the pens inscribed with the buyer's business name, so this situation falls under UCC 2–709. Gem Point is required to make the pens available for Southern Realty, but can resell them (in the event that it can find a buyer) at any time prior to collecting the judgment from Southern Realty. ●

The Right to Recover Damages

If a buyer or lessee repudiates a contract or wrongfully refuses to accept the goods, a seller or lessor can maintain an action to recover the damages that were sustained. Ordinarily, the amount of damages equals the difference between the contract price or lease payments and the market price or lease payments at the time and place of tender of the goods, plus incidental damages [UCC 2–708(1), 2A–528(1)]. When the ordinary measure of damages is insufficient to put the seller or lessor in the same position as the buyer's or lessee's performance would have, the UCC provides an alternative. In that situation, the proper measure of damages is the lost profits of the seller or lessor, including a reasonable allowance for overhead and other expenses [UCC 2–708(2), 2A–528(2)].

When the Goods Are in Transit

If the seller or lessor has delivered the goods to a carrier or a bailee but the buyer or lessee has not yet received them, the goods are said to be *in transit.* If, while the goods are in transit, the seller or lessor learns that the buyer or lessee is insolvent, the seller or lessor can stop the carrier or bailee from delivering the goods. The seller or lessor can stop the delivery of goods in transit to an insolvent party regardless of the quantity of goods shipped, but this is not true if the buyer or lessee is only in breach. When the buyer or lessee is not insolvent, the seller or lessor can stop delivery of goods in transit only if the quantity shipped is at least a carload, a truckload, a planeload, or a larger shipment [UCC 2–705(1), 2A–526(1)].

EXAMPLE 16.12 Arturo Ortega orders a truckload of lumber from Timber Products, Inc., to be shipped to Ortega six weeks later. Ortega, who owes Timber Products for a past shipment, promises to pay the debt immediately and to pay for the current shipment as soon as it is received. After the lumber has been shipped, a bankruptcy court judge notifies Timber Products that Ortega has filed a petition in bankruptcy and listed Timber Products as one of his creditors (see Chapter 21). If the goods are still in transit, Timber Products can stop the carrier from delivering the lumber to Ortega. •

Requirements for Stopping Delivery

To stop delivery, the seller or lessor must *timely notify* the carrier or other bailee that the goods are to be returned or held for the seller or lessor. If the carrier has sufficient time to stop delivery, it must hold and deliver the goods according to the instructions of the seller or lessor, who is liable to the carrier for any additional costs incurred [UCC 2–705(3), 2A–526(3)].

The seller or lessor has the right to stop delivery of the goods under UCC 2–705(2) and 2A–526(2) until the time when the following occurs:

1. The buyer or lessee obtains possession of the goods.
2. The carrier or the bailee acknowledges the rights of the buyer or lessee in the goods (by reshipping or holding the goods for the buyer or lessee, for example).
3. A negotiable document of title covering the goods has been properly transferred to the buyer (in sales transactions only), giving the buyer ownership rights in the goods [UCC 2–702].

Remedies Once the Goods Are Reclaimed

Once the seller or lessor reclaims the goods in transit, she or he can pursue the remedies allowed to sellers and lessors when the goods are in their possession.

KNOW THIS

Incidental damages include all reasonable expenses incurred because of a breach of contract.

When the Goods Are in the Possession of the Buyer or Lessee

Suppose that the buyer or lessee breaches a sales or lease contract at a time when the goods are in the buyer's or lessee's possession. In that event, the seller or lessor can sue to recover the purchase price of the goods or the lease payments due, plus incidental damages [UCC 2–709(1), 2A–529(1)].

In some situations, a seller may also have a right to reclaim the goods from the buyer. For instance, in a sales contract, if the buyer has received the goods on credit and the seller discovers that the buyer is insolvent, the seller can demand return of the goods [UCC 2–702(2)]. Ordinarily, the demand must be made within ten days of the buyer's receipt of the goods.[4] The seller's right to reclaim the goods is subject to the rights of a good faith purchaser or other subsequent buyer in the ordinary course of business who purchases the goods from the buyer before the seller reclaims them.

In regard to lease contracts, if the lessee is in default (fails to make payments that are due, for example), the lessor may reclaim the leased goods that are in the lessee's possession [UCC 2A–525(2)].

4. The seller can demand and reclaim the goods at any time, though, if the buyer misrepresented his or her solvency in writing within three months prior to the delivery of the goods.

Remedies of the Buyer or Lessee

When the seller or lessor breaches the contract, the buyer or lessee has numerous remedies available under the UCC. Like the remedies available to sellers and lessors, the remedies of buyers and lessees depend on the circumstances existing at the time of the breach. (See the *Business Application* feature on pages 432 and 433 for some suggestions on what to do when a contract is breached.)

When the Seller or Lessor Refuses to Deliver the Goods

If the seller or lessor refuses to deliver the goods, or the buyer or lessee has rightfully rejected the goods, the remedies available to the buyer or lessee include the right to:

1. Cancel (rescind) the contract.
2. Obtain goods that have been paid for if the seller or lessor is insolvent.
3. Sue to obtain specific performance if the goods are unique or damages are an inadequate remedy.
4. Buy other goods (obtain *cover*—defined on page 427), and obtain damages from the seller.
5. Sue to obtain identified goods held by a third party (*replevy* goods—defined on page 427).
6. Sue to obtain damages.

KNOW THIS

A seller or lessor breaches a contract by wrongfully failing to deliver the goods, delivering nonconforming goods, making an improper tender of the goods, or repudiating the contract.

The Right to Cancel the Contract

When a seller or lessor fails to make proper delivery or repudiates the contract, the buyer or lessee can cancel, or rescind, the contract. On notice of cancellation, the buyer or lessee is relieved of any further obligations under the contract but retains all rights to other remedies against the seller [UCC 2–711(1), 2A–508(1)(a)]. (The right to cancel the contract is also available to a buyer or lessee who has rightfully rejected goods or revoked acceptance, as will be discussed shortly.)

The Right to Obtain the Goods on Insolvency

If a buyer or lessee has made a partial or full payment for goods that are in the possession of a seller or lessor who is or becomes insolvent, the buyer or lessee has a right to obtain the goods. For this right to be exercised, the goods must be identified to the contract and the buyer or lessee must pay any remaining balance of the price to the seller or lessor [UCC 2–502, 2A–522].

The Right to Obtain Specific Performance

A buyer or lessee can obtain specific performance when the goods are unique and the remedy at law is inadequate [UCC 2–716(1), 2A–521(1)]. Ordinarily, a successful suit for monetary damages is sufficient to place a buyer or lessee in the position he or she would have occupied if the seller or lessor had fully performed.

When the contract is for the purchase of a particular work of art or a similarly unique item, however, monetary damages may not be sufficient. Under these circumstances, equity will require that the seller or lessor perform exactly by delivering the particular goods identified to the contract (a remedy of specific performance).

CASE EXAMPLE 16.13 Doreen Houseman and Eric Dare together bought a house and a pedigreed dog. When the couple separated, they agreed that Dare would keep the house (and pay Houseman for her interest in it), and Houseman would keep the dog. Houseman allowed Dare to take the dog for visits, but after one visit, Dare kept the dog. Houseman filed a lawsuit seeking specific performance of their agreement. The court found that because pets have special subjective value to their owners, a dog can be considered a unique good. Thus, an award of specific performance was appropriate.[5] •

5. *Houseman v. Dare*, 405 N.J.Super. 538, 966 A.2d 24 (2009).

Cover A remedy that allows the buyer or lessee, on the seller's or lessor's breach, to obtain substitute goods from another seller or lessor.

The Right of Cover In certain situations, buyers and lessees can protect themselves by obtaining **cover**—that is, by purchasing or leasing other goods to substitute for those due under the contract. This option is available when the seller or lessor repudiates the contract or fails to deliver the goods, or when a buyer or lessee has rightfully rejected goods or revoked acceptance.

In obtaining cover, the buyer or lessee must act in good faith and without unreasonable delay [UCC 2–712, 2A–518]. After purchasing or leasing substitute goods, the buyer or lessee can recover damages from the seller or lessor. The measure of damages is the difference between the cost of cover and the contract price (or lease payments), plus incidental and consequential damages. Any expenses (such as delivery costs) that were saved as a result of the breach are subtracted [UCC 2–712, 2–715, 2A–518]. Consequential damages are any losses suffered by the buyer or lessee that the seller or lessor could have foreseen (had reason to know about) at the time of contract formation. In addition, consequential damages may include any injury to the buyer's or lessee's person or property proximately resulting from the contract's breach [UCC 2–715(2), 2A–520(2)].

Buyers and lessees are not required to cover, and failure to do so will not bar them from using any other remedies available under the UCC. A buyer or lessee who fails to cover, however, may *not* be able to collect consequential damages that could have been avoided by purchasing or leasing substitute goods.

Replevin An action that can be used by a buyer or lessee to recover identified goods from a third party, such as a bailee, who is wrongfully withholding them.

The Right to Replevy Goods Buyers and lessees also have the right to replevy goods. **Replevin**[6] is an action that a buyer or lessee can use to recover specific goods from a third party, such as a bailee, who is wrongfully withholding them. Under the UCC, the buyer or lessee can replevy goods subject to the contract if the seller or lessor has repudiated or breached the contract. To maintain an action to replevy goods, usually buyers and lessees must show that they are unable to cover for the goods after a reasonable effort [UCC 2–716(3), 2A–521(3)].

The Right to Recover Damages If a seller or lessor repudiates the sales contract or fails to deliver the goods, the buyer or lessee can sue for damages. The measure of recovery is the difference between the contract price (or lease payments) and the market price of (or lease payments that could be obtained for) the goods at the time the buyer (or lessee) *learned* of the breach. The market price or market lease payments are determined at the place where the seller or lessor was supposed to deliver the goods.

KNOW THIS

Consequential damages compensate for a loss (such as lost profits) that is not direct but was reasonably foreseeable at the time of the breach.

The buyer or lessee can also recover incidental and consequential damages, less the expenses that were saved as a result of the breach [UCC 2–713, 2A–519]. **CASE EXAMPLE 16.14** Les Entreprises Jacques Defour & Fils, Inc., contracted to buy a 30,000-gallon industrial tank from Dinsick Equipment Corporation for $70,000. Les Entreprises hired Xaak Transport, Inc., to pick up the tank, but when Xaak arrived at the pickup location, there was no tank. Les Entreprises paid Xaak $7,459 for its services and filed a suit against Dinsick. Here, the buyer can recover the contract price, plus the shipping costs. The court awarded compensatory damages of $70,000 for the tank and incidental damages of $7,459 for the transport. To establish a breach of contract requires an enforceable contract, substantial performance by the nonbreaching party, a breach by the other party, and damage to the nonbreaching party. Les Entreprises agreed to buy a tank and paid the price. Dinsick failed to tender or deliver the tank, or to refund the price. The shipping costs were a necessary part of performance, so this was a reasonable expense.[7] •

6. Pronounced ruh-*pleh*-vun. Note that outside the UCC, the term *replevin* refers to a process that takes place prior to a court's judgment that permits the seizure of specific personal property in which a party claims a right or an interest.

7. *Les Entreprises Jacques Defour & Fils, Inc. v. Dinsick Equipment Corp.*, 2011 WL 307501 (N.D.Ill. 2011).

When the Seller or Lessor Delivers Nonconforming Goods

When the seller or lessor delivers nonconforming goods, the buyer or lessee has several remedies available under the UCC.

The Right to Reject the Goods

If either the goods or the tender of the goods by the seller or lessor fails to conform to the contract *in any respect,* the buyer or lessee can reject the goods in whole or in part [UCC 2–601, 2A–509]. If the buyer or lessee rejects the goods, she or he may then obtain cover, cancel the contract, or sue for damages for breach of contract, just as if the seller or lessor had refused to deliver the goods (see the earlier discussion of these remedies).

CASE EXAMPLE 16.15 Jorge Jauregui contracted to buy a Kawai RX5 piano from Bobb's Piano Sales. Bobb's represented that the piano was in new condition and qualified for the manufacturer's warranty. Jauregui paid the contract price, but the piano was delivered with "unacceptable damage," according to Jauregui, who videotaped its condition. Jauregui rejected the piano and filed a lawsuit for breach of contract. The court ruled that Bobb's had breached the contract by delivering nonconforming goods. Jauregui was entitled to damages equal to the contract price, plus interest, the sales tax, delivery charge, and attorneys' fees.[8] •

Timeliness and Reason for Rejection Required The buyer or lessee must reject the goods within a reasonable amount of time after delivery and must *seasonably* (timely) notify the seller or lessor [UCC 2–602(1), 2A–509(2)]. If the buyer or lessee fails to reject the goods within a reasonable amount of time, acceptance will be presumed.

When rejecting goods, the buyer or lessee must also designate defects that would have been apparent to the seller or lessor on reasonable inspection. Failure to do so precludes the buyer or lessee from using such defects to justify rejection or to establish breach when the seller could have cured the defects if they had been disclosed in a timely fashion [UCC 2–605, 2A–514].

A worker inspects returned goods that will be sold at Overstock.com. Is such a resale of these goods commercially acceptable?

(AP Photo/Jim Urquhart)

Duties of Merchant Buyers and Lessees When Goods Are Rejected What happens if a *merchant buyer* or *lessee* rightfully rejects goods and the seller or lessor has no agent or business at the place of rejection? In that situation, the merchant buyer or lessee has a good faith obligation to follow any reasonable instructions received from the seller or lessor with respect to the goods [UCC 2–603, 2A–511]. The buyer or lessee is entitled to be reimbursed for the care and cost entailed in following the instructions. The same requirements hold if the buyer or lessee rightfully revokes his or her acceptance of the goods at some later time [UCC 2–608(3), 2A–517(5)]. (Revocation of acceptance will be discussed shortly.)

If no instructions are forthcoming and the goods are perishable or threaten to decline in value quickly, the buyer can resell the goods in good faith. The buyer can then take the appropriate reimbursement from the proceeds and a selling commission (not to exceed

8. *Jauregui v. Bobb's Piano Sales & Service, Inc.*, 922 So.2d 303 (Fla.App. 2006).

10 percent of the gross proceeds) [UCC 2–603(1), (2); 2A–511(1), (2)]. If the goods are not perishable, the buyer or lessee may store them for the seller or lessor or reship them to the seller or lessor [UCC 2–604, 2A–512].

Revocation of Acceptance

Acceptance of the goods precludes the buyer or lessee from exercising the right of rejection, but it does not necessarily prevent the buyer or lessee from pursuing other remedies. In certain circumstances, a buyer or lessee is permitted to *revoke* her or his acceptance of the goods. Acceptance of a lot or a commercial unit can be revoked if the nonconformity *substantially* impairs the value of the lot or unit and if one of the following factors is present:

1. Acceptance was predicated on the reasonable assumption that the nonconformity would be cured, and it has not been cured within a reasonable time [UCC 2–608(1)(a), 2A–517(1)(a)].
2. The buyer or lessee did not discover the nonconformity before acceptance, either because it was difficult to discover before acceptance or because assurances made by the seller or lessor that the goods were conforming kept the buyer or lessee from inspecting the goods [UCC 2–608(1)(b), 2A–517(1)(b)].

Revocation of acceptance is not effective until the seller or lessor is notified, which must occur within a reasonable time after the buyer or lessee either discovers or *should have discovered* the grounds for revocation. Additionally, revocation must occur before the goods have undergone any substantial change (such as spoilage) not caused by their own defects [UCC 2–608(2), 2A–517(4)]. Once acceptance is revoked, the buyer or lessee can pursue remedies, just as if the goods had been rejected. (See this chapter's *Beyond Our Borders* feature below for a glimpse at how international sales law deals with revocation of acceptance.)

The Right to Recover Damages for Accepted Goods

A buyer or lessee who has accepted nonconforming goods may also keep the goods and recover damages caused by the breach. To do so, the buyer or lessee must notify the seller or lessor of the breach within a reasonable time after the defect was or should have been discovered. Failure to give notice of the defects (breach) to the seller or lessor bars the buyer or lessee from pursuing any remedy [UCC 2–607(3), 2A–516(3)]. In addition, the parties to a sales or lease contract can insert a provision requiring the buyer or lessee to give notice of any defects in the goods within a set period.

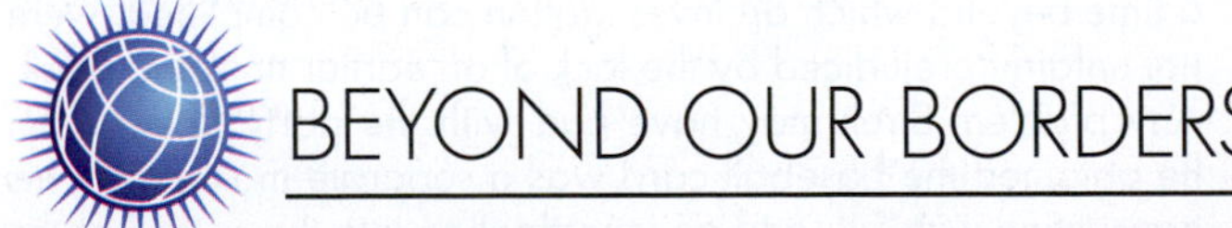

The CISG's Approach to Revocation of Acceptance

Under the UCC, a buyer or lessee who has accepted goods may be able to revoke acceptance under the circumstances mentioned in the text above. The United Nations Convention on Contracts for the International Sale of Goods (CISG) also allows buyers to rescind their contracts after they have accepted the goods.

The CISG, however, takes a somewhat different—and more direct—approach to the problem than the UCC does. In the same circumstances that permit a buyer to revoke acceptance under the UCC, under the CISG the buyer can simply declare that the seller has *fundamentally* breached the contract and proceed to sue the seller for the breach. Article 25 of the CISG states that a "breach of contract committed by one of the parties is fundamental if it results in such detriment to the other party as substantially to deprive him [or her] of what he [or she] is entitled to expect under the contract." For example, to revoke acceptance of a shipment under the CISG, a buyer need not prove that the nonconformity of one shipment substantially impaired the value of the whole lot. The buyer can simply file a lawsuit alleging that the seller is in breach.

Critical Thinking

What is the essential difference between revoking acceptance and bringing a suit for breach of contract?

When the goods delivered are not as promised, the measure of damages equals the difference between the value of the goods as accepted and their value if they had been delivered as warranted [UCC 2–714(2), 2A–519(4)]. The buyer or lessee is also entitled to incidental and consequential damages when appropriate [UCC 2–714(3), 2A–519(3)]. The UCC also permits the buyer or lessee, with proper notice to the seller or lessor, to deduct all or any part of the damages from the price or lease payments still due under the contract [UCC 2–717, 2A–516(1)].

Is two years after a sale of goods a reasonable time period in which to discover a defect in those goods and notify the seller or lessor of a breach? That was the question in the following *Spotlight Case*.

Spotlight on Baseball Cards

Case 16.3

Fitl v. Strek

Supreme Court of Nebraska, 269 Neb. 51, 690 N.W.2d 605 (2005).
caselaw.findlaw.com/courts/Nebraska[a]

A 1952 Mickey Mantle Topps baseball card.

(Terren in Virginia/Creative Commons)

FACTS Over the Labor Day weekend in 1995, James Fitl attended a sports-card show in San Francisco, California, where he met Mark Strek, doing business as Star Cards of San Francisco, an exhibitor at the show. Later, on Strek's representation that a certain 1952 Mickey Mantle Topps baseball card was in near-mint condition, Fitl bought the card from Strek for $17,750. Strek delivered the card to Fitl in Omaha, Nebraska, and Fitl placed it in a safe-deposit box. In May 1997, Fitl sent the card to Professional Sports Authenticators (PSA), a sports-card grading service. PSA told Fitl that the card was ungradable because it had been discolored and doctored. Fitl complained to Strek, who replied that Fitl should have returned the card within "a typical grace period for the unconditional return of a card, . . . 7 days to 1 month" of its receipt. In August, Fitl sent the card to ASA Accugrade, Inc. (ASA), another grading service, for a second opinion of the value. ASA also concluded that the card had been refinished and trimmed. Fitl filed a suit in a Nebraska state court against Strek, seeking damages. The court awarded Fitl $17,750, plus his court costs. Strek appealed to the Nebraska Supreme Court.

ISSUE Was two years after the sale of the baseball card a reasonable time to discover a defect and notify the seller of a breach?

DECISION Yes. The state supreme court affirmed the decision of the lower court.

REASON Section 2–607(3)(a) of the UCC states, "Where a tender has been accepted . . . the buyer must within a reasonable time after he discovers or should have discovered any breach notify the seller of breach or be barred from any remedy." "What is a reasonable time for taking any action depends on the nature, purpose and circumstances of such action" [UCC 1–205(a)]. The state supreme court concluded that the buyer (Fitl) had reasonably relied on the seller's (Strek's) representation that the goods were "authentic," which they were not, and when their defects were discovered, Fitl had given timely notice.

The court reasoned that "the policies behind the notice requirement, to allow the seller to correct a defect, to prepare for negotiation and litigation, and to protect against stale claims at a time beyond which an investigation can be completed, were not unfairly prejudiced by the lack of an earlier notice to Strek. Any problem Strek may have had with the party from whom he obtained the baseball card was a separate matter from his transaction with Fitl, and an investigation into the source of the altered card would not have minimized Fitl's damages."

WHAT IF THE FACTS WERE DIFFERENT? *Suppose that Fitl and Strek had included in their deal a written clause requiring Fitl to give notice of any defect in the card within "7 days to 1 month" of its receipt. Would the result have been different? Why or why not?*

a. Under "Browse Nebraska Courts," click on "Supreme Court of Nebraska." In the "Party name:" box, type "Fitl" and click on "Search." In the result, click on the name of the case to access the opinion.

Limitation of Remedies

LEARNING OBJECTIVE 5
In contracts subject to the UCC, are parties free to limit the remedies available to the nonbreaching party on a breach of contract? If so, in what ways?

The parties to a sales or lease contract can vary their respective rights and obligations by contractual agreement. For example, a seller and buyer can expressly provide for remedies in addition to those provided in the UCC. They can also provide remedies in lieu of those provided in the UCC, or they can change the measure of damages. The seller can provide that the buyer's only remedy on breach of warranty will be repair or replacement of the item, or the seller can limit the buyer's remedy to return of the goods and refund of the purchase price.

In sales and lease contracts, an agreed-on remedy is in addition to those provided in the UCC unless the parties expressly agree that the remedy is exclusive of all others [UCC 2–719(1), 2A–503(1), (2)].

Exclusive Remedies

(Andrey Snegirev/Shutterstock.com)

If this pipe-cutting machine has defective parts, can the buyer insist on replacement of the entire machine?

If the parties state that a remedy is exclusive, then it is the sole, or exclusive, remedy. **EXAMPLE 16.16** Standard Tool Company agrees to sell a pipe-cutting machine to United Pipe & Tubing Corporation. The contract limits United's remedy exclusively to repair or replacement of any defective parts. Thus, repair or replacement of defective parts is the buyer's exclusive remedy under this contract. •

When circumstances cause an exclusive remedy to fail in its essential purpose, however, it is no longer exclusive, and the buyer or lessee may pursue other remedies available under the UCC [UCC 2–719(2), 2A–503(2)]. **EXAMPLE 16.17** In *Example 16.16*, suppose that Standard Tool Company is unable to repair a defective part, and no replacement parts are available. In this situation, because the exclusive remedy failed in its essential purpose, the buyer normally will be entitled to seek other remedies provided to a buyer by the UCC. •

Limitations on Consequential Damages

As discussed in Chapter 14 on page 356, *consequential damages* are special damages that compensate for indirect losses (such as lost profits) resulting from a breach of contract that were reasonably foreseeable. Under the UCC, parties to a contract can limit or exclude consequential damages, provided the limitation is not unconscionable.

When the buyer or lessee is a consumer, any limitation of consequential damages for personal injuries resulting from consumer goods is *prima facie* (presumptively, or on its face) unconscionable. The limitation of consequential damages is not necessarily unconscionable when the loss is commercial in nature—for example, lost profits and property damage [UCC 2–719(3), 2A–503(3)].

Statute of Limitations

An action for breach of contract under the UCC must be commenced *within four years after the cause of action accrues*—that is, a buyer or lessee must file the lawsuit within four years after the breach occurs [UCC 2–725(1)]. In addition, a buyer or lessee who has accepted nonconforming goods usually must notify the breaching party of the breach within a reasonable time, or the aggrieved party is barred from pursuing any remedy [UCC 2–607(3)(a), 2A–516(3)].

The parties can agree in their contract to reduce this period to not less than one year, but cannot extend it beyond four years [UCC 2–725(1), 2A–506(1)]. A cause of action accrues for breach of warranty (to be discussed in Chapter 17) when the seller or lessor tenders delivery. This is the rule even if the aggrieved party is unaware that the cause of action has accrued [UCC 2–725(2), 2A–506(2)].

Reviewing . . . Performance and Breach of Sales and Lease Contracts

GFI, Inc., a Hong Kong company, makes audio decoder chips, one of the essential components used in the manufacture of MP3 players. Egan Electronics contracts with GFI to buy 10,000 chips on an installment contract, with 2,500 chips to be shipped every three months, F.O.B. Hong Kong via Air Express. At the time for the first delivery, GFI delivers only 2,400 chips but explains to Egan that even though the shipment is less than 5 percent short, the chips are of a higher quality than those specified in the contract and are worth 5 percent more than the contract price. Egan accepts the shipment and pays GFI the contract price. At the time for the second shipment, GFI makes a shipment identical to the first. Egan again accepts and pays for the chips. At the time for the third shipment, GFI ships 2,400 of the same chips, but this time GFI sends them via Hong Kong Air instead of Air Express. While in transit, the chips are destroyed. When it is time for the fourth shipment, GFI again sends 2,400 chips, but this time Egan rejects the chips without explanation. Using the information presented in the chapter, answer the following questions.

1. Did GFI have a legitimate reason to expect that Egan would accept the fourth shipment? Why or why not?
2. Does the substitution of carriers for the third shipment constitute a breach of the contract by GFI? Explain.
3. Suppose that the silicon used for the chips becomes unavailable for a period of time and that GFI cannot manufacture enough chips to fulfill the contract but does ship as many as it can to Egan. Under what doctrine might a court release GFI from further performance of the contract?
4. Under the UCC, does Egan have a right to reject the fourth shipment? Why or why not?

DEBATE THIS If a contract specifies a particular carrier, then the shipper must use that carrier or be in breach of the contract—no exceptions should ever be allowed.

BUSINESS APPLICATION

What Can You Do When a Contract Is Breached?*

A contract for the sale of goods has been breached. Can the dispute be settled without a trip to court? The answer depends on the willingness of the parties to agree on an appropriate remedy.

Contractual Clauses on Applicable Remedies

Often, the parties to sales and lease contracts agree in advance, in their contracts, on what remedies will be applicable in the event of a breach. This may take the form of a contract provision restricting or expanding remedies available under the Uniform Commercial Code [UCC 2–719]. Such clauses help to reduce uncertainty and the necessity for costly litigation.

When the Contract Is Silent on Applicable Remedies

If your agreement does not cover a breach and you are the nonbreaching party, the UCC gives you a variety of alternatives. You need to determine the available remedies, analyze them and rank them in order of priority, then predict how successful you might be in pursuing each remedy if you decide to go to court. Next, look at the position of the breaching party to determine the basis for negotiating a settlement.

*This *Business Application* is not meant to substitute for the services of an attorney who is licensed to practice law in your state.

For example, when defective goods are delivered and accepted, usually it is preferable for the buyer and seller to reach an agreement on a reduced purchase price. Practically speaking, though, the buyer may be unable to obtain a partial refund from the seller. In this situation, UCC 2–717 allows the buyer to give notice of the intention to deduct the damages from any part of the purchase price not yet paid. If you are a buyer who has accepted defective goods and has not yet paid in full, you may wish to exercise your rights under UCC 2–717 and deduct appropriate damages from your final payment. Remember that most breaches of contract do not end up in court—they are settled beforehand.

Checklist for the Nonbreaching Party to a Contract

1. *Ascertain if a remedy is explicitly written into your contract. Use that remedy, if possible, to avoid litigation.*
2. *If no specific remedy is available, look to the UCC.*
3. *Assess how successful you might be in pursuing a remedy if you go to court.*
4. *Analyze the position of the breaching party.*
5. *Determine whether a negotiated settlement is preferable to a lawsuit, which is best done by consulting your attorney.*

Key Terms

conforming goods 414
cover 427
incidental damages 424
installment contract 414
replevin 427
tender of delivery 414

Chapter Summary: Performance and Breach of Sales and Lease Contracts

REQUIREMENTS OF PERFORMANCE	
Obligations of the Seller or Lessor (See pages 414–421.)	1. The seller or lessor must tender *conforming* goods to the buyer or lessee. Tender must take place at a *reasonable hour* and in a *reasonable manner.* Under the perfect tender doctrine, the seller or lessor must tender goods that conform exactly to the terms of the contract [UCC 2–503(1), 2A–508(1)]. 2. If the seller or lessor tenders nonconforming goods prior to the performance date and the buyer or lessee rejects them, the seller or lessor may *cure* (repair or replace the goods) within the contract time for performance [UCC 2–508(1), 2A–513(1)]. If the seller or lessor had reasonable grounds to believe that the buyer or lessee would accept the tendered goods, on the buyer's or lessee's rejection the seller or lessor has a reasonable time to substitute conforming goods without liability [UCC 2–508(2), 2A–513(2)]. 3. If the agreed-on means of delivery becomes impracticable or unavailable, the seller must substitute an alternative means (such as a different carrier) if one is available [UCC 2–614(1)]. 4. If a seller or lessor tenders nonconforming goods in any one installment under an installment contract, the buyer or lessee may reject the installment only if its value is substantially impaired and cannot be cured. The entire installment contract is breached only when one or more nonconforming installments *substantially* impair the value of the *whole* contract [UCC 2–612, 2A–510]. 5. When performance becomes commercially impracticable owing to circumstances that were not foreseeable when the contract was formed, the perfect tender rule no longer holds [UCC 2–615, 2A–405].
Obligations of the Buyer or Lessee (See pages 421–422.)	1. On tender of delivery by the seller or lessor, the buyer or lessee must pay for the goods at the time and place the goods are *received,* unless the sale is made on credit. Payment may be made by any method generally acceptable in the commercial world unless the seller demands cash [UCC 2–310, 2–511]. In lease contracts, the lessee must make lease payments in accordance with the contract [UCC 2A–516(1)]. 2. Unless otherwise agreed, the buyer or lessee has an absolute right to inspect the goods before acceptance [UCC 2–513(1), 2A–515(1)]. 3. The buyer or lessee can manifest acceptance of delivered goods expressly in words or by conduct or by failing to reject the goods after a reasonable period of time following inspection or after having had a reasonable opportunity to inspect them [UCC 2–606(1), 2A–515(1)]. A buyer will be deemed to have accepted goods if he or she performs any act inconsistent with the seller's ownership [UCC 2–606(1)(c)]. 4. The buyer or lessee can make a partial acceptance if some of the goods do not conform to the contract and the seller or lessor failed to cure [2–601(c), 2A–509(1)].

Continued

Chapter Summary: Performance and Breach of Sales and Lease Contracts—Continued

Anticipatory Repudiation (See pages 422–423.)	If, before the time for performance, one party clearly indicates to the other an intention not to perform, under UCC 2–610 and 2A–402, the aggrieved party may do the following: 1. Await performance by the repudiating party for a commercially reasonable time. 2. Resort to any remedy for breach. 3. In either situation, suspend performance.
REMEDIES FOR BREACH OF CONTRACT	
Remedies of the Seller or Lessor (See pages 423–425.)	1. *When the goods are in the possession of the seller or lessor*—The seller or lessor may do the following: a. Cancel the contract [UCC 2–703(f), 2A–523(1)(a)]. b. Withhold delivery [UCC 2–703(a), 2A–523(1)(c)]. c. Resell or dispose of the goods [UCC 2–703(d), 2–706(1), 2A–523(1)(e), 2A–527(1)]. d. Sue to recover the purchase price or lease payments due [UCC 2–709(1), 2A–529(1)]. e. Sue to recover damages [UCC 2–708, 2A–528]. 2. *When the goods are in transit*—The seller or lessor may stop the carrier or bailee from delivering the goods under certain conditions [UCC 2–705, 2A–526]. 3. *When the goods are in the possession of the buyer or lessee*—The seller or lessor may do the following: a. Sue to recover the purchase price or lease payments due [UCC 2–709(1), 2A–529(1)]. b. Reclaim the goods. A seller may reclaim goods received by an insolvent buyer if the demand is made within ten days of receipt (reclaiming goods excludes all other remedies) [UCC 2–702(2)]. A lessor may repossess goods if the lessee is in default [UCC 2A–525(2)].
Remedies of the Buyer or Lessee (See pages 426–430.)	1. *When the seller or lessor refuses to deliver the goods*—The buyer or lessee may do the following: a. Cancel the contract [UCC 2–711(1), 2A–508(1)(a)]. b. Recover the goods if the seller or lessor becomes insolvent within ten days after receiving the first payment and the goods are identified to the contract [UCC 2–502, 2A–522]. c. Obtain specific performance (when the goods are unique and the remedy at law is inadequate) [UCC 2–716(1), 2A–521(1)]. d. Obtain cover [UCC 2–712, 2A–518]. e. Replevy the goods (if cover is unavailable) [UCC 2–716(3), 2A–521(3)]. f. Sue to recover damages [UCC 2–713, 2A–519]. 2. *When the seller or lessor delivers or tenders delivery of nonconforming goods*—The buyer or lessee may do the following: a. Reject the goods [UCC 2–601, 2A–509]. b. Revoke acceptance if the nonconformity *substantially* impairs the value of the unit or lot and if one of the following factors is present: (1) Acceptance was predicated on the reasonable assumption that the nonconformity would be cured, and it was not cured within a reasonable time [UCC 2–608(1)(a), 2A–517(1)(a)]. (2) The buyer or lessee did not discover the nonconformity before acceptance, either because it was difficult to discover before acceptance or because the seller's or lessor's assurance that the goods were conforming kept the buyer or lessee from inspecting the goods [UCC 2–608(1)(b), 2A–517(1)(b)]. c. Accept the goods and recover damages [UCC 2–607, 2–714, 2–717, 2A–519].
Limitation of Remedies (See page 431.)	1. Remedies may be limited in sales or lease contracts by agreement of the parties. If the contract states that a remedy is exclusive, then that is the sole remedy unless the remedy fails in its essential purpose. Sellers and lessors can also limit the rights of buyers and lessees to consequential damages unless the limitation is unconscionable [UCC 2–719, 2A–503]. 2. The UCC has a four-year statute of limitations for actions involving breach of contract. By agreement, the parties to a sales or lease contract can reduce this period to not less than one year, but they cannot extend it beyond four years [UCC 2–725(1), 2A–506(1)].

ExamPrep

ISSUE SPOTTERS

1. Country Fruit Stand orders eighty cases of peaches from Down Home Farms. Without stating a reason, Down Home untimely delivers thirty cases instead of eighty. Does Country have the right to reject the shipment? Explain. **(See page 415.)**

2. Brite Images, Inc. (BI), agrees to sell Catalog Corporation (CC) five thousand posters of celebrities, to be delivered on May 1. On April 1, BI repudiates the contract. CC informs BI that it expects delivery. Can CC sue BI without waiting until May 1? Why or why not? **(See pages 422–423.)**

—Check your answers to the Issue Spotters against the answers provided in Appendix E at the end of this text.

BEFORE THE TEST

Go to www.cengagebrain.com, enter the ISBN 9781133273561, and click on "Find" to locate this textbook's Web site. Then, click on "Access Now" under "Study Tools," and select Chapter 16 at the top. There, you will find a Practice Quiz that you can take to assess your mastery of the concepts in this chapter, as well as Flashcards, a Glossary of important terms, and Video Questions (when assigned).

For Review

Answers to the even-numbered questions in this For Review section can be found in Appendix F at the end of this text.

1. What are the respective obligations of the parties under a contract for the sale or lease of goods?
2. What is the perfect tender rule? What are some important exceptions to this rule that apply to sales and lease contracts?
3. What options are available to the nonbreaching party when the other party to a sales or lease contract repudiates the contract prior to the time for performance?
4. What remedies are available to a seller or lessor when the buyer or lessee breaches the contract? What remedies are available to a buyer or lessee if the seller or lessor breaches the contract?
5. In contracts subject to the UCC, are parties free to limit the remedies available to the nonbreaching party on a breach of contract? If so, in what ways?

Business Scenarios and Case Problems

16–1 **Remedies.** Genix, Inc., has contracted to sell Larson five hundred washing machines of a certain model at list price. Genix is to ship the goods on or before December 1. Genix produces one thousand washing machines of this model but has not yet prepared Larson's shipment. On November 1, Larson repudiates the contract. Discuss the remedies available to Genix in this situation. **(See page 423.)**

16–2 **Question with Sample Answer—Anticipatory Repudiation.** Moore contracted in writing to sell her 2010 Hyundai Santa Fe to Hammer for $16,500. Moore agreed to deliver the car on Wednesday, and Hammer promised to pay the $16,500 on the following Friday. On Tuesday, Hammer informed Moore that he would not be buying the car after all. By Friday, Hammer had changed his mind again and tendered $16,500 to Moore. Although Moore had not sold the car to another party, she refused the tender and refused to deliver. Hammer claimed that Moore had breached their contract. Moore contended that Hammer's repudiation released her from her duty to perform under the contract. Who is correct, and why? **(See page 422.)**

—For a sample answer to Question 16–2, go to Appendix G at the end of this text.

16–3 **Spotlight on Revocation of Acceptance—Remedies of the Buyer.** L.V.R.V., Inc., sells recreational vehicles (RVs) in Las Vegas, Nevada, as Wheeler's Las Vegas RV. In September 1997, Wheeler's sold a Santara RV made by Coachmen Recreational Vehicle Co. to Arthur and Roswitha Waddell. The Waddells hoped to spend two or three years driving around the country, but almost immediately—and repeatedly—they experienced problems with the RV. Its entry door popped open. Its cooling and heating systems did not work properly. Its batteries did not maintain a charge. Most significantly, its engine overheated when ascending a moderate grade. The Waddells brought it to Wheeler's service department for repairs. Over the next year and a half, the RV spent more than seven months at Wheeler's. In March 1999, the Waddells filed a complaint in a Nevada state court against the dealer to revoke their acceptance of the RV. What are the requirements for a buyer's revocation of acceptance? Were the requirements met in this case? In whose favor should the court rule? Why? [*Waddell v. L.V.R.V., Inc.*, 122 Nev. 15, 125 P.3d 1160 (2006)] **(See page 426.)**

16–4 **Breach and Damages.** Utility Systems of America, Inc., was doing roadwork when Chad DeRosier, a nearby landowner, asked Utility to dump 1,500 cubic yards of fill onto his property. Utility agreed but exceeded DeRosier's request by dumping 6,500 cubic yards. Utility offered to remove the extra fill for $9,500. DeRosier paid a different contractor $46,629 to remove the fill and do certain other work. He then filed a suit against Utility. Because Utility charged nothing for the fill, was there a breach of contract? If so, would the damages be greater than $9,500? Could consequential damages be justified? Discuss. [*DeRosier v. Utility Systems of America, Inc.*, 780 N.W.2d 1 (Minn.App. 2010)] **(See page 429.)**

16–5 Right of Inspection. Jessie Romero offered to deliver two trade-in vehicles—a 2003 Mitsubishi Montero and a 2002 Chevrolet Silverado pickup—to Scoggin-Dickey Chevrolet Buick, Inc., in exchange for a 2006 Silverado pickup. Scoggin-Dickey agreed. The parties negotiated a price, including a value for the trade-in vehicles, plus cash. Romero paid the cash and took the Silverado. On inspecting the trade-in vehicles, however, Scoggin-Dickey found that they had little value. The dealer repossessed the 2006 Silverado. Did the dealership have the right to inspect the goods and reject them when it did? Why or why not? [*Romero v. Scoggin-Dickey Chevrolet Buick, Inc.*, __ S.W.3d __ (Tex.Civ.App.—Amarillo 2010)] **(See page 421.)**

16–6 Right to Recover Damages. Woodridge USA Properties, L.P., bought eighty-seven commercial truck trailers from Southeast Trailer Mart, Inc. (STM). Gerald McCarty, an independent sales agent who arranged the deal, showed Woodridge the documents of title. They did not indicate that Woodridge was the buyer. Woodridge asked McCarty to sell the trailers, and within three months, they were sold. McCarty did not give the proceeds to Woodridge, however. Woodridge—without mentioning the title documents—asked STM to refund the contract price. STM refused. Does Woodridge have a right to recover damages from STM? Explain. [*Woodridge USA Properties, L.P. v. Southeast Trailer Mart, Inc.*, 2011 WL 303204 (11th Cir. 2011)] **(See page 424.)**

16–7 Case Problem with Sample Answer—Nonconforming Goods. Padma Paper Mills, Ltd., converts waste paper into usable paper. In 2007, Padma entered into a contract with Universal Exports, Inc., under which Universal Exports certified that it would ship white envelope cuttings, and Padma paid $131,000 for the paper. When the shipment arrived, however, Padma discovered that Universal Exports had sent multicolored paper plates and other brightly colored paper products. Padma accepted the goods but notified Universal Exports that they did not conform to the contract. Can Padma recover even though it accepted the goods knowing that they were nonconforming? If so, how? [*Padma Paper Mills, Ltd. v. Universal Exports, Inc.*, 34 Misc.3d 1236(A) (N.Y.Sup. 2012)] **(See pages 428–429.)**

—For a sample answer to Problem 16–7, go to Appendix H at the end of this text.

16–8 A Question of Ethics—Revocation of Acceptance. Scotwood Industries, Inc., sells calcium chloride flake for use in ice melt products. Between July and September 2004, Scotwood delivered thirty-seven shipments of flake to Frank Miller & Sons, Inc. After each delivery, Scotwood billed Miller, which paid thirty-five of the invoices and processed 30 to 50 percent of the flake. In August, Miller began complaining about the quality. Scotwood assured Miller that it would remedy the situation. Finally, in October, Miller told Scotwood, "This is totally unacceptable. We are willing to discuss Scotwood picking up the material." Miller claimed that the flake was substantially defective because it was chunked. Calcium chloride maintains its purity for up to five years, but if it is exposed to and absorbs moisture, it chunks, making it unusable. In response to Scotwood's suit to collect payment on the unpaid invoices, Miller filed a counterclaim in a federal district court for breach of contract, seeking to recover based on revocation of acceptance, among other things. [*Scotwood Industries, Inc. v. Frank Miller & Sons, Inc.*, 435 F.Supp.2d 1160 (D.Kan. 2006)] **(See page 429.)**

1. What is revocation of acceptance? How does a buyer effectively exercise this option? Do the facts in this case support this theory as a ground for Miller to recover damages? Why or why not?
2. Is there an ethical basis for allowing a buyer to revoke acceptance of goods and recover damages? If so, is there an ethical limit to this right? Discuss.

Critical Thinking and Writing Assignments

16–9 Critical Legal Thinking. Under what circumstances should courts not allow fully informed contracting parties to agree to limit remedies?

16–10 Business Law Writing. Suppose that you are a collector of antique cars and you need to purchase spare parts for a 1938 engine. These parts are not made anymore and are scarce. You discover that Beem has the spare parts that you need. To get the contract with Beem, you agree to pay 50 percent of the purchase price in advance. You send the payment on May 1, and Beem receives it on May 2. On May 3, Beem, having found another buyer willing to pay substantially more for the parts, informs you that he will not deliver as contracted. That same day, you learn that Beem is insolvent. Write three paragraphs fully discussing any possible remedies that would enable you to take possession of the parts.

16–11 Business Law Critical Thinking Group Assignment. Kodiak agrees to sell 1,000 espresso machines to Lin to be delivered on May 1. Due to a strike during the last week of April, there is a temporary shortage of delivery vehicles. Kodiak can deliver the espresso makers 200 at a time over a period of ten days, with the first delivery on May 1.

1. The first group will determine if Kodiak has the right to deliver the goods in five lots. What happens if Lin objects to delivery in lots?
2. A second group will analyze whether the doctrine of commercial impracticability applies to this scenario, and if it does, what the result will be.

CHAPTER 17

Warranties and Product Liability

(Lisa/Shutterstock.com)

CHAPTER OUTLINE

- Warranties
- Lemon Laws
- Product Liability
- Strict Product Liability
- Defenses to Product Liability

LEARNING OBJECTIVES

The five learning objectives below are designed to help improve your understanding of the chapter. After reading this chapter, you should be able to answer the following questions:

1. What factors determine whether a seller's or lessor's statement constitutes an express warranty or is mere puffery?
2. What implied warranties arise under the UCC?
3. Can a manufacturer be held liable to any person who suffers an injury proximately caused by the manufacturer's negligently made product?
4. What are the elements of a cause of action in strict product liability?
5. What defenses to liability can be raised in a product liability lawsuit?

"I'll warrant him heart-whole."

—William Shakespeare, 1564–1616 (English dramatist and poet)

Warranty is an age-old concept. In sales and lease law, a warranty is an assurance by the seller or lessor of certain facts concerning the goods being sold or leased. In the chapter-opening quotation, a character in William Shakespeare's play *As You Like It* warranted his friend "heart-whole." Likewise, in commercial law, sellers and lessors warrant to those who purchase or lease their goods that the goods are as represented or will be as promised.

The Uniform Commercial Code (UCC) has numerous rules governing product warranties as they occur in sales and lease contracts. Those rules are the subject matter of the first part of this chapter. A natural addition to the discussion is *product liability:* Who is liable to consumers, users, and bystanders for physical harm and property damage caused by a particular good or its use? In today's social environment of consumerism, businesspersons need to be keenly aware of how the sale or lease of defective products can lead to substantial liability.

Product liability encompasses not only the contract theory of warranty but also the tort theories of negligence and strict liability (discussed in Chapter 4). Warranty law is also part of the broad body of consumer protection law that will be discussed in Chapter 33.

Warranties

Most goods are covered by some type of warranty designed to protect consumers. Article 2 (on sales) and Article 2A (on leases) of the UCC designate several types of warranties that can arise in a sales or lease contract, including warranties of title, express warranties, and implied warranties.

Warranties of Title

Under the UCC, three types of title warranties—*good title, no liens,* and *no infringements*—can automatically arise in sales and lease contracts.

Good Title

In most sales, sellers warrant that they have good and valid title to the goods sold and that transfer of the title is rightful [UCC 2–312(1)(a)]. If the buyer subsequently learns that the seller did not have good title to goods that were purchased, the buyer can sue the seller for breach of this warranty.

EXAMPLE 17.1 Alexis steals a diamond ring from Calvin and sells it to Emma, who does not know that the ring is stolen. If Calvin discovers that Emma has the ring, then he has the right to reclaim it from Emma. When Alexis sold Emma the ring, Alexis automatically warranted to Emma that the title conveyed was valid and that its transfer was rightful. Because a thief has no title to stolen goods, Alexis breached the warranty of title imposed by the UCC and became liable to Emma for appropriate damages. • (There is no warranty of good title in lease contracts because title to the goods does not pass to the lessee, as discussed on page 399 of Chapter 15.)

Lien An encumbrance on a property to satisfy a debt or protect a claim for payment of a debt.

No Liens

A second warranty of title shields buyers and lessees who are *unaware* of any encumbrances, or **liens** (claims, charges, or liabilities—see Chapter 21), against goods at the time the contract is made [UCC 2–312(1)(b), 2A–211(1)]. This warranty protects buyers who, for example, unknowingly purchase goods that are subject to a creditor's *security interest* (an interest in the goods that secures payment or performance—see Chapter 20). If a creditor legally repossesses the goods from a buyer *who had no actual knowledge of the security interest,* the buyer can recover from the seller for breach of warranty.

No Infringements

A third type of title warranty is a warranty against infringement of any patent, trademark, or copyright. When the seller or lessor is a merchant, he or she automatically warrants that the buyer or lessee takes the goods *free of infringements.* In other words, a merchant promises that the goods delivered are free from any copyright, trademark, or patent claims of a third person [UCC 2–312(3), 2A–211(2)].

Express Warranty A promise that is included in a contract concerning the quality, condition, description, or performance of the goods being sold or leased.

Is this logo an express warranty?

(Arcady/Shutterstock.com)

Express Warranties

A seller or lessor can create an **express warranty** by making representations concerning the quality, condition, description, or performance potential of the goods. Under UCC 2–313 and 2A–210, express warranties arise when a seller or lessor indicates any of the following:

1. That the goods conform to any *affirmation* (declaration that something is true) or *promise* of fact that the seller or lessor makes to the buyer or lessee about the goods. Such affirmations or promises are usually made during the bargaining process. Statements such as "these drill bits will penetrate stainless steel—and without dulling" are express warranties.
2. That the goods conform to any *description* of them. For example, a label that reads "Crate contains one 150-horsepower diesel engine" or a contract that calls for the delivery of a "camel's hair coat" creates an express warranty.
3. That the goods conform to any *sample* or *model* of the goods shown to the buyer or lessee.

Basis of the Bargain

To create an express warranty, a seller or lessor does not have to use words such as *warrant* or *guarantee* [UCC 2–313(2), 2A–210(2)]. It is only necessary that a reasonable buyer or lessee would regard the representation of fact as part of the basis of the bargain [UCC 2–313(1), 2A–210(1)]. The UCC does not define the "basis of the bargain," however, and it is a question of fact in each case whether a representation was made at such a time and in such a way that it induced the buyer or lessee to enter into the contract.

LEARNING OBJECTIVE 1

What factors determine whether a seller's or lessor's statement constitutes an express warranty or is mere puffery?

Statements of Opinion and Value

Only statements of fact create express warranties. If the seller or lessor makes a statement about the supposed value or worth of the goods, or offers an opinion or recommendation about the goods, the seller or lessor is not creating an express warranty [UCC 2–313(2), 2A–210(2)].

EXAMPLE 17.2 A car salesperson claims that "this is the best used car to come along in years. It has four new tires and a 250-horsepower engine just rebuilt this year." The seller has made several *affirmations of fact* that can create a warranty: the automobile has an engine, the engine has 250 horsepower and was rebuilt this year, and there are four new tires on the automobile. The seller's *opinion* that the vehicle is "the best used car to come along in years," however, is known as "puffery" and creates no warranty. (*Puffery* is an expression of opinion by a seller or lessor that is not made as a representation of fact.) ●

A statement about the value of the goods, such as "this is worth a fortune" or "anywhere else you'd pay $10,000 for it," usually does not create a warranty. If the seller or lessor is an expert and gives an opinion as an expert to a layperson, though, then a warranty may be created.

It is not always easy to determine whether a statement constitutes an express warranty or puffery. Often, the reasonableness of the buyer's or lessee's reliance is the controlling criterion. For instance, a salesperson's statements that a ladder "will never break" and will "last a lifetime" are so clearly improbable that no reasonable buyer should rely on them. Courts also look at the context in which a statement is made to determine the reasonableness of the buyer's or lessee's reliance. For instance, a reasonable person is more likely to rely on a written statement made in an advertisement than on a statement made orally by a salesperson.

PREVENTING LEGAL DISPUTES

If you are in the business of selling or leasing goods, be careful about the words you use with customers, in writing and orally. If you do not intend to make an express warranty, do not make a promise or an affirmation of fact concerning the performance or quality of a product that you sell. Examine your firm's advertisements, brochures, and promotional materials, as well as any standard order forms and contracts, for statements that could be considered express warranties. To avoid unintended warranties, instruct all employees on how the promises they make to buyers during a sale can create warranties.

Implied Warranties

Implied Warranty A warranty that arises by law because of the circumstances of a sale rather than by the seller's express promise.

Implied Warranty of Merchantability A warranty that goods being sold or leased are reasonably fit for the general purpose for which they are sold or leased, are properly packaged and labeled, and are of proper quality.

An **implied warranty** is one that *the law derives* by implication or inference because of the circumstances of a sale, rather than by the seller's express promise. In an action based on breach of implied warranty, it is necessary to show that an implied warranty existed and that the breach of the warranty proximately caused[1] the damage sustained. We look here at some of the implied warranties that arise under the UCC.

Implied Warranty of Merchantability

Every sale or lease of goods made *by a merchant who deals in goods of the kind sold or leased* automatically gives rise to an **implied warranty of merchantability** [UCC 2–314, 2A–212]. **EXAMPLE 17.3** A

1. Proximate, or legal, cause exists when the connection between an act and an injury is strong enough to justify imposing liability—see Chapter 4 on page 114.

merchant who is in the business of selling ski equipment makes an implied warranty of merchantability every time she sells a pair of skis. A neighbor selling his skis at a garage sale does not (because he is not in the business of selling goods of this type). •

Merchantable Goods Goods that are *merchantable* are "reasonably fit for the ordinary purposes for which such goods are used." They must be of at least average, fair, or medium-grade quality. The quality must be comparable to a level that will pass without objection in the trade or market for goods of the same description. To be merchantable, the goods must also be adequately packaged and labeled, and they must conform to the promises or affirmations of fact made on the container or label, if any.

The warranty of merchantability may be breached even though the merchant did not know or could not have discovered that a product was defective (not merchantable). Of course, merchants are not absolute insurers against all accidents occurring in connection with their goods. For instance, a bar of soap is not unmerchantable merely because stepping on it could cause a user to slip and fall.

LEARNING OBJECTIVE 2
What implied warranties arise under the UCC?

CASE EXAMPLE 17.4 Darrell Shoop bought a Dodge Dakota truck that had been manufactured by DaimlerChrysler Corporation. Almost immediately, he had problems with the truck. During the first eighteen months, the truck's engine, suspension, steering, transmission, and other components required repairs twelve times, including at least five times for the same defect, which remained uncorrected. Shoop eventually traded in the truck and filed a lawsuit against DaimlerChrysler for breach of the implied warranty of merchantability. The court held that Shoop could maintain an action against DaimlerChrysler and use the fact that the truck had required a significant number of repairs as evidence that it was unmerchantable.[2] •

Merchantable Food The UCC recognizes the serving of food or drink to be consumed on or off the premises as a sale of goods subject to the implied warranty of merchantability [UCC 2–314(1)]. "Merchantable" food means food that is fit to eat.

Courts generally determine whether food is fit to eat on the basis of consumer expectations. The courts assume that consumers should reasonably expect on occasion to find bones in fish fillets, cherry pits in cherry pie, or a nutshell in a package of shelled nuts, for example—because such substances are natural incidents of the food. In contrast, consumers would not reasonably expect to find moth larvae in a can of peas or a piece of glass in a soft drink—because these substances are not natural to the food product.[3]

In the following *Classic Case*, the court had to determine whether a diner should reasonably expect to find a fish bone in fish chowder.

2. *Shoop v. DaimlerChrysler Corp.*, 371 Ill.App.3d 1058, 864 N.E.2d 785 (2007).
3. See, for example, *Ruvolo v. Homovich*, 149 Ohio App.3d 701, 778 N.E.2d 661 (2002).

Classic Case 17.1

Webster v. Blue Ship Tea Room, Inc.

Supreme Judicial Court of Massachusetts, 347 Mass. 421, 198 N.E.2d 309 (1964).

(hipokrat/iStockphoto.com)
Who is liable for fish bones in seafood chowder?

HISTORICAL AND CULTURAL SETTING *Chowder, a soup or stew made with fresh fish, possibly originated in the fishing villages of Brittany (a French province to the west of Paris) and was probably carried to Canada and New England by Breton immigrants. In the nineteenth century and earlier, recipes for chowder did not call for the removal of the fish bones. Chowder recipes in the first half of the twentieth century were the same as in previous centuries, sometimes*

Classic Case 17.1—Continued

specifying that the fish head, tail, and backbone were to be broken in pieces and boiled, with the "liquor thus produced . . . added to the balance of the chowder."[a] *By the middle of the twentieth century, there was a considerable body of case law concerning implied warranties and foreign and natural substances in food. It was perhaps inevitable that sooner or later, a consumer injured by a fish bone in chowder would challenge the merchantability of chowder containing fish bones.*

FACTS Blue Ship Tea Room, Inc., was located in Boston in an old building overlooking the ocean. Priscilla Webster, who had been born and raised in New England, went to the restaurant and ordered fish chowder. The chowder was milky in color. After three or four spoonfuls, she felt something lodged in her throat. As a result, she underwent two esophagoscopies; in the second esophagoscopy, a fish bone was found and removed. Webster filed a lawsuit against the restaurant in a Massachusetts state court for breach of the implied warranty of merchantability. The jury rendered a verdict for Webster, and the restaurant appealed to the state's highest court.

ISSUE Does serving fish chowder that contains a bone constitute a breach of an implied warranty of merchantability by the restaurant?

DECISION No. The Supreme Judicial Court of Massachusetts held that Webster could not recover against Blue Ship Tea Room because no breach of warranty had occurred.

REASON The court, citing UCC Section 2–314, stated that "a warranty that goods shall be merchantable is implied in a contract for their sale if the seller is a merchant with respect to goods of that kind. Under this section the serving for value of food or drink to be consumed either on the premises or elsewhere is a sale. . . . Goods to be merchantable must at least be . . . fit for the ordinary purposes for which such goods are used." The question here was whether a fish bone made the chowder unfit for eating. In the judge's opinion, "the joys of life in New England include the ready availability of fresh fish chowder. We should be prepared to cope with the hazards of fish bones, the occasional presence of which in chowders is, it seems to us, to be anticipated, and which, in the light of a hallowed tradition, do not impair their fitness or merchantability."

IMPACT OF THIS CASE ON TODAY'S LAW *This classic case, phrased in memorable language, was an early application of the UCC's implied warranty of merchantability to food products. The case established the rule that consumers should expect to occasionally find elements of food products that are natural to the product (such as fish bones in fish chowder). Courts today still apply this rule.*

a. Fannie Farmer, *The Boston Cooking School Cook Book* (Boston: Little, Brown, 1937), p. 166.

Implied Warranty of Fitness for a Particular Purpose A warranty that goods sold or leased are fit for the particular purpose for which the buyer or lessee will use the goods.

Implied Warranty of Fitness for a Particular Purpose

The **implied warranty of fitness for a particular purpose** arises when any seller or lessor (merchant or nonmerchant) knows the particular purpose for which a buyer or lessee will use the goods *and* knows that the buyer or lessee is relying on the skill and judgment of the seller or lessor to select suitable goods [UCC 2–315, 2A–213].

A "particular purpose" of the buyer or lessee differs from the "ordinary purpose for which goods are used" (merchantability). Goods can be merchantable but unfit for a particular purpose. **EXAMPLE 17.5** Cheryl needs a gallon of paint to match the color of her living room walls—a light shade between coral and peach. She takes a sample to the local hardware store and requests a gallon of paint of that color. Instead, she is given a gallon of bright blue paint. Here, the salesperson has not breached any warranty of implied merchantability—the bright blue paint is of high quality and suitable for interior walls—but he has breached an implied warranty of fitness for a particular purpose. •

A seller or lessor is not required to have actual knowledge of the buyer's or lessee's particular purpose, so long as the seller or lessor "has reason to know" the purpose. For an implied warranty to be created, however, the buyer or lessee must have *relied* on the skill or judgment of the seller or lessor in selecting or furnishing suitable goods.

Warranties Implied from Prior Dealings or Trade Custom

Implied warranties can also arise (or be excluded or modified) as a result of course of dealing or usage of trade [UCC 2–314(3), 2A–212(3)]. In the absence of evidence to the contrary, when both parties to a sales or lease contract have knowledge of a well-recognized trade custom, the courts will infer that both parties intended for that trade custom to apply to their contract.

EXAMPLE 17.6 Suppose that it is an industry-wide custom to lubricate new cars before they are delivered to buyers. Latoya buys a new car from Bender Chevrolet. After the purchase, Latoya discovers that Bender failed to lubricate the car before delivering it to her. In this situation, Latoya can hold the dealer liable for damages resulting from the breach of an implied warranty. (This, of course, would also be negligence on the part of the dealer.) •

Overlapping Warranties

KNOW THIS

Express and implied warranties do not necessarily displace each other. More than one warranty can cover the same goods in the same transaction.

Sometimes, two or more warranties are made in a single transaction. An implied warranty of merchantability, an implied warranty of fitness for a particular purpose, or both can exist in addition to an express warranty. For instance, when a sales contract for a new car states that "this car engine is warranted to be free from defects for 36,000 miles or thirty-six months, whichever occurs first," the seller has made an express warranty against all defects and an implied warranty that the car will be fit for normal use.

The rule under the UCC is that express and implied warranties are construed as *cumulative* if they are consistent with one another [UCC 2–317, 2A–215]. In other words, courts interpret two or more warranties as being in agreement with each other unless this construction is unreasonable. If it is unreasonable, then a court will hold that the warranties are inconsistent and apply the following rules to interpret which warranty is most important:

1. *Express* warranties displace inconsistent *implied* warranties, except for implied warranties of fitness for a particular purpose.
2. Samples take precedence over inconsistent general descriptions.
3. Exact or technical specifications displace inconsistent samples or general descriptions.

Warranty Disclaimers

The UCC generally permits warranties to be disclaimed or limited by specific and unambiguous language, provided that the buyer or lessee is protected from surprise. The manner in which a seller or lessor can disclaim warranties varies depending on the type of warranty.

Express Warranties

A seller or lessor can disclaim all oral express warranties by including in the contract a written (or an electronically recorded) disclaimer that is expressed in clear language, is conspicuous, and calls the buyer's or lessee's attention to the disclaimer [UCC 2–316(1), 2A–214(1)]. This allows the seller or lessor to avoid false allegations that oral warranties were made, and it ensures that only representations made by properly authorized individuals are included in the bargain.

Note, however, that a buyer or lessee must be made aware of any warranty disclaimers or modifications *at the time the contract is formed.* In other words, any oral or written warranties—or disclaimers—made during the bargaining process as part of a contract's formation cannot be modified at a later time by the seller or lessor.

Implied Warranties

Generally, unless circumstances indicate otherwise, the implied warranties of merchantability and fitness are disclaimed by the expressions "as is" or "with all faults," or other similar phrases. The phrase must be one that, in common understanding for both parties, calls the buyer's or lessee's attention to the fact that there are no implied warranties [UCC 2–316(3)(a), 2A–214(3)(a)]. (Note, however, that some states have laws that forbid "as is" sales. Other states do not allow disclaimers of warranties of merchantability for consumer goods.)

CASE EXAMPLE 17.7 Mandy Morningstar advertised a "lovely, eleven-year-old mare" with extensive jumping ability for sale. After examining the mare twice, Sue Hallett contracted to buy the horse. The contract she signed described the horse as an eleven-year-old mare, but indicated that the horse was being sold "as is." Shortly after the purchase, a veterinarian determined that the horse was actually sixteen years old and in no condition for jumping. Hallett stopped payment and tried to return the horse and cancel the contract. Morningstar sued for breach of contract. The court held that the statement in the contract describing the horse as eleven years old constituted an express warranty, which Morningstar had breached. Although the "as is" clause effectively disclaimed any implied warranties (of merchantability and fitness for a particular purpose, such as jumping), the court ruled that it did not disclaim the express warranty concerning the horse's age.[4] •

KNOW THIS

Courts generally view warranty disclaimers unfavorably, especially when consumers are involved.

Disclaimer of the Implied Warranty of Merchantability To specifically disclaim an implied warranty of merchantability, a seller or lessor must mention the word *merchantability* [UCC 2–316(2), 2A–214(2)]. The disclaimer need not be written, but if it is, the writing (or record) must be conspicuous [UCC 2–316(2), 2A–214(4)].

Under the UCC, a term or clause is conspicuous when it is written or displayed in such a way that a reasonable person would notice it. Words are conspicuous when they are in capital letters, in a larger font size, or in a different color than the surrounding text.

Disclaimer of the Implied Warranty of Fitness To specifically disclaim an implied warranty of fitness for a particular purpose, the disclaimer *must* be in a writing (or record) and must be conspicuous. The word *fitness* does not have to be mentioned. It is sufficient if, for example, the disclaimer states, "THERE ARE NO WARRANTIES THAT EXTEND BEYOND THE DESCRIPTION ON THE FACE HEREOF."

Buyer's or Lessee's Examination or Refusal to Inspect If a buyer or lessee actually examines the goods (or a sample or model) as fully as desired before entering into a contract, or if the buyer or lessee refuses to examine the goods on the seller's or lessor's request, *there is no implied warranty with respect to defects that a reasonable examination would reveal or defects that are actually found* [UCC 2–316(3)(b), 2A–214(2)(b)].

EXAMPLE 17.8 Azumi buys a lamp at Gershwin's Store. No express warranties are made. Gershwin asks Azumi to inspect the lamp before buying it, but she refuses. Had Azumi inspected the lamp, she would have noticed that the base was obviously cracked and the electrical cord was loose. If the lamp later cracks or starts a fire in Azumi's home and she is injured, she normally will not be able to hold Gershwin's liable for breach of the warranty of merchantability. Because Azumi refused to examine the lamp when asked by Gershwin, Azumi will be deemed to have assumed the risk that it was defective. •

Warranty Disclaimers and Unconscionability The UCC sections dealing with warranty disclaimers do not refer specifically to unconscionability as a factor. Ultimately, however, the courts will test warranty disclaimers with reference to the UCC's unconscionability standards [UCC 2–302, 2A–108]. Such factors as lack of bargaining position, take-it-or-leave-it choices, and a buyer's or lessee's failure to understand or know of a warranty disclaimer will be relevant to the issue of unconscionability.

Magnuson-Moss Warranty Act

The Magnuson-Moss Warranty Act of 1975[5] was designed to prevent deception in warranties by making them easier to understand. The act modifies UCC warranty rules to some extent when *consumer* transactions are involved. The UCC, however, remains the primary codification of warranty rules for commercial transactions.

4. *Morningstar v. Hallett*, 858 A.2d 125 (Pa.Super.Ct. 2004).

5. 15 U.S.C. Sections 2301–2312.

Under the Magnuson-Moss Act, a seller is not required to give an express written warranty for consumer goods sold. If a seller chooses to make an express written warranty, however, and the goods are priced at more than $25, the warranty must be labeled as "full" or "limited."

A *full warranty* requires free repair or replacement of any defective part. If the product cannot be repaired within a reasonable time, the consumer has the choice of a refund or a replacement without charge. A full warranty can be for an unlimited or limited time period, such as a "full twelve-month warranty." With a *limited warranty,* the buyer's recourse is limited in some fashion, such as to replacement of the item. The fact that only a limited warranty is being given must be conspicuously stated.

KNOW THIS

When a buyer or lessee is a consumer, a limitation on consequential damages for personal injuries resulting from nonconforming goods is *prima facie* unconscionable.

The Magnuson-Moss Act further requires the warrantor to make certain disclosures fully and conspicuously in a single document in "readily understood language." The document must state the names and addresses of all warrantors, indicate specifically what is warranted, and explain the procedures for enforcing the warranty. It must also clarify that the buyer has legal rights and explain any limitations on warranty relief.

Lemon Laws

Some purchasers of defective automobiles—called "lemons"—found that the remedies provided by the UCC were inadequate due to limitations imposed by the seller. In response to the frustrations of these buyers, all of the states have enacted *lemon laws.*

Coverage of Lemon Laws

Basically, state lemon laws provide remedies to consumers who buy automobiles that repeatedly fail to meet standards of quality and performance because they are "lemons." Although lemon laws vary by state, typically they apply to automobiles under warranty that are defective in a way that significantly affects the vehicle's value or use. Lemon laws do not necessarily cover used-car purchases (unless the car is covered by a manufacturer's extended warranty) or vehicles that are leased.[6]

Generally, the seller or manufacturer is given a number of opportunities to remedy the defect (usually four). If the seller fails to cure the problem despite a reasonable number of attempts (as specified by state law), the buyer is entitled to a new car, replacement of defective parts, or return of all consideration paid. Buyers who prevail in a lemon-law dispute may also be entitled to reimbursement of their attorneys' fees.

Arbitration Is Typical Procedure

When do lemon laws apply?

(Monkey Business Images/Shutterstock)

In most states, lemon laws require an aggrieved new-car owner to give the dealer or manufacturer an opportunity to solve the problem. If the problem persists, the owner must then submit complaints to the arbitration program specified in the manufacturer's warranty before taking the case to court. Decisions by arbitration panels are binding on the manufacturer—that is, cannot be appealed by the manufacturer to the courts—but usually are not binding on the purchaser.

Most major automobile companies operate their own arbitration panels, but some use independent arbitration services, such as those provided by the Better Business Bureau. Because industry-sponsored arbitration boards have been criticized for not being truly impartial,

6. Note that in some states, such as California, these laws may extend beyond automobile purchases and apply to other consumer goods.

some states have established mandatory, state government-sponsored arbitration programs for lemon-law disputes.

Product Liability

Product Liability The legal liability of manufacturers, sellers, and lessors of goods for injuries or damage caused by the goods to consumers, users, or bystanders.

Those who make, sell, or lease goods can be held liable for physical harm or property damage caused by those goods to a consumer, user, or bystander. This is called **product liability.** Product liability claims may be based on the warranty theories just discussed, as well as on the theories of negligence, misrepresentation, and strict liability. We look here at product liability based on negligence and misrepresentation.

Negligence

Chapter 4 defined *negligence* as the failure to exercise the degree of care that a reasonable, prudent person would have exercised under the circumstances. If a manufacturer fails to exercise "due care" to make a product safe, a person who is injured by the product may sue the manufacturer for negligence.

Due Care Must Be Exercised The manufacturer must exercise due care in designing the product, selecting the materials, using the appropriate production process, assembling the product, and placing adequate warnings on the label informing the user of dangers of which an ordinary person might not be aware. The duty of care also extends to the inspection and testing of any purchased products that are used in the final product sold by the manufacturer.

LEARNING OBJECTIVE 3
Can a manufacturer be held liable to any person who suffers an injury proximately caused by the manufacturer's negligently made product?

Privity of Contract Not Required A product liability action based on negligence does not require *privity of contract* between the injured plaintiff and the defendant manufacturer. As discussed in Chapter 13, *privity of contract* refers to the relationship that exists between the promisor and the promisee of a contract. Privity is the reason that normally only the parties to a contract can enforce that contract.

In the context of product liability law, privity is not required. A person who is injured by a defective product can bring a negligence suit against the product's manufacturer or seller, even though that person is not the one who actually purchased the product—and thus is not in privity. A manufacturer is liable for its failure to exercise due care to *any person* who sustains an injury proximately caused by a negligently made (defective) product.

Relative to the long history of the common law, this exception to the privity requirement is a fairly recent development, dating to the early part of the twentieth century. A leading case in this respect is *MacPherson v. Buick Motor Co.*, which is presented as this chapter's *Landmark in the Law* feature on the following page.

Misrepresentation

When a user or consumer is injured as a result of a manufacturer's or seller's fraudulent misrepresentation, the basis of liability may be the tort of fraud. The intentional mislabeling of packaged cosmetics, for instance, or the intentional concealment of a product's defects constitutes fraudulent misrepresentation.

The misrepresentation must be of a material fact, and the seller must have intended to induce the buyer's reliance on the misrepresentation. Misrepresentation on a label or advertisement is enough to show an intent to induce reliance. Of course, to bring a lawsuit on this ground, the buyer must have relied on the misrepresentation.

LANDMARK IN THE LAW

MacPherson v. Buick Motor Co. (1916)

In the landmark case of *MacPherson v. Buick Motor Co.*,[a] the New York Court of Appeals—New York's highest court—considered the liability of a manufacturer that failed to exercise reasonable care in manufacturing a finished product.

Case Background Donald MacPherson suffered injuries while riding in a Buick automobile that suddenly collapsed because one of the wheels was made of defective wood. The spokes crumbled into fragments, throwing MacPherson out of the vehicle and injuring him.

MacPherson had purchased the car from a Buick dealer, but he brought a lawsuit against the manufacturer, Buick Motor Company. Buick itself had not made the wheel but had bought it from another manufacturer. There was evidence, though, that the defects could have been discovered by a reasonable inspection by Buick and that no such inspection had taken place. MacPherson charged Buick with negligence for putting a human life in imminent danger.

The Issue before the Court and the Court's Ruling The primary issue was whether Buick owed a duty of care to anyone except the immediate purchaser of the car—that is, the Buick dealer. In deciding the issue, Justice Benjamin Cardozo stated that "if the nature of a thing is such that it is reasonably certain to place life and limb in peril when negligently made, it is then a thing of danger. . . . If to the element of danger there is added knowledge that the thing will be used by persons other than the purchaser, and used without new tests, then, irrespective of contract, the manufacturer of this thing of danger is under a duty to make it carefully."

The court concluded that "beyond all question, the nature of an automobile gives warning of probable danger if its construction is defective. This automobile was designed to go 50 miles an hour. Unless its wheels were sound and strong, injury was almost certain." Although Buick itself had not manufactured the wheel, the court held that Buick had a duty to inspect the wheels and that Buick "was responsible for the finished product." Therefore, Buick was liable to MacPherson for the injuries he sustained when he was thrown from the car.

Application to Today's World *This landmark decision was a significant step in creating the legal environment of the modern world. As often happens, technological developments necessitated changes in the law. Today, automobile manufacturers are commonly held liable when their negligence causes automobile users to be injured.*

a. 217 N.Y. 382, 111 N.E. 1050 (1916).

Strict Product Liability

Under the doctrine of strict liability (discussed in Chapter 4), people may be liable for the results of their acts regardless of their intentions or their exercise of reasonable care. In addition, liability does not depend on privity of contract. The injured party does not have to be the buyer or a *third party beneficiary* (see page 335 in Chapter 13), as required under contract warranty theory. In the 1960s, courts applied the doctrine of strict liability in several landmark cases involving manufactured goods, and this doctrine has since become a common method of holding manufacturers liable.

Strict Product Liability and Public Policy

The law imposes strict product liability as a matter of public policy. This public policy rests on the threefold assumption that:

1. Consumers should be protected against unsafe products.
2. Manufacturers and distributors should not escape liability for faulty products simply because they are not in privity of contract with the ultimate user of those products.
3. Manufacturers, sellers, and lessors of products are generally in a better position than consumers to bear the costs associated with injuries caused by their products—costs that they can ultimately pass on to all consumers in the form of higher prices.

California was the first state to impose strict product liability in tort on manufacturers. In a landmark decision, *Greenman v. Yuba Power Products, Inc.*,[7] the California Supreme Court set out the reason for applying tort law rather than contract law in cases involving consumers injured by defective products. According to the court, the "purpose of such liability is to [e]nsure that the costs of injuries resulting from defective products are borne by the manufacturers . . . rather than by the injured persons who are powerless to protect themselves."

Public policy may be expressed in a statute or in the common law. Sometimes, public policy may be revealed in a court's interpretation of a statute, as in the following *Spotlight Case*.

7. 59 Cal.2d 57, 377 P.2d 897, 27 Cal.Rptr. 697 (1963).

Spotlight on Injuries from Vaccinations

Case 17.2

Bruesewitz v. Wyeth, LLC

Supreme Court of the United States, __ U.S. __, 131 S.Ct. 1068, 179 L.Ed.2d 1 (2011).
www.supremecourt.gov[a]

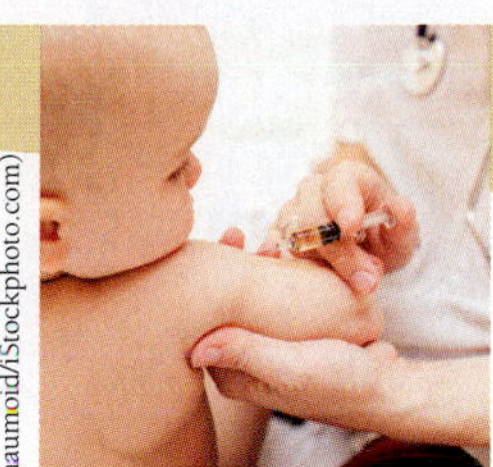
(naumoid/iStockphoto.com)

What happens when a vaccine causes adverse side effects?

FACTS When Hannah Bruesewitz was six months old, her pediatrician administered a dose of the diphtheria, tetanus, and pertussis (DTP) vaccine according to the Centers for Disease Control and Prevention's recommended childhood immunization schedule. Within twenty-four hours, Hannah began to experience seizures. She suffered more than one hundred seizures during the next month. Her doctors diagnosed her with "residual seizure disorder" and "developmental delay." Hannah's parents, Russell and Robalee Bruesewitz, filed a claim for relief in the U.S. Court of Federal Claims under the National Childhood Vaccine Injury Act (NCVIA) of 1986. The NCVIA set up a no-fault compensation program for persons injured by vaccines. The claim was denied. The Bruesewitzes then filed a suit in a Pennsylvania state court against Wyeth, LLC, the maker of the vaccine, alleging strict product liability. The suit was moved to a federal district court. The court held that the claim was preempted by the NCVIA, which includes provisions protecting manufacturers from liability for "a vaccine's unavoidable, adverse side effects." A federal appellate court affirmed the district court's judgment. The Bruesewitzes appealed to the United States Supreme Court.

ISSUE Was the Bruesewitzes' strict product liability claim against Wyeth for the injuries that their child suffered from vaccination preempted by the National Childhood Vaccine Injury Act?

DECISION Yes. The United States Supreme Court affirmed the lower court's judgment. The NCVIA preempted the Bruesewitzes' claim against Wyeth for injury to their daughter caused by the DTP vaccine's side effects.

REASON The Court reasoned that Congress enacted the NCVIA as a matter of public policy to stabilize the vaccine market and facilitate compensation. In the no-fault compensation program set up by the NCVIA, a person with a vaccine-related claim files a petition with the U.S. Court of Federal Claims. The court may award compensation for legal, medical, rehabilitation, counseling, special education, and vocational training expenses, as well as for diminished earning capacity, pain and suffering, and death. The awards are funded by a tax on the vaccine. In exchange for the "informal, efficient" compensation program, vaccine manufacturers that comply with the regulatory requirements are "immunized" from liability. The statute thus strikes a balance between paying victims harmed by vaccines and protecting the vaccine industry from collapsing under the costs of tort liability.

CRITICAL THINKING—Political Consideration *If the public wants to change the policy outlined in this case, which branch of the government—and at what level—should be lobbied to make the change? Explain.*

a. In the "Supreme Court Documents" column, in the "Opinions" pull-down menu, select "Bound Volumes." On the next page, in the "For Search Term:" box, type "Bruesewitz" and click on "Search." In the result, click on the name of the case to access the opinion. The United States Supreme Court maintains this Web site.

Requirements for Strict Liability

After the *Restatement (Second) of Torts* was issued in 1964, Section 402A became a widely accepted statement of how the doctrine of strict liability should be applied to sellers of goods (including manufacturers, processors, assemblers, packagers, bottlers, wholesalers, distributors, retailers, and lessors).

LEARNING OBJECTIVE 4
What are the elements of a cause of action in strict product liability?

The bases for an action in strict liability that are set forth in Section 402A of the *Restatement* can be summarized as the following six requirements. Depending on the jurisdiction, if these requirements are met, a manufacturer's liability to an injured party can be almost unlimited.

1. The product must have been in a *defective condition* when the defendant sold it.
2. The defendant must normally be engaged in the *business of selling* (or otherwise distributing) that product.
3. The product must be *unreasonably dangerous* to the user or consumer because of its defective condition (in most states).
4. The plaintiff must incur *physical harm* to self or property by use or consumption of the product.
5. The defective condition must be the *proximate cause* of the injury or damage.
6. The *goods must not have been substantially changed* from the time the product was sold to the time the injury was sustained.

(Michael Temchine/AFP/Getty Images)

Under what circumstances can a consumer prove that tires were sold in a defective condition?

Proving a Defective Condition

Under these requirements, in any action against a manufacturer, seller, or lessor, the plaintiff does not have to show why or how the product became defective. The plaintiff does, however, have to prove that the product was defective at the time it left the seller or lessor and that this defective condition made it "unreasonably dangerous" to the user or consumer. (See this chapter's *Beyond Our Borders* feature on the facing page for a discussion of how foreign suppliers were held liable for defective goods sold in the United States.)

Unless evidence can be presented that will support the conclusion that the product was defective when it was sold or leased, the plaintiff normally will not succeed. If the product was delivered in a safe condition and subsequent mishandling made it harmful to the user, the seller or lessor usually is not strictly liable.

Unreasonably Dangerous Products

The *Restatement* recognizes that many products cannot possibly be made entirely safe for all uses. Thus, sellers or lessors are held liable only for products that are *unreasonably* dangerous. A court may consider a product so defective as to be an **unreasonably dangerous product** in either of the following situations.

Unreasonably Dangerous Product A product that is so defective that it is dangerous beyond the expectation of an ordinary consumer or a product for which a less dangerous alternative was feasible but the manufacturer failed to produce it.

1. The product is dangerous beyond the expectation of the ordinary consumer.
2. A less dangerous alternative was economically feasible for the manufacturer, but the manufacturer failed to produce it.

As will be discussed next, a product may be unreasonably dangerous due to a flaw in the manufacturing process or in the design, or due to an inadequate warning.

Product Defects—*Restatement (Third) of Torts*

The *Restatement (Third) of Torts: Products Liability* defines the three types of product defects that have traditionally been recognized in product liability law—manufacturing defects, design defects, and inadequate warnings.

Manufacturing Defects

According to Section 2(a) of the *Restatement (Third) of Torts: Products Liability*, a product "contains a manufacturing defect when the product

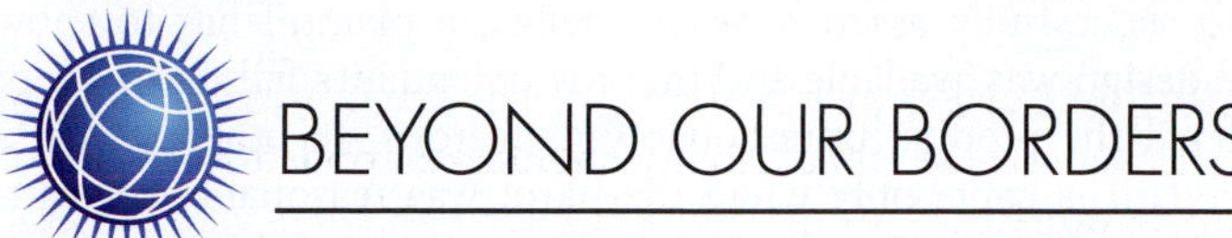

Imposing Product Liability as Far Away as China

Chinese drywall started being used in the construction of houses in the United States in 2003. By 2007, thousands of homes had been constructed with this product in Alabama, Florida, Louisiana, Mississippi, and a few other states. There was a problem, though—use of the Chinese drywall caused blackening and pitting of electrical wires. Homeowners began to notice an odor similar to rotten eggs. Air-conditioning units started failing, as did ceiling fans, alarm systems, refrigerators, and other appliances.

Numerous lawsuits were filed against the Chinese drywall manufacturers, which initially fought the claims. When the number of lawsuits ran into the thousands, however, the Chinese companies decided to settle.

The estimated value of the settlement is between $800 million and $1 billion. It includes an uncapped fund to pay for repairs for about 4,500 homes and a separate fund capped at $30 million that will be used to pay for health problems stemming from the defective Chinese drywall.

Critical Thinking

Could U.S. companies that sold Chinese drywall to consumers also be held liable for damages? Why or why not?

departs from its intended design even though all possible care was exercised in the preparation and marketing of the product." Basically, a manufacturing defect is a departure from a product unit's design specifications that results in products that are physically flawed, damaged, or incorrectly assembled. A glass bottle that is made too thin, causing it to explode in a consumer's face, is an example of a product with a manufacturing defect.

Usually, such defects occur when a manufacturer fails to assemble, test, or adequately check the quality of a product. Liability is imposed on the manufacturer (and on the wholesaler and retailer) regardless of whether the manufacturer's quality control efforts were "reasonable." The idea behind holding defendants strictly liable for manufacturing defects is to encourage greater investment in product safety and stringent quality control standards. (For more information on how effective quality control procedures can help businesses reduce their potential legal liability for breached warranties and defective products, see the *Linking Business Law to Corporate Management* feature on page 457.)

CASE EXAMPLE 17.9 Kevin Schmude purchased an eight-foot stepladder and used it to install radio-frequency shielding in a hospital room. While Schmude was standing on the ladder, it collapsed, and he was seriously injured. He filed a lawsuit against the ladder's maker, Tricam Industries, Inc., based on a manufacturing defect. Experts testified that when the ladder was assembled, the preexisting holes in the top cap did not properly line up with the holes in the rear right rail and backing plate. As a result of the misalignment, the rivet at the rear legs of the ladder was more likely to fail. A jury concluded that this manufacturing defect made the ladder unreasonably dangerous and awarded Schmude more than $677,000 in damages.[8] ●

Design Defects Unlike a product with a manufacturing defect, a product with a design defect is made in conformity with the manufacturer's design specifications, but it nevertheless results in injury to the user because the design itself is flawed. The product's design creates an unreasonable risk to the user. A product "is defective in design when the foreseeable risks of harm posed by the product could have been reduced or avoided by the adoption of a reasonable alternative design by the seller or other distributor, or a predecessor in the commercial chain of distribution, and the omission of the alternative design renders the product not reasonably safe."[9]

8. *Schmude v. Tricam Industries, Inc.*, 550 F.Supp.2d 846 (E.D.Wis. 2008).
9. *Restatement (Third) of Torts: Products Liability,* Section 2(b).

(antos777/iStockphoto.com)

If this ladder collapses and the worker is injured, who could be held liable?

Test for Design Defects To successfully assert a design defect, a plaintiff has to show that a reasonable alternative design was available and that the defendant's failure to adopt the alternative design rendered the product unreasonably dangerous. In other words, a manufacturer or other defendant is liable only when the harm was reasonably preventable. **CASE EXAMPLE 17.10** After Gillespie cut off several of his fingers while operating a table saw, he filed a lawsuit against the maker of the saw. Gillespie alleged that the blade guards on the saw were defectively designed. At trial, however, an expert testified that the alternative design for blade guards used for table saws could not have been used for the particular cut that Gillespie was performing at the time he was injured. The court found that Gillespie's claim about defective blade guards must fail because there was no proof that the "better" design of guard would have prevented his injury.[10] •

Factors to Be Considered According to the Official Comments accompanying the *Restatement (Third) of Torts,* a court can consider a broad range of factors in deciding claims of design defects. These factors include the magnitude and probability of the foreseeable risks, as well as the relative advantages and disadvantages of the product as designed and as it alternatively could have been designed. Basically, most courts engage in a risk-utility analysis, determining whether the risk of harm from the product as designed outweighs its utility to the user and to the public

CASE EXAMPLE 17.11 Jodie Bullock smoked cigarettes manufactured by Philip Morris for forty-five years. When she was diagnosed with lung cancer, Bullock brought a product liability suit against Philip Morris. She presented evidence that by the late 1950s, scientists had proved that smoking caused lung cancer. Nonetheless, Philip Morris had issued full-page announcements stating that there was no proof that smoking caused cancer and that "numerous scientists" questioned "the validity of the statistics." At trial, the judge instructed the jury to consider the gravity of the danger posed by the design, as well as the likelihood that the danger would cause injury.

The jury found that there was a defect in the design of the cigarettes and that they had been negligently designed. It awarded Bullock $850,000 in compensatory damages and $28 million in punitive damages. Philip Morris appealed, claiming that no evidence had been offered to show that there was a safer design for cigarettes. The reviewing court affirmed the jury's verdict but remanded the case for a reconsideration of the proper amount of punitive damages.[11] •

Inadequate Warnings

A product may also be deemed defective because of inadequate instructions or warnings. A product will be considered defective "when the foreseeable risks of harm posed by the product could have been reduced or avoided by the provision of reasonable instructions or warnings by the seller or other distributor, or a predecessor in the commercial chain of distribution, and the omission of the instructions or warnings renders the product not reasonably safe."[12] Generally, a seller must also warn consumers of the harm that can result from the *foreseeable misuse* of its product.

Content of Warnings Important factors for a court to consider include the risks of a product, the "content and comprehensibility" and "intensity of expression" of warnings and instructions, and the "characteristics of expected user groups."[13] Courts apply a "reasonableness" test to determine if the warnings adequately alert consumers to the

---

10. *Gillespie v. Sears, Roebuck & Co.,* 386 F.3d 21 (1st Cir. 2004).

11. *Bullock v. Philip Morris USA, Inc.,* 159 Cal.App.4th 655, 71 Cal.Rptr.3d 775 (2008). The California Court of Appeal subsequently upheld a punitive damages award of $13.8 million. See *Bullock v. Philip Morris USA, Inc.,* 198 Cal.App.4th 543, 131 Cal.Rptr.3d 382 (2011).

12. *Restatement (Third) of Torts: Products Liability,* Section 2(c).

13. *Restatement (Third) of Torts: Products Liability,* Section 2, Comment h.

product's risks. For example, children will likely respond more readily to bright, bold, simple warning labels, while educated adults might need more detailed information.

In the following case, a patient filed a product liability suit alleging that a product had a design defect and that the manufacturer had provided inadequate warnings. The court had to decide whether the plaintiff could pursue either theory of recovery.

Case 17.3

Johnson v. Medtronic, Inc.

Missouri Court of Appeals, 365 S.W.3d 226 (2012). www.courts.mo.gov[a]

(Munshi Ahmed/Bloomberg via Getty Images)

Medtronic manufactures medical devices, including defibrillators.

FACTS In 2005, Jeffrey Johnson was taken to the emergency room for an episode of atrial fibrillation, a heart rhythm disorder. Dr. David Hahn used a defibrillator manufactured by Medtronic, Inc., to deliver electric shocks to Johnson's heart. The defibrillator had synchronous and asynchronous modes, and it reverted to the asynchronous mode after each use. Hahn intended to deliver synchronized shocks, which required him to select the synchronous mode for each shock. Hahn did not read the device's instructions, which Medtronic had provided in both a manual and on the device itself. As a result, he delivered a synchronized shock, followed by twelve asynchronous shocks that endangered Johnson's life. Johnson and his wife filed a product liability suit against Medtronic asserting that Medtronic had provided inadequate warnings about the defibrillator and that the device had a design defect. The trial court found for Medtronic under both product liability theories, and the Johnsons appealed.

ISSUE Could the Johnsons pursue a product liability claim alleging either that Medtronic's warnings were inadequate or that the device had a design defect?

DECISION No and yes, respectively. The Missouri appellate court held that the Johnsons could not pursue a claim based on the inadequacy of Medtronic's warnings, but that they could pursue a claim alleging a design defect. Thus, the trial court's decision was affirmed in part and reversed in part.

REASON The court first held that the Johnsons could not pursue a claim alleging that Medtronic provided inadequate warnings. Johnson offered no evidence that he was harmed because the defibrillator was sold without an adequate warning. Instead, the record showed that Medtronic's instructions would have prevented Johnson's injuries, but Hahn had failed to follow or even read them. Nevertheless, the court held that the Johnsons could pursue their design defect claim. The Johnsons had provided evidence that Hahn's misuse was reasonably foreseeable. Importantly, Medtronic had known that other users had inadvertently delivered asynchronous shocks after failing to reset the device. The court concluded that the Johnsons were not precluded from bringing a claim for design defect simply because they could not pursue a claim of inadequate warnings. In some cases, "a manufacturer may be held liable where it chooses to warn of the danger . . . rather than preclude the danger by design."

CRITICAL THINKING—Legal Consideration *What could Medtronic do to avoid possible liability to plaintiffs like the Johnsons? Was there a reasonable alternative design for the defibrillator?*

a. In the right-hand column, click on "Opinions & Minutes." In the middle of the next page, after "Missouri Court of Appeals, Western District," click on "opinions." In the "Search Opinions . . ." box, type "Johnson v. Medtronic," and click on "Search." In the result, click on the case name to access the opinion.

ETHICAL ISSUE

Should tobacco companies be required to use graphic warnings to discourage smoking? Scientists long ago established that smoking is injurious to one's health and that nicotine is highly addictive. For decades, cigarette manufacturers have been required to put explicit warning labels on packages of cigarettes sold in the United States to discourage people from smoking. Although the number of smokers has declined over time, the Centers for Disease Control and Prevention estimates that more than 45 million adults still smoke and that 443,000 deaths each year can be attributed to smoking. Smoking also contributes substantially to the nation's health-care costs.

Continued

In an attempt to reduce smoking further, the U.S. Food and Drug Administration (FDA) issued a new rule requiring U.S. tobacco companies to include large graphic images on cigarette packages that show how smoking can kill. The images include pictures of diseased lungs and a cadaver on an autopsy table. In 2012, the U.S. District Court for the District of Columbia ruled against the FDA. The judge stated that the required labels did not convey facts to inform, but rather would force cigarette makers to display the government's antismoking message more prominently than the tobacco companies' own branding. In other words, the FDA requirement was "the impermissible expropriation of a company's advertising space for government advocacy." Though cigarette smoking may be harmful, it is not illegal. Therefore, tobacco companies have free speech rights.[14]

Of course, antismoking advocacy groups are unhappy with the district court's ruling. Matthew L. Meyers, president of the Campaign for Tobacco-Free Kids, said the decision was "wrong on the science and the law. The warnings unequivocally tell the truth about cigarette smoking."

Obvious Risks There is no duty to warn about risks that are obvious or commonly known. Warnings about such risks do not add to the safety of a product and could even detract from it by making other warnings seem less significant. The obviousness of a risk and a user's decision to proceed in the face of that risk may be a defense in a product liability suit based on a warning defect. (This defense and other defenses in product liability suits will be discussed later in this chapter.)

An action alleging that a product is defective due to an inadequate label can be based on state law. (For a discussion of a case involving a state law that required warning labels on violent video games, see this chapter's *Adapting the Law to the Online Environment* feature on the facing page.)

Market-Share Liability

Generally, in cases involving product liability, a plaintiff must prove that the defective product that caused her or his injury was made by a specific defendant. In a few situations, however, courts have dropped this requirement when a plaintiff cannot prove which of many distributors of a harmful product supplied the particular product that caused the injury. Under a theory of **market-share liability**, all firms that manufactured and distributed the product during the period in question are held liable for the plaintiff's injury in proportion to the firms' respective shares of the market for that product during that period.

Market-Share Liability A theory under which liability is shared among all firms that manufactured and distributed a particular product during a certain period of time. This form of liability sharing is used only when the true source of the harmful product is unidentifiable.

CASE EXAMPLE 17.12 John Smith suffered from hemophilia (a blood-clotting disorder). Because of his condition, he received injections of a blood protein known as antihemophiliac factor (AHF) concentrate. When he later tested positive for the AIDS (acquired immune deficiency syndrome) virus, he sued. Because it was not known which manufacturer was responsible for the particular AHF received by the plaintiff, the court held that all of the manufacturers of AHF could be held liable under a market-share theory of liability.[15] •

Courts in many jurisdictions do not recognize this theory of liability, believing that it deviates too significantly from traditional legal principles.[16] In jurisdictions that do recognize market-share liability, it is usually applied in cases involving drugs or

14. *R.J. Reynolds Tobacco Co. v. U.S. Food and Drug Administration*, 2012 WL 653828 (D.D.C. 2012).

15. *Smith v. Cutter Biological, Inc.*, 72 Haw. 416, 823 P.2d 717 (1991). See also *Sutowski v. Eli Lilly & Co.*, 92 Ohio St.3d 347, 696 N.E.2d 187 (1998); and *In re Methyl Tertiary Butyl Ether (MTBE) Products Liability Litigation*, 447 F.Supp.2d 289 (S.D.N.Y. 2006).

16. For the Illinois Supreme Court's position on market-share liability, see *Smith v. Eli Lilly Co.*, 137 Ill.2d 252, 560 N.E.2d 324, 148 Ill.Dec. 22 (1990). Pennsylvania law also does not recognize market-share liability. See *Bortell v. Eli Lilly & Co.*, 406 F.Supp.2d 1 (D.D.C. 2005).

ADAPTING THE LAW TO THE ONLINE ENVIRONMENT

THE SUPREME COURT TAKES A STAND ON WARNING LABELS FOR VIDEO GAMES

Almost every product that you purchase in the physical world has one or more warning labels. Indeed, some critics argue that these labels have become so long and ubiquitous that consumers ignore them. In other words, putting warnings on just about everything defeats their original purpose. In the online environment, warning labels are not so extensive—at least not yet.

Until now, video games have largely escaped mandated warning labels, although the video game industry has instituted a voluntary rating system to provide information about a video game's content. Each video game is assigned one of six age-specific ratings, ranging from "Early Childhood" to "Adults Only."

Should video games, whether downloaded or bought on a CD-ROM or DVD, have additional warnings to advise potential users (or their parents) that the games might be overly violent? When the California legislature enacted a law imposing restrictions and a labeling requirement on the sale or rental of "violent video games" to minors, this issue became paramount.[a]

Video Software Dealers Sue the State

The Video Software Dealers Association, along with the Entertainment Software Association, immediately brought a suit in federal district court seeking to invalidate the law. The court granted summary judgment in favor of the plaintiffs.

The act defined a violent video game as one in which "the range of options available to a player includes killing, maiming, dismembering, or sexually assaulting an image of a human being." While agreeing that some video games are unquestionably violent by everyday standards, the trial court pointed out that many video games are based on popular novels or motion pictures and have extensive plot lines.

Accordingly, the court found that the definition of a violent video game was unconstitutionally vague and thus violated the First Amendment's guarantee of freedom of speech. The court also noted the existence of the voluntary rating system. The U.S. Court of Appeals for the Ninth Circuit affirmed the district court's decision.[b]

The United States Supreme Court's Decision

The state of California appealed to the United States Supreme Court, but in 2011 the Court affirmed the decision in favor of the video game and software industries. The Court noted that video games are entitled to First Amendment protection. Because California had failed to show that the statute was justified by a compelling government interest and that the law was narrowly tailored to serve that interest, the Court ruled that the statute was unconstitutional.[c]

Critical Thinking

Why do you think that some legislators believe that the six-part, age-specific voluntary labeling system for video games is not sufficient to protect minors?

a. California Civil Code Sections 1746–1746.5.

b. *Video Software Dealers Association v. Schwarzenegger*, 556 F.3d 950 (9th Cir. 2009).

c. *Brown v. Entertainment Merchants Association*, ___ U.S. ___, 131 S.Ct. 2729, 180 L.Ed.2d 708 (2011).

chemicals, when it is difficult or impossible to determine which company made a particular product.

Other Applications of Strict Liability

Almost all courts extend the strict liability of manufacturers and other sellers to injured bystanders. **EXAMPLE 17.13** A forklift that Trent is operating will not go into reverse, and as a result, it runs into a bystander. In this situation, the bystander can sue the manufacturer of the defective forklift under strict liability (and possibly bring a negligence action against the forklift operator as well). •

Strict liability also applies to suppliers of component parts. **EXAMPLE 17.14** Toyota buys brake pads from a subcontractor and puts them in Corollas without changing their composition. If those pads are defective, both the supplier of the brake pads and Toyota will be held strictly liable for the injuries caused by the defects. •

Defenses to Product Liability

LEARNING OBJECTIVE 5
What defenses to liability can be raised in a product liability lawsuit?

Defendants in product liability suits can raise a number of defenses. One defense, of course, is to show that there is no basis for the plaintiff's claim. For instance, in a product liability case based on negligence, if a defendant can show that the plaintiff has *not* met the requirements (such as causation) for an action in negligence, generally the defendant will not be liable.

Similarly, in a case involving strict product liability, a defendant can claim that the plaintiff failed to meet one of the requirements. If the defendant establishes that the goods were altered after they were sold, for instance, the defendant normally will not be held liable.[17] A defendant may also assert that the *statute of limitations* (see page 15 in Chapter 1) for a product liability claim has lapsed.[18] Several other defenses may also be available to defendants, as discussed next.

Preemption

Today, some defendants are raising the defense of preemption—that government regulations preempt claims for product liability (see *Spotlight Case 17.2* on page 447, for example). The federal government has instituted numerous regulations that attempt to ensure the safety of products distributed to the public (consumer law is discussed in Chapter 33). In the past, a person who was injured by a product could assert a product liability claim regardless of whether the product was subject to government regulations. But that changed in 2008 when the United States Supreme Court held that an injured party may not be able to sue the manufacturer of defective products that are subject to federal regulatory schemes.

CASE EXAMPLE 17.15 In *Riegel v. Medtronic, Inc.*,[19] the United States Supreme Court held that a man who was injured by an approved medical device (in this case, a balloon catheter) could not sue its maker for negligence or strict product liability, or claim that the device was defectively designed. The Court observed that the Medical Device Amendments of 1976 (MDA) created a comprehensive scheme of federal safety oversight for medical devices. The MDA requires the U.S. Food and Drug Administration to review the design, labeling, and manufacturing of these devices before they are marketed to make sure that they are safe and effective. The Court reasoned that because premarket approval is a "rigorous process," it preempts all common law claims challenging the safety or effectiveness of a medical device that has been approved. •

Since the *Medtronic* decision, some courts have extended the preemption defense to other product liability actions. Other courts have been unwilling to deny an injured party relief simply because the federal government was supposed to ensure the product's safety.[20] Even the United States Supreme Court refused to extend the preemption defense to preclude a drug maker's liability in one subsequent case.[21]

Assumption of Risk

Assumption of risk can sometimes be used as a defense in a product liability action. To establish such a defense, the defendant must show that (1) the plaintiff knew and appreciated the risk created by the product defect and (2) the plaintiff voluntarily assumed the

---

17. See, for example, *Edmondson v. Macclesfield L-P Gas Co.*, 642 S.E.2d 265 (N.C.App. 2007); and *Pichardo v. C. S. Brown Co.*, 35 A.D.3d 303, 827 N.Y.S.2d 131 (N.Y.App. 2006).

18. Similar state statutes, called *statutes of repose*, place outer time limits on product liability actions.

19. 552 U.S. 312, 128 S.Ct. 999, 169 L.Ed.2d 892 (2008).

20. See, for example, *Paduano v. American Honda Motor Co.*, 169 Cal.App.4th 1453, 88 Cal.Rptr.3d 90 (2009), which was presented as the *Business Case Study with Dissenting Opinion* for Unit 1 on page 233; and *McDarby v. Merck & Co.*, 402 N.J.Super. 10, 949 A.2d 223 (2008).

21. *Wyeth v. Levine*, 555 U.S. 555, 129 S.Ct. 1187, 173 L.Ed.2d 51 (2009).

risk, even though it was unreasonable to do so. (See Chapter 4 for a more detailed discussion of assumption of risk.)

Although assumption of the risk is a defense in product liability actions, some courts do not allow it to be used as a defense to strict product liability claims. **CASE EXAMPLE 17.16** Executive Tans operated an upright tanning booth that had been manufactured by Sun Ergoline, Inc. Before using the booth, Savannah Boles signed a release form that contained an *exculpatory clause* (see page 297 in Chapter 11). The clause stated that she was using the booth at her own risk and that she released the manufacturer, among others, from any liability for injuries. After Boles entered the booth, several of her fingers came in contact with an exhaust fan located at the top of the booth, partially amputating them. Boles sued Sun Ergoline alleging strict product liability. Sun Ergoline argued that Boles's claims were barred by the release that she had signed. The lower courts agreed that Boles's claims were barred. The Supreme Court of Colorado reversed, however, because it concluded that, as a matter of public policy, assumption of risk (via the exculpatory clause) was not appropriate in a strict liability context. Therefore, Boles could sue Sun Ergoline to recover for her injuries.[22] •

Product Misuse

Similar to the defense of voluntary assumption of risk is that of product misuse, which occurs when a product is used for a purpose for which it was not intended. The courts have severely limited this defense, however, and it is now recognized as a defense only when the particular use was not reasonably foreseeable. If the misuse is foreseeable, the seller must take measures to guard against it.

Comparative Negligence (Fault)

Developments in the area of comparative negligence, or fault (discussed in Chapter 4), have also affected the doctrine of strict liability. In the past, the plaintiff's conduct was not a defense to liability for a defective product. Today, courts in many jurisdictions consider the negligent or intentional actions of both the plaintiff and the defendant when apportioning liability and awarding damages.[23] A defendant may be able to limit at least some of its liability for injuries caused by its defective product if it can show that the plaintiff's misuse of the product contributed to the injuries.

When proved, comparative negligence differs from other defenses in that it does not completely absolve the defendant of liability, but it can reduce the amount of damages that will be awarded to the plaintiff.

CASE EXAMPLE 17.17 Dan Smith, a mechanic in Alaska, was not wearing a hard hat at work when he was asked to start a diesel engine of an air compressor. Because the compressor was an older model, he had to prop open a door to start it. When Smith got the engine started, the door fell from its position and hit his head. The injury caused him to suffer from seizures and epilepsy. Smith sued the manufacturer, claiming that the engine was defectively designed. The manufacturer argued that Smith had been negligent by failing to wear his hard hat and by propping the door open in an unsafe manner. Smith's attorney claimed that the plaintiff's ordinary negligence could not be used as a defense in product liability cases, but the Alaska Supreme Court disagreed. Alaska, like many other states, allows comparative negligence to be raised as a defense in product liability lawsuits.[24] •

---

22. *Boles v. Sun Ergoline, Inc.*, 222 P.3d 724 (Co.Sup.Ct. 2010).

23. See, for example, *State Farm Insurance Companies v. Premier Manufactured Systems, Inc.*, 213 Ariz. 419, 142 P.3d 1232 (2006); and *Industrial Risk Insurers v. American Engineering Testing, Inc.*, 318 Wis.2d 148, 769 N.W.2d 82 (Wis.App. 2009).

24. *Smith v. Ingersoll-Rand Co.*, 14 P.3d 990 (Alaska 2000). See also *Winschel v. Brown*, 171 P.3d 142 (Alaska 2007).

Commonly Known Dangers

The dangers associated with certain products (such as sharp knives and guns) are so commonly known that manufacturers need not warn users of those dangers. If a defendant succeeds in convincing the court that a plaintiff's injury resulted from a *commonly known danger,* the defendant normally will not be liable.

CASE EXAMPLE 17.18 A classic case on this issue involved a plaintiff who was injured when an elastic exercise rope that she had purchased slipped off her foot and struck her in the eye, causing a detachment of the retina. The plaintiff claimed that the manufacturer should be liable because it had failed to warn users that the exercise rope might slip off a foot in this manner. The court stated that to hold the manufacturer liable in these circumstances "would go beyond the reasonable dictates of justice in fixing the liabilities of manufacturers." After all, stated the court, "[a]lmost every physical object can be inherently dangerous or potentially dangerous in a sense. . . . A manufacturer cannot manufacture a knife that will not cut or a hammer that will not mash a thumb or a stove that will not burn a finger. The law does not require [manufacturers] to warn of such common dangers."[25] ●

Knowledgeable User

A related defense is the *knowledgeable user* defense. If a particular danger (such as electrical shock) is or should be commonly known by particular users of the product (such as electricians), the manufacturer of electrical equipment need not warn these users of the danger.

CASE EXAMPLE 17.19 The parents of a group of teenagers who had become overweight and developed health problems filed a product liability lawsuit against McDonald's. The teenagers claimed that the well-known fast-food chain should be held liable for failing to warn customers of the adverse health effects of eating its food products. The court rejected this claim, however, based on the *knowledgeable user defense.* The court found that it is well known that the food at McDonald's contains high levels of cholesterol, fat, salt, and sugar and is therefore unhealthful. The court's opinion, which thwarted numerous future lawsuits against fast-food restaurants, stated: "If consumers know (or reasonably should know) the potential ill health effects of eating at McDonald's, they cannot blame McDonald's if they, nonetheless, choose to satiate [satisfy] their appetite with a surfeit [excess] of supersized McDonald's products."[26] ●

25. *Jamieson v. Woodward & Lothrop,* 247 F.2d 23, 101 D.C.App. 32 (1957).

26. *Pelman v. McDonald's Corp.,* 237 F.Supp.2d 512 (S.D.N.Y. 2003).

Reviewing . . . Warranties and Product Liability

Shalene Kolchek bought a Great Lakes Spa from Val Porter, a dealer who was selling spas at the state fair. Porter told Kolchek that Great Lakes spas are "top of the line" and "the Cadillac of spas" and indicated that the spa she was buying was "fully warranted for three years." After Kolchek signed an installment sale contract, Porter gave her the manufacturer's paperwork and arranged for the spa to be delivered and installed for her. Three months later, Kolchek noticed that one corner of the spa was leaking onto her new deck and causing damage. She complained to Porter, but he did nothing about the problem. Kolchek's family continued to use the spa. Using the information presented in the chapter, answer the following questions.

1. Did Porter's statement that the spa was "top of the line" and "the Cadillac of spas" create any type of warranty? Why or why not?
2. Did Porter breach the implied warranty of merchantability? Why or why not?

3. One night, Kolchek's six-year-old daughter, Litisha, was in the spa with her mother. Litisha's hair became entangled in the spa's drain, and she was sucked down and held under water for a prolonged period, causing her to suffer brain damage. Under which theory or theories of product liability can Kolchek sue Porter to recover for Litisha's injuries?
4. If Kolchek had negligently left Litisha alone in the spa before the incident described in the previous question, what defense to liability might Porter assert?

DEBATE THIS No express warranties should be created by the oral statements made by salespersons about a product.

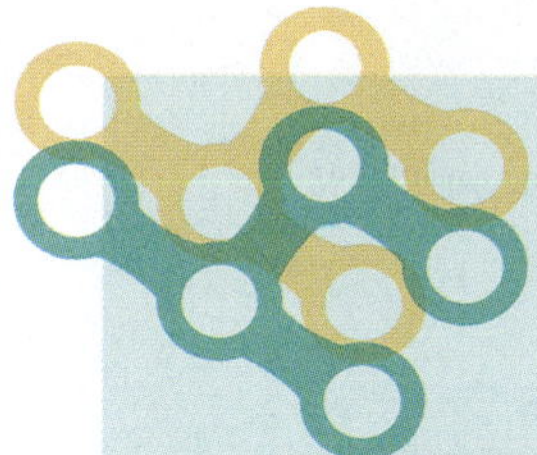

LINKING BUSINESS LAW to Corporate Management

Quality Control

In this chapter, you learned that breaches of warranties and manufacturing and design defects can give rise to liability. Although it is possible to minimize liability through warranty disclaimers and various defenses to product liability claims, all businesspersons know that such disclaimers and defenses do not necessarily fend off expensive lawsuits.

The legal issues surrounding product liability and warranties relate directly to quality control. As all of your management courses will emphasize, quality control is a major issue facing every manager in all organizations. Companies that have cost-effective quality control systems produce products with fewer manufacturing and design defects. As a result, these companies incur fewer potential and actual warranty and product liability lawsuits.

Three Types of Quality Control

Most management systems involve three types of quality control—preventive, concurrent, and feedback. They apply at different stages of the manufacturing process: preventive quality control occurs before the process begins, concurrent control takes place during the process, and feedback control occurs after it is finished.

In a typical manufacturing process, for example, preventive quality control might involve inspecting raw materials before they are put into the production process. Once the process begins, measuring and monitoring devices constantly assess quality standards as part of a concurrent quality control system. When the standards are not being met, employees correct the problem.

Once the manufacturing is completed, the products undergo a final quality inspection as part of the feedback quality control system. Of course, there are economic limits to how complete the final inspection will be. A refrigerator can be tested for an hour, a day, or a year. Management faces a trade-off. The less the refrigerator is tested, the sooner it gets to market and the faster the company receives its payment. The shorter the testing period, however, the higher the probability of a defect that will cost the manufacturer because of its expressed or implied warranties.

Total Quality Management (TQM)

Some managers attempt to reduce warranty and product liability costs by relying on a concurrent quality control system known as total quality management (TQM). This is an organization-wide effort to infuse quality into every activity in a company through continuous improvement.

Quality circles are a popular TQM technique. These are groups of six to twelve employees who volunteer to meet regularly to discuss problems and how to solve them. In a continuous stream manufacturing process, for example, a quality circle might consist of workers from different phases in the production process. Quality circles force changes in the production process that affect workers who are actually on the production line.

Benchmarking is another technique used in TQM. In benchmarking, a company continuously measures its products against those of its toughest competitors or the industry leaders in order to identify areas for improvement. In the automobile industry, benchmarking enabled several Japanese firms to overtake U.S. automakers in terms of quality. Some argue that Toyota gained worldwide market share by effectively using this type of quality control management system.

Another TQM system is called *Six Sigma*. Motorola introduced the quality principles in this system in the late 1980s, but Six Sigma has now become a generic term for a quality control approach that takes nothing for granted. It is based on

Continued

a five-step methodology: define, measure, analyze, improve, and control. Six Sigma controls emphasize discipline and a relentless attempt to achieve higher quality (and lower costs). A possible impediment to the institution of a Six Sigma program is that it requires a major commitment from top management because it may involve widespread changes throughout the entire organization.

Critical Thinking

Quality control leads to fewer defective products and fewer lawsuits. Consequently, managers know that quality control is important to their company's long-term financial health. At the same time, the more quality control managers impose on their organization, the higher the average cost per unit of whatever is produced and sold. How does a manager decide how much quality control to undertake?

Key Terms

express warranty 438
implied warranty 439
implied warranty of fitness for a particular purpose 441
implied warranty of merchantability 439
lien 438
market-share liability 452
product liability 445
unreasonably dangerous product 448

Chapter Summary: Warranties and Product Liability

WARRANTIES	
Warranties of Title (See page 438.)	In most sales, sellers warrant that they have good and valid title to the goods sold and that transfer of the title is rightful [UCC 2–312(1)(a)]. A second warranty of title shields buyers and lessees who are *unaware* of any encumbrances, or liens, against goods at the time the contract is made [UCC 2–312(1)(b), 2A–211(1)]. Third, when the seller or lessor is a merchant, he or she automatically warrants that the buyer or lessee takes the goods *free of infringements* [UCC 2–312(3), 2A–211(2)].
Express Warranties (See pages 438–439.)	1. *Under the UCC*—An express warranty arises under the UCC when a seller or lessor indicates, as part of the basis of the bargain, any of the following [UCC 2–313, 2A–210]: a. An affirmation or promise of fact. b. A description of the goods. c. A sample shown as conforming to the contract goods. 2. *Under the Magnuson-Moss Warranty Act*—Express written warranties covering consumer goods priced at more than $25, *if made,* must be labeled as one of the following: a. Full warranty—Free repair or replacement of defective parts. Or, if the goods cannot be repaired in a reasonable time, refund or replacement is available. b. Limited warranty—When less than a full warranty is being offered.
Implied Warranty of Merchantability (See pages 439–440.)	When a seller or lessor is a merchant who deals in goods of the kind sold or leased, the seller or lessor warrants that the goods sold or leased are properly packaged and labeled, are of proper quality, and are reasonably fit for the ordinary purposes for which such goods are used [UCC 2–314, 2A–212].
Implied Warranty of Fitness for a Particular Purpose (See page 441.)	Arises when the buyer's or lessee's purpose or use is expressly or impliedly known by the seller or lessor, and the buyer or lessee purchases or leases the goods in reliance on the seller's or lessor's selection [UCC 2–315, 2A–213]. Other implied warranties can arise as a result of course of dealing or usage of trade [UCC 2–314(3), 2A–212(3)].
Overlapping Warranties (See page 442.)	The UCC construes warranties as cumulative if they are consistent with each other. If warranties are inconsistent, then express warranties take precedence over implied warranties, except for the implied warranty of fitness for a particular purpose. Also, samples take precedence over general descriptions, and exact or technical specifications displace inconsistent samples or general descriptions.
Warranty Disclaimers (See pages 442–443.)	Express warranties can be disclaimed if the disclaimer is written in clear language, conspicuous, and called to the buyer's or lessee's attention at the time the contract is formed. A disclaimer of the implied warranty of merchantability must specifically mention the word *merchantability*. The disclaimer need not be in writing, but if it is written, it must be conspicuous. A disclaimer of the implied warranty of fitness *must* be in writing and be conspicuous, though it need not mention the word *fitness*.

Chapter Summary: Warranties and Product Liability—Continued

PRODUCT LIABILITY	
Liability Based on Negligence (See page 445.)	1. The manufacturer must use due care in designing the product, selecting materials, using the appropriate production process, assembling and testing the product, and placing adequate warnings on the label or product. 2. Privity of contract is not required. A manufacturer is liable for failure to exercise due care to any person who sustains an injury proximately caused by a negligently made (defective) product. 3. Fraudulent misrepresentation of a product may result in product liability based on the tort of fraud.
Strict Liability—Requirements (See pages 446–448.)	1. The defendant must have sold the product in a defective condition. 2. The defendant must normally be engaged in the business of selling that product. 3. The product must be unreasonably dangerous to the user or consumer because of its defective condition (in most states). 4. The plaintiff must incur physical harm to self or property by use or consumption of the product. 5. The defective condition must be the proximate cause of the injury or damage. 6. The goods must not have been substantially changed from the time the product was sold to the time the injury was sustained.
Strict Liability—Product Defects (See pages 448–452.)	A product may be defective in three basic ways: 1. In its manufacture. 2. In its design. 3. In the instructions or warnings that come with it.
Market-Share Liability (See pages 452–453.)	When plaintiffs cannot prove which of many distributors of a defective product supplied the particular product that caused the plaintiffs' injuries, some courts apply market-share liability. All firms that manufactured and distributed the harmful product during the period in question are then held liable for the plaintiffs' injuries in proportion to the firms' respective shares of the market, as directed by the court.
Other Applications of Strict Liability (See page 453.)	1. Manufacturers and other sellers are liable for harms suffered by bystanders as a result of defective products. 2. Suppliers of component parts are strictly liable for defective parts that, when incorporated into a product, cause injuries to users.
Defenses to Product Liability (See pages 454–456.)	1. *Preemption*—An injured party may not be able to sue the manufacturer of a product that is subject to comprehensive federal safety regulations, such as medical devices. 2. *Assumption of risk*—The user or consumer knew of the risk of harm and voluntarily assumed it. 3. *Product misuse*—The user or consumer misused the product in a way unforeseeable by the manufacturer. 4. *Comparative negligence*—Liability may be distributed between the plaintiff and the defendant under the doctrine of comparative negligence if the plaintiff's misuse of the product contributed to the risk of injury. 5. *Commonly known dangers*—If a defendant succeeds in convincing the court that a plaintiff's injury resulted from a commonly known danger, such as the danger associated with using a sharp knife, the defendant will not be liable. 6. *Knowledgeable user*—If a particular danger is or should be commonly known by particular users of the product, the manufacturer of the product need not warn these users of the danger.

ExamPrep

ISSUE SPOTTERS

1. Rim Corporation makes tire rims that it sells to Superior Vehicles, Inc., which installs them on cars. One set of rims is defective, which an inspection would reveal. Superior does not inspect the rims. The car with the defective rims is sold to Town Auto Sales, which sells the car to Uri. Soon, the car is in an accident caused by the defective rims, and Uri is injured. Is Superior Vehicles liable? Explain your answer. **(See page 445.)**
2. Real Chocolate Company makes a box of candy, which it sells to Sweet Things, Inc., a distributor. Sweet sells the box to a Tasty Candy store, where Jill buys it. Jill gives it to Ken, who breaks a tooth on a stone the same size and color as a piece of the candy. If Real, Sweet, and Tasty were not negligent, can they be liable for the injury? Why or why not? **(See page 445.)**

—Check your answers to the Issue Spotters against the answers provided in Appendix E at the end of this text.

BEFORE THE TEST

Go to www.cengagebrain.com, enter the ISBN 9781133273561, and click on "Find" to locate this textbook's Web site. Then, click on "Access Now" under "Study Tools," and select Chapter 17 at the top. There, you will find a Practice Quiz that you can take to assess your mastery of the concepts in this chapter, as well as Flashcards, a Glossary of important terms, and Video Questions (when assigned).

For Review

Answers to the even-numbered questions in this For Review section can be found in Appendix F at the end of this text.

1. What factors determine whether a seller's or lessor's statement constitutes an express warranty or is mere puffery?
2. What implied warranties arise under the UCC?
3. Can a manufacturer be held liable to any person who suffers an injury proximately caused by the manufacturer's negligently made product?
4. What are the elements of a cause of action in strict product liability?
5. What defenses to liability can be raised in a product liability lawsuit?

Business Scenarios and Case Problems

17–1 Product Liability. Carmen buys a television set manufactured by AKI Electronics. She is going on vacation, so she takes the set to her mother's house for her mother to use. Because the set is defective, it explodes, causing considerable damage to her mother's house. Carmen's mother sues AKI for the damage to her house. Discuss the theories under which Carmen's mother can recover from AKI. **(See page 445.)**

17–2 Question with Sample Answer—Implied Warranties. Tandy purchased a washing machine from Marshall Appliances. The sales contract included a provision explicitly disclaiming all express and implied warranties, including the implied warranty of merchantability. The disclaimer was printed in the same size and color as the rest of the contract. The machine turned out to be a "lemon" and never functioned properly. Tandy sought a refund of the purchase price, claiming that Marshall had breached the implied warranty of merchantability. Can Tandy recover her payment, notwithstanding the warranty disclaimer in the contract? Explain. **(See page 441.)**

—For a sample answer to Question 17–2, go to Appendix G at the end of this text.

17–3 Product Liability. Jason Clark, an experienced hunter, bought a paintball gun. Clark practiced with the gun and knew how to screw in the carbon dioxide cartridge, pump the gun, and use its safety and trigger. Although Clark was aware that he could purchase protective eyewear, he chose not to buy it. Clark had taken gun safety courses and understood that it was "common sense" not to shoot anyone in the face. Clark's friend, Chris Wright, also owned a paintball gun and was similarly familiar with the gun's use and its risks. Clark, Wright, and their friends played a game that involved shooting paintballs at cars whose occupants also had the guns. One night, while Clark and Wright were cruising with their guns, Wright shot at Clark's car, but hit Clark in the eye. Clark filed a product liability lawsuit against the manufacturer of Wright's paintball gun to recover for the injury. Clark claimed that the gun was defectively designed. During the trial, Wright testified that his gun "never malfunctioned." In whose favor should the court rule? Why? **(See pages 455–456.)**

17–4 Defenses to Product Liability. Brandon Stroud was driving a golf car made by Textron, Inc. The golf car did not have lights, but Textron did not warn against using it on public roads at night. When Stroud attempted to cross a road at 8:30 P.M., his golf car was struck by a vehicle driven by Joseph Thornley. Stroud was killed. His estate filed a suit against Textron, alleging strict product liability and product liability based on negligence. The charge was that the golf car was defective and unreasonably dangerous. What defense might Textron assert? Explain. [*Moore v. Barony House Restaurant,* LLC, 382 S.C. 35, 674 S.E.2d 500 (S.C.App. 2009)] **(See pages 454–456.)**

17–5 Product Misuse. Five-year-old Cheyenne Stark was riding in the backseat of her parents' Ford Taurus. Cheyenne was not sitting in a booster seat. Instead, she was using a seatbelt designed by Ford, but was wearing the shoulder belt behind her back. The car was involved in a collision. As a result, Cheyenne suffered a spinal cord injury and was paralyzed from the waist down. The family filed a suit against Ford Motor Co., alleging that the seatbelt was defectively designed. Could Ford successfully claim that Cheyenne had misused the seatbelt? Why or why not? [*Stark v. Ford Motor Co.,* 693 S.E.2d 253 (N.C.App. 2010)] **(See page 455.)**

17–6 Product Liability. Yun Tung Chow tried to unclog a floor drain in the kitchen of the restaurant where he worked. He used a drain cleaner called Lewis Red Devil Lye that contained crystalline sodium hydroxide. The product label said to wear eye protection, to put one tablespoon of lye directly into the drain, and to keep your face away from the drain because there could be dangerous backsplash. Not wearing eye protection, Chow mixed three spoonfuls of lye in a can and poured that mixture down the drain while bending over it. Liquid splashed back into his face, causing injury. He sued for product liability based on inadequate warnings and a design defect. The trial court granted summary judgment to the manufacturer. Chow appealed. An expert for Chow stated that the product was defective because it had a tendency to backsplash. Is that a convincing argument? Why or why not? [*Yun Tung Chow v. Reckitt & Coleman, Inc.*, 69 A.D.3d 413, 891 N.Y.S.2d 402 (N.Y.A.D. 1 Dept. 2010)] **(See pages 449–452.)**

17–7 **Case Problem with Sample Answer—Product Liability.** David Dobrovolny bought a new Ford F-350 pickup truck. A year later, the truck spontaneously caught fire in Dobrovolny's driveway. The truck was destroyed, but no other property was damaged, and no one was injured. Dobrovolny filed a suit in a Nebraska state court against Ford Motor Co. on a theory of strict product liability to recover the cost of the truck. Nebraska limits the application of strict product liability to situations involving personal injuries. Is Dobrovolny's claim likely to succeed? Why or why not? Is there another basis for liability on which he might recover? Explain. [*Dobrovolny v. Ford Motor Co.*, 281 Neb. 86, 793 N.W.2d 445 (2011)] **(See pages 446–453.)**

—For a sample answer to Problem 17–7, go to Appendix H at the end of this text.

17–8 **Spotlight on Apple—Implied Warranties.** Alan Vitt purchased an iBook G4 laptop computer from Apple, Inc. Shortly after the one-year warranty expired, the laptop failed to work due to a weakness in the product manufacture. Vitt sued Apple, arguing that the laptop should have lasted "at least a couple of years," which Vitt believed was a reasonable consumer expectation for a laptop. Vitt claimed that Apple's descriptions of the laptop as "durable," "rugged," "reliable," and "high performance" were affirmative statements concerning the quality and performance of the laptop, which Apple did not meet. How should the court rule? Why? [*Vitt v. Apple Computer, Inc.*, 2012 WL 627702 (9th Cir. 2011)] **(See pages 439–442.)**

17–9 **A Question of Ethics—Strict Product Liability.** Susan Calles lived with her four daughters, Amanda, age 11, Victoria, age 5, and Jenna and Jillian, age 3. In March 1998, Calles bought an Aim N Flame utility lighter, which she stored on the top shelf of her kitchen cabinet. A trigger can ignite the Aim N Flame after an "ON/OFF" switch is slid to the "on" position. On the night of March 31, Calles and Victoria left to get videos. Jenna and Jillian were in bed, and Amanda was watching television. Calles returned to find fire trucks and emergency vehicles around her home. Robert Finn, a fire investigator, determined that Jenna had started a fire using the lighter. Jillian suffered smoke inhalation, was hospitalized, and died on April 21. Calles filed a suit in an Illinois state court against Scripto-Tokai Corp., which distributed the Aim N Flame, and others. In her suit, which was grounded, in part, in strict liability claims, Calles alleged that the lighter was an "unreasonably dangerous product." Scripto filed a motion for summary judgment. [*Calles v. Scripto-Tokai Corp.*, 224 Ill.2d 247, 864 N.E.2d 249, 309 Ill.Dec. 383 (2007)] **(See pages 448–452.)**

1. A product is "unreasonably dangerous" when it is dangerous beyond the expectation of the ordinary consumer. Whose expectation—Calles's or Jenna's—applies here? Why? Does the lighter pass this test? Explain.
2. A product is also "unreasonably dangerous" when a less dangerous alternative was economically feasible for its maker, which failed to produce it. Scripto contended that because its product was "simple" and the danger was "obvious," it should not be liable under this test. Do you agree? Why or why not?
3. Calles presented evidence as to the likelihood and seriousness of injury from lighters that do not have child-safety devices. Scripto argued that the Aim N Flame is a useful, inexpensive, alternative source of fire and is safer than a match. Calles admitted that she was aware of the dangers presented by lighters in the hands of children. Scripto admitted that it had been a defendant in at least twenty-five suits for injuries that occurred under similar circumstances. With these factors in mind, how should the court rule? Why?

Critical Thinking and Writing Assignments

17–10 **Business Law Critical Thinking Group Assignment.** Bret D'Auguste was an experienced skier when he rented equipment to ski at Hunter Mountain Ski Bowl in New York. When D'Auguste entered an extremely difficult trail, he noticed immediately that the surface consisted of ice with almost no snow. He tried to exit the steeply declining trail by making a sharp right turn, but in the attempt, his left ski snapped off. D'Auguste lost his balance, fell, and slid down the mountain, striking his face and head against a fence along the trail. According to a report by a rental shop employee, one of the bindings on D'Auguste's skis had a "cracked heel housing." D'Auguste filed a lawsuit against the bindings' manufacturer on a theory of strict product liability. The manufacturer filed a motion for summary judgment.

1. The first group will take the position of the manufacturer and develop an argument why the court should *grant* the summary judgment motion and dismiss the strict product liability claim.
2. The second group will take the position of D'Auguste and formulate a basis for why the court should *deny* the motion and allow the strict product liability claim.

18 CHAPTER

Negotiable Instruments: Transferability and Liability

CHAPTER OUTLINE

- Types of Instruments
- Requirements for Negotiability
- Transfer of Instruments
- Holder in Due Course (HDC)
- Signature and Warranty Liability
- Defenses, Limitations, and Discharge

LEARNING OBJECTIVES

The five learning objectives below are designed to help improve your understanding of the chapter. After reading this chapter, you should be able to answer the following questions:

1. What requirements must an instrument meet to be negotiable?
2. What are the requirements for attaining the status of a holder in due course (HDC)?
3. What is the difference between signature liability and warranty liability?
4. Certain defenses are valid against all holders, including HDCs. What are these defenses called? Name four defenses that fall within this category.
5. Certain defenses can be used against an ordinary holder but are not effective against an HDC. What are these defenses called? Name four defenses that fall within this category.

(DNY59/iStockphoto.com)

"It took many generations for people to feel comfortable accepting paper in lieu of gold or silver."
—Alan Greenspan, 1926–present
(Chair of the Board of Governors of the Federal Reserve System, 1987–2006)

Negotiable Instrument A signed writing (record) that contains an unconditional promise or order to pay an exact sum on demand or at a specified future time to a specific person or order, or to bearer.

Most commercial transactions would be inconceivable without negotiable instruments. A **negotiable instrument** is a signed writing (record) that contains an unconditional promise or order to pay an exact sum on demand or at a specified future time to a specific person or order, or to bearer. Most negotiable instruments are paper documents, which is why they are sometimes referred to as *commercial paper*. The checks you write are negotiable instruments.

A negotiable instrument can function as a substitute for cash or as an extension of credit. As indicated in the chapter-opening quotation, "many generations" passed before paper became an acceptable substitute for gold or silver in commerce. For a negotiable instrument to operate *practically* as either a substitute for cash or a credit device, or both, it is essential that the instrument be *easily transferable without danger of being uncollectible*. Each rule described in the following pages can be examined in light of this essential function of negotiable instruments.

Types of Instruments

Section 3–104(b) of the Uniform Commercial Code (UCC) defines *instrument* as a "negotiable instrument."[1] For that reason, whenever the term *instrument* is used in this book, it refers to a negotiable instrument. The UCC specifies four types of negotiable instruments: *drafts, checks, promissory notes,* and *certificates of deposit* (CDs).

These instruments, which are summarized briefly in Exhibit 18.1 below, are frequently divided into the two classifications that we will discuss in the following subsections: *orders to pay* (drafts and checks) and *promises to pay* (promissory notes and CDs).

Negotiable instruments may also be classified as either demand instruments or time instruments. A *demand instrument* is payable on demand. In other words, it is payable immediately after it is issued and thereafter for a reasonable period of time. All checks are demand instruments because, by definition, they must be payable on demand. A *time instrument* is payable at a future date.

Drafts and Checks (Orders to Pay)

Draft Any instrument drawn on a drawee that orders the drawee to pay a certain amount of funds, usually to a third party (the payee), on demand or at a definite future time.

Drawer The party that initiates a draft (such as a check), thereby ordering the drawee to pay.

Drawee The party that is ordered to pay a draft or check. With a check, a bank or a financial institution is always the drawee.

Payee A person to whom an instrument is made payable.

Acceptance In negotiable instruments law, a drawee's signed agreement to pay a draft when it is presented.

A **draft** is an unconditional written order to pay rather than a promise to pay. Drafts involve three parties. The party creating the draft (the **drawer**) orders another party (the **drawee**) to pay funds, usually to a third party (the **payee**). The most common type of draft is a check, but drafts other than checks may be used in commercial transactions.

Time Drafts and Sight Drafts

A *time draft* is payable at a definite future time. A *sight draft* (or demand draft) is payable on sight—that is, when it is presented to the drawee (usually a bank or financial institution) for payment. A sight draft may be payable on acceptance. **Acceptance** is the drawee's written promise to pay the draft when it

1. Note that all of the references to Article 3 of the UCC in this chapter are to the 1990 version of Article 3, which has been adopted by nearly every state.

Exhibit 18.1 Basic Types of Negotiable Instruments

INSTRUMENTS	CHARACTERISTICS	PARTIES
ORDERS TO PAY:		
Draft	An order by one person to another person or to bearer [UCC 3–104(e)].	Drawer—The person who signs or makes the order to pay [UCC 3–103(a)(3)].
Check	A draft drawn on a bank and payable on demand [UCC 3–104(f)].[a] (With certain types of checks, such as cashier's checks, the bank is both the drawer and the drawee—see Chapter 19 for details.)	Drawee—The person to whom the order to pay is made [UCC 3–103(a)(2)]. Payee—The person to whom payment is ordered.
PROMISES TO PAY:		
Promissory note	A promise by one party to pay funds to another party or to bearer [UCC 3–104(e)].	Maker—The person who promises to pay [UCC 3–103(a)(5)]. Payee—The person to whom the promise is made.
Certificate of deposit	A note issued by a bank acknowledging a deposit of funds and made payable to the holder of the note [UCC 3–104(j)].	

a. Under UCC 4–105(1), banks include savings banks, savings and loan associations, credit unions, and trust companies. (Trust companies are organizations that perform the fiduciary functions of trusts and agencies.)

comes due. Usually, an instrument is accepted by writing the word *accepted* across its face, followed by the date of acceptance and the signature of the drawee. A draft can be both a time and a sight draft. Such a draft is payable at a stated time after sight (a draft that states it is payable ninety days after sight, for instance).

Exhibit 18.2 below shows a typical time draft. For the drawee to be obligated to honor (pay) the order, the drawee must be obligated to the drawer either by agreement or through a debtor-creditor relationship. **EXAMPLE 18.1** On January 16, OurTown Real Estate orders $1,000 worth of office supplies from Eastman Supply Company, with payment due in ninety days. Also on January 16, OurTown sends Eastman a draft drawn on its account with the First National Bank of Whiteacre as payment. In this scenario, the drawer is OurTown, the drawee is OurTown's bank (First National Bank of Whiteacre), and the payee is Eastman Supply Company. ●

"The two most beautiful words in the English language are 'check enclosed.'"

Dorothy Parker, 1893–1967 (American author and poet)

Trade Acceptances A *trade acceptance* is a type of draft that is commonly used in the sale of goods. In this draft, the seller is both the drawer and the payee. The buyer to whom credit is extended is the drawee. **EXAMPLE 18.2** Jackson Street Bistro buys its restaurant supplies from Osaka Industries. When Jackson requests supplies, Osaka creates a draft ordering Jackson to pay Osaka for the supplies within ninety days. Jackson accepts the draft by signing its face and is then obligated to make the payment. This is a trade acceptance and can be sold to a third party if Osaka is in need of cash before the payment is due. ● (If the draft orders the buyer's bank to pay, it is called a *banker's acceptance.*)

Check A draft drawn by a drawer ordering the drawee bank or financial institution to pay a certain amount of funds to the payee on demand.

Checks As mentioned, the most commonly used type of draft is a **check.** The writer of the check is the drawer, the bank on which the check is drawn is the drawee, and the person to whom the check is payable is the payee. Checks are demand instruments because they are payable on demand.

Checks will be discussed more fully in Chapter 19, but it should be noted here that with certain types of checks, such as *cashier's checks,* the bank is both the drawer and the drawee. The bank customer purchases a cashier's check from the bank—that is, pays the bank the amount of the check—and indicates to whom the check should be made payable. The bank, not the customer, is the drawer of the check, as well as the drawee.

Exhibit 18.2 A Typical Time Draft

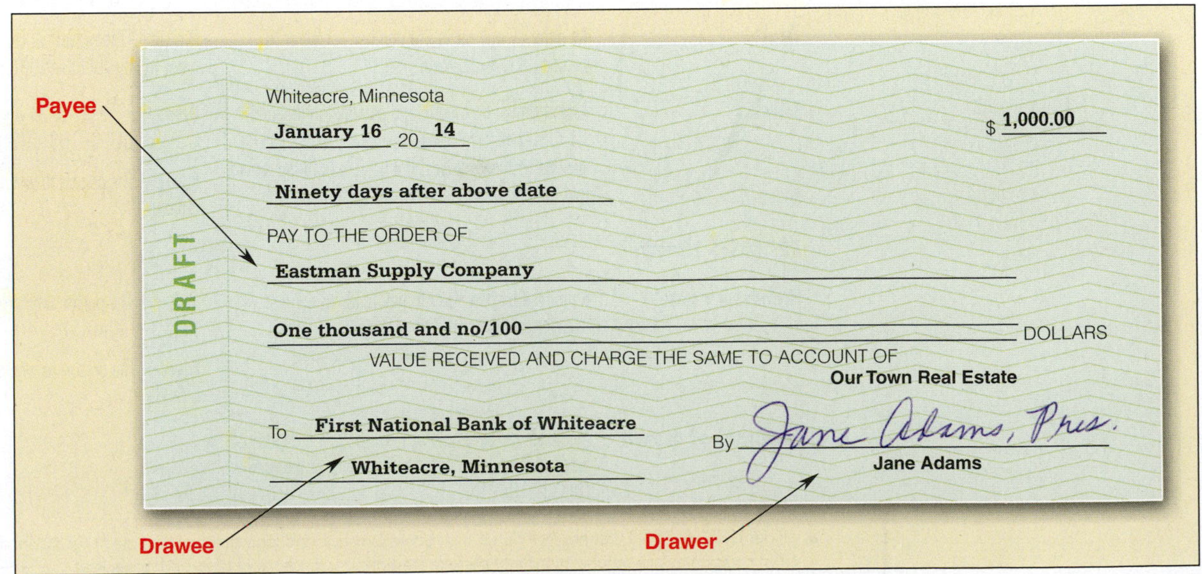

A cashier's check functions the same as cash because the bank has committed itself to paying the stated amount on demand.

Promissory Notes (Promises to Pay)

Promissory Note A written promise made by one person (the maker) to pay a fixed amount of funds to another person (the payee or a subsequent holder) on demand or on a specified date.

Maker One who promises to pay a fixed amount of funds to the holder of a promissory note or a certificate of deposit (CD).

A **promissory note** is a written promise made by one person (the **maker** of the promise to pay) to another (usually a payee). A promissory note, which is often referred to simply as a *note*, can be made payable at a definite time or on demand. It can name a specific payee or merely be payable to bearer (bearer instruments will be discussed later in this chapter). **EXAMPLE 18.3** On April 30, Laurence and Margaret Roberts sign a writing unconditionally promising to pay "to the order of" the First National Bank of Whiteacre $3,000 (with 8 percent interest) on or before June 29. This writing is a promissory note. •

A typical promissory note is shown in Exhibit 18.3 below.

CASE EXAMPLE 18.4 Joseph Cotton borrowed funds from a bank for his education and signed a promissory note for their repayment. The bank assigned the note to the U.S. Department of Education, and Cotton failed to pay the debt. The government then obtained a court order allowing it to garnish (take a percentage of) Cotton's wages and his federal income tax refund. Cotton filed a lawsuit seeking to avoid payment and claiming that the debt was invalid because he had not signed any document promising to pay the government. The court found that the signature on Cotton's employment records matched the one on the bank's note, which had been validly assigned to the government. Thus, the government was entitled to enforce the note.[2] •

Certificates of Deposit (Promises to Pay)

Certificate of Deposit (CD) A note issued by a bank in which the bank acknowledges the receipt of funds from a party and promises to repay that amount, with interest, to the party on a certain date.

A **certificate of deposit (CD)** is a type of note. A CD is issued when a party deposits funds with a bank that the bank promises to repay, with interest, on a certain date [UCC 3–104(j)]. The bank is the maker of the note, and the depositor is the payee. **EXAMPLE 18.5** On February 15, Sara Levin deposits $5,000 with the First National Bank of Whiteacre. The bank issues a CD, in which it promises to repay the $5,000, plus 3.25 percent annual interest, on August 15. •

2. *Cotton v. U.S. Department of Education,* 2006 WL 3313753 (M.D.Fla. 2006).

Exhibit 18.3 A Typical Promissory Note

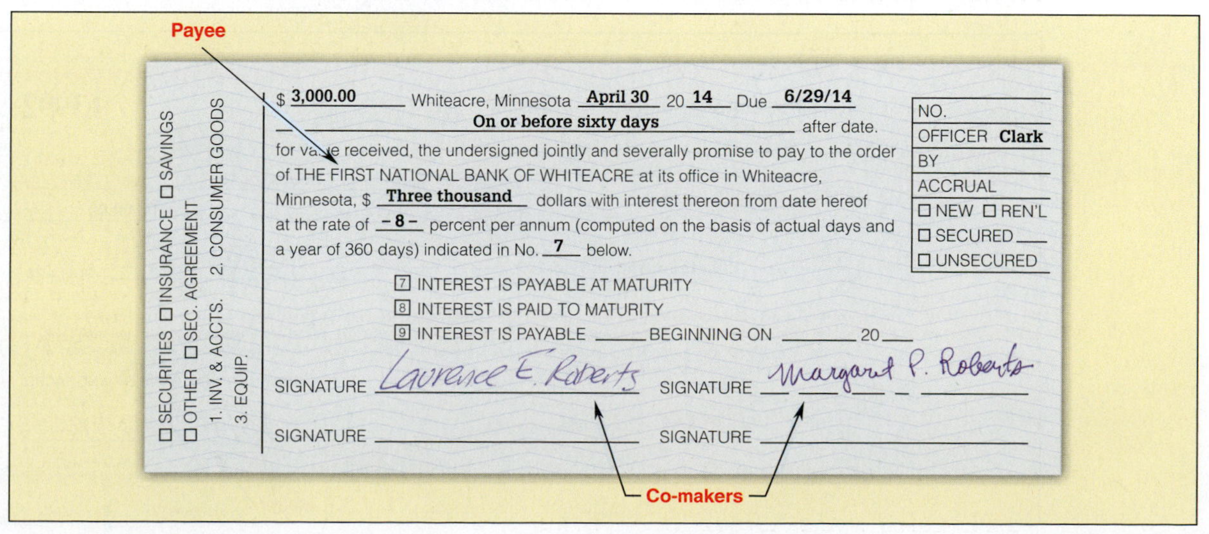

(Photo by George Frey/Bloomberg via Getty Images)

Before Washington Mutual's demise in 2008, it was offering 4.25 percent certificates of deposit.

Certificates of deposit in small denominations (for amounts up to \$100,000) are often sold by savings and loan associations, savings banks, commercial banks, and credit unions. Certificates of deposit for amounts over \$100,000 are called large or jumbo CDs.

Because CDs are time deposits, the purchaser-payee typically is not allowed to withdraw the funds before the date of maturity (except in limited circumstances, such as disability or death). If a payee wants to access the funds prior to the maturity date, he or she can sell (negotiate) the CD to a third party.

Exhibit 18.4 below shows a typical small CD.

Requirements for Negotiability

For an instrument to be negotiable, it must meet the following requirements:

LEARNING OBJECTIVE 1

What requirements must an instrument meet to be negotiable?

1. Be in writing.
2. Be signed by the maker or the drawer.
3. Be an unconditional promise or order to pay.
4. State a fixed amount of money.
5. Be payable on demand or at a definite time.
6. Be payable to order or to bearer, unless the instrument is a check.

Written Form

Negotiable instruments must be in written form [UCC 3–103(a)(6), (9)]. This is because negotiable instruments must possess the quality of certainty that only formal, written expression can give. The writing must have the following qualities:

1. The writing must be on material that lends itself to *permanence.* Instruments carved in blocks of ice or recorded on other impermanent surfaces would not qualify as negotiable instruments. **EXAMPLE 18.6** Suzanne writes in the sand, "I promise to pay \$500 to the order of Jack." This cannot be a negotiable instrument because, although it is in writing, it lacks permanence. ●

Exhibit 18.4 **A Typical Small Certificate of Deposit**

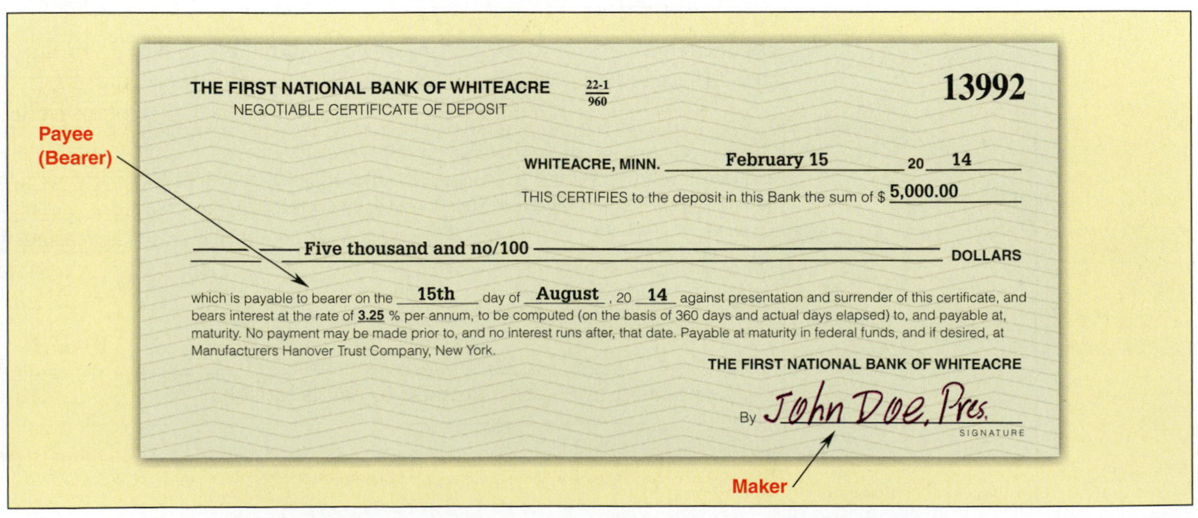
THE FIRST NATIONAL BANK OF WHITEACRE 22-1/960 13992
NEGOTIABLE CERTIFICATE OF DEPOSIT

WHITEACRE, MINN. February 15 20 14

THIS CERTIFIES to the deposit in this Bank the sum of \$ 5,000.00

Five thousand and no/100 DOLLARS

which is payable to bearer on the 15th day of August, 20 14 against presentation and surrender of this certificate, and bears interest at the rate of 3.25 % per annum, to be computed (on the basis of 360 days and actual days elapsed) to, and payable at, maturity. No payment may be made prior to, and no interest runs after, that date. Payable at maturity in federal funds, and if desired, at Manufacturers Hanover Trust Company, New York.

THE FIRST NATIONAL BANK OF WHITEACRE

By John Doe, Pres.
SIGNATURE

2. The writing must also have *portability.* Although the UCC does not explicitly state this requirement, if an instrument is not movable, it obviously cannot meet the requirement that it be freely transferable. **EXAMPLE 18.7** Charles writes on the side of a cow, "I promise to pay $500 to the order of Jason." Technically, this would meet the requirements of a negotiable instrument—except for portability. A cow cannot easily be transferred in the ordinary course of business. Thus, the "instrument" is nonnegotiable. •

The UCC nevertheless gives considerable leeway as to what can be a negotiable instrument. Courts have found checks and notes written on napkins, menus, tablecloths, shirts, and a variety of other materials to be negotiable instruments.

"I'm a writer. I write checks. They're not very good."

Wendy Liebman, 1961–present (American comedian)

Signatures

For an instrument to be negotiable, it must be signed by (1) the maker, if it is a note or a certificate of deposit, or (2) the drawer, if it is a draft or a check [UCC 3–103(a)(3)]. If a person signs an instrument as an authorized agent of the maker or drawer, the maker or drawer has effectively signed the instrument. (Agents' signatures will be discussed in Chapter 23.)

The UCC is quite lenient with regard to what constitutes a signature. Nearly any symbol executed or adopted by a person with the intent to authenticate a written document can be a signature. A signature can be made manually or by some device, such as a rubber stamp or thumbprint, and can consist of any name, including a trade or assumed name, or a word, mark, or symbol [UCC 3–401(b)]. If necessary, *parol evidence* (see page 320 in Chapter 12) is admissible to identify the signer. When the signer is identified, the signature becomes effective.

The location of the signature on the document is unimportant, although the usual place is the lower right-hand corner. A *handwritten* statement on the body of the instrument, such as "I, Jerome Garcia, promise to pay Elena Greer," is sufficient to act as a signature.

PREVENTING LEGAL DISPUTES

Although there are almost no limitations on the manner in which a signature can be made, be careful about receiving an instrument that has been signed in an unusual way. Oddities on a negotiable instrument can open the door to disputes and lead to litigation. Furthermore, an unusual signature clearly decreases the *marketability* of an instrument because it creates uncertainty.

Unconditional Promise or Order to Pay

The terms of the promise or order must be included in the writing on the face of a negotiable instrument. The terms must also be *unconditional*—that is, they cannot be conditioned on the occurrence or nonoccurrence of some other event or agreement [UCC 3–104(a)].

KNOW THIS

Negotiable instruments are classified as promises to pay or orders to pay.

Promise or Order

For an instrument to be negotiable, it must contain an express order or promise to pay. If a buyer executes a promissory note using the words "I promise to pay Jonas $1,000 on demand for the purchase of these goods," then this requirement for a negotiable instrument is satisfied. A mere acknowledgment of the debt, such as an I.O.U. ("I owe you"), might logically *imply* a promise, but it is not sufficient under the UCC because the promise must be an affirmative (express) undertaking [UCC 3–103(a)(9)]. If such words as "to be paid on demand" or "due on demand" are added to an I.O.U., however, the need for an express promise to pay is satisfied.[3]

3. A certificate of deposit (CD) is an exception in this respect. A CD does not have to contain an express promise because the bank's acknowledgment of the deposit and the other terms of the instrument clearly indicate a promise by the bank to repay the funds [UCC 3–104(j)].

An *order* is associated with three-party instruments, such as checks, drafts, and trade acceptances. An order directs a third party to pay the instrument as drawn. In the typical check, for example, the word "pay" (to the order of a payee) is a command to the drawee bank to pay the check when presented—thus, it is an order. A command, such as "pay," is mandatory even if it is accompanied by courteous words as in "Please pay" or "Kindly pay." Stating "I wish you would pay" does not fulfill this requirement. An order may be addressed to one party or to more than one party, either jointly ("to A *and* B") or alternatively ("to A *or* B") [UCC 3–103(a)(6)].

Unconditionality of Promise or Order

Only unconditional promises or orders can be negotiable. A promise or order is conditional (and therefore *not* negotiable) if it states (1) an express condition to payment, (2) that the promise or order is subject to or governed by another writing, or (3) that the rights or obligations with respect to the promise or order are stated in another writing.

A mere reference to another writing, however, does not make the promise or order conditional [UCC 3–106(a)]. For example, the words "As per contract" or "This debt arises from the sale of goods X and Y" do not render an instrument nonnegotiable. Similarly, a statement in the instrument that payment can be made only out of a particular fund or source will not render the instrument nonnegotiable [UCC 3–106(b)(ii)]. **EXAMPLE 18.8** The terms of Biggs's note state that payment will be made out of the proceeds of next year's cotton crop. This does not make the note nonnegotiable—although the payee of such a note may find the note commercially unacceptable and refuse to take it. ●

A Fixed Amount of Money

KNOW THIS

Interest payable on an instrument normally cannot exceed the maximum limit on interest under a state's usury statute.

Negotiable instruments must state with certainty a fixed amount of money to be paid at any time the instrument is payable [UCC 3–104(a)]. The term *fixed amount* means an amount that is ascertainable from the face of the instrument. A demand note payable with 8 percent interest meets the requirement of a fixed amount because its amount can be determined at the time it is payable or at any time thereafter [UCC 3–104(a)].

The rate of interest may also be determined from information that is not contained in the instrument if that information is readily ascertainable by use of a formula or a source described in the instrument [UCC 3–112(b)]. For instance, an instrument that is payable at the *legal rate of interest* (a rate of interest fixed by statute) is negotiable. Mortgage notes tied to a variable rate of interest (a rate that fluctuates as a result of market conditions) are also negotiable.

UCC 3–104(a) provides that a fixed amount is to be *payable in money*. The UCC defines money as "a medium of exchange authorized or adopted by a domestic or foreign government as a part of its currency" [UCC 1–201(24)]. Thus, a note that promises "to pay on demand $1,000 in gold" is not negotiable because gold is not a medium of exchange adopted by the U.S. government. An instrument payable in the United States with a face amount stated in a foreign currency is negotiable, however, and can be paid in the foreign currency or in the equivalent amount of U.S. dollars [UCC 3–107].

Some instruments pay interest rates that are tied to the Federal Funds Rate, shown below.

(AP Photo/Seth Wenig)

Payable on Demand or at a Definite Time

Acceptor A drawee that accepts, or promises to pay, an instrument when it is presented later for payment.

To determine the value of a negotiable instrument, it is necessary to know when the maker, drawee, or acceptor (an **acceptor** is a drawee that promises to pay an instrument when it is presented later for payment) is required to pay the instrument. A negotiable instrument must therefore "be payable on demand or at a definite time" [UCC 3–104(a)(2)].

Presentment The act of presenting an instrument to the party liable on the instrument in order to collect payment. Presentment also occurs when a person presents an instrument to a drawee for a required acceptance.

Payable on Demand

Instruments that are payable on demand include those that contain the words "Payable at sight" or "Payable upon presentment." **Presentment** means a demand made by or on behalf of a person entitled to enforce an instrument to either pay or accept the instrument [UCC 3–501]. Thus, presentment occurs when a person brings the instrument to the appropriate party for payment or acceptance.

The very nature of the instrument may indicate that it is payable on demand. For example, a check, by definition, is payable on demand [UCC 3–104(f)]. If no time for payment is specified and the person responsible for payment must pay on the instrument's presentment, the instrument is payable on demand [UCC 3–108(a)].

In the following case, the issue before the court was whether a promissory note was a demand note.

Case 18.1

Reger Development, LLC v. National City Bank

United States Court of Appeals, Seventh Circuit, 592 F.3d 759 (2010).
www.ca7.uscourts.gov[a]

(AlexSkopje/Shutterstock.com)

Many promissory notes are payable on demand.

FACTS Kevin Reger is the principal and sole member of Reger Development, LLC. Reger Development borrowed funds from National City Bank for several projects. National City then offered the company a line of credit to finance potential development opportunities, and Reger Development signed a promissory note requiring it to "pay this loan in full immediately upon Lender's demand." About a year later, the bank asked Reger Development to pay down some of the loan and stated that it would be reducing the amount of cash available through the line of credit. Kevin Reger "expressed surprise" at these developments and asked if the bank would call in the line of credit if Reger Development did not agree to the requests. The bank said that there was a possibility that it would demand payment of the credit line. Reger Development then sued National City, alleging that the bank had breached the terms of the note. A federal district court granted the bank's motion to dismiss, and Reger Development appealed. The main question before the court was whether the note entitled National City to demand payment from Reger Development at will.

ISSUE Was a note for a line of credit that stated it was a promissory note, but required the borrower (Reger Development) to pay the loan on the lender's demand, a demand instrument?

DECISION Yes. The U.S. Court of Appeals for the Seventh Circuit affirmed the district court's dismissal of Reger Development's complaint. The promissory note was a demand instrument, and thus National City had the right to collect payment from Reger Development at any time on demand.

REASON The appellate court reasoned that although a covenant of fair dealing and good faith is implied in every contract, "the duty to act in good faith does not apply to lenders seeking payment on demand notes." Reger alleged that National City had arbitrarily and capriciously demanded payment, even though Reger was not in default, and that National City had unilaterally changed the fundamental terms of the contract. The appellate court, however, pointed out that explicit contract language set forth the lender's right to demand payment at any time. National City had the "right to collect scheduled monthly interest payments and [did] not deviate from the structure of a demand note."

CRITICAL THINKING—Ethical Consideration *In its opinion, the court pointed out "the duty to act in good faith does not apply to lenders seeking payment on demand notes." Why is this so?*

a. Select "Opinions" under the "Case Information" heading. When the page opens, enter "09" and "2821" in the "Case Number" boxes, respectively, and click on "List Case(s)." On the page that appears next, click on the link to the case number to access the opinion (filed 01/20/2010). The U.S. Court of Appeals for the Seventh Circuit maintains this Web site.

Payable at a Definite Time

If an instrument is not payable on demand, to be negotiable it must be payable at a definite time. An instrument is payable at a definite time if it states that it is payable (1) on a specified date, (2) within a definite period of time (such as thirty days) after being presented for payment, or (3) on a date or time readily ascertainable at the time the promise or order is issued [UCC 3–108(b)]. The maker or drawee in a time draft, for example, is under no obligation to pay until the specified time.

When an instrument is payable by the maker or drawer on or before a stated date, it is clearly payable at a definite time. The maker or drawer has the *option* of paying before the stated maturity date, but the payee can still rely on payment being made by the maturity date. The option to pay early does not violate the definite-time requirement.

In contrast, an instrument that is undated and made payable "one month after date" is clearly nonnegotiable. There is no way to determine the maturity date from the face of the instrument.

Acceleration Clause A clause that allows a payee or other holder of a time instrument to demand payment of the entire amount due, with interest, if a certain event occurs, such as a default in the payment of an installment when due.

Holder Any person in possession of an instrument drawn, issued, or indorsed to him or her, to his or her order, to bearer, or in blank.

Acceleration Clause

An **acceleration clause** allows a payee or other holder of a time instrument to demand payment of the entire amount due, with interest, if a certain event occurs, such as a default in the payment of an installment when due. (A **holder** is any person in possession of an instrument drawn, issued, or indorsed to him or her, to his or her order, to bearer, or in blank [UCC 1–201(20)].)

Under the UCC, instruments that include acceleration clauses are negotiable because (1) the exact value of the instrument can be ascertained and (2) the instrument will be payable on a specified date if the event allowing acceleration does not occur [UCC 3–108(b)(ii)]. Thus, the specified date is the outside limit used to determine the value and negotiability of the instrument.

Extension Clause A clause in a time instrument that allows the instrument's date of maturity to be extended into the future.

Extension Clause

The reverse of an acceleration clause is an **extension clause**, which allows the date of maturity to be extended into the future [UCC 3–108(b)(iii), (iv)]. To keep the instrument negotiable, the interval of the extension must be specified if the right to extend the time of payment is given to the maker or drawer of the instrument. If, however, the holder of the instrument can extend the time of payment, the extended maturity date does not have to be specified.

Payable to Order or to Bearer

Because one of the functions of a negotiable instrument is to serve as a substitute for cash, freedom to transfer is essential. To ensure a proper transfer, the instrument must be "payable to order or to bearer" at the time it is issued or first comes into the possession of the holder [UCC 3–104(a)(1)]. An instrument is not negotiable unless it meets this requirement.

Order Instrument A negotiable instrument that is payable "to the order of an identified person" or "to an identified person or order."

Order Instruments

An **order instrument** is an instrument that is payable (1) "to the order of an identified person" or (2) "to an identified person or order" [UCC 3–109(b)]. An identified person is the person "to whom the instrument is initially payable" as determined by the intent of the maker or drawer [UCC 3–110(a)]. The identified person, in turn, may transfer the instrument to whomever he or she wishes. Thus, the maker or drawer is agreeing to pay either the person specified on the instrument or whomever that person might designate. In this way, the instrument retains its transferability.

Note that in order instruments, the person specified must be identified with *certainty* because the transfer of an order instrument requires the *indorsement,* or signature, of the payee (*indorsements* will be discussed at length later in this chapter). An order instrument made "Payable to the order of my nicest cousin," for instance, is not negotiable because it does not clearly specify the payee.

Bearer Instrument Any instrument that is not payable to a specific person, including instruments payable to the bearer or to "cash."

Bearer A person in possession of an instrument payable to bearer or indorsed in blank.

Bearer Instruments

A **bearer instrument** is an instrument that does not designate a specific payee [UCC 3–109(a)]. The term **bearer** refers to a person in possession of an instrument that is payable to bearer or indorsed in blank (with a signature only, as will be discussed shortly) [UCC 1–201(5), 3–109(a), 3–109(c)]. This means that the maker or drawer agrees to pay anyone who presents the instrument for payment.

Any instrument containing terms such as "Payable to Kathy Esposito or bearer" or "Pay to the order of cash" is a bearer instrument. In addition, an instrument that "indicates that it is not payable to an identified person" is a bearer instrument [UCC 3–109(a)(3)]. Thus, an instrument "payable to X" or "payable to Batman" can be negotiated as a bearer instrument, just as though it were payable to cash. An instrument made payable to a *nonexistent organization* or company is not a negotiable bearer instrument, however [UCC 3–109, Comment 2].

The bearer instrument at the center of the following *Spotlight Case* was a *gambling marker*—that is, a credit instrument that allows a gambler to receive tokens or chips from a casino based on a prior credit application. The court had to decide whether the gambling marker was negotiable.

Spotlight on Casino Markers

Case 18.2

Las Vegas Sands, LLC v. Nehme

United States Court of Appeals, Ninth Circuit, 632 F.3d 526 (2011).
www.ca9.uscourts.gov[a]

(nito/Shutterstock.com)

The Venetian Resort Hotel Casino in Las Vegas.

FACTS Amine Nehme, a California resident, applied for credit at the Venetian Resort Hotel Casino in Las Vegas, Nevada. Nehme was granted $500,000 in credit. He soon accrued more than $1.2 million in gambling debts to the Venetian, which he paid. About a year later, Nehme deposited $1,000 with the Venetian and signed a gambling marker for $500,000. Generally, a gambling marker is an instrument that is dated, bears the gambler's name—and the name and account number of the gambler's bank—and states the instruction "Pay to the Order of" the casino. In this case, though, the line following "Pay to the Order of" was apparently left blank, which made the marker a bearer instrument. Nehme quickly lost $500,000 gambling and left the casino. The Venetian presented the marker for payment to Bank of America, Nehme's bank, which returned it for insufficient funds. The casino's owner, Las Vegas Sands, LLC, applied Nehme's deposit against the marker and filed a suit against him to recover the remainder—$499,000—plus interest, claiming that he had failed to pay a negotiable instrument. A federal district court issued a summary judgment in the Venetian's favor. Nehme appealed.

ISSUE Was the gambling marker under which Nehme borrowed funds from a casino a negotiable instrument?

DECISION Yes. The U.S. Court of Appeals for the Ninth Circuit agreed with the lower court that the marker was a negotiable instrument. To determine whether Nehme could establish a defense to liability, the appellate court reversed the lower court's judgment and remanded the case for a trial.

REASON In Nevada, a negotiable instrument is defined as an unconditional order to pay a fixed amount of money, payable on demand or at a definite time, and stating no "undertaking" in addition to the payment of money [Nevada Revised Statutes Section 104.3104, Nevada's version of UCC 3–104]. A check is defined as a draft "payable on demand and drawn on a bank." The court reasoned that the gambling marker fit these definitions. It specified a fixed amount of money, $500,000. It did not state a time for payment and thus was payable on demand. It was unconditional and stated no "undertaking" by Nehme in addition to the payment of a fixed sum. Thus, the Venetian could enforce the marker against Nehme unless he could establish a defense to liability.

WHAT IF THE FACTS WERE DIFFERENT? *Suppose that the marker had stated "Payable to the Order of the Venetian." Could the casino have transferred it for collection? If so, how?*

a. In the left column, in the "Opinions" pull-out menu, click on "Published." On the next page, click on "Advanced Search." In the "by Case No.:" box, type "09-16740," and click on "Search." In the result, click on the name of the case to access the opinion. The U.S. Court of Appeals for the Ninth Circuit maintains this Web site.

Factors That Do Not Affect Negotiability

Certain ambiguities or omissions will not affect the negotiability of an instrument. The UCC provides the following rules for clearing up ambiguous terms:

KNOW THIS

An instrument that purports to be payable both to order and to bearer is a contradiction in terms. Such an instrument is a bearer instrument.

1. Unless the date of an instrument is necessary to determine a definite time for payment, the fact that an instrument is *undated* does not affect its negotiability. A typical example is an undated check, which is still negotiable. If a check is not dated, its date is the date of its issue, meaning the date the maker first delivers the check to another person to give that person rights in the check [UCC 3–113(b)].
2. Antedating or postdating an instrument does not affect the instrument's negotiability [UCC 3–113(a)]. *Antedating* occurs when a party puts a date on the instrument that is before the actual date, and *postdating* occurs when a party puts a date on an instrument that is after the actual date.

   EXAMPLE 18.9 On May 1, Avery draws a check on her account with First State Bank made payable to Consumer Credit Corporation. Avery postdates the check "May 15." Consumer Credit can negotiate the check, and, unless Avery tells First State otherwise, the bank can charge the amount of the check to Avery's account before May 15 [UCC 4–401(c)]. •
3. Handwritten terms outweigh typewritten and printed terms (preprinted terms on forms, for example), and typewritten terms outweigh printed terms [UCC 3–114]. **EXAMPLE 18.10** Like most checks, your check is printed "Pay to the order of" followed by a blank line. In handwriting, you insert in the blank, "Anita Delgado or bearer." The handwritten terms will outweigh the printed form (an order instrument), and the check will be a bearer instrument. •
4. Words outweigh figures unless the words are ambiguous [UCC 3–114]. This rule is important when the numerical amount and the written amount on a check differ. **EXAMPLE 18.11** Rob issues a check payable to Standard Appliance Company. For the amount, he fills in the numbers "$100" but writes in the words "One thousand and 00/100" dollars. The check is payable in the amount of $1,000. •
5. When an instrument does not specify a particular interest rate but simply states "with interest," the interest rate is the *judgment rate of interest* (a rate of interest fixed by statute that is applied to a monetary judgment awarded by a court until the judgment is paid or terminated) [UCC 3–112(b)].
6. A check is negotiable even if there is a notation on it stating that it is "nonnegotiable" or "not governed by Article 3." Any other instrument, in contrast, can be made nonnegotiable if the maker or drawer conspicuously notes on it that it is "nonnegotiable" or "not governed by Article 3" [UCC 3–104(d)].

Transfer of Instruments

Once issued, a negotiable instrument can be transferred by *assignment* or by *negotiation.* The party receiving the instrument obtains the rights of a holder only if the transfer is by negotiation.

Transfer by Assignment

Recall from page 328 of Chapter 13 that an assignment is a transfer of rights under a contract. Under general contract principles, a transfer by assignment to an assignee gives the assignee only those rights that the assignor possessed. Any defenses that can be raised against an assignor can normally be raised against the assignee. This same principle applies when a negotiable instrument, such as a promissory note, is transferred by assignment. The transferee is then an *assignee* rather than a *holder.*

Sometimes, a transfer fails to qualify as a negotiation because it fails to meet one or more of the requirements of a negotiable instrument, just discussed. When this occurs, the transfer becomes an assignment.

Transfer by Negotiation

Negotiation The transfer of an instrument in such form that the transferee (the person to whom the instrument is transferred) becomes a holder.

Negotiation is the transfer of an instrument in such form that the transferee (the person to whom the instrument is transferred) becomes a holder [UCC 3–201(a)]. Under UCC principles, a transfer by negotiation creates a holder who, at the very least, receives the rights of the previous possessor [UCC 3–203(b)].

Unlike an assignment, a transfer by negotiation can make it possible for a holder to receive more rights in the instrument than the prior possessor had [UCC 3–202(b), 3–305, 3–306]. A holder who receives greater rights is known as a *holder in due course,* a concept we will discuss later in this chapter.

There are two methods of negotiating an instrument so that the receiver becomes a holder. The method used depends on whether the instrument is an order instrument or a bearer instrument.

"Money has little value to its possessor unless it also has value to others."

Leland Stanford, 1824–1893 (U.S. senator and founder of Stanford University)

Negotiating Order Instruments

An order instrument contains the name of a payee capable of indorsing it, as in "Pay to the order of Lloyd Sorenson." If the instrument is an order instrument, it is negotiated by delivery with any necessary indorsements.

EXAMPLE 18.12 National Express Corporation issues a payroll check "to the order of Lloyd Sorenson." Sorenson takes the check to the bank, signs his name on the back (an indorsement), gives it to the teller (a delivery), and receives cash. Sorenson has *negotiated* the check to the bank [UCC 3–201(b)]. •

Negotiating order instruments requires both delivery and indorsement (indorsements will be discussed shortly). If Sorenson had taken the check to the bank and delivered it to the teller without signing it, the transfer would not qualify as a negotiation. In that situation, the transfer would be treated as an assignment, and the bank would become an assignee rather than a holder.

Negotiating Bearer Instruments

If an instrument is payable to bearer, it is negotiated by delivery—that is, by transfer into another person's possession. Indorsement is not necessary [UCC 3–201(b)]. The use of bearer instruments thus involves more risk through loss or theft than the use of order instruments.

EXAMPLE 18.13 Richard Kray writes a check "payable to cash" and hands it to Jessie Arnold (a delivery). Kray has issued the check (a bearer instrument) to Arnold. Arnold places the check in her wallet, which is subsequently stolen. The thief has possession of the check. At this point, the thief has no rights to the check. If the thief "delivers" the check to an innocent third person, however, negotiation will be complete. All rights to the check will be passed absolutely to that third person, and Arnold will lose all rights to recover the proceeds of the check from that person [UCC 3–306]. Of course, Arnold could attempt to recover the amount from the thief if the thief can be found. •

Indorsements

Indorsement A signature placed on an instrument for the purpose of transferring one's ownership rights in the instrument.

Indorsements are required whenever the instrument being negotiated is classified as an order instrument. An **indorsement** is a signature with or without additional words or statements. It is most often written on the back of the instrument itself. If there is no room on the instrument, the indorsement can be on a separate piece of paper that is firmly affixed to the instrument, such as with staples [UCC 3–204(a)]. (See this chapter's *Beyond Our Borders* feature on the following page for a discussion of the approach to indorsements in France.)

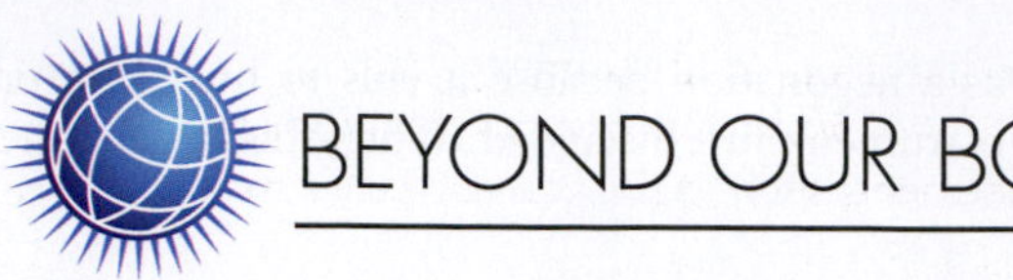

Severe Restrictions on Check Indorsements in France

If you were reading a business law textbook in France, you would find very little on check indorsements. The reason is that checks rarely, if ever, can be indorsed. That means that almost all checks must be deposited in a bank account, rather than transferred to another individual or entity.

On the back of every French check are two parallel lines printed by the bank. These lines mean that the check can be transferred only to a bank employee or the head of a postal bank. In other words, you cannot indorse and transfer checks the way we do in the United States. The French government says that these restrictions on indorsements reduce the risk of loss and theft.

Critical Thinking

What would be the cost to individuals and businesses that use checks if a similar law were passed in this country?

A person who transfers an instrument by signing (indorsing) it and delivering it to another person is an *indorser.* The person to whom the check is indorsed and delivered is the *indorsee.*

We examine here the four categories of indorsements: blank, special, qualified, and restrictive. Note that a single indorsement may have characteristics of more than one category. In other words, these categories are not mutually exclusive.

Blank Indorsement An indorsement that specifies no particular indorsee and can consist of a mere signature. An order instrument that is indorsed in blank becomes a bearer instrument.

Blank Indorsements

A **blank indorsement** does not specify a particular indorsee and can consist of a mere signature [UCC 3–205(b)]. Hence, a check payable "to the order of Alan Luberda" is indorsed in blank if Luberda simply writes his signature on the back of the check, as shown in Exhibit 18.5 alongside. An order instrument indorsed in blank becomes a bearer instrument and can be negotiated by delivery alone, as already discussed. In other words, a blank indorsement converts an order instrument to a bearer instrument, which anybody can cash.

Exhibit 18.5 A Blank Indorsement

Alan Luberda

Special Indorsement An indorsement on an instrument that identifies the specific person to whom the indorser intends to make the instrument payable. Thus, it names the indorsee.

Special Indorsements

A **special indorsement** contains the signature of the indorser and identifies the person to whom the instrument is made payable—that is, it names the indorsee [UCC 3–205(a)]. For instance, words such as "Pay to the order of Clay" or "Pay to Clay," followed by the signature of the indorser, create a special indorsement. When an instrument is indorsed in this way, it is an order instrument.

To avoid the risk of loss from theft, a holder may convert a blank indorsement to a special indorsement by writing, above the signature of the indorser, words identifying the indorsee [UCC 3–205(c)]. This changes the bearer instrument back to an order instrument.

EXAMPLE 18.14 A check is made payable to Peter Rabe. He indorses the check in blank by simply signing his name on the back and delivers the check to Anthony Bartomo. Anthony is unable to cash the check immediately and wants to avoid any risk should he lose the check. He therefore prints "Pay to Anthony Bartomo" above Peter's blank indorsement (see Exhibit 18.6 on the left). By doing this, Anthony has converted Peter's blank indorsement into a special indorsement. Further negotiation now requires Anthony Bartomo's indorsement plus delivery. •

Exhibit 18.6 A Special Indorsement

Pay to Anthony Bartomo
Peter Rabe

Qualified Indorsements

Generally, an indorser, *merely by indorsing,* impliedly promises to pay the holder or any subsequent indorser, the amount of the instrument in the event that the drawer or maker defaults on the payment [UCC 3–415(a)]. Usually, then, indorsements are *unqualified indorsements,* which means that the indorser is guaranteeing payment of the instrument in addition to transferring title to it.

Qualified Indorsement An indorsement on a negotiable instrument in which the indorser disclaims any contract liability on the instrument. The notation "without recourse" is commonly used to create a qualified indorsement.

An indorser who does not wish to be liable on an instrument can use a **qualified indorsement** to disclaim this liability [UCC 3–415(b)]. The notation "without recourse" is commonly used to create a qualified indorsement, such as the one shown in Exhibit 18.7.

Exhibit 18.7 A Qualified Indorsement

Pay to Elvie Ling, without recourse.
Bridgett Cage

The Effect of Qualified Indorsements

Qualified indorsements are often used by persons (agents) acting in a representative capacity, such as insurance agents who receive checks payable to them that are really intended as payment to the insurance company. The "without recourse" indorsement relieves the agent from any liability on a check. If the instrument is dishonored, the holder cannot recover from the agent who indorsed "without recourse" unless the indorser has breached one of the transfer warranties (relating to title, signature, and material alteration) that will be discussed later in this chapter.

Special versus Blank Qualified Indorsements

A qualified indorsement can be accompanied by either a special indorsement or a blank indorsement. A special qualified indorsement includes the name of the indorsee as well as the words *without recourse.* The special indorsement makes the instrument an order instrument, and it requires an indorsement, plus delivery, for negotiation. A blank qualified indorsement makes the instrument a bearer instrument, and only delivery is required for negotiation. In either situation, the instrument can be further negotiated.

The case that follows illustrates the effect of a blank qualified indorsement.

Case 18.3

Hammett v. Deutsche Bank National Co.

United States District Court, Eastern District of Virginia, 2010 WL 1225849 (2010).

(Imaginechina via AP Images)

Deutsche Bank National Company received delivery of a promissory note.

FACTS Vernon Hammett and others (the plaintiffs) purchased a residential property in Alexandria, Virginia. As part of that transaction, the plaintiffs executed a promissory note in favor of Encore Credit Corporation in the amount of $475,000. The note was secured by the property being purchased. Subsequently, the note was negotiated by delivery to Deutsche Bank National Company. The note had an attached allonge,[a] which contained a blank indorsement reading as follows: "Pay to The Order of ____ without Recourse Encore Credit Corp. A California Corporation."

At some point after executing the note, the plaintiffs refused to continue making the payments due under the note. As the holder of the note, Deutsche Bank initiated foreclosure proceedings on the property and subsequently purchased the property at the foreclosure sale. The plaintiffs brought an action against Deutsche Bank, alleging that the bank had no rights in the note. Deutsche Bank filed a motion to dismiss the case.

ISSUE If a borrower executes a note with a blank indorsement to purchase a home, can the current holder of the note enforce it by foreclosing on the homeowner?

DECISION Yes. The court granted the motion to dismiss the case. Deutsche Bank, as holder of the note, was entitled to enforce the instrument.

REASON The court reasoned that the note had included a blank qualified indorsement and thus only delivery of the instrument was required for negotiation. "If an instrument has a blank [i]ndorsement, it is considered 'payable to bearer' and it may be negotiated by transfer of possession alone." Because the face of the note showed that it had a blank indorsement, it was indeed negotiable by a simple change in possession. Thus, it

a. An *allonge* (pronounced uh-lonj) is a piece of paper firmly attached to a negotiable instrument on which indorsements can be made if there is no room on the instrument.

Case 18.3—Continues next page

Case 18.3—Continued

was enforceable by its current possessor, Deutsche Bank. The court further stated that "by their own allegations, Plaintiffs admit that they 'refused to pay' on the Note. To permit parties to the [instrument] to object to its payment, on any of the grounds stated, would greatly impair the negotiability of bills and notes, their most distinguishing, most useful, and most valued feature."

WHAT IF THE FACTS WERE DIFFERENT? *Suppose that the indorsement at issue in this case had been written on a separate document that was not firmly affixed to the note. Would this document have constituted an allonge? Would Deutsche Bank have been entitled to enforce the note? Explain.*

Restrictive Indorsement Any indorsement on a negotiable instrument that requires the indorsee to comply with certain instructions regarding the funds involved. A restrictive indorsement does not prohibit the further negotiation of the instrument.

Restrictive Indorsements

A **restrictive indorsement** requires the indorsee to comply with certain instructions regarding the funds involved, but it does not prohibit further negotiation of the instrument [UCC 3–206(a)]. Although most indorsements are nonrestrictive because there are no instructions or conditions attached to the payment of funds, many forms of restrictive indorsements do exist, including those discussed here.

Conditional Indorsements When payment depends on the occurrence of some event specified in the indorsement, the instrument has a conditional indorsement. **EXAMPLE 18.15** Ken Barton indorses a check, "Pay to Lars Johansen if he completes the renovation of my kitchen by June 1, 2014. [Signed] Ken Barton." Barton has created a conditional indorsement. • A conditional indorsement (on the back of the instrument) does not prevent further negotiation of the instrument.

Indorsements for Deposit or Collection A common type of restrictive indorsement is one that makes the indorsee (almost always a bank) a collecting agent of the indorser [UCC 3–206(c)]. **EXAMPLE 18.16** Stephanie Mallak has received a check and wants to deposit it into her checking account at the bank. She can indorse the check "For deposit [or collection] only. [Signed] Stephanie Mallak" (see Exhibit 18.8 below). She may also wish to write her bank account number on the check. A "For deposit" or "For Collection" indorsement locks the instrument into the bank-collection process and thus prohibits further negotiation except by the bank. Following this indorsement, only the bank can acquire the rights of a holder. •

Exhibit 18.8 "For Deposit" and "For Collection" Indorsements

For deposit only Stephanie Mallak	or	For collection only Stephanie Mallak

Trust Indorsement An indorsement to a person who is to hold or use funds for the benefit of the indorser or a third person. It is also known as an *agency indorsement.*

Trust (Agency) Indorsements An indorsement to a person who is to hold or use the funds for the benefit of the indorser or a third party is called a **trust indorsement** (also known as an *agency indorsement*) [UCC 3–206(d), (e)].

EXAMPLE 18.17 Robert Emerson asks his accountant, Ada Johnson, to pay some bills for his invalid wife, Sarah, while he is out of the country. He indorses a check as follows: "Pay to Ada Johnson as Agent for Sarah Emerson." This agency indorsement obligates Johnson to use the funds only for the benefit of Sarah Emerson. •

Exhibit 18.9 on the facing page shows sample trust (agency) indorsements.

Misspelled Names

An indorsement should be identical to the name that appears on the instrument. A payee or indorsee whose name is misspelled can indorse with the

Exhibit 18.9 Trust (Agency) Indorsements

Pay to Ada Johnson in trust for Sarah Emerson Robert Emerson	or	Pay to Ada Johnson as Agent for Sarah Emerson Robert Emerson

misspelled name, the correct name, or both [UCC 3–204(d)]. For example, if Sheryl Kruger receives a check payable to the order of Sherrill Krooger, she can indorse the check either "Sheryl Kruger" or "Sherrill Krooger," or both.

The usual practice is to indorse with the name as it appears on the instrument, followed by the correct name. (See the *Business Application* feature on pages 488–489 for suggestions to help businesspersons avoid problems with indorsements.)

Alternative or Joint Payees

An instrument payable to two or more persons *in the alternative* (for example, "Pay to the order of Tuan or Johnson") requires the indorsement of only one of the payees. In contrast, if an instrument is made payable to two or more persons *jointly* (for example, "Pay to the order of Sharrie and Bob Covington"), all of the payees' indorsements are necessary for negotiation.

If an instrument payable to two or more persons does not clearly indicate whether it is payable in the alternative or jointly (for example, "Pay to the order of John and/or Sara Fitzgerald"), then the instrument is payable to the persons alternatively [UCC 3–110(d)]. The same principles apply to special indorsements that indicate more than one identified person to whom the indorser intends to make the instrument payable [UCC 3–205(a)].

CASE EXAMPLE 18.18 Hyatt Corporation hired Skyscraper Building Maintenance, LLC, to perform maintenance services at some of its Florida hotels. Under an agreement with Skyscraper, J & D Financial Corporation asked Hyatt to make checks for the services payable to Skyscraper and J & D. Hyatt issued many checks to the two payees, but two of the checks were made payable to "J & D Financial Corp. Skyscraper Building Maint." Parties listed in this manner—without including an "and" or "or" between them—are referred to as *stacked payees*. A bank negotiated the two checks, which were indorsed only by Skyscraper.

J & D and Hyatt filed a lawsuit against the bank, claiming that the checks were payable *jointly* and thus required indorsement by both payees. The bank argued that the checks were payable to J & D and Skyscraper *alternatively*. A state court found that the bank was not liable because a check payable to stacked payees is ambiguous (unclear) and thus is payable alternatively under UCC 3–110(d). Consequently, the bank could negotiate the checks even though they were indorsed by only one of the two payees.[4] ●

Holder in Due Course (HDC)

Often, whether a holder is entitled to obtain payment will depend on whether the holder is a *holder in due course*. An ordinary holder obtains only those rights that the transferor had in the instrument, as mentioned previously. In this respect, a holder has the same status as an assignee (see Chapter 13). Like an assignee, a holder normally is subject to the same defenses that could be asserted against the transferor.

4. *Hyatt Corp. v. Palm Beach National Bank*, 840 So.2d 300 (Fla.App. 2003).

Holder in Due Course (HDC) A holder who acquires a negotiable instrument for value, in good faith, and without notice that the instrument is defective (such as that it is overdue, has been dishonored, is subject to a defense against it or a claim to it, contains unauthorized signatures, has been altered, or is so irregular or incomplete as to call its authenticity into question).

In contrast, a **holder in due course** is a holder who, by meeting certain acquisition requirements (to be discussed shortly), takes an instrument *free* of most of the defenses and claims that could be asserted against the transferor.

EXAMPLE 18.19 Marcia Cambry signs a $1,000 note payable to Alex Jerrod in payment for some ancient Roman coins. Jerrod negotiates the note to Alicia Larson, who promises to pay Jerrod for it in thirty days. During the next month, Larson learns that Jerrod has breached his contract with Cambry by delivering coins that were not from the Roman era, as promised, and that for this reason Cambry will not honor the $1,000 note. Whether Larson can hold Cambry liable on the note depends on whether Larson has met the requirements for HDC status. If Larson has met these requirements and thus has HDC status, Larson is entitled to payment on the note. If Larson has not met these requirements, she has the status of an ordinary holder, and Cambry's defense of breach of contract against payment to Jerrod will also be effective against Larson. •

Requirements for HDC Status

LEARNING OBJECTIVE 2
What are the requirements for attaining the status of a holder in due course (HDC)?

The basic requirements for attaining HDC status are set forth in UCC 3–302. A holder of a negotiable instrument is an HDC if she or he takes the instrument (1) for value, (2) in good faith, and (3) without notice that it is defective (such as when the instrument is overdue, dishonored, irregular, or incomplete). We now examine each of these requirements.

Taking for Value

An HDC must have given *value* for the instrument [UCC 3–302(a)(2)(i)]. A person who receives an instrument as a gift or inherits it has not met the requirement of value. In these situations, the person becomes an ordinary holder and does not possess the rights of an HDC.

Under UCC 3–303(a), a holder takes an instrument for value if the holder has done any of the following:

1. Performed the promise for which the instrument was issued or transferred.
2. Acquired a security interest or other lien in the instrument, excluding a lien obtained by a judicial proceeding (see Chapters 20 and 21).
3. Taken the instrument in payment of, or as security for, a preexisting claim. **EXAMPLE 18.20** Zon owes Dwyer $2,000 on a past-due account. If Zon negotiates a $2,000 note signed by Gordon to Dwyer and Dwyer accepts it to discharge the overdue account balance, Dwyer has given value for the instrument. •
4. Given a negotiable instrument as payment for the instrument. **EXAMPLE 18.21** Justin issued a $500 negotiable promissory note to Paulene. The note is due six months from the date issued. Paulene needs cash and does not want to wait for the maturity date to collect. She negotiates the note to her friend Kristen, who pays her $200 in cash and writes her a check—a negotiable instrument—for the balance of $300. Kristen has given full value for the note by paying $200 in cash and issuing Paulene the check for $300. •
5. Given an irrevocable commitment (such as a letter of credit) as payment for the instrument.

If a person promises to perform or give value in the future, that person is not an HDC. A holder takes an instrument for value *only to the extent that the promise has been performed* [UCC 3–303(a)(1)]. Therefore, in the Larson-Cambry scenario, which was presented earlier as *Example 18.19* above, Larson is not an HDC because she did not take the instrument (Cambry's note) for value—she has not yet paid Jerrod for the note. Thus, Cambry's defense of breach of contract is valid against Larson as well as Jerrod.

Exhibit 18.10 on the facing page illustrates these concepts.

Taking in Good Faith

To qualify as an HDC, a holder must take the instrument in *good faith* [UCC 3–302(a)(2)(ii)]. This means that the holder must have acted honestly in

Exhibit 18.10 Taking for Value

By exchanging defective goods for the note, Jerrod breached his contract with Cambry. Cambry could assert this defense if Jerrod presented the note to her for payment. Jerrod exchanged the note for Larson's promise to pay in thirty days, however. Because Larson did not take the note for value, she is not a holder in due course. Thus, Cambry can assert against Larson the defense of Jerrod's breach when Larson submits the note to Cambry for payment. In contrast, if Larson had taken the note for value, Cambry could not assert that defense and would be liable to pay the note.

"Carpe per diem—seize the check."

Robin Williams, 1952–present (Comedian and actor)

the process of acquiring the instrument. UCC 3–103(a)(4) defines *good faith* as "honesty in fact and the observance of reasonable commercial standards of fair dealing."

The good faith requirement applies only to the *holder.* It is immaterial whether the transferor acted in good faith. Thus, even a person who takes a negotiable instrument from a thief may become an HDC if the person acquired the instrument in good faith and had no reason to be suspicious of the transaction.

Because of the good faith requirement, courts must examine whether the purchaser, when acquiring the instrument, honestly believed that the instrument was not defective. **CASE EXAMPLE 18.22** Cassandra Demery worked as a bookkeeper at Clinton Georg's business, Freestyle, until she embezzled more than $200,000. Georg fired Demery and demanded repayment. Demery went to work for her parents' firm, Metro Fixtures, where she had some authority to write checks. Without specific authorization, however, she wrote a check to Freestyle for $189,000 on Metro's account and deposited it into Freestyle's account. She told Georg that the check was a loan to her from her family.

When Metro discovered Demery's theft, it filed a suit against Georg and Freestyle. Freestyle argued that it had taken the check in good faith and was an HDC. The Colorado Supreme Court agreed. Demery was the wrongdoer. Even though Metro did not authorize Demery to issue the check for $189,000, she had the authority to issue checks for Metro. Georg had no reason to know that Demery had lied about this check. Therefore, Metro would bear the loss.[5] •

Taking without Notice The final requirement for HDC status involves *notice* [UCC 3–302]. A person will not qualify for HDC protection if he or she is *on notice* (knows or has reason to know) that the instrument being acquired is defective in any one of the following ways [UCC 3–302(a)]:

1. It is overdue.
2. It has been dishonored.
3. It is part of a series of which at least one instrument has an uncured (uncorrected) default.
4. It contains an unauthorized signature or has been altered.
5. There is a defense against the instrument or a claim to it.
6. The instrument is so irregular or incomplete as to call its authenticity into question.

5. *Georg v. Metro Fixtures Contractors, Inc.*, 178 P.3d 1209 (Colo.Sup.Ct. 2008).

What Constitutes Notice? A holder will be deemed to have notice if she or he (1) has actual knowledge of the defect, (2) has received written notice (such as a letter listing the serial numbers of stolen bearer instruments), or (3) has reason to know that a defect exists, given all the facts and circumstances known at the time in question [UCC 1–201(25)].

The holder must also have received the notice "at a time and in a manner that gives a reasonable opportunity to act on it" [UCC 3–302(f)]. Facts that a purchaser might know but that do not necessarily make the instrument defective, such as bankruptcy proceedings against the maker or drawer, do not constitute notice that the instrument is defective [UCC 3–302(b)].

Overdue Instruments What constitutes notice that an instrument is overdue depends on whether it is a demand instrument (payable on demand) or a time instrument (payable at a definite time). A purchaser has notice that a *demand instrument* is overdue if she or he either takes the instrument knowing that demand has been made or takes the instrument an unreasonable length of time after its issue. For a check, a "reasonable time" is within ninety days after the date of the check. For all other demand instruments, what will be considered a reasonable time depends on the circumstances [UCC 3–304(a)].

Normally, a *time instrument* is overdue the day after its due date. Therefore, anyone who takes a time instrument after the due date is on notice that it is overdue [UCC 3–304(b)(2)]. Thus, if a promissory note due on May 15 is purchased on May 16, the purchaser will be an ordinary holder, not an HDC. If an instrument states that it is "Payable in thirty days," counting begins the day after the instrument is dated. Thus, a note dated December 1 that is payable in thirty days is due by midnight on December 31. If the payment date falls on a Sunday or holiday, the instrument is payable on the next business day.

Dishonor To refuse to pay or accept a negotiable instrument, whichever is required, even though the instrument is presented in a timely and proper manner.

Dishonored Instruments An instrument is **dishonored** when it is presented in a timely manner for payment or acceptance, whichever is required, and payment or acceptance is refused. The holder is on notice if he or she (1) has actual knowledge of the dishonor or (2) has knowledge of facts that would lead him or her to suspect that an instrument has been dishonored [UCC 3–302(a)(2)]. Conversely, if a person purchasing an instrument does not know and has no reason to know that it has been dishonored, the person is not put on notice and therefore can become an HDC.

KNOW THIS

A difference between the handwriting in the body of a check and the handwriting in the signature does not affect the validity of the check.

Notice of Claims or Defenses A holder cannot become an HDC if she or he has notice of any claim to the instrument or any defense against it [UCC 3–302(a)(2)]. Any obvious irregularity on the face of an instrument that calls into question its validity or terms of ownership, or that creates an ambiguity as to the party to pay, will bar HDC status.

For instance, if an instrument is so incomplete on its face that an element of negotiability is lacking (for example, the amount is not filled in), the purchaser cannot become an HDC. A good forgery of a signature or the careful alteration of an instrument, however, can go undetected by reasonable examination. In that situation, the purchaser can qualify as an HDC.

Holder through an HDC

A person who does not qualify as an HDC but who derives his or her title through an HDC can acquire the rights and privileges of an HDC. This rule, which is sometimes called the **shelter principle**, is set out in UCC 3–203(b).

Shelter Principle The principle that the holder of a negotiable instrument who cannot qualify as a holder in due course (HDC), but who derives his or her title through an HDC, acquires the rights of an HDC.

The shelter principle extends the benefits of HDC status and is designed to aid the HDC in readily disposing of the instrument. Under this rule, anyone—no matter how far removed from an HDC—who can ultimately trace his or her title back to an HDC may acquire the rights of an HDC. By extending the benefits of HDC status, the shelter principle promotes the marketability and free transferability of negotiable instruments.

There are some limitations on the shelter principle, though. Certain persons who formerly held instruments cannot improve their positions by later reacquiring the instruments from HDCs [UCC 3–203(b)]. If a holder participated in fraud or illegality affecting the instrument, or had notice of a claim or defense against an instrument, that holder is not allowed to improve her or his status by repurchasing the instrument from a later HDC.

"Most men are admirers of justice—when justice happens to be on their side."

Richard Whately, 1787–1863 (English theologian and logician)

Signature and Warranty Liability

Liability on negotiable instruments can arise either from a person's signature or from the warranties that are implied when the person presents the instrument for negotiation. Signature liability requires the transferor's signature, but no signature is required to impose warranty liability. We discuss signature liability (both primary and secondary) and warranty liability in the subsections that follow.

Signature Liability

The general rule is that every party, except a qualified indorser,[6] who signs a negotiable instrument is either primarily or secondarily liable for payment of that instrument when it comes due. Signature liability is contractual liability—no person will be held contractually liable for an instrument that he or she has not signed.

Primary Liability A person who is primarily liable on a negotiable instrument is absolutely required to pay the instrument—unless, of course, he or she has a valid defense to payment [UCC 3–305]. Only *makers* and *acceptors* of instruments are primarily liable.

The maker of a promissory note unconditionally promises to pay the note. It is the maker's promise to pay that makes the note a negotiable instrument. If the instrument was incomplete when the maker signed it, the maker is obligated to pay it according to its stated terms or according to terms that were agreed on and later filled in to complete the instrument [UCC 3–115, 3–407(a), 3–412].

EXAMPLE 18.23 Tristan executes a preprinted promissory note to Sharon, without filling in the blank for a due date. If Sharon does not complete the form by adding the date, the note will be payable on demand. If Sharon subsequently fills in a due date that Tristan authorized, the note is payable on the stated due date. In either situation, Tristan (the maker) is obligated to pay the note. •

KNOW THIS

A drawee is the party ordered to pay a draft or check, such as a bank or financial institution.

As mentioned earlier, an *acceptor* is a drawee that promises to pay an instrument, such as a *trade acceptance* or a *certified check* (to be discussed in Chapter 19), when it is presented for payment. Once a drawee indicates acceptance by signing the draft, the drawee becomes an acceptor and is obligated to pay the draft when it is presented for payment [UCC 3–409(a)]. Failure to pay an accepted draft when presented leads to primary signature liability.

Secondary Liability *Drawers* and *indorsers* are secondarily liable. On a negotiable instrument, secondary liability is similar to the liability of a guarantor in a simple contract in the sense that it is *contingent liability.* In other words, a drawer or an indorser will be liable only if the party that is responsible for paying the instrument refuses to do so (dishonors the instrument). The drawer's secondary liability on drafts and checks does not arise until the drawee fails to pay or to accept the instrument, whichever is required [UCC 3–412, 3–415].

6. A qualified indorser—one who indorses "without recourse"—undertakes no contractual obligation to pay. A qualified indorser merely assumes warranty liability, which will be discussed later in this chapter.

Dishonor of an instrument thus triggers the liability of parties who are secondarily liable on the instrument—that is, the drawer and *unqualified* indorsers. **EXAMPLE 18.24** Nina Lee writes a check on her account at Universal Bank payable to the order of Stephen Miller. Universal Bank refuses to pay the check when Miller presents it for payment, thus dishonoring the check. In this situation, Lee will be liable to Miller on the basis of her secondary liability. ● Drawers are secondarily liable on drafts unless they disclaim their liability by drawing the instruments "without recourse" (if the draft is a check, however, a drawer cannot disclaim liability) [UCC 3–414(e)].

KNOW THIS

A guarantor is liable on a contract to pay the debt of another only if the party who is primarily liable fails to pay.

Parties are secondarily liable on a negotiable instrument only if the following events occur:[7]

1. The instrument is properly and timely presented.
2. The instrument is dishonored.
3. Timely notice of dishonor is given to the secondarily liable party.

Proper Presentment As previously explained, *presentment* occurs when a person presents an instrument either to the party liable on the instrument for payment or to a drawee for acceptance. The UCC requires that a holder present the instrument to the appropriate party, in a timely fashion, and give reasonable identification if requested [UCC 3–414(f), 3–415(e), 3–501].

The party to whom the instrument must be presented depends on the type of instrument involved. A note or CD must be presented to the maker for payment. A draft is presented to the drawee for acceptance, payment, or both. A check is presented to the drawee for payment [UCC 3–501(a), 3–502(b)].

Presentment can be made by any commercially reasonable means, including oral, written, or electronic communication [UCC 3–501(b)]. Ordinarily, it is effective when the demand for payment or acceptance is received (if presentment takes place after an established cutoff hour, it may be treated as occurring the next business day).

Timely Presentment Timeliness is important for proper presentment [UCC 3–414(f), 3–415(e), 3–501(b)(4)]. Failure to present an instrument on time is the most common reason for improper presentment and leads to unqualified indorsers being discharged from secondary liability.

The holder of a domestic check must present that check for payment or collection within thirty days of its *date* to hold the drawer secondarily liable, and within thirty days after its indorsement to hold the indorser secondarily liable. The time for proper presentment for different types of instruments is shown in Exhibit 18.11 on the facing page.

Dishonor As mentioned previously, an instrument is dishonored when the required acceptance or payment is refused or cannot be obtained within the prescribed time. An instrument is also dishonored when the required presentment is excused (as it would be, for example, if the maker had died) and the instrument is not properly accepted or paid [UCC 3–502(e), 3–504].

In certain situations, postponement of payment or refusal to pay an instrument will *not* dishonor the instrument. When presentment is made after an established cutoff hour (not earlier than 2:00 P.M.), for instance, a bank can postpone payment until the following business day without dishonoring the instrument. In addition, when the holder refuses to exhibit the instrument, provide reasonable identification (such as a thumbprint), or sign a receipt for the payment, a bank's refusal to pay does not dishonor the instrument.

7. These requirements are necessary for a secondarily liable party to have signature liability on a negotiable instrument, but they are not necessary for a secondarily liable party to have warranty liability (to be discussed later in the chapter).

Exhibit 18.11 Time for Proper Presentment

TYPE OF INSTRUMENT	FOR ACCEPTANCE	FOR PAYMENT
Time	On or before due date.	On due date.
Demand	Within a reasonable time (after date of issue or after secondary party becomes liable on the instrument).	Within a reasonable time.
Check	Not applicable.	Within thirty days of its date, to hold drawer secondarily liable. Within thirty days of indorsement, to hold indorser secondarily liable.

Proper Notice Once an instrument has been dishonored, proper notice must be given to secondary parties (drawers and indorsers) for them to be held contractually liable. Notice may be given in any reasonable manner, including an oral, written, e-mail, or other electronic communication, as well as notice written or stamped on the instrument itself. A bank must give any necessary notice before its midnight deadline (midnight of the next banking day after receipt). Notice by any party other than a bank must be given within thirty days following the day of dishonor or the day on which the person who is secondarily liable receives notice of dishonor [UCC 3–503].

Unauthorized Signatures

Unauthorized signatures arise in two situations—when a person forges another person's name on a negotiable instrument and when an *agent* (see Chapter 23) who lacks authority signs an instrument on behalf of a principal. The general rule is that an unauthorized signature is wholly inoperative and will not bind the person whose name is signed or forged.

(Bluestocking/iStockphoto.com)

Who is responsible for validating the signature on a check?

EXAMPLE 18.25 Parker finds Dolby's checkbook lying in the street, writes out a check to himself, and forges Dolby's signature. Banks normally have a duty to determine whether a person's signature on a check is forged. If a bank fails to determine that Dolby's signature is not genuine and cashes the check for Parker, the bank will generally be liable to Dolby for the amount. ● (The liability of banks for paying checks with forged signatures will be discussed further in Chapter 19.) Similarly, if an agent lacks the authority to sign the principal's name or has exceeded the authority given by the principal, the signature does not bind the principal but will bind the "unauthorized signer" [UCC 3–403(a)].

There are two exceptions to the general rule that an unauthorized signature will not bind the person whose name is signed:

1. When the person whose name is signed ratifies (affirms) the signature, he or she will be bound [UCC 3–403(a)].
2. When the negligence of the person whose name was forged substantially contributed to the forgery, a court may not allow the person to deny the effectiveness of an unauthorized signature [UCC 3–115, 3–406, 4–401(d)(2)].

Special Rules for Unauthorized Indorsements

Generally, when an instrument has a forged or unauthorized indorsement, the burden of loss falls on the first party to take the instrument. The reason for this general rule is that the first party to take an instrument is in the best position to prevent the loss.

EXAMPLE 18.26 Jen Nilson steals a check that is payable to Inga Leed and drawn on Universal Bank. Nilson indorses the check "Inga Leed" and presents the check to Universal

Bank for payment. The bank, without asking Nilson for identification, pays the check, and Nilson disappears. In this situation, Leed will not be liable on the check because her indorsement was forged. The bank will bear the loss, which it might have avoided if it had asked Nilson for identification. ●

This general rule has two important exceptions that cause the loss to fall on the maker or drawer. These exceptions arise when an indorsement is made by an imposter or by a fictitious payee.

Imposter One who, by use of the mails, Internet, telephone, or personal appearance, induces a maker or drawer to issue an instrument in the name of an impersonated payee. Indorsements by imposters are treated as authorized indorsements under Article 3 of the UCC.

Imposter Rule An **imposter** is someone who pretends to be someone else and, by appearing in person or using the mails, Internet, telephone, or other electronic communication, induces a maker or drawer to issue an instrument in the name of the impersonated payee. If the maker or drawer believes the imposter to be the named payee at the time of issue, the indorsement by the imposter is not treated as unauthorized when the instrument is transferred to an innocent party. This is because the maker or drawer *intended* the imposter to receive the instrument.

In these situations, the unauthorized indorsement of a payee's name can be as effective as if the real payee had signed. The *imposter rule* provides that an imposter's indorsement will be effective—that is, not a forgery—insofar as the drawer or maker is concerned [UCC 3–404(a)].

EXAMPLE 18.27 Carol impersonates Donna and induces Edward to write a check payable to the order of Donna. Carol, continuing to impersonate Donna, negotiates the check to First National Bank as payment on her loan there. As the drawer of the check, Edward is liable for its amount to First National. ●

Fictitious Payee A payee on a negotiable instrument whom the maker or drawer did not intend to have an interest in the instrument. Indorsements by fictitious payees are treated as authorized indorsements under Article 3 of the UCC.

Fictitious Payee Rule When a person causes an instrument to be issued to a payee who will have *no interest* in the instrument, the payee is referred to as a **fictitious payee.** A fictitious payee can be a person or firm that does not truly exist, or it may be an identifiable party that will not acquire any interest in the instrument. Under the UCC's *fictitious payee rule,* the payee's indorsement is not treated as a forgery, and an innocent holder can hold the maker or drawer liable on the instrument [UCC 3–404(b), 3–405].

Situations involving fictitious payees most often arise when (1) a dishonest employee deceives the employer into signing an instrument payable to a party with no right to receive payment on the instrument or (2) a dishonest employee or agent has the authority to issue an instrument on behalf of the employer. For example, an employee might open a bank account in the name of a fictitious company and then deceive her or his employer into signing checks payable to that company. Regardless of whether the dishonest employee actually signs the check or merely supplies the employer with names of fictitious creditors (or with true names of creditors having fictitious debts), the result is the same under the UCC.

"Life is unfair."

Milton Friedman, 1912–2006
(American economist)

Warranty Liability

LEARNING OBJECTIVE 3
What is the difference between signature liability and warranty liability?

In addition to signature liability, transferors make certain implied warranties regarding the instruments that they are negotiating. Warranty liability arises even when a transferor does not indorse (sign) the instrument [UCC 3–416, 3–417].

Warranty liability is particularly important when a holder cannot hold a party liable on her or his signature, such as when a person delivers a bearer instrument. Unlike secondary signature liability, warranty liability is not subject to the conditions of proper presentment, dishonor, or notice of dishonor.

Warranties fall into two categories: those that arise on the *transfer* of a negotiable instrument and those that arise on *presentment.* Both transfer and presentment warranties attempt to shift liability back to a wrongdoer or to the person who dealt face to face with the wrongdoer and thus was in the best position to prevent the wrongdoing.

Transfer Warranties Five implied warranties made by any person who transfers an instrument for consideration to the transferee and, if the transfer is by indorsement, to all subsequent transferees and holders who take the instrument in good faith.

Transfer Warranties

A person who transfers an instrument *for consideration* makes certain warranties to the transferee and, if the transfer is by *indorsement,* to all subsequent transferees and holders who take the instrument in good faith. There are five **transfer warranties** [UCC 3–416]:[8]

1. The transferor is entitled to enforce the instrument.
2. All signatures are authentic and authorized.
3. The instrument has not been altered.
4. The instrument is not subject to a defense or claim of any party that can be asserted against the transferor.
5. The transferor has no knowledge of any insolvency (bankruptcy) proceedings against the maker, the acceptor, or the drawer of the instrument.

Presentment Warranties Implied warranties, made by any person who presents an instrument for payment or acceptance, that (1) the person is entitled to enforce the instrument or is authorized to act on behalf of a person who is so entitled, (2) the instrument has not been altered, and (3) the person has no knowledge that the drawer's signature is unauthorized.

Presentment Warranties

Any person who presents an instrument for payment or acceptance makes the following **presentment warranties** to any other person who in good faith pays or accepts the instrument [UCC 3–417(a), 3–417(d)]:

1. The person obtaining payment or acceptance is entitled to enforce the instrument or is authorized to obtain payment or acceptance on behalf of a person who is entitled to enforce the instrument. (This is, in effect, a warranty that there are no missing or unauthorized indorsements.)
2. The instrument has not been altered.
3. The person obtaining payment or acceptance has no knowledge that the signature of the issuer of the instrument is unauthorized.[9]

These warranties are referred to as presentment warranties because they protect the person to whom the instrument is presented. They often have the effect of shifting liability back to the party that was in the best position to prevent the wrongdoing.

The second and third presentment warranties do not apply to makers, acceptors, and drawers when the presenter is an HDC. It is assumed that a drawer or a maker will recognize his or her own signature and that a maker or an acceptor will recognize whether an instrument has been materially altered.

LEARNING OBJECTIVE 4

Certain defenses are valid against all holders, including HDCs. What are these defenses called? Name four defenses that fall within this category.

Defenses, Limitations, and Discharge

Defenses can bar collection from persons who would otherwise be primarily or secondarily liable on a negotiable instrument. There are two general categories of defenses—*universal defenses* and *personal defenses.*

Universal Defenses

Universal Defenses Defenses that are valid against all holders of a negotiable instrument, including holders in due course (HDCs) and holders with the rights of HDCs.

Universal defenses (also called *real defenses*) are valid against *all* holders, including HDCs and holders who take through an HDC. Universal defenses include those described here.

1. *Forgery of a signature on the instrument.* A forged signature cannot bind the person whose name is used unless that person ratifies (approves or validates) the signature or is barred from denying it (because the forgery was made possible by the maker's or drawer's negligence, for example) [UCC 3–403(a)]. Thus, when an instrument is forged, the person

---

8. A 2002 amendment to UCC 3–416(a) adds a sixth warranty: "with respect to a remotely created consumer item," such as an electronic check, drawn on a consumer account, which is not created by the payor bank and does not contain the drawer's handwritten signature. Under this amendment, a bank that accepts and pays the instrument warrants to the next bank in the collection chain that the consumer authorized the item in that amount.

9. As discussed in Footnote 8, amendments to Article 3 of the UCC provide additional protection for "remotely created" consumer items in the context of presentment also [see Amended UCC 3–417(a)(4)].

whose name is forged normally has no liability to pay any holder or any HDC the value of the instrument.

2. *Fraud in the execution.* If a person is deceived into signing a negotiable instrument, believing that she or he is signing something other than a negotiable instrument (such as a receipt), fraud in the execution is committed against the signer [UCC 3–305(a)(1)]. Fraud in the execution is a universal defense that can be asserted unless a reasonable inquiry would have revealed the nature and terms of the instrument.
3. *Material alteration.* An alteration is material if it changes the obligations of the parties in the instrument *in any way.* Material alterations include completing an instrument, adding words or numbers, or making any unauthorized changes that affect the obligation of a party [UCC 3–407(a)]. It is not a material alteration, however, to correct the maker's address or to change the figures on a check so that they agree with the written amount. Material alteration is a *complete defense* against an ordinary holder, but only a partial defense against an HDC.

KNOW THIS

Words outweigh figures on a negotiable instrument if the written amount and the amount given in figures are different.

4. *Discharge in bankruptcy.* Discharge in bankruptcy (see Chapter 21) is an absolute defense on any instrument, regardless of the status of the holder, because the purpose of bankruptcy is to settle finally all of the insolvent party's debts [UCC 3–305(a)(1)].
5. *Minority.* Minority, or infancy, is a universal defense only to the extent that state law recognizes it as a defense to a simple contract (see page 288 of Chapter 11) [UCC 3–305(a)(1)(i)].
6. *Illegality, mental incapacity, or extreme duress.* When the law declares an instrument to be void because it was issued in connection with illegal conduct, illegality is a universal defense. Similarly, if a person who signed the instrument has been declared by a court to be mentally incompetent, or was a under an immediate threat of force or violence (such as at gunpoint), the defense is universal [UCC 3–305(a)(1)(ii)].

Personal Defenses

Personal Defense A defense that can be used to avoid payment to an ordinary holder of a negotiable instrument but not a holder in due course (HDC) or a holder with the rights of an HDC.

Personal defenses (sometimes called *limited defenses*), such as those described here, can be used to avoid payment to an ordinary holder of a negotiable instrument, but not to an HDC or a holder with the rights of an HDC.

LEARNING OBJECTIVE 5

Certain defenses can be used against an ordinary holder but are not effective against an HDC. What are these defenses called? Name four defenses that fall within this category.

1. *Breach of contract or breach of warranty.* When there is a breach of the underlying contract for which the negotiable instrument was issued, the maker of a note can refuse to pay it, or the drawer of a check can stop payment.
2. *Lack or failure of consideration.* The absence of consideration (value) may be a successful personal defense in some instances [UCC 3–303(b), 3–305(a)(2)]. **EXAMPLE 18.28** Tara gives Clem, as a gift, a note that states, "I promise to pay you $100,000." Clem accepts the note. Because there is no consideration for Tara's promise, a court will not enforce the promise. ●
3. *Fraud in the inducement (ordinary fraud).* A person who issues a negotiable instrument based on false statements by the other party will be able to avoid payment on that instrument, unless the holder is an HDC.
4. *Illegality, mental incapacity, or ordinary duress.* If the law declares that an instrument is voidable because of illegality, mental incapacity, or ordinary duress, the defense is personal [UCC 3–305(a)(1)(ii)].

Federal Limitations on the Rights of HDCs

Under the HDC doctrine, a consumer who purchased a defective product (such as a defective automobile) would continue to be liable to HDCs even if the consumer returned the defective product to the retailer. To protect consumers, in 1976 the Federal Trade

Commission (FTC) issued a rule that effectively abolished the HDC doctrine in consumer transactions. How does this rule curb the rights of HDCs? See this chapter's *Landmark in the Law* feature below.

Discharge from Liability

Discharge from liability on an instrument can come from payment, cancellation, or material alteration. The liability of all parties is discharged when the party primarily liable on the instrument pays to the holder the full amount due [UCC 3–602, 3–603]. Payment by any other party discharges only the liability of that party and subsequent parties.

Intentional cancellation by the holder of an instrument discharges the liability of all parties [UCC 3–604]. Intentionally writing "Paid" across the face of an instrument cancels it, as does intentionally tearing it up. If a holder intentionally crosses out a party's signature, that party's liability and the liability of subsequent indorsers who have already indorsed the instrument are discharged. Materially altering an instrument may discharge the liability of any party affected by the alteration, as previously discussed [UCC 3–407(b)]. (An HDC may be able to enforce a materially altered instrument against its maker or drawer according to the instrument's original terms, however.)

LANDMARK IN THE LAW

Federal Trade Commission Rule 433

In 1976, the Federal Trade Commission (FTC) issued Rule 433,[a] which severely limited the rights of HDCs that purchase instruments arising out of *consumer credit* transactions. The rule, entitled "Preservation of Consumers' Claims and Defenses," applies to any seller or lessor of goods or services who takes or receives a consumer credit contract. The rule also applies to a seller or lessor who accepts as full or partial payment for a sale or lease the proceeds of any purchase-money loan[b] made in connection with any consumer credit contract.

Under the rule, these parties must include the following provision in the consumer credit contract:

NOTICE

ANY HOLDER OF THIS CONSUMER CREDIT CONTRACT IS SUBJECT TO ALL CLAIMS AND DEFENSES WHICH THE DEBTOR COULD ASSERT AGAINST THE SELLER OF GOODS OR SERVICES OBTAINED PURSUANT HERETO OR WITH THE PROCEEDS HEREOF. RECOVERY HEREUNDER BY THE DEBTOR SHALL NOT EXCEED AMOUNTS PAID BY THE DEBTOR HEREUNDER.

Thus, a consumer who is a party to a consumer credit transaction can bring any defense she or he has against the seller of a product against a subsequent holder as well. In essence, the FTC rule places an HDC of the negotiable instrument in the position of a contract assignee. The rule makes the buyer's duty to pay conditional on the seller's full performance of the contract. Finally, the rule clearly reduces the degree of transferability of negotiable instruments resulting from consumer credit contracts.

What if the seller does not include the notice in a promissory note and then sells the note to a third party, such as a bank? In this situation, the seller has violated the rule, but the bank has not. Because the FTC rule does not prohibit third parties from purchasing notes or credit contracts that do *not* contain the required provision, the third party does not become subject to the buyer's defenses against the seller. Thus, a few consumers remain unprotected by the FTC rule.

Application to Today's World *The FTC rule has been invoked in many cases involving automobiles that turned out to be "lemons," even when the consumer credit contract did not contain the FTC notice. In these and other actions to collect on notes issued to finance purchases, when the notice was not included in the accompanying documents, the courts have generally implied its existence as a contract term.*

---

a. 16 C.F.R. Section 433.2. The rule was enacted pursuant to the FTC's authority under the Federal Trade Commission Act, 15 U.S.C. Sections 41–58.

b. In a *purchase-money loan,* a seller or lessor advances funds to a buyer or lessee, through a credit contract, for the purchase or lease of goods.

Discharge of liability can also occur when a holder impairs another party's right of recourse (right to seek reimbursement) on the instrument [UCC 3–605]. This occurs when, for example, the holder releases, or agrees not to sue, a party against whom the indorser has a right of recourse.

Reviewing . . . Negotiable Instruments: Transferability and Liability

Robert Durbin, a student, borrowed funds from a bank for his education and signed a promissory note for their repayment. The bank loaned the funds under a federal program designed to assist students at postsecondary institutions. Under this program, repayment ordinarily begins nine to twelve months after the student borrower fails to carry at least one-half of the normal full-time course load at his or her school. The federal government guarantees that the note will be fully paid. If the student defaults on the payments, the lender presents the current balance—principal, interest, and costs—to the government. When the government pays the balance, it becomes the lender, and the borrower owes the government directly. After Durbin defaulted on his note, the government paid the lender the balance due and took possession of the note. Durbin then refused to pay the government, claiming that the government was not the holder of the note. The government filed a suit in a federal district court against Durbin to collect the amount due. Using the information presented in the chapter, answer the following questions.

1. Using the categories discussed in the chapter, what type of negotiable instrument was the note that Durbin signed (an order to pay or a promise to pay)? Explain.
2. Suppose that the note did not state a specific interest rate but instead referred to a statute that established the maximum interest rate for government-guaranteed student loans. Would the note fail to meet the requirements for negotiability in that situation? Why or why not?
3. How does a party who is not named by a negotiable instrument (in this situation, the government) obtain a right to enforce the instrument?
4. Suppose that, in court, Durbin argues that because the school closed down before he could finish his education, there was a failure of consideration: he did not get something of value in exchange for his promise to pay. Assuming that the government is a holder of the promissory note, would this argument likely be successful against it? Why or why not?

DEBATE THIS We should eliminate the status of holder in due course for those who possess negotiable instruments.

BUSINESS APPLICATION

Pitfalls When Writing and Indorsing Checks*

As a businessperson (and as a consumer), you will certainly be writing and receiving checks. Both activities can involve pitfalls.

Checks Drawn in Blank

The danger in signing a blank check is clear. Anyone can write in an unauthorized amount and cash the check. Although you may be able to assert lack of authorization against the person who filled in the check, subsequent holders of the properly indorsed check may be able to enforce the check as completed. While you are haggling with the person who inserted the unauthorized amount and who may not be able to repay it, you will also have to honor the check for the unauthorized amount to a subsequent holder in due course.

*This *Business Application* is not meant to substitute for the services of an attorney who is licensed to practice law in your state.

Checks Payable to "Cash"

It is equally dangerous to write out and sign a check payable to "cash" until you are actually at the bank. Remember that checks payable to "cash" are bearer instruments. This means that if you lose or misplace the check, anybody who finds it can present it (with proper identification) to the bank for payment.

Checks Indorsed in Blank

A negotiable instrument with a blank indorsement also has dangers. As a bearer instrument, it may be as easily transferred as cash. Therefore, when you make a bank deposit, you should sign (indorse) the back of the check in blank only in the presence of a teller. If you choose to indorse the check ahead of time, always insert the words "For deposit only" before you sign your name. As a precaution, you should consider obtaining an indorsement stamp from your bank. Then, when you receive a check payable to your business, you can indorse it immediately. The stamped indorsement will indicate that the check is for deposit only to your business account specified by the number.

Checklist for the Use of Negotiable Instruments

1. *A good rule of thumb is never to sign a blank check.*
2. *Another good rule of thumb is never to write and sign a check payable to "cash" until you are actually at the bank. If you must write the check ahead of time, consider making the check payable to the bank rather than to "cash."*
3. *Be wary of indorsing a check in blank unless a bank teller is simultaneously giving you a receipt for your deposit.*
4. *Consider obtaining an indorsement stamp from your bank so that when you receive checks, you can immediately indorse them "for deposit only" to your account.*

Key Terms

acceleration clause 470
acceptance 463
acceptor 469
bearer 471
bearer instrument 471
blank indorsement 474
certificate of deposit (CD) 465
check 464
dishonor 480
draft 463
drawee 463
drawer 463
extension clause 470
fictitious payee 484
holder 470
holder in due course (HDC) 478
imposter 484
indorsement 473
maker 465
negotiable instrument 462
negotiation 473
order instrument 470
payee 463
personal defense 486
presentment 469
presentment warranties 485
promissory note 465
qualified indorsement 475
restrictive indorsement 476
shelter principle 480
special indorsement 474
transfer warranties 485
trust indorsement 476
universal defenses 485

Chapter Summary: Negotiable Instruments: Transferability and Liability

Types of Instruments (See pages 463–466.)	The UCC specifies four types of negotiable instruments: drafts, checks, promissory notes, and certificates of deposit (CDs). These instruments fall into two basic classifications: 1. *Demand instruments versus time instruments*—A demand instrument is payable on demand (when the holder presents it to the maker or drawer). A time instrument is payable at a future date. 2. *Orders to pay versus promises to pay*—Checks and drafts are *orders* to pay. Promissory notes and CDs are *promises* to pay.
Requirements for Negotiability (See pages 466–472.)	To be negotiable, an instrument must meet the requirements stated below. 1. *Be in writing*—A writing can be on anything that is readily transferable and has a degree of permanence [UCC 3–103(a)(6), (9)]. 2. *Be signed by the maker or drawer*—The signature can be anyplace on the face of the instrument, can be in any form (including a rubber stamp), and can be made in a representative capacity [UCC 3–103(a)(3), 3–401(b)]. 3. *Be an unconditional promise or order to pay*— a. A promise must be more than a mere acknowledgment of a debt [UCC 3–103(a)(6), (9)]. b. The words "I/We promise" or "Pay" meet this criterion. c. Payment cannot be expressly conditioned on the occurrence of an event and cannot be made subject to or governed by another contract [UCC 3–106].

Continued

Chapter Summary: Negotiable Instruments: Transferability and Liability—Continued

Requirements for Negotiability—Continued	4. *State a fixed amount of money*— a. An amount is considered a fixed sum if it is ascertainable from the face of the instrument or (for the interest rate) readily determinable by a formula described in the instrument [UCC –104(a), 3–112(b)]. b. Any medium of exchange recognized as the currency of a government as money [UCC 3—201(24)]. 5. *Be payable on demand or at a definite time*— a. Any instrument that is payable on sight, presentation, or issue, or that does not state any time for payment, is a demand instrument [UCC 3—104(a)(2)]. b. An instrument is still payable at a definite time, even if it is payable on or before a stated date or within a fixed period after sight or if the drawer or maker has an option to extend the time for a definite period [UCC 3–108(a), (b), (c)]. c. Acceleration clauses do not affect the negotiability of the instrument. 6. *Be payable to order or bearer*— a. An order instrument must identify the payee with certainty. b. An instrument that indicates it is not payable to an identified person is payable to bearer [UCC 3–109(a)(3)].
Factors That Do Not Affect Negotiability (See page 472.)	Certain ambiguities or omissions will not affect an instrument's negotiability. See page 472 for a list of these factors.
Transfer of Instruments (See pages 472–477.)	1. *Transfer by assignment*—A transfer by assignment to an assignee gives the assignee only those rights that the assignor possessed. Any defenses against payment that can be raised against an assignor normally can be raised against the assignee. 2. *Transfer by negotiation*—An order instrument is negotiated by indorsement and delivery. A bearer instrument is negotiated by delivery only. 3. *Indorsements*— a. *Blank indorsements* do not specify a particular indorsee and can consist of a mere signature (see Exhibit 18.5 on page 474). b. *Special indorsements* contain the signature of the indorser and identify the indorsee (see Exhibit 18.6 on page 474). c. *Qualified indorsements* contain language, such as the notation "without recourse," that indicates the indorser is not guaranteeing payment of the instrument (see Exhibit 18.7 on page 475). d. *Restrictive indorsements,* such as "For deposit only," require the indorsee to comply with certain instructions regarding the funds involved, but do not prohibit further negotiation of the instrument.
Holder in Due Course (HDC) (See pages 477–481.)	1. *Holder*—A person in possession of an instrument drawn, issued, or indorsed to him or her, to his or her order, to bearer, or in blank. A holder obtains only those rights that the transferor had in the instrument. 2. *Holder in due course (HDC)*—A holder who, by meeting certain acquisition requirements (summarized next), takes an instrument free of most defenses and claims to which the transferor was subject. 3. *Requirements for HDC status*—To be an HDC, a holder must take the instrument: a. For value—A holder must give value to become an HDC and can take an instrument for value in any of the five ways listed on page 478 [UCC 3–303]. b. In good faith—Good faith is defined as "honesty in fact and the observance of reasonable commercial standards of fair dealing" [UCC 3–103(a)(4)]. c. Without notice—To be an HDC, a holder must not be on notice that the instrument is defective because it is overdue, has been dishonored, is part of a series of which at least one instrument has a uncured defect, contains an unauthorized signature or has been altered, or is so irregular or incomplete as to call its authenticity into question. 4. *Shelter principle*—A holder who cannot qualify as an HDC has the *rights* of an HDC if the holder derives her or his title through an HDC, unless the holder engaged in fraud or illegality affecting the instrument [UCC 3–203(b)].
Signature and Warranty Liability (See pages 481–485.)	Liability on negotiable instruments can arise either from a person's signature or from the (transfer and presentment) warranties that are implied when a person presents the instrument for negotiation. 1. *Signature liability*—Every party (except a qualified indorser) who signs a negotiable instrument is either primarily or secondarily liable for payment of the instrument when it comes due. a. Primary liability—Makers and acceptors are primarily liable (an *acceptor* is a drawee that promises in writing to pay an instrument when it is presented for payment at a later time) [UCC 3–115, 3–407, 3–409, 3–412].

Chapter Summary: Negotiable Instruments: Transferability and Liability—Continued

Signature and Warranty Liability—Continued	b. Secondary liability—Drawers and indorsers are secondarily liable [UCC 3–412, 3–414, 3–415, 3–501, 3–502, 3–503]. Parties are secondarily liable on an instrument only if (1) presentment is proper and timely, (2) the instrument is dishonored, and (3) they received timely notice of dishonor. 2. *Transfer warranties*—Any person who transfers an instrument for consideration makes five warranties to subsequent transferees and holders [UCC 3–416]. See the list on page 485. 3. *Presentment warranties*—Any person who presents an instrument for payment or acceptance makes three warranties to any person who in good faith pays or accepts the instrument [UCC 3–417(a), 3–417(d)]. See the list on page 485.
Defenses, Limitations, and Discharge (See pages 485–488.)	1. *Universal (real) defenses*—The following defenses are valid against all holders, including HDCs and holders with the rights of HDCs [UCC 3–305, 3–403, 3–407]: a. Forgery. b. Fraud in the execution. c. Material alteration. d. Discharge in bankruptcy. e. Minority—if the contract is voidable under state law. f. Illegality, mental incapacity, or extreme duress—if the contract is void under state law. 2. *Personal (limited) defenses*—The following defenses are valid against ordinary holders but not against HDCs or holders with the rights of HDCs [UCC 3–303, 3–305]: a. Breach of contract or breach of warranty. b. Lack or failure of consideration (value). c. Fraud in the inducement. d. Illegality and mental incapacity—if the contract is voidable. e. Ordinary duress or undue influence that renders the contract voidable. 3. *Federal limitations on the rights of HDCs*—Rule 433 of the Federal Trade Commission, issued in 1976, limits the rights of HDCs who purchase instruments arising out of consumer credit transactions. The rule allows a consumer who is a party to a consumer credit transaction to bring any defense he or she has against the seller against a subsequent holder as well, even if the subsequent holder is an HDC. 4. *Discharge from liability*—All parties to a negotiable instrument will be discharged when the party primarily liable on it pays to the holder the full amount due. Discharge can also occur in other circumstances (if the instrument has been canceled or materially altered, for example) [UCC 3–602 through 3–605].

ExamPrep

ISSUE SPOTTERS

1. Sabrina owes $600 to Yale, who asks Sabrina to sign an instrument for the debt. If included on that instrument, which of the following would prevent its negotiability—"I.O.U. $600," "I promise to pay $600," or an instruction to Sabrina's bank stating, "I wish you would pay $600 to Yale"? Why? **(See page 467.)**
2. Rye signs corporate checks for Suchin Corporation. Rye writes a check payable to U-All Company, even though Suchin does not owe U-All anything. Rye signs the check, forges U-All's indorsement, and cashes the check at Viceroy Bank, the drawee. Does Suchin have any recourse against the bank for the payment? Why or why not? **(See page 484.)**

–Check your answers to the Issue Spotters against the answers provided in Appendix E at the end of this text.

BEFORE THE TEST

Go to www.cengagebrain.com, enter the ISBN 9781133273561 and click on "Find" to locate this textbook's Web site. Then, click on "Access Now" under "Study Tools," and select Chapter 18 at the top. There, you will find a Practice Quiz that you can take to assess your mastery of the concepts in this chapter, as well as Flashcards, a Glossary of important terms, and Video Questions (when assigned).

For Review

Answers to the even-numbered questions in this For Review section can be found in Appendix F at the end of this text.

1. What requirements must an instrument meet to be negotiable?
2. What are the requirements for attaining the status of a holder in due course (HDC)?
3. What is the difference between signature liability and warranty liability?
4. Certain defenses are valid against all holders, including HDCs. What are these defenses called? Name four defenses that fall within this category.
5. Certain defenses can be used against an ordinary holder but are not effective against an HDC. What are these defenses called? Name four defenses that fall within this category.

Business Scenarios and Case Problems

18–1 Indorsements. A check drawn by David for $500 is made payable to the order of Matthew and issued to Matthew. Matthew owes his landlord $500 in rent and transfers the check to his landlord with the following indorsement: "For rent paid. [Signed] Matthew." Matthew's landlord has contracted to have Lambert do some landscaping on the property. When Lambert insists on immediate payment, the landlord transfers the check to Lambert without indorsement. Later, to pay for some palm trees purchased from Green's Nursery, Lambert transfers the check with the following indorsement: "Pay to Green's Nursery, without recourse. [Signed] Lambert." Green's Nursery sends the check to its bank indorsed "For deposit only. [Signed] Green's Nursery." **(See pages 473–477.)**

1. Classify each of these indorsements.
2. Was the transfer from Matthew's landlord to Lambert, without indorsement, an assignment or a negotiation? Explain.

18–2 Question with Sample Answer—Negotiable Instruments. Muriel Evans writes the following note on the back of an envelope: "I, Muriel Evans, promise to pay Karen Marvin or bearer $100 on demand." Is this a negotiable instrument? Discuss fully. **(See page 466.)**

—For a sample answer to Question 18–2, go to Appendix G at the end of this text.

18–3 Signature Liability. Marion makes a promissory note payable to the order of Perry. Perry indorses the note by writing "without recourse, Perry" and transfers the note for value to Steven. Steven, in need of cash, negotiates the note to Harriet by indorsing it with the words "Pay to Harriet, [signed] Steven." On the due date, Harriet presents the note to Marion for payment, only to learn that Marion has filed for bankruptcy and will have all debts (including the note) discharged in bankruptcy. Discuss fully whether Harriet can hold Marion, Perry, or Steven liable on the note. **(See pages 481–484.)**

18–4 Holder. Germanie Fequiere signed a note payable to BNC Mortgage. As security for the note, Fequiere signed a mortgage on certain real property. BNC indorsed the note in blank. Later, Chase Home Finance, LLC, became a holder in due course of the note and the holder of the mortgage. When Fequiere failed to make payments on the note, Chase sought to foreclose on the property. Fequiere argued that the mortgage had not been properly transferred to Chase. If that is true, can Chase obtain payment on the note? Why or why not? [*Chase Home Finance, LLC v. Fequiere,* 119 Conn.App. 570, 989 A.2d 606 (2010)] **(See pages 477–478.)**

18–5 Negotiability. Michael Scotto borrowed $2,970 from Cindy Vinueza. Both of their signatures appeared at the bottom of a note that stated, "I Michael Scotto owe Cindy Vinueza $2,970 (two thousand and nine-hundred & seventy dollars) & agree to pay her back in full. Signed on this 26th day of September 2009." More than a year later, Vinueza filed a suit against Scotto to recover on the note. Scotto admitted that he had borrowed the funds, but he contended—without proof—that he had paid Vinueza in full. Is this note negotiable? Which party is likely to prevail? Why? [*Vinueza v. Scotto,* 30 Misc.3d 1229, 924 N.Y.S.2d 312 (1 Dist. 2011)] **(See pages 466–472.)**

18–6 Case Problem with Sample Answer—Payable on Demand or at a Definite Time. Abby Novel signed a handwritten note that read, "Glen Gallwitz 1-8-2002 loaned me $5,000 at 6 percent interest a total of $10,000.00." The note did not state a time for repayment. Novel used the funds to manufacture and market a patented jewelry display design. More than seven years after Novel signed the note, Gallwitz filed a suit to recover the stated amount. Novel claimed that she did not have to pay because the note was not negotiable—it was incomplete. Is she correct? Explain. [*Gallwitz v. Novel,* 2011 Ohio 297 (5 Dist. 2011)] **(See page 469.)**

—For a sample answer to Problem 18–6, go to Appendix H at the end of this text.

18–7 Defenses. Thomas Klutz obtained a franchise from Kahala Franchise Corp. to operate a Samurai Sam's restaurant. Under their agreement, Klutz could transfer the franchise only if he obtained Kahala's approval and paid a transfer fee. Without telling Kahala, Klutz sold the restaurant to William Thorbecke. Thorbecke signed a note for the price. When Kahala learned of the deal, the franchisor told Thorbecke to stop using the Samurai Sam's name. Thorbecke stopped paying on the note, and Klutz filed a claim for the unpaid amount. In defense, Thorbecke asserted breach of contract and fraud. Are these defenses effective against Klutz? Explain. [*Kahala Franchise Corp. v. Hit Enterprises,* LLC, 159 Wash. App. 1013 (Div. 2 2011)] **(See page 486.)**

18–8 Defenses. Damion and Kiya Carmichael took out a loan from Ameriquest Mortgage Co. to refinance their mortgage. They signed a note to make monthly payments on the loan. Later, Deutsche Bank National Trust Co. acquired the note. The Carmichaels stopped making payments and filed for bankruptcy. Deutsche asked the court to foreclose on the mortgage. The Carmichaels asserted that they had been fraudulently induced to make the loan and sign the note. Was the bank free of this defense? Explain. [*In re Carmichael,* 443 Bankr. 698 (E.D.Pa. 2011)] **(See page 486.)**

18–9 A Question of Ethics—Promissory Notes. Clarence Morgan, Jr., owned Easy Way Automotive, a car dealership in D'Lo, Mississippi. Easy Way sold a truck to Loyd Barnard, who signed a note for the amount of the price payable to Trustmark National Bank in six months. Before the note came due, Barnard returned the truck to Easy Way, which sold it to another buyer. Using some of the proceeds from the second sale, Easy Way sent a check to Trustmark to pay Barnard's note. Meanwhile, Barnard obtained another truck from Easy Way financed through another six-month note payable to Trustmark. After eight of these deals, some of which involved more than one truck, an Easy Way check to Trustmark was dishonored. In a suit in a Mississippi state court, Trustmark sought to recover the amounts of two of the notes from Barnard. Trustmark had not secured titles to two of the trucks covered by the notes, however, and this complicated Barnard's efforts to reclaim the vehicles from the later buyers. [*Trustmark National Bank v. Barnard,* 930 So.2d 1281 (Miss.App. 2006)] **(See pages 465, 481–483.)**

1. On what basis might Barnard be liable on the Trustmark notes? Would he be primarily or secondarily liable? Could this liability be discharged on the theory that Barnard's right of recourse had been impaired when Trustmark did not secure titles to the trucks covered by the notes? Explain.
2. Easy Way's account had been subject to other recent overdrafts, and a week after the check to Trustmark was returned for insufficient funds, Morgan committed suicide. At the same time, Barnard was unable to obtain a mortgage because the unpaid notes affected his credit rating. How do the circumstances of this case underscore the importance of practicing business ethics?

Critical Thinking and Writing Assignments

18–10 Business Law Critical Thinking Group Assignment. Peter Gowin was an employee of a granite countertop business owned by Joann Stathis. In November 2012, Gowin signed a promissory note agreeing to pay $12,500 in order to become a co-owner of the business. The note was dated January 15, 2012 (ten months before it was signed) and required him to make installment payments starting in February 2012. Stathis told Gowin not to worry about the note and never requested any payments. Gowin continued to work at the business until 2014 when he quit, claiming that he owned half of the business. Stathis argued that Gowin was not a co-owner because he had never paid the $12,500 into the business.

1. The first group will formulate an argument in favor of Stathis that Gowin did not own any interest in the business because he had never paid the $12,500.
2. The second group will evaluate the strength of Gowin's argument. Gowin claimed that because compliance with the stated dates was impossible, the note effectively did not state a date for its payment and therefore was a demand note under UCC 3–108(a). Because no demand for payment had been made, Gowin argued that his obligation to pay had not arisen and the termination of his ownership interest in the granite business was improper.

19 CHAPTER

Checks and Banking in the Digital Age

(Paul Paladin/Shutterstock.com)

CHAPTER OUTLINE

- Checks
- The Bank-Customer Relationship
- Bank's Duty to Honor Checks
- Bank's Duty to Accept Deposits
- Electronic Fund Transfers
- E-Money and Online Banking

LEARNING OBJECTIVES

The five learning objectives below are designed to help improve your understanding of the chapter. After reading this chapter, you should be able to answer the following questions:

1. What type of check does a bank agree in advance to accept when the check is presented for payment?
2. When may a bank properly dishonor a customer's check without being liable to the customer?
3. What duties does the Uniform Commercial Code impose on a bank's customers with regard to forged and altered checks? What are the consequences if a customer is negligent in performing those duties?
4. What is electronic check presentment, and how does it differ from the traditional check-clearing process?
5. What are the four most common types of electronic fund transfers?

"Money is just what we use to keep tally."
—Henry Ford, 1863–1947 (American automobile manufacturer)

Checks are the most common type of negotiable instruments regulated by the Uniform Commercial Code (UCC). Checks are convenient to use because they serve as a substitute for cash. Thus, as Henry Ford said in the chapter-opening quotation, checks help us to "keep tally." To be sure, most students today tend to use debit cards rather than checks for many retail transactions. Not only do debit cards now account for more retail payments than checks, but payments are increasingly being made via smartphones, iPads, and other mobile devices, as we discuss later in this chapter. Nonetheless, commercial checks remain an integral part of the U.S. economic system.

Articles 3 and 4 of the UCC govern issues relating to checks. Article 4 of the UCC governs bank deposits and collections as well as bank-customer relationships. Article 4 also regulates the relationships of banks with one another as they process checks for payment, and it establishes a framework for deposit and checking agreements between a bank and its customers. A check therefore may fall within the scope of Article 3 and yet be subject to the provisions of Article 4 while in the course of collection. If a conflict between Article 3 and Article 4 arises, Article 4 controls [UCC 4–102(a)].

Checks

As explained in Chapter 18 on page 464, a *check* is a special type of draft that is drawn on a bank, ordering the bank to pay a fixed amount of funds on demand [UCC 3–104(f)]. Article 4 defines a *bank* as "a person engaged in the business of banking, including a savings bank, savings and loan association, credit union or trust company" [UCC 4–105(1)]. If any other institution (such as a brokerage firm) handles a check for payment or for collection, the check is not covered by Article 4.

Recall from the preceding chapter that a person who writes a check is called the *drawer*. The drawer is a depositor in the bank on which the check is drawn. The person to whom the check is payable is the *payee*. The bank or financial institution on which the check is drawn is the *drawee*. When Anita Cruzak writes a check from her checking account to pay her college tuition, she is the drawer, her bank is the drawee, and her college is the payee. We now look at some special types of checks.

Cashier's Checks

Cashier's Check A check drawn by a bank on itself.

Checks usually are three-party instruments, but on certain types of checks, the bank can serve as both the drawer and the drawee. For example, when a bank draws a check on itself, the check is called a **cashier's check** and is a negotiable instrument at the moment it is issued (see Exhibit 19.1 below) [UCC 3–104(g)]. Normally, a cashier's check indicates a specific payee. In effect, with a cashier's check, the bank assumes responsibility for paying the check, thus making the check more readily acceptable as a substitute for cash.

EXAMPLE 19.1 Kramer needs to pay a moving company $8,000 for moving his household goods to his new home in another state. The moving company requests payment in the form of a cashier's check. Kramer goes to a bank (he does not need to have an account at the bank) and purchases a cashier's check, payable to the moving company, in the amount of $8,000. Kramer has to pay the bank the $8,000 for the check, plus a small service fee. He then gives the check to the moving company. ●

Exhibit 19.1 A Cashier's Check

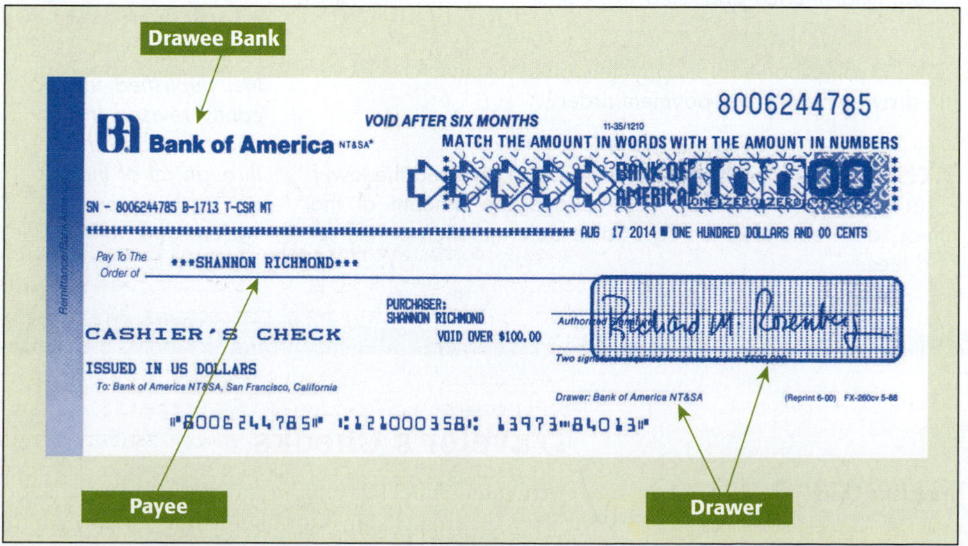

*The abbreviation *NT&SA* stands for National Trust and Savings Association. The Bank of America NT&SA is a subsidiary of Bank of America Corporation, which is engaged in financial services, insurance, investment management, and other businesses.

Cashier's checks are sometimes used in the business community as nearly the equivalent of cash. Except in very limited circumstances, the issuing bank must honor its cashier's checks when they are presented for payment. If a bank wrongfully dishonors a cashier's check, a holder can recover from the bank all expenses incurred, interest, and consequential damages [UCC 3–411]. This same rule applies if a bank wrongfully dishonors a certified check (to be discussed shortly).

Rather than being treated as the equivalent of cash, should a cashier's check be treated as a note with all of the applicable defenses? That was the question in the following case.

Case 19.1

MidAmerica Bank v. Charter One Bank

Illinois Supreme Court,
232 Ill.2d 560, 905 N.E.2d 839 (2009).

(John Quinn/Bloomberg via Getty Images)

A Charter One Bank branch.

FACTS Mary Christelle was the mother of David Hernandez, president of Essential Technologies of Illinois (ETI). Christelle bought a $50,000 cashier's check from Charter One Bank payable to ETI. ETI deposited the check into its account with MidAmerica Bank, FSB. Four days later, Christelle asked Charter One to *stop payment* (see the discussion on page 499). Charter One agreed and refused to honor the check. MidAmerica returned the check to ETI. Within two weeks, ETI's account had a negative balance of $52,000. MidAmerica closed the account and filed a suit in an Illinois state court against Charter One, alleging that the defendant wrongfully dishonored the cashier's check. Charter One argued that a cashier's check should be treated as a note subject to the defense of fraud. The court ruled in MidAmerica's favor, but a state intermediate appellate court reversed the ruling. MidAmerica appealed.

ISSUE Can a bank obtain payment on a cashier's check over the drawee bank's stop-payment order?

DECISION Yes. The Illinois Supreme Court reversed the lower court's decision, awarded MidAmerica the amount of the check, and remanded the case for a determination of interest and fees.

REASON A bank's refusal to pay a cashier's check based on its customer's request to stop payment is wrongful under UCC 3–411 because a customer has no right to stop payment on a cashier's check under UCC 4–403, which permits payment to be stopped only on items drawn "on the customer's account." A cashier's check is drawn on the issuing bank, not on the customer's account. Thus, Christelle had no right to stop payment after she gave the check to ETI. As for Charter One's argument that the check should be treated as a note, the court agreed that the drawer of a cashier's check has the same liability as the maker of a note "because a bank issuing a cashier's check is both the drawer and drawee of the check." But "the UCC provides that cashier's checks are drafts, not notes." Besides, the bank cannot assert fraud as a defense because it did not know of any fraud when it dishonored the check.

WHY IS THIS CASE IMPORTANT? *As noted earlier in the text, the UCC has been amended periodically since it was first published in 1952. In particular, Article 3 was significantly revised in 1990 when many sections were rewritten and renumbered. The reasoning in this case underscores that through all of the changes, the treatment of cashier's checks as "cash equivalents" in the world of commerce has never varied, and none of the amendments to Article 3 have been intended to alter that status.*

Traveler's Checks

Traveler's Check A check that is payable on demand, drawn on or payable through a financial institution, and designated as a traveler's check.

A **traveler's check** is an instrument that is payable on demand, drawn on or payable at or through a financial institution (such as a bank), and designated as a traveler's check. The issuing institution is directly obligated to accept and pay its traveler's check according to the check's terms.

Traveler's checks are designed to be a safe substitute for cash when a person is on vacation or traveling. They are issued for a fixed amount, such as $20, $50, or $100. The purchaser is required to sign the check at the time it is bought and again at the time it is used [UCC 3–104(i)]. Most major banks today do not issue their own traveler's checks but, instead, purchase and issue American Express traveler's checks for their customers (see Exhibit 19.2 below).

Certified Checks

Certified Check A check that has been accepted in writing by the bank on which it is drawn. By certifying (accepting) the check, the bank promises to pay the check at the time it is presented.

LEARNING OBJECTIVE 1

What type of check does a bank agree in advance to accept when the check is presented for payment?

A **certified check** is a check that has been *accepted* in writing by the bank on which it is drawn [UCC 3–409(d)]. When a drawee bank *certifies* (accepts) a check, it immediately charges the drawer's account with the amount of the check and transfers those funds to its own certified check account. In effect, the bank is agreeing in advance to accept that check when it is presented for payment and to make payment from those funds reserved in the certified check account. Essentially, certification prevents the bank from denying liability. It is a promise that sufficient funds are on deposit *and have been set aside* to cover the check.

To certify a check, the bank writes or stamps the word *certified* on the face of the check and typically writes the amount that it will pay.[1] Either the drawer or the holder (payee) of a check can request certification, but the drawee bank is not required to certify a check. (Note, though, that a bank's refusal to certify a check is not a dishonor of the check [UCC 3–409(d)].) Once a check is certified, the drawer and any prior indorsers are completely discharged from liability on the check [UCC 3–414(c), 3–415(d)]. Only the certifying bank is required to pay the instrument.

The Bank-Customer Relationship

The bank-customer relationship begins when the customer opens a checking account and deposits funds that the bank will use to pay for checks written by the customer. Essentially, three types of relationships come into being, as discussed next.

---

1. If the certification does not state an amount, and the amount is later increased and the instrument negotiated to a holder in due course (HDC), the obligation of the certifying bank is the amount of the instrument when it was taken by the HDC [UCC 3–413(b)].

Exhibit 19.2 A Traveler's Check

(Goodluz/Shutterstock.com)

When you open a checking account with your local bank, you are establishing a contractual relationship.

Creditor-Debtor Relationship

A creditor-debtor relationship is created between a customer and a bank when, for example, the customer makes cash deposits into a checking account. When a customer makes a deposit, the customer becomes a creditor, and the bank a debtor, for the amount deposited.

Agency Relationship

An agency relationship also arises between the customer and the bank when the customer writes a check on his or her account. In effect, the customer is ordering the bank to pay the amount specified on the check to the holder when the holder presents the check to the bank for payment. In this situation, the bank becomes the customer's agent and is obligated to honor the customer's request.

Similarly, if the customer deposits a check into his or her account, the bank, as the customer's agent, is obligated to collect payment on the check from the bank on which the check was drawn. To transfer checking account funds among different banks, each bank acts as the agent of collection for its customer [UCC 4–201(a)].

Contractual Relationship

Whenever a bank-customer relationship is established, certain contractual rights and duties arise. The specific rights and duties of the bank and its customer depend on the nature of the transaction. The respective rights and duties of banks and their customers are discussed in detail in the following pages. Another aspect of the bank-customer relationship—deposit insurance—is examined in the *Linking Business Law to Accounting and Finance* feature on pages 513–514.

Bank's Duty to Honor Checks

LEARNING OBJECTIVE 2
When may a bank properly dishonor a customer's check without being liable to the customer?

When a banking institution provides checking services, it agrees to honor the checks written by its customers, with the usual stipulation that the account must have sufficient funds available to pay each check [UCC 4–401(a)]. When a drawee bank *wrongfully* fails to honor a check, it is liable to its customer for damages resulting from its refusal to pay [UCC 4–402(b)]. The customer does not have to prove that the bank breached its contractual commitment or was negligent.

The customer's agreement with the bank includes a general obligation to keep sufficient funds on deposit to cover all checks written. The customer is liable to the payee or to the holder of a check in a civil suit if a check is dishonored for insufficient funds. If intent to defraud can be proved, the customer can also be subject to criminal prosecution for writing a bad check.

When the bank properly dishonors a check for insufficient funds, it has no liability to the customer. The bank may rightfully refuse payment on a customer's check in other circumstances as well. We look here at the rights and duties of both the bank and its customers in specific situations.

Overdrafts

Overdraft A check that is paid by the bank when the checking account on which the check is written contains insufficient funds to cover the check.

When the bank receives an item properly payable from its customer's checking account but the account contains insufficient funds to cover the amount of the check, the bank has two options. It can dishonor the item, or it can pay the item and charge the customer's account, thus creating an **overdraft**. The bank can subtract the amount of the overdraft (plus a service charge) from the customer's next deposit or other customer funds because a check carries with it an enforceable implied promise to reimburse the bank. With a joint account, however, the bank cannot hold any joint-account owner liable for payment of the overdraft unless that customer signed the check or benefited from its proceeds.

A bank can expressly agree with a customer to accept overdrafts through what is sometimes called an "overdraft protection agreement." If such an agreement is formed, any failure of the bank to honor a check because it would create an overdraft breaches this agreement and is treated as a wrongful dishonor [UCC 4–402(a)].

Postdated Checks

A bank may charge a postdated check against a customer's account, unless the customer notifies the bank, in a timely manner, not to pay the check until the stated date. The notice of postdating must be given in time to allow the bank to act on the notice before it pays the check. If the bank fails to act on the customer's notice and charges the customer's account before the date on the postdated check, the bank may be liable for any damages incurred by the customer [UCC 4–401(c)].[2]

Stale Checks

Stale Check A check, other than a certified check, that is presented for payment more than six months after its date.

Commercial banking practice regards a check that is presented for payment more than six months from its date as a **stale check.** A bank is not obligated to pay an uncertified check presented more than six months from its date [UCC 4–404]. When receiving a stale check for payment, the bank has the option of paying or not paying the check. The bank may consult the customer before paying the check. If a bank pays a stale check in good faith without consulting the customer, nonetheless, the bank has the right to charge the customer's account for the amount of the check.

Stop-Payment Orders

Stop-Payment Order An order by a bank customer to his or her bank not to pay or certify a certain check.

A **stop-payment order** is an order by a customer to his or her bank not to pay or certify a certain check. Only a customer (or a person authorized to draw on the account) can order the bank not to pay the check when it is presented for payment [UCC 4–403(a)].[3] A customer has no right to stop payment on a check that has been certified or accepted by a bank, however. In addition, the customer-drawer must have a *valid legal ground* for issuing such an order, or the holder can sue the customer-drawer for payment.

The customer must issue the stop-payment order within a reasonable time and in a reasonable manner to permit the bank to act on it [UCC 4–403(a)]. Most banks allow stop-payment orders to be submitted electronically via the bank's Web site. A written or electronic stop-payment order is effective for six months, at which time it must be renewed in writing [UCC 4–403(b)]. Although a stop-payment order can be given orally over the phone, it is binding on the bank for only fourteen calendar days unless confirmed in writing (or record).[4]

If the bank pays the check in spite of a stop-payment order, the bank will be obligated to recredit the customer's account. In addition, if the bank's payment over a stop-payment order causes subsequent checks written on the drawer's account to "bounce," the bank will be liable for the resultant costs the drawer incurs. The bank is liable only for the amount of actual damages suffered by the drawer, however [UCC 4–403(c)].

---

2. As noted in Chapter 18, postdating does not affect the negotiability of a check. A check is usually paid without respect to its date.
3. For a deceased customer, any person claiming a legitimate interest in the account may issue a stop-payment order [UCC 4–405].
4. Some states do not recognize oral stop-payment orders. They must be in writing.

Death or Incompetence of a Customer

Neither the death nor the incompetence of a customer revokes a bank's authority to pay an item until the bank is informed of the situation and has had a reasonable amount of time to act on the notice. Thus, if a bank is unaware that the customer who wrote a check has been declared incompetent or has died, the bank can pay the item without incurring liability [UCC 4–405]. Even when a bank knows of the death of its customer, for ten days after the *date of death*, it can pay or certify checks drawn on or before the date of death.

An exception to this rule is made if a person claiming an interest in that account, such as an heir, orders the bank to stop payment. Without this provision, banks would constantly be required to verify the continued life and competence of their drawers.

Checks Bearing Forged Drawers' Signatures

When a bank pays a check on which the drawer's signature is forged, generally the bank is liable. A bank may be able to recover at least some of the loss from the customer, however, if the customer's negligence contributed to the making of the forgery. A bank may also obtain partial recovery from the forger of the check (if he or she can be found) or from the holder who presented the check for payment (if the holder knew that the signature was forged).

"Canceled checks will be to future historians and cultural anthropologists what the Dead Sea Scrolls and hieroglyphics are to us."

Brent Staples, 1951–present (American journalist)

The General Rule A forged signature on a check has no legal effect as the signature of a customer-drawer [UCC 3–403(a)]. For this reason, banks require a signature card from each customer who opens a checking account. Signature cards allow the bank to verify whether the signatures on its customers' checks are genuine.

The general rule is that the bank must recredit the customer's account when it pays a check with a forged signature. (Note that banks today normally verify signatures only on checks that exceed a certain threshold, such as $2,500 or some higher amount. Even though a bank sometimes incurs liability costs when it has paid forged checks, the costs of verifying every check's signature would be much higher.)

A bank may contractually shift to the customer the risk of forged checks created by the use of facsimile or other nonmanual signatures. For instance, the contract might stipulate that the customer is solely responsible for maintaining security over any device affixing a signature to the customer's checks.

Customer Negligence When the customer's negligence substantially contributed to the forgery, the bank normally will not be obligated to recredit the customer's account for the amount of the check [UCC 3–406]. The customer's liability may be reduced, however, by the amount of loss caused by negligence on the part of the bank (or other "person") paying the instrument or taking it for value if the negligence substantially contributed to the loss [UCC 3–406(b)].

EXAMPLE 19.2 Gemco Corporation uses special check-writing equipment to write its payroll and business checks. Gemco discovers that an employee used the equipment to write himself a check for $10,000 and that the bank subsequently honored it. Gemco asks the bank to recredit $10,000 to its account for improperly paying the forged check. If the bank can show that Gemco failed to take reasonable care in controlling access to the check-writing equipment, the bank will not be required to recredit Gemco's account for the $10,000. If Gemco can show that negligence by the bank contributed substantially to the loss, however, then Gemco's liability may be reduced proportionately. •

(DNY59/iStockphoto.com)

What are the duties of a bank customer with respect to the examination of monthly bank statements?

Timely Examination of Bank Statements Required Banks typically either mail customers monthly statements detailing activity in their checking accounts, or they make these statements available in some other way—for example, online. In the past, banks routinely included the canceled checks themselves (or copies of them) with the statement sent to the customer.

Today, most banks simply provide the customer with information (check number, amount, and date of payment) on the statement that will allow the customer to reasonably identify the checks that the bank has paid [UCC 4–406(a), (b)]. If the bank retains the canceled checks, it must keep the checks—or legible copies of the checks—for seven years [UCC 4–406(b)]. The customer can obtain a copy of a canceled check during this period of time.

The customer has a duty to promptly examine bank statements (and canceled checks or copies) with reasonable care and to report any alterations or forged signatures [UCC 4–406(c)]. This includes forged signatures of indorsers, if discovered (to be discussed shortly). If the customer fails to fulfill this duty and the bank suffers a loss as a result, the customer will be liable for the loss [UCC 4–406(d)].

Consequences of Failing to Detect Forgeries Sometimes, the same wrongdoer has forged the customer's signature on a series of checks. To recover for all the forged items, the customer must discover and report the *first* forged check to the bank within thirty calendar days of the receipt of the bank statement [UCC 4–406(d)(2)]. Failure to notify the bank within this period of time discharges the bank's liability for *all* of the forged checks that it pays prior to notification.

CASE EXAMPLE 19.3 Joseph Montanez, an employee at Espresso Roma Corporation, used stolen software and blank checks to generate company checks on his home computer. The series of forged checks spanned a period in excess of two years and totaled more than $330,000. When the bank statements containing the forged checks arrived in the mail, Montanez removed the checks so that the forgeries would go undetected. Eventually, Espresso Roma discovered the forgeries and asked the bank to recredit its account. The bank refused, and litigation ensued. The court held that the bank was not liable for the forged checks because Espresso Roma had failed to report the first forgeries within the UCC's time period of thirty days.[5] •

KNOW THIS

If a bank is forced to recredit a customer's account, the bank may recover from the forger or from the party that cashed the check (usually a different customer or a collecting bank).

When the Bank Is Also Negligent

A bank customer can escape liability, at least in part, for failing to notify the bank of forged or altered checks within the required thirty-day period if the bank was also negligent—that is, failed to exercise ordinary care. In this situation, the loss will be allocated between the bank and the customer on the basis of *comparative negligence* (see page 117 in Chapter 4) [UCC 4–406(e)].

Ordinary Care The UCC defines *ordinary care* as the "observance of reasonable commercial standards, prevailing in . . . the business in which that person is engaged" [UCC 3–103]. As mentioned earlier, it is customary in the banking industry to manually examine signatures only on checks over a certain amount. Thus, if a bank fails to examine a signature on a particular check, the bank has not necessarily breached its duty to exercise ordinary care.

One-Year Time Limit Regardless of the degree of care exercised by the customer or the bank, the UCC places an absolute time limit on the liability of a bank for paying a check with a forged customer signature. A customer who fails to report a forged signature

5. *Espresso Roma Corp. v. Bank of America, N.A.*, 100 Cal.App.4th 525, 124 Cal.Rptr.2d 549 (2002).

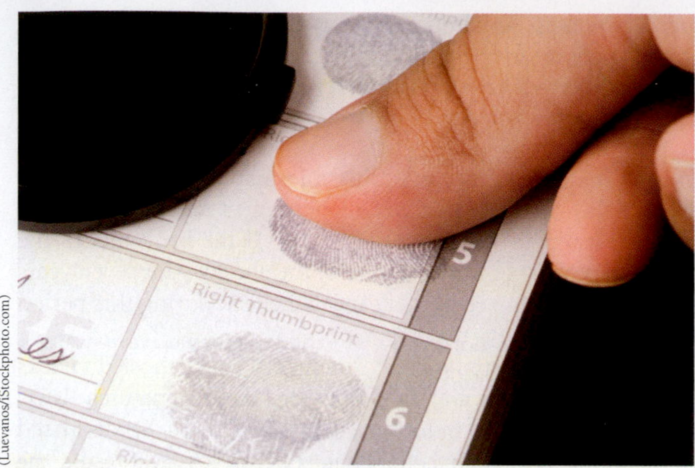

(Luevanos/iStockphoto.com)

Sometimes, when a person attempts to cash a check at a banking institution, the bank requests a thumb print on the back of the check. Why?

within one year from the date that the statement was made available for inspection loses the legal right to have the bank recredit his or her account [UCC 4–406(f)]. The parties can also agree in their contract to a lower time limit.

CASE EXAMPLE 19.4 Wanda Williamson, a clerk at Visiting Nurses Association (VNA), was responsible for making VNA bank deposits. Over a four-year period, Williamson embezzled more than $250,000 from VNA by forging its indorsement on checks and cashing them at the bank. Williamson was eventually arrested and convicted. VNA then filed a lawsuit against the bank, claiming that it had been negligent in allowing Williamson to cash the checks. The court found that the bank was not liable because VNA had failed to report the forged indorsements within the prescribed time period. Not only did UCC 4–406(f) preclude the action, but the bank's contract with VNA included a clause requiring customers to report a forgery within sixty days.[6] ●

PREVENTING LEGAL DISPUTES

Forgery of checks by employees and embezzlement of company funds are disturbingly common in today's business world. To avoid significant losses due to forgery or embezzlement, as well as litigation, use care in maintaining business bank accounts. Limit access to your business's bank accounts. Never leave company checkbooks or signature stamps in unsecured areas. Use passwords to limit access to computerized check-writing software. Examine bank statements in a timely fashion and be on the lookout for suspicious transactions. Remember that if a forgery is not reported within thirty days of the first statement in which the forged item appears, you, as the account holder, normally lose the right to hold the bank liable.

Checks Bearing Forged Indorsements

A bank that pays a customer's check bearing a forged indorsement must recredit the customer's account or be liable to the customer-drawer for breach of contract. **EXAMPLE 19.5** Simon issues a $500 check "to the order of Antonio." Juan steals the check, forges Antonio's indorsement, and cashes the check. When the check reaches Simon's bank, the bank pays it and debits Simon's account. The bank must recredit the $500 to Simon's account because it failed to carry out Simon's order to pay "to the order of Antonio" [UCC 4–401(a)]. Of course, Simon's bank can in turn recover—for breach of warranty (see Chapter 18)—from the bank that cashed the check when Juan presented it [UCC 4–207(a)(2)]. ●

Eventually, the loss usually falls on the first party to take the instrument bearing the forged indorsement because, as discussed in Chapter 18, a forged indorsement does not transfer title. Thus, whoever takes an instrument with a forged indorsement cannot become a holder.

In any event, the customer has a duty to report forged indorsements promptly. Failure to report forged indorsements within a three-year period after the forged items have been made available to the customer relieves the bank of liability [UCC 4–111].

In the following case, a bank's contract with its customer altered its statutory duties concerning forged indorsements. The court had to decide whether to follow the UCC or enforce the contract as written.

6. *Security State Bank v. Visiting Nurses Association of Telfair County, Inc.*, 568 S.E.2d 491 (Ga.App. 2002).

Case 19.2

Michigan Basic Property Insurance Association v. Washington

Court of Appeals of Michigan,
2012 WL 205753 (2012).
coa.courts.mi.gov[a]

(BlueNemo/iStockphoto.com)
Checks can be made out to more than one payee.

FACTS The Michigan Basic Property Insurance Association (MBP) issued a check for $69,559.06 from its account with Fifth Third Bank to Joyce Washington, Countrywide Home Loans, and T&C Federal Credit Union as co-payees. Washington indorsed the check herself by signing all three payees' names and did not distribute the proceeds to the co-payees. When the check reached Fifth Third Bank, it notified MBP of the payment through a daily account statement. MBP did not object, so Fifth Third Bank withdrew the funds from MBP's account. Fifth Third Bank also sent information about the check in a monthly account statement, and MBP still failed to object, even though the account agreement required it to provide prompt notice of any forgeries. MBP was forced to issue a second check to Countrywide, so it sued Fifth Third Bank and sought to have its account recredited. The trial court found that Fifth Third Bank was liable to MBP, and another party appealed on Fifth Third Bank's behalf.

ISSUE Was Fifth Third Bank liable to MBP for paying a check with forged indorsements?

DECISION No. The Michigan appellate court reversed the trial court's judgment.

REASON The court noted that, under the Uniform Commercial Code (UCC), the check was not properly payable because it had two forged indorsements. When a bank pays a check bearing a forged indorsement, the UCC ordinarily requires the bank to recredit the customer's account. Nevertheless, the court pointed out that the UCC allows parties to change their duties by contract. In this case, the account agreement obligated MBP to carefully review its checking account statements and to notify Fifth Third Bank of any problems within thirty days. In the absence of such notice, the contract provided that MBP, not Fifth Third Bank, was liable for any forged indorsements. Because MBP did not provide prompt notice of the forgeries, Fifth Third Bank was not required to recredit MBP's account.

CRITICAL THINKING—Legal Consideration *As a practical matter, does it make sense for the customer to bear primary responsibility for discovering instances of fraud? Which party is in a better position to detect any irregularities? Explain.*

a. Under "Resources," in the pull-down menu, select "Court Opinions/MSC Orders" and then "Search Options." On the next page, click on "Docket Number." When that page opens, select "Court of Appeals," type "299597" in the search box, and click on "Search." In the result, click on the case name to access the opinion.

Altered Checks

LEARNING OBJECTIVE 3
What duties does the Uniform Commercial Code impose on a bank's customers with regard to forged and altered checks? What are the consequences if a customer is negligent in performing those duties?

The customer's instruction to the bank is to pay the exact amount on the face of the check to the holder. The bank has a duty to examine each check before making final payment. If the bank fails to detect an alteration, it is liable to its customer for the loss because it did not pay as the customer ordered.

The bank's loss is the difference between the original amount of the check and the amount actually paid [UCC 4–401(d)(1)]. **EXAMPLE 19.6** A check written for $11 is altered to $111. The customer's account will be charged $11 (the amount the customer ordered the bank to pay). The bank normally will be responsible for the $100 difference. •

Customer Negligence

As in a situation involving a forged drawer's signature, a customer's negligence can shift the loss when payment is made on an altered check (unless the bank was also negligent). For example, a person may carelessly write a check leaving large gaps around the numbers and words where additional numbers and words can be inserted (see Exhibit 19.3 on the next page).

Exhibit 19.3 A Poorly Filled-Out Check

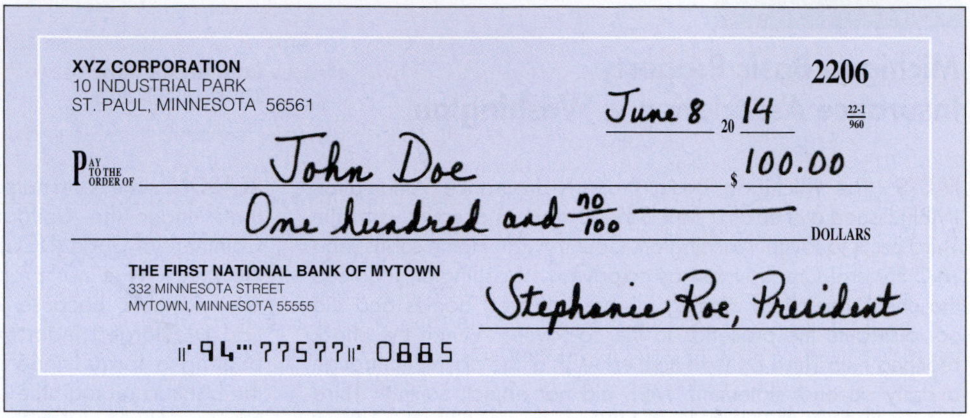

XYZ CORPORATION
10 INDUSTRIAL PARK
ST. PAUL, MINNESOTA 56561

2206

June 8 20 14

22-1/960

PAY TO THE ORDER OF John Doe $ 100.00

One hundred and 00/100 DOLLARS

THE FIRST NATIONAL BANK OF MYTOWN
332 MINNESOTA STREET
MYTOWN, MINNESOTA 55555

Stephanie Roe, President

⑈94⑈ 77577⑈ 0885

Similarly, a person who signs a check and leaves the dollar amount for someone else to fill in is barred from protesting when the bank unknowingly and in good faith pays whatever amount is shown [UCC 4–401(d)(2)]. Finally, if the bank can trace its loss on successive altered checks to the customer's failure to discover the initial alteration, the bank can reduce its liability for reimbursing the customer's account [UCC 4–406].

In every situation involving a forged drawer's signature or an alteration, a bank must observe reasonable commercial standards of care in paying on a customer's checks [UCC 4–406(e)]. The customer's negligence can be used as a defense only if the bank has exercised ordinary care.

Other Parties from Whom the Bank May Recover The bank is entitled to recover the amount of loss from the transferor who, by presenting the check for payment, warrants that the check has not been materially altered (warranty liability was discussed in Chapter 18). This rule has two exceptions, though. If the bank is also the drawer (as it is on a cashier's check), it cannot recover from the presenting party if the party is a holder in due course (HDC) acting in good faith [UCC 3–417(a)(2), 4–208(a)(2)]. The reason is that an instrument's drawer is in a better position than an HDC to know whether the instrument has been altered.

Similarly, an HDC who presents a certified check for payment in good faith will not be held liable under warranty principles if the check was altered before the HDC acquired it [UCC 3–417(a)(2), 4–207(a)(2)]. **EXAMPLE 19.7** Jordan draws a check for $500 payable to David. David alters the amount to $5,000. The drawee bank, First National, certifies the check for $5,000. David negotiates the check to Ethan, an HDC. The drawee bank pays Ethan $5,000. On discovering the mistake, the bank cannot recover from Ethan the $4,500 paid by mistake, even though the bank was not in a superior position to detect the alteration. This is in accord with the purpose of certification, which is to obtain the definite obligation of a bank to honor a definite instrument. •

Bank's Duty to Accept Deposits

A bank has a duty to its customer to accept the customer's deposits of cash and checks. When checks are deposited, the bank must make the funds represented by those checks available within certain time frames. A bank also has a duty to collect payment on any checks payable or indorsed to its customers and deposited by them into their accounts. Cash deposits made in U.S. currency are received into customers' accounts without being subject to further collection procedures.

(Yin Yang/iStockphoto.com)

If you deposit a check at your bank that is written on another bank, can you withdraw those funds in cash immediately? Why or why not?

Availability Schedule for Deposited Checks

The Expedited Funds Availability Act of 1987[7] and Regulation CC,[8] which was issued by the Federal Reserve Board of Governors (the *Federal Reserve System* will be discussed shortly) to implement the act, require that any local check deposited must be available for withdrawal by check or as cash within one business day from the date of deposit.

A check is classified as a local check if the first bank to receive the check for payment and the bank on which the check is drawn are located in the same check-processing region (check-processing regions are designated by the Federal Reserve Board of Governors). For nonlocal checks, the funds must be available for withdrawal within not more than five business days. Note that under the Check Clearing in the 21st Century Act (Check 21),[9] a bank has to credit a customer's account as soon as the bank receives the funds (Check 21 is discussed in this chapter's *Landmark in the Law* feature on the following page).

In addition, the Expedited Funds Availability Act requires the following:

1. That funds be available on the next business day for cash deposits and wire transfers, government checks, the first $100 of a day's check deposits, cashier's checks, certified checks, and checks for which the depositary and payor banks are branches of the same institution (*depositary* and *payor banks* will be discussed shortly).
2. That the first $100 of any deposit be available for cash withdrawal on the opening of the next business day after deposit. If a local check is deposited, the next $400 is to be available for withdrawal by no later than 5:00 p.m. the next business day. If, for example, you deposit a local check for $500 on Monday, you can withdraw $100 in cash at the opening of the business day on Tuesday, and an additional $400 must be available for withdrawal by no later than 5:00 P.M. on Wednesday.

A different availability schedule applies to deposits made at *nonproprietary* automated teller machines (ATMs). These are ATMs that are not owned or operated by the bank receiving the deposits. Basically, a five-day hold is permitted on all deposits, including cash deposits, made at nonproprietary ATMs.

The Traditional Collection Process

Usually, deposited checks involve parties that do business at different banks, but sometimes checks are written between customers of the same bank. Either situation brings into play the bank collection process as it operates within the statutory framework of Article 4 of the UCC. Note that the check-collection process described in the following subsections will be modified as the banking industry continues to implement Check 21.

Depositary Bank The first bank to receive a check for payment.

Payor Bank The bank on which a check is drawn (the drawee bank).

Collecting Bank Any bank handling an item for collection, except the payor bank.

Intermediary Bank Any bank to which an item is transferred in the course of collection, except the depositary or payor bank.

Designations of Banks Involved in the Collection Process

The first bank to receive a check for payment is the **depositary bank.**[10] For example, when a person deposits a tax-refund check into a personal checking account at the local bank, that bank is the depositary bank. The bank on which a check is drawn (the drawee bank) is called the **payor bank.** Any bank except the payor bank that handles a check during some phase of the collection process is a **collecting bank.** Any bank except the payor bank or the depositary bank to which an item is transferred in the course of this collection process is called an **intermediary bank.**

7. 12 U.S.C. Sections 4001–4010.
8. 12 C.F.R. Sections 229.1–229.42.
9. 12 U.S.C. Sections 5001–5018.
10. All definitions in this section are found in UCC 4–105. The terms *depositary* and *depository* have different meanings in the banking context. A depository bank refers to a *physical place* (a bank or other institution) in which deposits or funds are held or stored.

LANDMARK IN THE LAW

Check Clearing in the 21st Century Act (Check 21)

In the traditional collection process, paper checks had to be physically transported before they could be cleared. To streamline this costly and time-consuming process and improve the overall efficiency of the nation's payment system, Congress passed the Check Clearing in the 21st Century Act (Check 21) in 2003.

Purpose of Check 21 Before the implementation of Check 21, banks generally had to present the original paper check for payment because there was no broad-based system of electronic presentment. Check 21 has changed this situation by creating a new negotiable instrument called a *substitute check.* Although the act does not require banks to change their check-collection practices, the creation of substitute checks facilitates the use of electronic check processing.

Substitute Checks A substitute check is a paper reproduction of the front and back of an original check that contains all of the same information required on checks for automated processing. Banks create a substitute check from a digital image of an original check. Financial institutions that exchange digital images of checks do not have to send the original paper checks. They can simply transmit the information electronically and replace the original checks with the substitute checks. Banks that do not exchange checks electronically are required to accept substitute checks in the same way that they accept original checks.

By eliminating the original check after a substitute check is created, the financial system can prevent the check from being paid twice and reduce the expense of paper storage and retrieval. Nevertheless, at least for quite a while, not all checks will be converted to substitute checks. Thus, if a bank returns canceled checks to deposit holders at the end of each month, some of those returned checks may be substitute checks, and some may be original canceled paper checks.

Faster Access to Funds The Expedited Funds Availability Act requires the Federal Reserve Board to revise the availability schedule for funds from deposited checks to correspond to reductions in check-processing time.[a] Therefore, as the speed of check processing increases under Check 21, the Federal Reserve Board will reduce the maximum time that a bank can hold funds from deposited checks before making them available to the depositor. Thus, account holders will have faster access to their deposited funds, but they will also have less *float time*—the time between when a check is written and when the amount is actually deducted from the account.

Application to Today's World *As more financial institutions make agreements to transfer digital images of checks, the check-processing system will become more efficient and therefore less costly. Customers increasingly will be unable to rely on banking float when they are low on funds, so they should make sure that funds are available to cover checks when they are written. Customers cannot opt out of Check 21 and demand that their original canceled checks be returned with their monthly statements. Nor can they refuse to accept a substitute check as proof of payment.*

---

a. 12 U.S.C. Sections 4001–4010.

During the collection process, any bank can take on one or more of the various roles of depositary, payor, collecting, and intermediary bank. **EXAMPLE 19.8** A buyer in New York writes a check on her New York bank and sends it to a seller in San Francisco. The seller deposits the check in her San Francisco bank account. The seller's bank is both a *depositary bank* and a *collecting bank*. The buyer's bank in New York is the *payor bank*. As the check travels from San Francisco to New York, any collecting bank handling the item in the collection process (other than the depositary bank and the payor bank) is also called an *intermediary bank*. Exhibit 19.4 on the facing page illustrates how various banks function in the collection process in the context of this example. •

Check Collection between Customers of the Same Bank An item that is payable by the depositary bank (also the payor bank) that receives it is called an "on-us item." Usually, the bank issues a "provisional credit" for on-us items within the same day. If the bank does not dishonor the check by the opening of the second banking day following its receipt, the check is considered paid [UCC 4–215(e)(2)].

Exhibit 19.4 The Check-Collection Process

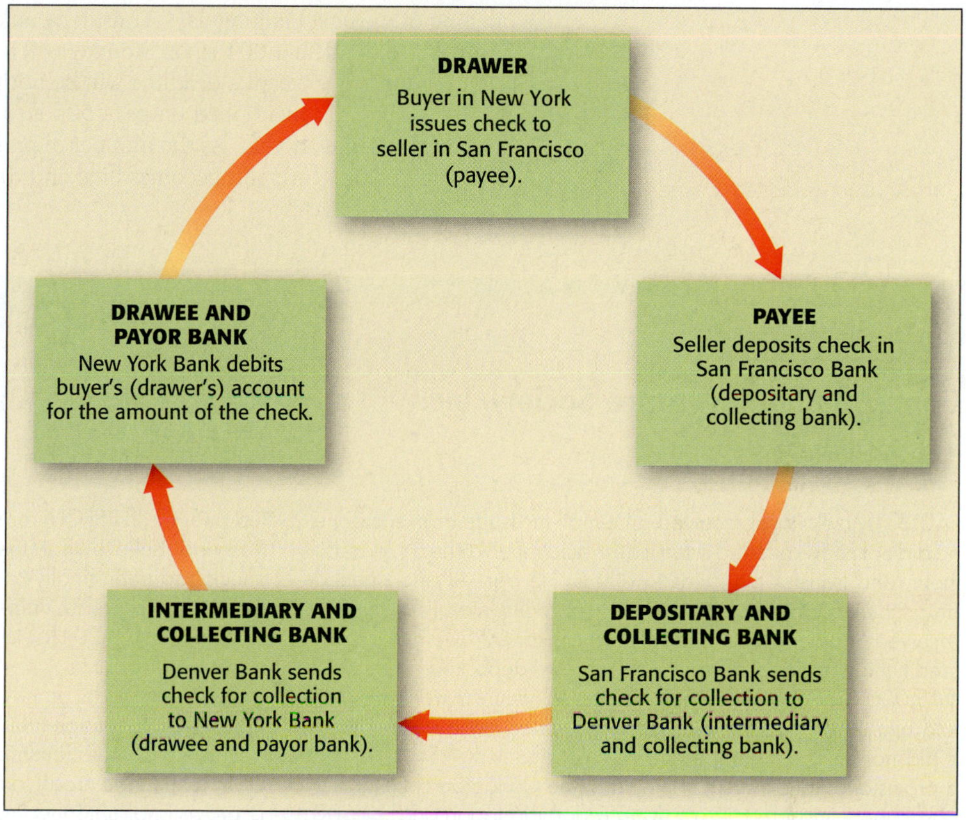

DRAWER
Buyer in New York issues check to seller in San Francisco (payee).

PAYEE
Seller deposits check in San Francisco Bank (depositary and collecting bank).

DEPOSITARY AND COLLECTING BANK
San Francisco Bank sends check for collection to Denver Bank (intermediary and collecting bank).

INTERMEDIARY AND COLLECTING BANK
Denver Bank sends check for collection to New York Bank (drawee and payor bank).

DRAWEE AND PAYOR BANK
New York Bank debits buyer's (drawer's) account for the amount of the check.

Check Collection between Customers of Different Banks

Once a depositary bank receives a check, it must arrange to present it either directly or through intermediary banks to the appropriate payor bank.

> "I saw a bank that said '24-Hour Banking,' but I don't have that much time."
>
> Steven Wright, 1955–present (American comedian)

Deadline Is Midnight of the Next Banking Day Each bank in the collection chain must pass the check on before midnight of the next banking day following its receipt [UCC 4–202(b)].[11] A "banking day" is any part of a day that the bank is open to carry on substantially all of its banking functions. Thus, if only a bank's drive-through facilities are open, a check deposited on Saturday will not trigger the bank's midnight deadline until the following Monday. When the check reaches the payor bank, that bank is liable for the face amount of the check, unless the payor bank dishonors the check or returns it by midnight on the next banking day following receipt [UCC 4–302].[12]

Deferred Posting after Cutoff Hour Because of this deadline and because banks need to maintain an even workflow in the many items they handle daily, the UCC permits what is called *deferred posting*. According to UCC 4–108, "a bank may fix an afternoon hour of

11. A bank may take a "reasonably longer time" in certain circumstances, such as when the bank's computer system is down due to a power failure, but the bank must show that its action is still timely [UCC 4–202(b)].

12. Most checks are cleared by a computerized process, and communication and computer facilities may fail because of electrical outages, equipment malfunction, or other conditions. A bank may be "excused" from liability for failing to meet its midnight deadline if such conditions arise and the bank has exercised "such diligence as the circumstances require" [UCC 4–109(d)].

2:00 P.M. or later as a cutoff hour for the handling of money and items and the making of entries on its books." Any checks received after that hour "may be treated as being received at the opening of the next banking day." Thus, if a bank's "cutoff hour" is 3:00 P.M., a check received by a payor bank at 4:00 P.M. on Monday will be deferred for posting until Tuesday. In this situation, the payor bank's deadline will be midnight Wednesday.

The provisional credit mentioned on page 506 also applies to checks presented to one bank for collection from another. As the number of banks in the collection chain increases, so does the time before the credit becomes final and the check is considered paid, as illustrated in the following case.

Case 19.3

Cumis Mutual Insurance Society, Inc. v. Rosol

Superior Court of New Jersey, Appellate Division, 2011 WL 589397 (2011).

(sshepard/iStockphoto.com)

The Polish & Slavic Federal Credit Union.

FACTS Mizek Rosol received an e-mail message from someone he did not know, offering a fee if he would receive checks, deposit them, and transfer the funds to others. He agreed and opened an account at Polish & Slavic Federal Credit Union (PSFCU). He received and deposited a cashier's check for $9,800 issued by a credit union in Florida. Three days later, he deposited a check for $45,000 drawn on a Canadian bank. Within a week, PSFCU told him that payment on the first check had been stopped, but it did not disclose that the check was fraudulent. PSFCU issued a provisional credit for the amount of the Canadian check. After Rosol had transferred $36,240 to a party in Japan and $4,500 to a party in Great Britain, the Canadian check was dishonored. PSFCU demanded that Rosol repay the transferred funds. He refused. PSFCU filed a claim with its insurer, Cumis Mutual Insurance Society, Inc. Cumis paid the claim and filed a suit against Rosol to recover the amount. The court issued a summary judgment in Cumis's favor. Rosol appealed.

ISSUE Were the funds that Rosol deposited from the Canadian check provisional at the time he transferred them to the parties in Japan and Great Britain?

DECISION Yes. A state intermediate appellate court reversed the lower court's judgment and remanded the case because "there were genuine issues of material fact precluding summary judgment." If PSFCU reasonably led Rosol to believe that the Canadian check had been finally credited to his account, the credit union could not rely on UCC 4–201(a) to recover the transferred funds.

REASON The appellate court explained that UCC 4–201(a) governed the relationship between PSFCU and Rosol. Under that provision, a credit to the account of "the owner" of a check is provisional until the final settlement of the check. The credit to Rosol's account for the checks was thus provisional between the time of their deposit and the time of their dishonor. During that period, PSFCU had a "right of recoupment" for the funds that Rosol had transferred. But Rosol contended that he would not have transferred those funds if PSFCU had told him that the first check was fraudulent—not just that it had been stopped. The court reasoned that "the state of his knowledge" about the first check could bear on the question of whether Rosol had acted reasonably in relying on what he was told about the second check.

CRITICAL THINKING—Ethical Consideration *In what ways was Rosol's apparent motive similar to the most common reason that ethical problems occur in business?*

Has the Expedited Funds Availability Act (EFAA) encouraged fraud? Since the EFAA was enacted in 1987, millions of people have fallen prey to a variety of check-fraud scams. The fraudsters contact a person—via e-mail, social media, telephone, or letter—and say that they will send that person a check for a certain amount if he or she agrees to wire some of the funds back to them, typically to cover "fees and taxes." The victim receives a check, deposits it into his or her account, and waits to see if the check "clears." A day or so later, when the law says the funds must be made available, the victim confirms that the funds are in his or her bank account and then wires the requested amount back to the fraudsters.

Unfortunately, by the time the bank discovers that the check is a fake and notifies the customer that the check has "bounced," the customer has already sent thousands of dollars to the fraudsters. Because the check was counterfeit, the bank has no liability on it, and the loss falls on the customer. The incidence of these scams is increasing, largely because the fraudsters know that the law requires U.S. banks to make the funds available almost immediately on deposited checks, even if those checks later prove to be counterfeit. Although the EFAA was intended to protect bank customers, it now appears to be having the opposite effect—making them a target for fraud.

Federal Reserve System A network of twelve district banks and related branches located around the country and headed by the Federal Reserve Board of Governors. Most banks in the United States have Federal Reserve accounts.

Clearinghouse A system or place where banks exchange checks and drafts drawn on each other and settle daily balances.

How the Federal Reserve System Clears Checks The **Federal Reserve System** is a network of twelve district banks, which are located around the country and headed by the Federal Reserve Board of Governors. Most banks in the United States have Federal Reserve accounts. The Federal Reserve System has greatly simplified the check-collection process by acting as a **clearinghouse**—a system or place where banks exchange checks and drafts drawn on each other and settle daily balances.

EXAMPLE 19.9 Pamela Moy of Philadelphia writes a check to Jeanne Sutton in San Francisco. When Sutton receives the check in the mail, she deposits it in her bank. Her bank then deposits the check in the Federal Reserve Bank of San Francisco, which transfers it to the Federal Reserve Bank of Philadelphia. That Federal Reserve bank then sends the check to Moy's bank, which deducts the amount of the check from Moy's account. •

LEARNING OBJECTIVE 4

What is electronic check presentment, and how does it differ from the traditional check-clearing process?

Electronic Check Presentment In the past, most checks were processed manually. The employees of each bank in the collection chain would physically handle each check that passed through the bank for collection or payment. Today, most checks are processed electronically—a practice that has been facilitated by Check 21, as described in the *Landmark in the Law* feature on page 506. Whereas manual check processing can take days, *electronic check presentment* can be done on the day of deposit. Items are encoded with information (such as the amount of the check) that is read and processed by other banks' computers. Sometimes, a check is retained at its place of deposit, and only its image or description is presented for payment under an electronic presentment agreement [UCC 4–110].[13]

A bank that encodes information on an item warrants to any subsequent bank or payor that the encoded information is correct [UCC 4–209]. This is also true for a bank that retains an item while transmitting its image or description as presentation for payment.

Regulation CC provides that a returned check must be encoded with the routing number of the depositary bank, the amount of the check, and other information and adds that this "does not affect a paying bank's responsibility to return a check within the deadlines required by the U.C.C." Under UCC 4–301(d)(2), an item is returned "when it is sent or delivered to the bank's customer or transferor or pursuant to his [or her] instructions."

Electronic Fund Transfers

Electronic Fund Transfer (EFT) A transfer of funds through the use of an electronic terminal, a telephone, a computer, or magnetic tape.

By utilizing computer technology in the form of electronic fund transfer systems, banking institutions no longer have to move mountains of paperwork to process fund transfers. An **electronic fund transfer (EFT)** is a transfer of funds through the use of an electronic terminal, a telephone, a computer, a tablet device, or a smartphone.

13. This section of the UCC assumes that no bank will participate in an electronic presentment program without an express agreement (which is no longer true since Check 21 went into effect). See Comment 2 to UCC 4–110.

KNOW THIS
The EFTA does not provide for the reversal of an electronic transfer of funds once it has occurred.

The law governing EFTs depends on the type of transfer involved. Consumer fund transfers are governed by the Electronic Fund Transfer Act (EFTA) of 1978.[14] Commercial fund transfers are governed by Article 4A of the UCC.

Although electronic banking offers numerous benefits, it also poses difficulties on occasion. It is difficult to issue stop-payment orders with electronic banking. Also, fewer records are available to prove or disprove that a transaction took place. The possibilities for tampering with a person's private banking information have also increased.

Types of EFT Systems

Most banks today offer EFT services to their customers. The following are the most common types of EFT systems used by bank customers:

LEARNING OBJECTIVE 5
What are the four most common types of electronic fund transfers?

1. *Automated teller machines* (ATMs)—The machines are connected online to the bank's computers. A customer inserts a plastic card (called an ATM or debit card) issued by the bank and keys in a *personal identification number* (PIN) to access her or his accounts and conduct banking transactions.
2. *Point-of-sale systems*—Online terminals allow consumers to transfer funds to merchants to pay for purchases using a debit card.
3. *Direct deposits and withdrawals*—Customers can authorize the bank to allow another party—such as the government or an employer—to make direct deposits into their accounts. Similarly, customers can request the bank to make automatic payments to a third party at regular, recurrent intervals from the customer's funds (insurance premiums or loan payments, for example).
4. *Internet payment systems*—Many financial institutions permit their customers to access the institution's computer system via the Internet and direct a transfer of funds between accounts or pay a particular bill.

Consumer Fund Transfers

The Electronic Fund Transfer Act (EFTA) provides a basic framework for the rights, liabilities, and responsibilities of users of EFT systems. Additionally, the act gave the Federal Reserve Board authority to issue rules and regulations to help implement the act's provisions. The Federal Reserve Board's implemental regulation is called **Regulation E.**

Regulation E A set of rules issued by the Federal Reserve System's Board of Governors to protect users of electronic fund transfer systems.

The EFTA governs financial institutions that offer electronic fund transfers involving consumer accounts. The types of accounts covered include checking accounts, savings accounts, and any other asset accounts established for personal, family, or household purposes. Telephone transfers are covered by the EFTA only if they are made in accordance with a prearranged plan under which periodic or recurring transfers are contemplated.

Disclosure Requirements

The EFTA is essentially a disclosure law benefiting consumers. The act requires financial institutions to inform consumers of their rights and responsibilities, including those listed here, with respect to EFT systems.

1. If a customer's debit card is lost or stolen and used without his or her permission, the customer shall be required to pay no more than $50 if he or she notifies the bank of the loss or theft within two days of learning about it. Otherwise, the liability increases to $500. The customer may be liable for more than $500 if he or she fails to report the unauthorized use within sixty days after it appears on the customer's statement. (If a customer voluntarily gives her or his debit card to another, who then uses it improperly, the protections just mentioned do not apply.)

14. 15 U.S.C. Sections 1693–1693r. The EFTA amended Title IX of the Consumer Credit Protection Act.

2. The customer must discover any error on the monthly statement within sixty days and notify the bank. The bank then has ten days to investigate and must report its conclusions to the customer in writing. If the bank takes longer than ten days, it must return the disputed amount to the customer's account until it finds the error. If there is no error, the customer has to return the disputed funds to the bank.
3. The bank must provide a monthly statement for every month in which there is an electronic transfer of funds. The statement must show the amount and date of the transfer, the names of the retailers or other third parties involved, the location or identification of the terminal, and the fees.

Violations and Damages

Unauthorized access to an EFT system constitutes a federal felony, and those convicted may be fined up to $10,000 and sentenced to as long as ten years in prison. Banks must strictly comply with the terms of the EFTA and are liable for any failure to adhere to its provisions.

For a bank's violation of the EFTA, a consumer may recover both actual damages (including attorneys' fees and costs) and punitive damages of not less than $100 and not more than $1,000. Even when a customer has sustained no actual damage, the bank may be liable for legal costs and punitive damages if it fails to follow the proper procedures outlined by the EFTA in regard to error resolution.

Commercial Transfers

KNOW THIS

If any part of an electronic fund transfer is covered by the EFTA, the entire transfer is excluded from UCC Article 4A.

Funds are also transferred electronically "by wire" between commercial parties. In fact, the dollar volume of payments by wire transfer is more than $1 trillion a day—an amount that far exceeds the dollar volume of payments made by other means. The two major wire payment systems are the Federal Reserve's wire transfer network (Fedwire) and the New York Clearing House Interbank Payments Systems (CHIPS).

Commercial wire transfers are governed by Article 4A of the UCC, which has been adopted by most states (and is included in Appendix C at the end of this text). **EXAMPLE 19.10** Jellux, Inc., owes $5 million to Perot Corporation. Instead of sending Perot a check or some other instrument that would enable Perot to obtain payment, Jellux instructs its bank, East Bank, to credit $5 million to Perot's account in West Bank. East Bank debits Jellux's East Bank account and wires $5 million to Perot's West Bank account. In more complex transactions, additional banks would be involved. •

E-Money and Online Banking

New forms of electronic payments (e-payments) have the potential to replace *physical* cash—coins and paper currency—with *virtual* cash in the form of electronic impulses. This is the unique promise of **digital cash,** which consists of funds stored on microchips and on other computer devices. Online banking has also become commonplace in today's world.

Digital Cash Funds contained on computer software, in the form of secure programs stored on microchips and on other computer devices.

In a few minutes, anybody with the proper software can access his or her account, transfer funds, write "checks," pay bills, monitor investments, and often even buy and sell stocks. (For a discussion of how smartphones are being used to make payments, see this chapter's *Adapting the Law to the Online Environment* feature on the next page.)

Forms of E-Money

E-Money Prepaid funds recorded on a computer or a card (such as a smart card or a stored-value card).

Stored-Value Card A card bearing a magnetic strip that holds magnetically encoded data, providing access to stored funds.

Various forms of electronic money, or **e-money,** are emerging. The simplest kind of e-money system uses **stored-value cards.** These are plastic cards embossed with magnetic strips containing magnetically encoded data. In some applications, a stored-value card can be used only to purchase specific goods and services offered by the card issuer.

Smart Card A card containing a microprocessor that permits storage of funds via security programming, can communicate with other computers, and does not require online authorization for fund transfers.

Smart cards are plastic cards containing computer microchips that can hold more information than a magnetic strip can. A smart card carries and processes security programming. This capability gives smart cards a technical advantage over stored-value cards. The microprocessors on smart cards can also authenticate the validity of transactions. Retailers can program electronic cash registers to confirm the authenticity of a smart card by examining a unique digital signature stored on its microchip.

Online Banking Services

Most customers use three kinds of online banking services: bill consolidation and payment, transferring funds among accounts, and applying for loans. Customers typically have to appear in person to finalize the terms of a loan, however. Generally, customers are not yet able to deposit and withdraw funds online, although some mobile-banking applications allow checks up to a certain amount to be deposited when a user e-mails an image of the front and back of the check. Smart cards may also eventually be used for withdrawing and depositing funds.

Since the late 1990s, several banks have operated exclusively on the Internet. These "virtual banks" have no physical branch offices. Because few people are equipped to send funds to virtual banks via smart-card technology, the virtual banks accept deposits through physical delivery systems, such as the U.S. Postal Service or FedEx.

ADAPTING THE LAW TO THE ONLINE ENVIRONMENT

SMARTPHONE-BASED PAYMENT SYSTEMS

In 2009, customers at certain Starbucks locations in New York, San Francisco, and Seattle began downloading an iPhone app to pay for their cappuccinos. Once the app is downloaded, the customer pays by simply flashing a bar code that appears on the iPhone's screen. By 2012, more than seven thousand Starbucks locations were accepting payments from all types of smartphone-based operating systems.

The Competition Will Become Fierce

The promise of a "mobile or digital wallet" is becoming reality. Banks, credit-card issuers, and, of course, AT&T, T-Mobile, and Verizon Wireless want to be part of the smartphone payment system revolution. All wireless carriers have agreements with American Express, Discovery, MasterCard, and Visa. In fact, Visa has its own e-wallet service.

Mobile payments can take many forms. American Express's digital payment system, Serve, allows person-to-person payments over mobile phones. Some merchants that already accept American Express cards accept payments via mobile phones. In addition, Bank of America, JPMorgan Chase, and Wells Fargo have created ClearXchange, which also allows bank customers to make person-to-person payments using mobile phone numbers.

Linking Digital Wallets to Other Apps on a Smartphone

According to those in this burgeoning field, the Holy Grail is a link from a digital wallet to another app within a single smartphone. Google, for example, is combining its Google Wallet with its Google Offers (a discount-deal app). Presumably, when more app-enabled "stores" are linked to digital wallets within smartphones, mobile payment systems will grow rapidly. Today, mobile pay volume is only about $150 billion, but that is expected to explode as the mass market adopts these systems.

Critical Thinking

Does having a digital wallet in an iPhone, Android-based phone, or other smartphone entail more security risks than carrying a physical wallet? Explain.

Reviewing . . . Checks and Banking in the Digital Age

RPM Pizza, Inc., issued a check for $96,000 to Systems Marketing for an advertising campaign. A few days later, RPM decided not to go through with the deal and placed a written stop-payment order on the check. RPM and Systems had no further contact for many months. Three weeks after the stop-payment order expired, however, Toby Rierson, an employee at Systems, cashed the check. Bank One Cambridge, RPM's bank, paid the check with funds from RPM's account. Because the check was more than six months old, it was stale. Thus, according to standard banking procedures as well as Bank One's own policies, the signature on the check should have been specially verified, but it was not. RPM filed a suit in a federal district court against Bank One to recover the amount of the check. Using the information presented in the chapter, answer the following questions.

1. How long is a written stop-payment order effective? What else could RPM have done to prevent this check from being cashed?
2. What would happen if it turned out that RPM did not have a legitimate reason for stopping payment on the check?
3. What are a bank's obligations with respect to stale checks?
4. Would a court be likely to hold the bank liable for the amount of the check because it failed to verify the signature on the check? Why or why not?

DEBATE THIS To reduce fraud, checks that utilize mechanical or electronic signature systems should not be honored.

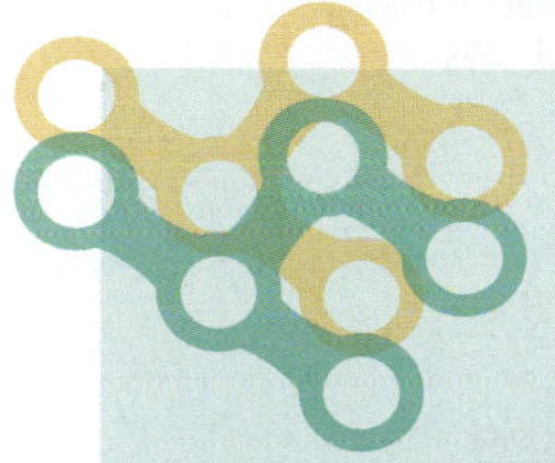

LINKING BUSINESS LAW to Accounting and Finance

Banking in a Period of Crisis

In this chapter, you learned about the bank-customer relationship as well as a bank's duty to honor checks and accept deposits. In the macroeconomics courses that your business school offers, the focus on the banking sector is quite different. Among other things, the courses examine banking panics and bank runs and their effects on the economy.

Bank Runs during the Great Depression

A *bank run* occurs when depositors simultaneously rush to convert their bank deposits into currency because they believe that the assets of their bank are not sufficient to cover its liabilities—the customers' deposits. The largest number of bank runs in modern history occurred during the Great Depression in the 1930s, when nine thousand banks failed.

Enter Deposit Insurance

To prevent bank runs, the federal government set up a system of deposit insurance to assure depositors that their deposits would be safe. The Federal Deposit Insurance Corporation (FDIC) and the Federal Savings and Loan Insurance Corporation (FSLIC) were created in the 1930s to insure deposits. In 1971, the National Credit Union Shares Insurance Fund (NCUSIF) was added to insure credit union deposits. Although the names and form of some of these organizations have changed over the years, the principle remains the same: to insure all accounts in these financial institutions against losses up to a specified limit. In 1933, each account was insured up to $2,500. During the recession that started in December 2007, the federal government wanted to make sure that no banking panics would occur. Therefore, in 2008 the insurance limit was raised to $250,000. Although federal insurance for bank deposits may seem like a good idea, some problems are associated with it.

Moral Hazard: An Unintended Consequence of Deposit Insurance

In your finance courses, you learn that the riskier a loan is, the higher the interest rate that a lending institution can charge the borrower. Bank managers must weigh the trade-off between risk and return

Continued

when deciding which loan applicants should receive funds. Loans to poor credit risks offer high profits, assuming that the borrowers actually pay off their debts. Good credit risks are more likely to pay their debts, but can obtain loans at lower rates.

Particularly since the fall of 2008, when the federal deposit insurance limit was increased to $250,000 per account, managers have had a greater incentive to make risky loans. By doing so, in the short run the banks make higher profits, and the managers receive higher salaries and bonuses. If some of these risky loans are not repaid, what is the likely outcome? A bank's losses are limited because the federal government—you, the taxpayer—will cover any shortfall between the bank's assets and its liabilities. Consequently, federal deposit insurance means that banks get to enjoy all of the profits of risk taking without bearing all of the consequences of that risk taking.

Thus, an unintended consequence of federal deposit insurance is to encourage *moral hazard*. It creates an incentive for bank managers to take more risks in their lending policies than they would otherwise.

Critical Thinking

Imagine the United States without federal deposit insurance. What are some of the mechanisms that would arise to "punish" bank managers who acted irresponsibly?

Key Terms

cashier's check 495
certified check 497
clearinghouse 509
collecting bank 505
depositary bank 505
digital cash 511
electronic fund transfer (EFT) 509
e-money 511
Federal Reserve System 509
intermediary bank 505
overdraft 498
payor bank 505
Regulation E 510
smart card 512
stale check 499
stop-payment order 499
stored-value card 511
traveler's check 496

Chapter Summary: Checks and Banking in the Digital Age

Checks (See pages 495–497.)	1. *Cashier's check*—A check drawn by a bank on itself (the bank is both the drawer and the drawee) and purchased by a customer. In effect, the bank assumes responsibility for paying the check, thus making the check nearly the equivalent of cash. 2. *Traveler's check*—An instrument on which a financial institution is both the drawer and the drawee. The purchaser must provide his or her signature as a countersignature for a traveler's check to become a negotiable instrument. 3. *Certified check*—A check for which the drawee bank certifies in writing that it has set aside funds from the drawer's account to ensure payment of the check on presentation. On certification, the drawer and all prior indorsers are completely discharged from liability on the check.
The Bank-Customer Relationship (See pages 497–498.)	1. *Creditor-debtor relationship*—A customer and a bank have a creditor-debtor relationship (the bank is the debtor because it holds the customer's funds on deposit). 2. *Agency relationship*—Because a bank must act in accordance with the customer's orders in regard to the customer's deposited money, an agency relationship also arises—the bank is the agent for the customer, who is the principal. 3. *Contractual relationship*—The bank's relationship with its customer is also contractual. Both the bank and the customer assume certain contractual duties when a customer opens a bank account.
Bank's Duty to Honor Checks (See pages 499–504.)	Generally, a bank has a duty to honor its customers' checks, provided that the customers have sufficient funds on deposit to cover the checks [UCC 4–401(a)]. The bank is liable to its customers for actual damages proved to be due to wrongful dishonor [UCC 4–402]. 1. *Overdraft*—The bank has a right to charge a customer's account for any item properly payable, even if the charge results in an overdraft. [UCC 4–401] 2. *Postdated check*—The bank may charge a postdated check against a customer's account, unless the customer notifies the bank of the postdating in time to allow the bank to act on the customer's notice before paying on the check [UCC 4–401]. 3. *Stale check*—The bank is not obligated to pay an uncertified check presented more than six months after its date, but the bank may do so in good faith without liability [UCC 4–404].

Chapter Summary: Checks and Banking in the Digital Age—Continued

Bank's Duty to Honor Checks —Continued	4. *Stop-payment order*—The customer (or a person authorized to draw on the account) must make a stop-payment order in time for the bank to have a reasonable opportunity to act. Oral orders are binding for only fourteen days unless they are confirmed in writing. Written or electronic orders are effective for only six months unless renewed in writing [UCC 4–403]. The bank is liable for wrongful payment over a timely stop-payment order to the extent that the customer suffers a loss. 5. *Death or incompetence of a customer*—So long as the bank does not know of the death or incompetence of a customer, the bank can pay an item without liability. Even with knowledge of a customer's death, a bank can honor or certify checks (in the absence of a stop-payment order) for ten days after the date of the customer's death [UCC 4–405]. 6. *Forged signature or alteration*—The customer has a duty to examine account statements with reasonable care on receipt and to notify the bank promptly of any forged signatures or alterations. On a series of forged signatures or alterations by the same wrongdoer, examination and report must be made within thirty calendar days of receipt of the first statement containing a forged or altered item[UCC 4–406]. The customer's failure to comply with these rules releases the bank from liability unless the bank failed to exercise reasonable care, in which case liability may be apportioned according to a comparative negligence standard. Regardless of care or lack of care, the customer is barred from holding the bank liable after one year for forged customer signatures or alterations and after three years for forged indorsements.
Bank's Duty to Accept Deposits (See pages 504–509.)	A bank has a duty to accept deposits made by its customers into their accounts. Funds from deposited checks must be made available to customers according to a schedule mandated by the Expedited Funds Availability Act of 1987 and Regulation CC. A bank also has a duty to collect payment on any checks deposited by its customers. When checks deposited by customers are drawn on other banks, the check-collection process comes into play. 1. *Definitions of banks*—UCC 4–105 provides the following definitions of banks involved in the collection process: a. Depositary bank—The first bank to accept a check for payment. b. Payor bank—The bank on which a check is drawn. c. Collecting bank—Any bank except the payor bank that handles a check during the collection process. d. Intermediary bank—Any bank except the payor bank or the depositary bank to which an item is transferred in the course of the collection process. 2. *Check collection between customers of the same bank*—A check payable by the depositary bank that receives it is an "on-us item." If the bank does not dishonor the check by the opening of the second banking day following its receipt, the check is considered paid [UCC 4–215(e)(2)]. 3. *Check collection between customers of different banks*—Each bank in the collection process must pass the check on to the next appropriate bank before midnight of the next banking day following its receipt [UCC 4–108, 4–202(b), 4–302]. 4. *How the Federal Reserve System clears checks*—The Federal Reserve System facilitates the check-clearing process by serving as a clearinghouse for checks. 5. *Electronic check presentment*—When checks are presented electronically, items are encoded with information (such as the amount of the check) that is read and processed by other banks' computers. Sometimes, a check is retained at its place of deposit, and only its image or description is presented for payment under a Federal Reserve agreement, clearinghouse rule, or other agreement [UCC 4–110].
Electronic Fund Transfers (See pages 509–511.)	1. *Types of EFT systems*— a. Automated teller machines (ATMs). b. Point-of-sale systems. c. Direct deposits and withdrawals. d. Internet payment systems. 2. *Consumer fund transfers*—Consumer fund transfers are governed by the Electronic Fund Transfer Act (EFTA) of 1978. The EFTA is basically a disclosure law that sets forth the rights and duties of the bank and the customer with respect to EFT systems. Banks must comply strictly with EFTA requirements. 3. *Commercial transfers*—Article 4A of the UCC, which has been adopted by almost all of the states, governs fund transfers not subject to the EFTA or other federal or state statutes.
E-Money and Online Banking (See pages 511–512.)	1. *New forms of e-payments*—These include stored-value cards and smart cards. 2. *Current online banking services*— a. Bill consolidation and payment. b. Transferring funds among accounts. c. Applying for loans.

ExamPrep

ISSUE SPOTTERS

1. Lyn writes a check for $900 to Mac, who indorses the check in blank and transfers it to Nan. She presents the check to Omega Bank, the drawee bank, for payment. Omega does not honor the check. Is Lyn liable to Nan? Could Lyn be subject to criminal prosecution? Why or why not? **(See page 498.)**
2. Roni writes a check for $700 to Sela. Sela indorses the check in blank and transfers it to Titus, who alters the check to read $7,000 and presents it to Union Bank, the drawee, for payment. The bank cashes it. Roni discovers the alteration and sues the bank. How much, if anything, can Roni recover? From whom can the bank recover this amount? **(See page 503.)**

– Check your answers to the Issue Spotters against the answers provided in Appendix E at the end of this text.

BEFORE THE TEST

Go to www.cengagebrain.com, enter the ISBN 9781133273561, and click on "Find" to locate this textbook's Web site. Then, click on "Access Now" under "Study Tools," and select Chapter 19 at the top. There, you will find a Practice Quiz that you can take to assess your mastery of the concepts in this chapter, as well as Flashcards, a Glossary of important terms, and Video Questions (when assigned).

For Review

Answers to the even-numbered questions in this For Review section can be found in Appendix F at the end of this text.

1. What type of check does a bank agree in advance to accept when the check is presented for payment?
2. When may a bank properly dishonor a customer's check without being liable to the customer?
3. What duties does the Uniform Commercial Code impose on a bank's customers with regard to forged and altered checks? What are the consequences if a customer is negligent in performing those duties?
4. What is electronic check presentment, and how does it differ from the traditional check-clearing process?
5. What are the four most common types of electronic fund transfers?

Business Scenarios and Case Problems

19–1 Forged Checks. Roy Supply, Inc., and R. M. R. Drywall, Inc., had checking accounts at Wells Fargo Bank. Both accounts required all checks to carry two signatures—that of Edward Roy and that of Twila June Moore, both of whom were executive officers of both companies. Between January 2006 and March 2008, the bank honored hundreds of checks on which Roy's signature was forged by Moore. On January 31, 2009, Roy and the two corporations notified the bank of the forgeries and then filed a suit in a California state court against the bank, alleging negligence. Who is liable for the amounts of the forged checks? Why? **(See pages 500–502.)**

19–2 Question with Sample Answer—Customer Negligence. Gary goes grocery shopping and carelessly leaves his checkbook in his shopping cart. His checkbook, with two blank checks remaining, is stolen by Dolores. On May 5, Dolores forges Gary's name on a check for $100 and cashes the check at Gary's bank, Citizens Bank of Middletown. Gary has not reported the loss of his blank checks to his bank. On June 1, Gary receives his monthly bank statement from Citizens Bank that includes the forged check, but he does not notice the item nor does he examine his bank statement. On June 20, Dolores forges Gary's last check. This check is for $1,000 and is cashed at Eastern City Bank, a bank with which Dolores has previously done business. Eastern City Bank puts the check through the collection process, and Citizens Bank honors it. On July 1, on receipt of his bank statement and canceled checks covering June transactions, Gary discovers both forgeries and immediately notifies Citizens Bank. Dolores cannot be found. Gary claims that Citizens Bank must recredit his account for both checks, as his signature was forged. Discuss fully Gary's claim. **(See pages 500–501.)**

—For a sample answer to Question 19–2, go to Appendix G at the end of this text.

19–3 Spotlight on Embezzlement—Forged Drawers' Signatures. In December 1999, Spacemakers of America, Inc., hired Jenny Triplett as a bookkeeper. Triplett was responsible for maintaining the company checkbook and reconciling it with the monthly statements from SunTrust Bank. She also handled invoices from vendors. Spacemakers' president, Dennis Rose, reviewed the invoices and signed the checks to pay them, but no other employee checked Triplett's work. By the end of her first full month of employment, Triplett had forged six checks totaling more than $22,000, all payable to Triple M Entertainment, which was not a Spacemakers vendor. By October 2000, Triplett had forged fifty-nine more checks, totaling more than $475,000. A SunTrust employee became suspicious of an item that required sight inspection under the bank's fraud detection standards, which exceeded those of other banks in the area. Triplett was arrested. Spacemakers sued SunTrust Bank, which filed a motion for summary judgment. On what basis could the bank avoid liability? In whose favor should the court rule, and why? [*Spacemakers of America, Inc. v. SunTrust Bank,* 271 Ga.App. 335, 609 S.E.2d 683 (2005)] **(See pages 500–502.)**

19–4 **Bank's Duty of Care.** When Arnett Gertrude was diagnosed with cancer, she added her nephew, Jack Scriber, as an authorized signatory to her checking account. Before Gertrude died, Scriber wrote checks on the account to transfer nearly all of the $600,000 in the account to his own account. After Gertrude's death, Bobbie Caudill, the administrator of her estate, discovered the withdrawals and filed a suit against the bank. What is the relationship between a bank and its customer? Is the bank liable in this case? Why or why not? [*Caudill v. Salyersville National Bank,* 2010 WL 45882 (Ky.App. 2010)] **(See page 500.)**

19–5 **Forged Drawers' Signatures.** Debbie Brooks and Martha Tingstrom lived together. Tingstrom handled their finances. For five years, Brooks did not look at any statements concerning her accounts. When she finally reviewed the statements, she discovered that Tingstrom had taken $85,500 from Brooks's checking account with Transamerica Financial Advisors. Tingstrom had forged Brooks's name on six checks paid between one and two years earlier. Another year passed before Brooks filed a suit against Transamerica. Who is most likely to suffer the loss for the checks paid with Brooks's forged signature? Why? [*Brooks v. Transamerica Financial Advisors,* 57 So.3d 1153 (La.App. 2 Cir. 2011)] **(See pages 500–502.)**

19–6 **Case Problem with Sample Answer—Honoring Checks.** Adley Abdulwahab (Wahab) opened an account on behalf of W Financial Group, LLC, with Wells Fargo Bank. Wahab was one of three authorized signers on the account. Five months later, Wahab withdrew $1,701,250 from W Financial's account to buy a cashier's check payable to Lubna Lateef. Wahab visited a different Wells Fargo branch and deposited the check into the account of CA Houston Investment Center, LLC. Wahab was the only authorized signer on this account. Lateef never received or indorsed the check. W Financial filed a suit to recover the amount. Applying the rules for payment on a forged indorsement, who is liable? [*Jones v. Wells Fargo Bank,* 666 F.3d 955 (5th Cir. 2012)] **(See page 502.)**

—For a sample answer to Problem 19–6, go to Appendix H at the end of this text.

19–7 **A Question of Ethics—Forged Signatures.** From the 1960s, James Johnson served as Bradley Union's personal caretaker and assistant, and was authorized by Union to handle his banking transactions. Louise Johnson, James's wife, wrote checks on Union's checking account to pay his bills, normally signing the checks "Brad Union." Branch Banking & Trust Co. (BB&T) managed Union's account. In December 2000, on the basis of Union's deteriorating mental and physical condition, a North Carolina state court declared him incompetent. Douglas Maxwell was appointed as Union's guardian. Maxwell "froze" Union's checking account and asked BB&T for copies of the canceled checks, which were provided by July 2001. Maxwell believed that Union's signature on the checks had been forged. In August 2002, Maxwell contacted BB&T, which refused to recredit Union's account. Maxwell filed a suit on Union's behalf in a North Carolina state court against BB&T. [*Union v. Branch Banking & Trust Co.,* 176 N.C.App. 711, 627 S.E.2d 276 (2006)] **(See pages 500–502.)**

1. Before Maxwell's appointment, BB&T sent monthly statements and canceled checks to Union, and Johnson reviewed them, but no unauthorized signatures were ever reported. On whom can liability be imposed in the case of a forged drawer's signature on a check? What are the limits set by Section 4–406(f) of the Uniform Commercial Code? Should Johnson's position, Union's incompetence, or Maxwell's appointment affect the application of these principles? Explain.
2. Why was this suit brought against BB&T? Is BB&T liable? If not, who is? Why? Regardless of any violations of the law, did anyone act unethically in this case? If so, who and why?

Critical Thinking and Writing Assignments

19–8 **Critical Legal Thinking.** Since the 1990 revision of Article 4, a bank is no longer required to include the customer's canceled checks when it sends monthly statements to the customer. A bank may simply itemize the checks (by number, date, and amount). It may provide photocopies of the checks as well but is not required to do so. What implications do the revised rules have for bank customers in terms of liability for unauthorized signatures and indorsements? **(See pages 500–501.)**

19–9 **Business Law Critical Thinking Group Assignment.** On January 5, Brian drafts a check for $3,000 drawn on Southern Marine Bank and payable to his assistant,

Shanta. Brian puts last year's date on the check by mistake. On January 7, before Shanta has had a chance to go to the bank, Brian is killed in an automobile accident. Southern Marine Bank is aware of Brian's death. On January 10, Shanta presents the check to the bank, and the bank honors the check by payment to Shanta. Later, Brian's widow, Joyce, claims that because the bank knew of Brian's death and also because the check was by date over one year old, the bank acted wrongfully when it paid Shanta. Joyce, as executor of Brian's estate and sole heir by his will, demands that Southern Marine Bank recredit Brian's estate for the check paid to Shanta.

1. The first group will determine whether the bank acted wrongfully by honoring Brian's check and paying Shanta.
2. The second group will assess whether Joyce has a valid claim against Southern Marine Bank for the amount of the check paid to Shanta.
3. A third group will assume that the check Brian drafted was on his business account rather than on his personal bank account and that he had two partners in the business. Would a business partner be in a better position to force Southern Marine Bank to recredit Brian's account than his widow? Why or why not?

19–10 Case Analysis Question. Go to Appendix I at the end of this text and examine the excerpt of Case No. 4, *NBT Bank, N.A. v. First National Community Bank.* Review and then brief the case, making sure that your brief answers the following questions.

1. **Issue:** The main issue in this case concerned the effect of an item on the face of a check and a specific time period. What was the item, what was the time period, and what was the question?
2. **Rule of Law:** Liability was assessed in this case according to what rule of law?
3. **Applying the Rule of Law:** What was most significant to the court's determination of the measure of damages?
4. **Conclusion:** How did the court resolve the dispute among the parties in this case?

CHAPTER 20

(Ying Geng/Shutterstock.com)

Secured Transactions

CHAPTER OUTLINE

- The Terminology of Secured Transactions
- Creation of a Security Interest
- Perfection of a Security Interest
- The Scope of a Security Interest
- Priorities
- Rights and Duties of Debtors and Creditors
- Default

LEARNING OBJECTIVES

The five learning objectives below are designed to help improve your understanding of the chapter. After reading this chapter, you should be able to answer the following questions:

1. What is a security interest? Who is a secured party? What is a security agreement? What is a financing statement?
2. What three requirements must be met to create an enforceable security interest?
3. What is the most common method of perfecting a security interest under Article 9?
4. If two secured parties have perfected security interests in the collateral of the debtor, which party has priority to the collateral on the debtor's default?
5. What rights does a secured creditor have on the debtor's default?

"I will pay you some, and, as most debtors do, promise you infinitely."
—William Shakespeare, 1564–1616 (English dramatist and poet)

When buying or leasing goods, debtors frequently pay some portion of the price now and promise to pay the remainder in the future, as William Shakespeare observed in the chapter-opening quotation. Logically, sellers and lenders do not want to risk nonpayment, so they usually will not sell goods or lend funds unless the payment is somehow guaranteed.

Secured Transaction Any transaction in which the payment of a debt is guaranteed, or secured, by personal property owned by the debtor or in which the debtor has a legal interest.

Whenever the payment of a debt is guaranteed, or *secured,* by personal property owned or held by the debtor, the transaction becomes known as a **secured transaction.** The concept of the secured transaction is as essential to modern business practice as the concept of credit. As you will see later in this chapter, secured transactions can now take place online.

Article 9 of the Uniform Commercial Code (UCC) governs secured transactions in personal property. Personal property includes accounts, agricultural liens, *chattel paper* (documents or records evidencing a debt secured by personal property), and *fixtures* (certain property that is attached to land—see Chapter 36). Personal property also includes other types of intangible property, such as negotiable instruments and patents.

LEARNING OBJECTIVE 1
What is a security interest? Who is a secured party? What is a security agreement? What is a financing statement?

Secured Party A creditor who has a security interest in the debtor's collateral, including a seller, lender, cosigner, or buyer of accounts or chattel paper.

Debtor Under Article 9 of the UCC, any party who owes payment or performance of a secured obligation.

Security Interest Any interest in personal property or fixtures that secures payment or performance of an obligation.

Security Agreement An agreement that creates or provides for a security interest between the debtor and a secured party.

Collateral Under Article 9 of the UCC, the property subject to a security interest.

Financing Statement A document filed by a secured creditor with the appropriate official to give notice to the public of the creditor's security interest in collateral belonging to the debtor named in the statement.

Default Failure to pay a debt when it is due.

LEARNING OBJECTIVE 2
What three requirements must be met to create an enforceable security interest?

The Terminology of Secured Transactions

In every state, the UCC's terminology is now uniformly used in all documents that involve secured transactions. A brief summary of the UCC's definitions of terms relating to secured transactions follows.

1. A **secured party** is any creditor who has a *security interest* in the *debtor's collateral.* This creditor can be a seller, a lender, a cosigner, or even a buyer of accounts or chattel paper [UCC 9–102(a)(72)].
2. A **debtor** is the "person" who *owes payment* or other performance of a secured obligation [UCC 9–102(a)(28)].
3. A **security interest** is the *interest* in the collateral (such as personal property or fixtures) that *secures payment or performance of an obligation* [UCC 1–201(37)].
4. A **security agreement** is an *agreement* that *creates* or provides for a *security interest* [UCC 9–102(a)(73)]. (In other words, it is the contract in which a debtor agrees to give a creditor the right to take his or her property in the event of default.)
5. **Collateral** is the subject of the *security interest* [UCC 9–102(a)(12)].
6. A **financing statement**—referred to as the UCC-1 form—is the *instrument normally filed to give public notice to third parties* of the *secured party's security interest* [UCC 9–102(a)(39)].

These basic definitions form the concept under which a debtor-creditor relationship becomes a secured transaction relationship (see Exhibit 20.1 below).

Creation of a Security Interest

A creditor has two main concerns if the debtor **defaults** (fails to pay the debt as promised): (1) Can the debt be satisfied through the possession and (usually) sale of the collateral? (2) Will the creditor have priority over any other creditors or buyers who may have rights in the same collateral? These two concerns are met through the creation and perfection of a security interest. We begin by examining how a security interest is created.

To become a secured party, the creditor must obtain a security interest in the collateral of the debtor. Three requirements must be met for a creditor to have an enforceable security interest:

1. Unless the creditor has possession of the collateral, there must be a written or authenticated security agreement that clearly describes the collateral subject to the security interest and is signed or authenticated by the debtor.
2. The secured party must give something of value to the debtor.
3. The debtor must have "rights" in the collateral.

Exhibit 20.1 Secured Transactions—Concept and Terminology

In a security agreement, a debtor and a creditor agree that the creditor will have a security interest in collateral in which the debtor has rights. In essence, the collateral secured the loan and ensures the creditor of payment should the debtor default.

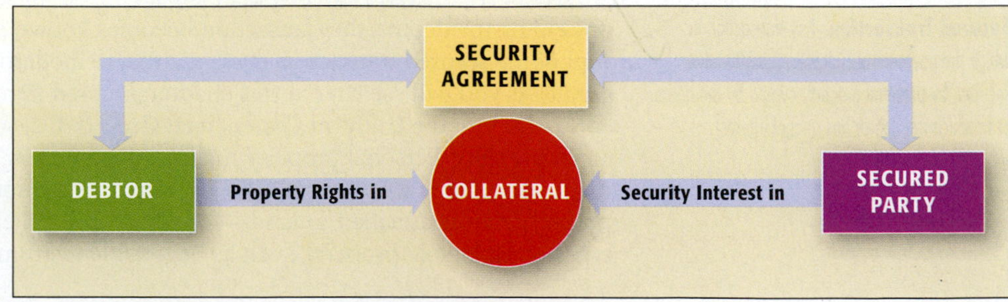

Attachment In a secured transaction, the process by which a secured creditor's interest "attaches" to the collateral and the creditor's security interest becomes enforceable.

Once these requirements have been met, the creditor's rights are said to attach to the collateral. **Attachment** gives the creditor an enforceable security interest in the collateral [UCC 9–203].[1]

EXAMPLE 20.1 To furnish his new office suite, Yuri applies for a credit card at an office supply store. The application contains a clause stating that the store will retain a security interest in the goods that he buys with the card until he has paid for the goods in full. This application would be considered a *written security agreement,* which is the first requirement for an enforceable security interest. The goods that Yuri buys with the card are the *something of value* from the secured party (the second requirement), and his ownership interest in those goods is the *right* that he has in them (the third requirement). Thus, the requirements for an enforceable security interest are met. When Yuri buys something with the card, the store's rights attach to the purchased goods. •

Written or Authenticated Security Agreement

When the collateral is *not* in the possession of the secured party, the security agreement must be either written or authenticated, and it must describe the collateral. Here, *authentication* means to sign, execute, or adopt any symbol on an electronic record that verifies that the person signing has the intent to adopt or accept the record [UCC 9–102(a)(7)(69)].

The reason authentication is acceptable is to provide for electronic filing (the filing process will be discussed later). (See this chapter's *Adapting the Law to the Online Environment* feature below for a discussion of a type of secured transaction that is performed online.)

A security agreement must contain a description of the collateral that reasonably identifies it. Generally, such phrases as "all the debtor's personal property" or "all the

1. Note that in the context of judicial liens, to be discussed in Chapter 21, the term *attachment* has a different meaning. In that context, it refers to a court-ordered seizure and taking into custody of property before the securing of a court judgment for a past-due debt.

ADAPTING THE LAW TO THE ONLINE ENVIRONMENT

SECURED TRANSACTIONS ONLINE

When you buy something online, you typically have to use your credit card, make an electronic fund transfer, or send a check before the goods that you bought are sent to you. If you are buying a large-ticket item, such as a car, you are not about to send funds without being assured that you will receive the car in the condition promised. Enter the concept of escrow.

Escrow Accounts

Escrow accounts are commonly used in real estate transactions (see Chapter 22), but they are also useful for smaller transactions, particularly those done on the Internet. An escrow account involves three parties—the buyer, the seller, and a trusted third party that collects, holds, and disperses funds according to instructions from the buyer and seller. Escrow services are provided by licensed and regulated escrow companies. For example, if you buy a car on the Internet, you and the seller agree on an escrow company to which you send the funds. When you receive the car and are satisfied with it, the escrow company releases the funds to the seller. This is a type of secured transaction.

Enter Escrow.com

One of the best-known online escrow firms is Escrow.com, which had provided escrow services for more than $1 billion in secured transactions by 2012. All of its escrow services are offered via its Web site and provided independently by Internet Escrow Services, one of its operating subsidiaries. Escrow.com is particularly useful for transactions that involve an international buyer or seller. It has become the recommended transaction settlement service for AutoTrader, Resale Weekly, Cars.com, eBay Motors, and Flippa.com.

Critical Thinking

How do online escrow services reduce Internet fraud?

(Gedhau67/iStockphoto.com)

Most clothing retailers do not pay cash for their inventories. What do they do instead?

debtor's assets" would *not* constitute a sufficient description [UCC 9–108(c)].

Secured Party Must Give Value

The secured party must give something of value to the debtor. Some examples of value include a binding commitment to extend credit or consideration to support a simple contract [UCC 1–204]. Normally, the value given by a secured party is in the form of a direct loan or a commitment to sell goods on credit.

Debtor Must Have Rights in the Collateral

The debtor must have rights in the collateral, which means that the debtor must have a current or a future ownership interest in or right to obtain possession of that collateral. For instance, a retail seller-debtor can give a secured party a security interest not only in existing inventory owned by the retailer but also in *future* inventory to be acquired by the retailer. (A common misconception is that the debtor must have title to the collateral to have rights in it, but this is not a requirement.)

Perfection of a Security Interest

Perfection The legal process by which secured parties protect themselves against the claims of third parties who may wish to have their debts satisfied out of the same collateral. It is usually accomplished by filing a financing statement with the appropriate government official.

Perfection is the legal process by which secured parties protect themselves against the claims of third parties who may wish to have their debts satisfied out of the same collateral. Whether a secured party's security interest is perfected or unperfected can have serious consequences for the secured party if, for example, the debtor defaults on the debt or files for bankruptcy.

What if the debtor has borrowed from two different creditors, using the same property as collateral for both loans? If the debtor defaults on both loans, which of the two creditors has first rights to the collateral? In this situation, the creditor with a perfected security interest will prevail.

LEARNING OBJECTIVE 3
What is the most common method of perfecting a security interest under Article 9?

Perfection can be accomplished in several ways, although the usual method is by filing a financing statement in the appropriate government office. Where or how a security interest is perfected sometimes depends on the type of collateral. Collateral is generally divided into *tangible collateral* (collateral that can be seen, felt, and touched) and *intangible collateral* (collateral that consists of or generates rights).

Exhibit 20.2 on the facing page summarizes various classifications of collateral and the methods of perfecting a security interest in collateral falling within each classification.[2]

Perfection by Filing

The most common means of perfection is by filing a *financing statement*—a document that gives public notice to third parties of the secured party's security interest—with the office of the appropriate government official. The security agreement itself can also be filed to perfect the security interest. The financing statement must provide the names of the debtor and the secured party, and must indicate the collateral covered by the financing statement. A uniform financing statement form is now used in all states [see UCC 9–521].

---

2. There are additional classifications, such as agricultural liens, investment property, and commercial tort claims. For definitions of these types of collateral, see UCC 9–102(a)(5), (a)(13), and (a)(49).

Exhibit 20.2 Selected Types of Collateral and Their Methods of Perfection

TANGIBLE COLLATERAL		METHOD OF PERFECTION
All things that are movable at the time the security interest attaches (such as livestock) or that are attached to the land, including timber to be cut and growing crops.		
1. Consumer Goods [UCC 9–301, 9–303, 9–309(1), 9–310(a), 9–313(a)]	Goods used or bought primarily for personal, family, or household purposes—for example, household furniture [UCC 9–102(a)(23)].	For purchase-money security interest, attachment (that is, the creation of a security interest) is sufficient. For boats, motor vehicles, and trailers, filing or compliance with a certificate-of-title statute is required. For other consumer goods, general rules of filing or possession apply.
2. Equipment [UCC 9–301, 9–310(a), 9–313(a)]	Goods bought for or used primarily in business (and not part of inventory or farm products)—for example, a delivery truck [UCC 9–102(a)(33)].	Filing or (rarely) possession by secured party.
3. Farm Products [UCC 9–301, 9–310(a), 9–313(a)]	Crops (including aquatic goods), livestock, or supplies produced in a farming operation—for example, ginned cotton, milk, eggs, and maple syrup [UCC 9–102(a)(34)].	Filing or (rarely) possession by secured party.
4. Inventory [UCC 9–301, 9–310(a), 9–313(a)]	Goods held by a person for sale or under a contract of service or lease; raw materials held for production and work in progress [UCC 9–102(a)(48)].	Filing or (rarely) possession by secured party.
5. Accessions [UCC 9–301, 9–310(a), 9–313(a)]	Personal property that is so attached, installed, or fixed to other personal property (goods) that it becomes a part of these goods—for example, a DVD player installed in an automobile [UCC 9–102(a)(1)].	Filing or (rarely) possession by secured party (same as personal property being attached).
INTANGIBLE COLLATERAL		**METHOD OF PERFECTION**
Nonphysical property that exists only in connection with something else.		
1. Chattel Paper [UCC 9–301, 9–310(a), 9–312(a), 9–313(a), 9–314(a)]	A writing or writings (record or records) that evidence both a monetary obligation and a security interest in goods and software used in goods—for example, a security agreement or a security agreement and promissory note. *Note:* If the record or records consist of information stored in an electronic medium, the collateral is called *electronic chattel paper.* If the information is inscribed on a tangible medium, it is called *tangible chattel paper* [UCC 9–102(a)(11), (a)(31), and (a)(78)].	Filing or possession or control by secured party.
2. Instruments [UCC 9–301, 9–309(4), 9–310(a), 9–312(a) and (e), 9–313(a)]	A negotiable instrument, such as a check, note, certificate of deposit, draft, or other writing that evidences a right to the payment of money and is not a security agreement or lease but rather a type that can ordinarily be transferred (after indorsement, if necessary) by delivery [UCC 9–102(a)(47)].	Except for temporary perfected status, filing or possession. For the sale of promissory notes, perfection can be by attachment (automatically on the creation of the security interest).
3. Accounts [UCC 9–301, 9–309(2) and (5), 9–310(a)]	Any right to receive payment for the following: (a) any property, real or personal, sold, leased, licensed, assigned, or otherwise disposed of, including intellectual licensed property; (b) services rendered or to be rendered, such as contract rights; (c) policies of insurance; (d) secondary obligations incurred; (e) use of a credit card; (f) winnings of a government-sponsored or government-authorized lottery or other game of chance; and (g) health-care insurance receivables, defined as an interest or claim under a policy of insurance to payment for health-care goods or services provided [UCC 9–102(a)(2) and (a)(46)].	Filing required except for certain assignments that can be perfected by attachment (automatically on the creation of the security interest).
4. Deposit Accounts [UCC 9–104, 9–304, 9–312(b), 9–314(a)]	Any demand, time, savings, passbook, or similar account maintained with a bank [UCC 9–102(a)(29)].	Perfection by control, such as when the secured party is the bank in which the account is maintained or when the parties have agreed that the secured party can direct the disposition of funds in a particular account.
5. General Intangibles [UCC 9–301, 9–309(3), 9–310(a) and (b)(8)]	Any personal property (or debtor's obligation to make payments on such) other than that defined above [UCC 9–102(a)(42)], including software that is independent from a computer or other good [UCC 9–102(a)(44), (a)(61), and (a)(75)].	Filing only (for copyrights, with the U.S. Copyright Office), except a sale of a payment intangible by attachment (automatically on the creation of the security interest).

(SimplyCreativePhotography/iStockphoto.com)

When a bank finances the purchase of a tractor, how does it perfect its security interest in that tractor?

Communication of the financing statement to the appropriate filing office, together with the correct filing fee, or the acceptance of the financing statement by the filing officer constitutes a filing [UCC 9–516(a)]. The word *communication* means that the filing can be accomplished electronically [UCC 9–102(a)(18)]. Once completed, filings are indexed in the name of the debtor so that they can be located by subsequent searchers. A financing statement may be filed even before a security agreement is made or a security interest attaches [UCC 9–502(d)].

The Debtor's Name The UCC requires that a financing statement be filed under the name of the debtor [UCC 9–502(a)(1)]. Slight variations in names normally will not be considered misleading if a search of the filing office's records, using a standard computer search engine routinely used by that office, would disclose the filings [UCC 9–506(c)].[3]

If the debtor is identified by the correct name at the time the financing statement is filed, the secured party's interest retains its priority even if the debtor later changes his or her name. Because most states use electronic filing systems, UCC 9–503 sets out some detailed rules for determining when the debtor's name as it appears on a financing statement is sufficient.

1. *Corporations.* For corporations, which are organizations that have registered with the state, the debtor's name on the financing statement must be "the name of the debtor indicated on the public record of the debtor's jurisdiction of organization" [UCC 9–503(a)(1)].
2. *Trusts.* If the debtor is a trust or a trustee with respect to property held in trust, the financing statement must disclose this information and provide the trust's name as specified in its official documents [UCC 9–503(a)(3)].
3. *Individuals and organizations.* For all others, the financing statement must disclose "the individual or organizational name of the debtor" [UCC 9–503(a)(4)(A)]. The word *organization* includes unincorporated associations, such as clubs, churches, joint ventures, and general partnerships. If an organizational debtor does not have a group name, the names of the individuals in the group must be listed.
4. *Trade names.* Providing only the debtor's trade name (or a fictitious name), such as the name Pete's Plumbing when it is not a distinct legal entity, in a financing statement is *not* sufficient for perfection [UCC 9–503(c)].

Changes in the Debtor's Name If the debtor's name changes, the financing statement remains effective for collateral the debtor acquired before or within four months after the name change. Unless an amendment to the financing statement is filed within this four-month period, collateral acquired by the debtor after the four-month period is unperfected [UCC 9–507(b) and (c)]. A one-page uniform financing statement amendment form is available for filing name changes and for other purposes.

PREVENTING LEGAL DISPUTES

Debtors frequently identify themselves by and change their trade names. This can make it difficult to find out whether an individual debtor's collateral is subject to a prior perfected security interest. For instance, a business named Bob's Automotive has two owners, but when one of them decides to leave, the trade name might become Specialized Auto Repair. Searching the records using the existing owner's name and the new trade name might not reveal a prior perfected security interest

3. If the name listed in the financing statement is so inaccurate that a search using the standard search engine will not disclose the debtor's name, then the financing statement is deemed seriously misleading under UCC 9–506. See also UCC 9–507, which governs the effectiveness of financing statements found to be seriously misleading.

from when the business was jointly owned and operating under a different name. Keep this in mind when making loans or extending credit. When searching the records, find out if the business has used any other names in the past and include those former names in your search. Remember that the key to determining if a security interest has been perfected is whether the financing statement adequately notifies other potential creditors that a security interest exists. If a search of the records using the debtor's correct name would disclose the interest, the filing is generally sufficient. To prevent legal problems, make sure that no other creditor has a prior interest in the property being used as collateral, and file the financing statement under the correct name.

"O.K., folks, let's move along. I'm sure you've all seen someone qualify for a loan before."

Description of the Collateral

Both the security agreement and the financing statement must describe the collateral in which the secured party has a security interest. The security agreement must describe the collateral because no security interest in goods can exist unless the parties agree on which goods are subject to the security interest. The financing statement must also describe the collateral because the purpose of filing the statement is to give public notice of the fact that certain goods of the debtor are subject to a security interest. For land-related security interests, a legal description of the realty is also required [UCC 9–502(b)].

Sometimes, the descriptions in the two documents vary. The description in the security agreement must be more precise than the description in the financing statement, which is allowed to be more general. **EXAMPLE 20.2** A security agreement for a commercial loan to a manufacturer may list all of the manufacturer's equipment subject to the loan by serial number. The financing statement for the equipment may simply state "all equipment owned or hereafter acquired." •

The UCC permits broad, general descriptions in the financing statement, such as "all assets" or "all personal property." Generally, whenever the description in a financing statement accurately describes the agreement between the secured party and the debtor, the description is sufficient [UCC 9–504].

In the following case, a secured party filed a financing statement claiming a security interest in livestock. The court had to decide if the secured party had perfected her security interest even though the collateral could not be identified by the security agreement alone.

Case 20.1

In re Baker

United States Bankruptcy Court, Northern District of New York, 465 Bankr. 359 (2012).
www.nynb.uscourts.gov[a]

How can cows be properly identified for a financing statement?

FACTS In 2006, Jeanne Angell sold fifty-eight dairy cows to Richard and Amanda Baker. Angell gave the Bakers a certificate of registration for each cow. Each certificate listed the cow's name, provided a diagram with the animal's distinctive markings, and identified Angell as a former owner. In 2008,

a. In the left-hand column, click on "Judges' Court Decisions." In the result, click on "Judge Davis" and, then, on "2012 Decisions." When that page opens, scroll down to February 29, 2012, and click on the link to access the opinion.

Case 20.1—Continues next page

Case 20.1—Continued

the parties executed a security agreement, and Angell attempted to perfect her security interest by filing a financing statement. Both documents identified the cows by name and by their ear tag identification numbers. The Bakers then sold twenty-two of the cows at auction, and Angell was entitled to the proceeds because of what the Bakers owed her. Sixteen of the cows, however, either did not have ear tags or had tag numbers that did not match the financing statement. The auction company therefore identified the cows using their names—which appeared on both the certificates and the financing statement—and the diagrams on the certificates. The Bakers later filed for bankruptcy. In court, the trustee argued that Angell had not perfected her security interest because the financing statement did not describe the cows in sufficient detail.

ISSUE Did Angell's financing statement describe the cows in enough detail for Angell to perfect her security interest?

DECISION Yes. The bankruptcy court determined that Angell had perfected her security interest and was entitled to the proceeds from the auction.

REASON UCC Section 9–108 provides that a description of the collateral "is sufficient . . . if it reasonably identifies what is described" in a way that makes it "objectively determinable." A financing statement, the court noted, need only provide "notice that a person may have a security interest." Once a third party has such notice, he or she is obligated to inquire further to determine which specific property is covered. In this case, Angell's financing statement provided notice that Angell might have a security interest in the cows. Although the financing statement contained incorrect ear tag identification numbers, a third party could have reasonably identified the cows using their names and the diagrams on their certificates of registration. In fact, the auction company did precisely that. Thus, Angell's financing statement had reasonably identified the cows and perfected her security interest.

CRITICAL THINKING—Legal Consideration *Do the UCC's rules concerning collateral descriptions encourage parties to enter into security agreements? Why or why not?*

Where to File

In most states, a financing statement must be filed centrally in the appropriate state office, such as the office of the secretary of state, in the state where the debtor is located. An exception occurs when the collateral consists of timber to be cut, fixtures, or items to be extracted—such as oil, coal, gas, and minerals [UCC 9–301(3) and (4), 9–502(b)]. In those circumstances, the financing statement is filed in the county where the collateral is located.

The state in which a financing statement should be filed depends on the *debtor's location,* not the location of the collateral [UCC 9–301]. The debtor's location is determined as follows [UCC 9–307]:

1. For *individual debtors,* it is the state of the debtor's principal residence.
2. For an *organization that is registered with the state,* such as a corporation or limited liability company, it is the state in which the organization is registered. Thus, if a debtor is incorporated in Maryland and has its chief executive office in New York, a secured party would file the financing statement in Maryland—the state of the debtor's organizational formation.
3. For *all other entities,* it is the state in which the business is located or, if the debtor has more than one office, the place from which the debtor manages its business operations and affairs.

Consequences of an Improper Filing

Any improper filing renders the security interest unperfected and reduces the secured party's claim in bankruptcy to that of an unsecured creditor. For instance, if the debtor's name on the financing statement is seriously misleading or if the collateral is not sufficiently described in the financing statement, the filing may not be effective.

CASE EXAMPLE 20.3 Corona Fruits & Veggies, Inc., loaned funds to Armando Munoz Juarez, a strawberry farmer. The documents set out Juarez's full name, but Juarez generally went by the name "Munoz" and signed the documents "Armando Munoz." Corona filed financing statements that identified the debtor as "Armando Munoz." In December, using some of the same collateral, Juarez obtained funds from Frozsun Foods, Inc., which filed a financing statement that identified the debtor as "Armando Juarez."

By the next July, Juarez owed Corona $230,482.52 and Frozsun $19,648.52. When Juarez did not repay his debts, Corona and Frozsun filed a suit against him. The court concluded that the identification of the debtor as "Armando Munoz" in Corona's financing statement was seriously misleading. Frozsun's interest thus took priority because its financing statement was recorded properly.[4]

The UCC financing statement includes a section for listing an "Additional Debtor." Is it misleading to include the names of additional debtors on an attached list but not refer to that list in the financing statement? The court in the following case considered this question.

4. *Corona Fruits & Veggies, Inc. v. Frozsun Foods, Inc.*, 143 Cal.App.4th 319, 48 Cal.Rptr.3d 868 (2006).

Case 20.2

In re Camtech Precision Manufacturing, Inc.

United States Bankruptcy Court,
Southern District of Florida,
443 Bankr. 190 (2011).

(ewg3D/iStockphoto.com)

Camtech Precision Manufacturing makes precision parts for military equipment.

FACTS Camtech Precision Manufacturing, Inc., makes precision parts and assemblies for aerospace and defense customers. Camtech is a subsidiary of R&J National Enterprises, Inc. (R&J). R&J had a nearly $4 million line of credit with Regions Bank in 2010. Regions Bank filed a series of financing statements with the appropriate state offices in Florida and New York to perfect security interests in the assets of R&J and its related companies. All of the statements were filed on the UCC financing statement form used in all states. The forms listed R&J as the debtor in the "Debtor" box and Avstar Aircraft Accessories, Inc., another R&J subsidiary, as an additional debtor in the "Additional Debtor" box.

Neither box, however, indicated that there were more debtors. Attached to each form was a sheet of plain paper that listed Camtech Precision Manufacturing, Inc., and Avstar Fuel Systems, Inc., as additional debtors. In 2010, R&J and the others filed a petition in a federal bankruptcy court to declare bankruptcy (discussed in Chapter 21). A committee of the companies' unsecured creditors asked the court to rule that Regions' financing statements failed to perfect the bank's security interest in the assets of Camtech and Avstar Fuel.

ISSUE Was each financing statement seriously misleading because it did not mention or refer to the additional debtors (including Camtech) that were listed on an attached page?

DECISION Yes. The court found that Regions' statements were seriously misleading and ineffective to perfect security interests in the assets of Camtech and Avstar Fuel. Because Regions failed to perfect its security interests, the bank was an unsecured creditor with respect to those two companies' assets.

REASON Florida and New York have approved the use of a standard UCC form for listing additional debtors. Regions did not use this form, but merely listed Camtech and Avstar Fuel as additional debtors on a single sheet of plain paper attached to each financing statement. Minor errors in a financing statement do not undercut its effectiveness. Appending a list of additional debtors without a reference in the "Additional Debtor" box on the financing statement, however, was "an error and an omission that made the financing statements seriously misleading." Searches of the two states' records failed to reveal any financing statement that identified Regions as a secured creditor of Camtech or Avstar Fuel. This failure rendered Regions' financing statements ineffective to perfect its security interests in the assets of Camtech and Avstar Fuel. With respect to these assets, the bank's claim was reduced to that of an unsecured creditor.

WHAT IF THE FACTS WERE DIFFERENT? *Suppose that searches of the Florida and New York records had revealed that Regions was a secured creditor of Camtech and Avstar Fuel. Would the result have been different in this case? Explain.*

Perfection without Filing

In two types of situations, security interests can be perfected without filing a financing statement. The first occurs when the collateral is transferred into the possession of the secured party. The second occurs when the security interest can be perfected on attachment (without a filing and without having to possess the goods) [UCC 9–309].

The phrase *perfected on attachment* means that these security interests are automatically perfected at the time of their creation. Two of the more common security interests that are perfected on attachment are a *purchase-money security interest* in consumer goods (defined and explained shortly) and an assignment of a beneficial interest in a decedent's estate [UCC 9–309(1), (13)].

Perfection by Possession

In the past, one of the most common means of obtaining financing was to **pledge** certain collateral as security for the debt and transfer the collateral into the creditor's possession. When the debt was paid, the collateral was returned to the debtor. Article 9 of the UCC retained the common law pledge and the principle that the security agreement need not be in writing to be enforceable if the collateral is transferred to the secured party [UCC 9–310, 9–312(b), 9–313].

Pledge A security device in which personal property is transferred into the possession of the creditor as security for the payment of a debt and retained by the creditor until the debt is paid.

EXAMPLE 20.4 Sheila needs cash to pay for a medical procedure. She gets a loan for $4,000 from Trent. As security for the loan, she gives him a promissory note on which she is the payee. Even though the agreement to hold the note as collateral was oral, Trent has a perfected security interest and does not need to file a financing statement. No other creditor of Sheila's can attempt to recover the promissory note from Trent in payment for other debts. •

For most collateral, possession by the secured party is impractical because it denies the debtor the right to use or derive income from the property to pay off the debt. **EXAMPLE 20.5** Jed, a farmer, takes out a loan to finance the purchase of a large corn harvester and uses the equipment as collateral. Clearly, the purpose of the purchase would be defeated if Jed transferred the collateral into the creditor's possession, because he would not be able to use the equipment to harvest his corn. • Certain items, however, such as stocks, bonds, negotiable instruments, and jewelry, are commonly transferred into the creditor's possession when they are used as collateral for loans.

Perfection by Attachment—The Purchase-Money Security Interest in Consumer Goods

Under the UCC, fourteen types of security interests are perfected automatically at the time they are created [UCC 9–309]. The most common is the **purchase-money security interest (PMSI)** in *consumer goods* (items bought primarily for personal, family, or household purposes). A PMSI in consumer goods is created when a person buys goods and the seller or lender agrees to extend credit for part or all of the purchase price of the goods. The entity that extends the credit and obtains the PMSI can be either the seller (a store, for example) or a financial institution that lends the buyer the funds with which to purchase the goods [UCC 9–102(a)(2)].

Purchase-Money Security Interest (PMSI) A security interest that arises when a seller or lender extends credit for part or all of the purchase price of goods purchased by a buyer.

Automatic Perfection A PMSI in consumer goods is perfected automatically at the time of a credit sale—that is, at the time the PMSI is created. The seller in this situation does not need to do anything more to perfect her or his interest. **EXAMPLE 20.6** To purchase a high-definition 3D television from ABC Television, Inc., for $2,500, Jamie signs an agreement to pay $1,000 down and $100 per month until the balance, plus interest, is fully paid. ABC is to retain a security interest in the television until full payment has been made. Because the security interest was created as part of the purchase agreement, it is a PMSI in consumer goods. ABC does not need to do anything else to perfect its security interest. •

"People may live as much retired from the world as they like, but sooner or later, they find themselves debtor or creditor to someone."

Johann Wolfgang von Goethe, 1749–1832 (German writer)

Exceptions to the Rule of Automatic Perfection There are exceptions to the rule of automatic perfection. First, certain types of security interests that are subject to other federal or

(Yuri Arcurs/Shutterstock.com)

If this couple pays for a TV on credit, does the creditor automatically obtain a security interest?

state laws may require additional steps to be perfected [UCC 9–311]. For instance, most states have certificate-of-title statutes that establish perfection requirements for specific goods, such as automobiles, trailers, boats, mobile homes, and farm tractors. If a consumer in these jurisdictions purchases a boat, for example, the secured party will need to file a certificate of title with the appropriate state official to perfect the PMSI.

A second exception involves PMSIs in nonconsumer goods, such as livestock or a business's inventory, which are not automatically perfected.

Effective Time Duration of Perfection

Continuation Statement A statement that, if filed within six months prior to the expiration date of the original financing statement, continues the perfection of the security interest for another five years.

A financing statement is effective for five years from the date of filing [UCC 9–515]. If a **continuation statement** is filed within six months *prior to* the expiration date, the effectiveness of the original statement is continued for another five years, starting with the expiration date of the first five-year period [UCC 9–515(d), (e)]. The effectiveness of the statement can be continued in the same manner indefinitely. Any attempt to file a continuation statement outside the six-month window will render the continuation ineffective, and the perfection will lapse at the end of the five-year period.

If a financing statement lapses, the security interest that had been perfected by the filing now becomes unperfected. A purchaser for value can acquire the collateral as if the security interest had never been perfected [UCC 9–515(c)].

The Scope of a Security Interest

As previously mentioned, a security interest can cover property that the debtor has ownership or possessory rights in the present or in the future. Therefore, security agreements can cover the proceeds from the sale of collateral, after-acquired property, and future advances, as discussed next.

Proceeds

Proceeds Under Article 9 of the UCC, whatever is received when collateral is sold or disposed of in some other way.

Proceeds are whatever cash or property is received when collateral is sold or disposed of in some other way [UCC 9–102(a)(64)]. A security interest in the collateral gives the secured party a security interest in the proceeds acquired from the sale of that collateral. **EXAMPLE 20.7** People's Bank has a perfected security interest in the inventory of a retail seller of heavy farm machinery. The retailer sells a tractor out of this inventory to Jacob Dunn, a farmer, who is by definition a *buyer in the ordinary course of business* (this term will be discussed later in the chapter). Dunn agrees, in a security agreement, to make monthly payments to the retailer for a period of twenty-four months. If the retailer goes into default on the loan from the bank, the bank is entitled to the remaining payments Dunn owes to the retailer as proceeds. •

A security interest in proceeds perfects automatically on the *perfection* of the secured party's security interest in the original collateral and remains perfected for twenty days after the debtor receives the proceeds. One way to extend the twenty-day automatic perfection period is to provide for extended coverage in the original security agreement [UCC 9–315(c), (d)]. This is typically done when the collateral is the type that is likely to be sold, such as a retailer's inventory—for example, of computers or cell phones. The UCC also permits a security interest in identifiable cash proceeds to remain perfected after twenty days [UCC 9–315(d)(2)].

After-Acquired Property

After-Acquired Property Property that is acquired by the debtor after the execution of a security agreement.

After-acquired property is property that the debtor acquired after the execution of the security agreement. The security agreement may provide for a security interest in after-acquired property, such as a debtor's inventory [UCC 9–204(1)]. Generally, the debtor will purchase new inventory to replace the inventory sold. The secured party wants this newly acquired inventory to be subject to the original security interest. Thus, the after-acquired property clause continues the secured party's claim to any inventory acquired thereafter. (This is not to say that the original security interest will always take priority over the rights of all other creditors with regard to this after-acquired inventory, as will be discussed later.)

EXAMPLE 20.8 Amato buys factory equipment from Bronson on credit, giving as security an interest in all of her equipment—both what she is buying and what she already owns. The security interest with Bronson contains an after-acquired property clause. Six months later, Amato pays cash to another seller of factory equipment for more equipment. Six months after that, Amato goes out of business before she has paid off her debt to Bronson. Bronson has a security interest in all of Amato's equipment, even the equipment bought from the other seller. •

Future Advances

Often, a debtor will arrange with a bank to have a *continuing line of credit* under which the debtor can borrow funds intermittently. Advances against lines of credit can be subject to a properly perfected security interest in certain collateral. The security agreement may provide that any future advances made against that line of credit are also subject to the security interest in the same collateral [UCC 9–204(c)]. Future advances do not have to be of the same type or otherwise related to the original advance to benefit from this type of **cross-collateralization.**[5] Cross-collateralization occurs when an asset that is not the subject of a loan is used to secure that loan.

Cross-Collateralization The use of an asset that is not the subject of a loan to collateralize that loan.

EXAMPLE 20.9 Stroh is the owner of a small manufacturing plant with equipment valued at $1 million. He has an immediate need for $50,000 of working capital, so he obtains a loan from Midwestern Bank and signs a security agreement, putting up all of his equipment as security. The bank properly perfects its security interest. The security agreement provides that Stroh can borrow up to $500,000 in the future, using the same equipment as collateral for any future advances. In this situation, Midwestern Bank does not have to execute a new security agreement and perfect a security interest in the collateral each time an advance is made, up to a cumulative total of $500,000. For priority purposes, each advance is perfected as of the date of the *original* perfection. •

The Floating-Lien Concept

A security agreement that provides for a security interest in proceeds, in after-acquired property, or in collateral subject to future advances by the secured party (or in all three) is often characterized as a **floating lien.** This type of security interest continues in the collateral or proceeds even if the collateral is sold, exchanged, or disposed of in some other way.

Floating Lien A security interest in proceeds, after-acquired property, or collateral subject to future advances by the secured party (or all three). The security interest is retained even when the collateral changes in character, classification, or location.

A Floating Lien in Inventory

Floating liens commonly arise in the financing of inventories. A creditor is not interested in *specific* pieces of inventory, which are constantly changing, so the lien "floats" from one item to another, as the inventory changes.

EXAMPLE 20.10 Cascade Sports, Inc., is an Oregon corporation that operates as a cross-country ski dealer and has a line of credit with Portland First Bank to finance its inventory of cross-country skis. Cascade and Portland First enter into a security agreement

5. See official Comment 5 to UCC 9–204.

that provides for coverage of proceeds, after-acquired inventory, present inventory, and future advances. Portland First perfects its security interest in the inventory by filing centrally with the office of the secretary of state in Oregon. One day, Cascade sells a new pair of the latest cross-country skis and receives a used pair in trade. That same day, Cascade purchases two new pairs of cross-country skis from a local manufacturer for cash. Later that day, to meet its payroll, Cascade borrows $8,000 from Portland First Bank under the security agreement.

Portland First gets a perfected security interest in the used pair of skis under the proceeds clause, has a perfected security interest in the two new pairs of skis purchased from the local manufacturer under the after-acquired property clause, and has the new amount of funds advanced to Cascade secured on all of the above collateral by the future-advances clause. All of this is accomplished under the original perfected security interest. The various items in the inventory have changed, but Portland First still has a perfected security interest in Cascade's inventory. Hence, it has a floating lien in the inventory. ●

A Floating Lien in a Shifting Stock of Goods The concept of the floating lien can also apply to a shifting stock of goods. The lien can start with raw materials, follow them as they become finished goods and inventories, and continue as the goods are sold and are turned into accounts receivable, chattel paper, or cash.

Priorities

When more than one party claims an interest in the same collateral, which has priority? The UCC sets out detailed rules to answer this question. Although in many situations the party who has a perfected security interest will have priority, there are exceptions.

KNOW THIS

Secured creditors—perfected or not—have priority over unsecured creditors.

General Rules of Priority

The basic rule is that when more than one security interest has been perfected in the same collateral, the first security interest to be perfected (or filed) has priority over any security interests that are perfected later. If only one of the conflicting security interests has been perfected, then that security interest has priority. If none of the security interests have been perfected, then the first security interest that attaches has priority. The UCC's rules of priority can be summarized as follows:

LEARNING OBJECTIVE 4

If two secured parties have perfected security interests in the collateral of the debtor, which party has priority to the collateral on the debtor's default?

1. *A perfected security interest has priority over unsecured creditors and unperfected security interests*. When two or more parties have claims to the same collateral, a perfected secured party's interest has priority over the interests of most other parties [UCC 9–322(a)(2)]. This includes priority to the proceeds from a sale of collateral resulting from a bankruptcy (giving the perfected secured party rights superior to that of the bankruptcy trustee, which will be discussed in Chapter 21).
2. *Conflicting perfected security interests.* When two or more secured parties have perfected security interests in the same collateral, the first to perfect (by filing or taking possession of the collateral) generally has priority [UCC 9–322(a)(1)].
3. *Conflicting unperfected security interests*. When two conflicting security interests are unperfected, the first to attach (be created) has priority [UCC 9–322(a)(3)]. This is sometimes called the "first-in-time" rule.

In the following case, the court had to determine which of two conflicting security interests in a mobile home took priority.

Case 20.3

Citizens National Bank of Jessamine County v. Washington Mutual Bank

Court of Appeals of Kentucky, 309 S.W.3d 792 (2010).

(Shank_ali/iStockphoto.com)
Do mobile homes need a title certificate?

FACTS Rose Day transferred land and a mobile home to Anthony and Kim Reynolds. The deed was recorded at the appropriate county office. The deed description did not mention the mobile home, but it was clear that the Reynoldses were purchasing both from Day. The Reynoldses executed a mortgage conveying a security interest in the property to Washington Mutual Bank. There was no mention of the mobile home in the mortgage. The Reynoldses also did not obtain a title certificate to the mobile home in their names, and the mobile home remained personal property rather than real property.

Several years later, the Reynoldses obtained a second mortgage from Citizens National Bank of Jessamine County. Again, there was no description of the mobile home in the mortgage. When the Reynoldses subsequently defaulted on both loans, Washington Mutual filed a complaint claiming lien priority on both the real estate and the mobile home. Citizens was listed as an interested party and was served with the complaint. After being served, Citizens and the Reynoldses executed a title lien statement regarding the mobile home, which was recorded in the county clerk's office. The trial court ruled that the filing of the complaint and notice of the lawsuit by Washington Mutual created a priority claim in the mobile home. Citizens appealed that decision, claiming that its security interest in the mobile home had priority.

ISSUE Was Citizens' security interest in the mobile home the first in time to attach?

DECISION Yes. The state appellate court reversed the trial court's decision. Washington Mutual's filing of a complaint and notice of a pending lawsuit did *not* create a priority lien on the mobile home but applied only to the interest in the real estate. Citizens' security interest in the mobile home had priority because it was perfected when Citizens recorded the title lien.

REASON The UCC explicitly "provides that the sole means of perfecting a security interest in personal property for which a certificate of title is issued is by placing a notation of the lien on the certificate of title." The court reasoned that Citizens (and the Reynoldses) had so perfected its lien, but Washington Mutual had not. "It is fundamental that unperfected security interests are subordinate to perfected security interests." It was irrelevant that Citizens had knowledge that Washington Mutual had filed a notice of a claim to both the real property and the mobile home. "Because Washington Mutual failed to perfect its lien under the mandates of the [UCC], its interest in the Reynoldses' manufactured [mobile] home must necessarily give way to Citizens' perfected claim."

WHAT IF THE FACTS WERE DIFFERENT? *Suppose that the mobile home had been permanently affixed to the land and was regarded as real property. In that situation, which of the two security interests would have taken priority? Discuss.*

Exceptions to the General Rules of Priority

Under some circumstances, on the debtor's default, the perfection of a security interest will not protect a secured party against certain other third parties having claims to the collateral. For example, the UCC provides that in some instances a PMSI, properly perfected,[6] will prevail over another security interest in after-acquired collateral, even though the other was perfected first. We discuss some significant exceptions to the general rules of priority in the following subsections.

Buyers in the Ordinary Course of Business

Under the UCC, a person who buys "in the ordinary course of business" takes the goods free from any security interest created by the seller *even if the security interest is perfected and the buyer knows of its*

6. Recall that, with some exceptions (such as motor vehicles), a PMSI in *consumer goods* is automatically perfected—no filing is necessary. A PMSI that is *not* in consumer goods must still be perfected, however.

existence [UCC 9–320(a)]. In other words, a buyer in the ordinary course will have priority even if a previously perfected security interest exists as to the goods. The rationale for this rule is obvious: if buyers could not obtain the goods free and clear of any security interest the merchant had created—for example, in inventory—the free flow of goods in the marketplace would be hindered.

A *buyer in the ordinary course of business* is a person who in good faith, and without knowledge that the sale violates the rights of another in the goods, buys goods in the ordinary course from a person in the business of selling goods of that kind [UCC 1–201(9)]. Note that the buyer can know about the existence of a perfected security interest, so long as he or she does not know that buying the goods violates the rights of any third party.

CASE EXAMPLE 20.11 Dublin Auto Sales granted a security interest in its inventory to Heartland Bank for a $300,000 line of credit. Heartland perfected its security interest by filing financing statements with the appropriate state offices. Dublin Auto used $9,000 of its credit to buy a Ford F-150 and $13,000 to buy a Jeep Cherokee and delivered the certificates of title, which designated Dublin Auto as the owner, to Heartland. Later, Dublin Auto sold the F-150 for $15,386.63 and the Jeep for $14,045. National City Bank financed both purchases. New certificates of title designated the buyers as the owners and Heartland as the "first lienholder." Heartland received none of the funds from the sales and sued National City, claiming that Heartland's security interest in the vehicles took priority. The court, however, ruled in National City's favor. Because the purchasers were buyers in the ordinary course of business, Heartland's security interest in the vehicles was extinguished at the time they were sold.[7] •

"A man who pays his bills on time is soon forgotten."

Oscar Wilde, 1854–1900
(Irish author and poet)

Buyers of the Collateral The UCC recognizes that there are certain types of buyers whose interests in purchased goods could conflict with those of a perfected secured party on the debtor's default. These include not only buyers in the ordinary course of business (as just discussed), but also buyers of farm products, chattel paper, instruments, documents, or securities. The UCC sets down special rules of priority for these types of buyers. See Exhibit 20.3 on the following page for a review of the rules on the priority of claims to a debtor's collateral.

Rights and Duties of Debtors and Creditors

The security agreement itself determines most of the rights and duties of the debtor and the secured party. The UCC, however, imposes some rights and duties that are applicable unless the security agreement states otherwise.

Information Requests

At the time of filing, a secured party has the option of furnishing a copy of the financing statement being filed to the filing officer and requesting that the filing officer make a note of the file number, the date, and the hour of the original filing on the copy [UCC 9–523(a)]. The filing officer must send this copy to the person designated by the secured party or to the debtor, if the debtor makes the request.

Under UCC 9–523(c) and (d), a filing officer must also give information to a person who is contemplating obtaining a security interest from a prospective debtor. The filing officer must issue a certificate that provides information on possible perfected financing statements with respect to the named debtor.

7. *Heartland Bank v. National City Bank,* 171 Ohio App.3d 132, 869 N.E.2d 746 (2007).

Exhibit 20.3 Priority of Claims to a Debtor's Collateral

PARTIES	PRIORITY
Perfected Secured Party versus Unsecured Parties and Creditors	A perfected secured party's interest has priority over the interests of most other parties, including unsecured creditors, unperfected secured parties, subsequent lien creditors, trustees in bankruptcy, and buyers who do not purchase the collateral in the ordinary course of business.
Perfected Secured Party versus Perfected Secured Party	Between two perfected secured parties in the same collateral, the general rule is that the first in time of perfection is the first in right to the collateral [UCC 9–322(a)(1)].
Perfected Secured Party versus Perfected PMSI	A PMSI, even if second in time of perfection, has priority in certain situations if it is perfected within twenty days after the debtor takes possession [UCC 9–324(a)].
Perfected Secured Party versus Purchaser of Debtor's Collateral	1. *Buyer of goods in the ordinary course of the seller's business*—Buyer prevails over a secured party's security interest, even if perfected and even if the buyer knows of the security interest [UCC 9–320(a)]. 2. *Buyer of consumer goods purchased outside the ordinary course of business*—Buyer prevails over a secured party's interest, even if perfected by attachment, providing the buyer purchased as follows: a. For value. b. Without actual knowledge of the security interest. c. For use as a consumer good. d. Prior to the secured party's perfection by *filing* [UCC 9–320(b)]. 3. *Buyer of chattel paper*—Buyer prevails if the buyer: a. Gave new value in making the purchase. b. Took possession in the ordinary course of the buyer's business. c. Took without knowledge of the security interest [UCC 9–330]. 4. *Buyer of instruments, documents, or securities*—Buyer who is a holder in due course, a holder to whom negotiable documents have been duly negotiated, or a bona fide purchaser of securities has priority over a previously perfected security interest [UCC 9–330(d), 9–331(a)]. 5. *Buyer of farm products*—Buyer from a farmer takes free and clear of perfected security interests unless, where permitted, a secured party files centrally an effective financing statement (EFS) or the buyer receives proper notice of the security interest before the sale.
Unperfected Secured Party versus Unsecured Creditor	An unperfected secured party prevails over unsecured creditors and creditors who have obtained judgments against the debtor but who have not begun the legal process to collect on those judgments [UCC 9–201(a)].

Release and Assignment

A secured party can release all or part of any collateral described in the financing statement, thereby terminating its security interest in that collateral. The release is recorded by filing a uniform amendment form [UCC 9–512, 9–521(b)]. A secured party can also assign all or part of the security interest to a third party (the assignee). The assignee becomes the secured party of record if the assignment is filed by use of a uniform amendment form [UCC 9–514, 9–521(a)].

Confirmation or Accounting Request by Debtor

The debtor may believe that the amount of the unpaid debt or the list of collateral subject to the security interest is inaccurate. The debtor has the right to request a confirmation of the unpaid debt or list of collateral [UCC 9–210]. The debtor is entitled to one request without charge every six months.

The secured party must comply with the debtor's confirmation request by authenticating and sending to the debtor an accounting within fourteen days after the request is received. Otherwise, the secured party will be held liable for any loss suffered by the debtor, plus $500 [UCC 9–210, 9–625(f)].

Termination Statement

When the debtor has fully paid the debt, if the secured party perfected the security interest by filing, the debtor is entitled to have a termination statement filed. Such a statement demonstrates to the public that the filed perfected security interest has been terminated [UCC 9–513].

Whenever consumer goods are involved, the secured party *must* file a termination statement (or, alternatively, a release) within one month of the final payment or within twenty days of receiving the debtor's authenticated demand, whichever is earlier [UCC 9–513(b)].

Default

LEARNING OBJECTIVE 5
What rights does a secured creditor have on a debtor's default?

Article 9 defines the rights, duties, and remedies of the secured party and of the debtor on the debtor's default. Should the secured party fail to comply with her or his duties, the debtor is afforded various rights and remedies.

The topic of default is one of great concern to secured lenders and to the lawyers who draft security agreements. What constitutes default is not always clear. In fact, Article 9 does not define the term. Consequently, parties are encouraged in practice—and by the UCC—to include in their security agreements the conditions that will constitute a default [UCC 9–601, 9–603]. Often, these critical terms are shaped by the creditor in an attempt to provide the maximum protection possible. The ultimate terms, however, may not go beyond the limitations imposed by the good faith requirement and the unconscionability provisions of the UCC.

Any breach of the terms of the security agreement can constitute default. Nevertheless, default occurs most commonly when the debtor fails to meet the scheduled payments or becomes bankrupt.

KNOW THIS

A trespass to land occurs when a person, without permission, enters onto another's land and is established as a trespasser.

Basic Remedies

The rights and remedies set out in UCC 9–601(a) and (b) are *cumulative* [UCC 9–601(c)]. Therefore, if a creditor is unsuccessful in enforcing rights by one method, he or she can pursue another method. Generally, a secured party's remedies can be divided into the two basic categories discussed next.

What does the self-help remedy mean?

(Photo by John Moore/Getty Images)

Repossession of the Collateral—The Self-Help Remedy On the debtor's default, a secured party can take peaceful possession of the collateral without the use of judicial process [UCC 9–609(b)]. This provision is often referred to as the "self-help" provision of Article 9. The UCC does not define *peaceful possession,* however. The general rule is that the collateral has been taken peacefully if the secured party can take possession without committing (1) trespass onto land, (2) assault and/or battery, or (3) breaking and entering.

On taking possession, the secured party may either retain the collateral for satisfaction of the debt [UCC 9–620] or resell the goods and apply the proceeds toward the debt [UCC 9–610].

Judicial Remedies Alternatively, a secured party can relinquish the security interest and use any judicial remedy available, such as obtaining a judgment on the underlying

Execution The implementation of a court's decree or judgment.

Levy The legal process of obtaining funds through the seizure and sale of nonexempt property, usually done after a writ of execution has been issued.

debt, followed by execution and levy. (**Execution** is the implementation of a court's decree or judgment. **Levy** is the legal process of obtaining funds through the seizure and sale of nonexempt property, usually done after a writ of execution has been issued.)

Execution and levy are rarely undertaken unless the collateral is no longer in existence or has substantially declined in value and the debtor has other assets available that may be legally seized to satisfy the debt [UCC 9–601(a)].[8]

(AP Photo/Paul Efird, Knoxville News Sentinel)

Sometimes when a secured party keeps the collateral after default, it sells the goods at a public auction, as shown above.

Disposition of Collateral

Once default has occurred and the secured party has obtained possession of the collateral, the secured party has several options. The secured party can (1) retain the collateral in full or partial satisfaction of the debt, or (2) sell, lease, license, or otherwise dispose of the collateral in any commercially reasonable manner and apply the proceeds toward satisfaction of the debt [UCC 9–602(7), 9–603, 9–610(a), 9–613, 9–620]. Any sale is always subject to procedures established by state law.

Retention of Collateral by the Secured Party

The UCC acknowledges that parties are sometimes better off if they do not sell the collateral. Therefore, a secured party may retain the collateral unless it consists of consumer goods and the debtor has paid 60 percent or more of the purchase price in a PMSI or debt in a non-PMSI—as will be discussed shortly [UCC 9–620(e)].

This general right, however, is subject to the following conditions:

1. The secured party must notify the debtor of its proposal to retain the collateral.
2. Notice is required unless the debtor has signed a statement renouncing or modifying her or his rights *after default* [UCC 9–620(a), 9–621].
3. If the collateral is consumer goods, the secured party does not need to give any other notice. In all other situations, the secured party must send notice to *any other secured party* from whom the secured party has received written or authenticated notice of a claim of interest in the collateral.
4. The secured party must also send notice to any other **junior lienholder** (one holding a lien that is subordinate to one or more other liens on the same property) who held a security interest (or statutory lien) in the collateral ten days before the debtor consented to the retention [UCC 9–621].

Junior Lienholder A party that holds a lien that is subordinate to one or more other liens on the same property.

If, within twenty days after the notice is sent, the secured party receives an objection sent by a person entitled to receive notification, the secured party must sell or otherwise dispose of the collateral (disposition procedures will be discussed shortly). If no written objection is received, the secured party may retain the collateral in full or partial satisfaction of the debtor's obligation [UCC 9–620(a), 9–621].

KNOW THIS

Conversion is a tort that involves depriving an owner of personal property without the owner's permission.

Consumer Goods

When the collateral is consumer goods and the debtor has paid 60 percent or more of the purchase price or loan amount, the secured party must sell or otherwise dispose of the repossessed collateral within ninety days [UCC 9–620(e), (f)]. Failure to comply opens the secured party to an action for conversion or other liability under UCC 9–625(b) and (c) unless the consumer-debtor signed a written statement *after default* renouncing or modifying the right to demand the sale of the goods [UCC 9–624].

8. Some assets are exempt from creditors' claims—see Chapter 21.

Disposition Procedures A secured party who chooses not to retain the collateral or who is required to sell it must resort to the disposition procedures prescribed in the UCC. The UCC allows substantial flexibility with regard to disposition. A secured party may sell, lease, license, or otherwise dispose of any or all of the collateral in its present condition or following any commercially reasonable preparation or processing [UCC 9–610(a)].

Notice Requirement The secured party must notify the debtor and other specified parties in writing ahead of time about the sale or disposition of the collateral. Notification is not required if the collateral is perishable, will decline rapidly in value, or is a type customarily sold on a recognized market [UCC 9–611(b), (c)]. The debtor may waive the right to receive this notice, but only after default [UCC 9–624(a)].

Must Be Done in a Commercially Reasonable Manner The collateral can be disposed of at public or private proceedings, but every aspect of the disposition's method, manner, time, and place must be commercially reasonable [UCC 9–610(b)]. Although the purpose of requiring a commercially reasonable disposition is to obtain a satisfactory price, the courts look at other factors besides price in determining reasonableness.

"If you think nobody cares if you're alive, try missing a couple of car payments."

Earl Wilson, 1907–1987
(American journalist)

CASE EXAMPLE 20.12 Shannon Hicklin bought a used Ford Explorer under an installment sales contract. When she fell three payments behind—still owing $5,741.65—Onyx Acceptance Corporation repossessed the car and sold it for $1,500 at a private auction. After deducting the costs of repossession and sale, there was a deficiency under the contract of $5,018.88. Onyx filed a suit to collect this amount from Hicklin.

Onyx claimed that the sale was commercially reasonable because the auction price ($1,500) was more than 50 percent of the estimated market value ($2,335). The court, however, found that the price alone was not enough to prove reasonableness. To do that, Onyx would have to show that every aspect of the sale was conducted in a commercially reasonable manner or, under UCC 9–627(b)(3), that the sale conformed with the reasonable commercial practices among dealers in that type of property. Onyx did not do either.[9] •

Proceeds from the Disposition

Proceeds from the disposition of collateral after default on the underlying debt are distributed in the following order:

1. Reasonable expenses incurred by the secured party in repossessing, storing, and reselling the collateral.
2. Balance of the debt owed to the secured party.
3. Junior lienholders who have made written or authenticated demands.
4. Unless the collateral consists of accounts, payment intangibles, promissory notes, or chattel paper, any surplus goes to the debtor [UCC 9–608(a); 9–615(a), (e)].

Noncash Proceeds

Whenever the secured party receives noncash proceeds from the disposition of collateral after default, the secured party must make a value determination and apply this value in a commercially reasonable manner [UCC 9–608(a)(3), 9–615(c)].

Deficiency Judgment

Deficiency Judgment A judgment against a debtor for the amount of a debt remaining unpaid after the collateral has been repossessed and sold.

Often, after proper disposition of the collateral, the secured party has not collected all that the debtor still owes. Unless otherwise agreed, the debtor is liable for any deficiency, and the creditor can obtain a **deficiency judgment** from a court to collect the deficiency.[10] Note, however, that if the underlying transaction was, for

9. *Hicklin v. Onyx Acceptance Corp.*, 970 A.2d 244 (Del.Sup.Ct. 2009).
10. As noted previously, the amount of the deficiency judgment may be reduced if the secured party failed to act in a commercially reasonable manner in disposing of the collateral.

instance, a sale of accounts or chattel paper, the debtor is entitled to any surplus or is liable for any deficiency only if the security agreement so provides [UCC 9–615(d), (e)].

How long should a secured party have to seek a deficiency judgment? Because of depreciation, the amount received from the sale of collateral is frequently less than the amount the debtor owes the secured party. As noted, the secured party can file a suit against the debtor in an attempt to collect the balance due. Practically speaking, however, debtors who have defaulted on a loan rarely have the cash to pay any deficiency. Article 9 does not contain a statute of limitations provision, so it is not clear how long secured parties have after default to file a deficiency suit against debtors. If a secured party waits until the debtor becomes solvent again, the court sometimes may not allow the suit. Is this fair? When creditors have sued debtors for deficiencies owed on repossessed cars, for instance, many courts apply the four-year limitation period in Article 2 because the transaction was a sale of goods, even though a security interest was involved.[11]

Redemption Rights

At any time before the secured party disposes of the collateral or enters into a contract for its disposition, or before the debtor's obligation has been discharged through the secured party's retention of the collateral, the debtor or any other secured party can exercise the right of *redemption* of the collateral. The debtor or other secured party can do this by tendering performance of all obligations secured by the collateral and by paying the expenses reasonably incurred by the secured party in retaking and maintaining the collateral [UCC 9–623].

11. See, for example, *Credit Acceptance Corp. v. Coates*, 2008 WL 3889424 (2008), in which the court observed that nine of the eleven states that have considered the issue concluded that installment contracts for the sale of a motor vehicle were governed by the limitations period of Article 2.

Reviewing . . . Secured Transactions

Paul Barton owned a small property-management company, doing business as Brighton Homes. In October, Barton went on a spending spree. First, he bought a Bose surround-sound system for his home from KDM Electronics. The next day, he purchased a Wilderness Systems kayak from Outdoor Outfitters, and the day after that he bought a new Toyota 4-Runner financed through Bridgeport Auto. Two weeks later, Barton purchased six new iMac computers for his office, also from KDM Electronics. Barton bought all of these items under installment sales contracts. Six months later, Barton's property-management business was failing, and he could not make the payments due on any of these purchases and thus defaulted on the loans. Using the information presented in the chapter, answer the following questions.

1. For which of Barton's purchases (the surround-sound system, the kayak, the 4-Runner, and the six iMacs) would the creditor need to file a financing statement to perfect its security interest?
2. Suppose that Barton's contract for the office computers mentioned only the name *Brighton Homes*. What would be the consequences if KDM Electronics filed a financing statement that listed only Brighton Homes as the debtor's name?
3. Which of these purchases would qualify as a PMSI in consumer goods?
4. Suppose that after KDM Electronics repossesses the surround-sound system, it decides to keep the system rather than sell it. Can KDM do this under Article 9? Why or why not?

DEBATE THIS A financing statement that does not have the debtor's exact name should still be effective because creditors should always be protected when debtors default.

Key Terms

after-acquired property 529
attachment 521
collateral 520
continuation statement 529
cross-collateralization 530
debtor 520
default 520
deficiency judgment 537
execution 536
financing statement 520
floating lien 530
junior lienholder 536
levy 536
perfection 522
pledge 528
proceeds 529
purchase-money security interest (PMSI) 528
secured party 520
secured transaction 519
security agreement 520
security interest 520

Chapter Summary: Secured Transactions

Creation of a Security Interest (See pages 520–522.)	1. Unless the creditor has possession of the collateral, there must be a written or authenticated security agreement that is signed or authenticated by the debtor and describes the collateral subject to the security interest. 2. The secured party must give value to the debtor. 3. The debtor must have rights in the collateral—some ownership interest in or right to obtain possession of the specified collateral.
Perfection of a Security Interest (See pages 522–529.)	The classification of collateral determines how and where a security interest is perfected (see Exhibit 20.2 on page 523). 1. *Perfection by filing*—The most common method of perfection is by filing a financing statement containing the names of the secured party and the debtor and indicating the collateral covered by the financing statement. The financing statement must be filed under the name of the debtor. Fictitious (trade) names normally are not sufficient. 2. *Perfection without filing*— a. By transfer of collateral—The debtor can transfer possession of the collateral to the secured party. A *pledge* is an example of this type of transfer. b. By attachment, such as the attachment of a purchase-money security interest (PMSI) in consumer goods. If the secured party has a PMSI in consumer goods, the secured party's security interest is perfected automatically. In all, fourteen types of security interests can be perfected by attachment.
The Scope of a Security Interest (See pages 529–531.)	A security agreement can cover the following types of property: 1. *Collateral in the present possession or control of the debtor.* 2. *Proceeds from a sale, exchange, or disposition of secured collateral.* 3. *After-acquired property*—A security agreement may provide that property acquired after execution of the agreement will also be secured by the agreement. This provision is often included in security agreements covering a debtor's inventory. 4. *Future advances*—A security agreement may provide that any future advances made against a line of credit will be subject to the initial security interest in the same collateral.
Priorities (See pages 531–533.)	See Exhibit 20.3 on page 534.
Rights and Duties of Debtors and Creditors (See pages 533–535.)	1. *Information request*—On request, the filing officer must send a statement listing the file number, the date, and the hour of the filing of the financing statement and other documents covering collateral of a particular debtor. 2. *Release and assignment*—A secured party may (a) release part or all of the collateral described in a filed financing statement, thus ending the creditor's security interest, or (b) assign part or all of the security interest to another party. 3. *Confirmation or accounting request by debtor*—If the debtor requests a confirmation of the unpaid debt or a list of the collateral, the secured party must send the debtor an authenticated accounting within fourteen days. 4. *Termination statement*—When a debt is paid, the secured party generally must file a *termination statement.* If the financing statement covers consumer goods, the termination statement must be filed by the secured party within one month after the debt is paid.
Default (See pages 535–538.)	On the debtor's default, the secured party may do either of the following: 1. Take possession (peacefully or by court order) of the collateral covered by the security agreement and then pursue one of two alternatives: a. Retain the collateral (unless the secured party has a PMSI in consumer goods and the debtor has paid 60 percent or more of the selling price or loan). This right is subject to the conditions listed on page 535. b. Dispose of the collateral in a commercially reasonable manner in accordance with the requirements of UCC 9–602(7), 9–603, 9–610(a), and 9–613. The proceeds are applied in the order listed on page 537. 2. Relinquish the security interest and use any judicial remedy available, such as proceeding to judgment on the underlying debt, followed by execution and levy on the nonexempt assets of the debtor.

ExamPrep

ISSUE SPOTTERS

1. Nero needs $500 to buy textbooks and other supplies. Olivia agrees to loan Nero $500, accepting Nero's computer as collateral. They put their agreement in writing. How can Olivia let other creditors know of her interest in the computer? **(See pages 522–529.)**
2. Liberty Bank loans Michelle $5,000 to buy a car, which is used as collateral to secure the loan. After repaying less than 50 percent of the loan, Michelle defaults. Liberty could repossess and keep the car, but the bank does not want it. What are the alternatives? **(See page 536.)**

—Check your answers to the Issue Spotters against the answers provided in Appendix E at the end of this text.

BEFORE THE TEST

Go to www.cengagebrain.com, enter the ISBN 9781133273561, and click on "Find" to locate this textbook's Web site. Then, click on "Access Now" under "Study Tools," and select Chapter 20 at the top. There, you will find a Practice Quiz that you can take to assess your mastery of the concepts in this chapter, as well as Flashcards, a Glossary of important terms, and Video Questions (when assigned).

For Review

Answers to the even-numbered questions in this For Review section can be found in Appendix F at the end of this text.

1. What is a security interest? Who is a secured party? What is a security agreement? What is a financing statement?
2. What three requirements must be met to create an enforceable security interest?
3. What is the most common method of perfecting a security interest under Article 9?
4. If two secured parties have perfected security interests in the collateral of the debtor, which party has priority to the collateral on the debtor's default?
5. What rights does a secured creditor have on the debtor's default?

Business Scenarios and Case Problems

20–1 Priority Disputes. Redford is a seller of electric generators. He purchases a large quantity of generators from a manufacturer, Mallon Corp., by making a down payment and signing an agreement to pay the balance over a period of time. The agreement gives Mallon Corp. a security interest in the generators and the proceeds. Mallon Corp. properly files a financing statement on its security interest. Redford receives the generators and immediately sells one of them to Garfield on an installment contract with payment to be made in twelve equal installments. At the time of the sale, Garfield knows of Mallon's security interest. Two months later, Redford goes into default on his payments to Mallon. Discuss Mallon's rights against purchaser Garfield in this situation. **(See page 531.)**

20–2 Question with Sample Answer—Perfection. Marsh has a prize horse named Arabian Knight. In need of working capital, Marsh borrows $5,000 from Mendez, who takes possession of Arabian Knight as security for the loan. No written agreement is signed. Discuss whether, in the absence of a written agreement, Mendez has a security interest in Arabian Knight. If Mendez does have a security interest, is it a perfected security interest? Explain. **(See page 522.)**

—For a sample answer to Question 20–2, go to Appendix G at the end of this text.

20–3 Spotlight on Radio Shack—Priorities. In June 1995, Michael and Debra Boudreaux, doing business as D&J Enterprises, Inc., bought a retail electronics store operated under a franchise from Radio Shack. The Boudreauxes borrowed from Cabool State Bank to pay for the business and signed loan documents and a financing statement, which identified the Boudreauxes as "Debtors." Elsewhere on the financing statement, the bank identified "D&J Enterprises, Inc., Radio Shack, Dealer, Debra K. Boudreaux, Michael C. Boudreaux" as "Debtors." The statement covered, in part, the store inventory. Before the end of the year, the Boudreauxes changed the name of their business to Tri-B Enterprises, Inc. In January 1998, the store closed. The next month, Radio Shack terminated the franchise and, despite the lack of a security interest, took possession of the inventory, claiming the Boudreauxes and Tri-B owed Radio Shack $6,394.73. The bank filed a suit in a Missouri state court against Radio Shack, claiming a perfected security interest in the inventory with priority over Radio Shack's claim. Did the bank's security interest take priority over Radio Shack's claim? Why or why not? [*Cabool State Bank v. Radio Shack,* 65 S.W.3d 613 (Mo.App. 2002)] **(See page 531.)**

20–4 **Case Problem with Sample Answer—Default.** Primesouth Bank issued a loan to Okefenokee Aircraft, Inc. (OAI), to buy a plane. OAI executed a note in favor of Primesouth in the amount of $161,306.25, plus interest. The plane secured the note. When OAI defaulted, Primesouth repossessed the plane. Instead of disposing of the collateral and seeking a deficiency judgment, however, the bank retained possession of the plane and filed a suit in a Georgia state court against OAI to enforce the note. OAI did not deny defaulting on the note or dispute the amount due. Instead, OAI argued that Primesouth Bank was not acting in a commercially reasonable manner. According to OAI, the creditor must sell the collateral and apply the proceeds against the debt. What is a secured creditor's obligation in these circumstances? Can the creditor retain the collateral and seek a judgment for the amount of the underlying debt, or is a sale required? Discuss. [*Okefenokee Aircraft, Inc. v. Primesouth Bank,* 296 Ga.App. 872, 676 S.E.2d 394 (2009)] **(See page 535.)**

—For a sample answer to Problem 20–4, go to Appendix H at the end of this text.

20–5 **Disposition of Collateral.** PRA Aviation, LLC, borrowed $3 million from Center Capital Corp. to buy a Gates Learjet 55B. Center perfected a security interest in the plane. Later, PRA defaulted on the loan, and Center obtained possession of the jet. The market, design, and mechanical condition of similar aircraft were reviewed to estimate the jet's value at $1.45 million. The jet was marketed in trade publications, on the Internet, and by direct advertising to select customers for $1.595 million. There were three offers. Center sold the jet to the high bidder for $1.3 million. Was the sale commercially reasonable? Explain. [*Center Capital Corp. v. PRA Aviation, LLC,* 2011 WL 867516 (E.D.Pa. 2011)] **(See page 536.)**

20–6 **Perfecting a Security Interest.** Thomas Tille owned M.A.T.T. Equipment Co. To operate the business, Tille borrowed funds from Union Bank. For each loan, Union filed a financing statement that included Tille's signature and address, the bank's address, and a description of the collateral. The first loan covered all of Tille's equipment, including "any after-acquired property." The second loan covered a truck crane "whether owned now or acquired later." The third loan covered a "Bobcat mini-excavator." Did these financing statements perfect Union's security interests? Explain. [*Union Bank Co. v. Heban,* 2012 WL 32102 (Ohio App. 2012) **(See pages 522–529.)**

20–7 **A Question of Ethics—Priorities.** In 1995, Mark Denton cosigned on a $101,250 loan that First Interstate Bank (FIB) made to his friend Eric Anderson. Denton's business assets—a mini-warehouse operation—secured the loan, because Anderson had no assets to use as collateral. Anderson also obtained a $260,000 U.S. Small Business Administration (SBA) loan from FIB at the same time. The purpose of both loans was to buy logging equipment with which Anderson could start a business. In 1997, the logging business failed and FIB repossessed and sold the equipment and used the funds to pay off the SBA loan. FIB then asked Denton to pay the other loan's outstanding balance ($98,460) plus interest. When Denton refused, FIB initiated proceedings to obtain his business assets. Denton claimed that Anderson's equipment was the collateral for the loan [*Denton v. First Interstate Bank of Commerce,* 2006 MT 193, 333 Mont. 169, 142 P.3d 797 (2006)] **(See page 531.)**

1. When the parties signed the loan, FIB's loan officer explained to them that if Anderson defaulted, the proceeds from the sale of the logging equipment would be applied to the SBA loan first. Is it fair to hold Denton liable for the unpaid balance of Anderson's loan? Why or why not?
2. Denton argued that the loan contract should not be enforceable because it was unconscionable and an adhesion contract. Is he correct? Explain.

Critical Thinking and Writing Assignments

20–8 **Business Law Critical Thinking Group Assignment.** Nick Sabol, doing business in the recording industry as Sound Farm Productions, applied to Morton Community Bank for a $58,000 loan to expand his business. Besides the loan application, Sabol signed a promissory note that referred to the bank's rights in "any collateral." Sabol also signed a letter authorizing Morton Community Bank to execute, file, and record all financing statements, amendments, and other documents required by Article 9 to establish a security interest in his state. Sabol did not sign any other documents, including the financing statement, which contained a description of the collateral. Two years later, without having repaid the loan, Sabol filed for bankruptcy. The bank claimed a security interest in Sabol's sound equipment.

1. The first group will list all the requirements of an enforceable security interest and explain why each of these elements is necessary.
2. The second group will determine if Morton Community Bank had a valid security interest.
3. The third group will discuss whether a bank should be able to execute financing statements on a debtor's behalf without the debtor being present or signing them. Are there are any drawbacks to this practice?

21 CHAPTER

Creditors' Rights and Bankruptcy

CHAPTER OUTLINE

- Laws Assisting Creditors
- Protection for Debtors
- Bankruptcy Proceedings
- Chapter 7—Liquidation
- Chapter 11—Reorganization
- Bankruptcy Relief under Chapter 12 and Chapter 13

LEARNING OBJECTIVES

The five learning objectives below are designed to help improve your understanding of the chapter. After reading this chapter, you should be able to answer the following questions:

1. What is a writ of execution? What is a prejudgment attachment? How does a creditor use these remedies?
2. What is garnishment? When might a creditor undertake a garnishment proceeding?
3. In a bankruptcy proceeding, what constitutes the debtor's estate in property? What property is exempt from the estate under federal bankruptcy law?
4. What is the difference between an exception to discharge and an objection to discharge?
5. In a Chapter 11 reorganization, what is the role of the debtor in possession?

(Kameleon007/iStockphoto.com)

"Capitalism without bankruptcy is like Christianity without hell."
—Frank Borman, 1928–present (U.S. astronaut and businessman)

Many people in today's economy are struggling to pay their monthly debts. Although in the old days, debtors were punished and sometimes even sent to jail for failing to pay their debts, people today rarely go to jail. They have many other options. In this chapter, we discuss some basic laws that assist the debtor and creditor in resolving disputes.

We then turn to the topic of bankruptcy—a last resort in resolving debtor-creditor problems. As implied by the chapter-opening quotation, bankruptcy may be a necessary evil in our capitalistic society. Hence, every businessperson should have some understanding of the bankruptcy process. Our discussion in this chapter specifically includes changes resulting from the 2005 Bankruptcy Reform Act. We also discuss in a feature on page 551 how some bankruptcy courts are now using social media to communicate with the public.

Laws Assisting Creditors

Both the common law and statutory laws other than Article 9 of the Uniform Commercial Code (UCC) create various rights and remedies for creditors. Here we discuss some of these rights and remedies.

Liens

As noted in Chapter 20, a *lien* is an encumbrance on (claim against) property to satisfy a debt or protect a claim for the payment of a debt. Creditors' liens may arise under the common law or under statutory law. Statutory liens include *mechanic's liens,* whereas *artisan's liens* were recognized by common law. *Judicial liens* arise when a creditor attempts to collect on a debt before or after a judgment is entered by a court.

Mechanic's and artisan's liens can be an important tool for creditors because these liens normally take priority over perfected security interests—unless a statute provides otherwise. Other types of liens can also be useful because a lien creditor generally has priority over an unperfected secured party. In other words, if a creditor obtains a lien *before* another party perfects a security interest in the same property, the lienholder has priority. If the lien is not obtained until *after* another's security interest in the property is perfected, the perfected security interest has priority.

Mechanic's Lien

If a person contracts for labor, services, or materials to be furnished for making improvements on real property (land and things attached to it, such as buildings and trees—see Chapter 36) and does not immediately pay for the improvements, the creditor can file a **mechanic's lien** on the property. This creates a special type of debtor-creditor relationship in which the real estate itself becomes security for the debt.

Mechanic's Lien A statutory lien on the real property of another to ensure payment to a person who has performed work and furnished materials for the repair or improvement of that property.

EXAMPLE 21.1 Jeff paints a house for Becky, a homeowner, for an agreed-on price to cover labor and materials. If Becky refuses to pay for the work or pays only a portion of the charges, a mechanic's lien against the property can be created. Jeff is the lienholder, and the real property is encumbered (burdened) with a mechanic's lien for the amount owed. If Becky does not pay the lien, the property can be sold to satisfy the debt. ●

State law governs the procedures that must be followed to create a mechanic's lien. Generally, the lienholder must file a written notice of lien within a specific time period (usually 60 to 120 days) from the last date labor or materials were provided. Notice of the foreclosure and sale must be given to the debtor in advance, however. (*Foreclosure* is the process by which the creditor deprives the debtor of the property.)

Artisan's Lien A possessory lien on personal property of another person to ensure payment to a person who has made improvements on and added value to that property.

If the homeowner does not pay this painter, what can he do to recover payment?

(PhilAugustavo/iStockphoto.com)

Artisan's Lien

When a debtor fails to pay for labor and materials furnished for the repair or improvement of personal property, a creditor can recover payment through an **artisan's lien.** In contrast to a mechanic's lien, an artisan's lien is *possessory*. The lienholder ordinarily must have retained possession of the property and have expressly or impliedly agreed to provide the services on a cash, not a credit, basis. The lien remains in existence as long as the lienholder maintains possession of the property, and the lien is terminated once possession is voluntarily surrendered—unless the surrender is only temporary.

EXAMPLE 21.2 Selena leaves her diamond ring at the jeweler's to be repaired and to have her initials engraved on the band. In the absence of an agreement, the jeweler can keep the ring until Selena pays for the services. Should Selena fail to pay, the jeweler has a lien on Selena's ring for the amount of the bill and normally can sell the ring in satisfaction of the lien. ●

Modern statutes permit the holder of an artisan's lien to foreclose and sell the property subject to the lien to satisfy payment of the debt. As with a mechanic's lien, the holder of an artisan's lien must give notice to the owner of the property prior to foreclosure and sale. The sale proceeds are used to pay the debt and the costs of the legal proceedings, and the surplus, if any, is paid to the former owner.

Judicial Liens

A creditor can bring a legal action against a debtor to collect a past-due debt. If the creditor is successful, the court awards the creditor a judgment against a debtor (usually for the amount of the debt plus any interest and legal costs incurred). Frequently, however, the creditor is unable to collect the awarded amount.

To ensure that a judgment will be collectible, the creditor can request that certain nonexempt property of the debtor be seized to satisfy the debt. (As will be discussed later in this chapter, under state or federal statutes, certain property is exempt from attachment by creditors.) A court's order to seize the debtor's property is known as a *writ of attachment* if it is issued before a judgment. If the court's order is issued after a judgment, it is referred to as a *writ of execution.*

LEARNING OBJECTIVE 1
What is a writ of execution? What is a prejudgment attachment? How does a creditor use these remedies?

Attachment The legal process of seizing another's property under a court order to secure satisfaction of a judgment yet to be rendered.

Writ of Attachment In the context of judicial liens, **attachment** is a court-ordered seizure of property before a judgment is secured for a past-due debt. Attachment rights are created by state statutes. Normally, attachment is a *prejudgment* remedy occurring either at the time a lawsuit is filed or immediately afterwards. The due process clause of the Fourteenth Amendment to the U.S. Constitution requires that the debtor be given notice and an opportunity to be heard (see Chapter 2).

To attach before judgment, a creditor must comply with the specific state's statutory requirements. The creditor must have an enforceable right to payment of the debt under law and must follow certain procedures or risk liability for wrongful attachment. Typically, the creditor must file an *affidavit*—that is, a written statement, made under oath—with the court and post a bond. The affidavit states that the debtor is in default and indicates the statutory grounds under which attachment is sought. The bond covers at least the court costs, the value of the debtor's loss of use of the goods, and the value of the property attached.

Writ of Attachment A writ used to enforce obedience to an order or judgment of the court.

When the court is satisfied that all of the requirements have been met, it issues a **writ of attachment,** which directs the sheriff or other public officer to seize nonexempt property. If the creditor prevails at trial, the seized property can be sold to satisfy the judgment.

Writ of Execution A writ that puts in force a court's decree or judgment.

Writ of Execution If the creditor wins at trial and the debtor will not or cannot pay the judgment, the creditor is entitled to go back to the court and request a **writ of execution.** This writ is a court order directing the sheriff to seize (levy) and sell any of the debtor's nonexempt real or personal property that is within the court's geographic jurisdiction (usually the county in which the courthouse is located).

The proceeds of the sale are used to pay off the judgment, accrued interest, and the costs of the sale. Any excess is paid to the debtor. The debtor can pay the judgment and redeem the nonexempt property any time before the sale takes place. (Because of exemption laws and bankruptcy laws, however, many judgments are uncollectible.)

LEARNING OBJECTIVE 2
What is garnishment? When might a creditor undertake a garnishment proceeding?

Garnishment A legal process whereby a creditor appropriates a debtor's property or wages that are in the hands of a third party.

Garnishment

Garnishment occurs when a creditor is permitted to collect a debt by seizing property of the debtor (such as wages or funds in a bank account) that is being held by a third party. As a result of a garnishment proceeding, the debtor's employer may be ordered by the court to turn over a portion of the debtor's wages to pay the debt.

Under what conditions could a creditor obtain a writ of attachment on this speed boat?

(dans_prat/iStockphoto.com)

CASE EXAMPLE 21.3 Helen Griffin failed to pay a debt she owed to Indiana Surgical Specialists. When Indiana Surgical filed a lawsuit to collect, the court issued a judgment in favor of Indiana Surgical and a garnishment order to withhold the appropriate amount from Griffin's earnings until her debt was paid. At the time, Griffin was working as an independent contractor (see Chapter 23 for a discussion of independent-contractor status) driving for a courier service. She claimed that her wages could not be garnished because she was not an employee. The court held that payments for the services of an independent contractor fall within the definition of earnings and can be garnished.[1] ●

Procedures

Garnishment can be a prejudgment remedy, requiring a hearing before a court, but it is most often a postjudgment remedy. State law governs garnishment, so the

1. *Indiana Surgical Specialists v. Griffin,* 867 N.E.2d 260 (Ind.App. 2007).

Creditors' Composition Agreement An agreement formed between a debtor and his or her creditors in which the creditors agree to accept a lesser sum than that owed by the debtor in full satisfaction of the debt.

Suretyship An express contract in which a third party (the surety) promises to be primarily responsible for a debtor's obligation to a creditor.

Surety A third party who agrees to be primarily responsible for the debt of another.

procedure varies. In some states, the creditor needs to obtain only one order of garnishment, which will then apply continuously to the debtor's wages until the entire debt is paid. In other states, the judgment creditor must go back to court for a separate order of garnishment for each pay period.

Limitations Both federal and state laws limit the amount that can be taken from a debtor's weekly take-home pay through garnishment proceedings.[2] Federal law provides a framework to protect debtors from suffering unduly when paying judgment debts.[3] State laws also provide dollar exemptions, and these amounts are often larger than those provided by federal law.

Under federal law, an employer cannot dismiss an employee because his or her wages are being garnished.

Creditors' Composition Agreements

Creditors may contract with the debtor for discharge of the debtor's liquidated debts (debts that are definite, or fixed, in amount) on payment of a sum less than that owed. These agreements are called **creditors' composition agreements**, or simply *composition agreements*, and usually are held to be enforceable.

Exhibit 21.1 Suretyship and Guaranty Parties

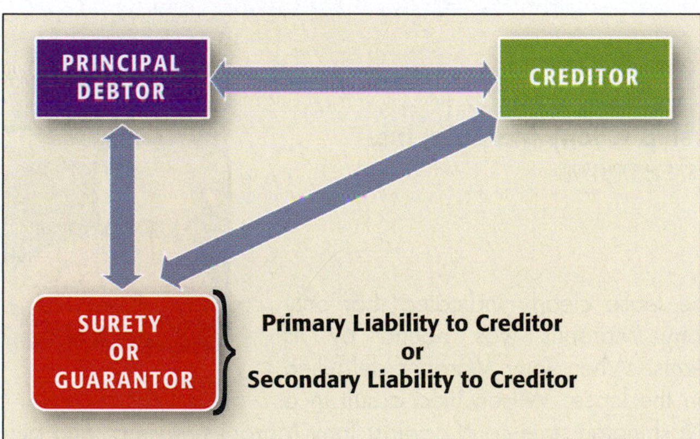

Suretyship and Guaranty

When a third person promises to pay a debt owed by another in the event the debtor does not pay, either a *suretyship* or a *guaranty* relationship is created. Exhibit 21.1 to the left illustrates these relationships. The third person's income and assets become the security for the debt owed.

Suretyship and guaranty provide creditors with the right to seek payment from the third party if the primary debtor defaults on her or his obligations. At common law, there were significant differences in the liability of a surety and a guarantor, as discussed in the following subsections. Today, however, the distinctions outlined here have been abolished in some states.

Surety A contract of strict **suretyship** is a promise made by a third person to be responsible for the debtor's obligation. It is an express contract between the **surety** (the third party) and the creditor. The surety in the strictest sense is primarily liable for the debt of the principal. The creditor need not exhaust all legal remedies against the principal debtor before holding the surety responsible for payment. The creditor can demand payment from the surety from the moment the debt is due.

How can a minor with little or no income convince a car dealer to sell him or her a car?

(Callietat/iStockphoto.com)

EXAMPLE 21.4 Roberto Delmar wants to borrow from the bank to buy a used car. Because Roberto is still in college, the bank will not lend him the funds unless his father, José Delmar, who has dealt with the bank before, will cosign the note (add his signature to the note, thereby becoming a surety and thus jointly liable for payment of the debt). When José cosigns the note, he becomes primarily liable to the bank. On the note's due date, the bank can seek payment from either Roberto or José, or both jointly. •

2. Some states (for example, Texas) do not permit garnishment of wages by private parties except under a child-support order.
3. For example, the federal Consumer Credit Protection Act of 1968, 15 U.S.C. Sections 1601–1693r, provides that a debtor can retain either 75 percent of disposable earnings per week or a sum equivalent to thirty hours of work paid at federal minimum-wage rates, whichever is greater.

Guarantor A person who agrees to satisfy the debt of another (the debtor) only after the principal debtor defaults. Thus, a guarantor's liability is secondary.

Guaranty

With a suretyship arrangement, the surety is *primarily* liable for the debtor's obligation. With a guaranty arrangement, the **guarantor**—the third person making the guaranty—is *secondarily* liable. The guarantor can be required to pay the obligation *only after the principal debtor defaults,* and default usually takes place only after the creditor has made an attempt to collect from the debtor.

EXAMPLE 21.5 BX Enterprises, a small corporation, needs to borrow funds to meet its payroll. The bank is skeptical about the creditworthiness of BX and requires Dawson, its president, who is a wealthy businessperson and the owner of 70 percent of BX Enterprises, to sign an agreement making himself personally liable for payment if BX does not pay off the loan. As a guarantor of the loan, Dawson cannot be held liable until BX Enterprises is in default. •

Under the Statute of Frauds, a guaranty contract between the guarantor and the creditor must be in writing to be enforceable unless the *main purpose rule* applies (see Chapter 12 on page 316).[4] Under common law, a suretyship agreement did not need to be in writing to be enforceable, and oral surety agreements were sufficient. Today, however, some states require a writing (record) to enforce a suretyship.

In the following *Spotlight Case,* the issue was whether a guaranty of a lease signed by the president of a corporation was enforceable against the officer personally, although he claimed to have signed the guaranty only as a representative of the corporation.

4. Briefly, the main purpose rule, or exception, provides that if the main purpose of the guaranty agreement is to benefit the guarantor, then the contract need not be in writing to be enforceable.

Spotlight on Personal Guaranties

Case 21.1

Wilson Court Limited Partnership v. Tony Maroni's, Inc.

Supreme Court of Washington, 134 Wash.2d 692, 952 P.2d 590 (1998).

(cristianl/iStockphoto.com)

Tony Maroni's pizza.

COMPANY PROFILE *Tony Riviera founded Tony Maroni's, Inc., to sell Tony Maroni's Famous Gourmet Pizza in Seattle, Washington, in the late 1980s. Tony Maroni's began by offering pizzas, salads, calzones, and lasagna for delivery only. By 1995, the firm had begun franchising its brand (franchising will be discussed in Chapter 28). Two years later, with eleven locations in the Seattle area, including six franchise outlets, and ten more stores in development, the company announced plans to open five hundred locations nationwide before 2002. Despite these plans, by the end of 1997, the firm had yet to turn a profit and was nearly $1 million in debt.*

FACTS Tony Maroni's, Inc., agreed to lease retail space owned by Wilson Court Limited Partnership. Tony Riviera, Tony Maroni's president, signed the lease for 1,676 square feet of space for a sixty-month term. When he signed the lease, Riviera also signed a guaranty agreement that was incorporated by reference in the lease.

On the signature line of the guaranty, Riviera wrote "President" after his name. The guaranty did not specifically identify who was bound, referring only to "the undersigned" or "Guarantor." Riviera also signed the lease in a representative capacity, but the lease clearly indicated that only Tony Maroni's was bound by its terms. When Tony Maroni's defaulted on the lease, Wilson filed a suit in a Washington state court against Tony Maroni's, Riviera, and others. Riviera asserted, in part, that he was not personally liable on the guaranty because he signed only in his capacity as a corporate officer. The court issued a summary judgment in favor of Wilson. Riviera appealed to the Washington Supreme Court.

ISSUE Was Riviera personally liable on the guaranty?

DECISION Yes. The Washington Supreme Court affirmed the judgment of the lower court.

REASON The state supreme court reasoned that if Riviera, the president, were not personally liable, the corporation would be the guarantor of its own lease. That conclusion would be commercially unreasonable because a party cannot be the guarantor of its own contract. The court pointed out that "any ambiguity in the Guaranty was created by Riviera" and "such ambiguity will be construed against Riviera as the party who drafted

Spotlight Case 21.1—Continued

this language." The court noted that the "combination of circumstances" made the guaranty ambiguous. Nevertheless, by referring to three parties, including the "Guarantor," "the language of the Guaranty itself compels the view Riviera is personally liable." The court explained that "[i]f Riviera signed the Guaranty only in his representative capacity, Tony Maroni's would be both Tenant and Guarantor, rendering the Guaranty provisions absurd." Thus, "the very nature of a guaranty is such that Riviera created personal liability by his signature."

CRITICAL THINKING—Ethical Consideration *Are there any circumstances in which a collateral document signed by a corporate officer to secure a corporate debt might not create personal liability? Explain.*

Actions That Release the Surety and Guarantor

Basically, the same actions will release a surety or a guarantor from an obligation. In general, the same rules apply to both sureties and guarantors. So, for simplicity, this subsection and the following subsections will refer just to sureties.

If a material modification is made in the terms of the original contract between the principal debtor and the creditor—without the surety's consent—the surety's obligation will be discharged. (The extent to which the surety is discharged depends on whether he or she was compensated and the amount of the loss suffered a result of the modification.) Similarly, if a debt is secured by collateral and the creditor surrenders the collateral to the debtor or impairs the collateral without the surety's consent, these acts can reduce the surety's obligation.

Naturally, any payment of the principal obligation by the debtor or by another person on the debtor's behalf will discharge the surety from the obligation. Even if the creditor refused to accept payment of the principal debt when it was tendered, the surety's obligation can be discharged.

Defenses of the Surety and the Guarantor

Generally, the surety (or guarantor) can also assert any of the defenses available to a principal debtor to avoid liability on the obligation to the creditor. A few exceptions do exist, however. The surety cannot assert the principal debtor's incapacity or bankruptcy as a defense, nor can the surety assert the statute of limitations as a defense.

Obviously, a surety may also have her or his own defenses—for example, her or his own incapacity or bankruptcy. If the creditor fraudulently induced the surety to guarantee the debt of the debtor, the surety can assert fraud as a defense. In most states, the creditor has a legal duty to inform the surety, before the formation of the suretyship contract, of material facts known by the creditor that would substantially increase the surety's risk. Failure to so inform may constitute fraud and renders the suretyship obligation voidable.

Rights of the Surety and the Guarantor

Usually, when the surety (or guarantor) pays the debt owed to the creditor, the surety (or guarantor) is entitled to certain rights.

Right of Subrogation The right of a surety or guarantor to stand in the place of (be substituted for) the creditors, giving the surety or guarantor the same legal rights against the debtor that the creditor had.

The Right of Subrogation The surety has the legal **right of subrogation,** which means that any right the creditor had against the debtor now becomes the right of the surety. Included are creditor rights in bankruptcy, rights to collateral possessed by the creditor, and rights to judgments secured by the creditor. In short, the surety stands in the shoes of the creditor and may pursue any remedies that were available to the creditor against the debtor.

Right of Reimbursement The legal right of a person to be repaid or indemnified for costs, expenses, or losses incurred or expended on behalf of another.

Co-Surety A person who assumes liability jointly with another surety for the payment of an obligation.

Right of Contribution The right of a co-surety who pays more than her or his proportionate share on a debtor's default to recover the excess paid from other co-sureties.

The Right of Reimbursement The surety has a **right of reimbursement** from the debtor. Basically, the surety is entitled to receive from the debtor all outlays made on behalf of the suretyship arrangement. Such outlays can include expenses incurred as well as the actual amount of the debt paid to the creditor.

The Right of Contribution Two or more sureties are called **co-sureties.** When one co-surety pays more than her or his proportionate share on a debtor's default, she or he is entitled to recover from the other co-sureties the amount paid above that surety's obligation. This is the **right of contribution.** Generally, a co-surety's liability either is determined by agreement between the co-sureties or, in the absence of an agreement, is specified in the suretyship contract itself.

EXAMPLE 21.6 Two co-sureties—Yasser and Itzhak—are obligated under a suretyship contract to guarantee the debt of Jules. Itzhak's maximum liability is $15,000, and Yasser's is $10,000. Jules owes $10,000 and is in default. Itzhak pays the creditor the entire $10,000. In the absence of an agreement to the contrary, Itzhak can recover $4,000 from Yasser. The amount of the debt that Yasser agreed to cover is divided by the total amount that Itzhak and Yasser together agreed to cover. The result is multiplied by the amount of the default, yielding the amount that Yasser owes—($10,000 ÷ $25,000) × $10,000 = $4,000. ●

PREVENTING LEGAL DISPUTES

Be careful when signing guaranty contracts. In particular, explicitly indicate if you are signing on behalf of a company rather than personally. If you are a corporate officer or director and you sign your name on a guaranty without indicating that you are signing as a representative of the corporation, you might be held personally liable. Although a guaranty contract may be preferable to a suretyship contract, in some states, because it creates secondary rather than primary liability, a guaranty still involves substantial risk. Depending on the wording used in a guaranty contract, the extent of the guarantor's liability may be unlimited or may continue over a series of transactions. Be absolutely clear about the potential liability before agreeing to serve as a guarantor, and contact an attorney for guidance.

Protection for Debtors

The law protects debtors as well as creditors. Certain property of the debtor, for example, is exempt from creditors' actions. Of course, bankruptcy laws, which will be discussed shortly, are designed specifically to assist debtors.

In most states, certain types of real and personal property are exempt from execution or attachment. State exemption statutes usually include both real and personal property.

Exempted Real Property

Homestead Exemption A law permitting a debtor to retain the family home, either in its entirety or up to a specified dollar amount, free from the claims of unsecured creditors or trustees in bankruptcy.

Probably the most familiar real property exemption is the **homestead exemption.** Each state permits the debtor to retain the family home, either in its entirety or up to a specified dollar amount, free from the claims of unsecured creditors or trustees in bankruptcy (discussed later in this chapter).

The General Rule

The purpose of the homestead exemption is to ensure that the debtor will retain some form of shelter. (Note that federal bankruptcy law now places a cap on the amount that debtors can claim under a state's homestead exemption—see page 558.)

EXAMPLE 21.7 Van Cleave owes Acosta $40,000. The debt is the subject of a lawsuit, and the court awards Acosta a judgment of $40,000 against Van Cleave. Van Cleave's home is valued at $50,000, and the state exemption on homesteads is $25,000. There are no

(KLH49/iStockphoto.com)

If a house is sold at auction to satisfy a debt, can the creditor always keep the full proceeds from that sale?

outstanding mortgages or other liens. To satisfy the judgment debt, Van Cleave's family home is sold at public auction for $45,000. The proceeds of the sale are distributed as follows:

1. Van Cleave is given $25,000 as his homestead exemption.
2. Acosta is paid $20,000 toward the judgment debt, leaving a $20,000 deficiency judgment that can be satisfied from any other nonexempt property (personal or real) that Van Cleave may have, if allowed by state law. •

Limitations In a few states, statutes allow the homestead exemption only if the judgment debtor has a family. If a judgment debtor does not have a family, a creditor may be entitled to collect the full amount realized from the sale of the debtor's home. In addition, the homestead exemption interacts with other areas of law and can sometimes operate to cancel out a portion of a lien on a debtor's real property.

CASE EXAMPLE 21.8 Antonio Stanley purchased a modular home from Yates Mobile Services Corporation. When Stanley failed to pay the purchase price of the home, Yates obtained a judicial lien against Stanley's property in the amount of $165,138.05. Stanley then filed for bankruptcy and asserted the homestead exemption. The court found that Stanley was entitled to avoid the lien to the extent that it impaired his exemption. Using a bankruptcy law formula, the court determined that the total impairment was $143,639.05 and that Stanley could avoid paying this amount to Yates. Thus, Yates was left with a judicial lien on Stanley's home in the amount of $21,499.[5] •

Exempted Personal Property

Personal property that is most often exempt under state law includes the following:

1. Household furniture up to a specified dollar amount.
2. Clothing and certain personal possessions, such as family pictures or a religious text.
3. A vehicle (or vehicles) for transportation (at least up to a specified dollar amount).
4. Certain classified animals, usually livestock but including pets.
5. Equipment that the debtor uses in a business or trade, such as tools or professional instruments, up to a specified dollar amount.

Bankruptcy Proceedings

Bankruptcy law in the United States has two goals—to protect a debtor by giving him or her a fresh start, free from creditors' claims, and to ensure equitable treatment to creditors who are competing for the debtor's assets. Bankruptcy law is federal law, but state laws on secured transactions, liens, judgments, and exemptions also play a role in federal bankruptcy proceedings.

Bankruptcy law before 2005 was based on the Bankruptcy Reform Act of 1978, as amended (called the Bankruptcy Code, or simply, the Code). In 2005, Congress enacted bankruptcy reform legislation that significantly overhauled certain provisions of the Bankruptcy Code for the first time in twenty-five years.[6] Because of its significance for creditors and debtors alike, we present the Bankruptcy Reform Act of 2005 as this chapter's *Landmark in the Law* feature on the following page.

5. *In re Stanley,* 2010 WL 2103441 (M.D.N.C. 2010).
6. The full title of the act is the Bankruptcy Abuse Prevention and Consumer Protection Act of 2005, Pub. L. No. 109-8, 119 Stat. 23 (April 20, 2005).

LANDMARK IN THE LAW

The Bankruptcy Reform Act of 2005

When Congress enacted the Bankruptcy Reform Act of 1978, many claimed that the new act made it too easy for debtors to file for bankruptcy protection. The Bankruptcy Reform Act of 2005 was passed, in part, in response to businesses' concerns about the rise in personal bankruptcy filings. From 1978 to 2005, personal bankruptcy filings increased dramatically. Various business groups—including credit-card companies, retailers, and banks—claimed that the bankruptcy process was being abused and that reform was necessary.

More Repayment Plans, Fewer Liquidation Bankruptcies

One of the major goals of the Bankruptcy Reform Act of 2005 is to require consumers to pay as many of their debts as they possibly can instead of having those debts fully discharged in bankruptcy. Before the reforms, the vast majority of bankruptcies were filed under Chapter 7 of the Bankruptcy Code, which permits debtors, with some exceptions, to have *all* of their debts discharged in bankruptcy. Only about 20 percent of personal bankruptcies were filed under Chapter 13 of the Bankruptcy Code. As you will read later in this chapter, this part of the Bankruptcy Code requires the debtor to establish a repayment plan and pay off as many of his or her debts as possible over a maximum period of five years. Under the 2005 legislation, more debtors have to file for bankruptcy under Chapter 13.

Other Significant Provisions of the Act

Another important provision of the Bankruptcy Reform Act of 2005 involves the homestead exemption. Before the passage of the act, some states allowed debtors petitioning for bankruptcy to exempt all of the *equity* (the market value minus the outstanding mortgage owed) in their homes during bankruptcy proceedings. The 2005 act leaves these exemptions in place but puts some limits on their use. The 2005 act also included a number of other changes. For example, one provision gives child-support obligations priority over other debts and allows enforcement agencies to continue efforts to collect child-support payments.

Application to Today's World *Under the Bankruptcy Reform Act of 2005, fewer debtors are allowed to have their debts discharged in Chapter 7 liquidation proceedings. At the same time, the act makes it more difficult for debtors to obtain a "fresh start" financially—one of the major goals of bankruptcy law in the United States. Today, more debtors are forced to file under Chapter 13. Additionally, the bankruptcy process has become more time consuming and costly because it requires more extensive documentation and certification. These changes in the law, in conjunction with the global financial crisis that began in 2007, have left many Americans unable to obtain relief from their debts.*

KNOW THIS

Congress regulates the jurisdiction of the federal courts, within the limits set by the U.S. Constitution. Congress can expand or reduce the number of federal courts at any time.

Bankruptcy Courts

Bankruptcy proceedings are held in federal bankruptcy courts, which are under the authority of U.S. district courts. Rulings by bankruptcy courts can be appealed to the district courts. The bankruptcy court holds proceedings dealing with the procedures required to administer the debtor's estate in bankruptcy (the debtor's assets, as will be discussed shortly). For a discussion of how bankruptcy courts are adapting to the use of social media, see this chapter's *Adapting the Law to the Online Environment* feature on the facing page.

Types of Bankruptcy Relief

The Bankruptcy Code is contained in Title 11 of the *United States Code* (U.S.C.) and has eight "chapters." Chapters 1, 3, and 5 of the Code include general definitional provisions and provisions governing case administration and procedures, creditors, the debtor, and the estate. These three chapters of the Code normally apply to all types of bankruptcies.

Four chapters of the Code set forth the most important types of relief that debtors can seek.

1. Chapter 7 provides for *liquidation* proceedings—that is, the selling of all nonexempt assets and the distribution of the proceeds to the debtor's creditors.

ADAPTING THE LAW TO THE ONLINE ENVIRONMENT

LIVE CHATTING WITH YOUR STATE'S BANKRUPTCY COURT

Chatting on social media has become a way of life for most younger people in this country and elsewhere. Online chats preceded social media and are still used at retail Web sites. Today, some tech-savvy employees at bankruptcy courts are using the retail online chat model to answer questions about bankruptcy.

Arizona Was First to Use Live Chats

The U.S. Bankruptcy Court for the District of Arizona started live chatting several years ago. It added live chat to its Web site as part of a strategic initiative to educate the public about bankruptcy. Rather than leaving voice messages, people who access the court's Web site can send and receive text messages via an easy-to-use chat box. The court's goal is to respond to a live chat request within thirty seconds.

In 2011, New Mexico became the second state to add online chatting to its bankruptcy court's Web site. Nevada followed with its live chat in 2012.

The courts that have adopted online chatting average about ten chats a day. Most chats last less than ten minutes.

Who Uses Bankruptcy Court Chat Rooms?

At first, only individuals interested in filing for bankruptcy without an attorney used the live chat services. When paralegals learned that they could get quick answers to their questions online, they also began to use the services.

Then, during the real estate meltdown of the last few years, many real estate lawyers expanded into the area of bankruptcy law, often as a way to help their clients avoid foreclosure through bankruptcy filings. Many of these lawyers also have used live chat to expand their knowledge of bankruptcy law.

Critical Thinking

Are there any downsides to live chats with bankruptcy courts? If so, what are they?

2. Chapter 11 governs reorganizations.
3. Chapter 12 (for family farmers and family fishermen) and Chapter 13 (for individuals) provide for adjustment of the debts of parties with regular income.[7]

Note that a debtor (except for a municipality) need not be insolvent[8] to file for bankruptcy relief under the Bankruptcy Code. Anyone obligated to a creditor can declare bankruptcy.

Special Treatment of Consumer-Debtors

Consumer-Debtor One whose debts result primarily from the purchases of goods for personal, family, or household use.

A **consumer-debtor** is a debtor whose debts result primarily from the purchase of goods for personal, family, or household use. The Bankruptcy Code requires that the clerk of the court give all consumer-debtors written notice of the general purpose, benefits, and costs of each chapter of bankruptcy under which they may proceed. In addition, the clerk must provide consumer-debtors with information on the types of services available from credit counseling agencies.

Chapter 7—Liquidation

Liquidation The sale of the nonexempt assets of a debtor and the distribution of the funds received to creditors.

Liquidation under Chapter 7 is the most familiar type of bankruptcy proceeding and is often referred to as an *ordinary, or straight, bankruptcy.* Put simply, a debtor in a liquidation bankruptcy turns all assets over to a trustee. The trustee sells the nonexempt assets and

7. There are no Chapters 2, 4, 6, 8, or 10 in Title 11. Such "gaps" are not uncommon in the *United States Code*. They occur because, when a statute is enacted, chapter numbers (or other subdivisional unit numbers) are sometimes reserved for future use. (A gap may also appear if a law has been repealed.)

8. The inability to pay debts as they come due is known as *equitable* insolvency. A *balance-sheet* insolvency, which exists when a debtor's liabilities exceed assets, is not the test. Thus, it is possible for debtors to petition voluntarily for bankruptcy even though their assets far exceed their liabilities. This situation may occur when a debtor's cash-flow problems become severe.

distributes the proceeds to creditors. With certain exceptions, the remaining debts are then **discharged** (extinguished), and the debtor is relieved of the obligation to pay the debts.

Discharge The termination of a bankruptcy debtor's obligation to pay debts.

Any "person"—defined as including individuals, partnerships, and corporations[9]—may be a debtor under Chapter 7. Railroads, insurance companies, banks, savings and loan associations, investment companies licensed by the U.S. Small Business Administration, and credit unions *cannot* be Chapter 7 debtors, however. Other chapters of the Code or other federal or state statutes apply to them. A husband and wife may file jointly for bankruptcy under a single petition.

A straight bankruptcy may be commenced by the filing of either a voluntary or an involuntary **petition in bankruptcy**—the document that is filed with a bankruptcy court to initiate bankruptcy proceedings. If a debtor files the petition, then it is a *voluntary bankruptcy*. If one or more creditors file a petition to force the debtor into bankruptcy, then it is called an *involuntary bankruptcy*. We discuss both voluntary and involuntary bankruptcy proceedings under Chapter 7 in the following subsections.

Petition in Bankruptcy The document that is filed with a bankruptcy court to initiate bankruptcy proceedings.

Voluntary Bankruptcy

To bring a voluntary petition in bankruptcy, the debtor files official forms designated for that purpose in the bankruptcy court. The law now requires that *before* debtors can file a petition, they must receive credit counseling from an approved nonprofit agency within the 180-day period preceding the date of filing. Debtors filing a Chapter 7 petition must include a certificate proving that they have received individual or group counseling from an approved agency within the last 180 days (roughly six months).

(WendellandCarolyn/iStockphoto.com)

Which creditors have claims on the proceeds from liquidation sales?

A consumer-debtor who is filing a liquidation bankruptcy must confirm the accuracy of the petition's contents. The debtor must also state in the petition, at the time of filing, that he or she understands the relief available under other chapters of the Code and has chosen to proceed under Chapter 7. Attorneys representing consumer-debtors must file an affidavit stating that they have informed the debtors of the relief available under each chapter of the Code. In addition, the attorneys must reasonably attempt to verify the accuracy of the consumer-debtors' petitions and schedules (described below). Failure to do so is considered perjury.

Chapter 7 Schedules

The voluntary petition contains the following schedules:

1. A list of both secured and unsecured creditors, their addresses, and the amount of debt owed to each.
2. A statement of the financial affairs of the debtor.
3. A list of all property owned by the debtor, including property claimed by the debtor to be exempt.
4. A list of current income and expenses.
5. A certificate of credit counseling (as discussed previously).
6. Proof of payments received from employers within sixty days prior to the filing of the petition.
7. A statement of the amount of monthly income, itemized to show how the amount is calculated.
8. A copy of the debtor's federal income tax return for the most recent year ending immediately before the filing of the petition.

The official forms must be completed accurately, sworn to under oath, and signed by the debtor. To conceal assets or knowingly supply false information on these schedules is a crime under the bankruptcy laws.

9. The definition of *corporation* includes unincorporated companies and associations. It also covers labor unions.

With the exception of tax returns, failure to file the required schedules within forty-five days after the filing of the petition (unless an extension is granted) will result in an automatic dismissal of the petition. The debtor has up to seven days before the date of the first creditors' meeting to provide a copy of the most recent tax returns to the trustee.

Tax Returns during Bankruptcy

In addition, a debtor may be required to file a tax return at the end of each tax year while the case is pending and to provide a copy to the court. This may be done at the request of the court or of the **U.S. trustee**—a government official who performs administrative tasks that a bankruptcy judge would otherwise have to perform, including supervising the work of the bankruptcy trustee.

U.S. Trustee A government official who performs certain administrative tasks that a bankruptcy judge would otherwise have to perform.

Any *party in interest* (a party, such as a creditor, who has a valid interest in the outcome of the proceedings) may make this request as well. Debtors may also be required to file tax returns during Chapter 11 and 13 bankruptcies.

Substantial Abuse and the Means Test

In the past, a bankruptcy court could dismiss a Chapter 7 petition for relief (discharge of debts) if the use of Chapter 7 would constitute a "substantial abuse" of bankruptcy law. Today, the law provides a *means test* to determine a debtor's eligibility for Chapter 7. The purpose of the test is to keep upper-income people from abusing the bankruptcy process by filing for Chapter 7, as was thought to have happened in the past. The test forces more people to file for Chapter 13 bankruptcy rather than have their debts discharged under Chapter 7.

The Basic Formula

A debtor wishing to file for bankruptcy must complete the means test to determine whether she or he qualifies for Chapter 7. The debtor's average monthly income in recent months is compared with the median income in the geographic area in which the person lives. (The U.S. Trustee Program provides these data at its Web site.) If the debtor's income is below the median income, the debtor usually is allowed to file for Chapter 7 bankruptcy, as there is no presumption of bankruptcy abuse.

Applying the Means Test to Future Disposable Income

If the debtor's income is above the median income, then further calculations must be made to determine whether the person will have sufficient disposable income in the future to repay at least some of his or her unsecured debts. *Disposable income* is calculated by subtracting living expenses and interest payments on secured debt, such as mortgage payments, from monthly income.

In making this calculation, the debtor's recent monthly income is presumed to continue for the next sixty months. Living expenses are the amounts allowed under formulas used by the Internal Revenue Service (IRS). The IRS allowances include modest allocations for food, clothing, housing, utilities, transportation (including car payments), health care, and other necessities. (The U.S. Trustee Program's Web site also provides these amounts.) The allowances do not include expenditures for items such as cell phones and cable television service.

Can the Debtor Afford to Pay Unsecured Debts?

Once future disposable income has been estimated, that amount is used to determine whether the debtor will have income that could be applied to unsecured debts. The court may also consider the debtor's bad faith or other circumstances indicating abuse.

CASE EXAMPLE 21.9 At thirty-three years old, Lisa Hebbring owned a home and a car, but had $11,124 in credit-card debt. Hebbring was earning $49,000 per year when she filed for Chapter 7 bankruptcy. Her petition listed monthly net income of $2,813 and expenditures of $2,897, for a deficit of $84.

In calculating her income, Hebbring excluded a $313 monthly deduction for contributions to retirement plans. The U.S. trustee filed a motion to dismiss Hebbring's petition due to substantial abuse, claiming that the retirement contributions should be disallowed. The court agreed and dismissed the Chapter 7 petition. Because Hebbring's retirement contributions were not reasonably necessary based on her age and financial circumstances, the court found that she was capable of paying her unsecured debts.[10]

Additional Grounds for Dismissal

As noted, a debtor's voluntary petition for Chapter 7 relief may be dismissed for substantial abuse or for failing to provide the necessary documents (such as schedules and tax returns) within the specified time.

In addition, a motion to dismiss a Chapter 7 filing may be granted in two other situations. First, if the debtor has been convicted of a violent crime or a drug-trafficking offense, the victim can file a motion to dismiss the voluntary petition.[11] Second, if the debtor fails to pay postpetition domestic-support obligations (which include child and spousal support), the court may dismiss the debtor's Chapter 7 petition.

Order for Relief

If the voluntary petition for bankruptcy is found to be proper, the filing of the petition will itself constitute an order for relief. (An **order for relief** is the court's grant of assistance to a debtor.) Once a consumer-debtor's voluntary petition has been filed, the clerk of the court (or other appointee) must give the trustee and creditors notice of the order for relief by mail not more than twenty days after the entry of the order.

Order for Relief A court's grant of assistance to a complainant. In bankruptcy proceedings, the order relieves the debtor of the immediate obligation to pay the debts listed in the bankruptcy petition.

Involuntary Bankruptcy

An involuntary bankruptcy occurs when the debtor's creditors force the debtor into bankruptcy proceedings. An involuntary case cannot be filed against a farmer[12] or a charitable institution. For an involuntary action to be filed against other debtors, the following requirements must be met: If the debtor has twelve or more creditors, three or more of those creditors having unsecured claims totaling at least $14,425 must join in the petition. If a debtor has fewer than twelve creditors, one or more creditors having a claim of $14,425 or more may file.

If the debtor challenges the involuntary petition, a hearing will be held, and the debtor's challenge will fail if the bankruptcy court finds either of the following:

1. The debtor generally is not paying debts as they become due.
2. A general receiver, assignee, or custodian took possession of, or was appointed to take charge of, substantially all of the debtor's property within 120 days before the filing of the involuntary petition.

If the court allows the bankruptcy to proceed, the debtor will be required to supply the same information in the bankruptcy schedules as in a voluntary bankruptcy.

An involuntary petition should not be used as an everyday debt-collection device, and the Code provides penalties for the filing of frivolous (unjustified) petitions against debtors. If the court dismisses an involuntary petition, the petitioning creditors may be required to pay the costs and attorneys' fees incurred by the debtor in defending against the petition. If the petition was filed in bad faith, damages can be awarded for injury to the debtor's reputation. Punitive damages may also be awarded.

"I hope that after I die, people will say of me: 'That guy sure owed me a lot of money.'"

Jack Handey, 1949–present (American humorist)

10. *Hebbring v. U.S. Trustee*, 463 F.3d 902 (9th Cir. 2006).
11. Note that the court may not dismiss a case on this ground if the debtor's bankruptcy is necessary to satisfy a claim for a domestic-support obligation.
12. The definition of *farmer* includes persons who receive more than 50 percent of their gross income from farming operations, such as tilling the soil; dairy farming; ranching; or the production or raising of crops, poultry, or livestock. Corporations and partnerships, as well as individuals, can be farmers.

Automatic Stay

Automatic Stay In bankruptcy proceedings, the suspension of almost all litigation and other action by creditors against the debtor or the debtor's property. The stay is effective the moment the debtor files a petition in bankruptcy.

The moment a petition, either voluntary or involuntary, is filed, an **automatic stay,** or suspension, of almost all actions by creditors against the debtor or the debtor's property normally goes into effect. In other words, once a petition has been filed, creditors cannot contact the debtor by phone or mail or start any legal proceedings to recover debts or to repossess property.

If a creditor *knowingly* violates the automatic stay (a willful violation), any injured party, including the debtor, is entitled to recover actual damages, costs, and attorneys' fees and may be entitled to punitive damages as well.

Until the bankruptcy proceeding is closed or dismissed, the automatic stay prohibits a creditor from taking any act to collect, assess, or recover a claim against the debtor that arose before the filing of the petition.

CASE EXAMPLE 21.10 Stefanie Kuehn filed for bankruptcy. When she requested a transcript from the university at which she obtained her master's degree, the university refused because she owed more than $6,000 in tuition. Kuehn complained to the court. The court ruled that the university had violated the automatic stay when it refused to provide a transcript because it was attempting to collect an unpaid tuition debt.[13] •

Exceptions to the Automatic Stay

The Code provides several exceptions to the automatic stay. Collection efforts can continue for domestic-support obligations, which include any debt owed to or recoverable by a spouse, former spouse, child of the debtor, a child's parent or guardian, or a governmental unit. In addition, proceedings against the debtor related to divorce, child custody or visitation, domestic violence, and support enforcement are not stayed. Also excepted are investigations by a securities regulatory agency (see Chapter 31) and certain statutory liens for property taxes.

Limitations on the Automatic Stay

A secured creditor or other party in interest can petition the bankruptcy court for relief from the automatic stay. If a creditor or other party requests relief from the stay, the stay will automatically terminate sixty days after the request, unless the court grants an extension[14] or the parties agree otherwise. Also, the automatic stay on secured debts normally will terminate thirty days after the petition is filed if the debtor had filed a bankruptcy petition that was dismissed within the prior year.

If the debtor had two or more bankruptcy petitions dismissed during the prior year, the Code presumes bad faith, and the automatic stay does not go into effect until the court determines that the petition was filed in good faith. In addition, the automatic stay on secured property terminates forty-five days after the creditors' meeting (see page 558) unless the debtor redeems or reaffirms certain debts (*reaffirmation* will be discussed on page 561). In other words, the debtor cannot keep the secured property (such as a financed automobile), even if she or he continues to make payments on it, without reinstating the rights of the secured party to collect on the debt.

Estate in Bankruptcy

Estate in Property All of the property owned by a person, including real estate and personal property.

On the commencement of a liquidation proceeding under Chapter 7, an **estate in property** is created. The estate consists of all the debtor's interests in property currently held, wherever located, together with *community property* (property jointly owned by a husband and wife in certain states—see Chapter 36), property transferred in a transaction voidable by

13. *In re Kuehn*, 563 F.3d 289 (7th Cir. 2009).

14. The court might grant an extension, for example, on a motion by the trustee that the property is of value to the estate.

the trustee, proceeds and profits from the property of the estate, and certain after-acquired property.

LEARNING OBJECTIVE 3

In a bankruptcy proceeding, what constitutes the debtor's estate in property? What property is exempt from the estate under federal bankruptcy law?

Interests in certain property—such as gifts, inheritances, property settlements (from divorce), and life insurance death proceeds—to which the debtor becomes entitled *within 180 days after filing* may also become part of the estate. Withholdings for employee benefit plan contributions are excluded from the estate.

Generally, though, the filing of a bankruptcy petition fixes a dividing line: property acquired before the filing of the petition becomes property of the estate, and property acquired after the filing of the petition, except as just noted, remains the debtor's.

The Bankruptcy Trustee

Promptly after the order for relief has been entered, a bankruptcy trustee is appointed. The basic duty of the trustee is to collect the debtor's available estate and reduce it to cash for distribution, preserving the interests of both the debtor and the unsecured creditors. This requires that the trustee be accountable for administering the debtor's estate.

To enable the trustee to accomplish this duty, the Code gives the trustee certain powers, stated in both general and specific terms. These powers must be exercised within two years of the order for relief.

Duties for Means Testing The trustee is required to review promptly all materials filed by the debtor to determine if there is substantial abuse. Within ten days after the first meeting of the creditors (discussed shortly), the trustee must file a statement as to whether the case is presumed to be an abuse under the means test. The trustee must provide all creditors with a copy of this statement.

When there is a presumption of abuse, the trustee must either file a motion to dismiss the petition (or convert it to a Chapter 13 case) or file a statement setting forth the reasons why the motion would not be appropriate.

Trustee's Powers The trustee has the power to require persons holding the debtor's property at the time the petition is filed to deliver the property to the trustee.[15] To enable the trustee to implement this power, the Code provides that the trustee has rights *equivalent* to those of certain other parties, such as a creditor who has a judicial lien. This power of a trustee, which is equivalent to that of a lien creditor, is known as the *strong-arm power.*

In addition, the trustee also has specific *powers of avoidance*—that is, the trustee can set aside (avoid) a sale or other transfer of the debtor's property, taking it back as a part of the debtor's estate. These powers of avoidance extend to any voidable rights available to the debtor, preferences, and fraudulent transfers by the debtor (these will each be discussed next). A trustee can also avoid certain statutory liens (creditors' claims against the debtor's property).

The debtor shares most of the trustee's avoidance powers. Thus, if the trustee does not take action to enforce one of these rights, the debtor in a liquidation bankruptcy can enforce it.

Voidable Rights A trustee steps into the shoes of the debtor. Thus, any reason that a debtor can use to obtain the return of his or her property can be used by the trustee as well. The grounds for recovery include fraud, duress, incapacity, and mutual mistake.

EXAMPLE 21.11 Blane sells his boat to Inga. Inga gives Blane a check, knowing that she has insufficient funds in her bank account to cover the check. Inga has committed fraud.

15. Usually, though, the trustee takes constructive, rather than actual, possession of the debtor's property. For instance, a trustee might change the locks on the doors and hire a security guard to constructively take possession of a business's inventory.

Blane has the right to avoid that transfer and recover the boat from Inga. If Blane files for Chapter 7 bankruptcy, the trustee can exercise the same right to recover the boat from Inga, and the boat becomes part of the debtor's estate. •

Preference In bankruptcy proceedings, a property transfer or payment made by the debtor that favors one creditor over others.

Preferences

A debtor is not permitted to make a property transfer or a payment that favors—or gives a **preference** to—one creditor over others. The trustee is allowed to recover payments made both voluntarily and involuntarily to one creditor in preference over another.

To have made a preferential payment that can be recovered, an *insolvent* debtor generally must have transferred property, for a *preexisting* debt, during the *ninety days* before the filing of the petition in bankruptcy. The transfer must have given the creditor more than the creditor would have received as a result of the bankruptcy proceedings. The Code presumes that the debtor is insolvent during the ninety-day period before filing a petition.

Preferred Creditor In the context of bankruptcy, a creditor who has received a preferential transfer from a debtor.

If a **preferred creditor** (one who has received a preferential transfer from the debtor) has sold the property to an innocent third party, the trustee cannot recover the property from the innocent party. The trustee can generally force the preferred creditor to pay the value of the property, however.

Preferences to Insiders

Sometimes, the creditor receiving the preference is an *insider*. An insider is any individual, partner, partnership, or officer or director of a corporation (or a relative of one of these) who has a close relationship with the debtor. In this situation, the avoidance power of the trustee is extended to transfers made within *one year* before filing. (If the transfer was fraudulent, as will be discussed shortly, the trustee can avoid transfers made within *two years* before filing.)

KNOW THIS

Usually, when property is recovered as a preference, the trustee sells it and distributes the proceeds to the debtor's creditors.

Note, however, that if the transfer occurred before the ninety-day period, the trustee is required to prove that the debtor was insolvent at the time it occurred or that the transfer was made to or for the benefit of an insider.

Transfers That Do Not Constitute Preferences

Not all transfers are preferences. To be a preference, the transfer must be made in exchange for something other than current consideration.

Most courts do not consider a debtor's payment for services rendered within fifteen days prior to the payment to be a preference. If a creditor receives payment in the ordinary course of business, such as payment of last month's cell phone bill, the trustee in bankruptcy cannot recover the payment.

To be recoverable, a preference must be a transfer for an antecedent (preexisting) debt, such as a year-old landscaping bill. In addition, the Code permits a consumer-debtor to transfer any property to a creditor up to a total value of $5,850, without the transfer constituting a preference. Payments of domestic-support debts do not constitute a preference. Neither do payments required under a plan created by an approved credit-counseling agency.

When is the sale of gold jewelry considered a fraudulent transfer?

(lissart/iStockphoto.com)

Fraudulent Transfers

A trustee can avoid (set aside or cancel) fraudulent transfers or obligations if (1) they were made within two years of the filing of the petition or (2) they were made with actual intent to hinder, delay, or defraud a creditor. **EXAMPLE 21.12** April is planning to petition for bankruptcy, so she sells her gold jewelry, worth $10,000, to a friend for $500. The friend agrees that in the future he will "sell" the jewelry back to April for the same amount. This is a fraudulent transfer that the trustee can undo. •

Exemptions

The trustee takes control over the debtor's property, but an individual debtor is entitled to exempt certain property from the bankruptcy. The Code exempts the following property:[16]

1. Up to $21,625 in equity in the debtor's residence and burial plot (the homestead exemption).
2. Interest in a motor vehicle up to $3,450.
3. Interest, up to $550 for a particular item, in household goods and furnishings, wearing apparel, appliances, books, animals, crops, and musical instruments (the aggregate total of all items is limited to $11,525).
4. Interest in jewelry up to $1,450.
5. Interest in any other property up to $1,150, plus any unused part of the $21,625 homestead exemption up to $10,825.
6. Interest in any tools of the debtor's trade up to $2,175.
7. A life insurance contract owned by the debtor (other than a credit life insurance contract).
8. Certain interests in accrued dividends and interest under life insurance contracts owned by the debtor, not to exceed $11,525.
9. Professionally prescribed health aids.
10. The right to receive Social Security and certain welfare benefits, alimony and support, certain retirement funds and pensions, and education savings accounts held for specific periods of time.
11. The right to receive certain personal-injury and other awards up to $21,625.

Individual states have the power to pass legislation precluding debtors from using the federal exemptions within the state. A majority of the states have done this, as mentioned earlier in this chapter. In those states, debtors may use only state, not federal, exemptions. In the rest of the states, an individual debtor (or a husband and wife filing jointly) may choose either the exemptions provided under state law or the federal exemptions.

The Homestead Exemption

The Bankruptcy Code limits the amount that can be claimed under the homestead exemption in bankruptcy. In general, if the debtor acquired the home within three and one-half years preceding the date of filing, the maximum equity exempted is $146,450 even if state law would permit a higher amount.

In addition, the state homestead exemption is available only if the debtor has lived in the state for two years before filing the petition. Furthermore, a debtor who has violated securities law, been convicted of a felony, or engaged in certain other intentional misconduct may not be permitted to claim the homestead exemption at all.

Creditors' Meeting and Claims

Within a reasonable time after the order of relief has been granted (not more than forty days), the trustee must call a meeting of the creditors listed in the schedules filed by the debtor. The bankruptcy judge does not attend this meeting, but the debtor must attend and submit to an examination under oath. At the meeting, the trustee ensures that the debtor is aware of the potential consequences of bankruptcy and the possibility of filing under a different chapter of the Code.

---

16. The dollar amounts stated in the Bankruptcy Code are adjusted automatically every three years on April 1 based on changes in the Consumer Price Index. The adjusted amounts are rounded to the nearest $25. The amounts stated in this chapter are in accordance with those computed on April 1, 2010.

To be entitled to receive a portion of the debtor's estate, each creditor normally files a *proof of claim* with the bankruptcy court clerk within ninety days of the creditors' meeting. The proof of claim lists the creditor's name and address, as well as the amount that the creditor asserts is owed to the creditor by the debtor.

In a bankruptcy case in which the debtor has no assets (called a "no-asset case"), creditors are notified of the debtor's petition for bankruptcy but are instructed not to file a claim. In no-asset cases, the unsecured creditors will receive no payment, and most, if not all, of these debts will be discharged.

Distribution of Property

The Code provides specific rules for the distribution of the debtor's property to secured and unsecured creditors. If any amount remains after the priority classes of creditors have been satisfied, it is turned over to the debtor. Exhibit 21.2 below illustrates the collection and distribution of property in most voluntary bankruptcies.

Distribution to Secured Creditors

The rights of perfected secured creditors were discussed in Chapter 20. The Code requires that consumer-debtors file a statement of intention with respect to the secured collateral. They can choose to pay off the debt and redeem the collateral, claim it is exempt, reaffirm the debt and continue making payments, or surrender the property to the secured party. If the collateral is surrendered to the secured party, the secured creditor can enforce the security interest either by accepting the property in full satisfaction of the debt or by selling the collateral and using the proceeds to pay off the debt.

Thus, the secured party has priority over unsecured parties as to the proceeds from the disposition of the collateral. Should the collateral be insufficient to cover the secured debt owed, the secured creditor becomes an unsecured creditor for the difference.

Distribution to Unsecured Creditors

Bankruptcy law establishes an order of priority for classes of debts owed to *unsecured* creditors, and they are paid in the order of their priority. Each class must be fully paid before the next class is entitled to any of the remaining proceeds.

Exhibit 21.2 Collection and Distribution of Property in Most Voluntary Bankruptcies

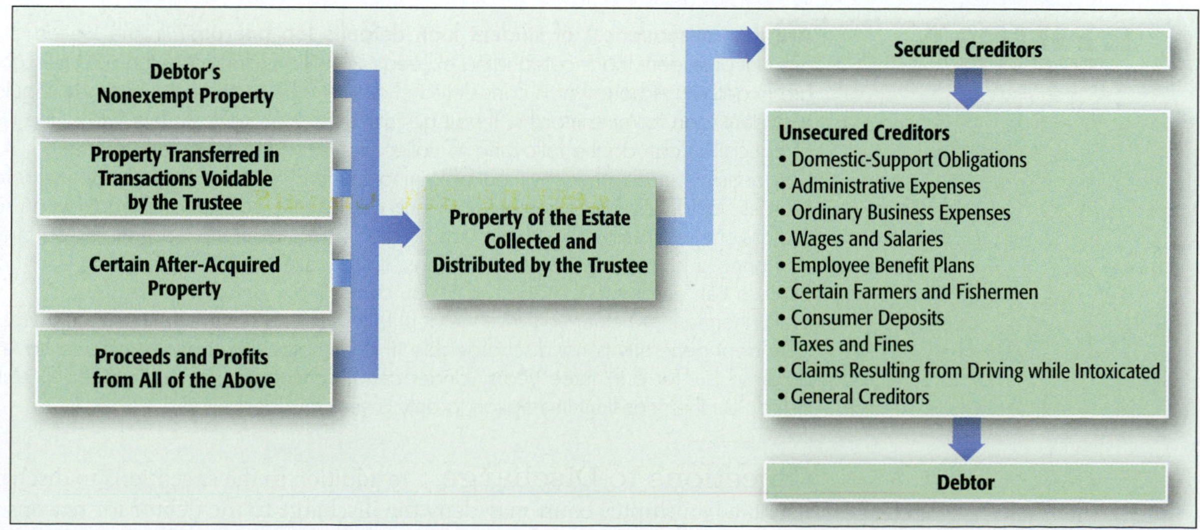

If there are insufficient proceeds to pay the full amount to all the creditors in a class, the proceeds are distributed *proportionately* to the creditors in that class, and classes lower in priority receive nothing. If there is any balance remaining after all the creditors are paid, it is returned to the debtor.

In almost all Chapter 7 bankruptcies, the funds will be insufficient to pay all creditors. Note that claims for domestic-support obligations, such as child support and alimony, have the highest priority among unsecured claims, so these debts must be paid first. If any amount remains after the priority classes of creditors have been satisfied, it is turned over to the debtor.

Discharge

KNOW THIS

Often, a discharge in bankruptcy—even under Chapter 7—does not free a debtor of *all* of her or his debts.

From the debtor's point of view, the primary purpose of liquidation is to obtain a fresh start through the discharge of debts. A discharge voids, or sets aside, any judgment on a discharged debt and prevents any action to collect it. Certain debts, however, are not dischargeable in bankruptcy. Also, certain debtors may not qualify to have all debts discharged in bankruptcy. These situations are discussed next.

LEARNING OBJECTIVE 4

What is the difference between an exception to discharge and an objection to discharge?

Exceptions to Discharge

The most important claims that are not dischargeable under Chapter 7 include the following:

1. Claims for back taxes accruing within two years prior to bankruptcy.
2. Claims for amounts borrowed by the debtor to pay federal taxes or any nondischargeable taxes.
3. Claims against property or funds obtained by the debtor under false pretenses or by false misrepresentations.
4. Claims based on fraud or misuse of funds by the debtor or claims involving the debtor's *embezzlement* or *larceny* (see pages 164 and 161, respectively, in Chapter 6).
5. Domestic-support obligations and property settlements.
6. Claims for amounts due on a retirement loan account.
7. Claims based on willful or malicious conduct by the debtor toward another or the property of another.
8. Certain government fines and penalties.
9. Certain student loans, unless payment of the loans causes an undue hardship for the debtor and the debtor's dependents.

Are the consequences of student loan defaults too onerous? In the United States today, the amount of student loans outstanding exceeds $1 trillion, and more than 20 percent of these loans are in default. A borrower is considered in default if he or she has not made regular payments on a student loan for nine months. If you go into default on your student loans, the U.S. Department of Education can do the following to collect the debt: (1) keep your tax refund, if you have one, (2) garnish your paycheck without obtaining a court judgment, and (3) take your federal benefits, such as Social Security retirement payments or disability payments. In addition, in some states, any professional license that you have can be revoked. Last but not least, the Department of Education can bring a lawsuit against you. If it wins, it can collect the judgment from your bank accounts or place a lien on any real property that you own.

Furthermore, whether you owe the debt to the federal government or to a private lender, student loan debt generally is *not* dischargeable in bankruptcy. You may be able to have your payments deferred but for only three years. Under certain circumstances, student loan debts may be canceled, but the rules limit this option to only a very few borrowers.

Objections to Discharge

In addition to the exceptions to discharge previously listed, a bankruptcy court may deny the discharge to the debtor for reasons relating to the debtor's *conduct* and not to the debt. The situations in which a court can deny discharge include the following:

1. The debtor's concealment or destruction of property with the intent to hinder, delay, or defraud a creditor.
2. The debtor's fraudulent concealment or destruction of financial records.
3. The granting of a discharge to the debtor within eight years prior to the filing of the petition.
4. The debtor's failure to complete the required consumer education course (unless such a course was not available).
5. Proceedings in which the debtor could be found guilty of a felony. (Basically, a court may not discharge any debt until the completion of the felony proceedings against the debtor.)

When a discharge is denied under these circumstances, the debtor's assets are still distributed to the creditors. After the bankruptcy proceeding, however, the debtor remains liable for the unpaid portions of all claims.

A discharge may be revoked (taken back) within one year if it is discovered that the debtor acted fraudulently or dishonestly during the bankruptcy proceeding. If that occurs, a creditor whose claim was not satisfied in the distribution of the debtor's property can proceed with his or her claim against the debtor.

Reaffirmation Agreement An agreement between a debtor and a creditor in which the debtor voluntarily agrees to pay a debt dischargeable in bankruptcy.

Reaffirmation of Debt

An agreement to pay a debt dischargeable in bankruptcy is called a **reaffirmation agreement.** A debtor may wish to pay a debt—for example, a debt owed to a family member, physician, bank, or some other creditor—even though the debt could be discharged in bankruptcy. Also, as noted previously, a debtor cannot retain secured property while continuing to pay without entering into a reaffirmation agreement.

Procedures To be enforceable, reaffirmation agreements must be made before the debtor is granted a discharge. The agreement must be signed and filed with the court (along with the original disclosure documents, as you will read shortly). Court approval is required unless the debtor is represented by an attorney during the negotiation of the reaffirmation agreement and submits the proper documents and certifications. Even when the debtor is represented by an attorney, court approval may be required if it appears that the reaffirmation will result in undue hardship to the debtor.

When court approval is required, a separate hearing will take place. The court will approve the reaffirmation only if it finds that the agreement will not result in undue hardship to the debtor and that the reaffirmation is consistent with the debtor's best interests.

Required Disclosures To discourage creditors from engaging in abusive reaffirmation practices, the law provides specific language for disclosures that must be given to debtors entering reaffirmation agreements. Among other things, these disclosures explain that the debtor is not required to reaffirm any debt, but that liens on secured property, such as mortgages and cars, will remain in effect even if the debt is not reaffirmed.

The reaffirmation agreement must disclose the amount of the debt reaffirmed, the rate of interest, the date payments begin, and the right to rescind. The disclosures also caution the debtor: "Only agree to reaffirm a debt if it is in your best interest. Be sure you can afford the payments you agree to make."

The original disclosure documents must be signed by the debtor, certified by the debtor's attorney, and filed with the court at the same time as the reaffirmation agreement. A reaffirmation agreement that is not accompanied by the original signed disclosures will not be effective.

Chapter 11—Reorganization

KNOW THIS

Chapter 11 proceedings are typically prolonged and costly. Whether a firm survives depends on its size and its ability to attract new investors despite its Chapter 11 status.

The type of bankruptcy proceeding used most commonly by corporate debtors is the Chapter 11 *reorganization*. In a reorganization, the creditors and the debtor formulate a plan under which the debtor pays a portion of its debts and the rest of the debts are discharged. The debtor is allowed to continue in business. Although this type of bankruptcy is generally a corporate reorganization, any debtors (including individuals but excluding stockbrokers and commodities brokers) who are eligible for Chapter 7 relief are eligible for relief under Chapter 11.

In 1994, Congress established a "fast-track" Chapter 11 procedure for small-business debtors whose liabilities do not exceed $2.19 million and who do not own or manage real estate. The fast track enables a debtor to avoid the appointment of a creditors' committee and also shortens the filing periods and relaxes certain other requirements. Because the process is shorter and simpler, it is less costly (see the *Linking Business Law to Corporate Management* feature on page 569 for suggestions on how small businesses can prepare for Chapter 11).

The same principles that govern the filing of a liquidation (Chapter 7) petition apply to reorganization (Chapter 11) proceedings. The case may be brought either voluntarily or involuntarily. The automatic-stay provision and its exceptions apply in reorganizations as well, as do the provisions regarding substantial abuse and additional grounds for dismissal (or conversion) of bankruptcy petitions.

Workouts

Workout An out-of-court agreement between a debtor and creditors that establishes a payment plan for discharging the debtor's debts.

In some instances, to avoid bankruptcy proceedings, creditors may prefer private, negotiated adjustments of creditor-debtor relations, also known as a **workout.** Often, these out-of-court workouts are much more flexible and thus conducive to a speedy settlement. Speed is critical because delay is one of the most costly elements in any bankruptcy proceeding. Another advantage of workouts is that they avoid the various administrative costs of bankruptcy proceedings.

Creditors' Best Interests

Once a petition for Chapter 11 has been filed, a bankruptcy court, after notice and a hearing, can dismiss or suspend all proceedings in a case at any time if dismissal or suspension would better serve the interests of the creditors. The Bankruptcy Code also allows a court, after notice and a hearing, to dismiss a case under reorganization "for cause." Cause includes the absence of a reasonable likelihood of rehabilitation, the inability to effect a plan, and an unreasonable delay by the debtor that is prejudicial to (may harm the interests of) creditors.[17]

LEARNING OBJECTIVE 5

In a Chapter 11 reorganization, what is the role of the debtor in possession?

Debtor in Possession

Debtor in Possession (DIP) In Chapter 11 bankruptcy proceedings, a debtor who is allowed to continue in possession of the estate in property (the business) and to continue business operations.

On entry of the order for relief, the debtor in Chapter 11 generally continues to operate the business as a **debtor in possession (DIP).** The court, however, may appoint a trustee (often referred to as a *receiver*) to operate the debtor's business if gross mismanagement of the business is shown or if appointing a trustee is in the best interests of the estate.

The DIP's role is similar to that of a trustee in a liquidation. The DIP is entitled to avoid preferential payments made to creditors and fraudulent transfers of assets. The DIP has the power to decide whether to cancel or assume prepetition *executory contracts* (those that are

17. See 11 U.S.C. Section 1112(b). A debtor whose petition is dismissed under this provision can file a new Chapter 11 petition (which may be granted unless it is filed in bad faith).

not yet performed—see page 246) or unexpired leases. Cancellation of executory contracts or unexpired leases can be a substantial benefit to a Chapter 11 debtor.

EXAMPLE 21.13 Five years ago, before a national recession, APT Corporation leased an office building for a twenty-year term. Now, APT can no longer pay the rent due under the lease and has filed for Chapter 11 reorganization. In this situation, the debtor in possession could cancel the lease so that APT will not be required to continue paying the substantial rent due for fifteen more years. •

Creditors' Committees

As soon as practicable after the entry of the order for relief, a committee of unsecured creditors is appointed. If the debtor has filed a plan accepted by the creditors, however, the trustee may decide not to call a meeting of the creditors. The committee may consult with the trustee or the debtor concerning the administration of the case or the formulation of the plan. Additional creditors' committees may be appointed to represent special interest creditors, and a court may order the trustee to change a committee's membership as needed to ensure adequate representation of the creditors.

Generally, no orders affecting the estate will be entered without the consent of the committee or a hearing in which the judge is informed of the position of the committee. As mentioned earlier, businesses with debts of less than $2.19 million that do not own or manage real estate can avoid creditors' committees. In these fast-track proceedings, orders can be entered without a committee's consent.

The Reorganization Plan

A reorganization plan is established to conserve and administer the debtor's assets in the hope of an eventual return to successful operation and solvency. The plan must be fair and equitable and must do the following:

1. Designate classes of claims and interests.
2. Specify the treatment to be afforded the classes. (The plan must provide the same treatment for all claims in a particular class.)
3. Provide an adequate means for execution. (Individual debtors must utilize postpetition assets as necessary to execute the plan.)
4. Provide for payment of tax claims over a five-year period.

Filing the Plan

Only the debtor may file a plan within the first 120 days after the date of the order for relief. This period may be extended up to eighteen months from the date of the order for relief. If the debtor does not meet the 120-day deadline or obtain an extension, or if the debtor fails to obtain the required creditor consent (discussed below) within 180 days, any party may propose a plan. If a small-business debtor chooses to avoid a creditors' committee, the time for the debtor's filing is 180 days.

Acceptance and Confirmation of the Plan

Once the plan has been developed, it is submitted to each class of creditors for acceptance. Each class must accept the plan unless the class is adversely affected by it. The plan need not provide for full repayment to unsecured creditors. Instead, creditors receive a percentage of each dollar owed to them by the debtor.

A class has accepted the plan when a majority of the creditors, representing two-thirds of the amount of the total claim, vote to approve it. Confirmation is conditioned on the debtor's certifying that all postpetition domestic-support obligations have been paid in full. For small-business debtors, if the plan meets the listed requirements, the court must confirm the plan within forty-five days (unless this period is extended).

Even when all classes of creditors accept the plan, the court may refuse to confirm it if it is not "in the best interests of the creditors." The plan can also be modified upon the request of the debtor, DIP, trustee, U.S. trustee, or holder of an unsecured claim. If an unsecured creditor objects to the plan, specific rules apply to the value of property to be distributed under the plan. Tax claims must be paid over a five-year period.

Even if only one class of creditors has accepted the plan, the court may still confirm the plan under the Code's so-called **cram-down provision.** In other words, the court may confirm the plan over the objections of a class of creditors. Before the court can exercise this right of cram-down confirmation, it must be demonstrated that the plan is fair and equitable, and does not discriminate unfairly against any creditors.

Cram-Down Provision A provision of the Bankruptcy Code that allows a court to confirm a debtor's Chapter 11 reorganization plan even though only one class of creditors has accepted it.

Discharge The plan is binding on confirmation. The law provides, however, that confirmation of a plan does not discharge an individual debtor. *For individual debtors, the plan must be completed before discharge will be granted,* unless the court orders otherwise. For all other debtors, the court may order discharge at any time after the plan is confirmed. The debtor is given a reorganization discharge from all claims not protected under the plan. This discharge does not apply to any claims that would be denied discharge under liquidation.

Bankruptcy Relief under Chapter 12 and Chapter 13

In addition to bankruptcy relief through liquidation (Chapter 7) and reorganization (Chapter 11), the Code also provides for family-farmer and family-fisherman debt adjustments (Chapter 12) and individuals' repayment plans (Chapter 13) .

Family Farmers and Fishermen—Chapter 12

In 1986, to help relieve economic pressure on small farmers, Congress created Chapter 12 of the Bankruptcy Code. In 2005, Congress extended this protection to family fishermen, modified its provisions somewhat, and made it a permanent chapter in the Bankruptcy Code (previously, it had to be periodically renewed by Congress).

For purposes of Chapter 12, a *family farmer* is one whose gross income is at least 50 percent farm dependent and whose debts are at least 50 percent farm related.[18] The total debt must not exceed $3,792,650. A partnership or a close corporation (see Chapter 29) that is at least 50 percent owned by the farm family can also qualify as a family farmer.[19]

A *family fisherman* is one whose gross income is at least 50 percent dependent on commercial fishing operations and whose debts are at least 80 percent related to commercial fishing. The total debt for a family fisherman must not exceed $1,757,475. As with family farmers, a partnership or close corporation can also qualify.

Filing the Petition The procedure for filing a family-farmer or family-fisherman bankruptcy plan is similar to the procedure for filing a repayment plan under Chapter 13, which will be discussed in detail later in the chapter. The debtor must file a plan not later than ninety days after the order for relief. The filing of the petition acts as an automatic stay against creditors' and co-obligors' actions against the estate.

---

18. Note that the Bankruptcy Code defines a *family farmer* and a *farmer* differently. To be a farmer, a person or business must receive 50 percent of gross income from a farming operation that the person or business owns or operates—see footnote 12.

19. Note that for a corporation or partnership to qualify under Chapter 12, at least 80 percent of the value of the firm's assets must consist of assets related to the farming operation.

A farmer or fisherman who has already filed a reorganization or repayment plan may convert the plan to a Chapter 12 plan. The debtor may also convert a Chapter 12 plan to a liquidation plan.

Content and Confirmation of the Plan

The content of a plan under Chapter 12 is basically the same as that of a Chapter 13 repayment plan (described below). The plan can be modified by the debtor but, except for cause, must be confirmed or denied within forty-five days of the filing of the plan.

The plan must provide for payment of secured debts at the value of the collateral. If the secured debt exceeds the value of the collateral, the remaining debt is unsecured. For unsecured debtors, the plan must be confirmed if either the value of the property to be distributed under the plan equals the amount of the claim or the plan provides that all of the debtor's disposable income to be received in a three-year period (or longer, by court approval) will be applied to making payments. Completion of payments under the plan discharges all debts provided for by the plan.

Individuals' Repayment Plan—Chapter 13

Chapter 13 of the Bankruptcy Code provides for the "Adjustment of Debts of an Individual with Regular Income." Individuals (not partnerships or corporations) with regular income who owe fixed unsecured debts of less than $360,475 or fixed secured debts of less than $1,081,400 may take advantage of bankruptcy repayment plans.

Many small-business debtors have a choice of filing under either Chapter 11 or Chapter 13. Repayment plans offer some advantages because they are typically less expensive and less complicated than reorganization or liquidation proceedings.

Filing the Petition

A Chapter 13 repayment plan case can be initiated only by the filing of a voluntary petition by the debtor or by the conversion of a Chapter 7 petition (because of a finding of substantial abuse under the means test, for instance). Certain liquidation and reorganization cases may be converted to Chapter 13 with the consent of the debtor.[20] A trustee, who will make payments under the plan, must be appointed. On the filing of a repayment plan petition, the automatic stay previously discussed takes effect. Although the stay applies to all or part of the debtor's consumer debt, it does not apply to any business debt incurred by the debtor or to any domestic-support obligations.

Good Faith Requirement

The Bankruptcy Code imposes the requirement of good faith on a debtor in both the filing of the petition and the filing of the plan. The Code does not define good faith, but if the circumstances as a whole indicate bad faith, a court can dismiss a debtor's Chapter 13 petition.

CASE EXAMPLE 21.14 Roger and Pauline Buis formed an air show business called Otto Airshows that included a helicopter decorated as "Otto the Clown." After a competitor won a defamation lawsuit against the Buises and Otto Airshows, the Buises stopped doing business as Otto Airshows and formed a new firm, Prop and Rotor Aviation, Inc., to which they leased the Otto equipment. Within a month, they filed a bankruptcy petition under Chapter 13. The plan and the schedules did not mention the lawsuit, the equipment lease, and several other items. The court therefore dismissed the Buises' petition due to bad faith. The debtors had not included all of their assets and liabilities on their initial petition, and they had timed its filing to avoid payment on the defamation judgment.[21]

20. A Chapter 13 repayment plan may be converted to a Chapter 7 liquidation either at the request of the debtor or, under certain circumstances, "for cause" by a creditor. A Chapter 13 case may be converted to a Chapter 11 case after a hearing.

21. *In re Buis,* 337 Bankr. 243 (N.D.Fla. 2006).

The Repayment Plan A plan of rehabilitation by repayment must provide for the following:

1. The turning over to the trustee of future earnings or income of the debtor as necessary for execution of the plan.
2. Full payment through deferred cash payments of all claims entitled to priority, such as taxes.[22]
3. Identical treatment of all claims within a particular class. (The Code permits the debtor to list co-debtors, such as guarantors or sureties, as a separate class.)

The repayment plan may provide for payment of all obligations in full or for payment of a lesser amount. The debtor must begin making payments under the proposed plan within thirty days after the plan has been filed and must continue to make "timely" payments from her or his disposable income. If the debtor fails to make timely payments or does not commence payments within the thirty-day period, the court can convert the case to a liquidation bankruptcy or dismiss the petition.

In putting together a repayment plan, a debtor must apply the means test to identify the amount of disposable income that will be available to repay creditors. The debtor is allowed to deduct certain expenses from monthly income to arrive at this amount. Can a debtor who owns a car outright claim the costs of car ownership as an expense? That was the issue in the following case.

22. As with a Chapter 11 reorganization plan, full repayment of all claims is not always required.

Case 21.2

Ransom v. FIA Card Services, N.A.

Supreme Court of the United States, __ U.S. __, 131 S.Ct. 716, 178 L.Ed.2d 603 (2011). www.supremecourt.gov [a]

(CraigRJD/iStockphoto.com)

A debtor owns a Toyota Camry free and clear. Can he claim a car-ownership deduction on the repayment plan?

FACTS Jason Ransom filed a petition in a federal bankruptcy court to declare bankruptcy under Chapter 13. Among his assets, Ransom reported a Toyota Camry that he owned free of any debt. In listing monthly expenses for the means test, he claimed a deduction of $471 for car ownership and a separate deduction of $388 for car-operating costs. Based on his means-test calculations, Ransom proposed a five-year plan that would repay about 25 percent of his unsecured debt. He listed FIA Card Services, N.A., as an unsecured creditor. FIA objected to Ransom's plan, arguing that he should not have claimed the car-ownership allowance because he did not make payments on his car. The court agreed with FIA and issued a decision in its favor. A Bankruptcy Appellate Panel and the U.S. Court of Appeals for the Ninth Circuit affirmed the decision. Ransom appealed to the United States Supreme Court.

ISSUE Can a debtor in bankruptcy claim the car-ownership deduction even though the debtor owns the car outright and does not make payments on it?

DECISION No. The United States Supreme Court affirmed the lower court's decision.

REASON The Supreme Court referred to tables of standardized expense amounts that a debtor could claim as reasonable living expenses and shield from creditors. The Bankruptcy Code limits a debtor's expense amounts to those that are "applicable," or appropriate. A deduction is appropriate only if the debtor will incur that expense during the life of the Chapter 13 plan. Because Ransom owned the car free and clear, the "Ownership Costs" category was not "applicable" to him, and he could not claim such an expense. The ultimate result was that confirmation of his repayment plan was denied. (Confirmation of repayment plans will be discussed shortly.)

CRITICAL THINKING—Economic Consideration *Should debtors with older vehicles be allowed to take an additional deduction for operating expenses? Explain.*

a. In the "Supreme Court Documents" column, in the "Opinions" pull-down menu, select "Bound Volumes." On the next page, in the "For Search Term:" box, type "Ransom" and click on "Search." In the result, click on the name of the case to access the opinion. The United States Supreme Court maintains this Web site.

The Length of the Plan The length of the payment plan can be three or five years, depending on the debtor's family income. If the debtor's family income is less than the median family income in the relevant geographic area under the means test, the term of the proposed plan must be three years.[23] The term may not exceed five years.

Confirmation of the Plan After the plan is filed, the court holds a confirmation hearing, at which interested parties (such as creditors) may object to the plan. The hearing must be held at least twenty days, but no more than forty-five days, after the meeting of the creditors. The debtor must have filed all prepetition tax returns and paid all postpetition domestic-support obligations before a court will confirm any plan. The court will confirm a plan with respect to each claim of a secured creditor under any of the following circumstances:

1. If the secured creditors have accepted the plan.
2. If the plan provides that secured creditors retain their liens until there is payment in full or until the debtor receives a discharge.
3. If the debtor surrenders the property securing the claims to the creditors.

KNOW THIS

Courts, trustees, and creditors carefully monitor Chapter 13 debtors. If payments are not made, a court can require that the debtor explain why and may allow a creditor to take back the property.

Discharge After the completion of all payments, the court grants a discharge of all debts provided for by the repayment plan. Except for allowed claims not provided for by the plan, certain long-term debts provided for by the plan, certain tax claims, payments on retirement accounts, and claims for domestic-support obligations, all other debts are dischargeable. Under current law, debts related to injury or property damage caused while driving under the influence of alcohol or drugs are nondischargeable.

In the following case, a debtor had proposed to discharge some of his student loan debt in a Chapter 13 repayment plan. Certain student loan debts can be discharged under Chapter 13, but only if the court finds that payment of the debt would constitute an "undue hardship" for the debtor. Due to an oversight by the creditor and an error by the bankruptcy court, the plan was approved and subsequently confirmed without the required finding of "undue hardship." The United States Supreme Court had to decide whether these problems rendered the discharge of the debt void.

23. See 11 U.S.C. Section 1322(d) for details.

Case 21.3

United Student Aid Funds, Inc. v. Espinosa

Supreme Court of the United States, __ U.S. __, 130 S.Ct. 1367, 176 L.Ed.2d 158 (2010). www.supremecourt.gov[a]

(YinYang/iStockphoto.com)

Can student loan debts be avoided in a bankruptcy proceeding?

FACTS Francisco Espinosa filed a petition for an individual repayment plan under Chapter 13 of the Bankruptcy Code. His plan proposed to pay only the principal on his student loan and to discharge the interest. United Student Aid Funds, Inc. (the creditor), had notice of the plan and did not object. Without finding that payment of the interest would cause undue hardship (as required under the Code), the court confirmed the plan. Years later, however, United filed a motion under Federal Rule of Civil Procedure 60(b)(4) asking the bankruptcy court to rule that its order confirming the plan was void because the order was issued in violation of the laws and rules governing bankruptcy. The court denied United's petition and ordered the creditor to cease its collection efforts. United appealed, and the case ultimately reached the United States Supreme Court.

a. In the "Supreme Court Documents" column, in the "Opinions" pull-down menu, select "Bound Volumes." On the next page, in the "For Search Term:" box, type "Espinosa" and click on "Search." In the result, click on the name of the case to access the opinion. The United States Supreme Court maintains this Web site.

Case 21.3—Continues next page

Case 21.3—Continued

ISSUE If a bankruptcy court committed a legal error by confirming a debtor's repayment plan to discharge student loan debt without the required finding of undue hardship, but the creditor did not object, is the court's judgment void?

DECISION No. The United States Supreme Court affirmed the decision of the lower court that the bankruptcy court's order was not void and that the student loan debt was thus discharged.

REASON The Supreme Court pointed out that the bankruptcy court's order confirming Espinosa's proposed plan was a final judgment from which United did not appeal. Federal Rule of Civil Procedure 60(b)(4) authorizes a court to relieve a party from a final judgment if that judgment is void, but a judgment is not void simply because it is or may have been erroneous. Moreover, a motion under this rule is not a substitute for a timely appeal. "The Bankruptcy Court's failure to find undue hardship before confirming Espinosa's plan was a legal error. But the order remains enforceable and binding on United because United had notice of the error and failed to object or timely appeal."

CRITICAL THINKING—Ethical Consideration *At one point, United argued that if the Court did not declare the bankruptcy court's order void, dishonest debtors would be encouraged to abuse the Chapter 13 process. How might such abuse occur, and should the possibility of such abuse affect the Court's decision? Discuss your answer.*

Reviewing . . . Creditors' Rights and Bankruptcy

Three months ago, Janet Hart's husband of twenty years died of cancer. Although he had medical insurance, he left Janet with outstanding medical bills of more than $50,000. Janet has worked at the local library for the past ten years, earning $1,500 per month. Since her husband's death, Janet also has received $1,500 in Social Security benefits and $1,100 in life insurance proceeds every month, giving her a monthly income of $4,100. After she pays the mortgage payment of $1,500 and the amounts due on other debts each month, Janet barely has enough left over to buy groceries for her family (she has two teenage daughters at home). She decides to file for Chapter 7 bankruptcy, hoping for a fresh start. Using the information provided in the chapter, answer the following questions.

1. Under the Bankruptcy Code after the reform act, what must Janet do before filing a petition for relief under Chapter 7?
2. How much time does Janet have after filing the bankruptcy petition to submit the required schedules? What happens if Janet does not meet the deadline?
3. Assume that Janet files a petition under Chapter 7. Further assume that the median family income in the state in which Janet lives is $49,300. What steps would a court take to determine whether Janet's petition is presumed to be "substantial abuse" under the means test?
4. Suppose that the court determines that no presumption of substantial abuse applies in Janet's case. Nevertheless, the court finds that Janet does have the ability to pay at least a portion of the medical bills out of her disposable income. What would the court likely order in that situation?

DEBATE THIS Rather than being allowed to file Chapter 7 bankruptcy petitions, individuals and couples should always be forced to make an effort to pay off their debts through Chapter 13.

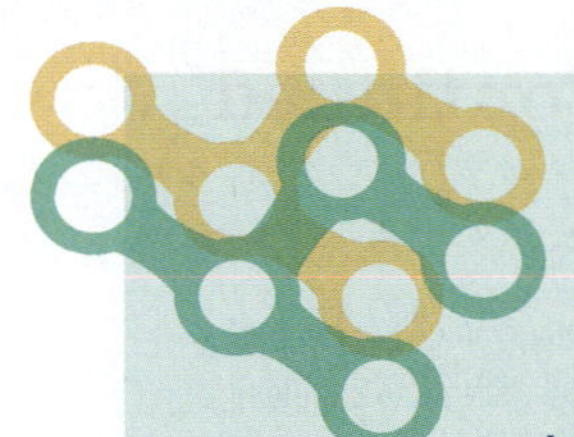

LINKING BUSINESS LAW to Corporate Management

What Can You Do to Prepare for a Chapter 11 Reorganization?

Chapter 11 of the Bankruptcy Code expresses the broad public policy of encouraging commerce. To this end, Chapter 11 allows a financially troubled business firm to petition for reorganization in bankruptcy while it is still solvent so that the firm's business can continue. Small businesses, however, do not fare very well under Chapter 11. Although a few corporations that enter into Chapter 11 emerge as functioning entities, only a small number of companies survive the process.

Plan Ahead

If you ever are a small-business owner contemplating Chapter 11 reorganization, you can improve your chances of being among the survivors by planning ahead. To ensure the greatest possibility of success, you should take action before, not after, entering bankruptcy proceedings. Discuss your financial troubles openly and cooperatively with creditors to see if you can agree on a workout or some other arrangement.

If you appear to have no choice but to file for a Chapter 11 protection, try to persuade a lender to loan you funds to see you through the bankruptcy. If your business is a small corporation, you might try to negotiate a favorable deal with a major investor. For example, a small business could offer to transfer ownership of stock to the investor in return for a loan to pay the costs of the bankruptcy proceedings and an option to repurchase the stock when the firm becomes profitable again.

Consult with Creditors

Most important, you should form a Chapter 11 plan before entering bankruptcy proceedings. Consult with creditors in advance to see what kind of plan would be acceptable to them, and prepare your plan accordingly. Having an acceptable plan prepared before you file will expedite the proceedings and thus save substantially on costs.

Critical Thinking

More bankruptcy filings are under Chapter 11, which may increase the time needed to complete the proceedings. How might this affect the likelihood that a firm will be able to negotiate a workout agreement with its creditors?

Key Terms

artisan's lien 543
attachment 544
automatic stay 555
consumer-debtor 551
co-surety 548
cram-down provision 564
creditors' composition agreement 545
debtor in possession (DIP) 562
discharge 552
estate in property 555
garnishment 544
guarantor 546
homestead exemption 548
liquidation 551
mechanic's lien 543
order for relief 554
petition in bankruptcy 552
preference 557
preferred creditor 557
reaffirmation agreement 561
right of contribution 548
right of reimbursement 548
right of subrogation 547
surety 545
suretyship 545
U.S. trustee 553
workout 562
writ of attachment 544
writ of execution 544

Chapter Summary: Creditors' Rights and Bankruptcy

LAWS ASSISTING CREDITORS	
Liens (See pages 543–544.)	1. *Mechanic's lien*—A nonpossessory, filed lien on an owner's real estate for labor, services, or materials furnished for making improvements on the realty. 2. *Artisan's lien*—A possessory lien on an owner's personal property for labor performed or value added.

Continued

Chapter Summary: Creditors' Rights and Bankruptcy—Continued

Liens—Continued	3. *Judicial liens*— a. Writ of attachment—A court order to seize a debtor's nonexempt property prior to a court's final determination of the creditor's rights to the property. Attachment is available only if the creditor posts a bond and complies with the applicable state statutes. b. Writ of execution—A court order directing the sheriff to seize (levy) and sell a debtor's nonexempt real or personal property to satisfy a court's judgment in the creditor's favor.
Garnishment (See pages 544–545.)	A collection remedy that allows a creditor to attach a debtor's funds (such as wages owed or bank accounts) and property that are held by a third person.
Creditors' Composition Agreements (See page 545.)	A contract between a debtor and his or her creditors by which the debtor's debts are discharged by payment of a sum less than the amount actually owed.
Suretyship and Guaranty (See pages 545–548.)	Under contract, a third person agrees to be primarily or secondarily liable for the debt owed by the principal debtor. A creditor can turn to this third person for satisfaction of the debt.
PROTECTION FOR DEBTORS	
Exemptions (See pages 548–549.)	Certain property of a debtor is exempt from creditors' actions under state laws. Each state permits a debtor to retain the family home, either in its entirety or up to a specified dollar amount, free from the claims of unsecured creditors or trustees in bankruptcy (homestead exemption).

BANKRUPTCY—A COMPARISON OF CHAPTERS 7, 11, 12, AND 13

Issue	Chapter 7	Chapter 11	Chapters 12 and 13
Who Can Petition	Debtor (voluntary) or creditors (involuntary).	Debtor (voluntary) or creditors (involuntary).	Debtor (voluntary) only.
Who Can Be a Debtor	Any "person" (including partnerships and corporations) except railroads, insurance companies, banks, savings and loan institutions, investment companies licensed by the U.S. Small Business Administration, and credit unions. Farmers and charitable institutions cannot be involuntarily petitioned.	Any debtor eligible for Chapter 7 relief; railroads are also eligible.	*Chapter 12*—Any family farmer (one whose gross income is at least 50 percent farm dependent and whose debts are at least 50 percent farm related) or family fisherman (one whose gross income is at least 50 percent dependent on and whose debts are at least 80 percent related to commercial fishing) or any partnership or close corporation at least 50 percent owned by a family farmer or fisherman, when total debt does not exceed $3,792,650 for a family farmer and $1,757,475 for a family fisherman. *Chapter 13*—Any individual (not partnerships or corporations) with regular income who owes fixed (liquidated) unsecured debts of less than $360,475 or fixed secured debts of less than $1,081,400.
Procedure Leading to Discharge	Nonexempt property is sold with proceeds to be distributed (in order) to priority groups. Dischargeable debts are terminated.	Plan is submitted. If it is approved and followed, debts are discharged.	Plan is submitted and must be approved if the value of the property to be distributed equals the amount of the claims or if the debtor turns over disposable income for a three-year or five-year period. If the plan is followed, debts are discharged.
Advantages	On liquidation and distribution, most debts are discharged, and the debtor has an opportunity for a fresh start.	Debtor continues in business. Creditors can either accept the plan, or it can be "crammed down" on them. The plan allows for the reorganization and liquidation of debts over the plan period.	Debtor continues in business or possession of assets. If the plan is approved, most debts are discharged after a three-year period.

ExamPrep

ISSUE SPOTTERS

1. Joe contracts with Larry of Midwest Roofing to fix Joe's roof. Joe pays half of the contract price in advance. Larry and Midwest complete the job, but Joe refuses to pay the rest of the price. What can Larry and Midwest do? **(See page 543.)**
2. Ogden is a vice president of Plumbing Service, Inc. (PSI). On May 1, Ogden loans PSI $10,000. On June 1, the firm repays the loan. On July 1, PSI files for bankruptcy. Quentin is appointed trustee. Can Quentin recover the $10,000 paid to Ogden on June 1? Why or why not? **(See page 557.)**

—Check your answers to the Issue Spotters against the answers provided in Appendix E at the end of this text.

BEFORE THE TEST

Go to www.cengagebrain.com, enter the ISBN 9781133273561, and click on "Find" to locate this textbook's Web site. Then, click on "Access Now" under "Study Tools," and select Chapter 21 at the top. There, you will find a Practice Quiz that you can take to assess your mastery of the concepts in this chapter, as well as Flashcards, a Glossary of important terms, and Video Questions (when assigned).

For Review

Answers to the even-numbered questions in this For Review section can be found in Appendix F at the end of this text.

1. What is a writ of execution? What is a prejudgment attachment? How does a creditor use these remedies?
2. What is garnishment? When might a creditor undertake a garnishment proceeding?
3. In a bankruptcy proceeding, what constitutes the debtor's estate in property? What property is exempt from the estate under federal bankruptcy law?
4. What is the difference between an exception to discharge and an objection to discharge?
5. In a Chapter 11 reorganization, what is the role of the debtor in possession?

Business Scenarios and Case Problems

21–1 Artisan's Lien. Air Ruidoso, Ltd., operated a commuter airline and air charter service between Ruidoso, New Mexico, and airports in Albuquerque and El Paso. Executive Aviation Center, Inc., provided services for airlines at the Albuquerque International Airport. When Air Ruidoso failed to pay more than $10,000 that it owed for fuel, oil, and oxygen, Executive Aviation took possession of Air Ruidoso's plane. Executive Aviation claimed that it had a lien on the plane and filed a suit in a New Mexico state court to foreclose. Do supplies such as fuel, oil, and oxygen qualify as "materials" for the purpose of creating an artisan's lien? Why or why not? **(See page 543.)**

21–2 Question with Sample Answer—Voluntary versus Involuntary Bankruptcy. Burke has been a rancher all her life, raising cattle and crops. Her ranch is valued at $500,000, almost all of which is exempt under state law. Burke has eight creditors and a total indebtedness of $70,000. Two of her largest creditors are Oman ($30,000 owed) and Sneed ($25,000 owed). The other six creditors have claims of less than $5,000 each. A drought has ruined all of Burke's crops and forced her to sell many of her cattle at a loss. She cannot pay off her creditors. **(See pages 552–554.)**

1. Under the Bankruptcy Code, can Burke, with a $500,000 ranch, voluntarily petition herself into bankruptcy? Explain.
2. Could either Oman or Sneed force Burke into involuntary bankruptcy? Explain.

—For a sample answer to Question 21–2, go to Appendix G at the end of this text.

21–3 Discharge in Bankruptcy. Cathy Coleman took out loans to complete her college education. After graduation, Coleman worked as a teacher before she filed a Chapter 13 bankruptcy petition. The court confirmed a five-year plan that required Coleman to commit all of her disposable income to paying the student loans. Less than a year later, she was laid off. Still owing more than $100,000 in student loans, Coleman asked the court to discharge the debt on the ground that paying it would be an undue hardship for her. Under Chapter 13, are student loans dischargeable? Should the court grant her request? What argument could be made in support of Coleman's request? [*In re Coleman,* 560 F.3d 1000 (9th Cir. 2009)] **(See pages 552–554.)**

21–4 Discharge. Caroline McAfee loaned $400,000 to Carter Oaks Crossing. Joseph Harman, Carter's president, signed a personal guaranty for the loan. Later, Harman obtained a discharge in bankruptcy under Chapter 7 for his personal debts. His petition did not list the guaranty among the debts. When Carter defaulted on the loan, McAfee sought to collect the unpaid amount from Harman based on the guaranty. Harman argued that the guaranty had been discharged in his bankruptcy. Is Harman correct? Why or why not? [*Harman v. McAfee*, 302 Ga.App. 698, 691 S.E.2d 586 (2010)] **(See pages 546–548.)**

21–5 Liens. Autolign Manufacturing Group, Inc., borrowed funds from Wamco 34, Ltd., to operate its auto parts business. The loan was secured by the molds that were used to form the parts. Autolign contracted with Delta Engineered Plastics, LLC, to make the parts and provided Delta with the molds. When Autolign defaulted on its obligations to Wamco and Delta, Delta asserted a "molder's lien" against the molds in its possession. A molder's lien is similar to an artisan's lien. Wamco argued that the molds were its property. Which claim had priority? Explain. [*Delta Engineered Plastics, LLC v. Autolign Manufacturing Group, Inc.*, 286 Mich.App. 115, 777 N.W.2d 502 (2010)] **(See page 543.)**

21–6 Guaranty. Majestic Group Korea, Ltd., borrowed $1.5 million from Overseas Private Investment Corp. (OPIC) to finance a Ruby Tuesday's restaurant. Nam Koo Kim, the sole owner of Majestic, and his spouse Hee Sun Kim signed personal guaranties for full payment of the loan. Majestic defaulted. OPIC filed a suit against the Kims to recover. Hee claimed that she did not understand the extent of her liability when she signed the guaranty. Was Hee liable for the debt? Explain. [*Overseas Private Investment Corp. v. Kim*, 69 A.D.3d 1185, 895 N.Y.S.2d 217 (2010)] **(See pages 546–548.)**

21–7 Protection for Debtors. Bill and Betty Ma owned half of a two-unit residential building. Betty lived in the unit, but Bill did not. To collect a judgment against the Mas, Mei-Fang Zhang obtained a writ of execution directing the sheriff to seize and sell the building. State law allowed a $100,000 homestead exemption if the debtor lived in the home and $175,000 if the debtor was also disabled and "unable to engage in gainful employment." Bill argued that he could not work because of "gout and dizziness." How much of an exemption were the Mas allowed? Why? [*Zhang v. Tse*, __ F.Supp.2d __ (N.D.Cal. 2011)] **(See pages 548–549.)**

21–8 Case Problem with Sample Answer—Automatic Stay. Michelle Gholston leased a Chevy Impala from EZ Auto Van Rentals. In November 2011, Gholston filed for bankruptcy. Around November 21, the bankruptcy court notified EZ Auto of Gholston's bankruptcy and the imposition of an automatic stay. Nevertheless, because Gholston had fallen behind on her payments, EZ Auto repossessed the vehicle on November 28. Gholston's attorney then reminded EZ Auto about the automatic stay, but the company failed to return the car. As a result of the car's repossession, Gholston suffered damages that included emotional distress, lost wages, attorneys' fees, and car rental expenses. Can Gholston recover from EZ Auto? Why or why not? [*In re Gholston*, ___ Bankr. ___, 2012 WL 639288 (M.D.Fla. 2012)] **(See page 555.)**

—For a sample answer to Problem 21–8, go to Appendix H at the end of this text.

21–9 A Question of Ethics—Guaranty Contracts. 73-75 Main Avenue, LLC, agreed to lease commercial property to PP Door Enterprise, Inc. if its principal officers executed personal guaranties and provided credit information. Nan Zhang signed the lease as manager of PP Door. The principals of PP Door signed the lease and guaranty agreements. When PP Door failed to make monthly payments, the lessor sued PP Door and its owner, Ping Ying Li. Li testified that she was the sole owner of PP Door but denied that Zhang was its manager. She also denied signing the guaranty agreement. She claimed that she had signed the credit authorization form because Zhang had told her he was too young to have good credit. Li claimed to have no knowledge of the lease agreement. She did admit, however, that she had paid the rent because Zhang had been in a car accident and had asked her to help pay his bills, including the rent. [73-75 *Main Avenue, LLC v. PP Door Enterprise, Inc.*, 120 Conn.App. 150, 991 A.2d 650 (2010)] **(See pages 546–548.)**

1. Li argued that she was not liable on the lease agreement because Zhang was not authorized to bind her to the lease. Do the facts support Li? Why or why not?
2. Li claimed that the guaranty for rent was not enforceable against her. Why might the court agree?

Critical Thinking and Writing Assignments

21–10 Business Law Writing. Write a few sentences describing the circumstances in which a creditor would resort to each of the following remedies when trying to collect on debt. **(See pages 543–544.)**

1. Mechanic's lien
2. Artisan's lien
3. Writ of attachment

21–11 Business Law Critical Thinking Group Assignment. Grant owns an older home valued at $45,000. He contracts with Jane's Plumbing to replace the bathtubs and fixtures in both bathrooms. Jane replaces them, and on June 1 she submits her bill of $4,000 to Grant. Because of financial difficulties, Grant does not pay the bill. Grant's only asset is his home, but his state's homestead exemption is $40,000.

1. The first group will determine whether Jane's Plumbing can obtain a lien to pay for the renovations. What type of lien would it be, and how is it created?
2. A second group will determine what would happen if Grant filed for Chapter 7 bankruptcy before Jane took any legal action to collect on her claim. Would Jane be a secured or unsecured creditor? Would Jane's position be different if she had obtained a lien before Grant's petition for bankruptcy? Explain.

CHAPTER 22

Mortgages and Foreclosures after the Recession

(wavebreakmedia/Shutterstock.com)

CHAPTER OUTLINE

- Mortgages
- Real Estate Financing Law
- Foreclosures

LEARNING OBJECTIVES

The five learning objectives below are designed to help improve your understanding of the chapter. After reading this chapter, you should be able to answer the following questions:

1. What is a subprime mortgage? How does it differ from a standard fixed-rate mortgage? What is a home equity loan?
2. When is private mortgage insurance required? Which party does it protect?
3. Does the Truth-in-Lending Act (TILA) apply to all mortgages? How do the TILA provisions protect borrowers and curb abusive practices by mortgage lenders?
4. What is a short sale? What advantages over mortgage foreclosure might it offer borrowers? Does the lender receive the full balance due on the mortgage loan in a short sale?
5. In a mortgage foreclosure, what legal rights do mortgage holders have if the sale proceeds are insufficient to pay the underlying debt?

"These days America is looking like the Bernie Madoff of economies: For many years it was held in respect, even awe, but it turns out to have been a fraud all along."
—Paul Krugman, 1953–present (U.S. columnist and winner of Nobel Prize in Economics)

During the first decade of the 2000s, the United States experienced one of the biggest real estate bubbles in its history as housing prices in many areas increased at unprecedented rates. The bubble started to shrink in 2006 and was still deflating in 2013. As a result of the collapse of the housing market and the financial crisis that accompanied it, the United States and much of the rest of the world suffered through what is now called the Great Recession.

Today, the real estate market is still in turmoil. Many people have lost their homes to foreclosure because they could not make the payments on their *mortgages*—the loans that borrowers obtain to purchase homes. Others can afford the payments but choose not to pay because they owe more on the properties than those properties are worth. The ongoing flood of foreclosures led the Obama administration in 2012 to propose an extension (for another few years) of the laws that were aimed at temporarily modifying mortgages.

It has become apparent that some of the mortgage process during the bubble years was fraught with fraud, as the chapter-opening quotation on the previous page suggests. Bank of America, for instance, paid nearly $20 billion in 2011 to settle claims involving mortgage-backed securities that it had designated as safe investments. In reality, many of the securities were based on mortgages granted to borrowers who could not afford to repay them. Other major mortgage companies, including Chase, Citigroup, JPMorgan, and Wells Fargo, faced similar fraud claims. Furthermore, the U.S. Justice Department has accused some mortgage lenders of engaging in discriminatory practices—see this chapter's *Law, Diversity, and Business: Managerial Implications* feature below.

Mortgage A written document that gives a creditor (the mortgagee) an interest in, or lien on, the debtor's (mortgagor's) real property as security for a debt. If the debt is not paid, the property can be sold by the creditor and the proceeds used to pay the debt.

Mortgagee Under a mortgage agreement, the creditor who takes a security interest in the debtor's property.

Mortgagor Under a mortgage agreement, the debtor who gives the creditor a security interest in the debtor's property in return for a mortgage loan.

Mortgages

When individuals purchase real property, they typically borrow funds from a financial institution for part or all of the purchase price. A **mortgage** is a written instrument that gives a creditor (the **mortgagee**) an interest in, or lien on, the debtor's (the **mortgagor's**) real property as security for the payment of a debt. Here, we look first at the different types of mortgages, including some new varieties that helped to inflate the housing bubble. Then we consider some of the ways that creditors protect their interest in the property and examine some of the more important provisions in a typical mortgage document.

LAW, DIVERSITY, AND BUSINESS: MANAGERIAL IMPLICATIONS

REVERSE REDLINING IN THE MORTGAGE MARKET

In December 2011, Bank of America reached a settlement with the U.S. Department of Justice in which it agreed to pay $335 million to compensate 200,000 borrowers who allegedly were discriminated against by Countrywide Financial, a subsidiary that Bank of America had acquired in 2008 when Countrywide was collapsing under its burden of bad loans. The Justice Department alleged that Countrywide had engaged in reverse redlining.

First, There Was Redlining For decades, the mortgage lending industry was accused of *redlining*—that is, drawing a red line on a map around poorer neighborhoods and refusing to offer mortgages to borrowers, often members of minority groups, who wished to purchase homes in those areas. In 1977, Congress passed the Community Reinvestment Act to require lenders to make mortgages more readily obtainable in redlined areas. Nonetheless, in the mid-1990s African American and Hispanic applicants for mortgages were still being rejected at a rate 1.6 times higher than white applicants with similar credit histories. Under the Clinton administration, organizations in redlined areas increasingly pressured banks to make more loans available. The lenders responded with *reverse redlining*.

Then, Reverse Redlining Became Profitable *Reverse redlining* is the opposite of redlining—instead of denying mortgages to members of minority groups, lenders targeted them. During the housing boom, lenders aggressively marketed their subprime mortgages in poorer areas. Wells Fargo, for instance, enlisted pastors in churches in African American communities to offer wealth-building seminars. The bank would make a donation to the church for every new mortgage application it received.

Why were lenders suddenly so interested in these borrowers? The answer is that subprime mortgages carry much higher interest rates than standard mortgages and are usually accompanied by higher up-front fees. In many instances, the Justice Department asserted, mortgage companies pushed African American and Hispanic borrowers into high-cost subprime mortgages even when they could qualify for standard mortgages. Other borrowers were given mortgages that they would not be able to pay—the lender pocketed the fees and sold the worthless mortgages to investors. As a result of such practices, minority groups have incurred a disproportionate percentage of foreclosures.

Business Implications *As a result of numerous charges of reverse redlining, banks and other financial institutions have increased their requirements for home loans. Bank managers have told their loan officers to make sure that all mortgage applicants can prove that they will be able to stay current on their mortgage payments.*

(AP Photo/Robert F. Bukaty)

Why do many home buyers opt for thirty-year mortgages?

Types of Mortgages

Mortgage loans are contracts and, as such, come in a variety of forms. Lenders offer several types of mortgage loans to meet the needs of borrowers. In recent decades, the expansion of home ownership became a political goal, and lenders were encouraged to become more creative in devising new types of mortgages. In many instances, these new mortgages were aimed at borrowers who could not qualify for traditional mortgages and lacked the funds to make a **down payment** (the part of the purchase price that is paid up front).

In general, these mortgages, which include some adjustable-rate mortgages, interest-only mortgages, and balloon mortgages, feature a low initial interest rate. Often, the borrower hopes to refinance—pay off the original mortgage and obtain a new one with more favorable terms—within a few years. When the housing bubble burst and house prices began to decline, however, refinancing became more difficult than many borrowers had anticipated.

Down Payment The part of the purchase price of real property that is paid up front, reducing the amount of the loan or mortgage.

Fixed-Rate Mortgage A standard mortgage with a fixed, or unchanging, rate of interest. The loan payments remain the same for the duration of the loan, which ranges between fifteen and forty years.

Fixed-Rate Mortgages

Fixed-rate mortgages are the simplest mortgage loans. A **fixed-rate mortgage** is a standard mortgage with a fixed, or unchanging, rate of interest. Payments on the loan remain the same for the duration of the mortgage, which ranges from fifteen to forty years.

Lenders determine the interest rate based on a variety of factors, including the borrower's credit history, credit score, income, and debts. Today, for a borrower to qualify for a standard fixed-rate mortgage loan, lenders typically require that the monthly mortgage payment (including principal, interest, taxes, and insurance) not exceed 28 percent of the person's gross income.

Adjustable-Rate Mortgage (ARM) A mortgage with a rate of interest that changes periodically, often with reference to a predetermined government interest rate (the index).

Adjustable-Rate Mortgages

With an **adjustable-rate mortgage (ARM),** the rate of interest paid by the borrower changes periodically. Typically, the interest rate is set at a relatively low fixed rate for a specified period, such as a year or three years. After that time, the interest rate adjusts annually or by some other period, such as biannually or monthly.

ARMs generally are described in terms of the initial fixed period and the adjustment period. For instance, if the interest rate is fixed for three years and then adjusts annually, the mortgage is called a 3/1 ARM, whereas if the rate adjusts annually after five years, the mortgage is a 5/1 ARM.

The interest rate adjustment is calculated by adding a certain number of percentage points (called the margin) to an index rate (one of various government interest rates). The margin and index rate are specified in the mortgage loan documents. **EXAMPLE 22.1** Greta and Marcus obtain a 3/1 ARM to purchase a home. After three years, when the first adjustment is to be made, the index rate is 6 percent. If the margin specified in the loan documents is 3 percentage points, the fully indexed interest rate for the ARM would be 9 percent. • Most ARMs, however, have lifetime interest rate caps that limit the amount that the rate can rise over the duration of the loan.

"Mortgage: a house with a guilty conscience."

Anonymous

Some ARMs also have caps that stipulate the maximum increase that can occur in any particular adjustment period. **EXAMPLE 22.2** In the Greta and Marcus example above, if the initial interest rate was 5 percent and the loan stipulated that the rate could rise no more than 3 percentage points in one adjustment period, the interest rate after three years would increase to 8 percent, not 9 percent, because of the cap. • Note that the interest rate could be adjusted downward as well as upward. If the index rate was 1 percent, the adjusted rate would potentially fall to 4 percent, although some ARMs also limit the amount that the rate can fall.

Interest-Only (IO) Mortgage A mortgage that allows the borrower to pay only the interest portion of the monthly payment and forgo paying any principal for a specified period of time, such as five years.

Interest-Only (IO) Mortgages

With an **interest-only (IO) mortgage**, the borrower can choose to pay only the interest portion of the monthly payments and forgo paying any of the principal for a specified period of time. (IO loans can be for fixed-rate or adjustable-rate mortgages.) This IO payment usually is available for three to ten years. After the IO payment option is exhausted, the borrower's payment increases to include payments on the principal.

LEARNING OBJECTIVE 1

What is a subprime mortgage? How does it differ from a standard fixed-rate mortgage? What is a home equity loan?

Subprime Mortgage A high-risk loan made to a borrower who does not qualify for a standard mortgage because of a poor credit rating or high debt-to-income ratio. Lenders typically charge a higher interest rate on subprime mortgages.

Subprime Mortgages

During the late 1990s and the first decade of the 2000s, *subprime lending* increased significantly. A **subprime mortgage** is a loan made to a borrower who does not qualify for a standard mortgage. Often, such borrowers have poor credit scores or a high current *debt-to-income ratio*—that is, the total amount owed as a percentage of current after-tax income. Subprime mortgages are riskier than traditional mortgages and have a higher default rate. Consequently, lenders charge a higher interest rate for subprime loans. Subprime mortgages can be fixed-rate, adjustable-rate, or IO loans. Subprime lending allows many people who could not otherwise purchase real property to do so, but at a higher risk to the lender.

Balloon Mortgage A mortgage that allows the borrower to make small monthly payments for an initial period, such as eight years, but then requires the entire remaining balance of the mortgage loan to be paid at the end of that period.

Balloon Mortgages

Like an ARM, a **balloon mortgage** starts with low payments for a specified period, usually seven to ten years. At the end of that period, a large balloon payment for the entire balance of the mortgage loan is due. Because the balloon payment is often very large, many borrowers refinance when it is due. A potential disadvantage is that the market interest rate may have risen by the time the loan is refinanced. As a result, the payments may be higher than they would have been if the buyer had initially obtained a fixed-rate mortgage instead of a balloon mortgage.

Who should benefit when a mortgage-participating bank fails? During the heyday of mortgage lending in the first decade of the 2000s, many banks wanted a "piece of the action." A bank could do this by becoming a *participating* bank when another bank contemplated making a multimillion-dollar mortgage and wanted to share the risk. In this way, Silverton Bank participated in half of a $4 million loan that Renasant Bank made to Eric and Tricia Ericson for the construction of a house in Tennessee.

By the time the construction was completed, however, the housing market had started to collapse, and ultimately the Ericsons defaulted on the $4 million loan. In the meantime, Silverton Bank, the participating bank, had failed and been taken over by the Federal Deposit Insurance Corporation. The principal lender, Renasant Bank, orally promised the Ericsons that if it could purchase Silverton's participating loan at a discount, it would credit the Ericsons with the full discount. When Renasant acquired the loan at a $475,000 discount, however, it refused to grant the Ericsons the credit.

Renasant argued that it did not have to apply the discount to the Ericsons' loan balance until they had repaid the entire balance, but the court ruled in favor of the Ericsons. Renasant had breached the oral agreement by refusing to give the Ericsons the $475,000 discount that it had obtained when it repurchased Silverton's participating loan.[1]

Home Equity Loans

Home Equity Loan A loan for which the borrower's home equity (the portion of the home's value that is paid off) is the collateral.

Home equity refers to the portion of a home's value that is "paid off." **EXAMPLE 22.3** If Susanna has a home valued at $200,000 and owes the bank $120,000 on her mortgage, she has 40 percent equity in her house ($80,000/$200,000 = 40 percent). With a **home equity loan,** a bank accepts the borrower's equity as *collateral,* which can be seized if the loan is not repaid on time. If Susanna takes out a $30,000 home equity loan, the amount is added to the amount of her mortgage ($30,000 + $120,000 = $150,000), so she now has only $50,000 (25 percent) equity in her $200,000 home. ●

1. *Renasant Bank v. Ericson,* 2012 WL 640659 (M.D.Tenn. 2012).

(AP Photo/Ben Margot)

Who can qualify for a home equity loan?

Borrowers often take out home equity loans to obtain funds to renovate the property itself. Others obtain home equity loans to pay off debt, such as credit-card debt, that carries a higher interest rate than they will pay on the home equity loan. This strategy can lead to problems, however, if the borrower cannot keep up the payments. Many Americans who lost their homes during the latest major recession were able to pay their original mortgage loans, but not their home equity loans.

From the lender's perspective, a home equity loan is riskier than a mortgage loan because home equity loans are *subordinated,* which means that they take a lower priority in any proceeding that occurs if the homeowner fails to make the payments on the primary mortgage.

Creditor Protection

When creditors grant mortgages, they are advancing a significant amount of funds for a number of years. Consequently, creditors take a number of steps to protect their interest.

LEARNING OBJECTIVE 2

When is private mortgage insurance required? Which party does it protect?

One precaution is to require debtors to obtain private mortgage insurance if they do not make a down payment of at least 20 percent of the purchase price. If a borrower makes a down payment of only 5 percent of the purchase price, the creditor might require insurance covering 15 percent of the cost. Then, if the debtor defaults, the creditor repossesses the house and receives reimbursement from the insurer for the covered portion of the loan.

In addition, the creditor will record the mortgage with the appropriate office in the county where the property is located. Recording "perfects" the security interest (see page 522 of Chapter 20) and ensures that the creditor is officially on record as holding an interest in the property. A lender that fails to record a mortgage could find itself in the position of an unsecured creditor.

Mortgages normally are lengthy documents that include a number of provisions. Many of these provisions are aimed at protecting the creditors' investment.

Statute of Frauds

Because a mortgage involves a transfer of real property, it must be in writing to comply with the Statute of Frauds (see page 313 in Chapter 12). Most mortgages today are highly formal documents with similar formats, but a mortgage is not required to follow any particular form. Indeed, as long as the mortgage satisfies the Statute of Frauds, it generally will be effective.

Important Mortgage Provisions

Mortgage documents ordinarily contain all or most of the following terms:

Prepayment Penalty Clause A clause in a mortgage loan contract that requires the borrower to pay a penalty if the mortgage is repaid in full within a certain period.

1. *The terms of the underlying loan.* These include the loan amount, the interest rate, the period of repayment, and other important financial terms, such as the margin and index rate for an ARM. Many lenders include a **prepayment penalty clause,** which requires the borrower to pay a penalty if the mortgage is repaid in full within a certain period. A prepayment penalty helps to protect the lender should the borrower refinance within a short time after obtaining a mortgage.
2. *Provisions relating to the maintenance of the property.* Because the mortgage conveys an interest in the property to the lender, the lender will require the borrower to maintain the property in such a way that the lender's investment is protected.
3. *A statement obligating the borrower to maintain homeowners' insurance on the property.* **Homeowner's insurance** (also known as *hazard insurance*) protects the lender's interest in the event of a loss due to certain hazards, such as fire or storm damage.

Homeowners' Insurance Insurance that protects a homeowner's property against damage from storms, fire, and other hazards.

4. *A list of the nonloan financial obligations to be borne by the borrower.* For instance, the borrower typically is required to pay all property taxes, assessments, and other claims against the property.
5. *A provision requiring that the borrower pay certain obligations in a specific way.* For instance, a borrower may be required to pay some or all of the taxes, insurance, assessments, or other expenses associated with the property in advance or through the lender. In this way, the lender is assured that the funds for these expenses will be available when the bills come due.

Although a record number of homeowners have failed to keep up with their mortgage payments in recent years, courts have continued to enforce the terms of plainly written financing documents. Even in today's more protective environment, borrowers cannot avoid the clear meaning of terms in financing documents, although the effect may be harsh.

Real Estate Financing Law

During the real estate boom in the first years of the 2000s, some lenders were less than honest with borrowers about the loan terms that they were signing. As a result, many individuals failed to understand how much the monthly payments on ARMs, interest-only mortgages, and other exotic types of loans might increase. In addition, fees and penalties were not always properly disclosed.

In an effort to provide more protection for borrowers, Congress and the Federal Reserve Board have instituted a number of new requirements, mostly in the form of required disclosures. Here, we examine the most important statutes that provide protection for borrowers. First, though, we look at some of the practices that led to the enactment of these statutes.

Predatory Lending and Other Improper Practices

The general term *predatory lending* is often used to describe situations in which borrowers are the victims of loan terms or lending procedures that are excessive, deceptive, or not properly disclosed. Predatory lending typically occurs during the loan origination process. It includes a number of practices ranging from failure to disclose terms to providing misleading information to outright dishonesty.

Two specific types of improper practices are often at the core of a violation. *Steering and targeting* occurs when the lender manipulates a borrower into accepting a loan product that benefits the lender but is not the best loan for the borrower. For instance, a lender may steer a borrower toward an ARM, even though the buyer qualifies for a fixed-rate mortgage. *Loan flipping* occurs when a lender convinces a homeowner to refinance soon after obtaining a mortgage. Such early refinancing rarely benefits the homeowner and may, in fact, result in prepayment penalties.

The Truth-in-Lending Act (TILA)

LEARNING OBJECTIVE 3
Does the Truth-in-Lending Act (TILA) apply to all mortgages? How do the TILA provisions protect borrowers and curb abusive practices by mortgage lenders?

The Truth-in-Lending Act (TILA) of 1968[2] requires lenders to disclose the terms of a loan in clear, readily understandable language so that borrowers can make rational choices. (We will discuss the TILA in more detail in Chapter 33 in the context of consumer law.) With respect to real estate transactions, the TILA applies only to residential loans.

Annual Percentage Rate (APR) The cost of credit on a yearly basis, typically expressed as an annual percentage.

Required Disclosures The major terms that must be disclosed under the TILA include the loan principal, the interest rate at which the loan is made, the **annual percentage rate,** or **APR** (the actual cost of the loan on a yearly basis), and all fees and

2. 15 U.S.C. Sections 1601–1693r.

costs associated with the loan. The TILA requires that these disclosures be made on standardized forms and based on uniform calculation formulas.

Certain types of loans—including ARMs, open-ended home equity loans, and high-interest loans—have specially tailored disclosure requirements. The Mortgage Disclosure Improvement Act of 2008[3] amended the TILA to strengthen the disclosures required for ARMs, which, as mentioned earlier, played a leading role in the recent real estate meltdown.

Prohibitions and Requirements

The TILA prohibits certain lender abuses and creates certain borrower rights. Among the prohibited practices is the charging of prepayment penalties on most subprime mortgages and home equity loans.

Appraiser An individual who specializes in determining the value of specified real or personal property.

The TILA also addresses other unfair, abusive, or deceptive home mortgage–lending practices. It provides that lenders may not coerce an **appraiser** (an individual who specializes in determining the value of specified real or personal property) into misstating the value of a property on which a loan is to be issued. Also, a loan cannot be advertised as a fixed-rate loan if, in fact, its rate or payment amounts will change.

Right to Rescind

A mortgage cannot be finalized until at least seven days after a borrower has received the TILA paperwork. Even if all required disclosures are provided, the TILA gives the borrower the right to rescind (cancel) a mortgage *within three business days*. Sunday is the only day of the week that is not a business day. If the lender fails to provide material TILA disclosures, including the three-day right to rescind, the rescission period lasts up to three years.

"The things that will destroy America are prosperity-at-any-price, peace-at-any-price, safety-first instead of duty-first, the love of soft living, and the get-rich-quick theory of life."

Theodore Roosevelt, 1858–1919
(Twenty-sixth president of the United States, 1901–1909)

Written Representations

The TILA requirements apply to the written materials the lender provides, not to any oral representations. If a lender provides the required TILA disclosures, a borrower who fails to read the relevant documents cannot claim fraud, even if the lender orally misrepresented the terms of the loan. **CASE EXAMPLE 22.4** Patricia Ostolaza and José Diaz owned a home on which they had two mortgage loans provided by Bank of America. Anthony Falcone told them that he could refinance their mortgages in a manner that would reduce their monthly payments. Falcone said that he represented Bank of America when in fact he represented Countrywide Home Loans, Inc.

At the closing of the new loan, the homeowners were given all of the relevant documents, including the TILA disclosure statement. The documents accurately stated the monthly payment under the new loan, which was higher than the couple's original payments. The homeowners later sued Falcone and Countrywide Bank, alleging fraud, but the court dismissed the suit because the homeowners had been given the opportunity to read all of the relevant documents, but had not done so.[4] •

Protection for High-Cost Mortgage Loan Recipients

In the last twenty years, lenders have provided many high-cost and high-fee mortgage products to people who could not easily obtain credit under other loan programs. These loans are commonly known as HOEPA loans, named after the Home Ownership and Equity Protection Act (HOEPA) of 1994,[5] which amended the TILA to create this special category of loans.

A loan can qualify for protection under HOEPA either because it carries a high rate of interest or because it entails high fees for the borrower. HOEPA applies if the APR disclosed

3. This act was contained in Sections 2501 through 2503 of the Housing and Economic Recovery Act of 2008, Pub. L. No. 110-289, enacted on July 30, 2008. Congress then amended its provisions as part of the Emergency Economic Stabilization Act of 2008 (also known as the Bailout Bill), Pub. L. No. 110-343, enacted on October 3, 2008.
4. *Ostolaza-Diaz v. Countrywide Bank, N.A.*, 2010 WL 95145 (4th Cir. 2010).
5. 15 U.S.C. Sections 1637 and 1647.

Treasury Securities Government debt issued by the U.S. Department of the Treasury. The interest rate on Treasury securities is often used as a baseline for measuring the rate on loan products with higher interest rates.

for the loan exceeds the interest rates of **Treasury securities** (or bonds) of comparable maturity by more than 8 percentage points for a first mortgage and 10 percentage points for a second mortgage. HOEPA can also apply when the total fees paid by the consumer exceed 8 percent of the loan amount or a set dollar amount (based on changes in the Consumer Price Index), whichever is larger.

Special Consumer Protections

If a loan qualifies for HOEPA protection, the consumer must receive several disclosures in addition to those required by the TILA. The lender must disclose the APR, the regular payment amount, and any required balloon payments. For loans with a variable rate of interest, the lender must disclose that the rate and monthly payments may increase and state the potential maximum monthly payment. These disclosures must be provided at least three business days before the loan is finalized.

In addition, the lender must provide a written notice stating that the consumer is not required to complete the loan process simply because he or she received the disclosures or signed the loan application. Borrowers must also be informed that they could lose their home (and all funds invested in it) if they default on the loan.

HOEPA also prohibits lenders from engaging in certain practices, such as requiring balloon payments for loans with terms of five years or less. Loans that result in negative amortization are also prohibited. **Negative amortization** occurs when the monthly payments are insufficient to cover the interest due on the loan. The difference is then added to the principal, so the balance owed on the loan increases over time.

Negative Amortization The condition when the payment made by the borrower is less than the interest due on the loan and the difference is added to the principal, thereby increasing the balance owed on the loan over time.

Remedies and Liabilities

For HOEPA violations, consumers can obtain damages in an amount equal to all finance charges and fees paid if the lender's failure to disclose is deemed material. Any failure to comply with HOEPA provisions also extends the borrower's right to rescind the loan for up to three years.

Whether a particular loan is covered by HOEPA and thus is entitled to the statute's significant protections can have important ramifications because it can determine whether a borrower can recover on a lender's failure to comply with HOEPA's provisions and the amount of the recovery. In the following case, a consumer attempted to recover from a lender for alleged violations of the TILA and HOEPA.

Case 22.1

In re Kitts

United States Bankruptcy Court, District of Utah, Central Division, 447 Bankr. 330 (2011).

(Oxford/iStockphoto.com)

Many financial institutions offer home refinancing.

FACTS Facing the loss of his family's home in Park City, Utah, to creditors, Brian Kitts sought to refinance the debt. He entered into two mortgage loan agreements for $1.35 million and $39,603.47, respectively, with Winterfox, LLC. As part of the deal, Kitts paid $87,500 in "loan origination fees." Kitts defaulted on the loans and filed a petition to declare bankruptcy. He also filed a complaint against Winterfox to recover damages for alleged violations of the federal Truth-in-Lending Act (TILA). The bankruptcy court dismissed the action, but on appeal, a federal district court ruled that Winterfox had failed to make certain required disclosures. The district court remanded the case for "further fact finding concerning damages" for violation of the TILA, as well as for Kitts's request for attorneys' fees.

ISSUE Was Kitts entitled to recover damages and attorneys' fees because Winterfox charged him $87,500 in finance charges in violation of HOEPA and TILA provisions?

DECISION Yes. The court concluded that HOEPA covered the Winterfox loans because they were high-cost mortgages. Because Winterfox did not provide any disclosures, Kitts was awarded statutory TILA damages of $4,000, compensatory damages of $87,500 under HOEPA for the finance charges paid in connection with the loans, and $150,000 for attorneys' fees.

Case 22.1—Continued

REASON The parties did not dispute that Winterfox had charged $87,500 in fees. The dispute was whether those fees qualified as "finance charges paid by the consumer" under TILA even though the funds were paid from the loan proceeds rather than coming out of the debtor's pocket. The court reasoned that because Kitts was obligated to pay the fees, they qualified as finance charges paid by the debtor. Thus, Winterfox violated the TILA by failing to provide disclosures on these high-cost loans, and Kitts was entitled to the statutory damages under the TILA. The court further reasoned that Winterfox's failure to provide notice of the required disclosures (under TILA) constituted a material failure to comply with HOEPA. Under the HOEPA, the plaintiff is entitled to compensatory damages, so the court awarded damages in the amount of the fees paid ($87,500), plus reasonable attorneys' fees ($150,000, calculated as 750 hours at $200 per hour).

CRITICAL THINKING—Legal Consideration *The TILA, HOEPA, and other consumer protection laws exist to protect purchasers from "unscrupulous" lenders or sellers. As consumers become better informed about these issues, will these laws still be needed? Discuss.*

Protection for Higher-Priced Mortgage Loans

The Federal Reserve Board enacted a rule that created a second category of expensive loans, called Higher-Priced Mortgage Loans (HPMLs). Only mortgages secured by a consumer's principal home qualify to receive the HPML designation.

Average Prime Offer Rate The mortgage rate offered to the best-qualified borrowers as established by a survey of lenders.

Bridge Loan A short-term loan that allows a buyer to make a down payment on a new home before selling the current home, which is used as collateral for the loan.

Requirements to Qualify

To be an HPML, a mortgage must have an APR that exceeds the *average prime offer rate* for a comparable transaction by 1.5 percentage points or more if the loan is a first lien on a dwelling. (The **average prime offer rate** is the rate offered to the best-qualified borrowers as established by a survey of lenders.) If the loan is secured by a subordinate lien on a home, then the APR must exceed the average prime offer rate by 3.5 percentage points or more in order for the loan to be considered an HPML.

Mortgages excluded from coverage include those for the initial construction of a home, temporary or *bridge loans* that are one year or shorter in duration, and home equity lines of credit. (**Bridge loans** are short-term loans that allow a buyer to make a down payment on a new home before selling her or his current home.)

Special Protections for Consumers

As with a HOEPA loan, consumers receiving an HPML receive additional protections. First, lenders cannot make an HPML based on the value of the consumer's home without verifying the consumer's ability to repay the loan. This verification is typically accomplished through review of the consumer's financial records such as tax returns, bank account statements, and payroll records. The creditor must also verify the consumer's other credit obligations.

Second, prepayment penalties are severely restricted for HPMLs. Prepayment penalties are allowed only if they are limited to two years, and they will not apply if the source of the prepayment funds is a refinancing by the creditor or the creditor's affiliate. Additionally, lenders must establish *escrow accounts* for borrowers' payments for homeowners' insurance and property taxes for all first mortgages. (An escrow account holds funds to be paid to a third party.) Finally, lenders cannot structure a loan specifically to evade the HPML protections.

Foreclosures

Foreclosure A proceeding in which a mortgagee either takes title to or forces the sale of the mortgagor's property in satisfaction of the debt.

If a homeowner defaults, or fails to make mortgage payments, the lender has the right to foreclose on the mortgaged property. **Foreclosure** is a process that allows a lender to legally repossess and auction off the property that is securing a loan.

(Olivier Le Queinec/Shutterstock.com)

When banks foreclose, they often end up owning the property.

Foreclosure is expensive and time consuming, however, and generally benefits neither the borrower, who loses his or her home, nor the lender, which faces the prospect of a loss on its loans. Therefore, various methods to avoid foreclosure have been developed. We look first at some of these methods and then turn to the foreclosure process itself.

How to Avoid Foreclosure

In the past, especially during the Great Depression of the 1930s, a number of alternatives to foreclosure were developed. More recently, as foreclosures have become more common than at any time since the Great Depression, Congress has intervened to aid in the modification of mortgage loans.

Forbearance An agreement between the lender and the borrower in which the lender agrees to temporarily cease requiring mortgage payments, to delay foreclosure, or to accept smaller payments than previously scheduled.

Workout Agreement A formal contract between a debtor and his or her creditors in which the parties agree to negotiate a payment plan for the amount due on the loan instead of proceeding to foreclosure.

Forbearance and Workout Agreements

The first preforeclosure option a borrower has is called forbearance. **Forbearance** is the postponement, for a limited time, of part or all of the payments on a loan in jeopardy of foreclosure. A lender grants forbearance when it expects that, during the forbearance period, the borrower can solve the problem by securing a new job, selling the property, or finding another acceptable solution.

When a borrower fails to make payments as required, the lender may attempt to negotiate a workout. As noted in Chapter 21, a *workout* is a voluntary process to cure the default in some fashion. The parties may even create a formal **workout agreement**—a written document that describes the rights and responsibilities of the parties as they try to resolve the default without proceeding to foreclosure. In such an agreement, the lender will likely agree to delay seeking foreclosure or other legal rights. In exchange, the borrower may agree to provide the lender with financial information on which a workout might be constructed.

Whether a workout is possible or preferable to foreclosure depends on many factors, including the value of the property, the amount of the unpaid principal, the market in which the property will be sold, the relationship of the lender and the borrower, and the financial condition of the borrower.

Housing and Urban Development Assistance

A lender may be able to work with the borrower to obtain an interest-free loan from the U.S. Department of Housing and Urban Development (HUD) to bring the mortgage current. HUD assistance may be available if the loan is at least four months (but not more than twelve months) delinquent, if the property is not in foreclosure, and if the borrower is able to make full mortgage payments. When the lender files a claim, HUD pays the lender the amount necessary to make the mortgage current. The borrower executes a note to HUD, and a lien for the second loan is placed on the property. The promissory note is interest free and comes due if the property is sold.

Short Sale A sale of real property for an amount that is less than the balance owed on the mortgage loan. The lender must consent to the sale and receives the proceeds, and the borrower still owes the balance of the mortgage debt to the lender unless the lender agrees to forgive it.

LEARNING OBJECTIVE 4

What is a short sale? What advantages over mortgage foreclosure might it offer borrowers? Does the lender receive the full balance due on the mortgage loan in a short sale?

Short Sales

When a borrower is unable to make mortgage payments, the lender may agree to a **short sale**—that is, a sale of the property for less than the balance due on the mortgage loan. The borrower must obtain the lender's permission for the short sale and typically has to show some hardship, such as the loss of a job, a decline in the value of the home, a divorce, or a death in the household. The lender receives the proceeds of the sale, and the borrower still owes the balance of the debt to the lender, unless the lender specifically agrees to forgive the remaining debt.

A short sale can offer several advantages. Although the borrower's credit rating is affected, the negative impact is less than it would be with a foreclosure, which generally remains on the borrower's credit report for seven years. The short sale process also avoids the expense of foreclosure for the lender and the trauma of being evicted from the home for the homeowner. But because the lender often has approval rights in a short sale, the sale process can take much longer than a standard real estate transaction. In addition, although the parties' losses are mitigated, the borrower still loses her or his home.

(Andy Dean Photography/Shutterstock.com)

Why would mortgage holders agree to short sales?

Sale and Leaseback

In some situations, the homeowner may be able to sell the property to an investor who is looking for an income property. The owner sells the property to the investor and then leases it back at an amount that is less than the monthly mortgage payment. The owner-seller uses the proceeds of the sale to pay off the mortgage and still has the use and possession of the property. In some circumstances, this strategy can also be used to raise capital when there is no risk of loss of the property.

Home Affordable Modification Program

In 2009, the U.S. Treasury Department launched the Home Affordable Modification Program (HAMP) to encourage private lenders to modify mortgages so as to lower the monthly payments of borrowers who are in default. The purpose of HAMP is not to force lenders to forgive all high-risk mortgages, but rather to reduce monthly mortgage payments to a level that the homeowner can reasonably pay. The program may share in the costs of modifying the loan and provides incentives to lenders based on successful loan modification.

Qualifications HAMP modifications are not available for every mortgage. To qualify for a HAMP modification, all of the following must be true:

1. The loan must have originated on or before January 1, 2009.
2. The home must be occupied by the owner and must be the homeowner's primary residence.[6]
3. The unpaid balance may not exceed $729,750 for a single-unit property.[7]
4. The homeowner must be facing financial hardship and be either more than sixty days late on mortgage payments or at risk of imminent default. Homeowners are required to verify their hardship through appropriate documentation.

"People are living longer than ever before, a phenomenon undoubtedly made necessary by the 30-year mortgage."

Doug Larson, 1926–present (U.S. columnist)

Restructuring the Mortgage The goal is to reduce the debtor's mortgage payment to 31 percent of his or her gross monthly income. The loan is restructured by adding any delinquencies (such as accrued interest, past-due taxes, or unpaid insurance premiums) to the principal amount. This increases the number of payments but eliminates the delinquencies by spreading them over the life of the loan.

Once the loan is restructured, lenders try to incrementally lower the mortgage interest rate to a level at which the payments are less than 31 percent of the debtor's income. If the lender cannot reach the 31 percent target by lowering the interest rate to 2 percent, then the lender can **reamortize** the loan (change the way the payments are configured), extending the schedule of payments for up to forty years.

Reamortize To change the way mortgage payments are configured, extending the term over which payments will be made.

The borrower then begins a ninety-day trial period to determine his or her ability to make three modified monthly payments. If the borrower succeeds, the lender offers permanent modifications.

Voluntary Conveyance

Under some circumstances, the parties may benefit from a **deed in lieu of foreclosure,** by which the property is voluntarily conveyed (transferred) to the lender in satisfaction of the mortgage. A property that has a current market value close to the outstanding loan principal, and on which no other loans have been taken, might be the subject of such a conveyance.

Deed in Lieu of Foreclosure An alternative to foreclosure in which the mortgagor voluntarily conveys the property to the lender in satisfaction of the mortgage.

Although the lender faces the risk that it may ultimately sell the property for less than the loan amount, the lender avoids the time, risk, and expense of foreclosure litigation. The borrower who gives the property to the lender without a fight also avoids the foreclosure process and may preserve a better credit rating than if he or she had been forced to give up the property involuntarily.

6. Investor-owned homes, vacant homes, and condemned properties are not eligible under the program.
7. Higher limits are allowed for properties with two to four units.

Friendly Foreclosure Another way for the parties to avoid a contested foreclosure is to engage in a friendly foreclosure. In such a transaction, the borrower in default agrees to submit to the court's jurisdiction, to waive any defenses as well as the right to appeal, and to cooperate with the lender. This process takes longer than a voluntary conveyance, but all of the parties have greater certainty as to the finality of the transaction with respect to others who might have a financial interest in the property.

The Foreclosure Procedure

If all efforts to find another solution fail, the lender will proceed to foreclosure—a process that dates back to English law. A formal foreclosure is necessary to extinguish the borrower's equitable *right of redemption* (see page 586).

To bring a foreclosure action, a creditor must have *standing to sue* (see page 69 in Chapter 3). In the following *Spotlight Case,* the court had to decide whether a bank could foreclose on a mortgage even though it could not prove when it became the owner of the debtor's promissory note.

Spotlight on Foreclosures

Case 22.2

McLean v. JPMorgan Chase Bank, N.A.

District Court of Appeal of Florida, 79 So.3d 170 (2012).

caselaw.findlaw.com[a]

(RiverNorthPhotography/iStockphoto.com)

How can Chase Bank foreclose on delinquent mortgages?

FACTS On May 11, 2009, JPMorgan Chase Bank (Chase) filed a foreclosure action against Robert McLean. The complaint alleged that Chase was entitled to enforce the mortgage and promissory note on which McLean had defaulted. Nevertheless, the attached mortgage identified a different mortgagee and lender, and Chase claimed that the note had been "lost, stolen, or destroyed." When McLean filed a motion to dismiss, Chase produced a mortgage assignment dated May 14, 2009, which was three days after it had filed the lawsuit. Eventually, Chase also filed the original note. Although the indorsement to Chase was undated, Chase then filed a motion for summary judgment. The trial court granted Chase's motion even though the accompanying affidavit failed to show that Chase owned the mortgage or note when it had filed the complaint. McLean appealed.

ISSUE Did Chase prove that it had standing to bring a foreclosure action against McLean?

DECISION No. The Florida appellate court reversed the trial court's grant of summary judgment to Chase.

REASON A party seeking foreclosure must have standing to foreclose when it files its complaint. In this case, the mortgage was assigned after Chase had filed its complaint, so Chase argued that it had standing because the promissory note was indorsed in its name. The indorsement was undated, however, and Chase's affidavit also did not show that Chase owned the note when it filed its lawsuit. The court therefore reversed summary judgment and instructed the trial court to find for Chase only if it proved that it had owned the note at the time of the complaint. Otherwise, the case would have to be dismissed and Chase would need to file a new complaint.

CRITICAL THINKING—Legal Consideration *If Chase cannot prove that it had owned the note at the time of its complaint, what will happen next? Will Chase prevail? Why or why not?*

a. Under "Popular State Resources," click on "Florida Caselaw." When the page opens, click on "District Court of Appeal of Florida." On the next page, type "McLean" in the "Party name:" box and click on "Search." In the result, click on the case name to access the opinion.

Judicial Foreclosure A court-supervised foreclosure proceeding in which the court determines the validity of the debt and, if the borrower is in default, issues a judgment for the lender.

Power of Sale Foreclosure A foreclosure procedure that is not court supervised and is available only in some states.

Types of Foreclosures

Generally, two types of foreclosure are used in the United States: **judicial foreclosure** and **power of sale foreclosure.** In a judicial foreclosure, which is available in all states, a court supervises the process. In a power of sale foreclosure, the lender is allowed to foreclose on and sell the property without judicial supervision.

Only a few states permit power of sale foreclosures because borrowers have less protection when a court does not supervise the process. In these states, lenders must strictly comply with the terms of the state statute governing power of sale foreclosures. Failure to follow the statutory requirements can lead to the foreclosure being invalidated. **CASE EXAMPLE 22.5** Antonio Ibanez obtained a home loan, as did Mark and Tammy LaRace. Each of the loans subsequently changed hands several times through various banks, as is common in the mortgage-lending industry. Both Ibanez and the LaRaces defaulted on their mortgages.

U.S. Bank, N.A. foreclosed on the Ibanez mortgage, and Wells Fargo foreclosed on the LaRace mortgage. Both banks published notices of the foreclosure sales in a newspaper, as required by statute, and then bought the homes at the foreclosure auctions. Both banks purchased the properties for significantly less than the purported market value. At the time of the foreclosures, each bank represented that it was the "owner and holder" of the mortgage. When the banks later filed for a court declaration stating that they owned the properties, however, the court ruled against them. The court found that the banks had failed to show that they were holders of the mortgages at the time of the foreclosures. Therefore, they did not have the authority to foreclose, and the foreclosure sales were invalid.[8] ●

Acceleration Clause In a mortgage loan contract, a clause that makes the entire loan balance become due if the borrower misses or is late making the monthly payments.

Acceleration Clauses

In a strict foreclosure, the lender may seek only the amount of the missed payments, not the entire loan amount. Therefore, lenders often include an *acceleration clause* in their loan documents. An **acceleration clause** allows the lender to call the entire loan due—even if only one payment is late or missed. Thus, with an acceleration clause, the lender can foreclose only once on the entire amount of the loan rather than having to foreclose on smaller amounts over a period of time as each payment is missed.

Notice of Default A formal notice to a borrower who is behind in making mortgage payments that the borrower is in default and may face foreclosure. The notice is filed by the lender in the county where the property is located.

Notice of Sale A formal notice to a borrower who is in default on a mortgage that the mortgaged property will be sold in a foreclosure proceeding.

Notice of Default and Notice of Sale

To initiate a foreclosure, a lender must record a **notice of default** with the appropriate county office. The borrower is then on notice of a possible foreclosure and can take steps to pay the loan and cure the default. If the loan is not paid within a reasonable time (usually three months), the borrower will receive a **notice of sale.** In addition, the notice of sale usually is posted on the property, recorded with the county, and published in a newspaper.

The property is then sold in an auction on the courthouse steps at the time and location indicated in the notice of sale. The buyer generally has to pay cash within twenty-four hours for the property. If the procedures are not followed precisely, the parties may have to resort to litigation to establish clear ownership of the property. The following case illustrates how the notice requirements work.

---

8. These two foreclosure cases were consolidated on appeal and ruled on jointly by the Massachusetts Supreme Court in *U.S. Bank, N.A. v. Ibanez*, 458 Mass. 637, 941 N.E.2d 40 (2011).

Case 22.3

Mitchell v. Valteau[a]

Court of Appeal of Louisiana, Fourth Circuit,
30 So.3d 1108 (2010).
www.la4th.org/Opinions.aspx[b]

(Jb Reed/Bloomberg via Getty Images)

A branch of Washington Mutual Bank.

FACTS Dr. Pamela Mitchell borrowed $143,724 to buy a house and lot. A mortgage on the property secured the loan and provided for the sale of the house on default. When Mitchell defaulted, the mortgage holder, Washington Mutual Bank, obtained a court order to seize and sell the property and notified Mitchell. The parties negotiated a new agreement that postponed the seizure and sale. After making two payments, Mitchell again defaulted, and the court issued an amended order of seizure. Despite several attempts, Mitchell was not notified of this order personally. The house was seized and sold. Several months later, Mitchell filed a petition to invalidate the judicial sale and request damages for wrongful seizure.

ISSUE Is Mitchell—who received the notice of seizure and sale in a foreclosure proceeding and then entered into a repayment agreement with the lender—entitled to receive a second notice of sale if she defaults again?

DECISION No. The Louisiana appellate court affirmed the lower court's decision in favor of the bank. Mitchell was not entitled to another notice of seizure and sale under Louisiana law.

REASON After examining Louisiana law and other cases, the reviewing court concluded that there was "no Louisiana authority for requiring a creditor to provide a debtor with notice of a rescheduled judicial sale." Further, it was clear from the repayment agreement that the seizure and sale proceedings would be placed on hold only during the time the repayment agreement was in place. "The agreement also provided for the resumption of the foreclosure in the event of a default in its terms, which Dr. Mitchell acknowledged occurred. There was no obligation to serve Dr. Mitchell with another notice of seizure."

CRITICAL THINKING—Ethical Consideration *What is the underlying purpose for requiring lenders to serve a written notice of seizure of property? Was the court's holding fair to Mitchell? Why or why not?*

---

a. Paul Valteau, in his capacity of civil sheriff, was named as one of the defendants.

b. From the search mode choices, select "Search Cases by Published Date." When that page opens, select "Click for Calendar." Using the arrow at the top of the calendar, go to January 2010, select "27," and then click on "Search." Scroll through the list at the bottom of the page to the case title and click on "Download" to access the opinion. The Louisiana court system maintains this Web site.

LEARNING OBJECTIVE 5
In a mortgage foreclosure, what legal rights do mortgage holders have if the sale proceeds are insufficient to pay the underlying debt?

Deficiency Judgments

If any equity remains after the foreclosed property is sold, the borrower is often able to keep the difference between the sale price and the mortgage amount. If the sale amount is not enough to cover the loan amount, the lender (in the majority of states) can ask a court for a *deficiency judgment*. A deficiency judgment is a judgment against the borrower for the amount of debt remaining unpaid after the collateral is sold. A deficiency judgment requires the borrower to make up the difference to the lender over time. Note that some states do not allow deficiency judgments for mortgaged residential real estate.

Redemption Rights

Equitable Right of Redemption The right of a borrower who is in default on a mortgage loan to redeem or purchase the property before foreclosure.

Statutory Right of Redemption A right provided by statute in some states under which mortgagors can buy back their property after a judicial foreclosure for a limited period of time, such as one year.

Every state allows a homeowner to buy the property *after default and before the foreclosure sale* by paying the full amount of the debt, plus any interest and costs that have accrued. This **equitable right of redemption** allows a defaulting borrower to gain title and regain possession of a property, but it ends when the property is sold at a foreclosure auction.

The **statutory right of redemption**, in contrast, entitles the borrower to repurchase property even *after a judicial foreclosure*. In other words, in states that provide for statutory redemption, the homeowner has a right to buy the property back from a third party who bought it at a foreclosure sale. Generally, the borrower may exercise this right for up to one year from the time the house is sold at a foreclosure sale.[9]

The borrower[10] must pay the price at which the house was sold at the foreclosure sale (the redemption price), plus taxes, interest, and assessments, as opposed to the balance owed on the foreclosed loan. Some states allow the borrower to retain possession of the property after the foreclosure sale and up until the statutory redemption period ends. If the borrower does not exercise the right of redemption, the new buyer receives title to and possession of the property.

9. Some states do not allow a borrower to waive the statutory right of redemption. This means that a buyer at auction must wait one year to obtain title to, and possession of, a foreclosed property.

10. Some states also allow spouses of a defaulting borrower or creditors holding liens on the property to purchase the property under the statutory right of redemption.

Reviewing . . . Mortgages and Foreclosures after the Recession

Al and Betty Smith own their home, which is valued at $200,000, completely—they have 100 percent home equity. They lost most of their savings in the stock market during the Great Recession. Needing funds to start a new business, they decide to take out a home equity loan. They borrow $150,000 for ten years at an interest rate of 12 percent. On the date they take out the loan, a ten-year Treasury bond is yielding 3 percent. The Smiths pay a total of $10,000 in "points and fees" to Alpha Bank. The Smiths are not given any notices that they can lose their home if they do not meet their obligations under the loan. Two weeks after consummating the loan, the Smiths change their minds and want to rescind the loan. Using the information presented in the chapter, answer the following questions.

1. Is the Smiths' loan covered by the Truth-in-Lending Act as amended by the Home Ownership and Equity Protection Act? Why or why not?
2. Do the Smiths have a right to rescind the loan two weeks after the fact, or is it too late? Explain.
3. Assume now that Alpha Bank had given the Smiths all of the required notices before the loan was consummated. If all other facts remain the same, would the Smiths have a right to rescind? Why or why not?
4. Suppose now that the Smiths never rescind the loan and that they default four years later while still owing Alpha Bank $120,000. The bank forecloses and raises only $110,000 when the house is sold at auction. In the majority of states, what options does Alpha Bank have to recover the difference? Explain.

DEBATE THIS Federal legislation enacted in the past few years has unfairly benefited those who should not have bought such expensive houses and taken on so much debt.

Key Terms

acceleration clause 585
adjustable-rate mortgage (ARM) 575
annual percentage rate (APR) 578
appraiser 579
average prime offer rate 581
balloon mortgage 576
bridge loan 581
deed in lieu of foreclosure 583
down payment 575
equitable right of redemption 586
fixed-rate mortgage 575
forbearance 582
foreclosure 581
home equity loan 576
homeowners' insurance 577
interest-only (IO) mortgage 576
judicial foreclosure 585
mortgage 574
mortgagee 574
mortgagor 574

negative amortization 580
notice of default 585
notice of sale 585
power of sale foreclosure 585
prepayment penalty clause 577
reamortize 583
short sale 582
statutory right of redemption 586
subprime mortgage 576
Treasury securities 580
workout agreement 582

Chapter Summary: Mortgages and Foreclosures after the Recession

Mortgages (See pages 574–578.)	1. *Types of mortgages*—A mortgage loan is a contract between a creditor (mortgagee) and a borrower (mortgagor). A down payment is the part of the purchase price that is paid up front. There are many types of mortgages, including: a. Fixed-rate mortgages, which are standard mortgages with a fixed rate of interest and payments that stay the same for the duration of the loan. b. Adjustable-rate mortgages (ARMs), in which the interest rate changes periodically, usually starting low and increasing over time. c. Interest-only mortgages, which allow borrowers to pay only the interest portion of the monthly payments for a limited time, after which the size of the payment increases. d. Subprime mortgages, which carry higher rates of interest because they are made to borrowers who do not qualify for standard mortgages. 2. *Creditor protection*—To protect its interests, a creditor may (a) require private mortgage insurance if the down payment is less than 20 percent of the purchase price, (b) perfect its security interest by recording the mortgage in the appropriate office, and (c) include a prepayment penalty clause and a clause requiring the borrower to maintain homeowners' insurance in the mortgage contract.
Real Estate Financing Law (See pages 578–581.)	1. *Predatory lending*—The practice of using loan terms or lending procedures that are excessive, deceptive, or not properly disclosed. Examples include steering and targeting, and loan flipping. 2. *Truth-in-Lending Act (TILA)*—This federal statute requires mortgage lenders to disclose the terms of a loan in clear, readily understandable language on standardized forms. a. Terms that must be disclosed include the loan principal, the interest rate at which the loan is made, the annual percentage rate, and all fees and costs. b. The TILA prohibits certain unfair lender practices, such as charging prepayment penalties on most subprime mortgages and home equity loans and coercing an appraiser into misstating the value of property. c. A borrower has the right to rescind a mortgage within three business days. If a lender does not provide the required disclosures, the rescission period runs for three years. 3. *High-cost mortgages*—The Home Ownership and Equity Protection Act (HOEPA) of 1994 creates special rules for high-cost and high-fee mortgage products. a. In addition to the TILA disclosures, HOEPA requires lenders to disclose the APR, the regular payment amount, and any balloon payments. Lenders must also disclose that the home may be lost if the borrower defaults, that the rate and payment amounts of variable-rate loans may increase, and what the maximum increase could be. HOEPA also prohibits short-term loans requiring balloon payments and loans that result in negative amortization. b. On a lender's material failure to disclose, a consumer may receive damages equal to all finance charges and fees paid. If a lender fails to comply with HOEPA, the borrower's right to rescind is extended to three years. 4. *Higher-priced mortgages*—Special protections apply to Higher-Priced Mortgage Loans (HPMLs). To qualify as an HPML, a mortgage must have an APR that exceeds the average prime offer rate by a certain amount for a comparable transaction.
Foreclosures (See pages 581–587.)	If the borrower defaults, the lender can foreclose on the mortgaged property. The foreclosure process allows a lender to repossess and auction the property. 1. *Ways to avoid foreclosure proceedings*—Foreclosure can sometimes be avoided through a forbearance or a workout agreement, an interest-free loan from the U.S. Department of Housing and Urban Development, a short sale, a sale and leaseback, a modification under the Home Affordable Modification Program, a deed in lieu of foreclosure, or a friendly foreclosure. 2. *Foreclosure procedures*—In a judicial foreclosure, which is available in all states, a court supervises the process. In a power of sale foreclosure, which is permitted in only a few states, the lender can foreclose on and sell the property without judicial supervision. a. To initiate a foreclosure, the lender records a notice of default with the county. If the loan is not paid, the borrower receives a notice of sale, and the property is sold at auction. b. In most states, if the sale proceeds do not cover the loan amount, the lender can obtain a deficiency judgment for the amount due. 3. *Redemption rights*— a. Equitable right of redemption—In all states, the borrower has the right to purchase the property after default by paying the full amount of the debt, plus interest and costs, before the foreclosure sale. b. Statutory right of redemption—In some states, the borrower has the right to repurchase the property even after a judicial foreclosure.

ExamPrep

ISSUE SPOTTERS

1. Ruth Ann borrows $175,000 from Sunny Valley Bank to buy a home. What are the major terms of the mortgage that must be disclosed in the writing under the Truth-in-Lending Act? **(See page 578.)**
2. Tanner borrows $150,000 from Southeast Credit Union to buy a home, which secures the loan. Two years into the term, Tanner stops making payments on the mortgage. After six months without payments, Southeast informs Tanner that he is in default and that it will proceed to foreclosure. What is foreclosure, and what is the usual procedure? **(See pages 584–586.)**

—Check your answers to the Issue Spotters against the answers provided in Appendix E at the end of this text.

BEFORE THE TEST

Go to www.cengagebrain.com, enter the ISBN 9781133273561, and click on "Find" to locate this textbook's Web site. Then, click on "Access Now" under "Study Tools," and select Chapter 22 at the top. There, you will find a Practice Quiz that you can take to assess your mastery of the concepts in this chapter, as well as Flashcards, a Glossary of important terms, and Video Questions (when assigned).

For Review

Answers to the even-numbered questions in this For Review section can be found in Appendix F at the end of this text.

1. What is a subprime mortgage? How does it differ from a standard fixed-rate mortgage? What is a home equity loan?
2. When is private mortgage insurance required? Which party does it protect?
3. Does the Truth-in-Lending Act (TILA) apply to all mortgages? How do the TILA provisions protect borrowers and curb abusive practices by mortgage lenders?
4. What is a short sale? What advantages over mortgage foreclosure might it offer borrowers? Does the lender receive the full balance due on the mortgage loan in a short sale?
5. In a mortgage foreclosure, what legal rights do mortgage holders have if the sale proceeds are insufficient to pay the underlying debt?

Business Scenarios and Case Problems

22–1 Disclosure Requirements. Rancho Mortgage, Inc., wants to launch a new advertising campaign designed to attract homebuyers in a difficult economic environment. Rancho plans to promote its new loan product, which offers a fixed interest rate for the first five years and then switches to a variable interest rate. Rancho believes that Spanish-speaking homebuyers have been underserved in recent years, and it wants to advertise particularly to that market. What must Rancho say (and not say) in its advertising campaigns about the structure of the loan product? Why? **(See pages 578–579.)**

22–2 Question with Sample Answer—Real Estate Financing. Jane Lane refinanced her mortgage with Central Equity, Inc. Central Equity split the transaction into two separate loan documents with separate Truth-in-Lending disclosure statements and settlement statements. Two years later, Lane tried to exercise her right to rescission under the Home Ownership and Equity Protection Act (HOEPA), but Central Equity refused. Central Equity said that the loans were two separate loan transactions and because neither loan imposed sufficient fees and costs to trigger HOEPA, its protections did not apply. Lane claimed that the costs and fees combined into a single transaction (which Lane expected the loan to be) would surpass the HOEPA threshold and trigger its protections. Because Central Equity did not provide the necessary disclosures under HOEPA, Lane argues that she can properly rescind under its provisions. Is Lane correct? Does loan splitting allow the lender to count each loan transaction with a borrower separately for purposes of HOEPA? Why or why not? **(See page 578.)**

—For a sample answer to Question 22–2, go to Appendix G at the end of this text.

22–3 Lender's Options. In 2011, Frank relocates and purchases a five-year-old house for $450,000. He pays $90,000 as a down payment and finances the remaining $360,000 of the purchase price with a loan from Bank of Town. Frank signs mortgage paperwork, giving Bank of Town a mortgage interest in the home. Frank pays on the loan for three years. At that point, the housing market has declined significantly. Frank's home is now valued at $265,000. The balance due on his loan is $354,000. In addition, the economy has slowed, and the booming business that Frank started when he bought the home has seen a decrease in revenues. It seems inevitable that Frank will not be able to make his payments. Discuss Bank of Town's options in this situation. **(See pages 582–584.)**

22–4 Right of Rescission. George and Mona Antanuos obtained a mortgage loan secured with rental property from the First National Bank of Arizona. At the closing, First National provided the Antanuoses with a "Notice of Right to Cancel," informing them about their TILA three-day rescission period. The following day, according to the Antanuoses, they informed the bank via fax that they wished to exercise their right to rescind. When First National refused to rescind the agreement, the Antanuoses sued the bank. The Antanuoses did not dispute that a consumer's right to rescind under the TILA applies only to the consumer's original dwelling and that they used their commercial property as a security interest. Instead, the Antanuoses argued that the bank was prohibited from denying them the rescission right because they relied on the bank's disclosure, which would have been required under the TILA, to their detriment. Would the court be convinced? Explain. [*Antanuos v. First National Bank of Arizona,* 508 F.Supp.2d 466 (E.D.Va. 2007)] **(See page 579.)**

22–5 Mortgage Foreclosure. In January 2003, Gary Ryder and Washington Mutual Bank, F.A., executed a note in which Ryder promised to pay $2,450,000, plus interest at a rate that could vary from month to month. The amount of the first payment was $10,933. The note was to be paid in full by February 1, 2033. A mortgage on Ryder's real property at 345 Round Hill Road in Greenwich, Connecticut, in favor of the bank secured his obligations under the note. The note and mortgage required Ryder to pay the taxes on the property, which he did not do in 2004 and 2005. The bank notified him that he was in default and, when he failed to act, paid $50,095.92 in taxes, penalties, interest, and fees. Other disputes arose between the parties, and Ryder filed a suit against the bank, alleging, in part, breach of contract. He charged, among other things, that some of his timely payments were not processed and were subjected to incorrect late fees, forcing him to make excessive payments and ultimately resulting in "non-payment by Ryder." The bank filed a counterclaim, seeking to foreclose on the mortgage. What should a creditor be required to prove to foreclose on mortgaged property? What would be a debtor's most effective defense? Which party in this case is likely to prevail on the bank's counterclaim? Why? [*Ryder v. Washington Mutual Bank, F.A.,* 501 F.Supp.2d 311 (D.Conn. 2007)] **(See pages 581–586.)**

22–6 Foreclosures. Roderick and Linda Sharpe borrowed $51,300 secured by a mortgage on their home. About six years later, with more than $68,000 needed to pay off the mortgage, the Sharpes defaulted. The mortgage holder, Wells Fargo Home Mortgage, foreclosed on the property. Immediately before and after the foreclosure sale, Wells Fargo obtained two separate real estate brokers' opinions as to the property's fair market value. Each opinion was based on the prices of three comparable houses then on the market and three comparable houses that had sold within the previous six months. Both opinions set the value at $33,500. This was the price at the sale. The Sharpes objected, arguing that the value of the property was $65,000 based on an appraisal that they could not provide. Was the sale price fair? Explain. [*In re Sharpe,* 425 Bankr. 620 (N.D.Ala. 2010)] **(See pages 585–586.)**

22–7 Foreclosure on Mortgage and Liens. LaSalle Bank loaned $8 million to Cypress Creek 1, LP, to build an apartment complex. The loan was secured by a mortgage. Cypress Creek hired contractors to provide concrete work, plumbing, carpentry, and other construction services. Cypress Creek went bankrupt, owing LaSalle $3 million. The contractors recorded *mechanic's liens* (see page 543 in Chapter 21) when they did not get paid for their work. The property was sold to LaSalle at a sheriff's sale for $1.3 million. The contractors claimed that they should be paid the amounts they were owed out of the $1.3 million and that the mechanic's liens should be satisfied before any funds were distributed to LaSalle for its mortgage. The trial court distributed the $1.3 million primarily to LaSalle, with only a small fraction going to the contractors. Do the liens come before the mortgage in priority of payment? Discuss. [*LaSalle Bank National Association v. Cypress Creek 1, LP,* 242 Ill.2d 231, 950 N.E.2d 1109 (2011)] **(See pages 584–586.)**

22–8 Case Problem with Sample Answer—Deficiency Judgment. First Brownsville Co. executed a promissory note secured by a mortgage so that it could build and operate a mini-warehouse storage business. When First Brownsville defaulted on the loan, Beach Community Bank sought to foreclose on the property in Florida state court. The court determined that First Brownsville owed $1,224,475, entered judgment for Beach Community, and scheduled a foreclosure sale. Beach Community was the only interested bidder at the foreclosure sale, so it bought the property for a mere $1,300. Pursuant to Florida law, Beach Community then sought a deficiency judgment. At the hearing, expert testimony established that the property's fair market value had been $1,480,000 a year earlier, but that the property was worth only $770,000 at the time of the sale. What should be the amount of Beach Community's deficiency judgment? Why? [*Beach Community Bank v. First Brownsville Co.,* 85 So.3d 1119 (Fla.App. 1st Dist. 2012)] **(See page 586.)**

—For a sample answer to Problem 22–8, go to Appendix H at the end of this text.

22–9 A Question of Ethics—Predatory Lending. Peter Sutton's home was subject to two mortgages with payments of more than $1,400 per month, but his only source of income was $1,080 monthly from Social Security. Hoping to reduce the size of the payments, Sutton contacted Apex Mortgage Services. According to Sutton, the broker led him to believe that he could refinance with Countrywide Home Loans, Inc., for payments of $428 per month. In the end, the broker arranged an adjustable-rate loan from Countrywide with initial payments of about $1,000 per month subject to future increases. The loan included a prepayment penalty. Sutton paid the broker a fee and signed the agreement, but later claimed that he did not understand the terms. The payments proved too much for Sutton to afford, and he defaulted on the loan. Sutton sued the broker and lender claiming violations of federal law. [*Sutton v. Countrywide Home Loans, Inc.*, ___ F.3d ___ (11th Cir. 2009)] **(See page 578.)**

1. Who is ethically responsible for Sutton's predicament? To what extent did Sutton have a duty to read and understand what he signed? Discuss.
2. Sutton argued that he should not have to pay the broker's fee because the broker did not provide any services that were of value. Do you agree? Why or why not?
3. Did Countrywide, the lender, have any ethical obligation to monitor the activities of the broker? Would the result have been different if Countrywide had intervened before the documents were signed? Explain.

Critical Thinking and Writing Assignments

22–10 **Business Law Critical Thinking Group Assignment.** Mr. and Mrs. Jones owned a home that went into foreclosure. During this time, they received a brochure from Rees-Max that read: "There are only a few months to go in your redemption period! Your options to save the equity in your home are fading. Call me immediately for a no-bull, no-obligation assessment of your situation. Even if you have been 'promised' by a mortgage broker or investor that they will help, CALL ME . . . ." The Joneses contacted Rees-Max, and they entered into an agreement. Rees-Max would buy the property from the Joneses, the Joneses would lease the property for a few months, and then the Joneses would purchase the property back from Rees-Max on a contract for deed. The agreement did not use the terms *debt, security,* or *mortgage,* and the documents stated that no security interest was granted. The Joneses property was appraised at $278,000 and purchased by Rees-Max for $214,000 with more than $30,000 in fees. When the Joneses complained about the fees, Rees-Max started eviction proceedings.

1. The first group will use the chapter materials to identify what type of transaction the Joneses entered into with Rees-Max.
2. The second group will determine whether this transaction constituted a mortgage that would receive TILA and HOEPA protection. Do the Joneses have any right to complain about the fees? Why or why not?

UNIT 3 Commercial Transactions

Business Case Study with Dissenting Opinion

First Bank v. Fischer & Frichtel, Inc.

As discussed in Chapter 22, when a borrower defaults on a mortgage, the lender may recover the remaining debt by foreclosing on the mortgaged property. In a judicial foreclosure—the method used in most states—the property is sold at auction under court supervision. If the proceeds are enough to cover the borrower's debt, the lender gets the proceeds, and the debt is satisfied. But if the proceeds are insufficient to cover the debt, the lender may obtain a deficiency judgment for the difference between the sale price and the amount owed.

In this *Business Case Study with Dissenting Opinion,* we review *First Bank v. Fischer & Frichtel, Inc.*[1] In this case, the lender was the only bidder at a judicial sale and bought the mortgaged property for far less than its fair market value. The Missouri Supreme Court had to determine the amount of the deficiency.

Case Background

Fischer & Frichtel, Inc., is an experienced real estate developer based in Missouri. In June 2000, Fischer & Frichtel borrowed $2.58 million from First Bank in order to buy twenty-one lots of property for a residential development. Over the next five years, Fischer & Frichtel paid First Bank as it sold the lots, which served as collateral for the loan. When the housing market collapsed, however, Fischer & Frichtel was unable to pay First Bank for nine unsold lots.

Through a series of negotiations, First Bank extended the loan's maturity date from July 1, 2003, to September 1, 2008. When the loan matured, Fischer & Frichtel defaulted, still owing $1.13 million. First Bank foreclosed on the unsold lots and was the only bidder at the judicial sale. First Bank's winning bid of $466,000 was based on its estimate of the lots' value, the depressed state of the real estate market, and the fact that it would have to sell the lots in bulk rather than individually.

First Bank filed a suit seeking to recover the unpaid principal and interest on the loan. At trial, Fischer & Frichtel presented expert testimony showing that the lots' fair market value was $918,000. The trial judge instructed the jury that, if it found for First Bank, it "must award . . . the balance due . . . on the date of maturity, less the fair market value of the property at the time of the foreclosure sale, plus interest." Following the judge's instructions, the jury awarded First Bank $215,875. First Bank then moved for a new trial, arguing that it was entitled to the full difference between the sale price and the amount owed. The trial court granted First Bank's motion, and Fischer & Frichtel appealed to the Missouri Supreme Court.

Majority Opinion

Laura Denvir *STITH*, Judge.

* * * *

Missouri and many * * * other states * * * require a debtor to pay as a deficiency the full difference between the debt and the foreclosure sale price. They do not permit a debtor to attack the sufficiency of the foreclosure sale price *as part of the deficiency proceeding* even if the debtor believes that the foreclosure sale price was inadequate.

This does not mean Missouri does not give a debtor a mechanism for attacking an inadequate foreclosure sale price. Rather, a debtor who believes that the foreclosure sale price was inadequate can bring an action to void the *foreclosure sale* itself. If the sale stands, then it has been thought fair to require the debtor to pay any deficiency remaining based on the foreclosure sale price.

* * * *

Missouri permits the debtor to void a properly noticed and carried out foreclosure sale only by showing that "the inadequacy * * * [of the sale price is] so gross that it shocks the conscience * * * and is in itself evidence of fraud." * * * Missouri's standard for proving that a foreclosure sale "shocks the conscience" is among the strictest in the country; more than one Missouri case has refused to set aside a sale that was only 20 to 30 percent of the fair market value * * * .

1. 364 S.W.3d 216 (Mo. 2012).

Business Case Study with Dissenting Opinion—Continued

Fischer & Frichtel argues that this standard * * * almost inevitably leads to windfalls for lenders. Fischer & Frichtel suggests that the foreclosure process is unfair in part because cash must be offered for the property by the bidder. This is a problem for the ordinary bidder, particularly a homeowner or small business owner, because the statutory minimum time period between notice of foreclosure and the actual sale is often less than a month, an insufficient amount of time to allow potential bidders to secure financing.

Fischer & Frichtel notes that the lender does not have this financing problem, as it does not have to pay with cash, but instead simply may deduct the purchase price from the amount of principal the borrower owes. Because realistically the lender often will be the sole bidder, it can buy the foreclosed property for far less than market value, sell the property at a profit and then collect a deficiency from the borrower based on the below-market value it paid for the property.

* * * *

* * * While the foreclosure sale price was barely more than 50 percent of the fair market value later determined by the jury, the lender gave cogent reasons for its lower bid due to the depressed real estate market and the bulk nature of the sale, as of trial the lender had not been able to sell the property, and Fischer & Frichtel has not argued it could not have purchased the property at the foreclosure sale * * * .

This is not a case, therefore, in which to consider a modification of the standard for setting aside a foreclosure sale solely due to inadequacy of price or whether a change should be made in the manner of determining a deficiency where the foreclosure price is less than the fair market value.

* * * *

For the reasons stated, the judgment of the trial court awarding a new trial is affirmed.

Dissenting Opinion

Richard B. *TEITELMAN*, Chief Justice.

I respectfully dissent. The purpose of a damage award is to make the injured party whole without creating a windfall. Accordingly, in nearly every context in which a party sustains damage to or the loss of a property or business interest, Missouri law measures damages by reference to fair market value. Yet in the foreclosure context, Missouri law ignores the fair market value of the foreclosed property and, instead, measures the lender's damages with reference to the foreclosure sale price. Rather than making the injured party whole, this anomaly in the law of damages, in many cases, will require the defaulting party to subsidize a substantial windfall to the lender. Aside from the fact that this anomaly long has been a part of Missouri law, there is no other compelling reason for continued adherence to a measure of damages that too often enriches one party at the expense of another. Consequently, I would hold that damages in a deficiency action should be measured by reference to the fair market value of the foreclosed property.

* * * *

I would reverse the judgment sustaining First Bank's motion for a new trial and order the trial court to enter judgment consistent with the jury's finding that the fair market value of the foreclosed property was $918,000 and that Fischer & Fritchel therefore owed First Bank a deficiency of $215,875.

Questions for Analysis

1. **Law** What was the majority's decision? What were the reasons for its decision?
2. **Law** Why did the dissent disagree with the majority? If the court had adopted the dissent's position, how would this have affected the result?
3. **Ethics** Suppose that First Bank, the only bidder at the judicial sale, had submitted a winning bid of $1,000. Would First Bank's conduct have been ethical? Why or why not?
4. **Economic Dimensions** Are there any reasons why the dissent's position might be more favorable for economic recovery from a recession? Explain your answer.
5. **Implications for the Businessperson** What does the majority's ruling mean for a mortgagee that bids on a foreclosed property at a judicial sale? Explain your answer.

UNIT 3 Commercial Transactions

Business Scenario

Sonja owns a bakery in San Francisco.

1. **Performance of Sales Contracts.** Sonja orders two new model X23 McIntyre ovens from Western Heating Appliances for $16,000. Sonja and Western Heating agree orally, via the telephone, that Western will deliver the ovens within two weeks and that Sonja will pay for the ovens when they are delivered. Two days later, Sonja receives a fax from Western confirming her order. Before delivery, Sonja learns that she can obtain the same ovens from another company at a much lower price. Sonja wants to cancel her order, but Western refuses. Is the contract enforceable against Sonja? Why or why not? **(See page 395.)**
2. **Product Liability.** One day, Sonja is baking a batch of croissants in one of the new ovens when part of the door detaches from the oven. As a result, Sonja's hands are badly burned, and she is unable to do any baking for several months. Sonja later learns that the hinge mechanism on the door was improperly installed. Sonja wants to sue the manufacturer to recover damages, including consequential damages for lost profits. Under what legal principles and doctrines might Sonja be able to recover damages? Discuss fully. **(See pages 445–449.)**
3. **Checks and Banking.** To pay a supplier, Sonja issues a check to Milled Grains Co. that is drawn on United First Bank. A Milled Grains employee, with authorization, indorses the check and transfers it to Milled Grains' financial institution, Second Federal Bank. Second Federal puts the check into the regular bank collection process. If United First refuses to honor the check, who will ultimately suffer the loss? Could Sonja be subject to criminal prosecution if United First refuses to honor the check? **(See page 498.)**
4. **Secured Transactions.** Sonja wants to borrow $40,000 from Credit National Bank to buy coffee-brewing equipment. If Credit National accepts Sonja's equipment as collateral for the loan, how does it let other potential creditors know of its interest? If Sonja fails to repay the loan, what are Credit National's alternatives with respect to collecting the amount due? **(See pages 522 and 535.)**
5. **Creditors' Rights.** Sonya borrows $20,000 from Ace Loan Co. to remodel the bakery and gives it to Jones Construction, a contractor, to do the work. The amount covers only half of the cost, but when Jones finishes the work, Sonja fails to pay the rest. Sonja also does not repay Ace for the loan. What can Jones do to collect what it is owed? What can Ace do? **(See page 543.)**

UNIT 3 Commercial Transactions

Group Project

Sara contracted to buy a new Steinway grand piano for $52,400 from InTune Pianos. InTune delivered a piano that had been in storage for a year and moved at least six times. Sara considered the piano to be unacceptably damaged.

1. The first group will determine whether Sara can reject the piano.
2. The second group will assume that Sara sued InTune and decide what would be the proper measure of recovery (types of damages and to cover what costs).
3. A third group will determine what types of warranties were implied in the sale of the piano and consider whether Sara could sue InTune based on breach of warranty.

UNIT 4

(P_Wei/iStockphoto.com)

Agency and Employment Law

UNIT CONTENTS

23. Agency Relationships in Business

24. Employment, Immigration, and Labor Law

25. Employment Discrimination and Diversity

CHAPTER 23

Agency Relationships in Business

(Goodluz/iStockphoto.com)

CHAPTER OUTLINE

- Agency Relationships
- How Agency Relationships Are Formed
- Duties of Agents and Principals
- Agent's Authority
- Liability in Agency Relationships
- How Agency Relationships Are Terminated

LEARNING OBJECTIVES

The five learning objectives below are designed to help improve your understanding of the chapter. After reading this chapter, you should be able to answer the following questions:

1 What is the difference between an employee and an independent contractor?

2 How do agency relationships arise?

3 What duties do agents and principals owe to each other?

4 When is a principal liable for the agent's actions with respect to third parties? When is the agent liable?

5 What are some of the ways in which an agency relationship can be terminated?

"[It] is a universal principle in the law of agency, that the powers of the agent are to be exercised for the benefit of the principal only, and not of the agent or of third parties."
—Joseph Story, 1779–1845 (Associate justice of the United States Supreme Court, 1811–1844)

Agency A relationship between two parties in which one party (the agent) agrees to represent or act for the other (the principal).

One of the most common, important, and pervasive legal relationships is that of **agency.** In an agency relationship between two parties, one of the parties, called the *agent,* agrees to represent or act for the other, called the *principal*. The principal has the right to control the agent's conduct in matters entrusted to the agent, and the agent must exercise his or her powers "for the benefit of the principal only," as Justice Joseph Story indicated in the chapter-opening quotation.

By using agents, a principal can conduct multiple business operations, such as entering contracts, at the same time in different locations. Using agents provides clear benefits to principals, but agents also create liability for their principals. For this reason, small businesses sometimes attempt to retain workers as independent contractors or "permalancers," but this strategy may lead to problems with federal and state tax authorities, as you will read later in this chapter.

Agency relationships are crucial to the business world. Indeed, the only way that some business entities—including corporations and limited liability companies—can function is through their agents. A familiar example of an agent is a corporate officer who serves in a representative capacity for the owners of the corporation. In this capacity, the officer has the authority to bind the principal (the corporation) to a contract.

Agency Relationships

Section 1(1) of the *Restatement (Third) of Agency*[1] defines agency as "the fiduciary relation which results from the manifestation of consent by one person to another that the other shall act in his [or her] behalf and subject to his [or her] control, and consent by the other so to act." In other words, in a principal-agent relationship, the parties have agreed that the agent will act *on behalf and instead of* the principal in negotiating and transacting business with third parties.

Fiduciary As a noun, a person having a duty created by his or her undertaking to act primarily for another's benefit in matters connected with the undertaking. As an adjective, a relationship founded on trust and confidence.

The term **fiduciary** is at the heart of agency law. The term can be used both as a noun and as an adjective. When used as a noun, it refers to a person having a duty created by her or his undertaking to act primarily for another's benefit in matters connected with the undertaking. When used as an adjective, as in "fiduciary relationship," it means that the relationship involves trust and confidence.

Agency relationships commonly exist between employers and employees. Agency relationships may sometimes also exist between employers and independent contractors who are hired to perform special tasks or services.

(Lisegagne/iStockphoto.com)

Corporations could not operate without employing agents.

Employer-Employee Relationships

Normally, all employees who deal with third parties are deemed to be agents. A salesperson in a department store, for instance, is an agent of the store's owner (the principal) and acts on the owner's behalf. Any sale of goods made by the salesperson to a customer is binding on the principal. Similarly, most representations of fact made by the salesperson with respect to the goods sold are binding on the principal.

Because employees who deal with third parties are generally deemed to be agents of their employers, agency law and employment law overlap considerably. Agency relationships, however, can exist outside an employer-employee relationship, so agency law has a broader reach than employment law. Additionally, agency law is based on the common law, whereas much employment law is statutory law.

Employment laws (state and federal) apply only to the employer-employee relationship. Statutes governing Social Security, withholding taxes, workers' compensation, unemployment compensation, workplace safety, employment discrimination, and the like (see Chapters 24 and 25) are applicable only if employer-employee status exists. *These laws do not apply to an independent contractor.*

LEARNING OBJECTIVE 1

What is the difference between an employee and an independent contractor?

Employer–Independent Contractor Relationships

Independent Contractor One who works for, and receives payment from, an employer but whose working conditions and methods are not controlled by the employer. An independent contractor is not an employee but may be an agent.

Independent contractors are not employees because, by definition, those who hire them have no control over the details of their physical performance. Section 2 of the *Restatement (Third) of Agency* defines an **independent contractor** as follows:

> [An independent contractor is] a person who contracts with another to do something for him [or her] but who is not controlled by the other nor subject to the other's right to control with

1. The *Restatement (Third) of Agency* is an authoritative summary of the law of agency and is often referred to by judges and other legal professionals.

respect to his [or her] physical conduct in the performance of the undertaking. *He [or she] may or may not be an agent.* [Emphasis added.]

Building contractors and subcontractors are independent contractors. A property owner does not control the acts of either of these professionals. Truck drivers who own their equipment and hire themselves out on a per-job basis are independent contractors, but truck drivers who drive company trucks on a regular basis are usually employees.

The relationship between a person or firm and an independent contractor may or may not involve an agency relationship. To illustrate: An owner of real estate who hires a real estate broker to negotiate a sale of the property not only has contracted with an independent contractor (the broker) but also has established an agency relationship for the specific purpose of selling the property. Another example is an insurance agent, who is both an independent contractor and an agent of the insurance company for which she or he sells policies. (Note that an insurance *broker,* in contrast, normally is an agent of the person obtaining insurance and not of the insurance company.)

"I'd like to think of you as a person, David, but it's my job to think of you as personnel."

Determining Employee Status

The courts are frequently asked to determine whether a particular worker is an employee or an independent contractor. How a court decides this issue can have a significant effect on the rights and liabilities of the parties. Employers are required to pay certain taxes, such as Social Security and unemployment insurance taxes, for employees but not for independent contractors.

Criteria Used by the Courts

In determining whether a worker has the status of an employee or an independent contractor, the courts often consider the following questions:

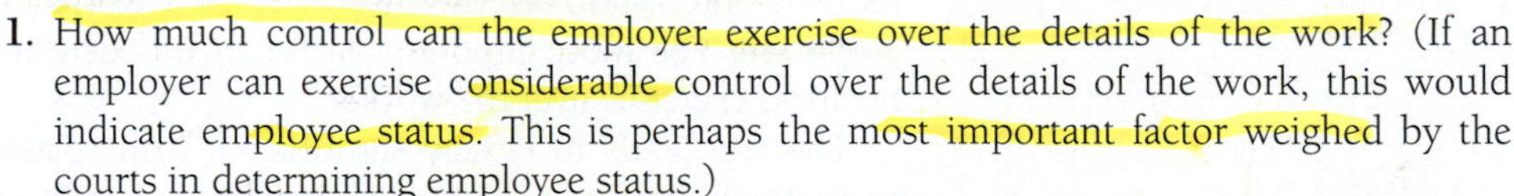

1. How much control can the employer exercise over the details of the work? (If an employer can exercise considerable control over the details of the work, this would indicate employee status. This is perhaps the most important factor weighed by the courts in determining employee status.)
2. Is the worker engaged in an occupation or business distinct from that of the employer? (If so, this points to independent-contractor status, not employee status.)
3. Is the work usually done under the employer's direction or by a specialist without supervision? (If the work is usually done under the employer's direction, this would indicate employee status.)
4. Does the employer supply the tools at the place of work? (If so, this would indicate employee status.)
5. For how long is the person employed? (If the person is employed for a long period of time, this would indicate employee status.)
6. What is the method of payment—by time period or at the completion of the job? (Payment by time period, such as once every two weeks or once a month, would indicate employee status.)
7. What degree of skill is required of the worker? (If little skill is required, this may indicate employee status.)

Disputes Involving Employment Law Sometimes, workers may benefit from having employee status—for tax purposes and to be protected under certain employment laws, for example. As mentioned earlier, federal statutes governing employment discrimination apply only when an employer-employee relationship exists. Protection under antidiscrimination statutes provides a significant incentive for workers to claim that they are employees rather than independent contractors.

CASE EXAMPLE 23.1 A Puerto Rican television station, WIPR, contracted with a woman to co-host a television show. The woman signed a new contract for each episode and was committed to work for WIPR only during the filming of the episodes. WIPR paid her a lump sum for each contract and did not withhold any taxes.

When the woman became pregnant, WIPR stopped contracting with her. She filed a lawsuit claiming that WIPR was discriminating against her in violation of federal antidiscrimination laws, but the court found in favor of WIPR. Because the parties had structured their relationship through repeated fixed-length contracts and had described the woman as an independent contractor on tax documents, she could not maintain an employment-discrimination suit.[2] •

Disputes Involving Tort Liability Whether a worker is an employee or an independent contractor can also affect the employer's liability for the worker's actions. **CASE EXAMPLE 23.2** El Palmar Taxi, Inc., requires its drivers to supply their own cabs, which must display El Palmar's logo. The drivers pay gas, maintenance, and insurance costs, and a fee to El Palmar. They can work when they want for as long as they want. Mario Julaju drove a taxi under a contract with El Palmar that described him as an independent contractor.

El Palmar sent Julaju to pick up Maria Lopez and her children. During the ride, Julaju's cab collided with a truck. To recover for their injuries, the Lopezes sued El Palmar. The employer argued that it was not liable because Julaju was an independent contractor. The court held in favor of El Palmar. An employer normally is not responsible for the actions of an independent contractor with whom the employer contracts. Here, the employment contract had clearly specified that Julaju was an independent contractor, and there were no facts indicating that he was an employee (or that the employer controlled his activities).[3] •

Criteria Used by the IRS

The Internal Revenue Service (IRS) has established its own criteria for determining whether a worker is an independent contractor or an employee. The most important factor in this determination is the degree of control the business exercises over the worker.

The IRS tends to closely scrutinize a firm's classification of its workers because, as mentioned, employers can avoid certain tax liabilities by hiring independent contractors instead of employees. Even when a firm classifies a worker as an independent contractor, the IRS may decide that the worker is actually an employee. In that situation, the employer will be responsible for paying any applicable Social Security, withholding, and unemployment taxes. Microsoft Corporation, for example, was once ordered to pay back payroll taxes for hundreds of workers that the IRS determined had been misclassified as independent contractors.[4] (The *Business Application* feature on page 619 offers suggestions on using independent contractors.)

ETHICAL ISSUE

Should small businesses be allowed to hire "permalancers"? Freelancers, of course, are independent contractors. Now small businesses across the country are turning increasingly to *permalancers*—freelancers who stay on a business's payroll for years. From the business's perspective, the advantages are obvious—the cost savings from using freelancers rather than employees can be as much as 30 percent because the business does not have to pay payroll and unemployment taxes or workers' compensation. Additionally, freelancers do not receive health-care and

2. *Alberty-Vélez v. Corporación de Puerto Rico para la Difusión Pública*, 361 F.3d 1 (1st Cir. 2004).
3. *Lopez v. El Palmar Taxi, Inc.*, 297 Ga.App. 121, 676 S.E.2d 460 (2009).
4. See *Vizcaino v. U.S. District Court for the Western District of Washington*, 173 F.3d 713 (9th Cir. 1999).

other benefits offered to employees. Finally, during an economic downturn, the business has more flexibility—it can let freelancers go quickly and usually without cost.

The IRS and state tax authorities, however, view permalancers differently. In early 2010, the IRS launched an ongoing program that will examine six thousand companies to make sure that permanent workers have not been misclassified as independent contractors. The Obama administration also revised some regulations to make it harder for businesses to classify workers as freelancers. The IRS is targeting small businesses not only because they hire lots of freelancers but also because, unlike larger companies, they usually do not have on-staff attorneys to defend them and thus are likely to acquiesce when the IRS clamps down.

But these efforts raise some ethical issues. Certainly, the tax authorities will gain some revenues but at the cost of reducing the flexibility of small businesses. If the businesses hire fewer workers as a result, are the taxes collected worth the possible increase in unemployment? Another trade-off to consider is between the advantages that a business obtains from hiring permalancers and the disadvantages to those workers of having no employee benefits.

Employee Status and "Works for Hire" Under the Copyright Act of 1976, any copyrighted work created by an employee within the scope of her or his employment at the request of the employer is a "work for hire," and the *employer* owns the copyright to the work. When an employer hires an independent contractor—a freelance artist, writer, or computer programmer, for example—the independent contractor owns the copyright *unless* the parties agree in writing that the work is a "work for hire" and the work falls into one of nine specific categories, including audiovisual and other works.

CASE EXAMPLE 23.3 Artisan House, Inc., hired a professional photographer, Steven H. Lindner, owner of SHL Imaging, Inc., to take pictures of its products for the creation of color slides to be used by Artisan's sales force. Lindner controlled his own work and carefully chose the lighting and angles used in the photographs. When Artisan published the photographs in a catalogue without Lindner's permission, SHL filed a lawsuit for copyright infringement. Artisan claimed that its publication of the photographs was authorized because they were works for hire. The court, however, held that SHL was an independent contractor and owned the copyrights to the photographs. Because SHL had not given Artisan permission (a license) to reproduce the photographs in other publications, Artisan was liable for copyright infringement.[5] •

How Agency Relationships Are Formed

Agency relationships normally are consensual. They come about by voluntary consent and agreement between the parties. Generally, the agreement need not be in writing,[6] and consideration is not required.

A person must have contractual capacity to be a principal. Those who cannot legally enter into contracts directly should not be allowed to do so indirectly through an agent. Any person can be an agent, though, regardless of whether he or she has the capacity to enter a contract (including minors).

An agency relationship can be created for any legal purpose. An agency relationship that is created for an illegal purpose or that is contrary to public policy is unenforceable. **EXAMPLE 23.4** Sharp (as principal) contracts with McKenzie (as agent) to sell illegal narcotics. This agency relationship is unenforceable because selling illegal narcotics is a felony and is contrary to public policy. • It is also illegal for physicians and other licensed professionals to employ unlicensed agents to perform professional actions.

---

5. *SHL Imaging, Inc. v. Artisan House, Inc.*, 117 F.Supp.2d 301 (S.D.N.Y. 2000).

6. The following are two main exceptions to the statement that agency agreements need not be in writing: (1) Whenever agency authority empowers the agent to enter into a contract that the Statute of Frauds requires to be in writing, the agent's authority from the principal must likewise be in writing (this is called the *equal dignity rule*—see page 607), and (2) a power of attorney, which confers authority to an agent, must be in writing.

LEARNING OBJECTIVE 2
How do agency relationships arise?

Generally, an agency relationship can arise in four ways: by agreement of the parties, by ratification, by estoppel, or by operation of law.

If a homeowner contracted with a landscaper to hire this gardener, who is the agent of whom?

(Jamievanbuskirk/iStockphoto.com)

Agency by Agreement

Most agency relationships are based on an express or implied agreement that the agent will act for the principal and that the principal agrees to have the agent so act. An agency agreement can take the form of an express written contract or be created by an oral agreement. **EXAMPLE 23.5** Reese asks Cary, a gardener, to contract with others for the care of his lawn on a regular basis. Cary agrees. An agency relationship is established between Reese (the principal) and Cary (the agent) for the lawn care. •

An agency agreement can also be implied by conduct. **EXAMPLE 23.6** A hotel expressly allows only Boris Koontz to park cars, but Boris has no employment contract there. The hotel's manager tells Boris when to work, as well as where and how to park the cars. The hotel's conduct amounts to a manifestation of its willingness to have Boris park its customers' cars, and Boris can infer from the hotel's conduct that he has authority to act as a parking valet. It can be inferred that Boris is an agent-employee for the hotel, his purpose being to provide valet parking services for hotel guests. •

In the following case, the court had to decide whether an agency relationship arose when a man who was being hospitalized asked his wife to sign the admissions papers for him.

Case 23.1

Laurel Creek Health Care Center v. Bishop

Court of Appeals of Kentucky, 2010 WL 985299 (2010).

(Franck-Boston/iStockphoto.com)

Hospitals require patients to sign admissions papers.

FACTS Gilbert Bishop was admitted to Laurel Creek Health Care Center suffering from various physical ailments. During an examination, Bishop told Laurel Creek staff that he could not use his hands well enough to write or hold a pencil, but he was otherwise found to be mentally competent. Bishop's sister, Rachel Combs, testified that when she arrived at the facility she offered to sign the admissions forms, but Laurel Creek employees told her that it was their policy to have a patient's spouse sign the admissions papers if the patient was unable to do so. Combs also testified that Bishop asked her to get his wife, Anna, so that she could sign his admissions papers.

Combs then brought Anna to the hospital, and Anna signed the admissions paperwork, which contained a provision for mandatory arbitration. Subsequently, Bishop went into cardiopulmonary arrest and died. Following his death, Bishop's family filed a negligence lawsuit against Laurel Creek, which asked the court to compel arbitration in accordance with the provision in the admissions paperwork signed by Anna. The trial court denied the request on the ground that Anna was not Bishop's agent and had no legal authority to make decisions for him. Laurel Creek appealed.

ISSUE Did Anna Bishop become her husband's agent by agreeing to sign the hospital admission papers on his behalf?

DECISION Yes. The Kentucky Court of Appeals reversed the lower court's judgment and remanded the case. An actual agency relationship between Bishop and his wife, Anna, had been formed, and the trial court had erred when it found otherwise.

REASON The court reasoned that to establish an agency relationship, a principal must voluntarily consent to be affected by the agent's actions, and the agent's actions must express consent to act on the principal's behalf. The court noted that "according to his sister, Rachel, Gilbert [Bishop] specifically asked that his wife be brought to the nursing home so that she could sign the admissions documents for him, and [his wife] acted upon that delegation of authority and signed the admissions papers." Another requirement is that the agent's actions affect the principal's legal relations. Clearly here, the court concluded, Anna's actions "affected Gilbert's relations

Case 23.1—Continued

with Laurel Creek, a third party." Therefore, "Gilbert had created an agency relationship upon which Laurel Creek justifiably relied."

CRITICAL THINKING—Legal Consideration *Laurel Creek argued that even if there was no actual agency relationship, an implied agency relationship existed. Is this argument valid? Why or why not?*

Agency by Ratification

Ratification A party's act of accepting or giving legal force to a contract or other obligation entered into by another that previously was not enforceable.

On occasion, a person who is in fact not an agent (or who is an agent acting outside the scope of her or his authority) may make a contract on behalf of another (a principal). If the principal affirms that contract by word or by action, an agency relationship is created by **ratification.** Ratification involves a question of intent, and intent can be expressed by either words or conduct. The basic requirements for ratification will be discussed later in this chapter.

Agency by Estoppel

When a principal causes a third person to believe that another person is his or her agent, and the third person deals with the supposed agent, the principal is "estopped to deny" the agency relationship. In such a situation, the principal's actions create the *appearance* of an agency that does not in fact exist. The third person must prove that she or he *reasonably* believed that an agency relationship existed, though.[7] Facts and circumstances must show that an ordinary, prudent person familiar with business practice and custom would have been justified in concluding that the agent had authority.

CASE EXAMPLE 23.7 Marsha and Jerry Wiedmaier owned Wiedmaier, Inc., a corporation that operated a truck stop. Their son, Michael, did not own any interest in the corporation but had worked at the truck stop as a fuel operator. Michael decided to form his own business called Extreme Diecast, LLC. To obtain a line of credit with Motorsport Marketing, Inc., Michael asked his mother to sign the credit application form. After Marsha had signed as "Secretary-Owner" of Wiedmaier, Inc., Michael added his name to the list of corporate owners and faxed the form to Motorsport. Later, when Michael stopped making payments on merchandise he had ordered, Motorsport sued Wiedmaier for the unpaid balance. The court ruled that Michael was an apparent agent of Wiedmaier, Inc., because the credit application had caused Motorsport to reasonably believe that Michael was acting as Wiedmaier's agent in ordering merchandise.[8] •

Note that the acts or declarations of a purported *agent* in and of themselves do not create an agency by estoppel. Rather, it is the deeds or statements *of the principal* that create an agency by estoppel. In other words, in *Case Example 23.7* above, if Marsha Wiedmaier had not signed the credit application on behalf of the principal-corporation, it would not have been reasonable for Motorsport to believe that Michael was Wiedmaier's agent.

Agency by Operation of Law

The courts may find an agency relationship in the absence of a formal agreement in other situations as well. This can occur in the family setting. When one spouse purchases certain necessaries and charges them to the other spouse's account, for example, the courts will

---

7. These concepts also apply when an agent undertakes an action that is beyond the scope of her or his authority, as will be discussed later in this chapter.

8. *Motorsport Marketing, Inc. v. Wiedmaier, Inc.*, 195 S.W.3d 492 (Mo.App. 2006).

often rule that the second spouse is liable to pay for the necessaries, either because of a social policy of promoting the general welfare of a spouse or because of a legal duty to supply necessaries to family members.

Agency by operation of law may also occur in emergency situations, when the agent's failure to act outside the scope of his or her authority would cause the principal substantial loss. If the agent is unable to contact the principal, the courts will often grant this emergency power. For instance, a railroad engineer may contract on behalf of her or his employer for medical care for an injured motorist hit by the train.

LEARNING OBJECTIVE 3
What duties do agents and principals owe to each other?

Duties of Agents and Principals

Once the principal-agent relationship has been created, both parties have duties that govern their conduct. As mentioned previously, an agency relationship is *fiduciary*—one of trust. In a fiduciary relationship, each party owes the other the duty to act with the utmost good faith.

(sjlocke/iStockphoto.com)

What five duties does this real estate agent owe to his clients?

In general, for every duty of the principal, the agent has a corresponding right, and vice versa. When one party to the agency relationship violates his or her duty to the other party, the remedies available to the nonbreaching party arise out of contract and tort law. These remedies include monetary damages, termination of the agency relationship, an injunction, and required accountings.

Agent's Duties to the Principal

Generally, the agent owes the principal five duties: (1) performance, (2) notification, (3) loyalty, (4) obedience, and (5) accounting.

Performance

An implied condition in every agency contract is the agent's agreement to use reasonable diligence and skill in performing the work. When an agent fails entirely to perform her or his duties, liability for breach of contract normally will result. The degree of skill or care required of an agent is usually that expected of a reasonable person under similar circumstances. Generally, this is interpreted to mean ordinary care. If an agent has claimed to possess special skill, however, failure to exercise that degree of skill constitutes a breach of the agent's duty.

Not all agency relationships are based on contract. In some situations, an agent acts gratuitously—that is, not for monetary compensation. A gratuitous agent cannot be liable for breach of contract, as there is no contract, but he or she can be subject to tort liability. Once a gratuitous agent has begun to act in an agency capacity, he or she has the duty to continue to perform in that capacity in an acceptable manner and is subject to the same standards of care and duty to perform as other agents.

Notification

An agent is required to notify the principal of all matters that come to her or his attention concerning the subject matter of the agency. This is the duty of notification, or the duty to inform. **EXAMPLE 23.8** Lang, an artist, is about to negotiate a contract to sell a series of paintings to Barber's Art Gallery for $25,000. Lang's agent learns that Barber is insolvent and will be unable to pay for the paintings. The agent has a duty to inform Lang of this fact because it is relevant to the subject matter of the agency—the sale of Lang's paintings. •

> "If God had an agent, the world wouldn't be built yet. It'd only be about Thursday."
>
> Jerry Reynolds, 1940–present (National Basketball Association executive)

Generally, the law assumes that the principal knows of any information acquired by the agent that is relevant to the agency—regardless of whether the agent actually passes on this information to the principal. It is a basic tenet of agency law that notice to the agent is notice to the principal.

Loyalty

Loyalty is one of the most fundamental duties in a fiduciary relationship. Basically, the agent has the duty to act *solely for the benefit of his or her principal* and not in the interest of the agent or a third party. For instance, an agent cannot represent two principals in the same transaction unless both know of the dual capacity and consent to it.

KNOW THIS

An agent's disclosure of confidential information could constitute the business tort of misappropriation of trade secrets.

The duty of loyalty also means that any information or knowledge acquired through the agency relationship is considered confidential. It would be a breach of loyalty to disclose such information either during the agency relationship or after its termination. Typical examples of confidential information are trade secrets and customer lists compiled by the principal.

In short, the agent's loyalty must be undivided. The agent's actions must be strictly for the benefit of the principal and must not result in any secret profit for the agent. **CASE EXAMPLE 23.9** Don Cousins contracts with Leo Hodgins, a real estate agent, to negotiate the purchase of an office building. While working for Cousins, Hodgins discovers that the property owner will sell the building only as a package deal with another parcel, so he buys the two properties, intending to resell the building to Cousins. Hodgins has breached his fiduciary duties. As a real estate agent, Hodgins has a duty to communicate all offers to his principal and not to purchase the property secretly and then resell it to his principal. Hodgins is required to act in Cousins's best interests and can become the purchaser in this situation only with Cousins's knowledge and approval.[9] •

Obedience

When acting on behalf of a principal, an agent has a duty to follow all lawful and clearly stated instructions of the principal. Any deviation from such instructions is a violation of this duty. During emergency situations, however, when the principal cannot be consulted, the agent may deviate from the instructions without violating this duty. Whenever instructions are not clearly stated, the agent can fulfill the duty of obedience by acting in good faith and in a manner reasonable under the circumstances.

Accounting

Unless an agent and a principal agree otherwise, the agent has the duty to keep and make available to the principal an account of all property and funds received and paid out on behalf of the principal. This includes gifts from third parties in connection with the agency. For example, a gift from a customer to a salesperson for prompt deliveries made by the salesperson's firm, in the absence of a company policy to the contrary, belongs to the firm. The agent has a duty to maintain separate accounts for the principal's funds and for the agent's personal funds, and the agent must not intermingle these accounts.

Principal's Duties to the Agent

The principal also owes certain duties to the agent. These duties relate to compensation, reimbursement and indemnification, cooperation, and safe working conditions.

Compensation

In general, when a principal requests services from an agent, the agent reasonably expects payment. The principal therefore has a duty to pay the agent for services rendered. For instance, when an accountant or an attorney is asked to act as an agent, an agreement to compensate the agent for service is implied. The principal also has a duty to pay that compensation in a timely manner. Except in a *gratuitous agency* relationship, in which an agent does not act for payment in return, the principal must pay the agreed-on value for an agent's services. If no amount has been expressly agreed on, the principal owes the agent the customary compensation for such services.

---

9. *Cousins v. Realty Ventures, Inc.*, 844 So.2d 860 (La.App. 5th Cir. 2003).

PREVENTING LEGAL DISPUTES

Many disputes arise because the principal and agent did not specify how much the agent would be paid. To avoid such disputes, always state in advance, and in writing, the amount or rate of compensation that you will pay your agents. Even when dealing with salespersons, such as real estate agents, who customarily are paid a percentage of the value of the sale, it is best to explicitly state the rate of compensation.

Reimbursement and Indemnification Whenever an agent disburses funds at the request of the principal or to pay for necessary expenses in the reasonable performance of his or her agency duties, the principal has the duty to reimburse the agent for these payments. Agents cannot recover for expenses incurred through their own misconduct or negligence, though.

Subject to the terms of the agency agreement, the principal has the duty to compensate, or *indemnify,* an agent for liabilities incurred because of authorized and lawful acts and transactions. For instance, if the principal fails to perform a contract formed by the agent with a third party and the third party then sues the agent, the principal must compensate the agent for any costs incurred in defending against the lawsuit.

Additionally, the principal must indemnify (pay) the agent for the value of benefits that the agent confers on the principal. The amount of indemnification is usually specified in the agency contract. If it is not, the courts will look to the nature of the business and the type of loss to determine the amount. Note that this rule applies to acts by gratuitous agents (see page 604) as well. If the finder of a dog that becomes sick takes the dog to a veterinarian and pays the required fees for the veterinarian's services, the (gratuitous) agent is entitled to be reimbursed by the dog's owner for those fees.

Cooperation A principal has a duty to cooperate with the agent and to assist the agent in performing her or his duties. The principal must do nothing to prevent that performance.

When a principal grants an agent an exclusive territory, for instance, the principal creates an *exclusive agency* and cannot compete with the agent or appoint or allow another agent to so compete. If the principal does so, she or he may be liable for the agent's lost sales or profits. **EXAMPLE 23.10** A newspaper (the principal) grants Emir (the agent) the right to sell its newspapers at a busy downtown intersection to the exclusion of all other vendors. This creates an exclusive territory within which only Emir has the right to sell that newspaper. If the newspaper allows another vendor to sell its paper in that area, Emir can sue for lost profits. •

Safe Working Conditions A principal is required to provide safe working premises, equipment, and conditions for all agents and employees. The principal has a duty to inspect the working conditions and to warn agents and employees about any hazards. When the agent is an employee, the employer's liability is frequently covered by state workers' compensation insurance, and federal and state statutes often require the employer to meet certain safety standards (to be discussed in Chapter 24).

"Let every eye negotiate for itself and trust no agent."

William Shakespeare, 1564–1616
(English poet and playwright)

Agent's Authority

An agent's authority to act can be either *actual* (express or implied) or *apparent.* If an agent contracts outside the scope of his or her authority, the principal may still become liable by ratifying the contract.

Express Authority

Express authority is authority declared in clear, direct, and definite terms. Express authority can be given orally or in writing.

Equal Dignity Rule A rule requiring that an agent's authority be in writing if the contract to be made on behalf of the principal must be in writing.

Equal Dignity Rule

In most states, the **equal dignity rule** requires that if the contract being executed is or must be in writing, then the agent's authority must also be in writing. Failure to comply with the equal dignity rule can make a contract voidable *at the option of the principal.* The law regards the contract at that point as a mere offer. If the principal decides to accept the offer, the agent's authority must be ratified, or affirmed, in writing.

EXAMPLE 23.11 Lee (the principal) orally asks Parkinson (the agent) to sell a ranch that Lee owns. Parkinson finds a buyer and signs a sales contract (a contract for an interest in realty must be in writing) on behalf of Lee to sell the ranch. The buyer cannot enforce the contract unless Lee subsequently ratifies Parkinson's agency status *in writing.* Once Parkinson's agency status is ratified, either party can enforce rights under the contract. •

Modern business practice allows exceptions to the equal dignity rule. An executive officer of a corporation normally is not required to obtain written authority from the corporation to conduct *ordinary* business transactions. The equal dignity rule also does not apply when an agent acts in the presence of a principal or when the agent's act of signing is merely perfunctory (automatic). Thus, if the principal negotiates a contract but is called out of town the day it is to be signed and orally authorizes his or her agent to sign the contract, the oral authorization is sufficient.

Power of Attorney Authorization for another to act as one's agent or attorney in either specified circumstances (special) or in all situations (general).

Notary Public A public official authorized to attest to the authenticity of signatures.

Power of Attorney

Giving an agent a **power of attorney** confers express authority.[10] The power of attorney normally is a written document and is usually notarized. (A document is notarized when a **notary public**—a person authorized by the state to attest to the authenticity of signatures—signs and dates the document and imprints it with his or her seal of authority.) Most states have statutory provisions for creating a power of attorney.

A power of attorney can be special (permitting the agent to do specified acts only), or it can be general (permitting the agent to transact all business for the principal). Because a general power of attorney grants extensive authority to an agent to act on behalf of the principal in many ways, it should be used with great caution. Ordinarily, a power of attorney terminates on the incapacity or death of the person giving the power.[11]

(Lucky Business/Shutterstock.com)

What functions does a notary public perform?

Implied Authority

An agent has the *implied authority* to do what is reasonably necessary to carry out his or her express authority and accomplish the objectives of the agency. Authority can also be implied by custom or inferred from the position the agent occupies.

EXAMPLE 23.12 Mueller is employed by Al's Supermarket to manage one of its stores. Al's has not expressly stated that Mueller has authority to contract with third persons. In this situation, though, authority to manage a business implies authority to do what is reasonably required (as is customary or can be inferred from a manager's position) to operate the business. This includes forming contracts to hire employees, to buy merchandise and equipment, and to advertise the products sold in the store. •

---

10. An agent who holds the power of attorney is called an *attorney-in-fact* for the principal. The holder does not have to be an attorney-at-law (and often is not).

11. A *durable* power of attorney, however, continues to be effective despite the principal's incapacity. An elderly person, for example, might grant a durable power of attorney to provide for the handling of property and investments or specific health-care needs should she or he become incompetent.

If an employee-agent makes unauthorized use of his employer's computer data, has he committed a crime? See this chapter's *Adapting the Law to the Online Environment* feature below for a discussion of this issue.

Apparent Authority

Apparent Authority Authority that is only apparent, not real. An agent's apparent authority arises when the principal causes a third party to believe that the agent has authority, even though she or he does not.

Actual authority (express or implied) arises from what the principal manifests *to the agent*. An agent has **apparent authority** when the principal, by either words or actions, causes a *third party* reasonably to believe that an agent has authority to act, even though the agent has no express or implied authority. If the third party changes his or her position in reliance on the principal's representations, the principal may be *estopped* (prevented) from denying that the agent had authority.

ADAPTING THE LAW TO THE ONLINE ENVIRONMENT

WHAT HAPPENS WHEN AN AGENT BREACHES COMPANY POLICY ON THE USE OF ELECTRONIC DATA?

Suppose that an employee-agent who is authorized to access company trade secrets contained in computer files takes those secrets to a competitor for whom the employee is about to begin working. Clearly, the agent has violated the ethical—and legal—duty of loyalty to the principal. Does this breach of loyalty mean that the employee's act of accessing the trade secrets was unauthorized?

The question has significant implications for both parties. If the act was unauthorized, the employee will be subject to state and federal laws prohibiting unauthorized access to computer information and data, including the Computer Fraud and Abuse Act (CFAA, discussed on page 184 in Chapter 6). If the act was authorized, these laws will not apply.

Employees "Exceed Authorized Access" to Their Company's Database

David Nosal once worked for Korn/Ferry and had access to the company's confidential database. When he left, he encouraged several former colleagues who still worked there to join him in starting a competing firm. He asked them to access Korn/Ferry's database and download source lists, names, and client contact information before they quit. The employees had authority to access the database, but Korn/Ferry's policy forbade disclosure of confidential information.

The government filed charges against Nosal and his colleagues for violating the CFAA, among other things.

A Court Rules That Violating an Employer's Use Restrictions Is Not a Crime

The U.S. Court of Appeals for the Ninth Circuit refused to find that the defendants had violated the CFAA. The court ruled that the phrase "exceed authorized access" in the CFAA refers to restrictions on access, not restrictions on use. The court reasoned that Congress's intent in enacting the CFAA was to prohibit people from hacking into computers without authorization.

The court also stated that the CFAA should not be used to criminally prosecute persons who use data in an unauthorized or unethical way. The court pointed out that "adopting the government's interpretation would turn vast numbers of teens and preteens into juvenile delinquents—and their parents and teachers into delinquency contributors." Furthermore, "the effect this broad construction of the CFAA has on workplace conduct pales by comparison with its effect on everyone else who uses a computer, smart-phone, iPad, Kindle, Nook, X-box, Blu-Ray player or any other Internet-enabled device."[a]

Critical Thinking

If an employee accesses Facebook at work even though personal use of a workplace computer is against the employer's stated policies, can the employee be criminally prosecuted? Why or why not?

a. *United States v. Nosal*, 676 F.3d 854 (9th Cir. 2012).

Apparent authority usually comes into existence through a principal's pattern of conduct over time. **EXAMPLE 23.13** Bailey is a traveling salesperson. She solicits orders for goods but does not carry them with her. She normally would not have the implied authority to collect payments from customers on behalf of the principal. Suppose that she does accept payments from Corgley Enterprises, however, and submits them to the principal's accounting department for processing. If the principal does nothing to stop Bailey from continuing this practice, a pattern develops over time, and the principal confers apparent authority on Bailey to accept payments from Corgley. •

At issue in the following *Spotlight Case* was whether the manager of a horse breeding operation had the authority to bind the farm's owner in a contract guaranteeing breeding rights.

Spotlight on Apparent Authority of Managers

Case 23.2

Lundberg v. Church Farm, Inc.

Court of Appeals of Illinois, 502 N.E.2d 806, 151 Ill.App.3d 452 (1986).

(Somogyvari/iStockphoto.com)

Who can guarantee a minimum number of foals during a limited time period?

FACTS Gilbert Church owned a horse breeding farm in Illinois managed by Herb Bagley. Advertisements for the breeding rights to one of Church Farm's stallions, Imperial Guard, directed all inquiries to "Herb Bagley, Manager." Vern and Gail Lundberg bred Thoroughbred horses. The Lundbergs contacted Bagley and executed a preprinted contract giving them breeding rights to Imperial Guard "at Imperial Guard's location," subject to approval of the mares by Church. Bagley handwrote a statement on the contract that guaranteed the Lundbergs "six live foals in the first two years." He then signed it "Gilbert G. Church by H. Bagley."

The Lundbergs bred four mares, which resulted in one live foal. Church then moved Imperial Guard from Illinois to Oklahoma. The Lundbergs sued Church for breaching the contract by moving the horse. Church claimed that Bagley was not authorized to sign contracts for Church or to change or add terms, but only to present preprinted contracts to potential buyers. Church testified that although Bagley was his farm manager and the contact person for breeding rights, Bagley had never before modified the preprinted forms or signed Church's name on these contracts. The jury found in favor of the Lundbergs and awarded $147,000 in damages. Church appealed.

ISSUE Was Bagley authorized to sign and modify contracts on behalf of Church?

DECISION Yes. The state appellate court affirmed the lower court's award of $147,000 to the Lundbergs. Because Church allowed circumstances to lead the Lundbergs to believe Bagley had authority, Church was bound by Bagley's actions.

REASON A principal may be bound by the unauthorized acts of an agent if the principal leads a third party to believe, or allows a third party to believe, that the agent has authority to perform the act. In this case, Church approved the advertisement listing Bagley as Church Farm's manager and point of contact. Bagley generally was the only person available to visitors to the farm. Bagley answered the farm's phone, and the breeding contract had a preprinted signature line for him. Church was not engaged in the actual negotiation or signing of the contracts but left that business for Bagley to complete. Based on Church's actions, a reasonable third party would believe that Bagley had authority to sign and modify contracts.

CRITICAL THINKING—Legal Consideration *What duties to Church might Bagley have violated in this situation?*

KNOW THIS

An agent who exceeds his or her authority and enters into a contract that the principal does not ratify may be liable to the third party on the ground of misrepresentation.

Ratification

As already mentioned, ratification occurs when the principal affirms an agent's *unauthorized* act. When ratification occurs, the principal is bound to the agent's act, and the act is treated as if it had been authorized by the principal *from the outset.* Ratification can be either express or implied.

If the principal does not ratify the contract, the principal is not bound, and the third party's agreement with the agent is viewed as merely an unaccepted offer. Because the third party's agreement is an unaccepted offer, the third party can revoke the offer at any time, without liability, before the principal ratifies the contract.

The requirements for ratification can be summarized as follows:

1. The agent must have acted on behalf of an identified principal who subsequently ratifies the action.
2. The principal must know of all material facts involved in the transaction. If a principal ratifies a contract without knowing all of the facts, the principal can rescind (cancel) the contract.
3. The principal must affirm the agent's act in its entirety.
4. The principal must have the legal capacity to authorize the transaction at the time the agent engages in the act and at the time the principal ratifies. The third party must also have the legal capacity to engage in the transaction.
5. The principal's affirmation must occur before the third party withdraws from the transaction.
6. The principal must observe the same formalities when approving the act done by the agent as would have been required to authorize it initially.

Liability in Agency Relationships

Frequently, a question arises as to which party, the principal or the agent, should be held liable for contracts formed by the agent or for torts or crimes committed by the agent. We look here at these aspects of agency law.

LEARNING OBJECTIVE 4

When is a principal liable for the agent's actions with respect to third parties? When is the agent liable?

Liability for Contracts

Liability for contracts formed by an agent depends on how the principal is classified and on whether the actions of the agent were authorized or unauthorized. Principals are classified as disclosed, partially disclosed, or undisclosed.[12]

Disclosed Principal A principal whose identity is known to a third party at the time the agent makes a contract with the third party.

Partially Disclosed Principal A principal whose identity is unknown by a third party, but the third party knows that the agent is or may be acting for a principal at the time the agent and the third party form a contract.

Undisclosed Principal A principal whose identity is unknown by a third party, and that person has no knowledge that the agent is acting for a principal at the time the agent and the third party form a contract.

A **disclosed principal** is a principal whose identity is known by the third party at the time the contract is made by the agent. A **partially disclosed principal** is a principal whose identity is not known by the third party, but the third party knows that the agent is or may be acting for a principal at the time the contract is made. **EXAMPLE 23.14** Sarah has contracted with a real estate agent to sell certain property. She wishes to keep her identity a secret, but the agent makes it clear to potential buyers of the property that the agent is acting in an agency capacity. In this situation, Sarah is a partially disclosed principal. • An **undisclosed principal** is a principal whose identity is totally unknown by the third party, and the third party has no knowledge that the agent is acting in an agency capacity at the time the contract is made.

Authorized Acts

If an agent acts within the scope of her or his authority, normally the principal is obligated to perform the contract regardless of whether the principal was disclosed, partially disclosed, or undisclosed. Whether the agent may also be held liable under the contract, however, depends on the status of the principal.

12. *Restatement (Third) of Agency,* Section 1.04(2).

Disclosed or Partially Disclosed Principal A disclosed or partially disclosed principal is liable to a third party for a contract made by an agent who is acting within the scope of her or his authority. If the principal is disclosed, an agent has no contractual liability for the nonperformance of the principal or the third party. If the principal is partially disclosed, in most states the agent is also treated as a party to the contract, and the third party can hold the agent liable for contractual nonperformance.[13]

KNOW THIS An agent who signs a negotiable instrument on behalf of a principal may be personally liable on the instrument. Liability depends, in part, on whether the identity of the principal is disclosed and whether the parties intend the agent to be bound by her or his signature.

CASE EXAMPLE 23.15 Walgreens leased commercial property to operate a drugstore at a mall owned by Kedzie Plaza Associates. A property management company, Taxman Corporation, signed the lease on behalf of the principal, Kedzie. The lease required the landlord to keep the sidewalks free of snow and ice, so Taxman, on behalf of Kedzie, contracted with another company to clear the sidewalks surrounding the Walgreens store. When a Walgreens employee slipped on ice outside the store and was injured, she sued Walgreens, Kedzie, and Taxman for negligence. Because the principal's identity (Kedzie) was fully disclosed in the snow-removal contract, the Illinois court ruled that the agent, Taxman, could not be held liable. Taxman did not assume a contractual obligation to remove the snow but merely retained a contractor to do so on behalf of the owner.[14] •

Undisclosed Principal When neither the fact of agency nor the identity of the principal is disclosed, the undisclosed principal is bound to perform just as if the principal had been fully disclosed at the time the contract was made. The agent is also liable as a party to the contract.

When a principal's identity is undisclosed and the agent is forced to pay the third party, the agent is entitled to be indemnified (compensated) by the principal. The principal had a duty to perform, even though his or her identity was undisclosed, and failure to do so will make the principal ultimately liable.

Once the undisclosed principal's identity is revealed, the third party generally can elect to hold either the principal or the agent liable on the contract. Conversely, the undisclosed principal can require the third party to fulfill the contract, *unless* (1) the undisclosed principal was expressly excluded as a party in the contract, (2) the contract is a negotiable instrument signed by the agent with no indication of signing in a representative capacity, or (3) the performance of the agent is personal to the contract, allowing the third party to refuse the principal's performance.

In the following case, three parties involved in an auto sales transaction were embroiled in a dispute over who was liable when the car's engine caught fire.

13. *Restatement (Third) of Agency,* Section 6.02.
14. *McBride v. Taxman Corp.*, 327 Ill.App.3d 992, 765 N.E.2d 51 (2002).

Case 23.3

Williams v. Pike

Court of Appeal of Louisiana, Second Circuit, 58 So.3d 525 (2011).
www.lacoa2.org[a]

(WoodenDinosaur/iStockphoto.com)

FACTS Bobby Williams bought a car for $3,000 at Sherman Henderson's auto repair business in Monroe, Louisiana. Although the car's owner was Joe Pike, the owner of Justice Wrecker Service, Henderson negotiated the sale, accepted Williams's payment, and gave him two receipts. Williams drove the car to Memphis, Tennessee, where his daughter

a. At the top, click on "Opinions." On the next page, in the "Search:" box, type "Williams v. Pike." In the result, click on the case number to access the opinion. The Court of Appeal of Louisiana for the Second Circuit maintains this Web site.

Case 23.3—Continues next page

Case 23.3—Continued

was a student. Three days after the sale, the car began to emit smoke and flames from under the hood. Williams extinguished the blaze and contacted Henderson. The next day, Williams's daughter had the vehicle towed at her expense to her apartment's parking lot, from which it was soon stolen. Williams filed a suit in a Louisiana state court against Pike and Henderson. The court awarded Williams $2,000, plus the costs of the suit, adding that if Williams had returned the car, it would have awarded him the entire price. Pike and Henderson appealed.

ISSUE Can the buyer of a defective car (Williams), hold both the agent and the principal liable when the agent (Henderson) sold the car for an undisclosed principal (Pike)?

DECISION Yes. A state intermediate appellate court affirmed the ruling of the lower court, including its judgment and the assessment of costs against both defendants. The appellate court added the costs of the appeal to the amount. Both Pike and Henderson were liable to Williams.

REASON The court noted that a state permit to sell the car had been issued to Pike and it showed that he was the owner. The car was displayed for sale at Henderson's business, however, and he actually sold it. The court reasoned that this made Pike the principal and Henderson his agent. The fact that their agency relationship was not made clear to Williams made Pike an undisclosed principal. Williams could thus choose to hold either Pike or Henderson liable for the condition of the car, which constituted a breach of implied warranty because the car did not fulfill the purpose for which it was intended. The loss of the use of the car, the "inconvenience" caused by the defect, the price, and the cost of the tow were among the factors that supported the award.

WHAT IF THE FACTS WERE DIFFERENT? *Suppose that Henderson had fully disclosed the fact of his agency relationship and the identity of his principal. Would the result have been different? Why or why not?*

Unauthorized Acts

If an agent has no authority but nevertheless contracts with a third party, the principal cannot be held liable on the contract. It does not matter whether the principal was disclosed, partially disclosed, or undisclosed. The *agent* is liable, however. **EXAMPLE 23.16** Scranton signs a contract for the purchase of a truck, purportedly acting as an agent under authority granted by Johnson. In fact, Johnson has not given Scranton any such authority. Johnson refuses to pay for the truck, claiming that Scranton had no authority to purchase it. The seller of the truck is entitled to hold Scranton liable for payment. •

If the principal is disclosed or partially disclosed, the agent is liable to the third party as long as the third party relied on the agency status. The agent's liability here is based on the breach of an *implied warranty of authority* (an agent impliedly warrants that he or she has the authority to enter a contract on behalf of the principal), not on breach of the contract itself.[15] If the third party knows at the time the contract is made that the agent does not have authority—or if the agent expresses to the third party *uncertainty* as to the extent of her or his authority—then the agent is not personally liable.

When ski patrollers help an injured skier, is there an agency involved?

(LifeJourneys/iStockphoto.com)

Liability for Torts and Crimes

Obviously, any person, including an agent, is liable for her or his own torts and crimes. Whether a principal can also be held liable for an agent's torts and crimes depends on several factors. In some situations, a principal may be held liable not only for the torts of an agent but also for the torts committed by an independent contractor.

Principal's Tortious Conduct

A principal conducting an activity through an agent may be liable for harm resulting from the principal's own negligence or recklessness. Thus, a principal may be liable for giving improper instructions, authorizing the use

15. The agent is not liable on the contract because the agent was never intended personally to be a party to the contract.

of improper materials or tools, or establishing improper rules that resulted in the agent's committing a tort. **EXAMPLE 23.17** Jack knows that Suki is not qualified to drive large trucks but nevertheless tells her to use the company truck to deliver some equipment to a customer. If someone is injured as a result, Jack (the principal) will be liable for his own negligence in giving improper instructions to Suki. •

Principal's Authorization of Agent's Tortious Conduct A principal who authorizes an agent to commit a tort may be liable to persons or property injured thereby, because the act is considered to be the principal's. **EXAMPLE 23.18** Selkow directs his agent, Warren, to cut the corn on specific acreage, which neither of them has the right to do. The harvest is therefore a trespass (a tort), and Selkow is liable to the owner of the corn. •

Note also that an agent acting at the principal's direction can be liable as a *tortfeasor* (one who commits a wrong, or tort), along with the principal, for committing the tortious act even if the agent was unaware of the wrongfulness of the act. Assume in the above example that Warren, the agent, did not know that Selkow had no right to harvest the corn. Warren can be held liable to the owner of the field for damages, along with Selkow, the principal.

Liability for Agent's Misrepresentation A principal is exposed to tort liability whenever a third person sustains a loss due to the agent's misrepresentation. The principal's liability depends on whether the agent was actually or apparently authorized to make representations and whether the representations were made within the scope of the agency. The principal is always directly responsible for an agent's misrepresentation made within the scope of the agent's authority. **EXAMPLE 23.19** Bassett is a demonstrator for Moore's products. Moore sends Bassett to a home show to demonstrate the products and to answer questions from consumers. Moore has given Bassett authority to make statements about the products. If Bassett makes only true representations, all is fine, but if he makes false claims, Moore will be liable for any injuries or damages sustained by third parties in reliance on Bassett's false representations. •

Respondeat Superior A doctrine under which a principal or an employer is held liable for the wrongful acts committed by agents or employees while acting within the course and scope of their agency or employment.

Vicarious Liability Indirect liability imposed on a supervisory party (such as an employer) for the actions of a subordinate (such as an employee) because of the relationship between the two parties.

Liability for Agent's Negligence As mentioned, an agent is liable for his or her own torts. A principal may also be liable for harm an agent caused to a third party under the doctrine of ***respondeat superior,***[16] a Latin term meaning "let the master respond."

Under what circumstances can a school bus driver be charged individually with negligence?

(AP Photo/Burlington Times-News, Scott Muthersbaugh)

This doctrine, which is discussed in this chapter's *Landmark in the Law* feature on the following page, is similar to the theory of strict liability discussed in Chapters 4 and 17. It imposes **vicarious liability,** or indirect liability, on the employer—that is, liability without regard to the personal fault of the employer—for torts committed by an employee in the course or scope of employment.

When an agent commits a negligent act, both the agent and the principal are liable. **CASE EXAMPLE 23.20** Aegis Communications hired Southwest Desert Images (SDI) to provide landscaping services for its property. An herbicide sprayed by SDI employee David Hoggatt entered the Aegis building through the air-conditioning system and caused Catherine Warner, an Aegis employee, to suffer a heart attack. Warner sued SDI and Hoggatt for negligence, but the lower court dismissed the suit against Hoggatt. On appeal, the court found that Hoggatt was

16. Pronounced ree-*spahn*-dee-uht soo-*peer*-ee-your.

LANDMARK IN THE LAW

The Doctrine of *Respondeat Superior*

The idea that a master (employer) must respond to third persons for losses negligently caused by the master's servant (employee) first appeared in Lord Holt's opinion in *Jones v. Hart* (1698).[a] By the early nineteenth century, this maxim had been adopted by most courts and was referred to as the doctrine of *respondeat superior.*

Theories of Liability The vicarious (indirect) liability of the master for the acts of the servant has been supported primarily by two theories. The first theory rests on the issue of *control,* or *fault*—the master has control over the acts of the servant and is thus responsible for injuries arising out of such service. The second theory is economic in nature—the master receives the benefits or profits of the servant's service and therefore should also suffer the losses. Moreover, the master is better able than the servant to absorb such losses.

The control theory is clearly recognized in the *Restatement (Third) of Agency,* which defines a master as "a principal who employs an agent to perform service in his [or her] affairs and who controls, or has the right to control, the physical conduct of the other in the performance of the service." Accordingly, a servant is defined as "an agent employed by a master to perform service in his [or her] affairs whose physical conduct in his [or her] performance of the service is controlled, or is subject to control, by the master."

Limitations on the Employer's Liability There are limitations on the master's liability for the acts of the servant, however. As discussed in the text, an employer (master) is responsible only for the wrongful conduct of an employee (servant) that occurs in "the scope of employment." Generally, the act must be of a kind that the servant was employed to do, it must have occurred within "authorized time and space limits," and it must have been "activated, at least in part, by a purpose to serve the master."

Application to Today's World *The courts have accepted the doctrine of* respondeat superior *for some two centuries. This theory of vicarious liability has practical implications in all situations in which a principal-agent (master-servant, employer-employee) relationship exists. Today, the small-town grocer with one clerk and the multinational corporation with thousands of employees are equally subject to the doctrine.*

a. K.B. 642, 90 Eng.Rep. 1255 (1698).

also liable. An agent is not excused from responsibility for tortious conduct just because he is working for a principal.[17] ●

Determining the Scope of Employment The key to determining whether a principal may be liable for the torts of an agent under the doctrine of *respondeat superior* is whether the torts are committed within the scope of the agency or employment. The factors that courts consider in determining whether a particular act occurred within the course and scope of employment are as follows:

1. Whether the employee's act was authorized by the employer.
2. The time, place, and purpose of the act.
3. Whether the act was one commonly performed by employees on behalf of their employers.
4. The extent to which the employer's interest was advanced by the act.
5. The extent to which the private interests of the employee were involved.
6. Whether the employer furnished the means or instrumentality (for example, a truck or a machine) by which the injury was inflicted.
7. Whether the employer had reason to know that the employee would do the act in question and whether the employee had ever done it before.
8. Whether the act involved the commission of a serious crime.

17. *Warner v. Southwest Desert Images, LLC,* 218 Ariz. 121, 180 P.3d 986 (2008).

The Distinction between a "Detour" and a "Frolic" A useful insight into the "scope of employment" concept may be gained from the judge's classic distinction between a "detour" and a "frolic" in the case of *Joel v. Morison.*[18] In this case, the English court held that if a servant merely took a detour from his master's business, the master is responsible. If, however, the servant was on a "frolic of his own" and not in any way "on his master's business," the master is not liable.

EXAMPLE 23.21 While driving his employer's vehicle to call on a customer, Mandel decides to stop at the post office—which is one block off his route—to mail a personal letter. Mandel then negligently runs into a parked vehicle owned by Chan. In this situation, because Mandel's detour from the employer's business is not substantial, he is still acting within the scope of employment, and the employer is liable.

The result would be different if Mandel had decided to pick up a few friends for cocktails in another city and in the process had negligently run into Chan's vehicle. In that situation, the departure from the employer's business would be substantial, and the employer normally would not be liable to Chan for damages. Mandel would be considered to have been on a "frolic" of his own. •

KNOW THIS

An agent-employee going to or from work or meals usually is not considered to be within the scope of employment. An agent-employee whose job requires travel, however, is considered to be within the scope of employment for the entire trip, including the return.

Employee Travel Time An employee going to and from work or to and from meals is usually considered outside the scope of employment. If travel is part of a person's position, however, such as a traveling salesperson or a regional representative of a company, then travel time is normally considered within the scope of employment. Thus, the duration of the business trip, including the return trip home, is within the scope of employment unless there is a significant departure from the employer's business.

Notice of Dangerous Conditions The employer is charged with knowledge of any dangerous conditions discovered by an employee and pertinent to the employment situation. **EXAMPLE 23.22** Brad, a maintenance employee in Martin's apartment building, notices a lead pipe protruding from the ground in the building's courtyard. Brad neglects either to fix the pipe or to inform Martin of the danger. John trips on the pipe and is injured. The employer is charged with knowledge of the dangerous condition regardless of whether or not Brad actually informed him. That knowledge is imputed to the employer by virtue of the employment relationship. •

Liability for Agent's Intentional Torts

Most intentional torts that employees commit have no relation to their employment. Thus, their employers will not be held liable. Nevertheless, under the doctrine of *respondeat superior,* the employer can be liable for an employee's intentional torts that are committed within the course and scope of employment, just as the employer is liable for negligence. For instance, an employer is liable when an employee (such as a "bouncer" at a nightclub or a security guard at a department store) commits the tort of assault and battery or false imprisonment while acting within the scope of employment.

In addition, an employer who knows or should know that an employee has a propensity for committing tortious acts is liable for the employee's acts even if they ordinarily would not be considered within the scope of employment. For instance, if the employer hires a bouncer knowing that he has a history of arrests for assault and battery, the employer may be liable if the employee viciously attacks a patron in the parking lot after hours.

An employer may also be liable for permitting an employee to engage in reckless actions that can injure others. **EXAMPLE 23.23** The owner of Bates Trucking observes an employee smoking while filling containerized trucks with highly flammable liquids. Failure to stop the employee will cause the employer to be liable for any injuries that result if a truck

18. 6 Car. & P. 501, 172 Eng.Rep. 1338 (1834).

explodes. ● (See this chapter's *Beyond Our Borders* feature below for a discussion of another approach to an employer's liability for an employee's acts.)

Liability for Independent Contractor's Torts Generally, an employer is not liable for physical harm caused to a third person by the negligent act of an independent contractor in the performance of the contract. This is because the employer does not have *the right to control* the details of an independent contractor's performance.

Exceptions to this rule are made in certain situations, though, such as when unusually hazardous activities are involved. Typical examples of such activities include blasting operations, the transportation of highly volatile chemicals, or the use of poisonous gases. In these situations, an employer cannot be shielded from liability merely by using an independent contractor. Strict liability is imposed on the employer-principal as a matter of law. Also, in some states, strict liability may be imposed by statute.

Liability for Agent's Crimes An agent is liable for his or her own crimes. A principal or employer is not liable for an agent's crime even if the crime was committed within the scope of authority or employment—unless the principal participated by conspiracy or other action. In some jurisdictions, under specific statutes, a principal may be liable for an agent's violation—in the course and scope of employment—of regulations, such as those governing sanitation, prices, weights, and the sale of liquor.

How Agency Relationships Are Terminated

Agency law is similar to contract law in that both an agency and a contract can be terminated *by an act of the parties* or *by operation of law.* Once the relationship between the principal and the agent has ended, the agent no longer has the right (*actual* authority) to bind the principal. For an agent's *apparent* authority to be terminated, though, third persons may also need to be notified that the agency has been terminated.

Termination by Act of the Parties

An agency may be terminated by act of the parties in any of the following ways:

1. *Lapse of time.* When an agency agreement specifies the time period during which the agency relationship will exist, the agency ends when that period expires. If no definite

BEYOND OUR BORDERS **Islamic Law and *Respondeat Superior***

The doctrine of *respondeat superior* is well established in the legal systems of the United States and most Western countries. As you have already read, under this doctrine employers can be held liable for the acts of their agents, including employees. The doctrine of *respondeat superior* is not universal, however. Most Middle Eastern countries, for example, do not follow this doctrine.

Islamic law, as codified in the *sharia,* holds to a strict belief that responsibility for human actions lies with the individual and cannot be vicariously extended to others. This belief and other concepts of Islamic law are based on the writings of Muhammad, the seventh-century prophet whose revelations form the basis of the Islamic religion and, by extension, the *sharia.* Muhammad's prophecies are documented in the Koran (Qur'an), which is the principal source of the *sharia.*

Critical Thinking

How would U.S. society be affected if employers could not be held vicariously liable for their employees' torts?

time is stated, the agency continues for a reasonable time and can be terminated at will by either party. What constitutes a "reasonable time" depends, of course, on the circumstances and the nature of the agency relationship.

2. *Purpose achieved.* If an agent is employed to accomplish a particular objective, such as the purchase of breeding stock for a cattle rancher, the agency automatically ends after the cattle have been purchased. If more than one agent is employed to accomplish the same purpose, such as the sale of real estate, the first agent to complete the sale automatically terminates the agency relationship for all the others.

LEARNING OBJECTIVE 5

What are some of the ways in which an agency relationship can be terminated?

3. *Occurrence of a specific event.* When an agency relationship is to terminate on the happening of a certain event, the agency automatically ends when the event occurs. If Posner appoints Rubik to handle her business affairs while she is away, the agency terminates when Posner returns.
4. *Mutual agreement.* The parties to an agency can cancel (rescind) their contract by mutually agreeing to terminate the agency relationship, even if it is for a specific duration.
5. *Termination by one party.* As a general rule, either party can terminate the agency relationship (the act of termination is called *revocation* if done by the principal and *renunciation* if done by the agent). Although both parties have the *power* to terminate the agency, they may not possess the *right*.

Wrongful Termination

Wrongful termination can subject the canceling party to a suit for breach of contract (this topic will be discussed further in Chapter 24). **EXAMPLE 23.24** Rawlins has a one-year employment contract with Munro to act as an agent in return for $65,000. Although Munro has the *power* to discharge Rawlins before the contract period expires, if he does so, he can be sued for breaching the contract because he had no *right* to terminate the agency. •

Notice of Termination

When an agency has been terminated by act of the parties, it is the principal's duty to inform any third parties who know of the existence of the agency that it has been terminated (although notice of the termination may be given by others). Although an agent's actual authority ends when the agency is terminated, an agent's *apparent authority* continues until the third party receives notice (from any source) that such authority has been terminated. If the principal knows that a third party has dealt with the agent, the principal is expected to notify that person *directly*. For third parties who have heard about the agency but have not yet dealt with the agent, *constructive notice* is sufficient.[19]

No particular form is required for notice of agency termination to be effective. The principal can personally notify the agent, or the agent can learn of the termination through some other means. **EXAMPLE 23.25** Manning bids on a shipment of steel, and Stone is hired as an agent to arrange transportation of the shipment. When Stone learns that Manning has lost the bid, Stone's authority to make the transportation arrangement terminates. • If the agent's authority is written, however, it normally must be revoked in writing.

Termination by Operation of Law

Termination of an agency by operation of law occurs in the circumstances discussed here. Note that when an agency terminates by operation of law, there is no duty to notify third persons.

1. *Death or insanity.* The general rule is that the death or mental incompetence of either the principal or the agent automatically and immediately terminates an ordinary agency relationship. Knowledge of the death is not required. **EXAMPLE 23.26** Geer sends Tyron

19. *Constructive notice* is information or knowledge of a fact imputed by law to a person if he or she could have discovered the fact by proper diligence. Constructive notice is often accomplished by newspaper publication.

to China to purchase a rare painting. Before Tyron makes the purchase, Geer dies. Tyron's agent status is terminated at the moment of Geer's death, even though Tyron does not know that Geer has died. • Some states, however, have enacted statutes changing this common law rule to make knowledge of the principal's death a requirement for agency termination.

2. *Impossibility*. When the specific subject matter of an agency is destroyed or lost, the agency terminates. **EXAMPLE 23.27** Bullard employs Gonzalez to sell Bullard's house, but before any sale, the house is destroyed by fire. In this situation, Gonzalez's agency and authority to sell Bullard's house terminate. • Similarly, when it is impossible for the agent to perform the agency lawfully because of a change in the law, the agency terminates.
3. *Changed circumstances*. When an event occurs that has such an unusual effect on the subject matter of the agency that the agent can reasonably infer that the principal will not want the agency to continue, the agency terminates. **EXAMPLE 23.28** Roberts hires Mullen to sell a tract of land for $20,000. Subsequently, Mullen learns that there is oil under the land and that the land is worth $1 million. The agency and Mullen's authority to sell the land for $20,000 are terminated. •
4. *Bankruptcy*. If either the principal or the agent petitions for bankruptcy, the agency is *usually* terminated. In certain circumstances, as when the agent's financial status is irrelevant to the purpose of the agency, the agency relationship may continue. Insolvency (defined as the inability to pay debts when they become due or when liabilities exceed assets), as distinguished from bankruptcy, does not necessarily terminate the relationship.
5. *War*. When the principal's country and the agent's country are at war with each other, the agency is terminated. In this situation, the agency is automatically suspended or terminated because there is no way to enforce the legal rights and obligations of the parties.

Reviewing . . . Agency Relationships in Business

Lynne Meyer, on her way to a business meeting and in a hurry, stopped by a Buy-Mart store for a new pair of nylons to wear to the meeting. There was a long line at one of the checkout counters, but a cashier, Valerie Watts, opened another counter and began loading the cash drawer. Meyer told Watts that she was in a hurry and asked Watts to work faster. Watts, however, only slowed her pace. At this point, Meyer hit Watts. It is not clear from the record whether Meyer hit Watts intentionally or, in an attempt to retrieve the nylons, hit her inadvertently. In response, Watts grabbed Meyer by the hair and hit her repeatedly in the back of the head, while Meyer screamed for help. Management personnel separated the two women and questioned them about the incident. Watts was immediately fired for violating the store's no-fighting policy. Meyer subsequently sued Buy-Mart, alleging that the store was liable for the tort (assault and battery) committed by its employee. Using the information presented in the chapter, answer the following questions.

1. Under what doctrine discussed in this chapter might Buy-Mart be held liable for the tort committed by Watts?
2. What is the key factor in determining whether Buy-Mart is liable under this doctrine?
3. How is Buy-Mart's potential liability affected depending on whether Watts's behavior constituted an intentional tort or a tort of negligence?
4. Suppose that when Watts applied for the job at Buy-Mart, she disclosed in her application that she had previously been convicted of felony assault and battery. Nevertheless, Buy-Mart hired Watts as a cashier. How might this fact affect Buy-Mart's liability for Watts's actions?

DEBATE THIS The doctrine of *respondeat superior* should be modified to make agents solely liable for some of their tortious (wrongful) acts.

BUSINESS APPLICATION

How Can an Employer Use Independent Contractors?*

As an employer, you may at some time consider hiring an independent contractor. Hiring workers as independent contractors instead of as employees may help you reduce both your potential tort liability and your tax liability.

Minimizing Potential Tort Liability

One reason for using an independent contractor is that employers usually are not liable for torts that independent contractors commit against third parties. Nevertheless, there are exceptions. If an employer exercises significant control over the activities of the independent contractor, for example, the contractor may be considered an employee, and the employer can then be liable for the contractor's torts.

To minimize possible liability, you should check an independent contractor's qualifications before hiring him or her. How extensively you need to investigate depends, of course, on the nature of the work. Hiring an independent contractor to maintain the landscaping should require a relatively limited investigation. A more thorough investigation will be necessary when employing an independent contractor to install the electrical systems that you sell. Complete investigations should also be performed anytime the contractor's activities present a potential danger to the public (as in delivering explosives).

Generally, the independent contractor should assume, in a written contract, liability for harms caused to third parties by the contractor's negligence. You should also require that the independent contractor purchase liability insurance to cover these costs.

Reducing Tax Liability and Other Costs

Another reason for hiring an independent contractor is that you do not need to pay or withhold Social Security, income, or unemployment taxes on his or her behalf. The independent contractor is responsible for paying these taxes. Additionally, an independent contractor is not eligible for any retirement or medical plans you provide to your employees, and this is a cost saving to you. Make sure that your contract with an independent contractor spells out that the contractor is responsible for paying taxes and is not entitled to any employment benefits.

A word of caution, though: simply designating a person as an independent contractor does not make her or him one. The Internal Revenue Service (IRS) will reclassify individuals as employees if it determines that they are "in fact" employees, regardless of how you have designated them. Keep proper documentation of the independent contractor's business identification number, business cards, and letterhead so that you can show the IRS that the contractor works independently.

If you improperly designate an employee as an independent contractor, the penalty may be high. Usually, you will be liable for back Social Security and unemployment taxes, plus interest and penalties. When in doubt, seek professional assistance in such matters.

Checklist for the Employer

1. *Check the qualifications of any independent contractor you plan to use to reduce the possibility that you might be legally liable for the contractor's negligence.*
2. *Require in any contract with an independent contractor that the contractor assume liability for harm to a third person caused by the contractor's negligence.*
3. *Require that independent contractors carry liability insurance. Examine the policy to make sure that it is current, particularly when the contractor will be undertaking actions that are more than normally hazardous to the public.*
4. *Do not do anything that would lead a third person to believe that an independent contractor is your employee, and do not allow independent contractors to represent themselves as your employees.*
5. *Regularly inspect the work of the independent contractor to make sure that it is being performed in accordance with contract specifications. Such supervision on your part will not change the worker's status as an independent contractor.*

*This *Business Application* is not meant to substitute for the services of an attorney who is licensed to practice law in your state.

Key Terms

agency 597
apparent authority 608
disclosed principal 610
equal dignity rule 607
fiduciary 598
independent contractor 598
notary public 607
partially disclosed principal 610
power of attorney 607
ratification 603
respondeat superior 613
undisclosed principal 610
vicarious liability 613

Chapter Summary: Agency Relationships in Business

Agency Relationships (See pages 598–601.)	In a *principal-agent* relationship, an agent acts on behalf of and instead of the principal in dealing with third parties. An employee who deals with third parties is normally an agent. An independent contractor is not an employee, and the employer has no control over the details of the person's physical performance. An independent contractor may or may not be an agent.
How Agency Relationships Are Formed (See pages 601–604.)	Agency relationships may be formed by the following methods: 1. *Agreement*—The agency relationship is formed through express consent (oral or written) or implied by conduct. 2. *Ratification*—The principal either by act or by agreement ratifies the conduct of a person who is not in fact an agent. 3. *Estoppel*—The principal causes a third person to believe that another person is the principal's agent, and the third person acts to his or her detriment in reasonable reliance on that belief. 4. *Operation of law*—The agency relationship is based on a social duty (such as the need to support family members) or formed in emergency situations when the agent is unable to contact the principal and failure to act outside the scope of the agent's authority would cause the principal substantial loss.
Duties of Agents and Principals (See pages 604–606.)	1. *Duties of the agent*— a. Performance—The agent must use reasonable diligence and skill in performing her or his duties or use the special skills that the agent has claimed to possess. b. Notification—The agent is required to notify the principal of all matters that come to his or her attention concerning the subject matter of the agency. c. Loyalty—The agent has a duty to act solely for the benefit of the principal and not in the interest of the agent or a third party. d. Obedience—The agent must follow all lawful and clearly stated instructions of the principal. e. Accounting—The agent has a duty to make available to the principal records of all property and funds received and paid out on behalf of the principal. 2. *Duties of the principal*— a. Compensation—Except in a gratuitous agency relationship, the principal must pay the agreed-on value (or reasonable value) for the agent's services. b. Reimbursement and indemnification—The principal must reimburse the agent for all funds disbursed at the request of the principal and for all funds that the agent disburses for necessary expenses in the reasonable performance of his or her agency duties. c. Cooperation—A principal must cooperate with and assist an agent in performing her or his duties. d. Safe working conditions—A principal must provide safe working conditions for agents and employees.
Agent's Authority (See pages 606–610.)	1. *Express authority*—Can be oral or in writing. Authorization must be in writing if the agent is to execute a contract that must be in writing. 2. *Implied authority*—Authority customarily associated with the position of the agent or authority that is deemed necessary for the agent to carry out expressly authorized tasks. 3. *Apparent authority*—Exists when the principal, by word or action, causes a third party reasonably to believe that an agent has authority to act, even though the agent has no express or implied authority. 4. *Ratification*—The affirmation by the principal of an agent's unauthorized action or promise. For the ratification to be effective, the principal must be aware of all material facts.
Liability in Agency Relationships (See pages 610–616.)	1. *Liability for contracts*—If the principal's identity is disclosed or partially disclosed at the time the agent forms a contract with a third party, the principal is liable to the third party under the contract if the agent acted within the scope of his or her authority. If the principal's identity is undisclosed at the time of contract formation, the agent is personally liable to the third party, but if the agent acted within the scope of his or her authority, the principal is also bound by the contract. 2. *Liability for agent's negligence*—Under the doctrine of *respondeat superior,* the principal is liable for any harm caused to another through the agent's torts if the agent was acting within the scope of her or his employment at the time the harmful act occurred. 3. *Liability for agent's intentional torts*—Usually, employers are not liable for the intentional torts that their agents commit, unless: a. The acts are committed within the scope of employment, and thus the doctrine of *respondeat superior* applies. b. The employer knows or should know that the employee has a propensity for committing tortious acts. c. The employer allowed the employee to engage in reckless acts that caused injury to another. d. The agent's misrepresentation causes a third party to sustain damage, and the agent had either actual or apparent authority to act. 4. *Liability for independent contractor's torts*—A principal is not liable for harm caused by an independent contractor's negligence, unless hazardous activities are involved or other exceptions apply. 5. *Liability for agent's crimes*—An agent is responsible for his or her own crimes, even if the crimes were committed while the agent was acting within the scope of authority or employment. A principal will be liable for an agent's crime only if the principal participated by conspiracy or other action or (in some jurisdictions) if the agent violated certain government regulations in the course of employment.

Chapter Summary: Agency Relationships in Business—Continued

How Agency Relationships Are Terminated (See pages 616–618.)	1. *By act of the parties—* Notice to third parties is required when an agency is terminated by act of the parties. Direct notice is required for those who have previously dealt with the agency, but constructive notice will suffice for all other third parties. See pages 616–617 for a list of the ways that an agency may be terminated by act of the parties. 2. *By operation of law—* Notice to third parties is not required when an agency is terminated by operation of law. See pages 617–618 for a list of the ways that an agency can be terminated by operation of law.

ExamPrep

ISSUE SPOTTERS

1. Vivian, owner of Wonder Goods Company, employs Xena as an administrative assistant. In Vivian's absence, and without authority, Xena represents herself as Vivian and signs a promissory note in Vivian's name. In what circumstance is Vivian liable on the note? **(See page 610.)**
2. Davis contracts with Estee to buy a certain horse on her behalf. Estee asks Davis not to reveal her identity. Davis makes a deal with Farmland Stables, the owner of the horse, and makes a down payment. Estee does not pay the rest of the price. Farmland Stables sues Davis for breach of contract. Can Davis hold Estee liable for whatever damages he has to pay? Why or why not? **(See page 606.)**

—Check your answers to the Issue Spotters against the answers provided in Appendix E at the end of this text.

BEFORE THE TEST

Go to www.cengagebrain.com, enter the ISBN 9781133273561, and click on "Find" to locate this textbook's Web site. Then, click on "Access Now" under "Study Tools," and select Chapter 23 at the top. There, you will find a Practice Quiz that you can take to assess your mastery of the concepts in this chapter, as well as Flashcards, a Glossary of important terms, and Video Questions (when assigned).

For Review

Answers to the even-numbered questions in this For Review section can be found in Appendix F at the end of this text.

1. What is the difference between an employee and an independent contractor?
2. How do agency relationships arise?
3. What duties do agents and principals owe to each other?
4. When is a principal liable for the agent's actions with respect to third parties? When is the agent liable?
5. What are some of the ways in which an agency relationship can be terminated?

Business Scenarios and Case Problems

23–1 Ratification by Principal. Springer, who was running for Congress, instructed his campaign staff not to purchase any campaign materials without his explicit authorization. In spite of these instructions, one of his campaign workers ordered Dubychek Printing Co. to print some promotional materials for Springer's campaign. When the printed materials arrived, Springer did not return them but instead used them during his campaign. When Springer failed to pay for the materials, Dubychek sued for recovery of the price. Springer contended that he was not liable on the sales contract because he had not authorized his agent to purchase the printing services. Dubychek argued that the campaign worker was Springer's agent and that the worker had authority to make the printing contract. Additionally, Dubychek claimed that even if the purchase was unauthorized, Springer's use of the materials constituted ratification of his agent's unauthorized purchase. Is Dubychek correct? Explain. **(See page 603.)**

23–2 Question with Sample Answer—Formation of an Agency. Paul Gett is a well-known, wealthy financial expert living in the city of Torris. Adam Wade, Gett's friend, tells Timothy Brown that he is Gett's agent for the purchase of rare coins. Wade even shows Brown a local newspaper clipping mentioning Gett's interest in coin collecting. Brown, knowing of Wade's friendship with Gett, contracts with Wade to sell a rare coin valued at $25,000 to Gett. Wade takes the coin and disappears with it. On the payment due date, Brown seeks to collect from Gett, claiming that Wade's agency made Gett liable. Gett does not deny that Wade was a friend, but he claims that Wade was never his agent. Discuss fully whether an agency was in existence at the time the contract for the rare coin was made. **(See pages 601–604.)**

—For a sample answer to Question 23–2, go to Appendix G at the end of this text.

23–3 **Employee versus Independent Contractor.** Stephen Hemmerling was a driver for the Happy Cab Co. Hemmerling paid certain fixed expenses and abided by a variety of rules relating to the use of the cab, the hours that could be worked, and the solicitation of fares, among other things. Rates were set by the state. Happy Cab did not withhold taxes from Hemmerling's pay. While driving the cab, Hemmerling was injured in an accident and filed a claim against Happy Cab in a Nebraska state court for workers' compensation benefits. Such benefits are not available to independent contractors. On what basis might the court hold that Hemmerling is an employee? Explain. **(See pages 598–601.)**

23–4 **Spotlight on Agency—Independent Contractors.** Frank Frausto delivered newspapers for Phoenix Newspapers, Inc., under a renewable six-month contract called a "Delivery Agent Agreement." The agreement identified Frausto as an independent contractor. Phoenix collected payments from customers and took complaints about delivery. Frausto was assigned the route for his deliveries and was required to deliver the papers within a certain time period each day. Frausto used his own vehicle to deliver the papers and had to provide proof of insurance to Phoenix. Phoenix provided him with health and disability insurance but did not withhold taxes from his weekly income. One morning while delivering papers, Frausto collided with a motorcycle ridden by William Santiago. Santiago filed a negligence action against Frausto and Phoenix. Phoenix argued that it should not be liable because Frausto was an independent contractor. What factors should the court consider in making its ruling? [*Santiago v. Phoenix Newspapers, Inc.,* 794 P.2d 138 (Ariz. 1990)] **(See pages 598–601.)**

23–5 **Loyalty.** Taser International, Inc., develops and makes video and audio recording devices. Steve Ward was Taser's vice president of marketing when he began to explore the possibility of developing and marketing devices of his own design, including a clip-on camera. Ward talked to patent attorneys and a product development company and completed most of a business plan before he resigned from Taser. He then formed Vievu, LLC, to market the clip-on camera. Did Ward breach the duty of loyalty? Could he have taken any steps toward starting his own firm without breaching this duty? Discuss. [*Taser International, Inc. v. Ward,* 224 Ariz. 389, 231 P.3d 921 (App. Div. 1 2010)] **(See page 605.)**

23–6 **Employment Relationships.** William Moore owned Moore Enterprises, a wholesale tire business. William's son, Jonathan, worked as a Moore Enterprises employee while he was in high school. Later, Jonathan started his own business, called Morecedes Tire. Morecedes regrooved tires and sold them to businesses, including Moore Enterprises. A decade after Jonathan started Morecedes, William offered him work with Moore Enterprises. On the first day, William told Jonathan to load certain tires on a trailer but did not tell him how to do it. Was Jonathan an independent contractor? Discuss. [*Moore v. Moore,* __ P.3d __ (Idaho 2011)] **(See pages 598–601.)**

23–7 **Disclosed Principal.** To display desserts in restaurants, Mario Sclafani ordered refrigeration units from Felix Storch, Inc. Felix faxed a credit application to Sclafani. The application was faxed back with a signature that appeared to be Sclafani's. Felix delivered the units. When they were not paid for, Felix filed a suit against Sclafani to collect. Sclafani denied that he had seen the application or signed it. He testified that he referred all credit questions to "the girl in the office." Who was the principal? Who was the agent? Who is liable on the contract? Explain. [*Felix Storch, Inc. v. Martinucci Desserts USA, Inc.,* 30 Misc.2d 1217, 924 N.Y.S.2d 308 (Suffolk Co. 2011)] **(See page 611.)**

23–8 **Case Problem with Sample Answer—Liability for Contracts.** Thomas Huskin and his wife entered into a contract to have their home remodeled by House Medic Handyman Service. Todd Hall signed the contract as an authorized representative of House Medic. It turned out that House Medic was a fictitious name for Hall Hauling, Ltd. The contract did not indicate this, however, and Hall did not inform the Huskins about Hall Hauling. When a contract dispute later arose, the Huskins sued Todd Hall personally for breach of contract. Can Hall be held personally liable? Why or why not? [*Huskin v. Hall,* 2012 WL 553136 (Ohio Ct.App. 2012)] **(See pages 611–612.)**

—For a sample answer to Problem 23–8, go to Appendix H at the end of this text.

23–9 **A Question of Ethics—Agency.** Emergency One, Inc. (EO), makes fire and rescue vehicles. Western Fire Truck, Inc., contracted with EO to be its exclusive dealer in Colorado and Wyoming through December 2003. James Costello, a Western salesperson, was authorized to order EO vehicles for his customers. Without informing Western, Costello e-mailed EO about Western's financial difficulties, discussed the viability of Western's contract, and asked about the possibility of working for EO. On EO's request, and in disregard of Western's instructions, Costello sent some payments for EO vehicles directly to EO. In addition, Costello, with EO's help, sent a competing bid to a potential Western customer. EO's representative e-mailed Costello, "You have my permission to kick [Western's] ass." In April 2002, EO terminated its contract with Western, which, after reviewing Costello's e-mail, fired Costello. Western filed a lawsuit against Costello and EO, alleging that Costello breached his duty as an agent and that EO aided and abetted the breach. [*Western Fire Truck, Inc. v. Emergency One, Inc.*, 134 P.3d 570 (Colo.App. 2006)] **(See pages 601–606.)**

1. Was there an agency relationship between Western and Costello? Western required monthly reports from its sales staff, but Costello did not report regularly. Does this indicate that Costello was *not* Western's agent? In determining whether an agency relationship exists, is the *right* to control or the *fact* of control more important? Explain.
2. Did Costello owe Western a duty? If so, what was the duty? Did Costello breach it? How?
3. A Colorado state statute allows a court to award punitive damages in "circumstances of fraud, malice, or willful and wanton conduct." Did any of these circumstances exist in this case? Should punitive damages be assessed against either defendant? Why or why not?

Critical Thinking and Writing Assignments

23–10 Critical Legal Thinking. What policy is served by the law that employers do not own the copyrights for works created by independent contractors (unless there is a written "work for hire" agreement)? **(See page 601.)**

23–11 Business Law Critical Thinking Group Assignment. Dean Brothers Corp. owns and operates a steel drum manufacturing plant. Lowell Wyden, the plant superintendent, hired Best Security Patrol, Inc. (BSP), a security company, to guard Dean property and "deter thieves and vandals." Some BSP security guards, as Wyden knew, carried firearms. Pete Sidell, a BSP security guard, was not certified as an armed guard but nevertheless took his gun to work. While working at the Dean plant on October 31, 2014, Sidell fired his gun at Tyrone Gaines, in the belief that Gaines was an intruder. The bullet struck and killed Gaines. Gaines's mother filed a lawsuit claiming that her son's death was the result of BSP's negligence, for which Dean was responsible.

1. The first group will determine what the plaintiff's best argument is to establish that Dean is responsible for BSP's actions.
2. The second group will discuss Dean's best defense and formulate arguments in support of it.

24 CHAPTER

Employment, Immigration, and Labor Law

CHAPTER OUTLINE

- Employment at Will
- Wages, Hours, and Layoffs
- Family and Medical Leave
- Worker Health and Safety
- Income Security
- Employee Privacy Rights
- Immigration Law
- Labor Unions

LEARNING OBJECTIVES

The five learning objectives below are designed to help improve your understanding of the chapter. After reading this chapter, you should be able to answer the following questions:

1. What is the employment-at-will doctrine? When and why are exceptions to this doctrine made?
2. What federal statute governs working hours and wages?
3. Under the Family and Medical Leave Act, in what circumstances may an employee take family or medical leave?
4. What are the two most important federal statutes governing immigration and employment today?
5. What federal statute gave employees the right to organize unions and engage in collective bargaining?

(Photo by Scott Olson/iStockPhoto)

"The employer generally gets the employees he deserves."
—Sir Walter Gilbey, 1831–1914 (English merchant)

Until the early 1900s, most employer-employee relationships were governed by the common law. Even today, as we will see, private employers have considerable freedom to hire and fire workers under the common law. (This is one reason that employers generally get the employees they deserve, as the chapter-opening quotation observed.)

In addition, however, numerous statutes and administrative agency regulations now govern the workplace. In this chapter and the next, we look at the most significant laws regulating employment relationships and at how these laws are changing to adapt to new technologies and new problems such as the influx of illegal immigrants. We also consider some current controversies, such as the degree to which employers can regulate their employees' use of social media and whether the states can enact their own laws to regulate immigration.

Of course, an important aspect of the employment relationship is the right to strike, and labor laws authorize both strikes by employees and lockouts by employers. In 2011, for instance, the owners of the teams in both the National Football League and the National Basketball Association imposed lockouts against the players during disputes over salaries and other issues (discussed on page 648).

Employment at Will

Employment at Will A common law doctrine under which either party may terminate an employment relationship at any time for any reason, unless a contract specifies otherwise.

Employment relationships have traditionally been governed by the common law doctrine of **employment at will**, which allows either the employer or the employee to end the relationship at any time and for any reason. Thus, employers can fire workers for any reason or for no reason, unless doing so violates an employee's statutory or contractual rights. Today, the majority of U.S. workers continue to have the legal status of "employees at will." Indeed, only one state (Montana) does not apply this doctrine. Nonetheless, federal and state statutes prevent the doctrine from being applied in a number of circumstances, and the courts have also created several exceptions.

LEARNING OBJECTIVE 1
What is the employment-at-will doctrine? When and why are exceptions to this doctrine made?

Exceptions to the Employment-at-Will Doctrine

Because of the sometimes harsh effects of the employment-at-will doctrine for employees, the courts have carved out various exceptions to it. These exceptions are based on contract theory, tort theory, and public policy.

Exceptions Based on Contract Theory

Some courts have held that an *implied* employment contract exists between an employer and an employee. If an employee is fired outside the terms of the implied contract, he or she may succeed in an action for breach of contract even though no written employment contract exists. **EXAMPLE 24.1** BDI Enterprise's employment manual and personnel bulletin both state that, as a matter of policy, workers will be dismissed only for good cause. If an employee reasonably expects BDI to follow this policy, a court may find that there is an implied contract based on the terms stated in the manual and bulletin.[1] • Generally, the employee's reasonable expectations are the key to whether an employment manual creates an implied contractual obligation.

An employer's oral promises to employees regarding discharge policy may also be considered part of an implied contract. If the employer fires a worker in a manner contrary to what was promised, a court may hold that the employer has violated the implied contract and is liable for damages. Most state courts will judge a claim of breach of an implied employment contract by traditional contract standards.

KNOW THIS
An implied contract may exist if a party furnishes a service expecting to be paid, and the other party, who knows (or should know) of this expectation, has a chance to reject the service and does not.

Exceptions Based on Tort Theory

In a few situations, the discharge of an employee may give rise to an action for wrongful discharge under tort theories. Abusive discharge procedures may result in a suit for intentional infliction of emotional distress or defamation.

In addition, some courts have permitted workers to sue their employers under the tort theory of fraud. **EXAMPLE 24.2** Goldfinch, Inc., induces a prospective employee to leave a lucrative job and move to another state by offering "a long-term job with a thriving business." In fact, Goldfinch is not only having significant financial problems but is also planning a merger that will result in the elimination of the position offered to the prospective employee. If the employee takes the job in reliance on Goldfinch's representations and is fired shortly thereafter, the employee may be able to bring an action against the employer for fraud. •

Exceptions Based on Public Policy

The most common exception to the employment-at-will doctrine is made on the basis that the worker was fired for reasons that violate a fundamental public policy of the jurisdiction. Generally, the public policy involved must be expressed clearly in the jurisdiction's statutory law.

1. See, for example, *Ross v. May Co.*, 377 Ill.App.3d 387, 880 N.E.2d 210 (1 Dist. 2007).

Whistleblowing An employee's disclosure to government authorities, upper-level managers, or the media that the employer is engaged in unsafe or illegal activities.

The public-policy exception may also apply to an employee who is discharged for **whistleblowing**—that is, telling government authorities, upper-level managers, or the media that her or his employer is engaged in some unsafe or illegal activity.

CASE EXAMPLE 24.3 Rebecca Wendeln was the staff coordinator at a nursing home. When Wendeln discovered that a patient at the home had been improperly moved and had been injured as a result, she reported the incident to state authorities, as she was required to do by state law. Wendeln's supervisor was angry about the report, and Wendeln was fired shortly thereafter. When Wendeln brought a lawsuit, the court held that although she was an employee at will, she was protected in this instance from retaliatory firing because a very clear mandate of public policy had been violated.[2] • Normally, however, whistleblowers seek protection from retaliatory discharge under federal and state statutory laws, such as the Whistleblower Protection Act of 1989.[3]

In the following case, an employee was fired after he complained to his supervisor about how she performed her job. The court had to decide whether the employee was protected by the employer's whistleblower policy even though it was implemented after he was hired.

2. *Wendeln v. The Beatrice Manor, Inc.*, 271 Neb. 373, 712 N.W.2d 226 (2006).

3. 5 U.S.C. Section 1201.

Case 24.1

Waddell v. Boyce Thompson Institute for Plant Research, Inc.

Supreme Court of New York, Appellate Division, 940 N.Y.S.2d 331 (2012).

(Galushko Sergey/Shutterstock.com)

To criticize one's supervisor is a difficult decision.

FACTS Donald Waddell worked as a business office supervisor for the Boyce Thompson Institute for Plant Research, Inc. Waddell did not have an employment contract for a fixed term, and the institute's employee manual said that his job was "terminable at the will of either the employee or [the Institute], at any time, with or without cause." Several months after hiring Waddell, the institute implemented a whistleblower policy designed to encourage "the highest standards of financial reporting and lawful and ethical behavior." The whistleblower policy stated that the institute would not retaliate against an employee for making a complaint "in good faith pursuant to this policy."

Beginning in May 2010, Waddell repeatedly told his supervisor, Sophia Darling, that she needed to file certain financial documents more promptly. In August 2010, Darling fired Waddell, telling him that his disrespectful and insubordinate conduct violated the institute's Code of Conduct. Waddell then sued the institute, and the trial court dismissed the lawsuit for failure to state a claim. Waddell appealed.

ISSUE Could Waddell's employment be terminated at will?

DECISION Yes. The New York appellate court found that Waddell did not state a claim for breach of an implied contract based on the institute's whistleblower policy. It therefore affirmed the trial court's judgment for the institute.

REASON Because Waddell did not have an employment contract with a fixed term, the court presumed that he was employed at will. An employee may overcome a presumption of employment at will if "the employer made the employee aware of [an] express written policy limiting its rights of discharge and . . . the employee detrimentally relied on that policy in accepting the employment." In this case, the institute had a written whistleblower policy, but it was implemented several months after Waddell was hired. Moreover, Waddell failed to allege that he passed up other job opportunities based on the policy. Because Waddell could not prove that he detrimentally relied on the whistleblower policy, he was employed at will. Waddell therefore failed to state a proper claim for breach of an implied contract.

CRITICAL THINKING—Ethical Consideration *Suppose that Waddell had been allowed to bring a claim for breach of contract. How might his supervisor, Darling, defend her conduct? Explain your answer.*

Wrongful Discharge

Whenever an employer discharges an employee in violation of an employment contract or a statute protecting employees, the employee may bring an action for **wrongful discharge**. Even if an employer's actions do not violate any provisions in an employment contract or a statute, the employer may still be subject to liability under a common law doctrine, such as a tort theory or agency. Note that in today's business world, an employment contract may be established or modified via e-mail exchanges.[4]

Wrongful Discharge An employer's termination of an employee's employment in violation of the law or an employment contract.

KNOW THIS

In today's business world, an employment contract may be established or modified via e-mail exchanges.

Wages, Hours, and Layoffs

LEARNING OBJECTIVE 2
What federal statute governs working hours and wages?

In the 1930s, Congress enacted several laws regulating the wages and working hours of employees. In 1931, Congress passed the Davis-Bacon Act,[5] which requires contractors and subcontractors working on federal government construction projects to pay "prevailing wages" to their employees. In 1936, the Walsh-Healey Act[6] was passed. This act requires that a minimum wage, as well as overtime pay at 1.5 times regular pay rates, be paid to employees of manufacturers or suppliers that enter into contracts with agencies of the federal government.

In 1938, Congress passed the Fair Labor Standards Act[7] (FLSA), which extended wage and hour requirements to cover all employers engaged in interstate commerce or in the production of goods for interstate commerce, plus certain other businesses. More than 130 million American workers are protected (or covered) by the FLSA, which is enforced by the Wage and Hour Division of the U.S. Department of Labor. Here, we examine the FLSA's provisions in regard to child labor, maximum hours, and minimum wages.

Child Labor

"All I've ever wanted was an honest week's pay for an honest day's work."

Steve Martin, 1945–present
(American actor and comedian)

The FLSA prohibits oppressive child labor. Children under fourteen years of age are allowed to do certain types of work, such as deliver newspapers or work for their parents. They may also work in the entertainment industry and (with some exceptions) in agriculture. Children who are fourteen or fifteen years of age are allowed to work, but not in hazardous occupations. There are also numerous restrictions on how many hours per day (particularly on school days) and per week they can work.

Working times and hours are not restricted for persons between the ages of sixteen and eighteen, but they cannot be employed in hazardous jobs or in jobs detrimental to their health and well-being. None of these restrictions apply to individuals over the age of eighteen.

Wages and Hours

Minimum Wage The lowest wage, either by government regulation or union contract, that an employer may pay an hourly worker.

The FLSA provides that a **minimum wage** (now $7.25 per hour) must be paid to employees in covered industries. Congress periodically revises this minimum wage. Additionally, many states have minimum wages. When the state minimum wage is greater than the federal minimum wage, the employee is entitled to the higher wage.

When an employee receives tips while on the job, the employer is required to pay only $2.13 an hour in direct wages—but only if that amount, plus the tips received, equals at least the federal minimum wage (because under the FLSA every covered employee must

4. See, for example, *Moroni v. Medco Health Solutions, Inc.*, 2008 WL 3539476 (E.D.Mich. 2008).
5. 40 U.S.C. Sections 276a–276a-5.
6. 41 U.S.C. Sections 35–45.
7. 29 U.S.C. Sections 201–260.

be paid $7.25 per hour). If an employee's tips combined with the employer's direct wages do not equal the federal minimum wage, the employer must make up the difference. If employers pay at least the federal minimum wage, the FLSA allows them to take employee tips and make other arrangements for their distribution.

Overtime Exemptions

Under the FLSA, employees who work more than forty hours per week normally must be paid 1.5 times their regular pay for all hours over forty. Note that the FLSA overtime provisions apply only after an employee has worked more than forty hours per *week*. Thus, employees who work for ten hours a day, four days per week, are not entitled to overtime pay because they do not work more than forty hours per week.

"By working faithfully eight hours a day, you may eventually get to be a boss and work twelve hours a day."

Robert Frost, 1875–1963
(American poet)

Certain employees—usually executive, administrative, and professional employees, as well as outside salespersons and computer programmers—are exempt from the FLSA's overtime provisions. Employers are not required to pay overtime wages to exempt employees. Employers can voluntarily pay overtime to ineligible employees but cannot waive or reduce the overtime requirements of the FLSA. (Smartphones and other technology have raised new issues concerning overtime wages, as discussed in this chapter's *Beyond Our Borders* feature below.)

Administrative Employees To qualify under the administrative employee exemption, the employee must be paid a salary, not hourly wages, and the employee's primary duty must be directly related to the management or general business operations of the employer. In addition, the employee's primary duty must include the exercise of discretion and independent judgment with respect to matters of significance.

CASE EXAMPLE 24.4 Patty Lee Smith was a pharmaceutical sales representative at Johnson and Johnson (J&J). She traveled to ten physicians' offices a day to promote the benefits of J&J's drug Concerta. Smith's work was unsupervised, she controlled her own schedule, and she received a salary of $66,000. When she filed a claim for overtime pay, the court held that she was an administrative employee and therefore exempt from the FLSA's overtime provisions.[8] ●

8. *Smith v. Johnson and Johnson*, 593 F.3d 280 (3d Cir. 2010).

BEYOND OUR BORDERS

Brazil Requires Employers to Pay Overtime for Use of Smartphones after Work Hours

Workers in the United States are increasingly arguing that they should receive overtime pay for the time they spend staying connected to work through their iPads,, smartphones, or other electronic devices. Indeed, many employers require their employees to carry a mobile device (BlackBerry, iPhone, or other smartphone or tablet) to keep in contact.

Checking e-mail, responding to text messages, tweeting, and using LinkedIn or other employment-related apps can be considered work. If employees who are not exempt under the overtime regulations are required to use mobile devices after office hours, the workers may have a valid claim to overtime wages. The FLSA is not clear about what constitutes work, however, so workers have difficulty showing they are entitled to overtime wages.

In Brazil, however, workers who answer work e-mails on their smartphones or other electronic devices after work are now entitled to receive overtime wages. Under legislation enacted in 2012 and approved by President Dilma Rousseff, e-mail from an employer is considered the equivalent of orders given directly to an employee, so it constitutes work. A few other nations also require payment to workers for staying connected through smartphones and other devices after hours.

Critical Thinking

What are the pros and cons of paying overtime wages to workers who check e-mail and perform other work-related tasks electronically after hours?

Executive Employees

An executive employee is one whose primary duty is management. An employee's primary duty is determined by what he or she does that is of principal value to the employer, not by how much time the employee spends doing particular tasks. An employer cannot deny overtime wages to an employee based only on the employee's job title, however, and must be able to show that the employee's primary duty qualifies her or him for an exemption.[9]

CASE EXAMPLE 24.5 Kevin Keevican, a manager at a Starbucks store, worked seventy hours a week for $650 to $800, a 10 to 20 percent bonus, and paid sick leave. Keevican (and other former managers) filed a claim against Starbucks for unpaid overtime, claiming that he had spent 70 to 80 percent of his time waiting on customers and thus was not an executive employee. The court, however, found that Keevican was "the single highest-ranking employee" in his particular store and was responsible on site for that store's day-to-day overall operations. Because his primary duty was managerial, Starbucks was not required to pay overtime.[10]

Layoffs

During the latest economic recession in the United States, hundreds of thousands of workers lost their jobs as many businesses disappeared. Other companies struggling to keep afloat reduced costs by restructuring their operations and downsizing their workforces, which meant layoffs. In this section, we discuss the laws pertaining to employee layoffs—an area that is increasingly the subject of litigation.

The Worker Adjustment and Retraining Notification Act

Federal law requires large employers to provide sixty days' notice before implementing a mass layoff or closing a plant that employs more than fifty full-time workers. The Worker Adjustment and Retraining Notification Act,[11] or WARN Act, applies to employers with at least one hundred full-time employees. Employers must notify workers of mass layoffs, which means a layoff of at least one-third of the full-time employees at a particular job site.

The WARN Act is intended to give workers advance notice so that they can start looking for a new job while they are still employed and to alert state agencies so that they can provide training and other resources for displaced workers. Employers must provide advance notice of the layoff to the affected workers *or* their representative (if the workers are members of a labor union), as well as to state and local government authorities. Even companies that anticipate filing for bankruptcy normally must provide notice under the WARN Act before implementing a mass layoff.

If sued, an employer that orders a mass layoff or plant closing in violation of the WARN Act can be fined up to $500 for each day of the violation. Employees can recover back pay for each day of the violation (up to sixty days), plus reasonable attorneys' fees.

State Laws May Also Require Layoff Notices

Many states also have statutes requiring employers to provide notice before initiating mass layoffs, and these laws may have different and even stricter requirements than the WARN Act. In New York, for

9. See, for example, *Slusser v. Vantage Builders, Inc.*, 576 F.Supp.2d 1207 (D.N.M. 2008).
10. *Mims v. Starbucks Corp.*, 2007 WL 10369 (S.D.Tex. 2007).
11. 29 U.S.C. Sections 2101 *et seq.*

instance, companies with fifty or more employees must provide ninety days' notice before any layoff that affects twenty-five or more full-time employees.

Family and Medical Leave

LEARNING OBJECTIVE 3
Under the Family and Medical Leave Act, in what circumstances may an employee take family or medical leave?

In 1993, Congress passed the Family and Medical Leave Act (FMLA)[12] to allow employees to take time off from work for family or medical reasons. A majority of the states have similar legislation, and many employers maintain private family-leave plans for their workers. Recently, additional categories of FMLA leave have been created for military caregivers and for qualifying exigencies (emergencies) that arise due to military service.

Coverage and Applicability

The FMLA requires employers who have fifty or more employees to provide employees with up to twelve weeks of unpaid family or medical leave during any twelve-month period. The FMLA expressly covers private and public (government) employees who have worked for their employers for at least a year. An employee may take *family leave* to care for a newborn baby or a child recently placed for adoption or foster care. An employee can take *medical leave* when the employee or the employee's spouse, child, or parent has a "serious health condition" requiring care.

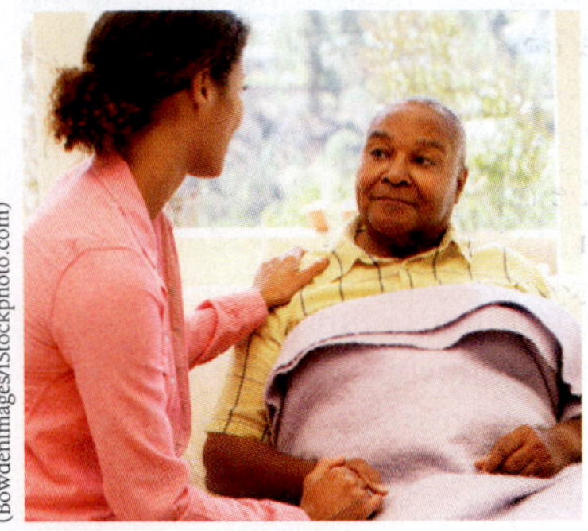

(Bowdenimages/iStockphoto.com)

A daughter helps her ailing father. Under what circumstances will she be protected by the Family and Medical Leave Act?

In addition, an employee caring for a family member with a serious injury or illness incurred as a result of military duty can take up to *twenty-six weeks of military caregiver leave* within a twelve-month period.[13] Also, an employee can take up to twelve weeks of *qualifying exigency leave* to handle specified *nonmedical* emergencies when a spouse, parent, or child is in, or called to, active military duty.[14] For instance, when a spouse is deployed to Afghanistan, an employee may take exigency leave to arrange for child care or to deal with financial or legal matters.

When an employee takes FMLA leave, the employer must continue the worker's health-care coverage on the same terms as if the employee had continued to work. On returning from FMLA leave, most employees must be restored to their original position or to a comparable position (with nearly equivalent pay and benefits, for example). An important exception allows the employer to avoid reinstating a *key employee*—defined as an employee whose pay falls within the top 10 percent of the firm's workforce.

Violations

An employer that violates the FMLA can be required to provide various remedies, including the following:

1. Damages to compensate an employee for lost benefits, denied compensation, and actual monetary losses (such as the cost of providing for care of the family member) up to an amount equivalent to the employee's wages for twelve weeks (twenty-six weeks for military caregiver leave).
2. Job reinstatement.
3. Promotion, if a promotion has been denied.

A successful plaintiff is entitled to court costs and attorneys' fees, and, in cases involving bad faith on the part of the employer, two times the amount of damages awarded by a judge or jury. Supervisors can also be held personally liable, as employers, for violations of the act.

---

12. 29 U.S.C. Sections 2601, 2611–2619, 2651–2654.
13. 29 C.F.R. Section 825.200.
14. 29 C.F.R. Section 825.126.

Employers generally are required to notify employees when an absence will be counted against leave authorized under the act. If an employer fails to provide such notice, and the employee consequently suffers an injury because he or she did not receive notice, the employer may be sanctioned.

Worker Health and Safety

Under the common law, employees who were injured on the job had to file lawsuits against their employers to obtain recovery. Today, numerous state and federal statutes protect employees and their families from the risk of accidental injury, death, or disease resulting from employment and provide a right to compensation for on-the-job injuries.

The Occupational Safety and Health Act

At the federal level, the primary legislation protecting employees' health and safety is the Occupational Safety and Health Act of 1970,[15] which is administered by the Occupational Safety and Health Administration (OSHA). The act imposes on employers a general duty to keep workplaces safe. In addition, the act prohibits employers from firing or discriminating against any employee who refuses to work when he or she believes a workplace is unsafe. OSHA has established specific safety standards for various industries that employers must follow. For instance, OSHA regulations require the use of safety guards on certain mechanical equipment and set maximum levels of exposure to substances in the workplace that may be harmful to a worker's health.

Notices, Records, and Reports

The act also requires that employers post certain notices in the workplace, perform prescribed record keeping, and submit specific reports. For instance, employers with eleven or more employees are required to keep occupational injury and illness records for each employee. Each record must be made available for inspection when requested by an OSHA compliance officer.

Whenever a work-related injury or disease occurs, employers must make reports directly to OSHA. If an employee dies or three or more employees are hospitalized because of a work-related incident, the employer must notify OSHA within eight hours. A company that fails to do so will be fined and may also be prosecuted under state law. Following the incident, a complete inspection of the premises is mandatory.

Inspections

OSHA compliance officers may enter and inspect facilities of any establishment covered by the Occupational Safety and Health Act. Employees may also file complaints of violations and cannot be fired by their employers for doing so.

State Workers' Compensation Laws

Workers' Compensation Laws State statutes that establish an administrative process for compensating workers for injuries that arise in the course of their employment, regardless of fault.

State **workers' compensation laws** establish an administrative procedure for compensating workers injured on the job. Instead of suing, an injured worker files a claim with the administrative agency or board that administers local workers' compensation claims.

Most workers' compensation statutes are similar. No state covers all employees. Typically, domestic workers, agricultural workers, temporary employees, and employees of common carriers (companies that provide transportation services to the public) are excluded, but minors are covered. Usually, the statutes allow employers to purchase insurance from a

15. 29 U.S.C. Sections 553, 651–678.

private insurer or a state fund to pay workers' compensation benefits in the event of a claim. Most states also allow employers to be self-insured—that is, employers that show an ability to pay claims do not need to buy insurance.

Requirements for Receiving Workers' Compensation In general, there are only two requirements for an employee to receive benefits under a state workers' compensation law:

1. The existence of an employment relationship.
2. An *accidental* injury that *occurred on the job or in the course of employment,* regardless of fault. (An injury that occurs while an employee is commuting to or from work usually is not considered to have occurred on the job or in the course of employment and hence is not covered.)

An injured employee must notify her or his employer promptly (usually within thirty days of the accident). Generally, an employee must also file a workers' compensation claim with the appropriate state agency or board within a certain period (sixty days to two years) from the time the injury is first noticed, rather than from the time of the accident.

Workers' Compensation versus Litigation An employee's acceptance of workers' compensation benefits bars the employee from suing for injuries caused by the employer's negligence. By barring lawsuits for negligence, workers' compensation laws also prevent employers from raising common law defenses to negligence, such as contributory negligence, assumption of risk, or injury caused by a "fellow servant" (another employee). A worker may sue an employer who *intentionally* injures the worker, however.

Income Security

Federal and state governments participate in insurance programs designed to protect employees and their families by covering the financial impact of retirement, disability, death, hospitalization, and unemployment. The key federal law on this subject is the Social Security Act of 1935.[16]

Social Security

The Social Security Act provides for old-age (retirement), survivors', and disability insurance. Hence, the act is often referred to as OASDI. Both employers and employees must "contribute" under the Federal Insurance Contributions Act (FICA)[17] to help pay for benefits that will partially make up for the employees' loss of income on retirement.

The basis for the employee's and the employer's contributions is the employee's annual wage base—the maximum amount of the employee's wages that are subject to the tax. The employer withholds the employee's FICA contribution from the employee's wages and ordinarily matches this contribution.

Almost every aspect of Social Security programs is now online.

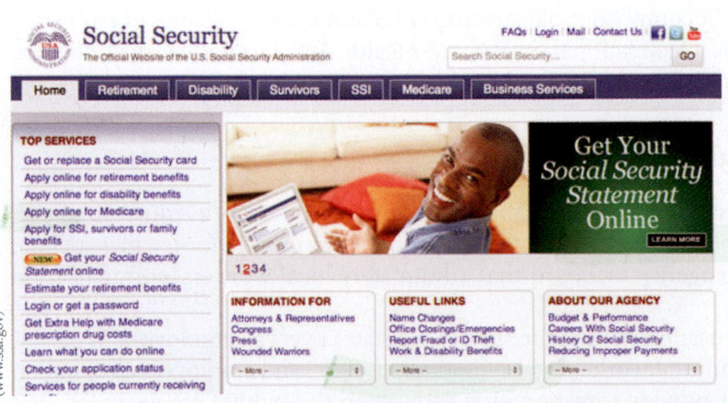

(www.ssa.gov)

16. 42 U.S.C. Sections 301–1397e.
17. 26 U.S.C. Sections 3101–3125.

KNOW THIS

Social Security covers almost all jobs in the United States. Nine out of ten workers "contribute" to this protection for themselves and their families.

Retired workers are then eligible to receive monthly payments from the Social Security Administration, which administers the Social Security Act. Social Security benefits are fixed by statute but increase automatically with increases in the cost of living.

Medicare

Medicare is a federal government health-insurance program that is administered by the Social Security Administration for people sixty-five years of age and older and for some under the age of sixty-five who are disabled. It originally had two parts, one pertaining to hospital costs and the other to nonhospital medical costs, such as visits to physicians' offices.

Additional Coverage Options Medicare now offers additional coverage options and a prescription-drug plan. People who have Medicare hospital insurance can also obtain additional federal medical insurance if they pay small monthly premiums, which increase as the cost of medical care increases.

Tax Contributions As with Social Security contributions, both the employer and the employee "contribute" to Medicare, but unlike Social Security, there is no cap on the amount of wages subject to the Medicare tax. In 2012, both the employer and the employee were required to pay 1.45 percent of *all* wages and salaries to finance Medicare.[18]

Thus, for Social Security and Medicare together, typically the employer and the employee each pay 7.65 percent (6.2 percent for Social Security + 1.45 percent for Medicare) of the wage base, up to the maximum, for a combined total of 15.3 percent.[19] In addition, all wages and salaries above the maximum wage base are taxed at a combined (employer and employee) rate of 2.9 percent for Medicare.

Self-employed persons pay both the employer and the employee portions of the Social Security and Medicare taxes (13.3 percent of income up to $110,100 and 2.9 percent of income above that amount in 2012). In addition, starting in 2013, a Medicare tax of 3.8 percent is applied to all investment income for those making more than $200,000.

Private Pension Plans

The major federal act regulating employee retirement plans is the Employee Retirement Income Security Act (ERISA) of 1974.[20] This act empowers a branch of the U.S. Department of Labor to enforce its provisions governing employers that have private pension funds for their employees.

ERISA created the Pension Benefit Guaranty Corporation (PBGC), an independent federal agency, to provide timely and uninterrupted payment of voluntary private pension benefits. The pension plans pay annual insurance premiums (at set rates adjusted for inflation) to the PBGC, which then pays benefits to participants in the event that a plan is unable to do so.

ERISA does not require an employer to establish a pension plan. When a plan exists, however, ERISA specifies standards for its management, including investment of funds and record-keeping requirements. A key provision of ERISA concerns vesting. **Vesting** gives an employee a legal right to receive pension benefits at some future date when he or she stops

Vesting The creation of an absolute or unconditional right or power.

18. As a result of the Health Care and Education Reconciliation Act of 2010, Medicare tax rates are expected to rise, and the applicable compensation base will expand to include more than just wage and salary income.

19. For 2012, the employee's contribution for Social Security was reduced to 4.2 percent, so the combined total was 13.3 percent. The maximum wage base in 2012 was $110,100.

20. 29 U.S.C. Sections 1001 *et seq.*

working. ERISA establishes complex vesting rules. Generally, however, all employee contributions to pension plans vest immediately, and employee rights to employer contributions to a plan vest after five years of employment.

Unemployment Insurance

KNOW THIS

If an employer does not pay unemployment taxes, a state government can place a lien (claim) on the business's property to secure the debt. (Liens were discussed in Chapter 21.)

To ease the financial impact of unemployment, the United States has a system of unemployment insurance. The Federal Unemployment Tax Act (FUTA) of 1935[21] created a state-administered system that provides unemployment compensation to eligible individuals. Under this system, employers pay into a fund, and the proceeds are paid out to qualified unemployed workers. The FUTA and state laws require employers that fall under the provisions of the act to pay unemployment taxes at regular intervals.

To be eligible for unemployment compensation, a worker must be willing and able to work. Workers who have been fired for misconduct or who have voluntarily left their jobs are not eligible for benefits. In the past, workers had to be actively seeking employment to continue receiving benefits. This rule was changed, however, in response to the high unemployment rates after the latest economic recession. President Barack Obama took measures that allow jobless persons to retain their unemployment benefits while pursuing additional education and training (rather than seeking employment).

COBRA

Federal law also enables workers to continue their health-care coverage after their jobs have been terminated—and the workers are thus no longer eligible for their employers' group health-insurance plans. The Consolidated Omnibus Budget Reconciliation Act (COBRA) of 1985[22] prohibits an employer from eliminating a worker's medical, optical, or dental insurance on the voluntary or involuntary termination of the worker's employment. The former employee—not the employer—pays the premiums under COBRA.

Employers, with some exceptions, must inform an employee of COBRA's provisions when the employee faces termination or a reduction of hours that would affect his or her eligibility for coverage under the plan. Only workers fired for gross misconduct are excluded from protection. An employer that does not comply with COBRA risks substantial penalties, such as a tax of up to 10 percent of the annual cost of the group plan or $500,000, whichever is less.

Employer-Sponsored Group Health Plans

The Health Insurance Portability and Accountability Act (HIPAA),[23] which was discussed in Chapter 2 in the context of privacy protections, contains provisions that affect employer-sponsored group health plans. HIPAA does not require employers to provide health insurance, but it does establish requirements for those that do provide such coverage. For instance, HIPAA strictly limits an employer's ability to exclude coverage for *preexisting conditions*, except pregnancy.

In addition, HIPAA restricts the manner in which covered employers collect, use, and disclose the health information of employees and their families. Employers must train employees, designate privacy officials, and distribute privacy notices to ensure that employees' health information is not disclosed to unauthorized parties. Failure to comply with HIPAA regulations can result in civil penalties of up to $100 per person per violation (with a cap of $25,000 per year). The employer is also subject to criminal prosecution for certain

21. 26 U.S.C. Sections 3301–3310.
22. 29 U.S.C. Sections 1161–1169.
23. 29 U.S.C.A. Sections 1181 *et seq.*

types of HIPAA violations and can face up to $250,000 in criminal fines and imprisonment for up to ten years if convicted.

(AP Photo/The Capital, Joshua McKerrow)

Employers often use video surveillance services to monitor employees. In addition, some employers engage in monitoring employee-generated e-mails.

Employee Privacy Rights

In the last thirty years, concerns about the privacy rights of employees have arisen in response to the sometimes invasive tactics used by employers to monitor and screen workers. Perhaps the greatest privacy concern in today's employment arena has to do with electronic performance monitoring.

Electronic Monitoring in the Workplace

More than half of employers engage in some form of surveillance of their employees. Many employers review employees' e-mail, blogs, instant messages, tweets, social media, smartphone, and Internet use. Employers also take digital video recordings of employees to assess job performance and record and review telephone conversations, voice mail, and text messages.

Although employees of private (nongovernment) employers have some privacy protection under tort law (see Chapter 4), state constitutions, and a number of state and federal statutes, employers have considerable leeway to monitor employees in the workplace. When determining whether an employer should be held liable for violating an employee's privacy rights, the courts generally weigh the employer's interests against the employee's reasonable expectation of privacy.

Normally, if employees have been informed that their communications are being monitored, they cannot reasonably expect those interactions to be private. If employees are not informed that certain communications are being monitored, however, the employer may be held liable for invading their privacy.

In addition, private employers generally can use specially designed software to track employees' Internet use and block access to certain Web sites without violating the First Amendment's protection of free speech, which applies only to government employees. In other words, the First Amendment generally prevents only *government employers* from restraining speech by blocking Web sites.

"We are rapidly entering the age of no privacy, where everyone is open to surveillance at all times; where there are no secrets."

William O. Douglas, 1898–1980 (Associate justice of the United States Supreme Court, 1939–1975)

The Electronic Communications Privacy Act Employers must comply with the Electronic Communications Privacy Act (ECPA) of 1986.[24] This act amended existing federal wiretapping law to cover electronic forms of communications, such as communications via cell phones or e-mail.

The ECPA prohibits the intentional interception of any wire, oral, or electronic communication and the intentional disclosure or use of the information obtained by the interception. Excluded from coverage, however, are any electronic communications through devices that are "furnished to the subscriber or user by a provider of wire or electronic communication service" and that are being used by the subscriber or user, or by the provider of the service, "in the ordinary course of its business." In other words, if a company provided the electronic device (cell phone, laptop, tablet) to the employee for ordinary business use, the company is not prohibited from intercepting business communications made on it.

24. 18 U.S.C. Sections 2510–2521.

This "business-extension exception" to the ECPA permits employers to monitor employees' electronic communications made in the ordinary course of business. It does not, however, permit employers to monitor employees' personal communications. Under another exception to the ECPA, however, an employer may avoid liability under the act if the employees consent to having their electronic communications intercepted by the employer. Thus, an employer may be able to avoid liability under the ECPA by requiring employees to sign forms indicating that they consent to the monitoring of personal as well as business communications.

The Stored Communications Act

Part of the ECPA is known as the Stored Communications Act (SCA).[25] The SCA prohibits intentional and unauthorized access to *stored* electronic communications and sets forth criminal and civil sanctions for violators. A person can violate the SCA by intentionally accessing a stored electronic communication. The SCA also prevents "providers" of communication services (such as cell phone companies and social media networks) from divulging private communications to certain entities and individuals.

For a discussion of how some employers are creating their own social media networks, see this chapter's *Adapting the Law to the Online Environment* feature below.

25. 18 U.S.C. Sections 2701–2711.

ADAPTING THE LAW TO THE ONLINE ENVIRONMENT

SOCIAL MEDIA IN THE WORKPLACE COME OF AGE

What do corporate giant Dell, Inc., and relatively small Nikon Instruments have in common? They—and many other companies—have created internal social media networks using enterprise social networking software and systems, such as Salesforce.com, Chatter, Yammer, and Socialcast. A glance at the posts on these internal networks reveals that they are quite different from typical posts on Facebook, LinkedIn, and Twitter. Rather than being personal, the tone is businesslike, and the posts deal with workplace concerns such as how a team is solving a problem or how to sell a new product.

Benefits and Pitfalls of Internal Social Media Networks

Internal social media networks offer businesses several advantages. Perhaps the most important is that employees can obtain real-time information about important issues such as production glitches. They can also exchange tips about how to deal with problems, such as difficult customers. News about the company's new products or those of a competitor is available immediately. Furthermore, employees spend much less time sorting through e-mail. Rather than wasting their fellow employees' time by sending mass e-mailings, workers can post messages or collaborate on presentations via the company's internal network.

Of course, the downside is that these networks may become polluted with annoying "white noise." If employees start posting comments about what they ate for lunch, for example, the system will lose much of its utility. Companies can prevent this from happening, though, by establishing explicit guidelines on what can be posted.

Keeping the Data Safe

Another concern is how to keep all that data and those corporate secrets safe. When a company sets up a social media network, it usually decides which employees can see which files and which employees will belong to each specific "social" group within the company. Often, the data created through a social media network are kept on the company's own servers in secure "clouds."

Critical Thinking

What problems might arise if data from an internal social media system are stored on third party servers?

PREVENTING LEGAL DISPUTES

To avoid legal disputes, exercise caution when monitoring employees and make sure that any monitoring is conducted in a reasonable place and manner. Establish written policies that include all types of electronic devices used by your employees—including employee-owned devices as well as those that the firm provides—and notify employees of how and when they may be monitored on these devices. Consider informing employees of the reasons for the monitoring. Explain what the concern is, what job repercussions could result, and what recourse employees have in the event that a negative action is taken against them. By providing more privacy protection to employees than is legally required, you can both avoid potential privacy complaints and give employees a sense that they retain some degree of privacy in their workplace, which can lead to greater job satisfaction.

Other Types of Monitoring

In addition to monitoring their employees' activities electronically, employers also engage in other types of monitoring. These practices, which have included lie-detector tests, drug tests, and genetic testing, have often been subject to challenge as violations of employee privacy rights.

Lie-Detector Tests At one time, many employers required employees or job applicants to take lie-detector (polygraph) tests in connection with their employment. Then, in 1988 Congress passed the Employee Polygraph Protection Act (EPPA).[26] The EPPA generally prohibits employers from requiring or even requesting that employees or job applicants take lie-detector tests. It also prevents employers from asking about or taking any negative employment action based on the results of a polygraph.

The act applies to most private employers (those with at least two employees and an annual volume of business of $500,000), but not to public employers (federal, state, and local government employers). Also exempt from the EPPA are security services firms and companies that manufacture and distribute controlled substances. Other employers may use lie-detector tests when investigating losses attributable to theft, including embezzlement and the theft of trade secrets.

Drug Testing In the interests of public safety, many employers, including government employers, require their employees to submit to drug testing.

Public Employers Government (public) employers are constrained in drug testing by the Fourth Amendment to the U.S. Constitution, which prohibits unreasonable searches and seizures (see Chapter 6). Drug testing of public employees is allowed by statute for transportation workers and is normally upheld by the courts when drug use in a particular job may threaten public safety. Also, when there is a reasonable basis for suspecting government employees of using drugs, courts often find that drug testing does not violate the Fourth Amendment.

Private Employers The Fourth Amendment does not apply to drug testing conducted by private employers. Hence, the privacy rights and drug testing of private-sector employees are governed by state law, which varies widely. Many states have statutes that allow drug testing by private employers but place restrictions on when and how the testing may be performed. A collective bargaining agreement may also provide protection against drug testing (or authorize drug testing under certain conditions).

Whether a private employer's drug tests are permissible typically depends on whether the tests are reasonable. Random drug tests and even "zero-tolerance" policies (that deny a "second chance" to employees who test positive for drugs) have been held to be reasonable.[27]

---

26. 29 U.S.C. Sections 2001 *et seq.*

27. See, for example, *CITGO Asphalt Refining Co. v. Paper, Allied-Industrial, Chemical, and Energy Workers International Union Local No. 2-991*, 385 F.3d 809 (3d Cir. 2004).

A related issue involves the inclusion of questions about drug use in background checks. Federal government employees have long been required to submit to background checks as a condition of employment. Many workers who work at U.S. government facilities are employees of private contractors, not of the government. They generally have not been subject to background checks. Recent standards, however, now require background checks for all federal workers, including contract employees. In the following case, several contract workers asserted that their privacy rights had been violated.

Case 24.2

National Aeronautics and Space Administration v. Nelson

Supreme Court of the United States, __U.S.__, 131 S.Ct. 746, 178 L.Ed.2d 667 (2011). www.supremecourt.gov[a]

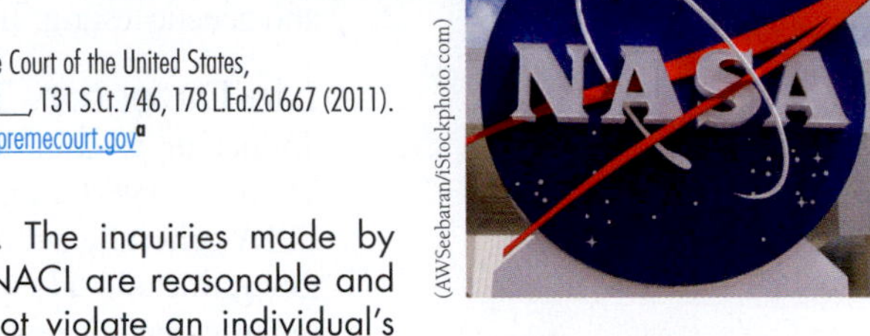

(AWSeebaran/iStockphoto.com)

FACTS The National Aeronautics and Space Administration (NASA) is an independent federal agency charged with planning and conducting "space activities." One of NASA's facilities is the Jet Propulsion Laboratory (JPL) in Pasadena, California, which is staffed exclusively by contract employees.

In 2007, under newly implemented standards, contract employees with long-term access to federal facilities were ordered to complete a standard background check—the National Agency Check with Inquiries (NACI). The NACI is designed to obtain information on such matters as counseling and treatment for illegal drug use, as well as mental and financial stability.

Robert Nelson and other JPL employees filed a lawsuit in a federal district court against NASA, claiming that the NACI violated their privacy rights. NASA argued that the employees' privacy rights were already protected by the Privacy Act of 1974, which allows the government to retain information only for "relevant and necessary" purposes and requires written consent before disclosure. The trial court ruled in favor of NASA, but the U.S. Court of Appeals for the Ninth Circuit reversed. NASA appealed to the United States Supreme Court.

ISSUE Does subjecting private employees who work at government facilities to a standard (NACI) background investigation violate their privacy rights?

DECISION No. The United States Supreme Court reversed the judgment of the federal appellate court and remanded the case. The inquiries made by the NACI are reasonable and do not violate an individual's right to privacy. The Privacy Act protects against the disclosure of private information.

REASON The Court reasoned that even presuming that the government's inquiries implicated a constitutional right to privacy, that does not prevent the government from asking reasonable questions as part of an employment background check. The Privacy Act provides safeguards against the public disclosure of an individual's private information without the individual's consent. The government has conducted employment investigations of applicants for the federal civil service for more than fifty years, and it simply extended this requirement to contract employees with long-term access to federal facilities. "Reasonable investigations of applicants and employees aid the Government in ensuring the security of its facilities and in employing a competent, reliable workforce." The Court concluded that a government employer's reasonable questions as part of a background check do not violate the right to privacy.

CRITICAL THINKING—Social Consideration *Suppose that after the decision in this case, a JPL employee refused to cooperate in an NACI background check. What would be the most likely consequences?*

a. In the "Supreme Court Documents" column, in the "Opinions" pull-down menu, select "Bound Volumes." On the next page, in the "For Search Term:" box, type "NASA v. Nelson" and click on "Search." In the results, click on the name of the case to access the opinion. The United States Supreme Court maintains this Web site. The United States Supreme Court maintains this Web site.

Genetic Testing A serious privacy issue arose when some employers began conducting genetic testing of employees or prospective employees in an effort to identify individuals who might develop significant health problems in the future. To prevent the improper use of genetic information in employment and health insurance, in 2008 Congress passed the Genetic Information Nondiscrimination Act (GINA).[28]

Under GINA, employers cannot make decisions about hiring, firing, job placement, or promotion based on the results of genetic testing. GINA also prohibits group health plans and insurers from denying coverage or charging higher premiums based solely on a genetic predisposition to developing a specific disease in the future.

Immigration Law

LEARNING OBJECTIVE 4

What are the two most important federal statutes governing immigration and employment today?

The United States had no laws restricting immigration until the late nineteenth century. Today, the most important laws governing immigration and employment are the Immigration Reform and Control Act[29] (IRCA) of 1986 and the Immigration Act of 1990.[30] Immigration law has become increasingly important in recent years. An estimated 12 million illegal immigrants now live in the United States, many of whom came to find jobs. Because U.S. employers face serious penalties if they hire illegal immigrants, it is necessary for businesspersons to have an understanding of immigration laws.

Immigration Reform and Control Act (IRCA)

When the IRCA was enacted in 1986, it provided amnesty to certain groups of illegal aliens living in the United States at the time. It also established a system that sanctions employers who hire illegal immigrants lacking work authorization.

The IRCA makes it illegal to hire, recruit, or refer for a fee someone not authorized to work in this country. Through Immigration and Customs Enforcement officers, the federal government conducts random compliance audits and engages in enforcement actions against employers who hire illegal immigrants.

I-9 Verification The process of verifying the employment eligibility and identity of a new worker. It must be completed within three days after the worker commences employment.

I-9 Employment Verification To comply with the IRCA, an employer must perform **I-9 verifications** for new hires, including those hired as "contractors" or "day workers" if they work under the employer's direct supervision. Form I-9, Employment Eligibility Verification, which is available from U.S. Citizenship and Immigration Services,[31] must be completed *within three days* of a worker's commencement of employment. The three-day period is to allow the employer to check the form's accuracy and to review and verify documents establishing the prospective worker's identity and eligibility for employment in the United States.

The employer must declare, under penalty of perjury, that an employee produced documents establishing his or her identity and legal employability. Acceptable documents include a U.S. passport establishing the person's citizenship or a document authorizing a foreign citizen to work in the United States, such as a Permanent Resident Card or an Alien Registration Receipt (discussed on the next page).

Most legal actions for violations of I-9 rules are brought against employees who provide false information or documentation. If the employee enters false information on an I-9 form or presents false documentation, the employer can fire the worker, who then may be subject to deportation. Nevertheless, employers must be honest when verifying

Who is eligible for a permanent residence card?

(Konstantin L/Shutterstock.com)

28. 26 U.S.C. Section 9834; 42 U.S.C. Sections 300gg-53, 1320d-9, 2000ff-1 to 2000ff-11.
29. 29 U.S.C. Section 1802.
30. This act amended various provisions of the Immigration and Nationality Act of 1952, 8 U.S.C. Sections 1101 *et seq.*
31. U.S. Citizenship and Immigration Services is a federal agency that is part of the U.S. Department of Homeland Security.

an employee's documentation: if an employer "should have known" that the worker was unauthorized, the employer has violated the rules.

Enforcement U.S. Immigration and Customs Enforcement (ICE) is the largest investigative arm of the U.S. Department of Homeland Security. ICE has a general inspection program that conducts random compliance audits. Other audits may occur if the agency receives a written complaint alleging an employer's violations. Government inspections include a review of an employer's file of I-9 forms. The government does not need a subpoena or a warrant to conduct such an inspection.

If an investigation reveals a possible violation, ICE will bring an administrative action and issue a Notice of Intent to Fine, which sets out the charges against the employer. The employer has a right to a hearing on the enforcement action if a request is filed within thirty days. This hearing is conducted before an *administrative law judge* (see Chapter 1), and the employer has a right to counsel and to *discovery* (see Chapter 3). The typical defense in such actions is good faith or substantial compliance with the documentation provisions.

Penalties An employer who violates the law by hiring an unauthorized alien is subject to substantial penalties. The employer may be fined up to $2,200 for each unauthorized employee for a first offense, $5,000 per employee for a second offense, and up to $11,000 for subsequent offenses. Criminal penalties, including additional fines and imprisonment for up to ten years, apply to employers who have engaged in a "pattern or practice of violations." A company may also be barred from future government contracts for violations.

KNOW THIS

If an employer had any reason to suspect that a worker's documents were forged or inaccurate at the time of hiring, the employer can be fined for violating the IRCA.

In determining the penalty, ICE considers the seriousness of the violation (such as intentional falsification of documents) and the employer's past compliance. ICE regulations also provide for mitigation or aggravation of the penalty under certain circumstances, such as whether the employer cooperated in the investigation or is a small business.

The Immigration Act

Often, U.S. businesses find that they cannot hire sufficient domestic workers with specialized skills. For this reason, U.S. immigration laws have long made provisions for businesses to hire specially qualified foreign workers. The Immigration Act of 1990 placed caps on the number of visas (entry permits) that can be issued to immigrants each year.

Most temporary visas are set aside for workers who can be characterized as "persons of extraordinary ability," members of the professions holding advanced degrees, or other skilled workers and professionals. To hire such an individual, an employer must submit a petition to ICE, which determines whether the job candidate meets the legal standards. Each visa is for a specific job, and there are legal limits on the employee's ability to change jobs once in the United States.

I-551 Alien Registration Receipts A company seeking to hire a noncitizen worker may do so if the worker is self-authorized. This means that the worker either is a lawful permanent resident or has a valid temporary Employment Authorization Document. A lawful permanent resident can prove his or her status to an employer by presenting an **I-551 Alien Registration Receipt**, known as a "green card," or a properly stamped foreign passport.

I-551 Alien Registration Receipt A document, known as a "green card," that shows that a foreign-born individual can legally work in the United States.

Many immigrant workers are not already self-authorized, and employers may attempt to obtain labor certification, or green cards, for the immigrants they wish to hire. Approximately fifty thousand new green cards are issued each year. A green card can be obtained only for a person who is being hired for a permanent, full-time position. (A separate authorization system provides for the temporary entry and hiring of nonimmigrant visa workers.)

> "Immigration is the sincerest form of flattery."
>
> Jack Paar, 1918–2004 (American entertainer)

The employer must show that no U.S. worker is qualified, willing, and able to take the job. The government has detailed regulations governing the advertising of positions as well as the certification process.[32] Any U.S. applicants who meet the stated job qualifications must be interviewed for the position. The employer must also be able to show that the qualifications required for the job are a business necessity.

The H-1B Visa Program

The most common and controversial visa program today is the H-1B visa system. To obtain an H-1B visa, the potential employee must be qualified in a "specialty occupation," meaning that the individual has highly specialized knowledge and has attained a bachelor's or higher degree or its equivalent. Individuals with H-1B visas can stay in the United States for three to six years and can work only for the sponsoring employer.

The recipients of these visas include many high-tech workers, such as computer programmers and electronics specialists. A maximum of sixty-five thousand H-1B visas are set aside each year for new immigrants. That limit is typically reached within the first few weeks of the year. Consequently, many businesses, such as Microsoft, continue to lobby Congress to expand the number of H-1B visas available to immigrants.

Labor Certification

A common criticism of the H-1B visa system is that it depresses the wages of U.S. workers because H-1B workers may be willing to work for less. The law addresses this complaint by requiring employers to pay H-1B workers the prevailing wage. Before submitting an H-1B application, an employer must file a Labor Certification application on a form known as ETA 9035.

The employer must agree to provide a wage level at least equal to the wages offered to other individuals with similar experience and qualifications and attest that the hiring will not adversely affect other workers similarly employed. The employer must also inform U.S. workers of the intent to hire a foreign worker by posting the form. The U.S. Department of Labor reviews the applications and may reject them for omissions or inaccuracies.

H-2, O, L, and E Visas

Other specialty temporary visas are available for other categories of employees. H-2 visas provide for workers performing agricultural labor of a seasonal nature. O visas provide entry for persons who have "extraordinary ability in the sciences, arts, education, business or athletics which has been demonstrated by sustained national or international acclaim." L visas allow a company's foreign managers or executives to work inside the United States. E visas permit the entry of certain foreign investors or entrepreneurs.

Should Arizona and other states be allowed to engage in cooperative immigration law enforcement? As the unemployment rate has remained stubbornly high since the recession, public resentment toward illegal immigrants has been growing, especially because some believe that illegal immigrants have taken job opportunities that otherwise would have gone to U.S. citizens. With state budgets under increasing pressure, there is also concern about the cost of providing education and other services for illegal immigrants.

Until recently, the laws governing immigration and the treatment of illegal immigrants have been federal. In 2010, however, Governor Jan Brewer of Arizona signed state legislation that required Arizona law enforcement officials to identify, charge, and possibly deport immigrants

32. The most relevant regulations can be found at 20 C.F.R. Section 655 (for temporary employment) and 20 C.F.R. Section 656 (for permanent employment).

who were in the state illegally. Under the Arizona law, immigrants would have to carry their papers at all times. Police officers could also verify an individual's immigration status during any law enforcement action or whenever the officers had a "reasonable suspicion" that someone was an illegal alien. In addition, Arizona citizens could sue police officers for not enforcing the law.

The federal government, however, insisted that federal immigration laws preempted state legislation. The United States Supreme Court ruled on the legality of the Arizona law in 2012—though not before several other states had passed similar legislation.

In *Arizona v. United States*,[33] the Court upheld the controversial "show-me-your-papers" provision that requires police to check the immigration status of persons stopped for another violation. All the other provisions of Arizona's law, however, were struck down as preempted by federal laws. States cannot pass laws that make it a crime for immigrants not to carry their registration documents, or make it a crime for those without work permits to seek employment. States also cannot authorize law enforcement to arrest people based solely on a reasonable suspicion that they are in the country illegally.

(EdStock/iStockphoto.com)

These construction workers argue for more jobs.

Labor Unions

In the 1930s, in addition to wage-hour laws, the government also enacted the first of several labor laws. These laws protect employees' rights to join labor unions, to bargain with management over the terms and conditions of employment, and to conduct strikes.

Federal Labor Laws

Federal labor laws governing union-employer relations have developed considerably since the first law was enacted in 1932. Initially, the laws were concerned with protecting the rights and interests of workers. Subsequent legislation placed some restraints on unions and granted rights to employers. We look here at four major federal statutes regulating union-employer relations.

Norris-LaGuardia Act In 1932, Congress protected peaceful strikes, picketing, and boycotts in the Norris-LaGuardia Act.[34] The statute restricted the power of federal courts to issue injunctions against unions engaged in peaceful strikes. In effect, this act established a national policy permitting employees to organize.

LEARNING OBJECTIVE 5
What federal statute gave employees the right to organize unions and engage in collective bargaining?

National Labor Relations Act One of the foremost statutes regulating labor is the National Labor Relations Act (NLRA) of 1935.[35] This act established the rights of employees to engage in collective bargaining and to strike. The act also specifically defined a number of employer practices as unfair to labor:

1. Interference with the efforts of employees to form, join, or assist labor organizations or to engage in concerted activities for mutual aid or protection.
2. An employer's domination of a labor organization or contribution of financial or other support to it.
3. Discrimination in the hiring or awarding of tenure to employees based on union affiliation.

33. ___ U.S. ___, 132 S.Ct. 2492, 183 L.Ed.2d 351 (2012).
34. 29 U.S.C. Sections 101–110, 113–115.
35. 20 U.S.C. Section 151.

4. Discrimination against employees for filing charges under the act or giving testimony under the act.
5. Refusal to bargain collectively with the duly designated representative of the employees.

The National Labor Relations Board (NLRB) The NLRA also created the National Labor Relations Board to oversee union elections and to prevent employers from engaging in unfair and illegal union activities and unfair labor practices.

The NLRB has the authority to investigate employees' charges of unfair labor practices and to file complaints against employers in response to these charges. When violations are found, the NLRB may also issue a cease-and-desist order compelling the employer to stop engaging in the unfair practices. Cease-and-desist orders can be enforced by a federal appellate court if necessary. After the NLRB rules on claims of unfair labor practices, its decision may be appealed to a federal court.

CASE EXAMPLE 24.6 Roundy's, Inc., which operates a chain of stores in Wisconsin, became involved in a dispute with a local construction union. When union members started distributing "extremely unflattering" flyers outside the stores, Roundy's ejected them from the property. The NLRB filed a complaint against Roundy's for unfair labor practices. An administrative law judge ruled that Roundy's had violated the law by discriminating against the union, and a federal appellate court affirmed. It is an unfair labor practice for an employer to prohibit union members from distributing flyers outside a store when it allows nonunion members to do so.[36] •

Good Faith Bargaining Under the NLRA, employers and unions have a duty to bargain in good faith. Bargaining over certain subjects is mandatory, and a party's refusal to bargain over these subjects is an unfair labor practice that can be reported to the NLRB. In one case, for instance, an employer was required to bargain with the union over the use of hidden video surveillance cameras.[37]

Workers Protected by the NLRA To be protected under the NLRA, an individual must be an *employee,* as that term is defined in the statute. Courts have long held that job applicants fall within the definition (otherwise, the NLRA's ban on discrimination in hiring would mean nothing). Additionally, the United States Supreme Court has held that individuals who are hired by a union to organize a company are to be considered employees of the company for NLRA purposes.[38]

ETHICAL ISSUE

Should employers be able to fire employees for posting criticisms of the employers on social media? A new issue that has recently emerged in employment and labor law concerns the steps that employers can legally take when their employees post critical comments about them on Facebook, Twitter, Google+, and other social media sites. An employer that reacts to highly critical posts by firing the employees may find that it has violated the law.

In 2011, the National Labor Relations Board (NLRB) received its first complaint related to social media. An employee at American Medical Response of Connecticut claimed that she had been fired after she criticized her boss on Facebook. She posted the critical comments after she had asked for a union representative but had been denied. The NLRB issued a complaint against the firm because federal labor law protects covered employees when they are engaged in "concerted activity" even when their union, if they have one, is not directly involved. The NLRB defines *concerted activity* as "two or more employees discussing pay or other work-related issues with each other." Therefore, an employee who merely posts a nasty comment about the employer

36. *Roundy's, Inc. v. NLRB,* 647 F.3d 638 (7th Cir. 2012).
37. *National Steel Corp. v. NLRB,* 324 F.3d 928 (7th Cir. 2003).
38. *NLRB v. Town & Country Electric, Inc.,* 516 U.S. 85, 116 S.Ct. 450, 133 L.Ed.2d 371 (1995).

on Facebook for all his or her "friends" to see would not be engaging in a protected activity. But if one or more co-workers respond to the post and add their comments about the employer, the posts would likely constitute a protected concerted activity.

Many companies have created policies for posts on Facebook and other social media sites. Stop & Shop, a supermarket chain, for example, established a policy that prohibited employees from having conversations about "confidential information" via social media. The employees' union filed a complaint with the NLRB. The union argued that Stop & Shop's policy violated federal labor law because it was so broad that it would prevent employees from engaging in protected activity, such as discussing wages and benefits. Stop & Shop subsequently withdrew the policy. In similar cases, the NLRB has consistently ruled in favor of the employees. (See the *Business Application* feature at the end of this chapter for some tips on creating a social media policy for employees.)

Labor-Management Relations Act

The Labor-Management Relations Act (LMRA) of 1947 (also called the Taft-Hartley Act)[39] was passed to proscribe certain unfair union practices, such as the *closed shop*. A **closed shop** requires union membership by its workers as a condition of employment.

Closed Shop A firm that requires union membership by its workers as a condition of employment, which is illegal.

Although the act made the closed shop illegal, it preserved the legality of the union shop. A **union shop** does not require membership as a prerequisite for employment but can, and usually does, require that workers join the union after a specified amount of time on the job.

Union Shop A firm that requires all workers, once employed, to become union members within a specified period of time as a condition of their continued employment.

The LMRA also prohibited unions from refusing to bargain with employers, engaging in certain types of picketing, and *featherbedding*—causing employers to hire more employees than necessary. The act also allowed individual states to pass their own **right-to-work laws**, which make it illegal for union membership to be required for *continued* employment in any establishment. Thus, union shops are technically illegal in the twenty-three states that have right-to-work laws.

Right-to-Work Law A state law providing that employees may not be required to join a union as a condition of retaining employment.

Labor-Management Reporting and Disclosure Act

In 1959, Congress enacted the Labor-Management Reporting and Disclosure Act (LMRDA).[40] The act established an employee bill of rights and reporting requirements for union activities. The act strictly regulates unions' internal business procedures, including union elections. For example, the LMRDA requires a union to hold regularly scheduled elections of officers using secret ballots. Ex-convicts are prohibited from holding union office. Moreover, union officials are accountable for union property and funds. Members have the right to attend and to participate in union meetings, to nominate officers, and to vote in most union proceedings.

The act also outlawed **hot-cargo agreements**, in which employers voluntarily agree with unions not to handle, use, or deal in goods produced by nonunion employees working for other employers.

Hot-Cargo Agreement An illegal agreement in which employers voluntarily agree with unions not to handle, use, or deal in the nonunion-produced goods of other employers.

Union Organization

Typically, the first step in organizing a union at a particular firm is to have the workers sign authorization cards. An **authorization card** usually states that the worker desires to have a certain union, such as the United Auto Workers, represent the workforce. If a majority of the workers sign authorization cards, the union organizers (unionizers) present the cards to the employer and ask for formal recognition of the union.

Authorization Card A card signed by an employee that gives a union permission to act on his or her behalf in negotiations with management.

The employer is not required to recognize the union at this point in the process, but it may do so voluntarily on a showing of majority support. (Under pro-labor legislation that has been proposed repeatedly in recent years, the employer would be required to recognize the union as soon as a majority of the workers had signed authorization cards—without holding an election, as described next.)[41]

39. 29 U.S.C. Sections 141 *et seq.*

40. 29 U.S.C. Sections 401 *et seq.*

41. If the proposed Employee Free Choice Act ever becomes law, some of the information stated here may change.

Union Elections

If the employer refuses to voluntarily recognize the union after a majority of the workers sign authorization cards—or if less than 50 percent of the workers sign authorization cards—the union organizers present the cards to the NLRB with a petition for an election. For an election to be held, the unionizers must demonstrate that at least 30 percent of the workers to be represented support a union or an election on unionization.

The proposed union must also represent an *appropriate bargaining unit.* Not every group of workers can form a single union. One key requirement of an appropriate bargaining unit is a *mutuality of interest* among all the workers to be represented by the union. Factors considered in determining whether there is a mutuality of interest include the *similarity of the jobs* of all the workers to be unionized and their physical location.

If all of these requirements are met, an election is held. The NLRB supervises the election and ensures secret voting and voter eligibility. If the proposed union receives majority support in a fair election, the NLRB certifies the union as the bargaining representative for the employees.

Union Election Campaigns

KNOW THIS

It is illegal for employers to require union membership as a prerequisite to employment, but not illegal to require that workers join the union after being employed for a period of time.

Many disputes between labor and management arise during union election campaigns. Generally, the employer has control over unionizing activities that take place on company property during working hours. Employers may thus limit the campaign activities of union supporters as long as the employer has a legitimate business reason for doing so. The employer may also reasonably limit the times and places that union solicitation occurs so long as the employer is not discriminating against the union.

EXAMPLE 24.7 A union is seeking to organize clerks at a department store owned by Amanti Enterprises. Amanti can prohibit all union solicitation in areas of the store open to the public because that activity could seriously interfere with the store's business. If Amanti allows solicitation for charitable causes in the workplace, however, it may not prohibit union solicitation. •

An employer may campaign among its workers against the union, but the NLRB carefully monitors and regulates the tactics used by management. Otherwise, management might use its economic power to coerce the workers into voting against unionization. If the employer issued threats ("If the union wins, you'll all be fired") or engaged in other unfair labor practices, the NLRB may certify the union even though it lost the election. Alternatively, the NLRB may ask a court to order a new election.

In the following case, the question was whether managers' brief interruptions of unionizing activities constituted illegal surveillance in violation of the National Labor Relations Act.

Case 24.3

Local Joint Executive Board of Las Vegas v. National Labor Relations Board

United States Court of Appeals, Ninth Circuit, 515 F.3d 942 (2008).

(Lingbeek/iStockphoto.com)

The Aladdin hotel before it became the Planet Hollywood Resort and Casino in Las Vegas.

FACTS Aladdin Gaming, LLC, operates a hotel and casino in Las Vegas, Nevada. On May 30, 2003, Local Joint Executive Board of Las Vegas and two other unions began an open campaign to organize Aladdin's housekeeping, food, and beverage departments. On two occasions during this campaign, human resources managers at Aladdin (Tracy Sapien and Stacey Briand) approached union organizers who were discussing unionization with employees in an employee dining room during a lunch break. Sapien and Briand interrupted the organizers while they were obtaining signatures on authorization cards and asked whether the employees were fully informed of the facts before signing. The unions filed a complaint with the National Labor Relations Board (NLRB) claiming that the

Case 24.3—Continues next page

Case 24.3—Continued

managers' actions were illegal surveillance in violation of the National Labor Relations Act (NLRA). The NLRB ruled in favor of Aladdin, and the unions appealed.

ISSUE Did the managers' conduct violate the NLRA?

DECISION No. The federal appellate court denied the unions' petition for review, concluding that the managers' brief interruptions of organizing activity did not constitute illegal surveillance.

REASON The NLRA states that an observation of union activity becomes unlawful when that surveillance "goes beyond casual and becomes unduly intrusive." The court found no evidence that Sapien and Briand used threats or other blatant, coercive means to strip union organizers of their rights under the act. The court noted that in both instances Sapien and Briand only attempted to give workers additional information to consider before signing the union cards. Once they were finished speaking to the employees, they left the area.

WHAT IF THE FACTS WERE DIFFERENT? *If management employees had interrupted union-organizing activities twenty-five times rather than just twice, would the outcome of this case have been different? Why or why not?*

Collective Bargaining

Collective Bargaining The process by which labor and management negotiate the terms and conditions of employment, including working hours and workplace conditions.

If the NLRB certifies the union, the union becomes the *exclusive bargaining representative* of the workers. The central legal right of a union is to engage in collective bargaining on the members' behalf. **Collective bargaining** is the process by which labor and management negotiate the terms and conditions of employment, including wages, benefits, working conditions, and other matters.

The Union Negotiates with Management

Collective bargaining allows union representatives elected by union members to speak on behalf of the members at the bargaining table. When a union is officially recognized, it may demand to bargain with the employer and negotiate new terms or conditions of employment. In collective bargaining, as in most other business negotiations, each side uses its economic power to pressure or persuade the other side to grant concessions.

Both Sides Must Bargain in Good Faith

Bargaining does not mean that one side must give in to the other or that compromises must be made. It does mean that a demand to bargain with the employer must be taken seriously and that both sides must bargain in "good faith."

Good faith bargaining means that management, for instance, must be willing to meet with union representatives and consider the union's wishes when negotiating a contract. It would be bad faith for management to engage in a campaign to undermine the union among workers or to constantly shift position on disputed contract terms. Another example of bad faith would be for management to send bargainers who lack authority to commit the company to a contract.

If an employer (or a union) refuses to bargain in good faith without justification, it has committed an unfair labor practice. The other party may then petition the NLRB for an order requiring good faith bargaining.

Strikes

Even when labor and management have bargained in good faith, they may be unable to reach a final agreement. When extensive collective bargaining has been conducted and an impasse results, the union may call a strike against the employer to pressure it into making

Strike An action undertaken by unionized workers when collective bargaining fails. The workers leave their jobs, refuse to work, and (typically) picket the employer's workplace.

concessions. In a **strike**, the unionized workers leave their jobs and refuse to work. The workers also typically picket the workplace, standing outside the facility with signs stating their complaints.

A strike is an extreme action. Striking workers lose their rights to be paid, and management loses production and may lose customers when orders cannot be filled. Labor law regulates the circumstances and conduct of strikes. Most strikes take the form of "economic strikes," which are initiated because the union wants a better contract. **EXAMPLE 24.8** Teachers in Eagle Point, Oregon, engaged in an economic strike in 2012 after contract negotiations with the school district failed to bring an agreement on pay, working hours, and subcontracting jobs. The unionized teachers picketed outside the school building. Classes were canceled for a few weeks until the district could find substitute teachers who would fill in during the strike. •

The Right to Strike

The right to strike is guaranteed by the NLRA, within limits, and strike activities, such as picketing, are protected by the free speech guarantee of the First Amendment to the U.S. Constitution. Nonworkers have a right to participate in picketing an employer.

The NLRA also gives workers the right to refuse to cross a picket line of fellow workers who are engaged in a lawful strike. Employers are permitted to hire replacement workers to substitute for the workers who are on strike.

Illegal Strikes

In the following situations, the conduct of the strikers may cause the strikes to be illegal:

1. *Violent strikes.* The use of violence (including the threat of violence) against management employees or substitute workers is illegal.
2. *Massed picketing.* If the strikers form a barrier and deny management or other nonunion workers access to the plant, the strike is illegal.
3. *Sit-down strikes.* Strikes in which employees simply stay in the plant without working are illegal.
4. *No-strike clause.* A strike may be illegal if it contravenes a no-strike clause that was in the previous collective bargaining agreement between the employer and the union.
5. *Secondary boycotts.* A **secondary boycott** is another type of illegal strike that is directed against someone other than the strikers' employer, such as the companies that sell materials to the employer. **EXAMPLE 24.9** The unionized workers of SemiCo go out on strike. To increase their economic leverage, the workers picket the leading suppliers and customers of SemiCo in an attempt to hurt the company's business. SemiCo is considered the primary employer, and its suppliers and customers are considered secondary employers. Picketing of the suppliers or customers is a secondary boycott, which was made illegal by the Labor-Management Relations Act (Taft-Hartley Act). •
6. *Wildcat strikes.* A *wildcat strike* occurs when a small number of workers, perhaps dissatisfied with a union's representation, call their own strike. The union is the exclusive bargaining representative of a group of workers, and only the union can call a strike. Therefore, a wildcat strike, unauthorized by the certified union, is illegal.

Secondary Boycott An illegal strike directed at suppliers and customers of the primary employer with whom the union has a labor dispute.

The Rights of Strikers after a Strike Ends

An important issue concerns the rights of strikers after the strike ends. In a typical economic strike over working conditions, the employer has a right to hire permanent replacements during the strike and need not terminate the replacement workers when the economic strikers seek to return to work. In other words, striking workers are not guaranteed the right to return to their jobs after the strike if satisfactory replacement workers have been found.

If the employer has not hired replacement workers to fill the strikers' positions, however, then the employer must rehire the economic strikers to fill any vacancies. Employers may not discriminate against former economic strikers, and those who are rehired retain their seniority rights. Different rules apply when a union strikes because the employer has engaged in unfair labor practices. In this situation, the employer may still hire replacements but must give the strikers back their jobs once the strike is over.

Lockouts

Lockout Occurs when an employer shuts down to prevent employees from working typically because it cannot reach a collective bargaining agreement with the union.

Lockouts are the employer's counterpart to the worker's right to strike. A **lockout** occurs when the employer shuts down to prevent employees from working.

Employer's Response to Imminent Strike

Lockouts usually are used when the employer believes that a strike is imminent. A lockout may be a legal employer response when a union and an employer have reached a stalemate in collective bargaining.

EXAMPLE 24.10 In 2011, the owners of the teams in the National Football League (NFL) imposed a lockout on the NFL players' union after negotiations on a new collective bargaining agreement broke down. The NFL owners had proposed to reduce players' salaries and extend the season by two games because of decreased profits due to the struggling economy. When the lockout was imposed, the union requested decertification, which cleared the way for a group of players to file an antitrust lawsuit (see Chapter 32). A settlement was reached before the start of the 2011 football season. The players accepted 3 percent less of the revenue generated (47 percent rather than 50 percent) in exchange for better working conditions and more retirement benefits. The owners agreed to keep the same number of games per season.

The owners of the teams in the National Basketball Association (NBA) also locked out their players in 2011 after the two sides failed to reach a collective bargaining agreement. The dispute involved the division of revenue and a salary cap. During the lockout, the players could not access NBA facilities, trainers, or staff, and the owners could not trade, sign, or contract with players. The lockout lasted 161 days and resulted in the cancellation of all preseason games and several weeks of regular season games before it was finally resolved. •

Illegal Lockouts

Some lockouts are illegal, however. An employer may not use a lockout as a tool to break the union and pressure employees into decertification. Consequently, an employer must be able to show some economic justification for instituting a lockout.

Reviewing . . . Employment, Immigration, and Labor Law

Rick Saldona began working as a traveling salesperson for Aimer Winery in 1991. Sales constituted 90 percent of Saldona's work time. Saldona worked an average of fifty hours per week but received no overtime pay. In June 2014, Saldona's new supervisor, Caesar Braxton, claimed that Saldona had been inflating his reported sales calls and required Saldona to submit to a polygraph test. Saldona reported Braxton to the U.S. Department of Labor, which prohibited Aimer from requiring Saldona to take a polygraph test for this purpose. In August 2014, Saldona's wife, Venita, fell from a ladder and sustained a head injury while employed as a full-time agricultural harvester. Saldona delivered to Aimer's human resources department a letter from his wife's physician indicating that she would need daily care for several months, and Saldona took leave until December 2014. Aimer had sixty-three employees at that time. When Saldona returned to Aimer, he was informed that his position had been eliminated because his sales territory had been combined with an adjacent territory. Using the information presented in the chapter, answer the following questions.

1. Would Saldona have been legally entitled to receive overtime pay at a higher rate? Why or why not?
2. What is the maximum length of time Saldona would have been allowed to take leave to care for his injured spouse?
3. Under what circumstances would Aimer have been allowed to require an employee to take a lie-detector test?
4. Would Aimer likely be able to avoid reinstating Saldona under the *key employee* exception? Why or why not?

DEBATE THIS: The U.S. labor market is highly competitive, so state and federal laws that require overtime pay are unnecessary and should be abolished.

BUSINESS APPLICATION

How to Develop a Policy on Employee Use of the Internet and Social Media*

Employers that make available the Internet, e-mail, smartphones, and social networking sites to their employees face some obvious risks. The employer could be liable if an employee harasses another employee via e-mail or a social networking site such as Facebook. Similarly, the employer could be liable if an employee uses the Internet to violate copyright and other intellectual property laws. Another risk is that an outside party might intercept confidential information or trade secrets contained in communications transmitted via the Internet. But if the employer monitors employees' use of the Internet and social media in an attempt to avoid these problems, the employer risks being held liable for violating employees' privacy.

Remember that a small company can be bankrupted by just one successful lawsuit against it. Even if the company wins the suit, it will likely have incurred substantial legal fees. Therefore, if you are an employer and find it necessary to monitor your employees' use of the Internet and social media, you should take care when creating your policy.

Inform Employees of the Monitoring and Obtain Their Consent

First, notify your employees that you will be monitoring their online communications and specify what will be monitored (e-mail, cell phones, text messages, posts on Facebook and other social media, and the like). Also state clearly whether you will monitor all work-related communications, even those sent via the employees' own devices, or whether you will monitor only communications sent via devices furnished by the company. Second, ask all employees to consent, in writing, to this monitoring.

Spell Out Permissible and Impermissible Uses

To ensure that employees understand what they may and may not do, develop comprehensive guidelines for Internet and social media use. Include specific examples of prohibited activities. Remember that the National Labor Relations Board has interpreted federal labor law to mean that employers cannot ban all use of social media by their employees (see page 636). Therefore, particularly if your employees are union members, it is a good idea to consult an attorney to ensure that your policy is legal.

Policies for Social Media Such As Facebook, Google+, LinkedIn, and Twitter

Be careful when creating policies on social media use. Employees have free speech and privacy rights, so make sure that you have a legitimate business reason for any restrictions you impose. Do not attempt to interfere with employees' discussions of wages and working conditions on social media sites—these are protected under federal labor law.

An employer can encourage employees to use discretion in posts on social media and can discourage them from making negative comments about co-workers. You probably can prohibit employees from disclosing confidential or personal information about customers, clients, co-workers, and possibly suppliers. You might also be able to restrict employees from making negative statements about the firm or its products and services.

Continued

---

*This *Business Application* is not meant to substitute for the services of an attorney who is licensed to practice law in your state.

Checklist for the Employer

1. Inform employees that their Internet and social media communications will be monitored, and indicate which communications and which devices will be monitored.
2. Obtain employees' written consent to having their electronic communications monitored.
3. Develop a comprehensive policy statement that explains how the Internet and social media should and should not be used.
4. Designate a person at the company that employees can go to if they have questions or concerns about the firm's policies on Internet or social media use.

Key Terms

authorization card 644
closed shop 644
collective bargaining 646
employment at will 625
hot-cargo agreement 644
I-9 verification 639
I-551 Alien Registration Receipt 640
lockout 648
minimum wage 627
right-to-work law 644
secondary boycott 647
strike 647
union shop 644
vesting 633
whistleblowing 626
workers' compensation laws 631
wrongful discharge 627

Chapter Summary: Employment, Immigration, and Labor Law

Employment at Will (See pages 625–627.)	1. *Employment-at-will doctrine*—Under this common law doctrine, either party may terminate the employment relationship at any time and for any reason ("at will"). 2. *Exceptions to the employment-at-will doctrine*—Courts have made exceptions to the doctrine on the basis of contract theory, tort theory, and public policy. Whistleblowers have occasionally received protection under the common law for reasons of public policy. 3. *Wrongful discharge*—Whenever an employer discharges an employee in violation of an employment contract or statutory law protecting employees, the employee may bring a suit for wrongful discharge.
Wages, Hours, and Layoffs (See pages 627–630.)	1. *Davis-Bacon Act (1931)*—Requires contractors and subcontractors working on federal government construction projects to pay their employees "prevailing wages." 2. *Walsh-Healey Act (1936)*—Requires firms that contract with federal agencies to pay their employees a minimum wage and overtime pay. 3. *Fair Labor Standards Act (1938)*—Extended wage and hour requirements to cover all employers whose activities affect interstate commerce plus certain other businesses. The act has specific requirements in regard to child labor, maximum hours, and minimum wages. 4. *The Worker Adjustment and Retraining Notification (WARN) Act*—Applies to employers with at least one hundred full-time employees and requires that sixty days' advance notice of mass layoffs (defined on page 629) be given to affected employees or their representative (if workers are in a labor union). Employers who violate the WARN Act can be fined up to $500 for each day of the violation. 5. *State layoff notice requirements*—May be different from and even stricter than the WARN Act's requirements.
Family and Medical Leave (See pages 630–631.)	The Family and Medical Leave Act (FMLA) requires employers with fifty or more employees to provide employees with up to twelve weeks of unpaid leave (twenty-six weeks for military caregiver leave) during any twelve-month period. 1. *Family leave*—May be taken to care for a newborn baby, an adopted child, or a foster child. 2. *Medical leave*—May be taken when the employee or the employee's spouse, child, or parent has a serious health condition requiring care. 3. *Military caregiver leave*—May be taken to care for a family member with a serious injury or illness incurred as a result of military duty. 4. *Qualifying exigency leave*—May be taken to handle specified nonmedical emergencies when a spouse, parent, or child is in, or called to, active military duty.
Worker Health and Safety (See pages 631–632.)	1. *Occupational Safety and Health Act (1970)*—Requires employers to meet specific safety and health standards that are established and enforced by the Occupational Safety and Health Administration (OSHA). 2. *State workers' compensation laws*—Establish an administrative procedure for compensating workers who are injured in accidents that occur on the job, regardless of fault.

Chapter Summary: Employment, Immigration, and Labor Law—Continued

Income Security (See pages 632–635.)	1. *Social Security and Medicare*—The Social Security Act of 1935 provides for old-age (retirement), survivors', and disability insurance. Both employers and employees must make contributions under the Federal Insurance Contributions Act (FICA). The Social Security Administration also administers Medicare, a health-insurance program for older or disabled persons. 2. *Private pension plans*—The federal Employee Retirement Income Security Act (ERISA) of 1974 establishes standards for the management of employer-provided pension plans. 3. *Unemployment insurance*—The Federal Unemployment Tax Act (FUTA) of 1935 created a system that provides unemployment compensation to eligible individuals. Employers are taxed to cover the costs. 4. *COBRA*—The Consolidated Omnibus Budget Reconciliation Act (COBRA) of 1985 requires employers to give employees, on termination of employment, the option of continuing their medical, optical, or dental insurance coverage for a certain period. 5. *HIPAA*—The Health Insurance Portability and Accountability Act (HIPAA) establishes requirements for employer-sponsored group health plans. The plans must also comply with various safeguards to ensure the privacy of employees' health information.
Employee Privacy Rights (See pages 635–639.)	In addition to the U.S. Constitution, tort law, state constitutions, and federal and state statutes may provide some protection for employees' privacy rights. Employer practices that are often challenged by employees as invasive of their privacy rights include electronic performance monitoring, lie-detector tests, drug testing, and genetic testing.
Immigration Law (See pages 639–642.)	1. *Immigration Reform and Control Act (1986)*—Prohibits employers from hiring illegal immigrants. The act is administered by U.S. Citizenship and Immigration Services. Compliance audits and enforcement actions are conducted by U.S. Immigration and Customs Enforcement. 2. *Immigration Act (1990)*—Limits the number of legal immigrants entering the United States by capping the number of visas (entry permits) that are issued each year.
Labor Unions (See pages 642–648.)	1. *Federal labor laws*— a. Norris-LaGuardia Act (1932)—Protects peaceful strikes, picketing, and primary boycotts. b. National Labor Relations Act (1935)—Established the rights of employees to engage in collective bargaining and to strike. It also defined specific employer practices as unfair to labor. The National Labor Relations Board (NLRB) was created to administer and enforce the act. c. Labor-Management Relations Act (1947)—Proscribes certain unfair union practices, such as the closed shop. d. Labor-Management Reporting and Disclosure Act (1959)—Established an employee bill of rights and reporting requirements for union activities. 2. *Union organization*—Union campaign activities and elections must comply with the requirements established by federal labor laws and the NLRB. 3. *Collective bargaining*—The process by which labor and management negotiate the terms and conditions of employment (such as wages, benefits, and working conditions). The central legal right of a labor union is to engage in collective bargaining on the members' behalf. 4. *Strikes*—When collective bargaining reaches an impasse, union members may use their ultimate weapon in labor-management struggles—the strike. A strike occurs when unionized workers leave their jobs and refuse to work.

ExamPrep

ISSUE SPOTTERS

1. Erin, an employee of Fine Print Shop, is injured on the job. For Erin to obtain workers' compensation, does her injury have to have been caused by Fine Print's negligence? Does it matter whether the action causing the injury was intentional? Explain. **(See page 631.)**
2. Onyx applies for work with Precision Design Company, which tells her that it requires union membership as a condition of employment. She applies for work with Quality Engineering, Inc., which does not require union membership as a condition of employment but requires employees to join a union after six months on the job. Are these conditions legal? Why or why not? **(See page 644.)**

—Check your answers to the Issue Spotters against the answers provided in Appendix E at the end of this text.

BEFORE THE TEST

Go to www.cengagebrain.com, enter the ISBN 9781133273561, and click on "Find" to locate this textbook's Web site. Then, click on "Access Now" under "Study Tools," and select Chapter 24 at the top. There, you will find a Practice Quiz that you can take to assess your mastery of the concepts in this chapter, as well as Flashcards, a Glossary of important terms, and Video Questions (when assigned).

For Review

Answers to the even-numbered questions in this For Review section can be found in Appendix F at the end of this text.

1. What is the employment-at-will doctrine? When and why are exceptions to this doctrine made?
2. What federal statute governs working hours and wages?
3. Under the Family and Medical Leave Act, in what circumstances may an employee take family or medical leave?
4. What are the two most important federal statutes governing immigration and employment today?
5. What federal statute gave employees the right to organize unions and engage in collective bargaining?

Business Scenarios and Case Problems

24–1 Wages and Hours. Calzoni Boating Co. is an interstate business engaged in manufacturing and selling boats. The company has five hundred nonunion employees. Representatives of these employees are requesting a four-day, ten-hours-per-day workweek, and Calzoni is concerned that this would require paying time and a half after eight hours per day. Which federal act is Calzoni thinking of that might require this? Will the act in fact require paying time and a half for all hours worked over eight hours per day if the employees' proposal is accepted? Explain. **(See page 628.)**

24–2 Question with Sample Answer—Wrongful Discharge. Denton and Carlo were employed at an appliance plant. Their job required them to do occasional maintenance work while standing on a wire mesh twenty feet above the plant floor. Other employees had fallen through the mesh, and one was killed by the fall. When Denton and Carlo were asked by their supervisor to do work that would likely require them to walk on the mesh, they refused due to their fear of bodily harm or death. Because of their refusal to do the requested work, the two employees were fired from their jobs. Was their discharge wrongful? If so, under what federal employment law? To what federal agency or department should they turn for assistance? **(See page 631.)**

—For a sample answer to Question 24–2, go to Appendix G at the end of this text.

24–3 Unfair Labor Practices. Consolidated Stores is undergoing a unionization campaign. Prior to the union election, management states that the union is unnecessary to protect workers. Management also provides bonuses and wage increases to the workers during this period. The employees reject the union. Union organizers protest that the wage increases during the election campaign unfairly prejudiced the vote. Should these wage increases be regarded as an unfair labor practice? Discuss. **(See page 645.)**

24–4 Employment at Will. Thomas Ellis signed an agreement with the BlueSky Charter School to serve as its director for one year, from July 1 to June 30. A sentence in bold type stated that the employment was "at will." The agreement included a provision for automatic annual renewal unless the school's board acted before April 15. On May 7, the board terminated the arrangement. Was Ellis an at-will employee? If so, what effect did this status have on the board's authority to terminate his employment? [*Ellis v. BlueSky Charter School*, __ N.W.2d __ (Mn.App. 2010)] **(See page 625.)**

24–5 Unfair Labor Practices. The Laborers' International Union of North America and Shaw Stone & Webster Construction, Inc., agreed on a provision that required all employees to pay dues to the union. Sebedeo Lopez went to work for Shaw Stone without paying the union dues. When the union pressed the company to fire him, Lopez agreed to pay. The union continued to demand his discharge, however, and Shaw Stone fired him. Was the union guilty of unfair labor practices? Why or why not? [*Laborers' International Union of North America, Local 578 v. NLRB*, 594 F.3d 732 (10th Cir. 2010)] **(See pages 644–645.)**

24–6 Case Problem with Sample Answer—Minimum Wage. Misty Cumbie worked as a waitress in Vita Café in Portland, Oregon. The café was owned and operated by Woody Woo, Inc. Woody Woo paid its servers an hourly wage that was higher than the state's minimum wage, but the servers were required to contribute their tips to a "tip pool." Approximately one-third of the tip-pool funds went to the servers, and the rest was distributed to kitchen staff members, who otherwise rarely received tips for their services. Did this tip-pooling arrangement violate the minimum wage provisions of the Fair Labor Standards Act? Explain. [*Cumbie v. Woody Woo, Inc.*, 596 F.3d 577 (9th Cir. 2010)] **(See pages 627–628.)**

—For a sample answer to Problem 24–6, go to Appendix H at the end of this text.

24–7 Workers' Compensation. As a safety measure, Dynea USA, Inc., required an employee, Tony Fairbanks, to wear steel-toed boots. One of the boots caused a sore on Fairbanks's leg. The skin over the sore broke, and within a week, Fairbanks was hospitalized with a methicillin-resistant staphylococcus aureus (MRSA) infection. He filed a workers' compensation claim. Dynea argued that the MRSA bacteria that caused the infection had been on Fairbanks's skin before he came to work. What are the requirements to recover workers' compensation benefits? Does this claim qualify? Explain. [*Dynea USA, Inc. v. Fairbanks*, 241 Or.App. 311, 250 P.3d 389 (2011)] **(See pages 631–632.)**

24–8 Exceptions to the Employment-at-Will Doctrine. Li Li worked for Packard Bioscience, and Mark Schmeizl was her supervisor. In March 2000, Schmeizl told Li to call Packard's competitors, pretend to be a potential customer, and request "pricing information and literature." Li refused to perform the assignment. She told Schmeizl that she thought the work was illegal and recommended that he contact Packard's legal department. Although a lawyer recommended against the practice, Schmeizl insisted that Li perform the calls. Moreover, he later wrote negative performance reviews because she was unable to get the requested information when she called competitors and identified herself as a Packard employee. On June 1, 2000, Li was terminated on Schmeizl's recommendation. Can Li bring a claim for wrongful discharge? Why or why not? [*Li v. Canberra Industries*, 134 Conn.App. 448, 39 A.3d 789 (2012)] **(See pages 625–627.)**

24–9 A Question of Ethics—Workers' Compensation. Beverly Tull had worked for Atchison Leather Products, Inc., for ten years when she began to complain of hand, wrist, and shoulder pain. Atchison recommended that she contact a certain physician, who in April 2000 diagnosed the condition as carpal tunnel syndrome "severe enough" for surgery. In August, Tull filed a claim with the state workers' compensation board. Because Atchison changed workers' compensation insurance companies every year, a dispute arose as to which company should pay Tull's claim. Fearing liability, no insurer would authorize treatment, and Tull was forced to delay surgery until December. The board granted her temporary total disability benefits for the subsequent six weeks that she missed work. On April 23, 2002, Berger Co. bought Atchison. The new employer adjusted Tull's work to be less demanding and stressful, but she continued to suffer pain. In July, a physician diagnosed her condition as permanent. The board granted her permanent partial disability benefits. By May 2005, the bickering over the financial responsibility for Tull's claim involved five insurers—four of which had each covered Atchison for a single year and one of which covered Berger. [*Tull v. Atchison Leather Products, Inc.*, 37 Kan.App.2d 87, 150 P.3d 316 (2007)] **(See pages 631–632.)**

1. When an injured employee files a claim for workers' compensation, there is a proceeding to assess the injury and determine the amount of compensation. Should a dispute between insurers over the payment of the claim be resolved in the same proceeding? Why or why not?
2. The board designated April 23, 2002, as the date of Tull's injury. What is the reason for determining the date of a worker's injury? Should the board in this case have selected this date or a different date? Why?
3. How should the board assess liability for the payment of Tull's medical expenses and disability benefits? Would it be appropriate to impose joint and several liability on the insurers, or should the individual liability of each of them be determined? Explain.

Critical Thinking and Writing Assignments

24–10 Business Law Critical Thinking Group Assignment. Nicole Tipton and Sadik Seferi owned and operated a restaurant in Iowa. Acting on a tip from the local police, agents of Immigration and Customs Enforcement executed search warrants at the restaurant and at an apartment where some restaurant workers lived. The agents discovered six undocumented aliens working at the restaurant and living together. When the I-9 forms for the restaurant's employees were reviewed, none were found for the six aliens. They were paid in cash while other employees were paid by check. Tipton and Seferi were charged with hiring and harboring illegal aliens.

1. The first group will develop an argument that Tipton and Seferi were guilty of hiring and harboring illegal aliens.
2. The second group will assess whether Tipton and Seferi can assert a defense by claiming that they did not know that the workers were unauthorized aliens.

25 CHAPTER

Employment Discrimination and Diversity

(Andresr/Shutterstock.com)

CHAPTER OUTLINE

- Title VII of the Civil Rights Act of 1964
- Discrimination Based on Age
- Discrimination Based on Disability
- Defenses to Employment Discrimination
- Affirmative Action

LEARNING OBJECTIVES

The five learning objectives below are designed to help improve your understanding of the chapter. After reading this chapter, you should be able to answer the following questions:

1. Generally, what kind of conduct is prohibited by Title VII of the Civil Rights Act of 1964, as amended?
2. What is the difference between disparate-treatment discrimination and disparate-impact discrimination?
3. What remedies are available under Title VII of the 1964 Civil Rights Act, as amended?
4. What federal act prohibits discrimination based on age?
5. What are three defenses to claims of employment discrimination?

"Equal rights for all, special privileges for none."
—Thomas Jefferson, 1743–1826 (Third president of the United States, 1801–1809)

Protected Class A group of persons protected by specific laws because of the group's defining characteristics, including race, color, religion, national origin, gender, age, and disability.

Out of the civil rights movement of the 1960s grew a body of law protecting employees against discrimination in the workplace. Legislation, judicial decisions, and administrative agency actions restrict employers from discriminating against workers on the basis of race, color, religion, national origin, gender, age, or disability. A class of persons defined by one or more of these criteria is known as a **protected class.** The laws designed to protect these individuals embody the sentiment expressed by Thomas Jefferson in the chapter-opening quotation above.

A person does not have to be a member of a minority group to be in a protected class. Women form a protected class although they outnumber men in the United States and thus are not statistically a minority. Conversely, not every minority group is protected. In 2012, the U.S. Census Bureau announced that for the first time the majority of babies born in the United States were not white. Instead, they were members of various other racial or ethnic groups. Although whites still make up the majority of the population—and will to do so for several

(Lyndon Baines Johnson Presidential Library and Museum)

President Lyndon B. Johnson signs the 1964 Civil Rights Act. This legislation represented the most far-reaching set of antidiscrimination laws in modern times. Which groups in our country benefited most from this act?

decades to come—at some point, whites will simply form the largest minority group among many other minority groups. Thus, protected classes are based not on rigid statistical definitions of minority versus majority but on whether a group is subject to discrimination.

The federal statutes discussed in this chapter prohibit **employment discrimination** against members of protected classes. Although this chapter focuses on federal statutes, many states have their own laws that protect employees against discrimination, and some provide more protection to employees than federal laws do.

Title VII of the Civil Rights Act of 1964

Employment Discrimination Treating employees or job applicants unequally on the basis of race, color, national origin, religion, gender, age, or disability.

LEARNING OBJECTIVE 1
Generally, what kind of conduct is prohibited by Title VII of the Civil Rights Act of 1964, as amended?

The most important statute covering employment discrimination is Title VII of the Civil Rights Act of 1964.[1] Title VII prohibits discrimination against employees, applicants, and union members on the basis of race, color, national origin, religion, or gender at any stage of employment. (Although federal law prohibits job discrimination only if it is based on these specific categories, some jurisdictions are expanding their laws to include other types of discrimination. See this chapter's *Law, Diversity, and Business: Managerial Implications* feature on the following page for a discussion on this issue.)

Title VII applies to employers with fifteen or more employees and labor unions with fifteen or more members. Title VII also applies to labor unions that operate hiring halls (to which members go regularly to be rationed jobs as they become available), employment agencies, and state and local governing units or agencies A special section of the act prohibits discrimination in most federal government employment.

The Equal Employment Opportunity Commission

Compliance with Title VII is monitored by the Equal Employment Opportunity Commission (EEOC). A victim of alleged discrimination must file a claim with the EEOC before bringing a suit against the employer. The EEOC may investigate the dispute and attempt to arrange an out-of-court settlement. If a voluntary agreement cannot be reached, the EEOC may file a suit against the employer on the employee's behalf. If the EEOC decides not to investigate the claim, the victim may bring her or his own lawsuit against the employer.

The EEOC does not investigate every claim of employment discrimination, regardless of the merits of the claim. Generally, it investigates only "priority cases," such as cases involving retaliatory discharge (firing an employee in retaliation for submitting a claim to the EEOC) and cases involving types of discrimination that are of particular concern to the EEOC.

Note that in 2011, the United States Supreme Court issued an important decision that limits the rights of employees—as a group, or class— to bring discrimination claims against their employer. **CASE EXAMPLE 25.1** A group of female employees sued Wal-Mart, the nation's largest private employer, alleging that store managers who had discretion over pay and promotions were biased against women and disproportionately favored men. The United States Supreme Court ruled in favor of Wal-Mart, effectively blocking the class

1. 42 U.S.C. Sections 2000e–2000e-17.

LAW, DIVERSITY, AND BUSINESS: MANAGERIAL IMPLICATIONS

COMBATING APPEARANCE-BASED DISCRIMINATION

Research has shown that short men make less income than tall men. Statistical research has also shown that compared with attractive individuals, less attractive people generally receive poorer performance reviews, lower salaries, and smaller damages awards if they win lawsuits. Should something be done about this?

Can "Lookism" Be Prohibited?

Although there is certainly evidence that appearance-based discrimination exists in the workplace and elsewhere, it is not so clear that it can be prohibited. In the 1970s, Michigan decided to do something about "lookism" and passed a law barring various kinds of appearance-based discrimination.[a] Whether because of the cost or the difficulty of proving this type of discrimination, however, only a few lawsuits based on the law have been filed each year. At least six cities have similar laws, but these laws also have not given rise to many lawsuits.

Federal and state laws prohibit discrimination against people who are clinically obese, but discrimination against those who are merely overweight is usually not illegal. Given that one study found that more than 40 percent of overweight women felt stigmatized by their employers, this remains a serious problem.

A Double Standard for Grooming

Women sometimes complain that they are held to different grooming standards in the workplace than their male counterparts. A female bartender at a casino in Nevada brought a lawsuit after she was fired for not complying with rules that required her to wear makeup and teased hair while male bartenders were just told to "look neat." The court ruled, however, that these allegations were not enough to outweigh an at-will employment contract.[b]

At the same time, women in senior management positions find that they can look "too sexy." A few years ago, a Citibank employee made headlines when she claimed that she was fired for her excessive sexiness, which supposedly distracted her male co-workers.

Business Implications

The United States has fought racism, sexism, and homophobia, and it seems likely that businesses will see an effort to combat "lookism." Managers should make sure that the jurisdiction in which their business operates does not already have laws against appearance-based discrimination. Moreover, even without such laws, female employees who suffer appearance-based discrimination may be able to assert a valid claim of gender discrimination instead.

a. Michigan Compiled Laws Section 37.2202.

b. *Jespersen v. Harrah's Operating Co.,* 444 F.3d 1104 (9th Cir. 2006).

action (a lawsuit in which a small number of plaintiffs sue on behalf of a larger group). The Court held that the women could not maintain a class action because they had failed to prove a company-wide policy of discrimination that had a common effect on all women covered by the class action.[2] This decision did not affect the rights of individual employees to sue under Title VII, however.

Intentional and Unintentional Discrimination

Title VII prohibits both intentional and unintentional discrimination.

Disparate-Treatment Discrimination A form of employment discrimination that results when an employer intentionally discriminates against employees who are members of protected classes.

Intentional Discrimination

Intentional discrimination by an employer against an employee is known as **disparate-treatment discrimination.** Because intent can be difficult to prove, courts have established certain procedures for resolving disparate-treatment cases. **EXAMPLE 25.2** Barbara applies for employment with a construction firm and is rejected. If she sues on the basis of disparate-treatment discrimination in hiring, she

2. *Wal-Mart Stores, Inc. v. Dukes,* ___ U.S. ___, 131 S.Ct. 2541, 180 L.Ed.2d 374 (2011).

must show that (1) she is a member of a protected class, (2) she applied and was qualified for the job in question, (3) she was rejected by the employer, and (4) the employer continued to seek applicants for the position or filled the position with a person not in a protected class. •

Prima Facie Case A case in which the plaintiff has produced sufficient evidence of his or her claim that the case will be decided for the plaintiff unless the defendant produces no evidence to rebut it.

If the woman can meet these relatively easy requirements, she has made out a ***prima facie* case** of illegal discrimination. *Prima facie* is Latin for "at first sight." Legally, it refers to a fact that is presumed to be true unless contradicted by evidence. Making out a *prima facie* case of discrimination means that the plaintiff has met her initial burden of proof and will win in the absence of a legally acceptable employer defense. (Defenses will be discussed later in this chapter.)

The burden then shifts to the employer-defendant, who must articulate a legal reason for not hiring the plaintiff. To prevail, the plaintiff must then show that the employer's reason is a *pretext* (not the true reason) and that the employer's decision was actually motivated by discriminatory intent.

Unintentional Discrimination

Employers often use interviews and tests to choose from among a large number of applicants for job openings. Minimum educational requirements are also common. These practices and procedures may have an unintended discriminatory impact on a protected class. (For tips on how human resources managers can prevent these types of discrimination claims, see the *Linking Business Law to Corporate Management* feature on page 674.)

Disparate-Impact Discrimination Discrimination that results from certain employer practices or procedures that, although not discriminatory on their face, have a discriminatory effect.

LEARNING OBJECTIVE 2
What is the difference between disparate-treatment discrimination and disparate-impact discrimination?

Disparate-impact discrimination occurs when a protected group of people is adversely affected by an employer's practices, procedures, or tests, even though they do not appear to be discriminatory. In a disparate-impact discrimination case, the complaining party must first show statistically that the employer's practices, procedures, or tests are discriminatory in effect. Once the plaintiff has made out a *prima facie* case, the burden of proof shifts to the employer to show that the practices or procedures in question were justified. There are two ways of proving that disparate-impact discrimination exists, as discussed next.

Pool of Applicants

A plaintiff can prove a disparate impact by comparing the employer's workforce to the pool of qualified individuals available in the local labor market. The plaintiff must show that (1) as a result of educational or other job requirements or hiring procedures, (2) the percentage of nonwhites, women, or members of other protected classes in the employer's workforce (3) does not reflect the percentage of that group in the pool of qualified applicants. If the plaintiff can show a connection between the practice and the disparity, he or she has made out a *prima facie* case and need not provide evidence of discriminatory intent.

Rate of Hiring

A plaintiff can also prove disparate-impact discrimination by comparing the selection rates of whites and nonwhites (or members of another protected class). When a job requirement or hiring procedure excludes members of a protected class from an employer's workforce at a substantially higher rate than nonmembers, discrimination occurs, regardless of the racial balance in the employer's workforce.

The EEOC has devised a test, called the "four-fifths rule," to determine whether an employment selection procedure is discriminatory on its face. Under this rule, a selection rate for protected classes that is less than four-fifths, or 80 percent, of the rate for the group with the highest rate will generally be regarded as evidence of disparate impact. **EXAMPLE 25.3** One hundred white applicants take an employment test, and fifty pass the test and are hired. One hundred minority applicants take the test, and twenty pass the test and are hired. Because twenty is less than four-fifths (80 percent) of fifty, the test would be considered discriminatory under the EEOC guidelines. •

ETHICAL ISSUE

Is there an implicit bias against job applicants who have been unemployed long term? Even though the recession that started in December 2007 has officially ended, the national unemployment rate has remained around 8 percent. As a result, many individuals have been unable to find work for several years. Now, the long-term unemployed are facing apparent discrimination when they apply for jobs. Some employers have indicated that they will not consider an applicant who has been unemployed longer than six months, especially if he or she has not pursued additional training or education during the period of unemployment.

Because the long-term unemployed do not form a protected class, they cannot sue for discrimination under federal law. They may soon get help from the states, however. At least thirteen states are considering legislation to prohibit discrimination against the unemployed in help-wanted ads. The New York–based National Employment Law Project is urging legislation that would explicitly prohibit employers and employment agencies from eliminating long-term unemployed applicants from consideration for jobs.

Discrimination Based on Race, Color, and National Origin

Title VII prohibits employers from discriminating against employees or job applicants on the basis of race, color, or national origin. If an employer's standards for selecting or promoting employees have a discriminatory effect on job applicants or employees in these protected classes, then a presumption of illegal discrimination arises. To avoid liability, the employer must then show that its standards have a substantial, demonstrable relationship to realistic qualifications for the job in question.

CASE EXAMPLE 25.4 Jiann Min Chang was an instructor at Alabama Agricultural and Mechanical University (AAMU). When AAMU terminated his employment, Chang filed a lawsuit claiming discrimination based on national origin. Chang established a *prima facie* case because he (1) was a member of a protected class, (2) was qualified for the job, (3) suffered an adverse employment action, and (4) was replaced by someone outside his protected class (a non-Asian instructor). AAMU, however, showed that Chang had argued with a university vice president and refused to comply with her instructions. The court ruled that the university had not renewed Chang's contract for a legitimate reason— insubordination—and therefore was not liable for unlawful discrimination.[3] •

Reverse Discrimination

Note that discrimination based on race can also take the form of *reverse discrimination,* or discrimination against "majority" individuals, such as white males. **CASE EXAMPLE 25.5** An African American woman fired four white men from their management positions at a school district. The men filed a lawsuit for racial discrimination, alleging that the woman was trying to eliminate white males from the department. The woman claimed that the terminations were part of a reorganization plan to cut costs. The jury sided with the men and awarded them nearly $3 million in damages. The verdict was upheld on appeal (though the damages award was reduced slightly).[4] •

In 2009, the United States Supreme Court issued a decision that has had a significant impact on disparate-impact and reverse discrimination litigation. **CASE EXAMPLE 25.6** The fire department in New Haven, Connecticut, administered a test to identify firefighters eligible for promotions. No African Americans and only two Hispanic firefighters passed the test. Fearing that it would be sued for discrimination if it based promotions on the test results, the city refused to use the results. The white firefighters (and one Hispanic) who had passed the test then sued the city, claiming reverse discrimination.

The United States Supreme Court held that an employer can engage in intentional discrimination to remedy an unintentional disparate impact only if the employer has "a strong

3. *Jiann Min Chang v. Alabama Agricultural and Mechanical University,* 2009 WL 3403180 (11th Cir. 2009).
4. *Johnston v. School District of Philadelphia,* 2006 WL 999966 (E.D.Pa. 2006).

basis in evidence" to believe that it will be successfully sued for disparate-impact discrimination "if it fails to take the race-conscious, discriminatory action." Mere fear of litigation was not sufficient reason for the city to discard its test results.[5] Subsequently, the city certified the test results and promoted the firefighters.

Potential "Section 1981" Claims Victims of racial or ethnic discrimination may also have a cause of action under 42 U.S.C. Section 1981. This section, which was enacted as part of the Civil Rights Act of 1866 to protect the rights of freed slaves, prohibits discrimination on the basis of race or ethnicity in the formation or enforcement of contracts. Because employment is often a contractual relationship, Section 1981 can provide an alternative basis for a plaintiff's action and is potentially advantageous because it does not place a cap on damages.

(Juanmonino/iStockphoto.com)

Under Title VII, can employers prohibit employees from participating in religious activities such as reciting prayers? Why or why not?

Discrimination Based on Religion

Title VII also prohibits government employers, private employers, and unions from discriminating against persons because of their religion. Employers cannot treat their employees more or less favorably based on their religious beliefs or practices and cannot require employees to participate in any religious activity (or forbid them from participating in one). **EXAMPLE 25.7** Jason Sewell claimed that his employer, a car dealership, fired him for not attending the weekly prayer meetings of dealership employees. If the dealership did require its employees to attend prayer gatherings and fired Sewell for not attending, he has a valid claim of religious discrimination.

Reasonable Accommodation An employer must "reasonably accommodate" the religious practices of its employees, unless to do so would cause undue hardship to the employer's business. Employers must reasonably accommodate an employee's religious belief even if the belief is not based on the doctrines of a traditionally recognized religion, such as Christianity or Judaism, or a denomination, such as Baptist. The only requirement is that the belief be sincerely held by the employee.

Undue Hardship If an employee's religion prohibits him or her from working on a certain day of the week or at a certain type of job, for instance, the employer must make a reasonable attempt to accommodate these religious requirements. A reasonable attempt to accommodate does not necessarily require the employer to permanently give an employee the requested day off, if to do so would cause the employer undue hardship.

CASE EXAMPLE 25.8 Miguel Sánchez–Rodríguez sold cell phones in shopping malls for AT&T in Puerto Rico. After six years, Sánchez informed his supervisors that he had become a Seventh Day Adventist and could no longer work on Saturdays for religious reasons. AT&T responded that his inability to work on Saturdays would cause it hardship.

As a reasonable accommodation, the company suggested that Sánchez swap schedules with others and offered him two other positions that did not require work on Saturdays. Sánchez could not find workers to swap shifts with him, however, and he declined the other jobs because they would result in less income. He began missing work on Saturdays. After a time, AT&T indicated that it would discipline him for any additional Saturdays that he missed. Eventually, he was placed on active disciplinary status. Sánchez resigned and filed a religious discrimination lawsuit against AT&T. The court found in favor of AT&T, and a federal appellate court affirmed. The company had made adequate efforts at accommodation by allowing Sánchez to swap shifts and offering him other positions that did not require work on Saturdays.[6]

5. *Ricci v. DeStefano*, 557 U.S. 557, 129 S.Ct. 2658, 174 L.Ed.2d 490 (2009).

6. *Sánchez-Rodríquez v. AT&T Mobility Puerto Rico, Inc.*, 673 F.3d 1 (1st Cir. 2012).

Discrimination Based on Gender

Under Title VII, as well as other federal acts (including the Equal Pay Act of 1963, which we also discuss here), employers are forbidden from discriminating against employees on the basis of gender. Employers are prohibited from classifying jobs as male or female and from advertising positions as male or female unless the employer can prove that the gender of the applicant is essential to the job. Employers also cannot have separate male and female seniority lists or refuse to promote employees based on gender.

"A sign that says 'men only' looks very different on a bathroom door than a courthouse door."

Thurgood Marshall, 1908–1993 (Associate justice of the United States Supreme Court, 1967–1991)

Gender Must Be a Determining Factor Generally, to succeed in a suit for gender discrimination, a plaintiff must demonstrate that gender was a determining factor in the employer's decision to fire or refuse to hire or promote her or him. Typically, this involves looking at all of the surrounding circumstances.

CASE EXAMPLE 25.9 Wanda Collier worked for Turner Industries Group, LLC, in the maintenance department. She complained to her supervisor that Jack Daniell, the head of the department, treated her unfairly. Her supervisor told her that Daniell had a problem with her gender and was harder on women. The supervisor talked to Daniell but did not take any disciplinary action.

A month later, Daniell confronted Collier, pushing her up against a wall and berating her. After this incident, Collier filed a formal complaint and kept a male co-worker with her at all times. A month later, she was fired. She subsequently filed a lawsuit alleging gender discrimination. The court concluded that there was enough evidence that gender was a determining factor in Daniell's conduct to allow Collier's claims to go to a jury.[7] •

Pregnancy Discrimination The Pregnancy Discrimination Act of 1978,[8] which amended Title VII, expanded the definition of gender discrimination to include discrimination based on pregnancy. Women affected by pregnancy, childbirth, or related medical conditions must be treated—for all employment-related purposes, including the receipt of benefits under employee benefit programs—the same as other persons not so affected but similar in ability to work.

Wage Discrimination Several laws prohibit employers from gender-based wage discrimination. The Equal Pay Act of 1963 requires equal pay for male and female employees doing similar work at the same establishment (a barber and a hair stylist, for example). To determine whether the Equal Pay Act has been violated, a court will look to the primary duties of the two jobs—the job content rather than the job description controls. If the wage differential is due to "any factor other than gender," such as a seniority or merit system, then it does not violate the Equal Pay Act.

President Obama signed the Lilly Ledbetter Fair Act in 2009. How does this act differ from the Paycheck Fairness Act?

(AP Photo/Pablo Martinez Monsivais)

The continuing disparity between the wages of men and women prompted Congress to pass the Paycheck Fairness Act of 2009, which closed some of the loopholes in the Equal Pay Act. The Paycheck Fairness Act clarified employers' defenses and prohibited the use of gender-based differentials in assessing an employee's education, training, or experience. It also provided additional remedies for wage discrimination similar to those available for discrimination based on race and national origin.

Congress also enacted the Lilly Ledbetter Fair Pay Act of 2009, which made discriminatory wages actionable under federal law regardless of when the discrimination began.[9] This act overturned a previous decision by the United States Supreme Court that had

7. *Collier v. Turner Industries Group, LLC*, 797 F.Supp.2d 1029 (D. Idaho 2011).
8. 42 U.S.C. Section 2000e(k).
9. Pub. L. No. 111-2, 123 Stat. 5 (January 5, 2009), amending 42 U.S.C. Section 2000e-5[e].

limited plaintiffs' time period to file a wage discrimination complaint to 180 days after the employer's decision.[10] Today, if a plaintiff continues to work for the employer while receiving discriminatory wages, the time period for filing a complaint is basically unlimited.

Constructive Discharge

Constructive Discharge A termination of employment brought about by making the employee's working conditions so intolerable that the employee reasonably feels compelled to leave.

The majority of Title VII complaints involve unlawful discrimination in decisions to hire or fire employees. In some situations, however, employees who leave their jobs voluntarily can claim that they were "constructively discharged" by the employer. **Constructive discharge** occurs when the employer causes the employee's working conditions to be so intolerable that a reasonable person in the employee's position would feel compelled to quit.

Proving Constructive Discharge

The plaintiff must present objective proof of intolerable working conditions, which the employer knew or had reason to know about yet failed to correct within a reasonable time period. Courts generally also require the employee to show causation—that the employer's unlawful discrimination caused the working conditions to be intolerable. Put a different way, the employee's resignation must be a foreseeable result of the employer's discriminatory action.

Although courts weigh the facts on a case-by-case basis, employee demotion is one of the most frequently cited reasons for a finding of constructive discharge, particularly when the employee was subjected to humiliation. **EXAMPLE 25.10** Khalil's employer humiliates him in front of his co-workers by informing him that he is being demoted to an inferior position. Khalil's co-workers then continually insult and harass him about his national origin (he is from Iran). The employer is aware of this discriminatory treatment but does nothing to remedy the situation, despite repeated complaints from Khalil. After several months, Khalil quits his job and files a Title VII claim. In this situation, Khalil would likely have sufficient evidence to maintain an action for constructive discharge in violation of Title VII. •

Applies to All Title VII Discrimination

Note that constructive discharge is a theory that plaintiffs can use to establish any type of discrimination claims under Title VII, including race, color, national origin, religion, gender, pregnancy, and sexual harassment. Constructive discharge has also been successfully used in situations involving discrimination based on age or disability (both of which will be discussed later in this chapter). Constructive discharge is most commonly asserted in cases involving sexual harassment, however.

When constructive discharge is claimed, the employee can pursue damages for loss of income, including back pay. These damages ordinarily are not available to an employee who left a job voluntarily.

Sexual Harassment

Sexual Harassment The demanding of sexual favors in return for job promotions or other benefits, or language or conduct that is so sexually offensive that it creates a hostile working environment.

Title VII also protects employees against **sexual harassment** in the workplace. Sexual harassment can take two forms: *quid pro quo* harassment and hostile-environment harassment. *Quid pro quo* is a Latin phrase that is often translated to mean "something in exchange for something else." *Quid pro quo* harassment occurs when sexual favors are demanded in return for job opportunities, promotions, salary increases, and the like. According to the United States Supreme Court, hostile-environment harassment occurs when "the workplace is permeated with discriminatory intimidation, ridicule, and insult, that is sufficiently severe or pervasive to alter the conditions of the victim's employment and create an abusive working environment." [11]

---

10. *Ledbetter v. Goodyear Tire Co.,* 550 U.S. 618, 127 S.Ct. 2162, 167 L.Ed.2d 982 (2007).

11. *Harris v. Forklift Systems,* 510 U.S. 17, 114 S.Ct. 367, 126 L.Ed.2d 295 (1993). See also *Billings v. Town of Grafton,* 515 F.3d 39 (1st Cir. 2008).

The courts determine whether the sexually offensive conduct was sufficiently severe or pervasive to create a hostile environment on a case-by-case basis. Typically, a single incident of sexually offensive conduct is not enough to create a hostile environment (although there have been exceptions when the conduct was particularly objectionable). Note also that if the employee who is alleging sexual harassment has signed an employment contract with an arbitration clause (see Chapter 3), she or he will most likely be required to arbitrate the claim.[12]

PREVENTING LEGAL DISPUTES

To avoid sexual-harassment complaints, you should be proactive in preventing sexual harassment in the workplace. Establish written policies, distribute them to employees, and review them annually. Make it clear that the policies prohibiting harassment and discrimination apply to everyone at all levels of your organization. Provide training. Assure employees that no one will be punished for making a complaint. If you receive complaints, always take them seriously and investigate—no matter how trivial they might seem.

Prompt remedial action is key, but it must not include any adverse action against the complainant (such as immediate termination). Also, never discourage employees from seeking the assistance of government agencies (such as the EEOC) or threaten or punish them for doing so. It is generally best to obtain the advice of counsel when you receive a sexual-harassment complaint.

Tangible Employment Action A significant change in employment status or benefits, such as occurs when an employee is fired, refused a promotion, or reassigned to a lesser position.

Harassment by Supervisors

For an employer to be held liable for a supervisor's sexual harassment, the supervisor normally must have taken a *tangible employment action* against the employee. A **tangible employment action** is a significant change in employment status or benefits, such as when an employee is fired, refused a promotion, demoted, or reassigned to a position with significantly different responsibilities. Only a supervisor, or another person acting with the authority of the employer, can cause this sort of injury. A constructive discharge also qualifies as a tangible employment action.[13]

The *Ellerth/Faragher* Affirmative Defense

In 1998, the United States Supreme Court issued several important rulings that have had a lasting impact on cases alleging sexual harassment by supervisors.[14] The Court held that an employer (a city) was liable for a supervisor's harassment of employees even though the employer was unaware of the behavior. Although the city had a written policy against sexual harassment, it had not distributed the policy to its employees and had not established any complaint procedures for employees who felt that they had been sexually harassed. In another case, the Court held that an employer can be liable for a supervisor's sexual harassment even though the employee does not suffer adverse job consequences.

A presumed victim of sexual harassment (on the right) attends a press conference with her attorney. What hurdles will she face in such litigation?

(AP Photo/Bay Area News Group, Oakland Tribune, Laura A. Oda)

The Court's decisions in these cases established what has become known as the "*Ellerth/Faragher* affirmative defense" to charges of sexual harassment. The defense has two elements:

1. That the employer has taken reasonable care to prevent and promptly correct any sexually harassing behavior (by establishing effective antiharassment policies and complaint procedures, for example).

12. See, for example, *EEOC v. Cheesecake Factory, Inc.*, 2009 WL 1259359 (D.Ariz. 2009).
13. See, for example, *Pennsylvania State Police v. Suders*, 542 U.S. 129, 124 S.Ct. 2342, 159 L.Ed.2d 204 (2004).
14. *Burlington Industries, Inc. v. Ellerth*, 524 U.S. 742, 118 S.Ct. 2257, 141 L.Ed.2d 633 (1998); and *Faragher v. City of Boca Raton*, 524 U.S. 775, 118 S.Ct. 2275, 141 L.Ed.2d 662 (1998).

"Sexual harassment at work: Is it a problem for the self-employed?"

Victoria Wood, 1953–present (English comedian and actor)

2. That the plaintiff-employee unreasonably failed to take advantage of any preventive or corrective opportunities provided by the employer to avoid harm.

An employer that can prove both elements will not be liable for a supervisor's harassment.

Retaliation by Employers Employers sometimes retaliate against employees who complain about sexual harassment or other Title VII violations. Retaliation can take many forms. An employer might demote or fire the person, or otherwise change the terms, conditions, and benefits of employment. Title VII prohibits retaliation, and employees can sue their employers. In a *retaliation claim,* an individual asserts that she or he has suffered a harm as a result of making a charge, testifying, or participating in a Title VII investigation or proceeding.

Plaintiffs do not have to prove that the challenged action adversely affected their workplace or employment.[15] Instead, to prove retaliation, plaintiffs must show that the challenged action was one that would likely have dissuaded a reasonable worker from making or supporting a charge of discrimination. Title VII's retaliation protection extends to an employee who speaks out about discrimination against another employee during an employer's internal investigation.[16] A court also held that it protected an employee who was fired after his fiancée filed a gender discrimination claim against their employer.[17]

In the following case, a female law professor lost her job after she complained about comments made by her dean and colleagues. The court had to decide whether she had been retaliated against for engaging in protected conduct.

15. *Burlington Northern and Santa Fe Railroad Co. v. White,* 548 U.S. 53, 126 S.Ct. 2405, 165 L.Ed.2d 345 (2006). (See the *Case Analysis Question* on page 677).

16. See *Crawford v. Metropolitan Government of Nashville and Davidson County, Tennessee,* 555 U.S. 271, 129 S.Ct. 846, 172 L.Ed.2d 650 (2009).

17. See *Thompson v. North American Stainless, LP,* ___ U.S. ___, 131 S.Ct. 863, 178 L.Ed.2d 694 (2011).

Case 25.1

Morales-Cruz v. University of Puerto Rico

United States Court of Appeals, First Circuit, 676 F.3d 220 (2012). www.ca1.uscourts.gov[a]

(Diego Cervo/Shutterstock.com)

FACTS In 2003, Myrta Morales-Cruz began a tenure-track teaching position at the University of Puerto Rico School of Law. During her probationary period, one of her colleagues in a law school clinic had an affair with one of their students that resulted in a pregnancy. In 2008, Morales-Cruz asked the university's administrative committee to approve a one-year extension for her tenure review. The law school's dean criticized Morales-Cruz for failing to report her colleague's affair. He later recommended granting the extension but called Morales-Cruz "insecure," "immature," and "fragile." Similarly, a law school committee recommended granting the extension, but a dissenting professor commented that Morales-Cruz had shown poor judgment, had "personality flaws," and had trouble with "complex and sensitive" situations.

Morales-Cruz soon learned about the negative comments and complained in writing to the university's chancellor. The dean then recommended denying the one-year extension, and the administrative committee ultimately did so. When her employment was terminated, Morales-Cruz sued the university under Title VII. Among other things, she asserted that the dean had retaliated against her for complaining to the chancellor. A federal district court found that Morales-Cruz had not stated a proper retaliation claim under Title VII, and she appealed.

ISSUE Can Morales-Cruz bring a retaliation claim under Title VII because the law school's dean retaliated against her for complaining to the university's chancellor?

a. In the right-hand column, click on "Opinions." On the next page, in the "Short Title *contains*" box, type "Morales-Cruz," and click on "Submit Search." In the result, click on the link to access the opinion.

Case 25.1—Continues next page

Case 25.1—Continued

DECISION No. The appellate court affirmed the district court's judgment for the University of Puerto Rico.

REASON Under Title VII, an employer may not retaliate against an employee because he or she has opposed a practice prohibited by Title VII. In this case, Morales-Cruz argued that the dean recommended against the one-year extension because she had complained about "discriminatory" comments. The court found that Morales-Cruz did not allege any facts that could be construed as gender-based discrimination. While the comments were hardly flattering, they were entirely gender-neutral. After all, the dean and dissenting professor said only that Morales-Cruz had shown poor judgment, had personality flaws, and was fragile, insecure, and immature. Thus, even if the dean retaliated against Morales-Cruz, it was not for engaging in conduct protected by Title VII.

CRITICAL THINKING—Ethical Consideration *Could the dean have had legitimate reasons for changing his mind about the one-year extension? If so, what were they?*

Harassment by Co-Workers and Nonemployees

When the harassment of co-workers, rather than supervisors, creates a hostile working environment, an employee may still have a cause of action against the employer. Normally, though, the employer will be held liable only if the employer knew, or should have known, about the harassment and failed to take immediate remedial action.

Occasionally, a court may also hold an employer liable for harassment by *nonemployees* if the employer knew about the harassment and failed to take corrective action. **EXAMPLE 25.11** Gordon, who owns and manages a Great Bites restaurant, knows that one of his regular customers, Dean, repeatedly harasses Sharon, a waitress. If Gordon does nothing and permits the harassment to continue, he may be liable under Title VII even though Dean is not an employee of the restaurant. •

Same-Gender Harassment

In *Oncale v. Sundowner Offshore Services, Inc.*,[18] the United States Supreme Court held that Title VII protection extends to individuals who are sexually harassed by members of the same gender. Proving that the harassment in same-gender cases is "based on sex" can be difficult, though. It is usually easier to establish a case of same-gender harassment when the harasser is homosexual.

Sexual Orientation Harassment

Although federal law (Title VII) does not prohibit discrimination or harassment based on a person's sexual orientation, a growing number of states have enacted laws that prohibit sexual orientation discrimination in private employment. Some states, such as Michigan, explicitly prohibit discrimination based on a person's gender identity or expression. Also, many companies have voluntarily established nondiscrimination policies that include sexual orientation. (Workers in the United States often have more protection against sexual harassment in the workplace than workers in other countries, as this chapter's *Beyond Our Borders* feature on the facing page explains.)

Online Harassment

Employees' online activities can create a hostile working environment in many ways. Racial jokes, ethnic slurs, or other comments contained in e-mail, text or instant messages, and social media or blog posts can become the basis for a claim of hostile-environment harassment or other forms of discrimination. A worker who regularly sees sexually explicit and

18. 523 U.S. 75, 118 S.Ct. 998, 140 L.Ed.2d 207 (1998).

BEYOND OUR BORDERS Sexual Harassment in Other Nations

The problem of sexual harassment in the workplace is not confined to the United States. Indeed, it is a worldwide problem for female workers. In Argentina, Brazil, Egypt, Turkey, and many other countries, there is no legal protection against any form of employment discrimination.

Even in those countries that do have laws prohibiting discriminatory employment practices, including gender-based discrimination, those laws often do not specifically include sexual harassment as a discriminatory practice.

Several countries have attempted to remedy this omission by passing new laws or amending others to specifically prohibit sexual harassment in the workplace. Japan, for example, has amended its Equal Employment Opportunity Law to include a provision making sexual harassment illegal. Thailand has also passed its first sexual-harassment law. The European Union has adopted a directive that specifically identifies sexual harassment as a form of discrimination.

Nevertheless, women's groups throughout Europe contend that corporations in European countries tend to view sexual harassment with "quiet tolerance." They contrast this attitude with that of most U.S. corporations, which have implemented specific procedures to deal with harassment claims.

Critical Thinking

Why do you think U.S. corporations are more aggressive than European companies in taking steps to prevent sexual harassment in the workplace?

---

offensive images on a co-worker's computer screen or tablet device may claim that they create a hostile working environment.[19]

Nevertheless, employers may be able to avoid liability for online harassment if they take prompt remedial action. **EXAMPLE 25.12** While working at TriCom, Shonda Dean receives racially harassing e-mailed jokes from another employee. Shortly afterward, the company issues a warning to the offending employee about the proper use of the e-mail system and holds two meetings to discuss company policy on the use of the system. If Dean sues TriCom for racial discrimination, a court may find that because the employer took prompt remedial action, TriCom should not be held liable for its employee's racially harassing e-mails. •

Remedies under Title VII

LEARNING OBJECTIVE 3
What remedies are available under Title VII of the 1964 Civil Rights Act, as amended?

Employer liability under Title VII may be extensive. If the plaintiff successfully proves that unlawful discrimination occurred, he or she may be awarded reinstatement, back pay, retroactive promotions, and damages. Compensatory damages are available only in cases of intentional discrimination. Punitive damages may be recovered against a private employer only if the employer acted with malice or reckless indifference to an individual's rights.

The statute limits the total amount of compensatory and punitive damages that the plaintiff can recover from specific employers, depending on the size of the employer. The cap ranges from $50,000 for employers with one hundred or fewer employees to $300,000 for employers with more than five hundred employees.

Discrimination Based on Age

Age discrimination is potentially the most widespread form of discrimination, because anyone—regardless of race, color, national origin, or gender—could eventually be a victim. The Age Discrimination in Employment Act (ADEA) of 1967[20] prohibits employment

---

19. See, for example, *Doe v. XYC Corp.*, 382 N.J.Super. 122 (App.Div. 2005).
20. 29 U.S.C. Sections 621–634.

LEARNING OBJECTIVE 4
What federal act prohibits discrimination based on age?

discrimination on the basis of age against individuals forty years of age or older. The act also prohibits mandatory retirement for nonmanagerial workers.

For the act to apply, an employer must have twenty or more employees, and the employer's business activities must affect interstate commerce. The EEOC administers the ADEA, but the act also permits private causes of action against employers for age discrimination.

The ADEA includes a provision that extends protections against age discrimination to federal government employees.[21] This provision encompasses not only claims of age discrimination, but also claims of retaliation for complaining about age discrimination, which are not specifically mentioned in the statute.[22] Thus, the ADEA protects federal and private-sector employees from retaliation based on age-related complaints.

Procedures under the ADEA

KNOW THIS
The Fourteenth Amendment prohibits any state from denying any person "the equal protection of the laws." This prohibition applies to the *federal* government through the due process clause of the Fifth Amendment.

The burden-shifting procedure under the ADEA differs from the procedure under Title VII as a result of a United States Supreme Court decision in 2009, which dramatically changed the burden of proof in age discrimination cases.[23] As explained earlier, if the plaintiff in a Title VII case can show that the employer was motivated, at least in part, by unlawful discrimination, the burden of proof shifts to the employer to articulate a legitimate nondiscriminatory reason. Thus, in cases in which the employer has a "mixed motive" for discharging an employee, the employer has the burden of proving its reason was legitimate.

Under the ADEA, in contrast, a plaintiff must show that the unlawful discrimination was not just a reason but *the* reason for the adverse employment action. In other words, the employee has the burden of establishing "but for" causation—that is, but for the plaintiff's age, the adverse action would not have happened.

Thus, to establish a *prima facie* case, the plaintiff must show that he or she (1) was a member of the protected age group, (2) was qualified for the position from which he or she was discharged, and (3) was discharged because of age discrimination. Then the burden shifts to the employer. If the employer offers a legitimate reason for its action, then the plaintiff must show that the stated reason is only a pretext and that the plaintiff's age was the real reason for the employer's decision. The following case illustrates this procedure.

---

21. See 29 U.S.C. Section 632(a) (2000 ed., Supp. V).

22. *Gomez-Perez v. Potter,* 553 U.S. 474, 128 S.Ct. 1931, 170 L.Ed.2d 887 (2008).

23. *Gross v. FBL Financial Services,* 557 U.S. 167, 129 S.Ct. 2343, 174 L.Ed.2d 119 (2009).

Case 25.2

Mora v. Jackson Memorial Foundation, Inc.

United States Court of Appeals, Eleventh Circuit,
597 F.3d 1201 (2010).
www.ca11.uscourts.gov/opinions/search.php[a]

(StockLite/Shutterstock.com)
When is firing an older worker considered age discrimination?

FACTS Josephine Mora, a fund-raiser for Jackson Memorial Foundation, Inc., was sixty-two years old when the foundation's chief executive officer (CEO) fired her, citing errors and issues with professionalism. Mora filed a suit against the foundation, alleging age discrimination. She asserted that when she was fired, the CEO told her, "I need someone younger I can pay less." She had a witness who had heard that statement as well as another in which the CEO said that Mora was "too old to be working

---

a. In the "Search by Keyword:" box, type "Jackson Memorial," and click on "Search." When that page opens, click on the link to access the opinion.

Case 25.2—Continued

here anyway." The foundation moved for summary judgment, arguing that Mora was fired chiefly because she was incompetent. The district court granted the motion, and Mora appealed.

ISSUE Did Mora present sufficient evidence that the employer's stated reason for firing her was only a pretext?

DECISION Yes. The U.S. Court of Appeals for the Eleventh Circuit vacated (set aside) the decision of the trial court and remanded the case for a trial.

REASON Because there was a "disputed question of material fact" as to whether the plaintiff had been fired because of her age, the defendant was not entitled to summary judgment. The district court should *not* have examined the question of whether Mora would have been fired no matter what her age was simply because she had become incompetent. "The resolution of this case depends on whose account of the pertinent conversations a jury would credit. A reasonable juror could accept that [the CEO] made the discriminatory-sounding remarks and that the remarks are sufficient evidence of a discriminatory motive." A reasonable juror could conclude that that the CEO fired Mora because of her age.

CRITICAL THINKING—Ethical Consideration *Is the court's decision fair to employers? Why or why not?*

State Employees Not Covered by the ADEA

Generally, the states are immune from lawsuits brought by private individuals in federal court—unless a state consents to the suit. This immunity stems from the United States Supreme Court's interpretation of the Eleventh Amendment (the text of this amendment is included in Appendix B of this text). **CASE EXAMPLE 25.13** In two Florida cases, professors and librarians contended that their employers—two Florida state universities—denied them salary increases and other benefits because they were getting old and their successors could be hired at lower cost. The universities claimed that as agencies of a sovereign state, they could not be sued in federal court without the state's consent. The cases ultimately reached the United States Supreme Court, which held that the Eleventh Amendment bars private parties from suing state employers for violations of the ADEA.[24] •

"Growing old is like being increasingly penalized for a crime you have not committed."

Anthony Powell, 1905–2000
(English novelist)

State immunity under the Eleventh Amendment is not absolute, however. In some situations, such as when fundamental rights are at stake, Congress has the power to abrogate (abolish) state immunity to private suits through legislation that unequivocally shows Congress's intent to subject states to private suits.[25]

As a general rule, though, the Court has found that state employers are immune from private suits brought by employees under the ADEA (for age discrimination, as noted above), the Americans with Disabilities Act[26] (for disability discrimination), and the Fair Labor Standards Act[27] (which relates to wages and hours—see Chapter 24). In contrast, states are not immune from the requirements of the Family and Medical Leave Act[28] (see Chapter 24).

Discrimination Based on Disability

The Americans with Disabilities Act (ADA) of 1990[29] prohibits disability-based discrimination in workplaces with fifteen or more workers (with the exception of state government employers, who are generally immune under the Eleventh Amendment, as just discussed).

---

24. *Kimel v. Florida Board of Regents,* 528 U.S. 62, 120 S.Ct. 631, 145 L.Ed.2d 522 (2000).
25. *Tennessee v. Lane,* 541 U.S. 509, 124 S.Ct. 1978, 158 L.Ed.2d 820 (2004).
26. *Board of Trustees of the University of Alabama v. Garrett,* 531 U.S. 356, 121 S.Ct. 955, 148 L.Ed.2d 866 (2001).
27. *Alden v. Maine,* 527 U.S. 706, 119 S.Ct. 2240, 144 L.Ed.2d 636 (1999).
28. *Nevada Department of Human Resources v. Hibbs,* 538 U.S. 721, 123 S.Ct. 1972, 155 L.Ed.2d 953 (2003).
29. 42 U.S.C. Sections 12102–12118.

Basically, the ADA requires that employers reasonably accommodate the needs of persons with disabilities unless to do so would cause the employer to suffer an undue hardship. In 2008, Congress broadened the coverage of the ADA's protections in the ADA Amendments Act,[30] which will be discussed shortly.

Procedures under the ADA

To prevail on a claim under the ADA, a plaintiff must show that he or she (1) has a disability, (2) is otherwise qualified for the employment in question, and (3) was excluded from the employment solely because of the disability. As in Title VII cases, a plaintiff must pursue her or his claim through the EEOC before filing an action in court for a violation of the ADA.

The EEOC may decide to investigate and perhaps even sue the employer on behalf of the employee. If the EEOC decides not to sue, then the employee is entitled to sue in court. According to the United States Supreme Court, the EEOC can bring a suit against an employer for disability-based discrimination even though the employee previously agreed to submit any job-related disputes to arbitration (see Chapter 3).[31]

Plaintiffs in lawsuits brought under the ADA may obtain many of the same remedies available under Title VII. These include reinstatement, back pay, a limited amount of compensatory and punitive damages (for intentional discrimination), and certain other forms of relief. Repeat violators may be ordered to pay fines of up to $100,000.

"Jobs are physically easier, but the worker now takes home worries instead of an aching back."

Homer Bigart, 1907–1991
(American journalist)

What Is a Disability?

The ADA is broadly drafted to cover persons with a wide range of disabilities. Specifically, the ADA defines *disability* to include any of the following:

1. A physical or mental impairment that substantially limits one or more of an individual's major life activities.
2. A record of such impairment.
3. Being regarded as having such an impairment.

Health conditions that have been considered disabilities under the federal law include blindness, alcoholism, heart disease, cancer, muscular dystrophy, cerebral palsy, paraplegia, diabetes, acquired immune deficiency syndrome (AIDS), testing positive for the human immunodeficiency virus (HIV), and morbid obesity (defined as existing when an individual's weight is two times the normal weight for his or her height).

A separate provision in the ADA prevents employers from taking adverse employment actions based on stereotypes or assumptions about individuals who associate with people who have disabilities.[32] At one time, the courts focused on whether a person was disabled *after* the use of corrective devices or medication. With this approach, a person with severe myopia, or nearsightedness, which can be corrected with lenses, for instance, would not qualify as disabled because that individual's major life activities were not substantially impaired. In 2008, Congress amended the ADA to strengthen its protections and prohibit employers from considering mitigating measures or medications when determining if an individual has a disability. Disability is now determined on a case-by-case basis.

---

30. 42 U.S.C. Sections 12103 and 12205a.

31. *EEOC v. Waffle House, Inc.*, 534 U.S. 279, 122 S.Ct. 754, 151 L.Ed.2d 755 (2002).

32. 42 U.S.C. Section 12112(b)(4). Under this provision, an employer cannot, for instance, refuse to hire the parent of a child with a disability based on the assumption that the parent will miss work too often or be unreliable.

A condition may fit the definition of disability in one set of circumstances, but not in another. What makes the difference in a particular situation? The court in the following case answered that question.

Case 25.3

Rohr v. Salt River Project Agricultural Improvement and Power District

United States Court of Appeals, Ninth Circuit,
555 F.3d 850 (2009).
www.ca9.uscourts.gov[a]

(Lightpoet/Shutterstock.com)

Can this man's diabetes be considered a disability?

HISTORICAL AND SOCIAL SETTING *Diabetes is a chronic and incurable disease associated with an increased risk of heart disease, stroke, high blood pressure, blindness, kidney disease, and many other disorders. Type 1 diabetes, or juvenile diabetes, results from the body's failure to produce insulin—a hormone that is needed to convert food into energy. Type 2 results from the body's failure to properly use insulin. If left untreated, type 2 can cause seizures and a coma. In the United States, approximately 23.6 million children and adults, or 7.8 percent of the population, have diabetes.*

FACTS Larry Rohr has type 2 diabetes. If he fails to follow a complex regimen of daily insulin injections, blood tests, and a strict diet, his blood sugar rises to a level that aggravates his disease. At the time of his diagnosis, he was a welding metallurgy specialist for the Salt River Project Agricultural Improvement and Power District, which provides utility services to homes in Arizona. Due to the effort required to manage his diabetes, particularly his strict diet, Rohr's physician forbade his assignment to tasks involving overnight, out-of-town travel. Salt River told Rohr that this would prevent him from performing the essential functions of his job, such as responding to power outages. Rohr was asked to transfer, apply for disability benefits, or take early retirement. He filed a suit against Salt River, alleging discrimination. The court issued a summary judgment in the employer's favor. Rohr appealed.

ISSUE Is diabetes a disability under the ADA if it significantly restricts an individual's eating?

DECISION Yes. The U.S. Court of Appeals for the Ninth Circuit vacated the lower court's judgment and remanded the case for trial.

REASON The ADA's definition of disability includes physical impairments that substantially limit a major life activity. Diabetes is a physical impairment because it affects the digestive, hemic (blood), and endocrine systems. Major life activities include eating patterns. Thus, if the symptoms of diabetes and the efforts to manage the disease significantly restrict an individual's eating, the definition of disability is met. In many instances, failure to take insulin can result in severe health problems and even death. Determining how much insulin to take can require frequent, self-administered blood tests and adjustments in activity and food levels. Rohr must follow these steps. Because insulin alone does not stabilize his blood sugar levels, he must strictly monitor what, and when, he eats every day. Failure to do so would endanger his health. "Straying from a diet for more than one or two meals is not a cause for medical concern for most people, and skipping a meal, or eating a large one, does not expose them to the risk of fainting." But for Rohr the effort to control his diet is substantially limiting.

CRITICAL THINKING—Technological Consideration *If Rohr could have monitored his condition and regimen through a cell phone or other portable Internet connection, would the result in this case likely have been affected? Explain.*

a. In the left-hand column, in the "Opinions" pull-out menu, click on "Published." On that page, click on "Advanced Search." In the "by Case No.:" box, type "06-16527" and click on "Search." In the result, click on the case title to access the opinion.

Reasonable Accommodation

The ADA does not require that employers accommodate the needs of job applicants or employees with disabilities who are not otherwise qualified for the work. If a job applicant or an employee with a disability can perform essential job functions with a reasonable accommodation, however, the employer must make the accommodation.

Required modifications may include installing ramps for a wheelchair, establishing more flexible working hours, creating or modifying job assignments, and creating or improving training materials and procedures. Generally, employers should give primary consideration to employees' preferences in deciding what accommodations should be made.

Undue Hardship

Employers who do not accommodate the needs of persons with disabilities must demonstrate that the accommodations will cause "undue hardship" in terms of being significantly difficult or expensive for the employer. Usually, the courts decide whether an accommodation constitutes an undue hardship on a case-by-case basis by looking at the employer's resources in relation to the specific accommodation.

EXAMPLE 25.14 Bryan Lockhart, who uses a wheelchair, works for a cell phone company that provides parking for its employees. Lockhart informs the company supervisors that the parking spaces are so narrow that he is unable to extend the ramp on his van that allows him to get in and out of the vehicle. Lockhart therefore requests that the company reasonably accommodate his needs by paying a monthly fee for him to use a larger parking space in an adjacent lot. In this situation, a court would likely find that it would not be an undue hardship for the employer to pay for additional parking for Lockhart. •

Job Applications and Preemployment Physical Exams

KNOW THIS

Preemployment screening procedures must be applied equally in regard to all job applicants.

Employers must modify their job-application process so that those with disabilities can compete for jobs with those who do not have disabilities. For instance, a job announcement might be modified to allow job applicants to respond by e-mail or letter, as well as by telephone, so that it does not discriminate against potential applicants with hearing impairments.

Employers are restricted in the kinds of questions they may ask on job-application forms and during preemployment interviews. Furthermore, they cannot require persons with disabilities to submit to preemployment physicals unless such exams are required of all other applicants. Employers can condition an offer of employment on the applicant's successfully passing a medical examination, but can disqualify the applicant only if the medical problems they discover would render the applicant unable to perform the job.

CASE EXAMPLE 25.15 When filling the position of delivery truck driver, a company cannot automatically screen out all applicants who are unable to meet the U.S. Department of Transportation's hearing standard. The company would first have to prove that drivers who are deaf are not qualified to perform the essential job function of driving safely and pose a higher risk of accidents than drivers who are not deaf.[33] •

Substance Abusers

Drug addiction is a disability under the ADA because drug addiction is a substantially limiting impairment. Those who are actually using illegal drugs are not protected by the act, however. The ADA protects only persons with *former* drug addictions—those who have completed or are now in a supervised drug-rehabilitation program. Individuals who have used drugs casually in the past are not protected under the act. They are not considered addicts and therefore do not have a disability (addiction).

People suffering from alcoholism are protected by the ADA. Employers cannot legally discriminate against employees simply because they are suffering from alcoholism. Of course, employers have the right to prohibit the use of alcohol in the workplace and can require that employees not be under the influence of alcohol while working. Employers can also fire or refuse to hire a person who is an alcoholic if he or she poses a substantial risk of harm either to himself or herself or to others and the risk cannot be reduced by reasonable accommodation.

---

33. *Bates v. United Parcel Service, Inc.*, 465 F.3d 1069 (9th Cir. 2006).

Health-Insurance Plans Workers with disabilities must be given equal access to any health insurance provided to other employees. Under 2010 health-care reforms, employers cannot exclude preexisting health conditions from coverage. An employer can also put a limit, or cap, on health-care payments under its group health policy—as long as such caps are "applied equally to all insured employees" and do not "discriminate on the basis of disability." Whenever a group health-care plan makes a disability-based distinction in its benefits, the plan violates the ADA (unless the employer can justify its actions under the business necessity defense, which will be discussed shortly).

Defenses to Employment Discrimination

LEARNING OBJECTIVE 5
What are three defenses to claims of employment discrimination?

The first line of defense for an employer charged with employment discrimination is, of course, to assert that the plaintiff has failed to meet his or her initial burden of proving that discrimination occurred. Once a plaintiff succeeds in proving discrimination, the burden shifts to the employer to justify the discriminatory practice.

Possible justifications include that the discrimination was the result of a business necessity, a bona fide occupational qualification, or a seniority system. In some situations, as noted earlier, an effective antiharassment policy and prompt remedial action when harassment occurs may shield employers from liability for sexual harassment under Title VII.

Business Necessity

Business Necessity A defense to an allegation of employment discrimination in which the employer demonstrates that an employment practice that discriminates against members of a protected class is related to job performance.

An employer may defend against a claim of disparate-impact (unintentional) discrimination by asserting that a practice that has a discriminatory effect is a **business necessity**. EXAMPLE 25.16 If requiring a high school diploma is shown to have a discriminatory effect, an employer might argue that a high school education is necessary for workers to perform the job at a required level of competence. If the employer can demonstrate a definite connection between a high school education and job performance, the employer normally will succeed in this business necessity defense. •

Bona Fide Occupational Qualification

Bona Fide Occupational Qualification (BFOQ) Identifiable characteristics reasonably necessary to the normal operation of a particular business. These characteristics can include gender, national origin, and religion, but not race.

Another defense applies when discrimination against a protected class is essential to a job—that is, when a particular trait is a **bona fide occupational qualification (BFOQ)**. Race, however, can never be a BFOQ.

Generally, courts have restricted the BFOQ defense to instances in which the employee's gender is essential to the job. EXAMPLE 25.17 A women's clothing store might legitimately hire only female sales attendants if part of an attendant's job involves assisting clients in the store's dressing rooms. Similarly, the Federal Aviation Administration can legitimately impose age limits for airline pilots—but an airline cannot impose weight limits only on female flight attendants. •

Seniority Systems

Seniority System A system in which those who have worked longest for an employer are first in line for promotions, salary increases, and other benefits, and are last to be laid off if the workforce must be reduced.

An employer with a history of discrimination might have no members of protected classes in upper-level positions. Even if the employer now seeks to be unbiased, some employees may bring a lawsuit asking a court to order that minorities be promoted ahead of schedule to compensate for past discrimination. If no present intent to discriminate is shown, however, and if promotions or other job benefits are distributed according to a fair **seniority system** (in which workers with more years of service are promoted first or laid off last), the employer normally has a good defense against the suit.

CASE EXAMPLE 25.18 According to the United States Supreme Court, this defense may also apply to alleged discrimination under the ADA. The case involved a baggage handler who had injured his back and asked to be reassigned to a mailroom at U.S. Airways, Inc. The airline refused to give the employee the position because another employee had seniority. The Court sided with U.S. Airways. If an employee with a disability requests an accommodation that conflicts with an employer's seniority system, the accommodation generally will not be considered "reasonable" under the act.[34] •

After-Acquired Evidence of Employee Misconduct

In some situations, employers have attempted to avoid liability for employment discrimination on the basis of "after-acquired evidence"—that is, evidence that the employer discovers after a lawsuit is filed—of an employee's misconduct. **EXAMPLE 25.19** An employer fires a worker who then sues the employer for employment discrimination. During pretrial investigation, the employer learns that the employee made material misrepresentations on his employment application—misrepresentations that, had the employer known about them, would have served as grounds to fire the individual. •

According to the United States Supreme Court, after-acquired evidence of wrongdoing cannot shield an employer entirely from liability for employment discrimination. It may, however, be used to limit the amount of damages for which the employer is liable.[35]

Affirmative Action

Affirmative Action Job-hiring policies that give special consideration to members of protected classes in an effort to overcome present effects of past discrimination.

Federal statutes and regulations providing for equal opportunity in the workplace were designed to reduce or eliminate discriminatory practices with respect to hiring, retaining, and promoting employees. **Affirmative action** programs go further and attempt to "make up" for past patterns of discrimination by giving members of protected classes preferential treatment in hiring or promotion. During the 1960s, all federal and state government agencies, private companies that contracted to do business with the federal government, and institutions that received federal funding were required to implement affirmative action policies.

Title VII of the Civil Rights Act of 1964 neither requires nor prohibits affirmative action. Thus, most private firms have not been required to implement affirmative action policies, though many have voluntarily done so. Affirmative action programs have been controversial, however, particularly when they have resulted in reverse discrimination (discussed on page 658).

Constitutionality of Affirmative Action Programs

Because of their inherently discriminatory nature, affirmative action programs may violate the equal protection clause of the Fourteenth Amendment to the U.S. Constitution. The United States Supreme Court has held that any federal, state, or local affirmative action program that uses racial or ethnic classifications as the basis for making decisions is subject to strict scrutiny by the courts.[36] Recall from Chapter 2 that strict scrutiny is the highest standard, which means that most affirmative action programs do not survive a court's analysis under this test.

Today, an affirmative action program normally is constitutional only if it attempts to remedy past discrimination and does not make use of quotas or preferences. Furthermore, once such a program has succeeded in the goal of remedying past discrimination, it must be changed or dropped.

34. *U.S. Airways, Inc. v. Barnett*, 535 U.S. 391, 122 S.Ct. 1516, 152 L.Ed.2d 589 (2002).

35. *McKennon v. Nashville Banner Publishing Co.*, 513 U.S. 352, 115 S.Ct. 879, 130 L.Ed.2d 852 (1995).

36. See the landmark decision in *Adarand Constructors, Inc. v. Peña*, 515 U.S. 200, 115 S.Ct. 2097, 132 L.Ed.2d 158 (1995).

Affirmative Action in Schools

Most of the affirmative action cases that have reached the United States Supreme Court in the last twenty years have involved university admissions programs and schools, rather than employment. Generally, the Court has found that a school admissions policy that *automatically* awards minority applicants a specified number of points needed to guarantee admission violates the equal protection clause.[37]

A school can, however, "consider race or ethnicity more flexibly as a 'plus' factor in the context of individualized consideration of each and every applicant."[38] In other words, it is unconstitutional for schools to apply a mechanical formula that gives "diversity bonuses" based on race or ethnicity.

CASE EXAMPLE 25.20 School districts in Seattle, Washington, and Jefferson County, Kentucky, adopted plans that relied on race to assign certain children to schools. The Seattle plan classified children as "white" or "nonwhite" and used the racial classifications as a "tiebreaker" to determine which high school students would attend. The school district in Jefferson County classified students as "black" or "other" to assign children to elementary schools. Parent groups filed lawsuits claiming that the racial preferences violated the equal protection clause.

The United States Supreme Court held that the school districts had failed to show that the use of racial classifications in their student assignment plans was necessary to achieve their stated goal of racial diversity. Hence, the affirmative action programs of both school districts were unconstitutional.[39] ●

---

37. *Gratz v. Bollinger,* 539 U.S. 244, 123 S.Ct. 2411, 156 L.Ed.2d 257 (2003).

38. *Grutter v. Bollinger,* 539 U.S. 306, 123 S.Ct. 2325, 156 L.Ed.2d 304 (2003).

39. The Court consolidated the two cases and issued one opinion for both. See *Parents Involved in Community Schools v. Seattle School District No. 1,* 551 U.S. 701, 127 S.Ct. 2738, 168 L.Ed.2d 508 (2007).

Reviewing . . . Employment Discrimination and Diversity

Amaani Lyle, an African American woman, took a job as a scriptwriters' assistant at Warner Brothers Television Productions. She worked for the writers of *Friends,* a popular, adult-oriented television series. One of her essential job duties was to type detailed notes for the scriptwriters during brainstorming sessions in which they discussed jokes, dialogue, and story lines. The writers then combed through Lyle's notes after the meetings for script material. During these meetings, the three male scriptwriters told lewd and vulgar jokes and made sexually explicit comments and gestures. They often talked about their personal sexual experiences and fantasies, and some of these conversations were then used in episodes of *Friends*.

During the meetings, Lyle never complained that she found the writers' conduct offensive. After four months, she was fired because she could not type fast enough to keep up with the writers' conversations during the meetings. She filed a suit against Warner Brothers alleging sexual harassment and claiming that her termination was based on racial discrimination. Using the information presented in the chapter, answer the following questions.

1. Would Lyle's claim of racial discrimination be for intentional (disparate-treatment) or unintentional (disparate-impact) discrimination? Explain.
2. Can Lyle establish a *prima facie* case of racial discrimination? Why or why not?
3. When she was hired, Lyle was told that typing speed was extremely important to her position. At the time, she maintained that she could type eighty words per minute, so she was not given a typing test. It later turned out that Lyle could type only fifty words per minute. What impact might typing speed have on Lyle's lawsuit?

Continued

4. Lyle's sexual-harassment claim is based on the hostile work environment created by the writers' sexually offensive conduct at meetings that she was required to attend. The writers, however, argue that their behavior was essential to the "creative process" of writing *Friends*, a show that routinely contained sexual innuendos and adult humor. Which defense discussed in the chapter might Warner Brothers assert using this argument?

DEBATE THIS: Members of minority groups and women have made enough economic progress in the last several decades that they no longer need special legislation to protect them.

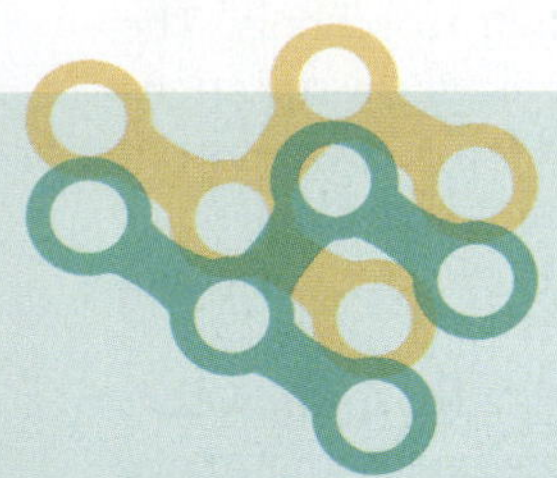

LINKING BUSINESS LAW to Corporate Management

Human Resource Management

Your career may lead to running a small business, managing a small part of a larger business, or making decisions for the operations of a big business. In any context, you may be responsible for employment decisions. As this chapter has suggested, an ill-conceived hiring or firing process can lead to a lawsuit. As a manager, you must also ensure that employees do not practice discrimination on the job. Enter the human resource management specialist.

What Is Human Resource Management?

Human resource management (HRM) is the acquisition, maintenance, and development of an organization's employees. HRM involves the design and application of formal systems in an organization to ensure the effective and efficient use of human talent to accomplish organizational goals.

All managers need to be skilled in HRM. Some firms require managers to play an active role in recruiting and selecting personnel, as well as in developing training programs. Those who work in a human resources department should be especially aware of the issues outlined in this chapter (and in Chapters 23 and 24).

The Acquisition Phase of HRM

Acquiring talented employees is the first step in an HRM system. All recruitment must be done without violating any of the laws and regulations outlined in this chapter. Obviously, recruitment must be colorblind, as well as indifferent to gender, religion, national origin, and age. Devise recruitment methods that do not have even the slightest hint of discriminatory basis. Recruitment methods must also give an equal chance to people with disabilities. Only the applicant's qualifications can be considered, not his or her disability. If a candidate with a disability is rejected, make sure to document that the rejection is based solely on the applicant's lack of training or ability.

On-the-Job HRM Issues

In addition, the HRM professional must also monitor the working environment. Sexual harassment is a major concern. You may need to work closely with an employment law specialist to develop antiharassment rules and policies. You also need to publish them and provide training to ensure that all employees are familiar with the firm's policy. In addition, you should create and supervise a grievance system so that any harassment can be stopped before it becomes actionable.

HRM Issues concerning Employee Termination

Even in employment-at-will jurisdictions, lawsuits can arise for improper termination. Develop a system to protect your company from lawsuits, such as procedures for documenting an employee's misconduct and the employer's warnings or other disciplinary actions. The company should also have an established policy for dealing with improper or incompetent behavior, and should be clear about the amount of severance pay that terminated employees will receive. Sometimes, it is better to err on the side of generosity to maintain the goodwill of terminated employees.

Critical Thinking

What are some types of actions that an HRM professional can take to reduce the probability of harassment lawsuits against her or his company?

Key Terms

affirmative action 672
bona fide occupational qualification (BFOQ) 671
business necessity 671
constructive discharge 661
disparate-impact discrimination 657
disparate-treatment discrimination 656
employment discrimination 655
prima facie case 657
protected class 654
seniority system 671
sexual harassment 661
tangible employment action 662

Chapter Summary: Employment Discrimination and Diversity

Title VII of the Civil Rights Act of 1964 (See pages 655–658.)	Title VII prohibits employment discrimination based on race, color, national origin, religion, or gender. 1. *Procedures*—Employees must file a claim with the Equal Employment Opportunity Commission (EEOC). The EEOC may sue the employer on the employee's behalf. If not, the employee may sue the employer directly. 2. *Types of discrimination*—Title VII prohibits both intentional (disparate-treatment) and unintentional (disparate-impact) discrimination. Disparate-impact discrimination occurs when an employer's practice, such as requiring a certain level of education, has the effect of discriminating against a protected class. Title VII also extends to discriminatory practices, such as various forms of harassment, in the online environment. 3. *Remedies for discrimination under Title VII*—Remedies include reinstatement, back pay, and retroactive promotions. Damages (both compensatory and punitive) may be awarded for intentional discrimination.
Discrimination Based on Age (See pages 665–667.)	The Age Discrimination in Employment Act (ADEA) of 1967 prohibits employment discrimination on the basis of age against individuals forty years of age or older. Procedures for bringing a case under the ADEA are similar to those for bringing a case under Title VII.
Discrimination Based on Disability (See pages 667–671.)	The Americans with Disabilities Act (ADA) of 1990 prohibits employment discrimination against persons with disabilities who are otherwise qualified to perform the essential functions of the jobs for which they apply. 1. *Procedures and remedies*—To prevail on a claim, the plaintiff must show that she or he has a disability, is otherwise qualified for the employment in question, and was excluded from it solely because of the disability. Procedures and remedies under the ADA are similar to those in Title VII cases. 2. *Definition of disability*—The ADA defines the term *disability* as a physical or mental impairment that substantially limits one or more major life activities, a record of such impairment, or being regarded as having such an impairment. 3. *Reasonable accommodation*—Employers are required to reasonably accommodate the needs of persons with disabilities through such measures as modifying the physical work environment and permitting more flexible work schedules. Employers are not required to accommodate the needs of all workers with disabilities, such as who pose a definite threat to health and safety in the workplace or who are not otherwise qualified for their jobs.
Defenses to Employment Discrimination (See pages 671–672.)	As defenses to claims of employment discrimination, employers may assert that the discrimination was required for reasons of business necessity, to meet a bona fide occupational qualification, or to maintain a legitimate seniority system. Evidence of prior employee misconduct acquired after the employee has been fired is not a defense to discrimination.
Affirmative Action (See pages 672–673.)	Affirmative action programs attempt to "make up" for past patterns of discrimination by giving members of protected classes preferential treatment in hiring or promotion. Such programs are subject to strict scrutiny by the courts and are often struck down for violating the Fourteenth Amendment.

ExamPrep

ISSUE SPOTTERS

1. Ruth is a supervisor for a Subs & Suds restaurant. Tim is a Subs & Suds employee. The owner announces that some employees will be discharged. Ruth tells Tim that if he has sex with her, he can keep his job. Is this sexual harassment? Why or why not? **(See pages 661–665.)**
2. Koko, a person with a disability, applies for a job at Lively Sales Corporation for which she is well qualified, but she is rejected. Lively continues to seek applicants and eventually fills the position with a person who does not have a disability. Could Koko succeed in a suit against Lively for discrimination? Explain. **(See page 668.)**

— Check your answers to the Issue Spotters against the answers provided in Appendix E at the end of this text.

BEFORE THE TEST

Go to www.cengagebrain.com, enter the ISBN 9781133273561, and click on "Find" to locate this textbook's Web site. Then, click on "Access Now" under "Study Tools," and select Chapter 25 at the top. There, you will find a Practice Quiz that you can take to assess your mastery of the concepts in this chapter, as well as Flashcards, a Glossary of important terms, and Video Questions (when assigned).

For Review

Answers to the even-numbered questions in this For Review section can be found in Appendix F at the end of this text.

1. Generally, what kind of conduct is prohibited by Title VII of the Civil Rights Act of 1964, as amended?
2. What is the difference between disparate-treatment discrimination and disparate-impact discrimination?
3. What remedies are available under Title VII of the 1964 Civil Rights Act, as amended?
4. What federal act prohibits discrimination based on age?
5. What are three defenses to claims of employment discrimination?

Business Scenarios and Case Problems

25–1 Title VII Violations. Discuss fully whether either of the following actions would constitute a violation of Title VII of the 1964 Civil Rights Act, as amended.

1. Tennington, Inc., is a consulting firm and has ten employees. These employees travel on consulting jobs in seven states. Tennington has an employment record of hiring only white males. **(See page 657.)**
2. Novo Films, Inc., is making a film about Africa and needs to employ approximately one hundred extras for this picture. To hire these extras, Novo advertises in all major newspapers in Southern California. The ad states that only African Americans need apply. **(See page 671.)**

25–2 Question with Sample Answer—Disparate-Impact Discrimination. Chinawa, a major processor of cheese sold throughout the United States, employs one hundred workers at its principal processing plant. The plant is located in Heartland Corners, which has a population that is 50 percent white and 25 percent African American, with the balance Hispanic American, Asian American, and others. Chinawa requires a high school diploma as a condition of employment for its cleaning crew. Three-fourths of the white population complete high school, compared with only one-fourth of those in the minority groups. Chinawa has an all-white cleaning crew. Has Chinawa violated Title VII of the Civil Rights Act of 1964? Explain. **(See pages 657 and 671.)**

—For a sample answer to Question 25–2, go to Appendix G at the end of this text.

25–3 Religious Discrimination. Gina Gomez, a devout Roman Catholic, worked for Sam's Department Stores, Inc., in Phoenix, Arizona. Sam's considered Gomez a productive employee because her sales exceeded $200,000 per year. At the time, the store gave its managers the discretion to grant unpaid leave to employees but prohibited vacations or leave during the holiday season—October through December. Gomez felt that she had a "calling" to go on a "pilgrimage" in October to Bosnia where some persons claimed to have had visions of the Virgin Mary. The Catholic Church had not designated the site an official pilgrimage site, the visions were not expected to be stronger in October, and tours were available at other times. The store managers denied Gomez's request for leave, but she had a nonrefundable ticket and left anyway. Sam's terminated her employment, and she could not find another job. Can Gomez establish a *prima facie* case of religious discrimination? Explain. **(See page 659.)**

25–4 Spotlight on the Civil Rights Act—Discrimination Based on Gender. Burlington Coat Factory Warehouse, Inc., had a dress code that required male salesclerks to wear business attire consisting of slacks, shirt, and a necktie. Female salesclerks, by contrast, were required to wear a smock so that customers could readily identify them. Karen O'Donnell and other female employees refused to wear the smock. Instead they reported to work in business attire and were suspended. After numerous suspensions, the female employees were fired for violating Burlington's dress code policy. All other conditions of employment, including salary, hours, and benefits, were the same for female and male employees. Was the dress code policy discriminatory? Why or why not? [*O'Donnell v. Burlington Coat Factory Warehouse, Inc.,* 656 F.Supp. 263 (S.D. Ohio 1987)] **(See page 660.)**

25–5 Case Problem with Sample Answer—Retaliation by Employers. Entek International hired Shane Dawson, a male homosexual. Some of Dawson's co-workers, including his supervisor, made derogatory comments about his sexual orientation. Dawson's work deteriorated. He filed a complaint with Entek's human resources department. Two days later, he was fired. State law made it unlawful for an employer to discriminate against an individual based on sexual orientation. Could Dawson establish a claim for retaliation? Explain. [*Dawson v. Entek International*, 630 F.3d 928 (9th Cir. 2011)] **(See page 663.)**

—For a sample answer to Problem 25–5, go to Appendix H at the end of this text.

25–6 **Sexual Harassment by Co-Worker.** Billie Bradford worked for the Kentucky Department of Community Based Services (DCBS). One of Bradford's co-workers, Lisa Stander, routinely engaged in extreme sexual behavior (such as touching herself and making crude comments) in Bradford's presence. Bradford and others regularly complained about Stander's conduct to their supervisor, Angie Taylor. Rather than resolve the problem, Taylor nonchalantly told Stander to stop, encouraged Bradford to talk to Stander, and suggested that Stander was just having fun. Assuming that Bradford was subjected to a hostile-work environment, could DCBS be liable? Why or why not? [*Bradford v. Department of Community Based Services*, 2012 WL 360032 (E.D.Ky. 2012)] **(See page 664.)**

25–7 **A Question of Ethics—Discrimination Based on Disability.** Titan Distribution, Inc., employed Quintak, Inc., to run its tire mounting and distribution operation in Des Moines, Iowa. Robert Chalfant worked for Quintak as a second-shift supervisor at Titan. He suffered a heart attack in 1992 and underwent heart bypass surgery in 1997. He also had arthritis. In July 2002, Titan decided to terminate Quintak. Chalfant applied to work at Titan. On his application, he described himself as having a disibility. After a physical exam, Titan's doctor concluded that Chalfant could work in his current capacity, and he was notified that he would be hired. Despite the notice, Nadis Barucic, a Titan employee, wrote "not pass px" at the top of Chalfant's application, and he was not hired. He took a job with AMPCO Systems, a parking ramp management company. This work involved walking up to five miles a day and lifting more weight than he had at Titan. In September, Titan eliminated its second shift. Chalfant filed a suit in a federal district court against Titan, in part, under the Americans with Disabilities Act (ADA). Titan argued that the reason it had not hired Chalfant was not that he did not pass the physical, but no one—including Barucic—could explain why she had written "not pass px" on his application. Later, Titan claimed that Chalfant was not hired because the entire second shift was going to be eliminated. [*Chalfant v. Titan Distribution, Inc.*, 475 F.3d 982 (8th Cir. 2007)] **(See pages 667–671.)**

1. What must Chalfant establish to make his case under the ADA? Can he meet these requirements? Explain.
2. In employment-discrimination cases, punitive damages can be appropriate when an employer acts with malice or reckless indifference to an employee's protected rights. Would an award of punitive damages to Chalfant be appropriate in this case? Discuss.

Critical Thinking and Writing Assignments

25–8 **Critical Legal Thinking.** Why has the federal government limited the application of the statutes discussed in this chapter to firms with a specified number of employees, such as fifteen or twenty? Should these laws apply to all employers, regardless of size? Why or why not?

25–9 **Case Analysis Question.** Go to Appendix I at the end of this text and examine the excerpt of Case No. 5, *Burlington Northern and Santa Fe Railway Co. v. White*. Review and then brief the case, making sure that your brief answers the following questions.

1. **Issue:** What was the plaintiff's complaint, the defendant's response, and the chief legal dispute between them?
2. **Rule of Law:** Which provisions of Title VII did the Supreme Court consider here, and which rule of statutory interpretation governed the Court's consideration?
3. **Applying the Rule of Law:** How did the Court interpret these provisions, and how did that interpretation apply to the circumstances in this case?
4. **Conclusion:** Based on its application of the principles in this case, what did the Court conclude?

25–10 **Business Law Critical Thinking Group Assignment.** Two African American plaintiffs sued the producers of the reality television series *The Bachelor* and *The Bachelorette* for racial discrimination. The plaintiffs claimed that the shows have never featured a person of color in the lead role. Plaintiffs also alleged that the producers failed to provide people of color who auditioned for lead roles with the same opportunities to compete as white people who auditioned.

1. The first group will assess whether the plaintiffs can establish a *prima facie* case of disparate-treatment (intentional) discrimination.
2. The second group will consider whether the plaintiffs can establish disparate-impact discrimination.
3. The third group will assume that the plaintiffs established a *prima facie* case and that the burden has shifted to the employer to articulate a legal reason for not hiring the plaintiffs. What legitimate reasons might the employer assert for not hiring the plaintiffs in this situation? Should the law require television producers to hire persons of color for lead roles in reality television shows? Explain your answer.

UNIT 4 Agency and Employment Law

Business Case Study with Dissenting Opinion

EEOC v. Greater Baltimore Medical Center, Inc.

As discussed in Chapter 25, the Americans with Disabilities Act (ADA) prohibits employment discrimination based on a disability. Although an employer is often required to reasonably accommodate the needs of an employee with a disability, the ADA does not protect an employee who cannot perform the essential functions of a job even when given a reasonable accommodation.

In this *Business Case Study with Dissenting Opinion*, we review *EEOC v. Greater Baltimore Medical Center, Inc.*[1] In this case, the Equal Employment Opportunity Commission (EEOC) filed an enforcement action on behalf of a disabled employee who was receiving Social Security Disability Income benefits. To receive the benefits, the employee had to state that he was incapable of working. The issue for the court was whether, despite the employee's representations, the EEOC could still show that he was capable of performing the job's essential functions.

Case Background

Michael Turner worked as a secretary for Greater Baltimore Medical Center (GBMC). Beginning in January 2005, Turner was hospitalized for five months because of a life-threatening condition called necrotizing fasciitis. Turner returned to work in November 2005 with his doctor's permission, but he soon suffered a stroke and was hospitalized again until late December.

On December 29, 2005, with his mother's help, Turner applied to the Social Security Administration (SSA) for Social Security Disability Income (SSDI) benefits. The application stated, "I became unable to work because of my disabling condition on January 15, 2005. I am still disabled." The application also said that Turner would tell the SSA if his condition improved to the point that he could work. A few days later, Turner's mother also submitted a report stating that Turner could not work because of his disabilities. Turner began receiving SSDI benefits in January 2006.

That same month, Turner told GBMC that he wanted to return to work as a part-time secretary. Turner submitted a form from his physician, but GBMC concluded that his conditions prevented him from performing his old job. As a result, GBMC said that it was not obligated to give Turner a position. By May 2006, Turner's condition had improved, and his doctor found that he could work full-time without any restrictions. But GBMC disagreed, and it terminated Turner in June 2006, when his leave expired. Afterward, Turner did more than 1,100 hours of volunteer work for GBMC. All the while, he continued to receive SSDI benefits.

In February 2007, Turner filed a discrimination charge with the EEOC. In September 2009, the EEOC filed an enforcement action in federal court on Turner's behalf. The district court granted summary judgment for GBMC because it found that, given Turner's SSDI benefits, the EEOC could not show that Turner could perform his old job's essential functions. The EEOC appealed.

Majority Opinion

O'GRADY, District Judge:

* * * *

The ADA prohibits a covered employer from discriminating "against a qualified individual with a disability because of the disability of such individual." *Among other things, EEOC must show that Mr. Turner is a "qualified individual with a disability," that is, "an individual with a disability who, with or without reasonable accommodation, can perform the essential functions of the employment position* * * *." [Emphasis added.]

Many persons who experience disabling medical problems become eligible for programs like SSDI, at least temporarily, during medical leave. If such a person seeks SSDI benefits and attempts to bring a claim under the ADA, he may assert disability in an application for SSDI benefits while simultaneously asserting that he is a "qualified individual" under the ADA, that is, he is able to work with or without reasonable accommodation. A conflict of this sort may appear to bar the claimant from receiving both disability benefits and ADA coverage.

1. 2012 WL 1302604 (4th Cir. 2012).

Business Case Study with Dissenting Opinion—Continued

* * * *

* * * There can be little doubt that the conflict between Mr. Turner's SSDI application and his ability to work with or without reasonable accommodation is genuine. Mr. Turner's SSDI application, submitted on December 29, 2005, states, "I became unable to work because of my disabling condition on January 15, 2005," and, "I am still disabled." Moreover, "I [Mr. Turner] agree to notify the Social Security Administration * * * [i]f my medical condition improves so that I would be able to work, even though I have not yet returned to work." The record indicates without contradiction that Mr. Turner was unable to work after he left the hospital on December 27, 2005. Mrs. Turner later submitted a form called a "Function Report" * * * in which she described Mr. Turner's symptoms and impairment. She noted severe disability in his left arm or hand, use of a bedside commode with hand rails, left-sided weakness requiring assistance, leg bracing, inability to drive, inability to lift more than 2–3 pounds, severely limited ability to stand, bend over and back, and walking. * * * Taken together, the SSDI application and documentation reasonably communicated that Mr. Turner was and would continue to be [unable to work].

Consistent with the application, the SSA awarded benefits to Mr. Turner on January 22, 2006. Mr. Turner continued to receive SSDI benefits at the time of the district court's decision. Mr. Turner did not revise his statements to SSDI, and apparently never notified the SSA about a change in his condition.

These reported disabilities conflict with the multiple work releases provided by [Turner's doctor] * * * . * * * They all indicated that Mr. Turner could have returned to work, directly contradicting the assertion in his SSDI application that he was and continued to be unable to work. * * * If Mr. Turner told GBMC in good faith that he could return to work, then he had no reason to believe that his earlier representations of disability were still accurate.

* * * *

* * * We in no way condone GBMC's refusal to reinstate Mr. Turner. Quite the contrary. We are deeply concerned about GBMC's attempts to prevent a partially disabled former employee from returning to work after he was cleared to return without restriction. Our result is nonetheless mandated by the plain language of the ADA and the relevant case law. The district court's judgment is therefore affirmed.

Dissenting Opinion

GREGORY, Circuit Judge, dissenting:

* * * *

This case * * * involves two different parties' context-related legal representations—*Turner's* assertion in the proceedings before the SSA and the *EEOC's* assertion in this action. While it is true that the EEOC is seeking relief on Turner's behalf, it cannot be said that the EEOC made a prior inconsistent statement in Turner's SSDI application. Its action should not be barred through the happenstance of an unemployed victim having applied for and received SSDI benefits. Moreover, the Supreme Court has repeatedly recognized that "the EEOC is not merely a proxy" for the individuals for whom it seeks relief. Rather, the Court has observed, "[w]hen the EEOC acts, albeit at the behest of and for the benefit of specific individuals, it acts also to vindicate the public interest in preventing employment discrimination." [Emphasis in original.]

Barring EEOC enforcement actions based on a charging party's legal assertions of disability in SSA proceedings * * * is also contrary to public policy. The EEOC's enforcement actions typically seek not only victim-specific relief but also injunctive relief such as training, posting of notices, and reporting requirements. As discussed above, these enforcement actions not only benefit the individuals on whose behalf the agency sues, but also benefit the public, which has an interest in the eradication of employment discrimination.

* * * *

Business Case Study with Dissenting Opinion—Continues next page

Business Case Study with Dissenting Opinion—Continued

Questions for Analysis

1. **Law** What was the majority's decision in this case? What were the reasons for its decision?
2. **Law** Why did the dissent disagree with the majority? If the court had adopted the dissent's position, how would this have affected the result?
3. **Ethics** Does the majority express any ethical reservations about its decision? If so, what are they? Do you have any ethical concerns about the majority's decision?
4. **Economic Dimensions** Based on this case, what do you think is the purpose of SSDI benefits? Did Turner need them?
5. **Implications for the Businessperson** What does the majority's ruling mean for employers who have disabled employees? Are the repercussions of disability discrimination more or less serious? Explain your answer.

UNIT 4 Agency and Employment Law

Business Scenario

Two brothers, Ray and Paul Ashford, start a business—Ashford Brothers, Inc.—manufacturing a new type of battery system for hybrid automobiles. The batteries hit the market at the perfect time and are in great demand.

1. **Agency.** Loren, one of Ashford's salespersons, anxious to make a sale, intentionally quotes a price to a customer that is $500 lower than Ashford had authorized for that particular product. The customer purchases the product at the quoted price. When Ashford learns of the deal, it claims that it is not legally bound to the sales contract because it did not authorize Loren to sell the product at that price. Is Ashford bound to the contract? Discuss fully. **(See pages 610–612.)**
2. **Workers' Compensation.** One day Gina, an Ashford employee, suffered a serious burn when she accidentally spilled some acid on her hand. The accident occurred because another employee, who was suspected of using illegal drugs, carelessly bumped into her. Gina's hand required a series of skin grafts before it healed sufficiently to allow her to return to work. Gina wants to obtain compensation for her lost wages and medical expenses. Can she do that? If so, how? **(See pages 631–632.)**
3. **Drug Testing.** After Gina's injury, Ashford decides to conduct random drug tests on all of its employees. Several employees claim that the testing violates their privacy rights and bring a lawsuit. What factors will the court consider in deciding whether the random drug testing is legally permissible? **(See page 637.)**
4. **COBRA.** Ashford provides health insurance for its two hundred employees, including Dan. For personal medical reasons, Dan takes twelve weeks' leave. During this period, can Dan continue his coverage under Ashford's health-insurance plan? After Dan returns to work, Ashford closes Dan's division and terminates the employees, including Dan. Can Dan continue his coverage under Ashford's health-insurance plan? Explain. **(See page 634.)**
5. **Sexual Harassment.** Aretha, another employee at Ashford, is disgusted by the sexually offensive behavior of several male employees. She has complained to her supervisor on several occasions about the behavior, but the supervisor merely laughs at

Business Scenario—Continued

her concerns. Aretha decides to bring a legal action against the company for sexual harassment. Does Aretha's complaint concern *quid pro quo* harassment or hostile-environment harassment? What federal statute protects employees from sexual harassment? What remedies are available under that statute? What procedures must Aretha follow in pursuing her legal action? **(See pages 661–665.)**

UNIT 4 Agency and Employment Law

Group Project

Hasna Azad, an Iranian, worked at Gold Standard, Inc., and was issued a smartphone for her business use.

1. One group will assume that Azad received harassing e-mails from another employee that disparaged her Iranian origin. Decide whether Gold Standard can be held liable for these e-mails.
2. A second group will assume that Gold Standard issued a warning to the offending employee immediately after the incident was reported and held two meetings about the proper use of the company's e-mail system. This group will determine how this might affect Gold Standard's liability.
3. A third group will assume that when Azad exceeded the company's limit on text messages, Gold Standard read her stored messages without her knowledge to determine whether they were work related or personal. This group will determine whether Azad can sue Gold Standard for violating her privacy rights.

UNIT 5

Business Organizations

UNIT CONTENTS

26. Sole Proprietorships and Private Franchises
27. All Forms of Partnership
28. Limited Liability Companies and Special Business Forms
29. Corporate Formation, Merger, and Termination
30. Corporate Directors, Officers, and Shareholders
31. Investor Protection, Insider Trading, and Corporate Governance

CHAPTER 26

Sole Proprietorships and Private Franchises

(AP Photo/Carlos Osorio)

CHAPTER OUTLINE

- Sole Proprietorships
- Franchises
- The Franchise Contract
- Termination of the Franchise

LEARNING OBJECTIVES

The five learning objectives below are designed to help improve your understanding of the chapter. After reading this chapter, you should be able to answer the following questions:

1. What advantages and disadvantages are associated with the sole proprietorship?
2. What are the most common types of franchises?
3. What laws govern a franchising relationship?
4. What terms and conditions are typically included in a franchise contract?
5. What is wrongful termination? In what types of situations do courts typically find that a franchisor has wrongfully terminated a franchise?

"Why not go out on a limb? Isn't that where the fruit is?"
Frank Scully, 1892–1964 (American author)

Entrepreneur One who initiates and assumes the financial risk of a new business enterprise and undertakes to provide or control its management.

Many Americans would agree with Frank Scully's comment in the chapter-opening quotation that to succeed in business one must "go out on a limb." Certainly, an entrepreneur's primary motive for undertaking a business enterprise is to make profits. An **entrepreneur** is one who initiates and assumes the financial risks of a new enterprise and undertakes to provide or control its management.

A question faced by anyone who wishes to start a business is what form of business organization to use. In making this determination, the entrepreneur needs to consider a number of important factors, including (1) ease of creation, (2) liability of the owners, (3) tax considerations, and (4) the need for capital. In studying this unit on business organizations, keep these factors in mind as you read about the various organizational forms available to entrepreneurs.

Traditionally, entrepreneurs have used three major forms to structure their business enterprises—the sole proprietorship, the partnership, and the corporation. In this chapter, we examine sole proprietorships and discuss franchises as well. Although the franchise is not really a business organizational form, it is widely used today by entrepreneurs.

Sole Proprietorships

Sole Proprietorship The simplest form of business organization, in which the owner is the business. The owner reports business income on his or her personal income tax return and is legally responsible for all debts and obligations incurred by the business.

The simplest form of business organization is a **sole proprietorship.** In this form, the owner is the business. Thus, anyone who does business without creating a separate business organization has a sole proprietorship. More than two-thirds of all U.S. businesses are sole proprietorships. They are usually small enterprises—about 99 percent of the sole proprietorships in the United States have revenues of less than $1 million per year. A sole proprietorship can be any type of business, ranging from an informal, home-office or Internet undertaking to a large restaurant or construction firm. (See this chapter's *Adapting Law to the Online Environment* feature below for a discussion of a sole proprietor who tried to change his name to match his business's Web site.)

Advantages of the Sole Proprietorship

LEARNING OBJECTIVE 1
What advantages and disadvantages are associated with the sole proprietorship?

A major advantage of the sole proprietorship is that the proprietor owns the entire business and has a right to receive all of the profits (because he or she assumes all of the risk). In addition, it is often easier and less costly to start a sole proprietorship than to start any

ADAPTING THE LAW TO THE ONLINE ENVIRONMENT

CAN A SOLE PROPRIETOR CHANGE HIS NAME TO MATCH HIS DOMAIN NAME?

Because of the ease of formation and inherent flexibility, many online businesses start out as sole proprietorships. Often, a Web site's domain name can contribute substantially to the business's success.

One sole proprietor thought his business would benefit from another name change. After he was assigned a domain name by the Internet Corporation for Assigned Names and Numbers (ICANN—see page 135 in Chapter 5), he asked the courts to allow him to change his name to that of his domain name.

Introducing Mr. NJweedman.com . . .

Robert Edward Forchion, Jr., has devoted his life to promoting the legalization of marijuana. While living in New Jersey, he became popularly known as NJweedman, after his Web site *NJweedman.com,* which discusses his efforts to legalize marijuana. In 2009, claiming that he was being persecuted in New Jersey, Forchion moved to California where he has managed a Rastafarian temple and a medical marijuana dispensary. (California is one of nearly twenty states that allow the legal distribution of medical marijuana.)

Petitioning the Courts for a Name Change

In 2001, while still living in New Jersey, Forchion tried to change his name legally to "NJweedman.com." When his petition was denied, he appealed, but the New Jersey Superior Court agreed with the lower court "that 'in his zeal to legalize marijuana . . . [Forchion seeks] to glamorize, persuade others to use marijuana, and to violate the law.'" The court concluded that Forchion's requested name change "implied glamorization by name of a substance that is illegal and prohibited to possess or to use."[a]

After Forchion moved to California, he tried again to change his name legally to "NJweedman.com." Again, his petition was denied, and the appellate court upheld the denial.

The court said that even if Forchion spelled his name "NJweedman DOT COM," it could lead to confusion if Forchion ever lost control of his domain name and someone else used the same name for a Web site. A "DOT COM" personal name could also create confusion because it might be similar to another domain name or a trademark. Finally, the court said that granting Forchion a new personal name that is the same as a Web site that advocates that individuals violate the law was not permissible, even in California where medical marijuana is legal.[b]

Critical Thinking

If a sole proprietor's Web site did not advocate any illegal action, would the courts be likely to allow the proprietor to change his or her name to match the site's domain name? Why or why not?

a. *State v. Forchion,* 182 N.J. 150, 862 A.2d 58 (2004).
b. *In re Forchion,* 198 Cal.App.4th 1284, 130 Cal.Rptr.3d 690 (2011).

other kind of business, as few legal formalities are involved.[1] No documents need to be filed with the government to start a sole proprietorship (though a state business license may be required to operate certain types of businesses).

Flexibility A sole proprietorship also offers more flexibility than does a partnership or a corporation. The sole proprietor is free to make any decision she or he wishes concerning the business—including whom to hire, when to take a vacation, and what kind of business to pursue. In addition, the proprietor can sell or transfer all or part of the business to another party at any time without seeking approval from anyone else. In contrast, approval is typically required from partners in a partnership (see Chapter 27) and from shareholders in a corporation (see Chapter 29).

"Always tell yourself: The difference between running a business and ruining a business is *I*."

Anonymous

Sometimes, a sole proprietor can benefit in a lawsuit from the fact that the business is indistinguishable from the owner. **CASE EXAMPLE 26.1** James Ferguson operated "Jim's 11-E Auto Sales" as a sole proprietorship and obtained insurance from Consumers Insurance Company. The policy was issued to "Jim Ferguson, Jim's 11-E Auto Sales."

Later, Ferguson bought a motorcycle in his own name, intending to repair and sell it through his dealership. One day when he was riding the motorcycle, he was struck by a car and seriously injured. When Ferguson sued Consumers Insurance, the insurer argued that because Ferguson bought the motorcycle in own name and was riding it at the time of the accident, it was his personal vehicle and was not covered under the dealership's policy. The court, however, held that the policy covered Ferguson's injuries. "Because the business is operated as a sole proprietorship, Jim Ferguson and 'Jim's 11-E Auto Sales' are one and the same."[2] •

Taxes A sole proprietor pays only personal income taxes (including Social Security and Medicare taxes) on the business's profits, which are reported as personal income on the proprietor's personal income tax return. Sole proprietors are also allowed to establish retirement accounts that are tax-exempt until the funds are withdrawn.

This sole proprietor enjoys full flexibility about how she runs her business. What are the downsides of this form of business organization?

(YinYang/iStockphoto)

Disadvantages of the Sole Proprietorship

The major disadvantage of the sole proprietorship is that the proprietor alone bears the burden of any losses or liabilities incurred by the business enterprise. In other words, the sole proprietor has unlimited liability, or legal responsibility, for all obligations incurred in doing business. Any lawsuit against the business or its employees can lead to unlimited personal liability for the owner of a sole proprietorship.

The personal liability of a sole proprietorship's owner was at issue in the following *Spotlight Case*. The case involved the federal Cable Communications Act, which prohibits a commercial establishment from broadcasting television programs to its patrons without authorization. The court had to decide whether the owner of the sole proprietorship that had installed a satellite television system was personally liable for violating this act by identifying a restaurant as a "residence" for billing purposes.

1. Although starting a sole proprietorship involves relatively few legal formalities compared with other business organizational forms, even small sole proprietorships may need to comply with certain zoning requirements, obtain appropriate licenses, and the like.
2. *Ferguson v. Jenkins*, 204 S.W.3d 779 (Tenn.App. 2006).

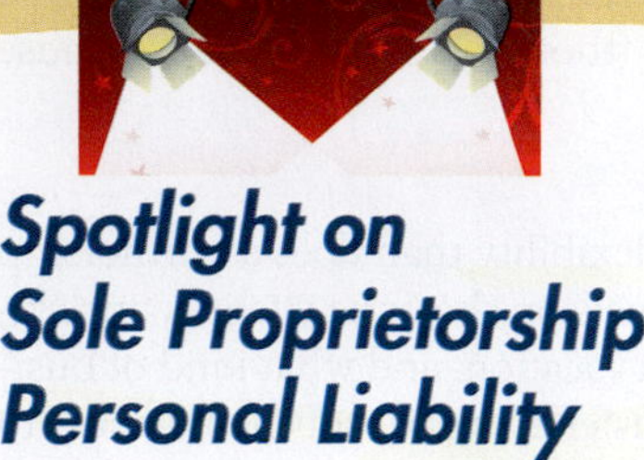

Spotlight on Sole Proprietorship Personal Liability

Case 26.1

Garden City Boxing Club, Inc. v. Dominguez

United States District Court, Northern District of Illinois, Eastern Division, 2006 WL 1517775 (2006).

(AP Photo/Laura Rauch)

Who is liable for paying the fee for closed-circuit broadcast rights to a prizefight?

FACTS Garden City Boxing Club, Inc. (GCB), owned the exclusive right to broadcast several prizefights via closed-circuit television, including the match between Oscar De La Hoya and Fernando Vargas on September 14, 2002. GCB sold the right to receive the broadcasts to bars and other commercial venues. The fee was $20 multiplied by an establishment's maximum fire code occupancy. Antenas Enterprises in Chicago, Illinois, sells and installs satellite television systems under a contract with DISH Network. After installing a system, Antenas sends the buyer's address and other identifying information to DISH. In January 2002, Luis Garcia, an Antenas employee, identified a new customer as José Melendez at 220 Hawthorn Commons in Vernon Hills. The address was a restaurant—Mundelein Burrito—but Garcia designated the account as residential. Mundelein's patrons watched the De La Hoya–Vargas match, as well as three other fights on other dates, for which the restaurant paid only the residential rate to DISH and nothing to GCB. GCB filed a suit in a federal district court against Luis Dominguez, the sole proprietor of Antenas, to collect the fee.

ISSUE Was Dominguez personally liable for the restaurant's commercial fee to GCB?

DECISION Yes. The court issued a summary judgment in GCB's favor, holding that the plaintiff was entitled to the amount of the fee, plus damages and attorneys' fees.

REASON The court found that Mundelein Burrito was clearly a commercial establishment. "The structure of the building, an exterior identification sign, and its location in a strip mall made this obvious." Under the Cable Communications Act, "an authorized intermediary of a communication violates the Act when it divulges communication through an electronic channel to one other than the addressee." Antenas's improper designation of Mundelein Burrito as residential allowed the unauthorized broadcast of four prizefights to the restaurant. Antenas is a sole proprietorship. Furthermore, a sole proprietorship has no legal identity apart from that of the individual who owns it. A sole proprietor is personally responsible for the acts that his or her employees commit within the scope of their employment. Dominguez owns Antenas, and Garcia is Dominguez's employee. "Accordingly, Dominguez is personally liable for the damages caused by the violation of . . . the [Cable Communications] Act."

WHAT IF THE FACTS WERE DIFFERENT? *If Mundelein Burrito had identified itself as a residence when ordering the satellite system, how might the result have been different?*

Personal Assets at Risk Creditors can go after the owner's personal assets to satisfy any business debts. Although sole proprietors may obtain insurance to protect the business, liability can easily exceed policy limits. This unlimited liability is a major factor to be considered in choosing a business form.

EXAMPLE 26.2 Sheila Fowler operates a golf shop near a world-class golf course as a sole proprietorship. One of Fowler's employees fails to secure a display of golf clubs, and they fall on Dean Maheesh, a professional golfer, and seriously injure him. If Maheesh sues Fowler's shop and wins, Fowler's personal liability could easily exceed the limits of her insurance policy. Fowler could lose not only her business, but also her house, car, and any other personal assets that can be attached to pay the judgment. ●

Lack of Continuity The sole proprietorship also has the disadvantage of lacking continuity on the death of the proprietor. When the owner dies, so does the business—it is automatically dissolved. Another disadvantage is that the proprietor's opportunity to raise capital is limited to personal funds and the funds of those who are willing to make loans.

Franchises

Franchise Any arrangement in which the owner of a trademark, trade name, or copyright licenses another to use that trademark, trade name, or copyright in the selling of goods or services.

Franchisee One receiving a license to use another's (the franchisor's) trademark, trade name, or copyright in the sale of goods and services.

Franchisor One licensing another (the franchisee) to use the owner's trademark, trade name, or copyright in the selling of goods or services.

Instead of setting up a business to market their own products or services, many entrepreneurs opt to purchase a franchise. A **franchise** is defined as any arrangement in which the owner of a trademark, a trade name, or a copyright licenses others to use the trademark, trade name, or copyright in the selling of goods or services. A **franchisee** (a purchaser of a franchise) is generally legally independent of the **franchisor** (the seller of the franchise). At the same time, the franchisee is economically dependent on the franchisor's integrated business system. In other words, a franchisee can operate as an independent businessperson but still obtain the advantages of a regional or national organization.

Today, franchising companies and their franchisees account for a significant portion of all retail sales in this country. Well-known franchises include McDonald's, 7-Eleven, and Holiday Inn. Franchising has also become a popular way for businesses to expand their operations internationally, as discussed in this chapter's *Beyond Our Borders* feature on the following page.

Types of Franchises

LEARNING OBJECTIVE 2
What are the most common types of franchises?

Many different kinds of businesses now sell franchises, and numerous types of franchises are available. Generally, though, the majority of franchises fall into one of three classifications: distributorships, chain-style business operations, or manufacturing or processing-plant arrangements.

KNOW THIS

Because a franchise involves the licensing of a trademark, a trade name, or a copyright, the law governing intellectual property may apply in some situations.

Distributorship

In a *distributorship,* a manufacturer (the franchisor) licenses a dealer (the franchisee) to sell its product. Often, a distributorship covers an exclusive territory. Automobile dealerships and beer distributorships are examples of this type of franchise.

EXAMPLE 26.3 Black Snow Beer Company distributes its brands of beer through a network of authorized wholesale distributors, each with an assigned territory. Marik signs a distributorship contract for the area from Gainesville to Ocala, Florida. If the contract states that Marik is the exclusive distributor in that area, then no other franchisee may distribute Black Snow beer in that region. ●

Many franchises operate worldwide. McDonald's is what type of franchise?

(Imaginechina via AP Images)

Chain-Style Business Operation

In a *chain-style business operation,* a franchise operates under a franchisor's trade name and is identified as a member of a select group of dealers that engage in the franchisor's business. The franchisee is generally required to follow standardized or prescribed methods of operation. Often, the franchisor requires that the franchisee maintain certain standards of operation.

In addition, the franchisee may be required to obtain materials and supplies exclusively from the franchisor. McDonald's and most other fast-food chains are examples of this type of franchise. Chain-style franchises are also common in service-related businesses, including real estate brokerage firms such as Century 21 and tax-preparing services such as H&R Block, Inc.

BEYOND OUR BORDERS Franchising in Foreign Nations

In the last twenty years, many U.S. companies (particularly fast-food chains and coffeehouses) have successfully expanded through franchising in nations around the globe. Target locations include Asia and Central and South America, as well as Canada and Mexico in North America. Franchises offer businesses a way to expand internationally without violating the legal restrictions that many nations impose on foreign ownership of businesses.

Cultural and Legal Differences Are Important

Businesspersons must exercise caution when entering international franchise relationships, however. Differences in language, culture, laws, and business practices can seriously complicate the franchising relationship. If a U.S. franchisor's quality control standards do not mesh with local business practices, for example, how can the franchisor maintain the quality of its product and protect its good reputation? If the law in China, for instance, does not provide for a high level of intellectual property protection, how can a U.S. franchisor protect its trademark rights or prevent its secret recipe or formula from being copied?

The Need to Assess the Market

Because of the complexities of international franchising, a company seeking to franchise overseas needs to conduct thorough research to determine whether its business will be well received in the target country. It is important to know the political and cultural climate, as well as the economic trends. Marketing surveys to assess the potential success of the franchise location are crucial.

Also, because compliance with U.S. disclosure laws may not satisfy the legal requirements of other nations, most successful franchisors retain attorneys knowledgeable in the laws of the target location. The attorneys can draft dispute-settlement provisions (such as an arbitration clause) for international franchising contracts and advise the franchisor about the tax implications of operating a foreign franchise (such as import taxes and customs duties).

Critical Thinking

Should a U.S.–based franchisor be allowed to impose contract terms and quality control standards on franchisees in foreign nations that are different from those imposed on domestic franchisees? Why or why not?

Manufacturing or Processing-Plant Arrangement In a *manufacturing or processing-plant arrangement,* the franchisor transmits to the franchisee the essential ingredients or formula to make a particular product. The franchisee then markets the product either at wholesale or at retail in accordance with the franchisor's standards. Examples of this type of franchise are Pepsi-Cola and other soft-drink bottling companies.

Laws Governing Franchising

Because a franchise relationship is primarily a contractual relationship, it is governed by contract law. If the franchise exists primarily for the sale of products manufactured by the franchisor, the law governing sales contracts as expressed in Article 2 of the Uniform Commercial Code applies (see Chapters 15 through 17).

LEARNING OBJECTIVE 3
What laws govern a franchising relationship?

Additionally, the federal government and most states have enacted laws governing certain aspects of franchising. Generally, these laws are designed to protect prospective franchisees from dishonest franchisors and to prohibit franchisors from terminating franchises without good cause.

Federal Regulation of Franchising The federal government regulates franchising through laws that apply to specific industries and through the Franchise Rule, created by the Federal Trade Commission (FTC).

Industry-Specific Standards Congress has enacted laws that protect franchisees in certain industries, such as automobile dealerships and service stations. These laws protect the franchisee from unreasonable demands and bad faith terminations of the franchise by the franchisor. If an automobile manufacturer–franchisor terminates a franchise because of a dealer-franchisee's failure to comply with unreasonable demands (for example, failure to

"You have written more than a book, Ms. McBean—you have written a franchise."

attain an unrealistically high sales quota), the manufacturer may be liable for damages.[3]

Similarly, federal law prescribes the conditions under which a franchisor of service stations can terminate the franchise.[4] Federal antitrust laws (to be discussed in Chapter 32) also apply in certain circumstances to prohibit certain types of anticompetitive agreements.

The Franchise Rule The FTC's Franchise Rule requires franchisors to disclose certain material facts that a prospective franchisee needs to make an informed decision concerning the purchase of a franchise.[5] It was designed to enable potential franchisees to weigh the risks and benefits of an investment. The rule requires the franchisor to make numerous written disclosures to prospective franchisees.

All representations made to a prospective franchisee must have a reasonable basis. For instance, if a franchisor provides projected earnings figures, the franchisor must indicate whether the figures are based on actual data or hypothetical examples. If a franchisor makes sales or earnings projections based on actual data for a specific franchise location, the franchisor must disclose the number and percentage of its existing franchises that have achieved this result.

Franchisors are also required to explain termination, cancellation, and renewal provisions of the franchise contract to potential franchisees before the agreement is signed. Those who violate the Franchise Rule are subject to substantial civil penalties, and the FTC can sue on behalf of injured parties to recover damages.

Online Disclosures The FTC's Franchise Rule has been amended to apply to franchise opportunities advertised on Web sites and communications sent electronically by franchisors. Prospective franchisees must be able to download or save all electronic disclosure documents. Additional disclosures are required about lawsuits that the franchisor has filed and any past settlement agreements.

A franchisor must also disclose whether the franchisor or an affiliate has the right to use other channels of distribution, such as the Internet, to make sales within the franchisee's territory. These amendments bring the federal rule into closer alignment with state franchise disclosure laws. Even as amended, however, the rule does not require franchisors to disclose information about potential earnings.

ETHICAL ISSUE

Should the law require franchisors to give prospective franchisees information about potential earnings? The most common question that entrepreneurs who are thinking about starting a franchise ask is, "How much will I make?" Surprisingly, the law does not require franchisors to provide any estimate of, or actual data on, the earnings potential of a franchise. Franchisors can voluntarily choose to provide earnings data—and if they do, they must follow specific rules, as previously mentioned—but they are not required to do so. About 75 percent of franchisors choose *not* to provide information about earnings potential.

The failure of the latest version of the FTC's Franchise Rule to require disclosure of earnings potential has led to many complaints from franchisees.[6] After all, some franchisees invest their life

---

3. Automobile Dealers' Franchise Act of 1965, also known as the Automobile Dealers' Day in Court Act, 15 U.S.C. Sections 1221 *et seq.*

4. Petroleum Marketing Practices Act (PMPA) of 1979, 15 U.S.C. Sections 2801 *et seq.*

5. 16 C.F.R. Part 436.

6. For example, Beth Tomei and nine other franchisees filed a class-action arbitration claim against their franchisor, Butterfly Life, a women's fitness company, for failure to disclose financial information. The arbitration was dismissed in 2009, however, because the plaintiff-franchisees reportedly failed to pay their allocated share of the arbitration fees.

savings in franchises that ultimately fail because of unrealistic earnings expectations. Moreover, the franchisee may be legally responsible to continue operating and paying the franchisor even when the business is not turning a profit. For instance, Thomas Anderson asked the franchisor, Rocky Mountain Chocolate Factory, Inc. (RMCF), and five of its franchisees for earnings information before he entered into a franchise agreement, but he did not receive any data. Even though his franchise failed to become profitable, Anderson and his partner were ordered by a court to pay $33,109 in past-due royalties and interest to RMCF (plus court costs and expenses).[7]

State Regulation of Franchising State legislation varies but often is aimed at protecting franchisees from unfair practices and bad faith terminations by franchisors. A number of states have laws similar to the federal rules requiring franchisors to provide presale disclosures to prospective franchisees.[8]

Many state laws also require that a disclosure document (known as the Franchise Disclosure Document, or FDD) be registered or filed with a state official, or they may require that the franchisor's advertising be submitted to the state for review or approval. To protect franchisees, a state law may require the disclosure of information such as the actual costs of operation, recurring expenses, and profits earned, along with data substantiating these figures. State deceptive trade practices acts (see Chapter 33) may also apply and prohibit certain types of actions on the part of franchisors.

When a franchisor rebrands its products, does that franchisor have remaining obligations to long-time franchisees who were selling the previous brand?

(Imaginechina via AP Images)

To prevent arbitrary or bad faith terminations, state law may prohibit termination without "good cause" or require that certain procedures be followed in terminating a franchising relationship. **CASE EXAMPLE 26.4** FMS, Inc., entered into a franchise agreement to become an authorized dealership for the sale of Samsung brand construction equipment. Then, Samsung sold its construction-equipment business to Volvo Construction Equipment North America, Inc., which was to continue selling Samsung brand equipment.

Later, Volvo rebranded the construction equipment under its own name and canceled FMS's franchise. FMS sued, claiming Volvo had terminated the franchise without "good cause" in violation of state law. Because Volvo was no longer manufacturing the Samsung brand equipment, however, the court found Volvo did have good cause to terminate FMS's franchise. If Volvo had continued making the Samsung brand equipment, it could not have terminated the FMS franchise, but the statute did not prohibit it from discontinuing the dealership as to the rebranded equipment.[9] ●

The Franchise Contract

LEARNING OBJECTIVE 4
What terms and conditions are typically included in a franchise contract?

The franchise relationship is defined by a contract between the franchisor and the franchisee. The franchise contract specifies the terms and conditions of the franchise and spells out the rights and duties of the franchisor and the franchisee. If either party fails to perform the contractual duties, that party may be subject to a lawsuit for breach of contract. Generally, statutes and case law governing franchising tend to emphasize the importance of good faith and fair dealing in franchise relationships.

7. *Rocky Mountain Chocolate Factory, Inc. v. SDMS, Inc.*, 2009 WL 579516 (D.Colo. 2009).
8. These states include California, Florida, Hawaii, Illinois, Indiana, Maryland, Michigan, Minnesota, New York, North Dakota, Oregon, Rhode Island, South Dakota, Texas, Utah, Virginia, Washington, and Wisconsin.
9. *FMS, Inc. v. Volvo Construction Equipment North America, Inc.*, 557 F.3d 758 (7th Cir. 2009).

Each type of franchise relationship has its own characteristics. We discuss some of the major issues typically found in franchise contracts next. (The *Business Application* feature on page 698 describes some steps a franchisee can take to avoid problems common in franchise agreements.)

Payment for the Franchise

The franchisee ordinarily pays an initial fee or lump-sum price for the franchise license (the privilege of being granted a franchise). This fee is separate from the various products that the franchisee purchases from or through the franchisor. In some industries, the franchisor relies heavily on the initial sale of the franchise for realizing a profit. In other industries, the continued dealing between the parties brings profit to both. In most situations, the franchisor will receive a stated percentage of the annual (or monthly) sales or annual volume of business done by the franchisee. The franchise agreement may also require the franchisee to pay a percentage of advertising costs and certain administrative expenses.

"Business opportunities are like buses, there's always another one coming."

Richard Branson, 1950–present (British entrepreneur)

Business Premises

The franchise agreement may specify whether the premises for the business must be leased or purchased outright. Sometimes, a building must be constructed or remodeled to meet the terms of the agreement. The agreement usually will specify whether the franchisor supplies equipment and furnishings for the premises or whether this is the responsibility of the franchisee.

Location of the Franchise

Typically, the franchisor will determine the territory to be served. Some franchise contracts give the franchisee exclusive rights, or "territorial rights," to a certain geographic area. Other franchise contracts, though they define the territory allotted to a particular franchise, either specifically state that the franchise is nonexclusive or are silent on the issue of territorial rights.

Many franchise cases involve disputes over territorial rights, and the implied covenant of good faith and fair dealing often comes into play in this area of franchising. If the franchise contract does not grant exclusive territorial rights to a franchisee and the franchisor allows a competing franchise to be established nearby, the franchisee may suffer a significant loss in profits. In this situation, a court may hold that the franchisor's actions breached an implied covenant of good faith and fair dealing (see page 695).

Quality Control by the Franchisor

Although the daily operation of the franchise is normally left to the franchisee, the franchise agreement may specify that the franchisor will provide some amount of supervision and control. When the franchisee prepares a product, such as food, or provides a service, such as a motel, the contract often provides that the franchisor will establish certain standards. Typically, the contract will state that the franchisor is permitted to make periodic inspections to ensure that the standards are being maintained so as to protect the franchise's name and reputation.

KNOW THIS

Under the doctrine of *respondeat superior,* an employer may be liable for the torts of employees if they occur within the scope of employment, without regard to the personal fault of the employer.

As a general rule, the validity of a provision permitting the franchisor to establish and enforce certain quality standards is unquestioned. Because the franchisor has a legitimate interest in maintaining the quality of the product or service to protect its name and reputation, it can exercise greater control in this area than would otherwise be tolerated. (Recall from Chapter 23 that in agency relationships the amount of control a principal has over its agent helps to determine whether that principal or franchisor is liable for an agent's actions.)

Pricing Arrangements

Franchises provide the franchisor with an outlet for the firm's goods and services. Depending on the nature of the business, the franchisor may require the franchisee to purchase certain supplies from the franchisor at an established price.[10] A franchisor cannot, however, set the prices at which the franchisee will resell the goods because such price setting may be a violation of state or federal antitrust laws, or both. A franchisor can suggest retail prices but cannot mandate them.

Termination of the Franchise

The duration of the franchise is a matter to be determined between the parties. Sometimes, a franchise will start out for a short period, such as a year, so that the franchisor can determine whether it wants to stay in business with the franchisee. Other times, the duration of the franchise contract correlates with the term of the lease for the business premises, and both are renewable at the end of that period.

Usually, the franchise agreement will specify that termination must be "for cause," such as death or disability of the franchisee, insolvency of the franchisee, breach of the franchise agreement, or failure to meet specified sales quotas. Most franchise contracts provide that notice of termination must be given. If no set time for termination is specified, then a reasonable time, with notice, will be implied. A franchisee must be given reasonable time to wind up the business—that is, to do the accounting and return any property of the franchisor, including confidential proprietary information and trade secrets.

PREVENTING LEGAL DISPUTES

To avoid potential disputes regarding franchise termination, always do preliminary research on a franchisor before agreeing to enter into a franchise contract. Find out whether the franchisor has terminated franchises in the past, how many times, and for what reasons. Contact five to ten franchisees of the same franchisor and ask questions about their relationships and any problems. If the franchisor has been honest, reliable, and reasonable with its franchisees in the past, you will have a better chance of avoiding disputes over wrongful termination in the future.

Wrongful Termination

LEARNING OBJECTIVE 5
What is wrongful termination? In what types of situations do courts typically find that a franchisor has wrongfully terminated a franchise?

Because a franchisor's termination of a franchise often has adverse consequences for the franchisee, much franchise litigation involves claims of wrongful termination. Generally, the termination provisions of contracts are more favorable to the franchisor. This means that the franchisee, who normally invests a substantial amount of time and funds to make the franchise operation successful, may receive little or nothing for the business on termination. The franchisor owns the trademark and hence the business.

It is in this area that statutory and case law become important. The federal and state laws discussed earlier attempts, among other things, to protect franchisees from arbitrary or unfair termination of their franchises by the franchisors.

In the following case, a group of service-station franchisees claimed that their franchisor had violated the Petroleum Marketing Practices Act (PMPA) of 1979, which limits the circumstances in which petroleum franchisors may terminate a franchise. The franchisees contended that changes in the rental provisions of the franchise contract had effectively

10. Although a franchisor can require franchisees to purchase supplies from it, requiring a franchisee to purchase exclusively from the franchisor may violate federal antitrust laws (see Chapter 32).

increased their fuel costs, thereby "constructively" (in effect) terminating the franchises. The franchisees, however, had continued to operate their service stations. Under the PMPA, must a franchisee abandon its franchise in order to recover for constructive termination? That was the issue facing the United States Supreme Court.

Case 26.2

Mac's Shell Service, Inc. v. Shell Oil Products Co.

Supreme Court of the United States,
___ U.S. ___, 130 S.Ct. 1251, 176 L.Ed.2d 36 (2010).
www.supremecourt.gov[a]

(GorazdBertalanic/iStockphoto)

Most Shell gas stations are franchises.

FACTS Shell Oil Company had franchise agreements with various gasoline stations in Massachusetts. Each franchisee was required to pay Shell monthly rent for use of the service-station premises. Shell offered the franchisees a rent subsidy that was dependent on how much gas they sold each month. Shell renewed the subsidies annually through notices that provided for cancellation with thirty days' notice. Later, Shell joined with two other oil companies to create Motiva Enterprises, LLC, and Shell assigned to Motiva its rights and obligations under the relevant franchise agreements.

On January 1, 2000, Motiva ended all volume-based rent subsidies. Sixty-three Shell franchisees filed suit against Shell and Motiva, alleging that the discontinuation of the rent subsidies constituted a breach of contract under state law as well as under the Petroleum Marketing Practices Act (PMPA). They claimed that by eliminating the rent subsidies, Shell and Motiva had "constructively terminated" their franchises in violation of federal law. At trial, the jury found in favor of the plaintiffs-franchisees, and the court entered judgment for the plaintiffs. Shell and Motiva appealed, arguing that they could not be found liable for constructive termination because none of the dealers had abandoned their franchises in response to Motiva's elimination of the rent subsidies. The lower courts affirmed. Shell and Motiva appealed to the United States Supreme Court.

ISSUE Under the PMPA, must a franchisee abandon its franchise in order to recover for constructive termination?

DECISION Yes. The United States Supreme Court reversed the lower court's judgment in favor of the plaintiffs and remanded the case for further proceedings.

REASON The Court focused solely on the question of whether a service-station franchisee may recover for constructive termination when the franchisor's allegedly wrongful conduct did not force the franchisee to abandon its franchise. "We conclude that a necessary element of any constructive termination claim . . . is that the franchisor's conduct forced an end to the franchisee's use of the franchisor's trademark, purchase of the franchisor's fuel, or occupation of the franchisor's service station." The Court held that the Petroleum Marketing Practices Act can be violated "only if an agreement for the use of a trademark, purchase of motor fuel, or lease of a premises is 'put [to] an end' . . . . Conduct that does not force an end to the franchise, in contrast, is not prohibited by the Act's plain terms."

WHAT IF THE FACTS WERE DIFFERENT? *Suppose that this case had involved restaurant franchises rather than gas stations, and that the restaurants continued to operate after Motiva ended volume-based rent subsidies. Could the franchisees claim constructive termination of the franchise in that situation? Explain.*

a. Select "Opinions" under "Supreme Court Documents" in the left column. On the page that opens, under "2009 Term," select "2009 Term Opinions of the Court." In the list of cases that appears, scroll down to "30" and click on the case title to access the opinion. The United States Supreme Court maintains this Web site.

The Importance of Good Faith and Fair Dealing

In determining whether a franchisor has acted in good faith when terminating a franchise agreement, the courts generally try to balance the rights of both parties. If a court perceives that a franchisor has arbitrarily or unfairly terminated a franchise, the franchisee will be provided with a remedy for wrongful termination. If a franchisor's decision to terminate a franchise was made in the normal course of the franchisor's business operations, however, and reasonable notice of termination was given to the franchisee, generally a court will not consider termination wrongful.

CASE EXAMPLE 26.5 Chapin Miller acquired Chic Miller's Chevrolet, a General Motors Corporation (GM) dealership. Chic Miller's entered into financing agreements to enable it to buy new vehicles from GM. At first, the dealership obtained financing through GM, but then it switched to Chase Manhattan Bank. Later, Chase declined to provide further financing, and Chic Miller's was unable to obtain a loan from any other lender, including GM. Under the franchise agreement, GM could terminate a dealership for "Failure of Dealer to maintain the line of credit." GM therefore terminated Chic Miller's franchise. Chic Miller's sued, claiming that GM had failed to act in good faith, but the court held in GM's favor. GM had good cause to terminate the dealership because Chic Miller's failed to maintain financing, which was a material requirement under the franchise agreement.[11] ●

The importance of good faith and fair dealing in a franchise relationship is underscored by the consequences of the franchisor's acts in the following case.

11. *Chic Miller's Chevrolet, Inc. v. General Motors Corp.*, 352 F.Supp.2d 241 (D.Conn. 2005).

Case 26.3

Holiday Inn Franchising, Inc. v. Hotel Associates, Inc.

Court of Appeals of Arkansas, 2011 Ark.App. 147 (2011). opinions.aoc.arkansas.gov[a]

(Photo by Bill Stryker)

What actions by franchisors might constitute fraud?

FACTS Buddy House was in the construction business. For decades, he collaborated on projects with Holiday Inn Franchising, Inc. Their relationship was characterized by good faith—many projects were undertaken without written contracts. At Holiday Inn's request, House inspected a hotel in Wichita Falls, Texas, to estimate the cost of getting it into shape. Holiday Inn wanted House to renovate the hotel and operate it as a Holiday Inn. House estimated that recovering the cost of renovation would take him more than ten years, so he asked for a franchise term longer than Holiday Inn's usual ten years. Holiday Inn refused, but said that if he ran the hotel "appropriately," the term would be extended at the end of ten years. House bought the hotel, renovated it, and operated it as Hotel Associates, Inc. (HAI), generating substantial profits. He refused offers to sell it for as much as $15 million.

Before the ten years had passed, Greg Aden, a Holiday Inn executive, developed a plan to license a different local hotel as a Holiday Inn instead of renewing House's franchise license. Aden stood to earn a commission from licensing the other hotel. No one informed House of Aden's plan. When the time came, HAI applied for an extension of its franchise, and Holiday Inn asked for major renovations. HAI spent $3 million to comply with this request. Holiday Inn did not renew the term for HAI, however, and granted a franchise to the other hotel instead. HAI sold its hotel for $5 million and filed a suit against Holiday Inn, asserting fraud. The court awarded HAI compensatory and punitive damages. Holiday Inn appealed.

ISSUE Did Holiday Inn's failure to inform House that it intended to grant the franchise to a different local hotel constitute fraud?

DECISION Yes. A state intermediate appellate court affirmed the lower court's judgment.

REASON The court recognized that a failure to volunteer information normally does not constitute fraud. But silence can amount to fraud when parties are in a relationship of trust and there is an "inequality" of knowledge between them—for example, when one party has information that the other party is justified in assuming does not exist. In this case, House's relationship with Holiday Inn was characterized by "honesty,

a. In the "Search All Opinions" section, click on "Search Opinions by Docket Number." On that page, in the "Enter Docket Number:" box, type "CA10-21." In the result, click on the name of the case to access the opinion. The Arkansas Judiciary maintains this Web site.

Case 26.3—Continued

trust, and the free flow of pertinent information." With respect to the Wichita Falls hotel, Holiday Inn assured HAI that its franchise would be renewed after ten years if it ran the hotel "appropriately." House was thus justified in assuming that his franchise was not in jeopardy. Holiday Inn, however, knew of Aden's plan to license a different facility in the same area and did not inform House. In these circumstances, the failure to inform was fraud. Even Holiday Inn personnel, including Aden, admitted that House should have been informed. The appellate court also upheld the lower court's award of compensatory damages and increased the amount of punitive damages, citing Holiday Inn's "degree of reprehensibility."

CRITICAL THINKING—Legal Consideration *Why should House and HAI have been advised of Holiday Inn's plan to grant a franchise to a different hotel in their territory?*

Reviewing . . . Sole Proprietorships and Private Franchises

Carlos Del Rey decided to open a fast-food Mexican restaurant and signed a franchise contract with a national chain called La Grande Enchilada. Under the franchise agreement, Del Rey purchased the building, and La Grande Enchilada supplied the equipment. The contract required the franchisee to strictly follow the franchisor's operating manual and stated that failure to do so would be grounds for terminating the franchise contract. The manual set forth detailed operating procedures and safety standards, and provided that a La Grande Enchilada representative would inspect the restaurant monthly to ensure compliance.

Nine months after Del Rey began operating his restaurant, a spark from the grill ignited an oily towel in the kitchen. No one was injured, but by the time firefighters put out the fire, the kitchen had sustained extensive damage. The cook told the fire department that the towel was "about two feet from the grill" when it caught fire, which was in compliance with the franchisor's manual that required towels to be at least one foot from the grills. Nevertheless, the next day La Grande Enchilada notified Del Rey that his franchise would terminate in thirty days for failure to follow the prescribed safety procedures. Using the information presented in the chapter, answer the following questions.

1. What type of franchise was Del Rey's La Grande Enchilada restaurant?
2. If Del Rey operates the restaurant as a sole proprietorship, who bears the loss for the damaged kitchen? Explain.
3. Assume that Del Rey files a lawsuit against La Grande Enchilada, claiming that his franchise was wrongfully terminated. What is the main factor a court would consider in determining whether the franchise was wrongfully terminated?
4. Would a court be likely to rule that La Grande Enchilada had good cause to terminate Del Rey's franchise in this situation? Why or why not?

DEBATE THIS All franchisors should be required by law to provide a comprehensive estimate of the profitability of a prospective franchise based on the experiences of their existing franchisors.

BUSINESS APPLICATION

What Problems Can a Franchisee Anticipate?*

A franchise arrangement appeals to many prospective businesspersons for several reasons. Entrepreneurs who purchase franchises can operate independently and without the risks associated with products that have never before been marketed. Additionally, the franchisee can usually rely on the assistance and guidance of a management network that is regional or national in scope and has been in place for some time.

Franchisees do face potential problems, however. Generally, to avoid possibly significant economic and legal difficulties, it is imperative that you obtain all relevant details about the business and ask an attorney to evaluate the franchise contract for possible pitfalls.

The Franchise Fee

Almost all franchise contracts require a franchise fee payable up front or in installments. This fee often ranges between $10,000 and $50,000. For nationally known franchises, such as McDonald's, the fee may be $500,000 or more. To calculate the true cost of the franchise, however, you must also include the fees that are paid once the franchise opens for business. For example, as a franchisee, you would probably pay 2 to 8 percent of your gross sales as royalties to the franchisor (for the use of the franchisor's trademark, for example). Another 1 to 2 percent of gross sales might go to the franchisor to cover advertising costs. Although your business would benefit from the advertising, the cost of that advertising might exceed the benefits you would realize.

Electronic Encroachment and Termination Provisions

Even when the franchise contract gives the franchisee exclusive territorial rights, many franchisees face problems from so-called electronic encroachment. Encroachment usually occurs when nothing in the franchise agreement prevents the franchisor from selling its products to customers located within the franchisee's territory via the Internet. As a prospective franchisee, you should make sure that your franchise contract covers such contingencies and that its provisions protect you against any losses you might incur from this type of competition.

A major economic consequence, usually of a negative nature, will occur if the franchisor terminates your franchise agreement. Before you sign a franchise contract, make sure that the provisions regarding termination are reasonable, are clearly specified, and provide you with adequate notice and sufficient time to wind up the business.

*This *Business Application* is not meant to substitute for the services of an attorney who is licensed to practice law in your state.

Checklist for the Franchisee

1. *Find out all you can about the franchisor: How long has the franchisor been in business? How profitable is the business? Is there a growing market for the product?*
2. *Obtain the most recent financial statement from the franchisor and a complete description of the business.*
3. *Obtain a clear and complete statement of all fees that you will be required to pay.*
4. *Determine whether the franchisor will help you find a suitable location, train managers and employees, assist with promotion and advertising, and supply capital or credit.*
5. *Visit other franchisees in the same business. Ask them about their profitability and their experiences with the product, the market, and the franchisor.*
6. *Carefully examine the franchise contract provisions relating to termination of the franchise agreement. Find out how many franchises have been terminated in the past several years.*
7. *Will you have an exclusive geographic territory and, if so, for how many years? Does the franchisor have a right to engage in Internet sales to customers within this territory?*
8. *Finally, the most important way to protect yourself is to have an attorney familiar with franchise law examine the contract before you sign it.*

Key Terms

entrepreneur 685
franchise 689
franchisee 689
franchisor 689
sole proprietorship 686

Chapter Summary: Sole Proprietorships and Private Franchises

Sole Proprietorships (See pages 686–689.)	The simplest form of business organization, the sole proprietorship is used by anyone who does business without creating a separate organization. The owner is the business. The owner pays personal income taxes on all profits and is personally liable for all business debts.
Franchises (See pages 689–692.)	1. *Types of franchises*— a. Distributorship (for example, automobile dealerships). b. Chain-style operation (for example, fast-food chains). c. Manufacturing/processing-plant arrangement (for example, soft-drink bottling companies, such as Pepsi-Cola). 2. *Laws governing franchising*—Franchises are governed by contract law. They are also governed by federal and state statutory laws and agency regulation.
The Franchise Contract (See pages 692–694.)	The franchise relationship is defined by a contract between the franchisor and the franchisee. The contract normally spells out the following terms: 1. *Payment for the franchise*—Ordinarily, the contract requires the franchisee (purchaser) to pay an initial fee or lump-sum price for the franchise license. 2. *Business premises*—Specifies whether the business premises will be leased or purchased by the franchisee. 3. *Location of the franchise*—Specifies the territory to be served by the franchisee. 4. *Quality control*—The franchisor may require the franchisee to abide by certain standards of quality relating to the product or service offered. 5. *Pricing arrangements*—The franchisor may require the franchisee to purchase certain supplies from the franchisor at an established price but cannot set retail resale prices.
Termination of the Franchise (See pages 694–697.)	Usually, the contract provides for the date and/or conditions of termination of the franchise arrangement. Both federal and state statutes attempt to protect franchisees from franchisors who unfairly or arbitrarily terminate franchises.

ExamPrep

ISSUE SPOTTERS

1. Frank plans to open a sporting goods store and to hire Gogi and Hap. Frank will invest only his own funds. He expects that he will not make a profit for at least eighteen months and will make only a small profit in the three years after that. He hopes to expand eventually. Would a sole proprietorship be an appropriate form for Frank's business? Why or why not? **(See pages 686–689.)**
2. Thirsty Bottling Company and U.S. Beverages, Inc. (USB), enter into a franchise agreement that states that the franchise may be terminated at any time "for cause." Thirsty fails to meet USB's specified sales quota. Does this constitute "cause" for termination? Why or why not? **(See pages 694–696.)**

—Check your answers to the Issue Spotters against the answers provided in Appendix E at the end of this text.

BEFORE THE TEST

Go to www.cengagebrain.com, enter the ISBN 9781133273561, and click on "Find" to locate this textbook's Web site. Then, click on "Access Now" under "Study Tools," and select Chapter 26 at the top. There, you will find a Practice Quiz that you can take to assess your mastery of the concepts in this chapter, as well as Flashcards, a Glossary of important terms, and Video Questions (when assigned).

For Review

Answers to the even-numbered questions in this For Review section can be found in Appendix F at the end of this text.

1. What advantages and disadvantages are associated with the sole proprietorship?
2. What are the most common types of franchises?

3. What laws govern a franchising relationship?
4. What terms and conditions are typically included in a franchise contract?
5. What is wrongful termination? In what types of situations do courts typically find that a franchisor has wrongfully terminated a franchise?

Business Scenarios and Case Problems

26–1 Franchising. Maria, Pablo, and Vicky are recent college graduates who would like to go into business for themselves. They are considering purchasing a franchise. If they enter into a franchising arrangement, they would have the support of a large company that could answer any questions they might have. Also, a firm that has been in business for many years would be experienced in dealing with some of the problems that novice businesspersons might encounter. These and other attributes of franchises can lessen some of the risks of the marketplace. What other aspects of franchising—positive and negative—should Maria, Pablo, and Vicky consider before committing themselves to a particular franchise? **(See pages 689–692.)**

26–2 Question with Sample Answer—Control of a Franchise. National Foods, Inc., sells franchises to its fast-food restaurants, known as Chicky-D's. Under the franchise agreement, franchisees agree to hire and train employees strictly according to Chicky-D's standards, and Chicky-D's regional supervisors must approve all new hires and policies, though this is routinely done. Chicky-D's reserves the right to terminate a franchise for violating the franchisor's rules. After several incidents of racist comments and conduct by Tim, a recently hired assistant manager at a Chicky-D's, Sharon, a counterperson at the restaurant, resigns. Sharon files a suit against National. National files a motion for summary judgment, arguing that it is not liable for harassment by franchise employees. Will the court grant National's motion? Why or why not? **(See page 693.)**

—For a sample answer to Question 26–2, go to Appendix G at the end of this text.

26–3 Spotlight on McDonald's—Franchise Termination. C.B. Management, Inc., had a franchise agreement with McDonald's Corp to operate McDonald's restaurants in Cleveland, Ohio. The agreement required C.B. to make monthly payments of certain percentages of the gross sales to McDonald's. If any payment was more than thirty days late, McDonald's had the right to terminate the franchise. The agreement also stated that even if McDonald's accepted a late payment, that would not "constitute a waiver of any subsequent breach." McDonald's sometimes accepted C.B.'s late payments, but when C.B. defaulted on the payments in July 2010, McDonald's gave notice of thirty days to comply or surrender possession of the restaurants. C.B. missed the deadline. McDonald's demanded that C.B. vacate the restaurants, but C.B. refused. McDonald's alleged that C.B. had violated the franchise agreement. C.B. claimed that McDonald's had breached the implied covenant of good faith and fair dealing. Which party should prevail and why? [*McDonald's Corp. v. C.B. Management Co.*, 13 F.Supp.2d 705 (N.D.Ill. 1998)] **(See pages 695–696.)**

26–4 Sole Proprietorship. Julie Anne Gaskill is an oral and maxillofacial surgeon in Bowling Green, Kentucky. Her medical practice is a sole proprietorship consisting of her as the sole surgeon, with office staff. She sees every patient, exercises all professional judgment and skill, and manages the business. When Gaskill and her spouse, John Robbins, initiated divorce proceedings in a Kentucky state court, her accountant estimated the value of the practice at $221,610, excluding goodwill. Robbins's accountant estimated the value at $669,075, including goodwill. Goodwill is the ability or reputation of a business to draw customers, get them to return, and contribute to future profitability. How can a sole proprietor's reputation, skill, and relationships with customers be valued? Could these qualities be divided into "personal" and "enterprise" goodwill, with some goodwill associated with the business and some solely due to the personal qualities of the proprietor? If so, what might comprise each type? Is this an effective method for valuing Gaskill's practice? Discuss. [*Gaskill v. Robbins*, 282 S.W.3d 306 (Ky. 2009)] **(See pages 686–689.)**

26–5 Franchise Disclosure. Peaberry Coffee, Inc., owned and operated about twenty company stores in the Denver area. The company began a franchise program and prepared a disclosure document as required by the Federal Trade Commission (FTC). Peaberry sold ten franchises, and each franchisee received a disclosure document. Later, when the franchises did not do well, the franchisees sued Peaberry, claiming that its FTC disclosure document had been fraudulent. Specifically, the franchisees claimed that Peaberry had not disclosed that most of the company stores were unprofitable and that its parent company had suffered significant financial losses over the years. In addition, Peaberry had included, in the franchisees' information packets, an article from the *Denver Business Journal* in which an executive had said that Peaberry was profitable. The FTC disclosure document had also contained an exculpatory clause (see Chapter 13), which said that the buyers should not rely on any material that was not in the franchise contract itself. Can a franchisor disclaim the relevance of the information it provides to franchisees? Why or why not? [*Colorado Coffee Bean, LLC v. Peaberry Coffee, Inc.*, 2010 WL 3031448 (Colo.App. 2010)] **(See pages 691–692.)**

26–6 The Franchise Contract. Kubota Tractor Corp. makes farm, industrial, and outdoor equipment. Its franchise contracts allow Kubota to enter into dealership agreements with "others at any location." Kejzar Motors, Inc., is a Kubota dealer in Nacogdoches and Jasper, Texas. These two Kejzar stores operate as one dealership with two locations. Kubota granted a dealership to Michael Hammer in Lufkin, Texas, which lies between Kejzar's two store locations. Kejzar filed a suit in a Texas state court against Kubota. Kejzar asked for an injunction to prevent Kubota from locating a dealership in the same market area. Kejzar argued that the new location would cause it to suffer a significant loss of profits. Which party in a franchise relationship typically determines the territory served by a franchisee? Which legal principles come into play in this area? How do these concepts most likely apply in this case? Discuss. [*Kejzar Motors, Inc. v. Kubota Tractor Corp.*, 334 S.W.3d 351 (Tex.App.—Tyler 2011)] **(See page 693.)**

26–7 **Case Problem with Sample Answer—Wrongful Termination of Franchise.** George Oshana and GTO Investments, Inc., operated a Mobil gas station franchise in Itasca, Illinois. In 2010, Oshana and GTO became involved in a rental dispute with Buchanan Energy, to which Mobil had assigned the lease. In November 2011, Buchanan terminated the franchise because Oshana and GTO had failed to pay the rent. Oshana and GTO, however, alleged that they were "ready, willing, and able to pay the rent" but that Buchanan failed to accept their electronic funds transfer. Have Oshana and GTO stated a claim for wrongful termination of their franchise? Why or why not? [*Oshana v. Buchanan Energy*, 2012 WL 426921 (N.D.Ill. 2012)] **(See pages 694–695.)**

—For a sample answer to Problem 26–7, go to Appendix H at the end of this text.

26–8 **A Question of Ethics—Sole Proprietorships.** In August 2004, Ralph Vilardo contacted Travel Center, Inc., in Cincinnati, Ohio, to buy a trip to Florida in December for his family to celebrate his fiftieth wedding anniversary. Vilardo paid $6,900 to David Sheets, the sole proprietor of Travel Center. Vilardo also paid $195 to Sheets for a separate trip to Florida in February 2005. Sheets assured Vilardo that everything was set, but in fact no arrangements were made. Later, two unauthorized charges for travel services totaling $1,182.35 appeared on Vilardo's credit-card statement. Vilardo filed a suit in an Ohio state court against Sheets and his business, alleging, among other things, fraud and violations of the state consumer protection law. Vilardo served Sheets and Travel Center with copies of the complaint, the summons, a request for admissions, and other documents filed with the court, including a motion for summary judgment. Responses to each of these filings were subject to certain time limits. Sheets responded once on his own behalf with a denial of all of Vilardo's claims. Travel Center did not respond. [*Vilardo v. Sheets*, 2006 WL 1843585 (12 Dist. 2006)] **(See pages 686–689.)**

1. Almost four months after Vilardo filed his complaint, Sheets decided that he was unable to adequately represent himself and retained an attorney who asked the court for more time. Should the court grant this request? Why or why not? Ultimately, what should the court rule in this case?
2. Sheets admitted that "Travel Center" was a sole proprietorship. He also argued that liability might be imposed on his business but not on himself. How would you rule with respect to this argument? Would there be anything unethical about allowing Sheets to avoid liability on this basis? Explain.

Critical Thinking and Writing Assignments

26–9 **Business Law Writing.** Jordan Mendelson is interested in starting a kitchen franchise business. Customers will come to the business to assemble gourmet dinners and then take the prepared meals to their homes for cooking. The franchisor requires each store to use a specific layout and provides the recipes for various dinners, but the franchisee is not required to purchase the food products from the franchisor. What general factors should Mendelson consider before entering into a contract to start such a franchise? Is location important? Are there any laws that Mendelson should consider, given that this franchise involves food preparation and sales? Should Mendelson operate this business as a sole proprietorship? Why or why not?

26–10 **Business Law Critical Thinking Group Assignment.** Walid Elkhatib, an Arab American, bought a Dunkin' Donuts franchise in Illinois. Ten years later, Dunkin' Donuts began offering breakfast sandwiches with bacon, ham, or sausage through its franchises. Elkhatib refused to sell these items at his store on the ground that his religion forbade the handling of pork. Elkhatib then opened a second franchise, at which he also refused to sell pork products. The next year, at both locations, Elkhatib began selling meatless sandwiches. He also opened a third franchise. When he proposed to relocate this franchise, Dunkin' Donuts refused to approve the new location and informed him that it would not renew any of his franchise agreements because he did not carry the full sandwich line. Elkhatib filed a lawsuit against Dunkin' Donuts.

1. The first group will argue on behalf of Elkhatib that Dunkin' Donuts wrongfully terminated his franchises.
2. The second group will take the side of Dunkin' Donuts and justify its decision to terminate the franchises.
3. The third group will assess whether Dunkin' Donuts acted in good faith in its relationship with Elkhatib. Also, consider whether Dunkin' Donuts should be required to accommodate Elkhatib's religious beliefs and allow him not to serve pork in these three locations.

27 CHAPTER

All Forms of Partnership

CHAPTER OUTLINE

- Basic Partnership Concepts
- Partnership Formation
- Partnership Operation, Dissociation, and Termination
- Limited Liability Partnerships
- Limited Partnerships

LEARNING OBJECTIVES

The five learning objectives below are designed to help improve your understanding of the chapter. After reading this chapter, you should be able to answer the following questions:

1 What are the three essential elements of a partnership?

2 What are the rights and duties of partners in an ordinary partnership?

3 What is meant by joint and several liability? Why is this often considered to be a disadvantage of the partnership form of business?

4 What advantages do limited liability partnerships offer to businesspersons that are not offered by general partnerships?

5 What are the key differences between the rights and liabilities of general partners and those of limited partners?

(lisegagne/iStockphoto.com)

"All men's gains . . . are the fruit of venturing."
—Herodotus, Fifth Century B.C.E. (Greek historian)

Traditionally, the two most common forms of business organization selected when two or more persons go into business together have been the partnership and the corporation. A *partnership* arises from an agreement, express or implied, between two or more persons to carry on a business for profit. Partners are co-owners of a business and have joint control over its operation and the right to share in its profits. As the chapter-opening quotation indicates, all gains are the "fruit of venturing," and partnerships—to the extent that they encourage business ventures—contribute to those gains.

The chapter opens with an examination of ordinary partnerships, or *general partnerships*, and the rights and duties of partners in this traditional business entity. We then examine some special forms of partnerships known as *limited liability partnerships* and *limited partnerships*, which receive different treatment under the law.

Although general partnerships are less common today than in the past, the limited liability forms of partnership are quite prevalent. Accountants and attorneys frequently organize as limited liability partnerships. Dewey & LeBoeuf, LLP, for instance, was one of the largest global law firms in New York before it filed for bankruptcy in 2012. Those entering the business world need to understand the rights and liabilities associated with the various types of partnerships discussed in this chapter.

Basic Partnership Concepts

Partnerships are governed both by common law concepts—in particular, those relating to agency—and by statutory law. As in so many other areas of business law, the National Conference of Commissioners on Uniform State Laws has drafted uniform laws for partnerships, and these uniform laws have been widely adopted by the states.

Agency Concepts and Partnership Law

KNOW THIS

Two or more persons are required to form a partnership. Other forms of business can be organized by a single individual.

When two or more persons agree to do business as partners, they enter into a special relationship with one another. To an extent, their relationship is similar to an agency relationship because each partner is deemed to be the agent of the other partners and of the partnership. Thus, the common law agency concepts outlined in Chapter 23 apply—specifically, the imputation of knowledge of, and responsibility for, acts done within the scope of the partnership relationship. In their relationships with one another, partners, like agents, are bound by fiduciary ties.

In one important way, however, partnership law is distinct from agency law. A partnership is based on a voluntary contract between two or more competent persons who agree to commit financial capital, labor, and skill to a business with the understanding that profits and losses will be shared. In a nonpartnership agency relationship, the agent usually does not have an ownership interest in the business, and he or she is not obliged to bear a portion of the ordinary business losses.

The Uniform Partnership Act

The Uniform Partnership Act (UPA) governs the operation of partnerships *in the absence of an express agreement* and has done much to reduce controversies concerning the law relating to partnerships. In other words, the partners are free to establish rules for their partnership that differ from those stated in the UPA. Except for Louisiana, every state has adopted the UPA, but if they do not, the UPA governs.

The majority of the states have adopted the most recent version of the UPA, which was issued in 1994 and amended in 1997 to provide limited liability for partners in a limited liability partnership.[1] We therefore base our discussion of the UPA in this chapter on the 1997 version of the act and refer to older versions of the UPA in footnotes when appropriate.

Definition of a Partnership

Partnership An agreement by two or more persons to carry on, as co-owners, a business for profit.

The UPA defines a **partnership** as "an association of two or more persons to carry on as co-owners a business for profit" [UPA 101(6)]. Note that the UPA's definition of *person* includes corporations, so a corporation can be a partner in a partnership [UPA 101(10)]. The *intent* to associate is a key element of a partnership, and a person cannot join a partnership unless all of the other partners consent [UPA 401(i)].

1. At the time this book went to press, more than two-thirds of the states, as well as the District of Columbia, Puerto Rico, and the U.S. Virgin Islands, had adopted the UPA with the 1997 amendments. Excerpts from the latest version of the UPA are presented on the Web site that accompanies this text.

When Does a Partnership Exist?

Parties sometimes find themselves in conflict over whether their business enterprise is a legal partnership, especially when there is no formal, written partnership agreement. In determining whether a partnership exists, courts usually look for the following three essential elements, which are implicit in the UPA's definition of a general partnership:

LEARNING OBJECTIVE 1
What are the three essential elements of a partnership?

1. A sharing of profits and losses.
2. A joint ownership of the business.
3. An equal right to be involved in the management of the business.

If the evidence in a particular case is insufficient to establish all three factors, the UPA provides a set of guidelines to be used.

Joint Ownership and Shared Profits Are Usually Not Sufficient

Joint ownership of property does not in and of itself create a partnership. In fact, the sharing of gross revenues and even profits from such ownership "does not by itself establish a partnership" [UPA 202(c)(1), (2)]. **EXAMPLE 27.1** Chiang and Burke jointly own farmland and lease it to a farmer for a share of the profits from the farming operation in lieu of fixed rental payments. This arrangement normally would not make Chiang, Burke, and the farmer partners. ●

In addition, a partnership will not be presumed to exist if shared profits were received as payment of any of the following [UPA 202(c)(3)]:

1. A debt by installments or interest on a loan.
2. Wages of an employee or payment for the services of an independent contractor.
3. Rent to a landlord.
4. An annuity to a surviving spouse or representative of a deceased partner.
5. A sale of the **goodwill**—the valuable reputation of a business viewed as an intangible asset—of a business or property.

Goodwill The market value of the good reputation of any company, partnership, or other business entity.

EXAMPLE 27.2 A debtor, Mason Snopel, owes a creditor, Alice Burns, $5,000 on an unsecured debt. They agree that Mason will pay 10 percent of his monthly business profits to Alice until the loan with interest has been paid. Although Mason and Alice are sharing profits from the business, they are not presumed to be partners. ●

Sharing Profits and Losses Usually Does Create a Partnership

While the sharing of profits from the joint ownership of property does not prove the existence of a partnership, sharing *both profits and losses* usually does.

EXAMPLE 27.3 Two sisters, Zoe and Cienna, buy a restaurant together, open a joint bank account from which they pay for expenses and supplies, and share the net profits (and losses) that the restaurant generates. Zoe manages the restaurant and Cienna handles the bookkeeping. After eight years, Cienna stops doing the bookkeeping and does no other work for the restaurant. Zoe, who is now operating the restaurant by herself, no longer wants to share the profits with Cienna. Zoe claims that she and Cienna did not establish a partnership. A court would probably find that a partnership existed because the sisters shared management responsibilities, had a joint bank account, and shared the profits *and losses* of the restaurant equally. ●

What determines if a partnership exists between two individuals working together in the same business?

(kzenon/iStockphoto)

Entity versus Aggregate Theory of Partnerships

At common law, a partnership was treated only as an aggregate of individuals and never as a separate legal entity. Thus, at common law a lawsuit could never be brought by or against the firm in its own name. Each individual partner had to sue or be sued.

Today, in contrast, a majority of the states follow the UPA and treat a partnership as an entity for most purposes. For example, a partnership usually can sue or be sued, collect judgments, and have all accounting procedures in the name of the partnership entity [UPA 201, 307(a)]. As an entity, a partnership may hold the title to real or personal property in its name rather than in the names of the individual partners. Additionally, federal procedural laws permit the partnership to be treated as an entity in suits in federal courts and bankruptcy proceedings.

Tax Treatment of Partnerships

Pass-Through Entity A business entity that has no tax liability. The entity's income is passed through to the owners, and they pay taxes on the income.

Information Return A tax return submitted by a partnership that only reports the business's income and losses. The partnership itself does not pay taxes on the income, but each partner's share of the profit (whether distributed or not) is taxed as individual income to that partner.

Modern law does treat a partnership as an aggregate of the individual partners rather than as a separate legal entity in one situation—for federal income tax purposes. The partnership is a pass-through entity and not a taxpaying entity. A **pass-through entity** is a business entity that has no tax liability—the entity's income is passed through to the owners of the entity, who pay income taxes on it.

Thus, the income or losses the partnership incurs are "passed through" the entity framework and attributed to the partners on their individual tax returns. The partnership itself has no tax liability and is responsible only for filing an **information return** with the Internal Revenue Service. The firm itself pays no taxes. A partner's profit from the partnership (whether distributed or not) is taxed as individual income to the individual partner. Similarly, partners can deduct a share of the partnership's losses on their individual tax returns (in proportion to their partnership interests).

Partnership Formation

Articles of Partnership A written agreement that sets forth each partner's rights and obligations with respect to the partnership.

As a general rule, agreements to form a partnership can be *oral, written,* or *implied by conduct.* Some partnership agreements, however, must be in writing (or an electronic record) to be legally enforceable under the Statute of Frauds (see Chapter 12 for details).

A partnership agreement, called **articles of partnership**, can include any terms that the parties wish, unless they are illegal or contrary to public policy or statute [UPA 103]. The terms commonly included in a partnership agreement are listed in Exhibit 27.1 on the following page. (Creating a partnership agreement in another country may involve additional requirements, as this chapter's *Beyond Our Borders* feature below explains.)

BEYOND OUR BORDERS Doing Business with Foreign Partners

U.S. businesspersons who wish to operate a partnership in another country often discover that the country requires local participation. This means that nationals of the host country must own a specific share of the business. In other words, the partnership will have to include one or more partners who live in the host country. Sometimes, U.S. businesspersons are reluctant to establish partnerships in a country that requires local participation. They fear that if the partnership breaks up, the technology and expertise developed by the partnership business may end up in the hands of a future competitor. In that event, the U.S. parties may have little recourse under the host country's laws against their former partners' use of the intellectual property.

Critical Thinking

Do local participation rules benefit countries in the long run? Explain.

Exhibit 27.1 **Common Terms Included in a Partnership Agreement**

TERM	DESCRIPTION
Basic Structure	1. Name of the partnership. 2. Names of the partners. 3. Location of the business and the state law under which the partnership is organized. 4. Purpose of the partnership. 5. Duration of the partnership.
Capital Contributions	1. Amount of capital that each partner is contributing. 2. The agreed-on value of any real or personal property that is contributed instead of cash. 3. How losses and gains on contributed capital will be allocated, and whether contributions will earn interest.
Sharing of Profits and Losses	1. Percentage of the profits and losses of the business that each partner will receive. 2. When distributions of profit will be made and how net profit will be calculated.
Management and Control	1. How management responsibilities will be divided among the partners. 2. Name(s) of the managing partner or partners, and whether other partners have voting rights.
Accounting and Partnership Records	1. Name of the bank in which the partnership will maintain its business and checking accounts. 2. Statement that an accounting of partnership records will be maintained and that any partner or her or his agent can review these records at any time. 3. The dates of the partnership's fiscal year (if used) and when the annual audit of the books will take place.
Dissociation and Dissolution	1. Events that will cause the dissociation of a partner or dissolve the partnership, such as the retirement, death, or incapacity of any partner. 2. How partnership property will be valued and apportioned on dissociation and dissolution. 3. Whether an arbitrator will determine the value of partnership property on dissociation and dissolution and whether that determination will be binding.
Arbitration	1. Whether arbitration is required for any dispute relating to the partnership agreement.

Duration of the Partnership

The partnership agreement can specify the duration of the partnership by stating that it will continue until a certain date or the completion of a particular project. A partnership that is specifically limited in duration is called a *partnership for a term.* Generally, withdrawing prematurely (before the expiration date) from a partnership for a term constitutes a breach of the agreement, and the responsible partner can be held liable for any resulting losses [UPA 602(b)(2)]. If no fixed duration is specified, the partnership is a *partnership at will.*

Partnership by Estoppel

Partnership by Estoppel Partnership liability imposed by a court on persons who have held themselves out to be partners, even though they were not, and others have detrimentally relied on their representations.

Occasionally, persons who are not partners may nevertheless hold themselves out as partners and make representations that third parties rely on in dealing with them. In such a situation, a court may conclude that a **partnership by estoppel** exists. The law does not confer any partnership rights on these persons, but it may impose liability on them. This is also true when a partner represents, expressly or impliedly, that a nonpartner is a member of the firm. Whenever a third person has reasonably and detrimentally relied on the representation that a nonpartner was part of the partnership, a partnership by estoppel is deemed to exist. When this occurs, the nonpartner is regarded as an agent whose acts are binding on the partnership [UPA 308].

CASE EXAMPLE 27.4 Jackson Paper Manufacturing Company makes paper that is used by Stonewall Packaging, LLC. Jackson and Stonewall have officers and directors in common, and they share employees, property, and equipment. In reliance on Jackson's business reputation, Best Cartage, Inc., agreed to provide transportation services for Stonewall and bought thirty-seven tractor-trailers to use in fulfilling the contract. Best provided the services until Stonewall terminated the agreement.

Best filed a suit for breach of contract against Stonewall and Jackson, seeking $500,678 in unpaid invoices and consequential damages of $1,315,336 for the tractor-trailers it had purchased. Best argued that Stonewall and Jackson had a partnership by estoppel. The court agreed, finding that "defendants combined labor, skills, and property to advance their alleged business partnership." Jackson had negotiated the agreement on Stonewall's behalf, and a news release stated that Jackson had sought tax incentives for Stonewall. Jackson also had bought real estate, equipment, and general supplies for Stonewall with no expectation of payment. This was sufficient to prove a partnership by estoppel.[2]

Partnership Operation, Dissociation, and Termination

The rights and duties of partners are governed largely by the specific terms of their partnership agreement. In the absence of provisions to the contrary in the partnership agreement, the law imposes the rights and duties discussed here. The character and nature of the partnership business generally influence the application of these rights and duties.

Rights of Partners

The rights of partners in a partnership relate to the following areas: management, interest in the partnership, compensation, inspection of books, accounting, and property.

LEARNING OBJECTIVE 2
What are the rights and duties of partners in an ordinary partnership?

Management Rights

In a general partnership, all partners have equal rights in managing the partnership [UPA 401(f)]. Unless the partners agree otherwise, each partner has one vote in management matters *regardless of the proportional size of his or her interest in the firm.* Often, in a large partnership, partners will agree to delegate daily management responsibilities to a management committee made up of one or more of the partners.

The majority rule controls decisions in ordinary matters connected with partnership business, unless otherwise specified in the agreement. Decisions that significantly affect the nature of the partnership or that are not apparently for carrying on the ordinary course of the partnership business, or business of the partnership's kind, however, require the *unanimous* consent of the partners [UPA 301(2), 401(i), (j)].

Unanimous consent is likely to be required for a decision to undertake any of the following actions:

1. Alter the essential nature of the firm's business as expressed in the partnership agreement or alter the capital structure of the partnership.
2. Admit new partners or enter a wholly new business.
3. Assign partnership property to a trust for the benefit of creditors.
4. Dispose of the partnership's *goodwill* (defined on page 704).
5. Confess judgment against the partnership or submit partnership claims to arbitration. (A **confession of judgment** is the act of a debtor permitting a judgment to be entered against her or him by a creditor, for an agreed sum, without the institution of legal proceedings.)
6. Undertake any act that would make further conduct of partnership business impossible.
7. Amend the partnership agreement.

Confession of Judgment The act or agreement of a debtor permitting a judgment to be entered against him or her by a creditor, for an agreed sum, without the institution of legal proceedings.

Interest in the Partnership

Each partner is entitled to the proportion of business profits and losses designated in the partnership agreement. If the agreement does not apportion profits (indicate how the profits will be shared), the UPA provides that profits will be shared equally. If the agreement does not apportion losses, losses will be shared in the same ratio as profits [UPA 401(b)].

2. *Best Cartage, Inc. v. Stonewall Packaging, LLC*, 727 S.E.2d 291 (N.C.App. 2012).

EXAMPLE 27.5 The partnership agreement for Rico and Brent provides for capital contributions of $60,000 from Rico and $40,000 from Brent, but it is silent as to how Rico and Brent will share profits or losses. In this situation, Rico and Brent will share both profits and losses equally. If their partnership agreement provided for profits to be shared in the same ratio as capital contributions, however, 60 percent of the profits would go to Rico, and 40 percent would go to Brent. If this partnership agreement was silent as to losses, losses would be shared in the same ratio as profits (60 percent and 40 percent, respectively). •

> "Forty for you, sixty for me—and equal partners we will be."
>
> Anonymous

Compensation

Devoting time, skill, and energy to partnership business is a partner's duty and generally is not a compensable service. Rather, as mentioned, a partner's income from the partnership takes the form of a distribution of profits according to the partner's share in the business. Partners can, of course, agree otherwise. For instance, the managing partner of a law firm often receives a salary—in addition to her or his share of profits—for performing special administrative or managerial duties.

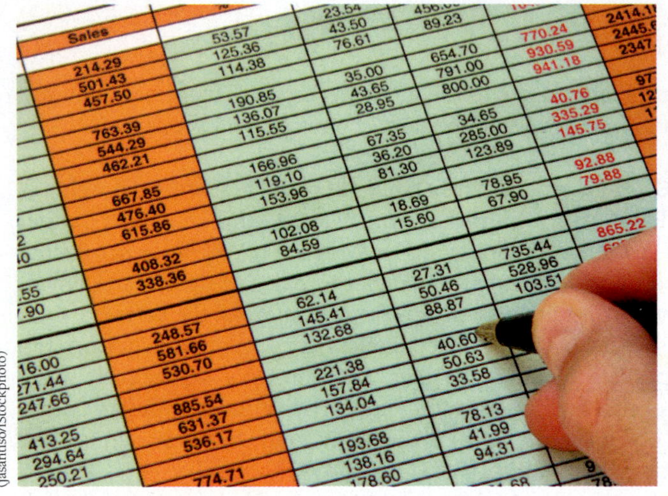

(jasantiso/iStockphoto)

Who has the right to inspect a partnership's books and records?

Inspection of Books

Partnership books and records must be accessible to all partners. Each partner has the right to receive (and the corresponding duty to produce) full and complete information concerning the conduct of all aspects of partnership business [UPA 403]. Each firm keeps books for recording and preserving such information. Partners contribute the information, and a bookkeeper or an accountant typically has the duty to preserve it. The books must be kept at the firm's principal business office and cannot be removed without the consent of all of the partners.

Every partner, whether active or inactive, is entitled to inspect all books and records on demand and can make copies of the materials. The personal representative of a deceased partner's estate has the same right of access to partnership books and records that the decedent would have had [UPA 403].

Accounting of Partnership Assets or Profits

An accounting of partnership assets or profits is required to determine the value of each partner's share in the partnership. An accounting can be performed voluntarily, or it can be compelled by court order. Under UPA 405(b), a partner has the right to bring an action for an accounting during the term of the partnership, as well as on the partnership's *dissolution* and *winding up* (see pages 713–715).

Property Rights

Property acquired *by* a partnership is the property of the partnership and not of the partners individually [UPA 203]. Partnership property includes all property that was originally contributed to the partnership and anything later purchased by the partnership or in the partnership's name (except in rare circumstances) [UPA 204]. A partner may use or possess partnership property only on behalf of the partnership [UPA 401(g)]. A partner is *not* a co-owner of partnership property and has no right to sell, mortgage, or transfer partnership property.

In other words, partnership property is owned by the partnership as an entity and not by the individual partners. Thus, partnership property cannot be used to satisfy the personal debt of an individual partner. That partner's creditor, however, can petition a court for a **charging order** to attach the partner's *interest* in the partnership (her or his proportionate share of the profits and losses and right to receive distributions) to satisfy the partner's obligation. (A partner can also assign her or his right to a share of the partnership profits to another to satisfy a debt.)

Charging Order In partnership law, an order granted by a court to a judgment creditor that entitles the creditor to attach a partner's interest in the partnership.

Duties and Liabilities of Partners

The duties and liabilities of partners are basically derived from agency law. Each partner is an agent of every other partner and acts as both a principal and an agent in any business transaction within the scope of the partnership agreement.

Each partner is also a general agent of the partnership in carrying out the usual business of the firm "or business of the kind carried on by the partnership" [UPA 301(1)]. Thus, every act of a partner concerning partnership business, or "business of the kind," and every contract signed in the partnership's name bind the firm.

Fiduciary Duties

The fiduciary duties a partner owes to the partnership and the other partners are the *duty of care* and the *duty of loyalty* [UPA 404(a)]. Under the UPA, a partner's duty of care involves refraining from "grossly negligent or reckless conduct, intentional misconduct, or a knowing violation of law" [UPA 404(c)]. A partner is not liable to the partnership for simple negligence or honest errors in judgment in conducting partnership business, though.

The duty of loyalty requires a partner to account to the partnership for "any property, profit, or benefit" derived by the partner from the partnership's business or the use of its property [UPA 404(b)]. A partner must also refrain from competing with the partnership in business or dealing with the firm as an adverse party.

The duty of loyalty can be breached by self-dealing, misusing partnership property, disclosing trade secrets, or usurping a partnership business opportunity, as the following *Classic Case* illustrates.

Classic Case 27.1

Meinhard v. Salmon

Court of Appeals of New York,
249 N.Y. 458, 164 N.E. 545 (1928).
www.nycourts.gov/reporter/Index.htm[a]

(olaser/iStockphoto)

What fiduciary duties does a partner have with respect to renewing a hotel lease?

FACTS Walter Salmon negotiated a twenty-year lease for the Hotel Bristol in New York City. To pay for the conversion of the building into shops and offices, Salmon entered into an agreement with Morton Meinhard to assume half of the cost. They agreed to share the profits and losses from the joint venture (a *joint venture* is similar to a partnership but typically is created for a single project, whereas a partnership usually involves an ongoing business), but Salmon was to have the sole power to manage the building. Less than four months before the end of the lease term, the building's owner approached Salmon about a project to raze the converted structure and construct a new building. Salmon agreed and signed a new lease in the name of his own business, Midpoint Realty Company, without telling Meinhard. When Meinhard learned of the deal, he filed a suit against Salmon. From a judgment in Meinhard's favor, Salmon appealed.

ISSUE Did Salmon breach his fiduciary duty of loyalty to Meinhard?

DECISION Yes. The Court of Appeals of New York held that Salmon had breached his fiduciary duty by failing to inform Meinhard of the business opportunity and secretly taking advantage of it for himself. The court therefore granted Meinhard an interest "measured by the value of half of the entire lease."

REASON The court stated, "Joint adventurers, like copartners, owe to one another, while the enterprise continues, the duty of the finest loyalty." Salmon's conduct excluded Meinhard from any chance to compete and from any chance to enjoy the opportunity for benefit. As a partner, Salmon was bound by his "obligation to his copartners in such dealings not to separate his interest from theirs, but, if he acquires any benefit, to communicate it to them." Salmon was also the managing coadventurer, and thus the court found that "for him and for those like him the rule of undivided loyalty is relentless and supreme."

a. In the links at the bottom of the page, click on "Archives." In the result, scroll to the name of the case and click on it to access the opinion. The New York State Law Reporting Bureau maintains this Web site.

Classic Case 27.1—Continues next page

Classic Case 27.1—Continued

WHAT IF THE FACTS WERE DIFFERENT? *Suppose that Salmon had disclosed the proposed deal to Meinhard, who had said that he was not interested. Would the result in this case have been different? Explain.*

IMPACT OF THIS CASE ON TODAY'S LAW *This landmark case involved a joint venture, not a partnership. At the time, a member of a joint venture had only the duty to refrain from actively subverting the rights of the other members. The decision in this case imposed the highest standard of loyalty on joint-venture members. The duty is now the same in both joint ventures and partnerships. The eloquent language in this case that describes the standard of loyalty is frequently quoted approvingly by courts in cases involving partnerships.*

Breach and Waiver of Fiduciary Duties A partner's fiduciary duties may not be waived or eliminated in the partnership agreement, and in fulfilling them each partner must act consistently with the obligation of good faith and fair dealing [UPA 103(b), 404(d)]. The agreement can specify acts that the partners agree will violate a fiduciary duty.

Note that a partner may pursue his or her own interests without automatically violating these duties [UPA 404(e)]. The key is whether the partner has disclosed the interest to the other partners. **EXAMPLE 27.6** Jayne Trell, a partner at Jacoby & Meyers, owns a shopping mall. Trell may vote against a partnership proposal to open a competing mall, provided that she has fully disclosed her interest in the existing shopping mall to the other partners at the firm. ● A partner cannot make secret profits or put self-interest before his or her duty to the interest of the partnership, however.

"Surround yourself with partners who are better than you are."

David Ogilvy, 1911–1999
(Scottish advertising executive)

Authority of Partners The UPA affirms general principles of agency law that pertain to the authority of a partner to bind a partnership in contract. A partner may also subject the partnership to tort liability under agency principles. When a partner is carrying on partnership business with third parties in the usual way, both the partner and the firm share liability.

If a partner acts within the scope of her or his authority, the partnership is legally bound to honor the partner's commitments to third parties. The partnership will not be liable, however, if the third parties know that the partner had no authority to commit the partnership. A partnership may limit the capacity of a partner to act as the firm's agent or transfer property on its behalf by filing a "statement of partnership authority" in a designated state office [UPA 105, 303].

Agency concepts that we explored in Chapter 23 relating to actual (express and implied) authority, apparent authority, and ratification also apply to partnerships. *The extent of implied authority is generally broader for partners than for ordinary agents, though.*

Some customarily implied powers include the authority to make warranties on goods in the retail sales business and the power to enter into contracts consistent with the firm's ordinary course of business. **EXAMPLE 27.7** Jamie Schwab is a partner in a firm that operates a retail tire store and regularly promises that "each tire will be warranted for normal wear for 40,000 miles." Because Schwab has authority to make warranties, the partnership is bound to honor the warranty. Schwab would not, however, have the authority to sell the partnership's office equipment, fixtures, or other property without the consent of all of the other partners. ●

Liability of Partners One significant disadvantage associated with a traditional partnership is that partners are *personally* liable for the debts of the partnership. In most states, the liability is essentially unlimited because the acts of one partner in the ordinary course of business subject the other partners to personal liability [UPA 305].

Joint Liability In partnership law, the partners' shared liability for partnership obligations and debts. A third party must sue all of the partners as a group, but each partner can be held liable for the full amount.

Joint Liability Each partner in a partnership is jointly liable for the partnership's obligations. **Joint liability** means that a third party must sue all of the partners as a group, but each partner can be held liable for the full amount. (Under the prior version of the UPA, which is still in effect in a few states, partners were subject to joint liability on partnership debts and contracts, but not on partnership debts arising from torts.)

If, for instance, a third party sues one individual partner on a partnership contract, that partner has the right to demand that the other partners be sued with her or him. In fact, if the third party does not name all of the partners in the lawsuit, the assets of the partnership cannot be used to satisfy the judgment. With joint liability, the partnership's assets must be exhausted before creditors can reach the partners' individual assets.[3]

LEARNING OBJECTIVE 3

What is meant by joint and several liability? Why is this often considered to be a disadvantage of the partnership form of business?

Joint and Several Liability In partnership law, a doctrine under which a plaintiff may sue, and collect a judgment from, all of the partners together (jointly) or one or more of the partners separately (severally, or individually). A partner can be held liable even if she or he did not participate in, ratify, or know about the conduct that gave rise to the lawsuit.

Joint and Several Liability In the majority of the states, under UPA 306(a), partners are jointly and severally (separately or individually) liable for all partnership obligations, including contracts, torts, and breaches of trust. **Joint and several liability** means that a third party has the option of suing all of the partners together (jointly) or one or more of the partners separately (severally). All partners in a partnership can be held liable regardless of whether a particular partner participated in, knew about, or ratified the conduct that gave rise to the lawsuit. Normally, though, the partnership's assets must be exhausted before a creditor can enforce a judgment against a partner's personal assets [UPA 307(d)].

A judgment against one partner severally (separately) does not extinguish the others' liability. (Similarly, a release of one partner does not discharge the partners' several liability.) Those not sued in the first action may be sued subsequently, unless the court in the first action held that the partnership was not liable. If a plaintiff is successful in a suit against a partner or partners, he or she may collect on the judgment only against the assets of those partners named as defendants. A partner who commits a tort may be required to indemnify (reimburse) the partnership for any damages it pays—unless the tort was committed in the ordinary course of the partnership's business.

CASE EXAMPLE 27.8 Nicole Moren, a partner in Jax Restaurant, was called back to the restaurant to help in the kitchen. She brought her two-year-old son, Remington, with her. While she was making pizzas, Remington reached into the dough press. His hand was crushed, causing permanent injuries. Through his father, Remington filed a suit against the partnership for negligence. The partnership filed a complaint against Moren, arguing that it was entitled to indemnity from Moren for her negligence. The court held in favor of Moren and ordered the partnership to pay damages to Remington. Moren was not required to indemnify the partnership because her negligence occurred in the ordinary course of the partnership's business.[4] •

Under what circumstances can partners be held personally liable for someone injured on partnership property?

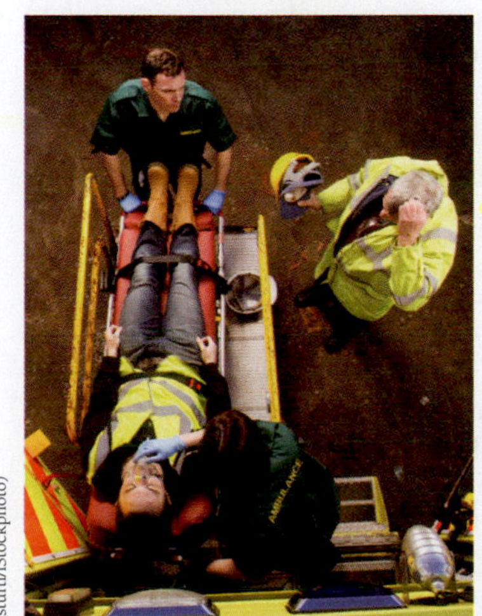

(sturti/iStockphoto)

Liability of an Incoming Partner A partner newly admitted to an existing partnership is not personally liable for any partnership obligations incurred before the person became a partner [UPA 306(b)]. The new partner's liability to existing creditors of the partnership is limited to her or his capital contribution to the firm. **EXAMPLE 27.9** Smartclub, an existing partnership with four members, admits a new partner, Alex Jaff. He contributes $100,000 to the partnership. Smartclub has debts amounting to $600,000 at the time Jaff joins the firm. Although Jaff's capital contribution of $100,000 can be used to satisfy Smartclub's prior obligations, Jaff is not personally liable for those debts. Thus, his personal assets cannot be used to satisfy the partnership's preexisting debts. If, however, the managing partner at Smartclub borrows funds from a bank for the partnership after Jaff becomes a partner, Jaff will be personally liable for those amounts, along with all other partners. •

3. For a case applying joint liability to a partnership, see *Shar's Cars, LLC v. Elder,* 97 P.3d 724 (Utah App. 2004).
4. *Moren v. Jax Restaurant,* 679 N.W.2d 165 (Minn.App. 2004).

Partner's Dissociation

Dissociation The severance of the relationship between a partner and a partnership when the partner ceases to be associated with the carrying on of the partnership business.

Dissociation occurs when a partner ceases to be associated in the carrying on of the partnership business. Although a partner always has the *power* to dissociate from the firm, he or she may not have the *right* to do so. Dissociation terminates the partner's actual authority to act for the partnership and to participate with the partners in running the business. Otherwise, the partnership continues to do business without the dissociating partner.[5]

Events Causing Dissociation

Under UPA 601, a partner can be dissociated from a partnership in any of the following ways:

1. By the partner's voluntarily giving notice of an "express will to withdraw."
2. By the occurrence of an event agreed to in the partnership agreement.
3. By a unanimous vote of the other partners under certain circumstances, such as when a partner transfers substantially all of her or his interest in the partnership, or when it becomes unlawful to carry on partnership business with that partner.
4. By order of a court or arbitrator if the partner has engaged in wrongful conduct that affects the partnership business, breached the partnership agreement or violated a duty owed to the partnership or the other partners, or engaged in conduct that makes it "not reasonably practicable to carry on the business in partnership with the partner" [UPA 601(5)].
5. By the partner's declaring bankruptcy, assigning his or her interest in the partnership for the benefit of creditors, or becoming physically or mentally incapacitated, or by the partner's death. Note that although the bankruptcy or death of a partner results in that partner's "dissociation" from the partnership, it is not an *automatic* ground for the partnership's dissolution (*dissolution* will be discussed on the next two pages).

Wrongful Dissociation

As mentioned, a partner has the power to dissociate from a partnership at any time, but if she or he lacks the right to dissociate, then the dissociation is considered wrongful under the law [UPA 602]. When a partner's dissociation is in breach of the partnership agreement, for instance, it is wrongful. **EXAMPLE 27.10** Jensen & Whalen's partnership agreement states that it is a breach of the agreement for any partner to assign partnership property to a creditor without the consent of the other partners. If Janis, a partner, makes such an assignment, she not only has breached the agreement but also has wrongfully dissociated from the partnership. •

Similarly, if a partner refuses to perform duties required by the partnership agreement—such as accounting for profits earned from the use of partnership property—this breach can be treated as a wrongful dissociation. A partner who wrongfully dissociates is liable to the partnership and to the other partners for damages caused by the dissociation.

Effects of Dissociation

Dissociation (rightful or wrongful) terminates some of the rights of the dissociated partner, requires that the partnership purchase his or her interest, and alters the liability of the parties to third parties.

Rights and Duties On a partner's dissociation, his or her right to participate in the management and conduct of the partnership business terminates [UPA 603]. The partner's duty of loyalty also ends. A partner's duty of care continues only with respect to events that occurred before dissociation, unless the partner participates in *winding up* the partnership's business (to be discussed shortly). **EXAMPLE 27.11** Debbie Pearson, a partner who leaves an accounting firm, Bubb & Ferngold, can immediately compete with that firm for new

---

5. Under the previous version of the UPA, when a partner withdrew from a partnership, the partnership was considered dissolved, its business had to be wound up, and the proceeds had to be distributed to creditors and among the partners. The new UPA dramatically changed the law governing partnership breakups and does not require that a partnership be dissolved just because one partner has left the firm.

clients. She must exercise care in completing ongoing client transactions, however, and must account to Bubb & Ferngold for any fees received from the former clients based on those transactions. ●

Buyout Price The amount payable to a partner on his or her dissociation from a partnership, based on the amount distributable to that partner if the firm were wound up on that date, and offset by any damages for wrongful dissociation.

Buyouts After a partner's dissociation, the partnership must purchase his or her partnership interest according to the rules in UPA 701. The **buyout price** is based on the amount that would have been distributed to the partner if the partnership had been wound up on the date of dissociation. Offset against the price are any amounts owed by the partner to the partnership, including any damages to the firm for the partner's wrongful dissociation. **CASE EXAMPLE 27.12** Wilbur and Dee Warnick and their son, Randall, bought a ranch for $335,000 and formed a partnership to operate it. The partners' initial capital contributions totaled $60,000, of which Randall paid 34 percent. Over the next twenty years, each partner contributed funds to the operation and received cash distributions from the partnership. In 1999, Randall dissociated from the partnership. When the parties could not agree on a buyout price, Randall filed a lawsuit. The court awarded Randall $115,783.13—the amount of his cash contributions, plus 34 percent of the increase in the value of the partnership's assets above all partners' cash contributions. Randall's parents appealed, arguing that $50,000 should be deducted from the appraised value of the assets for the estimated expenses of selling them. The court affirmed the buyout price, however, because "purely hypothetical costs of sale are not a required deduction in valuing partnership assets" to determine a buyout price.[6] ●

Liability to Third Parties For two years after a partner dissociates from a continuing partnership, the partnership may be bound by the acts of the dissociated partner based on apparent authority [UPA 702]. In other words, the partnership may be liable to a third party with whom a dissociated partner enters into a transaction if the third party reasonably believed that the dissociated partner was still a partner. Similarly, a dissociated partner may be liable for partnership obligations entered into during a two-year period following dissociation [UPA 703].

To avoid this possible liability, a partnership should notify its creditors, customers, and clients of a partner's dissociation. Also, either the partnership or the dissociated partner can file a statement of dissociation in the appropriate state office to limit the dissociated partner's authority to ninety days after the filing [UPA 704].

Partnership Termination

Dissolution The formal disbanding of a partnership or a corporation. It can take place by (1) acts of the partners or, in a corporation, acts of the shareholders and board of directors; (2) the subsequent illegality of the firm's business; (3) the expiration of a time period stated in a partnership agreement or a certificate of incorporation; or (4) judicial decree.

Winding Up The second of two stages in the termination of a partnership or corporation, in which the firm's assets are collected, liquidated, and distributed, and liabilities are discharged.

The same events that cause dissociation can result in the end of the partnership if the remaining partners no longer wish to (or are unable to) continue the partnership business. Only certain departures of a partner will end the partnership, though, and generally the partnership can continue if the remaining partners consent [UPA 801].

The termination of a partnership is referred to as **dissolution**, which essentially means the commencement of the winding up process. **Winding up** is the actual process of collecting, liquidating, and distributing the partnership assets.[7]

Dissolution

Dissolution of a partnership generally can be brought about by acts of the partners, by operation of law, or by judicial decree [UPA 801]. Any partnership (including one for a fixed term) can be dissolved by the partners' agreement. Similarly, if the partnership agreement states that it will dissolve on a certain event, such as a partner's death or

6. *Warnick v. Warnick*, 2006 WY 58, 133 P.3d 997 (2006).

7. Although "winding down" would seem to more accurately describe the process of settling accounts and liquidating the assets of a partnership, "winding up" has been traditionally used in English and U.S. statutory and case law to denote this final stage of a partnership's existence.

bankruptcy, then the occurrence of that event will dissolve the partnership. A partnership for a fixed term or a particular undertaking is dissolved by operation of law at the expiration of the term or on the completion of the undertaking.

Each partner must exercise good faith when dissolving a partnership. Some state statutes allow partners injured by another partner's bad faith to file a tort claim for wrongful dissolution of a partnership. **CASE EXAMPLE 27.13** Attorneys Randall Jordan and Mary Helen Moses formed a two-member partnership in 2003. Although the partnership was for an indefinite term, Jordan ended the partnership in 2006 and asked the court for declarations concerning the partners' financial obligations. Moses, who had objected to ending the partnership, filed a claim against Jordan for wrongful dissolution and for appropriating $180,000 in fees that should have gone to the partnership. Ultimately, the court held in favor of Moses. A claim for wrongful dissolution of a partnership may be based on damages arising from the excluded partner's loss of "an existing, or continuing, business opportunity" or of income and material assets. Because Jordan had attempted to appropriate partnership assets through dissolution, Moses could sue for wrongful dissolution.[8] •

Under the UPA, a court may order dissolution when it becomes obviously impractical for the firm to continue—for example, if the business can only be operated at a loss [UPA 801(5)]. Even when one partner has brought a court action seeking to dissolve a partnership, the partnership continues to exist until it is legally dissolved by the court or by the parties' agreement.[9]

In the following case, a family partnership began to experience serious problems because of a dispute between two partners. The court had to decide whether it was practicable for the firm to continue.

8. *Jordan v. Moses*, 291 Ga. 39, 727 S.E.2d 460 (2012).

9. See, for example, *Curley v. Kaiser*, 112 Conn.App. 213, 962 A.2d 167 (2009).

Case 27.2

Russell Realty Associates v. Russell

Supreme Court of Virginia,
724 S.E.2d 690 (2012).
www.courts.state.va.us[a]

(GorazdBertalanic/iStockphoto)

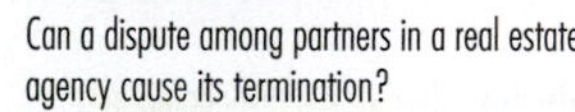

Can a dispute among partners in a real estate agency cause its termination?

FACTS In 1978, members of the Russell family began operating Russell Realty Associates as a partnership. Eddie Russell had decision-making authority over the partnership's business, which involved buying, holding, leasing, and selling investment properties. After several years, Eddie and his sister, Nina Russell, became involved in several heated disputes over whether to develop or sell particular properties and whether and how to include Nina's son in the partnership. Nina began to routinely question Eddie's business decisions, and she insisted on recording business meetings and editing the partnership's official minutes. Because of their disagreements, Russell Realty experienced two years of delays relating to zoning approval and appraisals before it could sell one piece of property. It also was unable to accept an attractive offer for another property. Despite the siblings' disputes, Russell Realty continued to profit and make distributions to its partners. Nevertheless, in 2008, Eddie filed a complaint seeking a judicial dissolution of Russell Realty. The court granted the dissolution, and Nina appealed.

ISSUE Can a court judicially dissolve Russell Realty?

DECISION Yes. The Virginia Supreme Court affirmed the judgment of the lower court.

REASON Under Virginia law, a partnership may be judicially dissolved if, among other reasons, the "economic purpose of the

a. In the search box at the right, type "Russell Realty Associates v. Russell" and click on "Go." In the result, click on the heading "Supreme Court of Virginia Opinions." When that page opens, scroll down to "110380" and click on the number to access the opinion.

Case 27.2—Continued

partnership is likely to be unreasonably frustrated" or it "is not . . . reasonably practicable to carry on the partnership business in conformity with the partnership agreement." In this case, the court found that Russell Realty's economic purpose was unreasonably frustrated because the partnership could no longer conduct its business "in an efficient and productive manner." Although the firm continued to profit, it experienced a significant delay in selling one piece of property and failed to accept a lucrative offer for another. Eddie and Nina's dispute also imposed several additional costs for the partnership, including costs associated with addressing litigation and having business meetings recorded. Moreover, the court concluded that it was not reasonably practicable to carry on the partnership business in conformity with the partnership agreement. Despite Eddie's decision-making authority under the agreement, the partnership operated very slowly and inefficiently. There was no reason to believe that Eddie and Nina's relationship would improve, so judicial dissolution was appropriate.

CRITICAL THINKING—Ethical Consideration *Does the judicial power to dissolve partnerships encourage partners to be more respectful toward each other? Why or why not?*

Winding Up

After dissolution, the partnership continues for the limited purpose of the winding up process. The partners cannot create new obligations on behalf of the partnership. They have authority only to complete transactions begun but not finished at the time of dissolution and to wind up the business of the partnership [UPA 803, 804(1)].

Winding up includes collecting and preserving partnership assets, discharging liabilities (paying debts), and accounting to each partner for the value of her or his interest in the partnership. Partners continue to have fiduciary duties to one another and to the firm during this process. UPA 401(h) provides that a partner is entitled to compensation for services in winding up partnership affairs (and reimbursement for expenses incurred in the process) above and apart from his or her share in the partnership profits.

KNOW THIS

Secured creditors have priority over unsecured creditors to any assets that serve as collateral for a partnership's debts.

Both creditors of the partnership and creditors of the individual partners can make claims on the partnership's assets. In general, partnership creditors and the partners' personal creditors share proportionately in the partners' assets, which include their interests in the partnership. A partnership's assets are distributed according to the following priorities [UPA 807]:

1. Payment of debts, including those owed to partner and nonpartner creditors.
2. Return of capital contributions and distribution of profits to partners.

If the partnership's liabilities are greater than its assets, the partners bear the losses—in the absence of a contrary agreement—in the same proportion in which they shared the profits (rather than, for example, in proportion to their contributions to the partnership's capital).

PREVENTING LEGAL DISPUTES

Before entering a partnership, agree on how the assets will be valued and divided in the event the partnership dissolves. Make express arrangements that will provide for a smooth dissolution. Your partners and you can enter into a buy-sell, or buyout, agreement, which provides that one or more partners will buy out the other or others, should the relationship deteriorate. Agreeing beforehand on who buys what, under which circumstances, and, if possible, at what price may eliminate costly negotiations or litigation later. Alternatively, your agreement can specify that one or more partners will determine the value of the interest being sold and that the other or others will decide whether to buy or sell.

Limited Liability Partnerships

Limited Liability Partnership (LLP)
A hybrid form of business organization that is used mainly by professionals who normally do business in a partnership. An LLP is a pass-through entity for tax purposes, but a partner's personal liability for the malpractice of other partners is limited.

LEARNING OBJECTIVE 4
What advantages do limited liability partnerships offer to businesspersons that are not offered by general partnerships?

The **limited liability partnership (LLP)** is a hybrid form of business designed mostly for professionals who normally do business as partners in a partnership. The first state to enact an LLP statute was Texas, in 1991. Other states quickly followed suit, and by 1997, almost all of the states had enacted LLP statutes.

The major advantage of the LLP is that it allows a partnership to continue as a pass-through entity for tax purposes but limits the personal liability of the partners. The LLP is especially attractive for two categories of businesses: professional service firms and family businesses. In fact, the largest international accountancy and professional services firms are organized as LLPs, including Ernst & Young, LLP, and PricewaterhouseCoopers, LLP.

Formation of an LLP

LLPs must be formed and operated in compliance with state statutes, which may include provisions of the UPA. The appropriate form must be filed with a central state agency, usually the secretary of state's office, and the business's name must include either "Limited Liability Partnership" or "LLP" [UPA 1001, 1002]. In addition, an LLP must file an annual report with the state to remain qualified as an LLP in that state [UPA 1003].

In most states, it is relatively easy to convert a traditional partnership into an LLP because the firm's basic organizational structure remains the same. Additionally, all of the statutory and common law rules governing partnerships still apply (apart from those modified by the LLP statute). Normally, LLP statutes are simply amendments to a state's already existing partnership law.

Liability in an LLP

An LLP allows professionals, such as attorneys and accountants, to avoid personal liability for the malpractice of other partners. A partner in an LLP is still liable for her or his own wrongful acts, such as negligence, however. Also liable is the partner who supervised the individual who committed a wrongful act. (This supervisory liability generally applies to all types of partners and partnerships, not just LLPs.)

EXAMPLE 27.14 Five lawyers are operating a law firm as a partnership. One of the attorneys, Dan Kolcher, is sued for malpractice and loses. The firm's malpractice insurance is now insufficient to pay the judgment. If the firm had been organized as a general partnership, the personal assets of the other attorneys could be used to satisfy the obligation. Because the firm is organized as an LLP, however, no other partner at the law firm can be held *personally* liable for Kolcher's malpractice, unless she or he acted as Kolcher's supervisor. In the absence of a supervisor, only Kolcher's personal assets can be used to satisfy the judgment. •

Although LLP statutes vary from state to state, generally each state statute limits the liability of partners in some way. For instance, Delaware law protects each innocent partner from the "debts and obligations of the partnership arising from negligence, wrongful acts, or misconduct." The UPA more broadly exempts partners from personal liability for any partnership obligation, "whether arising in contract, tort, or otherwise" [UPA 306(c)]. Although the language of some of these statutes may seem to apply specifically to attorneys, any group of professionals can organize an LLP.

Liability outside the State of Formation

When an LLP formed in one state wishes to do business in another state, it may be required to register in the second state—for example, by filing a statement of foreign qualification [UPA 1102]. Because state LLP statutes are not uniform, a question sometimes arises as to which law applies if the LLP statutes in the two states provide different liability protection. Most states apply the law of the state in which the LLP was formed, even when the firm does business in another state, which is also the rule under UPA 1101.

Sharing Liability among Partners

When more than one partner in an LLP is negligent, there is a question as to how liability is to be shared. Is each partner jointly and severally liable for the entire result, as a general partner would be in most states?

Some states provide for proportionate liability—that is, for separate determinations of the negligence of the partners. **EXAMPLE 27.15** Accountants Raj and Jane are partners in an LLP, with Raj supervising Jane. Jane negligently fails to file tax returns for their client, Centaur Tools. Centaur files a suit against Raj and Jane. In a state that does not allow for proportionate liability, Raj can be held liable for the entire loss. Under a proportionate liability statute, Raj will be liable for no more than his portion of the responsibility for the missed tax deadline. (Even if Jane settles the case quickly, Raj will still be liable for his portion.) •

LEARNING OBJECTIVE 5
What are the key differences between the rights and liabilities of general partners and those of limited partners?

Limited Partnerships

Limited Partnership (LP) A partnership consisting of one or more general partners (who manage the business and are personally liable for debts of the partnership) and one or more limited partners (who contribute only assets and are liable only up to the extent of their contributions).

General Partner In a limited partnership, a partner who assumes responsibility for the management of the partnership and has full liability for all partnership debts.

Limited Partner In a limited partnership, a partner who contributes capital to the partnership but has no right to participate in its management. The partner has no liability for partnership debts beyond the amount of her or his investment.

We now look at a business organizational form that limits the liability of *some* of its owners—the **limited partnership (LP).** Limited partnerships originated in medieval Europe and have been in existence in the United States since the early 1800s. Limited partnerships differ from general partnerships in several ways.

A limited partnership consists of at least one **general partner** and one or more **limited partners.** A general partner assumes management responsibility for the partnership and so has full responsibility for the partnership and for all of its debts. A limited partner contributes cash or other property and owns an interest in the firm but does not undertake any management responsibilities and is not personally liable for partnership debts beyond the amount of his or her investment. A limited partner can forfeit limited liability by taking part in the management of the business. Exhibit 27.2 on the next page compares characteristics of general and limited partnerships.[10]

Most states and the District of Columbia have adopted the Revised Uniform Limited Partnership Act (RULPA), which we refer to in the following discussion of limited partnerships. Note, however, that a minority of states have adopted some amendments that were proposed in 2001 to make the RULPA more flexible.

Formation of an LP

Certificate of Limited Partnership The document that must be filed with a designated state official to form a limited partnership.

In contrast to the informal, private, and voluntary agreement that usually suffices for a general partnership, the formation of a limited partnership is a public and formal proceeding that must follow statutory requirements. Not only must a limited partnership have at least one general partner and one limited partner, but the partners must also sign a **certificate of limited partnership.** Like articles of incorporation (see Chapter 28), this certificate must include certain information such as the name, mailing address, and capital contribution of each general and limited partner. The certificate must be filed with the designated state official—under the RULPA, the secretary of state. The certificate is usually open to public inspection.

10. Under the UPA, a general partnership can be converted into a limited partnership and vice versa [UPA 902, 903]. The UPA also provides for the merger of a general partnership with one or more general or limited partnerships under rules that are similar to those governing corporate mergers [UPA 905].

Exhibit 27.2 A Comparison of General Partnerships and Limited Partnerships

CHARACTERISTIC	GENERAL PARTNERSHIP (UPA)	LIMITED PARTNERSHIP (RULPA)
Creation	By agreement of two or more persons to carry on a business as co-owners for profit.	By agreement of two or more persons to carry on a business as co-owners for profit. Must include one or more general partners and one or more limited partners. Filing of a certificate with the secretary of state is required.
Sharing of Profits and Losses	By agreement. In the absence of agreement, profits are shared equally by the partners, and losses are shared in the same ratio as profits.	Profits are shared as required in the certificate agreement, and losses are shared likewise, up to the amount of the limited partners' capital contributions. In the absence of a provision in the certificate agreement, profits and losses are shared on the basis of percentages of capital contributions.
Liability	Unlimited personal liability of all partners.	Unlimited personal liability of all general partners; limited partners liable only to the extent of their capital contributions.
Capital Contribution	No minimum or mandatory amount; set by agreement.	Set by agreement.
Management	By agreement. In the absence of agreement, all partners have an equal voice.	Only the general partner (or the general partners). Limited partners have no voice or else are subject to liability as general partners (but only if a third party has reason to believe that the limited partner is a general partner). A limited partner may act as an agent or employee of the partnership and vote on amending the certificate or on the sale or dissolution of the partnership.
Duration	Terminated by agreement of the partners, but can continue to do business even when a partner dissociates from the partnership.	Terminated by agreement in the certificate or by retirement, death, or mental incompetence of a general partner in the absence of the right of the other general partners to continue the partnership. Death of a limited partner does not terminate the partnership, unless he or she is the only remaining limited partner.
Distribution of Assets on Liquidation—Order of Priorities	1. Payment of debts, including those owed to partner and nonpartner creditors. 2. Return of capital contributions and distribution of profit to partners.	1. Outside creditors and partner creditors. 2. Partners and former partners entitled to distributions of partnership assets. 3. Unless otherwise agreed, return of capital contributions and distribution of profit to partners.

Liabilities of Partners in an LP

KNOW THIS

A limited partner is liable only to the extent of any contribution that she or he made to the partnership, but can lose this limited liability by participating in management.

General partners, unlike limited partners, are personally liable to the partnership's creditors. Thus, at least one general partner is necessary in a limited partnership so that someone has personal liability. This policy can be circumvented in states that allow a corporation to be the general partner in a partnership. Because the corporation has limited liability by virtue of corporate laws, if a corporation is the general partner, no one in the limited partnership has personal liability.

In contrast to the personal liability of general partners, the liability of a limited partner is limited to the capital that she or he contributes or agrees to contribute to the partnership [RULPA 502]. Limited partners enjoy this limited liability only so long as they do not participate in management [RULPA 303]. A limited partner who participates in management will be just as liable as a general partner to any creditor who transacts business with the limited partnership and believes, based on the limited partner's conduct, that the limited partner is a general partner [RULPA 303]. The extent of review and advisement a limited partner can engage in before being exposed to liability remains rather vague, though.

ETHICAL ISSUE

Should an innocent partner be jointly liable for fraud? When general partners in a limited partnership jointly engage in fraud, there generally is no question that they are jointly liable. But if one general partner engages in fraud and the other is unaware of the wrongdoing, is it fair to make the innocent partner share in the liability? Many states' limited partnership laws protect innocent general partners from suits for fraud brought by limited partners. The law is less clear, however, when one general partner, by fraud and misrepresentation, induces a third party to invest in the limited partnership and thereby become a limited partner.

For example, Robert Bisno and James Coxeter formed two limited partnerships to develop property in Berkeley, California. Without Coxeter's knowledge, Bisno took almost $500,000 from one of the partnerships to buy a personal home. He also made material misrepresentations to potential investors. One of those investors, George Miske, discovered the fraud and brought suit. Coxeter argued that Miske was a limited partner, not an innocent third party, and therefore Coxeter should be protected from liability under the state's limited partnership law.

The court disagreed. The fraud at issue had induced Miske to purchase the limited partnership interest. Therefore, at the time the fraud was perpetrated by Bisno, Miske was an innocent third party. As a result, Coxeter, though innocent of any wrongdoing, was jointly liable.[11]

Dissociation and Dissolution

"A friendship founded on business is a good deal better than a business founded on friendship."

John D. Rockefeller, 1839–1937 (American industrialist)

A general partner has the power to voluntarily dissociate, or withdraw, from a limited partnership unless the partnership agreement specifies otherwise. A limited partner can withdraw from the partnership by giving six months' notice *unless* the partnership agreement specifies a term, which most do. Also, some states have passed laws prohibiting the withdrawal of limited partners.

Events That Cause Dissociation In a limited partnership, a general partner's voluntary dissociation from the firm normally will lead to dissolution *unless* all partners agree to continue the business. Similarly, the bankruptcy, retirement, death, or mental incompetence of a general partner will cause the dissociation of that partner and the dissolution of the limited partnership unless the other members agree to continue the firm [RULPA 801].

Bankruptcy of a limited partner, however, does not dissolve the partnership unless it causes the bankruptcy of the firm. Death or an assignment of the interest of a limited partner does not dissolve a limited partnership [RULPA 702, 704, 705]. A limited partnership can be dissolved by court decree [RULPA 802].

Distribution of Assets On dissolution, creditors' claims, including those of partners who are creditors, take first priority. After that, partners and former partners receive unpaid distributions of partnership assets and, except as otherwise agreed, amounts representing returns of their capital contributions and proportionate distributions of profits [RULPA 804].

Disputes commonly arise about how the partnership's assets should be valued and distributed and whether the business should be sold. **CASE EXAMPLE 27.16** Actor Kevin Costner was a limited partner in Midnight Star Enterprises, LP, which runs a casino, bar, and restaurant in South Dakota. There were two other limited partners, Carla and Francis Caneva, who owned a small percentage of the partnership (3.25 units each) and received salaries for managing its operations. Another company owned by Costner, Midnight Star Enterprises, Limited (MSEL), was the general partner. Costner thus controlled a majority of the partnership (93.5 units). When communications broke down between the partners, MSEL asked a court to dissolve the partnership. MSEL's accountant determined that the firm's fair market value was $3.1 million. The Canevas presented evidence that a competitor would buy the business for $6.2 million. The Canevas wanted the court to force Costner to either buy the business for that price within ten days or sell it on the open market to the highest bidder.

Ultimately, the state's highest court held in favor of Costner. A partner cannot force the sale of a limited partnership when the other partners want to continue the business. The court also accepted the $3.1 million buyout price of MSEL's accountant and ordered Costner to pay the Canevas the value of their 6.5 partnership units.[12]

---

11. *Miske v. Bisno*, 204 Cal.App.4th 1249, 139 Cal.Rptr.3d 626 (2012).

12. *In re Dissolution of Midnight Star Enterprises, LP*, 2006 SD 98, 724 N.W.2d 334 (2006).

Buy-Sell Agreements As mentioned earlier in the *Preventing Legal Disputes* feature on page 715, partners can agree ahead of time how the assets will be valued and divided if the partnership dissolves. Buy-sell agreements can help the partners avoid disputes. Nonetheless, buy-sell agreements do not eliminate all potential for litigation, especially if the terms are subject to more than one interpretation.

The limited partners in the following case dissociated from their partnership by giving notice. The dissociation triggered the provisions of a partnership buy-sell agreement. The withdrawing partners and the partnership, however, read those provisions somewhat differently. Which interpretation the court accepted would determine whether the partnership was required to buy the partners' interests.

Case 27.3

Craton Capital, LP v. Natural Pork Production II, LLP

Court of Appeals of Iowa, 797 N.W.2d 623 (2011).

(narvikk/iStockphoto)

When does a hog-raising limited partnership have to buy out a dissociating partner?

FACTS Natural Pork Production II, LLP (NPP), an Iowa limited liability partnership, raises hogs. Under a partnership buy-sell agreement, NPP was obligated to buy a dissociating partner's interests (units) but could defer the purchase if, in the judgment of the managing partners, the purchase would "adversely affect the working capital, cash flow or other financial means, condition or operation of the Partnership." Once this "impairment circumstance" was "no longer applicable," NPP was to make the purchase within thirty days. Craton Capital, LP, and Kruse Investment Company were among NPP's limited partners.

When they notified NPP of their dissociation, a wave of similar notices from other partners followed. NPP declared an impairment circumstance. Craton and Kruse filed a suit in an Iowa state court against NPP, asking the court to order the partnership to buy their units. NPP responded that the impairment circumstance still existed. Both parties filed motions for summary judgment on the issue of whether NPP was obligated to buy. The court issued a summary judgment in NPP's favor. Craton and Kruse appealed.

ISSUE Was Natural Pork Production (NPP) required under the buy-sell agreement to buy the dissociating partners' interests?

DECISION Yes. A state intermediate appellate court reversed the lower court's judgment in favor of NPP and remanded the case for the entry of a summary judgment in favor of Craton and Kruse.

REASON The court pointed out that the "Dissociation Notice" provision of the partnership agreement states that NPP shall buy a dissociating partner's units. This is mandatory. The only restriction is set out in the "impairment circumstance" provision. This provision applies when NPP is obligated to buy a dissociating partner's units and an impairment circumstance arises. Payment is then postponed, but the partnership is still obligated to buy the units. That is what occurred in this case. NPP argued that under the impairment circumstance provision, an obligation to buy a partner's units would never arise if the purchase would materially impair or adversely affect the financial condition of the partnership. But this interpretation, the court reasoned, was not consistent with "the actual wording." The word "shall" is mandatory. Thus, once Craton and Kruse gave their dissociation notice, NPP was obligated to buy their units. The declaration of an impairment circumstance only deferred the purchase.

WHAT IF THE FACTS WERE DIFFERENT? *Suppose that Craton and Kruse had been general partners rather than limited partners. In that circumstance, what might their dissociation have meant for NPP?*

Reviewing . . . All Forms of Partnership

Grace Tarnavsky and her sons, Manny and Jason, bought a ranch known as the Cowboy Palace in March 2009, and the three orally agreed to share the business for five years. Grace contributed 50 percent of the investment, and each son contributed 25 percent. Manny agreed to handle the livestock, and Jason agreed to do the bookkeeping. The Tarnavskys took out joint loans and opened a joint bank account into which they deposited the ranch's proceeds and from which they made payments for property, cattle, equipment, and supplies. In September 2013, Manny severely injured his back while baling hay and became permanently unable to handle livestock. Manny therefore hired additional laborers to tend the livestock, causing the Cowboy Palace to incur significant debt. In September 2014, Al's Feed Barn filed a lawsuit against Jason to collect $12,400 in unpaid debts. Using the information presented in the chapter, answer the following questions.

1. Was this relationship a partnership for a term or a partnership at will?
2. Did Manny have the authority to hire additional laborers to work at the ranch after his injury? Why or why not?
3. Under the UPA, can Al's Feed Barn bring an action against Jason individually for the Cowboy Palace's debt? Why or why not?
4. Suppose that after his back injury in 2013, Manny sent his mother and brother a notice indicating his intent to withdraw from the partnership. Can he still be held liable for the debt to Al's Feed Barn? Why or why not?

DEBATE THIS A partnership should automatically end when one partner dissociates from the firm.

Key Terms

articles of partnership 705
buyout price 713
certificate of limited partnership 717
charging order 708
confession of judgment 707
dissociation 712
dissolution 713
general partner 717
goodwill 704
information return 705
joint and several liability 711
joint liability 711
limited liability partnership (LLP) 716
limited partner 717
limited partnership (LP) 717
partnership 703
partnership by estoppel 706
pass-through entity 705
winding up 713

Chapter Summary: All Forms of Partnership

Partnerships (See pages 703–715.)	1. A partnership is created by agreement of the parties. 2. A partnership is treated as an entity except for limited purposes. 3. Each partner pays a proportionate share of income taxes on the net profits of the partnership, whether or not they are distributed. The partnership files only an information return with the Internal Revenue Service. 4. Each partner has an equal voice in management unless the partnership agreement provides otherwise. 5. In the absence of an agreement, partners share profits equally and share losses in the same ratio as they share profits. 6. The capital contribution of each partner is determined by agreement. 7. Partners have unlimited liability for partnership debts. 8. A partnership can be terminated by agreement or can be dissolved by action of the partners (dissociation from a partnership at will), operation of law (subsequent illegality), or court decree.

Continued

Chapter Summary: All Forms of Partnership—Continued

Limited Liability Partnerships (LLPs) (See pages 716–717.)	1. *Formation*—The appropriate form must be filed with a state agency, usually the secretary of state's office. Typically, an LLP is formed by professionals who work together as partners in a partnership. Under most state LLP statutes, it is relatively easy to convert a traditional partnership into an LLP. 2. *Liabilities of partners*—LLP statutes vary, but under the UPA, professionals generally can avoid personal liability for acts committed by other partners. Partners in an LLP continue to be liable for their own wrongful acts and for the wrongful acts of those whom they supervise.
Limited Partnerships (LP) (See pages 717–720.)	1. *Formation*—A certificate of limited partnership must be filed with the secretary of state's office or other designated state official. The certificate must include information about the business, similar to the information included in a articles of incorporation. The partnership consists of one or more general partners and one or more limited partners. 2. *Liabilities of partners*—General partners have unlimited liability for partnership obligations. Limited partners are liable only to the extent of their contributions. 3. *Limited partners and management*—Only general partners can participate in management. Limited partners have no voice in management. If they do participate in management, they risk having general-partner liability. 4. *Dissolution*—A general partner's voluntary dissociation, bankruptcy, death, or mental incompetence will cause the partnership's dissolution unless all partners agree to continue the business. The death or assignment of the interest of a limited partner does not dissolve the partnership. Bankruptcy of a limited partner also will not dissolve the partnership unless it causes the bankruptcy of the firm.

ExamPrep

ISSUE SPOTTERS

1. Darnell and Eliana are partners in D&E Designs, an architectural firm. When Darnell dies, his widow claims that as Darnell's heir, she is entitled to take his place as Eliana's partner or to receive a share of the firm's assets. Is she right? Why or why not? **(See pages 712–713.)**
2 Finian and Gloria are partners in F&G Delivery Service. When business is slow, without Gloria's knowledge, Finian leases the delivery vehicles as moving vans. Because the delivery vehicles would otherwise be sitting idle in a parking lot, can Finian keep the income that results from leasing the vehicles? Explain your answer. **(See page 709.)**

—Check your answers to the Issue Spotters against the answers provided in Appendix E at the end of this text.

BEFORE THE TEST

Go to www.cengagebrain.com, enter the ISBN 9781133273561, and click on "Find" to locate this textbook's Web site. Then, click on "Access Now" under "Study Tools," and select Chapter 27 at the top. There, you will find a Practice Quiz that you can take to assess your mastery of the concepts in this chapter, as well as Flashcards, a Glossary of important terms, and Video Questions (when assigned).

For Review

Answers to the even-numbered questions in this For Review section can be found in Appendix F at the end of this text.

1. What are the three essential elements of a partnership?
2. What are the rights and duties of partners in an ordinary partnership?
3. What is meant by joint and several liability? Why is this often considered to be a disadvantage of the partnership form of business?
4. What advantages do limited liability partnerships offer to businesspersons that are not offered by general partnerships?
5. What are the key differences between the rights and liabilities of general partners and those of limited partners?

Business Scenarios and Case Problems

27–1 Partnership Formation. Daniel is the owner of a chain of shoe stores. He hires Rubya to be the manager of a new store, which is to open in Grand Rapids, Michigan. Daniel, by written contract, agrees to pay Rubya a monthly salary and 20 percent of the profits. Without Daniel's knowledge, Rubya represents himself to Classen as Daniel's partner, showing Classen the agreement to share profits. Classen extends credit to Rubya. Rubya defaults. Discuss whether Classen can hold Daniel liable as a partner. **(See pages 705–707.)**

27–2 Question with Sample Answer—Limited Partnership. Dorinda, Luis, and Elizabeth form a limited partnership. Dorinda is a general partner, and Luis and Elizabeth are limited partners. Discuss fully whether each of the separate events below constitutes a dissolution of the limited partnership. **(See pages 717–719.)**

1. Luis assigns his partnership interest to Ashley.
2. Elizabeth is petitioned into involuntary bankruptcy.
3. Dorinda dies.

—For a sample answer to Question 27–2, go to Appendix G at the end of this text.

27–3 Distribution of Partnership Assets. Shawna and David formed a partnership. At the time of the partnership's formation, Shawna's capital contribution was $10,000, and David's was $15,000. Later, Shawna made a $10,000 loan to the partnership when it needed working capital. The partnership agreement provided that profits were to be shared with 40 percent for Shawna and 60 percent for David. The partnership was dissolved after David's death. At the end of the dissolution and the winding up of the partnership, the partnership's assets were $50,000, and the partnership's debts were $8,000. Discuss fully how the assets should be distributed. **(See page 715.)**

27–4 Limited Partnership. James Carpenter contracted with Austin Estates, LP, to buy property in Texas. Carpenter asked Sandra McBeth to invest in the deal. He admitted that a dispute had arisen with the city of Austin over water for the property, but he assured her that it would not be a significant obstacle. McBeth agreed to invest $800,000 to hold open the option to buy the property. She became a limited partner in StoneLake Ranch, LP. Carpenter acted as the firm's general partner. Despite his statements to McBeth, the purchase was delayed due to the water dispute. Unable to complete the purchase in a timely manner, Carpenter paid the $800,000 to Austin Estates without notifying McBeth. Later, Carpenter and others—*excluding* McBeth—bought the property and sold it at a profit. McBeth filed a suit in a Texas state court against Carpenter. What is the nature of the fiduciary duty that a general partner owes a limited partner? Did Carpenter breach that duty in this case? Explain. [*McBeth v. Carpenter,* 565 F.3d 171 (5th Cir. 2009)] **(See pages 709–710.)**

27–5 Partnership Dissolution. George Chaney and William Dickerson were partners in Bowen's Mill Landing, which purchased a large piece of land in the 1980s. The partners had planned to develop the property, but nothing was ever done. Chaney died in 1990, and his wife inherited his interest. When she died in 2004, her two sons, John and Dewey Lynch, inherited the half-interest in the partnership. Dickerson died in 1995, and his daughter, Billie Thompson, inherited his half-interest. In 2006, the Lynches filed a petition for partition, asking that a commission be appointed to make a fair division of the land, giving the Lynches half and Thompson half. In 2007, the commission reported on how to divide the land into two parts. Thompson objected that the land belonged to Bowen's Mill Landing and could not be divided. The trial court ordered Thompson to "effectuate the dissolution of any partnership entity and . . . to wind up the business and affairs of any partnership" so that the land could be divided. Thompson appealed. Can the court order the partnership to dissolve? Why or why not? [*Thompson v. Lynch,* 990 A.2d 432 (Sup.Ct.Del. 2010)] **(See pages 713–714.)**

27–6 Fiduciary Duties of Partners. Karl Horvath, Hein Rüsen, and Carl Thomas formed a partnership, HRT Enterprises, to buy a manufacturing plant. Rüsen and Thomas leased the plant to their own company, Merkur Steel. Merkur then sublet the premises to other companies owned by Rüsen and Thomas. The rent that these companies paid to Merkur was higher than the rent from the arrangement. Rüsen and Thomas did not tell Horvath about the subleases. Did Rüsen and Thomas breach their fiduciary duties to HRT and Horvath? Discuss. [*Horvath v. HRT Enterprises,* 489 Mich.App. 992, 800 N.W.2d 595 (2011)] **(See pages 709–710.)**

27–7 Case Problem with Sample Answer—Partnership Formation. Patricia Garcia and Bernardo Lucero were in a romantic relationship. While they were seeing each other, Garcia and Lucero acquired an electronics service center, paying $30,000 each. Two years later, they purchased an apartment complex. The property was deeded to Lucero, but neither Garcia nor Lucero made a down payment. The couple considered both properties to be owned "50/50," and they agreed to share profits, losses, and management rights. When the couple's romantic relationship ended, Garcia asked a court to declare that she and Lucero had a partnership. In court, Lucero argued that the couple did not have a written partnership agreement and thus did not have a partnership. Did they have a partnership? Why or why not? [*Garcia v. Lucero,* 366 S.W.3d 275 (Tex.App.—El Paso 2012)] **(See pages 705–706.)**

—For a sample answer to Problem 27–7, go to Appendix H at the end of this text.

27–8 A Question of Ethics—Dissociation. Elliot Willensky and Beverly Moran formed a partnership to buy, renovate, and sell a house. Moran agreed to finance the effort, which was to cost no more than $60,000. Willensky agreed to oversee the work, which was to be done in six months. Willensky lived in the house during the renovation. As the project progressed, Willensky incurred excessive and unnecessary expenses, misappropriated funds for his personal use, did not pay bills on time, and did not keep Moran informed of the costs. More than a year later, the renovation was still not completed and Willensky walked off the project. Moran completed the renovation, which ultimately cost $311,222, and sold the house. Moran then sued to dissolve the partnership and recover damages from Willensky for breach of contract and wrongful dissociation. [*Moran v. Willensky,* 339 S.W.3d 651 (Tenn.App. 2010)] **(See pages 712–713.)**

1. Moran alleged that Willensky had wrongfully dissociated from the partnership. When did this dissociation occur? Why was his dissociation wrongful?
2. Which of Willensky's actions breached the partnership agreement? Which of his acts were unethical or bad management?

Critical Thinking and Writing Assignments

27–9 **Business Law Writing.** Sandra Lerner and Patricia Holmes were friends. One evening, while applying nail polish to Lerner, Holmes layered a raspberry color over black to produce a new color, which Lerner liked. Later, the two created other colors with names like "Bruise," "Smog," and "Oil Slick," and titled their concept "Urban Decay." Lerner and Holmes started a firm to produce and market the polishes but never discussed the sharing of profits and losses. They agreed to build the business and then sell it. Together, they did market research, worked on a logo and advertising, obtained capital, and hired employees. Then Lerner began scheming to edge Holmes out of the firm.

1. Lerner claimed that there was no partnership agreement because there was no agreement on how to divide profits. Was Lerner right? Why or why not?
2. Suppose that Lerner, but not Holmes, had contributed a significant amount of personal funds to developing and marketing the new nail polish. Would this entitle Lerner to receive more of the profit? Explain.
3. Did Lerner violate her fiduciary duty? Why or why not?

27–10 **Business Law Critical Thinking Group Assignment.** At least six months before the 1996 Summer Olympic Games in Atlanta, Georgia, Stafford Fontenot, Steve Turner, Mike Montelaro, Joe Sokol, and Doug Brinsmade agreed to sell Cajun food at the games and began making preparations. On May 19, the group (calling themselves Prairie Cajun Seafood Catering of Louisiana) applied for a business license with the county health department. Later, Ted Norris sold a mobile kitchen for an $8,000 check drawn on the "Prairie Cajun Seafood Catering of Louisiana" account and two promissory notes, one for $12,000 and the other for $20,000. The notes, which were dated June 12, listed only Fontenot "d/b/a Prairie Cajun Seafood" as the maker (*d/b/a* is an abbreviation for "doing business as"). On July 31, Fontenot and his friends signed a partnership agreement, which listed specific percentages of profits and losses. They drove the mobile kitchen to Atlanta, but business was disastrous. When the notes were not paid, Norris filed a suit in a Louisiana state court against Fontenot, seeking payment.

1. The first group will discuss the elements of a partnership and determine whether there was a partnership among Fontenot and the others.
2. The second group will determine who can be held liable on the notes and why.

CHAPTER 28

Limited Liability Companies and Special Business Forms

(track5/iStockphoto.com)

CHAPTER OUTLINE

- Limited Liability Companies
- LLC Operation and Management
- Dissociation and Dissolution of an LLC
- Special Business Forms

LEARNING OBJECTIVES

The five learning objectives below are designed to help improve your understanding of the chapter. After reading this chapter, you should be able to answer the following questions:

1. How are limited liability companies formed, and who decides how they will be managed and operated?
2. What advantages do limited liability companies offer to businesspersons that are not offered by sole proprietorships or partnerships?
3. What are the two options for managing limited liability companies?
4. What is a joint venture? How is it similar to a partnership? How is it different?
5. What are the essential characteristics of joint stock companies, syndicates, business trusts, and cooperatives, respectively?

"To play it safe is not to play."
—Robert Altman, 1925–2006 (American film director)

In the United States, public policy encourages commerce and profit-making activities. Our government allows entrepreneurs to choose from a variety of business organizational forms. Many businesspersons would agree with the chapter-opening quotation that in business "to play it safe is not to play." Because risk is associated with the potential for higher profits, businesspersons are motivated to choose organizational forms that limit their liability while allowing them to take risks that may lead to greater profits.

In this chapter, we examine a relatively new and increasingly common form of business organization, the *limited liability company* (LLC). LLCs are becoming an organizational form of choice among businesspersons—a trend encouraged by state statutes permitting their use.

We begin by examining the origins and evolution of the LLC in the *Landmark in the Law* feature on the next page. Then we look at important characteristics of the LLC, discuss operation and management options in an LLC, and consider how the business is dissolved. The chapter concludes with a discussion of various other special business forms, such as joint ventures and cooperatives.

LANDMARK IN THE LAW

Limited Liability Company (LLC) Statutes

In 1977, Wyoming became the first state to pass legislation authorizing the creation of a limited liability company (LLC). Although LLCs did not emerge in the United States until the late 1970s, they have been used for more than a century in various foreign jurisdictions, including several European and South American nations.

Taxation of LLCs In the United States, after Wyoming's adoption of an LLC statute, it still was unclear how the Internal Revenue Service (IRS) would treat LLCs for tax purposes. In 1988, however, the IRS ruled that Wyoming LLCs would be taxed as partnerships instead of corporations, providing that certain requirements were met. Before this ruling, only one other state—Florida, in 1982—had authorized LLCs. The 1988 ruling encouraged additional states to enact LLC statutes, and in less than a decade, all states had done so.

Other IRS rules also encouraged more widespread use of LLCs in the business world. Under these rules, any unincorporated business with more than one owner is automatically taxed as a partnership unless it indicates otherwise on the tax form or fits into one of the exceptions. The exceptions involve publicly traded companies, companies formed under a state incorporation statute, and certain foreign-owned companies. If a business chooses to be taxed as a corporation, it can indicate this preference by checking a box on the IRS form.

Foreign Entities May Be LLC Members Part of the impetus behind the creation of LLCs in this country is that foreign investors are allowed to become LLC members. In an era increasingly characterized by global business efforts and investments, the LLC often offers U.S. firms and potential investors from other countries greater flexibility and opportunities than are available through partnerships or corporations.

Application to Today's World *Once it became clear that LLCs could be taxed as partnerships, the LLC form of business organization was widely adopted. Members could avoid the personal liability associated with the partnership form of business as well as the double taxation of the corporate form of business (see Chapter 29). Today, LLCs are a common form of business organization.*

Limited Liability Companies

Limited Liability Company (LLC) A hybrid form of business enterprise that offers the limited liability of a corporation and the tax advantages of a partnership.

A **limited liability company (LLC)** is a hybrid that combines the limited liability aspects of a corporation and the tax advantages of a partnership. LLCs are governed by state LLC statutes, which vary, of course, from state to state. Although the National Conference of Commissioners on Uniform State Laws (NCCUSL) issued the Uniform Limited Liability Company Act (ULLCA) in an attempt to create more uniformity among the states, less than one-fifth of the states have adopted it. Thus, the law governing LLCs remains far from uniform. Some provisions are common to most state statutes, however, and we base our discussion of LLCs in this section on these common elements.

KNOW THIS

A uniform law is a "model" law. It does not become the law of any state until the state legislature adopts it, either in part or in its entirety.

The Nature of the LLC

Member A person who has an ownership interest in a limited liability company.

LLCs share many characteristics with corporations. Like corporations, LLCs are creatures of the state. In other words, they must be formed and operated in compliance with state law. Like shareholders in a corporation, owners of an LLC, who are called **members**, enjoy limited liability [ULLCA 303].

Members are shielded from personal liability in many situations, even sometimes when sued by employees of the firm. **CASE EXAMPLE 28.1** Penny McFarland was the activities director at a retirement community in Virginia that was owned by an LLC. Her supervisor told her to take the residents outside for a walk on a day when the temperature was 95 degrees. McFarland complained to the state health department and was fired from

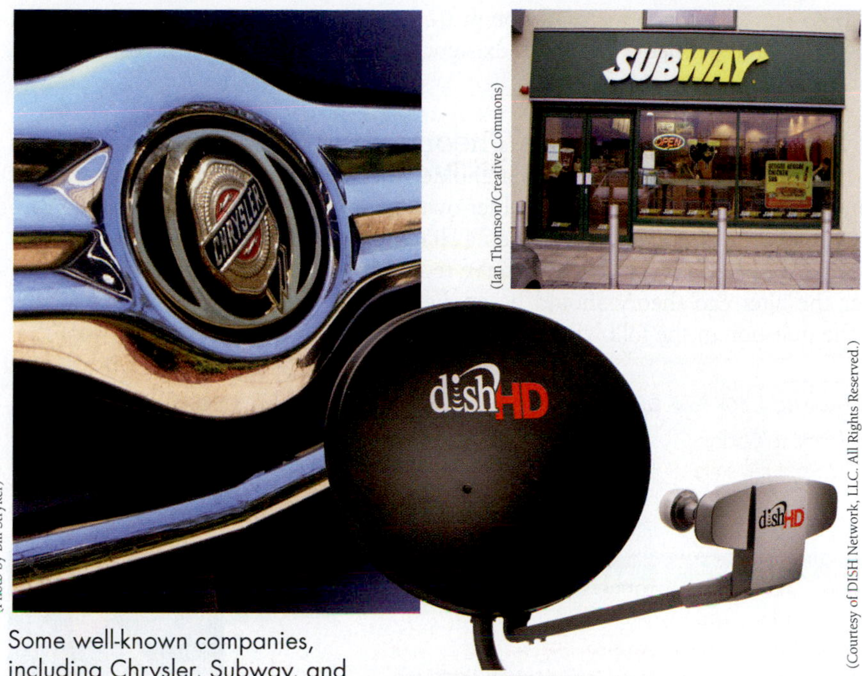

(Photo by Bill Stryker)
(Ian Thomson/Creative Commons)
(Courtesy of DISH Network, LLC. All Rights Reserved.)

Some well-known companies, including Chrysler, Subway, and Dish Network, are limited liability companies.

her job. She sued a number of managers and members of the LLC for wrongful discharge. The court held that under Virginia law, members, managers, and agents of an LLC are not responsible for its liabilities "solely" by virtue of their status. The court dismissed the action against all but one defendant, concluding that only those who "have played a key role in contributing to the company's tortious conduct" can be part of a wrongful discharge claim.[1] •

Like corporations, LLCs are legal entities apart from their members. As a legal person, an LLC can sue or be sued, enter into contracts, and hold title to property [ULLCA 201]. The terminology used to describe LLCs formed in other states or nations is also similar to the terminology used in corporate law. For example, an LLC formed in one state but doing business in another state is referred to in the second state as a *foreign LLC*.

LLC Formation

Articles of Organization The document filed with a designated state official by which a limited liability company is formed.

To form an LLC, **articles of organization** must be filed with a central state agency—usually the secretary of state's office [ULLCA 202].[2] Typically, the articles are required to include such information as the name of the business, its principal address, the name and address of a registered agent, the names of the members, and information on how the LLC will be managed [ULLCA 203]. Although a majority of the states permit one-member LLCs, some states require at least two members. The business's name must include the words *Limited Liability Company* or the initials *LLC* [ULLCA 105(a)].

Preformation Contracts

Sometimes, the future members of an LLC may enter into contracts on the entity's behalf before the LLC is formally formed. As you will read in Chapter 29, a similar process often occurs with corporations. Persons forming a corporation may enter into contracts during the process of incorporation but before the corporation becomes a legal entity. These contracts are referred to as preincorporation contracts. Once the corporation is formed and adopts the preincorporation contract (by means of a *novation*—see page 344 in Chapter 13), it can then enforce the contract terms.

LEARNING OBJECTIVE 1

How are limited liability companies formed, and who decides how they will be managed and operated?

In dealing with the preorganization contracts of LLCs, courts may apply the well-established principles of corporate law relating to preincorporation contracts. **CASE EXAMPLE 28.2** 607 South Park, LLC, entered into an agreement to sell a hotel to 607 Park View Associates, Ltd., which then assigned the rights to the purchase to another company, 02 Development, LLC. At the time, 02 Development did not yet exist—it was legally created several months later. 607 South Park subsequently refused to sell the hotel to 02 Development, and 02 Development sued for breach of the purchase agreement. A California appellate court ruled that LLCs should be treated the same as corporations with

1. *McFarland v. Virginia Retirement Services of Chesterfield, LLC,* 477 F.Supp.2d 727 (D.Va. 2007).
2. In addition to requiring the filing of articles of organization, a few states require that a notice of the intention to form an LLC be published in a local newspaper.

respect to preorganization contracts. Although 02 Development did not exist when the agreement was executed, once it came into existence, it could enforce any preorganization contract made on its behalf.[3]

Liability under the Alter Ego Theory

Sometimes, when a corporation is deemed to be merely an "alter ego" of the shareholder-owner, a court will *pierce the corporate veil* of limited liability and hold the shareholder-owner liable (see page 756 in Chapter 29). A court may apply the alter ego theory when a shareholder commingles (mixes together) personal and corporate funds or fails to observe required corporate formalities.

Whether the alter ego theory should be applied to hold an LLC member personally liable was the question in the following case.

3. *02 Development, LLC v. 607 South Park, LLC,* 159 Cal.App.4th 609, 71 Cal.Rptr.3d 608 (2008).

Case 28.1

ORX Resources, Inc. v. MBW Exploration, LLC

Court of Appeal of Louisiana, Fourth Circuit, 32 So.3d 931 (2010).

(SimplyCreativePhotography/iStockphoto)

Oil exploration companies are often LLCs.

FACTS To share the expenses and profits of a venture to develop oil and gas deposits, ORX Resources, Inc., partnered with MBW Exploration, LLC. Mark Washauer signed the agreement with ORX as "managing member" on behalf of MBW Exploration, LLC, which had not yet been formed. MBW did not have a bank account. Initially, Washauer paid for its expenditures with personal checks. He then paid MBW's participation fee with a check drawn on another of his business entities. When MBW's share of unpaid partnership expenses amounted to more than $84,220, ORX demanded payment from Washauer, who refused to pay. ORX sued both MBW Exploration, LLC, and Washauer for breach of contract. The trial court determined that Washauer had operated MBW as his *alter ego,* and it allowed ORX to "pierce the veil" of the LLC and hold the members jointly and severally liable for the debt. Washauer and MBW appealed the judgment.

ISSUE Should the court apply the alter ego theory from corporate law and "pierce the veil" of the LLC when its members have commingled funds and failed to observe LLC formalities?

DECISION Yes. A state intermediate appellate court affirmed the judgment of the trial court that the alter ego theory applied to LLCs in Louisiana.

REASON The court reasoned that Washauer had used MBW Exploration, LLC, as a shell and had attempted to avoid paying a legitimate debt of the LLC. "We find that Washauer's activities on behalf of MBW do merit the piercing of the veil of this LLC." Washauer had commingled the MBW funds with his personal funds and those of one of his separate companies. MBW had not even had a separate bank account to transact its own affairs. "Furthermore, when MBW began contracting with ORX, it had not yet been recognized as an LLC by the Louisiana Secretary of State." The court determined that "piercing the veil of an LLC is justified to prevent the use of the LLC form to defraud creditors." Washauer was operating MBW "at his leisure and discretion" and could be held personally liable jointly and severally with MBW.

CRITICAL THINKING—Legal Consideration *What does "jointly and severally" mean in terms of liability (see page 711 in Chapter 27)? Would ORX prefer that Washauer and MBW be held personally liable jointly and severally, rather than that Washauer alone be held personally liable? Explain.*

Jurisdictional Requirements

One of the significant differences between LLCs and corporations involves federal jurisdictional requirements (see the discussion of diversity-of-citizenship jurisdiction on page 66 of Chapter 3). Under federal law, a corporation is deemed to be a citizen of the state where it is incorporated and maintains its principal place of business.[4] The statute does not mention the citizenship of partnerships, LLCs, and other unincorporated associations, but the courts have tended to regard these entities as citizens of every state of which their members are citizens.

"Business is the salt of life."

Voltaire, 1694–1778
(French author and intellectual)

The state citizenship of LLCs may come into play when a party sues an LLC based on diversity of citizenship. Remember from Chapter 3 that when parties to a lawsuit are from different states, a federal court can exercise diversity jurisdiction if the amount in controversy exceeds $75,000. *Total* diversity of citizenship must exist, however.

EXAMPLE 28.3 Jen Fong, a citizen of New York, wishes to bring a lawsuit against Skycel, an LLC formed under the laws of Connecticut. One of Skycel's members also lives in New York. Fong will not be able to bring the action against Skycel in federal court—on the basis of diversity jurisdiction—because the defendant LLC is also considered a citizen of New York. The same would be true if Fong was filing a suit against multiple defendants and one of the defendants lived in New York. ●

Advantages of the LLC

The LLC offers many advantages to businesspersons, which is why this form of business organization has become increasingly popular. See the *Business Application* feature on page 739 for a discussion of the factors that entrepreneurs need to consider when choosing between LLCs and limited liability partnerships (LLPs).

Limited Liability

A key advantage of the LLC is that the liability of members is limited to the amount of their investments. Although the LLC as an entity can be held liable for any loss or injury caused by the wrongful acts or omissions of its members, the members themselves generally are not personally liable.

Taxation

Another advantage is the flexibility of the LLC in regard to taxation. An LLC that has *two or more members* can choose to be taxed either as a partnership or as a corporation. As you will read in Chapter 29, a corporate entity must pay income taxes on its profits, and the shareholders then pay personal income taxes on profits distributed as dividends. An LLC that wants to distribute profits to its members may prefer to be taxed as a partnership to avoid the "double taxation" that is characteristic of the corporate entity.

LEARNING OBJECTIVE 2
What advantages do limited liability companies offer to businesspersons that are not offered by sole proprietorships or partnerships?

Unless an LLC indicates that it wishes to be taxed as a corporation, the IRS automatically taxes it as a partnership. This means that the LLC as an entity pays no taxes. Rather, as in a partnership, profits are "passed through" the LLC to the members who then personally pay taxes on the profits. If an LLC's members want to reinvest the profits in the business, however, rather than distribute the profits to members, they may prefer that the LLC be taxed as a corporation. Corporate income tax rates may be lower than personal tax rates.

For federal income tax purposes, one-member LLCs are automatically taxed as sole proprietorships unless they indicate that they wish to be taxed as corporations. With respect to state taxes, most states follow the IRS rules.

Management and Foreign Investors

Still another advantage of the LLC for businesspersons is the flexibility it offers in terms of business operations and

4. 28 U.S.C. Section 1332.

(Photo Courtesy of ECD Ovonics)

Stan Ovshinsky, founder of Ovonic Hydrogen Systems, LLC. What are some of the advantages of doing business as an LLC instead of a corporation? Are there any disadvantages?

management—as will be discussed shortly. Finally, because foreign investors can participate in an LLC, the LLC form of business is attractive as a way to encourage investment. For a discussion of business organizations in other nations that are similar to the LLC, see this chapter's *Beyond Our Borders* feature on the facing page.

Disadvantages of the LLC

The main disadvantage of the LLC is that state LLC statutes are not uniform. Therefore, businesses that operate in more than one state may be treated differently in different states.

Generally, most states apply to a foreign LLC (an LLC formed in another state) the law of the state where the LLC was formed. Difficulties can arise, though, when one state's court must interpret and apply another state's laws.

LLC Operation and Management

As mentioned, an advantage of the LLC form of business is the flexibility it offers in terms of operation and management. We discuss the operating agreement, management options, and general operating procedures of LLCs next.

The LLC Operating Agreement

Operating Agreement An agreement in which the members of a limited liability company set forth the details of how the business will be managed and operated.

The members of an LLC can decide how to operate the various aspects of the business by forming an **operating agreement** [ULLCA 103(a)]. Operating agreements typically contain provisions relating to management, how profits will be divided, the transfer of membership interests, whether the LLC will be dissolved on the death or departure of a member, and other important issues.

A Writing Is Preferred In many states, an operating agreement is not required for an LLC to exist, and if there is one, it need not be in writing. Generally, though, LLC members should protect their interests by creating a written operating agreement. As in any business, disputes may arise over any number of issues. If there is no agreement covering the topic under dispute, such as how profits will be divided, the state LLC statute will govern the outcome. For example, most LLC statutes provide that if the members have not specified how profits will be divided, they will be divided equally among the members.

Partnership Law May Apply When an issue, such as the authority of individual members, is not covered by an operating agreement or by an LLC statute, the courts often apply principles of partnership law. These principles can give the members of an LLC broad authority to bind the LLC unless the operating agreement provides otherwise.

CASE EXAMPLE 28.4 Clifford Kuhn, Jr., and Joseph Tumminelli formed a limousine service as an LLC. They did not create a written operating agreement but orally agreed that Kuhn would provide the financial backing and procure customers, and that Tumminelli would manage the day-to-day operations. Tumminelli embezzled $283,000 from the company after cashing customers' checks at Quick Cash, Inc., a local check-cashing service. Kuhn filed a lawsuit against Tumminelli, the banks, and Quick Cash to recover the embezzled funds. He argued that Quick Cash and the banks were liable because Tumminelli did not have the authority to cash the company's checks. The court, however, held that in the absence of a written operating agreement to the contrary, a member of an LLC, like a partner in a partnership, does have the authority to cash the firm's checks.[5] ●

5. *Kuhn v. Tumminelli*, 366 N.J.Super. 431, 841 A.2d 496 (2004).

Limited Liability Companies in Other Nations

Limited liability companies are not unique to the United States. Many nations have business forms that provide limited liability, although these organizations may differ significantly from our domestic limited liability companies (LLCs). In Germany, the *GmbH*, or *Gesellschaft mit beschränkter Haftung* (which means "company with limited liability"), is a type of business entity that resembles the LLC. The GmbH is now the most widely used business form in Germany. A GmbH, however, is owned by shareholders and thus resembles a U.S. corporation in certain respects. German laws also impose numerous restrictions on the operations and business transactions of GmbHs, whereas LLCs in the United States are not even required to have an operating agreement.

Business forms that limit the liability of owners can also be found in various other countries. Limited liability companies known as *limitadas* are common in many Latin American nations. In France, a *société à responsabilité limitée* (meaning "society with limited liability") is an entity that provides business owners with limited liability. Although laws in the United Kingdom and Ireland use the term *limited liability partnership*, the entities are similar to our domestic LLCs. Japan has created a new type of business organization called the *godo kaisha (GK)*, which is also quite similar to an LLC in the United States.

Critical Thinking

Clearly, limited liability is an important aspect of doing business globally. Why might a nation limit the number of member-owners in a limited liability entity?

Management of an LLC

LEARNING OBJECTIVE 3
What are the two options for managing limited liability companies?

Basically, the members of an LLC have two options for managing the firm. It can be either a "member-managed" LLC or a "manager-managed" LLC. Most LLC statutes and the ULLCA provide that unless the articles of organization specify otherwise, an LLC is assumed to be member managed [ULLCA 203(a)(6)].

In a *member-managed* LLC, all of the members participate in management, and decisions are made by majority vote [ULLCA 404(a)]. In a *manager-managed* LLC, the members designate a group of persons to manage the firm. The management group may consist of only members, both members and nonmembers, or only nonmembers.

Managers of LLCs need to be cognizant of the firm's potential liability under the employment-discrimination laws discussed in Chapter 25. Those laws may also extend to individuals who are not members of a protected class, as discussed in this chapter's *Law, Diversity, and Business: Managerial Implications* feature on the following page.

Fiduciary Duties

"Business without profit is not business any more than a pickle is candy."

Charles Abbott, 1762–1832
(British jurist)

Under the ULLCA, managers in a manager-managed LLC owe fiduciary duties (the duty of loyalty and the duty of care) to the LLC and to its members, just as corporate directors and officers owe fiduciary duties to the corporation and to its shareholders [ULLCA 409(a), (h)]. Because not all states have adopted the ULLCA, though, some state statutes provide that managers owe fiduciary duties only to the LLC and not to its members.

Although to whom the duty is owed may seem insignificant at first glance, it can have a dramatic effect on the outcome of litigation. In North Carolina and Virginia, for instance, the LLC statutes do not explicitly create fiduciary duties for managers to members. Because the statutes are silent on a manager's duty to members, courts in those two states held that a manager-member owes fiduciary duties only to the LLC and not to the members.[6] In contrast, courts in Idaho and Kentucky held that a manager-member owes

6. *Kaplan v. O.K. Technologies, LLC*, 675 S.E.2d 133 (N.C.App. 2009); North Carolina General Statutes Section 57C-3-22(b); and *Remora Investments, LLC v. Orr*, 277 Va. 316, 673 S.E.2d 845 (2009); Virginia Code Section 13.1-1024.1.

LAW, DIVERSITY, AND BUSINESS: MANAGERIAL IMPLICATIONS

CAN A PERSON WHO IS NOT A MEMBER OF A PROTECTED CLASS SUE FOR DISCRIMINATION?

Under federal law and the laws of most states, discrimination in employment based on race, color, religion, national origin, gender, age, or disability is prohibited. Persons who are members of these protected classes can sue if they are subjected to discrimination. But can a person subjected to discrimination bring a lawsuit if he is not a member of a protected class, even though managers and other employees think that he is? This somewhat unusual situation occurred in New Jersey.

A Hostile Work Environment Myron Cowher worked at Carson & Roberts Site Construction & Engineering, Inc. For more than a year, at least two of his supervisors directed an almost daily barrage of anti-Semitic remarks at him. They believed that he was Jewish, although his actual background was German-Irish and Lutheran.

Cowher brought a suit against the supervisors and the construction company, claiming a hostile work environment. The trial court, however, ruled that he did not have *standing to sue* (see page 69 in Chapter 3) under New Jersey law because he was not Jewish and, thus, was not a member of a protected class. Cowher appealed.

Anti-Semitic Slurs Are Actionable—Even When Mistaken The appellate court disagreed. The court ruled that if Cowher can prove that the discrimination "would not have occurred but for the perception that he was Jewish," his claim is covered by New Jersey's antidiscrimination law.[a] The case was remanded for trial. Thus, in the appellate court's view, the nature of the discriminatory remarks, and not the actual characteristics of the plaintiff (Cowher), determines whether the remarks are actionable.

Business Implications *The New Jersey appellate court's ruling clearly indicates that even misdirected personal slurs in the workplace are unacceptable. What might have been considered playful banter in the past may be actionable today under various states' antidiscrimination laws.*

a. *Cowher v. Carson & Roberts Site Construction & Engineering, Inc.,* 425 N.J.Super 285, 40 A.3d 1171 (2012).

fiduciary duties to the LLC's members and that the members can sue the manager for breaching fiduciary duties.[7]

In Alabama, where the following case arose, managers owe fiduciary duties to the LLC and to its members.

7. *Bushi v. Sage Health Care, LLC,* 146 Idaho 764, 203 P.3d 694 (2009); Idaho Code Sections 30-6-101 *et seq.*; and *Patmon v. Hobbs,* 280 S.W.3d 589 (Ky.App. 2009); Kentucky Revised Statutes Section 275.170.

Case 28.2

Polk v. Polk

Court of Civil Appeals of Alabama,
70 So.3d 363 (2011).

(temis/iStockphoto)

A member of a plumbing LLC.

FACTS Leslie Polk and his children, Yurii and Dusty Polk and Lezanne Proctor, formed Polk Plumbing, LLC, in Alabama. Leslie, Dusty, and Yurii performed commercial plumbing work, and Lezanne, an accountant, maintained the financial records and served as the office manager. After a couple of years, Yurii quit the firm. Eighteen months later, Leslie "fired" Dusty and Lezanne. He denied them access to the LLC's books and offices but continued to operate the business.

Dusty and Lezanne filed a suit in an Alabama state court against Leslie, claiming breach of fiduciary duty. The court submitted the claim to a jury with the instruction that in Alabama employment relationships are "at will" (see Chapter 24). The court also told the jury that it could not consider the plaintiffs' "firing" as part of their claim. The jury awarded Dusty and Lezanne one dollar

Case 28.2—Continued

each in damages. They appealed, arguing that the judge's instructions to the jury were prejudicial—that is, that the instructions had substantially affected the outcome of the trial.

ISSUE Did the trial court properly instruct the jury on which evidence could be considered in Dusty and Lezanne's claim for breach of fiduciary duty?

DECISION No. A state intermediate appellate court reversed the lower court's judgment on the claim for breach of fiduciary duty and remanded the case for a new trial. The lower court erred by instructing the jury that Dusty and Lezanne's employment as managers was at will and by failing to instruct the jury that it could consider their "firing" as evidence in support of their claim.

REASON The court reasoned that the lower court had committed reversible errors that had "probably injuriously affected substantial rights of Dusty and Lezanne." Dusty and Lezanne served as managers of the LLC. The operating agreement provided that managers served until replaced or recalled by a vote of the majority of the members. Therefore, their employment as managers was not at will. Because no vote had been taken to recall or replace Dusty and Lezanne, their father did not have the authority to terminate their employment. His attempted "firing" of them was in violation of the LLC's operating agreement. If the jury had considered all of this evidence, the amount of damages might have been higher.

WHAT IF THE FACTS WERE DIFFERENT? *Suppose that Leslie had owned a majority of the shares in Polk Plumbing. Could his "firing" of Dusty and Lezanne still be considered as evidence of a breach of fiduciary duty? Explain.*

Decision-Making Procedures

The members of an LLC can also include provisions governing decision-making procedures in their operating agreement. For instance, the agreement can include procedures for choosing or removing managers. Although most LLC statutes are silent on this issue, the ULLCA provides that members may choose and remove managers by majority vote [ULLCA 404(b)(3)].

The members are also free to include provisions designating when and for what purposes they will hold formal members' meetings. In contrast to state laws governing corporations, which generally provide for shareholders' meetings (see Chapter 29), most state LLC statutes have no provisions regarding members' meetings.

Members may also specify in their agreement how voting rights will be apportioned. If they do not, LLC statutes in most states provide that voting rights are apportioned according to the members' capital contributions. Some states provide that, in the absence of an agreement to the contrary, each member has one vote.

Dissociation and Dissolution of an LLC

Recall from Chapter 27 that in the context of partnerships, *dissociation* occurs when a partner ceases to be associated in the carrying on of the business. The same concept applies to LLCs. A member of an LLC has the *power* to dissociate from the LLC at any time, but she or he may not have the *right* to dissociate.

Under the ULLCA, the events that trigger a member's dissociation from an LLC are similar to the events causing a partner to be dissociated under the Uniform Partnership Act (UPA). These include voluntary withdrawal, expulsion by other members or by court order, bankruptcy, incompetence, and death. Generally, if a member dies or otherwise dissociates from an LLC, the other members may continue to carry on the LLC's business, unless the operating agreement provides otherwise.

ETHICAL ISSUE

After selling real estate to their LLC, can its owners still claim a homestead exemption for the property when filing for bankruptcy? Although an LLC offers many advantages, a potential disadvantage may manifest itself if the members of an LLC file for personal bankruptcy after selling their home to their LLC. James and Susan Kane deeded their home to their two-member LLC and recorded ownership of the property in the LLC's name. The Kanes subsequently filed for personal bankruptcy and claimed a *homestead exemption* (see page 548 in Chapter 21) for the property on the basis that the LLC had been administratively dissolved and that since they were its only members, the property had reverted to them.

When one of the couple's debtors objected to the exemption, the court discovered that the LLC still maintained a bank account in its name and had taken out a mortgage on the property. Hence, the court said that the LLC still existed in the *winding up phase* (see facing page),and that the property belonged to the LLC because no deed had been executed transferring the property back to the Kanes. The Kanes' membership interests in the LLC were personal property and thus the property of their bankruptcy estate. Therefore, they could not claim the homestead exemption.[8]

The Effect of Dissociation

When a member dissociates from an LLC, he or she loses the right to participate in management and the right to act as an agent for the LLC. The member's duty of loyalty to the LLC also terminates, and the duty of care continues only with respect to events that occurred before dissociation. Generally, the dissociated member also has a right to have his or her interest in the LLC bought out by the other members. The LLC's operating agreement may contain provisions establishing a buyout price, but if it does not, the member's interest is usually purchased at a fair value. In states that have adopted the ULLCA, the LLC must purchase the interest at "fair" value within 120 days after the dissociation.

"Business is more exciting than any game."

Lord Beaverbrook, 1879–1964 (Canadian-British business tycoon)

If the member's dissociation violates the LLC's operating agreement, it is considered legally wrongful, and the dissociated member can be held liable for damages caused by the dissociation. **EXAMPLE 28.5** Chadwick and Barrel are members of an LLC. Chadwick manages the accounts, and Barrel, who has many connections in the community and is a skilled investor, brings in the business. If Barrel wrongfully dissociates from the LLC, the LLC's business will suffer, and Chadwick can hold Barrel liable for the loss of business resulting from her withdrawal. •

Dissolution

Regardless of whether a member's dissociation was wrongful or rightful, normally the dissociated member has no right to force the LLC to dissolve. The remaining members can opt to either continue or dissolve the business. Members can also stipulate in their operating agreement that certain events will cause dissolution, or they can agree that they have the power to dissolve the LLC by vote. As with partnerships, a court can order an LLC to be dissolved in certain circumstances, such as when the members have engaged in illegal or oppressive conduct, or when it is no longer feasible to carry on the business.

In the following case, three members formed an LLC to develop real estate. The court had to decide whether the LLC could be dissolved because continuing the business was impracticable.

8. *In re Kane*, 2011 WL 2119015 (Bank.D.Mass. 2011).

Case 28.3

Venture Sales, LLC v. Perkins

Supreme Court of Mississippi, 86 So. 3d 910 (2012).

(jml5571/iStockphoto)

An undeveloped subdivision.

FACTS Walter Perkins, Gary Fordham, and David Thompson formed Venture Sales, LLC, to develop a subdivision in Petal, Mississippi. All three men contributed land and funds to Venture Sales, resulting in total holdings of 466 acres of land and about $158,000 in cash.

Perkins was an assistant coach for the Cleveland Browns, so he trusted Fordham and Thompson to develop the property. More than a decade later, however, Fordham and Thompson still had not done

Case 28.3—Continued

anything with the property, although they had developed at least two other subdivisions in the area. Fordham and Thompson suggested selling the property, but Perkins disagreed with the proposed listing price of $3.5 million. Perkins then sought a judicial dissolution of Venture Sales. Fordham and Thompson told the court that they did not know when they could develop the property and that they had been unable to get the additional funds that they needed to proceed. The trial court ordered the company dissolved. Fordham, Thompson, and Venture Sales appealed.

ISSUE Can Venture Sales be judicially dissolved?

DECISION Yes. The Mississippi Supreme Court affirmed the judgment of the trial court.

REASON Under Mississippi law, an LLC may be judicially dissolved if, among other reasons, "it is not reasonably practicable to carry on the business in conformity with . . . the limited liability company agreement." The statute does not explain when continuing an LLC is "not reasonably practicable." The court therefore followed decisions from other jurisdictions recognizing that dissolution is appropriate when an LLC "is not meeting the economic purpose for which it was established." According to Venture Sales' operating agreement, the company's purpose was "to initially acquire, develop and [sell] commercial and residential properties near Petal, Forrest County, Mississippi."

Nevertheless, more than a decade later, the LLC's property remained undeveloped. Fordham and Thompson pointed to a number of reasons, including the financial crisis and Hurricane Katrina. But regardless of the reasons, Fordham and Thompson lacked the funds needed to proceed and did not know when they could develop the property as planned. Finally, it was immaterial that Perkins did not agree to other business opportunities, such as possibly selling the whole property for $3.5 million. After all, Venture Sales was formed to develop a subdivision. Because the LLC was not meeting that purpose, dissolution was warranted.

CRITICAL THINKING—Legal Consideration *Would dissolution be appropriate if the parties had formed a partnership rather than an LLC? Explain your answer.*

Winding Up

When an LLC is dissolved, any members who did not wrongfully dissociate may participate in the winding up process. To wind up the business, members must collect, liquidate, and distribute the LLC's assets.

Members may preserve the assets for a reasonable time to optimize their return, and they continue to have the authority to perform reasonable acts in conjunction with winding up. In other words, the LLC will be bound by the reasonable acts of its members during the winding up process.

Once all the LLC's assets have been sold, the proceeds are distributed to pay off debts to creditors first (including debts owed to members who are creditors of the LLC). The members' capital contributions are returned next, and any remaining amounts are then distributed to members in equal shares or according to their operating agreement.

PREVENTING LEGAL DISPUTES

When forming an LLC, carefully draft the operating agreement. Stipulate the events that will cause dissociation and how the fair-value buyout price will be calculated. Set a time limit within which the LLC must compensate the dissociated member (or her or his estate) in the event of withdrawal, disability, or death. Include provisions that clearly limit the authority of dissociated members to act on behalf of the LLC and provide a right to seek damages from members who exceed the agreed-on parameters. Also, notify third parties if any member dissociates and file a notice of dissociation with the state to limit the extent of the former member's apparent authority to act on behalf of the LLC. The operating agreement should specify any events that will automatically cause a dissolution, as well as which members will have a right to participate in—or make decisions about—the winding up process.

Special Business Forms

Besides the traditional business forms and limited liability companies discussed in this unit, several other forms can be used to organize a business. For the most part, these special business forms are hybrid organizations—that is, they have characteristics similar to those of partnerships or corporations or combine features of both. These forms include joint ventures, syndicates, joint stock companies, business trusts, and cooperatives.

Joint Ventures

Joint Venture A joint undertaking for a specific commercial enterprise by two or more persons or business entities. A joint venture is treated like a partnership for federal income tax purposes.

A **joint venture**, sometimes referred to as a *joint adventure*, is a relationship in which two or more persons or business entities combine their efforts or their property for a single transaction or project or for a related series of transactions or projects. Unless otherwise agreed, joint venturers share profits and losses equally. For instance, when several contractors combine their resources to build and sell houses in a single development, their relationship is a joint venture.

Joint ventures range in size from very small activities to multimillion-dollar joint actions carried out by some of the world's largest corporations. Large organizations often investigate new markets or new ideas by forming joint ventures with other enterprises. For instance, Intel Corporation and Micron Technology, Inc., formed a joint venture to manufacture NAND flash memory. NAND is a data-storage chip widely used in digital cameras, cell phones, and portable music players.

LEARNING OBJECTIVE 4
What is a joint venture? How is it similar to a partnership? How is it different?

Similarities to Partnerships

The joint venture resembles a partnership and is taxed like a partnership. For this reason, most courts apply the same principles to joint ventures as they apply to partnerships. Joint venturers owe to each other the same fiduciary duties, including the duty of loyalty, that partners owe each other. Thus, if one of the venturers secretly buys land that was supposed to be acquired by the joint venture, the other joint venturers may be awarded damages for the breach of loyalty.

A joint venturer can also be held personally liable for the venture's debts (because joint venturers share profits and *losses*). Like partners, joint venturers have equal rights to manage the activities of the enterprise, but they can agree to give control of the operation to one of the members.

Joint venturers also have authority as agents to enter into contracts for the business that will bind the joint venture. **CASE EXAMPLE 28.6** Murdo Cameron developed components for replicas of vintage P-51 Mustang planes. Cameron and Douglas Anderson agreed in writing to collaborate on the design and manufacture of two P-51s, one for each of them.

Without Cameron's knowledge, Anderson borrowed funds from SPW Associates, LLP, to finance the construction, using the first plane as security for the loan. After Anderson built one plane, he defaulted on the loan. SPW filed a lawsuit to obtain possession of the aircraft. The court ruled that Anderson and Cameron had entered into a joint venture and that the plane was the venture's property. Under partnership law, partners have the power as agents to bind the partnership. Because this principle applies to joint ventures, Anderson had the authority to grant SPW a security interest in the plane, and SPW was entitled to take possession of the plane.[9] •

KNOW THIS
A partnership involves a continuing relationship of the partners. A joint venture is often a one-time association.

Differences from Partnerships

Joint ventures differ from partnerships in several important ways. The members of a joint venture have less implied and apparent

9. *SPW Associates, LLP v. Anderson*, 2006 ND 159, 718 N.W.2d 580 (N.D.Sup.Ct. 2006).

authority than the partners in a partnership. As discussed in Chapter 27, each partner is treated as an agent of the other partners.

Because the activities of a joint venture are more limited than the business of a partnership, the members of a joint venture are presumed to have less power to bind their coventurers. In *Case Example 28.6* on the facing page, for instance, if Anderson's contract had not been directly related to the business of building vintage planes, the court might have concluded that Anderson lacked the authority to bind the joint venture. Also, unlike most partnerships, a joint venture normally terminates when the project or the transaction for which it was formed has been completed, though the members can specify how long the relationship will last.

LEARNING OBJECTIVE 5

What are the essential characteristics of joint stock companies, syndicates, business trusts, and cooperatives, respectively?

Syndicates

Syndicate A group of individuals or firms that join together to finance a project. A syndicate is also called an *investment group*.

A group of individuals or firms that join together to finance a particular project, such as the building of a shopping center or the purchase of a professional basketball franchise, is called a **syndicate** or an *investment group*. The form of such groups varies considerably. A syndicate may exist as a corporation or as a general or limited partnership. In some instances, the members do not have a legally recognized business arrangement but merely purchase and own property jointly.

Joint Stock Companies

Joint Stock Company A hybrid form of business organization that combines characteristics of a corporation and a partnership. Usually, a joint stock company is regarded as a partnership for tax and other legal purposes.

A **joint stock company** is a true hybrid of a partnership and a corporation. It has many characteristics of a corporation in that (1) its ownership is represented by transferable shares of stock, (2) it is usually managed by directors and officers of the company or association, and (3) it can have a perpetual existence. Most of its other features, however, are more characteristic of a partnership, and it is usually treated like a partnership.

As with a partnership, a joint stock company is formed by agreement (not statute), property is usually held in the names of the members, shareholders have personal liability, and the company generally is not treated as a legal entity for purposes of a lawsuit. In a joint stock company, however, shareholders are not considered to be agents of one another, as they are in a partnership (see Chapter 27).

Business Trusts

Business Trust A form of business organization, created by a written trust agreement, that resembles a corporation. Legal ownership and management of the trust's property stay with the trustees, and the profits are distributed to the beneficiaries, who have limited liability.

A **business trust** is created by a written trust agreement that sets forth the interests of the beneficiaries and the obligations and powers of the trustees. With a business trust, legal ownership and management of the property of the business stay with one or more of the trustees, and the profits are distributed to the beneficiaries.

The business trust was started in Massachusetts in an attempt to obtain the limited liability advantage of corporate status while avoiding certain restrictions on a corporation's ownership of, and ability to develop, real property. A business trust resembles a corporation in many respects. Beneficiaries of the trust, for example, are not personally responsible for the debts or obligations of the business trust. In fact, in a number of states, business trusts must pay corporate taxes.

Cooperatives

Cooperative An association, which may or may not be incorporated, that is organized to provide an economic service to its members. Unincorporated cooperatives are often treated like partnerships for tax and other legal purposes.

A **cooperative** is an association that is organized to provide an economic service to its members (or shareholders). It may or may not be incorporated. Most cooperatives are organized under state statutes for cooperatives, general business corporations, or LLCs.

(AP Photo/Brian Kersey)

Most people believe that cooperatives are small enterprises, but not all are. Ace Hardware is a nationwide "co-op" that has been in operation for more than eighty years. Ray Griffith, its chief executive officer (above), stands in the company's headquarters in Illinois.

Generally, an incorporated cooperative will distribute dividends, or profits, to its owners on the basis of their transactions with the cooperative rather than on the basis of the amount of capital they contributed. Members of incorporated cooperatives have limited liability, as do shareholders of corporations and members of LLCs. Cooperatives that are unincorporated are often treated like partnerships. The members have joint liability for the cooperative's acts.

This form of business generally is adopted by groups of individuals who wish to pool their resources to gain some advantage in the marketplace. Consumer purchasing co-ops are formed to obtain lower prices through quantity discounts. Seller marketing co-ops are formed to control the market and thereby enable members to sell their goods at higher prices. Co-ops range in size from small, local, consumer cooperatives to national businesses such as Ace Hardware and Land O' Lakes, a well-known producer of dairy products.

Reviewing . . . Limited Liability Companies and Special Business Forms

The city of Papagos, Arizona, had a deteriorating bridge in need of repair on a prominent public roadway. The city posted notices seeking proposals for an artistic bridge design and reconstruction. Davidson Masonry, LLC—owned and managed by Carl Davidson and his wife, Marilyn Rowe—decided to submit a bid for a decorative concrete project that incorporated artistic metalwork. They contacted Shana Lafayette, a local sculptor who specialized in large-scale metal creations, to help them design the bridge. The city selected their bridge design and awarded them the contract for a commission of $184,000.

Davidson Masonry and Lafayette then entered into an agreement to work together on the bridge project. Davidson Masonry agreed to install and pay for concrete and structural work, and Lafayette agreed to install the metalwork at her expense. They agreed that overall profits would be split, with 25 percent going to Lafayette and 75 percent going to Davidson Masonry. Lafayette designed numerous metal salmon sculptures that were incorporated into colorful decorative concrete forms designed by Rowe, while Davidson performed the structural engineering. The group worked together successfully until the completion of the project. Using the information presented in the chapter, answer the following questions.

1. Would Davidson Masonry automatically be taxed as a partnership or a corporation? Why or why not?
2. Is Davidson Masonry member managed or manager managed?
3. When Davidson Masonry and Lafayette entered into an agreement to work together, what kind of special business form was created? Explain.
4. Suppose that during construction, Lafayette had entered into an agreement to rent space in a warehouse that was close to the bridge so that she could work on her sculptures near the location where they would be installed. She entered into the contract without the knowledge or consent of Davidson Masonry. In this situation, would a court be likely to hold that Davidson Masonry was bound by the contract that Lafayette entered? Why or why not?

DEBATE THIS Because LLCs are essentially just partnerships with limited liability for members, all partnership laws should apply.

BUSINESS APPLICATION

How Do You Choose between an LLC and an LLP?*

One of the most important decisions that an entrepreneur makes is the selection of the form in which to do business. To make the best decision, a businessperson needs to consider all the legal, tax, licensing, and business consequences.

New forms of business organizations, including limited liability partnerships (LLPs—discussed in Chapter 27) and limited liability companies (LLCs), provide additional options. An initial consideration in choosing between these forms is the number of participants. An LLP must have two or more partners, but in many states, an LLC can have a single member (owner).

Liability Considerations

The members of an LLC are not liable for the obligations of the organization. Members' liability is limited to the amount of their property (investment) interest. The liability of the partners in an LLP varies from state to state. About half of the states exempt the partners from liability for any obligation of the firm. In some states, the partners are individually liable for the contractual obligations of the firm but are not liable for obligations arising from the torts of others. In either situation, a partner who is sued for malpractice may be on his or her own with respect to liability unless the other partners agree to help.

Distributions from the Firm

Members and partners generally are paid by allowing them to withdraw funds from the firm against their share of the profits. In many states, a member of an LLC must repay so-called wrongful distributions even if she or he did not know that the distributions were wrongful (wrongful distributions include those made when the LLC is insolvent). Under most LLP statutes, by contrast, the partners must repay only distributions that were fraudulent.

Management Structure

Both LLPs and LLCs can set up whatever management structure the participants desire. Also, all unincorporated business organizations, including LLPs and LLCs with two or more members, are treated as partnerships for federal income tax purposes (unless an LLC elects to be treated as a corporation[a]).

This means that the firms are not taxed at the entity level. Their income is passed through to the partners or members, who report it on their individual income tax returns. Some states impose additional taxes on LLCs.

Financial and Personal Relationships

Although the legal consequences of choosing a business form are certainly important, they are often secondary to the financial and personal relationships among the participants. Work effort, motivation, ability, and other personal attributes can be significant factors, as may fundamental business concerns such as the expenses and debts of the firm—and the extent of personal liability for these obligations.

Another practical factor to consider is the willingness of others to do business with an LLP or an LLC. A supplier, for example, may not be willing to extend credit to a firm whose partners or members will not accept personal liability for the debt.

Checklist for Choosing a Limited Liability Business Form

1. *Determine the number of participants a state requires, the forms it allows, and the limits on liability the state provides for the participants.*
2. *Evaluate the tax considerations.*
3. *Weigh such practical concerns as the financial and personal relationships among the participants and the willingness of others to do business with a particular organizational form.*

*This *Business Application* is not meant to substitute for the services of an attorney who is licensed to practice law in your state.

a. The chief benefits of electing corporate status for tax purposes are that the members generally are not subject to self-employment taxes and that fringe benefits may be provided to employee-members on a tax-reduced basis. The tax laws are complicated, however, and a professional should be consulted about the details.

Key Terms

articles of organization 727
business trust 737
cooperative 737
joint stock company 737
joint venture 736
limited liability company (LLC) 726
member 726
operating agreement 730
syndicate 737

Chapter Summary: Limited Liability Companies and Special Business Forms

Limited Liability Companies (See pages 726–730.)	1. *Formation*—Articles of organization must be filed with the appropriate state office—usually the office of the secretary of state—setting forth the name of the business, its principal address, the names of the owners (called *members*), and other relevant information. 2. *Advantages and disadvantages of the LLC*—Advantages of the LLC include limited liability, the option to be taxed as a partnership or as a corporation, and flexibility in deciding how the business will be managed and operated. The main disadvantage is the absence of uniformity in state LLC statutes.
LLC Operation and Management (See pages 730–733.)	1. *Operating agreement*—When an LLC is formed, the members decide, in an operating agreement, how the business will be managed and what rules will apply to the organization. 2. *Management*—An LLC may be managed by members only, by some members and some nonmembers, or by nonmembers only.
Dissociation and Dissolution of an LLC (See pages 733–735.)	Members of an LLC have the power to dissociate from the LLC at any time, but they may not have the right to dissociate. Dissociation does not always result in the dissolution of an LLC. The remaining members can choose to continue the business. Dissociated members have a right to have their interest purchased by the other members. If the LLC is dissolved, the business must be wound up and the assets sold. Creditors are paid first, and then members' capital investments are returned. Any remaining proceeds are distributed to members.
Special Business Forms (See pages 736–738.)	1. *Joint venture*—An organization created by two or more persons in contemplation of a limited activity or a single transaction. A joint venture is similar to a partnership in many respects. 2. *Syndicate*—An investment group that undertakes to finance a particular project. A syndicate may exist as a corporation or as a general or limited partnership. 3. *Joint stock company*—A business form similar to a corporation in some respects (transferable shares of stock, management by directors and officers, perpetual existence) but otherwise resembling a partnership. 4. *Business trust*—A business form created by a written trust agreement that sets forth the interests of the beneficiaries and the obligations and powers of the trustee(s). Beneficiaries are not personally liable for the debts or obligations of the business trust, which is similar to a corporation in many respects. 5. *Cooperative*—An association organized to provide an economic service, without profit, to its members. A co-op may take the form of a corporation or a partnership.

ExamPrep

ISSUE SPOTTERS

1. Gomer, Harry, and Ida are members of Jeweled Watches, LLC. What are their options with respect to the management of their firm? **(See page 731.)**
2. Greener Delivery Company and Hiway Trucking, Inc., form a business trust. Insta Equipment Company and Jiffy Supply Corporation form a joint stock company. Kwik Mart, Inc., and Luscious Produce, Inc., form an incorporated cooperative. What do these forms of business organization have in common? **(See pages 736–738.)**

—Check your answers to the Issue Spotters against the answers provided in Appendix E at the end of this text.

BEFORE THE TEST

Go to www.cengagebrain.com, enter the ISBN 9781133273561, and click on "Find" to locate this textbook's Web site. Then, click on "Access Now" under "Study Tools," and select Chapter 28 at the top. There, you will find a Practice Quiz that you can take to assess your mastery of the concepts in this chapter, as well as Flashcards, a Glossary of important terms, and Video Questions (when assigned).

For Review

Answers to the even-numbered questions in this For Review section can be found in Appendix F at the end of this text.

1. How are limited liability companies formed, and who decides how they will be managed and operated?
2. What advantages do limited liability companies offer to businesspersons that are not offered by sole proprietorships or partnerships?

3. What are the two options for managing limited liability companies?
4. What is a joint venture? How is it similar to a partnership? How is it different?
5. What are the essential characteristics of joint stock companies, syndicates, business trusts, and cooperatives, respectively?

Business Scenarios and Case Problems

28–1 Limited Liability Companies. John, Lesa, and Trevor form a limited liability company. John contributes 60 percent of the capital, and Lesa and Trevor each contribute 20 percent. Nothing is decided about how profits will be divided. John assumes that he will be entitled to 60 percent of the profits, in accordance with his contribution. Lesa and Trevor, however, assume that the profits will be divided equally. A dispute over the profits arises, and ultimately a court has to decide the issue. What law will the court apply? In most states, what will result? How could this dispute have been avoided in the first place? Discuss fully. **(See page 730.)**

28–2 Question with Sample Answer—Special Business Forms. Faraway Corp. is considering entering into two contracts, one with a joint stock company that distributes home products east of the Mississippi River and the other with a business trust formed by a number of sole proprietors who are sellers of home products on the West Coast. Both contracts involve large capital outlays for Faraway, which will supply each business with soft-drink dispensers. In both business organizations, at least two shareholders or beneficiaries are personally wealthy, but each organization has limited financial resources. The owner-managers of Faraway are not familiar with either form of business organization. Because each form resembles a corporation, they are concerned about whether they will be able to collect payments from the wealthy members of the business organizations in the event that either organization breaches the contract by failing to make the payments. Discuss fully Faraway's concern. **(See page 737.)**

—For a sample answer to Question 28–2, go to Appendix G at the end of this text.

28–3 Jurisdiction. Joe, a resident of New Jersey, wants to open a restaurant. He asks his friend Kay, who is an experienced attorney and a New Yorker, for her business and legal advice in exchange for a 20 percent ownership interest in the restaurant. Kay helps Joe negotiate a lease for the restaurant premises and advises Joe to organize the business as a limited liability company (LLC). Joe forms Café Olé, LLC, and, with Kay's help, obtains financing. Then, the night before the restaurant opens, Joe tells Kay that he is "cutting her out of the deal." The restaurant proves to be a success. Kay wants to file a suit in a federal district court against Joe and the LLC. Can a federal court exercise jurisdiction over the parties based on diversity of citizenship? Explain. **(See page 729.)**

28–4 Limited Liability Companies. A limited liability company (LLC) owned a Manhattan apartment building that was sold. The owners of 25 percent of the membership interests in the LLC filed a lawsuit on behalf of the company (the LLC)—called a derivative suit—claiming that those in majority control of the LLC sold the building for less than its market value and personally profited from the deal. The trial court dismissed the suit, holding that the plaintiffs individually could not bring a derivative suit "to redress wrongs suffered by the corporation" because such actions were permitted only for corporations and could not be brought for an LLC. The appellate court reversed, holding that derivative suits on behalf of LLCs are permitted. That decision was appealed. A key problem was that the state law governing LLCs did not address the issue. How should such matters logically be resolved? Are the minority owners in an LLC at the mercy of the decisions of the majority owners? Discuss fully. [*Tzolis v. Wolff,* 10 N.Y.3d 100, 884 N.E.2d 1005 (2008)] **(See pages 731–733.)**

28–5 Joint Ventures. Holiday Isle Resort & Marina, Inc., operated four restaurants, five bars, and various food kiosks at its resort in Islamorada, Florida. Holiday entered into a "joint venture agreement" with Rip Tosun to operate a fifth restaurant called Rip's—A Place For Ribs. The agreement gave Tosun authority over the employees and "full authority as to the conduct of the business." It also prohibited Tosun from competing with Rip's without Holiday's approval but did not prevent Holiday from competing. Later, Tosun sold half of his interest in Rip's to Thomas Hallock. Soon, Tosun and Holiday opened the Olde Florida Steakhouse next to Rip's. Holiday stopped serving breakfast at Rip's and diverted employees and equipment from Rip's to the Steakhouse, which then started offering breakfast. Hallock filed a suit in a Florida state court against Holiday. Did Holiday breach the joint-venture agreement? Did it breach the duties that joint venturers owe each other? Explain. [*Hallock v. Holiday Isle Resort & Marina, Inc.,* 4 So.3d 17 (Fla.App. 3 Dist. 2009)] **(See pages 736–737.)**

28–6 LLC Dissolution. Walter Van Houten and John King formed 1545 Ocean Avenue, LLC, with each managing 50 percent of the business. Its purpose was to renovate an existing building and build a new commercial building. Van Houten and King quarreled over many aspects of the work on the properties. King claimed that Van Houten paid contractors too much for the work performed. As the project neared completion, King demanded that the LLC be dissolved and that Van Houten agree to a buyout. Because the parties could not agree on a buyout, King sued for dissolution. The trial court prevented further work on the project while the dispute was settled. As the ground for dissolution, King cited the fights over management decisions. There was no claim of fraud or frustration of purpose. The trial court ordered that the LLC be dissolved. Van Houten appealed. Should either of the owners be forced to dissolve the LLC before completion of its purpose—that is, finishing the building projects? Discuss. [*In re 1545 Ocean*

Avenue, LLC, 893 N.Y.S.2d 590 (N.Y.A.D. 2 Dept. 2010)] **(See pages 733–734.)**

28–7 Case Problem with Sample Answer—LLC Operation. After Hurricane Katrina, James Williford, Patricia Mosser, Marquetta Smith, and Michael Floyd formed Bluewater Logistics, LLC, to bid on construction contracts. Under Mississippi law, every member of a member-managed LLC is entitled to participate in managing the business. The operating agreement provided for a "super majority" 75 percent vote to remove a member "under any other circumstances that would jeopardize the company status" as a contractor. After Bluewater had completed more than $5 million in contracts, Smith told Williford that she, Mosser, and Floyd were exercising their "super majority" vote to fire him. No reason was provided. Williford sued Bluewater and the other members. Did Smith, Mosser, and Floyd breach the state LLC statute, their fiduciary duties, or the Bluewater operating agreements? Discuss. [*Bluewater Logistics, LLC v. Williford,* 55 So.3d 148 (Miss. 2011)] **(See pages 730–732.)**

—For a sample answer to Problem 28–7, go to Appendix H at the end of this text.

28–8 Jurisdictional Requirements. Fadal Machining Centers, LLC, and MAG Industrial Automation Centers, LLC, sued a New Jersey–based corporation, Mid-Atlantic CNC, Inc., in federal district court. Ten percent of MAG was owned by SP MAG Holdings, a Delaware LLC. SP MAG had six members, including a Delaware limited partnership called Silver Point Capital Fund and a Delaware LLC called SPCP Group III. In turn, Silver Point and SPCP Group had a common member, Robert O'Shea, who was a New Jersey citizen. Assuming that the amount in controversy exceeds $75,000, does the district court have diversity jurisdiction? Why or why not? [*Fadal Machining Centers, LLC v. Mid-Atlantic CNC, Inc.,* 2012 WL 8669 (9th Cir. 2012)] **(See page 729.)**

28–9 A Question of Ethics—LLC Operation. Blushing Brides, LLC, a publisher of wedding planning magazines in Columbus, Ohio, opened an account with Gray Printing Co. in July 2000. On behalf of Blushing Brides, Louis Zacks, the firm's member-manager, signed a credit agreement that identified the firm as the "purchaser" and required payment within thirty days. Despite the agreement, Blushing Brides typically took up to six months to pay the full amount for its orders. Gray printed and shipped 10,000 copies of a fall/winter 2001 issue for Blushing Brides but had not been paid when the firm ordered 15,000 copies of a spring/summer 2002 issue. Gray refused to print the new order without an assurance of payment. Zacks signed a promissory note for $14,778, plus interest at 6 percent per year, payable to Gray on June 22. Gray printed the new order but by October had been paid only $7,500. Gray filed a suit in an Ohio state court against Blushing Brides and Zacks to collect the balance. [*Gray Printing Co. v. Blushing Brides, LLC,* 2006 WL 832587 (Ohio App. 2006)]

1. Under what circumstances is a member of an LLC liable for the firm's debts? In this case, is Zacks personally liable under the credit agreement for the unpaid amount on Blushing Brides' account? Did Zacks's promissory note affect the parties' liability on the account? Explain.
2. Does a member of an LLC have an ethical responsibility to meet the obligations of the firm? Discuss.
3. Gray shipped only 10,000 copies of the spring/summer 2002 issue of Blushing Brides' magazine, waiting for the publisher to identify a destination for the other 5,000 copies. The magazine had a retail price of $4.50 per copy. Did Gray have a legal or ethical duty to "mitigate the damages" by attempting to sell or otherwise distribute these copies itself? Why or why not?

Critical Thinking and Writing Assignments

28–10 Business Law Critical Thinking Group Assignment. Although a limited liability company (LLC) may be the best organizational form for most businesses, a significant number of firms may be better off as a corporation or some other form of organization.

1. The first group will outline several reasons why a firm might be better off as a corporation than as an LLC.
2. The second group will discuss whether it is preferable for a five-member LLC to be member managed or manager managed and will identify some of the factors that should be taken into consideration.

CHAPTER 29

Corporate Formation, Merger, and Termination

(pixhook/iStockphoto.com)

CHAPTER OUTLINE

- Corporate Nature and Classification
- Corporate Formation and Powers
- Piercing the Corporate Veil
- Corporate Financing
- Mergers and Acquisitions
- Corporate Termination

LEARNING OBJECTIVES

The five learning objectives below are designed to help improve your understanding of the chapter. After reading this chapter, you should be able to answer the following questions:

1 What is a close corporation?

2 What steps are involved in bringing a corporation into existence?

3 In what circumstances might a court disregard the corporate entity ("pierce the corporate veil") and hold the shareholders personally liable?

4 What are the basic differences between a merger, a consolidation, and a share exchange?

5 What are the two ways in which a corporation can be voluntarily dissolved?

"A corporation is an artificial being, invisible, intangible, and existing only in contemplation of law."
—John Marshall, 1755–1835 (Chief justice of the United States Supreme Court, 1801–1835)

The corporation is a creature of statute. As John Marshall indicated in the chapter-opening quotation, a corporation is an artificial being, existing only in law and neither tangible nor visible. Its existence generally depends on state law.

Each state has its own body of corporate law, and these laws are not entirely uniform. The Model Business Corporation Act (MBCA) is a codification of modern corporation law that has been influential in the drafting and revision of state corporation statutes. Today, the majority of state statutes are guided by the revised version of the MBCA, which is often referred to as the Revised Model Business Corporation Act (RMBCA). You should keep in mind, however, that there is considerable variation among the statutes of the states that have used the MBCA or the RMBCA as a basis for their statutes, and several states do not follow either act. Consequently, individual state corporation laws should be relied on rather than the MBCA or the RMBCA.

(AP Photo/April L. Brown)

Musicians celebrate Walmart at its shareholders' meeting in Fayetteville, Arkansas.

Corporate Nature and Classification

A **corporation** is a legal entity created and recognized by state law. It can consist of one or more *natural persons* (as opposed to the artificial *legal person* of the corporation) identified under a common name. A corporation can be owned by a single person, or it can have hundreds, thousands, or even millions of owners (shareholders). The corporation substitutes itself for its shareholders in conducting corporate business and in incurring liability, yet its authority to act and the liability for its actions are separate and apart from the individuals who own it.

A corporation is recognized as a "person," and it enjoys many of the same rights and privileges under state and federal law that natural persons enjoy. For instance, corporations possess the same right of access to the courts as natural persons and can sue or be sued. The constitutional guarantees of due process, free speech, and freedom from unreasonable searches and seizures also apply to corporations. In addition, corporations have a right under the First Amendment to fund political broadcasts—a topic discussed in this chapter's *Landmark in Law* feature on the facing page.

Corporate Personnel

Corporation A legal entity formed in compliance with statutory requirements that is distinct from its shareholder-owners.

Dividend A distribution of corporate profits to the corporation's shareholders in proportion to the number of shares held.

Retained Earnings The portion of a corporation's profits that has not been paid out as dividends to shareholders.

In a corporation, the responsibility for the overall management of the firm is entrusted to a *board of directors*, whose members are elected by the shareholders. The board of directors hires *corporate officers* and other employees to run the corporation's daily business operations of the corporation.

When an individual purchases a share of stock in a corporation, that person becomes a shareholder and thus an owner of the corporation. Unlike the members of a partnership, the body of shareholders can change constantly without affecting the continued existence of the corporation. A shareholder can sue the corporation, and the corporation can sue a shareholder. Also, under certain circumstances, a shareholder can sue on behalf of a corporation. The rights and duties of corporate personnel will be examined in detail in Chapter 30.

The Limited Liability of Shareholders

One of the key advantages of the corporate form is the limited liability of its owners (shareholders). Corporate shareholders normally are not personally liable for the obligations of the corporation beyond the extent of their investments. In certain limited situations, however, a court can *pierce the corporate veil* (see pages 756 and 757) and impose liability on shareholders for the corporation's obligations. Additionally, to enable the firm to obtain credit, shareholders in small companies sometimes voluntarily assume personal liability, as guarantors, for corporate obligations.

Who hires corporate personnel?

(bowdenimages/iStockphoto.com)

Corporate Earnings and Taxation

When a corporation earns profits, it can either pass them on to its shareholders in the form of **dividends** or retain them as profits. These **retained earnings**, if invested properly, will yield higher corporate profits in the future and thus cause the price of the company's stock to rise.

LANDMARK IN THE LAW

Citizens United v. Federal Election Commission

In *Citizens United v. Federal Election Commission*,[a] the United States Supreme Court held that the First Amendment prevents limits from being placed on corporate funding of independent political broadcasts. The case involved broadcasts of political material by Citizens United, a nonprofit corporation that has a *political action committee* (an organization that is registered with the government and campaigns for political candidates).

Background In 2002, in an effort to reform campaign financing, Congress enacted the Bipartisan Campaign Reform Act (BCRA), also known as the McCain-Feingold Act. One provision of the BCRA prohibited corporations and labor unions from using their general treasury funds to make independent expenditures for speech that is an "electioneering communication" or for speech that expressly advocates the election or defeat of a candidate.[b] The act defined an electioneering communication as "any broadcast, cable, or satellite communication" that "refers to a clearly identified candidate for Federal office" and is made within thirty days of a primary election.

In 2008, Citizens United produced a film called *Hillary: The Movie* that was critical of Hillary Clinton, who at the time was a candidate for the Democratic presidential nomination. As part of its distribution plans for *Hillary*, Citizens United wanted to make the film available on television through video-on-demand systems within thirty days of primary elections, but it was concerned about potential civil and criminal penalties for violating the BCRA.

Citizens United filed an action in federal court against the Federal Election Commission (FEC) seeking a declaratory judgment that the BCRA was unconstitutional as applied to *Hillary*. The court, however, ruled in favor of the FEC, finding that the film had no purpose except to discredit Clinton's candidacy. Citizens United appealed.

A Surprising Decision To the surprise of many commentators, the United States Supreme Court explicitly overruled two of its earlier decisions on campaign financing.[c] In a five-to-four decision, the Court struck down the provision of the BCRA that prohibited both for-profit and nonprofit corporations, as well as labor unions, from broadcasting "electioneering communications." Other provisions of the BCRA were upheld, however, including the provision that requires disclosures that identify the person or entity responsible for the content of electioneering communications.

Justice Anthony Kennedy, writing for the majority, said, "All speakers, including individuals and the media, use money amassed from the economic marketplace to fund their speech. The First Amendment protects the resulting speech, even if it was enabled by economic transactions with persons or entities who disagree with the speaker's ideas."

In dissent, Justice John Paul Stevens argued that the Court's ruling "threatens to undermine the integrity of elected institutions across the Nation. The path it has taken to reach its outcome will, I fear, do damage to this institution."

Application to Today's World *Many critics of the decision argued that it opens the door for corporations, including foreign owned corporations, to spend without limit to influence our elections. Although federal law still prohibits corporations and unions from giving funds directly to political campaigns, these entities can fund advertising and other actions that seek to persuade the voting public.*

---

a. 558 U.S. 310, 130 S.Ct. 876, 175 L.Ed.2d 753 (2010).
b. 2 U.S.C. Section 441b.
c. *Austin v. Michigan Chamber of Commerce*, 494 U.S. 652, 110 S.Ct. 1391, 108 L.Ed.2d 652 (1990); and *McConnell v. Federal Election Commission*, 540 U.S. 93, 124 S.Ct. 619, 157 L.Ed.2d 491 (2003).

Individual shareholders can then reap the benefits of these retained earnings in the capital gains that they receive when they sell their stock.

Corporate Taxation Whether a corporation retains its profits or passes them on to the shareholders as dividends, those profits are subject to income tax by various levels of government. As you will read later in this chapter, failure to pay taxes can lead to severe consequences. The state can suspend the entity's corporate status until the taxes are paid or even dissolve the corporation for failing to pay taxes.

Another important aspect of corporate taxation is that corporate profits can be subject to double taxation. The company pays tax on its profits, and then if the profits are passed on to the shareholders as dividends, the shareholders must also pay income tax on them. The corporation normally does not receive a tax deduction for dividends it distributes to shareholders. This double-taxation feature is one of the major disadvantages of the corporate business form.

ETHICAL ISSUE

Should online retailers be required to pay state taxes? In 1992, the United States Supreme Court ruled that an individual state cannot compel an out-of-state business that lacks a substantial physical presence within that state to collect and remit state taxes.[1] Although Congress has the power to pass legislation requiring out-of-state corporations to collect and remit state sales taxes, it has not done so.[2] Thus, only online retailers that also have a physical presence within a state must collect state taxes on any Web sales made to residents of that state. (State residents are required to self-report their purchases and pay use taxes to the state, which they rarely do.)

Several states have found a way to collect taxes on Internet sales made to state residents by out-of-state corporations—by redefining *physical presence.* In 2008, New York changed its tax laws to provide that if an online retailer pays any party within New York to solicit business for its products, that retailer has a physical presence in the state and must collect state taxes.[3] Since then, at least seventeen other states have made similar changes in their laws in an effort to increase their revenues by collecting sales tax from online retailers. These new laws, often called the "Amazon tax" because they are largely aimed at Amazon.com, affect all online sellers, including Overstock.com and Drugstore.com. These tax laws especially affect those retailers that pay affiliates to direct traffic to their Web sites. They allow states to tax online commerce even though Congress has explicitly chosen not to tax Internet sales.

Holding Companies

Holding Company A company whose business activity is holding shares in another company.

Some U.S. corporations use holding companies to reduce—or at least defer—their U.S. income taxes. At its simplest, a **holding company** (sometimes referred to as a *parent company*) is a company whose business activity consists of holding shares in another company. Typically, the holding company is established in a low-tax or no-tax offshore jurisdiction. Among the best known are the Cayman Islands, Dubai, Hong Kong, Luxembourg, Monaco, and Panama.

Sometimes, a U.S. corporation sets up a holding company in a low-tax offshore environment and then transfers its cash, bonds, stocks, and other investments to the holding company. In general, any profits received by the holding company on these investments are taxed at the rate of the offshore jurisdiction where the company is registered, not the rates applicable to the parent company or its shareholders in their country of residence. Thus, deposits of cash, for example, may earn interest that is taxed at only a minimal rate. Once the profits are brought "onshore," though, they are taxed at the federal corporate income tax rate, and any payments received by the shareholders are also taxable at the full U.S. rates.

What are some of the reasons that these demonstrators believe that large corporations are not paying enough taxes?

(AP Photo/The Casper Star-Tribune, Tim Kupsick)

Torts and Criminal Acts

A corporation is liable for the torts committed by its agents or officers within the course and scope of their employment. This principle applies to a corporation exactly as it applies to the ordinary agency relationships discussed in Chapter 23. It follows the doctrine of *respondeat superior.*

Recall from Chapter 6 that under modern criminal law, a corporation may be held liable for the criminal acts of its agents and employees. Although corporations cannot be imprisoned, they can be fined. (Of course, corporate directors and officers can be imprisoned, and many have been in recent years.)

1. *Quill Corp. v. North Dakota,* 504 U.S. 298, 112 S.Ct. 1904, 119 L.Ed.2d 91 (1992).
2. In fact, Congress temporarily prohibited the states from taxing Internet sales through 2014. See Internet Tax Freedom Act, Pub. L. No. 110-108.
3. New York Tax Law Section 1101(b)(8)(vi).

In addition, under sentencing guidelines for crimes committed by corporate employees (white-collar crimes), corporations can face fines amounting to hundreds of millions of dollars.[4]

CASE EXAMPLE 29.1 Brian Gauthier drove a dump truck for Angelo Todesca Corporation. The truck was missing its back-up alarm, but Angelo allowed Gauthier to continue driving it. At a worksite, Gauthier backed up the truck and struck and killed a police officer who was directing traffic. The state charged Angelo and Gauthier with the crime of vehicular homicide. Angelo argued that a "corporation" could not be guilty of vehicular homicide because it cannot "operate" a vehicle. The court ruled that if an employee commits a crime "while engaged in corporate business that the employee has been authorized to conduct," a corporation can be held liable for the crime. Hence, Angelo was liable for Gauthier's negligent operation of its truck, which resulted in a person's death.[5] •

Classification of Corporations

Corporations can be classified in several ways. The classification of a corporation normally depends on its location, purpose, and ownership characteristics, as described in the following subsections.

Domestic, Foreign, and Alien Corporations

A corporation is referred to as a **domestic corporation** by its home state (the state in which it incorporates). A corporation formed in one state but doing business in another is referred to in the second state as a **foreign corporation.** A corporation formed in another country (say, Mexico) but doing business in the United States is referred to in the United States as an **alien corporation.**

Domestic Corporation In a given state, a corporation that is organized under the law of that state.

Foreign Corporation In a given state, a corporation that does business in that state but is not incorporated there.

Alien Corporation A corporation formed in another country but doing business in the United States.

A corporation does not have an automatic right to do business in a state other than its state of incorporation. In some instances, it must obtain a *certificate of authority* in any state in which it plans to do business. Once the certificate has been issued, the corporation generally can exercise in that state all of the powers conferred on it by its home state. If a foreign corporation does business in a state without obtaining a certificate of authority, the state can impose substantial fines and sanctions on the corporation, and sometimes even on its officers, directors, or agents.

Note that most state statutes specify certain activities, such as soliciting orders via the Internet, that are not considered doing business within the state. Thus, a foreign corporation normally does not need a certificate of authority to sell goods or services via the Internet or by mail.

Is AMTRAK a public or publicly held corporation?

(EdStock/iStockphoto.com)

Public and Private Corporations

A public corporation is one formed by the government to meet some political or governmental purpose. Cities and towns that incorporate are common examples. In addition, many federal government organizations—such as the U.S. Postal Service, the Tennessee Valley Authority, and AMTRAK—are public corporations. Note that a public corporation is not the same as a *publicly held* corporation (often called a *public company*). A publicly held corporation is any corporation whose shares are publicly traded in securities markets, such as the New York Stock Exchange or the over-the-counter market.

In contrast to public corporations (*not* public companies), private corporations are created either wholly or in part for private benefit. Most corporations are private. Although they may

4. Note that the Sarbanes-Oxley Act, discussed in Chapter 7, stiffened the penalties for certain types of corporate crime and ordered the U.S. Sentencing Commission to revise the sentencing guidelines accordingly.

5. *Commonwealth v. Angelo Todesca Corp.*, 446 Mass. 128, 842 N.E.2d 930 (2006).

serve a public purpose, as a public electric or gas utility does, they are owned by private persons rather than by the government.[6]

KNOW THIS

A private corporation is a voluntary association, but a public corporation is not.

Nonprofit Corporations

Corporations formed for purposes other than making a profit are called *nonprofit* or *not-for-profit* corporations. Private hospitals, educational institutions, charities, and religious organizations, for example, are frequently organized as nonprofit corporations. The nonprofit corporation is a convenient form of organization that allows various groups to own property and to form contracts without exposing the individual members to personal liability.

Close Corporations

Close Corporation A corporation whose shareholders are limited to a small group of persons, often only family members.

Most corporate enterprises in the United States fall into the category of close corporations. A **close corporation** is one whose shares are held by members of a family or by relatively few persons. Close corporations are also referred to as *closely held, family,* or *privately held* corporations. Usually, the members of the small group constituting a close corporation are personally known to one another. Because the number of shareholders is so small, there is no trading market for the shares.

In practice, a close corporation is often operated like a partnership. Some states have enacted special statutory provisions that permit close corporations to depart significantly from certain formalities required by traditional corporation law.[7]

LEARNING OBJECTIVE 1
What is a close corporation?

Additionally, the RMBCA gives close corporations considerable flexibility in determining their operating rules [RMBCA 7.32]. If all of a corporation's shareholders agree in writing, the corporation can operate without directors, bylaws, annual or special shareholders' or directors' meetings, stock certificates, or formal records of shareholders' or directors' decisions.[8]

Management of Close Corporations

A close corporation has a single shareholder or a closely knit group of shareholders, who usually hold the positions of directors and officers. Management of a close corporation resembles that of a sole proprietorship or a partnership. As a corporation, however, the firm must meet all specific legal requirements set forth in state statutes.

To prevent a majority shareholder from dominating a close corporation, the corporation may require that more than a simple majority of the directors approve any action taken by the board. Typically, such a requirement would apply only to extraordinary actions, such as changing the amount of dividends or dismissing an employee-shareholder, and not to ordinary business decisions.

Transfer of Shares in Close Corporations

By definition, a close corporation has a small number of shareholders. Thus, the transfer of one shareholder's shares to someone else can cause serious management problems. The other shareholders may find themselves required to share control with someone they do not know or like.

EXAMPLE 29.2 Three brothers—Terry, Damon, and Henry Johnson—are the only shareholders of Johnson's Car Wash, Inc. Terry and Damon do not want Henry to sell his shares to an unknown third person. To avoid this situation, the corporation could restrict the transferability of shares to outside persons. Shareholders could be required to offer their shares to the corporation or the other shareholders before selling them to an outside purchaser. In fact, a few states have statutes that prohibit the transfer of close corporation shares unless certain persons—including shareholders, family members, and the corporation—are first given the opportunity to purchase the shares for the same price. •

6. The United States Supreme Court first recognized the property rights of private corporations and clarified the distinction between public and private corporations in the landmark case *Trustees of Dartmouth College v. Woodward*, 17 U.S. (4 Wheaton) 518, 4 L.Ed. 629 (1819).

7. For example, in some states (such as Maryland), a close corporation need not have a board of directors.

8. Shareholders cannot agree, however, to eliminate certain rights of shareholders, such as the right to inspect corporate books and records or the right to bring *derivative actions* (lawsuits on behalf of the corporation—see Chapter 30).

Control of a close corporation can also be stabilized through the use of a *shareholder agreement.* A shareholder agreement can provide that when one of the original shareholders dies, her or his shares of stock in the corporation will be divided in such a way that the proportionate holdings of the survivors, and thus their proportionate control, will be maintained. Courts are generally reluctant to interfere with private agreements, including shareholder agreements.

Misappropriation of Close Corporation Funds Sometimes, a majority shareholder in a close corporation takes advantage of his or her position and misappropriates company funds. In such situations, the normal remedy for the injured minority shareholders is to have their shares appraised and to be paid the fair market value for them.

In the following case, a minority shareholder charged that the majority shareholders paid themselves excessive compensation in breach of their fiduciary duty.

Case 29.1

Rubin v. Murray

Appellate Court of Massachusetts,
79 Mass.App.Ct. 64, 943 N.E.2d 949 (2011).

(rarpleti/iStockphoto.com)

FACTS Olympic Adhesives, Inc., makes and sells industrial adhesives. John Murray, Stephen Hopkins, and Paul Ryan were the controlling shareholders of the company, as well as officers, directors, and employees. Merek Rubin was a minority shareholder. Murray, Hopkins, and Ryan were paid salaries. Under Olympic's profit-sharing plan, one-third of its net operating income was paid into a fund that was distributed to employees, including Murray, Hopkins, and Ryan.

Twice a year, Murray, Hopkins, and Ryan also paid themselves additional compensation—a percentage of the net profits after profit sharing, allocated according to their stock ownership. Over a fifteen-year period, the percentage grew from 75 percent to between 92 and 98 percent. During this time, the additional compensation totaled nearly $15 million. Rubin filed a suit in a Massachusetts state court against Murray, Hopkins, and Ryan, alleging that they had paid themselves excessive compensation and deprived him of his share of Olympic's profits in violation of their fiduciary duty to him as a minority shareholder. The court ordered the defendants to repay Olympic nearly $6 million to be distributed among its shareholders. The defendants appealed.

ISSUE Did the majority shareholders in a close corporation breach their fiduciary duty to the minority shareholder by paying themselves a large percentage of the company's net profits twice a year, allocated according to their stock ownership?

DECISION Yes. A state intermediate appellate court affirmed the lower court's judgment. The trial court had discretion to determine what constituted reasonable compensation for the defendants, and its findings were based on sufficient evidence. The compensation of these majority shareholders was excessive and deprived Rubin of his share of Olympic profits in breach of their fiduciary duty to him as a minority shareholder.

REASON The court reasoned that a salary should reasonably relate to a corporate officer's ability and the quantity and quality of services the officer renders. Profits resulting from an officer's performance may also affect the amount of compensation. In this case, the trial judge found that a reasonable amount of compensation for each officer would have been 4 to 7 percent of net sales, plus a "success premium" related to individual contributions, for a total of 10 percent of Olympic's average annual net sales. This amount was comparable to the average compensation for officers in similar firms. The appellate court also pointed out that Murray was vague when he attempted to explain the basis for distributing the profits among the defendants. Those amounts seemed to correspond only to the percentage of the officers' stock ownership, rather than to any aspect of their performance.

WHAT IF THE FACTS WERE DIFFERENT? *Suppose that Murray could have pinpointed a job-related basis for the distribution of the net profits among the defendants. Would the result have been different? Explain.*

S Corporation A close business corporation that has most corporate attributes, including limited liability, but qualifies under the Internal Revenue Code to be taxed as a partnership.

S Corporations

A close corporation that meets the qualifying requirements specified in Subchapter S of the Internal Revenue Code can operate as an **S corporation.** If a corporation has S corporation status, it can avoid the imposition of income taxes at the corporate level while retaining many of the advantages of a corporation, particularly limited liability.

Important Requirements Among the numerous requirements for S corporation status, the following are the most important:

1. The corporation must be a domestic corporation.
2. The corporation must not be a member of an affiliated group of corporations.
3. The shareholders of the corporation must be individuals, estates, or certain trusts. Partnerships and nonqualifying trusts cannot be shareholders. Corporations can be shareholders under certain circumstances.
4. The corporation must have no more than one hundred shareholders.
5. The corporation must have only one class of stock, although all shareholders do not have to have the same voting rights.
6. No shareholder of the corporation may be a nonresident alien.

Effect of the S Election An S corporation is treated differently from a regular corporation for tax purposes. An S corporation is taxed like a partnership, so the corporate income passes through to the shareholders, who pay personal income tax on it. This treatment enables the S corporation to avoid the double taxation that is imposed on regular corporations. In addition, the shareholders' tax brackets may be lower than the tax bracket that the corporation would have been in if the tax had been imposed at the corporate level.

This tax saving is particularly attractive when the corporation wants to accumulate earnings for some future business purpose. If the corporation has losses, the S election allows the shareholders to use the losses to offset other taxable income. Nevertheless, because the limited liability company (see Chapter 28) and the limited liability partnership (see Chapter 27) offer similar tax advantages and greater flexibility, the S corporation has lost much of its significance.

KNOW THIS

Unlike the shareholders of most other corporations, the shareholders of professional corporations generally must be licensed professionals.

Professional Corporations

Professionals such as physicians, lawyers, dentists, and accountants can incorporate. Professional corporations typically are identified by the letters *S.C.* (service corporation), *P.C.* (professional corporation), or *P.A.* (professional association).

In general, the laws governing the formation and operation of professional corporations are similar to those governing ordinary business corporations. There are some differences in terms of liability, however, because the shareholder-owners are professionals who are held to a higher standard of conduct.

For liability purposes, some courts treat a professional corporation somewhat like a partnership and hold each professional liable for any malpractice committed within the scope of the business by the others in the firm. With the exception of malpractice or a breach of duty to clients or patients, a shareholder in a professional corporation generally cannot be held liable for the torts committed by other professionals at the firm.

Corporate Formation and Powers

Often, entrepreneurs start their business as a sole proprietorship or a partnership, but as the business grows and they wish to expand, they may decide to incorporate because a corporation can obtain more capital by issuing shares of stock. Incorporating a business is much simpler today than it was twenty years ago, and many states allow businesses to incorporate via the Internet. Here, we examine the process by which a corporation comes into existence.

Promotional Activities

> "A man to carry on a successful business must have imagination. He must see things as in a vision, a dream of the whole thing."
>
> Charles M. Schwab, 1862–1939 (American industrialist)

In the past, preliminary steps were taken to organize and promote the business prior to incorporating. Contracts were made with investors and others on behalf of the future corporation. Today, due to the relative ease of forming a corporation in most states, persons incorporating their business rarely, if ever, engage in preliminary promotional activities.

Nevertheless, it is important for businesspersons to understand that they are personally liable for all preincorporation contracts made with investors, accountants, or others on behalf of the future corporation. This personal liability continues until the corporation assumes the preincorporation contracts by *novation* (discussed on page 344 in Chapter 13). **EXAMPLE 29.3** Jade Sorrel contracts with an accountant, Ray Cooper, to provide tax advice for a proposed corporation, Blackstone, Inc. Cooper provides the services to Sorrel, knowing that the corporation has not yet been formed. Once Blackstone, Inc., is formed, Cooper sends an invoice to the corporation and to Sorrel personally, but the bill is not paid. Because Sorrel is personally liable for the preincorporation contract, Cooper can file a lawsuit against Sorrel for breaching the contract. Cooper cannot hold Blackstone, Inc., liable unless he has entered into a novation contract with the corporation. •

Incorporation Procedures

LEARNING OBJECTIVE 2
What steps are involved in bringing a corporation into existence?

Exact procedures for incorporation differ among states, but the basic steps are as follows: (1) select a state of incorporation, (2) secure the corporate name by confirming its availability, (3) prepare the articles of incorporation, and (4) file the articles of incorporation with the secretary of state and pay the specified fees. These steps are discussed in more detail in the following subsections.

Select the State of Incorporation

The first step in the incorporation process is to select a state in which to incorporate. Because state corporation laws differ, individuals may look for the states that offer the most advantageous tax or other provisions. Another consideration is the fee that a particular state charges to incorporate, as well as the annual fees and the fees for specific transactions (such as stock transfers).

Delaware has historically had the least restrictive laws and provisions that favor corporate management. Consequently, many corporations, including a number of the largest, have incorporated there. Delaware's statutes permit firms to incorporate in that state and conduct business and locate their operating headquarters elsewhere. Most other states now permit this as well.

Note, though, that close corporations, particularly those of a professional nature, generally incorporate in the state where their principal shareholders live and work. For reasons of convenience and cost, businesses often choose to incorporate in the state in which the corporation's business will primarily be conducted.

Secure the Corporate Name

The choice of a corporate name is subject to state approval to ensure against duplication or deception. State statutes usually require that the secretary of state (or sometimes the incorporators themselves) run a check on the proposed name in the state of incorporation. Once cleared, a name can be reserved for a short time, for a fee, pending the completion of the articles of incorporation. All corporate statutes require the corporation name to include the word *Corporation, Incorporated, Company,* or *Limited,* or abbreviations of these terms.

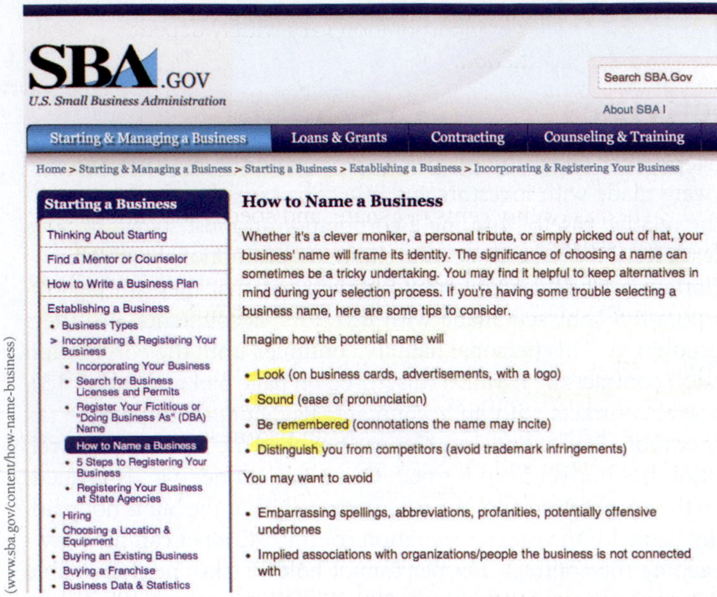

What is the most important requirement for naming new companies that is not mentioned in the above list from the SBA.gov Web site?

First Check Available Domain Names All corporations need to have an online presence to compete effectively in today's business climate. The corporate name should be one that can be used as the business's Internet domain name. Therefore, it is advisable to check what domain names are available *before* securing a corporate name with the state. Incorporators can do this by going to one of the many companies that issue domain names, such as Network Solutions, and finding out if the preferred name is available. If another business is using that name, incorporators will have to select an alternative name that can be used as the business's URL, and then they should seek approval from the state.

Trade Name Disputes A new corporation's name cannot be the same as (or deceptively similar to, see page 132) the name of an existing corporation doing business within the state. **EXAMPLE 29.4** If an existing corporation is named Digital Synergy, Inc., you cannot choose the name Digital Synergy Company because that name is deceptively similar to the first. The state will be unlikely to allow the corporate name because it could impliedly transfer a part of the goodwill established by the first corporate user to the second corporation. In addition, you would not want the name Digital Synergy Company because you would be unable to acquire an Internet domain name using even part of that name. ●

If those incorporating a firm contemplate doing business in other states—or over the Internet—they also need to check on existing corporate names in those states as well. Otherwise, if the firm does business under a name that is the same as or deceptively similar to an existing company's name, it may be liable for trade name infringement.

PREVENTING LEGAL DISPUTES

Be cautious when choosing a corporate name. Always check on the availability of a particular domain name before selecting a corporate name and clearing it with the state. Recognize that even if a particular state does not require the incorporator to run a name check, doing so can help prevent future disputes. Trade name disputes may also arise if your business's name is deceptively similar to the name of a partnership or limited liability company. Disputes are even more likely to arise among online firms. It is often worth incurring the additional cost of hiring a professional to conduct a name search.

Articles of Incorporation The document containing basic information about the corporation that is filed with the appropriate state official, usually the secretary of state, when a business is incorporated.

Prepare the Articles of Incorporation

The primary document needed to incorporate a business is the **articles of incorporation.** The articles include basic information about the corporation and serve as a primary source of authority for its future organization and business functions. The person or persons who execute (sign) the articles are called *incorporators.* Generally, the articles of incorporation *must* include the following information [RMBCA 2.02]:

1. The name of the corporation.
2. The number of shares the corporation is authorized to issue.
3. The name and address of the corporation's initial registered agent.
4. The name and address of each incorporator.

In addition, the articles *may* include other information, such as the names and addresses of the initial directors, the duration and purpose of the corporation, the par value of the corporation's shares, and other information pertinent to the rights and duties of the corporation's shareholders and directors. Articles of incorporation vary widely depending on the size and type of corporation and the jurisdiction.

Shares of the Corporation The articles must specify the number of shares of stock authorized for issuance. For instance, a company might state that the aggregate number of shares that the corporation has the authority to issue is five thousand. Large corporations often state a par value of each share, such as twenty cents per share, and specify the various types or classes of stock authorized for issuance (see the discussion of *common* and *preferred stock* later in this chapter). Sometimes, the articles set forth the capital structure of the corporation and other relevant information concerning equity, shares, and credit.

Registered Office and Agent The corporation must indicate the location and address of its registered office within the state. Usually, the registered office is also the principal office of the corporation. The corporation must also give the name and address of a specific person who has been designated as an *agent* and can receive legal documents (such as orders to appear in court) on behalf of the corporation.

Incorporators Each incorporator must be listed by name and address. The incorporators need not have any interest at all in the corporation, and sometimes signing the articles is their only duty. Many states do not have residency or age requirements for incorporators. States vary on the required number of incorporators. It can be as few as one or as many as three. Incorporators frequently participate in the first organizational meeting of the corporation.

Duration and Purpose A corporation has perpetual existence unless the articles state otherwise. The RMBCA does not require a specific statement of purpose to be included in the articles. A corporation can be formed for any lawful purpose. Although some incorporators choose to specify the intended business activities ("to engage in the production and sale of agricultural products," for example), it is increasingly common for the articles to state that the corporation is organized for "any legal business," with no mention of specifics, to avoid the need for future amendments.

Bylaws The internal rules of management adopted by a corporation at its first organizational meeting.

Internal Organization The articles can describe the internal structure of the corporation, although this is usually included in the **bylaws,** which are the internal rules of management adopted by the corporation at its first organizational meeting. The articles of incorporation commence the corporation, whereas the bylaws are formed after commencement by the board of directors. Bylaws cannot conflict with the corporation statute or the articles of incorporation [RMBCA 2.06].

Under the RMBCA, shareholders may amend or repeal the bylaws. The board of directors may also amend or repeal the bylaws unless the articles of incorporation or provisions of the corporation statute reserve this power to the shareholders exclusively [RMBCA 10.20]. Typical bylaw provisions describe such matters as voting requirements for shareholders, the election of the board of directors, the methods of replacing directors, and the manner and time of holding shareholders' and board meetings (these corporate activities will be discussed in Chapter 30).

KNOW THIS

Unlike the articles of incorporation, bylaws do not need to be filed with a state official.

File the Articles with the State Once the articles of incorporation have been prepared, signed, and authenticated by the incorporators, they are sent to the appropriate state official, usually the secretary of state, along with the required filing fee. In most states, the secretary of state then stamps the articles as "Filed" and returns a copy of the articles to the incorporators. Once this occurs, the corporation officially exists.

First Organizational Meeting to Adopt Bylaws

After incorporation, the first organizational meeting must be held. Usually, the most important function of this meeting is the adoption of the bylaws. If the articles of incorporation named the initial board of directors, then the directors, by majority vote, call the meeting to adopt the bylaws and complete the company's organization.

If the articles did not name the directors (as is typical), then the incorporators hold the meeting to elect the directors, adopt the bylaws, and complete the routine business of incorporation (authorizing the issuance of shares and hiring employees, for example). The business transacted depends on the requirements of the state's corporation statute, the nature of the corporation, the provisions made in the articles, and the desires of the incorporators.

(spxChrome/iStockphoto.com)

What are the routine aspects of forming a corporation?

Improper Incorporation

The procedures for incorporation are very specific. If they are not followed precisely, others may be able to challenge the existence of the corporation. Errors in the incorporation procedures can become important when, for example, a third party who is attempting to enforce a contract or bring a suit for a tort injury learns of them.

De Jure Corporations

If a corporation has substantially complied with all requirements for incorporation, the corporation is said to have *de jure* (rightful and lawful) existence. In most states and under the RMBCA, the secretary of state's filing of the articles of incorporation is conclusive proof that all mandatory statutory provisions have been met [RMBCA 2.03(b)].

Sometimes, there is a defect in complying with statutory mandates. If the defect is minor, such as an incorrect address listed on the articles of incorporation, most courts will overlook the defect and find that a corporation (*de jure*) exists.

De Facto Corporations

If the defect in formation is substantial, however, such as a corporation's failure to hold an organizational meeting to adopt bylaws, the outcome will vary depending on the court. Some states, including Mississippi, New York, Ohio, and Oklahoma, still recognize the common law doctrine of *de facto* corporation.[9] In those states, the courts will treat a corporation as a legal corporation despite the defect in its formation if all three of the following requirements are met:

1. A state statute exists under which the corporation can be validly incorporated.
2. The parties have made a good faith attempt to comply with the statute.
3. The parties have already undertaken to do business as a corporation.

Courts in many states, however, have interpreted their states' version of the RMBCA as abolishing the common law doctrine of *de facto* corporations. These states include Alaska, Arizona, Minnesota, New Mexico, Oregon, South Dakota, Tennessee, Utah, and Washington, as well as the District of Columbia. In those states, if there is a substantial defect in complying with the statutory mandates, the corporation does not legally exist, and the incorporators are personally liable.

Corporation by Estoppel

Sometimes, a business association holds itself out to others as being a corporation when it has made no attempt to incorporate. In those

9. See, for example, *In re Hausman*, 13 N.Y.3d 408, 921 N.E.2d 191, 893 N.Y.S.2d 499 (2009).

situations, the firm normally will be estopped (prevented) from denying corporate status in a lawsuit by a third party. The estoppel doctrine most commonly applies when a third party contracts with an entity that claims to be a corporation but has not filed articles of incorporation. It may also be applied when a third party contracts with a person claiming to be an agent of a corporation that does not in fact exist.

When justice requires, the courts treat an alleged corporation as if it were an actual corporation for the purpose of determining the rights and liabilities in a particular circumstance. Recognition of corporate status does not extend beyond the resolution of the problem at hand.

CASE EXAMPLE 29.5 W.P. Media, Inc., and Alabama MBA, Inc., agreed to form a wireless Internet services company. W.P. Media was to create a wireless network, and Alabama MBA was to contribute the capital. Hugh Brown signed the parties' contract on behalf of Alabama MBA as the chair of its board. At the time, however, Alabama MBA's articles of incorporation had not yet been filed. Brown filed the articles of incorporation the following year. Later, Brown and Alabama MBA filed a suit alleging that W.P. Media had breached their contract by not building the wireless network. The Supreme Court of Alabama held that because W.P. Media had treated Alabama MBA as a corporation, W.P. Media was estopped from denying Alabama MBA's corporate existence.[10] ●

Corporate Powers

When a corporation is created, the express and implied powers necessary to achieve its purpose also come into existence. The express powers of a corporation are found in its articles of incorporation, in the law of the state of incorporation, and in the state and federal constitutions.

Corporate bylaws also establish the express powers of the corporation. Because state corporation statutes frequently provide default rules that apply if the company's bylaws are silent on an issue, it is important that the bylaws set forth the specific operating rules of the corporation. In addition, after the bylaws are adopted, the corporation's board of directors will pass resolutions that also grant or restrict corporate powers.

The following order of priority is used when conflicts arise among documents involving corporations:

1. The U.S. Constitution.
2. State constitutions.
3. State statutes.
4. The articles of incorporation.
5. Bylaws.
6. Resolutions of the board of directors.

Implied Powers

When a corporation is created, it acquires certain implied powers. Barring express constitutional, statutory, or other prohibitions, the corporation has the implied power to perform all acts reasonably appropriate and necessary to accomplish its corporate purposes. For this reason, a corporation has the implied power to borrow funds within certain limits, to lend funds, and to extend credit to those with whom it has a legal or contractual relationship.

To borrow funds, the corporation acts through its board of directors to authorize the loan. Most often, the president or chief executive officer of the corporation will execute the necessary papers on behalf of the corporation. In so doing, corporate officers have the implied power to bind the corporation in matters directly connected with the *ordinary*

---

10. *Brown v. W.P. Media, Inc.*, 17 So.3d 1167 (2009).

business affairs of the enterprise. There is a limit to what a corporate officer can do, though. A corporate officer does not have the authority to bind the corporation to an action that will greatly affect the corporate purpose or undertaking, such as the sale of substantial corporate assets.

Ultra Vires Acts of a corporation that are beyond its express and implied powers to undertake (the Latin phrase means "beyond the powers").

Ultra Vires Doctrine

The term ***ultra vires*** means "beyond the powers." In corporate law, acts of a corporation that are beyond its express and implied powers are *ultra vires* acts.

When Corporate Actions Exceed Stated Purpose In the past, most cases dealing with *ultra vires* acts involved contracts made for unauthorized purposes. Now, however, most private corporations are organized for "any legal business" and not for a specific purpose, so the *ultra vires* doctrine has declined in importance. Today, cases that allege *ultra vires* acts usually involve nonprofit corporations or municipal (public) corporations.

CASE EXAMPLE 29.6 Four men formed a nonprofit corporation to create the Armenian Genocide Museum & Memorial (AGM&M). The bylaws appointed them as trustees (similar to corporate directors) for life. One of the trustees, Gerard L. Cafesjian, became the chair and president of AGM&M. Eventually, the relationship among the trustees deteriorated, and Cafesjian resigned. The corporation then brought a suit claiming that Cafesjian had engaged in numerous *ultra vires* acts, self-dealing, and mismanagement. Among other things, although the bylaws required an 80 percent affirmative vote of the trustees to take action, Cafesjian had taken many actions without the board's approval. He had also entered into contracts for real estate transactions in which he had a personal interest. Because Cafesjian had taken actions that exceeded his authority and had failed to follow the rules in the bylaws for board meetings, the court ruled that the corporation could go forward with its suit.[11] •

Remedies for Ultra Vires Acts Under Section 3.04 of the RMBCA, the shareholders can seek an injunction from a court to prevent (or stop) the corporation from engaging in *ultra vires* acts. The attorney general in the state of incorporation can also bring an action to obtain an injunction against the *ultra vires* transactions or to institute dissolution proceedings against the corporation on the basis of *ultra vires* acts. The corporation or its shareholders (on behalf of the corporation) can seek damages from the officers and directors who were responsible for the *ultra vires* acts.

Piercing the Corporate Veil

Piercing the Corporate Veil The action of a court to disregard the corporate entity and hold the shareholders personally liable for corporate debts and obligations.

Occasionally, the owners use a corporate entity to perpetrate a fraud, circumvent the law, or in some other way accomplish an illegitimate objective. In these situations, the court will ignore the corporate structure by **piercing the corporate veil** and exposing the shareholders to personal liability.

Generally, courts pierce the veil when the corporate privilege is abused for personal benefit or when the corporate business is treated so carelessly that it is indistinguishable from that of a controlling shareholder. In short, when the facts show that great injustice would result from the use of a corporation to avoid individual responsibility, a court will look behind the corporate structure to the individual shareholder. The shareholder/owner is then required to assume personal liability to creditors for the corporation's debts.

11. *Armenian Assembly of America, Inc. v. Cafesjian*, 692 F.Supp.2d 20 (D.C. 2010).

LEARNING OBJECTIVE 3

In what circumstances might a court disregard the corporate entity ("pierce the corporate veil") and hold the shareholders personally liable?

Factors That Lead Courts to Pierce the Corporate Veil

The following are some of the factors that frequently cause the courts to pierce the corporate veil:

1. A party is tricked or misled into dealing with the corporation rather than the individual.
2. The corporation is set up never to make a profit or always to be insolvent, or it is too "thinly" capitalized—that is, it has insufficient capital at the time of formation to meet its prospective debts or other potential liabilities.
3. Statutory corporate formalities, such as holding required corporation meetings, are not followed.
4. Personal and corporate interests are **commingled** to such an extent that the corporation has no separate identity.

Commingle To put funds or goods together into one mass so that they are mixed to such a degree that they no longer have separate identities, as when personal and corporate interests are mixed together to the extent that the corporation has no separate identity.

A Potential Problem for Close Corporations

The potential for corporate assets to be used for personal benefit is especially great in a *close corporation* (see page 748), in which the shares are held by a single person or by only a few individuals, usually family members. In such a situation, the separate status of the corporate entity and the sole shareholder (or family-member shareholders) must be carefully preserved. Certain practices invite trouble for the one-person or family-owned corporation: the commingling of corporate and personal funds, the failure to hold board of directors' meetings and record the minutes, or the shareholders' continuous personal use of corporate property (for example, vehicles).

In the following case, when a close corporation failed to pay its legal fees, its attorneys sought to hold the family-member shareholders personally liable. Could the attorneys pierce the corporate veil?

Case 29.2

Brennan's, Inc. v. Colbert

Court of Appeal of Louisiana, 85 So.3d 787 (2012).

(batman12/iStockphoto.com)

Can the shareholders of a close corporation be sued individually?

FACTS Three brothers—Pip, Jimmy, and Theodore Brennan—are shareholders of Brennan's, Inc., which owns and operates New Orleans' famous Brennan's Restaurant. The Brennan brothers retained attorney Edward Colbert and his firm, Kenyon & Kenyon, LLP, to represent Brennan's, Inc., in a dispute. All invoices were sent to Brennan's, Inc., and the Brennan brothers' payments came from the corporation's checking accounts.

As a close corporation, Brennan's, Inc., did not hold formal corporate meetings with agendas and minutes. Nevertheless, it did maintain corporate books, hold corporate bank accounts, and file corporate tax returns. In 2005, Brennan's, Inc., sued Colbert and Kenyon & Kenyon for legal malpractice. In its answer, Kenyon & Kenyon demanded unpaid legal fees both from Brennan's, Inc., and from the Brennan brothers personally. The court found that the Brennan brothers could not be held personally liable. On appeal, Kenyon & Kenyon argued that it should be allowed to pierce the corporate veil because Brennan's, Inc., did not observe corporate formalities and because the Brennan brothers did not honor their promises to pay their legal bills.

ISSUE Should the court pierce the corporate veil and allow Kenyon & Kenyon to hold the Brennan brothers personally liable?

DECISION No. The Louisiana appellate court affirmed the trial court's judgment for the Brennan brothers.

REASON Corporate shareholders generally may not be held personally liable, but a court may pierce the corporate veil if the shareholders fail to observe corporate formalities or use

Case 29.2—Continues next page

Case 29.2—Continued

the corporation to perpetrate a fraud. In this case, the Brennan brothers never agreed to personally pay Kenyon & Kenyon's legal fees. Instead, they simply spoke as shareholders for the firm's real client, Brennan's, Inc. Moreover, Kenyon & Kenyon knew that Brennan's, Inc., was a close corporation that operated somewhat informally. Although the corporation did not hold formal corporate meetings, it maintained corporate books, held corporate bank accounts, filed corporate tax returns, and even paid Kenyon & Kenyon with its own checks. Finally, the Brennan brothers did not defraud Kenyon & Kenyon by failing to pay their legal fees. "[I]f a broken promise to pay was sufficient to establish fraud," the court reasoned, "then every lawsuit against a corporation for a debt would automatically allow for the piercing of the corporate veil."

CRITICAL THINKING—Ethical Consideration *Should the Brennan brothers be held personally liable because they misled their attorneys? Why or why not?*

Corporate Financing

Securities Generally, stocks, bonds, or other items that represent an ownership interest in a corporation or a promise of repayment of debt by a corporation.

Stock An ownership (equity) interest in a corporation, measured in units of shares.

Bond A security that evidences a corporate (or government) debt.

Part of the process of corporate formation involves corporate financing. Corporations normally are financed by the issuance and sale of corporate securities. **Securities** (stocks and bonds) evidence the right to participate in earnings and the distribution of corporate property or the obligation to pay funds. (See the *Adapting the Law to the Online Environment* feature on the facing page for a discussion of how start-ups can seek financing online.)

Stocks, or *equity securities,* represent the purchase of ownership in the business firm. **Bonds** (debentures), or *debt securities,* represent the borrowing of funds by firms (and governments). Of course, not all debt is in the form of debt securities. For instance, some debt is in the form of accounts payable and notes payable, which typically are short-term debts. Bonds are simply a way for the corporation to split up its long-term debt so that it can be more easily marketed. (See this chapter's *Linking Business Law to Accounting and Finance* feature on page 768 for further discussion of corporate financing.)

"Gentlemen prefer bonds."

Andrew Mellon, 1855–1937 (American banker)

Bonds

Bonds are issued by business firms and by governments at all levels as evidence of the funds they are borrowing from investors. Bonds normally have a designated *maturity date*—the date when the principal, or face, amount of the bond is returned to the investor. They are sometimes referred to as *fixed-income securities* because their owners (that is, the creditors) receive fixed-dollar interest payments, usually semiannually, during the period of time before maturity.

Bond Indenture The agreement between the issuer of a bond and the bondholder that sets out the terms and features of the bond issue.

Because debt financing represents a legal obligation on the part of the corporation, various features and terms of a particular bond issue are specified in a lending agreement called a **bond indenture.** A corporate trustee, often a commercial bank trust department, acts on behalf of all bondholders in ensuring that the corporation meets the terms of the bond issue. The bond indenture specifies the maturity date of the bond and the pattern of interest payments until maturity.

Stocks

Issuing stocks is another way that corporations can obtain financing. The ways in which stocks differ from bonds are summarized in Exhibit 29.1 on the top of page 760. Basically, as mentioned, stocks represent ownership in a business firm, whereas bonds represent borrowing by the firm.

Exhibit 29.2 on the bottom of page 760 summarizes the types of stocks issued by corporations. We look now at the two major types of stock—*common stock* and *preferred stock.*

ADAPTING THE LAW TO THE ONLINE ENVIRONMENT

THE NEW ERA OF CROWDFUNDING

Every new company needs funds to grow, but banks are generally unwilling to finance a company with prospects but no profits as of yet. Venture capitalists do finance young companies, but there are not enough of them to fund all the companies looking for help. Now, start-ups that are unable to attract venture capitalists have a new way to obtain funding—crowdfunding.

What Is Crowdfunding?

Crowdfunding is a cooperative activity in which people network and pool funds and other resources via the Internet to assist a cause or invest in a venture. Sometimes, crowdfunding is used to raise funds for charitable purposes, such as disaster relief, but increasingly it is being used to finance budding entrepreneurs. Several rock bands have financed tours in this way, and now ventures of all kinds are trying to raise funds through crowdfunding.

Crowdfunding Becomes More Specialized

In a very short time, crowdfunding Web sites have proliferated. They offer partial ownership of start-ups in exchange for cash investments. At first, there were mostly generalized sites, such as Profounder.com and Startup Addict, but today the sites have become specialized. If you are interested only in new mobile apps, for example, you can go to the Apps Funder (www.appsfunder.com). As you might imagine, many of the apps are games, but this site also has a serious side. For instance, one new app that was funded involves sharing music scores. NewJelly (www.newjelly.com) raises funds for "dream" projects for artists and filmmakers.

Less Regulation Increases Crowdfunding's Appeal

Crowdfunding has taken off in many other countries, including France and Germany. Other countries' investor protection laws and regulations are often less stringent than U.S. laws, so we can expect to see more crowdfunding sites based abroad.

In 2012, President Barack Obama signed the JOBS Act (the acronym stands for "Jump-Start Our Business Start-Ups"), which relieved some of the regulatory burdens that you will read about in Chapter 31. Before this legislation, start-ups could look for financing only from investors who were "accredited," meaning that they had investment experience and a high net worth. If companies sought investment funds from the general public, they had to meet expensive and lengthy disclosure requirements. Under the new legislation, investing in start-ups will be more accessible to so-called nonaccredited investors.

Critical Thinking

What risks might be involved in crowdfunding investments?

Common Stock Shares of ownership in a corporation that give the owner of the stock a proportionate interest in the corporation with regard to control, earnings, and net assets. Common stock is lowest in priority with respect to payment of dividends and distribution of the corporation's assets on dissolution.

Common Stock

The true ownership of a corporation is represented by **common stock.** Common stock provides a proportionate interest in the corporation with regard to (1) control, (2) earnings, and (3) net assets. A shareholder's interest is generally in proportion to the number of shares he or she owns out of the total number of shares issued.

Voting Rights Voting rights in a corporation apply to the election of the firm's board of directors and to any proposed changes in the ownership structure of the firm. For example, a holder of common stock generally has the right to vote in a decision on a proposed merger, as mergers can change the proportion of ownership. State corporation law specifies the types of actions for which shareholder approval must be obtained.

Earnings Firms are not obligated to return a principal amount per share to each holder of common stock because no firm can ensure that the market price per share of its common stock will not decline over time. The issuing firm also does not have to guarantee a dividend. Indeed, some corporations never pay dividends.

Holders of common stock are investors who assume a *residual* position in the overall financial structure of a business. In terms of receiving payment for their investments, they are last in line. They are entitled to the earnings that are left after preferred stockholders, bondholders, suppliers, employees, and other groups have been paid. Once those groups

Exhibit 29.1 How Do Stocks and Bonds Differ?

STOCKS	BONDS
1. Stocks represent ownership.	1. Bonds represent debt.
2. Stocks (common) do not have a fixed dividend rate.	2. Interest on bonds must always be paid, whether or not any profit is earned.
3. Stockholders can elect the board of directors, which controls the corporation.	3. Bondholders usually have no voice in, or control over, management of the corporation.
4. Stocks do not have a maturity date. The corporation usually does not repay the stockholder.	4. Bonds have a maturity date, when the corporation is to repay the bondholder the face value of the bond.
5. All corporations issue or offer to sell stocks. This is the usual definition of a corporation.	5. Corporations do not necessarily issue bonds.
6. Stockholders have a claim against the property and income of a corporation after all creditors' claims have been met.	6. Bondholders have a claim against the property and income of a corporation that must be met *before* the claims of stockholders.

are paid, however, the owners of common stock may be entitled to *all* the remaining earnings as dividends. (The board of directors normally is not under any duty to declare the remaining earnings as dividends, however.)

Preferred Stock Stock that has priority over common stock as to payment of dividends and distribution of assets on the corporation's dissolution.

Preferred Stock

Preferred stock is stock with *preferences*. Usually, this means that holders of preferred stock have priority over holders of common stock as to dividends and payment on dissolution of the corporation. Holders of preferred stock may or may not have the right to vote.

Preferred stock is not included among the corporation's liabilities because it is equity. Like other equity securities, preferred shares have no fixed maturity date on which the firm must pay them off. Although firms occasionally buy back preferred stock, they are not legally obligated to do so.

Holders of preferred stock are investors who have assumed a rather cautious position in their relationship to the corporation. They have a stronger position than common shareholders with respect to dividends and claims on assets, but they will not share in the full prosperity of the firm if it grows successfully over time. Preferred stockholders do receive fixed dividends periodically, however, and they may benefit to some extent from changes in the market price of the shares.

Venture Capital and Private Equity Capital

As discussed, corporations traditionally obtain financing through issuing and selling securities (stocks and bonds) in the capital market. In reality, however, many investors do not

Exhibit 29.2 Types of Stocks

TYPE OF STOCK	DEFINITION
Common stock	Voting shares that represent ownership interest in a corporation. Common stock has the lowest priority with respect to payment of dividends and distribution of assets on the corporation's dissolution.
Preferred stock	Shares of stock that have priority over common-stock shares as to payment of dividends and distribution of assets on dissolution. Dividend payments are usually a fixed percentage of the face value of the share.
Cumulative preferred stock	Preferred shares on which required dividends not paid in a given year must be paid in a subsequent year before any common-stock dividends are paid.
Participating preferred stock	Preferred shares entitling the owner to receive the preferred-stock dividend and additional dividends if the corporation has paid dividends on common stock.
Convertible preferred stock	Preferred shares that, under certain conditions, can be converted into a specified number of common shares either in the issuing corporation or, sometimes, in another corporation.
Redeemable, or callable, preferred stock	Preferred shares issued with the express condition that the issuing corporation has the right to repurchase the shares as specified.

want to purchase stock in a business that lacks a track record, and banks are generally reluctant to extend loans to high-risk enterprises. Numerous corporations fail because they are undercapitalized. Therefore, to obtain sufficient financing, many entrepreneurs seek alternative financing.

Venture Capital Financing provided by professional, outside investors (venture capitalists) to new business ventures.

Venture Capital

Start-up businesses and high-risk enterprises often obtain venture capital financing. **Venture capital** is capital provided by professional, outside investors (*venture capitalists,* usually groups of wealthy investors and securities firms) to new business ventures. Venture capital investments are high risk—the investors must be willing to lose all of their invested funds—but offer the potential for well-above-average returns at some point in the future.

To obtain venture capital financing, the start-up business typically gives up a share of its ownership to the venture capitalists. In addition to funding, venture capitalists may provide managerial and technical expertise, and they nearly always are given some control over the new company's decisions. Many Internet-based companies, such as Google, were initially financed by venture capital.

Private Equity Capital Funds invested by a private equity firm in an existing corporation, usually to purchase and reorganize it.

Private Equity Capital

Private equity firms obtain their capital from wealthy investors in private markets. The firms use their **private equity capital** to invest in existing—often, publicly traded—corporations. Usually, they buy an entire corporation and then reorganize it. Sometimes, divisions of the purchased company are sold off to pay down debt. Ultimately, the private equity firm may sell shares in the reorganized (and perhaps more profitable) company to the public in an *initial public offering* (usually called an IPO—see Chapter 31). In this way, the private equity firm can make profits by selling its shares in the company to the public.

(sd619/iStockphoto.com)

Facebook acquired Instagram. Did Instagram cease to exist?

Mergers and Acquisitions

A corporation typically extends its operations by combining with another corporation through a merger, a consolidation, a share exchange, a purchase of assets, or a purchase of a controlling interest in the other corporation. The terms *merger* and *consolidation* traditionally referred to two legally distinct proceedings—although some people today use the term *consolidation* to refer to all types of combinations, including mergers and acquisitions.

Whether a combination is a merger, a consolidation, or a share exchange, the rights and liabilities of shareholders, the corporation, and the corporation's creditors are the same.

Merger

Merger The legal combination of two or more corporations in such a way that only one corporation (the surviving corporation) continues to exist, having acquired all of the assets and liabilities of the other corporation.

A **merger** involves the legal combination of two or more corporations in such a way that only one of the corporations continues to exist. **EXAMPLE 29.7** Corporation A and Corporation B decide to merge. They agree that A will absorb B. Therefore, on merging, B ceases to exist as a separate entity, and A continues as the *surviving corporation.* • Exhibit 29.3 on the top of the next page graphically illustrates this process.

LEARNING OBJECTIVE 4

What are the basic differences between a merger, a consolidation, and a share exchange?

One of the Firms Survives

After the merger, Corporation A is recognized as a single corporation, possessing all the rights, privileges, and powers of itself and Corporation B. It automatically acquires all of B's property and assets without the necessity of a formal transfer. Additionally, A becomes liable for all of B's debts and obligations.

Exhibit 29.3 Merger

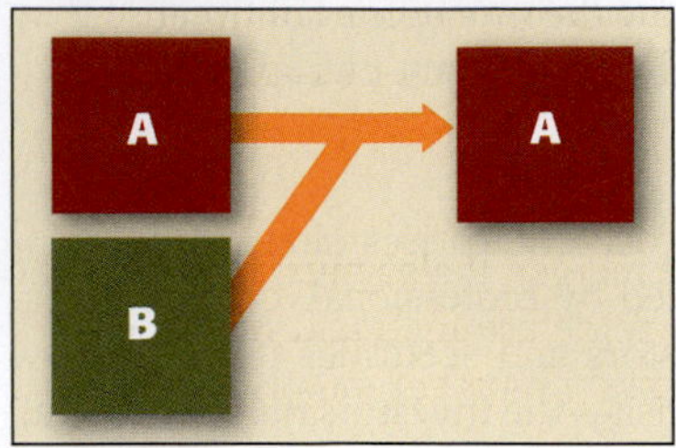

Finally, A's articles of incorporation are deemed amended to include any changes that are stated in the *articles of merger* (a document setting forth the terms and conditions of the merger that is filed with the secretary of state).

It Inherits Legal Rights and Obligations

In a merger, the surviving corporation inherits the disappearing corporation's preexisting legal rights and obligations. If the disappearing corporation had a right of action against a third party under tort or property law, for example, the surviving corporation can bring a suit after the merger to recover the disappearing corporation's damages.

Consolidation

Consolidation The legal combination of two or more corporations in such a way that the original corporations cease to exist, and a new corporation emerges with all their assets and liabilities.

In a **consolidation,** two or more corporations combine in such a way that each corporation ceases to exist and a new one emerges. EXAMPLE 29.8 Corporation A and Corporation B consolidate to form an entirely new organization, Corporation C. In the process, A and B both terminate, and C comes into existence as an entirely new entity. • Exhibit 29.4 on the left graphically illustrates this process.

Exhibit 29.4 Consolidation

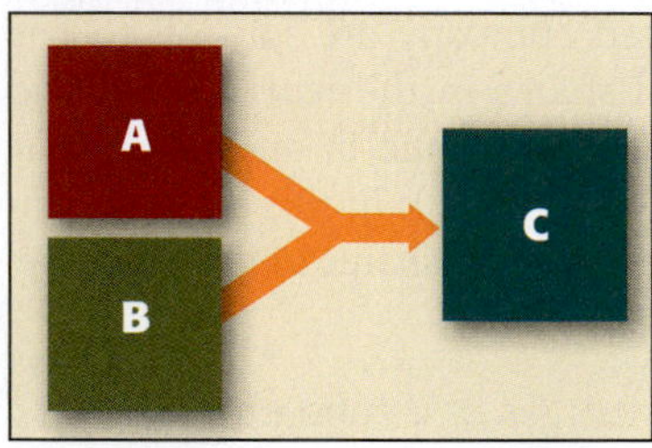

A New Corporation Is Formed

The results of a consolidation are essentially the same as the results of a merger. Corporation C is recognized as a new corporation and a single entity, while A and B cease to exist.

It Inherits All Rights and Liabilities of Both Predecessors

Corporation C inherits all of the rights, privileges, and powers previously held by A and B. Title to any property and assets owned by A and B passes to C without a formal transfer. Corporation C assumes liability for all of the debts and obligations owed by A and B. The *articles of consolidation,* which state the terms of the consolidation, take the place of A's and B's original corporate articles and are thereafter regarded as C's corporate articles.

When a merger or consolidation takes place, the surviving corporation or newly formed corporation will issue shares or pay some fair consideration to the shareholders of the corporation or corporations that cease to exist. True consolidations have become less common among for-profit corporations because it is often advantageous for one of the firms to survive. In contrast, nonprofit corporations and associations may prefer consolidation because it suggests a new beginning in which neither of the two initial entities is dominant.

Share Exchange

Share Exchange A transaction in which some or all of the shares of one corporation are exchanged for some or all of the shares of another corporation, but both corporations continue to exist.

In a **share exchange,** some or all of the shares of one corporation are exchanged for some or all of the shares of another corporation, but both companies continue to exist. Share exchanges are often used to create holding companies (discussed earlier in this chapter). For example, UAL Corporation is a large holding company that owns United Airlines. If one corporation owns *all* of the shares of another corporation, it is referred to as the *parent corporation,* and the wholly owned company is the *subsidiary corporation.*

Merger, Consolidation, or Share Exchange Procedures

All states have statutes authorizing mergers, consolidations, and share exchanges for domestic (in-state) and foreign (out-of-state) corporations. The procedures vary somewhat among jurisdictions. In some states, a consolidation resulting in an entirely new corporation simply follows the initial incorporation procedures discussed earlier in this chapter, whereas other business combinations must follow the procedures outlined below.

The RMBCA sets forth the following basic requirements [RMBCA 11.01–11.07]:

1. The board of directors of *each* corporation involved must approve the merger or consolidation plan.
2. The plan must specify any terms and conditions of the merger. It also must state how the value of the shares of each merging corporation will be determined and how they will be converted into shares or other securities, cash, property, or other interests in another corporation.
3. The majority of the shareholders of *each* corporation must vote to approve the plan at a shareholders' meeting. If any class of stock is entitled to vote as a separate group, the majority of each separate voting group must approve the plan.

   Although RMBCA 11.04(e) requires only a simple majority of the shareholders entitled to vote once a quorum is present, frequently a corporation's articles of incorporation or bylaws require approval by more than a simple majority (Chapter 30 will discuss *quorums* and other voting requirements). In addition, some state statutes require the approval of two-thirds of the outstanding shares of voting stock, and others require a four-fifths vote.
4. Once the plan is approved by the directors and the shareholders of both corporations, the surviving corporation files the plan (articles of merger, consolidation, or share exchange) with the appropriate official, usually the secretary of state.
5. When state formalities are satisfied, the state issues a certificate of merger to the surviving corporation or a certificate of consolidation to the newly consolidated corporation.

"There are two times in a man's life when he should not speculate: when he can't afford it and when he can."

Samuel Clemens (Mark Twain), 1835–1919 (American author and humorist)

Short-Form Mergers

RMBCA 11.04 provides a simplified procedure for the merger of a substantially owned subsidiary corporation into its parent corporation. Under these provisions, a **short-form merger**—also referred to as a **parent-subsidiary merger**—can be accomplished *without* the approval of the shareholders of either corporation.

Short-Form (Parent-Subsidiary) Merger A merger that can be accomplished without the approval of the shareholders of either corporation because one company (the parent corporation) owns at least 90 percent of the outstanding shares of each class of stock of the other corporation (the subsidiary corporation).

The short-form merger can be used only when the parent corporation owns at least 90 percent of the outstanding shares of each class of stock of the subsidiary corporation. Once the board of directors of the parent corporation approves the plan, it is filed with the state, and copies are sent to each shareholder of record in the subsidiary corporation.

Shareholder Approval

As mentioned, except in a short-form merger, the shareholders of both corporations must approve a merger or consolidation plan. Shareholders invest in a corporation with the expectation that the board of directors will manage the enterprise and make decisions on ordinary business matters. For *extraordinary* matters, normally both the board of directors and the shareholders must approve the transaction.

KNOW THIS

State statutes, articles of incorporation, and corporate bylaws can require the approval of more than a simple majority of shares for some extraordinary matters.

Mergers and other combinations are extraordinary business matters, meaning that the board of directors must normally obtain the shareholders' approval and provide appraisal rights (discussed next). Amendments to the articles of incorporation and the dissolution of the corporation also generally require shareholder approval.

Sometimes, a transaction can be structured in such a way that shareholder approval is not required, but if the shareholders challenge the transaction, a court might use its equity powers to require shareholder approval. For this reason, the board of directors may request shareholder approval even when it might not be legally required.

Appraisal Rights

What if a shareholder disapproves of a merger or a consolidation but is outvoted by the other shareholders? The law recognizes that a dissenting shareholder should not be forced to become an unwilling shareholder in a corporation that is new or different from the one in which the shareholder originally invested. Dissenting shareholders therefore are given a statutory right to be paid the fair value of the shares they held on the date of the merger or consolidation. This right is referred to as the shareholder's **appraisal right**. So long as the transaction does not involve fraud or other illegal conduct, appraisal rights are the exclusive remedy for a shareholder who is dissatisfied with the price received for the stock.

Appraisal Right The right of a dissenting shareholder, who objects to a merger or consolidation of the corporation, to have his or her shares appraised and to be paid the fair value of those shares by the corporation.

Appraisal rights normally extend to regular mergers, consolidations, share exchanges, short-form mergers, and sales of substantially all of the corporate assets not in the ordinary course of business. Such rights can be particularly important in a short-form merger because the minority stockholders do not receive advance notice of the merger, the directors do not consider or approve it, and there is no vote. Appraisal rights are often the only recourse available to shareholders who object to parent-subsidiary mergers.

Each state establishes the procedures for asserting appraisal rights in that jurisdiction. Shareholders may lose their appraisal rights if they do not adhere precisely to the procedures prescribed by statute. When they lose the right to an appraisal, dissenting shareholders must go along with the transaction despite their objections.

Purchase of Assets

When a corporation acquires all or substantially all of the assets of another corporation by direct purchase, the purchasing, or *acquiring*, corporation simply extends its ownership and control over more physical assets. Because no change in the legal entity occurs, the acquiring corporation is not required to obtain shareholder approval for the purchase.[12]

Note that the corporation that is *selling* all of its assets is substantially changing its business position and perhaps its ability to carry out its corporate purposes. For that reason, the corporation whose assets are being sold must obtain the approval of both the board of directors and the shareholders. In most states and under RMBCA 13.02, a dissenting shareholder of the selling corporation can demand appraisal rights.

Successor Liability in Purchases of Assets

KNOW THIS

In a merger or consolidation, the surviving corporation inherits the disappearing corporation's rights and obligations.

Generally, a corporation that purchases the assets of another corporation is not responsible for the liabilities of the selling corporation. Exceptions to this rule are made in certain circumstances, however.

In any of the following situations, the acquiring corporation will be held to have assumed *both* the assets and the liabilities of the selling corporation.

1. When the purchasing corporation impliedly or expressly assumes the seller's liabilities.
2. When the sale transaction is actually a merger or consolidation of the two companies.
3. When the purchaser continues the seller's business and retains the same personnel (same shareholders, directors, and officers).
4. When the sale is fraudulently executed to escape liability.

The following case involved a sale of corporate assets. Although the parties agreed that the purchasing corporation was assuming the seller's liabilities, the parties disagreed as to whether the liabilities being assumed were limited to those that were existing and outstanding as of the closing date. That was the question before the court.

12. Shareholder approval may be required in a few situations. If the acquiring corporation plans to pay for the assets with its own corporate stock and not enough authorized unissued shares are available, the shareholders must vote to approve the issuance of additional shares by amendment of the corporate articles. Also, if the acquiring corporation is a company whose stock is traded on a national stock exchange and it will be issuing a significant number (at least 20 percent) of its outstanding shares, shareholder approval can be required.

Case 29.3

American Standard, Inc. v. OakFabco, Inc.

Court of Appeals of New York,
14 N.Y.3d 399, 901 N.Y.S.2d 572 (2010).
www.courts.state.ny.us/decisions/index.shtml[a]

(ultramarinfoto/iStockphoto.com)

When does the purchase of a boiler division create ongoing liabilities for past acts?

FACTS American Standard, Inc., sold its Kewanee Boiler division to Kewanee Boiler Corporation, which is known as OakFabco, Inc. The agreement stated that OakFabco would purchase Kewanee assets subject to Kewanee liabilities. "Kewanee liabilities" were defined as "all the debts, liabilities, obligations, and commitments (fixed or contingent) connected with or attributable to Kewanee existing and outstanding at the Closing Date." The boilers manufactured by Kewanee had been insulated with asbestos, and as a result, many tort claims had been made in the years following the purchase of the business. Some of those claims were brought by plaintiffs who had suffered injuries after the closing of the transaction, allegedly attributable to boilers manufactured and sold before the closing. American Standard brought an action against OakFabco, asking the court for a declaratory judgment on the issue of whether liabilities for such injuries were among the "Kewanee liabilities" that OakFabco had assumed. The trial court held that OakFabco had assumed the liabilities, and an intermediate appellate court affirmed. OakFabco appealed.

ISSUE When a corporation purchases all of another corporation's assets and existing liabilities and debts, does that limit the purchasing corporation's liability for tort claims that arose *after* the closing date?

DECISION No. The New York Court of Appeals affirmed the intermediate appellate court's decision. The court concluded that the contract expressed the intention that OakFabco was to assume the liabilities of the selling corporation, including claims that arose after the closing date.

REASON The transaction in question "was a purchase and sale of substantially all of the assets of the Kewanee Boiler business 'subject to all debts, liabilities, and obligations connected with or attributable to such business and operations.' Nothing in the nature of the transaction suggested that the parties intended OakFabco, which got all the assets, to escape any of the related obligations." OakFabco pointed to the fact that the definition of Kewanee liabilities specified the debts, liabilities, obligations, and commitments existing and outstanding at the closing date. It argued that a tort claim could not be "existing and outstanding" before the tort plaintiff has been injured, because a tort lawsuit cannot be brought until after the injury.

The court, however, found that no clause in the agreement indicated an intention to adopt this meaning. Rather, the language in the agreement "clearly meant that the buyer would deal with any problems customers had after the closing date with boilers that had been installed previously." Consequently, the liabilities assumed by OakFabco included claims brought by tort claimants injured after the closing date by boilers installed before that date.

CRITICAL THINKING—Legal Consideration *Generally, a corporation that purchases the assets of another is not automatically responsible for the liabilities of the selling corporation, with some exceptions. Which exception applied in this case? Explain.*

a. In the left-hand column, select "Court of Appeals." On the page that opens, click on "Court of Appeals Content Search." In the results, in the "Search by Official Reports Citation for Opinions" boxes, type "14" and "399," and click on "Find." Click on the resulting link to access this case. The New York State court system maintains this Web site.

Purchase of Stock and Tender Offers

Target Corporation The corporation to be acquired in a corporate takeover.

Takeover The acquisition of control over a corporation through the purchase of a substantial number of the voting shares of the corporation.

Tender Offer An offer made by one company directly to the shareholders of another (target) company to purchase their shares of stock.

An alternative to the purchase of another corporation's assets is the purchase of a substantial number of the voting shares of its stock. This enables the acquiring corporation to control the **target corporation** (the corporation being acquired). The process of acquiring control over a corporation in this way is commonly referred to as a corporate **takeover**.

The acquiring corporation deals directly with the target company's shareholders in seeking to purchase the shares they hold. It does this by making a **tender offer** to all of the shareholders of the target corporation. The tender offer can be conditioned on receiving a specified number of shares by a certain date. The price offered is generally higher than the market price of the target corporation's stock prior to the announcement of the tender offer as a means of inducing shareholders to accept the offer.

"In the takeover business, if you want a friend, you buy a dog."

Carl Icahn, 1936–present (American financier)

EXAMPLE 29.9 In a merger of two Fortune 500 pharmaceutical companies, Pfizer, Inc., paid $68 billion to acquire its rival Wyeth. Wyeth shareholders reportedly received approximately $50.19 per share (part in cash and part in Pfizer stock), which amounted to a 15 percent premium over the market price of the stock. • Federal securities laws strictly control the terms, duration, and circumstances under which most tender offers are made. In addition, many states have passed antitakeover statutes.

Responses to Tender Offers

A firm may respond to a tender offer in numerous ways. Sometimes, a target firm's board of directors will see a tender offer as favorable and will recommend to the shareholders that they accept it. To resist a takeover, a target company can make a *self-tender,* which is an offer to acquire stock from its own shareholders and thereby retain corporate control.

Alternatively, a target corporation might resort to one of several other defensive tactics to resist a takeover (see Exhibit 29.5 below). In one commonly used tactic, known as a "poison pill," a target company gives its shareholders rights to purchase additional shares at low prices when there is a takeover attempt. The use of poison pills is an attempt to prevent takeovers by making a takeover prohibitively expensive.

Corporate Termination

Dissolution The formal disbanding of a corporation, which can take place by (1) an act of the state, (2) an agreement of the shareholders and the board of directors, (3) the expiration of a time period stated in the certificate of incorporation, or (4) a court order.

The termination of a corporation's existence has two phases—dissolution and winding up. **Dissolution** is the legal death of the artificial "person" of the corporation. *Winding up* is the process by which corporate assets are liquidated, or converted into cash and distributed among creditors and shareholders.[13]

Voluntary Dissolution

Dissolution can be brought about voluntarily by the directors and the shareholders. State corporation statutes establish the procedures required to voluntarily dissolve a corporation. Basically, there are two possible methods: (1) by the shareholders' unanimous vote

13. Some prefer to call this phase *liquidation,* but we use the term *winding up* to mean all acts needed to bring the legal and financial affairs of the business to an end, including liquidating the assets and distributing them among creditors and shareholders. See RMBCA 14.05.

Exhibit 29.5 The Terminology of Takeover Defenses

TERM	DEFINITION
Crown jewel	When threatened with a takeover, management makes the company less attractive to the raider by selling the company's most valuable asset (the "crown jewel") to a third party.
Golden parachute	When a takeover is successful, top management usually is changed. With this in mind, a company may establish special termination or retirement benefits that must be paid to top managers if they are "retired." In other words, a departing high-level manager's parachute will be "golden" when he or she is forced to "bail out" of the company.
Greenmail	To regain control, a target company may pay a higher-than-market price to repurchase the stock that the acquiring corporation bought. When a takeover is attempted through a gradual accumulation of target stock rather than a tender offer, the intent may be to get the target company to buy back the shares at a premium price—a concept similar to blackmail.
Pac-Man	Named after the Atari video game, this is an aggressive defense in which the target corporation attempts its own takeover of the acquiring corporation.
Poison pill	The target corporation issues to its stockholders rights to purchase additional shares at low prices when there is a takeover attempt. This makes the takeover undesirably or even prohibitively expensive for the acquiring corporation.
White knight	The target corporation solicits a merger with a third party, which then makes a better (often simply a higher) tender offer to the target's shareholders. The third party that "rescues" the target is the "white knight."

LEARNING OBJECTIVE 5
What are the two ways in which a corporation can be voluntarily dissolved?

to initiate dissolution proceedings[14] or (2) by a proposal of the board of directors that is submitted to the shareholders at a shareholders' meeting.

When a corporation is dissolved voluntarily, the corporation must file *articles of dissolution* with the state and notify its creditors of the dissolution. The corporation must also establish a date (at least 120 days after the date of dissolution) by which all claims against the corporation must be received [RMBCA 14.06].

Involuntary Dissolution

Because corporations are creatures of statute, the state can also dissolve a corporation in certain circumstances. The secretary of state or the state attorney general can bring an action to dissolve a corporation that has failed to pay its annual taxes or to submit required annual reports, for example. A state court can also dissolve a corporation that has engaged in *ultra vires* acts or committed fraud or misrepresentation to the state during incorporation.

KNOW THIS

The death of a sole proprietor or a partner can result in the dissolution of a business. The death of a corporate shareholder, however, rarely causes the dissolution of a corporation.

Sometimes, a shareholder or a group of shareholders petitions a court for corporate dissolution. A court may dissolve a corporation if the controlling shareholders or directors have engaged in fraudulent, illegal, or oppressive conduct. Shareholders may also petition a court for dissolution when the board of directors is deadlocked and the affairs of the corporation can no longer be conducted because of the deadlock.[15]

Winding Up

When dissolution takes place by voluntary action, the members of the board of directors act as trustees of the corporate assets. As trustees, they are responsible for winding up the affairs of the corporation for the benefit of corporate creditors and shareholders. This makes the board members personally liable for any breach of their fiduciary trustee duties.

Receiver In a corporate dissolution, a court-appointed person who winds up corporate affairs and liquidates corporate assets.

When the dissolution is involuntary—or if board members do not wish to act as trustees of the assets—the court will appoint a **receiver** to wind up the corporate affairs and liquidate corporate assets. Courts may also appoint a receiver when shareholders or creditors can show that the board of directors should not be permitted to act as trustees of the corporate assets.

14. Only some states allow shareholders to initiate corporate dissolution. See, for example, Delaware Code Section 275(c).
15. See, for example, *Sartori v. S&S Trucking, Inc.*, 2006 MT 164, 322 Mont. 503, 139 P.3d 806 (2006).

Reviewing . . . Corporate Formation, Merger, and Termination

William Sharp was the sole shareholder and manager of Chickasaw Club, Inc., an S corporation that operated a popular nightclub of the same name in Columbus, Georgia. Sharp maintained a corporate checking account but paid the club's employees, suppliers, and entertainers in cash out of the club's proceeds. Sharp owned the property on which the club was located. He rented it to the club but made mortgage payments out of the club's proceeds and often paid other personal expenses with Chickasaw corporate funds.

At 12:45 A.M. on July 31, eighteen-year-old Aubrey Lynn Pursley, who was already intoxicated, entered the Chickasaw Club. Chickasaw employees did not check Pursley's identification to verify her age, as required by a city ordinance. Pursley drank more alcohol at Chickasaw and was visibly intoxicated when she left the club at 3:00 A.M. with a beer in her hand. Shortly afterward, Pursley lost control of her car, struck a tree, and was killed. Joseph Dancause, Pursley's stepfather, filed a tort lawsuit against Chickasaw Club and William Sharp. Using the information presented in the chapter, answer the following questions.

Continued

1. Under what theory might the court in this case make an exception to the limited liability of shareholders and hold Sharp personally liable for the damages? What factors would be relevant to the court's decision?
2. Suppose that Chickasaw's articles of incorporation failed to describe the corporation's purpose or management structure as required by state law. Would the court be likely to rule that Sharp is personally liable to Dancause on that basis? Why or why not?
3. Suppose that the club extended credit to its regular patrons in an effort to maintain a loyal clientele, although neither the articles of incorporation nor the corporate bylaws authorized this practice. Would the corporation likely have the power to engage in this activity? Explain.
4. How would the court classify Chickasaw Club, Inc.—domestic or foreign, public or private?

DEBATE THIS The sole shareholder of an S corporation should not be able to avoid liability for the torts of her or his employees.

LINKING BUSINESS LAW to Accounting and Finance

Sources of Funds

Your career may take you from business intern or management trainee through other corporate positions to finance manager. A finance manager helps corporate directors and officers determine the sources of funds for ongoing corporate expenses and, hopefully, continued business expansion and growth.

Stocks and Bonds

Corporate finance managers have a variety of options for sources of funds. They include issuing shares of stock (equity) and selling corporate debt. A finance manager must weigh the advantages and disadvantages of each of these alternatives.

For instance, an issue of common stock does not create an obligation to make fixed interest payments to investors every year, as a sale of bonds would, but the additional shares dilute the holdings of current stockholders. In the case of preferred stock, a sale of shares creates additional preferences. For instance, holders of preferred stock have priority over holders of common stock with respect to dividends and to payment on the dissolution of the corporation.

Lines of Credit

Another option for a source of corporate funds is to borrow the funds. Commercial banks loan funds to all types of businesses. A bank typically provides a successful corporation with a line of credit that can be drawn on at any time and can be repaid when the business's cash flow warrants it. A commercial bank's line of credit, however, normally costs more in terms of interest than an issuance of corporate bonds.

Self-Financing

Finance managers sometimes decide that the best type of financing is self- financing. To accomplish this type of financing, a corporation retains its earnings on sales and uses those earnings for additional investments. The use of retained earnings is not without cost—there is an *opportunity cost* involved. That opportunity cost is the value that could have been earned if the retained earnings had been used for other investments, such as U.S. Treasury bonds. Retained earnings might also otherwise have been used to pay dividends to shareholders.

Critical Thinking

What is the benefit of paying dividends to shareholders rather than using retained earnings to expand?

Key Terms

alien corporation 747
appraisal right 764
articles of incorporation 752
bond 758
bond indenture 758
bylaws 753
close corporation 748
commingle 757
common stock 759
consolidation 762
corporation 744
dissolution 766
dividend 744
domestic corporation 747
foreign corporation 747
holding company 746
merger 761
piercing the corporate veil 756
preferred stock 760
private equity capital 761
receiver 767
retained earnings 744
S corporation 750
securities 758
share exchange 762
short-form (parent-subsidiary) merger 763
stock 758
takeover 765
target corporation 765
tender offer 765
ultra vires 756
venture capital 761

Chapter Summary: Corporate Formation, Merger, and Termination

Corporate Nature and Classification (See pages 744–750.)	A corporation is a legal entity distinct from its owners. Formal statutory requirements, which vary somewhat from state to state, must be followed in forming a corporation. 1. *Corporate personnel*—The shareholders own the corporation. They elect a board of directors to govern the corporation. The board of directors hires corporate officers and other employees to run the firm's daily business. 2. *Corporate taxation*—The corporation pays income tax on net profits, and shareholders pay income tax on the disbursed dividends that they receive from the corporation (double-taxation feature). 3. *Torts and criminal acts*—The corporation is liable for the torts committed by its agents or officers within the course and scope of their employment (under the doctrine of *respondeat superior*). A corporation can be held liable (and be fined) for the criminal acts of its agents and employees. 4. *Domestic, foreign, and alien corporations*—A corporation is referred to as a *domestic corporation* within its home state (the state in which it incorporates), as a *foreign corporation* by any state that is not its home state, and as an *alien corporation* if it originates in another country but does business in the United States. 5. *Public and private corporations*—A public corporation is formed by a government. A private corporation is formed wholly or in part for private benefit. Most corporations are private corporations. 6. *Nonprofit corporations*—Corporations formed without a profit-making purpose. 7. *Close corporations*—Corporations owned by a family or a relatively small number of individuals. Transfer of shares is usually restricted. 8. *S corporations*—Small domestic corporations that, under Subchapter S of the Internal Revenue Code, are taxed like partnerships, thereby allowing shareholders to enjoy limited liability while avoiding double taxation. 9. *Professional corporations*—Corporations formed by professionals (for example, physicians and lawyers). For liability purposes, some courts disregard the corporate form and treat the shareholders as partners.
Corporate Formation and Powers (See pages 750–756.)	1. *Promotional activities*—A person who enters contracts on behalf of the future corporation is personally liable on all preincorporation contracts until the corporation is formed and assumes the contracts by novation. 2. *Incorporation procedures*—Procedures vary among the states, but the basic steps are as follows: (a) select a state of incorporation, (b) secure the corporate name, (c) prepare the articles of incorporation, and (d) file the articles with the secretary of state. 3. *Articles of incorporation*—The articles must include the corporate name, the number of shares of stock the corporation is authorized to issue, the registered office and agent, and the names and addresses of the incorporators. The state's filing of the articles authorizes the corporation to conduct business. 4. *First organizational meeting*—The main function of the meeting is to adopt the bylaws, or internal rules of the corporation, but other business, such as election of the board of directors, may also take place. 5. *De jure or de facto corporation*—If a corporation has been improperly incorporated, the courts will sometimes impute corporate status to the firm by holding that it is a *de jure* or a *de facto* corporation. 6. *Corporation by estoppel*—If a firm is not incorporated but represents itself to be a corporation and is sued as such by a third party, it may be held to be a corporation by estoppel. 7. *Express powers*—These powers are granted by the (listed in order of priority): federal constitution, state constitutions, state statutes, articles of incorporation, bylaws, and resolutions of the board of directors. 8. *Implied powers*—Barring express constitutional, statutory, or other prohibitions, the corporation has the implied power to do all acts reasonably appropriate and necessary to accomplish its corporate purposes. 9. *Ultra vires doctrine*—Any act of a corporation that is beyond its express or implied powers is an *ultra vires* act and may lead to a lawsuit by the shareholders, corporation, or state attorney general to enjoin or recover damages for the *ultra vires* acts.

Continued

Chapter Summary: Corporate Formation, Merger, and Termination—Continued

Piercing the Corporate Veil (See pages 756–758.)	To avoid injustice, courts may "pierce the corporate veil" and hold a shareholder or shareholders personally liable. This usually occurs only when the corporation was established to circumvent the law, when the corporate form is used for an illegitimate or fraudulent purpose, or when the controlling shareholder commingles his or her own interests with those of the corporation to such an extent that the corporation no longer has a separate identity.
Corporate Financing (See pages 758–761.)	1. *Bonds*—Securities representing *corporate debt*—funds borrowed by a corporation. 2. *Stocks*—Equity securities issued by a corporation that represent the purchase of ownership in the firm. Exhibit 29.1 on page 760 describes how stocks differ from bonds, and Exhibit 29.2 on page 760 describes the types of stocks issued by corporations.
Mergers and Acquisitions (See pages 761–766.)	1. *Merger*—The legal combination of two or more corporations, with the result that the surviving corporation acquires all the assets and obligations of the other corporation, which then ceases to exist. 2. *Consolidation*—The legal combination of two or more corporations, with the result that each corporation ceases to exist and a new one emerges. The new corporation assumes all the assets and obligations of the former corporations. 3. *Share exchange*—Some or all of the shares of one corporation are exchanged for some or all of the shares of another corporation, but both corporations continue to exist. 4. *Procedures*—Determined by state statutes. The basic requirements are listed on page 763. 5. *Short-form (parent-subsidiary) merger*—Possible when the parent corporation owns at least 90 percent of the outstanding shares of each class of stock of the subsidiary corporation. Shareholder approval is not required. The merger need be approved only by the board of directors of the parent corporation. 6. *Appraisal rights*—Statutory rights of dissenting shareholders (given by state statute) to receive the *fair value* for their shares when a merger or consolidation takes place. 7. *Purchase of assets*—When one corporation acquires all or substantially all of the assets of another corporation, the acquiring (purchasing) corporation is not required to obtain shareholder approval, but the selling corporation must obtain the approval of both its directors and its shareholders for the asset sale. 8. *Purchase of stock and tender offers*—One corporation may acquire a substantial number of the voting shares of the stock of another (target) corporation through a tender offer, which is a public offer to all shareholders of the target corporation to purchase its stock at a price that generally is higher than the market price. 9. *Target responses*—Responses to takeover bids include self-tender (the target firm's offer to acquire its own shareholders' stock) and the strategies listed in Exhibit 29.5 on page 766.
Corporate Termination (See pages 766–767.)	The termination of a corporation involves the following two phases: 1. *Dissolution*—The legal death of the artificial "person" of the corporation. Dissolution can be brought about voluntarily by the directors and shareholders or involuntarily by the state or through a court order. 2. *Winding up (liquidation)*—The process by which corporate assets are converted into cash and distributed to creditors and shareholders. May be supervised by members of the board of directors (when dissolution is voluntary) or by a receiver appointed by the court.

ExamPrep

ISSUE SPOTTERS

1. Name Brand, Inc., is a small business. Twelve members of a single family own all of its stock. Ordinarily, corporate income is taxed at the corporate and shareholder levels. How can Name Brand avoid this double taxation of income? **(See page 750.)**
2. ABC Corporation combines with DEF, Inc. ABC ceases to exist. DEF is the surviving firm. Global Corporation and Hometown Company combine. Afterward, Global and Hometown cease to exist. GH, Inc., a new firm, functions in their place. Which of these combinations is a merger and which is a consolidation? **(See pages 761–762.)**

—Check your answers to the Issue Spotters against the answers provided in Appendix E at the end of this text.

BEFORE THE TEST

Go to www.cengagebrain.com, enter the ISBN 9781133273561, and click on "Find" to locate this textbook's Web site. Then, click on "Access Now" under "Study Tools," and select Chapter 29 at the top. There, you will find a Practice Quiz that you can take to assess your mastery of the concepts in this chapter, as well as Flashcards, a Glossary of important terms, and Video Questions (when assigned).

For Review

Answers to the even-numbered questions in this For Review section can be found in Appendix F at the end of this text.

1. What is a close corporation?
2. What steps are involved in bringing a corporation into existence?
3. In what circumstances might a court disregard the corporate entity ("pierce the corporate veil") and hold the shareholders personally liable?
4. What are the basic differences between a merger, a consolidation, and a share exchange?
5. What are the two ways in which a corporation can be voluntarily dissolved?

Business Scenarios and Case Problems

29–1 **Preincorporation.** Cummings, Okawa, and Taft are recent college graduates who want to form a corporation to manufacture and sell personal computers. Peterson tells them he will set in motion the formation of their corporation. First, Peterson makes a contract with Owens for the purchase of a piece of land for $20,000. Owens does not know of the prospective corporate formation at the time the contract is signed. Second, Peterson makes a contract with Babcock to build a small plant on the property being purchased. Babcock's contract is conditional on the corporation's formation. Peterson secures all necessary capitalization and files the articles of incorporation. Discuss whether the newly formed corporation, Peterson, or both are liable on the contracts with Owens and Babcock. Is the corporation automatically liable to Babcock on formation? Explain. **(See page 751.)**

29–2 **Question with Sample Answer—Corporate Powers.** Kora Nayenga and two business associates formed a corporation called Nayenga Corp. for the purpose of selling computer services. Kora, who owned 50 percent of the corporate shares, served as the corporation's president. Kora wished to obtain a personal loan from his bank for $250,000, but the bank required the note to be cosigned by a third party. Kora cosigned the note in the name of the corporation. Later, Kora defaulted on the note, and the bank sued the corporation for payment. The corporation asserted, as a defense, that Kora had exceeded his authority when he cosigned the note. Had he? Explain. **(See pages 755–756.)**

—For a sample answer to Question 29–2, go to Appendix G at the end of this text.

29–3 **Spotlight on Smart Inventions—Piercing the Corporate Veil.** Thomas Persson and Jon Nokes founded Smart Inventions, Inc., to market household consumer products. The success of their first product, the Smart Mop, continued with later products, which were sold through infomercials. Persson and Nokes were the firm's officers and equal shareholders, with Persson responsible for product development and Nokes in charge of day-to-day activities. By 1998, they had become dissatisfied with each other's efforts. Nokes represented the firm as financially "dying," "in a grim state, . . . worse than ever," and offered to buy all of Persson's shares for $1.6 million. Persson accepted. On the day that they signed the agreement to transfer the shares, Smart Inventions began marketing a new product—the Tap Light. It was an instant success, generating millions of dollars in revenues. In negotiating with Persson, Nokes had intentionally kept the Tap Light a secret. Persson sued Smart Inventions, asserting fraud and other claims. Under what principle might Smart Inventions be liable for Nokes's fraud? Is Smart Inventions liable in this case? Explain. [*Persson v. Smart Inventions, Inc.*, 125 Cal.App.4th 1141, 23 Cal.Rptr.3d 335 (2 Dist. 2005)] **(See pages 756–758.)**

29–4 **Piercing the Corporate Veil.** Smith Services, Inc., a trucking business owned by Tony Smith, charged its fuel purchases to an account at Laker Express. When Smith Services was not paid on several contracts, it ceased doing business and was dissolved. Smith continued to provide trucking services, however, as a sole proprietor. Laker Express sought to recover Smith Services' unpaid fuel charges, which amounted to about $35,000, from Smith. He argued that he was not personally liable for a corporate debt. Should the court pierce the corporate veil? Explain. [*Bear, Inc. v. Smith*, 303 S.W.3d 137 (Ky.App. 2010)] **(See pages 756–758.)**

29–5 **Close Corporations.** Mark Burnett and Kamran Pourgol were the only shareholders in a corporation that built and sold a house. When the buyers discovered that the house exceeded the amount of square footage allowed by the building permit, Pourgol agreed to renovate the house to conform to the permit. No work was done, however, and Burnett filed a suit against Pourgol. Burnett claimed that without his knowledge, Pourgol had submitted incorrect plans to obtain the building permit, misrepresented the extent of the renovation, and failed to fix the house. Was Pourgol guilty of misconduct? If so, how might it have been avoided? Discuss. [*Burnett v. Pourgol*, 83 A.D.3d 756, 921 N.Y.S.2d 280 (2 Dept. 2011)] **(See pages 748–749.)**

29–6 **Purchase of Stock.** Air Products & Chemicals, Inc., made a tender offer of $70 per share to the shareholders of Airgas, Inc. The Airgas board rejected the offer as inadequate and took defensive measures to block the bid. Some Airgas shareholders filed a suit against Airgas, seeking an order to compel the board to allow the shareholders to decide whether to accept Air Products' offer. Who should have the power to accept or reject a tender offer? Why? How can directors best fulfill their duty to act in the interest of their shareholders? (For more on the duties of directors, see Chapter 30.) [*Air Products & Chemicals, Inc. v. Airgas, Inc.*, 16 A.3d 48 (Del.Ch. 2011)] **(See pages 765–766.)**

29–7 **Case Problem with Sample Answer—Purchase of Assets.** Grand Adventures Tour & Travel Publishing Corp. (GATT) provided travel services. Duane Boyd, a former GATT director, incorporated Interline Travel & Tour, Inc. At a public sale, Interline bought GATT's assets. Interline moved into GATT's office building, hired former GATT employees, and began to serve GATT's customers. A GATT creditor, Call Center Technologies, Inc., sought to collect the unpaid amount on a contract with GATT from Interline. Is Interline liable? Why or why not? [*Call Center Technologies, Inc. v. Grand Adventures Tour & Travel Publishing Corp.*, 635 F.3d 48 (2d Cir. 2011)] **(See page 764.)**

—For a sample answer to Problem 29–7, go to Appendix H at the end of this text.

29–8 **Piercing the Corporate Veil.** In 1997, Leon Greenblatt, Andrew Jahelka, and Richard Nichols incorporated Loop Corp. with only $1,000 of capital. Three years later, Banco Panamericano, Inc., which was run entirely by Greenblatt and owned by a Greenblatt family trust, extended a large line of credit to Loop. Loop's subsidiaries then participated in the credit, giving $3 million to Loop while acquiring a security interest in Loop itself. Loop then opened an account with Wachovia Securities, LLC, to buy stock shares using credit provided by Wachovia. When the stock values plummeted, Loop owed Wachovia $1.89 million. Loop also defaulted on its loan from Banco, but Banco agreed to lend Loop millions of dollars more. Rather than repay Wachovia with the influx of funds, Loop gave the funds to closely related entities and "compensated" Nichols and Jahelka without issuing any W-2 forms (forms reporting compensation to the Internal Revenue Service). The evidence also showed that Loop made loans to other related entities and shared office space, equipment, and telephone and fax numbers with related entities. Loop also moved employees among related entities, failed to file its tax returns on time (or sometimes at all), and failed to follow its own bylaws. In a lawsuit brought by Wachovia, can the court hold Greenblatt, Jahelka, and Nichols personally liable by piercing the corporate veil? Why or why not? [*Wachovia Securities, LLC v. Banco Panamericano, Inc.*, 674 F.3d 743 (9th Cir. 2012)] **(See pages 756–758.)**

29–9 **A Question of Ethics—Improper Incorporation.** Mike Lyons incorporated Lyons Concrete, Inc., in Montana, but did not file its first annual report, so the state involuntarily dissolved the firm in 1996. Unaware of the dissolution, Lyons continued to do business as Lyons Concrete. In 2003, he signed a written contract with William Weimar to form and pour a certain amount of concrete on Weimar's property in Lake County for $19,810. Weimar was in a rush to complete the entire project, and he and Lyons orally agreed to additional work on a time-and-materials basis. When scheduling conflicts arose, Weimar had his own employees set some of the forms, which proved deficient. Weimar also directed Lyons to pour concrete in the rain, which undercut its quality. Midproject, Lyons submitted an invoice for $14,389, which Weimar paid. After the work was complete, Lyons billed Weimar for $25,731, but he refused to pay, claiming that the $14,389 covered everything. To recover the unpaid amount, Lyons filed a mechanic's lien as "Mike Lyons d/b/a Lyons Concrete, Inc." against Weimar's property. Weimar filed a suit to strike the lien, and Lyons filed a counterclaim. [*Weimar v. Lyons*, 338 Mont. 242, 164 P.3d 922 (2007)] **(See pages 750–756.)**

1. Before the trial, Weimar asked for a change of venue on the ground that a sign on the courthouse lawn advertised "Lyons Concrete." How might the sign affect a trial on the parties' dispute? Should the court grant this request?
2. Weimar asked the court to dismiss the counterclaim on the ground that the state had dissolved Lyons Concrete in 1996. Lyons immediately filed new articles of incorporation for "Lyons Concrete, Inc." Under what doctrine might the court rule that Weimar could not deny the existence of Lyons Concrete? What ethical values underlie this doctrine? Should the court make this ruling?
3. At the trial, Weimar argued, in part, that there was no "fixed price" contract between the parties and that even if there was, the poor quality of the work, which required repairs, amounted to a breach, excusing Weimar's further performance. Should the court rule in Weimar's favor on this basis?

Critical Thinking and Writing Assignments

29–10 **Business Law Critical Thinking Group Assignment.** Angie Jolson is the chair of the board of directors of Artel, Inc., and Sam Douglas is the chair of the board of directors of Fox Express, Inc. Jolson and Douglas meet to consider the possibility of combining their corporations and activities into a single corporate entity. They consider two alternative courses of action: Artel could acquire all of the stock and assets of Fox Express, or the corporations could combine to form a new corporation, called A&F Enterprises, Inc. Both Jolson and Douglas are concerned about the necessity of a formal transfer of property, liability for existing debts, and the need to amend the articles of incorporation.

1. The first group will identify the first proposed combination and outline its legal effect on the transfer of property, the liabilities of the combined corporations, and the need to amend the articles of incorporation.
2. The second group will do the same for the second proposed combination—determine what it is called and describe its legal effect on the transfer of property, the liabilities of the combined corporations, and the need to amend the articles of incorporation.

CHAPTER 30

Corporate Directors, Officers, and Shareholders

(Bershadsky Yuri/Shutterstock.com)

CHAPTER OUTLINE

- Directors and Officers
- Duties and Liabilities of Directors and Officers
- Shareholders
- Rights of Shareholders
- Duties and Liabilities of Shareholders
- Major Business Forms Compared

LEARNING OBJECTIVES

The five learning objectives below are designed to help improve your understanding of the chapter. After reading this chapter, you should be able to answer the following questions:

1. What are the duties of corporate directors and officers?
2. Directors are expected to use their best judgment in managing the corporation. What must directors do to avoid liability for honest mistakes of judgment and poor business decisions?
3. What is a voting proxy?
4. From what sources may dividends be paid legally? In what circumstances is a dividend illegal? What happens if a dividend is illegally paid?
5. If a group of shareholders perceives that the corporation has suffered a wrong and the directors refuse to take action, can the shareholders compel the directors to act? If so, how?

"They [Corporations] cannot commit treason, nor be outlawed nor excommunicated, because they have no soul."
—Sir Edward Coke, 1552–1634 (English jurist and legal scholar)

When Sir Edward Coke observed, in the chapter-opening quotation, that a corporation has no "soul," he was referring to the fact that a corporation is not a "natural" person but a legal fiction. No one individual shareholder or director bears sole responsibility for the corporation and its actions. Rather, a corporation joins the efforts and resources of a large number of individuals for the purpose of producing greater returns than those persons could have obtained individually.

Corporate directors, officers, and shareholders all play different roles within the corporate entity. Sometimes, actions that benefit the corporation as a whole do not coincide with the separate interests of the individuals making up the corporation. In such situations, it is important to know the rights and duties of all participants in the corporate enterprise.

This chapter focuses on the rights and duties of directors, officers, and shareholders and the ways in which conflicts among them are resolved. You will also read about the ongoing debate over whether shareholders should be able to access corporate proxy materials effortlessly and without cost.

Directors and Officers

The board of directors is the ultimate authority in every corporation. Directors have responsibility for all policymaking decisions necessary to the management of all corporate affairs. The board selects and removes the corporate officers, determines the capital structure of the corporation, and declares dividends. Each director has one vote, and customarily the majority rules. The general areas of responsibility of the board of directors are shown in Exhibit 30.1 below.

Directors are sometimes inappropriately characterized as *agents* because they act on behalf of the corporation. No *individual* director, however, can act as an agent to bind the corporation. As a group, directors collectively control the corporation in a way that no agent is able to control a principal. In addition, although directors occupy positions of trust and control over the corporation, they are not *trustees* because they do not hold title to property for the use and benefit of others.

There are few legal requirements concerning directors' qualifications. Only a handful of states impose minimum age and residency requirements. A director may be a shareholder, but this is not necessary (unless the articles of incorporation or bylaws require ownership interest).

Election of Directors

Subject to statutory limitations, the number of directors is set forth in the corporation's articles or bylaws. Historically, the minimum number of directors has been three, but today many states permit fewer. Normally, the incorporators appoint the first board of directors at the time the corporation is created. The initial board serves until the first annual shareholders' meeting. Subsequent directors are elected by a majority vote of the shareholders.

A director usually serves for a term of one year—from annual meeting to annual meeting. Most state statutes permit longer and staggered terms. A common practice is to elect one-third of the board members each year for a three-year term. In this way, there is greater management continuity.

KNOW THIS

The articles of incorporation may provide that a director can be removed only for cause.

Removal of Directors

A director can be removed *for cause*—that is, for failing to perform a required duty—either as specified in the articles or bylaws or by shareholder action. The board of directors may also have the power to remove a director for cause, subject to shareholder review. In most states, a director cannot be removed without cause unless the shareholders have reserved the right to do so at the time of his or her election.

Vacancies on the Board of Directors

If a director dies or resigns or if a new position is created through amendment of the articles or bylaws, either the shareholders

Exhibit 30.1 Directors' Management Responsibilities

AUTHORIZE MAJOR CORPORATE POLICY DECISIONS	SELECT AND REMOVE CORPORATE OFFICERS AND OTHER MANAGERIAL EMPLOYEES, AND DETERMINE THEIR COMPENSATION	MAKE CORPORATE FINANCIAL DECISIONS
Examples: • Oversee major contract negotiations and management-labor negotiations. • Initiate negotiations on the sale or lease of corporate assets outside the regular course of business. • Decide whether to pursue new product lines or business opportunities.	*Examples:* • Search for and hire corporate executives and determine the elements of their compensation packages, including stock options. • Supervise managerial employees and make decisions regarding their termination.	*Examples:* • Make decisions regarding the issuance of authorized shares and bonds. • Decide when to declare dividends that are to be paid to shareholders.

(sjlocke/iStockphoto.com)

Are directors of a corporation agents of that corporation? Why or why not?

or the board itself can fill the vacant position, depending on state law or the provisions of the bylaws. Note, however, that even when an election appears to be authorized by the bylaws, a court can invalidate it if the directors were attempting to manipulate the election in order to reduce the shareholders' influence.

CASE EXAMPLE 30.1 The bylaws of Liquid Audio, a Delaware corporation, authorized a board of five directors. Two directors on the board were elected each year. Another company offered to buy all of Liquid Audio's stock, but the board of directors rejected this offer. To prevent the shareholders from electing new directors who would allow the sale, the directors amended the bylaws to increase the number of directors to seven, thereby diminishing the shareholders' influence. The shareholders filed an action challenging the election. The Delaware Supreme Court ruled that the directors' action was illegal because they had attempted to diminish the shareholders' right to vote effectively in an election of directors.[1] •

Compensation of Directors

In the past, corporate directors rarely were compensated, but today they are often paid at least nominal sums and may receive more substantial compensation in large corporations because of the time, work, effort, and especially the risk involved. Most states permit the corporate articles or bylaws to authorize compensation for directors. In fact, the Revised Model Business Corporation Act (RMBCA) states that unless the articles or bylaws provide otherwise, the board of directors itself may set directors' compensation [RMBCA 8.11]. Directors also gain through indirect benefits, such as business contacts and prestige, and other rewards, such as stock options.

In many corporations, directors are also chief corporate officers (president or chief executive officer, for example) and receive compensation in their managerial positions. A director who is also an officer of the corporation is referred to as an **inside director,** whereas a director who does not hold a management position is an **outside director.** Typically, a corporation's board of directors includes both inside and outside directors.

Inside Director A person on the board of directors who is also an officer of the corporation.

Outside Director A person on the board of directors who does not hold a management position at the corporation.

Board of Directors' Meetings

The board of directors conducts business by holding formal meetings with recorded minutes. The dates of regular meetings are usually established in the articles or bylaws or by board resolution, and ordinarily no further notice is required. Special meetings can be called, with notice sent to all directors. Today, most states allow directors to participate in board meetings from remote locations via telephone, Web conferencing, or Skype, provided that all the directors can simultaneously hear each other during the meeting [RMBCA 8.20].

Unless the articles of incorporation or bylaws specify a greater number, a majority of the board of directors normally constitutes a quorum [RMBCA 8.24]. (A **quorum** is the minimum number of members of a body of officials or other group that must be present in order for business to be validly transacted.) Some state statutes specifically allow corporations to set a quorum at less than a majority but not less than one-third of the directors.[2]

Quorum The minimum number of members of a decision-making body that must be present before business may be transacted.

Once a quorum is present, the directors transact business and vote on issues affecting the corporation. Each director present at the meeting has one vote.[3] Ordinary matters generally require a simple majority vote, but certain extraordinary issues may require a greater-than-majority vote.

1. *MM Companies v. Liquid Audio, Inc.*, 813 A.2d 1118 (Del.Sup. 2003).
2. See, for example, Delaware Code Annotated Title 8, Section 141(b); and New York Business Corporation Law Section 707.
3. Except in Louisiana, which allows a director to authorize another person to cast a vote in his or her place under certain circumstances.

Committees of the Board of Directors

"I often feel like the director of a cemetery. I have a lot of people under me, but nobody listens!"

General James Gavin, 1907–1990 (U.S. Army lieutenant general)

When a board of directors has a large number of members and must deal with myriad complex business issues, meetings can become unwieldy. Therefore, the boards of large, publicly held corporations typically create committees of directors and delegate certain tasks to these committees. Committees focus on individual subjects and increase the efficiency of the board.

Two common types of committees are the *executive committee* and the *audit committee.* An executive committee handles interim management decisions between board meetings. It is limited to making decisions about ordinary business matters, though, and does not have the power to declare dividends, amend the bylaws, or authorize the issuance of stock. The Sarbanes-Oxley Act requires all publicly held corporations to have an audit committee. The audit committee is responsible for the selection, compensation, and oversight of the independent public accountants that audit the firm's financial records.

Rights of Directors

A corporate director must have certain rights to function properly in that position and make informed policy decisions for the company. The *right to participation* means that directors are entitled to participate in all board of directors' meetings and have a right to be notified of these meetings. Because the dates of regular board meetings are usually specified in the bylaws, as noted earlier, no notice of these meetings is required. If special meetings are called, however, notice is required unless waived by the director.

A director also has the *right of inspection,* which means that each director can access the corporation's books and records, facilities, and premises. Inspection rights are essential for directors to make informed decisions and to exercise the necessary supervision over corporate officers and employees. This right of inspection is almost absolute and cannot be restricted (by the articles, bylaws, or any act of the board).

When a director becomes involved in litigation by virtue of her or his position or actions, the director may also have a right to indemnification (reimbursement) for legal costs, fees, and damages incurred. Most states allow corporations to indemnify and purchase liability insurance for corporate directors [RMBCA 8.51].

PREVENTING LEGAL DISPUTES

Whenever businesspersons serve as corporate directors or officers, they may at some point become involved in litigation as a result of their positions. To protect against personal liability, directors or officers should take several steps. First, they should make sure that the corporate bylaws explicitly give them a right to indemnification (reimbursement) for any costs incurred as a result of litigation, as well as for any judgments or settlements. Second, they should have the corporation purchase directors' and officers' liability insurance (D&O insurance). Having D&O insurance enables the corporation to avoid paying the substantial costs involved in defending a particular director or officer. The D&O policies offered by most insurance companies have maximum coverage limits. It is therefore important to make sure that directors and officers will be indemnified in the event that the costs exceed the policy limits.

Corporate Officers and Executives

Corporate officers and other executive employees are hired by the board of directors. At a minimum, most corporations have a president, one or more vice presidents, a secretary, and a treasurer. In most states, an individual can hold more than one office, such as president and secretary, and can be both an officer and a director of the corporation. In addition

KNOW THIS

Shareholders own the corporation and directors make policy decisions, but the officers who run the corporation's daily business often have significant decision-making power.

to carrying out the duties articulated in the bylaws, corporate and managerial officers act as agents of the corporation, and the ordinary rules of agency (discussed in Chapter 23) normally apply to their employment.

Corporate officers and other high-level managers are employees of the company, so their rights are defined by employment contracts. The board of directors, though, normally can remove corporate officers at any time with or without cause and regardless of the terms of the employment contracts—although in so doing, the corporation may be liable for breach of contract.

Duties and Liabilities of Directors and Officers

LEARNING OBJECTIVE 1
What are the duties of corporate directors and officers?

The duties of directors and corporate officers are the same because both groups are involved in decision making and are in similar positions of control. Directors and officers are deemed fiduciaries of the corporation because their relationship with the corporation and its shareholders is one of trust and confidence. As fiduciaries, directors and officers owe ethical—and legal—duties to the corporation and to the shareholders as a whole. These fiduciary duties include the duty of care and the duty of loyalty.

(Directors and officers also have a duty not to destroy evidence in the event of a lawsuit involving the corporation. The *Business Application* feature on page 794 discusses how due care can be exercised to preserve electronic evidence by creating a retention policy for e-documents.)

Duty of Care

Directors and officers must exercise due care in performing their duties. The standard of *due care* has been variously described in judicial decisions and codified in many state corporation codes. Generally, a director or officer is expected to act in good faith, to exercise the care that an ordinarily prudent person would exercise in similar circumstances, and to act in what he or she considers to be the best interests of the corporation [RMBCA 8.30].

Directors and officers whose failure to exercise due care results in harm to the corporation or its shareholders can be held liable for negligence (unless the *business judgment rule* applies, as will be discussed shortly). The prospect of liability may be one reason why corporate officers are using special software to help identify employees who might commit embezzlement. (See this chapter's *Adapting the Law to the Online Environment* feature on the next page for a discussion of this topic.)

Duty to Make Informed and Reasonable Decisions

Directors and officers are expected to be informed on corporate matters and to conduct a reasonable investigation of the situation before making a decision. This means that they must do what is necessary to keep adequately informed: attend meetings and presentations, ask for information from those who have it, read reports, and review other written materials. In other words, directors and officers must investigate, study, and discuss matters and evaluate alternatives before making a decision. They cannot decide on the spur of the moment without adequate research.

Although directors and officers are expected to act in accordance with their own knowledge and training, they are also normally entitled to rely on information given to them by certain other persons. Most states and Section 8.30(b) of the RMBCA allow a director to make decisions in reliance on information furnished by competent officers or employees, professionals such as attorneys and accountants, and committees of the board of directors (on which the director does not serve). The reliance must be in good faith, of course, to insulate a director from liability if the information later proves to be inaccurate or unreliable.

ADAPTING THE LAW TO THE ONLINE ENVIRONMENT

SOFTWARE TO HELP OFFICERS SPOT POTENTIAL EMBEZZLERS

Every year, dishonest employees embezzle millions of dollars from corporations around the world, and those funds are rarely recovered. Consequently, corporate officers are always looking for ways to prevent embezzlement. The typical way to "catch a thief" is to hire an accountant to look for anomalies in the firm's financial records. An alternative is to use linguistic software.

Linguistic Software Looks for Future Embezzlers

Accountants can detect embezzlers only after the crime, but linguistic software looks for employees who may become embezzlers in the future. The software scans e-mails for signs that employees are having financial troubles and thus might be prone to embezzlement. For example, if the software suddenly finds the phrase "under the gun" and similar phrases in a rash of e-mails sent by an employee, a red flag is raised.

The software also looks for signs that employees are unhappy in their jobs, such as e-mails with numerous references to the "evil" or "immoral" corporation. Another red flag is raised if an employee sends many messages asking the recipients to "call my cell phone," or to "come by my office." Such messages suggest that the employee wants to communicate without the call being recorded or without leaving a written record.

Insider Traders Can Be Detected, Too

Financial firms also have to be concerned that brokers might be obtaining inside information and using it for their own benefit. Financial Tracking Technologies developed a software program that combs through employees' calendars and travel expense claims. The goal is to find out which employees have come into contact with certain outside investors.

Critical Thinking

What motivates corporate directors and officers to purchase linguistic software?

Duty to Exercise Reasonable Supervision Directors are also expected to exercise a reasonable amount of supervision when they delegate work to corporate officers and employees. **EXAMPLE 30.2** Dale, a corporate bank director, fails to attend any board of directors' meetings for five years. In addition, Dale never inspects any of the corporate books or records and generally fails to supervise the efforts of the bank president and the loan committee. Meanwhile, Brennan, the bank president, who is a corporate officer, makes various improper loans and permits large overdrafts. In this situation, Dale (the corporate director) can be held liable to the corporation for losses resulting from the unsupervised actions of the bank president and the loan committee. •

Dissenting Directors Directors are expected to attend board of directors' meetings, and their votes should be entered into the minutes of the meetings. Sometimes, an individual director disagrees with the majority's vote (which becomes an act of the board of directors). Unless a dissent is entered, the director is presumed to have assented. If a decision later leads to the directors being held liable for mismanagement, dissenting directors are rarely held individually liable to the corporation. For this reason, a director who is absent from a given meeting sometimes registers a dissent with the secretary of the board regarding actions taken at the meeting.

Business Judgment Rule A rule that immunizes corporate directors and officers from liability for decisions that result in corporate losses or damages as long as the decision makers took reasonable steps to become informed, had a rational basis for their decisions, and did not have a conflict of interest with the corporation.

The Business Judgment Rule

Directors and officers are expected to exercise due care and to use their best judgment in guiding corporate management, but they are not insurers of business success. Under the **business judgment rule**, a corporate director or officer will not be liable to the corporation or to its shareholders for honest mistakes of judgment and bad business decisions.

LEARNING OBJECTIVE 2
Directors are expected to use their best judgment in managing the corporation. What must directors do to avoid liability for honest mistakes of judgment and poor business decisions?

Courts give significant deference to the decisions of corporate directors and officers, and consider the reasonableness of a decision at the time it was made, without the benefit of hindsight. Thus, corporate decision makers are not subjected to second-guessing by shareholders or others in the corporation. The business judgment rule will apply as long as the director or officer did the following:

1. Took reasonable steps to become informed about the matter.
2. Had a rational basis for his or her decision.
3. Did not have a conflict of interest between his or her personal interest and that of the corporation.

In fact, unless there is evidence of bad faith, fraud, or a clear breach of fiduciary duties, most courts will apply the rule and protect directors and officers who make bad business decisions from liability for those choices. **CASE EXAMPLE 30.3** After a foreign firm announced its intention to acquire Lyondell Chemical Company, Lyondell's directors did nothing to prepare for a possible merger. They failed to research Lyondell's market value and made no attempt to seek out other potential buyers. The $13 billion cash merger was negotiated and finalized in less than a week—and the directors met for only seven hours to discuss it. Shareholders sued, claiming that the directors had breached their fiduciary duties by failing to maximize the sale price of the corporation. The Delaware Supreme Court ruled that the directors were protected by the business judgment rule.[4] •

Does the business judgment rule protect directors and officers from liability for all mistakes in judgment and bad decisions, except those that constitute gross negligence? Gross negligence is more than a mere failure to exercise ordinary care—it is an intentional failure to perform a duty in reckless disregard of the consequences. In the following case, the defendant argued that without a finding of gross negligence, the business judgment rule should apply.

4. *Lyondell Chemical Co. v. Ryan*, 970 A.2d 235 (Del.Sup. 2009).

Case 30.1

Henrichs v. Chugach Alaska Corp.

Supreme Court of Alaska,
250 P.3d 531 (2011).
government.westlaw.com/akcases[a]

(Photo by Bill Stryker)

When do bylaws become important?

FACTS The board of Chugach Alaska Corporation (CAC, a corporation of Alaska Natives) split into two factions—one led by Sheri Buretta, who had chaired the board for several years, and the other by director Robert Henrichs. A coalition of directors voted to remove Buretta and install Henrichs as the board's chair. During his term, Henrichs held mini-board meetings and made decisions with only his supporters present. He refused to comply with bylaws that required a special meeting of shareholders in response to a shareholder petition. In addition, he acted without board discussion or approval and ignored board rules in the conduct of meetings. He also personally mistreated directors, shareholders, and employees, and retaliated against directors who challenged his decisions by excluding them from the board and spending corporate funds to file meritless complaints against them with state authorities. After six months, the board voted to reinstall Buretta. CAC filed a suit in an Alaska state court against Henrichs, alleging a breach of fiduciary duty. A jury found Henrichs liable, and the court banned him from serving on CAC's board for five years. Henrichs appealed.

a. In the left-hand column, in the "Search" section, click on "By Word." On the next page, in the "Search for:" box, type "Henrichs." In the result, click on the name of the case with the citation 250 P.3d 531 to view the opinion. The Alaska State Court Law Library maintains this Web site.

Case 30.1—Continues next page ➡

Case 30.1—Continued

ISSUE Does the business judgment rule protect a director who acted in breach of his fiduciary duties?

DECISION No. The Alaska Supreme Court affirmed the lower court's decision. The business judgment rule did not protect Henrichs. A director or officer can be held liable for a breach of fiduciary duty without a finding of gross negligence.

REASON Henrichs contended that, under the business judgment rule, he could not be found liable unless he had been grossly negligent. The court agreed that the business judgment rule affords some protection for corporate directors, but added, "We have never measured the degree of protection afforded by the business judgment rule in terms of gross negligence." If there is evidence of bad faith, breach of a fiduciary duty, or acts in violation of public policy, the rule will not protect a director who makes bad business decisions from liability for those choices. The jury and the lower court had found that Henrichs committed a breach of fiduciary duty. The conduct was "volitional"—that is, Henrichs chose to act as he did and knew that his actions exceeded the rules. The misconduct was serious and egregious (outstandingly bad). In light of these findings, the business judgment rule did not protect Henrichs.

CRITICAL THINKING—Ethical Consideration *Does misbehavior such as the conduct at the heart of this case constitute a breach of business ethics? Discuss.*

Duty of Loyalty

Loyalty can be defined as faithfulness to one's obligations and duties. In the corporate context, the duty of loyalty requires directors and officers to subordinate their personal interests to the welfare of the corporation. Directors cannot use corporate funds or confidential corporate information for personal advantage and must refrain from self-dealing. For instance, a director should not oppose a tender offer (see Chapter 29) that is in the corporation's best interest simply because its acceptance may cost the director her or his position. Cases dealing with the duty of loyalty typically involve one or more of the following:

1. Competing with the corporation.
2. Usurping (taking advantage of) a corporate opportunity.
3. Having an interest that conflicts with the interest of the corporation.
4. Engaging in insider trading (using information that is not public to make a profit trading securities, as will be discussed in Chapter 31).
5. Authorizing a corporate transaction that is detrimental to minority shareholders.
6. Selling control over the corporation.

The following *Classic Case* illustrates the conflict that can arise between a corporate official's personal interest and his or her duty of loyalty.

Classic Case 30.2

(Dalton Rowe/ Creative Commons)

Pepsi-Cola got its start when the head of Loft Candy Company usurped a corporate opportunity.

Guth v. Loft, Inc.

Supreme Court of Delaware, 23 Del.Ch. 255, 5 A.2d 503 (1939).

HISTORICAL SETTING *In the 1920s, Loft Candy Company (Loft, Inc.), based in Long Island City, New York, was a publicly held company with a $13 million candy-and-restaurant chain. The company manufactured its own candies, syrups, and beverages and sold its products in its more than one hundred retail locations throughout the Northeast. The retail stores featured old-fashioned soda fountains and were very popular. In 1930, Charles Guth became Loft's president after a contentious stockholders' meeting. His position there set the stage for the rise of the soft drink Pepsi-Cola.*

FACTS At the time Charles Guth became Loft's president, Guth and his family owned Grace Company, which made syrups for soft drinks in a plant in Baltimore, Maryland. Coca-Cola

Classic Case 30.2—Continued

Company supplied Loft with cola syrup. Unhappy with what he felt was Coca-Cola's high price, Guth entered into an agreement with Roy Megargel to acquire the trademark and formula for Pepsi-Cola and form Pepsi-Cola Corporation. Neither Guth nor Megargel could finance the new venture, however, and Grace Company was insolvent. Without the knowledge of Loft's board of directors, Guth used Loft's capital, credit, facilities, and employees to further the Pepsi enterprise. At Guth's direction, a Loft employee made the concentrate for the syrup, which was sent to Grace Company to add sugar and water. Loft charged Grace Company for the concentrate but allowed forty months' credit. Grace charged Pepsi for the syrup but also granted substantial credit. Grace sold the syrup to Pepsi's customers, including Loft, which paid on delivery or within thirty days. Loft also paid for Pepsi's advertising.

Finally, losing profits at its stores as a result of switching from Coca-Cola, Loft filed a suit in a Delaware state court against Guth, Grace, and Pepsi, seeking their Pepsi stock and an accounting. The court entered a judgment in the plaintiff's favor. The defendants appealed to the Delaware Supreme Court.

ISSUE Did Guth violate his duty of loyalty to Loft, Inc., by acquiring the Pepsi-Cola trademark and formula for himself without the knowledge of Loft's board of directors?

DECISION Yes. The Delaware Supreme Court upheld the judgment of the lower court. The state supreme court was "convinced that the opportunity to acquire the Pepsi-Cola trademark and formula, goodwill and business belonged to [Loft], and that Guth, as its president, had no right to appropriate the opportunity to himself."

REASON The court pointed out that the officers and directors of a corporation stand in a fiduciary relationship to that corporation and to its shareholders. Corporate officers and directors must protect the corporation's interest at all times. They must also "refrain from doing anything that works injury to the corporation." In other words, corporate officers and directors must provide undivided and unselfish loyalty to the corporation, and "there should be no conflict between duty and self-interest." Whenever an opportunity is presented to the corporation, officers and directors with knowledge of that opportunity cannot seize it for themselves. "The corporation may elect to claim all of the benefits of the transaction for itself, and the law will impress a trust in favor of the corporation upon the property, interest, and profits required."

Guth clearly created a conflict between his self-interest and his duty to Loft—the corporation of which he was president and director. Guth illegally appropriated the Pepsi-Cola opportunity for himself and thereby placed himself in the position of competing with the company for which he worked.

WHAT IF THE FACTS WERE DIFFERENT? *Suppose that Loft's board of directors had approved Pepsi-Cola's use of its personnel and equipment. Would the court's decision have been different? Discuss.*

IMPACT OF THIS CASE ON TODAY'S LAW *This early Delaware decision was one of the first to set forth a test for determining when a corporate officer or director has breached the duty of loyalty. The test has two basic parts—whether the opportunity was reasonably related to the corporation's line of business, and whether the corporation was financially able to undertake the opportunity. The court also considered whether the corporation had an interest or expectancy in the opportunity and recognized that when the corporation had "no interest or expectancy, the officer or director is entitled to treat the opportunity as his own."*

Disclosure of Conflicts of Interest

"If it is not in the interest of the public, it is not in the interest of the business."

Joseph H. Defrees, 1812–1885 (U.S. congressman)

Corporate directors often have many business affiliations, and a director may sit on the board of more than one corporation. Of course, directors are precluded from entering into or supporting businesses that operate in direct competition with corporations on whose boards they serve. Their fiduciary duty requires them to make a full disclosure of any potential conflicts of interest that might arise in any corporate transaction [RMBCA 8.60].

Sometimes, a corporation enters into a contract or engages in a transaction in which an officer or director has a personal interest. The director or officer must make a *full disclosure* of that interest and must abstain from voting on the proposed transaction.

EXAMPLE 30.4 Southwood Corporation needs office space. Lambert Alden, one of its five directors, owns the building adjoining the corporation's main office building. He negotiates a lease with Southwood for the space, making a full disclosure to Southwood and the other four directors. The lease arrangement is fair and reasonable, and it is unanimously approved by the other four directors. In this situation, Alden has not breached his duty of loyalty to the corporation, and thus the contract is valid. If it were otherwise, directors would be prevented from ever transacting business with the corporations they serve. ●

Liability of Directors and Officers

Directors and officers are exposed to liability on many fronts. They may be held liable for the crimes and torts committed by themselves or by corporate employees under their supervision, as discussed in Chapter 6 and Chapter 23, respectively.

Additionally, if shareholders perceive that the corporate directors are not acting in the best interests of the corporation, they may sue the directors, in what is called a *shareholder's derivative suit,* on behalf of the corporation. (This type of action will be discussed later in this chapter, in the context of shareholders' rights.) Directors and officers can also be held personally liable under a number of statutes, such as those enacted to protect consumers or the environment (see Chapter 33).

Shareholders

The acquisition of a share of stock makes a person an owner and shareholder in a corporation. Shareholders thus own the corporation. Although they have no legal title to corporate property, such as buildings and equipment, they do have an equitable (ownership) interest in the firm.

KNOW THIS

Shareholders normally are not agents of the corporation.

As a general rule, shareholders have no responsibility for the daily management of the corporation, even if they are ultimately responsible for choosing the board of directors, which does have such control. Ordinarily, corporate officers and directors owe no duty to individual shareholders unless some contract or special relationship exists between them in addition to the corporate relationship. The duty of the officers and directors is to act in the best interests of the corporation and its shareholder-owners as a whole. In turn, as you will read later in this chapter, controlling shareholders owe a fiduciary duty to minority shareholders. Normally, there is no legal relationship between shareholders and creditors of the corporation. (Shareholders can be creditors of the corporation, though, and they have the same rights of recovery against the corporation as any other creditor.)

In this section, we look at the powers and voting rights of shareholders, which are generally established in the articles of incorporation and by the state's general corporation law.

Can shareholders vote at a shareholders' meeting?

(AP Photo/Sue Ogrocki)

Shareholders' Powers

Shareholders must approve fundamental changes affecting the corporation before the changes can be implemented. Hence, shareholders are empowered to amend the articles of incorporation and bylaws, approve a merger or the dissolution of the corporation, and approve the sale of all or substantially all of the corporation's assets. Some of these powers are subject to prior board approval.

Members of the board of directors are elected and removed by a vote of the shareholders. As mentioned earlier, the incorporators choose the first directors, who serve until the first shareholders' meeting. From that time on, the selection and retention of directors are exclusively shareholder functions.

Directors usually serve their full terms. If the shareholders judge them unsatisfactory, they are simply not reelected. Shareholders have the inherent power, however, to remove a director from office for cause (such as for breach of duty or misconduct) by a majority vote.[5] Some state statutes (and

5. A director can often demand court review of removal for cause.

(AP Photo/Rob Carr, File)

Who has the right to speak at a shareholders' meeting?

some corporate articles) permit removal of directors without cause by the vote of a majority of the holders of outstanding shares entitled to vote.

Shareholders' Meetings

Shareholders' meetings must occur at least annually. In addition, special meetings can be called to deal with urgent matters.

Notice of Meetings

A corporation must notify its shareholders of the date, time, and place of an annual or special shareholders' meeting at least ten days, but not more than sixty days, before the meeting date [RMBCA 7.05].[6] Notice of a special meeting must include a statement of the purpose of the meeting, and business transacted at the meeting is limited to that purpose.

Proxies

It is usually not practical for owners of only a few shares of stock of publicly traded corporations to attend shareholders' meetings. Therefore, the law allows stockholders to either vote in person or appoint another person as their agent to vote their shares at the meeting. The signed appointment form or electronic transmission authorizing an agent to vote the shares is called a **proxy** (from the Latin *procurare*, meaning "to manage, take care of").

Proxy In corporate law, a written or electronically transmitted form in which a stockholder authorizes another party to vote the stockholder's shares in a certain manner.

LEARNING OBJECTIVE 3
What is a voting proxy?

Management often solicits proxies, but any person can solicit proxies to concentrate voting power. Proxies have been used by a group of shareholders as a device for taking over a corporation (corporate takeovers were discussed in Chapter 29). Proxies normally are revocable (that is, they can be withdrawn), unless they are specifically designated as irrevocable. Under RMBCA 7.22(c), proxies last for eleven months, unless the proxy agreement provides for a longer period.

Proxy Materials and Shareholder Proposals

When shareholders want to change a company policy, they can put their idea up for a shareholder vote. They can do this by submitting a shareholder proposal to the board of directors and asking the board to include the proposal in the proxy materials that are sent to all shareholders before meetings.

The Securities and Exchange Commission (SEC), which regulates the purchase and sale of securities (see Chapter 31), has special provisions relating to proxies and shareholder proposals. SEC Rule 14a-8 provides that all shareholders who own stock worth at least $1,000 are eligible to submit proposals for inclusion in corporate proxy materials. The corporation is required to include information on whatever proposals will be considered at the shareholders' meeting along with proxy materials. Only those proposals that relate to significant policy considerations rather than ordinary business operations must be included.

Electronic Proxy Materials

In the past, corporations had to send large packets of paper documents to shareholders, but today, the SEC requires all publicly held companies to distribute electronic proxy (e-proxy) materials. Although companies must post their proxy materials on the Internet, they may still choose among several options—including paper documents sent by mail—for actually delivering the materials to shareholders.[7]

6. A shareholder can waive the requirement of written notice by signing a waiver form. In some states, a shareholder who does not receive written notice, but who learns of the meeting and attends without protesting the lack of notice, is said to have waived notice by such conduct. State statutes and corporate bylaws typically set forth the time within which notice must be sent, what methods can be used, and what the notice must contain.

7. 17 C.F.R. Parts 240, 249, and 274.

If a company wishes to distribute proxy materials only via the Internet, it can choose the notice-and-access delivery option. Under this model, the corporation posts the proxy materials on a Web site and notifies the shareholders that the proxy materials are available online. If a shareholder requests paper proxy materials, the company must send them within three business days. Shareholders can permanently elect to receive all future proxy materials on paper or by e-mail.

ETHICAL ISSUE

Should interest groups have free access to proxy materials in order to nominate their own candidates for corporate boards? During many years of lobbying, unions, pension funds, and other institutional investors sought a rule that would allow them access to corporate proxy materials without cost. The SEC ultimately passed a rule that required companies' proxy materials to include information about shareholder-nominated candidates for boards of directors. In the past, investor groups that wanted to replace directors had to mail separate ballots to all shareholders and then conduct a costly campaign. Before this new rule went into effect, however, the U.S. Chamber of Commerce and the Business Roundtable challenged it in court. The U.S. Court of Appeals for the District of Columbia Circuit struck down the rule, holding that the SEC "acted arbitrarily and capriciously for having failed . . . adequately to assess economic effects of a new rule."[8]

Ann Yerger, head of the Council of Institutional Investors, said, "We think the court got it wrong. We will continue to advocate for proxy access." Other shareholder advocates agreed. Shareholder groups believe that the proxy access rule would make boards of directors more accountable and would allow shareholders to have more say in corporations' strategic and financial decisions.

Shareholder Voting

Shareholders exercise ownership control through the power of their votes. Corporate business matters are presented in the form of *resolutions*, which shareholders vote to approve or disapprove. Each common shareholder is entitled to one vote per share, although the voting techniques to be discussed shortly all enhance the power of the shareholder's vote. The articles of incorporation can exclude or limit voting rights, particularly for certain classes of shares. For example, owners of preferred shares are usually denied the right to vote [RMBCA 7.21]. If a state statute requires specific voting procedures, the corporation's articles or bylaws must be consistent with the statute.

Quorum Requirements

For shareholders to conduct business at a meeting, a quorum must be present. Generally, a quorum exists when shareholders holding more than 50 percent of the outstanding shares are present. In some states, obtaining the unanimous written consent of shareholders is a permissible alternative to holding a shareholders' meeting [RMBCA 7.25].

KNOW THIS

Once a quorum is present, a vote can be taken even if some shareholders leave without casting their votes.

Once a quorum is present, voting can proceed. A majority vote of the shares represented at the meeting usually is required to pass resolutions. **EXAMPLE 30.5** Novo Pictures, Inc., has 10,000 outstanding shares of voting stock. Its articles of incorporation set the quorum at 50 percent of outstanding shares and provide that a majority vote of the shares present is necessary to pass resolutions concerning ordinary matters. Therefore, for this firm, a quorum of shareholders representing 5,000 outstanding shares must be present at a shareholders' meeting to conduct business. If exactly 5,000 shares are represented at the meeting, a vote of at least 2,501 of those shares is needed to pass a resolution. If 6,000 shares are represented, a vote of 3,001 will be required. •

At times, more than a simple majority vote will be required either by a state statute or by the corporate articles. Extraordinary corporate matters, such as a merger, consolidation, or dissolution of the corporation (as discussed in Chapter 29), require a higher percentage of all corporate shares entitled to vote [RMBCA 7.27].

8. *Business Roundtable v. SEC*, 647 F.3d 1144 (2011).

Voting Lists

The corporation prepares voting lists before each meeting of the shareholders. Ordinarily, only persons whose names appear on the corporation's shareholder records as owners are entitled to vote.[9]

The voting list contains the name and address of each shareholder as shown on the corporate records on a given cutoff, or record, date. (Under RMBCA 7.07, the record date may be as early as seventy days before the meeting.) The voting list also includes the number of voting shares held by each owner. The list is usually kept at the corporate headquarters and is available for shareholder inspection [RMBCA 7.20].

Cumulative Voting

Most states permit, and some require, shareholders to elect directors by *cumulative voting,* which is a voting method designed to allow minority shareholders to be represented on the board of directors.[10]

Formula

With cumulative voting, each shareholder is entitled to a total number of votes equal to the number of board members to be elected multiplied by the number of voting shares a shareholder owns. The shareholder can cast all of these votes for one candidate or split them among several nominees for director. All nominees stand for election at the same time. When cumulative voting is not required either by statute or under the articles, the entire board can be elected by a simple majority of shares at a shareholders' meeting.

Example of Cumulative Voting

Cumulative voting can best be understood by an example. **EXAMPLE 30.6** A corporation has 10,000 shares issued and outstanding. The minority shareholders hold 3,000 shares, and the majority shareholders hold the other 7,000 shares. Three members of the board are to be elected. The majority shareholders' nominees are Acevedo, Barkley, and Craycik. The minority shareholders' nominee is Drake. Can Drake be elected by the minority shareholders?

If cumulative voting is allowed, the answer is yes. Together, the minority shareholders have 9,000 votes (the number of directors to be elected times the number of shares held by the minority shareholders equals 3 times 3,000, which equals 9,000 votes). All of these votes can be cast to elect Drake. The majority shareholders have 21,000 votes (3 times 7,000 equals 21,000 votes), but these votes have to be distributed among their three nominees. The principle of cumulative voting is that no matter how the majority shareholders cast their 21,000 votes, they will not be able to elect all three directors if the minority shareholders cast all of their 9,000 votes for Drake, as illustrated in Exhibit 30.2 below. •

Other Voting Techniques

Before a shareholders' meeting, a group of shareholders can agree in writing to vote their shares together in a specified manner. Such agreements,

9. When the legal owner is bankrupt, incompetent, deceased, or in some other way under a legal disability, his or her vote can be cast by a person designated by law to control and manage the owner's property.

10. See, for example, California Corporations Code Section 708. Under RMBCA 7.28, however, no cumulative voting rights exist unless the articles of incorporation provide for them.

Exhibit 30.2 Results of Cumulative Voting

BALLOT	MAJORITY SHAREHOLDERS' VOTES			MINORITY SHAREHOLDERS' VOTES	DIRECTORS ELECTED
	Acevedo	Barkley	Craycik	Drake	
1	10,000	10,000	1,000	9,000	Acevedo/Barkley/Drake
2	9,001	9,000	2,999	9,000	Acevedo/Barkley/Drake
3	6,000	7,000	8,000	9,000	Barkley/Craycik/Drake

called *shareholder voting agreements,* usually are held to be valid and enforceable. A shareholder can also appoint a voting agent and vote by proxy.

CASE EXAMPLE 30.7 Several shareholders of Cryo-Cell International, Inc., mounted a proxy contest in an effort to replace the board of directors. Another stockholder, Andrew Filipowski, entered into a shareholder voting agreement to support management in exchange for being included in management's slate of directors. The company's chief executive officer, Mercedes Walton, secretly promised Filipowski that if management's slate won, the board of directors would add another board seat to be filled by a Filipowski designee.

After management won the election, Walton prepared to add Filipowski's designee to the board. Dissident shareholders challenged the election's results. The court held that although the voting agreement to include Filipowski on the management slate was legal, the board's actions and Walton's secret agreement constituted serious breaches of fiduciary duty that had tainted the election. The court therefore ordered a new election to be held.[11] •

(PhotoDisc)

Stock certificates are displayed. To be a shareholder, is it necessary to have physical possession of a certificate? Why or why not?

Rights of Shareholders

Shareholders possess numerous rights. A significant right—the right to vote their shares—has already been discussed. We now look at some additional rights of shareholders.

Stock Certificates

In the past, corporations typically issued a **stock certificate** that evidenced ownership of a specified number of shares in the corporation. Only a few jurisdictions still require physical stock certificates, and shareholders there have the right to demand that the corporation issue certificates (or replace those that were lost or destroyed). Stock is intangible personal property, however, and the ownership right exists independently of the certificate itself.

In most states and under RMBCA 6.26, boards of directors may provide that shares of stock will be uncertificated, or "paperless"—that is, no actual, physical stock certificates will be issued. When shares are uncertificated, the corporation may be required to send each shareholder a letter or some other form of notice that contains the same information that traditionally appeared on the face of stock certificates. Notice of shareholders' meetings, dividends, and operational and financial reports are all distributed according to the recorded ownership listed in the corporation's books.

Stock Certificate A certificate issued by a corporation evidencing the ownership of a specified number of shares in the corporation.

Preemptive Rights Rights that entitle shareholders to purchase newly issued shares of a corporation's stock, equal in percentage to shares already held, before the stock is offered to outside buyers. Preemptive rights enable shareholders to maintain their proportionate ownership and voice in the corporation.

Preemptive Rights

Sometimes, the articles of incorporation grant preemptive rights to shareholders [RMBCA 6.30]. With **preemptive rights,** a shareholder receives a preference over all other purchasers to subscribe to or purchase a prorated share of a new issue of stock.

Generally, preemptive rights apply only to additional, newly issued stock sold for cash, and the preemptive rights must be exercised within a specified time period, which is usually thirty days.

Allow a Shareholder to Maintain Proportionate Interest

A shareholder who is given preemptive rights can purchase the same percentage of the new shares being issued as she or he already holds in the company. This allows each shareholder

11. *Portnoy v. Cryo-Cell International, Inc.,* 940 A.2d 43 (Del.Ch. 2008).

to maintain her or his proportionate control, voting power, or financial interest in the corporation.

EXAMPLE 30.8 Tran Corporation authorizes and issues 1,000 shares of stock. Lebow purchases 100 shares, making her the owner of 10 percent of the company's stock. Subsequently, Tran, by vote of its shareholders, authorizes the issuance of another 1,000 shares (by amending the articles of incorporation). This increases its capital stock to a total of 2,000 shares.

If preemptive rights have been provided, Lebow can purchase one additional share of the new stock being issued for each share she already owns—or 100 additional shares. Thus, she can own 200 of the 2,000 shares outstanding, and she will maintain her relative position as a shareholder. If preemptive rights are not allowed, her proportionate control and voting power may be diluted from that of a 10 percent shareholder to that of a 5 percent shareholder because of the issuance of the additional 1,000 shares. ●

Important in Close Corporations

Preemptive rights are most important in close corporations because each shareholder owns a relatively small number of shares but controls a substantial interest in the corporation. Without preemptive rights, it would be possible for a shareholder to lose his or her proportionate control over the firm. Nevertheless, preemptive rights can hinder a corporation from raising capital from new, outside investors who can provide needed expertise as well as capital.

Stock Warrants

Stock Warrant The right to buy a given number of shares of stock at a specified price, usually within a set time period.

Stock warrants are rights to buy stock at a stated price by a specified date that are created by the company. Usually, when preemptive rights exist and a corporation is issuing additional shares, it issues its shareholders stock warrants. Warrants are often publicly traded on securities exchanges.

Dividends

LEARNING OBJECTIVE 4

From what sources may dividends be paid legally? In what circumstances is a dividend illegal? What happens if a dividend is illegally paid?

As mentioned in Chapter 29, a *dividend* is a distribution of corporate profits or income *ordered by the directors* and paid to the shareholders in proportion to their respective shares in the corporation. Dividends can be paid in cash, property, stock of the corporation that is paying the dividends, or stock of other corporations.[12]

State laws vary, but each state determines the general circumstances and legal requirements under which dividends are paid. State laws also control the sources of revenue to be used. Only certain funds are legally available for paying dividends. Depending on state law, dividends may be paid from the following sources:

1. *Retained earnings.* All states allow dividends to be paid from the undistributed net profits earned by the corporation, including capital gains from the sale of fixed assets. As mentioned in Chapter 29, the undistributed net profits are called *retained earnings.*
2. *Net profits.* A few states allow dividends to be issued from current net profits without regard to deficits in prior years.
3. *Surplus.* A number of states allow dividends to be paid out of any kind of surplus.

Illegal Dividends

Sometimes, dividends are improperly paid from an unauthorized account, or their payment causes the corporation to become insolvent. Generally, shareholders must return illegal dividends only if they knew that the dividends were illegal when the payment was received (or if the dividends were paid when the corporation was insolvent).

12. Technically, dividends paid in stock are not dividends. They maintain each shareholder's proportionate interest in the corporation. On one occasion, a distillery declared and paid a "dividend" in bonded whiskey.

Whenever dividends are illegal or improper, the board of directors can be held personally liable for the amount of the payment.

Directors' Failure to Declare a Dividend

When directors fail to declare a dividend, shareholders can ask a court to compel the directors to meet and to declare a dividend. To succeed, the shareholders must show that the directors have acted so unreasonably in withholding the dividend that their conduct is an abuse of their discretion.

Often, a corporation accumulates large cash reserves for a legitimate corporate purpose, such as expansion or research. The mere fact that the firm has sufficient earnings or surplus available to pay a dividend is not enough to compel directors to distribute funds that, in the board's opinion, should not be distributed. The courts are reluctant to interfere with corporate operations and will not compel directors to declare dividends unless abuse of discretion is clearly shown.

Inspection Rights

Shareholders in a corporation enjoy both common law and statutory inspection rights. The RMBCA provides that every shareholder is entitled to examine specified corporate records. The shareholder's right of inspection is limited, however, to the inspection and copying of corporate books and records for a *proper purpose,* provided the request is made in advance. The shareholder can inspect in person, or an attorney, accountant, or other authorized assistant can do so as the shareholder's agent.

"Executive ability is deciding quickly and getting somebody else to do the work."

J. C. Pollard, 1946–present (British businessman)

The power of inspection is fraught with potential abuses, and the corporation is allowed to protect itself from them. For instance, a shareholder can properly be denied access to corporate records to prevent harassment or to protect trade secrets or other confidential corporate information. In some states, a shareholder must have held his or her shares for a minimum period of time immediately preceding the demand to inspect or must hold a minimum number of outstanding shares. A shareholder who is denied the right of inspection can seek a court order to compel the inspection.

Transfer of Shares

Corporate stock represents an ownership right in intangible personal property. The law generally recognizes the right to transfer stock to another person unless there are valid restrictions on its transferability. Although stock certificates are negotiable and freely transferable by indorsement and delivery, transfer of stock in closely held corporations usually is restricted. These restrictions must be reasonable and may be set out in the bylaws or in a shareholder agreement. The existence of any restrictions on transferability must always be indicated on the face of the stock certificate.

When shares are transferred, a new entry is made in the corporate stock book to indicate the new owner. Until the corporation is notified and the entry is complete, all rights—including voting rights, the right to notice of shareholders' meetings, and the right to dividend distributions—remain with the current record owner.

Rights on Dissolution

When a corporation is dissolved and its outstanding debts and the claims of its creditors have been satisfied, the remaining assets are distributed to the shareholders in proportion to the percentage of shares owned by each shareholder. Certain classes of preferred stock can be given priority. If no class of stock has been given preference in the distribution of assets on liquidation, then all of the stockholders share the remaining assets.

As noted in Chapter 29, in some situations, shareholders can petition a court to have the corporation dissolved. The RMBCA permits any shareholder to initiate a dissolution proceeding in any of the following circumstances [RMBCA 14.30]:

1. The directors are deadlocked in the management of corporate affairs. The shareholders are unable to break that deadlock, and irreparable injury to the corporation is being suffered or threatened.
2. The acts of the directors or those in control of the corporation are illegal, oppressive, or fraudulent.
3. Corporate assets are being misapplied or wasted.
4. The shareholders are deadlocked in voting power and have failed, for a specified period (usually two annual meetings), to elect successors to directors whose terms have expired or would have expired with the election of successors.

The Shareholder's Derivative Suit

Shareholder's Derivative Suit A suit brought by a shareholder to enforce a corporate cause of action against a third person.

When the corporation is harmed by the actions of a third party, the directors can bring a lawsuit in the name of the corporation against that party. If the corporate directors fail to bring a lawsuit, shareholders can do so "derivatively" in what is known as a **shareholder's derivative suit.**

A shareholder cannot bring a derivative suit until ninety days after making a written demand on the corporation (the board of directors) to take suitable action [RMBCA 7.40]. Only if the directors refuse to take appropriate action can the derivative suit go forward.

LEARNING OBJECTIVE 5
If a group of shareholders perceives that the corporation has suffered a wrong and the directors refuse to take action, can the shareholders compel the directors to act? If so, how?

Typical When Acts of Directors and Officers Caused Harm to the Corporation

The right of shareholders to bring a derivative action is especially important when the wrong suffered by the corporation results from the actions of corporate directors or officers. This is because the directors and officers would probably be unwilling to take any action against themselves.

Nevertheless, a court will dismiss a derivative suit if the majority of directors or an independent panel determines in good faith that the lawsuit is not in the best interests of the corporation [RMBCA 7.44]. (Derivative actions are less common in other countries than in the United States, as this chapter's *Beyond Our Borders* feature below explains.)

Any Damages Recovered Go into Corporate Funds

When shareholders bring a derivative suit, they are not pursuing rights or benefits for themselves

BEYOND OUR BORDERS Derivative Actions in Other Nations

Today, shareholders' derivative suits account for most of the claims brought against directors and officers in the United States. Other nations, however, put more restrictions on the use of such suits. German law, for example, does not provide for derivative litigation, and a corporation's duty to its employees is just as significant as its duty to its shareholder-owners. The United Kingdom has no statute authorizing derivative actions, which are permitted only to challenge directors' actions that the shareholders could not legally ratify. Japan authorizes derivative actions but also permits a company to sue the plaintiff-shareholder for damages if the action is unsuccessful.

Critical Thinking

Do corporations benefit from shareholders' derivative suits? If so, how?

personally but are acting as guardians of the corporate entity. Therefore, if the suit is successful, any damages recovered normally go into the corporation's treasury, not to the shareholders personally.[13]

EXAMPLE 30.9 Zeon Corporation is owned by two shareholders, each holding 50 percent of the corporate shares. One of the shareholders wants to sue the other for misusing corporate assets or usurping corporate opportunities. In this situation, the plaintiff-shareholder will have to bring a shareholder's derivative suit (not a suit in his or her own name) because the alleged harm was suffered by Zeon, not by the plaintiff personally. Any damages awarded will go to the corporation, not to the plaintiff-shareholder. •

In the following case, the plaintiff was a minority shareholder who alleged that the directors of the corporation had denied him the benefits of his ownership interest in breach of their fiduciary duties. The trial court determined that the plaintiff's lawsuit had to be brought as a derivative action, which would mean that any damages obtained would go to the corporation. The state's highest court had to decide whether the shareholder could bring an individual claim rather than a derivative suit.

13. The shareholders may be entitled to reimbursement for reasonable expenses involved in the derivative suit, however, including attorneys' fees.

Case 30.3

McCann v. McCann

Supreme Court of Idaho, 275 P.3d 824 (2012).

(spxChrome/iStockphoto.com)

The McCann Ranch and Livestock Company.

FACTS In the 1970s, William McCann gave his sons, Bill and Ron, each 36.7 percent of the shares of his close corporation, McCann Ranch and Livestock Company. The remaining shares went to William's wife, Gertrude. When William died, Bill became the corporation's president and chief executive officer. The corporation paid Gertrude's personal expenses in an amount that represented about 75 percent of the net corporate income. Bill received regular salary increases. The corporation did not issue a dividend. In 2008, Ron filed a lawsuit alleging that the corporation's directors had breached the fiduciary duty they owed him as a minority shareholder. According to the complaint, the directors had subjected Ron to a "squeeze-out" designed to deprive him of the benefits of being a shareholder.

Ron alleged that the directors refused to give him a corporate job or board membership, failed to pay him dividends, and deprived him of other income through a series of business decisions that benefited only Bill and Gertrude. The court granted judgment for the defendants, finding that Ron had essentially filed a derivative suit without making a written demand on the corporation. Ron appealed.

ISSUE Can Ron sue Bill and Gertrude directly for breach of fiduciary duty rather than bringing a derivative action?

DECISION Yes. The Idaho Supreme Court reversed the trial court's decision and held that Ron could proceed with his suit for breach of fiduciary duty.

REASON Ordinarily, a shareholder must bring a derivative suit for claims arising from harm to a corporation. Nevertheless, a minority shareholder of a close corporation may bring an individual suit "if the shareholder alleges harm to himself distinct from that suffered by other shareholders." In this case, McCann Ranch's payments to Gertrude hurt the corporation as a whole. Nevertheless, Ron could sue individually under the theory that he had been subjected to a squeeze-out. Unlike Bill and Gertrude, who were the only other shareholders, Ron did not benefit from any of the decisions at issue. Thus, Ron could bring an individual suit for breach of fiduciary duty because he could show that he had been uniquely harmed.

CRITICAL THINKING—Legal Consideration *If this case proceeds to trial, how might the directors try to defend their decisions? What rule concerning director liability might protect them? Explain your answer.*

Duties and Liabilities of Shareholders

One of the hallmarks of the corporate form of business organization is that shareholders are not personally liable for the debts of the corporation. If the corporation fails, shareholders can lose their investments, but generally that is the limit of their liability. In certain instances of fraud, undercapitalization, or careless observance of corporate formalities, a court will pierce the corporate veil (disregard the corporate entity) and hold the shareholders individually liable. These situations are the exception, however, not the rule.

A shareholder can also be personally liable in certain other rare instances. One relates to illegal dividends, which were discussed previously. Another relates to *watered stock,* discussed next. Finally, in certain instances, a majority shareholder who engages in oppressive conduct or attempts to exclude minority shareholders from receiving certain benefits can be held personally liable.

Watered Stock

Watered Stock Shares of stock issued by a corporation for which the corporation receives, as payment, less than the stated value of the shares.

When a corporation issues shares for less than their fair market value, the shares are referred to as **watered stock.**[14] Usually, the shareholder who receives watered stock must pay the difference to the corporation (the shareholder is personally liable). In some states, the shareholder who receives watered stock may be liable to creditors of the corporation for unpaid corporate debts.

EXAMPLE 30.10 During the formation of a corporation, Gomez, one of the incorporators, transfers his property, Sunset Beach, to the corporation for 10,000 shares of stock. The stock has a specific face value *(par value)* of $100 per share, and thus the total price of the 10,000 shares is $1 million. After the property is transferred and the shares are issued, Sunset Beach is carried on the corporate books at a value of $1 million. On appraisal, it is discovered that the market value of the property at the time of transfer was only $500,000. The shares issued to Gomez are therefore watered stock, and he is liable to the corporation for the difference between the value of the shares and the value of the property. •

Duties of Majority Shareholders

In some instances, a majority shareholder is regarded as having a fiduciary duty to the corporation and to the minority shareholders. This occurs when a single shareholder (or a few shareholders acting in concert) owns a sufficient number of shares to exercise *de facto* (actual) control over the corporation. In these situations, majority shareholders owe a fiduciary duty to the minority shareholders.

When a majority shareholder breaches her or his fiduciary duty to a minority shareholder, the minority shareholder can sue for damages. A breach of fiduciary duties by those who control a close corporation normally constitutes what is known as *oppressive conduct.* A common example of a breach of fiduciary duty occurs when the majority shareholders "freeze out" the minority shareholders and exclude them from certain benefits of participating in the firm.

CASE EXAMPLE 30.11 Brodie, Jordan, and Barbuto formed a close corporation to operate a machine shop. Each owned one-third of the shares in the company, and all three were directors. Brodie served as the corporate president for twelve years but thereafter

14. The phrase *watered stock* was originally used to describe cattle that were kept thirsty during a long drive and then were allowed to drink large quantities of water just prior to their sale. The increased weight of the "watered stock" allowed the seller to reap a higher profit.

met with the other shareholders only a few times a year. After disagreements arose, Brodie asked the company to purchase his shares, but his requests were refused. A few years later, Brodie died, and his wife inherited his shares in the company. Jordan and Barbuto refused to perform a valuation of the company, denied her access to the corporate information she requested, did not declare any dividends, and refused to elect her as a director. In this situation, a court found that the majority shareholders had violated their fiduciary duty to Brodie's wife.[15] ●

Major Business Forms Compared

As mentioned in Chapter 26, when deciding which form of business organization would be most appropriate, businesspersons normally take into account several factors, including ease of creation, the liability of the owners, tax considerations, and the need for capital. Each major form of business organization offers distinct advantages and disadvantages with respect to these and other factors. Exhibit 30.3 below and on the facing page summarizes the essential advantages and disadvantages of each of the forms of business organization discussed in Chapters 26 through 30.

15. *Brodie v. Jordan*, 447 Mass. 866, 857 N.E.2d 1076 (2006).

Exhibit 30.3 Major Forms of Business Compared

CHARACTERISTIC	SOLE PROPRIETORSHIP	PARTNERSHIP	CORPORATION
Method of Creation	Created at will by owner.	Created by agreement of the parties.	Authorized by the state under the state's corporation law.
Legal Position	Not a separate entity; owner is the business.	A general partnership is a separate legal entity in most states.	Always a legal entity separate and distinct from its owners—a legal fiction for the purposes of owning property and being a party to litigation.
Liability	Unlimited liability.	Unlimited liability.	Limited liability of shareholders—shareholders are not liable for the debts of the corporation.
Duration	Determined by owner; automatically dissolved on owner's death.	Terminated by agreement of the partners, but can continue to do business even when a partner dissociates from the partnership.	Can have perpetual existence.
Transferability of Interest	Interest can be transferred, but individual's proprietorship then ends.	Although partnership interest can be assigned, assignee does not have full rights of a partner.	Shares of stock can be transferred.
Management	Completely at owner's discretion.	Each partner has a direct and equal voice in management unless expressly agreed otherwise in the partnership agreement.	Shareholders elect directors, who set policy and appoint officers.
Taxation	Owner pays personal taxes on business income.	Each partner pays pro rata share of income taxes on net profits, whether or not they are distributed.	Double taxation—corporation pays income tax on net profits, with no deduction for dividends, and shareholders pay income tax on disbursed dividends they receive.
Organizational Fees, Annual License Fees, and Annual Reports	None or minimal.	None or minimal.	All required.
Transaction of Business in Other States	Generally no limitation.	Generally no limitation.[a]	Normally must qualify to do business and obtain certificate of authority.

a. A few states have enacted statutes requiring that foreign partnerships qualify to do business there.

Exhibit 30.3 Major Forms of Business Compared—Continued

CHARACTERISTIC	LIMITED PARTNERSHIP	LIMITED LIABILITY COMPANY	LIMITED LIABILITY PARTNERSHIP
Method of Creation	Created by agreement to carry on a business for profit. At least one party must be a general partner and the other(s) limited partner(s). Certificate of limited partnership is filed. Charter must be issued by the state.	Created by an agreement of the member-owners of the company. Articles of organization are filed. Charter must be issued by the state.	Created by agreement of the partners. A statement of qualification for the limited liability partnership is filed.
Legal Position	Treated as a legal entity.	Treated as a legal entity.	Generally, treated same as a general partnership.
Liability	Unlimited liability of all general partners. Limited partners are liable only to the extent of capital contributions.	Member-owners' liability is limited to the amount of capital contributions or investments.	Varies, but under the Uniform Partnership Act, liability of a partner for acts committed by other partners is limited.
Duration	By agreement in certificate, or by termination of the last general partner (retirement, death, and the like) or last limited partner.	Unless a single-member LLC, can have perpetual existence (same as a corporation).	Remains in existence until cancellation or revocation.
Transferability of Interest	Interest can be assigned (same as a general partnership), but if assignee becomes a member with consent of other partners, certificate must be amended.	Member interests are freely transferable.	Interest can be assigned same as in a general partnership.
Management	General partners have equal voice or by agreement. Limited partners may not retain limited liability if they actively participate in management.	Member-owners can fully participate in management or can designate a group of persons to manage on behalf of the members.	Same as a general partnership.
Taxation	Generally taxed as a partnership.	LLC is not taxed, and members are taxed personally on profits "passed through" the LLC.	Same as a general partnership.
Organizational Fees, Annual License Fees, and Annual Reports	Organizational fee required; usually not others.	Organizational fee required. Others vary with states.	Fees are set by each state for filing statements of qualification, statements of foreign qualification, and annual reports.
Transaction of Business in Other States	Generally no limitations.	Generally no limitations, but may vary depending on state.	Must file a statement of foreign qualification before doing business in another state.

Reviewing . . . Corporate Directors, Officers, and Shareholders

David Brock is on the board of directors of Firm Body Fitness, Inc., which owns a string of fitness clubs in New Mexico. Brock owns 15 percent of the Firm Body stock, and he is also employed as a tanning technician at one of the fitness clubs. After the January financial report showed that Firm Body's tanning division was operating at a substantial net loss, the board of directors, led by Marty Levinson, discussed terminating the tanning operations. Brock successfully convinced a majority of the board that the tanning division was necessary to market the club's overall fitness package. By April, the tanning division's financial losses had risen. The board hired a business analyst who conducted surveys and determined that the tanning operations did not significantly increase membership. A shareholder, Diego Peñada, discovered that Brock owned stock in Sunglow, Inc., the company from which Firm Body purchased its tanning equipment. Peñada notified Levinson, who privately reprimanded Brock. Shortly thereafter, Brock and Mandy Vail, who owned 37 percent of the Firm Body stock and also held shares of Sunglow, voted to replace Levinson on the board of directors. Using the information presented in the chapter, answer the following questions.

1. What duties did Brock, as a director, owe to Firm Body?
2. Does the fact that Brock owned shares in Sunglow establish a conflict of interest? Why or why not?

Continued

3. Suppose that Firm Body brought an action against Brock claiming that he had breached the duty of loyalty by not disclosing his interest in Sunglow to the other directors. What theory might Brock use in his defense?
4. Now suppose that Firm Body did not bring an action against Brock. What type of lawsuit might Peñada be able to bring based on these facts?

DEBATE THIS Because most shareholders never bother to vote for directors, shareholders have no real control over corporations.

BUSINESS APPLICATION

Creating a Retention Policy for E-Documents*

If a corporation becomes the target of a civil lawsuit or criminal investigation, the company may be required to turn over any documents in its files relating to the matter during the discovery stage of litigation. These may include paper documents, e-contracts, e-mail messages, faxes, posts on social media networks or blogs, texts, tweets, voice mail, and other materials. It may even include information in personal files or on personal devices such as iPads kept in the homes of directors or officers. Under the current Federal Rules of Civil Procedure, which govern civil litigation procedures (see Chapter 3), a defendant in a lawsuit must disclose all relevant electronic data compilations and documents, as well as all relevant paper documents.

Although certain documents or data might free a company of any liability arising from a claim, others might substantiate a civil claim or criminal charge. It is also possible that information contained in a document—an interoffice e-mail memo, for example (or even a memo referring to that memo)—could be used to convince a jury that the company or its directors or officers had condoned a certain action that they later denied condoning.

Which E-Documents Should Be Retained?

How does a company decide which e-documents should be retained and which should be destroyed? By law, corporations are required to keep certain types of documents, such as those specified in the *Code of Federal Regulations* and in regulations issued by government agencies, such as the Occupational Safety and Health Administration. Most businesses today have a document-retention policy. Generally, any records that the company is not legally required to keep or that the company is sure it will have no legal need for should be removed from the files and destroyed. A joint-venture agreement, for example, should be kept. A memo about last year's company picnic should not.

Modifications May Be Necessary during an Investigation

Companies that are under investigation usually must modify their document-retention policy until the investigation has been completed. After receiving a subpoena to produce specific types of documents, company officers should instruct the appropriate employees not to destroy relevant papers or e-documents that would otherwise be disposed of as part of the company's normal document-retention program.

To avoid being charged with obstruction of justice, company officials must always exercise good faith in deciding which documents should or should not be destroyed when attempting to comply with a subpoena. The specter of criminal prosecution would appear to encourage the retention of even those documents that are only remotely related to the dispute—at least until it has been resolved.

Checklist for an E-Document-Retention Policy

1. *Develop guidelines that let employees know not only which e-documents should be retained and deleted but also which types of documents should not be created in the first place.*
2. *Find out which documents must be retained under the* Code of Federal Regulations *and other government agency regulations to which your corporation is subject.*
3. *Retain other e-documents only if their retention is in the corporation's interest.*
4. *If certain corporate documents are subpoenaed, modify your document-retention policy to retain any documents that are even remotely related to the dispute until it has been resolved.*

---

*This *Business Application* is not meant to substitute for the services of an attorney who is licensed to practice law in your state.

Key Terms

business judgment rule 778
inside director 775
outside director 775
preemptive rights 786
proxy 783
quorum 775
shareholder's derivative suit 789
stock certificate 786
stock warrant 787
watered stock 791

Chapter Summary: Corporate Directors, Officers, and Shareholders

Directors and Officers (See pages 774–777.)	1. *Directors' qualifications and responsibilities*—Few qualifications are required. A director may be a shareholder but is not required to be. Directors are responsible for all policymaking decisions necessary to the management of all corporate affairs (see Exhibit 30.1 on page 774). 2. *Election of directors*—The first board of directors is usually appointed by the incorporators. After that, directors are elected by the shareholders. Directors usually serve a one-year term, although their terms can be longer or staggered. Compensation is usually specified in the corporate articles or bylaws. 3. *Board of directors' meetings*—The board of directors holds formal meetings with recorded minutes. The date of regular meetings is usually established in the corporate articles or bylaws. Special meetings can be called, with notice sent to all directors. Quorum requirements vary from state to state. Usually, a quorum is a majority of the directors. Voting usually must be done in person, and in ordinary matters only a majority vote is required. 4. *Directors' committees*—A board of directors may create committees of directors and delegate various responsibilities to them. An executive committee and an audit committee are common types of committees. 5. *Rights of directors*—Directors' rights include the rights of participation, inspection, and indemnification. 6. *Corporate officers and executives*—Corporate officers and other executive employees are normally hired by the board of directors and have the rights defined by their employment contracts.
Duties and Liabilities of Directors and Officers (See pages 777–782.)	1. *Duty of care*—Directors and officers are obligated to act in good faith, to use prudent business judgment in the conduct of corporate affairs, and to act in the corporation's best interests. If a director fails to exercise this duty of care, she or he can be answerable to the corporation and to the shareholders for breaching the duty. 2. *The business judgment rule*—This rule immunizes directors and officers from liability when they acted in good faith, acted in the best interests of the corporation, and exercised due care. For the rule to apply, the directors and officers must have made an informed, reasonable, and loyal decision. 3. *Duty of loyalty*—Directors and officers have a fiduciary duty to subordinate their own interests to those of the corporation in matters relating to the corporation. 4. *Conflicts of interest*—To fulfill their duty of loyalty, directors and officers must make a full disclosure of any potential conflicts between their personal interests and those of the corporation. 5. *Liability of directors and officers*—Corporate directors and officers are personally liable for their own torts and crimes. Additionally, they may be held personally liable for the torts and crimes committed by corporate personnel under their supervision (see Chapters 6 and 23).
Shareholders (See pages 782–786.)	1. *Shareholders' powers*—Shareholders' powers include the approval of all fundamental changes affecting the corporation and the election of the board of directors. 2. *Shareholders' meetings*—Shareholders' meetings must occur at least annually, and special meetings can be called when necessary. Notice of the date, time, and place of the meeting (and its purpose, if it is specially called) must be sent to shareholders. Shareholders may vote by proxy (authorizing someone else to vote their shares) and may submit proposals to be included in the company's proxy materials sent to shareholders before meetings. 3. *Shareholder voting*—Shareholder voting requirements and procedures are as follows: a. A minimum number of shareholders (a quorum—generally, shareholders holding more than 50 percent of the outstanding shares) must be present at a meeting for business to be conducted. Resolutions are passed (usually) by a simple majority vote. b. The corporation must prepare voting lists of shareholders of record before each shareholders' meeting. c. Cumulative voting may or may not be required or permitted. Cumulative voting gives minority shareholders a better chance to be represented on the board of directors. d. A shareholder voting agreement (an agreement of shareholders to vote their shares together) is usually held to be valid and enforceable.

Continued

Chapter Summary: Corporate Directors, Officers, and Shareholders—Continued

Rights of Shareholders (See pages 786–790.)	In addition to voting rights, shareholders have numerous rights, which may include the following: 1. The right to a stock certificate, preemptive rights, and the right to stock warrants (depending on the articles of incorporation). 2. The right to obtain a dividend (at the discretion of the directors). 3. The right to inspect the corporate records. 4. The right to transfer shares (this right may be restricted in close corporations). 5. The right to a share of corporate assets when the corporation is dissolved. 6. The right to sue on behalf of the corporation (bring a shareholder's derivative suit) when the directors fail to do so.
Duties and Liabilities of Shareholders (See pages 791–792.)	Shareholders may be liable for the retention of illegal dividends and for the value of watered stock. In certain situations, majority shareholders may be regarded as having a fiduciary duty to minority shareholders and will be liable if that duty is breached.

ExamPrep

ISSUE SPOTTERS

1. Wonder Corporation has an opportunity to buy stock in XL, Inc. The directors decide that instead of Wonder buying the stock, the directors will buy it. Yvon, a Wonder shareholder, learns of the purchase and wants to sue the directors on Wonder's behalf. Can she do it? Explain. **(See page 789.)**
2. Nico is Omega Corporation's majority shareholder. He owns enough stock in Omega that if he were to sell it, the sale would be a transfer of control of the firm. Discuss whether Nico owes a duty to Omega or the minority shareholders in selling his shares. **(See page 791.)**

—Check your answers to the Issue Spotters against the answers provided in Appendix E at the end of this text.

BEFORE THE TEST

Go to www.cengagebrain.com, enter the ISBN 9781133273561, and click on "Find" to locate this textbook's Web site. Then, click on "Access Now" under "Study Tools," and select Chapter 30 at the top. There, you will find a Practice Quiz that you can take to assess your mastery of the concepts in this chapter, as well as Flashcards, a Glossary of important terms, and Video Questions (when assigned).

For Review

Answers to the even-numbered questions in this For Review section can be found in Appendix F at the end of this text.

1. What are the duties of corporate directors and officers?
2. Directors are expected to use their best judgment in managing the corporation. What must directors do to avoid liability for honest mistakes of judgment and poor business decisions?
3. What is a voting proxy?
4. From what sources may dividends be paid legally? In what circumstances is a dividend illegal? What happens if a dividend is illegally paid?
5. If a group of shareholders perceives that the corporation has suffered a wrong and the directors refuse to take action, can the shareholders compel the directors to act? If so, how?

Business Scenarios and Case Problems

30–1 Voting Techniques. Algonquin Corp. has issued and has outstanding 100,000 shares of common stock. Four stockholders own 60,000 of these shares, and for the past six years they have nominated a slate of candidates for membership on the board, all of whom have been elected. Sergio and twenty other shareholders, owning 20,000 shares, are dissatisfied with corporate management and want a representative on the board who shares their views. Explain under what circumstances Sergio and the twenty other shareholders can elect their representative to the board. **(See pages 784–786.)**

30–2 **Question with Sample Answer—Liability of Directors.** Starboard, Inc., has a board of directors consisting of three members (Ellsworth, Green, and Morino) and approximately five hundred shareholders. At a regular meeting of the board, the board selects Tyson as president of the corporation by a two-to-one vote, with Ellsworth dissenting. The minutes of the meeting do not register Ellsworth's dissenting vote. Later, during an audit, it is discovered that Tyson is a former convict and has openly embezzled $500,000 from Starboard. This loss is not covered by insurance. The corporation wants to hold directors Ellsworth, Green, and Morino liable. Ellsworth claims no liability. Discuss the personal liability of the directors to the corporation. **(See pages 777–779.)**

—For a sample answer to Question 30–2, go to Appendix G at the end of this text.

30–3 **Rights of Shareholders.** Lucia has acquired one share of common stock of a multimillion-dollar corporation with more than 500,000 shareholders. Lucia's ownership is so small that she is wondering what her rights are as a shareholder. For example, she wants to know whether owning this one share entitles her to (a) attend and vote at shareholders' meetings, (b) inspect the corporate books, and (c) receive yearly dividends. Discuss Lucia's rights in these three matters. **(See pages 786–790.)**

30–4 **Duties of Majority Shareholders.** Steve and Marie Venturini each owned half the stock of their family corporation, which had operated Steve's Sizzling Steakhouse since the 1930s. Steve, Marie, and her husband, Joe, ran the business until Steve died in 2001, leaving his stock in equal shares to his sons Steve and Gregg. Son Steve had never worked there. Gregg did occasional maintenance work until his father's death. Despite their lack of participation, the sons were paid more than $750 per week each. In 2002, Marie's son Blaise, who had obtained a college degree in restaurant management while working part-time at the steakhouse, took over its management. When his cousins became threatening, Blaise denied them access to the business and its books. Marie refused Gregg and Steve's offer of about $1.4 million for her stock in the restaurant, and they refused her offer of about $800,000 for theirs. They filed a suit against her, claiming, among other things, a breach of fiduciary duty. Should the court order the aunt to buy out the nephews or the nephews to buy out the aunt, or neither? Why? [*Venturini v. Steve's Steakhouse, Inc.*, 2006 WL 445059 (N.J.Super. Ch.Div. 2006)] **(See pages 791–792.)**

30–5 **Duties of Directors and Officers.** First Niles Financial, Inc., is a company whose sole business is to own and operate a bank, Home Federal Savings and Loan Association of Niles, Ohio. First Niles' directors include bank officers William Stephens, Daniel Csontos, and Lawrence Safarek; James Kramer, president of an air-conditioning company that services the bank; and Ralph Zuzolo, whose law firm serves the bank and whose title company participates in most of its real estate deals. First Niles' board put the bank up for sale. There were three bids. Farmers National Bank Corp. stated that it would not retain the board. Cortland Bancorp indicated that it would terminate the directors but consider them for future service. First Financial Corp. said nothing about the directors. The board did not pursue Farmers' offer, failed to respond timely to Cortland's request, and rejected First Financial's bid. Leonard Gantler and other First Niles shareholders filed a suit in a Delaware state court against Stephens and the others. What duties do directors and officers owe to a corporation and its shareholders? How might those duties have been breached here? Discuss. [*Gantler v. Stephens*, 965 A.2d 695 (Del.Sup. 2009)] **(See pages 777–782.)**

30–6 **Case Problem with Sample Answer—Rights of Shareholders.** Stanka Woods is the sole member of Hair Ventures, LLC. Hair Ventures owns 3 million shares of stock in Biolustré, Inc. For several years, Woods and other Biolustré shareholders did not receive notice of shareholders' meetings or financial reports. When Woods learned that Biolustré planned to issue more stock, Woods, through Hair Ventures, demanded to see Biolustré's books and records. Biolustré asserted that the request was not for a proper purpose. Does Woods have a right to inspect Biolustré's books and records? If so, what are the limits? Do any of those limits apply in this case? Explain. [*Biolustré, Inc. v. Hair Ventures, LLC*, 2011 WL 540574 (Tex.App.—San Antonio 2011)] **(See page 788.)**

—For a sample answer to Problem 30–6, go to Appendix H at the end of this text.

30–7 **Duty of Loyalty.** Kids International Corp. produced children's wear for Walmart and other retailers. Gila Dweck was a Kids director and its chief executive officer. Because she felt that she was not paid enough for the company's success, she started another firm, Success Apparel, to compete with Kids. Success operated out of Kids' premises, used its employees, borrowed on its credit, took advantage of its business opportunities, and capitalized on its customer relationships. As an "administrative fee," Dweck paid Kids 1 percent of Success's total sales. Did Dweck breach any fiduciary duties? Explain. [*Dweck v. Nasser*, 2012 WL 3194069 (Del.Ch. 2012)] **(See page 780.)**

30–8 **A Question of Ethics—Duties of Directors and Officers.** New Orleans Paddlewheels, Inc. (NOP), is a Louisiana corporation formed in 1982, when James Smith, Sr., and Warren Reuther were its only shareholders, with each holding 50 percent of the stock. NOP is part of a sprawling enterprise of tourism and hospitality companies in New Orleans. The positions on the board of each company were split equally between the Smith and Reuther families. At Smith's request, his son James Smith, Jr. (JES), became involved in the businesses. In 1999, NOP's board elected JES as president, in charge of day-to-day operations, and Reuther as chief executive officer (CEO), in charge of marketing and development. Over the next few years, animosity developed between Reuther and JES. In October 2001, JES terminated Reuther as CEO and denied him access to the offices and books of NOP and the other companies, literally changing the locks on the doors. At the next meetings of the boards of NOP and the overall enterprise, deadlock ensued, with the directors voting along family lines on every issue. Complaining that the meetings were a "waste of time," JES began to run the entire enterprise by taking advantage of an unequal balance of power on the companies' executive committees. In NOP's subsequent bankruptcy proceeding, Reuther filed a motion for the appointment of a trustee to formulate a plan for the firm's reorganization, alleging, among other things, misconduct by NOP's management. [*In re New Orleans Paddlewheels, Inc.*, 350 Bankr. 667 (E.D.La. 2006)] **(See pages 777–781.)**

1. Was Reuther legally entitled to have access to the books and records of NOP and the other companies? JES maintained, among other things, that NOP's books were "a mess." Was JES's denial of that access unethical? Explain.
2. How would you describe JES's attempt to gain control of NOP and the other companies? Were his actions deceptive and self-serving in the pursuit of personal gain or legitimate and reasonable in the pursuit of a business goal? Discuss.

Critical Thinking and Writing Assignments

30–9 Critical Legal Thinking. In general, courts are reluctant to grant shareholders' petitions for corporate dissolution except in extreme circumstances, such as when corporate directors or shareholders are deadlocked and the corporation suffers as a result. Instead, a court will attempt to "save" the corporate entity whenever possible. Why is this?

30–10 Business Law Critical Thinking Group Assignment. Milena Weintraub and Larry Griffith were shareholders in Grand Casino, Inc., which operated a casino in South Dakota. Griffith owned 51 percent of the stock and Weintraub 49 percent. Weintraub managed the casino, which Griffith typically visited once a week. At the end of 2012, an accounting audit showed that the cash on hand was less than the amount posted in the casino's books. Later, more shortfalls were discovered. In October 2014, Griffith did a complete audit. Weintraub was unable to account for $200,500 in missing cash. Griffith then kept all of the casino's most recent profits, including Weintraub's $90,447.20 share, and, without telling Weintraub, sold the casino for $400,000 and kept all of the proceeds. Weintraub filed a suit against Griffith, asserting a breach of fiduciary duty. Griffith countered with evidence of Weintraub's misappropriation of corporate cash.

1. The first group will discuss the duties that these parties owed to each other, and determine whether Weintraub or Griffith, or both, breached those duties.
2. The second group will decide how this dispute should be resolved and who should pay what to whom to reconcile the finances.
3. A third group will discuss whether Weintraub or Griffin violated any ethical duties to each other or to the corporation.

CHAPTER 31

(TommL/iStockphoto.com)

Investor Protection, Insider Trading, and Corporate Governance

CHAPTER OUTLINE

- Securities Act of 1933
- Securities Exchange Act of 1934
- State Securities Laws
- Corporate Governance
- Online Securities Fraud

LEARNING OBJECTIVES

The five learning objectives below are designed to help improve your understanding of the chapter. After reading this chapter, you should be able to answer the following questions:

1. What is meant by the term *securities?*
2. What are the two major statutes regulating the securities industry?
3. What is insider trading? Why is it prohibited?
4. What are some of the features of state securities laws?
5. What certification requirements does the Sarbanes-Oxley Act impose on corporate executives?

"You are remembered for the rules you break."
—General Douglas MacArthur, 1880–1964 (U.S. Army general)

Security Generally, a stock, bond, note, debenture, warrant, or other instrument representing an ownership interest in a corporation or a promise of repayment of debt by a corporation.

After the stock market crash of 1929, Congress enacted legislation to regulate securities markets. **Securities** generally are defined as any instruments representing corporate ownership (stock) or debts (bonds). The goal of regulation was to provide investors with more information to help them make buying and selling decisions about securities and to prohibit deceptive, unfair, and manipulative practices.

Today, the sale and transfer of securities are heavily regulated by federal and state statutes and by government agencies. Moreover, the Securities and Exchange Commission (SEC) has implemented new regulations since Congress passed the Dodd-Frank Wall Street Reform and Consumer Protection Act,[1] in reaction to the economic recession. We discuss the role of the SEC in the regulation of securities laws in this chapter's *Landmark in the Law* feature on the next page.

Despite all efforts to regulate the securities markets, people continue to break the rules and are often remembered for it, as observed in the chapter-opening quotation above. Violations are not always clear, though. Consider what happened when Facebook went

1. Pub. L. No. 111-203, July 21, 2010, 124 Stat. 1376; 12 U.S.C. Sections 5301 *et seq.*

LANDMARK IN THE LAW

The Securities and Exchange Commission

In 1931, in the wake of the stock market crash of 1929, the U.S. Senate passed a resolution calling for an extensive investigation of securities trading. The investigation led, ultimately, to the enactment of the Securities Act of 1933, which is also known as the *truth-in-securities* bill. In the following year, Congress passed the Securities Exchange Act. This 1934 act created the Securities and Exchange Commission (SEC).

Major Responsibilities of the SEC The SEC was created as an independent regulatory agency with the function of administering the 1933 and 1934 acts. Its major responsibilities in this respect are as follows:

1. Interprets federal securities laws and investigates securities law violations.
2. Issues new rules and amends existing rules.
3. Oversees the inspection of securities firms, brokers, investment advisers, and ratings agencies.
4. Oversees private regulatory organizations in the securities, accounting, and auditing fields.
5. Coordinates U.S. securities regulation with federal, state, and foreign authorities.

The SEC's Expanding Regulatory Powers Since its creation, the SEC's regulatory functions have gradually been increased by legislation granting it authority in different areas. For example, to curb further securities fraud, the Securities Enforcement Remedies and Penny Stock Reform Act of 1990[a] was enacted to expand the SEC's enforcement options and allow SEC administrative law judges to hear cases involving more types of alleged securities law violations. In addition, the act provides that courts can prevent persons who have engaged in securities fraud from serving as officers and directors of publicly held corporations. The Securities Acts Amendments of 1990 authorized the SEC to seek sanctions against those who violate foreign securities laws.[b]

The National Securities Markets Improvement Act of 1996 expanded the power of the SEC to exempt persons, securities, and transactions from the requirements of the securities laws.[c] (This part of the act is also known as the Capital Markets Efficiency Act.) The act also limited the authority of the states to regulate certain securities transactions and particular investment advisory firms.[d] The Sarbanes-Oxley Act of 2002,[e] which you will read about later in this chapter, further expanded the authority of the SEC by directing the agency to issue new rules relating to corporate disclosure requirements and by creating an oversight board to regulate public accounting firms.

Application to Today's World *The SEC is working to make the regulatory process more efficient and more relevant to today's securities trading practices. To this end, the SEC has embraced modern technology and communications methods, especially the Internet, more completely than many other federal agencies have. For example, the agency now requires—not just allows—companies to file certain information electronically so that it can be posted on the SEC's EDGAR (Electronic Data Gathering, Analysis, and Retrieval) database.*

a. 15 U.S.C. Section 77g.

b. 15 U.S.C. Section 78a.

c. 15 U.S.C. Sections 77z-3, 78mm.

d. 15 U.S.C. Section 80b-3a.

e. 15 U.S.C. Sections 7201 *et seq.*

public and issued stock in 2012. Facebook and its underwriters at Morgan Stanley determined that there was enough interest by investors to justify an opening price of $38 per share. Within a few weeks, however, the value of a share was $25.75—30 percent below the original price. A rash of lawsuits were filed, and government regulators began an investigation. Many suspected that Facebook had provided information only to underwriters and certain (institutional) investors rather than making it available to all investors. Such an action is a violation of the securities laws, as you will read in this chapter.

Securities Act of 1933

The Securities Act of 1933[2] governs initial sales of stock by businesses. The act was designed to prohibit various forms of fraud and to stabilize the securities industry by requiring that all essential information concerning the issuance of securities be made available to the investing public. Basically, the purpose of this act is to require disclosure. The 1933 act provides that

2. 15 U.S.C. Sections 77–77aa.

(National Archives)

During the stock market crash of 1929, hordes of investors crowded Wall Street to find out the latest news. How did the "crash" affect stock trading in the years thereafter?

all securities transactions must be registered with the SEC or be exempt from registration requirements.

What Is a Security?

Section 2(1) of the Securities Act of 1933 contains a broad definition of securities, which generally include the following:[3]

1. Instruments and interests commonly known as securities, such as preferred and common stocks, treasury stocks, bonds, debentures, and stock warrants.
2. Any interests, such as stock options, puts, calls, or other types of privilege on a security or on the right to purchase a security or a group of securities in a national security exchange.
3. Notes, instruments, or other evidence of indebtedness, including certificates of interest in a profit-sharing agreement and certificates of deposit.
4. Any fractional undivided interest in oil, gas, or other mineral rights.
5. Investment contracts, which include interests in limited partnerships and other investment schemes.

Investment Contract In securities law, a transaction in which a person invests in a common enterprise reasonably expecting profits that are derived primarily from the efforts of others.

LEARNING OBJECTIVE 1
What is meant by the term *securities*?

The *Howey* Test

In interpreting the act, the United States Supreme Court has held that an **investment contract** is any transaction in which a person (1) invests (2) in a common enterprise (3) reasonably expecting profits (4) derived *primarily* or *substantially* from others' managerial or entrepreneurial efforts. Known as the *Howey* test, this definition continues to guide the determination of what types of contracts can be considered securities.[4]

CASE EXAMPLE 31.1 Alpha Telcom sold, installed, and maintained pay-phone systems. As part of its pay-phone program, Alpha guaranteed buyers a 14 percent return on their investment. Alpha was operating at a net loss, however, and continually borrowed funds to pay investors the fixed rate of return it had promised. Eventually, the company filed for bankruptcy, and the SEC brought an action alleging that Alpha had violated the Securities Act of 1933. A federal court concluded that Alpha's pay-phone program was a security because it involved an investment contract.[5] •

Many Types of Securities

For our purposes, it is probably convenient to think of securities in their most common forms—stocks and bonds issued by corporations. Bear in mind, though, that securities can take many forms, including interests in whiskey, cosmetics, worms, beavers, boats, vacuum cleaners, muskrats, and cemetery lots. Almost any stake in the ownership or debt of a company can be considered a security. Investment contracts in condominiums, franchises, limited partnerships in real estate, and oil or gas or other mineral rights have qualified as securities.

PREVENTING LEGAL DISPUTES

Securities are not limited to stocks and bonds but can encompass a wide variety of legal claims. The analysis hinges on the nature of the transaction rather than on the particular instrument or rights involved. Because Congress enacted securities laws to regulate investments, in whatever form and by whatever name they are called, almost any type of security that might be sold as an investment can be subject to securities laws. When in doubt about whether an investment transaction involves securities, seek the advice of a specialized attorney.

3. 15 U.S.C. Section 77b(1). Amendments in 1982 added stock options.
4. *SEC v. W. J. Howey Co.*, 328 U.S. 293, 66 S.Ct. 1100, 90 L.Ed. 1244 (1946).
5. *SEC v. Alpha Telcom, Inc.*, 187 F.Supp.2d 1250 (2002). See also *SEC v. Edwards*, 540 U.S. 389, 124 S.Ct. 892, 157 L.Ed.2d 813 (2004), in which the United States Supreme Court held that an investment scheme offering contractual entitlement to a fixed rate of return can be an investment contract and therefore can be considered a security under federal law.

Registration Statement

Section 5 of the Securities Act of 1933 broadly provides that a security must be *registered* before being offered to the public unless it qualifies for an exemption. The issuing corporation must file a *registration statement* with the SEC and must provide all investors with a *prospectus*.

Prospectus A written document required by securities laws when a security is being sold. The prospectus describes the security, the financial operations of the issuing corporation, and the risk attaching to the security so that investors will have sufficient information to evaluate the risk involved in purchasing the security.

A **prospectus** is a written disclosure document that describes the security being sold, the financial operations of the issuing corporation, and the investment or risk attaching to the security. The prospectus also serves as a selling tool for the issuing corporation. The SEC now allows an issuer to deliver its prospectus to investors electronically via the Internet.[6]

In principle, the registration statement and the prospectus supply sufficient information to enable unsophisticated investors to evaluate the financial risk involved.

Contents of the Registration Statement

The registration statement must be written in plain English and fully describe the following:

1. The securities being offered for sale, including their relationship to the issuer's other capital securities.
2. The corporation's properties and business (including a financial statement certified by an independent public accounting firm).
3. The management of the corporation, including managerial compensation, stock options, pensions, and other benefits. Any interests of directors or officers in any material transactions with the corporation must be disclosed.
4. How the corporation intends to use the proceeds of the sale.
5. Any pending lawsuits or special risk factors.

KNOW THIS

The purpose of the Securities Act of 1933 is disclosure. The SEC does not consider whether a security is worth the investment price.

All companies, both domestic and foreign, must file their registration statements electronically so that they can be posted on the SEC's EDGAR (Electronic Data Gathering, Analysis, and Retrieval) database. The EDGAR database includes material on initial public offerings, proxy statements, corporations' annual reports, registration statements, and other documents that have been filed with the SEC. Investors can access the database via the Internet (**www.sec.gov/edgar.shtml**) to obtain information that can be used to make investment decisions.

What act requires securities to be registered?

(PictureLake/iStockphoto.com)

Registration Process

The registration statement does not become effective until after it has been reviewed and approved by the SEC (unless it is filed by a *well-known seasoned issuer,* as will be discussed shortly). The 1933 act restricted the types of activities that an issuer can engage in at each stage in the registration process.

Prefiling Period During the *prefiling period* (before filing the registration statement), the issuer normally cannot sell or offer to sell the securities. Once the registration statement has been filed, a waiting period begins while the SEC reviews the registration statement for completeness.[7]

6. Basically, an electronic prospectus must meet the same requirements as a printed prospectus. The SEC has special rules that address situations in which the graphics, images, or audio files in a printed prospectus cannot be reproduced in an electronic form. 17 C.F.R. Section 232.304.

7. The waiting period must last at least twenty days but always extends much longer because the SEC invariably requires numerous changes and additions to the registration statement.

Waiting Period During the *waiting period,* the securities can be offered for sale but cannot be sold by the issuing corporation. Only certain types of offers are allowed. All issuers can distribute a *preliminary prospectus,* which contains most of the information that will be included in the final prospectus but often does not include a price.

Most issuers can also use a *free-writing prospectus* during this period (although some inexperienced issuers will need to file a preliminary prospectus first).[8] A **free-writing prospectus** is any type of written, electronic, or graphic offer that describes the issuer or its securities and includes a legend indicating that the investor may obtain the prospectus at the SEC's Web site.

Free-Writing Prospectus A written, electronic, or graphic offer that is used during the waiting period and describes securities that are being offered for sale, or describes the issuing corporation and includes a legend indicating that the investor may obtain the prospectus at the Securities and Exchange Commission's Web site.

Posteffective Period Once the SEC has reviewed and approved the registration statement and the waiting period is over, the registration is effective, and the *posteffective period* begins. The issuer can now offer and sell the securities without restrictions. If the company issued a preliminary or free-writing prospectus to investors, it must provide those investors with a final prospectus either before or at the time they purchase the securities. The issuer can require investors to download the final prospectus from a Web site if it notifies them of the appropriate Internet address.

Well-Known Seasoned Issuers

In 2005, the SEC revised the registration process and loosened some of the restrictions on large, experienced issuers.[9] The rules created new categories of issuers depending on their size and presence in the market and provided a simplified registration process for these issuers. The large, well-known securities firms that issue most securities have the greatest flexibility.

A firm that has issued at least $1 billion in securities in the previous three years or has at least $700 million of value of outstanding stock in the hands of the public is considered a *well-known seasoned issuer* (WKSI). WKSIs can file registration statements the day they announce a new offering and are not required to wait for SEC review and approval. They can also use a free-writing prospectus at any time, even during the prefiling period.

Exempt Securities and Transactions

Certain types of securities are exempt from the registration requirements of the Securities Act of 1933. These securities—which generally can also be resold without being registered—are summarized in Exhibit 31.1 on the next page under the "Exempt Securities" heading.[10] The exhibit also lists and describes certain transactions that are exempt from registration requirements under various SEC regulations.

The transaction exemptions are the most important because they are very broad and can enable an issuer to avoid the high cost and complicated procedures associated with registration. Because the coverage of the exemptions overlaps somewhat, an offering may qualify for more than one. Therefore, many sales of securities occur without registration. Even when a transaction is exempt from the registration requirements, the offering is still subject to the antifraud provisions of the 1933 act (as well as those of the 1934 act, to be discussed later in this chapter).

KNOW THIS

The issuer of an exempt security does not have to disclose the same information as other issuers.

Regulation A Offerings

Securities issued by an issuer that has offered less than $5 million in securities during any twelve-month period are exempt from registration.[11] Under Regulation A,[12] the issuer must file with the SEC a notice of the issue and an offering

8. See SEC Rules 164 and 433.
9. Securities Offering Reform, codified at 17 C.F.R. Sections 200, 228, 229, 230, 239, 240, 243, 249, and 274.
10. 15 U.S.C. Section 77c.
11. 15 U.S.C. Section 77c(b).
12. 17 C.F.R. Sections 230.251–230.263.

Exhibit 31.1 Exemptions for Securities Offerings under the 1933 Securities Act

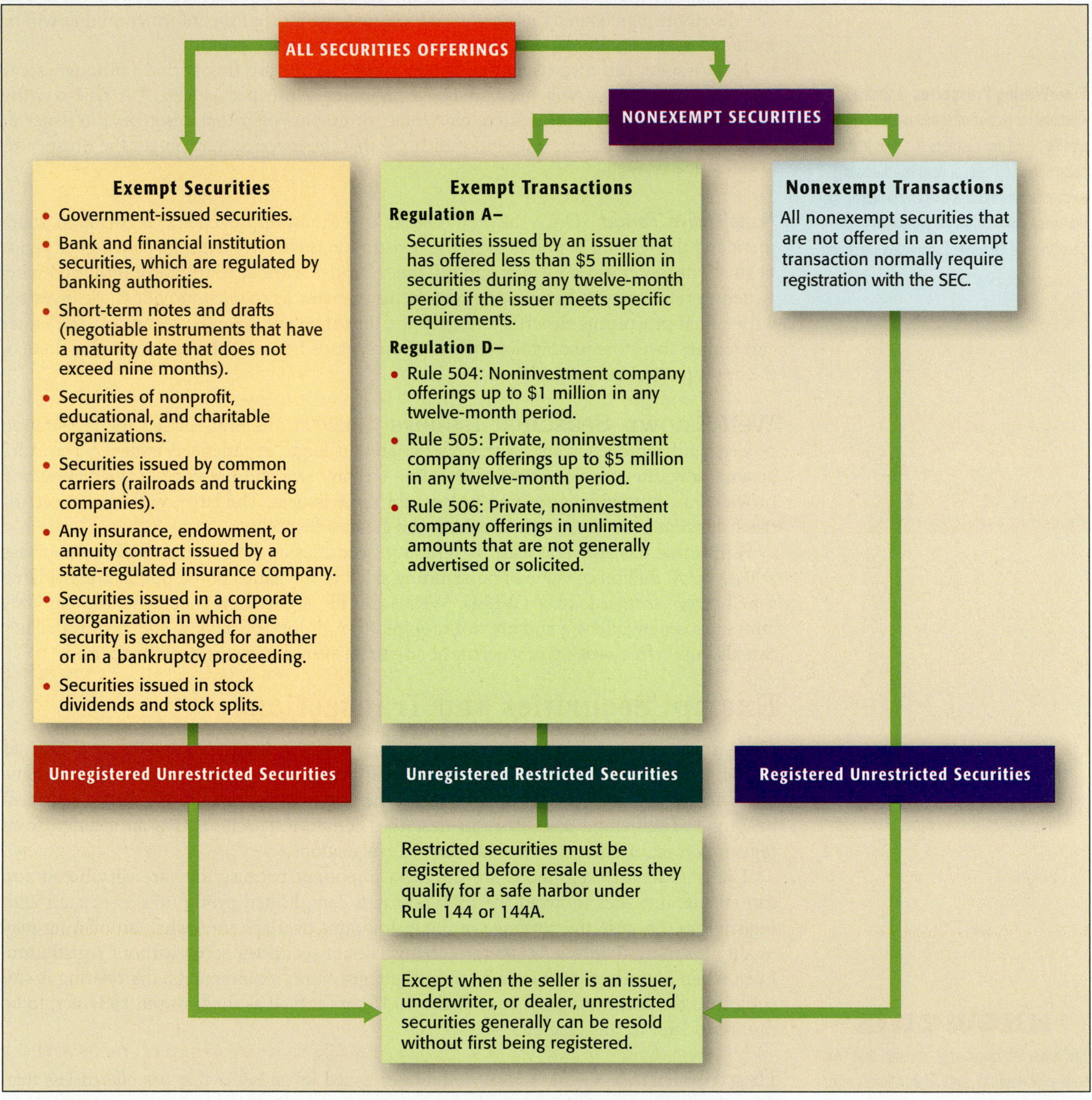

circular, which must also be provided to investors before the sale. This is a much simpler and less expensive process than the procedures associated with full registration.

Testing the Waters Companies are allowed to "test the waters" for potential interest before preparing the offering circular. To *test the waters* means to determine potential interest without actually selling any securities or requiring any commitment on the part of those who express interest. Small-business issuers (companies with annual revenues of less than $25 million) can use an integrated registration and reporting system that uses simpler forms than the full registration system.

Using the Internet Some companies have sold their securities via the Internet using Regulation A. **EXAMPLE 31.2** The Spring Street Brewing Company became the first company to sell securities via an online initial public offering (IPO). Spring Street raised about $1.6 million—without having to pay any commissions to brokers or underwriters. • Such online IPOs are particularly attractive to small companies and start-up ventures that may find it difficult to raise capital from institutional investors or through underwriters.

Small Offerings—Regulation D

The SEC's Regulation D contains several exemptions from registration requirements (Rules 504, 504a, 505, and 506) for offers that either involve a small dollar amount or are made in a limited manner.

Rule 504 Rule 504 is the exemption used by most small businesses. It provides that noninvestment company offerings up to $1 million in any twelve-month period are exempt. Noninvestment companies are firms that are not engaged primarily in the business of investing or trading in securities. (In contrast, an **investment company** is a firm that buys a large portfolio of securities and professionally manages it on behalf of many smaller shareholders/owners. A **mutual fund** is a type of investment company.)

Investment Company A company that acts on the behalf of many smaller shareholders-owners by buying a large portfolio of securities and professionally managing that portfolio.

Mutual Fund A specific type of investment company that continually buys or sells to investors shares of ownership in a portfolio.

EXAMPLE 31.3 Zeta Enterprises is a limited partnership that develops commercial property. Zeta intends to offer $600,000 of its limited partnership interests for sale between June 1 and next May 31. Because an interest in a limited partnership meets the definition of a security (discussed earlier in this chapter), this offering would be subject to the registration and prospectus requirements of the Securities Act of 1933. Under Rule 504, however, the sales of Zeta's interests are exempt from these requirements because Zeta is a noninvestment company making an offering of less than $1 million in a twelve-month period. Therefore, Zeta can sell its limited partnership interests without filing a registration statement with the SEC or issuing a prospectus to any investor. •

Rule 505 Another exemption is available under Rule 505 for private, noninvestment company offerings up to $5 million in any twelve-month period. The offer may be made to an unlimited number of *accredited investors* and up to thirty-five unaccredited investors. **Accredited investors** include banks, insurance companies, investment companies, employee benefit plans, the issuer's executive officers and directors, and persons whose income or net worth exceeds a certain threshold.

Accredited Investor In the context of securities offerings, "sophisticated" investors, such as banks, insurance companies, investment companies, the issuer's executive officers and directors, and persons whose income or net worth exceeds certain limits.

The SEC must be notified of the sales, and precautions must be taken because these restricted securities may be resold only by registration or in an exempt transaction. No general solicitation or advertising is allowed. The issuer must provide any unaccredited investors with disclosure documents that generally are the same as those used in registered offerings.

KNOW THIS

An investor can be "sophisticated" by virtue of his or her education and experience or by investing through a knowledgeable, experienced representative.

Rule 506—Private Placement Exemption Rule 506 exempts private, noninvestment company offerings in unlimited amounts that are not generally solicited or advertised. This exemption is often referred to as the *private placement* exemption because it exempts "transactions not involving any public offering."[13] To qualify for the exemption, the issuer must believe that each unaccredited investor has sufficient knowledge or experience in financial matters to be capable of evaluating the investment's merits and risks.[14]

13. 15 U.S.C. Section 77d(2).

14. 17 C.F.R. Section 230.506.

The private placement exemption is perhaps most important to firms that want to raise funds through the sale of securities without registering them. **EXAMPLE 31.4** Citco Corporation needs to raise capital to expand its operations. Citco decides to make a private $10 million offering of its common stock directly to two hundred accredited investors and thirty highly sophisticated, but unaccredited, investors. Citco provides all of these investors with a prospectus and material information about the firm, including its most recent financial statements.

As long as Citco notifies the SEC of the sale, this offering will likely qualify for the private placement exemption. The offering is nonpublic and not generally advertised. There are fewer than thirty-five unaccredited investors, and each of them possesses sufficient knowledge and experience to evaluate the risks involved. The issuer has provided all purchasers with the material information. Thus, Citco will *not* be required to comply with the registration requirements of the Securities Act of 1933. •

Resales and Safe Harbor Rules

Most securities can be resold without registration. The Securities Act of 1933 provides exemptions for resales by most persons other than issuers or underwriters. The average investor who sells shares of stock does not have to file a registration statement with the SEC.

Resales of restricted securities, however, trigger the registration requirements unless the party selling them complies with Rule 144 or Rule 144A. These rules are sometimes referred to as "safe harbors."

Rule 144 Rule 144 exempts restricted securities from registration on resale if all of the following conditions are met:

1. There is adequate current public information about the issuer. ("Adequate current public information" refers to the reports that certain companies are required to file under the Securities Exchange Act of 1934.)
2. The person selling the securities has owned them for at least six months if the issuer is subject to the reporting requirements of the 1934 act.[15] If the issuer is not subject to the 1934 act's reporting requirements, the seller must have owned the securities for at least one year.
3. The securities are sold in certain limited amounts in unsolicited brokers' transactions.
4. The SEC is notified of the resale.[16]

KNOW THIS

Securities do not have to be held for a specific period (six months or one year) to be exempt from registration on a resale under Rule 144A, as they do under Rule 144.

Rule 144A Securities that at the time of issue are not of the same class as securities listed on a national securities exchange or quoted in a U.S. automated interdealer quotation system may be resold under Rule 144A.[17] They may be sold only to a qualified institutional buyer (an institution, such as an insurance company or a bank that owns and invests at least $100 million in securities). The seller must take reasonable steps to ensure that the buyer knows that the seller is relying on the exemption under Rule 144A.

Violations of the 1933 Act

It is a violation of the Securities Act of 1933 to intentionally defraud investors by misrepresenting or omitting facts in a registration statement or prospectus. Liability is also imposed on those who are negligent for not discovering the fraud. Selling securities before the

15. Before 2008, when amendments to Rule 144 became effective, the holding period was one year if the issuer was subject to the reporting requirements of the 1934 act. See the revised SEC Rules and Regulations at 72 Federal Rules 71546-01, 2007 WL 4368599, Release No. 33-8869. This reduced holding period allows nonpublic issuers to raise capital electronically from private and overseas sources more quickly.

16. 17 C.F.R. Section 230.144.

17. 17 C.F.R. Section 230.144A.

effective date of the registration statement or under an exemption for which the securities do not qualify also results in liability.

Remedies Criminal violations are prosecuted by the U.S. Department of Justice. Violators may be fined up to $10,000, imprisoned for up to five years, or both.

The SEC is authorized to seek civil sanctions against those who willfully violate the 1933 act. It can request an injunction to prevent further sales of the securities involved or ask the court to grant other relief, such as an order to a violator to refund profits. Parties who purchase securities and suffer harm as a result of false or omitted statements may also bring suits in a federal court to recover their losses and other damages.

Defenses There are three basic defenses to charges of violations under the 1933 act. A defendant can avoid liability by proving that (1) the statement or omission was not material, (2) the plaintiff knew about the misrepresentation at the time of purchasing the stock, or (3) the defendant exercised *due diligence* in preparing the registration and reasonably believed at the time that the statements were true.

The due diligence defense is the most important because it can be asserted by any defendant, except the issuer of the stock. The defendant must prove that she or he reasonably believed, at the time the registration statement became effective, that the statements in it were true and there were no omissions of material facts.

The following case involved allegations of omissions of material information from an issuing company's registration statement. The defendants contended that the omissions were not material.

Case 31.1

Litwin v. Blackstone Group, LP

United States Court of Appeals, Second Circuit,
634 F.3d 706 (2011).
www.ca2.uscourts.gov[a]

(AP Photo/Mary Altaffer)

FACTS Blackstone Group, LP, manages investments. Its Corporate Private Equity Division accounts for nearly 40 percent of the assets under the company's management. In preparation for an initial public offering (IPO), Blackstone filed a registration statement with the Securities and Exchange Commission (SEC). At the time, Blackstone's investments included FGIC Corporation—a company that insured investments in subprime mortgages—and Freescale Semiconductor, Inc., which made wireless 3G chipsets for cell phones.

Before the IPO, FGIC's mortgage insurance experienced problems, and Freescale lost an exclusive contract with Motorola, Inc. (its largest customer). Consequently, both FGIC and Freescale began to generate substantial losses for Blackstone. Blackstone's registration statement did not mention the impact on its revenue of the investments in FGIC and Freescale. Martin Litwin and others who invested in the IPO filed a suit against Blackstone and its officers, alleging material omissions from the statement. Blackstone filed a motion to dismiss, which the court granted. The plaintiffs appealed.

ISSUE Was the fact that Blackstone had recently suffered substantial losses on two of its investments sufficient proof of material information that should have been disclosed in its registration statement?

DECISION Yes. The federal appellate court vacated the lower court's dismissal and remanded the case. The plaintiffs had provided sufficient allegations that Blackstone had omitted material information that it was required to disclose under securities law for the case to go to trial.

a. In the left column, click on "Decisions." On the next page, in the "Enter Docket #, Date, Party Name or find decisions that contain:" box, type "09-4426" and click on "Search." In the result, click on the docket number to access the opinion (the case name is shown as *Landmen Partners, Inc. v. Blackstone Group, LP*). The U.S. Court of Appeals for the Second Circuit maintains this Web site.

Case 31.1—Continues next page

Case 31.1—Continued

REASON Information is material if a reasonable investor would consider it significant in making an investment decision. A complaint can be dismissed on the ground that an omission is not material only if it would be "so obviously unimportant to a reasonable investor that reasonable minds could not differ on the question." In this case, the information concerned the extent to which known events and trends could reasonably be expected to affect Blackstone's investments and revenue. The plaintiffs alleged that Blackstone should have disclosed this information. In particular, a reasonable investor would want to know the expected effect on the corporate private equity sector's future revenue. Thus "the alleged . . . omissions relating to FGIC and Freescale were plausibly material."

CRITICAL THINKING—Legal Consideration *Litwin alleged that Blackstone had negligently omitted material information from the registration statement. What will he and the others have to show to prove their case?*

Securities Exchange Act of 1934

LEARNING OBJECTIVE 2
What are the two major statutes regulating the securities industry?

The Securities Exchange Act of 1934 provides for the regulation and registration of securities exchanges, brokers, dealers, and national securities associations, such as the National Association of Securities Dealers (NASD). Unlike the 1933 act, which is a one-time disclosure law, the 1934 act provides for continuous periodic disclosures by publicly held corporations to enable the SEC to regulate subsequent trading.

The Securities Exchange Act of 1934 applies to companies that have assets in excess of $10 million and five hundred or more shareholders. These corporations are referred to as Section 12 companies because they are required to register their securities under Section 12 of the 1934 act. Section 12 companies must file reports with the SEC annually and quarterly, and sometimes even monthly if specified events occur (such as a merger). Other provisions in the 1934 act require all securities brokers and dealers to be registered, to keep detailed records of their activities, and to file annual reports with the SEC.

The act also authorizes the SEC to engage in market surveillance to deter undesirable market practices such as fraud, market manipulation (attempts at illegally influencing stock prices), and misrepresentation. In addition, the act provides for the SEC's regulation of proxy solicitations for voting (discussed in Chapter 30).

Section 10(b), SEC Rule 10b-5, and Insider Trading

Section 10(b) is one of the more important sections of the Securities Exchange Act of 1934. This section proscribes the use of any manipulative or deceptive mechanism in violation of SEC rules and regulations. Among the rules that the SEC has promulgated pursuant to the 1934 act is **SEC Rule 10b-5**, which prohibits the commission of fraud in connection with the purchase or sale of any security.

SEC Rule 10b-5 A rule of the Securities and Exchange Commission that prohibits the commission of fraud in connection with the purchase or sale of any security. It is unlawful to make any untrue statement of a material fact or to omit a material fact if doing so causes the statement to be misleading.

SEC Rule 10b-5 applies to almost all cases concerning the trading of securities, whether on organized exchanges, in over-the-counter markets, or in private transactions. Generally, the rule covers just about any form of security, and the securities need not be registered under the 1933 act for the 1934 act to apply.

Private parties can sue for securities fraud under the 1934 act and SEC rules. The basic elements of a securities fraud action are as follows:

KNOW THIS
A required element in any fraud claim is reliance. The innocent party must justifiably have relied on the misrepresentation.

1. A *material misrepresentation* (or omission) in connection with the purchase and sale of securities.
2. *Scienter* (a wrongful state of mind).
3. *Reliance* by the plaintiff on the material misrepresentation.
4. An *economic loss*.
5. *Causation,* meaning that there is a causal connection between the misrepresentation and the loss.

Insider Trading The purchase or sale of securities on the basis of information that has not been made available to the public.

LEARNING OBJECTIVE 3

What is insider trading? Why is it prohibited?

Insider Trading

One of the major goals of Section 10(b) and SEC Rule 10b-5 is to prevent so-called **insider trading**, which occurs when persons buy or sell securities on the basis of information that is not available to the public. Corporate directors, officers, and others such as majority shareholders, for instance, often have advance inside information that can affect the future market value of the corporate stock. Obviously, if they act on this information, their positions give them a trading advantage over the general public and other shareholders.

The 1934 Securities Exchange Act defines inside information and extends liability to those who take advantage of such information in their personal transactions when they know that the information is unavailable to those with whom they are dealing. Section 10(b) of the 1934 act and SEC Rule 10b-5 apply to anyone who has access to or receives information of a nonpublic nature on which trading is based—not just to corporate "insiders."

A government official outlines what he believes was an insider trading scandal that involved computer company Dell, Inc.

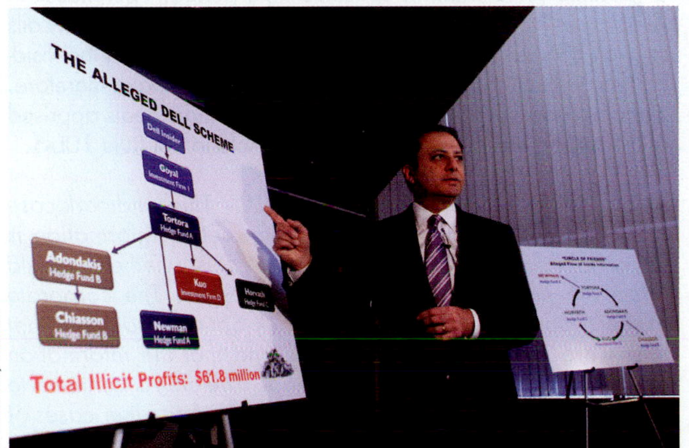

(AP Photo/Mary Altaffer)

Disclosure under SEC Rule 10b-5

Any material omission or misrepresentation of material facts in connection with the purchase or sale of a security may violate not only the Securities Act of 1933 but also the antifraud provisions of Section 10(b) of the 1934 act and SEC Rule 10b-5. The key to liability (which can be civil or criminal) under Section 10(b) and SEC Rule 10b-5 is whether the insider's information is *material*.

The following are some examples of material facts calling for disclosure under SEC Rule 10b-5:

1. Fraudulent trading in the company's stock by a broker-dealer.
2. A dividend change (whether up or down).
3. A contract for the sale of corporate assets.
4. A new discovery, a new process, or a new product.
5. A significant change in the firm's financial condition.
6. Potential litigation against the company.

Note that any one of these facts, by itself, is not *automatically* considered a material fact. Rather, it will be regarded as a material fact if it is significant enough that it would likely affect an investor's decision as to whether to purchase or sell the company's securities.

EXAMPLE 31.5 Sheen, Inc., is the defendant in a class-action product liability suit that its attorney, Paula Frasier, believes that the company will lose. Frasier has advised Sheen's directors, officers, and accountants that the company will likely have to pay a substantial damages award. Sheen plans to make a $5 million offering of newly issued stock before the date when the trial is expected to end. Sheen's potential liability and the financial consequences to the firm are material facts that must be disclosed because they are significant enough to affect an investor's decision as to whether to purchase the stock. •

The following is one of the *Classic Cases* interpreting materiality under SEC Rule 10b-5.

Classic Case 31.2

Securities and Exchange Commission v. Texas Gulf Sulphur Co.

United States Court of Appeals, Second Circuit, 401 F.2d 833 (1968).

(©Dmitri Melnik, 2009. Used under license from Shutterstock.com)

After sample drilling revealed potential mineral deposits, company executives made substantial stock purchases. Did they violate insider-trading laws?

HISTORICAL AND ENVIRONMENTAL SETTING *In 1957, the Texas Gulf Sulphur Company began exploring for minerals in eastern Canada. In March 1959, aerial geophysical surveys were conducted over more than fifteen thousand square miles of the area. The operations revealed numerous variations in the conductivity of the rock, which indicated a remarkable concentration of commercially exploitable minerals. One site of such variations was near Timmins, Ontario. On October 29 and 30, 1963, a ground survey of the site near Timmins indicated a need to drill for further evaluation.*

Classic Case 31.2—Continues next page

Classic Case 31.2—Continued

FACTS On November 12, 1963, the Texas Gulf Sulphur Company (TGS) drilled a hole that appeared to yield a core with an exceedingly high mineral content, although further drilling would be necessary to establish whether there was enough ore to be mined commercially. TGS kept secret the results of the core sample. After learning of the ore discovery, officers and employees of the company made substantial purchases of TGS's stock or accepted stock options (rights to purchase stock). On April 11, 1964, an unauthorized report of the mineral find appeared in the newspapers. On the following day, April 12, TGS issued a press release that played down the discovery and stated that it was too early to tell whether the ore find would be significant.

Later on, TGS announced a strike of at least 25 million tons of ore. The news led to a substantial increase in the price of TGS stock. The Securities and Exchange Commission (SEC) brought a suit in a federal district court against the officers and employees of TGS for violating the insider-trading prohibition of SEC Rule 10b-5. The officers and employees argued that the prohibition did not apply. They reasoned that the information on which they had traded was not material, as the find had not been commercially proved. The trial court held that most of the defendants had not violated SEC Rule 10b-5, and the SEC appealed.

ISSUE Did the officers and employees of TGS violate SEC Rule 10b-5 by buying the stock, even though they did not know the full extent and profit potential of the ore discovery at the time of their purchases?

DECISION Yes. The U.S. Court of Appeals for the Second Circuit reversed the lower court's decision and remanded the case for further proceedings, holding that the employees and officers had violated SEC Rule 10b-5's prohibition against insider trading.

REASON For SEC Rule 10b-5 purposes, the test of materiality is whether the information would affect the judgment of reasonable investors. Reasonable investors include speculative as well as conservative investors. "A major factor in determining whether the . . . discovery [of the ore] was a material fact is the importance attached to the drilling results by those who knew about it. . . . The timing by those who knew of it of their stock purchases and their purchases of short-term calls [rights to buy shares at a specified price within a specified time period]—purchases in some cases by individuals who had never before purchased calls or even TGS stock—virtually compels the inference that the insiders were influenced by the drilling results. . . . We hold, therefore, that all transactions in TGS stock or calls by individuals apprised of the drilling results . . . were made in violation of Rule 10b-5."

IMPACT OF THIS CASE ON TODAY'S LAW *This landmark case affirmed the principle that the test of whether information is "material," for SEC Rule 10b-5 purposes, is whether it would affect the judgment of reasonable investors. The corporate insiders' purchases of stock and stock options indicated that they were influenced by the results and that the information about the drilling results was material. The courts continue to cite this case when applying SEC Rule 10b-5 to other cases of alleged insider trading.*

Outsiders and SEC Rule 10b-5

The traditional insider-trading case involves true insiders—corporate officers, directors, and majority shareholders who have access to (and trade on) inside information. Increasingly, liability under Section 10(b) of the 1934 act and SEC Rule 10b-5 is being extended to certain "outsiders"—those persons who trade on inside information acquired indirectly. Two theories have been developed under which outsiders may be held liable for insider trading: the *tipper/tippee theory* and the *misappropriation theory.*

Tipper/Tippee Theory

Anyone who acquires inside information as a result of a corporate insider's breach of his or her fiduciary duty can be liable under SEC Rule 10b-5. This liability extends to **tippees** (those who receive "tips" from insiders) and even remote tippees (tippees of tippees).

Tippee A person who receives inside information.

The key to liability under this theory is that the inside information must be obtained as a result of someone's breach of a fiduciary duty to the corporation whose shares are involved in the trading. The tippee is liable under this theory only if (1) there is a breach of a duty not to disclose inside information, (2) the disclosure is in exchange for personal benefit, and (3) the tippee knows (or should know) of this breach and benefits from it.[18]

18. See, for example, *Chiarella v. United States*, 445 U.S. 222, 100 S.Ct. 1108, 63 L.Ed.2d 348 (1980); and *Dirks v. SEC*, 463 U.S. 646, 103 S.Ct. 3255, 77 L.Ed.2d 911 (1983).

"The way to stop financial 'joy-riding' is to arrest the chauffeur, not the automobile."

Woodrow Wilson, 1856–1924 (Twenty-eighth president of the United States, 1913–1921)

Misappropriation Theory Liability for insider trading may also be established under the misappropriation theory. This theory holds that an individual who wrongfully obtains (misappropriates) inside information and trades on it for her or his personal gain should be held liable because, in essence, she or he stole information rightfully belonging to another.

The misappropriation theory has been controversial because it significantly extends the reach of SEC Rule 10b-5 to outsiders who ordinarily would *not* be deemed fiduciaries of the corporations in whose stock they trade. The United States Supreme Court, however, has held that liability under SEC Rule 10b-5 can be based on the misappropriation theory.[19]

It is not always wrong to disclose material, nonpublic information about a company to another person. Nevertheless, a person who obtains the information and trades securities on it can be liable.

Insider Reporting and Trading—Section 16(b)

Section 16(b) of the 1934 act provides for the recapture by the corporation of all profits realized by an insider on any purchase and sale or sale and purchase of the corporation's stock within any six-month period.[20] It is irrelevant whether the insider actually uses inside information—*all such* **short-swing profits** *must be returned to the corporation.*

Short-Swing Profits Profits earned by a purchase and sale, or sale and purchase, of the same security within a six-month period. Under Section 16(b) of the 1934 Securities Exchange Act, the profits must be returned to the corporation if earned by company insiders from transactions in the company's stock.

In this context, *insiders* means officers, directors, and large stockholders of Section 12 corporations (those owning at least 10 percent of the class of equity securities registered under Section 12 of the 1934 act). To discourage such insiders from using nonpublic information about their companies for their personal benefit in the stock market, they must file reports with the SEC concerning their ownership and trading of the corporation's securities.

Section 16(b) applies not only to stock but also to warrants, options (see page 816), and securities convertible into stock. In addition, the courts have fashioned complex rules for determining profits. Note that the SEC exempts a number of transactions under Rule 16b-3.[21] For all of these reasons, corporate insiders are wise to seek specialized counsel before trading in the corporation's stock. Exhibit 31.2 below compares the effects of SEC Rule 10b-5 and Section 16(b).

19. *United States v. O'Hagan*, 521 U.S. 642, 117 S.Ct. 2199, 138 L.Ed.2d 724 (1997).

20. A person who expects the price of a particular stock to decline can realize profits by "selling short"—selling at a high price and repurchasing later at a lower price to cover the "short sale."

21. 17 C.F.R. Section 240.16b-3.

Exhibit 31.2 Comparison of Coverage, Application, and Liability under SEC Rule 10b-5 and Section 16(b)

AREA OF COMPARISON	SEC RULE 10b-5	SECTION 16(b)
What is the subject matter of the transaction?	Any security (does not have to be registered).	Any security (does not have to be registered).
What transactions are covered?	Purchase or sale.	Short-swing purchase and sale or short-swing sale and purchase.
Who is subject to liability?	Almost anyone with inside information under a duty to disclose—including officers, directors, controlling shareholders, and tippees.	Officers, directors, and certain shareholders who earn 10 percent or more.
Is omission or misrepresentation necessary for liability?	Yes.	No.
Are there any exempt transactions?	No.	Yes, there are a number of exemptions.
Who may bring an action?	A person transacting with an insider, the SEC, or a purchaser or seller damaged by a wrongful act.	A corporation or a shareholder by derivative action.

The Private Securities Litigation Reform Act of 1995

The disclosure requirements of SEC Rule 10b-5 had the unintended effect of deterring the disclosure of forward-looking information. To understand why, consider an example. **EXAMPLE 31.6** QT Company announces that its projected earnings in a future time period will be a certain amount, but the forecast turns out to be wrong. The earnings are in fact much lower, and the price of QT's stock is affected—negatively. The shareholders then file suit against the company, alleging that the directors violated SEC Rule 10b-5 by disclosing misleading financial information. •

In an attempt to rectify this problem and promote disclosure, Congress passed the Private Securities Litigation Reform Act of 1995.

Safe Harbor Provisions The Private Securities Litigation Reform Act provides a "safe harbor" for publicly held companies that make forward-looking statements, such as financial forecasts. Those who make such statements are protected against liability for securities fraud as long as the statements are accompanied by "meaningful cautionary statements identifying important factors that could cause actual results to differ materially from those in the forward-looking statement."[22]

Pleading Requirements The Private Securities Litigation Reform Act also affected the level of detail required in securities fraud complaints. Plaintiffs must specify each misleading statement and say how it led them to a mistaken belief. A plaintiff must also state facts that give "rise to a strong inference that the defendant acted with the required state of mind," and indicate how the defendant's misrepresentations "caused the loss for which the plaintiff seeks to recover."[23]

In the following *Spotlight Case,* the plaintiffs claimed that the company's misrepresentations about a new product had artificially inflated the price of the stock that the plaintiffs had purchased. The issue was whether the allegations in the complaint were sufficient to show that the defendant's misrepresentations had caused the plaintiffs' economic loss.

22. 15 U.S.C. Sections 77z-2, 78u-5.
23. 15 U.S.C. Section 78u-4(b)(1).

Spotlight on Proving Securities Fraud

Case 31.3

Dura Pharmaceuticals, Inc. v. Broudo

Supreme Court of the United States, 544 U.S. 336, 125 S.Ct. 1627, 161 L.Ed.2d 577 (2005).

(pagadesign/iStockphoto.com)

How can the FDA affect a drug company's stock price?

FACTS Michael Broudo and other investors purchased stock in Dura Pharmaceuticals, Inc. The company represented that its drug sales were profitable and that the U.S. Food and Drug Administration (FDA) would soon approve the sale of its new asthmatic spray device. Both statements turned out to be untrue. Dura's stock price fell by almost half after the company announced lower earnings due to slow drug sales. When Dura announced that the FDA would not approve its spray device, the price fell again, although it soon rebounded close to its previous level. The investors sued Dura under Section 10(b).

The investors argued that Dura's statements had inflated the price of the stock, causing them to suffer a greater loss when the bad news was disclosed. The investors provided no other evidence about the connection between the statements and the loss. The trial court dismissed the case, in part, because the investors failed to sufficiently prove that their loss was caused by Dura's statements. The appellate court reversed, and the case was appealed to the United States Supreme Court.

Spotlight Case 31.3—Continued

ISSUE Can the investors prove that Dura's misstatements caused the loss simply by establishing that the price on the date of purchase was inflated because of the misrepresentations?

DECISION No. The fact that the stock price dropped after the firm's disclosure of bad news, without other evidence, is not sufficient to prove that the misrepresentations caused the economic loss under Section 10(b) of the 1934 act.

REASON Although an inflated share price can cause a later economic loss, that causation cannot be assumed in every situation. When a purchaser resells shares at a lower price, that price might reflect other factors besides the earlier misrepresentation. Changed economic circumstances, industry-specific challenges, and investor expectations can all affect the price of a stock. The longer the time between the purchase and the sale, the more likely it is that other factors besides the misrepresentation caused the loss. Investors must show not only that had they known the truth about the stock they would not have purchased it, but also that they suffered an actual economic loss.

CRITICAL THINKING—Financial Consideration *How does the decision in this case make it more difficult for plaintiffs to prove fraud?*

Limitations on Class Actions

After the Private Securities Litigation Reform Act was passed, a number of securities class-action suits were filed in state courts to skirt its requirements. In response to this problem, Congress passed the Securities Litigation Uniform Standards Act of 1998 (SLUSA).[24] The act placed stringent limits on the ability of plaintiffs to bring class-action suits in state courts against firms whose securities are traded on national stock exchanges. SLUSA not only prevents the purchasers and sellers of securities from bringing class-action fraud claims under state securities laws, but also applies to investors who are fraudulently induced to hold on to their securities.[25]

Regulation of Proxy Statements

Section 14(a) of the Securities Exchange Act of 1934 regulates the solicitation of proxies (see Chapter 30) from shareholders of Section 12 companies. The SEC regulates the content of proxy statements. Whoever solicits a proxy must fully and accurately disclose in the proxy statement all of the facts that are pertinent to the matter on which the shareholders are to vote. SEC Rule 14a-9 is similar to the antifraud provisions of SEC Rule 10b-5. Remedies for violations are extensive, ranging from injunctions to prevent a vote from being taken to monetary damages.

Violations of the 1934 Act

As mentioned earlier, violations of Section 10(b) of the Securities Exchange Act of 1934 and SEC Rule 10b-5, including insider trading, may be subject to criminal or civil liability.

Scienter Requirement

For either criminal or civil sanctions to be imposed, *scienter* must exist—that is, the violator must have had an intent to defraud or knowledge of her or his misconduct (see Chapter 12). *Scienter* can be proved by showing that the defendant made false statements or wrongfully failed to disclose material facts. In some situations, *scienter* can even be proved by showing that the defendant was consciously reckless as to the truth or falsity of his or her statements.

24. Pub. L. No. 105-353. This act amended many sections of Title 15 of the *United States Code*.

25. *Merrill Lynch, Pierce, Fenner & Smith, Inc. v. Dabit*, 547 U.S. 71, 126 S.Ct. 1503, 164 L.Ed.2d 179 (2006). This Supreme Court decision forms the basis of the *Case Analysis Question* on page 826.

CASE EXAMPLE 31.7 Alvin Gebhart and Jack Archer started a business venture purchasing mobile home parks (MHPs) from owners and converting them to resident ownership. They formed MHP Conversions, LP, to facilitate the conversion process and issue promissory notes that were sold to investors to raise funds for the purchases. Archer ran the MHP program, and Gebhart sold the promissory notes. Gebhart sold nearly $2.4 million in MHP promissory notes to clients, who bought notes based on the Gebhart's positive statements about the investment.

During the time Gebhart was selling the notes, however, he never actually looked into the finances of the MHP program. He relied entirely on information that Archer gave him, some of which was not true. When Gebhart was later sued for securities fraud, a federal appellate court concluded that there was sufficient evidence of *scienter* (see page 311). Gebhart knew that he had no knowledge of the financial affairs of MHP, and he had been consciously reckless as to the truth or falsity of his statements about investing in MHP.[26] •

Scienter Not Required for Section 16(b) Violations

Violations of Section 16(b) include the sale by insiders of stock acquired less than six months before the sale (or less than six months after the sale if selling short). These violations are subject to civil sanctions. Liability under Section 16(b) is strict liability. Neither *scienter* nor negligence is required.

Criminal Penalties

For violations of Section 10(b) and Rule 10b-5, an individual may be fined up to $5 million, imprisoned for up to twenty years, or both. A partnership or a corporation may be fined up to $25 million. Section 807 of the Sarbanes-Oxley Act provides that for a *willful* violation of the 1934 act, the violator may be imprisoned for up to twenty-five years in addition to being fined.

For a defendant to be convicted in a criminal prosecution under the securities laws, there can be no reasonable doubt that the defendant knew he or she was acting wrongfully. A jury is not allowed merely to speculate that the defendant may have acted willfully. **CASE EXAMPLE 31.8** Martha Stewart, founder of a well-known media and homemaking empire, was charged with intentionally deceiving investors based on public statements she made. In 2001, Stewart's stockbroker allegedly had informed Stewart that the head of ImClone Systems, Inc., was selling his shares in that company. Stewart then sold her ImClone shares. The next day, ImClone announced that the U.S. Food and Drug Administration had not approved Erbitux, the company's greatly anticipated medication.

After the government began investigating Stewart's ImClone trades, she publicly stated that she had previously instructed her stockbroker to sell her ImClone stock if the price fell to $60 per share. The government prosecutor claimed that Stewart's statement showed she had the intent to deceive investors. The court, however, acquitted Stewart on this charge because "to find the essential element of criminal intent beyond a reasonable doubt, a rational juror would have to speculate."[27] •

Civil Sanctions

The SEC can also bring suit in a federal district court against anyone violating or aiding in a violation of the 1934 act or SEC rules by purchasing or selling a security while in the possession of material nonpublic information.[28] The violation must occur on or through the facilities of a national securities exchange or from or through a broker or dealer.

---

26. *Gebhart v. SEC*, 595 F.3d 1034 (9th Cir. 2010).

27. *United States v. Stewart*, 305 F.Supp.2d 368 (S.D.N.Y. 2004). Stewart was later convicted on other charges relating to her ImClone trading that did not require proof of intent.

28. The Insider Trading Sanctions Act of 1984, 15 U.S.C. Section 78u(d)(2)(A).

A court may assess a penalty for as much as triple the profits gained or the loss avoided by the guilty party.[29] The Insider Trading and Securities Fraud Enforcement Act of 1988 increased the number of persons who may be subject to civil liability for insider trading and gave the SEC authority to pay monetary rewards to informants.[30]

Private parties may also sue violators of Section 10(b) and Rule 10b-5. A private party may obtain rescission (cancellation) of a contract to buy securities or damages to the extent of the violator's illegal profits. Those found liable have a right to seek contribution from those who share responsibility for the violations, including accountants, attorneys, and corporations. For violations of Section 16(b), a corporation can bring an action to recover the short-swing profits.

State Securities Laws

Today, every state has its own corporate securities laws, or "blue sky laws," that regulate the offer and sale of securities within its borders. (As mentioned in Chapter 11, the phrase *blue sky laws* dates to a 1917 decision by the United States Supreme Court in which the Court declared that the purpose of such laws was to prevent "speculative schemes which have no more basis than so many feet of 'blue sky.' ")[31] Article 8 of the Uniform Commercial Code, which has been adopted by all of the states, also imposes various requirements relating to the purchase and sale of securities.

LEARNING OBJECTIVE 4
What are some of the features of state securities laws?

Requirements under State Securities Laws

Typically, state laws have disclosure requirements and antifraud provisions, many of which are patterned after Section 10(b) of the Securities Exchange Act of 1934 and SEC Rule 10b-5. State laws also provide for the registration of securities offered or issued for sale within the state and impose disclosure requirements.

Methods of registration, required disclosures, and exemptions from registration vary among states. Unless an exemption from registration is applicable, issuers must register or qualify their stock with the appropriate state official, often called a *corporations commissioner.* Additionally, most state securities laws regulate securities brokers and dealers.

Concurrent Regulation

State securities laws apply mainly to intrastate transactions. Since the adoption of the 1933 and 1934 federal securities acts, the state and federal governments have regulated securities concurrently. Issuers must comply with both federal and state securities laws, and exemptions from federal law are not exemptions from state laws.

The dual federal and state system has not always worked well, particularly during the early 1990s, when the securities markets underwent considerable expansion. Today, most of the duplicate regulations have been eliminated, and the SEC has exclusive power to regulate most national securities activities. The National Conference of Commissioners on Uniform State Laws also substantially revised the Uniform Securities Act in 2002 to coordinate state and federal securities regulation and enforcement efforts. Seventeen states have adopted the most recent version of the Uniform Securities Act.[32]

KNOW THIS

Federal securities laws do not take priority over state securities laws.

---

29. Profit or loss is defined as "the difference between the purchase or sale price of the security and the value of that security as measured by the trading price of the security at a reasonable period of time after public dissemination of the nonpublic information." 15 U.S.C. Section 78u(d)(2)(C).

30. 15 U.S.C. Section 78u-1.

31. *Hall v. Geiger-Jones Co.,* 242 U.S. 539, 37 S.Ct. 217, 61 L.Ed. 480 (1917).

32. At the time this book went to press, the Uniform Securities Act had been adopted in Georgia, Hawaii, Idaho, Indiana, Iowa, Kansas, Maine, Michigan, Minnesota, Mississippi, Missouri, New Mexico, Oklahoma, South Carolina, South Dakota, Vermont, and Wisconsin, as well as in the U.S. Virgin Islands.

Corporate Governance

Corporate Governance A set of policies specifying the rights and responsibilities of the various participants in a corporation and spelling out the rules and procedures for making corporate decisions.

Corporate governance can be narrowly defined as the relationship between a corporation and its shareholders. Some argue for a broader definition—that corporate governance specifies the rights and responsibilities among different participants in the corporation, such as the board of directors, managers, shareholders, and other stakeholders, and spells out the rules and procedures for making decisions on corporate affairs. Regardless of the way it is defined, effective corporate governance requires more than just compliance with laws and regulations. (For a discussion of corporate governance in other nations, see this chapter's *Beyond Our Borders* feature below.)

Effective corporate governance is essential in large corporations because corporate ownership (by shareholders) is separated from corporate control (by officers and managers). Under these circumstances, officers and managers may attempt to advance their own interests at the expense of the shareholders. The well-publicized corporate scandals in the first decade of the 2000s clearly illustrate the reasons for concern about managerial opportunism.

Attempts at Aligning the Interests of Officers with Those of Shareholders

Stock Option A right to buy a given number of shares of stock at a set price, usually within a specified time period.

Some corporations have sought to align the financial interests of their officers with those of the company's shareholders by providing the officers with **stock options,** which enable them to purchase shares of the corporation's stock at a set price. When the market price rises above that level, the officers can sell their shares for a profit. Because a stock's market price generally increases as the corporation prospers, the options give the officers a financial stake in the corporation's well-being and supposedly encourage them to work hard for the benefit of the shareholders.

Options have turned out to be an imperfect device for providing effective governance, however. Executives in some companies have been tempted to "cook" the company's books in order to keep share prices higher so that they could sell their stock for a profit. Executives in other corporations have experienced no losses when share prices dropped because their options were "repriced" so that they did not suffer from the share price decline. Thus, although stock options theoretically can motivate officers to protect shareholder interests, stock option plans have sometimes become a way for officers to take advantage of shareholders.

With stock options generally failing to work as planned, there has been an outcry for more "outside" directors (those with no formal employment affiliation with the company). The theory is that independent directors will more closely monitor the actions of corporate

BEYOND OUR BORDERS Corporate Governance in Other Nations

Corporate governance has become an issue of concern not only for U.S. corporations, but also for corporate entities around the world. With the globalization of business, a corporation's bad acts (or lack of control systems) can have far-reaching consequences.

Different models of corporate governance exist, often depending on the degree of capitalism in the particular nation. In the United States, corporate governance tends to give priority to shareholders' interests. This approach encourages significant innovation and cost and quality competition.

In contrast, the coordinated model of governance that prevails in continental Europe and Japan gives priority to the interests of so-called stakeholders—employees, managers, suppliers, customers, and the community. The coordinated model still encourages innovation and cost and quality competition, but not to the same extent as the U.S. model.

Critical Thinking

Why does the presence of a capitalist system affect a nation's perspective on corporate governance?

officers. Hence, today we see more boards with outside directors. Note, though, that outside directors may not be truly independent of corporate officers. They may be friends or business associates of the leading officers.

ETHICAL ISSUE

Should shareholders have more control over corporate officers' compensation? Over the last several years, executive compensation has become a hotly debated issue. Many critics argue that the chief executive officers (CEOs) of public companies are paid too much, especially in comparison with the wages earned by the average worker.

The Dodd-Frank Wall Street Reform and Consumer Protection Act includes a "say-on-pay" provision that gives shareholders the right to vote on executive compensation for senior executives at every public U.S. company. In 2009, shareholders defeated a pay package for a CEO for the first time, voting against proposed compensation of more than $50 million for Ray Irani, the head of Occidental Petroleum. Two years later, shareholders voted to reject executive pay arrangements at thirty-five U.S. firms.

These votes on executive pay are nonbinding, however—the board of directors does not have to abide by them. Furthermore, more than 90 percent of shareholder votes on executive pay have been in favor of the proposed compensation plans. Despite the "say on pay" provision, the average compensation for a CEO in 2011 was almost $10 million, up 6 percent from the previous year. The average U.S. employee would have to work almost 250 years to match that salary.

The Goal Is to Promote Accountability

> "Honesty is the single most important factor having a direct bearing on the final success of an individual, corporation, or product."
>
> Ed McMahon, 1923–2009 (American entertainer)

Effective corporate governance standards are designed to address problems (such as those briefly discussed above) and to motivate officers to make decisions that promote the financial interests of the company's shareholders. Generally, corporate governance entails corporate decision-making structures that monitor employees (particularly officers) to ensure that they are acting for the benefit of the shareholders. Thus, corporate governance involves, at a minimum:

1. The audited reporting of financial progress at the corporation, so managers can be evaluated.
2. Legal protections for shareholders, so violators of the law, who attempt to take advantage of shareholders, can be punished for misbehavior and victims may recover damages for any associated losses.

The Company Benefits

Effective corporate governance may have considerable practical significance. Firms that are more accountable to shareholders typically report higher profits, higher sales growth, higher firm value, and other economic advantages. Thus, a corporation that provides better corporate governance in the form of greater accountability to investors may also have a higher valuation than a corporation that is less concerned about governance.

Corporations that promote diversity in the workplace, and especially in management, may also experience increased profits, growth, and value. Nevertheless, one aspect of corporations around the world still is not very diverse—see this chapter's *Law, Diversity, and Business: Managerial Implications* feature on the following page.

Stock options are valuable when the market price of a company's share rises greatly. Why?

(AP Photo/Richard Drew, File)

Governance and Corporation Law

State corporation statutes set up the legal framework for corporate governance. Under the corporate law of Delaware, where most major companies incorporate, all corporations must have certain structures of corporate governance in place. The most important

LAW, DIVERSITY, AND BUSINESS: MANAGERIAL IMPLICATIONS

THE WORLDWIDE LACK OF WOMEN ON BOARDS OF DIRECTORS

Certainly, the saying "It's a man's world" applies to corporate boardrooms around the world. In France, Germany, Great Britain, and the United States, women account for only 10 to 15 percent of the directors of publicly traded companies. The average for the twenty-seven members of the European Union (EU) is slightly above 10 percent. In Europe, Norway and Sweden stand out with more than 30 percent and 25 percent, respectively. Elsewhere, boards of directors in Brazil, China, India, and Russia average only about 5 percent female members.

More Female Board Members Lead to Higher Profits The absence of women from corporate boards is somewhat surprising because there is evidence that suggests companies may benefit when they have more female board members. The consulting firm McKinsey & Company looked at almost one hundred public companies in Europe that had a high proportion of women in senior management positions. Comparing the financial performance of those firms with the average for firms in the same industry, McKinsey concluded that firms with more women in "high places" had a higher rate of return on investment, higher operating profits, and higher share prices for their stock.

Are Mandatory Quotas the Way to Go? One way to increase the number of women on corporate boards is to mandate that companies add more women. Some countries are doing exactly that. France recently passed a law that requires public companies to reserve 40 percent of board seats for women by 2017. Norway and Spain already have similar legislation, and Germany is considering such a law. The European Parliament recently passed a resolution calling for all nations in the EU to enact legislation that would require major public companies to have a minimum of 40 percent female board members by 2020.

Those in favor of such quotas believe that they are long overdue. They argue that women bring a different perspective to board meetings and that the current dearth of women in boardrooms is due to subtle gender discrimination.

Others point out that quotas might harm some companies. If companies cannot find sufficient well-trained women to fill their quotas, they may have to appoint inexperienced women to their boards. In Norway, for example, women accounted for only 9 percent of directors in 2003. When Norwegian companies were required to increase this percentage to 40 percent within five years, many firms had to promote women who were less experienced than the directors they were replacing. Some of those companies subsequently suffered a drop in their market capitalization.

Business Implications *In the United States today, women earn the majority of master's degrees and hold more than half of the entry-level jobs in major U.S. companies. Corporate managers need to develop more flexible schedules and career paths for women who want to balance work and family. In the process, the "fast track" to upper management positions could be modified to enable more women to eventually become board members.*

structure, of course, is the board of directors because the board makes the major decisions about the future of the corporation.

The Board of Directors Under corporate law, a corporation must have a board of directors elected by the shareholders. Almost anyone can become a director, though some organizations, such as the New York Stock Exchange, require certain standards of service for directors of their listed corporations.

Directors are responsible for ensuring that the corporation's officers are operating wisely and in the exclusive interest of shareholders. The directors receive reports from the officers and give them managerial directions. In reality, though, corporate directors devote a relatively small amount of time to monitoring officers.

Ideally, shareholders would monitor the directors' supervision of the officers. In practice, however, it can be difficult for shareholders to monitor directors and hold them responsible for corporate failings. Although the directors can be sued for failing to do their jobs effectively, directors are rarely held personally liable.

The Audit Committee A crucial committee of the board of directors is the *audit committee,* which oversees the corporation's accounting and financial reporting processes, including both internal and outside auditors. Unless the committee members have sufficient expertise and are willing to spend the time to carefully examine the corporation's bookkeeping methods, however, the audit committee may be ineffective.

The audit committee also oversees the corporation's "internal controls," which are the measures taken to ensure that reported results are accurate. As an example, these controls—carried out largely by the company's internal auditing staff—help to determine whether a corporation's debts are collectible. If the debts are not collectible, it is up to the audit committee to make sure that the corporation's financial officers do not simply pretend that payment will eventually be made.

The Compensation Committee Another important committee of the board of directors is the *compensation committee.* This committee monitors and determines the compensation the company's officers are paid. As part of this process, it is responsible for assessing the officers' performance and for designing a compensation system that will better align the officers' interests with those of the shareholders.

The Sarbanes-Oxley Act

As discussed in Chapter 7, in 2002 following a series of corporate scandals, Congress passed the Sarbanes-Oxley Act. The act separately addresses certain issues relating to corporate governance. Generally, the act attempts to increase corporate accountability by imposing strict disclosure requirements and harsh penalties for violations of securities laws. Among other things, the act requires chief corporate executives to take responsibility for the accuracy of financial statements and reports that are filed with the SEC.

Additionally, the act requires that certain financial and stock-transaction reports be filed with the SEC earlier than was required under the previous rules. The act also created a new entity, called the Public Company Accounting Oversight Board, which regulates and oversees public accounting firms. Other provisions of the act established private civil actions and expanded the SEC's remedies in administrative and civil actions.

Because of the importance of this act for corporate leaders and for those dealing with securities transactions, we present excerpts and explanatory comments in Appendix D at the end of this text. We also highlight some of its key provisions relating to corporate accountability in Exhibit 31.3 on the next page.

Michael Oxley is a former member of the U.S. House of Representatives and vice president of NASDAQ, the over-the-counter stock exchange. When in Congress, he cosponsored legislation that imposed large compliance costs on publicly held companies. What is the name of that legislation?

(Fred Prouser/Reuters/Landov)

More Internal Controls and Accountability The Sarbanes-Oxley Act also introduced direct *federal* corporate governance requirements for public companies (companies whose shares are traded in the public securities markets). The law addressed many of the corporate governance procedures just discussed and created new requirements in an attempt to make the system work more effectively. The requirements deal with independent monitoring of company officers by both the board of directors and auditors.

Sections 302 and 404 of Sarbanes-Oxley require high-level managers (the most senior officers) to establish and maintain an effective system of internal controls, including "disclosure controls and procedures" to ensure that company financial reports are accurate and timely and to document financial results prior to reporting. Moreover, senior management must reassess the system's effectiveness annually. Some companies

Exhibit 31.3 Some Key Provisions of the Sarbanes-Oxley Act Relating to Corporate Accountability

Certification Requirements—Under Section 906 of the Sarbanes-Oxley Act, the chief executive officers (CEOs) and chief financial officers (CFOs) of most major companies listed on public stock exchanges must certify financial statements that are filed with the SEC. CEOs and CFOs have to certify that filed financial reports "fully comply" with SEC requirements and that all of the information reported "fairly represents in all material respects, the financial conditions and results of operations of the issuer."

Under Section 302 of the act, CEOs and CFOs of reporting companies are required to certify that a signing officer reviewed each quarterly and annual filing with the SEC and that none contained untrue statements of material fact. Also, the signing officer or officers must certify that they have established an internal control system to identify all material information and that any deficiencies in the system were disclosed to the auditors.

Effectiveness of Internal Controls on Financial Reporting—Under Section 404(a), all public companies are required to assess the effectiveness of their internal control over financial reporting. Section 404(b) requires independent auditors to report on management's assessment of internal controls, but companies with a public float of less than $75 million are exempted from this requirement.

Loans to Directors and Officers—Section 402 prohibits any reporting company, as well as any private company that is filing an initial public offering, from making personal loans to directors and executive officers (with a few limited exceptions, such as for certain consumer and housing loans).

Protection for Whistleblowers—Section 806 protects "whistleblowers"—employees who report ("blow the whistle" on) securities violations by their employers—from being fired or in any way discriminated against by their employers.

Blackout Periods—Section 306 prohibits certain types of securities transactions during "blackout periods"—periods during which the issuer's ability to purchase, sell, or otherwise transfer funds in individual account plans (such as pension funds) is suspended.

Enhanced Penalties for—

- *Violations of Section 906 Certification Requirements*—A CEO or CFO who certifies a financial report or statement filed with the SEC knowing that the report or statement does not fulfill all of the requirements of Section 906 will be subject to criminal penalties of up to $1 million in fines, ten years in prison, or both. *Willful* violators of the certification requirements may be subject to $5 million in fines, twenty years in prison, or both.
- *Violations of the Securities Exchange Act of 1934*—Penalties for securities fraud under the 1934 act were also increased (as discussed earlier in this chapter). Individual violators may be fined up to $5 million, imprisoned for up to twenty years, or both. *Willful* violators may be imprisoned for up to twenty-five years in addition to being fined.
- *Destruction or Alteration of Documents*—Anyone who alters, destroys, or conceals documents or otherwise obstructs any official proceeding will be subject to fines, imprisonment for up to twenty years, or both.
- *Other Forms of White-Collar Crime*—The act stiffened the penalties for certain criminal violations, such as federal mail and wire fraud, and ordered the U.S. Sentencing Commission to revise the sentencing guidelines for white-collar crimes (see Chapter 6).

Statute of Limitations for Securities Fraud—Section 804 provides that a private right of action for securities fraud may be brought no later than two years after the discovery of the violation or five years after the violation, whichever is earlier.

had to take expensive steps to bring their internal controls up to the new federal standard. After the act was passed, hundreds of companies reported that they had identified and corrected shortcomings in their internal control systems.

Exemptions for Smaller Companies

The Sarbanes-Oxley Act initially required all public companies to have an independent auditor file a report with the SEC on management's assessment of internal controls. In 2010, however, Congress enacted an exemption for smaller companies in an effort to reduce compliance costs. Public companies with a market capitalization, or public float (price times total shares publicly owned), of less than $75 million no longer need to have an auditor report on management's assessment of internal controls.

LEARNING OBJECTIVE 5
What certification requirements does the Sarbanes-Oxley Act impose on corporate executives?

Certification and Monitoring Requirements

Section 906 requires that chief executive officers (CEOs) and chief financial officers (CFOs) certify that the information in the corporate financial statements "fairly represents in all material respects, the financial conditions and results of operations of the issuer." These corporate officers are subject to both civil and criminal penalties for violation of this section. This requirement makes officers directly accountable for the accuracy of their financial reporting and avoids any "ignorance defense" if shortcomings are later discovered.

Sarbanes-Oxley also includes requirements to improve directors' monitoring of officers' activities. All members of the corporate audit committee for public companies must be outside directors. The New York Stock Exchange has a similar rule that also extends to the board's compensation committee. The audit committee must have a written charter that sets out its duties and provides for performance appraisal. At least one "financial expert" must serve on the audit committee, which must hold executive meetings without company officers being present. The audit committee must establish procedures to encourage "whistleblowers" to report violations. In addition to reviewing the internal controls, the committee also monitors the actions of the outside auditor.

Online Securities Fraud

A major problem facing the SEC today is how to enforce the antifraud provisions of the securities laws in the online environment. In 1999, in the first cases involving illegal online securities offerings, the SEC filed suit against three individuals for illegally offering securities on an Internet auction site.[33] In essence, all three indicated that their companies would go public soon and attempted to sell unregistered securities via the Web auction site. Since then, the SEC has brought a variety of Internet-related fraud cases and regularly issues interpretive releases to explain how securities laws apply in the online environment.

Online Investment Scams

"Make money your God and it will plague you like the devil."

Henry Fielding, 1707–1754 (English author)

An ongoing problem is how to curb online investment scams. As discussed in Chapter 6, the Internet has created a new vehicle for criminals to use to commit fraud and has provided them with new ways of targeting innocent investors. The criminally inclined can use spam, online newsletters and bulletin boards, chat rooms, blogs, social media, and tweets to spread false information and perpetrate fraud. For a relatively small cost, criminals can even build sophisticated Web pages to facilitate their investment scams.

Fraudulent E-Mails

There are countless variations of investment scams, most of which promise spectacular returns for small investments. A person might receive spam e-mail that falsely claims the earnings potential of a home business can "turn $5 into $60,000 in just three to six weeks." A few years ago, an investment scam claimed "your stimulus package has arrived" and promised recipients that they could make $100,000 a year using their home computers.

Although most people are dubious of the bogus claims made in spam messages, such offers can be more attractive during times of economic recession. Often, investment scams are simply the electronic version of pyramid schemes in which the participants attempt to profit solely by recruiting new participants.

Online Investment Newsletters and Forums

Hundreds of online investment newsletters provide free information on stocks. Legitimate online newsletters can help investors gather valuable information, but some of these newsletters are used for fraud. The law allows companies to pay people who write these newsletters to tout their securities, but the newsletters are required to disclose who paid for the advertising.

33. *In re Davis,* SEC Administrative File No. 3-10080 (October 20, 1999); *In re Haas,* SEC Administrative File No. 3-10081 (October 20, 1999); *In re Sitaras,* SEC Administrative File No. 3-10082 (October 20, 1999).

Many fraudsters either fail to disclose or lie about who paid them. Thus, an investor reading an online newsletter may believe that the information is unbiased, when in fact the fraudsters will directly profit by convincing investors to buy or sell particular stocks.

The same deceptive tactics can be used on online bulletin boards (such as newsgroups and usenet groups), blogs, and social networking sites, including Twitter and Facebook. While hiding their true identity, fraudsters may falsely pump up a company or reveal some "inside" information about a new product or lucrative contract to convince people to invest. By using multiple aliases on an online forum, a single person can easily create the illusion of widespread interest in a small stock.

Ponzi Schemes

Although securities fraud is increasingly occurring online, schemes conducted primarily offline have not disappeared. In recent years, the SEC has filed an increasing number of enforcement actions against perpetrators of *Ponzi schemes* (discussed on page 190 of Chapter 7).

Since 2010, the SEC has brought more than a hundred enforcement actions against nearly two hundred individuals and two hundred and fifty entities for carrying out Ponzi schemes. It has also barred more than sixty-five persons from working in the securities industry.

Offshore Fraud

Ponzi schemes sometimes target U.S. residents and convince them to invest in offshore companies or banks. **CASE EXAMPLE 31.9** In 2012, Texas billionaire R. Allen Stanford, of the Stanford Financial Group, was convicted for orchestrating a $7 billion scheme to defraud more than five thousand investors. Stanford had advised clients to buy certificates of deposit with improbably high interest rates from his Antigua-based Stanford International Bank. Although some early investors were paid returns from the funds provided by later investors, Stanford used $1.6 billion of the funds for personal purchases. He also falsified financial statements that were filed with the SEC and reportedly paid more than $100,000 in bribes to an Antigua official to ensure that the bank would not be audited.[34] •

"Risk-Free" Fraud

Another type of fraud scheme offers risk-free or low-risk investments to lure investors. **EXAMPLE 31.10** Debi Mitchom used her firm, Mitchom & Company, to fraudulently obtain at least $10 million from dozens of investors by selling securities in her special investment fund. Mitchom told investors that she had a proven track record of successful securities trading and showed them false account statements that showed artificially high balances.

In reality, Mitchom was not a registered investment adviser, had not traded any securities for several years, and had suffered substantial losses on investments she did make. Mitchom promised investors returns averaging 20 percent with minimal risk to their principal and claimed to be using an investment strategy based on short-term price trends. She used less than half of the funds entrusted to her for trading purposes and spent at least $5 million for her personal expenses. The SEC filed a complaint alleging that Mitchom and her company had engaged in a multimillion-dollar Ponzi scheme. Mitchom agreed to settle the case and return more than $7 million (plus interest) of the wrongfully acquired funds. •

34. *United States v. Stanford*, 2012 WL 1699459 (S.D.Tex. 2012).

Reviewing . . . Investor Protection, Insider Trading, and Corporate Governance

Dale Emerson served as the chief financial officer for Reliant Electric Company, a distributor of electricity serving portions of Montana and North Dakota. Reliant was in the final stages of planning a takeover of Dakota Gasworks, Inc., a natural gas distributor that operated solely within North Dakota. Emerson went on a weekend fishing trip with his uncle, Ernest Wallace. Emerson mentioned to Wallace that he had been putting in a lot of extra hours at the office planning a takeover of Dakota Gasworks. When he returned from the fishing trip, Wallace purchased $20,000 worth of Reliant stock. Three weeks later, Reliant made a tender offer to Dakota Gasworks stockholders and purchased 57 percent of Dakota Gasworks stock. Over the next two weeks, the price of Reliant stock rose 72 percent before leveling out. Wallace then sold his Reliant stock for a gross profit of $14,400. Using the information presented in the chapter, answer the following questions.

1. Would registration with the SEC be required for Dakota Gasworks securities? Why or why not?
2. Did Emerson violate Section 10(b) of the Securities Exchange Act of 1934 and SEC Rule 10b-5? Why or why not?
3. What theory or theories might a court use to hold Wallace liable for insider trading?
4. Under the Sarbanes-Oxley Act, who would be required to certify the accuracy of financial statements filed with the SEC?

DEBATE THIS Insider trading should be legalized.

Key Terms

accredited investor 805
corporate governance 816
free-writing prospectus 803
insider trading 809
investment company 805
investment contract 801
mutual fund 805
prospectus 802
SEC Rule 10b-5 808
security 799
short-swing profits 811
stock option 816
tippee 810

Chapter Summary: Investor Protection, Insider Trading, and Corporate Governance

Securities Act of 1933 (See pages 800–808.)	Prohibits fraud and stabilizes the securities industry by requiring disclosure of all essential information relating to the issuance of securities to the investing public. 1. *Registration requirements*—Securities, unless exempt, must be registered with the SEC before being offered to the public. The *registration statement* must include detailed financial information about the issuing corporation; the intended use of the proceeds of the securities being issued; and certain disclosures, such as interests of directors or officers and pending lawsuits. 2. *Prospectus*—The issuer must provide investors with a *prospectus* that describes the security being sold, the issuing corporation, and the risk attaching to the security. 3. *Exemptions*—The SEC has exempted certain offerings from the requirements of the Securities Act of 1933. Exemptions may be determined on the basis of the size of the issue, whether the offering is private or public, and whether advertising is involved. Exemptions are summarized in Exhibit 31.1 on page 804.
Securities Exchange Act of 1934 (See pages 808–815.)	Provides for the regulation and registration of securities exchanges, brokers, dealers, and national securities associations (such as the NASD). Maintains a continuous disclosure system for all corporations with securities on the securities exchanges and for those companies that have assets in excess of $10 million and five hundred or more shareholders (Section 12 companies).

Continued

Chapter Summary: Investor Protection, Insider Trading, and Corporate Governance—Continued

Securities Exchange Act of 1934—Continued	1. *SEC Rule 10b-5 [under Section 10(b) of the 1934 act]*— a. Applies to almost all trading of securities—a firm's securities do not have to be registered under the 1933 act for the 1934 act to apply. b. Applies to insider trading by corporate officers, directors, majority shareholders, and any persons receiving inside information (information not available to the public) who base their trading on this information. c. Liability for insider trading may be based on the tipper/tippee or the misappropriation theory. d. May be violated by failing to disclose "material facts" that must be disclosed under this rule. e. Liability for violations can be civil or criminal. 2. *Insider trading [under Section 16(b) of the 1934 act]*—To prevent corporate insiders from taking advantage of inside information, the 1934 act requires officers, directors, and shareholders owning 10 percent or more of the issued stock of a corporation to turn over to the corporation all short-term profits (called *short-swing profits*) realized from the purchase and sale or sale and purchase of corporate stock within any six-month period. 3. *Regulation of proxies*—The SEC regulates the content of proxy statements sent to shareholders of Section 12 companies. Section 14(a) is essentially a disclosure law, with provisions similar to the antifraud provisions of SEC Rule 10b-5.
State Securities Laws (See page 815.)	All states have corporate securities laws (*blue sky laws*) that regulate the offer and sale of securities within state borders. These laws are designed to prevent "speculative schemes which have no more basis than so many feet of 'blue sky.'" States regulate securities concurrently with the federal government. The Uniform Securities Act of 2002, which has been adopted by seventeen states and is being considered by several others, is designed to promote coordination and reduce duplication between state and federal securities regulation.
Corporate Governance (See pages 816–821.)	1. *Definition*—Corporate governance involves a set of policies specifying the rights and responsibilities of the various participants in a corporation and spelling out the rules and procedures for making decisions on corporate affairs. 2. *The need for corporate governance*—Corporate governance is necessary in large corporations because corporate ownership (by the shareholders) is separated from corporate control (by officers and managers). This separation of corporate ownership and control can often result in conflicting interests. Corporate governance standards address such issues. 3. *Sarbanes-Oxley Act*—This act attempts to increase corporate accountability by imposing strict disclosure requirements and harsh penalties for violations of securities laws.
Online Securities Fraud (See pages 821–822.)	A major problem facing the SEC today is how to enforce the antifraud provisions of the securities laws in the online environment. Internet-related forms of securities fraud include numerous types of investment scams. The SEC has brought numerous enforcement actions against perpetrators of Ponzi schemes, both online and offline.

ExamPrep

ISSUE SPOTTERS

1. When a corporation wishes to issue certain securities, it must provide sufficient information for an unsophisticated investor to evaluate the financial risk involved. Specifically, the law imposes liability for making a false statement or omission that is "material." What sort of information would an investor consider material? **(See page 809.)**
2. Lee is an officer of Magma Oil, Inc. Lee knows that a Magma geologist has just discovered a new deposit of oil. Can Lee take advantage of this information to buy and sell Magma stock? Why or why not? **(See page 809.)**

—Check your answers to the Issue Spotters against the answers provided in Appendix E at the end of this text.

BEFORE THE TEST

Go to www.cengagebrain.com, enter the ISBN 9781133273561, and click on "Find" to locate this textbook's Web site. Then, click on "Access Now" under "Study Tools," and select Chapter 31 at the top. There, you will find a Practice Quiz that you can take to assess your mastery of the concepts in this chapter, as well as Flashcards, a Glossary of important terms, and Video Questions (when assigned).

For Review

Answers to the even-numbered questions in this For Review section can be found in Appendix F at the end of this text.

1. What is meant by the term *securities*?
2. What are the two major statutes regulating the securities industry?
3. What is insider trading? Why is it prohibited?
4. What are some of the features of state securities laws?
5. What certification requirements does the Sarbanes-Oxley Act impose on corporate executives?

Business Scenarios and Case Problems

31–1 Registration Requirements. Langley Brothers, Inc., a corporation incorporated and doing business in Kansas, decides to sell common stock worth $1 million to the public. The stock will be sold only within the state of Kansas. Joseph Langley, the chair of the board, says the offering need not be registered with the Securities and Exchange Commission. His brother, Harry, disagrees. Who is right? Explain. **(See page 802.)**

31–2 Question with Sample Answer—Registration of Stock. Huron Corp. has 300,000 common shares outstanding. The owners of these outstanding shares live in several different states. Huron has decided to split the 300,000 shares two for one. Will Huron Corp. have to file a registration statement and prospectus on the 300,000 new shares to be issued as a result of the split? Explain. **(See page 802.)**

—For a sample answer to Question 31–2, go to Appendix G at the end of this text.

31–3 Violations of the 1934 Act. To comply with accounting principles, a company that engages in software development must either "expense" the cost (record it immediately on the company's financial statement) or "capitalize" it (record it as a cost incurred in increments over time). If the project is in the pre- or post-development stage, the cost must be expensed. Otherwise it may be capitalized. Capitalizing a cost makes a company look more profitable in the short term. Digimarc Corp. announced that it had improperly capitalized software development costs over at least the previous eighteen months. The errors resulted in $2.7 million in overstated earnings, requiring a restatement of prior financial statements. Zucco Partners, LLC, which had bought Digimarc stock within the relevant period, filed a suit in a federal district court against the firm. Zucco claimed that it could show that there had been disagreements within Digimarc over its accounting. Is this sufficient to establish a violation of SEC Rule 10b-5? Why or why not? [*Zucco Partners, LLC v. Digimarc Corp.*, 552 F.3d 981 (9th Cir. 2009)] **(See pages 813–815.)**

31–4 Insider Trading. Jabil Circuit, Inc., is a publicly traded electronics and technology company. A group of shareholders who owned Jabil stock from 2001 to 2007 sued the company and its auditors, directors, and officers for insider trading. Stock options were a part of Jabil's compensation for executives. Sometimes, stock options were backdated to a point in time when the stock price was lower, so the options would be worth more to certain company executives. Backdating is not illegal so long as it is reported, but Jabil did not report the fact that backdating had occurred. Thus, expenses were underreported, and net income was overstated by millions of dollars. The shareholders claimed that by rigging the stock price through backdating, the executives had engaged in insider trading and could pick favorable purchase prices and that there was a general practice of selling stock before unfavorable news about the company was reported to the public. The shareholders, however, had no specific information about these stock trades or when (or even if) a particular executive was aware of any accounting errors during the time of any backdating purchases. Were the shareholders' allegations sufficient to assert that insider trading had occurred under Rule 10b-5? Why or why not? [*Edward J. Goodman Life Income Trust v. Jabil Circuit, Inc.*, 594 F.3d 783 (11th Cir. 2010)] **(See page 809.)**

31–5 Case Problem with Sample Answer—Violations of the 1934 Act. Matrixx Initiatives, Inc., makes and sells over-the-counter pharmaceutical products. Its core brand is Zicam, which accounts for 70 percent of its sales. Matrixx received reports that some consumers had lost their sense of smell (a condition called *anosmia*) after using Zicam Cold Remedy. Four product liability suits were filed against Matrixx, seeking damages for anosmia. In public statements relating to revenues and product safety, however, Matrixx did not reveal this information. James Siracusano and other Matrixx investors filed a suit in a federal district court against the company and its executives under Section 10(b) of the Securities Exchange Act of 1934 and SEC Rule 10b-5, claiming that the statements were misleading because they did not disclose the information about the product liability suits. Matrixx argued that to be material, information must consist of a statistically significant number of adverse events that require disclosure. Because Siracusano's claim did not allege that Matrixx knew of a statistically significant number of adverse events, the company contended that the claim should be dismissed. What is the standard for materiality in this context? Should Siracusano's claim be dismissed? Explain. [*Matrixx Initiatives, Inc. v. Siracusano*, __ U.S. __, 131 S.Ct. 1309, 179 L.Ed.2d 398 (2011)] **(See pages 813–815.)**

—For a sample answer to Problem 31–5, go to Appendix H at the end of this text.

31–6 **Disclosure under SEC Rule 10b-5.** Dodona I, LLC, invested $4 million in two securities offerings from Goldman, Sachs & Co. The investments were in collateralized debt obligations (CDOs). Their value depended on residential mortgage-backed securities (RMBS), whose value in turn depended on the performance of subprime residential mortgages. Before marketing the CDOs, Goldman had noticed several "red flags" relating to investments in the subprime market, in which it had invested heavily. To limit its risk, Goldman began betting against subprime mortgages, RMBS, and CDOs, including the CDOs it had sold to Dodona. In an internal e-mail, one Goldman official commented that the company had managed to "make some lemonade from some big old lemons." Nevertheless, Goldman's marketing materials provided only boilerplate statements about the risks of investing in the securities. The CDOs were later downgraded to junk status, and Dodona suffered a major loss while Goldman profited. Assuming that Goldman did not affirmatively misrepresent any facts about the CDOs, can Dodona still recover under SEC Rule 10b-5? If so, how? [*Dodona I, LLC v. Goldman, Sachs & Co.,* 847 F.Supp.2d 624 (S.D.N.Y. 2012)] **(See page 809.)**

31–7 **A Question of Ethics—Violations of the 1934 Act.** Melvin Lyttle told John Montana and Paul Knight about a "Trading Program" that purportedly would buy and sell securities in deals that were fully insured, as well as monitored and controlled by the Federal Reserve Board. Without checking the details or even verifying whether the Program existed, Montana and Knight, with Lyttle's help, began to sell interests in the Program to investors. For a minimum investment of $1 million, the investors were promised extraordinary rates of return—from 10 percent to as much as 100 percent per week—without risk. They were also told that the Program would "utilize banks that can ensure full bank integrity of The Transaction whose undertaking[s] are in complete harmony with international banking rules and protocol and who [sic] guarantee maximum security of a Funder's Capital Placement Amount." Nothing was required but the investors' funds and their silence—the Program was to be kept secret. Over a four-month period, Montana raised nearly $23 million from twenty-two investors. The promised gains did not accrue, however. Instead, Montana, Lyttle, and Knight depleted the investors' funds in high-risk trades or spent the funds on themselves. [*SEC v. Montana,* 464 F.Supp.2d 772 (S.D.Ind. 2006)] **(See pages 813–815.)**

1. The Securities and Exchange Commission (SEC) filed a suit against Montana alleging violations of Section 10(b) and SEC Rule 10b-5. What is required to establish a violation of these laws? Explain how and why the facts in this case meet, or fail to meet, these requirements.
2. Ultimately, about half of the investors recouped the amount they had invested. Should the others be considered at least partly responsible for their own losses? Discuss.

Critical Thinking and Writing Assignments

31–8 **Case Analysis Question.** Go to Appendix I at the end of this text and examine the excerpt of Case No. 6, *Merrill Lynch, Pierce, Fenner & Smith, Inc. v. Dabit.* Review and then brief the case, making sure that your brief answers the following questions.

1. **Issue:** The dispute in this case centered on whether a certain federal statute covered the claims of a certain class of investors who had allegedly been the victims of fraud. What was the statute, who were the investors, and how were they allegedly defrauded?
2. **Rule of Law:** On what "requisite showing" did the United States Supreme Court base its decision?
3. **Applying the Rule of Law:** What were the reasons for the Court's conclusion? What rule of statutory interpretation supported this reasoning? How did the purpose of the statute influence its application?
4. **Conclusion:** How did the Court's ruling affect the investors' claims?

31–9 **Business Law Critical Thinking Group Assignment.** Karel Svoboda, a credit officer for Rogue Bank, evaluated and approved his employer's extensions of credit to clients. These responsibilities gave Svoboda access to nonpublic information about the clients' earnings, performance, acquisitions, and business plans from confidential memos, e-mail, and other sources. Svoboda devised a scheme with Alena Robles, an independent accountant, to use this information to trade securities. Pursuant to their scheme, Robles traded in the securities of more than twenty different companies and profited by more than $2 million. Svoboda also executed trades for his own profit of more than $800,000, despite their agreement that Robles would do all of the trading. Aware that their scheme violated Rogue Bank's policy, they attempted to conduct their trades to avoid suspicion. When the bank questioned Svoboda about his actions, he lied, refused to cooperate, and was fired.

1. The first group will determine whether Svoboda or Robles committed any crimes.
2. The second group will decide whether Svoboda or Robles are subject to civil liability. If so, who could file a suit and on what ground? What are the possible sanctions?
3. A third group will identify any defenses that Svoboda or Robles could raise, and determine their likelihood of success.

UNIT 5 Business Organizations

Business Case Study with Dissenting Opinion

Notz v. Everett Smith Group, Ltd.

This *Business Case Study with Dissenting Opinion* examines *Notz v. Everett Smith Group, Ltd.*,[1] in which a minority shareholder claimed that he was excluded from some of the benefits of participating in the corporation. The shareholder asserted that the majority shareholder and the board of directors, which was controlled by the majority shareholder, had breached their fiduciary duties to the minority shareholder and to the firm (see pages 791 and 792 in Chapter 30). The court had to decide whether the minority shareholder could bring a suit directly to recover personally from the directors or whether he was limited to bringing a shareholder's derivative suit on behalf of the corporation (see pages 789 and 790 in Chapter 30).

Case Background

Albert Trostel & Sons (ATS) began as a tannery in Milwaukee, Wisconsin, in the 1800s. Over the decades, ATS acquired subsidiaries and expanded into the production of rubber and plastics. Everett Smith came to work for ATS in 1938, later became its president, and eventually gained control of the company. Smith formed Everett Smith Group, Ltd., which owned 88.9 percent of ATS by 2003. Edward Notz owned 5.5 percent, and others owned the rest. All of the members of ATS's board of directors were either officers or directors of the Smith Group.

In 2004, ATS had an opportunity to acquire Dickten & Masch, a competing thermoplastics maker. The ATS board chose not to act. Instead, the Smith Group, which had no direct holdings in the plastics field, acquired Dickten & Masch. Within months, the Smith Group's new affiliate bought the assets of ATS's plastics subsidiary, Trostel Specialty Elastomers Group, Inc. (Trostel SEG), from ATS.

Notz filed a suit in a Wisconsin state court against the Smith Group, alleging breach of fiduciary duty for stripping ATS of its most important assets and diverting the corporate opportunity to buy Dickten & Masch. The court dismissed the claim, and a state intermediate appellate court affirmed. Notz appealed to the Wisconsin Supreme Court.

Majority Opinion

N. Patrick *CROOKS*, J. [Judge]

* * * *

Notz's claims of breach of fiduciary duty are primarily based on the series of transactions in which the Smith Group acquired two plastics companies. The allegations are that the Smith Group, as ATS's majority shareholder, rejected the opportunity ATS had to buy Dickten & Masch; the Smith Group subsequently bought Dickten & Masch itself; and the Smith Group, in its capacity as majority shareholder, orchestrated the sale of ATS's valuable plastics group, Trostel SEG, to its own new acquisition.

The question is whether those allegations support direct claims for breach of fiduciary duty to a minority shareholder. * * * The Smith Group argues that * * * these are derivative claims; Notz argues that * * * these are direct claims.

* * * *Though each shareholder has an individual right to be treated fairly by the board of directors, when the injury from such actions is primarily to the corporation, there can be no direct claim by minority shareholders.* [Emphasis added.]

* * * It is true the fiduciary duty of a director is owed to the individual stockholders as well as to the corporation. Directors in this state may not use their position of trust to further their private interests. Thus, where some individual right of a stockholder is being impaired by the improper acts of a director, the stockholder can bring a direct suit

1. 316 Wis.2d 640, 764 N.W.2d 904 (2009).

Business Case Study with Dissenting Opinion—Continues next page

Business Case Study with Dissenting Opinion—Continued

on his own behalf because it is his individual right that is being violated. However, a right of action that belongs to the corporation cannot be pursued as a direct claim by an individual stockholder. * * * *Even where the injury to the corporation results in harm to a shareholder, it won't transform an action from a derivative to a direct one* * * * . That such primary and direct injury to a corporation may have a subsequent impact on the value of the stockholders' shares is clear, but that is not enough to create a right to bring a direct, rather than derivative, action. Where the injury to the corporation is the primary injury, and any injury to stockholders secondary, it is the derivative action alone that can be brought and maintained. That is the general rule, and, if it were to be abandoned, there would be no reason left for the concept of derivative actions for the redress of wrongs to a corporation. [Emphasis added.]

* * * *

Notz alleges self-dealing on the part of the majority shareholder, but * * * a shareholder-director's self-dealing [does not] transform an action that primarily injures the corporation into one that primarily injures a shareholder.

We agree with the Smith Group that breach of fiduciary duty claims, based on the lost opportunity to purchase one company and the sale of a subsidiary with great growth potential, are [derivative claims]. Our analysis * * * centers on a determination of whether the primary injury is to the corporation or to the shareholder. * * * An injury primarily * * * to an individual shareholder [is] one which affects a shareholder's rights in a manner distinct from the effect upon other shareholders. We agree with the court of appeals that the allegations here are essentially that the Smith Group stripped ATS of its most important assets and engaged in various acts of self-dealing, and that those are allegations of injury primarily to ATS. * * * All of the shareholders of ATS were affected equally by the loss of the opportunity to acquire Dickten & Masch and by the sale of Trostel SEG, the plastics division.

* * * *

* * * We agree with the court of appeals that the claims of harm alleged—the loss of a corporate opportunity and the sale of a subsidiary with high growth potential—caused harm primarily to the corporation, and thus we affirm the dismissal of Notz's direct claim of breach of fiduciary duty as to those allegations.

Dissenting Opinion

Ann Walsh *BRADLEY*, J. [Judge] (* * * DISSENTING * * *).

* * * *

* * * I disagree with the majority * * * that Notz's claim for breach of fiduciary duty arising out of corporate usurpation is a derivative rather than a direct claim and that it thus must be dismissed.

Instead, * * * I conclude that Notz states a direct claim for breach of fiduciary duty arising out of the defendants' usurpation of a corporate opportunity.

* * * *

* * * Officers and directors owe a fiduciary duty to shareholders to act in good faith and to treat each shareholder fairly. The directors and officers of a corporation owe a fiduciary duty to not use their positions for their own personal advantage * * * to the detriment of the interests of the stockholders of the corporation.

That same fiduciary duty is also owed by majority shareholders to minority shareholders.

Officers, directors, and controlling shareholders breach their fiduciary duties when they treat minority shareholders differently, and inequitably, or when they use their position of trust to further their private interests. If through that control a sale of the corporate property is made and the property acquired by the majority, the minority may not be excluded from a fair participation in the fruits of the sale.

* * * *

[The majority's] conclusion is antithetical to the facts. It is true that all shareholders suffered a common injury in that the value of their investment in ATS depreciated. Nonetheless, Notz suffered an additional injury that was unique to the minority shareholders. The Smith Group who planned and executed these transactions received a net gain, but Notz suffered a net loss. * * * Notz's injury was distinct from the injury to the controlling shareholder—unlike the defendants, Notz was denied continued participation in a thriving growth industry.

Business Case Study with Dissenting Opinion—Continued

Questions for Analysis

1. **Law** What did the majority rule with respect to the dispute before the court? On what reasoning did the majority base its ruling?
2. **Law** What was the dissent's interpretation of the facts in this case? How would the dissent have applied the law to these facts? Why?
3. **Ethics** From an ethical perspective, should ATS's directors have made different decisions on the choices that came before the board? Discuss.
4. **Economic Dimensions** Could a shareholder in the position of the minority shareholder in this case seek a judicial dissolution? If so, what would be the likely result?
5. **Implications for the Shareholder** Can a shareholder pursue a derivative claim on behalf of a corporation? If so, what steps must the shareholder take? Why might a shareholder be reluctant to take these steps?

UNIT 5 Business Organizations

Business Scenario

John leases an office and buys computer equipment. Initially, to pay for the lease and the equipment, he goes into the business of designing Web pages. He also has an idea for a new software product that he hopes will be more profitable than designing Web pages. Whenever he has time, he works on the software.

1. **Selecting a Business Organization.** After six months, Mary and Paul come to work in the office to help develop John's idea. John continues to pay the rent and other expenses, including salaries for Mary and Paul. John does not expect to make a profit until the software is developed, which could take months. Even then, there may be very little profit unless the product is marketed successfully. If the software is successful, though, John believes that the firm will be able to follow up with other products. In choosing a form of business organization for this firm, what are the important considerations? What are the advantages and disadvantages of each basic option? **(See pages 792–793.)**
2. **Corporate Nature and Classification.** It is decided that the organizational form for this firm should provide limited liability for the owners. The owners will include John, Mary, Paul, and some members of their respective families. One of the features of the corporate form is limited liability. Ordinarily, however, corporate income is taxed at both the corporate level and the shareholder level. Which corporate form could the firm use to avoid this double taxation? Which other forms of business organization provide limited liability? What factors, other than liability and taxation, influence a firm's choice among these forms? **(See pages 744–750.)**
3. **Duties of Corporate Directors.** The firm is incorporated as Digital Software, Inc. (DSI). The software is developed and marketed successfully, and DSI prospers. John, Mary, and Paul become directors of DSI. At a board meeting, Paul proposes a marketing strategy for DSI's next product, and John and Mary approve it. Implementing the strategy causes DSI's profits to drop. If the shareholders accuse Paul of breaching his fiduciary duty to DSI, what is Paul's most likely defense? If the shareholders accuse John and Mary of the same breach, what is their best defense? In either case, if the shareholders file a suit, how is a court likely to rule? **(See pages 777–782.)**

Business Scenario—Continues next page

Business Scenario—Continued

4. **Securities Regulation.** Mary and Paul withdraw from DSI to set up their own firm. To obtain operating capital, they solicit investors who agree to become "general partners." Mary and Paul designate themselves "managing partners." The investors are spread over a wide area geographically and do not know anything about Mary and Paul's business until they are contacted. Are Mary and Paul truly soliciting partners, or are they selling securities? What are the criteria for determining whether an investment is a security? What are the advantages and disadvantages of selling securities versus soliciting partners? **(See page 801.)**

UNIT 5 Business Organizations

Group Project

Jeremy incorporated FormFit Concrete, Inc., but did not file its first annual report, so the state involuntarily dissolved the firm. Unaware of this, Jeremy contracted with Market Square to lay the foundations for a commercial building project. After Jeremy completed the concrete work, Market Square refused to pay. To recover, Jeremy filed a claim as "FormFit Concrete, Inc." Market Square asked the court to dismiss the claim on the ground that the state had dissolved that firm. Jeremy immediately filed new articles of incorporation for FormFit Concrete, Inc.

1. The first group will identify the doctrine of corporate law under which Jeremy might be able to recover from Market Square.
2. A second group will decide whether a court is likely to allow Jeremy to recover and the reasons why or why not.
3. A third group will determine whether FormFit Concrete, Inc., is more likely to be a close corporation or an S corporation. Explain why, and describe the differences.

UNIT 6

(steinphoto/iStockphoto.com)

Government Regulation

UNIT CONTENTS

32. Antitrust Law and Promoting Competition

33. Consumer and Environmental Law

34. Liability of Accountants and Other Professionals

CHAPTER 32

(J-Elgaard/iStockphoto.com)

Antitrust Law and Promoting Competition

CHAPTER OUTLINE

- The Sherman Antitrust Act
- Section 1 of the Sherman Act
- Section 2 of the Sherman Act
- The Clayton Act
- Enforcement and Exemptions
- U.S. Antitrust Laws in the Global Context

LEARNING OBJECTIVES

The five learning objectives below are designed to help improve your understanding of the chapter. After reading this chapter, you should be able to answer the following questions:

1. What is a monopoly? What is market power? How do these concepts relate to each other?
2. What anticompetitive activities are prohibited by Section 1 of the Sherman Act?
3. What type of activity is prohibited by Section 2 of the Sherman Act?
4. What are the four major provisions of the Clayton Act, and what types of activities do these provisions prohibit?
5. What agencies of the federal government enforce the federal antitrust laws?

"Competition is not only the basis of protection to the consumer but is the incentive to progress."
—Herbert Hoover, 1874–1964 (Thirty-first president of the United States, 1929–1933)

Antitrust Law Laws protecting commerce from unlawful restraints and anticompetitive practices.

The laws regulating economic competition in the United States are referred to as **antitrust laws.** They include the Sherman Antitrust Act of 1890[1] and the Clayton Act[2] and the Federal Trade Commission Act,[3] passed by Congress in 1914 to further curb anticompetitive or unfair business practices. Congress later amended the 1914 acts to broaden and strengthen their coverage. We examine these major federal antitrust statutes in this chapter.

The basis of antitrust legislation is the desire to foster competition. Antitrust legislation was initially created—and continues to be enforced—because of our society's belief that competition leads to lower prices and generates more product information. As President Herbert Hoover indicated in the chapter-opening quotation, competition not only protects the consumer, but also provides "the incentive to progress."

1. 15 U.S.C. Sections 1–7.
2. 15 U.S.C. Sections 12–27.
3. 15 U.S.C. Sections 41–58.

Consumers and society as a whole benefit when producers strive to develop better products that they can sell at lower prices to beat the competition. This is still true today, which is why the government is concerned about the pricing of e-books, as you will read later in this chapter.

The Sherman Antitrust Act

Today's antitrust laws are the direct descendants of common law actions intended to limit *restraints of trade* (agreements between or among firms that have the effect of reducing competition in the marketplace). Such actions date to the fifteenth century in England.

In the United States, concern over monopolistic practices arose after the Civil War with the growth of large corporate enterprises and their attempts to reduce competition. To thwart competition, they legally tied themselves together in business trusts. As discussed in Chapter 28 on page 737, a business trust is a form of business organization in which trustees hold title to property for the benefit of others. The most powerful of these trusts, the Standard Oil trust, is examined in this chapter's *Landmark in the Law* feature on the facing page.

In 1890, Congress passed "An Act to Protect Trade and Commerce against Unlawful Restraints and Monopolies"—commonly known as the Sherman Antitrust Act or, more simply, as the Sherman Act. The Sherman Act became (and still is) one of the government's most powerful weapons in the effort to maintain a competitive economy.

Major Provisions of the Sherman Act

Sections 1 and 2 contain the main provisions of the Sherman Act:

1. Every contract, combination in the form of trust or otherwise, or conspiracy, in restraint of trade or commerce among the several States, or with foreign nations, is hereby declared to be illegal [and is a felony punishable by a fine and/or imprisonment].
2. Every person who shall monopolize, or attempt to monopolize, or combine or conspire with any other person or persons, to monopolize any part of the trade or commerce among the several States, or with foreign nations, shall be deemed guilty of a felony [and is similarly punishable].

Differences Between Section 1 and Section 2

These two sections of the Sherman Act are quite different. Violation of Section 1 requires two or more persons, as a person cannot contract or combine or conspire alone. Thus, the essence of the illegal activity is *the act of joining together.* Section 2, though, can apply either to one person or to two or more persons because it refers to "every person." Thus, unilateral conduct can result in a violation of Section 2.

The cases brought under Section 1 of the Sherman Act differ from those brought under Section 2. Section 1 cases are often concerned with finding an agreement (written or oral)

One of Standard Oil's refineries in Richmond, California, around 1900.

(Library of Congress)

LANDMARK IN THE LAW

The Sherman Antitrust Act of 1890

The author of the Sherman Antitrust Act of 1890, Senator John Sherman, was the brother of the famous Civil War general William Tecumseh Sherman and a recognized financial authority. Sherman had been concerned for years about diminishing competition in U.S. industry and the emergence of monopolies, such as the Standard Oil trust.

The Standard Oil Trust By 1890, the Standard Oil trust had become the foremost petroleum refining and marketing combination in the United States. Streamlined, integrated, and centrally controlled, Standard Oil maintained an indisputable monopoly over the industry. The trust controlled 90 percent of the U.S. market for refined petroleum products, making it impossible for small producers to compete with such a leviathan.

The increasing consolidation in U.S. industry, and particularly the Standard Oil trust, came to the attention of the public in March 1881. Henry Demarest Lloyd, a young journalist from Chicago, published an article in the *Atlantic Monthly* entitled "The Story of a Great Monopoly." The article argued that the U.S. petroleum industry was dominated by one firm—Standard Oil. Lloyd's article was so popular that the issue was reprinted six times. It marked the beginning of the U.S. public's growing concern over monopolies.

The Passage of the Sherman Antitrust Act The common law regarding trade regulation was not always consistent. Certainly, it was not very familiar to the members of Congress. The public concern over large business integrations and trusts was familiar, however. In 1888, 1889, and again in 1890, Senator Sherman introduced in Congress bills designed to destroy the large combinations of capital that, he felt, were creating a lack of balance within the nation's economy.

Sherman told Congress that the Sherman Act "does not announce a new principle of law, but applies old and well-recognized principles of the common law."[a] In 1890, the Fifty-First Congress enacted the bill into law. Generally, the act prohibits business combinations and conspiracies that restrain trade and commerce, as well as certain monopolistic practices.

Application to Today's World *The Sherman Antitrust Act remains very relevant to today's world. Since the widely publicized monopolization case against Microsoft Corporation in 2001,*[b] *the U.S. Department of Justice and state attorneys general have brought numerous Sherman Act cases against other corporations, including eBay, Intel, and Philip Morris.*[c]

---

a. 21 *Congressional Record* 2456 (1890).

b. *United States v. Microsoft Corp.*, 253 F.3d 34 (D.C.Cir. 2001). This case will be discussed in *Case Example 32.7* on page 843.

c. See, for example, *United States v. Philip Morris USA, Inc.*, 566 F.3d 1095 (D.C.Cir. 2009); *In re eBay Seller Antitrust Litigation*, 545 F.Supp.2d 1027 (N.D.Cal. 2008); and *In re Intel Corp. Microprocessor Antitrust Litigation*, 2007 WL 137152 (D.Del. 2007).

LEARNING OBJECTIVE 1
What is a monopoly? What is market power? How do these concepts relate to each other?

Monopoly A market in which there is a single seller or a very limited number of sellers.

Monopoly Power The ability of a monopoly to dictate what takes place in a given market.

Market Power The power of a firm to control the market price of its product. A monopoly has the greatest degree of market power.

that leads to a restraint of trade. Section 2 cases deal with the structure of a monopoly that already exists in the marketplace. The term **monopoly** generally is used to describe a market in which there is a single seller or a very limited number of sellers. Whereas Section 1 focuses on agreements that are restrictive—that is, agreements that have a wrongful purpose—Section 2 addresses the misuse of **monopoly power** in the marketplace.

Monopoly power exists when a firm has an extreme amount of **market power**—the power to affect the market price of its product. Both Section 1 and Section 2 seek to curtail market practices that result in undesired monopoly pricing and output behavior. For a case to be brought under Section 2, however, the "threshold" or "necessary" amount of monopoly power must already exist. We will return to a discussion of these two sections of the Sherman Act after we look at the act's jurisdictional requirements.

Jurisdictional Requirements

The Sherman Act applies only to restraints that have a substantial impact on interstate commerce. Generally, any activity that substantially affects interstate commerce falls within the scope of the Sherman Act. As will be discussed later in this chapter, the Sherman Act also extends to U.S. nationals abroad who are engaged in activities that have an effect on U.S. foreign commerce. Federal courts have exclusive jurisdiction over antitrust cases brought under the Sherman Act. State laws regulate local restraints on competition, and state courts decide claims brought under those laws.

Section 1 of the Sherman Act

LEARNING OBJECTIVE 2
What anticompetitive activities are prohibited by Section 1 of the Sherman Act?

The underlying assumption of Section 1 of the Sherman Act is that society's welfare is harmed if rival firms are permitted to join in an agreement that consolidates their market power or otherwise restrains competition. The types of trade restraints that Section 1 of the Sherman Act prohibits generally fall into two broad categories: *horizontal restraints* and *vertical restraints,* both of which will be discussed shortly. First, though, we look at the rules that the courts may apply when assessing the anticompetitive impact of alleged restraints on trade.

Per Se Violations versus the Rule of Reason

***Per Se* Violation** A restraint of trade that is so anticompetitive that it is deemed inherently (*per se*) illegal.

Rule of Reason A test used to determine whether an anticompetitive agreement constitutes a reasonable restraint on trade. Courts consider such factors as the purpose of the agreement, its effect on competition, and whether less restrictive means could have been used.

Some restraints are so blatantly and substantially anticompetitive that they are deemed ***per se* violations**—illegal *per se* (on their face, or inherently)—under Section 1. Other agreements, however, even though they result in enhanced market power, do not *unreasonably* restrain trade. Using what is called the **rule of reason,** the courts analyze anticompetitive agreements that allegedly violate Section 1 of the Sherman Act to determine whether they actually constitute reasonable restraints on trade.

Why the Rule of Reason Was Developed The need for a rule-of-reason analysis of some agreements in restraint of trade is obvious—if the rule of reason had not been developed, almost any business agreement could conceivably be held to violate the Sherman Act. Justice Louis Brandeis effectively phrased this sentiment in *Chicago Board of Trade v. United States,* a case decided in 1918:

> Every agreement concerning trade, every regulation of trade, restrains. To bind, to restrain, is of their very essence. The true test of legality is whether the restraint imposed is such as merely regulates and perhaps thereby promotes competition or whether it is such as may suppress or even destroy competition.[4]

Factors Courts Consider under the Rule of Reason When analyzing an alleged Section 1 violation under the rule of reason, a court will consider several factors. These factors include the purpose of the agreement, the parties' market ability to implement the agreement to achieve that purpose, and the effect or potential effect of the agreement on competition. Another factor that a court might consider is whether the parties could have relied on less restrictive means to achieve their purpose.

"I don't know what a monopoly is until somebody tells me."

Steve Ballmer, 1956–present (Chief executive officer of Microsoft Corporation)

CASE EXAMPLE 32.1 The National Football League (NFL) includes thirty-two separately owned professional football teams. Each team has its own name, colors, and logo, and owns related intellectual property that it markets through National Football League Properties (NFLP). Until 2000, the NFLP granted nonexclusive licenses to a number of vendors, permitting them to manufacture and sell apparel bearing NFL team insignias. American Needle, Inc., was one of those licensees.

In late 2000, the teams authorized the NFLP to grant exclusive licenses, and the NFLP granted Reebok International, Ltd., an exclusive ten-year license to manufacture and sell trademarked headwear for all thirty-two teams. It then declined to renew American Needle's

4. 246 U.S. 231, 38 S.Ct. 242, 62 L.Ed. 683 (1918).

nonexclusive license. American Needle sued, claiming that the NFL teams, the NFLP, and Reebok had violated Section 1 of the Sherman Act. The United States Supreme Court agreed. The Court concluded that the agreement among the NFL teams to license their intellectual property exclusively through the NFLP to Reebok constituted concerted activity.[5]

Should TV programmers and distributors be held in violation of the Sherman Act? When consumers want cable or satellite television programming, they can choose among various cable and satellite providers, or distributors, but each distributor will offer multichannel packages. In other words, a consumer cannot order just the channels that she or he watches regularly. All of the multichannel packages include some very popular channels and some other channels that have very low viewership. Thus, consumers are forced to pay for some unwanted channels in order to get the ones they do want.

A group of consumers sued NBC Universal, the Walt Disney Company, and other programmers, as well as cable and satellite distributors. The consumers claimed that the defendants, because of their full or partial ownership of broadcast channels and their ownership or control of multiple cable or satellite channels, had a higher degree of market power vis-à-vis all distributors. They also claimed that the programmers had exploited this power by requiring the "bundling" of numerous channels in each multichannel package offered to consumers.

The U.S. Court of Appeals for the Ninth Circuit disagreed. The court pointed out that the Sherman Act applies to actions that diminish competition and, in this instance, there was still competition among programmers and distributors.[6]

Horizontal Restraints

Horizontal Restraint Any agreement that restrains competition between rival firms competing in the same market.

The term **horizontal restraint** is encountered frequently in antitrust law. A horizontal restraint is any agreement that in some way restrains competition between rival firms competing in the same market.

Price-Fixing Agreement An agreement between competitors to fix the prices of products or services at a certain level.

Price Fixing

Any **price-fixing agreement**—an agreement among competitors to fix prices—constitutes a *per se* violation of Section 1. The agreement on price need not be explicit: as long as it restricts output or artificially fixes price, it violates the law. The U.S. government is concerned that price fixing is occurring in the e-book industry. See this chapter's *Adapting the Law to the Online Environment* feature on the following page.

Price Fixing Is Never Reasonable Perhaps the definitive case involving price-fixing agreements is still the 1940 case of *United States v. Socony-Vacuum Oil Co.*[7] In that case, a group of independent oil producers in Texas and Louisiana were caught between falling demand due to the Great Depression of the 1930s and increasing supply from newly discovered oil fields in the region. In response to these conditions, a group of major refining companies agreed to buy "distress" gasoline (excess supplies) from the independents so as to dispose of it in an "orderly manner." Although there was no explicit agreement as to price, it was clear that the purpose of the agreement was to limit the supply of gasoline on the market and thereby raise prices.

The United States Supreme Court recognized the effects that such an agreement could have on open and free competition. The Court held that the reasonableness of a price-fixing agreement is never a defense. Any agreement that restricts output or artificially fixes price is a *per se* violation of Section 1. The rationale of the *per se* rule was best stated in what is now the most famous portion of the Court's opinion—footnote 59. In that footnote, Justice William O. Douglas compared a freely functioning price system to a body's central nervous

5. *American Needle, Inc. v. National Football League,* ___ U.S. ___, 130 S.Ct. 2201, 176 L.Ed.2d 947 (2010).
6. *Brantley v. NBC Universal, Inc.,* 675 F.3d 1192 (9th Cir. 2012).
7. 310 U.S. 150, 60 S.Ct. 811, 84 L.Ed. 1129 (1940).

ADAPTING THE LAW TO THE ONLINE ENVIRONMENT

THE JUSTICE DEPARTMENT GOES AFTER E-BOOK PRICING

In 2012, the U.S. Justice Department filed a lawsuit against five major book publishers and Apple, Inc., charging that they had conspired to fix the prices of e-books. According to the thirty-six-page complaint, publishing executives met "in private rooms for dinner in upscale Manhattan restaurants" to discuss ways to limit e-book price competition. As a result, claims the Justice Department, consumers paid "tens of millions of dollars more for e-books than they otherwise would have paid."

The E-Book Market Explodes

E-books were only a niche product until a few years ago when Amazon.com released its first Kindle e-book reader. To sell more Kindles, Amazon offered thousands of popular books for downloading at $9.99 per e-book. Amazon kept 50 percent and gave 50 percent to the publishers, who had to agree to Amazon's pricing. Although Amazon lost on its e-book sales, it made up the losses by selling more Kindles.

Enter Apple's iPad

When the iPad entered the scene, Apple and the book publishers agreed to use Apple's "agency" model, which allowed the publishers to set their own prices while Apple kept 30 percent as a commission. Apple was already using this model for games and apps for its iPhones and iPads.

The Justice Department, however, decided that because the publishers chose prices that were relatively similar, price fixing was evident. Nowhere in the Justice Department's complaint did it acknowledge that the agency model is the standard approach for many types of sales. Indeed, the Justice Department claimed that the agency model is *per se* illegal and "would not have occurred without the conspiracy among the defendants." Yet the model is used in many industries and has been upheld by federal courts for years.

(Photo by Bill Stryker)

Amazon Still Leads but Not by Much

When the Kindle was king, Amazon had 90 percent of the e-book market. Since the advent of the the iPad, Barnes & Noble's Nook, and other e-book readers, Kindle's market share has fallen to 60 percent because of increased competition. E-books now cost anywhere from zero to $14.99.

It's *Gone with the Wind* All Over Again

During the Great Depression, the federal government brought a similar antitrust lawsuit. At the time, Macy's, the department store chain, sold books at a steep discount. It was selling *Gone with the Wind* for the equivalent of $15 in today's dollars, whereas smaller stores charged double or triple that price. Publishers and booksellers lobbied for protection from what they called predatory pricing. Ultimately, the federal government did not prevail, but for a while, retail book prices remained high.

Critical Thinking

The publishing business is in dire straits today with retail bookstores going bankrupt and publishers laying off hundreds of employees. Why do you think the declining book business was worthy of so much attention from the Justice Department?

What major company tried to fix LCD prices?

(Peter J. Kovacs / Shutterstock.com)

system, condemning price-fixing agreements as threats to "the central nervous system of the economy."

Price Fixing Today Price-fixing cartels (groups) are still commonplace in today's business world, particularly among global companies (see page 850 for a discussion of the extraterritorial application of the Sherman Act). For instance, in 2011, Samsung Electronics, Sharp Corporation, and five other makers of liquid crystal displays (LCDs) for notebooks and other devices agreed to pay more than $553 million to settle price-fixing claims against them. Price-fixing accusations are also frequently made against drug manufacturers.

CASE EXAMPLE 32.2 The manufacturer of the prescription drug Cardizem CD, which can help prevent heart attacks, was about to lose its patent on the drug. Another company developed a generic version in anticipation of the patent expiring. After the two firms became involved in litigation over the patent, the first company agreed to pay the second company $40 million per year not to market the generic version until their dispute was resolved. This agreement was held to be a *per se* violation of the Sherman Act because it restrained competition between rival firms and delayed the entry of generic versions of Cardizem into the market.[8] •

Group Boycott An agreement by two or more sellers to refuse to deal with a particular person or firm.

Group Boycotts

A **group boycott** is an agreement by two or more sellers to refuse to deal with (boycott) a particular person or firm. Such group boycotts have been held to constitute *per se* violations of Section 1 of the Sherman Act. Section 1 has been violated if it can be demonstrated that the boycott or joint refusal to deal was undertaken with the intention of eliminating competition or preventing entry into a given market. Some boycotts, such as group boycotts against a supplier for political reasons, may be protected under the First Amendment right to freedom of expression, however.

Horizontal Market Division

It is a *per se* violation of Section 1 of the Sherman Act for competitors to divide up territories or customers. **EXAMPLE 32.3** Alred Office Supply, Belmont Business, and Carlson's, Inc., compete against each other in the states of Kansas, Nebraska, and Oklahoma. The three firms agree that Alred will sell products only in Kansas, Belmont will sell only in Nebraska, and Carlson's will sell only in Oklahoma. This concerted action reduces marketing costs and allows all three (assuming there is no other competition) to raise the price of the goods sold in their respective states.

The same violation would take place if the three firms agreed to divide up their customers by having Alred sell only to institutional purchasers (such as governments and schools) in all three states, Belmont only to wholesalers, and Carlson only to retailers. •

Trade Associations

Businesses in the same general industry or profession frequently organize trade associations to pursue common interests. A trade association may engage in various joint activities such as exchanging information, representing the members' business interests before governmental bodies, conducting advertising campaigns, and setting regulatory standards to govern the industry or profession.

Generally, the rule of reason is applied to many of these horizontal actions. If a court finds that a trade association practice or agreement that restrains trade is sufficiently beneficial both to the association and to the public, it may deem the restraint reasonable.

Concentrated Industry An industry in which a single firm or a small number of firms control a large percentage of market sales.

In concentrated industries, however, trade associations can be, and have been, used as a means to facilitate anticompetitive actions, such as fixing prices or allocating markets. A **concentrated industry** is one in which either a single firm or a small number of firms control a large percentage of market sales. When trade association agreements have substantially anticompetitive effects, a court will consider them to be in violation of Section 1 of the Sherman Act.

Vertical Restraints

Vertical Restraint A restraint of trade created by an agreement between firms at different levels in the manufacturing and distribution process.

Vertically Integrated Firm A firm that carries out two or more functional phases (manufacturing, distribution, and retailing, for example) of the chain of production.

A **vertical restraint** of trade results from an agreement between firms at different levels in the manufacturing and distribution process. In contrast to horizontal relationships, which occur at the same level of operation, vertical relationships encompass the entire chain of production. The chain of production normally includes the purchase of inventory, basic manufacturing, distribution to wholesalers, and eventual sale of a product at the retail level. When a single firm carries out two or more of the separate functional phases, it is considered to be a **vertically integrated firm.**

---

8. *In re Cardizem CD Antitrust Litigation,* 332 F.3d 896 (6th Cir. 2003).

Even though firms operating at different functional levels are not in direct competition with one another, they are in competition with other firms. Thus, agreements between firms standing in a vertical relationship may affect competition. Some vertical restraints are *per se* violations of Section 1. Others are judged under the rule of reason.

Territorial or Customer Restrictions

In arranging for the distribution of its products, a manufacturing firm often wishes to insulate dealers from direct competition with other dealers selling the product. To do so, it may institute territorial restrictions or attempt to prohibit wholesalers or retailers from reselling the product to certain classes of buyers, such as competing retailers.

Territorial and customer restrictions were once considered *per se* violations of Section 1, but in 1977, the United States Supreme Court held that they should be judged under the rule of reason. **CASE EXAMPLE 32.4** GTE Sylvania, Inc., limited the number of retail franchises that it granted in any given geographic area and required them to sell only Sylvania products. Sylvania retained sole discretion to increase the number of retailers in an area. When Sylvania decided to open a new franchise, it terminated the franchise of Continental T.V., Inc. Continental sued, claiming that Sylvania's vertically restrictive franchise system violated Section 1. The Supreme Court found that "vertical restrictions promote interbrand competition by allowing the manufacturer to achieve certain efficiencies in the distribution of his products." Therefore, Sylvania's vertical system, which was not price restrictive, did not constitute a *per se* violation of Section 1 of the Sherman Act.[9] •

The decision in the *Continental* case marked a definite shift from rigid characterization of these kinds of vertical restraints to a more flexible, economic analysis of the restraints under the rule of reason. A firm may have legitimate reasons for imposing territorial or customer restrictions, and not all such restrictions harm competition.

Resale Price Maintenance Agreements

Resale Price Maintenance Agreement An agreement between a manufacturer and a retailer in which the manufacturer specifies what the retail prices of its products must be.

An agreement between a manufacturer and a distributor or retailer in which the manufacturer specifies what the retail prices of its products must be is referred to as a **resale price maintenance agreement.** Such agreements were also once considered to be *per se* violations of Section 1, but the United States Supreme Court ruled in 1997 that *maximum* resale price maintenance agreements should be judged under the rule of reason.[10] The setting of a maximum price that retailers and distributors can charge for a manufacturer's products may sometimes increase competition and benefit consumers. In 2007, the Supreme Court held that *minimum* resale price maintenance agreements should also be judged under the rule of reason.[11]

Section 2 of the Sherman Act

LEARNING OBJECTIVE 3
What type of activity is prohibited by Section 2 of the Sherman Act?

Section 1 of the Sherman Act prohibits certain concerted, or joint, activities that restrain trade. In contrast, Section 2 condemns "every person who shall monopolize, or attempt to monopolize." Thus, two distinct types of behavior are subject to sanction under Section 2: *monopolization* and *attempts to monopolize*.

Predatory Pricing The pricing of a product below cost with the intent to drive competitors out of the market.

One tactic that may be involved in either offense is **predatory pricing.** Predatory pricing involves an attempt by one firm to drive its competitors from the market by selling its product at prices substantially *below* the normal costs of production. Once the competitors are eliminated, the firm will presumably attempt to recapture its losses and go on to earn higher profits by driving prices up far above their competitive levels.

9. *Continental T.V., Inc. v. GTE Sylvania, Inc.*, 433 U.S. 36, 97 S.Ct. 2549, 53 L.Ed.2d 568 (1977).
10. *State Oil Co. v. Khan*, 522 U.S. 3, 118 S.Ct. 275, 139 L.Ed.2d 199 (1997).
11. *Leegin Creative Leather Products, Inc. v. PSKS, Inc.*, 551 U.S. 877, 127 S.Ct. 2705, 168 L.Ed.2d 623 (2007).

Monopolization

Monopolization The possession of monopoly power in the relevant market and the willful acquisition or maintenance of that power, as distinguished from growth or development as a consequence of a superior product, business acumen, or historic accident.

The United States Supreme Court has defined the offense of **monopolization** as involving two elements: "(1) the possession of monopoly power in the relevant market and (2) the willful acquisition or maintenance of [that] power as distinguished from growth or development as a consequence of a superior product, business acumen, or historic accident."[12] A violation of Section 2 requires that both these elements—monopoly power and an intent to monopolize—be established.

Monopoly Power

The Sherman Act does not define *monopoly.* In economic theory, monopoly refers to control of a single market by a single entity. It is well established in antitrust law, however, that a firm may be deemed a monopolist even though it is not the sole seller in a market. Additionally, size alone does not determine whether a firm is a monopoly.

EXAMPLE 32.5 A "mom and pop" grocery located in the isolated town of Happy Camp, Idaho, is a monopolist if it is the only grocery serving that particular market. Size in relation to the market is what matters because monopoly involves the power to affect prices. •

Monopoly power may be proved by direct evidence that the firm used its power to control prices and restrict output.[13] Usually, however, there is not enough evidence to show that the firm was intentionally controlling prices, so the plaintiff has to offer indirect, or circumstantial, evidence of monopoly power. To prove monopoly power indirectly, the plaintiff must show that the firm has a dominant share of the relevant market and that there are significant barriers for new competitors entering that market.

In the following case, the court had to decide whether there was sufficient evidence to show that the company possessed monopoly power in the relevant market.

12. *United States v. Grinnell Corp.*, 384 U.S. 563, 86 S.Ct. 1698, 16 L.Ed.2d 778 (1966).

13. See, for example, *Broadcom Corp. v. Qualcomm, Inc.*, 501 F.3d 297 (3d Cir. 2007).

Case 32.1

E. I. du Pont de Nemours and Co. v. Kolon Industries, Inc.

United States Court of Appeals, Fourth Circuit, 637 F.3d 435 (2011).

(AP Photo/Seth Perlman)

COMPANY PROFILE *DuPont, founded in 1802, started as a gunpowder manufacturer. Today, it operates in ninety countries in the fields of agriculture, apparel, communications, electronics, home construction, nutrition, and transportation. Its latest major investment was in a biodegradable ingredient used in cosmetics, liquid detergents, and antifreeze.*

FACTS DuPont manufactures and sells para-aramid fiber, which is a complex synthetic fiber used to make body armor, fiber-optic cables, and tires, among other things. Only three producers of this fiber—DuPont (based in the United States), Teijin (based in the Netherlands), and Kolon Industries, Inc. (based in South Korea)—sell it in the U.S. market. DuPont is the industry leader, accounting for more than 70 percent of all para-aramid fibers purchased in the United States. In 2009, DuPont brought a lawsuit against Kolon for misappropriation of trade secrets. Kolon counterclaimed that DuPont had monopolized and attempted to monopolize the para-aramid market in violation of Section 2 of the Sherman Act.

Kolon claimed that DuPont illegally used multiyear supply agreements requiring its high-volume para-aramid fiber customers to purchase from 80 to 100 percent of their needs from DuPont. Kolon alleged that these agreements limited the other producers' ability to compete. DuPont moved to dismiss

Case 32.1—Continues next page

Case 32.1—Continued

the counterclaim, arguing, in part, that Kolon's allegations of unlawful exclusionary conduct were insufficient. A federal district court agreed and dismissed Kolon's counterclaim. Kolon appealed. The U.S. Court of Appeals for the Fourth Circuit examined the trial court's reasoning.

ISSUE Did Kolon present sufficient evidence that DuPont possessed monopoly power in the para-aramid market to maintain a claim for monopolization and attempted monopolization?

DECISION Yes. The U.S. Court of Appeals for the Fourth Circuit reversed the district court's decision, finding that Kolon had alleged sufficient facts to show that DuPont's behavior violated Section 2 of the Sherman Act.

REASON The federal appellate court reasoned that DuPont's control of more than 70 percent of the U.S. para-aramid fiber market showed its monopoly power. "A monopolist is not free to take certain actions that a company in a competitive . . . market may take because there is no market constraint on a monopolist's behavior." The multiyear contracts that DuPont imposed on its highest-volume purchasers severely limited Kolon from competing for the most important customers. "DuPont's conduct has had a direct, substantial, and adverse effect on competition . . . [and] has constrained the only potential entrant [Kolon] to the United States in decades from effectively entering the market." Because DuPont's conduct reduced or eliminated additional competition and preserved DuPont's monopoly position, the court concluded that it violated Section 2.

WHAT IF THE FACTS WERE DIFFERENT? *Assume that DuPont had 45 percent of the market and Kolon, along with numerous other competitors, had the remaining 65 percent. Would the appellate court have ruled the same? Why or why not?*

Relevant Market

Before a court can determine whether a firm has a dominant market share, it must define the relevant market. The relevant market consists of two elements: a relevant product market and a relevant geographic market.

Relevant Product Market The relevant product market includes all products that, although produced by different firms, have identical attributes, such as sugar. It also includes products that are reasonably interchangeable for the purpose for which they are produced. Products will be considered reasonably interchangeable if consumers treat them as acceptable substitutes.[14]

Establishing the relevant product market is often a key issue in monopolization cases because the way the market is defined may determine whether a firm has monopoly power. By defining the product market narrowly, the degree of a firm's market power is enhanced.

CASE EXAMPLE 32.6 Whole Foods Market, Inc., wished to acquire Wild Oats Markets, Inc., its main competitor in nationwide high-end organic food supermarkets. The Federal Trade Commission (FTC) filed a Section 2 claim against Whole Foods to prevent the merger. The FTC argued that the relevant product market consisted of only "premium natural and organic supermarkets" rather than all supermarkets, as Whole Foods maintained. An appellate court accepted the FTC's narrow definition of the relevant market and remanded the case to the lower court to decide what remedies were appropriate, as the merger had already taken place. Whole Foods and the FTC later entered into a settlement that required Whole Foods to divest (sell or give up control over) thirteen stores, most of which were formerly Wild Oats outlets.[15] •

Relevant Geographic Market The second component of the relevant market is the geographic extent of the market. For products that are sold nationwide, the geographic market encompasses the entire United States. If transportation costs are significant or a producer and its competitors sell in only a limited area (one in which customers have no access to

14. See, for example, *HDC Medical, Inc. v. Minntech Corp.*, 474 F.3d 543 (8th Cir. 2007).

15. *FTC v. Whole Foods Market, Inc.*, 548 F.3d 1028 (D.C.Cir. 2008); and 592 F.Supp.2d 107 (D.D.C. 2009).

other sources of the product), the geographic market is limited to that area. A national firm may thus compete in several distinct areas and have monopoly power in one area but not in another.

Generally, the geographic market is that section of the country within which a firm can increase its price a bit without attracting new sellers or without losing many customers to alternative suppliers outside that area. Of course, the Internet and e-commerce are changing the notion of the size and limits of a geographic market. It may become difficult to perceive any geographic market as local, except for products that are not easily transported, such as concrete. The reality is that we live in a global world, including one for commerce.

KNOW THIS

Section 2 of the Sherman Act essentially condemns the *act* of monopolizing, not the possession of monopoly power.

The Intent Requirement

Monopoly power, in and of itself, does not constitute the offense of monopolization under Section 2 of the Sherman Act. The offense also requires an *intent* to monopolize.

Why Intent Is Required A dominant market share may be the result of business acumen or the development of a superior product. It may simply be the result of a historic accident. In these situations, the acquisition of monopoly power is not an antitrust violation. Indeed, it would be contrary to society's interest to condemn every firm that acquired a position of power because it was well managed and efficient and marketed a product desired by consumers.

Why did Netscape sue Microsoft?

(AP Photo)

Inferred from Anticompetitive Conduct If a firm possesses market power as a result of carrying out some purposeful act to acquire or maintain that power through anticompetitive means, then it is in violation of Section 2. In most monopolization cases, intent may be inferred from evidence that the firm had monopoly power and engaged in anticompetitive behavior.

CASE EXAMPLE 32.7 When Navigator, the first popular graphical Internet browser by Netscape Communications Corporation, was introduced, Microsoft, Inc., perceived a threat to its dominance of the operating-system market. Microsoft developed a competing browser, Internet Explorer, and then began to require computer makers that wanted to install the Windows operating system to also install Explorer and exclude Navigator. Microsoft included codes in Windows that would cripple the operating system if Explorer was deleted, and paid Internet service providers to distribute Explorer and exclude Navigator. Because of this pattern of exclusionary conduct, a court found Microsoft guilty of monopolization. Microsoft's pattern of conduct could be rational only if the firm knew that it possessed monopoly power.[16]

PREVENTING LEGAL DISPUTES

Because exclusionary conduct can have legitimate efficiency-enhancing effects, it can be difficult to determine when conduct will be viewed as anticompetitive and a violation of Section 2 of the Sherman Act. Thus, a business that possesses monopoly power must be careful that its actions cannot be inferred to be evidence of intent to monopolize. Even if your business does not have a dominant market share, you would be wise to take precautions.

Make sure that you can articulate clear, legitimate reasons for the particular conduct or contract and that you do not provide any direct evidence (damaging e-mails, for example) of an intent to exclude competitors. A court will be less likely to infer the intent to monopolize if the specific conduct was aimed at increasing output and lowering per-unit costs, improving product quality, or protecting a patented technology or innovation.

16. *United States v. Microsoft Corp.*, 253 F.3d 34 (D.C.Cir. 2001). Microsoft has faced numerous antitrust claims and has settled a number of lawsuits in which it was accused of antitrust violations and anticompetitive tactics.

(mkaminski/iStockphoto.com)

Why did the smallest Aspen ski resort sue Aspen Skiing Company?

Unilateral Refusals to Deal

Group boycotts, discussed earlier, are also joint refusals to deal—sellers acting as a group jointly refuse to deal with another business or individual. These group refusals are subject to close scrutiny under Section 1 of the Sherman Act. A single manufacturer acting unilaterally, though, normally is free to deal, or not to deal, with whomever it wishes.[17]

Nevertheless, in limited circumstances, a unilateral refusal to deal will violate antitrust laws. These instances involve offenses proscribed under Section 2 of the Sherman Act and occur only if (1) the firm refusing to deal has—or is likely to acquire—monopoly power and (2) the refusal is likely to have an anticompetitive effect on a particular market.

CASE EXAMPLE 32.8 Aspen Skiing Company, the owner of three of the four major downhill ski areas in Aspen, Colorado, refused to continue participating in a jointly offered six-day "all Aspen" lift ticket. The Supreme Court ruled that Aspen Skiing's refusal to cooperate with its smaller competitor was a violation of Section 2 of the Sherman Act. Because the company owned three-fourths of the local ski areas, it had monopoly power, and thus its unilateral refusal had an anticompetitive effect on the market.[18] •

Attempts to Monopolize

Attempted Monopolization An action by a firm that involves anticompetitive conduct, the intent to gain monopoly power, and a "dangerous probability" of success in achieving monopoly power.

Section 2 also prohibits **attempted monopolization** of a market, which requires proof of the following three elements:

1. Anticompetitive conduct.
2. The specific intent to exclude competitors and garner monopoly power.
3. A "dangerous" probability of success in achieving monopoly power. The probability cannot be dangerous unless the alleged offender possesses some degree of market power. Only *serious* threats of monopolization are condemned as violations.

As mentioned earlier, predatory pricing is a form of anticompetitive conduct that, in theory, could be used by firms that are attempting to monopolize. (Predatory pricing may also lead to claims of price discrimination, discussed next.) Predatory bidding involves the acquisition and use of *monopsony power,* which is market power on the *buy* side of a market. This may occur when a buyer bids up the price of an input too high for its competitors to pay, causing them to leave the market. The predatory bidder may then attempt to drive down input prices to reap above-competitive profits and recoup any losses it suffered in bidding up the prices.

The question in the following *Spotlight Case* was whether a claim of predatory bidding was sufficiently similar to a claim of predatory pricing so that the same antitrust test should apply to both.

17. See, for example, *Pacific Bell Telephone Co. v. Linkline Communications, Inc.*, 555 U.S. 438, 129 S.Ct. 1109, 172 L.Ed.2d 836 (2009).

18. *Aspen Skiing Co. v. Aspen Highlands Skiing Corp.*, 472 U.S. 585, 105 S.Ct. 2847, 86 L.Ed.2d 467 (1985).

Spotlight on Weyerhaeuser Co.

Case 32.2

Weyerhaeuser Co. v. Ross-Simmons Hardwood Lumber Co.

Supreme Court of the United States, 549 U.S. 312, 127 S.Ct. 1069, 166 L.Ed.2d 911 (2007).
www.findlaw.com/casecode/supreme.html[a]

(Claire L. Evans/Creative Commons)

Was predatory bidding on the price of alder logs tantamount to predatory pricing and therefore illegal?

FACTS Weyerhaeuser Company entered the Pacific Northwest's hardwood lumber market in 1980. By 2000, Weyerhaeuser owned six mills processing 65 percent of the red alder logs in the region. Meanwhile, Ross-Simmons Hardwood Lumber Company operated a single

a. In the "Browse Supreme Court Opinions" section, click on "2007." On that page, scroll to the name of the case and click on it to access the opinion.

Spotlight Case 32.2—Continued

competing mill. When the prices of the logs rose and those for the lumber fell, Ross-Simmons suffered heavy losses. Several million dollars in debt, the mill closed in 2001. Ross-Simmons filed a suit in a federal district court against Weyerhaeuser, alleging attempted monopolization under Section 2 of the Sherman Act. Ross-Simmons claimed that Weyerhaeuser used its dominant position in the market to bid up the prices of logs and prevent its competitors from being profitable. Weyerhaeuser argued that the antitrust test for predatory pricing applies to a claim of predatory bidding and that Ross-Simmons had not met this standard. The district court ruled in favor of the plaintiff, the U.S. Court of Appeals for the Ninth Circuit affirmed, and Weyerhaeuser appealed to the United States Supreme Court.

ISSUE Does the antitrust test that applies to a claim of predatory pricing also apply to a claim of predatory bidding?

DECISION Yes. Because Ross-Simmons conceded that it had not met this standard, the Supreme Court vacated the lower court's judgment and remanded the case.

REASON Both predatory pricing and predatory bidding involve a company's intentional use of pricing for an anticompetitive purpose. Both actions require a company to incur a short-term loss on the possibility of later making a "supracompetitive" profit. Because a "rational" firm is unlikely to "make this sacrifice," both schemes are "rarely tried and even more rarely successful." A failed scheme of either type can benefit consumers. Thus, the two-part predatory-pricing test should apply to predatory-bidding claims. A plaintiff alleging predatory bidding must then prove that the defendant's "bidding on the buy side caused the cost of the relevant output to rise above the revenues generated in the sale of those outputs." The plaintiff must also prove that "the defendant has a dangerous probability of recouping the losses incurred in bidding up input prices through the exercise of monopsony power."

WHY IS THIS CASE IMPORTANT? *Predatory-bidding schemes of the type that Ross-Simmons alleged Weyerhaeuser had committed are rare. Under the standard that the Court imposed in this case, a plaintiff's successful claim will likely be even more rare. But this may not be a negative development, at least for consumers. A predatory-bidding scheme can actually benefit consumers—a predator's high bidding can cause it to acquire more inputs, which can lead to the manufacture of more outputs, and increases in output generally result in lower prices to consumers.*

The Clayton Act

LEARNING OBJECTIVE 4
What are the four major provisions of the Clayton Act, and what types of activities do these provisions prohibit?

In 1914, Congress attempted to strengthen federal antitrust laws by enacting the Clayton Act. The Clayton Act was aimed at specific anticompetitive or monopolistic practices that the Sherman Act did not cover. The substantive provisions of the act deal with four distinct forms of business behavior, which are declared illegal but not criminal. In each instance, the act states that the behavior is illegal only if it tends to substantially lessen competition or to create monopoly power.

The major offenses under the Clayton Act are set out in Sections 2, 3, 7, and 8 of the act.

Section 2 (The Robinson-Patman Act)—Price Discrimination

Price Discrimination A seller's act of charging competing buyers different prices for identical products or services.

Section 2 of the Clayton Act prohibits **price discrimination**, which occurs when a seller charges different prices to competing buyers for identical goods or services. Congress strengthened this section by amending it with the passage of the Robinson-Patman Act in 1936.

As amended, Section 2 prohibits price discrimination that cannot be justified by differences in production costs, transportation costs, or cost differences due to other reasons. In short, a seller is prohibited from charging a lower price to one buyer than is charged to that buyer's competitor.

Requirements

To violate Section 2, the seller must be engaged in interstate commerce, the goods must be of like grade and quality, and goods must have been sold to

> "Becoming number one is easier than remaining number one."
>
> Bill Bradley, 1943–present (American politician and athlete)

two or more purchasers. In addition, the effect of the price discrimination must be to substantially lessen competition, tend to create a monopoly, or otherwise injure competition. Without proof of an actual injury resulting from the price discrimination, the plaintiff cannot recover damages.

Note that price discrimination claims can arise from discounts, offsets, rebates, or allowances given to one buyer over another. Giving favorable credit terms, delivery, or freight charges to only some buyers can also lead to allegations of price discrimination. For instance, offering goods to different customers at the same price but including free delivery for certain buyers may violate Section 2 in some circumstances.

Defenses

There are several statutory defenses to liability for price discrimination.

1. *Cost justification.* If the seller can justify the price reduction by demonstrating that a particular buyer's purchases saved the seller costs in producing and selling the goods, the seller will not be liable for price discrimination.
2. *Meeting competitor's prices.* If the seller charged the lower price in a good faith attempt to meet an equally low price of a competitor, the seller will not be liable for price discrimination. **CASE EXAMPLE 32.9** Water Craft was a retail dealership of Mercury Marine outboard motors in Baton Rouge, Louisiana. Mercury Marine also sold its motors to other dealers in the Baton Rouge area. When Water Craft discovered that Mercury was selling its outboard motors at a substantial discount to Water Craft's largest competitor, it filed a price discrimination lawsuit against Mercury. The court ruled in favor of Mercury Marine, however, because it was able to show that the discounts given to Water Craft's competitor were made in good faith to meet the low price charged by another manufacturer of marine motors.[19] •
3. *Changing market conditions.* A seller may lower its price on an item in response to changing conditions affecting the market for or the marketability of the goods concerned. Thus, if an advance in technology makes a particular product less marketable than it was previously, a seller can lower the product's price.

Section 3—Exclusionary Practices

Under Section 3 of the Clayton Act, sellers or lessors cannot condition the sale or lease of goods on the buyer's or lessee's promise not to use or deal in the goods of the seller's competitor. In effect, this section prohibits two types of vertical agreements involving exclusionary practices—*exclusive-dealing contracts* and *tying arrangements*.

Exclusive-Dealing Contracts

Exclusive-Dealing Contract An agreement under which a seller forbids a buyer to purchase products from the seller's competitors.

A contract under which a seller forbids a buyer to purchase products from the seller's competitors is called an **exclusive-dealing contract.** A seller is prohibited from making an exclusive-dealing contract under Section 3 if the effect of the contract is "to substantially lessen competition or tend to create a monopoly." **CASE EXAMPLE 32.10** In a classic case decided by the United States Supreme Court in 1949, Standard Oil Company, the largest gasoline seller in the nation at that time, made exclusive-dealing contracts with independent stations in seven western states. The contracts involved 16 percent of all retail outlets, with sales amounting to approximately 7 percent of all retail sales in that market. The market was substantially concentrated because the seven largest gasoline suppliers all used exclusive-dealing contracts with their independent retailers. Together, these suppliers controlled 65 percent of the market. The Court looked at market conditions after the arrangements were instituted and found that market shares were extremely stable and entry into the market was apparently restricted. Because

19. *Water Craft Management, LLC v. Mercury Marine*, 457 F.3d 484 (5th Cir. 2006).

competition was "foreclosed in a substantial share" of the relevant market, the Court held that Section 3 of the Clayton Act had been violated.[20] • Note that since the Supreme Court's 1949 decision, a number of subsequent decisions have called the holding in this case into doubt.[21]

Today, it is clear that to violate antitrust law, an exclusive-dealing agreement (or *tying arrangement,* discussed next) must qualitatively and substantially harm competition. To prevail, a plaintiff must present affirmative evidence that the performance of the agreement will foreclose competition and harm consumers.

Tying Arrangement A seller's act of conditioning the sale of a product or service on the buyer's agreement to purchase another product or service from the seller.

Tying Arrangements

When a seller conditions the sale of a product (the tying product) on the buyer's agreement to purchase another product (the tied product) produced or distributed by the same seller, a **tying arrangement** results. The legality of a tying arrangement (or *tie-in sales agreement)* depends on many factors, particularly the purpose of the agreement and its likely effect on competition in the relevant markets (the market for the tying product and the market for the tied product).

EXAMPLE 32.11 Morshigi Precision, Inc., manufactures laptop hardware and provides repair service for the hardware. Morshigi also makes and markets software, but the company will provide support for buyers of the software only if they also buy its hardware service. This is a tying arrangement. Depending on the purpose of the agreement and the effect of the agreement on competition in the market for the two products, the agreement may be illegal. •

Section 3 of the Clayton Act has been held to apply only to commodities, not to services. Some tying arrangements, however, can also be considered agreements that restrain trade in violation of Section 1 of the Sherman Act. Thus, cases involving tying arrangements of services have been brought under Section 1 of the Sherman Act. Although earlier cases condemned tying arrangements as illegal *per se*, courts now evaluate tying agreements under the rule of reason.[22]

Section 7—Mergers

Under Section 7 of the Clayton Act, a person or business organization cannot hold stock and/or assets in another entity "where the effect . . . may be to substantially lessen competition." Section 7 is the statutory authority for preventing mergers or acquisitions (discussed in Chapter 29 on pages 761–763) that could result in monopoly power or a substantial lessening of competition in the marketplace.

Market Concentration The degree to which a small number of firms control a large percentage of a relevant market.

A crucial consideration in most merger cases is the **market concentration** of a product or business. Determining market concentration involves allocating percentage market shares among the various companies in the relevant market. When a small number of companies control a large share of the market, the market is concentrated. **EXAMPLE 32.12** If the four largest grocery stores in Chicago accounted for 80 percent of all retail food sales, the market clearly would be concentrated in those four firms. If one of these stores absorbed the assets and liabilities of another, so the other ceased to exist, the result would be a merger that would further concentrate the market and thereby possibly diminish competition. •

Competition, however, is not necessarily diminished solely as a result of market concentration, and courts will consider other factors in determining whether a merger will violate Section 7. One factor of particular importance in evaluating the effects of a merger is whether the merger will make it more difficult for *potential* competitors to enter the relevant market.

---

20. *Standard Oil Co. of California v. United States*, 337 U.S. 293, 69 S.Ct. 1051, 93 L.Ed. 1371 (1949).
21. See, for example, *Illinois Tool Works, Inc. v. Independent Ink, Inc.*, 547 U.S. 28, 126 S.Ct. 1281, 164 L.Ed.2d 26 (2006); and *Stop & Shop Supermarket Co. v. Blue Cross & Blue Shield of Rhode Island*, 373 F.3d 57 (1st Cir. 2004).
22. See, for example, *Illinois Tool Works, Inc. v. Independent Ink, Inc.*, cited in footnote 21.

Horizontal Merger A merger between two firms that are competing in the same market.

Horizontal Mergers

Mergers between firms that compete with each other in the same market are called **horizontal mergers.** If a horizontal merger creates an entity with a significant market share, the merger will be presumed illegal because it increases market concentration.

When analyzing the legality of a horizontal merger, the courts also consider three other factors: the overall concentration of the relevant product market, the relevant market's history of tending toward concentration, and whether the apparent design of the merger is to establish market power or to restrict competition.

Vertical Merger The acquisition by a company at one stage of production of a company at a higher or lower stage of production (such as a company merging with one of its suppliers or retailers).

Vertical Mergers

A **vertical merger** occurs when a company at one stage of production acquires a company at a higher or lower stage of production. An example of a vertical merger is a company merging with one of its suppliers or retailers. Whether a vertical merger is illegal generally depends on several factors, such as whether the merger would produce a firm controlling an undue percentage share of the relevant market.

The courts also analyze whether the merger would result in a significant increase in the concentration of firms in that market, the barriers to entry into the market, and the apparent intent of the merging parties. Mergers that do not prevent competitors of either merging firm from competing in a segment of the market are legal.

Section 8—Interlocking Directorates

Section 8 of the Clayton Act deals with *interlocking directorates*—that is, the practice of having individuals serve as directors on the boards of two or more competing companies simultaneously. Specifically, no person may be a director in two or more competing corporations at the same time if either of the corporations has capital, surplus, or undivided profits aggregating more than $27,784,000 or competitive sales of $2,778,100 or more. The FTC adjusts the threshold amounts each year. (The amounts given here are those announced by the FTC in 2012.)

The reasoning behind the FTC's prohibition of interlocking directorates is that if two competing businesses share the same officers and directors, the firms are unlikely to compete with one another, or to compete aggressively. If directors or officers do not comply with this prohibition, they may be liable under the Clayton Act.

LEARNING OBJECTIVE 5

What agencies of the federal government enforce the federal antitrust laws?

Enforcement and Exemptions

The federal agencies that enforce the federal antitrust laws are the U.S. Department of Justice (DOJ) and the Federal Trade Commission (FTC). The FTC was established by the Federal Trade Commission Act of 1914. Section 5 of that act condemns all forms of anticompetitive behavior that are not covered under other federal antitrust laws.

KNOW THIS

Section 5 of the Federal Trade Commission Act is broader than the other antitrust laws. It covers nearly all anticompetitive behavior, including conduct that does not violate either the Sherman Act or the Clayton Act.

Enforcement by Federal Agencies

Only the DOJ can prosecute violations of the Sherman Act, which can be either criminal or civil offenses. Violations of the Clayton Act are not crimes, but the act can be enforced by either the DOJ or the FTC through civil proceedings.

Divestiture A company's sale of one or more of its divisions' operating functions under court order as part of the enforcement of the antitrust laws.

The DOJ or the FTC may ask the courts to impose various remedies, including **divestiture** (making a company give up one or more of its operating functions) and dissolution. A meatpacking firm, for instance, might be forced to divest itself of control or ownership of butcher shops. (To find out how you can avoid antitrust problems, see the *Business Application* feature on pages 852 and 853.)

The FTC has the sole authority to enforce violations of Section 5 of the Federal Trade Commission Act. FTC actions are effected through administrative orders, but if a firm violates an FTC order, the FTC can seek court sanctions for the violation.

Enforcement by Private Parties

Treble Damages Damages that, by statute, are three times the amount of actual damages suffered.

A private party who has been injured as a result of a violation of the Sherman Act or the Clayton Act can sue for **treble damages** (three times the actual damages suffered) and attorneys' fees. In some instances, private parties may also seek injunctive relief to prevent antitrust violations. A party wishing to sue under the Sherman Act must prove that

1. The antitrust violation either caused or was a substantial factor in causing the injury that was suffered.
2. The unlawful actions of the accused party affected business activities of the plaintiff that were protected by the antitrust laws.

Exemptions from Antitrust Laws

There are many legislative and constitutional limitations on antitrust enforcement. Most of the statutory or judicially created exemptions to antitrust laws apply in such areas as labor, insurance, and foreign trade, and are listed in Exhibit 32.1 below.

Exhibit 32.1 Exemptions to Antitrust Enforcement

EXEMPTION	SOURCE AND SCOPE
Labor	Clayton Act—Permits unions to organize and bargain without violating antitrust laws and specifies that strikes and other labor activities normally do not violate any federal law.
Agricultural associations	Clayton Act and Capper-Volstead Act of 1922—Allow agricultural cooperatives to set prices.
Fisheries	Fisheries Cooperative Marketing Act of 1976—Allows the fishing industry to set prices.
Insurance companies	McCarran-Ferguson Act of 1945—Exempts the insurance business in states in which the industry is regulated.
Exporters	Webb-Pomerene Act of 1918—Allows U.S. exporters to engage in cooperative activity to compete with similar foreign associations. Export Trading Company Act of 1982—Permits the U.S. Department of Justice to exempt certain exporters.
Professional baseball	The United States Supreme Court has held that professional baseball is exempt because it is not "interstate commerce."[a]
Oil marketing	Interstate Oil Compact of 1935—Allows states to set quotas on oil to be marketed in interstate commerce.
Defense activities	Defense Production Act of 1950—Allows the president to approve, and thereby exempt, certain activities to further the military defense of the United States.
Small businesses' cooperative research	Small Business Administration Act of 1958—Allows small firms to undertake cooperative research.
State actions	The United States Supreme Court has held that actions by a state are exempt if the state clearly articulates and actively supervises the policy behind its action.[b]
Regulated industries	Industries (such as airlines) are exempt when a federal administrative agency (such as the Federal Aviation Administration) has primary regulatory authority.
Businesspersons' joint efforts to seek government action	Cooperative efforts by businesspersons to obtain legislative, judicial, or executive action are exempt unless it is clear that an effort is "objectively baseless" and is an attempt to make anticompetitive use of government processes.[c]

a. *Federal Baseball Club of Baltimore, Inc. v. National League of Professional Baseball Clubs,* 259 U.S. 200, 42 S.Ct. 465, 66 L.Ed. 898 (1922). A federal district court has held that this exemption applies only to the game's reserve system. (Under the reserve system, teams hold players' contracts for the players' entire careers. The reserve system generally is being replaced by the free agency system.) See *Piazza v. Major League Baseball,* 831 F.Supp. 420 (E.D.Pa. 1993).

b. See *Parker v. Brown,* 317 U.S. 341, 63 S.Ct. 307, 87 L.Ed. 315 (1943).

c. *Eastern Railroad Presidents Conference v. Noerr Motor Freight, Inc.,* 365 U.S. 127, 81 S.Ct. 523, 5 L.Ed.2d 464 (1961); and *United Mine Workers of America v. Pennington,* 381 U.S. 657, 89 S.Ct. 1585, 14 L.Ed.2d 626 (1965). These two cases established the exception often referred to as the *Noerr-Pennington* doctrine.

One of the most significant of these exemptions covers joint efforts by businesspersons to obtain legislative, judicial, or executive action. Under this exemption, Blu-ray producers can jointly lobby Congress to change the copyright laws without being held liable for attempting to restrain trade. Another exemption covers professional baseball teams.

U.S. Antitrust Laws in the Global Context

U.S. antitrust laws have a broad application. Not only may persons in foreign nations be subject to their provisions, but the laws may also be applied to protect foreign consumers and competitors from violations committed by U.S. business firms. Consequently, *foreign persons,* a term that by definition includes foreign governments, may sue under U.S. antitrust laws in U.S. courts.

The Extraterritorial Application of U.S. Antitrust Laws

Section 1 of the Sherman Act provides for the extraterritorial effect of the U.S. antitrust laws. The United States is a major proponent of free competition in the global economy, and thus any conspiracy that has a *substantial effect* on U.S. commerce is within the reach of the Sherman Act. The violation may even occur outside the United States, and foreign persons including governments can be sued for violation of U.S. antitrust laws. Before U.S. courts will exercise jurisdiction and apply antitrust laws, it must be shown that the alleged violation had a substantial effect on U.S. commerce. U.S. jurisdiction is automatically invoked, however, when a *per se* violation occurs.

If a domestic firm, for example, joins a foreign cartel to control the production, price, or distribution of goods, and this cartel has a *substantial effect* on U.S. commerce, a *per se* violation may exist. Hence, both the domestic firm and the foreign cartel could be sued for violation of the U.S. antitrust laws. Likewise, if a foreign firm doing business in the United States enters into a price-fixing or other anticompetitive agreement to control a portion of U.S. markets, a *per se* violation may exist.

In the following case, the court had to decide whether an alleged anticompetitive conspiracy had a substantial effect on U.S. commerce.

Case 32.3

Carrier Corp. v. Outokumpu Oyj

United States Court of Appeals, Sixth Circuit, 673 F.3d 430 (2012). www.ca6.uscourts.gov[a]

(tbabasade/iStockphoto.com)

Why did Carrier sue Outokumpu Oyj?

FACTS Carrier Corporation is a U.S. firm that manufactures air-conditioning and refrigeration (ACR) equipment. To make these products, Carrier uses ACR copper tubing bought from Outokumpu Oyj, a Finnish company. Carrier is one of the world's largest purchasers of ACR copper tubing. The Commission of the European Communities (EC) found that Outokumpu had conspired with other companies to fix ACR tubing prices in Europe. Carrier then filed a suit in a U.S. court, alleging that the cartel (group) had also conspired to fix prices in the United States by agreeing that only Outokumpu would sell ACR tubing in the U.S. market. The district court dismissed Carrier's claim for lack of jurisdiction. Carrier appealed.

ISSUE Did the Finnish company's anticompetitive actions have a sufficient effect on U.S. commerce to enable a U.S. court to exercise jurisdiction over it under the Sherman Act?

a. In the left-hand column, under "Opinions," click on "Opinions Search." When that page opens, type "Outokumpu Oyj" in the "Short Title *contains*" box, and click on "Submit Query." In the result, click on the opinion number to access the opinion. The U.S. Court of Appeals for the Sixth Circuit maintains this Web site.

Case 32.3—Continued

DECISION Yes. The federal appellate court reversed the district court's judgment for the defendant.

REASON Carrier's complaint sufficiently alleged that Outokumpu's conspiracy had a substantial effect on U.S. commerce. Carrier alleged that Outokumpu had conspired to divide up U.S. customers, which caused higher prices for ACR copper tubing. The complaint also alleged specific details about the conspiracy by drawing from the EC's decisions. It did not matter that the EC did not identify a conspiracy aimed at the United States because that was beyond the scope of its decision. Carrier had some evidence that the conspiracy reached the United States because Outokumpu's competitors solicited its business only after the conspiracy ended. Therefore, the district court had jurisdiction over Carrier's Sherman Act claims.

CRITICAL THINKING—Legal Consideration *When this case proceeds, should the district court apply the rule of reason? Why or why not?*

The Application of Foreign Antitrust Laws

Large U.S. companies increasingly need to worry about the application of foreign antitrust laws as well. The European Union, in particular, has stepped up its enforcement actions against antitrust violators, as discussed in this chapter's *Beyond Our Borders* feature below.

Many other nations also have laws that promote competition and prohibit trade restraints. For instance, Japanese antitrust laws forbid unfair trade practices, monopolization, and restrictions that unreasonably restrain trade. China's antitrust rules restrict monopolization and price fixing (although China has claimed that the government may set prices on exported goods without violating these rules). Indonesia, Malaysia, South Korea, and Vietnam all have statutes protecting competition. Argentina, Brazil, Chile, Peru, and several other Latin American countries have adopted modern antitrust laws as well.

Most of these antitrust laws apply extraterritorially, as U.S. antitrust laws do. This means that a U.S. company may be subject to another nation's antitrust laws if the company's conduct has a substantial effect on that nation's commerce. For instance, South Korea fined Intel, Inc., the world's largest semiconductor chip maker, $25 million for antitrust violations in 2008. Japan settled an antitrust case against Intel in 2005.

BEYOND OUR BORDERS — The European Union's Expanding Role in Antitrust Litigation

The European Union (EU) has laws promoting competition that are stricter in many respects than those of the United States. Although the EU's laws provide only for civil, rather than criminal, penalties, the rules define more conduct as anticompetitive than U.S. laws do.

The EU actively pursues antitrust violators, especially individual companies and cartels that engage in alleged monopolistic conduct. For example, in 2009, the EU fined chip-making giant Intel, Inc., $1.44 billion in an antitrust case. According to European regulators, Intel offered computer manufacturers and retailers price discounts and marketing subsidies if they agreed to buy Intel's chips rather than the chips produced by Intel's main competitor in Europe. The EU has also fined Microsoft Corporation more than $2 billion in the last twelve years for anticompetitive conduct.

The EU is investigating Google, Inc., for potentially violating European antitrust laws by thwarting competition in Internet search engines. Ironically, in 2011, Microsoft—which has paid substantial fines to the EU for anticompetitive conduct—filed its own complaint with the EU against Google. Among other things, Microsoft claims that Google has unlawfully restricted competing search engines from accessing YouTube, content from book publishers, advertiser data, and more. (A similar case brought against Google in the United States, for monopolizing or attempting to monopolize Internet search engines, was dismissed in 2011.[a])

Critical Thinking

Some commentators argue that EU regulators are too focused on reining in powerful U.S. technology companies, such as Microsoft and Intel. How might the large fines imposed by the EU on successful U.S. technology firms affect competition in the United States?

a. See *TradeComet.com, LLC v. Google, Inc.*, 647 F.3d 472 (2d Cir. 2011).

Reviewing . . . Antitrust Law and Promoting Competition

The Internet Corporation for Assigned Names and Numbers (ICANN) is a nonprofit entity that organizes Internet domain names. It is governed by a board of directors elected by various groups with commercial interests in the Internet. One of ICANN's functions is to authorize an entity to serve as a registrar for certain "top level domains" (TLDs). ICANN entered into an agreement with VeriSign to provide registry services for the ".com" TLD in accordance with ICANN's specifications. VeriSign complained that ICANN was restricting the services that it could make available as a registrar and was blocking new services, imposing unnecessary conditions on those services, and setting prices at which the services were offered. VeriSign claimed that ICANN's control of the registry services for domain names violated Section 1 of the Sherman Act. Using the information presented in the chapter, answer the following questions.

1. Should ICANN's actions be judged under the rule of reason or be deemed a *per se* violation of Section 1 of the Sherman Act? Explain.
2. Should ICANN's actions be viewed as a horizontal or a vertical restraint of trade? Explain.
3. Does it matter that ICANN's directors are chosen by groups with a commercial interest in the Internet? Why or why not?
4. If the dispute is judged under the rule of reason, what might be ICANN's defense for having a standardized set of registry services that must be used?

DEBATE THIS The Internet and the rise of e-commerce have rendered our antitrust concepts and laws obsolete.

BUSINESS APPLICATION

How Can You Avoid Antitrust Problems?*

Business managers need to be aware of how antitrust legislation may affect their activities. In addition to the federal antitrust laws covered in this chapter, the states also have antitrust and unfair competition laws. Moreover, state authorities have the power to bring civil lawsuits to enforce federal antitrust laws. Additionally, antitrust law is subject to various interpretations by the courts. Unless a businessperson exercises caution, a court may decide that his or her actions are in violation of a federal or state statute.

Pricing Issues

Almost all businesses have competitors and want to outsell those competitors. The pricing of a business's goods or services is extremely important not only for its volume of sales, but also for its bottom-line profit. When setting or changing prices, businesses frequently hire a cost accountant to perform an analysis. This is only a start because a firm must also consider the prices of a competitor's similar or identical products. Most businesses do not want a "price war" with rapidly declining prices.

Thus, it is not uncommon for a business to charge basically the same price as its competitors. A problem arises when there is an agreement (express or implied) to fix the price. This is a *per se* violation of Section 1 of the Sherman Act and can result in criminal or civil actions (including treble damages).

Knowing the price a competitor charges—and meeting that price—is not a violation in and of itself. Frequently, the legality depends on how the information was obtained. Violations occur when there is a communication (regardless of purpose) between a business owner (or employee) and a direct competitor. If concerned that a communication may cause antitrust pricing problems, businesspersons should consult with an attorney who can explain what is legal when dealing with competitors.

*This *Business Application* is not meant to substitute for the services of an attorney who is licensed to practice law in your state.

Implications of Foreign Law

Antitrust issues are not limited to domestic firms doing business in the United States. In today's global economy, many companies conduct business in other nations and with foreign businesses. Antitrust laws in other countries differ from U.S. law and can apply to a U.S. firm that has dealings with businesses located in a foreign nation even though the firm does not have a physical presence there. Always be aware of the antitrust laws of any country in which you are doing business. Generally, any businessperson who is considering doing business overseas should seek counsel from a competent attorney concerning potential antitrust violations.

Checklist for Avoiding Antitrust Problems

1. *Exercise caution when communicating and dealing with competitors.*
2. *Seek the advice of an attorney specializing in antitrust law to ensure that your business practices and agreements do not violate antitrust laws.*
3. *If you conduct business in other nations, obtain the advice of an attorney who is familiar with the antitrust laws of those nations.*

Key Terms

antitrust law 833
attempted monopolization 844
concentrated industry 839
divestiture 848
exclusive-dealing contract 846
group boycott 839
horizontal merger 848
horizontal restraint 837
market concentration 847
market power 835
monopolization 841
monopoly 835
monopoly power 835
per se violation 836
predatory pricing 840
price discrimination 845
price-fixing agreement 837
resale price maintenance agreement 840
rule of reason 836
treble damages 849
tying arrangement 847
vertical merger 848
vertical restraint 839
vertically integrated firm 839

Chapter Summary: Antitrust Law and Promoting Competition

The Sherman Antitrust Act (1890) **(See pages 834–845.)**	1. *Major provisions*— a. Section 1—Prohibits contracts, combinations, and conspiracies in restraint of trade. (1) Horizontal restraints subject to Section 1 include price-fixing agreements, group boycotts (joint refusals to deal), horizontal market divisions, and trade association agreements. (2) Vertical restraints subject to Section 1 include territorial or customer restrictions, resale price maintenance agreements, and refusals to deal. b. Section 2—Prohibits monopolies and attempts to monopolize. 2. *Jurisdictional requirements*—The Sherman Act applies only to activities that have a significant impact on interstate commerce. 3. *Interpretive rules*— a. *Per se* rule—Applied to restraints on trade that are so inherently anticompetitive that they cannot be justified and are deemed illegal as a matter of law. b. Rule of reason—Applied when an anticompetitive agreement may be justified by legitimate benefits. Under the rule of reason, the lawfulness of a trade restraint will be determined by the purpose and effects of the restraint.
The Clayton Act (1914) **(See pages 845–848.)**	The major provisions are as follows: 1. *Section 2*—As amended in 1936 by the Robinson-Patman Act, prohibits a seller engaged in interstate commerce from price discrimination that substantially lessens competition. 2. *Section 3*—Prohibits exclusionary practices, such as exclusive-dealing contracts and tying arrangements, when the effect may be to substantially lessen competition. 3. *Section 7*—Prohibits mergers when the effect may be to substantially lessen competition or to tend to create a monopoly. a. A horizontal merger will be presumed unlawful if the entity created by the merger will have a significant market share. b. A vertical merger will be unlawful if the merger prevents competitors of either merging firm from competing in a segment of the market that otherwise would be open to them, resulting in a substantial lessening of competition. 4. *Section 8*—Prohibits interlocking directorates.

Continued

Chapter Summary: Antitrust Law and Promoting Competition—Continued

Enforcement and Exemptions (See pages 848–850.)	1. *Enforcement*—The U.S. Department of Justice and the Federal Trade Commission enforce the federal antitrust laws. Private parties who have been injured as a result of violations of the Sherman Act or Clayton Act may bring civil suits, and, if successful, they may be awarded treble damages and attorneys' fees. 2. *Exemptions*—Numerous exemptions from the antitrust laws have been created. See Exhibit 32.1 on page 849 for a list of significant exemptions.
U.S. Antitrust Laws in the Global Context (See pages 850–852.)	1. *Application of U.S. laws*—U.S. antitrust laws can be applied in foreign nations to protect foreign consumers and competitors. Foreign governments and persons can also bring actions under U.S. antitrust laws. Section 1 of the Sherman Act applies to any conspiracy that has a substantial effect on U.S. commerce. 2. *Application of foreign laws*—Many other nations also have laws that promote competition and prohibit trade restraints, and some are more restrictive than U.S. laws. These foreign antitrust laws are increasingly being applied to U.S. firms.

ExamPrep

ISSUE SPOTTERS

1. Under what circumstances would Pop's Market, a small store in a small, isolated town, be considered a monopolist? If Pop's is a monopolist, is it in violation of Section 2 of the Sherman Act? Why or why not? **(See page 841.)**
2. Maple Corporation conditions the sale of its syrup on the buyer's agreement to buy Maple's pancake mix. What factors would a court consider to decide whether this arrangement violates the Clayton Act? **(See page 847.)**

—Check your answers to the Issue Spotters against the answers provided in Appendix E at the end of this text.

BEFORE THE TEST

Go to www.cengagebrain.com, enter the ISBN 9781133273561, and click on "Find" to locate this textbook's Web site. Then, click on "Access Now" under "Study Tools," and select Chapter 32 at the top. There, you will find a Practice Quiz that you can take to assess your mastery of the concepts in this chapter, as well as Flashcards, a Glossary of important terms, and Video Questions (when assigned).

For Review

Answers to the even-numbered questions in this For Review section can be found in Appendix F at the end of this text.

1. What is a monopoly? What is market power? How do these concepts relate to each other?
2. What anticompetitive activities are prohibited by Section 1 of the Sherman Act?
3. What type of activity is prohibited by Section 2 of the Sherman Act?
4. What are the four major provisions of the Clayton Act, and what types of activities do these provisions prohibit?
5. What agencies of the federal government enforce the federal antitrust laws?

Business Scenarios and Case Problems

32–1 Sherman Act. An agreement that is blatantly and substantially anticompetitive is deemed a *per se* violation of Section 1 of the Sherman Act. Under what rule is an agreement analyzed if it appears to be anticompetitive but is not a *per se* violation? In making this analysis, what factors will a court consider? **(See page 836.)**

32–2 Question with Sample Answer—Antitrust Laws. Allitron, Inc., and Donovan, Ltd., are interstate competitors selling similar appliances, principally in the states of Illinois, Indiana, Kentucky, and Ohio. Allitron and Donovan agree that Allitron will no longer sell in Indiana and Ohio and that Donovan will no longer sell in Illinois and Kentucky. Have Allitron and Donovan violated any antitrust laws? If so, which law? Explain. **(See pages 836–840.)**

—For a sample answer to Question 32–2, go to Appendix G at the end of this text.]

32–3 Tying Arrangement. John Sheridan owned a Marathon gas station franchise. He sued Marathon Petroleum Co. under Section 1 of the Sherman Act and Section 3 of the Clayton Act, charging it with illegally tying the processing of credit-card sales to the gas station. As a condition of obtaining a Marathon dealership, dealers had to agree to let the franchisor process credit cards. They could not shop around to see if credit-card processing could be obtained at a lower price from another source. The district court dismissed the case for failure to state a claim. Sheridan appealed. Is there a tying arrangement? If so, does it violate the law? [*Sheridan v. Marathon Petroleum Co.*, 530 F.3d 590 (7th Cir. 2008)] **(See page 847.)**

32–4 **Case Problem with Sample Answer—Section 2 of the Sherman Act.** When Deer Valley Resort Co. (DVRC) was developing its ski resort in the Wasatch Mountains near Park City, Utah, it sold parcels of land in the resort village to third parties. Each sales contract reserved the right of approval over the conduct of certain businesses on the property, including ski rentals. For fifteen years, DVRC permitted Christy Sports, LLC, to rent skis in competition with DVRC's ski rental outlet. When DVRC opened a new midmountain ski rental outlet, it revoked Christy's permission to rent skis. This meant that most skiers who flew into Salt Lake City and shuttled to Deer Valley had few choices: they could carry their ski equipment onto their flights, take a shuttle into Park City and look for cheaper ski rentals there, or rent from DVRC. Christy filed a suit against DVRC. Was DVRC's action an attempt to monopolize in violation of Section 2 of the Sherman Act? Why or why not? [*Christy Sports, LLC v. Deer Valley Resort Co.*, 555 F.3d 1188 (10th Cir. 2009)] **(See pages 840–844.)**

—For a sample answer to Problem 32–4, go to Appendix H at the end of this text.

32–5 **The Sherman Act.** Together, EMI, Sony BMG Music Entertainment, Universal Music Group Recordings, Inc., and Warner Music Group Corp. produced, licensed, and distributed 80 percent of the digital music sold in the United States. The companies formed MusicNet to sell music to online services that sold the songs to consumers. MusicNet required all of the services to sell the songs at the same price and subject to the same restrictions. Digitization of music became cheaper, but MusicNet did not change its prices. Did MusicNet violate the antitrust laws? Explain. [*Starr v. Sony BMG Music Entertainment*, 592 F.3d 314 (2d Cir. 2010)] **(See pages 836–840.)**

32–6 **Price Discrimination.** Dayton Superior Corp. sells its products in interstate commerce to several companies, including Spa Steel Products, Inc. The purchasers often compete directly with each other for customers. From 2005 to 2007, one of Spa Steel's customers purchased Dayton Superior's products from two of Spa Steel's competitors. According to the customer, Spa Steel's prices were always 10 to 15 percent higher even though they were for the same products. As a result, Spa Steel lost sales to at least that customer and perhaps others. Spa Steel wants to sue Dayton Superior for price discrimination. Which requirements for such a claim under Section 2 of the Clayton Act does Spa Steel satisfy? What additional facts will it need to prove? [*Dayton Superior Corp. v. Spa Steel Products, Inc.*, 2012 WL 113663 (N.D.N.Y. 2012)] **(See page 845.)**

32–7 **A Question of Ethics—Section 1 of the Sherman Act.** In the 1990s, DuCoa, LP, made choline chloride, a B-complex vitamin essential for the growth and development of animals. The U.S. market for choline chloride was divided into thirds among DuCoa, Bioproducts, Inc., and Chinook Group, Ltd. To stabilize the market and keep the price of the vitamin higher than it would otherwise be, the companies agreed to fix the price and allocate market share by deciding which of them would offer the lowest price to each customer. At times, however, the companies disregarded the agreement. During an increase in competitive activity in 1997, Daniel Rose became president of DuCoa and found out about the conspiracy. In 1998, Rose implemented a strategy to persuade DuCoa's competitors to rejoin the conspiracy. By April, the three companies had reallocated their market shares and increased their prices. In June, the U.S. Department of Justice began to investigate allegations of price fixing in the vitamin market. Ultimately, Rose was convicted of conspiracy to violate Section 1 of the Sherman Act. [*United States v. Rose*, 449 F.3d 627 (5th Cir. 2006)] **(See pages 836–840.)**

1. The court "enhanced" Rose's sentence to thirty months' imprisonment, one year of supervised release, and a $20,000 fine because of his role as "a manager or supervisor" in the conspiracy. Rose appealed this enhancement. Was it fair to increase Rose's sentence on this ground? Why or why not?
2. Was Rose's participation in the conspiracy unethical? If so, how might Rose have behaved ethically instead? Explain.

Critical Thinking and Writing Assignments

32–8 **Business Law Writing.** Write two paragraphs explaining some ways that antitrust laws might place too great of a burden on commerce in the global marketplace.

32–9 **Business Law Critical Thinking Group Assignment.** Residents of the city of Madison, Wisconsin, became concerned about overconsumption of liquor near the campus of the University of Wisconsin (UW). The city initiated a new policy, imposing conditions on area bars to discourage reduced-price "specials" that were believed to encourage high-volume and dangerous drinking. In 2012, the city began to draft an ordinance to ban all drink specials. Bar owners responded by announcing that they had "voluntarily" agreed to discontinue drink specials on Friday and Saturday nights after 8:00 P.M. The city put its ordinance on hold. Several UW students filed a lawsuit against the local bar owners' association alleging violations of antitrust law.

1. The first group will identify the grounds on which the plaintiffs might base their claim for relief and formulate an argument on behalf of the plaintiffs.
2. The second group will determine whether the defendants are exempt from the antitrust laws.
3. The third group will decide how the court should rule in this dispute and provide reasons for its answer.

33 CHAPTER

Consumer and Environmental Law

CHAPTER OUTLINE

- Consumer Law
- Environmental Law

LEARNING OBJECTIVES

The five learning objectives below are designed to help improve your understanding of the chapter. After reading this chapter, you should be able to answer the following questions:

1. When will advertising be deemed deceptive?
2. What are the major federal statutes providing for consumer protection in credit transactions?
3. Under what common law theories can polluters be held liable?
4. What is contained in an environmental impact statement, and who must file one?
5. What major federal statutes regulate air and water pollution?

(AVTG/iStockphoto.com)

"The good of the people is the greatest law."

—Marcus Tullius Cicero, 106–43 B.C.E. (Roman politician and orator)

During the heyday of the consumer movement in the 1960s and 1970s, Congress enacted a substantial amount of legislation to protect "the good of the people," to borrow a phrase from Marcus Tullius Cicero (see the chapter-opening quotation above). All statutes, agency rules, and common law judicial decisions that attempt to protect the interests of consumers are classified as *consumer law.*

Since the financial crisis that started in 2008, there has been a renewed interest in protecting consumers from credit-card companies, financial institutions, and insurance companies. Congress enacted new credit-card regulations, as well as certain financial reforms to regulate the nation's largest banks. Congress also enacted health-care reforms, including a law that requires chain restaurants to post the caloric content of foods on their menus.

In the first part of this chapter, we examine some of the major laws and regulations protecting consumers. We then turn to a discussion of environmental law, which consists of all of the laws and regulations designed to protect and preserve the environment.

(LauriPatterson/iStockphoto.com)

Were Campbell's claims truthful?

Consumer Law

Sources of consumer protection exist at all levels of government. At the federal level, a number of laws have been passed to define the duties of sellers and the rights of consumers. Exhibit 33.1 below indicates many of the areas of consumer law that are regulated by statutes. Federal administrative agencies, such as the Federal Trade Commission (FTC), also provide an important source of consumer protection. Nearly every agency and department of the federal government has an office of consumer affairs, and most states have one or more such offices, including the offices of state attorneys general, to assist consumers.

Deceptive Advertising

LEARNING OBJECTIVE 1
When will advertising be deemed deceptive?

One of the earliest—and still one of the most important—federal consumer protection laws is the Federal Trade Commission Act (mentioned in Chapter 32). The act created the FTC to carry out the broadly stated goal of preventing unfair and deceptive trade practices, including deceptive advertising.

Deceptive Advertising Advertising that misleads consumers, either by making unjustified claims about a product's performance or by omitting a material fact concerning the product's composition or performance.

Generally, **deceptive advertising** occurs if a reasonable consumer would be misled by the advertising claim. Vague generalities and obvious exaggerations (that a reasonable person would not believe to be true) are permissible. These claims are known as *puffery* (see page 439 in Chapter 17). When a claim has the appearance of authenticity, however, it may create problems. Advertising that *appears* to be based on factual evidence but that in fact cannot be scientifically supported will be deemed deceptive. A classic example occurred in a 1944 case in which the claim that a skin cream would restore youthful qualities to aged skin was deemed deceptive.[1]

Half-Truths

Some advertisements contain "half-truths," meaning that the information is true but incomplete and, therefore, leads consumers to a false conclusion. **EXAMPLE 33.1** The maker of Campbell's soups advertised that "most" Campbell's soups were low in fat and cholesterol and thus were helpful in fighting heart disease. What the ad did not say was that Campbell's soups were also high in sodium and that high-sodium diets may increase the risk of heart disease. Hence, the FTC ruled that the company's claims were deceptive. ● Advertising featuring an endorsement by a celebrity may be deemed deceptive if the celebrity does not actually use the product.

Exhibit 33.1 Selected Areas of Consumer Law Regulated by Statutes

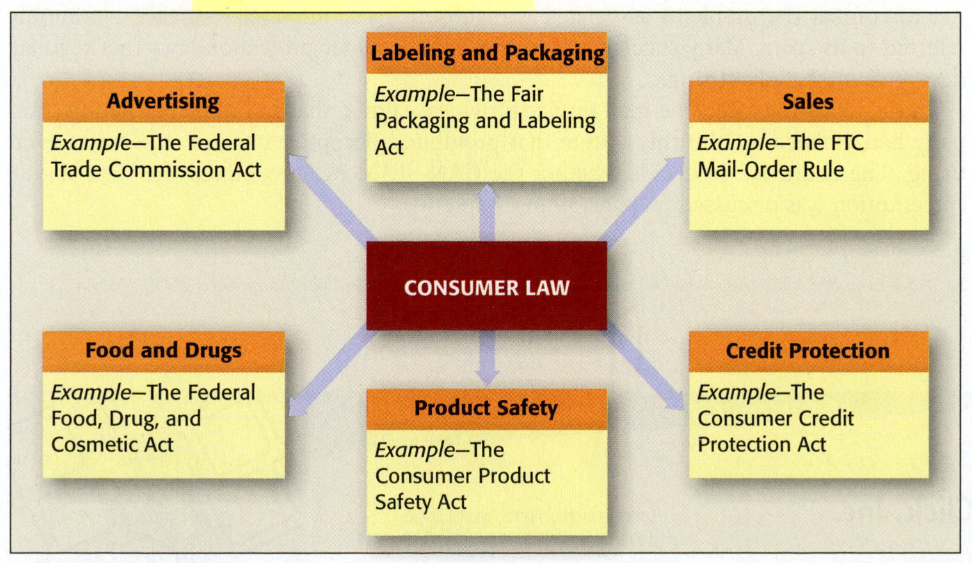

Bait-and-Switch Advertising

The FTC has issued rules that govern specific advertising techniques. One of the more important rules is contained in the

1. *Charles of the Ritz Distributors Corp. v. FTC*, 143 F.2d 676 (2d Cir. 1944).

Bait-and-Switch Advertising Advertising a product at an attractive price and then telling the consumer that the advertised product is not available or is of poor quality and encouraging her or him to purchase a more expensive item.

FTC's "Guides Against Bait Advertising."[2] The rule is designed to prevent **bait-and-switch advertising**—that is, advertising a very low price for a particular item that will likely be unavailable to the consumer and then encouraging him or her to purchase a more expensive item.

The low price is the "bait" to lure the consumer into the store. The salesperson is instructed to "switch" the consumer to a different, more expensive item. According to the FTC guidelines, bait-and-switch advertising occurs if the seller refuses to show the advertised item, fails to have reasonable quantities of it available, fails to promise to deliver the advertised item within a reasonable time, or discourages employees from selling the item.

"Ads are the cave art of the twentieth century."

Marshall McLuhan, 1911–1980 (Canadian academic and commentator)

Online Deceptive Advertising Deceptive advertising can occur in the online environment as well. The FTC actively monitors online advertising and has identified numerous Web sites that have made false or deceptive claims for products ranging from medical treatments for various diseases to exercise equipment and weight-loss aids.

The FTC has issued guidelines to help online businesses comply with the laws prohibiting deceptive advertising.[3] These guidelines include the following three basic requirements:

1. All ads—both online and offline—must be truthful and not misleading.
2. The claims made in an ad must be substantiated—that is, advertisers must have evidence to back up their claims.
3. Ads cannot be unfair, which the FTC defines as "likely to cause substantial consumer injury that consumers could not reasonably avoid and that is not outweighed by the benefit to consumers or competition."

Clear and Conspicuous Disclosure The guidelines also call for "clear and conspicuous" disclosure of any qualifying or limiting information. Because consumers may not read an entire Web page, the disclosure should be placed as close as possible to the claim being qualified. The next-best location is on a section of the page to which a consumer can easily scroll. Generally, hyperlinks to a disclosure are recommended only for lengthy disclosures.

Spam As discussed on page 120 in Chapter 4, Congress passed the federal CAN-SPAM Act to combat the problems associated with unsolicited commercial e-mails, commonly referred to as spam. Many states have also passed consumer protection laws that regulate deceptive online advertising.

In the following case, an e-mail service provider claimed that an online marketing company had violated a California statute that prohibited deceptive content in e-mail advertising. The court had to decide whether the CAN-SPAM Act preempted the state statute (preemption was discussed on page 39 in Chapter 2).

2. 16 C.F.R. Section 288.
3. *"Advertising and Marketing on the Internet: Rules of the Road,"* Federal Trade Commission, Sept. 2000, Web.

Case 33.1

Hypertouch, Inc. v. ValueClick, Inc.

California Court of Appeal, Second District, 192 Cal.App.4th 805, 123 Cal.Rptr.3d 8 (2011).

(pressureUA/Shutterstock.com)

FACTS Hypertouch, Inc., provides e-mail service to customers located inside and outside California. ValueClick, Inc., and its subsidiaries provide online marketing services to third party advertisers that promote retail products. ValueClick contracts with these advertisers to place offers on its Web sites. ValueClick also contracts with affiliates that send out commercial e-mail advertisements. The advertisements include links redirecting consumers to promotions on ValueClick's

Case 33.1—Continued

Web sites. If a consumer clicks through an e-mail advertisement and participates in a promotional offer, the affiliate that sent the initial e-mail is compensated for generating a customer "lead." The affiliate, rather than ValueClick, controls the content and headers of the e-mails. Hypertouch filed a complaint against ValueClick, its subsidiaries, and others for violating a California state statute that prohibits e-mail advertising that contains deceptive content and headings. The trial court held that the federal CAN-SPAM Act preempts the California statute and granted a summary judgment in favor of ValueClick. Hypertouch appealed.

ISSUE Does the federal CAN-SPAM Act preempt California's statute on deceptive e-mail advertising (spam)?

DECISION No. The California Court of Appeal held that California's anti-spam statute is not preempted by the federal CAN-SPAM Act.

REASON The CAN-SPAM Act expressly exempts from preemption state laws that prohibit "falsity or deception" in commercial e-mail. The trial court had interpreted this exemption to apply only to state statutes that require a plaintiff to establish the elements of common law fraud. But the appellate court disagreed, finding that "sections of the CAN-SPAM Act indicate that the phrase 'falsity and deception' was not intended to apply only to common law fraud." According to the court, the states are "free to regulate the use of deceptive practices in commercial e-mails in whatever manner they [choose]." The California statute imposes strict liability on anyone who advertises in a commercial e-mail that contains false, deceptive, or misleading information, whether or not the advertiser has knowledge of the violation. Evidence showed that ValueClick had advertised in more than 45,000 e-mails received by Hypertouch customers that contained deceptive "header information" in violation of the statute. Therefore, the court reversed the lower court's decision and remanded the case for trial.

CRITICAL THINKING—Social Consideration *How might the heading of an e-mail advertisement be deceptive? Describe several ways.*

Federal Trade Commission Actions

If the FTC concludes that a given advertisement is unfair or deceptive, it sends a formal complaint to the alleged offender. The company may agree to settle the complaint without further proceedings. If not, the FTC can conduct a hearing before an *administrative law judge* (see page 10 in Chapter 1) in which the company can present its defense.

FTC Orders and Remedies

If the FTC succeeds in proving that an advertisement is unfair or deceptive, it usually issues a **cease-and-desist order** requiring the company to stop the challenged advertising. In some circumstances, the FTC may also require **counteradvertising** in which the company advertises anew—in print, on the Internet, on radio, and on television—to inform the public about the earlier misinformation. The FTC sometimes institutes a **multiple product order**, which requires a firm to cease and desist from false advertising in regard to all of its products, not just the product that was the subject of the action.

Cease-and-Desist Order An administrative or judicial order prohibiting a person or business firm from conducting activities that an agency or court has deemed illegal.

Counteradvertising New advertising that is undertaken to correct earlier false claims that were made about a product.

Multiple Product Order An order requiring a firm that has engaged in deceptive advertising to cease and desist from false advertising in regard to all the firm's products.

Damages When Consumers Are Injured

When a company's deceptive ad involves wrongful charges to consumers, the FTC may seek other remedies, including restitution. **CASE EXAMPLE 33.2** Verity International, Ltd., billed phone-line subscribers who accessed certain online pornography sites at the rate for international calls to Madagascar. When consumers complained about the charges, Verity employees told them that the charges were valid and had to be paid, or the consumers would face further collection action. A federal appellate court held that this representation of "uncontestability" was deceptive and a violation of the FTC Act and ordered Verity to pay nearly $18 million in restitution to consumers.[4]

4. *FTC v. Verity International, Ltd.*, 443 F.3d 48 (2d Cir. 2006).

The Telemarketing Sales Rule

The FTC's Telemarketing Sales Rule (TSR)[5] requires a telemarketer to identify the seller, describe the product being sold, and disclose all material facts related to the sale. Material facts include the total cost of the goods being sold, any restrictions on obtaining or using the goods, and whether a sale will be considered final and nonrefundable. The act makes it illegal for telemarketers to misrepresent information (including facts about their goods or services and earnings potential, for example).

Changes in technology often require changes in the law.

A telemarketer must also remove a consumer's name from its list of potential contacts if the consumer so requests. An amendment to the Telemarketing Sales Rule established the national Do Not Call Registry. Telemarketers may not call consumers who have placed their names on the list.

Labeling and Packaging

In general, labels must be accurate, and they must use words that are understood by the ordinary consumer. In some instances, labels must specify the raw materials used in the product, such as the percentage of cotton, nylon, or other fibers used in a garment. In other instances, the product must carry a warning, such as those required on cigarette packages and advertising.[6]

(AP Photo/Reed Saxon)

Does federal law preempt state deceptive advertising laws with respect to published fuel economy estimates?

Fuel Economy Labels on Automobiles

The Energy Policy and Conservation Act (EPCA)[7] requires automakers to attach an information label to every new car. This label must include the Environmental Protection Agency's fuel economy estimate for the vehicle. **CASE EXAMPLE 33.3** Gaetano Paduano bought a new Honda Civic Hybrid in California. The information label on the car included the fuel economy estimate from the Environmental Protection Agency (EPA). Honda's sales brochure added, "Just drive the Hybrid like you would a conventional car and save on fuel bills."

When Paduano discovered that the car's fuel economy was less than half of the EPA's estimate, he sued Honda for deceptive advertising. The automaker claimed that the federal law (the EPCA) preempted the state's deceptive advertising law, but the court held in Paduano's favor, finding that the federal statute did not preempt a claim for deceptive advertising made under state law.[8] ●

Food Labeling

Several statutes deal specifically with food labeling. The Fair Packaging and Labeling Act requires that food product labels identify (1) the product, (2) the net quantity of the contents, (3) the manufacturer, and (4) the packager or distributor.[9] The Nutrition Labeling and Education Act requires food labels to provide standard nutrition facts and regulates the use of such terms as *fresh* and *low fat*. The U.S. Food and Drug Administration (FDA) and the U.S. Department of Agriculture (USDA) are the primary agencies that issue regulations on food labeling. These rules are updated annually and require the labels on fresh meats, vegetables, and fruits to indicate where the food originated.

---

5. 16 C.F.R. Sections 310.1–310.8.

6. 15 U.S.C. Sections 1331 *et seq.*

7. 49 U.S.C. Section 32908(b)(1).

8. *Paduano v. American Honda Motor Co.*, 169 Cal.App. 4th 1453, 88 Cal.Rptr.3d 90 (2009). This case is also featured in Unit 1's *Business Case Study with Dissenting Opinion* on pages 233–235.

9. 15 U.S.C. Sections 4401–4408.

Menu Labeling Regulations The health-care reform bill enacted in 2010 (see page 864) included a provision aimed at combating the problem of obesity in the United States. The provision requires all restaurant chains with twenty or more locations to post the caloric content of the foods on their menus so that customers will know how many calories they are eating.[10] In addition, restaurants are required to post guidelines on the number of calories that an average person requires daily. Customers can use this information to determine what portion of a day's calories a particular food choice will provide. The new federal law supersedes all state and local laws already in existence.

Any restaurant to which the law applies must post the caloric content of the foods listed on its standard menu, menu boards, or menu lists for drive-thru windows. Signs also have to be posted near salad bars and buffets, providing information on the foods offered there. Exempt from the rules are condiments, daily specials, and foods offered for only a limited period (less than sixty days). The FDA is developing specific regulations supporting the standards for menu labeling.

Sales

"Cooling-Off" Laws Laws that allow buyers to cancel door-to-door sales contracts within a certain period of time, such as three business days.

A number of statutes protect consumers by requiring the disclosure of certain terms in sales transactions and providing rules governing specific types of sales and unsolicited merchandise. Many states and the FTC, for example, have **"cooling-off" laws** that permit the buyers of goods sold door to door to cancel their contracts within three business days. The FTC rule further requires that consumers be notified in Spanish of this right if the oral negotiations for the sale were in that language.

Telephone and Mail-Order Sales The FTC's Mail or Telephone Order Merchandise Rule[11] protects consumers who purchase goods over the phone, through the mail or fax machine, or via the Internet. Merchants are required to ship orders within the time promised in their advertisements and to notify consumers when orders cannot be shipped on time. Merchants must also issue a refund within a specified period of time when a consumer cancels an order.

"A consumer is a shopper who is sore about something."

Harold Coffin, 1905–1981
(American humorist)

Online Sales The FTC and other federal agencies have brought numerous enforcement actions against perpetrators of online fraud. Nonetheless, protecting consumers from fraudulent and deceptive sales practices conducted via the Internet has proved to be a challenging task. Faced with economic recession, job losses, mounting debt, and dwindling savings, consumers have increasingly fallen prey to Internet fraud in recent years. Complaints to the FTC about sales of business opportunities, such as work-at-home offers, have grown dramatically in the last ten years.

Many consumers also complain that companies are tracking their online purchases. You can read about a new bill of rights for consumer privacy in this chapter's *Adapting the Law to the Online Environment* feature on the following page.

Protection of Health and Safety

Although labeling and packaging laws (discussed earlier) promote consumer health and safety, there is a significant distinction between regulating the information dispensed about a product and regulating the actual content of the product. The classic example is tobacco products. Producers of tobacco products are required to warn consumers about the hazards associated with the use of their products, but the sale of tobacco products has not

---

10. See Section 4205 of the Patient Protection and Affordable Care Act, Pub. L. No.111-148, March 23, 2010, 124 Stat. 119.

11. 16 C.F.R. Sections 435.1–435.2.

ADAPTING THE LAW TO THE ONLINE ENVIRONMENT

A CONSUMER PRIVACY BILL OF RIGHTS

Whenever consumers purchase items from an online retailer, such as Amazon.com, or a retailer that sells both offline and online, such as Target Brands, Inc., the retailer collects information about the consumer. Over time, the retailer can amass considerable data about a person's shopping habits. Does collecting this information violate a consumer's right to privacy? Should the retailers be able to pass on the data they have collected to their affiliates? Should they be able to use the information to predict what a consumer might want and then create online "coupons" customized to fit the person's buying history?

The President Proposes a Consumer Privacy Bill of Rights

To protect consumers' personal information, the Obama administration drafted a consumer privacy bill of rights that would apply both online and offline. In introducing the bill of rights and asking Congress to enact it into law, President Obama said that "American consumers can't wait any longer for clear rules of the road that ensure their personal information is safe online."

The following is the bill of rights proposed by the president:

1. Individual Control—Consumers have a right to exercise control over what personal data organizations collect from them and how they use it.
2. Transparency—Consumers have the right to easily understandable information about privacy and security practices.
3. Respect for Context—Consumers have a right to expect that organizations will collect, use, and disclose personal data in ways that are consistent with the context in which consumers provide the data.
4. Security—Consumers have the right to secure and responsible handling of personal data.
5. Access and Accuracy—Consumers have a right to access and correct personal data in usable formats, in a manner that is appropriate to the sensitivity of the data and the risk of adverse consequences to consumers if the data are inaccurate.
6. Focus Collection—Consumers have a right to reasonable limits on the personal data that companies collect and retain.
7. Accountability—Consumers have a right to have personal data handled by companies with appropriate measures in place to assure that they adhere to the Consumer Privacy Bill of Rights.

The Implications of the Consumer Privacy Bill of Rights

If this proposed privacy bill of rights becomes law, retailers will have to change some of their procedures:

1. Retailers will have to give customers better choices about what data are collected and how the data are used for marketing.
2. Retailers will have to take into account consumers' expectations about how their information will be used once it is collected.
3. Retailers will have to allow consumers to set reasonable limits on the personal information that is collected about them.

Critical Thinking

Some argue that restricting retailers' tracking ability will actually make consumers worse off. How would this be possible?

been subjected to significant restrictions or banned outright despite the obvious dangers to health. (See this chapter's *Law, Diversity, and Business: Managerial Implications* feature on the facing page for a discussion of a safety issue facing airlines.) We now examine various laws that regulate the actual products made available to consumers.

KNOW THIS

The U.S. Food and Drug Administration is authorized to obtain, among other things, orders for the recall and seizure of certain products.

Food and Drugs The most important legislation regulating food and drugs is the Federal Food, Drug, and Cosmetic Act (FDCA).[12] To protect consumers against adulterated (contaminated) and misbranded foods and drugs, the FDCA establishes food standards, specifies safe levels of potentially hazardous food additives, and sets classifications of food and food advertising. Most of these statutory requirements are enforced by the U.S. Food and Drug Administration (FDA).

12. 21 U.S.C. Section 301.

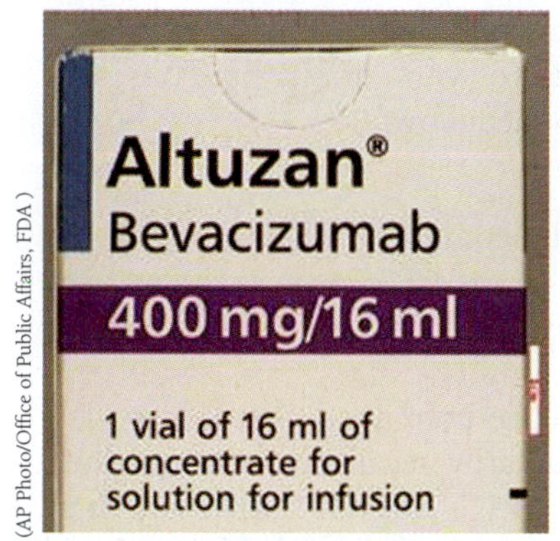

(AP Photo/Office of Public Affairs, FDA)

Can the FDA prevent fake drugs from being sold to consumers?

Under the FDCA, the FDA is also responsible for ensuring that drugs are safe, as well as effective, before they are marketed to the public. The FDA has established extensive procedures that drug manufacturers must follow to show that their drugs are safe.

CASE EXAMPLE 33.4 A group of terminally ill patients claimed that they were entitled, under the U.S. Constitution, to better access to experimental drugs before the FDA completed its clinical tests. The court, however, found that the FDA's policy of limiting access to drugs that were undergoing tests was rationally related to protecting patients from potentially unsafe drugs. Therefore, the court held that terminally ill patients do not have a fundamental constitutional right of access to experimental drugs.[13]

The FDA also has the authority to regulate medical devices, such as pacemakers, and to withdraw from the market any such device that is mislabeled.[14]

Consumer Product Safety In 1972, the Consumer Product Safety Act[15] created the first comprehensive scheme of regulation over matters concerning consumer safety. The act also established the Consumer Product Safety Commission (CPSC).

13. *Abigail Alliance for Better Access to Developmental Drugs v. von Eschenbach*, 495 F.3d 695 (D.C.Cir. 2007).
14. 21 U.S.C. Sections 352(o), 360(j), 360(k), and 360c–360k.
15. 15 U.S.C. Section 2051.

LAW, DIVERSITY, AND BUSINESS: MANAGERIAL IMPLICATIONS

HOW SHOULD AIRLINES DEAL WITH "CUSTOMERS OF SIZE"?

Anyone who travels on commercial airlines is aware that planes are crowded and seats are narrow. For some, they are too narrow. Airlines face a particular problem with "customers of size" because they may impinge on the comfort of those seated next to them. The issue involves more than comfort, however—it can also be a matter of safety.

Challenging Southwest Airlines Southwest Airlines has a policy for "customers of size." When an agent believes that a passenger will reduce the comfort of anyone seated next to her or him, the agent can ask that a second seat be purchased. Kenlie Tiggeman, an overweight passenger, however, was allowed to proceed to the gate. A gate attendant looked at her and told her, in the presence of other passengers, that she would have to purchase a second seat because of her size. Tiggeman refused and filed a lawsuit against Southwest, asserting that the airline's employees "did not follow their company policy and chose to discriminate, humiliate, and harass."

Further, she argued that Southwest takes "discriminatory action . . . toward obese customers." Tiggeman did not ask for damages. Rather, she wanted a court to order Southwest to clarify its policy with respect to larger passengers.

The Airlines Also Face a Safety Issue In 2010, to adjust for Americans' increasing weight, the Federal Aviation Administration (FAA) revised the passenger weights that it uses to calculate a flight's total weight and balance. The FAA now requires the airlines to use an average weight of 200 pounds for men and 179 pounds for women.

Yet the government's regulations for the strength of airline seats and seatbelts have not been revised since they were written about seventy years ago. They are based on a passenger weight of 170 pounds, even though today the average U.S. man weighs 194 pounds. Engineers and scientists claim that airline seats are unsafe for today's heavier passengers.

The safety implications are obvious. Airlines have a unique challenge of protecting larger passengers. Dr. Dietrich Jehle, a professor of emergency medicine at the State University of New York at Buffalo, says, "Since a third of the population is obese, we need to be doing some of our crash testing with obese dummies."

Business Implications *Government experts predict that by the year 2030, 44 percent of adult Americans will be obese—a development that businesses will have to take into consideration. Persons of size represent a significant segment of Americans, and businesses must adapt.*

The CPSC's Authority The CPSC conducts research on the safety of individual products and maintains a clearinghouse on the risks associated with various products. The Consumer Product Safety Act authorizes the CPSC to do the following:

1. Set safety standards for consumer products.
2. Ban the manufacture and sale of any product that the commission believes poses an "unreasonable risk" to consumers. (Products banned by the CPSC have included various types of fireworks, cribs, and toys, as well as many products containing asbestos or vinyl chloride.)
3. Remove from the market any products it believes to be imminently hazardous. The CPSC frequently works with manufacturers to voluntarily recall defective products from stores. **EXAMPLE 33.5** In cooperation with the CPSC, Kolcraft Enterprises, Inc., recalled one million infant play yards because of a defective latch that could cause a rail to fall, posing a risk to children. ●
4. Require manufacturers to report any products already sold or intended for sale that have proved to be hazardous.
5. Administer other product-safety legislation, including the Child Protection and Toy Safety Act[16] and the Federal Hazardous Substances Act.[17]

Notification Requirements The Consumer Product Safety Act imposes notification requirements on distributors of consumer products. Distributors must immediately notify the CPSC when they receive information that a product "contains a defect which . . . creates a substantial risk to the public" or "an unreasonable risk of serious injury or death."

Health-Care Reforms

In 2010, the health-care reforms enacted by Congress went into effect and gave Americans new rights and benefits with regard to health care.[18] By 2014, these laws will prohibit certain insurance company practices, such as denying coverage for preexisting conditions.

Expanded Coverage for Children and Seniors The reforms expanded access to health care by enabling more children to obtain health-insurance coverage and allowing young adults (under age twenty-six) to stay on their parents' health-insurance policies. The act also ended lifetime and most annual limits on care and gave patients access to recommended preventive services (such as cancer screening, vaccinations, and well-baby checks) without cost. Medicare recipients now receive a 50 percent discount on name-brand drugs, and the gap in Medicare's prescription drug coverage will be eliminated by 2020.

Controlling Costs of Health Insurance In an attempt to control the rising costs of health insurance, the law requires insurance companies to spend at least 85 percent of all premium dollars collected from large employers—and 80 percent of the premiums collected from individuals and small employers—on benefits and quality improvement. If insurance companies do not meet these goals, they must provide rebates to consumers. Additionally, states can require insurance companies to justify their premium increases to be eligible to participate in the new health-insurance exchanges.

---

16. 15 U.S.C. Section 1262(e).
17. 15 U.S.C. Sections 1261–1273.
18. Patient Protection and Affordable Health Care Act of 2010, Pub. L. No.111-148, March 23, 2010, 124 Stat. 119; and the Health Care and Education Reconciliation Act of 2010, Pub. L. No. 111-152, March 30, 2010, 124 Stat. 1029.

Credit Protection

Credit protection is one of the most important aspects of consumer protection legislation. Nearly 80 percent of U.S. consumers have credit cards, and most carry a balance on these cards, which amounts to about $2.5 trillion of debt nationwide. In 2010, Congress established a new agency, the Consumer Financial Protection Bureau, to oversee the practices of banks, mortgage lenders, and credit-card companies.

LEARNING OBJECTIVE 2
What are the major federal statutes providing for consumer protection in credit transactions?

Truth-in-Lending Act

A key statute regulating the credit and credit-card industries is the Truth-in-Lending Act (TILA), the name commonly given to Title 1 of the Consumer Credit Protection Act (CCPA), as amended.[19] The TILA is basically a *disclosure law.* It is administered by the Federal Reserve Board and requires sellers and lenders to disclose credit terms or loan terms (such as the annual percentage rate, or APR, and any finance charges) so that individuals can shop around for the best financing arrangements.

Application TILA requirements apply only to persons who, in the ordinary course of business, lend funds, sell on credit, or arrange for the extension of credit. Thus, sales or loans made between two consumers do not come under the act. Additionally, this law protects only debtors who are *natural* persons (as opposed to the artificial "person" of a corporation) and does not extend to other legal entities.

Regulation Z A set of rules issued by the Federal Reserve Board of Governors to implement the provisions of the Truth-in-Lending Act.

Disclosure The disclosure requirements are found in **Regulation Z,** issued by the Federal Reserve Board of Governors. If the contracting parties are subject to the TILA, the requirements of Regulation Z apply to any transaction involving an installment sales contract that calls for payment to be made in more than four installments. Transactions subject to Regulation Z typically include installment loans, retail and installment sales, car loans, home-improvement loans, and certain real estate loans if the amount of financing is less than $25,000.

KNOW THIS

The Federal Reserve Board is part of the Federal Reserve System, which influences the lending and investing activities of commercial banks and the cost and availability of credit.

Equal Credit Opportunity The Equal Credit Opportunity Act (ECOA) amended the TILA in 1974. The ECOA prohibits the denial of credit solely on the basis of race, religion, national origin, color, gender, marital status, or age. The act also prohibits credit discrimination on the basis of whether an individual receives certain forms of income, such as public-assistance benefits.

Under the ECOA, a creditor may not require the signature of an applicant's spouse, or a cosigner, on a credit instrument if the applicant qualifies under the creditor's standards of creditworthiness for the amount requested. **CASE EXAMPLE 33.6** Tonja, an African American, applied for financing with a used-car dealer. The dealer reviewed Tonja's credit report and, without submitting the application to the lender, decided that she would not qualify. Instead of informing Tonja that she did not qualify, the dealer told her that she needed a cosigner on the loan to purchase the car. According to a federal appellate court, the dealership qualified as a creditor in this situation because it unilaterally denied credit. Thus, the dealer could be held liable under the ECOA.[20] •

Which federal law prohibits discrimination for credit-card applications?

(teekid/iStockphoto.com)

Credit-Card Rules The TILA also contains provisions regarding credit cards. One provision limits the liability of a cardholder to $50 per card for unauthorized charges made before the creditor is notified that the card has

19. 15 U.S.C. Sections 1601–1693r. The TILA was amended in 1980 by the Truth-in-Lending Simplification and Reform Act and again in 2009 by the Credit Card Accountability Responsibility and Disclosure Act of 2009.

20. *Treadway v. Gateway Chevrolet Oldsmobile, Inc.,* 362 F.3d 971 (7th Cir. 2004).

been lost. If a consumer received an *unsolicited* credit card in the mail that is later stolen, the company that issued the card cannot charge the consumer for any unauthorized charges.

Another provision requires credit-card companies to disclose the balance computation method that is used to determine the outstanding balance, and to state when finance charges begin to accrue. Other provisions set forth procedures for resolving billing disputes with the credit-card company. These procedures may be used if, for instance, a cardholder wishes to withhold payment for a faulty product purchased with a credit card.

Amendments to Credit-Card Rules Amendments to TILA's credit-card rules that became effective in 2010 added the following protections:

1. Protect consumers from retroactive increases in interest rates on existing card balances unless the account is sixty days delinquent.
2. Require companies to provide forty-five days' advance notice to consumers before changing credit-card terms, such as the annual percentage rate.
3. Require companies to send out monthly bills to cardholders twenty-one days before the due date.
4. Prevent companies from increasing the interest rate charged on a customer's credit-card balance except in specific situations, such as when a promotional rate ends.
5. Prevent companies from charging overlimit fees except in specified situations.
6. Require companies to apply payments in excess of the minimum amount due to the customer's higher-interest balances first when the borrower has balances with different rates (such as the higher interest rates commonly charged for cash advances).
7. Prevent companies from computing finance charges based on the previous billing cycle (known as double-cycle billing, which hurts consumers because they are charged interest for the previous cycle even though they have paid the bill in full).

Fair Credit Reporting Act

The Fair Credit Reporting Act (FCRA)[21] protects consumers against inaccurate credit reporting and requires that lenders and other creditors report correct, relevant, and up-to-date information. The act provides that consumer credit reporting agencies may issue credit reports to users only for specified purposes, including the extension of credit, the issuance of insurance policies, and compliance with a court order, or in response to a consumer's request for a copy of her or his own credit report. (See the *Business Application* feature on page 877 for tips on how businesspersons can use credit reporting services.)

How does the Fair Credit Reporting Act protect consumers?

(teekid/iStockphoto.com)

Consumer Notification and Inaccurate Information Any time a consumer is denied credit or insurance on the basis of his or her credit report, the consumer must be notified of that fact and of the name and address of the credit reporting agency that issued the report. The same notice must be sent to consumers who are charged more than others ordinarily would be for credit or insurance because of their credit reports.

Under the FCRA, consumers can request the source of any information used by the credit agency, as well as the identity of anyone who has received an agency's report. Consumers are also permitted to have access to the information contained about them in a credit reporting agency's files. If a consumer discovers that the agency's files contain inaccurate information, the agency, on the consumer's written request, must investigate the disputed information. Any unverifiable or erroneous information must be deleted within a reasonable period of time.

21. 15 U.S.C. Sections 1681 *et seq.*

Remedies for Violations An agency that fails to comply with the act is liable for actual damages, plus additional damages not to exceed $1,000 and attorneys' fees.[22] Creditors and other companies that use information from credit reporting agencies may also be liable for violations of the FCRA. The United States Supreme Court has held that an insurance company's failure to notify new customers that they were paying higher insurance rates as a result of their credit scores was a *willful* violation of the FCRA.[23]

CASE EXAMPLE 33.7 Branch Banking & Trust Company of Virginia (BB&T) gave Rex Saunders an auto loan but failed to give him a payment coupon book and rebuffed his attempts to make payments on the loan. Eventually, BB&T discovered its mistake and demanded full payment, plus interest and penalties. When payment was not immediately forthcoming, BB&T declared that Saunders was in default. It then repossessed the car and forwarded adverse credit information about Saunders to credit reporting agencies without noting that Saunders disputed the information. Saunders filed a lawsuit alleging violations of the FCRA and was awarded $80,000 in punitive damages. An appellate court found that the damages award was reasonable, given BB&T's willful violation.[24] •

"Credit is a system whereby a person who can't pay gets another person who can't pay to guarantee that he can pay."

Charles Dickens, 1812–1870 (English novelist)

Fair and Accurate Credit Transactions Act

Congress passed the Fair and Accurate Credit Transactions (FACT) Act to combat identity theft.[25] The act established a national fraud alert system so that consumers who suspect that they have been or may be victimized by identity theft can place an alert in their credit files. The act also requires the major credit reporting agencies to provide consumers with a free copy of their credit reports every twelve months.

Another provision requires account numbers on credit-card receipts to be truncated (shortened) so that merchants, employees, and others who have access to the receipts cannot obtain a consumer's name and full credit-card number. The act also mandates that financial institutions work with the FTC to identify "red flag" indicators of identity theft and to develop rules for disposing of sensitive credit information.

Fair Debt-Collection Practices

The Fair Debt Collection Practices Act (FDCPA)[26] attempts to curb abuses by collection agencies. The act applies only to specialized debt-collection agencies and attorneys who regularly attempt to collect debts on behalf of someone else, usually for a percentage of the amount owed. Creditors attempting to collect debts are not covered by the act unless, by misrepresenting themselves, they cause the debtors to believe that they are collection agencies. A debt collector who fails to comply with the act is liable for actual damages, plus additional damages not to exceed $1,000[27] and attorneys' fees.

Under the FDCPA, a collection agency may not do any of the following:

1. Contact the debtor at the debtor's place of employment if the debtor's employer objects.
2. Contact the debtor at inconvenient or unusual times (such as three o'clock in the morning), or at any time if the debtor is being represented by an attorney.
3. Contact third parties other than the debtor's parents, spouse, or financial adviser about payment of a debt unless a court authorizes such action.
4. Harass or intimidate the debtor (by using abusive language or threatening violence, for instance) or make false or misleading statements (such as posing as a police officer).

---

22. 15 U.S.C. Section 1681n.
23. *Safeco Insurance Co. of America v. Burr*, 551 U.S. 47, 127 S.Ct. 2201, 167 L.Ed.2d 1045 (2007).
24. *Saunders v. Branch Banking & Trust Co. of Virginia*, 526 F.3d 142 (4th Cir. 2008).
25. Pub. L. No. 108-159, 117 Stat. 1952 (December 4, 2003).
26. 15 U.S.C. Section 1692.
27. According to the U.S. Court of Appeals for the Sixth Circuit, the $1,000 limit on damages applies to each lawsuit, not to each violation. See *Wright v. Finance Service of Norwalk, Inc.*, 22 F.3d 647 (6th Cir. 1994).

5. Communicate with the debtor at any time after receiving notice that the debtor is refusing to pay the debt, except to advise the debtor of further action to be taken by the collection agency.

The FDCPA also requires a collection agency to include a *validation notice* whenever it initially contacts a debtor for payment of a debt or within five days of that initial contact. The notice must state that the debtor has thirty days in which to dispute the debt and to request a written verification of the debt from the collection agency. The debtor's request for debt validation must be in writing.

ETHICAL ISSUE

Does leaving voice mail messages for a debtor violate the Fair Debt Collection Practices Act? Debt-collection practices have often raised privacy concerns. There have been many lawsuits against collection agencies over voice messages or voice mails left by debt collectors. The FDCPA prohibits disclosures about a debt to third parties. Does leaving a voice message regarding a debt collection on an answering machine constitute such a disclosure? That depends on the jurisdiction and the situation. In one example, a Florida court ruled in favor of the debtor. It stated that if a collection agency leaves a voice message for a consumer on an answering machine—even at home—other people (third parties) could hear the message.[28]

In contrast, a federal court in Minnesota held that leaving voice messages on a debtor's cell phone did not violate the FDCPA, even though the debtor's children listened to them. Because the messages did not identify the debtor or the debt, the court reasoned that "they conveyed no more information than would have been obvious in caller ID." The suit against the debt collector was dismissed.[29]

Environmental Law

We now turn to a discussion of the various ways in which businesses are regulated by the government in the interest of attempting to protect the environment. Environmental protection is not without a price, however. For many businesses, the costs of complying with environmental regulations are high, and for some, they may seem too high.

Common Law Actions

LEARNING OBJECTIVE 3
Under what common law theories can polluters be held liable?

Common law remedies against environmental pollution originated centuries ago in England. Those responsible for operations that created dirt, smoke, noxious odors, noise, or toxic substances were sometimes held liable under common law theories of nuisance or negligence. Today, injured individuals continue to rely on the common law to obtain damages and injunctions against business polluters.

Nuisance A common law doctrine under which persons may be held liable for using their property in a manner that unreasonably interferes with others' rights to use or enjoy their own property.

Nuisance

Under the common law doctrine of **nuisance,** persons may be held liable if they use their property in a manner that unreasonably interferes with others' rights to use or enjoy their own property. In these situations, the courts commonly balance the harm caused by the pollution against the costs of stopping it.

Courts have often denied injunctive relief on the ground that the hardships that would be imposed on the polluter and on the community are relatively greater than the hardships suffered by the plaintiff. **EXAMPLE 33.8** Hewitt's Factory causes neighboring landowners to suffer from smoke, soot, and vibrations. The factory, however, may be left in operation if it is the core of the local economy. The injured parties may be awarded only monetary damages, which may include compensation for the decrease in the value of their property caused by Hewitt's operation. ●

To obtain relief from pollution under the nuisance doctrine, a property owner may have to identify a distinct harm separate from that affecting the general public. This harm is referred to as a "private" nuisance. Under the common law, individuals were denied

---

28. *Berg v. Merchants Association Collection Division, Inc.*, 586 F.Supp.2d 1336 (S.D.Fla. 2008).

29. *Zortman v. J.C. Christensen & Associates, Inc.*, 2012 WL 1563918 (D.Minn. 2012).

standing (access to the courts—see Chapter 3) unless they suffered a harm distinct from the harm suffered by the public at large. Some states still require this. A public authority (such as a state's attorney general), though, can sue to abate a "public" nuisance.

Negligence and Strict Liability

An injured party may sue a business polluter in tort under the negligence and strict liability theories discussed in Chapter 4. The basis for a negligence action is the business's failure to use reasonable care toward the party whose injury was foreseeable and caused by the lack of reasonable care. For instance, employees might sue an employer whose failure to use proper pollution controls contaminated the air and caused the employees to suffer respiratory illnesses. Lawsuits for personal injuries caused by exposure to a toxic substance, such as asbestos, radiation, or hazardous waste, have given rise to a growing body of tort law known as **toxic torts.**

Toxic Tort A civil wrong arising from exposure to a toxic substance, such as asbestos, radiation, or hazardous waste.

Businesses that engage in ultrahazardous activities—such as the transportation of radioactive materials—are strictly liable for any injuries the activities cause. In a strict liability action, the injured party does not need to prove that the business failed to exercise reasonable care.

Federal Regulation

All levels of government in the United States regulate some aspect of the environment. Congress has enacted a number of statutes to control the impact of human activities on the environment. Some of these laws have been passed in an attempt to improve the quality of air and water. Other laws specifically regulate toxic chemicals, including pesticides, herbicides, and hazardous wastes.

Environmental Regulatory Agencies

The primary agency regulating environmental law is the Environmental Protection Agency (EPA). Other federal agencies with authority to regulate specific environmental matters include the Department of the Interior, the Department of Defense, the Department of Labor, the Food and Drug Administration, and the Nuclear Regulatory Commission. All agencies of the federal government must take environmental factors into consideration when making significant decisions. In addition, state and local agencies also play an important role in enforcing federal environmental legislation.

Most federal environmental laws provide that private parties can sue to enforce environmental regulations if government agencies fail to do so. Typically, a threshold hurdle in such suits is meeting the requirements for standing to sue.

LEARNING OBJECTIVE 4
What is contained in an environmental impact statement, and who must file one?

Environmental Impact Statements

The National Environmental Policy Act (NEPA) of 1969[30] requires that an **environmental impact statement (EIS)** be prepared for every major federal action that significantly affects the quality of the environment. An EIS must analyze the following:

Environmental Impact Statement (EIS) A formal analysis required for any major federal action that will significantly affect the quality of the environment to determine the action's impact and explore alternatives.

1. The impact on the environment that the action will have.
2. Any adverse effects on the environment and alternative actions that might be taken.
3. Irreversible effects the action might generate.

An action qualifies as "major" if it involves a substantial commitment of resources (monetary or otherwise). An action is "federal" if a federal agency has the power to control it. Construction by a private developer of a ski resort on federal land, for example, may require an EIS. Building or operating a nuclear plant, which requires a federal permit, requires an EIS. If an agency decides that an EIS is unnecessary, it must issue a statement supporting this conclusion. Private individuals, consumer interest groups, businesses, and others who believe that a federal agency's actions threaten the environment often use EISs as a means of challenging those actions.

30. 42 U.S.C. Sections 4321–4370d.

(AP Photo/David J. Phillip)

Why are stationary sources of pollution regulated differently than mobile sources?

Air Pollution

Congress first authorized funds for air-pollution research and enacted the Clean Air Act to address multistate air pollution in the 1950s and 1960s.[31] The Clean Air Act provides the basis for issuing regulations to control pollution coming from mobile sources (such as automobiles and other vehicles) and stationary sources (such as electric utilities and industrial plants).

Mobile Sources of Air Pollution Regulations governing air pollution from automobiles and other mobile sources specify pollution standards and establish time schedules for meeting the standards. The EPA periodically updates the pollution standards to reduce the amount of emissions allowed in light of new developments and data.

LEARNING OBJECTIVE 5
What major federal statutes regulate air and water pollution?

Reducing Emissions over the Long Term The Obama administration announced a long-term goal of reducing emissions of nitrogen oxide and other pollutants, including those from automobiles, by 80 percent by 2050. In 2010, the administration ordered the EPA to develop national standards regulating fuel economy and emissions for medium- and heavy-duty trucks, starting with 2014 models.

Greenhouse Gases A growing concern is that greenhouse gases, such as carbon dioxide (CO_2), may contribute to global warming. The Clean Air Act, as amended, however, does not specifically mention CO_2 emissions. Therefore, until 2009, the EPA did not regulate CO_2 emissions from motor vehicles. **CASE EXAMPLE 33.9** Environmental groups and several states sued the EPA in an effort to force the agency to regulate CO_2 emissions. When the case reached the United States Supreme Court, the EPA argued that the plaintiffs lacked standing (see page 69 of Chapter 3). The agency claimed that because global warming has widespread effects, an individual plaintiff could not show the particularized harm required for standing. The agency also maintained that it did not have authority under the Clean Air Act to address global climate change and regulate CO_2.

The Court, however, ruled that Massachusetts had standing because its coastline, including state-owned lands, faced a threat from rising sea levels potentially caused by global warming. The Court also held that the Clean Air Act's broad definition of air pollutant gives the EPA authority to regulate CO_2 and requires the EPA to regulate any air pollutants that might "endanger public health or welfare." Accordingly, the Court ordered the EPA to determine whether CO_2 was a pollutant that endangered the public health.[32] • The EPA later concluded that greenhouse gases, including CO_2 emissions, do constitute a public danger.

"There's so much pollution in the air now that if it weren't for our lungs, there'd be no place to put it all."

Robert Orben, 1927–present (American comedian)

Stationary Sources of Air Pollution The Clean Air Act authorizes the EPA to establish air-quality standards for stationary sources (such as manufacturing plants) but recognizes that the primary responsibility for preventing and controlling air pollution rests with state and local governments.

The EPA sets primary and secondary levels of ambient standards— that is, the maximum permissible levels of certain pollutants—and the states formulate plans to achieve those standards. Different standards apply depending on whether the sources of pollution are located in clean areas or polluted areas and whether they are existing sources or major new sources.

31. 42 U.S.C. Sections 7401 *et seq.*
32. *Massachusetts v. EPA*, 549 U.S. 497, 127 S.Ct. 1438, 167 L.Ed.2d 248 (2007).

Hazardous Air Pollutants The EPA standards are aimed at controlling hazardous air pollutants—those likely to cause death or serious irreversible or incapacitating illness such as cancer or neurological and reproductive damage. The Clean Air Act requires the EPA to list all regulated hazardous air pollutants on a prioritized schedule. In all, nearly two hundred substances, including asbestos, benzene, beryllium, cadmium, and vinyl chloride, have been classified as hazardous. They are emitted from stationary sources by a variety of business activities, including smelting (melting ore to produce metal), dry cleaning, house painting, and commercial baking.

Maximum Achievable Control Technology Instead of establishing specific emissions standards for each hazardous air pollutant, the Clean Air Act requires major sources of pollutants to use pollution-control equipment that represents the *maximum achievable control technology,* or MACT, to reduce emissions. The EPA issues guidelines as to what equipment meets this standard.[33]

Violations of the Clean Air Act

For violations of emission limits under the Clean Air Act, the EPA can assess civil penalties of up to $25,000 per day. Additional fines of up to $5,000 per day can be assessed for other violations, such as failing to maintain the required records. To penalize those who find it more cost-effective to violate the act than to comply with it, the EPA is authorized to obtain a penalty equal to the violator's economic benefits from noncompliance. Persons who provide information about violators may be paid up to $10,000. Private individuals can also sue violators.

Those who knowingly violate the act may be subject to criminal penalties, including fines of up to $1 million and imprisonment for up to two years (for false statements or failures to report violations). Corporate officers are among those who may be subject to these penalties.

Water Pollution

Water pollution stems mostly from industrial, municipal, and agricultural sources. Pollutants entering streams, lakes, and oceans include organic wastes, heated water, sediments from soil runoff, nutrients (including fertilizers and human and animal wastes), and toxic chemicals and other hazardous substances. We look here at laws and regulations governing water pollution.

"Among the treasures of our land is water—fast becoming our most valuable, most prized, most critical resource."

Dwight D. Eisenhower, 1890–1969
(Thirty-fourth president of the United States, 1953–1961)

Federal regulations governing the pollution of water can be traced back to the Rivers and Harbors Appropriations Act of 1899.[34] These regulations prohibited ships and manufacturers from discharging or depositing refuse in navigable waterways without a permit. In 1948, Congress passed the Federal Water Pollution Control Act (FWPCA),[35] but its regulatory system and enforcement powers proved to be inadequate.

The Clean Water Act

In 1972, amendments to the FWPCA—known as the Clean Water Act (CWA)—established the following goals: (1) make waters safe for swimming, (2) protect fish and wildlife, and (3) eliminate the discharge of pollutants into the water. The amendments set specific time schedules, which were extended by amendment and by the Water Quality Act.[36] Under these schedules, the EPA limits the discharge of various types of pollutants based on the technology available for controlling them.

Permit System for Point Source Emissions The CWA established a permit system, called the *National Pollutant Discharge Elimination System (NPDES),* for regulating discharges

33. The EPA has also issued rules to regulate hazardous air pollutants emitted by landfills. See 40 C.F.R. Sections 60.750–60.759.
34. 33 U.S.C. Sections 401–418.
35. 33 U.S.C. Sections 1251–1387.
36. This act amended 33 U.S.C. Section 1251.

from "point sources" of pollution. Point sources include industrial, municipal (such as sewer pipes and sewage treatment plants), and agricultural facilities.[37] Under this system, industrial, municipal, and agricultural polluters must apply for permits before discharging wastes into surface waters.

NPDES permits can be issued by the EPA and authorized state agencies and Indian tribes, but only if the discharge will not violate water-quality standards (both federal and state standards). Special requirements must be met to discharge toxic chemicals and residue from oil spills. NPDES permits must be renewed every five years. Although initially the NPDES system focused mainly on industrial wastewater, it was later expanded to cover storm water discharges.

When water from rainstorms flows over streets, parking lots, commercial sites, and other developed areas, the water collects sediments, trash, used motor oil, raw sewage, pesticides, and other toxic contaminants. This polluted runoff flows into urban storm sewers, which often empty into rivers or oceans. In the following case, the plaintiffs claimed that Los Angeles County, California, was responsible for heavily polluted storm water runoff flowing into navigable rivers in the surrounding area.

37. 33 U.S.C. Section 1342.

Case 33.2

Natural Resources Defense Council, Inc. v. County of Los Angeles

United States Court of Appeals, Ninth Circuit, 673 F.3d 880 (2011).

(Ju-Lee/iStockphoto.com)

Which entities can be sued for discharge of urban storm water into navigable waters?

FACTS Two environmental organizations—the Natural Resources Defense Council (NRDC) and the Santa Monica Baykeeper—brought a lawsuit against the county of Los Angeles and the Los Angeles County Flood Control District, which included eighty-four cities and some unincorporated areas. The NRDC and Santa Monica alleged that the county and the district were discharging urban storm water runoff into navigable waters in violation of the Clean Water Act. The levels of pollutants detected in four rivers—the Santa Clara River, the Los Angeles River, the San Gabriel River, and Malibu Creek—exceeded the limits allowed in the National Pollutant Discharge Elimination System (NPDES) permit that governs municipal storm water discharges in Los Angeles County.

All parties agreed that the rivers did not meet water-quality standards. The issue was whether the NRDC and Santa Monica had proved that the county and the district were responsible. The defendants claimed that there was no evidence establishing their responsibility for discharging storm water carrying pollutants into the rivers. The federal district court held in favor of the defendants (the county and district agencies), and the NRDC and Santa Monica appealed.

ISSUE Were Los Angeles County and its Flood Control District responsible for discharging pollutants into navigable rivers?

DECISION Yes. The federal appellate court held that the agencies were liable for discharging polluted storm water into two of the four waterways. The court reversed the district court's decision regarding the Los Angeles River and the San Gabriel River

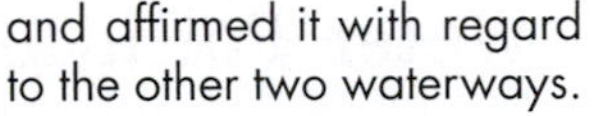
and affirmed it with regard to the other two waterways.

REASON The court noted that in Los Angeles County, storm water runoff is collected by thousands of storm drains and channeled to a main storm-sewer system, or MS4. The Los Angeles River and San Gabriel River Monitoring Stations are located in a channelized portion of the MS4 that is owned and operated by the district. Storm water known to contain standards-exceeding pollutants passes through these monitoring stations and is discharged into the two rivers. Because the monitoring makes the district aware of the pollution levels in the water, the court found that there was sufficient evidence to establish liability. The district (along with the county) was responsible for exceeding the amount of pollutants it was permitted to discharge from the storm-sewer systems into the Los Angeles River and the San Gabriel River. Evidence did not establish that the district was responsible for excess pollution in the Santa Clara River and Malibu Creek, because those monitoring stations were not located within the channelized portion of the MS4, and thus they were not under the district's control.

WHAT IF THE FACTS WERE DIFFERENT? *Suppose that Los Angeles County had moved all of its monitoring stations outside the "channelized portion of the MS4." If none of the stations that monitored pollution in the four waterways was located within the district's MS4 system, how might the outcome have been changed?*

Standards for Equipment Regulations generally specify that the *best available control technology*, or BACT, be installed. The EPA issues guidelines as to what equipment meets this standard. Essentially, the guidelines require the most effective pollution-control equipment available.

New sources must install BACT equipment before beginning operations. Existing sources are subject to timetables for the installation of BACT equipment and must immediately install equipment that utilizes the *best practical control technology*, or BPCT. The EPA also issues guidelines as to what equipment meets this standard.

Wetlands Water-saturated, protected areas of land that support wildlife and cannot be filled in or dredged without a permit.

Wetlands

The CWA prohibits the filling or dredging of **wetlands** unless a permit is obtained from the Army Corps of Engineers. The EPA defines *wetlands* as "those areas that are inundated or saturated by surface or ground water at a frequency and duration sufficient to support . . . vegetation typically adapted for life in saturated soil conditions."

Wetlands are thought to be vital to the ecosystem because they filter streams and rivers and provide habitat for wildlife. In the past, the EPA's broad interpretation of what constitutes a wetland generated substantial controversy, but the courts have considerably scaled back the CWA's protection of wetlands in recent years.[38]

Violations of the Clean Water Act

Under the CWA, violators are subject to a variety of civil and criminal penalties. Depending on the violation, civil penalties range from $10,000 per day to $25,000 per day, but not more than $25,000 per violation. Criminal penalties, which apply only if a violation was intentional, range from a fine of $2,500 per day and imprisonment for up to one year to a fine of $1 million and fifteen years' imprisonment. Injunctive relief and damages can also be imposed. The polluting party can be required to clean up the pollution or pay for the cost of doing so.

In the following case, landowners filed a lawsuit challenging an EPA order finding that they had violated the CWA. The United States Supreme Court had to decide whether the federal courts could review the EPA's decision.

38. See, for example, *Rapanos v. United States*, 547 U.S. 715, 126 S.Ct. 2208, 165 L.Ed.2d 159 (2006).

Case 33.3

Sackett v. Environmental Protection Agency

Supreme Court of the United States,
___ U.S. ___, 132 S.Ct. 1367, 182 L.Ed.2d 367 (2012).
www.supremecourt.gov/opinions[a]

(wbritten/iStockphoto.com)

FACTS To build a home in Idaho, Michael and Chantell Sackett filled in part of their residential lot with dirt and rock. A few months later, they received a compliance order from the Environmental Protection Agency (EPA). The order stated that, because their property was near a major lake, the Sacketts had polluted wetlands in violation of the Clean Water Act. The order required the Sacketts to restore their property immediately and told them that they faced fines of $75,000 a day until they complied. The Sacketts requested a hearing with the EPA. When a hearing was denied, they sued the EPA in federal district court, asserting, among other things, that the compliance order was "arbitrary and capricious" under the Administrative Procedure Act. The district court found that it could not review the EPA's compliance order. On appeal, a federal appellate court affirmed, concluding that the Sacketts had to wait for the EPA to bring an enforcement action against them. The Sacketts appealed to the United States Supreme Court.

ISSUE Under the Administrative Procedure Act, could the Sacketts challenge the EPA's compliance order in federal court?

a. Under "Current Term," click on "Latest Slip Opinions." In the resulting list, scroll down to "35" in the first column, and click on the case name to access the opinion. The United States Supreme Court maintains this Web site.

Case 33.3—Continues next page

Case 33.3—Continued

DECISION Yes. The United States Supreme Court held that the Sacketts could challenge the EPA's compliance order in federal court. The Court reversed the judgment of the federal appellate court.

REASON The Administrative Procedure Act (APA) allows courts to review any "final agency action for which there is no other adequate remedy in court." The Court concluded that the EPA's compliance order was a "final" agency action because it determined the Sacketts' rights and obligations. The compliance order required the Sacketts to restore their property to its previous condition, and they could not seek further review with the EPA. In fact, the EPA denied them that opportunity when it rejected their request for a hearing. Second, the Court found that the Sacketts had "no other adequate remedy in court." Given that they faced such heavy daily fines, the Sacketts could not realistically wait for the EPA to bring an enforcement action. Finally, the Clean Water Act itself did not preclude judicial review under the APA. The courts are not prevented from reviewing compliance orders simply because the EPA also has the option of bringing enforcement actions.

CRITICAL THINKING—Legal Consideration *What does the Court's decision in this case mean for people and businesses that face compliance orders? Are they more or less likely to acquiesce to orders they find objectionable?*

Drinking Water

The Safe Drinking Water Act[39] requires the EPA to set maximum levels for pollutants in public water systems. Public water system operators must come as close as possible to meeting the EPA's standards by using the best available technology that is economically and technologically feasible.

Under the act, each supplier of drinking water is required to send every household that it supplies with water an annual statement describing the source of its water. Suppliers must also disclose the level of any contaminants contained in the water and any possible health concerns associated with the contaminants.

The EPA is particularly concerned about contamination from underground sources, such as pesticides and wastes leaked from landfills or disposed of in underground injection wells. Many of these substances are associated with cancer and may cause damage to the central nervous system, liver, and kidneys. Although some evidence suggests that trace amounts of pharmaceuticals may be entering the nation's drinking water, the law does not yet require suppliers to test for or report these substances. The drugs come from prescription medications taken by humans and antibiotics and other medications given to livestock.

Oil Pollution

When more than 10 million gallons of oil leaked into Alaska's Prince William Sound from the *Exxon Valdez* supertanker in 1989, Congress responded by passing the Oil Pollution Act.[40] (At that time, the *Exxon Valdez* disaster was the worst oil spill in U.S. history, but the British Petroleum oil spill in the Gulf of Mexico in 2010 surpassed it.) Under this act, any onshore or offshore oil facility, oil shipper, vessel owner, or vessel operator that discharges oil into navigable waters or onto an adjoining shore can be liable for clean-up costs and damages.

Toxic Chemicals

Today, the control of toxic chemicals used in agriculture and in industry has become increasingly important.

Pesticides and Herbicides

Under the Federal Insecticide, Fungicide, and Rodenticide Act (FIFRA),[41] pesticides and herbicides must be (1) registered before they can

39. 42 U.S.C. Sections 300f to 300j-25.

40. 33 U.S.C. Sections 2701–2761.

41. 7 U.S.C. Sections 135–136y.

be sold, (2) certified and used only for approved applications, and (3) used in limited quantities when applied to food crops. The EPA can cancel or suspend registration of substances that are identified as harmful and may also inspect factories where the chemicals are made. There must be no more than a one-in-a-million risk to people of developing cancer from any kind of exposure to the substance, including eating food that contains pesticide residues.[42]

It is a violation of FIFRA to sell a pesticide or herbicide that is unregistered or has had its registration canceled or suspended. It is also a violation to sell a pesticide or herbicide with a false or misleading label or to destroy or deface any labeling required under the act. Penalties for commercial dealers include imprisonment for up to one year and a fine of up to $25,000. Farmers and other private users of pesticides or herbicides who violate the act are subject to a $1,000 fine and incarceration for up to thirty days.

Note that a state can also regulate the sale and use of federally registered pesticides. **CASE EXAMPLE 33.10** The EPA conditionally registered Strongarm, a weed-killing pesticide, in 2000. Dow Agrosciences, LLC, immediately sold Strongarm to Texas peanut farmers. When the farmers applied it, however, Strongarm damaged their crops while failing to control the growth of weeds. The farmers sued Dow, but the lower courts ruled that FIFRA preempted their claims. The farmers appealed to the United States Supreme Court. The Supreme Court held that under a specific provision of FIFRA, a state can regulate the sale and use of federally registered pesticides so long as the regulation does not permit anything that FIFRA prohibits.[43] •

Toxic Substances

The Toxic Substances Control Act[44] was passed to regulate chemicals and chemical compounds that are known to be toxic and to institute investigation of any possible harmful effects from new chemical compounds. The act applies to compounds such as asbestos and polychlorinated biphenyls, popularly known as PCBs.

The regulations authorize the EPA to require that manufacturers, processors, and other organizations planning to use chemicals first determine their effects on human health and the environment. The EPA can regulate substances that potentially pose an imminent hazard or an unreasonable risk of injury to health or the environment. The EPA may require special labeling, limit the use of a substance, set production quotas, or prohibit the use of a substance altogether.

Hazardous Waste Disposal

Some industrial, agricultural, and household wastes pose more serious threats than others. If not properly disposed of, these toxic chemicals may present a substantial danger to human health and the environment. If released into the environment, they may contaminate public drinking water resources.

Resource Conservation and Recovery Act

In 1976, Congress passed the Resource Conservation and Recovery Act (RCRA)[45] in reaction to concern over the effects of hazardous waste materials on the environment. The RCRA required the EPA to determine which forms of solid waste should be considered hazardous and to establish regulations to monitor and control hazardous waste disposal.

The act also requires all producers of hazardous waste materials to label and package properly any hazardous waste to be transported. Amendments to the RCRA decrease the use of land containment in the disposal of hazardous waste and require smaller generators of hazardous waste to comply with the act.

---

42. 21 U.S.C. Section 346a.

43. *Bates v. Dow Agrosciences, LLC,* 544 U.S. 431, 125 S.Ct. 1788, 161 L.Ed.2d 687 (2005).

44. 15 U.S.C. Sections 2601–2692.

45. 42 U.S.C. Sections 6901 *et seq.*

Under the RCRA, a company may be assessed a civil penalty of up to $25,000 for each violation.[46] Penalties are based on the seriousness of the violation, the probability of harm, and the extent to which the violation deviates from RCRA requirements. Criminal penalties include fines of up to $50,000 for each day of violation, imprisonment for up to two years (in most instances), or both.[47] Criminal fines and the period of imprisonment can be doubled for certain repeat offenders.

Superfund

In 1980, Congress passed the Comprehensive Environmental Response, Compensation, and Liability Act (CERCLA),[48] commonly known as Superfund, to regulate the clean-up of leaking hazardous waste–disposal sites. A special federal fund was created for that purpose.

CERCLA, as amended, has four primary elements:

1. It established an information-gathering and analysis system that enables the government to identify chemical dump sites and determine the appropriate action.
2. It authorized the EPA to respond to hazardous substance emergencies and to arrange for the clean-up of a leaking site directly if the persons responsible for the problem fail to clean up the site.
3. It created a Hazardous Substance Response Trust Fund (also called Superfund) to pay for the clean-up of hazardous sites using funds obtained through taxes on certain businesses.
4. It allowed the government to recover the cost of clean-up from the persons who were (even remotely) responsible for hazardous substance releases.

Potentially Responsible Parties under Superfund

Superfund provides that when a release or a threatened release of hazardous chemicals from a site occurs, the EPA can clean up the site and recover the cost of the clean-up from the following persons: (1) the person who generated the wastes disposed of at the site, (2) the person who transported the wastes to the site, (3) the person who owned or operated the site at the time of the disposal, or (4) the current owner or operator.

Potentially Responsible Party (PRP)
A party liable for the costs of cleaning up a hazardous waste–disposal site under the Comprehensive Environmental Response, Compensation, and Liability Act.

A person falling within one of these categories is referred to as a **potentially responsible party (PRP).** If the PRPs do not clean up the site, the EPA can clean up the site and recover the clean-up costs from the PRPs.

Joint and Several Liability under Superfund

Liability under Superfund is usually joint and several—that is, a person who generated *only a fraction of the hazardous waste* disposed of at the site may nevertheless be liable for *all* of the clean-up costs. CERCLA authorizes a party who has incurred clean-up costs to bring a "contribution action" against any other person who is liable or potentially liable for a percentage of the costs.

---

46. 42 U.S.C. Section 6928(a).
47. 42 U.S.C. Section 6928(d).
48. 42 U.S.C. Sections 9601–9675.

Reviewing . . . Consumer and Environmental Law

Residents of Lake Caliopa, Minnesota, began noticing an unusually high number of lung ailments among their population. Several concerned local citizens pooled their resources and commissioned a study of the frequency of these health conditions per capita in Lake Caliopa as compared with national averages. The study concluded that residents of Lake Caliopa experienced four to seven times the rate of frequency of asthma, bronchitis, and emphysema as the population nationwide. During the study period, citizens began expressing concerns about the large volumes of smog emitted by the Cotton Design apparel manufacturing plant on the outskirts of town. The plant had opened its production facility two miles east of town beside the Tawakoni River and employed seventy workers.

Just downstream on the Tawakoni River, the city of Lake Caliopa operated a public waterworks facility, which supplied all city residents with water. The Minnesota Pollution Control Agency required Cotton Design to install new equipment to control air and water pollution. Later, citizens brought a lawsuit in a Minnesota state court against Cotton Design for various respiratory ailments allegedly caused or compounded by smog from Cotton Design's factory. Using the information presented in the chapter, answer the following questions.

1. Under the common law, what would each plaintiff be required to identify in order to be given relief by the court?
2. What standard for limiting emissions into the air does Cotton Design's pollution-control equipment have to meet?
3. If Cotton Design's emissions violated the Clean Air Act, how much can the EPA assess in fines per day?
4. What information must the city send to every household that it supplies with water?

DEBATE THIS Laws against bait-and-switch advertising should be abolished because no consumer is ever forced to buy anything.

BUSINESS APPLICATION

The Proper Way to Use Credit Reporting Services*

As explained in the chapter, the Fair Credit Reporting Act (FCRA) protects consumers against inaccurate credit reporting. Many credit reporting agencies provide much more than just credit reports, however. Increasingly, they are providing employers with employment history, information on educational attainment, and criminal records for current employees and job applicants.

Disclosure Issues When Making Background Checks

If a company uses credit reporting agencies, it must disclose this to current employees and to applicants. If a company does not conform to the requirements of advance notice, disclosure, and consent, it can become involved in litigation.

For example, Vitran Express used credit reporting agencies to determine whether prospective employees had criminal records without disclosing this practice to applicants as required by the FCRA. One applicant lost a job offer because the credit reporting agency forwarded inaccurate information indicating that he had a criminal history when he did not. When he and other job applicants brought a class-action lawsuit against Vitran Express, the company ultimately agreed to pay millions of dollars to settle the case.

Steps That Employers Should Take to Avoid Litigation

All companies must make sure that they comply with federal law when they do background checks. Employers must give advance notice and disclosure, and obtain each employee's or applicant's consent to any background check that exceeds a simple credit check.

To ensure that there are no legal problems, an employer should certify in writing to each credit reporting agency that it will follow federal rules concerning notice, authorization, disclosure, and adverse action notices (letters rejecting applicants).

Each prospective employee should be given a clear disclosure—in a separate document—stating that a background report may be requested from a consumer reporting service. At that time, the company should obtain the person's written consent.

Whenever a consumer report influences the company's decision not to hire someone, to avoid a lawsuit, the company should provide the following documents to the individual *before* rejecting him or her:

- The Federal Trade Commission document called "A Summary of Your Rights under the Fair Credit Reporting Act."
- A copy of the consumer report on which the company based its negative decision.

Checklist for the Businessperson

1. *Your in-house counsel or you should carefully review federal law in this matter.*
2. *Always let prospective employees know that you're going to use a consumer reporting service's report as part of the process of evaluating their application.*
3. *Create a separate document that indicates that you are going to use a consumer reporting service.*

---

*This *Business Application* is not meant to substitute for the services of an attorney who is licensed to practice law in your state.

Key Terms

bait-and-switch advertising 858
cease-and-desist order 859
"cooling-off" laws 861
counteradvertising 859
deceptive advertising 857
environmental impact statement (EIS) 869
multiple product order 859
nuisance 868
potentially responsible party (PRP) 876
Regulation Z 865
toxic tort 869
wetlands 873

Chapter Summary: Consumer and Environmental Law

CONSUMER LAW	
Deceptive Advertising (See pages 857–860.)	1. *Definition of deceptive advertising*—Generally, an advertising claim will be deemed deceptive if it would mislead a reasonable consumer. 2. *Bait-and-switch advertising*—Advertising a lower-priced product (the bait) to lure consumers into the store and then telling them the product is unavailable and urging them to buy a higher-priced product (the switch) is prohibited by the FTC. 3. *Online deceptive advertising*—The FTC has issued guidelines to help online businesses comply with the laws prohibiting deceptive advertising. 4. *FTC actions against deceptive advertising*— a. Cease-and-desist orders—Requiring the advertiser to stop the challenged advertising. b. Counteradvertising—Requiring the advertiser to advertise to correct the earlier misinformation.
Labeling and Packaging (See pages 860–861.)	Manufacturers must comply with the labeling or packaging requirements for their specific products. In general, all labels must be accurate and not misleading.
Sales (See page 861.)	Federal and state statutes and regulations govern certain practices of sellers who solicit over the telephone or through the mails and protect consumers to some extent against fraudulent and deceptive online sales practices.
Protection of Health and Safety (See pages 861–864.)	1. *Food and drugs*—The Federal Food, Drug, and Cosmetic Act protects consumers against adulterated and misbranded foods and drugs. The act establishes food standards, specifies safe levels of potentially hazardous food additives, and sets classifications of food and food advertising. 2. *Consumer product safety*—The Consumer Product Safety Act seeks to protect consumers from injury from hazardous products. The Consumer Product Safety Commission has the power to remove products that are deemed imminently hazardous from the market and to ban the manufacture and sale of hazardous products.
Credit Protection (See pages 865–868.)	1. *Consumer Credit Protection Act, Title I (Truth-in-Lending Act, or TILA)*—A disclosure law that requires sellers and lenders to disclose credit terms or loan terms in certain transactions, including retail and installment sales and loans, car loans, home-improvement loans, and certain real estate loans. Additionally, the TILA provides for the following: a. Equal credit opportunity—Creditors are prohibited from discriminating on the basis of race, religion, marital status, gender, national origin, color, or age. b. Credit-card protection—Liability of cardholders for unauthorized charges is limited to $50, providing notice requirements are met. Consumers are not liable for unauthorized charges made on unsolicited credit cards. The act also sets out procedures to be used in settling disputes between credit-card companies and their cardholders. 2. *Fair Credit Reporting Act*—Entitles consumers to request verification of the accuracy of a credit report and to have unverified or false information removed from their files. 3. *Fair and Accurate Credit Transaction Act*—Combats identity theft by establishing a national fraud alert system. Requires account numbers to be truncated and credit reporting agencies to provide one free credit report per year to consumers. 4. *Fair Debt Collection Practices Act*—Prohibits debt collectors from using unfair debt-collection practices, such as contacting the debtor at his or her place of employment if the employer objects or at unreasonable times, contacting third parties about the debt, and harassing the debtor.
ENVIRONMENTAL LAW	
Common Law Actions (See pages 868–869.)	1. *Nuisance*—A common law doctrine under which persons may be held liable if their use of their property unreasonably interferes with others' rights to use their own property. 2. *Negligence and strict liability*—Parties may recover damages for injuries sustained as a result of a firm's pollution-causing activities if they can demonstrate that the harm was a foreseeable result of the firm's failure to exercise reasonable care (negligence). Businesses engaging in ultrahazardous activities are liable for whatever injuries the activities cause, regardless of whether the firms exercise reasonable care.

Chapter Summary: Consumer and Environmental Law—Continued

Federal Regulation (See pages 869–876.)	1. *Environmental protection agencies*—The primary agency regulating environmental law is the federal Environmental Protection Agency (EPA), which administers most federal environmental policies and statutes. 2. *Assessing environmental impact*—The National Environmental Policy Act requires the preparation of an environmental impact statement (EIS) for every major federal action. An EIS must analyze the action's impact on the environment, its adverse effects and possible alternatives, and its irreversible effects on environmental quality. 3. *Important areas regulated by the federal government*—These include the following: a. Air pollution—Regulated under the authority of the Clean Air Act and its amendments. b. Water pollution—Regulated under the authority of the Rivers and Harbors Appropriations Act and the Federal Water Pollution Control Act, as amended by the Clean Water Act. c. Toxic chemicals and hazardous waste—Pesticides and herbicides, toxic substances, and hazardous waste are regulated under the authority of the Federal Insecticide, Fungicide, and Rodenticide Act, the Toxic Substances Control Act, and the Resource Conservation and Recovery Act, respectively. The Comprehensive Environmental Response, Compensation, and Liability Act (CERCLA), as amended, regulates the clean-up of hazardous waste–disposal sites.

ExamPrep

ISSUE SPOTTERS

1. Gert buys a notebook computer from EZ Electronics. She pays for it with her credit card. When the computer proves defective, she asks EZ to repair or replace it, but EZ refuses. What can Gert do? **(See page 866.)**
2. Resource Refining Company's plant emits smoke and fumes. Resource's operation includes a short railway system, and trucks enter and exit the grounds continuously. Constant vibrations from the trains and trucks rattle nearby residential neighborhoods. The residents sue Resource. Are there any reasons that the court might refuse to enjoin Resource's operation? Explain. **(See page 868.)**

—Check your answers to the Issue Spotters against the answers provided in Appendix E at the end of this text.

BEFORE THE TEST

Go to www.cengagebrain.com, enter the ISBN 9781133273561, and click on "Find" to locate this textbook's Web site. Then, click on "Access Now" under "Study Tools," and select Chapter 33 at the top. There, you will find a Practice Quiz that you can take to assess your mastery of the concepts in this chapter, as well as Flashcards, a Glossary of important terms, and Video Questions (when assigned).

For Review

Answers to the even-numbered questions in this For Review section can be found in Appendix F at the end of this text.

1. When will advertising be deemed deceptive?
2. What are the major federal statutes providing for consumer protection in credit transactions?
3. Under what common law theories can polluters be held liable?
4. What is contained in an environmental impact statement, and who must file one?
5. What major federal statutes regulate air and water pollution?

Business Scenarios and Case Problems

33–1 Environmental Laws. Fruitade, Inc., is a processor of a soft drink called Freshen Up. Fruitade uses returnable bottles, which it cleans with a special acid to allow for further beverage processing. The acid is diluted with water and then allowed to pass into a navigable stream. Fruitade crushes its broken bottles and throws the crushed glass into the stream. Discuss fully any environmental laws that Fruitade has violated. **(See pages 871–874.)**

33–2 **Question with Sample Answer—Credit Protection.** Maria Ochoa receives two new credit cards on May 1. She had solicited one of them from Midtown Department Store, and the other arrived unsolicited from High-Flying Airlines. During the month of May, Ochoa makes numerous credit-card purchases from Midtown Department Store, but she does not use the High-Flying Airlines card. On May 31, a burglar breaks into Ochoa's home and steals both credit cards, along with other items. Ochoa notifies Midtown Department Store of the theft on June 2, but she fails to notify High-Flying Airlines. Using the Midtown credit card, the burglar makes a $500 purchase on June 1 and a $200 purchase on June 3. The burglar then charges a vacation flight on the High-Flying Airlines card for $1,000 on June 5. Ochoa receives the bills for these charges and refuses to pay them. Discuss Ochoa's liability in these situations. **(See page 866.)**

—For a sample answer to Question 33–2, go to Appendix G at the end of this text.

33–3 **Case Problem with Sample Answer—Food Labeling.** The Nutrition Labeling and Education Act (NLEA) requires packaged food to have a "Nutrition Facts" panel that sets out "nutrition information," including "the total number of calories" per serving. Restaurants are exempt from this requirement. Before the 2010 health-care reforms provisions on menu labeling (see page 861), the NLEA also regulated nutrition-content claims, such as "low sodium," that a purveyor might choose to add to a label. The NLEA permitted a state or local law to require restaurants to disclose nutrition information about the food they serve, but expressly preempted state or local attempts to regulate nutrition-content claims. New York City Health Code Section 81.50 required 10 percent of the restaurants in the city, including McDonald's, Burger King, and Kentucky Fried Chicken, to post calorie-content information on their menus. The New York State Restaurant Association (NYSRA) filed a suit in a federal district court, contending that the NLEA preempted Section 81.50. (Under the U.S. Constitution, state or local laws that conflict with federal laws are preempted.) Was the NYSRA correct? Explain. [*New York State Restaurant Association v. New York City Board of Health,* 556 F.3d 114 (2d Cir. 2009)] **(See pages 860–861.)**

—For a sample answer to Problem 33–3, go to Appendix H at the end of this text.

33–4 **Deceptive Advertising.** Brian Cleary and Rita Burke filed a suit against cigarette maker Philip Morris USA, Inc., seeking class-action status for a claim of deceptive advertising. They claimed that "light" cigarettes, such as Marlboro Lights, were advertised as safer than regular cigarettes, even though the health effects are the same. They contended that the tobacco companies concealed the true nature of light cigarettes. Philip Morris correctly claimed that it was authorized by the government to advertise cigarettes, including light cigarettes. Assuming that is true, should Cleary and Burke still be able to bring a deceptive advertising claim against the tobacco company? Why or why not? [*Cleary v. Philip Morris USA, Inc.,* 683 F.Supp.2d 730 (N.D.Ill. 2010)] **(See pages 857–860.)**

33–5 **Environmental Impact Statement.** The U.S. National Park Service (NPS) manages the Grand Canyon National Park in Arizona under a management plan that is subject to periodic review. In 2006, after nine years of background work and the completion of a comprehensive environmental impact statement, the NPS issued a new management plan for the park. One part of the plan allowed for the continued use of rafts on the Colorado River, which runs through the Grand Canyon. The number of the rafts was limited, however. Several environmental groups criticized the plan because they felt that it still allowed too many rafts on the river. The groups asked a federal appellate court to overturn the plan, claiming that it violated the wilderness status of the national park. When can a federal court overturn a determination by an agency such as the NPS? Explain. [*River Runners for Wilderness v. Martin,* 593 F.3d 1064 (9th Cir. 2010)] **(See page 869.)**

33–6 **Fair Debt-Collection Practices.** Bank of America hired Atlantic Resource Management, LLC, to collect a debt from Michael Engler. Atlantic called Engler's employer and asked his supervisor about the company's policy concerning the execution of warrants. It then told the supervisor that, to stop the process, Engler needed to call Atlantic about "Case Number 37291 NY0969" during the first three hours of his next shift. When Engler's supervisor told him about the call, Engler feared that he might be arrested, and he experienced discomfort, embarrassment, and emotional distress at work. Can Engler recover under the Fair Debt Collection Practices Act? Why or why not? [*Engler v. Atlantic Resource Management, LLC,* 2012 WL 464728 (W.D.N.Y. 2012)] **(See pages 867–868.)**

33–7 **A Question of Ethics—Clean Air Act.** In the Clean Air Act, Congress allowed California, which has particular problems with clean air, to adopt its own standard for emissions from cars and trucks, subject to the approval of the Environmental Protection Agency (EPA) according to certain criteria. Congress also allowed other states to adopt California's standard after the EPA's approval. In 2004, in an effort to address global warming, the California Air Resources Board amended the state's standard to attain "the maximum feasible and cost-effective reduction of GHG [greenhouse gas] emissions from motor vehicles." The regulation, which applies to new passenger vehicles and light-duty trucks for 2009 and later, imposes decreasing limits on emissions of carbon dioxide through 2016. While EPA approval was pending, Vermont and other states adopted similar standards. Green Mountain Chrysler Plymouth Dodge Jeep and other auto dealers, automakers, and associations of automakers filed a suit in a federal district court against George Crombie (secretary of the Vermont Agency of Natural Resources) and others, seeking relief from the state regulations. [*Green Mountain Chrysler Plymouth Dodge Jeep v. Crombie,* 508 F.Supp.2d 295 (D.Vt. 2007)] **(See pages 870–871.)**

1. Under the Environmental Policy and Conservation Act (EPCA), the National Highway Traffic Safety Administration sets fuel economy standards for new cars. The plaintiffs argued, among other things, that the EPCA, which prohibits states from adopting fuel economy standards, preempts Vermont's GHG regulation. Do the GHG rules equate to the fuel economy standards? Discuss.
2. Do Vermont's rules tread on the efforts of the federal government to address global warming internationally? Who should regulate GHG emissions? The federal government? The state governments? Both? Neither? Why?
3. The plaintiffs claimed that they would go bankrupt if they were forced to adhere to the state's GHG standards. Should they be granted relief on this basis? Does history support their claim? Explain.

Critical Thinking and Writing Assignments

33–8 **Business Law Critical Thinking Group Assignment.** Many states have enacted laws that go even further than federal laws to protect consumers. These laws vary tremendously from state to state.

1. The first group will decide whether having different laws is fair to sellers who may be prohibited from engaging in a practice in one state that is legal in another.
2. The second group will consider how these different laws might affect a business.
3. A third group will determine whether it is fair that residents of one state have more protection than residents of another.

34 CHAPTER

Liability of Accountants and Other Professionals

(damircudic/iStockphoto.com)

CHAPTER OUTLINE

- Potential Common Law Liability to Clients
- Potential Liability to Third Parties
- The Sarbanes-Oxley Act
- Potential Statutory Liability of Accountants under Securities Laws
- Potential Criminal Liability
- Confidentiality and Privilege

LEARNING OBJECTIVES

The five learning objectives below are designed to help improve your understanding of the chapter. After reading this chapter, you should be able to answer the following questions:

1. Under what common law theories may professionals be liable to clients?
2. What are the rules concerning an auditor's liability to third parties?
3. How might an accountant violate federal securities laws?
4. What crimes might an accountant commit under the Internal Revenue Code?
5. What constrains professionals to keep communications with their clients confidential?

"A member should observe the profession's technical and ethical standards . . . and discharge professional responsibility to the best of the member's ability."

—Article V, *Code of Professional Conduct,* American Institute of Certified Public Accountants

Professionals are obligated to adhere to standards of performance commonly accepted within their professions. The standard of due care to which the members of the American Institute of Certified Public Accountants are expected to adhere is set out in the chapter-opening quotation above. Investors rely heavily on the opinions of certified public accountants when making decisions about whether to invest in a company.

The Ponzi scheme perpetrated by Bernard Madoff that bilked investors out of $65 billion (see page 190 in Chapter 7) demonstrates the importance of adhering to professional accounting standards. Madoff's investment firm was "audited" by accountant David Friehling, who admitted that he never verified the existence of the assets that Madoff claimed to have, never checked to see that the stock trades that Madoff reported actually took place, and never examined the bank account in which billions of dollars in client funds were supposedly deposited. Had Friehling taken any of these basic steps, Madoff's scheme would have come to light. Friehling pleaded guilty to securities fraud, investment adviser fraud, and obstructing the administration of the tax law—offenses that could result in decades in prison.

Accountants, attorneys, physicians, and other professionals have found themselves increasingly subject to liability in the past twenty years. In this chapter, we examine the potential sources of professional liability.

Potential Common Law Liability to Clients

Under the common law, professionals may be liable to clients for breach of contract, negligence, or fraud.

Liability for Breach of Contract

LEARNING OBJECTIVE 1
Under what common law theories may professionals be liable to clients?

Accountants and other professionals face liability under the common law for any breach of contract. A professional owes a duty to his or her client to honor the terms of their contract and to perform the contract within the stated time period. If the professional fails to perform as agreed, then he or she has breached the contract, and the client has the right to recover damages. A professional may be held liable for expenses incurred by the client in securing another professional to provide the contracted-for services, for penalties imposed on the client for failure to meet deadlines, and for any other reasonable and foreseeable monetary losses that arise from the breach.

Liability for Negligence

Accountants and other professionals may also be held liable under the common law for negligence in the performance of their services. To establish negligence, the following elements must be proved:

1. A duty of care existed.
2. That duty of care was breached.
3. The plaintiff suffered an injury.
4. The injury was proximately caused by the defendant's breach of the duty of care.

All professionals are subject to standards of conduct established by codes of professional ethics, by state statutes, and by judicial decisions. In addition, in their performance of contracts, professionals must exercise the established standards of care, knowledge, and judgment generally accepted by members of their professional group. Here, we look at the duty of care owed by two groups of professionals that frequently perform services for business firms: accountants and attorneys.

Generally Accepted Accounting Principles (GAAP) The conventions, rules, and procedures developed by the Financial Accounting Standards Board to define accepted accounting practices at a particular time.

Generally Accepted Auditing Standards (GAAS) Standards established by the American Institute of Certified Public Accountants to define the professional qualities and judgment that should be exercised by an auditor in performing an audit.

Accountant's Duty of Care

Accountants play a major role in a business's financial system. They maintain the firm's financial records; design, control, and audit its record-keeping systems; prepare reliable statements that reflect the business's financial status; and give tax advice and prepare tax returns.

GAAP and GAAS In performing their services, accountants must comply with **generally accepted accounting principles (GAAP)** and **generally accepted auditing standards (GAAS).** The Financial Accounting Standards Board (FASB, usually pronounced "faz-bee") determines what accounting conventions, rules, and procedures constitute GAAP at a given point in time. GAAS are standards concerning the professional qualities and judgment that an auditor should exercise in performing an audit. The American Institute of Certified Public Accountants established GAAS.

As long as an accountant conforms to generally accepted standards and acts in good faith, he or she normally will not be held liable to the client for incorrect judgment. (For a discussion of how GAAP is being replaced by global accounting rules, see this chapter's *Landmark in the Law* feature below.)

A violation of GAAP and GAAS is considered *prima facie* evidence of negligence on the part of the accountant. Compliance with GAAP and GAAS, however, does not *necessarily* relieve an accountant from potential legal liability. An accountant may be held to a higher standard of conduct established by state statute and by judicial decisions.

LANDMARK IN THE LAW

The SEC Adopts Global Accounting Rules

At one time, investors and companies considered U.S. accounting rules, known as generally accepted accounting principles (GAAP), to be the gold standard—the best system for reporting earnings and other financial information. Then came the subprime mortgage meltdown and the global economic crisis, which caused many to question the effectiveness and superiority of GAAP.

In 2008, the Securities and Exchange Commission (SEC) unanimously approved a plan to require U.S. companies to use a set of global accounting rules, known as International Financial Reporting Standards (IFRS), for all of the financial reports that they must file with the commission. The plan called for the use of GAAP to be phased out.

Why Shift to Global Accounting Standards? The SEC decided to replace the rules-based GAAP with the principles-based IFRS for several reasons. GAAP rules are detailed and fill nearly 25,000 pages. The IFRS are simpler and more straightforward, spanning only 2,500 pages, and they focus more on over-riding principles than on specific rules.

Consequently, companies should eventually find it less difficult to comply with the international rules, and this should lead to cost savings. Another benefit is that investors will find it easier to make cross-country comparisons between, say, a technology company in Silicon Valley and one in Germany or Japan.

Furthermore, having uniform accounting rules that apply to all nations makes sense in a global economy. The European Union and 113 other nations, including Australia, Canada, China, India, and Mexico, have already adopted the IFRS. In fact, most of the United States' trading partners use the global rules.

The Downside to Adopting Global Rules Despite these benefits, the shift to the global rules has some drawbacks. It will be both costly and time consuming. Companies will have to upgrade their communications and software systems, study and implement the new rules, and train their employees, accountants, and tax attorneys.

To ease the transition, the SEC has set up a multiyear timetable for converting to the IFRS. The largest multinational companies are required to use the global rules by 2014, and the smallest publicly reporting companies must make the shift by 2016. Nonetheless, some of the smaller U.S. firms may find it difficult to absorb the costs of converting to the IFRS.

Another concern is that although the IFRS are simpler, they may not be better than GAAP. Because the global rules are broader and less detailed, they give companies more leeway in reporting, so less financial information may be disclosed. There are also indications that using the IFRS can lead to wide variances in profit reporting and tends to boost earnings above what they would have been under GAAP. Finally, the role of the U.S. Financial Accounting Standards Board and the SEC in shaping and overseeing accounting standards will necessarily be reduced because the London-based International Accounting Standards Board sets the IFRS.

Application to Today's World *The shift to IFRS received broad bipartisan political support even during the economic recession. Nevertheless, it will take years for the United States to completely implement global accounting rules. Business students should study and understand the IFRS so that they are prepared to use these rules in their future careers.*

Defalcation Embezzlement or misappropriation of funds.

Discovering Improprieties As a general rule, an accountant is not required to discover every impropriety, **defalcation**[1] (embezzlement), or fraud, in her or his client's books. If, however, the impropriety, defalcation, or fraud has gone undiscovered because of the accountant's negligence or failure to perform an express or implied duty, the accountant will be liable for any resulting losses suffered by the client. Therefore, an accountant who uncovers suspicious financial transactions and fails to investigate the matter fully or to inform the client of the discovery can be held liable to the client for the resulting loss.

Audits One of the most important tasks that an accountant may perform for a business is an audit. An *audit* is a systematic inspection, by analyses and tests, of a business's financial records.

The purpose of an audit is to provide the auditor with evidence to support an opinion on the reliability of the business's financial statements. A normal audit is not intended to uncover fraud or other misconduct. Nevertheless, an accountant may be liable for failing to detect misconduct if a normal audit would have revealed it. Also, if the auditor agreed to examine the records for evidence of fraud or other obvious misconduct and then failed to detect it, he or she may be liable. After performing an audit, the auditor issues an opinion letter stating whether, in his or her opinion, the financial statements fairly present the business's financial position.

Qualified Opinions and Disclaimers In issuing an opinion letter, an auditor may *qualify* the opinion or include a disclaimer. In a disclaimer, the auditor basically is stating that she or he does not have sufficient information to issue an opinion. An opinion or disclaimer that disclaims any liability for false or misleading financial statements is too general, however. A qualified opinion or a disclaimer must be specific and identify the reason for the qualification or disclaimer.

EXAMPLE 34.1 Richard Zehr performs an audit of Lacey Corporation. In the opinion letter, Zehr qualifies his opinion by stating that there is uncertainty about how a lawsuit against the firm will be resolved. In this situation, Zehr will not be liable if the outcome of the suit is unfavorable for the firm. Zehr could still be liable, however, for failing to discover other problems that an audit in compliance with GAAS and GAAP would have revealed. •

Defenses to Negligence If an accountant is found guilty of negligence, the client can collect damages for losses that arose from the accountant's negligence. An accountant facing a claim of negligence, however, has several possible defenses, including the following:

1. The accountant was not negligent.
2. If the accountant was negligent, this negligence was not the proximate cause of the client's losses.
3. The client was also negligent (depending on whether state law allows contributory negligence as a defense).

> "Never call an accountant a credit to his profession; a good accountant is a debit to his profession."
>
> Attributed to Charles J.C. Lyell, 1943–1996 (American commentator)

CASE EXAMPLE 34.2 Coopers & Lybrand, LLP, provided accounting services for Oregon Steel Mills (OSM), Inc. Coopers advised OSM to report a certain transaction as a $12.3 million gain on its financial statements. Later, when OSM planned to make a public offering of its stock, the Securities and Exchange Commission (SEC) reviewed its financial statements and concluded that the transaction was treated improperly. Because of the delay while OSM corrected its statements, the public offering did not occur on May 2, when OSM's stock

---

1. This term, pronounced deh-fal-*kay*-shun, is derived from the Latin *de* ("off") amd *falx* ("sickle"—a tool from cutting grain or tall grass). As used here, the term refers to the act of an embezzler.

was selling for $16 per share, but on June 13, when, due to unrelated factors, the price was $13.50. OSM filed a lawsuit against Coopers claiming that the negligent accounting resulted in the stock's being sold at a lower price. The court held, however, that although the accountant's negligence had delayed the stock offering, the negligence was not the proximate cause of the decline in the stock price. Thus, Coopers could not be held liable for damages based on the price decline.[2] ●

Attorney's Duty of Care

The conduct of attorneys is governed by rules established by each state and by the American Bar Association's Code of Professional Responsibility and Model Rules of Professional Conduct. All attorneys owe a duty to provide competent and diligent representation. Attorneys are required to be familiar with well-settled principles of law applicable to a case and to discover law that can be found through a reasonable amount of research.

Normally, an attorney's performance is expected to be that of a reasonably competent general practitioner of ordinary skill, experience, and capacity. An attorney who holds himself or herself out as having expertise in a particular area of law (such as intellectual property) is held to a higher standard of care in that area of the law than attorneys without such expertise.

When does an attorney's recreational use of illegal drugs rise to the level of disregarding professional obligations?

(keeweeboy/iStockphoto.com)

Misconduct

Typically, a state's rules of professional conduct for attorneys provide that committing a criminal act that reflects adversely on the person's "honesty or trustworthiness, or fitness as a lawyer in other respects" is professional misconduct. The rules often further provide that a lawyer should not engage in conduct involving "dishonesty, fraud, deceit, or misrepresentation." Under these rules, state authorities can discipline attorneys for many types of misconduct.

CASE EXAMPLE 34.3 Michael Inglimo, who was licensed to practice law in Wisconsin, occasionally used marijuana with a person who later became his client in a criminal case. After the trial, the client claimed that Inglimo had been high on drugs during the trial and had not adequately represented him. Two years later, Inglimo was convicted for misdemeanor possession of marijuana. State authorities also discovered that Inglimo had commingled client funds and written several checks for personal expenses out of his client trust account.

The state initiated disciplinary proceedings to have Inglimo's license to practice suspended. Inglimo argued that he should not be suspended because his misconduct was related to his past use of controlled substances and he no longer used drugs. The court, however, concluded that the suspension was necessary to protect the public in light of Inglimo's "disturbing pattern of disregard" for his professional obligations.[3] ●

Malpractice Professional negligence, or failure to exercise reasonable care and professional judgment, that results in injury, loss, or damage to those relying on the professional.

Liability for Malpractice

When an attorney fails to exercise reasonable care and professional judgment, she or he breaches the duty of care and can be held liable for **malpractice** (professional negligence).

In malpractice cases—as in all cases involving allegations of negligence—the plaintiff must prove that the attorney's breach actually caused the plaintiff to suffer some injury. **EXAMPLE 34.4** Attorney Lynette Boehmer allows the statute of limitations to lapse on the claim of Karen Anderson, a client. Boehmer can be held liable for malpractice because Anderson can no longer pursue her claim and has lost a potential award of damages. ●

Allegations of malpractice gave rise to the following case.

---

2. *Oregon Steel Mills, Inc. v. Coopers & Lybrand, LLP*, 336 Or. 329, 83 P.3d 322 (2004).
3. *In re Disciplinary Proceedings against Inglimo*, 2007 WI 126, 305 Wis.2d 71, 740 N.W.2d 125 (2007).

Case 34.1

Kelley v. Buckley

Court of Appeals of Ohio, Eighth District, 193 Ohio App.3d 11, 2011 Ohio 1362 (2011). www.sconet.state.oh.us/rod[a]

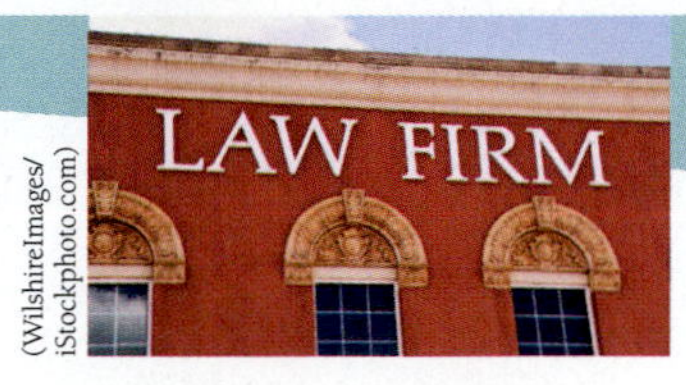

(Wilshirelmages/ iStockphoto.com)

FACTS Attorneys Michael Kelley and James Ferraro founded Kelley & Ferraro, LLP (K&F), an Ohio law firm. When Kelley died, his widow, Lynn Kelley, contacted lawyer Brent Buckley of Buckley King, LPA, who had drafted the K&F partnership agreement. The agreement provided that on Michael's death, Lynn was to be paid 40 percent of the firm's gross revenues. Buckley King had recently been retained by Ferraro to represent his interests in any dispute with Michael's estate, however, and Buckley advised Lynn, the executor of the estate, to settle with Ferraro quickly.

Despite Lynn's repeated requests, Buckley did not give her a copy of the partnership agreement. Meanwhile, she became embroiled in litigation with lawyer John Sivinski, who had worked for K&F and claimed a share of Michael's profits. Buckley King represented Ferraro and K&F in this dispute and withheld copies of an employment contract between K&F and Sivinski. When Lynn eventually obtained a copy of Sivinski's contract, it revealed that his claim against the estate was fraudulent. She then filed a malpractice suit against Brent Buckley and Buckley King. The court issued a summary judgment in favor of Buckley and the firm. Lynn appealed.

ISSUE Did Lynn Kelley present sufficient evidence that attorney Buckley had committed malpractice to allow her claim to go forward to trial?

DECISION Yes. A state intermediate appellate court reversed the summary judgment in the defendants' favor and remanded the case for additional discovery and a trial. The court also awarded Lynn the costs of the appeal.

REASON The court reasoned that there were genuine issues of material fact relating to all of Lynn's claims. For example, she claimed that the defendants had breached a duty of care owed to Michael when they negotiated the original partnership agreement. They argued that Michael had limited the scope of their representation when he allegedly told Buckley over the phone that he was handling the negotiations and choosing the business entity and that Buckley should follow his instructions. The court, however, noted that any oral statements supposedly made by Michael were hearsay evidence that was not admissible for the purpose of showing he had limited the attorney's representation.

The court also reasoned that there were genuine issues of fact concerning Lynn's allegation that the defendants had drafted Sivinski's contract and could have ended his suit by producing a copy. The defendants denied that they had created the contract. They also contended that Lynn had consented to their representation of Ferraro and K&F in her claims against them, but she denied this. The defendants argued that Lynn had failed to show that her allegations of malpractice caused her to suffer any damages. She had asserted, however, that their failure to give her a copy of the partnership agreement and their advice to settle with Ferraro quickly had caused her emotional distress.

CRITICAL THINKING—Ethical Consideration *Suppose that Buckley and the Buckley King firm are held legally liable at trial on all of Lynn's claims for malpractice. What acts of ethical misconduct might this indicate?*

a. Click on "8th Appellate District Opinions." On the next page, select "In the Year 2011" from the "Decided:" menu, type "2011-Ohio-1362" in the "WebCite No:" box, and click on "Submit." In the result, click on the name of the case to access the opinion. The Ohio Supreme Court and judicial system maintain this Web site.

Liability for Fraud

An accountant may be found liable for either actual fraud or constructive fraud. Recall from Chapter 12 that fraud, or misrepresentation, involves the following elements:

1. A misrepresentation of a material fact.
2. An intent to deceive.
3. Justifiable reliance by the innocent party on the misrepresentation.
4. To obtain damages, the innocent party must have been injured.

A professional may be held liable for *actual fraud* when he or she intentionally misstates a material fact to mislead a client and the client is injured as a result of her or his justifiable reliance on the misstated fact. A material fact is one that a reasonable person would consider important in deciding whether to act.

In contrast, a professional may be held liable for *constructive* fraud whether or not he or she acted with fraudulent intent. **EXAMPLE 34.5** Paula, an accountant, is conducting an audit of National Computing Company (NCC). Paula accepts the explanations of Ron, an NCC officer, regarding certain financial irregularities, despite evidence that contradicts those explanations and indicates that the irregularities may be illegal. Paula's conduct could be characterized as an intentional failure to perform a duty in reckless disregard of the consequences of such failure. This would constitute gross negligence and could be held to be constructive fraud. • Both actual and constructive fraud are potential sources of legal liability for an accountant or other professional.

For fraudulent conduct, an accountant may also suffer penalties imposed by a state board of accountancy, as the following case illustrates.

Case 34.2

Walsh v. State

Nebraska Supreme Court,
276 Neb. 1034, 759 N.W.2d 100 (2009).

(VisualField/iStockphoto.com)

FACTS Stephen Teiper wrote a letter to the Nebraska Board of Public Accountancy to accuse his brother-in-law, Michael Walsh, a certified public accountant (CPA), of impersonating Teiper on the phone to obtain financial information from Teiper's insurance company. The board filed a complaint against Walsh for a violation of its rules. At a hearing, Walsh admitted that he had impersonated Teiper, but argued that Teiper had provided his personal information to Walsh for this purpose. The board found that Walsh had committed a "discreditable act" and concluded that his conduct reflected adversely on his fitness to engage in the practice of public accountancy. As sanctions, the board reprimanded Walsh, placed him on probation for three months, and ordered him to attend four hours of continuing education in ethics. The board also ordered him to pay the costs of the hearing. Walsh petitioned a Nebraska state court, which affirmed the orders. Walsh appealed.

ISSUE Was there a sufficient connection between the practice of public accountancy and Walsh's conduct to allow the board to discipline him?

DECISION Yes. The Nebraska Supreme Court affirmed the lower court's decision. Walsh's actions reflected adversely on the accountancy profession, which demands a high level of honesty and integrity.

REASON A CPA cannot impersonate another person and "make false statements," or otherwise commit fraud, without "tainting" the CPA's reputation and the reputation of the accountancy profession. Like attorneys and other professionals, CPAs are held to "a high degree of moral and ethical integrity" because laypersons depend on CPAs' "honesty, integrity, sound professional judgment, and compliance with government regulations." The Nebraska Board of Public Accountancy has the authority to issue rules to "establish and maintain a high standard of integrity and dignity in the profession of public accountancy." Under these rules, a CPA "shall not commit an act that reflects adversely" on his or her fitness to practice the profession. The board can discipline CPAs who do not follow these standards and can impose various sanctions, including those levied on Walsh.

CRITICAL THINKING—Ethical Consideration *Was the specific reason for Walsh's impersonation significant to the result in this case? Why or why not?*

Potential Liability to Third Parties

Traditionally, an accountant or other professional did not owe any duty to a third person with whom she or he had no direct contractual relationship—that is, to any person not in *privity of contract*. A professional's duty was only to her or his client. Violations of statutes, fraud, and other intentional or reckless acts of wrongdoing were the only exceptions to this general rule.

Today, numerous third parties—including investors, shareholders, creditors, corporate managers and directors, and regulatory agencies—rely on professional opinions, such as those of auditors, when making decisions. In view of this extensive reliance, many courts have all but abandoned the privity requirement in regard to accountants' liability to third parties.

LEARNING OBJECTIVE 2
What are the rules concerning an auditor's liability to third parties?

In this section, we focus primarily on the potential liability of auditors to third parties. Understanding an auditor's common law liability to third parties is critical because often, when a business fails, its independent auditor (accountant) is one of the few potentially solvent defendants. The majority of courts now hold that auditors can be held liable to third parties for negligence, but the standard for the imposition of this liability varies. There generally are three different views of accountants' liability to third parties, each of which we discuss below.

The *Ultramares* Rule

The traditional rule regarding an accountant's liability to third parties was enunciated by Chief Judge Benjamin Cardozo in *Ultramares Corp. v. Touche,* a case decided in 1931.[4]

CASE EXAMPLE 34.6 Fred Stern & Company hired the public accounting firm of Touche, Niven & Company to review Stern's financial records and prepare a balance sheet for the year ending December 31, 1923.[5] Touche prepared the balance sheet and supplied Stern with thirty-two certified copies. According to the certified balance sheet, Stern had a net worth (assets less liabilities) of $1,070,715.26.

In reality, however, Stern's liabilities exceeded its assets—the company's records had been falsified by insiders at Stern to reflect a positive net worth (assets exceed liabilities). In reliance on the certified balance sheets, Ultramares Corporation loaned substantial amounts to Stern. After Stern was declared bankrupt, Ultramares brought an action against Touche for negligence in an attempt to recover damages. ●

(blackred/iStockphoto.com)

To what extent is an accounting firm liable for incorrect balance sheet information that is distributed to the public?

The Requirement of Privity

The New York Court of Appeals (that state's highest court) refused to impose liability on the Touche accountants and concluded that they owed a duty of care only to those persons for whose "primary benefit" the statements were intended. In this case, Stern was the only person for whose primary benefit the statements were intended. The court held that in the absence of privity or a relationship "so close as to approach that of privity," a party could not recover from an accountant. The court's requirement of privity has since been referred to as the *Ultramares* rule, or the New York rule.

CASE EXAMPLE 34.7 Toro Company supplied equipment and credit to Summit Power Equipment Distributors and required Summit to submit audited reports so that Toro could

4. 255 N.Y. 170, 174 N.E. 441 (1931).
5. Banks, creditors, stockholders, purchasers, or sellers often rely on a balance sheet as a basis for making decisions relating to a company's business.

evaluate its financial condition. Summit supplied Toro with reports prepared by accountants at Krouse, Kern & Company, which allegedly contained mistakes and omissions regarding Summit's financial condition. Toro extended large amounts of credit to Summit in reliance on the audited reports. When Summit was unable to repay the loans, Toro brought a negligence action against the accounting firm and proved that accountants at Krouse knew the reports it furnished would be used by Summit to induce Toro to extend credit. Nevertheless, under the *Ultramares* rule, the court refused to hold the accounting firm liable because the firm was not in privity with Toro.[6] •

Modified to Allow "Near Privity" The *Ultramares* rule was somewhat modified in a 1985 New York case, *Credit Alliance Corp. v. Arthur Andersen & Co.*[7] In that case, the court held that if a third party has a sufficiently close relationship or nexus (link or connection) with an accountant, then the *Ultramares* privity requirement may be satisfied even if no accountant-client relationship is established. The rule enunciated in the *Credit Alliance* case is often referred to as the "near privity" rule. Only a minority of states have adopted this rule, however.

The *Restatement* Rule

The *Ultramares* rule has been severely criticized because much of the work performed by auditors is intended for use by persons who are not parties to the contract. Thus, it is asserted that the auditors owe a duty to these third parties. Consequently, there has been an erosion of the *Ultramares* rule, and accountants have increasingly been exposed to potential liability to third parties.

The majority of courts have adopted the position taken by the *Restatement (Third) of Torts,* which states that accountants are subject to liability for negligence not only to their clients but also to foreseen, or *known,* users—or classes of users—of their reports or financial statements. Under the *Restatement (Third) of Torts,* an accountant's liability extends to the following:

1. Persons for whose benefit and guidance the accountant intends to supply the information or knows that the recipient intends to supply it.
2. Persons that the accountant intends the information to influence or knows that the recipient so intends.

EXAMPLE 34.8 Steve, an accountant, prepares a financial statement for Tech Software, Inc., a client, knowing that Tech Software will submit the statement to First National Bank with an application for a loan. If Steve makes negligent misstatements or omissions in the statement, he may be held liable by the bank because he knew that the bank would rely on his work product when deciding whether to make the loan. •

The "Reasonably Foreseeable Users" Rule

A small minority of courts hold accountants liable to any users whose reliance on an accountant's statements or reports was *reasonably foreseeable*. This standard has been criticized as extending liability too far and exposing accountants to massive liability..

The majority of courts have concluded that the *Restatement's* approach is more reasonable because it allows accountants to control their exposure to liability. Liability is "fixed by the accountants' particular knowledge at the moment the audit is published," not by the foreseeability of the harm that might occur to a third party after the report is released.

6. *Toro Co. v. Krouse, Kern & Co.*, 827 F.2d 155 (7th Cir. 1987).
7. 66 N.Y.2d 812, 489 N.E.2d 249, 498 N.Y.S.2d 362 (1985).

Liability of Attorneys

Like accountants, attorneys may be held liable under the common law to third parties who rely on legal opinions to their detriment. Generally, an attorney is not liable to a nonclient unless there is fraud (or malicious conduct) by the attorney. The liability principles stated in the *Restatement (Third) of Torts*, however, may apply to attorneys as well as to accountants.

(tupungato/iStockphoto.com)

To the extent that Deloitte & Touche engages in auditing public companies, its procedures are overseen by the Public Company Accounting Oversight Board.

The Sarbanes-Oxley Act

The Sarbanes-Oxley Act (discussed on page 196 of Chapter 7 and page 820 of Chapter 31) imposes a number of strict requirements on both domestic and foreign public accounting firms. These requirements apply to firms that provide auditing services to companies ("issuers") whose securities are sold to public investors. The act defines an *issuer* as a company that has securities that are registered under Section 12 of the Securities Exchange Act of 1934, that is required to file reports under Section 15(d) of the 1934 act, or that files—or has filed—a registration statement that has not yet become effective under the Securities Act of 1933.

The Public Company Accounting Oversight Board

The Sarbanes-Oxley Act increased government oversight of public accounting practices by creating the Public Company Accounting Oversight Board, which reports to the Securities and Exchange Commission. The board oversees the audit of public companies that are subject to securities laws. The goal is to protect public investors and to ensure that public accounting firms comply with the provisions of the act. The act defines *public accounting firms* as firms "engaged in the practice of public accounting or preparing or issuing audit reports."

The key provisions relating to the duties of the oversight board and the requirements relating to public accounting firms are summarized in Exhibit 34.1 on the next page. (Provisions relating to corporate fraud and the responsibilities of corporate officers and directors were described and listed in Exhibit 31.3 on page 820.)

Requirements for Maintaining Working Papers

Working Papers The documents used and developed by an accountant during an audit, such as notes, computations, and memoranda.

Performing an audit for a client involves an accumulation of **working papers**—the various documents used and developed during the audit. These include notes, computations, memoranda, copies, and other papers that make up the work product of an accountant's services to a client.

Under the common law, which in this instance has been codified in a number of states, working papers remain the accountant's property. It is important for accountants to retain such records in the event that they need to defend against lawsuits for negligence or other actions in which their competence is challenged. The client also has a right to access an accountant's working papers because they reflect the client's financial situation. On a client's request, an accountant must return to the client any of the client's records or journals, and failure to do so may result in liability.

"Destroy the old files, but make copies first."

Samuel Goldwyn, 1879–1974 (American motion picture producer)

Section 802(a)(1) of the Sarbanes-Oxley Act provides that accountants must maintain working papers relating to an audit or review for five years—subsequently increased to seven years—from the end of the fiscal period in which the audit or review was concluded. A knowing violation of this requirement will subject the accountant to a fine, imprisonment for up to ten years, or both.

Are the high costs of complying with the Sarbanes-Oxley Act justified by more ethical conduct? Since its enactment, critics have complained that the costs of complying with the Sarbanes-Oxley Act greatly outweigh the perceived benefits. In fact, studies estimate that a public company spends, on average, at least $2.9 million annually complying with the act's provisions. These funds could otherwise have been distributed as dividends to shareholders or reinvested to finance the company's growth and thereby provide more jobs.

The burdens of complying with the Sarbanes-Oxley Act have also led many companies to go private, turning over control to private equity firms (businesses that own shares in companies that are not listed on a public stock exchange). There is also some doubt as to whether the act has been effective in improving corporate ethics and accountability.

Potential Statutory Liability of Accountants under Securities Laws

LEARNING OBJECTIVE 3
How might an accountant violate federal securities laws?

Both civil and criminal liability may be imposed on accountants under the Securities Act of 1933, the Securities Exchange Act of 1934, and the Private Securities Litigation Reform Act of 1995.[8]

8. Civil and criminal liability may also be imposed on accountants and other professionals under other statutes, including the Racketeer Influenced and Corrupt Organizations Act (RICO). RICO was discussed in Chapter 6.

Exhibit 34.1 Key Provisions of the Sarbanes-Oxley Act Relating to Public Accounting Firms

AUDITOR INDEPENDENCE

To help ensure that auditors remain independent of the firms that they audit, Title II of the Sarbanes-Oxley Act does the following:

1. Makes it unlawful for Registered Public Accounting Firms (RPAFs) to perform both audit and nonaudit services for the same company at the same time. Nonaudit services include the following:
   - Bookkeeping or other services related to the accounting records or financial statements of the audit client.
   - Financial information systems design and implementation.
   - Appraisal or valuation services.
   - Fairness opinions.
   - Management functions.
   - Broker or dealer, investment adviser, or investment banking services.
2. Requires preapproval for most auditing services from the issuer's (the corporation's) audit committee.
3. Requires audit partner rotation by prohibiting RPAFs from providing audit services to an issuer if either the lead audit partner or the audit partner responsible for reviewing the audit has provided such services to that corporation in each of the prior five years.
4. Requires RPAFs to make timely reports to the audit committees of the corporations. The report must indicate all critical accounting policies and practices to be used; all alternative treatments of financial information within generally accepted accounting principles that have been discussed with the corporation's management officials, the ramifications of the use of such alternative treatments, and the treatment preferred by the auditor; and other material written communications between the auditor and the corporation's management.
5. Makes it unlawful for an RPAF to provide auditing services to an issuer if the corporation's chief executive officer, chief financial officer, chief accounting officer, or controller was previously employed by the auditor and participated in any capacity in the audit of the corporation during the one-year period preceding the date that the audit began.

DOCUMENT RETENTION AND DESTRUCTION

The Sarbanes-Oxley Act provides that anyone who destroys, alters, or falsifies records with the intent to obstruct or influence a federal investigation or in relation to bankruptcy proceedings can be criminally prosecuted and sentenced to a fine, imprisonment for up to twenty years, or both.

The act also requires accountants who audit or review publicly traded companies to retain all working papers related to the audit or review for a period of five years (now amended to seven years). Violators can be sentenced to a fine, imprisonment for up to ten years, or both.

Liability under the Securities Act of 1933

The Securities Act of 1933 requires registration statements to be filed with the Securities and Exchange Commission (SEC) prior to an offering of securities (see Chapter 31).[9] Accountants frequently prepare and certify the issuer's financial statements that are included in the registration statement.

Liability under Section 11

Section 11 of the Securities Act of 1933 imposes civil liability on accountants for misstatements and omissions of material facts in registration statements. An accountant may be liable if he or she prepared any financial statements included in the registration statement that "contained an untrue statement of a material fact or omitted to state a material fact required to be stated therein or necessary to make the statements therein not misleading."[10]

Under Section 11, an accountant's liability for a misstatement or omission of a material fact in a registration statement extends to anyone who acquires a security covered by the registration statement. A purchaser of a security need only demonstrate that she or he has suffered a loss on the security. Proof of reliance on the materially false statement or misleading omission ordinarily is not required. Nor is there a requirement of privity between the accountant and the security purchasers.

Due Diligence A required standard of care that certain professionals, such as accountants, must meet to avoid liability for securities violations.

The Due Diligence Standard Section 11 imposes a duty on accountants to use **due diligence** in preparing the financial statements included in the filed registration statements. Failure to follow GAAP and GAAS is proof of a lack of due diligence. After a purchaser has proved a loss on the security, the accountant has the burden of showing that he or she exercised due diligence in preparing the financial statements.

To avoid liability, the accountant must show that he or she

1. Conducted a reasonable investigation.
2. Had reasonable grounds to believe and did believe, at the time the registration statement became effective, that the financial statements therein were true and that there was no omission of a material fact that would be misleading.[11]

In particular, the due diligence standard places a burden on accountants to verify information furnished by a corporation's officers and directors. Merely asking questions is not always sufficient to satisfy the requirement. Accountants can be held liable for failing to detect danger signals in documents furnished by corporate officers that, under GAAS, require further investigation under the circumstances.[12]

PREVENTING LEGAL DISPUTES

When "danger signals" exist, you must investigate the situation further. Remember that persons other than accountants, such as corporate directors, officers, and managers, can also be liable for failing to perform due diligence. Courts are more likely to impose liability when someone has ignored warning signs or red flags that suggest accounting errors or misstatements are present. To avoid liability, always investigate the facts underlying financial statements that appear "too good to be true." Compare recent financial statements with earlier ones, read minutes of shareholders' and directors' meetings, and inspect changes in material contracts, bad debts, and newly discovered liabilities. Know what is required to meet due diligence standards in the particular jurisdiction and conduct yourself in a manner that is above reproach.

9. Many securities and transactions are expressly exempted from the 1933 act.

10. 15 U.S.C. Section 77k(a).

11. 15 U.S.C. Section 77k(b)(3).

12. See *In re Cardinal Health, Inc. Securities Litigation*, 426 F.Supp.2d 688 (S.D. Ohio 2006); and *In re WorldCom, Inc. Securities Litigation*, 352 F.Supp.2d 472 (S.D.N.Y. 2005).

Defenses to Liability Besides proving that he or she has acted with due diligence, an accountant can raise the following defenses to Section 11 liability:

1. There were no misstatements or omissions.
2. The misstatements or omissions were not of material facts.
3. The misstatements or omissions had no causal connection to the plaintiff's loss.
4. The plaintiff-purchaser invested in the securities knowing of the misstatements or omissions.

Liability under Section 12(2)

Section 12(2) of the Securities Act of 1933 imposes civil liability for fraud in relation to offerings or sales of securities.[13] Liability is based on communication to an investor, whether orally or in the written prospectus,[14] of an untrue statement or omission of a material fact.

Penalties and Sanctions for Violations

Those who purchase securities and suffer harm as a result of a false or omitted statement, or some other violation, may bring a suit in a federal court to recover their losses and other damages. The U.S. Department of Justice brings criminal actions against those who commit willful violations. The penalties include fines of up to $10,000, imprisonment for up to five years, or both. The SEC is authorized to seek an injunction against a willful violator to prevent further violations. The SEC can also ask a court to grant other relief, such as an order to a violator to refund profits derived from an illegal transaction.

Liability under the Securities Exchange Act of 1934

Under Sections 18 and 10(b) of the Securities Exchange Act of 1934 and SEC Rule 10b-5, an accountant may be found liable for fraud. A plaintiff has a substantially heavier burden of proof under the 1934 act than under the 1933 act because an accountant does not have to prove due diligence to escape liability under the 1934 act.

Liability under Section 18

Section 18 of the 1934 act imposes civil liability on an accountant who makes or causes to be made in any application, report, or document a statement that at the time and in light of the circumstances was false or misleading with respect to any material fact.[15]

Section 18 liability is narrow in that it applies only to applications, reports, documents, and registration statements filed with the SEC. This remedy is further limited in that it applies only to sellers and purchasers. Under Section 18, a seller or purchaser must prove one of the following:

1. That the false or misleading statement affected the price of the security.
2. That the purchaser or seller relied on the false or misleading statement in making the purchase or sale and was not aware of the inaccuracy of the statement.

An accountant will not be liable for violating Section 18 if he or she acted in good faith in preparing the financial statement. To demonstrate good faith, an accountant must show that he or she had no knowledge that the financial statement was false and misleading. Acting in good faith also requires that the accountant lacked any intent to deceive, manipulate, defraud, or seek unfair advantage over another party. (Note that "mere" negligence in

13. 15 U.S.C. Section 77ℓ.
14. As discussed in Chapter 31, a *prospectus* contains financial disclosures about the corporation for the benefit of potential investors.
15. 15 U.S.C. Section 78r(a).

preparing a financial statement does not lead to liability under the 1934 act. This differs from the 1933 act, under which an accountant is liable for *all* negligent acts.)

Liability under Section 10(b) and Rule 10b-5

Accountants additionally face potential legal liability under the antifraud provisions contained in the Securities Exchange Act of 1934 and SEC Rule 10b-5. The scope of these antifraud provisions is very broad and allows private parties to bring civil actions against violators.

Prohibited Conduct Section 10(b) makes it unlawful for any person, including accountants, to use, in connection with the purchase or sale of any security, any manipulative or deceptive device or contrivance in contravention of SEC rules and regulations.[16] Rule 10b-5 further makes it unlawful for any person, by use of any means or instrumentality of interstate commerce, to do the following:

1. Employ any device, scheme, or artifice (pretense) to defraud.
2. Make any untrue statement of a material fact or omit a material fact necessary to ensure that the statements made were not misleading, in light of the circumstances.
3. Engage in any act, practice, or course of business that operates or would operate as a fraud or deceit on any person, in connection with the purchase or sale of any security.[17]

Extent of Liability Accountants may be held liable only to sellers or purchasers of securities under Section 10(b) and Rule 10b-5. Privity is not necessary for a recovery. An accountant may be found liable not only for fraudulent misstatements of material facts in written material filed with the SEC, but also for any fraudulent oral statements or omissions made in connection with the purchase or sale of any security.

For a plaintiff to succeed in recovering damages under these antifraud provisions, however, he or she must prove intent (*scienter*) to commit the fraudulent or deceptive act. Ordinary negligence is not enough.

Do accountants have a duty to correct misstatements that they discover in *previous* financial statements? What if they know that potential investors are relying on those statements? Those were the questions in the following *Spotlight Case.*

16. 15 U.S.C. Section 78j(b)
17. 17 C.F.R. Section 240.10b-5.

Spotlight on an Accountant's Duty to Correct Mistakes in Financial Statements

Case 34.3
Overton v. Todman & Co., CPAs
United States Court of Appeals, Second Circuit, 478 F.3d 479 (2007).

(©Atanas Bezov, 2009. Used under license from Shutterstock.com)
Must an accounting firm make public its new knowledge of prior misstatements?

FACTS From 1999 through 2002, Todman & Company, CPAs, audited the financial statements of Direct Brokerage, Inc. (DBI), a broker-dealer in New York registered with the Securities and Exchange Commission (SEC). Each year, Todman issued an unqualified opinion that DBI's financial statements were accurate. DBI filed its statements and Todman's opinions with the SEC. Despite the certifications of accuracy, Todman made significant errors that concealed DBI's largest liability—its payroll taxes—in the 1999 and 2000 audits. The errors came to light in 2003 when the New York State subpoenaed DBI's payroll records, and it became clear that the company had not filed or paid its payroll taxes for 1999 and 2000. This put DBI in a precarious financial position, owing the state more than $3 million in unpaid taxes, interest, and penalties.

To meet its needs, DBI sought outside investors, including David Overton, who relied on DBI's statements and Todman's

Spotlight Case 34.3—Continues next page

Spotlight Case 34.3—Continued

opinion for 2002 to invest in DBI. When DBI collapsed under the weight of its liabilities in 2004, Overton and others filed a suit in a federal district court against Todman, asserting, among other things, fraud under Section 10(b) and Rule 10b-5. The court dismissed the complaint. The plaintiffs appealed.

ISSUE Is an accountant liable for securities fraud if the accountant certified a financial statement containing a misstatement and later learned of the misstatement but failed to correct it, even though the accountant knew that investors were relying on the statement?

DECISION Yes. The federal appellate court held that an accountant is liable in these circumstances under Section 10(b) and Rule 10b-5. The court vacated the lower court's dismissal and remanded the case for further proceedings.

REASON The court pointed out that any person or entity, including an accountant, "who employs a manipulative device or makes a material misstatement (or omission) on which a purchaser or seller of securities relies may be liable as a primary violator under [Section] 10b-5, assuming all of the requirements for primary liability under Rule 10b-5 are met." To be liable, one of the requirements is a "duty to speak." Such a duty arises "when one party has information that the other party is entitled to know because of a fiduciary or other similar relation of trust and confidence between them."

When accountants issue a certified opinion, they create the required special relationship with investors. Thus, accountants have a duty to take reasonable steps to correct misstatements that they discover in previous financial statements on which they know the public is relying. Silence in this situation can constitute a false or misleading statement under Section 10(b) and Rule 10b-5. Among other authorities, the court cited Section 10(b), which covers "any person," a United States Supreme Court decision that "labeled a critical element under [Section] 10(b) and Rule 10b-5: reliance by potential investors on the accountant's omission."[a]

WHAT IF THE FACTS WERE DIFFERENT? *If Todman had conducted an audit for DBI but had not issued a certified opinion about DBI's financial statements, would the result have been the same? Explain.*

a. See *Central Bank of Denver v. First Interstate Bank of Denver*, 511 U.S. 164, 114 S.Ct. 1439, 128 L.Ed.2d 119 (1994).

The Private Securities Litigation Reform Act

The Private Securities Litigation Reform Act made some changes to the potential liability of accountants and other professionals in securities fraud cases. Among other things, the act imposed a statutory obligation on accountants. An auditor must use adequate procedures in an audit to detect any illegal acts of the company being audited. If something illegal is detected, the auditor must disclose it to the company's board of directors, the audit committee, or the SEC, depending on the circumstances.[18]

Proportionate Liability

The act provides that, in most situations, a party is liable only for the proportion of damages for which he or she is responsible.[19] An accountant who participates in, but is unaware of, illegal conduct may not be liable for the entire loss caused by the illegality.

EXAMPLE 34.9 Nina, an accountant, helps the president and owner of Midstate Trucking company draft financial statements that misrepresent Midstate's financial condition, but Nina is not actually aware of the fraud. Nina might be held liable, but the amount of her liability could be proportionately less than the entire loss. •

Aiding and Abetting

The act also made it a separate crime to aid and abet a violation of the Securities Exchange Act of 1934, such as by knowingly participating in or assisting some improper activity or keeping quiet about such illegal activity.

If an accountant knowingly aids and abets a primary violator, the SEC can seek an injunction or monetary damages. **EXAMPLE 34.10** Smith & Jones, an accounting firm,

18. 15 U.S.C. Section 78j-1.
19. 15 U.S.C. Section 78u-4(g).

performs an audit for ABC Sales Company that is so inadequate as to constitute gross negligence. ABC uses the materials provided by Smith & Jones as part of a scheme to defraud investors. When the scheme is uncovered, the SEC can bring an action against Smith & Jones for aiding and abetting on the ground that the firm knew or should have known of the material misrepresentations that were in its audit and on which investors were likely to rely. ●

Potential Criminal Liability

An accountant may be found criminally liable for violations of securities laws and tax laws. In addition, in most states, criminal penalties may be imposed for actions such as knowingly certifying false or fraudulent reports, and falsifying, altering, or destroying books of account. Accountants may also be held criminally liable for obtaining property or credit through the use of false financial statements.

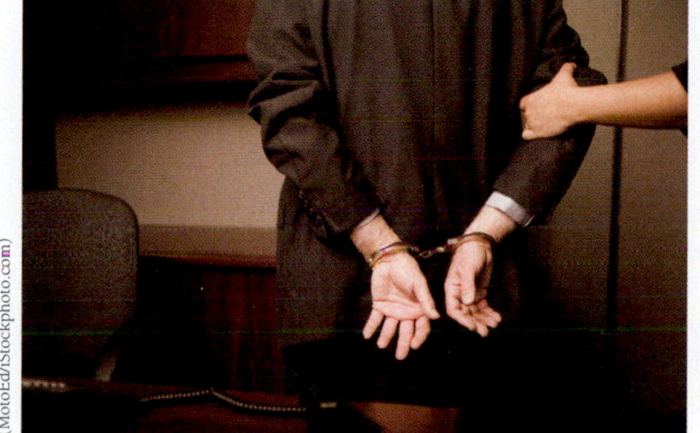

(MotoEd/iStockphoto.com)

The Securities and Exchange Acts of 1933 and 1934 created accountants' violations that can be criminally prosecuted.

Criminal Violations of Securities Laws

Accountants may be subject to criminal penalties for *willful* violations of the Securities Act of 1933 and the Securities Exchange Act of 1934. If convicted, they face imprisonment for up to five years and/or a fine of up to $10,000 under the 1933 act, and imprisonment for up to ten years and a fine of $100,000 under the 1934 act.

Under the Sarbanes-Oxley Act, if an accountant's false or misleading certified audit statement is used in a securities filing, the accountant may be fined up to $5 million, imprisoned for up to twenty years, or both.

Criminal Violations of Tax Laws

LEARNING OBJECTIVE 4
What crimes might an accountant commit under the Internal Revenue Code?

The Internal Revenue Code makes aiding or assisting in the preparation of a false tax return a felony punishable by a fine of $100,000 ($500,000 in the case of a corporation) and imprisonment for up to three years.[20] This provision applies to anyone who prepares tax returns for others for compensation, and not just to accountants.[21] A penalty of $250 per tax return is levied on tax preparers for negligent understatement of the client's tax liability. For willful understatement of tax liability or reckless or intentional disregard of rules or regulations, a penalty of $1,000 is imposed.[22]

A tax preparer may also be subject to penalties for failing to furnish the taxpayer with a copy of the return, failing to sign the return, or failing to furnish the appropriate tax identification numbers.[23] In addition, those who prepare tax returns for others may be fined $1,000 per document for aiding and abetting another's understatement of tax liability (the penalty is increased to $10,000 in corporate cases).[24] The tax preparer's liability is limited to one penalty per taxpayer per tax year.

LEARNING OBJECTIVE 5
What constrains professionals to keep communications with their clients confidential?

Confidentiality and Privilege

Professionals are restrained by the ethical tenets of their professions to keep all communications with their clients confidential.

20. 26 U.S.C. Section 7206(2).
21. 26 U.S.C. Section 7701(a)(36).
22. 26 U.S.C. Section 6694.
23. 26 U.S.C. Section 6695.
24. 26 U.S.C. Section 6701.

Attorney-Client Relationships

The confidentiality of attorney-client communications is protected by law, which confers a privilege on such communications. This privilege is granted because of the client's need to fully disclose the facts of his or her case to the attorney. To encourage frankness, confidential attorney-client communications relating to representation are normally held in strictest confidence and protected by law. The attorney and her or his employees may not discuss the client's case with anyone—even under court order—without the client's permission. The client holds the privilege, and only the client may waive it—by disclosing privileged information to someone outside the privilege, for example.

Note, however, that since the Sarbanes-Oxley Act was enacted, the SEC has implemented new rules requiring attorneys who become aware that a client has violated securities laws to report the violation to the SEC. Reporting a client's misconduct could be a breach of the attorney-client privilege, however, so the new rules have aroused controversy in the legal community.

Accountant-Client Relationships

In a few states, accountant-client communications are privileged by state statute. In these states, accountant-client communications may not be revealed even in court or in court-sanctioned proceedings without the client's permission. The majority of states, however, abide by the common law, which provides that, if a court so orders, an accountant must disclose information about his or her client to the court. Physicians and other professionals may similarly be compelled to disclose in court information given to them in confidence by patients or clients.

Communications between professionals and their clients—other than those between an attorney and her or his client—are not privileged under federal law. In cases involving federal law, state-provided rights to confidentiality of accountant-client communications are not recognized. Thus, in those cases, an accountant must provide all information requested in a court order.

Reviewing . . . Liability of Accountants and Other Professionals

Superior Wholesale Corporation planned to purchase Regal Furniture, Inc., and wished to determine Regal's net worth. Superior hired Lynette Shuebke, of the accounting firm Shuebke Delgado, to review an audit that had been prepared by Norman Chase, the accountant for Regal. Shuebke advised Superior that Chase had performed a high-quality audit and that Regal's inventory on the audit dates was stated accurately on the general ledger. As a result of these representations, Superior went forward with its purchase of Regal. After the purchase, Superior discovered that the audit by Chase had been materially inaccurate and misleading, primarily because the inventory had been grossly overstated on the balance sheet. Later, a former Regal employee who had begun working for Superior exposed an e-mail exchange between Chase and former Regal chief executive officer Buddy Gantry. The exchange revealed that Chase had cooperated in overstating the inventory and understating Regal's tax liability. Using the information presented in the chapter, answer the following questions.

1. If Shuebke's review was conducted in good faith and conformed to generally accepted accounting principles, could Superior hold Shuebke Delgado liable for negligently failing to detect material omissions in Chase's audit? Why or why not?
2. According to the rule adopted by the majority of courts to determine accountants' liability to third parties, could Chase be liable to Superior? Explain.

3. Generally, what requirements must be met before Superior can recover damages under Section 10(b) of the Securities Exchange Act of 1934 and SEC Rule 10b-5? Can Superior meet these requirements?
4. Suppose that a court determined that Chase had aided Regal in willfully understating its tax liability. What is the maximum penalty that could be imposed on Chase?

DEBATE THIS Only the largest publicly held companies should be subject to the Sarbanes-Oxley Act.

Key Terms

defalcation 885
due diligence 893
generally accepted accounting principles (GAAP) 883
generally accepted auditing standards (GAAS) 883
malpractice 886
working papers 891

Chapter Summary: Liability of Accountants and Other Professionals

COMMON LAW LIABILITY	
Potential Common Law Liability to Clients (See pages 883–888.)	1. *Breach of contract*—A professional who fails to fulfill contractual obligations can be held liable for breach of contract and resulting damages. 2. *Negligence*—An accountant, attorney, or other professional, in performing of her or his duties, must use the care, knowledge, and judgment generally used by professionals in the same or similar circumstances. Failure to do so is negligence. An accountant's violation of generally accepted accounting principles and generally accepted auditing standards is *prima facie* evidence of negligence. 3. *Fraud*—Intentionally misrepresenting a material fact to a client, when the client relies on the misrepresentation, is fraud. Gross negligence in performance of duties is constructive fraud.
Potential Liability to Third Parties (See pages 889–891.)	An accountant may be liable for negligence to any third person the accountant knows or should have known will benefit from the accountant's work. The standard for imposing this liability varies, but generally courts follow one of the following rules: 1. *Ultramares rule*—Liability will be imposed only if the accountant is in privity, or near privity, with the third party. 2. *Restatement rule*—Liability will be imposed only if the third party's reliance is foreseen, or known, or if the third party is among a class of foreseen, or known, users. The majority of courts have adopted this rule. 3. *"Reasonably foreseeable user" rule*—Liability will be imposed if the third party's use was reasonably foreseeable.
STATUTORY LIABILITY	
The Sarbanes-Oxley Act (See pages 891–892.)	1. *Purpose*—This act imposed requirements on public accounting firms that provide auditing services to companies whose securities are sold to public investors. 2. *Government oversight*—The act created the Public Company Accounting Oversight Board to provide government oversight over public accounting practices. 3. *Working papers*—The act requires accountants to maintain working papers relating to an audit or review for seven years from the end of the fiscal period in which the audit or review was concluded. 4. *Other requirements*—See Exhibit 34.1 on page 892.
Securities Act of 1933—Section 11 (See pages 893–894.)	An accountant who makes a false statement or omits a material fact in audited financial statements required for registration of securities under the law may be liable to anyone who acquires securities covered by the registration statement. The accountant's defense is basically the use of due diligence and the reasonable belief that the work was complete and correct. The burden of proof is on the accountant. Willful violations of this act may be subject to criminal penalties.

Continued

Chapter Summary: Liability of Accountants and Other Professionals—Continued

Securities Act of 1933—Section 12(2) (See page 894.)	An accountant may be liable when a prospectus or other communication presented to an investor contained an untrue statement or omission of a material fact.
Securities Exchange Act of 1934—Sections 10(b) and 18 (See pages 894–895.)	Accountants may be held liable for false and misleading applications, reports, and documents required under the act. The burden is on the plaintiff, and the accountant has numerous defenses, including good faith and lack of knowledge that what was submitted was false.
Potential Criminal Liability (See page 897.)	1. Willful violations of the Securities Act of 1933 and the Securities Exchange Act of 1934 may be subject to criminal penalties. 2. Aiding or assisting in the preparation of a false tax return is a felony. Aiding and abetting an individual's understatement of tax liability is a separate crime. Tax preparers who negligently or willfully understate a client's tax liability or who recklessly or intentionally disregard Internal Revenue rules or regulations are subject to criminal penalties.

ExamPrep

ISSUE SPOTTERS

1. Dave, an accountant, prepares a financial statement for Excel Company, a client, knowing that Excel will use the statement to obtain a loan from First National Bank. Dave makes negligent omissions in the statement that result in a loss to the bank. Can the bank successfully sue Dave? Why or why not? **(See page 890.)**
2. Nora, an accountant, prepares a financial statement as part of a registration statement that Omega, Inc., files with the Securities and Exchange Commission before making a public offering of securities. The statement contains a misstatement of material fact that is not attributable to Nora's fraud or negligence. Pat relies on the misstatement, buys some of the securities, and suffers a loss. Can Nora be held liable to Pat? Explain. **(See page 893.)**

—Check your answers to the Issue Spotters against the answers provided in Appendix E at the end of this text.

BEFORE THE TEST

Go to www.cengagebrain.com, enter the ISBN 9781133273561, and click on "Find" to locate this textbook's Web site. Then, click on "Access Now" under "Study Tools," and select Chapter 34 at the top. There, you will find a Practice Quiz that you can take to assess your mastery of the concepts in this chapter, as well as Flashcards, a Glossary of important terms, and Video Questions (when assigned).

For Review

Answers to the even-numbered questions in this For Review section can be found in Appendix F at the end of this text.

1. Under what common law theories may professionals be liable to clients?
2. What are the rules concerning an auditor's liability to third parties?
3. How might an accountant violate federal securities laws?
4. What crimes might an accountant commit under the Internal Revenue Code?
5. What constrains professionals to keep communications with their clients confidential?

Business Scenarios and Case Problems

34–1 The *Ultramares* Rule. Larkin, Inc., retains Howard Perkins to manage its books and prepare its financial statements. Perkins, a certified public accountant, lives in Indiana and practices there. After twenty years, Perkins has become a bit bored with generally accepted accounting principles (GAAP) and has adopted more creative accounting methods. Now, though, Perkins has a problem, as he is being sued by Molly Tucker, one of Larkin's creditors. Tucker alleges that Perkins either knew or should have known that Larkin's financial statements would be distributed to various individuals. Furthermore, she asserts that these financial statements were negligently prepared and seriously inaccurate. What are the consequences of Perkins's failure to follow GAAP? Under the traditional *Ultramares* rule, can Tucker recover damages from Perkins? Explain. **(See pages 889–890.)**

34–2 **Question with Sample Answer—The *Ultramares* Rule.** The accounting firm of Goldman, Walters, Johnson & Co. prepared financial statements for Lucy's Fashions, Inc. After reviewing the financial statements, Happydays State Bank agreed to loan Lucy's Fashions $35,000 for expansion. When Lucy's Fashions declared bankruptcy under Chapter 11 six months later, Happydays State Bank filed an action against Goldman, Walters, Johnson & Co., alleging negligent preparation of financial statements. Assuming that the court has abandoned the *Ultramares* approach, what is the result? What are the policy reasons for holding accountants liable to third parties with whom they are not in privity? **(See pages 889–890.)**

—For a sample answer to Question 34–2, go to Appendix G at the end of this text.

34–3 **Accountant's Liability under Rule 10b-5.** In early 2014, Bennett, Inc., offered a substantial number of new common shares to the public. Harvey Helms had a long-standing interest in Bennett because his grandfather had once been president of the company. On receiving Bennett's prospectus, Helms was dismayed by the pessimism it embodied, so he decided to delay purchasing stock in the company. Later, Helms asserted that the prospectus prepared by the accountants was overly pessimistic and contained materially misleading statements. Discuss fully how successful Helms would be in bringing a suit under Rule 10b-5 against Bennett's accountants of Bennett, Inc. **(See page 895.)**

34–4 **Accountant's Liability for Audit.** A West Virginia bank ran its asset value from $100 million to $1 billion over seven years by aggressively marketing subprime loans. The Office of the Comptroller of the Currency, a federal regulator, audited the bank and discovered that the books had been falsified for several years and that the bank was insolvent. The Comptroller closed the bank and brought criminal charges against its managers. The Comptroller fined Grant Thornton, LLP, the bank's accounting firm, $300,000 for recklessly failing to meet generally accepted auditing standards during the years it audited the bank. The Comptroller claimed Thornton violated federal law by "participating in . . . unsafe and unsound banking practice." Thornton appealed, contending that it was not involved in bank operations to that extent based on its audit function. What would be the key to determining if the accounting firm could be held liable for that violation of federal law? [*Grant Thornton, LLP v. Office of the Comptroller of the Currency,* 514 F.3d 1328 (D.C.Cir. 2008)] **(See page 895.)**

34–5 **Professional's Liability.** Soon after Teresa DeYoung's husband died, her mother-in-law also died, leaving an inheritance of more than $400,000 for DeYoung's children. DeYoung hired John Ruggerio, an attorney, to ensure that her children would receive it. Ruggerio advised her to invest the funds in his real estate business. She declined. A few months later, $300,000 of the inheritance was sent to Ruggerio. Without telling DeYoung, he deposited the $300,000 in his account and began to use the funds in his real estate business. Nine months later, $109,000 of the inheritance was sent to Ruggerio. He paid this to DeYoung. She asked about the remaining amount. Ruggerio lied to hide his theft. Unable to access these funds, DeYoung's children changed their college plans to attend less expensive institutions. Nearly three years later, DeYoung learned the truth. Can she bring a suit against Ruggerio? If so, on what ground? If not, why not? Did Ruggerio violate any standard of professional ethics? Discuss. [*DeYoung v. Ruggerio,* 2009 VT 9, 971 A.2d 627 (2009)] **(See page 886.)**

34–6 **Professional Malpractice.** Jeffery Guerrero hired James McDonald, a certified public accountant, to represent him and his business in an appeal to the Internal Revenue Service. The appeal was about audits that showed Guerrero owed more taxes. When the appeal failed, McDonald assisted in preparing materials for an appeal to the Tax Court, which was also not successful. Guerrero then sued McDonald for professional negligence in the preparation of his evidence for the court. Specifically, Guerrero claimed that McDonald had failed to adequately prepare witnesses and to present all the arguments that could have been made on his behalf and would have enabled him to win the case. Guerrero contended that McDonald was liable for all of the additional taxes he was required to pay. Is Guerrero's claim likely to result in liability on McDonald's part? What factors would the court consider? [*Guerrero v. McDonald,* 302 Ga.App. 164, 690 S.E.2d 486 (2010)] **(See page 886.)**

34–7 **Case Problem with Sample Answer—Potential Liability to Third Parties.** In 2006, twenty-seven people and entities became limited partners in two hedge funds that had invested with Bernard Madoff and his investment firm. The partners' investment adviser gave them various investment information, including a memorandum indicating that an independent certified public accountant, KPMG, LLP, had audited the hedge funds' annual reports. Since 2004, KPMG had also prepared annual reports addressed to the funds' "Partners." Each report stated that KPMG had investigated the funds' financial statements, had followed generally accepted auditing principles, and had concluded that the statements fairly summarized the funds' financial conditions. Moreover, KPMG used the information from its audits to prepare individual tax statements for each fund partner. In 2008, Madoff was charged with securities fraud for running a massive Ponzi scheme. In a 2009 report, the Securities and Exchange Commission identified numerous "red flags" that should have been discovered by investment advisers and auditors. Unfortunately, they were not, and the hedge funds' partners lost millions of dollars. Is KPMG potentially liable to the funds' partners under the *Restatement (Third) of Torts*? Why or why not? [*Askenazy v. Tremont Group Holdings, Inc.*, 2012 WL 440675 (Mass.Super. 2012)] **(See pages 889–891.)**

—For a sample answer to Problem 34–7, go to Appendix H at the end of this text.

34–8 **A Question of Ethics—Securities Laws.** Portland Shellfish Co. processes live shellfish in Maine. As one of the firm's two owners, Frank Wetmore held 300 voting and 150 nonvoting shares of the stock. Donna Holden held the other 300 voting shares. Donna's husband, Jeff, managed the company's daily operations, including production, procurement, and sales. The board of directors consisted of Frank and Jeff. In 2001, disagreements arose over the company's management. The Holdens invoked the "Shareholders' Agreement," which provided that "[i]n the event of a deadlock, the directors shall hire an accountant at [MacDonald, Page, Schatz, Fletcher & Co., LLC] to determine the value of the outstanding shares. . . . [E]ach shareholder shall have the right to buy out the other shareholder(s)' interest." MacDonald Page estimated the stock's "fair market value" to be $1.09 million. Donna offered to buy Frank's shares at a price equal to his proportionate share. Frank countered by offering $1.25 million for Donna's shares. Donna rejected Frank's offer and insisted that he sell his shares to her or she would sue. In the face of this threat, Frank sold his shares to Donna for $750,705. Believing the stock to be worth more than twice MacDonald Page's estimate, Frank filed a suit in a federal district court against the accountant. [*Wetmore v. MacDonald, Page, Schatz, Fletcher & Co., LLC*, 476 F.3d 1 (1st Cir. 2007)]

1. Frank claimed that in valuing the stock, the accountant disregarded "commonly accepted and reliable methods of valuation in favor of less reliable methods." He alleged negligence, among other things. MacDonald Page filed a motion to dismiss the complaint. What are the elements that establish negligence? Which is the most critical element in this case?
2. MacDonald Page evaluated the company's stock by identifying its "fair market value," defined as "[t]he price at which the property would change hands between a willing buyer and a willing seller, neither being under a compulsion to buy or sell and both having reasonable knowledge of relevant facts." The accountant knew that the shareholders would use its estimate to determine the price that one would pay to the other. Under these circumstances, was Frank's injury foreseeable? Explain.
3. What factor might have influenced Frank to sell his shares to Donna even if he thought that MacDonald Page's "fair market value" figure was less than half what it should have been? Does this factor represent an unfair, or unethical, advantage? Why or why not?

Critical Thinking and Writing Assignments

34–9 **Business Law Critical Thinking Group Assignment.** Napster, Inc., offered a service that allowed its users to browse digital music files on other users' computers and download selections for free. Music industry principals sued Napster for copyright infringement, and the court ordered Napster to remove from its service files that were identified as infringing. When Napster failed to comply, it was shut down.

A few months later, Bertelsmann, a German corporation, loaned Napster $85 million to fund its anticipated transition to a licensed digital music distribution system. The terms allowed Napster to spend the loan on "general, administrative and overhead expenses." In an e-mail, Napster's chief executive officer referred to a "side deal" under which Napster could use up to $10 million of the loan to pay litigation expenses. Napster failed to launch the new system before declaring bankruptcy. The plaintiffs filed a suit against Bertelsmann, alleging that by its loan, it prolonged Napster's infringement. The plaintiffs asked the court to order the disclosure of all attorney-client communications related to the loan.

1. The first group will identify the principle that Bertelsmann could assert to protect these communications and outline the purpose of this protection.
2. The second group will decide whether this principle should protect a client who consults an attorney for advice that will help the client commit fraud.
3. A third group will determine whether the court should grant the plaintiffs' request.

UNIT 6 Government Regulation

Business Case Study with Dissenting Opinion

Department of Environmental Quality v. Worth Township

As mentioned in Chapter 33, many states have enacted environmental protection laws, including laws that prohibit water pollution. Most water pollution comes from industrial, municipal, and agricultural sources, but private citizens can also cause water pollution.

In this *Business Case Study with Dissenting Opinion,* we review *Department of Environmental Quality v. Worth Township.*[1] In this case, the Michigan Department of Environmental Quality argued that a municipality, Worth Township, was responsible for raw sewage that had been discharged within its borders by private citizens. The Michigan Supreme Court had to decide whether the municipality could be held liable even though it had not polluted the state's waters.

Case Background

Worth Township, Michigan, is located on the shore of Lake Huron. Over several years, raw sewage originating in Worth Township contaminated the surface waters of Lake Huron and several of its tributaries. All the contamination came from private properties with failing septic systems. At the time of the pollution, Worth Township did not have a municipal sewerage system. The municipality agreed to construct one by June 2008, but it never did because it lacked the funds.

As a result, the Michigan Department of Environmental Quality (DEQ) sought an injunction requiring Worth Township to prevent raw sewage from being discharged from within its borders. Worth Township argued that it was not liable for private citizens' conduct under the Michigan Natural Resources and Environmental Protection Act (NREPA). The trial court granted summary judgment to the DEQ, but a state appellate court held that Worth Township could not be held liable because it did not itself pollute state waters. The DEQ appealed to the Michigan Supreme Court.

Majority Opinion

HATHAWAY, J. [Justice]

* * * *

We begin by examining the language of [subsection (1) of the statute]. This subsection sets forth the manner in which a "person" is deemed to have violated part 31 of NREPA. * * * A "person" is defined as "an individual, partnership, corporation, association, governmental entity, or other legal entity." *Thus, the term "person" includes a governmental entity such as Worth Township. * * * A person violates [the statute] if the person "directly or indirectly discharge[s] into the waters of the state a substance that is or may become injurious to * * * the public health, safety, or welfare."* Accordingly, [the statute] is applicable to a governmental entity such as Worth Township if the governmental entity directly or indirectly discharges into state waters a substance that is or may become injurious to public safety. [Emphasis added.]

Next, [subsection] (2) provides specific language with regard to violations by governmental entities. Its first sentence provides that the

> discharge of any raw sewage * * *, directly or indirectly, into any of the waters of the state shall be considered prima facie evidence of a violation of this part by the municipality in which the discharge originated unless the discharge is permitted by an order or rule of the [DEQ].

There is no dispute that raw sewage is being discharged into state waters from within Worth Township. Nor is this discharge permitted by an order or rule of the DEQ. Thus, the phrase "*shall be considered prima facie evidence of a violation of this part by the municipality in which the discharge originated*" is at the core of the dispute before us. [Emphasis in original.]

* * * *

1. 491 Mich. 227, 814 N.W.2d 646 (2012).

Business Case Study with Dissenting Opinion—Continues next page

Business Case Study with Dissenting Opinion—Continued

* * * It is clear that, historically, the Legislature intended that a local unit of government, such as a township, be responsible for discharges into state waters involving raw sewage originating within its boundaries. It is also clear that, historically, the Legislature intended to hold a local unit of government responsible for such a discharge regardless of whether the governmental unit itself caused the discharge or whether the discharge was caused by "inhabitants or persons occupying lands from which" the raw sewage originated.

Additionally, we note that the most localized form of government involved, such as a township, has the authority to prevent the discharge of raw sewage. Historically, townships have been responsible for overseeing the disposal of sewage generated within the township. * * * A township has the power to finance, construct, and maintain a sewerage system. A township also has the power to condemn individual properties that are injurious to public health, and a township has the authority to grant franchises to public utilities within its boundaries. Moreover, townships have the authority to adopt ordinances regulating public health, safety, and welfare, including ordinances that require individual property owners to hook up to a sewerage system. *There is simply no reason why a township, as a "municipality," cannot be deemed a responsible entity under the language of [subsection] (2) when a discharge occurs within its borders.* The Court of Appeals * * * erred by concluding otherwise. [Emphasis added.]

Dissenting Opinion

YOUNG, C.J., [Chief Justice], *(dissenting).*

I respectfully dissent from the majority's interpretation of [subsection] (2). [Subsection] (2) prohibits the discharge of raw human sewage into state waters and states that such a discharge "shall be considered prima facie evidence of a violation of this part by the municipality in which the discharge originated * * * ." The majority interprets [subsection (2)] to mean that a municipality is presumed responsible for a discharge of raw human sewage that originated within its borders, that the municipality may *only* rebut the presumption of liability by showing that the discharge of raw human sewage was not injurious, and that the municipality may *not* rebut the presumption of liability by showing that it did not cause the discharge. The majority's decision thus imposes *strict liability* on a municipality for every injurious or potentially injurious discharge of raw human sewage that originates within its borders, even if the municipality can conclusively establish that some other entity caused the pollutant discharge.

* * * *

One example will suffice to show the broad implications of the majority's interpretation. Suppose that a portable toilet company regularly, but surreptitiously [secretly], dumps its collected human waste into state waters within a township and the township can conclusively establish that the company, and not the township, caused the discharges. Under the majority's interpretation of [subsection] (2), the township may not avoid liability for the actions of polluters who are under an *independent* statutory obligation to refrain from discharging waste into state waters. Thus, under the majority's interpretation, the underlying municipality is *always* responsible for *every* injurious discharge of human waste into state waters, even though individuals *actually* responsible for the discharges have themselves violated [subsection] (1) and are liable for the penalties provided by law.

Questions for Analysis

1. **Law** What was the majority's decision in this case? What were the reasons for its decision?
2. **Law** Why did the dissent disagree with the majority? If the court had adopted the dissent's position, how would this have affected the result?
3. **Ethics** Do you have any ethical concerns about the majority's decision? Explain your answer.
4. **Economic Dimensions** Legally, does it matter whether Worth Township was able to pay for a sewerage system? Why or why not?
5. **Implications for the Businessperson** What does the majority's ruling mean for businesses? Does it give them a greater incentive to avoid polluting? Why or why not?

UNIT 6 Government Regulation

Business Scenario

Alpha Software, Inc., and Beta Products Corporation—both small firms—are competitors in the business of software research, development, and production.

1. **Antitrust Law.** Alpha and Beta form a joint venture to research, develop, and produce new software for a particular line of computers. Does this business combination violate the antitrust laws? If so, is it a *per se* violation, or is it subject to the rule of reason? Alpha and Beta decide to merge. After the merger, Beta is the surviving firm. What aspect of this firm's presence in the market will be assessed to decide whether this merger is in violation of any antitrust laws? **(See pages 836–840.)**
2. **Consumer Law.** To market its products profitably, Beta considers a number of advertising and labeling proposals. One proposal is that Beta suggest in its advertising that one of its software products has a certain function even though the product does not actually have that capability. Another suggestion is that Beta sell half of a certain program in packaging that misleads the buyer into believing the entire program is included. To obtain the entire program, customers would need to buy a second product. Can Beta implement these suggestions or otherwise market its products in any way it likes? If not, why not? **(See pages 857–868.)**
3. **Environmental Law.** The production part of Beta's operations generates hazardous waste. Gamma Transport Company transports the waste to Omega Waste Corporation, which owns and operates a hazardous waste–disposal site. At the site, some containers leak hazardous waste, and the Environmental Protection Agency (EPA) cleans it up. From whom can the EPA recover the cost of the clean-up? **(See pages 868–876.)**
4. **Liability of Accountants.** Beta hires a certified public accountant, Aaron Schleger, to prepare its financial reports and issue opinion letters based on those reports. One year, Beta falls into serious financial trouble, but this is not reflected in Schleger's reports and opinion letters. Relying on Schleger's portrayal of the company's fiscal health, Beta borrows substantial amounts to develop a new product. The bank, in lending funds to Beta, relies on an opinion letter from Schleger, and Schleger is aware of the bank's reliance. Assuming that Schleger was negligent but did not engage in intentional fraud, what is his potential liability in this situation? Discuss fully. **(See pages 892–897.)**

UNIT 6 Government Regulation

Group Project

Pharma, Inc., made Cancera, a prescription drug that helped in the treatment of certain forms of cancer. When Cancera's patent was about to expire, Synthetic Chemix Corporation developed a generic version of Cancera and prepared to enter the market. Within weeks of this drug's debut, Pharma offered to pay Synthetic $50 million per year *not* to market the generic version. Synthetic accepted the offer.

1. The first group will determine whether the agreement between Pharma and Synthetic was a violation of antitrust law.
2. The second group will examine the impact of delaying entry of the generic version of Cancera into the market and determine its effect on competition.
3. The third group will decide whether a court, in considering these issues, would apply the *per se* rule or the rule of reason.

UNIT 7

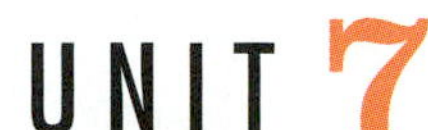

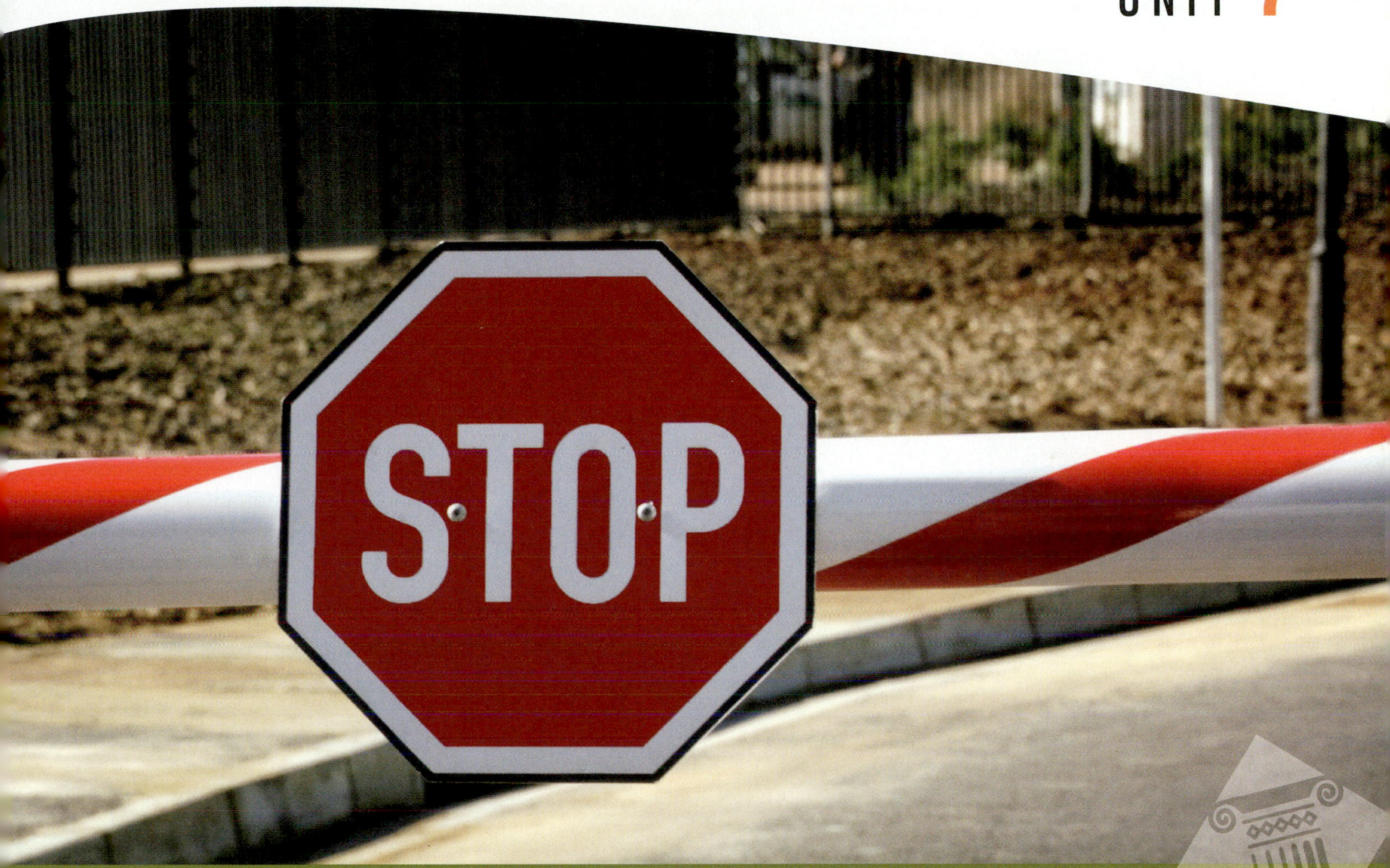

(volschenkh/iStockphoto.com)

Property and Its Protection

UNIT CONTENTS

35. Personal Property and Bailments

36. Real Property and Landlord-Tenant Law

37. Insurance, Wills, and Trusts

CHAPTER 35

(Iakov Filimonov/Shutterstock.com)

Personal Property and Bailments

CHAPTER OUTLINE

- Property Ownership
- Acquiring Ownership of Personal Property
- Mislaid, Lost, and Abandoned Property
- Bailments

LEARNING OBJECTIVES

The five learning objectives below are designed to help improve your understanding of the chapter. After reading this chapter, you should be able to answer the following questions:

1. What is real property? What is personal property?
2. What is the difference between a joint tenancy and a tenancy in common?
3. What are the three necessary elements for an effective gift?
4. What are the three elements of a bailment?
5. What are the basic rights and duties of a bailee? What are the rights and duties of a bailor?

"The great . . . end . . . of men united into commonwealths, and putting themselves under government, is the preservation of their property."
—John Locke, 1632–1704 (English political philosopher)

Property Legally protected rights and interests in anything with an ascertainable value that is subject to ownership.

Real Property Land and everything attached to it, such as trees and buildings.

Personal Property Property that is movable. Any property that is not real property.

Chattel All forms of personal property.

Property consists of the legally protected rights and interests a person has in anything with an ascertainable value that is subject to ownership. For instance, virtual property has become quite valuable in today's world, as you will read later in this chapter. Property would have little value, however, if the law did not define the owner's rights to use her or his property, to sell or dispose of it, and to prevent trespass on it. Indeed, John Locke, as indicated in the chapter-opening quotation above, considered the preservation of property to be the primary reason for the establishment of government.

Property is divided into real property and personal property. **Real property** (sometimes called *realty* or *real estate*—see Chapter 36) consists of land and everything permanently attached to it. Everything else is **personal property,** or *personalty*. Attorneys sometimes refer to personal property as **chattel,** a term used under the common law to denote all forms of personal property. Personal property can be tangible or intangible. *Tangible* personal property, such as a television set or a car, has physical substance. *Intangible* personal property represents some set of rights and interests but has no real physical existence. Stocks and bonds, patents, and copyrights are examples of intangible personal property.

Property Ownership

LEARNING OBJECTIVE 1
What is real property?
What is personal property?

Ownership of property—both real and personal property—can be viewed as a bundle of rights, including the right to possess the property and to dispose of it by sale, gift, lease, or other means. As discussed on page 399 in Chapter 15, the right of ownership in property is often referred to as *title*.

Fee Simple

Fee Simple An absolute form of property ownership entitling the property owner to use, possess, or dispose of the property as he or she chooses during his or her lifetime. On death, the interest in the property descends to the owner's heirs.

A person who holds the entire bundle of rights to property is said to be an owner in **fee simple.** An owner in fee simple is entitled to use, possess, or dispose of the property as he or she chooses during his or her lifetime, and on this owner's death, the interests in the property descend to his or her heirs. We will return to this form of property ownership in Chapter 36, in the context of ownership rights in real property.

Concurrent Ownership

Concurrent Ownership Joint ownership.

Persons who share ownership rights simultaneously in a particular piece of property are said to be *concurrent* owners. There are two principal types of **concurrent ownership:** *tenancy in common* and *joint tenancy.* Additionally, in some states, married persons can hold property together as *community property.*

Tenancy in Common Co-ownership of property in which each party owns an undivided interest that passes to her or his heirs at death.

Tenancy in Common

A **tenancy in common** is a form of co-ownership in which each of two or more persons owns an *undivided* interest in the property. The interest is undivided because each tenant has rights in the *whole* property. On the death of a tenant in common, that tenant's interest in the property passes to her or his heirs.

EXAMPLE 35.1 Sofia and Greg own a rare art collection together as tenants in common. This means that Sofia and Greg each have rights in the *entire* collection. (If Sofia owned some of the paintings and Greg owned others, then the interest would be *divided.*) If Sofia dies before Greg, a one-half interest in the art collection will become the property of Sofia's heirs. If Sofia sells her interest to Jorge before she dies, Jorge and Greg will be co-owners as tenants in common. If Jorge dies, his interest in the personal property will pass to his heirs, and they in turn will own the property with Greg as tenants in common. ●

LEARNING OBJECTIVE 2
What is the difference between a joint tenancy and a tenancy in common?

Joint Tenancy Co-ownership of property in which each party owns an undivided portion of the property. On the death of a joint tenant, his or her interest automatically passes to the surviving joint tenant(s).

Joint Tenancy

In a **joint tenancy,** each of two or more persons owns an undivided interest in the property, but a deceased joint tenant's interest passes to the surviving joint tenant or tenants.[1] The rights of a surviving joint tenant to inherit a deceased joint tenant's ownership interest—referred to as *survivorship rights*—distinguish the joint tenancy from the tenancy in common. A joint tenancy can be terminated before a tenant's death by gift or by sale. In this situation, the person who receives the property as a gift or who purchases the property becomes a tenant in common, not a joint tenant.

EXAMPLE 35.2 In *Example 35.1,* suppose that Sofia and Greg hold their art collection in a joint tenancy. In this situation, if Sofia dies before Greg, the entire collection will become the property of Greg. Sofia's heirs will receive no interest in the collection. If Sofia, while living, sells her interest to Jorge, however, the sale will terminate the joint tenancy, and Jorge and Greg will become co-owners as tenants in common. ●

1. See, for example, *In re Estate of Grote,* 766 N.W.2d 82 (Minn.App. 2009).

(©ratafon, 2009. Used under license from Shutterstock.com)

Will this couple necessarily share equally in all income earned during their marriage?

In most states, it is presumed that a co-tenancy is a tenancy in common unless there is a clear intention to establish a joint tenancy. In those states, specific language is necessary to create a joint tenancy.

Community Property

A married couple is allowed to own property as **community property** in a limited number of states.[2] If property is held as community property, each spouse technically owns an undivided one-half interest in property acquired during the marriage. Generally, community property does *not* include property acquired before the marriage or property acquired by gift or inheritance as separate property during the marriage. After a divorce, community property is divided equally in some states and according to the discretion of the court in other states.

Community Property A form of concurrent ownership of property in which each spouse owns an undivided one-half interest in property acquired during the marriage.

Acquiring Ownership of Personal Property

The most common way of acquiring personal property is by purchasing it. (Today, even virtual property is often purchased—see this chapter's *Adapting the Law to the Online Environment* feature on the following page for a discussion.)

We have already discussed the purchase and sale of personal property (goods) in Chapters 15 through 17. Often, property is acquired by will or inheritance, a topic we will cover in Chapter 37. Here, we look at additional ways in which ownership of personal property can be acquired, including acquisition by possession, production, gifts, accession, and confusion.

Possession

Sometimes, a person can become the owner of personal property merely by possessing it. An example of acquiring ownership by possession is the capture of wild animals. Wild animals belong to no one in their natural state, and the first person to take possession of a wild animal normally owns it. A hunter who kills a deer, for instance, has assumed ownership of it (unless he or she acted in violation of the law).

Those who find lost or abandoned property can also acquire ownership rights through mere possession of the property, as will be discussed later in the chapter. (Ownership rights in real property can also be acquired through possession, such as *adverse possession*—see page 939 in Chapter 36.)

How does a person acquire ownership of wild animals?

(njmcc/iStockphoto.com)

Production

Production—the fruits of labor—is another means of acquiring ownership of personal property. For instance, writers, inventors, and manufacturers all produce personal property and thereby acquire title to it. (In some situations, though, as when a researcher is hired to invent a new product or technique, the researcher-producer may not own what is produced—see Chapter 23.)

2. These states include Alaska, Arizona, California, Idaho, Louisiana, Nevada, New Mexico, Texas, Washington, and Wisconsin. Puerto Rico allows property to be owned as community property as well.

ADAPTING THE LAW TO THE ONLINE ENVIRONMENT

THE EXPLODING WORLD OF VIRTUAL AND DIGITAL PROPERTY

Jon Jacobs took out a real mortgage on his real house so that he could pay $100,000 in real dollars for a virtual asteroid near the virtual Planet Calypso in the virtual world Entropia Universe. A few years later, he sold Club Neverdie, the virtual space resort he had constructed on the virtual asteroid, for more than $600,000. At the time, Jacobs was making $200,000 per year from players' purchases of virtual goods at the resort.

If the prospect of paying real funds for virtual property seems disconcerting, remember that property does not have to be tangible. Property consists of a bundle of rights in anything that has an ascertainable value and is subject to ownership—a definition that encompasses virtual property, including all the intangible objects used in virtual worlds like Entropia Universe and Second Life.

Digital Goods Have Value, Too

Digital goods include virtual goods, but more important, they include digital books, music libraries, and movie downloads. Like virtual property, digital property has real value. Some digital music libraries, for example, cost thousands of dollars.

Who Gets to Keep the Digital Goods?

Domain names, expensively created Web sites, digital music, and virtual real estate all create property interests. The growing value of virtual and digital goods raises some legal questions, though.

For example, what are the respective rights of the creator/owner of a virtual world Web site and the players at that site? And what happens when a husband and wife decide to divorce after they have purchased virtual real estate or digital goods with real-world dollars? The couple—or a court—will have to figure out a way to divide the goods, particularly in a community property state. Property and divorce laws will have to adapt to take this changing world into account.

Critical Thinking

How might a couple who enjoy purchasing virtual and digital goods together avoid property division issues in the event of a divorce?

Gifts

Gift A voluntary transfer of property made without consideration, past or present.

A **gift** is another fairly common means of acquiring and transferring ownership of real and personal property. A gift is essentially a *voluntary* transfer of property ownership for which no consideration is given. As discussed in Chapter 11, the presence of consideration is what distinguishes a contract from a gift.

LEARNING OBJECTIVE 3

What are the three necessary elements for an effective gift?

For a gift to be effective, three requirements must be met: (1) donative intent on the part of the *donor* (the one giving the gift), (2) delivery, and (3) acceptance by the *donee* (the one receiving the gift). We examine each of these requirements here, as well as the requirements of a gift made in contemplation of imminent death. Until these three requirements are met, no effective gift has been made. **EXAMPLE 35.3** Your aunt tells you that she *intends* to give you a new Mercedes-Benz for your next birthday. This is simply a promise to make a gift. It is not considered a gift until the Mercedes-Benz is delivered and accepted. •

ETHICAL ISSUE

Who owns the engagement ring? Often, when two people decide to marry, one party (traditionally the man in an opposite-sex relationship) gives the other an engagement ring. What if the engagement is called off? Etiquette authorities routinely counsel that if the woman breaks the engagement, she should return the ring, but if the man calls the wedding off, the woman is entitled to keep the ring. When the party who gave the ring (the donor) sues for its return after a breakup, the courts are split.

Courts in a majority of states, including Kansas, Michigan, New York, and Ohio, hold that an engagement ring is not a real gift. Rather, it is a "conditional gift" that becomes final only if the marriage occurs. If the marriage does not take place, the ring is returned to the donor regardless of who broke the engagement. This position is similar to the law of ancient Rome, which mandated that when an engagement was broken, the woman had to return the ring, as a penalty, regardless

(jmalov/iStockphoto.com)

Can a woman keep her engagement ring if the wedding is called off?

of who was at fault. Some judges, however, disagree with the conditional-gift theory and contend that an engagement ring is a gift and, as such, it belongs to the donee, even if the engagement is broken.

Donative Intent When a gift is challenged in court, the court will determine whether donative intent exists by looking at the language of the donor and the surrounding circumstances. A court may look at the relationship between the parties and the size of the gift in relation to the donor's other assets. When a person has given away a large portion of her or his assets, the court will scrutinize the transaction closely to determine the donor's mental capacity and look for indications of fraud or duress.

In the following case, the court examined the intent and capacity of a woman who gave more than $50,000 to her dogs' veterinarian.

Case 35.1

Goodman v. Atwood

Appeals Court of Massachusetts,
78 Mass.App.Ct. 655, 940 N.E.2d 514 (2011).

(joanek/iStockphoto.com)

FACTS Jean Knowles Goodman, who was eighty-five years old, gave Dr. Steven Atwood several checks over a period of three months that totaled $56,100. Atwood was a veterinarian who had cared for Goodman's dogs for nearly twenty years. Atwood and Goodman had become friends, and he had regularly visited her house to care for her dogs and socialize with her. Shortly after writing the last check, Goodman was hospitalized and diagnosed with dementia (loss of brain function) and alcohol dependency. A guardian was appointed for Goodman. The guardian filed a lawsuit against Atwood to invalidate the gifts, claiming that Goodman had lacked mental capacity and donative intent. At trial, a psychiatrist who had examined Goodman testified on behalf of Atwood that while Goodman lacked the capacity to care for herself, she would have understood that she was giving away her funds. The trial judge ruled that Goodman had the capacity and intent to make the gifts to Atwood. The guardian appealed.

ISSUE Was there sufficient proof that Goodman had donative intent to make the gifts to Atwood even though she was later found to be mentally incompetent?

DECISION Yes. The state appellate court affirmed the lower court's judgment in favor of Atwood.

REASON In a civil action, the plaintiff has the burden of proving the essential elements of a claim—in this case, the lack of capacity and intent. The court found that the trial judge had used the proper standard of evidence and had kept the burden of proof on the plaintiff (the guardian). There was sufficient evidence of the donor's capacity and intent to support the trial judge's findings. "The plaintiff's own witness conceded the possibility that the donor experienced periods of mental awareness in addition to her lucidity [clarity] regarding financial affairs." The appellate court acknowledged "that a reasonable and conscientious finder of fact could have reached a different conclusion." Nonetheless, it is not the task of an appellate court "to substitute our judgment for that of the fact finder, and on this record we do not conclude that a mistake has clearly been made."

WHAT IF THE FACTS WERE DIFFERENT? *If there had been a jury trial, and the jury had concluded that Goodman lacked mental capacity and intent at the time she made the gifts to Atwood, would the appellate court still have affirmed the decision? Why or why not?*

Delivery The gift must be delivered to the donee. Delivery may be accomplished by means of a third person who is the agent of either the donor or the donee. Naturally, no delivery is necessary if the gift is already in the hands of the donee. Delivery is obvious in most cases, but some objects cannot be relinquished physically. Then the question of delivery depends on the surrounding circumstances.

Constructive Delivery A symbolic delivery of property that cannot be physically delivered. Constructive delivery confers the right to possession of the property, but not the actual possession.

Constructive Delivery When the object itself cannot be physically delivered, a symbolic, or constructive, delivery will be sufficient. **Constructive delivery** confers the right to take possession of the object in question, but not the actual possession. **EXAMPLE 35.4** Angela wants to make a gift of various rare coins that she has stored in a safe-deposit box. She obviously cannot deliver the box itself to the donee and does not want to take the coins out of the bank. Angela can simply deliver the key to the box to the donee and authorize the donee's access to the box and its contents. This action constitutes a constructive delivery of the contents of the box. •

Constructive delivery is always necessary for gifts of intangible property, such as stocks, bonds, insurance policies, and contracts. What will be delivered are documents that represent rights and are not, in themselves, the true property.

Dominion Ownership rights in property, including the right to possess and control the property.

Relinquishing Dominion and Control An effective delivery also requires giving up complete control and **dominion** (ownership rights) over the subject matter of the gift. The outcome of disputes often turns on whether control has actually been relinquished. The Internal Revenue Service scrutinizes transactions between relatives, especially when one claims to have given income-producing property to another who is in a lower marginal tax bracket. Unless complete control over the property has been relinquished, the "donor"—not the family member who received the "gift"—will have to pay taxes on the income from that property.

In the following *Classic Case,* the court focused on the requirement that a donor must relinquish complete control and dominion over property given to the donee before a gift can be effectively delivered.

Classic Case 35.2

In re Estate of Piper

Missouri Court of Appeals, 676 S.W.2d 897 (1984).

(©Ingvar Bjork, 2009. Used under license from Shutterstock.com)

How can two diamond rings have been gifted if they remain in the owner's purse after her death?

FACTS Gladys Piper died intestate (without a will) in 1982. At her death, she owned miscellaneous personal property worth $5,000 and had in her purse $200 in cash and two diamond rings. Wanda Brown, Piper's niece, took the contents of the purse, allegedly to preserve the items for the estate. Clara Kaufmann, a friend of Piper's, filed a claim against the estate for $4,800. From October 1974 until Piper's death, Kaufmann had taken Piper to the doctor, beauty shop, and grocery store. Kaufmann had also written Piper's checks to pay her bills and had helped her care for her home. Kaufmann maintained that Piper had promised to pay her for these services and had given her the diamond rings as a gift. A Missouri state trial court denied her request for payment. The court found that her services had been voluntary. Kaufmann then filed a petition for delivery of personal property—the rings—which was granted by the trial court. Brown, other heirs, and the administrator of Piper's estate appealed.

ISSUE Had Gladys Piper made an effective gift of the rings to Clara Kaufmann?

DECISION No. The state appellate court reversed the judgment of the trial court on the ground that Piper had never delivered the rings to Kaufmann.

REASON Kaufmann claimed that the rings belonged to her by reason of a "consummated gift long prior to the death of Gladys Piper." Two witnesses testified at the trial that Piper had told them that she was going to wear the rings until she died but that the rings belonged to Kaufmann. The appellate court, however, found "no evidence of any actual delivery." The court pointed out that the essentials of a gift are (1) a present intention to make a gift on the part of the donor, (2) a delivery of the property by the donor to the donee, and (3) an acceptance by the donee. Here, the evidence showed only an intent to make a gift. Because there was no delivery—either actual or constructive—no valid gift was made.

Classic Case 35.2—Continued

WHAT IF THE FACTS WERE DIFFERENT? *Suppose that Gladys Piper had told Clara Kaufmann that she was giving the rings to Clara but wished to keep them in her possession for a few more days. Would this have affected the court's decision in this case? Explain.*

IMPACT OF THIS CASE ON TODAY'S LAW *This case clearly illustrates the delivery requirement when making a gift. Assuming that Piper did, indeed, intend for Kaufmann to have the rings, it was unfortunate that Kaufmann had no right to receive them after Piper's death. Yet the alternative could lead to perhaps even more unfairness. The policy behind the delivery requirement is to protect property owners and their heirs from fraudulent claims based solely on parol evidence. If not for this policy, a person could easily claim that a gift had been made when, in fact, it had not.*

Acceptance

The final requirement of a valid gift is acceptance by the donee. This rarely presents any problem, as most donees readily accept their gifts. The courts generally assume acceptance unless the circumstances indicate otherwise.

Gift *Inter Vivos* A gift made during lifetime and not in contemplation of imminent death, in contrast to a gift *causa mortis.*

Gift *Causa Mortis* A gift made in contemplation of imminent death. The gift is revoked if the donor does not die as contemplated.

Gifts *Inter Vivos* and Gifts *Causa Mortis*

A gift made during one's lifetime is termed a **gift *inter vivos.*** **Gifts *causa mortis*** (so-called *deathbed gifts*) are made in contemplation of imminent death. To be effective, a gift *causa mortis* must not only meet the three requirements discussed earlier—donative intent, delivery, and acceptance by the donee—but is also subject to some special rules.

Automatically Revoked If Donor Recovers

A gift *causa mortis* does not become absolute until the donor dies from the contemplated event, and it is automatically revoked if the donor survives. **EXAMPLE 35.5** Yang, who is about to undergo surgery to remove a cancerous tumor, delivers an envelope to Chao, a close business associate. The envelope contains a letter saying, "I want to give you this check for $1 million in the event of my death from this operation." Chao cashes the check. The surgeon performs the operation and removes the tumor. Yang recovers fully. Several months later, Yang dies from a heart attack that is totally unrelated to the operation.

If the administrator of Yang's estate (see Chapter 37) tries to recover the $1 million, she will normally succeed. The gift *causa mortis* to Chao is automatically revoked if Yang recovers. The *specific event* that was contemplated in making the gift was death from a particular operation. Because Yang's death was not the result of this event, the gift is revoked, and the $1 million passes to Yang's estate. •

Automatically Revoked If Donee Dies

A gift *causa mortis* is also revoked if the prospective donee dies before the donor. Therefore, even if Yang in *Example 35.5* had died during the operation, the gift would have been revoked if Chao had died a few minutes earlier. In that event, the $1 million would have passed to Yang's estate, and not to Chao's heirs.

Accession

Accession The addition of value to personal property by the use of labor or materials. In some situations, a person may acquire ownership rights in another's property through accession.

Accession means "something added." Accession occurs when someone adds value to an item of personal property by the use of either labor or materials. Generally, there is no dispute about who owns the property after the accession occurs, especially when the accession is accomplished with the owner's consent. **EXAMPLE 35.6** Hoshi buys all the materials necessary to customize his Corvette. He hires Zach, a customizing specialist, to come to his house to perform the work. Hoshi pays Zach for the value of the labor, obviously retaining title to the property. •

Bad Faith

If the improvement was made wrongfully—without the permission of the owner—the owner retains title to the property and normally does not have to pay for the improvement. This is true even if the accession increased the value of the property substantially. **EXAMPLE 35.7** Patti steals a car and puts expensive new tires on it. If the rightful owner later recovers the car, he obviously will not be required to compensate Patti, a car thief, for the value of the new tires. •

Good Faith

If the accession is performed in good faith—and the improvement was made due to an honest mistake of judgment—the owner normally still retains title to the property but usually must pay for the improvement. In rare instances, when the improvement greatly increases the value of the property or changes its identity, the court may rule that ownership has passed to the improver. In those rare situations, the improver must compensate the original owner for the value of the property before the accession occurred.

Confusion

Confusion The mixing together of goods belonging to two or more owners to such an extent that the separately owned goods cannot be identified.

Confusion is the commingling (mixing together) of goods to such an extent that one person's personal property cannot be distinguished from another's. Confusion frequently occurs with *fungible goods*, such as grain or oil, which consist of identical units.

If confusion occurs as a result of agreement, an honest mistake, or the act of some third party, the owners share ownership as tenants in common and will share any loss in proportion to their ownership interests in the property. **EXAMPLE 35.8** Five farmers in a small Iowa community enter into a cooperative arrangement. Each fall, the farmers harvest the same amount of number 2–grade yellow corn and store it in silos that are held by the cooperative. Each farmer thus owns one-fifth of the total corn in the silos. If a fire burns down one of the silos, each farmer will bear one-fifth of the loss. • When goods are confused due to an intentional wrongful act, then the innocent party ordinarily acquires title to the whole.

Mislaid, Lost, and Abandoned Property

As already mentioned, one of the methods of acquiring ownership of property is to possess it. Simply finding something and holding on to it, however, does not necessarily give the finder any legal rights in the property. Different rules apply, depending on whether the property was mislaid, lost, or abandoned.

Mislaid Property

Mislaid Property Property that the owner has voluntarily parted with and then has inadvertently forgotten.

Property that has voluntarily been placed somewhere by the owner and then inadvertently forgotten is **mislaid property.** A person who finds mislaid property does not obtain title to it. Instead, the owner of the place where the property was mislaid becomes the caretaker of the property because it is highly likely that the true owner will return.[3] **EXAMPLE 35.9** You go to a movie theater. While paying for popcorn at the concessions stand, you set your iPhone on the counter and then leave it there. The iPhone is mislaid property, and the theater owner is entrusted with the duty of reasonable care for it. •

3. The finder of mislaid property is an involuntary bailee (see page 919 of this chapter).

Lost Property

Lost Property Property that the owner has involuntarily parted with and then cannot find or recover.

Property that is *involuntarily* left is **lost property.** A finder of the property can claim title to the property against the whole world—*except the true owner.*[4] The adage "Finders keepers, losers weepers" is actually written into law—provided that the loser (the rightful owner) cannot be found. If the true owner is identified and demands that the lost property be returned, the finder must return it. In contrast, if a third party attempts to take possession of the lost property, the finder will have a better title than the third party.

EXAMPLE 35.10 Khalia works in a large library at night. As she crosses the courtyard on her way home, she finds a gold bracelet set with what seem to be precious stones. She takes the bracelet to a jeweler to have it appraised. While pretending to weigh the bracelet, the jeweler's employee removes several of the stones. If Khalia brings an action to recover the stones from the jeweler, she normally will win because she found lost property and holds title against everyone *except the true owner.* •

KNOW THIS

A finder who appropriates the personal property of another, knowing who the true owner is, can be guilty of conversion.

Conversion of Lost Property

When a finder of lost property knows the true owner and fails to return the property to that person, the finder has committed the tort of *conversion* (the wrongful taking of another's property—see Chapter 4). **EXAMPLE 35.11** In *Example 35.10,* suppose that Khalia knows that the gold bracelet she found belongs to Geneva. If Khalia does not return the bracelet, she can be held liable for conversion. • Many states require the finder to make a reasonably diligent search to locate the true owner of lost property. (The *Business Application* feature on page 926 discusses the obligations that states often impose on finders of lost property.)

Estray Statute A statute defining finders' rights in property when the true owners are unknown.

Estray Statutes

Many states have **estray statutes,** which encourage and facilitate the return of property to its true owner and then reward the finder for honesty if the property remains unclaimed. These laws provide an incentive for finders to report their discoveries by making it possible for them, after a specified period of time, to acquire legal title to the property they have found. Generally, the item must be lost property, not merely mislaid property, for estray statutes to apply. Estray statutes usually require the finder or the county clerk to advertise the property in an attempt to help the owner recover it.

CASE EXAMPLE 35.12 Drug smugglers often enter the United States illegally from Canada via a frozen river that flows through Van Buren, Maine. When two railroad employees walking near the railroad tracks in Van Buren found a duffel bag that contained $165,580 in cash, they reported their find to U.S. Customs agents, who took custody of the bag and cash. A drug-sniffing dog gave a positive alert on the bag for the scent of drugs. The federal government filed a lawsuit claiming title to the property under forfeiture laws, which provide that cash and property involved in illegal drug transactions are forfeited to the government.

The two employees argued that they were entitled to the $165,580 under Maine's estray statute. The statute required finders to (1) provide written notice to the town clerk within seven days after finding the property, (2) post a public notice in the town, and (3) advertise in the town's newspaper for one month. Because the employees had not fulfilled these requirements, the court ruled that they had not acquired title to the property. Thus, the federal government had a right to seize the cash.[5] •

4. For a classic English case establishing this principle, see *Armory v. Delamirie,* 93 Eng.Rep. 664 (K.B. [King's Bench] 1722).

5. *United States v. One Hundred Sixty-Five Thousand Five Hundred Eighty Dollars ($165,580) in U.S. Currency,* 502 F.Supp.2d 114 (D.Me. 2007).

Abandoned Property

Abandoned Property Property that has been discarded by the owner, who has no intention of reclaiming it.

Abandoned property has been discarded by the true owner, who has no intention of reclaiming title to it. Someone who finds abandoned property acquires title to it that is good against the whole world, *including the original owner.* If a person finds abandoned property while trespassing on the property of another, however, the owner of the land, not the finder, will acquire title to the property.

An owner of lost property who eventually gives up any further attempt to find it is frequently held to have abandoned the property. **EXAMPLE 35.13** As Aleka is driving on the freeway, her valuable designer-label scarf blows out the window. She retraces her route and searches for the scarf but cannot find it. She finally gives up her search and proceeds to her destination five hundred miles away. When Frye later finds the scarf, he acquires title to it that is good even against Aleka. By completely giving up her search, Aleka abandoned the scarf just as effectively as if she had intentionally discarded it. •

Bailment A situation in which the personal property of one person (a bailor) is entrusted to another (a bailee), who is obligated to return the bailed property to the bailor or dispose of it as directed.

Bailor One who entrusts goods to a bailee.

Bailee One to whom goods are entrusted by a bailor.

Bailments

Many routine personal and business transactions involve bailments. A **bailment** is formed by the delivery of personal property, without transfer of title, by one person, called a **bailor,** to another, called a **bailee.** Usually, a bailment is formed for a particular purpose—for example, to loan, lease, store, repair, or transport the property. What distinguishes a bailment from a sale or a gift is that there is no passage of title and no intent to transfer title. On completion of the purpose, the bailee is obligated to return the bailed property in the same or better condition to the bailor or a third person or to dispose of it as directed.

(sturti/iStockphoto.com)

Is the bailment relationship between a dry cleaner and a customer based on contract?

Bailments usually are created by agreement, but not necessarily by contract because in many bailments not all of the elements of a contract (such as mutual assent and consideration) are present. **EXAMPLE 35.14** If Amy lends her bicycle to a friend, a bailment is created, but not by contract, because there is no consideration. Many commercial bailments, such as the delivery of clothing to the cleaners for dry cleaning, are based on contract, though. •

PREVENTING LEGAL DISPUTES

The law of bailments applies to many routine personal and business transactions. When a transaction involves a bailment, whether you realize it or not, you are subject to the obligations and duties that arise from the bailment relationship. Consequently, knowing how bailment relationships are created, and what rights, duties, and liabilities flow from ordinary bailments, is critical in avoiding legal disputes. Also important is understanding that bailees can limit the dollar amount of their liability by contract.

Elements of a Bailment

LEARNING OBJECTIVE 4
What are the three elements of a bailment?

Not all transactions involving the delivery of property from one person to another create a bailment. For such a transfer to become a bailment, the following three elements must be present:

1. Personal property.
2. Delivery of possession (without title).
3. Agreement that the property will be returned to the bailor or otherwise disposed of according to its owner's directions.

Personal Property Requirement

Only personal property, not real property or persons, can be the subject of a bailment. Although bailments commonly involve *tangible* items—jewelry, cattle, automobiles, and the like—*intangible* personal property, such as promissory notes and shares of corporate stock, may also be bailed.

Delivery of Possession

Delivery of possession means the transfer of possession of the property to the bailee. For delivery to occur, the bailee must be given exclusive possession and control over the property, and the bailee must *knowingly* accept the personal property.[6] In other words, the bailee must *intend* to exercise control over it.

If either delivery of possession or knowing acceptance is lacking, there is no bailment relationship. **EXAMPLE 35.15** Olga goes to a five-star restaurant and checks her coat at the door. In the pocket of the coat is a diamond necklace worth $20,000. In accepting the coat, the bailee does not *knowingly* also accept the necklace. Thus, a bailment of the coat exists—because the restaurant has exclusive possession and control over the coat and knowingly accepted it—but not a bailment of the necklace. •

Physical versus Constructive Delivery

Either *physical* or *constructive* delivery will result in the bailee's exclusive possession of and control over the property. As discussed earlier in the context of gifts, constructive delivery is a substitute, or symbolic, delivery. What is delivered to the bailee is not the actual property bailed (such as a car) but something so related to the property (such as the car keys) that the requirement of delivery is satisfied.

Involuntary Bailments

In certain situations, a bailment is found despite the apparent lack of the requisite elements of control and knowledge. One instance occurs when the bailee acquires the property accidentally or by mistake—as in finding someone else's lost or mislaid property. A bailment is created even though the bailor did not voluntarily deliver the property to the bailee. Such bailments are called *constructive* or *involuntary* bailments.

EXAMPLE 35.16 Several corporate managers attend an urgent meeting at the law firm of Jacobs & Matheson. One of the corporate officers, Kyle Gustafson, inadvertently leaves his briefcase at the firm at the conclusion of the meeting. In this situation, a court could find that an involuntary bailment was created, even though Gustafson did not voluntarily deliver the briefcase and the law firm did not intentionally accept it. If an involuntary bailment existed, the firm would be responsible for taking care of the briefcase and returning it to Gustafson. •

Bailment Agreement

A bailment agreement can be express or implied. Although a written contract is not required for bailments of less than one year (that is, the Statute of Frauds does not apply—see Chapter 12), it is a good idea to have one, especially when valuable property is involved.

The bailment agreement expressly or impliedly provides for the return of the bailed property to the bailor or to a third person, or for the disposal of the property by the bailee. The agreement presupposes that the bailee will return the identical goods originally given by the bailor. (In certain types of bailments, though, such as bailments of fungible goods, the property returned need only be equivalent property.)

EXAMPLE 35.17 A bailment is created when Holman stores his grain (fungible goods) in Joe's Warehouse. At the end of the storage period, however, the warehouse is not obligated to return to Holman exactly the same grain that he stored. As long as the warehouse returns grain of the same *type, grade,* and *quantity,* the warehouse—the bailee—has performed its obligation. •

6. We are dealing here with *voluntary bailments.* This does not apply to *involuntary bailments.*

Ordinary Bailments

Bailments are either *ordinary* or *special (extraordinary)*. There are three types of ordinary bailments. They are distinguished according to *which party receives a benefit from the bailment*. This factor will dictate the rights and liabilities of the parties, and the courts use it to determine the standard of care required of the bailee in possession of the personal property. The three types of ordinary bailments are as follows:

1. *Bailment for the sole benefit of the bailor.* This is a gratuitous bailment (a bailment without consideration) for the convenience and benefit of the bailor. Basically, the bailee is caring for the bailor's property as a favor. **EXAMPLE 35.18** Allen asks Sumi, his friend, to store his car in her garage while he is away. If Sumi agrees to do so, this is a gratuitous bailment because the bailment of the car is for the sole benefit of the bailor (Allen). ●
2. *Bailment for the sole benefit of the bailee.* This type of bailment typically occurs when one person lends an item to another person (the bailee) solely for the bailee's convenience and benefit. **EXAMPLE 35.19** Allen asks to borrow Sumi's boat so that he can go sailing over the weekend. The bailment of the boat is for Allen's (the bailee's) sole benefit. ●
3. *Bailment for the mutual benefit of the bailee and the bailor.* This is the most common kind of bailment and involves some form of compensation for storing items or holding property while it is being serviced. It is a contractual bailment and may be referred to as a *bailment for hire* or a *commercial bailment*. **EXAMPLE 35.20** Allen leaves his car at a service station for an oil change. Because the service station will be paid to change Allen's oil, this is a mutual-benefit bailment. ●

Rights of the Bailee

Certain rights are implicit in the bailment agreement. Generally, the bailee has the right to take possession of the property, to utilize the property for accomplishing the purpose of the bailment, to receive some form of compensation, and to limit her or his liability for the bailed goods. These rights of the bailee are present (with some limitations) in varying degrees in all bailment transactions.

Right of Possession A hallmark of the bailment agreement is that the bailee acquires the *right to control and possess the property temporarily*. The bailee's right of possession permits the bailee to recover damages from any third person for damage or loss of the property. **EXAMPLE 35.21** No-Spot Dry Cleaners sends all suede leather garments to Cleanall Company for special processing. If Cleanall loses or damages any leather goods, No-Spot has the right to recover against Cleanall. ● If the bailed property is stolen, the bailee has a legal right to regain possession of it.

Right to Use Bailed Property Depending on the type of bailment and the terms of the bailment agreement, a bailee may also have a right to use the bailed property. When no provision is made, the extent of use depends on how necessary it is for the goods to be at the bailee's disposal for the ordinary purpose of the bailment to be carried out. **EXAMPLE 35.22** If you borrow a friend's car to drive to the airport, you, as the bailee, would obviously be expected to use the car. In a bailment involving the long-term storage of a car, however, the bailee is not expected to use the car because the ordinary purpose of a storage bailment does not include use of the property. ●

Right of Compensation Except in a gratuitous bailment, a bailee has a right to be compensated as provided for in the bailment agreement. The bailee also has a right to be reimbursed for costs incurred and services rendered in the keeping of the bailed property—even in a gratuitous bailment. **EXAMPLE 35.23** Margo loses her pet dog, and Justine finds it. Justine takes Margo's dog to her home and feeds it. Even though she takes good care of the dog, it becomes ill and she takes it to a veterinarian. Justine pays the bill for the veterinarian's services and the medicine. Justine normally will be entitled to be reimbursed by Margo for all reasonable costs incurred in the keeping of Margo's dog. •

To enforce the right of compensation, the bailee has a right to place a *possessory lien* on the bailed property until he or she has been fully compensated. A lien on bailed property is referred to as a **bailee's lien**, or *artisan's lien* (see page 543 in Chapter 21). If the bailor refuses to pay or cannot pay the charges (compensation), in most states the bailee is entitled to foreclose on the lien and sell the property to recover the amount owed.

Bailee's Lien A possessory (artisan's) lien that a bailee entitled to compensation can place on the bailed property to ensure that he or she will be paid for the services provided.

Right to Limit Liability In ordinary bailments, bailees have the right to limit their liability, provided that the limitations are called to the attention of the bailor and are not against public policy. It is essential that the bailor be informed of the limitation in some way.

Even when the bailor knows of the limitation, courts consider certain types of disclaimers of liability to be against public policy and therefore illegal. The courts carefully scrutinize *exculpatory clauses*, which limit a person's liability for her or his own wrongful acts, and in bailments they are often held to be illegal. This is particularly true in bailments for the mutual benefit of the bailor and the bailee.

EXAMPLE 35.24 A receipt from a parking garage expressly disclaims liability for any damage to parked cars, regardless of the cause. Because the bailee has attempted to exclude liability for the bailee's own negligence, including the parking attendant's negligence, the clause will likely be deemed unenforceable because it is against public policy. •

Can a valet parking service disclaim all liability for any actions of its parking attendants?

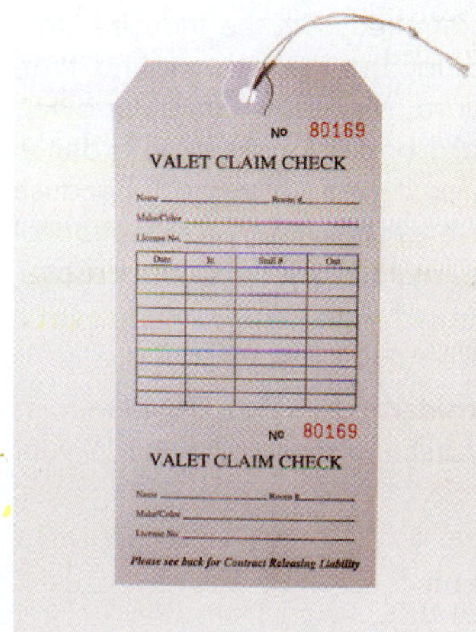

(AdShooter/iStockphoto.com)

Duties of the Bailee

The bailee has two basic responsibilities: (1) to take appropriate care of the property and (2) to surrender the property to the bailor or dispose of it in accordance with the bailor's instructions at the end of the bailment.

The Duty of Care The bailee must exercise reasonable care in preserving the bailed property. What constitutes reasonable care in a bailment situation normally depends on the nature and specific circumstances of the bailment.

LEARNING OBJECTIVE 5
What are the basic rights and duties of a bailee? What are the rights and duties of a bailor?

The courts determine the appropriate standard of care on the basis of the type of bailment involved. In a bailment for the sole benefit of the bailor, the bailee need exercise only a slight degree of care. In a bailment for the sole benefit of the bailee, however, the bailee must exercise great care. In a mutual-benefit bailment, courts normally impose a reasonable standard of care—that is, the bailee must exercise the degree of care that a reasonable and prudent person would exercise in the same circumstances.

Exhibit 35.1 below illustrates these concepts. A bailee's failure to exercise appropriate care in handling the bailor's property results in tort liability.

Exhibit 35.1 Degree of Care Required of a Bailee

In the following case, a bailee lost computer data while he was replacing a hard drive. The court had to decide whether the bailee was negligent.

Case 35.3

Bridge Tower Dental, P.A. v. Meridian Computer Center, Inc.

Supreme Court of Idaho, 152 Idaho 569, 272 P.3d 541 (2012). www.isc.idaho.gov[a]

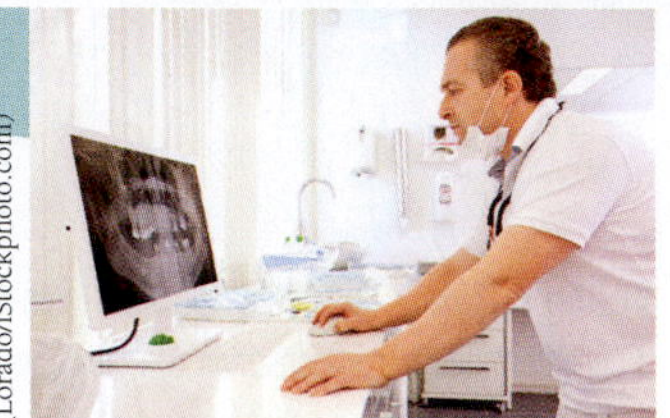
(Lorado/iStockphoto.com)

FACTS Bridge Tower Dental, P.A., contracted with Meridian Computer Center, Inc., to develop a computer system for its dental practice. Bridge Tower then paid a computer consultant, Al Colson, to install the system and provide maintenance and support. In 2004, Colson noticed that one of the server's two hard drives had stopped working and that the system was backing up data only on the mirrored hard drive. After telling Bridge Tower about the problem, Colson took the server to Meridian Computer to be repaired. The owner of Meridian Computer, Jason Patten, agreed to replace the failing hard drive under the warranty.

In attempting to copy data from the mirrored hard drive, however, Patten accidentally erased all the data. Following the industry standard, Patten had not backed up the mirrored drive because he was not asked to do so. As a result, Bridge Tower lost all of its patients' records and contact information. Bridge Tower sued Meridian Computer for negligence, and the jury found for Meridian Computer. Bridge Tower appealed.

ISSUE Did Meridian Computer breach its duty of care?

DECISION Yes. The Idaho Supreme Court reversed the judgment for Meridian Computer and held that Bridge Tower was entitled to recover.

REASON The parties agreed that a bailment existed because Colson acted as Bridge Tower's agent when he entrusted the server to Meridian Computer. The court found that the bailment included both the machine and its contents, including the data that Meridian Computer lost. The court presumed that Meridian Computer was negligent because it damaged the property by erasing all the data on the mirrored hard drive. That presumption was especially appropriate here because Patten admitted that he erased the data by mistake. Meridian Computer argued that it had complied with the industry standard in not backing up the data, but the court found that, regardless of the industry standard, Meridian Computer owed "a duty to protect and safeguard bailed property in order to return it in the same condition as it was delivered." Because Meridian Computer could not overcome the presumption of negligence, Bridge Tower was entitled to judgment as a matter of law.

CRITICAL THINKING—Legal Consideration *Based on the facts presented here, what kind of bailment existed? Explain your answer.*

a. Under "Supreme Court Appeals," select "Opinions" and then "Supreme Court Civil Opinions" from the menu. When that page opens, scroll down to March 5, 2012, and click on the case name to access the opinion. The Supreme Court of Idaho maintains this Web site.

Duty to Return Bailed Property At the end of the bailment, the bailee normally must hand over the original property to the bailor or to someone the bailor designates, or must otherwise dispose of it as directed. This is usually a *contractual* duty arising from the bailment agreement (contract). Failure to give up possession at the time the bailment ends is a breach of contract and could result in the tort of conversion or an action based on bailee negligence. A bailee may also be liable for conversion if the goods being held are delivered to the wrong person. Hence, the bailee should verify that the person (other than the bailor) to whom the goods are given is authorized to take possession.

Lost or Damaged Property If the bailed property has been lost or is returned damaged, a court will presume that the bailee was negligent. The bailee's obligation is excused, however, if the property was destroyed, lost, or stolen through no fault of the bailee (or claimed by a third party with a superior claim). In other words, the bailee can rebut the presumption of negligence by showing that he or she exercised due care.

CASE EXAMPLE 35.25 Michael LaPlace boarded a horse at Pierre Briere's stable, where Charlene Bridgwood also boarded a horse. LaPlace had previously boarded horses at the farm owned by Bridgwood's husband, and Bridgwood had often exercised LaPlace's horses there. One day, Bridgwood helped exercise the horses at Briere's stable.

During the exercise, LaPlace's horse suddenly collapsed and died. LaPlace sued Briere for negligence. The court found that there was a presumption of negligence because the horse died in Briere's care during its bailment. Nevertheless, Briere had successfully rebutted that presumption by showing that Bridgwood was an experienced handler and exercised the horse in an ordinary manner. Thus, Briere was not liable for the horse's death.[7] •

Duties of the Bailor

The duties of a bailor are essentially the same as the rights of a bailee. A bailor has a duty to compensate the bailee either as agreed or as reimbursement for costs incurred by the bailee in keeping the bailed property. A bailor also has an all-encompassing duty to provide the bailee with goods or chattels that are free from known defects that could cause injury to the bailee.

Bailor's Duty to Reveal Defects

The bailor's duty to reveal defects to the bailee translates into two rules:

1. In a *mutual-benefit bailment*, the bailor must notify the bailee of all known defects and any hidden defects that the bailor knows of or could have discovered with reasonable diligence and proper inspection.
2. In a *bailment for the sole benefit of the bailee*, the bailor must notify the bailee of any known defects.

The bailor's duty to reveal defects is based on a negligence theory of tort law. A bailor who fails to give the appropriate notice is liable to the bailee and to any other person who might reasonably be expected to come into contact with the defective article.

EXAMPLE 35.26 Rentco (the bailor) rents a tractor to Hal Iverson. Unknown to Rentco, the brake mechanism on the tractor is defective at the time the bailment is made. Rentco could have discovered the defect on reasonable inspection. Iverson uses the defective tractor without knowledge of the brake problem and is injured, along with two other field workers, when the tractor rolls downhill out of control after failing to stop. In this situation, Rentco is liable for the injuries sustained by Iverson and the other workers because it negligently failed to discover the defect and notify Iverson. •

Warranty Liability for Defective Goods

A bailor can also incur *warranty liability* based on contract law (see Chapter 17) for injuries resulting from the bailment of defective articles. Property leased by a bailor must be *fit for the intended purpose of the bailment.* Warranties of fitness arise by law in sales contracts and leases, and judges have extended these warranties to situations in which the bailees are compensated for the bailment (such as when one leaves a car with a parking attendant). Article 2A of the Uniform Commercial Code (UCC) extends the implied warranties of merchantability and fitness for a particular purpose to bailments whenever the bailments include rights to use the bailed goods.[8]

Special Types of Bailments

A business is also likely to engage in some special types of bailment transactions in which the bailee's duty of care is *extraordinary* and the bailee's liability for loss or damage to the property is absolute. These special situations usually involve bailments made by common carriers and hotel operators. Warehouse companies have the same duty of care as ordinary

7. *LaPlace v. Briere*, 404 N.J.Super. 585, 962 A.2d 1139 (2009).
8. UCC 2A–212, 2A–213.

bailees, but, like carriers, they are subject to extensive regulation under federal and state laws, including Article 7 of the UCC.

Common Carriers

Common carriers are publicly licensed to transport goods or passengers on regular routes at set rates. They provide transportation services to the general public, in contrast to private carriers, which operate transportation facilities for a select clientele.

Common carriers are legally bound to carry all passengers or freight as long as there is enough space, the fee is paid, and there are no reasonable grounds to refuse to do so. A private carrier is not required to provide service to every person or company making a request.

Strict Liability Applies The delivery of goods to a common carrier creates a bailment relationship between the shipper (bailor) and the common carrier (bailee). Unlike ordinary bailees, the common carrier is held to a standard of care based on *strict liability,* rather than reasonable care, in protecting the bailed personal property. This means that the common carrier is absolutely liable, regardless of due care, for all loss or damage to goods except in limited circumstances, such as when damage was caused by a natural disaster or war.

Limitations on Liability Common carriers cannot contract away their liability for damaged goods. Subject to government regulations, however, they are permitted to limit their dollar liability to an amount stated on the shipment contract or rate filing.[9] **CASE EXAMPLE 35.27** A jewelry store used UPS to ship a diamond ring worth $105,000. The owner of the jewelry store arranged for the shipment on UPS's Web site, which required him to click on two on-screen boxes to agree to "My UPS Terms and Conditions." Among these terms, UPS and its insurer limited their liability and the amount of insurance coverage on packages to $50,000 and refused to ship items worth more than $50,000. Both UPS and its insurer disclaimed liability *entirely* for such items.

When the ring was lost, the jewelry store filed suit against UPS to recover $50,000 under the insurance policy. The court held that UPS's disclaimer of liability was enforceable. It also found that the jewelry store had breached the contract by indicating that the shipment was worth less than $50,000 when the ring was worth a lot more.[10]

Warehouse Companies

Warehousing is the business of storing property for compensation.[11] Like ordinary bailees, warehouse companies are liable for loss or damage to property resulting from *negligence*. A warehouse company, though, is a professional bailee and is therefore expected to exercise a high degree of care to protect and preserve the goods. A warehouse company can limit the dollar amount of its liability, but the bailor must be given the option of paying an increased storage rate for an increase in the liability limit.

Unlike ordinary bailees, a warehouse company can issue *documents of title*—in particular, *warehouse receipts*—and is subject to extensive government regulation, including Article 7 of the UCC.[12] A warehouse receipt describes the bailed property and the terms of the bailment contract. It can be negotiable or nonnegotiable, depending on how it is written. It is negotiable if its terms provide that the warehouse company will deliver the goods "to the bearer" of the receipt or "to the order of" a person named on the receipt.[13]

---

9. Federal laws require common carriers to offer shippers the opportunity to obtain higher dollar limits for loss by paying a higher fee for the transport.

10. *Treiber & Straub, Inc. v. United Parcel Service, Inc.*, 474 F.3d 379 (7th Cir. 2007).

11. UCC 7–102(h) refers to the person engaged in the storing of goods for hire as a "warehouseman."

12. A *document of title* is defined in UCC 1–201(15) as any "document which in the regular course of business or financing is treated as adequately evidencing that the person in possession of it is entitled to receive, hold, and dispose of the document and the goods it covers." A *warehouse receipt* is a document of title issued by a person engaged for hire in the business of storing goods for hire.

13. UCC 7–104.

The warehouse receipt represents the goods (that is, it indicates title) and hence has value and utility in financing commercial transactions.

EXAMPLE 35.28 Ossip delivers 6,500 cases of canned corn to Chaney, the owner of a warehouse. Chaney issues a negotiable warehouse receipt payable "to bearer" and gives it to Ossip. Ossip sells and delivers the warehouse receipt to Better Foods, Inc. Better Foods is now the owner of the corn and has the right to obtain the cases by simply presenting the warehouse receipt to Chaney. •

Hotel Operators At common law, hotel owners were strictly liable for the loss of any cash or property that guests brought into their rooms. Today, state statutes continue to apply strict liability to hotel operators for any loss or damage to their guests' personal property.

In many states, hotel operators can avoid strict liability for loss of guests' cash and valuables by (1) providing a safe in which to keep them and (2) notifying guests that a safe is available. In addition, statutes often limit the liability of hotels with regard to articles that are not kept in the safe and may limit the availability of damages in the absence of negligence. Most statutes require that the hotel post these limitations on the doors of the rooms or otherwise notify the guest. The failure of the hotel to follow the state statutory requirements can lead to liability.

EXAMPLE 35.29 A guest at the Four Seasons hotel in Washington, D.C., was traveling with jewelry valued at $1.2 million. She put the jewelry in the safe in her room, but someone came into the room and removed the jewelry from the safe without the use of force. The woman sued the hotel, which asserted that it was not liable under the state statute. A court ruled that the Four Seasons had not complied with the state statute, which required it to post the law in the guest rooms and public rooms. Therefore, the hotel could not assert the statute's limitation on liability. •

Reviewing . . . Personal Property and Bailments

Vanessa Denai owned forty acres of land in rural Louisiana with a 1,600-square-foot house on it and a metal barn near the house. Denai met Lance Finney, who had been seeking a small plot of rural property to rent. After several meetings, Denai invited Finney to live on a corner of her land in exchange for Finney's assistance in cutting wood and tending her property. Denai agreed to store Finney's sailboat in her barn. With Denai's consent, Finney constructed a concrete and oak foundation on Denai's property and purchased a 190-square-foot dome from Dome Baja for $3,395. The dome was shipped by Doty Express, a transportation company licensed to serve the public. When it arrived, Finney installed the dome frame and fabric exterior so that the dome was detachable from the foundation. A year after Finney installed the dome, Denai wrote Finney a note stating, "I've decided to give you four acres of land surrounding your dome as drawn on this map." This gift violated no local land-use restrictions. Using the information presented in the chapter, answer the following questions.

1. Is the dome real property or personal property? Explain.
2. Is Denai's gift of land to Finney a testamentary gift, a gift *causa mortis,* or a gift *inter vivos?*
3. What type of bailment relationship was created when Denai agreed to store Finney's boat? What degree of care was Denai required to exercise in storing the boat?
4. What standard of care applied to the shipment of the dome by Doty Express?

DEBATE THIS: Common carriers should not be able to limit their liability.

BUSINESS APPLICATION

What Should You Do with Lost Property?*

If you are walking down a street in New York City and come across a valuable diamond ring lying in the gutter, what should you do? You might be tempted to keep the ring or sell it and enjoy the proceeds, but that would be unethical. It would also be illegal under New York law—and under the laws of many other states as well.

An Example—New York Laws

New York law defines *lost property* to include lost property, mislaid property, and abandoned property, whether it is cash, goods, or some other type of tangible personal property. Generally, the finder of property worth $20 or more must either return it to the rightful owner or report the find to the police and deposit the property at a police station within ten days. Failure to do so is a misdemeanor, subject to a fine and imprisonment for not more than six months. When the finder delivers the property to the authorities, he or she is given a receipt, and the statutory waiting period begins (ranging from three months for property valued at less than $100 to three years for property valued at more than $5,000). The police then attempt to find the rightful owner.

Other States' Lost-Property Laws

Many other states have also enacted lost-property statutes. The statutes differ greatly from state to state, but typically they eliminate the distinctions among lost, mislaid, and abandoned property, as the New York statute does. Many statutes also require the finder to deposit found property with local authorities, although the penalty imposed for failure to do so may not be as severe as under New York's statute. Lost-property statutes also typically require the police to attempt to find the true owner through such measures as calling the owner of the premises where the property was found. Sometimes, the finder must advertise the property and its discovery through the county court.

Generally, if the true owner cannot be located within a certain period of time, which varies depending on the value of the property and whether the property is perishable, the finder gets the property. If the finder does not appear after the period of time has lapsed, the property may be sold and the proceeds disposed of as specified by statute. In California, for instance, the proceeds from such a sale go into a state fund (if the state police had custody of the lost property) or become the property of the city, county, town, or village (if other police had custody).

*This *Business Application* is not meant to substitute for the services of an attorney who is licensed to practice law in your state.

Checklist for the Finder of Lost Property

1. *To maximize your chances of legally keeping lost property, take the found property to the nearest police station.*
2. *Make sure you follow the statutory requirements of the jurisdiction, which may require you to advertise the found property.*

Key Terms

abandoned property 918
accession 915
bailee 918
bailee's lien 921
bailment 918
bailor 918
chattel 909
community property 911
concurrent ownership 910
confusion 916
constructive delivery 914
dominion 914
estray statute 917
fee simple 910
gift 912
gift *causa mortis* 915
gift *inter vivos* 915
joint tenancy 910
lost property 917
mislaid property 916
personal property 909
property 909
real property 909
tenancy in common 910

Chapter Summary: Personal Property and Bailments

PERSONAL PROPERTY	
Definition of Personal Property (See page 909.)	Personal property (personalty or chattel) includes all property not classified as real property (realty). Personal property can be tangible (such as a TV or a car) or intangible (such as stocks or bonds).

Chapter Summary: Personal Property and Bailments—Continued

Property Ownership (See pages 910–911.)	1. *Fee simple*—The fullest ownership rights in property. Owners can use, possess, or dispose of the property as they choose during their lifetimes and pass on the property to their heirs at death. 2. *Tenancy in common*—Co-ownership in which two or more persons own an undivided interest in property. On a tenant's death, that tenant's property interest passes to his or her heirs. 3. *Joint tenancy*—Co-ownership in which two or more persons own an undivided interest in property. On the death of a joint tenant, that tenant's property interest transfers to the remaining tenant(s), *not* to the heirs of the deceased. 4. *Community property*—A form of co-ownership between a husband and wife in which each spouse technically owns an undivided one-half interest in property acquired during the marriage. This type of ownership exists only in certain states.
Acquiring Ownership of Personal Property (See pages 911–916.)	The most common way of acquiring ownership in personal property is by purchasing it. The following are additional methods of acquiring personal property: 1. *Possession*—Property may be acquired by possession if no other person has title to it (for example, capturing wild animals or finding abandoned property). 2. *Production*—Any product or item produced by an individual (with minor exceptions) becomes the property of that individual. 3. *Gifts*—A gift is effective when the following conditions exist: a. There is evidence of *intent* to make a gift of the property in question. b. The gift is *delivered* (physically or constructively) to the donee or the donee's agent. c. The gift is *accepted* by the donee. 4. *Accession*—When value is added to personal property by the use of labor or materials, the added value generally becomes the property of the owner of the original property (although the owner sometimes must pay for good faith accessions). In rare situations, good faith accessions that substantially increase the value of the property or change its identity may cause title to pass to the improver. 5. *Confusion*—If a person wrongfully and willfully commingles fungible goods with those of another in order to render them indistinguishable, the innocent party acquires title to the whole. Otherwise, the owners become tenants in common of the commingled goods.
Mislaid, Lost, and Abandoned Property (See pages 916–918.)	The finder of property acquires different rights depending on whether the property was mislaid, lost, or abandoned. 1. *Mislaid property*—Property that is placed somewhere voluntarily by the owner and then inadvertently forgotten. The finder does not acquire title. 2. *Lost property*—Property that is involuntarily left and forgotten. The finder can claim title to the property against the whole world *except the true owner.* 3. *Abandoned property*—Property that is discarded by the owner with no intention of claiming it in the future. The finder can claim title to the property against the whole world *including the original owner.*
	BAILMENTS
Elements of a Bailment (See pages 918–919.)	1. *Personal property*—Bailments involve only personal property. 2. *Delivery of possession*—For an effective bailment to exist, the bailee (the one receiving the property) must be given exclusive possession and control over the property, and in a voluntary bailment, the bailee must knowingly accept the personal property. 3. *The bailment agreement*—Expressly or impliedly provides for the return of the bailed property to the bailor or a third party, or for the disposal of the bailed property by the bailee.
Ordinary Bailments (See pages 920–923.)	1. *Types of bailments*— a. Bailment for the sole benefit of the bailor—A gratuitous bailment undertaken for the sole benefit of the bailor (for example, as a favor to the bailor). b. Bailment for the sole benefit of the bailee—A gratuitous loan of an article to a person (the bailee) solely for the bailee's benefit. c. Mutual-benefit (contractual) bailment—The most common kind of bailment. It involves compensation between the bailee and bailor for the service provided. 2. *Rights of a bailee (duties of a bailor)*— a. The right of possession—Allows a bailee to sue any third persons who damage, lose, or convert the bailed property. b. The right to be compensated and reimbursed for expenses—In the event of nonpayment, the bailee has the right to place a possessory (bailee's) lien on the bailed property. c. The right to limit liability—An ordinary bailee can limit his or her liability for loss or damage, provided proper notice is given and the limitation is not against public policy. In special bailments, limitations on liability for negligence or on types of losses usually are not allowed, but limitations on the monetary amount of liability are permitted.

Continued

Chapter Summary: Personal Property and Bailments—Continued

Ordinary Bailments—Continued	3. *Duties of a bailee (rights of a bailor)*— a. A bailee must exercise appropriate care over property entrusted to her or him. What constitutes appropriate care normally depends on the nature and circumstances of the bailment. See Exhibit 35.1 on page 921. b. Bailed goods in a bailee's possession must be either returned to the bailor or disposed of according to the bailor's directions. A bailee's failure to return the bailed property creates a presumption of negligence and constitutes a breach of contract or the tort of conversion of goods.
Special Types of Bailments (See pages 923–925.)	1. *Common carriers*—Carriers that are publicly licensed to provide transportation services to the general public. A common carrier is held to a standard of care based on *strict liability.* 2. *Warehouse companies*—Warehouse operators differ from ordinary bailees in that they (a) can issue documents of title (warehouse receipts) and (b) are subject to state and federal statutes, including Article 7 of the UCC (as are common carriers). They must exercise a high degree of care over the bailed property and are liable for loss of or damage to property if they fail to do so. 3. *Hotel operators*—Operators of hotels are subject to strict liability for any loss or damage to their guests' personal property. State statutes may limit liability if the hotel provides a safe and properly notifies its guests.

ExamPrep

ISSUE SPOTTERS

1. Quintana Corporation sends important documents to Regal Nursery, Inc., via Speedy Messenger Service. While the documents are in Speedy's care, a third party causes an accident to Speedy's delivery vehicle that results in the loss of the documents. Does Speedy have a right to recover from the third party for the loss of the documents? Why or why not? **(See page 920.)**
2. Rosa de la Mar Corporation ships a load of goods via Southeast Delivery Company. The load of goods is lost in a hurricane in Florida. Who suffers the loss? Explain your answer. **(See page 924.)**

—Check your answers to the Issue Spotters against the answers provided in Appendix E at the end of this text.

BEFORE THE TEST

Go to www.cengagebrain.com, enter the ISBN 9781133273561, and click on "Find" to locate this textbook's Web site. Then, click on "Access Now" under "Study Tools," and select Chapter 35 at the top. There, you will find a Practice Quiz that you can take to assess your mastery of the concepts in this chapter, as well as Flashcards, a Glossary of important terms, and Video Questions (when assigned).

For Review

Answers to the even-numbered questions in this For Review section can be found in Appendix F at the end of this text.

1. What is real property? What is personal property?
2. What is the difference between a joint tenancy and a tenancy in common?
3. What are the three necessary elements for an effective gift?
4. What are the three elements of a bailment?
5. What are the basic rights and duties of a bailee? What are the rights and duties of a bailor?

Business Scenarios and Case Problems

35–1 Duties of the Bailee. Discuss the standard of care traditionally required of the bailee for the bailed property in each of the following situations, and determine whether the bailee breached that duty. **(See pages 921–923.)**

1. Ricardo borrows Steve's lawn mower because his own lawn mower needs repair. Ricardo mows his front yard. To mow the backyard, he needs to move some hoses and lawn furniture. He leaves the mower in front of his house

while doing so. When he returns to the front yard, he discovers that the mower has been stolen.

2. Alicia owns a valuable speedboat. She is going on vacation and asks her neighbor, Maureen, to store the boat in one stall of Maureen's double garage. Maureen consents, and the boat is moved into the garage. Maureen needs some grocery items for dinner and drives to the store. She leaves the garage door open while she is gone, as is her custom, and the speedboat is stolen during that time.

35–2 **Gifts.** Jaspal has a severe heart attack and is taken to the hospital. He is aware that he is not expected to live. Because he is a bachelor with no close relatives nearby, Jaspal gives his car keys to his close friend Friedrich, telling Friedrich that he is expected to die and that the car is Friedrich's. Jaspal survives the heart attack, but two months later he dies from pneumonia. Sam, Jaspal's uncle and the executor of his estate, wants Friedrich to return the car. Friedrich refuses, claiming that the car was a gift from Jaspal. Discuss whether Friedrich will be required to return the car to Jaspal's estate. **(See pages 912–915.)**

35–3 **Question with Sample Answer—Bailments.** Curtis is an executive on a business trip to the West Coast. He has driven his car on this trip and checks into the Hotel Ritz. The hotel has a guarded underground parking lot. Curtis gives his car keys to the parking lot attendant but fails to notify the attendant that his wife's $10,000 fur coat is in a box in the trunk. The next day, on checking out, he discovers that his car has been stolen. Curtis wants to hold the hotel liable for both the car and the coat. Discuss the probable success of his claim. **(See pages 920–923.)**

—For a sample answer to Question 35–3, go to Appendix G at the end of this text.

35–4 **Found Property.** A. D. Lock owned Lock Hospitality, Inc., which in turn owned the Best Western Motel in Conway, Arkansas. Joe Terry and David Stocks were preparing the motel for renovation. As they were removing the ceiling tiles in room 118, with Lock present in the room, they noticed a dusty cardboard box near the heating and air-supply vent where it had apparently been concealed. Terry climbed a ladder to reach the box, opened it, and handed it to Stocks. The box was filled with more than $38,000 in old currency. Lock took possession of the box and its contents. Terry and Stocks filed a suit in an Arkansas state court against Lock and his corporation to obtain the currency. Should the cash be characterized as lost, mislaid, or abandoned property? To whom should the court award it? Explain. [*Terry v. Lock,* 343 Ark. 452, 37 S.W.3d 202 (2001)] **(See pages 916–918.)**

35–5 **Spotlight on Joint Tenancy—Property Ownership.** Vincent Slavin was a partner at Cantor Fitzgerald Securities in the World Trade Center (WTC) in New York City. In 1998, Slavin and Anna Baez became engaged and began living together. They placed both of their names on three accounts at Chase Manhattan Bank according to the bank's terms, which provided that "accounts with multiple owners are joint, payable to either owner or the survivor." Slavin arranged for the direct deposit of his salary and commissions into one of the accounts. On September 11, 2001, Slavin died when two planes piloted by terrorists crashed into the WTC towers, causing their collapse. At the time, the balance in the three accounts was $656,944.36. On September 14, Cantor Fitzgerald deposited an additional $58,264.73 into the direct-deposit account. Baez soon withdrew the entire amount from all of the accounts. Mary Jelnek, Slavin's mother, filed a suit against Baez to determine the ownership of the funds that had been in the accounts. In what form of ownership were the accounts held? Who is entitled to which of the funds and why? [*In re Jelnek,* 3 Misc.3d 725, 777 N.Y.S.2d 871 (2004)] **(See pages 910–916.)**

35–6 **Gifts.** John Wasniewski opened a brokerage account with Quick and Reilly, Inc., in his son James's name. Twelve years later, when the balance was $52,085, the account was closed, and the funds were transferred to a joint account in the names of John and James's brother. James did not learn of the existence of the account in his name until the transfer, when he received a tax form for the account's final year. He filed a suit in a Connecticut state court against Quick and Reilly, alleging breach of contract and seeking to recover the account's principal and interest. What are the elements of a valid gift? Did John's opening of the account with Quick and Reilly constitute a gift to James? What is the likely result in this case, and why? [*Wasniewski v. Quick and Reilly, Inc.,* 292 Conn. 98, 971 A.2d 8 (Conn. 2009)] **(See pages 912–915.)**

35–7 **Case Problem with Sample Answer—Bailment Obligation.** Bob Moreland left his plane at Don Gray's aircraft repair shop to be painted. When Moreland picked up the airplane, he was disappointed in the quality of the work and pointed out numerous defects. Moreland refused to pay Gray and flew the plane to another shop to have the work redone. Gray sued to collect, contending that Moreland had no right to take the plane to another shop without giving Gray a chance to fix any defects. Gray further argued that by taking the plane, Moreland had accepted Gray's work. Moreland counterclaimed for his expenses. Which party should be awarded damages and why? [*Gray v. Moreland,* 2010 Ark.App. 207 (2010)] **(See pages 920–923.)**

—For a sample answer to Problem 35–7, go to Appendix H at the end of this text.

35–8 **A Question of Ethics—Gifts.** Marcella Lashmett was engaged in farming in Illinois. Her daughter Christine Montgomery was also a farmer. Christine often borrowed Marcella's farm equipment. More than once, Christine used the equipment as a trade-in on the purchase of new equipment titled in Christine's name alone. After each transaction, Christine paid Marcella an agreed-to amount, and Marcella filed a gift tax return. Marcella died on December 19, 1999. Her heirs included Christine and Marcella's other daughter, Cheryl Thomas. Marcella's will gave whatever farm equipment remained on her death to Christine. If Christine chose to sell or trade any of the items, however, the proceeds were to be split equally with Cheryl. The will named Christine to handle the disposition of the estate, but she did nothing. Eventually, Cheryl filed a petition with an Illinois state court, which appointed her to administer the will. Cheryl then filed a suit against her sister to discover what assets their mother had owned. [*In re Estate of Lashmett,* 369 Ill.App.3d 1013, 874 N.E.2d 65 (4 Dist. 2007)] **(See pages 912–915.)**

1. Cheryl learned that three months before Marcella's death, Christine had used Marcella's tractor as a trade-in on the purchase of a new tractor. The trade-in credit had been $55,296.28. Marcella had been paid nothing, and no gift tax return had been filed. Christine claimed, among other things, that the old tractor had been a gift. What is a "gift"? What are the elements of a gift? What do the facts suggest on this claim? Discuss.
2. Christine also claimed that she had tried to pay Marcella $20,000 on the trade-in of the tractor but that her mother had refused to accept it. Christine showed a check made out to Marcella for that amount and marked "void." Would you rule in Christine's favor on this claim? Why or why not?

Critical Thinking and Writing Assignments

35–9 **Business Law Critical Thinking Group Assignment.** On learning that Sébastien planned to travel abroad, Roslyn asked him to deliver $25,000 in cash to her family in Mexico. During a customs inspection at the border, Sébastien told the customs inspector that he carried less than $10,000. The officer discovered the actual amount of cash that Sébastien was carrying, seized it, and arrested Sébastien. Roslyn asked the government to return what she claimed were her funds, arguing that the arrangement with Sébastien was a bailment and that she still held title to the cash.

1. The first group will argue that Roslyn is entitled to the cash.
2. The second group will take the position of the government and develop an argument that Roslyn's agreement with Sébastien does not qualify as a bailment.

CHAPTER 36

Real Property and Landlord-Tenant Law

CHAPTER OUTLINE

- The Nature of Real Property
- Ownership Interests in Real Property
- Transfer of Ownership
- Leasehold Estates
- Landlord-Tenant Relationships

LEARNING OBJECTIVES

The five learning objectives below are designed to help improve your understanding of the chapter. After reading this chapter, you should be able to answer the following questions:

1. What is a fixture, and how does it relate to real property rights?
2. What is an easement? Describe three ways that easements are created.
3. What are the requirements for acquiring property by adverse possession?
4. What is a leasehold estate? What types of leasehold estates, or tenancies, can be created when real property is leased?
5. What are the respective duties of the landlord and the tenant concerning the use and maintenance of leased property?

"The right of property is the most sacred of all the rights of citizenship."
—Jean-Jacques Rousseau, 1712–1778 (French writer and philosopher)

From earliest times, property has provided a means for survival. Primitive peoples lived off the fruits of the land, eating the vegetation and wildlife. Later, as the vegetation was cultivated and the wildlife domesticated, property provided farmland and pasture. Throughout history, property has continued to be an indicator of family wealth and social position. Indeed, an individual's right to his or her property has become, in the words of Jean-Jacques Rousseau, one of the "most sacred of all the rights of citizenship."

In this chapter, we examine the nature of real property and the ways in which it can be owned and transferred. We even consider the sale of a haunted house in this chapter's *Spotlight Case.* We also discuss leased property and landlord-tenant relationships.

The Nature of Real Property

Real property consists of land and the buildings, plants, and trees that are on it. Real property also includes subsurface and airspace rights, as well as personal property that has become permanently attached to real property. Whereas personal property is movable, real property—also called *real estate* or *realty*—is immovable.

Land

Land includes the soil on the surface of the earth and the natural or artificial structures that are attached to it. It further includes all the waters contained on or under the surface and much, but not necessarily all, of the airspace above it. The exterior boundaries of land extend down to the center of the earth and up to the farthest reaches of the atmosphere (subject to certain qualifications).

(Steve Mann/Shutterstock.com)

Who owns the airspace above residential land?

Airspace and Subsurface Rights

The owner of real property has rights to the airspace above the land, as well as to the soil and minerals underneath it. Limitations on either airspace rights or subsurface rights normally must be indicated on the document that transfers title at the time of purchase. When no such limitations, or *encumbrances,* are noted, a purchaser generally can expect to have an unlimited right to possession of the property.

Airspace Rights

Disputes concerning airspace rights may involve the right of commercial and private planes to fly over property and the right of individuals and governments to seed clouds and produce rain artificially. Flights over private land normally do not violate property rights unless the flights are so low and so frequent that they directly interfere with the owner's enjoyment and use of the land.[1] Leaning walls or buildings and projecting eave spouts or roofs may also violate the airspace rights of an adjoining property owner.

Subsurface Rights

In many states, land ownership may be separated, in that the surface of a piece of land and the subsurface may have different owners. Subsurface rights can be extremely valuable, as these rights include the ownership of minerals, oil, and natural gas. Subsurface rights would be of little value, however, if the owner could not use the surface to exercise those rights. Hence, a subsurface owner has a right (called a *profit,* to be discussed later in this chapter) to go onto the surface of the land to, for example, discover and mine minerals.

When ownership is separated into surface and subsurface rights, each owner can pass title to what she or he owns without the consent of the other owner. Of course, conflicts can arise between the surface owner's use of the property and the subsurface owner's need to extract minerals, oil, or natural gas. In that situation, one party's interest may become subservient (secondary) to the other party's interest either by statute or by case law. If the owners of the subsurface rights excavate (dig), they are absolutely liable if their excavation causes the surface to collapse. Many states have statutes that also make the excavators liable for any damage to structures on the land. Typically, these statutes provide precise requirements for excavations of various depths.

"The meek shall inherit the earth, but not the mineral rights."

J. Paul Getty, 1892–1976 (American entrepreneur and industrialist)

Plant Life and Vegetation

Plant life, both natural and cultivated, is also considered to be real property. In many instances, the natural vegetation, such as trees, adds greatly to the value of the realty. When a parcel of land is sold and the land has growing crops on it, the sale includes the crops, unless otherwise specified in the sales contract. When crops are sold by themselves,

1. *United States v. Causby,* 328 U.S. 256, 66 S.Ct. 1062, 90 L.Ed. 1206 (1946).

however, they are considered to be personal property or goods. Consequently, the sale of crops is a sale of goods and thus is governed by the Uniform Commercial Code (UCC) rather than by real property law.[2]

LEARNING OBJECTIVE 1

What is a fixture, and how does it relate to real property rights?

Fixture An item of personal property that has become so closely associated with real property that it is legally regarded as part of that real property.

Fixtures

Certain personal property can become so closely associated with the real property to which it is attached that the law views it as real property. Such property is known as a **fixture**—an item *affixed* to realty, meaning that it is attached to the real property in a permanent way. The item may be attached, embedded into, or permanently situated on the property by means of cement, plaster, bolts, nails, roots, or screws. The fixture can be physically attached to the real property, be attached to another fixture, or even be without any actual physical attachment to the land (such as a statue). As long as the owner intends the property to be a fixture, normally it will be a fixture.

Fixtures are included in the sale of land if the sales contract does not provide otherwise. The sale of a house includes the land and the house and the garage on the land, as well as the cabinets, plumbing, and windows. Because these are permanently affixed to the property, they are considered to be a part of it. Certain items, such as drapes and window-unit air conditioners, are difficult to classify. Thus, a contract for the sale of a house or commercial realty should indicate which items of this sort are included in the sale.

(Songbird839/iStockphoto.com)

Under what circumstances is an industrial-quality irrigation system considered a fixture?

CASE EXAMPLE 36.1 Sand & Sage Farm had an eight-tower center-pivot irrigation system bolted to a cement slab and connected to an underground well. The bank held a mortgage note on the farm secured by "all buildings, improvements, and fixtures." The farm's owners had also used the property as security for other loans, but the contracts for those loans did not specifically mention fixtures or the irrigation system. Later, when Sand & Sage filed for bankruptcy, a dispute arose between the bank and another creditor over the irrigation system. The court held that the irrigation system was a fixture because it was firmly attached to the land and integral to the operation of the farm. Therefore, the bank's security interest had priority over the other creditor's interest.[3] •

PREVENTING LEGAL DISPUTES

When real property is being sold, transferred, or subjected to a security interest, make sure that any contract specifically lists which fixtures are to be included. Without such a list, the parties may have very different ideas as to what is being transferred with the real property (or included as collateral for a loan). It is much simpler and less expensive to itemize fixtures in a contract than to engage in litigation.

Ownership Interests in Real Property

"Few . . . men own their property. The property owns them."

Robert G. Ingersoll, 1833–1899 (American politician and lecturer)

Ownership of property is an abstract concept that cannot exist independently of the legal system. No one can actually possess or *hold* a piece of land, the airspace above it, the earth below it, and all the water contained on it. The legal system therefore recognizes certain rights and duties that constitute ownership interests in real property.

Recall from Chapter 35 that property ownership is often viewed as a bundle of rights. One who possesses the entire bundle of rights is said to hold the property in *fee simple*,

2. See UCC 2–107(2), discussed in Chapters 15 and 16.

3. *In re Sand & Sage Farm & Ranch, Inc.*, 266 Bankr. 507 (D.Kans. 2001).

which is the most complete form of ownership. When only some of the rights in the bundle are transferred to another person, the effect is to limit the ownership rights of both the transferor of the rights and the recipient.

Ownership in Fee Simple

Fee Simple Absolute An ownership interest in land in which the owner has the greatest possible aggregation of rights, privileges, and power.

In a **fee simple absolute**, the owner has the greatest aggregation of rights, privileges, and power possible. The owner can give the property away or dispose of the property by *deed* (the instrument used to transfer property, as will be discussed later in this chapter) or by will. When there is no will, the fee simple ownership interest passes to the owner's legal heirs on her or his death. A fee simple is potentially infinite in duration and is assigned forever to a person and her or his heirs without limitation or condition. The owner has the rights of *exclusive* possession and use of the property.

The rights that accompany a fee simple include the right to use the land for whatever purpose the owner sees fit. Of course, other laws, including applicable zoning, noise, and environmental laws, may limit the owner's ability to use the property in certain ways. A person who uses his or her property in a manner that unreasonably interferes with others' right to use or enjoy their own property can be liable for the tort of *nuisance* (discussed in Chapter 33).

CASE EXAMPLE 36.2 Nancy and James Biglane owned and lived in a building in Natchez, Mississippi. Next door to the Biglanes' property was a popular bar called the Under the Hill Saloon that featured live music. During the summer, the Saloon, which had no air-conditioning, opened its windows and doors, and live music echoed up and down the street. Although the Biglanes installed extra insulation, thicker windows, and air-conditioning units in their building, the noise from the Saloon kept them awake at night. Eventually, the Biglanes sued the owners of the Saloon for nuisance. The court held that the noise from the bar unreasonably interfered with the Biglanes' right to enjoy their property and enjoined (prevented) the Saloon from opening its windows and doors while playing music.[4] •

Life Estates

Life Estate An interest in land that exists only for the duration of the life of a specified individual, usually the holder of the estate.

Conveyance The transfer of title to real property from one person to another by deed or other document.

A **life estate** is an estate that lasts for the life of some specified individual. A **conveyance**, or transfer of real property, "to A for his life" creates a life estate. In a life estate, the life tenant's ownership rights cease to exist on the life tenant's death. The life tenant has the right to use the land, provided that he or she commits no waste (injury to the land). In other words, the life tenant cannot use the land in a manner that would adversely affect its value.

The life tenant is entitled to any rents generated by the land and can harvest crops from the land. If mines and oil wells are already on the land, the life tenant can extract minerals and oil and is entitled to the royalties, but he or she cannot exploit the land by creating new wells or mines.

The life tenant can create liens, *easements* (discussed below), and leases, but none can extend beyond the life of the tenant. In addition, with few exceptions, the owner of a life estate has an exclusive right to possession during her or his life.

Along with these rights, the life tenant also has some duties—to keep the property in repair and to pay property taxes. In short, the owner of the life estate has the same rights as a fee simple owner except that the life tenant must maintain the value of the property during her or his tenancy.

4. *Biglane v. Under the Hill Corp.*, 949 So.2d 9 (Miss.Sup.Ct. 2007).

Nonpossessory Interests

Nonpossessory Interest In the context of real property, an interest that involves the right to use land but not the right to possess it.

Easement A nonpossessory right, established by express or implied agreement, to make limited use of another's property without removing anything from the property.

Profit In real property law, the right to enter onto another's property and remove something of value from that property.

In contrast to the types of property interests just described, some interests in land do not include any rights to possess the property. These interests are therefore known as **nonpossessory interests.** They include easements, profits, and licenses.

An **easement** is the right of a person to make limited use of another person's real property without taking anything from the property. An easement, for instance, can be the right to walk or drive across another's property. In contrast, a **profit**[5] is the right to go onto land owned by another and take away some part of the land itself or some product of the land. EXAMPLE 36.3 Akmed owns The Dunes. Akmed gives Carmen the right to go there to remove all the sand and gravel that she needs for her cement business. Carmen has a profit. ●

Easements and profits can be classified as either *appurtenant* or *in gross.* Because easements and profits are similar and the same rules apply to both, we discuss them together.

Easement or Profit Appurtenant

An easement or profit *appurtenant* arises when the owner of one piece of land has a right to go onto (or remove something from) an adjacent piece of land owned by another. The land that is benefited by the easement is called the *dominant estate,* and the land that is burdened is called the *servient estate.*

Because easements appurtenant are intended to *benefit the land,* they run (are conveyed) with the land when it is transferred. EXAMPLE 36.4 Acosta has a right to drive his car across Green's land, which is adjacent to Acosta's land. This right-of-way over Green's property is an easement appurtenant to Acosta's property and can be used only by Acosta. If Acosta sells his land, the easement runs with the land to benefit the new owner. ●

KNOW THIS

An easement appurtenant requires two adjacent pieces of land owned by two different persons, but an easement in gross needs only one piece of land owned by someone other than the owner of the easement.

Easement or Profit in Gross

In an easement or profit *in gross,* the right to use or take things from another's land is given to one who does not own an adjacent tract of land. These easements are intended to *benefit a particular person or business,* not a particular piece of land, and cannot be transferred.

EXAMPLE 36.5 Avery owns a parcel of land with a marble quarry. Avery conveys (transfers) to Classic Stone Corporation the right to come onto her land and remove up to five hundred pounds of marble per day. Classic Stone owns a profit in gross and cannot transfer this right to another. ● Similarly, when a utility company is granted an easement to run its power lines across another's property, it obtains an easement in gross.

LEARNING OBJECTIVE 2

What is an easement? Describe three ways that easements are created.

Creation of an Easement or Profit

Most easements and profits are created by an express grant in a contract, deed (discussed shortly), or will (see Chapter 37). This allows the parties to include terms defining the extent and length of time of use. In some situations, an easement or profit can also be created without an express agreement.

An easement or profit may arise by *implication* when the circumstances surrounding the division of a parcel of property imply its existence. EXAMPLE 36.6 Barrow divides a parcel of land that has only one well for drinking water. If Barrow conveys the half without a well to Jarad, a profit by implication arises because Jarad needs drinking water. ●

An easement may also be created by *necessity.* An easement by necessity does not require a division of property for its existence. A person who rents an apartment, for example, has an easement by necessity in the private road leading up to the apartment building.

An easement arises by *prescription* when one person exercises an easement, such as a right-of-way, on another person's land without the landowner's consent, and the use is apparent and continues for the length of time required by the applicable statute of

5. As used here, the term *profit* does not refer to the profits made by a business firm. Rather, it means a gain or an advantage.

limitations. (In much the same way, title to property may be obtained by *adverse possession,* as will be discussed on pages 939 and 940.)

Termination of an Easement or Profit

An easement or profit can be terminated or extinguished in several ways. The simplest way is to deed it back to the owner of the land that is burdened by it. Another way is to abandon it and create evidence of intent to relinquish the right to use it. Mere nonuse will not extinguish an easement or profit *unless the nonuse is accompanied by an overt act showing the intent to abandon.* Also, if the owner of an easement or profit becomes the owner of the property burdened by it, then it is merged into the property.

License In the context of real property, a revocable right or privilege to enter onto another person's land.

License

In the context of real property, a **license** is the revocable right to enter onto another person's land. It is a personal privilege that arises from the consent of the owner of the land and can be revoked by the owner. A ticket to attend a movie at a theater or a concert is an example of a license.

In essence, a license grants a person the authority to enter the land of another and perform a specified act or series of acts without obtaining any permanent interest in the land. When a person with a license exceeds the authority granted and undertakes an action that is not permitted, the property owner can sue that person for trespass (discussed in Chapter 4).

CASE EXAMPLE 36.7 A Catholic church granted Prince Realty Management, LLC, a three-month license to use a three-foot strip of its property adjacent to Prince's property. The license authorized Prince to "put up plywood panels," creating a temporary fence to protect Prince's property during the construction of a new building. During the license's term, Prince installed steel piles and beams on the licensed property. When Prince ignored the church's demands that these structures be removed, the church sued Prince for trespass. The court held that because the license allowed only temporary structures and Prince had exceeded its authority by installing steel piles and beams, the church was entitled to damages.[6]

Transfer of Ownership

Ownership interests in real property are frequently transferred (conveyed) by sale, and the terms of the transfer are specified in a real estate sales contract. Often, real estate brokers or agents who are licensed by the state assist the buyers and sellers during the sales transaction.

Real property ownership can also be transferred by gift, by will or inheritance, by possession, or by *eminent domain.* When ownership rights in real property are transferred, the type of interest being transferred and the conditions of the transfer normally are set forth in a *deed* executed by the person who is conveying the property.

Real Estate Sales Contracts

In some ways, a sale of real estate is similar to a sale of goods because it involves a transfer of ownership, often with specific warranties. A sale of real estate, however, is generally a more complicated transaction that involves certain formalities that are not required in a sale of goods. Usually, after lengthy negotiations (involving offers, counteroffers, and responses), the parties enter into a detailed contract setting forth their agreement. A contract for a sale of land includes such terms as the purchase price, the type of deed the buyer will receive, the condition of the premises, and any items that will be included.

6. *Roman Catholic Church of Our Lady of Sorrows v. Prince Realty Management, LLC,* 47 A.D.3d 909, 850 N.Y.S.2d 569 (2008).

Unless the buyer pays cash for the property, he or she must obtain financing through a mortgage loan (see page 574 of Chapter 22). Real estate sales contracts are often contingent on the buyer's ability to obtain financing at or below a specified rate of interest. The contract may also be contingent on the buyer's sale of other real property, the seller's acquisition of title insurance, or the completion of a survey of the property and its passing one or more inspections. Normally, the buyer is responsible for having the premises inspected for physical or mechanical defects and for insect infestation.

Implied Warranty of Habitability
An implied promise by a seller of a new house that the house is fit for human habitation. Also, the implied promise by a landlord that rented residential premises are habitable.

Implied Warranties in the Sale of New Homes

Most states recognize a warranty—the **implied warranty of habitability**—in the sale of new homes. The seller of a new house warrants that it will be fit for human habitation even if the deed or contract of sale does not include such a warranty.

Essentially, the seller is warranting that the house is in reasonable working order and is of reasonably sound construction. Thus, under this warranty, the seller of a new home is in effect a guarantor of its fitness. In some states, the warranty protects not only the first purchaser but any subsequent purchaser as well.

Seller's Duty to Disclose Hidden Defects

In most jurisdictions, courts impose on sellers a duty to disclose any known defect that materially affects the value of the property and that the buyer could not reasonably discover. Failure to disclose such a material defect gives the buyer the right to rescind the contract and to sue for damages based on fraud or misrepresentation. There is usually a limit to the time within which the buyer can bring a suit against the seller based on the defect, however.

CASE EXAMPLE 36.8 Matthew Humphrey partially renovated a house in Louisiana and sold it to Terry and Tabitha Whitehead for $67,000. A few months after the Whiteheads moved in, they discovered rotten wood behind the tile in the bathroom and experienced problems with the fireplace and the plumbing. Two years later, the Whiteheads filed a suit against Humphrey seeking to rescind the sale. They argued that the plumbing problems were a latent defect that the seller had failed to disclose. Evidence revealed that prior to the sale, the parties were made aware of issues regarding the sewer system and that corrective actions were taken. At the time of the sale, the toilets flushed, and neither side realized that the latent defects had not been resolved. The court ruled that rescission was not warranted because the Whiteheads had waited too long after their discovery to file a claim against Humphrey.[7] •

In the following *Spotlight Case*, the court had to decide whether a buyer—who was not told that the house he had purchased was allegedly haunted—had the right to rescind the sales contract.

7. *Whitehead v. Humphrey*, 954 So.2d 859 (La.App. 2007).

Spotlight on Sales of Haunted Houses

Case 36.1

Stambovsky v. Ackley

Supreme Court, Appellate Division, New York, 572 N.Y.S.2d 672, 169 A.D.2d 254 (1991).

(ccahill/iStockphoto.com)

FACTS Jeffrey Stambovsky signed a contract to buy Helen Ackley's house in Nyack, New York. After the contract was signed, Stambovsky discovered that the house was widely reputed to be haunted. The Ackley family claimed to have seen poltergeists on numerous occasions over the previous nine years. The Ackleys had been interviewed about the house in both a national publication *(Reader's Digest)* and the local newspaper. The house was included on a walking tour of Nyack, New York, as "a riverfront Victorian (with ghost)." When Stambovsky learned of the

Spotlight Case 36.1—Continues next page

Spotlight Case 36.1—Continued

house's reputation, he sued to rescind the contract, alleging that Ackley and her real estate agent had made material misrepresentations when they failed to disclose Ackley's belief that the home was haunted.

ISSUE Was the omission of the alleged haunted nature of the house a material misrepresentation that would allow Stambovsky to rescind the contract?

DECISION Yes. The court allowed Stambovsky to rescind the contract.

REASON Ackley and her family had created the house's reputation as haunted and profited from that reputation over a number of years. That reputation harmed the resale value of the home, however. Because the Ackleys had created the impairment and knew that it was not likely to be discovered by a purchaser from out of town, they had an obligation to disclose it. They should have brought the impairment to the attention of all prospective buyers, including Stambovsky. Even though the Ackleys did not actively mislead Stambovsky, they allowed him to sign the contract knowing that he was unaware of the home's haunted reputation. Because they unfairly took advantage of his ignorance, they could not enforce the contract.

CRITICAL THINKING—Ethical Consideration *Assuming that Ackley's behavior was unethical, was it unethical because she failed to tell Stambovsky something about the house that he did not know, or was it unethical because of the nature of the information she omitted? What if Ackley had failed to mention that the roof leaked or that the well was dry—conditions that a buyer would normally investigate? Explain your answer.*

Deeds

Deed A document by which title to real property is passed.

Possession and title to land are passed from person to person by means of a **deed**—the instrument of conveyance of real property. Unlike a contract, a deed does not have to be supported by legally sufficient consideration. To be valid, a deed must include the following:

KNOW THIS

Gifts of real property are common, and they require deeds even though there is no consideration for the gift.

1. The names of the buyer *(grantee)* and the seller *(grantor)*.
2. Words indicating an intent to convey the property (for example, "I hereby bargain, sell, grant, or give").
3. A legally sufficient description of the land.
4. The grantor's (and usually her or his spouse's) signature.
5. Delivery of the deed.

Warranty Deed A deed that provides the greatest amount of protection for the grantee, in that the grantor promises that she or he has title to the property conveyed in the deed, that there are no undisclosed encumbrances on the property, and that the grantee will enjoy quiet possession of the property.

Warranty Deeds

Different types of deeds provide different degrees of protection against defects of title. A **warranty deed** makes the greatest number of *covenants*, or promises, from the grantor to the grantee and thus provides the greatest protection against defects of title. In most states, special language is required to create a general warranty deed.

Warranty deeds commonly include the following:

1. A covenant that the grantor has the title to, and the power to convey, the property.
2. A covenant of quiet enjoyment (a warranty that the buyer will not be disturbed in her or his possession of the land).
3. A covenant that transfer of the property is made without knowledge of adverse claims of third parties.

Generally, the warranty deed makes the grantor liable for all defects of title during the time that the property was held by the grantor and previous titleholders. **EXAMPLE 36.9** Julio sells a two-acre lot and office building by warranty deed to Daniel. Subsequently, a third person shows up who has better title than Julio had and forces Daniel off the property. Here, the covenant of quiet enjoyment has been breached. Daniel can sue Julio to recover the purchase price of the land, plus any other damages incurred as a result. ●

Special Warranty Deed A deed that warrants only that the grantor held good title during his or her ownership of the property and does not warrant that there were no defects of title when the property was held by previous owners.

Special Warranty Deeds

In contrast to a warranty deed, a **special warranty deed,** which is also referred to as a *limited warranty deed,* warrants only that the grantor or seller held good title during his or her ownership of the property. In other words, the grantor is not warranting that there were no defects of title when the property was held by previous owners.

If the special warranty deed discloses all liens or other encumbrances, the seller will not be liable to the buyer if a third person subsequently interferes with the buyer's ownership. If the third person's claim arises out of, or is related to, some act of the seller, however, the seller will be liable to the buyer for damages.

Quitclaim Deed A deed that conveys only whatever interest the grantor had in the property and therefore offers the least amount of protection against defects of title.

Quitclaim Deeds

A **quitclaim deed** offers the least amount of protection against defects of title. Basically, a quitclaim deed conveys to the grantee whatever interest the grantor had. Therefore, if the grantor had no interest, then the grantee receives no interest.

Quitclaim deeds are often used when the seller, or grantor, is uncertain as to the extent of his or her rights in the property. They may also be used to release a party's interest in a particular parcel of property, such as in divorce settlements or business dissolutions when the grantors are dividing up their interests in real property.

Recording Statutes Statutes that allow deeds, mortgages, and other real property transactions to be recorded so as to provide notice to future purchasers or creditors of an existing claim on the property.

Recording Statutes

Every jurisdiction has **recording statutes,** which allow deeds to be recorded for a fee. Deeds are recorded in the county where the property is located. Recording a deed gives notice to the public that a certain person is now the owner of a particular parcel of real estate. Thus, prospective buyers can check the public records to see whether there have been earlier transactions creating interests or rights in specific parcels of real property.

Will or Inheritance

Property that is transferred on an owner's death is passed either by will or by state inheritance laws. If the owner of land dies with a will, the land passes in accordance with the terms of the will. If the owner dies without a will, state inheritance statutes prescribe how and to whom the property will pass. Transfers of property by will or inheritance will be examined in detail in Chapter 37.

Adverse Possession

Adverse Possession The acquisition of title to real property by occupying it openly, without the consent of the owner, for a period of time specified by a state statute. The occupation must be actual, exclusive, open, continuous, and in opposition to all others, including the owner.

Adverse possession is a means of obtaining title to land without delivery of a deed. Essentially, when one person possesses the property of another for a certain statutory period of time (three to thirty years, with ten years being most common), that person, called the *adverse possessor,* acquires title to the land and cannot be removed from it by the original owner. The adverse possessor may ultimately obtain a perfect title just as if there had been a conveyance by deed.

LEARNING OBJECTIVE 3

What are the requirements for acquiring property by adverse possession?

Requirements for Adverse Possession

For property to be held adversely, four elements must be satisfied:

1. Possession must be *actual and exclusive*—that is, the possessor must take sole physical occupancy of the property.
2. The possession must be *open, visible, and notorious,* not secret or clandestine. The possessor must occupy the land for all the world to see.
3. Possession must be *continuous and peaceable for the required period of time.* This requirement means that the possessor must not be interrupted in the occupancy by the true owner or by the courts.

4. Possession must be *hostile and adverse.* In other words, the possessor must claim the property as against the whole world. He or she cannot be living on the property with the permission of the owner.

Purpose of the Doctrine There are a number of public-policy reasons for the adverse possession doctrine. These include society's interest in resolving boundary disputes, determining title when title to property is in question, and ensuring that real property remains in the stream of commerce. More fundamentally, policies behind the doctrine include rewarding possessors for putting land to productive use and punishing owners who sit on their rights too long and do not take action when they see adverse possession.

CASE EXAMPLE 36.10 Charles Scarborough and Mildred Rollins were adjoining landowners, sharing one common boundary. Based on Rollins's survey of the property, Rollins believed that she owned a portion of a gravel road located to the south of the apartment buildings she owned. In contrast, Scarborough believed that the gravel road was located totally on his property and that he owned some property north of the gravel road toward Rollins's apartment buildings. Scarborough filed a complaint seeking to receive quiet title to the property and prove he was the sole owner. The court ruled that Rollins owned a portion of the gravel road by adverse possession. She had used it openly for more than thirty-five years, it was generally thought to be part of her apartment complex, and she had paid taxes on it.[8] ●

Eminent Domain

Eminent Domain The power of a government to take land from private citizens for public use on the payment of just compensation.

Even ownership in fee simple absolute is limited by a superior ownership. The U.S. government has an ultimate ownership right in all land. This right, known as **eminent domain,** is sometimes referred to as the *condemnation power* of government to take land for public use. It gives the government the right to acquire possession of real property in the manner directed by the U.S. Constitution and the laws of the state whenever the public interest requires it. Property may be taken only for public use, not for private benefit.

EXAMPLE 36.11 When a new public highway is to be built, the government must decide where to build it and how much land to condemn. After the government determines that a particular parcel of land is necessary for public use, it will first offer to buy the property. If the owner refuses the offer, the government brings a judicial (**condemnation**) proceeding to obtain title to the land. Then, in another proceeding, the court determines the *fair value* of the land, which usually is approximately equal to its market value. ●

Condemnation The process of taking private property for public use through the government's power of eminent domain.

Taking The taking of private property by the government for public use through the power of eminent domain.

When the government uses its power of eminent domain to acquire land owned by a private party, a **taking** occurs. Under the *takings clause* of the Fifth Amendment to the U.S. Constitution, the government must pay "just compensation" to the property owner. State constitutions contain similar provisions.

The following case involved condemnation actions brought by a town to acquire rights-of-way for a natural gas pipeline to be constructed through the town. The issue was whether the pipeline was for public use, even though it was not built to furnish natural gas to the residents of that town.

8. *Scarborough v. Rollins,* 44 So.3d 381 (2010).

Case 36.2

Town of Midland v. Morris

Court of Appeals of North Carolina, 704 S.E.2d 329 (2011).

(Lingbeek/iStockphoto.com)

FACTS The Transcontinental Pipeline transports and distributes natural gas from the Gulf of Mexico to the northeastern United States. The city of Monroe, North Carolina, decided to supply its citizens and the surrounding area with natural gas by constructing a direct connection between its natural gas distribution system and the Transcontinental Pipeline. To construct the connecting

Case 36.2—Continued

pipeline, Monroe needed to acquire the rights to property along a forty-two-mile route. To do this, Monroe entered into an agreement with the town of Midland under which Midland would acquire the property (either by voluntary transfer or by eminent domain) and grant an easement to Monroe. In exchange, Midland would have the right to install a tap on the pipeline and receive discounted natural gas services.

In 2008, Midland began the process of acquiring the property necessary for construction of the pipeline. When negotiations for voluntary acquisitions of the rights-of-way failed, Midland exercised its eminent domain authority to condemn the needed property. Midland filed fifteen condemnation actions, which the property owners (including Harry Morris) challenged. The trial court ruled in favor of Midland, and the property owners appealed. The property owners claimed, among other things, that Midland had not condemned the property for public use or benefit because Midland had no concrete plans to furnish natural gas services from the pipeline to the city and its citizens.

ISSUE Was Midland's condemnation of property to construct a natural gas pipeline a taking for public use even though the city had no immediate plan to furnish gas to its residents?

DECISION Yes. The appellate court affirmed the lower court's decision that Midland had lawfully exercised its eminent domain power.

REASON The court chose to interpret the relevant state statutes broadly rather than narrowly. A narrow interpretation would have limited the city's power to establish a public utility to situations in which the city had a concrete plan to furnish services. Under the court's broader interpretation, the city had the power to establish a public utility when the city had a plan to develop the infrastructure and capability but no immediate plan to actually furnish the services. The agreement with Monroe gave Midland control over a tap on the pipeline and the right to receive a specific amount of natural gas per day at a discounted cost.

Even though Midland might never tap into the pipeline, the court found that the condemnation satisfied the public use test because it gave the citizens of Midland a right to a definite use of the condemned property. Furthermore, the court reasoned that the availability of natural gas benefited the public by contributing to the general welfare and prosperity of the public at large. "Midland's tap on the Pipeline, and its potential to provide natural gas service, likely will spur growth, as well as provide Midland with an advantage in industrial recruitment. These opportunities must be seen as public benefits accruing to the citizens of Midland, such that Midland's condemnations are for the public benefit."

CRITICAL THINKING—Ethical Consideration *Is it fair that a city can exercise its eminent domain power to take property even though the property will not be used immediately to benefit the city's residents? Why or why not?*

ETHICAL ISSUE

Should eminent domain be used to promote private development? Issues of fairness often arise when the government takes private property for public use. One issue is whether it is fair for a government to take property by eminent domain and then convey it to private developers. For example, suppose that a city government decides that it is in the public interest to have a larger parking lot for a local, privately owned sports stadium or to have a manufacturing plant locate in the city to create more jobs. The government may condemn certain tracts of existing housing or business property and then convey the land to the privately owned stadium or manufacturing plant. Such actions may bring in private developers and businesses that provide jobs and increase tax revenues, thus revitalizing communities. But is the land really being taken for "public use," as required by the Fifth Amendment to the U.S. Constitution?

Although the United States Supreme Court has approved this type of taking, the Court also recognized that individual states have the right to pass laws that prohibit takings for economic development.[9] Thirty-five states have done exactly that, limiting the government's ability to take private property and give it to private developers. At least eight states have amended their state constitutions, and a number of other states have passed ballot measures. Thus, the debate over whether it is fair for a government to take its citizens' property for economic redevelopment continues.

9. See *Kelo v. City of New London, Connecticut,* 545 U.S. 469, 125 S.Ct. 2655, 162 L.Ed.2d 439 (2005). The *Kelo* case forms the basis of the *Case Analysis Question* on page 948, and an excerpt of the case appears in Appendix I.

LEARNING OBJECTIVE 4
What is a leasehold estate? What types of leasehold estates, or tenancies, can be created when real property is leased?

Leasehold Estate An interest in real property that gives a tenant a qualified right to possess and/or use the property for a limited time under a lease.

Leasehold Estates

A **leasehold estate** is created when a real property owner or lessor (landlord) agrees to convey the right to possess and use the property to a lessee (tenant) for a certain period of time. The tenant has a *qualified* right to exclusive possession—it is qualified because the landlord has a right to enter on the premises to ensure that waste is not being committed. The *temporary* nature of possession, under a lease, is what distinguishes a tenant from a purchaser, who acquires title to the property. The tenant can use the land—for example, by harvesting crops—but cannot injure it by such activities as cutting down timber for sale or extracting oil.

Fixed-Term Tenancy

Fixed-Term Tenancy A type of tenancy under which property is leased for a specified period of time, such as a month, a year, or a period of years.

A **fixed-term tenancy**, also called a *tenancy for years,* is created by an express contract by which property is leased for a specified period of time, such as a day, a month, a year, or a period of years. Signing a one-year lease to occupy an apartment, for instance, creates a fixed-term tenancy.

Note that the term need not be specified by date and can be conditioned on the occurrence of an event, such as leasing a cabin for the summer or an apartment during Mardi Gras. At the end of the period specified in the lease, the lease ends (without notice), and possession of the property returns to the lessor. If the tenant dies during the period of the lease, the lease interest passes to the tenant's heirs as personal property. Often, leases include renewal or extension provisions.

Periodic Tenancy

Periodic Tenancy A type of tenancy created by lease for an indefinite period with payment of rent at fixed intervals, such as week to week, month to month, or year to year.

A **periodic tenancy** is created by a lease that does not specify how long it is to last but does specify that rent is to be paid at certain intervals. This type of tenancy is automatically renewed for another rental period unless properly terminated. **EXAMPLE 36.12** Kayla enters into a lease with Capital Properties. The lease states, "Rent is due on the tenth day of every month." This provision creates a periodic tenancy from month to month. • This type of tenancy can also extend from week to week or from year to year.

Under the common law, to terminate a periodic tenancy, the landlord or tenant must give at least one period's notice to the other party. If the tenancy extends from month to month, for example, one month's notice must be given prior to the last month's rent payment. Today, however, many state's statutes require a different period for notice of termination in a periodic tenancy.

Tenancy at Will

Tenancy at Will A type of tenancy that either the landlord or the tenant can terminate without notice.

With a **tenancy at will,** either party can terminate the tenancy without notice. This type of tenancy can arise if a landlord allows a person to live on the premises without paying rent or rents property to a tenant "for as long as both agree." Tenancies at will are rare today because most state statutes require a landlord to provide some period of notice to terminate a tenancy (as previously noted). States may also require a landowner to have sufficient cause (reason) to end a residential tenancy.

Tenancy at Sufferance

Tenancy at Sufferance A type of tenancy under which a tenant continues wrongfully to occupy leased property after the lease has terminated.

The mere possession of land without right is called a **tenancy at sufferance.** A tenancy at sufferance is not a true tenancy because it is created when a tenant *wrongfully* retains possession of property. Whenever a tenancy for years or a periodic tenancy ends and the tenant continues to retain possession of the premises without the owner's permission, a tenancy at sufferance is created.

When a commercial or residential tenant wrongfully retains possession, the landlord is entitled to damages. Typically, the damages are based on the fair market rental value of the premises after the expiration of the lease.

Landlord-Tenant Relationships

KNOW THIS Sound business practice dictates that a lease for commercial property should be written carefully and should clearly define the parties' rights and obligations.

A landlord-tenant relationship is established by a lease contract. In most states, statutes require leases for terms exceeding one year to be in writing. The lease should describe the property and indicate the length of the term, the amount of the rent, and how and when it is to be paid.

State or local law often dictates permissible lease terms. For example, a statute or ordinance might prohibit the leasing of a structure that is in a certain physical condition or is not in compliance with local building codes. As in other areas of law, the National Conference of Commissioners on Uniform State Laws has issued an act to create more uniformity in the laws governing landlord-tenant relationships. Twenty-one states have adopted variations of the Uniform Residential Landlord and Tenant Act (URLTA).

Rights and Duties

LEARNING OBJECTIVE 5

What are the respective duties of the landlord and the tenant concerning the use and maintenance of leased property?

The rights and duties of landlords and tenants generally pertain to four broad areas of concern—the possession, use, maintenance, and, of course, rent of leased property.

Possession A landlord is obligated to give a tenant possession of the property that the tenant has agreed to lease. After obtaining possession, the tenant retains the property exclusively until the lease expires, unless the lease states otherwise.

The covenant of quiet enjoyment mentioned previously also applies to leased premises. Under this covenant, the landlord promises that during the lease term, neither the landlord nor anyone having a superior title to the property will disturb the tenant's use and enjoyment of the property. This covenant forms the essence of the landlord-tenant relationship, and if it is breached, the tenant can terminate the lease and sue for damages.

Eviction A landlord's act of depriving a tenant of possession of the leased premises.

Constructive Eviction A form of eviction that occurs when a landlord fails to perform adequately any of the duties required by the lease, thereby making the tenant's further use and enjoyment of the property exceedingly difficult or impossible.

If the landlord deprives the tenant of possession of the leased property or interferes with the tenant's use or enjoyment of it, an eviction occurs. An **eviction** arises, for instance, when the landlord changes the lock and refuses to give the tenant a new key. A **constructive eviction** occurs when the landlord wrongfully performs or fails to perform any of the duties the lease requires, thereby making the tenant's further use and enjoyment of the property exceedingly difficult or impossible. Examples of constructive eviction include a landlord's failure to provide heat in the winter, electricity, or other essential utilities.

Use and Maintenance of the Premises The tenant normally may make any use of the leased property, provided the use is legal and does not injure the landlord's interest. The parties are free to limit by agreement the uses to which the property may be put.

The tenant is responsible for any damage to the premises that he or she causes, intentionally or negligently, and may be held liable for the cost of returning the property to the physical condition it was in at the lease's inception. The tenant is not responsible for ordinary wear and tear and the property's consequent depreciation in value. Also, the tenant is not entitled to create a *nuisance* by substantially interfering with others' quiet enjoyment of their property rights (nuisance was discussed on page 868 of Chapter 33 and is illustrated in *Case Example 36.2* on page 934).

In some jurisdictions, landlords of residential property are required by statute to maintain the premises in good repair. Landlords must also comply with any applicable state statutes and city ordinances regarding maintenance and repair of buildings.

Implied Warranty of Habitability

The implied warranty of habitability (see page 937) also applies to *residential* leases. It requires a landlord who leases residential property to ensure that the premises are habitable—that is, a safe and suitable place for people to live. Also, the landlord must make repairs to maintain the premises in that condition for the lease's duration. Generally, this warranty applies to major, or *substantial*, physical defects that the landlord knows or should know about and has had a reasonable time to repair—for example, a large hole in the roof.

KNOW THIS

Options that may be available to a tenant on a landlord's breach of the implied warranty of habitability include repairing the defect and deducting the cost from the rent, canceling the lease, and suing for damages.

Rent

Rent is the tenant's payment to the landlord for the tenant's occupancy or use of the landlord's real property. Usually, the tenant must pay the rent even if she or he refuses to occupy the property or moves out, as long as the refusal or the move is unjustified and the lease is in force. Under the common law, if the leased premises were destroyed by fire or flood, the tenant still had to pay rent. Today, however, if an apartment building burns down, most state's laws do not require tenants to continue to pay rent.

In some situations, such as when a landlord breaches the implied warranty of habitability, a tenant may be allowed to withhold rent as a remedy. When rent withholding is authorized under a statute, the tenant must usually put the amount withheld into an *escrow account*. The funds are held in the name of the tenant and are returned to the tenant if the landlord fails to make the premises habitable.

Transferring Rights to Leased Property

Either the landlord or the tenant may wish to transfer her or his rights to the leased property during the term of the lease. If a landlord transfers complete title to the leased property to another, the tenant becomes the tenant of the new owner. The new owner may collect subsequent rent but must abide by the terms of the existing lease.

"Even in hell the peasant will have to serve the landlord, for, while the landlord is boiling in a cauldron, the peasant will have to put wood under it."

Russian Proverb

Assignment

The tenant's transfer of his or her entire interest in the leased property to a third person is an *assignment of the lease*. Many leases require the landlord's written consent for an assignment to be valid. An assignment made without such consent can be avoided (nullified). State statutes may specify that the landlord may not unreasonably withhold consent, though. Also, a landlord who knowingly accepts rent from the assignee may be held to have waived the consent requirement.

When an assignment is valid, the assignee acquires all of the tenant's rights under the lease. Nevertheless, an assignment does not release the original tenant (the assignor) from the obligation to pay rent should the assignee default. Also, if the assignee exercises an option under the original lease to extend the term, the assigning tenant remains liable for the rent during the extension, unless the landlord agrees otherwise.

Subleases

The tenant's transfer of all or part of the premises for a period shorter than the lease term is a **sublease**. Many leases also require the landlord's written consent for a sublease. If the landlord's consent is required, a sublease without such permission is ineffective. Also, like an assignment, a sublease does not release the tenant from her or his obligations under the lease.

Sublease A tenant's transfer of all or part of the leased premises to a third person for a period shorter than the lease term.

EXAMPLE 36.13 Derek, a student, leases an apartment for a two-year period. Although Derek had planned on attending summer school, he decides to accept a job offer in Europe for the summer months instead. Derek therefore obtains his landlord's consent to sublease the apartment to Ava. Ava is bound by the same terms of the lease as Derek, and the landlord can hold Derek liable if Ava violates the lease terms. ●

Reviewing . . . Real Property and Landlord-Tenant Law

Vern Shoepke bought a two-story home in Roche, Maine. The warranty deed did not specify what covenants would be included in the conveyance. The property was adjacent to a public park that included a popular Frisbee golf course. (Frisbee golf is a sport similar to golf but using Frisbees.) Wayakichi Creek ran along the north end of the park and along Shoepke's property. The deed allowed Roche citizens the right to walk across a five-foot-wide section of the lot beside Wayakichi Creek as part of a two-mile public trail system.

Teenagers regularly threw Frisbee golf discs from the walking path behind Shoepke's property over his yard to the adjacent park. Shoepke habitually shouted and cursed at the teenagers, demanding that they not throw the discs over his yard.

Two months after moving into his Roche home, Shoepke leased the second floor to Lauren Slater for nine months. (The lease agreement did not specify that Shoepke's consent would be required to sublease the second floor.) After three months of tenancy, Slater sublet the second floor to a local artist, Javier Indalecio. Over the remaining six months, Indalecio's use of oil paints damaged the carpeting in Shoepke's home. Using the information presented in the chapter, answer the following questions.

1. What is the term for the right of Roche citizens to walk across Shoepke's land on the trail?
2. What covenants would most courts infer were included in the warranty deed that Shoepke received when he bought his house?
3. Can Shoepke hold Slater financially responsible for the damage to the carpeting caused by Indalecio? Explain.
4. Suppose that Slater—to offset her liability for the carpet damage caused by Indalecio—files a counterclaim against Shoepke for breach of the covenant of quiet enjoyment. Could the fact that teenagers continually throw Frisbees over Shoepke's yard outside the second-floor windows arguably be a breach of the covenant of quiet enjoyment? Why or why not?

DEBATE THIS Under no circumstances should a local government be able to condemn property in order to sell it later to real estate developers for private use.

Key Terms

adverse possession 939
condemnation 940
constructive eviction 943
conveyance 934
deed 938
easement 935
eminent domain 940
eviction 943
fee simple absolute 934
fixed-term tenancy 942
fixture 933
implied warranty of habitability 937
leasehold estate 942
license 936
life estate 934
nonpossessory interest 935
periodic tenancy 942
profit 935
quitclaim deed 939
recording statutes 939
special warranty deed 939
sublease 944
taking 940
tenancy at sufferance 942
tenancy at will 942
warranty deed 938

Chapter Summary: Real Property and Landlord-Tenant Law

The Nature of Real Property (See pages 931–933.)	Real property (also called real estate or realty) is immovable. It includes land, subsurface and airspace rights, plant life and vegetation, and fixtures.
Ownership Interests in Real Property (See pages 933–936.)	1. *Fee simple absolute*—The most complete form of ownership. 2. *Life estate*—An estate that lasts for the life of a specified individual, during which time the individual is entitled to possess, use, and benefit from the estate. The life tenant's ownership rights cease to exist on her or his death. 3. *Nonpossessory interest*—An interest that involves the right to use real property but not to possess it. Easements, profits, and licenses are nonpossessory interests.

Continued

Chapter Summary: Real Property and Landlord-Tenant Law—Continued

Transfer of Ownership (See pages 936–941.)	1. *By deed*—When real property is sold or transferred as a gift, title to the property is conveyed by means of a deed. A deed must meet specific legal requirements. A *warranty deed* provides the most extensive protection against defects of title. A *quitclaim deed* conveys to the grantee only whatever interest the grantor had in the property. A deed may be recorded in the manner prescribed by *recording statutes* in the appropriate jurisdiction to give third parties notice of the owner's interest. 2. *By will or inheritance*—If the owner dies after having made a valid will, the land passes as specified in the will. If the owner dies without having made a will, the heirs inherit according to state inheritance statutes. 3. *By adverse possession*—When a person possesses the property of another for a statutory period of time (ten years is the most common), that person acquires title to the property, provided the possession is actual and exclusive, open and visible, continuous and peaceable, and hostile and adverse (without the permission of the owner). 4. *By eminent domain*—The government can take land for public use, with just compensation, when the public interest requires the taking.
Leasehold Estates (See pages 942–943.)	A leasehold estate is an interest in real property that is held for only a limited period of time, as specified in the lease agreement. Types of tenancies include the following: 1. *Fixed-term tenancy*—Tenancy for a period of time stated by express contract. 2. *Periodic tenancy*—Tenancy for a period determined by the frequency of rent payments and automatically renewed unless proper notice is given. 3. *Tenancy at will*—Tenancy for as long as both parties agree. No notice of termination is required. 4. *Tenancy at sufferance*—Possession of land without legal right.
Landlord-Tenant Relationships (See pages 943–944.)	1. *Lease agreement*—The landlord-tenant relationship is created by a lease agreement. State or local laws may dictate whether the lease must be in writing and what lease terms are permissible. 2. *Rights and duties*—The rights and duties that arise under a lease agreement generally pertain to the following areas: a. Possession—The tenant has an exclusive right to possess the leased premises. Under the covenant of quiet enjoyment, the landlord promises that during the lease term, neither the landlord nor anyone having superior title to the property will disturb the tenant's use and enjoyment of the property. b. Use and maintenance of the premises—Unless the parties agree otherwise, the tenant may make any legal use of the property. The tenant is responsible for any damage that he or she causes. The landlord must comply with laws that set specific standards for the maintenance of real property. The implied warranty of habitability requires that the landlord furnish and maintain residential premises in a habitable condition (that is, in a condition safe and suitable for human life). c. Rent—The tenant must pay the rent as long as the lease is in force, unless the tenant justifiably refuses to occupy the property or withholds the rent because of the landlord's failure to maintain the premises properly. 3. *Transferring rights to leased property*— a. If the landlord transfers complete title to the leased property, the tenant becomes the tenant of the new owner. The new owner may then collect the rent but must abide by the existing lease. b. Generally, in the absence of an agreement to the contrary, tenants may assign their rights (but not their duties) under a lease contract to a third person. Tenants may also sublease leased property to a third person, but the original tenant is not relieved of any obligations to the landlord under the lease. In either situation, the landlord's consent may be required, but statutes may prohibit the landlord from unreasonably withholding consent.

ExamPrep

ISSUE SPOTTERS

1. Bernie sells his house to Consuela under a warranty deed. Later, Delmira appears, holding a better title to the house than Consuela has. Delmira wants Consuela off the property. What can Consuela do? **(See page 938.)**
2. Grey owns a commercial building in fee simple. Grey transfers temporary possession of the building to Haven Corporation. Can Haven transfer possession for even less time to Idyll Company? Explain. **(See page 934.)**

—Check your answers to the Issue Spotters against the answers provided in Appendix E at the end of this text.

BEFORE THE TEST

Go to www.cengagebrain.com, enter the ISBN 9781133273561, and click on "Find" to locate this textbook's Web site. Then, click on "Access Now" under "Study Tools," and select Chapter 36 at the top. There, you will find a Practice Quiz that you can take to assess your mastery of the concepts in this chapter, as well as Flashcards, a Glossary of important terms, and Video Questions (when assigned).

For Review

Answers to the even-numbered questions in this* For Review *section can be found in Appendix F at the end of this text.

1. What is a fixture, and how does it relate to real property rights?
2. What is an easement? Describe three ways that easements are created.
3. What are the requirements for acquiring property by adverse possession?
4. What is a leasehold estate? What types of leasehold estates, or tenancies, can be created when real property is leased?
5. What are the respective duties of the landlord and the tenant concerning the use and maintenance of leased property?

Business Scenarios and Case Problems

36–1 Property Ownership. Twenty-two years ago, Lorenz was a wanderer. At that time, he decided to settle down on an unoccupied, three-acre parcel of land that he did not own. People in the area told him that they had no idea who owned the property. Lorenz built a house on the land, got married, and raised three children while living there. He fenced in the land, installed a gate with a sign above it that read "Lorenz's Homestead," and removed trespassers. Lorenz is now confronted by Joe Reese, who has a deed in his name as owner of the property. Reese, claiming ownership of the land, orders Lorenz and his family off the property. Discuss who has the better "title" to the property. **(See pages 938–939.)**

36–2 Question with Sample Answer—Deeds. Wiley and Gemma are neighbors. Wiley's lot is extremely large, and his present and future use of it will not involve the entire area. Gemma wants to build a single-car garage and driveway along the present lot boundary. Because the placement of her existing structures makes it impossible for her to comply with an ordinance requiring buildings to be set back fifteen feet from an adjoining property line, Gemma cannot build the garage. Gemma contracts to purchase ten feet of Wiley's property along their boundary line for $3,000. Wiley is willing to sell but will give Gemma only a quitclaim deed, whereas Gemma wants a warranty deed. Discuss the differences between these deeds as they would affect the rights of the parties if the title to this ten feet of land later proves to be defective. **(See pages 938–939.)**

—For a sample answer to Question 36–2, go to Appendix G at the end of this text.

36–3 Eviction. James owns a three-story building. He leases the ground floor to Juan's Mexican restaurant. The lease is to run for a five-year period and contains an express covenant of quiet enjoyment. One year later, James leases the top two stories to the Upbeat Club, which features live music. The club's hours run from 7:00 P.M. to 1:00 A.M. The noise from the Upbeat Club is so loud that it is driving customers away from Juan's restaurant. Juan has notified James of the interference and has called the police on a number of occasions. James refuses to talk to the owners of the Upbeat Club or to do anything to remedy the situation. Juan abandons the premises. James files a suit for breach of the lease agreement and for the rental payments still due under the lease. Juan claims that he was constructively evicted and files a countersuit for damages. Discuss who will be held liable. **(See page 943.)**

36–4 Ownership in Fee Simple. Thomas and Teresa Cline built a house on 76 acres next to Roy Berg's home in Virginia. The homes were about 1,800 feet apart but in view of each other. After several disagreements between the parties, Berg equipped an 11-foot tripod with motion sensors and floodlights that intermittently illuminated the Clines' home. Berg also installed surveillance cameras that tracked some of the movement on the Clines' property. The cameras transmitted on an open frequency, which could be received by any television within range. The Clines asked Berg to turn off, or at least redirect, the lights. When he refused, they erected a fence for 200 feet along the parties' common property line. The 32-foot-high fence consisted of 20 utility poles spaced 10 feet apart with plastic wrap stretched between the poles. This effectively blocked the lights and cameras. Berg filed a suit against the Clines in a Virginia state court, complaining that the fence interfered unreasonably with his use and enjoyment of his property. He asked the court to order the Clines to take the fence down. What are the limits on an owner's use of property? How should the court rule in this case? Why? [*Cline v. Berg*, 273 Va. 142, 639 S.E.2d 231 (2007)] **(See page 934.)**

36–5 Commercial Lease Terms. Gi Hwa Park entered into a lease with Landmark HHH, LLC, for retail space in the Plaza at Landmark, a shopping center in Virginia. The lease provided that the landlord would keep the roof "in good repair" and that the tenant would obtain insurance on her inventory and absolve the landlord from any losses to the extent of the insurance proceeds. Park opened a store—The Four Seasons—in the space, specializing in imported men's suits and accessories. Within a month of the store's opening and continuing for nearly eight years, water intermittently leaked through the roof, causing damage. Landmark eventually had a new roof installed, but water continued to leak into The Four Seasons. On a night of record rainfall, the store suffered substantial water damage, and Park was forced to close the store. On what basis might Park seek to recover from Landmark? What might Landmark assert in response? Which party's argument is more likely to succeed, and why? [*Landmark HHH, LLC v. Gi Hwa Park,* 277 Va. 50, 671 S.E.2d 143 (2009)] **(See page 943.)**

36–6 **Case Problem with Sample Answer—Adverse Possession.** The McKeag family operated a marina on their lakefront property in Bolton, New York. For more than forty years, the McKeags used a section of property belonging to their neighbors, the Finleys, as a beach for the marina's customers. The McKeags also stored a large float on the beach during the winter months, built their own retaining wall, and planted bushes and flowers there. The McKeags prevented others from using the property, including the Finleys. Nevertheless, the families always had a friendly relationship, and one of the Finleys gave the McKeags permission to continue using the beach in 1992. He also reminded them of his ownership several times, to which they said nothing. The McKeags also asked for permission to mow grass on the property and once apologized for leaving a jet ski there. Can the McKeags establish adverse possession over the statutory period of ten years? Why or why not? [*McKeag v. Finley,* 939 N.Y.S.2d 644 (N.Y.App.Div. 2012)] **(See pages 939–940.)**

—For a sample answer to Problem 36–6, go to Appendix H at the end of this text.

36–7 **A Question of Ethics—Adverse Possession.** Alana Mansell built a garage on her property that encroached on the property of her neighbor, Betty Hunter, by fourteen feet. Hunter knew of the encroachment and informally agreed to it, but she did not transfer ownership of the property to Mansell. A survey twenty-eight years later confirmed the encroachment, and Hunter sought the removal of the garage. Mansell asked a court to declare that she was the owner of the property by adverse possession. [*Hunter v. Mansell,* 240 P.3d 469 (Colo.App. 2010)] **(See pages 939–940.)**

1. Did Mansell obtain title by adverse possession? Would the open occupation of the property for nearly thirty years be in Mansell's favor? Why or why not?
2. Was her conduct in any way unethical? Discuss.

Critical Thinking and Writing Assignments

36–8 **Case Analysis Question.** Go to Appendix I at the end of this text and examine the excerpt of Case No. 7, *Kelo v. City of New London, Connecticut.* Review and then brief the case, making sure that your brief answers the following questions.

1. **Issue:** On what issue did the United States Supreme Court focus in this case?
2. **Rule of Law:** What does the Fifth Amendment to the U.S. Constitution, which the Court applied, require with respect to the legal issue in this case?
3. **Applying the Rule of Law:** How did the Court apply the rule of law to the facts of this case?
4. **Conclusion:** What was the Court's conclusion concerning the issue in this case?

36–9 **Business Law Critical Thinking Group Assignment.** The Wallen family owned a cabin on Lummi Island in the state of Washington. A driveway ran from the cabin across their property to South Nugent Road. Floyd Massey bought the adjacent lot and built a cabin on it in 1980. To gain access to his property, Massey used a bulldozer to extend the driveway, without the Wallens' permission but also without their objection. In 2005, the Wallens sold their property to Wright Fish Company. Massey continued to use and maintain the driveway without permission or objection. In 2010, Massey sold his property to Robert Drake. Drake and his employees continued to use and maintain the driveway without permission or objection, although Drake knew it was located largely on Wright's property. In 2012, Wright sold its lot to Robert Smersh. The next year, Smersh told Drake to stop using the driveway. Drake filed a suit against Smersh, claiming an easement by prescription (which is created by meeting the same requirements as adverse possession).

1. The first group will decide whether Drake's use of the driveway meets all of the requirements for adverse possession (easement by prescription).
2. The second group will determine how the court should rule in this case and why. Does it matter that Drake knew the driveway was located largely on Wright's (and then Smersh's) property? Should it matter?
3. A third group will evaluate the underlying policy and fairness of adverse possession laws. Should the law reward persons who take possession of someone else's land for their own use? Does it make sense to punish owners who allow someone else to use their land without complaint?

CHAPTER 37

(AnthiaCumming/iStockphoto.com)

Insurance, Wills, and Trusts

CHAPTER OUTLINE

- Insurance
- Wills
- Trusts

LEARNING OBJECTIVES

The five learning objectives below are designed to help improve your understanding of the chapter. After reading this chapter, you should be able to answer the following questions:

1. Is an insurance broker the agent of the insurance applicant or the agent of the insurer?
2. What is an insurable interest? When must an insurable interest exist—at the time the insurance policy is obtained, at the time the loss occurs, or both?
3. What are the basic requirements for executing a will?
4. What is the difference between a *per stirpes* distribution and a *per capita* distribution of an estate to the grandchildren of the deceased?
5. What are the four essential elements of a trust? What is the difference between an express trust and an implied trust?

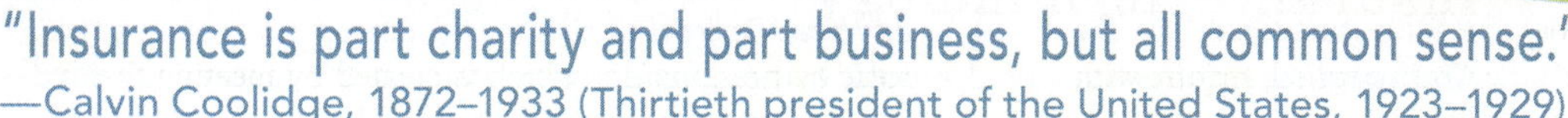
"Insurance is part charity and part business, but all common sense."
—Calvin Coolidge, 1872–1933 (Thirtieth president of the United States, 1923–1929)

Most individuals insure both real and personal property (as well as their lives). As Calvin Coolidge asserted in the chapter-opening quotation, insurance is "all common sense"—by insuring our property, we protect ourselves against damage and loss.

The first part of this chapter focuses on insurance, which is a foremost concern of all property owners. We then examine how property is transferred on the death of its owner. Certainly, the laws of succession are a necessary corollary to the concept of private ownership of property. Our laws require that on death, title to the property of the decedent (one who has recently died) must be delivered in full somewhere. In this chapter, we see that this can be done by will, through trusts, or through state laws prescribing distribution of property among heirs or next of kin. We also discuss social media estate planning later in this chapter.

Insurance

Many precautions may be taken to protect against the hazards of life. For instance, an individual may wear a seat belt to protect against injuries from automobile accidents or install smoke detectors to guard against injury from fire. Of course, no one can predict whether an accident or a fire will ever occur, but individuals and businesses must establish plans to protect their personal and financial interests should some event threaten to undermine their security.

Insurance A contract in which, for a stipulated consideration, one party agrees to compensate the other for loss on a specific subject by a specified peril.

Risk A prediction concerning potential loss based on known and unknown factors.

Risk Management In the context of insurance, the transfer of certain risks from the insured to the insurance company by contractual agreement.

Insurance is a contract by which the insurance company (the insurer) promises to pay an amount or to give something of value to another (either the insured or the beneficiary) in the event that the insured is injured, dies, or sustains damage to her or his property as a result of particular, stated contingencies. Basically, insurance is an arrangement for *transferring and allocating risk.* In many instances, **risk** can be described as a prediction concerning potential loss based on known and unknown factors. Insurance, however, involves much more than a game of chance.

Risk management normally involves the transfer of certain risks from the individual to the insurance company by a contractual agreement. The insurance contract and its provisions will be examined shortly. First, however, we look at the different types of insurance that can be obtained, insurance terminology, and the concept of insurable interest.

Classifications of Insurance

Insurance is classified according to the nature of the risk involved. For instance, fire insurance, casualty insurance, life insurance, and title insurance apply to different types of risk. Furthermore, policies of these types protect different persons and interests. This is reasonable because the types of losses that are expected and that are foreseeable or unforeseeable vary with the nature of the activity.

Exhibit 37.1 on the facing page presents a list of selected insurance classifications. (For a discussion of insurance policies designed to cover the special kinds of risks faced by online businesses, see the *Business Application* feature on pages 970 and 971.)

Insurance Terminology

Policy In insurance law, the contract between the insurer and the insured.

Premium In insurance law, the price paid by the insured for insurance protection for a specified period of time.

Underwriter In insurance law, the insurer, or the one assuming a risk in return for the payment of a premium.

An insurance contract is called a **policy,** the consideration paid to the insurer is called a **premium,** and the insurance company is sometimes called an **underwriter.** The parties to an insurance policy are the *insurer* (the insurance company) and the *insured* (the person covered by its provisions or the holder of the policy).

Insurance contracts are usually obtained through an *agent,* who ordinarily works for the insurance company, or through a *broker,* who is ordinarily an *independent contractor.* When a broker deals with an applicant for insurance, the broker is, in effect, the applicant's agent and not an agent of the insurance company. In contrast, an insurance agent is an agent of the insurance company, not of the applicant. Thus, the agent owes fiduciary duties to the insurer (the insurance company), but not to the person who is applying for insurance.

LEARNING OBJECTIVE 1

Is an insurance broker the agent of the insurance applicant or the agent of the insurer?

As a general rule, the insurance company is bound by the acts of its insurance agents when they act within the agency relationship (discussed in Chapter 23). In most situations, state law determines the status of all parties writing or obtaining insurance.

Insurable Interest

Insurable Interest An interest that exists when a person benefits from the preservation of the health or life of the insured or the property to be insured.

A person can insure anything in which she or he has an **insurable interest.** In regard to real and personal property, an insurable interest exists when the insured derives a pecuniary (monetary) benefit from the preservation and continued existence of the property. Put another way, a person has an insurable interest in property when she or he would sustain a

Exhibit 37.1 Selected Insurance Classifications

TYPE OF INSURANCE	COVERAGE
Accident	Covers expenses, losses, and suffering incurred by the insured because of accidents causing physical injury and any consequent disability; sometimes includes a specified payment to heirs of the insured if death results from an accident.
All-risk	Covers all losses that the insured may incur except those that are specifically excluded. Typical exclusions are war, pollution, earthquakes, and floods.
Automobile	May cover damage to automobiles resulting from specified hazards or occurrences (such as fire, vandalism, theft, or collision); normally provides protection against liability for personal injuries and property damage resulting from the operation of the vehicle.
Casualty	Protects against losses incurred by the insured as a result of being held liable for personal injuries or property damage sustained by others.
Decreasing-term life	Provides life insurance; requires uniform payments over the life (term) of the policy, but with a decreasing face value (amount of coverage).
Disability	Replaces a portion of the insured's monthly income from employment in the event that illness or injury causes a short- or long-term disability. Some states require employers to provide short-term disability insurance. Benefits typically last a set period of time, such as six months for short-term coverage or five years for long-term coverage.
Employer's liability	Insures an employer against liability for injuries or losses sustained by employees during the course of their employment; covers claims not covered under workers' compensation insurance.
Fidelity or guaranty	Provides indemnity against losses in trade or losses caused by the dishonesty of employees, the insolvency of debtors, or breaches of contract.
Fire	Covers losses incurred by the insured as a result of fire.
Floater	Covers movable property, as long as the property is within the territorial boundaries specified in the contract.
Homeowners'	Protects homeowners against some or all risks of loss to their residences and the residences' contents or liability arising from the use of the property.
Key-person	Protects a business in the event of the death or disability of a key employee.
Liability	Protects against liability imposed on the insured as a result of injuries to the person or property of another.
Life	Covers the death of the policyholder. On the death of the insured, the insurer pays the amount specified in the policy to the insured's beneficiary.
Major medical	Protects the insured against major hospital, medical, or surgical expenses.
Malpractice	Protects professionals (physicians, lawyers, and others) against malpractice claims brought against them by their patients or clients; a form of liability insurance.
Term life	Provides life insurance for a specified period of time (term) with no cash surrender value; usually renewable.

financial loss from its destruction. Without an insurable interest, there is no enforceable contract, and a transaction to purchase insurance coverage would have to be treated as a wager.

LEARNING OBJECTIVE 2

What is an insurable interest? When must an insurable interest exist—at the time the insurance policy is obtained, at the time the loss occurs, or both?

Life Insurance In regard to life insurance, a person must have a reasonable expectation of benefit from the continued life of another in order to have an insurable interest in that person's life. The insurable interest must exist *at the time the policy is obtained.* The benefit may be pecuniary (as with so-called *key-person insurance,* which insures the lives of important employees, usually in small companies), or it may be founded on the relationship between the parties (by blood or affinity).

Property Insurance For property insurance, the insurable interest must exist at the time the loss occurs but need not exist when the policy is purchased. The existence of an insurable interest is a primary concern in determining liability under an insurance policy.

CASE EXAMPLE 37.1 ABM Industries, Inc., leased office and storage space in the World Trade Center (WTC) in New York City in 2001. ABM also ran the building's heating, ventilation, and air-conditioning systems, and maintained all of the WTC's common areas. At the time, ABM employed more than eight hundred workers at the WTC. Zurich American Insurance Company insured ABM against losses resulting from "business interruption" caused by direct physical loss or damage "to property owned, controlled, used, leased or intended for use" by ABM.

After the terrorist attacks on September 11, 2001, ABM filed a claim with Zurich to recover for the loss of all income derived from ABM's WTC operations. Zurich argued that ABM's recovery should be limited to the income lost as a result of the destruction of ABM's office and storage space and supplies. A court, however, ruled that ABM was entitled to compensation for the loss of all of its WTC operations. The court reasoned that the "policy's scope expressly includes real or personal property that the insured 'used,' 'controlled,' or 'intended for use.'" Because ABM's income depended on "the common areas and leased premises in the WTC complex," it had an insurable interest in that property at the time of the loss.[1]

The Insurance Contract

An insurance contract is governed by the general principles of contract law, although the insurance industry is heavily regulated by each state. Here, we discuss the application for insurance, the date when the contract takes effect, and some of the important provisions typically found in insurance contracts. We also discuss the cancellation of an insurance policy and defenses that insurance companies can raise against payment on a policy.

KNOW THIS

The federal government has the power to regulate the insurance industry under the commerce clause of the U.S. Constitution. Instead of exercising this power itself, Congress allows the states to regulate insurance.

Application

The filled-in application form for insurance is usually attached to the policy and made a part of the insurance contract. Thus, an insurance applicant is bound by any false statements that appear in the application (subject to certain exceptions). Because the insurance company evaluates the risk factors based on the information included in the insurance application, misstatements or misrepresentations can void a policy, especially if the insurance company can show that it would not have extended insurance if it had known the true facts.

Effective Date

The effective date of an insurance contract—that is, the date on which the insurance coverage begins—is important. In some situations, the insurance applicant is not protected until a formal written policy is issued. For instance, if the parties agree that the policy will be issued and delivered at a later time, the contract is not effective until the policy is issued and delivered. Thus, any loss sustained between the time of application and the delivery of the policy is not covered.

Also, remember that a broker is an agent of the applicant, not an agent of the insurance company. Therefore, if a person hires a broker to obtain insurance, and the broker fails to procure a policy, the applicant normally is not insured.

Binder

In other situations, the applicant is protected between the time the application is received and the time the insurance company either accepts or rejects it. A person who seeks insurance from an insurance company's agent is usually protected from the moment the application is made, provided—for life insurance—that some form of premium has been paid. Usually, the agent will write a memorandum, or **binder**, indicating that a policy is pending and stating its essential terms.

Binder A written, temporary insurance policy.

Life Insurance

Parties may agree that a life insurance policy will be binding at the time the insured pays the first premium, or the policy may be expressly contingent on the applicant's passing a physical examination. If the applicant pays the premium but dies before having the physical examination, then in order to collect, the applicant's estate normally must show that the applicant *would have passed* the examination had he or she not died.

Coinsurance Clauses

Often, when taking out fire insurance policies, property owners insure their property for less than full value because most fires do not result in a

1. *Zurich American Insurance Co. v. ABM Industries, Inc.*, 397 F.3d 158 (2d Cir. 2005).

total loss. To encourage owners to insure their property for an amount as close to full value as possible, fire insurance policies commonly include a coinsurance clause.

Typically, a *coinsurance clause* provides that if the owner insures the property up to a specified percentage—usually 80 percent—of its value, she or he will recover any loss up to the face amount of the policy. If the insurance is for less than the fixed percentage, the owner is responsible for a proportionate share of the loss.

Coinsurance applies only in instances of partial loss. The amount of the recovery is calculated by using the following formula:

$$\text{Loss} \times \left(\frac{\text{Amount of Insurance Coverage}}{\text{Coinsurance Percentage} \times \text{Property Value}} \right) = \text{Amount of Recovery}$$

EXAMPLE 37.2 Madison, who owns property valued at $200,000, takes out a policy in the amount of $100,000. If Madison then suffers a loss of $80,000, her recovery will be $50,000. Madison will be responsible for (coinsure) the balance of the loss, or $30,000, which is the amount of loss ($80,000) minus the amount of recovery ($50,000).

$$\$80{,}000 \times \left(\frac{\$100{,}000}{0.8 \times \$200{,}000} \right) = \$50{,}000$$

If Madison had taken out a policy in the amount of 80 percent of the value of the property, or $160,000, then according to the same formula, she would have recovered the full amount of the loss (the face amount of the policy). ●

Incontestability Clause A clause in a policy for life or health insurance stating that after the policy has been in force for a specified length of time (usually two or three years), the insurer cannot contest statements made in the policyholder's application.

Incontestability Clauses

Statutes commonly require that a policy for life or health insurance include an **incontestability clause.** Under this clause, after the policy has been in force for a specified length of time—often two or three years—the insurer cannot contest statements made in the application. Once a policy becomes incontestable, the insurer cannot later avoid a claim on the basis of, for instance, fraud on the part of the insured, unless the clause provides an exception for that circumstance.

Some other important provisions and clauses that are frequently included in insurance contracts are described in Exhibit 37.2 below.

Exhibit 37.2 Insurance Contract Provisions and Clauses

TYPE OF CLAUSE	DESCRIPTION
Antilapse clause	An antilapse clause provides that the policy will not automatically lapse if no payment is made on the date due. Ordinarily, under such a provision, the insured has a *grace period* of thirty or thirty-one days within which to pay an overdue premium before the policy is canceled.
Appraisal clause	Insurance policies frequently provide that if the parties cannot agree on the amount of a loss covered under the policy or the value of the property lost, an appraisal, or estimate, by an impartial and qualified third party can be demanded.
Arbitration clause	Many insurance policies include clauses that call for arbitration of any disputes that arise between the insurer and the insured concerning the settlement of claims.
Incontestability clause	An incontestability clause provides that after a policy has been in force for a specified length of time—usually two or three years—the insurer cannot contest statements made in the application.
Multiple insurance	Many insurance policies include a clause providing that if the insured has multiple insurance policies that cover the same property and the amount of coverage exceeds the loss, the loss will be shared proportionately by the insurance companies.

Interpreting the Insurance Contract The courts are aware that most people do not have the special training necessary to understand the intricate terminology used in insurance policies. Therefore, when disputes arise, the courts will interpret the words used in an insurance contract according to their ordinary meanings in light of the nature of the coverage involved.

When there is an ambiguity in the policy, the provision generally is interpreted *against* the insurance company. Also, when it is unclear whether an insurance contract actually exists because the written policy has not been delivered, the uncertainty normally is resolved against the insurance company. The court presumes that the policy is in effect unless the company can show otherwise. Similarly, an insurer must make sure that the insured is adequately notified of any change in coverage under an existing policy.

Disputes over insurance often focus on the application of an exclusion in the policy, as the following case illustrates.

Case 37.1

Valero v. Florida Insurance Guaranty Association, Inc.

District Court of Appeal of Florida, Fourth District, 59 So.3d 1166 (2011).

(KLH49/iStockphoto.com)

FACTS Alberto and Karelli Mila were insured under a homeowners' liability policy. "Exclusion k" of the policy stated that coverage did not apply to "bodily injury arising out of sexual molestation, corporal punishment or physical or mental abuse." Verushka Valero, on behalf of her child, filed a suit in a Florida state court against the Milas, charging them with negligent supervision of a perpetrator who had sexually molested Valero's child.

The Milas filed a claim asking their insurer to defend against the charges. The insurer had become insolvent, so the claim was submitted to the Florida Insurance Guaranty Association, Inc. (FIGA). FIGA is a nonprofit corporation created by the Florida legislature to evaluate and resolve claims when insurance companies become insolvent (a similar insurance guaranty association exists in nearly every state). FIGA refused to pay the Milas' claim and asked the court to rule that it had no obligation under the policy to provide such a defense. The court issued a summary judgment in FIGA's favor. Valero and the Milas appealed, arguing that exclusion k was ambiguous.

ISSUE Was the term of the Milas' insurance policy that excluded coverage for "bodily injury arising out of sexual molestation" ambiguous as to whether it covered acts by someone under their supervision?

DECISION No. A state intermediate appellate court affirmed the lower court's judgment. The exclusion applied to preclude coverage in this case.

REASON The Milas pointed out that a different exclusion, exclusion l, used the phrase "by any person" and exclusion k did not. Thus, the Milas contended, it was not clear whether exclusion k applied only to acts of an insured. The court read the entire list of twelve exclusions together and concluded that the phrase in exclusion l was "superfluous." Even if the phrase "by any person" had been used in exclusion k, coverage might still have been denied, as in this case. Valero and the Milas also cited decisions from other jurisdictions to support their argument. The court found these decisions to be "not helpful" because they considered exclusions in isolation, not in the context of other exclusions.

WHAT IF THE FACTS WERE DIFFERENT? *Suppose that exclusion k, instead of exclusion l, had used the phrase "by any person." Would the result have been different? Explain.*

Cancellation The insured can cancel a policy at any time, and the insurer can cancel under certain circumstances. When an insurance company can cancel its insurance contract, the policy or a state statute usually requires that the insurer give advance written notice of the cancellation to the insured. The same requirement applies when only part of a policy is canceled. Any premium paid in advance may be refundable on the policy's cancellation. The insured may also be entitled to a life insurance policy's cash surrender value.

Auto and Property Insurance The insurer may cancel an insurance policy for various reasons, depending on the type of insurance. For instance, automobile insurance can be canceled for nonpayment of premiums or suspension of the insured's driver's license. Property insurance can be canceled for nonpayment of premiums, for the insured's fraud or misrepresentation, and for certain other reasons that would increase the risk assumed by the insurer.

Life and Health Insurance Life and health policies can be canceled because of false statements made by the insured in the application, but the cancellation must take place before the effective date of an incontestability clause. An insurer cannot cancel—or refuse to renew—a policy for discriminatory reasons or other reasons that violate public policy, or because the insured has appeared as a witness in a case against the company.

Good Faith Obligations

Both parties to an insurance contract are responsible for the obligations they assume under the contract (contract law was discussed in Chapters 9 through 14). In addition, both the insured and the insurer have an implied duty to act in good faith.

Good faith requires the party who is applying for insurance to reveal everything necessary for the insurer to evaluate the risk. In other words, the applicant must disclose all material facts, including all facts that an insurer would consider in determining whether to charge a higher premium or to refuse to issue a policy altogether. Many insurance companies today require that an applicant give the company permission to access other information, such as private medical records and credit ratings, for the purpose of evaluating the risk.

Duty to Investigate Once the insurer has accepted the risk and some event occurs that gives rise to a claim, the insurer has a duty to investigate to determine the facts. When a policy provides insurance against third party claims, the insurer is obligated to make reasonable efforts to settle such a claim. If a settlement cannot be reached, then regardless of the claim's merit, the insurer must defend any suit against the insured. Usually, a policy provides that in this situation the insured must cooperate in the defense and attend hearings and trials if necessary.

Duty to Defend An insurer has a duty to provide or pay an attorney to defend its insured when a complaint alleges facts that could, if proved, impose liability on the insured within the policy's coverage.

CASE EXAMPLE 37.3 Dentist Robert Woo installed implants for one of his employees, Tina Alberts, whose family raised potbellied pigs. As a joke, while Alberts was anesthetized, Woo installed a set of "flippers" (temporary partial bridges) shaped like boar tusks and took photos. A month later, Woo's staff showed the photos to Alberts at a party. Alberts refused to return to work. She filed a suit against Woo for battery. Woo's insurance company refused to defend him in the suit, and he ended up paying Alberts $250,000 to settle her claim. Woo then sued the insurance company and won. The court held that the insurance company had a duty to defend Woo under the professional liability provision of his policy because Woo's practical joke took place during a routine dental procedure.[2] ●

Bad Faith Actions Although the law of insurance generally follows contract law, most states now recognize a "bad faith" tort action against insurers. Thus, if an insurer in bad faith denies coverage of a claim, the insured may recover in tort in an amount exceeding the policy's coverage limits and may also recover punitive damages. Some courts have held insurers liable for bad faith refusals to settle claims for reasonable amounts within the policy limits.

---

2. *Woo v. Fireman's Fund Insurance Co.*, 161 Wash.2d 43, 164 P.3d 454 (2007).

Defenses against Payment An insurance company can raise any of the defenses that would be valid in an ordinary action on a contract, as well as some defenses that do not apply in ordinary contract actions.

1. *Fraud or misrepresentation*. If the insurance company can show that the policy was procured by fraud or misrepresentation, it may have a valid defense for not paying on a claim. (The insurance company may also have the right to disaffirm or rescind the insurance contract.)
2. *Lack of an insurable interest*. An absolute defense exists if the insurer can show that the insured lacked an insurable interest—thus rendering the policy void from the beginning.
3. *Illegal actions of the insured*. Improper actions, such as those that are against public policy or that are otherwise illegal, can also give the insurance company a defense against the payment of a claim or allow it to rescind the contract.

An insurance company can be prevented, or estopped, from asserting some defenses that are usually available, however. For instance, an insurance company normally cannot escape payment on the death of an insured on the ground that the person's age was stated incorrectly on the application. Also, incontestability clauses prevent the insurer from asserting certain defenses.

Who should create a will?

(skynesher/iStockphoto.com)

Wills

Not only do the owners of property want to protect it during their lifetime through insurance coverage, but they typically also wish to transfer it to their loved ones at the time of their death. A **will** is the final declaration of how a person desires to have her or his property disposed of after death. It is a formal instrument that must follow exactly the requirements of state law to be effective. A will is referred to as a *testamentary disposition* of property, and one who dies after having made a valid will is said to have died **testate.**

A will can serve other purposes besides the distribution of property. It can appoint a guardian for minor children or incapacitated adults. It can also appoint a personal representative to settle the affairs of the deceased. Exhibit 37.3 on the facing page presents excerpts from the will of Michael Jackson, the "King of Pop," who died from cardiac arrest in 2009 at the age of fifty. Jackson held a substantial amount of tangible and intangible property, including the publishing rights to most of The Beatles' music catalogue. The will is a "pour-over" will, meaning that it transfers all of his property (that is not already held in the name of the trust) into the Michael Jackson Family Trust (trusts are discussed on page 965). Jackson's will also appoints his mother, Katherine Jackson, as the guardian of his three minor children.

A person who dies without having created a valid will is said to have died **intestate.** In this situation, state **intestacy laws** prescribe the distribution of the property among heirs or next of kin. If no heirs or kin can be found, title to the property will be transferred to the state.

Will An instrument made by a testator directing what is to be done with her or his property after death.

Testate Having left a will at death.

Intestate As a noun, one who has died without having created a valid will. As an adjective, the state of having died without a will.

Intestacy Laws State statutes that specify how property will be distributed when a person dies intestate (without a valid will).

Terminology of Wills

A person who makes out a will is known as a **testator** (from the Latin *testari*, "to make a will"). The court responsible for administering any legal problems surrounding a will is called a *probate court*, as mentioned in Chapter 3. When a person dies, a personal representative administers the estate and settles all of the decedent's (deceased person's) affairs.

An **executor** is a personal representative named in the will, whereas an **administrator** is a personal representative appointed by the court for a decedent who dies without a will. The court will also appoint an administrator if the will does not name an executor or if the named person lacks the capacity to serve as an executor.

Testator One who makes and executes a will.

Executor A person appointed by a testator in a will to administer her or his estate.

Administrator One who is appointed by a court to administer a person's estate if the decedent died without a valid will or if the executor named in the will cannot serve.

Exhibit 37.3 Excerpts from Michael Jackson's Will

LAST WILL OF MICHAEL JOSEPH JACKSON

I, MICHAEL JOSEPH JACKSON, a resident of the State of California, declare this to be my last Will, and do hereby revoke all former wills and codicils made by me.

I. I declare that I am not married. My marriage to DEBORAH JEAN ROWE JACKSON has been dissolved. I have three children now living, PRINCE MICHAEL JACKSON, JR., PARIS MICHAEL KATHERINE JACKSON and PRINCE MICHAEL JOSEPH JACKSON, II. I have no other children, living or deceased.

II. It is my intention by this Will to dispose of all property which I am entitled to dispose of by will. I specifically refrain from exercising all powers of appointment that I may possess at the time of my death.

III. I give my entire estate to the Trustee or Trustees then acting under that certain Amended and Restated Declaration of Trust executed on March 22, 2002 by me as Trustee and Trustor which is called the MICHAEL JACKSON FAMILY TRUST, giving effect to any amendments thereto made prior to my death. All such assets shall be held, managed and distributed as a part of said Trust according to its terms and not as a separate testamentary trust.

If for any reason this gift is not operative or is invalid, or if the aforesaid Trust fails or has been revoked, I give my residuary estate to the Trustee or Trustees named to act in the MICHAEL JACKSON FAMILY TRUST, as Amended and Restated on March 22, 2002, and I direct said Trustee or Trustees to divide, administer, hold and distribute the trust estate pursuant to the provisions of said Trust * * * .

* * * *

IV. I direct that all federal estate taxes and state inheritance or succession taxes payable upon or resulting from or by reason of my death (herein "Death Taxes") attributable to property which is part of the trust estate of the MICHAEL JACKSON FAMILY TRUST, including property which passes to said trust from my probate estate shall be paid by the Trustee of said trust in accordance with its terms. Death Taxes attributable to property passing outside this Will, other than property constituting the trust estate of the trust mentioned in the preceding sentence, shall be charged against the taker of said property.

V. I appoint JOHN BRANCA, JOHN McCLAIN and BARRY SIEGEL as co-Executors of this Will. In the event of any of their deaths, resignations, inability, failure or refusal to serve or continue to serve as a co-Executor, the other shall serve and no replacement need be named. The co-Executors serving at any time after my death may name one or more replacements to serve in the event that none of the three named individuals is willing or able to serve at any time.

The term "my executors" as used in this Will shall include any duly acting personal representative or representatives of my estate. No individual acting as such need past a bond.

I hereby give to my Executors, full power and authority at any time or times to sell, lease, mortgage, pledge, exchange or otherwise dispose of the property, whether real or personal comprising my estate, upon such terms as my Executors shall deem best, to continue any business enterprises, to purchase assets from my estate, to continue in force and pay any insurance policy * * * .

VI. Except as otherwise provided in this Will or in the Trust referred to in Article III hereof, I have intentionally omitted to provide for my heirs. I have intentionally omitted to provide for my former wife, DEBORAH JEAN ROWE JACKSON.

* * * *

VIII. If any of my children are minors at the time of my death, I nominate my mother, KATHERINE JACKSON as guardian of the persons and estates of such minor children. If KATHERINE JACKSON fails to survive me, or is unable or unwilling to act as guardian, I nominate DIANA ROSS as guardian of the persons and estates of such minor children.

* * * *

Devise A gift of real property by will, or the act of giving real property by will.

Bequest A gift of personal property by will (from the verb *to bequeath*).

Legacy A gift of personal property under a will.

Devisee One designated in a will to receive a gift of real property.

Legatee One designated in a will to receive a gift of personal property.

A gift of real estate by will is generally called a **devise**, and a gift of personal property by will is called a **bequest**, or **legacy**. The recipient of a gift by will is a **devisee** or a **legatee**, depending on whether the gift was a devise or a legacy.

Types of Gifts

Gifts by will can be specific, general, or residuary. A *specific* devise or bequest (legacy) describes particular property (such as "Eastwood Estate" or "my gold pocket watch") that can be distinguished from all the rest of the testator's property.

A *general* devise or bequest (legacy) uses less restrictive terminology. For instance, "I devise all my lands" is a general devise. A general bequest often specifies a dollar amount instead of a particular item of property, such as a watch or an automobile. "I give to my nephew, Carleton, $30,000," for example, is a general bequest.

Abatement If the assets of an estate are insufficient to pay in full all general bequests provided for in the will, an *abatement* takes place, meaning the legatees receive reduced benefits. **EXAMPLE 37.4** Yusuf's will leaves $15,000 each to his children, Tamara and Kwame. On Yusuf's death, only $10,000 is available to honor these bequests. By abatement, each child will receive $5,000. ●

If bequests are more complicated, abatement may be more complex. The testator's intent, as expressed in the will, controls.

Residuary Clause

Sometimes, a will provides that any assets remaining after the estate's debts have been paid and specific gifts have been made are to be distributed in a specific way through a *residuary clause.* Residuary clauses are often used when the exact amount to be distributed cannot be determined until all of the other gifts and payouts have been made. If the testator has *not* indicated what party or parties should receive the residuary of the estate, the residuary passes according to state laws of intestacy.

LEARNING OBJECTIVE 3
What are the basic requirements for executing a will?

Requirements for a Valid Will

A will must comply with statutory formalities designed to ensure that the testator understood his or her actions at the time the will was made. These formalities are intended to help prevent fraud. Unless they are followed, the will is declared void, and the decedent's property is distributed according to the laws of intestacy of that state, as discussed later in this chapter.

Although the required formalities vary among jurisdictions, most states uphold certain basic requirements for executing a will. The National Conference of Commissioners on Uniform State Laws has issued the Uniform Probate Code (UPC). Almost half of the states have enacted some part of the UPC and incorporated it into their own probate codes.

For a valid will, most states require proof of (1) the testator's capacity, (2) testamentary intent, (3) a written document, (4) the testator's signature, and (5) the signatures of persons who witnessed the testator sign the will.

KNOW THIS

In most states, the age of majority for contractual purposes is eighteen years.

Testamentary Capacity and Intent

To have testamentary capacity, a testator must be of legal age and sound mind *at the time the will is made.* The minimum legal age for executing a will in most states and under the UPC is eighteen years [UPC 2–501]. Thus, the will of a twenty-one-year-old decedent written when the person was sixteen is invalid if, under state law, the legal age for executing a will is eighteen.

The concept of "being of sound mind" refers to the testator's ability to formulate and to comprehend a personal plan for the disposition of property. Persons who have been declared incompetent in a legal proceeding do not meet the sound mind requirement.

A valid will is one that represents the maker's intention to transfer and distribute her or his property. Generally, a testator must:

1. Know the nature of the act (of making a will).
2. Comprehend and remember the "natural objects of his or her bounty" (usually, family members and persons for whom the testator has affection).
3. Know the nature and extent of her or his property.
4. Understand the distribution of assets called for by the will.

"If you want to see a man's true character, watch him divide an estate."

Benjamin Franklin, 1706–1790
(American diplomat, author, and scientist)

Undue Influence When it can be shown that the decedent's plan of distribution was the result of fraud or of undue influence, the will is declared invalid. A court may sometimes infer undue influence when the named beneficiary was in a position to influence the making of the will. If the testator ignored blood relatives and named as a beneficiary a nonrelative who was in constant close contact with the testator, for instance, a court might infer undue influence.

EXAMPLE 37.5 Frieda is a nurse who was responsible for caring for Julie, the testator, during the last years of her life. After Julie's death, her family discovers that her will names Frieda as a beneficiary and excludes all family members. If Julie's family challenges the validity of the will on the basis of undue influence, the court might infer that Frieda unduly influenced Julie and declare the will invalid. ●

In the following case, a testator's children and grandchildren claimed that his third wife had unduly influenced him to create a new will that did not provide for them. After a jury trial, the court declared the will invalid. An appellate court had to determine if there was sufficient evidence of undue influence to support the jury's verdict.

Case 37.2

In re Estate of Johnson

Court of Appeals of Texas, San Antonio, 340 S.W.3d 769 (2011).

(AP Photo/Paul Iverson)

FACTS Belton Kleberg Johnson was a descendant of the founders of the King Ranch, a famous ranch in Texas that dates back to the 1850s. He was married three times and had three children from his first marriage, as well as eight grandchildren. Johnson was a long-term alcoholic, who had received both inpatient and outpatient treatment at alcohol rehabilitation facilities during his life. While married to his second wife, Johnson executed a will that provided for her during her lifetime and left the remainder of his estate in a trust for his children and grandchildren. When his second wife died, he changed the will to give $1 million to each grandchild and the remainder to five charities. His children were provided for in a separate trust. While married to his third wife, Laura, he executed a will that left $1 million to each grandchild and the rest to Laura. Two years later, in 1999, another will left his entire estate in trust to Laura for her life and then to a foundation that she controlled.

ISSUE Was Johnson's 1999 will, which left his entire estate to Laura and excluded his children and grandchildren, a result of undue influence?

DECISION Yes. The state appellate court affirmed the lower court's judgment in favor of the plaintiffs. The court concluded that Johnson's last will was invalid due to Laura's undue influence.

REASON To prevail on an undue influence claim in Texas, the plaintiff must prove that (1) undue influence was exerted, (2) the influence overpowered the mind of the testator, and (3) the will would not have been executed but for the undue influence. The court reasoned that Johnson was an admitted alcoholic with permanent cognitive defects and memory problems that would have caused him to be more susceptible to undue influence. Because the exertion of undue influence is usually subtle, the court considered the extended course of dealings and circumstances in this case. Evidence suggested that Laura had exerted substantial control over many aspects of Johnson's life, and her in-court testimony denying Johnson's drinking problem cast doubt on her truthfulness. Evidence also established that Johnson was quite proud of his heritage and wanted to provide for his descendants, as well as for the charities named in the earlier will.

WHAT IF THE FACTS WERE DIFFERENT? *Suppose that Johnson, in his 1999 will, had specifically mentioned that it was his intention that his children and grandchildren not receive any portion of his estate. Would that have changed the outcome? Why or why not?*

Disinheritance There is no requirement that testators give their estate to the natural objects of their bounty. A testator may decide to disinherit, or leave nothing to, an individual for various reasons. Most states have laws that attempt to prevent accidental disinheritance, however. There are also laws that protect minor children from loss of the family residence. Therefore, the testator's intent to disinherit needs to be clear.

The following case involved a will in the form of a testamentary letter that left the decedent's entire estate to a friend and explicitly disinherited his family. The friend died before the decedent, so the court had to decide whether to follow the state's intestacy laws or enforce the disinheritance clause.

Case 37.3

In re Estate of Melton

Supreme Court of Nevada, 272 P.3d 668 (2012). caselaw.findlaw.com[a]

(stockcreations/iStockphoto.com)

Can a person disinherit his or her daughter?

FACTS In 1975, William Melton executed a will that, among other things, stated that his daughter, Vicki Palm, was to receive nothing. In 1979, he added a handwritten note to the will, saying that his friend, Alberta Kelleher, was to receive a small portion of his estate. In 1995, Melton sent a

a. Under "State Supreme, Appellate, and Trial Courts," click on "Nevada." When that page opens, click on "Supreme Court of Nevada." In the "Party name:" box, type "Melton," and click on "Search." In the result, click on the case name to access the opinion. FindLaw maintains this Web site.

Case 37.3—Continues next page

Case 37.3—Continued

signed, handwritten letter to Kelleher. In the letter, Melton said he was returning from his mother's funeral and, because she had died in an automobile accident, he wanted to put "something in writing" leaving Kelleher his "entire estate." Melton also said, "I do not want my brother Larry J. Melton or Vicki Palm or any of my other relatives to have one penny of my estate." When Melton died in 2008, Kelleher had already passed away, and Palm was his only natural heir. The state of Nevada argued that it should receive everything because Palm had been disinherited. Nevertheless, the trial court applied the state's intestacy laws and distributed the entire estate to Palm. The state appealed.

ISSUE Could Melton bypass Nevada's intestacy laws through a will that disinherited his family but failed to dispose of his property?

DECISION Yes. The Nevada Supreme Court reversed the judgment of the lower court. It held that the disinheritance clause was enforceable and that Melton's estate should go to the state of Nevada.

REASON Under the common law, the courts have developed two rules to determine whether a disinheritance clause should apply to any property that is not distributed by the will. Under the English rule, a disinheritance clause is enforceable only if "at least one . . . heir remained eligible to receive the intestate property." Under the American rule, the testator must "affirmatively dispos[e] of the entire estate through a will." Many courts follow the American rule because disinheritance clauses create complications when they are applied to intestate property. For example, some courts say that such clauses "create an undesirable 'mixing' of the probate and intestacy systems by requiring courts to alter the distribution scheme provided in the intestacy statute." The state of Nevada, however, has rejected the common law rule by defining a will to include a "testamentary instrument that merely . . . excludes or limits the right of an individual or class to succeed to property of the decedent passing by intestate succession." As a result, Melton could disinherit his family without giving his property to someone else. Therefore, the state was entitled to Melton's property.

CRITICAL THINKING—Legal Consideration *Based on the information presented here, did Melton have testamentary intent when he wrote his letter? Why or why not?*

Holographic Will A will written entirely in the testator's handwriting.

Noncupative Will An oral will (often called a *deathbed will*) made before witnesses. Usually, such wills are limited to transfers of personal property.

Writing Requirements

Generally, a will must be in writing. The writing itself can be informal as long as it substantially complies with the statutory requirements. In some states, a will can be handwritten in crayon or ink. It can be written on a sheet or scrap of paper, on a paper bag, or on a piece of cloth. A will that is completely in the handwriting of the testator is called a **holographic will** (sometimes referred to as an *olographic will*).

In some instances, a court may find an oral will valid. A **nuncupative will** is an oral will made before witnesses. It is not permitted in most states. Where authorized by statute, such wills are generally valid only if made during the last illness of the testator and are therefore sometimes referred to as *deathbed wills*. Normally, only personal property can be transferred by a nuncupative will. Statutes frequently permit members of the military to make nuncupative wills when on active duty.

Signature Requirements

A fundamental requirement is that the testator's signature must appear on the will, generally at the end. Each jurisdiction dictates by statute and court decision what constitutes a signature. Initials, an X or other mark, and words such as "Mom" have all been upheld as valid when it was shown that the testators *intended* them to be signatures.

Witness Requirements

A will usually must be attested (sworn to) by two, and sometimes three, witnesses. The number of witnesses, their qualifications, and the manner in which the witnessing must be done are generally set out in a statute. A witness can be required to be disinterested—that is, not a beneficiary under the will. The UPC, however, provides that a will is valid even if it is attested by an interested witness [UPC 2–505]. There are no age requirements for witnesses, but they must be mentally competent.

The purpose of the witnesses is to verify that the testator actually executed (signed) the will and had the requisite intent and capacity at the time. A witness does not have to read

(©mr. Brightside, 2009. Used under license from Shutterstock.com)

Is tearing up a will a legally recognized method of revoking that will?

the contents of the will. Usually, the testator and all witnesses sign in the sight or the presence of one another, but there are exceptions.[3] The UPC does not require all parties to sign in the presence of one another and deems it sufficient if the testator acknowledges her or his signature to the witnesses [UPC 2–502]. The UPC also provides an alternative to traditional witnesses—the signature may be acknowledged by the testator before a notary public.

Publication

A will is *published* by an oral declaration by the maker to the witnesses that the document they are about to sign is his or her "last will and testament." In most states, publication is an unnecessary formality, and it is not required under the UPC.

Revocation of Wills

The testator can revoke a will at any time during his or her life, either by a physical act, such as tearing up the will, or by a subsequent writing. Wills can also be revoked by operation of law. Revocation can be partial or complete, and it must follow certain strict formalities.

Revocation by a Physical Act of the Maker

A testator can revoke a will by *intentionally* burning, tearing, canceling, obliterating, or otherwise destroying it, or by having someone else do so in the testator's presence and at the testator's direction.[4]

In some states, partial revocation by physical act of the testator is recognized. Thus, those portions of a will lined out or torn away are dropped, and the remaining parts of the will are valid. In no circumstances, however, can a provision be crossed out and an additional or substitute provision written in. Such altered portions require reexecution (resigning) and reattestation (rewitnessing).

To revoke a will by physical act, it is necessary to follow the mandates of a state statute exactly. When a state statute prescribes the specific methods for revoking a will by physical act, only those methods can be used to revoke the will.

Codicil A written supplement or modification to a will. A codicil must be executed with the same formalities as a will.

Revocation by a Subsequent Writing

A will may also be wholly or partially revoked by a **codicil,** a written instrument separate from the will that amends or revokes provisions in the will. A codicil eliminates the necessity of redrafting an entire will merely to add to it or amend it. A codicil can also be used to revoke an entire will. The codicil must be executed with the same formalities required for a will, and it must refer expressly to the will. In effect, it updates a will because the will is "incorporated by reference" into the codicil.

A new will (second will) can be executed that may or may not revoke the first or a prior will, depending on the language used. To revoke a prior will, the second will must use language specifically revoking other wills, such as "This will hereby revokes all prior wills." If the second will is otherwise valid and properly executed, it will revoke all prior wills. If the express *declaration of revocation* is missing, then both wills are read together. If there are any discrepancies between the wills, the second will controls.

Revocation by Operation of Law

Revocation by *operation of law* occurs when marriage, divorce or annulment, or the birth of a child takes place after a will has been executed.

Marriage and Divorce

In most states, when a testator marries after executing a will that does not include the new spouse, on the testator's death, the spouse will receive a share of the testator's estate. The surviving spouse normally receives the amount that he or she

3. See, for example, *Slack v. Truitt,* 368 Md. 2, 791 A.2d 129 (2000).

4. The destruction cannot be inadvertent. The testator must have the intent to revoke the will.

would have taken had the testator died intestate—that is, without a will (see page 964 on intestate succession). This is called an *elective share,* or a *forced share,* and it is often one-third of the estate or an amount equal to a spouse's share under intestacy laws.

In effect, the will is revoked to the point of providing the spouse with an intestate share. The rest of the estate is passed under the will [UPC 2–301, 2–508]. If, however, the new spouse is otherwise provided for in the will (or by transfer of property outside the will), he or she will not be given an intestate amount. Also, if the parties had a valid *prenuptial agreement* (see page 316 of Chapter 12), its provisions dictate what the surviving spouse receives.

Divorce does not necessarily revoke the entire will.[5] A divorce or an annulment occurring after a will has been executed revokes those dispositions of property made under the will to the former spouse [UPC 2–508].

Children If a child is born after a will has been executed and if it appears that the deceased parent would have made a provision for the child, that child may be entitled to a portion of the estate. Most state laws allow a child to receive some portion of a parent's estate even if no provision is made in the parent's will. This is true *unless it is clear from the will's terms that the testator intended to disinherit the child* (see Case 37.3 on page 959 for an example of disinheritance). Under the UPC, the rule is the same.

Probate Procedures and Estate Planning

Probate The process of proving and validating a will and settling all matters pertaining to an estate.

To **probate** a will means to establish its validity and to carry the administration of the estate through a court process. Probate laws vary from state to state. Typically, the procedure depends on the size and complexity of the decedent's estate.

People commonly engage in estate planning in an attempt to avoid formal probate procedures and to maximize the value of their estate by reducing taxes and other expenses. Individuals should also consider formulating a social media estate plan, as discussed in this chapter's *Adapting the Law to the Online Environment* feature on the facing page.

Informal Probate

For smaller estates, most state statutes provide for the distribution of assets without formal probate proceedings. Faster and less expensive methods are then used. Property can be transferred by *affidavit* (a written statement taken before a person who has authority to affirm it), and problems or questions can be handled during an administrative hearing. Some state statutes allow title to cars, savings and checking accounts, and certain other property to be transferred simply by filling out forms.

A majority of states also provide for *family settlement agreements,* which are private agreements among the beneficiaries. Once a will is admitted to probate, the family members can agree among themselves on how to distribute the decedent's assets. Although a family settlement agreement speeds the settlement process, a court order is still needed to protect the estate from future creditors and to clear title to the assets involved.

Formal Probate

For larger estates, formal probate proceedings normally are undertaken, and the probate court supervises every aspect of the process. Additionally, in some situations—such as when a guardian for minor children must be appointed—more formal probate procedures cannot be avoided.

Formal probate proceedings may take several months or several years to complete, depending on the size and complexity of the estate and whether the will is contested. As a result, a sizable portion of the decedent's assets (as much as 10 percent) may go toward payment of court costs and fees charged by attorneys and personal representatives.

5. Note that the 2008 amendments to the UPC, which have been adopted by only a few states, provide for automatic revocation of testamentary devises on divorce [amended UPC 2–804].

ADAPTING THE LAW TO THE ONLINE ENVIRONMENT

SOCIAL MEDIA ESTATE PLANNING

People are generally quite careful about choosing the personal representatives who will deal with their real estate, bank accounts, and investments after they are gone. Today, the same care should be taken in choosing an online executor to deal with a deceased's online identity, particularly in social media.

What an Online Executor Should Do

An online executor is responsible for dealing with a decedent's e-mail addresses, social media profiles, and blogs. E-mail accounts should be closed, but some people do not want their social media profiles to be erased after they die. They want the profiles to be maintained, at least for some specified time after death, so that family and friends can visit them. Some people ask that the online executor place a memorial profile in their social media accounts.

Why Social Media Estate Planning Is Important

Online estate planning is essential because the deceased can still be a victim of identity theft. Unscrupulous fraudsters often use dead people's online identities to defraud private companies, individuals, and federal and state governments. If all of a person's e-mail addresses and social media accounts are closed, it is harder for online fraudsters to use them for identity theft.

In addition, closing an e-mail account not only protects family members from being harassed with continuing spam after the person's death but also prevents spammers from hijacking the account. Spammers can use a dead person's e-mail account as the sender of billions of unwanted bulk e-mails.

Critical Thinking

Why might an online executor need a copy of the deceased's death certificate?

Will Substitutes Various instruments, such as living trusts or life insurance plans, that may be used to avoid the formal probate process.

Property Transfers outside the Probate Process Often, a person can avoid the cost of probate by employing various **will substitutes**—for example, *living trusts* (see page 966), life insurance policies or individual retirement accounts (IRAs) with named beneficiaries, or joint-tenancy arrangements.[6] Not all alternatives to formal probate administration are suitable to every estate, however.

PREVENTING LEGAL DISPUTES

For most people, estate planning involves not only ensuring that, after they die, their property goes to the intended recipients, but also avoiding probate and maximizing their estates. To this end, many choose to set up a living trust, arrange for a joint tenancy, or name beneficiaries of an IRA or an insurance policy.

If you use these will substitutes, though, you should be aware that a court will not apply the same principles in reviewing a transfer outside the probate process as it would apply to a testamentary transfer. Therefore, any such arrangements must be carefully drafted by your attorney and must comply with all legal requirements. To avoid disputes between beneficiaries after your death, make sure that your words and actions in such property transfers are clear and represent the final expression of your intent.

Intestacy Laws

As mentioned earlier, each state regulates by statute how property will be distributed when a person dies intestate (without a valid will). Intestacy laws attempt to carry out the likely intent and wishes of the decedent.

These laws assume that deceased persons would have intended that their natural heirs (spouses, children, grandchildren, or other family members) inherit their property.

6. Recall from Chapters 35 and 36 that in a joint tenancy, when one joint tenant dies, the other joint tenant or tenants automatically inherit the deceased tenant's share of the property.

Therefore, intestacy statutes set out rules and priorities under which these heirs inherit the property. If no heirs exist, the state will assume ownership of the property. The rules of descent vary widely from state to state.

"You cannot live without the lawyers, and certainly you cannot die without them."

Joseph H. Choate, 1832–1917 (American lawyer and diplomat)

Surviving Spouse and Children Usually, state statutes provide that the estate must be used to satisfy first the debts of the decedent. Then, the remaining assets pass to the surviving spouse and to the children. A surviving spouse usually receives only a share of the estate—one-half if there is also a surviving child and one-third if there are two or more children. Only if no children or grandchildren survive the decedent will a surviving spouse be entitled to the entire estate.

EXAMPLE 37.6 Allen dies intestate and is survived by his wife, Beth, and his children, Duane and Tara. Allen's property passes according to intestacy laws. After his outstanding debts are paid, Beth will receive the homestead (either in fee simple or as a life estate) and ordinarily a one-third interest in all other property. The remaining real and personal property will pass to Duane and Tara in equal portions. •

Under most state intestacy laws and under the UPC, in-laws do not share in an estate. If a child dies before his or her parents, the child's spouse will not receive an inheritance on the parents' death. For instance, if Duane died before his father (Allen) in *Example 37.6,* Duane's spouse would not inherit Duane's share of Allen's estate.

When There Is No Surviving Spouse or Child When there is no surviving spouse or child, the order of inheritance is grandchildren, then brothers and sisters, and, in some states, parents of the decedent. These relatives are usually called *lineal descendants.*

If there are no lineal descendants, then *collateral heirs*—nieces, nephews, aunts, and uncles of the decedent—make up the next group to share. If there are no survivors in any of these groups, most statutes provide for the property to be distributed among the next of kin of the collateral heirs.

Stepchildren, Adopted Children, and Illegitimate Children Under intestacy laws, stepchildren are not considered kin. Legally adopted children, however, are recognized as lawful heirs of their adoptive parents (as are children who are in the process of being adopted at the time of death). Statutes vary from state to state in regard to the inheritance rights of illegitimate children (children born out of wedlock).

Generally, an illegitimate child is treated as the child of the mother and can inherit from her and her relatives. Traditionally, the child was not regarded as the legal child of the father for inheritance purposes—unless paternity was established through some legal proceeding.

Because of the dramatic increase in the number of children born out of wedlock today, many states have relaxed their laws of inheritance. A majority of states now consider a child born of any union that has the characteristics of a formal marriage relationship (such as unmarried parents who cohabit) to be legitimate. Under the revised UPC, a child is the child of his or her natural (biological) parents, regardless of their marital status, as long as the natural parent has openly treated the child as her or his child [UPC 2–114]. Although illegitimate children may have inheritance rights in most states, their rights are not necessarily identical to those of legitimate children.

LEARNING OBJECTIVE 4
What is the difference between a *per stirpes* distribution and a *per capita* distribution of an estate to the grandchildren of the deceased?

Grandchildren Usually, a will provides for how the decedent's estate will be distributed to descendants of deceased children—that is, to the decedent's grandchildren. If a will does not include such a provision—or if a person dies intestate—the question arises as to what share the grandchildren of the decedent will receive. Each state designates one of two methods of distributing the assets of intestate decedents.

Per Stirpes A method of distributing an intestate's estate so that each heir in a certain class (such as grandchildren) takes the share to which her or his deceased ancestor (such as a mother or father) would have been entitled.

Per Stirpes *Distribution* One method of dividing an intestate's estate is ***per stirpes***.[7] Under this method, within a class or group of distributees (for example, grandchildren), the children of any one descendant take the share that their deceased parent *would have been* entitled to inherit.

EXAMPLE 37.7 Michael, a widower, has two children, Scott and Jonathan. Scott has two children (Becky and Holly), and Jonathan has one child (Paul). Scott and Jonathan die before their father, and then Michael dies. If Michael's estate is distributed *per stirpes,* Becky and Holly each receive one-fourth of the estate (dividing Scott's one-half share). Paul receives one-half of the estate (taking Jonathan's one-half share). Exhibit 37.4 below illustrates the *per stirpes* method of distribution. •

Per Capita A method of distributing an intestate's estate so that each heir in a certain class (such as grandchildren) receives an equal share.

Per Capita *Distribution* An estate may also be distributed on a ***per capita***[8] basis, which means that each person in a class or group takes an equal share of the estate. If Michael's estate is distributed *per capita,* Becky, Holly, and Paul each receive a one-third share. Exhibit 37.5 on the next page illustrates the *per capita* method of distribution.

Trusts

Trust An arrangement in which title to property is held by one person (a trustee) for the benefit of another (a beneficiary).

A **trust** is any arrangement through which property is transferred from one person to a trustee to be administered for the transferor's or another party's benefit. It can also be defined as a right of property held by one party for the benefit of another. A trust can be created for any purpose that is not illegal or against public policy, and it can be express or implied.

The essential elements of a trust are as follows:

LEARNING OBJECTIVE 5
What are the four essential elements of a trust? What is the difference between an express trust and an implied trust?

1. A designated beneficiary.
2. A designated trustee.
3. A fund sufficiently identified to enable title to pass to the trustee.
4. Actual delivery by the *settlor* or *grantor* (the person creating the trust) to the trustee with the intention of passing title.

7. *Per stirpes* is a Latin term meaning "by the roots" or "by stock." When used in estate law, it means proportionally divided between beneficiaries according to their deceased ancestor's share.
8. *Per capita* is a Latin term meaning "per person" or "for each head." When used in estate law, it means equally divided between beneficiaries.

Exhibit 37.4 *Per Stirpes* Distribution

Under this method of distribution, an heir takes the share that his or her deceased parent would have been entitled to inherit had the parent lived. This may mean that a class of distributees—the grandchildren in this example—will not inherit in equal portions. Note that Becky and Holly receive only one-fourth of Michael's estate while Paul inherits one-half.

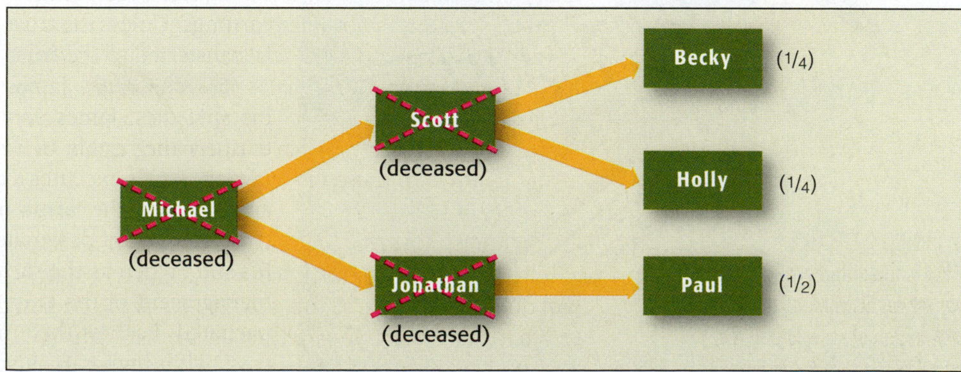

Exhibit 37.5 ***Per Capita* Distribution**

Under this method of distribution, all heirs in a certain class—in this example, the grandchildren—inherit equally. Note that Becky and Holly in this situation each inherit one-third, as does Paul.

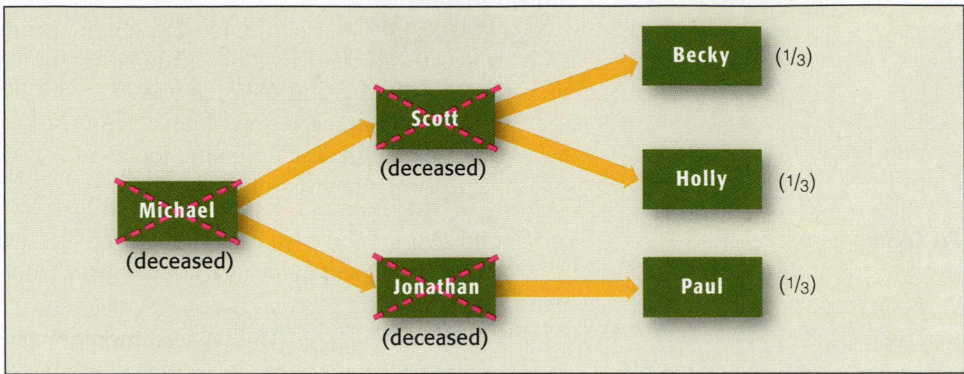

Express Trusts

An express trust is created or declared in explicit terms, usually in writing. There are many types of express trusts, each with its own special characteristics.

Living *(Inter Vivos)* Trust A trust created by the grantor (settlor) and effective during his or her lifetime.

Living Trusts

A ***living trust***—or *inter vivos trust* (*inter vivos* is Latin for "between or among the living")—is a trust created by a grantor during her or his lifetime. Living trusts have become a popular estate-planning option because at the grantor's death, assets held in a living trust can pass to the heirs without going through probate.

Note, however, that living trusts do not shelter assets from estate taxes, and the grantor may still have to pay income taxes on trust earnings—depending on whether the trust is revocable or irrevocable.

Revocable Living Trusts Living trusts can be revocable or irrevocable. In a *revocable* living trust, which is the most common type, the grantor retains control over the trust property during her or his lifetime. The grantor deeds the property to the trust but retains the power to amend, alter, or revoke the trust during her or his lifetime.

The grantor may also serve as a trustee or co-trustee and can arrange to receive income earned by the trust assets during her or his lifetime. Because the grantor is in control of the funds, she or he is required to pay income taxes on the trust earnings. Unless the trust is revoked, the principal of the trust is transferred to the trust beneficiary on the grantor's death.

EXAMPLE 37.8 James Cortez owns a large farm. After his wife dies, James contacts his attorney to create a living trust for the benefit of his three children, Alicia, Emma, and Jayden. James executes a deed conveying the farm to the trust and transfers the farm's bank accounts into the name of the trust. The trust designates James as the trustee and names his son Jayden as the *successor trustee,* who will take over the management of the trust when James dies or becomes incapacitated. Each of the children will receive income from the trust while James is alive. When James dies, the farm will

Who would want to create a living trust?

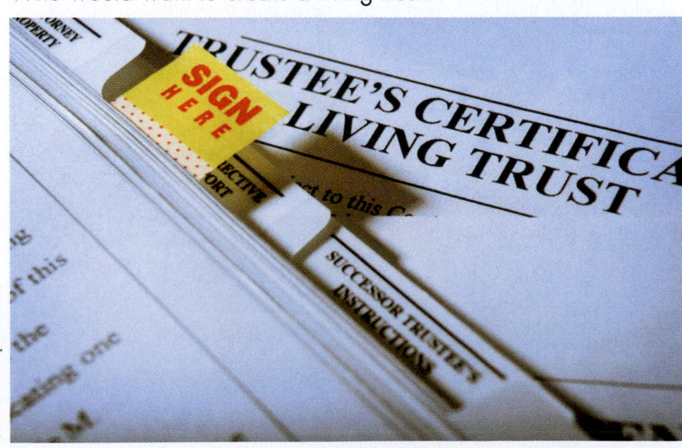

(DNY59/iStockphoto.com)

pass to them without having to go through probate. By holding the property in a revocable living trust, James still has control over the farm during his life. This trust arrangement is illustrated in Exhibit 37.6 below. •

Irrevocable Living Trusts In an *irrevocable* living trust, in contrast, the grantor permanently gives up control over the property to the trustee. The grantor executes a trust deed, and legal title to the trust property passes to the named trustee. The trustee has a duty to administer the property as directed by the grantor for the benefit and in the interest of the beneficiaries.

The trustee must preserve the trust property, make it productive, and pay income to the beneficiaries if required by the terms of the trust agreement. Because the grantor has, in effect, given over the property for the benefit of the beneficiaries, he or she is no longer responsible for paying income taxes on the trust earnings.

Testamentary Trust A trust that is created by will and therefore does not take effect until the death of the testator.

Testamentary Trusts

A **testamentary trust** is created by will and comes into existence on the settlor's death. Although a testamentary trust has a trustee who maintains legal title to the trust property, the trustee's actions are subject to judicial approval. This trustee can be named in the will or be appointed by the court. Thus, a testamentary trust does not fail because a trustee has not been named in the will. The legal responsibilities of the trustee are the same as in an *inter vivos* trust.

If a court finds that the will setting up a testamentary trust is invalid, then the trust will also be invalid. The property that was supposed to be in the trust will then pass according to intestacy laws, not according to the terms of the trust.

Charitable Trust A trust in which the property held by the trustee must be used for a charitable purpose, such as the advancement of health, education, or religion.

Charitable Trusts

A **charitable trust** is an express trust designed for the benefit of a segment of the public or the public in general. It differs from other types of trusts in that the identities of the beneficiaries are uncertain and it can be established to last indefinitely. Usually, to be deemed a charitable trust, a trust must be created for charitable, educational, religious, or scientific purposes.

Spendthrift Trust A trust created to protect the beneficiary from spending all the funds to which she or he is entitled. Only a certain portion of the total amount is given to the beneficiary at any one time, and most states prohibit creditors from attaching assets of the trust.

Spendthrift Trusts

A **spendthrift trust** is created to provide for the maintenance of a beneficiary by preventing him or her from being careless with the bestowed funds. Unlike the beneficiaries of other trusts, the beneficiary in a spendthrift trust is not permitted to transfer or assign his or her right to the trust's principal or future payments from the trust (*assignments* were discussed in Chapter 13).

Essentially, the beneficiary can withdraw only a certain portion of the total amount to which he or she is entitled at any one time. The majority of states allow spendthrift trust provisions that prohibit creditors from attaching such trusts.

Exhibit 37.6 A Revocable Living Trust Arrangement

Totten Trust A trust created when a person deposits funds in his or her own name for a specific beneficiary, who will receive the funds of the depositor's death. The trust is revocable at will until the depositor dies or completes the gift.

Totten Trusts

A **Totten trust**[9] is created when one person deposits funds in her or his own name with instructions that on the settlor's death, whatever is in that account should go to a specific beneficiary. This trust is revocable at will until the depositor dies or completes the gift during her or his lifetime (by delivering the funds to the intended beneficiary, for example). The beneficiary has no access to the funds until the depositor's death, when the beneficiary obtains property rights to the balance on hand.

Implied Trusts

Sometimes, a trust will be imposed (implied) by law, even in the absence of an express trust. Implied trusts include resulting trusts and constructive trusts.

Constructive Trust An equitable trust that is imposed in the interests of fairness and justice when someone wrongfully holds legal title to property.

Constructive Trusts

A **constructive trust** is an equitable trust imposed by a court in the interests of fairness and justice. In a constructive trust, the owner is declared to be a trustee for the parties who are, in equity, actually entitled to the benefits that flow from the trust. Courts often impose constructive trusts when someone who is in a confidential or fiduciary relationship with another person, such as a guardian to a ward, has breached a duty to that person.

If someone wrongfully holds legal title to property—because the property was obtained through fraud or in breach of a legal duty, for example—a court may impose a constructive trust. **CASE EXAMPLE 37.9** Stella Jankowski added her niece Genevieve Viarengo as a joint owner on bank accounts and other financial assets valued at $500,000. Jankowski also executed a will that divided her estate equally among her ten nieces, nephews, and cousins, and named Viarengo and Richard Golebiewski as coexecutors. She did not tell the attorney who drafted the will about the jointly held accounts.

When Jankowski died, Viarengo emptied her safe, removed her financial records, and claimed that the funds in the accounts were hers. Jankowski's other relatives filed a suit and asked the court to impose a constructive trust. The court found that Viarengo had committed fraud in obtaining the assets that she had held jointly with Jankowski and would be unjustly enriched if she were allowed to retain them. Therefore, the court imposed a constructive trust.[10] ●

Resulting Trust An implied trust arising from the conduct of the parties. When one party holds the actual legal title to another's property only for that other person's benefit.

Resulting Trust

A **resulting trust** arises from the conduct of the parties. When circumstances raise an inference that one party holds legal title to the property for the benefit of another, a court may infer a resulting trust.

EXAMPLE 37.10 Fuentes wants to put one acre of land she owns on the market for sale. Because she is going out of the country for two years and will not be able to deed the property to a buyer during that period, Fuentes conveys (transfers) the property to her good friend Oswald. Oswald can then attempt to sell the property while Fuentes is gone. Because the intent of the transaction in which Fuentes conveyed the property to Oswald is neither a sale nor a gift, the property will be held in trust (a resulting trust) by Oswald for the benefit of Fuentes. Therefore, on Fuentes's return, Oswald will be required either to deed back the property to Fuentes or, if the property has been sold, to turn over the proceeds (held in trust) to her. ●

---

9. This type of trust derives its unusual name from the case, *In re Totten,* 179 N.Y. 112, 71 N.E. 748 (1904).

10. *Garrigus v. Viarengo,* 112 Conn.App. 655, 963 A.2d 1065 (2009).

The Trustee

The *trustee* is the person holding the trust property. Anyone legally capable of holding title to, and dealing in, property can be a trustee. If the settlor of a trust fails to name a trustee, or if a named trustee cannot or will not serve, the trust does not fail—an appropriate court can appoint a trustee.

Trustee's Duties

A trustee must act with honesty, good faith, and prudence in administering the trust and must exercise a high degree of loyalty toward the trust beneficiary. The general standard of care is the degree of care a prudent person would exercise in his or her personal affairs.[11] The duty of loyalty requires that the trustee act in the exclusive interest of the beneficiary.

A trustee's specific duties include the following:

1. Maintain clear and accurate accounts of the trust's administration.
2. Furnish complete and correct information to the beneficiary.
3. Keep trust assets separate from her or his own assets.
4. Pay to an income beneficiary the net income of the trust assets at reasonable intervals.
5. Distribute the risk of loss from investments by reasonable diversification and dispose of assets that do not represent prudent investments. (Prudent investment choices might include federal, state, or municipal bonds and some corporate bonds and stocks.)

Trustee's Powers

When a settlor creates a trust, he or she may set forth the trustee's powers and performance. State law governs in the absence of specific terms in the trust, and the states often restrict the trustee's investment of trust funds.

> "Put not your trust in money, but put your money in trust."
>
> Oliver Wendell Holmes, Jr., 1841–1935 (Associate justice of the United States Supreme Court, 1902–1932)

Typically, statutes confine trustees to investments in conservative debt securities such as government, utility, and railroad bonds. Frequently, though, a settlor grants a trustee discretionary investment power. In that circumstance, any statute may be considered only advisory, with the trustee's decisions subject in most states to the prudent person rule. Of course, a trustee is responsible for carrying out the purposes of the trust. If the trustee fails to comply with the terms of the trust or the controlling statute, he or she is personally liable for any loss.

Allocations between Principal and Income

Often, a settlor will provide one beneficiary with a life estate and another beneficiary with the remainder interest in a trust. A farmer, for instance, may create a testamentary trust providing that the farm's income be paid to her surviving spouse and that on the surviving spouse's death, the farm be given to their children. In this example, the surviving spouse has a *life estate* in the farm's income, and the children have a *remainder interest* in the farm (the principal).

When a trust is set up in this manner, questions may arise as to how the receipts and expenses for the farm's management and the trust's administration should be allocated between income and principal. When a trust instrument does not provide instructions, a trustee must refer to applicable state law. The general rule is that ordinary receipts and expenses are chargeable to the income beneficiary, whereas extraordinary receipts and expenses are allocated to the principal beneficiaries.[12] For example, the receipt of rent from trust realty would be ordinary, as would the expense of paying the property's taxes. The cost of long-term improvements and proceeds from the property's sale, however, would be extraordinary.

---

11. Revised Uniform Principal and Income Act, Section 2(a)(3); *Restatement (Third) of Trusts (Prudent Investor Rule),* Section 227. This rule is in force in the majority of states by statute and in a small number of states under the common law.

12. Revised Uniform Principal and Income Act, Sections 3, 6, 8, and 13; *Restatement (Second) of Trusts,* Section 233.

Reviewing . . . Insurance, Wills, and Trusts

In June 2013, Bernard Ramish set up a $48,000 trust fund through West Plains Credit Union to provide tuition for his nephew, Nathan Covacek, to attend Tri-State Polytechnic Institute. The trust was established under Ramish's control and went into effect that August. In December, Ramish suffered a brain aneurysm that caused frequent, severe headaches but no other symptoms. In August 2014, Ramish developed heat stroke and collapsed on the golf course at La Prima Country Club.

After recuperating at the clubhouse, Ramish quickly wrote his will on the back of a wine list. It stated, "My last will and testament: Upon my death, I give all of my personal property to my friend Bernard Eshom and my home to Lizzie Johansen." He signed the will at the bottom in the presence of five men in the La Prima clubhouse, and all five men signed as witnesses.

A week later, Ramish suffered a second aneurysm and died in his sleep. He was survived by his mother (Dorris Ramish), his nephew (Nathan Covacek), his son-in-law (Bruce Lupin), and his granddaughter (Tori Lupin). Using the information presented in the chapter, answer the following questions.

1. Does Ramish's testament on the back of the wine list meet the requirements for a valid will?
2. Suppose that after Ramish's first aneurysm in 2014, Covacek contacted an insurance company to obtain a life insurance policy on Ramish's life. Would Covacek have had an insurable interest in his uncle's life? Why or why not?
3. What would the order of inheritance have been if Ramish had died intestate?
4. What will most likely happen to the trust fund established for Covacek on Ramish's death?

DEBATE THIS Any changes to existing, fully witnessed wills should also have to be witnessed.

BUSINESS APPLICATION

How Can You Manage Risk in Cyberspace?*

Companies doing business online face many risks that are not covered by traditional types of insurance (see Exhibit 37.1 on page 951). Not surprisingly, a growing number of companies are now offering policies designed to cover Web-related risks.

Insurance Coverage for Web-Related Risks

Insurance to cover Web-related incidents is frequently referred to as *network intrusion insurance*. Such insurance protects companies from losses stemming from hacking and computer viruses, programming errors, and network and Web site disruptions. It also protects against losses from theft of electronic data and assets, including intellectual property, and losses arising from claims of Web-related defamation, copyright infringement, false advertising, and violations of users' privacy rights.

InsureTrust.com, an insurer affiliated with three leading insurance companies—American International Group, Lloyd's of London, and Reliance National—is a leading provider of cyberinsurance. Other insurers, such as Hartford Insurance and the Chubb Group of Insurance Companies, have also added insurance for Web-related perils to their offerings. Clearly, the market for cyberinsurance is evolving rapidly, and new policies will continue to appear.

Customized Policies

Unlike traditional insurance policies, which are generally drafted by insurance companies and presented to insurance applicants on a take-it-or-leave-it basis, cyberinsurance policies are usually customized to provide protection against specific risks faced by a particular

*This *Business Application* is not meant to substitute for the services of an attorney who is licensed to practice law in your state.

type of business. For example, an Internet service provider will face different risks than an online merchant, and a banking institution will face different risks than a law firm. The specific business-related risks are taken into consideration when determining the policy premium.

Qualifying Criteria

Many companies that offer network intrusion insurance require applicants to meet high security standards. In other words, to qualify for a policy under an insurance company's risk management processes, a business must have Web-related security measures in place. Several companies assess the applicant's security system before underwriting a policy.

For example, an insurer might assess the applicant's security measures and refuse to provide coverage unless the business scores higher than 60 percent. If the business does not score that high, it can contract with the company to improve its Web-related security.

Checklist for the Businessperson

1. *Determine the types of risks that your Web business is exposed to and try to obtain an insurance policy that protects you against those specific risks.*
2. *As when procuring any type of insurance, read the policy carefully, including any exclusions contained in the fine print, before committing to it.*
3. *Do not be "penny wise and pound foolish" when it comes to insurance protection. Though insurance coverage may seem expensive, it may be much less costly than the loss of intellectual property or the cost of defending against a lawsuit. Opting for a higher deductible can reduce the amount you pay in premiums.*
4. *Find out what the company's underwriting standards are and determine whether your Web security measures meet its standards.*

Key Terms

administrator 956
bequest 957
binder 952
charitable trust 967
codicil 961
constructive trust 968
devise 957
devisee 957
executor 956
holographic will 960
incontestability clause 953
insurable interest 950
insurance 950
intestacy laws 956
intestate 956
legacy 957
legatee 957
living (*inter vivos*) trust 966
nuncupative will 960
per capita 965
per stirpes 965
policy 950
premium 950
probate 962
resulting trust 968
risk 950
risk management 950
spendthrift trust 967
testamentary trust 967
testate 956
testator 956
Totten trust 968
trust 965
underwriter 950
will 956
will substitutes 963

Chapter Summary: Insurance, Wills, and Trusts

INSURANCE	
Classifications (See page 950.)	See Exhibit 37.1 on page 951.
Terminology (See page 950.)	1. *Policy*—The insurance contract. 2. *Premium*—The consideration paid to the insurer for a policy. 3. *Underwriter*—The insurance company. 4. *Parties*—Include the insurer (the insurance company), the insured (the person covered by insurance), an agent (a representative of the insurance company) or a broker (ordinarily an independent contractor), and a beneficiary (a person to receive proceeds under the policy).
Insurable Interest (See pages 950–952.)	An insurable interest exists whenever an individual or entity benefits from the preservation of the health or life of the insured or the property to be insured. For life insurance, an insurable interest must exist at the time the policy is issued. For property insurance, an insurable interest must exist at the time of the loss.
The Insurance Contract (See pages 952–956.)	1. *Laws governing*—The general principles of contract law are applied. The insurance industry is also heavily regulated by the states. 2. *Application*—An insurance applicant is bound by any false statements that appear in the application (subject to certain exceptions), which is part of the insurance contract. Misstatements or misrepresentations may be grounds for voiding the policy.

Continued

Chapter Summary: Insurance, Wills, and Trusts—Continued

The Insurance Contract—Continued	3. *Effective date*—Coverage on an insurance policy can begin when a *binder* (a written memorandum indicating that a formal policy is pending and stating its essential terms) is written; when the policy is issued; at the time of contract formation; or depending on the terms of the contract, when certain conditions are met. 4. *Provisions and clauses*—See Exhibit 37.2 on page 953. Words will be given their ordinary meanings, and any ambiguity in the policy will be interpreted against the insurance company. When the written policy has not been delivered and it is unclear whether an insurance contract actually exists, the uncertainty will be resolved against the insurance company. The court will presume that the policy is in effect unless the company can show otherwise. 5. *Defenses against payment to the insured*—Defenses include misrepresentation or fraud by the applicant.
WILLS	
Terminology (See pages 956–957.)	1. *Intestate*—One who dies without a valid will. 2. *Testator*—A person who makes out a will. 3. *Personal representative*—A person appointed in a will or by a court to settle the affairs of a decedent. A personal representative named in the will is an *executor.* A personal representative appointed by the court for an intestate decedent is an *administrator.* 4. *Devise*—A gift of real estate by will; may be general or specific. The recipient of a devise is a *devisee.* 5. *Bequest, or legacy*—A gift of personal property by will; may be general or specific. The recipient of a bequest (legacy) is a *legatee.*
Requirements for a Valid Will (See pages 958–961.)	1. The testator must have testamentary capacity (be of legal age and sound mind at the time the will is made). 2. A will must be in writing (except for nuncupative wills). A holographic will is completely in the handwriting of the testator. 3. A will must be signed by the testator. What constitutes a signature varies from jurisdiction to jurisdiction. 4. A nonholographic will (an attested will) must be witnessed in the manner prescribed by state statute.
Revocation of Wills (See pages 961–962.)	1. *By physical act of the maker*—Tearing up, canceling, obliterating, or deliberately destroying part or all of a will. 2. *By subsequent writing*— a. Codicil—A formal, separate document to amend or revoke an existing will. b. Second will or new will—A new, properly executed will expressly revoking the existing will. 3 *By operation of law*— a. Marriage—Generally revokes part of a will written before the marriage. b. Divorce or annulment—Revokes dispositions of property made under a will to a former spouse. c. Subsequently born child—Most states allow the child to receive a portion of the estate.
Probate Procedures and Estate Planning (See pages 962–963.)	To probate a will means to establish its validity and to carry the administration of the estate through a state court process. Probate procedures may be informal or formal, depending on the size of the estate and other factors, such as whether a guardian for minor children must be appointed.
Intestacy Laws (See pages 963–965.)	1. Intestacy laws vary widely from state to state. Usually, the law provides that the surviving spouse and children inherit the property of the decedent (after the decedent's debts are paid). The spouse usually inherits the entire estate if there are no children, one-half of the estate if there is one child, and one-third of the estate if there are two or more children. 2. If there is no surviving spouse or child, then, in order, lineal descendants (grandchildren, brothers and sisters, and—in some states—parents of the decedent) inherit. If there are no lineal descendants, then collateral heirs (nieces, nephews, aunts, and uncles of the decedent) inherit.
TRUSTS	
Definition (See page 965.)	A trust is any arrangement through which property is transferred from one person to a trustee to be administered for another party's benefit. The essential elements of a trust are (1) a designated beneficiary, (2) a designated trustee, (3) a fund sufficiently identified to enable title to pass to the trustee, and (4) actual delivery to the trustee with the intention of passing title.
Express Trusts (See pages 966–968.)	Express trusts are created by explicit terms, usually in writing, and include the following: 1. *Living (inter vivos) trust*—A trust created by a grantor during her or his lifetime. 2. *Testamentary trust*—A trust that is created by will and comes into existence on the death of the grantor. 3. *Charitable trust*—A trust designed for the benefit of a public group or the public in general.

Chapter Summary: Insurance, Wills, and Trusts—Continued

Express Trusts—Continued	4. *Spendthrift trust*—A trust created to provide for a beneficiary by allowing the beneficiary to withdraw only a certain amount at any one time. 5. *Totten trust*—A trust created when one person deposits funds in his or her own name as a trustee for another.
Implied Trusts (See page 968.)	Implied trusts, which are imposed by law in the interests of fairness and justice, include the following: 1. *Constructive trust*—Arises by operation of law when a person wrongfully takes title to property. A court may require the owner to hold the property in trust for those who, in equity, are entitled to enjoy the benefits from the trust. 2. *Resulting trust*—Arises from the conduct of the parties when an apparent intention to create a trust is present.

ExamPrep

ISSUE SPOTTERS

1. Sheila makes out a will, leaving her property in equal thirds to Toby and Umeko, her children, and Velda, her niece. Two years later, Sheila is adjudged mentally incompetent, and that same year, she dies. Can Toby and Umeko have Sheila's will revoked on the ground that she did not have the capacity to make a will? Why or why not? **(See page 958.)**
2. Ralph dies without having made a will. He is survived by many relatives—a spouse, children, adopted children, sisters, brothers, uncles, aunts, cousins, nephews, and nieces. What determines who gets what? **(See pages 963–965.)**

—Check your answers to the Issue Spotters against the answers provided in Appendix E at the end of this text.

BEFORE THE TEST

Go to www.cengagebrain.com, enter the ISBN 9781133273561, and click on "Find" to locate this textbook's Web site. Then, click on "Access Now" under "Study Tools," and select Chapter 37 at the top. There, you will find a Practice Quiz that you can take to assess your mastery of the concepts in this chapter, as well as Flashcards, a Glossary of important terms, and Video Questions (when assigned).

For Review

Answers to the even-numbered questions in this For Review section can be found in Appendix F at the end of this text.

1. Is an insurance broker the agent of the insurance applicant or the agent of the insurer?
2. What is an insurable interest? When must an insurable interest exist—at the time the insurance policy is obtained, at the time the loss occurs, or both?
3. What are the basic requirements for executing a will?
4. What is the difference between a *per stirpes* distribution and a *per capita* distribution of an estate to the grandchildren of the deceased?
5. What are the four essential elements of a trust? What is the difference between an express trust and an implied trust?

Business Scenarios and Case Problems

37–1 Timing of Insurance Coverage. On October 10, Joleen Vora applied for a $50,000 life insurance policy with Magnum Life Insurance Co. She named her husband, Jay, as the beneficiary. Joleen paid the insurance company the first year's premium on making the application. Two days later, before she had a chance to take the physical examination required by the insurance company and before the policy was issued, Joleen was killed in an automobile accident. Jay submitted a claim to the insurance company for the $50,000. Can Jay collect? Explain. **(See pages 952–956.)**

37–2 Question with Sample Answer—Wills and Intestacy Laws. Benjamin is a widower who has two married children, Edward and Patricia. Patricia has two children, Perry and Paul. Edward has no children. Benjamin dies, and his will leaves all his property equally to his children, Edward and Patricia, and provides that should a child predecease him, the grandchildren are to take *per stirpes*. The will was witnessed by Patricia and by Benjamin's lawyer and was signed by Benjamin in their presence. Patricia has predeceased Benjamin. Edward claims the will is invalid.

1. Discuss whether the will is valid. **(See pages 958–961.)**
2. Discuss the distribution of Benjamin's estate if the will is invalid. **(See pages 963–965.)**
3. Discuss the distribution of Benjamin's estate if the will is valid. **(See pages 964–965.)**

—For a sample answer to Question 37–2, go to Appendix G at the end of this text.

37–3 Intestacy Laws. A Florida statute provides that the right of election of a surviving spouse can be waived by written agreement: "A waiver of 'all rights,' or equivalent language, in the property or estate of a present or prospective spouse . . . is a waiver of all rights to elective share." The day before Mary Ann Taylor married Louis Taylor in Florida, they entered into a prenuptial agreement. The agreement stated that all property belonging to each spouse would "forever remain his or her personal estate," "said property shall remain forever free of claim by the other," and the parties would retain "full rights and authority" over their property as they would have as "if not married." After Louis's death, his only child, Joshua Taylor, filed a petition in a Florida state court for a determination of the beneficiaries of Louis's estate. How much of the estate can Mary Ann elect to receive? Explain. [*Taylor v. Taylor,* 1 So.3d 348 (Fla.App. 1 Dist. 2009)] **(See pages 963–965.)**

37–4 Requirements of a Will. Katherine Hagan executed a will that left her estate to various charitable organizations, such as the Humane Society, and expressly excluded her relatives. When Hagan died, her estate was worth $1.48 million. Janice Benjamin and other Hagan relatives objected to the will. They argued that it was invalid because Hagan had not been of "sound mind" and that the funds should pass to them by intestacy. Should the will be declared void? Why or why not? [*Benjamin v. JPMorgan Chase Bank, N.A.,* 305 S.W.3d 446 (Ky.App. 2010)] **(See pages 958–959.)**

37–5 Case Problem with Sample Answer—Revocation of a Will. Marion Peterson executed a will that contained a bequest to Vasta Lucas in the form of a trust. On Lucas's death, the trustee was to distribute the assets to four beneficiaries, including Peterson's brother and sister, Arvin and Carolyn. Later, without witnesses, Peterson crossed out the beneficiaries' names, but she left the bequest to Lucas intact. After Peterson's death, Arvin and Carolyn contended that the will had been completely revoked. Were they correct? Explain. [*Peterson v. Harrell,* 286 Ga. 546, 690 S.E.2d 151 (2010)] **(See pages 961–962.)**

—For a sample answer to Problem 37–5, go to Appendix H at the end of this text.

37–6 Bad Faith Actions. Leo and Mary Deters owned Deters Tower Service, Inc., in Iowa. Deters Tower serviced television and radio towers and antennas in a multistate area. The firm obtained a commercial general liability policy issued by USF Insurance Co. to provide coverage for its officers, including Leo. One afternoon, Leo and two Deters Tower employees were working on a TV tower in Council Bluffs when they fell from the tower to their deaths. The workers' families filed a negligence suit against Leo's estate. USF refused to defend the Deters estate against the suit and pay any resulting claim and did not provide a reason for this response. Is USF liable to the Deters estate for this refusal? If so, on what basis might the Deters estate recover, and how much? [*Deters v. USF Insurance Co.,* 797 N.W.2d 621 (Iowa App. 2011)] **(See page 955.)**

37–7 Undue Influence. Susie Walker executed a will that left her entire estate to her grandson. When her grandson died, Susie executed a new will that named her great-grandson as her sole beneficiary and specifically disinherited her son, Tommy. At the time, Tommy's ex-wife was living with Susie. After Susie died, Tommy filed a suit, claiming that her will was the product of undue influence on the part of his ex-wife. Several witnesses testified that Susie had been mentally competent when she executed her will. Does undue influence appear likely based on these facts? Why or why not? [*In re Estate of Walker,* 80 A.D.3d 865, 914 N.Y.S.2d 379 (3 Dept. 2011)] **(See page 958.)**

37–8 Insurance Provisions and Clauses. Darling's Rent-a-Car carried property insurance on its cars under a policy issued by Philadelphia Indemnity Insurance Co. The policy listed Darling's as the "insured." Darling's rented a car to Joshuah Farrington. In the rental contract, Farrington agreed to be responsible for any damage to the car and declined the optional insurance. Later, Farrington collided with a moose. Philadelphia paid Darling's for the damage to the car and sought to collect this amount from Farrington. Farrington argued that he was an "insured" under Darling's policy. How should "insured" be interpreted in this case? Why? [*Philadelphia Indemnity Insurance Co. v. Farrington,* 37 A.3d 305 (Me. 2012) **(See pages 950–952, 954.)**

37–9 A Question of Ethics—Will Requirements. Vickie Lynn Smith, an actress and model also known as Anna Nicole Smith, met J. Howard Marshall II in 1991. During their courtship, J. Howard lavished gifts and large sums of money on Anna Nicole, and they married on June 27, 1994. J. Howard died on August 4, 1995. According to Anna Nicole, J. Howard intended to provide for her financial security through a trust, but under the terms of his will, all of his assets were transferred to a trust for the benefit of E. Pierce Marshall, one of J. Howard's sons. While J. Howard's estate was subject to probate proceedings in a Texas state court, Anna Nicole filed for bankruptcy in a federal bankruptcy court. Pierce filed a claim in the bankruptcy proceeding, alleging that Anna Nicole had defamed him when her lawyers told the media that Pierce had engaged in forgery and fraud to gain control of his father's assets. Anna Nicole filed a counterclaim, alleging that Pierce prevented the transfer of his father's assets to a trust for her by, among other things, imprisoning J. Howard against his wishes, surrounding him with security guards to prevent contact with her, and transferring property against his wishes. [*Marshall v. Marshall,* 547 U.S. 293, 126 S.Ct. 1735, 164 L.Ed.2d 480 (2006)] **(See pages 958–962.)**

1. What is the purpose underlying the requirements for a valid will? Which of these requirements might be at issue in this case? How should it apply here? Why?
2. State courts generally have jurisdiction over the probate of a will and the administration of an estate. Does the Texas state court thus have the sole authority to adjudicate all of the claims in this case? Why or why not?
3. How should Pierce's claim against Anna Nicole and her counterclaim be resolved?
4. Anna Nicole executed her will in 2001. The beneficiary—Daniel, her son, who was not J. Howard's child—died in 2006, shortly after Anna Nicole gave birth to a daughter, Dannielynn. In 2007, before executing a new will, Anna Nicole died. What happens if a will's beneficiary dies before the testator? What happens if a child is born after a will is executed?

Critical Thinking and Writing Assignments

37–10 **Business Law Critical Thinking Group Assignment.** PAJ, Inc., a jewelry company, had a commercial general liability (CGL) policy from Hanover Insurance Company. The policy required PAJ to notify Hanover of any claim or suit against PAJ "as soon as practicable." Yurman Designs sued PAJ for copyright infringement because of the design of a particular jewelry line. Because PAJ did not realize that the CGL policy had a clause that covered infringement claims, it did not notify Hanover of the suit until four to six months after litigation began. Hanover contended that the policy did not apply to this incident because the late notification had violated its terms. PAJ sued Hanover, seeking a declaration that it was obligated to defend and indemnify PAJ.

1. The first group will decide whether Hanover had an obligation to provide PAJ with legal assistance.
2. The second group will determine the effect that PAJ's late notice to the insurance company had on its ability to provide assistance and mount a defense. Should the court require the insurance company to indemnify PAJ in this situation? Why or why not?

UNIT 7 Property and Its Protection

Business Case Study with Dissenting Opinion

Kovarik v. Kovarik

When a couple divorces, the division of the marital estate—all of the property that the parties accumulated during their marriage—often leads to disputes. Questions of ownership frequently arise in divorce proceedings: Who owned what property, and how did she or he acquire it? If property was allegedly acquired by gift, did the transfer satisfy the requirements for a valid gift?

Those questions arose in *Kovarik v. Kovarik*,[1] which we examine in this *Business Case Study with Dissenting Opinion.* During a divorce, a dispute arose over whether the couple's marital estate included several certificates of deposit (discussed in Chapter 18) worth about $60,000 in which one spouse allegedly had an interest. The acquisition, division, and transfer of ownership of personal property were discussed in Chapter 35, and other types of property transfers were covered in Chapter 36.

Case Background

Jennifer Stahl and Bradly Kovarik were married in North Dakota in July 2001. A few months later, Bradly's parents, Dennis and Marlene, liquidated their farm business, and invested the proceeds in certificates of deposit (CDs). Four of the CDs were in the names of Bradly and his sister, Wanda Morstad, but were retained by their parents.

Jennifer and Bradly separated in August 2007. Jennifer filed for divorce in a North Dakota state court. In a list of their marital property, she included the four CDs. Bradly denied any interest in those items.

At the trial, Bradly testified that he learned about the CDs from his sister, who cashed one without giving him any of the proceeds after Jennifer filed for divorce. At their mother's request, his sister also negotiated the other three CDs before the divorce trial. The court did not include the CDs in valuing and distributing the Kovariks' marital estate. Jennifer appealed to the North Dakota Supreme Court, arguing that Bradly's interest in the CDs should have been included.

Majority Opinion

SANDSTROM, Justice.

* * * *

A [trial] court's decisions regarding the division of marital property are findings of fact and may be reversed on appeal only if clearly erroneous. A finding of fact is clearly erroneous if it is induced by an erroneous view of the law, if there is no evidence to support it, or if, after reviewing the entirety of the evidence, this Court is left with a definite and firm conviction a mistake has been made. A [trial] court's findings of fact are presumed correct, and we view the evidence in the light most favorable to its findings.

Division of marital property upon divorce must be equitable. Although the division does not have to be equal, a substantial disparity must be explained. *All of the real and personal property accumulated by the parties, regardless of source, must be included in the marital estate.* [Emphasis added.]

* * * *

A * * * court may consider property to be part of the marital estate, if supported by evidence, even if a party claims it is owned by a nonparty. The principles applicable to *inter vivos* gifts in general apply as well to purported gifts of certificates of deposit. A valid gift made during the donor's lifetime must satisfy certain requirements—donative intent, delivery, actual or constructive, and acceptance by donee. A donor's intent is a question of fact. The actual or constructive delivery must be

1. 2009 ND 82, 765 N.W.2d 511 (2009).

Business Case Study with Dissenting Opinion—Continued

of a nature sufficient to divest the owner of all dominion [control] over the property and to invest the donee therewith.

Bradly Kovarik's parents testified that after liquidating their farm and equipment * * *, they placed four certificates of deposit in Bradly Kovarik's and his sister's names—"Wanda Morstad or Bradly Kovarik." They also testified they did not intend to give Bradly Kovarik and Morstad any present interest in the certificates. Moreover, Bradly Kovarik's father testified that the certificates, prior to having been cashed out, had been locked in a safe in their home and neither Bradly Kovarik nor his sister could just come and take the certificates.

Bradly Kovarik testified he had no knowledge of the certificates' existence until his sister told him she cashed one out and used some of the proceeds for home repairs. He also testified he did not receive any of the remaining proceeds. Wanda Morstad testified she did not expect the certificates of deposit to belong to her. When requested, she assisted her parents in cashing out the certificates, which she did with respect to the remaining three certificates.

The [trial] court found Bradly Kovarik's parents did not intend to gift the certificates to him and his sister. The court further found the certificates were never delivered to either Bradly Kovarik or his sister but were retained in their parents' possession. The record does not reflect donative intent or delivery of the certificates to Bradly Kovarik, either actual or constructive. *In the absence of a donative intent and delivery, the [trial] court's finding that there was no valid gift is not clearly erroneous.* [Emphasis added.]

* * * *

We hold the [trial] court's property distribution and property valuation is not clearly erroneous, and affirm.

Dissenting Opinion

MARING, Justice, dissenting.

I respectfully dissent from * * * the Majority opinion because the [trial] court * * * erred in concluding Bradly Kovarik's parents never gave him the certificates of deposit.

* * * *

First, the [trial] court found Bradly Kovarik's parents did not intend to give the certificates of deposit to Bradly Kovarik or his sister. This finding is not supported by the record. Bradly Kovarik admits that he and his sister were the co-owners of the certificates of deposit. Bradly Kovarik's sister also testified * * * that she was the co-owner of the certificates of deposit with her brother.

* * * *

Dennis Kovarik's testimony establishes that he knew Bradly Kovarik was a joint owner of the certificates of deposit * * *. Marlene Kovarik's testimony establishes that Bradly Kovarik was the joint owner of the certificates of deposit.

These admissions by Bradly Kovarik and his family that he owned the certificates of deposits are supported by the law. The parties do not dispute that Bradly Kovarik's name was on the certificate of deposit together with his sister's name or that neither of his parents' names were on the certificates of deposit. It is presumed that a certificate of deposit belongs to the person whose name appears on the certificate. * * * Bradly Kovarik's parents gave up their exclusive dominion and control over their assets when they placed the money in certificates of deposit in their children's names.

* * * *

The [trial] court found the certificates of deposit were never delivered to Bradly Kovarik or his sister because the parents kept possession of the certificates of deposit. This finding is not supported by the record.

* * * *

* * * Bradly Kovarik's parents divested themselves of the control of the certificates of deposit by first solely placing their children's names on the certificates of deposit and then delivering the certificates of deposit to Wanda Morstad to be cashed.

* * * *

In conclusion, I dissent because the certificates of deposit were completed gifts to Bradly Kovarik and must be included in the marital estate.

Business Case Study with Dissenting Opinion—Continues next page

Business Case Study with Dissenting Opinion—Continued

Questions for Analysis

1. **Law** How does the majority respond to the appellant's argument in this case? What is the majority's reasoning?
2. **Law** How does the dissent analyze the issue before the court?
3. **Ethics** According to Marlene Kovarik, the CDs were obtained in her children's names in an effort to avoid the parents' tax obligations, rather than to give the funds to the children. Is this ethical? Explain.
4. **Social Dimensions** If the Kovariks had invested their funds in real estate in their children's names, instead of CDs, would the result in this case have been the same? Why or why not?
5. **Implications for the Estate Planner** How might Marlene and Dennis Kovarik have avoided the question that Jennifer raised here? Discuss.

UNIT 7 Property and Its Protection

Business Scenario

Dave graduates from State University with an engineering degree and goes into business as a self-employed computer programmer.

1. **Ownership of Personal Property.** To advertise his services on the Internet, Dave creates and produces a short digital video. Hollywood Films, Inc., sees the video and hires Dave to program the special effects for a short sequence in a Hollywood movie. Their contract states that all rights to the sequence belong to Hollywood. Does the digital video, the movie sequence, both, or neither belong to Dave? Explain. **(See pages 911–916.)**
2. **Landlord-Tenant Law.** Dave leases an office in Carl's Riverside Plaza office building for a two-year term. What is Dave's obligation for the rent if he moves out before the end of the term? If Dave dies during the term, who is entitled to possession of the office? What is Dave's obligation for the rent if Carl sells the building to Commercial Investments, Inc., before Dave's lease is up? **(See pages 942–944.)**
3. **Real Property Deeds.** At the end of the lease term, Dave buys the office building from Carl, who gives Dave a warranty deed. Commercial Investments later challenges Dave's ownership of the building and presents its own allegedly valid deed. What will it mean if a court rules that Dave owns the building in fee simple? If Commercial Investments is successful, can Dave recover anything from Carl? Explain. **(See pages 933–939.)**
4. **Insurance.** Dave's programming business expands, and he hires Mary as an employee. Mary becomes invaluable to the business, and Dave obtains a key-person insurance policy on her life. She dies six years later. If the insurance company discovers that Dave understated Mary's age when applying for the policy (which includes an incontestability clause), can the insurer legitimately refuse payment? If Mary had resigned to start her own programming firm one year before she died, can Dave collect payment under the policy? Why or why not? **(See pages 950–956.)**
5. **Wills and Trusts.** Over time, Dave acquires other commercial property, which eventually becomes the most lucrative part of his business. Dave wants his adult children, Frank and Terry, to get the benefit of this property when he dies. Dave does not think that Frank and Terry can manage the property, however, because they have their own careers and live in other states. How can Dave provide for them to get the benefit of the property under someone else's management? In his will, Dave designates Hal, his attorney, as executor. What does an executor do? **(See pages 956–969.)**

UNIT 7 Property and Its Protection

Group Project

Hobie and Colleen designed and developed a smartphone app called Do It. Do It is a game in which players cooperate rather than compete to complete a task, such as draw a picture, play a tune, or score a point.

Documents evidence each party's investment, ownership, and share of profits and losses in the app. In the documents, Hobie and Colleen are referred to as "joint owners" and "tenants."

1. The first group will determine whether the ownership interest of each party is a tenancy in common or a joint tenancy. Is there a presumption that applies? Discuss.
2. The second group will describe the differences between a tenancy in common and a joint tenancy. What happens to Colleen's interest if Hobie dies?
3. A third group will assume that Hobie and Colleen were not married but lived together and held the property as tenants in common. If Hobie has no children and dies without a will, does Colleen inherit his interest in the Do It app? Why or why not? How would most states' intestate succession laws distribute Hobie's property?

APPENDIX **A**

How to Brief Cases and Analyze Case Problems

How to Brief Cases

To fully understand the law with respect to business, you need to be able to read and understand court decisions. To make this task easier, you can use a method of case analysis that is called *briefing*. There is a fairly standard procedure that you can follow when you "brief" any court case. You must first read the case opinion carefully. When you feel you understand the case, you can prepare a brief of it.

Although the format of the brief may vary, typically it will present the essentials of the case under headings such as those listed below.

1. **Citation.** Give the full citation for the case, including the name of the case, the date it was decided, and the court that decided it.
2. **Facts.** Briefly indicate (a) the reasons for the lawsuit; (b) the identity and arguments of the plaintiff(s) and defendant(s), respectively; and (c) the lower court's decision—if appropriate.
3. **Issue.** Concisely phrase, in the form of a question, the essential issue before the court. (If more than one issue is involved, you may have two—or even more—questions here.)
4. **Decision.** Indicate here—with a "yes" or "no," if possible—the court's answer to the question (or questions) in the Issue section above.
5. **Reason.** Summarize as briefly as possible the reasons given by the court for its decision (or decisions) and the case or statutory law relied on by the court in arriving at its decision.

For a case-specific example of what should be included under each of the above headings when briefing a case, see the review of the sample court case presented in the appendix to Chapter 1 of this text on pages 31 and 32.

Analyzing Case Problems

In addition to learning how to brief cases, students of business law and the legal environment also find it helpful to know how to analyze case problems. Part of the study of business law and the legal environment usually involves analyzing case problems, such as those included in this text at the end of each chapter.

For each case problem in this book, we provide the relevant background and facts of the lawsuit and the issue before the court. When you are assigned one of these problems, your job will be to determine how the court should decide the issue, and why. In other words, you will need to engage in legal analysis and reasoning. Here, we offer some suggestions on how to make this task less daunting. We begin by presenting a sample case problem:

> While Janet Lawson, a famous pianist, was shopping in Quality Market, she slipped and fell on a wet floor in one of the aisles. The floor had recently been mopped by one of the store's employees, but there were no signs warning customers that the floor in that area was wet. As a result of the fall, Lawson injured her right arm and was unable to perform piano concerts for the next six months. Had she been able to perform the scheduled concerts, she would have earned approximately $60,000 over that period of time. Lawson sued Quality Market for this amount, plus another $10,000 in medical expenses. She claimed that the store's failure to warn customers of the wet floor constituted negligence and therefore the market was liable for her injuries. Will the court agree with Lawson? Discuss.

Understand the Facts

This may sound obvious, but before you can analyze or apply the relevant law to a specific set of facts, you must clearly understand those facts. In other words, you should read through the case problem carefully—more than once, if necessary—to make sure you understand the identity of the plaintiff(s) and defendant(s) in the case and the progression of events that led to the lawsuit.

In the sample case problem just given, the identity of the parties is fairly obvious. Janet Lawson is the one bringing the suit; therefore, she is the plaintiff. Lawson is bringing the suit against Quality Market, so it is the defendant. Some of the case problems you may work on have multiple plaintiffs or defendants. Often, it is helpful to use abbreviations for the parties. To indicate a reference to a plaintiff, for example, the *pi* symbol—π—is often used, and a defendant is denoted by a *delta*—Δ—a triangle.

The events leading to the lawsuit are also fairly straightforward. Lawson slipped and fell on a wet floor, and she contends that Quality Market should be liable for her injuries because it was negligent in not posting a sign warning customers of the wet floor.

When you are working on case problems, realize that the facts should be accepted as they are given. For instance, in our sample problem, it should be accepted that the floor was wet and that there was no sign. In other words, avoid making conjectures, such as "Maybe the floor wasn't too wet," or "Maybe an employee was getting a sign to put up," or "Maybe someone stole the sign." Questioning the facts as they are presented only adds confusion to your analysis.

Legal Analysis and Reasoning

Once you understand the facts given in the case problem, you can begin to analyze the case. Recall from Chapter 1 that the **IRAC method** is a helpful tool to use in the legal analysis and reasoning process. IRAC is an acronym for **I**ssue, **R**ule, **A**pplication, **C**onclusion. Applying this method to our sample problem would involve the following steps:

1. First, you need to decide what legal **issue** is involved in the case. In our sample case, the basic issue is whether Quality Market's failure to warn customers of the wet floor constituted negligence. As discussed in Chapter 4, negligence is a *tort*—a civil wrong. In a tort lawsuit, the plaintiff seeks to be compensated for another's wrongful act. A defendant will be deemed negligent if he or she breached a duty of care owed to the plaintiff and the breach of that duty caused the plaintiff to suffer harm.
2. Once you have identified the issue, the next step is to determine what **rule of law** applies to the issue. To make this determination, you will want to carefully review the text discussion relating to the issue involved in the problem. Our sample case problem involves the tort of negligence, which is covered in Chapter 4. The applicable rule of law is the tort law principle that business owners owe a duty to exercise reasonable care to protect their customers *(business invitees)*. Reasonable care, in this context, includes either removing—or warning customers of—*foreseeable* risks about which the owner *knew* or *should have known*. Business owners need not warn customers of "open and obvious" risks, however. If a business owner breaches this duty of care (fails to exercise the appropriate degree of care toward customers), and the breach of duty causes a customer to be injured, the business owner will be liable to the customer for the customer's injuries.
3. The next—and usually the most difficult—step in analyzing case problems is the **application** of the relevant rule of law to the specific facts of the case you are studying. In our sample problem, applying the tort law principle just discussed presents few difficulties. An employee of the store had mopped the floor in the aisle where Lawson slipped and fell, but no sign was present indicating that the floor was wet. That a customer might fall on a wet floor is clearly a foreseeable risk. Therefore, the failure to warn customers about the wet floor was a breach of the duty of care owed by the business owner to the store's customers.
4. Once you have completed Step 3 in the IRAC method, you should be ready to draw your **conclusion.** In our sample problem, Quality Market is liable to Lawson for her injuries because the market's breach of its duty of care caused Lawson's injuries.

The fact patterns in the case problems presented in this text are not always as simple as those presented in our sample problem. Often, a case has more than one plaintiff or defendant. A case may also involve more than one issue and have more than one applicable rule of law. Furthermore, in some case problems the facts may indicate that the general rule of law should not apply. Suppose that a store employee told Lawson about the wet floor and advised her not to walk in that aisle, but Lawson decided to walk there anyway. This fact could alter the outcome of the case because the store could then raise the defense of *assumption of risk* (see Chapter 4).

Nonetheless, a careful review of the chapter should always provide you with the knowledge you need to analyze the problem thoroughly and arrive at accurate conclusions.

APPENDIX **B**

The Constitution of the United States

Preamble

We the People of the United States, in Order to form a more perfect Union, establish Justice, insure domestic Tranquility, provide for the common defence, promote the general Welfare, and secure the Blessings of Liberty to ourselves and our Posterity, do ordain and establish this Constitution for the United States of America.

Article I

Section 1. All legislative Powers herein granted shall be vested in a Congress of the United States, which shall consist of a Senate and House of Representatives.

Section 2. The House of Representatives shall be composed of Members chosen every second Year by the People of the several States, and the Electors in each State shall have the Qualifications requisite for Electors of the most numerous Branch of the State Legislature.

No Person shall be a Representative who shall not have attained to the Age of twenty five Years, and been seven Years a Citizen of the United States, and who shall not, when elected, be an Inhabitant of that State in which he shall be chosen.

Representatives and direct Taxes shall be apportioned among the several States which may be included within this Union, according to their respective Numbers, which shall be determined by adding to the whole Number of free Persons, including those bound to Service for a Term of Years, and excluding Indians not taxed, three fifths of all other Persons. The actual Enumeration shall be made within three Years after the first Meeting of the Congress of the United States, and within every subsequent Term of ten Years, in such Manner as they shall by Law direct. The Number of Representatives shall not exceed one for every thirty Thousand, but each State shall have at Least one Representative; and until such enumeration shall be made, the State of New Hampshire shall be entitled to chuse three, Massachusetts eight, Rhode Island and Providence Plantations one, Connecticut five, New York six, New Jersey four, Pennsylvania eight, Delaware one, Maryland six, Virginia ten, North Carolina five, South Carolina five, and Georgia three.

When vacancies happen in the Representation from any State, the Executive Authority thereof shall issue Writs of Election to fill such Vacancies.

The House of Representatives shall chuse their Speaker and other Officers; and shall have the sole Power of Impeachment.

Section 3. The Senate of the United States shall be composed of two Senators from each State, chosen by the Legislature thereof, for six Years; and each Senator shall have one Vote.

Immediately after they shall be assembled in Consequence of the first Election, they shall be divided as equally as may be into three Classes. The Seats of the Senators of the first Class shall be vacated at the Expiration of the second Year, of the second Class at the Expiration of the fourth Year, and of the third Class at the Expiration of the sixth Year, so that one third may be chosen every second Year; and if Vacancies happen by Resignation, or otherwise, during the Recess of the Legislature of any State, the Executive thereof may make temporary Appointments until the next Meeting of the Legislature, which shall then fill such Vacancies.

No Person shall be a Senator who shall not have attained to the Age of thirty Years, and been nine Years a Citizen of the United States, and who shall not, when elected, be an Inhabitant of that State for which he shall be chosen.

The Vice President of the United States shall be President of the Senate, but shall have no Vote, unless they be equally divided.

The Senate shall chuse their other Officers, and also a President pro tempore, in the Absence of the Vice President, or when he shall exercise the Office of President of the United States.

The Senate shall have the sole Power to try all Impeachments. When sitting for that Purpose, they shall be on Oath or Affirmation. When the President of the United States is tried, the Chief Justice shall preside: And no Person shall be convicted without the Concurrence of two thirds of the Members present.

Judgment in Cases of Impeachment shall not extend further than to removal from Office, and disqualification to hold and enjoy any Office of honor, Trust, or Profit under the United States: but the Party convicted shall nevertheless be liable and subject to Indictment, Trial, Judgment, and Punishment, according to Law.

Section 4. The Times, Places and Manner of holding Elections for Senators and Representatives, shall be prescribed in each State by the Legislature thereof; but the Congress may at any time by Law make or alter such Regulations, except as to the Places of chusing Senators.

The Congress shall assemble at least once in every Year, and such Meeting shall be on the first Monday in December, unless they shall by Law appoint a different Day.

Section 5. Each House shall be the Judge of the Elections, Returns, and Qualifications of its own Members, and a Majority of each shall constitute a Quorum to do Business; but a smaller Number may adjourn from day to day, and may be authorized to compel the Attendance of absent Members, in such Manner, and under such Penalties as each House may provide.

Each House may determine the Rules of its Proceedings, punish its Members for disorderly Behavior, and, with the Concurrence of two thirds, expel a Member.

Each House shall keep a Journal of its Proceedings, and from time to time publish the same, excepting such Parts as may in their Judgment require Secrecy; and the Yeas and Nays of the Members of either House on any question shall, at the Desire of one fifth of those Present, be entered on the Journal.

Neither House, during the Session of Congress, shall, without the Consent of the other, adjourn for more than three days, nor to any other Place than that in which the two Houses shall be sitting.

Section 6. The Senators and Representatives shall receive a Compensation for their Services, to be ascertained by Law, and paid out of the Treasury of the United States. They shall in all Cases, except Treason, Felony and Breach of the Peace, be privileged from Arrest during their Attendance at the Session of their respective Houses, and in going to and returning from the same; and for any Speech or Debate in either House, they shall not be questioned in any other Place.

No Senator or Representative shall, during the Time for which he was elected, be appointed to any civil Office under the Authority of the United States, which shall have been created, or the Emoluments whereof shall have been increased during such time; and no Person holding any Office under the United States, shall be a Member of either House during his Continuance in Office.

Section 7. All Bills for raising Revenue shall originate in the House of Representatives; but the Senate may propose or concur with Amendments as on other Bills.

Every Bill which shall have passed the House of Representatives and the Senate, shall, before it become a Law, be presented to the President of the United States; If he approve he shall sign it, but if not he shall return it, with his Objections to the House in which it shall have originated, who shall enter the Objections at large on their Journal, and proceed to reconsider it. If after such Reconsideration two thirds of that House shall agree to pass the Bill, it shall be sent together with the Objections, to the other House, by which it shall likewise be reconsidered, and if approved by two thirds of that House, it shall become a Law. But in all such Cases the Votes of both Houses shall be determined by Yeas and Nays, and the Names of the Persons voting for and against the Bill shall be entered on the Journal of each House respectively. If any Bill shall not be returned by the President within ten Days (Sundays excepted) after it shall have been presented to him, the Same shall be a Law, in like Manner as if he had signed it, unless the Congress by their Adjournment prevent its Return in which Case it shall not be a Law.

Every Order, Resolution, or Vote, to which the Concurrence of the Senate and House of Representatives may be necessary (except on a question of Adjournment) shall be presented to the President of the United States; and before the Same shall take Effect, shall be approved by him, or being disapproved by him, shall be repassed by two thirds of the Senate and House of Representatives, according to the Rules and Limitations prescribed in the Case of a Bill.

Section 8. The Congress shall have Power To lay and collect Taxes, Duties, Imposts and Excises, to pay the Debts and provide for the common Defence and general Welfare of the United States; but all Duties, Imposts and Excises shall be uniform throughout the United States;

To borrow Money on the credit of the United States;

To regulate Commerce with foreign Nations, and among the several States, and with the Indian Tribes;

To establish an uniform Rule of Naturalization, and uniform Laws on the subject of Bankruptcies throughout the United States;

To coin Money, regulate the Value thereof, and of foreign Coin, and fix the Standard of Weights and Measures;

To provide for the Punishment of counterfeiting the Securities and current Coin of the United States;

To establish Post Offices and post Roads;

To promote the Progress of Science and useful Arts, by securing for limited Times to Authors and Inventors the exclusive Right to their respective Writings and Discoveries;

To constitute Tribunals inferior to the supreme Court;

To define and punish Piracies and Felonies committed on the high Seas, and Offenses against the Law of Nations;

To declare War, grant Letters of Marque and Reprisal, and make Rules concerning Captures on Land and Water;

To raise and support Armies, but no Appropriation of Money to that Use shall be for a longer Term than two Years;

To provide and maintain a Navy;

To make Rules for the Government and Regulation of the land and naval Forces;

To provide for calling forth the Militia to execute the Laws of the Union, suppress Insurrections and repel Invasions;

To provide for organizing, arming, and disciplining, the Militia, and for governing such Part of them as may be employed in the Service of the United States, reserving to the States respectively, the Appointment of the Officers, and the Authority of training the Militia according to the discipline prescribed by Congress;

To exercise exclusive Legislation in all Cases whatsoever, over such District (not exceeding ten Miles square) as may, by Cession of particular States, and the Acceptance of Congress, become the Seat of the Government of the United States, and to exercise like Authority over all Places purchased by the Consent of the Legislature of the State in which the Same shall be, for the Erection of Forts, Magazines, Arsenals, dock-Yards, and other needful Buildings;—And

To make all Laws which shall be necessary and proper for carrying into Execution the foregoing Powers, and all other Powers vested by this Constitution in the Government of the United States, or in any Department or Officer thereof.

Section 9. The Migration or Importation of such Persons as any of the States now existing shall think proper to admit, shall not be prohibited by the Congress prior to the Year one thousand eight hundred and eight, but a Tax or duty may be imposed on such Importation, not exceeding ten dollars for each Person.

The privilege of the Writ of Habeas Corpus shall not be suspended, unless when in Cases of Rebellion or Invasion the public Safety may require it.

No Bill of Attainder or ex post facto Law shall be passed.

No Capitation, or other direct, Tax shall be laid, unless in Proportion to the Census or Enumeration herein before directed to be taken.

No Tax or Duty shall be laid on Articles exported from any State.

No Preference shall be given by any Regulation of Commerce or Revenue to the Ports of one State over those of another: nor shall Vessels bound to, or from, one State be obliged to enter, clear, or pay Duties in another.

No Money shall be drawn from the Treasury, but in Consequence of Appropriations made by Law; and a regular Statement and Account of the Receipts and Expenditures of all public Money shall be published from time to time.

No Title of Nobility shall be granted by the United States: And no Person holding any Office of Profit or Trust under them, shall, without the Consent of the Congress, accept of any present, Emolument, Office, or Title, of any kind whatever, from any King, Prince, or foreign State.

Section 10. No State shall enter into any Treaty, Alliance, or Confederation; grant Letters of Marque and Reprisal; coin Money; emit Bills of Credit; make any Thing but gold and silver Coin a Tender in Payment of Debts; pass any Bill of Attainder, ex post facto Law, or Law impairing the Obligation of Contracts, or grant any Title of Nobility.

No State shall, without the Consent of the Congress, lay any Imposts or Duties on Imports or Exports, except what may be absolutely necessary for executing its inspection Laws: and the net Produce of all Duties and Imposts, laid by any State on Imports or Exports, shall be for the Use of the Treasury of the United States; and all such Laws shall be subject to the Revision and Controul of the Congress.

No State shall, without the Consent of Congress, lay any Duty of Tonnage, keep Troops, or Ships of War in time of Peace, enter into any Agreement or Compact with another State, or with a foreign Power, or engage in War, unless actually invaded, or in such imminent Danger as will not admit of delay.

Article II

Section 1. The executive Power shall be vested in a President of the United States of America. He shall hold his Office during the Term of four Years, and, together with the Vice President, chosen for the same Term, be elected, as follows:

Each State shall appoint, in such Manner as the Legislature thereof may direct, a Number of Electors, equal to the whole Number of Senators and Representatives to which the State may be entitled in the Congress; but no Senator or Representative, or Person holding an Office of Trust or Profit under the United States, shall be appointed an Elector.

The Electors shall meet in their respective States, and vote by Ballot for two Persons, of whom one at least shall not be an Inhabitant of the same State with themselves. And they shall make a List of all the Persons voted for, and of the Number of Votes for each; which List they shall sign and certify, and transmit sealed to the Seat of the Government of the United States, directed to the President of the Senate. The President of the Senate shall, in the Presence of the Senate and House of Representatives, open all the Certificates, and the Votes shall then be counted. The Person having the greatest Number of Votes shall be the President, if such Number be a Majority of the whole Number of Electors appointed; and if there be more than one who have such Majority, and have an equal Number of Votes, then the House of Representatives shall immediately chuse by Ballot one of them for President; and if no Person have a Majority, then from the five highest on the List the said House shall in like Manner chuse the President. But in chusing the President, the Votes shall be taken by States, the Representation from each State having one Vote; A quorum for this Purpose shall consist of a Member or Members from two thirds of the States, and a Majority of all the States shall be necessary to a Choice. In every Case, after the Choice of the President, the Person having the greater Number of Votes of the Electors shall be the Vice President. But if there should remain two or more who have equal Votes, the Senate shall chuse from them by Ballot the Vice President.

The Congress may determine the Time of chusing the Electors, and the Day on which they shall give their Votes; which Day shall be the same throughout the United States.

No person except a natural born Citizen, or a Citizen of the United States, at the time of the Adoption of this Constitution, shall be eligible to the Office of President; neither shall any Person be eligible to that Office who shall not have attained to the Age of thirty five Years, and been fourteen Years a Resident within the United States.

In Case of the Removal of the President from Office, or of his Death, Resignation or Inability to discharge the Powers and Duties of the said Office, the same shall devolve on the Vice President, and the Congress may by Law provide for the Case of Removal, Death, Resignation or Inability, both of the President and Vice President, declaring what Officer shall then act as President, and such Officer shall act accordingly, until the Disability be removed, or a President shall be elected.

The President shall, at stated Times, receive for his Services, a Compensation, which shall neither be increased nor diminished during the Period for which he shall have been elected, and he shall not receive within that Period any other Emolument from the United States, or any of them.

Before he enter on the Execution of his Office, he shall take the following Oath or Affirmation: "I do solemnly swear (or affirm) that I will faithfully execute the Office of President of the United States, and will to the best of my Ability, preserve, protect and defend the Constitution of the United States."

Section 2. The President shall be Commander in Chief of the Army and Navy of the United States, and of the Militia of the several States, when called into the actual Service of the United States; he may require the Opinion, in writing, of the principal Officer in each of the executive Departments, upon any Subject relating to the Duties of their respective Offices, and he shall have Power to grant Reprieves and Pardons for Offenses against the United States, except in Cases of Impeachment.

He shall have Power, by and with the Advice and Consent of the Senate to make Treaties, provided two thirds of the Senators present concur; and he shall nominate, and by and with the Advice and Consent of the Senate, shall appoint Ambassadors, other public Ministers and Consuls, Judges of the supreme Court, and all other Officers of the United States, whose Appointments are not herein otherwise provided for, and which shall be established by Law; but the Congress may by Law vest the Appointment of such inferior Officers, as they think proper, in the President alone, in the Courts of Law, or in the Heads of Departments.

The President shall have Power to fill up all Vacancies that may happen during the Recess of the Senate, by granting Commissions which shall expire at the End of their next Session.

Section 3. He shall from time to time give to the Congress Information of the State of the Union, and recommend to their Consideration such Measures as he shall judge necessary and expedient; he may, on extraordinary Occasions, convene both Houses, or either of them, and in Case of Disagreement between them, with Respect to the Time of Adjournment, he may adjourn them to such Time as he shall think proper; he shall receive Ambassadors and other public Ministers; he shall take Care that the Laws be faithfully executed, and shall Commission all the Officers of the United States.

Section 4. The President, Vice President and all civil Officers of the United States, shall be removed from Office on Impeachment for, and Conviction of, Treason, Bribery, or other high Crimes and Misdemeanors.

Article III

Section 1. The judicial Power of the United States, shall be vested in one supreme Court, and in such inferior Courts as the Congress may from time to time ordain and establish. The Judges, both of the supreme and inferior Courts, shall hold their Offices during good Behaviour, and shall, at stated Times, receive for their Services a Compensation, which shall not be diminished during their Continuance in Office.

Section 2. The judicial Power shall extend to all Cases, in Law and Equity, arising under this Constitution, the Laws of the United States, and Treaties made, or which shall be made, under their Authority;—to all Cases affecting Ambassadors, other public Ministers and Consuls;—to all Cases of admiralty and maritime Jurisdiction;—to Controversies to which the United States shall be a Party;—to Controversies between two or more States;—between a State and Citizens of another State;—between Citizens of different States;—between Citizens of the same State claiming Lands under Grants of different States, and between a State, or the Citizens thereof, and foreign States, Citizens or Subjects.

In all Cases affecting Ambassadors, other public Ministers and Consuls, and those in which a State shall be a Party, the supreme Court shall have original Jurisdiction. In all the other Cases before mentioned, the supreme Court shall have appellate Jurisdiction, both as to Law and Fact, with such Exceptions, and under such Regulations as the Congress shall make.

The Trial of all Crimes, except in Cases of Impeachment, shall be by Jury; and such Trial shall be held in the State where the said Crimes shall have been committed; but when not committed within any State, the Trial shall be at such Place or Places as the Congress may by Law have directed.

Section 3. Treason against the United States, shall consist only in levying War against them, or, in adhering to their Enemies, giving them Aid and Comfort. No Person shall be convicted of Treason unless on the Testimony of two Witnesses to the same overt Act, or on Confession in open Court.

The Congress shall have Power to declare the Punishment of Treason, but no Attainder of Treason shall work Corruption of Blood, or Forfeiture except during the Life of the Person attainted.

Article IV

Section 1. Full Faith and Credit shall be given in each State to the public Acts, Records, and judicial Proceedings of every other State. And the Congress may by general Laws prescribe the Manner in which such Acts, Records and Proceedings shall be proved, and the Effect thereof.

Section 2. The Citizens of each State shall be entitled to all Privileges and Immunities of Citizens in the several States.

A Person charged in any State with Treason, Felony, or other Crime, who shall flee from Justice, and be found in another State, shall on Demand of the executive Authority of the State from which he fled, be delivered up, to be removed to the State having Jurisdiction of the Crime.

No Person held to Service or Labour in one State, under the Laws thereof, escaping into another, shall, in Consequence of any Law or Regulation therein, be discharged from such Service or Labour, but shall be delivered up on Claim of the Party to whom such Service or Labour may be due.

Section 3. New States may be admitted by the Congress into this Union; but no new State shall be formed or erected within the Jurisdiction of any other State; nor any State be formed by the Junction of two or more States, or Parts of States, without the Consent of the Legislatures of the States concerned as well as of the Congress.

The Congress shall have Power to dispose of and make all needful Rules and Regulations respecting the Territory or other Property belonging to the United States; and nothing in this Constitution shall be so construed as to Prejudice any Claims of the United States, or of any particular State.

Section 4. The United States shall guarantee to every State in this Union a Republican Form of Government, and shall protect each of them against Invasion; and on Application of the Legislature, or of the Executive (when the Legislature cannot be convened) against domestic Violence.

Article V

The Congress, whenever two thirds of both Houses shall deem it necessary, shall propose Amendments to this Constitution, or, on the Application of the Legislatures of two thirds of the several States, shall call a Convention for proposing Amendments, which, in either Case, shall be valid to all Intents and Purposes, as part of this Constitution, when ratified by the Legislatures of three fourths of the several States, or by Conventions in three fourths thereof, as the one or the other Mode of Ratification may be proposed by the Congress; Provided that no Amendment which may be made prior to the Year One thousand eight hundred and eight shall in any Manner affect the first and fourth Clauses in the Ninth Section of the first Article; and that no State, without its Consent, shall be deprived of its equal Suffrage in the Senate.

Article VI

All Debts contracted and Engagements entered into, before the Adoption of this Constitution shall be as valid against the United States under this Constitution, as under the Confederation.

This Constitution, and the Laws of the United States which shall be made in Pursuance thereof; and all Treaties made, or which shall be made, under the Authority of the United States, shall be the supreme Law of the Land; and the Judges in every State shall be bound thereby, any Thing in the Constitution or Laws of any State to the Contrary notwithstanding.

The Senators and Representatives before mentioned, and the Members of the several State Legislatures, and all executive and judicial Officers, both of the United States and of the several States, shall be bound by Oath or Affirmation, to support this Constitution; but no religious Test shall ever be required as a Qualification to any Office or public Trust under the United States.

Article VII

The Ratification of the Conventions of nine States shall be sufficient for the Establishment of this Constitution between the States so ratifying the Same.

Amendment I [1791]

Congress shall make no law respecting an establishment of religion, or prohibiting the free exercise thereof; or abridging the freedom of speech, or of the press; or the right of the people peaceably to assembly, and to petition the Government for a redress of grievances.

Amendment II [1791]

A well regulated Militia, being necessary to the security of a free State, the right of the people to keep and bear Arms, shall not be infringed.

Amendment III [1791]

No Soldier shall, in time of peace be quartered in any house, without the consent of the Owner, nor in time of war, but in a manner to be prescribed by law.

Amendment IV [1791]

The right of the people to be secure in their persons, houses, papers, and effects, against unreasonable searches and seizures, shall not be violated, and no Warrants shall issue, but upon probable cause, supported by Oath or affirmation, and particularly describing the place to be searched, and the persons or things to be seized.

Amendment V [1791]

No person shall be held to answer for a capital, or otherwise infamous crime, unless on a presentment or indictment of a Grand Jury, except in cases arising in the land or naval forces, or in the Militia, when in actual service in time of War or public danger; nor shall any person be subject for the same offence to be twice put in jeopardy of life or limb; nor shall be compelled in any criminal case to be a witness against himself, nor be deprived of life, liberty, or property, without due process of law; nor shall private property be taken for public use, without just compensation.

Amendment VI [1791]

In all criminal prosecutions, the accused shall enjoy the right to a speedy and public trial, by an impartial jury of the State and district wherein the crime shall have been committed, which district shall have been previously ascertained by law, and to be informed of the nature and cause of the accusation; to be confronted with the witnesses against him; to have compulsory process for obtaining witnesses in his favor, and to have the Assistance of Counsel for his defence.

Amendment VII [1791]

In Suits at common law, where the value in controversy shall exceed twenty dollars, the right of trial by jury shall be preserved, and no fact tried by jury, shall be otherwise re-examined in any Court of the United States, than according to the rules of the common law.

Amendment VIII [1791]

Excessive bail shall not be required, nor excessive fines imposed, nor cruel and unusual punishments inflicted.

Amendment IX [1791]

The enumeration in the Constitution, of certain rights, shall not be construed to deny or disparage others retained by the people.

Amendment X [1791]

The powers not delegated to the United States by the Constitution, nor prohibited by it to the States, are reserved to the States respectively, or to the people.

Amendment XI [1798]

The Judicial power of the United States shall not be construed to extend to any suit in law or equity, commenced or prosecuted against one of the United States by Citizens of another State, or by Citizens or Subjects of any Foreign State.

Amendment XII [1804]

The Electors shall meet in their respective states, and vote by ballot for President and Vice-President, one of whom, at least, shall not be an inhabitant of the same state with themselves; they shall name in their ballots the person voted for as President, and in distinct ballots the person voted for as Vice-President, and they shall make distinct lists of all persons voted for as President, and of all persons voted for as Vice-President, and of the number of votes for each, which lists they shall sign and certify, and transmit sealed to the seat of the government of the United States, directed to the President of the Senate;—The President of the Senate shall, in the presence of the Senate and House of Representatives, open all the certificates and the votes shall then be counted;—The person having the greatest number of votes for President, shall be the President, if such number be a majority of the whole number of Electors appointed; and if no person have such majority, then from the persons having the highest numbers not exceeding three on the list of those voted for as President, the House of Representatives shall choose immediately, by ballot, the President. But in choosing the President, the votes shall be taken by states, the representation from each state having one vote; a quorum for this purpose shall consist of a member or members from two-thirds of the states, and a majority of all states shall be necessary to a choice. And if the House of Representatives shall not choose a President whenever the right of choice shall devolve upon them, before the fourth day of March next following, then the Vice-President shall act as President, as in the case of the death or other constitutional disability of the President.—The person having the greatest number of votes as Vice-President, shall be the Vice-President, if such number be a majority of the whole number of Electors appointed, and if no person have a majority, then from the two highest numbers on the list, the Senate shall choose the Vice-President; a quorum for the purpose shall consist of two-thirds of the whole number of Senators, and a majority of the whole number shall be necessary to a choice. But no person constitutionally ineligible to the office of President shall be eligible to that of Vice-President of the United States.

Amendment XIII [1865]

Section 1. Neither slavery nor involuntary servitude, except as a punishment for crime whereof the party shall have been duly convicted, shall exist within the United States, or any place subject to their jurisdiction.

Section 2. Congress shall have power to enforce this article by appropriate legislation.

Amendment XIV [1868]

Section 1. All persons born or naturalized in the United States, and subject to the jurisdiction thereof, are citizens of the United States and of the State wherein they reside. No State shall make or enforce any law which shall abridge the privileges or immunities of citizens of the United States; nor shall any State deprive any person of life, liberty, or property, without due process of law; nor deny to any person within its jurisdiction the equal protection of the laws.

Section 2. Representatives shall be apportioned among the several States according to their respective numbers, counting the whole number of persons in each State, excluding Indians not taxed. But when the right to vote at any election for the choice of electors for President and Vice President of the United States, Representatives in Congress, the Executive and Judicial officers of a State, or the members of the Legislature thereof, is denied to any of the male inhabitants of such State, being twenty-one years of age, and citizens of the United States, or in any way abridged, except for participation in rebellion, or other crime, the basis of representation therein shall be reduced in the proportion which the number of such male citizens shall bear to the whole number of male citizens twenty-one years of age in such State.

Section 3. No person shall be a Senator or Representative in Congress, or elector of President and Vice President, or hold any office, civil or military, under the United States, or under any State, who having previously taken an oath, as a member of Congress, or as an officer of the United States, or as a member of any State legislature, or as an executive or judicial officer of any State, to support the Constitution of the United States, shall have engaged in insurrection or rebellion against the same, or given aid or comfort to the enemies thereof. But Congress may by a vote of two-thirds of each House, remove such disability.

Section 4. The validity of the public debt of the United States, authorized by law, including debts incurred for payment of pensions and bounties for services in suppressing insurrection or rebellion, shall not be questioned. But neither the United States nor any State shall assume or pay any debt or obligation incurred in aid of insurrection or rebellion against the United States, or any claim for the loss or emancipation of any slave; but all such debts, obligations and claims shall be held illegal and void.

Section 5. The Congress shall have power to enforce, by appropriate legislation, the provisions of this article.

Amendment XV [1870]

Section 1. The right of citizens of the United States to vote shall not be denied or abridged by the United States or by any State on account of race, color, or previous condition of servitude.

Section 2. The Congress shall have power to enforce this article by appropriate legislation.

Amendment XVI [1913]

The Congress shall have power to lay and collect taxes on incomes, from whatever source derived, without apportionment among the several States, and without regard to any census or enumeration.

Amendment XVII [1913]

Section 1. The Senate of the United States shall be composed of two Senators from each State, elected by the people thereof, for six years; and each Senator shall have one vote. The electors in each State shall have the qualifications requisite for electors of the most numerous branch of the State legislatures.

Section 2. When vacancies happen in the representation of any State in the Senate, the executive authority of such State shall issue writs of election to fill such vacancies: *Provided,* That the legislature of any State may empower the executive thereof to make temporary appointments until the people fill the vacancies by election as the legislature may direct.

Section 3. This amendment shall not be so construed as to affect the election or term of any Senator chosen before it becomes valid as part of the Constitution.

Amendment XVIII [1919]

Section 1. After one year from the ratification of this article the manufacture, sale, or transportation of intoxicating liquors within, the importation thereof into, or the exportation thereof from the United States and all territory subject to the jurisdiction thereof for beverage purposes is hereby prohibited.

Section 2. The Congress and the several States shall have concurrent power to enforce this article by appropriate legislation.

Section 3. This article shall be inoperative unless it shall have been ratified as an amendment to the Constitution by the legislatures of the several States, as provided in the Constitution, within seven years from the date of the submission hereof to the States by the Congress.

Amendment XIX [1920]

Section 1. The right of citizens of the United States to vote shall not be denied or abridged by the United States or by any State on account of sex.

Section 2. Congress shall have power to enforce this article by appropriate legislation.

Amendment XX [1933]

Section 1. The terms of the President and Vice President shall end at noon on the 20th day of January, and the terms of Senators and Representatives at noon on the 3d day of January, of the years in which such terms would have ended if this article had not been ratified; and the terms of their successors shall then begin.

Section 2. The Congress shall assemble at least once in every year, and such meeting shall begin at noon on the 3d day of January, unless they shall by law appoint a different day.

Section 3. If, at the time fixed for the beginning of the term of the President, the President elect shall have died, the Vice President elect shall become President. If the President shall not have been chosen before the time fixed for the beginning of his term, or if the President elect shall have failed to qualify, then the Vice President elect shall act as President until a President shall have qualified; and the Congress may by law provide for the case wherein neither a President elect nor a Vice President elect shall have qualified, declaring who shall then act as President, or the manner in which one who is to act shall be selected, and such person shall act accordingly until a President or Vice President shall have qualified.

Section 4. The Congress may by law provide for the case of the death of any of the persons from whom the House of Representatives may choose a President whenever the right of choice shall have devolved upon them, and for the case of the death of any of the persons from whom the Senate may choose a Vice President whenever the right of choice shall have devolved upon them.

Section 5. Sections 1 and 2 shall take effect on the 15th day of October following the ratification of this article.

Section 6. This article shall be inoperative unless it shall have been ratified as an amendment to the Constitution by the legislatures of three-fourths of the several States within seven years from the date of its submission.

Amendment XXI [1933]

Section 1. The eighteenth article of amendment to the Constitution of the United States is hereby repealed.

Section 2. The transportation or importation into any State, Territory, or possession of the United States for delivery or use therein of intoxicating liquors, in violation of the laws thereof, is hereby prohibited.

Section 3. This article shall be inoperative unless it shall have been ratified as an amendment to the Constitution by conventions in the several States, as provided in the Constitution, within seven years from the date of the submission hereof to the States by the Congress.

Amendment XXII [1951]

Section 1. No person shall be elected to the office of the President more than twice, and no person who has held the office of President, or acted as President, for more than two years of a term to which some other person was elected President shall be elected to the office of President more than once. But this Article shall not apply to any person holding the office of President when this Article was proposed by the Congress, and shall not prevent any person who may be holding the office of President, or acting as President, during the term within which this Article becomes operative from holding the office of President or acting as President during the remainder of such term.

Section 2. This article shall be inoperative unless it shall have been ratified as an amendment to the Constitution by the legislatures of three-fourths of the several States within seven years from the date of its submission to the States by the Congress.

Amendment XXIII [1961]

Section 1. The District constituting the seat of Government of the United States shall appoint in such manner as the Congress may direct:

A number of electors of President and Vice President equal to the whole number of Senators and Representatives in Congress to which the District would be entitled if it were a State, but in no event more than the least populous state; they shall be in addition to those appointed by the states, but they shall be considered, for the purposes of the election of President and Vice President, to be electors appointed by a state; and they shall meet in the District and perform such duties as provided by the twelfth article of amendment.

Section 2. The Congress shall have power to enforce this article by appropriate legislation.

Amendment XXIV [1964]

Section 1. The right of citizens of the United States to vote in any primary or other election for President or Vice President, for electors for President or Vice President, or for Senator or Representative in Congress, shall not be denied or abridged by the United States, or any State by reason of failure to pay any poll tax or other tax.

Section 2. The Congress shall have power to enforce this article by appropriate legislation.

Amendment XXV [1967]

Section 1. In case of the removal of the President from office or of his death or resignation, the Vice President shall become President.

Section 2. Whenever there is a vacancy in the office of the Vice President, the President shall nominate a Vice President who shall take office upon confirmation by a majority vote of both Houses of Congress.

Section 3. Whenever the President transmits to the President pro tempore of the Senate and the Speaker of the House of Representatives his written declaration that he is unable to discharge the powers and duties of his office, and until he transmits to them a written declaration to the contrary, such powers and duties shall be discharged by the Vice President as Acting President.

Section 4. Whenever the Vice President and a majority of either the principal officers of the executive departments or of such other body as Congress may by law provide, transmit to the President pro tempore of the Senate and the Speaker of the House of Representatives their written declaration that the President is unable to discharge the powers and duties of his office, the Vice President shall immediately assume the powers and duties of the office as Acting President.

Thereafter, when the President transmits to the President pro tempore of the Senate and the Speaker of the House of Representatives his written declaration that no inability exists, he shall resume the powers and duties of his office unless the Vice President and a majority of either the principal officers of the executive department or of such other body as Congress may by law provide, transmit within four days to the President pro tempore of the Senate and the Speaker of the House of Representatives their written declaration that the President is unable to discharge the powers and duties of his office. Thereupon Congress shall decide the issue, assembling within forty-eight hours for that purpose if not in session. If the Congress, within twenty-one days after receipt of the latter written declaration, or, if Congress is not in session, within twenty-one days after Congress is required to assemble, determines by two-thirds vote of both Houses that the President is unable to discharge the powers and duties of his office, the Vice President shall continue to discharge the same as Acting President; otherwise, the President shall resume the powers and duties of his office.

Amendment XXVI [1971]

Section 1. The right of citizens of the United States, who are eighteen years of age or older, to vote shall not be denied or abridged by the United States or by any State on account of age.

Section 2. The Congress shall have power to enforce this article by appropriate legislation.

Amendment XXVII [1992]

No law, varying the compensation for the services of the Senators and Representatives, shall take effect, until an election of Representatives shall have intervened.

APPENDIX **C**

The Uniform Commercial Code (Excerpts)

(Adopted in fifty-two jurisdictions; all fifty States, although Louisiana has adopted only Articles 1, 3, 4, 7, 8, and 9; the District of Columbia; and the Virgin Islands.)

The Uniform Commercial Code consists of the following articles:

Articles:

1. **General Provisions**
2. **Sales**

2A. **Leases**

3. **Negotiable Instruments**
4. **Bank Deposits and Collections**

4A. **Fund Transfers**

5. **Letters of Credit**
6. **Repealer of Article 6—Bulk Transfers and [Revised] Article 6—Bulk Sales**
7. **Warehouse Receipts, Bills of Lading and Other Documents of Title**
8. **Investment Securities**
9. **Secured Transactions**
10. **Effective Date and Repealer**
11. **Effective Date and Transition Provisions**

Article 1 GENERAL PROVISIONS

Part 1 General Provisions

§ 1–101. Short Titles.

(a) This [Act] may be cited as Uniform Commercial Code.

(b) This article may be cited as Uniform Commercial Code–Uniform Provisions.

§ 1–102. Scope of Article.

This article applies to a transaction to the extent that it is governed by another article of [the Uniform Commercial Code].

§ 1–103. Construction of [Uniform Commercial Code] to Promote Its Purpose and Policies; Applicability of Supplemental Principles of Law.

(a) [The Uniform Commercial Code] must be liberally construed and applied to promote its underlying purposes and policies, which are:

(1) to simplify, clarify, and modernize the law governing commercial transactions;

(2) to permit the continued expansion of commercial practices through custom, usage, and agreement of the parties; and

(3) to make uniform the law among the various jurisdictions.

(b) Unless displaced by the particular provisions of [the Uniform Commercial Code], the principles of law and equity, including the law merchant and the law relative to capacity to contract, principal and agent, estoppel, fraud, misrepresentation, duress, coercion, mistake, bankruptcy, and other validating or invalidating cause, supplement its provisions.

§ 1–104. Construction Against Implicit Repeal.

This Act being a general act intended as a unified coverage of its subject matter, no part of it shall be deemed to be impliedly repealed by subsequent legislation if such construction can reasonably be avoided.

§ 1–105. Severability.

If any provision or clause of [the Uniform Commercial Code] or its application to any person or circumstance is held invalid, the invalidity does not affect other provisions or applications of [the Uniform Commercial Code] which can be given effect without the invalid provision or application, and to this end the provisions of [the Uniform Commercial Code] are severable.

§ 1–106. Use of Singular and Plural; Gender.

In [the Uniform Commercial Code], unless the statutory context otherwise requires:

(1) words in the singular number include the plural, and those in the plural include the singular; and

(2) words of any gender also refer to any other gender.

§ 1–107. Section Captions.

Section captions are part of [the Uniform Commercial Code].

§ 1–108. Relation to Electronic Signatures in Global and National Commerce Act.

This article modifies, limits, and supersedes the Federal Electronic Signatures in Global and National Commerce Act, 15 U.S.C. Sections 7001 *et seq.*, except that nothing in this article modifies, limits, or supersedes section 7001(c) of that act or authorizes electronic delivery of any of the notices described in section 7003(b) of that Act.

Part 2 General Definitions and Principles of Interpretation

§ 1–201. General Definitions.

Subject to additional definitions contained in the subsequent Articles of this Act which are applicable to specific Articles or Parts thereof, and unless the context otherwise requires, in this Act:

(1) "Action", in the sense of a judicial proceeding, includes recoupment, counterclaim, set-off, suit in equity, and any other proceedings in which rights are determined.

(2) "Aggrieved party" means a party entitled to resort to a remedy.

(3) "Agreement", as distinguished from "contract", means the bargain of the parties in fact, as found in their language or by implication from other circumstances, including course of performance, course of dealing, or usage of trade as provided in Section 1–303.

(4) "Bank" means a person engaged in the business of banking and includes a savings bank, savings and loan association, credit union, and trust company.

(5) "Bearer" means a person in control of a negotiable electronic document of title or a person in possession of a negotiable instrument, negotiable tangible document of title, or certificated security that is payable to bearer or indorsed in blank.

(6) "Bill of lading" means a document of title evidencing the receipt of goods for shipment issued by a person engaged in the business of directly or indirectly transporting or forwarding goods. The term does not include a warehouse receipt.

(7) "Branch" includes a separately incorporated foreign branch of a bank.

(8) "Burden of establishing" a fact means the burden of persuading the trier of fact that the existence of the fact is more probable than its nonexistence.

(9) "Buyer in ordinary course of business" means a person that buys goods in good faith, without knowledge that the sale violates the rights of another person in the goods, and in the ordinary course from a person, other than a pawnbroker, in the business of selling goods of that kind. A person buys goods in the ordinary course if the sale to the person comports with the usual or customary practices in the kind of business in which the seller is engaged or with the seller's own usual or customary practices. A person that sells oil, gas, or other minerals at the wellhead or minehead is a person in the business of selling goods of that kind. A buyer in ordinary course of business may buy for cash, by exchange of other property, or on secured or unsecured credit, and may acquire goods or documents of title under a pre-existing contract for sale. Only a buyer that takes possession of the goods or has a right to recover the goods from the seller under Article 2 may be a buyer in ordinary course of business. A person that acquires goods in a transfer in bulk or as security for or in total or partial satisfaction of a money debt is not a buyer in ordinary course of business.

(10) "Conspicuous", with reference to a term, means so written, displayed, or presented that a reasonable person against which it is to operate ought to have noticed it. Whether a term is "conspicuous" or not is a decision for the court. Conspicuous terms include the following:

(A) a heading in capitals equal to or greater in size than the surrounding text, or in contrasting type, font, or color to the surrounding text of the same or lesser size; and

(B) language in the body of a record or display in larger type than the surrounding text, or in contrasting type, font, or color to the surrounding text of the same size, or set off from surrounding text of the same size by symbols or other marks that call attention to the language.

(11) "Consumer" means an individual who enters into a transaction primarily for personal, family, or household purposes.

(12) "Contract", as distinguished from "agreement", means the total legal obligation that results from the parties' agreement as determined by [the Uniform Commercial Code] as supplemented by any other laws.

(13) "Creditor" includes a general creditor, a secured creditor, a lien creditor and any representative of creditors, including an assignee for the benefit of creditors, a trustee in bankruptcy, a receiver in equity and an executor or administrator of an insolvent debtor's or assignor's estate.

(14) "Defendant" includes a person in the position of defendant in a counterclaim, cross-action, or third-party claim.

(15) "Delivery" with respect to an electronic document of title means voluntary transfer of control and with respect to an instrument, a tangible document of title, or chattel paper means voluntary transfer of possession.

(16) "Document of title" means a record (i) that in regular course of business or financing is treated as adequately evidencing that the person in possession or control of the record is entitled to receive, control, hold, and dispose of the record and the goods the record covers and (ii) that purports to be issued by or addressed to a bailee and to cover goods in the bailee's possession which are either identified or are fungible portions of an identified mass. The term includes a bill of lading, transport document, dock warrant, dock receipt, warehouse receipt, and order for delivery of goods. An electronic document of title means a document of title evidenced by a record consisting of information stored in an electronic medium. A tangible document of title means a document of title evidenced by a record consisting of information that is inscribed on a tangible medium.

(17) "Fault" means a default, breach, or wrongful act or omission.

(18) "Fungible goods" means:

(A) goods of which any unit, by nature or usage of trade, is the equivalent of any other like unit; or

(B) goods that by agreement are treated as equivalent.

(19) "Genuine" means free of forgery or counterfeiting.

(20) "Good faith," except as otherwise provided in Article 5, means honesty in fact and the observance of reasonable commercial standards of fair dealing.

(21) "Holder" means:

(A) the person in possession of a negotiable instrument that is payable either to bearer or to an identified person that is the person in possession;

(B) the person in possession of a negotiable tangible document of title if the goods are deliverable either to bearer or to the order of the person in possession; or

(C) the person in control of a negotiable electronic document of title.

(22) "Insolvency proceeding" includes an assignment for the benefit of creditors or other proceeding intended to liquidate or rehabilitate the estate of the person involved.

(23) "Insolvent" means:

(A) having generally ceased to pay debts in the ordinary course of business other than as a result of bona fide dispute;

(B) being unable to pay debts as they become due; or

(C) being insolvent within the meaning of federal bankruptcy law.

(24) "Money" means a medium of exchange currently authorized or adopted by a domestic or foreign government. The term includes a monetary unit of account established by an intergovernmental organization or by agreement between two or more countries.

(25) "Organization" means a person other than an individual.

(26) "Party", as distinguished from "third party", means a person that has engaged in a transaction or made an agreement subject to [the Uniform Commercial Code].

(27) "Person" means an individual, corporation, business trust, estate, trust, partnership, limited liability company, association, joint venture, government, governmental subdivision, agency, or instrumentality, public corporation, or any other legal or commercial entity.

(28) "Present value" means the amount as of a date certain of one or more sums payable in the future, discounted to the date certain by use of either an interest rate specified by the parties if that rate is not manifestly unreasonable at the time the transaction is entered into or, if an interest rate is not so specified, a commercially reasonable rate that takes into account the facts and circumstances at the time the transaction is entered into.

(29) "Purchase" means taking by sale, lease, discount, negotiation, mortgage, pledge, lien, security interest, issue or reissue, gift, or any other voluntary transaction creating an interest in property.

(30) "Purchaser" means a person that takes by purchase.

(31) "Record" means information that is inscribed on a tangible medium or that is stored in an electronic or other medium and is retrievable in perceivable form.

(32) "Remedy" means any remedial right to which an aggrieved party is entitled with or without resort to a tribunal.

(33) "Representative" means a person empowered to act for another, including an agent, an officer of a corporation or association, and a trustee, executor, or administrator of an estate.

(34) "Right" includes remedy.

(35) "Security interest" means an interest in personal property or fixtures which secures payment or performance of an obligation. "Security interest" includes any interest of a consignor and a buyer of accounts, chattel paper, a payment intangible, or a promissory note in a transaction that is subject to Article 9. "Security interest" does not include the special property interest of a buyer of goods on identification of those goods to a contract for sale under Section 2–401, but a buyer may also acquire a "security interest" by complying with Article 9. Except as otherwise provided in Section 2–505, the right of a seller or lessor of goods under Article 2 or 2A to retain or acquire possession of the goods is not a "security interest", but a seller or lessor may also acquire a "security interest" by complying with Article 9. The retention or reservation of title by a seller of goods notwithstanding shipment or delivery to the buyer under Section 2–401 is limited in effect to a reservation of a "security interest." Whether a transaction in the form of a lease creates a "security interest" is determined pursuant to Section 1–203.

(36) "Send" in connection with a writing, record, or notice means:

(A) to deposit in the mail or deliver for transmission by any other usual means of communication with postage or cost of transmission provided for and properly addressed and, in the case of an instrument, to an address specified thereon or otherwise agreed, or if there be none to any address reasonable under the circumstances; or

(B) in any other way to cause to be received any record or notice within the time it would have arrived if properly sent.

(37) "Signed" includes using any symbol executed or adopted with present intention to adopt or accept a writing.

(38) "State" means a State of the United States, the District of Columbia, Puerto Rico, the United States Virgin Islands, or any territory or insular possession subject to the jurisdiction of the United States.

(39) "Surety" includes a guarantor or other secondary obligor.

(40) "Term" means a portion of an agreement that relates to a particular matter.

(41) "Unauthorized signature" means a signature made without actual, implied, or apparent authority. The term includes a forgery.

(42) "Warehouse receipt" means a document of title issued by a person engaged in the business of storing goods for hire.

(43) "Writing" includes printing, typewriting, or any other intentional reduction to tangible form. "Written" has a corresponding meaning.

As amended in 2003.

* * * *

§ 1–205. Reasonable Time; Seasonableness.

(a) Whether a time for taking an action required by [the Uniform Commercial Code] is reasonable depends on the nature, purpose, and circumstances of the action.

(b) An action is taken seasonably if it is taken at or within the time agreed or, if no time is agreed, at or within a reasonable time.

* * * *

Part 3 Territorial Applicability and General Rules

* * * *

§ 1–303. Course of Performance, Course of Dealing, and Usage of Trade.

(a) A "course of performance" is a sequence of conduct between the parties to a particular transaction that exists if:

(1) the agreement of the parties with respect to the transaction involves repeated occasions for performance by a party; and

(2) the other party, with knowledge of the nature of the performance and opportunity for objection to it, accepts the performance or acquiesces in it without objection.

(b) A "course of dealing" is a sequence of conduct concerning previous transactions between the parties to a particular transaction that is fairly to be regarded as establishing a common basis of understanding for interpreting their expressions and other conduct.

(c) A "usage of trade" is any practice or method of dealing having such regularity of observance in a place, vocation, or trade as to justify an expectation that it will be observed with respect to the transaction in question. The existence and scope of such a usage must be proved as facts. If it is established that such a usage is embodied in a trade code or similar record, the interpretation of the record is a question of law.

(d) A course of performance or course of dealing between the parties or usage of trade in the vocation or trade in which they are engaged or of which they are or should be aware is relevant in ascertaining the meaning of the parties' agreement, may give particular meaning to specific terms of the agreement, and may supplement or qualify the terms of the agreement. A usage of trade applicable in the place in which part of the performance under the agreement is to occur may be so utilized as to that part of the performance.

(e) Except as otherwise provided in subsection (f), the express terms of an agreement and any applicable course of performance, course of dealing, or usage of trade must be construed whenever reasonable as consistent with each other. If such a construction is unreasonable:

(1) express terms prevail over course of performance, course of dealing, and usage of trade;

(2) course of performance prevails over course of dealing and usage of trade; and

(3) course of dealing prevails over usage of trade.

(f) Subject to Section 2–209 and Section 2A–208, a course of performance is relevant to show a waiver or modification of any term inconsistent with the course of performance.

(g) Evidence of a relevant usage of trade offered by one party is not admissible unless that party has given the other party notice that the court finds sufficient to prevent unfair surprise to the other party.

§ 1–304. Obligation of Good Faith.

Every contract or duty within [the Uniform Commercial Code] imposes an obligation of good faith in its performance and enforcement.

* * * *

§ 1–309. Option to Accelerate at Will.

A term providing that one party or that party's successor in interest may accelerate payment or performance or require collateral or additional collateral "at will" or when the party "deems itself insecure," or words of similar import, means that the party has power to do so only if that party in good faith believes that the prospect of payment or performance is impaired. The burden of establishing lack of good faith is on the party against which the power has been exercised.

§ 1–310. Subordinated Obligations.

An obligation may be issued as subordinated to performance of another obligation of the person obligated, or a creditor may subordinate its right to performance of an obligation by agreement with either the person obligated or another creditor of the person obligated. Subordination does not create a security interest as against either the common debtor or a subordinated creditor.

Article 2 SALES

Part 1 Short Title, General Construction and Subject Matter

§ 2–101. Short Title.

This Article shall be known and may be cited as Uniform Commercial Code—Sales.

§ 2–102. Scope; Certain Security and Other Transactions Excluded From This Article.

Unless the context otherwise requires, this Article applies to transactions in goods; it does not apply to any transaction which although in the form of an unconditional contract to sell or present sale is intended to operate only as a security transaction nor does this Article impair or repeal any statute regulating sales to consumers, farmers or other specified classes of buyers.

§ 2–103. Definitions and Index of Definitions.

(1) In this Article unless the context otherwise requires

(a) "Buyer" means a person who buys or contracts to buy goods.

(b) "Good faith" in the case of a merchant means honesty in fact and the observance of reasonable commercial standards of fair dealing in the trade.

(c) "Receipt" of goods means taking physical possession of them.

(d) "Seller" means a person who sells or contracts to sell goods.

(2) Other definitions applying to this Article or to specified Parts thereof, and the sections in which they appear are:

"Acceptance". Section 2–606.
"Banker's credit". Section 2–325.
"Between merchants". Section 2–104.
"Cancellation". Section 2–106(4).
"Commercial unit". Section 2–105.
"Confirmed credit". Section 2–325.
"Conforming to contract". Section 2–106.
"Contract for sale". Section 2–106.
"Cover". Section 2–712.
"Entrusting". Section 2–403.
"Financing agency". Section 2–104.
"Future goods". Section 2–105.
"Goods". Section 2–105.
"Identification". Section 2–501.
"Installment contract". Section 2–612.
"Letter of Credit". Section 2–325.

"Lot". Section 2–105.
"Merchant". Section 2–104.
"Overseas". Section 2–323.
"Person in position of seller". Section 2–707.
"Present sale". Section 2–106.
"Sale". Section 2–106.
"Sale on approval". Section 2–326.
"Sale or return". Section 2–326.
"Termination". Section 2–106.

(3) The following definitions in other Articles apply to this Article:

"Check". Section 3–104.
"Consignee". Section 7–102.
"Consignor". Section 7–102.
"Consumer goods". Section 9–109.
"Dishonor". Section 3–507.
"Draft". Section 3–104.

(4) In addition Article 1 contains general definitions and principles of construction and interpretation applicable throughout this Article.

As amended in 1994 and 1999.

§ 2–104. Definitions: "Merchant"; "Between Merchants"; "Financing Agency".

(1) "Merchant" means a person who deals in goods of the kind or otherwise by his occupation holds himself out as having knowledge or skill peculiar to the practices or goods involved in the transaction or to whom such knowledge or skill may be attributed by his employment of an agent or broker or other intermediary who by his occupation holds himself out as having such knowledge or skill.

(2) "Financing agency" means a bank, finance company or other person who in the ordinary course of business makes advances against goods or documents of title or who by arrangement with either the seller or the buyer intervenes in ordinary course to make or collect payment due or claimed under the contract for sale, as by purchasing or paying the seller's draft or making advances against it or by merely taking it for collection whether or not documents of title accompany the draft. "Financing agency" includes also a bank or other person who similarly intervenes between persons who are in the position of seller and buyer in respect to the goods (Section 2–707).

(3) "Between merchants" means in any transaction with respect to which both parties are chargeable with the knowledge or skill of merchants.

§ 2–105. Definitions: Transferability; "Goods"; "Future" Goods; "Lot"; "Commercial Unit".

(1) "Goods" means all things (including specially manufactured goods) which are movable at the time of identification to the contract for sale other than the money in which the price is to be paid, investment securities (Article 8) and things in action. "Goods" also includes the unborn young of animals and growing crops and other identified things attached to realty as described in the section on goods to be severed from realty (Section 2–107).

(2) Goods must be both existing and identified before any interest in them can pass. Goods which are not both existing and identified are "future" goods. A purported present sale of future goods or of any interest therein operates as a contract to sell.

(3) There may be a sale of a part interest in existing identified goods.

(4) An undivided share in an identified bulk of fungible goods is sufficiently identified to be sold although the quantity of the bulk is not determined. Any agreed proportion of such a bulk or any quantity thereof agreed upon by number, weight or other measure may to the extent of the seller's interest in the bulk be sold to the buyer who then becomes an owner in common.

(5) "Lot" means a parcel or a single article which is the subject matter of a separate sale or delivery, whether or not it is sufficient to perform the contract.

(6) "Commercial unit" means such a unit of goods as by commercial usage is a single whole for purposes of sale and division of which materially impairs its character or value on the market or in use. A commercial unit may be a single article (as a machine) or a set of articles (as a suite of furniture or an assortment of sizes) or a quantity (as a bale, gross, or carload) or any other unit treated in use or in the relevant market as a single whole.

§ 2–106. Definitions: "Contract"; "Agreement"; "Contract for Sale"; "Sale"; "Present Sale"; "Conforming" to Contract; "Termination"; "Cancellation".

(1) In this Article unless the context otherwise requires "contract" and "agreement" are limited to those relating to the present or future sale of goods. "Contract for sale" includes both a present sale of goods and a contract to sell goods at a future time. A "sale" consists in the passing of title from the seller to the buyer for a price (Section 2–401). A "present sale" means a sale which is accomplished by the making of the contract.

(2) Goods or conduct including any part of a performance are "conforming" or conform to the contract when they are in accordance with the obligations under the contract.

(3) "Termination" occurs when either party pursuant to a power created by agreement or law puts an end to the contract otherwise than for its breach. On "termination" all obligations which are still executory on both sides are discharged but any right based on prior breach or performance survives.

(4) "Cancellation" occurs when either party puts an end to the contract for breach by the other and its effect is the same as that of "termination" except that the cancelling party also retains any remedy for breach of the whole contract or any unperformed balance.

§ 2–107. Goods to Be Severed From Realty: Recording.

(1) A contract for the sale of minerals or the like (including oil and gas) or a structure or its materials to be removed from realty is a contract for the sale of goods within this Article if they are to be severed by the seller but until severance a purported present sale thereof which is not effective as a transfer of an interest in land is effective only as a contract to sell.

(2) A contract for the sale apart from the land of growing crops or other things attached to realty and capable of severance without material harm thereto but not described in subsection (1) or of timber to be cut is a contract for the sale of goods within this

Article whether the subject matter is to be severed by the buyer or by the seller even though it forms part of the realty at the time of contracting, and the parties can by identification effect a present sale before severance.

(3) The provisions of this section are subject to any third party rights provided by the law relating to realty records, and the contract for sale may be executed and recorded as a document transferring an interest in land and shall then constitute notice to third parties of the buyer's rights under the contract for sale.

As amended in 1972.

Part 2 Form, Formation and Readjustment of Contract

§ 2–201. Formal Requirements; Statute of Frauds.

(1) Except as otherwise provided in this section a contract for the sale of goods for the price of $500 or more is not enforceable by way of action or defense unless there is some writing sufficient to indicate that a contract for sale has been made between the parties and signed by the party against whom enforcement is sought or by his authorized agent or broker. A writing is not insufficient because it omits or incorrectly states a term agreed upon but the contract is not enforceable under this paragraph beyond the quantity of goods shown in such writing.

(2) Between merchants if within a reasonable time a writing in confirmation of the contract and sufficient against the sender is received and the party receiving it has reason to know its contents, its satisfies the requirements of subsection (1) against such party unless written notice of objection to its contents is given within ten days after it is received.

(3) A contract which does not satisfy the requirements of subsection (1) but which is valid in other respects is enforceable

(a) if the goods are to be specially manufactured for the buyer and are not suitable for sale to others in the ordinary course of the seller's business and the seller, before notice of repudiation is received and under circumstances which reasonably indicate that the goods are for the buyer, has made either a substantial beginning of their manufacture or commitments for their procurement; or

(b) if the party against whom enforcement is sought admits in his pleading, testimony or otherwise in court that a contract for sale was made, but the contract is not enforceable under this provision beyond the quantity of goods admitted; or

(c) with respect to goods for which payment has been made and accepted or which have been received and accepted (Sec. 2–606).

§ 2–202. Final Written Expression: Parol or Extrinsic Evidence.

Terms with respect to which the confirmatory memoranda of the parties agree or which are otherwise set forth in a writing intended by the parties as a final expression of their agreement with respect to such terms as are included therein may not be contradicted by evidence of any prior agreement or of a contemporaneous oral agreement but may be explained or supplemented

(a) by course of dealing or usage of trade (Section 1–205) or by course of performance (Section 2–208); and

(b) by evidence of consistent additional terms unless the court finds the writing to have been intended also as a complete and exclusive statement of the terms of the agreement.

§ 2–203. Seals Inoperative.

The affixing of a seal to a writing evidencing a contract for sale or an offer to buy or sell goods does not constitute the writing a sealed instrument and the law with respect to sealed instruments does not apply to such a contract or offer.

§ 2–204. Formation in General.

(1) A contract for sale of goods may be made in any manner sufficient to show agreement, including conduct by both parties which recognizes the existence of such a contract.

(2) An agreement sufficient to constitute a contract for sale may be found even though the moment of its making is undetermined.

(3) Even though one or more terms are left open a contract for sale does not fail for indefiniteness if the parties have intended to make a contract and there is a reasonably certain basis for giving an appropriate remedy.

§ 2–205. Firm Offers.

An offer by a merchant to buy or sell goods in a signed writing which by its terms gives assurance that it will be held open is not revocable, for lack of consideration, during the time stated or if no time is stated for a reasonable time, but in no event may such period of irrevocability exceed three months; but any such term of assurance on a form supplied by the offeree must be separately signed by the offeror.

§ 2–206. Offer and Acceptance in Formation of Contract.

(1) Unless other unambiguously indicated by the language or circumstances

(a) an offer to make a contract shall be construed as inviting acceptance in any manner and by any medium reasonable in the circumstances;

(b) an order or other offer to buy goods for prompt or current shipment shall be construed as inviting acceptance either by a prompt promise to ship or by the prompt or current shipment of conforming or nonconforming goods, but such a shipment of non-conforming goods does not constitute an acceptance if the seller seasonably notifies the buyer that the shipment is offered only as an accommodation to the buyer.

(2) Where the beginning of a requested performance is a reasonable mode of acceptance an offeror who is not notified of acceptance within a reasonable time may treat the offer as having lapsed before acceptance.

§ 2–207. Additional Terms in Acceptance or Confirmation.

(1) A definite and seasonable expression of acceptance or a written confirmation which is sent within a reasonable time operates as an acceptance even though it states terms additional to or different from those offered or agreed upon, unless acceptance is expressly made conditional on assent to the additional or different terms.

(2) The additional terms are to be construed as proposals for addition to the contract. Between merchants such terms become part of the contract unless:

(a) the offer expressly limits acceptance to the terms of the offer;

(b) they materially alter it; or

(c) notification of objection to them has already been given or is given within a reasonable time after notice of them is received.

(3) Conduct by both parties which recognizes the existence of a contract is sufficient to establish a contract for sale although the writings of the parties do not otherwise establish a contract. In such case the terms of the particular contract consist of those terms on which the writings of the parties agree, together with any supplementary terms incorporated under any other provisions of this Act.

§ 2–208. Course of Performance or Practical Construction.

(1) Where the contract for sale involves repeated occasions for performance by either party with knowledge of the nature of the performance and opportunity for objection to it by the other, any course of performance accepted or acquiesced in without objection shall be relevant to determine the meaning of the agreement.

(2) The express terms of the agreement and any such course of performance, as well as any course of dealing and usage of trade, shall be construed whenever reasonable as consistent with each other; but when such construction is unreasonable, express terms shall control course of performance and course of performance shall control both course of dealing and usage of trade (Section 1–205).

(3) Subject to the provisions of the next section on modification and waiver, such course of performance shall be relevant to show a waiver or modification of any term inconsistent with such course of performance.

§ 2–209. Modification, Rescission and Waiver.

(1) An agreement modifying a contract within this Article needs no consideration to be binding.

(2) A signed agreement which excludes modification or rescission except by a signed writing cannot be otherwise modified or rescinded, but except as between merchants such a requirement on a form supplied by the merchant must be separately signed by the other party.

(3) The requirements of the statute of frauds section of this Article (Section 2–201) must be satisfied if the contract as modified is within its provisions.

(4) Although an attempt at modification or rescission does not satisfy the requirements of subsection (2) or (3) it can operate as a waiver.

(5) A party who has made a waiver affecting an executory portion of the contract may retract the waiver by reasonable notification received by the other party that strict performance will be required of any term waived, unless the retraction would be unjust in view of a material change of position in reliance on the waiver.

§ 2–210. Delegation of Performance; Assignment of Rights.

(1) A party may perform his duty through a delegate unless otherwise agreed or unless the other party has a substantial interest in having his original promisor perform or control the acts required by the contract. No delegation of performance relieves the party delegating of any duty to perform or any liability for breach.

(2) Except as otherwise provided in Section 9–406, unless otherwise agreed, all rights of either seller or buyer can be assigned except where the assignment would materially change the duty of the other party, or increase materially the burden or risk imposed on him by his contract, or impair materially his chance of obtaining return performance. A right to damages for breach of the whole contract or a right arising out of the assignor's due performance of his entire obligation can be assigned despite agreement otherwise.

(3) The creation, attachment, perfection, or enforcement of a security interest in the seller's interest under a contract is not a transfer that materially changes the duty of or increases materially the burden or risk imposed on the buyer or impairs materially the buyer's chance of obtaining return performance within the purview of subsection (2) unless, and then only to the extent that, enforcement actually results in a delegation of material performance of the seller. Even in that event, the creation, attachment, perfection, and enforcement of the security interest remain effective, but (i) the seller is liable to the buyer for damages caused by the delegation to the extent that the damages could not reasonably by prevented by the buyer, and (ii) a court having jurisdiction may grant other appropriate relief, including cancellation of the contract for sale or an injunction against enforcement of the security interest or consummation of the enforcement.

(4) Unless the circumstances indicate the contrary a prohibition of assignment of "the contract" is to be construed as barring only the delegation to the assignee of the assignor's performance.

(5) An assignment of "the contract" or of "all my rights under the contract" or an assignment in similar general terms is an assignment of rights and unless the language or the circumstances (as in an assignment for security) indicate the contrary, it is a delegation of performance of the duties of the assignor and its acceptance by the assignee constitutes a promise by him to perform those duties. This promise is enforceable by either the assignor or the other party to the original contract.

(6) The other party may treat any assignment which delegates performance as creating reasonable grounds for insecurity and may without prejudice to his rights against the assignor demand assurances from the assignee (Section 2–609).

As amended in 1999.

Part 3 General Obligation and Construction of Contract

§ 2–301. General Obligations of Parties.

The obligation of the seller is to transfer and deliver and that of the buyer is to accept and pay in accordance with the contract.

§ 2–302. Unconscionable Contract or Clause.

(1) If the court as a matter of law finds the contract or any clause of the contract to have been unconscionable at the time it was made

the court may refuse to enforce the contract, or it may enforce the remainder of the contract without the unconscionable clause, or it may so limit the application of any unconscionable clause as to avoid any unconscionable result.

(2) When it is claimed or appears to the court that the contract or any clause thereof may be unconscionable the parties shall be afforded a reasonable opportunity to present evidence as to its commercial setting, purpose and effect to aid the court in making the determination.

§ 2–303. Allocations or Division of Risks.

Where this Article allocates a risk or a burden as between the parties "unless otherwise agreed", the agreement may not only shift the allocation but may also divide the risk or burden.

§ 2–304. Price Payable in Money, Goods, Realty, or Otherwise.

(1) The price can be made payable in money or otherwise. If it is payable in whole or in part in goods each party is a seller of the goods which he is to transfer.

(2) Even though all or part of the price is payable in an interest in realty the transfer of the goods and the seller's obligations with reference to them are subject to this Article, but not the transfer of the interest in realty or the transferor's obligations in connection therewith.

§ 2–305. Open Price Term.

(1) The parties if they so intend can conclude a contract for sale even though the price is not settled. In such a case the price is a reasonable price at the time for delivery if

(a) nothing is said as to price; or

(b) the price is left to be agreed by the parties and they fail to agree; or

(c) the price is to be fixed in terms of some agreed market or other standard as set or recorded by a third person or agency and it is not so set or recorded.

(2) A price to be fixed by the seller or by the buyer means a price for him to fix in good faith.

(3) When a price left to be fixed otherwise than by agreement of the parties fails to be fixed through fault of one party the other may at his option treat the contract as cancelled or himself fix a reasonable price.

(4) Where, however, the parties intend not to be bound unless the price be fixed or agreed and it is not fixed or agreed there is no contract. In such a case the buyer must return any goods already received or if unable so to do must pay their reasonable value at the time of delivery and the seller must return any portion of the price paid on account.

§ 2–306. Output, Requirements and Exclusive Dealings.

(1) A term which measures the quantity by the output of the seller or the requirements of the buyer means such actual output or requirements as may occur in good faith, except that no quantity unreasonably disproportionate to any stated estimate or in the absence of a stated estimate to any normal or otherwise comparable prior output or requirements may be tendered or demanded.

(2) A lawful agreement by either the seller or the buyer for exclusive dealing in the kind of goods concerned imposes unless otherwise agreed an obligation by the seller to use best efforts to supply the goods and by the buyer to use best efforts to promote their sale.

§ 2–307. Delivery in Single Lot or Several Lots.

Unless otherwise agreed all goods called for by a contract for sale must be tendered in a single delivery and payment is due only on such tender but where the circumstances give either party the right to make or demand delivery in lots the price if it can be apportioned may be demanded for each lot.

§ 2–308. Absence of Specified Place for Delivery.

Unless otherwise agreed

(a) the place for delivery of goods is the seller's place of business or if he has none his residence; but

(b) in a contract for sale of identified goods which to the knowledge of the parties at the time of contracting are in some other place, that place is the place for their delivery; and

(c) documents of title may be delivered through customary banking channels.

§ 2–309. Absence of Specific Time Provisions; Notice of Termination.

(1) The time for shipment or delivery or any other action under a contract if not provided in this Article or agreed upon shall be a reasonable time.

(2) Where the contract provides for successive performances but is indefinite in duration it is valid for a reasonable time but unless otherwise agreed may be terminated at any time by either party.

(3) Termination of a contract by one party except on the happening of an agreed event requires that reasonable notification be received by the other party and an agreement dispensing with notification is invalid if its operation would be unconscionable.

§ 2–310. Open Time for Payment or Running of Credit; Authority to Ship Under Reservation.

Unless otherwise agreed

(a) payment is due at the time and place at which the buyer is to receive the goods even though the place of shipment is the place of delivery; and

(b) if the seller is authorized to send the goods he may ship them under reservation, and may tender the documents of title, but the buyer may inspect the goods after their arrival before payment is due unless such inspection is inconsistent with the terms of the contract (Section 2–513); and

(c) if delivery is authorized and made by way of documents of title otherwise than by subsection (b) then payment is due at the time and place at which the buyer is to receive the documents regardless of where the goods are to be received; and

(d) where the seller is required or authorized to ship the goods on credit the credit period runs from the time of shipment but post-dating the invoice or delaying its dispatch will correspondingly delay the starting of the credit period.

§ 2–311. Options and Cooperation Respecting Performance.

(1) An agreement for sale which is otherwise sufficiently definite (subsection (3) of Section 2–204) to be a contract is not made invalid by the fact that it leaves particulars of performance to be specified

by one of the parties. Any such specification must be made in good faith and within limits set by commercial reasonableness.

(2) Unless otherwise agreed specifications relating to assortment of the goods are at the buyer's option and except as otherwise provided in subsections (1)(c) and (3) of Section 2–319 specifications or arrangements relating to shipment are at the seller's option.

(3) Where such specification would materially affect the other party's performance but is not seasonably made or where one party's cooperation is necessary to the agreed performance of the other but is not seasonably forthcoming, the other party in addition to all other remedies

(a) is excused for any resulting delay in his own performance; and

(b) may also either proceed to perform in any reasonable manner or after the time for a material part of his own performance treat the failure to specify or to cooperate as a breach by failure to deliver or accept the goods.

§ 2–312. Warranty of Title and Against Infringement; Buyer's Obligation Against Infringement.

(1) Subject to subsection (2) there is in a contract for sale a warranty by the seller that

(a) the title conveyed shall be good, and its transfer rightful; and

(b) the goods shall be delivered free from any security interest or other lien or encumbrance of which the buyer at the time of contracting has no knowledge.

(2) A warranty under subsection (1) will be excluded or modified only by specific language or by circumstances which give the buyer reason to know that the person selling does not claim title in himself or that he is purporting to sell only such right or title as he or a third person may have.

(3) Unless otherwise agreed a seller who is a merchant regularly dealing in goods of the kind warrants that the goods shall be delivered free of the rightful claim of any third person by way of infringement or the like but a buyer who furnishes specifications to the seller must hold the seller harmless against any such claim which arises out of compliance with the specifications.

§ 2–313. Express Warranties by Affirmation, Promise, Description, Sample.

(1) Express warranties by the seller are created as follows:

(a) Any affirmation of fact or promise made by the seller to the buyer which relates to the goods and becomes part of the basis of the bargain creates an express warranty that the goods shall conform to the affirmation or promise.

(b) Any description of the goods which is made part of the basis of the bargain creates an express warranty that the goods shall conform to the description.

(c) Any sample or model which is made part of the basis of the bargain creates an express warranty that the whole of the goods shall conform to the sample or model.

(2) It is not necessary to the creation of an express warranty that the seller use formal words such as "warrant" or "guarantee" or that he have a specific intention to make a warranty, but an affirmation merely of the value of the goods or a statement purporting to be merely the seller's opinion or commendation of the goods does not create a warranty.

§ 2–314. Implied Warranty: Merchantability; Usage of Trade.

(1) Unless excluded or modified (Section 2–316), a warranty that the goods shall be merchantable is implied in a contract for their sale if the seller is a merchant with respect to goods of that kind. Under this section the serving for value of food or drink to be consumed either on the premises or elsewhere is a sale.

(2) Goods to be merchantable must be at least such as

(a) pass without objection in the trade under the contract description; and

(b) in the case of fungible goods, are of fair average quality within the description; and

(c) are fit for the ordinary purposes for which such goods are used; and

(d) run, within the variations permitted by the agreement, of even kind, quality and quantity within each unit and among all units involved; and

(e) are adequately contained, packaged, and labeled as the agreement may require; and

(f) conform to the promises or affirmations of fact made on the container or label if any.

(3) Unless excluded or modified (Section 2–316) other implied warranties may arise from course of dealing or usage of trade.

§ 2–315. Implied Warranty: Fitness for Particular Purpose.

Where the seller at the time of contracting has reason to know any particular purpose for which the goods are required and that the buyer is relying on the seller's skill or judgment to select or furnish suitable goods, there is unless excluded or modified under the next section an implied warranty that the goods shall be fit for such purpose.

§ 2–316. Exclusion or Modification of Warranties.

(1) Words or conduct relevant to the creation of an express warranty and words or conduct tending to negate or limit warranty shall be construed wherever reasonable as consistent with each other; but subject to the provisions of this Article on parol or extrinsic evidence (Section 2–202) negation or limitation is inoperative to the extent that such construction is unreasonable.

(2) Subject to subsection (3), to exclude or modify the implied warranty of merchantability or any part of it the language must mention merchantability and in case of a writing must be conspicuous, and to exclude or modify any implied warranty of fitness the exclusion must be by a writing and conspicuous. Language to exclude all implied warranties of fitness is sufficient if it states, for example, that "There are no warranties which extend beyond the description on the face hereof."

(3) Notwithstanding subsection (2)

(a) unless the circumstances indicate otherwise, all implied warranties are excluded by expressions like "as is", "with all faults" or other language which in common understanding calls the buyer's attention to the exclusion of warranties and makes plain that there is no implied warranty; and

(b) when the buyer before entering into the contract has examined the goods or the sample or model as fully as he desired or has refused to examine the goods there is no implied warranty with regard to defects which an examination ought in the circumstances to have revealed to him; and

(c) an implied warranty can also be excluded or modified by course of dealing or course of performance or usage of trade.

(4) Remedies for breach of warranty can be limited in accordance with the provisions of this Article on liquidation or limitation of damages and on contractual modification of remedy (Sections 2–718 and 2–719).

§ 2–317. Cumulation and Conflict of Warranties Express or Implied.

Warranties whether express or implied shall be construed as consistent with each other and as cumulative, but if such construction is unreasonable the intention of the parties shall determine which warranty is dominant. In ascertaining that intention the following rules apply:

(a) Exact or technical specifications displace an inconsistent sample or model or general language of description.

(b) A sample from an existing bulk displaces inconsistent general language of description.

(c) Express warranties displace inconsistent implied warranties other than an implied warranty of fitness for a particular purpose.

§ 2–318. Third Party Beneficiaries of Warranties Express or Implied.

Note: If this Act is introduced in the Congress of the United States this section should be omitted. (States to select one alternative.)

Alternative A

A seller's warranty whether express or implied extends to any natural person who is in the family or household of his buyer or who is a guest in his home if it is reasonable to expect that such person may use, consume or be affected by the goods and who is injured in person by breach of the warranty. A seller may not exclude or limit the operation of this section.

Alternative B

A seller's warranty whether express or implied extends to any natural person who may reasonably be expected to use, consume or be affected by the goods and who is injured in person by breach of the warranty. A seller may not exclude or limit the operation of this section.

Alternative C

A seller's warranty whether express or implied extends to any person who may reasonably be expected to use, consume or be affected by the goods and who is injured by breach of the warranty. A seller may not exclude or limit the operation of this section with respect to injury to the person of an individual to whom the warranty extends.

As amended 1966.

§ 2–319. F.O.B. and F.A.S. Terms.

(1) Unless otherwise agreed the term F.O.B. (which means "free on board") at a named place, even though used only in connection with the stated price, is a delivery term under which

(a) when the term is F.O.B. the place of shipment, the seller must at that place ship the goods in the manner provided in this Article (Section 2–504) and bear the expense and risk of putting them into the possession of the carrier; or

(b) when the term is F.O.B. the place of destination, the seller must at his own expense and risk transport the goods to that place and there tender delivery of them in the manner provided in this Article (Section 2–503);

(c) when under either (a) or (b) the term is also F.O.B. vessel, car or other vehicle, the seller must in addition at his own expense and risk load the goods on board. If the term is F.O.B. vessel the buyer must name the vessel and in an appropriate case the seller must comply with the provisions of this Article on the form of bill of lading (Section 2–323).

(2) Unless otherwise agreed the term F.A.S. vessel (which means "free alongside") at a named port, even though used only in connection with the stated price, is a delivery term under which the seller must

(a) at his own expense and risk deliver the goods alongside the vessel in the manner usual in that port or on a dock designated and provided by the buyer; and

(b) obtain and tender a receipt for the goods in exchange for which the carrier is under a duty to issue a bill of lading.

(3) Unless otherwise agreed in any case falling within subsection (1)(a) or (c) or subsection (2) the buyer must seasonably give any needed instructions for making delivery, including when the term is F.A.S. or F.O.B. the loading berth of the vessel and in an appropriate case its name and sailing date. The seller may treat the failure of needed instructions as a failure of cooperation under this Article (Section 2–311). He may also at his option move the goods in any reasonable manner preparatory to delivery or shipment.

(4) Under the term F.O.B. vessel or F.A.S. unless otherwise agreed the buyer must make payment against tender of the required documents and the seller may not tender nor the buyer demand delivery of the goods in substitution for the documents.

§ 2–320. C.I.F. and C. & F. Terms.

(1) The term C.I.F. means that the price includes in a lump sum the cost of the goods and the insurance and freight to the named destination. The term C. & F. or C.F. means that the price so includes cost and freight to the named destination.

(2) Unless otherwise agreed and even though used only in connection with the stated price and destination, the term C.I.F. destination or its equivalent requires the seller at his own expense and risk to

(a) put the goods into the possession of a carrier at the port for shipment and obtain a negotiable bill or bills of lading covering the entire transportation to the named destination; and

(b) load the goods and obtain a receipt from the carrier (which may be contained in the bill of lading) showing that the freight has been paid or provided for; and

(c) obtain a policy or certificate of insurance, including any war risk insurance, of a kind and on terms then current at the port of shipment in the usual amount, in the currency of the contract, shown to cover the same goods covered by the bill of lading and providing for payment of loss to the order of the buyer or for the account of whom it may concern; but the seller may add to the price the amount of the premium for any such war risk insurance; and

(d) prepare an invoice of the goods and procure any other documents required to effect shipment or to comply with the contract; and

(e) forward and tender with commercial promptness all the documents in due form and with any indorsement necessary to perfect the buyer's rights.

(3) Unless otherwise agreed the term C. & F. or its equivalent has the same effect and imposes upon the seller the same obligations and risks as a C.I.F. term except the obligation as to insurance.

(4) Under the term C.I.F. or C. & F. unless otherwise agreed the buyer must make payment against tender of the required documents and the seller may not tender nor the buyer demand delivery of the goods in substitution for the documents.

§ 2–321. C.I.F. or C. & F.: "Net Landed Weights"; "Payment on Arrival"; Warranty of Condition on Arrival.

Under a contract containing a term C.I.F. or C. & F.

(1) Where the price is based on or is to be adjusted according to "net landed weights", "delivered weights", "out turn" quantity or quality or the like, unless otherwise agreed the seller must reasonably estimate the price. The payment due on tender of the documents called for by the contract is the amount so estimated, but after final adjustment of the price a settlement must be made with commercial promptness.

(2) An agreement described in subsection (1) or any warranty of quality or condition of the goods on arrival places upon the seller the risk of ordinary deterioration, shrinkage and the like in transportation but has no effect on the place or time of identification to the contract for sale or delivery or on the passing of the risk of loss.

(3) Unless otherwise agreed where the contract provides for payment on or after arrival of the goods the seller must before payment allow such preliminary inspection as is feasible; but if the goods are lost delivery of the documents and payment are due when the goods should have arrived.

§ 2–322. Delivery "Ex-Ship".

(1) Unless otherwise agreed a term for delivery of goods "ex-ship" (which means from the carrying vessel) or in equivalent language is not restricted to a particular ship and requires delivery from a ship which has reached a place at the named port of destination where goods of the kind are usually discharged.

(2) Under such a term unless otherwise agreed

(a) the seller must discharge all liens arising out of the carriage and furnish the buyer with a direction which puts the carrier under a duty to deliver the goods; and

(b) the risk of loss does not pass to the buyer until the goods leave the ship's tackle or are otherwise properly unloaded.

§ 2–323. Form of Bill of Lading Required in Overseas Shipment; "Overseas".

(1) Where the contract contemplates overseas shipment and contains a term C.I.F. or C. & F. or F.O.B. vessel, the seller unless otherwise agreed must obtain a negotiable bill of lading stating that the goods have been loaded on board or, in the case of a term C.I.F. or C. & F., received for shipment.

(2) Where in a case within subsection (1) a bill of lading has been issued in a set of parts, unless otherwise agreed if the documents are not to be sent from abroad the buyer may demand tender of the full set; otherwise only one part of the bill of lading need be tendered. Even if the agreement expressly requires a full set

(a) due tender of a single part is acceptable within the provisions of this Article on cure of improper delivery (subsection (1) of Section 2–508); and

(b) even though the full set is demanded, if the documents are sent from abroad the person tendering an incomplete set may nevertheless require payment upon furnishing an indemnity which the buyer in good faith deems adequate.

(3) A shipment by water or by air or a contract contemplating such shipment is "overseas" insofar as by usage of trade or agreement it is subject to the commercial, financing or shipping practices characteristic of international deep water commerce.

§ 2–324. "No Arrival, No Sale" Term.

Under a term "no arrival, no sale" or terms of like meaning, unless otherwise agreed,

(a) the seller must properly ship conforming goods and if they arrive by any means he must tender them on arrival but he assumes no obligation that the goods will arrive unless he has caused the non-arrival; and

(b) where without fault of the seller the goods are in part lost or have so deteriorated as no longer to conform to the contract or arrive after the contract time, the buyer may proceed as if there had been casualty to identified goods (Section 2–613).

§ 2–325. "Letter of Credit" Term; "Confirmed Credit".

(1) Failure of the buyer seasonably to furnish an agreed letter of credit is a breach of the contract for sale.

(2) The delivery to seller of a proper letter of credit suspends the buyer's obligation to pay. If the letter of credit is dishonored, the seller may on seasonable notification to the buyer require payment directly from him.

(3) Unless otherwise agreed the term "letter of credit" or "banker's credit" in a contract for sale means an irrevocable credit issued by a financing agency of good repute and, where the shipment is overseas, of good international repute. The term "confirmed credit"

means that the credit must also carry the direct obligation of such an agency which does business in the seller's financial market.

§ 2–326. Sale on Approval and Sale or Return; Rights of Creditors.

(1) Unless otherwise agreed, if delivered goods may be returned by the buyer even though they conform to the contract, the transaction is

(a) a "sale on approval" if the goods are delivered primarily for use, and

(b) a "sale or return" if the goods are delivered primarily for resale.

(2) Goods held on approval are not subject to the claims of the buyer's creditors until acceptance; goods held on sale or return are subject to such claims while in the buyer's possession.

(3) Any "or return" term of a contract for sale is to be treated as a separate contract for sale within the statute of frauds section of this Article (Section 2–201) and as contradicting the sale aspect of the contract within the provisions of this Article or on parol or extrinsic evidence (Section 2–202).

As amended in 1999.

§ 2–327. Special Incidents of Sale on Approval and Sale or Return.

(1) Under a sale on approval unless otherwise agreed

(a) although the goods are identified to the contract the risk of loss and the title do not pass to the buyer until acceptance; and

(b) use of the goods consistent with the purpose of trial is not acceptance but failure seasonably to notify the seller of election to return the goods is acceptance, and if the goods conform to the contract acceptance of any part is acceptance of the whole; and

(c) after due notification of election to return, the return is at the seller's risk and expense but a merchant buyer must follow any reasonable instructions.

(2) Under a sale or return unless otherwise agreed

(a) the option to return extends to the whole or any commercial unit of the goods while in substantially their original condition, but must be exercised seasonably; and

(b) the return is at the buyer's risk and expense.

§ 2–328. Sale by Auction.

(1) In a sale by auction if goods are put up in lots each lot is the subject of a separate sale.

(2) A sale by auction is complete when the auctioneer so announces by the fall of the hammer or in other customary manner. Where a bid is made while the hammer is falling in acceptance of a prior bid the auctioneer may in his discretion reopen the bidding or declare the goods sold under the bid on which the hammer was falling.

(3) Such a sale is with reserve unless the goods are in explicit terms put up without reserve. In an auction with reserve the auctioneer may withdraw the goods at any time until he announces completion of the sale. In an auction without reserve, after the auctioneer calls for bids on an article or lot, that article or lot cannot be withdrawn unless no bid is made within a reasonable time. In either case a bidder may retract his bid until the auctioneer's announcement of completion of the sale, but a bidder's retraction does not revive any previous bid.

(4) If the auctioneer knowingly receives a bid on the seller's behalf or the seller makes or procures such as bid, and notice has not been given that liberty for such bidding is reserved, the buyer may at his option avoid the sale or take the goods at the price of the last good faith bid prior to the completion of the sale. This subsection shall not apply to any bid at a forced sale.

Part 4 Title, Creditors and Good Faith Purchasers

§ 2–401. Passing of Title; Reservation for Security; Limited Application of This Section.

Each provision of this Article with regard to the rights, obligations and remedies of the seller, the buyer, purchasers or other third parties applies irrespective of title to the goods except where the provision refers to such title. Insofar as situations are not covered by the other provisions of this Article and matters concerning title became material the following rules apply:

(1) Title to goods cannot pass under a contract for sale prior to their identification to the contract (Section 2–501), and unless otherwise explicitly agreed the buyer acquires by their identification a special property as limited by this Act. Any retention or reservation by the seller of the title (property) in goods shipped or delivered to the buyer is limited in effect to a reservation of a security interest. Subject to these provisions and to the provisions of the Article on Secured Transactions (Article 9), title to goods passes from the seller to the buyer in any manner and on any conditions explicitly agreed on by the parties.

(2) Unless otherwise explicitly agreed title passes to the buyer at the time and place at which the seller completes his performance with reference to the physical delivery of the goods, despite any reservation of a security interest and even though a document of title is to be delivered at a different time or place; and in particular and despite any reservation of a security interest by the bill of lading

(a) if the contract requires or authorizes the seller to send the goods to the buyer but does not require him to deliver them at destination, title passes to the buyer at the time and place of shipment; but

(b) if the contract requires delivery at destination, title passes on tender there.

(3) Unless otherwise explicitly agreed where delivery is to be made without moving the goods,

(a) if the seller is to deliver a document of title, title passes at the time when and the place where he delivers such documents; or

(b) if the goods are at the time of contracting already identified and no documents are to be delivered, title passes at the time and place of contracting.

(4) A rejection or other refusal by the buyer to receive or retain the goods, whether or not justified, or a justified revocation of acceptance revests title to the goods in the seller. Such revesting occurs by operation of law and is not a "sale".

§ 2–402. Rights of Seller's Creditors Against Sold Goods.

(1) Except as provided in subsections (2) and (3), rights of unsecured creditors of the seller with respect to goods which have been identified to a contract for sale are subject to the buyer's rights to recover the goods under this Article (Sections 2–502 and 2–716).

(2) A creditor of the seller may treat a sale or an identification of goods to a contract for sale as void if as against him a retention of possession by the seller is fraudulent under any rule of law of the state where the goods are situated, except that retention of possession in good faith and current course of trade by a merchant-seller for a commercially reasonable time after a sale or identification is not fraudulent.

(3) Nothing in this Article shall be deemed to impair the rights of creditors of the seller

(a) under the provisions of the Article on Secured Transactions (Article 9); or

(b) where identification to the contract or delivery is made not in current course of trade but in satisfaction of or as security for a pre-existing claim for money, security or the like and is made under circumstances which under any rule of law of the state where the goods are situated would apart from this Article constitute the transaction a fraudulent transfer or voidable preference.

§ 2–403. Power to Transfer; Good Faith Purchase of Goods; "Entrusting".

(1) A purchaser of goods acquires all title which his transferor had or had power to transfer except that a purchaser of a limited interest acquires rights only to the extent of the interest purchased. A person with voidable title has power to transfer a good title to a good faith purchaser for value. When goods have been delivered under a transaction of purchase the purchaser has such power even though

(a) the transferor was deceived as to the identity of the purchaser, or

(b) the delivery was in exchange for a check which is later dishonored, or

(c) it was agreed that the transaction was to be a "cash sale", or

(d) the delivery was procured through fraud punishable as larcenous under the criminal law.

(2) Any entrusting of possession of goods to a merchant who deals in goods of that kind gives him power to transfer all rights of the entruster to a buyer in ordinary course of business.

(3) "Entrusting" includes any delivery and any acquiescence in retention of possession regardless of any condition expressed between the parties to the delivery or acquiescence and regardless of whether the procurement of the entrusting or the possessor's disposition of the goods have been such as to be larcenous under the criminal law.

(4) The rights of other purchasers of goods and of lien creditors are governed by the Articles on Secured Transactions (Article 9), Bulk Transfers (Article 6) and Documents of Title (Article 7).

As amended in 1988.

Part 5 Performance

§ 2–501. Insurable Interest in Goods; Manner of Identification of Goods.

(1) The buyer obtains a special property and an insurable interest in goods by identification of existing goods as goods to which the contract refers even though the goods so identified are non-conforming and he has an option to return or reject them. Such identification can be made at any time and in any manner explicitly agreed to by the parties. In the absence of explicit agreement identification occurs

(a) when the contract is made if it is for the sale of goods already existing and identified;

(b) if the contract is for the sale of future goods other than those described in paragraph (c), when goods are shipped, marked or otherwise designated by the seller as goods to which the contract refers;

(c) when the crops are planted or otherwise become growing crops or the young are conceived if the contract is for the sale of unborn young to be born within twelve months after contracting or for the sale of crops to be harvested within twelve months or the next normal harvest season after contracting whichever is longer.

(2) The seller retains an insurable interest in goods so long as title to or any security interest in the goods remains in him and where the identification is by the seller alone he may until default or insolvency or notification to the buyer that the identification is final substitute other goods for those identified.

(3) Nothing in this section impairs any insurable interest recognized under any other statute or rule of law.

§ 2–502. Buyer's Right to Goods on Seller's Insolvency.

(1) Subject to subsections (2) and (3) and even though the goods have not been shipped a buyer who has paid a part or all of the price of goods in which he has a special property under the provisions of the immediately preceding section may on making and keeping good a tender of any unpaid portion of their price recover them from the seller if:

(a) in the case of goods bought for personal, family, or household purposes, the seller repudiates or fails to deliver as required by the contract; or

(b) in all cases, the seller becomes insolvent within ten days after receipt of the first installment on their price.

(2) The buyer's right to recover the goods under subsection (1)(a) vests upon acquisition of a special property, even if the seller had not then repudiated or failed to deliver.

(3) If the identification creating his special property has been made by the buyer he acquires the right to recover the goods only if they conform to the contract for sale.

As amended in 1999.

§ 2–503. Manner of Seller's Tender of Delivery.

(1) Tender of delivery requires that the seller put and hold conforming goods at the buyer's disposition and give the buyer any notification reasonably necessary to enable him to take delivery. The manner, time and place for tender are determined by the agreement and this Article, and in particular

(a) tender must be at a reasonable hour, and if it is of goods they must be kept available for the period reasonably necessary to enable the buyer to take possession; but

(b) unless otherwise agreed the buyer must furnish facilities reasonably suited to the receipt of the goods.

(2) Where the case is within the next section respecting shipment tender requires that the seller comply with its provisions.

(3) Where the seller is required to deliver at a particular destination tender requires that he comply with subsection (1) and also in any appropriate case tender documents as described in subsections (4) and (5) of this section.

(4) Where goods are in the possession of a bailee and are to be delivered without being moved

(a) tender requires that the seller either tender a negotiable document of title covering such goods or procure acknowledgment by the bailee of the buyer's right to possession of the goods; but

(b) tender to the buyer of a non-negotiable document of title or of a written direction to the bailee to deliver is sufficient tender unless the buyer seasonably objects, and receipt by the bailee of notification of the buyer's rights fixes those rights as against the bailee and all third persons; but risk of loss of the goods and of any failure by the bailee to honor the non-negotiable document of title or to obey the direction remains on the seller until the buyer has had a reasonable time to present the document or direction, and a refusal by the bailee to honor the document or to obey the direction defeats the tender.

(5) Where the contract requires the seller to deliver documents

(a) he must tender all such documents in correct form, except as provided in this Article with respect to bills of lading in a set (subsection (2) of Section 2–323); and

(b) tender through customary banking channels is sufficient and dishonor of a draft accompanying the documents constitutes non-acceptance or rejection.

§ 2–504. Shipment by Seller.

Where the seller is required or authorized to send the goods to the buyer and the contract does not require him to deliver them at a particular destination, then unless otherwise agreed he must

(a) put the goods in the possession of such a carrier and make such a contract for their transportation as may be reasonable having regard to the nature of the goods and other circumstances of the case; and

(b) obtain and promptly deliver or tender in due form any document necessary to enable the buyer to obtain possession of the goods or otherwise required by the agreement or by usage of trade; and

(c) promptly notify the buyer of the shipment.

Failure to notify the buyer under paragraph (c) or to make a proper contract under paragraph (a) is a ground for rejection only if material delay or loss ensues.

§ 2–505. Seller's Shipment under Reservation.

(1) Where the seller has identified goods to the contract by or before shipment:

(a) his procurement of a negotiable bill of lading to his own order or otherwise reserves in him a security interest in the goods. His procurement of the bill to the order of a financing agency or of the buyer indicates in addition only the seller's expectation of transferring that interest to the person named.

(b) a non-negotiable bill of lading to himself or his nominee reserves possession of the goods as security but except in a case of conditional delivery (subsection (2) of Section 2–507) a non-negotiable bill of lading naming the buyer as consignee reserves no security interest even though the seller retains possession of the bill of lading.

(2) When shipment by the seller with reservation of a security interest is in violation of the contract for sale it constitutes an improper contract for transportation within the preceding section but impairs neither the rights given to the buyer by shipment and identification of the goods to the contract nor the seller's powers as a holder of a negotiable document.

§ 2–506. Rights of Financing Agency.

(1) A financing agency by paying or purchasing for value a draft which relates to a shipment of goods acquires to the extent of the payment or purchase and in addition to its own rights under the draft and any document of title securing it any rights of the shipper in the goods including the right to stop delivery and the shipper's right to have the draft honored by the buyer.

(2) The right to reimbursement of a financing agency which has in good faith honored or purchased the draft under commitment to or authority from the buyer is not impaired by subsequent discovery of defects with reference to any relevant document which was apparently regular on its face.

§ 2–507. Effect of Seller's Tender; Delivery on Condition.

(1) Tender of delivery is a condition to the buyer's duty to accept the goods and, unless otherwise agreed, to his duty to pay for them. Tender entitles the seller to acceptance of the goods and to payment according to the contract.

(2) Where payment is due and demanded on the delivery to the buyer of goods or documents of title, his right as against the seller to retain or dispose of them is conditional upon his making the payment due.

§ 2–508. Cure by Seller of Improper Tender or Delivery; Replacement.

(1) Where any tender or delivery by the seller is rejected because non-conforming and the time for performance has not yet expired,

the seller may seasonably notify the buyer of his intention to cure and may then within the contract time make a conforming delivery.

(2) Where the buyer rejects a non-conforming tender which the seller had reasonable grounds to believe would be acceptable with or without money allowance the seller may if he seasonably notifies the buyer have a further reasonable time to substitute a conforming tender.

§ 2–509. Risk of Loss in the Absence of Breach.

(1) Where the contract requires or authorizes the seller to ship the goods by carrier

(a) if it does not require him to deliver them at a particular destination, the risk of loss passes to the buyer when the goods are duly delivered to the carrier even though the shipment is under reservation (Section 2–505); but

(b) if it does require him to deliver them at a particular destination and the goods are there duly tendered while in the possession of the carrier, the risk of loss passes to the buyer when the goods are there duly so tendered as to enable the buyer to take delivery.

(2) Where the goods are held by a bailee to be delivered without being moved, the risk of loss passes to the buyer

(a) on his receipt of a negotiable document of title covering the goods; or

(b) on acknowledgment by the bailee of the buyer's right to possession of the goods; or

(c) after his receipt of a non-negotiable document of title or other written direction to deliver, as provided in subsection (4) (b) of Section 2–503.

(3) In any case not within subsection (1) or (2), the risk of loss passes to the buyer on his receipt of the goods if the seller is a merchant; otherwise the risk passes to the buyer on tender of delivery.

(4) The provisions of this section are subject to contrary agreement of the parties and to the provisions of this Article on sale on approval (Section 2–327) and on effect of breach on risk of loss (Section 2–510).

§ 2–510. Effect of Breach on Risk of Loss.

(1) Where a tender or delivery of goods so fails to conform to the contract as to give a right of rejection the risk of their loss remains on the seller until cure or acceptance.

(2) Where the buyer rightfully revokes acceptance he may to the extent of any deficiency in his effective insurance coverage treat the risk of loss as having rested on the seller from the beginning.

(3) Where the buyer as to conforming goods already identified to the contract for sale repudiates or is otherwise in breach before risk of their loss has passed to him, the seller may to the extent of any deficiency in his effective insurance coverage treat the risk of loss as resting on the buyer for a commercially reasonable time.

§ 2–511. Tender of Payment by Buyer; Payment by Check.

(1) Unless otherwise agreed tender of payment is a condition to the seller's duty to tender and complete any delivery.

(2) Tender of payment is sufficient when made by any means or in any manner current in the ordinary course of business unless the seller demands payment in legal tender and gives any extension of time reasonably necessary to procure it.

(3) Subject to the provisions of this Act on the effect of an instrument on an obligation (Section 3–310), payment by check is conditional and is defeated as between the parties by dishonor of the check on due presentment.

As amended in 1994.

§ 2–512. Payment by Buyer Before Inspection.

(1) Where the contract requires payment before inspection non-conformity of the goods does not excuse the buyer from so making payment unless

(a) the non-conformity appears without inspection; or

(b) despite tender of the required documents the circumstances would justify injunction against honor under this Act (Section 5–109(b)).

(2) Payment pursuant to subsection (1) does not constitute an acceptance of goods or impair the buyer's right to inspect or any of his remedies.

As amended in 1995.

§ 2–513. Buyer's Right to Inspection of Goods.

(1) Unless otherwise agreed and subject to subsection (3), where goods are tendered or delivered or identified to the contract for sale, the buyer has a right before payment or acceptance to inspect them at any reasonable place and time and in any reasonable manner. When the seller is required or authorized to send the goods to the buyer, the inspection may be after their arrival.

(2) Expenses of inspection must be borne by the buyer but may be recovered from the seller if the goods do not conform and are rejected.

(3) Unless otherwise agreed and subject to the provisions of this Article on C.I.F. contracts (subsection (3) of Section 2–321), the buyer is not entitled to inspect the goods before payment of the price when the contract provides

(a) for delivery "C.O.D." or on other like terms; or

(b) for payment against documents of title, except where such payment is due only after the goods are to become available for inspection.

(4) A place or method of inspection fixed by the parties is presumed to be exclusive but unless otherwise expressly agreed it does not postpone identification or shift the place for delivery or for passing the risk of loss. If compliance becomes impossible, inspection shall be as provided in this section unless the place or method fixed was clearly intended as an indispensable condition failure of which avoids the contract.

§ 2–514. When Documents Deliverable on Acceptance; When on Payment.

Unless otherwise agreed documents against which a draft is drawn are to be delivered to the drawee on acceptance of the draft if it is payable more than three days after presentment; otherwise, only on payment.

§ 2–515. Preserving Evidence of Goods in Dispute.

In furtherance of the adjustment of any claim or dispute

(a) either party on reasonable notification to the other and for the purpose of ascertaining the facts and preserving evidence has the right to inspect, test and sample the goods including such of them as may be in the possession or control of the other; and

(b) the parties may agree to a third party inspection or survey to determine the conformity or condition of the goods and may agree that the findings shall be binding upon them in any subsequent litigation or adjustment.

Part 6 Breach, Repudiation and Excuse

§ 2–601. Buyer's Rights on Improper Delivery.

Subject to the provisions of this Article on breach in installment contracts (Section 2–612) and unless otherwise agreed under the sections on contractual limitations of remedy (Sections 2–718 and 2–719), if the goods or the tender of delivery fail in any respect to conform to the contract, the buyer may

(a) reject the whole; or

(b) accept the whole; or

(c) accept any commercial unit or units and reject the rest.

§ 2–602. Manner and Effect of Rightful Rejection.

(1) Rejection of goods must be within a reasonable time after their delivery or tender. It is ineffective unless the buyer seasonably notifies the seller.

(2) Subject to the provisions of the two following sections on rejected goods (Sections 2–603 and 2–604),

(a) after rejection any exercise of ownership by the buyer with respect to any commercial unit is wrongful as against the seller; and

(b) if the buyer has before rejection taken physical possession of goods in which he does not have a security interest under the provisions of this Article (subsection (3) of Section 2–711), he is under a duty after rejection to hold them with reasonable care at the seller's disposition for a time sufficient to permit the seller to remove them; but

(c) the buyer has no further obligations with regard to goods rightfully rejected.

(3) The seller's rights with respect to goods wrongfully rejected are governed by the provisions of this Article on Seller's remedies in general (Section 2–703).

§ 2–603. Merchant Buyer's Duties as to Rightfully Rejected Goods.

(1) Subject to any security interest in the buyer (subsection (3) of Section 2–711), when the seller has no agent or place of business at the market of rejection a merchant buyer is under a duty after rejection of goods in his possession or control to follow any reasonable instructions received from the seller with respect to the goods and in the absence of such instructions to make reasonable efforts to sell them for the seller's account if they are perishable or threaten to decline in value speedily. Instructions are not reasonable if on demand indemnity for expenses is not forthcoming.

(2) When the buyer sells goods under subsection (1), he is entitled to reimbursement from the seller or out of the proceeds for reasonable expenses of caring for and selling them, and if the expenses include no selling commission then to such commission as is usual in the trade or if there is none to a reasonable sum not exceeding ten per cent on the gross proceeds.

(3) In complying with this section the buyer is held only to good faith and good faith conduct hereunder is neither acceptance nor conversion nor the basis of an action for damages.

§ 2–604. Buyer's Options as to Salvage of Rightfully Rejected Goods.

Subject to the provisions of the immediately preceding section on perishables if the seller gives no instructions within a reasonable time after notification of rejection the buyer may store the rejected goods for the seller's account or reship them to him or resell them for the seller's account with reimbursement as provided in the preceding section. Such action is not acceptance or conversion.

§ 2–605. Waiver of Buyer's Objections by Failure to Particularize.

(1) The buyer's failure to state in connection with rejection a particular defect which is ascertainable by reasonable inspection precludes him from relying on the unstated defect to justify rejection or to establish breach

(a) where the seller could have cured it if stated seasonably; or

(b) between merchants when the seller has after rejection made a request in writing for a full and final written statement of all defects on which the buyer proposes to rely.

(2) Payment against documents made without reservation of rights precludes recovery of the payment for defects apparent on the face of the documents.

§ 2–606. What Constitutes Acceptance of Goods.

(1) Acceptance of goods occurs when the buyer

(a) after a reasonable opportunity to inspect the goods signifies to the seller that the goods are conforming or that he will take or retain them in spite of their nonconformity; or

(b) fails to make an effective rejection (subsection (1) of Section 2–602), but such acceptance does not occur until the buyer has had a reasonable opportunity to inspect them; or

(c) does any act inconsistent with the seller's ownership; but if such act is wrongful as against the seller it is an acceptance only if ratified by him.

(2) Acceptance of a part of any commercial unit is acceptance of that entire unit.

§ 2–607. Effect of Acceptance; Notice of Breach; Burden of Establishing Breach After Acceptance; Notice of Claim or Litigation to Person Answerable Over.

(1) The buyer must pay at the contract rate for any goods accepted.

(2) Acceptance of goods by the buyer precludes rejection of the goods accepted and if made with knowledge of a non-conformity cannot be revoked because of it unless the acceptance was on the reasonable assumption that the non-conformity would be seasonably cured but acceptance does not of itself impair any other remedy provided by this Article for non-conformity.

(3) Where a tender has been accepted

(a) the buyer must within a reasonable time after he discovers or should have discovered any breach notify the seller of breach or be barred from any remedy; and

(b) if the claim is one for infringement or the like (subsection (3) of Section 2–312) and the buyer is sued as a result of such a breach he must so notify the seller within a reasonable time after he receives notice of the litigation or be barred from any remedy over for liability established by the litigation.

(4) The burden is on the buyer to establish any breach with respect to the goods accepted.

(5) Where the buyer is sued for breach of a warranty or other obligation for which his seller is answerable over

(a) he may give his seller written notice of the litigation. If the notice states that the seller may come in and defend and that if the seller does not do so he will be bound in any action against him by his buyer by any determination of fact common to the two litigations, then unless the seller after seasonable receipt of the notice does come in and defend he is so bound.

(b) if the claim is one for infringement or the like (subsection (3) of Section 2–312) the original seller may demand in writing that his buyer turn over to him control of the litigation including settlement or else be barred from any remedy over and if he also agrees to bear all expense and to satisfy any adverse judgment, then unless the buyer after seasonable receipt of the demand does turn over control the buyer is so barred.

(6) The provisions of subsections (3), (4) and (5) apply to any obligation of a buyer to hold the seller harmless against infringement or the like (subsection (3) of Section 2–312).

§ 2–608. Revocation of Acceptance in Whole or in Part.

(1) The buyer may revoke his acceptance of a lot or commercial unit whose non-conformity substantially impairs its value to him if he has accepted it

(a) on the reasonable assumption that its nonconformity would be cured and it has not been seasonably cured; or

(b) without discovery of such non-conformity if his acceptance was reasonably induced either by the difficulty of discovery before acceptance or by the seller's assurances.

(2) Revocation of acceptance must occur within a reasonable time after the buyer discovers or should have discovered the ground for it and before any substantial change in condition of the goods which is not caused by their own defects. It is not effective until the buyer notifies the seller of it.

(3) A buyer who so revokes has the same rights and duties with regard to the goods involved as if he had rejected them.

§ 2–609. Right to Adequate Assurance of Performance.

(1) A contract for sale imposes an obligation on each party that the other's expectation of receiving due performance will not be impaired. When reasonable grounds for insecurity arise with respect to the performance of either party the other may in writing demand adequate assurance of due performance and until he receives such assurance may if commercially reasonable suspend any performance for which he has not already received the agreed return.

(2) Between merchants the reasonableness of grounds for insecurity and the adequacy of any assurance offered shall be determined according to commercial standards.

(3) Acceptance of any improper delivery or payment does not prejudice the party's right to demand adequate assurance of future performance.

(4) After receipt of a justified demand failure to provide within a reasonable time not exceeding thirty days such assurance of due performance as is adequate under the circumstances of the particular case is a repudiation of the contract.

§ 2–610. Anticipatory Repudiation.

When either party repudiates the contract with respect to a performance not yet due the loss of which will substantially impair the value of the contract to the other, the aggrieved party may

(a) for a commercially reasonable time await performance by the repudiating party; or

(b) resort to any remedy for breach (Section 2–703 or Section 2–711), even though he has notified the repudiating party that he would await the latter's performance and has urged retraction; and

(c) in either case suspend his own performance or proceed in accordance with the provisions of this Article on the seller's right to identify goods to the contract notwithstanding breach or to salvage unfinished goods (Section 2–704).

§ 2–611. Retraction of Anticipatory Repudiation.

(1) Until the repudiating party's next performance is due he can retract his repudiation unless the aggrieved party has since the repudiation cancelled or materially changed his position or otherwise indicated that he considers the repudiation final.

(2) Retraction may be by any method which clearly indicates to the aggrieved party that the repudiating party intends to perform, but must include any assurance justifiably demanded under the provisions of this Article (Section 2–609).

(3) Retraction reinstates the repudiating party's rights under the contract with due excuse and allowance to the aggrieved party for any delay occasioned by the repudiation.

§ 2–612. "Installment Contract"; Breach.

(1) An "installment contract" is one which requires or authorizes the delivery of goods in separate lots to be separately accepted, even though the contract contains a clause "each delivery is a separate contract" or its equivalent.

(2) The buyer may reject any installment which is non-conforming if the non-conformity substantially impairs the value of that installment

and cannot be cured or if the non-conformity is a defect in the required documents; but if the non-conformity does not fall within subsection (3) and the seller gives adequate assurance of its cure the buyer must accept that installment.

(3) Whenever non-conformity or default with respect to one or more installments substantially impairs the value of the whole contract there is a breach of the whole. But the aggrieved party reinstates the contract if he accepts a non-conforming installment without seasonably notifying of cancellation or if he brings an action with respect only to past installments or demands performance as to future installments.

§ 2–613. Casualty to Identified Goods.

Where the contract requires for its performance goods identified when the contract is made, and the goods suffer casualty without fault of either party before the risk of loss passes to the buyer, or in a proper case under a "no arrival, no sale" term (Section 2–324) then

(a) if the loss is total the contract is avoided; and

(b) if the loss is partial or the goods have so deteriorated as no longer to conform to the contract the buyer may nevertheless demand inspection and at his option either treat the contract as voided or accept the goods with due allowance from the contract price for the deterioration or the deficiency in quantity but without further right against the seller.

§ 2–614. Substituted Performance.

(1) Where without fault of either party the agreed berthing, loading, or unloading facilities fail or an agreed type of carrier becomes unavailable or the agreed manner of delivery otherwise becomes commercially impracticable but a commercially reasonable substitute is available, such substitute performance must be tendered and accepted.

(2) If the agreed means or manner of payment fails because of domestic or foreign governmental regulation, the seller may withhold or stop delivery unless the buyer provides a means or manner of payment which is commercially a substantial equivalent. If delivery has already been taken, payment by the means or in the manner provided by the regulation discharges the buyer's obligation unless the regulation is discriminatory, oppressive or predatory.

§ 2–615. Excuse by Failure of Presupposed Conditions.

Except so far as a seller may have assumed a greater obligation and subject to the preceding section on substituted performance:

(a) Delay in delivery or non-delivery in whole or in part by a seller who complies with paragraphs (b) and (c) is not a breach of his duty under a contract for sale if performance as agreed has been made impracticable by the occurrence of a contingency the nonoccurrence of which was a basic assumption on which the contract was made or by compliance in good faith with any applicable foreign or domestic governmental regulation or order whether or not it later proves to be invalid.

(b) Where the causes mentioned in paragraph (a) affect only a part of the seller's capacity to perform, he must allocate production and deliveries among his customers but may at his option include regular customers not then under contract as well as his own requirements for further manufacture. He may so allocate in any manner which is fair and reasonable.

(c) The seller must notify the buyer seasonably that there will be delay or non-delivery and, when allocation is required under paragraph (b), of the estimated quota thus made available for the buyer.

§ 2–616. Procedure on Notice Claiming Excuse.

(1) Where the buyer receives notification of a material or indefinite delay or an allocation justified under the preceding section he may by written notification to the seller as to any delivery concerned, and where the prospective deficiency substantially impairs the value of the whole contract under the provisions of this Article relating to breach of installment contracts (Section 2–612), then also as to the whole,

(a) terminate and thereby discharge any unexecuted portion of the contract; or

(b) modify the contract by agreeing to take his available quota in substitution.

(2) If after receipt of such notification from the seller the buyer fails so to modify the contract within a reasonable time not exceeding thirty days the contract lapses with respect to any deliveries affected.

(3) The provisions of this section may not be negated by agreement except in so far as the seller has assumed a greater obligation under the preceding section.

Part 7 Remedies

§ 2–701. Remedies for Breach of Collateral Contracts Not Impaired.

Remedies for breach of any obligation or promise collateral or ancillary to a contract for sale are not impaired by the provisions of this Article.

§ 2–702. Seller's Remedies on Discovery of Buyer's Insolvency.

(1) Where the seller discovers the buyer to be insolvent he may refuse delivery except for cash including payment for all goods theretofore delivered under the contract, and stop delivery under this Article (Section 2–705).

(2) Where the seller discovers that the buyer has received goods on credit while insolvent he may reclaim the goods upon demand made within ten days after the receipt, but if misrepresentation of solvency has been made to the particular seller in writing within three months before delivery the ten day limitation does not apply. Except as provided in this subsection the seller may not base a right to reclaim goods on the buyer's fraudulent or innocent misrepresentation of solvency or of intent to pay.

(3) The seller's right to reclaim under subsection (2) is subject to the rights of a buyer in ordinary course or other good faith purchaser under this Article (Section 2–403). Successful reclamation of goods excludes all other remedies with respect to them.

§ 2–703. Seller's Remedies in General.

Where the buyer wrongfully rejects or revokes acceptance of goods or fails to make a payment due on or before delivery or repudiates with respect to a part or the whole, then with respect to any goods directly affected and, if the breach is of the whole contract (Section 2–612), then also with respect to the whole undelivered balance, the aggrieved seller may

(a) withhold delivery of such goods;

(b) stop delivery by any bailee as hereafter provided (Section 2–705);

(c) proceed under the next section respecting goods still unidentified to the contract;

(d) resell and recover damages as hereafter provided (Section 2–706);

(e) recover damages for non-acceptance (Section 2–708) or in a proper case the price (Section 2–709);

(f) cancel.

§ 2–704. Seller's Right to Identify Goods to the Contract Notwithstanding Breach or to Salvage Unfinished Goods.

(1) An aggrieved seller under the preceding section may

(a) identify to the contract conforming goods not already identified if at the time he learned of the breach they are in his possession or control;

(b) treat as the subject of resale goods which have demonstrably been intended for the particular contract even though those goods are unfinished.

(2) Where the goods are unfinished an aggrieved seller may in the exercise of reasonable commercial judgment for the purposes of avoiding loss and of effective realization either complete the manufacture and wholly identify the goods to the contract or cease manufacture and resell for scrap or salvage value or proceed in any other reasonable manner.

§ 2–705. Seller's Stoppage of Delivery in Transit or Otherwise.

(1) The seller may stop delivery of goods in the possession of a carrier or other bailee when he discovers the buyer to be insolvent (Section 2–702) and may stop delivery of carload, truckload, planeload or larger shipments of express or freight when the buyer repudiates or fails to make a payment due before delivery or if for any other reason the seller has a right to withhold or reclaim the goods.

(2) As against such buyer the seller may stop delivery until

(a) receipt of the goods by the buyer; or

(b) acknowledgment to the buyer by any bailee of the goods except a carrier that the bailee holds the goods for the buyer; or

(c) such acknowledgment to the buyer by a carrier by reshipment or as warehouseman; or

(d) negotiation to the buyer of any negotiable document of title covering the goods.

(3) (a) To stop delivery the seller must so notify as to enable the bailee by reasonable diligence to prevent delivery of the goods.

(b) After such notification the bailee must hold and deliver the goods according to the directions of the seller but the seller is liable to the bailee for any ensuing charges or damages.

(c) If a negotiable document of title has been issued for goods the bailee is not obliged to obey a notification to stop until surrender of the document.

(d) A carrier who has issued a non-negotiable bill of lading is not obliged to obey a notification to stop received from a person other than the consignor.

§ 2–706. Seller's Resale Including Contract for Resale.

(1) Under the conditions stated in Section 2–703 on seller's remedies, the seller may resell the goods concerned or the undelivered balance thereof. Where the resale is made in good faith and in a commercially reasonable manner the seller may recover the difference between the resale price and the contract price together with any incidental damages allowed under the provisions of this Article (Section 2–710), but less expenses saved in consequence of the buyer's breach.

(2) Except as otherwise provided in subsection (3) or unless otherwise agreed resale may be at public or private sale including sale by way of one or more contracts to sell or of identification to an existing contract of the seller. Sale may be as a unit or in parcels and at any time and place and on any terms but every aspect of the sale including the method, manner, time, place and terms must be commercially reasonable. The resale must be reasonably identified as referring to the broken contract, but it is not necessary that the goods be in existence or that any or all of them have been identified to the contract before the breach.

(3) Where the resale is at private sale the seller must give the buyer reasonable notification of his intention to resell.

(4) Where the resale is at public sale

(a) only identified goods can be sold except where there is a recognized market for a public sale of futures in goods of the kind; and

(b) it must be made at a usual place or market for public sale if one is reasonably available and except in the case of goods which are perishable or threaten to decline in value speedily the seller must give the buyer reasonable notice of the time and place of the resale; and

(c) if the goods are not to be within the view of those attending the sale the notification of sale must state the place where the goods are located and provide for their reasonable inspection by prospective bidders; and

(d) the seller may buy.

(5) A purchaser who buys in good faith at a resale takes the goods free of any rights of the original buyer even though the seller fails to comply with one or more of the requirements of this section.

(6) The seller is not accountable to the buyer for any profit made on any resale. A person in the position of a seller (Section 2–707)

or a buyer who has rightfully rejected or justifiably revoked acceptance must account for any excess over the amount of his security interest, as hereinafter defined (subsection (3) of Section 2–711).

§ 2–707. "Person in the Position of a Seller".

(1) A "person in the position of a seller" includes as against a principal an agent who has paid or become responsible for the price of goods on behalf of his principal or anyone who otherwise holds a security interest or other right in goods similar to that of a seller.

(2) A person in the position of a seller may as provided in this Article withhold or stop delivery (Section 2–705) and resell (Section 2–706) and recover incidental damages (Section 2–710).

§ 2–708. Seller's Damages for Non-Acceptance or Repudiation.

(1) Subject to subsection (2) and to the provisions of this Article with respect to proof of market price (Section 2–723), the measure of damages for non-acceptance or repudiation by the buyer is the difference between the market price at the time and place for tender and the unpaid contract price together with any incidental damages provided in this Article (Section 2–710), but less expenses saved in consequence of the buyer's breach.

(2) If the measure of damages provided in subsection (1) is inadequate to put the seller in as good a position as performance would have done then the measure of damages is the profit (including reasonable overhead) which the seller would have made from full performance by the buyer, together with any incidental damages provided in this Article (Section 2–710), due allowance for costs reasonably incurred and due credit for payments or proceeds of resale.

§ 2–709. Action for the Price.

(1) When the buyer fails to pay the price as it becomes due the seller may recover, together with any incidental damages under the next section, the price

(a) of goods accepted or of conforming goods lost or damaged within a commercially reasonable time after risk of their loss has passed to the buyer; and

(b) of goods identified to the contract if the seller is unable after reasonable effort to resell them at a reasonable price or the circumstances reasonably indicate that such effort will be unavailing.

(2) Where the seller sues for the price he must hold for the buyer any goods which have been identified to the contract and are still in his control except that if resale becomes possible he may resell them at any time prior to the collection of the judgment. The net proceeds of any such resale must be credited to the buyer and payment of the judgment entitles him to any goods not resold.

(3) After the buyer has wrongfully rejected or revoked acceptance of the goods or has failed to make a payment due or has repudiated (Section 2–610), a seller who is held not entitled to the price under this section shall nevertheless be awarded damages for non-acceptance under the preceding section.

§ 2–710. Seller's Incidental Damages.

Incidental damages to an aggrieved seller include any commercially reasonable charges, expenses or commissions incurred in stopping delivery, in the transportation, care and custody of goods after the buyer's breach, in connection with return or resale of the goods or otherwise resulting from the breach.

§ 2–711. Buyer's Remedies in General; Buyer's Security Interest in Rejected Goods.

(1) Where the seller fails to make delivery or repudiates or the buyer rightfully rejects or justifiably revokes acceptance then with respect to any goods involved, and with respect to the whole if the breach goes to the whole contract (Section 2–612), the buyer may cancel and whether or not he has done so may in addition to recovering so much of the price as has been paid

(a) "cover" and have damages under the next section as to all the goods affected whether or not they have been identified to the contract; or

(b) recover damages for non-delivery as provided in this Article (Section 2–713).

(2) Where the seller fails to deliver or repudiates the buyer may also

(a) if the goods have been identified recover them as provided in this Article (Section 2–502); or

(b) in a proper case obtain specific performance or replevy the goods as provided in this Article (Section 2–716).

(3) On rightful rejection or justifiable revocation of acceptance a buyer has a security interest in goods in his possession or control for any payments made on their price and any expenses reasonably incurred in their inspection, receipt, transportation, care and custody and may hold such goods and resell them in like manner as an aggrieved seller (Section 2–706).

§ 2–712. "Cover"; Buyer's Procurement of Substitute Goods.

(1) After a breach within the preceding section the buyer may "cover" by making in good faith and without unreasonable delay any reasonable purchase of or contract to purchase goods in substitution for those due from the seller.

(2) The buyer may recover from the seller as damages the difference between the cost of cover and the contract price together with any incidental or consequential damages as hereinafter defined (Section 2–715), but less expenses saved in consequence of the seller's breach.

(3) Failure of the buyer to effect cover within this section does not bar him from any other remedy.

§ 2–713. Buyer's Damages for Non-Delivery or Repudiation.

(1) Subject to the provisions of this Article with respect to proof of market price (Section 2–723), the measure of damages for non-delivery or repudiation by the seller is the difference between the market price at the time when the buyer learned of the breach and the contract price together with any incidental and consequential damages provided in this Article (Section 2–715), but less expenses saved in consequence of the seller's breach.

(2) Market price is to be determined as of the place for tender or, in cases of rejection after arrival or revocation of acceptance, as of the place of arrival.

§ 2–714. Buyer's Damages for Breach in Regard to Accepted Goods.

(1) Where the buyer has accepted goods and given notification (subsection (3) of Section 2–607) he may recover as damages for any non-conformity of tender the loss resulting in the ordinary course of events from the seller's breach as determined in any manner which is reasonable.

(2) The measure of damages for breach of warranty is the difference at the time and place of acceptance between the value of the goods accepted and the value they would have had if they had been as warranted, unless special circumstances show proximate damages of a different amount.

(3) In a proper case any incidental and consequential damages under the next section may also be recovered.

§ 2–715. Buyer's Incidental and Consequential Damages.

(1) Incidental damages resulting from the seller's breach include expenses reasonably incurred in inspection, receipt, transportation and care and custody of goods rightfully rejected, any commercially reasonable charges, expenses or commissions in connection with effecting cover and any other reasonable expense incident to the delay or other breach.

(2) Consequential damages resulting from the seller's breach include

(a) any loss resulting from general or particular requirements and needs of which the seller at the time of contracting had reason to know and which could not reasonably be prevented by cover or otherwise; and

(b) injury to person or property proximately resulting from any breach of warranty.

§ 2–716. Buyer's Right to Specific Performance or Replevin.

(1) Specific performance may be decreed where the goods are unique or in other proper circumstances.

(2) The decree for specific performance may include such terms and conditions as to payment of the price, damages, or other relief as the court may deem just.

(3) The buyer has a right of replevin for goods identified to the contract if after reasonable effort he is unable to effect cover for such goods or the circumstances reasonably indicate that such effort will be unavailing or if the goods have been shipped under reservation and satisfaction of the security interest in them has been made or tendered. In the case of goods bought for personal, family, or household purposes, the buyer's right of replevin vests upon acquisition of a special property, even if the seller had not then repudiated or failed to deliver.

As amended in 1999.

§ 2–717. Deduction of Damages From the Price.

The buyer on notifying the seller of his intention to do so may deduct all or any part of the damages resulting from any breach of the contract from any part of the price still due under the same contract.

§ 2–718. Liquidation or Limitation of Damages; Deposits.

(1) Damages for breach by either party may be liquidated in the agreement but only at an amount which is reasonable in the light of the anticipated or actual harm caused by the breach, the difficulties of proof of loss, and the inconvenience or nonfeasibility of otherwise obtaining an adequate remedy. A term fixing unreasonably large liquidated damages is void as a penalty.

(2) Where the seller justifiably withholds delivery of goods because of the buyer's breach, the buyer is entitled to restitution of any amount by which the sum of his payments exceeds

(a) the amount to which the seller is entitled by virtue of terms liquidating the seller's damages in accordance with subsection (1), or

(b) in the absence of such terms, twenty per cent of the value of the total performance for which the buyer is obligated under the contract or $500, whichever is smaller.

(3) The buyer's right to restitution under subsection (2) is subject to offset to the extent that the seller establishes

(a) a right to recover damages under the provisions of this Article other than subsection (1), and

(b) the amount or value of any benefits received by the buyer directly or indirectly by reason of the contract.

(4) Where a seller has received payment in goods their reasonable value or the proceeds of their resale shall be treated as payments for the purposes of subsection (2); but if the seller has notice of the buyer's breach before reselling goods received in part performance, his resale is subject to the conditions laid down in this Article on resale by an aggrieved seller (Section 2–706).

§ 2–719. Contractual Modification or Limitation of Remedy.

(1) Subject to the provisions of subsections (2) and (3) of this section and of the preceding section on liquidation and limitation of damages,

(a) the agreement may provide for remedies in addition to or in substitution for those provided in this Article and may limit or alter the measure of damages recoverable under this Article, as by limiting the buyer's remedies to return of the goods and repayment of the price or to repair and replacement of nonconforming goods or parts; and

(b) resort to a remedy as provided is optional unless the remedy is expressly agreed to be exclusive, in which case it is the sole remedy.

(2) Where circumstances cause an exclusive or limited remedy to fail of its essential purpose, remedy may be had as provided in this Act.

(3) Consequential damages may be limited or excluded unless the limitation or exclusion is unconscionable. Limitation of consequential damages for injury to the person in the case of consumer goods is prima facie unconscionable but limitation of damages where the loss is commercial is not.

§ 2–720. Effect of "Cancellation" or "Rescission" on Claims for Antecedent Breach.

Unless the contrary intention clearly appears, expressions of "cancellation" or "rescission" of the contract or the like shall not be construed as a renunciation or discharge of any claim in damages for an antecedent breach.

§ 2–721. Remedies for Fraud.

Remedies for material misrepresentation or fraud include all remedies available under this Article for non-fraudulent breach. Neither rescission or a claim for rescission of the contract for sale nor rejection or return of the goods shall bar or be deemed inconsistent with a claim for damages or other remedy.

§ 2–722. Who Can Sue Third Parties for Injury to Goods.

Where a third party so deals with goods which have been identified to a contract for sale as to cause actionable injury to a party to that contract

(a) a right of action against the third party is in either party to the contract for sale who has title to or a security interest or a special property or an insurable interest in the goods; and if the goods have been destroyed or converted a right of action is also in the party who either bore the risk of loss under the contract for sale or has since the injury assumed that risk as against the other;

(b) if at the time of the injury the party plaintiff did not bear the risk of loss as against the other party to the contract for sale and there is no arrangement between them for disposition of the recovery, his suit or settlement is, subject to his own interest, as a fiduciary for the other party to the contract;

(c) either party may with the consent of the other sue for the benefit of whom it may concern.

§ 2–723. Proof of Market Price: Time and Place.

(1) If an action based on anticipatory repudiation comes to trial before the time for performance with respect to some or all of the goods, any damages based on market price (Section 2–708 or Section 2–713) shall be determined according to the price of such goods prevailing at the time when the aggrieved party learned of the repudiation.

(2) If evidence of a price prevailing at the times or places described in this Article is not readily available the price prevailing within any reasonable time before or after the time described or at any other place which in commercial judgment or under usage of trade would serve as a reasonable substitute for the one described may be used, making any proper allowance for the cost of transporting the goods to or from such other place.

(3) Evidence of a relevant price prevailing at a time or place other than the one described in this Article offered by one party is not admissible unless and until he has given the other party such notice as the court finds sufficient to prevent unfair surprise.

§ 2–724. Admissibility of Market Quotations.

Whenever the prevailing price or value of any goods regularly bought and sold in any established commodity market is in issue, reports in official publications or trade journals or in newspapers or periodicals of general circulation published as the reports of such market shall be admissible in evidence. The circumstances of the preparation of such a report may be shown to affect its weight but not its admissibility.

§ 2–725. Statute of Limitations in Contracts for Sale.

(1) An action for breach of any contract for sale must be commenced within four years after the cause of action has accrued. By the original agreement the parties may reduce the period of limitation to not less than one year but may not extend it.

(2) A cause of action accrues when the breach occurs, regardless of the aggrieved party's lack of knowledge of the breach. A breach of warranty occurs when tender of delivery is made, except that where a warranty explicitly extends to future performance of the goods and discovery of the breach must await the time of such performance the cause of action accrues when the breach is or should have been discovered.

(3) Where an action commenced within the time limited by subsection (1) is so terminated as to leave available a remedy by another action for the same breach such other action may be commenced after the expiration of the time limited and within six months after the termination of the first action unless the termination resulted from voluntary discontinuance or from dismissal for failure or neglect to prosecute.

(4) This section does not alter the law on tolling of the statute of limitations nor does it apply to causes of action which have accrued before this Act becomes effective.

Article 2A LEASES

Part 1 General Provisions

§ 2A–101. Short Title.

This Article shall be known and may be cited as the Uniform Commercial Code—Leases.

§ 2A–102. Scope.

This Article applies to any transaction, regardless of form, that creates a lease.

§ 2A–103. Definitions and Index of Definitions.

(1) In this Article unless the context otherwise requires:

(a) "Buyer in ordinary course of business" means a person who in good faith and without knowledge that the sale to him [or her] is in violation of the ownership rights or security interest or leasehold interest of a third party in the goods buys in ordinary course from a person in the business of selling goods of that kind but does not include a pawnbroker. "Buying" may be for cash or by exchange of other property or on secured or unsecured credit and includes receiving goods or documents of title under a pre-existing contract for sale but does not include a transfer in bulk or as security for or in total or partial satisfaction of a money debt.

(b) "Cancellation" occurs when either party puts an end to the lease contract for default by the other party.

(c) "Commercial unit" means such a unit of goods as by commercial usage is a single whole for purposes of lease and division of which materially impairs its character or value on the market or in use. A commercial unit may be a single article, as a machine, or a set of articles, as a suite of furniture or a line of machinery, or a quantity, as a gross or carload, or any other unit treated in use or in the relevant market as a single whole.

(d) "Conforming" goods or performance under a lease contract means goods or performance that are in accordance with the obligations under the lease contract.

(e) "Consumer lease" means a lease that a lessor regularly engaged in the business of leasing or selling makes to a lessee who is an individual and who takes under the lease primarily for a personal, family, or household purpose [, if the total payments to be made under the lease contract, excluding payments for options to renew or buy, do not exceed $______].

(f) "Fault" means wrongful act, omission, breach, or default.

(g) "Finance lease" means a lease with respect to which:

(i) the lessor does not select, manufacture or supply the goods;

(ii) the lessor acquires the goods or the right to possession and use of the goods in connection with the lease; and

(iii) one of the following occurs:

(A) the lessee receives a copy of the contract by which the lessor acquired the goods or the right to possession and use of the goods before signing the lease contract;

(B) the lessee's approval of the contract by which the lessor acquired the goods or the right to possession and use of the goods is a condition to effectiveness of the lease contract;

(C) the lessee, before signing the lease contract, receives an accurate and complete statement designating the promises and warranties, and any disclaimers of warranties, limitations or modifications of remedies, or liquidated damages, including those of a third party, such as the manufacturer of the goods, provided to the lessor by the person supplying the goods in connection with or as part of the contract by which the lessor acquired the goods or the right to possession and use of the goods; or

(D) if the lease is not a consumer lease, the lessor, before the lessee signs the lease contract, informs the lessee in writing (a) of the identity of the person supplying the goods to the lessor, unless the lessee has selected that person and directed the lessor to acquire the goods or the right to possession and use of the goods from that person, (b) that the lessee is entitled under this Article to any promises and warranties, including those of any third party, provided to the lessor by the person supplying the goods in connection with or as part of the contract by which the lessor acquired the goods or the right to possession and use of the goods, and (c) that the lessee may communicate with the person supplying the goods to the lessor and receive an accurate and complete statement of those promises and warranties, including any disclaimers and limitations of them or of remedies.

(h) "Goods" means all things that are movable at the time of identification to the lease contract, or are fixtures (Section 2A–309), but the term does not include money, documents, instruments, accounts, chattel paper, general intangibles, or minerals or the like, including oil and gas, before extraction. The term also includes the unborn young of animals.

(i) "Installment lease contract" means a lease contract that authorizes or requires the delivery of goods in separate lots to be separately accepted, even though the lease contract contains a clause "each delivery is a separate lease" or its equivalent.

(j) "Lease" means a transfer of the right to possession and use of goods for a term in return for consideration, but a sale, including a sale on approval or a sale or return, or retention or creation of a security interest is not a lease. Unless the context clearly indicates otherwise, the term includes a sublease.

(k) "Lease agreement" means the bargain, with respect to the lease, of the lessor and the lessee in fact as found in their language or by implication from other circumstances including course of dealing or usage of trade or course of performance as provided in this Article. Unless the context clearly indicates otherwise, the term includes a sublease agreement.

(l) "Lease contract" means the total legal obligation that results from the lease agreement as affected by this Article and any other applicable rules of law. Unless the context clearly indicates otherwise, the term includes a sublease contract.

(m) "Leasehold interest" means the interest of the lessor or the lessee under a lease contract.

(n) "Lessee" means a person who acquires the right to possession and use of goods under a lease. Unless the context clearly indicates otherwise, the term includes a sublessee.

(o) "Lessee in ordinary course of business" means a person who in good faith and without knowledge that the lease to him [or her] is in violation of the ownership rights or security interest or leasehold interest of a third party in the goods, leases in ordinary course from a person in the business of selling or leasing goods of that kind but does not include a pawnbroker. "Leasing" may be for cash or by exchange of other property or on secured or unsecured credit and includes receiving goods or documents of title under a pre-existing lease contract but does not include a transfer in bulk or as security for or in total or partial satisfaction of a money debt.

(p) "Lessor" means a person who transfers the right to possession and use of goods under a lease. Unless the context clearly indicates otherwise, the term includes a sublessor.

(q) "Lessor's residual interest" means the lessor's interest in the goods after expiration, termination, or cancellation of the lease contract.

(r) "Lien" means a charge against or interest in goods to secure payment of a debt or performance of an obligation, but the term does not include a security interest.

(s) "Lot" means a parcel or a single article that is the subject matter of a separate lease or delivery, whether or not it is sufficient to perform the lease contract.

(t) "Merchant lessee" means a lessee that is a merchant with respect to goods of the kind subject to the lease.

(u) "Present value" means the amount as of a date certain of one or more sums payable in the future, discounted to the date certain. The discount is determined by the interest rate specified by the parties if the rate was not manifestly unreasonable at the time the transaction was entered into; otherwise, the discount is determined by a commercially reasonable rate that takes into account the facts and circumstances of each case at the time the transaction was entered into.

(v) "Purchase" includes taking by sale, lease, mortgage, security interest, pledge, gift, or any other voluntary transaction creating an interest in goods.

(w) "Sublease" means a lease of goods the right to possession and use of which was acquired by the lessor as a lessee under an existing lease.

(x) "Supplier" means a person from whom a lessor buys or leases goods to be leased under a finance lease.

(y) "Supply contract" means a contract under which a lessor buys or leases goods to be leased.

(z) "Termination" occurs when either party pursuant to a power created by agreement or law puts an end to the lease contract otherwise than for default.

(2) Other definitions applying to this Article and the sections in which they appear are:

"Accessions". Section 2A–310(1).

"Construction mortgage". Section 2A–309(1)(d).

"Encumbrance". Section 2A–309(1)(e).

"Fixtures". Section 2A–309(1)(a).

"Fixture filing". Section 2A–309(1)(b).

"Purchase money lease". Section 2A–309(1)(c).

(3) The following definitions in other Articles apply to this Article:

"Accounts". Section 9–106.

"Between merchants". Section 2–104(3).

"Buyer". Section 2–103(1)(a).

"Chattel paper". Section 9–105(1)(b).

"Consumer goods". Section 9–109(1).

"Document". Section 9–105(1)(f).

"Entrusting". Section 2–403(3).

"General intangibles". Section 9–106.

"Good faith". Section 2–103(1)(b).

"Instrument". Section 9–105(1)(i).

"Merchant". Section 2–104(1).

"Mortgage". Section 9–105(1)(j).

"Pursuant to commitment". Section 9–105(1)(k).

"Receipt". Section 2–103(1)(c).

"Sale". Section 2–106(1).

"Sale on approval". Section 2–326.

"Sale or return". Section 2–326.

"Seller". Section 2–103(1)(d).

(4) In addition Article 1 contains general definitions and principles of construction and interpretation applicable throughout this Article.

As amended in 1990 and 1999.

§ 2A–104. Leases Subject to Other Law.

(1) A lease, although subject to this Article, is also subject to any applicable:

(a) certificate of title statute of this State: (list any certificate of title statutes covering automobiles, trailers, mobile homes, boats, farm tractors, and the like);

(b) certificate of title statute of another jurisdiction (Section 2A–105); or

(c) consumer protection statute of this State, or final consumer protection decision of a court of this State existing on the effective date of this Article.

(2) In case of conflict between this Article, other than Sections 2A–105, 2A–304(3), and 2A–305(3), and a statute or decision referred to in subsection (1), the statute or decision controls.

(3) Failure to comply with an applicable law has only the effect specified therein.

As amended in 1990.

§ 2A–105. Territorial Application of Article to Goods Covered by Certificate of Title.

Subject to the provisions of Sections 2A–304(3) and 2A–305(3), with respect to goods covered by a certificate of title issued under a statute of this State or of another jurisdiction, compliance and the effect of compliance or noncompliance with a certificate of title statute are governed by the law (including the conflict of laws rules) of the jurisdiction issuing the certificate until the earlier of (a) surrender of the certificate, or (b) four months after the goods are removed from that jurisdiction and thereafter until a new certificate of title is issued by another jurisdiction.

§ 2A–106. Limitation on Power of Parties to Consumer Lease to Choose Applicable Law and Judicial Forum.

(1) If the law chosen by the parties to a consumer lease is that of a jurisdiction other than a jurisdiction in which the lessee resides at the time the lease agreement becomes enforceable or within 30 days thereafter or in which the goods are to be used, the choice is not enforceable.

(2) If the judicial forum chosen by the parties to a consumer lease is a forum that would not otherwise have jurisdiction over the lessee, the choice is not enforceable.

§ 2A–107. Waiver or Renunciation of Claim or Right After Default.

Any claim or right arising out of an alleged default or breach of warranty may be discharged in whole or in part without consideration by a written waiver or renunciation signed and delivered by the aggrieved party.

§ 2A–108. Unconscionability.

(1) If the court as a matter of law finds a lease contract or any clause of a lease contract to have been unconscionable at the time it was made the court may refuse to enforce the lease contract, or it may enforce the remainder of the lease contract without the

unconscionable clause, or it may so limit the application of any unconscionable clause as to avoid any unconscionable result.

(2) With respect to a consumer lease, if the court as a matter of law finds that a lease contract or any clause of a lease contract has been induced by unconscionable conduct or that unconscionable conduct has occurred in the collection of a claim arising from a lease contract, the court may grant appropriate relief.

(3) Before making a finding of unconscionability under subsection (1) or (2), the court, on its own motion or that of a party, shall afford the parties a reasonable opportunity to present evidence as to the setting, purpose, and effect of the lease contract or clause thereof, or of the conduct.

(4) In an action in which the lessee claims unconscionability with respect to a consumer lease:

(a) If the court finds unconscionability under subsection (1) or (2), the court shall award reasonable attorney's fees to the lessee.

(b) If the court does not find unconscionability and the lessee claiming unconscionability has brought or maintained an action he [or she] knew to be groundless, the court shall award reasonable attorney's fees to the party against whom the claim is made.

(c) In determining attorney's fees, the amount of the recovery on behalf of the claimant under subsections (1) and (2) is not controlling.

§ 2A–109. Option to Accelerate at Will.

(1) A term providing that one party or his [or her] successor in interest may accelerate payment or performance or require collateral or additional collateral "at will" or "when he [or she] deems himself [or herself] insecure" or in words of similar import must be construed to mean that he [or she] has power to do so only if he [or she] in good faith believes that the prospect of payment or performance is impaired.

(2) With respect to a consumer lease, the burden of establishing good faith under subsection (1) is on the party who exercised the power; otherwise the burden of establishing lack of good faith is on the party against whom the power has been exercised.

Part 2 Formation and Construction of Lease Contract

§ 2A–201. Statute of Frauds.

(1) A lease contract is not enforceable by way of action or defense unless:

(a) the total payments to be made under the lease contract, excluding payments for options to renew or buy, are less than $1,000; or

(b) there is a writing, signed by the party against whom enforcement is sought or by that party's authorized agent, sufficient to indicate that a lease contract has been made between the parties and to describe the goods leased and the lease term.

(2) Any description of leased goods or of the lease term is sufficient and satisfies subsection (1)(b), whether or not it is specific, if it reasonably identifies what is described.

(3) A writing is not insufficient because it omits or incorrectly states a term agreed upon, but the lease contract is not enforceable under subsection (1)(b) beyond the lease term and the quantity of goods shown in the writing.

(4) A lease contract that does not satisfy the requirements of subsection (1), but which is valid in other respects, is enforceable:

(a) if the goods are to be specially manufactured or obtained for the lessee and are not suitable for lease or sale to others in the ordinary course of the lessor's business, and the lessor, before notice of repudiation is received and under circumstances that reasonably indicate that the goods are for the lessee, has made either a substantial beginning of their manufacture or commitments for their procurement;

(b) if the party against whom enforcement is sought admits in that party's pleading, testimony or otherwise in court that a lease contract was made, but the lease contract is not enforceable under this provision beyond the quantity of goods admitted; or

(c) with respect to goods that have been received and accepted by the lessee.

(5) The lease term under a lease contract referred to in subsection (4) is:

(a) if there is a writing signed by the party against whom enforcement is sought or by that party's authorized agent specifying the lease term, the term so specified;

(b) if the party against whom enforcement is sought admits in that party's pleading, testimony, or otherwise in court a lease term, the term so admitted; or

(c) a reasonable lease term.

§ 2A–202. Final Written Expression: Parol or Extrinsic Evidence.

Terms with respect to which the confirmatory memoranda of the parties agree or which are otherwise set forth in a writing intended by the parties as a final expression of their agreement with respect to such terms as are included therein may not be contradicted by evidence of any prior agreement or of a contemporaneous oral agreement but may be explained or supplemented:

(a) by course of dealing or usage of trade or by course of performance; and

(b) by evidence of consistent additional terms unless the court finds the writing to have been intended also as a complete and exclusive statement of the terms of the agreement.

§ 2A–203. Seals Inoperative.

The affixing of a seal to a writing evidencing a lease contract or an offer to enter into a lease contract does not render the writing a sealed instrument and the law with respect to sealed instruments does not apply to the lease contract or offer.

§ 2A–204. Formation in General.

(1) A lease contract may be made in any manner sufficient to show agreement, including conduct by both parties which recognizes the existence of a lease contract.

(2) An agreement sufficient to constitute a lease contract may be found although the moment of its making is undetermined.

(3) Although one or more terms are left open, a lease contract does not fail for indefiniteness if the parties have intended to make a lease contract and there is a reasonably certain basis for giving an appropriate remedy.

§ 2A–205. Firm Offers.

An offer by a merchant to lease goods to or from another person in a signed writing that by its terms gives assurance it will be held open is not revocable, for lack of consideration, during the time stated or, if no time is stated, for a reasonable time, but in no event may the period of irrevocability exceed 3 months. Any such term of assurance on a form supplied by the offeree must be separately signed by the offeror.

§ 2A–206. Offer and Acceptance in Formation of Lease Contract.

(1) Unless otherwise unambiguously indicated by the language or circumstances, an offer to make a lease contract must be construed as inviting acceptance in any manner and by any medium reasonable in the circumstances.

(2) If the beginning of a requested performance is a reasonable mode of acceptance, an offeror who is not notified of acceptance within a reasonable time may treat the offer as having lapsed before acceptance.

§ 2A–207. Course of Performance or Practical Construction.

(1) If a lease contract involves repeated occasions for performance by either party with knowledge of the nature of the performance and opportunity for objection to it by the other, any course of performance accepted or acquiesced in without objection is relevant to determine the meaning of the lease agreement.

(2) The express terms of a lease agreement and any course of performance, as well as any course of dealing and usage of trade, must be construed whenever reasonable as consistent with each other; but if that construction is unreasonable, express terms control course of performance, course of performance controls both course of dealing and usage of trade, and course of dealing controls usage of trade.

(3) Subject to the provisions of Section 2A–208 on modification and waiver, course of performance is relevant to show a waiver or modification of any term inconsistent with the course of performance.

§ 2A–208. Modification, Rescission and Waiver.

(1) An agreement modifying a lease contract needs no consideration to be binding.

(2) A signed lease agreement that excludes modification or rescission except by a signed writing may not be otherwise modified or rescinded, but, except as between merchants, such a requirement on a form supplied by a merchant must be separately signed by the other party.

(3) Although an attempt at modification or rescission does not satisfy the requirements of subsection (2), it may operate as a waiver.

(4) A party who has made a waiver affecting an executory portion of a lease contract may retract the waiver by reasonable notification received by the other party that strict performance will be required of any term waived, unless the retraction would be unjust in view of a material change of position in reliance on the waiver.

§ 2A–209. Lessee under Finance Lease as Beneficiary of Supply Contract.

(1) The benefit of the supplier's promises to the lessor under the supply contract and of all warranties, whether express or implied, including those of any third party provided in connection with or as part of the supply contract, extends to the lessee to the extent of the lessee's leasehold interest under a finance lease related to the supply contract, but is subject to the terms warranty and of the supply contract and all defenses or claims arising therefrom.

(2) The extension of the benefit of supplier's promises and of warranties to the lessee (Section 2A–209(1)) does not: (i) modify the rights and obligations of the parties to the supply contract, whether arising therefrom or otherwise, or (ii) impose any duty or liability under the supply contract on the lessee.

(3) Any modification or rescission of the supply contract by the supplier and the lessor is effective between the supplier and the lessee unless, before the modification or rescission, the supplier has received notice that the lessee has entered into a finance lease related to the supply contract. If the modification or rescission is effective between the supplier and the lessee, the lessor is deemed to have assumed, in addition to the obligations of the lessor to the lessee under the lease contract, promises of the supplier to the lessor and warranties that were so modified or rescinded as they existed and were available to the lessee before modification or rescission.

(4) In addition to the extension of the benefit of the supplier's promises and of warranties to the lessee under subsection (1), the lessee retains all rights that the lessee may have against the supplier which arise from an agreement between the lessee and the supplier or under other law.

As amended in 1990.

§ 2A–210. Express Warranties.

(1) Express warranties by the lessor are created as follows:

(a) Any affirmation of fact or promise made by the lessor to the lessee which relates to the goods and becomes part of the basis of the bargain creates an express warranty that the goods will conform to the affirmation or promise.

(b) Any description of the goods which is made part of the basis of the bargain creates an express warranty that the goods will conform to the description.

(c) Any sample or model that is made part of the basis of the bargain creates an express warranty that the whole of the goods will conform to the sample or model.

(2) It is not necessary to the creation of an express warranty that the lessor use formal words, such as "warrant" or "guarantee," or that the lessor have a specific intention to make a warranty, but

an affirmation merely of the value of the goods or a statement purporting to be merely the lessor's opinion or commendation of the goods does not create a warranty.

§ 2A–211. Warranties Against Interference and Against Infringement; Lessee's Obligation Against Infringement.

(1) There is in a lease contract a warranty that for the lease term no person holds a claim to or interest in the goods that arose from an act or omission of the lessor, other than a claim by way of infringement or the like, which will interfere with the lessee's enjoyment of its leasehold interest.

(2) Except in a finance lease there is in a lease contract by a lessor who is a merchant regularly dealing in goods of the kind a warranty that the goods are delivered free of the rightful claim of any person by way of infringement or the like.

(3) A lessee who furnishes specifications to a lessor or a supplier shall hold the lessor and the supplier harmless against any claim by way of infringement or the like that arises out of compliance with the specifications.

§ 2A–212. Implied Warranty of Merchantability.

(1) Except in a finance lease, a warranty that the goods will be merchantable is implied in a lease contract if the lessor is a merchant with respect to goods of that kind.

(2) Goods to be merchantable must be at least such as

(a) pass without objection in the trade under the description in the lease agreement;

(b) in the case of fungible goods, are of fair average quality within the description;

(c) are fit for the ordinary purposes for which goods of that type are used;

(d) run, within the variation permitted by the lease agreement, of even kind, quality, and quantity within each unit and among all units involved;

(e) are adequately contained, packaged, and labeled as the lease agreement may require; and

(f) conform to any promises or affirmations of fact made on the container or label.

(3) Other implied warranties may arise from course of dealing or usage of trade.

§ 2A–213. Implied Warranty of Fitness for Particular Purpose.

Except in a finance of lease, if the lessor at the time the lease contract is made has reason to know of any particular purpose for which the goods are required and that the lessee is relying on the lessor's skill or judgment to select or furnish suitable goods, there is in the lease contract an implied warranty that the goods will be fit for that purpose.

§ 2A–214. Exclusion or Modification of Warranties.

(1) Words or conduct relevant to the creation of an express warranty and words or conduct tending to negate or limit a warranty must be construed wherever reasonable as consistent with each other; but, subject to the provisions of Section 2A–202 on parol or extrinsic evidence, negation or limitation is inoperative to the extent that the construction is unreasonable.

(2) Subject to subsection (3), to exclude or modify the implied warranty of merchantability or any part of it the language must mention "merchantability", be by a writing, and be conspicuous. Subject to subsection (3), to exclude or modify any implied warranty of fitness the exclusion must be by a writing and be conspicuous. Language to exclude all implied warranties of fitness is sufficient if it is in writing, is conspicuous and states, for example, "There is no warranty that the goods will be fit for a particular purpose".

(3) Notwithstanding subsection (2), but subject to subsection (4),

(a) unless the circumstances indicate otherwise, all implied warranties are excluded by expressions like "as is" or "with all faults" or by other language that in common understanding calls the lessee's attention to the exclusion of warranties and makes plain that there is no implied warranty, if in writing and conspicuous;

(b) if the lessee before entering into the lease contract has examined the goods or the sample or model as fully as desired or has refused to examine the goods, there is no implied warranty with regard to defects that an examination ought in the circumstances to have revealed; and

(c) an implied warranty may also be excluded or modified by course of dealing, course of performance, or usage of trade.

(4) To exclude or modify a warranty against interference or against infringement (Section 2A–211) or any part of it, the language must be specific, be by a writing, and be conspicuous, unless the circumstances, including course of performance, course of dealing, or usage of trade, give the lessee reason to know that the goods are being leased subject to a claim or interest of any person.

§ 2A–215. Cumulation and Conflict of Warranties Express or Implied.

Warranties, whether express or implied, must be construed as consistent with each other and as cumulative, but if that construction is unreasonable, the intention of the parties determines which warranty is dominant. In ascertaining that intention the following rules apply:

(a) Exact or technical specifications displace an inconsistent sample or model or general language of description.

(b) A sample from an existing bulk displaces inconsistent general language of description.

(c) Express warranties displace inconsistent implied warranties other than an implied warranty of fitness for a particular purpose.

§ 2A–216. Third-Party Beneficiaries of Express and Implied Warranties.

Alternative A

A warranty to or for the benefit of a lessee under this Article, whether express or implied, extends to any natural person who is in the family or household of the lessee or who is a guest in the lessee's home if it is reasonable to expect that such person may use, consume, or be affected by the goods and who is injured in person by breach of the warranty. This section does not displace principles of law and equity that extend a warranty to or for the benefit of a lessee to other persons. The operation of this section may not be excluded, modified, or limited, but an exclusion, modification, or limitation of the warranty, including any with respect to rights and remedies, effective against the lessee is also effective against any beneficiary designated under this section.

Alternative B

A warranty to or for the benefit of a lessee under this Article, whether express or implied, extends to any natural person who may reasonably be expected to use, consume, or be affected by the goods and who is injured in person by breach of the warranty. This section does not displace principles of law and equity that extend a warranty to or for the benefit of a lessee to other persons. The operation of this section may not be excluded, modified, or limited, but an exclusion, modification, or limitation of the warranty, including any with respect to rights and remedies, effective against the lessee is also effective against the beneficiary designated under this section.

Alternative C

A warranty to or for the benefit of a lessee under this Article, whether express or implied, extends to any person who may reasonably be expected to use, consume, or be affected by the goods and who is injured by breach of the warranty. The operation of this section may not be excluded, modified, or limited with respect to injury to the person of an individual to whom the warranty extends, but an exclusion, modification, or limitation of the warranty, including any with respect to rights and remedies, effective against the lessee is also effective against the beneficiary designated under this section.

§ 2A–217. Identification.

Identification of goods as goods to which a lease contract refers may be made at any time and in any manner explicitly agreed to by the parties. In the absence of explicit agreement, identification occurs:

(a) when the lease contract is made if the lease contract is for a lease of goods that are existing and identified;

(b) when the goods are shipped, marked, or otherwise designated by the lessor as goods to which the lease contract refers, if the lease contract is for a lease of goods that are not existing and identified; or

(c) when the young are conceived, if the lease contract is for a lease of unborn young of animals.

§ 2A–218. Insurance and Proceeds.

(1) A lessee obtains an insurable interest when existing goods are identified to the lease contract even though the goods identified are nonconforming and the lessee has an option to reject them.

(2) If a lessee has an insurable interest only by reason of the lessor's identification of the goods, the lessor, until default or insolvency or notification to the lessee that identification is final, may substitute other goods for those identified.

(3) Notwithstanding a lessee's insurable interest under subsections (1) and (2), the lessor retains an insurable interest until an option to buy has been exercised by the lessee and risk of loss has passed to the lessee.

(4) Nothing in this section impairs any insurable interest recognized under any other statute or rule of law.

(5) The parties by agreement may determine that one or more parties have an obligation to obtain and pay for insurance covering the goods and by agreement may determine the beneficiary of the proceeds of the insurance.

§ 2A–219. Risk of Loss.

(1) Except in the case of a finance lease, risk of loss is retained by the lessor and does not pass to the lessee. In the case of a finance lease, risk of loss passes to the lessee.

(2) Subject to the provisions of this Article on the effect of default on risk of loss (Section 2A–220), if risk of loss is to pass to the lessee and the time of passage is not stated, the following rules apply:

(a) If the lease contract requires or authorizes the goods to be shipped by carrier

(i) and it does not require delivery at a particular destination, the risk of loss passes to the lessee when the goods are duly delivered to the carrier; but

(ii) if it does require delivery at a particular destination and the goods are there duly tendered while in the possession of the carrier, the risk of loss passes to the lessee when the goods are there duly so tendered as to enable the lessee to take delivery.

(b) If the goods are held by a bailee to be delivered without being moved, the risk of loss passes to the lessee on acknowledgment by the bailee of the lessee's right to possession of the goods.

(c) In any case not within subsection (a) or (b), the risk of loss passes to the lessee on the lessee's receipt of the goods if the lessor, or, in the case of a finance lease, the supplier, is a merchant; otherwise the risk passes to the lessee on tender of delivery.

§ 2A–220. Effect of Default on Risk of Loss.

(1) Where risk of loss is to pass to the lessee and the time of passage is not stated:

(a) If a tender or delivery of goods so fails to conform to the lease contract as to give a right of rejection, the risk of their loss remains with the lessor, or, in the case of a finance lease, the supplier, until cure or acceptance.

(b) If the lessee rightfully revokes acceptance, he [or she], to the extent of any deficiency in his [or her] effective insurance coverage, may treat the risk of loss as having remained with the lessor from the beginning.

(2) Whether or not risk of loss is to pass to the lessee, if the lessee as to conforming goods already identified to a lease contract

repudiates or is otherwise in default under the lease contract, the lessor, or, in the case of a finance lease, the supplier, to the extent of any deficiency in his [or her] effective insurance coverage may treat the risk of loss as resting on the lessee for a commercially reasonable time.

§ 2A–221. Casualty to Identified Goods.

If a lease contract requires goods identified when the lease contract is made, and the goods suffer casualty without fault of the lessee, the lessor or the supplier before delivery, or the goods suffer casualty before risk of loss passes to the lessee pursuant to the lease agreement or Section 2A–219, then:

(a) if the loss is total, the lease contract is avoided; and

(b) if the loss is partial or the goods have so deteriorated as to no longer conform to the lease contract, the lessee may nevertheless demand inspection and at his [or her] option either treat the lease contract as avoided or, except in a finance lease that is not a consumer lease, accept the goods with due allowance from the rent payable for the balance of the lease term for the deterioration or the deficiency in quantity but without further right against the lessor.

Part 3 Effect of Lease Contract

§ 2A–301. Enforceability of Lease Contract.

Except as otherwise provided in this Article, a lease contract is effective and enforceable according to its terms between the parties, against purchasers of the goods and against creditors of the parties.

§ 2A–302. Title to and Possession of Goods.

Except as otherwise provided in this Article, each provision of this Article applies whether the lessor or a third party has title to the goods, and whether the lessor, the lessee, or a third party has possession of the goods, notwithstanding any statute or rule of law that possession or the absence of possession is fraudulent.

§ 2A–303. Alienability of Party's Interest Under Lease Contract or of Lessor's Residual Interest in Goods; Delegation of Performance; Transfer of Rights.

(1) As used in this section, "creation of a security interest" includes the sale of a lease contract that is subject to Article 9, Secured Transactions, by reason of Section 9–109(a)(3).

(2) Except as provided in subsections (3) and Section 9–407, a provision in a lease agreement which (i) prohibits the voluntary or involuntary transfer, including a transfer by sale, sublease, creation or enforcement of a security interest, or attachment, levy, or other judicial process, of an interest of a party under the lease contract or of the lessor's residual interest in the goods, or (ii) makes such a transfer an event of default, gives rise to the rights and remedies provided in subsection (4), but a transfer that is prohibited or is an event of default under the lease agreement is otherwise effective.

(3) A provision in a lease agreement which (i) prohibits a transfer of a right to damages for default with respect to the whole lease contract or of a right to payment arising out of the transferor's due performance of the transferor's entire obligation, or (ii) makes such a transfer an event of default, is not enforceable, and such a transfer is not a transfer that materially impairs the propsect of obtaining return performance by, materially changes the duty of, or materially increases the burden or risk imposed on, the other party to the lease contract within the purview of subsection (4).

(4) Subject to subsection (3) and Section 9–407:

(a) if a transfer is made which is made an event of default under a lease agreement, the party to the lease contract not making the transfer, unless that party waives the default or otherwise agrees, has the rights and remedies described in Section 2A–501(2);

(b) if paragraph (a) is not applicable and if a transfer is made that (i) is prohibited under a lease agreement or (ii) materially impairs the prospect of obtaining return performance by, materially changes the duty of, or materially increases the burden or risk imposed on, the other party to the lease contract, unless the party not making the transfer agrees at any time to the transfer in the lease contract or otherwise, then, except as limited by contract, (i) the transferor is liable to the party not making the transfer for damages caused by the transfer to the extent that the damages could not reasonably be prevented by the party not making the transfer and (ii) a court having jurisdiction may grant other appropriate relief, including cancellation of the lease contract or an injunction against the transfer.

(5) A transfer of "the lease" or of "all my rights under the lease", or a transfer in similar general terms, is a transfer of rights and, unless the language or the circumstances, as in a transfer for security, indicate the contrary, the transfer is a delegation of duties by the transferor to the transferee. Acceptance by the transferee constitutes a promise by the transferee to perform those duties. The promise is enforceable by either the transferor or the other party to the lease contract.

(6) Unless otherwise agreed by the lessor and the lessee, a delegation of performance does not relieve the transferor as against the other party of any duty to perform or of any liability for default.

(7) In a consumer lease, to prohibit the transfer of an interest of a party under the lease contract or to make a transfer an event of default, the language must be specific, by a writing, and conspicuous.

As amended in 1990 and 1999.

§ 2A–304. Subsequent Lease of Goods by Lessor.

(1) Subject to Section 2A–303, a subsequent lessee from a lessor of goods under an existing lease contract obtains, to the extent of the leasehold interest transferred, the leasehold interest in the goods that the lessor had or had power to transfer, and except as provided in subsection (2) and Section 2A–527(4), takes subject to the existing lease contract. A lessor with voidable title has power to transfer a good leasehold interest to a good faith subsequent lessee for value, but only to the extent set forth in the preceding sentence. If goods have been delivered under a transaction of purchase the lessor has that power even though:

(a) the lessor's transferor was deceived as to the identity of the lessor;

(b) the delivery was in exchange for a check which is later dishonored;

(c) it was agreed that the transaction was to be a "cash sale"; or

(d) the delivery was procured through fraud punishable as larcenous under the criminal law.

(2) A subsequent lessee in the ordinary course of business from a lessor who is a merchant dealing in goods of that kind to whom the goods were entrusted by the existing lessee of that lessor before the interest of the subsequent lessee became enforceable against that lessor obtains, to the extent of the leasehold interest transferred, all of that lessor's and the existing lessee's rights to the goods, and takes free of the existing lease contract.

(3) A subsequent lessee from the lessor of goods that are subject to an existing lease contract and are covered by a certificate of title issued under a statute of this State or of another jurisdiction takes no greater rights than those provided both by this section and by the certificate of title statute.

As amended in 1990.

§ 2A–305. Sale or Sublease of Goods by Lessee.

(1) Subject to the provisions of Section 2A–303, a buyer or sublessee from the lessee of goods under an existing lease contract obtains, to the extent of the interest transferred, the leasehold interest in the goods that the lessee had or had power to transfer, and except as provided in subsection (2) and Section 2A–511(4), takes subject to the existing lease contract. A lessee with a voidable leasehold interest has power to transfer a good leasehold interest to a good faith buyer for value or a good faith sublessee for value, but only to the extent set forth in the preceding sentence. When goods have been delivered under a transaction of lease the lessee has that power even though:

(a) the lessor was deceived as to the identity of the lessee;

(b) the delivery was in exchange for a check which is later dishonored; or

(c) the delivery was procured through fraud punishable as larcenous under the criminal law.

(2) A buyer in the ordinary course of business or a sublessee in the ordinary course of business from a lessee who is a merchant dealing in goods of that kind to whom the goods were entrusted by the lessor obtains, to the extent of the interest transferred, all of the lessor's and lessee's rights to the goods, and takes free of the existing lease contract.

(3) A buyer or sublessee from the lessee of goods that are subject to an existing lease contract and are covered by a certificate of title issued under a statute of this State or of another jurisdiction takes no greater rights than those provided both by this section and by the certificate of title statute.

§ 2A–306. Priority of Certain Liens Arising by Operation of Law.

If a person in the ordinary course of his [or her] business furnishes services or materials with respect to goods subject to a lease contract, a lien upon those goods in the possession of that person given by statute or rule of law for those materials or services takes priority over any interest of the lessor or lessee under the lease contract or this Article unless the lien is created by statute and the statute provides otherwise or unless the lien is created by rule of law and the rule of law provides otherwise.

§ 2A–307. Priority of Liens Arising by Attachment or Levy on, Security Interests in, and Other Claims to Goods.

(1) Except as otherwise provided in Section 2A–306, a creditor of a lessee takes subject to the lease contract.

(2) Except as otherwise provided in subsection (3) and in Sections 2A–306 and 2A–308, a creditor of a lessor takes subject to the lease contract unless the creditor holds a lien that attached to the goods before the lease contract became enforceable.

(3) Except as otherwise provided in Sections 9–317, 9–321, and 9–323, a lessee takes a leasehold interest subject to a security interest held by a creditor of the lessor.

As amended in 1990 and 1999.

§ 2A–308. Special Rights of Creditors.

(1) A creditor of a lessor in possession of goods subject to a lease contract may treat the lease contract as void if as against the creditor retention of possession by the lessor is fraudulent under any statute or rule of law, but retention of possession in good faith and current course of trade by the lessor for a commercially reasonable time after the lease contract becomes enforceable is not fraudulent.

(2) Nothing in this Article impairs the rights of creditors of a lessor if the lease contract (a) becomes enforceable, not in current course of trade but in satisfaction of or as security for a pre-existing claim for money, security, or the like, and (b) is made under circumstances which under any statute or rule of law apart from this Article would constitute the transaction a fraudulent transfer or voidable preference.

(3) A creditor of a seller may treat a sale or an identification of goods to a contract for sale as void if as against the creditor retention of possession by the seller is fraudulent under any statute or rule of law, but retention of possession of the goods pursuant to a lease contract entered into by the seller as lessee and the buyer as lessor in connection with the sale or identification of the goods is not fraudulent if the buyer bought for value and in good faith.

§ 2A–309. Lessor's and Lessee's Rights When Goods Become Fixtures.

(1) In this section:

(a) goods are "fixtures" when they become so related to particular real estate that an interest in them arises under real estate law;

(b) a "fixture filing" is the filing, in the office where a mortgage on the real estate would be filed or recorded, of a financing statement covering goods that are or are to become fixtures and conforming to the requirements of Section 9–502(a) and (b);

(c) a lease is a "purchase money lease" unless the lessee has possession or use of the goods or the right to possession or use of the goods before the lease agreement is enforceable;

(d) a mortgage is a "construction mortgage" to the extent it secures an obligation incurred for the construction of an improvement on land including the acquisition cost of the land, if the recorded writing so indicates; and

(e) "encumbrance" includes real estate mortgages and other liens on real estate and all other rights in real estate that are not ownership interests.

(2) Under this Article a lease may be of goods that are fixtures or may continue in goods that become fixtures, but no lease exists under this Article of ordinary building materials incorporated into an improvement on land.

(3) This Article does not prevent creation of a lease of fixtures pursuant to real estate law.

(4) The perfected interest of a lessor of fixtures has priority over a conflicting interest of an encumbrancer or owner of the real estate if:

(a) the lease is a purchase money lease, the conflicting interest of the encumbrancer or owner arises before the goods become fixtures, the interest of the lessor is perfected by a fixture filing before the goods become fixtures or within ten days thereafter, and the lessee has an interest of record in the real estate or is in possession of the real estate; or

(b) the interest of the lessor is perfected by a fixture filing before the interest of the encumbrancer or owner is of record, the lessor's interest has priority over any conflicting interest of a predecessor in title of the encumbrancer or owner, and the lessee has an interest of record in the real estate or is in possession of the real estate.

(5) The interest of a lessor of fixtures, whether or not perfected, has priority over the conflicting interest of an encumbrancer or owner of the real estate if:

(a) the fixtures are readily removable factory or office machines, readily removable equipment that is not primarily used or leased for use in the operation of the real estate, or readily removable replacements of domestic appliances that are goods subject to a consumer lease, and before the goods become fixtures the lease contract is enforceable; or

(b) the conflicting interest is a lien on the real estate obtained by legal or equitable proceedings after the lease contract is enforceable; or

(c) the encumbrancer or owner has consented in writing to the lease or has disclaimed an interest in the goods as fixtures; or

(d) the lessee has a right to remove the goods as against the encumbrancer or owner. If the lessee's right to remove terminates, the priority of the interest of the lessor continues for a reasonable time.

(6) Notwithstanding paragraph (4)(a) but otherwise subject to subsections (4) and (5), the interest of a lessor of fixtures, including the lessor's residual interest, is subordinate to the conflicting interest of an encumbrancer of the real estate under a construction mortgage recorded before the goods become fixtures if the goods become fixtures before the completion of the construction. To the extent given to refinance a construction mortgage, the conflicting interest of an encumbrancer of the real estate under a mortgage has this priority to the same extent as the encumbrancer of the real estate under the construction mortgage.

(7) In cases not within the preceding subsections, priority between the interest of a lessor of fixtures, including the lessor's residual interest, and the conflicting interest of an encumbrancer or owner of the real estate who is not the lessee is determined by the priority rules governing conflicting interests in real estate.

(8) If the interest of a lessor of fixtures, including the lessor's residual interest, has priority over all conflicting interests of all owners and encumbrancers of the real estate, the lessor or the lessee may (i) on default, expiration, termination, or cancellation of the lease agreement but subject to the agreement and this Article, or (ii) if necessary to enforce other rights and remedies of the lessor or lessee under this Article, remove the goods from the real estate, free and clear of all conflicting interests of all owners and encumbrancers of the real estate, but the lessor or lessee must reimburse any encumbrancer or owner of the real estate who is not the lessee and who has not otherwise agreed for the cost of repair of any physical injury, but not for any diminution in value of the real estate caused by the absence of the goods removed or by any necessity of replacing them. A person entitled to reimbursement may refuse permission to remove until the party seeking removal gives adequate security for the performance of this obligation.

(9) Even though the lease agreement does not create a security interest, the interest of a lessor of fixtures, including the lessor's residual interest, is perfected by filing a financing statement as a fixture filing for leased goods that are or are to become fixtures in accordance with the relevant provisions of the Article on Secured Transactions (Article 9).

As amended in 1990 and 1999.

§ 2A–310. Lessor's and Lessee's Rights When Goods Become Accessions.

(1) Goods are "accessions" when they are installed in or affixed to other goods.

(2) The interest of a lessor or a lessee under a lease contract entered into before the goods became accessions is superior to all interests in the whole except as stated in subsection (4).

(3) The interest of a lessor or a lessee under a lease contract entered into at the time or after the goods became accessions is superior to all subsequently acquired interests in the whole except as stated in subsection (4) but is subordinate to interests in the whole existing at the time the lease contract was made unless the holders of such interests in the whole have in writing consented to the lease or disclaimed an interest in the goods as part of the whole.

(4) The interest of a lessor or a lessee under a lease contract described in subsection (2) or (3) is subordinate to the interest of

(a) a buyer in the ordinary course of business or a lessee in the ordinary course of business of any interest in the whole acquired after the goods became accessions; or

(b) a creditor with a security interest in the whole perfected before the lease contract was made to the extent that the creditor makes subsequent advances without knowledge of the lease contract.

(5) When under subsections (2) or (3) and (4) a lessor or a lessee of accessions holds an interest that is superior to all interests in the whole, the lessor or the lessee may (a) on default, expiration, termination, or cancellation of the lease contract by the other party but subject to the provisions of the lease contract and this Article, or (b) if necessary to enforce his [or her] other rights and remedies under this Article, remove the goods from the whole, free and clear of all interests in the whole, but he [or she] must reimburse any holder of an interest in the whole who is not the lessee and who has not otherwise agreed for the cost of repair of any physical injury but not for any diminution in value of the whole caused by the absence of the goods removed or by any necessity for replacing them. A person entitled to reimbursement may refuse permission to remove until the party seeking removal gives adequate security for the performance of this obligation.

§ 2A–311. Priority Subject to Subordination.

Nothing in this Article prevents subordination by agreement by any person entitled to priority.

As added in 1990.

Part 4 Performance of Lease Contract: Repudiated, Substituted and Excused

§ 2A–401. Insecurity: Adequate Assurance of Performance.

(1) A lease contract imposes an obligation on each party that the other's expectation of receiving due performance will not be impaired.

(2) If reasonable grounds for insecurity arise with respect to the performance of either party, the insecure party may demand in writing adequate assurance of due performance. Until the insecure party receives that assurance, if commercially reasonable the insecure party may suspend any performance for which he [or she] has not already received the agreed return.

(3) A repudiation of the lease contract occurs if assurance of due performance adequate under the circumstances of the particular case is not provided to the insecure party within a reasonable time, not to exceed 30 days after receipt of a demand by the other party.

(4) Between merchants, the reasonableness of grounds for insecurity and the adequacy of any assurance offered must be determined according to commercial standards.

(5) Acceptance of any nonconforming delivery or payment does not prejudice the aggrieved party's right to demand adequate assurance of future performance.

§ 2A–402. Anticipatory Repudiation.

If either party repudiates a lease contract with respect to a performance not yet due under the lease contract, the loss of which performance will substantially impair the value of the lease contract to the other, the aggrieved party may:

(a) for a commercially reasonable time, await retraction of repudiation and performance by the repudiating party;

(b) make demand pursuant to Section 2A–401 and await assurance of future performance adequate under the circumstances of the particular case; or

(c) resort to any right or remedy upon default under the lease contract or this Article, even though the aggrieved party has notified the repudiating party that the aggrieved party would await the repudiating party's performance and assurance and has urged retraction. In addition, whether or not the aggrieved party is pursuing one of the foregoing remedies, the aggrieved party may suspend performance or, if the aggrieved party is the lessor, proceed in accordance with the provisions of this Article on the lessor's right to identify goods to the lease contract notwithstanding default or to salvage unfinished goods (Section 2A–524).

§ 2A–403. Retraction of Anticipatory Repudiation.

(1) Until the repudiating party's next performance is due, the repudiating party can retract the repudiation unless, since the repudiation, the aggrieved party has cancelled the lease contract or materially changed the aggrieved party's position or otherwise indicated that the aggrieved party considers the repudiation final.

(2) Retraction may be by any method that clearly indicates to the aggrieved party that the repudiating party intends to perform under the lease contract and includes any assurance demanded under Section 2A–401.

(3) Retraction reinstates a repudiating party's rights under a lease contract with due excuse and allowance to the aggrieved party for any delay occasioned by the repudiation.

§ 2A–404. Substituted Performance.

(1) If without fault of the lessee, the lessor and the supplier, the agreed berthing, loading, or unloading facilities fail or the agreed type of carrier becomes unavailable or the agreed manner of delivery otherwise becomes commercially impracticable, but a commercially reasonable substitute is available, the substitute performance must be tendered and accepted.

(2) If the agreed means or manner of payment fails because of domestic or foreign governmental regulation:

(a) the lessor may withhold or stop delivery or cause the supplier to withhold or stop delivery unless the lessee provides a means or manner of payment that is commercially a substantial equivalent; and

(b) if delivery has already been taken, payment by the means or in the manner provided by the regulation discharges the lessee's obligation unless the regulation is discriminatory, oppressive, or predatory.

§ 2A–405. Excused Performance.

Subject to Section 2A–404 on substituted performance, the following rules apply:

(a) Delay in delivery or nondelivery in whole or in part by a lessor or a supplier who complies with paragraphs (b) and (c) is not a default under the lease contract if performance as agreed has been made impracticable by the occurrence of a contingency the nonoccurrence of which was a basic assumption on which the lease contract was made or by compliance in good faith with any applicable foreign or domestic governmental regulation or order, whether or not the regulation or order later proves to be invalid.

(b) If the causes mentioned in paragraph (a) affect only part of the lessor's or the supplier's capacity to perform, he [or she] shall allocate production and deliveries among his [or her] customers but at his [or her] option may include regular customers not then under contract for sale or lease as well as his [or her] own requirements for further manufacture. He [or she] may so allocate in any manner that is fair and reasonable.

(c) The lessor seasonably shall notify the lessee and in the case of a finance lease the supplier seasonably shall notify the lessor and the lessee, if known, that there will be delay or nondelivery and, if allocation is required under paragraph (b), of the estimated quota thus made available for the lessee.

§ 2A–406. Procedure on Excused Performance.

(1) If the lessee receives notification of a material or indefinite delay or an allocation justified under Section 2A–405, the lessee may by written notification to the lessor as to any goods involved, and with respect to all of the goods if under an installment lease contract the value of the whole lease contract is substantially impaired (Section 2A–510):

(a) terminate the lease contract (Section 2A-505(2)); or

(b) except in a finance lease that is not a consumer lease, modify the lease contract by accepting the available quota in substitution, with due allowance from the rent payable for the balance of the lease term for the deficiency but without further right against the lessor.

(2) If, after receipt of a notification from the lessor under Section 2A–405, the lessee fails so to modify the lease agreement within a reasonable time not exceeding 30 days, the lease contract lapses with respect to any deliveries affected.

§ 2A–407. Irrevocable Promises: Finance Leases.

(1) In the case of a finance lease that is not a consumer lease the lessee's promises under the lease contract become irrevocable and independent upon the lessee's acceptance of the goods.

(2) A promise that has become irrevocable and independent under subsection (1):

(a) is effective and enforceable between the parties, and by or against third parties including assignees of the parties, and

(b) is not subject to cancellation, termination, modification, repudiation, excuse, or substitution without the consent of the party to whom the promise runs.

(3) This section does not affect the validity under any other law of a covenant in any lease contract making the lessee's promises irrevocable and independent upon the lessee's acceptance of the goods.

As amended in 1990.

Part 5 Default

A. In General

§ 2A–501. Default: Procedure.

(1) Whether the lessor or the lessee is in default under a lease contract is determined by the lease agreement and this Article.

(2) If the lessor or the lessee is in default under the lease contract, the party seeking enforcement has rights and remedies as provided in this Article and, except as limited by this Article, as provided in the lease agreement.

(3) If the lessor or the lessee is in default under the lease contract, the party seeking enforcement may reduce the party's claim to judgment, or otherwise enforce the lease contract by self-help or any available judicial procedure or nonjudicial procedure, including administrative proceeding, arbitration, or the like, in accordance with this Article.

(4) Except as otherwise provided in Section 1–106(1) or this Article or the lease agreement, the rights and remedies referred to in subsections (2) and (3) are cumulative.

(5) If the lease agreement covers both real property and goods, the party seeking enforcement may proceed under this Part as to the goods, or under other applicable law as to both the real property and the goods in accordance with that party's rights and remedies in respect of the real property, in which case this Part does not apply.

As amended in 1990.

§ 2A–502. Notice After Default.

Except as otherwise provided in this Article or the lease agreement, the lessor or lessee in default under the lease contract is not entitled to notice of default or notice of enforcement from the other party to the lease agreement.

§ 2A–503. Modification or Impairment of Rights and Remedies.

(1) Except as otherwise provided in this Article, the lease agreement may include rights and remedies for default in addition to or in substitution for those provided in this Article and may limit or alter the measure of damages recoverable under this Article.

(2) Resort to a remedy provided under this Article or in the lease agreement is optional unless the remedy is expressly agreed to be exclusive. If circumstances cause an exclusive or limited remedy to fail of its essential purpose, or provision for an exclusive remedy is unconscionable, remedy may be had as provided in this Article.

(3) Consequential damages may be liquidated under Section 2A–504, or may otherwise be limited, altered, or excluded unless the limitation, alteration, or exclusion is unconscionable. Limitation, alteration, or exclusion of consequential damages for injury to the person in the case of consumer goods is prima facie unconscionable but limitation, alteration, or exclusion of damages where the loss is commercial is not prima facie unconscionable.

(4) Rights and remedies on default by the lessor or the lessee with respect to any obligation or promise collateral or ancillary to the lease contract are not impaired by this Article.

As amended in 1990.

§ 2A–504. Liquidation of Damages.

(1) Damages payable by either party for default, or any other act or omission, including indemnity for loss or diminution of anticipated tax benefits or loss or damage to lessor's residual interest, may be liquidated in the lease agreement but only at an amount or by a formula that is reasonable in light of the then anticipated harm caused by the default or other act or omission.

(2) If the lease agreement provides for liquidation of damages, and such provision does not comply with subsection (1), or such provision is an exclusive or limited remedy that circumstances cause to fail of its essential purpose, remedy may be had as provided in this Article.

(3) If the lessor justifiably withholds or stops delivery of goods because of the lessee's default or insolvency (Section 2A–525 or 2A–526), the lessee is entitled to restitution of any amount by which the sum of his [or her] payments exceeds:

(a) the amount to which the lessor is entitled by virtue of terms liquidating the lessor's damages in accordance with subsection (1); or

(b) in the absence of those terms, 20 percent of the then present value of the total rent the lessee was obligated to pay for the balance of the lease term, or, in the case of a consumer lease, the lesser of such amount or $500.

(4) A lessee's right to restitution under subsection (3) is subject to offset to the extent the lessor establishes:

(a) a right to recover damages under the provisions of this Article other than subsection (1); and

(b) the amount or value of any benefits received by the lessee directly or indirectly by reason of the lease contract.

§ 2A–505. Cancellation and Termination and Effect of Cancellation, Termination, Rescission, or Fraud on Rights and Remedies.

(1) On cancellation of the lease contract, all obligations that are still executory on both sides are discharged, but any right based on prior default or performance survives, and the cancelling party also retains any remedy for default of the whole lease contract or any unperformed balance.

(2) On termination of the lease contract, all obligations that are still executory on both sides are discharged but any right based on prior default or performance survives.

(3) Unless the contrary intention clearly appears, expressions of "cancellation," "rescission," or the like of the lease contract may not be construed as a renunciation or discharge of any claim in damages for an antecedent default.

(4) Rights and remedies for material misrepresentation or fraud include all rights and remedies available under this Article for default.

(5) Neither rescission nor a claim for rescission of the lease contract nor rejection or return of the goods may bar or be deemed inconsistent with a claim for damages or other right or remedy.

§ 2A–506. Statute of Limitations.

(1) An action for default under a lease contract, including breach of warranty or indemnity, must be commenced within 4 years after the cause of action accrued. By the original lease contract the parties may reduce the period of limitation to not less than one year.

(2) A cause of action for default accrues when the act or omission on which the default or breach of warranty is based is or should have been discovered by the aggrieved party, or when the default occurs, whichever is later. A cause of action for indemnity accrues when the act or omission on which the claim for indemnity is based is or should have been discovered by the indemnified party, whichever is later.

(3) If an action commenced within the time limited by subsection (1) is so terminated as to leave available a remedy by another action for the same default or breach of warranty or indemnity, the other action may be commenced after the expiration of the time limited and within 6 months after the termination of the first action unless the termination resulted from voluntary discontinuance or from dismissal for failure or neglect to prosecute.

(4) This section does not alter the law on tolling of the statute of limitations nor does it apply to causes of action that have accrued before this Article becomes effective.

§ 2A–507. Proof of Market Rent: Time and Place.

(1) Damages based on market rent (Section 2A–519 or 2A–528) are determined according to the rent for the use of the goods concerned for a lease term identical to the remaining lease term of the original lease agreement and prevailing at the times specified in Sections 2A–519 and 2A–528.

(2) If evidence of rent for the use of the goods concerned for a lease term identical to the remaining lease term of the original lease agreement and prevailing at the times or places described in this Article is not readily available, the rent prevailing within any reasonable time before or after the time described or at any other place or for a different lease term which in commercial judgment or under usage of trade would serve as a reasonable substitute for the one described may be used, making any proper allowance for the difference, including the cost of transporting the goods to or from the other place.

(3) Evidence of a relevant rent prevailing at a time or place or for a lease term other than the one described in this Article offered by one party is not admissible unless and until he [or she] has given the other party notice the court finds sufficient to prevent unfair surprise.

(4) If the prevailing rent or value of any goods regularly leased in any established market is in issue, reports in official publications or trade journals or in newspapers or periodicals of general circulation published as the reports of that market are admissible in evidence. The circumstances of the preparation of the report may be shown to affect its weight but not its admissibility.

As amended in 1990.

B. Default by Lessor

§ 2A–508. Lessee's Remedies.

(1) If a lessor fails to deliver the goods in conformity to the lease contract (Section 2A–509) or repudiates the lease contract (Section 2A–402), or a lessee rightfully rejects the goods (Section 2A–509) or justifiably revokes acceptance of the goods (Section 2A–517), then with respect to any goods involved, and with respect to all

of the goods if under an installment lease contract the value of the whole lease contract is substantially impaired (Section 2A–510), the lessor is in default under the lease contract and the lessee may:

(a) cancel the lease contract (Section 2A–505(1));

(b) recover so much of the rent and security as has been paid and is just under the circumstances;

(c) cover and recover damages as to all goods affected whether or not they have been identified to the lease contract (Sections 2A–518 and 2A–520), or recover damages for non-delivery (Sections 2A–519 and 2A–520);

(d) exercise any other rights or pursue any other remedies provided in the lease contract.

(2) If a lessor fails to deliver the goods in conformity to the lease contract or repudiates the lease contract, the lessee may also:

(a) if the goods have been identified, recover them (Section 2A–522); or

(b) in a proper case, obtain specific performance or replevy the goods (Section 2A–521).

(3) If a lessor is otherwise in default under a lease contract, the lessee may exercise the rights and pursue the remedies provided in the lease contract, which may include a right to cancel the lease, and in Section 2A–519(3).

(4) If a lessor has breached a warranty, whether express or implied, the lessee may recover damages (Section 2A–519(4)).

(5) On rightful rejection or justifiable revocation of acceptance, a lessee has a security interest in goods in the lessee's possession or control for any rent and security that has been paid and any expenses reasonably incurred in their inspection, receipt, transportation, and care and custody and may hold those goods and dispose of them in good faith and in a commercially reasonable manner, subject to Section 2A–527(5).

(6) Subject to the provisions of Section 2A–407, a lessee, on notifying the lessor of the lessee's intention to do so, may deduct all or any part of the damages resulting from any default under the lease contract from any part of the rent still due under the same lease contract.

As amended in 1990.

§ 2A–509. Lessee's Rights on Improper Delivery; Rightful Rejection.

(1) Subject to the provisions of Section 2A–510 on default in installment lease contracts, if the goods or the tender or delivery fail in any respect to conform to the lease contract, the lessee may reject or accept the goods or accept any commercial unit or units and reject the rest of the goods.

(2) Rejection of goods is ineffective unless it is within a reasonable time after tender or delivery of the goods and the lessee seasonably notifies the lessor.

§ 2A–510. Installment Lease Contracts: Rejection and Default.

(1) Under an installment lease contract a lessee may reject any delivery that is nonconforming if the nonconformity substantially impairs the value of that delivery and cannot be cured or the nonconformity is a defect in the required documents; but if the nonconformity does not fall within subsection (2) and the lessor or the supplier gives adequate assurance of its cure, the lessee must accept that delivery.

(2) Whenever nonconformity or default with respect to one or more deliveries substantially impairs the value of the installment lease contract as a whole there is a default with respect to the whole. But, the aggrieved party reinstates the installment lease contract as a whole if the aggrieved party accepts a nonconforming delivery without seasonably notifying of cancellation or brings an action with respect only to past deliveries or demands performance as to future deliveries.

§ 2A–511. Merchant Lessee's Duties as to Rightfully Rejected Goods.

(1) Subject to any security interest of a lessee (Section 2A–508(5)), if a lessor or a supplier has no agent or place of business at the market of rejection, a merchant lessee, after rejection of goods in his [or her] possession or control, shall follow any reasonable instructions received from the lessor or the supplier with respect to the goods. In the absence of those instructions, a merchant lessee shall make reasonable efforts to sell, lease, or otherwise dispose of the goods for the lessor's account if they threaten to decline in value speedily. Instructions are not reasonable if on demand indemnity for expenses is not forthcoming.

(2) If a merchant lessee (subsection (1)) or any other lessee (Section 2A–512) disposes of goods, he [or she] is entitled to reimbursement either from the lessor or the supplier or out of the proceeds for reasonable expenses of caring for and disposing of the goods and, if the expenses include no disposition commission, to such commission as is usual in the trade, or if there is none, to a reasonable sum not exceeding 10 percent of the gross proceeds.

(3) In complying with this section or Section 2A–512, the lessee is held only to good faith. Good faith conduct hereunder is neither acceptance or conversion nor the basis of an action for damages.

(4) A purchaser who purchases in good faith from a lessee pursuant to this section or Section 2A–512 takes the goods free of any rights of the lessor and the supplier even though the lessee fails to comply with one or more of the requirements of this Article.

§ 2A–512. Lessee's Duties as to Rightfully Rejected Goods.

(1) Except as otherwise provided with respect to goods that threaten to decline in value speedily (Section 2A–511) and subject to any security interest of a lessee (Section 2A–508(5)):

(a) the lessee, after rejection of goods in the lessee's possession, shall hold them with reasonable care at the lessor's or the supplier's disposition for a reasonable time after the lessee's seasonable notification of rejection;

(b) if the lessor or the supplier gives no instructions within a reasonable time after notification of rejection, the lessee may store the rejected goods for the lessor's or the supplier's account or ship them to the lessor or the supplier or dispose of them for the lessor's or the supplier's account with reimbursement in the manner provided in Section 2A–511; but

(c) the lessee has no further obligations with regard to goods rightfully rejected.

(2) Action by the lessee pursuant to subsection (1) is not acceptance or conversion.

§ 2A–513. Cure by Lessor of Improper Tender or Delivery; Replacement.

(1) If any tender or delivery by the lessor or the supplier is rejected because nonconforming and the time for performance has not yet expired, the lessor or the supplier may seasonably notify the lessee of the lessor's or the supplier's intention to cure and may then make a conforming delivery within the time provided in the lease contract.

(2) If the lessee rejects a nonconforming tender that the lessor or the supplier had reasonable grounds to believe would be acceptable with or without money allowance, the lessor or the supplier may have a further reasonable time to substitute a conforming tender if he [or she] seasonably notifies the lessee.

§ 2A–514. Waiver of Lessee's Objections.

(1) In rejecting goods, a lessee's failure to state a particular defect that is ascertainable by reasonable inspection precludes the lessee from relying on the defect to justify rejection or to establish default:

(a) if, stated seasonably, the lessor or the supplier could have cured it (Section 2A–513); or

(b) between merchants if the lessor or the supplier after rejection has made a request in writing for a full and final written statement of all defects on which the lessee proposes to rely.

(2) A lessee's failure to reserve rights when paying rent or other consideration against documents precludes recovery of the payment for defects apparent on the face of the documents.

§ 2A–515. Acceptance of Goods.

(1) Acceptance of goods occurs after the lessee has had a reasonable opportunity to inspect the goods and

(a) the lessee signifies or acts with respect to the goods in a manner that signifies to the lessor or the supplier that the goods are conforming or that the lessee will take or retain them in spite of their nonconformity; or

(b) the lessee fails to make an effective rejection of the goods (Section 2A–509(2)).

(2) Acceptance of a part of any commercial unit is acceptance of that entire unit.

§ 2A–516. Effect of Acceptance of Goods; Notice of Default; Burden of Establishing Default after Acceptance; Notice of Claim or Litigation to Person Answerable Over.

(1) A lessee must pay rent for any goods accepted in accordance with the lease contract, with due allowance for goods rightfully rejected or not delivered.

(2) A lessee's acceptance of goods precludes rejection of the goods accepted. In the case of a finance lease, if made with knowledge of a nonconformity, acceptance cannot be revoked because of it. In any other case, if made with knowledge of a nonconformity, acceptance cannot be revoked because of it unless the acceptance was on the reasonable assumption that the nonconformity would be seasonably cured. Acceptance does not of itself impair any other remedy provided by this Article or the lease agreement for nonconformity.

(3) If a tender has been accepted:

(a) within a reasonable time after the lessee discovers or should have discovered any default, the lessee shall notify the lessor and the supplier, if any, or be barred from any remedy against the party notified;

(b) except in the case of a consumer lease, within a reasonable time after the lessee receives notice of litigation for infringement or the like (Section 2A–211) the lessee shall notify the lessor or be barred from any remedy over for liability established by the litigation; and

(c) the burden is on the lessee to establish any default.

(4) If a lessee is sued for breach of a warranty or other obligation for which a lessor or a supplier is answerable over the following apply:

(a) The lessee may give the lessor or the supplier, or both, written notice of the litigation. If the notice states that the person notified may come in and defend and that if the person notified does not do so that person will be bound in any action against that person by the lessee by any determination of fact common to the two litigations, then unless the person notified after seasonable receipt of the notice does come in and defend that person is so bound.

(b) The lessor or the supplier may demand in writing that the lessee turn over control of the litigation including settlement if the claim is one for infringement or the like (Section 2A–211) or else be barred from any remedy over. If the demand states that the lessor or the supplier agrees to bear all expense and to satisfy any adverse judgment, then unless the lessee after seasonable receipt of the demand does turn over control the lessee is so barred.

(5) Subsections (3) and (4) apply to any obligation of a lessee to hold the lessor or the supplier harmless against infringement or the like (Section 2A–211).

As amended in 1990.

§ 2A–517. Revocation of Acceptance of Goods.

(1) A lessee may revoke acceptance of a lot or commercial unit whose nonconformity substantially impairs its value to the lessee if the lessee has accepted it:

(a) except in the case of a finance lease, on the reasonable assumption that its nonconformity would be cured and it has not been seasonably cured; or

(b) without discovery of the nonconformity if the lessee's acceptance was reasonably induced either by the lessor's assurances or, except in the case of a finance lease, by the difficulty of discovery before acceptance.

(2) Except in the case of a finance lease that is not a consumer lease, a lessee may revoke acceptance of a lot or commercial unit

if the lessor defaults under the lease contract and the default substantially impairs the value of that lot or commercial unit to the lessee.

(3) If the lease agreement so provides, the lessee may revoke acceptance of a lot or commercial unit because of other defaults by the lessor.

(4) Revocation of acceptance must occur within a reasonable time after the lessee discovers or should have discovered the ground for it and before any substantial change in condition of the goods which is not caused by the nonconformity. Revocation is not effective until the lessee notifies the lessor.

(5) A lessee who so revokes has the same rights and duties with regard to the goods involved as if the lessee had rejected them.

As amended in 1990.

§ 2A–518. Cover; Substitute Goods.

(1) After a default by a lessor under the lease contract of the type described in Section 2A–508(1), or, if agreed, after other default by the lessor, the lessee may cover by making any purchase or lease of or contract to purchase or lease goods in substitution for those due from the lessor.

(2) Except as otherwise provided with respect to damages liquidated in the lease agreement (Section 2A–504) or otherwise determined pursuant to agreement of the parties (Sections 1–102(3) and 2A–503), if a lessee's cover is by lease agreement substantially similar to the original lease agreement and the new lease agreement is made in good faith and in a commercially reasonable manner, the lessee may recover from the lessor as damages (i) the present value, as of the date of the commencement of the term of the new lease agreement, of the rent under the new lease agreement applicable to that period of the new lease term which is comparable to the then remaining term of the original lease agreement minus the present value as of the same date of the total rent for the then remaining lease term of the original lease agreement, and (ii) any incidental or consequential damages, less expenses saved in consequence of the lessor's default.

(3) If a lessee's cover is by lease agreement that for any reason does not qualify for treatment under subsection (2), or is by purchase or otherwise, the lessee may recover from the lessor as if the lessee had elected not to cover and Section 2A–519 governs.

As amended in 1990.

§ 2A–519. Lessee's Damages for Non-Delivery, Repudiation, Default, and Breach of Warranty in Regard to Accepted Goods.

(1) Except as otherwise provided with respect to damages liquidated in the lease agreement (Section 2A–504) or otherwise determined pursuant to agreement of the parties (Sections 1–102(3) and 2A–503), if a lessee elects not to cover or a lessee elects to cover and the cover is by lease agreement that for any reason does not qualify for treatment under Section 2A–518(2), or is by purchase or otherwise, the measure of damages for non-delivery or repudiation by the lessor or for rejection or revocation of acceptance by the lessee is the present value, as of the date of the default, of the then market rent minus the present value as of the same date of the original rent, computed for the remaining lease term of the original lease agreement, together with incidental and consequential damages, less expenses saved in consequence of the lessor's default.

(2) Market rent is to be determined as of the place for tender or, in cases of rejection after arrival or revocation of acceptance, as of the place of arrival.

(3) Except as otherwise agreed, if the lessee has accepted goods and given notification (Section 2A–516(3)), the measure of damages for non-conforming tender or delivery or other default by a lessor is the loss resulting in the ordinary course of events from the lessor's default as determined in any manner that is reasonable together with incidental and consequential damages, less expenses saved in consequence of the lessor's default.

(4) Except as otherwise agreed, the measure of damages for breach of warranty is the present value at the time and place of acceptance of the difference between the value of the use of the goods accepted and the value if they had been as warranted for the lease term, unless special circumstances show proximate damages of a different amount, together with incidental and consequential damages, less expenses saved in consequence of the lessor's default or breach of warranty.

As amended in 1990.

§ 2A–520. Lessee's Incidental and Consequential Damages.

(1) Incidental damages resulting from a lessor's default include expenses reasonably incurred in inspection, receipt, transportation, and care and custody of goods rightfully rejected or goods the acceptance of which is justifiably revoked, any commercially reasonable charges, expenses or commissions in connection with effecting cover, and any other reasonable expense incident to the default.

(2) Consequential damages resulting from a lessor's default include:

(a) any loss resulting from general or particular requirements and needs of which the lessor at the time of contracting had reason to know and which could not reasonably be prevented by cover or otherwise; and

(b) injury to person or property proximately resulting from any breach of warranty.

§ 2A–521. Lessee's Right to Specific Performance or Replevin.

(1) Specific performance may be decreed if the goods are unique or in other proper circumstances.

(2) A decree for specific performance may include any terms and conditions as to payment of the rent, damages, or other relief that the court deems just.

(3) A lessee has a right of replevin, detinue, sequestration, claim and delivery, or the like for goods identified to the lease contract if after reasonable effort the lessee is unable to effect cover for those goods or the circumstances reasonably indicate that the effort will be unavailing.

§ 2A–522. Lessee's Right to Goods on Lessor's Insolvency.

(1) Subject to subsection (2) and even though the goods have not been shipped, a lessee who has paid a part or all of the rent and

security for goods identified to a lease contract (Section 2A–217) on making and keeping good a tender of any unpaid portion of the rent and security due under the lease contract may recover the goods identified from the lessor if the lessor becomes insolvent within 10 days after receipt of the first installment of rent and security.

(2) A lessee acquires the right to recover goods identified to a lease contract only if they conform to the lease contract.

C. Default by Lessee

§ 2A–523. Lessor's Remedies.

(1) If a lessee wrongfully rejects or revokes acceptance of goods or fails to make a payment when due or repudiates with respect to a part or the whole, then, with respect to any goods involved, and with respect to all of the goods if under an installment lease contract the value of the whole lease contract is substantially impaired (Section 2A–510), the lessee is in default under the lease contract and the lessor may:

(a) cancel the lease contract (Section 2A–505(1));

(b) proceed respecting goods not identified to the lease contract (Section 2A–524);

(c) withhold delivery of the goods and take possession of goods previously delivered (Section 2A–525);

(d) stop delivery of the goods by any bailee (Section 2A–526);

(e) dispose of the goods and recover damages (Section 2A–527), or retain the goods and recover damages (Section 2A–528), or in a proper case recover rent (Section 2A–529)

(f) exercise any other rights or pursue any other remedies provided in the lease contract.

(2) If a lessor does not fully exercise a right or obtain a remedy to which the lessor is entitled under subsection (1), the lessor may recover the loss resulting in the ordinary course of events from the lessee's default as determined in any reasonable manner, together with incidental damages, less expenses saved in consequence of the lessee's default.

(3) If a lessee is otherwise in default under a lease contract, the lessor may exercise the rights and pursue the remedies provided in the lease contract, which may include a right to cancel the lease. In addition, unless otherwise provided in the lease contract:

(a) if the default substantially impairs the value of the lease contract to the lessor, the lessor may exercise the rights and pursue the remedies provided in subsections (1) or (2); or

(b) if the default does not substantially impair the value of the lease contract to the lessor, the lessor may recover as provided in subsection (2).

As amended in 1990.

§ 2A–524. Lessor's Right to Identify Goods to Lease Contract.

(1) After default by the lessee under the lease contract of the type described in Section 2A–523(1) or 2A–523(3)(a) or, if agreed, after other default by the lessee, the lessor may:

(a) identify to the lease contract conforming goods not already identified if at the time the lessor learned of the default they were in the lessor's or the supplier's possession or control; and

(b) dispose of goods (Section 2A–527(1)) that demonstrably have been intended for the particular lease contract even though those goods are unfinished.

(2) If the goods are unfinished, in the exercise of reasonable commercial judgment for the purposes of avoiding loss and of effective realization, an aggrieved lessor or the supplier may either complete manufacture and wholly identify the goods to the lease contract or cease manufacture and lease, sell, or otherwise dispose of the goods for scrap or salvage value or proceed in any other reasonable manner.

As amended in 1990.

§ 2A–525. Lessor's Right to Possession of Goods.

(1) If a lessor discovers the lessee to be insolvent, the lessor may refuse to deliver the goods.

(2) After a default by the lessee under the lease contract of the type described in Section 2A–523(1) or 2A–523(3)(a) or, if agreed, after other default by the lessee, the lessor has the right to take possession of the goods. If the lease contract so provides, the lessor may require the lessee to assemble the goods and make them available to the lessor at a place to be designated by the lessor which is reasonably convenient to both parties. Without removal, the lessor may render unusable any goods employed in trade or business, and may dispose of goods on the lessee's premises (Section 2A–527).

(3) The lessor may proceed under subsection (2) without judicial process if that can be done without breach of the peace or the lessor may proceed by action.

As amended in 1990.

§ 2A–526. Lessor's Stoppage of Delivery in Transit or Otherwise.

(1) A lessor may stop delivery of goods in the possession of a carrier or other bailee if the lessor discovers the lessee to be insolvent and may stop delivery of carload, truckload, planeload, or larger shipments of express or freight if the lessee repudiates or fails to make a payment due before delivery, whether for rent, security or otherwise under the lease contract, or for any other reason the lessor has a right to withhold or take possession of the goods.

(2) In pursuing its remedies under subsection (1), the lessor may stop delivery until

(a) receipt of the goods by the lessee;

(b) acknowledgment to the lessee by any bailee of the goods, except a carrier, that the bailee holds the goods for the lessee; or

(c) such an acknowledgment to the lessee by a carrier via reshipment or as warehouseman.

(3) (a) To stop delivery, a lessor shall so notify as to enable the bailee by reasonable diligence to prevent delivery of the goods.

(b) After notification, the bailee shall hold and deliver the goods according to the directions of the lessor, but the lessor is liable to the bailee for any ensuing charges or damages.

(c) A carrier who has issued a nonnegotiable bill of lading is not obliged to obey a notification to stop received from a person other than the consignor.

§ 2A–527. Lessor's Rights to Dispose of Goods.

(1) After a default by a lessee under the lease contract of the type described in Section 2A–523(1) or 2A–523(3)(a) or after the lessor refuses to deliver or takes possession of goods (Section 2A–525 or 2A–526), or, if agreed, after other default by a lessee, the lessor may dispose of the goods concerned or the undelivered balance thereof by lease, sale, or otherwise.

(2) Except as otherwise provided with respect to damages liquidated in the lease agreement (Section 2A–504) or otherwise determined pursuant to agreement of the parties (Sections 1–102(3) and 2A–503), if the disposition is by lease agreement substantially similar to the original lease agreement and the new lease agreement is made in good faith and in a commercially reasonable manner, the lessor may recover from the lessee as damages (i) accrued and unpaid rent as of the date of the commencement of the term of the new lease agreement, (ii) the present value, as of the same date, of the total rent for the then remaining lease term of the original lease agreement minus the present value, as of the same date, of the rent under the new lease agreement applicable to that period of the new lease term which is comparable to the then remaining term of the original lease agreement, and (iii) any incidental damages allowed under Section 2A–530, less expenses saved in consequence of the lessee's default.

(3) If the lessor's disposition is by lease agreement that for any reason does not qualify for treatment under subsection (2), or is by sale or otherwise, the lessor may recover from the lessee as if the lessor had elected not to dispose of the goods and Section 2A–528 governs.

(4) A subsequent buyer or lessee who buys or leases from the lessor in good faith for value as a result of a disposition under this section takes the goods free of the original lease contract and any rights of the original lessee even though the lessor fails to comply with one or more of the requirements of this Article.

(5) The lessor is not accountable to the lessee for any profit made on any disposition. A lessee who has rightfully rejected or justifiably revoked acceptance shall account to the lessor for any excess over the amount of the lessee's security interest (Section 2A–508(5)).

As amended in 1990.

§ 2A–528. Lessor's Damages for Non-acceptance, Failure to Pay, Repudiation, or Other Default.

(1) Except as otherwise provided with respect to damages liquidated in the lease agreement (Section 2A–504) or otherwise determined pursuant to agreement of the parties (Section 1–102(3) and 2A–503), if a lessor elects to retain the goods or a lessor elects to dispose of the goods and the disposition is by lease agreement that for any reason does not qualify for treatment under Section 2A–527(2), or is by sale or otherwise, the lessor may recover from the lessee as damages for a default of the type described in Section 2A–523(1) or 2A–523(3)(a), or if agreed, for other default of the lessee, (i) accrued and unpaid rent as of the date of the default if the lessee has never taken possession of the goods, or, if the lessee has taken possession of the goods, as of the date the lessor repossesses the goods or an earlier date on which the lessee makes a tender of the goods to the lessor, (ii) the present value as of the date determined under clause (i) of the total rent for the then remaining lease term of the original lease agreement minus the present value as of the same date of the market rent as the place where the goods are located computed for the same lease term, and (iii) any incidental damages allowed under Section 2A–530, less expenses saved in consequence of the lessee's default.

(2) If the measure of damages provided in subsection (1) is inadequate to put a lessor in as good a position as performance would have, the measure of damages is the present value of the profit, including reasonable overhead, the lessor would have made from full performance by the lessee, together with any incidental damages allowed under Section 2A–530, due allowance for costs reasonably incurred and due credit for payments or proceeds of disposition.

As amended in 1990.

§ 2A–529. Lessor's Action for the Rent.

(1) After default by the lessee under the lease contract of the type described in Section 2A–523(1) or 2A–523(3)(a) or, if agreed, after other default by the lessee, if the lessor complies with subsection (2), the lessor may recover from the lessee as damages:

(a) for goods accepted by the lessee and not repossessed by or tendered to the lessor, and for conforming goods lost or damaged within a commercially reasonable time after risk of loss passes to the lessee (Section 2A–219), (i) accrued and unpaid rent as of the date of entry of judgment in favor of the lessor (ii) the present value as of the same date of the rent for the then remaining lease term of the lease agreement, and (iii) any incidental damages allowed under Section 2A–530, less expenses saved in consequence of the lessee's default; and

(b) for goods identified to the lease contract if the lessor is unable after reasonable effort to dispose of them at a reasonable price or the circumstances reasonably indicate that effort will be unavailing, (i) accrued and unpaid rent as of the date of entry of judgment in favor of the lessor, (ii) the present value as of the same date of the rent for the then remaining lease term of the lease agreement, and (iii) any incidental damages allowed under Section 2A–530, less expenses saved in consequence of the lessee's default.

(2) Except as provided in subsection (3), the lessor shall hold for the lessee for the remaining lease term of the lease agreement any goods that have been identified to the lease contract and are in the lessor's control.

(3) The lessor may dispose of the goods at any time before collection of the judgment for damages obtained pursuant to subsection (1). If the disposition is before the end of the remaining lease term of the lease agreement, the lessor's recovery against the lessee for damages is governed by Section 2A–527 or Section 2A–528, and the lessor will cause an appropriate credit to be provided against a judgment for damages to the extent that the amount of the judgment exceeds the recovery available pursuant to Section 2A–527 or 2A–528.

(4) Payment of the judgment for damages obtained pursuant to subsection (1) entitles the lessee to the use and possession of the

goods not then disposed of for the remaining lease term of and in accordance with the lease agreement.

(5) After default by the lessee under the lease contract of the type described in Section 2A–523(1) or Section 2A–523(3)(a) or, if agreed, after other default by the lessee, a lessor who is held not entitled to rent under this section must nevertheless be awarded damages for non-acceptance under Sections 2A–527 and 2A–528.

As amended in 1990.

§ 2A–530. Lessor's Incidental Damages.

Incidental damages to an aggrieved lessor include any commercially reasonable charges, expenses, or commissions incurred in stopping delivery, in the transportation, care and custody of goods after the lessee's default, in connection with return or disposition of the goods, or otherwise resulting from the default.

§ 2A–531. Standing to Sue Third Parties for Injury to Goods.

(1) If a third party so deals with goods that have been identified to a lease contract as to cause actionable injury to a party to the lease contract (a) the lessor has a right of action against the third party, and (b) the lessee also has a right of action against the third party if the lessee:

(i) has a security interest in the goods;

(ii) has an insurable interest in the goods; or

(iii) bears the risk of loss under the lease contract or has since the injury assumed that risk as against the lessor and the goods have been converted or destroyed.

(2) If at the time of the injury the party plaintiff did not bear the risk of loss as against the other party to the lease contract and there is no arrangement between them for disposition of the recovery, his [or her] suit or settlement, subject to his [or her] own interest, is as a fiduciary for the other party to the lease contract.

(3) Either party with the consent of the other may sue for the benefit of whom it may concern.

§ 2A–532. Lessor's Rights to Residual Interest.

In addition to any other recovery permitted by this Article or other law, the lessor may recover from the lessee an amount that will fully compensate the lessor for any loss of or damage to the lessor's residual interest in the goods caused by the default of the lessee.

As added in 1990.

Revised Article 3 NEGOTIABLE INSTRUMENTS

Part 1 General Provisions and Definitions

§ 3–101. Short Title.

This Article may be cited as Uniform Commercial Code–Negotiable Instruments.

§ 3–102. Subject Matter.

(a) This Article applies to negotiable instruments. It does not apply to money, to payment orders governed by Article 4A, or to securities governed by Article 8.

(b) If there is conflict between this Article and Article 4 or 9, Articles 4 and 9 govern.

(c) Regulations of the Board of Governors of the Federal Reserve System and operating circulars of the Federal Reserve Banks supersede any inconsistent provision of this Article to the extent of the inconsistency.

§ 3–103. Definitions.

(a) In this Article:

(1) "Acceptor" means a drawee who has accepted a draft.

(2) "Drawee" means a person ordered in a draft to make payment.

(3) "Drawer" means a person who signs or is identified in a draft as a person ordering payment.

(4) "Good faith" means honesty in fact and the observance of reasonable commercial standards of fair dealing.

(5) "Maker" means a person who signs or is identified in a note as a person undertaking to pay.

(6) "Order" means a written instruction to pay money signed by the person giving the instruction. The instruction may be addressed to any person, including the person giving the instruction, or to one or more persons jointly or in the alternative but not in succession. An authorization to pay is not an order unless the person authorized to pay is also instructed to pay.

(7) "Ordinary care" in the case of a person engaged in business means observance of reasonable commercial standards, prevailing in the area in which the person is located, with respect to the business in which the person is engaged. In the case of a bank that takes an instrument for processing for collection or payment by automated means, reasonable commercial standards do not require the bank to examine the instrument if the failure to examine does not violate the bank's prescribed procedures and the bank's procedures do not vary unreasonably from general banking usage not disapproved by this Article or Article 4.

(8) "Party" means a party to an instrument.

(9) "Promise" means a written undertaking to pay money signed by the person undertaking to pay. An acknowledgment of an obligation by the obligor is not a promise unless the obligor also undertakes to pay the obligation.

(10) "Prove" with respect to a fact means to meet the burden of establishing the fact (Section 1–201(8)).

(11) "Remitter" means a person who purchases an instrument from its issuer if the instrument is payable to an identified person other than the purchaser.

(b) [Other definitions' section references deleted.]

(c) [Other definitions' section references deleted.]

(d) In addition, Article 1 contains general definitions and principles of construction and interpretation applicable throughout this Article.

§ 3–104. Negotiable Instrument.

(a) Except as provided in subsections (c) and (d), "negotiable instrument" means an unconditional promise or order to pay a fixed amount of money, with or without interest or other charges described in the promise or order, if it:

(1) is payable to bearer or to order at the time it is issued or first comes into possession of a holder;

(2) is payable on demand or at a definite time; and

(3) does not state any other undertaking or instruction by the person promising or ordering payment to do any act in addition to the payment of money, but the promise or order may contain (i) an undertaking or power to give, maintain, or protect collateral to secure payment, (ii) an authorization or power to the holder to confess judgment or realize on or dispose of collateral, or (iii) a waiver of the benefit of any law intended for the advantage or protection of an obligor.

(b) "Instrument" means a negotiable instrument.

(c) An order that meets all of the requirements of subsection (a), except paragraph (1), and otherwise falls within the definition of "check" in subsection (f) is a negotiable instrument and a check.

(d) A promise or order other than a check is not an instrument if, at the time it is issued or first comes into possession of a holder, it contains a conspicuous statement, however expressed, to the effect that the promise or order is not negotiable or is not an instrument governed by this Article.

(e) An instrument is a "note" if it is a promise and is a "draft" if it is an order. If an instrument falls within the definition of both "note" and "draft," a person entitled to enforce the instrument may treat it as either.

(f) "Check" means (i) a draft, other than a documentary draft, payable on demand and drawn on a bank or (ii) a cashier's check or teller's check. An instrument may be a check even though it is described on its face by another term, such as "money order."

(g) "Cashier's check" means a draft with respect to which the drawer and drawee are the same bank or branches of the same bank.

(h) "Teller's check" means a draft drawn by a bank (i) on another bank, or (ii) payable at or through a bank.

(i) "Traveler's check" means an instrument that (i) is payable on demand, (ii) is drawn on or payable at or through a bank, (iii) is designated by the term "traveler's check" or by a substantially similar term, and (iv) requires, as a condition to payment, a countersignature by a person whose specimen signature appears on the instrument.

(j) "Certificate of deposit" means an instrument containing an acknowledgment by a bank that a sum of money has been received by the bank and a promise by the bank to repay the sum of money. A certificate of deposit is a note of the bank.

§ 3–105. Issue of Instrument.

(a) "Issue" means the first delivery of an instrument by the maker or drawer, whether to a holder or nonholder, for the purpose of giving rights on the instrument to any person.

(b) An unissued instrument, or an unissued incomplete instrument that is completed, is binding on the maker or drawer, but nonissuance is a defense. An instrument that is conditionally issued or is issued for a special purpose is binding on the maker or drawer, but failure of the condition or special purpose to be fulfilled is a defense.

(c) "Issuer" applies to issued and unissued instruments and means a maker or drawer of an instrument.

§ 3–106. Unconditional Promise or Order.

(a) Except as provided in this section, for the purposes of Section 3–104(a), a promise or order is unconditional unless it states (i) an express condition to payment, (ii) that the promise or order is subject to or governed by another writing, or (iii) that rights or obligations with respect to the promise or order are stated in another writing. A reference to another writing does not of itself make the promise or order conditional.

(b) A promise or order is not made conditional (i) by a reference to another writing for a statement of rights with respect to collateral, prepayment, or acceleration, or (ii) because payment is limited to resort to a particular fund or source.

(c) If a promise or order requires, as a condition to payment, a countersignature by a person whose specimen signature appears on the promise or order, the condition does not make the promise or order conditional for the purposes of Section 3–104(a). If the person whose specimen signature appears on an instrument fails to countersign the instrument, the failure to countersign is a defense to the obligation of the issuer, but the failure does not prevent a transferee of the instrument from becoming a holder of the instrument.

(d) If a promise or order at the time it is issued or first comes into possession of a holder contains a statement, required by applicable statutory or administrative law, to the effect that the rights of a holder or transferee are subject to claims or defenses that the issuer could assert against the original payee, the promise or order is not thereby made conditional for the purposes of Section 3–104(a); but if the promise or order is an instrument, there cannot be a holder in due course of the instrument.

§ 3–107. Instrument Payable in Foreign Money.

Unless the instrument otherwise provides, an instrument that states the amount payable in foreign money may be paid in the foreign money or in an equivalent amount in dollars calculated by using the current bank-offered spot rate at the place of payment for the purchase of dollars on the day on which the instrument is paid.

§ 3–108. Payable on Demand or at Definite Time.

(a) A promise or order is "payable on demand" if it (i) states that it is payable on demand or at sight, or otherwise indicates that it is payable at the will of the holder, or (ii) does not state any time of payment.

(b) A promise or order is "payable at a definite time" if it is payable on elapse of a definite period of time after sight or acceptance or at a fixed date or dates or at a time or times readily ascertainable at the time the promise or order is issued, subject to rights of (i) prepayment, (ii) acceleration, (iii) extension at the option of the holder, or (iv) extension to a further definite time at the option of the maker or acceptor or automatically upon or after a specified act or event.

(c) If an instrument, payable at a fixed date, is also payable upon demand made before the fixed date, the instrument is payable on demand until the fixed date and, if demand for payment is not made before that date, becomes payable at a definite time on the fixed date.

§ 3–109. Payable to Bearer or to Order.

(a) A promise or order is payable to bearer if it:

(1) states that it is payable to bearer or to the order of bearer or otherwise indicates that the person in possession of the promise or order is entitled to payment;

(2) does not state a payee; or

(3) states that it is payable to or to the order of cash or otherwise indicates that it is not payable to an identified person.

(b) A promise or order that is not payable to bearer is payable to order if it is payable (i) to the order of an identified person or (ii) to an identified person or order. A promise or order that is payable to order is payable to the identified person.

(c) An instrument payable to bearer may become payable to an identified person if it is specially indorsed pursuant to Section 3–205(a). An instrument payable to an identified person may become payable to bearer if it is indorsed in blank pursuant to Section 3–205(b).

§ 3–110. Identification of Person to Whom Instrument Is Payable.

(a) The person to whom an instrument is initially payable is determined by the intent of the person, whether or not authorized, signing as, or in the name or behalf of, the issuer of the instrument. The instrument is payable to the person intended by the signer even if that person is identified in the instrument by a name or other identification that is not that of the intended person. If more than one person signs in the name or behalf of the issuer of an instrument and all the signers do not intend the same person as payee, the instrument is payable to any person intended by one or more of the signers.

(b) If the signature of the issuer of an instrument is made by automated means, such as a check-writing machine, the payee of the instrument is determined by the intent of the person who supplied the name or identification of the payee, whether or not authorized to do so.

(c) A person to whom an instrument is payable may be identified in any way, including by name, identifying number, office, or account number. For the purpose of determining the holder of an instrument, the following rules apply:

(1) If an instrument is payable to an account and the account is identified only by number, the instrument is payable to the person to whom the account is payable. If an instrument is payable to an account identified by number and by the name of a person, the instrument is payable to the named person, whether or not that person is the owner of the account identified by number.

(2) If an instrument is payable to:

(i) a trust, an estate, or a person described as trustee or representative of a trust or estate, the instrument is payable to the trustee, the representative, or a successor of either, whether or not the beneficiary or estate is also named;

(ii) a person described as agent or similar representative of a named or identified person, the instrument is payable to the represented person, the representative, or a successor of the representative;

(iii) a fund or organization that is not a legal entity, the instrument is payable to a representative of the members of the fund or organization; or

(iv) an office or to a person described as holding an office, the instrument is payable to the named person, the incumbent of the office, or a successor to the incumbent.

(d) If an instrument is payable to two or more persons alternatively, it is payable to any of them and may be negotiated, discharged, or enforced by any or all of them in possession of the instrument. If an instrument is payable to two or more persons not alternatively, it is payable to all of them and may be negotiated, discharged, or enforced only by all of them. If an instrument payable to two or more persons is ambiguous as to whether it is payable to the persons alternatively, the instrument is payable to the persons alternatively.

§ 3–111. Place of Payment.

Except as otherwise provided for items in Article 4, an instrument is payable at the place of payment stated in the instrument. If no place of payment is stated, an instrument is payable at the address of the drawee or maker stated in the instrument. If no address is stated, the place of payment is the place of business of the drawee or maker. If a drawee or maker has more than one place of business, the place of payment is any place of business of the drawee or maker chosen by the person entitled to enforce the instrument. If the drawee or maker has no place of business, the place of payment is the residence of the drawee or maker.

§ 3–112. Interest.

(a) Unless otherwise provided in the instrument, (i) an instrument is not payable with interest, and (ii) interest on an interest-bearing instrument is payable from the date of the instrument.

(b) Interest may be stated in an instrument as a fixed or variable amount of money or it may be expressed as a fixed or variable rate or rates. The amount or rate of interest may be stated or described in the instrument in any manner and may require reference to information not contained in the instrument. If an instrument provides for interest, but the amount of interest payable cannot be ascertained from the description, interest is payable at the judgment rate in effect at the place of payment of the instrument and at the time interest first accrues.

§ 3–113. Date of Instrument.

(a) An instrument may be antedated or postdated. The date stated determines the time of payment if the instrument is payable at a fixed period after date. Except as provided in Section 4–401(c), an instrument payable on demand is not payable before the date of the instrument.

(b) If an instrument is undated, its date is the date of its issue or, in the case of an unissued instrument, the date it first comes into possession of a holder.

§ 3–114. Contradictory Terms of Instrument.

If an instrument contains contradictory terms, typewritten terms prevail over printed terms, handwritten terms prevail over both, and words prevail over numbers.

§ 3–115. Incomplete Instrument.

(a) "Incomplete instrument" means a signed writing, whether or not issued by the signer, the contents of which show at the time of signing that it is incomplete but that the signer intended it to be completed by the addition of words or numbers.

(b) Subject to subsection (c), if an incomplete instrument is an instrument under Section 3–104, it may be enforced according to its terms if it is not completed, or according to its terms as augmented by completion. If an incomplete instrument is not an instrument under Section 3–104, but, after completion, the requirements of Section 3–104 are met, the instrument may be enforced according to its terms as augmented by completion.

(c) If words or numbers are added to an incomplete instrument without authority of the signer, there is an alteration of the incomplete instrument under Section 3–407.

(d) The burden of establishing that words or numbers were added to an incomplete instrument without authority of the signer is on the person asserting the lack of authority.

§ 3–116. Joint and Several Liability; Contribution.

(a) Except as otherwise provided in the instrument, two or more persons who have the same liability on an instrument as makers, drawers, acceptors, indorsers who indorse as joint payees, or anomalous indorsers are jointly and severally liable in the capacity in which they sign.

(b) Except as provided in Section 3–419(e) or by agreement of the affected parties, a party having joint and several liability who pays the instrument is entitled to receive from any party having the same joint and several liability contribution in accordance with applicable law.

(c) Discharge of one party having joint and several liability by a person entitled to enforce the instrument does not affect the right under subsection (b) of a party having the same joint and several liability to receive contribution from the party discharged.

§ 3–117. Other Agreements Affecting Instrument.

Subject to applicable law regarding exclusion of proof of contemporaneous or previous agreements, the obligation of a party to an instrument to pay the instrument may be modified, supplemented, or nullified by a separate agreement of the obligor and a person entitled to enforce the instrument, if the instrument is issued or the obligation is incurred in reliance on the agreement or as part of the same transaction giving rise to the agreement. To the extent an obligation is modified, supplemented, or nullified by an agreement under this section, the agreement is a defense to the obligation.

§ 3–118. Statute of Limitations.

(a) Except as provided in subsection (e), an action to enforce the obligation of a party to pay a note payable at a definite time must be commenced within six years after the due date or dates stated in the note or, if a due date is accelerated, within six years after the accelerated due date.

(b) Except as provided in subsection (d) or (e), if demand for payment is made to the maker of a note payable on demand, an action to enforce the obligation of a party to pay the note must be commenced within six years after the demand. If no demand for payment is made to the maker, an action to enforce the note is barred if neither principal nor interest on the note has been paid for a continuous period of 10 years.

(c) Except as provided in subsection (d), an action to enforce the obligation of a party to an unaccepted draft to pay the draft must be commenced within three years after dishonor of the draft or 10 years after the date of the draft, whichever period expires first.

(d) An action to enforce the obligation of the acceptor of a certified check or the issuer of a teller's check, cashier's check, or traveler's check must be commenced within three years after demand for payment is made to the acceptor or issuer, as the case may be.

(e) An action to enforce the obligation of a party to a certificate of deposit to pay the instrument must be commenced within six years after demand for payment is made to the maker, but if the instrument states a due date and the maker is not required to pay before that date, the six-year period begins when a demand for payment is in effect and the due date has passed.

(f) An action to enforce the obligation of a party to pay an accepted draft, other than a certified check, must be commenced (i) within six years after the due date or dates stated in the draft or acceptance if the obligation of the acceptor is payable at a definite time, or (ii) within six years after the date of the acceptance if the obligation of the acceptor is payable on demand.

(g) Unless governed by other law regarding claims for indemnity or contribution, an action (i) for conversion of an instrument, for money had and received, or like action based on conversion, (ii) for breach of warranty, or (iii) to enforce an obligation, duty, or right arising under this Article and not governed by this section must be commenced within three years after the [cause of action] accrues.

§ 3–119. Notice of Right to Defend Action.

In an action for breach of an obligation for which a third person is answerable over pursuant to this Article or Article 4, the defendant may give the third person written notice of the litigation, and the person notified may then give similar notice to any other person who is answerable over. If the notice states (i) that the person notified may come in and defend and (ii) that failure to do so will bind the person notified in an action later brought by the person giving the notice as to any determination of fact common to the two litigations, the person notified is so bound unless after seasonable receipt of the notice the person notified does come in and defend.

Part 2 Negotiation, Transfer, and Indorsement

§ 3–201. Negotiation.

(a) "Negotiation" means a transfer of possession, whether voluntary or involuntary, of an instrument by a person other than the issuer to a person who thereby becomes its holder.

(b) Except for negotiation by a remitter, if an instrument is payable to an identified person, negotiation requires transfer of possession of the instrument and its indorsement by the holder. If an instrument is payable to bearer, it may be negotiated by transfer of possession alone.

§ 3–202. Negotiation Subject to Rescission.

(a) Negotiation is effective even if obtained (i) from an infant, a corporation exceeding its powers, or a person without capacity, (ii) by fraud, duress, or mistake, or (iii) in breach of duty or as part of an illegal transaction.

(b) To the extent permitted by other law, negotiation may be rescinded or may be subject to other remedies, but those remedies may not be asserted against a subsequent holder in due course or a person paying the instrument in good faith and without knowledge of facts that are a basis for rescission or other remedy.

§ 3–203. Transfer of Instrument; Rights Acquired by Transfer.

(a) An instrument is transferred when it is delivered by a person other than its issuer for the purpose of giving to the person receiving delivery the right to enforce the instrument.

(b) Transfer of an instrument, whether or not the transfer is a negotiation, vests in the transferee any right of the transferor to enforce the instrument, including any right as a holder in due course, but the transferee cannot acquire rights of a holder in due course by a transfer, directly or indirectly, from a holder in due course if the transferee engaged in fraud or illegality affecting the instrument.

(c) Unless otherwise agreed, if an instrument is transferred for value and the transferee does not become a holder because of lack of indorsement by the transferor, the transferee has a specifically enforceable right to the unqualified indorsement of the transferor, but negotiation of the instrument does not occur until the indorsement is made.

(d) If a transferor purports to transfer less than the entire instrument, negotiation of the instrument does not occur. The transferee obtains no rights under this Article and has only the rights of a partial assignee.

§ 3–204. Indorsement.

(a) "Indorsement" means a signature, other than that of a signer as maker, drawer, or acceptor, that alone or accompanied by other words is made on an instrument for the purpose of (i) negotiating the instrument, (ii) restricting payment of the instrument, or (iii) incurring indorser's liability on the instrument, but regardless of the intent of the signer, a signature and its accompanying words is an indorsement unless the accompanying words, terms of the instrument, place of the signature, or other circumstances unambiguously indicate that the signature was made for a purpose other than indorsement. For the purpose of determining whether a signature is made on an instrument, a paper affixed to the instrument is a part of the instrument.

(b) "Indorser" means a person who makes an indorsement.

(c) For the purpose of determining whether the transferee of an instrument is a holder, an indorsement that transfers a security interest in the instrument is effective as an unqualified indorsement of the instrument.

(d) If an instrument is payable to a holder under a name that is not the name of the holder, indorsement may be made by the holder in the name stated in the instrument or in the holder's name or both, but signature in both names may be required by a person paying or taking the instrument for value or collection.

§ 3–205. Special Indorsement; Blank Indorsement; Anomalous Indorsement.

(a) If an indorsement is made by the holder of an instrument, whether payable to an identified person or payable to bearer, and the indorsement identifies a person to whom it makes the instrument payable, it is a "special indorsement." When specially indorsed, an instrument becomes payable to the identified person and may be negotiated only by the indorsement of that person. The principles stated in Section 3–110 apply to special indorsements.

(b) If an indorsement is made by the holder of an instrument and it is not a special indorsement, it is a "blank indorsement." When indorsed in blank, an instrument becomes payable to bearer and may be negotiated by transfer of possession alone until specially indorsed.

(c) The holder may convert a blank indorsement that consists only of a signature into a special indorsement by writing, above the signature of the indorser, words identifying the person to whom the instrument is made payable.

(d) "Anomalous indorsement" means an indorsement made by a person who is not the holder of the instrument. An anomalous indorsement does not affect the manner in which the instrument may be negotiated.

§ 3–206. Restrictive Indorsement.

(a) An indorsement limiting payment to a particular person or otherwise prohibiting further transfer or negotiation of the instrument is not effective to prevent further transfer or negotiation of the instrument.

(b) An indorsement stating a condition to the right of the indorsee to receive payment does not affect the right of the indorsee to enforce the instrument. A person paying the instrument or taking it for value or collection may disregard the condition, and the rights and liabilities of that person are not affected by whether the condition has been fulfilled.

(c) If an instrument bears an indorsement (i) described in Section 4–201(b), or (ii) in blank or to a particular bank using the words "for deposit," "for collection," or other words indicating a purpose of having the instrument collected by a bank for the indorser or for a particular account, the following rules apply:

(1) A person, other than a bank, who purchases the instrument when so indorsed converts the instrument unless the amount paid for the instrument is received by the indorser or applied consistently with the indorsement.

(2) A depositary bank that purchases the instrument or takes it for collection when so indorsed converts the instrument unless the amount paid by the bank with respect to the instrument is received by the indorser or applied consistently with the indorsement.

(3) A payor bank that is also the depositary bank or that takes the instrument for immediate payment over the counter from a person other than a collecting bank converts the instrument unless the proceeds of the instrument are received by the indorser or applied consistently with the indorsement.

(4) Except as otherwise provided in paragraph (3), a payor bank or intermediary bank may disregard the indorsement and is not liable if the proceeds of the instrument are not received by the indorser or applied consistently with the indorsement.

(d) Except for an indorsement covered by subsection (c), if an instrument bears an indorsement using words to the effect that payment is to be made to the indorsee as agent, trustee, or other fiduciary for the benefit of the indorser or another person, the following rules apply:

(1) Unless there is notice of breach of fiduciary duty as provided in Section 3–307, a person who purchases the instrument from the indorsee or takes the instrument from the indorsee for collection or payment may pay the proceeds of payment or the value given for the instrument to the indorsee without regard to whether the indorsee violates a fiduciary duty to the indorser.

(2) A subsequent transferee of the instrument or person who pays the instrument is neither given notice nor otherwise affected by the restriction in the indorsement unless the transferee or payor knows that the fiduciary dealt with the instrument or its proceeds in breach of fiduciary duty.

(e) The presence on an instrument of an indorsement to which this section applies does not prevent a purchaser of the instrument from becoming a holder in due course of the instrument unless the purchaser is a converter under subsection (c) or has notice or knowledge of breach of fiduciary duty as stated in subsection (d).

(f) In an action to enforce the obligation of a party to pay the instrument, the obligor has a defense if payment would violate an indorsement to which this section applies and the payment is not permitted by this section.

§ 3–207. Reacquisition.

Reacquisition of an instrument occurs if it is transferred to a former holder, by negotiation or otherwise. A former holder who reacquires the instrument may cancel indorsements made after the reacquirer first became a holder of the instrument. If the cancellation causes the instrument to be payable to the reacquirer or to bearer, the reacquirer may negotiate the instrument. An indorser whose indorsement is canceled is discharged, and the discharge is effective against any subsequent holder.

Part 3 Enforcement of Instruments

§ 3–301. Person Entitled to Enforce Instrument.

"Person entitled to enforce" an instrument means (i) the holder of the instrument, (ii) a nonholder in possession of the instrument who has the rights of a holder, or (iii) a person not in possession of the instrument who is entitled to enforce the instrument pursuant to Section 3–309 or 3–418(d). A person may be a person entitled to enforce the instrument even though the person is not the owner of the instrument or is in wrongful possession of the instrument.

§ 3–302. Holder in Due Course.

(a) Subject to subsection (c) and Section 3–106(d), "holder in due course" means the holder of an instrument if:

(1) the instrument when issued or negotiated to the holder does not bear such apparent evidence of forgery or alteration or is not otherwise so irregular or incomplete as to call into question its authenticity; and

(2) the holder took the instrument (i) for value, (ii) in good faith, (iii) without notice that the instrument is overdue or has been dishonored or that there is an uncured default with respect to payment of another instrument issued as part of the same series, (iv) without notice that the instrument contains an unauthorized signature or has been altered, (v) without notice of any claim to the instrument described in Section 3–306, and (vi) without notice that any party has a defense or claim in recoupment described in Section 3–305(a).

(b) Notice of discharge of a party, other than discharge in an insolvency proceeding, is not notice of a defense under subsection (a), but discharge is effective against a person who became a holder in due course with notice of the discharge. Public filing or recording of a document does not of itself constitute notice of a defense, claim in recoupment, or claim to the instrument.

(c) Except to the extent a transferor or predecessor in interest has rights as a holder in due course, a person does not acquire rights of a holder in due course of an instrument taken (i) by legal process or by purchase in an execution, bankruptcy, or creditor's sale or similar proceeding, (ii) by purchase as part of a bulk transaction not in ordinary course of business of the transferor, or (iii) as the successor in interest to an estate or other organization.

(d) If, under Section 3–303(a)(1), the promise of performance that is the consideration for an instrument has been partially performed, the holder may assert rights as a holder in due course of the instrument only to the fraction of the amount payable under the instrument equal to the value of the partial performance divided by the value of the promised performance.

(e) If (i) the person entitled to enforce an instrument has only a security interest in the instrument and (ii) the person obliged to pay the instrument has a defense, claim in recoupment, or claim to the instrument that may be asserted against the person who granted the security interest, the person entitled to enforce the instrument may assert rights as a holder in due course only to an amount payable under the instrument which, at the time of enforcement of the instrument, does not exceed the amount of the unpaid obligation secured.

(f) To be effective, notice must be received at a time and in a manner that gives a reasonable opportunity to act on it.

(g) This section is subject to any law limiting status as a holder in due course in particular classes of transactions.

§ 3–303. Value and Consideration.

(a) An instrument is issued or transferred for value if:

(1) the instrument is issued or transferred for a promise of performance, to the extent the promise has been performed;

(2) the transferee acquires a security interest or other lien in the instrument other than a lien obtained by judicial proceeding;

(3) the instrument is issued or transferred as payment of, or as security for, an antecedent claim against any person, whether or not the claim is due;

(4) the instrument is issued or transferred in exchange for a negotiable instrument; or

(5) the instrument is issued or transferred in exchange for the incurring of an irrevocable obligation to a third party by the person taking the instrument.

(b) "Consideration" means any consideration sufficient to support a simple contract. The drawer or maker of an instrument has a defense if the instrument is issued without consideration. If an instrument is issued for a promise of performance, the issuer has a defense to the extent performance of the promise is due and the promise has not been performed. If an instrument is issued for value as stated in subsection (a), the instrument is also issued for consideration.

§ 3–304. Overdue Instrument.

(a) An instrument payable on demand becomes overdue at the earliest of the following times:

(1) on the day after the day demand for payment is duly made;

(2) if the instrument is a check, 90 days after its date; or

(3) if the instrument is not a check, when the instrument has been outstanding for a period of time after its date which is unreasonably long under the circumstances of the particular case in light of the nature of the instrument and usage of the trade.

(b) With respect to an instrument payable at a definite time the following rules apply:

(1) If the principal is payable in installments and a due date has not been accelerated, the instrument becomes overdue upon default under the instrument for nonpayment of an installment, and the instrument remains overdue until the default is cured.

(2) If the principal is not payable in installments and the due date has not been accelerated, the instrument becomes overdue on the day after the due date.

(3) If a due date with respect to principal has been accelerated, the instrument becomes overdue on the day after the accelerated due date.

(c) Unless the due date of principal has been accelerated, an instrument does not become overdue if there is default in payment of interest but no default in payment of principal.

§ 3–305. Defenses and Claims in Recoupment.

(a) Except as stated in subsection (b), the right to enforce the obligation of a party to pay an instrument is subject to the following:

(1) a defense of the obligor based on (i) infancy of the obligor to the extent it is a defense to a simple contract, (ii) duress, lack of legal capacity, or illegality of the transaction which, under other law, nullifies the obligation of the obligor, (iii) fraud that induced the obligor to sign the instrument with neither knowledge nor reasonable opportunity to learn of its character or its essential terms, or (iv) discharge of the obligor in insolvency proceedings;

(2) a defense of the obligor stated in another section of this Article or a defense of the obligor that would be available if the person entitled to enforce the instrument were enforcing a right to payment under a simple contract; and

(3) a claim in recoupment of the obligor against the original payee of the instrument if the claim arose from the transaction that gave rise to the instrument; but the claim of the obligor may be asserted against a transferee of the instrument only to reduce the amount owing on the instrument at the time the action is brought.

(b) The right of a holder in due course to enforce the obligation of a party to pay the instrument is subject to defenses of the obligor stated in subsection (a)(1), but is not subject to defenses of the obligor stated in subsection (a)(2) or claims in recoupment stated in subsection (a)(3) against a person other than the holder.

(c) Except as stated in subsection (d), in an action to enforce the obligation of a party to pay the instrument, the obligor may not assert against the person entitled to enforce the instrument a defense, claim in recoupment, or claim to the instrument (Section 3–306) of another person, but the other person's claim to the instrument may be asserted by the obligor if the other person is joined in the action and personally asserts the claim against the person entitled to enforce the instrument. An obligor is not obliged to pay the instrument if the person seeking enforcement of the instrument does not have rights of a holder in due course and the obligor proves that the instrument is a lost or stolen instrument.

(d) In an action to enforce the obligation of an accommodation party to pay an instrument, the accommodation party may assert against the person entitled to enforce the instrument any defense or claim in recoupment under subsection (a) that the accommodated party could assert against the person entitled to enforce the instrument, except the defenses of discharge in insolvency proceedings, infancy, and lack of legal capacity.

§ 3–306. Claims to an Instrument.

A person taking an instrument, other than a person having rights of a holder in due course, is subject to a claim of a property or possessory right in the instrument or its proceeds, including a claim to rescind a negotiation and to recover the instrument or its proceeds. A person having rights of a holder in due course takes free of the claim to the instrument.

§ 3–307. Notice of Breach of Fiduciary Duty.

(a) In this section:

(1) "Fiduciary" means an agent, trustee, partner, corporate officer or director, or other representative owing a fiduciary duty with respect to an instrument.

(2) "Represented person" means the principal, beneficiary, partnership, corporation, or other person to whom the duty stated in paragraph (1) is owed.

(b) If (i) an instrument is taken from a fiduciary for payment or collection or for value, (ii) the taker has knowledge of the fiduciary status of the fiduciary, and (iii) the represented person makes a claim to the instrument or its proceeds on the basis that the transaction of the fiduciary is a breach of fiduciary duty, the following rules apply:

(1) Notice of breach of fiduciary duty by the fiduciary is notice of the claim of the represented person.

(2) In the case of an instrument payable to the represented person or the fiduciary as such, the taker has notice of the breach of fiduciary duty if the instrument is (i) taken in payment of or as security for a debt known by the taker to be the personal debt of the fiduciary, (ii) taken in a transaction known by the taker to be for the personal benefit of the fiduciary, or (iii) deposited to an account other than an account of the fiduciary, as such, or an account of the represented person.

(3) If an instrument is issued by the represented person or the fiduciary as such, and made payable to the fiduciary personally, the taker does not have notice of the breach of fiduciary duty unless the taker knows of the breach of fiduciary duty.

(4) If an instrument is issued by the represented person or the fiduciary as such, to the taker as payee, the taker has notice of the breach of fiduciary duty if the instrument is (i) taken in payment of or as security for a debt known by the taker to be the personal debt of the fiduciary, (ii) taken in a transaction known by the taker to be for the personal benefit of the fiduciary, or (iii) deposited to an account other than an account of the fiduciary, as such, or an account of the represented person.

§ 3–308. Proof of Signatures and Status as Holder in Due Course.

(a) In an action with respect to an instrument, the authenticity of, and authority to make, each signature on the instrument is admitted unless specifically denied in the pleadings. If the validity of a signature is denied in the pleadings, the burden of establishing validity is on the person claiming validity, but the signature is presumed to be authentic and authorized unless the action is to enforce the liability of the purported signer and the signer is dead or incompetent at the time of trial of the issue of validity of the signature. If an action to enforce the instrument is brought against a person as the undisclosed principal of a person who signed the instrument as a party to the instrument, the plaintiff has the burden of establishing that the defendant is liable on the instrument as a represented person under Section 3–402(a).

(b) If the validity of signatures is admitted or proved and there is compliance with subsection (a), a plaintiff producing the instrument is entitled to payment if the plaintiff proves entitlement to enforce the instrument under Section 3–301, unless the defendant proves a defense or claim in recoupment. If a defense or claim in recoupment is proved, the right to payment of the plaintiff is subject to the defense or claim, except to the extent the plaintiff proves that the plaintiff has rights of a holder in due course which are not subject to the defense or claim.

§ 3–309. Enforcement of Lost, Destroyed, or Stolen Instrument.

(a) A person not in possession of an instrument is entitled to enforce the instrument if (i) the person was in possession of the instrument and entitled to enforce it when loss of possession occurred, (ii) the loss of possession was not the result of a transfer by the person or a lawful seizure, and (iii) the person cannot reasonably obtain possession of the instrument because the instrument was destroyed, its whereabouts cannot be determined, or it is in the wrongful possession of an unknown person or a person that cannot be found or is not amenable to service of process.

(b) A person seeking enforcement of an instrument under subsection (a) must prove the terms of the instrument and the person's right to enforce the instrument. If that proof is made, Section 3–308 applies to the case as if the person seeking enforcement had produced the instrument. The court may not enter judgment in favor of the person seeking enforcement unless it finds that the person required to pay the instrument is adequately protected against loss that might occur by reason of a claim by another person to enforce the instrument. Adequate protection may be provided by any reasonable means.

§ 3–310. Effect of Instrument on Obligation for Which Taken.

(a) Unless otherwise agreed, if a certified check, cashier's check, or teller's check is taken for an obligation, the obligation is discharged to the same extent discharge would result if an amount of money equal to the amount of the instrument were taken in payment of the obligation. Discharge of the obligation does not affect any liability that the obligor may have as an indorser of the instrument.

(b) Unless otherwise agreed and except as provided in subsection (a), if a note or an uncertified check is taken for an obligation, the obligation is suspended to the same extent the obligation would be discharged if an amount of money equal to the amount of the instrument were taken, and the following rules apply:

(1) In the case of an uncertified check, suspension of the obligation continues until dishonor of the check or until it is paid or certified. Payment or certification of the check results in discharge of the obligation to the extent of the amount of the check.

(2) In the case of a note, suspension of the obligation continues until dishonor of the note or until it is paid. Payment of the note results in discharge of the obligation to the extent of the payment.

(3) Except as provided in paragraph (4), if the check or note is dishonored and the obligee of the obligation for which the instrument was taken is the person entitled to enforce the instrument, the obligee may enforce either the instrument or the obligation. In the case of an instrument of a third person which

is negotiated to the obligee by the obligor, discharge of the obligor on the instrument also discharges the obligation.

(4) If the person entitled to enforce the instrument taken for an obligation is a person other than the obligee, the obligee may not enforce the obligation to the extent the obligation is suspended. If the obligee is the person entitled to enforce the instrument but no longer has possession of it because it was lost, stolen, or destroyed, the obligation may not be enforced to the extent of the amount payable on the instrument, and to that extent the obligee's rights against the obligor are limited to enforcement of the instrument.

(c) If an instrument other than one described in subsection (a) or (b) is taken for an obligation, the effect is (i) that stated in subsection (a) if the instrument is one on which a bank is liable as maker or acceptor, or (ii) that stated in subsection (b) in any other case.

§ 3–311. Accord and Satisfaction by Use of Instrument.

(a) If a person against whom a claim is asserted proves that (i) that person in good faith tendered an instrument to the claimant as full satisfaction of the claim, (ii) the amount of the claim was unliquidated or subject to a bona fide dispute, and (iii) the claimant obtained payment of the instrument, the following subsections apply.

(b) Unless subsection (c) applies, the claim is discharged if the person against whom the claim is asserted proves that the instrument or an accompanying written communication contained a conspicuous statement to the effect that the instrument was tendered as full satisfaction of the claim.

(c) Subject to subsection (d), a claim is not discharged under subsection (b) if either of the following applies:

(1) The claimant, if an organization, proves that (i) within a reasonable time before the tender, the claimant sent a conspicuous statement to the person against whom the claim is asserted that communications concerning disputed debts, including an instrument tendered as full satisfaction of a debt, are to be sent to a designated person, office, or place, and (ii) the instrument or accompanying communication was not received by that designated person, office, or place.

(2) The claimant, whether or not an organization, proves that within 90 days after payment of the instrument, the claimant tendered repayment of the amount of the instrument to the person against whom the claim is asserted. This paragraph does not apply if the claimant is an organization that sent a statement complying with paragraph (1)(i).

(d) A claim is discharged if the person against whom the claim is asserted proves that within a reasonable time before collection of the instrument was initiated, the claimant, or an agent of the claimant having direct responsibility with respect to the disputed obligation, knew that the instrument was tendered in full satisfaction of the claim.

§ 3–312. Lost, Destroyed, or Stolen Cashier's Check, Teller's Check, or Certified Check.

(a) In this section:

(1) "Check" means a cashier's check, teller's check, or certified check.

(2) "Claimant" means a person who claims the right to receive the amount of a cashier's check, teller's check, or certified check that was lost, destroyed, or stolen.

(3) "Declaration of loss" means a written statement, made under penalty of perjury, to the effect that (i) the declarer lost possession of a check, (ii) the declarer is the drawer or payee of the check, in the case of a certified check, or the remitter or payee of the check, in the case of a cashier's check or teller's check, (iii) the loss of possession was not the result of a transfer by the declarer or a lawful seizure, and (iv) the declarer cannot reasonably obtain possession of the check because the check was destroyed, its whereabouts cannot be determined, or it is in the wrongful possession of an unknown person or a person that cannot be found or is not amenable to service of process.

(4) "Obligated bank" means the issuer of a cashier's check or teller's check or the acceptor of a certified check.

(b) A claimant may assert a claim to the amount of a check by a communication to the obligated bank describing the check with reasonable certainty and requesting payment of the amount of the check, if (i) the claimant is the drawer or payee of a certified check or the remitter or payee of a cashier's check or teller's check, (ii) the communication contains or is accompanied by a declaration of loss of the claimant with respect to the check, (iii) the communication is received at a time and in a manner affording the bank a reasonable time to act on it before the check is paid, and (iv) the claimant provides reasonable identification if requested by the obligated bank. Delivery of a declaration of loss is a warranty of the truth of the statements made in the declaration. If a claim is asserted in compliance with this subsection, the following rules apply:

(1) The claim becomes enforceable at the later of (i) the time the claim is asserted, or (ii) the 90th day following the date of the check, in the case of a cashier's check or teller's check, or the 90th day following the date of the acceptance, in the case of a certified check.

(2) Until the claim becomes enforceable, it has no legal effect and the obligated bank may pay the check or, in the case of a teller's check, may permit the drawee to pay the check. Payment to a person entitled to enforce the check discharges all liability of the obligated bank with respect to the check.

(3) If the claim becomes enforceable before the check is presented for payment, the obligated bank is not obliged to pay the check.

(4) When the claim becomes enforceable, the obligated bank becomes obliged to pay the amount of the check to the claimant if payment of the check has not been made to a person entitled to enforce the check. Subject to Section 4–302(a)(1), payment to the claimant discharges all liability of the obligated bank with respect to the check.

(c) If the obligated bank pays the amount of a check to a claimant under subsection (b)(4) and the check is presented for payment by a person having rights of a holder in due course, the claimant is obliged to (i) refund the payment to the obligated bank if the check is paid, or (ii) pay the amount of the check to the person having rights of a holder in due course if the check is dishonored.

(d) If a claimant has the right to assert a claim under subsection (b) and is also a person entitled to enforce a cashier's check, teller's check, or certified check which is lost, destroyed, or stolen, the claimant may assert rights with respect to the check either under this section or Section 3–309.

Added in 1991.

Part 4 Liability of Parties

§ 3–401. Signature.

(a) A person is not liable on an instrument unless (i) the person signed the instrument, or (ii) the person is represented by an agent or representative who signed the instrument and the signature is binding on the represented person under Section 3–402.

(b) A signature may be made (i) manually or by means of a device or machine, and (ii) by the use of any name, including a trade or assumed name, or by a word, mark, or symbol executed or adopted by a person with present intention to authenticate a writing.

§ 3–402. Signature by Representative.

(a) If a person acting, or purporting to act, as a representative signs an instrument by signing either the name of the represented person or the name of the signer, the represented person is bound by the signature to the same extent the represented person would be bound if the signature were on a simple contract. If the represented person is bound, the signature of the representative is the "authorized signature of the represented person" and the represented person is liable on the instrument, whether or not identified in the instrument.

(b) If a representative signs the name of the representative to an instrument and the signature is an authorized signature of the represented person, the following rules apply:

(1) If the form of the signature shows unambiguously that the signature is made on behalf of the represented person who is identified in the instrument, the representative is not liable on the instrument.

(2) Subject to subsection (c), if (i) the form of the signature does not show unambiguously that the signature is made in a representative capacity or (ii) the represented person is not identified in the instrument, the representative is liable on the instrument to a holder in due course that took the instrument without notice that the representative was not intended to be liable on the instrument. With respect to any other person, the representative is liable on the instrument unless the representative proves that the original parties did not intend the representative to be liable on the instrument.

(c) If a representative signs the name of the representative as drawer of a check without indication of the representative status and the check is payable from an account of the represented person who is identified on the check, the signer is not liable on the check if the signature is an authorized signature of the represented person.

§ 3–403. Unauthorized Signature.

(a) Unless otherwise provided in this Article or Article 4, an unauthorized signature is ineffective except as the signature of the unauthorized signer in favor of a person who in good faith pays the instrument or takes it for value. An unauthorized signature may be ratified for all purposes of this Article.

(b) If the signature of more than one person is required to constitute the authorized signature of an organization, the signature of the organization is unauthorized if one of the required signatures is lacking.

(c) The civil or criminal liability of a person who makes an unauthorized signature is not affected by any provision of this Article which makes the unauthorized signature effective for the purposes of this Article.

§ 3–404. Impostors; Fictitious Payees.

(a) If an impostor, by use of the mails or otherwise, induces the issuer of an instrument to issue the instrument to the impostor, or to a person acting in concert with the impostor, by impersonating the payee of the instrument or a person authorized to act for the payee, an indorsement of the instrument by any person in the name of the payee is effective as the indorsement of the payee in favor of a person who, in good faith, pays the instrument or takes it for value or for collection.

(b) If (i) a person whose intent determines to whom an instrument is payable (Section 3–110(a) or (b)) does not intend the person identified as payee to have any interest in the instrument, or (ii) the person identified as payee of an instrument is a fictitious person, the following rules apply until the instrument is negotiated by special indorsement:

(1) Any person in possession of the instrument is its holder.

(2) An indorsement by any person in the name of the payee stated in the instrument is effective as the indorsement of the payee in favor of a person who, in good faith, pays the instrument or takes it for value or for collection.

(c) Under subsection (a) or (b), an indorsement is made in the name of a payee if (i) it is made in a name substantially similar to that of the payee or (ii) the instrument, whether or not indorsed, is deposited in a depositary bank to an account in a name substantially similar to that of the payee.

(d) With respect to an instrument to which subsection (a) or (b) applies, if a person paying the instrument or taking it for value or for collection fails to exercise ordinary care in paying or taking the instrument and that failure substantially contributes to loss resulting from payment of the instrument, the person bearing the loss may recover from the person failing to exercise ordinary care to the extent the failure to exercise ordinary care contributed to the loss.

§ 3–405. Employer's Responsibility for Fraudulent Indorsement by Employee.

(a) In this section:

(1) "Employee" includes an independent contractor and employee of an independent contractor retained by the employer.

(2) "Fraudulent indorsement" means (i) in the case of an instrument payable to the employer, a forged indorsement purporting to be that of the employer, or (ii) in the case of an instrument with respect to which the employer is the issuer, a forged indorsement purporting to be that of the person identified as payee.

(3) "Responsibility" with respect to instruments means authority (i) to sign or indorse instruments on behalf of the employer, (ii) to process instruments received by the employer for bookkeeping purposes, for deposit to an account, or for other disposition, (iii) to prepare or process instruments for issue in the name of the employer, (iv) to supply information determining the names or addresses of payees of instruments to be issued in the name of the employer, (v) to control the disposition of instruments to be issued in the name of the employer, or (vi) to act otherwise with respect to instruments in a responsible capacity. "Responsibility" does not include authority that merely allows an employee to have access to instruments or blank or incomplete instrument forms that are being stored or transported or are part of incoming or outgoing mail, or similar access.

(b) For the purpose of determining the rights and liabilities of a person who, in good faith, pays an instrument or takes it for value or for collection, if an employer entrusted an employee with responsibility with respect to the instrument and the employee or a person acting in concert with the employee makes a fraudulent indorsement of the instrument, the indorsement is effective as the indorsement of the person to whom the instrument is payable if it is made in the name of that person. If the person paying the instrument or taking it for value or for collection fails to exercise ordinary care in paying or taking the instrument and that failure substantially contributes to loss resulting from the fraud, the person bearing the loss may recover from the person failing to exercise ordinary care to the extent the failure to exercise ordinary care contributed to the loss.

(c) Under subsection (b), an indorsement is made in the name of the person to whom an instrument is payable if (i) it is made in a name substantially similar to the name of that person or (ii) the instrument, whether or not indorsed, is deposited in a depositary bank to an account in a name substantially similar to the name of that person.

§ 3–406. Negligence Contributing to Forged Signature or Alteration of Instrument.

(a) A person whose failure to exercise ordinary care substantially contributes to an alteration of an instrument or to the making of a forged signature on an instrument is precluded from asserting the alteration or the forgery against a person who, in good faith, pays the instrument or takes it for value or for collection.

(b) Under subsection (a), if the person asserting the preclusion fails to exercise ordinary care in paying or taking the instrument and that failure substantially contributes to loss, the loss is allocated between the person precluded and the person asserting the preclusion according to the extent to which the failure of each to exercise ordinary care contributed to the loss.

(c) Under subsection (a), the burden of proving failure to exercise ordinary care is on the person asserting the preclusion. Under subsection (b), the burden of proving failure to exercise ordinary care is on the person precluded.

§ 3–407. Alteration.

(a) "Alteration" means (i) an unauthorized change in an instrument that purports to modify in any respect the obligation of a party, or (ii) an unauthorized addition of words or numbers or other change to an incomplete instrument relating to the obligation of a party.

(b) Except as provided in subsection (c), an alteration fraudulently made discharges a party whose obligation is affected by the alteration unless that party assents or is precluded from asserting the alteration. No other alteration discharges a party, and the instrument may be enforced according to its original terms.

(c) A payor bank or drawee paying a fraudulently altered instrument or a person taking it for value, in good faith and without notice of the alteration, may enforce rights with respect to the instrument (i) according to its original terms, or (ii) in the case of an incomplete instrument altered by unauthorized completion, according to its terms as completed.

§ 3–408. Drawee Not Liable on Unaccepted Draft.

A check or other draft does not of itself operate as an assignment of funds in the hands of the drawee available for its payment, and the drawee is not liable on the instrument until the drawee accepts it.

§ 3–409. Acceptance of Draft; Certified Check.

(a) "Acceptance" means the drawee's signed agreement to pay a draft as presented. It must be written on the draft and may consist of the drawee's signature alone. Acceptance may be made at any time and becomes effective when notification pursuant to instructions is given or the accepted draft is delivered for the purpose of giving rights on the acceptance to any person.

(b) A draft may be accepted although it has not been signed by the drawer, is otherwise incomplete, is overdue, or has been dishonored.

(c) If a draft is payable at a fixed period after sight and the acceptor fails to date the acceptance, the holder may complete the acceptance by supplying a date in good faith.

(d) "Certified check" means a check accepted by the bank on which it is drawn. Acceptance may be made as stated in subsection (a) or by a writing on the check which indicates that the check is certified. The drawee of a check has no obligation to certify the check, and refusal to certify is not dishonor of the check.

§ 3–410. Acceptance Varying Draft.

(a) If the terms of a drawee's acceptance vary from the terms of the draft as presented, the holder may refuse the acceptance and treat the draft as dishonored. In that case, the drawee may cancel the acceptance.

(b) The terms of a draft are not varied by an acceptance to pay at a particular bank or place in the United States, unless the acceptance states that the draft is to be paid only at that bank or place.

(c) If the holder assents to an acceptance varying the terms of a draft, the obligation of each drawer and indorser that does not expressly assent to the acceptance is discharged.

§ 3–411. Refusal to Pay Cashier's Checks, Teller's Checks, and Certified Checks.

(a) In this section, "obligated bank" means the acceptor of a certified check or the issuer of a cashier's check or teller's check bought from the issuer.

(b) If the obligated bank wrongfully (i) refuses to pay a cashier's check or certified check, (ii) stops payment of a teller's check, or (iii) refuses to pay a dishonored teller's check, the person asserting the right to enforce the check is entitled to compensation for expenses and loss of interest resulting from the nonpayment and may recover consequential damages if the obligated bank refuses to pay after receiving notice of particular circumstances giving rise to the damages.

(c) Expenses or consequential damages under subsection (b) are not recoverable if the refusal of the obligated bank to pay occurs because (i) the bank suspends payments, (ii) the obligated bank asserts a claim or defense of the bank that it has reasonable grounds to believe is available against the person entitled to enforce the instrument, (iii) the obligated bank has a reasonable doubt whether the person demanding payment is the person entitled to enforce the instrument, or (iv) payment is prohibited by law.

§ 3–412. Obligation of Issuer of Note or Cashier's Check.

The issuer of a note or cashier's check or other draft drawn on the drawer is obliged to pay the instrument (i) according to its terms at the time it was issued or, if not issued, at the time it first came into possession of a holder, or (ii) if the issuer signed an incomplete instrument, according to its terms when completed, to the extent stated in Sections 3–115 and 3–407. The obligation is owed to a person entitled to enforce the instrument or to an indorser who paid the instrument under Section 3–415.

§ 3–413. Obligation of Acceptor.

(a) The acceptor of a draft is obliged to pay the draft (i) according to its terms at the time it was accepted, even though the acceptance states that the draft is payable "as originally drawn" or equivalent terms, (ii) if the acceptance varies the terms of the draft, according to the terms of the draft as varied, or (iii) if the acceptance is of a draft that is an incomplete instrument, according to its terms when completed, to the extent stated in Sections 3–115 and 3–407. The obligation is owed to a person entitled to enforce the draft or to the drawer or an indorser who paid the draft under Section 3–414 or 3–415.

(b) If the certification of a check or other acceptance of a draft states the amount certified or accepted, the obligation of the acceptor is that amount. If (i) the certification or acceptance does not state an amount, (ii) the amount of the instrument is subsequently raised, and (iii) the instrument is then negotiated to a holder in due course, the obligation of the acceptor is the amount of the instrument at the time it was taken by the holder in due course.

§ 3–414. Obligation of Drawer.

(a) This section does not apply to cashier's checks or other drafts drawn on the drawer.

(b) If an unaccepted draft is dishonored, the drawer is obliged to pay the draft (i) according to its terms at the time it was issued or, if not issued, at the time it first came into possession of a holder, or (ii) if the drawer signed an incomplete instrument, according to its terms when completed, to the extent stated in Sections 3–115 and 3–407. The obligation is owed to a person entitled to enforce the draft or to an indorser who paid the draft under Section 3–415.

(c) If a draft is accepted by a bank, the drawer is discharged, regardless of when or by whom acceptance was obtained.

(d) If a draft is accepted and the acceptor is not a bank, the obligation of the drawer to pay the draft if the draft is dishonored by the acceptor is the same as the obligation of an indorser under Section 3–415(a) and (c).

(e) If a draft states that it is drawn "without recourse" or otherwise disclaims liability of the drawer to pay the draft, the drawer is not liable under subsection (b) to pay the draft if the draft is not a check. A disclaimer of the liability stated in subsection (b) is not effective if the draft is a check.

(f) If (i) a check is not presented for payment or given to a depositary bank for collection within 30 days after its date, (ii) the drawee suspends payments after expiration of the 30-day period without paying the check, and (iii) because of the suspension of payments, the drawer is deprived of funds maintained with the drawee to cover payment of the check, the drawer to the extent deprived of funds may discharge its obligation to pay the check by assigning to the person entitled to enforce the check the rights of the drawer against the drawee with respect to the funds.

§ 3–415. Obligation of Indorser.

(a) Subject to subsections (b), (c), and (d) and to Section 3–419(d), if an instrument is dishonored, an indorser is obliged to pay the amount due on the instrument (i) according to the terms of the instrument at the time it was indorsed, or (ii) if the indorser indorsed an incomplete instrument, according to its terms when completed, to the extent stated in Sections 3–115 and 3–407. The obligation of the indorser is owed to a person entitled to enforce the instrument or to a subsequent indorser who paid the instrument under this section.

(b) If an indorsement states that it is made "without recourse" or otherwise disclaims liability of the indorser, the indorser is not liable under subsection (a) to pay the instrument.

(c) If notice of dishonor of an instrument is required by Section 3–503 and notice of dishonor complying with that section is not given to an indorser, the liability of the indorser under subsection (a) is discharged.

(d) If a draft is accepted by a bank after an indorsement is made, the liability of the indorser under subsection (a) is discharged.

(e) If an indorser of a check is liable under subsection (a) and the check is not presented for payment, or given to a depositary bank for collection, within 30 days after the day the indorsement was made, the liability of the indorser under subsection (a) is discharged.

As amended in 1993.

§ 3–416. Transfer Warranties.

(a) A person who transfers an instrument for consideration warrants to the transferee and, if the transfer is by indorsement, to any subsequent transferee that:

(1) the warrantor is a person entitled to enforce the instrument;

(2) all signatures on the instrument are authentic and authorized;

(3) the instrument has not been altered;

(4) the instrument is not subject to a defense or claim in recoupment of any party which can be asserted against the warrantor; and

(5) the warrantor has no knowledge of any insolvency proceeding commenced with respect to the maker or acceptor or, in the case of an unaccepted draft, the drawer.

(b) A person to whom the warranties under subsection (a) are made and who took the instrument in good faith may recover from the warrantor as damages for breach of warranty an amount equal to the loss suffered as a result of the breach, but not more than the amount of the instrument plus expenses and loss of interest incurred as a result of the breach.

(c) The warranties stated in subsection (a) cannot be disclaimed with respect to checks. Unless notice of a claim for breach of warranty is given to the warrantor within 30 days after the claimant has reason to know of the breach and the identity of the warrantor, the liability of the warrantor under subsection (b) is discharged to the extent of any loss caused by the delay in giving notice of the claim.

(d) A [cause of action] for breach of warranty under this section accrues when the claimant has reason to know of the breach.

§ 3–417. Presentment Warranties.

(a) If an unaccepted draft is presented to the drawee for payment or acceptance and the drawee pays or accepts the draft, (i) the person obtaining payment or acceptance, at the time of presentment, and (ii) a previous transferor of the draft, at the time of transfer, warrant to the drawee making payment or accepting the draft in good faith that:

(1) the warrantor is, or was, at the time the warrantor transferred the draft, a person entitled to enforce the draft or authorized to obtain payment or acceptance of the draft on behalf of a person entitled to enforce the draft;

(2) the draft has not been altered; and

(3) the warrantor has no knowledge that the signature of the drawer of the draft is unauthorized.

(b) A drawee making payment may recover from any warrantor damages for breach of warranty equal to the amount paid by the drawee less the amount the drawee received or is entitled to receive from the drawer because of the payment. In addition, the drawee is entitled to compensation for expenses and loss of interest resulting from the breach. The right of the drawee to recover damages under this subsection is not affected by any failure of the drawee to exercise ordinary care in making payment. If the drawee accepts the draft, breach of warranty is a defense to the obligation of the acceptor. If the acceptor makes payment with respect to the draft, the acceptor is entitled to recover from any warrantor for breach of warranty the amounts stated in this subsection.

(c) If a drawee asserts a claim for breach of warranty under subsection (a) based on an unauthorized indorsement of the draft or an alteration of the draft, the warrantor may defend by proving that the indorsement is effective under Section 3–404 or 3–405 or the drawer is precluded under Section 3–406 or 4–406 from asserting against the drawee the unauthorized indorsement or alteration.

(d) If (i) a dishonored draft is presented for payment to the drawer or an indorser or (ii) any other instrument is presented for payment to a party obliged to pay the instrument, and (iii) payment is received, the following rules apply:

(1) The person obtaining payment and a prior transferor of the instrument warrant to the person making payment in good faith that the warrantor is, or was, at the time the warrantor transferred the instrument, a person entitled to enforce the instrument or authorized to obtain payment on behalf of a person entitled to enforce the instrument.

(2) The person making payment may recover from any warrantor for breach of warranty an amount equal to the amount paid plus expenses and loss of interest resulting from the breach.

(e) The warranties stated in subsections (a) and (d) cannot be disclaimed with respect to checks. Unless notice of a claim for breach of warranty is given to the warrantor within 30 days after the claimant has reason to know of the breach and the identity of the warrantor, the liability of the warrantor under subsection (b) or (d) is discharged to the extent of any loss caused by the delay in giving notice of the claim.

(f) A [cause of action] for breach of warranty under this section accrues when the claimant has reason to know of the breach.

§ 3–418. Payment or Acceptance by Mistake.

(a) Except as provided in subsection (c), if the drawee of a draft pays or accepts the draft and the drawee acted on the mistaken belief that (i) payment of the draft had not been stopped pursuant to Section 4–403 or (ii) the signature of the drawer of the draft was authorized, the drawee may recover the amount of the draft from the person to whom or for whose benefit payment was made or, in the case of acceptance, may revoke the acceptance. Rights of the drawee under this subsection are not affected by failure of the drawee to exercise ordinary care in paying or accepting the draft.

(b) Except as provided in subsection (c), if an instrument has been paid or accepted by mistake and the case is not covered by subsection (a), the person paying or accepting may, to the extent permitted by the law governing mistake and restitution, (i) recover the payment from the person to whom or for whose benefit payment was made or (ii) in the case of acceptance, may revoke the acceptance.

(c) The remedies provided by subsection (a) or (b) may not be asserted against a person who took the instrument in good faith and for value or who in good faith changed position in reliance on the payment or acceptance. This subsection does not limit remedies provided by Section 3–417 or 4–407.

(d) Notwithstanding Section 4–215, if an instrument is paid or accepted by mistake and the payor or acceptor recovers payment or revokes acceptance under subsection (a) or (b), the instrument is deemed not to have been paid or accepted and is treated as dishonored, and the person from whom payment is recovered has rights as a person entitled to enforce the dishonored instrument.

§ 3–419. Instruments Signed for Accommodation.

(a) If an instrument is issued for value given for the benefit of a party to the instrument ("accommodated party") and another party to the instrument ("accommodation party") signs the instrument for the purpose of incurring liability on the instrument without being a direct beneficiary of the value given for the instrument, the instrument is signed by the accommodation party "for accommodation."

(b) An accommodation party may sign the instrument as maker, drawer, acceptor, or indorser and, subject to subsection (d), is obliged to pay the instrument in the capacity in which the accommodation party signs. The obligation of an accommodation party may be enforced notwithstanding any statute of frauds and whether or not the accommodation party receives consideration for the accommodation.

(c) A person signing an instrument is presumed to be an accommodation party and there is notice that the instrument is signed for accommodation if the signature is an anomalous indorsement or is accompanied by words indicating that the signer is acting as surety or guarantor with respect to the obligation of another party to the instrument. Except as provided in Section 3–605, the obligation of an accommodation party to pay the instrument is not affected by the fact that the person enforcing the obligation had notice when the instrument was taken by that person that the accommodation party signed the instrument for accommodation.

(d) If the signature of a party to an instrument is accompanied by words indicating unambiguously that the party is guaranteeing collection rather than payment of the obligation of another party to the instrument, the signer is obliged to pay the amount due on the instrument to a person entitled to enforce the instrument only if (i) execution of judgment against the other party has been returned unsatisfied, (ii) the other party is insolvent or in an insolvency proceeding, (iii) the other party cannot be served with process, or (iv) it is otherwise apparent that payment cannot be obtained from the other party.

(e) An accommodation party who pays the instrument is entitled to reimbursement from the accommodated party and is entitled to enforce the instrument against the accommodated party. An accommodated party who pays the instrument has no right of recourse against, and is not entitled to contribution from, an accommodation party.

§ 3–420. Conversion of Instrument.

(a) The law applicable to conversion of personal property applies to instruments. An instrument is also converted if it is taken by transfer, other than a negotiation, from a person not entitled to enforce the instrument or a bank makes or obtains payment with respect to the instrument for a person not entitled to enforce the instrument or receive payment. An action for conversion of an instrument may not be brought by (i) the issuer or acceptor of the instrument or (ii) a payee or indorsee who did not receive delivery of the instrument either directly or through delivery to an agent or a co-payee.

(b) In an action under subsection (a), the measure of liability is presumed to be the amount payable on the instrument, but recovery may not exceed the amount of the plaintiff's interest in the instrument.

(c) A representative, other than a depositary bank, who has in good faith dealt with an instrument or its proceeds on behalf of one who was not the person entitled to enforce the instrument is not liable in conversion to that person beyond the amount of any proceeds that it has not paid out.

Part 5 Dishonor

§ 3–501. Presentment.

(a) "Presentment" means a demand made by or on behalf of a person entitled to enforce an instrument (i) to pay the instrument made to the drawee or a party obliged to pay the instrument or, in the case of a note or accepted draft payable at a bank, to the bank, or (ii) to accept a draft made to the drawee.

(b) The following rules are subject to Article 4, agreement of the parties, and clearing-house rules and the like:

(1) Presentment may be made at the place of payment of the instrument and must be made at the place of payment if the instrument is payable at a bank in the United States; may be made by any commercially reasonable means, including an oral, written, or electronic communication; is effective when the demand for payment or acceptance is received by the person to whom presentment is made; and is effective if made to any one of two or more makers, acceptors, drawees, or other payors.

(2) Upon demand of the person to whom presentment is made, the person making presentment must (i) exhibit the instrument, (ii) give reasonable identification and, if presentment is made on behalf of another person, reasonable evidence of authority to do so, and (. . .) sign a receipt on the instrument for any payment made or surrender the instrument if full payment is made.

(3) Without dishonoring the instrument, the party to whom presentment is made may (i) return the instrument for lack of a necessary indorsement, or (ii) refuse payment or acceptance for failure of the presentment to comply with the terms of the instrument, an agreement of the parties, or other applicable law or rule.

(4) The party to whom presentment is made may treat presentment as occurring on the next business day after the day of presentment if the party to whom presentment is made has established a cut-off hour not earlier than 2 p.m. for the receipt

and processing of instruments presented for payment or acceptance and presentment is made after the cut-off hour.

§ 3–502. Dishonor.

(a) Dishonor of a note is governed by the following rules:

(1) If the note is payable on demand, the note is dishonored if presentment is duly made to the maker and the note is not paid on the day of presentment.

(2) If the note is not payable on demand and is payable at or through a bank or the terms of the note require presentment, the note is dishonored if presentment is duly made and the note is not paid on the day it becomes payable or the day of presentment, whichever is later.

(3) If the note is not payable on demand and paragraph (2) does not apply, the note is dishonored if it is not paid on the day it becomes payable.

(b) Dishonor of an unaccepted draft other than a documentary draft is governed by the following rules:

(1) If a check is duly presented for payment to the payor bank otherwise than for immediate payment over the counter, the check is dishonored if the payor bank makes timely return of the check or sends timely notice of dishonor or nonpayment under Section 4–301 or 4–302, or becomes accountable for the amount of the check under Section 4–302.

(2) If a draft is payable on demand and paragraph (1) does not apply, the draft is dishonored if presentment for payment is duly made to the drawee and the draft is not paid on the day of presentment.

(3) If a draft is payable on a date stated in the draft, the draft is dishonored if (i) presentment for payment is duly made to the drawee and payment is not made on the day the draft becomes payable or the day of presentment, whichever is later, or (ii) presentment for acceptance is duly made before the day the draft becomes payable and the draft is not accepted on the day of presentment.

(4) If a draft is payable on elapse of a period of time after sight or acceptance, the draft is dishonored if presentment for acceptance is duly made and the draft is not accepted on the day of presentment.

(c) Dishonor of an unaccepted documentary draft occurs according to the rules stated in subsection (b)(2), (3), and (4), except that payment or acceptance may be delayed without dishonor until no later than the close of the third business day of the drawee following the day on which payment or acceptance is required by those paragraphs.

(d) Dishonor of an accepted draft is governed by the following rules:

(1) If the draft is payable on demand, the draft is dishonored if presentment for payment is duly made to the acceptor and the draft is not paid on the day of presentment.

(2) If the draft is not payable on demand, the draft is dishonored if presentment for payment is duly made to the acceptor and payment is not made on the day it becomes payable or the day of presentment, whichever is later.

(e) In any case in which presentment is otherwise required for dishonor under this section and presentment is excused under Section 3–504, dishonor occurs without presentment if the instrument is not duly accepted or paid.

(f) If a draft is dishonored because timely acceptance of the draft was not made and the person entitled to demand acceptance consents to a late acceptance, from the time of acceptance the draft is treated as never having been dishonored.

§ 3–503. Notice of Dishonor.

(a) The obligation of an indorser stated in Section 3–415(a) and the obligation of a drawer stated in Section 3–414(d) may not be enforced unless (i) the indorser or drawer is given notice of dishonor of the instrument complying with this section or (ii) notice of dishonor is excused under Section 3–504(b).

(b) Notice of dishonor may be given by any person; may be given by any commercially reasonable means, including an oral, written, or electronic communication; and is sufficient if it reasonably identifies the instrument and indicates that the instrument has been dishonored or has not been paid or accepted. Return of an instrument given to a bank for collection is sufficient notice of dishonor.

(c) Subject to Section 3–504(c), with respect to an instrument taken for collection by a collecting bank, notice of dishonor must be given (i) by the bank before midnight of the next banking day following the banking day on which the bank receives notice of dishonor of the instrument, or (ii) by any other person within 30 days following the day on which the person receives notice of dishonor. With respect to any other instrument, notice of dishonor must be given within 30 days following the day on which dishonor occurs.

§ 3–504. Excused Presentment and Notice of Dishonor.

(a) Presentment for payment or acceptance of an instrument is excused if (i) the person entitled to present the instrument cannot with reasonable diligence make presentment, (ii) the maker or acceptor has repudiated an obligation to pay the instrument or is dead or in insolvency proceedings, (iii) by the terms of the instrument presentment is not necessary to enforce the obligation of indorsers or the drawer, (iv) the drawer or indorser whose obligation is being enforced has waived presentment or otherwise has no reason to expect or right to require that the instrument be paid or accepted, or (v) the drawer instructed the drawee not to pay or accept the draft or the drawee was not obligated to the drawer to pay the draft.

(b) Notice of dishonor is excused if (i) by the terms of the instrument notice of dishonor is not necessary to enforce the obligation of a party to pay the instrument, or (ii) the party whose obligation is being enforced waived notice of dishonor. A waiver of presentment is also a waiver of notice of dishonor.

(c) Delay in giving notice of dishonor is excused if the delay was caused by circumstances beyond the control of the person giving the notice and the person giving the notice exercised reasonable diligence after the cause of the delay ceased to operate.

§ 3–505. Evidence of Dishonor.

(a) The following are admissible as evidence and create a presumption of dishonor and of any notice of dishonor stated:

(1) a document regular in form as provided in subsection (b) which purports to be a protest;

(2) a purported stamp or writing of the drawee, payor bank, or presenting bank on or accompanying the instrument stating that acceptance or payment has been refused unless reasons for the refusal are stated and the reasons are not consistent with dishonor;

(3) a book or record of the drawee, payor bank, or collecting bank, kept in the usual course of business which shows dishonor, even if there is no evidence of who made the entry.

(b) A protest is a certificate of dishonor made by a United States consul or vice consul, or a notary public or other person authorized to administer oaths by the law of the place where dishonor occurs. It may be made upon information satisfactory to that person. The protest must identify the instrument and certify either that presentment has been made or, if not made, the reason why it was not made, and that the instrument has been dishonored by nonacceptance or nonpayment. The protest may also certify that notice of dishonor has been given to some or all parties.

Part 6 Discharge and Payment

§ 3–601. Discharge and Effect of Discharge.

(a) The obligation of a party to pay the instrument is discharged as stated in this Article or by an act or agreement with the party which would discharge an obligation to pay money under a simple contract.

(b) Discharge of the obligation of a party is not effective against a person acquiring rights of a holder in due course of the instrument without notice of the discharge.

§ 3–602. Payment.

(a) Subject to subsection (b), an instrument is paid to the extent payment is made (i) by or on behalf of a party obliged to pay the instrument, and (ii) to a person entitled to enforce the instrument. To the extent of the payment, the obligation of the party obliged to pay the instrument is discharged even though payment is made with knowledge of a claim to the instrument under Section 3–306 by another person.

(b) The obligation of a party to pay the instrument is not discharged under subsection (a) if:

(1) a claim to the instrument under Section 3–306 is enforceable against the party receiving payment and (i) payment is made with knowledge by the payor that payment is prohibited by injunction or similar process of a court of competent jurisdiction, or (ii) in the case of an instrument other than a cashier's check, teller's check, or certified check, the party making payment accepted, from the person having a claim to the instrument, indemnity against loss resulting from refusal to pay the person entitled to enforce the instrument; or

(2) the person making payment knows that the instrument is a stolen instrument and pays a person it knows is in wrongful possession of the instrument.

§ 3–603. Tender of Payment.

(a) If tender of payment of an obligation to pay an instrument is made to a person entitled to enforce the instrument, the effect of tender is governed by principles of law applicable to tender of payment under a simple contract.

(b) If tender of payment of an obligation to pay an instrument is made to a person entitled to enforce the instrument and the tender is refused, there is discharge, to the extent of the amount of the tender, of the obligation of an indorser or accommodation party having a right of recourse with respect to the obligation to which the tender relates.

(c) If tender of payment of an amount due on an instrument is made to a person entitled to enforce the instrument, the obligation of the obligor to pay interest after the due date on the amount tendered is discharged. If presentment is required with respect to an instrument and the obligor is able and ready to pay on the due date at every place of payment stated in the instrument, the obligor is deemed to have made tender of payment on the due date to the person entitled to enforce the instrument.

§ 3–604. Discharge by Cancellation or Renunciation.

(a) A person entitled to enforce an instrument, with or without consideration, may discharge the obligation of a party to pay the instrument (i) by an intentional voluntary act, such as surrender of the instrument to the party, destruction, mutilation, or cancellation of the instrument, cancellation or striking out of the party's signature, or the addition of words to the instrument indicating discharge, or (ii) by agreeing not to sue or otherwise renouncing rights against the party by a signed writing.

(b) Cancellation or striking out of an indorsement pursuant to subsection (a) does not affect the status and rights of a party derived from the indorsement.

§ 3–605. Discharge of Indorsers and Accommodation Parties.

(a) In this section, the term "indorser" includes a drawer having the obligation described in Section 3–414(d).

(b) Discharge, under Section 3–604, of the obligation of a party to pay an instrument does not discharge the obligation of an indorser or accommodation party having a right of recourse against the discharged party.

(c) If a person entitled to enforce an instrument agrees, with or without consideration, to an extension of the due date of the obligation of a party to pay the instrument, the extension discharges an indorser or accommodation party having a right of recourse against the party whose obligation is extended to the extent the indorser or accommodation party proves that the extension caused loss to the indorser or accommodation party with respect to the right of recourse.

(d) If a person entitled to enforce an instrument agrees, with or without consideration, to a material modification of the obligation of a party other than an extension of the due date, the modification discharges the obligation of an indorser or accommodation party having a right of recourse against the person whose obligation is modified to the extent the modification causes loss to the indorser or accommodation party with respect to the right of recourse. The loss suffered by the indorser or accommodation party as a result of the modification is equal to the amount of the right of recourse unless the person enforcing the instrument proves that no loss was caused by the modification or that the loss caused by the modification was an amount less than the amount of the right of recourse.

(e) If the obligation of a party to pay an instrument is secured by an interest in collateral and a person entitled to enforce the instrument impairs the value of the interest in collateral, the obligation of an indorser or accommodation party having a right of recourse against the obligor is discharged to the extent of the impairment. The value of an interest in collateral is impaired to the extent (i) the value of the interest is reduced to an amount less than the amount of the right of recourse of the party asserting discharge, or (ii) the reduction in value of the interest causes an increase in the amount by which the amount of the right of recourse exceeds the value of the interest. The burden of proving impairment is on the party asserting discharge.

(f) If the obligation of a party is secured by an interest in collateral not provided by an accommodation party and a person entitled to enforce the instrument impairs the value of the interest in collateral, the obligation of any party who is jointly and severally liable with respect to the secured obligation is discharged to the extent the impairment causes the party asserting discharge to pay more than that party would have been obliged to pay, taking into account rights of contribution, if impairment had not occurred. If the party asserting discharge is an accommodation party not entitled to discharge under subsection (e), the party is deemed to have a right to contribution based on joint and several liability rather than a right to reimbursement. The burden of proving impairment is on the party asserting discharge.

(g) Under subsection (e) or (f), impairing value of an interest in collateral includes (i) failure to obtain or maintain perfection or recordation of the interest in collateral, (ii) release of collateral without substitution of collateral of equal value, (iii) failure to perform a duty to preserve the value of collateral owed, under Article 9 or other law, to a debtor or surety or other person secondarily liable, or (iv) failure to comply with applicable law in disposing of collateral.

(h) An accommodation party is not discharged under subsection (c), (d), or (e) unless the person entitled to enforce the instrument knows of the accommodation or has notice under Section 3–419(c) that the instrument was signed for accommodation.

(i) A party is not discharged under this section if (i) the party asserting discharge consents to the event or conduct that is the basis of the discharge, or (ii) the instrument or a separate agreement of the party provides for waiver of discharge under this section either specifically or by general language indicating that parties waive defenses based on suretyship or impairment of collateral.

ADDENDUM TO REVISED ARTICLE 3

Notes to Legislative Counsel

1. If revised Article 3 is adopted in your state, the reference in Section 2–511 to Section 3–802 should be changed to Section 3–310.

2. If revised Article 3 is adopted in your state and the Uniform Fiduciaries Act is also in effect in your state, you may want to consider amending Uniform Fiduciaries Act § 9 to conform to Section 3–307(b)(2)(iii) and (4)(iii). See Official Comment 3 to Section 3–307.

Revised Article 4
BANK DEPOSITS AND COLLECTIONS

Part 1 General Provisions and Definitions

§ 4–101. Short Title.

This Article may be cited as Uniform Commercial Code—Bank Deposits and Collections.

As amended in 1990.

§ 4–102. Applicability.

(a) To the extent that items within this Article are also within Articles 3 and 8, they are subject to those Articles. If there is conflict, this Article governs Article 3, but Article 8 governs this Article.

(b) The liability of a bank for action or non-action with respect to an item handled by it for purposes of presentment, payment, or collection is governed by the law of the place where the bank is located. In the case of action or non-action by or at a branch or separate office of a bank, its liability is governed by the law of the place where the branch or separate office is located.

§ 4–103. Variation by Agreement; Measure of Damages; Action Constituting Ordinary Care.

(a) The effect of the provisions of this Article may be varied by agreement, but the parties to the agreement cannot disclaim a bank's responsibility for its lack of good faith or failure to exercise ordinary care or limit the measure of damages for the lack or failure. However, the parties may determine by agreement the standards by which the bank's responsibility is to be measured if those standards are not manifestly unreasonable.

(b) Federal Reserve regulations and operating circulars, clearing-house rules, and the like have the effect of agreements under subsection (a), whether or not specifically assented to by all parties interested in items handled.

(c) Action or non-action approved by this Article or pursuant to Federal Reserve regulations or operating circulars is the exercise of ordinary care and, in the absence of special instructions, action or non-action consistent with clearing-house rules and the like or with a general banking usage not disapproved by this Article, is prima facie the exercise of ordinary care.

(d) The specification or approval of certain procedures by this Article is not disapproval of other procedures that may be reasonable under the circumstances.

(e) The measure of damages for failure to exercise ordinary care in handling an item is the amount of the item reduced by an amount that could not have been realized by the exercise of ordinary care. If there is also bad faith it includes any other damages the party suffered as a proximate consequence.

As amended in 1990.

§ 4–104. Definitions and Index of Definitions.

(a) In this Article, unless the context otherwise requires:

(1) "Account" means any deposit or credit account with a bank, including a demand, time, savings, passbook, share draft, or like account, other than an account evidenced by a certificate of deposit;

(2) "Afternoon" means the period of a day between noon and midnight;

(3) "Banking day" means the part of a day on which a bank is open to the public for carrying on substantially all of its banking functions;

(4) "Clearing house" means an association of banks or other payors regularly clearing items;

(5) "Customer" means a person having an account with a bank or for whom a bank has agreed to collect items, including a bank that maintains an account at another bank;

(6) "Documentary draft" means a draft to be presented for acceptance or payment if specified documents, certificated securities (Section 8–102) or instructions for uncertificated securities (Section 8–102), or other certificates, statements, or the like are to be received by the drawee or other payor before acceptance or payment of the draft;

(7) "Draft" means a draft as defined in Section 3–104 or an item, other than an instrument, that is an order;

(8) "Drawee" means a person ordered in a draft to make payment;

(9) "Item" means an instrument or a promise or order to pay money handled by a bank for collection or payment. The term does not include a payment order governed by Article 4A or a credit or debit card slip;

(10) "Midnight deadline" with respect to a bank is midnight on its next banking day following the banking day on which it receives the relevant item or notice or from which the time for taking action commences to run, whichever is later;

(11) "Settle" means to pay in cash, by clearing-house settlement, in a charge or credit or by remittance, or otherwise as agreed. A settlement may be either provisional or final;

(12) "Suspends payments" with respect to a bank means that it has been closed by order of the supervisory authorities, that a public officer has been appointed to take it over, or that it ceases or refuses to make payments in the ordinary course of business.

(b) [Other definitions' section references deleted.]

(c) [Other definitions' section references deleted.]

(d) In addition, Article 1 contains general definitions and principles of construction and interpretation applicable throughout this Article.

§ 4–105. "Bank"; "Depositary Bank"; "Payor Bank"; "Intermediary Bank"; "Collecting Bank"; "Presenting Bank".

In this Article:

(1) "Bank" means a person engaged in the business of banking, including a savings bank, savings and loan association, credit union, or trust company;

(2) "Depositary bank" means the first bank to take an item even though it is also the payor bank, unless the item is presented for immediate payment over the counter;

(3) "Payor bank" means a bank that is the drawee of a draft;

(4) "Intermediary bank" means a bank to which an item is transferred in course of collection except the depositary or payor bank;

(5) "Collecting bank" means a bank handling an item for collection except the payor bank;

(6) "Presenting bank" means a bank presenting an item except a payor bank.

§ 4–106. Payable Through or Payable at Bank: Collecting Bank.

(a) If an item states that it is "payable through" a bank identified in the item, (i) the item designates the bank as a collecting bank and does not by itself authorize the bank to pay the item, and (ii) the item may be presented for payment only by or through the bank.

Alternative A

(b) If an item states that it is "payable at" a bank identified in the item, the item is equivalent to a draft drawn on the bank.

Alternative B

(b) If an item states that it is "payable at" a bank identified in the item, (i) the item designates the bank as a collecting bank and does not by itself authorize the bank to pay the item, and (ii) the item may be presented for payment only by or through the bank.

(c) If a draft names a nonbank drawee and it is unclear whether a bank named in the draft is a co-drawee or a collecting bank, the bank is a collecting bank.

As added in 1990.

§ 4–107. Separate Office of Bank.

A branch or separate office of a bank is a separate bank for the purpose of computing the time within which and determining the place at or to which action may be taken or notices or orders shall be given under this Article and under Article 3.

As amended in 1962 and 1990.

§ 4–108. Time of Receipt of Items.

(a) For the purpose of allowing time to process items, prove balances, and make the necessary entries on its books to determine its position for the day, a bank may fix an afternoon hour of 2 p.m. or later as a cutoff hour for the handling of money and items and the making of entries on its books.

(b) An item or deposit of money received on any day after a cutoff hour so fixed or after the close of the banking day may be treated as being received at the opening of the next banking day.

As amended in 1990.

§ 4–109. Delays.

(a) Unless otherwise instructed, a collecting bank in a good faith effort to secure payment of a specific item drawn on a payor other than a bank, and with or without the approval of any person involved, may waive, modify, or extend time limits imposed or permitted by this [act] for a period not exceeding two additional banking days without discharge of drawers or indorsers or liability to its transferor or a prior party.

(b) Delay by a collecting bank or payor bank beyond time limits prescribed or permitted by this [act] or by instructions is excused if (i) the delay is caused by interruption of communication or computer facilities, suspension of payments by another bank, war, emergency conditions, failure of equipment, or other circumstances beyond the control of the bank, and (ii) the bank exercises such diligence as the circumstances require.

§ 4–110. Electronic Presentment.

(a) "Agreement for electronic presentment" means an agreement, clearing-house rule, or Federal Reserve regulation or operating circular, providing that presentment of an item may be made by transmission of an image of an item or information describing the item ("presentment notice") rather than delivery of the item itself. The agreement may provide for procedures governing retention, presentment, payment, dishonor, and other matters concerning items subject to the agreement.

(b) Presentment of an item pursuant to an agreement for presentment is made when the presentment notice is received.

(c) If presentment is made by presentment notice, a reference to "item" or "check" in this Article means the presentment notice unless the context otherwise indicates.

As added in 1990.

§ 4–111. Statute of Limitations.

An action to enforce an obligation, duty, or right arising under this Article must be commenced within three years after the [cause of action] accrues.

As added in 1990.

Part 2 Collection of Items: Depositary and Collecting Banks

§ 4–201. Status of Collecting Bank as Agent and Provisional Status of Credits; Applicability of Article; Item Indorsed "Pay Any Bank".

(a) Unless a contrary intent clearly appears and before the time that a settlement given by a collecting bank for an item is or becomes final, the bank, with respect to an item, is an agent or sub-agent of the owner of the item and any settlement given for the item is provisional. This provision applies regardless of the form of indorsement or lack of indorsement and even though credit given for the item is subject to immediate withdrawal as of right or is in fact withdrawn; but the continuance of ownership of an item by its owner and any rights of the owner to proceeds of the item are subject to rights of a collecting bank, such as those resulting from outstanding advances on the item and rights of recoupment or setoff. If an item is handled by banks for purposes of presentment, payment, collection, or return, the relevant provisions of this Article apply even though action of the parties clearly establishes that a particular bank has purchased the item and is the owner of it.

(b) After an item has been indorsed with the words "pay any bank" or the like, only a bank may acquire the rights of a holder until the item has been:

(1) returned to the customer initiating collection; or

(2) specially indorsed by a bank to a person who is not a bank.

As amended in 1990.

§ 4–202. Responsibility for Collection or Return; When Action Timely.

(a) A collecting bank must exercise ordinary care in:

(1) presenting an item or sending it for presentment;

(2) sending notice of dishonor or nonpayment or returning an item other than a documentary draft to the bank's transferor after learning that the item has not been paid or accepted, as the case may be;

(3) settling for an item when the bank receives final settlement; and

(4) notifying its transferor of any loss or delay in transit within a reasonable time after discovery thereof.

(b) A collecting bank exercises ordinary care under subsection (a) by taking proper action before its midnight deadline following receipt of an item, notice, or settlement. Taking proper action within a reasonably longer time may constitute the exercise of ordinary care, but the bank has the burden of establishing timeliness.

(c) Subject to subsection (a)(1), a bank is not liable for the insolvency, neglect, misconduct, mistake, or default of another bank or person or for loss or destruction of an item in the possession of others or in transit.

As amended in 1990.

§ 4–203. Effect of Instructions.

Subject to Article 3 concerning conversion of instruments (Section 3–420) and restrictive indorsements (Section 3–206), only a collecting bank's transferor can give instructions that affect the bank or constitute notice to it, and a collecting bank is not liable to prior parties for any action taken pursuant to the instructions or in accordance with any agreement with its transferor.

§ 4–204. Methods of Sending and Presenting; Sending Directly to Payor Bank.

(a) A collecting bank shall send items by a reasonably prompt method, taking into consideration relevant instructions, the nature of the item, the number of those items on hand, the cost of collection involved, and the method generally used by it or others to present those items.

(b) A collecting bank may send:

(1) an item directly to the payor bank;

(2) an item to a nonbank payor if authorized by its transferor; and

(3) an item other than documentary drafts to a nonbank payor, if authorized by Federal Reserve regulation or operating circular, clearing-house rule, or the like.

(c) Presentment may be made by a presenting bank at a place where the payor bank or other payor has requested that presentment be made.

As amended in 1990.

§ 4–205. Depositary Bank Holder of Unindorsed Item.

If a customer delivers an item to a depositary bank for collection:

(1) the depositary bank becomes a holder of the item at the time it receives the item for collection if the customer at the time of delivery was a holder of the item, whether or not the customer indorses the item, and, if the bank satisfies the other requirements of Section 3–302, it is a holder in due course; and

(2) the depositary bank warrants to collecting banks, the payor bank or other payor, and the drawer that the amount of the item was paid to the customer or deposited to the customer's account.

As amended in 1990.

§ 4–206. Transfer Between Banks.

Any agreed method that identifies the transferor bank is sufficient for the item's further transfer to another bank.

As amended in 1990.

§ 4–207. Transfer Warranties.

(a) A customer or collecting bank that transfers an item and receives a settlement or other consideration warrants to the transferee and to any subsequent collecting bank that:

(1) the warrantor is a person entitled to enforce the item;

(2) all signatures on the item are authentic and authorized;

(3) the item has not been altered;

(4) the item is not subject to a defense or claim in recoupment (Section 3–305(a)) of any party that can be asserted against the warrantor; and

(5) the warrantor has no knowledge of any insolvency proceeding commenced with respect to the maker or acceptor or, in the case of an unaccepted draft, the drawer.

(b) If an item is dishonored, a customer or collecting bank transferring the item and receiving settlement or other consideration is obliged to pay the amount due on the item (i) according to the terms of the item at the time it was transferred, or (ii) if the transfer was of an incomplete item, according to its terms when completed as stated in Sections 3–115 and 3–407. The obligation of a transferor is owed to the transferee and to any subsequent collecting bank that takes the item in good faith. A transferor cannot disclaim its obligation under this subsection by an indorsement stating that it is made "without recourse" or otherwise disclaiming liability.

(c) A person to whom the warranties under subsection (a) are made and who took the item in good faith may recover from the warrantor as damages for breach of warranty an amount equal to the loss suffered as a result of the breach, but not more than the amount of the item plus expenses and loss of interest incurred as a result of the breach.

(d) The warranties stated in subsection (a) cannot be disclaimed with respect to checks. Unless notice of a claim for breach of warranty is given to the warrantor within 30 days after the claimant has reason to know of the breach and the identity of the warrantor, the warrantor is discharged to the extent of any loss caused by the delay in giving notice of the claim.

(e) A cause of action for breach of warranty under this section accrues when the claimant has reason to know of the breach.

As amended in 1990.

§ 4–208. Presentment Warranties.

(a) If an unaccepted draft is presented to the drawee for payment or acceptance and the drawee pays or accepts the draft, (i) the person obtaining payment or acceptance, at the time of presentment, and (ii) a previous transferor of the draft, at the time of transfer, warrant to the drawee that pays or accepts the draft in good faith that:

(1) the warrantor is, or was, at the time the warrantor transferred the draft, a person entitled to enforce the draft or authorized to obtain payment or acceptance of the draft on behalf of a person entitled to enforce the draft;

(2) the draft has not been altered; and

(3) the warrantor has no knowledge that the signature of the purported drawer of the draft is unauthorized.

(b) A drawee making payment may recover from a warrantor damages for breach of warranty equal to the amount paid by the drawee less the amount the drawee received or is entitled to receive from the drawer because of the payment. In addition, the drawee is entitled to compensation for expenses and loss of interest resulting from the breach. The right of the drawee to recover damages under this subsection is not affected by any failure of the drawee to exercise ordinary care in making payment. If the drawee accepts the draft (i) breach of warranty is a defense to the obligation of the acceptor, and (ii) if the acceptor makes payment with respect to the draft, the acceptor is entitled to recover from a warrantor for breach of warranty the amounts stated in this subsection.

(c) If a drawee asserts a claim for breach of warranty under subsection (a) based on an unauthorized indorsement of the draft or an alteration of the draft, the warrantor may defend by proving that the indorsement is effective under Section 3–404 or 3–405 or the drawer is precluded under Section 3–406 or 4–406 from asserting against the drawee the unauthorized indorsement or alteration.

(d) If (i) a dishonored draft is presented for payment to the drawer or an indorser or (ii) any other item is presented for payment to a party obliged to pay the item, and the item is paid, the person obtaining payment and a prior transferor of the item warrant to the person making payment in good faith that the warrantor is, or was, at the time the warrantor transferred the item, a person entitled to enforce the item or authorized to obtain payment on behalf of a person entitled to enforce the item. The person making payment may recover from any warrantor for breach of warranty an amount equal to the amount paid plus expenses and loss of interest resulting from the breach.

(e) The warranties stated in subsections (a) and (d) cannot be disclaimed with respect to checks. Unless notice of a claim for breach of warranty is given to the warrantor within 30 days after the claimant has reason to know of the breach and the identity of the warrantor, the warrantor is discharged to the extent of any loss caused by the delay in giving notice of the claim.

(f) A cause of action for breach of warranty under this section accrues when the claimant has reason to know of the breach.

As amended in 1990.

§ 4–209. Encoding and Retention Warranties.

(a) A person who encodes information on or with respect to an item after issue warrants to any subsequent collecting bank and to the payor bank or other payor that the information is correctly encoded. If the customer of a depositary bank encodes, that bank also makes the warranty.

(b) A person who undertakes to retain an item pursuant to an agreement for electronic presentment warrants to any subsequent collecting bank and to the payor bank or other payor that retention and presentment of the item comply with the agreement. If a customer of a depositary bank undertakes to retain an item, that bank also makes this warranty.

(c) A person to whom warranties are made under this section and who took the item in good faith may recover from the warrantor as damages for breach of warranty an amount equal to the loss suffered as a result of the breach, plus expenses and loss of interest incurred as a result of the breach.

As added in 1990.

§ 4–210. Security Interest of Collecting Bank in Items, Accompanying Documents and Proceeds.

(a) A collecting bank has a security interest in an item and any accompanying documents or the proceeds of either:

(1) in case of an item deposited in an account, to the extent to which credit given for the item has been withdrawn or applied;

(2) in case of an item for which it has given credit available for withdrawal as of right, to the extent of the credit given, whether or not the credit is drawn upon or there is a right of charge-back; or

(3) if it makes an advance on or against the item.

(b) If credit given for several items received at one time or pursuant to a single agreement is withdrawn or applied in part, the security interest remains upon all the items, any accompanying documents or the proceeds of either. For the purpose of this section, credits first given are first withdrawn.

(c) Receipt by a collecting bank of a final settlement for an item is a realization on its security interest in the item, accompanying documents, and proceeds. So long as the bank does not receive final settlement for the item or give up possession of the item or accompanying documents for purposes other than collection, the security interest continues to that extent and is subject to Article 9, but:

(1) no security agreement is necessary to make the security interest enforceable (Section 9–203(1)(a));

(2) no filing is required to perfect the security interest; and

(3) the security interest has priority over conflicting perfected security interests in the item, accompanying documents, or proceeds.

As amended in 1990 and 1999.

§ 4–211. When Bank Gives Value for Purposes of Holder in Due Course.

For purposes of determining its status as a holder in due course, a bank has given value to the extent it has a security interest in an item, if the bank otherwise complies with the requirements of Section 3–302 on what constitutes a holder in due course.

As amended in 1990.

§ 4–212. Presentment by Notice of Item Not Payable by, Through, or at Bank; Liability of Drawer or Indorser.

(a) Unless otherwise instructed, a collecting bank may present an item not payable by, through, or at a bank by sending to the party to accept or pay a written notice that the bank holds the item for acceptance or payment. The notice must be sent in time to be received on or before the day when presentment is due and the bank must meet any requirement of the party to accept or pay under Section 3–501 by the close of the bank's next banking day after it knows of the requirement.

(b) If presentment is made by notice and payment, acceptance, or request for compliance with a requirement under Section 3–501 is not received by the close of business on the day after maturity or, in the case of demand items, by the close of business on the third banking day after notice was sent, the presenting bank may treat the item as dishonored and charge any drawer or indorser by sending it notice of the facts.

As amended in 1990.

§ 4–213. Medium and Time of Settlement by Bank.

(a) With respect to settlement by a bank, the medium and time of settlement may be prescribed by Federal Reserve regulations or circulars, clearing-house rules, and the like, or agreement. In the absence of such prescription:

(1) the medium of settlement is cash or credit to an account in a Federal Reserve bank of or specified by the person to receive settlement; and

(2) the time of settlement is:

(i) with respect to tender of settlement by cash, a cashier's check, or teller's check, when the cash or check is sent or delivered;

(ii) with respect to tender of settlement by credit in an account in a Federal Reserve Bank, when the credit is made;

(iii) with respect to tender of settlement by a credit or debit to an account in a bank, when the credit or debit is made or, in the case of tender of settlement by authority to charge an account, when the authority is sent or delivered; or

(iv) with respect to tender of settlement by a funds transfer, when payment is made pursuant to Section 4A–406(a) to the person receiving settlement.

(b) If the tender of settlement is not by a medium authorized by subsection (a) or the time of settlement is not fixed by subsection (a), no settlement occurs until the tender of settlement is accepted by the person receiving settlement.

(c) If settlement for an item is made by cashier's check or teller's check and the person receiving settlement, before its midnight deadline:

(1) presents or forwards the check for collection, settlement is final when the check is finally paid; or

(2) fails to present or forward the check for collection, settlement is final at the midnight deadline of the person receiving settlement.

(d) If settlement for an item is made by giving authority to charge the account of the bank giving settlement in the bank receiving settlement, settlement is final when the charge is made by the bank receiving settlement if there are funds available in the account for the amount of the item.

As amended in 1990.

§ 4–214. Right of Charge-Back or Refund; Liability of Collecting Bank: Return of Item.

(a) If a collecting bank has made provisional settlement with its customer for an item and fails by reason of dishonor, suspension of payments by a bank, or otherwise to receive settlement for the item which is or becomes final, the bank may revoke the settlement given by it, charge back the amount of any credit given for the item to its customer's account, or obtain refund from its customer, whether or not it is able to return the item, if by its midnight deadline or within a longer reasonable time after it learns the facts it returns the item or sends notification of the facts. If the return or notice is delayed beyond the bank's midnight deadline or a longer reasonable time after it learns the facts, the bank may revoke the settlement, charge back the credit, or obtain refund from its customer, but it is liable for any loss resulting from the delay. These rights to revoke, charge back, and obtain refund terminate if and when a settlement for the item received by the bank is or becomes final.

(b) A collecting bank returns an item when it is sent or delivered to the bank's customer or transferor or pursuant to its instructions.

(c) A depositary bank that is also the payor may charge back the amount of an item to its customer's account or obtain refund in accordance with the section governing return of an item received by a payor bank for credit on its books (Section 4–301).

(d) The right to charge back is not affected by:

(1) previous use of a credit given for the item; or

(2) failure by any bank to exercise ordinary care with respect to the item, but a bank so failing remains liable.

(e) A failure to charge back or claim refund does not affect other rights of the bank against the customer or any other party.

(f) If credit is given in dollars as the equivalent of the value of an item payable in foreign money, the dollar amount of any charge-back or refund must be calculated on the basis of the bank-offered spot rate for the foreign money prevailing on the day when the person entitled to the charge-back or refund learns that it will not receive payment in ordinary course.

As amended in 1990.

§ 4–215. Final Payment of Item by Payor Bank; When Provisional Debits and Credits Become Final; When Certain Credits Become Available for Withdrawal.

(a) An item is finally paid by a payor bank when the bank has first done any of the following:

(1) paid the item in cash;

(2) settled for the item without having a right to revoke the settlement under statute, clearing-house rule, or agreement; or

(3) made a provisional settlement for the item and failed to revoke the settlement in the time and manner permitted by statute, clearing-house rule, or agreement.

(b) If provisional settlement for an item does not become final, the item is not finally paid.

(c) If provisional settlement for an item between the presenting and payor banks is made through a clearing house or by debits or credits in an account between them, then to the extent that provisional debits or credits for the item are entered in accounts between the presenting and payor banks or between the presenting and successive prior collecting banks seriatim, they become final upon final payment of the item by the payor bank.

(d) If a collecting bank receives a settlement for an item which is or becomes final, the bank is accountable to its customer for the amount of the item and any provisional credit given for the item in an account with its customer becomes final.

(e) Subject to (i) applicable law stating a time for availability of funds and (ii) any right of the bank to apply the credit to an obligation of the customer, credit given by a bank for an item in a customer's account becomes available for withdrawal as of right:

(1) if the bank has received a provisional settlement for the item, when the settlement becomes final and the bank has had a reasonable time to receive return of the item and the item has not been received within that time;

(2) if the bank is both the depositary bank and the payor bank, and the item is finally paid, at the opening of the bank's second banking day following receipt of the item.

(f) Subject to applicable law stating a time for availability of funds and any right of a bank to apply a deposit to an obligation of the depositor, a deposit of money becomes available for withdrawal as of right at the opening of the bank's next banking day after receipt of the deposit.

As amended in 1990.

§ 4–216. Insolvency and Preference.

(a) If an item is in or comes into the possession of a payor or collecting bank that suspends payment and the item has not been finally paid, the item must be returned by the receiver, trustee, or agent in charge of the closed bank to the presenting bank or the closed bank's customer.

(b) If a payor bank finally pays an item and suspends payments without making a settlement for the item with its customer or the presenting bank which settlement is or becomes final, the owner of the item has a preferred claim against the payor bank.

(c) If a payor bank gives or a collecting bank gives or receives a provisional settlement for an item and thereafter suspends payments, the suspension does not prevent or interfere with the settlement's becoming final if the finality occurs automatically upon the lapse of certain time or the happening of certain events.

(d) If a collecting bank receives from subsequent parties settlement for an item, which settlement is or becomes final and the bank suspends payments without making a settlement for the item with its customer which settlement is or becomes final, the owner of the item has a preferred claim against the collecting bank.

As amended in 1990.

Part 3 Collection of Items: Payor Banks

§ 4–301. Deferred Posting; Recovery of Payment by Return of Items; Time of Dishonor; Return of Items by Payor Bank.

(a) If a payor bank settles for a demand item other than a documentary draft presented otherwise than for immediate payment over the counter before midnight of the banking day of receipt, the payor bank may revoke the settlement and recover the settlement if, before it has made final payment and before its midnight deadline, it

(1) returns the item; or

(2) sends written notice of dishonor or nonpayment if the item is unavailable for return.

(b) If a demand item is received by a payor bank for credit on its books, it may return the item or send notice of dishonor and may revoke any credit given or recover the amount thereof withdrawn by its customer, if it acts within the time limit and in the manner specified in subsection (a).

(c) Unless previous notice of dishonor has been sent, an item is dishonored at the time when for purposes of dishonor it is returned or notice sent in accordance with this section.

(d) An item is returned:

(1) as to an item presented through a clearing house, when it is delivered to the presenting or last collecting bank or to the clearing house or is sent or delivered in accordance with clearing-house rules; or

(2) in all other cases, when it is sent or delivered to the bank's customer or transferor or pursuant to instructions.

As amended in 1990.

§ 4–302. Payor Bank's Responsibility for Late Return of Item.

(a) If an item is presented to and received by a payor bank, the bank is accountable for the amount of:

(1) a demand item, other than a documentary draft, whether properly payable or not, if the bank, in any case in which it is not also the depositary bank, retains the item beyond midnight of the banking day of receipt without settling for it or, whether or not it is also the depositary bank, does not pay or return the item or send notice of dishonor until after its midnight deadline; or

(2) any other properly payable item unless, within the time allowed for acceptance or payment of that item, the bank either accepts or pays the item or returns it and accompanying documents.

(b) The liability of a payor bank to pay an item pursuant to subsection (a) is subject to defenses based on breach of a presentment warranty (Section 4–208) or proof that the person seeking enforcement of the liability presented or transferred the item for the purpose of defrauding the payor bank.

As amended in 1990.

§ 4–303. When Items Subject to Notice, Stop-Payment Order, Legal Process, or Setoff; Order in Which Items May Be Charged or Certified.

(a) Any knowledge, notice, or stop-payment order received by, legal process served upon, or setoff exercised by a payor bank comes too late to terminate, suspend, or modify the bank's right or duty to pay an item or to charge its customer's account for the item if the knowledge, notice, stop-payment order, or legal process is received or served and a reasonable time for the bank to act thereon expires or the setoff is exercised after the earliest of the following:

(1) the bank accepts or certifies the item;

(2) the bank pays the item in cash;

(3) the bank settles for the item without having a right to revoke the settlement under statute, clearing-house rule, or agreement;

(4) the bank becomes accountable for the amount of the item under Section 4–302 dealing with the payor bank's responsibility for late return of items; or

(5) with respect to checks, a cutoff hour no earlier than one hour after the opening of the next banking day after the banking day on which the bank received the check and no later than the close of that next banking day or, if no cutoff hour is fixed, the close of the next banking day after the banking day on which the bank received the check.

(b) Subject to subsection (a), items may be accepted, paid, certified, or charged to the indicated account of its customer in any order.

As amended in 1990.

Part 4 Relationship Between Payor Bank and Its Customer

§ 4–401. When Bank May Charge Customer's Account.

(a) A bank may charge against the account of a customer an item that is properly payable from the account even though the charge creates an overdraft. An item is properly payable if it is authorized by the customer and is in accordance with any agreement between the customer and bank.

(b) A customer is not liable for the amount of an overdraft if the customer neither signed the item nor benefited from the proceeds of the item.

(c) A bank may charge against the account of a customer a check that is otherwise properly payable from the account, even though payment was made before the date of the check, unless the customer has given notice to the bank of the postdating describing the check with reasonable certainty. The notice is effective for the period stated in Section 4–403(b) for stop-payment orders, and must be received at such time and in such manner as to afford the bank a reasonable opportunity to act on it before the bank takes any action with respect to the check described in Section 4–303. If a bank charges against the account of a customer a check before the date stated in the notice of postdating, the bank is liable for damages for the loss resulting from its act. The loss may include damages for dishonor of subsequent items under Section 4–402.

(d) A bank that in good faith makes payment to a holder may charge the indicated account of its customer according to:

(1) the original terms of the altered item; or

(2) the terms of the completed item, even though the bank knows the item has been completed unless the bank has notice that the completion was improper.

As amended in 1990.

§ 4–402. Bank's Liability to Customer for Wrongful Dishonor; Time of Determining Insufficiency of Account.

(a) Except as otherwise provided in this Article, a payor bank wrongfully dishonors an item if it dishonors an item that is properly payable, but a bank may dishonor an item that would create an overdraft unless it has agreed to pay the overdraft.

(b) A payor bank is liable to its customer for damages proximately caused by the wrongful dishonor of an item. Liability is limited to actual damages proved and may include damages for an arrest or prosecution of the customer or other consequential damages. Whether any consequential damages are proximately caused by the wrongful dishonor is a question of fact to be determined in each case.

(c) A payor bank's determination of the customer's account balance on which a decision to dishonor for insufficiency of available funds is based may be made at any time between the time the item is received by the payor bank and the time that the payor bank returns the item or gives notice in lieu of return, and no more than one determination need be made. If, at the election of the payor bank, a subsequent balance determination is made for the purpose of reevaluating the bank's decision to dishonor the item, the account balance at that time is determinative of whether a dishonor for insufficiency of available funds is wrongful.

As amended in 1990.

§ 4–403. Customer's Right to Stop Payment; Burden of Proof of Loss.

(a) A customer or any person authorized to draw on the account if there is more than one person may stop payment of any item drawn on the customer's account or close the account by an order to the bank describing the item or account with reasonable certainty received at a time and in a manner that affords the bank a reasonable opportunity to act on it before any action by the bank with respect to the item described in Section 4–303. If the signature of more than one person is required to draw on an account, any of these persons may stop payment or close the account.

(b) A stop-payment order is effective for six months, but it lapses after 14 calendar days if the original order was oral and was not confirmed in writing within that period. A stop-payment order may be renewed for additional six-month periods by a writing given to the bank within a period during which the stop-payment order is effective.

(c) The burden of establishing the fact and amount of loss resulting from the payment of an item contrary to a stop-payment order or order to close an account is on the customer. The loss from payment of an item contrary to a stop-payment order may include damages for dishonor of subsequent items under Section 4–402.

As amended in 1990.

§ 4–404. Bank Not Obliged to Pay Check More Than Six Months Old.

A bank is under no obligation to a customer having a checking account to pay a check, other than a certified check, which is presented more than six months after its date, but it may charge its customer's account for a payment made thereafter in good faith.

§ 4–405. Death or Incompetence of Customer.

(a) A payor or collecting bank's authority to accept, pay, or collect an item or to account for proceeds of its collection, if otherwise effective, is not rendered ineffective by incompetence of a customer of either bank existing at the time the item is issued or its collection is undertaken if the bank does not know of an adjudication of incompetence. Neither death nor incompetence of a customer revokes the authority to accept, pay, collect, or account until the bank knows of the fact of death or of an adjudication of incompetence and has reasonable opportunity to act on it.

(b) Even with knowledge, a bank may for 10 days after the date of death pay or certify checks drawn on or before the date unless ordered to stop payment by a person claiming an interest in the account.

As amended in 1990.

§ 4–406. Customer's Duty to Discover and Report Unauthorized Signature or Alteration.

(a) A bank that sends or makes available to a customer a statement of account showing payment of items for the account shall either return or make available to the customer the items paid or provide information in the statement of account sufficient to allow the customer reasonably to identify the items paid. The statement of account provides sufficient information if the item is described by item number, amount, and date of payment.

(b) If the items are not returned to the customer, the person retaining the items shall either retain the items or, if the items are destroyed, maintain the capacity to furnish legible copies of the items until the expiration of seven years after receipt of the items. A customer may request an item from the bank that paid the item, and that bank must provide in a reasonable time either the item or, if the item has been destroyed or is not otherwise obtainable, a legible copy of the item.

(c) If a bank sends or makes available a statement of account or items pursuant to subsection (a), the customer must exercise reasonable promptness in examining the statement or the items to determine whether any payment was not authorized because of an alteration of an item or because a purported signature by or on behalf of the customer was not authorized. If, based on the statement or items provided, the customer should reasonably have discovered the unauthorized payment, the customer must promptly notify the bank of the relevant facts.

(d) If the bank proves that the customer failed, with respect to an item, to comply with the duties imposed on the customer by subsection (c), the customer is precluded from asserting against the bank:

(1) the customer's unauthorized signature or any alteration on the item, if the bank also proves that it suffered a loss by reason of the failure; and

(2) the customer's unauthorized signature or alteration by the same wrongdoer on any other item paid in good faith by the bank if the payment was made before the bank received notice from the customer of the unauthorized signature or alteration and after the customer had been afforded a reasonable period of time, not exceeding 30 days, in which to examine the item or statement of account and notify the bank.

(e) If subsection (d) applies and the customer proves that the bank failed to exercise ordinary care in paying the item and that the failure substantially contributed to loss, the loss is allocated between the customer precluded and the bank asserting the preclusion according to the extent to which the failure of the customer to comply with subsection (c) and the failure of the bank to exercise ordinary care contributed to the loss. If the customer proves that the bank did not pay the item in good faith, the preclusion under subsection (d) does not apply.

(f) Without regard to care or lack of care of either the customer or the bank, a customer who does not within one year after the statement or items are made available to the customer (subsection (a)) discover and report the customer's unauthorized signature on or any alteration on the item is precluded from asserting against the bank the unauthorized signature or alteration. If there is a preclusion under this subsection, the payor bank may not recover for breach or warranty under Section 4–208 with respect to the unauthorized signature or alteration to which the preclusion applies.

As amended in 1990.

§ 4–407. Payor Bank's Right to Subrogation on Improper Payment.

If a payor has paid an item over the order of the drawer or maker to stop payment, or after an account has been closed, or otherwise under circumstances giving a basis for objection by the drawer or maker, to prevent unjust enrichment and only to the extent necessary to prevent loss to the bank by reason of its payment of the item, the payor bank is subrogated to the rights

(1) of any holder in due course on the item against the drawer or maker;

(2) of the payee or any other holder of the item against the drawer or maker either on the item or under the transaction out of which the item arose; and

(3) of the drawer or maker against the payee or any other holder of the item with respect to the transaction out of which the item arose.

As amended in 1990.

Part 5 Collection of Documentary Drafts

§ 4–501. Handling of Documentary Drafts; Duty to Send for Presentment and to Notify Customer of Dishonor.

A bank that takes a documentary draft for collection shall present or send the draft and accompanying documents for presentment and, upon learning that the draft has not been paid or accepted in due course, shall seasonably notify its customer of the fact even though it may have discounted or bought the draft or extended credit available for withdrawal as of right.

As amended in 1990.

§ 4–502. Presentment of "On Arrival" Drafts.

If a draft or the relevant instructions require presentment "on arrival", "when goods arrive" or the like, the collecting bank need not present until in its judgment a reasonable time for arrival of the goods has expired. Refusal to pay or accept because the goods have not arrived is not dishonor; the bank must notify its transferor of the refusal but need not present the draft again until it is instructed to do so or learns of the arrival of the goods.

§ 4–503. Responsibility of Presenting Bank for Documents and Goods; Report of Reasons for Dishonor; Referee in Case of Need.

Unless otherwise instructed and except as provided in Article 5, a bank presenting a documentary draft:

(1) must deliver the documents to the drawee on acceptance of the draft if it is payable more than three days after presentment, otherwise, only on payment; and

(2) upon dishonor, either in the case of presentment for acceptance or presentment for payment, may seek and follow instructions from any referee in case of need designated in the draft or, if the presenting bank does not choose to utilize the referee's services, it must use diligence and good faith to ascertain the reason for dishonor, must notify its transferor of the dishonor and of the results of its effort to ascertain the reasons therefor, and must request instructions.

However, the presenting bank is under no obligation with respect to goods represented by the documents except to follow any reasonable instructions seasonably received; it has a right to reimbursement for any expense incurred in following instructions and to prepayment of or indemnity for those expenses.

As amended in 1990.

§ 4–504. Privilege of Presenting Bank to Deal With Goods; Security Interest for Expenses.

(a) A presenting bank that, following the dishonor of a documentary draft, has seasonably requested instructions but does not receive them within a reasonable time may store, sell, or otherwise deal with the goods in any reasonable manner.

(b) For its reasonable expenses incurred by action under subsection (a) the presenting bank has a lien upon the goods or their proceeds, which may be foreclosed in the same manner as an unpaid seller's lien.

As amended in 1990.

Article 4A FUNDS TRANSFERS

Part 1 Subject Matter and Definitions

§ 4A–101. Short Title.

This Article may be cited as Uniform Commercial Code—Funds Transfers.

§ 4A–102. Subject Matter.

Except as otherwise provided in Section 4A–108, this Article applies to funds transfers defined in Section 4A–104.

§ 4A–103. Payment Order–Definitions.

(a) In this Article:

(1) "Payment order" means an instruction of a sender to a receiving bank, transmitted orally, electronically, or in writing, to pay, or to cause another bank to pay, a fixed or determinable amount of money to a beneficiary if:

(i) the instruction does not state a condition to payment to the beneficiary other than time of payment,

(ii) the receiving bank is to be reimbursed by debiting an account of, or otherwise receiving payment from, the sender, and

(iii) the instruction is transmitted by the sender directly to the receiving bank or to an agent, funds-transfer system, or communication system for transmittal to the receiving bank.

(2) "Beneficiary" means the person to be paid by the beneficiary's bank.

(3) "Beneficiary's bank" means the bank identified in a payment order in which an account of the beneficiary is to be credited pursuant to the order or which otherwise is to make payment to the beneficiary if the order does not provide for payment to an account.

(4) "Receiving bank" means the bank to which the sender's instruction is addressed.

(5) "Sender" means the person giving the instruction to the receiving bank.

(b) If an instruction complying with subsection (a)(1) is to make more than one payment to a beneficiary, the instruction is a separate payment order with respect to each payment.

(c) A payment order is issued when it is sent to the receiving bank.

§ 4A–104. Funds Transfer–Definitions.

In this Article:

(a) "Funds transfer" means the series of transactions, beginning with the originator's payment order, made for the purpose of making payment to the beneficiary of the order. The term includes any payment order issued by the originator's bank or an intermediary bank intended to carry out the originator's payment order. A funds transfer is completed by acceptance by the beneficiary's bank of a payment order for the benefit of the beneficiary of the originator's payment order.

(b) "Intermediary bank" means a receiving bank other than the originator's bank or the beneficiary's bank.

(c) "Originator" means the sender of the first payment order in a funds transfer.

(d) "Originator's bank" means (i) the receiving bank to which the payment order of the originator is issued if the originator is not a bank, or (ii) the originator if the originator is a bank.

§ 4A–105. Other Definitions.

(a) In this Article:

(1) "Authorized account" means a deposit account of a customer in a bank designated by the customer as a source of payment of payment orders issued by the customer to the bank. If a customer does not so designate an account, any account of the customer is an authorized account if payment of a payment order from that account is not inconsistent with a restriction on the use of that account.

(2) "Bank" means a person engaged in the business of banking and includes a savings bank, savings and loan association, credit union, and trust company. A branch or separate office of a bank is a separate bank for purposes of this Article.

(3) "Customer" means a person, including a bank, having an account with a bank or from whom a bank has agreed to receive payment orders.

(4) "Funds-transfer business day" of a receiving bank means the part of a day during which the receiving bank is open for the receipt, processing, and transmittal of payment orders and cancellations and amendments of payment orders.

(5) "Funds-transfer system" means a wire transfer network, automated clearing house, or other communication system of a clearing house or other association of banks through which a payment order by a bank may be transmitted to the bank to which the order is addressed.

(6) "Good faith" means honesty in fact and the observance of reasonable commercial standards of fair dealing.

(7) "Prove" with respect to a fact means to meet the burden of establishing the fact (Section 1–201(8)).

(b) Other definitions applying to this Article and the sections in which they appear are:

"Acceptance" Section 4A–209

"Beneficiary"	Section 4A–103
"Beneficiary's bank"	Section 4A–103
"Executed"	Section 4A–301
"Execution date"	Section 4A–301
"Funds transfer"	Section 4A–104
"Funds-transfer system rule"	Section 4A–501
"Intermediary bank"	Section 4A–104
"Originator"	Section 4A–104
"Originator's bank"	Section 4A–104
"Payment by beneficiary's bank to beneficiary"	Section 4A–405
"Payment by originator to beneficiary"	Section 4A–406
"Payment by sender to receiving bank"	Section 4A–403
"Payment date"	Section 4A–401
"Payment order"	Section 4A–103
"Receiving bank"	Section 4A–103
"Security procedure"	Section 4A–201
"Sender"	Section 4A–103

(c) The following definitions in Article 4 apply to this Article:

"Clearing house"	Section 4–104
"Item"	Section 4–104
"Suspends payments"	Section 4–104

(d) In addition, Article 1 contains general definitions and principles of construction and interpretation applicable throughout this Article.

§ 4A–106. Time Payment Order Is Received.

(a) The time of receipt of a payment order or communication cancelling or amending a payment order is determined by the rules applicable to receipt of a notice stated in Section 1–201(27). A receiving bank may fix a cut-off time or times on a funds-transfer business day for the receipt and processing of payment orders and communications cancelling or amending payment orders. Different cut-off times may apply to payment orders, cancellations, or amendments, or to different categories of payment orders, cancellations, or amendments. A cut-off time may apply to senders generally or different cut-off times may apply to different senders or categories of payment orders. If a payment order or communication cancelling or amending a payment order is received after the close of a funds-transfer business day or after the appropriate cut-off time on a funds-transfer business day, the receiving bank may treat the payment order or communication as received at the opening of the next funds-transfer business day.

(b) If this Article refers to an execution date or payment date or states a day on which a receiving bank is required to take action, and the date or day does not fall on a funds-transfer business day, the next day that is a funds-transfer business day is treated as the date or day stated, unless the contrary is stated in this Article.

§ 4A–107. Federal Reserve Regulations and Operating Circulars.

Regulations of the Board of Governors of the Federal Reserve System and operating circulars of the Federal Reserve Banks supersede any inconsistent provision of this Article to the extent of the inconsistency.

§ 4A–108. Exclusion of Consumer Transactions Governed by Federal Law.

This Article does not apply to a funds transfer any part of which is governed by the Electronic Fund Transfer Act of 1978 (Title XX, Public Law 95–630, 92 Stat. 3728, 15 U.S.C. § 1693 *et seq.*) as amended from time to time.

Part 2 Issue and Acceptance of Payment Order

§ 4A–201. Security Procedure.

"Security procedure" means a procedure established by agreement of a customer and a receiving bank for the purpose of (i) verifying that a payment order or communication amending or cancelling a payment order is that of the customer, or (ii) detecting error in the transmission or the content of the payment order or communication. A security procedure may require the use of algorithms or other codes, identifying words or numbers, encryption, callback procedures, or similar security devices. Comparison of a signature on a payment order or communication with an authorized specimen signature of the customer is not by itself a security procedure.

§ 4A–202. Authorized and Verified Payment Orders.

(a) A payment order received by the receiving bank is the authorized order of the person identified as sender if that person authorized the order or is otherwise bound by it under the law of agency.

(b) If a bank and its customer have agreed that the authenticity of payment orders issued to the bank in the name of the customer as sender will be verified pursuant to a security procedure, a payment order received by the receiving bank is effective as the order of the customer, whether or not authorized, if (i) the security procedure is a commercially reasonable method of providing security against unauthorized payment orders, and (ii) the bank proves that it accepted the payment order in good faith and in compliance with the security procedure and any written agreement or instruction of the customer restricting acceptance of payment orders issued in the name of the customer. The bank is not required to follow an instruction that violates a written agreement with the customer or notice of which is not received at a time and in a manner affording the bank a reasonable opportunity to act on it before the payment order is accepted.

(c) Commercial reasonableness of a security procedure is a question of law to be determined by considering the wishes of the customer expressed to the bank, the circumstances of the customer known to the bank, including the size, type, and frequency of payment orders normally issued by the customer to the bank, alternative security procedures offered to the customer, and security procedures in general use by customers and receiving banks similarly situated. A security procedure is deemed to be commercially reasonable if (i) the security procedure was chosen by the customer after the bank offered, and the customer refused, a security procedure that was commercially reasonable for that customer, and (ii) the customer expressly agreed in writing to be bound by any payment order, whether or not authorized, issued in its name and accepted by the bank in compliance with the security procedure chosen by the customer.

(d) The term "sender" in this Article includes the customer in whose name a payment order is issued if the order is the authorized order of the customer under subsection (a), or it is effective as the order of the customer under subsection (b).

(e) This section applies to amendments and cancellations of payment orders to the same extent it applies to payment orders.

(f) Except as provided in this section and in Section 4A–203(a)(1), rights and obligations arising under this section or Section 4A–203 may not be varied by agreement.

§ 4A–203. Unenforceability of Certain Verified Payment Orders.

(a) If an accepted payment order is not, under Section 4A–202(a), an authorized order of a customer identified as sender, but is effective as an order of the customer pursuant to Section 4A–202(b), the following rules apply:

(1) By express written agreement, the receiving bank may limit the extent to which it is entitled to enforce or retain payment of the payment order.

(2) The receiving bank is not entitled to enforce or retain payment of the payment order if the customer proves that the order was not caused, directly or indirectly, by a person (i) entrusted at any time with duties to act for the customer with respect to payment orders or the security procedure, or (ii) who obtained access to transmitting facilities of the customer or who obtained, from a source controlled by the customer and without authority of the receiving bank, information facilitating breach of the security procedure, regardless of how the information was obtained or whether the customer was at fault. Information includes any access device, computer software, or the like.

(b) This section applies to amendments of payment orders to the same extent it applies to payment orders.

§ 4A–204. Refund of Payment and Duty of Customer to Report with Respect to Unauthorized Payment Order.

(a) If a receiving bank accepts a payment order issued in the name of its customer as sender which is (i) not authorized and not effective as the order of the customer under Section 4A–202, or (ii) not enforceable, in whole or in part, against the customer under Section 4A–203, the bank shall refund any payment of the payment order received from the customer to the extent the bank is not entitled to enforce payment and shall pay interest on the refundable amount calculated from the date the bank received payment to the date of the refund. However, the customer is not entitled to interest from the bank on the amount to be refunded if the customer fails to exercise ordinary care to determine that the order was not authorized by the customer and to notify the bank of the relevant facts within a reasonable time not exceeding 90 days after the date the customer received notification from the bank that the order was accepted or that the customer's account was debited with respect to the order. The bank is not entitled to any recovery from the customer on account of a failure by the customer to give notification as stated in this section.

(b) Reasonable time under subsection (a) may be fixed by agreement as stated in Section 1–204(1), but the obligation of a receiving bank to refund payment as stated in subsection (a) may not otherwise be varied by agreement.

§ 4A–205. Erroneous Payment Orders.

(a) If an accepted payment order was transmitted pursuant to a security procedure for the detection of error and the payment order (i) erroneously instructed payment to a beneficiary not intended by the sender, (ii) erroneously instructed payment in an amount greater than the amount intended by the sender, or (iii) was an erroneously transmitted duplicate of a payment order previously sent by the sender, the following rules apply:

(1) If the sender proves that the sender or a person acting on behalf of the sender pursuant to Section 4A–206 complied with the security procedure and that the error would have been detected if the receiving bank had also complied, the sender is not obliged to pay the order to the extent stated in paragraphs (2) and (3).

(2) If the funds transfer is completed on the basis of an erroneous payment order described in clause (i) or (iii) of subsection (a), the sender is not obliged to pay the order and the receiving bank is entitled to recover from the beneficiary any amount paid to the beneficiary to the extent allowed by the law governing mistake and restitution.

(3) If the funds transfer is completed on the basis of a payment order described in clause (ii) of subsection (a), the sender is not obliged to pay the order to the extent the amount received by the beneficiary is greater than the amount intended by the sender. In that case, the receiving bank is entitled to recover from the beneficiary the excess amount received to the extent allowed by the law governing mistake and restitution.

(b) If (i) the sender of an erroneous payment order described in subsection (a) is not obliged to pay all or part of the order, and (ii) the sender receives notification from the receiving bank that the order was accepted by the bank or that the sender's account was debited with respect to the order, the sender has a duty to exercise ordinary care, on the basis of information available to the sender, to discover the error with respect to the order and to advise the bank of the relevant facts within a reasonable time, not exceeding 90 days, after the bank's notification was received by the sender. If the bank proves that the sender failed to perform that duty, the sender is liable to the bank for the loss the bank proves it incurred as a result of the failure, but the liability of the sender may not exceed the amount of the sender's order.

(c) This section applies to amendments to payment orders to the same extent it applies to payment orders.

§ 4A–206. Transmission of Payment Order through Funds-Transfer or Other Communication System.

(a) If a payment order addressed to a receiving bank is transmitted to a funds-transfer system or other third party communication system for transmittal to the bank, the system is deemed to be an agent of the sender for the purpose of transmitting the payment order to the bank. If there is a discrepancy between the terms of the payment order transmitted to the system and the terms of the payment order transmitted by the system to the bank, the terms of the payment order of the sender are those transmitted by the system. This section does not apply to a funds-transfer system of the Federal Reserve Banks.

(b) This section applies to cancellations and amendments to payment orders to the same extent it applies to payment orders.

§ 4A–207. Misdescription of Beneficiary.

(a) Subject to subsection (b), if, in a payment order received by the beneficiary's bank, the name, bank account number, or other identification of the beneficiary refers to a nonexistent or unidentifiable person or account, no person has rights as a beneficiary of the order and acceptance of the order cannot occur.

(b) If a payment order received by the beneficiary's bank identifies the beneficiary both by name and by an identifying or bank account number and the name and number identify different persons, the following rules apply:

(1) Except as otherwise provided in subsection (c), if the beneficiary's bank does not know that the name and number refer to different persons, it may rely on the number as the proper identification of the beneficiary of the order. The beneficiary's bank need not determine whether the name and number refer to the same person.

(2) If the beneficiary's bank pays the person identified by name or knows that the name and number identify different persons, no person has rights as beneficiary except the person paid by the beneficiary's bank if that person was entitled to receive payment from the originator of the funds transfer. If no person has rights as beneficiary, acceptance of the order cannot occur.

(c) If (i) a payment order described in subsection (b) is accepted, (ii) the originator's payment order described the beneficiary inconsistently by name and number, and (iii) the beneficiary's bank pays the person identified by number as permitted by subsection (b)(1), the following rules apply:

(1) If the originator is a bank, the originator is obliged to pay its order.

(2) If the originator is not a bank and proves that the person identified by number was not entitled to receive payment from the originator, the originator is not obliged to pay its order unless the originator's bank proves that the originator, before acceptance of the originator's order, had notice that payment of a payment order issued by the originator might be made by the beneficiary's bank on the basis of an identifying or bank account number even if it identifies a person different from the named beneficiary. Proof of notice may be made by any admissible evidence. The originator's bank satisfies the burden of proof if it proves that the originator, before the payment order was accepted, signed a writing stating the information to which the notice relates.

(d) In a case governed by subsection (b)(1), if the beneficiary's bank rightfully pays the person identified by number and that person was not entitled to receive payment from the originator, the amount paid may be recovered from that person to the extent allowed by the law governing mistake and restitution as follows:

(1) If the originator is obliged to pay its payment order as stated in subsection (c), the originator has the right to recover.

(2) If the originator is not a bank and is not obliged to pay its payment order, the originator's bank has the right to recover.

§ 4A–208. Misdescription of Intermediary Bank or Beneficiary's Bank.

(a) This subsection applies to a payment order identifying an intermediary bank or the beneficiary's bank only by an identifying number.

(1) The receiving bank may rely on the number as the proper identification of the intermediary or beneficiary's bank and need not determine whether the number identifies a bank.

(2) The sender is obliged to compensate the receiving bank for any loss and expenses incurred by the receiving bank as a result of its reliance on the number in executing or attempting to execute the order.

(b) This subsection applies to a payment order identifying an intermediary bank or the beneficiary's bank both by name and an identifying number if the name and number identify different persons.

(1) If the sender is a bank, the receiving bank may rely on the number as the proper identification of the intermediary or beneficiary's bank if the receiving bank, when it executes the sender's order, does not know that the name and number identify different persons. The receiving bank need not determine whether the name and number refer to the same person or whether the number refers to a bank. The sender is obliged to compensate the receiving bank for any loss and expenses incurred by the receiving bank as a result of its reliance on the number in executing or attempting to execute the order.

(2) If the sender is not a bank and the receiving bank proves that the sender, before the payment order was accepted, had notice that the receiving bank might rely on the number as the proper identification of the intermediary or beneficiary's bank even if it identifies a person different from the bank identified by name, the rights and obligations of the sender and the receiving bank are governed by subsection (b)(1), as though the sender were a bank. Proof of notice may be made by any admissible evidence. The receiving bank satisfies the burden of proof if it proves that the sender, before the payment order was accepted, signed a writing stating the information to which the notice relates.

(3) Regardless of whether the sender is a bank, the receiving bank may rely on the name as the proper identification of the

intermediary or beneficiary's bank if the receiving bank, at the time it executes the sender's order, does not know that the name and number identify different persons. The receiving bank need not determine whether the name and number refer to the same person.

(4) If the receiving bank knows that the name and number identify different persons, reliance on either the name or the number in executing the sender's payment order is a breach of the obligation stated in Section 4A–302(a)(1).

§ 4A–209. Acceptance of Payment Order.

(a) Subject to subsection (d), a receiving bank other than the beneficiary's bank accepts a payment order when it executes the order.

(b) Subject to subsections (c) and (d), a beneficiary's bank accepts a payment order at the earliest of the following times:

(1) When the bank (i) pays the beneficiary as stated in Section 4A–405(a) or 4A–405(b), or (ii) notifies the beneficiary of receipt of the order or that the account of the beneficiary has been credited with respect to the order unless the notice indicates that the bank is rejecting the order or that funds with respect to the order may not be withdrawn or used until receipt of payment from the sender of the order;

(2) When the bank receives payment of the entire amount of the sender's order pursuant to Section 4A–403(a)(1) or 4A–403(a)(2); or

(3) The opening of the next funds-transfer business day of the bank following the payment date of the order if, at that time, the amount of the sender's order is fully covered by a withdrawable credit balance in an authorized account of the sender or the bank has otherwise received full payment from the sender, unless the order was rejected before that time or is rejected within (i) one hour after that time, or (ii) one hour after the opening of the next business day of the sender following the payment date if that time is later. If notice of rejection is received by the sender after the payment date and the authorized account of the sender does not bear interest, the bank is obliged to pay interest to the sender on the amount of the order for the number of days elapsing after the payment date to the day the sender receives notice or learns that the order was not accepted, counting that day as an elapsed day. If the withdrawable credit balance during that period falls below the amount of the order, the amount of interest payable is reduced accordingly.

(c) Acceptance of a payment order cannot occur before the order is received by the receiving bank. Acceptance does not occur under subsection (b)(2) or (b)(3) if the beneficiary of the payment order does not have an account with the receiving bank, the account has been closed, or the receiving bank is not permitted by law to receive credits for the beneficiary's account.

(d) A payment order issued to the originator's bank cannot be accepted until the payment date if the bank is the beneficiary's bank, or the execution date if the bank is not the beneficiary's bank. If the originator's bank executes the originator's payment order before the execution date or pays the beneficiary of the originator's payment order before the payment date and the payment order is subsequently cancelled pursuant to Section 4A–211(b), the bank may recover from the beneficiary any payment received to the extent allowed by the law governing mistake and restitution.

§ 4A–210. Rejection of Payment Order.

(a) A payment order is rejected by the receiving bank by a notice of rejection transmitted to the sender orally, electronically, or in writing. A notice of rejection need not use any particular words and is sufficient if it indicates that the receiving bank is rejecting the order or will not execute or pay the order. Rejection is effective when the notice is given if transmission is by a means that is reasonable in the circumstances. If notice of rejection is given by a means that is not reasonable, rejection is effective when the notice is received. If an agreement of the sender and receiving bank establishes the means to be used to reject a payment order, (i) any means complying with the agreement is reasonable and (ii) any means not complying is not reasonable unless no significant delay in receipt of the notice resulted from the use of the noncomplying means.

(b) This subsection applies if a receiving bank other than the beneficiary's bank fails to execute a payment order despite the existence on the execution date of a withdrawable credit balance in an authorized account of the sender sufficient to cover the order. If the sender does not receive notice of rejection of the order on the execution date and the authorized account of the sender does not bear interest, the bank is obliged to pay interest to the sender on the amount of the order for the number of days elapsing after the execution date to the earlier of the day the order is cancelled pursuant to Section 4A–211(d) or the day the sender receives notice or learns that the order was not executed, counting the final day of the period as an elapsed day. If the withdrawable credit balance during that period falls below the amount of the order, the amount of interest is reduced accordingly.

(c) If a receiving bank suspends payments, all unaccepted payment orders issued to it are are deemed rejected at the time the bank suspends payments.

(d) Acceptance of a payment order precludes a later rejection of the order. Rejection of a payment order precludes a later acceptance of the order.

§ 4A–211. Cancellation and Amendment of Payment Order.

(a) A communication of the sender of a payment order cancelling or amending the order may be transmitted to the receiving bank orally, electronically, or in writing. If a security procedure is in effect between the sender and the receiving bank, the communication is not effective to cancel or amend the order unless the communication is verified pursuant to the security procedure or the bank agrees to the cancellation or amendment.

(b) Subject to subsection (a), a communication by the sender cancelling or amending a payment order is effective to cancel or amend the order if notice of the communication is received at a time and in a manner affording the receiving bank a reasonable opportunity to act on the communication before the bank accepts the payment order.

(c) After a payment order has been accepted, cancellation or amendment of the order is not effective unless the receiving bank agrees or a funds-transfer system rule allows cancellation or amendment without agreement of the bank.

(1) With respect to a payment order accepted by a receiving bank other than the beneficiary's bank, cancellation or amendment is not effective unless a conforming cancellation or amendment of the payment order issued by the receiving bank is also made.

(2) With respect to a payment order accepted by the beneficiary's bank, cancellation or amendment is not effective unless the order was issued in execution of an unauthorized payment order, or because of a mistake by a sender in the funds transfer which resulted in the issuance of a payment order (i) that is a duplicate of a payment order previously issued by the sender, (ii) that orders payment to a beneficiary not entitled to receive payment from the originator, or (iii) that orders payment in an amount greater than the amount the beneficiary was entitled to receive from the originator. If the payment order is cancelled or amended, the beneficiary's bank is entitled to recover from the beneficiary any amount paid to the beneficiary to the extent allowed by the law governing mistake and restitution.

(d) An unaccepted payment order is cancelled by operation of law at the close of the fifth funds-transfer business day of the receiving bank after the execution date or payment date of the order.

(e) A cancelled payment order cannot be accepted. If an accepted payment order is cancelled, the acceptance is nullified and no person has any right or obligation based on the acceptance. Amendment of a payment order is deemed to be cancellation of the original order at the time of amendment and issue of a new payment order in the amended form at the same time.

(f) Unless otherwise provided in an agreement of the parties or in a funds-transfer system rule, if the receiving bank, after accepting a payment order, agrees to cancellation or amendment of the order by the sender or is bound by a funds-transfer system rule allowing cancellation or amendment without the bank's agreement, the sender, whether or not cancellation or amendment is effective, is liable to the bank for any loss and expenses, including reasonable attorney's fees, incurred by the bank as a result of the cancellation or amendment or attempted cancellation or amendment.

(g) A payment order is not revoked by the death or legal incapacity of the sender unless the receiving bank knows of the death or of an adjudication of incapacity by a court of competent jurisdiction and has reasonable opportunity to act before acceptance of the order.

(h) A funds-transfer system rule is not effective to the extent it conflicts with subsection (c)(2).

§ 4A–212. Liability and Duty of Receiving Bank Regarding Unaccepted Payment Order.

If a receiving bank fails to accept a payment order that it is obliged by express agreement to accept, the bank is liable for breach of the agreement to the extent provided in the agreement or in this Article, but does not otherwise have any duty to accept a payment order or, before acceptance, to take any action, or refrain from taking action, with respect to the order except as provided in this Article or by express agreement. Liability based on acceptance arises only when acceptance occurs as stated in Section 4A–209, and liability is limited to that provided in this Article. A receiving bank is not the agent of the sender or beneficiary of the payment order it accepts, or of any other party to the funds transfer, and the bank owes no duty to any party to the funds transfer except as provided in this Article or by express agreement.

Part 3 Execution of Sender's Payment Order by Receiving Bank

§ 4A–301. Execution and Execution Date.

(a) A payment order is "executed" by the receiving bank when it issues a payment order intended to carry out the payment order received by the bank. A payment order received by the beneficiary's bank can be accepted but cannot be executed.

(b) "Execution date" of a payment order means the day on which the receiving bank may properly issue a payment order in execution of the sender's order. The execution date may be determined by instruction of the sender but cannot be earlier than the day the order is received and, unless otherwise determined, is the day the order is received. If the sender's instruction states a payment date, the execution date is the payment date or an earlier date on which execution is reasonably necessary to allow payment to the beneficiary on the payment date.

§ 4A–302. Obligations of Receiving Bank in Execution of Payment Order.

(a) Except as provided in subsections (b) through (d), if the receiving bank accepts a payment order pursuant to Section 4A–209(a), the bank has the following obligations in executing the order:

(1) The receiving bank is obliged to issue, on the execution date, a payment order complying with the sender's order and to follow the sender's instructions concerning (i) any intermediary bank or funds-transfer system to be used in carrying out the funds transfer, or (ii) the means by which payment orders are to be transmitted in the funds transfer. If the originator's bank issues a payment order to an intermediary bank, the originator's bank is obliged to instruct the intermediary bank according to the instruction of the originator. An intermediary bank in the funds transfer is similarly bound by an instruction given to it by the sender of the payment order it accepts.

(2) If the sender's instruction states that the funds transfer is to be carried out telephonically or by wire transfer or otherwise indicates that the funds transfer is to be carried out by the most expeditious means, the receiving bank is obliged to transmit its payment order by the most expeditious available means, and to instruct any intermediary bank accordingly. If a sender's instruction states a payment date, the receiving bank is obliged to transmit its payment order at a time and by means reasonably necessary to allow payment to the beneficiary on the payment date or as soon thereafter as is feasible.

(b) Unless otherwise instructed, a receiving bank executing a payment order may (i) use any funds-transfer system if use of that system is reasonable in the circumstances, and (ii) issue a payment order to the beneficiary's bank or to an intermediary bank through which a payment order conforming to the sender's order can expeditiously be issued to the beneficiary's bank if the receiving bank exercises ordinary care in the selection of the intermediary bank. A receiving bank is not required to follow an instruction of the sender designating a funds-transfer system to be used in carrying out the funds transfer if the receiving bank, in good faith, determines that it is not feasible to follow the instruction or that following the instruction would unduly delay completion of the funds transfer.

(c) Unless subsection (a)(2) applies or the receiving bank is otherwise instructed, the bank may execute a payment order by transmitting its payment order by first class mail or by any means reasonable in the circumstances. If the receiving bank is instructed to execute the sender's order by transmitting its payment order by a particular means, the receiving bank may issue its payment order by the means stated or by any means as expeditious as the means stated.

(d) Unless instructed by the sender, (i) the receiving bank may not obtain payment of its charges for services and expenses in connection with the execution of the sender's order by issuing a payment order in an amount equal to the amount of the sender's order less the amount of the charges, and (ii) may not instruct a subsequent receiving bank to obtain payment of its charges in the same manner.

§ 4A–303. Erroneous Execution of Payment Order.

(a) A receiving bank that (i) executes the payment order of the sender by issuing a payment order in an amount greater than the amount of the sender's order, or (ii) issues a payment order in execution of the sender's order and then issues a duplicate order, is entitled to payment of the amount of the sender's order under Section 4A–402(c) if that subsection is otherwise satisfied. The bank is entitled to recover from the beneficiary of the erroneous order the excess payment received to the extent allowed by the law governing mistake and restitution.

(b) A receiving bank that executes the payment order of the sender by issuing a payment order in an amount less than the amount of the sender's order is entitled to payment of the amount of the sender's order under Section 4A–402(c) if (i) that subsection is otherwise satisfied and (ii) the bank corrects its mistake by issuing an additional payment order for the benefit of the beneficiary of the sender's order. If the error is not corrected, the issuer of the erroneous order is entitled to receive or retain payment from the sender of the order it accepted only to the extent of the amount of the erroneous order. This subsection does not apply if the receiving bank executes the sender's payment order by issuing a payment order in an amount less than the amount of the sender's order for the purpose of obtaining payment of its charges for services and expenses pursuant to instruction of the sender.

(c) If a receiving bank executes the payment order of the sender by issuing a payment order to a beneficiary different from the beneficiary of the sender's order and the funds transfer is completed on the basis of that error, the sender of the payment order that was erroneously executed and all previous senders in the funds transfer are not obliged to pay the payment orders they issued. The issuer of the erroneous order is entitled to recover from the beneficiary of the order the payment received to the extent allowed by the law governing mistake and restitution.

§ 4A–304. Duty of Sender to Report Erroneously Executed Payment Order.

If the sender of a payment order that is erroneously executed as stated in Section 4A–303 receives notification from the receiving bank that the order was executed or that the sender's account was debited with respect to the order, the sender has a duty to exercise ordinary care to determine, on the basis of information available to the sender, that the order was erroneously executed and to notify the bank of the relevant facts within a reasonable time not exceeding 90 days after the notification from the bank was received by the sender. If the sender fails to perform that duty, the bank is not obliged to pay interest on any amount refundable to the sender under Section 4A–402(d) for the period before the bank learns of the execution error. The bank is not entitled to any recovery from the sender on account of a failure by the sender to perform the duty stated in this section.

§ 4A–305. Liability for Late or Improper Execution or Failure to Execute Payment Order.

(a) If a funds transfer is completed but execution of a payment order by the receiving bank in breach of Section 4A–302 results in delay in payment to the beneficiary, the bank is obliged to pay interest to either the originator or the beneficiary of the funds transfer for the period of delay caused by the improper execution. Except as provided in subsection (c), additional damages are not recoverable.

(b) If execution of a payment order by a receiving bank in breach of Section 4A–302 results in (i) noncompletion of the funds transfer, (ii) failure to use an intermediary bank designated by the originator, or (iii) issuance of a payment order that does not comply with the terms of the payment order of the originator, the bank is liable to the originator for its expenses in the funds transfer and for incidental expenses and interest losses, to the extent not covered by subsection (a), resulting from the improper execution. Except as provided in subsection (c), additional damages are not recoverable.

(c) In addition to the amounts payable under subsections (a) and (b), damages, including consequential damages, are recoverable to the extent provided in an express written agreement of the receiving bank.

(d) If a receiving bank fails to execute a payment order it was obliged by express agreement to execute, the receiving bank is liable to the sender for its expenses in the transaction and for incidental expenses and interest losses resulting from the failure to execute. Additional damages, including consequential damages, are recoverable to the extent provided in an express written agreement of the receiving bank, but are not otherwise recoverable.

(e) Reasonable attorney's fees are recoverable if demand for compensation under subsection (a) or (b) is made and refused before an action is brought on the claim. If a claim is made for breach of an agreement under subsection (d) and the agreement does not provide for damages, reasonable attorney's fees are recoverable if demand for compensation under subsection (d) is made and refused before an action is brought on the claim.

(f) Except as stated in this section, the liability of a receiving bank under subsections (a) and (b) may not be varied by agreement.

Part 4 Payment

§ 4A–401. Payment Date.

"Payment date" of a payment order means the day on which the amount of the order is payable to the beneficiary by the beneficiary's bank. The payment date may be determined by instruction of the sender but cannot be earlier than the day the order is received by the beneficiary's bank and, unless otherwise determined, is the day the order is received by the beneficiary's bank.

§ 4A–402. Obligation of Sender to Pay Receiving Bank.

(a) This section is subject to Sections 4A–205 and 4A–207.

(b) With respect to a payment order issued to the beneficiary's bank, acceptance of the order by the bank obliges the sender to pay the bank the amount of the order, but payment is not due until the payment date of the order.

(c) This subsection is subject to subsection (e) and to Section 4A–303. With respect to a payment order issued to a receiving bank other than the beneficiary's bank, acceptance of the order by the receiving bank obliges the sender to pay the bank the amount of the sender's order. Payment by the sender is not due until the execution date of the sender's order. The obligation of that sender to pay its payment order is excused if the funds transfer is not completed by acceptance by the beneficiary's bank of a payment order instructing payment to the beneficiary of that sender's payment order.

(d) If the sender of a payment order pays the order and was not obliged to pay all or part of the amount paid, the bank receiving payment is obliged to refund payment to the extent the sender was not obliged to pay. Except as provided in Sections 4A–204 and 4A–304, interest is payable on the refundable amount from the date of payment.

(e) If a funds transfer is not completed as stated in subsection (c) and an intermediary bank is obliged to refund payment as stated in subsection (d) but is unable to do so because not permitted by applicable law or because the bank suspends payments, a sender in the funds transfer that executed a payment order in compliance with an instruction, as stated in Section 4A–302(a)(1), to route the funds transfer through that intermediary bank is entitled to receive or retain payment from the sender of the payment order that it accepted. The first sender in the funds transfer that issued an instruction requiring routing through that intermediary bank is subrogated to the right of the bank that paid the intermediary bank to refund as stated in subsection (d).

(f) The right of the sender of a payment order to be excused from the obligation to pay the order as stated in subsection (c) or to receive refund under subsection (d) may not be varied by agreement.

§ 4A–403. Payment by Sender to Receiving Bank.

(a) Payment of the sender's obligation under Section 4A–402 to pay the receiving bank occurs as follows:

(1) If the sender is a bank, payment occurs when the receiving bank receives final settlement of the obligation through a Federal Reserve Bank or through a funds-transfer system.

(2) If the sender is a bank and the sender (i) credited an account of the receiving bank with the sender, or (ii) caused an account of the receiving bank in another bank to be credited, payment occurs when the credit is withdrawn or, if not withdrawn, at midnight of the day on which the credit is withdrawable and the receiving bank learns of that fact.

(3) If the receiving bank debits an account of the sender with the receiving bank, payment occurs when the debit is made to the extent the debit is covered by a withdrawable credit balance in the account.

(b) If the sender and receiving bank are members of a funds-transfer system that nets obligations multilaterally among participants, the receiving bank receives final settlement when settlement is complete in accordance with the rules of the system. The obligation of the sender to pay the amount of a payment order transmitted through the funds-transfer system may be satisfied, to the extent permitted by the rules of the system, by setting off and applying against the sender's obligation the right of the sender to receive payment from the receiving bank of the amount of any other payment order transmitted to the sender by the receiving bank through the funds-transfer system. The aggregate balance of obligations owed by each sender to each receiving bank in the funds-transfer system may be satisfied, to the extent permitted by the rules of the system, by setting off and applying against that balance the aggregate balance of obligations owed to the sender by other members of the system. The aggregate balance is determined after the right of setoff stated in the second sentence of this subsection has been exercised.

(c) If two banks transmit payment orders to each other under an agreement that settlement of the obligations of each bank to the other under Section 4A–402 will be made at the end of the day or other period, the total amount owed with respect to all orders transmitted by one bank shall be set off against the total amount owed with respect to all orders transmitted by the other bank. To the extent of the setoff, each bank has made payment to the other.

(d) In a case not covered by subsection (a), the time when payment of the sender's obligation under Section 4A–402(b) or 4A–402(c) occurs is governed by applicable principles of law that determine when an obligation is satisfied.

§ 4A–404. Obligation of Beneficiary's Bank to Pay and Give Notice to Beneficiary.

(a) Subject to Sections 4A–211(e), 4A–405(d), and 4A–405(e), if a beneficiary's bank accepts a payment order, the bank is obliged to pay the amount of the order to the beneficiary of the order. Payment is due on the payment date of the order, but if acceptance occurs on the payment date after the close of the funds-transfer business day of the bank, payment is due on the next funds-transfer business day. If the bank refuses to pay after demand by the beneficiary and receipt of notice of particular circumstances that will give rise to consequential damages as a result of nonpayment, the beneficiary may recover damages resulting from the refusal to pay to the extent the bank had notice of the damages, unless the bank proves that it did not pay because of a reasonable doubt concerning the right of the beneficiary to payment.

(b) If a payment order accepted by the beneficiary's bank instructs payment to an account of the beneficiary, the bank is obliged to notify the beneficiary of receipt of the order before midnight of the next funds-transfer business day following the payment date. If the payment order does not instruct payment to an account of the beneficiary, the bank is required to notify the beneficiary only if notice is required by the order. Notice may be given by first class mail or any other means reasonable in the circumstances. If the bank fails to give the required notice, the bank is obliged to pay interest to the beneficiary on the amount of the payment order from the day notice should have been given until the day the beneficiary learned of receipt of the payment order by the bank. No other damages are recoverable. Reasonable attorney's fees are also recoverable if demand for interest is made and refused before an action is brought on the claim.

(c) The right of a beneficiary to receive payment and damages as stated in subsection (a) may not be varied by agreement or a funds-transfer system rule. The right of a beneficiary to be notified as stated in subsection (b) may be varied by agreement of the beneficiary or by a funds-transfer system rule if the beneficiary is notified of the rule before initiation of the funds transfer.

§ 4A–405. Payment by Beneficiary's Bank to Beneficiary.

(a) If the beneficiary's bank credits an account of the beneficiary of a payment order, payment of the bank's obligation under Section 4A–404(a) occurs when and to the extent (i) the beneficiary is notified of the right to withdraw the credit, (ii) the bank lawfully applies the credit to a debt of the beneficiary, or (iii) funds with respect to the order are otherwise made available to the beneficiary by the bank.

(b) If the beneficiary's bank does not credit an account of the beneficiary of a payment order, the time when payment of the bank's obligation under Section 4A–404(a) occurs is governed by principles of law that determine when an obligation is satisfied.

(c) Except as stated in subsections (d) and (e), if the beneficiary's bank pays the beneficiary of a payment order under a condition to payment or agreement of the beneficiary giving the bank the right to recover payment from the beneficiary if the bank does not receive payment of the order, the condition to payment or agreement is not enforceable.

(d) A funds-transfer system rule may provide that payments made to beneficiaries of funds transfers made through the system are provisional until receipt of payment by the beneficiary's bank of the payment order it accepted. A beneficiary's bank that makes a payment that is provisional under the rule is entitled to refund from the beneficiary if (i) the rule requires that both the beneficiary and the originator be given notice of the provisional nature of the payment before the funds transfer is initiated, (ii) the beneficiary, the beneficiary's bank, and the originator's bank agreed to be bound by the rule, and (iii) the beneficiary's bank did not receive payment of the payment order that it accepted. If the beneficiary is obliged to refund payment to the beneficiary's bank, acceptance of the payment order by the beneficiary's bank is nullified and no payment by the originator of the funds transfer to the beneficiary occurs under Section 4A–406.

(e) This subsection applies to a funds transfer that includes a payment order transmitted over a funds-transfer system that (i) nets obligations multilaterally among participants, and (ii) has in effect a loss-sharing agreement among participants for the purpose of providing funds necessary to complete settlement of the obligations of one or more participants that do not meet their settlement obligations. If the beneficiary's bank in the funds transfer accepts a payment order and the system fails to complete settlement pursuant to its rules with respect to any payment order in the funds transfer, (i) the acceptance by the beneficiary's bank is nullified and no person has any right or obligation based on the acceptance, (ii) the beneficiary's bank is entitled to recover payment from the beneficiary, (iii) no payment by the originator to the beneficiary occurs under Section 4A–406, and (iv) subject to Section 4A–402(e), each sender in the funds transfer is excused from its obligation to pay its payment order under Section 4A–402(c) because the funds transfer has not been completed.

§ 4A–406. Payment by Originator to Beneficiary; Discharge of Underlying Obligation.

(a) Subject to Sections 4A–211(e), 4A–405(d), and 4A–405(e), the originator of a funds transfer pays the beneficiary of the originator's payment order (i) at the time a payment order for the benefit of the beneficiary is accepted by the beneficiary's bank in the funds transfer and (ii) in an amount equal to the amount of the order accepted by the beneficiary's bank, but not more than the amount of the originator's order.

(b) If payment under subsection (a) is made to satisfy an obligation, the obligation is discharged to the same extent discharge would result from payment to the beneficiary of the same amount in money, unless (i) the payment under subsection (a) was made by a means prohibited by the contract of the beneficiary with respect to the obligation, (ii) the beneficiary, within a reasonable time after receiving notice of receipt of the order by the beneficiary's bank, notified the originator of the beneficiary's refusal of the payment, (iii) funds with respect to the order were not withdrawn by the beneficiary or applied to a debt of the beneficiary, and (iv) the beneficiary would suffer a loss that could reasonably have been avoided if payment had been made by a means complying with the contract. If payment by the originator does not result in discharge under this section, the originator is subrogated to the rights of the beneficiary to receive payment from the beneficiary's bank under Section 4A–404(a).

(c) For the purpose of determining whether discharge of an obligation occurs under subsection (b), if the beneficiary's bank accepts a payment order in an amount equal to the amount of the originator's payment order less charges of one or more receiving banks in the funds transfer, payment to the beneficiary is deemed to be in the amount of the originator's order unless upon demand by the beneficiary the originator does not pay the beneficiary the amount of the deducted charges.

(d) Rights of the originator or of the beneficiary of a funds transfer under this section may be varied only by agreement of the originator and the beneficiary.

Part 5 Miscellaneous Provisions

§ 4A–501. Variation by Agreement and Effect of Funds-Transfer System Rule.

(a) Except as otherwise provided in this Article, the rights and obligations of a party to a funds transfer may be varied by agreement of the affected party.

(b) "Funds-transfer system rule" means a rule of an association of banks (i) governing transmission of payment orders by means of a funds-transfer system of the association or rights and obligations with respect to those orders, or (ii) to the extent the rule governs rights and obligations between banks that are parties to a funds transfer in which a Federal Reserve Bank, acting as an intermediary bank, sends a payment order to the beneficiary's bank. Except as otherwise provided in this Article, a funds-transfer system rule governing rights and obligations between participating banks using the system may be effective even if the rule conflicts with this Article and indirectly affects another party to the funds transfer who does not consent to the rule. A funds-transfer system rule may also govern rights and obligations of parties other than participating banks using the system to the extent stated in Sections 4A–404(c), 4A–405(d), and 4A–507(c).

§ 4A–502. Creditor Process Served on Receiving Bank; Setoff by Beneficiary's Bank.

(a) As used in this section, "creditor process" means levy, attachment, garnishment, notice of lien, sequestration, or similar process issued by or on behalf of a creditor or other claimant with respect to an account.

(b) This subsection applies to creditor process with respect to an authorized account of the sender of a payment order if the creditor process is served on the receiving bank. For the purpose of determining rights with respect to the creditor process, if the receiving bank accepts the payment order the balance in the authorized account is deemed to be reduced by the amount of the payment order to the extent the bank did not otherwise receive payment of the order, unless the creditor process is served at a time and in a manner affording the bank a reasonable opportunity to act on it before the bank accepts the payment order.

(c) If a beneficiary's bank has received a payment order for payment to the beneficiary's account in the bank, the following rules apply:

(1) The bank may credit the beneficiary's account. The amount credited may be set off against an obligation owed by the beneficiary to the bank or may be applied to satisfy creditor process served on the bank with respect to the account.

(2) The bank may credit the beneficiary's account and allow withdrawal of the amount credited unless creditor process with respect to the account is served at a time and in a manner affording the bank a reasonable opportunity to act to prevent withdrawal.

(3) If creditor process with respect to the beneficiary's account has been served and the bank has had a reasonable opportunity to act on it, the bank may not reject the payment order except for a reason unrelated to the service of process.

(d) Creditor process with respect to a payment by the originator to the beneficiary pursuant to a funds transfer may be served only on the beneficiary's bank with respect to the debt owed by that bank to the beneficiary. Any other bank served with the creditor process is not obliged to act with respect to the process.

§ 4A–503. Injunction or Restraining Order with Respect to Funds Transfer.

For proper cause and in compliance with applicable law, a court may restrain (i) a person from issuing a payment order to initiate a funds transfer, (ii) an originator's bank from executing the payment order of the originator, or (iii) the beneficiary's bank from releasing funds to the beneficiary or the beneficiary from withdrawing the funds. A court may not otherwise restrain a person from issuing a payment order, paying or receiving payment of a payment order, or otherwise acting with respect to a funds transfer.

§ 4A–504. Order in Which Items and Payment Orders May Be Charged to Account; Order of Withdrawals from Account.

(a) If a receiving bank has received more than one payment order of the sender or one or more payment orders and other items that are payable from the sender's account, the bank may charge the sender's account with respect to the various orders and items in any sequence.

(b) In determining whether a credit to an account has been withdrawn by the holder of the account or applied to a debt of the holder of the account, credits first made to the account are first withdrawn or applied.

§ 4A–505. Preclusion of Objection to Debit of Customer's Account.

If a receiving bank has received payment from its customer with respect to a payment order issued in the name of the customer as sender and accepted by the bank, and the customer received notification reasonably identifying the order, the customer is precluded from asserting that the bank is not entitled to retain the payment unless the customer notifies the bank of the customer's objection to the payment within one year after the notification was received by the customer.

§ 4A–506. Rate of Interest.

(a) If, under this Article, a receiving bank is obliged to pay interest with respect to a payment order issued to the bank, the amount payable may be determined (i) by agreement of the sender and receiving bank, or (ii) by a funds-transfer system rule if the payment order is transmitted through a funds-transfer system.

(b) If the amount of interest is not determined by an agreement or rule as stated in subsection (a), the amount is calculated by multiplying the applicable Federal Funds rate by the amount on which interest is payable, and then multiplying the product by the number of days for which interest is payable. The applicable Federal Funds rate is the average of the Federal Funds rates published by the Federal Reserve Bank of New York for each of the days for which interest is payable divided by 360. The Federal Funds rate for any day on which a published rate is not available is the same as the published rate for the next preceding day for which there is a published rate. If a receiving bank that accepted a payment order is required to refund payment to the sender of the order because the funds transfer was not completed, but the failure to complete was not due to any fault by the bank, the interest payable is reduced by a percentage equal to the reserve requirement on deposits of the receiving bank.

§ 4A–507. Choice of Law.

(a) The following rules apply unless the affected parties otherwise agree or subsection (c) applies:

(1) The rights and obligations between the sender of a payment order and the receiving bank are governed by the law of the jurisdiction in which the receiving bank is located.

(2) The rights and obligations between the beneficiary's bank and the beneficiary are governed by the law of the jurisdiction in which the beneficiary's bank is located.

(3) The issue of when payment is made pursuant to a funds transfer by the originator to the beneficiary is governed by the law of the jurisdiction in which the beneficiary's bank is located.

(b) If the parties described in each paragraph of subsection (a) have made an agreement selecting the law of a particular jurisdiction to govern rights and obligations between each other, the law of that jurisdiction governs those rights and obligations, whether or not the payment order or the funds transfer bears a reasonable relation to that jurisdiction.

(c) A funds-transfer system rule may select the law of a particular jurisdiction to govern (i) rights and obligations between participating banks with respect to payment orders transmitted or processed through the system, or (ii) the rights and obligations of some or all parties to a funds transfer any part of which is carried out by means of the system. A choice of law made pursuant to clause (i) is binding on participating banks. A choice of law made pursuant to clause (ii) is binding on the originator, other sender, or a receiving bank having notice that the funds-transfer system might be used in the funds transfer and of the choice of law by the system when the originator, other sender, or receiving bank issued or accepted a payment order. The beneficiary of a funds transfer is bound by the choice of law if, when the funds transfer is initiated, the beneficiary has notice that the funds-transfer system might be used in the funds transfer and of the choice of law by the system. The law of a jurisdiction selected pursuant to this subsection may govern, whether or not that law bears a reasonable relation to the matter in issue.

(d) In the event of inconsistency between an agreement under subsection (b) and a choice-of-law rule under subsection (c), the agreement under subsection (b) prevails.

(e) If a funds transfer is made by use of more than one funds-transfer system and there is inconsistency between choice-of-law rules of the systems, the matter in issue is governed by the law of the selected jurisdiction that has the most significant relationship to the matter in issue.

* * * *

Revised Article 9 SECURED TRANSACTIONS

Part 1 General Provisions

[Subpart 1. Short Title, Definitions, and General Concepts]

§ 9–101. Short Title.

This article may be cited as Uniform Commercial Code—Secured Transactions.

§ 9–102. Definitions and Index of Definitions.

(a) In this article:

(1) "Accession" means goods that are physically united with other goods in such a manner that the identity of the original goods is not lost.

(2) "Account", except as used in "account for", means a right to payment of a monetary obligation, whether or not earned by performance, (i) for property that has been or is to be sold, leased, licensed, assigned, or otherwise disposed of, (ii) for services rendered or to be rendered, (iii) for a policy of insurance issued or to be issued, (iv) for a secondary obligation incurred or to be incurred, (v) for energy provided or to be provided, (vi) for the use or hire of a vessel under a charter or other contract, (vii) arising out of the use of a credit or charge card or information contained on or for use with the card, or (viii) as winnings in a lottery or other game of chance operated or sponsored by a State, governmental unit of a State, or person licensed or authorized to operate the game by a State or governmental unit of a State. The term includes health-care insurance receivables. The term does not include (i) rights to payment evidenced by chattel paper or an instrument, (ii) commercial tort claims, (iii) deposit accounts, (iv) investment property, (v) letter-of-credit rights or letters of credit, or (vi) rights to payment for money or funds advanced or sold, other than rights arising out of the use of a credit or charge card or information contained on or for use with the card.

(3) "Account debtor" means a person obligated on an account, chattel paper, or general intangible. The term does not include persons obligated to pay a negotiable instrument, even if the instrument constitutes part of chattel paper.

(4) "Accounting", except as used in "accounting for", means a record:

(A) authenticated by a secured party;

(B) indicating the aggregate unpaid secured obligations as of a date not more than 35 days earlier or 35 days later than the date of the record; and

(C) identifying the components of the obligations in reasonable detail.

(5) "Agricultural lien" means an interest, other than a security interest, in farm products:

(A) which secures payment or performance of an obligation for:

(i) goods or services furnished in connection with a debtor's farming operation; or

(ii) rent on real property leased by a debtor in connection with its farming operation;

(B) which is created by statute in favor of a person that:

(i) in the ordinary course of its business furnished goods or services to a debtor in connection with a debtor's farming operation; or

(ii) leased real property to a debtor in connection with the debtor's farming operation; and

(C) whose effectiveness does not depend on the person's possession of the personal property.

(6) "As-extracted collateral" means:

(A) oil, gas, or other minerals that are subject to a security interest that:

(i) is created by a debtor having an interest in the minerals before extraction; and

(ii) attaches to the minerals as extracted; or

(B) accounts arising out of the sale at the wellhead or minehead of oil, gas, or other minerals in which the debtor had an interest before extraction.

(7) "Authenticate" means:

(A) to sign; or

(B) to execute or otherwise adopt a symbol, or encrypt or similarly process a record in whole or in part, with the present intent of the authenticating person to identify the person and adopt or accept a record.

(8) "Bank" means an organization that is engaged in the business of banking. The term includes savings banks, savings and loan associations, credit unions, and trust companies.

(9) "Cash proceeds" means proceeds that are money, checks, deposit accounts, or the like.

(10) "Certificate of title" means a certificate of title with respect to which a statute provides for the security interest in question to be indicated on the certificate as a condition or result of the security interest's obtaining priority over the rights of a lien creditor with respect to the collateral.

(11) "Chattel paper" means a record or records that evidence both a monetary obligation and a security interest in specific goods, a security interest in specific goods and software used in the goods, a security interest in specific goods and license of software used in the goods, a lease of specific goods, or a lease of specific goods and license of software used in the goods. In this paragraph, "monetary obligation" means a monetary obligation secured by the goods or owed under a lease of the goods and includes a monetary obligation with respect to software used in the goods. The term does not include (i) charters or other contracts involving the use or hire of a vessel or (ii) records that evidence a right to payment arising out of the use of a credit or charge card or information contained on or for use with the card. If a transaction is evidenced by records that include an instrument or series of instruments, the group of records taken together constitutes chattel paper.

(12) "Collateral" means the property subject to a security interest or agricultural lien. The term includes:

(A) proceeds to which a security interest attaches;

(B) accounts, chattel paper, payment intangibles, and promissory notes that have been sold; and

(C) goods that are the subject of a consignment.

(13) "Commercial tort claim" means a claim arising in tort with respect to which:

(A) the claimant is an organization; or

(B) the claimant is an individual and the claim:

(i) arose in the course of the claimant's business or profession; and

(ii) does not include damages arising out of personal injury to or the death of an individual.

(14) "Commodity account" means an account maintained by a commodity intermediary in which a commodity contract is carried for a commodity customer.

(15) "Commodity contract" means a commodity futures contract, an option on a commodity futures contract, a commodity option, or another contract if the contract or option is:

(A) traded on or subject to the rules of a board of trade that has been designated as a contract market for such a contract pursuant to federal commodities laws; or

(B) traded on a foreign commodity board of trade, exchange, or market, and is carried on the books of a commodity intermediary for a commodity customer.

(16) "Commodity customer" means a person for which a commodity intermediary carries a commodity contract on its books.

(17) "Commodity intermediary" means a person that:

(A) is registered as a futures commission merchant under federal commodities law; or

(B) in the ordinary course of its business provides clearance or settlement services for a board of trade that has been designated as a contract market pursuant to federal commodities law.

(18) "Communicate" means:

(A) to send a written or other tangible record;

(B) to transmit a record by any means agreed upon by the persons sending and receiving the record; or

(C) in the case of transmission of a record to or by a filing office, to transmit a record by any means prescribed by filing-office rule.

(19) "Consignee" means a merchant to which goods are delivered in a consignment.

(20) "Consignment" means a transaction, regardless of its form, in which a person delivers goods to a merchant for the purpose of sale and:

(A) the merchant:

(i) deals in goods of that kind under a name other than the name of the person making delivery;

(ii) is not an auctioneer; and

(iii) is not generally known by its creditors to be substantially engaged in selling the goods of others;

(B) with respect to each delivery, the aggregate value of the goods is $1,000 or more at the time of delivery;

(C) the goods are not consumer goods immediately before delivery; and

(D) the transaction does not create a security interest that secures an obligation.

(21) "Consignor" means a person that delivers goods to a consignee in a consignment.

(22) "Consumer debtor" means a debtor in a consumer transaction.

(23) "Consumer goods" means goods that are used or bought for use primarily for personal, family, or household purposes.

(24) "Consumer-goods transaction" means a consumer transaction in which:

(A) an individual incurs an obligation primarily for personal, family, or household purposes; and

(B) a security interest in consumer goods secures the obligation.

(25) "Consumer obligor" means an obligor who is an individual and who incurred the obligation as part of a transaction entered into primarily for personal, family, or household purposes.

(26) "Consumer transaction" means a transaction in which (i) an individual incurs an obligation primarily for personal, family, or household purposes, (ii) a security interest secures the obligation, and (iii) the collateral is held or acquired primarily for personal, family, or household purposes. The term includes consumer-goods transactions.

(27) "Continuation statement" means an amendment of a financing statement which:

(A) identifies, by its file number, the initial financing statement to which it relates; and

(B) indicates that it is a continuation statement for, or that it is filed to continue the effectiveness of, the identified financing statement.

(28) "Debtor" means:

(A) a person having an interest, other than a security interest or other lien, in the collateral, whether or not the person is an obligor;

(B) a seller of accounts, chattel paper, payment intangibles, or promissory notes; or

(C) a consignee.

(29) "Deposit account" means a demand, time, savings, passbook, or similar account maintained with a bank. The term does not include investment property or accounts evidenced by an instrument.

(30) "Document" means a document of title or a receipt of the type described in Section 7–201(2).

(31) "Electronic chattel paper" means chattel paper evidenced by a record or records consisting of information stored in an electronic medium.

(32) "Encumbrance" means a right, other than an ownership interest, in real property. The term includes mortgages and other liens on real property.

(33) "Equipment" means goods other than inventory, farm products, or consumer goods.

(34) "Farm products" means goods, other than standing timber, with respect to which the debtor is engaged in a farming operation and which are:

(A) crops grown, growing, or to be grown, including:

(i) crops produced on trees, vines, and bushes; and

(ii) aquatic goods produced in aquacultural operations;

(B) livestock, born or unborn, including aquatic goods produced in aquacultural operations;

(C) supplies used or produced in a farming operation; or

(D) products of crops or livestock in their unmanufactured states.

(35) "Farming operation" means raising, cultivating, propagating, fattening, grazing, or any other farming, livestock, or aquacultural operation.

(36) "File number" means the number assigned to an initial financing statement pursuant to Section 9–519(a).

(37) "Filing office" means an office designated in Section 9–501 as the place to file a financing statement.

(38) "Filing-office rule" means a rule adopted pursuant to Section 9–526.

(39) "Financing statement" means a record or records composed of an initial financing statement and any filed record relating to the initial financing statement.

(40) "Fixture filing" means the filing of a financing statement covering goods that are or are to become fixtures and satisfying Section 9–502(a) and (b). The term includes the filing of a financing statement covering goods of a transmitting utility which are or are to become fixtures.

(41) "Fixtures" means goods that have become so related to particular real property that an interest in them arises under real property law.

(42) "General intangible" means any personal property, including things in action, other than accounts, chattel paper, commercial tort claims, deposit accounts, documents, goods, instruments, investment property, letter-of-credit rights, letters of credit, money, and oil, gas, or other minerals before extraction. The term includes payment intangibles and software.

(43) "Good faith" means honesty in fact and the observance of reasonable commercial standards of fair dealing.

(44) "Goods" means all things that are movable when a security interest attaches. The term includes (i) fixtures, (ii) standing timber that is to be cut and removed under a conveyance or contract for sale, (iii) the unborn young of animals, (iv) crops grown, growing, or to be grown, even if the crops are produced on trees, vines, or bushes, and (v) manufactured homes. The term also includes a computer program embedded in goods and any supporting information provided in connection with a transaction relating to the program if (i) the program is associated with the goods in such a manner that it customarily is considered part of the goods, or (ii) by becoming the owner of the goods, a person acquires a right to use the program in connection with the goods. The term does not include a computer program embedded in goods that consist solely of the medium in which the program is embedded. The term also does not include accounts, chattel paper, commercial tort claims, deposit accounts, documents, general intangibles, instruments, investment property, letter-of-credit rights, letters of credit, money, or oil, gas, or other minerals before extraction.

(45) "Governmental unit" means a subdivision, agency, department, county, parish, municipality, or other unit of the government of the United States, a State, or a foreign country. The term includes an organization having a separate corporate existence if the organization is eligible to issue debt on which interest is exempt from income taxation under the laws of the United States.

(46) "Health-care-insurance receivable" means an interest in or claim under a policy of insurance which is a right to payment of a monetary obligation for health-care goods or services provided.

(47) "Instrument" means a negotiable instrument or any other writing that evidences a right to the payment of a monetary obligation, is not itself a security agreement or lease, and is of a type that in ordinary course of business is transferred by delivery with any necessary indorsement or assignment. The term does not include (i) investment property, (ii) letters of credit, or (iii) writings that evidence a right to payment arising out of the use of a credit or charge card or information contained on or for use with the card.

(48) "Inventory" means goods, other than farm products, which:

(A) are leased by a person as lessor;

(B) are held by a person for sale or lease or to be furnished under a contract of service;

(C) are furnished by a person under a contract of service; or

(D) consist of raw materials, work in process, or materials used or consumed in a business.

(49) "Investment property" means a security, whether certificated or uncertificated, security entitlement, securities account, commodity contract, or commodity account.

(50) "Jurisdiction of organization", with respect to a registered organization, means the jurisdiction under whose law the organization is organized.

(51) "Letter-of-credit right" means a right to payment or performance under a letter of credit, whether or not the beneficiary has demanded or is at the time entitled to demand payment or performance. The term does not include the right of a beneficiary to demand payment or performance under a letter of credit.

(52) "Lien creditor" means:

(A) a creditor that has acquired a lien on the property involved by attachment, levy, or the like;

(B) an assignee for benefit of creditors from the time of assignment;

(C) a trustee in bankruptcy from the date of the filing of the petition; or

(D) a receiver in equity from the time of appointment.

(53) "Manufactured home" means a structure, transportable in one or more sections, which, in the traveling mode, is eight body feet or more in width or 40 body feet or more in length, or, when erected on site, is 320 or more square feet, and which is built on a permanent chassis and designed to be used as a dwelling with or without a permanent foundation when connected to the required utilities, and includes the plumbing, heating, air-conditioning, and electrical systems contained therein. The term includes any structure that meets all of the requirements of this paragraph except the size requirements and with respect to which the manufacturer voluntarily files a certification required by the United States Secretary of Housing and Urban Development and complies with the standards established under Title 42 of the United States Code.

(54) "Manufactured-home transaction" means a secured transaction:

(A) that creates a purchase-money security interest in a manufactured home, other than a manufactured home held as inventory; or

(B) in which a manufactured home, other than a manufactured home held as inventory, is the primary collateral.

(55) "Mortgage" means a consensual interest in real property, including fixtures, which secures payment or performance of an obligation.

(56) "New debtor" means a person that becomes bound as debtor under Section 9–203(d) by a security agreement previously entered into by another person.

(57) "New value" means (i) money, (ii) money's worth in property, services, or new credit, or (iii) release by a transferee of

an interest in property previously transferred to the transferee. The term does not include an obligation substituted for another obligation.

(58) "Noncash proceeds" means proceeds other than cash proceeds.

(59) "Obligor" means a person that, with respect to an obligation secured by a security interest in or an agricultural lien on the collateral, (i) owes payment or other performance of the obligation, (ii) has provided property other than the collateral to secure payment or other performance of the obligation, or (iii) is otherwise accountable in whole or in part for payment or other performance of the obligation. The term does not include issuers or nominated persons under a letter of credit.

(60) "Original debtor", except as used in Section 9–310(c), means a person that, as debtor, entered into a security agreement to which a new debtor has become bound under Section 9–203(d).

(61) "Payment intangible" means a general intangible under which the account debtor's principal obligation is a monetary obligation.

(62) "Person related to", with respect to an individual, means:

(A) the spouse of the individual;

(B) a brother, brother-in-law, sister, or sister-in-law of the individual;

(C) an ancestor or lineal descendant of the individual or the individual's spouse; or

(D) any other relative, by blood or marriage, of the individual or the individual's spouse who shares the same home with the individual.

(63) "Person related to", with respect to an organization, means:

(A) a person directly or indirectly controlling, controlled by, or under common control with the organization;

(B) an officer or director of, or a person performing similar functions with respect to, the organization;

(C) an officer or director of, or a person performing similar functions with respect to, a person described in subparagraph (A);

(D) the spouse of an individual described in subparagraph (A), (B), or (C); or

(E) an individual who is related by blood or marriage to an individual described in subparagraph (A), (B), (C), or (D) and shares the same home with the individual.

(64) "Proceeds", except as used in Section 9–609(b), means the following property:

(A) whatever is acquired upon the sale, lease, license, exchange, or other disposition of collateral;

(B) whatever is collected on, or distributed on account of, collateral;

(C) rights arising out of collateral;

(D) to the extent of the value of collateral, claims arising out of the loss, nonconformity, or interference with the use of, defects or infringement of rights in, or damage to, the collateral; or

(E) to the extent of the value of collateral and to the extent payable to the debtor or the secured party, insurance payable by reason of the loss or nonconformity of, defects or infringement of rights in, or damage to, the collateral.

(65) "Promissory note" means an instrument that evidences a promise to pay a monetary obligation, does not evidence an order to pay, and does not contain an acknowledgment by a bank that the bank has received for deposit a sum of money or funds.

(66) "Proposal" means a record authenticated by a secured party which includes the terms on which the secured party is willing to accept collateral in full or partial satisfaction of the obligation it secures pursuant to Sections 9–620, 9–621, and 9–622.

(67) "Public-finance transaction" means a secured transaction in connection with which:

(A) debt securities are issued;

(B) all or a portion of the securities issued have an initial stated maturity of at least 20 years; and

(C) the debtor, obligor, secured party, account debtor or other person obligated on collateral, assignor or assignee of a secured obligation, or assignor or assignee of a security interest is a State or a governmental unit of a State.

(68) "Pursuant to commitment", with respect to an advance made or other value given by a secured party, means pursuant to the secured party's obligation, whether or not a subsequent event of default or other event not within the secured party's control has relieved or may relieve the secured party from its obligation.

(69) "Record", except as used in "for record", "of record", "record or legal title", and "record owner", means information that is inscribed on a tangible medium or which is stored in an electronic or other medium and is retrievable in perceivable form.

(70) "Registered organization" means an organization organized solely under the law of a single State or the United States and as to which the State or the United States must maintain a public record showing the organization to have been organized.

(71) "Secondary obligor" means an obligor to the extent that:

(A) the obligor's obligation is secondary; or

(B) the obligor has a right of recourse with respect to an obligation secured by collateral against the debtor, another obligor, or property of either.

(72) "Secured party" means:

(A) a person in whose favor a security interest is created or provided for under a security agreement, whether or not any obligation to be secured is outstanding;

(B) a person that holds an agricultural lien;

(C) a consignor;

(D) a person to which accounts, chattel paper, payment intangibles, or promissory notes have been sold;

(E) a trustee, indenture trustee, agent, collateral agent, or other representative in whose favor a security interest or agricultural lien is created or provided for; or

(F) a person that holds a security interest arising under Section 2–401, 2–505, 2–711(3), 2A–508(5), 4–210, or 5–118.

(73) "Security agreement" means an agreement that creates or provides for a security interest.

(74) "Send", in connection with a record or notification, means:

(A) to deposit in the mail, deliver for transmission, or transmit by any other usual means of communication, with postage or cost of transmission provided for, addressed to any address reasonable under the circumstances; or

(B) to cause the record or notification to be received within the time that it would have been received if properly sent under subparagraph (A).

(75) "Software" means a computer program and any supporting information provided in connection with a transaction relating to the program. The term does not include a computer program that is included in the definition of goods.

(76) "State" means a State of the United States, the District of Columbia, Puerto Rico, the United States Virgin Islands, or any territory or insular possession subject to the jurisdiction of the United States.

(77) "Supporting obligation" means a letter-of-credit right or secondary obligation that supports the payment or performance of an account, chattel paper, a document, a general intangible, an instrument, or investment property.

(78) "Tangible chattel paper" means chattel paper evidenced by a record or records consisting of information that is inscribed on a tangible medium.

(79) "Termination statement" means an amendment of a financing statement which:

(A) identifies, by its file number, the initial financing statement to which it relates; and

(B) indicates either that it is a termination statement or that the identified financing statement is no longer effective.

(80) "Transmitting utility" means a person primarily engaged in the business of:

(A) operating a railroad, subway, street railway, or trolley bus;

(B) transmitting communications electrically, electromagnetically, or by light;

(C) transmitting goods by pipeline or sewer; or

(D) transmitting or producing and transmitting electricity, steam, gas, or water.

(b) The following definitions in other articles apply to this article:

"Applicant."	Section 5–102
"Beneficiary."	Section 5–102
"Broker."	Section 8–102
"Certificated security."	Section 8–102
"Check."	Section 3–104
"Clearing corporation."	Section 8–102
"Contract for sale."	Section 2–106
"Customer."	Section 4–104
"Entitlement holder."	Section 8–102
"Financial asset."	Section 8–102
"Holder in due course."	Section 3–302
"Issuer" (with respect to a letter of credit or letter-of-credit right).	Section 5–102
"Issuer" (with respect to a security).	Section 8–201
"Lease."	Section 2A–103
"Lease agreement."	Section 2A–103
"Lease contract."	Section 2A–103
"Leasehold interest."	Section 2A–103
"Lessee."	Section 2A–103
"Lessee in ordinary course of business."	Section 2A–103
"Lessor."	Section 2A–103
"Lessor's residual interest."	Section 2A–103
"Letter of credit."	Section 5–102
"Merchant."	Section 2–104
"Negotiable instrument."	Section 3–104
"Nominated person."	Section 5–102
"Note."	Section 3–104
"Proceeds of a letter of credit."	Section 5–114
"Prove."	Section 3–103
"Sale."	Section 2–106
"Securities account."	Section 8–501
"Securities intermediary."	Section 8–102
"Security."	Section 8–102
"Security certificate."	Section 8–102
"Security entitlement."	Section 8–102
"Uncertificated security."	Section 8–102

(c) Article 1 contains general definitions and principles of construction and interpretation applicable throughout this article.

Amended in 1999 and 2000.

§ 9–103. Purchase-Money Security Interest; Application of Payments; Burden of Establishing.

(a) In this section:

(1) "purchase-money collateral" means goods or software that secures a purchase-money obligation incurred with respect to that collateral; and

(2) "purchase-money obligation" means an obligation of an obligor incurred as all or part of the price of the collateral or for value given to enable the debtor to acquire rights in or the use of the collateral if the value is in fact so used.

(b) A security interest in goods is a purchase-money security interest:

(1) to the extent that the goods are purchase-money collateral with respect to that security interest;

(2) if the security interest is in inventory that is or was purchase-money collateral, also to the extent that the security interest secures a purchase-money obligation incurred with respect to other inventory in which the secured party holds or held a purchase-money security interest; and

(3) also to the extent that the security interest secures a purchase-money obligation incurred with respect to software in which the secured party holds or held a purchase-money security interest.

(c) A security interest in software is a purchase-money security interest to the extent that the security interest also secures a purchase-money obligation incurred with respect to goods in which the secured party holds or held a purchase-money security interest if:

(1) the debtor acquired its interest in the software in an integrated transaction in which it acquired an interest in the goods; and

(2) the debtor acquired its interest in the software for the principal purpose of using the software in the goods.

(d) The security interest of a consignor in goods that are the subject of a consignment is a purchase-money security interest in inventory.

(e) In a transaction other than a consumer-goods transaction, if the extent to which a security interest is a purchase-money security interest depends on the application of a payment to a particular obligation, the payment must be applied:

(1) in accordance with any reasonable method of application to which the parties agree;

(2) in the absence of the parties' agreement to a reasonable method, in accordance with any intention of the obligor manifested at or before the time of payment; or

(3) in the absence of an agreement to a reasonable method and a timely manifestation of the obligor's intention, in the following order:

(A) to obligations that are not secured; and

(B) if more than one obligation is secured, to obligations secured by purchase-money security interests in the order in which those obligations were incurred.

(f) In a transaction other than a consumer-goods transaction, a purchase-money security interest does not lose its status as such, even if:

(1) the purchase-money collateral also secures an obligation that is not a purchase-money obligation;

(2) collateral that is not purchase-money collateral also secures the purchase-money obligation; or

(3) the purchase-money obligation has been renewed, refinanced, consolidated, or restructured.

(g) In a transaction other than a consumer-goods transaction, a secured party claiming a purchase-money security interest has the burden of establishing the extent to which the security interest is a purchase-money security interest.

(h) The limitation of the rules in subsections (e), (f), and (g) to transactions other than consumer-goods transactions is intended to leave to the court the determination of the proper rules in consumer-goods transactions. The court may not infer from that limitation the nature of the proper rule in consumer-goods transactions and may continue to apply established approaches.

§ 9–104. Control of Deposit Account.

(a) A secured party has control of a deposit account if:

(1) the secured party is the bank with which the deposit account is maintained;

(2) the debtor, secured party, and bank have agreed in an authenticated record that the bank will comply with instructions originated by the secured party directing disposition of the funds in the deposit account without further consent by the debtor; or

(3) the secured party becomes the bank's customer with respect to the deposit account.

(b) A secured party that has satisfied subsection (a) has control, even if the debtor retains the right to direct the disposition of funds from the deposit account.

§ 9–105. Control of Electronic Chattel Paper.

A secured party has control of electronic chattel paper if the record or records comprising the chattel paper are created, stored, and assigned in such a manner that:

(1) a single authoritative copy of the record or records exists which is unique, identifiable and, except as otherwise provided in paragraphs (4), (5), and (6), unalterable;

(2) the authoritative copy identifies the secured party as the assignee of the record or records;

(3) the authoritative copy is communicated to and maintained by the secured party or its designated custodian;

(4) copies or revisions that add or change an identified assignee of the authoritative copy can be made only with the participation of the secured party;

(5) each copy of the authoritative copy and any copy of a copy is readily identifiable as a copy that is not the authoritative copy; and

(6) any revision of the authoritative copy is readily identifiable as an authorized or unauthorized revision.

§ 9–106. Control of Investment Property.

(a) A person has control of a certificated security, uncertificated security, or security entitlement as provided in Section 8–106.

(b) A secured party has control of a commodity contract if:

(1) the secured party is the commodity intermediary with which the commodity contract is carried; or

(2) the commodity customer, secured party, and commodity intermediary have agreed that the commodity intermediary will

apply any value distributed on account of the commodity contract as directed by the secured party without further consent by the commodity customer.

(c) A secured party having control of all security entitlements or commodity contracts carried in a securities account or commodity account has control over the securities account or commodity account.

§ 9–107. Control of Letter-of-Credit Right.

A secured party has control of a letter-of-credit right to the extent of any right to payment or performance by the issuer or any nominated person if the issuer or nominated person has consented to an assignment of proceeds of the letter of credit under Section 5–114(c) or otherwise applicable law or practice.

§ 9–108. Sufficiency of Description.

(a) Except as otherwise provided in subsections (c), (d), and (e), a description of personal or real property is sufficient, whether or not it is specific, if it reasonably identifies what is described.

(b) Except as otherwise provided in subsection (d), a description of collateral reasonably identifies the collateral if it identifies the collateral by:

(1) specific listing;

(2) category;

(3) except as otherwise provided in subsection (e), a type of collateral defined in [the Uniform Commercial Code];

(4) quantity;

(5) computational or allocational formula or procedure; or

(6) except as otherwise provided in subsection (c), any other method, if the identity of the collateral is objectively determinable.

(c) A description of collateral as "all the debtor's assets" or "all the debtor's personal property" or using words of similar import does not reasonably identify the collateral.

(d) Except as otherwise provided in subsection (e), a description of a security entitlement, securities account, or commodity account is sufficient if it describes:

(1) the collateral by those terms or as investment property; or

(2) the underlying financial asset or commodity contract.

(e) A description only by type of collateral defined in [the Uniform Commercial Code] is an insufficient description of:

(1) a commercial tort claim; or

(2) in a consumer transaction, consumer goods, a security entitlement, a securities account, or a commodity account.

[Subpart 2. Applicability of Article]

§ 9–109. Scope.

(a) Except as otherwise provided in subsections (c) and (d), this article applies to:

(1) a transaction, regardless of its form, that creates a security interest in personal property or fixtures by contract;

(2) an agricultural lien;

(3) a sale of accounts, chattel paper, payment intangibles, or promissory notes;

(4) a consignment;

(5) a security interest arising under Section 2–401, 2–505, 2–711(3), or 2A–508(5), as provided in Section 9–110; and

(6) a security interest arising under Section 4–210 or 5–118.

(b) The application of this article to a security interest in a secured obligation is not affected by the fact that the obligation is itself secured by a transaction or interest to which this article does not apply.

(c) This article does not apply to the extent that:

(1) a statute, regulation, or treaty of the United States preempts this article;

(2) another statute of this State expressly governs the creation, perfection, priority, or enforcement of a security interest created by this State or a governmental unit of this State;

(3) a statute of another State, a foreign country, or a governmental unit of another State or a foreign country, other than a statute generally applicable to security interests, expressly governs creation, perfection, priority, or enforcement of a security interest created by the State, country, or governmental unit; or

(4) the rights of a transferee beneficiary or nominated person under a letter of credit are independent and superior under Section 5–114.

(d) This article does not apply to:

(1) a landlord's lien, other than an agricultural lien;

(2) a lien, other than an agricultural lien, given by statute or other rule of law for services or materials, but Section 9–333 applies with respect to priority of the lien;

(3) an assignment of a claim for wages, salary, or other compensation of an employee;

(4) a sale of accounts, chattel paper, payment intangibles, or promissory notes as part of a sale of the business out of which they arose;

(5) an assignment of accounts, chattel paper, payment intangibles, or promissory notes which is for the purpose of collection only;

(6) an assignment of a right to payment under a contract to an assignee that is also obligated to perform under the contract;

(7) an assignment of a single account, payment intangible, or promissory note to an assignee in full or partial satisfaction of a preexisting indebtedness;

(8) a transfer of an interest in or an assignment of a claim under a policy of insurance, other than an assignment by or to a health-care provider of a health-care-insurance receivable and any subsequent assignment of the right to payment, but Sections 9–315 and 9–322 apply with respect to proceeds and priorities in proceeds;

(9) an assignment of a right represented by a judgment, other than a judgment taken on a right to payment that was collateral;

(10) a right of recoupment or set-off, but:

(A) Section 9–340 applies with respect to the effectiveness of rights of recoupment or set-off against deposit accounts; and

(B) Section 9–404 applies with respect to defenses or claims of an account debtor;

(11) the creation or transfer of an interest in or lien on real property, including a lease or rents thereunder, except to the extent that provision is made for:

(A) liens on real property in Sections 9–203 and 9–308;

(B) fixtures in Section 9–334;

(C) fixture filings in Sections 9–501, 9–502, 9–512, 9–516, and 9–519; and

(D) security agreements covering personal and real property in Section 9–604;

(12) an assignment of a claim arising in tort, other than a commercial tort claim, but Sections 9–315 and 9–322 apply with respect to proceeds and priorities in proceeds; or

(13) an assignment of a deposit account in a consumer transaction, but Sections 9–315 and 9–322 apply with respect to proceeds and priorities in proceeds.

§ 9–110. Security Interests Arising under Article 2 or 2A.

A security interest arising under Section 2–401, 2–505, 2–711(3), or 2A–508(5) is subject to this article. However, until the debtor obtains possession of the goods:

(1) the security interest is enforceable, even if Section 9–203(b)(3) has not been satisfied;

(2) filing is not required to perfect the security interest;

(3) the rights of the secured party after default by the debtor are governed by Article 2 or 2A; and

(4) the security interest has priority over a conflicting security interest created by the debtor.

Part 2 Effectiveness of Security Agreement; Attachment of Security Interest; Rights of Parties to Security Agreement

[Subpart 1. Effectiveness and Attachment]

§ 9–201. General Effectiveness of Security Agreement.

(a) Except as otherwise provided in [the Uniform Commercial Code], a security agreement is effective according to its terms between the parties, against purchasers of the collateral, and against creditors.

(b) A transaction subject to this article is subject to any applicable rule of law which establishes a different rule for consumers and [insert reference to (i) any other statute or regulation that regulates the rates, charges, agreements, and practices for loans, credit sales, or other extensions of credit and (ii) any consumer-protection statute or regulation].

(c) In case of conflict between this article and a rule of law, statute, or regulation described in subsection (b), the rule of law, statute, or regulation controls. Failure to comply with a statute or regulation described in subsection (b) has only the effect the statute or regulation specifies.

(d) This article does not:

(1) validate any rate, charge, agreement, or practice that violates a rule of law, statute, or regulation described in subsection (b); or

(2) extend the application of the rule of law, statute, or regulation to a transaction not otherwise subject to it.

§ 9–202. Title to Collateral Immaterial.

Except as otherwise provided with respect to consignments or sales of accounts, chattel paper, payment intangibles, or promissory notes, the provisions of this article with regard to rights and obligations apply whether title to collateral is in the secured party or the debtor.

§ 9–203. Attachment and Enforceability of Security Interest; Proceeds; Supporting Obligations; Formal Requisites.

(a) A security interest attaches to collateral when it becomes enforceable against the debtor with respect to the collateral, unless an agreement expressly postpones the time of attachment.

(b) Except as otherwise provided in subsections (c) through (i), a security interest is enforceable against the debtor and third parties with respect to the collateral only if:

(1) value has been given;

(2) the debtor has rights in the collateral or the power to transfer rights in the collateral to a secured party; and

(3) one of the following conditions is met:

(A) the debtor has authenticated a security agreement that provides a description of the collateral and, if the security interest covers timber to be cut, a description of the land concerned;

(B) the collateral is not a certificated security and is in the possession of the secured party under Section 9–313 pursuant to the debtor's security agreement;

(C) the collateral is a certificated security in registered form and the security certificate has been delivered to the secured party under Section 8–301 pursuant to the debtor's security agreement; or

(D) the collateral is deposit accounts, electronic chattel paper, investment property, or letter-of-credit rights, and the secured party has control under Section 9–104, 9–105, 9–106, or 9–107 pursuant to the debtor's security agreement.

(c) Subsection (b) is subject to Section 4–210 on the security interest of a collecting bank, Section 5–118 on the security interest of a letter-of-credit issuer or nominated person, Section 9–110 on a security interest arising under Article 2 or 2A, and Section 9–206 on security interests in investment property.

(d) A person becomes bound as debtor by a security agreement entered into by another person if, by operation of law other than this article or by contract:

(1) the security agreement becomes effective to create a security interest in the person's property; or

(2) the person becomes generally obligated for the obligations of the other person, including the obligation secured under the security agreement, and acquires or succeeds to all or substantially all of the assets of the other person.

(e) If a new debtor becomes bound as debtor by a security agreement entered into by another person:

(1) the agreement satisfies subsection (b)(3) with respect to existing or after-acquired property of the new debtor to the extent the property is described in the agreement; and

(2) another agreement is not necessary to make a security interest in the property enforceable.

(f) The attachment of a security interest in collateral gives the secured party the rights to proceeds provided by Section 9–315 and is also attachment of a security interest in a supporting obligation for the collateral.

(g) The attachment of a security interest in a right to payment or performance secured by a security interest or other lien on personal or real property is also attachment of a security interest in the security interest, mortgage, or other lien.

(h) The attachment of a security interest in a securities account is also attachment of a security interest in the security entitlements carried in the securities account.

(i) The attachment of a security interest in a commodity account is also attachment of a security interest in the commodity contracts carried in the commodity account.

§ 9–204. After-Acquired Property; Future Advances.

(a) Except as otherwise provided in subsection (b), a security agreement may create or provide for a security interest in after-acquired collateral.

(b) A security interest does not attach under a term constituting an after-acquired property clause to:

(1) consumer goods, other than an accession when given as additional security, unless the debtor acquires rights in them within 10 days after the secured party gives value; or

(2) a commercial tort claim.

(c) A security agreement may provide that collateral secures, or that accounts, chattel paper, payment intangibles, or promissory notes are sold in connection with, future advances or other value, whether or not the advances or value are given pursuant to commitment.

§ 9–205. Use or Disposition of Collateral Permissible.

(a) A security interest is not invalid or fraudulent against creditors solely because:

(1) the debtor has the right or ability to:

(A) use, commingle, or dispose of all or part of the collateral, including returned or repossessed goods;

(B) collect, compromise, enforce, or otherwise deal with collateral;

(C) accept the return of collateral or make repossessions; or

(D) use, commingle, or dispose of proceeds; or

(2) the secured party fails to require the debtor to account for proceeds or replace collateral.

(b) This section does not relax the requirements of possession if attachment, perfection, or enforcement of a security interest depends upon possession of the collateral by the secured party.

§ 9–206. Security Interest Arising in Purchase or Delivery of Financial Asset.

(a) A security interest in favor of a securities intermediary attaches to a person's security entitlement if:

(1) the person buys a financial asset through the securities intermediary in a transaction in which the person is obligated to pay the purchase price to the securities intermediary at the time of the purchase; and

(2) the securities intermediary credits the financial asset to the buyer's securities account before the buyer pays the securities intermediary.

(b) The security interest described in subsection (a) secures the person's obligation to pay for the financial asset.

(c) A security interest in favor of a person that delivers a certificated security or other financial asset represented by a writing attaches to the security or other financial asset if:

(1) the security or other financial asset:

(A) in the ordinary course of business is transferred by delivery with any necessary indorsement or assignment; and

(B) is delivered under an agreement between persons in the business of dealing with such securities or financial assets; and

(2) the agreement calls for delivery against payment.

(d) The security interest described in subsection (c) secures the obligation to make payment for the delivery.

[Subpart 2. Rights and Duties]

§ 9–207. Rights and Duties of Secured Party Having Possession or Control of Collateral.

(a) Except as otherwise provided in subsection (d), a secured party shall use reasonable care in the custody and preservation of collateral in the secured party's possession. In the case of chattel paper or an instrument, reasonable care includes taking necessary steps to preserve rights against prior parties unless otherwise agreed.

(b) Except as otherwise provided in subsection (d), if a secured party has possession of collateral:

(1) reasonable expenses, including the cost of insurance and payment of taxes or other charges, incurred in the custody, preservation, use, or operation of the collateral are chargeable to the debtor and are secured by the collateral;

(2) the risk of accidental loss or damage is on the debtor to the extent of a deficiency in any effective insurance coverage;

(3) the secured party shall keep the collateral identifiable, but fungible collateral may be commingled; and

(4) the secured party may use or operate the collateral:

(A) for the purpose of preserving the collateral or its value;

(B) as permitted by an order of a court having competent jurisdiction; or

(C) except in the case of consumer goods, in the manner and to the extent agreed by the debtor.

(c) Except as otherwise provided in subsection (d), a secured party having possession of collateral or control of collateral under Section 9–104, 9–105, 9–106, or 9–107:

(1) may hold as additional security any proceeds, except money or funds, received from the collateral;

(2) shall apply money or funds received from the collateral to reduce the secured obligation, unless remitted to the debtor; and

(3) may create a security interest in the collateral.

(d) If the secured party is a buyer of accounts, chattel paper, payment intangibles, or promissory notes or a consignor:

(1) subsection (a) does not apply unless the secured party is entitled under an agreement:

(A) to charge back uncollected collateral; or

(B) otherwise to full or limited recourse against the debtor or a secondary obligor based on the nonpayment or other default of an account debtor or other obligor on the collateral; and

(2) subsections (b) and (c) do not apply.

§ 9–208. Additional Duties of Secured Party Having Control of Collateral.

(a) This section applies to cases in which there is no outstanding secured obligation and the secured party is not committed to make advances, incur obligations, or otherwise give value.

(b) Within 10 days after receiving an authenticated demand by the debtor:

(1) a secured party having control of a deposit account under Section 9–104(a)(2) shall send to the bank with which the deposit account is maintained an authenticated statement that releases the bank from any further obligation to comply with instructions originated by the secured party;

(2) a secured party having control of a deposit account under Section 9–104(a)(3) shall:

(A) pay the debtor the balance on deposit in the deposit account; or

(B) transfer the balance on deposit into a deposit account in the debtor's name;

(3) a secured party, other than a buyer, having control of electronic chattel paper under Section 9–105 shall:

(A) communicate the authoritative copy of the electronic chattel paper to the debtor or its designated custodian;

(B) if the debtor designates a custodian that is the designated custodian with which the authoritative copy of the electronic chattel paper is maintained for the secured party, communicate to the custodian an authenticated record releasing the designated custodian from any further obligation to comply with instructions originated by the secured party and instructing the custodian to comply with instructions originated by the debtor; and

(C) take appropriate action to enable the debtor or its designated custodian to make copies of or revisions to the authoritative copy which add or change an identified assignee of the authoritative copy without the consent of the secured party;

(4) a secured party having control of investment property under Section 8–106(d)(2) or 9–106(b) shall send to the securities intermediary or commodity intermediary with which the security entitlement or commodity contract is maintained an authenticated record that releases the securities intermediary or commodity intermediary from any further obligation to comply with entitlement orders or directions originated by the secured party; and

(5) a secured party having control of a letter-of-credit right under Section 9–107 shall send to each person having an unfulfilled obligation to pay or deliver proceeds of the letter of credit to the secured party an authenticated release from any further obligation to pay or deliver proceeds of the letter of credit to the secured party.

§ 9–209. Duties of Secured Party If Account Debtor Has Been Notified of Assignment.

(a) Except as otherwise provided in subsection (c), this section applies if:

(1) there is no outstanding secured obligation; and

(2) the secured party is not committed to make advances, incur obligations, or otherwise give value.

(b) Within 10 days after receiving an authenticated demand by the debtor, a secured party shall send to an account debtor that has received notification of an assignment to the secured party as assignee under Section 9–406(a) an authenticated record that releases the account debtor from any further obligation to the secured party.

(c) This section does not apply to an assignment constituting the sale of an account, chattel paper, or payment intangible.

§ 9–210. Request for Accounting; Request Regarding List of Collateral or Statement of Account.

(a) In this section:

(1) "Request" means a record of a type described in paragraph (2), (3), or (4).

(2) "Request for an accounting" means a record authenticated by a debtor requesting that the recipient provide an accounting of the unpaid obligations secured by collateral and reasonably identifying the transaction or relationship that is the subject of the request.

(3) "Request regarding a list of collateral" means a record authenticated by a debtor requesting that the recipient approve or correct a list of what the debtor believes to be the collateral

securing an obligation and reasonably identifying the transaction or relationship that is the subject of the request.

(4) "Request regarding a statement of account" means a record authenticated by a debtor requesting that the recipient approve or correct a statement indicating what the debtor believes to be the aggregate amount of unpaid obligations secured by collateral as of a specified date and reasonably identifying the transaction or relationship that is the subject of the request.

(b) Subject to subsections (c), (d), (e), and (f), a secured party, other than a buyer of accounts, chattel paper, payment intangibles, or promissory notes or a consignor, shall comply with a request within 14 days after receipt:

(1) in the case of a request for an accounting, by authenticating and sending to the debtor an accounting; and

(2) in the case of a request regarding a list of collateral or a request regarding a statement of account, by authenticating and sending to the debtor an approval or correction.

(c) A secured party that claims a security interest in all of a particular type of collateral owned by the debtor may comply with a request regarding a list of collateral by sending to the debtor an authenticated record including a statement to that effect within 14 days after receipt.

(d) A person that receives a request regarding a list of collateral, claims no interest in the collateral when it receives the request, and claimed an interest in the collateral at an earlier time shall comply with the request within 14 days after receipt by sending to the debtor an authenticated record:

(1) disclaiming any interest in the collateral; and

(2) if known to the recipient, providing the name and mailing address of any assignee of or successor to the recipient's interest in the collateral.

(e) A person that receives a request for an accounting or a request regarding a statement of account, claims no interest in the obligations when it receives the request, and claimed an interest in the obligations at an earlier time shall comply with the request within 14 days after receipt by sending to the debtor an authenticated record:

(1) disclaiming any interest in the obligations; and

(2) if known to the recipient, providing the name and mailing address of any assignee of or successor to the recipient's interest in the obligations.

(f) A debtor is entitled without charge to one response to a request under this section during any six-month period. The secured party may require payment of a charge not exceeding $25 for each additional response.

As amended in 1999.

Part 3 Perfection and Priority

[Subpart 1. Law Governing Perfection and Priority]

§ 9–301. Law Governing Perfection and Priority of Security Interests.

Except as otherwise provided in Sections 9–303 through 9–306, the following rules determine the law governing perfection, the effect of perfection or nonperfection, and the priority of a security interest in collateral:

(1) Except as otherwise provided in this section, while a debtor is located in a jurisdiction, the local law of that jurisdiction governs perfection, the effect of perfection or nonperfection, and the priority of a security interest in collateral.

(2) While collateral is located in a jurisdiction, the local law of that jurisdiction governs perfection, the effect of perfection or nonperfection, and the priority of a possessory security interest in that collateral.

(3) Except as otherwise provided in paragraph (4), while negotiable documents, goods, instruments, money, or tangible chattel paper is located in a jurisdiction, the local law of that jurisdiction governs:

(A) perfection of a security interest in the goods by filing a fixture filing;

(B) perfection of a security interest in timber to be cut; and

(C) the effect of perfection or nonperfection and the priority of a nonpossessory security interest in the collateral.

(4) The local law of the jurisdiction in which the wellhead or minehead is located governs perfection, the effect of perfection or nonperfection, and the priority of a security interest in as-extracted collateral.

§ 9–302. Law Governing Perfection and Priority of Agricultural Liens.

While farm products are located in a jurisdiction, the local law of that jurisdiction governs perfection, the effect of perfection or nonperfection, and the priority of an agricultural lien on the farm products.

§ 9–303. Law Governing Perfection and Priority of Security Interests in Goods Covered by a Certificate of Title.

(a) This section applies to goods covered by a certificate of title, even if there is no other relationship between the jurisdiction under whose certificate of title the goods are covered and the goods or the debtor.

(b) Goods become covered by a certificate of title when a valid application for the certificate of title and the applicable fee are delivered to the appropriate authority. Goods cease to be covered by a certificate of title at the earlier of the time the certificate of title ceases to be effective under the law of the issuing jurisdiction or the time the goods become covered subsequently by a certificate of title issued by another jurisdiction.

(c) The local law of the jurisdiction under whose certificate of title the goods are covered governs perfection, the effect of perfection or nonperfection, and the priority of a security interest in goods covered by a certificate of title from the time the goods become covered by the certificate of title until the goods cease to be covered by the certificate of title.

§ 9–304. Law Governing Perfection and Priority of Security Interests in Deposit Accounts.

(a) The local law of a bank's jurisdiction governs perfection, the effect of perfection or nonperfection, and the priority of a security interest in a deposit account maintained with that bank.

(b) The following rules determine a bank's jurisdiction for purposes of this part:

(1) If an agreement between the bank and the debtor governing the deposit account expressly provides that a particular jurisdiction is the bank's jurisdiction for purposes of this part, this article, or [the Uniform Commercial Code], that jurisdiction is the bank's jurisdiction.

(2) If paragraph (1) does not apply and an agreement between the bank and its customer governing the deposit account expressly provides that the agreement is governed by the law of a particular jurisdiction, that jurisdiction is the bank's jurisdiction.

(3) If neither paragraph (1) nor paragraph (2) applies and an agreement between the bank and its customer governing the deposit account expressly provides that the deposit account is maintained at an office in a particular jurisdiction, that jurisdiction is the bank's jurisdiction.

(4) If none of the preceding paragraphs applies, the bank's jurisdiction is the jurisdiction in which the office identified in an account statement as the office serving the customer's account is located.

(5) If none of the preceding paragraphs applies, the bank's jurisdiction is the jurisdiction in which the chief executive office of the bank is located.

§ 9–305. Law Governing Perfection and Priority of Security Interests in Investment Property.

(a) Except as otherwise provided in subsection (c), the following rules apply:

(1) While a security certificate is located in a jurisdiction, the local law of that jurisdiction governs perfection, the effect of perfection or nonperfection, and the priority of a security interest in the certificated security represented thereby.

(2) The local law of the issuer's jurisdiction as specified in Section 8–110(d) governs perfection, the effect of perfection or nonperfection, and the priority of a security interest in an uncertificated security.

(3) The local law of the securities intermediary's jurisdiction as specified in Section 8–110(e) governs perfection, the effect of perfection or nonperfection, and the priority of a security interest in a security entitlement or securities account.

(4) The local law of the commodity intermediary's jurisdiction governs perfection, the effect of perfection or nonperfection, and the priority of a security interest in a commodity contract or commodity account.

(b) The following rules determine a commodity intermediary's jurisdiction for purposes of this part:

(1) If an agreement between the commodity intermediary and commodity customer governing the commodity account expressly provides that a particular jurisdiction is the commodity intermediary's jurisdiction for purposes of this part, this article, or [the Uniform Commercial Code], that jurisdiction is the commodity intermediary's jurisdiction.

(2) If paragraph (1) does not apply and an agreement between the commodity intermediary and commodity customer governing the commodity account expressly provides that the agreement is governed by the law of a particular jurisdiction, that jurisdiction is the commodity intermediary's jurisdiction.

(3) If neither paragraph (1) nor paragraph (2) applies and an agreement between the commodity intermediary and commodity customer governing the commodity account expressly provides that the commodity account is maintained at an office in a particular jurisdiction, that jurisdiction is the commodity intermediary's jurisdiction.

(4) If none of the preceding paragraphs applies, the commodity intermediary's jurisdiction is the jurisdiction in which the office identified in an account statement as the office serving the commodity customer's account is located.

(5) If none of the preceding paragraphs applies, the commodity intermediary's jurisdiction is the jurisdiction in which the chief executive office of the commodity intermediary is located.

(c) The local law of the jurisdiction in which the debtor is located governs:

(1) perfection of a security interest in investment property by filing;

(2) automatic perfection of a security interest in investment property created by a broker or securities intermediary; and

(3) automatic perfection of a security interest in a commodity contract or commodity account created by a commodity intermediary.

§ 9–306. Law Governing Perfection and Priority of Security Interests in Letter-of-Credit Rights.

(a) Subject to subsection (c), the local law of the issuer's jurisdiction or a nominated person's jurisdiction governs perfection, the effect of perfection or nonperfection, and the priority of a security interest in a letter-of-credit right if the issuer's jurisdiction or nominated person's jurisdiction is a State.

(b) For purposes of this part, an issuer's jurisdiction or nominated person's jurisdiction is the jurisdiction whose law governs the liability of the issuer or nominated person with respect to the letter-of-credit right as provided in Section 5–116.

(c) This section does not apply to a security interest that is perfected only under Section 9–308(d).

§ 9–307. Location of Debtor.

(a) In this section, "place of business" means a place where a debtor conducts its affairs.

(b) Except as otherwise provided in this section, the following rules determine a debtor's location:

(1) A debtor who is an individual is located at the individual's principal residence.

(2) A debtor that is an organization and has only one place of business is located at its place of business.

(3) A debtor that is an organization and has more than one place of business is located at its chief executive office.

(c) Subsection (b) applies only if a debtor's residence, place of business, or chief executive office, as applicable, is located in a jurisdiction whose law generally requires information concerning the existence of a nonpossessory security interest to be made generally available in a filing, recording, or registration system as a condition or result of the security interest's obtaining priority over the rights of a lien creditor with respect to the collateral. If subsection (b) does not apply, the debtor is located in the District of Columbia.

(d) A person that ceases to exist, have a residence, or have a place of business continues to be located in the jurisdiction specified by subsections (b) and (c).

(e) A registered organization that is organized under the law of a State is located in that State.

(f) Except as otherwise provided in subsection (i), a registered organization that is organized under the law of the United States and a branch or agency of a bank that is not organized under the law of the United States or a State are located:

(1) in the State that the law of the United States designates, if the law designates a State of location;

(2) in the State that the registered organization, branch, or agency designates, if the law of the United States authorizes the registered organization, branch, or agency to designate its State of location; or

(3) in the District of Columbia, if neither paragraph (1) nor paragraph (2) applies.

(g) A registered organization continues to be located in the jurisdiction specified by subsection (e) or (f) notwithstanding:

(1) the suspension, revocation, forfeiture, or lapse of the registered organization's status as such in its jurisdiction of organization; or

(2) the dissolution, winding up, or cancellation of the existence of the registered organization.

(h) The United States is located in the District of Columbia.

(i) A branch or agency of a bank that is not organized under the law of the United States or a State is located in the State in which the branch or agency is licensed, if all branches and agencies of the bank are licensed in only one State.

(j) A foreign air carrier under the Federal Aviation Act of 1958, as amended, is located at the designated office of the agent upon which service of process may be made on behalf of the carrier.

(k) This section applies only for purposes of this part.

[Subpart 2. Perfection]

§ 9–308. When Security Interest or Agricultural Lien Is Perfected; Continuity of Perfection.

(a) Except as otherwise provided in this section and Section 9–309, a security interest is perfected if it has attached and all of the applicable requirements for perfection in Sections 9–310 through 9–316 have been satisfied. A security interest is perfected when it attaches if the applicable requirements are satisfied before the security interest attaches.

(b) An agricultural lien is perfected if it has become effective and all of the applicable requirements for perfection in Section 9–310 have been satisfied. An agricultural lien is perfected when it becomes effective if the applicable requirements are satisfied before the agricultural lien becomes effective.

(c) A security interest or agricultural lien is perfected continuously if it is originally perfected by one method under this article and is later perfected by another method under this article, without an intermediate period when it was unperfected.

(d) Perfection of a security interest in collateral also perfects a security interest in a supporting obligation for the collateral.

(e) Perfection of a security interest in a right to payment or performance also perfects a security interest in a security interest, mortgage, or other lien on personal or real property securing the right.

(f) Perfection of a security interest in a securities account also perfects a security interest in the security entitlements carried in the securities account.

(g) Perfection of a security interest in a commodity account also perfects a security interest in the commodity contracts carried in the commodity account.

Legislative Note: Any statute conflicting with subsection (e) must be made expressly subject to that subsection.

§ 9–309. Security Interest Perfected upon Attachment.

The following security interests are perfected when they attach:

(1) a purchase-money security interest in consumer goods, except as otherwise provided in Section 9–311(b) with respect to consumer goods that are subject to a statute or treaty described in Section 9–311(a);

(2) an assignment of accounts or payment intangibles which does not by itself or in conjunction with other assignments to the same assignee transfer a significant part of the assignor's outstanding accounts or payment intangibles;

(3) a sale of a payment intangible;

(4) a sale of a promissory note;

(5) a security interest created by the assignment of a health-care-insurance receivable to the provider of the health-care goods or services;

(6) a security interest arising under Section 2–401, 2–505, 2–711(3), or 2A–508(5), until the debtor obtains possession of the collateral;

(7) a security interest of a collecting bank arising under Section 4–210;

(8) a security interest of an issuer or nominated person arising under Section 5–118;

(9) a security interest arising in the delivery of a financial asset under Section 9–206(c);

(10) a security interest in investment property created by a broker or securities intermediary;

(11) a security interest in a commodity contract or a commodity account created by a commodity intermediary;

(12) an assignment for the benefit of all creditors of the transferor and subsequent transfers by the assignee thereunder; and

(13) a security interest created by an assignment of a beneficial interest in a decedent's estate; and

(14) a sale by an individual of an account that is a right to payment of winnings in a lottery or other game of chance.

§ 9–310. When Filing Required to Perfect Security Interest or Agricultural Lien; Security Interests and Agricultural Liens to Which Filing Provisions Do Not Apply.

(a) Except as otherwise provided in subsection (b) and Section 9–312(b), a financing statement must be filed to perfect all security interests and agricultural liens.

(b) The filing of a financing statement is not necessary to perfect a security interest:

(1) that is perfected under Section 9–308(d), (e), (f), or (g);

(2) that is perfected under Section 9–309 when it attaches;

(3) in property subject to a statute, regulation, or treaty described in Section 9–311(a);

(4) in goods in possession of a bailee which is perfected under Section 9–312(d)(1) or (2);

(5) in certificated securities, documents, goods, or instruments which is perfected without filing or possession under Section 9–312(e), (f), or (g);

(6) in collateral in the secured party's possession under Section 9–313;

(7) in a certificated security which is perfected by delivery of the security certificate to the secured party under Section 9–313;

(8) in deposit accounts, electronic chattel paper, investment property, or letter-of-credit rights which is perfected by control under Section 9–314;

(9) in proceeds which is perfected under Section 9–315; or

(10) that is perfected under Section 9–316.

(c) If a secured party assigns a perfected security interest or agricultural lien, a filing under this article is not required to continue the perfected status of the security interest against creditors of and transferees from the original debtor.

§ 9–311. Perfection of Security Interests in Property Subject to Certain Statutes, Regulations, and Treaties.

(a) Except as otherwise provided in subsection (d), the filing of a financing statement is not necessary or effective to perfect a security interest in property subject to:

(1) a statute, regulation, or treaty of the United States whose requirements for a security interest's obtaining priority over the rights of a lien creditor with respect to the property preempt Section 9–310(a);

(2) [list any certificate-of-title statute covering automobiles, trailers, mobile homes, boats, farm tractors, or the like, which provides for a security interest to be indicated on the certificate as a condition or result of perfection, and any non-Uniform Commercial Code central filing statute]; or

(3) a certificate-of-title statute of another jurisdiction which provides for a security interest to be indicated on the certificate as a condition or result of the security interest's obtaining priority over the rights of a lien creditor with respect to the property.

(b) Compliance with the requirements of a statute, regulation, or treaty described in subsection (a) for obtaining priority over the rights of a lien creditor is equivalent to the filing of a financing statement under this article. Except as otherwise provided in subsection (d) and Sections 9–313 and 9–316(d) and (e) for goods covered by a certificate of title, a security interest in property subject to a statute, regulation, or treaty described in subsection (a) may be perfected only by compliance with those requirements, and a security interest so perfected remains perfected notwithstanding a change in the use or transfer of possession of the collateral.

(c) Except as otherwise provided in subsection (d) and Section 9–316(d) and (e), duration and renewal of perfection of a security interest perfected by compliance with the requirements prescribed by a statute, regulation, or treaty described in subsection (a) are governed by the statute, regulation, or treaty. In other respects, the security interest is subject to this article.

(d) During any period in which collateral subject to a statute specified in subsection (a)(2) is inventory held for sale or lease by a person or leased by that person as lessor and that person is in the business of selling goods of that kind, this section does not apply to a security interest in that collateral created by that person.

Legislative Note: This Article contemplates that perfection of a security interest in goods covered by a certificate of title occurs upon receipt by appropriate State officials of a properly tendered application for a certificate of title on which the security interest is to be indicated, without a relation back to an earlier time. States whose certificate-of-title statutes provide for perfection at a different time or contain a relation-back provision should amend the statutes accordingly.

§ 9–312. Perfection of Security Interests in Chattel Paper, Deposit Accounts, Documents, Goods Covered by Documents, Instruments, Investment Property, Letter-of-Credit Rights, and Money; Perfection by Permissive Filing; Temporary Perfection without Filing or Transfer of Possession.

(a) A security interest in chattel paper, negotiable documents, instruments, or investment property may be perfected by filing.

(b) Except as otherwise provided in Section 9–315(c) and (d) for proceeds:

(1) a security interest in a deposit account may be perfected only by control under Section 9–314;

(2) and except as otherwise provided in Section 9–308(d), a security interest in a letter-of-credit right may be perfected only by control under Section 9–314; and

(3) a security interest in money may be perfected only by the secured party's taking possession under Section 9–313.

(c) While goods are in the possession of a bailee that has issued a negotiable document covering the goods:

(1) a security interest in the goods may be perfected by perfecting a security interest in the document; and

(2) a security interest perfected in the document has priority over any security interest that becomes perfected in the goods by another method during that time.

(d) While goods are in the possession of a bailee that has issued a nonnegotiable document covering the goods, a security interest in the goods may be perfected by:

(1) issuance of a document in the name of the secured party;

(2) the bailee's receipt of notification of the secured party's interest; or

(3) filing as to the goods.

(e) A security interest in certificated securities, negotiable documents, or instruments is perfected without filing or the taking of possession for a period of 20 days from the time it attaches to the extent that it arises for new value given under an authenticated security agreement.

(f) A perfected security interest in a negotiable document or goods in possession of a bailee, other than one that has issued a negotiable document for the goods, remains perfected for 20 days without filing if the secured party makes available to the debtor the goods or documents representing the goods for the purpose of:

(1) ultimate sale or exchange; or

(2) loading, unloading, storing, shipping, transshipping, manufacturing, processing, or otherwise dealing with them in a manner preliminary to their sale or exchange.

(g) A perfected security interest in a certificated security or instrument remains perfected for 20 days without filing if the secured party delivers the security certificate or instrument to the debtor for the purpose of:

(1) ultimate sale or exchange; or

(2) presentation, collection, enforcement, renewal, or registration of transfer.

(h) After the 20-day period specified in subsection (e), (f), or (g) expires, perfection depends upon compliance with this article.

§ 9–313. When Possession by or Delivery to Secured Party Perfects Security Interest without Filing.

(a) Except as otherwise provided in subsection (b), a secured party may perfect a security interest in negotiable documents, goods, instruments, money, or tangible chattel paper by taking possession of the collateral. A secured party may perfect a security interest in certificated securities by taking delivery of the certificated securities under Section 8–301.

(b) With respect to goods covered by a certificate of title issued by this State, a secured party may perfect a security interest in the goods by taking possession of the goods only in the circumstances described in Section 9–316(d).

(c) With respect to collateral other than certificated securities and goods covered by a document, a secured party takes possession of collateral in the possession of a person other than the debtor, the secured party, or a lessee of the collateral from the debtor in the ordinary course of the debtor's business, when:

(1) the person in possession authenticates a record acknowledging that it holds possession of the collateral for the secured party's benefit; or

(2) the person takes possession of the collateral after having authenticated a record acknowledging that it will hold possession of collateral for the secured party's benefit.

(d) If perfection of a security interest depends upon possession of the collateral by a secured party, perfection occurs no earlier than the time the secured party takes possession and continues only while the secured party retains possession.

(e) A security interest in a certificated security in registered form is perfected by delivery when delivery of the certificated security occurs under Section 8–301 and remains perfected by delivery until the debtor obtains possession of the security certificate.

(f) A person in possession of collateral is not required to acknowledge that it holds possession for a secured party's benefit.

(g) If a person acknowledges that it holds possession for the secured party's benefit:

(1) the acknowledgment is effective under subsection (c) or Section 8–301(a), even if the acknowledgment violates the rights of a debtor; and

(2) unless the person otherwise agrees or law other than this article otherwise provides, the person does not owe any duty to the secured party and is not required to confirm the acknowledgment to another person.

(h) A secured party having possession of collateral does not relinquish possession by delivering the collateral to a person other than the debtor or a lessee of the collateral from the debtor in the ordinary course of the debtor's business if the person was instructed before the delivery or is instructed contemporaneously with the delivery:

(1) to hold possession of the collateral for the secured party's benefit; or

(2) to redeliver the collateral to the secured party.

(i) A secured party does not relinquish possession, even if a delivery under subsection (h) violates the rights of a debtor. A person to which collateral is delivered under subsection (h) does not owe any duty to the secured party and is not required to confirm the delivery to another person unless the person otherwise agrees or law other than this article otherwise provides.

§ 9–314. Perfection by Control.

(a) A security interest in investment property, deposit accounts, letter-of-credit rights, or electronic chattel paper may be perfected by control of the collateral under Section 9–104, 9–105, 9–106, or 9–107.

(b) A security interest in deposit accounts, electronic chattel paper, or letter-of-credit rights is perfected by control under Section 9–104, 9–105, or 9–107 when the secured party obtains control and remains perfected by control only while the secured party retains control.

(c) A security interest in investment property is perfected by control under Section 9–106 from the time the secured party obtains control and remains perfected by control until:

(1) the secured party does not have control; and

(2) one of the following occurs:

(A) if the collateral is a certificated security, the debtor has or acquires possession of the security certificate;

(B) if the collateral is an uncertificated security, the issuer has registered or registers the debtor as the registered owner; or

(C) if the collateral is a security entitlement, the debtor is or becomes the entitlement holder.

§ 9–315. Secured Party's Rights on Disposition of Collateral and in Proceeds.

(a) Except as otherwise provided in this article and in Section 2–403(2):

(1) a security interest or agricultural lien continues in collateral notwithstanding sale, lease, license, exchange, or other disposition thereof unless the secured party authorized the disposition free of the security interest or agricultural lien; and

(2) a security interest attaches to any identifiable proceeds of collateral.

(b) Proceeds that are commingled with other property are identifiable proceeds:

(1) if the proceeds are goods, to the extent provided by Section 9–336; and

(2) if the proceeds are not goods, to the extent that the secured party identifies the proceeds by a method of tracing, including application of equitable principles, that is permitted under law other than this article with respect to commingled property of the type involved.

(c) A security interest in proceeds is a perfected security interest if the security interest in the original collateral was perfected.

(d) A perfected security interest in proceeds becomes unperfected on the 21st day after the security interest attaches to the proceeds unless:

(1) the following conditions are satisfied:

(A) a filed financing statement covers the original collateral;

(B) the proceeds are collateral in which a security interest may be perfected by filing in the office in which the financing statement has been filed; and

(C) the proceeds are not acquired with cash proceeds;

(2) the proceeds are identifiable cash proceeds; or

(3) the security interest in the proceeds is perfected other than under subsection (c) when the security interest attaches to the proceeds or within 20 days thereafter.

(e) If a filed financing statement covers the original collateral, a security interest in proceeds which remains perfected under subsection (d)(1) becomes unperfected at the later of:

(1) when the effectiveness of the filed financing statement lapses under Section 9–515 or is terminated under Section 9–513; or

(2) the 21st day after the security interest attaches to the proceeds.

§ 9–316. Continued Perfection of Security Interest Following Change in Governing Law.

(a) A security interest perfected pursuant to the law of the jurisdiction designated in Section 9–301(1) or 9–305(c) remains perfected until the earliest of:

(1) the time perfection would have ceased under the law of that jurisdiction;

(2) the expiration of four months after a change of the debtor's location to another jurisdiction; or

(3) the expiration of one year after a transfer of collateral to a person that thereby becomes a debtor and is located in another jurisdiction.

(b) If a security interest described in subsection (a) becomes perfected under the law of the other jurisdiction before the earliest time or event described in that subsection, it remains perfected thereafter. If the security interest does not become perfected under the law of the other jurisdiction before the earliest time or event, it becomes unperfected and is deemed never to have been perfected as against a purchaser of the collateral for value.

(c) A possessory security interest in collateral, other than goods covered by a certificate of title and as-extracted collateral consisting of goods, remains continuously perfected if:

(1) the collateral is located in one jurisdiction and subject to a security interest perfected under the law of that jurisdiction;

(2) thereafter the collateral is brought into another jurisdiction; and

(3) upon entry into the other jurisdiction, the security interest is perfected under the law of the other jurisdiction.

(d) Except as otherwise provided in subsection (e), a security interest in goods covered by a certificate of title which is perfected by any method under the law of another jurisdiction when the goods become covered by a certificate of title from this State remains perfected until the security interest would have become unperfected under the law of the other jurisdiction had the goods not become so covered.

(e) A security interest described in subsection (d) becomes unperfected as against a purchaser of the goods for value and is deemed never to have been perfected as against a purchaser of the goods for value if the applicable requirements for perfection under Section 9–311(b) or 9–313 are not satisfied before the earlier of:

(1) the time the security interest would have become unperfected under the law of the other jurisdiction had the goods not become covered by a certificate of title from this State; or

(2) the expiration of four months after the goods had become so covered.

(f) A security interest in deposit accounts, letter-of-credit rights, or investment property which is perfected under the law of the bank's jurisdiction, the issuer's jurisdiction, a nominated person's jurisdiction, the securities intermediary's jurisdiction, or the commodity intermediary's jurisdiction, as applicable, remains perfected until the earlier of:

(1) the time the security interest would have become unperfected under the law of that jurisdiction; or

(2) the expiration of four months after a change of the applicable jurisdiction to another jurisdiction.

(g) If a security interest described in subsection (f) becomes perfected under the law of the other jurisdiction before the earlier of the time or the end of the period described in that subsection, it remains perfected thereafter. If the security interest does not become perfected under the law of the other jurisdiction before the earlier of that time or the end of that period, it becomes unperfected and is deemed never to have been perfected as against a purchaser of the collateral for value.

[Subpart 3. Priority]

§ 9–317. Interests That Take Priority over or Take Free of Security Interest or Agricultural Lien.

(a) A security interest or agricultural lien is subordinate to the rights of:

(1) a person entitled to priority under Section 9–322; and

(2) except as otherwise provided in subsection (e), a person that becomes a lien creditor before the earlier of the time:

(A) the security interest or agricultural lien is perfected; or

(B) one of the conditions specified in Section 9–203(b)(3) is met and a financing statement covering the collateral is filed.

(b) Except as otherwise provided in subsection (e), a buyer, other than a secured party, of tangible chattel paper, documents, goods, instruments, or a security certificate takes free of a security interest or agricultural lien if the buyer gives value and receives delivery of the collateral without knowledge of the security interest or agricultural lien and before it is perfected.

(c) Except as otherwise provided in subsection (e), a lessee of goods takes free of a security interest or agricultural lien if the lessee gives value and receives delivery of the collateral without knowledge of the security interest or agricultural lien and before it is perfected.

(d) A licensee of a general intangible or a buyer, other than a secured party, of accounts, electronic chattel paper, general intangibles, or investment property other than a certificated security takes free of a security interest if the licensee or buyer gives value without knowledge of the security interest and before it is perfected.

(e) Except as otherwise provided in Sections 9–320 and 9–321, if a person files a financing statement with respect to a purchase-money security interest before or within 20 days after the debtor receives delivery of the collateral, the security interest takes priority over the rights of a buyer, lessee, or lien creditor which arise between the time the security interest attaches and the time of filing.

As amended in 2000.

§ 9–318. No Interest Retained in Right to Payment That Is Sold; Rights and Title of Seller of Account or Chattel Paper with Respect to Creditors and Purchasers.

(a) A debtor that has sold an account, chattel paper, payment intangible, or promissory note does not retain a legal or equitable interest in the collateral sold.

(b) For purposes of determining the rights of creditors of, and purchasers for value of an account or chattel paper from, a debtor that has sold an account or chattel paper, while the buyer's security interest is unperfected, the debtor is deemed to have rights and title to the account or chattel paper identical to those the debtor sold.

§ 9–319. Rights and Title of Consignee with Respect to Creditors and Purchasers.

(a) Except as otherwise provided in subsection (b), for purposes of determining the rights of creditors of, and purchasers for value of goods from, a consignee, while the goods are in the possession of the consignee, the consignee is deemed to have rights and title to the goods identical to those the consignor had or had power to transfer.

(b) For purposes of determining the rights of a creditor of a consignee, law other than this article determines the rights and title of a consignee while goods are in the consignee's possession if, under this part, a perfected security interest held by the consignor would have priority over the rights of the creditor.

§ 9–320. Buyer of Goods.

(a) Except as otherwise provided in subsection (e), a buyer in ordinary course of business, other than a person buying farm products from a person engaged in farming operations, takes free of a security interest created by the buyer's seller, even if the security interest is perfected and the buyer knows of its existence.

(b) Except as otherwise provided in subsection (e), a buyer of goods from a person who used or bought the goods for use primarily for personal, family, or household purposes takes free of a security interest, even if perfected, if the buyer buys:

(1) without knowledge of the security interest;

(2) for value;

(3) primarily for the buyer's personal, family, or household purposes; and

(4) before the filing of a financing statement covering the goods.

(c) To the extent that it affects the priority of a security interest over a buyer of goods under subsection (b), the period of effectiveness of a filing made in the jurisdiction in which the seller is located is governed by Section 9–316(a) and (b).

(d) A buyer in ordinary course of business buying oil, gas, or other minerals at the wellhead or minehead or after extraction takes free of an interest arising out of an encumbrance.

(e) Subsections (a) and (b) do not affect a security interest in goods in the possession of the secured party under Section 9–313.

§ 9–321. Licensee of General Intangible and Lessee of Goods in Ordinary Course of Business.

(a) In this section, "licensee in ordinary course of business" means a person that becomes a licensee of a general intangible in good faith, without knowledge that the license violates the rights of another person in the general intangible, and in the ordinary course from a person in the business of licensing general intangibles of that kind. A person becomes a licensee in the ordinary course if the license to the person comports with the usual or customary practices in the kind of business in which the licensor is engaged or with the licensor's own usual or customary practices.

(b) A licensee in ordinary course of business takes its rights under a nonexclusive license free of a security interest in the general intangible created by the licensor, even if the security interest is perfected and the licensee knows of its existence.

(c) A lessee in ordinary course of business takes its leasehold interest free of a security interest in the goods created by the lessor, even if the security interest is perfected and the lessee knows of its existence.

§ 9–322. Priorities among Conflicting Security Interests in and Agricultural Liens on Same Collateral.

(a) Except as otherwise provided in this section, priority among conflicting security interests and agricultural liens in the same collateral is determined according to the following rules:

(1) Conflicting perfected security interests and agricultural liens rank according to priority in time of filing or perfection. Priority dates from the earlier of the time a filing covering the collateral is first made or the security interest or agricultural lien is first perfected, if there is no period thereafter when there is neither filing nor perfection.

(2) A perfected security interest or agricultural lien has priority over a conflicting unperfected security interest or agricultural lien.

(3) The first security interest or agricultural lien to attach or become effective has priority if conflicting security interests and agricultural liens are unperfected.

(b) For the purposes of subsection (a)(1):

(1) the time of filing or perfection as to a security interest in collateral is also the time of filing or perfection as to a security interest in proceeds; and

(2) the time of filing or perfection as to a security interest in collateral supported by a supporting obligation is also the time of filing or perfection as to a security interest in the supporting obligation.

(c) Except as otherwise provided in subsection (f), a security interest in collateral which qualifies for priority over a conflicting security interest under Section 9–327, 9–328, 9–329, 9–330, or 9–331 also has priority over a conflicting security interest in:

(1) any supporting obligation for the collateral; and

(2) proceeds of the collateral if:

(A) the security interest in proceeds is perfected;

(B) the proceeds are cash proceeds or of the same type as the collateral; and

(C) in the case of proceeds that are proceeds of proceeds, all intervening proceeds are cash proceeds, proceeds of the same type as the collateral, or an account relating to the collateral.

(d) Subject to subsection (e) and except as otherwise provided in subsection (f), if a security interest in chattel paper, deposit accounts, negotiable documents, instruments, investment property, or letter-of-credit rights is perfected by a method other than filing, conflicting perfected security interests in proceeds of the collateral rank according to priority in time of filing.

(e) Subsection (d) applies only if the proceeds of the collateral are not cash proceeds, chattel paper, negotiable documents, instruments, investment property, or letter-of-credit rights.

(f) Subsections (a) through (e) are subject to:

(1) subsection (g) and the other provisions of this part;

(2) Section 4–210 with respect to a security interest of a collecting bank;

(3) Section 5–118 with respect to a security interest of an issuer or nominated person; and

(4) Section 9–110 with respect to a security interest arising under Article 2 or 2A.

(g) A perfected agricultural lien on collateral has priority over a conflicting security interest in or agricultural lien on the same collateral if the statute creating the agricultural lien so provides.

§ 9–323. Future Advances.

(a) Except as otherwise provided in subsection (c), for purposes of determining the priority of a perfected security interest under Section 9–322(a)(1), perfection of the security interest dates from the time an advance is made to the extent that the security interest secures an advance that:

(1) is made while the security interest is perfected only:

(A) under Section 9–309 when it attaches; or

(B) temporarily under Section 9–312(e), (f), or (g); and

(2) is not made pursuant to a commitment entered into before or while the security interest is perfected by a method other than under Section 9–309 or 9–312(e), (f), or (g).

(b) Except as otherwise provided in subsection (c), a security interest is subordinate to the rights of a person that becomes a lien creditor to the extent that the security interest secures an advance made more than 45 days after the person becomes a lien creditor unless the advance is made:

(1) without knowledge of the lien; or

(2) pursuant to a commitment entered into without knowledge of the lien.

(c) Subsections (a) and (b) do not apply to a security interest held by a secured party that is a buyer of accounts, chattel paper, payment intangibles, or promissory notes or a consignor.

(d) Except as otherwise provided in subsection (e), a buyer of goods other than a buyer in ordinary course of business takes free of a security interest to the extent that it secures advances made after the earlier of:

(1) the time the secured party acquires knowledge of the buyer's purchase; or

(2) 45 days after the purchase.

(e) Subsection (d) does not apply if the advance is made pursuant to a commitment entered into without knowledge of the buyer's purchase and before the expiration of the 45-day period.

(f) Except as otherwise provided in subsection (g), a lessee of goods, other than a lessee in ordinary course of business, takes the leasehold interest free of a security interest to the extent that it secures advances made after the earlier of:

(1) the time the secured party acquires knowledge of the lease; or

(2) 45 days after the lease contract becomes enforceable.

(g) Subsection (f) does not apply if the advance is made pursuant to a commitment entered into without knowledge of the lease and before the expiration of the 45-day period.

As amended in 1999.

§ 9–324. Priority of Purchase-Money Security Interests.

(a) Except as otherwise provided in subsection (g), a perfected purchase-money security interest in goods other than inventory or livestock has priority over a conflicting security interest in the same goods, and, except as otherwise provided in Section 9–327, a perfected security interest in its identifiable proceeds also has priority, if the purchase-money security interest is perfected when the debtor receives possession of the collateral or within 20 days thereafter.

(b) Subject to subsection (c) and except as otherwise provided in subsection (g), a perfected purchase-money security interest in inventory has priority over a conflicting security interest in the same inventory, has priority over a conflicting security interest in chattel paper or an instrument constituting proceeds of the inventory and in proceeds of the chattel paper, if so provided in Section 9–330, and, except as otherwise provided in Section 9–327, also has priority in identifiable cash proceeds of the inventory to the extent the identifiable cash proceeds are received on or before the delivery of the inventory to a buyer, if:

(1) the purchase-money security interest is perfected when the debtor receives possession of the inventory;

(2) the purchase-money secured party sends an authenticated notification to the holder of the conflicting security interest;

(3) the holder of the conflicting security interest receives the notification within five years before the debtor receives possession of the inventory; and

(4) the notification states that the person sending the notification has or expects to acquire a purchase-money security interest in inventory of the debtor and describes the inventory.

(c) Subsections (b)(2) through (4) apply only if the holder of the conflicting security interest had filed a financing statement covering the same types of inventory:

(1) if the purchase-money security interest is perfected by filing, before the date of the filing; or

(2) if the purchase-money security interest is temporarily perfected without filing or possession under Section 9–312(f), before the beginning of the 20-day period thereunder.

(d) Subject to subsection (e) and except as otherwise provided in subsection (g), a perfected purchase-money security interest in livestock that are farm products has priority over a conflicting security interest in the same livestock, and, except as otherwise provided in Section 9–327, a perfected security interest in their identifiable proceeds and identifiable products in their unmanufactured states also has priority, if:

(1) the purchase-money security interest is perfected when the debtor receives possession of the livestock;

(2) the purchase-money secured party sends an authenticated notification to the holder of the conflicting security interest;

(3) the holder of the conflicting security interest receives the notification within six months before the debtor receives possession of the livestock; and

(4) the notification states that the person sending the notification has or expects to acquire a purchase-money security interest in livestock of the debtor and describes the livestock.

(e) Subsections (d)(2) through (4) apply only if the holder of the conflicting security interest had filed a financing statement covering the same types of livestock:

(1) if the purchase-money security interest is perfected by filing, before the date of the filing; or

(2) if the purchase-money security interest is temporarily perfected without filing or possession under Section 9–312(f), before the beginning of the 20-day period thereunder.

(f) Except as otherwise provided in subsection (g), a perfected purchase-money security interest in software has priority over a conflicting security interest in the same collateral, and, except as otherwise provided in Section 9–327, a perfected security interest in its identifiable proceeds also has priority, to the extent that the purchase-money security interest in the goods in which the software was acquired for use has priority in the goods and proceeds of the goods under this section.

(g) If more than one security interest qualifies for priority in the same collateral under subsection (a), (b), (d), or (f):

(1) a security interest securing an obligation incurred as all or part of the price of the collateral has priority over a security interest securing an obligation incurred for value given to enable the debtor to acquire rights in or the use of collateral; and

(2) in all other cases, Section 9–322(a) applies to the qualifying security interests.

§ 9–325. Priority of Security Interests in Transferred Collateral.

(a) Except as otherwise provided in subsection (b), a security interest created by a debtor is subordinate to a security interest in the same collateral created by another person if:

(1) the debtor acquired the collateral subject to the security interest created by the other person;

(2) the security interest created by the other person was perfected when the debtor acquired the collateral; and

(3) there is no period thereafter when the security interest is unperfected.

(b) Subsection (a) subordinates a security interest only if the security interest:

(1) otherwise would have priority solely under Section 9–322(a) or 9–324; or

(2) arose solely under Section 2–711(3) or 2A–508(5).

§ 9–326. Priority of Security Interests Created by New Debtor.

(a) Subject to subsection (b), a security interest created by a new debtor which is perfected by a filed financing statement that is effective solely under Section 9–508 in collateral in which a new debtor has or acquires rights is subordinate to a security interest in the same collateral which is perfected other than by a filed financing statement that is effective solely under Section 9–508.

(b) The other provisions of this part determine the priority among conflicting security interests in the same collateral perfected by filed financing statements that are effective solely under Section 9–508. However, if the security agreements to which a new debtor became bound as debtor were not entered into by the same original debtor, the conflicting security interests rank according to priority in time of the new debtor's having become bound.

§ 9–327. Priority of Security Interests in Deposit Account.

The following rules govern priority among conflicting security interests in the same deposit account:

(1) A security interest held by a secured party having control of the deposit account under Section 9–104 has priority over a conflicting security interest held by a secured party that does not have control.

(2) Except as otherwise provided in paragraphs (3) and (4), security interests perfected by control under Section 9–314 rank according to priority in time of obtaining control.

(3) Except as otherwise provided in paragraph (4), a security interest held by the bank with which the deposit account is maintained has priority over a conflicting security interest held by another secured party.

(4) A security interest perfected by control under Section 9–104(a)(3) has priority over a security interest held by the bank with which the deposit account is maintained.

§ 9–328. Priority of Security Interests in Investment Property.

The following rules govern priority among conflicting security interests in the same investment property:

(1) A security interest held by a secured party having control of investment property under Section 9–106 has priority over a security interest held by a secured party that does not have control of the investment property.

(2) Except as otherwise provided in paragraphs (3) and (4), conflicting security interests held by secured parties each of which has control under Section 9–106 rank according to priority in time of:

(A) if the collateral is a security, obtaining control;

(B) if the collateral is a security entitlement carried in a securities account and:

(i) if the secured party obtained control under Section 8–106(d)(1), the secured party's becoming the person for which the securities account is maintained;

(ii) if the secured party obtained control under Section 8–106(d)(2), the securities intermediary's agreement to comply with the secured party's entitlement orders with respect to security entitlements carried or to be carried in the securities account; or

(iii) if the secured party obtained control through another person under Section 8–106(d)(3), the time on which priority would be based under this paragraph if the other person were the secured party; or

(C) if the collateral is a commodity contract carried with a commodity intermediary, the satisfaction of the requirement for control specified in Section 9–106(b)(2) with respect to commodity contracts carried or to be carried with the commodity intermediary.

(3) A security interest held by a securities intermediary in a security entitlement or a securities account maintained with the securities intermediary has priority over a conflicting security interest held by another secured party.

(4) A security interest held by a commodity intermediary in a commodity contract or a commodity account maintained with the commodity intermediary has priority over a conflicting security interest held by another secured party.

(5) A security interest in a certificated security in registered form which is perfected by taking delivery under Section 9–313(a) and not by control under Section 9–314 has priority over a conflicting security interest perfected by a method other than control.

(6) Conflicting security interests created by a broker, securities intermediary, or commodity intermediary which are perfected without control under Section 9–106 rank equally.

(7) In all other cases, priority among conflicting security interests in investment property is governed by Sections 9–322 and 9–323.

§ 9–329. Priority of Security Interests in Letter-of-Credit Right.

The following rules govern priority among conflicting security interests in the same letter-of-credit right:

(1) A security interest held by a secured party having control of the letter-of-credit right under Section 9–107 has priority to the extent of its control over a conflicting security interest held by a secured party that does not have control.

(2) Security interests perfected by control under Section 9–314 rank according to priority in time of obtaining control.

§ 9–330. Priority of Purchaser of Chattel Paper or Instrument.

(a) A purchaser of chattel paper has priority over a security interest in the chattel paper which is claimed merely as proceeds of inventory subject to a security interest if:

(1) in good faith and in the ordinary course of the purchaser's business, the purchaser gives new value and takes possession of the chattel paper or obtains control of the chattel paper under Section 9–105; and

(2) the chattel paper does not indicate that it has been assigned to an identified assignee other than the purchaser.

(b) A purchaser of chattel paper has priority over a security interest in the chattel paper which is claimed other than merely as proceeds of inventory subject to a security interest if the purchaser gives new value and takes possession of the chattel paper or obtains control of the chattel paper under Section 9–105 in good faith, in the ordinary course of the purchaser's business, and without knowledge that the purchase violates the rights of the secured party.

(c) Except as otherwise provided in Section 9–327, a purchaser having priority in chattel paper under subsection (a) or (b) also has priority in proceeds of the chattel paper to the extent that:

(1) Section 9–322 provides for priority in the proceeds; or

(2) the proceeds consist of the specific goods covered by the chattel paper or cash proceeds of the specific goods, even if the purchaser's security interest in the proceeds is unperfected.

(d) Except as otherwise provided in Section 9–331(a), a purchaser of an instrument has priority over a security interest in the instrument perfected by a method other than possession if the purchaser gives value and takes possession of the instrument in good faith and without knowledge that the purchase violates the rights of the secured party.

(e) For purposes of subsections (a) and (b), the holder of a purchase-money security interest in inventory gives new value for chattel paper constituting proceeds of the inventory.

(f) For purposes of subsections (b) and (d), if chattel paper or an instrument indicates that it has been assigned to an identified secured party other than the purchaser, a purchaser of the chattel paper or instrument has knowledge that the purchase violates the rights of the secured party.

§ 9–331. Priority of Rights of Purchasers of Instruments, Documents, and Securities under Other Articles; Priority of Interests in Financial Assets and Security Entitlements under Article 8.

(a) This article does not limit the rights of a holder in due course of a negotiable instrument, a holder to which a negotiable document of title has been duly negotiated, or a protected purchaser of a security. These holders or purchasers take priority over an earlier security interest, even if perfected, to the extent provided in Articles 3, 7, and 8.

(b) This article does not limit the rights of or impose liability on a person to the extent that the person is protected against the assertion of a claim under Article 8.

(c) Filing under this article does not constitute notice of a claim or defense to the holders, or purchasers, or persons described in subsections (a) and (b).

§ 9–332. Transfer of Money; Transfer of Funds from Deposit Account.

(a) A transferee of money takes the money free of a security interest unless the transferee acts in collusion with the debtor in violating the rights of the secured party.

(b) A transferee of funds from a deposit account takes the funds free of a security interest in the deposit account unless the transferee acts in collusion with the debtor in violating the rights of the secured party.

§ 9–333. Priority of Certain Liens Arising by Operation of Law.

(a) In this section, "possessory lien" means an interest, other than a security interest or an agricultural lien:

(1) which secures payment or performance of an obligation for services or materials furnished with respect to goods by a person in the ordinary course of the person's business;

(2) which is created by statute or rule of law in favor of the person; and

(3) whose effectiveness depends on the person's possession of the goods.

(b) A possessory lien on goods has priority over a security interest in the goods unless the lien is created by a statute that expressly provides otherwise.

§ 9–334. Priority of Security Interests in Fixtures and Crops.

(a) A security interest under this article may be created in goods that are fixtures or may continue in goods that become fixtures. A security interest does not exist under this article in ordinary building materials incorporated into an improvement on land.

(b) This article does not prevent creation of an encumbrance upon fixtures under real property law.

(c) In cases not governed by subsections (d) through (h), a security interest in fixtures is subordinate to a conflicting interest of an encumbrancer or owner of the related real property other than the debtor.

(d) Except as otherwise provided in subsection (h), a perfected security interest in fixtures has priority over a conflicting interest of an encumbrancer or owner of the real property if the debtor has an interest of record in or is in possession of the real property and:

(1) the security interest is a purchase-money security interest;

(2) the interest of the encumbrancer or owner arises before the goods become fixtures; and

(3) the security interest is perfected by a fixture filing before the goods become fixtures or within 20 days thereafter.

(e) A perfected security interest in fixtures has priority over a conflicting interest of an encumbrancer or owner of the real property if:

(1) the debtor has an interest of record in the real property or is in possession of the real property and the security interest:

(A) is perfected by a fixture filing before the interest of the encumbrancer or owner is of record; and

(B) has priority over any conflicting interest of a predecessor in title of the encumbrancer or owner;

(2) before the goods become fixtures, the security interest is perfected by any method permitted by this article and the fixtures are readily removable:

(A) factory or office machines;

(B) equipment that is not primarily used or leased for use in the operation of the real property; or

(C) replacements of domestic appliances that are consumer goods;

(3) the conflicting interest is a lien on the real property obtained by legal or equitable proceedings after the security interest was perfected by any method permitted by this article; or

(4) the security interest is:

(A) created in a manufactured home in a manufactured-home transaction; and

(B) perfected pursuant to a statute described in Section 9–311(a)(2).

(f) A security interest in fixtures, whether or not perfected, has priority over a conflicting interest of an encumbrancer or owner of the real property if:

(1) the encumbrancer or owner has, in an authenticated record, consented to the security interest or disclaimed an interest in the goods as fixtures; or

(2) the debtor has a right to remove the goods as against the encumbrancer or owner.

(g) The priority of the security interest under paragraph (f)(2) continues for a reasonable time if the debtor's right to remove the goods as against the encumbrancer or owner terminates.

(h) A mortgage is a construction mortgage to the extent that it secures an obligation incurred for the construction of an improvement on land, including the acquisition cost of the land, if a recorded record of the mortgage so indicates. Except as otherwise provided in subsections (e) and (f), a security interest in fixtures is subordinate to a construction mortgage if a record of the mortgage is recorded before the goods become fixtures and the goods become fixtures before the completion of the construction. A mortgage has this priority to the same extent as a construction mortgage to the extent that it is given to refinance a construction mortgage.

(i) A perfected security interest in crops growing on real property has priority over a conflicting interest of an encumbrancer or owner of the real property if the debtor has an interest of record in or is in possession of the real property.

(j) Subsection (i) prevails over any inconsistent provisions of the following statutes:

[List here any statutes containing provisions inconsistent with subsection (i).]

Legislative Note: States that amend statutes to remove provisions inconsistent with subsection (i) need not enact subsection (j).

§ 9–335. Accessions.

(a) A security interest may be created in an accession and continues in collateral that becomes an accession.

(b) If a security interest is perfected when the collateral becomes an accession, the security interest remains perfected in the collateral.

(c) Except as otherwise provided in subsection (d), the other provisions of this part determine the priority of a security interest in an accession.

(d) A security interest in an accession is subordinate to a security interest in the whole which is perfected by compliance with the requirements of a certificate-of-title statute under Section 9–311(b).

(e) After default, subject to Part 6, a secured party may remove an accession from other goods if the security interest in the accession has priority over the claims of every person having an interest in the whole.

(f) A secured party that removes an accession from other goods under subsection (e) shall promptly reimburse any holder of a security interest or other lien on, or owner of, the whole or of the other goods, other than the debtor, for the cost of repair of any physical injury to the whole or the other goods. The secured party need not reimburse the holder or owner for any diminution in value of the whole or the other goods caused by the absence of the accession removed or by any necessity for replacing it. A person entitled to reimbursement may refuse permission to remove until the secured party gives adequate assurance for the performance of the obligation to reimburse.

§ 9–336. Commingled Goods.

(a) In this section, "commingled goods" means goods that are physically united with other goods in such a manner that their identity is lost in a product or mass.

(b) A security interest does not exist in commingled goods as such. However, a security interest may attach to a product or mass that results when goods become commingled goods.

(c) If collateral becomes commingled goods, a security interest attaches to the product or mass.

(d) If a security interest in collateral is perfected before the collateral becomes commingled goods, the security interest that attaches to the product or mass under subsection (c) is perfected.

(e) Except as otherwise provided in subsection (f), the other provisions of this part determine the priority of a security interest that attaches to the product or mass under subsection (c).

(f) If more than one security interest attaches to the product or mass under subsection (c), the following rules determine priority:

(1) A security interest that is perfected under subsection (d) has priority over a security interest that is unperfected at the time the collateral becomes commingled goods.

(2) If more than one security interest is perfected under subsection (d), the security interests rank equally in proportion to the value of the collateral at the time it became commingled goods.

§ 9–337. Priority of Security Interests in Goods Covered by Certificate of Title.

If, while a security interest in goods is perfected by any method under the law of another jurisdiction, this State issues a certificate of title that does not show that the goods are subject to the security interest or contain a statement that they may be subject to security interests not shown on the certificate:

(1) a buyer of the goods, other than a person in the business of selling goods of that kind, takes free of the security interest if the buyer gives value and receives delivery of the goods after issuance of the certificate and without knowledge of the security interest; and

(2) the security interest is subordinate to a conflicting security interest in the goods that attaches, and is perfected under Section 9–311(b), after issuance of the certificate and without the conflicting secured party's knowledge of the security interest.

§ 9–338. Priority of Security Interest or Agricultural Lien Perfected by Filed Financing Statement Providing Certain Incorrect Information.

If a security interest or agricultural lien is perfected by a filed financing statement providing information described in Section 9–516(b)(5) which is incorrect at the time the financing statement is filed:

(1) the security interest or agricultural lien is subordinate to a conflicting perfected security interest in the collateral to the extent that the holder of the conflicting security interest gives value in reasonable reliance upon the incorrect information; and

(2) a purchaser, other than a secured party, of the collateral takes free of the security interest or agricultural lien to the extent that, in reasonable reliance upon the incorrect information, the purchaser gives value and, in the case of chattel paper, documents, goods, instruments, or a security certificate, receives delivery of the collateral.

§ 9–339. Priority Subject to Subordination.

This article does not preclude subordination by agreement by a person entitled to priority.

[Subpart 4. Rights of Bank]

§ 9–340. Effectiveness of Right of Recoupment or Set-Off against Deposit Account.

(a) Except as otherwise provided in subsection (c), a bank with which a deposit account is maintained may exercise any right of recoupment or set-off against a secured party that holds a security interest in the deposit account.

(b) Except as otherwise provided in subsection (c), the application of this article to a security interest in a deposit account does not affect a right of recoupment or set-off of the secured party as to a deposit account maintained with the secured party.

(c) The exercise by a bank of a set-off against a deposit account is ineffective against a secured party that holds a security interest in the deposit account which is perfected by control under Section 9–104(a)(3), if the set-off is based on a claim against the debtor.

§ 9–341. Bank's Rights and Duties with Respect to Deposit Account.

Except as otherwise provided in Section 9–340(c), and unless the bank otherwise agrees in an authenticated record, a bank's rights and duties with respect to a deposit account maintained with the bank are not terminated, suspended, or modified by:

(1) the creation, attachment, or perfection of a security interest in the deposit account;

(2) the bank's knowledge of the security interest; or

(3) the bank's receipt of instructions from the secured party.

§ 9–342. Bank's Right to Refuse to Enter into or Disclose Existence of Control Agreement.

This article does not require a bank to enter into an agreement of the kind described in Section 9–104(a)(2), even if its customer so requests or directs. A bank that has entered into such an agreement is not required to confirm the existence of the agreement to another person unless requested to do so by its customer.

Part 4 Rights of Third Parties

§ 9–401. Alienability of Debtor's Rights.

(a) Except as otherwise provided in subsection (b) and Sections 9–406, 9–407, 9–408, and 9–409, whether a debtor's rights in collateral may be voluntarily or involuntarily transferred is governed by law other than this article.

(b) An agreement between the debtor and secured party which prohibits a transfer of the debtor's rights in collateral or makes the transfer a default does not prevent the transfer from taking effect.

§ 9–402. Secured Party Not Obligated on Contract of Debtor or in Tort.

The existence of a security interest, agricultural lien, or authority given to a debtor to dispose of or use collateral, without more, does not subject a secured party to liability in contract or tort for the debtor's acts or omissions.

§ 9–403. Agreement Not to Assert Defenses against Assignee.

(a) In this section, "value" has the meaning provided in Section 3–303(a).

(b) Except as otherwise provided in this section, an agreement between an account debtor and an assignor not to assert against an assignee any claim or defense that the account debtor may have against the assignor is enforceable by an assignee that takes an assignment:

(1) for value;

(2) in good faith;

(3) without notice of a claim of a property or possessory right to the property assigned; and

(4) without notice of a defense or claim in recoupment of the type that may be asserted against a person entitled to enforce a negotiable instrument under Section 3–305(a).

(c) Subsection (b) does not apply to defenses of a type that may be asserted against a holder in due course of a negotiable instrument under Section 3–305(b).

(d) In a consumer transaction, if a record evidences the account debtor's obligation, law other than this article requires that the record include a statement to the effect that the rights of an assignee are subject to claims or defenses that the account debtor could assert against the original obligee, and the record does not include such a statement:

(1) the record has the same effect as if the record included such a statement; and

(2) the account debtor may assert against an assignee those claims and defenses that would have been available if the record included such a statement.

(e) This section is subject to law other than this article which establishes a different rule for an account debtor who is an individual and who incurred the obligation primarily for personal, family, or household purposes.

(f) Except as otherwise provided in subsection (d), this section does not displace law other than this article which gives effect to an agreement by an account debtor not to assert a claim or defense against an assignee.

§ 9–404. Rights Acquired by Assignee; Claims and Defenses against Assignee.

(a) Unless an account debtor has made an enforceable agreement not to assert defenses or claims, and subject to subsections (b) through (e), the rights of an assignee are subject to:

(1) all terms of the agreement between the account debtor and assignor and any defense or claim in recoupment arising from the transaction that gave rise to the contract; and

(2) any other defense or claim of the account debtor against the assignor which accrues before the account debtor receives a notification of the assignment authenticated by the assignor or the assignee.

(b) Subject to subsection (c) and except as otherwise provided in subsection (d), the claim of an account debtor against an assignor may be asserted against an assignee under subsection (a) only to reduce the amount the account debtor owes.

(c) This section is subject to law other than this article which establishes a different rule for an account debtor who is an individual and who incurred the obligation primarily for personal, family, or household purposes.

(d) In a consumer transaction, if a record evidences the account debtor's obligation, law other than this article requires that the record include a statement to the effect that the account debtor's recovery against an assignee with respect to claims and defenses against the assignor may not exceed amounts paid by the account debtor under the record, and the record does not include such a statement, the extent to which a claim of an account debtor against the assignor may be asserted against an assignee is determined as if the record included such a statement.

(e) This section does not apply to an assignment of a health-care-insurance receivable.

§ 9–405. Modification of Assigned Contract.

(a) A modification of or substitution for an assigned contract is effective against an assignee if made in good faith. The assignee acquires corresponding rights under the modified or substituted contract. The assignment may provide that the modification or substitution is a breach of contract by the assignor. This subsection is subject to subsections (b) through (d).

(b) Subsection (a) applies to the extent that:

(1) the right to payment or a part thereof under an assigned contract has not been fully earned by performance; or

(2) the right to payment or a part thereof has been fully earned by performance and the account debtor has not received notification of the assignment under Section 9–406(a).

(c) This section is subject to law other than this article which establishes a different rule for an account debtor who is an individual and who incurred the obligation primarily for personal, family, or household purposes.

(d) This section does not apply to an assignment of a health-care-insurance receivable.

§ 9–406. Discharge of Account Debtor; Notification of Assignment; Identification and Proof of Assignment; Restrictions on Assignment of Accounts, Chattel Paper, Payment Intangibles, and Promissory Notes Ineffective.

(a) Subject to subsections (b) through (i), an account debtor on an account, chattel paper, or a payment intangible may discharge its obligation by paying the assignor until, but not after, the account debtor receives a notification, authenticated by the assignor or the assignee, that the amount due or to become due has been assigned and that payment is to be made to the assignee. After receipt of the notification, the account debtor may discharge its obligation by paying the assignee and may not discharge the obligation by paying the assignor.

(b) Subject to subsection (h), notification is ineffective under subsection (a):

(1) if it does not reasonably identify the rights assigned;

(2) to the extent that an agreement between an account debtor and a seller of a payment intangible limits the account debtor's duty to pay a person other than the seller and the limitation is effective under law other than this article; or

(3) at the option of an account debtor, if the notification notifies the account debtor to make less than the full amount of any installment or other periodic payment to the assignee, even if:

(A) only a portion of the account, chattel paper, or payment intangible has been assigned to that assignee;

(B) a portion has been assigned to another assignee; or

(C) the account debtor knows that the assignment to that assignee is limited.

(c) Subject to subsection (h), if requested by the account debtor, an assignee shall seasonably furnish reasonable proof that the assignment has been made. Unless the assignee complies, the account debtor may discharge its obligation by paying the assignor, even if the account debtor has received a notification under subsection (a).

(d) Except as otherwise provided in subsection (e) and Sections 2A–303 and 9–407, and subject to subsection (h), a term in an agreement between an account debtor and an assignor or in a promissory note is ineffective to the extent that it:

(1) prohibits, restricts, or requires the consent of the account debtor or person obligated on the promissory note to the assignment or transfer of, or the creation, attachment, perfection, or enforcement of a security interest in, the account, chattel paper, payment intangible, or promissory note; or

(2) provides that the assignment or transfer or the creation, attachment, perfection, or enforcement of the security interest may give rise to a default, breach, right of recoupment, claim, defense, termination, right of termination, or remedy under the account, chattel paper, payment intangible, or promissory note.

(e) Subsection (d) does not apply to the sale of a payment intangible or promissory note.

(f) Except as otherwise provided in Sections 2A–303 and 9–407 and subject to subsections (h) and (i), a rule of law, statute, or regulation that prohibits, restricts, or requires the consent of a government, governmental body or official, or account debtor to the assignment or transfer of, or creation of a security interest in, an account or chattel paper is ineffective to the extent that the rule of law, statute, or regulation:

(1) prohibits, restricts, or requires the consent of the government, governmental body or official, or account debtor to the assignment or transfer of, or the creation, attachment, perfection, or enforcement of a security interest in the account or chattel paper; or

(2) provides that the assignment or transfer or the creation, attachment, perfection, or enforcement of the security interest may give rise to a default, breach, right of recoupment, claim, defense, termination, right of termination, or remedy under the account or chattel paper.

(g) Subject to subsection (h), an account debtor may not waive or vary its option under subsection (b)(3).

(h) This section is subject to law other than this article which establishes a different rule for an account debtor who is an individual and who incurred the obligation primarily for personal, family, or household purposes.

(i) This section does not apply to an assignment of a health-care-insurance receivable.

(j) This section prevails over any inconsistent provisions of the following statutes, rules, and regulations:

[List here any statutes, rules, and regulations containing provisions inconsistent with this section.]

Legislative Note: States that amend statutes, rules, and regulations to remove provisions inconsistent with this section need not enact subsection (j).

As amended in 1999 and 2000.

§ 9–407. Restrictions on Creation or Enforcement of Security Interest in Leasehold Interest or in Lessor's Residual Interest.

(a) Except as otherwise provided in subsection (b), a term in a lease agreement is ineffective to the extent that it:

(1) prohibits, restricts, or requires the consent of a party to the lease to the assignment or transfer of, or the creation, attachment, perfection, or enforcement of a security interest in an interest of a party under the lease contract or in the lessor's residual interest in the goods; or

(2) provides that the assignment or transfer or the creation, attachment, perfection, or enforcement of the security interest may give rise to a default, breach, right of recoupment, claim, defense, termination, right of termination, or remedy under the lease.

(b) Except as otherwise provided in Section 2A–303(7), a term described in subsection (a)(2) is effective to the extent that there is:

(1) a transfer by the lessee of the lessee's right of possession or use of the goods in violation of the term; or

(2) a delegation of a material performance of either party to the lease contract in violation of the term.

(c) The creation, attachment, perfection, or enforcement of a security interest in the lessor's interest under the lease contract or the lessor's residual interest in the goods is not a transfer that materially impairs the lessee's prospect of obtaining return performance or materially changes the duty of or materially increases the burden or risk imposed on the lessee within the purview of Section 2A–303(4) unless, and then only to the extent that, enforcement actually results in a delegation of material performance of the lessor.

As amended in 1999.

§ 9–408. Restrictions on Assignment of Promissory Notes, Health-Care-Insurance Receivables, and Certain General Intangibles Ineffective.

(a) Except as otherwise provided in subsection (b), a term in a promissory note or in an agreement between an account debtor and a debtor which relates to a health-care-insurance receivable or a general intangible, including a contract, permit, license, or franchise, and which term prohibits, restricts, or requires the consent of the person obligated on the promissory note or the account debtor to, the assignment or transfer of, or creation, attachment, or perfection of a security interest in, the promissory note, health-care-insurance receivable, or general intangible, is ineffective to the extent that the term:

(1) would impair the creation, attachment, or perfection of a security interest; or

(2) provides that the assignment or transfer or the creation, attachment, or perfection of the security interest may give rise to a default, breach, right of recoupment, claim, defense, termination, right of termination, or remedy under the promissory note, health-care-insurance receivable, or general intangible.

(b) Subsection (a) applies to a security interest in a payment intangible or promissory note only if the security interest arises out of a sale of the payment intangible or promissory note.

(c) A rule of law, statute, or regulation that prohibits, restricts, or requires the consent of a government, governmental body or official, person obligated on a promissory note, or account debtor to the assignment or transfer of, or creation of a security interest in, a promissory note, health-care-insurance receivable, or general intangible, including a contract, permit, license, or franchise between an account debtor and a debtor, is ineffective to the extent that the rule of law, statute, or regulation:

(1) would impair the creation, attachment, or perfection of a security interest; or

(2) provides that the assignment or transfer or the creation, attachment, or perfection of the security interest may give rise to a default, breach, right of recoupment, claim, defense, termination, right of termination, or remedy under the promissory note, health-care-insurance receivable, or general intangible.

(d) To the extent that a term in a promissory note or in an agreement between an account debtor and a debtor which relates to a health-care-insurance receivable or general intangible or a rule of law, statute, or regulation described in subsection (c) would be effective under law other than this article but is ineffective under subsection (a) or (c), the creation, attachment, or perfection of a security interest in the promissory note, health-care-insurance receivable, or general intangible:

(1) is not enforceable against the person obligated on the promissory note or the account debtor;

(2) does not impose a duty or obligation on the person obligated on the promissory note or the account debtor;

(3) does not require the person obligated on the promissory note or the account debtor to recognize the security interest, pay or render performance to the secured party, or accept payment or performance from the secured party;

(4) does not entitle the secured party to use or assign the debtor's rights under the promissory note, health-care-insurance receivable, or general intangible, including any related information or materials furnished to the debtor in the transaction giving rise to the promissory note, health-care-insurance receivable, or general intangible;

(5) does not entitle the secured party to use, assign, possess, or have access to any trade secrets or confidential information of the person obligated on the promissory note or the account debtor; and

(6) does not entitle the secured party to enforce the security interest in the promissory note, health-care-insurance receivable, or general intangible.

(e) This section prevails over any inconsistent provisions of the following statutes, rules, and regulations:

[List here any statutes, rules, and regulations containing provisions inconsistent with this section.]

Legislative Note: States that amend statutes, rules, and regulations to remove provisions inconsistent with this section need not enact subsection (e).

As amended in 1999.

§ 9–409. Restrictions on Assignment of Letter-of-Credit Rights Ineffective.

(a) A term in a letter of credit or a rule of law, statute, regulation, custom, or practice applicable to the letter of credit which prohibits, restricts, or requires the consent of an applicant, issuer, or nominated person to a beneficiary's assignment of or creation of a security interest in a letter-of-credit right is ineffective to the extent that the term or rule of law, statute, regulation, custom, or practice:

(1) would impair the creation, attachment, or perfection of a security interest in the letter-of-credit right; or

(2) provides that the assignment or the creation, attachment, or perfection of the security interest may give rise to a default, breach, right of recoupment, claim, defense, termination, right of termination, or remedy under the letter-of-credit right.

(b) To the extent that a term in a letter of credit is ineffective under subsection (a) but would be effective under law other than this article or a custom or practice applicable to the letter of credit, to the transfer of a right to draw or otherwise demand performance under the letter of credit, or to the assignment of a right to proceeds of the letter of credit, the creation, attachment, or perfection of a security interest in the letter-of-credit right:

(1) is not enforceable against the applicant, issuer, nominated person, or transferee beneficiary;

(2) imposes no duties or obligations on the applicant, issuer, nominated person, or transferee beneficiary; and

(3) does not require the applicant, issuer, nominated person, or transferee beneficiary to recognize the security interest, pay or render performance to the secured party, or accept payment or other performance from the secured party.

As amended in 1999.

Part 5 Filing

[Subpart 1. Filing Office; Contents and Effectiveness of Financing Statement]

§ 9–501. Filing Office.

(a) Except as otherwise provided in subsection (b), if the local law of this State governs perfection of a security interest or agricultural lien, the office in which to file a financing statement to perfect the security interest or agricultural lien is:

(1) the office designated for the filing or recording of a record of a mortgage on the related real property, if:

(A) the collateral is as-extracted collateral or timber to be cut; or

(B) the financing statement is filed as a fixture filing and the collateral is goods that are or are to become fixtures; or

(2) the office of [ ] [or any office duly authorized by [ ]], in all other cases, including a case in which the collateral is goods that are or are to become fixtures and the financing statement is not filed as a fixture filing.

(b) The office in which to file a financing statement to perfect a security interest in collateral, including fixtures, of a transmitting utility is the office of [ ]. The financing statement also constitutes a fixture filing as to the collateral indicated in the financing statement which is or is to become fixtures.

Legislative Note: The State should designate the filing office where the brackets appear. The filing office may be that of a governmental official (e.g., the Secretary of State) or a private party that maintains the State's filing system.

§ 9–502. Contents of Financing Statement; Record of Mortgage as Financing Statement; Time of Filing Financing Statement.

(a) Subject to subsection (b), a financing statement is sufficient only if it:

(1) provides the name of the debtor;

(2) provides the name of the secured party or a representative of the secured party; and

(3) indicates the collateral covered by the financing statement.

(b) Except as otherwise provided in Section 9–501(b), to be sufficient, a financing statement that covers as-extracted collateral or timber to be cut, or which is filed as a fixture filing and covers goods that are or are to become fixtures, must satisfy subsection (a) and also:

(1) indicate that it covers this type of collateral;

(2) indicate that it is to be filed [for record] in the real property records;

(3) provide a description of the real property to which the collateral is related [sufficient to give constructive notice of a mortgage under the law of this State if the description were contained in a record of the mortgage of the real property]; and

(4) if the debtor does not have an interest of record in the real property, provide the name of a record owner.

(c) A record of a mortgage is effective, from the date of recording, as a financing statement filed as a fixture filing or as a financing statement covering as-extracted collateral or timber to be cut only if:

(1) the record indicates the goods or accounts that it covers;

(2) the goods are or are to become fixtures related to the real property described in the record or the collateral is related to the real property described in the record and is as-extracted collateral or timber to be cut;

(3) the record satisfies the requirements for a financing statement in this section other than an indication that it is to be filed in the real property records; and

(4) the record is [duly] recorded.

(d) A financing statement may be filed before a security agreement is made or a security interest otherwise attaches.

Legislative Note: Language in brackets is optional. Where the State has any special recording system for real property other than the usual grantor-grantee index (as, for instance, a tract system or a title registration or Torrens system) local adaptations of subsection (b) and Section 9–519(d) and (e) may be necessary. See, e.g., Mass. Gen. Laws Chapter 106, Section 9–410.

§ 9–503. Name of Debtor and Secured Party.

(a) A financing statement sufficiently provides the name of the debtor:

(1) if the debtor is a registered organization, only if the financing statement provides the name of the debtor indicated on the public record of the debtor's jurisdiction of organization which shows the debtor to have been organized;

(2) if the debtor is a decedent's estate, only if the financing statement provides the name of the decedent and indicates that the debtor is an estate;

(3) if the debtor is a trust or a trustee acting with respect to property held in trust, only if the financing statement:

(A) provides the name specified for the trust in its organic documents or, if no name is specified, provides the name of the settlor and additional information sufficient to distinguish the debtor from other trusts having one or more of the same settlors; and

(B) indicates, in the debtor's name or otherwise, that the debtor is a trust or is a trustee acting with respect to property held in trust; and

(4) in other cases:

(A) if the debtor has a name, only if it provides the individual or organizational name of the debtor; and

(B) if the debtor does not have a name, only if it provides the names of the partners, members, associates, or other persons comprising the debtor.

(b) A financing statement that provides the name of the debtor in accordance with subsection (a) is not rendered ineffective by the absence of:

(1) a trade name or other name of the debtor; or

(2) unless required under subsection (a)(4)(B), names of partners, members, associates, or other persons comprising the debtor.

(c) A financing statement that provides only the debtor's trade name does not sufficiently provide the name of the debtor.

(d) Failure to indicate the representative capacity of a secured party or representative of a secured party does not affect the sufficiency of a financing statement.

(e) A financing statement may provide the name of more than one debtor and the name of more than one secured party.

§ 9–504. Indication of Collateral.

A financing statement sufficiently indicates the collateral that it covers if the financing statement provides:

(1) a description of the collateral pursuant to Section 9–108; or

(2) an indication that the financing statement covers all assets or all personal property.

As amended in 1999.

§ 9–505. Filing and Compliance with Other Statutes and Treaties for Consignments, Leases, Other Bailments, and Other Transactions.

(a) A consignor, lessor, or other bailor of goods, a licensor, or a buyer of a payment intangible or promissory note may file a financing statement, or may comply with a statute or treaty described in Section 9–311(a), using the terms "consignor", "consignee", "lessor", "lessee", "bailor", "bailee", "licensor", "licensee", "owner", "registered owner", "buyer", "seller", or words of similar import, instead of the terms "secured party" and "debtor".

(b) This part applies to the filing of a financing statement under subsection (a) and, as appropriate, to compliance that is equivalent to filing a financing statement under Section 9–311(b), but the filing or compliance is not of itself a factor in determining whether the collateral secures an obligation. If it is determined for another reason that the collateral secures an obligation, a security interest held by the consignor, lessor, bailor, licensor, owner, or buyer which attaches to the collateral is perfected by the filing or compliance.

§ 9–506. Effect of Errors or Omissions.

(a) A financing statement substantially satisfying the requirements of this part is effective, even if it has minor errors or omissions, unless the errors or omissions make the financing statement seriously misleading.

(b) Except as otherwise provided in subsection (c), a financing statement that fails sufficiently to provide the name of the debtor in accordance with Section 9–503(a) is seriously misleading.

(c) If a search of the records of the filing office under the debtor's correct name, using the filing office's standard search logic, if any, would disclose a financing statement that fails sufficiently to provide the name of the debtor in accordance with Section 9–503(a), the name provided does not make the financing statement seriously misleading.

(d) For purposes of Section 9–508(b), the "debtor's correct name" in subsection (c) means the correct name of the new debtor.

§ 9–507. Effect of Certain Events on Effectiveness of Financing Statement.

(a) A filed financing statement remains effective with respect to collateral that is sold, exchanged, leased, licensed, or otherwise disposed of and in which a security interest or agricultural lien continues, even if the secured party knows of or consents to the disposition.

(b) Except as otherwise provided in subsection (c) and Section 9–508, a financing statement is not rendered ineffective if, after the financing statement is filed, the information provided in the financing statement becomes seriously misleading under Section 9–506.

(c) If a debtor so changes its name that a filed financing statement becomes seriously misleading under Section 9–506:

(1) the financing statement is effective to perfect a security interest in collateral acquired by the debtor before, or within four months after, the change; and

(2) the financing statement is not effective to perfect a security interest in collateral acquired by the debtor more than four months after the change, unless an amendment to the financing statement which renders the financing statement not seriously misleading is filed within four months after the change.

§ 9–508. Effectiveness of Financing Statement If New Debtor Becomes Bound by Security Agreement.

(a) Except as otherwise provided in this section, a filed financing statement naming an original debtor is effective to perfect a security interest in collateral in which a new debtor has or acquires rights to the extent that the financing statement would have been effective had the original debtor acquired rights in the collateral.

(b) If the difference between the name of the original debtor and that of the new debtor causes a filed financing statement that is effective under subsection (a) to be seriously misleading under Section 9–506:

(1) the financing statement is effective to perfect a security interest in collateral acquired by the new debtor before, and within four months after, the new debtor becomes bound under Section 9B–203(d); and

(2) the financing statement is not effective to perfect a security interest in collateral acquired by the new debtor more than four months after the new debtor becomes bound under Section 9–203(d) unless an initial financing statement providing the name of the new debtor is filed before the expiration of that time.

(c) This section does not apply to collateral as to which a filed financing statement remains effective against the new debtor under Section 9–507(a).

§ 9–509. Persons Entitled to File a Record.

(a) A person may file an initial financing statement, amendment that adds collateral covered by a financing statement, or amendment that adds a debtor to a financing statement only if:

(1) the debtor authorizes the filing in an authenticated record or pursuant to subsection (b) or (c); or

(2) the person holds an agricultural lien that has become effective at the time of filing and the financing statement covers only collateral in which the person holds an agricultural lien.

(b) By authenticating or becoming bound as debtor by a security agreement, a debtor or new debtor authorizes the filing of an initial financing statement, and an amendment, covering:

(1) the collateral described in the security agreement; and

(2) property that becomes collateral under Section 9–315(a)(2), whether or not the security agreement expressly covers proceeds.

(c) By acquiring collateral in which a security interest or agricultural lien continues under Section 9–315(a)(1), a debtor authorizes the filing of an initial financing statement, and an amendment, covering the collateral and property that becomes collateral under Section 9–315(a)(2).

(d) A person may file an amendment other than an amendment that adds collateral covered by a financing statement or an amendment that adds a debtor to a financing statement only if:

(1) the secured party of record authorizes the filing; or

(2) the amendment is a termination statement for a financing statement as to which the secured party of record has failed to file or send a termination statement as required by Section 9–513(a) or (c), the debtor authorizes the filing, and the termination statement indicates that the debtor authorized it to be filed.

(e) If there is more than one secured party of record for a financing statement, each secured party of record may authorize the filing of an amendment under subsection (d).

As amended in 2000.

§ 9–510. Effectiveness of Filed Record.

(a) A filed record is effective only to the extent that it was filed by a person that may file it under Section 9–509.

(b) A record authorized by one secured party of record does not affect the financing statement with respect to another secured party of record.

(c) A continuation statement that is not filed within the six-month period prescribed by Section 9–515(d) is ineffective.

§ 9–511. Secured Party of Record.

(a) A secured party of record with respect to a financing statement is a person whose name is provided as the name of the secured party or a representative of the secured party in an initial financing statement that has been filed. If an initial financing statement is filed under Section 9–514(a), the assignee named in the initial financing statement is the secured party of record with respect to the financing statement.

(b) If an amendment of a financing statement which provides the name of a person as a secured party or a representative of a secured party is filed, the person named in the amendment is a secured party of record. If an amendment is filed under Section 9–514(b), the assignee named in the amendment is a secured party of record.

(c) A person remains a secured party of record until the filing of an amendment of the financing statement which deletes the person.

§ 9–512. Amendment of Financing Statement.

[Alternative A]

(a) Subject to Section 9–509, a person may add or delete collateral covered by, continue or terminate the effectiveness of, or, subject to subsection (e), otherwise amend the information provided in, a financing statement by filing an amendment that:

(1) identifies, by its file number, the initial financing statement to which the amendment relates; and

(2) if the amendment relates to an initial financing statement filed [or recorded] in a filing office described in Section 9–501(a)(1), provides the information specified in Section 9–502(b).

[Alternative B]

(a) Subject to Section 9–509, a person may add or delete collateral covered by, continue or terminate the effectiveness of, or, subject to subsection (e), otherwise amend the information provided in, a financing statement by filing an amendment that:

(1) identifies, by its file number, the initial financing statement to which the amendment relates; and

(2) if the amendment relates to an initial financing statement filed [or recorded] in a filing office described in Section 9–501(a)(1), provides the date [and time] that the initial financing statement was filed [or recorded] and the information specified in Section 9–502(b).

[End of Alternatives]

(b) Except as otherwise provided in Section 9–515, the filing of an amendment does not extend the period of effectiveness of the financing statement.

(c) A financing statement that is amended by an amendment that adds collateral is effective as to the added collateral only from the date of the filing of the amendment.

(d) A financing statement that is amended by an amendment that adds a debtor is effective as to the added debtor only from the date of the filing of the amendment.

(e) An amendment is ineffective to the extent it:

(1) purports to delete all debtors and fails to provide the name of a debtor to be covered by the financing statement; or

(2) purports to delete all secured parties of record and fails to provide the name of a new secured party of record.

Legislative Note: States whose real-estate filing offices require additional information in amendments and cannot search their records by both the name of the debtor and the file number should enact Alternative B to Sections 9–512(a), 9–518(b), 9–519(f), and 9–522(a).

§ 9–513. Termination Statement.

(a) A secured party shall cause the secured party of record for a financing statement to file a termination statement for the financing statement if the financing statement covers consumer goods and:

(1) there is no obligation secured by the collateral covered by the financing statement and no commitment to make an advance, incur an obligation, or otherwise give value; or

(2) the debtor did not authorize the filing of the initial financing statement.

(b) To comply with subsection (a), a secured party shall cause the secured party of record to file the termination statement:

(1) within one month after there is no obligation secured by the collateral covered by the financing statement and no commitment to make an advance, incur an obligation, or otherwise give value; or

(2) if earlier, within 20 days after the secured party receives an authenticated demand from a debtor.

(c) In cases not governed by subsection (a), within 20 days after a secured party receives an authenticated demand from a debtor, the secured party shall cause the secured party of record for a financing statement to send to the debtor a termination statement for the financing statement or file the termination statement in the filing office if:

(1) except in the case of a financing statement covering accounts or chattel paper that has been sold or goods that are the subject of a consignment, there is no obligation secured by the collateral covered by the financing statement and no commitment to make an advance, incur an obligation, or otherwise give value;

(2) the financing statement covers accounts or chattel paper that has been sold but as to which the account debtor or other person obligated has discharged its obligation;

(3) the financing statement covers goods that were the subject of a consignment to the debtor but are not in the debtor's possession; or

(4) the debtor did not authorize the filing of the initial financing statement.

(d) Except as otherwise provided in Section 9–510, upon the filing of a termination statement with the filing office, the financing statement to which the termination statement relates ceases to be effective. Except as otherwise provided in Section 9–510, for purposes of Sections 9–519(g), 9–522(a), and 9–523(c), the filing with the filing office of a termination statement relating to a financing statement that indicates that the debtor is a transmitting utility also causes the effectiveness of the financing statement to lapse.

As amended in 2000.

§ 9–514. Assignment of Powers of Secured Party of Record.

(a) Except as otherwise provided in subsection (c), an initial financing statement may reflect an assignment of all of the secured party's power to authorize an amendment to the financing statement by providing the name and mailing address of the assignee as the name and address of the secured party.

(b) Except as otherwise provided in subsection (c), a secured party of record may assign of record all or part of its power to authorize an amendment to a financing statement by filing in the filing office an amendment of the financing statement which:

(1) identifies, by its file number, the initial financing statement to which it relates;

(2) provides the name of the assignor; and

(3) provides the name and mailing address of the assignee.

(c) An assignment of record of a security interest in a fixture covered by a record of a mortgage which is effective as a financing statement filed as a fixture filing under Section 9–502(c) may be made only by an assignment of record of the mortgage in the manner provided by law of this State other than [the Uniform Commercial Code].

§ 9–515. Duration and Effectiveness of Financing Statement; Effect of Lapsed Financing Statement.

(a) Except as otherwise provided in subsections (b), (e), (f), and (g), a filed financing statement is effective for a period of five years after the date of filing.

(b) Except as otherwise provided in subsections (e), (f), and (g), an initial financing statement filed in connection with a public-finance transaction or manufactured-home transaction is effective for a period of 30 years after the date of filing if it indicates that it is filed in connection with a public-finance transaction or manufactured-home transaction.

(c) The effectiveness of a filed financing statement lapses on the expiration of the period of its effectiveness unless before the lapse a continuation statement is filed pursuant to subsection (d). Upon lapse, a financing statement ceases to be effective and any security interest or agricultural lien that was perfected by the financing statement becomes unperfected, unless the security interest is perfected otherwise. If the security interest or agricultural lien becomes unperfected upon lapse, it is deemed never to have been perfected as against a purchaser of the collateral for value.

(d) A continuation statement may be filed only within six months before the expiration of the five-year period specified in subsection (a) or the 30-year period specified in subsection (b), whichever is applicable.

(e) Except as otherwise provided in Section 9–510, upon timely filing of a continuation statement, the effectiveness of the initial financing statement continues for a period of five years commencing on the day on which the financing statement would have become ineffective in the absence of the filing. Upon the expiration of the five-year period, the financing statement lapses in the same manner as provided in subsection (c), unless, before the lapse, another continuation statement is filed pursuant to subsection (d). Succeeding continuation statements may be filed in the same manner to continue the effectiveness of the initial financing statement.

(f) If a debtor is a transmitting utility and a filed financing statement so indicates, the financing statement is effective until a termination statement is filed.

(g) A record of a mortgage that is effective as a financing statement filed as a fixture filing under Section 9–502(c) remains effective as a financing statement filed as a fixture filing until the mortgage is released or satisfied of record or its effectiveness otherwise terminates as to the real property.

§ 9–516. What Constitutes Filing; Effectiveness of Filing.

(a) Except as otherwise provided in subsection (b), communication of a record to a filing office and tender of the filing fee or acceptance of the record by the filing office constitutes filing.

(b) Filing does not occur with respect to a record that a filing office refuses to accept because:

(1) the record is not communicated by a method or medium of communication authorized by the filing office;

(2) an amount equal to or greater than the applicable filing fee is not tendered;

(3) the filing office is unable to index the record because:

(A) in the case of an initial financing statement, the record does not provide a name for the debtor;

(B) in the case of an amendment or correction statement, the record:

(i) does not identify the initial financing statement as required by Section 9–512 or 9–518, as applicable; or

(ii) identifies an initial financing statement whose effectiveness has lapsed under Section 9–515;

(C) in the case of an initial financing statement that provides the name of a debtor identified as an individual or an amendment that provides a name of a debtor identified as an individual which was not previously provided in the financing statement to which the record relates, the record does not identify the debtor's last name; or

(D) in the case of a record filed [or recorded] in the filing office described in Section 9–501(a)(1), the record does not provide a sufficient description of the real property to which it relates;

(4) in the case of an initial financing statement or an amendment that adds a secured party of record, the record does not provide a name and mailing address for the secured party of record;

(5) in the case of an initial financing statement or an amendment that provides a name of a debtor which was not previously provided in the financing statement to which the amendment relates, the record does not:

(A) provide a mailing address for the debtor;

(B) indicate whether the debtor is an individual or an organization; or

(C) if the financing statement indicates that the debtor is an organization, provide:

(i) a type of organization for the debtor;

(ii) a jurisdiction of organization for the debtor; or

(iii) an organizational identification number for the debtor or indicate that the debtor has none;

(6) in the case of an assignment reflected in an initial financing statement under Section 9–514(a) or an amendment filed under Section 9–514(b), the record does not provide a name and mailing address for the assignee; or

(7) in the case of a continuation statement, the record is not filed within the six-month period prescribed by Section 9–515(d).

(c) For purposes of subsection (b):

(1) a record does not provide information if the filing office is unable to read or decipher the information; and

(2) a record that does not indicate that it is an amendment or identify an initial financing statement to which it relates, as required by Section 9–512, 9–514, or 9–518, is an initial financing statement.

(d) A record that is communicated to the filing office with tender of the filing fee, but which the filing office refuses to accept for a reason other than one set forth in subsection (b), is effective as a filed record except as against a purchaser of the collateral which gives value in reasonable reliance upon the absence of the record from the files.

§ 9–517. Effect of Indexing Errors.

The failure of the filing office to index a record correctly does not affect the effectiveness of the filed record.

§ 9–518. Claim Concerning Inaccurate or Wrongfully Filed Record.

(a) A person may file in the filing office a correction statement with respect to a record indexed there under the person's name if the person believes that the record is inaccurate or was wrongfully filed.

[Alternative A]

(b) A correction statement must:

(1) identify the record to which it relates by the file number assigned to the initial financing statement to which the record relates;

(2) indicate that it is a correction statement; and

(3) provide the basis for the person's belief that the record is inaccurate and indicate the manner in which the person believes the record should be amended to cure any inaccuracy or provide the basis for the person's belief that the record was wrongfully filed.

[Alternative B]

(b) A correction statement must:

(1) identify the record to which it relates by:

(A) the file number assigned to the initial financing statement to which the record relates; and

(B) if the correction statement relates to a record filed [or recorded] in a filing office described in Section 9–501(a)(1), the date [and time] that the initial financing statement was filed [or recorded] and the information specified in Section 9–502(b);

(2) indicate that it is a correction statement; and

(3) provide the basis for the person's belief that the record is inaccurate and indicate the manner in which the person believes the record should be amended to cure any inaccuracy or provide the basis for the person's belief that the record was wrongfully filed.

[End of Alternatives]

(c) The filing of a correction statement does not affect the effectiveness of an initial financing statement or other filed record.

Legislative Note: States whose real-estate filing offices require additional information in amendments and cannot search their records by both the name of the debtor and the file number should enact Alternative B to Sections 9–512(a), 9–518(b), 9–519(f), and 9–522(a).

[Subpart 2. Duties and Operation of Filing Office]

§ 9–519. Numbering, Maintaining, and Indexing Records; Communicating Information Provided in Records.

(a) For each record filed in a filing office, the filing office shall:

(1) assign a unique number to the filed record;

(2) create a record that bears the number assigned to the filed record and the date and time of filing;

(3) maintain the filed record for public inspection; and

(4) index the filed record in accordance with subsections (c), (d), and (e).

(b) A file number [assigned after January 1, 2002,] must include a digit that:

(1) is mathematically derived from or related to the other digits of the file number; and

(2) aids the filing office in determining whether a number communicated as the file number includes a single-digit or transpositional error.

(c) Except as otherwise provided in subsections (d) and (e), the filing office shall:

(1) index an initial financing statement according to the name of the debtor and index all filed records relating to the initial financing statement in a manner that associates with one another an initial financing statement and all filed records relating to the initial financing statement; and

(2) index a record that provides a name of a debtor which was not previously provided in the financing statement to which the record relates also according to the name that was not previously provided.

(d) If a financing statement is filed as a fixture filing or covers as-extracted collateral or timber to be cut, [it must be filed for record and] the filing office shall index it:

(1) under the names of the debtor and of each owner of record shown on the financing statement as if they were the mortgagors under a mortgage of the real property described; and

(2) to the extent that the law of this State provides for indexing of records of mortgages under the name of the mortgagee, under the name of the secured party as if the secured party were the mortgagee thereunder, or, if indexing is by description, as if the financing statement were a record of a mortgage of the real property described.

(e) If a financing statement is filed as a fixture filing or covers as-extracted collateral or timber to be cut, the filing office shall index an assignment filed under Section 9–514(a) or an amendment filed under Section 9–514(b):

(1) under the name of the assignor as grantor; and

(2) to the extent that the law of this State provides for indexing a record of the assignment of a mortgage under the name of the assignee, under the name of the assignee.

[Alternative A]

(f) The filing office shall maintain a capability:

(1) to retrieve a record by the name of the debtor and by the file number assigned to the initial financing statement to which the record relates; and

(2) to associate and retrieve with one another an initial financing statement and each filed record relating to the initial financing statement.

[Alternative B]

(f) The filing office shall maintain a capability:

(1) to retrieve a record by the name of the debtor and:

(A) if the filing office is described in Section 9–501(a)(1), by the file number assigned to the initial financing statement to which the record relates and the date [and time] that the record was filed [or recorded]; or

(B) if the filing office is described in Section 9–501(a)(2), by the file number assigned to the initial financing statement to which the record relates; and

(2) to associate and retrieve with one another an initial financing statement and each filed record relating to the initial financing statement.

[End of Alternatives]

(g) The filing office may not remove a debtor's name from the index until one year after the effectiveness of a financing statement naming the debtor lapses under Section 9–515 with respect to all secured parties of record.

(h) The filing office shall perform the acts required by subsections (a) through (e) at the time and in the manner prescribed by filing-office rule, but not later than two business days after the filing office receives the record in question.

[(i) Subsection[s] [(b)] [and] [(h)] do[es] not apply to a filing office described in Section 9–501(a)(1).]

Legislative Notes:

1. States whose filing offices currently assign file numbers that include a verification number, commonly known as a "check digit," or can implement this requirement before the effective date of this Article should omit the bracketed language in subsection (b).

2. In States in which writings will not appear in the real property records and indices unless actually recorded the bracketed language in subsection (d) should be used.

3. States whose real-estate filing offices require additional information in amendments and cannot search their records by both the name of the debtor and the file number should enact Alternative B to Sections 9–512(a), 9–518(b), 9–519(f), and 9–522(a).

4. A State that elects not to require real-estate filing offices to comply with either or both of subsections (b) and (h) may adopt an applicable variation of subsection (i) and add "Except as otherwise provided in subsection (i)," to the appropriate subsection or subsections.

§ 9–520. Acceptance and Refusal to Accept Record.

(a) A filing office shall refuse to accept a record for filing for a reason set forth in Section 9–516(b) and may refuse to accept a record for filing only for a reason set forth in Section 9–516(b).

(b) If a filing office refuses to accept a record for filing, it shall communicate to the person that presented the record the fact of and reason for the refusal and the date and time the record would have been filed had the filing office accepted it. The communication must be made at the time and in the manner prescribed by filing-office rule but [, in the case of a filing office described in Section

9–501(a)(2),] in no event more than two business days after the filing office receives the record.

(c) A filed financing statement satisfying Section 9–502(a) and (b) is effective, even if the filing office is required to refuse to accept it for filing under subsection (a). However, Section 9–338 applies to a filed financing statement providing information described in Section 9–516(b)(5) which is incorrect at the time the financing statement is filed.

(d) If a record communicated to a filing office provides information that relates to more than one debtor, this part applies as to each debtor separately.

Legislative Note: A State that elects not to require real-property filing offices to comply with subsection (b) should include the bracketed language.

§ 9–521. Uniform Form of Written Financing Statement and Amendment.

(a) A filing office that accepts written records may not refuse to accept a written initial financing statement in the following form and format except for a reason set forth in Section 9–516(b):

[NATIONAL UCC FINANCING STATEMENT (FORM UCC1) (REV. 7/29/98)]

[NATIONAL UCC FINANCING STATEMENT ADDENDUM (FORM UCC1Ad)(REV. 07/29/98)]

(b) A filing office that accepts written records may not refuse to accept a written record in the following form and format except for a reason set forth in Section 9–516(b):

[NATIONAL UCC FINANCING STATEMENT AMENDMENT (FORM UCC3)(REV. 07/29/98)]

[NATIONAL UCC FINANCING STATEMENT AMENDMENT ADDENDUM (FORM UCC3Ad)(REV. 07/29/98)]

§ 9–522. Maintenance and Destruction of Records.

[Alternative A]

(a) The filing office shall maintain a record of the information provided in a filed financing statement for at least one year after the effectiveness of the financing statement has lapsed under Section 9–515 with respect to all secured parties of record. The record must be retrievable by using the name of the debtor and by using the file number assigned to the initial financing statement to which the record relates.

[Alternative B]

(a) The filing office shall maintain a record of the information provided in a filed financing statement for at least one year after the effectiveness of the financing statement has lapsed under Section 9–515 with respect to all secured parties of record. The record must be retrievable by using the name of the debtor and:

(1) if the record was filed [or recorded] in the filing office described in Section 9–501(a)(1), by using the file number assigned to the initial financing statement to which the record relates and the date [and time] that the record was filed [or recorded]; or

(2) if the record was filed in the filing office described in Section 9–501(a)(2), by using the file number assigned to the initial financing statement to which the record relates.

[End of Alternatives]

(b) Except to the extent that a statute governing disposition of public records provides otherwise, the filing office immediately may destroy any written record evidencing a financing statement. However, if the filing office destroys a written record, it shall maintain another record of the financing statement which complies with subsection (a).

Legislative Note: States whose real-estate filing offices require additional information in amendments and cannot search their records by both the name of the debtor and the file number should enact Alternative B to Sections 9–512(a), 9–518(b), 9–519(f), and 9–522(a).

§ 9–523. Information from Filing Office; Sale or License of Records.

(a) If a person that files a written record requests an acknowledgment of the filing, the filing office shall send to the person an image of the record showing the number assigned to the record pursuant to Section 9–519(a)(1) and the date and time of the filing of the record. However, if the person furnishes a copy of the record to the filing office, the filing office may instead:

(1) note upon the copy the number assigned to the record pursuant to Section 9–519(a)(1) and the date and time of the filing of the record; and

(2) send the copy to the person.

(b) If a person files a record other than a written record, the filing office shall communicate to the person an acknowledgment that provides:

(1) the information in the record;

(2) the number assigned to the record pursuant to Section 9–519(a)(1); and

(3) the date and time of the filing of the record.

(c) The filing office shall communicate or otherwise make available in a record the following information to any person that requests it:

(1) whether there is on file on a date and time specified by the filing office, but not a date earlier than three business days before the filing office receives the request, any financing statement that:

(A) designates a particular debtor [or, if the request so states, designates a particular debtor at the address specified in the request];

(B) has not lapsed under Section 9–515 with respect to all secured parties of record; and

(C) if the request so states, has lapsed under Section 9–515 and a record of which is maintained by the filing office under Section 9–522(a);

(2) the date and time of filing of each financing statement; and

(3) the information provided in each financing statement.

(d) In complying with its duty under subsection (c), the filing office may communicate information in any medium. However, if requested, the filing office shall communicate information by issuing [its written certificate] [a record that can be admitted into evidence in the courts of this State without extrinsic evidence of its authenticity].

(e) The filing office shall perform the acts required by subsections (a) through (d) at the time and in the manner prescribed by filing-office rule, but not later than two business days after the filing office receives the request.

(f) At least weekly, the [insert appropriate official or governmental agency] [filing office] shall offer to sell or license to the public on a nonexclusive basis, in bulk, copies of all records filed in it under this part, in every medium from time to time available to the filing office.

Legislative Notes:

1. States whose filing office does not offer the additional service of responding to search requests limited to a particular address should omit the bracketed language in subsection (c)(1)(A).

2. A State that elects not to require real-estate filing offices to comply with either or both of subsections (e) and (f) should specify in the appropriate subsection(s) only the filing office described in Section 9–501(a)(2).

§ 9–524. Delay by Filing Office.

Delay by the filing office beyond a time limit prescribed by this part is excused if:

(1) the delay is caused by interruption of communication or computer facilities, war, emergency conditions, failure of equipment, or other circumstances beyond control of the filing office; and

(2) the filing office exercises reasonable diligence under the circumstances.

§ 9–525. Fees.

(a) Except as otherwise provided in subsection (e), the fee for filing and indexing a record under this part, other than an initial financing statement of the kind described in subsection (b), is [the amount specified in subsection (c), if applicable, plus]:

(1) $[X] if the record is communicated in writing and consists of one or two pages;

(2) $[2X] if the record is communicated in writing and consists of more than two pages; and

(3) $[½X] if the record is communicated by another medium authorized by filing-office rule.

(b) Except as otherwise provided in subsection (e), the fee for filing and indexing an initial financing statement of the following kind is [the amount specified in subsection (c), if applicable, plus]:

(1) $______ if the financing statement indicates that it is filed in connection with a public-finance transaction;

(2) $______ if the financing statement indicates that it is filed in connection with a manufactured-home transaction.

[Alternative A]

(c) The number of names required to be indexed does not affect the amount of the fee in subsections (a) and (b).

[Alternative B]

(c) Except as otherwise provided in subsection (e), if a record is communicated in writing, the fee for each name more than two required to be indexed is $______.

[End of Alternatives]

(d) The fee for responding to a request for information from the filing office, including for [issuing a certificate showing] [communicating] whether there is on file any financing statement naming a particular debtor, is:

(1) $______ if the request is communicated in writing; and

(2) $______ if the request is communicated by another medium authorized by filing-office rule.

(e) This section does not require a fee with respect to a record of a mortgage which is effective as a financing statement filed as a fixture filing or as a financing statement covering as-extracted collateral or timber to be cut under Section 9–502(c). However, the recording and satisfaction fees that otherwise would be applicable to the record of the mortgage apply.

Legislative Notes:

1. To preserve uniformity, a State that places the provisions of this section together with statutes setting fees for other services should do so without modification.

2. A State should enact subsection (c), Alternative A, and omit the bracketed language in subsections (a) and (b) unless its indexing system entails a substantial additional cost when indexing additional names.

As amended in 2000.

§ 9–526. Filing-Office Rules.

(a) The [insert appropriate governmental official or agency] shall adopt and publish rules to implement this article. The filing-office rules must be[:

(1)] consistent with this article[; and

(2) adopted and published in accordance with the [insert any applicable state administrative procedure act]].

(b) To keep the filing-office rules and practices of the filing office in harmony with the rules and practices of filing offices in other jurisdictions that enact substantially this part, and to keep the technology used by the filing office compatible with the technology used by filing offices in other jurisdictions that enact substantially this part, the [insert appropriate governmental official or agency], so far as is consistent with the purposes, policies, and provisions of this article, in adopting, amending, and repealing filing-office rules, shall:

(1) consult with filing offices in other jurisdictions that enact substantially this part; and

(2) consult the most recent version of the Model Rules promulgated by the International Association of Corporate Administrators or any successor organization; and

(3) take into consideration the rules and practices of, and the technology used by, filing offices in other jurisdictions that enact substantially this part.

§ 9–527. Duty to Report.

The [insert appropriate governmental official or agency] shall report [annually on or before ______] to the [Governor and Legislature] on the operation of the filing office. The report must contain a statement of the extent to which:

(1) the filing-office rules are not in harmony with the rules of filing offices in other jurisdictions that enact substantially this part and the reasons for these variations; and

(2) the filing-office rules are not in harmony with the most recent version of the Model Rules promulgated by the International Association of Corporate Administrators, or any successor organization, and the reasons for these variations.

Part 6 Default

[Subpart 1. Default and Enforcement of Security Interest]

§ 9–601. Rights after Default; Judicial Enforcement; Consignor or Buyer of Accounts, Chattel Paper, Payment Intangibles, or Promissory Notes.

(a) After default, a secured party has the rights provided in this part and, except as otherwise provided in Section 9–602, those provided by agreement of the parties. A secured party:

(1) may reduce a claim to judgment, foreclose, or otherwise enforce the claim, security interest, or agricultural lien by any available judicial procedure; and

(2) if the collateral is documents, may proceed either as to the documents or as to the goods they cover.

(b) A secured party in possession of collateral or control of collateral under Section 9–104, 9–105, 9–106, or 9–107 has the rights and duties provided in Section 9–207.

(c) The rights under subsections (a) and (b) are cumulative and may be exercised simultaneously.

(d) Except as otherwise provided in subsection (g) and Section 9–605, after default, a debtor and an obligor have the rights provided in this part and by agreement of the parties.

(e) If a secured party has reduced its claim to judgment, the lien of any levy that may be made upon the collateral by virtue of an execution based upon the judgment relates back to the earliest of:

(1) the date of perfection of the security interest or agricultural lien in the collateral;

(2) the date of filing a financing statement covering the collateral; or

(3) any date specified in a statute under which the agricultural lien was created.

(f) A sale pursuant to an execution is a foreclosure of the security interest or agricultural lien by judicial procedure within the meaning of this section. A secured party may purchase at the sale and thereafter hold the collateral free of any other requirements of this article.

(g) Except as otherwise provided in Section 9–607(c), this part imposes no duties upon a secured party that is a consignor or is a buyer of accounts, chattel paper, payment intangibles, or promissory notes.

§ 9–602. Waiver and Variance of Rights and Duties.

Except as otherwise provided in Section 9–624, to the extent that they give rights to a debtor or obligor and impose duties on a secured party, the debtor or obligor may not waive or vary the rules stated in the following listed sections:

(1) Section 9–207(b)(4)(C), which deals with use and operation of the collateral by the secured party;

(2) Section 9–210, which deals with requests for an accounting and requests concerning a list of collateral and statement of account;

(3) Section 9–607(c), which deals with collection and enforcement of collateral;

(4) Sections 9–608(a) and 9–615(c) to the extent that they deal with application or payment of noncash proceeds of collection, enforcement, or disposition;

(5) Sections 9–608(a) and 9–615(d) to the extent that they require accounting for or payment of surplus proceeds of collateral;

(6) Section 9–609 to the extent that it imposes upon a secured party that takes possession of collateral without judicial process the duty to do so without breach of the peace;

(7) Sections 9–610(b), 9–611, 9–613, and 9–614, which deal with disposition of collateral;

(8) Section 9–615(f), which deals with calculation of a deficiency or surplus when a disposition is made to the secured party, a person related to the secured party, or a secondary obligor;

(9) Section 9–616, which deals with explanation of the calculation of a surplus or deficiency;

(10) Sections 9–620, 9–621, and 9–622, which deal with acceptance of collateral in satisfaction of obligation;

(11) Section 9–623, which deals with redemption of collateral;

(12) Section 9–624, which deals with permissible waivers; and

(13) Sections 9–625 and 9–626, which deal with the secured party's liability for failure to comply with this article.

§ 9–603. Agreement on Standards Concerning Rights and Duties.

(a) The parties may determine by agreement the standards measuring the fulfillment of the rights of a debtor or obligor and the duties of a secured party under a rule stated in Section 9–602 if the standards are not manifestly unreasonable.

(b) Subsection (a) does not apply to the duty under Section 9–609 to refrain from breaching the peace.

§ 9–604. Procedure If Security Agreement Covers Real Property or Fixtures.

(a) If a security agreement covers both personal and real property, a secured party may proceed:

(1) under this part as to the personal property without prejudicing any rights with respect to the real property; or

(2) as to both the personal property and the real property in accordance with the rights with respect to the real property, in which case the other provisions of this part do not apply.

(b) Subject to subsection (c), if a security agreement covers goods that are or become fixtures, a secured party may proceed:

(1) under this part; or

(2) in accordance with the rights with respect to real property, in which case the other provisions of this part do not apply.

(c) Subject to the other provisions of this part, if a secured party holding a security interest in fixtures has priority over all owners and encumbrancers of the real property, the secured party, after default, may remove the collateral from the real property.

(d) A secured party that removes collateral shall promptly reimburse any encumbrancer or owner of the real property, other than the debtor, for the cost of repair of any physical injury caused by the removal. The secured party need not reimburse the encumbrancer or owner for any diminution in value of the real property caused by the absence of the goods removed or by any necessity of replacing them. A person entitled to reimbursement may refuse permission to remove until the secured party gives adequate assurance for the performance of the obligation to reimburse.

§ 9–605. Unknown Debtor or Secondary Obligor.

A secured party does not owe a duty based on its status as secured party:

(1) to a person that is a debtor or obligor, unless the secured party knows:

(A) that the person is a debtor or obligor;

(B) the identity of the person; and

(C) how to communicate with the person; or

(2) to a secured party or lienholder that has filed a financing statement against a person, unless the secured party knows:

(A) that the person is a debtor; and

(B) the identity of the person.

§ 9–606. Time of Default for Agricultural Lien.

For purposes of this part, a default occurs in connection with an agricultural lien at the time the secured party becomes entitled to enforce the lien in accordance with the statute under which it was created.

§ 9–607. Collection and Enforcement by Secured Party.

(a) If so agreed, and in any event after default, a secured party:

(1) may notify an account debtor or other person obligated on collateral to make payment or otherwise render performance to or for the benefit of the secured party;

(2) may take any proceeds to which the secured party is entitled under Section 9–315;

(3) may enforce the obligations of an account debtor or other person obligated on collateral and exercise the rights of the debtor with respect to the obligation of the account debtor or other person obligated on collateral to make payment or otherwise render performance to the debtor, and with respect to any property that secures the obligations of the account debtor or other person obligated on the collateral;

(4) if it holds a security interest in a deposit account perfected by control under Section 9–104(a)(1), may apply the balance of the deposit account to the obligation secured by the deposit account; and

(5) if it holds a security interest in a deposit account perfected by control under Section 9–104(a)(2) or (3), may instruct the bank to pay the balance of the deposit account to or for the benefit of the secured party.

(b) If necessary to enable a secured party to exercise under subsection (a)(3) the right of a debtor to enforce a mortgage nonjudicially, the secured party may record in the office in which a record of the mortgage is recorded:

(1) a copy of the security agreement that creates or provides for a security interest in the obligation secured by the mortgage; and

(2) the secured party's sworn affidavit in recordable form stating that:

(A) a default has occurred; and

(B) the secured party is entitled to enforce the mortgage nonjudicially.

(c) A secured party shall proceed in a commercially reasonable manner if the secured party:

(1) undertakes to collect from or enforce an obligation of an account debtor or other person obligated on collateral; and

(2) is entitled to charge back uncollected collateral or otherwise to full or limited recourse against the debtor or a secondary obligor.

(d) A secured party may deduct from the collections made pursuant to subsection (c) reasonable expenses of collection and enforcement, including reasonable attorney's fees and legal expenses incurred by the secured party.

(e) This section does not determine whether an account debtor, bank, or other person obligated on collateral owes a duty to a secured party.

As amended in 2000.

§ 9–608. Application of Proceeds of Collection or Enforcement; Liability for Deficiency and Right to Surplus.

(a) If a security interest or agricultural lien secures payment or performance of an obligation, the following rules apply:

(1) A secured party shall apply or pay over for application the cash proceeds of collection or enforcement under Section 9–607 in the following order to:

(A) the reasonable expenses of collection and enforcement and, to the extent provided for by agreement and not prohibited by law, reasonable attorney's fees and legal expenses incurred by the secured party;

(B) the satisfaction of obligations secured by the security interest or agricultural lien under which the collection or enforcement is made; and

(C) the satisfaction of obligations secured by any subordinate security interest in or other lien on the collateral subject to the security interest or agricultural lien under which the collection or enforcement is made if the secured party receives an authenticated demand for proceeds before distribution of the proceeds is completed.

(2) If requested by a secured party, a holder of a subordinate security interest or other lien shall furnish reasonable proof of the interest or lien within a reasonable time. Unless the holder complies, the secured party need not comply with the holder's demand under paragraph (1)(C).

(3) A secured party need not apply or pay over for application noncash proceeds of collection and enforcement under Section 9–607 unless the failure to do so would be commercially unreasonable. A secured party that applies or pays over for application noncash proceeds shall do so in a commercially reasonable manner.

(4) A secured party shall account to and pay a debtor for any surplus, and the obligor is liable for any deficiency.

(b) If the underlying transaction is a sale of accounts, chattel paper, payment intangibles, or promissory notes, the debtor is not entitled to any surplus, and the obligor is not liable for any deficiency.

As amended in 2000.

§ 9–609. Secured Party's Right to Take Possession after Default.

(a) After default, a secured party:

(1) may take possession of the collateral; and

(2) without removal, may render equipment unusable and dispose of collateral on a debtor's premises under Section 9–610.

(b) A secured party may proceed under subsection (a):

(1) pursuant to judicial process; or

(2) without judicial process, if it proceeds without breach of the peace.

(c) If so agreed, and in any event after default, a secured party may require the debtor to assemble the collateral and make it available to the secured party at a place to be designated by the secured party which is reasonably convenient to both parties.

§ 9–610. Disposition of Collateral after Default.

(a) After default, a secured party may sell, lease, license, or otherwise dispose of any or all of the collateral in its present condition or following any commercially reasonable preparation or processing.

(b) Every aspect of a disposition of collateral, including the method, manner, time, place, and other terms, must be commercially reasonable. If commercially reasonable, a secured party may dispose of collateral by public or private proceedings, by one or more contracts, as a unit or in parcels, and at any time and place and on any terms.

(c) A secured party may purchase collateral:

(1) at a public disposition; or

(2) at a private disposition only if the collateral is of a kind that is customarily sold on a recognized market or the subject of widely distributed standard price quotations.

(d) A contract for sale, lease, license, or other disposition includes the warranties relating to title, possession, quiet enjoyment, and the like which by operation of law accompany a voluntary disposition of property of the kind subject to the contract.

(e) A secured party may disclaim or modify warranties under subsection (d):

(1) in a manner that would be effective to disclaim or modify the warranties in a voluntary disposition of property of the kind subject to the contract of disposition; or

(2) by communicating to the purchaser a record evidencing the contract for disposition and including an express disclaimer or modification of the warranties.

(f) A record is sufficient to disclaim warranties under subsection (e) if it indicates "There is no warranty relating to title, possession, quiet enjoyment, or the like in this disposition" or uses words of similar import.

§ 9–611. Notification before Disposition of Collateral.

(a) In this section, "notification date" means the earlier of the date on which:

(1) a secured party sends to the debtor and any secondary obligor an authenticated notification of disposition; or

(2) the debtor and any secondary obligor waive the right to notification.

(b) Except as otherwise provided in subsection (d), a secured party that disposes of collateral under Section 9–610 shall send to the persons specified in subsection (c) a reasonable authenticated notification of disposition.

(c) To comply with subsection (b), the secured party shall send an authenticated notification of disposition to:

(1) the debtor;

(2) any secondary obligor; and

(3) if the collateral is other than consumer goods:

(A) any other person from which the secured party has received, before the notification date, an authenticated notification of a claim of an interest in the collateral;

(B) any other secured party or lienholder that, 10 days before the notification date, held a security interest in or other lien on the collateral perfected by the filing of a financing statement that:

(i) identified the collateral;

(ii) was indexed under the debtor's name as of that date; and

(iii) was filed in the office in which to file a financing statement against the debtor covering the collateral as of that date; and

(C) any other secured party that, 10 days before the notification date, held a security interest in the collateral perfected by compliance with a statute, regulation, or treaty described in Section 9–311(a).

(d) Subsection (b) does not apply if the collateral is perishable or threatens to decline speedily in value or is of a type customarily sold on a recognized market.

(e) A secured party complies with the requirement for notification prescribed by subsection (c)(3)(B) if:

(1) not later than 20 days or earlier than 30 days before the notification date, the secured party requests, in a commercially reasonable manner, information concerning financing statements indexed under the debtor's name in the office indicated in subsection (c)(3)(B); and

(2) before the notification date, the secured party:

(A) did not receive a response to the request for information; or

(B) received a response to the request for information and sent an authenticated notification of disposition to each secured party or other lienholder named in that response whose financing statement covered the collateral.

§ 9–612. Timeliness of Notification before Disposition of Collateral.

(a) Except as otherwise provided in subsection (b), whether a notification is sent within a reasonable time is a question of fact.

(b) In a transaction other than a consumer transaction, a notification of disposition sent after default and 10 days or more before the earliest time of disposition set forth in the notification is sent within a reasonable time before the disposition.

§ 9–613. Contents and Form of Notification before Disposition of Collateral: General.

Except in a consumer-goods transaction, the following rules apply:

(1) The contents of a notification of disposition are sufficient if the notification:

(A) describes the debtor and the secured party;

(B) describes the collateral that is the subject of the intended disposition;

(C) states the method of intended disposition;

(D) states that the debtor is entitled to an accounting of the unpaid indebtedness and states the charge, if any, for an accounting; and

(E) states the time and place of a public disposition or the time after which any other disposition is to be made.

(2) Whether the contents of a notification that lacks any of the information specified in paragraph (1) are nevertheless sufficient is a question of fact.

(3) The contents of a notification providing substantially the information specified in paragraph (1) are sufficient, even if the notification includes:

(A) information not specified by that paragraph; or

(B) minor errors that are not seriously misleading.

(4) A particular phrasing of the notification is not required.

(5) The following form of notification and the form appearing in Section 9–614(3), when completed, each provides sufficient information:

NOTIFICATION OF DISPOSITION OF COLLATERAL

To: *[Name of debtor, obligor, or other person to which the notification is sent]*

From: *[Name, address, and telephone number of secured party]*

Name of Debtor(s): *[Include only if debtor(s) are not an addressee]*

[For a public disposition:]

We will sell [or lease or license, *as applicable]* the [*describe collateral*] [to the highest qualified bidder] in public as follows:

Day and Date: ______

Time: ______

Place: ______

[For a private disposition:]

We will sell [or lease or license, *as applicable*] the [*describe collateral*] privately sometime after [*day and date*].

You are entitled to an accounting of the unpaid indebtedness secured by the property that we intend to sell [or lease or license, *as applicable*] [for a charge of $______]. You may request an accounting by calling us at [*telephone number*].

[End of Form]

As amended in 2000.

§ 9–614. Contents and Form of Notification before Disposition of Collateral: Consumer-Goods Transaction.

In a consumer-goods transaction, the following rules apply:

(1) A notification of disposition must provide the following information:

(A) the information specified in Section 9–613(1);

(B) a description of any liability for a deficiency of the person to which the notification is sent;

(C) a telephone number from which the amount that must be paid to the secured party to redeem the collateral under Section 9–623 is available; and

(D) a telephone number or mailing address from which additional information concerning the disposition and the obligation secured is available.

(2) A particular phrasing of the notification is not required.

(3) The following form of notification, when completed, provides sufficient information:

[*Name and address of secured party*]

[*Date*]

NOTICE OF OUR PLAN TO SELL PROPERTY

[*Name and address of any obligor who is also a debtor*]

Subject: [*Identification of Transaction*]

We have your [*describe collateral*], because you broke promises in our agreement.

[*For a public disposition:*]

We will sell [*describe collateral*] at public sale. A sale could include a lease or license. The sale will be held as follows:

Date: _______

Time: _______

Place: _______

You may attend the sale and bring bidders if you want.

[*For a private disposition:*]

We will sell [*describe collateral*] at private sale sometime after [*date*]. A sale could include a lease or license.

The money that we get from the sale (after paying our costs) will reduce the amount you owe. If we get less money than you owe, you [*will or will not, as applicable*] still owe us the difference. If we get more money than you owe, you will get the extra money, unless we must pay it to someone else.

You can get the property back at any time before we sell it by paying us the full amount you owe (not just the past due payments), including our expenses. To learn the exact amount you must pay, call us at [*telephone number*].

If you want us to explain to you in writing how we have figured the amount that you owe us, you may call us at [telephone number] [or write us at [*secured party's address*]] and request a written explanation. [We will charge you $_______ for the explanation if we sent you another written explanation of the amount you owe us within the last six months.]

If you need more information about the sale call us at [*telephone number*] [or write us at [secured party's address]].

We are sending this notice to the following other people who have an interest in [*describe collateral*] or who owe money under your agreement:

[*Names of all other debtors and obligors, if any*]

[End of Form]

(4) A notification in the form of paragraph (3) is sufficient, even if additional information appears at the end of the form.

(5) A notification in the form of paragraph (3) is sufficient, even if it includes errors in information not required by paragraph (1), unless the error is misleading with respect to rights arising under this article.

(6) If a notification under this section is not in the form of paragraph (3), law other than this article determines the effect of including information not required by paragraph (1).

§ 9–615. Application of Proceeds of Disposition; Liability for Deficiency and Right to Surplus.

(a) A secured party shall apply or pay over for application the cash proceeds of disposition under Section 9–610 in the following order to:

(1) the reasonable expenses of retaking, holding, preparing for disposition, processing, and disposing, and, to the extent provided for by agreement and not prohibited by law, reasonable attorney's fees and legal expenses incurred by the secured party;

(2) the satisfaction of obligations secured by the security interest or agricultural lien under which the disposition is made;

(3) the satisfaction of obligations secured by any subordinate security interest in or other subordinate lien on the collateral if:

(A) the secured party receives from the holder of the subordinate security interest or other lien an authenticated demand for proceeds before distribution of the proceeds is completed; and

(B) in a case in which a consignor has an interest in the collateral, the subordinate security interest or other lien is senior to the interest of the consignor; and

(4) a secured party that is a consignor of the collateral if the secured party receives from the consignor an authenticated demand for proceeds before distribution of the proceeds is completed.

(b) If requested by a secured party, a holder of a subordinate security interest or other lien shall furnish reasonable proof of the interest or lien within a reasonable time. Unless the holder does so, the secured party need not comply with the holder's demand under subsection (a)(3).

(c) A secured party need not apply or pay over for application noncash proceeds of disposition under Section 9–610 unless the failure to do so would be commercially unreasonable. A secured party that applies or pays over for application noncash proceeds shall do so in a commercially reasonable manner.

(d) If the security interest under which a disposition is made secures payment or performance of an obligation, after making the payments and applications required by subsection (a) and permitted by subsection (c):

(1) unless subsection (a)(4) requires the secured party to apply or pay over cash proceeds to a consignor, the secured party shall account to and pay a debtor for any surplus; and

(2) the obligor is liable for any deficiency.

(e) If the underlying transaction is a sale of accounts, chattel paper, payment intangibles, or promissory notes:

(1) the debtor is not entitled to any surplus; and

(2) the obligor is not liable for any deficiency.

(f) The surplus or deficiency following a disposition is calculated based on the amount of proceeds that would have been realized in a disposition complying with this part to a transferee other than the secured party, a person related to the secured party, or a secondary obligor if:

(1) the transferee in the disposition is the secured party, a person related to the secured party, or a secondary obligor; and

(2) the amount of proceeds of the disposition is significantly below the range of proceeds that a complying disposition to a person other than the secured party, a person related to the secured party, or a secondary obligor would have brought.

(g) A secured party that receives cash proceeds of a disposition in good faith and without knowledge that the receipt violates the rights of the holder of a security interest or other lien that is not subordinate to the security interest or agricultural lien under which the disposition is made:

(1) takes the cash proceeds free of the security interest or other lien;

(2) is not obligated to apply the proceeds of the disposition to the satisfaction of obligations secured by the security interest or other lien; and

(3) is not obligated to account to or pay the holder of the security interest or other lien for any surplus.

As amended in 2000.

§ 9–616. Explanation of Calculation of Surplus or Deficiency.

(a) In this section:

(1) "Explanation" means a writing that:

(A) states the amount of the surplus or deficiency;

(B) provides an explanation in accordance with subsection (c) of how the secured party calculated the surplus or deficiency;

(C) states, if applicable, that future debits, credits, charges, including additional credit service charges or interest, rebates, and expenses may affect the amount of the surplus or deficiency; and

(D) provides a telephone number or mailing address from which additional information concerning the transaction is available.

(2) "Request" means a record:

(A) authenticated by a debtor or consumer obligor;

(B) requesting that the recipient provide an explanation; and

(C) sent after disposition of the collateral under Section 9–610.

(b) In a consumer-goods transaction in which the debtor is entitled to a surplus or a consumer obligor is liable for a deficiency under Section 9–615, the secured party shall:

(1) send an explanation to the debtor or consumer obligor, as applicable, after the disposition and:

(A) before or when the secured party accounts to the debtor and pays any surplus or first makes written demand on the consumer obligor after the disposition for payment of the deficiency; and

(B) within 14 days after receipt of a request; or

(2) in the case of a consumer obligor who is liable for a deficiency, within 14 days after receipt of a request, send to the consumer obligor a record waiving the secured party's right to a deficiency.

(c) To comply with subsection (a)(1)(B), a writing must provide the following information in the following order:

(1) the aggregate amount of obligations secured by the security interest under which the disposition was made, and, if the amount reflects a rebate of unearned interest or credit service charge, an indication of that fact, calculated as of a specified date:

(A) if the secured party takes or receives possession of the collateral after default, not more than 35 days before the secured party takes or receives possession; or

(B) if the secured party takes or receives possession of the collateral before default or does not take possession of the collateral, not more than 35 days before the disposition;

(2) the amount of proceeds of the disposition;

(3) the aggregate amount of the obligations after deducting the amount of proceeds;

(4) the amount, in the aggregate or by type, and types of expenses, including expenses of retaking, holding, preparing for disposition, processing, and disposing of the collateral, and attorney's fees secured by the collateral which are known to the secured party and relate to the current disposition;

(5) the amount, in the aggregate or by type, and types of credits, including rebates of interest or credit service charges, to which the obligor is known to be entitled and which are not reflected in the amount in paragraph (1); and

(6) the amount of the surplus or deficiency.

(d) A particular phrasing of the explanation is not required. An explanation complying substantially with the requirements of subsection (a) is sufficient, even if it includes minor errors that are not seriously misleading.

(e) A debtor or consumer obligor is entitled without charge to one response to a request under this section during any six-month period in which the secured party did not send to the debtor or consumer obligor an explanation pursuant to subsection (b)(1). The secured party may require payment of a charge not exceeding $25 for each additional response.

§ 9–617. Rights of Transferee of Collateral.

(a) A secured party's disposition of collateral after default:

(1) transfers to a transferee for value all of the debtor's rights in the collateral;

(2) discharges the security interest under which the disposition is made; and

(3) discharges any subordinate security interest or other subordinate lien [other than liens created under [cite acts or statutes providing for liens, if any, that are not to be discharged]].

(b) A transferee that acts in good faith takes free of the rights and interests described in subsection (a), even if the secured party fails to comply with this article or the requirements of any judicial proceeding.

(c) If a transferee does not take free of the rights and interests described in subsection (a), the transferee takes the collateral subject to:

(1) the debtor's rights in the collateral;

(2) the security interest or agricultural lien under which the disposition is made; and

(3) any other security interest or other lien.

§ 9–618. Rights and Duties of Certain Secondary Obligors.

(a) A secondary obligor acquires the rights and becomes obligated to perform the duties of the secured party after the secondary obligor:

(1) receives an assignment of a secured obligation from the secured party;

(2) receives a transfer of collateral from the secured party and agrees to accept the rights and assume the duties of the secured party; or

(3) is subrogated to the rights of a secured party with respect to collateral.

(b) An assignment, transfer, or subrogation described in subsection (a):

(1) is not a disposition of collateral under Section 9–610; and

(2) relieves the secured party of further duties under this article.

§ 9–619. Transfer of Record or Legal Title.

(a) In this section, "transfer statement" means a record authenticated by a secured party stating:

(1) that the debtor has defaulted in connection with an obligation secured by specified collateral;

(2) that the secured party has exercised its post-default remedies with respect to the collateral;

(3) that, by reason of the exercise, a transferee has acquired the rights of the debtor in the collateral; and

(4) the name and mailing address of the secured party, debtor, and transferee.

(b) A transfer statement entitles the transferee to the transfer of record of all rights of the debtor in the collateral specified in the statement in any official filing, recording, registration, or certificate-of-title system covering the collateral. If a transfer statement is presented with the applicable fee and request form to the official or office responsible for maintaining the system, the official or office shall:

(1) accept the transfer statement;

(2) promptly amend its records to reflect the transfer; and

(3) if applicable, issue a new appropriate certificate of title in the name of the transferee.

(c) A transfer of the record or legal title to collateral to a secured party under subsection (b) or otherwise is not of itself a disposition of collateral under this article and does not of itself relieve the secured party of its duties under this article.

§ 9–620. Acceptance of Collateral in Full or Partial Satisfaction of Obligation; Compulsory Disposition of Collateral.

(a) Except as otherwise provided in subsection (g), a secured party may accept collateral in full or partial satisfaction of the obligation it secures only if:

(1) the debtor consents to the acceptance under subsection (c);

(2) the secured party does not receive, within the time set forth in subsection (d), a notification of objection to the proposal authenticated by:

(A) a person to which the secured party was required to send a proposal under Section 9–621; or

(B) any other person, other than the debtor, holding an interest in the collateral subordinate to the security interest that is the subject of the proposal;

(3) if the collateral is consumer goods, the collateral is not in the possession of the debtor when the debtor consents to the acceptance; and

(4) subsection (e) does not require the secured party to dispose of the collateral or the debtor waives the requirement pursuant to Section 9–624.

(b) A purported or apparent acceptance of collateral under this section is ineffective unless:

(1) the secured party consents to the acceptance in an authenticated record or sends a proposal to the debtor; and

(2) the conditions of subsection (a) are met.

(c) For purposes of this section:

(1) a debtor consents to an acceptance of collateral in partial satisfaction of the obligation it secures only if the debtor agrees to the terms of the acceptance in a record authenticated after default; and

(2) a debtor consents to an acceptance of collateral in full satisfaction of the obligation it secures only if the debtor agrees to the terms of the acceptance in a record authenticated after default or the secured party:

(A) sends to the debtor after default a proposal that is unconditional or subject only to a condition that collateral not in the possession of the secured party be preserved or maintained;

(B) in the proposal, proposes to accept collateral in full satisfaction of the obligation it secures; and

(C) does not receive a notification of objection authenticated by the debtor within 20 days after the proposal is sent.

(d) To be effective under subsection (a)(2), a notification of objection must be received by the secured party:

(1) in the case of a person to which the proposal was sent pursuant to Section 9–621, within 20 days after notification was sent to that person; and

(2) in other cases:

(A) within 20 days after the last notification was sent pursuant to Section 9–621; or

(B) if a notification was not sent, before the debtor consents to the acceptance under subsection (c).

(e) A secured party that has taken possession of collateral shall dispose of the collateral pursuant to Section 9–610 within the time specified in subsection (f) if:

(1) 60 percent of the cash price has been paid in the case of a purchase-money security interest in consumer goods; or

(2) 60 percent of the principal amount of the obligation secured has been paid in the case of a non-purchase-money security interest in consumer goods.

(f) To comply with subsection (e), the secured party shall dispose of the collateral:

(1) within 90 days after taking possession; or

(2) within any longer period to which the debtor and all secondary obligors have agreed in an agreement to that effect entered into and authenticated after default.

(g) In a consumer transaction, a secured party may not accept collateral in partial satisfaction of the obligation it secures.

§ 9–621. Notification of Proposal to Accept Collateral.

(a) A secured party that desires to accept collateral in full or partial satisfaction of the obligation it secures shall send its proposal to:

(1) any person from which the secured party has received, before the debtor consented to the acceptance, an authenticated notification of a claim of an interest in the collateral;

(2) any other secured party or lienholder that, 10 days before the debtor consented to the acceptance, held a security interest in or other lien on the collateral perfected by the filing of a financing statement that:

(A) identified the collateral;

(B) was indexed under the debtor's name as of that date; and

(C) was filed in the office or offices in which to file a financing statement against the debtor covering the collateral as of that date; and

(3) any other secured party that, 10 days before the debtor consented to the acceptance, held a security interest in the collateral perfected by compliance with a statute, regulation, or treaty described in Section 9–311(a).

(b) A secured party that desires to accept collateral in partial satisfaction of the obligation it secures shall send its proposal to any secondary obligor in addition to the persons described in subsection (a).

§ 9–622. Effect of Acceptance of Collateral.

(a) A secured party's acceptance of collateral in full or partial satisfaction of the obligation it secures:

(1) discharges the obligation to the extent consented to by the debtor;

(2) transfers to the secured party all of a debtor's rights in the collateral;

(3) discharges the security interest or agricultural lien that is the subject of the debtor's consent and any subordinate security interest or other subordinate lien; and

(4) terminates any other subordinate interest.

(b) A subordinate interest is discharged or terminated under subsection (a), even if the secured party fails to comply with this article.

§ 9–623. Right to Redeem Collateral.

(a) A debtor, any secondary obligor, or any other secured party or lienholder may redeem collateral.

(b) To redeem collateral, a person shall tender:

(1) fulfillment of all obligations secured by the collateral; and

(2) the reasonable expenses and attorney's fees described in Section 9–615(a)(1).

(c) A redemption may occur at any time before a secured party:

(1) has collected collateral under Section 9–607;

(2) has disposed of collateral or entered into a contract for its disposition under Section 9–610; or

(3) has accepted collateral in full or partial satisfaction of the obligation it secures under Section 9–622.

§ 9–624. Waiver.

(a) A debtor or secondary obligor may waive the right to notification of disposition of collateral under Section 9–611 only by an agreement to that effect entered into and authenticated after default.

(b) A debtor may waive the right to require disposition of collateral under Section 9–620(e) only by an agreement to that effect entered into and authenticated after default.

(c) Except in a consumer-goods transaction, a debtor or secondary obligor may waive the right to redeem collateral under Section 9–623 only by an agreement to that effect entered into and authenticated after default.

[Subpart 2. Noncompliance with Article]

§ 9–625. Remedies for Secured Party's Failure to Comply with Article.

(a) If it is established that a secured party is not proceeding in accordance with this article, a court may order or restrain collection, enforcement, or disposition of collateral on appropriate terms and conditions.

(b) Subject to subsections (c), (d), and (f), a person is liable for damages in the amount of any loss caused by a failure to comply with this article. Loss caused by a failure to comply may include loss resulting from the debtor's inability to obtain, or increased costs of, alternative financing.

(c) Except as otherwise provided in Section 9–628:

(1) a person that, at the time of the failure, was a debtor, was an obligor, or held a security interest in or other lien on the collateral may recover damages under subsection (b) for its loss; and

(2) if the collateral is consumer goods, a person that was a debtor or a secondary obligor at the time a secured party failed to comply with this part may recover for that failure in any event an amount not less than the credit service charge plus 10 percent of the principal amount of the obligation or the time-price differential plus 10 percent of the cash price.

(d) A debtor whose deficiency is eliminated under Section 9–626 may recover damages for the loss of any surplus. However, a debtor or secondary obligor whose deficiency is eliminated or reduced under Section 9–626 may not otherwise recover under subsection (b) for noncompliance with the provisions of this part relating to collection, enforcement, disposition, or acceptance.

(e) In addition to any damages recoverable under subsection (b), the debtor, consumer obligor, or person named as a debtor in a filed record, as applicable, may recover $500 in each case from a person that:

(1) fails to comply with Section 9–208;

(2) fails to comply with Section 9–209;

(3) files a record that the person is not entitled to file under Section 9–509(a);

(4) fails to cause the secured party of record to file or send a termination statement as required by Section 9–513(a) or (c);

(5) fails to comply with Section 9–616(b)(1) and whose failure is part of a pattern, or consistent with a practice, of noncompliance; or

(6) fails to comply with Section 9–616(b)(2).

(f) A debtor or consumer obligor may recover damages under subsection (b) and, in addition, $500 in each case from a person that, without reasonable cause, fails to comply with a request under Section 9–210. A recipient of a request under Section 9–210 which never claimed an interest in the collateral or obligations that are the subject of a request under that section has a reasonable excuse for failure to comply with the request within the meaning of this subsection.

(g) If a secured party fails to comply with a request regarding a list of collateral or a statement of account under Section 9–210, the secured party may claim a security interest only as shown in the list or statement included in the request as against a person that is reasonably misled by the failure.

As amended in 2000.

§ 9–626. Action in Which Deficiency or Surplus Is in Issue.

(a) In an action arising from a transaction, other than a consumer transaction, in which the amount of a deficiency or surplus is in issue, the following rules apply:

(1) A secured party need not prove compliance with the provisions of this part relating to collection, enforcement, disposition, or acceptance unless the debtor or a secondary obligor places the secured party's compliance in issue.

(2) If the secured party's compliance is placed in issue, the secured party has the burden of establishing that the collection, enforcement, disposition, or acceptance was conducted in accordance with this part.

(3) Except as otherwise provided in Section 9–628, if a secured party fails to prove that the collection, enforcement, disposition, or acceptance was conducted in accordance with the provisions of this part relating to collection, enforcement, disposition, or acceptance, the liability of a debtor or a secondary obligor for a deficiency is limited to an amount by which the sum of the secured obligation, expenses, and attorney's fees exceeds the greater of:

(A) the proceeds of the collection, enforcement, disposition, or acceptance; or

(B) the amount of proceeds that would have been realized had the noncomplying secured party proceeded in accordance with the provisions of this part relating to collection, enforcement, disposition, or acceptance.

(4) For purposes of paragraph (3)(B), the amount of proceeds that would have been realized is equal to the sum of the secured obligation, expenses, and attorney's fees unless the secured party proves that the amount is less than that sum.

(5) If a deficiency or surplus is calculated under Section 9–615(f), the debtor or obligor has the burden of establishing that the amount of proceeds of the disposition is significantly below the range of prices that a complying disposition to a person other than the secured party, a person related to the secured party, or a secondary obligor would have brought.

(b) The limitation of the rules in subsection (a) to transactions other than consumer transactions is intended to leave to the court the determination of the proper rules in consumer transactions. The court may not infer from that limitation the nature of the proper rule in consumer transactions and may continue to apply established approaches.

§ 9–627. Determination of Whether Conduct Was Commercially Reasonable.

(a) The fact that a greater amount could have been obtained by a collection, enforcement, disposition, or acceptance at a different time or in a different method from that selected by the secured party is not of itself sufficient to preclude the secured party from establishing that the collection, enforcement, disposition, or acceptance was made in a commercially reasonable manner.

(b) A disposition of collateral is made in a commercially reasonable manner if the disposition is made:

(1) in the usual manner on any recognized market;

(2) at the price current in any recognized market at the time of the disposition; or

(3) otherwise in conformity with reasonable commercial practices among dealers in the type of property that was the subject of the disposition.

(c) A collection, enforcement, disposition, or acceptance is commercially reasonable if it has been approved:

(1) in a judicial proceeding;

(2) by a bona fide creditors' committee;

(3) by a representative of creditors; or

(4) by an assignee for the benefit of creditors.

(d) Approval under subsection (c) need not be obtained, and lack of approval does not mean that the collection, enforcement, disposition, or acceptance is not commercially reasonable.

§ 9–628. Nonliability and Limitation on Liability of Secured Party; Liability of Secondary Obligor.

(a) Unless a secured party knows that a person is a debtor or obligor, knows the identity of the person, and knows how to communicate with the person:

(1) the secured party is not liable to the person, or to a secured party or lienholder that has filed a financing statement against the person, for failure to comply with this article; and

(2) the secured party's failure to comply with this article does not affect the liability of the person for a deficiency.

(b) A secured party is not liable because of its status as secured party:

(1) to a person that is a debtor or obligor, unless the secured party knows:

(A) that the person is a debtor or obligor;

(B) the identity of the person; and

(C) how to communicate with the person; or

(2) to a secured party or lienholder that has filed a financing statement against a person, unless the secured party knows:

(A) that the person is a debtor; and

(B) the identity of the person.

(c) A secured party is not liable to any person, and a person's liability for a deficiency is not affected, because of any act or omission arising out of the secured party's reasonable belief that a transaction is not a consumer-goods transaction or a consumer transaction or that goods are not consumer goods, if the secured party's belief is based on its reasonable reliance on:

(1) a debtor's representation concerning the purpose for which collateral was to be used, acquired, or held; or

(2) an obligor's representation concerning the purpose for which a secured obligation was incurred.

(d) A secured party is not liable to any person under Section 9–625(c)(2) for its failure to comply with Section 9–616.

(e) A secured party is not liable under Section 9–625(c)(2) more than once with respect to any one secured obligation.

Part 7 Transition

§ 9–701. Effective Date.

This [Act] takes effect on July 1, 2001.

§ 9–702. Savings Clause.

(a) Except as otherwise provided in this part, this [Act] applies to a transaction or lien within its scope, even if the transaction or lien was entered into or created before this [Act] takes effect.

(b) Except as otherwise provided in subsection (c) and Sections 9–703 through 9–709:

(1) transactions and liens that were not governed by [former Article 9], were validly entered into or created before this [Act] takes effect, and would be subject to this [Act] if they had been entered into or created after this [Act] takes effect, and the rights, duties, and interests flowing from those transactions and liens remain valid after this [Act] takes effect; and

(2) the transactions and liens may be terminated, completed, consummated, and enforced as required or permitted by this [Act] or by the law that otherwise would apply if this [Act] had not taken effect.

(c) This [Act] does not affect an action, case, or proceeding commenced before this [Act] takes effect.

As amended in 2000.

§ 9–703. Security Interest Perfected before Effective Date.

(a) A security interest that is enforceable immediately before this [Act] takes effect and would have priority over the rights of a person that becomes a lien creditor at that time is a perfected security interest under this [Act] if, when this [Act] takes effect, the applicable requirements for enforceability and perfection under this [Act] are satisfied without further action.

(b) Except as otherwise provided in Section 9–705, if, immediately before this [Act] takes effect, a security interest is enforceable and would have priority over the rights of a person that becomes a lien creditor at that time, but the applicable requirements for enforceability or perfection under this [Act] are not satisfied when this [Act] takes effect, the security interest:

(1) is a perfected security interest for one year after this [Act] takes effect;

(2) remains enforceable thereafter only if the security interest becomes enforceable under Section 9–203 before the year expires; and

(3) remains perfected thereafter only if the applicable requirements for perfection under this [Act] are satisfied before the year expires.

§ 9–704. Security Interest Unperfected before Effective Date.

A security interest that is enforceable immediately before this [Act] takes effect but which would be subordinate to the rights of a person that becomes a lien creditor at that time:

(1) remains an enforceable security interest for one year after this [Act] takes effect;

(2) remains enforceable thereafter if the security interest becomes enforceable under Section 9–203 when this [Act] takes effect or within one year thereafter; and

(3) becomes perfected:

(A) without further action, when this [Act] takes effect if the applicable requirements for perfection under this [Act] are satisfied before or at that time; or

(B) when the applicable requirements for perfection are satisfied if the requirements are satisfied after that time.

§ 9–705. Effectiveness of Action Taken before Effective Date.

(a) If action, other than the filing of a financing statement, is taken before this [Act] takes effect and the action would have resulted in priority of a security interest over the rights of a person that becomes a lien creditor had the security interest become enforceable before this [Act] takes effect, the action is effective to perfect a security interest that attaches under this [Act] within one year after this [Act] takes effect. An attached security interest becomes unperfected one year after this [Act] takes effect unless the security interest becomes a perfected security interest under this [Act] before the expiration of that period.

(b) The filing of a financing statement before this [Act] takes effect is effective to perfect a security interest to the extent the filing would satisfy the applicable requirements for perfection under this [Act].

(c) This [Act] does not render ineffective an effective financing statement that, before this [Act] takes effect, is filed and satisfies the applicable requirements for perfection under the law of the jurisdiction governing perfection as provided in [former Section 9–103]. However, except as otherwise provided in subsections (d) and (e) and Section 9–706, the financing statement ceases to be effective at the earlier of:

(1) the time the financing statement would have ceased to be effective under the law of the jurisdiction in which it is filed; or

(2) June 30, 2006.

(d) The filing of a continuation statement after this [Act] takes effect does not continue the effectiveness of the financing statement filed before this [Act] takes effect. However, upon the timely filing of a continuation statement after this [Act] takes effect and in accordance with the law of the jurisdiction governing perfection as provided in Part 3, the effectiveness of a financing statement filed in the same office in that jurisdiction before this [Act] takes effect continues for the period provided by the law of that jurisdiction.

(e) Subsection (c)(2) applies to a financing statement that, before this [Act] takes effect, is filed against a transmitting utility and satisfies the applicable requirements for perfection under the law of the jurisdiction governing perfection as provided in [former Section 9–103] only to the extent that Part 3 provides that the law of a jurisdiction other than the jurisdiction in which the financing statement is filed governs perfection of a security interest in collateral covered by the financing statement.

(f) A financing statement that includes a financing statement filed before this [Act] takes effect and a continuation statement filed after this [Act] takes effect is effective only to the extent that it satisfies the requirements of Part 5 for an initial financing statement.

§ 9–706. When Initial Financing Statement Suffices to Continue Effectiveness of Financing Statement.

(a) The filing of an initial financing statement in the office specified in Section 9–501 continues the effectiveness of a financing statement filed before this [Act] takes effect if:

(1) the filing of an initial financing statement in that office would be effective to perfect a security interest under this [Act];

(2) the pre-effective-date financing statement was filed in an office in another State or another office in this State; and

(3) the initial financing statement satisfies subsection (c).

(b) The filing of an initial financing statement under subsection (a) continues the effectiveness of the pre-effective-date financing statement:

(1) if the initial financing statement is filed before this [Act] takes effect, for the period provided in [former Section 9–403] with respect to a financing statement; and

(2) if the initial financing statement is filed after this [Act] takes effect, for the period provided in Section 9–515 with respect to an initial financing statement.

(c) To be effective for purposes of subsection (a), an initial financing statement must:

(1) satisfy the requirements of Part 5 for an initial financing statement;

(2) identify the pre-effective-date financing statement by indicating the office in which the financing statement was filed and providing the dates of filing and file numbers, if any, of the financing statement and of the most recent continuation statement filed with respect to the financing statement; and

(3) indicate that the pre-effective-date financing statement remains effective.

§ 9–707. Amendment of Pre-Effective-Date Financing Statement.

(a) In this section, "Pre-effective-date financing statement" means a financing statement filed before this [Act] takes effect.

(b) After this [Act] takes effect, a person may add or delete collateral covered by, continue or terminate the effectiveness of, or otherwise amend the information provided in, a pre-effective-date financing statement only in accordance with the law of the jurisdiction governing perfection as provided in Part 3. However, the effectiveness of a pre-effective-date financing statement also may be terminated in accordance with the law of the jurisdiction in which the financing statement is filed.

(c) Except as otherwise provided in subsection (d), if the law of this State governs perfection of a security interest, the information in a pre-effective-date financing statement may be amended after this [Act] takes effect only if:

(1) the pre-effective-date financing statement and an amendment are filed in the office specified in Section 9–501;

(2) an amendment is filed in the office specified in Section 9–501 concurrently with, or after the filing in that office of, an initial financing statement that satisfies Section 9–706(c); or

(3) an initial financing statement that provides the information as amended and satisfies Section 9–706(c) is filed in the office specified in Section 9–501.

(d) If the law of this State governs perfection of a security interest, the effectiveness of a pre-effective-date financing statement may be continued only under Section 9–705(d) and (f) or 9–706.

(e) Whether or not the law of this State governs perfection of a security interest, the effectiveness of a pre-effective-date financing statement filed in this State may be terminated after this [Act] takes effect by filing a termination statement in the office in which the pre-effective-date financing statement is filed, unless an initial financing statement that satisfies Section 9–706(c) has been filed in the office specified by the law of the jurisdiction governing perfection as provided in Part 3 as the office in which to file a financing statement.

As amended in 2000.

§ 9–708. Persons Entitled to File Initial Financing Statement or Continuation Statement.

A person may file an initial financing statement or a continuation statement under this part if:

(1) the secured party of record authorizes the filing; and

(2) the filing is necessary under this part:

(A) to continue the effectiveness of a financing statement filed before this [Act] takes effect; or

(B) to perfect or continue the perfection of a security interest.

As amended in 2000.

§ 9–709. Priority.

(a) This [Act] determines the priority of conflicting claims to collateral. However, if the relative priorities of the claims were established before this [Act] takes effect, [former Article 9] determines priority.

(b) For purposes of Section 9–322(a), the priority of a security interest that becomes enforceable under Section 9–203 of this [Act] dates from the time this [Act] takes effect if the security interest is perfected under this [Act] by the filing of a financing statement before this [Act] takes effect which would not have been effective to perfect the security interest under [former Article 9]. This subsection does not apply to conflicting security interests each of which is perfected by the filing of such a financing statement.

As amended in 2000.

* * * *

The Sarbanes-Oxley Act (Excerpts and Explanatory Comments)

Note: The author's explanatory comments appear in italics following the excerpt from each section.

Section 302

Corporate responsibility for financial reports[1]

(a) Regulations required

The Commission shall, by rule, require, for each company filing periodic reports under section 13(a) or 15(d) of the Securities Exchange Act of 1934 (15 U.S.C. 78m, 78o(d)), that the principal executive officer or officers and the principal financial officer or officers, or persons performing similar functions, certify in each annual or quarterly report filed or submitted under either such section of such Act that—

(1) the signing officer has reviewed the report;

(2) based on the officer's knowledge, the report does not contain any untrue statement of a material fact or omit to state a material fact necessary in order to make the statements made, in light of the circumstances under which such statements were made, not misleading;

(3) based on such officer's knowledge, the financial statements, and other financial information included in the report, fairly present in all material respects the financial condition and results of operations of the issuer as of, and for, the periods presented in the report;

(4) the signing officers—

(A) are responsible for establishing and maintaining internal controls;

(B) have designed such internal controls to ensure that material information relating to the issuer and its consolidated subsidiaries is made known to such officers by others within those entities, particularly during the period in which the periodic reports are being prepared;

(C) have evaluated the effectiveness of the issuer's internal controls as of a date within 90 days prior to the report; and

(D) have presented in the report their conclusions about the effectiveness of their internal controls based on their evaluation as of that date;

(5) the signing officers have disclosed to the issuer's auditors and the audit committee of the board of directors (or persons fulfilling the equivalent function)—

(A) all significant deficiencies in the design or operation of internal controls which could adversely affect the issuer's ability to record, process, summarize, and report financial data and have identified for the issuer's auditors any material weaknesses in internal controls; and

(B) any fraud, whether or not material, that involves management or other employees who have a significant role in the issuer's internal controls; and

(6) the signing officers have indicated in the report whether or not there were significant changes in internal controls or in other factors that could significantly affect internal controls subsequent to the date of their evaluation, including any corrective actions with regard to significant deficiencies and material weaknesses.

(b) Foreign reincorporations have no effect

Nothing in this section shall be interpreted or applied in any way to allow any issuer to lessen the legal force of the statement required under this section, by an issuer having reincorporated or having engaged in any other transaction that resulted in the transfer of the corporate domicile or offices of the issuer from inside the United States to outside of the United States.

(c) Deadline

The rules required by subsection (a) of this section shall be effective not later than 30 days after July 30, 2002.

* * * *

Explanatory Comments:

Section 302 requires the chief executive officer (CEO) and chief financial officer (CFO) of each public company to certify that they have reviewed the company's quarterly and annual reports to be filed with the Securities and Exchange Commission (SEC). The CEO and CFO must certify that, based on their knowledge, the reports do not contain any untrue statement of a material fact or any half-truth that would make the report misleading, and that the information contained in the reports fairly presents the company's financial condition.

In addition, this section also requires the CEO and CFO to certify that they have created and designed an internal control system for their company and have recently evaluated that system to ensure that it is effectively providing them with relevant and accurate financial information. If the signing officers have found any significant deficiencies or weaknesses in the company's system or have discovered any evidence of fraud, they must have reported the situation, and any corrective actions they have taken, to the auditors and the audit committee.

1. This section of the Sarbanes-Oxley Act is codified at 15 U.S.C. Section 7241.

Section 306

Insider trades during pension fund blackout periods[2]

(a) Prohibition of insider trading during pension fund blackout periods

(1) In general

Except to the extent otherwise provided by rule of the Commission pursuant to paragraph (3), it shall be unlawful for any director or executive officer of an issuer of any equity security (other than an exempted security), directly or indirectly, to purchase, sell, or otherwise acquire or transfer any equity security of the issuer (other than an exempted security) during any blackout period with respect to such equity security if such director or officer acquires such equity security in connection with his or her service or employment as a director or executive officer.

(2) Remedy

(A) In general

Any profit realized by a director or executive officer referred to in paragraph (1) from any purchase, sale, or other acquisition or transfer in violation of this subsection shall inure to and be recoverable by the issuer, irrespective of any intention on the part of such director or executive officer in entering into the transaction.

(B) Actions to recover profits

An action to recover profits in accordance with this subsection may be instituted at law or in equity in any court of competent jurisdiction by the issuer, or by the owner of any security of the issuer in the name and in behalf of the issuer if the issuer fails or refuses to bring such action within 60 days after the date of request, or fails diligently to prosecute the action thereafter, except that no such suit shall be brought more than 2 years after the date on which such profit was realized.

(3) Rulemaking authorized

The Commission shall, in consultation with the Secretary of Labor, issue rules to clarify the application of this subsection and to prevent evasion thereof. Such rules shall provide for the application of the requirements of paragraph (1) with respect to entities treated as a single employer with respect to an issuer under section 414(b), (c), (m), or (o) of Title 26 to the extent necessary to clarify the application of such requirements and to prevent evasion thereof. Such rules may also provide for appropriate exceptions from the requirements of this subsection, including exceptions for purchases pursuant to an automatic dividend reinvestment program or purchases or sales made pursuant to an advance election.

(4) Blackout period

For purposes of this subsection, the term "blackout period", with respect to the equity securities of any issuer—

(A) means any period of more than 3 consecutive business days during which the ability of not fewer than 50 percent of the participants or beneficiaries under all individual account plans maintained by the issuer to purchase, sell, or otherwise acquire or transfer an interest in any equity of such issuer held in such an individual account plan is temporarily suspended by the issuer or by a fiduciary of the plan; and

(B) does not include, under regulations which shall be prescribed by the Commission—

(i) a regularly scheduled period in which the participants and beneficiaries may not purchase, sell, or otherwise acquire or transfer an interest in any equity of such issuer, if such period is—

(I) incorporated into the individual account plan; and

(II) timely disclosed to employees before becoming participants under the individual account plan or as a subsequent amendment to the plan; or

(ii) any suspension described in subparagraph (A) that is imposed solely in connection with persons becoming participants or beneficiaries, or ceasing to be participants or beneficiaries, in an individual account plan by reason of a corporate merger, acquisition, divestiture, or similar transaction involving the plan or plan sponsor.

(5) Individual account plan

For purposes of this subsection, the term "individual account plan" has the meaning provided in section 1002(34) of Title 29, except that such term shall not include a one-participant retirement plan (within the meaning of section 1021(i)(8)(B) of Title 29).

(6) Notice to directors, executive officers, and the Commission

In any case in which a director or executive officer is subject to the requirements of this subsection in connection with a blackout period (as defined in paragraph (4)) with respect to any equity securities, the issuer of such equity securities shall timely notify such director or officer and the Securities and Exchange Commission of such blackout period.

* * * *

Explanatory Comments:

Corporate pension funds typically prohibit employees from trading shares of the corporation during periods when the pension fund is undergoing significant change. Before 2002, however, these blackout periods did not affect the corporation's executives, who frequently received shares of the corporate stock as part of their compensation. Section 306 was Congress's solution to the basic unfairness of this situation. This section of the act required the SEC to issue rules that prohibit any director or executive officer from trading during pension fund blackout periods. (The SEC later issued these rules, entitled Regulation Blackout Trading Restriction, or Reg BTR.)

Section 306 also provided shareholders with a right to file a shareholder's derivative suit against officers and directors who have profited from trading during these blackout periods (provided that the corporation has failed to bring a suit). The officer or director can be forced to return to the corporation any profits received, regardless of whether the director or officer acted with bad intent.

2. Codified at 15 U.S.C. Section 7244.

Section 402

Periodical and other reports[3]

* * * *

(i) Accuracy of financial reports

Each financial report that contains financial statements, and that is required to be prepared in accordance with (or reconciled to) generally accepted accounting principles under this chapter and filed with the Commission shall reflect all material correcting adjustments that have been identified by a registered public accounting firm in accordance with generally accepted accounting principles and the rules and regulations of the Commission.

(j) Off-balance sheet transactions

Not later than 180 days after July 30, 2002, the Commission shall issue final rules providing that each annual and quarterly financial report required to be filed with the Commission shall disclose all material off-balance sheet transactions, arrangements, obligations (including contingent obligations), and other relationships of the issuer with unconsolidated entities or other persons, that may have a material current or future effect on financial condition, changes in financial condition, results of operations, liquidity, capital expenditures, capital resources, or significant components of revenues or expenses.

(k) Prohibition on personal loans to executives

(1) In general

It shall be unlawful for any issuer (as defined in section 7201 of this title), directly or indirectly, including through any subsidiary, to extend or maintain credit, to arrange for the extension of credit, or to renew an extension of credit, in the form of a personal loan to or for any director or executive officer (or equivalent thereof) of that issuer. An extension of credit maintained by the issuer on July 30, 2002, shall not be subject to the provisions of this subsection, provided that there is no material modification to any term of any such extension of credit or any renewal of any such extension of credit on or after July 30, 2002.

(2) Limitation

Paragraph (1) does not preclude any home improvement and manufactured home loans (as that term is defined in section 1464 of Title 12), consumer credit (as defined in section 1602 of this title), or any extension of credit under an open end credit plan (as defined in section 1602 of this title), or a charge card (as defined in section 1637(c)(4)(e) of this title), or any extension of credit by a broker or dealer registered under section 78o of this title to an employee of that broker or dealer to buy, trade, or carry securities, that is permitted under rules or regulations of the Board of Governors of the Federal Reserve System pursuant to section 78g of this title (other than an extension of credit that would be used to purchase the stock of that issuer), that is—

(A) made or provided in the ordinary course of the consumer credit business of such issuer;

(B) of a type that is generally made available by such issuer to the public; and

(C) made by such issuer on market terms, or terms that are no more favorable than those offered by the issuer to the general public for such extensions of credit.

(3) Rule of construction for certain loans

Paragraph (1) does not apply to any loan made or maintained by an insured depository institution (as defined in section 1813 of Title 12), if the loan is subject to the insider lending restrictions of section 375b of Title 12.

(l) Real time issuer disclosures

Each issuer reporting under subsection (a) of this section or section 78o(d) of this title shall disclose to the public on a rapid and current basis such additional information concerning material changes in the financial condition or operations of the issuer, in plain English, which may include trend and qualitative information and graphic presentations, as the Commission determines, by rule, is necessary or useful for the protection of investors and in the public interest.

Explanatory Comments:

Before this act, many corporate executives typically received extremely large salaries, significant bonuses, and abundant stock options, even when the companies for which they worked were suffering. Executives were also routinely given personal loans from corporate funds, many of which were never paid back. The average large company during that period loaned almost $1 million a year to top executives, and some companies loaned hundreds of millions of dollars to their executives every year. Section 402 amended the 1934 Securities Exchange Act to prohibit public companies from making personal loans to executive officers and directors.

There are a few exceptions to this prohibition, such as home-improvement loans made in the ordinary course of business. Note also that while loans are forbidden, outright gifts are not. A corporation is free to give gifts to its executives, including cash, provided that these gifts are disclosed on its financial reports. The idea is that corporate directors will be deterred from making substantial gifts to their executives by the disclosure requirement—particularly if the corporation's financial condition is questionable—because making such gifts could be perceived as abusing their authority.

Section 403

Directors, officers, and principal stockholders[4]

(a) Disclosures required

(1) Directors, officers, and principal stockholders required to file

Every person who is directly or indirectly the beneficial owner of more than 10 percent of any class of any equity security (other than an exempted security) which is registered pursuant to section 78l of this title, or who is a director or an officer

3. This section of the Sarbanes-Oxley Act amended some of the provisions of the 1934 Securities Exchange Act and added the paragraphs reproduced here at 15 U.S.C. Section 78m.

4. This section of the Sarbanes-Oxley Act amended the disclosure provisions of the 1934 Securities Exchange Act, at 15 U.S.C. Section 78p.

of the issuer of such security, shall file the statements required by this subsection with the Commission (and, if such security is registered on a national securities exchange, also with the exchange).

(2) Time of filing

The statements required by this subsection shall be filed—

(A) at the time of the registration of such security on a national securities exchange or by the effective date of a registration statement filed pursuant to section 78l(g) of this title;

(B) within 10 days after he or she becomes such beneficial owner, director, or officer;

(C) if there has been a change in such ownership, or if such person shall have purchased or sold a security-based swap agreement (as defined in section 206(b) of the Gramm-Leach-Bliley Act (15 U.S.C. 78c note)) involving such equity security, before the end of the second business day following the day on which the subject transaction has been executed, or at such other time as the Commission shall establish, by rule, in any case in which the Commission determines that such 2-day period is not feasible.

(3) Contents of statements

A statement filed—

(A) under subparagraph (A) or (B) of paragraph (2) shall contain a statement of the amount of all equity securities of such issuer of which the filing person is the beneficial owner; and

(B) under subparagraph (C) of such paragraph shall indicate ownership by the filing person at the date of filing, any such changes in such ownership, and such purchases and sales of the security-based swap agreements as have occurred since the most recent such filing under such subparagraph.

(4) Electronic filing and availability

Beginning not later than 1 year after July 30, 2002—

(A) a statement filed under subparagraph (C) of paragraph (2) shall be filed electronically;

(B) the Commission shall provide each such statement on a publicly accessible Internet site not later than the end of the business day following that filing; and

(C) the issuer (if the issuer maintains a corporate website) shall provide that statement on that corporate website, not later than the end of the business day following that filing.

* * * *

Explanatory Comments:

This section dramatically shortens the time period provided in the Securities Exchange Act of 1934 for disclosing transactions by insiders. The prior law stated that most transactions had to be reported within ten days of the beginning of the following month, although certain transactions did not have to be reported until the following fiscal year (within the first forty-five days).

In several instances, some insider trading was not disclosed (and was therefore not discovered) until long after the transactions. So Congress added this section to reduce the time period for making disclosures. Under Section 403, most transactions by insiders must be electronically filed with the SEC within two business days.

Also, any company that maintains a Web site must post these SEC filings on its site by the end of the next business day. Congress enacted this section in the belief that if insiders are required to file reports of their transactions promptly with the SEC, companies will do more to police themselves and prevent insider trading.

Section 404

Management assessment of internal controls[5]

(a) Rules required

The Commission shall prescribe rules requiring each annual report required by section 78m(a) or 78o(d) of this title to contain an internal control report, which shall—

(1) state the responsibility of management for establishing and maintaining an adequate internal control structure and procedures for financial reporting; and

(2) contain an assessment, as of the end of the most recent fiscal year of the issuer, of the effectiveness of the internal control structure and procedures of the issuer for financial reporting.

(b) Internal control evaluation and reporting

With respect to the internal control assessment required by subsection (a) of this section, each registered public accounting firm that prepares or issues the audit report for the issuer shall attest to, and report on, the assessment made by the management of the issuer. An attestation made under this subsection shall be made in accordance with standards for attestation engagements issued or adopted by the Board. Any such attestation shall not be the subject of a separate engagement.

* * * *

Explanatory Comments:

This section was enacted to prevent corporate executives from claiming they were ignorant of significant errors in their companies' financial reports. For instance, several CEOs testified before Congress that they simply had no idea that the corporations' financial statements were off by billions of dollars. Congress therefore passed Section 404, which requires each annual report to contain a description and assessment of the company's internal control structure and financial reporting procedures. The section also requires that an audit be conducted of the internal control assessment, as well as the financial statements contained in the report. This section goes hand in hand with Section 302 (which, as discussed previously, requires various certifications attesting to the accuracy of the information in financial reports).

Section 404 has been one of the more controversial and expensive provisions in the Sarbanes-Oxley Act because it requires companies to assess their own internal financial controls to make sure that their financial statements are reliable and accurate. A corporation might need to set up a disclosure committee and a coordinator, establish codes of conduct for accounting and financial personnel, create documentation procedures, provide train-

5. Codified at 15 U.S.C. Section 7262.

ing, and outline the individuals who are responsible for performing each of the procedures. Companies that were already well managed have not experienced substantial difficulty complying with this section. Other companies, however, have spent millions of dollars setting up, documenting, and evaluating their internal financial control systems. Although initially creating the internal financial control system is a one-time-only expense, the costs of maintaining and evaluating it are ongoing. Some corporations that spent considerable sums complying with Section 404 have been able to offset these costs by discovering and correcting inefficiencies or frauds within their systems. Nevertheless, it is unlikely that any corporation will find compliance with this section to be inexpensive.

Section 802(a)

Destruction, alteration, or falsification of records in Federal investigations and bankruptcy[6]

Whoever knowingly alters, destroys, mutilates, conceals, covers up, falsifies, or makes a false entry in any record, document, or tangible object with the intent to impede, obstruct, or influence the investigation or proper administration of any matter within the jurisdiction of any department or agency of the United States or any case filed under title 11, or in relation to or contemplation of any such matter or case, shall be fined under this title, imprisoned not more than 20 years, or both.

Destruction of corporate audit records[7]

(a) (1) Any accountant who conducts an audit of an issuer of securities to which section 10A(a) of the Securities Exchange Act of 1934 (15 U.S.C. 78j-1(a)) applies, shall maintain all audit or review workpapers for a period of 5 years from the end of the fiscal period in which the audit or review was concluded.

(2) The Securities and Exchange Commission shall promulgate, within 180 days, after adequate notice and an opportunity for comment, such rules and regulations, as are reasonably necessary, relating to the retention of relevant records such as workpapers, documents that form the basis of an audit or review, memoranda, correspondence, communications, other documents, and records (including electronic records) which are created, sent, or received in connection with an audit or review and contain conclusions, opinions, analyses, or financial data relating to such an audit or review, which is conducted by any accountant who conducts an audit of an issuer of securities to which section 10A(a) of the Securities Exchange Act of 1934 (15 U.S.C. 78j-1(a)) applies. The Commission may, from time to time, amend or supplement the rules and regulations that it is required to promulgate under this section, after adequate notice and an opportunity for comment, in order to ensure that such rules and regulations adequately comport with the purposes of this section.

(b) Whoever knowingly and willfully violates subsection (a)(1), or any rule or regulation promulgated by the Securities and Exchange Commission under subsection (a)(2), shall be fined under this title, imprisoned not more than 10 years, or both.

(c) Nothing in this section shall be deemed to diminish or relieve any person of any other duty or obligation imposed by Federal or State law or regulation to maintain, or refrain from destroying, any document.

* * * *

Explanatory Comments:

Section 802(a) enacted two new statutes that punish those who alter or destroy documents. The first statute is not specifically limited to securities fraud cases. It provides that anyone who alters, destroys, or falsifies records in federal investigations or bankruptcy may be criminally prosecuted and sentenced to a fine or to up to twenty years in prison, or both. The second statute requires auditors of public companies to keep all audit or review working papers for five years but expressly allows the SEC to amend or supplement these requirements as it sees fit. The SEC has, in fact, amended this section by issuing a rule that requires auditors who audit reporting companies to retain working papers for seven years from the conclusion of the review. Section 802(a) further provides that anyone who knowingly and willfully violates this statute is subject to criminal prosecution and can be sentenced to a fine, imprisoned for up to ten years, or both if convicted.

This portion of the Sarbanes-Oxley Act implicitly recognizes that persons who are under investigation often are tempted to respond by destroying or falsifying documents that might prove their complicity in wrongdoing. The severity of the punishment should provide a strong incentive for these individuals to resist the temptation.

Section 804

Time limitations on the commencement of civil actions arising under Acts of Congress[8]

(a) Except as otherwise provided by law, a civil action arising under an Act of Congress enacted after the date of the enactment of this section may not be commenced later than 4 years after the cause of action accrues.

(b) Notwithstanding subsection (a), a private right of action that involves a claim of fraud, deceit, manipulation, or contrivance in contravention of a regulatory requirement concerning the securities laws, as defined in section 3(a)(47) of the Securities Exchange Act of 1934 (15 U.S.C. 78c(a)(47)), may be brought not later than the earlier of—

(1) 2 years after the discovery of the facts constituting the violation; or

(2) 5 years after such violation.

* * * *

Explanatory Comments:

Before the enactment of this section, Section 10(b) of the Securities Exchange Act of 1934 had no express statute of limitations. The courts generally required plaintiffs to have filed suit within one year from the date that they should (using due diligence) have discovered that a fraud had been committed but no later than three years

6. Codified at 15 U.S.C. Section 1519.

7. Codified at 15 U.S.C. Section 1520.

8. Codified at 28 U.S.C. Section 1658.

after the fraud occurred. Section 804 extends this period by specifying that plaintiffs must file a lawsuit within two years after they discover (or should have discovered) a fraud but no later than five years after the fraud's occurrence. This provision has prevented the courts from dismissing numerous securities fraud lawsuits.

Section 806

Civil action to protect against retaliation in fraud cases[9]

(a) Whistleblower protection for employees of publicly traded companies.—

No company with a class of securities registered under section 12 of the Securities Exchange Act of 1934 (15 U.S.C. 78l), or that is required to file reports under section 15(d) of the Securities Exchange Act of 1934 (15 U.S.C. 78o(d)), or any officer, employee, contractor, subcontractor, or agent of such company, may discharge, demote, suspend, threaten, harass, or in any other manner discriminate against an employee in the terms and conditions of employment because of any lawful act done by the employee—

(1) to provide information, cause information to be provided, or otherwise assist in an investigation regarding any conduct which the employee reasonably believes constitutes a violation of section 1341, 1343, 1344, or 1348, any rule or regulation of the Securities and Exchange Commission, or any provision of Federal law relating to fraud against shareholders, when the information or assistance is provided to or the investigation is conducted by—

(A) a Federal regulatory or law enforcement agency;

(B) any Member of Congress or any committee of Congress; or

(C) a person with supervisory authority over the employee (or such other person working for the employer who has the authority to investigate, discover, or terminate misconduct); or

(2) to file, cause to be filed, testify, participate in, or otherwise assist in a proceeding filed or about to be filed (with any knowledge of the employer) relating to an alleged violation of section 1341, 1343, 1344, or 1348, any rule or regulation of the Securities and Exchange Commission, or any provision of Federal law relating to fraud against shareholders.

(b) Enforcement action.—

(1) In general.—A person who alleges discharge or other discrimination by any person in violation of subsection (a) may seek relief under subsection (c), by—

(A) filing a complaint with the Secretary of Labor; or

(B) if the Secretary has not issued a final decision within 180 days of the filing of the complaint and there is no showing that such delay is due to the bad faith of the claimant, bringing an action at law or equity for de novo review in the appropriate district court of the United States, which shall have jurisdiction over such an action without regard to the amount in controversy.

(2) Procedure.—

(A) In general.—An action under paragraph (1)(A) shall be governed under the rules and procedures set forth in section 42121(b) of title 49, United States Code.

(B) Exception.—Notification made under section 42121(b)(1) of title 49, United States Code, shall be made to the person named in the complaint and to the employer.

(C) Burdens of proof.—An action brought under paragraph (1)(B) shall be governed by the legal burdens of proof set forth in section 42121(b) of title 49, United States Code.

(D) Statute of limitations.—An action under paragraph (1) shall be commenced not later than 90 days after the date on which the violation occurs.

(c) Remedies.—

(1) In general.—An employee prevailing in any action under subsection (b)(1) shall be entitled to all relief necessary to make the employee whole.

(2) Compensatory damages.—Relief for any action under paragraph (1) shall include—

(A) reinstatement with the same seniority status that the employee would have had, but for the discrimination;

(B) the amount of back pay, with interest; and

(C) compensation for any special damages sustained as a result of the discrimination, including litigation costs, expert witness fees, and reasonable attorney fees.

(d) Rights retained by employee.—Nothing in this section shall be deemed to diminish the rights, privileges, or remedies of any employee under any Federal or State law, or under any collective bargaining agreement.

Explanatory Comments:

Section 806 is one of several provisions that were included in the Sarbanes-Oxley Act to encourage and protect whistleblowers—that is, employees who report their employer's alleged violations of securities law to the authorities. This section applies to employees, agents, and independent contractors who work for publicly traded companies or testify about such a company during an investigation. It sets up an administrative procedure at the U.S. Department of Labor for individuals who claim that their employer retaliated against them (fired or demoted them, for example) for blowing the whistle on the employer's wrongful conduct. It also allows the award of civil damages—including back pay, reinstatement, special damages, attorneys' fees, and court costs—to employees who prove that they suffered retaliation. Since this provision was enacted, whistleblowers have filed numerous complaints with the U.S. Department of Labor under this section.

Section 807

Securities fraud[10]

Whoever knowingly executes, or attempts to execute, a scheme or artifice—

9. Codified at 18 U.S.C. Section 1514A.

10. Codified at 18 U.S.C. Section 1348.

(1) to defraud any person in connection with any security of an issuer with a class of securities registered under section 12 of the Securities Exchange Act of 1934 (15 U.S.C. 78l) or that is required to file reports under section 15(d) of the Securities Exchange Act of 1934 (15 U.S.C. 78o(d)); or

(2) to obtain, by means of false or fraudulent pretenses, representations, or promises, any money or property in connection with the purchase or sale of any security of an issuer with a class of securities registered under section 12 of the Securities Exchange Act of 1934 (15 U.S.C. 78l) or that is required to file reports under section 15(d) of the Securities Exchange Act of 1934 (15 U.S.C. 78o(d)); shall be fined under this title, or imprisoned not more than 25 years, or both.

* * * *

Explanatory Comments:

Section 807 adds a new provision to the federal criminal code that addresses securities fraud. Before 2002, federal securities law had already made it a crime—under Section 10(b) of the Securities Exchange Act of 1934 and SEC Rule 10b-5, both of which were discussed in Chapter 31—to intentionally defraud someone in connection with a purchase or sale of securities, but the offense was not listed in the federal criminal code.

Also, paragraph 2 of Section 807 goes beyond what is prohibited under securities law by making it a crime to obtain by means of false or fraudulent pretenses any money or property from the purchase or sale of securities. This new provision allows violators to be punished by up to twenty-five years in prison, a fine, or both.

Section 906

Failure of corporate officers to certify financial reports[11]

(a) Certification of periodic financial reports.—Each periodic report containing financial statements filed by an issuer with the Securities Exchange Commission pursuant to section 13(a) or 15(d) of the Securities Exchange Act of 1934 (15 U.S.C. 78m(a) or 78o(d)) shall be accompanied by a written statement by the chief executive officer and chief financial officer (or equivalent thereof) of the issuer.

(b) Content.—The statement required under subsection (a) shall certify that the periodic report containing the financial statements fully complies with the requirements of section 13(a) or 15(d) of the Securities Exchange Act of 1934 (15 U.S.C. 78m or 78o(d)) and that information contained in the periodic report fairly presents, in all material respects, the financial condition and results of operations of the issuer.

(c) Criminal penalties.—Whoever—

(1) certifies any statement as set forth in subsections (a) and (b) of this section knowing that the periodic report accompanying the statement does not comport with all the requirements set forth in this section shall be fined not more than $1,000,000 or imprisoned not more than 10 years, or both; or

(2) willfully certifies any statement as set forth in subsections (a) and (b) of this section knowing that the periodic report accompanying the statement does not comport with all the requirements set forth in this section shall be fined not more than $5,000,000, or imprisoned not more than 20 years, or both.

Explanatory Comments:

As previously discussed, under Section 302 a corporation's CEO and CFO are required to certify that they believe the quarterly and annual reports their company files with the SEC are accurate and fairly present the company's financial condition. Section 906 adds "teeth" to these requirements by authorizing criminal penalties for those officers who intentionally certify inaccurate SEC filings.

Knowing violations of the requirements are punishable by a fine of up to $1 million, ten years' imprisonment, or both. Willful violators may be fined up to $5 million, sentenced to up to twenty years' imprisonment, or both. Although the difference between a knowing and a willful violation is not entirely clear, the section is obviously intended to remind corporate officers of the serious consequences of certifying inaccurate reports to the SEC.

11. Codified at 18 U.S.C. Section 1350.

APPENDIX E

Answers to *Issue Spotters*

Chapter 1

1A: No. The U.S. Constitution is the supreme law of the land and applies to all jurisdictions. A law in violation of the Constitution (in this question, the First Amendment to the Constitution) will be declared unconstitutional.

2A: Yes. Administrative rulemaking starts with the publication of a notice of the rulemaking in the *Federal Register*. Among other details, this notice states where and when the proceedings, such as a public hearing, will be held. Proponents and opponents can offer their comments and concerns regarding the pending rule. After reviewing all the comments from the proceedings, the agency's decision makers consider what was presented and draft the final rule.

Chapter 2

1A: No. Even if commercial speech is not related to illegal activities or misleading, it may be restricted if a state has a substantial government interest that cannot be achieved by less restrictive means. In this case, the interest in energy conservation is substantial, but it could be achieved by less restrictive means. That would be the utilities' defense against the enforcement of this state law.

2A: Yes. The tax would limit the liberty of some persons, such as out-of-state businesses, so it is subject to a review under the equal protection clause. Protecting local businesses from out-of-state competition is not a legitimate government objective. Thus, such a tax would violate the equal protection clause.

Chapter 3

1A: Yes. Submission of the dispute to mediation or nonbinding arbitration is mandatory, but compliance with the decision of the mediator or arbitrator is voluntary.

2A: Tom could file a motion for a directed verdict. This motion asks the judge to direct a verdict for Tom on the ground that Sue presented no evidence that would justify granting her relief. The judge grants the motion if there is insufficient evidence to raise an issue of fact.

Chapter 4

1A: Probably. To recover on the basis of negligence, the injured party as a plaintiff must show that the truck's owner owed the plaintiff a duty of care, that the owner breached that duty, that the plaintiff was injured, and that the breach caused the injury. In this problem, the owner's actions breached the duty of reasonable care. The billboard falling on the plaintiff was the direct cause of the injury, not the plaintiff's own negligence. Thus, liability turns on whether the plaintiff can connect the breach of duty to the injury. This involves the test of proximate cause—the question of foreseeability. The consequences to the injured party must have been a foreseeable result of the owner's carelessness.

2A: The company might defend against this electrician's claim by asserting that the electrician should have known of the risk and, therefore, the company had no duty to warn. According to the problem, the danger is common knowledge in the electrician's field and should have been apparent to this electrician, given his years of training and experience. In other words, the company most likely had no need to warn the electrician of the risk.

The firm could also raise comparative negligence. Both parties' negligence, if any, could be weighed and the liability distributed proportionately. The defendant could furthermore assert assumption of risk, claiming that the electrician voluntarily entered into a dangerous situation, knowing the risk involved.

Chapter 5

1A: This is patent infringement. A software maker in this situation might best protect its product, save litigation costs, and profit from its patent by the use of a license. In the context of this problem, a license would grant permission to sell a patented item. (A license can be limited to certain purposes and to the licensee only.)

2A: Yes. This may be an instance of trademark dilution. Dilution occurs when a trademark is used, without permission, in a way that diminishes the distinctive quality of the mark. Dilution does not require proof that consumers are likely to be confused by the use of the unauthorized mark. The products involved do not have to be similar. Dilution does require, however, that a mark be famous when the dilution occurs.

Chapter 6

1A: Yes. With respect to the gas station, Daisy has obtained goods by false pretenses. She might also be charged with the crimes of larceny and forgery, and most states have special statutes covering illegal use of credit cards.

2A: Yes. The Counterfeit Access Device and Computer Fraud and Abuse Act of 1984 provides that a person who accesses a computer online, without permission, to obtain classified data—such as consumer credit files in a credit agency's database—is subject to criminal prosecution. The crime has two elements: accessing the computer without permission and taking data. It is a felony if done for private financial gain. Penalties include fines and imprisonment for up to twenty years. The victim of the theft can also bring a civil suit against the criminal to obtain damages and other relief.

Chapter 7

1A: Maybe. On the one hand, it is not the company's "fault" when a product is misused. Also, keeping the product on the market is not a violation of the law, and stopping sales would hurt profits. On the other hand, suspending sales could reduce suffering and could prevent negative publicity that might occur if sales continued.

2A: When a corporation decides to respond to what it sees as a moral obligation to correct for past discrimination by adjusting pay differences among its employees, an ethical conflict is raised between the firm and its employees and between the firm and its shareholders. This dilemma arises directly out of the effect such a decision has on the firm's profits. If satisfying this obligation increases profitability, then the dilemma is easily resolved in favor of "doing the right thing."

Chapter 8

1A: Under the principle of comity, a U.S court would defer and give effect to foreign laws and judicial decrees that are consistent with U.S. law and public policy.

2A: The practice described in this problem is known as dumping, which is regarded as an unfair international trade practice. Dumping is the sale of imported goods at "less than fair value." Based on the price of those goods in the exporting country, an extra tariff—known as an antidumping duty—can be imposed on the imports.

Chapter 9

1A: Under the objective theory of contracts, if a reasonable person would have thought that Joli had accepted Keerin's offer when she signed and returned the letter, then a contract was made, and Joli is obligated to buy the book. This depends, in part, on what was said in the letter and what was said in response. For instance, did the letter contain a valid offer, and did the response constitute a valid acceptance? Under any circumstances, the issue is not whether either party subjectively believed that they did, or did not, have a contract.

2A: No. This contract, although not fully executed, is for an illegal purpose and therefore is void. A void contract gives rise to no legal obligation on the part of any party. A contract that is void is no contract. There is nothing to enforce.

Chapter 10

1A: No. Revocation of an offer may be implied by conduct inconsistent with the offer. When Fidelity Corporation rehired Monica, and Ron learned of the hiring, the offer was revoked. His acceptance was too late.

2A: First, it might be noted that the Uniform Electronic Transactions Act (UETA) does not apply unless the parties to a contract agree to use e-commerce in their transaction. In this deal, of course, the parties used e-commerce. The UETA removes barriers to e-commerce by giving the same legal effect to e-records and e-signatures as to paper documents and signatures. The UETA itself does not include rules for e-commerce transactions, however.

Chapter 11

1A: Yes. The original contract was executory—that is, not yet performed by both parties. The parties rescinded the original contract and agreed to a new contract.

2A: No. Generally, an exculpatory clause (a clause attempting to absolve a party of negligence or other wrongs) is not enforced if the party seeking its enforcement is involved in a business that is important to the public as a matter of practical necessity, such as an airline. Because of the essential nature of such services, the party would have an advantage in bargaining strength and could insist that anyone contracting for its services agree not to hold it liable.

Chapter 12

1A: Yes. Elle may be liable on the ground of negligent misrepresentation. A misrepresentation is negligent if a person fails to exercise reasonable care in disclosing material facts or does not use the skill and competence required by his or her business or profession.

2A: No. The memo would be a sufficient writing to enforce the contract against My-T if that party chose not to complete the deal, however. Letterhead stationery can constitute a signature. If the memo names the parties, the subject matter, the consideration, and the quantity involved in the transaction, it may be sufficient to be enforced against the party whose letterhead appears on it.

Chapter 13

1A: Yes. Generally, if a contract clearly states that a right is not assignable, no assignment will be effective, but there are exceptions. Assignment of the right to receive monetary payment cannot be prohibited.

2A: Contracts that are executory on both sides—contracts on which neither party has performed—can be rescinded solely by agreement. Contracts that are executed on one side—contracts on which one party has performed—can be rescinded only if the party who has performed receives consideration for the promise to call off the deal.

Chapter 14

1A: A nonbreaching party is entitled to her or his benefit of the bargain under the contract. Here, the innocent party is entitled to be put in the position she would have been in if the contract had been fully performed. The measure of the benefit is the cost to complete the work ($500). These are compensatory damages.

2A: No. To recover damages that flow from the consequences of a breach but that are caused by circumstances beyond the contract (consequential damages), the breaching party must know, or have reason to know, that special circumstances will cause the nonbreaching party to suffer the additional loss. That was not the circumstance in this problem.

Chapter 15

1A: A shipment of nonconforming goods constitutes an acceptance and a breach, unless the seller seasonably notifies the buyer that the nonconforming shipment does not constitute an acceptance and is offered only as an accommodation. Thus, since there was no notification in this problem, the shipment was both an acceptance and a breach.

2A: Yes. In a transaction between merchants, the requirement of a writing is satisfied if one of them sends to the other a signed written confirmation that indicates the terms of the agreement, and the merchant receiving it has reason to know of its contents. If the merchant who receives the confirmation does not object in writing within ten days after receipt, the writing will be enforceable against him or her even though he or she has not signed anything.

Chapter 16

1A: Yes. A seller is obligated to deliver goods in conformity with a contract in every detail. This is the perfect tender rule. The exception of the seller's right to cure does not apply here because the seller delivered too little too late to take advantage of this exception.

2A: Yes. When anticipatory repudiation occurs, a buyer (or lessee) can resort to any remedy for breach even if the buyer tells the seller (the repudiating party in this problem) that the buyer will wait for the seller's performance.

Chapter 17

1A: Yes. The manufacturer is liable for the injuries to the user of the product. A manufacturer is liable for its failure to exercise due care to any person who sustains an injury proximately caused by a negligently made (defective) product. In this problem, the failure to inspect is a failure to use due care. Of course, the maker of the component part may also be liable.

2A: Yes. Under the doctrine of strict liability, persons may be liable for the results of their acts regardless of their intentions or their exercise of reasonable care (that is, regardless of fault).

Chapter 18

1A: A statement that "I.O.U." money (or anything else) or an instruction to a bank stating, "I wish you would pay," would render any instrument nonnegotiable. To be negotiable, an instrument must contain an express promise to pay. An I.O.U. is only an acknowledgment of indebtedness. An order stating, "I wish you would pay," is not sufficiently precise.

2A: No. When a drawer's employee provides the drawer with the name of a fictitious payee (a payee whom the drawer does not actually intend to have any interest in an instrument), a forgery of the payee's name is effective to pass good title to subsequent transferees.

Chapter 19

1A: Yes, to both questions. In a civil suit, a drawer (Lyn) is liable to a payee (Nan) or to a holder of a check that is not honored. If intent to defraud can be proved, the drawer (Lyn) can also be subject to criminal prosecution for writing a bad check.

2A: The drawer is entitled to $6,300—the amount to which the check was altered ($7,000) less the amount that the drawer ordered the bank to pay ($700). The bank may recover this amount from the party who presented the altered check for payment.

Chapter 20

1A: A creditor can put other creditors on notice by perfecting her or his interest: by filing a financing statement in the appropriate public office, or by taking possession of the collateral until the debtor repays the loan.

2A: When collateral consists of consumer goods, and the debtor has paid less than 60 percent of the debt or the purchase price, the creditor has the option of disposing of the collateral in a commercially reasonable manner. This generally requires notice to the debtor of the place, time, and manner of sale. A debtor can waive the right to notice, but only after default. Before the disposal, a debtor can redeem the collateral by tendering performance of all of the obligations secured by the collateral and by paying the creditor's reasonable expenses in retaking and maintaining the collateral.

Chapter 21

1A: Each of the parties can place a mechanic's lien on the debtor's property. If the debtor does not pay what is owed, the property can be sold to satisfy the debt. The only requirements are that the lien be filed within a specific time from the time of the work, depending on the state statute, and that notice of the foreclosure and sale be given to the debtor in advance.

2A: Yes. A debtor's payment to a creditor made for a preexisting debt, within ninety days (one year in the case of an insider or fraud) of a bankruptcy filing, can be recovered if it gives the creditor more than he or she would have received in the bankruptcy proceedings. A trustee can recover this preference using her or his specific avoidance powers.

Chapter 22

1A: The major terms that must be disclosed under the Truth-in-Lending Act include the loan principal, the interest rate at which the loan is made, the annual percentage rate or APR (the actual cost of the loan on a yearly basis), and all fees and costs associated with the loan. These disclosures must be made on standardized forms and based on uniform formulas of calculation. Certain types of loans have special disclosure requirements.

2A: Foreclosure is the process that allows a lender to repossess and auction off property that is securing a loan. The two most common types of foreclosure are judicial foreclosure and power of sale foreclosure. In the former—available in all states—a court supervises the process. This is the more common method of foreclosure. In the latter—available in only a few states—a lender forecloses on and sells the property without court supervision.

If the sale proceeds cover the mortgage debt and foreclosure costs, the debtor receives any surplus. If the proceeds do not cover the debt and costs, the mortgagee can seek to recover the difference through a deficiency judgment, which is obtained in a separate action. A deficiency judgment entitles the creditor to recover this difference from a sale of the debtor's other nonexempt property. Before a foreclosure sale, a mortgagor can redeem the property by paying the debt, plus any interest and costs. This is called the equitable right of redemption.

Chapter 23

1A: When a person enters into a contract on another's behalf without the authority to do so, the other may be liable on the contract if he or she approves or affirms that contract. In other words, the employer-principal would be liable for the note in this problem on ratifying it. Whether the employer-principal ratifies the note or not, the unauthorized agent is most likely also liable for it.

2A: Yes. A principal has a duty to indemnify (reimburse) an agent for liabilities incurred because of authorized and lawful acts and transactions and for losses suffered because of the principal's failure to perform his or her duties.

Chapter 24

1A: Workers' compensation laws establish a procedure for compensating workers who are injured on the job. Instead of suing to collect benefits, an injured worker notifies the employer of the injury and files a claim with the appropriate state agency. The right to recover is normally determined without regard to negligence or fault, but intentionally inflicted injuries are not covered. Unlike the potential for recovery in a lawsuit based on negligence or fault, recovery under a workers' compensation statute is limited to the specific amount designated in the statute for the employee's injury.

2A: No. A closed shop (a company that requires union membership as a condition of employment) is illegal. A union shop (a company that does not require union membership as a condition of employment but requires workers to join the union after a certain time on the job) is illegal in a state with a right-to-work law, which makes it illegal to require union membership for continued employment.

Chapter 25

1A: Yes. One type of sexual harassment occurs when a request for sexual favors is a condition of employment, and the person making the request is a supervisor or acts with the authority of the employer. A tangible employment action, such as continued employment, may also lead to the employer's liability for the supervisor's conduct. That the injured employee is a male and the supervisor a female, instead of the other way around, would not affect the outcome. Same-gender harassment is also actionable.

2A: Yes, Koko could succeed in a discrimination suit if she can show that she was not hired solely because of her disability. The other elements for a discrimination suit based on a disability are that the plaintiff (1) has a disability and (2) is otherwise qualified for the job. Both of these elements appear to be satisfied in this scenario.

Chapter 26

1A: When a business is relatively small and is not diversified, employs relatively few people, has modest profits, and is not likely to expand significantly or require extensive financing in the immediate future, the most appropriate form for doing business may be a sole proprietorship.

2A: Yes. Failing to meet a specified sales quota can constitute a breach of a franchise agreement. If the franchisor is acting in good faith, "cause" may also include the death or disability of the franchisee, the insolvency of the franchisee, and a breach of another term of the franchise agreement.

Chapter 27

1A: No. A widow (or widower) has no right to take a dead partner's place. A partner's death causes dissociation after which the partnership must purchase the dissociated partner's partnership interest. Therefore, the surviving partners must pay the decedent's estate (for his widow) the value of the deceased partner's interest in the partnership.

2A: No. Under the partners' fiduciary duty, a partner must account to the partnership for any personal profits or benefits derived without the consent of all the partners in connection with the use of any partnership property. Here, the leasing partner may not keep the funds.

Chapter 28

1A: The members of a limited liability company (LLC) may designate a group to run their firm. In that situation, the firm would be a manager-managed LLC. The group may include only members, only nonmembers, or members and nonmembers. If, instead, all members participate in management, the firm would be a member-managed LLC. In fact, unless the members agree otherwise, all members are considered to participate in the management of the firm.

2A: Although there are differences, all of these forms of business organizations resemble corporations. A joint stock company, for example, features ownership by shares of stock, it is managed by directors and officers, and it has perpetual existence. A business trust, like a corporation, distributes profits to persons who are not personally responsible for the debts of the organization, and management of the business is in the hands of trustees, just as the management of a corporation is in the hands of directors and officers. An incorporated cooperative, which is subject to state laws covering nonprofit corporations, distributes profits to its owners.

Chapter 29

1A: Yes. Small businesses that meet certain requirements can qualify as S corporations, created specifically to permit small businesses to avoid double taxation. The six requirements of an S corporation are (1) the firm must be a domestic corporation; (2) the firm must not be a member of an affiliated group of corporations; (3) the firm must have fewer than a certain number of shareholders; (4) the shareholders must be individuals, estates, or qualified trusts (or corporations in some cases); (5) there can be only one class of stock; and (6) no shareholder can be a nonresident alien.

2A: The first combination is a merger. One of the previously existing corporations absorbed the other. The second combination is a consolidation. Neither of the combining corporations continue after the combination, and a new firm continues in their place.

Chapter 30

1A: Yes. A shareholder can bring a derivative suit on behalf of a corporation, if some wrong is done to the corporation. Normally, any damages recovered go into the corporate treasury.

2A: Yes. A single shareholder—or a few shareholders acting together—who owns enough stock to exercise *de facto* control over a corporation owes the corporation and the minority shareholders a fiduciary duty when transferring those shares.

Chapter 31

1A: The average investor is not concerned with minor inaccuracies but with facts that if disclosed would tend to deter him or her from buying the securities. These would include material facts that have an important bearing on the condition of the issuer and its business—such as liabilities, loans to officers and directors, customer delinquencies, and pending lawsuits.

2A: No. The Securities Exchange Act of 1934 extends liability to officers and directors in their personal transactions for taking advantage of inside information when they know it is unavailable to the persons with whom they are dealing.

Chapter 32

1A: Size alone does not determine whether a firm is a monopoly—size in relation to the market is what matters. A small store in a small, isolated town is a monopolist if it is the only store serving that market. Monopoly involves the power to affect prices and output. If a firm has sufficient market power to control prices and exclude competition, that firm has monopoly power. Monopoly power in itself is not a violation of Section 2 of the Sherman Act. The offense also requires an intent to acquire or maintain that power through anticompetitive means.

2A: This agreement is a tying arrangement. The legality of a tying arrangement depends on the purpose of the agreement, the agreement's likely effect on competition in the relevant markets (the market for the tying product and the market for the tied product), and other factors. Tying arrangements for commodities are subject to Section 3 of the Clayton Act. Tying arrangements for services can be agreements in restraint of trade in violation of Section 1 of the Sherman Act.

Chapter 33

1A: Under the Truth-in-Lending Act, a buyer who wishes to withhold payment for a faulty product purchased with a credit card must follow specific procedures to settle the dispute. The credit-card issuer then must intervene and attempt to settle the dispute.

2A: Yes. On the ground that the hardships to be imposed on the polluter and on the community are greater than the hardships suffered by the residents, the court might deny an injunction—if the plant is the core of the local economy, for instance, the residents may only be awarded damages.

Chapter 34

1A: Yes. In these circumstances, when the accountant knows that the bank will use the statement, the bank is a foreseeable user. A foreseeable user is a third party within the class of parties to whom an accountant may be liable for negligence.

2A: No. In the circumstances described, the accountant will not be held liable to a purchaser of the securities. Although an accountant may be liable under securities laws for including untrue statements or omitting material facts from financial statements, due diligence is a defense to liability. Due diligence requires an accountant to conduct a reasonable investigation and have reason to believe that the financial statements were true at the time. The facts say that the misstatement of material fact in Omega's financial statement was not attributable to any fraud or negligence on Nora's part. Therefore, Nora can show that she used due diligence and will not be held liable to Pat.

Chapter 35

1A: Yes. A bailee's right of possession, even though temporary, permits the bailee to recover damages from any third persons for damage or loss to the property.

2A: Rosa de la Mar Corporation, the shipper, suffers the loss. A common carrier is liable for damage caused by the willful acts of third persons or by an accident. Other losses must be borne by the shipper (or the recipient, depending on the terms of their contract). In this situation, this shipment was lost due to an act of God.

Chapter 36

1A: This is a breach of the warranty deed's covenant of quiet enjoyment. Consuela can sue Bernie and recover the purchase price of the house, plus any damages.

2A: Yes. An owner of a fee simple has the most rights possible—he or she can give the property away, sell it, transfer it by will, use it for almost any purpose, possess it to the exclusion of all the world, or, as in this case, transfer possession for any period of time. The party to whom possession is transferred can also transfer her or his interest (usually only with the owner's permission) for any lesser period of time.

Chapter 37

1A: No. To have testamentary capacity, a testator must be of legal age and sound mind *at the time the will is made*. Generally, the testator must (1) know the nature of the act, (2) comprehend and remember the "natural objects of his or her bounty," (3) know the nature and extent of her or his property, and (4) understand the distribution of assets called for by the will. In this situation, Sheila had testamentary capacity at the time she made the will. The fact that she was ruled mentally incompetent two years after making the will does not provide sufficient grounds to revoke it.

2A: The estate will pass according to the state's intestacy laws. Intestacy laws set out how property is distributed when a person dies without a will. Their purpose is to carry out the likely intent of the decedent. The laws determine which of the deceased's natural heirs (including, in this order, the surviving spouse, lineal descendants, parents, and collateral heirs) inherit his or her property.

APPENDIX F

Answers to Even-Numbered *For Review* Questions

Chapter 1

2. What is the common law tradition?

Because of our colonial heritage, much of American law is based on the English legal system. After the Norman Conquest of England in 1066, the king's courts sought to establish a uniform set of rules for the entire country. What evolved in these courts was the common law—a body of general legal principles that applied throughout the entire English realm. Courts developed the common law rules from the principles underlying judges' decisions in actual legal controversies.

4. What is the difference between remedies at law and remedies in equity?

An award of compensation in either money or property, including land, is a remedy at law. Remedies in equity include the following:

1. A decree for specific performance—that is, an order to perform what was promised.
2. An injunction, which is an order directing a party to do or refrain from doing a particular act.
3. A rescission, or cancellation, of a contract and a return of the parties to the positions that they held before the contract's formation.

As a rule, courts will grant an equitable remedy only when the remedy at law (monetary damages) is inadequate. Remedies in equity on the whole are more flexible than remedies at law.

Chapter 2

2. What constitutional clause gives the federal government the power to regulate commercial activities among the various states?

To prevent states from establishing laws and regulations that would interfere with trade and commerce among the states, the Constitution expressly delegated to the national government the power to regulate interstate commerce. The commerce clause—Article I, Section 8, of the U.S. Constitution—expressly permits Congress "to regulate Commerce with foreign Nations, and among the several States, and with the Indian Tribes."

4. What is the Bill of Rights? What freedoms does the First Amendment guarantee?

The Bill of Rights consists of the first ten amendments to the U.S. Constitution. Adopted in 1791, the Bill of Rights embodies protections for individuals against interference by the federal government. Some of the protections also apply to business entities. The First Amendment guarantees the freedoms of religion, speech, and the press, and the rights to assemble peaceably and to petition the government.

Chapter 3

2. Before a court can hear a case, it must have jurisdiction. Over what must it have jurisdiction? How are the courts applying traditional jurisdictional concepts to cases involving Internet transactions?

To hear a case, a court must have jurisdiction over the person against whom the suit is brought or over the property involved in the suit. The court must also have jurisdiction over the subject matter. Generally, courts apply a "sliding-scale" standard to determine when it is proper to exercise jurisdiction over a defendant whose only connection with the jurisdiction is the Internet.

4. What is discovery, and how does electronic discovery differ from traditional discovery?

Discovery is the process of obtaining information and evidence about a case from the other party or third parties. Discovery entails gaining access to witnesses, documents, records, and other types of evidence. Electronic discovery differs in its subject—that is, e-media, such as e-mail or text messages, rather than traditional sources of information, such as paper documents.

Chapter 4

2. What are two basic categories of torts?

Generally, the purpose of tort law is to provide remedies for the invasion of legally recognized and protected interests, such as personal safety, freedom of movement, property, and some intangibles, including privacy and reputation. The two broad categories of torts are intentional and unintentional.

4. Identify the four elements of negligence.

The four elements of negligence are as follows:

1. A duty of care owed by the defendant to the plaintiff.
2. The defendant's breach of that duty.
3. The plaintiff's suffering a legally recognizable injury.
4. The in-fact and proximate cause of that injury by the defendant's breach.

Chapter 5

2. Why is the protection of trademarks important?

Article I, Section 8, of the U.S. Constitution authorizes Congress "to promote the Progress of Science and useful Arts, by securing for limited Times to Authors and Inventors the exclusive Right to their respective Writings and Discoveries." Laws protecting trademarks—and patents and copyrights as well—are designed to protect and reward inventive and artistic creativity.

4. What laws protect authors' rights in the works they create?

Copyright law protects the rights of the authors of certain literary or artistic productions. The Copyright Act of 1976, as amended, covers these rights.

Chapter 6

2. What are five broad categories of crimes? What is white-collar crime?

Traditionally, crimes have been grouped into the following categories: violent crime (crimes against persons), property crime, public order crime, white-collar crime, and organized crime.

White-collar crime is an illegal act or series of acts committed by an individual or business entity using some nonviolent means, usually in the course of a legitimate occupation.

4. What constitutional safeguards exist to protect persons accused of crimes?

Under the Fourth Amendment, before searching or seizing private property, law enforcement officers must obtain a search warrant, which requires probable cause.

Under the Fifth Amendment, no one can be deprived of "life, liberty, or property without due process of law." The Fifth Amendment also protects persons against double jeopardy and self-incrimination.

The Sixth Amendment guarantees the right to a speedy trial, the right to a jury trial, the right to a public trial, the right to confront witnesses, and the right to counsel. Individuals who are arrested must be informed of certain constitutional rights, including their Fifth Amendment right to remain silent and their Sixth Amendment right to counsel. All evidence obtained in violation of the Fourth, Fifth, and Sixth Amendments, as well as all evidence derived from the illegally obtained evidence, must be excluded from the trial.

The Eighth Amendment prohibits excessive bail and fines, and cruel and unusual punishment.

Chapter 7

2. How can business leaders encourage their companies to act ethically?

Ethical leadership is important to create and maintain an ethical workplace. Managers can set standards and then apply those standards to themselves and their firm's employees.

4. What are six guidelines that an employee can use to evaluate whether his or her actions are ethical?

Guidelines for evaluating whether behavior is ethical can be found (1) in the law, (2) business rules and procedures, (3) social values, (4) an individual's conscience, (5) an individual's promises and obligations to others, and (6) personal or societal heroes.

An action is most likely ethical if it is consistent with the law, or at least the "spirit" of the law, as well as company policies, and if it can survive the scrutiny of one's conscience and the regard of one's heroes without betraying commitments to others.

Chapter 8

2. What is the act of state doctrine? In what circumstances is this doctrine applied?

The act of state doctrine is a judicially created doctrine that provides that the judicial branch of one country will not examine the validity of public acts committed by a recognized foreign government within its own territory. This doctrine is often employed in cases involving expropriation or confiscation.

4. What are three clauses commonly included in international business contracts?

Choice-of-language, forum-selection, and choice-of-law clauses are commonly used in international business contracts.

Chapter 9

2. What are the four basic elements necessary to the formation of a valid contract?

The basic elements for the formation of a valid contract are an agreement, consideration, contractual capacity, and legality.

4. How does a void contract differ from a voidable contract? What is an unenforceable contract?

A void contract is not a valid contract—it is not a contract at all. A voidable contract is a valid contract, but one that can be avoided at the option of one or both of the parties.

An unenforceable contract is one that cannot be enforced because of certain legal defenses against it.

Chapter 10

2. In what circumstances will an offer be irrevocable?

An offeror may not effectively revoke an offer if the offeree has changed position in justifiable reliance on the offer. Also, an option contract takes away the offeror's power to revoke an offer for the period of time specified in the option (or, if unspecified, for a reasonable time).

4. How do shrink-wrap and click-on agreements differ from other contracts? How have traditional laws been applied to these agreements?

With a shrink-wrap agreement, the terms are expressed inside the box in which the goods are packaged. A click-on agreement arises when a buyer, completing a transaction on a computer, is required to indicate assent to the terms by clicking on a button that says, for example, "I agree."

Generally, courts have enforced the terms of these agreements the same as the terms of other contracts, applying the traditional common law of contracts. Article 2 of the Uniform Commercial Code provides that acceptance can be made by conduct. The *Restatement (Second) of Contracts* has a similar provision. Under these provisions, a binding contract can be created by conduct, including conduct accepting the terms in a shrink-wrap or click-on agreement.

Chapter 11

2. In what circumstances might a promise be enforced despite a lack of consideration?

Under the doctrine of promissory estoppel (or detrimental reliance), a promisor (the offeror) is estopped, or prevented, from revoking a promise even in the absence of consideration. There are three required elements:

1. A clear and definite promise.
2. The promisee's justifiable reliance on the promise.
3. Reliance of a substantial and definite character.

4. Under what circumstances will a covenant not to compete be enforced? When will such covenants not be enforced?

A covenant not to compete can be enforced:

1. If it is ancillary (secondary) to an agreement to sell an ongoing business, thus enabling the seller to sell, and the purchaser to buy, the goodwill and reputation of the business.
2. If it is contained in an employment contract and is reasonable in terms of time and geographic area.

A covenant not to compete will be unenforceable if it does not protect a legitimate business interest or is broader than necessary to protect a legitimate interest. This is because such a covenant would unreasonably restrain trade and be contrary to public policy.

Chapter 12

2. What is the difference between a mistake of value or quality and a mistake of fact?

A mistake as to the value of a deal is an ordinary risk of business for which a court normally will not provide relief. A mistake concerning a fact important to the subject matter of a contract, however, may provide a basis for relief.

4. What contracts must be in writing to be enforceable?

Contracts that are normally required to be in writing or evidenced by a written memorandum include:

- Contracts involving interests in land.
- Contracts that cannot by their terms be performed within one year from the day after the date of formation.
- Collateral contracts, such as promises to answer for the debt or duty of another.
- Promises made in consideration of marriage.
- Contracts for the sale of goods priced at $500 or more.

Chapter 13

2. In what situations is the delegation of duties prohibited?

Delegation of duties is prohibited in the following situations:

1. When the performance depends on the personal skill or talents of the obligor.
2. When special trust has been placed in the obligor.
3. When performance by a third party will vary materially from that expected by the obligee under the contract.
4. When the contract expressly prohibits delegation.

4. How are most contracts discharged?

The most common way to discharge, or terminate, a contract is by the performance of contractual duties.

Chapter 14

2. What is the difference between compensatory damages and consequential damages? What are nominal damages, and when do courts award nominal damages?

Compensatory damages compensate an injured party for injuries or damages. Foreseeable damages that result from a party's breach of contract are consequential damages. Consequential damages differ from compensatory damages in that they are caused by special circumstances beyond the contract.

Nominal damages are awarded to an innocent party when no actual damage has been suffered. Nominal damages might be awarded as a matter of principle to establish fault or wrongful behavior.

4. When do courts grant specific performance as a remedy?

Specific performance might be granted as a remedy when damages offer an inadequate remedy and the subject matter of the contract is unique.

Chapter 15

2. In a sales contract, if an offeree includes additional or different terms in an acceptance, will a contract result? If so, what happens to these terms?

Under the Uniform Commercial Code, a contract can be formed, even if the offeree's acceptance includes additional or different terms. If one of the parties is a nonmerchant, the contract does not include the additional terms. If both parties are merchants, the additional terms automatically become part of the contract unless one of the following occurs:

1. The original offer expressly limits acceptance to the terms of the offer.
2. The new or changed terms materially alter the contract.
3. The offeror objects to the new or changed terms within a reasonable period of time.

(If the additional terms expressly require the offeror's assent, the offeree's response is not an acceptance, but a counteroffer.) Under some circumstances, a court might strike the additional terms.

4. Risk of loss does not necessarily pass with title. If the parties to a contract do not expressly agree when risk passes and the goods are to be delivered without movement by the seller, when does risk pass?

If the seller holds the goods and is a merchant, the risk of loss passes to the buyer when the buyer takes physical possession of the goods. If the seller holds the goods and is not a merchant, the risk of loss passes to the buyer on tender of delivery. When a bailee is holding the goods, the risk of loss passes to the buyer when (1) the buyer receives a negotiable document of title for the goods, (2) the bailee acknowledges the buyer's right to possess the goods, or (3) the buyer receives a nonnegotiable document of title and has had a reasonable time to present the document to the bailee and demand the goods.

Chapter 16

2. What is the perfect tender rule? What are some important exceptions to this rule that apply to sales and lease contracts?

Under the perfect tender rule, the seller or lessor has an obligation to ship or tender conforming goods. If the goods or tender of delivery fails in any respect, the buyer or lessee has the right to accept the goods, reject the entire shipment, or accept part and reject part. Exceptions to the rule may be established by agreement.

When goods are rejected because they are nonconforming and the time for performance has not expired, the seller or lessor can notify the buyer or lessee promptly of the intention to cure and then do so within the contract time for performance. If the time for performance has expired, the seller or lessor can still cure within a reasonable time if, at the time of delivery, he or she had reasonable grounds to believe that the nonconforming tender would be acceptable. When an agreed-on manner of delivery becomes impracticable or unavailable through no fault of either party, a seller may choose a commercially reasonable substitute.

4. What remedies are available to a seller or lessor when the buyer or lessee breaches the contract? What remedies are available to a buyer or lessee if the seller or lessor breaches the contract?

Depending on the circumstances at the time of a buyer's or lessee's breach, a seller or lessor may have the right to cancel the contract, withhold delivery, resell or dispose of the goods subject to the contract, recover the purchase price (or lease payments), recover damages, stop delivery in transit, or reclaim the goods.

Similarly, on a seller's or lessor's breach, a buyer or lessee may have the right to cancel the contract, recover the goods, obtain specific performance, obtain cover, replevy the goods, recover damages, reject the goods, withhold delivery, resell or dispose of the goods, stop delivery, or revoke acceptance.

Chapter 17

2. What implied warranties arise under the UCC?

Implied warranties that arise under the UCC include the implied warranty of merchantability, the implied warranty of fitness for a particular purpose, and implied warranties that may arise from, or be excluded or modified by, course of dealing, course of performance, or usage of trade.

4. What are the elements of a cause of action in strict product liability?

Under Section 402A of the *Restatement (Second) of Torts,* the elements of an action for strict product liability are as follows:

1. The product must be in a defective condition when the defendant sells it.
2. The defendant must normally be engaged in the business of selling (or distributing) that product.
3. The product must be unreasonably dangerous to the user or consumer because of its defective condition (in most states).
4. The plaintiff must incur physical harm to self or property by use or consumption of the product.
5. The defective condition must be the proximate cause of the injury or damage.
6. The goods must not have been substantially changed from the time the product was sold to the time the injury was sustained.

Chapter 18

2. What are the requirements for attaining the status of a holder in due course (HDC)?

A holder of a negotiable instrument becomes an HDC if he or she takes the instrument (1) for value; (2) in good faith; and (3) without notice that the instrument is overdue, that it has been dishonored, that any person has a defense against it or a claim to it, or that it contains unauthorized signatures or alterations, or is so irregular or incomplete as to call into question its authenticity.

4. Certain defenses are valid against all holders, including HDCs. What are these defenses called? Name four defenses that fall within this category.

Universal, or real, defenses are good against the claims of all holders, including HDCs. These defenses include forgery of a maker's or drawer's signature, fraud in the execution of an instrument, material alteration of an instrument, discharge in bankruptcy, minority to the extent recognized by state law, illegality to the extent that state law makes a transaction void, mental incapacity if a person has been so adjudged in a state proceeding, and extreme duress.

Chapter 19

2. When may a bank properly dishonor a customer's check without being liable to the customer?

A bank may dishonor a customer's check without liability to the customer when the customer's account contains insufficient funds to pay the check, providing the bank did not agree to cover overdrafts. A bank may also properly dishonor a stale check, a timely check subject to a valid stop-payment order, a check drawn after the customer's death, and forged or altered checks.

4. What is electronic check presentment, and how does it differ from the traditional check-clearing process?

With electronic check presentment, items are encoded with information (such as the amount of the check) that is read and processed by other banks' computers. A check may sometimes be retained at its place of deposit, and then only its image or description is presented for payment. A bank that encodes information on an item warrants to any subsequent bank or payor that the encoded information is correct.

This differs from the traditional check-clearing process because employees of each bank in the collection chain no longer have to physically handle each check that passes through the bank for collection or payment. Therefore, obtaining payment is much quicker. Whereas manual check processing can take days, electronic check presentment can be done on the day of deposit.

Chapter 20

2. What three requirements must be met to create an enforceable security interest?

The three requirements that must be met to create an enforceable security interest are as follows:

1. Either the collateral must be in the possession of the secured party in accordance with an agreement, or there must be a written or authenticated security agreement that describes the collateral subject to the security interest and is signed or authenticated by the debtor.
2. The secured party must give to the debtor something of value.
3. The debtor must have "rights" in the collateral.

4. If two secured parties have perfected security interests in the collateral of the debtor, which party has priority to the collateral on the debtor's default?

When two or more secured parties have perfected security interests in the same collateral, the first to perfect has priority, unless an applicable state statute provides otherwise.

Chapter 21

2. What is garnishment? When might a creditor undertake a garnishment proceeding?

Garnishment occurs when a creditor is permitted to collect a debt by seizing property of the debtor that is being held by a third party (such as a paycheck held by an employer or a checking account held by a bank). A creditor might use garnishment in a situation in which a debt has not been paid, but the process is closely regulated.

4. What is the difference between an exception to discharge and an objection to discharge?

An exception to discharge is a claim that is not dischargeable in bankruptcy, such as a government claim for unpaid taxes. An objection to discharge is a circumstance that causes a discharge to be denied, such as concealing assets.

Chapter 22

2. When is private mortgage insurance required? Which party does it protect?

A creditor may require private mortgage insurance if a mortgagor does not make a down payment of at least 20 percent of the purchase price for residential real property.

The creditor is protected if the borrower defaults because in that event the insurer reimburses the creditor for a portion of the loan.

4. What is a short sale? What advantages over mortgage foreclosure might it offer borrowers? Does the lender receive the full balance due on the mortgage loan in a short sale?

A short sale is a sale of real property for an amount that is less than the balance owed on the mortgage loan. Unlike a mortgage foreclosure, both the lender and the borrower must consent to a short sale. A short sale can be advantageous for a borrower because it has a less negative effect on the homeowner's credit than a foreclosure does and because the homeowner is not evicted from her or his home.

Following a short sale, and after the sale proceeds are applied, the borrower still owes the balance of the mortgage debt to the lender unless the lender agrees to forgive the remaining debt.

Chapter 23

2. How do agency relationships arise?

Agency relationships normally are consensual—that is, they arise by voluntary consent and agreement between the parties.

4. When is a principal liable for the agent's actions with respect to third parties? When is the agent liable?

A disclosed or partially disclosed principal is liable to a third party for a contract made by an agent who was acting within the scope of her or his authority. If the agent exceeds the scope of authority and the principal fails to ratify the contract, the agent may be liable (and the principal may not).

When neither the fact of agency nor the identity of the principal is disclosed, the agent is liable, and if the agent has acted within the scope of his or her authority, the undisclosed principal is also liable. Each party is liable for his or her own torts and crimes. A principal may also be liable for an agent's torts committed within the course or scope of employment. A principal is liable for an agent's crime if the principal participated by conspiracy or other action.

Chapter 24

2. What federal statute governs working hours and wages?

The Fair Labor Standards Act is the most significant federal statute governing working hours and wages.

4. What are the two most important federal statutes governing immigration and employment today?

The most important federal statutes governing immigration and the employment of noncitizens are the Immigration Reform and Control Act (IRCA) of 1986 and the Immigration Act of 1990.

Chapter 25

2. What is the difference between disparate-treatment discrimination and disparate-impact discrimination?

Intentional discrimination by an employer against an employee is known as disparate-treatment discrimination.

Disparate-impact discrimination occurs when, as a result of educational or other job requirements or hiring procedures, an employer's workforce does not reflect the percentage of nonwhites, women, or members of other protected classes that characterizes qualified individuals in the local labor market. Disparate-impact discrimination does not require evidence of intent.

4. What federal act prohibits discrimination based on age?

The Age Discrimination in Employment Act of 1967 prohibits discrimination on the basis of age.

Chapter 26

2. What are the most common types of franchises?

The majority of franchises are distributorships, chain-style business operations, or manufacturing or processing-plant arrangements.

4. What terms and conditions are typically included in a franchise contract?

A franchise contract typically covers such issues as the franchisee's payment for the franchise, any lease or purchase of the business premises, any lease or purchase of equipment, the location of the franchise, the territory to be served, the business organization of the franchisee, quality standards to be met, the degree of supervision and control by the franchisor, pricing arrangements, and termination of the franchise.

Chapter 27

2. What are the rights and duties of partners in an ordinary partnership?

The rights and duties of partners may be whatever the partners declare them to be. In the absence of partners' agreements to the contrary, the law imposes certain rights and duties. These include:

- A sharing of profits and losses in equal measure.
- The ability to assign a partnership interest.
- Equal rights in managing the firm (subject to majority rule).
- Access to all of the firm's books and records.
- An accounting of assets and profits.
- A sharing of the firm's property.

The duties include fiduciary duties, being bound to third parties through contracts entered into with other partners, and liability for the firm's debts and liabilities.

4. What advantages do limited liability partnerships offer to businesspersons that are not offered by general partnerships?

An advantage of a limited liability partnership over a general partnership is that, depending on the applicable state statute, the liability of the partners for partnership and partners' debts and torts can be limited to the amount of the partners' investments. Another advantage is that partners in a limited liability partnership generally are not liable for other partners' malpractice.

Chapter 28

2. What advantages do limited liability companies offer to businesspersons that are not offered by sole proprietorships or partnerships?

An important advantage of limited liability companies (LLCs) is that the liability of the members is limited to the amount of their investments. Another advantage of LLCs is the flexibility they offer in regard to taxation and management.

4. What is a joint venture? How is it similar to a partnership? How is it different?

A joint venture is an enterprise in which two or more persons or business entities combine their efforts or their property for a single transaction or project, or a related series of transactions or projects.

Generally, partnership law applies to joint ventures, although joint venturers have less implied and apparent authority than partners because they have less power to bind the members of their organization.

Chapter 29

2. What steps are involved in bringing a corporation into existence?

The steps to bring a corporation into existence are (1) preliminary organizational and promotional undertakings and (2) the legal process of incorporation. A promoter (one who takes the preliminary steps in organizing a corporation) is liable on preincorporation contracts unless the other contracting party agrees not to hold the promoter liable or the corporation assumes the contract by novation.

4. What are the basic differences between a merger, a consolidation, and a share exchange?

A merger involves the legal combination of two or more corporations so that only one of the original corporations remains after the merger is completed. The remaining company continues as the surviving corporation and possesses all the assets and liabilities of the disappearing corporation.

In a consolidation, two or more corporations combine to form an entirely new corporation. The original corporations cease to exist when the new corporation is formed. The new corporation also assumes any assets and liabilities previously possessed by the original corporations.

In a share exchange, some or all of the stock of a company is exchanged for some or all of the stock of another company, and both firms continue to exist.

Chapter 30

2. Directors are expected to use their best judgment in managing the corporation. What must directors do to avoid liability for honest mistakes of judgment and poor business decisions?

Directors and officers must exercise due care in performing their duties. They are expected to:

- Be informed on corporate matters.
- Act in accordance with their own knowledge and training.
- Exercise a reasonable amount of supervision when they delegate work to others.
- Attend board of directors' meetings.

In general, directors and officers must act in good faith, in what they consider to be the best interests of the corporation, and with the care that an ordinarily prudent person in a similar position would exercise in similar circumstances. This requires an informed decision, with a rational basis, and with no conflict between the decision maker's personal interest and the interest of the corporation.

4. From what sources may dividends be paid legally? In what circumstances is a dividend illegal? What happens if a dividend is illegally paid?

Depending on state law, dividends may be paid from retained earnings, current net profits, and any surplus. A dividend paid while the corporation is insolvent is an illegal dividend. Dividends improperly paid from an unauthorized account are illegal.

Shareholders must return illegal dividends if they knew that the dividends were illegal when they received them. Whenever dividends are illegal or improper, the board of directors can be held personally liable for the amount of the payment.

Chapter 31

2. What are the two major statutes regulating the securities industry?

The major statutes regulating the securities industry are the Securities Act of 1933 and the Securities Exchange Act of 1934, which created the Securities and Exchange Commission.

4. What are some of the features of state securities laws?

Typically, state laws have disclosure requirements and antifraud provisions patterned after Section 10(b) of the Securities Exchange Act of 1934 and SEC Rule 10b-5. State laws provide for the registration or qualification of securities offered or issued for sale within the state with the appropriate state official. Also, most state securities laws regulate securities brokers and dealers.

Chapter 32

2. What anticompetitive activities are prohibited by Section 1 of the Sherman Act?

Section 1 prohibits agreements that are anticompetitively restrictive—that is, agreements that have the wrongful purpose of restraining competition, such as price fixing.

4. What agencies of the federal government enforce the federal antitrust laws?

The federal agencies that enforce the antitrust laws are the U.S. Department of Justice and the Federal Trade Commission.

Chapter 33

2. What are the major federal statutes providing for consumer protection in credit transactions?

Federal statutes that protect consumers in credit transactions include the various titles of the Consumer Credit Protection Act—the Truth-in-Lending Act, of which the Equal Credit Opportunity Act and the Consumer Leasing Act are a part—as well as the Fair Credit Reporting Act and the Fair Debt Collection Practices Act.

4. What is contained in an environmental impact statement, and who must file one?

An environmental impact statement (EIS) analyzes the following:

- The impact on the environment that an action will have.
- Any adverse effects on the environment and alternative actions that might be taken.
- Irreversible effects the action might generate.

An EIS must be prepared for every major federal action that significantly affects the quality of the environment. An action is "major" if it involves a substantial commitment of resources (monetary or otherwise). An action is "federal" if a federal agency has the power to control it.

Chapter 34

2. What are the rules concerning an auditor's liability to third parties?

An auditor may be liable to a third party on the ground of negligence, when the auditor knew or should have known that the third party would benefit from the auditor's work. Depending on the jurisdiction, liability may be imposed only if one of the following occurs:

1. The auditor is in privity, or near privity, with the third party.
2. The third party's reliance on the auditor's work was foreseen, or the third party was within a class of known or foreseeable users.
3. The third party's use of the auditor's work was reasonably foreseeable.

4. What crimes might an accountant commit under the Internal Revenue Code?

Crimes under the Internal Revenue Code include the following:

1. Aiding or assisting in the preparation of a false tax return.
2. Aiding or abetting an individual's understatement of tax liability.
3. Negligently or willfully understating a client's tax liability, or recklessly or intentionally disregarding Internal Revenue Code rules or regulations.
4. Failing to provide a taxpayer with a copy of a tax return, failing to sign the return, or failing to furnish the appropriate tax identification numbers.

Chapter 35

2. What is the difference between a joint tenancy and a tenancy in common?

A tenancy in common is a form of co-ownership in which each of two or more persons owns an undivided interest in the whole property. On the death of a tenant in common, that tenant's interest passes to his or her heirs. In a joint tenancy, each of two or more persons owns an undivided interest in the property, and a deceased joint tenant's interest passes to the surviving joint tenant or tenants. This right distinguishes the joint tenancy from the tenancy in common.

4. What are the three elements of a bailment?

A bailment is formed (1) by the delivery of personal property without transfer of title, (2) by a bailor to a bailee, under an agreement, often for (3) a particular purpose.

Chapter 36

2. What is an easement? Describe three ways that easements are created.

An easement is the right of a person to make limited use of another person's real property without taking anything from the property, such as a right-of-way to cross another's property. Most easements are created by express grant in a contract.

An easement may also be created by the following:

1. *Implication* when surrounding circumstances imply its existence.
2. *Necessity* when an easement is required to access one's own property.
3. *Prescription* when authorized by a statute. Prescription occurs when someone utilizes an easement on property without the owner's permission and the use is apparent and continues for the length of time required by the applicable statute of limitations.

4. What is a leasehold estate? What types of leasehold estates, or tenancies, can be created when real property is leased?

A leasehold estate is property in the possession of a tenant. A leasehold estate can include a fixed-term tenancy, periodic tenancy, tenancy at will, and tenancy at sufferance.

Chapter 37

2. What is an insurable interest? When must an insurable interest exist—at the time the insurance policy is obtained, at the time the loss occurs, or both?

For real and personal property, an insurable interest exists when the insured derives a pecuniary (monetary) benefit from the existence of the property and would sustain a pecuniary loss from its destruction.

For a life, an insurable interest exists when a person has a reasonable expectation of benefit from the continued life of another. The benefit may be monetary, or it may be founded on the relationship between the parties (by blood or affinity).

For property insurance, the interest must exist at the time the loss occurs but need not exist when the policy is purchased. For life insurance, the interest must exist at the time the policy is obtained.

4. What is the difference between a *per stirpes* distribution and a *per capita* distribution of an estate to the grandchildren of the deceased?

Per stirpes distribution dictates that grandchildren share the part of the estate that their deceased parent (and descendant of the deceased grandparent) would have been entitled to inherit.

Per capita distribution dictates that each grandchild takes an equal share of the estate.

Sample Answers for *Questions with Sample Answer*

1–3A. Question with Sample Answer

The U.S. Constitution is the supreme law of the land. A law in violation of the Constitution, no matter what its source, will be declared unconstitutional and will not be enforced. In this problem, the court determined that a Massachusetts state statute was in conflict with the U.S. Constitution. The Constitution takes priority, so the statute will not be enforced.

In the actual case on which this problem is based, the trial court held that the statute violated the Constitution, and the U.S. Court of Appeals for the First Circuit affirmed this holding. Under the statute's definitions of large and small wineries, most of the small wineries were in state, and all of the large wineries were out of state. The court found that the purpose of the statute was to "ensure that Massachusetts' wineries obtained an advantage over their out-of-state counterparts."

2–2A. Question with Sample Answer

Thomas has a constitutionally protected right to the free exercise of his religion. In denying his claim for unemployment benefits, the state violated this right. Employers are obligated to make reasonable accommodations for their employees' beliefs that are openly and sincerely held, as were Thomas's beliefs. By moving him to a department that made military goods, his employer effectively forced him to choose between his job and his religious principles. This unilateral decision on the part of the employer was the reason Thomas left his job and why the company was required to compensate Thomas for his resulting unemployment.

3–2A. Question with Sample Answer

Marya can bring suit in all three courts. The trucking firm did business in Florida, and the accident occurred there. Thus, the state of Florida would have jurisdiction over the defendant. Because the firm was headquartered in Georgia and had its principal place of business in that state, Marya could also sue in a Georgia court. Finally, because the amount in controversy exceeds $75,000, the suit could be brought in federal court on the basis of diversity of citizenship.

4–2A. Question with Sample Answer

Yes. The *Restatement (Second) of Torts* defines *negligence* as "conduct that falls below the standard established by law for the protection of others against unreasonable risk of harm." The standard established by law is that of a reasonable person acting with due care in the circumstances. Shannon was well aware that the medication she took would make her drowsy, and her failure to observe due care—that is, refrain from driving—under the circumstances was negligent.

5–2A. Question with Sample Answer

1. Making a photocopy of an article in a scholarly journal "for purposes such as . . . scholarship, or research, is not an infringement of copyright" under Section 107 of the Copyright Act.
2. This is an example of trademark infringement. When a trademark is copied to a substantial degree or used in its entirety by one who is not entitled to use it, the trademark has been infringed.
3. This is the most likely example of copyright infringement. Generally, the determination of whether the reproduction of copyrighted material constitutes copyright infringement is made on a case-by-case basis under the "fair use" doctrine, as expressed in Section 107 of the Copyright Act. Courts consider such factors as the "purpose and character" of the use, such as whether it is "of a commercial nature"; "the amount and substantiality of the portion used in relation to the copyrighted work as a whole"; and "the effect of the use on the potential market" for the copied work. Here, the DVD storeowner is copying copyrighted works in their entirety for commercial purposes, thereby affecting the market for the works.

6–2A. Question with Sample Answer

Kayla has committed fraud in her e-mail. The elements of the tort of fraud are as follows:

1. The misrepresentation of material facts or conditions was made with knowledge that they were false or with reckless disregard for the truth.
2. There was an intent to induce another to rely on the misrepresentation.
3. There was justifiable reliance on the misrepresentation by the deceived party.
4. Damages were suffered as a result of the reliance.
5. There was a causal connection between the misrepresentation and the injury.

If any of Kayla's recipients reply to her false plea with cash, it is likely that all of these requirements for fraud will have been met.

7–2A. Question with Sample Answer

Factors for the firm to consider in making its decision include the appropriate ethical standard. Under the utilitarian standard, an action is correct, or "right," when, among the people it affects, it produces the greatest amount of good for the greatest number of people. When an action affects the majority adversely, it is morally wrong.

Applying the utilitarian standard requires three steps: (1) determine which individuals will be affected by the action in question; (2) perform an assessment, or cost-benefit analysis, of the negative and positive effects of alternative actions on these individuals; and (3) choose the alternative that will produce the maximum societal utility.

Ethical standards may also be based on a concept of duty, which suggests that the end can never justify the means and that human beings should not be treated as mere means to an end. But ethical decision making in a business context is not always simple. It is particularly difficult when an action will have different effects on different groups of people—shareholders, employees, society, and other stakeholders, such as the local community. Thus, another factor to consider is to whom the firm believes it owes a duty.

8–2A. Question with Sample Answer

Yes, it is reasonable to rely on the producers' financial records, which are reasonably reflective of their costs because their normal allocation methods were used for a number of years. These records are historically relied on to present important financial information to shareholders, lenders, tax authorities, auditors, and other third parties. Provided that the producers' records and books comply with generally accepted accounting principles and were verified by independent auditors, it is reasonable to use them to determine the production costs and fair market value of canned pineapple in the United States.

9–2A. Question with Sample Answer

Janine was unconscious or otherwise unable to agree to a contract for the nursing services she received while she was in the hospital. Under the doctrine of quasi contract, however, the law will sometimes create a fictional contract in order to prevent one party from unjustly receiving a benefit at the expense of another. Quasi contract provides a basis for Nursing Services to recover the value of the services it provided while Janine was in the hospital.

Nursing Services can recover for the at-home services under an implied contract because Janine was aware that the services were being provided for her. Under this type of contract, the conduct of the parties creates and defines the terms. Janine's acceptance of the services constitutes her agreement to form a contract, and she will probably be required to pay Nursing Services in full.

10–3A. Question with Sample Answer

1. Death of either the offeror or the offeree prior to acceptance automatically terminates a revocable offer. The basic legal reason is that the offer is personal to the parties and cannot be passed on to others, not even to the estate of the deceased. This rule applies even if the other party is unaware of the death. Thus, Cherneck's offer terminates on Cherneck's death, and Bollow's later acceptance does not constitute a contract.
2. An offer is automatically terminated by the destruction of the specific subject matter of the offer prior to acceptance. Thus, Bollow's acceptance after the fire does not constitute a contract.
3. When the offer is irrevocable, under an option contract, death of the offeror does not terminate the option contract, and the offeree can accept the offer to sell the equipment, binding the offeror's estate to performance. Performance is not personal to Cherneck, as the estate can transfer title to the equipment. Knowledge of the death is immaterial to the offeree's right of acceptance. Thus, Bollow can hold Cherneck's estate to a contract for the purchase of the equipment.
4. When the offer is irrevocable, under an option contract, death of the offeree also does not terminate the offer. Because the option is a separate contract, the contract survives and passes to the offeree's estate, which can exercise the option by acceptance within the option period. Thus, acceptance by Bollow's estate binds Cherneck to a contract for the sale of the equipment.

11–2A. Question with Sample Answer

Past consideration is no consideration. Therefore, a promise to pay for an event that has already taken place is not enforceable. There is nothing to bargain for in this situation. Also, there is no consideration if the promise is based on a moral duty (obligation) to pay. Because Daniel is presumed to be an adult responsible for his own care, Fred has no legal duty of care to Daniel. Because Fred had at best only a moral obligation to reimburse the elderly couple for the care rendered, and because the promise to pay was for an event already performed, Fred's promise cannot be enforced.

Because of the harshness of this rule, a few states have passed statutes enforcing such agreements (usually only up to the value of care received), or a court will enforce such a promise if the promisor received a substantial benefit (such as being saved from physical harm or financial disaster). In this situation, though, it is unlikely that the court would hold for the elderly couple, as the recipient of the benefit was Daniel, and not the promisor, Fred.

12–2A. Question with Sample Answer

In this situation, Gemma becomes a guarantor on the loan. That is, she guarantees the hardware store that she will pay for the mower if her brother fails to do so. This kind of collateral promise, in which the guarantor states that he or she will become responsible only if the primary party does not perform, must be in writing to be enforceable.

There is an exception, however. If the main purpose in accepting secondary liability is to secure a personal benefit—for example, if Gemma's brother bought the mower for her—the contract need not be in writing. The court will determine from the circumstances of the case whether the main purpose was to secure a personal benefit and thus, in effect, to answer for the guarantor's own debt.

13–2A. Question with Sample Answer

As a general rule, any rights flowing from a contract can be assigned. There are, however, exceptions, such as when the contract expressly prohibits or limits assignment. Under the principle of freedom of contract, such prohibitions are enforced—unless they are deemed contrary to public policy. For example, courts have held that a clause prohibiting assignment that restrains the alienation of property is invalid by virtue of being against public policy.

Authorities differ on how a case like Aron's should be decided. Some courts would enforce the prohibition and hold that Aron's assignment to Erica is ineffective without the landlord's consent. Others would permit the assignment to be effective and would limit the landlord's remedies to the normal contract remedies ensuing from Aron's breach.

14–2A. Question with Sample Answer

The question of whether a party has properly mitigated damages is a question of fact. Here, there is evidence to support a finding that Barton attempted to mitigate her damages—she apparently made reasonable efforts to find, and did find, employment. Because the position paid a significantly lower salary, it was not unreasonable for her to refuse it. Thus, under the circumstances, it was not unreasonable for her to choose to move to London.

A court should therefore award Barton $72,000 for the one year's salary she would have been paid if VanHorn had not repudiated their contract and the costs to move to London.

15–2A. Question with Sample Answer

Yes. Under UCC 2–205, a merchant offeror, who in a signed writing gives assurance that an offer will remain open, creates an irrevocable offer (without payment of consideration) for the time period stated in the assurance up to a period of three months. As a merchant, Jennings was obliged to hold the offer (which had been made in a signed writing—the letter) open until October 9. Wheeler's acceptance of the offer before October 9 created a valid contract, which Jennings breached when he sold the Thunderbird to a third party.

16–2A. Question with Sample Answer

Hammer is correct. Moore's refusal to deliver the car to Hammer on Friday, when Hammer tendered the $8,500 to Moore, constituted a breach of their contract. Moore could have canceled the contract on Hammer's anticipatory repudiation but did not do so and did not change her position in any way as a result of Hammer's anticipatory breach. Hammer could retract his repudiation of the contract at any time prior to the time performance was due.

Because Hammer did retract his repudiation and decided to buy the car at the time performance was due (and not later), Moore was obligated to abide by the terms of the contract

17–2A. Question with Sample Answer

Yes. To disclaim the implied warranty of fitness for a particular purpose, the disclaimer must be in writing and be conspicuous. Although the implied warranty of merchantability can be disclaimed orally, if the disclaimer is in writing, it must be conspicuously written. This means that through different color or size of type or some other technique, the disclaimer must stand out from the context in which it is printed so as to alert the reader of the document to the disclaimer.

In this case, the disclaimer was printed in the same size and color of type as the rest of the contract and was not conspicuous. If this was the only warranty disclaimer, it is not effective and Tandy can recover.

18–2A. Question with Sample Answer

For an instrument to be negotiable, it must meet the following requirements:

1. Be in writing.
2. Be signed by the maker or the drawer.
3. Be an unconditional promise or order to pay.
4. State a fixed amount of money.
5. Be payable on demand or at a definite time.
6. Be payable to order or to bearer, unless it is a check.

The instrument in this case meets the writing requirement because it is handwritten on something with a degree of permanence that is transferable. The instrument meets the requirement of being signed by the maker, as Muriel Evans's signature (her name in her handwriting) appears in the body of the instrument. The instrument's payment is not conditional and contains Muriel Evans's definite promise to pay.

In addition, the sum of $100 is both a fixed amount and payable in money (U.S. currency). Because the instrument is payable on demand and to bearer (Karen Marvin or any holder), the instrument is negotiable.

19–2A. Question with Sample Answer

Gary goes grocery shopping and carelessly leaves his checkbook in his shopping cart. His checkbook, with two blank checks remaining, is stolen by Dolores. On May 5, Dolores forges Gary's name on a check for $100 and cashes the check at Gary's bank, Citizens Bank of Middletown. Gary has not reported the loss of his blank checks to his bank.

On June 1, Gary receives his monthly bank statement from Citizens Bank that includes the forged check, but he does not notice the item nor does he examine his bank statement.

On June 20, Dolores forges Gary's last check. This check is for $1,000 and is cashed at Eastern City Bank, a bank with which Dolores has previously done business. Eastern City Bank puts the check through the collection process, and Citizens Bank honors it.

On July 1, on receipt of his bank statement and canceled checks covering June transactions, Gary discovers both forgeries and immediately notifies Citizens Bank. Dolores cannot be found. Gary claims that Citizens Bank must recredit his account for both checks, as his signature was forged. Discuss fully Gary's claim.

20–2A. Question with Sample Answer

Yes. Mendez has both a security interest in Arabian Knight and is a perfected secured party. He has met all the necessary criteria listed under UCC 9–203 to be a secured creditor. Mendez has given value of $5,000 and has taken possession of the collateral, Arabian Knight, owned by Marsh (who has rights in the collateral). Thus, Mendez has a security interest even though Marsh did not sign a security agreement. Once a security interest attaches, a transfer of possession of the collateral to the secured party can perfect the party's security interest without a filing [UCC 9–310(b)(6), 9–313]. Thus, a security interest was created and perfected at the time Marsh transferred Arabian Knight to Mendez as security for the loan.

21–2A. Question with Sample Answer

1. Any person, including a rancher or farmer, can voluntarily petition himself or herself into bankruptcy. The person has only to be a debtor. This includes partnerships and corporations that are liable on a claim held by a creditor, as well as individuals. The debtor does not have to be insolvent to file a petition. Under the Code, a debtor is presumed to be insolvent when his or her debts exceed the fair market value of nonexempt assets. Thus, even though Burke owns a $500,000 ranch and has debts of only $70,000, she can voluntarily petition herself into bankruptcy.
2. Neither Oman nor Sneed—nor any combination of Burke's creditors—can involuntarily petition Burke into bankruptcy. The Code provides that involuntary bankruptcy proceedings cannot be commenced against a farmer. The definition of a *farmer* includes a person who receives 50 percent of her or his gross income from farming operations, such as tilling the soil, ranching, or the production or raising of crops or livestock. Because Burke obviously fits the definition of a farmer, no creditor can force her into bankruptcy.

22–2A. Question with Sample Answer

The answer is likely no. If the loan was split without the consumer's consent, prior court cases have found that such practices violate the requirement of the Truth-in-Lending Act (TILA) that all disclosures for a single transaction must be grouped into a single writing.

Even if the plaintiff acquiesced to splitting the loan, the practice appears to circumvent the purpose of the Home Ownership and Equity Protection Act through an artificial restructuring of the loan transaction. If consumer protections could be circumvented by splitting loans, lenders would have a strong incentive to divide loans as necessary to keep individual loan costs as low as possible.

23–3A. Question with Sample Answer

Agency is usually a consensual relationship in that the principal and agent agree that the agent will have the authority to act for the principal, binding the principal to any contract with a third party. If no agency in fact exists, the purported agent's contracts with third parties are not binding on the principal. In this case, no agency by agreement was created.

Brown may claim that an agency by estoppel was created, but this argument will fail. Agency by estoppel is applicable only when a principal causes a third person to believe that another person is the principal's agent. In that situation, the principal's words or actions lead the third party to reasonably believe that the agent has authority. Hence, the principal is estopped (prevented) from claiming that no agency actually existed. Acts and declarations of the agent, however, do not in and of themselves create an agency by estoppel, because such actions should not reasonably lead a third person to believe that the purported agent has authority.

In this case, Wade's declarations and allegations alone led Brown to believe that Wade was an agent. Gett's actions were not involved. It is not reasonable to believe that someone is an agent solely because he or she is a friend of the principal. Therefore, Brown cannot hold Gett liable unless Gett ratifies Wade's contract—which is unlikely, as Wade has disappeared with the rare coin.

24–2A. Question with Sample Answer

The Occupational Safety and Health Act requires employers to provide safe working conditions for employees. The act prohibits employers from discharging or discriminating against any employee who refuses to work when the employee believes in good faith that he or she will risk death or great bodily harm by undertaking the employment activity. Denton and Carlo had sufficient reason to believe that the maintenance job required of them by their employer involved great risk.

Therefore, under the act, their discharge was wrongful. Denton and Carlo can turn to the Occupational Safety and Health Administration, which is part of the U.S. Department of Labor, for assistance.

25–2A. Question with Sample Answer

Educational requirements can be legally imposed as long as the requirement is directly related to, and necessary for, performance of the job. The requirement of a high school diploma is not a direct, job-related requirement in this case. Chinawa obviously comes under the 1964 Civil Rights Act, Title VII, as amended, and the educational requirement under the circumstances is definitely discriminatory against minorities.

26–2A. Question with Sample Answer

The court would likely conclude that National Foods was responsible for the acts of harassment by the manager at the franchised restaurant because the employees were the agents of National Foods. An agency relationship can be implied from the circumstances and conduct of the parties. The important question is the degree of control that a franchisor has over its franchisees. Whether the franchisor actually exercises that control is beside the point. Here, National Foods retained considerable control over new hires and the franchisee's policies, as well as the right to terminate the franchise for violations. That its supervisors routinely approved the policies would not undercut National Foods' liability.

27–2A. Question with Sample Answer

1. A limited partner's interest is assignable. In fact, assignment allows the assignee to become a substituted limited partner

with the consent of the remaining partners. The assignment does not dissolve the limited partnership.

2. Bankruptcy of the limited partnership itself causes dissolution, but bankruptcy of one of the limited partners does not dissolve the partnership unless it causes the bankruptcy of the firm.
3. The retirement, death, or insanity of a general partner dissolves the partnership unless the business can be continued by the remaining general partners. Because Dorinda was the only general partner, her death dissolves the limited partnership.

28–2A. Question with Sample Answer

Although a joint stock company has characteristics of a corporation, it is usually treated as a partnership. Therefore, although the joint stock company issues transferable shares of stock and is managed by directors and officers, the shareholders have personal liability. Unless the shareholders transfer their stock and ownership to a third party, not only are the joint stock company's assets available for damages caused by a breach, but the individual shareholders' assets are also subject to such liability.

A business trust resembles and is treated like a corporation in many respects. One is the limited liability of the beneficiaries. Unless state law treats the beneficiaries as partners, making them liable to the business trust's creditors, Faraway Corp. can look to only the business trust's assets in the event of a breach.

29–2A. Question with Sample Answer

It could be argued that Kora exceeded his authority when he cosigned the note on behalf of the corporation. The board of directors of a corporation delegates the authority to transact all ordinary business of the corporation to the president. If cosigning a note for a personal loan is not "ordinary business of the corporation," then the board, as principal, must ratify the act. There is no indication that the board did so in this instance.

30–2A. Question with Sample Answer

Directors are personally answerable to the corporation and the shareholders for breach of their duty to exercise reasonable care in conducting the affairs of the corporation. Reasonable care is the degree of care that a reasonably prudent person would use in the conduct of personal business affairs. When directors delegate the running of the corporate affairs to officers, the directors are expected to use reasonable care in selecting and supervising the officers. Failure to do so will make the directors liable for negligence or mismanagement. A director who dissents to an action by the board is not personally liable for losses resulting from that action. Unless the dissent is entered into the board meeting minutes, however, the director is presumed to have assented.

Therefore, the first issue in the case of Starboard, Inc., is whether the board members failed to use reasonable care in selecting the president, Tyson. If so, and particularly if the board failed to provide a reasonable amount of supervision (as openly embezzled funds would indicate), the directors will be personally liable. This liability will include Ellsworth unless she can prove that she dissented and that she tried to reasonably supervise Tyson. Considering the facts in this case, it is questionable that Ellsworth could prove this.

31–2A. Question with Sample Answer

No. Under federal securities law, a stock split is exempt from registration requirements because no stock is being sold. The existing shares are merely being split, and the corporation does not receive any consideration for the additional shares created.

32–2A. Question with Sample Answer

Yes. The major antitrust law being violated is the Sherman Act, Section 1. Allitron and Donovan are engaged in interstate commerce, and the agreement to divide marketing territories between them is a contract in restraint of trade. The U.S. Department of Justice could seek fines of up to $1 million from each corporation, and the officers or directors responsible could be imprisoned for up to three years.

33–2A. Question with Sample Answer

The Truth-in-Lending Act (TILA) deals specifically with lost or stolen credit cards and the unauthorized use of credit cards. For credit cards solicited by the cardholder and then lost or stolen, the act limits the liability of the cardholder to $50 for unauthorized charges made before the card issuer is notified. There is no liability for any unauthorized charges made after the date of notice.

Therefore, for the Midtown Department Store credit card stolen on May 31, Ochoa is liable for $50 of the $500 charge made on June 1, which occurred before Ochoa notified the card issuer. Ochoa has no liability for the $200 charge on June 3 because it was made after the issuer was notified.

TILA prohibits the issuance of unsolicited credit cards. Unless an individual accepts an unsolicited card (such as by using it), she or he is not liable for any unauthorized charges if the card is lost or stolen. The person does not have to notify the issuer of an unsolicited, unaccepted card to be relieved of all liability for unauthorized charges. Therefore, Ochoa owes $50 to Midtown Department Store and nothing to High-Flying Airlines.

34–2A. Question with Sample Answer

Assuming that the circuit court has abandoned the *Ultramares* rule, it is likely that the accounting firm of Goldman, Walters, Johnson & Co. will be held liable to Happydays State Bank for negligent preparation of financial statements.

As a side note, this hypothetical question is partially derived from the case, *Citizens State Bank v. Timm, Schmidt & Co.* In that case, the Supreme Court of Wisconsin enunciated various policy reasons for holding accountants liable to third parties even in the absence of privity. The court suggested that this potential liability would make accountants more careful in preparing financial statements.

Moreover, in some situations the accountants may be the only solvent defendants. Hence, unless liability is imposed on the accountants, third parties who reasonably rely on financial statements may go unprotected. The court also observed that if third parties, such as banks, have to absorb the costs of bad loans made as a result of negligently prepared financial statements, then the cost of credit to the public in general will increase. The court suggested that accountants are in a better position to absorb the risk by purchasing liability insurance.

35–3A. Question with Sample Answer

For Curtis to recover against the hotel, he must first prove that a bailment relationship was created between himself and the hotel as to the car or the fur coat, or both. For a bailment to exist, there must be a delivery of personal property that gives the bailee exclusive possession of the property, and the bailee must knowingly accept the bailed property. If either element is lacking, there is no bailment relationship and no liability on the part of the bailee hotel.

The facts clearly indicate that the bailee hotel took exclusive possession and control of Curtis's car. The hotel knowingly accepted the car when the attendant took the car from Curtis and parked it in the underground garage, retaining the keys. Thus, a bailment was created as to the car. Since this was a mutual-benefit bailment, the hotel owed Curtis the duty to exercise reasonable care over the car and to return it at the end of the bailment.

Failure to return the car creates a presumption of negligence (lack of reasonable care). Unless the hotel can rebut this presumption, the hotel is liable to Curtis for the loss of the car. As to the fur coat, the hotel neither knew nor expected that the trunk contained an expensive fur coat. Thus, although the hotel knowingly took exclusive possession of the car, the hotel did not do so with the fur coat. (But for a regular coat and other items likely to be in a car, the hotel would be liable.) Because no bailment of the expensive fur coat was created, the hotel has no liability for its loss.

36–2A. Question with Sample Answer

Wiley understandably wants a general warranty deed, as this type of deed will give him the most extensive protection against any defects of title claimed against the property transferred. The general warranty deed would have Gemma warranting the following:

1. That she has the title to, and the power to convey, the property.
2. A covenant of quiet enjoyment (a warranty that the buyer will not be disturbed in his possession of the land).
3. That transfer of the property is made without knowledge of adverse claims of third parties.

Gemma, however, is conveying only ten feet along a property line that may not even be accurately surveyed. Therefore, she does not wish to make these warranties.

Consequently, Gemma is offering a quitclaim deed, which does not convey any warranties but conveys only whatever interest, if any, the grantor owns. Although title is passed by a quitclaim deed, the quality of the title is not warranted. Because Wiley really needs the property, it appears that he has three choices. He can accept the quitclaim deed, he can increase his offer price to obtain the general warranty deed he wants, or he can offer to have a title search made, which should satisfy both parties.

37–2A. Question with Sample Answer

1. In most states, for a will to be valid, it must be in writing, signed by the testator, and witnessed (attested to) according to the statutes of the state. In this instance, Benjamin's will was unquestionably written (typewritten) and signed by the testator. The only problem is with the witnesses. Some states require three witnesses, and some states invalidate a will if a named beneficiary is also a witness. The Uniform Probate Code provides that a will is valid even if attested to by an interested witness. Therefore, whether the will is valid depends on the state laws dealing with witness qualifications.
2. If the will is declared invalid, Benjamin's estate will pass in accordance with the state's intestacy laws. These statutes provide for distribution of an estate when there is no valid will. The intent of the statutes is to distribute the estate in the way that the deceased person would have wished. Generally, the estate is divided between a surviving spouse and all surviving children. Because Benjamin is a widower, if his only surviving child is Edward, the entire estate will go to Edward, and Benjamin's grandchildren, Perry and Paul, will receive nothing from the estate.
3. If the will is valid, the estate will be divided between Benjamin's two children, Patricia and Edward. Should either or both predecease Benjamin, leaving children (Benjamin's grandchildren), the grandchildren take *per stirpes* the share that would have gone to their parent. In this situation, Edward, as a surviving child of Benjamin, would receive one-half of the estate, and Perry and Paul, as grandchildren, would each receive *per stirpes* one-fourth of the estate (one-half of the share that would have gone to their deceased mother, Patricia).

APPENDIX H

Sample Answers for *Case Problems with Sample Answer*

1–6A. Case Problem with Sample Answer

The common law system spread throughout medieval England after the Norman Conquest in 1066. Courts developed the common law rules from the principles behind the decisions in actual legal controversies. Judges attempted to be consistent. When possible, they based their decisions on the principles suggested by earlier cases. They sought to decide similar cases in a similar way and considered new cases with care because they knew that their decisions would make new law. Each interpretation became part of the law on the subject and served as a legal precedent. Later cases that involved similar legal principles or facts could be decided with reference to that precedent.

The practice of deciding new cases with reference to former decisions, or precedents, eventually became a cornerstone of the English and American judicial systems. It forms a doctrine called *stare decisis*. Under this doctrine, judges are obligated to follow the precedents established within their jurisdictions. Generally, those countries that were once colonies of Great Britain retained their English common law heritage after they achieved their independence. Today, common law systems exist in Australia, Canada, India, Ireland, and New Zealand, as well as the United States.

Most of the other European nations base their legal systems on Roman civil law. Civil law is codified law—an ordered grouping of legal principles enacted into law by a legislature or governing body. In a civil law system, the primary source of law is a statutory code, and case precedents are not judicially binding as they are in a common law system. Nonetheless, judges in such systems commonly refer to previous decisions as sources of legal guidance. The difference is that judges in a civil law system are not bound by precedent—in other words, the doctrine of *stare decisis* does not apply.

2–6A. Case Problem with Sample Answer

The establishment clause prohibits the government from passing laws or taking actions that promote religion or show a preference for one religion over another. In assessing a government action, the courts look at the predominant purpose for the action and ask whether the action has the effect of endorsing religion.

Although DeWeese claimed to have a nonreligious purpose for displaying the poster of the Ten Commandments in a courtroom, his own statements showed a religious purpose. These statements reflected his views about "warring" legal philosophies and his belief that "our legal system is based on moral absolutes from divine law handed down by God through the Ten Commandments." This plainly constitutes a religious purpose that violates the establishment clause because it has the effect of endorsing Judaism or Christianity over other religions. In the case on which this problem is based, the court ruled in favor of the American Civil Liberties Union.

3–4A. Case Problem with Sample Answer

Based on a recent holding by the Washington state supreme court, the federal appeals court held that the arbitration provision was *unconscionable* (see page 296 in Chapter 11) and therefore invalid. Because it was invalid, the restriction on class-action suits was also invalid. The state court reasoned that by offering a contract that restricted class actions and required arbitration, the company had improperly stripped consumers of rights they would normally have to attack certain industry practices.

Class-action suits are often brought in cases of deceptive or unfair industry practices when the losses suffered by an individual consumer are too small to warrant a consumer suing.

In this case, the alleged added cell phone fees are so small that no one consumer would be likely to litigate or arbitrate the matter due to the expenses involved. Because the arbitration agreement eliminates the possibility of class actions, it violates public policy and is void and unenforceable.

4–4A. Case Problem with Sample Answer

Defamation involves wrongfully hurting a person's good reputation. Doing so in writing is the tort of libel. The basis of the tort of defamation is the publication of a statement that holds an individual up to contempt, ridicule, or hatred. Publication means that the statement is communicated to someone other than the defamed party. A person who republishes defamatory statements is liable. The publication of information that places a person in a false light, such as a story that she did something she did not actually do, could also constitute an invasion of privacy. Truth normally is an absolute defense to a charge of defamation.

In this problem, the police communicated to the *Herald* that Eubanks was charged with a crime, and the paper published the information. Its publication might hold Eubanks up to contempt, ridicule, or hatred. The information was not correct, placing Eubanks in a false light. Yet the *Herald*'s publication of the information was an accurate, truthful summary of a police report. No information was changed. There is no indication that the paper was aware of the second e-mail before it published its summary of the first. Thus, truth is most likely an absolute defense to Eubanks's charges. In the actual case on which this problem is based, the court issued a judgment in favor of the newspaper.

5–5A. Case Problem with Sample Answer

Some business information that cannot be protected by trademark, patent, or copyright law is protected against appropriation by competitors as trade secrets. Trade secrets consist of anything that makes a company unique and that would have value to a competitor—customer lists, plans, research and development, pricing information, marketing techniques, and production techniques, for example. Theft of trade secrets is a federal crime.

In this problem, the documents in the boxes in the car could constitute trade secrets. But a number of factors suggest that a finding of theft and imposition of liability would not be appropriate. The boxes were not marked in any way that would indicate they contained confidential information. The boxes were stored in an employee's car. The alleged thief was the employee's spouse, not a CPR competitor, and she apparently had no idea what was in the boxes. Leaving trade secrets so accessible does not show an effort to protect the information.

In the case on which this problem is based, the court dismissed Jones's claim, in part, on the reasoning stated above.

6–5A. Case Problem with Sample Answer

Under the Fourth Amendment, a police officer must obtain a search warrant to search private property. In a traffic stop, however, it seems unreasonable to require an officer to obtain a warrant to search one of the vehicle's occupants. But it seems reasonable to apply some standard to prevent police misconduct. An officer might be held to a standard of probable cause, which consists of reasonable grounds to believe that a person should be searched.

In some situations, however, an officer may have a reasonable suspicion short of probable cause to believe that a person poses a risk of violence. In a traffic-stop setting, for example, the normal reaction of a person stopped for a driving infraction would not pose this risk, but it might arise if the person feared that evidence of a more serious crime might be discovered. A criminal's motivation to use violence to prevent the discovery could be great, and because the vehicle is already stopped, the additional intrusion is minimal. Under these circumstances, a limited search of the person for weapons would protect the officer, the individual, and the public. Thus, an officer who conducts a routine traffic stop could perform a pat-down search of a passenger on a reasonable suspicion that the person may be armed and dangerous.

7–4A. Case Problem with Sample Answer

The law does not codify all ethical requirements. A firm may have acted unethically but still not be legally accountable unless the party that was wronged can establish some basis for liability. Rules of law are designed to require plaintiffs to prove certain elements that establish a defendant's liability in order to recover for injuries or loss. Ethical codes and internal guidelines may have significance in evaluating a company's conduct, but they are not rules of law—a violation of a company policy is not a basis for liability.

In this case, Havensure had the burden of proving liability. Prudential's violation of its own company guideline was clearly wrongful—and might be a matter of concern for insurance regulators—but this misconduct did not create an obligation to Havensure. Havensure cannot establish a cause of action against Prudential for violating its own policy. In the actual case on which this problem is based, the court ruled in Prudential's favor.

8–3A. Case Problem with Sample Answer

The court ruled that it had jurisdiction over Voda's foreign patent infringement claims. Cordis appealed to a federal appellate court, which concluded that the lower court did not have jurisdiction. The appellate court found that "considerations of comity" "constitute compelling reasons to decline jurisdiction" in this case.

The court explained, "Comity, in the legal sense, is neither a matter of absolute obligation, on the one hand, nor of mere courtesy and good will, upon the other. But it is the recognition which one nation allows within its territory to the legislative, executive or judicial acts of another nation, having due regard both to international duty and convenience, and to the rights of its own citizens or of other persons who are under the protection of its laws.

Courts must also bear in mind that whatever laws are carried into execution, within the limits of any government, are considered as having the same effect everywhere, so far as they do not occasion a prejudice to the rights of the other governments, or their citizens."

Here, Voda did not identify any international duty that required the U.S. judicial system to adjudicate foreign patent infringement claims, and the court found none. Voda also did not show that it would be more convenient for U.S. courts to assume jurisdiction or that foreign courts would inadequately protect his foreign patent rights. Therefore, the court saw "no reason why American courts should supplant British, Canadian, French, or German courts in interpreting and enforcing British, Canadian, European, French, or German patents. . . . Because the purpose underlying comity is not furthered and potentially hindered in this case, adjudication of Voda's foreign patent infringement claims should be left to the sovereigns that create the property rights in the first instance."

9–7A. Case Problem with Sample Answer

Gutkowski does not have a valid claim for payment, nor should he recover on the basis of a quasi contract. Quasi contracts are imposed by courts on parties in the interest of fairness and justice. Usually, a quasi contract is imposed to avoid the unjust enrichment of one party at the expense of another. Gutkowski was compensated as a consultant. For him to establish a claim that he is due more compensation based on unjust enrichment, he must have proof. As it is, he has only his claim that there were discussions about him being a part owner of YES. Discussions and negotiations are not a basis for recovery on a quasi contract.

In the actual case on which this problem is based, the court dismissed Gutkowski's claim for payment.

10–6A. Case Problem with Sample Answer

An offer is a manifestation of willingness to enter into a bargain that is made in a way that justifies another person in understanding that his or her assent to that bargain is invited and will conclude it. The test for an offer is whether it induces a reasonable belief in the recipient that the recipient can, by accepting, bind the sender. In making an offer, the offeror may decide to whom to extend it.

In this situation, Prairie Meadows Casino is the offeror. It extends an offer to wager to its patrons, promising that if a patron accepts the offer by wagering an amount and wins, the casino will pay off the wager. Because the casino has the ability to determine the individuals to whom the offer is made, it may also exclude certain individuals. Blackford was banned from the casino. Under an objective test, unless the ban was lifted, Blackford could not reasonably believe that he was among the individuals invited to accept the offer. In addition, the ban against Blackford had not been lifted—the casino had not extended him an offer to wager. Because there was no offer to him, no contract could result.

In the actual case on which this problem is based, the court entered a judgment in the casino's favor on this reasoning.

11–6A. Case Problem with Sample Answer

In this case, the agreement that restricted the buyer's options for resolution of a dispute to arbitration and limited the amount of damages was both procedurally and substantively unconscionable. Procedural unconscionability concerns the manner in which the parties enter into a contract. Substantive unconscionability can occur when a contract leaves one party to the agreement without a remedy for the nonperformance of the other.

Here, GeoEx told customers that the arbitration terms in its release form were nonnegotiable and that climbers would encounter the same requirements with any other travel company. This amounted to procedural unconscionability, underscoring the customers' lack of bargaining power. The imbalance resulted in oppressive terms, with no real negotiation and an absence of meaningful choice. Furthermore, the restriction on forum (San Francisco) and the limitation on damages (the cost of the trip)—with no limitation on GeoEx's damages—amounted to substantive unconscionability.

In the actual case on which this problem is based, the court ruled that the agreement was unconscionable.

12–4A. Case Problem with Sample Answer

No. Generally, a contract for a sale of land must be in writing and state the essential terms (such as location and price) and describe the property with sufficient clarity to allow the terms to be determined from the writing, without reference to outside sources. In this problem, the parties' "Purchase Agreement" was void for lack of an adequate property description. The agreement merely provided the name of the business and a street address. Thus, the seller could not enforce it, and the prospective buyers could back out of the deal.

In the actual case on which this problem is based, the court ruled that the agreement was unenforceable because the description was not sufficient.

13–6A. Case Problem with Sample Answer

Maciel was not correct. In this problem, the performance of a legal obligation under the parties' contract was contingent on a condition—the occurrence of a certain event. If the condition was not satisfied, the obligations of the parties were discharged. Here, Regent University promised to provide an apartment in its housing facility to Maciel as long as he maintained his status as a Regent student. Maintaining student status was the condition for the university's provision of an apartment. On the termination of that status, Regent was entitled to require Maciel to vacate the apartment.

According to the facts in the problem, Maciel decided to withdraw from the university at the end of the spring semester. This rendered him ineligible to remain in the apartment. In other words, this decision resulted in noncompliance with the condition for the university's provision of an apartment, and the university was thus no longer bound to perform. Contrary to Maciel's argument, he did not have the "legal authority" to continue to occupy the apartment. In the actual case on which this problem is based, the court convicted Maciel of trespassing. In response to Maciel's argument, a state intermediate appellate court applied the reasoning set out above to affirm the conviction.

14–7A. Case Problem with Sample Answer

Simard is liable only for the losses and expenses related to the first resale. Simard could reasonably anticipate that his breach would require another sale and that the sales price might be less than what he agreed to pay. Therefore, he should be liable for the difference between his sales price and the first resale price ($29,000), plus any expenses arising from the first resale.

Simard is not liable, however, for any expenses and losses related to the second resale. After all, Simard did not cause the second purchaser's default, and he could not reasonably foresee that default as a probable result of his breach.

15–4A. Case Problem with Sample Answer

Altieri held title to the car that she was driving at the time of the accident in which Godfrey was injured. Once goods exist and are identified, title can be determined. Under the UCC, any explicit understanding between the buyer and the seller determines when title passes. If there is no such agreement, title passes to the buyer at the time and place that the seller physically delivers the goods.

In lease contracts, title to the goods is retained by the lessor-owner of the goods. The UCC's provisions relating to passage to title do not apply to leased goods. Here, Altieri originally leased the car from G.E. Capital Auto Lease, Inc., but by the time of the accident she had bought it. Even though she had not fully paid for the car or completed the transfer-of-title paperwork, she owned it. Title to the car passed to Altieri when she bought it and took delivery of it. Thus, Altieri, not G.E., was the owner of the car at the time of the accident.

In the actual case on which this problem is based, the court concluded that G.E. was not the owner of the vehicle when Godfrey was injured.

16–7A. Case Problem with Sample Answer

Padma notified Universal Exports about its breach, so Padma has two ways to recover even though it accepted the goods. Padma's first option is to argue that it revoked its acceptance, giving it the right to reject the goods. To revoke acceptance, Padma would have to show that:

1. The nonconformity substantially impaired the value of the shipment.
2. It predicated its acceptance on a reasonable assumption that Universal Exports would cure the nonconformity.
3. Universal Exports did not cure the nonconformity within a reasonable time.

Padma's second option is to keep the goods and recover for the damages caused by Universal Exports' breach. Under this option, Padma could recover at least the difference between the value of the goods as promised and their value as accepted.

17–7A. Case Problem with Sample Answer

No. Dobrovolny's claim is not likely to succeed. The majority of states recognize strict product liability. The purpose of strict product liability is to ensure that the costs of injuries resulting from defective products are borne by the manufacturers rather than by the injured persons. The law imposes this liability as a matter of public policy. Some state courts limit the application of the tort theory of strict product liability to situations involving personal injuries rather than property damage.

In this problem, Nebraska recognizes strict product liability, but the state's courts limit its application. The issue is whether these limits apply when a product self-destructs without causing damage to persons or other property. When a product injures only itself, the reasons for imposing liability in tort lose their significance. The consumer has not been injured, and the loss concerns the consumer's benefit of the bargain from the contract with the seller of the product.

Although a consumer with only a damaged product may not recover in tort, the consumer is not without other remedies. Recovery can be sought on a contract theory for breach of warranty. Product value and quality are the purposes of warranties. Thus, even though the court is likely to deny Dobrovolny's strict product liability claim, he might seek to recover for breach of warranty on contract principles for the loss of his truck. If there were no express warranties that the truck would not spontaneously combust, relief may be possible for breach of the implied warranty of merchantability or fitness for a particular purpose.

In the actual case on which this problem is based, the court issued a decision in Ford's favor.

18–6A. Case Problem with Sample Answer

No. Novel is not correct. The instrument is a note and Novel is bound to pay it. For an instrument to be negotiable under UCC 3–104, it must meet the following requirements: (1) be in writing, (2) be signed by the maker or the drawer, (3) be an unconditional promise or order to pay, (4) state a fixed amount of money, (5) be payable on demand or at a definite time, and (6) be payable to order or to bearer unless it is a check. When no time for payment is stated on an instrument, the instrument is payable on demand.

Applying these principles to the facts in this problem, all of the requirements to establish the instrument as negotiable are met:

1. The instrument is in writing.
2. It is signed by Novel.
3. There are no conditions or promises other than the unconditional promise to pay.
4. The instrument states a fixed amount—$10,000.
5. The instrument does not include a definite repayment date, which means that it is payable on demand.
6. The instrument is payable to Gallwitz.

In the actual case on which this problem is based, the court ruled in favor of Gallwitz for payment of the note.

19–6A. Case Problem with Sample Answer

Wells Fargo is liable to W Financial for the amount of the check. A bank that pays a customer's check bearing a forged indorsement must recredit the customer's account or be liable to the customer-drawer for breach of contract. The bank must recredit the account because it failed to carry out the drawer's order to pay to the order of the named party. Eventually, the loss falls on the first party to take the instrument bearing the forged indorsement because a forged indorsement does not transfer title. Thus, whoever takes an instrument with a forged indorsement cannot become a holder.

Under these rules, Wells Fargo is liable to W Financial for the amount of the check. The bank had an obligation to ensure that the check was properly indorsed. The bank did not pay the check to the order of Lateef, the named payee, but accepted the check for deposit into the account of CA Houston without Lateef's indorsement. The bank did not obtain title to the instrument and could not become a holder, nor was it entitled to enforce the instrument on behalf of any other party who was entitled to enforce it.

In the actual case on which this problem is based, the court held the bank liable to pay the amount of the check to W Financial.

20–4A. Case Problem with Sample Answer

A secured creditor can take various steps to satisfy a debt. Under the UCC, these remedies are cumulative and can be exercised simultaneously. A secured creditor can repossess and retain a debtor's collateral in full or partial satisfaction of the debt. The collateral does not have to be disposed of first unless the parties have agreed otherwise. If the collateral satisfies the debt only partially, the creditor can seek a judgment for the balance due. Of course, it would not be fair for a creditor to deprive the debtor of the possession of the collateral for an unreasonable length of time and not apply the property, or the proceeds from its sale, against the debt.

The creditor must act in a commercially reasonable manner and take steps to sell, lease, retain, or otherwise dispose of the collateral. In this problem, it does not appear that the bank failed to proceed in a commercially reasonable manner. The bank chose to retain the collateral and seek a judgment on the debt. The amount that OAI owes the bank might be at issue, but the facts state that the debtor did not dispute the amount due.

In the case on which this problem is based, the court issued a judgment in the bank's favor based on the principles stated here.

21–8A. Case Problem with Sample Answer

Gholston can recover damages because EZ Auto willfully violated the automatic stay. EZ Auto repossessed the car even though it received notice of the automatic stay from the bankruptcy court. Moreover, EZ Auto retained the car even after it was reminded of the stay by Gholston's attorney. Thus, EZ Auto knew about the automatic stay and violated it intentionally. Because Gholston suffered direct damages as a result, she can recover from EZ Auto.

22–8A. Case Problem with Sample Answer

Ordinarily, a deficiency judgment will be for the difference between the borrower's outstanding debt and the final sales price at the foreclosure sale. Courts will not apply the sales price, however, if the property sells for far less than its fair market value. That happened here, so Beach Community Bank is entitled to the difference between First Brownsville's outstanding debt and the property's fair market value at the time of the foreclosure sale. Based on the court's foreclosure judgment and the expert testimony at the deficiency judgment hearing, First Brownsville owes $454,475.

23–8A. Case Problem with Sample Answer

Hall may be held personally liable. Hall could not be an agent for House Medic because it was a fictitious name and not a real entity. Moreover, when the contract was formed, Hall did not disclose his true principal, which was Hall Hauling, Ltd. Thus, Hall may be held personally liable as a party to the contract.

24–6A. Case Problem with Sample Answer

No. Woody Woo's tip-pooling policy did not violate the minimum wage provisions of the Fair Labor Standards Act (FLSA). When tipping is a customary part of a business as it is in the restaurant industry, the tips—in the absence of an explicit agreement to the contrary—belong to the recipient. When another arrangement is made, however, it is likely valid unless there is a statutory limitation. The FLSA does not prevent employers, who are paying at least the minimum wage, from taking employee tips and making another arrangement for tip distributions.

Here, Woody Woo's tip-pool arrangement is fine so long as it does not reduce the servers' hourly wages to less than the state's minimum wage. That does not occur because Woody Woo pays its servers more than the state's minimum wage before tips.

25–5A. Case Problem with Sample Answer

Yes. Dawson could establish a claim for retaliation. Title VII prohibits retaliation. In a retaliation claim, an individual asserts that he or she suffered harm as a result of making a charge, testifying, or participating in a Title VII investigation or proceeding. To prove retaliation, a plaintiff must show that the challenged action was one that would likely have dissuaded a reasonable worker from making or supporting a charge of discrimination.

In this problem, under applicable state law, it was unlawful for an employer to discriminate against an individual based on sexual orientation. Dawson was subjected to derision on the part of co-workers, including his supervisor, based on his sexual orientation. He filed a complaint with his employer's human resources department. Two days later, he was fired. The proximity in time and the other circumstances, especially the supervisor's conduct, would support a retaliation claim. Also, the discharge would likely have dissuaded Dawson, or any reasonable worker, from making a claim of discrimination.

In the actual case on which this problem is based, the court held that Dawson offered enough evidence that "a reasonable trier of fact could find in favor of Dawson on his retaliation claim."

26–7A. Case Problem with Sample Answer

Oshana and GTO have stated a claim for wrongful termination of their franchise. A franchisor must act in good faith when terminating a franchise agreement. If the termination is arbitrary or unfair, a franchisee may have a claim for wrongful termination.

In this case, Oshana and GTO have alleged that Buchanan acted in bad faith. Their failure to pay rent would ordinarily be a valid basis for termination, but not if it was entirely precipitated by Buchanan. Thus, Oshana and GTO may recover if they can prove that their allegations are true.

27–7A. Case Problem with Sample Answer

Garcia and Lucero probably satisfied all three requirements for forming a partnership. They owned the two properties equally, agreed to share both profits and losses, and enjoyed equal management rights. Moreover, it is immaterial that they lacked a written partnership agreement. The Statute of Frauds does not apply to these facts, and a partnership agreement can be oral or implied by the parties' conduct.

28–7A. Case Problem with Sample Answer

No. One Bluewater member could not unilaterally "fire" another member without providing a reason. Part of the attractiveness of an LLC as a form of business enterprise is its flexibility. The members can decide how to operate the business through an operating agreement. For example, the agreement can set forth procedures for choosing or removing members or managers.

Here, the Bluewater operating agreement provided for a "super majority" vote to remove a member under circumstances that would jeopardize the firm's contractor status. Thus, one Bluewater member could not unilaterally "fire" another member without providing a reason. In fact, a majority of the members could not terminate the other's interest in the firm without providing a reason. Moreover, the only acceptable reason would be a circumstance that undercut the firm's status as a contractor.

The flexibility of the LLC business form relates to its framework, not to its members' capacity to violate its operating agreement. In the actual case on which this problem is based, Smith attempted to "fire" Williford without providing a reason. In Williford's suit, the court issued a judgment in his favor.

29–7A. Case Problem with Sample Answer

Yes. Most likely, Interline is liable for the unpaid amount on the GATT contract with Call Center. An acquiring corporation will be held to have assumed the liabilities of the selling corporation in the following situations:

1. The purchasing corporation expressly or impliedly assumes the seller's liabilities.
2. The sale transaction is in effect a merger or consolidation of the two companies.
3. The purchaser continues the seller's business and retains the same personnel (shareholders, directors, and officers).
4. The sale is entered into fraudulently for the purpose of escaping liability.

In this problem, Interline acquired GATT's assets at a public sale. There is no indication that Interline agreed to assume GATT's liabilities, there was no merger or other combination of the two companies, and it does not appear that the sale was fraudulently entered into to escape liability.

Thus, the focus is on the third item listed above—whether Interline was liable for GATT's debts because it continued GATT's business with the same personnel. Boyd was not a GATT employee, but he was a former GATT director. Other members of Interline's staff were former GATT employees. GATT and Interline operated out of the same office building. Both companies were in the business of providing travel services to many of the same customers. These factors indicate that Interline is responsible for GATT's liabilities, including its debt to Call Center.

In the actual case on which this problem is based, the court focused on the same principles discussed here to issue a judgment in Call Center's favor.

30–6A. Case Problem with Sample Answer

Yes. Woods has a right to inspect Biolustré's books and records. Every shareholder is entitled to examine corporate records. A shareholder can inspect the books in person or through an agent such as an attorney, accountant, or other authorized assistant.

The right of inspection is limited to the inspection and copying of corporate books and records for a proper purpose. This is because the power of inspection is fraught with potential for abuse—for example, it can involve the disclosure of trade secrets and other confidential information. Thus, a corporation is allowed to protect itself.

Here, Woods, through Hair Ventures, has the right to inspect Biolustré's books and records. She has a proper purpose for the inspection—to obtain information about Biolustré's financial situation. She, and other shareholders, had not received notice of shareholders' meetings or corporate financial reports for years, or notice of Biolustré's plan to issue additional stock. Hair Ventures had a substantial investment in the company.

In the actual case on which this problem is based, the court ordered Biolustré to produce its books and records for Hair Ventures' inspection.

31–5A. Case Problem with Sample Answer

An omission or misrepresentation of a material fact in connection with the purchase or sale of a security may violate Section 10(b) of the Securities Exchange Act of 1934 and SEC Rule 10b-5. The key question is whether the omitted or misrepresented information is material. A fact, by itself, is not automatically material. A fact will be regarded as material only if it is significant enough that it would likely affect an investor's decision as to whether to buy or sell the company's securities. For example, a company's potential liability in a product liability suit and the financial consequences to the firm are material facts that must be disclosed because they are significant enough to affect an investor's decision as to whether to buy stock in the company.

In this case, the plaintiffs' claim should not be dismissed. To prevail on their claim that the defendants made material omissions in violation of Section 10(b) and SEC Rule 10-5, the plaintiffs must prove that the omission was material. Their complaint alleged the omission of information linking Zicam and anosmia (a loss of the sense of smell) and plausibly suggested that reasonable investors would have viewed this information as material. Zicam products account for 70 percent of Matrixx's sales. Matrixx received reports of consumers who suffered anosia after using Zicam Cold Remedy.

In public statements discussing revenues and product safety, Matrixx did not disclose this information. But the information was significant enough to likely affect a consumer's decision to use the product, and this would affect revenue and ultimately the commercial viability of the product. The information was therefore significant enough to likely affect an investor's decision whether to buy or sell Matrixx's stock, and this would affect the stock price. Thus, the plaintiffs' allegations were sufficient. Contrary to the defendants' assertion, statistical sampling is not required to show materiality—reasonable investors could view reports of adverse events as material even if the reports did not provide statistically significant evidence.

32–4A. Case Problem with Sample Answer

No. DVRC's action does not represent an attempt to monopolize in violation of the Sherman Act. DVRC merely returned to a position that it had a right to have from the beginning. In their contract DVRC had expressly informed Christy that their relationship could change at any time. Thus, Christy knew from the beginning that its ski rental business could operate only with DVRC's permission, subject to DVRC's business judgment.

If DVRC had terminated a profitable relationship without any economic justification, it might have shown a willingness to forgo short-term profits to achieve an anticompetitive end. But there is no indication that DVRC terminated a profitable business relationship or that DVRC was motivated by anything other than a desire to increase profits. Rather than forgoing short-term profits, DVRC can expect to increase its short-term profits by operating its own ski rental facility.

The court in the case on which this problem is based dismissed Christy's suit, a decision that the U.S. Court of Appeals for the Tenth Circuit affirmed.

33–3A. Case Problem with Sample Answer

According to the facts set out in the problem, the Nutrition Labeling and Education Act (NLEA) does not regulate nutrition information labeling for restaurant food, and state and local governments can adopt their own rules. The NLEA does regulate nutrition content claims on restaurant food, however, and attempts by state and local governments to regulate those claims are expressly preempted.

The issue in this case is whether the calorie disclosures mandated for chain restaurants' menus and menu boards under New York City Health Code Section 81.50 are "information" or "claims." The types of information covered by the provision on "nutrition information" include "total number of calories." Thus, the calorie-content information required by Section 81.50 falls under this provision. Therefore, Section 81.50 is within the area that the NLEA leaves to state and local governments. In other words, the NLEA permits the information required by Section 81.50.

Therefore, federal law at the time of this dispute—before the new menu labeling requirements enacted in 2010 and discussed in the chapter—did not preempt this local regulation.

The court in the actual case on which this problem is based issued a summary judgment in the defendants' favor, and on the reasoning stated above, the U.S. Court of Appeals for the Second Circuit affirmed.

34–7A. Case Problem with Sample Answer

KPMG is potentially liable to the hedge funds' partners under the *Restatement (Third) of Torts.* Under Section 552 of the *Restatement,* an auditor owes a duty to "persons for whose benefit and guidance the accountant intends to supply . . . information."

In this case, KPMG prepared annual reports on the hedge funds and addressed them to the funds' "Partners." Additionally, KPMG knew who the partners were because it prepared individual tax forms for them each year. Thus, KPMG's annual reports were for the partners' benefit and guidance. The partners relied on the reports, including their representations that they complied with generally accepted accounting principles.

As a result, they lost millions of dollars, which exposes KPMG to possible liability under Section 552.

35–7A. Case Problem with Sample Answer

Moreland should be awarded damages, and Gray should take nothing. The bailee must exercise reasonable care in preserving the bailed property. What constitutes reasonable care in a bailment situation normally depends on the nature and specific circumstances of the bailment. If the bailed property has been lost or is returned damaged, a court will presume that the bailee was negligent.

In the circumstances of this problem, when the bailor (Moreland, the owner of the aircraft) entrusted the plane to the bailee's (Gray's) repair shop for painting, the work was not properly performed. This violated the bailee's duty to exercise reasonable care and breached the bailment contract. Because the plane was returned damaged, this may also constitute negligence. In the event of a breach, the bailor may sue for damages. The measure of damages is the difference between the value of the bailed property in its present condition and what it would have been worth if the work had been properly performed.

Thus, Gray is liable to Moreland for failing to properly paint the plane. In the actual case on which this problem is based, the court upheld a jury award to Moreland of damages and attorneys' fees.

36–6A. Case Problem with Sample Answer

The McKeags satisfied the first three requirements for adverse possession:

1. Their possession was actual and exclusive because they used the beach and prevented others from doing so, including the Finleys.
2. Their possession was open, visible, and notorious because they made improvements to the beach and regularly kept their belongings there.
3. Their possession was continuous and peaceable for the required ten years. They possessed the property for more than four decades, and they even kept a large float there during the winter months.

Nevertheless, the McKeags' possession was *not* hostile and adverse, which is the fourth requirement. The Finleys had substantial evidence that they gave the McKeags permission to use the beach. Rather than reject the Finleys' permission as unnecessary, the McKeags sometimes said nothing and other times seemingly affirmed that the property belonged to the Finleys. Thus, because the McKeags did not satisfy all four requirements, they cannot establish adverse possession.

37–5A. Case Problem with Sample Answer

Arvin and Carolyn were not correct. An executed will is revocable by the testator at any time during his or her life. The physical acts by which a testator may revoke a will include intentionally canceling it. In some states, partial revocation by physical act is recognized. Thus, those portions of a will lined out can be dropped, and the remaining parts of the will can be given effect.

Here, Peterson clearly altered her will by crossing out Arvin's and Carolyn's names as the beneficiaries of the trust. Apparently, Peterson intended to cancel only this portion of the will, not the entire will—her alterations left the bequest to Lucas intact. There is no indication in the facts of undue influence or other improper circumstances. Thus, the part of the will that Peterson lined out can be dropped, and the rest of the will can be given effect.

In the actual case on which this problem is based, the court held that the will was valid as altered.

APPENDIX I

Case Excerpts for *Case Analysis Questions*

CASE NO. 1 FOR CHAPTER 4

Lott v. Levitt, 469 F.Supp.2d 575 (E.D.Ill. 2007)

In 2005, well-known economist Steven Levitt ("Levitt") and journalist Stephen J. Dubner ("Dubner") coauthored the best-selling book *Freakonomics*[.] * * * In the book, Levitt and Dubner [discuss] * * * the theory for which fellow economist, * * * John R. Lott, Jr. ("Lott"), is known[:] * * * that laws permitting individuals to carry concealed weapons result in a statistically significant and provable reduction in serious crime rates. Lott filed the instant lawsuit against Levitt and [others] * * * . Lott claims [in part] that an email written by Levitt to another economist * * * constitutes defamation * * * . [Levitt filed a motion to dismiss this claim.]

* * * *

Lott is discussed in the following single paragraph in Chapter 4 of *Freakonomics*, entitled "Where Have All the Criminals Gone?":

> * * * There is an * * * argument—that we need more guns on the street, but in the hands of the right people * * * . The economist John R. Lott Jr. is the main champion of this idea. * * * [H]e argues that violent crime has decreased in areas where law abiding citizens are allowed to carry concealed weapons. His theory might be surprising, but it is sensible. If a criminal thinks his potential victim may be armed, he may be deterred from committing the crime. Handgun opponents call Lott a pro-gun ideologue * * * . There was the troubling allegation that Lott actually invented some of the survey data that support his more-guns/less-crime theory. Regardless of whether the data were faked, Lott's admittedly intriguing hypothesis doesn't seem to be true. When other scholars have tried to replicate his results, they found that right-to-carry laws simply don't bring down crime.

On May 24 or May 25, 2005, John McCall ("McCall"), described by Lott as an economist residing in Texas, sent Levitt an email regarding the above passage, stating:

> I * * * found the following citations—have not read any of them yet, but it appears they all replicate Lott's research. [McCall referred to a "Special Issue" of *The Journal of Law and Economics* published in October 2001 that contained a collection of articles delivered at an academic conference co-sponsored by the Center for Law, Economics and Public Policy at Yale Law School and the American Enterprise Institute, where Lott had recently been a resident scholar.] *The Journal of Law and Economics* is not chopped liver.

That same day, Levitt responded:

> It was not a peer refereed edition of the *Journal*. For $15,000 he was able to buy an issue and put in only work that supported him. My best friend was the editor and was outraged the press let Lott do this.

* * * *

A statement is considered defamatory if it tends to cause such harm to the reputation of another that it lowers that person in the eyes of the community or deters third persons from associating with that person. [Emphasis added.]

* * * *

* * * Lott contends that the statements about him in * * * the email * * * imply that his results were falsified or that his theories lack merit, and thus impute a lack of ability and integrity in his profession as an economist, academic, and researcher. Indeed, a claim that an academic or economist falsified his results and could only publish his theories by buying an issue of a journal and avoiding peer review would surely impute a lack of ability and prejudice that person in his profession.

* * * *

* * * *The First Amendment protects statements that cannot be reasonably interpreted as stating actual facts.* [Emphasis added.]

The test for whether a statement is a factual assertion is whether the statement is precise, readily understood, and susceptible of being verified as true or false. This test * * * is a reasonableness standard; whether a reasonable reader would understand the defendant to be informing him of a fact or opinion. Language that is loose, figurative, or hyperbolic negates the impression that a statement is asserting actual facts. Accordingly, *vague, unprovable statements and statements of opinion do not give rise to a defamation claim.* If it is plain that the speaker is expressing a subjective view, an interpretation, a theory, conjecture, or surmise, rather than claiming to be in possession of objectively verifiable facts, the statement is not actionable. [Emphasis added.]

In this case, however, Levitt's email sounds as if he was in possession of objectively verifiable facts. * * * First, it would be unreasonable to interpret Levitt's unqualified statement that the *Journal* edition was not "peer refereed" as Levitt [argues that he was] merely giving his opinion on the "peers" chosen to review, or referee, the Special Issue. Indeed, the editor of the *Journal* might be able to verify the truth or falsity of whether the Special Issue was reviewed by peers. * * * Second, a reasonable reader would not interpret Levitt's assertion that "For $15,000 [Lott] was able to buy an issue and put in only work that supported him" as simply a statement of Levitt's opinion. Levitt's email appears to state objectively verifiable facts: that Lott paid $15,000 to control the content of the Special Issue. The editor of the *Journal* again might be the source to verify the truth or falsity of this statement. Third, the same editor could verify whether he was "outraged" by the acts described in the foregoing statements. Therefore, the defamatory statements in Levitt's email to McCall are objectively verifiable * * *.

* * * *

* * * In his email to McCall, * * * Levitt made a string of defamatory assertions about Lott's involvement in the publication of the Special Issue of the *Journal* that—no matter how rash or shortsighted Levitt was when he made them—cannot be reasonably interpreted as innocent or mere opinion.

* * * Levitt's motion to dismiss [this part of Lott's] Complaint is denied.

CASE NO. 2 FOR CHAPTER 10

Feldman v. Google, Inc., 513 F.Supp.2d 229 (E.D.Pa. 2007)

Before the court is Defendant Google, Inc.'s Motion to * * * Transfer [the case to Santa Clara County]. Also before the court is Plaintiff Lawrence E. Feldman's Cross-Motion for Summary Judgment. The ultimate issues raised by the motions and determined by the court are whether a forum selection clause in an Internet "clickwrap" agreement is enforceable * * *.

Defendant's motion seeks to enforce the forum selection clause in an online "clickwrap" agreement, which provides for venue in Santa Clara County * * *.

On or about January 2003, Plaintiff, a lawyer with his own law firm, Lawrence E. Feldman & Associates, purchased advertising from Defendant Google, Inc.'s "AdWords" Program, to attract potential clients who may have been harmed by drugs under scrutiny by the U.S. Food and Drug Administration.

In the AdWords program, whenever an internet user searched on the internet search engine, Google.com, for keywords or "Adwords" purchased by Plaintiff, such as "Vioxx," "Bextra," and "Celebrex," Plaintiff's ad would appear. If the searcher clicked on Plaintiff's ad, Defendant would charge Plaintiff for each click made on the ad.

This procedure is known as "pay per click" advertising. The price per keyword is determined by a bidding process, wherein the highest bidder for a keyword would have its ad placed at the top of the list of results from a Google.com search by an Internet user.

Plaintiff claims that he was the victim of "click fraud." Click fraud occurs when entities or persons, such as competitors or pranksters, without any interest in Plaintiff's services, click repeatedly on Plaintiff's ad, the result of which drives up his advertising cost and discourages him from advertising. * * * Plaintiff alleges that twenty to thirty percent of all clicks for which he was charged were fraudulent. He claims that Google required him to pay for all clicks on his ads, including those which were fraudulent.

* * * *

The type of contract at issue here is commonly referred to as a "clickwrap" agreement. A clickwrap agreement appears on an Internet web page and requires that a user consent to any terms or conditions by clicking on a dialog box on the screen in order to proceed with the Internet transaction. *Even though they are electronic, clickwrap agreements are considered to be writings because they are printable and storable.* [Emphasis added.]

To determine whether a clickwrap agreement is enforceable, courts * * * apply traditional principles of contract law and focus on whether the plaintiffs had reasonable notice of and manifested assent to the clickwrap agreement. *Absent a showing of fraud, failure to read an enforceable clickwrap agreement, as with any binding contract, will not excuse compliance with its terms.* [Emphasis added.]

* * * *

Plaintiff [Feldman] claims he did not have notice or knowledge of the forum selection clause, and therefore that there was no "meeting of the minds" required for contract formation.

* * * *

* * * In order to activate an AdWords account, the user had to visit a Web page which displayed the Agreement in a scrollable text box. * * * The user did not have to scroll down to a submerged screen or click on a series of hyperlinks to view the Agreement. Instead, text of the AdWords Agreement was immediately visible to the user, as was a prominent admonition in boldface to read the terms and conditions carefully, and with instruction to indicate assent if the user agreed to the terms.

That the user would have to scroll through the text box of the Agreement to read it in its entirety does not defeat notice because there was sufficient notice of the Agreement itself and clicking "Yes" constituted assent to all of the terms. The preamble, which was immediately visible, also made clear that assent to the terms was binding. The Agreement was presented in readable 12-point font. It was only seven paragraphs long—not so long so as to render scrolling down to view all of the terms inconvenient or impossible. A printer-friendly, full-screen version was made readily available. The user had ample time to review the document.

* * * The user * * * had to take affirmative action and click the "Yes, I agree to the above terms and conditions" button in order to proceed to the next step. Clicking "Continue" without clicking the "Yes" button would have returned the user to the same Web page. If the user did not agree to all of the terms, he could not have activated his account, placed ads, or incurred charges.

* * * *

A reasonably prudent Internet user would have known of the existence of terms in the AdWords Agreement. Plaintiff had to have had reasonable notice of the terms. By clicking on "Yes, I agree to the above terms and conditions" button, Plaintiff indicated assent to the terms.

* * * *

For the foregoing reasons, * * * Defendant's motion to transfer is granted and Plaintiff's motion for summary judgment is denied.

CASE NO. 3 FOR CHAPTER 15

Spray-Tek, Inc. v. Robbins Motor Transportation, Inc., 426 F.Supp.2d 875 (W.D.Wis. 2006)

* * * *

Plaintiff Spray-Tek, Inc. is engaged in the business of commercial dehydration of food flavor, pharmaceutical and soft chemical products. In 2003 plaintiff entered into a contract with Niro, Inc. (hereinafter Niro) in which Niro was to design and manufacture a fourteen-foot diameter conebottom drying chamber * * * for plaintiff. Pursuant to the terms of the contract Niro was also responsible for shipping the drying chamber from its facility in Hudson, Wisconsin to plaintiff's facility in Bethlehem, Pennsylvania. The contract stated in relevant part:

* * * *

> For one (1) Niro-Bowen * * * drying chamber, * * * F.O.B. points of manufacture in the U.S.A. * * * Price * * * $1,161,500.00.
>
> * * * *
>
> IX. RISKS OF LOSS. The Purchaser shall bear the risk of loss of or damage to the equipment and parts after delivery of the equipment and parts to the job site or to the shipping point if delivery F.O.B. shipping point is specified.

On October 14, 2004, Niro's representative Mr. David Thoen contacted defendant Robbins Motor Transportation, Inc. to obtain an estimate for transporting the drying chamber to plaintiff. * * * Mr. Robert Kauffman, Jr. who serves as defendant's Southwest Regional Terminal Manager * * * prepared and sent an estimate to Niro.

Mr. Thoen signed the estimate and faxed it back to defendant * * *.

On October 18, 2004, defendant arrived at Niro's facility in Hudson, Wisconsin and the drying chamber was loaded onto its trailer. Niro prepared a Bill of Lading * * * .

* * * *

On or about October 28, 2004 the drying chamber was damaged while it was in transit * * * when it struck an overpass and became dislodged from defendant's vehicle. It was inspected and declared a total loss. Accordingly, Niro manufactured a replacement drying chamber for plaintiff and invoiced it $233,100.00 in replacement costs.

* * * *

[Spray-Tek filed a suit in a federal district court against Robbins under a federal statute known as the Carmack Amendment to recover the replacement cost and other expenses.] The Carmack Amendment * * * states in relevant part:

> A carrier providing transportation or service * * * shall issue a receipt or bill of lading for property it receives for transportation under this part. That carrier * * * [is] liable to the person entitled to recover under the receipt or bill of lading.

The purpose of the Carmack Amendment is to establish uniform federal guidelines designed in part to remove the uncertainty surrounding a carrier's liability when damage occurs to a shipper's interstate shipment.

Under the Carmack Amendment plaintiff bears the burden of establishing a *prima facie* [legally sufficient] case which requires it to demonstrate: (1) delivery to the carrier in good condition; (2) arrival in damaged condition; and (3) the amount of damages. * * * The excepted causes [relieving a carrier of liability] are: (1) acts of God; (2) the public enemy; (3) acts of the shipper himself; (4) public authority; or (5) the inherent vice or nature of the goods.

Defendant concedes that it received the drying chamber in good condition. Accordingly, plaintiff's first element of its *prima facie* case is established.

* * * *

It is undisputed that the drying chamber was damaged when it struck an overpass and became dislodged from defendant's vehicle. Additionally, it is undisputed that after the accident the drying chamber was inspected and declared a total loss.

An * * * argument defendant asserts concerning plaintiff's second element of its *prima facie* case is that plaintiff cannot demonstrate it owned the drying chamber during transport. However, the contract plaintiff entered into with Niro establishes that it was the owner of the drying chamber when it was damaged. The contract provided that the terms of sale were "F.O.B. points of manufacture in the U.S.A." According to * * * plaintiff's vice president and general manager "F.O.B. points of manufacture" means that the drying chamber became plaintiff's property once it was "placed on board the delivery truck at its point of manufacture in Hudson, Wisconsin."

[This] assertion * * * is reinforced by the provision in the contract concerning risks of loss. * * * [T]he "F.O.B. points of manufacture" language * * * demonstrates that plaintiff bore the risk of loss once the drying chamber departed from Niro's Hudson, Wisconsin facility. * * * Accordingly, plaintiff established the second element of its *prima facie* case.

Finally, defendant asserts plaintiff cannot meet its burden of establishing the third element of its *prima facie* case because it failed to demonstrate what "it is obligated to pay for the dryer." However, * * * Niro invoiced plaintiff $233,100.00 for the replacement dryer. Accordingly, plaintiff established the third element of its *prima facie* case because its amount of damages is $233,100.00.

Plaintiff met its burden of establishing a *prima facie* case under the Carmack Amendment. * * * Defendant concedes it failed to produce any evidence establishing that damage to the shipment was due to one of the excepted causes. Accordingly, plaintiff is entitled to summary judgment on the issue of defendant's liability under the Carmack Amendment.

* * * *

[The court allowed the case to go to trial on another issue, however.]

CASE NO. 4 FOR CHAPTER 19

NBT Bank, N.A. v. First National Community Bank, 393 F.3d 404 (3d Cir. 2004)

* * * *

* * * [A] small group of Pennsylvania business entities arranged to write checks on one account, drawing on non-existent funds, and then cover these overdrafts with checks drawn on another account that also lacked sufficient funds. * * * The scheme collapsed when three checks initially deposited at [NBT Bank, N.A.,] and subsequently presented for payment to [First National Community Bank (FNCB)] were discovered by FNCB to have been drawn on an FNCB account that lacked sufficient funds. There is no dispute between the parties that two of these three checks were properly returned by FNCB to the [Federal Reserve Bank of Philadelphia] prior to the applicable midnight deadline.

* * * *

[On March 8, 2001, the third check (the "Disputed Check"), which was drawn on an FNCB account in the amount of $706,000, was deposited at NBT by an entity called PA Health.] After the Disputed Check was presented for deposit at NBT, the bank gave provisional credit to the depositor, PA Health, for the amount of the Disputed Check. NBT also transmitted the Disputed Check to the Reserve Bank for presentment to FNCB. * * * The Reserve Bank then forwarded the Disputed Check to FNCB, and FNCB received it on March 12, 2001.

* * * *

On March 13, 2001, FNCB determined it would not pay the Disputed Check because of the absence of sufficient funds in the account on which the check was drawn. That same day, FNCB sought to return the Disputed Check to NBT through the Reserve Bank. * * * [T]he Disputed Check was physically delivered to the Reserve Bank prior to 11:59 P.M. on March 13.* * * FNCB also sent a notice of dishonor to NBT * * * in which FNCB indicated that it did not intend to pay the Disputed Check. NBT received this notice prior to the close of business on March 13.

* * * *

When FNCB sent the Disputed Check to the Reserve Bank on March 13, 2001, FNCB * * * erroneously encoded [it] with the routing number for PNC Bank instead of the routing number for NBT [Bank].

* * * Because the Disputed Check was improperly encoded, NBT did not receive it back * * * until March 16, 2001. * * * NBT suffered no damages or actual loss as a result of the encoding error * * * .

* * * *

NBT instituted this action [in a federal district court] against FNCB on May 25, 2001. * * * NBT claimed that FNCB's encoding error meant FNCB had failed to return the Disputed Check prior to the midnight deadline as required by the UCC, and that FNCB was therefore accountable to NBT for the full amount of the Disputed Check.

The District Court granted FNCB's motion [for summary judgment]. NBT appeals.

* * * *

* * * Federal law forms part of the legal framework within which check-processing activities take place. Of particular relevance to this appeal are the 1988 regulations adopted by the Federal Reserve implementing the Expedited Funds Availability Act. These regulations, referred to collectively as "Regulation CC," complement but do not necessarily replace the requirements of Article 4 of the UCC.

* * * *

* * * Regulation CC indisputably binds the parties, pursuant to both its own terms, as well as [13 Pennsylvania Consolidated Statutes Annotated Section 4103 (Pennsylvania's version of UCC 4–103)], which indicates that "Federal Reserve regulations" are to be treated as agreements that may vary the terms of the UCC.

Because Regulation CC * * * is binding on the parties, and because Regulation CC is the source of the encoding requirement invoked by NBT, the extent of FNCB's liability for its encoding error must be measured by the standards set forth in Regulation CC. *Regulation CC states that a bank that fails to exercise ordinary care in complying with the [encoding] provisions of * * * Regulation CC * * * "may be liable" to the depositary bank.* Then, in broad, unrestricted language, Regulation CC states: [Emphasis added.]

> The measure of damages for failure to exercise ordinary care is the amount of the loss incurred, up to the amount of the check, reduced by the amount of the loss that the [plaintiff bank] would have incurred even if the [defendant] bank had exercised ordinary care.

This provision does not provide an exception to this standard for measuring damages in instances where noncompliance with Regulation CC is alleged to have resulted in noncompliance with the UCC's midnight deadline rule. Here, the parties have stipulated that NBT suffered no loss as a result of FNCB's encoding error. Thus, under the plain language of Regulation CC, NBT may not recover from FNCB for the amount of the Disputed Check.

* * * *

Accordingly,* * * we affirm the order of the District Court * * * .

CASE NO. 5 FOR CHAPTER 25

Burlington Northern and Santa Fe Railway Co. v. White, 548 U.S. 53, 126 S.Ct. 2405, 165 L.Ed.2d 345 (2006)

* * * *

* * * Sheila White [was] the only woman working in the Maintenance of Way department at [Burlington Northern & Santa Fe Railway Company's] Tennessee Yard. In September 1997, White complained to Burlington officials that her * * * supervisor, Bill Joiner, had repeatedly told her that women should not be working

in the Maintenance of Way department. [Joiner was disciplined. White was reassigned from forklift duty to "track laborer" tasks.]

* * * *

On October 10, White filed a complaint with the Equal Employment Opportunity Commission (EEOC * * *).

[In December, White's supervisor, Percy Sharkey, complained to Burlington officials that White had been insubordinate. She was suspended without pay but reinstated after an investigation and awarded back pay for the period of the suspension. White filed a second charge with the EEOC.]

* * * *

* * * [Later] White filed this Title VII action against Burlington in federal [district] court. * * * [S]he claimed that Burlington's actions—(1) changing her job responsibilities, and (2) suspending her * * * without pay—amounted to unlawful retaliation in violation of Title VII. A jury found in White's favor * * * [and] awarded her $43,500 in * * * damages * * * .

* * * [On appeal, the U.S. Court of Appeals for the Sixth Circuit held that Title VII's antiretaliation ban is limited to acts that adversely affect the terms, conditions, or benefits of employment, and] affirmed the District Court's judgment in White's favor on both retaliation claims. [Burlington appealed to the United States Supreme Court.]

* * * *

* * * The language of the [antidiscrimination] provision differs from that of the antiretaliation provision in important ways.

The * * * words in the [antidiscrimination] provision—"hire," "discharge," "compensation, terms, conditions, or privileges of employment," "employment opportunities," and "status as an employee"—explicitly limit the scope of that provision to actions that affect employment or alter the conditions of the workplace. No such limiting words appear in the antiretaliation provision.

* * * The two provisions differ not only in language but in purpose as well. The antidiscrimination provision seeks a workplace where individuals are not discriminated against because of their racial, ethnic, religious, or gender-based status. *The antiretaliation provision seeks to secure that primary objective by preventing an employer from interfering (through retaliation) with an employee's efforts to secure or advance enforcement of the Act's basic guarantees.* The [antidiscrimination] provision seeks to prevent injury to individuals based on who they are, i.e., their status. *The antiretaliation provision seeks to prevent harm to individuals based on what they do, i.e., their conduct.* [Emphasis added.]

To secure the first objective, Congress did not need to prohibit anything other than employment related discrimination.

But one cannot secure the second objective by focusing only upon employer actions and harm that concern employment and the workplace. * * * *An employer can effectively retaliate against an employee by taking actions not directly related to his employment or by causing him harm outside the workplace.* [Emphasis added.]

* * * *

* * * We conclude that * * * the anti-retaliation provision extends beyond workplace related or employment-related retaliatory acts * * * .

* * * *

* * * A plaintiff must show that a reasonable employee would have found the challenged action materially adverse, which in this context means it well might have dissuaded a reasonable worker from making or supporting a charge of discrimination.

* * * *

* * * [In this case] the track labor duties were by all accounts more arduous and dirtier; * * * the forklift operator position required more qualifications, which is an indication of prestige; and * * * the forklift operator position was objectively considered a better job and the male employees resented White for occupying it. Based on this record, a jury could reasonably conclude that the reassignment of responsibilities would have been materially adverse to a reasonable employee.

* * * *

For these reasons, the judgment of the Court of Appeals is affirmed.

CASE NO. 6 FOR CHAPTER 31

Merrill Lynch, Pierce, Fenner & Smith, Inc. v. Dabit, 547 U.S. 71, 126 S.Ct. 1503, 164 L.Ed.2d 179 (2006)

* * * *

Petitioner Merrill Lynch, Pierce, Fenner & Smith, Inc. (Merrill Lynch), * * * offers research and brokerage services to investors.

Respondent, Shadi Dabit, is a former Merrill Lynch broker. He filed this class action in the United States District Court for the Western District of Oklahoma on behalf of himself and all other former or current brokers who, while employed by Merrill Lynch, purchased (for themselves and for their clients) certain stocks between December 1, 1999, and December 31, 2000. * * * Dabit * * * advanced his claims under Oklahoma state law.

* * * [Dabit's theory was that Merrill Lynch] research analysts * * * issued overly optimistic appraisals of the stocks' value; the brokers * * * relied on the analysts' reports in advising their investor clients * * * ; and the clients and brokers both continued to hold their stocks long beyond the point when, had the truth been known, they would have sold. * * * [W]hen the truth was actually revealed * * * , the stocks' prices plummeted.

* * * *

* * * [The case was transferred] to the United States District Court for the Southern District of New York * * * [which granted Merrill Lynch's motion to dismiss. The U.S. Court of Appeals for the Second Circuit reversed this ruling. Merrill Lynch appealed to the United States Supreme Court.]

* * * *

The magnitude of the federal interest in protecting the integrity and efficient operation of the market for nationally traded securities cannot be overstated. In response to the sudden and disastrous collapse in prices of listed stocks in 1929, and the Great Depression that followed, Congress enacted the Securities Act of 1933, and the Securities Exchange Act of 1934. Since their enactment, these two statutes have anchored federal regulation of vital elements of our economy.

* * * *

Policy considerations * * * prompted Congress, in 1995, to adopt [the Private Securities Litigation Reform Act] targeted at perceived abuses of the class-action vehicle in litigation involving nationally traded securities.

* * * *

* * * [P]laintiffs and their representatives began bringing class actions under state law, often in state court. * * * To stem this shift from Federal to State courts * * * , Congress enacted SLUSA.

* * * *

The core provision of SLUSA reads as follows:

> * * * No * * * class action based upon the * * * law of any State * * * may be maintained in any * * * court by any private party alleging—* * * a misrepresentation or omission of a material fact in connection with the purchase or sale of a * * * security * * * .

* * * *

* * * Under our precedents, it is enough that the fraud alleged "coincide" with a securities transaction—whether by the plaintiff or by someone else. *The requisite showing, in other words, is deception "in connection with the purchase or sale of any security," not deception of an identifiable purchaser or seller.* Notably, this broader interpretation of the statutory language comports [is consistent] with the longstanding views of the [Securities and Exchange Commission (SEC)]. [Emphasis added.]

Congress can hardly have been unaware of the broad construction adopted by both this Court and the SEC when it imported the key phrase—"in connection with the purchase or sale"—into SLUSA's core provision. *And when judicial interpretations have settled the meaning of an existing statutory provision, repetition of the same language in a new statute indicates * * * the intent to incorporate its * * * judicial interpretations as well.* [Emphasis added.]

* * * A narrow reading of the statute would undercut the effectiveness of the 1995 Reform Act and thus run contrary to SLUSA's stated purpose "to prevent certain State private securities class action lawsuits alleging fraud from being used to frustrate the objectives" of the 1995 Act.

* * * The prospect is raised, then, of parallel class actions proceeding in state and federal court, with different standards governing claims asserted on identical facts. That prospect * * * squarely conflicts with the congressional preference for national standards for securities class action lawsuits involving nationally traded securities.

* * * *

The judgment of the Court of Appeals for the Second Circuit is vacated, and the case is remanded * * * .

CASE NO. 7 FOR CHAPTER 36

Kelo v. City of New London, Connecticut, 545 U.S. 469, 125 S.Ct. 2655, 162 L.Ed.2d 439 (2005)

* * * *

The city of New London (hereinafter City) sits at the junction of the Thames River and the Long Island Sound in southeastern Connecticut. Decades of economic decline led a state agency in 1990 to designate the City a "distressed municipality." In 1996, the Federal Government closed the Naval Undersea Warfare Center, which had been located in the Fort Trumbull area of the City and had employed over 1,500 people. In 1998, the City's unemployment rate was nearly double that of the State, and its population of just under 24,000 residents was at its lowest since 1920.

These conditions prompted state and local officials to target New London * * * for economic revitalization. * * * In February [1998] the pharmaceutical company Pfizer Inc. announced that it would build a $300 million research facility on a site immediately adjacent to Fort Trumbull; local planners hoped that Pfizer would draw new business to the area * * *.

* * * *

The city council approved [a] plan in January 2000 [to redevelop the area that once housed the federal facility]. The [City] successfully negotiated the purchase of most of the real estate in the 90-acre area, but its negotiations with [some of the property owners] failed. As a consequence, in November 2000, the [City] initiated * * * condemnation proceedings * * *.

* * * *

* * * Susette Kelo has lived in the Fort Trumbull area since 1997. * * * [S]he prizes [her house] for its water view. * * *

In December 2000 [Kelo and others] brought this action in [a Connecticut state court against the City and others]. They claimed, among other things, that the taking of their properties would violate the "public use" restriction in the [U.S. Constitution's] Fifth Amendment. * * * [The court issued a ruling partly in favor of both sides].

* * * [B]oth sides took appeals to the Supreme Court of Connecticut [which] held * * * that all of the City's proposed takings were valid.

* * * *

We granted *certiorari* to determine whether a city's decision to take property for the purpose of economic development satisfies the "public use" requirement of the Fifth Amendment.

* * * *

* * * [T]his Court long ago rejected any literal requirement that condemned property be put into use for the general public. * * * Not only was the "use by the public" test difficult to administer (e.g., what proportion of the public need have access to the property? at what price?), but it proved to be impractical given the diverse and always evolving needs of society. Accordingly, * * * *this Court * * * embraced the broader and more natural interpretation of public use as "public purpose."* * * * [Emphasis added.]

The disposition of this case therefore turns on the question whether the City's development plan serves a "public purpose."

* * * *

Viewed as a whole, our jurisprudence has recognized that the needs of society have varied between different parts of the Nation, just as they have evolved over time in response to changed circumstances. * * * *For more than a century, our public use jurisprudence has wisely eschewed [avoided] rigid formulas and intrusive scrutiny in favor of affording legislatures broad latitude in* *determining what public needs justify the use of the takings power.* [Emphasis added.]

* * * *

Those who govern the City were not confronted with the need to remove blight in the Fort Trumbull area, but their determination that the area was sufficiently distressed to justify a program of economic rejuvenation is entitled to our deference. The City has carefully formulated an economic development plan that it believes will provide appreciable benefits to the community, including—but by no means limited to—new jobs and increased tax revenue. * * * To effectuate this plan, the City has invoked a state statute that specifically authorizes the use of eminent domain to promote economic development. Given the comprehensive character of the plan, the thorough deliberation that preceded its adoption, and the limited scope of our review, it is appropriate for us * * * to resolve the challenges of the individual owners, not on a piecemeal basis,but rather in light of the entire plan. *Because that plan unquestionably serves a public purpose, the takings challenged here satisfy the public use requirement of the Fifth Amendment.* [Emphasis added.]

* * * *

The judgment of the Supreme Court of Connecticut is affirmed.

Glossary

A

Abandoned Property Property that has been discarded by the owner, who has no intention of reclaiming it.

Acceleration Clause A clause that allows a payee or other holder of a time instrument to demand payment of the entire amount due, with interest, if a certain event occurs, such as a default in the payment of an installment when due. In a mortgage loan contract, a clause that makes the entire loan balance become due if the borrower misses or is late making the monthly payments.

Acceptance The act of voluntarily agreeing, through words or conduct, to the terms of an offer, thereby creating a contract. In negotiable instruments law, a drawee's signed agreement to pay a draft when it is presented.

Acceptor A drawee that accepts, or promises to pay, an instrument when it is presented later for payment.

Accession The addition of value to personal property by the use of labor or materials. In some situations, a person may acquire ownership rights in another's property through accession.

Accord and Satisfaction A common means of settling a disputed claim, whereby a debtor offers to pay a lesser amount than the creditor purports to be owed.

Accredited Investor In the context of securities offerings, "sophisticated" investors, such as banks, insurance companies, investment companies, the issuer's executive officers and directors, and persons whose income or net worth exceeds certain limits.

Actionable Capable of serving as the basis of a lawsuit. An actionable claim can be pursued in a lawsuit or other court action.

Act of State Doctrine A doctrine providing that the judicial branch of one country will not examine the validity of public acts committed by a recognized foreign government within its own territory.

Actual Malice The deliberate intent to cause harm that exists when a person makes a statement with either knowledge of its falsity or reckless disregard of the truth. Actual malice is required to establish defamation against public figures.

Actus reus A guilty (prohibited) act. The commission of a prohibited act is one of the two essential elements required for criminal liability, the other element being the intent to commit a crime.

Adhesion Contract A standard-form contract in which the stronger party dictates the terms.

Adjudicate To render a judicial decision. Adjudication is the trial-like proceeding in which an administrative law judge hears and resolves disputes involving an administrative agency's regulations.

Adjustable-Rate Mortgage (ARM) A mortgage with a rate of interest that changes periodically, often with reference to a predetermined government interest rate (the index).

Administrative Agency A federal or state government agency created by the legislature to perform a specific function, such as to make and enforce rules pertaining to the environment.

Administrative Law The body of law created by administrative agencies in order to carry out their duties and responsibilities.

Administrative Law Judge (ALJ) One who presides over an administrative agency hearing and has the power to administer oaths, take testimony, rule on questions of evidence, and make determinations of fact.

Administrative Process The procedure used by administrative agencies in administering the law.

Administrator One who is appointed by a court to administer a person's estate if the decedent died without a valid will or if the executor named in the will cannot serve.

Adverse Possession The acquisition of title to real property by occupying it openly, without the consent of the owner, for a period of time specified by a state statute. The occupation must be actual, exclusive, open, continuous, and in opposition to all others, including the owner.

Affirmative Action Job-hiring policies that give special consideration to members of protected classes in an effort to overcome present effects of past discrimination.

After-Acquired Property Property that is acquired by the debtor after the execution of a security agreement.

Agency A relationship between two parties in which one party (the agent) agrees to represent or act for the other (the principal).

Agreement A mutual understanding or meeting of the minds between two or more individuals regarding the terms of a contract.

Alienation The of transfer of land out of one's possession (thus "alienating" the land from oneself).

Alien Corporation A corporation formed in another country but doing business in the United States.

Alternative Dispute Resolution (ADR) The resolution of disputes in ways other than those involved in the traditional judicial process, such as negotiation, mediation, and arbitration.

Annual Percentage Rate (APR) The cost of credit on a yearly basis, typically expressed as an annual percentage.

Answer Procedurally, a defendant's response to the plaintiff's complaint.

Anticipatory Repudiation An assertion or action by a party indicating that he or she will not perform a contractual obligation.

Antitrust Law Laws protecting commerce from unlawful restraints and anticompetitive practices.

Apparent Authority Authority that is only apparent, not real. An agent's apparent authority arises when the principal causes a third party to believe that the agent has authority, even though she or he does not.

Appraisal Right The right of a dissenting shareholder, who objects to a merger or consolidation of the corporation, to have his or her shares appraised and to be paid the fair value of those shares by the corporation.

Appraiser An individual who specializes in determining the value of specified real or personal property.

Appropriation In tort law, the use by one person of another person's name, likeness, or other identifying characteristic without permission and for the benefit of the user.

Arbitration Clause A clause in a contract that provides that, in the event of a dispute, the parties will submit the dispute to arbitration rather than litigate the dispute in court.

Arbitration The settling of a dispute by submitting it to a disinterested third party (other than a court), who renders a decision.

Arson The intentional burning of a building.

Articles of Incorporation The document containing basic information about the corporation that is filed with the appropriate state official, usually the secretary of state, when a business is incorporated.

Articles of Organization The document filed with a designated state official by which a limited liability company is formed.

Articles of Partnership A written agreement that sets forth each partner's rights and obligations with respect to the partnership.

Artisan's Lien A possessory lien on personal property of another person to ensure payment to a person who has made improvements on and added value to that property.

Assault Any word or action intended to make another person fearful of immediate physical harm—a reasonably believable threat.

Assignee A party to whom the rights under a contract are transferred, or assigned.

Assignment The transfer to another of all or part of one's rights arising under a contract.

Assignor A party who transfers (assigns) his or her rights under a contract to another party (called the *assignee*).

Assumption of Risk A defense to negligence. A plaintiff may not recover for injuries or damage suffered from risks he or she knows of and has voluntarily assumed.

Attachment The legal process of seizing another's property under a court order to secure satisfaction of a judgment yet to be rendered. In a secured transaction, the process by which a secured creditor's interest "attaches" to the collateral and the creditor's security interest becomes enforceable.

Attempted Monopolization An action by a firm that involves anticompetitive conduct, the intent to gain monopoly power, and a "dangerous probability" of success in achieving monopoly power.

Authorization Card A card signed by an employee that gives a union permission to act on his or her behalf in negotiations with management.

Automatic Stay In bankruptcy proceedings, the suspension of almost all litigation and other action by creditors against the debtor or the debtor's property. The stay is effective the moment the debtor files a petition in bankruptcy.

Average Prime Offer Rate The mortgage rate offered to the best-qualified borrowers as established by a survey of lenders.

Award The monetary compensation given to a party at the end of a trial or other proceeding.

B

Bailee One to whom goods are entrusted by a bailor.

Bailee's Lien A possessory (artisan's) lien that a bailee entitled to compensation can place on the bailed property to ensure that he or she will be paid for the services provided.

Bailee Under the UCC, a party who, by a bill of lading, warehouse receipt, or other document of title, acknowledges possession of goods and/or contracts to deliver them.

Bailment A situation in which the personal property of one person (a bailor) is entrusted to another (a bailee), who is obligated to return the bailed property to the bailor or dispose of it as directed.

Bailor One who entrusts goods to a bailee.

Bait-and-Switch Advertising Advertising a product at an attractive price and then telling the consumer that the advertised product is not available or is of poor quality and encouraging her or him to purchase a more expensive item.

Balloon Mortgage A mortgage that allows the borrower to make small monthly payments for an initial period, such as eight years, but then requires the entire remaining balance of the mortgage loan to be paid at the end of that period.

Bankruptcy Court A federal court of limited jurisdiction that handles only bankruptcy proceedings, which are governed by federal bankruptcy law.

Battery Unexcused, harmful or offensive, physical contact with another that is intentionally performed.

Bearer A person in possession of an instrument payable to bearer or indorsed in blank.

Bearer Instrument Any instrument that is not payable to a specific person, including instruments payable to the bearer or to "cash."

Bequest A gift of personal property by will (from the verb *to bequeath*).

Beyond a Reasonable Doubt The standard of proof used in criminal cases.

Bilateral Contract A type of contract that arises when a promise is given in exchange for a return promise.

Bill of Rights The first ten amendments to the U.S. Constitution.

Binder A written, temporary insurance policy.

Binding Authority Any source of law that a court *must* follow when deciding a case.

Blank Indorsement An indorsement that specifies no particular indorsee and can consist of a mere signature. An order instrument that is indorsed in blank becomes a bearer instrument.

Blue Sky Laws State laws that regulate the offering and sale of securities for the protection of the public.

Bona Fide Occupational Qualification (BFOQ) Identifiable characteristics reasonably necessary to the normal operation of a particular business. These characteristics can include gender, national origin, and religion, but not race.

Bond A security that evidences a corporate (or government) debt.

Bond Indenture The agreement between the issuer of a bond and the bondholder that sets out the terms and features of the bond issue.

Botnet A network of compromised computers connected to the Internet that can be used to generate spam, relay viruses, or cause servers to fail.

Breach The failure to perform a legal obligation.

Breach of Contract The failure, without legal excuse, of a promisor to perform the obligations of a contract.

Bridge Loan A short-term loan that allows a buyer to make a down payment on a new home before selling the current home, which is used as collateral for the loan.

Brief A written summary or statement prepared by one side in a lawsuit to explain its case to the judge.

Browse-Wrap Term A term or condition of use that is presented when an online buyer downloads a product but the buyer does not have to agree to before installing or using the product.

Burglary The unlawful entry or breaking into a building with the intent to commit a felony.

Business Ethics What constitutes right or wrong behavior and the application of moral principles in a business context.

Business Invitee A person, such as a customer or a client, who is invited onto business premises by the owner of those premises for business purposes.

Business Judgment Rule A rule that immunizes corporate directors and officers from liability for decisions that result in corporate losses or damages as long as the decision makers took reasonable steps to become informed, had a rational basis for their decisions, and did not have a conflict of interest with the corporation.

Business Necessity A defense to an allegation of employment discrimination in which the employer demonstrates that an employment practice that discriminates against members of a protected class is related to job performance.

Business Tort Wrongful interference with another's business rights and relationships.

Business Trust A form of business organization, created by a written trust agreement, that resembles a corporation. Legal ownership and management of the trust's property stay with the trustees, and the profits are distributed to the beneficiaries, who have limited liability.

Buyout Price The amount payable to a partner on his or her dissociation from a partnership, based on the amount distributable to that partner if the firm were wound up on that date, and offset by any damages for wrongful dissociation.

Bylaws The internal rules of management adopted by a corporation at its first organizational meeting.

C

Case Law The rules of law announced in court decisions. Case law interprets statutes, regulations, constitutional provisions, and other case law.

Cashier's Check A check drawn by a bank on itself.

Categorical Imperative An ethical guideline developed by Immanuel Kant under which an action is evaluated in terms of what would happen if everybody else in the same situation, or category, acted the same way.

Causation in Fact An act or omission without which an event would not have occurred.

Cease-and-Desist Order An administrative or judicial order prohibiting a person or business firm from conducting activities that an agency or court has deemed illegal.

Certificate of Deposit (CD) A note issued by a bank in which the bank acknowledges the receipt of funds from a party and promises to repay that amount, with interest, to the party on a certain date.

Certificate of Limited Partnership The document that must be filed with a designated state official to form a limited partnership.

Certification Mark A mark used by one or more persons, other than the owner, to certify the region, materials, mode of manufacture, quality, or other characteristic of specific goods or services.

Certified Check A check that has been accepted in writing by the bank on which it is drawn. By certifying (accepting) the check, the bank promises to pay the check at the time it is presented.

Charging Order In partnership law, an order granted by a court to a judgment creditor that entitles the creditor to attach a partner's interest in the partnership.

Charitable Trust A trust in which the property held by the trustee must be used for a charitable purpose, such as the advancement of health, education, or religion.

Chattel All forms of personal property.

Check A draft drawn by a drawer ordering the drawee bank or financial institution to pay a certain amount of funds to the payee on demand.

Checks and Balances The principle under which the powers of the national government are divided among three separate branches—the executive, legislative, and judicial branches—each of which exercises a check on the actions of the others.

Choice-of-Language Clause A clause in a contract designating the official language by which the contract will be interpreted in the event of a disagreement over the contract's terms.

Choice-of-Law Clause A clause in a contract designating the law (such as the law of a particular state or nation) that will govern the contract.

Citation A reference to a publication in which a legal authority—such as a statute or a court decision—or other source can be found.

Civil Law The branch of law dealing with the definition and enforcement of all private or public rights, as opposed to criminal matters.

Civil Law System A system of law derived from Roman law that is based on codified laws (rather than on case precedents).

Clearinghouse A system or place where banks exchange checks and drafts drawn on each other and settle daily balances.

Click-on Agreement An agreement that arises when an online buyer clicks on "I agree," or otherwise indicates her or his assent to be bound by the terms of an offer.

Close Corporation A corporation whose shareholders are limited to a small group of persons, often only family members.

Closed Shop A firm that requires union membership by its workers as a condition of employment, which is illegal.

Cloud Computing A Web-based service that extends a computer's software or storage capabilities by allowing users to remotely access excess storage and computing capacity as needed.

Codicil A written supplement or modification to a will. A codicil must be executed with the same formalities as a will.

Collateral Under Article 9 of the UCC, the property subject to a security interest.

Collateral Promise A secondary promise to a primary transaction, such as a promise made by one person to pay the debts of another if the latter fails to perform. A collateral promise normally must be in writing to be enforceable.

Collecting Bank Any bank handling an item for collection, except the payor bank.

Collective Bargaining The process by which labor and management negotiate the terms and conditions of employment, including working hours and workplace conditions.

Collective Mark A mark used by members of a cooperative, association, union, or other organization to certify the region, materials, mode of manufacture, quality, or other characteristic of specific goods or services.

Comity The principle by which one nation defers to and gives effect to the laws and judicial decrees of another nation. This recognition is based primarily on respect.

Commerce Clause The provision in Article I, Section 8, of the U.S. Constitution that gives Congress the power to regulate interstate commerce.

Commercial Impracticability A doctrine that may excuse the duty to perform a contract when performance becomes much more difficult or costly due to forces that neither party could control or contemplate at the time the contract was formed.

Commingle To put funds or goods together into one mass so that they are mixed to such a degree that they no longer have separate identities, as when personal and corporate interests are mixed together to the extent that the corporation has no separate identity.

Common Law The body of law developed from custom or judicial decisions in English and U.S. courts, not attributable to a legislature.

Common Stock Shares of ownership in a corporation that give the owner of the stock a proportionate interest in the corporation with regard to control, earnings, and net assets. Common stock is lowest in priority with respect to payment of dividends and distribution of the corporation's assets on dissolution.

Community Property A form of concurrent ownership of property in which each spouse owns an undivided one-half interest in property acquired during the marriage.

Comparative Negligence A rule in tort law, used in the majority of states, that reduces the plaintiff's recovery in proportion to the plaintiff's degree of fault, rather than barring recovery completely.

Compelling Government Interest A test of constitutionality that requires the government to have convincing reasons for passing any law that restricts fundamental rights, such as free speech, or distinguishes between people based on a suspect trait.

Compensatory Damages A monetary award equivalent to the actual value of injuries or damage sustained by the aggrieved party.

Complaint The pleading made by a plaintiff alleging wrongdoing on the part of the defendant. When filed with a court, the complaint initiates a lawsuit.

Computer Crime The unlawful use of a computer or network to take or alter data, or to gain the use of computers or services without authorization.

Concentrated Industry An industry in which a single firm or a small number of firms control a large percentage of market sales.

Concurrent Conditions Conditions that must occur or be performed at the same time—they are mutually dependent. No obligations arise until these conditions are simultaneously performed.

Concurrent Jurisdiction Jurisdiction that exists when two different courts have the power to hear a case.

Concurrent Ownership Joint ownership.

Concurring Opinion A court opinion by one or more judges or justices who agree with the majority but want to make or emphasize a point that was not made or emphasized in the majority's opinion.

Condemnation The process of taking private property for public use through the government's power of eminent domain.

Condition A qualification, provision, or clause in a contractual agreement, the occurrence or nonoccurrence of which creates, suspends, or terminates the obligations of the contracting parties.

Condition Precedent A condition in a contract that must be met before a party's promise becomes absolute.

Condition Subsequent A condition in a contract that, if it occurs, operates to terminate a party's absolute promise to perform.

Confession of Judgment The act or agreement of a debtor permitting a judgment to be entered against him or her by a creditor, for an agreed sum, without the institution of legal proceedings.

Confiscation A government's taking of a privately owned business or personal property without a proper public purpose or an award of just compensation.

Conforming Goods Goods that conform to contract specifications.

Confusion The mixing together of goods belonging to two or more owners to such an extent that the separately owned goods cannot be identified.

Consequential Damages Special damages that compensate for a loss that does not directly or immediately result from a breach of contract (such as lost profits), but was reasonably foreseeable at the time the breach or injury occurred.

Consideration The value given in return for a promise or performance in a contractual agreement.

Consolidation The legal combination of two or more corporations in such a way that the original corporations cease to exist, and a new corporation emerges with all their assets and liabilities.

Constitutional Law The body of law derived from the U.S. Constitution and the constitutions of the various states.

Constructive Delivery A symbolic delivery of property that cannot be physically delivered. Constructive delivery confers the right to possession of the property, but not the actual possession.

Constructive Discharge A termination of employment brought about by making the employee's working conditions so intolerable that the employee reasonably feels compelled to leave.

Constructive Eviction A form of eviction that occurs when a landlord fails to perform adequately any of the duties required by the lease, thereby making the tenant's further use and enjoyment of the property exceedingly difficult or impossible.

Constructive Trust An equitable trust that is imposed in the interests of fairness and justice when someone wrongfully holds legal title to property.

Consumer-Debtor One whose debts result primarily from the purchases of goods for personal, family, or household use.

Continuation Statement A statement that, if filed within six months prior to the expiration date of the original financing statement, continues the perfection of the security interest for another five years.

Contract A set of promises constituting an agreement between parties, giving each a legal duty to the other and also the right to seek a remedy for the breach of the promises or duties.

Contractual Capacity The capacity required by the law for a party who enters into a contract to be bound by that contract.

Contributory Negligence A rule in tort law, used in only a few states, that completely bars the plaintiff from recovering any damages if the damage suffered is partly the plaintiff's own fault.

Conversion Wrongfully taking or retaining possession of an individual's personal property and placing it in the service of another.

Conveyance The transfer of title to real property from one person to another by deed or other document.

"Cooling-off" Laws Laws that allow buyers to cancel door-to-door sales contracts within a certain period of time, such as three business days.

Cooperative An association, which may or may not be incorporated, that is organized to provide an economic service to its members. Unincorporated cooperatives are often treated like partnerships for tax and other legal purposes.

Copyright The exclusive right of an author or originator of a literary or artistic production to publish, print, sell, or otherwise use that production for a statutory period of time.

Corporate Governance A set of policies specifying the rights and responsibilities of the various participants in a corporation and spelling out the rules and procedures for making corporate decisions.

Corporate Social Responsibility The idea that corporations can and should act ethically and be accountable to society for their actions.

Corporation A legal entity formed in compliance with statutory requirements that is distinct from its shareholder-owners.

Correspondent Bank A bank in which another bank has an account (and vice versa) for the purpose of facilitating fund transfers.

Cost-Benefit Analysis A decision-making technique that involves weighing the costs of a given action against the benefits of that action.

Co-Surety A person who assumes liability jointly with another surety for the payment of an obligation.

Counteradvertising New advertising that is undertaken to correct earlier false claims that were made about a product.

Counterclaim A claim made by a defendant in a civil lawsuit against the plaintiff. In effect, the defendant is suing the plaintiff.

Counteroffer An offeree's response to an offer in which the offeree rejects the original offer and at the same time makes a new offer.

Course of Dealing Prior conduct between the parties to a contract that establishes a common basis for their understanding.

Course of Performance The conduct that occurs under the terms of a particular agreement, which indicates what the parties to that agreement intended it to mean.

Covenant Not to Compete A contractual promise of one party to refrain from conducting business similar to that of another party for a certain period of time and within a specified geographical area.

Covenant Not to Sue An agreement to substitute a contractual obligation for some other type of legal action based on a valid claim.

Cover A remedy that allows the buyer or lessee, on the seller's or lessor's breach, to obtain substitute goods from another seller or lessor.

Cram-Down Provision A provision of the Bankruptcy Code that allows a court to confirm a debtor's Chapter 11 reorganization plan even though only one class of creditors has accepted it.

Creditors' Composition Agreement An agreement formed between a debtor and his or her creditors in which the creditors agree to accept a lesser sum than that owed by the debtor in full satisfaction of the debt.

Crime A wrong against society proclaimed in a statute and, if committed, punishable by society through fines, imprisonment, or death.

Criminal Law The branch of law that defines and punishes wrongful actions committed against the public.

Cross-Collateralization The use of an asset that is not the subject of a loan to collateralize that loan.

Cure The rights of a party who tenders nonconforming performance to correct his or her performance within the contract period.

Cyber Crime A crime that occurs in the online environment rather than in the physical world.

Cyber Fraud Any misrepresentation knowingly made over the Internet with the intention of deceiving another for the purpose of obtaining property or funds.

Cyberlaw An informal term used to refer to all laws governing electronic communications and transactions, particularly those conducted via the Internet.

Cyber Mark A trademark in cyberspace.

Cybersquatting The act of registering a domain name that is the same as, or confusingly similar to, the trademark of another and then offering to sell that domain name back to the trademark owner.

Cyber Tort A tort committed in cyberspace.

D

Damages A monetary award sought as a remedy for a breach of contract or a tortious action.

Debtor in Possession (DIP) In Chapter 11 bankruptcy proceedings, a debtor who is allowed to continue in possession of the estate in property (the business) and to continue business operations.

Debtor Under Article 9 of the Uniform Commercial Code, any party who owes payment or performance of a secured obligation.

Deceptive Advertising Advertising that misleads consumers, either by making unjustified claims about a product's performance or by omitting a material fact concerning the product's composition or performance.

Deed A document by which title to real property is passed.

Deed in Lieu of Foreclosure An alternative to foreclosure in which the mortgagor voluntarily conveys the property to the lender in satisfaction of the mortgage.

Defalcation Embezzlement or misappropriation of funds.

Defamation Anything published or publicly spoken that causes injury to another's good name, reputation, or character.

Default Failure to pay a debt when it is due.

Default Judgment A judgment entered by a court against a defendant who has failed to appear in court to answer or defend against the plaintiff's claim.

Defendant One against whom a lawsuit is brought, or the accused person in a criminal proceeding.

Defense A reason offered and alleged by a defendant in an action or lawsuit as to why the plaintiff should not recover or establish what she or he seeks.

Deficiency Judgment A judgment against a debtor for the amount of a debt remaining unpaid after the collateral has been repossessed and sold.

Delegatee A party to whom contractual obligations are transferred, or delegated.

Delegation of Duties The transfer to another of all or part of one's duties arising under a contract.

Delegator A party who transfers (delegates) her or his obligations under a contract to another party (called the *delegatee*).

Depositary Bank The first bank to receive a check for payment.

Deposition The testimony of a party to a lawsuit or a witness taken under oath before a trial.

Destination Contract A contract for the sale of goods in which the seller is required or authorized to ship the goods by carrier and tender delivery of the goods at a particular destination. The seller assumes liability for any losses or damage to the goods until they are tendered at the destination specified in the contract.

Devise A gift of real property by will, or the act of giving real property by will.

Devisee One designated in a will to receive a gift of real property.

Digital Cash Funds contained on computer software, in the form of secure programs stored on microchips and on other computer devices.

Disaffirmance The legal avoidance, or setting aside, of a contractual obligation.

Discharge The termination of an obligation, such as occurs when the parties to a contract have fully performed their contractual obligations.

Disclosed Principal A principal whose identity is known to a third party at the time the agent makes a contract with the third party.

Discovery A method by which the opposing parties obtain information from each other to prepare for trial.

Dishonor To refuse to pay or accept a negotiable instrument, whichever is required, even though the instrument is presented in a timely and proper manner.

Disparagement of Property An economically injurious falsehood about another's product or property.

Disparate-Impact Discrimination Discrimination that results from certain employer practices or procedures that, although not discriminatory on their face, have a discriminatory effect.

Disparate-Treatment Discrimination A form of employment discrimination that results when an employer intentionally discriminates against employees who are members of protected classes.

Dissenting Opinion A court opinion that presents the views of one or more judges or justices who disagree with the majority's decision.

Dissociation The severance of the relationship between a partner and a partnership when the partner ceases to be associated with the carrying on of the partnership business.

Dissolution The formal disbanding of a partnership or a corporation. It can take place by (1) acts of the partners or, in a corporation, acts of the shareholders and board of directors; (2) the subsequent illegality of the firm's business; (3) the expiration of a time period stated in a partnership agreement or a certificate of incorporation; or (4) a court order.

Distributed Network A network used by persons located (distributed) in different places to share computer files.

Distribution Agreement A contract between a seller and a distributor of the seller's products setting out the terms and conditions of the distributorship.

Diversity of Citizenship A basis for federal court jurisdiction over a lawsuit between citizens of different states and countries.

Divestiture A company's sale of one or more of its divisions' operating functions under court order as part of the enforcement of the antitrust laws.

Dividend A distribution of corporate profits to the corporation's shareholders in proportion to the number of shares held.

Docket The list of cases entered on a court's calendar and thus scheduled to be heard by the court.

Document of Title A paper exchanged in the regular course of business that evidences the right to possession of goods (for example, a bill of lading or a warehouse receipt).

Domain Name Part of an Internet address, such as *cengage.com*. The part to the right of the period is the top level domain and indicates the type of entity that operates the site, and the part to the left of the period, called the second level domain, is chosen by the entity.

Domestic Corporation In a given state, a corporation that is organized under the law of that state.

Dominion Ownership rights in property, including the right to possess and control the property.

Double Jeopardy The Fifth Amendment requirement that prohibits a person from being tried twice for the same criminal offense.

Down Payment The part of the purchase price of real property that is paid up front, reducing the amount of the loan or mortgage.

Draft Any instrument drawn on a drawee that orders the drawee to pay a certain amount of funds, usually to a third party (the payee), on demand or at a definite future time.

Dram Shop Act A state statute that imposes liability on the owners of bars and taverns, as well as those who serve alcoholic drinks to the public, for injuries resulting from accidents caused by intoxicated persons when the sellers or servers of alcoholic drinks contributed to the intoxication.

Drawee The party that is ordered to pay a draft or check. With a check, a bank or a financial institution is always the drawee.

Drawer The party that initiates a draft (such as a check), thereby ordering the drawee to pay.

Due Diligence A required standard of care that certain professionals, such as accountants, must meet to avoid liability for securities violations.

Due Process Clause The provisions in the Fifth and Fourteenth Amendments that guarantee that no person shall be deprived of life, liberty, or property without due process of law. State constitutions often include similar clauses.

Dumping The sale of goods in a foreign country at a price below the price charged for the same goods in the domestic market.

Duress Unlawful pressure brought to bear on a person, causing the person to perform an act that she or he would not otherwise perform.

Duty of Care The duty of all persons, as established by tort law, to exercise a reasonable amount of care in their dealings with others. Failure to exercise due care, which is normally determined by the reasonable person standard, constitutes the tort of negligence.

E

Easement A nonpossessory right, established by express or implied agreement, to make limited use of another's property without removing anything from the property.

E-Contract A contract that is formed electronically.

E-Evidence A type of evidence that consists of all computer-generated or electronically recorded information.

Electronic Fund Transfer (EFT) A transfer of funds through the use of an electronic terminal, a telephone, a computer, or magnetic tape.

Emancipation In regard to minors, the act of being freed from parental control.

Embezzlement The fraudulent appropriation of funds or other property by a person who was entrusted with the funds or property.

Eminent Domain The power of a government to take land from private citizens for public use on the payment of just compensation.

E-Money Prepaid funds recorded on a computer or a card (such as a smart card or a stored-value card).

Employment at Will A common law doctrine under which either party may terminate an employment relationship at any time for any reason, unless a contract specifies otherwise.

Employment Contract A contract between an employer and an employee in which the terms and conditions of employment are stated.

Employment Discrimination Treating employees or job applicants unequally on the basis of race, color, national origin, religion, gender, age, or disability.

Enabling Legislation A statute enacted by Congress that authorizes the creation of an administrative agency and specifies the name, composition, purpose, and powers of the agency being created.

Entrapment A defense in which a defendant claims that he or she was induced by a public official to commit a crime that he or she would otherwise not have committed.

Entrepreneur One who initiates and assumes the financial risk of a new business enterprise and undertakes to provide or control its management.

Entrustment Rule The rule that entrusting goods to a merchant who deals in goods of that kind gives that merchant the power to transfer those goods and all rights to them to a buyer in the ordinary course of business.

Environmental Impact Statement (EIS) A formal analysis required for any major federal action that will significantly affect the quality of the environment to determine the action's impact and explore alternatives.

Equal Dignity Rule A rule requiring that an agent's authority be in writing if the contract to be made on behalf of the principal must be in writing.

Equal Protection Clause The provision in the Fourteenth Amendment that requires state governments to treat similarly situated individuals in a similar manner.

Equitable Principles and Maxims General propositions or principles of law that have to do with fairness (equity).

Equitable Right of Redemption The right of a borrower who is in default on a mortgage loan to redeem or purchase the property before foreclosure.

E-Signature An electronic sound, symbol, or process attached to or logically associated with a record and adopted by a person with the intent to sign the record.

Establishment Clause The provision in the First Amendment that prohibits the government from establishing any state-sponsored religion or enacting any law that promotes religion or favors one religion over another.

Estate in Property All of the property owned by a person, including real estate and personal property.

Estopped Barred, impeded, or precluded.

Estray Statute A statute defining finders' rights in property when the true owners are unknown.

Ethical Reasoning A reasoning process in which an individual links his or her moral convictions or ethical standards to the particular situation at hand.

Ethics Moral principles and values applied to social behavior.

Eviction A landlord's act of depriving a tenant of possession of the leased premises.

Exclusionary Rule A rule that prevents evidence that is obtained illegally or without a proper search warrant—and any evidence derived from illegally obtained evidence—from being admissible in court.

Exclusive-Dealing Contract An agreement under which a seller forbids a buyer to purchase products from the seller's competitors.

Exclusive Jurisdiction Jurisdiction that exists when a case can be heard only in a particular court or type of court.

Exculpatory Clause A clause that releases a contractual party from liability in the event of monetary or physical injury, no matter who is at fault.

Executed Contract A contract that has been fully performed by both parties.

Execution The implementation of a court's decree or judgment.

Executor A person appointed by a testator in a will to administer her or his estate.

Executory Contract A contract that has not yet been fully performed.

Export The sale of goods and services by domestic firms to buyers located in other countries.

Express Contract A contract in which the terms of the agreement are stated in words, oral or written.

Express Warranty A promise that is included in a contract concerning the quality, condition, description, or performance of the goods being sold or leased.

Expropriation A government's seizure of a privately owned business or personal property for a proper public purpose and with just compensation.

Extension Clause A clause in a time instrument that allows the instrument's date of maturity to be extended into the future.

F

Federal Form of Government A system of government in which the states form a union and the sovereign power is divided between the central government and the member states.

Federal Question A question that pertains to the U.S. Constitution, an act of Congress, or a treaty and provides a basis for federal jurisdiction in a case.

Federal Reserve System A network of twelve district banks and related branches located around the country and headed by the Federal Reserve Board of Governors. Most banks in the United States have Federal Reserve accounts.

Fee Simple An absolute form of property ownership entitling the property owner to use, possess, or dispose of the property as he or she chooses during his or her lifetime. On death, the interest in the property descends to the owner's heirs.

Fee Simple Absolute An ownership interest in land in which the owner has the greatest possible aggregation of rights, privileges, and power.

Felony A crime—such as arson, murder, rape, or robbery—that carries the most severe sanctions, ranging from more than one year in a state or federal prison to the death penalty.

Fictitious Payee A payee on a negotiable instrument whom the maker or drawer did not intend to have an interest in the instrument. Indorsements by fictitious payees are treated as authorized indorsements under Article 3 of the UCC.

Fiduciary As a noun, a person having a duty created by his or her undertaking to act primarily for another's benefit in matters connected with the undertaking. As an adjective, a relationship founded on trust and confidence.

Filtering Software A computer program that is designed to block access to certain Web sites, based on their content. The software blocks the retrieval of a site whose URL or key words are on a list within the program.

Financing Statement A document filed by a secured creditor with the appropriate official to give notice to the public of the creditor's security interest in collateral belonging to the debtor named in the statement.

Firm Offer An offer (by a merchant) that is irrevocable without the necessity of consideration for a stated period of time or, if no definite period is stated, for a reasonable time (neither period to exceed three months).

Fixed-Rate Mortgage A standard mortgage with a fixed, or unchanging, rate of interest. The loan payments remain the same for the duration of the loan, which ranges between fifteen and forty years.

Fixed-Term Tenancy A type of tenancy under which property is leased for a specified period of time, such as a month, a year, or a period of years.

Fixture An item of personal property that has become so closely associated with real property that it is legally regarded as part of that real property.

Floating Lien A security interest in proceeds, after-acquired property, or collateral subject to future advances by the secured party (or all three). The security interest is retained even when the collateral changes in character, classification, or location.

Forbearance The act of refraining from an action that one has a legal right to undertake. In mortgages, an agreement between the lender and the borrower in which the lender agrees to temporarily cease requiring mortgage payments, to delay foreclosure, or to accept smaller payments than previously scheduled.

***Force Majeure* Clause** A provision in a contract stipulating that certain unforeseen events—such as war, political upheavals, or acts of God—will excuse a party from liability for nonperformance of contractual obligations.

Foreclosure A proceeding in which a mortgagee either takes title to or forces the sale of the mortgagor's property in satisfaction of the debt.

Foreign Corporation In a given state, a corporation that does business in that state but is not incorporated there.

Foreign Exchange Market A worldwide system in which foreign currencies are bought and sold.

Forgery The fraudulent making or altering of any writing in a way that changes the legal rights and liabilities of another.

Formal Contract An agreement that by law requires a specific form for its validity.

Forum-Selection Clause A provision in a contract designating the court, jurisdiction, or tribunal that will decide any disputes arising under the contract.

Franchise Any arrangement in which the owner of a trademark, trade name, or copyright licenses another to use that trademark, trade name, or copyright in the selling of goods or services.

Franchisee One receiving a license to use another's (the franchisor's) trademark, trade name, or copyright in the sale of goods and services.

Franchisor One licensing another (the franchisee) to use the owner's trademark, trade name, or copyright in the selling of goods or services.

Fraudulent Misrepresentation Any misrepresentation, either by misstatement or by omission of a material fact, knowingly made with the intention of deceiving another and on which a reasonable person would and does rely to his or her detriment.

Free Exercise Clause The provision in the First Amendment that prohibits the government from interfering with people's religious practices or forms of worship.

Free-Writing Prospectus A written, electronic, or graphic offer that is used during the waiting period and describes securities that are being offered for sale, or describes the issuing corporation and includes a legend indicating that the investor may obtain the prospectus at the Securities and Exchange Commission's Web site.

Frustration of Purpose A court-created doctrine under which a party to a contract will be relieved of her or his duty to perform when the objective purpose for performance no longer exists (due to reasons beyond that party's control).

Fungible Goods Goods that are alike by physical nature, agreement, or trade usage.

G

Garnishment A legal process whereby a creditor appropriates a debtor's property or wages that are in the hands of a third party.

Generally Accepted Accounting Principles (GAAP) The conventions, rules, and procedures developed by the Financial Accounting Standards Board to define accepted accounting practices at a particular time.

Generally Accepted Auditing Standards (GAAS) Standards established by the American Institute of Certified Public Accountants to define the professional qualities and judgment that should be exercised by an auditor in performing an audit.

General Partner In a limited partnership, a partner who assumes responsibility for the management of the partnership and has full liability for all partnership debts.

Gift A voluntary transfer of property made without consideration, past or present.

Gift *Causa Mortis* A gift made in contemplation of imminent death. The gift is revoked if the donor does not die as contemplated.

Gift *Inter Vivos* A gift made during lifetime and not in contemplation of imminent death, in contrast to a gift *causa mortis*.

Good Faith Purchaser A purchaser who buys without notice of any circumstance that would cause a person of ordinary prudence to inquire as to whether the seller has valid title to the goods being sold.

Good Samaritan Statute A state statute stipulating that persons who provide emergency services to, or rescue, someone in peril cannot be sued for negligence unless they act recklessly, thereby causing further harm.

Goodwill The market value of the good reputation of any company, partnership, or other business entity.

Grand Jury A group of citizens who decide, after hearing the state's evidence, whether a reasonable basis (probable cause) exists for believing that a crime has been committed and that a trial ought to be held.

Group Boycott An agreement by two or more sellers to refuse to deal with a particular person or firm.

Guarantor A person who agrees to satisfy the debt of another (the debtor) only after the principal debtor defaults. Thus, a guarantor's liability is secondary.

H

Hacker A person who uses computers to gain unauthorized access to data.

Historical School A school of legal thought that looks to the past to determine what the principles of contemporary law should be.

Holder Any person in possession of an instrument drawn, issued, or indorsed to him or her, to his or her order, to bearer, or in blank.

Holder in Due Course (HDC) A holder who acquires a negotiable instrument for value, in good faith, and without notice that the instrument is defective (such as that it is overdue, has been dishonored, is subject to a defense against it or a claim to it, contains unauthorized signatures, has been altered, or is so irregular or incomplete as to call its authenticity into question).

Holding Company A company whose business activity is holding shares in another company.

Holographic Will A will written entirely in the testator's handwriting.

Home Equity Loan A loan for which the borrower's home equity (the portion of the home's value that is paid off) is the collateral.

Homeowners' Insurance Insurance that protects a homeowner's property against damage from storms, fire, and other hazards.

Homestead Exemption A law permitting a debtor to retain the family home, either in its entirety or up to a specified dollar amount, free from the claims of unsecured creditors or trustees in bankruptcy.

Horizontal Merger A merger between two firms that are competing in the same market.

Horizontal Restraint Any agreement that restrains competition between rival firms competing in the same market.

Hot-Cargo Agreement An illegal agreement in which employers voluntarily agree with unions not to handle, use, or deal in the non-union-produced goods of other employers.

I

I-9 Verification The process of verifying the employment eligibility and identity of a new worker. It must be completed within three days after the worker commences employment.

I-551 Alien Registration Receipt A document, known as a "green card," that shows that a foreign-born individual can legally work in the United States.

Identification In a sale of goods, the express designation of the goods provided for in the contract.

Identity Theft The illegal use of someone else's personal information to access the victim's financial resources.

Implied Contract A contract formed in whole or in part from the conduct of the parties.

Implied Warranty A warranty that arises by law because of the circumstances of a sale rather than by the seller's express promise.

Implied Warranty of Fitness for a Particular Purpose A warranty that goods sold or leased are fit for the particular purpose for which the buyer or lessee will use the goods.

Implied Warranty of Habitability An implied promise by a seller of a new house that the house is fit for human habitation. Also, the implied promise by a landlord that rented residential premises are habitable.

Implied Warranty of Merchantability A warranty that goods being sold or leased are reasonably fit for the general purpose for which they are sold or leased, are properly packaged and labeled, and are of proper quality.

Impossibility of Performance A doctrine under which a party to a contract is relieved of his or her duty to perform when performance becomes objectively impossible or totally impracticable.

Imposter One who, by use of the mails, Internet, telephone, or personal appearance, induces a maker or drawer to issue an instrument in the name of an impersonated payee. Indorsements by imposters are treated as authorized indorsements under Article 3 of the UCC.

Incidental Beneficiary A third party who benefits from a contract even though the contract was not formed for that purpose. An incidental beneficiary has no rights in the contract and cannot sue to have it enforced.

Incidental Damages All costs resulting from a breach of contract, including all reasonable expenses incurred because of the breach.

Incontestability Clause A clause in a policy for life or health insurance stating that after the policy has been in force for a specified length of time (usually two or three years), the insurer cannot contest statements made in the policyholder's application.

Independent Contractor One who works for, and receives payment from, an employer but whose working conditions and methods are not controlled by the employer. An independent contractor is not an employee but may be an agent.

Indictment A formal charge by a grand jury that there is probable cause to believe that a named person has committed a crime.

Indorsement A signature placed on an instrument for the purpose of transferring one's ownership rights in the instrument.

Informal Contract A contract that does not require a specific form or method of creation to be valid.

Information A formal accusation or complaint (without an indictment) issued in certain types of actions (usually criminal actions involving lesser crimes) by a government prosecutor.

Information Return A tax return submitted by a partnership that only reports the business's income and losses. The partnership itself does not pay taxes on the income, but each partner's share of the profit (whether distributed or not) is taxed as individual income to that partner.

Inside Director A person on the board of directors who is also an officer of the corporation.

Insider Trading The purchase or sale of securities on the basis of information that has not been made available to the public.

Insolvent A condition in which a person cannot pay his or her debts as they become due or ceases to pay debts in the ordinary course of business.

Installment Contract A contract that requires or authorizes delivery in two or more separate lots to be accepted and paid for separately.

Insurable Interest An interest that exists when a person benefits from the preservation of the health or life of the insured or the property to be insured. In regards to sales and lease contracts, a property interest in goods being sold or leased that is sufficiently substantial to permit a party to insure against damage to the goods.

Insurance A contract in which, for a stipulated consideration, one party agrees to compensate the other for loss on a specific subject by a specified peril.

Intangible Property Property that cannot be seen or touched but exists only conceptually, such as corporate stocks. Such property is not governed by Article 2 of the UCC.

Integrated Contract A written contract that constitutes the final expression of the parties' agreement. Evidence extraneous to the contract that contradicts or alters the meaning of the contract in any way is inadmissible.

Intellectual Property Property resulting from intellectual and creative processes.

Intended Beneficiary A third party for whose benefit a contract is formed. An intended beneficiary can sue the promisor if the contract is breached.

Intentional Tort A wrongful act knowingly committed.

Interest-Only (IO) Mortgage A mortgage that allows the borrower to pay only the interest portion of the monthly payment and forgo paying any principal for a specified period of time, such as five years.

Intermediary Bank Any bank to which an item is transferred in the course of collection, except the depositary or payor bank.

International Law The law that governs relations among nations.

International Organization An organization that is composed mainly of member nations and usually established by treaty—for example, the United Nations. More broadly, the term also includes nongovernmental organizations (NGOs) such as the Red Cross.

Interpretive Rule A nonbinding rule or policy statement issued by an administrative agency that explains how it interprets and intends to apply the statutes it enforces.

Interrogatories A series of written questions for which written answers are prepared by a party to a lawsuit, usually with the assistance of the party's attorney, and then signed under oath.

Intestacy Laws State statutes that specify how property will be distributed when a person dies intestate (without a valid will).

Intestate As a noun, one who has died without having created a valid will. As an adjective, the state of having died without a will.

Investment Company A company that acts on the behalf of many smaller shareholders-owners by buying a large portfolio of securities and professionally managing that portfolio.

Investment Contract In securities law, a transaction in which a person invests in a common enterprise reasonably expecting profits that are derived primarily from the efforts of others.

J

Joint and Several Liability In partnership law, a doctrine under which a plaintiff may sue, and collect a judgment from, all of the partners together (jointly) or one or more of the partners separately (severally, or individually). A partner can be held liable even if she or he did not participate in, ratify, or know about the conduct that gave rise to the lawsuit.

Joint Liability In partnership law, the partners' shared liability for partnership obligations and debts. A third party must sue all of the partners as a group, but each partner can be held liable for the full amount.

Joint Stock Company A hybrid form of business organization that combines characteristics of a corporation and a partnership. Usually, a joint stock company is regarded as a partnership for tax and other legal purposes.

Joint Tenancy Co-ownership of property in which each party owns an undivided portion of the property. On the death of a joint tenant, his or her interest automatically passes to the surviving joint tenant(s).

Joint Venture A joint undertaking for a specific commercial enterprise by two or more persons or business entities. A joint venture is treated like a partnership for federal income tax purposes.

Judicial Foreclosure A court-supervised foreclosure proceeding in which the court determines the validity of the debt and, if the borrower is in default, issues a judgment for the lender.

Judicial Review The process by which a court decides on the constitutionality of legislative enactments and actions of the executive branch.

Junior Lienholder A party that holds a lien that is subordinate to one or more other liens on the same property.

Jurisdiction The authority of a court to hear and decide a specific case.

Jurisprudence The science or philosophy of law.

Justiciable Controversy A controversy that is not hypothetical or academic but real and substantial; a requirement that must be satisfied before a court will hear a case.

L

Larceny The wrongful taking and carrying away of another person's personal property with the intent to permanently deprive the owner of the property.

Law A body of enforceable rules governing relationships among individuals and between individuals and their society.

Lease Under Article 2A of the Uniform Commercial Code, a transfer of the right to possess and use goods for a period of time in exchange for payment.

Lease Agreement An agreement in which one person (the lessor) agrees to transfer the right to the possession and use of property to another person (the lessee) in exchange for rental payments.

Leasehold Estate An interest in real property that gives a tenant a qualified right to possess and/or use the property for a limited time under a lease.

Legacy A gift of personal property under a will.

Legal Positivism A school of legal thought centered on the assumption that there is no law higher than the laws created by a national government. Laws must be obeyed, even if they are unjust, to prevent anarchy.

Legal Realism A school of legal thought that holds that the law is only one factor to be considered when deciding cases and that social and economic circumstances should also be taken into account.

Legatee One designated in a will to receive a gift of personal property.

Legislative Rule An administrative agency's rule that carries the same weight as a congressionally enacted statute.

Lessee A person who acquires the right to the possession and use of another's goods in exchange for rental payments.

Lessor A person who transfers the right to the possession and use of goods to another in exchange for rental payments.

Letter of Credit A written document in which the issuer (usually a bank) promises to honor drafts or other demands for payment by third persons in accordance with the terms of the instrument.

Levy The legal process of obtaining funds through the seizure and sale of nonexempt property, usually done after a writ of execution has been issued.

Libel Defamation in writing or another form having the quality of permanence (such as a digital recording).

License An agreement by the owner of intellectual property to permit another to use a trademark, copyright, patent, or trade secret for certain limited purposes. In the context of real property, a revocable right or privilege to enter onto another person's land.

Lien An encumbrance on a property to satisfy a debt or protect a claim for payment of a debt.

Life Estate An interest in land that exists only for the duration of the life of a specified individual, usually the holder of the estate.

Limited Liability Company (LLC) A hybrid form of business enterprise that offers the limited liability of a corporation and the tax advantages of a partnership.

Limited Liability Partnership (LLP) A hybrid form of business organization that is used mainly by professionals who normally do business in a partnership. An LLP is a pass-through entity for tax purposes, but a partner's personal liability for the malpractice of other partners is limited.

Limited Partner In a limited partnership, a partner who contributes capital to the partnership but has no right to participate in its management. The partner has no liability for partnership debts beyond the amount of her or his investment.

Limited Partnership (LP) A partnership consisting of one or more general partners (who manage the business and are personally liable for debts of the partnership) and one or more limited partners (who contribute only assets and are liable only up to the extent of their contributions).

Liquidated Damages An amount, stipulated in a contract, that the parties to the contract believe to be a reasonable estimation of the damages that will occur in the event of a breach.

Liquidated Debt A debt whose amount has been ascertained, fixed, agreed on, settled, or exactly determined.

Liquidation The sale of the nonexempt assets of a debtor and the distribution of the funds received to creditors.

Litigation The process of resolving a dispute through the court system.

Living *(Inter Vivos)* Trust A trust created by the grantor (settlor) and effective during his or her lifetime.

Lockout Occurs when an employer shuts down to prevent employees from working typically because it cannot reach a collective bargaining agreement with the union.

Long Arm Statute A state statute that permits a state to exercise jurisdiction over nonresident defendants.

Lost Property Property that the owner has involuntarily parted with and then cannot find or recover.

M

Mailbox Rule A common law rule that acceptance takes effect, and thus completes formation of the contract, at the time the offeree sends or delivers the acceptance via the communication mode expressly or impliedly authorized by the offeror.

Majority Opinion A court opinion that represents the views of the majority (more than half) of the judges or justices deciding the case.

Maker One who promises to pay a fixed amount of funds to the holder of a promissory note or a certificate of deposit (CD).

Malpractice Professional negligence, or failure to exercise reasonable care and professional judgment, that results in injury, loss, or damage to those relying on the professional.

Malware Malicious software programs, such as viruses and worms, that are designed to cause harm to a computer, network, or other device.

Market Concentration The degree to which a small number of firms control a large percentage of a relevant market.

Market Power The power of a firm to control the market price of its product. A monopoly has the greatest degree of market power.

Market-Share Liability A theory under which liability is shared among all firms that manufactured and distributed a particular product during a certain period of time. This form of liability sharing is used only when the true source of the harmful product is unidentifiable.

Mechanic's Lien A statutory lien on the real property of another to ensure payment to a person who has performed work and furnished materials for the repair or improvement of that property.

Mediation A method of settling disputes outside the courts by using the services of a neutral third party, who acts as a communicating agent between the parties and assists them in negotiating a settlement.

Member A person who has an ownership interest in a limited liability company.

Mens rea The wrongful mental state ("guilty mind"), or intent, that is one of the key requirements to establish criminal liability for an act.

Merchant Under the UCC, a person who deals in goods of the kind involved in the sales contract or who holds herself or himself out as having skill or knowledge peculiar to the practices or goods being purchased or sold.

Merger The legal combination of two or more corporations in such a way that only one corporation (the surviving corporation) continues to exist, having acquired all of the assets and liabilities of the other corporation.

Meta Tag A key word in a document that can serve as an index reference to the document. On the Web, search engines return results based, in part, on the tags in Web documents.

Minimum Wage The lowest wage, either by government regulation or union contract, that an employer may pay an hourly worker.

Mirror Image Rule A common law rule that requires that the terms of the offeree's acceptance adhere exactly to the terms of the offeror's offer for a valid contract to be formed.

Misdemeanor A lesser crime than a felony, punishable by a fine or incarceration in jail for up to one year.

Mislaid Property Property that the owner has voluntarily parted with and then has inadvertently forgotten.

Mitigation of Damages The requirement that a plaintiff do whatever is reasonable to minimize the damages caused by the defendant.

Money Laundering Engaging in financial transactions to conceal the identity, source, or destination of illegally gained funds.

Monopolization The possession of monopoly power in the relevant market and the willful acquisition or maintenance of that power, as distinguished from growth or development as a consequence of a superior product, business acumen, or historic accident.

Monopoly A market in which there is a single seller or a very limited number of sellers.

Monopoly Power The ability of a monopoly to dictate what takes place in a given market.

Moral Minimum The minimum degree of ethical behavior expected of a business firm, which is usually defined as compliance with the law.

Mortgage A written document that gives a creditor (the mortgagee) an interest in, or lien on, the debtor's (mortgagor's) real property as security for a debt. If the debt is not paid, the property can be sold by the creditor and the proceeds used to pay the debt.

Mortgagee Under a mortgage agreement, the creditor who takes a security interest in the debtor's property.

Mortgagor Under a mortgage agreement, the debtor who gives the creditor a security interest in the debtor's property in return for a mortgage loan.

Motion for a Directed Verdict A motion for the judge to take the decision out of the hands of the jury and to direct a verdict for the party making the motion on the ground that the other party has not produced sufficient evidence to support her or his claim.

Motion for a New Trial A motion asserting that the trial was so fundamentally flawed (because of error, newly discovered evidence, prejudice, or another reason) that a new trial is necessary to prevent a miscarriage of justice.

Motion for Judgment *n.o.v.* A motion requesting the court to grant judgment in favor of the party making the motion on the ground that the jury's verdict against him or her was unreasonable and erroneous.

Motion for Judgment on the Pleadings A motion by either party to a lawsuit at the close of the pleadings requesting the court to decide the issue solely on the pleadings without proceeding to trial. The motion will be granted only if no facts are in dispute.

Motion for Summary Judgment A motion requesting the court to enter a judgment without proceeding to trial. The motion can be based on evidence outside the pleadings and will be granted only if no facts are in dispute.

Motion to Dismiss A pleading in which a defendant admits the facts as alleged by the plaintiff but asserts that the plaintiff's claim to state a cause of action has no basis in law.

Multiple Product Order An order requiring a firm that has engaged in deceptive advertising to cease and desist from false advertising in regard to all the firm's products.

Mutual Fund A specific type of investment company that continually buys or sells to investors shares of ownership in a portfolio.

N

National Law Law that pertains to a particular nation (as opposed to international law).

Natural Law The oldest school of legal thought, based on the belief that the legal system should reflect universal ("higher") moral and ethical principles that are inherent in human nature.

Necessaries Necessities required for life, such as food, shelter, clothing, and medical attention.

Negative Amortization The condition when the payment made by the borrower is less than the interest due on the loan and the difference is added to the principal, thereby increasing the balance owed on the loan over time.

Negligence The failure to exercise the standard of care that a reasonable person would exercise in similar circumstances.

Negligence *Per Se* An action or failure to act in violation of a statutory requirement.

Negotiable Instrument A signed writing (record) that contains an unconditional promise or order to pay an exact sum on demand or at a specified future time to a specific person or order, or to bearer.

Negotiation A process in which parties attempt to settle their dispute informally, with or without attorneys to represent them. Or, the transfer of an instrument in such form that the *transferee* (the person to whom the instrument is transferred) becomes a holder.

Nominal Damages A small monetary award (often one dollar) granted to a plaintiff when no actual damage was suffered.

Nonpossessory Interest In the context of real property, an interest that involves the right to use land but not the right to possess it.

Normal Trade Relations (NTR) Status A legal trade status granted to member countries of the World Trade Organization.

Notary Public A public official authorized to attest to the authenticity of signatures.

Notice of Default A formal notice to a borrower who is behind in making mortgage payments that the borrower is in default and may face foreclosure. The notice is filed by the lender in the county where the property is located.

Notice of Sale A formal notice to a borrower who is in default on a mortgage that the mortgaged property will be sold in a foreclosure proceeding.

Novation The substitution, by agreement, of a new contract for an old one, with the rights under the old one being terminated.

Nuisance A common law doctrine under which persons may be held liable for using their property in a manner that unreasonably interferes with others' rights to use or enjoy their own property.

Nuncupative Will An oral will (often called a *deathbed will*) made before witnesses. Usually, such wills are limited to transfers of personal property.

O

Objective Theory of Contracts The view that contracting parties shall only be bound by terms that can objectively be inferred from promises made.

Obligee One to whom an obligation is owed.

Obligor One who owes an obligation to another.

Offer A promise or commitment to perform or refrain from performing some specified act in the future.

Offeree A person to whom an offer is made.

Offeror A person who makes an offer.

Online Dispute Resolution (ODR) The resolution of disputes with the assistance of organizations that offer dispute-resolution services via the Internet.

Operating Agreement An agreement in which the members of a limited liability company set forth the details of how the business will be managed and operated.

Option Contract A contract under which the offeror cannot revoke the offer for a stipulated time period (because the offeree has given consideration for the offer to remain open).

Order for Relief A court's grant of assistance to a complainant. In bankruptcy proceedings, the order relieves the debtor of the immediate obligation to pay the debts listed in the bankruptcy petition.

Order Instrument A negotiable instrument that is payable "to the order of an identified person" or "to an identified person or order."

Ordinance A regulation enacted by a city or county legislative body that becomes part of that state's statutory law.

Output Contract An agreement in which a seller agrees to sell and a buyer agrees to buy all or up to a stated amount of what the seller produces.

Outside Director A person on the board of directors who does not hold a management position at the corporation.

Overdraft A check that is paid by the bank when the checking account on which the check is written contains insufficient funds to cover the check.

P

Parol Evidence Rule A rule of contracts under which a court will not receive into evidence prior or contemporaneous oral statements and agreements that contradict the terms of the parties' written contract.

Partially Disclosed Principal A principal whose identity is unknown by a third party, but the third party knows that the agent is or may be acting for a principal at the time the agent and the third party form a contract.

Partnering Agreement An agreement between a seller and a buyer who frequently do business with each other concerning the terms and conditions that will apply to all subsequently formed electronic contracts.

Partnership An agreement by two or more persons to carry on, as co-owners, a business for profit.

Partnership by Estoppel Partnership liability imposed by a court on persons who have held themselves out to be partners, even though they were not, and others have detrimentally relied on their representations.

Pass-Through Entity A business entity that has no tax liability. The entity's income is passed through to the owners, and they pay taxes on the income.

Past Consideration An act that takes place before the contract is made and that ordinarily, by itself, cannot be consideration for a later promise to pay for the act.

Patent A property right granted by the federal government that gives an inventor an exclusive right to make, use, sell, or offer to sell an invention in the United States for a limited time.

Payee A person to whom an instrument is made payable.

Payor Bank The bank on which a check is drawn (the drawee bank).

Peer-to-Peer (P2P) Networking The sharing of resources (such as files, hard drives, and processing styles) among multiple computers.

Penalty A contract clause that specifies a certain amount to be paid in the event of a default or breach of contract but is unenforceable because it is designed to punish the breaching party rather than to provide a reasonable estimate of damages.

Per Capita A method of distributing an intestate's estate so that each heir in a certain class (such as grandchildren) receives an equal share.

***Per Curiam* Opinion** A court opinion that does not indicate which judge or justice authored the opinion.

Perfection The legal process by which secured parties protect themselves against the claims of third parties who may wish to have their debts satisfied out of the same collateral. It is usually accomplished by filing a financing statement with the appropriate government official.

Performance The fulfillment of one's duties under a contract—the normal way of discharging one's contractual obligations.

Periodic Tenancy A type of tenancy created by lease for an indefinite period with payment of rent at fixed intervals, such as week to week, month to month, or year to year.

***Per Se* Violation** A restraint of trade that is so anticompetitive that it is deemed inherently (*per se*) illegal.

Personal Defense A defense that can be used to avoid payment to an ordinary holder of a negotiable instrument but not a holder in due course (HDC) or a holder with the rights of an HDC.

Personal Property Property that is movable. Any property that is not real property.

Per Stirpes A method of distributing an intestate's estate so that each heir in a certain class (such as grandchildren) takes the share to which her or his deceased ancestor (such as a mother or father) would have been entitled.

Persuasive Authority Any legal authority or source of law that a court may look to for guidance but need not follow when making its decision.

Petition in Bankruptcy The document that is filed with a bankruptcy court to initiate bankruptcy proceedings.

Petty Offense The least serious kind of criminal offense, such as a traffic or building-code violation.

Phishing An e-mail fraud scam in which the messages purport to be from legitimate businesses to induce individuals into revealing their personal financial data, passwords, or other information.

Piercing the Corporate Veil The action of a court to disregard the corporate entity and hold the shareholders personally liable for corporate debts and obligations.

Plaintiff One who initiates a lawsuit.

Plea Bargaining The process by which a criminal defendant and the prosecutor work out an agreement to dispose of the criminal case, subject to court approval.

Pleadings Statements by the plaintiff and the defendant that detail the facts, charges, and defenses of a case.

Pledge A security device in which personal property is transferred into the possession of the creditor as security for the payment of a debt and retained by the creditor until the debt is paid.

Plurality Opinion A court opinion that is joined by the largest number of the judges or justices hearing the case, but less than half of the total number.

Police Powers Powers possessed by the states as part of their inherent sovereignty. These powers may be exercised to protect or promote the public order, health, safety, morals, and general welfare.

Policy In insurance law, the contract between the insurer and the insured.

Potentially Responsible Party (PRP) A party liable for the costs of cleaning up a hazardous waste–disposal site under the Comprehensive Environmental Response, Compensation, and Liability Act.

Power of Attorney Authorization for another to act as one's agent or attorney in either specified circumstances (special) or in all situations (general).

Power of Sale Foreclosure A foreclosure procedure that is not court supervised and is available only in some states.

Precedent A court decision that furnishes an example or authority for deciding subsequent cases involving identical or similar facts.

Predatory Pricing The pricing of a product below cost with the intent to drive competitors out of the market.

Predominant-Factor Test A test courts use to determine whether a contract is primarily for the sale of goods or for the sale of services.

Preemption A doctrine under which certain federal laws preempt, or take precedence over, conflicting state or local laws.

Preemptive Rights Rights that entitle shareholders to purchase newly issued shares of a corporation's stock, equal in percentage to shares already held, before the stock is offered to outside buyers. Preemptive rights enable shareholders to maintain their proportionate ownership and voice in the corporation.

Preference In bankruptcy proceedings, a property transfer or payment made by the debtor that favors one creditor over others.

Preferred Creditor In the context of bankruptcy, a creditor who has received a preferential transfer from a debtor.

Preferred Stock Stock that has priority over common stock as to payment of dividends and distribution of assets on the corporation's dissolution.

Premium In insurance law, the price paid by the insured for insurance protection for a specified period of time.

Prenuptial Agreement An agreement made before marriage that defines each partner's ownership rights in the other partner's property. Prenuptial agreements must be in writing to be enforceable.

Prepayment Penalty Clause A clause in a mortgage loan contract that requires the borrower to pay a penalty if the mortgage is repaid in full within a certain period.

Presentment The act of presenting an instrument to the party liable on the instrument in order to collect payment. Presentment also occurs when a person presents an instrument to a drawee for a required acceptance.

Presentment Warranties Implied warranties, made by any person who presents an instrument for payment or acceptance, that (1) the person is entitled to enforce the instrument or is authorized to act on behalf of a person who is so entitled, (2) the instrument has not been altered, and (3) the person has no knowledge that the drawer's signature is unauthorized.

Price Discrimination A seller's act of charging competing buyers different prices for identical products or services.

Price-Fixing Agreement An agreement between competitors to fix the prices of products or services at a certain level.

***Prima Facie* Case** A case in which the plaintiff has produced sufficient evidence of his or her claim that the case will be decided for the plaintiff unless the defendant produces no evidence to rebut it.

Primary Source of Law A document that establishes the law on a particular issue, such as a constitution, a statute, an administrative rule, or a court decision.

Principle of Rights The belief that human beings have certain fundamental rights. Whether an action or decision is ethical depends on how it affects the rights of various groups, such as owners, employees, consumers, suppliers, the community, and society.

Private Equity Capital Funds invested by a private equity firm in an existing corporation, usually to purchase and reorganize it.

Privilege A special right, advantage, or immunity granted to a person or a class of persons, such as a judge's absolute privilege to avoid liability for defamation over statements made in the courtroom during a trial.

Privity of Contract The relationship that exists between the promisor and the promisee of a contract.

Probable Cause Reasonable grounds for believing that a search should be conducted or that a person should be arrested.

Probate The process of proving and validating a will and settling all matters pertaining to an estate.

Probate Court A state court of limited jurisdiction that conducts proceedings relating to the settlement of a deceased person's estate.

Procedural Law Law that establishes the methods of enforcing the rights established by substantive law.

Proceeds Under Article 9 of the UCC, whatever is received when collateral is sold or disposed of in some other way.

Product Liability The legal liability of manufacturers, sellers, and lessors of goods for injuries or damage caused by the goods to consumers, users, or bystanders.

Profit In real property law, the right to enter onto another's property and remove something of value from that property.

Promise A declaration that binds a person who makes it (the promisor) to do or not to do a certain act.

Promisee A person to whom a promise is made.

Promisor A person who makes a promise.

Promissory Estoppel A doctrine that can be used to enforce a promise when the promisee has justifiably relied on it and when justice will be better served by enforcing the promise.

Promissory Note A written promise made by one person (the maker) to pay a fixed amount of funds to another person (the payee or a subsequent holder) on demand or on a specified date.

Property Legally protected rights and interests in anything with an ascertainable value that is subject to ownership.

Prospectus A written document required by securities laws when a security is being sold. The prospectus describes the security, the financial operations of the issuing corporation, and the risk attaching to the security so that investors will have sufficient information to evaluate the risk involved in purchasing the security.

Protected Class A group of persons protected by specific laws because of the group's defining characteristics, including race, color, religion, national origin, gender, age, and disability.

Proximate Cause Legal cause. It exists when the connection between an act and an injury is strong enough to justify imposing liability.

Proxy In corporate law, a written or electronically transmitted form in which a stockholder authorizes another party to vote the stockholder's shares in a certain manner.

Puffery A salesperson's often exaggerated claims concerning the quality of property offered for sale. Such claims involve opinions rather than facts and are not legally binding promises or warranties.

Punitive Damages Monetary damages that may be awarded to a plaintiff to punish the defendant and deter similar conduct in the future.

Purchase-Money Security Interest (PMSI) A security interest that arises when a seller or lender extends credit for part or all of the purchase price of goods purchased by a buyer.

Qualified Indorsement An indorsement on a negotiable instrument in which the indorser disclaims any contract liability on the instrument. The notation "without recourse" is commonly used to create a qualified indorsement.

Quasi Contract An obligation or contract imposed by law (a court), in the absence of an agreement, to prevent the unjust enrichment of one party.

Question of Fact In a lawsuit, an issue that involves only disputed facts, and not what the law is on a given point.

Question of Law In a lawsuit, an issue involving the application or interpretation of a law.

Quitclaim Deed A deed that conveys only whatever interest the grantor had in the property and therefore offers the least amount of protection against defects of title.

Quorum The minimum number of members of a decision-making body that must be present before business may be transacted.

Quota A set limit on the amount of goods that can be imported.

R

Ratification A party's act of accepting or giving legal force to a contract or other obligation entered into by another that previously was not enforceable.

Reaffirmation Agreement An agreement between a debtor and a creditor in which the debtor voluntarily agrees to pay a debt dischargeable in bankruptcy.

Real Property Land and everything attached to it, such as trees and buildings.

Reamortize To change the way mortgage payments are configured, extending the term over which payments will be made.

Reasonable Person Standard The standard of behavior expected of a hypothetical "reasonable person." It is the standard against which negligence is measured and that must be observed to avoid liability for negligence.

Receiver In a corporate dissolution, a court-appointed person who winds up corporate affairs and liquidates corporate assets.

Record Information that is either inscribed on a tangible medium or stored in an electronic or other medium and is retrievable.

Recording Statutes Statutes that allow deeds, mortgages, and other real property transactions to be recorded so as to provide notice to future purchasers or creditors of an existing claim on the property.

Reformation A court-ordered correction of a written contract so that it reflects the true intentions of the parties.

Regulation E A set of rules issued by the Federal Reserve System's Board of Governors to protect users of electronic fund transfer systems.

Regulation Z A set of rules issued by the Federal Reserve Board of Governors to implement the provisions of the Truth-in-Lending Act.

Release An agreement in which one party gives up the right to pursue a legal claim against another party.

Remedy The relief given to an innocent party to enforce a right or compensate for the violation of a right.

Replevin An action that can be used by a buyer or lessee to recover identified goods from a third party, such as a bailee, who is wrongfully withholding them.

Reply Procedurally, a plaintiff's response to a defendant's answer.

Requirements Contract An agreement in which a buyer agrees to purchase and the seller agrees to sell all or up to a stated amount of what the buyer needs or requires.

Resale Price Maintenance Agreement An agreement between a manufacturer and a retailer in which the manufacturer specifies what the retail prices of its products must be.

Rescission A remedy whereby a contract is canceled and the parties are returned to the positions they occupied before the contract was made.

Res Ipsa Loquitur A doctrine under which negligence may be inferred simply because an event occurred, if it is the type of event that would not occur in the absence of negligence. Literally, the term means "the facts speak for themselves."

Respondeat Superior A doctrine under which a principal or an employer is held liable for the wrongful acts committed by agents or employees while acting within the course and scope of their agency or employment.

Restitution An equitable remedy under which a person is restored to his or her original position prior to loss or injury, or placed in the position he or she would have been in had the breach not occurred.

Restrictive Indorsement Any indorsement on a negotiable instrument that requires the indorsee to comply with certain instructions regarding the funds involved. A restrictive indorsement does not prohibit the further negotiation of the instrument.

Resulting Trust An implied trust arising from the conduct of the parties. When one party holds the actual legal title to another's property only for that other person's benefit.

Retained Earnings The portion of a corporation's profits that has not been paid out as dividends to shareholders.

Revocation The withdrawal of a contract offer by the offeror. Unless an offer is irrevocable, it can be revoked at any time prior to acceptance without liability.

Right of Contribution The right of a co-surety who pays more than her or his proportionate share on a debtor's default to recover the excess paid from other co-sureties.

Right of Reimbursement The legal right of a person to be repaid or indemnified for costs, expenses, or losses incurred or expended on behalf of another.

Right of Subrogation The right of a surety or guarantor to stand in the place of (be substituted for) the creditors, giving the surety or guarantor the same legal rights against the debtor that the creditor had.

Right-to-Work Law A state law providing that employees may not be required to join a union as a condition of retaining employment.

Risk A prediction concerning potential loss based on known and unknown factors.

Risk Management In the context of insurance, the transfer of certain risks from the insured to the insurance company by contractual agreement.

Robbery The act of forcefully and unlawfully taking personal property of any value from another.

Rulemaking The process by which an administrative agency formally adopts a new regulation or amends an old one.

Rule of Four A rule of the United States Supreme Court under which the Court will not issue a writ of *certiorari* unless at least four justices approve of the decision to issue the writ.

Rule of Reason A test used to determine whether an anticompetitive agreement constitutes a reasonable restraint on trade. Courts consider such factors as the purpose of the agreement, its effect on competition, and whether less restrictive means could have been used.

S

Sale The passing of title to property from the seller to the buyer for a price.

Sales Contract A contract for the sale of goods.

Scienter Knowledge by a misrepresenting party that material facts have been falsely represented or omitted with an intent to deceive.

S Corporation A close business corporation that has most corporate attributes, including limited liability, but qualifies under the Internal Revenue Code to be taxed as a partnership.

Search Warrant An order granted by a public authority, such as a judge, that authorizes law enforcement personnel to search particular premises or property.

Seasonably Within a specified time period or, if no period is specified, within a reasonable time.

Secondary Boycott An illegal strike directed at suppliers and customers of the primary employer with whom the union has a labor dispute.

Secondary Source of Law A publication that summarizes or interprets the law, such as a legal encyclopedia, a legal treatise, or an article in a law review.

SEC Rule 10b-5 A rule of the Securities and Exchange Commission that prohibits the commission of fraud in connection with the purchase or sale of any security. It is unlawful to make any untrue statement of a material fact or to omit a material fact if doing so causes the statement to be misleading.

Secured Party A creditor who has a security interest in the debtor's collateral, including a seller, lender, cosigner, or buyer of accounts or chattel paper.

Secured Transaction Any transaction in which the payment of a debt is guaranteed, or secured, by personal property owned by the debtor or in which the debtor has a legal interest.

Securities Generally, stocks, bonds, or other items that represent an ownership interest in a corporation or a promise of repayment of debt by a corporation.

Security Generally, a stock, bond, note, debenture, warrant, or other instrument representing an ownership interest in a corporation or a promise of repayment of debt by a corporation.

Security Agreement An agreement that creates or provides for a security interest between the debtor and a secured party.

Security Interest Any interest in personal property or fixtures that secures payment or performance of an obligation.

Self-Defense The legally recognized privilege to do what is reasonably necessary to protect oneself, one's property, or someone else against injury by another.

Self-Incrimination Giving testimony in a trial or other legal proceeding that could expose the person testifying to criminal prosecution.

Seniority System A system in which those who have worked longest for an employer are first in line for promotions, salary increases, and other benefits, and are last to be laid off if the workforce must be reduced.

Service Mark A trademark that is used to distinguish the services (rather than the products) of one person or company from those of another.

Sexual Harassment The demanding of sexual favors in return for job promotions or other benefits, or language or conduct that is so sexually offensive that it creates a hostile working environment.

Share Exchange A transaction in which some or all of the shares of one corporation are exchanged for some or all of the shares of another corporation, but both corporations continue to exist.

Shareholder's Derivative Suit A suit brought by a shareholder to enforce a corporate cause of action against a third person.

Shelter Principle The principle that the holder of a negotiable instrument who cannot qualify as a holder in due course (HDC), but who derives his or her title through an HDC, acquires the rights of an HDC.

Shipment Contract A contract for the sale of goods in which the seller is required or authorized to ship the goods by carrier. The seller assumes liability for any losses or damage to the goods until they are delivered to the carrier.

Short-Form (Parent-Subsidiary) Merger A merger that can be accomplished without the approval of the shareholders of either corporation because one company (the parent corporation) owns at least 90 percent of the outstanding shares of each class of stock of the other corporation (the subsidiary corporation).

Short Sale A sale of real property for an amount that is less than the balance owed on the mortgage loan. The lender must consent to the sale and receives the proceeds, and the borrower still owes the balance of the mortgage debt to the lender unless the lender agrees to forgive it.

Short-Swing Profits Profits earned by a purchase and sale, or sale and purchase, of the same security within a six-month period. Under Section 16(b) of the 1934 Securities Exchange Act, the profits must be returned to the corporation if earned by company insiders from transactions in the company's stock.

Shrink-Wrap Agreement An agreement whose terms are expressed in a document located inside a box in which goods (usually software) are packaged.

Slander Defamation in oral form.

Slander of Quality (Trade Libel) The publication of false information about another's product, alleging that it is not what its seller claims.

Slander of Title The publication of a statement that denies or casts doubt on another's legal ownership of any property, causing financial loss to that property's owner.

Small Claims Court A special court in which parties can litigate small claims without an attorney.

Smart Card A card containing a microprocessor that permits storage of funds via security programming, can communicate with other computers, and does not require online authorization for fund transfers.

Sole Proprietorship The simplest form of business organization, in which the owner is the business. The owner reports business income on his or her personal income tax return and is legally responsible for all debts and obligations incurred by the business.

Sovereign Immunity A doctrine that immunizes foreign nations from the jurisdiction of U.S. courts when certain conditions are satisfied.

Special Indorsement An indorsement on an instrument that identifies the specific person to whom the indorser intends to make the instrument payable. Thus, it names the indorsee.

Special Warranty Deed A deed that warrants only that the grantor held good title during his or her ownership of the property and does not warrant that there were no defects of title when the property was held by previous owners.

Specific Performance An equitable remedy in which a court orders the parties to perform as promised in the contract. This remedy normally is granted only when the legal remedy (monetary damages) is inadequate.

Spendthrift Trust A trust created to protect the beneficiary from spending all the funds to which she or he is entitled. Only a certain portion of the total amount is given to the beneficiary at any one time, and most states prohibit creditors from attaching assets of the trust.

Stale Check A check, other than a certified check, that is presented for payment more than six months after its date.

Standing to Sue The legal requirement that an individual must have a sufficient stake in a controversy before he or she can bring a lawsuit.

Stare Decisis A common law doctrine under which judges are obligated to follow the precedents established in prior decisions.

Statute of Frauds A state statute that requires certain types of contracts to be in writing to be enforceable.

Statutory Law The body of law enacted by legislative bodies (as opposed to constitutional law, administrative law, or case law).

Statutory Right of Redemption A right provided by statute in some states under which mortgagors can buy back their property after a judicial foreclosure for a limited period of time, such as one year.

Stock An ownership (equity) interest in a corporation, measured in units of shares.

Stock Buyback The purchase of shares of a company's own stock by that company on the open market.

Stock Certificate A certificate issued by a corporation evidencing the ownership of a specified number of shares in the corporation.

Stock Option A right to buy a given number of shares of stock at a set price, usually within a specified time period.

Stock Warrant The right to buy a given number of shares of stock at a specified price, usually within a set time period.

Stop-Payment Order An order by a bank customer to his or her bank not to pay or certify a certain check.

Stored-Value Card A card bearing a magnetic strip that holds magnetically encoded data, providing access to stored funds.

Strict Liability Liability regardless of fault, which is imposed on those engaged in abnormally dangerous activities, on persons who keep dangerous animals, and on manufacturers or sellers that introduce into commerce defective and unreasonably dangerous goods.

Strike An action undertaken by unionized workers when collective bargaining fails. The workers leave their jobs, refuse to work, and (typically) picket the employer's workplace.

Sublease A tenant's transfer of all or part of the leased premises to a third person for a period shorter than the lease term.

Subprime Mortgage A high-risk loan made to a borrower who does not qualify for a standard mortgage because of a poor credit rating or high debt-to-income ratio. Lenders typically charge a higher interest rate on subprime mortgages.

Substantive Law Law that defines, describes, regulates, and creates legal rights and obligations.

Summary Jury Trial (SJT) A method of settling disputes by holding a trial in which the jury's verdict is not binding but instead guides the parties toward reaching an agreement during the mandatory negotiations that immediately follow.

Summons A document informing a defendant that a legal action has been commenced against her or him and that the defendant must appear in court on a certain date to answer the plaintiff's complaint.

Supremacy Clause The requirement in Article VI of the U.S. Constitution that provides that the Constitution, laws, and treaties of the United States are "the supreme Law of the Land."

Surety A third party who agrees to be primarily responsible for the debt of another.

Suretyship An express contract in which a third party (the surety) promises to be primarily responsible for a debtor's obligation to a creditor.

Symbolic Speech Nonverbal expressions of beliefs. Symbolic speech, which includes gestures, movements, and articles of clothing, is given substantial protection by the courts.

Syndicate A group of individuals or firms that join together to finance a project. A syndicate is also called an *investment group*.

T

Takeover The acquisition of control over a corporation through the purchase of a substantial number of the voting shares of the corporation.

Taking The taking of private property by the government for public use through the power of eminent domain.

Tangible Employment Action A significant change in employment status or benefits, such as occurs when an employee is fired, refused a promotion, or reassigned to a lesser position.

Tangible Property Property that has physical existence and can be distinguished by the senses of touch and sight.

Target Corporation The corporation to be acquired in a corporate takeover.

Tariff A tax on imported goods.

Tenancy at Sufferance A type of tenancy under which a tenant continues wrongfully to occupy leased property after the lease has terminated.

Tenancy at Will A type of tenancy that either the landlord or the tenant can terminate without notice.

Tenancy in Common Co-ownership of property in which each party owns an undivided interest that passes to her or his heirs at death.

Tender An unconditional offer to perform an obligation by a person who is ready, willing, and able to do so.

Tender of Delivery A seller's or lessor's act of placing conforming goods at the disposal of the buyer or lessee and providing whatever notification is reasonably necessary to enable the buyer or lessee to take delivery.

Tender Offer An offer made by one company directly to the shareholders of another (target) company to purchase their shares of stock.

Testamentary Trust A trust that is created by will and therefore does not take effect until the death of the testator.

Testate Having left a will at death.

Testator One who makes and executes a will.

Third Party Beneficiary One for whose benefit a promise is made in a contract but who is not a party to the contract.

Tippee A person who receives inside information.

Tort A wrongful act (other than a breach of contract) that results in harm or injury to another and leads to civil liability.

Tortfeasor One who commits a tort.

Totten Trust A trust created when a person deposits funds in his or her own name for a specific beneficiary, who will receive the funds of the depositor's death. The trust is revocable at will until the depositor dies or completes the gift.

Toxic Tort A civil wrong arising from exposure to a toxic substance, such as asbestos, radiation, or hazardous waste.

Trade Dress The image and overall appearance ("look and feel") of a product that is protected by trademark law.

Trademark A distinctive word, symbol, or design that identifies the manufacturer as the source of particular goods and distinguishes its products from those made or sold by others.

Trade Name A name that a business uses to identify itself and its brand. A trade name is directly related to a business's reputation and goodwill and is protected under trademark law.

Trade Secret A formula, device, idea, process, or other information used in a business that gives the owner a competitve advantage in the marketplace.

Transfer Warranties Five implied warranties made by any person who transfers an instrument for consideration to the transferee and, if the transfer is by indorsement, to all subsequent transferees and holders who take the instrument in good faith.

Traveler's Check A check that is payable on demand, drawn on or payable through a financial institution, and designated as a traveler's check.

Treasury Securities Government debt issued by the U.S. Department of the Treasury. The interest rate on Treasury securities is often used as a baseline for measuring the rate on loan products with higher interest rates.

Treaty A formal international agreement negotiated between two nations or among several nations. In the United States, all treaties must be approved by the Senate.

Treble Damages Damages that, by statute, are three times the amount of actual damages suffered.

Trespass to Land Entry onto, above, or below the surface of land owned by another without the owner's permission or legal authorization.

Trespass to Personal Property Wrongfully taking or harming the personal property of another or otherwise interfering with the lawful owner's possession of personal property.

Trust An arrangement in which title to property is held by one person (a trustee) for the benefit of another (a beneficiary).

Trust Indorsement An indorsement to a person who is to hold or use funds for the benefit of the indorser or a third person. It is also known as an *agency indorsement*.

Tying Arrangement A seller's act of conditioning the sale of a product or service on the buyer's agreement to purchase another product or service from the seller.

U

Ultra Vires Acts of a corporation that are beyond its express and implied powers to undertake (the Latin phrase means "beyond the powers").

Unconscionable (Contract or Clause) A contract or clause that is void on the basis of public policy because one party was forced to accept terms that are unfairly burdensome and that unfairly benefit the stronger party.

Underwriter In insurance law, the insurer, or the one assuming a risk in return for the payment of a premium.

Undisclosed Principal A principal whose identity is unknown by a third party, and that person has no knowledge that the agent is acting for a principal at the time the agent and the third party form a contract.

Unenforceable Contract A valid contract rendered unenforceable by some statute or law.

Uniform Law A model law developed by the National Conference of Commissioners on Uniform State Laws for the states to consider enacting into statute.

Unilateral Contract A contract that results when an offer can be accepted only by the offeree's performance.

Union Shop A firm that requires all workers, once employed, to become union members within a specified period of time as a condition of their continued employment.

Universal Defenses Defenses that are valid against all holders of a negotiable instrument, including holders in due course (HDCs) and holders with the rights of HDCs.

Unreasonably Dangerous Product A product that is so defective that it is dangerous beyond the expectation of an ordinary consumer or a product for which a less dangerous alternative was feasible but the manufacturer failed to produce it.

Usage of Trade Any practice or method of dealing that is so regularly observed in a place, vocation, or trade that parties justifiably expect it will be observed in their transaction.

U.S. Trustee A government official who performs certain administrative tasks that a bankruptcy judge would otherwise have to perform.

Usury Charging an illegal rate of interest.

Utilitarianism An approach to ethical reasoning in which an action is evaluated in terms of its consequences for those whom it will affect. A "good" action is one that results in the greatest good for the greatest number of people.

V

Valid Contract A contract that results when the elements necessary for contract formation (agreement, consideration, legal purpose, and contractual capacity) are present.

Venture Capital Financing provided by professional, outside investors (*venture capitalists*) to new business ventures.

Venue The geographic district in which a legal action is tried and from which the jury is selected.

Vertically Integrated Firm A firm that carries out two or more functional phases (manufacturing, distribution, and retailing, for example) of the chain of production.

Vertical Merger The acquisition by a company at one stage of production of a company at a higher or lower stage of production (such as a company merging with one of its suppliers or retailers).

Vertical Restraint A restraint of trade created by an agreement between firms at different levels in the manufacturing and distribution process.

Vesting The creation of an absolute or unconditional right or power.

Vicarious Liability Indirect liability imposed on a supervisory party (such as an employer) for the actions of a subordinate (such as an employee) because of the relationship between the two parties.

Virus A software program that can replicate itself over a network and spread from one device to another, altering files and interfering with normal operations.

Voidable Contract A contract that may be legally avoided at the option of one or both of the parties.

Void Contract A contract having no legal force or binding effect.

Voir Dire An important part of the jury selection process in which the attorneys question prospective jurors about their backgrounds, attitudes, and biases to ascertain whether they can be impartial jurors.

W

Warranty Deed A deed that provides the greatest amount of protection for the grantee, in that the grantor promises that she or he has title to the property conveyed in the deed, that there are no undisclosed encumbrances on the property, and that the grantee will enjoy quiet possession of the property.

Watered Stock Shares of stock issued by a corporation for which the corporation receives, as payment, less than the stated value of the shares.

Wetlands Water-saturated, protected areas of land that support wildlife and cannot be filled in or dredged without a permit.

Whistleblowing An employee's disclosure to government authorities, upper-level managers, or the media that the employer is engaged in unsafe or illegal activities.

White-Collar Crime Nonviolent crime committed by individuals or corporations to obtain a personal or business advantage.

Will An instrument made by a testator directing what is to be done with her or his property after death.

Will Substitutes Various instruments, such as living trusts or life insurance plans, that may be used to avoid the formal probate process.

Winding Up The second of two stages in the termination of a partnership or corporation, in which the firm's assets are collected, liquidated, and distributed, and liabilities are discharged.

Workers' Compensation Laws State statutes that establish an administrative process for compensating workers for injuries that arise in the course of their employment, regardless of fault.

Working Papers The documents used and developed by an accountant during an audit, such as notes, computations, and memoranda.

Workout Agreement A formal contract between a debtor and his or her creditors in which the parties agree to negotiate a payment plan for the amount due on the loan instead of proceeding to foreclosure.

Worm A software program that automatically replicates itself over a network but does not alter files and is usually invisible to the user until it has consumed system resources.

Writ of Attachment A writ used to enforce obedience to an order or judgment of the court.

Writ of *Certiorari* A writ from a higher court asking a lower court for the record of a case.

Writ of Execution A writ that puts in force a court's decree or judgment.

Wrongful Discharge An employer's termination of an employee's employment in violation of the law or an employment contract.

Table of Cases

For your convenience and reference, here is a list of all the cases mentioned in this text, including those within the footnotes, features, and case problems. The summarized cases in the chapters of this text are given special emphasis by having their titles appear in **boldface.**

A

A&M Records, Inc. v. Napster, Inc., 146
Abdullahi v. Pfizer, Inc., 20
Abigail Alliance for Better Access to Developmental Drugs v. von Eschenbach, 863
Access Organics, Inc. v. Hernandez, 303
Aceves v. U.S. Bank, N.A., 304
Adams Associates, LLC v. Frank Pasquale Limited Partnership, 209
Adarand Constructors, Inc. v. Peña, 672
Adjani, United States v., 171
Air Products & Chemicals, Inc. v. Airgas, Inc., 772
Alberty-Vélez v. Corporación de Puerto Rico para la Difusión Pública, 600
Alden v. Maine, 667
Aleris International, Ltd. *In re,* 411
Alexander, State v., 390
Allan v. Nersesova, 336
Almeida v. Amazon.com, Inc., 120
Almog v. Arab Bank, PLC, 227
American Assembly of America, Inc. v. Cafesjian, 756
American Civil Liberties Union of Ohio Foundation, Inc. v. DeWeese, 59
American Civil Liberties Union v. Ashcroft, 46
American Civil Liberties Union v. National Security Agency, 55
American Isuzu Motors, Inc. v. Ntsebeza, 226
American Library Association, United States v., 46
American Needle, Inc. v. National Football League, 837
American Standard, Inc. v. OakFabco, Inc., 765
Angelos, United States v., 178
Anthony v. Yahoo, Inc., 120, 309
Antilles Cement Corp. v. Fortuno, 59
Apple, Inc. v. Samsung Electronics Co., 140
Arizona v. Johnson, 188
Arizona v. United States, 642
Armory v. Delamirie, 917
Ashcroft v. American Civil Liberties Union, 46
Ashley County, Arkansas v. Pfizer, Inc., 208
Askenazy v. Tremont Group Holdings, Inc., 901–902
Assicurazioni Generali, S.P.A., *In re,* 232
Atlanta, City of v. Hotels.com, L.P., 386
Aul v. Golden Rule Insurance Co., 297
Austin v. Michigan Chamber of Commerce, 745
Austin v. Nestle, Inc., 94

B

B-Sharp Musical Productions, Inc. v. Haber, 359
B.S. International, Ltd. v. JMAM, LLC, 411
Bad Frog Brewery, Inc. v. New York State Liquor Authority, 45
Baillie Estates Limited v. Du Pont (UK) Limited, 247
Baker, *In re,* 525–526
Balboa Island Village Inn, Inc. v. Lemen, 59
Barrand v. Whataburger, Inc., 261
Bartell v. Eli Lilly & Co., 452
Basis Technology Corp. v. Amazon.com, Inc., 262
Bates v. Dow Agrosciences, LLC, 875
Bates v. United Parcel Service, Inc., 670
Bazak International Corp. v. Tarrant Apparel Group, 395
Baze v. Rees, 174
Beach Community Bank v. First Brownsville Co., 590
Bear, Inc. v. Smith, 771
Bell Atlantic Corp. v. Twombly, 75
Bell Helicopter Textron, Inc. v. Islamic Republic of Iran, 232
Beneficial Homeowner Service Corp. v. Steele, 319–320
Benjamin v. JPMorgan Chase Bank, N.A., 974
Berg v. Merchants Association Collection Division, Inc., 868
Bessemer & Lake Erie Railroad Co. v. Seaway Marine Transport, 96
Best Cartage, Inc. v. Stonewall Packaging, LLC, 707
Beydoun, United States v., 134
Biglane v. Under the Hill Corp., 934
Billings v. Town of Grafton, 662
Bilski, *In re,* 138
Biolustré, Inc. v. Hair Ventures, LLC, 797
Blackford v. Prairie Meadows Racetrack and Casino, 279
Blackman v. Iverson, 285
Blackwell Publishing, Inc. v. Custom Copies, Inc., 154
Bluewater Logistics, LLC v. Williford, *In re,* 742
Board of Trustees of the University of Alabama v. Garrett, 667
Boles v. Sun Ergoline, Inc., 455
Bonilla v. Crystal Graphics Equipment, Inc., 411
Booker, United States v., 178
Boschetto v. Hansing, 67
Braddock v. Braddock, 376–378
Bradford v. Department of Community Based Services, 677
Brantley v. NBC Universal, Inc., 837
Brennan's, Inc. v. Colbert, 757–758
Bridge Tower Dental, P.A. v. Meridian Computer Center, Inc., 922

Bridgeport Music, Inc. v. Dimension Films, 144
Briefing.com v. Jones, 153
BRJM, LLC v. Output Systems, Inc., 326
Brodie v. Jordan, 792
Brooks v. Transamerica Financial Advisors, 517
Brown v. Board of Education of Topeka, 12
Brown v. Entertainment Merchants Association, 453
Brown v. W.P. Media, Inc., 755
Bruesewitz v. Wyeth, LLC, 447
BUC International Corp. v. International Yacht Council, Ltd., 142
Buckeye Check Cashing, Inc. v. Cordegna, 86
Buis, *In re,* 5
Bullock v. Philip Morris USA, Inc., 450
Burck v. Mars, Inc., 105
Burlington Industries, Inc. v. Ellerth, 662
Burlington Northern and Santa Fe Railroad Co. v. White, 663, 667
Burnett v. Pourgol, 771
Burson v. Simard, 369
Busch v. Viacom International, Inc., 100
Bush v. Department of Justice, 70
Bushi v. Sage Health Care, LLC, 732
Business Roundtable v. SEC, 784
Byrd v. Maricopa County Sheriff's Department, 188

C

Cabool State Bank v. Radio Shack, 541–542
Café Erotica v. Florida Department of Transportation, 44
Café Erotica/We Dare to Bare v. Florida Department of Transportation, 44
Call Center Technologies, Inc. v. Grand Adventures Tour & Travel Publishing Corp., 772
Calles v. Scripto-Tokai Corp., 461
Camtech Precision Manufacturing, Inc., *In re,* 527
Canfield v. Health Communications, Inc., 137
Cardinal Health, Inc. Securities Litigation, *In re,* 893
Cardizem CD Antitrust Litigation, *In re,* 839
Carmichael, *In re,* 493
Carrier Corp. v. Outokumpu Oyj, 850–851
Castillo v. Tyson, 337
Caudill v. Salyersville National Bank, 517
Causby, United States v., 932
Center Capital Corp. v. PRA Aviation, LLC, 541
Chalfant v. Titan Distribution, Inc, 677
Charles of the Ritz Distributors Corp. v. FTC, 857
Chase Home Finance, LLC v. Fequiere, 492
Chevron Corp., *In re,* 224
Chiarella v. United States, 810
Chic Miller's Chevrolet, Inc. v. General Motors Corp., 696
Chicago Board of Trade v. United States, 836
Chicago Lawyers Committee for Civil Rights Under Law, Inc. v. Craigslist, Inc., 120
Chinasa, United States v., 165
Christy Sports, LLC v. Deer Valley Resort Co., 855
CITGO Asphalt Refining Co. v. Paper, Allied-Industrial, Chemical, and Energy Workers International Union Local No. 2-991, 637
Citizens National Bank of Jessamine County v. Washington Mutual Bank, 532
Citizens United v. Federal Election Commission, 44, 745
Citizens' Committee to Save Our Canyons v. Krueger, 11
City of __________. *See* name of city
CleanFlicks of Colorado, LLC v. Soderbergh, 209
Cleary v. Philip Morris USA, Inc., 880
Cleveland Construction, Inc. v. Levco Construction, Inc., 86
Cline v. Berg, 947
Coca-Cola Co. v. Babyback's International, Inc., 319–320
Coca-Cola Co. v. Koke Co. of America, 127, 137–138
Cohen v. Seinfeld, 369
Coleman, *In re,* 571
Collier v. Turner Industries Group, LLC, 660
Colorado Coffee Bean, LLC v. Peaberry Coffee, Inc., 700
Columbia Pictures v. Brunnell, 79
Comedy Club, Inc. v. Improv West Associates, 295
Commonwealth v. __________. *See* name of opposing party
Consolidated Edison Co. v. Public Service Commission, 44
Continental TV, Inc. v. GTE Sylvania, Inc., 840
Coral Construction, Inc. v. San Francisco, 261
Corona Fruits & Veggies, Inc. v. Frozsun Foods, Inc., 527
Cousins v. Realty Ventures, Inc., 605
Covenant Health and Rehabilitation of Picayune, LP v. Lumpkin, 94
Cowher v. Carson & Roberts Site Construction & Engineering, Inc., 732
Crane Ice Cream Co. v. Terminal Freezing & Heating Co., 334
Craton Capital, LP v. Natural Pork Production II, LLP, 720
Crawford v. Metropolitan Government of Nashville and Davidson County, Tennessee, 663
Credit Acceptance Corp. v. Coates, 538
Crespo, Commonwealth v., 134
Crummy v. Morgan, 67
Cumbie v. Woody Woo, Inc., 652–653
Cumis Mutual Insurance Society, Inc. v. Rosol, 508
Curley v. Kaiser, 714

D

Davis v. O'Melveny & Myers, LLC, 87
Davis, *In re,* 821
Dawson v. Entek International, 676–677
Dayton Superior Corp. v. Spa Steel Products, Inc., 855
De La Concha v. Fordham University, 358
Delta Engineered Plastics, LLC v. Autolign Manufacturing Group, Inc., 572
Denton v. First Interstate Bank of Commerce, 541
Department of Environmental Quality v. Worth Township, 903–904
DeRosier v. Utility Systems of America, Inc., 435–436
Deters v. USF Insurance Co., 974
Devine v. Roche Biomedical Laboratories, 350
DeYoung v. Ruggerio, 901
Dickerson v. United States, 175
Dirks v. SEC, 810
Disciplinary Proceedings against __________. *See* name of party

Dissolution of Midnight Star Enterprises, LP, *In re,* 719
District of Columbia v. Heller, 41
Dobrovolny v. Ford Motor Co., 461
Dodona I, LLC v. Goldman, Sachs & Co., 826
Dodson by Dodson v. Shrader, 289
Doe 1 v. AOL, LLC, 23
Doe v. SexSearch.com, 309
Doe v. XYC Corp., 665
Drew, United States v., 184
Drury v. Assisted Living Concepts, Inc., 304
Dura Pharmaceuticals, Inc. v. Broudo, 812–813
Dweck v. Nasser, 797
Dynea USA, Inc. v. Fairbanks, 653

E

E. I. du Pont de Nemours and Co. v. Kolon Industries, Inc., 79, 841–842
East Capitol View Community Development Corp. v. Robinson, 346
Eastern Railroad Presidents Conference v. Noerr Motor Freight, Inc., 849
eBay, Inc. v. MercExchange, LLC, 140
eBay Seller Antitrust Legislation, *In re,* 835
Edmondson v. Macclesfield LP Gas Co., 454
Edward J. Goodman Life Income Trust v. Jabil Circuit, Inc., 825
EEOC v. Cheesecake Factory, Inc., 661
EEOC v. Greater Baltimore Medical Center, Inc., 678–679
EEOC v. Waffle House, Inc., 668
Ehrenfeld v. Mahfouz, 102
Electronic Privacy Information Center v. U.S. Department of Homeland Security, 55
Ellis v. BlueSky Charter School, 652
Emerick v. Cardiac Study Center, Inc., 362–363
Engler v. Atlantic Resource Management, LLC, 880
ESPN, Inc. v. Quiksilver, Inc., 131
Espresso Roma Corp. v. Bank of America, N.A., 501
Estate of __________. *See* name of party
Eubanks v. Northwest Herald Newspapers, 124–125
Eurodif, S.A., United States v., 231

F

Facto v. Panagis, 346
Fadal Machining Centers, LLC v. Mid-Atlantic CNC, Inc., 742
Fair Housing Council of San Fernando Valley v. Roommate.com, LLC, 120, 308
Fallsview Glatt Kosher Caterers, Inc. v. Rosenfeld, 411
Family Winemakers of California v. Jenkins, 22
Faragher v. City of Boca Raton, 662
Farhang v. Indian Institute of Technology, 232
Fazio v. Cypress/GR Houston I, LP, 311
Federal Baseball Club of Baltimore, Inc. v. National League of Professional Baseball Clubs, 849
Federal Trade Commission. *See* FTC
Feldman v. Google, Inc., 280
Felix Storch, Inc. v. Martinucci Desserts USA, Inc., 622
Ferguson v. Jenkins, 687
1545 Ocean Avenue, LLC, *In re,* 741–742,
First Bank v. Fischer & Frichtel, Inc., 592–593
First National Bank of Boston v. Bellotti, 44
Fitl v. Strek, 430
FMS, Inc. v. Volvo Construction Equipment North America, Inc., 692
Forchion, *In re,* 686
Forchion, State v. 686
Fox & Lamberth Enterprises, Inc. v. Craftsmen Home Improvement, Inc., 411–412
Freeman v. Brown Hiller, Inc., 295
Frostifresh Corp. v. Reynoso, 398
FTC v. Verity International, Ltd., 859
FTC v. Whole Foods Market, Inc., 842
Fteja v. Facebook, Inc., 270

G

Gallwitz v. Novel, 492
Gaming Venture, Inc. v. Tastee Restaurant Corp., 292
Gantler v. Stephens, 797
Garcia v, Lucero, 723
Garden City Boxing Club, Inc. v. Dominguez, 688
Garrigus v. Viarengo, 968
Garware Polyester, Ltd. v. Intermax Trading Corp., 221
Gaskill v. Robbins, 700
Gatton v. T-Mobile USA, Inc., 297
Gebhart v. SEC, 814
Genger v. TR Investors, LLC, 79
Georg v. Metro Fixtures Contractors, Inc., 479
George V Restauration S.A. v. Little Rest Twelve, Inc., 135
Gholston, *In re,* 572
Gibbons v. Ogden, 36
Gillespie v. Sears, Roebuck & Co., 450
Gilmer v. Interstate Johnson Lane Corp., 87
Glacial Plains Cooperative v. Lindgren, 396
Gleeson v. Preferred Sourcing, LLC, 146
Godfrey v. G.E. Capital Auto Lease, Inc., 411, 412
Golan v. Holder, 149
Gold v. Ziff Communications Co., 332
Goldberg v. UBS AG, 22–23, 212, 227
Goldstein v. Lackard, 27
Gomez-Perez v. Potter, 666
Gonzales v. O Centro Espirito Beneficente Uniao Do Vegetal, 48
Gonzales v. Raich, 38
Goodlettsville, City of v. Priceline.com, Inc., 386
Goodman v. Atwood, 913
Gould & Lamb, LLC v. D'Alusio, 295
Grant Thornton, LLP v. Office of the Comptroller of the Currency, 901
Gratz v. Bollinger, 672
Gray Printing Co. v. Blushing Brides, LLC
Gray v. Moreland, 929
Great White Bear, LLC v. Mervyns, LLC, 395
Green Mountain Chrysler Plymouth Dodge Jeep v. Crombie, 881

Greenman v. Yuba Power Products, Inc., 447
Griswold v. Connecticut, 51
Gross v. FBL Financial Services, 666
Gross v. Miramax Film Corp., 141
Grote, *In re* Estate of, 910
Grutter v. Bollinger, 672
Gubbins v. Hurson, 117
Gucci America, Inc. v. Wong Huoqing, 68–69
Guerrero v. McDonald, 801
Gunasekera v. Irwin, 58
Guth v. Loft, Inc., 780–781
Gutkowski v. Steinbrenner, 255
Guzman, United States v., 28

H

Haas, *In re,* 821
Hadley v. Baxendale, 357
Hall v. Geigerjones Co., 815
Hallock v. Holiday Isle Resort & Marina, Inc., 741
Hamer v. Sidway, 282, 283
Hammett v. Deutsche Bank National Co., 475–476
Hanjuan Jin, United States v., 154
Harjo v. Pro-Football, Inc., 131
Harman v. McAfee, 571–572
Harris v. Forklift Systems, 661
Harvey v. Dow, 287–288
Hasbro, Inc. v. Internet Entertainment Group, Ltd., 137
Hausman, *In re,* 754
Havensure, LLC v. Prudential Insurance Co. of America, 208
Hawkins v. McGee, 259
HDC Medical, Inc. v. Minntech Corp., 842
Heart of Atlanta Motel v. United States, 37
Heartland Bank v. National City Bank, 538
Hebbring v. U.S. Trustee, 554
Henderson v. National Railroad Passenger Corp., 125
Henrichs v. Chugach Alaska Corp., 779–780
Hialeah Automotive, LLC v. Basulto, 303–304
Hicklin v. Onyx Acceptance Corp., 537
Hochster v. De La Tour, 343
Holiday Inn Franchising, Inc. v. Hotel Associates, Inc., 696–697
Horvath v. HRT Enterprises, 723
Hosch v. Colonial Pacific Leasing Corp., 329
Houseman v. Dare, 426
Hubbert v. Dell Corp., 279
Hunter v. Mansell, 948
Hurst v. Socialist People's Libyan Arab Jamahiriya, 232
Huskin v. Hall, 622
Hustler Magazine, Inc. v. Falwell, 100
Hyatt Corp. v. Palm Beach National Bank, 477
Hypertouch, Inc. v. ValueClick, Inc., 858–859

I

Illinois Tool Works, Inc. v. Independent Ink, Inc., 847
In re ________. *See* name of party
Indiana Surgical Specialists v. Griffin, 544
Industrial Risk Insurers v. American Engineering Testing, Inc., 455
Inglimo, Disciplinary Proceedings against, *In re,* 886
Intel Corp. Microprocessor Antitrust Litigation, *In re,* 79, 835
International Shoe Co. v. State of Washington, 63
Io Group, Inc. v. GLBT, 79
Isquierdo v. Gyroscope, Inc., 113

J

J.T. v. Monster Mountain, LLC, 304
Jabri v. Gaddura, 72
Jamieson v. Woodward & Lathrop, 456
Jamison Well Drilling, Inc. v. Pfeifer, 355
Jannusch v. Naffziger, 387
Jauregi v. Bobb's Piano Sales & Service, Inc., 428
Jaynes v. Commonwealth of Virginia, 179
Jelnek, *In re,* 929
Jensen v. International Business Machines Corp., 256
Jesmer v. Retail Magic, Inc., 272
Jespersen v. Harrah's Operating Co., 656
Ji-Haw Industrial Co. v. Broquet, 63
Jiann Min Chang v. Alabama Agricultural and Mechanical University, 658
Joel v. Morison, 615
Johnson Construction Co. v. Shaffer, 198
Johnson v. Medtronic, Inc., 451
Johnson, *In re* Estate of, 959
Johnston v. School District of Philadelphia, 658
Jones v. Hamilton, 153–154
Jones v. Hart, 614
Jones v. Star Credit Corp., 297, 398–399
Jones v. Wells Fargo Bank, 517
Jones, United States v., 31, 171
Jordan v. Moses, 714

K

Kahala Franchise Corp. v. Hit Enterprises, LLC, 492–493
Kane, *In re,* 734
Kaplan v. O.K. Technologies, LLC, 731
Kazery v. Wilkinson, 351
Kejzar Motors, Inc. v. Kubota Tractor Corp., 701
Kelley v. Buckley, 887
Kelo v. City of New London, Connecticut, 941, 948
Khulumani v. Barclay National Bank, Ltd., 226–227
Kim v. Park, 342
Kimel v. Florida Board of Regents, 667
Kirby v. Sega of America, Inc., 105
Kitts, *In re,* 580–581
Kiwanuka v. Bakilana, 125
Kizeart, United States v., 174
Klasch v. Walgreen Co., 112
Klimecek, United States v., 188
Koch Materials Co. v. Shore Slurry Seal, Inc., 420
Kovarik v. Kovarik, 976–978
Krasner v. HSH Nordbank AG, 208–209

KSR International Co. v. Teleflex, Inc., 138
Kuehn, *In re,* 555
Kuhn v. Tumminelli, 730
Kwan v. Clearwire Corp., 279

L

L&H Construction Co. v. Circle Redmont, Inc., 307–308
Laasko v. Xerox Corp., 221
Laboratory Corporation of America Holdings v. Metabolite Laboratories, Inc., 138
Laborers' International Union of North America, Local 578 v. NLRB, 652
Landmark HHH, LLC v. Gi Hwa Park, 947–948
Langdon v. United Restaurants, Inc., 251
LaPlace v. Briere, 923
Las Vegas Sands, LLC v. Nehme, 471
LaSalle Bank National Association v. Cypress Creek 1, L.P., 590
Lashmett, *In re* Estate of, 929–930
Laurel Creek Health Care Center v. Bishop, 602–603
Lawrence v. Fox, 335
Lawrence v. Texas, 42
Leadsinger, Inc. v. BMG Music Publishing, 143
Ledbetter v. Goodyear Tire Co., 661
Leegin Creative Leather Products, Inc. v. PSKS, Inc., 840
Les Enterprises Jacques Defour & Fils, Inc. v. Dinsick Equipment Corp., 427
Li v. Canberra Industries, 653
Lindquist Ford, Inc. v. Middleton Motors, Inc., 368–369
Litle v. Arab Bank, PLC, 227
Litwin v. Blackstone Group, LP, 807–808
Local Joint Executive Board of Las Vegas v. NLRB, 645–646
Loff v. Levitt, 100
Lohtka v. Geographic Expeditions, Inc., 304
Lopez v. El Palmar Taxi, Inc., 600
Lopez, United States v., 38
Lott v. Levitt, 100, 125
Lowden v. T-Mobile USA, Inc., 93
Lucy v. Zehmer, 259
Lumley v. Gye, 107
Lundberg v. Church Farm, Inc., 609
Lutfi v. Spears, 104
Lyondell Chemical Co. v. Ryan, 779

M

M'Naghten's Case, 169
Mac's Shell Service, Inc. v. Shell Oil Products Co., 695
Macias v. Excel Building Services, LLC, 87
Maciel v. Commonwealth, 350–351
MacPherson v. Buick Motor Co., 445, 446
Maple Farms, Inc. v. City School District of Elmira, 418–419
Marbury v. Madison, 35, 63
Marshall v. Marshall, 974–975
Massachusetts v. EPA, 870
Mathews v. B and K Foods, Inc., 194
Matrixx Initiatives, Inc. v. Siracusano, 825
McBeth v. Carpenter, 723
McBride v. Taxman Corp., 611
McCann v. McCann, 790
McConnell v. Federal Election Commission, 745
McDarby v. Merck & Co., 454
McDonald's Corp. v. C.B. Management Co., 700
McFarland v. Virginia Retirement Services of Chesterfield, LLC, 727
McKeag v. Finley, 948
McKennon v. Nashville Banner Publishing Co., 672
McLean v. JPMorgan Chase Bank, N.A., 584
Medtronic, Inc. v. Hughes, 125
Meinhard v. Salmon, 709–710
Melton, *In re* Estate of, 959–960
Merrill, Lynch, Pierce, Fenner & Smith v. Dabit, 813, 826
Messerschmidt v. Millender, 172–173
Methyl Tertiary Butyl Ether, *In re,* 452
Metro-Goldwyn-Mayer Studios, Inc. v. Grokster, Ltd., 146
Michigan Basic Property Insurance Association v. Washington, 503
Microsoft Corp. v. AT&T Corp., 139
Microsoft Corp., United States v., 835, 843
MidAmerica Bank v. Charter One Bank, 496
Midland, Town of v. Morris, 940–941
Miller v. California, 46
Miller v. Miller, 255
Mims v. Starbucks Corp., 629
Mineral Park Land Co. v. Howard, 346
Miranda v. Arizona, 175, 176
Miske v. Bisno, 719
Mitchell County v. Zimmerman, 48–49
Mitchell v. Valteau, 586
MM Companies v. Liquid Audio, Inc., 775
Monsanto Co. v. McFarling, 139
Monsanto Co. v. Scruggs, 139
Moon, United States v., 173
Moore v. Barony House Restaurant, LLC, 460
Moore v. Moore, 622
Mora v. Jackson Memorial Foundation, Inc., 666–667
Morales-Cruz v. University of Puerto Rico, 663–664
Moran v. Willensky, 723–724
Moren v. Jax Restaurant, 711
Morningstar v. Hallett, 443
Moroni v. Medco Health Solutions, Inc., 627
Morrison, United States v., 38
Morse v. Frederick, 43
Moseley v. V Secret Catalogue, Inc., 129
Motorsport Marketing, Inc. v. Wiedmaier, Inc., 603
Murphy v. McNamara, 398

N

Nagrampa v. MailCoups, Inc., 87
National Aeronautics and Space Administration v. Nelson, 638
National Federation of Independent Business v. Sibelius, 33
National Football League Players Association v. National Football League Management Council, 94

National Labor Relations Board. *See* NLRB
National Steel Corp. v. NLRB, 643
Natural Resources Defense Council, Inc. v. County of Los Angeles, 872
NBT Bank, N. A. v. First National Community Bank, 518
Nelson v. United States, 178
Net2Phone, Inc. v. eBay, Inc., 79
Nevada Department of Human Resources v. Hibbs, 667
New Orleans Paddlewheels, Inc., *In re,* 797–798
New York State Restaurant Association v. New York City Board of Health, 880
New York Times Co. v. Sullivan, 103
Newmark & Co. Real Estate, Inc. v. 2615 East 17 Street Realty, LLC, 326
NLRB v. Town & Country Electric, Inc., 643
Northpoint Properties, Inc. v. Charter One Bank, 325
Nosal, United States v., 608
Notz v. Everett Smith Group, Ltd., 827–829

O

O'Bryan v. Holy See, 215
O'Donnell v. Burlington Coat Factory Warehouse, Inc., 676
O'Hagan, United States v., 811
Old Carco, LLC, *In re,* 419
Oliver, United States v., 180–181
Olmstead v. United States, 51
Omole, United States v., 188–189
Oncale v. Sundowner Offshore Services, Inc., 664
One Hundred Sixty-Five Thousand Five Hundred Eighty Dollars, United States v., 917
Ontanuos v. First National Bank of Arizona, 590
Ora, Commonwealth v., 42
Oregon Steel Mills, Inc. v. Coopers & Lybrand, LLP, 886
Orlando v. Cole, 101
ORX Resources, Inc. v. MBW Exploration, LLC, 728
Ostolaza-Diaz v. Countrywide Bank, N.A., 579
Overseas Private Investment Corp. v. Kim, 572
Overton v. Todman & Co., CPAs, 895–896

P

Pack 2000, Inc. v. Cushman, 339
Padma Paper Mills, Ltd. v. Universal Exports, Inc., 436
Paduano v. American Honda Motor Co., 233–235, 454, **860**
Palsgraf v. Long Island Railroad Co., 115
Panenka v. Panenka, 255
Parents Involved in Community Schools v. Seattle School District No. 1, 673
Park, United States v., 160
Parker v. Brown, 849
Patmon v. Hobbs, 732
Payne v. Hurwitz, 346
Pelman v. McDonald's Corp., 456
PEMS Co. International, Inc. v. Temp-Air, Inc., 304
Pennsylvania State Police v. Suders, 662
People v. __________. *See* name of party
Perry v. Brown, 52
Persson v. Smart Inventions, Inc., 771
Peterson v. Ek, 368
Peterson v. Harrell, 974
Philadelphia Indemnity Insurance Co. v. Farrington, 974
Philip Morris USA, Inc., United States v., 835
PhoneDog v. Kravitz, 147
Piazza v. Major League Baseball, 849
PIC Group, Inc. v. LandCoast Insulation, Inc., 79
Pichardo v. C. S. Brown Co., 454
Piper, *In re* Estate of, 914–915
Planned Pethood Plus, Inc. v. KeyCorp, Inc., 369
Playboy Enterprises, Inc. v. Welles, 137
Plessy v. Ferguson, 12
Polk v. Polk, 732–733
Porterhouse Custom Homes, Inc. v. 84 Lumber Co., 266
Portnoy v. Cryo-Cell International, Inc., 786
Printz v. United States, 38
PRM Energy Systems v. Primenergy, LLC, 94
Pro-Football Inc. v. Harjo, 131
Purdue Frederick Co., United States v., 193

Q

Quill Corp. v. North Dakota, 746

R

R. J. Reynolds Tobacco Co. v. U.S. Food and Drug Administration, 452
Raffles v. Wichelhous, 307
Randy's, Inc. v. NLRB, 643
Ransom v. FIA Cord Services, N.A., 566
Rapanos v. United States, 873
Reger Development, LLC v. National City Bank, 469
Regina v. Dudley and Stephens, 23
Remora Investments, LLC v. Orr, 731
Renasant Bank v. Ericson, 576
Reno v. American Civil Liberties Union, 46
Republic of the Philippines v. Pimentel, 231
Ricci v. DeStefano, 659
Riegel v. Medtronic, Inc., 39, 454
River Runners for Wilderness v. Martin, 880
Rocky Mountain Chocolate Factory, Inc. v. SDMS, 692
Rogalski v. Little Poker League, LLC, 243
Rohr v. Salt River Project Agricultural Improvement and Power District, 669
Rolando S., *In re,* 184
Roman Catholic Church of Our Lady of Sorrows v. Prince Realty Management, LLC, 936
Romero v. Scoggin-Dickey Chevrolet Buick, Inc., 436
Roper v. Simmons, 42
Roscoe, People v., 160
Rose, United States v., 855
Rosendahl v. Bridgepoint Education, Inc., 269
Ross v. May Co., 625
RSN Properties, Inc. v. Engineering Consulting Services, Ltd., 364

Rubin v. Murray, 749
Russell Realty Associates v. Russell, 714–715
Ruvolo v. Homovich, 440
Ryder v. Washington Mutual Bank, F.A., 590

S

S&T Oil Equipment & Machinery, Ltd. v. Juridica Investments, Ltd., 222–223
Sackett v. EPA, 873–874
Safeco Insurance Co. of America v. Burr, 867
Salim v. Solaiman, 325
Sample v. Monsanto Co., 139
Sánchez-Rodríquez v. AT&T Mobility Puerto Rico, Inc., 659
Sand & Sage Farm & Ranch, Inc., *In re,* 933
Santiago v. Phoenix Newspapers, Inc., 622
Sarl Louis Feraud International v. Viewfinder, Inc., 224
Sartori v. S&S Trucking, Inc., 767
Sarvis v. Vermont State Colleges, 312
Scarborough v. Rollins, 940
Schmude v. Tricam Industries, Inc., 449
Schwarzrock v. Remote Technologies, Inc., 244
Scotwood Industries, Inc. v. Frank Miller & Sons, Inc., 436
Seal Polymer Industries v. Med-Express, Inc., 94
Seaver v. Ransom, 336
Seawest Services Association v. Copenhaver, 248
SEC v. Alpha Telcom, Inc., 801
SEC v. Edwards, 801
SEC v. Montana, 826
SEC v. Texas Gulf Sulphur Co., 809–810
SEC v. W. J. Howey Co., 801
Securities and Exchange Commission. *See* SEC
Security State Bank v. Visiting Nurses Association of Telfair County, Inc., 502
Selleck v. Cuenco, 310
Senna Hills, Ltd. v. Sonterra Energy Corp., 350
73-75 Main Avenue, LLC v. PP Door Enterprise, Inc., 572
Shar's Cars, LLC v. Elder, 711
Sharpe, *In re,* 590
Sheridan v. Marathon Petroleum Co., 854–855
SHL Imaging, Inc. v. Artisan House, Inc., 601
Shoop v. DaimlerChrysler Corp., 440
Shoyoye v. County of Los Angeles, 99
Simkin v. Blank, 325
Singh, United States v., 160
Singletary, III v. P&A Investments, Inc., 411
Sisuphan, People v., 164–165
Sitaras, *In re,* 821
Six Flags, Inc. v. Steadfast Insurance Co., 261
Slack v. Truitt, 961
Slayton, State v., 159
Slusser v. Vantage Builders, Inc., 629
Smith v. Cutter Biological, Inc., 452
Smith v. Eli Lilly Co., 452
Smith v. Ingersoll-Rand Co., 455
Smith v. Johnson and Johnson, 628
Socony-Vacuum Oil Co., United States v., 837
Southern Prestige Industries, Inc. v. Independence Plating Corp., 64–65
Spacemakers of America, Inc. v. SunTrust Bank, 516–517
Spectrum Stores, Inc. v. Citgo Petroleum Corp., 213
Spray-Tek, Inc. v. Robbins Motor Transportation, Inc., 412
Sprint Communications Co. v. APCC Services, Inc., 70
SPW Associates, LLP v. Anderson, 736
Stainbrook v. Law, 361
Stambovsky v. Ackley, 937–938
Standard Oil Co. of California v. United States, 847
Stanford, United States v., 822
Stanley, *In re,* 549
Starbucks Corp. v. Lundberg, 129
Stark v. Ford Motor Co., 460
Starr v. Sony BMG Music Entertainment, 855
State Farm Automobile Insurance Co. v. Campbell, 97
State Farm Insurance Companies v. Premier Manufactured Systems, Inc., 455
State Oil Co. v. Khan, 840
State v. __________. *See* name of party
Stewart, United States v., 814
Stop & Shop Supermarket Co. v. Blue Cross & Blue Shield of Rhode Island, 847
Stultz v. Safety and Compliance Management, Inc., 295
Sturdza v. United Arab Emirates, 293
Sunset Gold Realty, LLC v. Premier Building & Development, Inc., 351
Surowiec v. Capital Title Agency, Inc., 9
Sutowski v. Eli Lilly & Co., 452
Sutton v. Countrywide Home Loans, Inc., 590–591

T

T.V. *ex rel.* B.V. v. Smith-Green Community School Corp., 43
Taylor v. Baseball Club of Seattle, L.P., 116
Taylor v. Taylor, 974
Tennessee v. Lane, 667
Terry v. Lock, 929
Testa v. Ground Systems, Inc., 369
Texas v. Johnson, 41, 43
Thibodeau v. Comcast Corp., 297
Thompson v. Lynch, 723
Thompson v. North American Stainless, LP, 663
Thyroff v. Nationwide Mutual Insurance Co., 110
Toro Co. v. Krouse, Kern & Co., 890
Totten, *In re,* 968
TracFone Wireless, Inc. v. Bequator Corp., 279
Tractebel Energy Marketing, Inc. v. AEP Power Marketing, Inc., 261
TradeComet.com, LLC v. Google, Inc., 851
Travelscape, LLC v. South Carolina Department of Revenue, 386
Treadway v. Gateway Chevrolet Oldsmobile, Inc., 865
Treiber v. Straub, Inc. v. United Parcel Service, Inc., 924
Trell v. American Association for the Advancement of Science, 260
Tri-M Group, LLC v. Sharp, 39

Trunk v. City of San Diego, 47
Trustees of Dartmouth College v. Woodward, 748
Trustmark National Bank v. Barnard, 493
Tull v. Atchison Leather Products, Inc., 653
Turner v. State of Arkansas, 188
2007 Custom Motorcycle, United States v., 400–401
Tzolis v. Wolff, 741

U

U.S. Airways, Inc. v. Barnett, 672
U.S. Bank, N.A. v. Ibanez, 585
U.S. Bank, N.A. v. Tennessee Farmers Mutual Insurance Co., 252
Uhrhahn Construction & Design, Inc. v. Hopkins, 245
Ultramares Corp. v. Touche, 889
Union Bank Co. v. Heban, 541
Union v. Branch Banking & Trust Co., 517
United Fabrics International, Inc. v. C & J Wear, Inc., 154
United Mine Workers of America v. Pennington, 849
United States v. __________. *See* name of opposing party
United Student Aid Funds, Inc. v. Espinosa, 567–568

V

Vaks v. Ryan, 326
Van Horn v. Watson, 118
Van Orden v. Perry, 47
Van Zanen v. Qwest Wireless, LLC, 249
Vandeln v. The Beatrice Manor, Inc., 626
Venture Sales, LLC v. Perkins, 734–735
Venturini v. Steve's Steakhouse, Inc., 797
Verigy US, Inc. v. Mayder, 146
Video Software Dealers Association v. Schwarzenegger, 453
Vilardo v. Sheets, 701
Vinueza v. Scotto, 492
Vitt v. Apple Computer, Inc., 461
Vizcaino v. U.S. District Court for the Western District of Washington, 600
Voda v. Cordis Corp., 231
Vokes v. Arthur Murray, Inc., 310
Volero v. Florida Insurance Guaranty Association, Inc., 954

W

Wachovia Securities, LLC v. Banco Panamericano, Inc., 772
Waddell v. Boyce Thompson Institute for Plant Research, Inc., 626
Waddell v. L.V.R.V., Inc., 435
Wagner v. Columbia Pictures Industries, Inc., 251
Wal-Mart Stores, Inc. v. Dukes, 656
Walker, *In re* Estate of, 974
Walsh v. State, 188, **888**
Warner v. Southwest Desert Images, LLC, 614
Warnick v. Warnick, 713
Wasniewski v. Quick and Reilly, Inc., 929
Watercraft Management, LLC v. Mercury Marine, 846
Webster v. Blue Ship Tea Room, Inc., 440–441
Weidner v. Carroll, 142
Weimar v. Lyons, 772
Western Fire Truck, Inc. v. Emergency One, Inc., 623
Western Surety Co. v. APAC-Southeast, Inc., 350
Wetmore v. MacDonald, Page, Schatz, Fletcher & Co., LLC, 902
Weyerhaeuser Co. v. Ross-Simmons Hardwood Lumber Co., 844–845
White Plains Coat & Apron Co. v. Cintas Corp., 125
White v. Samsung Electronics America, Inc., 105
Whitehead v. Humphrey, 937
Wilchcombe v. TeeVee Toons, Inc., 153
Williams v. Pike, 611–612
Williams, United States v., 46
Wilson Court Limited Partnership v. Tony Maroni's, Inc., 546–547
Wilson Sporting Goods Co. v. U.S. Golf & Tennis Centers, Inc., 416
Winschel v. Brown, 455
Wisconsin Electric Power Co. v. Union Pacific Railroad Co., 341
Woo v. Fireman's Fund Insurance Co., 955
Wood Care Centers, Inc. v. Evangel Temple Assembly of God of Wichita Falls, 325
Woodbridge USA Properties, L.P. v. Southeast Trailer Mart, Inc., 436
WorldCom, Inc. Securities Litigation, *In re,* 893
WPS, Inc. v. Expro Americas, LLC, 392–393
Wrench, LLC v. Taco Bell Corp., 255
Wright v. Finance Service of Norwalk, Inc., 867
Wright v. Moore, 117
Wright v. Universal Maritime Service Corp., 87
Wyeth v. Levine, 454

Y

Yeagle v. Collegiate Times, 124
Yun Tung Chow v. Reckitt & Coleman, Inc., 461

Z

Z4 Technologies, Inc. v. Microsoft Corp., 140
Zhang v. Tse, 572
Zippo Manufacturing Co. v. Zippo Dot Com, Inc., 67
Zortman v. J. C. Christiansen & Associates, Inc., 868
Zucco Partners, LLC v. Digimarc Corp., 825
Zurich American Insurance Co. v. ABM Industries, Inc., 952

Index

A

Abatement, 957
Abnormally dangerous activities, 119
Abuse of process, 106
Acceleration clause, 470
Acceptance(s)
 banker's, 463
 of bribe, 165
 contractual. *See* Contract(s), acceptance in; Lease contract(s), acceptance in; Sales contract(s), acceptance in
 of delivered goods, 421–422
  revocation of, 429
 e-contracts and, 268
 of gift, 915
 medium of, 267n
 in negotiable instruments law, 463
 online, 270–272
 partial, 421–423
 trade, 464, 481
Acceptor, 481, 485
Accession, 915–916
Accord
 defined, 28, 344
 satisfaction and, 285–286
  contract discharge by, 344
  settlement of claims by, 285–286
Account party, to letter of credit, 224
Accountant(s)
 accountant-client relationship and, 897–898
 audits and, 885
 duty of care of, 883–886
 Foreign Corrupt Practices Act and, 205
 liability of, 882–902
  under common law, 883–886
  criminal, 897
  under securities laws, 891–897
  to third parties, 889–891
 opinions and disclaimers by, 885
 Sarbanes-Oxley Act and, 891
 working papers of, 891–892
Accounting
 agent's duty of, 605
 debtor's request for, 534–535
 managerial, 206
Act of state doctrine, 212, 213–214
Action
 affirmative, 672–673
 in equity, 14
 at law, 14
Actual malice, 103–104
Actus reus (guilty act), 158
Adjudication, 9
Administrative agency(ies), 8–11. *See also* Administrative law; Government regulation(s)
 adjudication by, 9–11
 authority of, 10
 creation of, 9
 defined, 9–10
 enforcement by, 10
 environmental regulatory, 869
 executive, 9
 federal, 9
 hearings by, 9
 independent regulatory, 9
 investigation by, 10, 20
 parallel (at state level), 9
 regulations of, 20
  as primary source of law, 6
 rulemaking by, 9–10, 20
 state and local, 9
Administrative law, 8–11
 dealing with, 20
 defined, 8
 finding, 25
Administrative Procedure Act (APA)(1946), 9, 55
Administrative process, 9
Admission(s)
 as exception to Statute of Frauds, 317, 395–396
 request for, during discovery, 77
ADR. *See* Alterative dispute resolution
Advertising, advertisement
 bait-and-switch, 857–858
 counteradvertising and, 859
 on Craigslist, to sell human organs, ethics and, 291
 deceptive, 857–860
 online, 291, 858–859
 restrictions on, 44
Affidavit, 544, 962
Affirmative action, 672–673
Affordable Care Act, 33
Age
 discrimination based on, 227, 655, 665–667, 732
 of majority, 288, 289n
Age Discrimination in Employment Act (ADEA)(1967), 227, 665–667
Agency relationship(s), 8–11, 597–623. *See also* Agent(s); Principal(s)
 bank-customer relationship as, 498
 defined, 8, 597
 determining existence of, 599–600
 duties in, 604–606
 employer-employee, 598
 employer–independent contractor, 598–599
 formation of, 601–604
 insurance broker versus insurance agent and, 599
 partnerships and, 703
 termination of, 616–618
Agent(s)
 authority of, 606–610
 authorized and unauthorized acts of, 610–612
 compensation and, 605–606
 duties of, to principal, 604–605
 gratuitous, 605
 insurance, 599
 liability of, 610–613
 misrepresentation by, 613
 offeree's, 263
 partner as, 706, 709
 principal's duties to, 604, 605–606
 real estate broker as, 599
 registered, 753
 torts and crimes of, 122, 612–616
 unauthorized signature of, 483
 use of employer's electronic data and, 608
Agreement(s). *See also* Contract(s)
 agency relationship created by, 602–603
 to agree, offer versus, 260–261
 bailment, 918, 919. *See also* Bailment(s)
 buy-sell, 720
 click-on, 270, 271
 contract discharge by, 343–344
 contractual, 241, 257
 creditors' composition, 545
 defined, 258
 family settlement, 962
 hot-cargo, 644
 illegal, withdrawal from, 299
 international, 211
 lease, 388. *See also* Lease contract(s)
 mutual, agency termination by, 617
 noncompetition, sample, illustrated, 372–375
 nondisclosure, sample, illustrated, 372–375
 operating (of LLC), 730
 overdraft protection, 499
 partnering, 272
 partnership, 706. *See also* Partnership(s)
 preliminary, offer versus, 260–261

prenuptial, 316
price-fixing, 837–839
reaffirmation, 561
rental, mitigation of damages and, 358
resale price maintenance, 840
security, 521–522, 523, 535. *See also* Security agreement(s)
shareholder, 749, 786
shrink-wrap, 270–271
trade association, 839
workout, 582

Agricultural associations, exemption of, from antitrust laws, 849
Aiding and abetting, securities laws and, 896–897
Alien Tort Claims Act (ATCA)(1789), 226, 227
Alienation, restraints against, 331
Alter ego theory, 727
Alteration, 344–345, 486, 503–504
Alternative Dispute Resolution (ADR), 83–90. *See also* Arbitration; Mediation; Negotiation(s)
defined, 83
lawsuit versus, 90
service providers for, 88

Amazon.com, customer relationship management (CRM) and, 276
America Invents Act (Leahy-Smith America Invents Act)(2011), 138
American International Group (AIG), 197
American law
in global context 225–227
sources of, 6–11

American Recovery and Reinvestment Act (ARRA)(2009), 53
Americans with Disabilities Act (ADA)(1990), 227, 667–669
Answer, 76
Anti-Counterfeiting Trade Agreement (ACTA), 148
Anti-Terrorism Act (ATA), 212, 227
Anticybersquatting Consumer Protection Act (ACPA)(1999), 136
Antilapse clause, 955
Antitrust law(s), 833–855
avoiding problems under, 852
defined, 833
enforcement of, 848–851
exclusionary practices and, 846–847
exemptions from, 848–850
extraterritoriality of, 225–226, 850–851
foreign, application of, 851
franchising and, 691, 694n
in global context, 225–226, 850–851
monopolization and, 841–845
origins of, 834, 835
per se violations under, 836, 839, 849
problems with, avoiding, 852
rule of reason and, 836–837

Appeals, 80–82
Appellant, 30
Appellate court(s), 25–28, 71–73, 81–82
federal, 27–29. *See also* United States Supreme Court
jurisdiction of, 65
options of, in disposition of cases, 81
state, 25–28, 71–73

Appellate review, 81–82
Appellee, 30
Appropriation, 104, 105
Arbitration, 84–89
arbitrability and, 87
binding versus nonbinding, 84
defined, 84
e-contracts and, 269
employment contracts and, 662
as form of ADR, 84–88
insurance contracts and, 955
international contracts and, 223, 224
lemon laws and, 444–445
mandatory, in employment context, 87
private proceedings and, 87–88
procedures for, compared to trial, 84–85
service providers of, 88

Arrest, 175–176
Arson, 163
Articles
of consolidation, 762, 763
of dissolution, 767
of incorporation, 753, 774, 775, 782
of merger, 762, 763
of organization, 727
of partnership, 705

Assault, 98
Assets
Assignee, 328, 330
Assignment(s), 328–332, 348
of "all rights," 334–335
defined, 328
law governing, summarized, 335
of leased property, 944
of limited partner's interest in partnership, 719
notice of, 331–332
relationship of parties and, illustrated, 329
rights not subject to, 330–331
of security interest, 534
transfer of negotiable instruments by, 472–473

Assignor, 328,
Assurance, right of, 420
Attachment, 521, 522n, 528–529, 544, 549
Attorney(s)
-at-law, 607n
attorney-client relationship and, 897–898
choosing and using, 228–229
district (DA), 17
duty of care of, 886–887
-in-fact, 607n
liability of, 891
for malpractice, 886–887
to third parties, 889–891
power of, 607
durable, 607

Attractive nuisance doctrine, 109
Attribution, 274
Auction, online, fraud and, 179
Audit committee, 819, 821
Auditing, ethics and, 196
Audits, 885
Authentication, 521–522, 535
Authority(ies)
actual, 606–607
of agent, 606–610
apparent, 608–609
binding, 12
certificate of, 747
express, 607
implied, 607–608, 710
of joint venturers, 736–737
of partner, 710
persuasive, 12

Authorization card, 644
Automated teller machines (ATMs), 510
Automobile Dealers' Franchise Act (Automobile Dealers' Day in Court Act) (1965), 691n
Award
jury, 80
arbitrator's, 85

B

Bailee
acknowledgment by, of buyer's or lessee's rights, 425
defined, 404, 918
degree of care required of, 920–922
duties of, 921–923
goods held by, 404
involuntary, 916n, 919n
rights of, 920–921

Bailment(s), 918–927
defined, 918
elements of, 918
involuntary (constructive), 916n, 919
lost or damaged property and, 922–923
for the mutual benefit of bailor and bailee, 920, 921
ordinary, 920–923
for the sole benefit of the bailee, 920, 921
for the sole benefit of the bailor, 920, 921
special types of (extraordinary), 923–925

Bailor
defined, 918
duties of, 923

Bank(s)
acceptance by, of certified check, 497
check collection process of, 505–509
under Check 21, 509
traditional, 505–509
collecting, 505
correspondent, 223
customer of. *See* Bank customer(s)
deferred posting by, 507–508
depositary, 505
depository, 505n
duty of
to accept deposits, 504–509
to honor checks, 498
failure of mortgage-participating, ethics and, 576
hacking accounts of, protecting against,185
intermediate, 505
letter of credit and, 224
liability of, 499–504
midnight deadline of, 507
negligence of, 501–502
one-year time limit of, for paying on forged check, 501–502
online banking and, 511–512

payor, 505
relationship of, with customer, 497–498
runs on, 513
Bank customer(s)
death or incompetence of, 500
of different banks, check collection between, 507
examination of bank statement by, 501
failure of, to detect forged checks, 501
negligence of, 500–501, 503–504
relationship of, with bank, 497–498
of same bank, check collection between, 506
Bankruptcy, 549–569
automatic stay in, 555, 562, 564, 574
cram-down provision in, 564
discharge in, 345, 486, 552, 560–561, 565, 567–568
estate in property and, 555, 559–560, 561
fraud in, 166, 557, 563
involuntary, 554, 562
law governing, 549–550
means test in, 553–554, 556
petition in, 552, 554, 562, 564, 565
preferences in, 557, 563
relief in, types of, 550–551. *See also* individual chapters of Bankruptcy Code
straight (ordinary), 553
student loans and, 560
substantial abuse presumption and, 553–554, 562, 565
trustee in, 556–557, 562, 564, 565, 566
voluntary, 552–554, 562, 565
Bankruptcy Code (Bankruptcy Reform Act of 1978). *See also* Bankruptcy
chapter "gaps" in, 551n
Chapter 7 (liquidation proceedings) of, 550, 551–561, 562
Chapter 11 (reorganization) of, 551, 562–564, 566, 569
Chapter 12 (adjustment of debts for family farmers and family fishermen) of, 551, 564–565
Chapter 13 (adjustment of debts for individuals) of, 565–568
Bankruptcy Reform Act (1978). *See* Bankruptcy Code
Bankruptcy Reform Act (Bankruptcy Abuse Prevention and Consumer Protection Act)(2005), 549, 550
Bankruptcy Reporter (Bankr.)(West), 27
Bargain, basis of, 439
Bargained-for exchange, 282–283
Bargaining, collective. *See* Collective bargaining
Baseball, professional, exemption of, from antitrust laws, 849
Battery, 98
Bearer, 470, 471
Bearer instrument(s), 470, 471, 473
Beneficiary(ies)
creditor, 336
defined, 335
donee, 336
incidental, 337–338
intended beneficiary versus, 337
of insurance policy, 950
intended, 335, 337–338
of letter of credit, 224
third party, 335–338
of trust, 965
Bequest, 957
Berne Convention (1886), 148–149
Beyond a reasonable doubt, 156, 177
Bids, invitation to submit, offer versus, 260
Bill of lading, 224, 401
Bill of Rights, 40–51. *See also* individual amendments
Binder, 952
Bipartisan Campaign Reform Act (BCRA) (McCain-Feingold Act)(2002), 745n
Board of directors. *See* Corporate director(s)
Bona fide occupational qualification (BFOQ), 671
Bond(s), 758, 768, 799
defined, 758
stock versus, summarized, 760
Bond indenture, 758
Books
"cooking" the, 816
inspection of
corporate director's right of, 776
partner's right of, 708
shareholder's right of, 788
Botnets, 182
Boycott, group, 839
Brady Handgun Violence Protection Act (1993), 38
Breach
of contract. *See* Contract(s), breach of; Lease contract(s) breach of; Sales contract(s), breach of
defined, 4
of duty of care, 111–113
of fiduciary duties, 710
of online testing service contract, 354
Bribery, 165–166
commercial, 165–166
of foreign officials, 165, 204–205, 220
of public officials, 165
Brief, 30–32, 81
Burden of proof
in civil cases, 104, 156
in criminal case, 156, 177
in defamation case, 104
Burglary, 161
Business
Bill of Rights and, 40–51
legal environment and, 4–6, 7
management of. *See* Management
mismanagement of, appointment of receiver and, 562
sale of, covenants not to compete and, 294
seller's place of, delivery and, 414–415
small, 8
cooperative research by, exemption of, from antitrust laws, 849
exemptions for, under Sarbanes-Oxley Act, 820
role of law in, 6
tort liability of, 122
wrongful interference with, 96, 106, 107
Business ethics, 191–198
attitude of top management and, 194
codes of ethics and, 195–196
defined, 191
ethical decision making and, 201
on global level, 201–205
importance of, 191
leadership and, 193–195
moral minimum and, 191–192
questions regarding, solutions to, 202
transgressions of, by financial institutions, 190–191, 196–198
Business invitee, 112
Business judgment rule, 777, 778–780
Business organization(s), 685–798
business trust as, 737
cooperative as, 737–738
franchises and. *See* Franchise(s)
joint stock company as, 737
joint venture as, 736
limited liability company (LLC) as. *See* Limited liability company(ies)
limited liability partnership (LLP) as. *See* Limited liability partnership(s)
limited partnership as. *See* Limited (special) partnership
major forms of, compared, 792–793
partnership as. *See* Partnership(s)
sole proprietorship as. *See* Sole proprietorship(s)
special forms of, 736–738
syndicate (investment group) as, 737
Business trust, 737
Buyer(s). *See also* Purchaser(s)
acceptance of goods by, 421–422
breach by, 405
of collateral, 533
goods in possession of, seller's remedies and, 425
insurable interest of, 405
obligations of, 421–422
in the ordinary course of business, 402, 529, 532–533
payment obligations of, 421
refusal by, to inspect goods, warranty and, 443
remedies of, on seller's breach, 426–431
right of inspection of, 421
Bystanders, strict product liability and, 453

C

Cable Communications Act, 687
CAN-SPAM (Controlling the Assault of Non-Solicited Pornography and Marketing) Act (2003), 120–121, 858
Cancellation, 14, 312, 360, 423, 426, 563, 954–955. *See also* Rescission
C&F (cost and freight), 404
Capacity
contractual, 242, 268, 288–291
defined, 288
testamentary, 958
Capital
private equity, 760–761
venture, 760–761
Capital Markets Efficiency Act (1996), 800
Capper-Volstead Act (1922), 849

Care
  due, 445
  duty of, 111–114
    accountant's, 883–886
    attorney's, 886–887
    bailee's, 921–922
    bank's, 501
    breach of, 111–114, 710
    of corporate directors and officers, 777–778
    defined, 111
    insurance agent's, 950
    joint venturer's, 736
    landowner's, 109, 112–113
    LLC managers and, 731–733
    manufacturer's, 445
    negligence and, 111–114
    partner's, 709, 712–713, 715
    of professionals,113, 883–887
    trustee's, 969
  ordinary, 501
  reasonable, 109, 111, 112–113
Carrier(s), 403–404
  common, 924
  delivery via, 415
  substitution of, 417
Case(s). *See also* Lawsuit(s); Litigation
  briefing a, 30–32
  carrier, 403–404
  criminal, major steps in, illustrated, 177
  decisions in. *See* Decision(s); Opinion(s)
  of first impression, 12
  following through state court system, 75–82
  how to read and analyze, 30–32
  major steps in processing, illustrated, 177
  old, 27
  prima facie, 657, 666
  sample, 30–32
  titles and terminology of, 27, 30
Case law, 11. *See also* Common law
  citations to, 25, 27, 28
  defined, 11
  finding, 25–30
  as primary source of law, 6
  reading and understanding, 27, 30
  stare decisis and, 12
Cash
  checks payable to, 489
  digital, 511
Catalogue, offer versus, 260
Categorical imperative, 198
Causation
  "but for," 666
  as element of negligence, 111, 113–114, 666
  in fact, 113–114
Cause
  franchise termination for, 692, 694
  probable, 172–173, 175, 176
  proximate (legal), 114, 439n
  removal of corporate director for, 774, 782
  superseding, 116
Central America–Dominican Republic–United States Free Trade Agreement (CAFTA-DR), 219–220
CERCLA (Comprehensive Environmental Response, Compensation, and Liability Act)(1980), 876
Certificate(s)
  of authority, 747
  of deposit (CD), 465, 466
  of limited partnership, 717
  stock, 786
Certification mark, 132
Chain-style business operation, as type of franchise, 689
Chancellor, 13
Chattel, 109, 909. *See also* Personal property
Chattel paper, 510
Check(s), 464–465, 497–497
  altered, 503–504
  cashier's, 465, 495–496
  certified, 481, 497
  clearance of, 509
  collection process and, 505–509
    under Check 21, 509
    traditional, 505–509
  defined, 464, 495
  deposited, availability schedule for, 505
  dishonored, 402
  electronic presentment of, 509
  forged drawers' signatures on, 500–502
  forged indorsements on, 502–503
  honoring of, 498
  indorsed in blank, 489
  overdrafts and, 498–499
  payable to "cash," 488
  pitfalls when writing and indorsing, 488–489
  poorly filled out, illustrated, 504
  postdating, 499
  stale, 499
  stop-payment orders and, 499
  traveler's, 496–497
Check 21 (Check Clearing in the 21st Century Act)(2003), 506, 509
Checks and balances system, 35
Child Online Protection Act (COPA)(1998), 46
Child Protection and Toy Safety Act, 864
Children
  adopted, intestacy laws and, 964
  child labor and, 627
  health care and, 864
  intestacy laws and, 964–965
  pornography and, 46
  revocation of will and, 961–962
  wages of, in foreign workplaces, 203
Children's Internet Protection Act (CIPA) (2000), 46
Choice-of-language clause, 221
Choice-of-law clause, 221, 270
C.I.F. (cost, insurance, and freight), 404
Circulars, offers versus, 260
Circumstances, changed, agency termination and, 618
CISG. *See* United Nations Convention on Contracts for the International Sale of Goods
Citation(s)
  defined, 8
  how to read, 24–29
  parallel, 25–26
Citizenship
  corporate, 200–201
  diversity of, 66
Civil law, criminal law versus, 156–157
  criminal law versus, 17
  defined, 17
Civil law system, 17, 18
Civil Rights Act
  of 1866, Section 1981 of, 659
  of 1964, Title VII of, 202, 227, 656, 658, 659, 660, 661. 663, 664, 668, 672
Claim(s)
  creditors', 558–559
  to debtor's collateral, priority of, summarized, 534
  of employment discrimination, 655
  international tort, 226–227
  potential "Section 1981," 658
  proof of, bankruptcy and, 558–559
  retaliation, 663
  workers' compensation, 631–632
Class, protected, 298, 654, 732
Class Action Fairness Act (CAFA)(2005), 97
Class actions, limitations on, 813
Clayton Act (1914), 833, 845–848, 849
Clean Air Act (1963), 870–871
Clean Water Act (CWA)(1972), 871–874
Clearinghouse, 509
Click-on agreement, 270, 271
Close corporation(s), 748–749
  misappropriation of funds of, 749–750
  preemptive shareholder rights and, 787
Closed shop, 644
Closing arguments, 80
Cloud computing, 145
Co-sureties, 548
COBRA (Consolidated Omnibus Budget Reconciliation Act), 634
Code of Federal Regulations (C.F.R.), 25
Collateral
  buyers of, 533
  classification of, and perfection of security interest, 523
  consumer goods as, 536–537. *See also* Purchase-money security interest(s)
  debtor's rights in, 522
  defined, 520
  description of, in financing statement, 525–526
  disposition of, 536–537
    in commercially reasonable manner, 537
    notice requirement and, 537
    procedures for, 537
  intangible, 522
  possession of, perfection without filing and, 528
  priority of claims to, summarized, 531–533, 534
  proceeds from disposition of, 529
  redemption of, 538
  release of, 534
  repossession of ("self-help"), 535
  retention of, by secured party, 536
  sale of, 536–537
  security agreement and, 521

tangible, 522
Collection agencies, 867–868
Collective bargaining, 643, 646
defined, 646
good faith and, 643, 646
Collective mark, 132
Color, discrimination based on, 227, 655, 658–659, 661, 732
Comity, principle of, 212–213
Commercial activity, 215
Commercial impracticability, 346, 347, 418–419
Commercial paper. *See* Negotiable instrument(s)
Commercial reasonableness, 389, 537
Commercial unit, 421–422
Commingling, of personal and corporate interests, 728, 757
Common law
defined, 11
early English courts and, 11
employment relationships and, 624
equitable remedies and, 13–15
stare decisis and, 11–12
tradition of, 11–15
Common law system, 12–15
Communication(s)
acceptance of offer and, 266–267
authorized means of, 267
of offer, 263
privileged, 101, 103
stored, 636–637
in workplace, monitoring of, 635–637
Communications Decency Act (ADA)(1996), 46, 309
Community Reinvestment Act (1977), 574
Compelling state interest, 42, 48, 51
Compensation
of agent, 605–606
bailee's right to, 920–921
of corporate directors, 775
of corporate officers, shareholders' control and, 817
just, for government taking, 940–941
partners and, 708
unemployment, 634
workers', 631–632
Competition
antitrust laws and, 833–855
covenants not to enter into. *See* Covenant(s) not to compete
predatory behavior versus, 107
unfair, 96
Compilations
of facts, 142
of law, 8
Complaint, 75–76
Comprehensive Environmental Response, Compensation, and Liability Act (CERCLA)(1980), 876
Computer Fraud and Abuse Act (CFAA), (Counterfeit Access Device and Computer Fraud and Abuse Act)(1984) 184, 608
Computer Software Copyright Act (1980), 143
Concentrated industry, 839
Condition
concurrent, 340
defined, 339
of performance, 338–340
precedent, 321, 339–340
subsequent, 340
Conduct
of corporate personnel, corporate dissolution and, 100, 767, 789
misrepresentation by, 309–310
of the parties, contract formation and, 245
partnership implied by, 705
foreign workplace and, 203
Confidentiality, professional-client relationships and, 897–898
Confirmation, debtor's request for, 534–535
Confiscation, 214, 217
Conflict
of interest, corporate decision making and, 781–782
ethical, how to resolve, 199
Confusion, acquiring personal property by, 916
Consideration
in contracts. *See* Contract(s), consideration in; Lease contract(s), consideration in; Sales contract(s), consideration in
insurance and, 950
negotiable instruments and, 485, 486
under UCC, 286n
Consolidated Omnibus Budget Reconciliation Act (COBRA), 634
Consolidation, 962
articles of, 762, 763
illustrated, 762
Consumer(s)
privacy bill of rights of, 862
protection for, mortgage loans and, 580–581
laws protecting. *See* Consumer law(s)
foreign, U.S. antitrust law and, 225
rights of holders in due course and, 487
Consumer Credit Protection Act (CCPA) (1968), 545, 865
Consumer Financial Protection Bureau, 865
Consumer goods
as collateral, 536–537. *See also* Purchase-money security interest(s)
"remotely created," UCC protection for, 485n
retention of collateral by secured party and, 539
Consumer law(s), 865–868
areas of, regulated by statutes, illustrated, 857
credit protection and, 865–868
deceptive advertising and, 857–860
defined, 856
health and safety protection and, 861–864
labeling and packaging and, 861–863
sales and, 861
telemarketing and, 860
Consumer Product Safety Commission (1972) (CPSC), 863–864
Consumer-debtors, 551–552
Contest, change of prize for, ethics and, 243
Contract(s), 240. *See also* Agreement(s)
acceptance in, 265, 268
communication of, 266–267
defined, 265
mode and timeliness of, 267
persons qualified for, 265
silence as, 265–266
substitute method of, 267
unequivocal, 265
adhesion, 296
agent's liability and, 610–612
agreement in, 241, 257–280
analysis of, 371
anticipatory repudiation of, 343, 422–423
arbitration clause in, 85
assignment prohibited by, 330–331
between merchants, special rules for, 395
bilateral, 242–244, 266n
breach of, 4, 352. 355–356
anticipatory, 343, 422–423
as defense to liability on negotiable instrument and, 486
material, 342
professional's liability and, 883
remedies for, 353–364. *See also* Remedy(ies)
cancellation of, 14, 312, 360, 423, 426, 563, 954–955. *See also* Rescission
capacity and, 242, 268, 288–291
collateral, 313, 314–315
consideration in, 241
adequacy of, 283
defined, 282
lack of, 284, 286
past, 284–285
as requirement for valid contract, 241
construction, 354–356, 359, 361n
contrary to public policy, 293–298
contrary to statute, 291–293
defined, 240–241
delegations prohibited by, 333
destination, 401, 404, 415
disaffirmance of, by minor, 289–290
discharge of, 291, 338–347
electronic. *See* E-contract(s)
elements of, 241–242
employment. *See* Employment contract(s)
enforceability of, 246–248, 299
agreement to agree and, 260–261
condition precedent and, 321
covenants not to compete and, 296
defenses to, 299, 305–326. *See also* Parol evidence rule; Statute of Frauds
e-mailed documents and, 247, 322
limitation-of-liability clauses and, 364–365
liquidated damages and, 358–359
shrink-wrap agreements and, 271
exclusive-dealing, 846–847
exculpatory clauses in, 297–298, 364
executed, 246
executory, 246, 563
express, 245
form of, 242
formal, 244–245
formation of, 242–247

franchise, 690, 692–694
freedom from, 241
freedom of, 241, 283
function of, 240
"home solicitation," 360n
implied (implied in fact), 245
implied in law (quasi contract), 248–249
incomplete, 320
informal (simple), 244–245
installment, 417
insurance. *See* Insurance, contract for
integrated, 321–322, 397
international. *See* International contract(s)
interpretation of, 249–252, 398
investment, 801
involving sale of land, Statute of Frauds and, 313–314
law governing
as civil law, 17
compared with law governing sales contracts, illustrated, 384
overview of, 240–241
sources of, 240
legality of, 242, 291–298
limitation of liability clauses in, 364–365
material alteration of, 344–345
mirror image rule and, 264, 392
objective theory of, 241
offer in, 258–265
communication of, to offeree, 263
defined, 258
irrevocable, 264–265
requirements of, 258–263
termination of, 263–265
option, 265, 391n
option-to-cancel clauses in, 285
oral, 318. *See also* Statute of Frauds
output, 390–391
performance of, 246
personal-service. *See* Personal-service contract(s)
plain language laws and, 249
preincorporation, 727
privity of, 327, 445, 889–890
quasi (implied in law), 248–249, 363–364
ratification of, 290
real estate sales and, 936–938
reformation and, 296, 360, 361, 362–363
repudiation of, anticipatory, 343, 422–423
requirements, 390–391
rescission of, 284, 343–344, 360, 423, 579
in restraint of trade, 293–296
severable (divisible), 299
shipment, 401, 403, 415
simple (implied), 245
subject to Statute of Frauds, 313–318
subsequent modification of, parol evidence rule and, 320
third party beneficiary, 335–338
types of, 242–246
unconscionability and, 296–297. *See also* Unconscionability
unilateral, 242–244
valid, 241–242, 246
void, 320
voidable, 246–247, 291, 320
voluntary consent to, 242, 305, 306–308
Contractual relationship
bank and bank customer as, 498
wrongful interference with, 106, 108
Contribution, right of, 548
Control, relinquishing, gifts and, 914–915
Controlled Substances Act, 48
Convention on Contracts for the International Sale of Goods (CISG) (1980), 406–407
acceptance and, 407
revocation of, 429
applicability of, 406
offer and, 406–407
Statute of Frauds and, 317, 406
UCC compared with, 406–407
Conversion, 110 , 917
Conveyance, 934
Cooperation, principal's duty of, 606
Cooperative, as business form, 737–738
Copyright Act (1976), 140–143, 145, 148
Copyrights, 140–146
Corporate director(s), 744, 773–782
agency concepts and, 774
approval of merger or consolidation plan by, 763
business judgment rule and, 778–780
committees of, 776
compensation of, 775
dissenting, 778
duties of, 777–782
election of, 774–776, 782
failure of, to declare dividend, 787
fraud by, corporate dissolution and, 767, 789
illegal conduct by, corporate dissolution and, 767
interlocking directorates and, 848
lack of women on boards of, 818
liability of, 160, 777, 782
liability insurance for, 776
management responsibilities of, 774. *See also* Management
meetings of, 775, 776, 778
negligence of, 777
oppressive conduct and, 767, 789
inside versus outside, 775, 816–817
qualifications of, 774
removal of, 774, 777, 782
rights of, 776
shareholder's derivative suit and, 782, 789–790
term of, 774
vacancies on board of, 774–775
Corporate officer(s), 744, 776–782
aligning interests of, with those of shareholders, 816–817
business judgment rule and, 778–780
duty of loyalty and, 780–781
liability of, 160, 777, 782
negligence of, 777
reasonable supervision by, 778
responsible corporate officer doctrine and, 160
shareholder's derivative suit and, 782, 789–790
Corporation(s)
acquiring (purchasing), 764
adverse publicity and, 203, 204
alien, 747
assets of, wasting, 789
board of directors of. *See* Corporate director(s)
bylaws of, 753, 774–775
classification of, 747–750
close. *See* Close corporation(s)
competing with, duty of loyalty and, 780–781
conflict in laws governing, priorities among, 755
consolidation and, 761–762, 962
corporate citizenship and, 200–201
corporate governance and, 17–21
corporate social responsibility and, 199–201
as creature of state, 743
de facto, 754
de jure, 754
defined, 552, 744
directors of. *See* Corporate director(s)
dissolution of, 766–767, 788–789
dividends of, 744–747, 759–760, 787–788
domestic (in-state), 747
duration and purpose of, 753
by estoppel, 754–755
executives of, 197–198, 776–777 *See also* Corporate director(s); Corporate officer(s)
financing of, 758–761, 766. *See also* Bond(s); Security(ies);
first organizational meeting of, 754
foreign (out-of-state), 747
formation of, 750–758
financing and. *See* Corporation(s), financing of
incorporation procedures and. *See* Incorporation
promotional activities and, 751
freedom of speech and, 44
initial public offering (IPO) of, 761, 805
internal organization of, 753
as "legal person," 64, 159–160, 744, 766, 773, 951
liability and, 727, 746–747
management of, 457, 569, 748–749, 761, 774, 776, 782,
mergers and acquisitions and, 761–766
name of, 524, 745–746
nature of, 744–747
net profits of, 787
nonprofit (not-for-profit), 748
officers of. *See* Corporate officer(s)
ownership of. *See* Shareholder(s)
parent, 746
personnel of, 744. *See also* Corporate director(s); corporate officer(s); Shareholder(s)
piercing corporate veil of, 728, 744, 756–758
powers of, 755–756
private, 747–748
professional (P.C.), 750
public, 747–748
purchase of assets and, 764–765
registered office and agent of, 753

reputation of, social media and, 203, 204, 206, 643
retained earnings of, 744–747, 759–760, 787
retention policy for e-documents of, 794
S, 750
service (S.C.), 750
shareholders of. *See* Shareholder(s)
shares of, 753
sources of funds for, 768
subsidiary, 217, 762–763
successor, liability of, 761–765
surplus of, 787
surviving, 761
target, 765
taxes and, 729, 744–747
termination of, 766–767
ultra vires actions by, 756–758
veil of, piercing, 728, 744, 756–758
wholly owned (subsidiary), 762–763
winding up of, 767

Cost-benefit analysis, 199
Counteradvertising, 859
Counterclaim, 76
Counterfeit goods, 133–134
Counteroffer, 264, 392
Course of performance, 252, 321, 397–398
Course of (prior) dealing, 252, 321, 397
Courts, 60–83
- appellate. *See* Appellate court(s)
- bankruptcy, 65, 550, 551
- criteria used by, in determining employee status, 599
- cyber, 83
- decisions of, common law tradition and, 13
- docket of, 83
- early English, 11
- electronic filing and, 82
- of equity, 13–14
- federal. *See* Federal court system
- Islamic law, 72
- jurisdiction and. *See* Jurisdiction
- king's (*curiae regis*), 13
- of law, 13
- online, 83
- probate, 65, 956, 962–963
- records of, privacy of, Internet and, 53–54
- rules of contract interpretation used by, 252
- small claims, 91
- state. *See* State court systems
- trial, 25, 70–73. *See also* Trial(s)

Covenant(s) not to compete
- defined, 294
- employment contracts and, 294–296
- and nondisclosure agreement, sample, illustrated, 372–375
- reformation of, 296, 362–363
- sale of ongoing business and, 294

Covenant not to sue, 286
Cover, 427
Craigslist, advertisements on, ethics and, 291
Credit
- consumer protection and, 865–868
- discrimination and, 865
- equal opportunity and, 865
- letter of. *See* Letter of credit
- line of, 530, 768

Credit card(s)
- identity theft and, 180, 181
- percentage of U.S. consumers having, 865
- rules for, 865–866

Credit Card Accountability, Responsibility, and Disclosure Act (2009), 865n
Credit reporting, 866–867, 877
Creditor(s)
- acceptance and confirmation of bankruptcy plan by, 564–567
- Chapter 11 reorganization and, 558–559, 562, 569
- claims of, in bankruptcy, 558–559
- committees of, 563
- composition agreements of, 545
- involuntary bankruptcy and, 554
- laws assisting, 542–548
- of limited liability company, winding up and, 735
- of limited partnership, dissolution and, 719
- meetings of, in bankruptcy, 558–559
- out-of-court workouts and, 562
- partnership dissolution and, 715
- petition for involuntary bankruptcy of debtor, 554
- preferred, 557
- protection for, mortgages and, 577–578
- relationship of, with debtor, bank-customer relationship as, 498
- remedies of, 542–548
- rights and duties of, 533, 542–548
- unsecured, 559–560

Crime(s)
- agent's liability for, 616
- classification of, 167–168
- computer, 162, 178–179. *See also* Cyber crime(s)
- cyber. *See* Cyber crime(s)
- defined, 156
- federal, 159, 166
- organized, 166–167
- property, 161–163
- prosecution for, tort lawsuit for same act versus, 157
- public order, 163–164
- state, 159
- types of, 161–168
- violent, 161
- white-collar, 163–164, 178

Criminal justice, Native Americans and, 162
Criminal law. 155–189. *See also* Crime(s)
- civil law versus, 17, 156–157
- criminal process and, 175–178
- defined, 17
- jurisdiction and, 162
- overcriminalization and, 159

Criminal liability, 158–160. *See also* Crime(s); Criminal law
- corporate, 159–160, 746–747
- defenses to, 168–175
- intent and, 158
- under securities laws, 897

Criminal trial, right to speedy and public, 40
Cross-collateralization, 530
Cruel and unusual punishment, 40
Cure, 405, 416–417
Customer restrictions, 840
Cyber crime(s), 178–185
- computer crimes and, 178–179
- cyber theft, 179–181
- defined, 179
- hacking and, 182
- identity theft and, 180–181
- prosecution of, 183–184

Cyber fraud, 179
Cyber marks, 135–137
Cyber torts, 119–181
Cyberlaw, 17
Cyberspace. *See* Internet
Cybersquatting, 135–136
Cyberterrorism, 183

D

Damages, 353–359
- accountant's negligence and, 885
- buyer's or lessee's right to recover, 427, 429
- compensatory, 96, 114, 353–356
- consequential (special), 356, 357, 431
- deceptive advertising and, 859
- defamation and, 102–103
- defined, 96
- general, 96, 102
- incidental, 353, 494
- liquidated, penalties versus, 358–359
- mitigation of, 357–358
- nominal, 356–357
- punitive, 96–97, 312, 356
- seller's or lessor's right to recover, 424
- special, 96, 102–103
- in tort actions, 96–97
- treble (triple), 849
- types of, 353–357

Danger(s)
- on business premises, 113
- commonly known, 455, 456
- "danger invites rescue" doctrine and, 118
- unreasonably dangerous products and, 448

Davis-Bacon Act (1931), 627
Death
- of bank customer, 499n, 500
- of contract party, contract discharge by, 345
- of general partner, dissolution of limited partnership and, 719
- of limited partner, partnership dissolution and, 719
- of offeror, offer termination and, 264–265
- of principal or agent, agency termination and, 617–618
- testate, 956

Debit card, lost or stolen, 510
Debt(s)
- collection agencies and, 867–868
- liquidated, 285–286
- of partnership, winding up partnership and, 715
- preexisting, 557
- reaffirmation of, 555, 461
- unliquidated, 286

Debtor(s)
- collateral of. *See* Collateral
- consumer, 551–552

default of, 520, 535
deficiency judgment and, 537–538
defined, 520
future disposable income of, 553
laws assisting, 548–549. *See also* Bankruptcy; Consumer law(s)
location of, filing of financing statement and, 526
name of, in financing statement, 524, 525–526
in possession (DIP), 562–563
property of
garnishment and, 544–545
liens and, 542–544
relationship of, with creditor, bank-customer relationship as, 498
requirements of, mortgages and, 577–578
right of, to accounting of unpaid debt or list of collateral, 534
rights and duties of, 533
Decisions, court
affirmation of, by appellate court, 81
appeal of, 80–82
appellate court, 30
federal court
citations to, 28, 29–30
finding, 28, 29–30
remandment of, 81
reversal of, 81
state court
citations to, 25–27, 28
finding, 25–27, 28
Deeds, 937, 938–939
Defalcation, 885
Defamation, 100–104
defenses against, 103–104
defined, 100
online, identifying author of, 119
Default of debtor, 520, 535, 560, 585
Default judgment, 76
Defendant, 14, 30, 76
Defense(s)
affirmative, 76, 114–117, 662
business necessity, 671
defined, 98
employment discrimination, 671–672
knowledgeable user, 456
negligence, 114–117
notice of, HDC status and, 480
of others, 98
personal, 485, 486
of property, 98
self-, 98, 168
universal (real), 485–486
Defense activities, exemption of, from antitrust laws, 849
Defense Production Act (1950), 849
Delegatee, 333
Delegation(s), 328, 332–335, 348
defined, 332
duties not subject to, 333
Delegator, 332
Delivery,
via carrier, 415
constructive, 914, 919
ex-ship, 404
of gift, 913–915
in installments, 414
with or without movement of goods, risk of loss and, 403–405
of negotiable instrument, 473
nonconforming goods, buyer's and lessee's remedies and, 428–430
physical, 919
place of, 414–415
of possession, 918–919
seller's or lessor's right
to stop, 425
to withhold, 494
tender of, 404, 414
when seller or lessor refuses to make, 426–428
Demand, payable on, 468
Deposit(s)
bank's duty to accept, 504–509
certificate of (CD), 465, 466
direct, 510
insurance for, 513–514
Deposited acceptance rule, 267
Depositions, 79
Descendants, intestacy laws and, 964
Destruction
of identified goods, 420
of subject matter
agency termination and, 618
impossibility of performance and, 345
offer termination and, 264–265
Detrimental reliance, 286–288, 318. *See also* Reliance
Devise, 957
Devisee, 957
Digital cash, 511
Digital Millennium Copyright Act (DMCA), 144, 145
"Digital wallet," 512
Dilution, trademark, 128–129
Disability(ies)
discrimination based on, 227, 655, 667–671, 732
reasonable accommodation of, 669–670, 732
Disaffirmance, 289–290
Discharge
in bankruptcy, 386, 441, 560–561, 565, 567–568
constructive, 661
of contract, 291, 338–347
defined, 338
from liability on negotiable instrument, 487–488
wrongful, 627
Disclaimer
by auditor, 885
of warranty, 442–443
Disclosure
full, of director's conflict of interest, 781–782
of nature of defect, right to cure and, 417
debt reaffirmation and, 561
under Rule 10b-5, 808–813
under TILA, 578–581
Discovery, 77–78
Discrimination
based on
appearance, 656
color, 227, 655, 658–659, 661, 732
disability, 227, 655, 667–671, 732
reasonable accommodation of, 669–670, 732
gender, 227, 655, 660–661, 662–665, 732
corporate boards of directors and, 818
genetic testing, 639
national origin, 227, 655, 658–659, 661, 732
pregnancy, 660, 661
race, 227, 655, 658–659, 661, 732
religion, 227, 655, 659, 661, 732
reasonable accommodation and, 659
sexual harassment, 661–665, 732
union affiliation, 642
wages, 660–661
credit, 865
disparate-impact (unintentional), 657–658, 671
disparate-treatment (intentional), 656–657
employment. *See* Employment discrimination
Equal Employment Opportunity Commission (EEOC) and, 655–656
laws prohibiting, extraterritorial application of of, 227–228
price, 845–846
prima facie case of, 657
reverse, 658–659
Dishonor, of negotiable instruments, 479, 480, 482
Disparagement of property, 110
Dissociation
in limited partnership, 719
of member of LLC, 733–735
of partner, 712–713, 719–720. *See also* Partnership(s)
Dissolution
defined, 766
of corporation, 766–767
of limited partnership, 719–720
of LLC, 733–735
of partnership, 719–720
Distributed network, 144–145
Distributorship, 689
Divestiture, 848
Dividends, 744–747, 759–760, 787–788
Do Not Call Registry, 860
Docket, 83
Document(s)
electronic. *See* E-document(s)
of title, 401, 404, 924n
Dodd-Frank Wall Street Reform and Consumer Protection Act, 799, 817
Domain names, 135–136
Dominion, relinquishing, gifts and, 914–915
Donor, donee, 912
Double jeopardy, 40, 173–174
Draft(s)
defined, 463
sight, 463–464
time, 463–464
Drawee
defined, 463, 495
liability of, 481

Drawer
defined, 463, 495
forged signature of, 500–502
liability of, 481, 482
Drugs
consumer protection and, 861–863
testing employees for, 637
Due diligence, 807, 893
Due process
attachment of property and, 544
constitutional guarantee of, 40, 41, 49–50
corporations and, 744
criminal procedures and, 173
procedural, 49–50, 173
punitive damages and, 97
substantive, 50, 80, 173
Dumping, 218
Duress, 313
criminal liability and, 169
as defense to liability on negotiable instrument, 486
defined, 169
illegal agreement and, 299
Duty(ies)
antidumping, 218
of care. *See* Care, duty of
of cooperation, 420–421
delegation of. *See* Delegation(s)
ethics and, 198–199
fiduciary. *See* Fiduciary duty(ies)
of loyalty. *See* Loyalty, duty of
preexisting, 284
to warn, of product risks, 452

E

Easements, 934–936
E-commerce, removing barriers to, 273
Economic Espionage Act (1996), 146, 166
Economic Recovery Act (2008), 579n
E-contract(s), 268–275
agreement in, 268–272
consideration in, 268
defined, 268
e-signatures on, 269
forum-selection clauses in, 270
licensing software and, 268
offer in, 268–270
requirements for, 268
E-discovery, 78
E-document(s)
creating retention policy for, 794
e-signatures and, 272
law governing, 272–275
E-evidence, 78
defined, 78
failure to preserve, 79
EFT. *See* Electronic fund transfer(s)
Eighth Amendment, 40, 174
Electronic Communications Privacy Act (ECPA)(1986), 635–636
Electronic contracts. *See* E-contract(s)
Electronic data, employer's, agent's use of, 608
Electronic discovery (e-discovery), 78
Electronic documents. *See* E-document(s)
Electronic evidence. *See* E-evidence
Electronic filing
federal courts and, 82
of financing statement, 524
Electronic fund transfer(s) (EFT), 509–511
commercial, 511
consumer, 510–511
defined, 509
disclosure requirements and, 510–511
types of, 510
Electronic Fund Transfer Act (EFTA)(1978), 510–511
Electronic monitoring, employee privacy rights and, 635–637
Eleventh Amendment, 667
E-mail
CAN-SPAM Act and, 120
contractual acceptance and, 267
contractual agreement and, 247
e-contracts and, 258. *See also* E-contract(s)
fraudulent, securities and, 821
harassment via, 664
sufficiency of writing and, 319, 323
Emancipation of minor, 288
Embezzlement, 164–165, 778
Eminent domain, 936, 940–941
Emissions, permit system for, 871–872
E-money, 511
Emotional distress, intentional infliction of, 99–100, 102
Employee(s)
administrative, 628
as agent of employer, 598
with disabilities, 669
reasonable accommodation of, 669–670
undue hardship and, 670
discrimination against. *See* Employment discrimination
drug testing and, 637–638
executive, overtime and, 628–629
family and medical leave for, 630–631
genetic testing and, 639
health of, 631–632
income security for, 632–634
independent contractor versus, 599–601
key, 630
lie-detector tests and, 637
misconduct of, after-acquired evidence and, 672
overtime for, 628–629
in Brazil, for use of smartphones after work, 628
exemptions from, 628–629
privacy rights of, 52, 635–639
private pension plans of, 633–634
protected by NLRA, 643
providing ethics training to, 195
safety of, 631–632
torts of, 122, 600, 615
unions and. *See* Union(s)
working for U.S. employers abroad, protections for, 227
works for hire of, copyright issues and, 601
wrongful discharge of, 627
wrongful termination of, 357–358, 627
Employee Free Choice Act, 644n
Employer(s)
criticism of, in social media, ethics and, 643
degree of control exercised by, 599
drug testing and, 637–638
group health plans sponsored by, 634–635
hiring of "permalancers" by, ethics and, 600–601
liability of
for employees' and agents' torts, *respondeat superior* and, 613–615
for independent contractors' torts, 600
retaliation by, 663–664
unions and. *See* Union(s)
Employer-employee relationship, 598
Employer–independent contractor relationship, 598–599
Employment. *See also* Workplace
discrimination and. *See* Employment discrimination
children and, 627
immigration laws and, 639–642
layoffs and, 627, 629–630
mandatory arbitration and, 87
OSHA and, 631–632
right-to-work laws and, 644
scope of, 613–615
wages and, 627–629
at will, 624–627
Employment contract(s), 357–358
arbitration clause in, 662
corporate officers and managers and, 777
covenant not to compete in, 294–296
defined, 294
mitigation of damages and, 357–358
sample, annotated, 370–375
Employment discrimination, 655–677
affirmative action and, 672–673
based on
age, 227, 655, 665–667, 732
color, 227, 655, 658–659, 661, 667–671, 732
disability, 227, 655, 667–671, 732
reasonable accommodation of, 669–670
gender, 227, 655, 660–661, 662–665, 732
national origin, 227, 655, 658–659, 661, 732
pregnancy, 660, 661
race, 227, 655, 658–659, 661, 732
religion, 227, 655, 659, 661, 732
reasonable accommodation of, 659
union affiliation, 642
defined, 655
disparate-impact (unintentional), 657–658, 671
disparate-treatment (intentional), 656–657
Equal Employment Opportunity Commission and, 10, 20, 655–656, 657, 661, 666, 668, 678
genetic testing and, 639
hostile-environment, 732
long-term unemployment of job applicant and, 658
prima facie case of, 657, 666
reasonable accommodation and, 659
undue hardship and, 659
remedies for under Title VII, 665
reverse, 658–659
sexual harassment as, 661–665, 732

wages and, 660–661
Employment Retirement Income Security Act (ERISA)(1974), 633–634
Enabling legislation, 9
Energy Policy and Conservation Act (EPCA), 860
Entrapment, 170
Entrepreneur, 685
Entrustment rule, 402
Environmental law, 868–876
common law actions and, 868–869
federal regulations and, 869–876
negligence and strict liability under, 869
Environmental Protection Agency (EPA), 860, 869–872, 873–874, 876
Equal Credit Opportunity Act (ECOA) (1974), 865
Equal dignity rule, 601n, 607
Equal Employment Opportunity Commission (EEOC), 10, 20, 655–656, 657, 661, 666, 668, 678
Equal Pay Act (1963), 660
Equal protection clause, 50–51, 672
Equitable principles and maxims, 15
Equitable remedies, 11–15, 359–363
Equitable right of redemption, 586
Equity
action in, 14
action at law versus, illustrated, 14
courts of, 13–14
home, 576–577
merging of, with law, 14
remedies in, 11–15, 359–363
Error(s). *See also* Mistake(s)
in bank statements, 511
in credit report, 866–867
effect of, under UETA, 272
obvious or clerical (or typographic), 321
Escrow account, 521
E-SIGN Act (Electronic signatures in Global and National Commerce Act)(2000), 272, 273–274
E-signature(s)
attribution of, 274
authorized, 272
defined, 272
e-contracts and, 269
law governing, 272–275
of notary public, 274
technology and, 272
Estate
life, 934, 969
in property, 555–556
distribution of, 559–560
leasehold, 942–943
Estate planning, social media and, 963
Estop, 287
Estoppel
agency by, 603
apparent authority and, 608–609
corporation by, 754–755
partnership by, 706–707
promissory. *See* Promissory estoppel
Ethics, 190–209
bias against long-unemployed job applicants and, 658
business. *See* Business ethics
codes of, 195–196
contractual obligations and, 419
costs of complying with Sarbanes-Oxley Act and, 892
criticism of employers in social media and, 643
debt-collection practices and, 868
debtor's insolvency after deficiency judgment and, 498
default on student loans and, 560
defined, 191
defining material breach of contract and, 342
duty-based, 198–199
employer's use of "permalancers" and, 600–601
ethical reasoning and, approaches to, 198–201
failure of mortgage-participating bank and, 576
federal versus state copyright law and, 141
free access to proxy materials by interest groups and, 784
graphic product warnings and, 451–452
high-tech tracking devices and, 171
immigration law enforcement and, 641–642
Kantian, 198
liability of innocent partners and, 717–718
limitation-of-liability clauses and, 365
market power of TV programmers and distributors and, 837
merchants' information about customers' buying patterns and, 388
online retailers and state taxes and, 746
outcome-based, 199
ownership of engagement rings and, 912–913
pharmacists' duty of care and, 111
religious standards and, 198
risks of reporting unethical behavior and, 201
terrorism v. privacy rights and, 55
training employees in, 195
underfunded courts and, 73
European Court of Human rights, 42
European Patent Office, 138
European Union (EU), antitrust litigation and, 219
Event, specific, occurrence of
agency termination and, 617
gift *causa mortis* and, 915
partnership dissolution and, 713–714
Eviction, 943
Evidence
after-acquired, 672
discovery and, 77
e- (electronic), 78–79
extrinsic (outside), 250, 251n
parol (oral). *See* Parol evidence rule
preponderance of, 156
prima facie, of negligence, 884
rules governing use of, 179
Examination. *See also* Inspection
of bank statement, 501
of goods, by buyer or lessee, 421–422, 443
physical, preemployment, 670
request for, during discovery, 78
Exchange, share, 762
Exclusionary rule, 174–175
Exculpatory clause, 297–298, 364
Execution, 535, 549
Executive agencies, 9. *See also* Government regulation(s)
Executive employees, 628
Executor, 956
Exemption(s)
from antitrust laws, 848–850
bankruptcy and, 558, 849
homestead, 549, 558, 733–734
personal property, 549
real property, 548–549
Sarbanes-Oxley Act and, 820
from securities registration, 803–806
Expedited Funds Availability Act (EFAA) (1987), 508–509
Export(s), exporting, 215–218
exemption of, from antitrust laws, 849
financing of, 217
promoting, 216
Export Promotion Cabinet, 216
Export Trading Company Act (1982), 849
Export-Import Bank, 216
Expression
freedom of, 141–142, 839. *See also* Speech, freedom of
of opinion, 259. *See also* Opinion(s), statement of
Expropriation, 214, 217
Extension clause, 470
Exxon Valdez, 874

F

Fact(s)
affirmations of, 438
causation in, 113–114
compilations of, copyrightability and, 142
finding of, by trial court, 72–73
future, representations of, fraud and, 310
justifiable ignorance of the, 298
material misrepresentation of, 306–307, 308–311, 445, 887–888
private, public disclosure of, 104
question of, 72–73
statements of, 106, 439
defamation and, 100–101, 106
express warranty and, 439
opinion versus. 106
Fair and Accurate Credit Transactions (FACT) Act, 867
Fair Credit Reporting Act (FCRA), 866–867
Fair Debt-Collection Practices Act (FDCPA), 867–868
Fair Labor Standards Act (FLSA)(1938), 627, 527, 667, 628–629
Fair Packaging and Labeling Act, 860
False imprisonment, 98–99
Family and Medical Leave Act (FMLA)(1993), 630–631, 667
Family farmer, defined, 564–565

Family fisherman, 564–565
Farmer, 554n, 564n, 564–565
F.A.S. (free alongside ship), 404
Featherbedding, 644
Federal Arbitration Act (FAA)(1925), 85–86
Federal Aviation Administration (FAA), 863
Federal Communications Commission (FCC), 9
Federal court system, 73–75
  appellate (reviewing) courts of,27–29, 73–74. *See also* United States Supreme Court
  bankruptcy courts and, 550
  decisions in
    citations to, 27. 28, 29–30
    finding, 27, 28, 29–30
  illustrated, 74
  judges in, 73
  jurisdiction of, 65–66
  trial courts (United States District Courts) in, 65, 73. *See also* Trial court(s)
Federal Deposit Insurance Corporation (FDIC), 513, 576
Federal Food, Drug, and Cosmetic Act (FDCA), 860–863
Federal form of government, 34
Federal Hazardous Substances Act (1960), 864
Federal Insecticide, Fungicide, and Rodenticide Act (FIFRA), 874–875
Federal Insurance Contributions Act (FICA), 632–633
Federal question, 65–66
Federal Register, 10
Federal Reporter (F. Fd., or F.3d)(West), 27
Federal Reserve System (Fed)
  Board of Governors of
    Regulation CC of, 509
    Regulation E of, 510
    Regulation Z of, 865
  check clearance by, 509
  check collection process and, 505–509
  electronic check presentment and, 509
  wire transfer network of (Fedwire), 511
Federal Rules of Appellate Procedure, 13
Federal Rules of Civil Procedure, 77, 78
Federal Savings and Loan Insurance Corporation (FSLIC), 513
Federal Supplement (F.Supp. or F.Supp.2d) (West), 27
Federal Trade Commission (FTC), 9, 842, 848, 849
  antitrust laws enforced by, 848–849
  creation of, 9, 848
  credit reporting and, 867, 877
  deceptive advertising and, 857–860
  Do Not Call Registry and, 860
  enabling legislation of, 9
  Franchise Rule of, 690–691
  identity theft and, 867
  as independent regulatory agency, 9
  interlocking directorate threshold amounts and, 848
  online sales and, 861
  orders and remedies of, 859
  purpose of, 9
  rule of, limiting rights of HDCs, 486–487
  Rule 433 of, 487
  as source of consumer protection, 857-860, 861, 867
  telemarketing and, 860
  telephone and mail-order sales and, 861
Federal Trade Commission Act (1914), 9, 333, 848
Federal Trademark Dilution Act (1995), 128
Federal Unemployment Tax Act (FUTA), 634
Federal Water Pollution Control Act (FWPCA), 871
Fedwire, 511
Fee simple, 910–911, 934
Felony, 167–168
Fictitious payee rule, 484
Fiduciary
  defined, 598
  at heart of agency law, 598
Fiduciary duty(ies)
  of agents and principals, 598
  of corporate directors and officers, 777–782
  duty of care as. *See* Care, duty of
  of insurance agent to insurer, 950
  of joint venturers, 736
  LLCs and, 731–733
  duty of loyalty as. *See* Loyalty, duty of
  of partners, 709, 710, 712–715
  securities violations and, 810–811
  of trustees, 969
Fifth Amendment, 40, 49, 50, 170, 173–174, 940–941
File-sharing technology, 144–145
Filing
  of appeal, 81
  electronic, 82
Filtering software, 46
Financial institutions, ethical transgressions by, 190–191, 196–198
Financing statement
  contents of, 523–526
  continuation statement and, 529
  debtor's name on, 524–525
  defined, 520
  description of collateral in, 525–526
  filing of, 521, 523–528
    improper, consequences of, 526–527
    place of, 526
  lapse of, 529
  request for information from, 533
Financing, corporate, 758–761, 766, 768
First Amendment, 40, 41–46, 47, 100, 749, 839
Fisheries, exemption of, from antitrust laws, 849
Fisheries Cooperative Marketing Act (1976), 849
Fixtures, 519, 933
F.O.B. (free on board), 404
Food
  consumer protection and, 862–863
  labeling and packaging of, 860–861
  merchantable, 440–441
Forbearance, 282, 582
Force
  deadly versus nondeadly, 168
  justifiable use of, 168
  reasonable, 98–99
Force majeure clause, 221
Foreclosure, 573
  deed in lieu of, 583–584
  defined, 581
  friendly, 584
  how to avoid, 582–584
  judicial, 585, 586
  power of sale, 585
  procedures for, 584–586
  strict, 585
  types of, 585
Foreign Corrupt Practices Act (FCPA)(1977), 204–205, 220
Foreign exchange rate, 223
Foreign investors, in LLC, 729–730
Foreign nations
  franchising in, 690
  shareholder's derivative suits and, 790
Foreign officials, bribery of, 165, 204–205, 220
Foreign Sovereign Immunities Act (FSIA) (1976), 214–215
Foreign suppliers, 195
  monitoring employment practices of, 202–203
Foreseeability
  of circumstances, commercial impracticability and, 418–419
  misuse of products and, 450
  proximate cause and, 114, 115
  of risk, product misuse and, 450
  of unforeseen difficulties, 284
  of users of accountant's statements or reports, 889–891
Forfeiture, 166
Forgery, 163
  consequences of failing to detect, 501
  as defense to liability on negotiable instrument, 485–486
  of drawer's signatures on checks, 500–502
  of indorsements, 502–503 of
Forum shopping, 97, 102, 227
Forum-selection clause, 221, 270
Fourteenth Amendment, 41, 49, 50, 672
Fourth Amendment, 40, 55, 171–173, 637
Franchisee, 689–697
Franchises, 689–692
Franchisor, 689–697
Fraud, 105–106. *See also* Misrepresentation
  accountant's liability for, 885, 886–887
  actual, 886–887
  auction, online, 179
  bankruptcy, 166, 557, 563
  constructive, 886–887
  corporate directors and officers and, 778–780
  cyber, 179
  elements of, 308–312
  in the execution, 486
  illegal agreement and, 299
  in the inducement (ordinary fraud), 486
  mail, 165
  offshore, 822
  online, 179, 821–823

product liability and, 445
purchase of corporate assets and, 764–765
"risk-free," 822
securities, 808–811, 821–823
wire, 165
Fraudulent misrepresentation. *See* Fraud; Misrepresentation
Free-writing prospectus, 803
Freelancer. *See* Independent contractor(s)
Frustration of purpose, 346
Fundamental right, 50–51
Future advances, 530

G

GAAP (generally accepted accounting principles), 883–884, 893
GAAS (generally accepted auditing standards), 883–884, 893
Gambling, 292, 294
Garnishee, 544
Garnishment, 544–545
Gender, discrimination based on, 202, 227, 655, 660–661, 662–665, 732. *See also* Sexual harassment
General partnerships, 703–715 . *See also* Partnership(s)
comparison of limited partnership with, 718
Genetic Information Nondiscrimination Act (GINA), 639
Genetic testing, discrimination and, 637
Gift(s)
acquiring personal property by, 912–915
causa mortis (deathbed gift), 915
defined, 912
engagement rings and, ethics and, 912
inter vivos, 915
by will, types of, 957–958
Global marketing strategies, cultural differences and, 202, 203
Good faith, 428
accession and, 916
arbitrator's decision and, 85
bankruptcy and, 562n, 565
buyer's resale of rejected goods and, 428–429
collective bargaining and, 643, 646
consideration and, 392
corporate directors and officers and, 777, 778–780
defined, 478
franchising and, 693, 695–697
insurance and, 955
open price term and, 389
of partners, on dissolution of partnership, 714
release and, 286
required by Bankruptcy Code, 565
right to cure and, 417
sales and lease contracts and, 389, 390
secured transactions and, 535
substantial performance and, 341
taking in, HDC status and, 478
UCC and, 389, 392, 402, 413, 417, 479, 535
Good faith purchaser for value, 289n, 402
Goods
acceptance of, 421–422
associated with real estate, 386
bailed. *See* Bailment(s)
buyer's and lessee's right
to inspect, 443
to reject, 428–429
to obtain, 426
to replevy, 427
combined with services, 386
conforming, 392
defined, 414
risk of loss and, 405
consumer
purchase-money security interest (PMSI) in, 528
retention of collateral by secured party and, 536
contracts involving sale of. *See* Sales contract(s)
contracts primarily for, 387
counterfeit, 133–134
defined, 384–387
delivery of. *See* Delivery
description of, warranties and, 438
digital, 912
existing, 399
fungible, 400
future, 399–400
identification of, 399–400, 405–406
identified, destruction of, 420
in possession of buyer or lessee, seller's or lessor's remedies and, 425
in possession of seller or lessor, risk of loss and, 404
inspection of, 443
insurable interest in, 405–406
lessor's right to reclaim, 425
location of, as place of delivery, 414–415
merchantable, 440
nonconforming, 392, 405, 428–430
partial acceptance of, 423
prompt shipment of, 266n
reclaimed, remedies and, 425
rejection of, 428–429, 443
sale of. *See* Sales contract(s)
sample or model of, warranties and, 438
seller's or lessor's remedies when resale price insufficient, 424
seller's or lessor's right
to resell or dispose of, 423–424
to reclaim, 425
severance of, from land, 386
specially manufactured, exception to Statute of Frauds and, 395
stolen, receiving, 162–163
tender of, 401, 415–416
that are part of a larger mass, 400
in transit, seller's or lessor's remedies and, 424–425
unfinished, at time of breach, 423–424
warranties concerning. *See* Implied warranty(ies); Warranty(ies)
Goodwill, 108, 704, 707
Government
federal form of, 34
judiciary's role in, 61
local, ordinances of, 8
powers of
checks and balances of, 35
commerce clause and, 35–39
constitutional, 34–39
limitations on, 34, 40
regulation by. *See* Government regulation(s)
separation of, 34–35
Government regulation(s)
antitrust laws and. *See* Antitrust law(s)
concurrent, 815
counterfeit goods and, 133–134
environmental, 869–877
export controls and, 217–218
of franchising, 690–692
of gambling, 292
import controls and, 218
of securities, 799–826. *See also* Security(ies),
of spam, 120–121
by states. *See* State(s), regulation by
Gramm-Leach-Bliley Act (1999), 56
Grand jury, 176
Grandchildren, intestacy laws and, 964–965
per capita distribution of decedent's estate to, 965, 966
per stirpes distribution of decedent's estate to, 965
Grantee, grantor, 965
"Green card" (I-555 Registration Receipt), 640–641
Greenhouse gases, 870
Group boycotts, 839
Guaranty, guarantor, 545–548
Gun-Free School Zones Act (1990), 38

H

Hackers, hacking, 182, 185
Hague Convention on the Law Applicable to Contracts for the International Sale of Goods (Choice-of-Law Convention) (1986), 221
Harassment, 661–665. *See also* Sexual harassment
Hazardous air pollution, 870
Hazardous waste disposal, 875–876
Health Care and Education Reconciliation Act (2010), 633, 864n
Health insurance, 34, 633, 634, 671, 864, 955
Health Insurance Portability and Accountability Act (HIPAA), 53, 634
Health-care reforms, 864
Herbicides, 874–875
Historical school of legal thought, 16
Holder, 478, 479
defined, 470
through an HDC, 480–481
Holder in due course (HDC), 477–481
defined, 478
holder through a, 480–481
federal limitations on rights of, 486–487
requirements for status of, 478
transfer warranties and, 485
Holding companies, offshore, taxes and, 746
Home Affordable Modification Program (HAMP), 583

Home equity, 576–577
Home Ownership and Equity Protection Act (HOEPA)(1994), 579–580
Homestead exemption, 549, 733–734
Horizontal market division, 839
Hostile-environment harassment, 661, 732
Hotel operators, liability of, 925
Howey test, 801

I

ICANN (Internet Corporation for Assigned Names and Numbers), 686
Identification
  of collateral, 521
  of goods, 399–400
  insurable interest and, 405–406
  of perpetrator, prosecuting cyber crime and, 183–184
Identified goods, destruction of, 420
Identity, appropriation of, 104
Identity theft, 180–181, 867
  credit cards and, 181
  phishing and, 181
Illegality
  of contract, 298–299. *See also* Contract(s), legality of
  contract discharge by, 291
  as defense to liability on negotiable instrument, 486
  effect of, 297–298
  supervening, of proposed contract, 264
Immigration, 639, 642
  enforcement of laws governing, 640
  federal laws and, 639–642
  I-9 employment verification and, 639
  I-551 Alien Registration Receipt ("green card") and, 640–641
  labor certification application and, 641
  state laws and, 624, 641–642
  visa programs and, 641–642
Immigration Act (1990), 640–642
Immigration and Customs Enforcement (ICE), 629n, 640
Immigration and Nationality Act (1952), 639n
Immigration Reform and Control Act (IRCA) (1986), 639–640
Immunity
  as defense to criminal liability, 170
  sovereign, 214–215
  state, 667
Implied warranty(ies), 439–442
  bailments and, 923
  based on prior dealings or trade custom, 441–442
  defined, 439
  disclaimers of, 442–443
  of fitness for a particular purpose, 439, 923
  overlapping warranties and, 442
  of habitability, 937, 944
  of merchantability, 439–441, 923
Imports, importing, 218
Impossibility
  agency termination and, 618
  in Germany, 346
  objective, 345
  of performance, 345–346
  subjective, 346
  temporary, 346
Imposter rule, 484
Incapacity, mental. *See* Mental incompetence
Incompetence. *See* Mental incompetence
Incorporation
  checking domain names for, 752
  improper, 754–755
  preincorporation contracts and, 727
  preparing articles of, 752–753
  procedures for, 751–753
  promotional activities and, 751
  securing the corporate name and, 751
  selecting state of, 751
  trade name disputes and, 752
Incorporators, 753
Indemnification
  of agent, 606
  corporate director's right to, 776
Independent contractor(s)
  agency relationships and, 598
  defined, 598
  employer's use of, 619
  insurance broker as, 950
  torts of, 600
  works for hire and, 601
independent regulatory agencies, 9. *See also* Government regulation(s)
Indictment, 40, 176
Individual retirement accounts (IRAs), 963
Indorsee, 449
Indorsement(s)
  in blank, 474, 475, 489
  conditional, 476
  defined, 473
  for deposit or collection, 476
  forged, 502–503
  misspelled names on, 476–477
  qualified, 474–476
  restrictive, 476
  severe restrictions on, in France, 474
  special, 474
  trust (agency), 476–477
  transfer warranties and, 485
  unauthorized, 483–484
Indorsers, 481, 482
Information,
  in criminal process, 176
  digital, copyrights in, 144
  electronically stored, 79
  on financing statement, request for, 533
  inside, 809
  requests for
    during discovery, 77–78
    by secured party or debtor, 533
Infringement
  copyright, 142
  patent, 139–140
  title warranties and, 438
  trademark, 129
Inheritance, 939
Initial public offering (IPO), 761, 805
Injury(ies)
  as requirement for damages, 114
  to consumers, caused by deceptive advertising, 859
  to innocent party, 111, 312, 887, 312
  legally recognizable, 111, 113, 114
  in workplace, 631–632
Insanity, as defense to criminal liability, 169
Inside information, 809
Insider trading, 808–811
  defined, 166
  detection of, software to assist, 778
Insider Trading and Securities Fraud Enforcement Act (1988), 815
Insider Trading Sanctions Act (1984), 814
Insiders, preferences to, 557
Insolvency
  balance-sheet, 551n
  of debtor after deficiency judgment, 498
  defined, 402
  of drawer or maker, 485
  equitable, 551n
  filing for bankruptcy and, 551
  of seller or lessor, 426
  transfer warranties and, 485
  UCC and, 402
Inspection
  buyer's or lessee's refusal to make, 443
  by OSHA, 631
  right of
    buyer's or lessee's, 421–422
    director's and officer's, 776
    partner's, 708
    shareholder's, 788
  warranties and, 443
Insurable interest, 405–406, 950–952
Insurance, 950–856
  auto, 955
  beneficiary of, 950
  classifications of, 950–952
    summarized, 951
  coinsurance clauses and, 952–953
  contract for (insurance policy), 952–956
    application and, 952
    appraisal clause and, 955
    cancellation of, 954–955
    clauses and provisions in, summarized, 953
    effective date of, 952
    good faith obligations under, 955
    incontestability clauses and, 953
    interpreting, 954
  defenses to payment of claims and, 956
  defined, 950
  deposit, 513–514
  for directors and officers (D&O insurance), 776
  duties of insurer under, 955
  group health, 634–635
  homeowners' (hazard), mortgage loans and, 577
  insurable interest and, 405–406, 950–952
  for investments abroad, 217 for
  key-person, 951
  life, 951, 952, 955
  for losses due to hacking, 185
  policy for. *See* Insurance, contract for
  preexisting condition and, 634
  premium for, 950, 952
  property, 951, 955
  terminology of, 950
  underwriter for, 950

unemployment, 634
Insurance companies, exemption of, from antitrust laws, 849
Insurer, 950
Insured, 950
Intellectual property, 126–154. *See also* specific forms of intellectual property
defined, 126
former partner's use of, 705
forms of, summarized, 147
international protection for, 127, 147–150
Intent, intention
to abandon easement or profit, 936
criminal liability and, 158
to deceive, 311–312, 887–888
donative, 913
future, statements of, 259–260
implied, 843
monopoly power and, 843
offer and, 258–262
of parties, contract interpretation and, 250–252
in tort law, 97
wills and, 958
Intentional tort(s)
agent's, 615
defined, 97
against persons, 97–98
against property, 107–110
Interest(s)
conflict of, 781–782
insurable, 405–406, 950–952
in land, contracts involving, 361
partner's, in partnership, 707–708
partnership, interest in the, 715
rate of
annual percentage (APR), 578–579
judgment, 472
mortgages and, 575–576
negotiable instruments and, 468
usury and, 292
security. *See* Security interest(s)
Interlocking directorates, 848
Intermediate scrutiny, 51
Internal Revenue Code, 750, 897
Internal Revenue Service (IRS), 600–601, 705, 729, 914
International business transactions
global marketing strategies and, 690
government regulation and, 217–220
making payment on, 223–225
International contract(s), 406–406
clauses in, 220–221, 222–223
dispute resolution and, 222–223, 224
jurisdictional issues and, 68–69
licensing and, 217
side payments and, 204–205
International customs, 211
International Financial Reporting Standards (IFRS), 884
International law(s), 18–19, 210–232
defined, 18–19, 210
in global context, 225–227
sources of, 211–212
Statute of Frauds and, 317
International organizations, 211–212
International principles and doctrines, 212–215
Internet
auction fraud and, 179
banking and, 511–512
bankruptcy court chat rooms and, 550
contract formation and, 247, 268–275. *See also* E-contract(s)
corporate reputations and, 203, 204, 206
court system and, 82
crowdfunding via, 759
cyber marks and, 135–137
dating sites on, misrepresentation and, 309
deceptive advertising and, 858–859
defamation and, 119, 120
dispute resolution and, 88–89
electronic (e-) proxies on, 783–784
employee use of, 635–637, 649–650
escrow services and, 521
estate planning and, 963
expansion of precedent and, 13
file-sharing technology and, 144–145
franchising and, 691
freedom of speech and, 43
gambling and, 294
hacking and, 182, 185
harassment and, 664
identity theft and, 180–181
initial public offering via, 805
investment newsletters and forums on, 821–822
investment scams via, 821
jurisdiction and, 66–68
licensing software and, 268
misrepresentation and, 309
obscene speech and, 46
payment systems on, 510
personal ads on, 309
posting false information on, 184
privacy rights and, 53–54
reporting systems and, 196
retail fraud and, 179
sales on, taxes and, 746
searchable patent databases on, 138
secured transactions and, 521
securities fraud and, 821–823
securities sold via, 805, 821–823
social networking and, 52
trademark dilution and, 137
trademark disputes and, 130
travel companies on, local taxation and, 386
Internet Corporation for Assigned Names and Numbers (ICANN), 138
Internet service providers (ISPs), 98, 119, 120, 145
Internet Tax Freedom Act (1998), 746n
Interpretative rules, 10
Interrogatories, 79
Interstate Oil Compact (1935), 849
Intestacy laws, 963–965
Intestate, 956
Intoxicated persons, 290, 300
Intrusion into an individual's affairs or seclusion, 104
Inventory
floating lien in, 530
security interest in, 530
Investigation, by administrative agencies, 10, 20
Investing in foreign nations, 217
Investment company, 805
Investor(s)
accredited, 805
protection for, 799–826
foreign, in LLC, 729–730
Invitation to submit bids, 260
Involuntary dissolution, of corporation, 767
Islamic law, 18, 72, 616

J

Joint stock companies, 737, 738
Joint ventures, 736
Judge(s)
administrative law (ALJ), 10
defined, 30
federal, appointment of, 73
justice versus, 30
sentencing guidelines and, 178
Judgment(s)
confession of, 707
default, 76
deficiency, 498, 537–538, 586
enforcement of, 82
on the pleadings, 76–77
summary, 77
Judicial review, 61, 63
Judiciary
federal, increased diversity in, 62
role of, in American government, 61
Judiciary Act (1789), 63
Jurisdiction, 61–69
antitrust laws and, 850
appellate, 65
concurrent, 66
in cyberspace, 66–68
defined, 61
exclusive, 66
of federal courts, 65–66
international issues concerning, 68–69
limited, 65–66
limited liability company and, 729
minimum contacts and, 62–64, 66–67
original, 65
over persons (*in personam*) 62–65
precedents and, 12
over property (*in rem*), 62–65
prosecuting cyber crime and, 183–184
of Sherman Act, 835–836
"sliding-scale" standard and, 67–68
over subject matter, 65
United States Constitution and, 65–66
Jurisprudence, 15–16
Jury(ies)
grand, 176
prospective jurors for, challenges to, 79–80
selection of (*voir dire*), 78–80
trial by, right to, 40, 174
Justice(s)
defined, 30
judge versus, 30
of United States Supreme Court, 74
Justiciable controversy, 69–70

K

Key person, 951
Knowledgeable user defense, 456

L

Labor
  child, 627
  exemption of, from antitrust laws, 849
Labor certification, 641
Labor law, 624, 642–649
Labor union(s). *See* Union(s)
Labor-Management Relations Act (Taft-Hartley Act)(1947), 644
Labor-Management Reporting and Disclosure Act (LMRDA)(1959), 644
Land. *See also* Real property
  defined, 932
  interests in, contracts involving, 313–314, 361
  sale of, disaffirmance and, 289
  "things attached" to, 933
  trespass to, 108–109
Landlord-tenant relationship, 943–944
  mitigation of damages and, 358
  rights and duties in, 943–944
Landowners, duty of, 112–113
Lanham Act (1946), 128, 129
Larceny, 161–162
Law(s)
  action at, versus action in equity, illustrated, 14
  administrative. *See* Administrative law
  affecting single business transaction, 4, 5
  antitrust. *See* Antitrust law(s)
  blue sky, 298, 815
  case. *See* Case law
  change in, illegal performance and, 346
  civil. *See* Civil law
  classifications of, 16–19
  "code," 17–18
  common. *See* Common law
  constitutional, 6–7
  consumer. *See* Consumer law(s)
  contract. *See* Contract(s)
  "cooling off," 861
  courts of, 13
  criminal. *See* Crime(s); Criminal law
  cyber-, 17
  defined, 3
  due process of. *See* Due process
  environmental. *See* Environmental law(s)
  foreign, 41
  governing franchising, 689–697. *See* also Franchise(s)
  "gray areas" in, 193
  immigration, 639–642. *See also* Immigration
  international. *See* International law(s)
  intestacy, 956, 963–965
  Islamic, 18, 72, 616
  labeling and packaging, 860–861
  labor. *See* Labor law(s)
  lemon, 444–445
  merging of, with equity, 14
  misrepresentation of, 310
  mistake of, 169
  national, 18–19, 210
  natural, 15
  operation of. *See* Operation of law
  partnership. *See* Partnership(s)
  plain-language, 249, 250
  primary sources of, 6
  procedural, 16–17
  questions of, 72
  right-to-work, 644
  secondary sources of, 6
  sources of, 6–11
  statutory, 7–8
  substantive, 16–17
  tort. *See* Tort(s)
  U.S., in global context, 225–227, 690
  uniform 8, 283
  workers' compensation. *See* Workers' compensation
Lawsuit(s). *See also* Case(s); Litigation
  ADR versus, 90
  basic judicial requirements for, 61–70
  class-action, 97
  covenant not to bring, 286
  parties to, 30
  sample, 30–32
  shareholder's derivative, 744, 782, 789–790
  standing to bring (standing to sue), 69–70
  tort, criminal prosecution for same act versus, 157
  workers' compensation versus, 632
Lawyers' Edition of the Supreme Court Reports (L.Ed. or L.Ed.2d), 27
Lease(s). *See also* Lease contract(s)
  consumer, 388
  defined, 388
  by nonowners, 402
Lease contract(s)
  acceptance in, 391–394
  breach of, 422–423
    anticipatory, 420, 422–423
  cancellation of, 423
  consideration and, 392, 394
  formation of, 383, 388–412
  good faith requirement and, 389
  modification of, 394
  offer in, 389–391
  performance obligations in, 396, 414–422
  remedies for breach of
    damages as, 494
    of lessee, 425–429
    of lessor, 423–425
  repudiation of, anticipatory, 420, 422–423
  rescission of, 423, 426
  risk of loss and, 399–405, 408
  Statute of Frauds and, 394–396
  transferring rights under, 944
  unconscionability and, 296, 398–399
Leased premises, use and maintenance of, 943
Legacy, 957
Legal encyclopedias, 6
Legal environment, business activities and, 4–6
Legal positivism, 16
Legal realism, 16
Legatee, 957
Legislative (substantive) rule, 9–10
Legitimate government interest, 51
Lender. *See* Creditor(s)
Lessee
  breach by, 405
  defined, 388
  goods in possession of, lessor's remedies and, 425
  insurable interest of, 405
  obligations of, 421-422
  payment obligations of, 421
  refusal of, to inspect goods, 443
  right of inspection of, 421
Lessor
  breach by, 405
  defined, 388
  goods in possession of, lessee's remedies and, 423–424
  insolvency of, 426
  insurable interest of, 405–406
  obligations of, 414–421
Letter of credit, 223–225
  defined, 223
  illustration of, 226
  parties to, 224
  value of, 224–225
Levy, 535
Liability
  contingent, 481
  contract clauses limiting, 297–298, 364–365
  joint, 711
  joint and several, 711, 876
  market share, 452–453
  primary, 481, 545, 547
  product. *See* Product liability
  proportionate, 896
  secondary, 481–483, 547–547
  signature, 481–484
  strict. *See* Strict liability
  vicarious (indirect), 146, 613
  warranty, 481, 484–485, 923
  without fault. *See* Strict liability
Libel, 100, 110
License, licensing, 134–135, 217, 936
  click-on agreements and, 270–271
  defined, 134
  of intellectual property, 217, 558, 689
  online contract formation and, 268
  shrink-wrap agreements and, 270–271
Licensee, 109, 268
Licensor, 268
Licensing statutes, 292–293
Lie-detector tests, 637
Lien(s), 438, 548–549
  artisan's, 109, 548
  bailee's, 921
  floating, 530–531
  judicial, 521n, 548–549
  mechanic's, 548
  on negotiable instrument, 478
  possessory, 548
  title warranties and, 438
Lilly Ledbetter Fair Pay Act (2009), 660–661
Limited liability company(ies) (LLC), 726–735
  compared with other business forms, 724, 739, 792–793
  defined, 726
  management of, 729–733

nature of, 726–727
taxation and, 726, 729
Limited liability partnership (LLP), 716, 717
compared with other business forms, 792–793
Limited (special) partnership (LP), 717–720
compared with other major business forms, 792–793
comparison of general partnership with, 718
defined, 717
Liquidation, under Chapter 7, 550, 551–561
Litigation
abusive or frivolous, 106
arbitration versus, 224
defined, 75
workers' compensation versus, 632
Loan(s)
home equity, 576–577
mortgage, 328. *See also* Mortgage(s)
student, bankruptcy and, 560
Truth-in-Lending Act and, 578–579
Loss(es)
defined, 815n
economic, 808
joint ventures and, 736
partnerships and, 704
risk of, 399–405, 408
Loyalty
defined, 780
duty of
agent's, 605
breach of, 709
corporate directors' and officers', 780–781
joint venturers', 736
LLC manager's, 731–733
partners', 709, 712

M

Madrid Protocol (2003), 150
Magnuson-Moss Warranty Act (1975), 443–444
Mail Fraud Act (1990), 165n
Mailbox rule, 267
"Main purpose" rule, 316, 546n
Majority, age of, 288, 289b
Maker, 465
act of, will revocation by, 961
defined, 465,
insolvency of, 485
liability of, 481
Malpractice, 113, 886–887
Malware, 182
Management
customer relationship (CRM), 276
human resource (HRM), 674
top, ethical attitudes and behavior of, 194–195
total quality (TQM), 457
Manufacturing
abroad, 216–217
defects in products and, 448–449
or processing plant arrangement, franchises and, 690
Marijuana, medical, 38, 686
Market, relevant, 842–843
Market concentration, 847
Market power, 835, 837
Marketing strategies, global, cultural differences and, 202, 203
Marriage, 52
promises made in consideration of, 313, 314
wills and, 961–962, 964
Marriage equality, 52
McCarran-Ferguson Act (1945), 849
Mediation, as form of ADR, 84
Medicare, 633
Member of LLC, 726, 727, 729, 731, 733–734
Mens rea (wrongful mental state), 158
Mental incapacity. *See* Mental incompetence
Mental incompetence
of agent or principal, agency termination and, 617–618
of bank customer, 500
contractual capacity and, 290–291
as defense to liability on negotiable instrument, 486
of general partner, limited partnership dissolution and, 719
of limited partner, partnership dissolution and, 719
of offeror, offer termination and, 264
of principal or agent, agency termination and, 617–618
Menus, labeling requirements for, 861
Merchant(s)
both parties as, 393
contracts between, special rules for, 395
customer buying patterns and, 388
defined, 387
entrustment of goods to, 402
firm offer of, 391
oral contracts between, 318
special standards for, under UCC, 265n, 387, 392–394
status as, 387
Mergers, 761–766, 847–848
Meta tags, 46, 136–137
Minimum contacts, 66
Minor(s)
contractual capacity and, 288–290
disaffirmance by, 289–290
emancipation of, 288
entering into contracts with, 300
status as, liability on negotiable instrument and, 486
Miranda rule, 174–175
Mirror image rule, 264, 392
Misappropriation theory, 810–811
Misdemeanors, 168
Misrepresentation
fraudulent, 308–312
intent to deceive and, 311–312
of law, 310
material, 808
negligent, 106
online personals and, 309
product liability based on, 445
professional's liability for, 887–888
reliance on, 312
voluntary consent and, 308–312
Mistake. *See also* Error(s)
bilateral (mutual), 306–308, 361
as defense to criminal liability, 169
of fact, 169, 306, 307
of law, 169
mathematical, 306
unilateral, 306
of value, 306
voluntary consent and, 306–313, 323
Model Business Corporation Act (MBCA), 743
Model Penal Code, 158n, 160n
Money
fixed amount of, 468
laundering of, 166–167
monetary systems and, 223
Monopolization, 840–844, 850
attempted, 840, 844–845
Monopoly, 835
Monopoly power, 835, 841–842
Moral minimum, 191–192
Mortgagee, 574
Mortgage(s), 328, 573–591. *See also* Loan(s)
acceleration clause and, 585
adjustable-rate (ARM), 576
balloon, 576
creditor protection and, 577–578
defined, 573, 574
fixed-rate, 575
foreclosure and. *See* Foreclosure(s)
high-cost mortgage loan (HCML) and, 579–581, 582
important provisions of, 577
interest-only (IO), 576
pre-payment penalty clause and, 577
property maintenance clause and, 577
protection for consumers and, 580
reamortizing, 582
recording of, 577
requirement of homeowners' insurance and, 577
restructuring of, 582
reverse redlining and, 574
right to rescind, 579
subprime, 576
types of, 575–576
writing requirement and, 577
Mortgage Disclosure Improvement Act (2008), 579
Mortgagor, 574
Motion(s)
for directed verdict, 80
to dismiss, 76
for judgment *n.o.v.*, 80
for judgment on the pleadings, 76–77
for new trial, 80
pretrial, 76–77, 80
for summary judgment, 77
MP3, 144–146
Music files, online sharing of, 144–146
Mutual fund, 805

N

National Credit Union Shares Insurance Fund (NCUSIF), 513
National Environmental Policy Act (NEPA) (1960), 869
National Export Initiative (NEI)(2010), 216
National Labor Relations Act (NLRA)(1935), 642–643, 645–646
National Conference of Commissioners on Uniform State Law (NCCUSL), 272, 273, 283, 285, 703, 726, 815, 943, 958
National law, 18–19, 210
National origin, discrimination based on, 227, 655, 658–659, 661, 732
National Pollutant Discharge Elimination System (NPDES), 871–872
National Reporter System (West), 25, 26
National Securities Markets Improvement Act (1996), 800
Native Americans, criminal justice and, 162
Natural law school, 15–16
Natural rights, 16
Necessaries, 290
Necessity
  as defense to criminal liability, 168
  easement by, 935
Negligence, 97, 111–122
  of agent, 613–615
  bank, 501–502
  comparative, 117, 455
  contributory, 116–117
  criminal, 158
  defenses to, 114–117
  defined, 111
  elements of, 111
  environmental law and, 869
  gross, 97
  per se, 117
  product liability based on, 445
  professional's liability and, 883–887
  special doctrines and statutes concerning, 117–118
Negotiable instrument(s), 462–493
  alteration of, 479
  assignment of, 331
  certificates of deposit (CDs) as, 465–466
  checks as. *See* Check(s)
  defense against, HDC status and, 479
  defined, 462
  incomplete, 479
  dishonored, 479, 480
  drafts as, 463–464
  as formal contract, 244–245
  indorsements on. *See* Indorsement(s)
  liability on
    defenses to, 485–486
    discharge from, 487–488
    signature, 481–484
    warranty, 481, 484–485
  negotiability of, 466–472
    factors not affecting, 472
    requirements for, 466
  notes as, 465–466
  overdue, 479, 480
  signatures on. *See* Signature(s)
  transfer of, 472
    by assignment, 472–473
    by negotiation, 472, 473
    warranties and, 484–485
  types of, 463–466
    summarized, 463
  UCC and, 467
  undated, 472
Negotiation(s)
  collective bargaining and, 646
  as form of ADR, 84
  preliminary, 260
  transfer of negotiable instruments by, 472, 473
Netflix, customer relationship management (CRM) and, 276
Network, distributed, 144–145
Networking, peer–to–peer (P2P), 144–145
New York Clearing House Interbank Payments Systems (CHIPS), 511
Ninth Amendment, 40
Nonconforming goods, 392, 405, 428–430
Nonmerchant, one or both parties as, 393
Normal trade relations (NTR) status, 219
Norris-LaGuardia Act (1932), 642
North American Free Trade Agreement (NAFTA), 218, 219
Notary public, 607
Notice(s)
  of acceptance, 392, 407
  agent's duty of, 604
  of assignment, 331–332
  of claims or defenses, HDC status and, 480
  constructive, 617n
  to consumer, credit reporting and, 866
  of dangerous conditions in workplace, 615
  to debtor and others, of disposition of collateral, 536, 537
  of default, 544, 585
  of layoff, 629–630
  posting of, in workplace, 631
  proper, of dishonor, 482
  of revocation of acceptance, 429
  of shareholder meetings, 783
  of special directors' meetings, 776
  taking without, HDC status and, 479–480
  of termination of agency, 617
  of termination of ongoing sales contract, 390
  validation, 868
Novation, 344
Nuisance, 868–869
Nutrition Labeling and Education Act, 860

O

Obedience, agent's duty of, 605
Obligation(s)
  performance, 414–422
  suspension of, on anticipatory repudiation, 422
  primary versus secondary, 315–316
Obligee, 328, 330, 333–334
Obligor, 328, 330, 333–334
Occupational Safety and Health Act (1970), 631
Occupational Safety and Health Administration (OSHA), 20, 631
Offer
  of bribe, 165
  CISG and, 406–407
  contractual, 258–265
  display of, online, 268
  merchant's firm, 391
  online, 268–270
  settlement, 366
  tender, 765–766
  for unilateral contract, 243
Offeree
  counteroffer by, 264
  defined, 242, 258
  death or incompetence of, offer termination and, 264–265
  duty of, to speak, 265–266
  inquiries about offer by, 264
  rejection of offer by, 263–264
Offerer
  assent of, to additional terms, 393–394
  death or incompetence of, offer termination and, 264–265
  defined, 242, 258
  intent of, 258–262
  revocation of offer by, 263
Officers, corporate. *See* Corporate officer(s)
Oil marketing, exemption of, from antitrust laws, 849
Oil Pollution Act (1990), 874
One-year rule, 313, 314–315, 363
Online contracts. *See* E-contracts(s)
Operating agreement, 734
  writing and, 730
Operation of law
  agency relationship formed by, 603–604
  agency terminated by, 617–618
  contract discharge by, 344–347
  termination of offer by, 264
  will revocation by, 961–962
Opinion(s)
  of appellate court, 30
  of auditor, 885
  concurring, 30
  dissenting, 30
  expressions of offer versus, 259
  majority, 30
  per curiam, 30
  plurality, 30
  statement of, 100, 106, 310, 439
  unanimous, 30
  unpublished, 13, 27
Order(s)
  cease-and-desist, 859
  charging, 708
  multiple product, 859
  to pay, 467–468. *See also* Check(s)
  payable to, 470
  for relief, 554
  stop-payment, 499
Order instrument(s)
  defined, 470

negotiating, 473
Ordinances, 8
OSHA (Occupational Safety and Health Administration), 20
Outsiders, SEC Rule 10b-5 and, 810–811
Ownership, of property. *See* Property, personal, ownership of; Property, ownership of; Real property, ownership of

P

PA (professional association), 750
PacMan defense to takeover, 766
Parent-subsidiary (short-form) merger, 763
Parents, liability of, for minor's contracts, 290
Paris Convention (1883), 147
Parol evidence rule, 320–322
  defined, 320
  exceptions to, 320–321
  sales and lease contracts and, 396–397
  identification of signer of negotiable instrument and, 467
Participation, corporate director's right to, 776
Partner(s)
  actions of, partnership dissolution and, 713–714
  admission of new, 707
  as agent, 706, 709
  authority of, agency law and, 710
  compensation of, 708
  dissociation of, 711, 712–713, 719–720
  fiduciary duties of, 709, 715
  foreign, 705
  incoming, 710–711
  interest of, in partnership, 707–708
  liability of, 710–711, 716–718
    joint, 711
    joint and several, 711
  in limited partnership, 716–720
  in limited liability partnership, 716–717
  management rights of, 707–708
  rights of, 707–708
  usurping of partnership business opportunity by, 709–710
Partnership(s), 702–724
  agency concepts and, 703
  articles of, 705
  assets or profits of, accounting of, 708
  basic concepts concerning, 703
  debts of, 710
  defined, 703, 704
  dissolution of, 713, 714
  duration of, 706
  entity versus aggregate theory of, 704–705
  by estoppel, 706–707
  formation of, 704–707
  general (ordinary), 702
  law governing, 703, 730
  limited. *See* Limited liability partnership(s); Limited partnership(s)
  management of, 704
  partner's interest in, 707–708
  partnership agreement and, 706
  as pass-through entity, 705, 716
  property rights and, 708
  shared profits and losses of, 704
  special. *See* Limited (special) partnership(s)
  tax treatment of, 705, 716
  for a term, 706
  at will, 706
  winding up of, 715
Party(ies)
  acts of
    offer termination by, 263–264
    agency termination by, 616–617
  agreement of
    exception to perfect tender rule and, 416
    to conduct transactions electronically, 273–274
  conduct of
    acceptance of e-contract and, 270
    implied contract created by, 245
  to contract, death or incapacity of, contract discharge by, 345
  innocent, injury to, 111, 312, 887, 312
  to lawsuits, 30
  to letter of credit, 224
  potentially responsible (PRP), 876
  secured. *See* Secured party(ies)
Pass-through entities, taxes and, 704, 716, 705, 716, 729
Patents, 138–140
Patient Protection and Affordable Care Act (2010), 861n, 864n
Payable
  to bearer, 470, 471
  to order, 470
Paycheck Fairness Act (2009), 660
Payee(s)
  alternative or joint, 477
  defined, 463
  fictitious, 484
Payment(s)
  accord and satisfaction and, 285
  bankruptcy plans and, 564–567
  to bearer, 470, 471
  buyer's obligation to make, 414
  to creditors, liquidation bankruptcy and, 553
  at a definite time, 463, 469–470
  on demand, 468
  down, 268, 575, 577
  insurance company's defenses against, 956
  international transactions and, 223–225
  Internet and, 510
  to order, 467, 468, 470
  side, international transactions and, 204–205
  smart-phone based systems for, 512
  tax, mortgages and, 577
  timely, 566
PCBs (polychlorinated biphenyls), 875
Peer–to–peer (P2P) networking, 144–145
Penalty(ies)
  defined, 358
  liquidated damages versus, 358–359
Pension Benefit Guaranty Corporation (PBGC), 633
Pension plans, private, 633–634
Per se, 117
Perfect tender rule, 415–421
Perfection, of security interest. *See* Security interest(s), perfection of
Performance
  agent's duty of, to principal, 604
  complete, 341
  conditions of, 338–340
  of contract, 246
  course of, 252, 321, 397–398
  defined, 338
  discharge by, 340–342
  impossibility of, 345–346. *See also* Impossibility
  obligations of, 414–422
  options and cooperation regarding, 390
  options to consider when you cannot perform and, 366
  partial
    as exception to perfect tender rule, 419
    as exception to Statute of Frauds, 317, 396, 419
  right of assurance and, 420
  to the satisfaction of another, 341–342
  substantial, 341
  tender of, 340
  time for, 416–417
"Permalancers," 600–601
Person(s)
  accused, constitutional protections for, 170–178
  intentional torts against, 97–98
  intoxicated, 290
  key, insurance for, 951
  "legal" (artificial)
    corporation as, 64, 159–160, 744, 766, 773, 951
    limited liability company as, 727
  natural, 744
Personal identification number (PIN), 510
Personal property, 909–918
  artisan's lien and, 548
  bailments and. *See* Bailment(s)
  conversion of, 110
  defined, 108, 909
  exempt, 549
  intangible, 523, 909–910
  ownership of, acquiring, 911–918
  security interests in, 519. *See also* Security interest(s)
  tangible, 523, 909–910, 919
  trespass to, 109
Personal representative, 956
Personal-service contract(s)
  assignment and, 330
  delegations and, 333
  specific performance and, 361
Personalty, 109. *See* Personal property
Persuasive authority, 12
Pesticides, 874–875
Petitioner, 30
Petroleum Marketing Practices Act (PMPA) (1979), 691n, 694–695
Petty offenses, 168
Phishing, 181
Piercing the corporate veil, 728, 756–758
Plain language laws, 249, 250
Plain meaning rule, 250–252
Plaintiff
  defined, 14, 30
  complaint of, 75–76

Plant life, as real property, 932 –933
Plea bargaining, 170
Pleadings, 75–76
  motion for judgment on, 76–77
Pledge, 528
Point-of-sale systems, 510
"Poison pill" defense to takeover, 768
Police powers, 38
Pollution, 874
  air, 870–871
  oil, 874
  water, 871–874
Polychlorinated biphenyls (PCBs), 875
Ponzi schemes, 180, 822
Pornography, 46
Possession
  acquiring personal property by, 911
  actual, 556
  adverse, 939–940
  bailee's right to, 918, 920
  of collateral, perfection without filing and, 528
  constructive, 556
  debtor in (DIP), 562–563
  of leased premises, 943
Power(s)
  of attorney, 601n, 607
  condemnation, 940
  market, 835
  monopoly, 835, 841–842
  government, 34. *See also* Government; Government regulation(s)
    checks and balances and, 35
  of shareholders, 782–783
  strong-arm, 556
Precedent, 11–12, 13
Predatory behavior, 107
Predatory lending, 578
Predatory pricing, 840
Predominant factor test, 386–387
Preemption
  defined, 38
  of claims for product liability, 454
Preferences
  bankruptcy and, 557, 563
  stock with, 758, 760
Preferred stock, 758, 760
Pregnancy, discrimination based on, 660, 661
Pregnancy Discrimination Act (1978), 660
Preponderance of the evidence, 156
Presentment
  electronic, 509
  of instrument, 469
  proper, 482, 483
  timely, 482
Presentment warranties, 484–485
"Pretexting," 56
Pretrial conference, 78
Price
  buyout, 713
  discrimination and, 845–846
  disposition of collateral and, 537
  open term for, CISG and, 406
  predatory pricing and, 840
  price fixing and, 837–839, 849
  purchase, seller's or lessor's right to recover, 424
  resale, 424
Primary sources of law, 6
Principal(s)
  agent's duties to, 604–605
  defined, 597
  disclosed, 610, 611
  duties of, to agent, 604, 605–606
  partially disclosed, 610, 611
  tortious conduct of, 612–613
  undisclosed, 610, 612
Prior dealing (course of dealing), 252, 321, 441–442
Privacy, invasion of, 104
Privacy Act (1974), 53
Privacy right(s), 34
  constitutional protection for, 51–52, 104
  consumers and, 862
  e-contracts and, 269
  of employees, 635–639
  federal laws protecting, 52–53, 54
  medical information and, 54
  social networks and, 108
  technological advances and, 53–55
  United States Constitution and, 51–52
  USA Patriot Act (2001) and, 54–55
  workplace monitoring and, 635–639
Private equity capital, 760–761
Private Securities Litigation Reform Act (1995), 812–813, 896
Privilege, 101
  accountant-client, 897–898
  attorney-client, 897–898
  defined, 103
  to detain, 98–99
  qualified, 103
Privity of contract, 327, 448, 889–890
Prize, changing in contest, ethics and, 243
Probable cause, 172–173, 175, 176
Probate, 962
  defined, 962
  formal, 962
  informal, 962
  property transfers outside the process of, 963
Procedural law, 16–17
Proceeds from disposition of collateral, 529, 535, 537
Product(s)
  defects in, 448–450
  labeling and packaging of, 860–861
  misuse of, 450, 455
  safety of, consumer protection and, 863–864
  unreasonably dangerous, 448
Product liability, 445–458
  based on
    misrepresentation, 445
    negligence, 445
  of Chinese sellers, for defective goods sold in United States, 449
  defenses to, 454–458
  defined, 444
  strict
    assumptions underlying, 446–447
    public policy and, 446–447
    requirements for, 448
Product market, relevant, 842
Production, acquiring personal property by, 911–912
Professional association (PA), 750
Professionals. *See also* Accountant(s); Attorney(s)
  duties of, 113, 883–887
  liability of, 882–902
Profit(s)
  defined, 815n
  in real property law, 935–936
  partnership, 708
  joint ventures and, 736
  distribution of, in joint stock companies, 738
  maximization of, business ethics and, 192–193
  net, of corporation, 787
  partnerships and, 704
  short-swing, 810
Promise(s)
  absolute, 338
  collateral, 315–316
  defined, 239
  enforcement of, to avoid injustice, 287
  illusory, 285
  made in consideration of marriage, 315
  to pay, 465–468
  to ship, as acceptance, 266n, 391
Promisee, 240
Promisor, 240, 335–336
Promissory estoppel, 286–288
  application of, 287–288
  detrimental reliance and, 286–288
  as exception to Statute of Frauds, 318
  requirements to establish, 287
Promissory note, 465, 481
Proof, burden of. *See* Burden of proof
Proper presentment, 482, 483
Property
  abandoned, 918
  after-acquired, 529–530
  bailed
    bailee's duty to return, 922
    bailee's right to use, 920
  community, 555–556, 911
  crimes involving, 161–163
  defined, 909
  disparagement of, 110
  distribution of, in bankruptcy, 559–560
  estate in, 555–556
  exempt, 536n, 544
  insurance for, 951–952, 955
  intangible, 384, 386
  intellectual. *See* Intellectual property
  lost, 917, 926
  mislaid, 916
  movable, 384, 386
  ownership of, 910–916
    concurrent, 910
    in fee simple, 910–911
  personal. *See* Personal property
  real. *See* Real property
  tangible, 384, 386
  testamentary disposition of, 956. *See also* Will(s)
  title to, 910
  virtual and digital, 912

Proposition 8, 52
Proposition 209, 261
Prosecution
  of cyber crime, 183–184
  malicious, 106
Prospectus, 802, 803, 894
Protect Act (Prosecutorial Remedies and Cyber Tools to End the Exploitation of Children Today Act)(2003), 46
Protect IP Act (PIPA), 144
Protected class, 298, 654, 732
Proximate (legal) cause, 114, 439n, 783
Proxy, 783
Proxy materials, 783–784
Prudent Investor Rule, 969n
Public Company Accounting Oversight Board, 819, 891
Public contracting, equal opportunity in, 261
Public figures, 103–104
Public policy, 241
  contract legality and, 242
  contracts contrary to, 293–298
  encouragement of commerce and, 725
  exception to at-will employment based on, 625–626
  freedom of contract and, 242
  product liability and, 446–447
  religion and, 47
Publication
  of administrative agency rules, 10
  of court decisions, 13
  of information placing person in false light, 104
  as requirement for defamation, 101
  of a will, 961
Puffery, 105, 310
Purchase(s)
  of assets, 764
  of stock, tender offer and, 765–766
Purchase price, seller's right to recover, 424
Purchase-money security interest (PMSI), 528–529
  automatic perfection of, 528–529
  defined, 528
  priority of, 532
Purchaser, good faith, 289n, 402
Purpose
  achieved, agency termination and, 617
  frustration of, 346
  particular, implied warranty of fitness and, 439
  proper, shareholder's right to inspection and, 788

Q

Quality, slander of, 110
Quality control, 457, 693
Quantum meruit, 364
Quasi contract (contract implied in law), 363–364
Question(s)
  corporate, business ethics and, 202
  of fact, 72–73
  federal, 65–66
  of law, 72 of
Quid pro quo harassment, 661
Quitclaim deed, 939
Quorum, 763, 775, 783
Quotas, 217, 818

R

Race, discrimination based on, 227, 655, 658–659, 661, 732
Racketeer Influenced and Corrupt Organizations Act (RICO)(1970), 167, 892n
Ratification
  agency by, 603
  defined, 290, 603
  by employer, of agent's unauthorized act, 610
"Rational basis" test, 51
Reaffirmation of debt, 555
Real estate. *See* Land; Real property
Real property, 108, 397. 583, 931–943
  defined, 108, 909
  exempt, 548–549
  financing law governing, 578–587
  fixtures and, 519, 933
  goods associated with, 386
  homestead exemption and, 548
  mechanic's lien and, 548
  mortgages and. *See* Mortgage(s)
  nature of, 931–933
  ownership interests in, 933–934
    nonpossessory, 935–936
    sale of, contracts for, 936–939
    transfer of, 936–941
  taking of, for public use, 940–941
  "things attached" to, 519, 933
Realty. *See* Land; Real property
Reasonable manner, 99, 414, 636
Reasonable person standard, 98, 99, 111–112, 241, 338
Reasonableness, commercial, 389
"Reasonably foreseeable users" rule, 890
Receiver, 562, 767
Recklessness, criminal negligence and, 158
Record(s). *See also* Books
  attribution and, 274
  e-contracts and, 274
  sending and receiving, 275
  corporate, shareholder's right to inspect, 788
  court, technology and, 53–54
  employment, OSHA and, 631
  court, privacy and, 53–54
  inspection of
    director's right of, 776
    partner's right of, 708
    shareholder's right of, 788
  shareholder, 784
Recording, of mortgages, 577
Redemption right of, 538, 584, 586–587
Redlining, reverse, 574
Reformation, 296, 361, 362–363
Refusal to deal, 844
Registration
  securities, 802–806
  trademark, 129
Regulated industries, exemption of, from antitrust laws, 849
Regulation. *See* Government regulation(s)
Reimbursement
  agent's right to, 606
  corporate director's right to, 776
  surety's right to, 548
Rejection
  duties of merchant buyers and lessees on, 428
  of goods, by buyer or lessee, 422, 428–429
  of offer, by offeree, 263–264
  reason for, 428
Release, 286, 547
Relevant market, 842–843
Reliance
  detrimental, 286–288, 706
  justifiable, 887–888
  on misrepresentation, 312, 445, 808
  reasonable, 706
Relief, order for, 554
Religion
  discrimination based on, 227, 655, 659, 661, 732
  of employees, reasonable accommodation of, 659
  establishment clause and, 47
  ethical standards and, 198
  free exercise clause and, 47–49
  freedom of, 40, 47–49
Remedy(ies)
  basic, creditor's, on debtor's default, 535
  defined, 13
  in equity, 11–15, 354, 359–363
  exclusive, 431
  judicial, 535–536
  at law, 14, 353–359. *See also* Damages
  limitation of, 269, 364–365, 431
  prejudgment, 544
  postjudgment, 544–545
  rescission, 360
  restitution, 360
  self-help (repossession of collateral) by creditor, 535
  summarized, 362
Rent, 944
Reorganization, in bankruptcy. *See* Bankruptcy
Replevin, 427
Reply, 76
Reports, reporters, 24–30
Repudiation, anticipatory, 420, 422–423
Res ipsa loquitur, 117
Rescission, 14. *See also* Cancellation
  for breach of contract, 284, 360, 426
  defined, 284
  "home solicitation contracts" and, 360n
  of mortgage, right to, 579
  mutual, contract discharge by, 343–344
  restitution and, 360
Resource Conservation and Recovery Act (RCRA)(1976), 875–876
Respondeat superior, 613–615, 746
Respondent, 30
Responsible corporate officer doctrine, 160
Restatement rule, 890

Restatement (Second) of Contracts, 243n, 244n, 270, 306n, 308n, 309n, 313n 316n, 318, 320, 322n, 328, 330, 334, 340, 342n, 344n, 345n, 346n, 352n, 353n, 358n, 360n, 448
Restatement (Second) of Trusts, 969n
Restatement (Third) of Agency, 598, 610n, 611n, 614
Restatement (Third) of Torts: Products Liability, 448, 449n, 450, 890
Restatement (Third) of Trusts, 969n
Restatements of the Law, 6, 244n *See also individual restatements*
Restitution, 360
Restraint(s)
 against alienation, 331
 of trade, contracts in, 293–296, 834. *See also* Antitrust law(s)
  horizontal, 837–839
  vertical, 839–840
Retaliation, 663–664
Reverse discrimination, 658–659
Reverse redlining, 574
Revised Model Business Corporation Act (RMBCA), 743, 775
Revised Principal and Income Act, 969n
Revised Uniform Limited Partnership Act (RULPA), 717
Revocation. *See also* Cancellation
 of acceptance, 429
 of gift, 915
 of living trust, 966
 of offer, 243, 263
RICO (Racketeer Influenced and Corrupt Organizations Act)(1970), 167, 892n
Right(s)
 airspace, 932
 appraisal, 764
 assignment of, 328–332
 of assurance, 420
 conflicting, ethics and, 199
 preemptive, 786–787
 principle of, 199
 redemption 538
 subsurface, 932
 survivorship, 910–911
Risk(s)
 assumption of, 115, 454–455
 defined, 950
 of loss, 399–405, 408
 commonly known, 452
 duty to warn of, 112, 452
 management of, 950
 of loss, 399–405, 408
 obvious, 112–113, 452
Rivers and Harbors Appropriations Act (1899), 871
Robbery, 161
Robinson-Patman Act (1914), 845–846
Rulemaking, 9–10, 20

S

Safe Drinking Water Act, 874
Safety
 consumer protection and, 861–864
 public, 175
 in workplace, 606, 631–632
Sale(s)
 of collateral, 537–538
 defined, 384
 door-to-door, 861
 and leaseback, 583
 mail-order, 861
 by nonowners, 402
 notice of, 585
 online, 861
 power of, foreclosure and, 585
 telephone, 861
 consumer protection and, 861
 "cooling off" laws and, 861
 "short," 582, 811
Sales contract(s)
 acceptance in, 391–394, 421–422
  additional terms and, 392–394
  mirror image rule and, 392
  revocation of, 429
 anticipatory repudiation of, 420, 422–423
 assignments and, 331
 breach of, 405, 422–423
  anticipatory, 420, 422–423
  remedies for
   of buyer, 425–429
   damages as, 354, 494
   limitation of, 431
   of seller, 423–425
  risk of loss and, 405
 cancellation of, 423, 426
 consideration in, 392, 394
 defined, 384
 duration of ongoing, 390
 duty of cooperation and, 420–421
 formation of, 383, 388–412
 good faith requirement and, 392, 389
 installment, 342n
 interpretation of, 398
 law governing, major differences between general contract law and, 384, 385
 between merchants, special rules for, 391, 392–394
 offer in, 389–391
  merchant's firm, 391
 parol evidence rule and, 396–398
 performance of, 414–422
  partial, 396
 repudiation of, 420, 422–423
 rescission of, 423, 426
 right of assurance and, 420
 risk of loss and, 399–405, 408
 rules of construction and, 398
 Statute of Frauds and, 316–317, 394–396
 terms of. *See* Term(s)
 title and, 399–403
 UCC and, 240
 unconscionability and, 296, 398–399
Sarbanes-Oxley Act (2002), 178, 196, 291, 747n, 776, 814, 819–821, 891, 892, 897
 key provisions of, 820
 Web-based reporting systems and, 196
Satisfaction
 accord and, 285–286, 344
 of another, performance to the, 341
 defined, 28, 344
Schools of legal thought, 15–16
Scienter (guilty knowledge), 808, 311–312, 835–814
Search warrant, 171–173
Second Amendment, 40, 41
Secondary sources of law, 6
Secured party(ies), 520, 536
 defined, 520
 priority of, over other creditors, 531–533
 release from, 534
 remedies of, 535–538
 retention of collateral by, 536
Secured transactions, 519, 541
 defined, 519
 online, 521
 terminology of, 520
 value given for, 522
Securing the Protection of Our Enduring and Established Constitutional Heritage Act (2010), 102
Securities Act (1933), 800–808, 815, 897, 898, 893–894
 amendments to (1990), 800
 Section 11 of, 893–894
Securities and Exchange Commission (SEC), 783, 784, 799
 adoption of global accounting rules by, 884
 civil actions by, for securities violations, 814–815
 creation of, 800
 EDGAR (Electronic Data Gathering, Analysis, and Retrieval) database of, 801, 802
 expanding regulatory powers of, 800
 as independent regulatory agency, 9
 as legal landmark, 800
 major responsibilities of, 800
 online securities fraud and, 821–823
 Public Company Accounting Oversight Board and, 819, 891
 Regulation A of, 803–805
 Regulation D of, 805–806
 Rule 10b-5 of, 808–813, 895–896
  compared with Section 16(b), 811
 Rule 14a-8 of, 783
 securities law violations enforced by, 806–808, 813–815
Securities Enforcement Remedies and Penny Stock Reform Act (1990), 800
Securities Exchange Act (1934), 800, 803, 808–815, 886–887
 professional's liability under, 894–896
 Section 10(b) of, 808–811, 813–814, 895–896
  Rule 16(b) compared with, 811
 Section 14(a) of, 813
 Section 16(b) of, 811, 814
  Rule 10b–5 compared with, 811
 Section 18 of, 894
Securities laws, accountant's liability under, 897
Securities Litigation Uniform Standards Act (SLUSA)(1998), 813
Security(ies). *See also* Bond(s); Securities Act; Securities and Exchange Commission, Securities Exchange Act; Stock(s)

corporate governance and, 816–821
debt, 758
defined, 758, 799, 801
equity (stocks), 758
fixed-income (bonds), 758
fraud and, 178
income. *See* Employee(s), income security for
insider trading and, 166
online fraud and, 821–823
registration of, 802–806
regulation of, 799–826
by state, 815
treasury, 580
types of, 801
Security agreement(s), 521–522, 525
authentication and, 522–523
description of collateral and, 525
writing requirement and, 522–523
Security interest(s)
in after-acquired property, 529–530
attachment and, 521
creation of, 520–522
debtor's default and, 535–536
defined, 520
floating lien and, 530–531
in future advances, 530
in inventory, 530
perfection of, 522–529
by attachment, 528–529
automatic, 532n
defined, 522
effective time duration of, 529
by filing, 522–527. *See also* Financing statement, filing of
methods of, summarized, 523
by possession, 528
without filing, 528
priorities among claims to debtor's collateral and, 531–533
in proceeds, 529
purchase-money (PMSI), 528–529
scope of, 529–531
termination of, 535
Self-incrimination, 40, 170, 173–174
Seller(s)
breach by, 405
goods held by, risk of loss and, 404
goods in possession of, seller's remedies and, 404, 423–424
insolvency of, 426
insurable interest of, 405–406
obligations of, 414–421
puffery and, 105, 310
right of, to reclaim goods, 425
Seniority systems, 671–672
Sentencing guidelines, 178n, 179
Sentencing Reform Act (1984), 178
Service(s)
of process, 76
goods combined with, 386
personal. *See* Personal-service contract(s)
Service mark, 132, 151
Settlement
of claims, by accord and satisfaction, 285–286
as option, when you cannot perform contract, 366
Settlor (grantor), of trust, 965
Seventh Amendment, 40
Sexual harassment, 661–665, 732
defined, 661
establishing complaint procedures for, 662
Ellerth-Faragher defense to, 662–663
hostile-environment, 661
in other countries, 202, 665
preventive policies and, 662
quid pro quo, 661
sexual orientation and, 664
by supervisors, 662–663
Sexual orientation, harassment and, 664
Share(s), 753
transfer of, 748–749, 788
Share exchange, 762–763
Shareholders, 200, 744, 773, 782–792
agreement of, to transfer shares, 749
aligning interests of, with those of officers, 816–817
appraisal rights of, 654
approval by
for extraordinary matters, 763, 782
of merger and consolidation plan, 763
deadlock of, 789
derivative suit by, 782, 789–790
duties and liabilities of, 791–792
election and removal of directors and, 774, 782
inspection rights of, 788
in joint stock companies, 737
liability of, 728, 744
majority, fiduciary duties of, 782, 791–792
meetings of, 783–784
minority, majority shareholders' duty to, 782, 791–792
powers of, 782–783
proposals by, 783
proxy materials and, 783
relationship of, with directors and officers, 782
rights of, 786–790
transfer of shares and, 748–749
voting by, 784–786
Sharia, 18
Shelter principle, 480
Sherman Antitrust Act (1890), 225, 833, 834–845, 847, 848, 849, 850–851
extraterritorial application of, 850–851
Shipment
accommodation, 392
prompt, as acceptance, 391
Shrink-wrap agreements, 270–271
Sight drafts, 463–464
Signature(s)
authentication of, 607
firm offer and, 391
on negotiable instruments
forged drawers', 486–487, 500–502
liability for, 481–485
location of, on instrument, 467
requirement of, 467
notary public and, 607
Statute of Frauds and, 318–319
UCC flexibility regarding, 467
unauthorized, 483–485
of agent, 483
HDC status and, 479
wills and, 960
Silence
as acceptance, 265–266
misrepresentation by, 310–311
Slander, 102–103, 110
Small Business Administration Act (1958), 849
Smart cards, 512
Social media
criticism of employers in, 643
employee use of, developing policy for, 649–650
trademark disputes and, 130
Social Security Act (Old-age, Survivors', and Disability Insurance)(1935), 632–633
Social Security Administration, 633
Software
"crimeware," 182–183
copyright protection for, 142–143
filtering, 46
gambling and, 294
licensing of, 268
via Internet, 268
malware and, 182
shrink-wrap agreement to purchase, 270–271
worm, 182
Sole proprietorship, 686–689
compared with other major business forms, 792–793
Sovereign immunity, doctrine of, 214–215
Spam, 120–121, 858–859
Specific performance, 317, 360–361
in land-sale contracts, 354
buyer's or lessee's right to obtain, 426
defined, 360
personal-service contracts and, 361
Speech
commercial, 44
constitutional limitations on, 100–101
corporate (political), 44, 744
freedom of, 40, 100
online speech and, 42
reasonable restrictions on, 41–44, 100–101
obscene, 46
by public figures, 100
symbolic, 41, 42
unprotected, 45–46. *See also* Defamation
Stakeholder approach, to corporate social responsibility, 200
Standard of proof. *See* Burden of proof
Standing to sue, 69
Starbucks Coffee Company, 406
Stare decisis, 11–12
State(s)
courts of. *See* State court systems
law codes of, citations to, 24–25
laws of
corporations and, 743, 751, 753, 767, 782, 817–818
crimes and, 159

immigration and, 624, 641–642
intestacy, 964
layoff notices and, 629–630
on lost property, 917, 926
marriage and, 52
privacy rights and, 635
trade secrets and, 146
uniform, adoption of, 8
on wills, 958
workers' compensation and, 631–632
police powers of, 7, 38, 40
regulation by
of advertising, 44
commerce clause and, 35–39
of franchising, 692
of securities, 815
of spam, 120
State court systems, 70–73. *See also* Court(s)
appellate courts of. *See* Appellate court(s)
courts of appeals in. *See* Appellate court(s)
decisions in
citations to, 25–27, 28
finding, 25–27, 28
following a case through, 75–82
highest (supreme) court of, 30, 73
trial courts in, 70–71
Statement(s)
bank, timely examination of, 501
constituting slander *per se,* 102–103
continuation, 529
environmental impact (EIS), 869
of fact
fraud and, 106
requirement for defamation, 100–101
financial, 885
financing. *See* Financing statement(s)
of opinion, 100, 106, 310, 439
registration, 802–803
termination, of security interest, 535
of value, 439
Statute(s)
arbitration, 85–86
assignments prohibited by, 330
contrary to public policy, 330
dram shop, 118
estray, 917, 926
of frauds. *See* Statute of Frauds
Good Samaritan, 118
licensing, 292–293
of limitations. *See* Statute of limitations
long arm, 62–64
as primary sources of law, 6
recording, 939
regulating gambling, 292
special negligence, 117–118
Statute of Frauds
CISG and, 406
contract between merchants, special rules for, 395
contracts subject to, 313–318
defined, 313
exceptions to, 317–318, 395–396
"main purpose" rule and, 316
merchant status and, 395
mortgages and, 577
one-year-rule and, 313, 314–315
sales contracts and, 394–396
special exceptions to, under UCC, 318
sufficiency of the writing and, 318–319, 323, 394
writing requirements of, 313–318, 601n
Statute of limitations, 51, 76
as defense to criminal liability, 170
lawsuit for breach of contract and, 344
under UCC, 431, 538
Statutory law
citations to, 8
defined, 7–8
finding, 24–25
Steering, 578
Stock(s), 758–760, 768, 799
acquisition of, shareholder status and, 782
bonds versus, summarized, 760
common, 758–759
defined, 758
as equity securities, 758
preferred, 758, 760
purchase of, tender offers and, 765–766
types of, listed, 760
watered, 791
Stock buyback, 196–196
Stock certificate, 786
Stock options, 197, 816
Stock warrant, 787
Stop Counterfeiting in Manufactured Goods Act (SCMGA)(2006), 133–134
Stop Online Piracy Act (SOPA), 144
Stop-payment order, 499
Stored Communications Act (SCA)(1986), 636
Stored-value cards, 511
Strict liability, 118–119
bailees and, 924
bystanders and, 453
common carriers and, 924
for crimes, 158
defined, 118
environmental law and, 869
hotel operators and, 925
product liability and. *See* Product liability
requirements for, 448
Strict scrutiny, 50–62
Strikes, 624, 646–648
Student loans, bankruptcy and, 560
Subject matter
destruction of
agency termination and, 618
impossibility of performance and, 345
offer termination and, 264–265
jurisdiction over, 65
Subleases, 944
Subrogation, surety's right of, 547
Substance abusers, ADA and, 670–671
Substantive law, 16–17
Summary jury trials (SJTs), 88
Summons, 76
Superfund (Comprehensive Environmental Response, Compensation, and Liability Act)(CERCLA)(1980), 876
Superseding cause, 116
Supervening illegality, 264
Supervisors, sexual harassment by, 662
Suppliers
of component parts, strict product liability and, 453
foreign, 195, 202–203
Support Our Law Enforcement and Safe Neighborhoods Act (2010), 641–642
Supremacy clause, 39
Supreme Court Reporter (S.Ct.)(West), 27
Suretyship, surety, 545–548
Suspect trait, 50–51
Syndicate (investment group), 737

T

Taft-Hartley Act (Labor-Management Relations Act)(1947), 644
Takeover
corporate, 765–766
defenses to, terminology of, 766
Taking
in good faith, HDC status and, 478
of private property for public use, 40, 940–941
for value, HDC status and, 478–479
without notice, HDC status and, 479–480
Tangible employment action, 662
Targeting, by lender, 578
Tariffs, 217
Tax(es), taxation
accountant's liability and, 897
"Amazon tax" and, 746
corporate, 744–747
double taxation and, 729, 745–746
gifts and, 914
joint venture and, 736
limited liability companies and, 726, 728
limited liability partnerships and, 716
Medicare and, 633
partnerships and, 705
pass-through entities and, 705, 716
payment of, mortgages and, 577
payroll, independent contractors and, 619
Social Security and, 633
sole proprietorship and, 687
state, online retailers and, 746
Tax return(s)
during bankruptcy, 553
of partnership, 705
Technology
contracts and. *See* E-contract(s)
e-signatures and, 272
file-sharing, 144–145
maximum achievable control (MACT), 871
privacy rights and, 53–55
Telemarketing, 860
Telephone Records and Privacy Protection Act, 56
Tenancy. *See also* Tenant(s)
in common, 910
fixed-term, 942
joint, 910–911
life estates and, 934
periodic, 942
at sufferance, 942–943
at will, 942
Tenant(s)
in common, 400
relationship of, with landlord, 358, 943–944

Tender
  of delivery, 401, 404, 414
  perfect, 415–416
    exceptions to, 416–421
  of performance, 340
  self-, 766
Tender offer, 765–766
Tenth Amendment, 7, 40
Term(s)
  additional
    in sales and lease contracts, 392–393
    CISG and, 407
    offeror's assent to, 393–394
    UCC and, 265n
  ambiguous, 250, 252, 320
  browse-wrap, 271–272
  in click-on agreement, ethics and, 271
  definiteness of, 262–263
  delivery, 403–404
  express, 252
  handwritten versus typewritten and printed, 472
  mortgage loans and, 577
  of online offer, 268–269
  of online contract, violation of, 354
  open delivery, 389
  open payment, 389–390
  open price, 389, 406
  open, 389–390, 406
  partnership for a, 707
  quantity, 389
  shrink-wrap agreement and, 270–271
Territorial restrictions, 840
Terrorism, aiding and abetting, forum-shopping plaintiffs and, 227
Terrorism Reform Act (2008), 102
Testamentary disposition of property, 956
Testate, 956
Testator, 956
Testing the waters, 804–805
Texting, harassment via, 664
Third Amendment, 40
Third party(ies)
  contract novation and, 344
  liability to
    of accountants and other professionals, 889–891
    of attorneys, 889–891
    on partner's dissociation, 713
  satisfaction of, performance to the, 341–342
Third party beneficiaries, 335–338
Time, timeliness
  buyer's rejection of goods and, 422
  contract formation, mental incompetence and, 291
  contractual acceptance and, 267
  duration of perfection of security interest and, 529
  lapse of
    agency termination and, 616–617
    offer termination and, 264
  payable at a definite, 469, 470
  for performance, 416–417
  for presentment, 482, 483
  reasonable, 99, 264, 404, 414
  rejection of goods and, 428
Time drafts, 463–464
Tipper/tippee theory, 810–811
Title, 399–408
  case, 27, 30
  document of. *See* Document(s), of title.
  good, 438
  passage of, 399–403
  to property, 910
  slander of, 110
  void, 402, 403
  voidable, 402, 403
  warranties of, 438
Tort(s), 95–125
  agent's, 612–616
  business, 95
  classification of, 97
  by corporation, 746–747
  cyber, 96
  defined, 95
  of employee, *respondeat superior* and, 746
  of independent contractor, 600
  international claims in, 226–227
  law of
    basis of, 96–97
    exception to at-will employment based on, 625
  privacy rights and, 52
  reform and, 97
  toxic, 869
  unintentional. *See* Negligence
Tortfeasor, 97
Toxic chemicals, 874–876
Toxic substances, 875
Toxic Substances Control Act, 875
Trade
  barriers to, minimizing, 219–220
  contracts in restraint of, 293–296
  restraints on. *See* Restraints, on trade
  usage of, 252, 321, 397
Trade acceptance, 464, 481
Trade associations, 839
Trade custom, warranties implied from, 441–442
Trade dress, 132–133
Trade libel, 110
Trade names, 134
  disputes over, 752
  financing statements and, 524
Trade secrets, 146–147
  in cyberspace, 146–147
  defined, 146
  federal and state laws on, 146
  theft of, 166
Trademark, 127–137,151, 217
Trademark dilution, 128–129
Trading, insider, 166, 808–811
Trading with the Enemy Act (1917), 218
Transportation Security Administration (TSA), 55
Treasury securities, 580
Treaties, 211
Treaty of Rome, 219
Trespass
  to land, 108–109
  to personal property, 109
Trial(s)
  criminal, 177–178
  jury, right to, 40, 174
  procedures at, 80
    compared to arbitration, 84–85
  right to speedy and public, 40, 174
  summary jury (SJTs), 88
Trial courts, 25, 70–73. *See also* Trial(s)
TRIPS (Trade-Related Aspects of Intellectual Property Rights) agreement, 148, 149–150
Troubled Asset Relief Program (TARP), 198
Trust(s), 966–969
  allocations between principal and income of, 969
  business 737
  charitable, 967
  constructive, 968
  express, 966–968
  implied, 968
  living (*inter vivos*), 966–967
  resulting, 968
  spendthrift, 967
  testamentary, 967
  Totten, 968
Trustee(s)
  bankruptcy and, 556–557
  corporate directors and, 774
  of trust, 965, 969
    duties of, 969
    powers of, 969
Truth-in-Lending Act (TILA)(1968), 578–579, 865–866
Truth-in-lending Simplification and Reform Act (1980), 865n
Twenty-seventh Amendment, 40n
Tying arrangements (tie-in sales agreement), 847

U

UCC. *See* Uniform Commercial Code
Ultra vires doctrine, 756
Ultramares rule, 889–890
Unconscionability, 398–399
  of contract or clause, 296–297
  defined, 296
  limitations on consequential damages and, 431
  procedural, 296–297
  substantive, 297
  warranty disclaimers and, 443
Underwriter, 950
Undue hardship, accommodating employees' needs and, 659, 670
Undue influence
  fraudulent misrepresentation and, 312
  illegal agreement and, 299
  wills and, 958
Unforeseeability of difficulties, rescission and, 284. *See also* Foreseeability
Uniform Arbitration Act (1955), 85
Uniform Commercial Code (UCC), 8, 383
  adoption of, by states, 384
  Article 2 of (Sales)
    franchising and, 690
    merchant status and, 387

puffery and, 105, 310
scope of, 384–388
UETA and, 273
warranties under, 437–444
Article 2A of (Leases)
bailments and, 923
scope of, 388
UETA and, 273
warranties under, 437–444
Article 3 of (Negotiable Instruments), 384, 463n, 494
Article 4 of (Bank Deposits and Collections), 384, 494, 495
Article 4A of (Funds Transfers), 284
Article 5 of (Letters of Credit), 384
Article 7 of (Documents of Title), 384, 924–925
Article 9 of (Secured Transactions), 519
CISG compared with, 406–407
citations to, 29
commercial reasonableness under, 389
consideration under, 394
entrustment rule under, 402
fictitious payee rule of, 484
good faith and, 389, 392, 402, 413, 417, 427, 535
imposter rule and, 484
as legal landmark, 385
limitation of remedies under, 364, 431
parol evidence rule and, 320–322, 396–397
passage of title under, 399–403
penalties and, 358–359
perfect tender rule under, 416–421
periodic changes and updates of, 385
rescission of contract under, 426
risk of loss and, 399, 403–405
rules of construction under, 398
signatures under, 391n
Statute of Frauds under, 316–317
statute of limitations under, 431
unconscionability and, 296, 398–399
warranties and, 437–444
Uniform Electronic Transactions Act (UETA), 272, 273, 267, 274–275
Uniform Limited Liability Company Act (ULLCA), 726
Uniform Partnership Act (UPA), 703, 713, 715–727, 733
Uniform Probate Code (UPC), 958, 960, 961, 962, 964
Uniform Residential Landlord and Tenant Act (URLTA), 943
Uniform Securities Act (2002), 815
Uniform Trade Secrets Act, 146
Union elections and campaigns, 645–646
appropriate bargaining unit and, 645–646
Union(s)
affiliation with, discrimination based on, 642
collective bargaining and, 643, 646
elections by, 645–646
illegal activities and, 643
labor laws and, 642–644
organization of, 644
strikes and, 624, 646–648
unfair labor practices and, 643, 646
Union shop, 644
United Nations Convention on Contracts for the International Sale of Goods, 221. *See also* CISG
United Nations Convention on the Recognition and Enforcement of Foreign Arbitral Awards (New York Convention), 222
United States Census Bureau, 654–655
United States Citizenship and Immigration Services, 629
United States Code (U.S.C.), 24, 551n
United States Code Annotated (U.S.C.A.), 24
United States Constitution
amendments to. *See* Bill of Rights; individual amendments
brevity of, 33
commerce clause of, 35–39
compulsory self-incrimination prohibited by, 40, 170, 173–174
due process clause of, 40, 41, 49–50, 173, 544, 744. *See also* Due process
equal protection clause of, 50–51, 672
establishment clause of, 47–49
exports and, 217–218
federal courts under, 65–66
freedom of contract protected by, 241
intellectual property protected by, 126
judicial review and, 61
marriage equality and, 52
safeguards under, for accused persons, 170–178
sentencing guidelines and, 179
speedy and public trial guaranteed by, 40
supremacy clause of, 39
takings clause of, 40
privacy rights and, 51–52
administrative agency rulemaking and, 10
amendments to, 7
as primary source of law, 6
privacy rights and, 51–52, 637
supremacy clause, 39
as supreme law of the land, 6–7
takings clause of, 940–941
unreasonable searches and seizures prohibited by, 40, 55, 448, 634–638, 744
United States Court of Federal Claims, 82
United States Court of International Trade, 82
United States Department of Agriculture, 860
United States Department of Homeland Security, 55, 629n, 640
United States Department of Housing and Urban Development (HUD), 582
United States Department of Justice, 178, 184, 294, 574, 807–808, 838, 894
United States Department of Labor, 641, 627
United States Department of the Treasury, 583, 768
United States Food and Drug Administration (FDA), 860–863
United States Immigration and Customs Enforcement (ICE), 639, 640
United States International Trade Commission, 140
United States Patent and Trademark Office, 129, 138
United States Reports, 27
United States Safe Web Act (Undertaking Spam, Spyware, and Fraud Enforcement with Enforcers Beyond Borders Act) (2006), 121
United States Sentencing Commission, 178, 477n
United States Statutes at Large, 24
United States Supreme Court
appeals to, 74–75
constitutional authority of, 74
as final interpreter of the United States Constitution, 41
impact of foreign law on, 42
justices of, 74
petitions granted by, 75
rule of four of, 75
writ of *certiorari* of, 74–75
United States Trustee Program, 553
Unjust enrichment, 363
Unlawful Internet Gambling Enforcement Act (2006), 294
Unreasonable searches and seizures, 40, 55, 448, 634–638, 744
USA Patriot Act (Uniting and Strengthening America by Providing Appropriate Tools Required to Intercept and Obstruct Terrorism Act)(2001), 54–55
Usage of trade, 252, 321, 397
Usury, 292
Utilitarianism, 199

V

Validation notice, 868
Value(s)
of digital goods, 912
face (par), stock, 791
fair, dumping and, 218
given by secured party, 522
good faith purchaser for, 289n
impaired, due to nonconformity 417
legally sufficient, 282
of letter of credit, 224–225
mistake of, 306
of partner's share in partnership, 708
statement of, 439
stored, e-money and, 511
taking for, HDC status and, 478, 479
Vegetation, as real property, 932–933
Venture capital, 760–761
Venue, 69
Verdict, 80, 156
Vertically integrated firm, 839–840
Vesting, under ERISA, 633–634
Video games, warning labels for, 453
Virus, 182
Visas, 641
Voluntary consent, 242, 268, 305, 323
Voting
by directors, 775
by shareholders, 733, 759, 782, 775, 784–786
voting agreements and, 786
voting lists and, 785

W

Wage(s), 627–629
    minimum, 627–628
    overtime and, 628–629
    discrimination and, 660–661
    garnishment of, 544–545
    labor certification and, 641
    minimum, 627–628
    workplaces abroad and, 203
Wage and hours laws, 627–629
Waiver, by partner, of fiduciary duties, 710
War, agency termination and, 618
Warehouse companies, 924
Warehouse receipt, 401, 924
Warning(s)
    design defects and, 450–451
    graphic, ethics and, 451–452
    video games and, 453
Warrant(s)
    search, 171–173
    stock, 787
Warranty(ies), 437–444
    breach of, as defense to liability on negotiable instrument, 486
    cumulative nature of, under UCC, 442
    disclaimers of, 442–443
    express, 438–439, 442
    full, 444
    implied. *See* Implied warranty(ies)
    limited, 444
    Magnuson-Moss Warranty Act and, 443–444
    negotiable instruments and, 481, 484–485
    overlapping, 442
    presentment, 484–485
    of title, 438
    transfer, 484–485
    under UCC, 437–444
Web-based reporting systems, 196
Webb-Pomerene Act (1918), 849
Westlaw®(WL)(West Group), 27
Wetlands, 873
Whistleblower Protection Act (1989), 626
Whistleblowers, 626
White knight defense to takeover , 766
Wild animals, strict liability and, 119
Will(s), 956–963
    codicil to, 961
    defined, 956
    disinheritance by, 959–960, 962
    employment at. *See* Employment, at will
    estate planning and, 963
    gifts by, 957–958
    holographic (olographic), 960
    intent and, 958
    legal age for executing, 958
    nuncupative, 960
    partnership at, 706
    probate procedures and, 962–963
    publication of, 961
    residuary clause in, 958
    revocation of, 961–962
    by operation of law, 961
        by physical act of maker, 961
        by subsequent writing, 961
    sample, excerpt from, 958
    substitutes for, 963
    terminology of, 956–957
    testamentary capacity and, 958
    transfer of real property by, 939
    valid, requirements for, 958–961
    writing requirement and, 960
Wire Act (1961), 294
Witness, examination of, 40
Worker Adjustment and Retraining Notification (WARN) Act, 629
Workers' compensation, 631–632
    litigation versus, 632
    requirements for receiving, 632
Working papers, 891–892
Workout agreement, 582
Workplace
    discrimination and. *See* Employment discrimination
    in foreign countries, cultural differences and, 203, 690
    harassment in, 661–665. *See also* Harassment
    intolerable conditions in, constructive discharge and, 661
    monitoring in, privacy rights and, 635–639
    notice of dangerous conditions in, 615
    OSHA inspections and, 631
    safety in, 606, 631–632
Works for hire, employee status and, copyright issues and, 601
World Intellectual Property Organization (WIPO), 145
World Trade Organization (WTO), 219
Worm, 182
Writ(s)
    of attachment, 549
    of *certiorari*, 74–75
    of execution, 549
    of *mandamus*, 63
Writing requirement(s)
    CISG and, 407
    equal dignity rule and, 601n, 607
    for mortgage loans, 577
    libel and, 10
    merchant's firm offer and, 391
    modification of sales contract and, 394
    negotiable instruments and, 466–467
    one-year rule and, 313, 314–315, 363
    operating agreement and, 730
    partnership agreement and, 705
    power of attorney and, 601n, 607
    security interests and, 521–522
    Statute of Frauds and 313–318
    sufficiency of, 318–320, 323, 394
    under UCC, 315, 316–317
    wills and, 960
Wrongful interference, 96, 106, 108

Y

Year Books, 13

LANDMARK IN THE LAW

Equitable Principles and Maxims 15

Gibbons v. Ogden (1824) 36

Marbury v. Madison (1803) 63

Palsgraf v. Long Island Railroad Co. (1928) 115

The Digital Millennium Copyright Act of 1998 145

Miranda v. Arizona (1966) 176

Hamer v. Sidway (1891) 283

Hadley v. Baxendale (1854) 357

The Uniform Commercial Code 385

MacPherson v. Buick Motor Co. (1916) 446

Federal Trade Commission Rule 433 487

Check Clearing in the 21st Century Act (Check 21) 506

The Bankruptcy Reform Act of 2005 550

The Doctrine of *Respondeat Superior* 614

Limited Liability Company (LLC) Statutes 726

Citizens United v. Federal Election Commission (2010) 745

The Securities and Exchange Commission 800

The Sherman Antitrust Act of 1890 835

The SEC Adopts Global Accounting Rules 884

BEYOND OUR BORDERS

National Law Systems 18

The Impact of Foreign Law on the United States Supreme Court 42

Islamic Law Courts Abroad and at Home 72

"Libel Tourism" 102

The Anti-Counterfeiting Trade Agreement 148

Hackers Hide in Plain Sight in Russia 182

Arbitration versus Litigation 224

The Statute of Frauds and International Sales Contracts 317

Impossibility or Impracticability of Performance in Germany 347

The CISG's Approach to Revocation of Acceptance 429

Imposing Product Liability as Far Away as China 449

Severe Restrictions on Check Indorsements in France 474

Islamic Law and *Respondeat Superior* 616

Brazil Requires Employers to Pay Overtime for Use of Smartphones after Work Hours 628

Sexual Harassment in Other Nations 665

Franchising in Foreign Nations 690

Doing Business with Foreign Partners 705

Limited Liability Companies in Other Nations 731

Derivative Actions in Other Nations 789

Corporate Governance in Other Nations 817

The European Union's Expanding Role in Antitrust Litigation 851